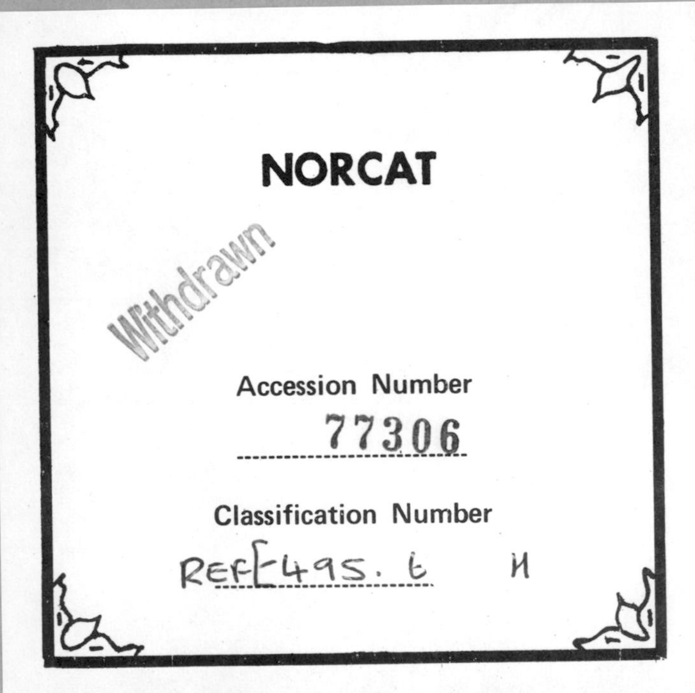

A
JAPANESE AND ENGLISH DICTIONARY WITH AN ENGLISH AND JAPANESE INDEX

A JAPANESE AND ENGLISH DICTIONARY WITH AN ENGLISH AND JAPANESE INDEX

by

JAMES CURTIS HEPBURN

CHARLES E. TUTTLE CO.: PUBLISHERS
Rutland, Vermont & Tokyo, Japan

Representatives
Continental Europe: BOXERBOOKS, INC., *Zurich*
British Isles: PRENTICE-HALL INTERNATIONAL, INC., *London*
Australasia: BOOK WISE (AUSTRALIA) PTY. LTD.
104–108 Sussex Street, Sydney 2000

Published by the Charles E. Tuttle Company, Inc.
of Rutland, Vermont & Tokyo, Japan
with editorial offices at
Suido 1-chome, 2–6, Bunkyo-ku, Tokyo, Japan

Library of Congress Catalog Card No. 81-52935
International Standard Book No. 0-8048-1441-4

First Tuttle edition, 1983

PRINTED IN JAPAN

PUBLISHER'S FOREWORD

THIS work stands as a monument in the study of Japan and the Japanese language by the Western world. First published in 1867, as Japan was just beginning to renew contact with the outside world after centuries of self-imposed isolation, the dictionary was of immense value to students of Japanese and of English. It constituted a remarkable feat on the part of its compiler, who based it largely upon his own studies of the language under native teachers in Japan.

Born in 1815, James Curtis Hepburn was graduated from Princeton College in 1832, and the Medical Department of the University of Pennsylvania in 1836. After practicing medicine in the United States, and serving as a medical missionary in Singapore and Amoy, Dr. Hepburn and his wife arrived in Japan in 1859 under the auspices of the Presbyterian Board of Foreign Missions. For more than thirty years thereafter he ministered to the spiritual and the medical needs of the Japanese people, as well as doing pioneering work in translation and the study of the Japanese language.

Dr. Hepburn was among the first foreign missionaries to enter Japan after Commodore Perry's "black ships" first came to "open" the country in 1853. It was only in 1868 that Japan made a definite commitment to modernization in the Meiji Restoration. Christian teaching was still under a government ban, and a Japanese was arrested in 1871 for the crime of possessing copies of the Gospel of Mark, in Dr. Hepburn's translation. The man died in prison in 1872, though the ban was relaxed the following year in response to Western pressure.

Dr. Hepburn is perhaps best remembered today as the originator of the Hepburn system for the romanization of Japanese, which remains the standard system. The romanization system can be seen in an early form in this dictionary; differences from present practice are surprisingly few. Dr. Hepburn also contributed to early efforts at Bible translation, and the writing of religious tracts. And of course he compiled this dictionary, which had to be published in Shanghai due to a lack of well-developed printing facilities in Japan.

A few words about Dr. Hepburn's busy medical practice, which he maintained amid his other labors, may be of interest. In 1861 he opened an infirmary in Kanagawa, where he operated a free clinic for eighteen years. Within a few months of the infirmary's opening, thirty-five hundred patients had consulted him. His office was filled with patients as well as Japanese doctors and medical students who had come great distances to inspect his methods. When the famous Kabuki actor Sawamura Tanosuke was stricken by gangrene, Dr. Hepburn successfully amputated his leg and replaced it with an artificial limb shipped from the United States. Sawamura's stage comeback caused a sensation, and convinced many Japanese of the efficacy of Western medicine.

In 1892 Dr. Hepburn retired from his work and returned to the United States. The *Japan Mail* wrote that "the beauty of his character, his untiring charity, his absolute self-negation, and his steady zeal in the cause of everything good, constitute a picture which could hardly fail to appeal to the Japanese people," and indeed he was greatly esteemed by Japanese and by foreign residents alike. In 1905, on Dr. Hepburn's ninetieth birthday, the emperor of Japan awarded him the Imperial Order of the Rising Sun, Third Class. At the end of a full and productive life, he died in 1911.

The present edition of Dr. Hepburn's dictionary is based upon the first edition, of 1867, published by the American Presbyterian Mission Press in Shanghai. The publisher takes special pleasure in making this classic available to the public once again.

PREFACE.

In introducing this Dictionary to the public the author feels no small degree of diffidence. Nothing but the great need of such a work, felt by all foreigners in Japan, and the constant demand upon those who were making the study of the language their special business to share their acquisitions with others, could have induced him to issue it at this stage of his acquaintance with the language. The conviction that it is a first step in the right direction, and that, with all its deficiencies, it will prove of some use, could alone have made him consent to its publication.

In compiling this work the author has labored under the very great difficulty of having had little to assist him from the works of predecessors in the same field. The only works of the kind within his reach were the small vocabulary of Dr. Medhurst published in Batavia in 1830; and the Japanese and Portuguese Dictionary published by the Jesuit missionaries in 1603. His principal dependence, however, has been upon the living teacher, so that he feels himself alone responsible for every thing in the work.

There are over 20,000 Japanese words defined in the dictionary. This number might have been considerably increased, if all the compound words of which the language is capable, and all the obsolete words had been inserted. Those here published have been collected, for the most part, in the course of his own reading, or heard in use among the people. A large number of the words are of Chinese origin, and used mainly in books and epistolary writings, and have a very limited range of meaning. The most common words, whether native or Chinese, he has endeavored to illustrate, as much as possible, with examples; some of them extracted from books, but generally with colloquial phrases.

He might have made it a less pretentious volume, confining himself to only such words as are in common use; but his desire has been to present the whole language to the eye of the scholar arranged in proper order; and though he may not have exhausted the meaning of the words, he has endeavored to make as near an approximation to it as possible.

To render the work more complete he has added the Japanese Kana, and Chinese characters. The spelling with the Kana is according to the best native authority. The Chinese characters attached to the native words are those commonly used as their equivalents.

It has also been attempted to designate the part of speech to which each word belongs. This with the native words is not a matter of much difficulty, but with the Chinese is impossible in most cases, as the same word may be viewed as a noun, verb, or adjective, according to it various relations.

The introduction of the synonymous words will also be found useful. This branch has been more fully carried out in the second part, or Index.

In Romanizing the words, the effort has been in every case to express the sound as pronounced by the most cultivated natives; and the system of orthography, with a few variations, is that generally adopted by the students of the language in Japan.

The printing has been accomplished under many difficulties, especially from the want of accented vowels and a proper supply of capital letters which could not be procured in Shanghai, and had to be manufactured under many disadvantages. This will account for the want of uniformity and irregularity observable.

Notwithstanding every care, not a few typographical errors are observed; but as most of them are unimportant and a little attention will enable the reader to rectify them for himself, it is not thought necessary to publish a list of errata.

With these apologies and explanations, the author commits this work, the fruit of nearly eight years of unremitting labor, to the kind indulgence of those who are making the language their study, and if he can in this way, lend them a helping hand out of some of the difficulties which he had so often to encounter alone, he will feel that his labor has not been in vain.

J. C. H.

	i	ro	ha	ba	pa	ni	ho	bo	po	he	be	pe	to	do	chi	ji	ri	nu
1	イ	ロ	ハ	バ	パ	ニ	ホ	ボ	ポ	ヘ	ベ	ペ	ト	ド	チ	ヂ	リ	ヌ
2	い	ろ	は	ば	ぱ	に	ほ	ぼ	ぽ	へ	べ	ぺ	と	ど	ち	ぢ	り	ぬ
3	い	ろ	は	ば	パ	に	ほ	ぼ	ぽ	へ	べ	ぺ	と	ど	ち	ぢ	り	ぬ
4	伊	呂	波	婆		爾	保	菩		閉	辨		登	杼	智	地	利	奴
5	膳	路	葉	羽		丹	穗	帆		經	邊		砥	度	千	道	里	沼

	ru	wo	wa	ka	ga	yo	ta	da	re	so	zo	tsz	dz	ne	na	ra	mu	u
1	ル	ヲ	ワ	カ	ガ	ヨ	タ	ダ	レ	ソ	ゾ	ツ	ヅ	子	ナ	ラ	ム	ウ
2	る	を	わ	か	が	よ	た	だ	れ	そ	ぞ	つ	づ	ね	な	ら	む	う
3	る	を	わ	か	が	よ	た	だ	れ	そ	ぞ	つ	づ	ね	な	ら	む	う
4	留	袁	和	加	鵞	與	多	陀	禮	曾	叙	都	頭	禰	奈	羅	無	宇
5	流	尾	輪	香	鹿	代	田	駄	連	十	存	津	圖	根	名	樂	六	卯

	i	no	o	ku	gu	ya	ma	ke	ge	fu	bu	pu	ko	go	ye	te	de	a
1	井	ノ	オ	ク	グ	ヤ	マ	ケ	ゲ	フ	ブ	プ	コ	ゴ	エ	テ	デ	ア
2	ゐ	の	れ	く	ぐ	や	ま	け	げ	ふ	ぶ	ぷ	こ	ご	に	て	で	あ
3	ゐ	の	お	く	ぐ	や	ま	け	げ	ふ	ぶ	ぷ	こ	ご	え	て	で	あ
4	爲	濃	於	苦	具	耶	麻	計	解	不	歩		古	呉	衣	低	泥	阿
5	猪	之	億	九	愚	屋	真	氣	毛	布	部		兒	五	江	而	手	吾

	sa	za	ki	gi	yu	me	mi	shi	ji	ye	hi	bi	mo	sc	ze	sz	dz	n
1	サ	ザ	キ	ギ	ユ	メ	ミ	シ	ジ	ヱ	ヒ	ビ	モ	セ	ゼ	ス	ズ	ン
2	さ	ざ	き	ぎ	ゆ	め	み	し	じ	ゑ	ひ	び	も	せ	ぜ	す	ず	ん
3	さ	ざ	き	ぎ	ゆ	め	み	し	じ	ゑ	ひ	び	も	せ	ぜ	す	ず	ん
4	佐	邪	紀	義	由	米	美	師	慈	恵	飛	備	毋	世	是	須	受	牟
5	狭	坐	木	杵	湯	女	三	石	次	穢	火	日	裳	瀬	背	酢	巣	将

INTRODUCTION.

THE ORTHOGRAPHY.

a has the sound of *a* in *father*.
e ,, ,, *e* in *they, prey*.
i ,, ,, *i* in *machine*.
o ,, ,, *o* in *no, so*.
u ,, ,, *u* in *rule, moon*.

The horizontal mark over the vowels; as, ā, ī, ō, ū, indicates merely that the sound is prolonged.

ai has the sound of *ai* in *aisle*, or *eye*.
au ,, *ow* in *cow, how*.
ch ,, *ch* in *church*.
sh ,, *sh* in *shall, ship*.

a, when followed by a syllable commencing with *y*, has the sound of *ai*, or *i* in *thine;* as, *hayaku*, is pronounced, *haiyaku; ayamachi, aiyamachi.*

f, has a close resemblance to the sound of the English, *f;* but differs from it in that the teeth do not touch the lip, but the sound is made by blowing *fu*, softly through the lips when nearly closed, something like the *wh* sound in *who*, or *why*.

g, in the Yedo dialect has the soft sound of *ng;* but in Nagasaki, Kiyoto, and the southern departments it is pronounced hard; as in *go, gain*.

r, in *ra, re, ro, ru*, has the sound of the English, *r;* but in *ri*, it is pronounced more like *d*. But this is not invariable as many natives give it the common *r* sound.

The vowel sound in *sz, tsz*, and *dz*, is the same. It has no equivalent in English, but as near as possible to the sound expressed by the letters. *Se* in Kiyoto, Nagasaki and the southern departments is pronounced, *she;* and *ze*, like *je*.

The final *n* (ン), when at the end of a word has always the sound of *ng;* as, *mon* = *mong, san* = *sang, shin* = *shing;* but in the body of a word, when followed by a syllable beginning with *b, m*, or *p*, it is pronounced like *m;* as, *ban-min* = *bamming, mon-ban* = *mombang, shin-pai* = *shimpai*. Before the other consonants it has the sound of *n;* as, *an-nai, an-raku, ban-dai*.

The sounds of the other consonants, viz. *b d h j k m n p s t w y z*, do not differ from their common English sounds.

THE WRITTEN CHARACTER OR KANA.

The native language of the Japanese seems not to have been reduced to writing before the introduction of the Chinese characters. Ancient written characters are spoken of, and their forms and sounds even given, but it is doubtful whether they were used. The only vestiges said to be still remaining are the inscriptions upon two stone tablets, preserved and regarded with superstitious veneration, one in a Sintoo temple in Miwa of the department of Yamato; the other in a temple in Kidzki in the department of Idzmo.

The most ancient writings in the native language still extant are the *Kojiki* (古事記), a history of Japan from the earliest ages to the time when it was written about A. D. 711; and the *Manyōshu* (萬葉集), a collection of native poetry made some fifty years later. In both of these wo.ks the square and unabbreviated form (*Kaisho*) of the Chinese characters is used phonetically to represent the sounds of the Japanese syllables. These characters were called *Kari-na*, (假字), or borrowed names, contracted afterwards into *Kana* (see 4 and 5 of the table). These characters, more or less abbreviated and simplified in form, are called *Hira-kana* (3 of the table), or plain letters, and are still the common symbols used in writing the native language.

The *Katakana*, (片假名), or side letters, (1 of the table) are also derived from the Chinese characters, where instead of taking the whole, only a part of the character is used. These are more ancient than the *Hirakana*, but have been little used except in Dictionaries, books intended for the learned, or to spell foreign names.

There is still another form used, called the *I-ro-ha kana*, said to have been invented by *Kūkai*, or *Kōbōdaishi*, a Buddhist priest and founder of the *Shingonshu* sect, who died in A. D. 835. This form of *Kana* was devised by its author in order to assimilate the letters, as much as possible, to the *Bonji*, or characters used in the sacred books of the Buddhists.

The Japanese syllabary consists of seventy-two syllables, as seen in the table; they are generally arranged according to the five vowel sounds; as follows :—

a ア	*ka* カ	*sa* サ	*ta* タ	*na* ナ	*ha* ハ	*ma* マ	*ya* ヤ	*ra* ラ	*wa* ワ	*ga* ガ	*za* ザ	*da* ダ	*ba* バ	*pa* パ
i イ	*ki* キ	*shi* シ	*chi* チ	*ni* ニ	*hi* ヒ	*mi* ミ	*i* イ	*ri* リ	*i* 井	*gi* ギ	*ji* ジ	*ji* ヂ	*bi* ビ	*pi* ピ
u ウ	*ku* ク	*sz* ス	*tsz* ツ	*nu* ヌ	*fu* フ	*mu* ム	*yu* ユ	*ru* ル	*u* ウ	*gu* グ	*dz* ズ	*dz* ヅ	*bu* ブ	*pu* プ
e エ	*ke* ケ	*se* セ	*te* テ	*ne* 子	*he* ヘ	*me* メ	*ye* エ	*re* レ	*ye* ヱ	*ge* ゲ	*ze* ゼ	*de* デ	*be* ベ	*pe* ペ
o オ	*ko* コ	*so* ソ	*to* ト	*no* ノ	*ho* ホ	*mo* モ	*yo* ヨ	*ro* ロ	*wo* ヲ	*go* ゴ	*zo* ゾ	*do* ド	*bo* ボ	*po* ポ

To complete this table the syllables, イ ウ and エ have to be repeated. There are also amongst them several syllables, as, ヱ and エ, イ and 井, ヲ and オ, ヂ and ジ, and ヅ and ズ, which are said to have represented different sounds in ancient times ; but at the present time they can no longer be distinguished; in correct spelling, however, care must be taken that they be not written indiscriminately; there is a rule, established by ancient usage, to be observed in their use.

THE SYLLABLES IN COMBINATION.

The syllables commencing with the soft asperates, *h* and *f*, and *y*, for the most part, loose their consonants, and their vowels combine with the vowel of the preceeding syllable; sometimes forming a diphthong; as, *a-hi*, *ai; afu*, *au*, or ō; sometimes lengthening the sound of the first vowel; as, *nu-fu*, *nū; to-ho*, *tō; i-hi*, *ī; yo-fu*, *yō; ho-ho*, *ō*.

Sometimes with the consonant of the first and the vowel of the second forming a new syllable, epecially in writing the sounds of Chinese words; as, *chi-ya*, *cha; shi-ya*, *sha; chi-yo*, *cho; shi-yo*, *sho; ji-yo*, *jo*; or by still greater changes; as, *chi-ya-u*, *chō; shi-ya-u*, *shō; shi-yo-u*, *shō*; or by forming an entirely new sound; as *t-eu*, *chō; he-u*, *hiyō; de-fu*, *jō; se-fu*, *shō*.

In the following table all these changes are given in regular order, for the sake of those who may wish to consult this dictionary, and who may have the Kana only without the voice of the living teacher to direct them to the proper sound.

イフ *iu*	トヒ *toi*	ヨヒ *yoi*	ウヱ *wiye*	コウ *ko*	ユヒ *yui*
イヒ *ī*	ドウ *dō*	タウ *tō*	ウヘ *wiye*	コヒ *koi*	メウ *miyō*
イイ *ī*	チヤ *cha*	タフ *tō*	ウヒ *ui*	コフ *kō*	メヒ *mei*
イハ *iwa*	チヨ *cho*	タヘ *taye*	ウハ *uwa*	ゴウ *gō*	シヤ *sha*
ロウ *rō*	チヤウ *chō*	タヒ *tai*	ウヲ *uwo*	ゴフ *gō*	シヨ *sho*
ハウ *hō*	チヨウ *chō*	ダウ *dō*	ノウ *nō*	エウ *yō*	シヤウ *shō*
ハフ *hō*	ヂヨ *jo*	レウ *riyō*	ノホ *nō*	テウ *chō*	シヤフ *shō*
ハヘ *haye*	ヂヤウ *jō*	レフ *riyō*	オフ *ō*	テフ *chō*	シヨウ *shō*
バウ *bō*	リフ *riu*	ソフ *sō*	オホ *ō*	デウ *jō*	シユ *shu*
バフ *bō*	ヌフ *nū*	ソウ *sō*	オオ *ō*	デフ *jō*	シユウ *shū*
ヘウ *hiyō*	ヌウ *nū*	ソホ *sō*	オウ *ō*	アウ *ō* or *au*	ジヤ *ja*
ベウ *biyō*	ヌヒ *nui*	ソヒ *soi*	オヒ *oi*	アフ *ō* or *au*	ジヨ *jo*
ホウ *hō*	ヲウ *ō*	ゾウ *zō*	クハ *kuwa*	アヒ *ai*	ジヤウ *jō*
ホフ *hō*	ヲヒ *oi*	ツヒ *tszi*	クヒ *kui*	アア *ā*	ジフ *jū*
ホホ *hō*	ワフ *ō*	ツウ *ts'ū*	クウ *kū*	アハ *awa*	ジユ *ju*
ボウ *bō*	ワウ *ō*	子ウ *niyō*	ヤウ *yō*	サウ *sō*	モウ *mō*
ニフ *niu*	カウ *kō*	ナウ *nō*	ヤフ *yō*	ザフ *sō*	モオ *mō*
ニホ *nio*	カフ *kō*	ナフ *nō*	マウ *mō*	ザウ *zō*	セウ *shō*
ニヒ *nī*	カヒ *kai*	ナホ *nao*	マヒ *mai*	ザフ *zō*	セフ *shō*
ニヘ *niye*	カホ *kao*	ナヘ *naye*	マヘ *maye*	キフ *kiu*	セハ *sewa*
トフ *tō*	ガウ *gō*	ラウ *rō*	ケウ *kiyō*	キハ *kiwa*	スヒ *szi*
トウ *tō*	ガフ *go*	ラフ *rō*	ケフ *kiyō*	ユウ *yū*	スフ *szu*
トホ *tō*	ヨフ *yō*	ウヤ *wiya*	フウ *fū*	ユフ *yū*	スハ *szwa*
トヲ *tō*	ヨウ *yō*				

In the system of orthography adopted in this work, the *y* has been retained before the vowels *a* and *o* whenever possible, in order to separate the vowels, render the syllables more distinct, and follow the *kana*.

The syllables *tsz*, (ツ) when preceeding the strong consonant, *k*, *s*, *p*, and *t*, is elided, and the consonant of the following syllable doubled; as *batsz-kun* becomes *bakkun; matsz-szgu* becomes *masszgu; tetszpō*, *teppō; matsz-taku*, *mattaku*.

Ku, (ク) when following by a syllable beginning with *k* looses its vowel; as, *baku-ka*, *bakka; biku-ko*, *bikko; koku-ka*, *kokka*.

The sound of the vowel *i*, is often elided; as in *h'to*, *sh'chi*, *sh'ta*, *sh'te*, *ch'sha*.

ABBREVIATIONS.

a.	stand for	adjective.
adv.	,,	adverb.
caust.	,,	the causative form of the verb.
dub.	,,	the dubitative or future form of the verb.
exclam.	,,	exclamation or interjection.
imp.	,,	imperative mood.
i.v.	,,	intransitive verb.
n.	,,	noun.
neg.	,,	negative form of the verb.
pass.	,,	passive ,,
pot.	,,	potential ,,
post-pos.	,,	post-position.
pp.	,,	perfect particle.
ppr.	,,	present particle.
pret.	,,	preterit tense.
sub.	,,	subjunctive mood.
syn.	,,	synonymous words.
t.v.	,,	transitive verb.
id. or *idem*	,,	the same.
†	,,	word used only in books or obsolete.
‖	,,	colloquial word little used, or not of the Yedo dialect.
=	,,	equal to.

— in the Dictionary stands for the repetition of the Japanese word; in the Index for the repetition of the English word.

JAPANESE AND ENGLISH DICTIONARY.

ABA

Ā, アア, 嗚呼. An exclamation or sigh expressive of grief, concern, pity, contempt, or admiration.=Ah! alas! oh! *Ā dō itashimashō.* Ah! what shall I do. *Ā kanashii kana*, alas! how sad. *Ā nasake nai*, oh! how unkind. Syn. SATEMO-SATEMO.

Ā, アア, 彼, *adv.* In that way, so, that. *Ā szru* to do in that way. *Ā shite iru to h'to ni togamerareru*, if you do so you will be blamed.

ABAI,*-au,-atta*, アハフ, *t.v.* To shield or screen from danger, to protect or defend. Syn. KABAU.

ABAKE,*-ru,-ta*, アハケル, 發, *i. v.* To break open of itself. fig. divulged, made public.

ABAKI,*-ku,-ita*, アハク, 發, *t. v.* To break or dig open that which confines or covers something else. fig. to expose or divulge a secret. *Tszka wo abaku*, to dig open a grave. *Hara wo —*, to cut open the belly. *Kōdzi ga dote wo abaita*, the inundation has broken open the dike. *Inji wo —*, to divulge a secret. Syn. HIRAKU.

ABARA, アハラ, 肋, *n.* The side of the chest.

ABARA-BONE, アハラボネ, 肋骨, *n.* A rib.

ABARA-YA, アハラヤ, 敗宅, *n.* A dilapidated house.

ABARE,*-ru,-ta*, アハレル, 暴亂, *i.v.* To act in a wild, violent, turbulent or destructive manner; to be mischievous, riotous. *Sake ni yotte abareru*, to be drunk and violent. Syn. RAMBŌ SZRU.

ABARE-MONO, アハレモノ, *n.* A riotous mischievous fellow.

ABARI, アハリ, 網針, *n.* A bamboo needle used for making nets.

ABATA, アハタ, 痘斑, *n.* Pock-marks. Syn. JANKO, MITCHA.

ABU

ABATA-DZRA, アハタツラ, 痲臉, *n.* Pock-marked face.

ABAYO, アハヨ, *interj.* Good bye (used only to children.)

ABEKOBE-NI, アベコベニ, *adv.* In a contrary or reversed manner, inside out, upside down. *Hashi wo — motsz*, to hold the chopsticks upside down, *Kimono wo — kiru*, to wear the coat inside out. Syn. ACHI-KOCHI, SAKA-SAMA.

ABI,*-ru,-ta*, アビル, 浴, *t. v.* To bathe by pouring water over one's self. *midz wo —*, to bathe with cold water. *Yu abi wo szru*, to bathe with warm water.

ABI-JIGOKU, アビヂゴク, 阿鼻地獄, *n.* The lowest of the eight hells of the Buddhists.

ABIKO, アビコ, 石龍, *n.* A kind of lizard.

ABISE,*-ru-ta*, アビセル, 潑, *t. v.* To pour water over or bathe another. *H'to ni midz wo abiseru*, to pour water over a person.

ABU, アブ, 虻, *n.* A horse-fly.

ABUKU, アブク, 泡, *n.* Bubbles, froth, foam. *coll.* for *Awa.*

ABUMI, アブミ, 鐙, *n.* A stirrup. *— wo fumbaru*, to stand on the stirrups, (in the manner of the Japanese.)

ABUMI-SHI, アブミシ, 鐙工, *n.* A stirrup-maker.

ABUNAGARI,*-ru-ta*, アブナガル, *i.v.* Timid, fearful, apprehensive of danger. Syn. AYABUMU.

ABUNAI,-KI,-SHI, アブナイ, 浮雲. *a.* Dangerous. *Abunai*, take care. *Abunai koto*, a dangerous thing. Syn. AYAUI, KENNON.

ABUNAKU, or ABUNŌ, アブナク, 浮雲, *adv. idem. Abunaku nai*, no danger.

ABUNASA, アブナサ, 浮雲, *n.* The dangerousness.

ABURA, アブラ, 油, *n.* Oil, grease, fat. — *no shimi*, a grease spot. — *wo tszgu* to pour oil, (into a lamp). — *wo shimeru*, to make oil (by pressing). — *de ageru*, to fry in oil. — *wo sasz*, to oil, (as machinery.)

ABURA-ASHI, アブラアシ, 膩足, *n.* Sweaty feet.

ABURA-DARU, アブラダル, 油樽, *n.* An oil-tub.

ABURA-DE, アブラデ, 膩手, *n.* Sweaty hands.

ABURAGE, アブラゲ, 油煎, *n.* Any thing fried in oil.

ABURA-GIRI, アブラギリ, 荏桐, *n.* The name of a tree from which oil is obtained.

ABURA-GIRI,*–ru,–tta*, アブラギル, 油切, *i.v.* To become oily on the surface, as boiled meat; to be covered with sweat.

ABURA-KASZ, アブラカス, 油枯餅, *n.* Oil-cake, (the refuse after the oil is pressed out.)

ABURA-KAWA, アブラカハ, 膜, *n.* The membrane that encloses the fat.

ABURAKE, アブラケ, 油氣, *n.* Oily, fatty, greasy, (in taste.)

ABURAMI, アブラミ, 膏肉, *n.* The fat or fatty part of flesh.

ABURA-MUSHI, アブラムシ, 滑蟲, *n.* A cockroach.

ABURA-NA, アブラナ, 油菜, *n.* The rape-seed plant.

ABURA-NUKI, アブラヌキ, 油拔, *n.* Any thing that extracts grease.

ABURA-SASHI, アブラサシ, 注子, *n.* An oil-can, (for machinery.)

ABURA-SHIME, アブラシメ, 油搾, *n.* An oil-press.

ABURA-TSZBO, アブラツボ, 油壺, *n.* An oil-jar.

ABURA-TSZGI, アブラツギ, 油釭 *n.* An oil-can, (for filling a lamp.)

ABURAYA, アブラヤ, 油屋, *n.* An oil-store, an oil seller.

ABURA-YE, アブラエ, 油畫, *n.* An oil-painting.

ABURA-ZARA, アブラザラ, 燈盞, *n.* A lamp-cup.

ABURE,*–ru,–ta*, アブレル, 溢, *i.v.* To overflow, to inundate, to cover with numbers. *Kawa ga abureta*, the river has overflown (its banks.) *Sake wo kai ni itta ga abureta.* I went to buy some wine but failed to get it. Syn. KOBORERU.

ABURE-MONO, アブレモノ, 溢者, *n.* A ruffian.

ABURI,*–ru,–tta*, アブル, 烘, *t. v.* To hold or place near a fire in order to warm, dry, roast or toast. *Te wo* —, to warm the hands at a fire.

ABURI-KAWAKASHI,*–sz,–sh'ta*, アブリカハカス, 焙乾, *t.v.* To dry at a fire.

ABURIKO, アブリコ, 焙籠, *n.* A gridiron.

ABURI-KOGASHI,*–sz,–sh'ta*, アブリコガス, 焙灼, *t. v.* To char, scorch, to blacken at the fire.

ABURI-KOROSHI,*–sz,–sh'ta*, アブリコロス, 烘殺, *t.v.* To roast to death, burn at the stake.

ACHI, アチ, 彼地, *adv.* There, that place, — *iki na*, get out of the way.

ACHI-KOCHI, アチコチ, 彼地此地, *adv.* Here and there, all about, more or less. — *wo sagash'te mo miyedz.* I searched all over but could not find it. — *ni san ri arimashō*, it is about three miles. *Fude wo — ni motta*, held the pen upside down.

ACHIRA, アチラ, 彼地. *adv.* There, that place, yonder, (same as *Achi.*) Syn. ASZKO.

ADA, アダ, 仇, *n.* An enemy, adversary, opponent, foe. *Ada szru*, to oppose. — *wo utsz*; — *wo muku*; — *wo kayesz*, to kill an enemy. *Ware ni ada szru mono totemo nikumi-sztszru koto naku*, we should by no means scorn those that oppose us. Syn. TEKI, KATAKI.

ADA-BANA, アダハナ, 徒花. *n.* Blossoms which bear no fruit.

ADA-GATAKI, アダガタキ, 仇敵, *n.* A private enemy.

ADA-GUCHI, アダグチ, 渾口, *n.* Empty trifling or foolish talk.

ADAKAMO, アダカモ, 恰, *adv.* (in comparing or contrasting one thing with another), just. *Tszki no hikari sayaka-ni sh'te adakamo hiru no gotoku*, the moonlight was just as bright as the day. *Adakamo shi-shitaru h'to no yomi-gayerishi gotoku*, just like the coming to life of a dead man. Syn. CHŌDO, SANAGARA.

ADAMEKI,*–ku,–ita*, アダメク, *i.v.* Fond of gayety and pleasure. *Ware wa kore made budō ni kori-katamarite adameku kokoro wa motadz.* I, until this, had been hardened in vice, and had no fondness for gayety.

ADA-NA, アダナ, 虛, *a.* False, empty, vain, deceitful; fleeting, transitory. — *kokoro*, false-hearted. *Tszyu yori mo adanaru inochi*, a life more fleeting than the dew.

ADA-NA, アダナ, 婀娜, *a.* Beautiful, pretty, gay. — *szgata*, beautiful person.

ADA-NA, アダナ, 虛名, *n.* A false name, nick-name.

ADA-NI, アダニ, 虛, *adv.* Falsely, vainly.

ADAPPOI, アダッポイ, *a.* Beautiful, pretty, gay. *Koye ga* —,

†ADASHI, アダシ, 他, *a.* Other, another, foreign. — *gami*, other gods, (not belonging to this country.) — *yo*, another world. — *kuni*, foreign country. — *h'to*, another person. — *kokoro*, falsehearted. Syn. TA, HOKA.

ADAYA, アダヤ, 浮矢, *n.* An arrow that has missed the mark.

ADAYAKA-NA, アダヤカナ, 婀娜, Beautiful.

ADOKENAI,-SHI,-KI, アドケナイ, *a.* Childlike, artless, simple.

ADOKENAKU, アドケナク, *adv. id.*

ADZCHI, アヅチ, 射垜, *n.* A bank of earth against which a target is placed.

ADZKARI,*-ru,-tta*, アヅカル, 預, *i.v.* To receive, to be intrusted with, to have committed to one's care, to take charge of. *Tabi-tabi o-sewa ni adzkari*, have often been favoured with your assistance. *Gochisō ni adzkari katajikenai*, thanks for your entertainment. *Shichiya mono wo adzkarite kane wo kasz*, the pawnbroker lends money on receiving any thing on deposit.

ADZKE,*-ru,-ta*, アヅケル, 預, *t. v.* To commit to the care of another, to entrust. to give in charge, to deposit. *Shichiya ye mono wo adzkete kane wo karu*, to borrow money at the pawnbrokers by depositing something.

ADZKI, アヅキ, 小豆, *n.* A small red bean.

ADZMA, アヅマ, 東, *n.* The eastern states of Japan, same as *K'wantō*.

ADZMAYA, アヅマヤ, 四阿屋, *n.* A shed open on the sides.

ADZSA, アヅサ, 梓, *n.* The name of a tree, the wood of which is used for block-cutting, and making bows.

AFURE,*-ru,-ta*, アフレル, 溢, *i. v.* Same as *Abure,-ru.*

AGAKI,*-ku,-ita*, アガク, 蹀, *i. v.* (comp. of *Ashi*, foot, and *kaku*, to scratch.) To paw with the feet, to gallop; to move the legs as a tortoise when lying on its back. *Mushi ga aomuite agaku*, the beetle lying on its back works its feet. *Agaite mo mogaite mo shiyō ga nai*, with all his pawing there is no help for him.

AGAKI, アガキ, 足掻, *n.* Galloping. *Uma no — wo hayameru*, to make the horse gallop faster.

AGAME,*-ru,-ta*, アガメル, 崇, *t. v.* (*lit.* make high.) To exalt, to adore, to glorify, to honor. *Kami wo* —, to adore the gods. *H'to wo kami ni* —, to exalt a man into a god. Syn. WIYAMAU, TATTOBU.

AGANAI,*-au*, or *ō,-atta*, アガナフ, 贖, *t.v.* To atone for, to make satisfaction for, to compensate, to redeem. *Kane wo motte tszmi wo* —, to make satisfaction for crime with money. *Moshi aganō-bekumba h'to sono mi wo momo ni sen*, people would cut themselves into a hundred pieces to redeem him.

AGARI,*-ru,-tta*, アガル, 上, *i.v.* To ascend, rise, go up. *Yama ni* —, to ascend a hill. *Gakumon ni* —, to advance in learning. *Nedan ga agatta*, the price has gone up. *Iro ga* —, the color is heightened. *Te ga agatta*, has become more expert. *Fune yori agaru*, to land from a boat. *Fushin deki-agatta*, the building is finished. *Tenki ga agatta*, it has cleared off. *O agari nasai*, used in inviting others to come in, to eat, &c. *Sakana ga agatta*, the fish is dead. *Yakume ga agatta*, removed from office, &c. *Shi-agatta*, finished. Syn. NOBORU.

AGARI-BA, アガリハ, 上場, *n.* The floor for standing on coming out of a bath.

AGARI-DAN, アガリダン, 上段, *n.* A ladder, steps. Syn. HASHIGO.

AGARI-GUCHI, アガリグチ, 上口, *n.* The entrance to a flight of steps.

AGARI-SAGARI, アガリサガリ, 上下, *n.* Rise and fall.

AGARI-YA, アガリヤ, 監倉, *n.* A gaol.

†AGATA, アガタ, 縣, *n.* obs. same as *Kori*, the division of a state,=a county.

AGE,*-ru,-ta*, アゲル, 上, *t.v.* To elevate, to raise, to give, to offer in sacrifice, to reckon, to tell, to finish. *Ho wo* —, to hoist a sail. *Koye wo agete yobu*, to call with a loud voice. *Iro wo* —, to heighten the color. *Na wo* —, to be famous. *Fune no ni wo* —, to unload a ship. *Kadz wo* —, to count up, to tell the number. *Shiageru*, to finish doing. *Nuri-ageru*, to finish painting.

AGE,*-ru,-ta*, アゲル, 煎, *t.v.* To fry. *Sakana wo* —, to fry fish.

AGECHI, アゲチ, 止乳, *n.* Weaning a child. — *wo szru.*

AGEGOSHI, アゲゴシ, 轝輿, *n.* A sedan chair raised on poles.

AGEGOTATSZ, アゲゴタツ, 上火閣, *n.* A brazier placed on a stand.

AGEKU-NI, アゲクニ, 上句, *adv.* At last, finally. Syn. SHIMAI-NI.

AGEKU-NO-HATE-NI, アゲクノハテニ, idem.

†AGATSZRAI,*-ō,-ōta*, アゲツラフ, 論, *t. v.* To discuss, to discourse on, to reason on.

AGI, アギ, 阿魏, *n.* Assafœtida.

AGI, or AGOTO, アギ, 顋, *n.* The lower jaw. *Uwa-agi,* the upper-jaw. *Aku riu no agito ni kakaru,* to fall into the jaws of an evil dragon.

AGO, or AGOTA, アゴ, 顋, *n.* The chin, lower jaw,— *ga hadzreru,* the jaw is dislocated. — *wo otosh'te miru,* to stare with open mouth, — *de ashirō,* to motion with the chin. *Amari agota wo tataku-na,* don't talk so much.

AGUMI,*-mu,-nda,* アグム, 楽倦, *i. v.* Tired, wearied, to have one's patience exhausted. *Ano h'to no naga-banashi ni wa agunda,* wearied with his long talking. *Agumi-hateru,* quite tired out. Syn. TAIKUTSZ.

AGURA, アグラ, 箕踞, *n.* Sitting with the legs crossed tailor fashion,—*wo kaku,* to sit cross-legged.

AGURU, アグル, same as *Ageru.*

AHEN, アヘン, 阿片, *n.* Opium.

AHIRU, アヒル, 家鴨, *n.* The domestic duck.

AHŌ, アホウ, 阿呆, *n.* A dunce, fool; foolish, silly. —*wo iu,* to tale foolishness. — *na koto,* a foolish affair. Syn. BAKA, OROKANARU.

AHŌRASHII,–KI,–KU, アホウラシイ, 阿呆敷, Foolish, silly, stupid in manner.

AI, アイ, exclam. used in answering a call. *Ai-ai to henji wo szru.*

AI, アイ, 藍, *n.* The polygonum Tinetorium. used for dying blue, *ai-iro,* blue color, — *de someru,* to dye blue.

†AI, アイ, 哀, (*kanashimu*). Sorrow, sadness, grief. — *wo omō,* to grieve.

AI, アイ, 間, *n.* Interval of time or space, time, during, between. *Ha no ai ni mono ga hasanda,* something is sticking between the teeth. *Tō ai,* present time, now. Syn. AIDA, MA.

AI, *au, atta,* アフ, 逢, *i. v.* To meet, to meet with, encounter, suffer. *To chiu de ame ni atta,* caught in the rain whilst in the way. *Hidoi me ni atta,* met with great abuse.

AI, *au, atta,* アフ, 合, *i. v.* To agree, correspond. accord, suit, fit. *Ki ni au,* to like, to suit one's mind. *Wari fu ga atta.* The seals correspond with each other. *Kono haori wa watakushi ni yoku ai-mas,* this coat fits me nicely.

AI, アヒ, 相, Together, mutual, (used only in compound words; and frequently prefixed to words, in epistolary composition, for elegance or politeness).

AI-AI-NI, アヒアヒニ, 間間, *adv.* At various intervals of time or space.

AI-BAN, アヒハン, 相番, *n.* Same watch, fellow watch-man.

AI-BETSZ, アイベツ, 哀別, Separation or parting at death. — *no kanashimi,* the sorrow of parting at death.

AIBIAI,*-au,-atta,* アイビアフ, 歩合, *t. v.* The same as *Ayumi-ai.*

AI-BIKI, アヒビキ, 相引, *n.* A mutual retreat or withdrawal, a drawn battle or game.

AI-BŌ, アイボウ, 相棒, *n.* A fellow chair-bearer or cooly.

AIBORE,*-ru,-ta,* アヒボレル, 相惚, *i. v.* To be in love with each other.

AIDA, アイダ, 間, *n.* Interval of space or time; time; space; between, while, during; since, as, because. *Yama to yama no* —, between the mountains. *Oya ko no — ga warui,* the parent and child are on bad terms. *H'to toki no* —, the space of one hour. *Ichi ri no* —, the space of a mile. *Szkoshi no* —, a littlewhile. *Kon seki tszmi okuri sōro* —, as the goods were sent this evening, &c. Syn. MA, NAKA.

AIDAGARA, アイダガラ, 間柄, *n.* Relations, connections. Syn. SHINRUI, TSZDZKIAI.

AIDZ, アヒヅ, 相圖, *n.* A signal. — *wo szru,* to make a signal. — *no kata,* a signal flag. — *no teppō,* a signal gun.

AI-DZCHI, アイツチ, 相鎚, *n.* A large sledge-hammer.

AI-DZRI, アイズリ, 藍摺, *n.* Printed with blue figures.

†AI-JAKU, アイヂヤク, 愛著. Love. *Fūfu no* —, conjugal love.

AI-JIRUSHI, アヒジルシ, 合印, *n.* An ensign, banner, badge.

AI-KAGI, アヒカギ, 印鍵, *n.* A false key, a fellow key to the same lock.

AI-KAMAYETE, アヒカマヘテ, 相搆, *adv.* Certainly, positively, by all means. Syn. KESSHITE.

AIKIYŌ, アイキヤウ, 愛敬. That which excites love, lovely, amiable. Syn. KAWAIRASHII.

†AI-KOKU, アイコク, 哀哭, *(Kanashimi naku).* To cry with sorrow.

AI-KOTOBA, アヒコトハ, 合詞, *n.* A signal, (by words or sound,) countersign. — *wo awasz,* to reply to a signal.

AI-KUCHI, アヒクチ, 匕首, *n.* A dirk, dagger.

AI-KUGI, アヒクギ, 合釘, *n.* A nail fixed in the edge of a board to join it with another.

†AI-MIN, アイミン, 哀愍, *(Kanashimi awaremu).* To compassionate.

†AI-MUKAI, *-au,-atta*, アヒムカフ, 相向, *i. v.* To be opposite each other.

AI-MUKAI-NI, アヒムカヒニ, 相向, *adv.* Opposite to each other, face to face.

AI-NEN, アイネン, 愛念, *n.* Love, affection.

AINIKU, アイニク, coll. corruption of *Ayaniku.*

AIRASHII,-KI, アイラシイ, 愛敷, *a.* Lovely, dear, darling, pretty, sweet. Syn. KAWAIRASHII.

†AI-REN, アイレン, 哀憐, Compassion, pity. Syn. FU-BIN, AWAREMI.

AIRO, アイロ, 文色, *n.* (cont. of *aya* and *iro.*) Figure and color. *Teppō no kemuri nite mono no airo mo wakaranu* owing to the smoke of the guns we could not discern any thing. Syn. AYAME.

AIRŌ, アイラフ, 藍蝋, *n.* A blue color, for painting.

AISATSZ, アイサツ, 挨拶, *n.* Salutation; acknowledgment of a favor, an answer. — *szru,* to salute. *Sewa ni natte* — *wo szru,* to pay a visit with a present in acknowledgment of a favor. *Kangayete* — *wo shiro,* when you have thought it over, give me your answer.

AISATSZ-NIN, アイサツニン, 挨拶人, *n.* A peace-maker, a mediator. Syn. ATSZKAI-NIN, CHIU-NIN.

AISHI, アイシ, 愛子, *n.* Beloved child.

AI-SHI, *-szru,-sh'ta*, アイスル, 愛, *t.v.* To love, to regard with affection, as a parent or friend. *H'to wo aiszru mono wa h'to ni aiserareru beshi,* he that loves others shall be loved. Syn. FU-BIN.

AI-SŌ, アイサウ, 愛相, *n.* Hospitable, courteous, or polite treatment of a guest, — *wo szru,* to treat hospitably, — *wo iu,* to welcome, — *mo nai h'to.*

AISŌNAGE-NI, アイサウナゲニ, 無愛相氣 *adv.* In an inhospitable, or unwelcome manner.

AISŌRASHII, アイサウラシイ, 愛相敷, *a.* Kind, welcome or hospitable manner or appearance.

AISŌRASHIKU,-U, アイサウラシク, 愛相敷, *adv. Idem.*

AITA, アイタ, exclamation of pain, = it hurts! it pains!

AITAI,-KI,-KU,-Ō, アイタイ, 逢度. Wish to meet, would like to see. *Watakushi aitai to itte kudasare,* please tell him I wish to see him. *Ano h'to ni yō ga aru kara zehi aitai,* as I have business with him I must see him whether or no.

AITAI, アヒタイ, 相對. Face to face, opposite to each other; between themselves without the presence or intervention of another. — *sh'te sake wo nomu. Aitaijini,* dying together by suicide.

AITAI-GAI, アヒタガイニ, 相互, *n.* Buying goods of each other without the intervention of a third person.

AITAI-NI, アヒタイニ, 相對, *adv.* Privately, by themselves, without the interposition or presence of others.

AITE, アヒテ, 相手, *n.* An opponent, antagonist, adversary, competitor, the other party in any affair. — *wo szru,* to act as an antagonist. — *wo shte kudasare,* join me in a match (game, &c.) *Aite hoshi ya to omō tokoro da.* I was just wishing I had some one to talk to (or to play with.)

AITEDORI, *-ru,-tta*, アヒテドル, 相手取. *t.v.* To accuse, to charge with crime, to criminate, to regard as the responsible person.

AITSZ, アイツ, 彼奴, (cont. of *Ano yatsz*). That low fellow.

AIYAKE, アヒヤケ, 婚姻. The daughter-in-law's or son-in-law's father.

AIYOME, アヒヨメ, 妯娌, *n.* The wives of two brothers.

AIZOME, アイゾメ, 藍染, *n.* Blue-dyed.

AJI, アヂ, 鰺, *n.* The name of a fish.

AJI, アヂ, 味, *n.* Taste, flavor. — *wo miru,* to try the flavor. — *wo tszkeru,* to flavor.

AJIGAMO, アヂガモ, 味鴨, *n.* The name of a wild duck.

†AJIKINAI,-KI,-KU, アヂキナイ, 無情, Unpleasant, unhappy, miserable. *Ajikinaku tszki hi wo okuru,* to pass the time unhappily. *Yo wo ajikinaku omō,* to be weary of the world.

AJINA, アヂナ, 奇怪, *a.* Strange, wonderful, surprising. Syn. AYASHII, HEN-NA.

AJINAI,-KI, アヂナイ, 無味, *a.* Without flavor, tasteless. *Kaze hiite tabemono ga ajinai,* when one has a cold food is tasteless.

AJINAKU, or AJINŌ, アヂナク, *adv. id.*

AJIRO, アジロ, 網代, *n.* A woven work of bamboo ratan or grass.

AJISAI, アヂサイ, 紫陽花, *n.* The Hydrangea.

AJIWAI, アヂハヒ, 味, *n.* Taste, flavor. — *ga yoi;* — *ga warui;* — *ga nai.*

AJIWAI,-Ō,-Ōta, アヂハフ, 味, *t. v.* To taste, fig. to try, examine. *Ajiwōte miru,* to try by tasting.

AKA, アカ, 阿伽, *n.* The water placed by the Buddhists before their idols, and in the hollow places cut in tomb stones. — *kudzru*, to offer up water. (This word is not Japanese, but a Pali word introduced by the Buddhists; its resemblance to theLat. aqua is striking.

AKA, アカ, 淦, *n.* Bilge-water. — *wo kayeru*, to bail out a boat or pump a ship.

AKA, アカ, 垢, *n.* The dirt or grease of the body, the dirt or slime of water. *Yuaka*, the incrustation on the inside of a teapot. — *wo otosz*, to clean off the dirt. — *ga tszita*, dirty.

AKA, アカ, 赤, Red, used only in compounds.

AKADAIKON, アカダイコン, 赤太根, *n.* A beet.

AKA-DAMA, アカダマ, 赤玉, *n.* The name of a secret medicine, made into red pills, and used for pain in the stomach.

AKAGAI, アカガイ, 赤蛤, *n.* The name of a species of red shell-fish.

AKAGANE, アカガ子, 銅, *n.* Copper. Syn. DŌ.

AKAGAO, アカガホ, 赤顔, *n.* A red face.

AKAGARI, アカガリ, *n.* The same as *Akagire.*

AKAGAYERU, アカガヘル 赤蛙, *n.* A species of frog, having a beautifully striped skin.

AKAGASHI, アカガシ, 赤橿, *n.* The name of tree, lit. red-oak.

AKAGIRE, アカギレ, 胝, *n.* Chaps, or cracks on the hands or feet produced by cold. *Te ni — ga dekita*, my hands are chapped.

AKAGO, アカゴ, 赤子, *n.* An infant.

AKAHADAKA, アカハダカ, 赤裸, Naked, bare of clothing, — *ni naru;* — *de soto ye deru*, to go out of the house naked, Syn. SZHADAKA.

AKAHARA, アカハラ, 赤痢, *n.* Dysentery. Syn. RI-BIYŌ.

AKAI,-KI, アカイ, 赤, *a.* Red. *Akai kimono*, red clothes. *Hana ga akai*, the flower is red. *Akai iro*, red color.

AKAJIMITA, アカジミタ, 垢染, *a.* Dirty, soiled. — *kimono*, dirty clothes.

AKAKU, アカク, *adv.* Red. — *szru*, to make red; — *naru*, to become red; — *nai*, it is not red.

AKAMATSZ, アカマツ, 赤松, *n.* Red pine.

AKAMBŌ, アカンボウ, 赤子, *n.* An infant. Syn. MIDORIGO.

AKAME,-*ru*,-*ta*, アカメル, 赤, *t. v.* To make red, to redden. *Kao wo*, to blush.

AKAMI, アカミ, 赤, *n.* A redness, a red color or tinge of red; the lean part of flesh.

AKAMI-DACHI,-*tsz*,-*tta*, アカミダツ, 立赤, *i.v.* To turn or become red, as the leaves or fruit.

AKAMI-WATARI, -*ru*, -*tta*, アカミワタル, 赤渡, *i. v.* To become red all over, as the sky at sunset.

AKANE, アカ子, 茜, *n.* The name of a root used for dyeing red.

AKANU, アカヌ, 不明, neg. of *Aki*, not open, or 不厭, not tired or weary, — *naka*, a delightful friendship. *Rachi ga* —, slow, not expeditious.

AKA-OTOSHI, アカオトシ, 垢落, *n.* Any thing that will cleanse or remove dirt.

AKARAGAO, アカラガホ, 赤顔, *n.* A red face.

AKARAMI,-*mu*,-*nda*, アカラム, 赤, *i.v.* To become red, to redden, to blush. *Kao ga* —, to blush.

AKARA-SAMA-NI, アカラサマニ, 赤地, *adv.* Without concealment or disguise, explicitly, plainly, clearly. — *iu*, to speak &c. Syn. MUKIDASHI.

AKARE,-*ru*,-*ta*, アカレル, 被厭, pass. of *Aki*. To be disliked, loathed.

AKARI, アカリ, 明, *n.* The light, a light. *Mado wo akete — wo toru*, to open the window and let in the light. — *ye deru*, to come to the light. *Mado kara — ga sasz* the light shines in through the window. — *wo tszkeru*, to light a lamp. *Mi no — ga tatsz*, my innocence is cleared up.

AKARISAKI, アカリサキ, 明前, *n.* Before one's light, in one's light. — *ni tatsz*, to stand in one's light.

AKARI-TORI, アカリトリ, 明取, *n.* A window, or any place for letting in light.

AKARŪ, アカルウ, same as *Akaruku.*

AKARUI,-KI, アカルイ, 明, *a.* Light, not dark. — *tokoro*, a light place.

AKARUKU, アカルク, 明, *adv.* Light. — *naru*, to become light, — *szru*, to make light, lighten, — *nai*, not light. *Mi no wiye — szru*, to make clear one's reputation.

AKARUMI, アカルミ, 明, *n.* A light place.

AKARUSA, アカルサ, 明, *n.* The light, the state or degree of light.

AKARUSHI, アカルシ, 明, *a.* It is light.

AKASA, アカサ, 赤, *n.* The redness.

AKASHI, アカシ, 赤, *a.* Red or it is red.

AKASHI,-*sz*,-*sh'ta*, アカス, 明, *t. v.* To declare or make known something concealed, to confess, reveal; to bring to light, to spend the whole night in doing anything, as. *Hon wo yonde yo wo* —, to spend the night in reading. *Naki* —, to cry all night. *Aritei ni* —, to confess the whole truth. *Yo wo akashi-kaneru*, to spend a miserable night.

AKASHI, アカシ, 證, *n.* Proof, evidence. *Furui uta wo hikite — to shi*, cited ancient poetry in proof. Syn. SHŌKO.

AKASZJI, アカスヂ, 赤筋, *n.* Red lines, or veins.

AKATORI, アカトリ, 淦取, *n.* A vessel for bailing a boat.

AKATSZKI, アカツキ, 曉, *n.* The dawn of day. Syn. YOAKE, AKEBONO.

AKE,*-ru,-ta*, アケル, 明, or 開, *t. v.* To open; to empty. *To wo —*, to open a door. *Kuchi wo —*, to open the mouth, *Michi wo —*, to open the way, clear the road. *Iye wo —*, to vacate a house, or to absent one's self from home. *Hako wo —*, to open a box, or to empty a box. *Ana wo —*, to make a hole. *Aida wo —*, to make an opening between. *Yo ga —*, the day has dawned. *Nen ga —*, the years or time of service is finished. *Toshi ga —*, the new year has begun. *Futa wo —*, to take off a lid. Syn. HIRAKU.

AKE, アケ, 朱, *n.* A red color.

AKEBONO, アケボノ, 曙, *n.* Day break, dawn.

AKEGATA, アケガタ, 曙方, idem.

AKE-HANASHI,*-sz,-sh'ta*, アケハナス, 明離, *t. v.* To leave open, *To wo —*, to leave the door open.

AKE-MUTSZ, アケムツ, 曙六, *n.* Six o'-clock in the morning.

AKENI, アケニ, *n.* A trunk, in which such things are kept as are of frequent use in travelling.

AKE-NO-KANE, アケノカネ, 曉鐘, *n.* The morning bell, struck about sunrise.

AKE-TATE, アケタテ, 開閉, *n.* Opening and shutting.

AKI, アキ, 秋, *n.* Autumn, fall.

AKI,*-ku, or kiru, aita*, アク, 飽, or 厭, *i. v.* To eat enough, to be full, satiated, to have enough, to be tired of, wearied. *Aku made taberu*, to eat to satiety. *Mo ki-ki aita.* I have heard enough, or I am tired of hearing. *Sakana ni aku*, to be tired of fish.
Syn. ITŌ, IYA NI NARU.

AKI, アキ, 厭, *n.* Satiety, fullness, enough. *— ga deru*, to get tired of anything. *— ga hayai*, soon weary of.

AKI, *aku, aita*, アク, 開 or 空, *i. v.* To be open, empty, vacant, unoccupied, to begin. *To ga aita*, the door is open. *Iye ga aita*, the house is vacant. *Hako ga aita*, the box is empty. *Akinai no kuchi ga aita*, the sale has commenced. *Me ga aku*, eyes are open. Syn. HIRAKU, KARA.

AKIBITO, アキビト, 商人, *n.* A merchant, trader. Syn. AKINDO.

AKI-CHI, アキチ, 空地, *n.* Vacant ground.

AKI-DANA, アキダナ, 空店, *n.* A vacant shop or house.

AKI-HATE,*-ru,-ta*, アキハテル, 厭果, *i.v.* To be completely satiated or tired of any-thing, disgusted. *Kono shigoto ni aki-hateta*, quite tired of this work.

AKI-IYE, アキイヘ, 空家, *n.* A vacant house.

AKIMEKURA, アキメクラ, 青盲 *n.* Amau-rosis.

AKINAI,*-au,-atta*, アキナフ, 商, *t. v.* To trade in, to traffic, to buy and sell. *Oma-ye wa nani wo akinai-nasaru*, what do you trade in? Syn. BAI-BAI, SHŌBAI SZRU.

AKINAI, アキナヒ, 商, *n.* Trade, traffic, commerce. *— wo szru*, to trade.
Syn. SHŌBAI.

AKINAI-BUNE, アキナヒブネ, 舩商, *(shō-sen,) n.* A merchant-ship.

AKINAI-MONO, アキナヒモノ, 商物, *n.* Merchandize.

AKINDO, アキンド, 商人, *n.* A merchant.

AKIPPOI, アキツポイ, *a.* Easily tired, soon satisfied, fickle.

AKIRAKA, アキラカ, 明. Clear, plain, in-telligent, luminous. *— naru hi*, a clear day.

AKIRAKA-NI, アキラカニ, 明, *adv.* Clearly, distinctly, plainly, evidently, intelligently. *— iu*, to speak plainly.

AKIRAME,*-ru,-ta*, アキラメル, 諦, *t.v.* To clear, to make plain, to understand, to clear, free or relieve the mind of doubt or perplexity, to be resigned or become easy in mind. *Dōri wo —*, to make the truth plain or to understand it. *Shikata ga nai to —*, finding there is no remedy to be resigned. Syn. OMOI-KIRU.

AKIRAME, アキラメ, 諦, *n.* Ease or relief of mind from doubt, perplexity or anxie-ty; resignation, satisfaction. *— no tame ni isha ni mite morau*, to ask a physician to see a patient merely for one's satisfac-tion. *— no warui onna*, a woman who will not be resigned or dismiss a matter from her mind.

AKIRE,*-ru,-ta*, アキレル, *i.v.* To be aston-ished, amazed, to wonder, to be surprised. *Akirete mono ga iwarenu*, not able to speak from astonishment. *Akireta hto*, a won-derful man.
Syn. ODOROKU, BŌZEN.

AKITARI,–*ru*,–*tta*, アキタル 飽足, *i.v.* To be satisfied, to have enough, contented. *Akitaradz*, neg. unsatisfied.

†AKITSZSHIMA, or AKITS-SZ, アキツシマ, 秋津洲, *n.* An ancient name of Japan.

AKIYA, アキヤ, 空屋, *n.* A vacant house.

AKKERAKAN, アツケラカン, *adv.* Yed. coll. In a vacant empty manner, having nothing to occupy one's self with. — *to sh'te hi wo kurasz*, to spend the day in a vacant idle manner.

AKKI, アクキ, 悪鬼, (*ashiki oni*) *n.* Evil spirits.

AKKI, アクキ, 悪氣, *n.* Noxious vapors, miasma.

AKKŌ, アクコウ, 悪口, (*ashiki kuchi,*) *n.* Vile, scurrilous or blackguard language. — *szru*, to blackguard, revile. Syn. NONOSHIRU, ZŌ-GON.

AKŌ, アカウ, 赤, *adv*, contraction of *Akaku*, Red.

AKOGARE,–*ru*,–*ta*, アコガレル, *i. v.* To be fond of, to love, as flowers.

AKOGI-NI, アコギニ, 阿漕, *adv.* In a contumacious manner, persistantly, obstinately. Syn. SHITSZKOI, HITASZRA-NI.

AKU, アク, the adjective or final form of *Aki* 飽 or 開.

AKU, アク, 灰汁, *n.* Lye, also the liquor obtained by slacking lime or steeping any thing in water.

AKU, アク, 悪, (*ashiki,*) *n.* Anything bad, wicked, evil, infamous, atrocious, hellish, malignant, noxious, virulent, foul. — *wo szru*, to commit evil. — *wo korasz*, to punish wickedness. — *ni fukeru*, to increase in evil, (used generally in comp. words as an adjective.)

AKUBI, アクビ, 欠, *n.* Yawning, gaping. — *wo szru*, to yawn, gape.

AKU-BIYŌ, アクビヤウ, 悪病, (*ashiki yamai.*) *n.* A malignant or foul disease.

AKU-CHI, アクチ, 悪血, *n.* Impure blood.

AKUDOI,–KI, アクドイ, *a.*, coll. Gross, coarse, not delicate, not refined, persistent, obstinate. Syn. SHITSZKOI.

AKU-FŪ, アクフウ, 悪風, (*ashiki narawashi,*) *n.* A bad custom.

AKU-GŌ, アクガフ, 悪業, (*ashiki waza,*) *n.* Evil deeds, (Budd.) — *wo tszkurite aku gō no mukui wo ukuru.*

AKU-GIAKU, アクギヤク, 悪逆, *n.* Any thing or person outrageously wicked, atrocious, nefarious, diabolical or impious.

AKU-JI, アクジ, 悪事, (*ashiki koto,*) *n.* A bad affair, wicked thing. — *sen ri*, a bad thing is known a thousand miles.

AKUJITSZ, アクジツ, 悪實, *n.* The seed of the *Gobō*, used as a medicine.

AKU-MA, アクマ, 悪魔, *n.* A demon, devil.

AKU-MIYŌ, アクミヤウ, 悪名, (*ashiki na,*) *n.* A bad name or reputation.

AKU-NEN, アクネン, 悪念, *n.* Evil thought.

AKU-NIN, アクニン, 悪人, (*warui h'to,*) *n.* An exceedingly wicked man.

AKU-RIYŌ, アクリヤウ, 悪靈, *n.* A malicious spirit of a dead person. — *ga toritszku*, possessed by a malicious spirit.

AKU-SŌ, アクサウ, 悪相, *n.* A bad or malicious physiognomy.

AKUTA, アクタ, 芥, *n.* Dirt, litter, filth. Syn. GOMI.

AKU-TAI, アクタイ, 悪體, *n.* Vile, foul, scurrilous language. Syn. AKKŌ.

AKU-TŌ, アクタウ, 悪黨, *n.* An atrociously wicked person or company.

AMA, アマ, 尼, *n.* A buddhist nun.

AMA, アマ, 漁人, *n.* A fisher-woman.

AMA, アマ, 天, *n.* Heaven, the sky, used only in compounds.

AMABOSHI, アマボシ, 甘干, *n.* Sun-dried, without being salted.

AMACHA, アマチヤ, 甘茶, *n.* The name of a sweet infusion, used as a medicine, and for washing the image of Shaka, on the anniversary of his birth.

AMADARI, アマダレ, 霤, *n.* The rain dropping from the eaves.

AMADERA, アマデラ, 尼寺, *n.* A convent or nunnery, (Budd.)

AMADO, アマド, 雨戸, *n.* Rain-door, the outside sliding doors.

AMAGAPPA, アマガツパ, 雨合羽, *n.* A raincoat.

AMAGASA, アマガサ, 雨笠, *n.* A rain hat, or 雨傘, an umbrella.

AMAGAYERU, アマガヘル, 雨蛙, *n.* A tree-frog.

AMAGOI, アマゴヒ, 雨乞, *n.* Prayers and sacrifices offered up, to procure rain.

AMAGU, アマグ, 雨具, *n.* Articles used to protect from rain.

AMAI,–KI, アマイ, 甘, *a.* Sweet. [淡], not enough salt; [弛], loose, not tight; [鈍], soft as metal; foolish. *Satō ga amai*, sugar is sweet. *Shiwo ga* —, there is not enough salt in it. *Nori ga* —, there is not enough starch in it, (clothes.) *Kusabi ga* —, the wedge is loose. *Katana no kane ga* —, the metal of the sword is soft. *Chiye ga* —, has but little wit.

AMAJIWO, アマジホ, 淡鹽, *n.* Slightly salted.

AMAKEDZKI,*-ku,-ita,* アマケツク, 雨氣付, *i. v.* To have the appearance of rain.

AMAKU, アマク, 甘, *adv.* Sweet, see *Amai.* — *szru,* to sweeten. — *nai,* it is not sweet. *Kane ga amakute kire nai,* the metal is so soft it will not cut.

AMA-KUDARI,*-aru,-atta,* アマクダル, 天降, *i. v.* To descend from heaven.

†AMA-MA, アママ, 雨間, *(ame no aida,) n.* Intervals between showers of rain.

AMA-MIDZ, アマミヅ, 雨水, *n.* Rain-water.

AMA-MORI, アマモリ, 雨漏, *n.* A leaking of rain through the roof.

AMA-MOYOI, アマモヨヒ, 雨催, *n.* A gathering of the clouds for rain. — *ga szru.*

AMANAI,*-au,-atta,* アマナフ, 甘, *t. v.* To relish, *ī wo amanawadz,* not to relish food.

AMANEKU, アマネク, 普, *adv.* Every where, universally, all, whole. *Hi wa — sekai wo terasz,* the sun shines over the whole earth. Syn. MAN-BEN-NI.

AMANJI,*-dzru,-jita,* アマンヅル, 甘, *i.v.* To relish, delight in. *Shoku wo —,* to relish food.

AMANOGAWA, アマノガハ, 天漢, *n.* The milky way.

AMA-ŌI, アマオホヒ, 雨覆, *n.* A covering or screen to keep off the rain.

AMARI,*-ru,-tta,* アマル, 餘, *i.v.* To exceed, to be more or greater than, to be beyond or above, to remain over, to be left over. *Toshi wa rokujū ni amaru,* he was more than sixty years old. *Kore dake amatta,* there is so much over, *Te ni amaru,* too strong for, too much for one's strength. *Me ni —,* cannot bear to look at, cannot see patiently. *Ureshisa ga mi ni —,* his happiness was excessive, (lit. too much for his body). Syn. NOKORU, SZGIRU.

AMARI, アマリ, *n.* That which is left over, the remainder, excess. *Danna no — wa watakushi itadakimas,* I receive what my master leaves.

AMARI, アマリ, 餘, *adv.* Very, exceedingly, more than, too, above. — *samui,* very cold. — *tanto,* too much. *Hatszka —,* more than twenty days. — *ōki,* too large. — *omoshiroku mo nai,* not very agreeable. Syn. HANAHADA, SZGI.

AMARI-NA, or AMARI-NO, アマリナ, 餘, *a.* Excessive. — *kurushisa ni koye wo hasszru,* cried out through excessive pain. — *koto wo iu,* to say that which is improper or unjust.

AMASA, アマサ, 甘, *n.* The degree of sweetness, &c., see *Amai.*

AMASHI, アマシ, 甘, *a.* Sweet, see *Amai.*

AMASHI,*-sz,-sh'ta,* アマス, 餘, *t.v.* To let remain, leave over. *Teki wo amasz na,* don't let any of the enemy remain. *Amasadz,* neg. without leaving any.
Syn. NOKOSZ.

AMASŌ-NA, アマサウナ, 甘相, *a.* Having the appearance of being sweet, &c., see *Amai.*

AMASSAE, アマツサヘ, 剰, *adv.* Moreover, besides, still more. Syn. SONO WIYE-NI.

AMATA, アマタ, 數多, *a.* Many, much. — *tabi,* many times. — *no h'to,* a great many persons.
Syn. ŌKU, OBITADASHII, TANTO.

†AMATSZ, アマツ, (comp. of *Ama,* heaven, and obs. gen. suffix, *tsz,* of.) .— *kami,* god of heaven. — *hi,* the sun. — *otome,* angels.

AMAYADORI, アマヤドリ, 雨休, *n.* Shelter from the rain.

AMAYAKASHI,*-sz,-sh'ta,* アマヤカス, *t. v.* To humor, pet or indulge, as a child; to dandle or amuse a child, *Kodomo wo —.*

AMAYE,*-ru,-ta,* アマエル, 嬌, *t. v.* To caress, fondle, to fawn upon in the manner of a child. *Kodomo ga oya ni —,* the child fondles upon its parents.

AMAYO, アマヨ, 雨夜, *n.* A rainy night.

AMAZAKE, アマザケ, 醴, *n.* Sweet *sake,* a kind of fermented rice.

AMBAI, アンバイ, 鹽梅, *n.* The seasoning or taste of food, the state, condition, way, manner. — *wo miru,* to taste or examine into the condition of anything. *Watakushi ambai ga warui,* I do not feel well. *Kiyō wa o — wa ikaga de gozarimas,* how do you feel to day. *Kono sztaji no — ga yoi,* this soup is nicely seasoned. *Kono fude wa ī — ni kakeru,* this pen writes well. *Biyōnin no — wo tadzneru,* to inquire how a sick person is.
Syn. KAGEN, GUWAI, YŌDAI.

AME, アメ, 飴, *n.* A kind of jelly made of wheat flour.

AME, アメ, 天, *n.* The sky, heavens. *Ametszchi* heaven and earth. — *ga sh'ta,* under the heavens, the Empire of Japan.

AME, アメ, 雨, *n.* Rain. — *ga furu,* it rains. — *ga hareta,* the rain has cleared off. — *ga yanda,* the rain has stopped. — *ga kakaru,* to get wet with rain. — *ga furisō da,* it looks like rain.

AME-FURI, アメフリ, 雨降, *(u-ten,) n.* Rainy weather.

AMEUSHI, アメウシ, 黄牛, *n* A yellow haired ox.

AMI, アミ, 網, *n.* A net, net work of any kind. — *no me*, the meshes of a net; — *wo szku*, to make a net; — *wo utsz*, to cast a net. — *wo hiku*, to draw a net; — *wo haru*, to spread a net; — *ni kakaru*, to be taken in a net.

AMI,*-mu,-nda*, アム, 編, *t.v.* To net, or make net work; to weave or bind together with strings; to compose. *Szdari wo* —, to make a bamboo shade. *Shomotsz wo* —, to compose a book.

AMI, アミ, *n.* A small kind of shrimp.

AMI-BA, アミハ, 網場, *n.* A place for drying nets.

AMIDA, アミダ, 阿彌陀, *n.* Buddha.

AMI-DO, アミド, 網戸, *n.* A door made of wire gauze.

AMIGASA, アミガサ, 編笠, *n.* A hat made of bamboo or ratan.

AMI-HIKI, アミヒキ, 網引, *n.* A fisherman.

AMI-JIBAN, アミジハン, 網襦, *n.* A net shirt.

AMMA, アンマ, 按摩, *n.* Shampooing, also a Shampooer. — *wo toru*, to shampoo. — *wo momu*, id. — *ni momaseru*, to be rubbed by a shampooer.

AMMARI, アンマリ, coll. same as *Amari*.

AMMATORI, アンマトリ, 按摩師, *n.* A shampooer. Syn. DŌIN.

AMMIN, アンミン, 安眠, *(yaszku nemuru,)* quiet and sound sleep.

AMMOCHI, アンモチ, 餡餅, *n.* A kind of cake stuffed with beans and sugar.

AMMON, アンモン, 案文, *n.* A first or rough copy. Syn. SH'TAGAKI, SŌKO.

AMPERA, アンペラ, *n.* A kind of chinese matting.

AMPI, アンピ, 安否, *(yaszku inaya,) n.* Whether well or not. — *wo tō*, to inquire after the health of any one or his family. — *wo shiraseru*, to inform as to one's health.

AMPUKU, アンプク, 按腹, *(hara wo momu,)* shampooing or rubbing the abdomen. — *szru.*

AN, アン, 庵, *n.* A small house inhabited by a retired Budd. priest.

AN, アン, 餡, *n.* Minced meat, or a mixture of beans and sugar used for baking in cakes.

AN, アン, 案, *n.* Opinion, thought, expectation. — *no gotoku*, just as was thought or expected. — *ni tagawadz*, not different from what was supposed. — *no hoka*, contrary to one's expectation. — *ni sōi szru*, idem. Syn. OMOI, KANGAYE.

†AN, アン, 安, *(yaszi.)* Freedom from trouble, sickness or calamity, ease, happiness, tranquility, (this word is only used in compounds.)

†AN, アン, 暗, *(yami, kurashi.)* Dark, (only used in compounds.)

ANA, アナ, 阿那, Exclamation of joy, sorrow, surprise, disgust, &c.,=how! oh! — *ureshi ya*, how delightful! — *osoroshi ya*, how fearful! — *ya to bakari sakebu*, could only exclaim, oh!

ANA, アナ, 穴, *n.* A hole, cave, pit, mine. — *wo horu*, to dig a hole. — *wo akeru*, to make a hole. *Fushi-ana*, a knot hole.

ANADORI,*-ru,-tta*, アナドル, 侮, *t.v.* To despise, contemn, scorn; look down upon, disdain. *Shō teki wo anadoru koto nakare*, don't despise a weak enemy. *H'to wo anadoru mono wa h'to ni anadorareru*, (prov.) he that despises others shall be despised. Syn. KARONDZRU, MISAGERU, IYASHIMERU.

ANADORI, アナドリ, 侮, *n.* Contempt, disdain, scorn. Syn. KEIBETSZ.

ANAGACHI-NI, アナガチニ, 强, *adv.* Without right or reason, unreasonably, willfully, stubbornly, obstinately. — *tatakai wo konomadz*, not fond of war merely for the sake of fighting. — *h'to no kokoro wo utagawadz*, must not be unreasonably suspicious of others.
Syn. SHITE, MURI-NI.

ANAGO, アナゴ, 海鰻, *n.* A species of eel.

ANA-GURA, アナグラ, 窨, *n.* A cellar or store-house underground.

ANAJI, アナジ, 牝痔, *n.* Fistula in ano.

†ANAKASH'KO, アナカシコ, 穴賢, Exclam. of fear, deep respect or admiration, used mostly at the close of a letter or a Budd. sermon.

ANATA, アナタ, 彼方, (cont. of *ano* and *kata.)* That side, there; you, (respectful). *Kawa no — ni*, on that or the other side of the river. — *konata*, here and there; both sides. — *doko ye*, where are you going. Syn. ATCHI, ACHIRA, OMAYE.

ANATAGATA, アナタガタ, plural of *Anata*, You, (respectful).

ANCHI, アンチ, 安置, *(Yasznji oku,)* — *szru*, to place an idol in a temple.

†ANDARA, アンダラ, *n.* Nonsense, foolishness. *Nani wo — tszkusz zo ye*, what nonsense are you saying?

ANDO, アンド, 安堵. Ease, happiness, tranquility, freedom from care or trouble. *Chichi haha no kokoro wo — saseru wo*

dai ichi to sz, it should be our principal care to make our parents happy.
Syn. OSHITSZKU.

ANDON, アンド, 行燈, *n.* A lamp.

ANDZ, アンズ, 杏子, *n.* Apricot.

ANE, アネ, 姊, *n.* Older sister.

ANE-BUN, アネブン, 義姊, *n.* One who acts the part of an older sister.

ANEGO, アネゴ, *n.* Sister; used by common people in familiarly addressing a woman.

ANE-MUKO, アネムコ, 姊壻, *n.* Older sister's husband, brother in law.

ANE-MUSZME, アネムスメ, 長女, *n.* The eldest daughter.

ANGA, アンガ, 晏駕, *n.* The death of the Mikado. Syn. HŌ-GIYO.

ANGIYA, アンギヤ, 行脚, *n.* Strolling, going about on foot, (as priests, musicians, &c.) — *szru*, to stroll or go about on foot. Syn. YŪ-REKI.

AN-G'WAI, アングワイ, 案外, *(omoi no hoka)* Contrary to expectation, unexpectedly. — *hayaku dekita*, done sooner than I expected. Syn. ZONG'WAI, AN-NO-HOKA.

ANI, アニ, 豈, exclam. always at the beginning of a sentence ending in *ya*. *Ani hakaran ya*, how unexpected!
Syn. IKADEKA.

ANI, アニ, 兄, *n.* Older brother.

ANI-BUN, アニブン, 義兄, *n.* One who acts the part of an older brother.

ANI-DESHI, アニデシ, 兄弟子, *n.* Older pupils.

ANIGO, アニゴ, *n.* Brother, used in familiar address to another.

ANIKI, アニキ, 兄, *n.* An older brother.

†AN-ITSZ, アンイツ, 安佚, *(kimama,)* *n.* Living at ease, without the necessity of work.

ANI-YOME, アニヨメ, 嫂, *n.* Older brother's wife, or sister in law.

†AN-JAKU, アンジヤク, 暗弱, *(kuraku yowashi.)* Imbecile, idiotic. — *nite katoku ni tatadz.*

ANJI, *-jiru*, or *dzru,-jita*, アンジル, 案, *i. v.* To think anxiously about, to be anxious, concerned. *Anjiru yori umu ga yaszi*, (prov.) a labor is less painful than the anxiety about it. *Oya ga ko wo anjiru*, parents are anxious about their children. Syn. KURŌ SZRU, SHIMPAI SZRU.

ANJI, アンジ, 案, *n.* An invention, contrivance, anxiety.

ANJI-DASHI, *-sz,-sh'ta*, アンジダス, 案出, *t. v.* To call to mind, to suddenly recollect. To plan, invent, to contrive, to excogitate. Syn. OMOI-DASZ.

ANJI-KURASHI, *-sz,-sh'ta*, アンジクラス, 案暮, *t. v.* To live in constant anxiety.

ANJI-MEGURASHI, *-sz,-sh'ta*, アンジメグラス, 案廻, *t. v.* To ponder anxiously about.

ANJITSZ, アンジツ, 庵室, *n* A small Budd. temple, or dwelling of a priest.

ANJI-WABI, *-ru,-ta*, アンジワビル, 案侘, *t. v.* To be anxious and distressed about.

ANJI-WADZRAI, *-au,-atta*, アンジワヅラフ, 案煩, *t. v.* To be painfully anxious about. *Ikaga sen to anji-wadzrau.*

ANJU, アンジユ, 安住, *(yaszku szmau)* Living in safety or free from trouble or calamity.

ANKAN, アンカン, 安閑, Free from business, without working. — *to sh'te hi wo kurasz*, to live as a man of leisure.

†ANKI, アンキ, 安危, *(yaszki, ayauki,)* *n.* Safety or danger, existence or ruin. *Kuni no — kono h'to ikusa ni kakaru*, the safety of the country depends on this battle.

ANKI, アンキ, 安氣, *n.* Peace or tranquility of mind, happiness.

†AN-KIYO, アンキヨ, 安居, *(yaszku oru.)* Living in ease, free from trouble.

†AN-KŌ, アンカウ, 安康, Free from trouble or calamity. Syn. BUJI.

ANNA, アンナ, (contr. of *Ano* and *Yō-na,*) *a.* That kind, manner or way; such.

AN-NAI, アンナイ, 案內, *n* Knocking at a door, or calling out *tanomō*, for admittance. Sending word or a messenger; to call a person to come, or show him the way. The way, the roads or natural features of a country; the streets and peculiar arrangement of a city or town; the inside arrangement of a castle or house. — *wo iu* or — *wo kō*, to call out for admittance. — *ga aru*, there is some one at the door. — *wo shiru*, to know the road or way, &c. — *wo szru*, to guide or show the way.

ANNAIJA, アンナイジヤ, 案內者, *n.* A guide, one acquainted with the roads or natural features of a country or place.

†AN-NEI, アンネイ, 安寧. *(Yaszku yaszshi,)* *n.* Tranquility, case, freedom from sickness, trouble or calamity.

AN-NON, アンオン, 安穩, *(Yaszku odayaka,)* peace, ease, quietness, freedom from danger or disturbance, safety. Syn. BUJI.

ANO, アノ, 彼, (comp. of *a* and *no,*) *a.* That. — *h'to*, that man, he. — *tōri*. that way. Son. KANO.

AN-RAKU, アンラク, 安樂, same as *Annon.*

AN-SHIN, アンシン, 安心, (*Yaszki kokoro,*) *n.* A mind free from care, anxiety or trouble; composure, ease, tranquility. Syn. ANDO.

†AN-SHŌ, アンシヨウ, 暗誦, Reciting from memory. Syn. SORANDZRU, CHIU DE YOMU,

†AN-SOKU, アンソク, 安息, Rest, ceasing from labor. -- *szru,* to rest. — *nichi,* a day of rest, sabbath-day. Syn. KIU-SOKU, YASZMU, IKŌ.

†AN-TAI, アンタイ, 安泰, *n.* same as *An-kō.*

ANZAN, アンザン, 安産, (*Yaszku umu,*) *n.* An easy or natural labor, — *szru.*

†AN-ZEN, アンゼン, 安全, (*Yaszku mattashi.*) Completely safe, free from all evil or harm; perfect peace and tranquility.

AO, アヲ, 青, Light green or sky blue, used only in compounds.

AOBA, アヲハ, 青葉, *n.* Green leaves.

AOBAI, アヲハイ, 青蠅, *n.* The blue-bottle fly.

AOBANA, アヲハナ, 青涕, *n.* A snotty nose. — *wo tareru.*

AOCHA, アヲチヤ, 青茶, *n.* A yellowish green color,

AODZKE, アヲヅケ, 青漬, *n.* Green plums pickled in salt.

AOGI,*-gu,-ida,* アフグ, 扇, *t.v.* To fan, to winnow. *Ōgi de aogu,* to fan with a fan. *Mugi wo* —, to fan wheat.

AOGI,*-gu,-ida,* アフグ, 仰, *t. v.* To look upwards, to turn the face upwards, to assume the attitude of veneration and supplication. *Ten wo* —, to look upwards at the sky. *Aogi-fusz,* to lie with the face turned upward. *Aogi-negau,* to supplicate with deep veneration. *Aogi-miru,* to look up at.

AOGI-NEGAWAKUBA, アフギネガハクハ, 仰願, *adv.* Most respectfully pray that.

AOGI-TATE,*-ru,-ta,* アフギタテル, 扇立, *t. v.* To fan. *Hi wo* —, to kindle fire by fanning.

AOHIKI, アヲヒキ, 青蟇, *n.* A small green, frog.

AOI, or AOKI, アヲイ, 青, *a.* Light green or blue; green, unripe, immature, inexperienced. *Aoi budō,* green grapes. — *koto wo iu,* to say something silly.

AOI, アフヒ, 葵, *n.* The holly-hock.

AOKU, アヲク, 青, *adv.* Green, see *Aoi.* — *naru,* to become green; — *szru,* to make green; — *miyeru,* to look green.

AOMI, アヲミ, 青, *n.* A tinge or shade of green, the green.

AOMI,*-mu,-nda,* アヲム, 青, *i. v.* To become green.

AOMI-DACHI,*-tsz,-tta,* アヲミダツ, 青立, *i. v.* To appear, or look green.

AOMUKI,*-ku,-ita,* アヲムク, 仰向, *i. v.* To turn the face upwards. *Aomuite hoshi wo miru,* to look up at the stars. *Aomuite neru,* to lie on the back.

AONA, アヲナ, 菁, *n.* Greens.

AONOKI,*-ku,-ita,* アヲノク, *i.v.* The same as *Aomuku.*

AORI, アフリ, 障泥, *n.* The flaps of a saddle. The fan used for winnowing grain.

AORI,*-ru,-tta,* アフル, *i. v.* To flap as any thing broad or loose in the wind, to slam to swing in the wind, as a door, shutter' &c., (*t. v.*) To flap, or beat with a flap., *To ga aoru,* the door slams. *Uma wo* —, to beat a horse by striking the stirrups against the saddle flaps. *Hi ni aorarete yane kara ochiru,* struck by the flame he fell from the roof.

AORI, アフリ, *n.* The blast of wind made by the flapping or slamming of any thing. — *wo kū,* to be struck by a sudden blast, as of a falling house.

AOSA, アヲサ, 青, *n.* The greenness.

AOSA, アヲサ, 陟釐, *n.* Seaweed, used for manure.

AOSHI, アヲシ, 青, *a.* Green, see *Aoi.*

AOSORA, アヲソラ, 青空, The sky.

AOSZJI, アヲスヂ, 青筋, *n.* The blue veins of the temples.

AOTA, アヲタ, 青田, *n.* The green paddy-fields, A dead-head, one who enters theatres and shows without paying. Syn. DEMBŌ.

AOTO, アヲト, 青砥, *n.* A kind of green stone, used for whetstones.

AOUMA, アヲウマ, 青馬, *n.* A black-horse.

†AOUNABARA, アヲウナハラ, 滄溟, *n.* The deep blue sea.

AOYAGI, アヲヤギ, 青柳, *n.* The willow. Syn. YANAGI.

AOZAME,*-ru,-ta,* アヲザメル, 青醒, *i. v.* to become livid. *Iro aozamete miyeru,* he became of a livid color.

APPARE, アツパレ, 憐, (same as *aware,*) exclam. of surprise and admiration. — *sayetaru o te no uchi,* what a splendid blow!

ARA, アラ, 骨, *n.* The bones of fish or fowl. — *wa inu ni yare,* gives the bones to the dog. Syn. HONE.

ARA, アラ, 新, (*shin,*) New. — *ka furu ka,* is it new or old? — *wa takai,* the new is dear.

ARA, アラ, 嗚呼, Exclam. of joy, fear, surprise, &c., same as *Ana.* — *osoroshii ya,* how dreadful!

Ara, アラ, 粗, *a.* Coarse, rough, crude, unwrought, unpolished, (used only in compounds.)

Ara-ara, アラアラ, 粗粗, *adv.* Coarsely, roughly, briefly, summarily, not minutely particularly or neatly, not with care or attention. Syn. ZATTO, SOMATSZ-NI.

Ara-arashii,-ki, アラアラシイ, 猛, or 粗, *a.* Coarse, rough, rude, harsh, violent, boisterous, fierce, vehement, ferocious, tempestuous. *Ara-arashiku, adv.* Syn. TAKESHII, HAGESHII.

Araba, アラハ, sub-mood of *Ari*, same as *Areba.* If I have, if there is.

Aradachi,-*tsz,-tta*, アラタツ, 荒立, *i. v.* To become enraged, exasperated, irritated. *Jin-ki ga* —, the people are exasperated. Syn. IKARU, HARA GA TATSZ.

Aradate,-*ru,-ta*, アラダテル, 荒立, *t. v.* To irritate, to exasperate, excite to anger. Syn. IKARASERU, HARA WO TATESASERU.

Arade, アラデ, (comp. of *Ari* and neg. gerund. suff. *de*,)=by the not having, if there is not. — *kanawanu*, cannot do without. *Anata ni — hoka ni szru h'to wa nai*, if you can't do it nobody else can.

Aradz, アラズ, 非, neg. of *Ari*, is not. *Ano h'to wa tszne-bito ni aradz*, he is not a common man.

Aradzmba, アラズンハ, (comp. of *Ari* and *wa*, with *m* euphonic), neg. subj. of *Ari*, if I have not, if there is not, same as *Arade*, or *nakereba*.

Ara-dzmori, アラヅモリ, 荒積, *n.* A rough estimate.

Aragai,-*au,-tta*, アラガフ, *t. v.* To irritate, to provoke, to tease. *Kodomo ni* —, to tease a child. Syn. IKARASERU.

Aragane, アラガ子, 荒金, *n.* Crude metal, ore.

Aragawa, アラガハ, 荒皮, *n.* A raw hide, undressed skin.

Ara-giyō, アラギヤウ, 荒行, *n.* Religious austerities.

Aragome, アラゴメ, 荒米, *n.* Uncleaned rice.

Arai, or **Araki**, アライ, 荒, Coarse in texture size or quality, rough, not smooth; harsh, rude, wild, boisterous, tempestuous, violent, *ji no arai kinu*, silk of coarse texture. *Ki no arai h'to*, a man of violent temper. *Nami ga* —, the sea is rough. *Kaze ga* —, the wind is strong. *Tszbu ga* —, the grains are coarse. *Hada ga* —, the skin or surface of any thing is rough.

Arai,-*au,-atta*, アラフ, 洗, *t.v.* To wash, to cleanse. *Te wo* —, to wash the hands. *Cha-wan wo araye*, wash the cups. *Kokoro wo* —, to cleanse the heart. *Kimono wo* —, to wash clothes. Syn. SZSZGU, SENTAKU SZRU.

Arai, アラヒ, 洗, *n.* The washing. *Kono kimono no — ga warui*, these clothes are badly washed.

Arai-guszri, アラヒグスリ, 洗薬, *n.* A medical wash.

Araiko, アラヒコ, 洗粉, *n.* A washing powder made of beans.

Arai-otoshi,-*sz,-sh'ta*, アラヒヲトス, 洗落, *t. v.* To wash out. *Shimi wo* —, to wash out a stain.

Arai-tade,-*ru,-ta*, アラヒタデル, *t. v.* To cleanse the bottom of a ship by burning and washing.

Arai-yone, アラヒヨ子, 洗米, *(semmai,) n.* Washed rice offered to idols.

Araji, アラジ, (comp. of *Ari* and fut. or dub. neg. suff. *ji.*) I think it is not, or I doubt whether it is.=coll. *Arumai*, or *Nakarō*.

Arakajime, アラカジメ, 豫, *adv.* Beforehand; summarily, in a general way; not particularly or minutely. — *yōi wo sh'te oku*, to make preparation beforehand. — *mi-tszmoru*, to make a rough estimate. Syn. MAYEMOTTE, TAI-RIYAKU.

Ara-kasegi, アラカセギ, *n.* Rough or coarse work.

Ara-kata, アラカタ, 荒方, *adv.* For the most part, in the main, mostly, generally. — *dekita*, mostly finished. Syn. TAIGAI, TAI-RIYAKU, TAI-TEI.

Arakenai, or **Arakenashi**, アラケナイ, 荒氣, *a.* Rough in temper, savage, cruel, churlish. — *h'to.*

Arakenaku, アラケナク, *adv.* id.

†**Aramahoshii**, or **Aramahoshiki**, アラマホシイ, *a.* That which one desires or longs for. — *ku, adv.*

Aramashi, アラマシ, *adv.* For the most part, in the main, mostly, generally, not minutely. *Fushin ga— dekita*, the building is mainly finished. Syn. TAI-TEI, ARA-KATA.

Arame, アラメ, 荒布, *n.* A kind of edible seaweed.

†**Arame**, アラメ, same as *Aran*, or coll. *aru de arō*, I think it is, I think there are.

Arami, アラミ, 新刀, *n.* An unfinished sword-blade.

Aramomi, アラモミ, 糲, *n.* Rice with the hulls on.

Ara-mono, アラモノ, 荒物, *n.* Coarse-wares, a general term for such things as wood, charcoal, brooms, clogs, &c.

Aran, アラン, fut. of *Ari*,=*Arô* of the coll. Will be, or would be. *Kaku aran to omoishi yuye*, because I thought it would be so. *Inochi no aran kagiri tatakau*, to fight as long as there is life.

Aranami, アラナミ, 荒波, *n.* Rough sea, boisterous waves.

†**Araneba**, アラネハ, (comp. of *aranu* and *wa*,) neg. subj of *Ari*, if there be not.= coll. *nakereba.*

†**Aranu**, アラヌ, 不有, neg. of *Ari*. — *koto wo iu*, to say what is not so.

Araraka-ni, アララカニ, 荒, *adv.* Roughly, rudely, harshly.

Arare, アラレ, 霰, *n.* Snow falling in round pellets. — *ga furu.*

†**Ararenu**, アラレヌ, neg. pot. of *Ari*. Cannot be. *Arare mo nai*, idem.

Arasa, アラサ, *n.* The coarseness, roughness, see *Arai.*

Arase,*-ru*,*-ta*, アラセル, 令有, caust. of *Ari*. To cause to be or exist.

†**Araserare**,*-ru*,*-ta*, アラセラレル, *i. v.* The same as *ari*, *aru*, *atta*, but used only of the most exalted persons. *Go buji ni araserare sôrô ya*, are you well?

†**Arashi**, アラシ, 荒, *a.* see *Arai.*

Arashi,*-sz*,*-sh'ta*, アラス, 荒, *t. v.* To spoil, ruin or injure by violence, to lay waste, destroy; to let go to ruin. *Inoshishi ga hatake wo* —, the wild hogs spoil the wheat fields.

Arashi, アラシ, 嵐, *n.* A tempest, storm.

Arashime,*-ru*, アラシメル, 令有, caust. and honorific of *Ari*. To cause or order to be or exist. *Kami wa arayuru mono wo* —. God caused all things to exist.

Arasoi,*-ō*,*-ōta*, アラソフ, 争, *t.v.* To contend, to strive or compete, to dispute about, to wrangle, quarrel. *Shōbu wo* —, to contend for victory. *Dōri wo* —, to dispute about the truth.

Arasoi, アラソヒ, 争, *n.* A dispute, contention, debate, wrangling. — *wo okosz*, to raise a dispute.

Arasoitagari,*-ru*,*-tta*, アラソヒタガル, *i.v.* (comp. of *Arasoi*, *taku* and *ari*.) To be fond of disputing or argument; contentious; disputatious.

†**Aratama**, アラタマ, 璞, *n.* An unpolished gem. — *no toshi*, the year.

Aratamari,*-ru*,*-tta*, アラタマル, 改, *i.v.* To be amended, overhauled, corrected, reformed, altered, changed to something better. *Nengō ga* —, the name of the year is changed. *Okite ga* —, the statutes are amended. Sny. KAWARU.

Aratame,*-ru*,*-ta*, アラタメル, 改, *t.v.* To amend, alter, change, make better, to improve, reform, to examine, inspect, overhaul. *Kokoro wo* —, to reform the heart. *Okonai wo* —, to amend the conduct. *Okite wo* —, to amend the laws. *Nimotsz wo* —, to inspect goods. *Chōmen wo* —, to examine an account book. *Na wo* —, to change the name.
Syn. KAYERU, SHIRABERU, GIMMI-SZRU.

Aratame, アラタメ 改, *n.* Examination, inspection. — *wo ukeru.* Syn. GIMMI, SHIRABE.

Aratamete, アタラメテ, 改而, *adv.* Especially, particularly. Syn. BETSZDAN-NI.

Arata-na, アラタナ, 新, *a.* New. — *iye*, a new house.

Arata-na, アラタナ, 奇驗, *a.* Wonderful in hearing prayer, or fearful in power, (used only in praying to Hotoke or Kami). — *go riyaku*, thy wonderful grace.

Arata-ni, アラタニ, 新, *adv.* Anew, newly, in a new manner.

Arate, アラテ, 新手, *n.* Fresh troops, a fresh hand. — *wo ire-kayeru*, to bring up fresh troops, in place of those exhausted.

Arato, アラト, 礪石, *n.* A coarse kind of whetstone.

Arawa-ni, アラハニ, 陽, *adv.* Openly, publicly. *Kakush'te mo* — *shirete oru*, you may try to conceal it but it is publicly known. — *iwarenu koto*, a thing which should not be openly talked about.

Araware,*-ru*,*-ta*, アラハレル, 顯, *i.v.* To be seen, to appear, to be manifest, visible; to be known, to be discovered, revealed. *Kurō ga kao ni* —, his trouble showed itself in his face. *Muhon ga* —, the conspiracy became known. *Kiri ga harete yama ga* —, the fog having cleared off the mountain is visible.

Arawase,*-ru*,*-ta*, アラハセル, 令洗, caust. of *Arai*. To make, order or let wash. *Te wo* —, to make a person wash his hands.

Arawashi,*-sz*,*-sh'ta*, アラハス, 著, *i. v.* To make to appear, cause to be seen, to display, disclose, manifest, to show, make known, reveal, declare, publish. *Ikari wo kao ni* —, to show anger in the countenance. *Makoto wo* —, to declare the truth. *Hon wo* —, to publish a book.
Syn. MISERU.

ARAYURU, アラユル, 所有, *a.* That which is, existing. — *mono,* all things that are. *ari to — mono mina ningen wo yashinau mono da,* all things conduce to the good of man.

ARAZARU, アラザル, 非, neg. adj. of *Ari.*

ARE, アレ, Exclam. in calling to another, or to draw attention. *Are, machina-yo,* hollo! wait a little.

ARE, アレ, 彼, *pro.* That. *Are wa nani,* what is that? *Are hodo,* that much. *Are wa dare no iye,* whose house is that?

†ARE, アレ, imp. of *Ari.* Be it, whether, *Oide are,* come here. *Kaku* —, so be it. *H'to ni mo are kedamono ni mo are mina kami no tszkutta mono,* whether man or animals all were made by God.

ARE,*–ru,–ta,* アレル, 荒, *i. v.* To be spoiled, ruined, laid waste, to be savage, ferocious, raging, tempestuous, stormy. *Ta ga kōdzi de areta,* the rice-fields were spoiled by the inundation. *Teoi sh'ka ga* —, the wounded stag is savage. *Umi ga* —, the sea is stormy. *Den-ji ga* —, the fields are waste.

ARE, アレ, 荒, *n.* A storm, tempest.

AREBA. アレバ, conj. of *Ari,* if there is, if he has.

ARE-CHI, アレチ, 荒地, *n.* Waste land.

AREDOMO, アレドモ, conj. mo. of *Ari.* Although there is.

†AREGASHI, アレガシ, (comp. of *Are,* imp. of *Ari,* and *Kashi.*) Be I pray you, I wish that. *Oya ni kō-kō aregashi,* I pray you be obedient to your parents. *On yurushi* —, I pray you pardon me.

ARI, アリ, *n.* A dove-tailed joint.

ARI, アリ, 蟻, *n.* An ant.

ARI, *aru, atta,* アル, 有, *i. v.* To be, to have, to exist. *Aru ka nai ka wakari masen,* I dont know whether there is or not; or, whether he has or not. *Kono koto hon ni aru,* this is in a book. *Sekai ni aru mono,* the things that are in the world. *Atta ka,* have you found it? or got it? *Atte mo yoi,* it is well to have it. *Kono sakana wa doku ga aru* this fish is poisonous, (lit. has poison in it.) *Kuwashiku kaite aru,* it is minutely written.

ARIAI,*–au,–atta,* アリアフ, 有合, *i.v.* To happen to be present, happen to have at hand. *Sono ba ni ariatte kīta,* happening to be at that place I heard it. *Soba ni ariō bō wo totte butta,* seizing a stick which happened to be near, I struck.

ARI-AKE, アリアケ, 有明, *n.* Lasting all night. — *no tszki,* a moon which shines all night. — *no ando,* a lamp which burns all night.

ARI-ARI-TO, アリアリト, 有有, *adv.* Just as it was or is, plainly, distinctly. *Yūrei ga — miyeta,* the ghost was distinctly visible.

ARI-AWASE,*–ru,–ta,* アリアハセル, 在合, *t. v.* same as *Ariai.*

ARI-DAKE, アリダケ, 有丈, *n.* All there is. — *motteyuke,* bring all there is.

ARI-DOKORO, アリドコロ, 在所, *n.* The place where anything is. — *ga shirenu,* don't know where it is.

ARI-FURE,*–ru,–ta,* アリフレル, 在舊, *t. v.* To be common, usual, ordinary, customary. *Ari-fureta tōri ni szru,* do it in the customary way. *Ari-fureta mono,* a common thing.

ARIGATAI,-KI, アリガタイ, 有難, (comp. of *Ari,* to be, and *katai,* difficult,) *a.* Difficult or hard to do; rare and excellent; exciting feelings of admiration, praise and thankfulness; grateful, thankful. *Tayaszku shime-otosz koto arigatashi,* to attack and take it (castle) will not be easy. *Yo ni arigataki on h'to,* a person whose like, for estimable qualities, is seldom seen in this world. *Arigatai koto wo shiranu,* devoid of gratitude. *Jōdo no arigataki,* the bliss of paradise. Syn. KATAJIKENAI.

ARIGATAGARI,*–ru,–tta,* アリガタガル, 有難, *i.v.* Grateful, thankful, or fond of expressing thanks.

ARIGATAKU, アリガタク, 有難, *adv.* Thankful, grateful. — *omō,* to feel grateful; — *naru,* to become grateful.

ARIGATASA, アリガタサ, 有難, *n.* The state or degree of gratitude, also things to be thankful for, favors, blessings, benefactions.

ARIGATŌ, アリガタウ, 有難, *adv.* I thank you. — *zonjimas,* or — *gozarimas,* id.

ARI-GIRI, アリギリ, 有切, *n.* All there is, the whole. *Kono abura — de gozarimas,* this is all the oil there is.

ARI-KA, アリカ, 在處, *n.* The place where any thing is. — *ga shiremasen,* dont know where it, he, or she, is.

†ARIKI,*–ku,* アリク, 歩行, *i. v.* To walk, to go, same as *Aruku.*

ARI-KITARI, アリキタリ, 在來, *a.* Something which has come down from ancient times, old, ancient, antique. *Arikitari no tōri,* antique style. *Arikitatta mono.*

ARI-MASZ, アリマス, (comp. of *Ari* and honorific *masz,*) same as *aru.* To be, to have. *Arimash'ta,* pret, have got or have found. *Arimasen,* neg. have not or is not. *Arimaszmai,* I think there is not, or has not, or will not.

ARI-NO-MAMA, アリノママ, 在儘, *n.* Just as it is; truly, without concealment. —*ni sh'ta oku*, let them be just as they are. —*ni hanasz*, to state or tell truly.

ARINOTOWATARI, アリノトワタリ, 會陰, *n.* The perinæum.

ARI-SAMA, アリサマ, 在様, *n.* The state, condition, circumstances, case.
Syn. YŌ-SZ, YŌ-DAI.

ARI-SHO, アリシヨ, 在所, *n.* The place in which any thing is. *Kataki no — ga shireta*, enemy's whereabouts is known.

ARI-SŌ, アリサウ, 有想, Appears to be or to have, looks as if there is. *Ano h'to kane ga* —, he appears to have money. — *na mon da*, I think it must be so. *Biyō ki no — na onna*, a sickly looking woman.

ARITAI, -KI, -SHI, アリタイ, 有度, *a.* Wish to be. *Sō aritai mono da*, I wish it were so. *Kotaru mono wa oya ni kōkō aritaki mono*, I wish that all children were obedient to their parents.

ARITEI, アリテイ, 在躰, *n.* The truth or real facts of the case, the circumstances just as they are. — *ni iu*, to tell the whole truth.

ARITSZKE, -*ru*, -*ta*, アリツケル, 在付, *t. v.* To settle a person in a place of service or business; to settle a daughter in marriage. *Yō-yaku muszme wo aritszketa*, have at length married off my daughter.

ARITSZKI, -*ku*, -*itta*, アリツク, 在付, *i. v.* To be settled in a place of service, to find a situation, to be married, (of a daughter.) *Hōkō ni aritszita*, settled in a place (as a servant.)

ARI-YŌ, アリヤウ, 在様, *n.* The true state of the case, all the circumstances, the facts. — *wo iu*, to tell, &c.

ARIZASHI, アリザシ, *n.* Dove-tailed, (in joinery.)

ARŌ, アラウ, (cont. of *Araku*,) *adv.* Coarse, rough, see *Arai*.

ARŌ, アラウ, coll. fut. or dub. of *Ari*, same as *Aran*. Will be, I think it will, I think it is or there is. *Ame ga furu de arō*, I think it will rain. *Sō de arō*, I think it is so. *Kono sake wa nai ga dōsh'ta de arō*, I wonder how it is this *sake* is all gone. *H'to ga nonda de arō*, I expect somebody has drunk it.

ARU, アル, 有, adj. and fin. form of *Ari*. To be, to have; a certain, some. *Aru h'to*, there was a man, or some men. *Aru-toki*, some times. *Aru tokoro ni*, in a certain place. *Aru ni mo ararenu omoi wo szru*, could not feel that it was so. *Moshi aru nara mise-nasare*, if you have it let us see it.

ARU-HEI-TŌ, アルヘイタウ, 有平糖, *n.* A kind of confectionary.

ARUIWA, アルイハ, 或, *adv.* Or, either, some, others; and; *Aruiwa uma ni nori — kago ni notte yuka*, some rode on horses, others went in chairs.

ARUJI, アルジ, 主人, (*shujin*,) *n.* Lord, master, landlord, owner. *Chiu-ji wo — to szru*, to make fidelity the principal thing.
Syn. NUSHI.

ARUKI, -*ku*, -*ita*, アルク, 歩行, *i. v.* To walk. *Aruite kuru*, to come on foot. *Kago de* —, to go by chair. Syn. AYUMU.

ASA, アサ, 麻, *n.* Hemp.

ASA, アサ, 朝, *n.* Morning, before 10 o'clock A.M. *Asa hayaku*, early in the morning. — *no uchi*, during the morning. *Asa osoku*, late in the morning.

ASA, アサ, 淺, Shallow, (used only in compounds.)

ASA-ASASHII, or ASA-ASASHIKI, アサアサシイ, 淺淺敷, *a.* Shallow, not deep, superficial.

ASA-BORAKE, アサボラケ, 朝朗, *n.* Day-break, dawn. Syn. AKATSZKI, YOAKE.

ASADE, アサデ, 淺手, *n.* A slight or superficial wound.

ASAGAO, アサガホ, 牽牛花, *n.* The morning glory.

ASA-GARA, アサガラ, 麻空, *n.* The refuse bark of hemp.

ASAGAREI, アサガレイ, 朝餉, *n.* An early morning lunch.

ASAGASZMI, アサガスミ, 朝霞, *n.* The morning haze.

ASAGI, アサギ, 淺黄, *n.* A light green color.

ASAGIYOME, アサギヨメ, 朝淨, *n.* The morning wash.

ASAHAKA-NA, アサハカナ, 淺墓, *a.* Shallow minded, not clever or shrewd, silly, foolish.

ASAHAN, アサハン, 朝飯, *n.* Breakfast.
Syn. ASAMESHI.

ASAI, or ASAKI, アサイ, 淺, *a.* Shallow, not deep. *Midz ga* —, the water is shallow. *Asai kawa*, a shallow river. *Ido ga* —, the well is not deep. — *iro*, a light shade of any color. *Chiye no — h'to*, a person of shallow understanding. — *chawan*, a shallow cup.

ASAKARANU, or ASAKARADZ, アサカラヌ, 不淺, Not shallow, deep. — *naka*, deep intimacy or friendship. *Asakaradz katajikenai*, deeply obliged.

Asake, アサケ, 朝明, (comp. of *Asa* and *ake*,) *n*. Day-break, dawn.

Asaku, アサク, 淺, *adv*. Shallow, not deep, see *Asai*.

Asa-madaki, アサマダキ, 朝未明, *n*. Before day-break.

Asamashii,-ki, アサマシイ, 淺猿, *a*. Shallow-brained, silly, foolish, not wise, of little judgment. — *ku, adv*.

Asameshi, アサメシ, 朝飯, *n*. Breakfast.

†Asana-yūna, アサナユウナ, 朝夕, (*asaban*,) *n*. Morning and evening.

Asane, アサネ, 朝寐, *n*. Sleeping late in the morning, — *bō*, a late sleeper.

Asa-nuno, アサヌノ, 麻布, *n*. Grass-cloth.

Asa-o, アサオ, 麻苧, *n*. Raw or unwrought hemp thread.

Asa-oki, アサオキ, 朝起, *n*. Rising from bed in the morning.

Asari, アサリ, 蜊, *n*. The name of a bivalve, Lima cardiformis?

Asari,-*ru*,-*tta*, アサル, 足探, (cont. of *Ashi* and *saguru*,) *t. v*. To scratch and search for food, as a fowl. *Ye wo* —, id.

Asasa, アササ, 淺, *n*. The shallowness. *Kawa no — ni fune ga tōranu*, boats cannot go up and down the river on account of its shallowness.

Asashi, アサシ, 淺, *a*. Shallow, see *Asai*.

Asatte, アサツテ, 明後日, (*Miyōgo nichi*,) *adv*. Day-after-to-morrow.

Ase, アセ, 汗, *n*. Sweat, perspiration — *wo kaku*, to sweat. — *ga deru*, he sweats.

Asebo, or Asemo, アセボ, *n*. Prickly heat.

Aseri,-*ru*,-*tta*, アセル, *i. v*. To be in a hurry, to be in hot haste, to be urgent, eager, vehement; to twist and turn, as in trying to escape. *Kayese kayese to aseredomo mimi ni kiki-iredz*, he cried urgently, "come back, come back," but he would not hear. *Ikura asette mo ma-ni-awanu*, hurry as much as I may, I cant do it. Syn. isogu, seku.

Asetori, アセトリ, 汗衫, *n*. An undershirt worn to protect the other garments from sweat.

Ashi, アシ, 足, *n*. The leg, foot. — *no yubi*, the toes. — *no kō*, the instep or back of the foot. — *no ura*, sole of the foot. *Hi no* —, the rays of the sun shining through a cloud. *Ame no* —, the appearance of rain falling in the distance. *Fune no* —, that part of a ship that is beneath the surface of the water. — *ni makasete yuku*, to go not knowing where. — *no ato*, the print of the feet.

Ashi, アシ, 蘆, *n*. A rush or flag.

Ashi, アシ, 悪, Evil. *Yoshi-ashi*, good and evil.

Ashi-aburi, アシアブリ, 脚爐, *n*. A foot-stove.

Ashiato, アシアト, 足跡, *n*. Foot prints.

Ashiba, アシハ, 足場, *n*. A scaffold.

Ashibaya, アシハヤ, 足早, *n*. Swift-footed, fleet.

Ashi-biyōshi, アシビヤウシ, 足柏子, *n*. Beating time or drumming with the feet. — *wo toru*, to beat time, &c.

Ashida, アシダ, 足駄, *n*. Wooden clogs.

Ashi-damari, アシダマリ, 足留, *n*. A foot hold, point d'appui, a base for military operations.

Ashi-dome, アシドメ, 足止, *n*. A stop in going or coming, a halt. — *wo szru*, to stop.

Ashidori, アシドリ, 跬步, *n*. The gait or manner of walking. —*ga warui*, his gait is bad.

Ashi-dzri, アシズリ, 足摺, *n*. Dancing and knocking the feet together in anger. — *wo sh'te naku*, to dance and cry (as a child.) Syn. jidanda.

Ashi-gakari, アシガカリ, 足掛, *n*. A foot hold, a place to step on.

Ashigane, アシガネ, 鈦, *n*. Fetters, shackles. Syn. hadashi.

Ashigaru, アシガル, 足輕, *n*. Foot soldiers. Syn. zōhiyō.

Ashigase, アシガセ, 桎, *n*. Stocks for confining the feet of criminals.

†Ashii, or Ashiki, アシキ, 悪, *a*. Bad, wicked, evil. Syn. warui.

Ashijiro, アシジロ, 足代, *n*. A scaffold. Syn. ashiba.

Ashika, アシカ, 海驢, *n*. A seal. Syn. ottosei.

Ashiku, アシク, 悪, *adv*. Bad, evil, see *Ashii*. — *iu*, to speak evil of.

Ashi-kubi, アシクビ, 足首, *n*. The ankle.

Ashi-matoi, アシマトヒ, 足綢, *n*. A clog, impediment, hindrance.

Ashimoto, アシモト, 足下, *n*. Near the feet. — *ni aru*, it is near your feet.

Ashi-motszre, アシモツレ, 足縺, *n*. A clog, impediment or hindrance in going. Syn. ashi-matoi.

Ashi-naka, アシナカ, 足半, *n*. Sandals which cover only about half the sole.

Ashi-nami, アシナミ, *n*. The line, or order of the feet, as in troops marching. — *wo soroyete aruku*, to walk keeping step with each other.

Ashi-naye, アシナヘ, 蹇, *n*. Crippled in the legs, or feet.

Ashi-oto, アシオト, 足音, *n.* The sound made by the feet in walking; sound of foot-steps.

Ashirai, *-au, -atta*, アシラフ, 會釋, *t. v.* To treat, to behave, or act towards; to amuse, to entertain; to set off, decorate. *Ta-nin wo kiyōdai no yōni* —, to treat a stranger like a brother. *Deshi ni ken-jutsz no kei-ko wo ashiratte yaru*, to fence with a pupil in order to instruct him. *Ki-yaku wo* —, to entertain a guest. *Kodomo wo* —, to amuse a child. *Sakana ni ao-mono wo* —, to decorate a fish with green leaves. *Matsz no ne ni sasa wo ashiratte wiyeru*, to plant small bamboo near a pine tree in order to set it off.
Syn. TORI-ATSZKAU.

Ashirai, アシラヒ, 遇, *n.* Treatment, entertainment; decoration.

Ashisa, アシサ, 悪, *n.* The badness, see *Ashii.*

Ashisama-ni, アシサマニ, 悪様, *adv.* In a bad manner. — *iu*, to speak evil of.

Ash'ta, アシタ, 明日, *(miyōnichi,) adv.* To-morrow, also 晨, this morning.
Syn. ASZ, ASA.

Ashi-tszgi, アシツギ, 凳, *n.* A stepping stool for reaching to a height.

Ashi-yowa, アシヨワ, 足弱, *n.* Weak in the legs, slow of foot, as a woman, child, or old person. — *dzre michi ga hakado-ranu.*

Ashi-zoroye, アジゾロヘ, 足揃, *n.* The feet in line. — *de aruku*, to walk with the feet in line, or to keep time in walking.

Asobase, *-ru, -ta*, アソハセル, 令遊, caust. of *Asobi.* To amuse, divert; to cause, or let be without work, or idle. *Hō-kō-nin wo asobasete oku*, to let a servant spend his time in idleness.

Asobashi, *-sz, -sh'ta*, アソハス, 遊, *t.v.* To amuse, divert; to let, or cause to be without work; to do, make, = *nasaru*, in this sense used only in speaking to honorable persons. *Shu-jin shuyen wo asobasz*, the prince makes a wine-banquet. *Kō asoba-se*, do it thus.

Asobi, *-bu, -nda*, アソブ, 遊, *i. v.* To sport, frolic; to divert, or amuse one's self; to be without work, to idle, to spend time idly. *Yama ni* —, to go for pleasure into the mountains. *Asonde kurasz*, to live in idleness, or pleasure.

Asobi, アソビ, 遊, *n.* Amusement, diversion, pleasure, sport, frolic, play, or room for motion. — *ni yuku*, to go any place for pleasure. — *no szki na h'to*, a person fond of pleasure.

Assari-to, アツサリト, 厚去, *adv.* Delicate in taste or color, neat. — *sh'ta tabe-mono*, food of delicate taste.
Syn. TAMPAKU.

Asz, アス, 翌日, *(yokujitsz,) adv.* To-morrow. — *no asa*, to-morrow morning.
Syn. ASH'TA.

Aszko, アスコ, 彼許, *adv.* Yonder, there.
Syn. ACHIRA.

Atafuta-to, アタフタト, *adv.* In an agitated flurried manner, hurriedly. — *ka-ke-dasz*, ran out in a great flurry.
Syn. AWATADASHIKU.

Atai, アタイ, 直, *n.* Price, value, worth. — *wa ikura*, what is the price? — *nashi*, price-less, (either invaluable, or worthless.) Syn. NEDAN.

Atama, アタマ, 頭, *n.* The head, the top, the highest part. — *ga itai*, the head pains. *Yama no* —, the top of a mountain. *Ki no* —, the top of a tree. — *wo haru*, to strike the head, to squeeze a certain percentage from the wages, (as a coolie master, &c.)
Syn. KASHIRA, ITADAKI.

Atamagachi, アタマガチ, 頭大, Large headed, larger at the top than at the bottom. *Shishi wa — na kedamono*, the wild hog is a large-headed animal.

Atara, アタラ, 可惜, *(oshimu beki,) a.* Any thing which one regrets to lose, to be regretted, too precious to lose. — *koto wo sh'ta*, have done what I deeply regret. — *hana wo kaze ga fuku*, the wind has blown away a flower, the loss of which I greatly regret.

Atarashii, *-ki*, アタラシイ, 新, *a.* New, fresh, not stale — *kimono*, new clothes. — *midz*, fresh water. — *sakana*, fresh fish. Syn. SHINKI.

Atarashiku, or **Atarashiu**, アタラシク, 新, *adv.* New, newly; fresh not stale. — *nai*, not new. — *dekita iye*, a house newly built. — *naru*, to become new.
Syn. ARATA-NI, SHINKI-NI.

Atarashisa, アタラシサ, *n.* The newness.

Atari, アタリ, 邊, *n.* Vicinity, neighborhood, near in place, or in time, about. *Nondo no — ni*, near the neck. *Kono — ni tera wa nai ka*, is there a temple in this vicinity? — *wo harau*, to clear away those near, (as with a sword.) *Kiyo-nen atari*, about last year.
Syn. KINJŌ, HEN, HOTORI.

Atari, *-ru, -tta*, アタル, 當, or 中, *i. v.* To hit, strike against; to touch; to reach, attain to; to turn out, or come to pass; to succeed, as by chance; to happen, hit upon, fall upon by chance. *Ya ga mato ni atatta*, the arrow has hit the mark. *Fune ga iwa ni* —, the ship struck on a rock. *Tszkuye ni ataru na*, dont touch the desk. *Watakushi no atama wa ano h'to no kata ni ataru*, my head reaches to his shoulder. *Nippon no g'wan-jitsz wa Igirisz no ni-g'watsz jū-go nichi ni* —, the Japanese new-year's-day falls upon the 15th day of the English 2nd month. *Yoropa wa Ajia no nishi ni ataru*, Europe lies on the west of Asia. *Watakushi ni wa itoko ni ataru*, he turns out to be my nephew. *Uranai ga atatta*, the prediction of the fortuneteller has fallen true. *Sono toki ni atatte ran ga okoru*, it happened at that time that a disturbance arose. *H'to no ki ni* —, to offend a person. *Atszsa ni* —, to be sun-struck, or overcome by the heat. *Tabemono ga atatta*, made sick by something he has eaten. *Shibai ga atatta*. the theatre has turned out a success. *Yama ga atatta*, the speculation has succeeded. *Hi no ataru tokoro ni oku*, lay it in a sunny place. *Ano h'to ni kuji ga atatta*, the lot has fallen upon him.

ATARI-HADZRE, アタリハヅレ, 當外, *n.* Hit and miss, success and failure.

ATARIMAYE, アタリマヘ, 當前, *n.* As it should be, right, proper, according to the law of nature, natural, of course; usual, common, ordinary. *Karita kane wo kayesz no wa — da*, it is right to return borrowed money. *Midz no shimo ye nagareru wa — da*, it is natural for water to flow downwards. — *no kimono*, clothes such as are usually worn. Syn. TŌZEN.

ATATAKAI,-KI,-SHI, アタタカイ, 暖, *a.* Warm. *Haru ga* —, the spring is warm. — *kimono*, warm clothing.

ATATAKAKU, or ATATAKŌ, アタタカク, 暖, *adv.* Warm, warmly. — *naru*, to become warm.

ATATAKA-NA, アタタカナ, 暖, *a.* Warm. — *tenki*, warm weather.

ATATAKA-NI, アタタカニ, 暖, *adv. idem.* — *naru*, to become warm.

ATATAKASA, アタタカサ, 暖, *n.* The warmth, warmness.

ATATAMARI,*-ru,-tta*, アタタマル, *i. v.* To be warm, or become warm.

ATATAME,*-ru,-ta*, アタタメル, 温, *t. v.* To make warm. *Hi wo taite heya wo* —, to make a fire and warm the room.

ATATTE, アタツテ, 當, ger. of *Atari*.

†ATAWADZ, アタハズ, 不能, Not able, cannot, impossible. Syn. DEKINU.

‖ATAYE,*-ru,-ta*, アタヘル, 與, *t. v.* To give. *Kojiki ni zeni wo* —, to give cash to a beggar. *H'to ni haji wo* —, to make a person ashamed.
Syn. YARU, SADZKERU, TSZKAWASZ.

‖ATAYE, アタヘ, 與, *n.* A gift. *Ten no* —, the gift of heaven. Syn. SADZKE.

ATE,*-ru,-ta*, アテル, 當, *t. v.* To hit, strike, touch; to apply one thing to another, to put; to direct towards as an object; to apportion. *Ya wo mato ni* —, to hit the mark with an arrow. *Ya wo mato ni atete nerau*, to aim an arrow at a mark. *Kao ni te wo* —, to touch the hand to the face. *Hi ni* —, to put anything in the sun. *Kono naka ni aru mono wo atete mi-nasai*, guess what is inside of this. *Mono-sashi wo* —, to measure with a foot measure, or yard-stick. *Mi ni atete omoi-yaru*, to feel for another remembering our own troubles. *Hinoshi wo* —, to iron, as clothes. *Yakume wo* —, to allot each one his duty. *H'totsz dztsz atete-yaru*, give them one apiece.

ATE, アテ, 當, *n.* A block, or anything placed for a thing in motion to strike against; a pad for protection against a blow or friction; a mark, target; object, aim; a clew; anything to look to, rely or depend on. — *ni szru*, to use as a block, or object, to depend on. *Tori wo ate ni teppō wo utsz*, to fire a gun at a bird. — *nashi ni yuku*, to go without an object, a clew, or without any one to depend on. — *ga hadzreru*, that on which reliance was placed has failed. *Ano h'to no yakusoku wa ate ni naranu*, his promise is not to be depended on. — *ga nai*, have no person to look to, or depend on. *Doru ichi mai ate ni yaru*, to give one dollar to each person.

ATEDO, アテド, 當所, *n.* Object, aim, clew. — *nashi ni yaku*, to go without any particular object.

ATEGAI,*-au,-atta*, アテガフ, 當合, *t. v.* To apply or fit one thing to another, to apportion, to assign, allot, appoint. *H'tori maye ni-jū dztsz wo* —, to apportion twenty to each man. *Ōki ka chīsai ka ategatte miru*, to see whether it is too large or too small, (by applying one on the other.)

ATEHAME,*-ru,-ta*, アテハメル, *t. v.* To appropriate, design, set apart for; assign, or devote to a particular use. *Kono kane wa shakkin ni atehamete aru*, this money is designed for the payment of a debt.

ATE-JI, アテジ, 當字, *n.* A character used merely for its sound, without regard to its meaning.

ATE-KOSZRI, アテコスリ, *n.* A hit, rebuke or censure administered indirectly, or by implication. — *wo iu.*

ATE-OKONAI,*–au,–atta*, アテオコナフ, 當行, *t.v.* To apportion, allot, grant. *Kerai ni chi-giyō wo* —, to grant a portion of land to a servant.

ATE-TSZKE,*–ru,–ta*, アテツケル, 當付, *t.v.* To allude, hint at, or refer to some one not directly mentioned. *H'to ni ate-tszkete mono wo iu*, to say anything intending it as a hit against another.

†ATEYAKANA, アテヤカナ, *a.* Refined, genteel, not vulgar.
Syn. MIYABIYAKA, JŌHIN.

ATO, アト, 跡, or 後, *n.* The mark, or impression left by anything, a track, trace, point, trail, scar, cicatrice. That which remains, as, ruins, remains, vestige, relic. That which comes after, succeeds or follows. With, *no, ni, de, ye* or *kara*, it means, behind, after, afterwards, last, before, ago, backwards. — *wo tszgu*, to succeed another in estate, business, &c. *Kodomo wa haka no* - *wo sh'tau.* a child longs to go after its mother. *Sake-nomi ga* — *wo hiku*, a drunkard stays long at his cups. *Rōshō wa* — *wo hiku yamai*, consumption is a disease which infects one's children. *Yobaiboshi ga* — *wo hiku*, a meteor leaves a train behind it. *wo tateru*, to raise up the ruins of a family. — *wo tszkeru*, to make a mark. — *wo sagasz*, to search for the trail or track. — *ye yoru*, to move back. *H'to no* — *ni tatsz*, to stand behind another. — *no tszki*, last month. — *ni hanash'ta koto*, that which was said before. *Gozen no* — *de cha wo nomu*, to drink tea after dinner. — *kara yuku*, to go after, or afterwards. *San nen ato*, three years ago.

ATO-GETSZ, アトゲツ, 後月, *n.* Last month.

ATO-HARA, アトハラ, 後腹, *n.* After-pains, (met.) after-clap.

ATO-KATA, アトカタ, 跡形, *n.* Mark, trace. *Tori wa tonde* — *mo nashi*, when a bird has flown it leaves no trace.

ATO-ME, アトメ, 跡目, *n.* A successor. — *wo tszgu*, to succeed to the place, or estate which another has left.

ATONIGIYAKASHI, アトニギヤカシ, 跡賑, *n.* A feast, or entertainment made after a person has gone on a journey, by the friends left behind.

ATO-SAKI, アトサキ, 後先, *n.* That which is before, and behind; the past, and the future. Antecedent, and consequence. — *wo kangayeru*, to examine a subject on all sides.

ATO-SHIZARI, アトシザリ, 却退, *n.* Moving backwards, shrinking back, as in fear.

ATO-TORI, アトトリ, 跡取, *n.* An heir, successor.

ATO-TSZGI, アトツギ, 後嗣, *n.* An heir, or successor.

†ATSZ ,or ATSZRU, アツル, 當, same as *Ateru. Shoku ni atszbeki mono*, a thing that would do for food.

ATSZ, アツ, 暑, hot, and 厚, thick, (used only in compounds.)

ATSZ-GAMI, アツガミ, 厚紙, *n.* A kind of thick, coarse paper.

ATSZ-GAN, アツガン, 熱燗, *n.* Hot *sake.*

ATSZ-GI, アツギ, 厚着, *n.* Thick, and warm clothing, putting on many garments one over the other.

ATSZI,–KI,–SHI, アツイ, 熱, *a.* Hot. — *hi* a hot day. *Yu ga* —, the water is hot.

ATSZI,–KI,–SHI, アツイ, 厚, *a.* Thick from side to side; fig. great, liberal. *Kawa ga* —, the skin, bark, or rind is thick. *Atszi hōbi*, a liberal reward.

ATSZITA, アツイタ, 厚板, *n.* A thick kind of silkgoods.

ATSZKAI,*–au,–atta*, アツカフ, 扱, *t.v.* To manage, negotiate, or transact a matter between two parties. *Ken-k'wa wo atszkatte naka wo naosz*, to mediate in a quarrel and restore friendship. Syn. HAKARAU.

ATSZKAI, アツカヒ, 和論, *n.* Mediation, intervention, negotiation. — *wo szru.*

ATSZKAI-NIN, アツカヒニン, 扱人, *n.* A mediatior, negotiator. Syu. AISATSZNIN.

ATSZKAWA-DZRA, アツカハヅラ, 厚皮面, *n.* Thick-skinned-face, brazen-faced, impudent.

ATSZKU, アツク, 熱, *adv.* Hot, — *szru*, to make hot. — *naru*, to become hot. — *nai*, not hot. — *te komaru*, it is so hot I don't know what to do.

ATSZKU, アツク, 厚, *adv.* Thick from side to side. — *sewa wo szru*, to render great services. *Pan wo* — *kiru*, to cut bread in thick slices. — *nai kami*, thin paper.

ATSZMARI,*–ru,–tta*, アツマル, 集, *i.v.* To be assembled, congregated, collected together. *Shibai wo mi ni h'to ga* —, people are assembled to see the theatre
Syn. YORU, MURAGARU.

ATSZMARI, アツマリ, 集, *n.* An assembly, congregation, collection.

ATSZME,*–ru,–ta*, アツメル, 集, *t. v.* To assemble, congregate, to collect, convene, to gather. *Hō-dan ni h'to wo* —, to as-

semble people to the preaching. *Hana wo* —, to gather flowers.
Syn. YOSERU, MATOMERU.

ATSZRAYE,*-ru,-ta*, アツラヘル, 誂, *t. v.* To order anything to be made, or purchased. *Tszkuye wo daiku ni* —, to order a desk of the carpenter. *O atszraye no shina ga Yedo kara dekite kimash'ta*, the article you ordered has come from Yedo.
Syn. CHŪ-MON SZRU.

ATSZRAYE, アツラヘ, 誂, *n.* An order for the making, or buying of anything. *Hoka no h'to no — da kara uraremasen*, as it was ordered by another person I cannot sell it. — *wo ukeru*, to receive an order.
Syn. CHŪ-MON.

ATSZSA, アツサ, 熱, *n.* The heat. *Konnichi no — wa iku do*, how hot is it to-day? — *ni makeru*, to be overcome by the heat.

ATSZSA, アツサ, 厚, *n.* Thickness. *Kono ita no — wa go bu*, this board is half an inch thick.

ATSZU, アツウ, same as *Atszku*.

ATTA, アツタ, pret. of *Ai, au, atta*, 逢, and 合, also pret. of *Ari*, 有.

ATTARA, アツタラ, coll. same as *Atara*.

ATTARA, アツタラ, coll. cont. of *Atte araba*, if there is, if you have. *Yu ga — motte-koi*, if there is any hot water bring it.

ATTE, アツテ, ger. of *Ai*, 逢, or 合, and *Ari* 有. *Atte mo nakute mo kamai-masen*, whether I have or not, it makes no difference.

ATTO, アツト, exclam. of sudden surprise, or in answering a call. — *sakebu.*

AWA, アハ, 粟, *n.* Millet.

AWA, アワ, 沫, *n.* Froth, foam, bubbles. — *wo fuku*, to froth at the mouth. — *ga tatsz*, it bubbles, it foams.

AWABI, アハビ, 鰒, *n.* The Haliotis tuberculata, or "sea-ear."

AWADZ, or AWANU, アハズ, 不逢, neg. of *Ai, au*, not to meet. — *ni kayeru*, to return without meeting.

AWA-GARA, アハガラ, 粟空, *n.* The shells, or bran of millet.

‖AWAI, アハイ, 間, *n.* The space between two things, between. *Yama no — no michi*, a road between the mountains.
Syn. AIDA.

AWA-MOCHI, アハモチ, 粟餅, *n.* Bread made of rice and millet.

AWAMORI, アワモリ, 泡盛, *n.* A kind of strong spirits made in Kiu-shū.

†AWARE, アハレ, exclam. of entreaty, of pity or admiration. —*inochi bakari wo tasz-ke tamaye*, I pray you only spare my life.

AWARE, アハレ, 哀, *n.* Pity, compassion, tenderness of heart. — *wo moyosz*, to feel compassion. — *ni omō, id.*
Syn. FU-BIN.

AWARE,*-ru,-ta*, アハレル, 被逢, pass. or pot. of *ai, au, atta*. Can meet. *Dōsh'tara awareru da-rō ka*, how shall I get an opportunity of meeting him?

AWAREMI,*-mu-nda*, アハレム, 憐, *t. v.* To pity, compassionate. *Awarende ishoku wo atayeru*, compassionating gave food and clothing.
Syn. FUBIN NI OMŌ, ITAWASHIKU OMŌ.

AWAREMI, アハレミ, 憐, *n.* Pity, compassion, mercy. — *no fukai h'to*, a person of great compassion. Syn. FUBIN, JIHI.

AWARE-NA, アハレナ, 憐, *a.* Exciting pity or compassion, pitiful, miserable. — *koto.*

AWARESA, アハレサ, 憐, *n.* A condition exciting pity, misery.

AWASE,*-ru,-ta*, アハセル, 合, *t.v.* To join together, to unite; to mix together, to compound as medicine. To make do, make suit, or answer the purpose. *Kami-sori wo* —, to hone a razor. *Kuszri wo* —, to compound medicines. *Te wo awasete haiszru*, to join the hands and worship. *Kokoro wo* —, to agree together. *Chikara wo* —, to unite strength, or do altogether. *Chōshi wo* —, to tune, to make to agree or harmonize as musical notes. *Ano h'to ni awasete kudasare*, pray introduce me to him.

AWASE, アハセ, 袷衣, *n.* A garment of double thickness or lined.

AWASEDO, アハセド, 合砥, *n.* A hone, whetstone.

AWASE-GUSZRI, アハセグスリ, 合藥 *n.* A medicine compounded of several ingredients.

AWASEME, アハセメ, 合目, *n.* A joint, or seam where two things are united.

AWATADASHI,*-KI,-SHI*, アハタダシイ, 遽, *a.* Agitated, excited, flurried in manner.

AWATADASHIKU, *adv.* In a flurried, excited manner.

AWATE,*-ru,-ta*, アハテル, 周章, *i.v.* To be excited, agitated, flurried, alarmed.
Syn. ODOROKU, UROTAYERU.

†AWAYA, アハヤ, exclam. of alarm, agitation, excitement, or surprise. — *to miru uchi ni.* — *teki yo.*

AWAZARU, アハザル, 不合, neg. of *Ai.*

†AYA, アヤ, exclam. of alarm, or excitement.

AYA, アヤ, 綾, *n.* Silk damask.

AYA, アヤ, *n.* Cat's-cradle, a puzzle made

with a string looped over the fingers, played by children. — *wo toru.*

AYA, アヤ, 文, *n.* A figure, or design of any kind wrought in cloth for ornament. — *wo nasz*, to ornament with figures, &c. *Haru no yo no yami wa, aya nashi, ume no hana, ka wo tadznete zo shiru-bekari-keru*, in the darkness of a spring night when no object can be distinguished, the plum-blossom may be found by its fragrance. Syn. BUN MOYŌ.

AYABUMI,*-mu,-nda*, アヤブム, 危, *i. v.* To suspect danger, to be timid, to be fearful, suspicious. Syn. ABUNAGARU.

AYADORI,*-ru,-tta*, アヤドル, 操, *t. v.* To form the figures or designs on cloth while in the loom, which is done by working a frame from which strings go to be attached to the warp; thus it also means, to embellish, ornament, also, to work the strings of a puppet, or to play balls. *Hata, ganshoku, bun-shō, nin-giyō, toma nado wo —*

AYAKARI,*-ru,-tta*, アヤカル, 肖, *t. v.* To resemble, to be like. *Harami onna ga usagi wo kuyeba sono ko ga usagi ni ayakatte mitsz-kuchi ni naru*, if a pregnant woman eats hare her child will have three lips like a hare. *Ano h'to ni ayakaritai*, I wish to be like that man. Syn. NIRU, RUI-SZRU.

AYAMACHI,*-tsz,-tta*, アヤマツ, 過, or 誤, *t. v.* To commit a mistake, error, blunder, or fault, to miss; to offend against, transgress, or violate unintentionally. *Ayamatte aratamuru ni habakaru koto nakare*, having committed a mistake don't be backward to rectify it. *Okite wo —*, to offend against the laws. *Ayamatte h'to wo korosz*, to kill a person by mistake. Syn. MACHIGAU, TAGAYERU.

AYAMACHI, アヤマチ, 過, *n.* A mistake, error, fault, a wrong. *Watakushi no — da*, it was my fault. — *wo kuyuru*, to be sorry for a mistake. — *wo aratameru*, to rectify a mistake, or reform one's faults. Syn. OCHIDO, MACHIGAI, SOSŌ.

AYAMARI,*-ru,-tta*, アヤマル, 過, *t. v.* To miss, mistake, err; to offend against. To acknowledge a fault, or mistake, to apologize. *Michi wo —*, to miss the way. *Burei wo —*, to apologize for a rudeness. *Ayamatadz mato wo iru*, to hit the target without missing. Syn. MACHIGAU, WABIRU.

AYAMARI, アヤマリ, 過, *n.* (same as *Ayamachi.*) A mistake, error, fault, a wrong, an apology, acknowledgement of an error. — *ni kita*, came to apologize.

AYAME, アヤメ, 菖蒲, *n.* The sweet flag, Calamus Aromaticus. Syn. SHŌBU.

†AYAME, アヤメ, 文目, *n.* The lines, or colors that define a figure, but generally used metaphorically, as, *mono no — mo wakanu yami yo*, a night so dark that things could not be distinguished one from another.

AYAME,*-ru,-ta*, アヤメル, *t. v.* To kill with the sword to slay, to murder. *H'to wo —*. Syn. KIRI-KOROSZ.

AYANIKU, アヤニク, 生憎, *adv.* (comp. of *Aya*, exclam. and *niku*, odious.) How unfortunate, unluckily. — *rusz da*, he is unfortunately out.

AYASHI,*-sz,-sh'ta*, アヤス 落, *t.v.* To spill, only used of blood. *Chi wo —*, to spill the blood of another.

AYASHI,*-sz,-sh'ta*, アヤス, *t.v.* To play with or amuse a child. *Ko wo —*, *id.*

AYASHII,-KI,-SHI, アヤシイ, 怪, *a.* Strange, marvellous, wonderful, suspicious, dubious, doubtful. *Ayashiki mo ayashimazareba ayashiki koto nashi*, even if a thing is strange, if we are not surprised at it, it ceases to be strange. Syn. MEDZRASHII, FUSHINGI.

AYASHIKU,-U, アヤシク, 怪, *adv. Id.* — *omō*, to consider strange, to feel suspicious of. — *nai*, not strange.

AYASHIMI,*-mu,-nda*, アヤシム, 怪, *t. v.* To think strange, to wonder at, to marvel at; to suspect. *H'to wo —*, to suspect a person. *Ayashimu ni taradz*, not a matter to be surprised at, or to be suspicious of. Syn. UTAGAU, FUSHIGI NI OMŌ.

AYASHIMI, アヤシミ, 怪, *n.* Wonder, surprise, suspicion, doubt. — *wo idaku*, to entertain suspicion. — *fukumu*, *id.* Syn. GINEN, UTAGAI.

AYASHISA, アヤシサ, 怪, *n.* The strangeness, wonderfulness.

AYATSZ, アヤツ, *n.* That scoundrel, that low fellow. Syn. AITSZ.

AYATSZRI,*-ru,-tta*, アヤツル, 操, *t.v.* The same as *Ayadori*, but used only for playing the strings of a puppet, or playing several balls at the same time, *Ningiyō wo —*

AYAUI,-KI,-SHI, アヤウイ, 危, *a.* Dangerous, perilous, full of risk. — *tokoro wo taszkatta*, saved from great peril. — *me ni atta*, was in a dangerous predicament. Syn. ABUNAI.

AYE,*-ru,-ta*, アヘル, 和, *t. v.* To dress as a salad. *Na wo ayeru*, to dress *na* with various articles and make a salad. *Ayemono*, a salad.

†Ayedz, アヘズ, 不敢, *adv.* Without stopping, or waiting to perform the action of the verb with which it is connected, as. *Iki mo tszki ayedz*, without waiting to take breath. *Hanashi wo kiki ayedz detta*, went out without stopping to hear what was said. *Toru mono mo tori ayedz*, not stopping to take anything.
Syn, MA MO NAKU.

‖Ayegi,*–gu,–ida*, アヘグ, 喘, *i.v.* To pant, to blow, as one out of breath. *Ayeide hashiru*, to run panting.

Ayen, アエン, 亞鉛, *n.* Zinc. *Ayen-k'wa*, flowers of zinc.

†Ayenai,–ki,–shi, アヘナイ, 無敢, *a.* Pitiful, sad; in a little while, (?) — *saigo*, sad end, (of life).

†Ayenaku, アヘナク, *adv. id.* — *iki wa taye ni keru*, in a moment the breath is cut off, (?)

†Ayete, アヘテ, 敢, *adv.* To dare, venture, presume, used only in Chinese composition. — *sedz*, dare not do. — *iru koto yurusadz*, dare not allow you to enter.

Ayu, アユ, 鮎, *n.* A kind of river fish.

Ayu, アユ, 阿諛, *(omoneri hetszrau,)* — *szru*, to flatter, adulate.

Āyu, アアイフ, 彼云, *a.* That way, or manner, that kind. Syn. ANNA, ANA-YŌ.

†Ayumi,*–mu,–nda*, アユム, 歩, *i.v.* To walk, to go on foot. Syn. ARUKU.

†Ayumi, アユミ, 歩, *n.* Walking, going on foot. *Seijin no — wo hakobu tokoro*, the places visited by the sage.

Ayumiai,*–au,–atta*, アユミアフ, 歩合, *t.v.* To split the difference in price, both parties (buyer and seller) to move a little in fixing the price of anything. *Nedan wo —, id.* Syn. AIBIAI.

Ayumi-ita, アユミイタ, 歩板, *n.* A board, or plank for walking on in order to enter a boat.

Aza, アザ, 痣, *n.* Maculæ, dark or red spots on the skin.

Azakeri,*–ru,–ta*, アザケル, 嘲, *t. v.* To laugh at, ridicule, deride, to scoff, jeer. *H'to wo —*,
Syn. SOSHIRU, GURŌ SZRU, BAKA NI SZRU.

Azakeri, アザケリ, 嘲, *n.* Ridicule, derision. *H'to no — wo ukeru*, to be laughed at by others.

Azami, アザミ, 薊, *n.* A thistle.

Azamuki,*–ku,–ita*, アザムク, 欺, *t.v.* To deceive, impose on, to hoax, cheat, delude, to beguile, defraud. *H'to wo azamuite kane wo toru*, to cheat a person and take his money. Syn. DAMASZ, TABAKARU.

Azamuki, アザムキ, 欺, *n.* Deception, imposition, guile, fraud.

Azana, アザナ, 字, *n.* The common name by which a person is called.

†Azanaye,*–ru*, アザナヘル, 糾, *t. v.* To twist as a rope. Syn. NAU.

Azarashi, アザラシ, 水豹, *n.* The otter.

†Azare,*–ru,–ta*, アザレル, 餒, *t.v.* To be spoiled, tainted, as fish or meat.
Syn. KUSARU, KUCHIRU.

Azawarai,*–au,–tta*, アザワラフ, 嘲笑, *t.v.* To laugh at in derision, scorn, or contempt. Syn. SESERAWARAI.

Azayaka-na, アザヤカナ, 粲, *a.* Clear, plain, distinct.
Syn. AKIRAKANA, HAKKIRI.

Azayaka-ni, アサヤカニ, 粲, *adv.* Clearly, distinctly. plainly.

Aze, アゼ, 畔, *n.* The mound, or dyke that separates rice-fields. Syn. KURO.

Aze, アゼ, 綜, *n.* The reed of a loom through which the warp is passed.

Aze-ito, アゼイト, 綜絲, *n.* The strings of the above.

B

Ba, バ, A conjunctive particle affixed to verbs.

Ba, バ, 場, *n.* A place, arena. *Ba wo toru.* to occupy a place, take up room *Ba ga nai*, there is no room. *Yokiba*, a good place. *Kassemba*, a field of battle. *Sono ba*, that place, or that time.
Syn. TOKORO.

Ba, バ, (impure *wa.*) 把, *n.* A numeral used in counting bundles, fowls, or birds. *Maki sam ba*, three bundles of wood. *Tori sam ba*, three fowls.

Baba, ババ, 馬場, *n.* A place for practising horsemanship. or training horses.

Baba, ババ, 祖母, *n.* Grand-mother. *Obaba san, (o·bā san,)* a polite name in speaking to an old woman.

Bachi, バチ, 撥, *n.* A drumstick, the stick used in playing the guitar, or striking a gong.

Bachi, バチ, 罰, *n.* Punishment inflicted by heaven. *Bachi ga ataru*, to be smitten of God. *Oya no bachi wo kōmuru*, to be punished of God for disobedience to parents. Syn. TOGAME, TATARI.

Bachi-men, バチメン, 撥面, *n.* The place on a banjo where it is played.

Ba-dai, バダイ, 馬代, *n.* Horse money; the price of a horse, made a present to high officials.

BA-DARAI, バダライ, 馬盥, *n.* A horse bason.

BA-FUN, バフン, 馬糞, *n.* Horse dung.

BA-GEI, バゲイ, 馬藝, *n.* Equestrian feats.

BA-GINU, バギヌ, 馬褐, *n.* A horse blanket.

BA-GU, バグ, 馬具, *n.* Articles necessary in using a horse, harness.

BAGU-YA, バグヤ, 馬具屋, *n.* A harness maker. A saddler.

BAHAN, バハン, 八幡, *n.* Smuggling. *Bahan szru*, to smuggle. *Bahan nin*, a smuggler. *Baham-mono*, smuggled goods. Syn. MITSZ-BAIKAI.

||BAHARE,*–ru,–ta*, バハレル, 場晴, *i. v.* To be public before the world, open. *Baharete szru*, to do publicly. *Bahareta koto*, a thing public and known.
Syn. OMOTE-MUKI.

BAHIFŪ, バヒフウ, 馬脾風, *n.* Croup.

BA-I, バイ, 馬醫, *n.* A horse doctor.

BAI, バイ, 唄, *n.* A kind of snail.

†BAI, バイ, 梅, *(ume,) n.* The plum.

BAI, バイ, 倍, Double, twice as much. *Bai ni szru*, to double. *Bai ni naru*, to be doubled. *Ni-sô-bai*, twice as much. *San-sō-bai*, three times as much.

||BAI-BAI, バイバイ, 賣買, *n.* Buying and selling, trade, traffic, commerce. *Bai-bai szru*, to buy and sell, to trade. *Kono shina wa baibai ni gozaimasen*, this is not an article of trade.
Syn. URI-KAI, AKINAI, SHŌ-BAI.

BAI-BOKU, バイボク, 賣卜, Fortune telling, soothsaying. *Bai-boku szru*, to tell fortunes. *Bai-boku sensei*, a fortune teller.
Syn. URANAI.

BAI-DOKU, バイドク, 黴毒, *n.* Syphilis.

BAI-KEN-JŌ, バイケンジヤウ, 賣券狀, *n.* A written contract, article of agreement. A Deed. *Bai-kenjō wo tori-yari szru*, to give and receive a deed of sale.

BAI-MASHI, バイマシ, 倍增, Doubled in quantity. *Baimashi ni szru*, to double the quantity, to increase in geometrical progression.

BAI-NIN, バイニン, 賣人, *(uru h'to,) n.* A seller, merchant.

BAI-SEN, バイセン, 賣舩, *(akinai-bune,) n.* Merchant ship.

BAISHAKU, バイシヤク, 媒妁, *n.* A go-between, middle-man, a match-maker.
Syn. NAKAUDO.

BAI-SHIN, バイシン, 倍臣, *n.* A vassal of a feudatory, a rear-vassal.
Syn. MATA-MONO.

BAI-TOKU, バイトク, 賣得, *n.* Profit from trading. *Bai-toku szru*, to make money by selling. Syn MŌKE.

BAITORI-GACHI, バイトリガチ, 奪取勝, *n.* Seizing pell mell; scrambling for anything, the best man foremost. *Baitori-gachi ni szru*, to scramble.
Syn. TORI-HŌDAI.

BAI-U, バイウ, 梅雨, *(ume no ame.)* The June rains, when things are apt to mould.

BAI-YAKU, バイヤク, 賣藥, *(uri-guszri,) n.* Medicines kept for sale. *Baiyaku mise*, an apothecary shop. *Bai-yaku wo seiszru*, to compound drugs for sale.

BAKA, バカ, 馬鹿, *n.* A fool, dunce, (a contemptous epithet.) A kind of clam. *Baka wo iu*, to talk nonsense. *Baka wo szru*, to act as a fool. *Baka ni tszkeru kuszri ga nai*, there is no medicine for a fool. — *ni szru*, to ridicule, make fun of.
Syn. TAWAKE, AHŌ.

BAKA-BAKASHII,–KI,–KU, バカバカシイ, 馬鹿敷, Like a fool; stupidly, foolish. *Baka-baka-shiku nagai*, very long

BAKA-NA, バカナ, *a.* Foolish, stupid.

BAKARASHII,–KI,–KU, バカラシイ, Foolish, like a dunce.

BAKARI, バカリ, 計, *adv.* Only; about; just as when. *H'tori bakari*, only one person. *H'yaku nin bakari*, about a hundred persons. *Soko ni deta bakari*, just as he went out. *Shiro deta bakari nite teppō ni ataru*, he was shot just as he left the castle. Syn. HODO, NOMI.

BAKASARE,*–ru,–ta*, バカサレル, pass of *Bakasz*,

BAKASHI,*–sz,–ta*, バカス, 魅, *t.v.* To cheat, delude, to bewitch. *Hitszne onna no katachi ni bakete h'to wo bakasz*, the fox assuming the appearance of a woman deludes man.
Syn. MAYOWASZ, TABURAKASZ, MADOWASZ, DAMASZ.

BAKE,*–ru,–ta*, バケル, 化, *i. v.* To be transformed, changed into another form, (used generally of the fox, or cat.) *Neko baba ni bakeru*, the cat is changed into an old woman.
Syn. HENDZRU, KAWARU.

BAKE, バケ, 化, *n.* Transformation, deception ,fraud, imposition. *Bake ga arawareta*, he shows the cloven foot; the deception is made to appear.

BAKE-MONO, バケモノ, 化物, *n.* An apparition, spectre. *Bakemono ga deta.* — *ni ai mash'ta.*

†BAKKA, バクカ, 幕下, *n.* A feudal chief or feudatory lord.

†BAKKIN, バツキン, 罰勤, *n.* Punishment by hard labor.

†BAKKO-*szru*, バツコ, 跋扈, To strut, to swagger.
Syn. FUMBATTAGARU, ŌGIYŌ.

BAKKUN, バツクン, 拔群, Pre-eminent, transcendent, surpassing others; exceeding great.
Syn. NUKINDZRU, MENITATSZ, HIIDERU.

†BAKU, バク, 麥, (*mugi*), *n.* Wheat.

BAKU, バク, 貘, *n.* A tapir.

BAKUCHI, バクチ, 博奕, Gambling. *Bakuchi wo utsz*, to gamble.

BAKUCHI-UCHI, バクチウチ, 博奕打, *n.* A gambler.

BAKUCHI-YADO, バクチヤド, 博奕宿, *n.* A gambling house.

BAKUHAN, バクハン, 麥飯, *n.* A kind of food made of rice and wheat.

BAKURŌ, バクラウ, 博勞, *n.* A horse-jockey. — *szru*, to trade in horses.

†BAKUSHI,–*szru*,–*sh'ta*, バクスル, 縛, To bind. *Ma wo* —, to bind evil spirits.

BAKUSHU, バクシユ, 麥酒, *n.* Spirits made of wheat, Whiskey.

BAKUTAI, バクタイ, 莫大, A great quantity. *Bakutai na mono-iri*, great expenditure. *Bakutai ni*, adv. greatly.
Syn. TÁKU-SAN.

BAKU-YEKI, バクエキ, 博奕, Gambling. — *wo szru*, to gamble. Syn. BAKUCHI.

BAMMIN, バンミン, 萬民, (*yorodz no h'to*) *n.* All people.

BAMMOTS, バンモツ, 萬物, (*yorodz no mono*) *n.* All things.

BAMPŌ, バンパウ, 萬方, *n.* Every where, all quarters.

BAN, バン, 鷭, *n.* A kind of snipe.

BAN, バン, 盤, *n.* A block, checker-table.

BAN, バン, 晚, *n.* Evening, night. *Konban*, this evening. *Asa ban*, morning and evening.

BAN, バン, 萬, (*yorodz.*) Ten thousand. All.

BAN, バン, 番, *n.* A guard, watch. The ordinal suffix to numbers. *Ban wo szru*, to keep watch. *Ban sh'te iru*, keeping watch. *Mon-ban*, a gate-keeper. *Ichi-ban*, number one; the first. *Ichi-ban me*, the first one. *Ni-ban*, the second. *Iku-ban*, or *Nam-ban*, what number?

BAN-BAN, バンバン, 萬萬, Ten thousand times ten thousand, very many. *Ban-ban medetaku zonjimaszru*, I wish you infinite joy.

BANCHA, バンチャ, 山茗, *n.* An inferior kind of tea.

BAN-DAI, バンダイ, 番代, *n.* A substitute in official, police, or watch duty, *Bandai wo tanomu*, to find a substitute.

BAN-DAI, バンダイ, 萬代, *n.* All generations, all the dynasties, for ever.

‖BAN-DATE, バンダテ, 番立, *n.* In numerical order. *Ban-date sh'te oku*, place in numerical order.

†BAN-GAKU, バンガク, 蕃學, *n.* Foreign literature and science, especially European.

†BAN-GAKU, バンガク, 晚學, (*osoku manabu*). Learning late in life.

BAN-GASHIRA, バンガシラ, 番頭, *n.* A captain.

BANGAWARI, バンガハリ, 番代, *n.* Change of watch. *Bangawari wo szru*, to change the watch.

†BAN-GO, バンゴ, 蠻語, *n.* Foreign language; (Dutch or western languages).

†BAN-I, バンイ, 蠻夷, *n.* (*yebisz*). Barbarian, applied to Western nations.

BAN-JAKU, バンジヤク, 磐石, *n.* A rock.

BAN-JI, バンジ, 萬事, (*yorodz no koto.*) Every thing done, every kind of affair whatever.

†BAN-JŌ, バンジヤウ, 番匠, *n.* A carpenter. Syn. DAIKU.

BAN-JŌ, バンジヨウ, 萬乘, *n.* The ruler of ten thousand chariots, the Emperor.

†BAN-KEI, バンケイ, 晚景, *n.* Evening.

BAN-KOKU, バンコク, 萬國, (*yorodz no kuni*) *n.* All countries.

BAN-NIN, バンニン, 守人, (*mamoru h'to*). *n.* A guard, watchman; a policeman; keeper.

†BAN-RIYŌ, バンリヨウ, 蟠龍, *n.* A kind of lizzard.

†BAN-SE, バンセ, 萬世, *n.* (*yorodz yo*). All ages.

BAN-SHO, バンシヨ, 蕃書, *n.* Foreign books.

BAN-SHO, バンシヨ, 番所, *n.* A guard house, watch house. police station.

BAN-SŌ, バンソウ, 伴僧, *n.* A young Buddhist priest.

BAN-TAN, バンタン, 萬端, Every thing, every particular.

BANTARŌ, バンタラウ, 番太郎, *n.* An inferior street watchman.

BANTŌ, バントウ, 番頭, *n.* The chief clerk in a mercantile house.

BAN-YA, バンヤ, 番屋, *n.* The watch-house of the *gishinban*.

†BAPPAI, バツパイ, 罰盃, *n.* The punishment inflicted on the losing party in a game by making him drink a large quantity of *sake*. *Bappai wo nomaszru.*

BARA, バラ, coll. *n.* A small iron cash.

BARA, バラ 茨, *n.* A rose bush. *Bara no hana*, a rose. *Bara no toge*, the thorn of a rose.

BARA, バラ, A plural suffix; used by a superior in addressing others. *Wakatono-bara*, young cavaliers. *H'yakshō-bara*, the farmers.

BARA-BARA, バラバラ, , *adv.* In a scattered manner; in a dispersed, separated way. Also, the sound of the falling of things scattered, as the pattering of rain, of hail, &c. — *to nigeru*, to scatter andflee away — *to kubaru*, to be scattered about in separate clusters. *Ame ga — to furu*, there is a slight sprinkle of rain. *Kami wo — ni saku*, to tear paper into bits. *Oke — to kudzreru*, the tub has fallen to pieces, *Toji ga kirete hon ga — ni naru*, when the thread is cut the leaves of a book fall to pieces.

BARA-MAKI,, バラマキ, Sowing broadcast.

BARA-MON, バラモン, 婆羅門, *n.* The disciples of Shaka Niurai.

BARASEN, バラセン, 零亂錢, *n.* Loose money not strung together.

BARARI-TO, バラリト, *adv.* Same as *Bara-bara. Barari-to kiru*, to cut in two. *Bara-ri-to oku*, to place separately. *Kami wo barari-to yaburu*, to tear paper into pieces.

†BAREKIJIN, バレキジン, 馬櫪神, The god of horses.

BAREN, バレン, 馴牙, *n.* A long fringe attached to a banner.

BARI, バリ 尿, *n.* The urine. Syn. SHŌBEN.

BA-RIKI, バリキ, 馬力, *n.* Horse-power.

BASA-BASA, バサバサ, *adv.* The sound, or appearance of any th ng very dry. (?)

BASHAKU, バシャク, 馬借, *n.* An office where horses and coolies are hired, a livery stable.

BASHI, バシ, A particle of no meaning, some times answering to *wo*, or *sh'te* of the colloquial. *Yudan bashi sh'tamō na*, don't be negligent, *Yudan sh'te h'to ni bashi ubawaru na*, let no one seize it through carelessness.

BA-SHO, バショ, 場所, *n.* A place. Syn. BA, TOKORO.

BASHŌ, バセウ, 芭蕉, *n.* The banana, or plantain.

BASSARE,*-ru,-ta*, バッサレル, pass. of *Batsz*, to be punished by heaven.

BASSEKI, ハッセキ, 末席, *n.* The lowest seat.

BASSHI, バッシ, 末子, *n.* (*szye no ko.*) The youngest child.

BASSHI,*-szru,-sh'ta*, バッスル, 罰, *t. v.* To punish. Syn. TSZMI-SZRU, KEIBATS.

BASSON, バッソン, 末孫, *n.* The latest descendant.

†BASSZI, ハッスイ, 拔萃, (*nuki-atszmeru.*) To make and collect extracts, (as from books.) To extract and collect together.

BATA-BATA, バタバタ, *adv.* The sound of the flapping of the wings of a bird flying, of the feet running, or the sound of flat things striking, or falling in rapid succession. *Bata-bata to hatataki wo szru. Korori de h'to ga bata-bata to shinuru*, people die of cholera in rapid succession.

†BATEI, バテイ, 馬蹄, (*uma no hidzme,*) *n.* A horse's hoof.

†BATSZ, バツ, 跋, The end of a book.

BATSZ, バツ, 罰, *n.* Punishment, (inflicted by heaven.) *Ten no batsz*, punishment of heaven. *Batsz wo kōmuru*, to be punished.

BATSGIN, バツギン, 罰銀, *n.* A fine in money, damages, forfeit paid in money.

BATSYŌ, バツエフ, 末葉, *n.* The last descendant of a family.

BATSZA, バツザ, 末座, *n.* The lowest seat.

BATTA, バッタ, 匾蛋, *n.* A grasshopper.

BATTARI-TO, バッタリト, *adv.* The same as *Bata-bata. To wo battari to shimeru*, to slam the door.

BATTO, バット, *adv.* Sudden opening out, or bursting into view. *Hi wa batto moyetatsz*, the fire suddenly blazed up. *Hana wa batto hiraku*, the flower suddenly burst open.

†BAYA, バヤ, A verb suffix, expressing desire, intention. *Oshiye wo ukete h'to to narabaya*, by receiving instruction would become a man. *Mida wo tanonde Hotoke ni narabaya*, worshiped *Amida* that he might become a god. *Jı-gai sebaya to omoi*, thought he would kill himself.

BEBE, ベベ, *n.* A child's clothes, (children's language.) *Bebe wo kisheru*, to dress a child.

BEI, ベイ, same as *Beki.*

BEI, ベイ, 米, *n.* (*Kome.*) Rice.

BEI-KOKU, ベイコク, 米穀, *n.* Rice and cereals.

BEKARADZ, or BEKARAZARU, ベカラズ, 不可, neg. of *Beki.* Must not, should not. *Mu-yō no mono iru bekaradz*, no admittance except on business.

BEKI,*-KU,-SHI*, ベキ, 可, An auxilliary verb, having the sense of would, should, shall, will. *Beshi*, is used also as an imperative. *Itasz-beki koto*, a thing that should be done. *Watakushi no kamau beki koto de wa nai*, it is not a thing that I should interfere (or meddle) with. *Naru-beku wa oite kudasare*, if possible let it be as it is. *Ono-ono zongi-yori wo iu beshi*, let each say what he thinks.

BEKKAKU, ベツカク, 別格, *n.* An exception, not included in the rule, excluded, excepted. *Bekkaku wo motte mōshi-tzkeru*, to order as an exception. *Kodomo wa bekkaku ni sh'te kamawa-nai*, children being excepted it matters not. *Onna to naga-sode wa nanigoto mo bekkaku*, women and those that wear long sleeves (doctors and priests) are at all times excepted.

BEKKE, ベツケ, 別家, (*wakare no iye,*) *n.* Separating from the family, and going to house keeping for one's self; as a younger son. A separate house. *Bekke wo szru. Bekke saseru. Bekke yori hon-ke wo tszgu.*
Syn. BUNKE.

†BEKKIU, ベツキウ, 別宮, *n.* A separate *Miya.*

†BEKKOKU, ベツコク, 別國, *n.* A different country.

BEKKON, ベツコン, 別魂, Especially dear, particularly intimate. *Bekkon no aidagara*, a particularly dear relationship.

BEKKŌ, ベツカフ, 鼈甲, *n.* Tortoise-shell.

BEM-BEN, ベンベン, 浼焉, *adv.* Dilatory, procrastinating, tardy, slow. *Bemben to nani wo sh'te iru*, why have you been so slow? *Bemben to sh'te iru iraremai*, it will not do to procrastinate.
Syn. YŪ-YŪ, YURU-YURU, SORO-SORO.

BEM-BETSZ, ベンベツ, 辨別, To discriminate, to distinguish. — *szru.*
Syn. WAKERU.

BEMPATSZ, ベンパツ, 辮髮, *n*, The Chinese cue.

†BEMPEI, ベンペイ, 便閉, Obstruction of either fecal or urinary discharge. *Dai-bempei*, constipation of bowels. *Shō-bempei*, retention of urine.

BEN, ベン, 辨, Fluent in talking, eloquent. *Ben no yoi h'to. Ben ga warui. Ben ni makash'te sama-zama ni sszmeru*, to persuade with all his eloquence.

BENDSZU, ベンズル, see *Benji.*

†BENDOKU, ベンドク, 便毒, *n.* A bubo.
Syn. YOKONE.

BENI, ベニ, 紅粉, *n.* Rouge. The saffron plant. *Beni no hana*, the saffron flower. *Beni wo tszkeru*, to rouge.

BENI-SASHI-YUBI, ベニサシユビ, 無名指, *n.* The ring-finger.

BENI-ZARA, ベニザラ, 紅皿, The saucer in which rouge is kept.

BENI-ZOME, ベニゾメ, 紅染, Dyed in red.

BENJI,*–ru*, or *dzru,–ta*, ベンズル, 辨, *t. v.* To discriminate, distinguish; to explain, to expound, to do, transact. *Ze ka hi ka benji-kaneru*, difficult to distinguish the right and the wrong. *Yō wo benjiru* to transact business.
Syn. WAKATSZ, TOKU, TSZTOMERU.

BENKE-JIMA, ベンケジマ, 辨慶縞, *n.* Plaid, or checkered figures in cloth.

†BEN-KETSZ, ベンケツ, 便血, *n.* Bloody flux.

BENKIYŌ, ベンキヤウ, 勉强, (*tsztome.*) Industrious, diligent.

†BENNEI, ベンネイ, 辨佞, (*Hetszrai mono.*) Flattery, adulation. *Bennei naru h'to.*

BENRI, ベンリ, 便利, Convenient, commodious, adapted to use. *Benri ga yoi*, convenient, well adapted to use. *Benri ga warui*, or *Fubenri*, inconvenient.
Syn. TSZGŌ.

BENSHA, ベンシヤ, 辨者, *n.* An eloquent person, one fluent, and good at talking.

BENTO, ベンタウ, 辨當, *n.* A small box for carrying boiled rice, also, the food contained in the box.

BENZAITEN, ベンザイテン, 辨財天, *n.* The name of a Buddhist idol, the god of wealth.

BEN-ZETSZ, ベンゼツ, 辨舌, *n.* Fluent and clever at talking, eloquent.

BEPPUKU, ベツプク, 別腹, *n.* A different mother, but the same father, step-children.

BERABŌ, ベラボウ, A vulgar coll. word. *n.* A fool, an idler.

BESOKAKU, ベソカク, The appearance of the face when about to cry.

BESSHI, ベツシ, 別紙, (*bets no kami.*) *n.* Another paper, a different sheet of paper.

BESSHIN, ベツシン, 別心, (*bets no kokoro.*) Another, or different mind; alienation of heart. *Besshin naku*, of the same mind.

BESSHITE, ベツシテ, 別而, *adv.* Especially, particularly. *Kaze ga aru kara bessh'te hi no moto yō-jin shiro*, as it is windy be especially careful of fire.
Syn. WAKETE, KAKUBETSZ NI, SASH'TE.

BESSHO, ベツシヨ, 別所, (*Hoka no-tokoro.*) Another, or different place.

BESSŌ, ベツサウ, 別莊, *n.* A pleasure house, a summer house.

BETA-BETA, ベタベタ, *adv.* Sticky, gluey adhesive, glutinous, viscid. *Nori ga beta-beta tszku*, the gum is sticky.

BETATSZKI,*–ku,–ita*, ベタツク, *t. v.* To

be sticky, adhesive, glutinous, to stick to,

BETO-BETO, ベトベト, *adv.* Sticky, adhesive. glutinous.

BETSZ, ベツ, 別, (*hoka.*) Another, different, separate. — *no h'to*, another person.
Syn. YO, TA.

BETSZ-BETSZ-NI, ベツベツニ, *adv.* Separately, apart. *Betsz-betsz ni szru*, to separate, put apart.

BETSZ-DAN, ベツダン, 別段, Another and different thing, something besides; separate, distinct, especial, exceptional, particular. *Kore wa — ni ageru*, give this over and above. — *ni*, particularly.
Syn. KABUBETS, KOTO-NI.

BETSZ-GI, ベツギ, 別義, Different, especial, besides, unusual, extraordinary. — *kore naku soro*, have nothing especial, or unusual (to say.) — *de wa nai*, nothing new, or strange. -- *mōshi-maji*, no objection to make.

BETSZI, ベツイ, 別意, Especial, strange, different from what is common. — *sara ni nashi*, nothing strange, or unusual.

BETSZ-JI, ベツジ, 別事, (*betsz no koto*,) (same as above.)

BETSZJŌ, ベツゼウ, 條別, Different, unusual, exceptional. *Kono yamai inochi ni wa — nai*, this disease will not shorten life.

BETSZJO,*–szru*, ベツジヨ, 蔑如, To make light of, slight, show contempt for.
Syn. KARONDSRU.

BETTAKU, ベツタク, 別宅, (*Hoka no iye.*) A separate house, — *szru*, to live in a house separate from the principal family.

BETTARI-TO, ベツタリ, *adv.* Sticking fast to, applied close against. — *tszku*, to stick fast to. *Dai ni — yori-kakaru*, to lean against the table.

BETTŌ, ベツタウ, 別當, *n.* A Buddhist priest who also observes the Shintoo worship.

BETTŌ, ベツタウ, *n.* A hostler, groom.
Syn. KUCHI-TORI.

BI, ビ, 美, Beautiful, elegant, fine, good, delicious, pleasant, excellent. — *na mono*, a beautiful thing. *Bi-fu*, 美婦, a beautiful woman. *Bi-fuku*, 美服, fine clothes. *Bi-giyoku*, 美玉, a precious stone. *Bi-jin*, 美人, a handsome person. *Bi-jo*, 美女, a beautiful woman. *Bi kei*, 美景, beautiful scenery. *Bi mei*, 美名, a good name. *Bi mi*, 美味, delicious taste. *Bi-sei*, 美聲, a fine voice. *Bi shoku*, 美色, beautiful color. *Bi-shoku*, 美食, delicious food. *Bi-sō*, a good physiognomy.
Syn. UMASHI, YOSHI, URUWASHI, UTSZKUSHI.

†BI, ビ, 微, Small, little in size, degree, or quantity, mean, trifling. *Bi-fū*, 微風, light wind. *Bi-jaku*, 微弱, weak, delicate, feeble. *Bi-kan*, 微寒, slight degree of cold. *Bi-riki*, 微力, little strength. *Bi-shō*, 微笑, a smile. *Bi-u*, 微雨, a fine rain. *Bi-un*, 微運, unlucky. *Bi-fuku*, 微服, mean clothes.
Syn. CHIISASHI, SZKUNASHI, SZKOSHI.

BI, ビ, 尾, (*hiki.*) Tail, the numeral used in counting fish. *Sakana ichi bi*, one fish.

||BIBIRI,*–ru*,*–ta*, ビビル, 縮, *i. v.* To contract, shrink. Syn. CHIJIMARU.

BIBISHII,–KI,–KU,–SHI, ビビイシ, 美美, Beautiful, handsome, fine, splendid. *Bibishiku yosōte shutsz-jin szru*, splendidly caparisoned they marched out.
Syn. UTSZKUSHII, URUWASHI.

BICHI-BICHI, ビチビチ, 鱍鱍, *adv.* The springing or leaping motion of a live fish when thrown on the ground. — *to haneru*, to spring and leap about, as a fish. — *ikiteiru uchi ni*, whilst yet alive and kicking.

BIIDORO, ビイドロ, 硝子, *n.* Glass.

BIJI, ビジ, 鼻痔, *n* Polypus of the nose.

BIKKO, ビクコ, 跛行, *n.* Lame, a cripple. — *wo hiku*, to walk lame. Syn. CHIMBA.

BIKKURI, ビツクリ, *adv.* Startled, as by sudden alarm; surprised, shocked. *Dashi-nuke no ji-shin de — shimash'ta*, startled by the sudden shock of an earthquake. *Ni san nen mi-nai uchi ni — szru hodo ni o nari da*, in the two or three years in which I have not seen you, you have changed surprisingly. Syn. ODOROKU, TAMAGERU.

BIKU, ビク, 比丘, *n.* A bonze, Buddhist priest.

BIKU-BIKU-*szru*, ビクビクスル, *i.v.* To start in alarm, or in sleep, to wince, to jerk as in a fit. *Moshi ya otte ga kuru ka to — szru*, to start as if the pursuer had come.

BIKUNI, ビクニ, 丘比尼, *n.* A nun.

BIKU-TSZKI,*–ku*,*–ita*, ビクツク, *i. v.* To start, jerk or wince involuntarily.

BIMBŌ, ビンバウ, 貧乏, Poor, destitute. — *na*, (*a.*) poor. — *ni naru*, to become poor. — *nin*, a poor man. — *szru*, to be poor. Syn. MADZSHIKI, HINKIU.

BI-MEI, ビメイ, 未明, (*imada akedz*). Before day-break.

BI-MOKU, ビモク, 眉目, (*mayu, me*), *n.* Eye-brows and eyes. — *wo odorokasz*, to startle or surprise a person.

BIN, ビン, 鬢, *n.* The temples, the hair on the temples. — *wo haru*, to slap a person on the temple. — *wo kaki-aguru*, to smooth back the hair on the temples. — *no hotszre*, the loose hair hanging from the temples.

BIN, ビン, 瓶, *n.* A phial, a small bottle.

BIN, ビン, 便, *n.* Opportunity; convenient time or way. — *wo ukagō*. to seek for an opportunity. — *wo kiku*, idem. — *ga yoi*, it is a good opportunity. *Go-bin*, a future opportunity. *Kō-bin*, a fortunate opportunity. Syn. TSZIDE, TAYORI.

BINGACHŌ, ビンガテウ, 頻伽鳥, *n.* A fabulous being of the Buddhists, having a human form covered with feathers, supposed to live in heaven.

BINGI, ビンギ, 便宜, *n.* Opportunity, convenient way or time. — *no chi de katte kudasare*, buy it wherever it is convenient. *Yen-ro yuye ni — ga mare*, because it is far opportunities are seldom.
Syn. BENRI, TAYORI.

BINRŌJI, ビンラウジ, 檳榔子, *n.* The betel-nut.

BIN-SASHI, ビンサシ, 鬢插, *n.* A hair-pin.

BIN-TSZKE, ビンツケ, 髮油, *n.* Pomatum.

BINZASARA, ビンザサラ, 拍板, *n.* A kind of musical instrument.

BIRA, ビラ, *n.* A handbill, placard, or notice posted up. — *wo haru*, to post a handbill

BIRA-BIRA, ビラビラ, *adv.* With a waving fluttering motion, (same as *Hira*). *Hata ga — ugoku*, the flag waves. *Szso wo — fuki-ageru*, to blow up the skirts of a dress.

BIRAN,*-szru*, ビラン, 糜爛, To be red and sore, inflammed. *Kidz ga —*, the wound is inflammed.
Syn. TADARERU.

BIRARĪ-TO, ビラリト, same as *Bira-bira*.

BIRA-TSZKI,*–ku,–ita*, ビラツク, *i.v.* To wave and flutter, as a flag in the wind.

BIRI-BIRI, ビリビリ, *adv.* Like the sound of anything dry, tearing or cracking open, A smarting, griping or pricking pain. Chapped, cracked, split. — *to wareru*. — *to sakeru*. — *to itamu*, *Ammari — ī-nasaru na*, dont talk so incessantly.

BIRITSZKI,*–ku–ita*, ビリツク, *i.v.* To smart, prick, gripe.

BIRŌ, ビロウ, 尾籠, *(oko)*. Indecent, indelicate, something of which one is ashamed to speak, mostly used apologetically. — *nagara go-ran kudasare*, excuse the indelicacy, but please look at this (something offensive or unsightly). — *na furu-mai*, indecent behaviour. — *wo wabiru*, to apologize for something indecent.
Syn. BUREI, SHITSZREI.

BIRŌDO, ビロウド, 天鵞絨, *n.* Velvet.

BISAI, ビサイ, 微細, *adv.* Minutely, particularly. — *ni shirusz*, to write down minutely. Syn. KOMAYAKA-NI, KUWASHIKU.

‖BI-SHŌ, ビセウ, 微小, Little, minute, trifling, few. Syn. CHIISAI, SZKUNAI.

BITA, ビタ, 鐚, *n.* An iron cash. — *ichi-mon*, one cash.

BITEIKOTSZ, ヒテイコツ, 尾底骨, *n.* The coccyx.

†BITŌ, ビトウ, 鼻頭, *(Hana-saki.)* *n.* Tip of the nose.

BIWA, ビハ 琵琶, *n.* A banjo with four strings. — *wo hiku*, to play on a banjo.

BIWA, ビハ, 枇杷, *n.* A loquat.

BIWABON, ビハボン, 口琴, *n.* A kind of wind-instrument.

BIWA-HŌSHI, ビハホウシ, 琵琶法師, *n.* A strolling player on the banjo.

BIWA-UCHI, ビハウチ, 琶琵打, *n.* A player on the banjo.

BIYAKKO, ビヤクコ, 白狐, *(shiroi kitsz-ne,)* *n.* A white fox.

BIYAKU-DAN, ビヤクダン, 白檀, *n.* Sandal-wood.

†BIYAKUGŌ, ビヤクガウ, 白毫, *n.* A protuberance on the forehead of Buddhist idols, supposed to be the organ of omniscience.

†BIYAKURI, ビヤクリ, 白痢, *n.* White mucous stools.

BIYAKURŌ, ビヤクラフ, 白蠟, *n.* White wax.

BIYAKURŌ, ビヤクラウ, 白勞, *n.* Pewter.

BIYŌ, ビヤウ, 鋲, *n.* A tack, a small nail with a large head.

†BIYŌ, ビヤウ, 廟, *n.* Imperial cemetery.

†BIYŌ-BIYŌ, ビヤウビヤウ, 渺渺, *adv.* Indistinct from distance, scarcely to be distinguished, as anything on the distant horizon.

BIYŌBU, ビヤウブ, 屏風, *n.* A folding screen. — *issō*, a pair of screens. — *hanzō*, one screen.

BIYŌ-CHIU, ビヤウチウ, 病中, Whilst sick, during sickness.

†BIYŌ-DAN, ビヤウダン, 廟壇, *n.* The altar where tablets are kept.

BIYŌ-DŌ, ビヤウダウ, 平等, *(tairaka-ni h'toshi.)* Even and equal, just and equal. — *ni kubaru*, to distribute equally.

BIYŌ-GAN, ビヤウガン, 病眼, *n.* Sore-eyes.

BIYŌ-GO, ビヤウゴ, 病後, (*Yami agari,*) *n.* After sickness, convalescence.

BIYŌ IN, ビヤウヰン, 病院 *n.* A hospital, infirmary.

BIYŌ-JA, ビヤウジヤ, 病者, *n.* A sick person.

BIYŌ-KA, ビヤウカ, 病家, *n.* A sick family, a house where there is sickness.

†BIYŌ-KAKU, ビヤウカク, 病客, *n.* A sick guest, a hospital patient.

BIYŌ-KI, ビヤウキ, 病氣, (*Yamai,*) *n.* Sickness, disease.

BIYŌ-KON, ビヤウコン, 病根, (*Yamai no moto,*) *n.* Origin of disease.

BIYŌ-KU, ビヤウク, 病苦, *n.* Sufferings from disease.

BIYŌ-NAN, ビヤウナン, 病難, *n.* Calamity, or affliction from disease.

BIYŌ-NIN, ビヤウニン, 病人, *n.* A sick person.

BIYŌ-NŌ, ビヤウナウ, 病惱, Faint and exhausted by disease.

BIYŌ-SHI, ビヤウシ, 病死, *n.* Died of sickness, a natural death.

BIYŌ-SHIN, ビヤウシン, 病身, *n.* Sickly, an invalid.

BIYŌ-SHŌ, ビヤウシヤウ, 病牀, *n.* A sick-bed.

BIYŌ-SHŌ, ビヤウシヤウ, 病症, *n.* Symptoms of disease.

BIYŌ-TEI, ビヤウテイ, 體病, *n.* Kind, or nature of disease.

BŌ, ボウ 棒, *n.* A pole, a club, stick, bludgeon; a blow with a stick. *Rok'shaku bō,* a six-foot pole. — *wo tszkau,* to fence with a pole. *Ichi-bō wo atayeru,* to give one blow (with a rod). *Saki-bō,* the foremost man where two are carrying with the same pole. *Ato-bō,* the hindmost man. — *wo hiku,* to draw a line across, to erase.

†BŌ, ボウ, 鵬, *n.* A fabulous bird of monstrous size.

†BŌ, バウ, 望, *n.* Full of the moon. *Tszki wa bō ni mitszru,* the moon is full.

†BŌ, バウ, 房, *n.* A chamber. Syn. NEYA.

BŌ, バウ, 坊, *n.* A small Buddhist temple, the small houses near a temple where the priests live. *Is-san no bō-shū,* all the priests of the temple.

BŌ, バウ, (coll.) A child under five years. — *wa nichi-nichi chiye-dzite airashiku narimash'ta,* the child daily growing in intelligence has become more loveable. *Obō san wa ōkiku o nari-nasaimash'ta,* how your child has grown. Syn. OSANAGO.

BŌ-AKU, バウアク, 暴惡, (*takeshiki aku.*) Fierce and wicked, atrociously wicked.

BŌ-BANA, バウバナ, 棒鼻, *n.* The end, or confines of a town, (*shiku no hadzre.*)

BŌ-BŌ, バウバウ, 茫茫, *adv.* Growing and spreading over thick and close, as the hair, beard, or grass when neglected. *Kusa — to oi-shigeri michi wakaradz,* the grass growing up thick the road could not be distinguished. — *to sh'ta sora,* cloudy and thick weather.

BŌ-BURA, ボウブラ, 南瓜, *n,* A pumpkin.

†BŌ-CHŌ, ボウチヤウ, 膨脹, Swollen. — *szru,* to be swollen. Syn. FUKURERU.

BODAI, ボダイ, 菩提, *n* Devotion, or mortification of all carnal affections, in order to obtain salvation. (Bud.) — *no michi ni iru,* to enter on a religious life. — *no nen yameru,* to cease having religious feelings. — *wo tomurau,* to say prayers for the dead.

BODAIJŪ, ボダイジユ, 菩提樹, *n.* The name of a tree, from which rosaries are made. (Bud.)

BODAI-SHIN, ボダイシン, 菩提心, *n.* A devotional mind, intent on seeking salvation by mortifying the carnal affections. — *wo okosz,* to excite to a devotional mind. (Bud.)

BODAI-SHO, ボダイシヨ, 菩提所, *n.* The temple, or cemetery where prayers and offerings are made for the dead. (Bud.)

BODŌ, ボダウ, 母堂, (*haha,*) *n.* Mother, (in speaking to another of his mother). *Go — sama,* your mother.

BŌDZ, バウズ, 坊主, *n.* A bonze, buddhist priest; one whose head is shaven.

BŌFURI-MUSHI, ボウフリムシ, 孑孓, *n.* The animalculæ found in stagnant water.

†BŌFŪ, バウフウ, 暴風, (*arakaze*). A violent wind, a tempest.
Syn. HAYATE, ARASHI.

BŌGAN, バウガン, 坊官, *n.* The servant of a two-sworded Buddhist priest.

BŌGASHIRA, ボウガシラ, 棒頭, *n.* The head-man of chair coolies.

†BŌGETSZ, バウゲツ, 望月, (*mochidzki*), *n.* The full-moon.

BOGI, ボギ, 母儀, *n.* Mother, (same as *bodō.*

†BŌ-GIYAKU, バウギヤク, 暴逆, Violent, and rebellious against master or parent.

BŌ-GIYO, バウギヨ, 防禦, To resist, or repel the attack of an enemy. — *no yōi szru,* to make preparations to resist an enemy. Syn. FUSEGU.

BŌ-GUI, ボウグイ, 界牌, *n.* Posts erected to mark a boundary, a sign-post. — *wo utsz,* to set up boundary posts.

BŌ-GUMI, ボウグミ, 棒組, *n.* Chair-bearers guild.

BŌHAN, ボウハン, 謀判, *n.* A forged seal. — *szru*, to forge a seal.

†BŌI, バウイ, 暴意, *n.* Violent, cruel, fierce.

BŌ-JAKU-BU-JIN, バウシヤクブジン, 傍若無人, Without fear, shame, or respect for others.

BŌJI, ボウシ, 炊夫, *n.* A cook, or kitchen servant,

BŌ-JITS, バウシツ, 望日, *n.* The 15th day of the month, when the moon is full.

BOKASHI, *-sz,-shta*, ボカス, *t.v.* To shade from a deep to a lighter color, to surround with a halo. or shaded border.

BOKE, ボケ, 木瓜, *n.* The Pirus Japonica.

BOKE, *-ru,-ta*, ボケル, 惚, *i.v.* To be shaded on the margin from a deep to a light color. (Met. To degenerate, to become childish from age). *Toshi ga yotte boketa*, to be old and childish. Syn. BOREKU.

BOKE-BOKE-TO, ボケボケト, 惚惚, *adv.* Stupid, silly, childish.

†BŌKEI, ボウケイ, 謀計, *n.* An artifice, trick, fraud, plot, stratagem. Syn. HAKARIGOTO.

BOKI-BOKI-TO, ボキボキト, *adv.* The sound of cracking the fingers, or breaking a radish. *Yubi wo — oru*, to crack the fingers. *Daikon wo — oru*, to snap a radish in two.

BŌ-KIYAKU, バウキヤク, 忘却, To forget. Syn. WASZRERU, SHITSZ-NEN.

†BOKKIYO, *-szru*, ボクキヨ, 卜居, *i.v.* To erect, or own a house.

†BŌKŌ, ボコウ, 母公, *n.* Mother.

†BŌKŌ, バウクワウ, 膀胱, *n.* The bladder.

BŌKON, バウコン, 亡魂, *n.* A ghost, spirit. Syn. YŪREI.

BOKU, ボク, 僕, *n.* A servant, also in speaking humbly of one'self, your servant, I. Syn. KERAI, KODZKAI.

BOKU, ボク, 木, *(ki)*, Wood, wooden. — *seki*, wood and stone.

BOKU, ボク 墨, *(szmi)*, Ink.

BOKU-DO, ボクドウ, 牧童, *(maki no warambe)*, A cowherd, herdsman.

BOKU-RI, ボクリ, 木履, *(geta)*, *n.* Wooden clogs.

BOKU-SEKI, ボクセキ, 墨跡, *(szmi no ato)*, Writing, penmanship.

BOKUSHA, ボクシヤ, 卜者, *(uranai-ja) n.* A fortune-teller.

†BOKUSHI, *-sz-,shta'* ボクス, 卜, *t.v.* To tell fortunes. Syn. URANAU.

BOKU-TŌ, ボクトウ, 木刀, *n.* A wooden sword.

BOKUZEI, ボクゼイ, 卜筮, *n.* Bamboo rods used by fortune-tellers.

BOM-BORI, ボンボリ, 雪洞, *n.* A candlestand.

BOM-BU, ボンブ, 凡夫, *(tada no h'to)*, *n.* A man, an ordinary man; human being. (Bud.) *Hotoke mo motowa — nari — mo satoreba hotoke nari, Amida* originally was only a man, a man also by fully knowing all things becomes a god. — *no uchi nite — ni aradz*, being in the form of a man yet not a man.

BOM-MATSZRI, ボンマツリ, 盆祭, *n.* The feast of lanterns, on the 13th, 14th, and 15th of the 7th month.

BŌ-MORI, バウモリ, 坊守, *n.* The wife of a priest of the Montoshu sect of Buddhists.

†BOMPI, ボンピ, 凡卑, *n.* A vulgar person.

BON, ボン, 盆, *n.* A wooden tray, a waiter

BON, ボン, 鬼節, *n.* The feast of lanterns.

†BŌ-NA, バウナ, 暴, *(arai,) a.* Fierce, violent, cruel, tempestuous.

†BON-CHI, ボンチ, 凡智, *n.* Ordinary wisdom or talent;. not extraordinary.

BON-DEN, ボンデン, 梵天, *n.* A festival celebrated, when any severe sickness prevails, to propitiate evil spirits.

†BON-GO, ボンゴ, 梵語, *n.* The sacred language of the Buddhists. The Pali.

BON-JI, ボンジ, 梵字, *n.* The sacred written character used by the Buddhists. Pali letters.

BON-KU, ボンク, 盆供, *n.* Offerings made during the feast of lanterns to the spirits of the dead.

BON-NIN, ボンニン, 凡人, *n.* A man or human being, not supernatural; a common person, an ordinary man in talent or ability. — *ni aradz*, not a common man.

BON-NŌ, ボンナウ, 煩悩, *n.* Lust, sensuality, sinful desires. *Bon-nō wo szku*, to save from sinful lusts. *Bon-nō ga okoru*, the rousing up of sinful desires. *Bon-nō no kidzna wo tatsz*, to cut off the first motion of lusts. *Bon-nō no inu oyedomo saradz*, though a lustful dog be driven away he will not leave.

BON-NO-KUBO, ボンノクボ, 頸凹, *n.* The hollow on the back of the neck.

†BON-RIYO, ボンリヨ, 凡慮, *n.* Ordinary human intellect, *Bon-riyo no oyobu tokoro ni aradz*, that which men of common minds cannot attain to.

†BON-SHIN, ボンシン, 凡身, *n.* Ordinary human body.

†BON-SHIN, ボンシン, 凡心, *n.* Common human intellect.

BONSŌ, ボンサウ, 凡僧, *n.* A common priest, an ignorant priest.

BONYARI, ボンヤリ, 漠然, *adv.* Dim, obscure, cloudy, hazy. *Me ga — sh'te yoku miye nai*, my eyes are dim and I cannot see well. *— sh'ta h'to*, a person of dull perception, Syn. UTTORI, BOTTO.

†BONZAI, ボンザイ, 犯罪, (*tszmi wo okasz*), To commit sin

†BON-ZOKU, ボンゾク, 凡俗, Common and mean; the common herd, the laity. *— no mi wa fugō ni sh'te kami ni chikayoru koto atawadz*, the common people being unholy cannot approach god.

†BŌ-OKU, バウオク, 茅屋, (*waraya*) *n.* A thatched house.

BORA, ボラ, 鯔, *n.* A kind of fish.

BORE,*–ru*,*–ta*, ボレル, 耄, *i.v.* To be old and childish, decrepit,

BOREI, ボレイ, 牡蠣, *n.* Lime made by burning shells, used as a medicine.

BORI-BORI-TO, ボリボリト, coll. *adv.* The sound of craunching, or crushing any hard substance with the teeth. *Inu ga — hone wo kamu*, the dog is gnawing a bone. *— nedzmi ga nani ka kūte iru*, what is the rat gnawing at?

†BŌ-RIYAKU, ボウリヤク, 謀略, *n.* An artifice, trick, stratagem. *— wo okonau*, to use a stratagem.
Syn. BŌKEI, HAKARIGOTO.

BORO, ボロ, *n.* Rags.

BORO-BORO-TO, ボロボロト, *adv.* In a crumbling or ragged manner. *Tszchi — ochiru*, the dirt falls crumbling.

BOROKE,*–ru*,*–ta*, ボロケル, same as *Boreru*.

BORONJI, ボロンジ, 梵論字, *n.* A person who goes about with his head and face concealed in a basket playing on a flageolet. Syn. KOMOSŌ:

BOROTSZCHI, ボロツチ,, *n.* Loose crumbling earth.

BOSATSZ, ボサツ, 菩薩, *n.* Name of Buddhist divinities inferior to Hotoke.

†BŌSEN, バウセン, 防戰, (*fusegi-tatakau*), To resist, repel, fight off.

†BŌSHA, バウシヤ, 茅舍, n. A thatched house.

BŌSHI, バウシ, 帽子, *n.* A white cap made of raw cotton, worn by the bride at her wedding, and by women at funerals.

†BO-SHIN, バウシン, 亡親, *n.* Deceased parents.

BŌSHO, ボウシヨ, 謀書, *n.* A forged letter, or writing.

†BŌSHOKU, バウシヨク, 暴食, Eating voraciously, or gluttonously.
Syn. MUYAMI TO KŪ.

†BOSSZRU, ボツスル, 沒, *i.v.* To die, end, perish. *Chi-chi bossh'te sono okonai wo miru*, when the father is dead, (the son) should observe his ways. *Hi wa nishi ni —*, the sun has sunk in the west.
Syn. SHINURU, OWARU, KURERU.

BOTAN, ボタン, 牡丹, *n.* The peony.

BOTAN, ボタン, 紐扣子, (derived from Eng. button), *n.* A button.

BOTAN-KIYO, ボタンキヨ, 巴旦杏, *n.* A kind of plum.

BOTEFURI, ボテフリ, 賣菜傭, *n.* A hawker, a pedler of goods in the streets.

BOTSZ-BOTSZ, ボツボツ, 勃勃, *adv.* Little by little, slowly, doing a little at a time, coll. *— to kusa wo mushiru*, to pull up weeds little by little.

†BOTSZ-DEKI, ボツデキ, 沒溺, Drowned.

†BOTSZ-ZEN-TO, ボツゼン, 勃然, *adv.* Sudden burst, or flash, as of anger.

BŌ-TSZKAI, ボウツカイ, 棍手, *n.* A pedler of quack medicines, who to attract buyers, exhibits his skill in the use of the club.

BOTSZ-RAKU, ボツラク, 沒落, Ruined, fallen and destroyed; broken and ended, (as a fortune, property,) bankrupt. *Kanemochi mo muri ga aru to — shimasz*, a man though he be rich will be ruined by dishonesty.

BOTTERI-TO, ボツテリト, 豐豔, *adv.* Fleshy, corpulent. *— f'tote iru*, to be large and corpulent. Syn. KOYERU, FUTORU.

BOTTO, ボツト, *adv.* Dull, stupid, flat, lifeless or sluggish in manner. *Me ga — sh'ta*, eyes have become dull.

BOTTORI, ボツトリ, *adv.* In a soft, quiet or silent manner, or like any thing soft and wet falling *— to sh'te iru*, to be quiet. *Yuki ga — to ochiru.*

BŌ-U, バウウ, 暴雨, (*hageshii ame*), *n.* A violent rain.

BŌ-YA, バウヤ, (same as *Bō*), A child, baby. *— kochi yokose na*, bring the baby here.

BŌZEN, バウゼン, 忙然, *adv.* Stupified. thunderstruck, astounded, aghast. *— to sh'te iru.*

BU, ブ, 武, Military. *— wo arasō*, to dispute about military affairs.

BU ブ, 分, *n.* A part, fraction, the tenth of an inch. *Ichi —* one part. *Sam — ichi*, one third. *H'yaku — ichi*, one hundredth part. *Is-szn go —*, one inch and a half.

BU, ブ, 部, A classifier for a class, set, or

kind; radicals. *Kono hon san satsz wo motte ichi — to szru*, this book is complete in three volumes. *Kono ji wa nan no — ni aru de arō*, what is the radical of this character?

BU, ブ, 無; 不, A syllable of negation. No, not, is not.

BU-AI, ブアイ, 步合, (*risoku*,) *n.* Interest on money, profit.

BU-AISATSZ, ブアイサツ, 不挨拶, Answering rudely, or ill-humoredly.

BU-ASHIRAI-NA, ブアシライナ, 不會釋, *a.* Rude, inhospitable, or uncivil in treatment of guests

BU-BARI,*–ru,–tta*, ブバル, 武張, *i. v.* To display, or show-off courage, to bully. *Bu-batta h'to*, one who struts and makes a martial show.

BU-BI, ブビ, 武備, Military preparations. — *genjū ni szru*, to make strong the military preparations.

BU-BIKI, ブビキ, 分引, Small reduction in price. — *wo szru*, to make a small reduction of price.

BUCHI, ブチ, 駁, *n.* Piebald. — *m'ma*, a piebald horse.

BUCHI,*–tsz,–tta*, ブツ, 打, *t. v.* To strike, beat, hit, knock, whip. This word is a coll. and vulgar form of *Utsz*, and much used joined with other verbs. *Te, kobushi, muchi, ishi, kanadzchi, take, ki nado de butsz*, to strike with the hand, fist, whip, stone, hammer, bamboo, or stick.
Syn. UTSZ, CHŌCHAKU SZRU.

BUCHI-AKE,*–ru,–ta*, ブチアケル, 打明, *t. v.* To knock or beat open; to empty out, as a bag, box, &c.

BUCHI-ATE,*–ru,–ta*, ブチアテル, 打當, *t.v.* To shoot at and hit, to strike, to hit.

BUCHI-DASHI,*–sz,–sh'ta*, ブチダス, 打出, *t. v.* To knock or beat out.

BUCHI-KACHI,*–tsz,–tta*, ブチカツ, 打勝, *i. v.* To win, or overcome in a fight.

BUCHI-KOROSHI,*–sz,–sh'ta*, ブチコロス, 打殺, *t. v.* To beat to death.

BUCHI-KOWASHI,*–sz,–sh'ta*, ブチコワス, 打壞, *t. v.* To break down by beating, to strike and break.

BUCHI-KOMI,*–mu,–nda*, ブチコム, 打込, *t. v.* To drive into, to hammer in.

BUCHI-KUDAKI,*–ku,–ita*, ブチクダク, 打碎, *t. v.* To beat into pieces.

BUCHI-MAKE,*–ru,–ta*, ブチマケル, 打潑, *t. v.* To empty and scatter, as water, or grain from a bag.

BUCHI-MAKE,*–ru,–ta*, ブチマケル, 打負, *i. v.* To be beaten, or lose in a fight.

BUCHI-NUKI,*–ku,–ita*, ブチヌク, 打拔, *t. v.* To drive, or hammer through.

BUCHI-SHIME,*–ru,–ta*, ブチシメル, 打占, *t. v.* To strike and kill, as a rat, snake; to seize and bind as a thief, to beat.

BUCHI-TAOSHI,*–sz,–sh'ta*, ブチタフス, 打倒, *t. v.* To knock down, as a man, or any thing standing.

BUCHI-TATAKI,*–ku,–ita*, ブチタタク, 打, 拷 *t. v.* To fight, box.

BUCHI-TOME,*–ru,–ta*, ブチトメル, 打止, *t.v.* To shoot and kill any thing in motion.

BUCHI-TSZKE,*–ru,–ta*, ブチツケル, 打付, *t. v.* To hit, to hammer fast, to nail fast.

BUCHI-YABURI,*–ru,–tta*, ブチャブル, 打破, *t. v.* To tear, or break by beating.

BU-CHŌ-HŌ, ブチヤウハウ, 不調法, Awkward, clumsy, bungling, inexperienced, stupid, foolish, bad, used mostly apologettically of one's self. — *wo szru*, to do a foolish or awkward thing. *Sake wo — de gozarimas*, (in declining to drink,) I am poor at drinking wine. — *mono nanibun yoroshiku otanomi mōshimasz*, as I am inexperienced please help me all you can.
Syn. SO-SŌ, FUTSZDZKA.

BUDŌ, ブダウ, 葡萄, *n.* Grapes. — *dzru*, grape-vine. — *shu*, grape-wine.

BU-DŌ, ブダウ, 無道, (*michi nashi*.) Devoid of principle, impious, vicious, unreasonable.

BU-DŌ, ブダウ, 武道, (*Samurai no michi*.) *n.* Military sciences.

BU-GAKU, ブガク, 舞樂, *n.* Pantomime and music.

BU-GEI, ブゲイ, 武藝, *n.* The military arts, of which the Jap reckon 14, such as the use of the sword, spear, bow, club, musket, horse, &c.

BU-GEN, ブゲン, 分限, Rich, wealthy. *Bu-gen-sha*, a rich man.

BU-GIN, ブギン, 步銀, *n.* Percentage, or profit from exchange.

BU-GIYŌ, ブギヤウ, 奉行, *n.* A superintendent, a governor. — *sho*, superintendent's office.

BU-GU, ブグ, 武具, *n.* Military arms and accoutrements.

BU-I, ブイ, 武威, *n.* Military power.

BU-I, ブイ, 無異, (*kawaru koto nashi*). Without any thing strange, or unusual; without accident.

BU-IKI-NA, ブイキナ, coll. Clownish, vulgar, coarse, rough in manners.

BU-IKU, ブイク, 撫育, (*sodateru.*) To bring up, to rear up, support, nourish. *Kodomo wo — szru,*

BU-IN, ブイン, 無音, (*tayori ga nai,*) No letter, no word, no communication. *makoto-ni go buin tszkamatszri soro,* I have not written to you for a long time.

BUJI, ブジ, 事無, (*nani goto mo nai*), without accident, without anything unusual occuring, safe, free from trouble. *Yedo kara buji ni uchi ye kayeri-mash'ta,* has returned home from Yedo in safety. Syn. SOKUSAI.

BU-JUTS, ブジユツ, 武術, *n.* Military art.

BUKE, ブケ, 武家, (*samurai.*) *n.* The military class, or gentry.

†BU-KEI, ブケイ, 無稽, Untrue, fictitious, fabrication.

BU-KI, ブキ, 武器, (*samurai no utszwa.*) *n.* Military arms.

BU-KIRIYŌ, ブキリヤウ, 無容色, Homely, ugly.

BU-KIYOKU, ブキヨク, 舞曲. *n.* Music and dancing.

BU-KIYŌ, ブキヨウ, 不器用. Of no ability talent or ingenuity, not clever, awkward, unskilful.

BUKKI, ブツキ, 佛器, (*Hotoke no utszwa*), *n.* Utensils used in the worship of Buddha.

BUKKIYO, ブツキヤウ, 佛經, *n.* The sacred books of the Buddhists.

BUKKOROSZ, ブツコロス. See *Buchikoroshi.*

BUKKOWASZ, ブツコワス, See *Buchikowashi.*

BUKKOMU, ブツコム. See *Buchikomi.*

BUKKU, ブツク, 佛供, *n.* Things offered up to *Hotoke*, in worship.

BUKKUDAKU, ブツクダク. See *Buchi-kudaki*

BUKK'WA, ブツクワ, 佛果. *n.* Buddhist perfection. The reward of a religious life.

†BU-KO, ブコ, 武庫, *n.* An armory, a house in which arms are kept.

BUKŌ, ブカウ, 武功. *n.* Military services worthy of praise; great military deeds or merit. *Bu-kō wo tateru.*

BU-KOTSZ, ブコツ, 無骨. Rude, coarse; clownish, rustic.

BUKURIYO, ブクリヤウ, 茯苓, *n.* The name of a medicine, a kind of fungus growing on the root of the pine. Syn. MATSZHODO.

BUMA, ブマ, 無間. Awkward, acting out of time and place, blundering.

BUM-BU, ブンブ, 文武. *n.* Literature and military art.

BU-MEI, ブメイ, 武名. *n.* Military fame. *Bumei no aru h'to.*

BUMMAKERU, ブンマケル. See *Buchi-make.*

†BUM-PA, ブンパ, 分派, (*wakare no nagare*). The streams branching from a fountain. Fig. of teaching, or doctrines transmitted from some person, or place, as its origin. *Hasshu wa mina tenjiku no shaka no bum-pa de gozarimasz.* The Buddhist sects all came down from the Indian *Shaka.*

†BUM-PITSZ, ブンピツ, 文筆. *n.* Literature and writing. — *Bum pitsz ni tassh'ta h'to,* one accomplished in literature, and the art of writing.

BHM-PŌ, ブンパウ, 文法. *n.* Rules of composition, style of writing.

BUN, ブン, 文, (*fumi*). *n.* Writing, letters, composition, literature. — *Bun ni tasszru h'to,* an accomplished writer.

BUN, ブン, 分, (*wakachi*). *n.* A part, portion, division, share, duty, station in life, circumstances, ability. *Kore wa watakushi no bun,* this is my share. *Bun no hoka,* besides one's proper part, duty or place. *Bun ni szgiru,* to exceed what is proper to one's station, or one's ability. *Oyabun,* the part of a parent. *Ichi gon no mōshi-bun gozarimasen,* had not a word to say.

BUN-BUN-NI, ブンブンニ, *adv.* Divided into portions. or shares, separately. *Bunbun ni oku,* to place in separate portions. *Bun-bun ni szru,* to apportion out, to divide into shares.

BUN-CHIN, ブンチン, 文鎮, *n.* A paper-weight.

BUN-CHŌ, ブンテウ, 文鳥, *n.* The name of a bird.

BUN-DŌ, ブンダウ, 文道, (*fumi no michi,*) *n.* Literature, learning. — *wo shiradz sh'te bu-dō tszi-ni shō-ri wo yezaru koto,* military science alone, without a knowledge of literature, can never be successful.

BUNDORI, ブンドリ, 分捕, *n.* Seizing the spoil of the vanquished. — *szru,* to seize the spoils.

BU-NEN, ブネン, 無念, Unmindful, heedless, inattentive, forgetful.

†BUN-GAKU, ブンガク, 文學, Learning to read, pursuing literary studies, especially the Chinese classics.

BUN-GEN, ブンゲン, 分限, *n.* Condition, place, social position, circumstances, station in life. — *wo hakaru,* to consider one's circumstances. — *sō-ō-na h'to,* a person of good position, or easy circumstances. Syn. MI-BUN.

BUNKE, ブンケ, 分家, *n.* Leaving the paternal home to set up house for one's self, (as a younger son). — *wo szru.*

BUNKEN, ブンケン, 分見, To survey, or measure the height, or distance. — *szru.*

BUN-KEN-DŌGU, ブンケンダウグ, 分見道具, *n.* Surveying instruments.

BUN-KEN-YEDZ, ブンケンヱヅ, 分見繪圖, *n.* The chart of a survey.

BUN-KO, ブンコ, 文庫, *n.* A library; a box for keeping books in.

BUN-MAWASHI, ブンマハシ, 筆硯, *n.* A pair of dividers, or compasses.

BU-NIYŌ, ブニヨウ, 豐饒, *n.* A fruitful year.

BUN-RI, ブンリ, 分離, (*wakare hanareru,*) To separate, to sunder, to analyze.

BUN-RIYŌ, ブンリヤウ, 分量, *n.* Weight proportion, quantity. *Kono kuszri wa ichi do ni — ikura nomi-mashō ka,* how much of this medicine shall I take at one time? Syn. MEKATA.

BUNSAN, *-szru*, ブンサン, 分散, (*wakare chiru.*) To break up and scatter, (as a family from poverty.) *Konkiu ni tski bunsan itashimash'ta. Gunzei shi hō ye bunsan szru.* The army broke and scattered in all directions.

BUNSHŌ, ブンシヤウ, 文章, *n.* A writing, composition, a document. Syn. FUMI.

†BUN-TATSZ, ブンタツ, 文達. To commit to writing, communicate in writing.

BUN-TEI, ブンテイ, 文躰. *n.* The style of a writing.

BUN-TSŪ, ブンツウ, 文通. To communicate by letter.

BUN-ZAI, ブンザイ, 分際, *n.* Condition, place, or social position, kind, used only of inferiors. *Chō-nin no bun-zai to sh'te furachina yatsz da.* Syn. BUNGEN.

BUPPŌ, ブツパウ, 佛法, *n.* The rites and ordinances of Buddhism. — *ni iru,* to become a Buddhist.

BURA-BURA-TO, ブラブラ, *adv.* In a swinging, or dangling way, idly, without object. — *sh'te aruku,* to roam about idly, without any particular business. *Bura-bura yamai,* a chronic state of ill health, neither sick nor well.

BURANKO, ブランコ, *n.* A swing. Syn. YUSAWARI,

BURARI, ブラリ, *adv.* Dangling, hanging loosely, and swinging to and fro; idly. *Burarito ugoku,* to swing backwards and forwards. — *san,* an idler.

†BU-RAI, ブライ, 無頼, (*tanomoshige nashi.*) Useless, good for nothing, profligate, abandoned to vice.

BU-REI, ブレイ, 無禮, Rude, impolite, vulgar, devoid of good manners. — *wo togameru,* to censure rudeness. — *na yats da,* a vulgar fellow. Syn. SHITSZREI.

BURI, ブリ, 鰤, *n.* Name of a fish.

BURI, ブリ, (same as *furi* 經,) *adv.* During, time since. *Mika-buri,* for three days. *Tō-ka-buri no kuszri wo kudasare,* give me medicine enough for ten days. *Hisashi-buri Yokohama ye kimash'ta,* it is a long time since I have been to Yokohama. *Hisashi-buri tenki yoku narimash'ta,* it is a long time since we have had pleasant weather, (before to-day.)

BURI-BURI, ブリブリ, *n.* A kind of toy.

†BU-RIYAKU, ブリヤク, 武略, *n.* Military plan, or stratagem.

BURU-BURU, ブルブル, 戰戰, *adv.* Trembling. *Kowagatte — furūta,* to tremble with fear. *Samukute — furuyeru,* to tremble with cold. Syn. WANA-WANA.

BU-RUI, ブルイ, 部類, *n.* Genera and species; class. — *wo wakette atszmeru,* to collect and arrange in classes.

BU-SAIKU, ブサイク, 不細工, Bad workmanship, badly made, unskilful. — *ni dekita,* badly made. — *na hako,* a badly made box.

BU-SA-HŌ, ブサハフ, 無作法, Not acting according to the rules of propriety. Impolite. Syn. SHITSZREI.

BU-SATA, ブサタ, 無沙汰, (*otodzre nashi.*) Remiss or negligent in writing, or visiting, (used by way of apology.) *ōi-ni go — itashimash'ta,* I have been very remiss in writing to you, or in visiting you.

BU-SEI, ブセイ, 不精, (*okotaru.*) Idle, lazy, not diligent, negligent. *Kono ko wa — da kara gakumon wa agarimasen,* this child, owing to his idleness, does not learn. Syn. RANDA.

BU-SHI, ブシ, 武士, (*samurai, mononofu.*) *n.* A cavalier, military class; soldier.

BU-SHIN-JIN, ブシンジン, 無信心, Infidel, unbelieving, not devout, irreligious.

BU-SHITSZKE, ブシツケ, 不躾, Rude, impolite, vulgar. Syn. BUREI. SHITSZREI.

BU-SHŌ, ブシヤウ, 不性, Idle, lazy, loafing, slovenly. — *na mono,* a loafer, lazy fellow. Syn. MONOGUSAI.

BU-SHŌ, ブシヤウ, 武將, *n.* A general, commander of an army.

BU-SHUBI, ブシユビ, 不首尾, Out of favor, disgraced, disapproved. *Hōkō-saki ye wa — de kao ga dasarenu,* as I am in disgrace with my employer, I cannot show myself.

BU-SHUKAN, ブシユカン, 佛手柑, *n.* A citron.

BU-SŌ, ブサウ, 無雙, (*narabi nashi.*) Without an equal or match, unequaled.

BUSSAN, ブツサン, 佛參, (*Hotoke mairi.*) To visit the temples, or graves, for worship. Syn. SANKEI.

BUSSHI, ブツシ, 佛師, (*Hotoke-tszkuri.*) *n.* A maker of idols.

BUSSHŌ, ブツシヤウ, 佛餉, *n.* Gifts of rice made to priests.

BUSSHŌYE, ブツシヤウヱ, 佛生會, *n.* The birth day of Shaka, the 8th day of the 8th month.

BUSSŌ, ブツサウ, 物躁, *n.* Commotion, disturbance, excitement. — *na koto,* commotion.
Syn. SŌDŌ, SAWAGASHII, DŌRAN.

BUTA, ブタ, 豚, *n.* A hog, pig. — *no niku,* pork. Syn. INOKO.

BUTA-BUTA-TO, ブタブタ, *adv.* Fat, corpulent. — *futotte iru,*

BU-TAI, ブタイ, 舞臺, *n.* The stage of a theatre. — *wo fumu,* to make a debut on the stage.

BUTARE,–*ru*,–*ta*, ブタレル, 被打, pass. or pot. of *Buchi* To be struck, hit, or beaten. *Bō de butareta,* struck by a club.

BUT-CHIMERU, ブツチメル, see *Buchi-shime.*

BUTCHŌDZRA, ブツチヤウヅラ, 佛頂面, *n.* A morose, surly countenance.

BUTSZ, ブツ, 佛, (*Hotoke,*) *n.* The supreme being of the Buddhists, Buddha.

BUTSZ, ブツ, 打, see *Buchi,* to strike.

BUTSZ, ブツ, 物, (*mono.*) *n.* A thing. *Banbutsz,* all things.

BUTSZ-BACHI, ブツバチ, 佛罰, *n.* Punishment inflicted by Buddha.

BUTSZ-BUTSZ-TO, ブツブツ, 沸沸, *adv.* The noise of water boiling, bursting of bubbles. — *wakitatsz,* to boil up with a bubbling noise. — *kogoto wo iu,* to grumble and scold to one's self.

BUTSZ-DAN, ブツダン, 佛壇, *n.* The shelf on which the family idol is placed.

BUTSZ-DŌ, ブツダウ, 佛道, (*Butsz no michi.*) *n.* Buddhism.

BUTSZ-DŌ, ブツダウ, 佛堂, *n.* A Buddhist temple.

BUTSZ-GU, ブツグ, 佛具, *n.* The furniture used in the worship of Buddha.

BUTSZ-JI, ブツジ, 佛事, *n.* Worship, or religious ceremonies performed for the dead.

BUTSZ-MA, ブツマ, 佛間, *n.* The room in which the idol is kept, and where religious services are performed; a chapel-room.

BUTSZ-YE, ブツエ, 佛衣, *n.* Clothes worn by Buddhist priests.

BUTSZ-YE, ブツヱ, 佛繪, *n.* Pictures of Buddha.

BUTSZ-ZAISE, ブツザイセ, 佛在世, Whilst Shaka lived.

BUTSZ-ZŌ, ブツザウ, 佛像, *n.* Image of Buddha.

BUTTAOSZ, ブツタフス, see *Buchi-taoshi*

BUTTATAKU, ブツタタク, see *Buchi-tataki.*

BUTTSZKERU,ブツツケル, see *Buchi-tszke.*

BU-WAKE, ブワケ, 部分, Divided into classes, arranged in classes. — *wo szru.*

BU-YAKU, ブヤク, 賦役, Public service rendered by the lower classes to government. — *ni dasz,* to go out on public service. Syn. YAKU.

BU-YEN, ブエン, 無鹽, Fresh. just caught, (as fish,) *Buyenzakana,* id.

BU-YENRIYO, ブエンリヨ, 無遠慮, Without diffidence, without backwardness, or restraint, forward, bold, pert, impudent.

BU-YŌ-JIN, ブヤウジン, 無用心, Careless, heedless, negligent, unmindful.

C

CHA, チヤ, 茶, *n.* Tea. — *wo irete kure,* make some tea (to a servant.) — *wo niru,* or — *wo senjiru,* to boil tea. — *wo tateru,* to make tea from the powdered leaf. — *wo iru,* to fire, or roast tea. — *wo hiku,* to powder tea. — *wo tszmu,* to pick tea. — *wo seiszru,* to prepare the tea for market. — *wo tszmeru,* to pack tea in boxes. — *wo furumō,* to serve out tea. — *wo sonayeru,* to make offerings of tea. — *no kai,* a tea-party.

CHA-BAKO, チヤバコ, 茶箱, *n.* A tea-chest, or box.

CHA-BAN, チヤバン, 茶番, *n.* A clown, buffoon.

CHA-BATAKE, チヤバタケ, 茶圃, *n.* A tea plantation.

CHA-BENTŌ, チヤベンタウ, 茶行厨, *n.* A portable chest with drawers and furnace for preparing tea when on a journey.

CHA-BIN, チヤビン, 茶瓶, *n.* A tea-pot.

CHA-BISHAKU, チヤビシヤク, 茶杓, *n.* A tea ladle.

CHA-BŌKI, チヤバウキ, 茶帚, *n.* A feather brush, used in sweeping up tea when grinding it in a mill.

CHA-BON, チヤボン, 茶盆, *n.* A tea-tray.

CHA-BUKURO, チヤブクロ, 茶袋, *n.* A

small hempen bag, used for holding the tea in boiling it.

CHA-DAI, チャダイ, 茶臺, *n.* A wooden stand for a tea-cup.

CHA-DANSZ, チャダンス, 茶厨, *n.* A cupboard for keeping tea and tea-utensils.

CHA-DŌGU, チャダウグ, 茶具, *n.* Vessels and utensils used in making tea.

CHA-DZKE, チャヅケ, 茶漬, *n.* A food made by mixing boiled rice in tea.

CHA-GARA, チャガラ, 茶滓, *n.* Tea-grounds.

CHA-GAMA, チャガマ, 茶釜, *n.* A pot for boiling tea.

CHA-G'WASHI, チャグワシ, 茶果, (pro. *Chagashi,*) *n.* Fruit, or sweetmeats eaten with tea.

CHA-HŌJI, チャハウジ, 茶焙, *n.* A vessel for heating tea leaves before drawing.

CHA-IRE, チャイレ, 茶入, *n.* A tea-caddy.

CHA-IRI, チャイリ, 茶煎, *n.* A pan for firing tea.

CHA-IRO, チャイロ, 茶色, *n.* Tea-color.

CHA-JIN, チャジン, 茶人, *n.* A master in the art of preparing powdered tea; an eccentric person.

CHA-KASZ, チャカス, 茶滓, *n.* Tea-grounds.

CHAKASHI,–*sz*,–*sh'ta*, チャカス, 嘲弄, *t.v.* To hoax, to befool, to trick, to impose on. Syn. GURŌ SZRU, AZAKERU.

CHA-KI, チャキ, 茶器, *n.* Utensils for preparing powdered tea.

CHA-KIN, チャキン, 茶巾, *n.* A tea-towel.

CHA-KOSHI, チャコシ, 茶漉, *n.* A tea-strainer.

CHAKU,–*szru*, チャク, 著, To arrive at, to wear. — *shidai*, upon arrival, as soon as he arrives.

CHAKU-FU, チャクフ, 著府, Arrival at Yedo.

CHAKU-GAN, チャクガン, 著岸, To arrive in port, to land.

CHAKU-NAN, チャクナン, 嫡男, *n.* The eldest son.

CHAKU-RIU, チャクリウ, 嫡流, *n.* The eldest son's line.

CHAKU-SEN, チャクセン, 著舩, Ship arrival. *Konnichi — itashimash'ta*, the ship arrived to-day.

CHAKU-SHI, チャクシ, 嫡子, *n.* The eldest son.

CHAKU,–*shi*,–*sz*,–*sh'ta*, チャクス, 著, *t. v.* To arrive, to wear. *Kon-nichi yedo kara — shi mashta*, I arrived from Yedo to-day. *Haori wo — szru*, to wear a coat. Syn. TSZKU, KIRU.

CHAKU-SON, チャクソン, 嫡孫, *n.* A descendant in the regular line of the eldest son.

CHAKU-TŌ,–*szru*, チャクタウ, 著到, *t. v.* To arrive.

CHAKU-YŌ, チャクヨウ, 著用, To wear, put on. *Kimono wo — szru.*

CHAKU-ZA, チャクザ, 著座, *(za ni tszku)*, To sit down.

CHA-MESHI, チャメシ, 茶飯, *n.* Rice boiled in tea.

CHA-MISE, チミセ, 茶店, *n.* A tea-house.

CHAN, チャン, 油脂, *n.* Tar, resin.

CHA-NO-FU, チャノフ, 茶譜, *n.* A tea price-current.

CHA-NOKO, チャノコ, 點心, *n.* Cake, sweetmeats, or any thing eaten with tea.

CHANOMA, チャノマ, 茶間, *n.* The dining room.

CHAN-TO, チャント, *adv.* Correctly, straight, right, perfectly, completely, fully. *Kimono wo — szru*, to settle, or rectify one's dress. — *sh'ta nari*, precise, or exact in dress and behaviour. — *szmi-mash'ta*, it is completely finished. — *sh'te ore*, sit straight.

CHAN, チャン, (Yed. coll.), *n.* Father, used only by the lower classes.

CHAN-CHAN-BŌDZ, チャンチャンボウズ, *n.* vul. coll. A Chinaman; (from the resemblance of his head to a poppy capsule.)

CHAPPO, チャッポ, 女裩, (coll.) The cloth worn around the loins by women.

CHARUMERA, チャルメラ, 喇叭, *n.* A trumpet, bugle.

CHA-SHAKU, チャシャク 茶匙, *n.* A tea-spoon.

CHA-SEKI, チャセキ, 茶席, *n.* A tea-party.

CHASEN, チャセン, 茶筌, *n.* A tea-stirrer made of bamboo.

CHA-SHI, チャシ, 茶師, *n.* A tea grower.

CHA-SHIBU, チャシブ, 茶澁, *n.* The deposit from tea on an old tea cup.

CHA-SHITSZ, チャシツ, 茶室, *n.* A tea-room.

CHA-TEI, チャテイ, 茶亭, *n.* A tea-stall.

CHA-TŌ, チャタウ, 茶湯, *n.* Offerings of tea made to idols.

CHA-TSZBO, チャツボ, 茶壺, *n.* A tea-jar.

CHATTO, チャット, *adv.* Quickly, instantly.

CHA-USZ, チャウス, 茶磨, *n.* A tea-mill, for pulverizing tea.

CHA-WAN, チャワン, 茶碗, *n.* A tea-cup.

CHAYA, チャヤ, 茶屋, *n.* A tea-store, tea-house.

CHA-YEN, チャエン, 茶園, *n.* A tea-garden, or plantation.

CHA-ZOME, チャゾメ, 茶染, *n.* Dyed of a tea-color.

CHI, チ, 千, (sen.) A thousand. — *tose*, a thousand years. — *tabi*, a thousand times.

CHI, チ, 地, *n.* The earth. a place or region of country. *Ten* —, heaven and earth. *Tō* —, this part or region of country.
Syn. TSZCHI, TOKORO.

CHI, チ, 血, *n.* Blood. — *wo haku*, to vomit blood. — *no michi*, the menses. — *no namida*, tears of blood. — *wo toru*, to take blood, to bleed. — *no meguri*, the circulation of the blood. — *ga sawagu*, derangement of the menses. — *ga kudaru*, discharge of blood. — *wo tomeru*, to stop the flow of blood. — *ga deru*, it bleeds. Syn. KETSZ.

CHI, チ, 乳, *n.* Milk (Coll. *chi-chi.*)

CHI, チ, 智, Wise, shrewd, clever, knowledge, intellect. (coll. *Chiye*). — *no naki h'to*, a person of no intelligence, — *aru h'to*, a clever person.
Syn. KASH'KOI, SATOSHI, MONOSHIRU,

CHI-BANARE, チバナレ, 乳離, *n.* Weaning. — *wo szru*, to wean.

CHIBI-CHIBI, チビチビ, 微微, *adv.* Little by little, a little at a time, in small quantities. *Kane wo — watasz*, to pay money a little at a time. Syn. SZKOSHI-DZTSZ.

‖CHIBI,*–ru,–ta*, チビル, 耗, *i.v.* To waste away, be consumed, grow less and less. *Mai nichi tszkatta kara toishi mo hōchō mo chibita*, the whetstone and knife from daily use waste away. *Noki no amadare de ishi ga chibita*, the stone is worn away by the rain dropping from the eaves. Syn. HERU.

CHI-BŌ, チボウ 智謀, *n.* Clever at planning, fertile in expedients.

CHI-BURUI, チブルイ, 血振, *n.* The shivering of lying-in women, the cold stage of milk-fever.

CHI-BUSA, チブサ, 乳房, *n.* The breasts.

CHI-CHI, チチ, 父, *n.* Father. — *haha*, father and mother. — *kata*, relations on the father's side.
Syn. TETE OYA, TO-TO, O-TOTTSAN, CHAN.

CHI-CHI, チチ, 乳, *n.* Milk. The breasts. — *ga deru*, the milk flows. — *ga haru*, the breast is swollen. — *wo amasz*, to throw up milk (as an infant). — *wo nomaseru*, to give suck. — *wo shiboru*, to milk. — *kusai*, smell of milk, babyish.

CHI-CHI,*–szru*, チチ, 遅遅, To be late, tardy, slow, to procrastinate.
Syn. GUDZ GUDZ SZRU, HIMADORU, RACHI NO AKANU.

†CHI-CHIU, チチウ, 踟蹰, *(tachi motōru)*, To be slow in deciding, to hesitate, to doubt. Syn. YEN-NIN, CHIU-CHO, TAMERAU.

CHI-DARAKE, チダラケ, (coll). Smeared with blood

CHIDORI, チドリ, 千鳥, *n.* A snipe. — *ashi ni aruku*, to walk with steps crossing each other. — *ni nu*, to cross stich.

CHIGAI,-ō, or-*au*,-*ōta*, or-*atta*, チガフ, 違, *i.v.* To be different; to mistake; to miss. *Nippun no fude to gai-koku no fude to — masz*, the Japanese pen differs from that of foreigners. *Doko no kuni demo h'to no kokoro chigawa-nai*, in every nation the heart of man is the same. *Iki* —, to miss in going. *Szre* —, to graze in passing. *Fumi* —, to make a false step.
Syn. TAGAU, KOTONARU, MACHGIAI.

CHIGAI, チガヒ, 違, *n.* Difference, mistake. — *wa nai*, there is no difference.

CHIGAI-DANA, チガヒダナ, 違棚, *n.* A shelf, one half of which is on a different plain from the other.

CHIGAYA, チガヤ, 茅 , *n.* A kind of coarse grass.

CHIGI, チギ, 杜秤, *(hakari,) n.* A weighing beam.

CHIGIRE,*–ru,–ta*, チギレル, 斷離, *i. v.* To be torn. *Kimono ga chigirete sagatta*, the clothes are torn and hanging down.

CHGIRE-CHIGIRE, チギレチギレ, 斷斷, *adv.* In a scattered manner; helter-skelter; broken and disorderly.

CHIGIRI,*–ru,–tta*, チキル, 拗切, *t. v.* To tear off. *Kaki wo chigitte toru*, to pluck off a persimmon. Syn. MUSHIRU.

CHIGIRI, チギリ, 契, *n.* An alliance, relation of marriage, or friendship; a union, compact, agreement. — *wo muszbu*, to make an alliance. *Shū-jū no — kono yo nomi ni aradz*, the relation of master and servant is not confined to this world.
Syn. YAK'SOKU, KEIYAKU, MAJIWARI.

CHIGIRI,*–ru,–tta*, チギル, 契, *i. v.* To form an alliance, have fellowship with, make a compact. *H'to to chigiru nara uszku chigirite szye woba toge-yo*, in our intercourse with others slight familiarity will conduce to long friendship.
Syn. MAJIWARU, YAK'SOKU SZRU.

CHIGI-YŌ, チギヤウ, 知行, *n.* The estate of a lord, or noble. — *wa sai-koku nite taku wa jū man goku*, his estate is in the western provinces, and revenue one hundred thousand *koku*.
Syn. RIYŌBUN, SHORIYO.

CHIGO, チゴ, 兒, *n.* An infant. A servant boy of the Emperor.
Syn. WAKAMBE, AKAMBO.

†CHI-HATSZ, ヂハツ, 薙髪, (*kami wo soru,*) *n.* Shaving the head, entering the priest-hood. Syn. KASHIRA-OROSZ, TEI-HATS, RAK'SHOKU.

†CHI-IN, チイン, 知音, *n.* An intimate friend, or acquaintance.
Syn. KONI-NA-H'TO, HŌYU.

CHIJIKAMARI,*–ru,–tta*, チヂカマル, 縮, *i. v.* To shrink, to contract, to shrug up. *Samukute chijikamatta*, shrunk with cold.

CHIJIMARI,*–ru,–tta*, チヂマル, 縮, *i. v.* To shrink, contract, diminish in size, shrug up, to be corrugated.

CHIJIME,*–ru,–ta*, チヂメル, 縮, *t. v.* To cause to contract, to shrink, lessen in bulk, to corrugate, wrinkle. *Inochi wo* —, to shorten life.

CHIJIMI,*–mu,–nda*, チヂム, 縮, *i. v.* To be contracted. shrunk, corrugated, shortened.

CHIJIMI, チヂミ, 縮, *n.* A kind of corrugated cloth.

CHIJIRE,*–ru,–ta*, チヂレル, 縮, *i. v,* To be curled, frizzled, corrugated, wrinkled. *Kami ga chijireru*, the hair is curled. *Chijirèke*, curly hair.

CHIJOKU, チジヨク, 恥辱, *n.* Ashamed, shame. — *wo toru*, to feel ashamed. — *wo atayeru*, to cause another to feel ashamed. Syn. HAJI, HADZKASHIME.

CHIKADZKE,*–ru,–ta*, チカヅケル, 暱, *t. v.* To bring near, cause to approach, make familiar with, cause to associate with. *Kodomo wo aku-nin ni chikadzkeru koto warui*, it is wrong to make children intimate with bad men.

CHIKADZKI,*–ku,–ita*, チカツク, 近著, *i. v.* To draw near, approach, associate, be familiar with. *Samusa ga dan-dan chikadzku*, cold weather is gradually drawing near. Syn. CHIKAYORU.

CHIKADZKI, チカツキ, 相識, *n.* An acquaintance, companion, friend.
Syn. TOMO-DACHI. HŌYU.

‖CHIKAGATSZYE, チカガツヱ, 近飢, Hungry, craving food.

CHIKAGORO, チカゴロ, 近項, *adv.* Lately, recently, very, indeed. — *wa hayari yamai ōku*, epidemic diseases have prevailed much of late. — *kita*, came lately. — *katajikenai*, very much obliged. — *ni nai medzrashii koto*, not for many years such a strange thing. Syn. KONOAIDA; KIN-RAI.

CHIKAI,–KI,–SHI, チカイ, 近, *a.* Near, not far; familiar. — *michi*, a near way. *Chikaku szru*, to bring near, be intimate with. *Chikaki toshi* in recent times. *Chikaki shinrui*, near relatives. *Chikō gozarimasz*, it is near. *Ammari chikaku gozarimasen* they are not much alike, (of two words).

CHIKAI, チカイ, 誓, *n.* An oath. — *Chikai wo muszbu*, to bind by an oath. *Chikai wo tateru*, to take an oath. *Chikai wo somuku*, to break an oath. Syn. SEIGON.

CHIKAI,*–au–atta*, チカフ, 誓, *i. v.* To take an oath, to swear. *Ware mato wo inukadzmba chicatte kono ba wo saraji*, I swear, if I do not hit the mark, I will not leave this place.

CHIKA-JIKA, チカヂカ, 近近, (*kin-kin*), *adv*, Soon, shortly, in a short time. — *Chikajika no uchi Yedo yc mairimasz.* I shall go to Yedo soon. Syn. TŌKARADZ, KIN-JITS.

†CHKAKU, チカク, 知覺, (*oboye*), *n.* Feeling, sensation; *sinke no chikaku wa don ni naru*, the sensibility of the nerves is blunted.

CHIKAKU, or CHIKŌ, チカク, 近, *adv.* Near, see *Chikai.*

CHIKAME, チカメ, 短視. Near-sighted.

CHIKARA, チカラ, 力, *n.* Strength, ability. *Chikara wo arasō*, to dispute about strength. *Kane wo chikara ni szru*, to rely on money. *Chikara wo awaszru*- to unite together with strength, money, or talent. in order to accomplish some thing. *Chikara ga ochiru*, to be discouraged, to lose heart. *Chikara wo otosz*, to dishearten, — *wo tszkeru*, to encourage. Syn. RIKI.

CHIKARA-DAKE, チカラダケ, 力竹, *n.* A bamboo used to give strength, or support to any thing.

CHIKARA-GANE, チカラガネ, 力金, *n.* A buckle.

CHIKARA-GAWA, チカラガハ, 靳, *n.* A stirrup-leather.

CHIKARAGE, チカラゲ, 力毛, *n.* The long hairs on the arms breast and legs, supposed to indicate strength.

CHICARAGI, チカラギ, 力木, *n.* A weaver's-beam.

CHICARA-KOBU, チカラコブ, 力瘤, *n.* The lump made on the arm above the elbow by the contraction of Biceps-flexor muscle.

CHIKARA-MOCHI, チカラモチ, 力持. Persons who exhibit their strength by lifting heavy weights.

CHICAYORI,*–ru,–tta*, チカヨル, 近依, *i. v.* To approach, draw near.

CHI-KEMURI, チケムリ, 血煙, *n.* Vapor of blood. *Chikemuri tatsz made tatakau,*

†CHIKI, チキ, 知已, *n.* An acquaintance, friend. Syn. CHIKADZKI.

CHIKIRI, チキリ, 縢, *n.* A weaver's beam.

CHI-KIU, チキウ, 地毬, *n.* A terrestrial-globe.

CHI-KIYŌDAI, チキヤウダイ, 乳兄弟, *n.* Nursed by the same nurse, or at the same breast.

CHIKKIYO, チツキヨ, 蟄居, *n.* Imprisonment in one's own house for some offence; — *saseru,* to imprison, &c.
Syn. OSHI-KOME.

CHIKKURI, チツクリ, *adv.* A little, in time or space. *Chikkuri magatta,* a little bent.

†CHIKU, チク, 竹, *(take), n.* Bamboo, only used in compounds words.

CHIKU-BA, チクバ, 竹馬, *n.* A bamboo horse. *Chikuba no tomo,* a play-fellow.

CHI-KUBI, チクビ, 乳頭, *n.* The nipples.

CHIKU-CHIKU, チクチク, *adv.* Pricking, sticking. — *itai,* a pricking pain. — *szru,* to prick, stick.

CHIKUDARE, チクダリ, 下血, *(geketsz.) n.* A bloody flux.

CHIKU-ICHI, チクイチ, 逐一, *adv.* Minutely, particularly, each and every one. — *ni hanashi wo szru,* to tell minutely, tell every particular. — *ni shōchi itashimash'ta,* have granted each and every thing.
Syn. KUWASHIKU, ISAI-NI, ICHI-ICHI.

†CHIKU-RIN, チクリン, 竹林, *n.* A bamboo-grove. Syn. YABU,

CHIKU-SHŌ, チクシヤウ, 畜生, *n.* A beast, brute.

CHIKUSHŌDŌ, チクシヤウダウ, 畜生道, *n.* A place of torment in the Buddhist infernum.

CHIKUTEN,–*szru,* チクテン, 逐電, *t. v.* To abscond, to run away. *Kuni wo — szru,* to abscond from one's country.
Syn, NIGERU, SHUPPON SZRU,

†CHI-K'WAN, チクワン, 遲緩, To delay, procrastinate, tardy, slow.

CHIMAKI, チマキ, 粽, *n.* A kind of rice cake.

CHIMAMIRE, チマミレ, 血塗, Smeared with blood. Syn. CHIDARAKE, CHIMIDORO.

CHIMATA, チマタ, 街, *n.* Forks of a road; a town, a place. *Kassen no —,* a field of battle.

CHI-MATSZRI, チマツリ, 釁, *n.* An offering of the blood of an enemy to the Kami, to insure victory.

CHI-MAYOI, チマヨヒ, 血迷, *n.* Faintness from loss of blood.

CHIMBA, チンバ, 跛, Lame. *Kata —,* lame in one leg. Syn. BIKKO.

†CHIM-BOTSZ,–*szru,* チンボツ, 沈沒, *(shidzmi horobu.)* Submerged and lost, ruined, destroyed.

CHIM-BUTSZ, チンブツ, 珍物, *(medzrashi mono,) n.* A rare thing, unusual and excellent, dainty and delicate food.

CHIMMARI, チンマリ, 約, *adv.* Abridged, condensed, reduced in size, in miniature. — *to sh'ta yoi iye da,* a small and neat house.

CHIMPI, チンピ, 陳皮, *n.* Dried orange peel.

CHIMPŌ, チンポウ, 珍寶, *n.* Rare and valuable, precious.

CHIMPO, チンポ, *n.* The male member.

†CHIN, チン, 朕, pro. I, me, only used by the Mikado, when speaking of himself.

CHIN, チン, 佛林狗, *n.* A small pet dog.

CHIN, チン, 亭, *(tei,) n.* A small summer-house.

CHIN, チン, 賃, *n.* Hire, fare, wages. *Tana-chin,* house rent. *Funa-chin,* boat hire, or freight. *Tema-chin,* price of labor. *Dachin,* fare for transporting on horse back. *Un-chin,* freight, fare. — *wo harau,* to pay the hire, &c.

CHINAMI, チナミ, 緣, *n.* Connection, relation, alliance, cause, reason. — *wo muszbu,* to form a connection. — *wo fukaku itasz,* to form an intimate alliance.
Syn. YEN, YUKARI, YŌSZGA.

CHINAMI-NI, チナミニ, 因, *adv.* (An illative word). In connection with, or taking this opportunity, taking this occasion, or apropos to this subject. *Sen-koku ikusabanashi no uchi ni uma no koto ga ari mash'ta ga, sono — yotte, uma no koto wo kuwashiku o hanashi moshimasz,* as there was something said about a horse in the war-story just told, I will avail myself of the opportunity to speak more particularly about it. Syn. TSZIDE-NI.

CHIN-CHŌ, チンチヨウ, 珍重, *n.* To felicitate, congratulate, to be glad of, to regard as a great delicacy, or of great value. — *ni zonji-tatematszri soro.*
Syn. KEKKŌ, MEDETAI.

†CHIN-DEKI チンデキ, 沈溺, *(shidzmi oboru,) n.* Ruined, destroyed.

CHIN-DAN, チンダン, 珍談, *(medzrashi hanashi,) n.* News.

CHIN-DZRU, チンズル, 陳, To state, relate, narrate. Syn. NOBERU.

CHIN-GIN,*-szru*, チンギン, 沈吟, To speak to one's self. *Ikaga sen to — szru*, "what shall I do" he said to himself.

CHIN-GO, チンゴ, 鎮護, (*shidzme mamoru*), To govern; to guard and keep in subjection; tranquilize.

CHIN-JI, チンジ, 珍事, (*medzrashi koto*), *n.* A strange thing, unwonted, uncommon affair, (generally in a bad sense).

CHIN-KIN-BORI, チンキンボリ, 沈金彫, *n.* Carved and gilt work.

‖CHIN-KŌ, チンカウ, 珍肴, *n.* Rare and fine fish.

CHIN-K'WA, チンクワ, 鎮火, *n.* Extinguished, (as a conflagration).

CHI-NOMI-GO, チノミゴ, 乳子, *n.* An infant, suckling.

†CHI-NORI, チノリ, 地利, *n.* The strong, or important places of a country. *Ten no toki wa — ni shikadz.* Syn. YŌ-GAI.

†CHINRIN, チンリン, 沈淪, (*shidzmi-shidzmaru*), Ruined, destroyed.

CHIN-SEN, チンセン, 賃錢, *n.* Hire, wages, money earned.

CHIN-SETSZ, チンセツ, 珍説, *n.* (*medzrashi hanashi*), News. *Nan-zo — wa gozarimasen ka*, is there any news?

CHIN-SHIGOTO, チンシゴト, 賃仕事, *n.* Taking in sewing, (for a living).

†CHIN-SHO, チンシヨ, 珍書, (*medzrashi shōmotsz*). A rare and valuable book.

CHIN-ZA, チンザ, 鎮座. To dwell, (as a *kami* in a *miya*), *— mashimas.*

CHIN-ZEN, チンゼン, 珍膳. A feast, entertainment.

CHINIZŌ, チンザウ, 珍藏, *n.* Property, property highly valued. *Kono hon wa soregashi uji no — de gozarimasz*, this book is the property of Mr. —

CHIRA-CHIRA, チラチラ, *adv.* In a flickering fluttering manner. *Yuki ga — to furu*, the snow falls with a fluttering motion.

†CHI-RAN, チラン, 治亂, (*osamuru, midareru*). Tranquility and disturbance, or peace and war.

CHIRARI-TO, チラリ, 瞥, *adv.* A glimpse, a short, transient view, or sound. *— miru*, to glance at.

CHIRATSKI,*-ku,-ita*, チラツク, 閃, *i. v.* To flicker, to twinkle, to be dazzled, flutter. *Hoshi ga chiradzku*, the stars twinkle. *Kaze ga fuite hi chiradzku*, the light flikers in the wind. *Iri hi ga sash'te me ga chiradzku*, the eyes are dazzled by looking at the setting sun. *Yuki ga —* the snow falls, Syn. HIRAMEKU.

CHIRASHI,*-sz,-sh'ta*, チラス, 散, *t.v.* To scatter, to disperse. *Kaze ga hana wo fuki-chirasz*, the wind scatters the flowers. *Hi-bana wo chirash'te tatakō*, they fought until they made the sparks fly.

CHIRI, チリ, 地理, *n.* Geography.

CHIRI,*-ru,-tta*, チル, 散, *i.v.* To be scattered, to be dispersed. *Szmi ga chiru*, the ink spreads (as in porous paper). *Momiji ga chiru*, the red leaves of autumn are scattered. Syn. SANDZRU.

CHIRI, チリ, 塵, *n.* Dirt, rubbish, litter, dust. *— wo harau*, to clean away dust. Syn. GOMI, AKUTA.

†CHIRIBAMI,*-mu,-nda*, チリバム, 鏤, *t.v.* To carve, to engrave. *Adzsa ni —*, to carve in blocks of *adzsa*, (for printing.) Syn. HORU, YERU.

CHIRI-GAMI, チリガミ, 塵紙, *n.* A kind of coarse paper made of the rubbish of a paper mill.

CHIRI-HARAI, チリハラヒ, 塵掃, *n.* A dusting brush.

CHIRI-CIRI, チリチリ, 散散, *adv.* Scattered, dispersed. Syn. BARA-BARA, SAN-ZAN.

CHIRIKE, チリケ, 身柱, *n.* Nape of the neck.

CHIRIMEN, チリメン, 縮緬, *n.* Crape.

CHIRI-TORI, チリトリ, 塵取, *n.* A dust pan.

CHI-RIYAKU, チリヤク, 智略, *n.* Wisdom, discretion, wisdom and sagacity in planning, or contriving.

†CHI-RIYOKU, チリヨク, 智力, Wise, shrewd, discreet.

CHIRO-CHIRO, チロチロ, *adv.* In a flickering manner, with a short, irregular motion. *— moyeru*, to burn in a slow and flickering manner.

CHIRORI, チロリ, 酒注, *n.* A metal pot for warming *sake.*

CHIRU, チル, See *Chiri.*

CHĪSAI,*-KI,-SHI*, チヒサイ, 小, *a.* Small, little in size; trifling, or of small importance. *— inu*, a small dog. *— koye*, a low voice. *— toki*, when one was little (or young). *— koto*, a small matter, unimportant. *— kidz*, a trifling wound.

CHĪSAKU, or CHĪSŌ, チヒサク, *adv.* Idem. *— naru*, to become small. *— szru*, to make small. *— nai*, not small.

CHISAN,*-szru*, チサン, 遲參, (*osoku mairu*), To be late in coming.

CHI-SHA, チシヤ, 智者, *n.* A wise, sagacious, or ingenious person.

CHISHA, チシヤ, 萵苣, *n.* Lettuce.

†CHISHI, チシ, 稚子, *n.* A child. Syn. KODOMO.

CHISHIKI, チシキ, 知識, Wise and learned,(applied only to Buddhist priests).

CHI-SHIRU, チシル, 乳汁, *n.* Milk.

CHISŌ, チソウ, 馳走, *n.* A feast, entertainment, amusement, pleasure. — *wo szru,* to make a feast. *Kiyaku ye — ni gei-sha wo yobu,* to call a ballad-singer for the amusement of guests. *Ōkini go — ni narimash'ta,* I thank you for your delightful entertainment. *Dan-dan go — ni ainarimash'te katajikenaku zonjimaszru* (id.) Syn. FURU-MAI, KIYŌ-Ō, MOTENASHI.

†CHI-SOKU, チソク, 遲速, *(ososhi hayashi),* Slow and fast, tardy and quick.

†CHISSZ, チツス, 蟄, *n.* To be imprisoned, or confined to the house for crime. Syn. CHIKKIYO.

CHI-SZJI, チスヂ, 血脈, Blood relation. — *ga tszdzite iru,* the family line is unbroken.

†CHI-TAI, チタイ, 遲滯, *(todokōru,)* Slow, failing to do. — *naku,* without fail, promptly and in time.

CHITSZ, チツ, 帙, *n.* A cover. or case for books, in the manner of the Chinese. Syn. FUMAKI.

CHITTO, チツト, 些小, *adv.* A little in quantity or time. — *bakari kudasaimase,* give me a little. — *o machi-nasare,* wait a little. Syn. SZKOSHI, WADZKA, ISASAKA.

CHIU, チウ, 中, *(naka.)* Middle, centre; middling in quality, medium, within, during, whilst. *Jō — ge,* the grades, or qualities, of superior, middling and inferior. Syn. MANNAKA.

CHIU, チウ, 宙, *n.* Empty space, air, — *wo tonde nigeta,* flew away. — *ni burarito sagatta,* hung dangling in the air. *Chiu-nori wo szru,* to ride in the air. — *ni agaru,* to ascend in the air. — *de yomu,* to recite from memory.

CHIU, チウ, 忠, *n.* Fidelity to a master; patriotism. — *wo tszkusz,* to be faithful to the utmost. Syn. MAMEYAKA.

CHIU, チウ, 註, *n.* Commentary, notes. — *wo kaku,* to write a commentary on a text.

CHIU,*–szru,* チウ, 誅, To kill, slay, to punish with death. Syn. KOROSZ.

CHIU, チウ, 晝, *n.* Day, day-time. *Chiu-ya,* day and night. Syn. HIRU.

CHIU-BATSZ, チウバツ, 誅罰, To punish with death, to slay.

CHIUBU, チウブ, 中風, *n.* Hemiphlegia.

†CHIU-CHO,*–szru,* チウチヨ, 躊躇, To hesitate, to be in doubt, or uncertainty. Syn. TAMERAU, YUYŌ SZRU, GUDSZ-GUDSZ SZRU.

CHIU-DŌ, チウダウ, 中道, *n.* Half-way, in the midst of, or while doing any thing. — *ni sh'te hai-sz,* to give up when only half done.

CHIU-DŌRI, チウダウリ, 中通, *n.* Medium quality.

CHIU-GEN, チウゲン, 仲間, *n.* Inferior servants of the Samurai. Syn. ORISZKE.

CHIU-GEN, チウゲン, 中元, *n.* The 15th day of the 7th month. The middle of the year, and last day of the Feast of Lanterns.

CHIUGOKU, チウゴク, 中國, *n.* The 8 central provinces of Japan, viz: Harima, Mimasaka, Bizen, Bitchiu, Bingo, Aki, Szwō, Nagato

CHIU-GOSHŌ, チウゴシヤウ, 中小性, *n.* The name of a military rank.

CHIU-GI, チウギ, 忠義, *n.* Fidelity, patriotism, loyalty.

CHIU-HAN, チウハン, 晝飯, *(hiru-meshi,) n.* Dinner.

CHIU-IN, チウイン, 中陰, *n.* The period of 49 days mourning.

CHIU-JIKI, チウジキ, 晝食, *(hiru-meshi,) n.* Dinner.

CHIU-JUN, チウジユン, 中旬, The middle decade of the month, from the 10th to the 20th day.

†CHIU-KA, チウカ, 仲夏, *n.* The middle of summer, 7th month.

†CHIU-KAI,*–szru,* チウカイ, 註解, To comment on, to explain with notes

†CHIU-KAN, チウクワン, 中浣, same as *Chiu-jun.*

†CHIU-KAN, チウカン, 忠諫, Faithful reproof from a servant, advice, or remonstrance.

CHIU-KI, チウキ, 中氣, *n.* Palsy.

CHIU-KO, チウコ, 中古, *(naka mukashi,) n.* Middle ages.

CHIU-KŌ, チウカウ, 忠孝, *n.* Fidelity to a master, and obedience to parents; than which the Japanese suppose there are no higher virtues.

CHIU-MON, チウモン, 中門, *n.* The inner door, or gate-way of a court.

CHIU-MON, チウモン, 註文, An order for goods. — *szru,* to send an order for goods. — *chō,* an order book. Syn. ATSZRAYERU.

CHIU-NA-GON, チウナゴン, 言納中, *n.* An order of nobility.

CHIU-NEN, チウネン, 中年, *n.* Middle age of life.

CHIU-NIN, チウニン, 仲人, *n.* A middleman, mediator, go-between. Syn. NAKA-

UDO, AISATSZ-NIN, ATSZKAI-NIN, BAI-SHAKU, KUCHI-KIKI.

CHIU-NORI, チウノリ, 宙乘, *n.* A play-actor who appears to walk in the air.

CHIUŌ, チウワウ, 中央, *n.* The centre, middle.
Syn. NAKABA, MANNAKA.

CHIU-RIKU, チウリク, 誅戮, To slay, to kill, to punish with death.

†CHIU-SAKU, チウサク, 籌策, *n.* A stratagem, plan, scheme.
Syn. HAKARIGOTO, SAKU-RIYAKU.

†CHIU-SHAKU, チウシヤク, 註釋, To explain with notes, or commentary.

CHIU-SETSZ, チウセツ, 忠節, *n.* Fidelity, loyalty.

CHIU-SHIN,–*szru*, チウシン, 註進, *t.v.* To report, to inform, tell, (to a superior). *Sai-koku yori hikiyaku wo motte Yedo omote ye — ni oyobu*, to report from the western provinces to Yedo by a courier.
Syn. TODOKERU.

CHIU-SHIN, チウシン, 忠心, *n.* Fidelity, loyalty.

CHIU-SHIN, チウシン, 忠臣, *n.* A faithful servant

CHIU-SHŌ, チウシヤウ, 中症, *n.* Palsy.

CHIU-SHU, チウシウ, 仲秋 *n.* The 15th day of 8th month, middle of autumn.

CHIU-SHUN, チウシユン, 仲春, *n.* The second month, middle month of spring.

CHIU-TO, チウト, 中途, *adv.* During, in the midst of doing anything. — *ni sh'te hai-sz*, to give up in the midst of doing anything. — *de yamerarete wa komaru*, if you give up before you have completed it, I shall be inconvenienced.
Syn. CHIU-DŌ, NAKABA, HAN-TO.

CHIU-TŌ, チウトウ, 仲冬, *n.* The 11th month, middle month of winter.

†CHIU-U, チウウ, 中有, The dark space intervening between earth and hades, (Budh) — *no yami ni mayō*, to wander about in outer darkness.

CHIU-ZETSZ, チウゼツ, 中絶, (*naka tayeru*,) Giving up, ceasing to do or breaking off anything, and resuming again, interruption. *Kei-ko wo — sh'te heta ni natta*, being interrupted in my study, I have become rusty.

CHI-WA, チワ, 千話, *n.* Love-talk, the flirting and coquetry of young people. *Chiwa-gen-ka inu mo kamawanu*, a dog even will not interfere in a love-quarrel.
Syn, IRO-GURUI.

CHIWA-BUMI, チワブミ, 艶書, *n.* A love-letter.

CHIWA-GURUI, チワグルイ, 婬戲, *n.* Love-sickness.

CHIYE, チヱ, 智慧, *n.* Intelligence, talent, cleverness, ingenious. — *aru h'to*, an intelligent person. — *no nai otoko da*, a man of no talent. — *no wa*, a puzzle made of rings. Syn. KASH'KOI, RIKŌ, SAI-CHI.

CHŌ, チヤウ, 町, *n.* A street, a division of a street, a measure of length = 60 *ken*, = 360 feet, also a land measure of 3,000 *tszbo*, = 108,000 sq feet.

CHŌ, チヤウ, 帳, *n.* A register, account-book, leger. — *ni tskeru*, to enter in an account-book.

CHŌ, チヤウ, 挺, *n.* The numeral for guns, ink, candles, poles, hoes. *Teppō it* —, one gun, one piece of cannon. *Szmi san* —, three sticks of ink. *Rōsoku ni* —, two candles.

†CHŌ, チヤウ, 腸, *n.* The intestines.
Syn. H'YAKUHIRO.

CHŌ, テウ, 朝, *n.* Morning, — *seki*, morning and evening. Syn. ASA.

CHŌ, テフ, 蝶, *n.* A butterfly.

CHŌ, チヤウ, 丁, *n.* Numeral for sedan-chairs. *Kago san* —, three sedan chairs.

CHŌ, チヤウ, 偶, Even number. — *han*, even and odd. Syn. GU.

CHŌ, チヤウ, 長, (*nagai.*) Long. old, senior, chief, principal eminent, superior. *Shishi wa hiyaku-jū no — nari*, the lion is the chief among beasts. *Sake wa h'yaku yaku no* —, wine is the best of medicines.
Syn. OSA, KASHIRA.

CHO-AI, チヤウアヒ, 帳合, Balancing, or comparing accounts, to audit accounts.
Syn. CHŌ-MEN WO HIKI-AWASERU.

CHŌ-AI, チヨウアイ, 寵愛, (*itszkushimu*). To love. Syn. KAWAIGARU, AI-SZRU,

CHŌ-BIYŌ, チヤウビヤウ, 長病, (*nagayamai*,) *n.* A chronic disease.

CHŌ-BŌ, テウバウ, 眺望, *n.* A view, prospect, — *szru*, to look at a landscape. *Kono yama no — ga yoi*, the view from this mountain is fine.
Syn. MI-WATASHI, NAGAME.

CHOBO, チヨボ, 點, *n.* A dot, point, speck. — *wo utsz*, to make a dot.

CHOBO-CHOBO, チヨボチヨボ, 點點, *adv.* Dotted, the sound of dropping of rain-drops. *Amadare ga — ochiru.*
Syn. POCHI-POCHI.

CHOBO-ICHI, チヨボイチ, 樗蒲, *n.* A kind of gambling played with dice. — *wo szru.*

CHOBOKURE, チヨボクレ, *n.* A kind of song sung by a beggar who goes about beating a wooden bell.

CHŌ-BŌN, チヤウボン, 張本, *n.* A ring leader. *Tōzoku no* —, chief of banditti. — *nin*, a ring-leader, chief.
Syn. HOTTŌ-NIN, KASHIRA.

CHO-BUKU, テウブク, 調伏, *n.* Enchantment, or incantations, used to bring evil on an enemy. — *szru*, to use magic arts &c. — *no inori*, incantation.
Syn. NŌRO, SHUSO.

CHŌ-CHAKU,–*szru*, チヤウチヤク, 打擲, *t.v.* To beat. whip, strike.
Syn. UCHI-TATAKU, BUTSZ.

CHŌ-CHIN, テウチン, 挑燈, *n.* A lantern.

CHO-CHO-TO, or CHOTO, チヤウチヤウ, 打打, *adv.* The sound or appearance of striking, clashing. — *utsz*, — *kiru*.

CHŌ-DAI,–*szru*, チヤウダイ, 頂戴, *i.v.* To receive from a superior. — *itashi-tai*, I would like to have this.
Syn. ITADAKU, MORAU.

CHŌ-DAI, チヤウダイ, 帳臺, *n.* A curtained bedstead.

†CHŌ-DAN, チヤウダン, 長談, (*naga banashi*), *n.* Long talk. *Ano hto no — ni wa komaru*, annoyed by his long-talking.

CHŌ-DANSZ, チヤウダンス, 帳廚, *n.* A chest or bureau in which account books are kept.

CHŌDATSZ, テウダツ, 調達, To make up, or collect together a sum of money, *Kon nichi-jū ni ichi man doru chō-datsz seneba naranu.* I must to day make up ten thousand dollars. Syn. TOTONOYERU. SAI-KAKUSZRU.

†CHŌ-DO, テウド, 調度, *n.* Kitchen utensils. — *no mono wo motomu.*

CHŌ-DO, テウド, 恰, *adv.* Just, exactly, — *yoi*, just right. — *yoi tokoro ye kita*, have come just at the right time.
Syn. ADAKAMO, HOTONDO.

CHŌ-DZ, テウヅ, 手水, *n.* Water used for washing the face, or hands. — *wo tszkau*, to wash the face, or hands. — *wo szru*, to make water.

CHŌDZ-BA, テウヅバ, 手水場, *n.* A privy, water-closet.

CHŌ-DZ-BACHI, テウヅバチ, 手水鉢, *n.* The bason of water kept near a privy.

CHŌ-DZRU, チヤウズル, 長, *i.v.* See *Chōji.*

CHŌ-GIN, チヤウギン, 錠銀, *n.* Silver-ingots, or bars.

CHŌ-GŌ, テウガフ, 調合, To compound medicines. — *szru.*

CHŌ-HŌ, チヨウハウ, 重寶, Convenient, useful, appropriate. — *na mono.*
Syn. BENRI.

CHOITO, チヨイト, 一寸, *adv.* For a moment, instant, little while. Same as *Chotto.* — *o mise kudasare*, just let me look at it. — *o yori nasai*, come in for a moment.

CHŌJA, チヤウジヤ, 長者, *n.* A rich-man, one in good circumstances.

CHŌJI, チヤウジ, 丁子, *n.* Cloves.

CHŌJI,–*ru*,–*ta*, チヤウズル, 長, *t. v.* To grow long or large, grow up, to excel, become great, surpass, to be more and more addicted to. *Bun-gei ni* —, excelling in literature and polite accomplishments. *Asobi ni* —, to be more and more fond of pleasure. Syn. NOBIRU, ŌKIKU, SZGURERU, FUKERU.

CHŌJI,–*szru*, チヤウジ, 停止, *t. v.* To forbid, prohibit, interdict, stop.
Syn. KINSDZRU, TODOMURU.

CHŌJI-AWASE,–*ru*,–*ta*, チヤウジアハセル, 打合, *i.v.* To consult and agree upon.
Syn. SŌDAN SZRU.

CHŌJITSZ, チヤウジツ, 長日, (*nagai hi*), *n.* A long day.

CHŌ-JO, チヤウジヤウ, 頂上, *n.* The highest point, the summit, top. *Yama no* —, top of a mountain. Syn. ITADAKI, ZETCHŌ.

CHŌJU, チヤウジユ, 長壽, *n.* Long life.

CHŌ-JUTSZ, チヨジユツ, 著述, To write or compose a work.

CHŌ-KEN, チヤウケン, 長絹, *n.* A long-sleeved coat worn by a *Kuge.*

CHOKIBUNE, チヨキブネ, 猪牙舩, *n.* A kind of small river boat.

CHŌ-KIRI, チヤウキリ, 帳切, Expunging the name from the town-register.

CHŌ-KIU, チヤウキウ, 長久, (*nagaki hisashii*), A long time, eternal.

†CHOKKAN,–*szru*, チヨクカン, 直諫, (*tadaci ni isamu*,) To reprove a superior to his face.

CHOKKIYO, チヨクキヨ, 勅許, *n.* Imperial permission.

CHOKKURA, チヨククラ, , *adv.* Just, merely, in a light easy way. — *itte kuru*, will come in a moment. — *dash'te miru.* just look and find it (as a word.) — *itte miyo*, just come and see. Syn. CHOITO, or CHOTTO.

CHOKO-CHOKO, チヨコチヨコ, *adv.* Frequently, often. — *mairimasz*, to go frequently. Syn. SHIBA-SHIBA, TABI-TABI.

CHOKOSAI, チヨコサイ, Vain, affected with a smattering of learning, pretending to learning. — *na yatsz.* Syn. KOSHAKU.

CHOKU, チヨク, 鍾, *n.* A small cup for drinking *sake.*

CHOKU, チヨク, 直, Right, just, upright, honest. — *na h'to*, an honest man.

†CHOKU, チヨク, 勅, *(mikotonori)*, Imperial, relating to the Mikado.

CHOKU-JŌ, チヨクヂヤウ, 勅定, Mikado's orders.

CHOKU-MEI, チヨクメイ, 勅命, *n.* id.

CHOKU-SHI, チヨクシ, 勅使, *n.* Imperial ambassador.

CHOKU-SHO, チヨクシヨ, 勅書, *n.* Mikado's letter.

CHŌ-MAN, チヤウマン, 脹滿, *n.* Dropsy of the abdomen.

CHOMBORI, チヨンボリ, Same as *Chobo*. A dot, speck, the least quantity. *Szdzri ni midz wo — irete kudasai*, just give me a speck of water on this inkstone.

CHŌMEI, チヤウメイ, 長命, *(naga-iki)*, *n.* Long-life.

CHŌ-MEN, チヤウメン, 帳面, *n.* An account book, register, record-book, ledger.

CHŌ-MON, *-szru*, チヤウモン, 聽聞, To listen to, to attend, (as preaching, a sermon). *Hōdan wo — szru*, to listen to a sermon. Syn. KIKU.

CHŌ-NAI, チヤウナイ, 町內, *(machi no uchi)*, In the street. *Kono h'to watakushi no — ni orimas*, this man lives in the same street with me.

†CHŌ-NAN, チヤウナン, 長男, *n.* Oldest son. Syn. CHAKUNAN, SŌRIYO.

CHŌ-NIN チヤウニン, 町人, *n.* Towns-people, citizen of a town, common-people, not *samurai*.

CHŌ-REN, *-szru*, テウレン, 調練, To drill, to parade, to go through military exercises. *Gunzei wo* —, to drill an army. Syn. SŌREN, JINDATE.

†CHO-RIU, チヨリツ, 佇立, To stand up, as if to look at something, to stand on tip-toe. Syn. TSZTATSZ, TSZMADATSZ.

CHŌ-RŌ, チヤウラウ, 長老, *n.* The superior in a monastery, of the Zen sect of Buddhists.

CHŌ-RŌ, *-szru*, テウロウ, 嘲哢, To make sport of, to quiz, to make a fool of, to treat with irony; to mock, ridicule. *Tenka no* —, a laughing- stock to the whole empire. Syn. AZAKERU, GURU SZRU, NABURU.

†CHŌ-SAI, テウサイ, 超歲, *(toshi wo kosz.)* To be growing old. Syn. OTSZNEN.

CHŌ-SAI-BŌ, テウサイバウ, *n.* A fool, dunce. *H'to wo chōsaibō ni szru*, to make a fool of a person.

†CHO-SAKU, *-szru*, チヨサク, 著作, To write, or make a book.

†CHŌ-SAN, チヨウサン, 重三, *n.* A holy-day on the 3rd day of the 3rd month.

CHŌSEI, *-szru*, チヤウセイ, 長生, *(nugai-ki,)* To live long.

CHŌ-SHI, テウシ, 銚子, *n.* A metal kettle used for warming *sake*.

†CHŌ-SHI, チヤウシ, 長子, *n.* Eldest child.

CHŌ SHI, テウシ, 調子, *n.* Tone of voice, or of an instrument; tune. (fig.) spirits, *Chō-shi hadzre no koye*, a voice that does not tune with others. *Chō-shi wo hadzreru*, to be out of tune. *Chō-shi wo awaseru*, to chord, to put in tune. — *ga warui*, spirits are bad, to be out of tune.

CHŌ-SHIN, *-szru*, テウシン, 調進, *(totonoye szszmuru,)* *t. v.* To prepare and offer sweetmeats or medicine to a superior.

CHŌ-TAN, チヤウタン, 長短, *(naga, mijika,)* Long and short.

CHŌ-TO, チヤウト, 長途, *(naga michi,)* *n.* A long journey.

CHŌ-TO, チヤウト, 打, *adv.* Sound or appearance of cutting and slashing, same as *Chō-chō-to*.

†CHŌ-TSZGAI, テフツガヒ, 蝶番, *n.* A hinge.

CHOTTO, チヨツト, 一寸, *adv.* A little while, a moment, same as *Choito*.

CHŌ-YA, チヤウヤ, 長夜, *(nagayo,)* *n.* Long night.

CHŌ-YAKU, チヤウヤク, 町役, *n.* Town officers, ward-officers including, *Nanushi. Toshyori*, *Kumigashira*.

CHŌ-YŌ, チヨウヤウ, 重陽, *n.* A holy-day on the 9th. day of the 9th. month.

D.

DA, ダ, *(yed coll.* contracted from *De aru*, same as *ja* of the southern dialects.) It is often used as a substitute for a sentence, or something understood. *Nan-da*, what is it? *Are wa dare-da*, who is that? *Matszri wa itsz da*, when is the festival? *Kore wa nan da*, what is this? *fude da*, it is a pencil, *Sayō da*, it is so? *Kiyō wa atszi hi da*, this is a hot day. *Sore da kara watakushi iya da*, so then I don't want it, or *da kara iyada*, *(idem.)* *Da to iute* (or *datte mo,)* *sonna warui koto wa dekinai*, even if it be so, I cannot do such a wicked thing. *Da ga ne*, still; granting it to be so; be it so; be it so, but; *Me no warui hodo kurushii koto wa nai*, there is nothing so painful as a sore eye; *da ga ne, ha no itai no mo kurushii ze*, but tooth-ache is quite as painful.

DA, ダ, 駄, *n.* Numeral for a horse-load, about 150 catties, or 200 pounds. *Nimotsz ichi da,* one horse-load of goods.

†DABI, ダビ, 茶毘, *n.* Burning the bodies of the dead. *Dabi wo szru. Dabi-sho,* the place where dead bodies are burned. Syn. K'WASŌ.

DACHI, ダチ, (a suffix, derived from *Tatsz.*) *Tomo-dachi,* a companion, *Ichi-nin-dachi,* one man alone,

DA-CHIN, ダチン, 駄賃, *n.* Fare for transportation on horses, or coolies.

DA-CHŌ, ダテウ, 駝鳥, *n.* The Ostrich.

DA-DA, ダダ, , *n.* Fretful, petulent, cross, as a child, *dada wo iu,* to fret and whine, (as a cross child.)

DADAKE,*-ru,-ta,* ダダケル, *i. v.* To fret, to be cross, ill-tempered.
Syn. JIRERU.

DADAKKO, ダダッコ, 驕兒, *n.* A cross, fretful child.

DAI, ダイ, 臺, *n,* A stand, a frame work for holding or supporting something else, a pedestal, *Chadai,* a cupstand. *Shoku-dai,* a candle stick. *Teppō-dai,* a gun-carriage; gun-stock, *Fumi-dai,* a foot stool.

DAI, ダイ, 代, (*yo*) *n.* Age, dynasty, reign, generation. *Ban-dai,* all generations, Always, eternal, *Dai-dai,* every generation, or every dynasty.

DAI, ダイ, 代, (*shiro,*) *n.* Money given in exchange for anything; cost, price; vicarious, substitute. *Dai wo harau,* to pay off the cost. *Wata no dai wo ūketoru,* to receive the price of cotton. *Dai ni tatsz,* to act as a substitute.

DAI, ダイ, 題, *n.* A theme, text, subject, topic. — *wo dasz,* to propose a theme. *Kono keshiki wo — ni sh'te uta wo yomu,* make a piece of poetry on this landscape. *Nan-dai,* a difficult text.

DAI, ダイ, 第, The ordinal prefix. — *ichi,* the first. *Dai-ni-ban,* the second.

DAI, ダイ, 大, (*ōkii,*) Large, great, big, used mostly in compound words. — *goku jō no shina,* a thing of the very highest quality. — *kichi nichi,* a most lucky-day.

DAI-BA, ダイバ, 臺場, *n.* A fort. — *wo kidzku,* to construct a fort. *Odaiba.*

DAI-BEN, ダイベン, 大便, *n.* Feces excrement. — *szru,* to go to stool.
Syn. DAI-YŌ, KUSO.

DAI-BUN, ダイブン, 大分, *adv.* Much, to a large degree, for the most part. — *yokunatta,* he is much better. — *szdzshikunatta,* it is much cooler.
Syn. YOHODO, HONTONDO, SZKOBURU.

DAI-CHŌ, ダイチヤウ, 大腸, *n,* The large intestines.

DAI-DAI, ダイダイ, 橙, *n.* A kind of bitter orange.

DAI-DŌ, ダイダウ, 大道, (*ōji,*) *n.* Highway, main-road.

DAIDOKORO, ダイドコロ 臺所, *n.* A kitchen.

DAI-DZ, ダイヅ, 大豆, *n.* A kind of large white bean. Soja hispida.

DAI-GA, ダイガ, 大河, (*ō kawa,*) *n.* A large river.

DAI-GAKU, ダイガク, 大學, *n.* The great learning,—one of the four books of Confucius.

DAI-GAKURIYŌ, ダイガクレウ, 大學寮, *n.* Imperial university at Kiyoto.

DAI-GAWARI, ダイガハリ, 代替,*n.* Change of dynasty, reign, or headship of a family.

DAI-GI, ダイギ, 臺木, *n.* The stump, or stem on which a graft is fixed.

DAI-GŌ, ダイガウ, 題號, *n.* The name, or title of a book. Syn. GE-DAI, HIYŌ-DAI.

DAI-G'WAN, ダイグワン, 大願, (*ō negai,*) *n.* Prayer, petition, desire. *Isshō no* —, the desire of one's whole life. — *wo kakeru,* to offer up prayer. Syn. NEGAI.

DAI-HACHI-GURUMA, ダイハチグルマ, 大八車, *n.* A car, or dray for hauling goods.

DAI-HAN-NIYA, ダイハンニャ, 大般若, *n.* The name of the six hundred Budh. sacred books. — *kiyō wo tendoku szru,* to chant these books through, reading only a little here and there, at one sitting by a general assembly of priests.

DAI-HITSZ, ダイヒツ, 代筆, *n* A secretary, amanuensis.

†DAI-JI, ダイジ, 題辭, *n.* The preface of a book. Syn. JOBUN, HASHIGAKI.

DAI-JI, ダイジ, 大事, Important; of consequence, careful. *Dai-ji-nai,* of no importance. — *ni kakeru,* to regard with care, careful of. *O — ni nasare,* take care of yourself. — *na shina de gozarimasz,* it is a thing of great consequence.
Syn. TAI-SETSZ.

DAI-JIN, ダイジン 大人, *u.* A rich man.

DAI-JŌ-BU, ダイヂヤウブ, 大丈夫, *a.* Strong, firm, solid; well fortified, able to resist, hale, robust, sound in body; fixed, settled; safe, secure.
Syn. TASH'KA, SHIKKARI TO SH'TA.

DAI-JŌ-YE, ダイジヤウヱ, 大嘗會, *n.* The ceremony of offering rice to the Kami by the Tenshi, on the first year of his ascension to the throne.

DAI-KAGURA, ダイカグラ, 大神樂, *n.* A kind of dancing in the street, by a person wearing a mask like a lion's head.

DAI-JŌ-DAI-JIN, ダイジヤウダイジン, 大政大臣, A title of the highest rank.

DAI-KAI, ダイカイ, 大海, *n.* The ocean. Syn. AOUNABARA, SOTO-UMI.

DAI-KAN, ダイカン, 大寒, *n.* The period of greatest cold, one of the 24th terms, extending from about Jan. 21st to Feb. 6th.

DAI-KIN, ダイキン, 代金, *n.* Price, value, money paid in exchange for goods.

DAI-KOKU, ダイコク, 梵嫂, *n.* The mistress of a priest.

DAI-KOKU-BASHIRA, ダイコクバシラ, 大極柱, *n.* The large pillar in the centre of a house.

DAI-KOKU-DEN, ダイコクデン, 大黒天, *n.* The god of wealth. *Fuku no kami.*

DAI-KON, ダイコン, 大根, *n.* A kind of large radish. Raphanus sativus.

DAIKU, ダイク, 大工, *n.* A carpenter. *Funa-daiku*, a ship builder. *Fune no* —, a ship's carpenter.

DAI-K'WAN, ダイクワン, 代官, *n.* A lieutenant, or deputy officer, who superintends the affairs of an estate or fief belonging to his master.

DAI-MIYŌ, ダイミヤウ, 大名, *n.* A feudal chief, a baron, a noble.

DAI-MOKU, ダイモク, 題目, *n.* The name, or title of a book.

DAIMON, ダイモン, 大紋, *n.* A kind of coat worn by nobles.

DAI-MOTSZ, ダイモツ, 代物, *n.* Money given in exchange for goods. — *wa ikura*, what is the price?

DAI-NAGON, ダイナゴン, 大納言, *n.* The title of a rank of nobility.

DAI-NAN, ダイナン, 大難, (*ō wazawai,*) *n.* Great calamity.

DAINASHI, ダイナシ, 無第, *adv.* Spoiled, out of order, disordered, dirty. — *ni naru*, to be spoiled. *Kimono ga — ni furukunatta*, the garment is old and spoiled. Syn. MUCHA-KUCHA.

DAI-Ō, ダイワウ, 大黄, *n.* Rhubarb.

DAIRI, ダイリ内, 裏, *n.* The palace of the Mikado. Syn. KIN-RI, KIN-CHIU.

DAI-RIKI, ダイリキ, 大力, (*ō-chikara.*) Powerful, great strength. Syn. GŌRIKI.

DAI-RIYŌ, ダイレウ, 代料, *n.* Money given in exchange for goods, price, cost. Syn. DAI-KIN, DAI-MOTSU.

DAI-SAN, ダイサン, 代參, (*kawari ni mairu.* To visit a temple by proxy.

DAI-SHŌ, ダイセウ, 大小, Large and small, long and short. — *wo sasz*, to wear the long and short sword. *Tszki no* —, the long and short months.

DAI-SŌ-JŌ, ダイソウジヤウ, 大僧正, *n.* The title of the highest grade in the Buddhist priesthood, an Arch-bishop.

DAI-SZ, ダイス, 臺子, *n.* A stand with a furnace used in making tea..

DAI-TAN, ダイタン, 大膽, (*kimo no f'toi.*) Great courage, courageous; bold, impudent.

DAI-ZAI, ダイザイ, 大罪, (*ōinaru tszmi.*) Great crime. — *nin*, a great offender.

DA-JAKU, ダジヤク, 惰弱, Infirm, or weak in body, and unable to attend to business, invalid. — *nite yakunitatanu*, being weak and sickly he is of no use. Syn. HI-NIYKAU, JŪ-JAKU.

DAKARE, *-ru, -ta*, ダカレル, (pass. of *Daku*), to be held in the arms.

DAKAYE, *-ru, -ta*, ダカヘル, 抱, *t. v.* To hold in the arms, to embrace, to hug. *Oya ga kodomo wo* —, the parent carries the child in the arms. Syn. KAKAYERU, IDAKU.

DAKAYE, ダカヘ, 抱, *n.* An armful. *H'to — hodo no ki*, an armfnl of wood.

DAKE, ダケ, 丈, *n.* Much, quantity. *Kore* —, so much. *Dore* —, how much? *Ari* —, all there are. Syn. HODO, GURAI.

DAKI, *-ku, -ita*, ダク, 抱, *t.v.* To hold in the arms, to embrace, to hug. *Kodomo wo f'tokoro ni daku*, to carry a child in the bosom.

DAKI-AI, *-au, -atta*, ダキアフ, 抱合, *i. v.* To embrace each other.

DAKI-KAKAYE, *-ru, -ta*, ダキカカヘル, 懷抱, *t.v.* To embrace, to hold in the arms.

DAKI-KOMI, *-mu, -nda*, ダキコム, 抱籠, *t.v.* To carry into, to gain over to one's party or interest; to make friends of; to subsidize. *Mai-nai wo motte h'to wo daki-komu*, to gain over a person with bribes.

DAKI-OKOSHI, *-sz, -sh'ta*, ダキオコス, 抱起, *t.v.* To lift up in the arms.

DAKI-SHIME, *-ru, -tu*, ダキシメル, 抱緊, *t.v.* To hug tightly.

DAKI-TSZKI, *-ku, -ita*, ダキツク, 抱著, *i.v.* To cling to with the arms, to hug up to. *Kodomo wa oya ni daki-tszku*, the child clings to its parent.

DAKIU, ダキウ, 打球, *n.* A game of ball played on horseback. — *wo szru*, to play the above game. — *saji*, a pole armed with a net with which the ball is caught.

DAKKŌ, ダツコウ, 脱肛, *n.* Prolapsus ani.

DAKU, ダク, See *Daki*.

DAKU-BOKU, ダクボク, 凸凹, *adv.* Full of ups and downs, or hills and hollows, uneven. *Michi ga — sh'te arukarenu*, the road is so uneven it can't be traveled.
Syn. TAKABIKU.

†DAKU,–*szru*, ダク, 諾, To assent, consent, to answer, or respond to a call.
Syn. NOMI-KOMU, UBENAU, SHŌ-CHI-SZRU. GATTEN-SZRU

DAMARI,–*ru*,–*atta*, ダマル, 默, *i.v.* To be silent, still, not to speak. *Damatte iru*, to be silent. *Damatte ita kudasare*, please say nothing about it. *Damare*, be still.
Syn. MOKUNEN, MODASZ.

DAMARI, ダマリ, 默, *n.* Silence, without speaking. — *de szru*, to do anything without telling. — *no maku*, a theatrical scene where the actors are silent. — *de kiku*, to hear in silence.

DAMASARE,–*ru*,–*ta*, ダマサレル, 被欺, (pass. of *Damasz*). To be deceived, cheated, &c.

DAMASHI,–*sz*,–*sh'ta*, ダマス, 欺, *t.v.* To cheat, hoax, take-in, deceive, circumvent. *H'to wo damash'te kane wo toru*, to cheat a man out of his money. *Kitszne wa h'to wo damasz mono da*, the fox is an animal which deceives men.
AZAMUKU, ITSWARU, TABURAKASZ.

DAMASHI-KOMI,–*mu*,–*nda*, ダマシコム, 欺籠, *t.v.* To take in, cheat, over-reach, victimize.

DAMASHI-TORI,–*ru*,–*tta*, ダマシトル, 欺取, *t.v.* To take by cheating.

DAME, ダメ, 徒目, Vain, useless. *Kuszri wo nomash'te mo — da*, it is useless to take medicine. Syn. MUDA.

DAM'MA, ダウマ, 駄馬, *n.* A pack-horse.

DAMMARI, ダンマリ, (Yed coll. for *Damari*).

DAMMATSZMA, ダンマツマ, 斷末魔, *n.* Articulo mortis, hour of death. (Bud).
Syn. MATSZGO, RIMMIYŌJŪ, RINJŪ.

DAMMETSZ, ダンメツ, 斷滅. To destroy.

DAMO, ダモ. Same as *demo, saye*.

DAMPAN, ダンパン, 談判, *n.* Conference on a serious or important subject, consultation, deliberation.
Syn. DANKO, SŌDAN, KAKE-AI.

DAMPŌ, ダンパウ, 檀方, *n.* The parishioners of a temple.
Syn. DANKE, DANNA, DAN-OTSZ.

DAN, ダン, 段, *n.* A step, a raised platform, *Hashigo no* —, the steps of a staircase or ladder. — *wo kidszku*, to throw up a platform, (of dirt or stones). *Butsz-dan*, an altar.

DAN, ダン, 段, *n.* Grade, rank, step, a section of a book, an act, or play in a theatre, thing or affair, subject. *Kono — no kokoro wa*, the meaning of this section. — *ga chigai*, of different grades. *Ichi-dan*, one act, &c., also completely, wholly.

DAN-BIRA, ダンビラ, 快刀, *n.* A broad sword.

DAN-DAN, ダンダン, 段段, *adv.* Step by step, gradually, by degrees. — *te ga agaru*, gradually becomes a better hand at,
Syn. OI-OI, SHIDAI-SHIDAI NI.

DAN-DARA, ダンダラ, *n.* Striped crosswise, marked or cut across in sections, irregular. — *no hata*. a flag with cross stirpes. — *ni someru*, dyed with cross stripes. — *biyōshi*, irregular sounds, loud and soft.

DANSZRU, ダンズル. See *Danji*.

DAN-GI, ダンギ, 談義, *n.* Preaching, a sermon by a Buddhist priest of the Monto sect. — *wo kiku*, to listen to a sermon. *Heta no naga* —. the long sermon of a tyro. Syn. SEPPŌ, HŌDAN, KŌSHAKU.

DANGO, ダンゴ, 團子, *n.* A dumpling.

DANI, ダニ, 木虱, *n.* A dog-tick.

DANI, ダニ, 駄荷, *n.* Goods carried by a pack-horse.

DANI, ダニ, *adv.* Even, only, as much as, *Nani kotayen kotoba — naku*, had not even a word to answer. *Oto — shedz*, not making even a sound.
Syn. SAYE, DEMO.

DANJI,–*ru*,–*ta*, ダンズル 談, *i. v.* To speak, talk, say. *O danji mōshitai koto ga aru.* I have something I should like to say. Syn. HANASZ. SODAN.

DAN-JIKI, ダンジキ, 斷食, *n.* Fasting, abstaining from food. — *wo szru*, to fast.

DANJIRI, ダンヂリ, *n.* An ornamented car drawn by oxen or men, at festivals.
Syn. DASHI.

DAN-KE, ダンケ, 檀家, *n.* The parishioners, or supporters of a temple.

DAN-KI, ダンキ, 暖氣, *n.* Warm weather.
Syn. ATATAKAI.

†DAN-KIN, ダンキン, 斷金, (*kane wo kiru.*) — *no majiwari*, strongest friendship.

DAN-KŌ, ダンカフ, 談合, (*hanashi-ai*,) To talk together, consult about.
Syn. SŌ-DAN.

DANNA, ダンナ, 檀那, *n.* The parishioners of a temple. Master. *Omaye no — wa dare ka*, whose servant are you? — *sama*, (respectful) master.
Syn. SHU-JIN, TEI-SHU, ARUJI.

DANNA-DERA, ダンナデラ, 檀那寺, *n.*

The temple of which a person is a parishioner.

†DAN-OTSZ, ダンオツ, 檀越, (same as *Danke.*)

DAN-RIN, ダンリン, 檀林, *n.* A Buddhist monastery.

DAN-ZAI, ダンザイ, 斷罪, (*Kiru-tszmi.*) *n.* Capital punishment. — *ni okonau,* to punish with decapitation.

DAN-ZETSZ, ダンゼツ, 斷絶, To cut off, destroy. *Ka-mei wo — szru* to cut off the family name.

DARA-DARA, ダラダラ, *adv.* In a slow sluggish manner. *Chi ga — to nagareru,* the blood flows in a sluggish current.

DARAKE,*–ru,–ta,* ダラケル, *i. v.* To be languid, dull, sluggish, drooping, indisposed to exertion. *Kiyō wa atszkute karada ga daraketa,* to day it is so hot I feel languid. *Daraketa nari,* a languid manner. Syn. SHIMARI GA NAI.

DARAKE, ダラケ, Used only in composition with nouns,=covered with, filled with; smeared with. *Kao ga szmi-darake da,* face is smeared over with ink. *Te ga chi-darake ni natta,* hands are covered with blood. *Kuni wa aku-nin-darake da,* the country is filled with bad men. *Yama-darake,* mountainous. Syn. MABURE.

DARAKU, ダラク, 墮落, (*ochiru.*) — *szru,* to fall, to fall away, to apostatize. (Budd.) *Jigoku ni — szru,* to fall into hell. *Daraku-sō,* an apostate priest.
Syn. GEN-ZOKU.

DARANI, ダラニ, 陀羅尼, *n.* A Buddhist sacred book written in the Pali character.

DARANISZKE, or DARASZKE, ダラニスケ, 陀羅尼介, *n.* A kind of bitter medicine.

DARE,*–ru,–ta,* ダレル, 低, *i.v.* (coll. same as *Tareru.*) To fall in price. *Wata mo szkoshi dareta,* cotton has fallen a little. *Kome-sōba mo chitto dare-kuchi da,* the price of rice has begun to fall a little.
Syn. SAGARU.

DARE, ダレ, 誰, (same as *Tare.*) pro. Who. — *ga itash'ta,* who did it? — *nite mo,* or *Dare-demo,* any body, every-body, whoever. *Soko ni iru no wa dare da,* who is in there. — *mo shitta mono wa nai,* no body knows it, or I don't know anybody. *Kore wa — no hon da,* whose book is this? — *ni yari mashō ka,* to whom shall I give it? Syn. NANI-BITO.

DARUI,– KI, – SHI, ダルイ, *a.* Languid, sluggish, dull, heavy, lifeless, weak and indisposed to exertion.

DARUKU, ダルク, *adv.* idem. *Haru-saki wa karada ga daruku-naru,* in the latter part of spring the body becomes languid.
Syn. NAMAKERU, TAIGI, KETTARUI.

DARUMA, ダルマ, 達磨, *n.* A follower of Shaka, and teacher of Buddhism in China.

DARUMAKI, ダルマキ, 達磨忌, *n.* A festival in honor of Daruma on the 5th day of the 10th month.

DARUMI,*–mu,–nda,* ダルム, 弛, *i. v.* To be slack, relaxed, loose, drooping; negligent, remiss. *Me no kawa ga darumu,* the skin of the eyelid is relaxed. *Toko no ito ga darunda,* the kite-string is slack.
Syn. KUTSZROGU, YURUMU.

DASHI, ダシ, *n.* Flavoring for soup. *Katsz-obushi no dashi,* a sauce made of dried fish.

DASHI, ダシ, 樂車, *n.* An ornamented car drawn at festivals. Same as *Danjiri.*

DASHI, ダシ, 託, *n.* Pretext, pretence, excuse. — *ni szru,* to do on pretence.
Syn. KAKOTSZKE.

DASHI,*–sz,–ta,* ダス, 出, *t. v.* To put out, take out, drive out, bring out, lead out, to cause to go out. *Cha wo dase,* bring in the tea. *Dash'te miru,* to take out and look. *Kane wo dash'te kau,* to pay out money and buy. *Bōya ga aruki-dash'ta,* the child has begun to walk. *Medzrashii koto kiki-dash'ta,* I have heard (found out by hearing) a strange thing. *Ji wo mi-dash'ta,* I have found the word. *Mise wo dasz,* to set up a new store. Syn. IDASZ.

DASHI-AI, ダシアヒ, 出合, *n.* Paying out together, investing in shares. *Ikura dztsz no —, de kono mise wo o dashi-nasatta,* how much capital has each person invested in this store?

DASHI-IRE, ダシイレ, 出納, *n.* Expenditures and receipts; the taking out and putting in. *Kane no — ga ōi,* to take in and pay out a great deal of money.

DASHI-NUKE-NI, ダシヌケニ, 出抜, *adv.* Suddenly, by surprise, unexpectedly. — *h'to wo tataku,* to suddenly strike a person, so as to make him start.
Syn. FUTO, FUI-NI, HAKARADZ, OMOI-GAKE-NAKU.

DASHI-NUKI,*–ku,–ita,* ダシヌク, 出拔, *t.v.* To play a trick on, to evade, dodge away; to circumvent. Syn. HADZSZ.

DASSO, ダッソ, 脫疽, *n.* Gangrene of the feet.

DATAI, ダタイ, 墮胎, *n.* Abortion, — *szru,* to cause abort on. — *no kuszri,* medicines which cause abortion.
Syn. KO WO OROSZ.

DATE, ダテ, 伊達, *n.* Ornament, tinsel,

finery, — *wo szru*, to adorn, decorate. — *otoko*, a fop. — *dōgu*, articles carried in the train of Daimio's for shew and ornament merely. — *moyō*, decorated with gay figures (as a dress). — *na*, gay, gaudy. Syn. HADE.

DATE-SHA, ダテシヤ, 艶妝者, *n.* One fond of wearing finery, a fop.

DAYUI, ダユイ, same as *Darui.*

†DA-UN, ダウン, 朶雲, *n.* A letter. — *kudasare arigataku zonji soro*, many thanks for your letter.

DE, デ, Post-pos. expressing the cause, manner or instrument, the place, or time, and sometimes answering to the sub. verb. With, by, at, of, in. *Te de butsz*, strike with the hand. *Fude de kaku*, to write with a pen. *Fune de yuku*, to go by ship. *H'tori de aru*, to be by one's self, (to be alone,) *Yedo de koshirayeru*, made at Yedo, *Take de koshirayeru*, made of bamboo, *Damari de yuku.* went without speaking, or in silence. *Kore wa nan de aru*, what is this? *Kami de aru*, it is paper. *Sayō de gozarimasz*, yes, it is so. *Dō de gozarimasz*, how is it? Syn. NITE, NI, WO-MOTTE.

DE, デ, 不, a neg. suffix; contraction of *dzte* or *dz sh'te.* *Shirade kanawanu*, must know. *Te mo furede oku*, to let be and not touch it. *Mono wo mo iwade nige-usetari*, without saying a word he disappeared

DE,*-ru,-ta*, デル, 出, *i, v.* To go out, issue-forth, proceed from; to arise, appear, *uchi kara dete yuku*, to go out of the house. *Date-koi*, come out. *Deta*, or *demash'ta*, has gone out- *Hi ga deta*, the sun has risen. *Hōki-boshi ga deta*, a comet has appeared, *Hima ga deru*, to be out of employment. *Yoi chiye ga deta*, has shown great wisdom. *Ka ga deta*, the musquitoes have come, *Ki no me ga deta*, the buds have sprouted. Syn. DERU, IDZRU.

DEAI,*-au,-atta*, デアフ, 出會, *i. v.* To meet while out, to meet with. *Michi de deatta*, to meet in the road. *Deaigashira ni atama wo utsz*, to bump heads just on going out. *Kai-jō nite nampū ni de-ai*, met with adverse winds at sea.

DEBA, テバ, 露歯, *n.* Projecting teeth.

DEBA, デバ, 出刃, *n.* A kitchen-knife.

DEBANA, デバナ, 出初, *n.* The period of greatest perfection, *Cha no debana*, that point in making an infusion of tea when it is best. *Midz no debana*, the highest point of a flood of water.

DEBARI,*-ru,-tta*, テバル, 出張, *i.v.* To leave home and attend on business, or duty at some fixed place. *Ken-jutsz-shi tzki rok-sai ni dōjō ye debaru*, the teacher of the sword exercise six times in a month attends at the gymnasium. *Ban-sho ye debaru*, to attend at the police station. *De-bari no isha*, a physician who has regular places away from home for prescribing for the sick. Syn. SHUT-CHO SZRU.

DE-BESO, デベソ, 突臍, *n.* Projecting navel, umbilical hernia.

DE-BITAI, デビタヒ, 出額, *n.* Projecting eye-brows.

DE-CHIGAI,*-au,-atta*, デチガフ, 出違, *i. v.* To miss by going out; to be out when another calls, and so miss seeing.

DE-DANA, デダナ, 出店, *n.* A shop in another place, a branch-shop.

DEDEMUSHI, デデムシ, 蝸牛, *n.* A snail.

DEGIRE, デギレ, 出切, *n.* Scraps of cloth left after cutting.

DE-HŌDAI, デハウダイ, 出放題, *adv.* Speaking off-hand; at random, without reflection, — *ni iu*, to speak at random. Syn. DETARAME.

†DEI, デイ, 泥, *(doro,) n.* Mud. — *chiu no hachisz no gotoku*, like a lotus flower growing in the mud, *(fig.)* of one who rises to high honor from a mean origin.

DEI-DEI, デイデイ, *n.* A class of people of very low grade, who make their living, the men by mending shoes, the women, by playing the guitar in the streets, the same as *Hi-nin.*

DE-IRI, デイリ, 出入, *n.* Going out and in, expenses and receipts; a dispute, suit at law. *Kane no — ga ōi*, the income and expenditures are large. — *ga aru*, to have a dispute. *De-iri-guchi*, a door, common passage way.

DEI-TO, デイト, 泥土, *(doro tszchi,) n.* Mud and clay.

DE-JIRO, デジロ, 出城, *n.* An out-castle. one besides the main-castle erected in another place.

DE-KAKARI,*-ru,-tta*, デカカル, 出掛, *i.v.* Ready, or about to go out. *Dekakatte oru kara noch'hodo o me ni kakarimashō*, as I am about to go out I will see you by and by.

DE-KASHI,*-sz,-ta*, デカス, 出來, *t. v.* To cause to do; mostly used in the perfect tense and implying surprise.) *Kore wa de-kash'ta*, how well you have done it! *Tonda koto de-kash'ta*, done a bad business. *Dekashigao*, proud or puffed up with success, boastful.

DE-KASEGI, デカセキ, 出稼, *n.* Business, or employment away from home. — *ni yuku*, to go away from home to work.

DE-KAWARI, デカハリ, 出替, *n.* Change in going out to service; doing duty in the place of one whose time has expired. — *no maye*, before one's time of service is up. — *ga kuru*, time of service is up. *Shibai no* —, the exchange of play actors from one theatre to another.

DEKI, *-ru,-ta*, デキル, 出來, *i.v.* To do, make, finish; can, able. *Dekiru-ka dekinu-ka*, can you do it, or not? *Dekinai*, can't. *Dekineba dekinakute mo yoi*, if you can't do it, never mind. *Iye ga dekita*, the house is finished. *Ko toshi wa kome ga yoku dekita*, this year the rice has done well. *Are wa yoku dek'ta h'to da*, that is an an accomplished man. *Nebuto ga dek'ta*, have got a boil. *Ko ga dek'ta*, has brought-forth a child. Syn. SHUTTAI SZRU, JO-JŪ SZRU, SZRU, ITASZ, NASZ.

DEKI, デキ, 出來, *n.* The product; what is done, or finished. — *ga warui*, it is badly made, or done. *Kome no — ga yoi*, the rice crop is good. *Shigoto no — wa ōi*, the work done is great. *Deki fudeki ga aru*, some times (the crop is) good, some times bad; good and bad. — *shidai mottekoi*, bring it as soon as it is done.

DEKI-AI, *-au,-utta*, デキアフ, 出來合, *i. v.* To be ready made, at hand, on hand. *Sai-wai dekiatta shina ga gozarimasz*, fortunately I have one ready made.

DEKI-AI, デキアヒ, *n.* Ready made articles. *do gozen wo dasz*, to put out just such food as there is at hand. — *no kimono*, ready-made clothing. — *no tszkuye gozarimasz ka*, have you any tables ready-made? Syn. MA-NI-AI, ARI-AI.

DEKI-BUGEN, デキブゲン, 暴富, *n.* Riches acquired suddenly.

DEKI-GOKORO, デキゴコロ, 出來心, *n.* Sudden notion, or fancy, sudden desire. *Futo sh'ta — de tszi warui koto itashimash'ta*, seized with a sudden notion I did wrong.

DEKI-MONO, デキモノ, 瘍腫, *n.* A sore, an ulcer. — *ga dek'ta*, I have an ulcer, it has ulcerated.

DEKI-SHI, デキシ, 溺死, *n.* Drowned. *Kesa h'to ga — sh'ta*, this morning there was a man drowned.
Syn. OBORE-JINI, MIWO NAGETE SHINURU.

DEKI-SOKONAI, *-au,-atta*, テキソコナヒ, 出來損, *i. v.* To be spoiled, or injured in making; to be badly made. *Kore wa deki-sokonai da kara tada agemasz*, as this is badly made I will not charge for it.

DEKO, デコ, 木偶人, *n.* A puppet with a large projecting forehead.

DEKUWASE, *-ru,-ta*, デクハセル, 出吃, *i. v.* To meet unexpectedly.

DE-MARU, デマル, 別堡, *n.* A fortress, or castle in another place, separate from the principal one.

DEMBATA, デンバタ, 田畑, *n.* Rice and wheat fields.

DEMBŌ, デンバウ, A low-fellow who pushes into theatres and bath-houses without paying. Syn. AOTA.

DEMBU, デンブ, *n.* Kind of food, made of fish.

DEMBU-YA-JIN, デンブヤジン, 田夫野人, *n.* A rustic, a clownish, ignorant fellow.

DEM-BUN, テンブン, 傳聞, (*tsztayete kiku.*) To know by hearsay, to hear from others, a report. — *de wa jissetsz ga shire nai*, knowing merely by report, I am not sure of it.

DEME, デメ, 眲目, *n.* Projecting eyes.

DE-MISE, デミセ, 出店, *n.* A branch store.

DEMO, デモ, (*de*, and *mo*,) conj. Either, or, whether, even if, soever. Found in compounds, as in *Nandemo Itszdemo, Dochirademo, Daredemo*, (which see.) *Inu demo neko demo niwatori wo toru ka shiranu*, I don't know whether it was a dog or cat which took the fowl. *Ame demo furu ka shiranu.* I don't know whether it will rain. *Yuki demo furaneba yoi ga*, it would be better if it did not snow. *Uso demo itte damash'te toru ga yoi*, if it is even by lying, better cheat him out of it. *Sore demo iya da*, I won't even for that. *Nedzmi demo hīta sō da*, it looks as if a rat had taken it. *O cha demo agare*, take some tea, (implying there is nothing else.) *Yama ye demo agatte miyō ka*, I think I will go up the hills and look about. *Yuku to demo yukanai to demo o ī yo*, say whether you will go or not, (it don't matter which.)

†DEM-PO, デンポ, 田圃, *n.* Fields.

DEM-PŌ, デンパウ, 傳法, *n.* Traditional religious rites, doctrines, or rules.

DEM-PŌ, デンパウ, 傳方, *n.* A medical receipt received from another.

DEM-PU, デンプ, 田夫, *n.* A farmer, hus bandman. Syn. H'YAK'SHŌ.

DE-MUKAI, デムカヒ, 出迎, *n.* Going out to welcome in a guest, going out to meet. — *ni yuku*, to go out to receive a friend.

DEN, デン, 傳, (*tsztaye*,) *n.* A record, history, rules, precepts, or doctrines, transmitted and received through others.

DEN, デン, 田, (*ta*,) *n.* Rice-field. — *ippo*, one field.

DE-NA, DENASAI, or DENASARE, デナ, The coll. imper. of *Deru.*

DEN-CHIU, デンチウ, 殿中, *n.* The dwelling place of the Shōgun, the Palace.

DEN-GAKU, デンガク, 田樂, *n.* A kind of food made of baked *tōfu*, also a kind of ancient theatre now obsolete.

DEN-GON, デンゴン, 傳言, *(tsztayeru kotoba), n.* Word, verbal message, transmitted from one person to another, — *wo ukeru*, to be informed of, or receive a message. *Go dengon kudasaru beku soro*, please inform others Syn. KOTODZTE.

DENJI, デンヂ, 田地, *n.* Rice-field, a farm, plantation.

DEN-JŌ, デンジヤウ, 殿上, *n.* The Mikado's audience chamber.

DEN-JU, デンジユ, 傳授, *(tsztaye sadzku), n.* Teaching, instruction, or precepts transmitted. — *szru*, to instruct, teach. — *wo ukeru*, to receive instruction.

DEN-KA, デンカ, 田家, *n.* A farm-house.

DEN-KA, デンカ, 殿下, *n.* The servants, or ministers of the Mikado.

DEN-KI, デンキ, 傳記, *(tsztaye shirusz), n.* Records, history, chronicle. *Tera no — ni kuwashiku noshete aru*, it is minutely related in the records of the temple.

†DEN-K'WA, デンクワ, 電火, *n.* Lightning. Syn. INADZMA.

DEN-RAI, デンライ, 傳來, (*tsztaye-kitaru*), Transmitted; handed down, come down by tradition. *Sen-sō yori denrai no hō-ken*, a valuable sword come-down from one's ancestors.

DEN-SETSZ, デンセツ, 傳說, *(tsztaye-banashi), n.* A story, saying or report, transmitted from one to another. — *nite kikimash'ta*, know it only by report.

†DEN-ZEM-BIYŌ, デンセンビヤウ, 傳染病, *n.* A hereditary disease, contagious disease.

†DEN-SEN, *–szru*, デンセン, 傳染, To transmit disease from one to another, to infect with disease.

†DEN-SHA, デンシヤ, 田舍, *n.* A farm house; the country.

DEN-SO, デンソ, 田租, *n.* Rice tax paid by farmers.

DEN-TATSZ, *–szru*, デンタツ, 傳達, To deliver a message.

DERARE, *–ru*, *–ta*, デラレル, 被出, pass of *Deru.*

DERO, デロ, (a vulgar coll. imp. of *Deru*) Get out, go out.

DERŌ, デラウ, coll. fut, or dub. of *Deru*, I shall go out, or, I think I shall go out.

DERU, デル, (see De.)

DE-SAKARI, デサカリ, 出盛, *n.* The time of being out in greatest numbers. *Yatsz doki ni h'to no* —, the greatest concourse, of people is at two o'clock. *Hōsō ga* —, the height of the eruption of small-pox.

DESHBARI, *–ru*, *–tta*, テシヤバル, *i. v.* To rudely interrupt others while talking, to obtrude, or interfere in speaking. *Temaye no deshabaru ni wa oyobanai*, there is no need of your interference. Syn. SASHIDERU, DESZGIRU.

DESHI, デシ, 弟子, *n.* A pupil, scholar, disciple, learner. — *domo*, pupils. Syn. MONJIN, MONTEI.

DESHI-HŌBAI, デシホウバイ, 同門, *n.* Fellow-pupils, school-mates.

DESHI-IRI, デシイリ, 入門, *(niu mon,) n.* Entering as a pupil, becoming a disciple. — *wo szru*, to enter as a pupil. — *no shū-gi*, tuition fee.

DESHI-KIYŌDAI, デシキヤウダイ, 師兄弟, *n.* Pupils of the same teacher.

DESŌ, デサウ, *u.* The appearance of going out, looks like going out. *Kaze ga desōna tenki*, it looks as if it would blow.

DE-SOROI, *–ō*, *–ōta*, デソロフ, 出揃, *i. v.* To come out fully, every one to appear. *Hōsō ga de-sōrōta*, the small pox eruption is fully out.

DE-SZGI, *–ru*, *–ta*, デスギル, 出過, *i. v.* To interrupt, to meddle, interfere; to intrude, — *mono*, a meddler, intruder. Syn. DESHABARU.

DE-TACHI, *–tsz*, *–tta*, デタツ, 出立, *i. v.* To start out, to start off, to set out. *Kesa mutsz doko ni detachi-mash'ta*, he started at 6 o'clock this morning. Syn. SHUTTATSZ, HOSSOKU.

DETARAME, デタラメ, *n.* Speaking at random, saying anything that comes first without reflection, — *wo iu, id.* Syn. DEHŌDAI.

DET-CHI, デツチ, 小奴, *n.* A shop boy.

DEYŌJŌ, デヤウジヤウ, 出養生, *n.* Leaving home on account of health, — *szru*, to go abroad for health.

DE-YU, デユ, 温泉, *n.* Hot springs. Syn. ONSEN, TŌJIBA.

DO, ド, 度, *n.* A degree in geometry, or division of a thermometer, right or just measure. *wo hakaru*, to count the degrees. *Kon-nichi no atszsa iku do*, how high is the thermometer to day? — *wo szgiru*, to exceed the proper degree. *In-shoku no do naki*, no regular times for eating and drinking, *Ichi do*, once, *Maido*, often. *Iku do*, how often? *Do-do*, frequently. — *wo ushinau*, to lose presence of mind, or to be disconcerted. Syn. TABI.

Dō, ドウ, 胴, *n.* The trunk, the body, that part of a coat of mail which covers the trunk. — *no ma*, the middle part of a ship between the fore and mizzen masts.

Dō, ダウ, 道, (*michi*,) *n.* A road, way, virtue, reason, doctrine, principle, truth, used only in comp. words.

Dō, ダウ, 堂, *n.* A temple, public hall, a chamber.

Dō, ドウ, 銅, (*akagane*,) *n.* Copper.

Dō, ドウ, 同, (*onaji*,) Alike, the same, together. — *jitsz*, 同日, same day. — *nen*, 同年, same year. — *getsz*, 同月, same month. — *chō*, 同町, same street. — *butsz*, 同物, same thing, alike.

Dō, ドウ, (*adv.*) How, in what manner, for what reason, by what cause, in what state, why, what. — *szru de arō zo*, what will become of him? or, what will he do? or, why are you making that? *Usaburo* — *sh'te iru ka*, how is *Usaburo* doing? — *sh'ta*, how was it done? how was it? where is it? — *sh'tara yokarō*, how had I better do? — *demo yoi*, anyhow will do. — *nari tomo itashimashō*, however it may be I will do it. — *shiyō*, what shall I do? or, how shall I do? — *sh'te mo dekinai*, do what I may I can't do it. *Kiyō wa* — *sh'te konai*, why don't he come to day? — *sh'ta mono de arō ka*, or, — *darōka*, what had I better do? — *sh'te mite mo omoshiroku nai*, let me try what I will, it is disagreeable. — *sh'ta koto yara mune ga itai*, how did I come by this pain in the breast? — *de gozarimasz*, — *desz*, or — *da*, how is it?, (in meeting) what's the news? or how are you? — *da ka obotszkanai*, I am doubtful about the result.— *iu wake*, for what reason. — *iu h'to*, what kind of a man. — *mo*, how! — *mo miyō da*, how beautiful! — *mo shiyō ga nai*, there is no help at all. — *mo miye nai*, can't see it at all. — *ka*, and — *zo*, (beseeching, intreating, desiring,) please, I pray, I wish. — *ka taszketai mono da*, I pray you to help me. — *ka yoi kufū ga arisō na mono da*, I wish I knew some good plan. — *zo kash'te kudasare*, please lend me. — *ka kōka deki-agatta*, I have at last some how or other finished. — *yara kōyara* (idem,) Syn. IKAGA, DONOYONI.

†DOBA, ドバ, 駑馬, *n.* A useless horse.

Dō-BACHI, ドウバチ, 銅鉢, *n.* A copper bowl.

Dō-BAN, ダウバン, 堂番, *n.* The keeper of a temple.

DO-BASHI, トバシ, 土橋, *n.* A bridge the floor of which is of earth.

DOBI, ドビ, 荼薇, *n* The white rose.

DO-BIN, ドビン, 土瓶, *n.* An earthen teapot.

Dō-Bō, ドウボウ, *n.* An inferior servant of the *Shō-gun*.

DO-BOKU, ドウボク, 僮僕, *n.* A servant boy.

DOBU, ドブ, 街渠, *n.* A ditch, trench, drain.

DOBU-DOBU, ドブドブ, *adv.* The sound made by a liquid flowing from a bottle, or of a small thing falling into water.

Dō-BUKU, ダウブク, 道服, *n.* A kind of coat worn by retired persons.

Dō-BURUI, ドウブルイ, 胴慄, *n.* Shivering, trembling. — *ga szru*, to tremble.

DOBUTSZ, ドブツ, *n.* A fat and silly person.

†Dō-BUTSZ, ドウブツ, 動物, (*ugokumono*). *n.* Things that have life and motion.

†DōCHI, ドウチ, 童稚, *n.* A child, a young person under 10 years. Syn, WARAMBE, KODOMO, OSANAGO.

DOCHIRA, ドチラ, 何地, pro. Where, which. — *ye ittaka shire nai*, I don't know where he has gone. — *kara oide nasatta*, where have you come from? — *ni i-nasaru*, where do you live? — *ga yoi*, which is the best? — *demo yoroshii*, either will do. — *mo yoroshii*, they are both good. Syn. IDZKATA, DOKO.

Dō-CHIU, ダウチウ, 道中, *n.* In the road, while on a journey, while traveling.

DODAI, ドダイ, 土臺, *n.* The foundation sill of a house.

Dō-DAN, ドウダン, 同斷, A word used to save repetition, ditto. *Migi* —, same as before,

Dō-Dō,-*szru*, ドウダウ, 同道, To travel together, to go together. *Go* — *mōshimasz*, I will go with you.

DODOITSZ, ドドイツ, 都都一, *n.* A kind of song.

Dō-DŌ-TO, ドウドウ, *adv.* The sound of rushing water, or wind. *Midz* — *hibiku*, the rushing sound of water.

†DO-FŪ, ドフウ, 土風, *n.* Local customs, or manners.

Dō-GAKU, ドウガク, 同學, Learning, or studying together with the same teacher.

Dō-GANE, ドウガネ, 銅金, *n.* The metal bands around a sword scabbard.

Dōgi, ドウギ, 胴著, *n.* A corset, or short jacket worn inside of the other clothes.

Dō-giri, ドウギリ, 胴功, *n.* Cutting the body in two by a side blow.

Dō-giyo, ドウギヤウ, 同行, *n.* Traveling together on a pilgrimage, or, going together on the same religious duties, as begging priests.

Dō-gu, ダウグ, 道具, *n.* Tools, implements, utensils, furniture, arms, weapons.

Dō-guszri, ドウグスリ, 火藥, *n.* Gunpowder. Syn. YENSHŌ.

Dō-guszri-ire, ドウグスリイレ, 火藥鑑, *n.* A powder flask.

Dō-guya, ダウグヤ, 道具屋, *n.* A shop where second-hand furniture is sold.

Dō-hai, ドウハイ, 同輩, *(onaji tomogara)*, *n.* Same rank or social position, equals. — *no aisatsz wo szru*, to salute as an equal.

Dōhan, ドウハン, 銅板, *n.* Copper plate for printing, engraved on copper plate. — *no ye*, a copper plate engraving.

Dō-han, ドウハン, 同藩, *n.* Fellow servants of the same *Daimiyo*.

Dō-han, ドウハン, 同伴, *(onajiku tomonau)*. Going along with, accompanying. *Go — itashimashō*, I will go with you. Syn. TSZRE.

Dō-hen, ドウヘン, 同變, *n.* In the same state, condition, without change, (said only of a sick person).

Do-hiyō, ドヒヤウ, 土俵, *n.* Bags filled with earth.

Dohiyō-ba, ドヒヤウバ, 土俵場, *n.* The ring made with earth-bags where wrestlers perform.

Dō-i, ドウイ, 同意, *(onaji kokoro)*, *n.* Of the same mind, like minded. — *szru*, to be of &c.

Dō-in, ダウイン, 導引, Shampooing. Syn. AMMA.

†**Dō-ji**, ドウジ, 童子, *n.* A boy.

Dōji, *-ru,-ta*, ドウズル, 動, *(ugoku,) i. v.* To move, affect, influence. — *taru keshi ki mo naku*, no appearance of being affected. Syn. KANDZRU.

Do-jin, ドジン, 土人, *n.* Aborigines, original inhabitants.

Do-jō, ドジヤウ, 鯲, *n.* A kind of small fish caught in rice fields, a lamprey?

Dō-jō, ダウジヤウ, 道場, *n.* A hall erected before Buddhist temples; a place where the art of fencing is taught.

Doka-doka, ドカドカ, *adv.* The sound of loud steps. — *to aruku.*

Dō-kaku, ドウカク, 同格, *(onaji kurai)*, Same in rank.

Dōke, *-ru,-ta*, ドウケル, *i. v.* To jest, to act the buffoon, to talk for the diversion of others. — *mono*, a jester, buffoon, clown. Syn. HIYŌ-GERU, KOKKEI, FUZAKERU.

Doke, *-ru,-ta*, ドケル, 退, *t.v.* Yed. coll. for *Nokeru*. To put out of the way, move to one side. *Doke*, go away, get out of the way. *Mono wo dokete szwaru*, to push anything aside and sit down.

Doki, *-ku,-ita*, ドク 退, *i.v.* To get out of the way, to move aside. *Watakushi dokimas anata o szwari nasare*, I will move out of the way do you sit down.

Dōki, ドウキ, 動氣, *n.* Palpitation of heart.

†**Doki**, ドキ, 土器, *n.* Earthenware.

†**Doki**, ドキ, 怒氣, *n.* Anger. — *wo nadameru*, to soothe anger. Syn. IKARI.

Doki-doki, ドキドキ, 悸悸, *adv.* Beating of the heart. *Mune ga — szru*, heart went pita-pat.

Dō-kin, ドウキン, 同勤, *(onaji tsztome)*, *n.* Same official employment.

Dō-kiyo, ドウキヨ, 同居. Living together in the same house, boarding together.

Dō-kiyō, ドウキヤウ, 同鄉, *(onaji sato)*. Natives of the same place. — *no h'to.*

Dokkari-to, ドツカリ, *adv.* In the manner of a sudden and violent fall. — *szwaru*, to sit down suddenly and with violence, to come down with a bang.

Dokkeshi, ドクケシ, 消毒, *n.* An antidote to poison.

Dokki, ドクキ, 毒氣, *n.* Poisonous air or gas.

†**Dokkiyo**, ドクキヨ, 獨居, *(h'tori oru)*, To live alone.

Dokkoi, ドツコイ, Exclamation of surprise, or of sudden alarm.

†**Dokkō**, *-szru*, ドクカウ, 獨行, *(hitori yuku)*. To travel alone.

Dōko, ドウコ, 銅壺, *n.* A copper boiler.

Doko, ドコ, 何處, *adv.* Where. — *no h'to da*, where is he from? what country is he of? *Kono hon — de dekimash'ta*, where was this book made? — *ye yuku*, where are you going? *Uchi wa — da*, where do you live? — *ye mo iku no wa iya da*, I wont go any where. — *demo yoi*, any place will do. *Hi wa — demo ataru*, the sun shines every where. — *zo ni aru de arō*, I think they are in some place. — *to mo nashi ni yuku*, to go, not knowing

where. — *ka ni* or *Dokka ni.* some where, some place or another.
Syn. IDZKU, DOCHIRA.

DOKŌ-JIN, ドコウジン, 土公神, *n.* The god of the kitchen.

DOKU, ドク 毒, *n.* Poison. — *ni ataru*, to be poisoned. — *wo kesz*, to counteract poison. — *na*, poisonous, hurtful. *Doku-ja*, 毒蛇, a venomous snake. *Doku-giyo*, 毒魚, poisonous fish. *Doku-mushi*, 毒蟲, poisonous insect. *Doku-shu*, 毒酒, poisonous liquor. *Doku-yaku*, 毒藥, poinous medicine. *Doku-ya*, 毒箭, poisoned arrow.

DOKU, ドク 獨. Alone, single, solitary, (only used in compounds).

DOKUDAMI, ドクダミ 蕺, *n.* Kind of plant. The Houttuynia cordata.

DOKUDATE, ドクダテ, 毒絶, *n.* Abstaining from hurtful food, regulating the diet. — *wo szru*, to diet, to abstain from hurtful food.

DOKU-DOKU-SHII, ドクドクシイ 毒毒敷, *a.* Poisonous in appearance.

DOKU-DOKU, ドクドク, *adv.* The sound of water flowing from a bottle, gurgling. *midz ga tokuri kara — to deru*, water flows from a bottle with a gurgling noise.

DOKU-GAI,*–szru*, ドクガイ, 毒害. To kill with poison, to poison.

†DOKU-GAKU, ドクガク 獨學, (*hitori manabi*). Studying, or learning by one's self, self-taught.

†DOKU-GIN, ドクギン, 獨吟, (*h'tori de utau*). Singing alone.

DOKU-IMI, ドクイミ, 毒忌 Avoiding hurtful food, dieting.

†DOKU-JU, ドクジユ, 讀誦. Reading the Buddisht sacred books.

DOKU-KIYŌ, ドクキヤウ 讀經, (*kiyō wo yomu*). Reading the Buddisht sacred books.

DOKU-MI, ドクミ, 毒味 *n.* Tasting to prove whether a thing is poisonous, or not.

†DOKU-RAKU, ドクラク, 獨樂, (*h'tori tanoshimu*). Happy by one's self.

†DOKU-RIU, ドクリフ, 獨立, (*h'tori-dachi*) Independent, free from the control of another. *Sho-koku da kara — wa dekinu*, it is too small to become independent.

†DOKURO, ドクロ, 髑髏, (*atama no hone*). The skull, (of a dead person).
Syn. SHARIKŌBE.

DOKU-SATSZ, ドクサツ, 毒殺. Killing with poison, poisoning.

†DOKU-SHAKU, ドクシヤク, 獨酌, (*h'tori kumu*). Drinking wine alone.

DOKU-SHIN, ドクシン, 獨身, (*h'tori mi*). Single person, unmarried, living alone.

†DOKU-SHO, ドクシヨ, 讀書, (*hon wo yomu*). To read books,

†DOKU-ZA, ドクザ, 獨座, (*h'tori szwaru*). Sitting alone.

DOMA, ドマ, 土間, *n.* The small court unfloored, at the entrance of. Japanese houses.

DŌ-MAKI, ドウマキ, 纒袋, *n.* A long wallet for carrying money, tied around the body.

DOM-BUTSZ, ドンブツ, 鈍物, *n.* A blockhead, a dunce.

DO-MIN, ドミン, 土民, *n.* A farmer belonging to any particular district.

DOMO, ドモ, 等, A plural ending, used in speaking of inferiors, or of many where the speaker is one. *Watakushi-domo*, we. *Onna-domo*, the women. *Muszme-domo*, the girls. *Omaye-domo*, you. *Fushigi no koto —*, many wonderful things.
Syn. RA, TACHI.

DOMO, ドモ, 共, Conjunctive suffix to verbs, though, although, but. *Miredomo miedsz, kikedomo kikoyedsz*, looking but not seeing, listening but not hearing. *Ame wa furu keredomo mairimash'ta*, he went although it rained.

†DŌMŌ, ドウモウ, 童蒙, *n.* A child.

DŌMORI,*–ru,–tta*, ドモル, 吃, *i.v.* To stutter, to stammer. *Ano h'to wa kuchi ga domoru*, that man stutters.

DŌMORI, ドモリ 吃. Stutterer.

DON, ドン, 鈍, (*nibui*). Dull, blunt, stupid, *Don to*, 鈍刀, a dull knife. *Donna h'to*, a stupid person.

DON, ドン, 殿, (contracted from *Dono*). A common title of address to servants, or inferiors, as *Kiu don*, Mr. Kiu, *Kame don*, Mr. Kame.

DO-NABE, ドナベ, 土鍋, *n.* An earthen pot

†DŌ-NAN, ドウナン, 童男, *n.* A boy.

DONATA, ドナタ, 阿誰, pron. Who. *Kore wa — no hon de gozarimasz*, whose book is this? *Donata-demo kitekudasare*, please one of you come here, (in speaking to several persons at once.)

DONCHAN, ドンチヤン, To be confused, to be thrown into disorder, or tumult.
Syn. AWATERU, SAWAGU.

DON-DON, ドンドン, 鼕鼕, *adv.* The sound of beating a drum, or rolling of a waggon; of a person running. *Wata Yokohama ni — hakobu*, cotton is brought to Yokohama in frequent and large quantities. *H'to ga*

— *kakette kuru.* *Tai-ko* — *to hibiki-wataru.*

DON-GAME, ドンカメ, 泥龜, *n.* A large kind of Tortoise.

†DŌ-NIYO, ドウニヨ, 童女, *n.* A young girl.

DONNA, ドンナ, (contr. of *Donoyōna.*) What kind? — *mono de gozarimasz,* what kind of a thing is it? — *ni bimbō darō,* I think he his very poor. — *ni omō koto ga attemo,* however difficult a matter it may be.

DONO, ドノ, 殿, (same as *Tono,*) *n.* A title, same as *sama,* used when speaking of superiors.

DONO, ドノ, Which? what? — *h'to* which person? — *kuni,* which country? — *yō ni,* in what way? *Dono kurai,* how much? Syn. DORE.

DON-TAKU, ドンタク, (a word derived from the Dutch, much used.) *n.* Sunday, a holyday.

DONSZ, ドンス, 緞子, *n.* A kind of silk fabric of which belts are made.

DŌ-ON, ドウオン, 同音, *(onaji koye), n.* One voice, same sound. — *ni,* with one voice.

DOPPO, ドクポ, 獨歩, To walk out alone, to take a walk alone. To be alone in talent or ability, above all others. *Ko-kon ni — szru no sai ari.*

DORA, ドラ, 銅鑼, *n,* A kind of gong suspended before idols and struck by worshipers to arouse the attention of the god.

DORA, ドラ, (coll. contr. of *Dōraku.*) Dissolute, profligate. viscious, abandoned. *Dora muszko. Dora muszme. Dora-neko,* a cat given to stealing.

DŌRAKU, ダウラク, 狹邪, Given to vice and dissipation, dissolute, vicious, profligate. — *mono,* a dissolute person. Syn. HŌTŌ.

DŌ-RAN, ドウラン, 動亂, Exciting disturbance, causing excitement and confusion. Syn. SŌDŌ, BUSSŌ.

DŌ-RAN, ドウラン, 銃卵, *n.* A leather bag, or wallet; knapsack; satchel.

DŌRE, ドウレ, A word used in the families of the nobility only in answering a call.

DORE, ドレ, Which. — *ga ī,* which is the best? — *mo onajikoto,* they are both alike. — *demo yoroshii,* either will do. *Kono hon no uchi — ni aru,* in which of these books is it? — *no hikidashi ni aru,* in which drawer is it? — *hodo,* or — *dake,* how much? Syn. DOCHIRA, DONO.

DORE, ドレ, exclam. of wonder, surprise. — *hai-ken itasō mise nasare,* I would like to see it, show it to me.

DŌRI, ダウリ, 道理, *(michi,) n.* Reason, right principle, truth, principles, doctrine, cause or reason, a natural rule or law. *Ten-chi no* —, the laws of nature. *Chiu-kō wa h'to no okonau beki* —, loyalty, and obedience to parents, are natural laws which men should obey. — *wo somuku,* to act contrary to what is right. *Dō-iu — de dekiru mono ka shiranu,* I don't know for what reason it was made.

†DORIYŌ, ドリヤウ, 度量, *n.* Talent, ability, capacity. Syn. KIRIYŌ, RIYŌKEN.

†DORIYŌ, ドリヨウ, 土龍, *n.* A mole. Syn. MUGURAMOCHI.

†DŌ-RO, ダウロ, 道路, *n.* A way, road. Syn. MICHI.

†DORO, ドロ, 泥, *n.* Mud. — *no umi,* chaos, *Doro-darake,* covered with mud. — *no yō ni yōta,* drunk as mud, (dead drunk.) *Doro-mabure,* smeared with mud.

DOROBŌ, ドロボウ, 盜, *n.* A thief, robber. Syn. NUSZBITO.

DORO-DORO, ドロドロ, 殷殷, *adv.* Rumbling sound, as of distant thunder, or cannon, of person walking. *O dztsz no oto ga — to hibiku,* the rumbling sound of (distant) cannon.

DŌ-RUI, ドウルイ, 同類, *n.* Same kind, same class, or sort.

DŌSA, ドウサ, 礬紗, *n.* The stuff, made of glue and alum, for glazing paper. — *wo hiku,* to glaze paper.

DOSAKUSA, ドサクサ, (coll.) *n.* Confusion, tumult, turmoil. — *magire ni mono wo toru,* taking advantage of the confusion to steal.

DO,*-shi,-szru,-sh'ta,* ドスル, 度, To save. (Bud.) *Shu-jō wo do szru,* to save all creatures.

DŌ-SHIN, ドウシン, 同心, *(onaji kokoro), n.* Of the same mind, like minded. Also, a constable or policeman.

DŌ-SHUKU, ドウシユク, 同宿, *n.* Stopping, or lodging together at the same inn. — *szru,*

DOSEI, ドセイ, 土星, *n.* The planet Saturn.

DŌ-SHA, ダウシヤ, 道者, *n.* A religionist, devotee, a pilgrim, one engaged in religious duties.

DŌSHI, ドホシ, 通, (impure *tōshi,* used only in compounds,) Constantly, without ceasing, or interval. *Yomi-dōshi,* constantly reading. *Yo-dōshi,* the whole night. *Kami wa mamori-dōshi nari,* the gods are constantly watching.

DŌSHI, ドウシ, 同士, Amongst themselves, with each other, together, in company with. *Doshi-ikusa*, a civil war. *Doshi-uchi*, (idem.) *Onna-dōshi tera ni mairu*, the women went together to the temple. *Tomo-dachi dōshi sake wo nomu*, the friends drink wine together.
Syn. AITOMONI, NAKAMA.

DOSZGOYE, ドスゴヱ, A fierce, harsh voice.

DOSZŪ, ドスウ, 度數, *n*. The degree of heat, temperature.

DOTE, ドテ, 堤, *n*. A mound, or bank of earth which separates rice-fields, a dike, embankment. — *wo kidzku*, to throw up a dike. Syn. TSZTSZMI.

DOTERA, ドテラ, *u*. A long wadded coat worn in winter by the lower classes.

DOTTO, ドツト, *adv*. Sudden burst of noise from many persons, as, — *warau*, to burst into laughter. — *homeru*, to burst out in praise. — *yobu*, all cried out at once.

DŌ-WA, ダウワ, 道話, *(michi no hanashi,) n*. Religious, or moral discourses. — *wo chō-mon szru*, to listen to religious discourses. Syn. SHINGAKU-BANASHI.

DO-WASZRE, ドワスレ, 偶忘, *n*. Suddenly forgetting, not able to recall what one knows well. — *wo sh'te omoi-dasenu*.

DŌ-YAKU, ドウヤク, 同役, *n*. Same office, same public service.

DŌ-YŌ, ドウエウ, 同搖, *(ugoku), n*. Motion. — *szru*, to move, shake.

DOYŌ, ドヨウ, 土用, *n*. A period of some 20 days in each of the four seasons.

DŌYŌ, ドウヤウ, 同樣, Same way, same manner, alike, same. Syn. ONAJIKOTO.

DŌ-YOKU-NA, ドウヨクナ, 胴欲, *a*. Greedy, covetous, avaricious. *Ammari — mono*, an exceedingly covetous person.
Syn. MUSABORU, YOKU-BARU, TONYOKU, HOSHIGARU.

DOYOMEKI,*-ku,-ita*, ドヨメク, 哄 or
DOYOMI,*-mu,-nda*, ドヨム. To make a loud noise, to raise a cry, or uproar; the call, or noise of many birds, or animals, the sound of a torrent of water. *Yama doyomu made naku sh'ka*, the loud noise of the stag crying in the mountains.
Syn. SODOROKU, HIBIKU.

†DŌ-YŪ, ドウユウ, 同遊, *n*. Companions in literary studies.

DOZAYEMON, ドザヱモン, 溺死人, *n*. The name of a man who was celebrated for giving a decent burial to the bodies of drowned persons; hence the name came to be used for, a drowned person.
Syn. DEKI-SHI-NIN.

DŌ-ZEN, ドウゼン, 同前, *(maye ni onaji)*. Same as before, ditto, alike, the same.

DŌ-ZO, ドザウ, 土藏, *n*. A mud fire-proof building, a store house. Syn. KURA.

†DŌ-ZOKU, ダウゾク, 道俗, *n*. Priest, and people, clergy and laity.

DZ, ズ, 不. A neg. suffix to verbs.

DZ, ツ, 頭, *n*. The head. — *ga takai*, your head is too high, (in scolding an inferior for want of good manners in holding his head up). — *ga omoi* my head feels heavy. Syn. KASHIRA, ATAMA, KŌBE,

DZ, ツ, 圖, *n*. A drawing, picture, sketch, a plan. — *szru*, to draw a sketch. — *wo hiku*, to draw a plan. — *wo toru*, to draw a picture. *Iye no* —, the plan of a house. *Kuni no* —, a map of a country.
Syn. YE, YEDZ, KATA.

DZ-BOSHI, ツボシ, 圖星, *n*. The black spot in the centre of a target, the crown of the head. *Omoi — wo hadzsanu*, not to fail in one's aim, or object.

DZ-BŌTO, ズボウト, 甘草, *n*. Extract of liquorice.

DZ-BU, ツブ, *adv*. The sound made by plunging into water. — *to midz ni tszkeru*, to plunge anything into water.

DZBUNURE, ツブヌレ, 渾濡, *n*. To be wet from head to foot, wet all over. — *ni naru*, (idem).

DZBUROKU, ツブロク, Drunk. — *ni natta*, to become drunk.

DZDA, ツダ, 頭陀, *n*. A Buddhist priest.

DZDA-BUKURO, ツダブクロ, 頭陀囊, *n*. The bag carried by begging priests.

DZDA-DZDA, ズダズダ, 寸寸, *adv*. Pieces. — *ni kiru* to cut into pieces.
Syn. SUN-ZUN-NI.

DZDZ, ズズ, 樹珠, *n*. A rosary. — *wo momu*, to roll the rosary between the hands. — *wo tszmaguru*, to push the beads of the rosary along with the nail.
Syn. JUDZ, NENJU.

DZDZ-DAMA, ズズダマ, 薏苡, or DZDZGO, ズズゴ, *n*. A plant vulgarly called Job's-tears. The Coix lacryma.

DZI, ズイ, 髓, *n*. Marrow, pith of wood.
Syn. KOTSZ-DZI.

DZI-BUN, ズイブン, 隨分, *adv*. Tolerably; as good as the circumstances will admit of, moderately, pretty well. — *yoku narimashō*, it will do pretty well. — *jōdz ni natta*, has become pretty skilful.
Syn. KANARI.

DZI-GEN, ズイケン, 瑞驗. A favorable token, a good omen.

DZI-HITSZ, ズイヒツ, 隨筆, *(fude-dzsame)*,

n. Miscellaneous writings. — *wo kaku.* Syn. MAMPITSZ.

DZI-I, ズイイ, 隨意, (*kokoro makase*). At one's pleasure, according to one's mind, or convenience. — *ni nasare*, do as you like. Syn. KOKORO-MOCHI SHIDAI, KATTE SHIDAI, OMŌ-MAMA, KI-MAMA.

DZI-ICHI, ズイイチ, 隨一, The best, the first. *Baka no* —, the greatest fool.

DZI-JŪ, ズイジウ, 隨從, *n.* A follower, attendant, a disciple, adherent. — *szru*, to obey, to follow. Syn. SH'TAGAU.

DZI-KI, ズイキ, 隨喜, *n.* Delightful assent, joyful approval. *Seppō wo chōmonshi — no namida wo moyōshikeri.*

DZI-KI, ズイキ, 芋莖, *n.* The stem of a species of artichoke, used as food. Syn. IMOGARA.

†DZI-MU, ズイム, 瑞夢, *n.* A lucky dream.

DZI-SHIN, ズイシン, 隨身, *n.* A follower, a disciple.

DZI-SŌ, ズイサウ, 瑞相, *n.* A lucky sign, a favorable sign. Syn. YOI-SHIRASE.

DZI-TO, ヅイト, *adv.* Directly, in a direct straight manner, without minding ceremony. — *hairu*, to go straight in, without saying anything, or minding any body.

DZKARA, ヅカラ. An affix, comp. of *dz* euphonic and *kara*, from, by, found in the words, *Kuchi* —, by one's own month, *Midzkara*, of one's self, *Yedzkara, Onodzkara.*

DZKI-DZKI,–*itamu*, ヅキヅキイタム, 炘衝痛. To throb with pain.

DZ-KIN, ヅキン, 頭巾, *n.* A bonnet, cap worn in cold weather.

DZKKARI, or DZPPARI, ズツカリ, *adv.* Apart, separate. — *to kiru*, to cut in two.

DZMI, ヅミ, *n.* A kind of yellow dyestuff.

DZN-DO, ズンド, *adv.* Particularly, especially, very. — *yoi*, very good. — *yoku nai*, very bad. Syn. KAKUBETSZ, BAKKUN, KOTO-NI.

DZN-DZN-NI, ズンズンニ, 寸寸, *adv.* Into small pieces. *Kami wo — hiki-saku*, to tear paper into small pieces. Syn. SZDA-DZDA.

DZN-DZN, ズンズン, 駸駸, *adv.* Rapidly, fast. *Fune ga — hashiru*, the ship sails fast. *Kodomo wa — sodatsz*, the child grows rapidly. Syn. SASSATO.

DZ-NI-NORI,–*ru*,–*tta*, ヅニノル, *i. v.* To be carried on by an impulse received, to go upon the strength of anything. *Saka wo kake-oritaru dz-ni-notte kawa wo tobikosz*, carried on by the impetus received from running down the declivity he jumped over the river.

DZRA-DZRA, ズラズラ, *adv.* Glibly, smoothly. — *hon wo yomu*, to read a book glibly.

DZRI,–*ru*,–*tta*, ズル, *t. v.* To slide down, to slip down. *Uma no ni ga* —, the horse's load slips-down. *Ji-shin de kawara ga dztta*, owing to the earthquake the tiles slip-down. Syn. SZBERU.

DZRI-KOMI,–*mu*,–*nda*, ズリコム, *i. v.* To slip, or slide down into. *Kawa ni* —, to slip into the river.

DZRI-OCHI,–*ru*,–*ta*, ズリオチル, *t. v.* To slip, or slide down any thing. *Uma kara* —, to slide down from a horse. *Yama wo* —, to slide down a hill.

DZRŌ, ズロウ, Cheating, knavish, cunning.

DZRU-DZRU, ズルズル, *adv.* Slippery, smoothly, in a slippery manner. — *to szberu*, to slide. — *ni natta*, to slip into the possession of anything.

DZRUI,-KI,-SHI, ズルイ, *a.* Cheating, knavish, sly, cunning, shirking. — *yatsz da*, a knavish fellow.

DZRUKU, ズルク, *adv.* idem. — *szru*, to cheat.

DZRUKE,–*ru*,–*ta*, ズルケル, *i. v.* To be idle, lazy, to shirk work. *Shō-ku-nin ga dzrukete komaru*, I am pestered by the laziness of the workmen. *Ano ko wa dzrukete gakkō ye yukadz ni asobu*, that child plays truant and does not go to school.

DZSA, ズサ, 從者, *n.* A follower, servant. Syn. JŪSHA, TOMO.

DZ-SHI, ヅシ, 廚子, *n.* A small shrine in which idols are kept.

DZ-SŌ, ヅサウ, 頭瘡, *n.* An eruption on the scalp.

DZSSHIRI, ヅスシリ, *adv.* The sound of a bag of money falling on the ground; very much.

DZ-TSZ, ヅツ, 充, *adv.* The number to which it is joined separately taken, as, *H'totsz-dztsz*, one by one, one at a time. *F'tatsz-dztsz*, two by two, or two at a time. *H'tori-dztsz*, one person at a time. *San-nin dztsz*, three persons at a time.

DZ-TS'Ū, ヅツウ, 頭痛, (*Kashira no itami,*) *n.* Head-ache. — *itashimash'ta*, have a head-ache.

DZTSZNAI,-KI,-SHI, ズツナシ, 無術, *a.* Painful, grievous, distressing, hard to bear. Syn. KURUSHII.

DZTTO, ヅツト, *adv.* In a direct, straight course, same as *Dzi-to.*

F

†Fu, フ, 腑, *n.* The abdominal viscera. *Roppu*, the six abdominal viscera.

Fu, フ, 歩, *n.* A pawn, in the game of chess. — *wo utsz*, to place a pawn. — *wo toru*, to take a pawn; — *wo tszku*, to move a pawn.

Fu, フ, 斑, *n.* White and black spots, (as on leaves, fish.) — *ga aru*, to be spotted —*iri*, spotted, speckled. Syn. MADARA.

Fu, フ, 麩, *n.* A kind of food, made of wheat-flour. — *ya*, the shop where the above is sold.

†Fu, フ, 婦, *n.* A woman, a wife. —*jin*, a woman. *Fū-fu*, husband and wife.

Fu, フ, 譜, *n.* A music book; musical notes. — *wo mite utau.* — *wo yomu.* — *ga chigai.*

Fu, フ, 不, A negative prefix, used only in compound words.

Fū, フウ, 夫, *n.* A husband. —*fu*, husband and wife. Syn. OTTO, TEISHU.

Fū, フウ, 封, *n.* The closing of a letter, an envelope, or seal. — *wo kiru.* — *wo hiraku*, to open a letter.

Fū, フウ, 風, (*kaze.*) *n.* The wind, manner, deportment, customs. — *u*, wind and rain. *Tai-fū*, a typhoon. *Koku-fū*, customs of a country. Syn. NARAWASHI.

Fu-annai, フアンナイ, 不案内, Unacquainted with the roads of a country; a stranger in. *Kono kuni wa — de gozarimasz*, I am not acquainted with this country, see *Annai*.

Fu-bako, フバコ, 文箱, *n.* A lacquered box, used for carrying letters.

Fu-ben, フベン, 不便, Inconvenient, incommodious, unsuitable.

Fu-benri, フベンリ, 不便利, idem.

Fu-ben, フベン, 不辯, Not eloquent, slow of speech, not good at talking.

Fubin, フビン, 不便, *n.* Compassion, pity. *H'to no nangi wo — ni omō*, feeling compassion for the afflictions of men. Syn. AWARE.

Fu-bo, フボ, 父母, (*chichi, haha,*) *n.* Father and mother, parents.

Fu-buki, フブキ, 吹雪, *n.* Wind and snow, snow-storm.

Fū-bun, フウブン, 風聞, *n.* A report, rumor. Syn. HIYŌBAN, UWASA.

Fuchi, フチ, 緣, *n.* A border, rim, edge, margin. — *wo tszkeru*, to make a border. Syn. HERI.

Fuchi, フチ, 淵, *n.* A deep pool or eddy of water.

Fuchi, フチ, 扶持, *n.* Rations in rice paid to officials, soldiers, &c.=5 go. about 1 quart. *Ichi nin fuchi*, rations for one man. *Go nin fuchi*, five rations. — *nin*, a person in government employ. — *mai*, rice served out for rations; *Fuchi-kata*, the officer who serves out rations; the number of rations.

Fu-chin, フチン, 浮沈, (*uki shidzmi,*) Float and sink, vicissitudes.

Fu-chiu, フチウ, 不忠, Unfaithful to a master, disloyal.

Fuda, フダ, 札, *n.* A card, ticket, label. *Ki-fuda*, a wooden ticket. —*tszki*, labeled, ticketed. *Bakuchi no* —, playing cards.

Fu-dai, フダイ, 譜代, For successive generations. — *no kerai*, a hereditary vassal.

Fu-dan, フダン, 不斷, (*tayedz,*) Uninterrupted, constant, continual; (coll.) usual, common. — *zakura*, a Japonica that blooms the whole year. — *no tōri*, the usual way. — *gi* every day clothes. Syn. ITSZMO, HEIZEI.

Fuda-sashi, フダサシ, 札差, *n.* A licensed merchant who exchanges the rice rations of government officials for money. Syn, KURAYADO.

Fude, フデ, 筆, *n.* A pencil, pen. — *no jiku*, the handle of a pen. — *no saya*, the sheath of a pen. — *no saki*, the point of a pen. —*wo yu*, to make a pencil. — *wo ireru*, to correct with a pen. — *wo orosz*, to break in a new pencil. Syn. HITSZ.

Fude-dzkai, フデヅカヒ, 用筆, *n.* Penmanship. — *ga arai*, the penmanship is coarse.

Fu-deki, フデキ, 不出來, Badly made; poor crop. *Kono dai wa — de gozarimasz*, this stand is badly made. *Ine ga* —, the rice crop is poor.

Fude-nose, フデノセ, 筆架, (*hikka.*) *n.* A pen-rack.

Fude-shi, フデシ, 筆師, *n.* A pen-maker.

Fude-ya, フデヤ, 筆屋, *n.* A pen-store.

Fudō-miyō-ō, フドウミヤウワウ, 不動明王, *n.* The name of a Buddhist divinity. Syn. FUDŌ-SAMA.

Fu-dō, フドウ, 不同, (*onajikaradz,*) Unlike, different, uneven.

Fū-doku, フウドク, 風毒, *n.* Rheumatism.

Fudoshi, フドシ, 犢鼻褌, Same as *Fundoshi.*

Fu-dztome, フツトメ, 不勤, *n.* Neglect of duty. —*wo szru*, to neglect duty.

FŪ-FU, フウフ, 夫婦, *n.* Husband and wife.

FU-FUMMIYŌ, フフンミヤウ, 不分明, (*akiraka naradz,*) Not clear, not plain, unintelligible.

FŪ-GA, フウガ, 風雅, Elegant, in good taste, genteel, refined, simple and neat style, chaste. — *na h'to*, a man of refined taste. Syn. MIYABI.

FUGAINAI, フガイナイ, A useless unprofitable person.

FŪ-GAN, フウガン, 風眼, *n.* Catarrhal ophthalmia.

FU-GI, フギ, 不義, Immoral, wicked, vicious, contrary to what is right, adulterous. —*naru mono*, a wicked person who violates morality.

FŪ-GI, フウギ, 風儀, *n.* Customs, manners, Syn. NARAWASHI.

FU-GIYŌ-GI, フギヤウギ, 不行儀, Rude, impolite, unmannerly, ill-bred.

FU-GIYŌ-JŌ, フギヤウジヤウ, 不行狀, Wicked, abandoned, profligate, dissolute.

FU-GIYŌ-SEKI, フギヤウセキ, 不行跡, id.

FU-GŌ, フガフ ,符合, Matching, corresponding like the two parts of a seal. —*itash'ta*, it matches.

†FU-GU, フグ, 不虞, (*omoi-gakenu,*) Unexpected, unthought of.

FUGU, フグ, 不具, (*sonawaradz,*) Maimed, deformed. Syn. KATAWA.

FUGU, フグ, 河豚, *n.* The porpoise.

FUGURI, フグリ 陰嚢, (*innō*), *n.* The testicles. Syn. KINTAMA.

†FU-HEI, フヘイ, 不平, (*tairakanaradz*), Displeasure, uneasiness, irritation, vexation. — *wo iu*, or, — *wo narasz*, to utter one's displeasure.

FU-HEN-JI, フヘンジ, 不返事, To make no answer, to answer roughly or uncourteously.

FU-HŌ, フハフ, 不法, Lawless, vicious, not conforming to rule or law. —*na h'to*, a lawless, abandoned person. — *wo szru*, to commit a trespass, or breach of law. Syn. FURACHI.

FU-I, フイ, 不意, (*omowadz*), *n.* By surprise, unexpected, accidental, off one's guard, not thinking. — *wo utareta*, to be surprised and beaten, or killed. — *no sonaye wo szru*, to provide against surprise. — *no sai-nan*, an unexpected calamity.
Syn. OMOI MO YORANU, FUTO, DASHI-NUKE.

FUICHŌ, フイチヤウ, 風聽. To proclaim, publish, promulgate.
Syn. HIROMERU.

FUIGO, フイゴ, 橐籥, *n.* A bellows. — *wo fuku*, to blow a bellows. — *matszri*, a festival on the 8th day of 11th month.

FŪ-IN, フウイン, 封印, *n.* A seal, or stamp. *Tegami ni* — *wo osz*, to seal a letter. —*tszki no tegami*, a sealed letter.

FŪ-JA, フウジヤ, 風邪, *n.* A cold. — *nite hikikomu*, confined with a cold.
Syn. HIKI-KAZE.

FU-JI, フジ, 不時, (*toki-naradz*). Out of season, out of the regular order or time, irregular, fortuitous, contingent, casual. — *no niu-yō*, contingent expenses. — *no hen*, accidental affair. Syn. RIN-JI.

FU-JI, フヂ, 籐, *n.* Wisteria chinensis.

FŪJI,–*ru*,–*ta*, フウジル, 封, To seal up a letter. *Tegami wo fūjiru*, to seal a letter. *Fūji komeru*, to inclose and seal up something inside of another.

†FU-JIN, フジン, 不仁, (*nasake no nai*). Unkind, inhuman, without love or pity. — *na h'to*, — *na koto*.

FU-JIN, フジン, 婦人, *n.* A woman.
Syn. ONNA.

FU-JITSZ, フジツ, 不實. False, untrue, insincere, hypocritical, unkind, inhuman. — *no h'to*. Syn. MAKOTO NO NAI, FUNINJŌ.

FU-JITSZ, フジツ, 不日, (*hodo naku*). In a short time, in a few days. — *ni dekimashō*, I will do it in a few days.
Syn. TŌKARADZ.

FU-JI-YŪ, or FUJŪ, フジユウ, 不自由. Not as a person would like, disagreeable, unpleasant, uncomfortable, inconvenient, annoying. — *na koto*,
Syn. MAMA NI NARA NAI.

FU-JŌ, フヂヤウ, 不定, (*sadamaradz*). Uncertain, not fixed, (mostly used of the length of life).

FU-JŌ, フジヤウ, 不淨. Unclean, filthy, dirty, foul, defiled. — *na mono*, an unclean person. — *wo yokeru*, to keep off an offensive smell.
Syn. KEGARE, KIYORAKA-NARANU, OYE.

†FU-JO, フジヨ, 扶助. Help, aid, assistance. — *szru* to help, &c.
Syn. TASZKERU, TETSZDAI WO SZRU.

FUKA, フカ, 富家, (*tomeru iye*), *n.* Wealthy family, rich.

FUKA, フカ, 鮫, *n.* A shark. Syn. SAME.

†FU-KA, フカ, 不可, Not right, should not be.

FUKAI,–KI,–SHI, フカイ, 深, *a.* Deep, profound. *Fukai ka asai ka*, is it deep or not? *Umi ga fukai*, the sea is deep. *Ano onna to kono otoko to fukai naka de aru sō na*, that woman and this man seem to be very intimate.

FUKAKU, or FUKŌ, フカク, 深, *adv.* Idem. — *szru*, to deepen. — *naru*, to be deep. *Fkō gozarimasz*, it is deep. *Yama fukaku sz ndeiru*, he lives far amongst the mountains. *Yo ga fukaku natta*, the night is far spent. — *tszki-ai-masen*, not intimate.

FUKAKU, フカク, 不覺, *n.* Loss, injury, defeat. — *wo toru*, to suffer defeat, to be worsted.

FUKAKUGO, フカクゴ, 不覺悟. Without fore-thought or preparation, careless, heedless, improvident. Syn. YO-JIN NASHI.

†FŪ-KAN, フウカン, 諷諫, *(mono ni yosoyete isamuru).* To reprove a superior indirectly as by a parable. — *szru.*

FUKARE, *-ru, -ta*, フカレル, 被吹. Pass. of *Fuku*. *Kaze ni* —, to be blown by the wind.

FUKASE, *-ru, -ta*, フカセル, The causative of *Fuku*. *Watakushi ni fuye wo fukash'te kudasare*, let me blow your flute. *Kami sama wa kaze wo fukaseru*, God makes the wind to blow. *Watakushi ni fukash'te kudasare*, let me wipe it, or (in speaking of roofing), let me roof the house.

FUKASA, フカサ, *n.* The depth. — *wa dono kurai*, how deep is it?

FUKASHI, *-sz, -sh'ta*, フカス, 蒸, *t.v.* To cook by steaming. *Meshi wo fukasz*, to steam rice. Syn. MUSZ.

FUKE, フケ, 頭垢, *n.* Dandruff, scurf on the head.

FUKE, *-ru, -ta*, フケル, 深, *i.v.* To grow old, to grow late. *Toshi ga fuketa*, has grown old. *Ano h'to yohodo fuketa*, he has grown quite old. *Yo ga fuketa*, it is late in the night. Syn. TAKERU.

FUKE, *-ru, -ta*, フケル 葺, *i.v.* Placed on a roof, roofed, can roof. *Nokiba ni fukeru ayame*, the sweet flag placed on the eaves. *Kono yane ichi nichi ni fukeru ka*, can you roof this house in a day?

†FUKEI, フケイ, 不敬, *(wiyamawanu.)* Disrespectful, irreverent, impolite.

FŪ-KEI, フウケイ, 風景, *(Keshiki,) n.* Landscape, scenery. — *ga yoi*, the landscape is beautiful.

FUKEIKI, フケイキ, 不景氣, *n.* Dull, no business or trade, no bustle, still, quiet; plain, coarse. *Kono setsz Yedo mo — da sōna*, there seems to be little trade now doing in Yedo. *Kamakura mo — na tokoro da, Kamakura* is a dull place. *Akinai — da*, trade is dull. *Fu-keiki no nari wo sh'te-kita*, he wore coarse clothes. Syn. SAMISHIKI.

FUKERI, *-ru, -tta*, フケル, 耽, *i. v.* To be addicted to, given up to, absorbed, or immersed in, fond of. *Iro ni* —, addicted to venery. *Shu shoku ni* —, fond of eating and drinking. Syn. OBORERU, SZSAMU, HAMARU.

FUKESŌ, フケサウ, 普化僧, *n.* A kind of strolling musician, same as *Komusō*.

FUKE-TA, フケタ, 深田, *n.* Marshy, swampy land.

FUKI, *-ku, -ita*, フク, 吹, *t. v.* To blow. *Kaze ga fuku*, the wind blows. *Fuye wo fuku*, to blow a flute. *Iki wo fuku*, to blow with the breath. *Midz wo fuku*, to sprinkle water with the mouth.

FUKI, *-ku, -ita*, フク, 葺, *t. v.* To roof, to cover with a roof. *Yane wo fuku*, to put on a roof.

FUKI, *-ku, -ita*, フク, 拭, *t. v.* To wipe. *Tenugui de te wo fuku*, to wipe the hands with a handkerchief. *Fukin de chawan wo fuku*, to wipe the cups with a napkin.

FUKI, フキ, 款冬, *n.* A kind of vegetable. The Nardosmia japonica.

FUKI-AGE, *-ru, -ta*, フキアゲル, 吹上, *t. v.* To blow up, to cause to ascend by blowing.

FUKI-CHIRASHI, *-sz, -sh'ta*, フキチラス, 吹散, *t. v.* To scatter by blowing.

FUKI-DASHI, *-sz, -sh'ta*, フキダス 吹出, *i. v.* To blow out. *Kaze ga fuki-dashta*, the wind has begun to blow.

FUKI-DE-MONO, フキデモノ, 吹出物, *n.* An eruption on the skin.

FUKI-HANACHI, *-tsz, -tta*, フキハナツ, 吹放, *t. v.* To blow apart, or separate by blowing.

FUKI-HARAI, *-au, -atta*, フキハラフ, 吹拂, *t. v.* To blow away, blow off.

FUKI-KAKE, *-ru, -ta*, フキカケル, 吹掛, *t. v.* To blow upon. *Midz wo* —, to sprinkle water by blowing it from the mouth.

FUKI-KAYE, *-ru, -ta*, フキカヘル, 葺替, *t. v.* To re-roof, put on a new roof. *Yane wo fuki-kayeru*, or *fuki-gaye wo szru*, idem.

FUKI-KAYESHI, *-sz, -sh'ta*, フキカヘス, 吹返, *t v.* To blow over, upset by blowing. To come to life, to begin to breathe again. *Biyōbu wo* —, to blow over a screen. *Yōyō iki wo fuki-kayesz*, at length came to life again.

FUKI-KESHI, *-sz, -sh'ta*, フキケス, 吹滅, *t. v.* To blow out, extinguish by blowing.

FUKI-KOMI, *-mu, -uda*, フキコム, 吹籠, *t. & i. t.* To blow into, blown in by the wind. *Iye ni kaze ga fuki-konda*, the wind blew into the house.

FUKI-KOWASHI,-sz-,sh'ta, フキコワス, 吹毀, To break by blowing, broken by the wind.

FUKIN, フキン, 拭巾, n. A towel, a napkin.

FUKI-NAGASHI, チキナガシ, 吹流, n. A streamer, a kind of flag.

FUKI-YA, フキヤ, 吹箭, n. An arrow blown out of a blow gun. — *no tsztsz*, a blow-gun.

FUKI-YAMI,-mu,-nda, フキヤム, 吹止, i. v. To cease blowing. *Kaze ya fuki-yanda*, the wind has stopped blowing.

FU-KIYŌ, フキヨウ, 不興, n. Displeasure. *go — wo kōmuru*, to incur the displeasure of one's lord.

FUKI-TAOSHI,-sz,-sh'ta, フキタフス, 吹倒, i v. To blow down any thing standing.

FUKI-TORI,-ru,-tta, フキトル, 吹取, t. v. To tear off by blowing, blown off by the wind. *Kaze ni fuki-torareta*, torn off by the wind; also to wipe off.

FUKI-TŌSHI,-sz,-sh'ta, フキトホス, 吹透, t v. To blow through, (as a tube.)

FU-KITSZ, フキツ, 不吉, Unlucky.

FUKI-WAKE,-ru,-ta, フキワケル, 吹分, t. v. To refine metals, to separate the dross. *Fuki-wakete miru*, to assay.

FUKKI, or FŪ-KI, フクキ, 富貴, (*tomi tattoki*.) Rich and noble, rich, wealthy.

FU-KŌ, フカウ, 不孝, Unfilial, disobedient to parents. *Oya ni fukō*, id.

FU-KŌ, フカウ, 不幸, n. Misfortune, calamity, ill-luck; a death in the family. — *ni au*, to meet with a misfortune. — *no naka no saiwai*. Syn. FU-SHI-AWASE.

FUKOSSO, フコツソ, 附骨疽, n. Caries of the bones.

FUKU, フク. See *Fuki*.

FUKU, フク, 腹. The belly, abdomen. *Dō fuku no kiyōdai*, children of the same mother. — *chiu ga itamu*, to have pain in the belly.

FUKU, フク, 福, Prosperity, luck, good fortune, earthly good. — *no kami*, the god of wealth, or of luck.

FUKU, フク, 服, n. Clothing; the numeral for doses of medicine. *Imi-buku* or *mo-fuku*, mourning clothes. *I-fuku*, clothes. *Kuszri ippuku, ni fuku, sam-buku.*

FUKU, フク, 幅, The numeral for pictures, maps, &c. *Kakemono ippuku*, one picture.

FUKUBE, フクベ, 瓢, n. A calabash, gourd. Syn. HIYŌTAN.

FUKU-BIKI, フクビキ, 福引, n. A kind of game in which prizes are drawn; a lottery.

FUKU-HEI, フクヘイ, 伏兵, n. An ambush, troops lying in ambush. Syn. FUSEZEI.

FUKU-JIN, フクジン, 福神, n. The god of good luck.

FUKUJŪ,-szru, フクジウ, 服從, (*tszki sh'tagau*). To follow, adhere to, obey, (as a teacher).

FUKU-JUSŌ, フクジユサウ, 福壽草. The name of a flower. The Adonis sibirica.

FUKUME,-ru,-ta, フクメル, 哺, t.v. To feed with the mouth, as a bird its young, *Tszbame wa ko ni ye wo fukumeru.* Syn. KUKUMERU.

FUKUMEN, フクメン, 覆面. Covering the face with a veil, a veil. — *szru*; — *wo kakeru.*

FUKUMI,-mu,-nda, フクム, 含, t.v. To hold in the mouth, to keep or hold in the mind, to entertain, to comprehend, to contain, to include. *Kuchi ni midz wo fukumu*, to hold water in the mouth. *Warai*, or *Yemi wo fukumu*, to smile. *Ikon wo fukumu*, to hate. *Fucunde oru*, to understand and keep to one's self, to include. Syn. KUKUMU, OBIRU.

FUKURAHAGI, ヲクラハギ, 腓, n. The calf of the leg.

FUKURASHI,-sz-,sh'ta, フクラス, or FUKURAKASHI,-sz,-sh'ta, フクラカス, 膨, caust. of *Fukureru*. To inflate, distend, to cause to swell. *Ki-kiu wo* —, to blow up a balloon.

FUKURE,-ru,-ta, フクレル, 膨, or 脹, i.v. To be inflated, distended, swollen, puffed up. *Pan ga fukureta*, the bread has risen. Syn. HAREKU, BŌ-CHŌ SZRU.

FUKURIN, フクリン, 覆輪, n. An ornamented border.

FUKU-RIU, フクリフ, 腹立, (*hara-tate*,) Anger. — *szru*, to be angry. Syn. RIPPUKU.

FUKURO, フクロ, 袋, n. A bag, sack, pouch. *Kobukuro*, a small bag, the womb. *O-fukuro*, mother, *Te-bukuro*, a glove.

FUKURŌ, フクラウ, 梟, n. An owl.

FUKUSA, フクサ, 服紗, n. A silk handkerchief, used for wrapping.

FUKUSHI,-sz,-sh'ta, フクス, 伏, (*sh'tagau*,) t. v. or i. v. To submit, yield, acquiesce in, to cause to submit, to subjugate, to bring into obedience. (服,) to take medicine. *Tszmi ni* —, to yield, or acknowledge one's guilt. *Dōri ni* —, to submit to reason. *Ten-ka wo*—, to subjugate the empire. *Kuszri wo* —, to take medicine.

FUKU-SHI, フクシ, 副使, *n.* Vice ambassador.

†FUKU-SHIN, フクシン, 腹心, Faithful, constant, true. — *no kerai*, a faithful servant.

†FUKU-SHŪ,*-szru*, フクシウ, 復讎, (*Kataki wo utsz,*) To take vengeance on an enemy.

FUKU-SHŌ, フクシヤウ, 副將, *n.* Vice Tykoon.

FUKUSZKE, フクスケ, 福助, *n.* A person of short stature and large head, a dwarf.

FUKU-SZRU, フクスル, 伏, (See *Fukushi.*)

FUKU-T'SU, フクツウ, 腹痛, (*Hara no itami.*) *n.* Colic, pain in the abdomen.

†FŪ-K'WA, フウクワ, 風化, Liquefaction, deliquescing. — *szru*, to deliquesce. Syn. TOKERU.

†FU-K'WAI, (pron. FUKAI,) フクワイ, 不快, (*kokoro yokaradz,*) Unwell, indisposed, sick; To be on bad terms. — *de gozarimasz*, do not feel well. *Go — de arimash'ta sō na*, you look as if you had not been well. Syn. BIYŌKI, AMBAI WARUI.

†FU-K'WAI, フクワイ, 附會, *n.* A forced comparison or analogy; straining or wresting the meaning of words. — *szru*, — *no setsz.* Syn. KOJITSZKE.

FUKU-YAKU, フクヤク, 服藥, (*kuszri wo nomu,*) To take medicine. — *szru.*

FUKU-ZŌNASHI, フクザウナシ, 無覆藏, (*ōi kakusz koto nashi,*) Without concealment. *Fukuzō naku ohanashi nasai*, speak without concealment.

FUMASE,*-ru,-ta*, フマセル, or FUMASHI, *-sz,-sh'ta*, フマス, 令踏, *t. v.* To cause to walk on, or tread.

FUMAYE,*-ru,-ta*, フマヘル, To tread on, to step on *Fumayete ugokasznai*, tread on it, and keep it from moving.

FUM-BARI,*-ru,-tta*, フンバル, 踏張, *i. v.* To spread out the legs, to strut. *Fumbatte aruku*, to walk, with long steps.

FUMBATAKARU, フンバタカル, 跋扈, *i. v.* To straddle, to strut, to walk with a proud gait, to swagger. Syn. BAKKO SZRU.

FUM-BETSZ, フンベツ, 分別, (*wakimaye,*) *n.* Judgment, discrimination, discernment; a plan, expedient. — *szru*, to judge of, discriminate. — *no nai h'to da*, a person of no judgment.

†FUM-BO, フンボ, 墳墓, *n.* A tomb, grave. Syn. HAKA.

FŪ-MI, フウミ, 風味, *n.* Flavor, taste, Syn. AJIWAI.

FUMI, フミ, 文, *n.* A writing of any kind, a book, a letter. —*wo kaku*; — *wo yaru*, — *wo hiraku*; — *wo tszkeru*; *wo yomu*; Syn. TEGAMI, SHOMOTSZ.

FUMI,*-mu,-nda*, フム, 踏, *t.v.* To tread on, to step on, walk on, trample on. *Kurai wo fumu*, to reign, sit on the throne. *Michi wo tōri nagara hebi wo funda*, whilst going along the road I trod on a snake. *Mekata wo funde-miru*, to guess at the weight.

FUMI-ARASHI,*-sz,-sh'ta*, フミアラス, 踏荒, *t. v.* To destroy or lay waste by treading over.

FUMI-BAKO, フミバコ, 文箱, *n.* A box used for carrying letters. Syn. FUBAKO.

FUMI-DAN, フミダン, 踏壇, *n.* A stepping block, a step-ladder, stool. Syn. FUMI-TSZGI.

FUMI-DZKI, フミヅキ, 文月, *u.* The 7th month.

FUMI HADZSHI,*-sz,-sh'ta*, フミハヅス, 踏外, *t. v.* To make a misstep, to trip, stumble.

FUMI-KATAME,*-ru,-ta*, フミカタメル, 踏堅, *t. v.* To harden by treading on.

FUMI-KOMI,*-mu,-nda*, フミコム, 踏込, *t. v.* To step into.

FUMI-KOROSHI,*-sz,-sh'ta*, フミコロス, 踏殺, *t. v.* To kill by treading on.

FUMI-KOYE,*-ru,-ta*, フミコエル, 踏越, *t. v.* To walk across, tread over. *Kōri wo* —, to tread over the ice.

FUMI KUDAKI, *ku,-ita*, フミクダク, 踏砕, To break by treading on, tread to pieces.

FUMI-MAYOI,*-ō,-otta*, フミマヨフ, 踏迷, To wander from the way.

FUMI-NARASHI,*-sz,-sh'ta*, フミナラス, 踏鳴, *t. v.* To make a noise with the feet in walking. (踏均,) to level by treading on.

FUMI-NIJIRI,*-ru,-tta*, フミニジル, 蹂躪, *t. v.* To crush, or grind with the foot or heel.

FUMI-OTOSHI,*-sz,-sh'ta*, フミオトス, 踏落, *t. v.* To throw down by treading on, as anything standing.

FUMI-TAOSHI,*-sz,-sh'ta*, フミタフス, 踏倒, *t. v.* To throw over by stepping on.

FUMI-TODOMARI,*-ru,-tta*, フミトドマル, 踏留, *i. v.* To halt, make a stand.

FUMI-TSZBUSHI,*-sz,-sh'ta*, フミツブス, 踏潰, *t. v.* To break, crush, or mash with the foot.

FUMI-TSZKE,*-ru,-ta*, フミツケル, 踏附, To tread on, step on, (fig.) to treat with contempt, to trample on. *H'to wo fumitszke ni szru*, to trample on others.

FUMMIYŌ, フンミヤウ, 分 明, Clear, plain, distinct. Syn. AKIRAKA.

FUMOTO, フモト, 麓, *n.* The base, or foot of a mountain. — *no chaya*, tea house at the foot of the hill.

†FUM-PATSZ,–*szru*, フンパツ, 奮 發, To become ardent, eager, zealous; to be excited, or roused to action from idleness, or inactivity. — *sh'te gakumon szru*, roused up to the pursuit of learning.
Syn. FUNGEKI.

†FUM-PUN, フンプン, 紛 紛, *adv.* In a confused manner, in a dispersed manner, scattered here and there. *Ki no ha kaze ni fum-pun to ochiru*, the leaves fell scattered by the wind. *Hana ga fum-pun to niyō*, the fragrance of flowers was diffused all around.

FUMU, フム, see *Fumi*.

FUN, フン, 分, *n.* The tenth part of a Monme,=16 grs. Troy. *Ippun*, one fun, *nifun*, two fun.

FUN, フン, 粉, *(ko.) n.* Fine powder. *Kimpun*, gold-dust, powdered gold. *Gim-pun*, powdered silver. *Mempun*, flour. *Teppun*, powdered iron.

FUN, フン, 糞, *n.* Dung, feces. *Kono neko fun-shi ga warui*, the cat is filthy in her habits. *Tori no* —. Syn. KUSŌ.

FUNA, フナ, 鮒, *n.* A kind of river fish, carp.

FUNA-ASOBI, フナアソビ, 舩遊, *n.* Boating for pleasure.

FUNABA, フナバ, 舩 場, *n.* A place where boats, or ships are used; sea port.
Syn. MINATO.

FUNA-BASHI, フナバシ, 舩 橋, *n.* A bridge of boats, a pontoon bridge.

FUNA-BATA, フナバタ, 舷, or FUNA-BERI, フナベリ, 船 緣, *n.* The gunwale of a boat, or bulwarks of a ship.

FUNABITO, フナビト, 舟 人, *n.* Sailors, boatmen. Syn. SENDŌ.

FUNA-CHIN, フナチン, 舟 貸, *n.* Boat fare, freight.

FUNA-DAIKU, フナダイク, 舟 大 工, *n.* A ship-carpenter, a ship-builder.

FUNA-DAMA, フナダマ, 舟 玉, *n.* The god of ships, worshiped by sailors.

FUNA-DAYORI, フナダヨリ, 舟 便, *(binsen)*, *n.* Ship-opportunity; by means of a ship. *Osaka ye funa-dayori ga aru*, there is an opportunity of going or sending to Osaka by ship, or, a ship is about to sail for Osaka.

FUNA-DOIYA, フナドイヤ, 舟 問 屋, *n.* A commission house for goods brought by ship.

FUNA-DZMI, フナヅミ, 舟 積, *n.* Loading a ship. *Kon-nichi funa-dzmi wo itashimasz*, I shall put in cargo to-day. *Kon-nichi funa-dzmi de gozarimasz*, this is the day for loading cargo.

FUNA-GAKARI, フナガカリ, 舟 繫, *n.* Anchoring, or making-fast a ship or boat. — *wo szru*, to anchor. — *sh'te oru*, to be at anchor.

FUNA-GASSEN, or FUNA-IKUSA, フナガッセン, 船 合 戰, *n.* A naval battle.

FUNA-JI, フナヂ, 船 路, *n.* The way, or distance by ship; The route of a ship. — *wa oyoso iku sen ri*, about how many thousand miles is it by ship? *Shanghai ye no funa-ji wa dochira wo yuku*, by what route does a ship go to Shanghai?

FUNA-KATA, フナカタ, 舟 力, *n.* Sailors, boatmen.

FUNA-KO, フナコ, 舟 子, *n.* idem.

FUNA-KOBORI, フナコボリ, 舩 溢, *n.* A person saved from a shipwreck.

FUNA-MANJŪ, フナマンヂウ, 舩 饅 頭, *n.* A ship's prostitute.

FUNA-MOCHI, フナモチ, 舩 持, *n.* A ship-owner.

FUNA-OROSHI, フナオロシ, 舩 卸, *n.* Launching a ship.

FUNA-OSA, フナオサ, 舩 長, *n.* The Captain of a ship.

FUNA-TSZKI, フナツキ, 船 著, *n.* A place where boats or ships stop, or anchor.
Syn. MINATO.

FUNA-UTA, フナウタ, 船 歌, *n.* A boat song.

FUNA-WATASHI, フナワタシ, 舩 渡, *n.* A ferry.

FUNA-YADO, フナヤド, 船 宿, *n.* A sailors-inn, a boat house. A person who keeps boats for hire.

FUNA-YOSOI, フナヨソヒ, 艤, *n.* Fitting out or preparing a ship for embarkation.

FUNA-YUSAN, フナユサン, 舩 遊 山, *n.* A boat excursion for pleasure.

FUNA-ZOKO, フナゾコ, 舟 底, *n.* A ship's bottom.

FUN-DEI, フンデイ, 粉 泥, *n.* A kind of gilt paint.

FUNDŌ, フンドウ, 分 銅, *n.* The weights of a weighing beam, or scales.

†FUNDO, フンド, 憤 怒, *n.* Anger.
Syn. IKIDŌRU, HARATATSZ.

FUN-DOSHI, フンドシ, 褌, *n.* The cloth worn around the loins by Japanese.

FUNE, フネ, 船, *n.* A boat, ship; a vat, the large tub in a bath house. — *no hogeta*, the yards of a ship; — *no hodzna*, the halyards of a ship; — *no kaji*, the rudder of a ship; — *no tomo*, the poop of a ship; — *no omote*, the bow of a ship; — *no ho*, the sail of a ship; — *no hobashira*, the masts of a ship; — *no aka*, bilge water. — *wo kogu*, to scull a boat. — *wo moyō*, to lash boats together. — *wo kakeru*, to anchor a ship; — *wo magiru*, to tack. — *wa itsz goro demasz*, when does the ship sail? *Itsz goro fune ga kochira ye tszkimashō ka*, when do you think the ship will arrive? — *ga yureru*, the boat rocks. — *ni noru*, to embark, or ride in a ship; — *ni yō*, to be sea-sick. — *de yuku*, to go by ship. *Ni wo fune ni tszmu*, to load cargo.

†FUNEI, フネイ, 不佞, *pro.* I. Syn SHESSHA.

FUN-GOMI, フンゴミ, 踏込, *n.* A kind of pantaloon tied around the knee.

†FUN-GEKI, フンゲキ, 憤激. Excited, roused into passion, animated, inflamed by anger. Syn. IKIDŌRU.

FUNIAI, フニアヒ, 不似合. Unbecoming, not to fit, unsuitable, improper.

†FUNIKU, フニク, 腐肉, *n.* Gangrene, mortification.

FU-NIN-JŌ, フニンジヤウ, 不人情, Unkind, inhuman, cruel, without natural affection. Syn. FUJITSZ, HAKUJŌ.

FU-NIN-SŌ, フニンサウ, 不人相, *n.* A bad physiognomy.

FU-N'YOI, フニヨイ 不如意, (*kokoro no omū yō ni naradz*). Not to one's mind, disagreeable, unpleasant, offensive, inconvenient. Syn. FUJIYŪ.

‖FU-N'YO-HŌ, フニヨハフ, 不如法, (*hō no gotoku naradz*). Contrary to rule, or law, immoral, depraved, dissolute.

FUN-JITSZ, フンジツ, 紛失. To lose. — *sh'ta*, have lost. Syn. USHINAU, NAKUNARU.

†FUN-KOTSZ, フンコツ, 粉骨, (*hone wo ko ni szru*). To pulverize the bones; fig. to exert to the utmost, to labor to do, do with one's might. Syn. HONE WO ORU.

FŪ-NORI, フウノリ, 封粘, *n.* A wafer, sealing wax, gum used for sealing letters.

FUNORI, フノリ, 海羅, *n.* A kind of seaweed, used for glazing, and starching.

FUN-RIN, フンリン, 分厘, *n.* A grain, the smallest particle. — *mo machigawanu*, not the slightest mistake.

†FUNRIU, フンリウ, 粉瘤, *n.* An encysted tumor.

FU-RACHI, フラチ, 不埒. Wicked, vicious, unprincipled, abandoned, lawless.

FURA-FURA, フラフラ, *adv.* In a limber manner, dizzy. — *to me-mai ga sh'te kita*, to swoon, or faint away. *Me ga — to szru*, eyes are dizzy.

FŪ-RAI, フウライ, 風來. Coming as if blown by the wind, having no owner or certain dwelling place.

FURARI-TO, フラリト, 偶然, *adv.* In a thoughtless, careless manner, ramblingly. *Kodomo wa — deta*, the child has wandered out. Syn. FUTO.

FURASHI, -*sz*, -*sh'ta*, フラス, 令降, or

FURASE, -*ru*, -*ta*, フラセル. Caust. of *Furu*. To cause to shake, &c. *Kami sama wa ame wo furaseru*, God makes it rain.

FURASZKO, フラスコ, 佛狼壺, *n.* A flask, bottle.

FURA-TSZKI, -*ku*, -*ita*, フラツク. To be shaky, trembling, unsteady, loose, tottering.

FURE, -*ru*, -*ta*, フレル, 觸, *t.v.* To touch, hit, strike against in passing; to graze, brush against; to publish, make known, promulgate. *Te wo —*, to touch the hand to anything. *Hei ni fureru*, to brush against a fence. *Me ni —*, to get a glimpse of. *Kimi no ikari ni fureta*, to incur the master's anger. *Jikō ni fureru* to be affected by the climate. *Yamai ni fureru*, to contract disease. *Ki ni —*, to offend, or hurt the feelings. *O fure wo fureru*, to publish a proclamation. *K'wai-jō de fureru*, to publish by a circular. *Ofure*, a government proclamation Syn. ATARU, TSZGERU, HIROMERU.

FURE, -*ru*, -*ta*, フレル, *i.v.* Turned or bent from the proper or straight line, deflected, canted, inclined. *Ki ga fureta*, to be out of one's mind. *Iye ga fureta*, the house is not trim. *Migi ye fureta*, canted toward the right. Syn. CHIGAU, MAGARU.

FURE-CHIRASHI, -*sz*, -*sh'ta*, フレチラス, 觸散, *t.v.* To circulate, give publicity, make known here and there.

FURE-DASHI, -*sz*, -*sh'ta*, フレダス 觸出, *t.v.* To publish, make proclamation, circulate a notice.

FURE-GAKI, フレガキ, 觸書, *n.* A proclamation.

FURE-SASE, -*ru*, -*ta*, フレサセル 令觸, or

FURESHIME, -*ru*, -*ta*, フレシメル. To cause to be published, to make another to publish.

FURE-SHIRASE, -*ru*, -*ta*, フレシラセル, 令觸知, To make known by proclamation, to publish abroad, to tell publicly.

FURI, -*ru*, -*tta*, フル, 降, (*kudaru*), *i.v.* To fall as rain. *Ame ga furu*, it rains. *Yuki ga futte kita*, it has begun to snow. *Sa-*

kuban shimo ga futta, there was frost last night.

FURI,*-ru,-tta*, フル, 振, *t.v.* To brandish, wave, flourish, to shake. *Katana wo furu*, to brandish a sword. *Te wo futte aruku*, to walk swinging the arms. *Iya da to kube wo futta*, shook his head, saying he would not.

FURI,*-ru,-tta*, フル, 經, *t.v.* To pass, or spend time. *Yokohama ni ite toshi wo furu koto go nen*, five years were spent living in Yokohama. Syn. HERU.

FURI, フリ, 振, *n.* Numeral for swords. *Naginata h'to furi*, one halberd. *Tachi sam-buri*, three long swords.

FURI, フリ, 態, *n.* Manners, behavior, deportment, air, gait, carriage. *Furi no warui h'to*, a person of bad manners. *Nari-furi*, the dress, style of dress. *Minu furi wo szru*, to act as if not seeing. Syn. YŌSZ, KATACHI, SZGATA, NARI.

FURI-AI, フリアヒ, 振合, *n.* Usual practice, usage, custom, example. Syn. REI.

FURI-DASHI,*-sz,-sh'ta*, フリダス 振出, *t.v.* To shake out, 降出. To begin to rain. *Koshō wo* —, to shake out pepper. *Ame ga furi-dashta*, it has begun to rain.

FURI-HANACHI,*-tsz,-tta*, フリハナフ, 振放, *t. v.* To shake off, shake loose.

FURI-HARAI,*-au,-atta*, フリハラフ, 振拂, *t. v.* To shake off. (as dust.)

FURI-KAKE,*-ru,-ta*, フリカケル, 振掛, *t. v.* To sprinkle.

FURI-KAYE,*-ru,-ta*, フリカヘル, 振返, To look round, to look back, (振替,) To turn anything round.

FURI-KIRI,*-ru,-tta*, フリキル, 振切, *t. v.* To part in two by shaking.

FURI-KOMERARE,*-ru,-ta*, フリコメラレル, 被降籠, Detained in the house by rain. *Ame ni furi-komerareta.* id.

FURI-MAWASHI,*-sz,-sh'ta*, フリマハス, 振廻, *t v.* To brandish about. *Katana wo* —, to brandish a sword.

FURI-MUKI,*-ku,-ita*, フリムク, 振向, *i. v.* To turn round towards, to turn and face.

FŪRIN, フウリン, 風鈴, *n.* A small bell hung up to be shaken by the wind.

†FURI-SAKE-MI,*-ru,-ta*, フリサケミル, 振, 仰見, To look up at. *Ama no hara furi-sake-mireba.*

FURI-SODE, フリソデ, 振袖, *n.* Long pendulous sleeves.

FURI-SŌ, フリサウ, 降相, Appearance of rain. — *de gozarimasz*, it looks like rain,

FURI-SZTE,*-ru,-ta*, フリステル, 振捨 *t. v.* To throw away, to fling away.

FURI-TSZDZKI,*-ku,-ita*, フリツヅク, 降續, *i. v.* To rain for several successive days.

FURI-TSZKE,*-ru,-ta*, フリツケル, 振著, *t. v.* To turn away from in dislike.

FŪ-RIU, フウリウ, 風流, Genteel, refined, elegant, classical, chaste. Syn. MIYABI-YAKA, SHARAKU, IKINA.

FURI-URI, フリウリ, 風賣, *n.* A peddler, one who hawks goods about. — *wo szru*, to peddle goods.

FURI-WAKE-GAMI, フリワケガミ, 振分髮, *n.* Long hair hanging down the back.

FU-RIYO, フリヨ, 不慮, (*omowadz*) Contrary to one's expectations, different from what was thought.

FURI-ZORA, フリゾラ, 降空, *n.* A cloudy sky that looks like rain.

FURO, フロ, 風呂, *n.* A bath-tub; A box for drying lacquered ware in, an oven, a small culinary furnace. — *ni iru*, to go into a bath-tub. *Mushi-buro*, a vapor-bath. Syn. YUDONO.

FURO-BA, フロバ, 風呂場, *n.* A bath-room.

FURO-FUKI, フロフキ, 風呂吹, *n.* A kind of food made of boiled radishes.

FUROSHIKI, フロシキ, 風呂敷, *n.* A cloth used for wrapping, a handkerchief.

FURU, フル, (See *Furi.*)

FURUBI,*-ru,-ta*, フルビル, 古, *i. v.* To be old, and faded; timeworn.

FURU-DŌGU, フルダウグ, 古道具, *n.* Old furniture. — *ya*, a shop where old furniture is sold.

FURUI,*-u,-utta*, フルウ, 振, To shake; to sift, to tremble, shiver, shudder. *Kimono wo* —, to shake one's clothes. *Samukute furū*, to shiver with cold. *Osorete furū*, to tremble with fear. *Iya de mi-burui ga szru*, to shudder with disgust. *Udonko wo* —, to sift flour. *Ji ga furū*, the earth quakes. *I wo tenka ni* —, to make one's power felt over the whole empire.

FURUI, フルヒ, 篩, *n.* A seive.

FURUI, フルヒ, 戰, *n.* A trembling, tremor, shaking, shivering. — *ga aru*, to have a trembling.

FURUKU, or FURŪ, フルク, 古, *adv.* Idem. *Furuku natta*, has become old. *Furū gozarimasz*, it is old. *Furuku szru*, to make look old and faded.

FURUI,-KI,-SHI, フルイ, 古, *a.* Old not new, ancient, stale, decayed by time. *Fu-*

rui iye, and old house. *Furui kimono*, old, worn out clothes.

FURUI-WAKERU, フルヒワケル, 振分, *t.v.* To separate by sifting.

FURU-GI, フルギ, 古衣, *n.* Old clothes.

FURU-GIRE, フルギレ, 古切, *n.* Old rags.

FURU-KANE, フルカチ, 古鉄, *n.* Old metal.

FURU-KUSAI,–KI, フルクサイ, 古臭, *a.* Old-fashioned, antiquated, ancient, obsolete. — *ūta*, an old song.

FURUMAI, フルマヒ, 振舞, *n.* Deportment. behaviour, conduct. *Tachi-furumai*, (idem) Syn. ŌKONAI.

FURUMAI,–*au*,–*atta*, フルマフ, 饗, *t.v.* To entertain, to treat, to feast. *H'to ni furumau*,, to give a feast to a person.
Syn. CHISO SZRU, MOTENASZ.

FURUMEKASHII,–KI, フルメカシイ, *a.* Old, antiquated, ancient, obsolete.

FURUMEKASHIKU, フルメカシク, *adv.* idem.

FURUSA, フルサ, 古, *n.* The oldness, antiquity.

FURU-SATO, フルサト, 古鄉, *n.* Native place, place of one's birth. Syn. KOKIYŌ.

FURUTE, フルテ, 古手, *n.* Old clothes. — *ya.* a second hand clothing store.
Syn- FURUGI.

FURUWASHI,–*sz*,–*sh'ta*, フルハス, 戰, *t. v.* To cause to tremble. *Mi wo furuwash'te iru*, was trembling.

FUSA, フサ, 總, *n.* A tassel; numeral for bunches of grapes. *Budō h'to fusa*, one bunch of grapes.

FUSAGARE,–*ru*,–*ta*, フサガレル, pass. of *Fusagu. Ano akindo Yokohama wo fusagareta*, that merchant has been shut out of Yokohama.

FUSAGARI,–*ru*,–*atta*, フサガル, 塞, *i. v.* To be shut, closed, obstructed, blocked up. *Cha-wan mina fusagatte oru*, the teacups are all in use. *Kuchi ga fusagaru*, the mouth is shut. *Michi ga fusagatte oru*, the roads are obstructed. *Ki ga fusagaru*, to be heavy at heart, gloomy. *Te ga* — to be busy, or occupied. Syn. TSZMARU.

FUSAGI,–*gu*,–*ida*, フサグ, 塞, *t. v.* To shut, close, to stop up, block up, obstruct, to plug up, to dam up. *Me wo fusagu*, to shut the eyes. *Kuchi wo* —, to shut the mouth. *Nedzmi no ana wo* —, to stop up a rat hole. *Kawa wo* —, to dam up a river. *Ki wo fusaide oru*, to feel gloomy, melancholy.
Syn. TSZMERU.

FU-SAI, フサイ, 夫妻, (*me-oto*,) *n.* Husband and wife.

†FU-SAI, フサイ, 不才, Without talent, no ability,

FU-SAN, フサン, 不參, (*kitaradz:*) Not come.

FUSE, フセ, 布施, *n.* Alms given to priests. — *wo szru*, to give alms. *Fuse-motsz*, alms.

FUSEGI,–*gu*,–*ida*, フセグ, 防, *t.v.* To ward off, to keep off, shut out, fend off, to resist, to repel, oppose. *Teki wo fusĕgu*, to resist the enemy. *Kaze wo* —, to keep off the wind. *Te de* — to ward off with the hand.
Syn. BŌGIYO SZRU.

FUSEGI-TATAKAI,–*au*,–*atta*, フセギタタカフ, 防戰, *t. v.* To fight off, to fight and oppose. Syn. BŌSEN SZRU.

FUSEGO, フセゴ, 伏籠, *n.* A large basket.

†FU-SEI, フセイ, 不精, Indolent, slothful, lazy.

FUSE-NUI, フセヌイ, 伏縫, *n.* A hem, to lay and sew a hem.

FUSERI,–*ru*–*tta*, フセル 覆, *t. v.* To turn bottom up. *Cha-wan wo fuseru*, to turn a tea-cup bottom up.

FUSERI,–*ru*,–*tta*, フセル, 臥, *t.v.* To lie down, recline. *Fusete oru*, is lying down, is in bed.

FUSE-ZEI, フセゼイ, 伏兵, *n.* An ambuscade. Syn. FUKU-HEI.

FUSHI,–*sz*,–*sh'ta*, フス, 臥, *i. v.* To lie down, recline. (伏,) to bend down, to stoop. (偃,) prostrated. *Kodomo ga fush'te oru*, the child is lying down. *Ki ga kaze de fushimash'ta*, the tree was thrown down by the wind. Syn. NERU.

FU-SHI, フシ, 父子, (*oya-ko*,) *n.* Father and child.

FU-SHI, フシ, 五倍子, *n.* Gall-nuts. Syn. GOBAISHI.

†FŪ-SHI, フウシ, 夫子, *n.* Teacher.

FU-SHI, フシ, 節, *n.* A joint, knot, notes, or tones of music. *Fushi-bushi*, the joints. *Fushi ana*, a knot hole. — *wo tszkeru*, to set to music, to make the musical marks. *Take no* —, the joint of a bamboo.

FU-SHI-AWASE, フシアハセ, 不仕合, Unfortunate, misfortune, bad luck, calamity. — *ni au*, to meet with misfortune.

FUSHI-DO, フシド, 臥房, *n.* A chamber. The lair of a wild beast.

FUSHI-DZKE, フシヅケ, 節附, *n.* Setting songs to music, affixing the musical notes. (also) the punishment of crucifixion by driving the nails through the joints.

FU-SHI-GI, フシギ, 不思議, Strange, wonderful, surprising, marvelous. miraculous, supernatural. —*na koto da*, it is a wonderful thing. — *na koto wo szru*, to work a miracle. Syn. AYASHII, KI-MIYŌ.

FUSHI-KURE-DACHI,*-tsz,-tta*,フシクレダツ, *i. v.* To be uneven, full of knots *Kono ita fushikuredatte iru*, this board is full of inequalities.

FUSHI-MAROBI,*-bu,-ta*, フシマロブ, 伏轉, *i. v.* To fall and roll over.

FUSHIME, フシメ, 節目, *n.* A knot in wood.

FU-SHIN, フシン, 不審, Doubtful, suspicious, not clear, dubious, strange.
Syn. IBUKASHII, UTAGAWASHII.

FUSHIN, フシン, 普請, *n.* A building. — *szru*, to construct, to build. *Iye wo fushin szru*, to build a house. Syn. ZŌ-SAKU SZRU, TATERU.

FUSHI-OGAMI,*-mu,-nda*, フシオガム, 伏拜, *t. v.* To bow down and worship.

FŪ-SHITSZ, フウシツ, 風濕, *n.* Rheumatism.

FUSHUBI, フシユビ, 不首尾, same as *Bushubi*.

FU-SHŌ, フシヨウ, 不勝, (*szguredz.*) Unpleasant. — *na otenki*, unpleasant weather. *Fushō-bushō ni*, nolens volens.

†FU-SHŌ, フセウ, 不肖, (*nidz,*) (a self depreciating expression.) Stupid, silly, awkward, not equal to you — *nagara*, although I am stupid. — *sh'te kudasare*, pardon my awkwardness.

FU-SHŌ-CHI, フシヨウチ, 不承知, Not consenting, not acquiescing, unwilling.

FU-SHO-ZON, フシヨゾン, 不所存, Thoughtless, heedless, careless, without right judgment.

†FUSO, フソ 父祖, *n.* Grandfather.

FUSŌKA, フサウクワ, *n.* Chinese hybiscus.

†FUSŌKOKU, フサウコク, 扶桑國, *n.* Japan.

FUSOKU, フソク, 不足, (*taranu.*) Deficient, not enough, inadequate, wanting. — *no kokoro*, discontented. — *wo iu*, to complain, find fault with one's condition. *H'totsz* — *szru*, to want one, deficient in one *Nani no* — *mo nai*, to be wanting in nothing, to be contented.

FU-SŌ-Ō, フサウオウ, 不相應, Unsuitable, unbecoming, incongruous, inconsistent with. *Bungen ni* —, unbecoming one's station.
Syn. FU-TSZRI-AI.

FU-SOROI, フソロヒ, 不揃, Uneven, not equal, not uniform.

FUSZ, フス, see *Fushi*.

FUSZBE,*-ru,-ta*, フスベル, 燻, *t. v.* To smoke, to expose to smoke, to fumigate. *Ka wo* —, to smoke out musquitoes.
Syn. IBUSZ, KUYORASZ.

FUSZBE-IRO, フスベイロ, *n.* Smoky color.

FUSZBORI,*-ru,-tta*, フスボル, 燻, *i. v.* To be smoked; color changed or made dirty by smoke, smoky. *Iye ga fuszbotta*, the house is tranished with smoke.
Syn. IBURU, KUYORU.

FUSZJI, フスヂ, 不理, Unjust, improper.

FUSZMA, フスマ, 衾, *n.* Sliding screens covered with wall paper, also, a bed quilt.

FUTA, フタ, 蓋, *n.* A lid, cover. — *wo szru*, to cover with a lid. — *wo toru*, to take off the lid.

FUTA, フタ, 痂, *n.* A scab. Syn. KASABUTA.

FUTA, フタ, 二, Two, (used only in comp. words.) *Futa-michi*, two ways.

FUTAGO, フタゴ, 孖, *n.* Twins. — *wo umu*, to beget twins

FŪ-TAI, フウタイ, 風袋, *n.* The tare of goods, the tassels of a pictures. — *ga ikura*, how much is the tare?

FUTA-GOKORO, フタゴコロ, 二心, Not sincere, unfaithful, treacherous. — *naku*, faithful, true, loyal.

FUTA-MATA, フタマタ, 二股, Divided into two branches, forked. — *daikon*, a forked radish. — *yari*, a double headed spear.

‖FUTAMEKI,*-ku,-ita*, フタメク, *i. v.* To pant with alarm or excitement, to be flurried, agitated. *Awate futameku*, to be flurried, alarmed, agitated.

FUTANO, フタノ, 脚布, *n.* A cloth worn by women around the loins.

FUTA-NARI, フタナリ, 二形, *n.* A hermaphrodite.

FUTAOYA, フタオヤ, 兩親, *n.* Father and mother, parents. Syn. RIYŌ SHIN.

FUTARI, フタリ, 二人, *n.* Two persons, both persons. — *dzre de yuku*, to go together.

FUTA-TABI, フタタビ, 再, *n.* Twice.
Syn. NI-DO.

FUTATSZ, フタツ, 二, Two. Syn. NI.

FUTAYE, フタヘ, 二重, Two ply, double, two layers. — *mawasz* to wrap round twice, make two turns (of a rope.) — *goshi*, bent in the loins, as old people with age.

FŪ-TEI, フウテイ, 風体, *n.* Manner, deportment, appearance. Syn. NARI-FURI.

FU-TEGIWA, フテギハ, 不手際, Badly made, coarsely finished, unskilled, bungling. Syn. BUSAIKU, HETA.

FU-TEKI, フテキ, 不敵, Fearless, bold, having no fear of man, daring, audacious. — *na mono da*.

FU-TE-MAWARI, フテマハリ, 不手廻,

Not turning the hand to all the work that is required of one, not able to do perfectly, completely or thoroughly, owing to being short-handed, or having too much to do. Syn, FUYUKITODOKI.

FUTO, フト, 不圖, *adv.* Suddenly, unexpectedly, by chance, accidentally, casually. — *de aimash'ta*, met unexpectedly. — *sh'ta koto*, accidental affair.
Syn. HAKARADZ, OMOWADZ.

†FUTO, フト, 浮圖, *n.* A Buddhist pagoda. *Futoshi*, a priest.

†FUTŌ, フタウ, 不當, Heinous, criminal, atrocious.

FU-TODOKI, フトドキ, 不屆, Audacious, atrocious, daring, despising the restraints of law or decorum. — *na yatsz da.*
Syn. FURACHI.

FUTOI,-KI,-SHI, フトイ, 太, *a.* Thick, or large in diameter, big, coarse, daring, audacious. — *ito*, coarse thread. *Ashi ga* —, his legs are big. *Futoi koto wo szru otoko da*, one who does a daring thing. *Kimo ga* —, bold, courageous. — *ki*, a large tree.

FUTOKU, or FUTŌ, フトク, 太, *adv.* idem. *Futoku natta*, has grown large. *Futō gozarimasz*, it is thick.

FUTOKU-TAKUMASHIKI, フトクタクマシキ, 太逞, Spirited, mettlesome, fiery, of a horse only. — *m'ma ni noru*, to ride a spirited horse.

FUTOKORO, フトコロ, 懷, *n.* The bosom, or pocket made by the folds of the clothes about the breast. — *ni ireru*, to put into the bosom. *Oya no futokoro ni ite nani mo shiranu*, always being in his mother's bosom is a dunce. Syn K'WAI CHIU.

FU-TOKUI, フトクイ, 不得意, Unskilled, not an adept in, not versed in.

FU-TOKU-SHIN, フトクシン, 不得心, Without consent, not assenting. Syn. FUSHŌCHI.

FUTO-MOMO, フトモモ, 太股, *n.* The thigh.

FUTO-MONO, フトモノ, 太物, *n.* A kind of silk-goods.

FUTON, フトン 蒲團, *n.* A mattrass, a quilted bed cover, a cushion. *Zabuton*, a cushion.

FUTORI,*-ru,-tta*, フトル, 肥, *i.v.* To be large, fat, fleshy. *Kono kodomo yoku futotta*, this child has grown very large.
Syn. KOYERU.

FUTŌRI, フトオリ, 太織, *n.* A thick kind of coarse silk goods.

FUTOSA, フトサ, 太, *n.* The largeness, the size. — *wa dono kurai*, what is the size? (in diameter).

FUTSZ, フツ, 佛, *n.* France. — *go*, the French language. — *no gunkan*, a French ship of war.

FU-TSZDZKA, フツヅカ, 不束, Improper, stupid, silly, ignorant, clownish, used in self depreciation.

FU-TSZ-GŌ, フツガフ, 不都合, Inconvenient, not suited to, incommodious.
Syn. KATE NO WARUI, FU-BENRI.

FUTSZ-KA, フツカ, 二日, The second day of the month; two days. *Go g'wats futszka*, the second day of the fifth month. *Futszka tateba yaszmu*, after two days I shall rest.

FU-TSZKI-AI, フツキアヒ, 不附合, No friendship, no intercourse, no intimacy. — *ni natta*, have broken off all intimacy.
Syn. NAKA GA WARUI, UTOKUSZRU.

FU-TSZRI-AI, フツリアヒ, 不釣合, Not matching, disproportioned, not balancing. *Chō-chin ni tszri-gane wa fu-tszri-ai da*, a lantern cannot balance a big bell. — *na fūfu*, a badly matched man and wife.
Syn. FU-SŌ-Ō.

FUTTEI, フツテイ, 拂底, *a* Scarce. *Ito wa kono setsz futtei de gozarimasz*, silk is at present very scarce. Syn. SZKUNAI.

FU-TS'Ū, フツウ, 不通, No communication, no intercourse, no dealings.
Syn. OTODZRE GA NAI, TAORI GA NAI.

FUTTSZRI, フツツリ, *adv.* The sound of anything snapping. — *to kireru*, to break with a snap. — *to omoi-kiru*, to dismiss entirely from one's thoughts.

FU-TS'Ū-YŌ, フツウヨウ, 不通用, Not current, not in use, or generally received.

FU-WA, フワ, 不和, *(yawaragadz).* On bad terms, unfriendly, disagreeing, no concord. *Naka — to naru.*

FUWA-FUWA, フワフワ, *adv.* In a light airy, buoyant manner, spongy, buoyantly. *Kami ga kaze ni — to agaru*, paper rises buoyantly in the air. *Pan ga — to fukureta*, the bread is spongy and light.

FUWAKE, フワケ, 腑分, *n.* Dissection of a dead body, an autopsy. — *wo szru*, to dissect a dead body. Syn. KAIBŌ

FUWARI-TO, フワリト, *adv.* In a light and airy manner, buoyantly, spongy. — *tonde kuru*, to come buoyantly, sailing (as a bird).

FUYASHI,*-sz,-sh'ta*, フヤス, 殖, *t.v.* To cause to increase, to augment, to make more. *Kiu-kin wo fuyash'te yaru*, to increase the wages. *Gunzei wo fuyashitara yokarō*, it would be better to increase the army. Syn. MASZ.

FUYE,-*ru*,-*ta*, フエル, 殖, *i.v.* To increase, multiply, spread, augment in number or bulk; to enlarge, swell. *Hana ga fuyeta*, the flowers have spread. *Nomi ga fuyeta*, the fleas have become thick. *Midz ni nurete fuyeta*, to swell from being wet. Syn. ŌKU-NARU.

FUYE, フエ, 笛, *n.* A flute, whistle. — *wo fuku*, to blow the flute.

FUYE, フエ, 管氣, *n.* The wind pipe. — *wo tatsz*, to cut the throat. Syn. NODOBUYE.

†FU-YEKI, フエキ, 不易, Without change, unchanging. *Ban-dai fuyeki*, never changing. Syn. KAWARA-NAI.

†FU-YEKI, フエキ, 不益, (*yeki mo nai*). Unprofitable, useless. Syn. MUYAKU, MUDA.

FU-YEN, フエン, 不緣, Divorce, separation of husband and wife. *Fuyen ni naru*, to be divorced. — *no gi nite oya moto ye kayeru*, being divorced she returned to her father's house.

†FUYETSZ, フエツ, 斧鉞, *n.* A kind of axe. Syn. ONO.

FU-YŌ, フヨウ, 芙蓉, *n.* (*hasz no hana*). The Lotus flower.

FU-YŌ, フヨウ, 不用, Not wanted, not needed, of no use, useless. — *nara watakushi chō-dai*, if you don't want it give it to me. Syn. IRANU. MUDA.

FUYŌI, フヨウイ, 不用意, (*kokoro mochīdz*). Improvident, neglect of preparation.

FUYŌJIN, フヨウジン, See *Buyōjin*.

FUYŌ-JŌ, フヤウジヤウ, 不養生, Careless of one's health.

FUYU, フユ, 冬, *n.* Winter.

FUYU-GOMORI, フユゴモリ, 冬籠, *n.* Kept in the house by the cold, confined by the winter.

FU-YUKI-TODOKI, フユキトドキ 不行届, Not reaching to, or doing all that is required, doing imperfectly, remissly, or not thoroughly. Syn. FUTEMAWARI.

FUYU-MEKI,-*ku*,-*ita*, フユメク, Wintery, having the appearance of winter. *Kono aida soro-soro fuyumeite mairimash'ta*, it has of late gradually been getting like winter.

FUZAKE,-*ru*,-*ta*, フザケル, 狎戲, *i.v.* To sport, romp, frolic. *Kodoma wa fuzakete oru*, the children are frolicking. Syn. TAWAMURERU.

FUZAKE,-*ru*,-*ta*フザケル, 膨裂, *i. v.* To swell and soften, (as rice when boiled.) *Kome ga fuzaketa*.

FUZEI, フゼイ, 風情, *n.* State, condition, manner, appearance, like. *Nan no — mo nai*, nothing very agreeable. Syn. ARISAMA, OMOMUKI, GOTOKU.

FŪ-ZETSZ, フウゼツ, 風説, *n.* A report, rumor. Syn. FŪBUN, HIYŌBAN, UWASA.

FŪ-ZOKU, フウゾク, 風俗, *n*, Customs, manners, usages. Syn. NARAWASHI, FUTEI,

G.

†GA, ガ, 駕, (*norimono,*) *n.* A carriage, or norimon, used now only in letters, without retaining the original meaning. — *wo todomeru*, to stop. — *wo unagasz*, to go. — *wo mageru*, to come.

GA, or GACHŌ, ガ, 鵞, *n.* A tame goose.

Ga, ガ, (1.) Sign of genitive case = of; *Watakushi ga tame ni*, for my sake. *Kare ga yorokobi*, his joy. *Soregashi ga mono*, my thing. (2.) As designating the subject of an intransitive verb, having also an indefinite sense; as, *Ame ga furu*, it rains; *Fune ga deta*, a ship has sailed. *To ga aita*, the door is open. *Sake ga agatta*, the price of *sake* has risen. *H'to ga nai*, there is nobody. (3) As a conjunctive particle = but. *Itte mo yoī ga, ikanai hō ga yoroshii*, you may go, but it would be better if you did not. *Watakushi wa yuku ga nani ka go-yō wa nai ka*, I shall go, then can't I do something for you? *Hōbō wo tadznemash'ta ga Gen-san wa i-masen yo*, I have inquired all about, but, I can't find any such person as Mr. *Gen*. (4.) Sometimes as designating the subject of a transitive verb, same as *wo*. *Chi-chi ga nomitai*, I wan't to nurse. *Hanashi ga kikitai*, I want to hear what is said.

GA, ガ, 賀, An occasion when congratulations, or felicitations are sent, a festival, holyday. *Ga-szru*, to congratulate, felicitate. *Nen-ga*, new year's day. *Sh'chijū no ga*, congratulations to a person who has attained his 70th year. *Ga no iwai*, congratulations on reaching an advanced age. Syn. IWAU.

GACHŌ, ガテウ, 鵞鳥, *n.* A tame goose.

GACHI, ガチ, 勝, (from *kachi* to prevail.) An affix, giving the word to which it is joined the predominance in quantity or influence, as, *Kome-gachi no meshi*, a food made of rice and wheat, where the rice is in the largest quantity. *Ma-tzchi-gachi*, soil which is for the most part good. *Kuromi-gachi*, black the prevailing color. *Tayema-gachi*, at long intervals. *Okotari gachi*, given to idleness. *Itszwari-gachi*, given to lying. *Kono tszki ame-gachi da*, this is a rainy month.

GA-I, ガイ, 我意, (*waga kokoro*,) One's own way, own will, own opiniom. — *wo hoshī-mama ni nasz*, obstinately to follow one's own opinion.

GAI, ガイ, 害, Injurious, hurtful. — *szru*, to kill, murder. — *ni naru*, to be hurtful, injurious. — *wo nozoku*, to abate an evil. *Gaishin*. 害心, cruel disposition. Syn. SOKONAU.

GAI-BUN, (See *G'wai-bun*.

GAI-KOTSZ, ガイコツ, 骸骨, *n*. The bones of dead persons.

GAIN-YAKU, ガンヤク, 丸藥, (See *Gwan-yuku*.

†GAI-SŌ, ガイサウ, 咳嗽, *n*. A cough. Syn. SEKI.

GAKE, ガケ, 絶壁, *n* A precipice; a steep, — *michi*, a road cut along a precipice. — *kara ochiru*, to fall from a precipice. Syn. ZEPPEKI.

GAKE, ガケ, coll. affix. = whilst. *Kayeri-gake*, whilst returning. *Ki-gake ni unjōsho ye yori-mash'ta*, whilst coming I called at the Custom-house. *Tōri-gake*. whilst passing. (2.) = quantity, as, *Sammai gake*, three times as much (in sheets), three fold. *G'wai-koku no kami no atszsa wa Nippon no kami no ni-mai-gake aru*, foreign paper is twice as thick as Japanese. Syn. SHINA, TSZIDE-NI.

GAKI, ガキ, 餓鬼, *n*. (*wiyetaru oni*,) A hungry spirit, or devil. The spirits of the dead punished with hunger in the Buddhist infernum. *Gaki-dō*, one of the eight divisions of the Buddhist Hades.

GAKKARI, ガクカリ, *adv*. Tired, fatigued, exhausted. — *sh'te oru*. to be exhausted.

GAKKI, ガクキ, 樂器, *n*. A musical instrument,

GAKKŌ, ガクカウ, 學校, *n*. A school, academy.

GAKKURI, ガククリ, *adv*. Suddenly sinking down or losing strength like a person fainting. — *ōjō wo sh'ta*, died suddenly. Syn. NIWAKA, BIKKURI.

GAKU, ガク, 樂, *n* Music. — *wo shiraberu*, to make music. *Gaku-nin*, a musician. *Saru-gaku*, a musical exhibition, or opera.

GAKU, ガク, 學, *n*. Learning, literature, science. — *ga aru*, to be learned. — *sai*, literary talents.

GAKU, ガク, 額, *n*. Tablets with painted figures or inscriptions on them, suspended in houses, for ornament, or in temples, as votive offerings; a picture. — *wo kakeru*, to hang up a tablet. *Gakudō*, 額堂, a small temple in which votive offerings of pictures are hung. A picture gallary.

GAKU-MON, ガクモン, 學問, *n*. Learning, literature, science. — *szru*, to study, to read, to apply one's self to learning. — *jo*, a school house. — *ga agatta*, to make progress in learning.

GAKU-RIYŌ, ガクレウ, 學寮, *n*. A school connected with a monastery.

GAKU-SHA, ガクシヤ, 學者, *n*. A scholar, learned man.

GAKU-TŌ, ガクトウ, 學頭, *n*. The head pupil of a school, a tutor, or usher.

†GAKUZEN, ガクゼン, 愕然, *adv*. In an alarmed, started manner. Syn. BIKKURI.

GAMA, ガマ, 蝦蟆, *n*. A bull-frog.

GAMA, ガマ, 蒲, *n*. A kind of rush. — *mushiro*, a mat made of rushes.

GA-MAN, ガマン, 我慢, *n*. Fortitude, patience, endurance,. — *szru*, to bear patiently, endure. — *sh'te i-nasare*, be patient. — *no tszyoi h'to*, a person of great fortitude. *Yase-gaman wo szru*, to assume or affect an appearance of fortitude. Syn. KORAYERU, SHIMBŌ SZRU.

GAMASAII, ガマシイ, 个間敷, an affix. similar to *rashii*, = like to, in the manner of. *Kurō-gamashiki*, troublesome. *Jō-dan-gamashiku*, waggish, mischievous. *Fu-jin-gamashii*, unkindly. Syn. SŌ-NA.

GAM-BIYO, ガンビヤウ, 眼病, (*me no yamai*,) *n*. Ophthalmia.

GAM-BUTSZ, ガンブツ, 贋物, (*nise mono*,) *n*. Counterfeit, spurious. *Kore wa — da*, this is a counterfeit.

†GAM-MOKU, ガンモク, 眼目, (*manako*,) *n*. The eye; (fig.) important. — *wo tszkeru*, to aim at, fix the attention on. — *na tokoro*, an important place.

GAN, ガン, 鳫, *n*. A wild goose. Syn. KARI.

GAN, ガン, 眼, (*manako*,) *n* The eye. *Nikugan*, fleshly eye. *Shingan*, spiritual eye, (Bud.) Syn. ME.

GAN, ガン, 願, See, *G'wan*.

GANA, ガナ, (impure *ka* of doubt, and *na* of desire,) exclam. of doubt and desire. *Nani-gana agetai*, I wish I had some thing to give him. *Ano h'to no iye ni koto gana arekashi*, I wish some evil might befal his family.

GAN-CHI, ガンチ, 瞎, *n*. Blind of one eye. Syn. KATAME, MEKKACHI.

GAN-GASA, ガンガサ, 鳫瘡, *n*. An eruption on the legs which appears in the fall and disappears in the spring.

GAN-GI, ガンギ, 鴈木, *n.* Steps up the side of a hill.

GAN-KA, ガンカ, 眼下, (*me no sh'ta*), Beneath or below the eye. — *ni h'to wo mi-kudasz*, to look down on, or despise others.

GAN-KUBI, ガンクビ, 鴈頸, *n.* The bowl of a tobacco pipe.

GAN-KUTSZ, ガンクツ, 巖窟, (*iwa ya,*) *n.* A cave in the rocks.

GAN-RAI, ガンライ, 元來, See *G'wanrai.*

GAN-RI, ガンリ, 元利, See *G'wanri.*

GANRIKI, ガンリキ, 眼力, Strength of eye, sharpness of sight. — *tszyoi h'to*, a person of strong eyes.

GAN-SHO, ガンシヨ, 願書, see *G'wansho.*

GAN-SHOKU, ガンシヨク, 顏色, (*kao no iro,*) *n.* The complexion, or color of the face, the countenance. — *wo kayete hara wo tatsz*, changed color and became angry. — *wo tszkurau*, to assume a pleasing expression of face. Syn. KESHIKI.

GAN-ZEKI, ガンゼキ, 巖石, *n.* Rocks.

GAN-ZEN, ガンゼン, 眼前, (*me no maye,*) Before the eyes, now, the present time.

‖GANZENAI,-KI,-SHI, ガンゼナイ, *a.* Cross, petulent, selfwilled, as a child.

‖GAORI,-*ru*,-*otta*, ガオル, 折我, *i. v.* To be humbled, crestfallen, mortified; dispirited, heartless, discouraged.

GAPPI, ガツピ, 月日, (*tszki hi,*) *n.* Month and day; date. — *wo kaku*, to write the date.

GARA, ガラ, 柄, A suffix to nouns, = kind, quality, appearance, figure. *H'to-gara ga yoi*, a person of good appearance. *Shima gara ga warui*, the kind of striping is bad.

GARA-GARA, ガラガラ, *adv.* The sound of rattling, like the falling of tiles, or of a waggon, rattling over stones. *Kawara ga — to ochiru.*

GARAN, ガラン, 伽藍, *n.* A Buddhist temple.

GA-RIU, ガリウ, 我流, Own peculiar style, self-taught method, or style. *Kenjutsz wo — ni tszkau. Ji wo — ni kaku.*

GA-SATSZ, ガサツ, Rough and coarse in manner, careless. — *na h'to*, a rough and careless person. Syn. SOMATSZ, ARA-ARASHII.

†GA-SHI, ガシ, 餓死, (*wiye-jini.*) Starved to death.

†GA-SHI,-*szru*,-*sh'ta*, ガスル, 駕, *i.v.* To ride. *Kumo ni gaszru*, to ride on a cloud. Syn. NORU.

GAS-SHI,-*szru*,-*sh'ta*, ガツスル, 合, *t. v.* To join together, to unite. Syn. AWASZRU.

GASSHŌ, ガツシヤウ, 合掌, (*te wo awaseru.*) Joined hands. *Kami ni mukai gasshō szru.*

‖GASSŌ, ガツソウ, 合僧, Unshaven headed, not having the hair cut. *Ano h'to wo gassō.*

GATA-GATA, ガタガタ, *adv.* The sound of rattling, slamming. *To ga — szru*, the door slams, or rattles (in the wind.) — *furu*, to rattle.

GATAPISHI, ガタピシ, *adv.* The sound of feet, or wooden clogs, a pattering, or rattling noise. — *to aruku.*

GATARI-TO, ガタリト, same as *Gata-gata.*

GATEN,-*szru*, ガテン, 合點, To consent, to assent, allow. To understand, perceive. *Gaten ga yukadz*, cannot understand, suspicious. Syn. SHŌCHI, WAKARU, YURUSZ.

GATERA, ガテラ, A suffix to verbs, same as *Nagara*,=while, at the same time that. *Hana-mi gatera*, while looking at the flowers. *Yuki-gatera*, while going. Syn. KATA-GATA, NAGARA.

GATTAI, ガツタイ, 合體, Like-minded, agreeing together. — *szru*,

GATTEN, ガツテン, same as *Gaten.*

†GAYENDZRU, ガヘンズル, 肯, *i. v.* To consent, assent, be willing. — *ya inaya*, are you willing or not?

GAZAMI, ガザミ, *n.* A kind of sea crab.

†GAZEN, ガゼン, 俄然, *adv.* Suddenly. Syn. NIWAKA-NI.

GE, ゲ, A syllable suffixed to adjectives and other words,=looks like, manner, appearance, as *Ureshi-ge na kao*, a joyful countenance. *Samu-ge*, looking as if cold, or a cold appearance. *Oshi-ge mo naku*, not appearing to regret, or grudge.

†GE, ゲ, 偈, *n.* Buddhist verses. — *wo yomu.*

GE, ゲ, 下, (*shimo, sh'ta*) Below, beneath, down, inferior, under. To descend. — *no shina*, an article of inferior quality. — *no maki*, the last volume.

GE-BA, ゲバ, 下馬, (*Uma yori oriru.*) To dismount from a horse.

GEBI,-*ru*,-*ta*, ゲビル, *i. v.* To be low, vulgar, mean, base.

GE-CHAKU, ゲチヤク, 下著, (*kudari tszku.*) To arrive at home from the capital.

GE-DAI, ゲダイ, 外題, *n.* The name, or title on the outside of a book. *Hon no* —, the name of a book. *Shibai no ge-dai*, the name of a play.

GE-DAN, ゲダン, 下段, *n.* Lower step,

grade, or degree. — *ni kamayeru*, to hold the sword in the lower guard.

†GE-DATSZ, ゲダツ, 解脱, *n.* Deliverance from evil, salvation. — *wo yeru*, to obtain deliverance from evil. (Bud.)

†GE-DEN, ゲデン, 外典, *n.* The title given by the Buddhist to books which treat only of outward conduct, as, the Chinese classics.

†GE-DŌ, ゲダウ, 外道, (*hoka no michi*). Contrary to the true way, heretical, heterodox. (Bud).

†GE-DOKU, ゲドク, 解毒, *n.* An antidote to poison.

†GE-GEN, ゲゲン, 下弦, *n.* The last quarter of the moon.

†GE-HAI, ゲハイ, 下輩, *n.* The lower classes of people.

GE-HIN, ゲヒン, 下品, *n.* Inferior quality.

GEI, ゲイ, 藝, *n.* Polite accomplishments. *Riku-gei*, the six ac. viz., etiquette, music, horsemanship, archery, writing and arithmetic.

GEI-GEI, ゲイゲイ, *adv.* The sound of belching. *Amari taberu to — ga deru.* Syn. OKUBI, KARAYEDZKI.

GEI-KO, ゲイコ, 藝子, *n.* A dancing girl.

GEISHA, ゲイシャ, 藝者, idem.

GE-JI, ゲヂ, 下知, *n.* Command, order, (from a superior.) — *wo szru*, to give orders — *wo ukeru*, to receive a command. Syn. MŌSHI-WATASHI, Ī-TSZKE.

GEJI-GEJI, ゲジゲジ, 蜓蚰, *n.* A kind of insect of the family of Miriapoda.

GE-JIKI, ゲヂキ, 下直, *n.* Low in price, cheap. *Ito ga ge-jiki ni natta*, silk has become low in price. — *na mono*, a low priced article. Syn. NEDAN YASZI.

GE-JO, ゲヂヨ, 下女, *n.* A servant girl.

GE-JŌ, ゲジヨウ, 下乗, To get out of a norimon. — *bashi*, the place where visitors to the palace leave the norimon.

GE-JUN, ゲジユン, 下旬, *n.* The last decade of the month.

†GE-KAI, ゲカイ, 下界, *n.* The lower world, this world. (Bud).

GE-KAN, ゲカン, 下疳, *n.* Disease of the genitals.

†GE-KETSZ, ゲケツ, 下血, *n.* (*chi kudari*). A bloody flux.

†GEKI-RAN, ゲキラン, 逆亂, *n.* Revolt, rebellion, insurrection. — *wo okosz*, to excite revolt.

†GEKIRIN, ゲキリン, 逆鱗, *n.* Imperial anger.

†GEKKŌ, ゲックワウ, 月光, (*tszki no hikari*). Moonlight.

GE-KO, ゲコ, 下戸, *n.* A temperate person, one who does not drink spirits.

GE-KŌ, ゲカウ, 下向, (*sh'ta ni mukō*). To go down from the Capital, or from a temple.

GE-K'WA, ゲクワ, 外科, *n.* Surgery. — *isha*, a surgeon. — *dōgu*, surgical instruments.

GEM-BUKU, ゲンブク, 元服, The ceremony of shaving off the forelock, and changing the name of a young man, on arriving at the age of 15, who then becomes a man. — *szru*, to perform the above ceremony.

†GEMMEI, ゲンメイ, 嚴命, Strict order.

GENA, ゲナ, I hear that, is it so that. *Sō da gena*, I hear it is so. *Ano h'to Yedo kara kayerimash'ta gena*, I hear that he has returned from Yedo. *Nikugena kao*, an ugly face.

GE-NAN, ゲナン, 下男, *n.* A man-servant.

GE-NI, or GENIMO, ゲニ, 實, *adv.* Indeed, truly. Syn. JITSZ-NI.

GE-NIN, ゲニン, 下人, (*shimobe*), *n.* A servant.

GENJI,-*ru* or *dzru*,-*jita*, ゲンズル, 現, *i.v.* To appear, to be visible, manifested. *Kō-dan no toki moro-moro no dzi-ō genjita*, when he was preaching many strange signs appeared. Syn. ARAWARERU, MIYERU.

GENJI,-*ru* or *dzru*,-*ta*, ゲンズル, 減, *t.v.* To lessen, diminish, retrench, curtail, abbreviate. *Kiu-kin wo* —, to diminish the wages. Syn. HERASZ, HABUKU.

GEN-JŪ, ゲンヂユウ, 嚴重, Strict, severe, rigorous, secure, strong, well-fortified. — *ni szru*, to make strong and secure. — *ni mamoru*, — *ni naru*. Syn. KIBISHII.

GEN-JUTSZ, ゲンジユツ, 幻術, *n.* Secret arts, magic arts, supernatural powers, (of becoming invisible, &c).

GENKA, ゲンクワ, 玄關, *n.* A porch at the entrance of a house.

†GENKAN, ゲンカン, 嚴寒, Severe cold.

GEN-KI, ゲンキ, 元氣, *n.* Natural vigor, strength, spirited, active, cheerful. — *naru h'to*, a person of vigorous constitution, or of high spirits. — *no nai h'to*, — *ga warui*. Syn. SEI, IKIOI.

GENKIN, ゲンキン, 現金, *n.* Ready money, money paid down on delivery of goods. *Gen-kin kake-ne nashi*, ready money and but one price.

GENKOTSZ, ゲンコ, *n.* The knuckles, fist.

GEN-SHŌ, ゲンセウ, 減少, To lessen, diminish.

GEN-SHO, ゲンショ, 嚴暑, Severe heat.

†GENSO, ゲンソ, 素元, The essence, active principle, extract, (of medicine.)

†GENSON, ゲンソン, 玄孫, Great-great-grand child.

GEN-ZAI, ゲンザイ, 現在, The present time, the present. — *no haha*, the mother one now has.

GEN-ZE, ゲンゼ 現世, *n.* The present world, the present life. (Budd.)

GEN-ZOKU, ゲンゾク, 還俗, To return to the world, to abandon the priesthood. — *szru.*

GEPPAKU, ゲツパク, 月迫, *n.* The last part of the 12th month.

GEPPU, ゲツプ, 噯氣, *n.* Belching. — *szru*, to belch. — *ga deru.* Syn. OKUBI.

GE-RAKU,-*szru*, ゲラク, 下落, To fall in price.

GERI, ゲリ, 下痢, *n.* Diarrhœa.

GERŌ, ゲラウ, 下郎, *n.* A low vulgar fellow.

GESAN, ゲサン, 下山, *(yama wo kudaru).* To descend a hill.

GESE,-*ru*,-*ta*, ゲセル, 解, *i.v.* To understand.

‖GE-SETSZ, ゲセツ, 下拙, *per. pro.* I, me, (humble).

GESEN, ゲセン, 下賤, Vulgar, low, mean, base. — *na mono.* Syn. IYASHII.

GESHI,-*szru*,-*ta*, ゲスル, 解, *t.v.* To explain.

GESHI, ゲシ, 夏至, *n.* The summer solstice.

GE-SHIKU, ゲシユク, 下宿, The quartering of the servants of Daimio's in private houses, billeting.

GESHI-NIN, ゲシニン, 下手人, *n.* A murderer.

GE-SHOKU, ゲショク, 下職, *n.* Low employment.

GESZ, ゲス, 下司, *n.* Low fellow, vulgar.

GE-SZI, ゲスイ, 下水, *n.* Dirty water, the water of a drain, spittoon, &c.

GETA, ゲタ, 下踏, *n.* Wooden clogs. — *no ha*, the two pieces of wood under the sole.

GETSZ, ゲツ, 月, *n.* The moon, month. This word is used only for reckoning time by months, as, *ichi getsz*, one month; *ni getsz*, two months; *gwatsz*, is used in naming the months, as *go gwatsz*, the fifth month, *kugwatsz*, the 9th month, &c.

GETSZ-YA, ゲツヤ, 月夜, A moonlight night. Syn. TSZKI-YO.

GEYA, ゲヤ, 下屋, *n.* A house or apartments built to connect with the main building.

GE-ZA, ゲザ, 下座, A lower seat.

GE-ZAI, ゲザイ, 下劑, *n.* Purgative medicine.

†GI, ギ, 妓, *n.* A prostitute, a singing girl.

GI, ギ, 義, Right, just, proper, faithful, patriotic; meaning, signification; affair, business, = *koto. Ichi gi ni mo oyobadz*, made no objection. *Gi ni szgireba kataku-na ni naru*, by being over much righteous we become bigoted. *Kono ji no gi wa ikaga*, what is the meaning of this word. — *wo haru*, to rouse up patriotic feelings. *Kono gi*, this business, or affair. *Miji no gi*, the above matter. *Sayō no gi de wa nai*, it is nothing of the kind.

GI-BUTSZ, ギブツ, 僞物, *n.* Counterfeit, spurious. Syn. GAMBUTSZ, NISE-MONO.

GI-HEI, ギヘイ, 義兵, *n.* A faithful or loyal soldier.

GI-HITSZ, ギヒツ, 僞筆, *n.* A forged writing, a forgery.

†GI-JO, ギヂヨ, 女妓, *n.* A singing girl.

GIKKURI-TO, ギククリト, *adv.* Startled, alarmed with sudden apprehension. — *hashiri-yoru.*

GIMMI, ギンミ, 味吟, *n.* Examination, inspection, judging, inquiry, choosing. *Tszmibito wo gimmi szru*, to examine a criminal, — *wo ukeru*, to be judged. Syn. SHIRABE. TADASHI.

†GI-MON, ギモン, 疑問, *(utagatte tō.)* Being in doubt about anything to inquire about it.

GIM-PAKU, ギンパク, 銀箔, *n.* Silver plated.

GIN, ギン, 銀, *(shirokane,) n.* Silver. — *de koshirayeru*, made of silver. *Gin-sekai*, 銀世界, ground covered with snow. *Gindei*, 銀泥, a kind of silvery paint.

†GIN-DZRU, ギンズル, 吟, To sing.

GI-NEN, ギネン, 疑念, (*utagau omoi,*) *n.* Doubt, suspicion.

†GIN-GA, ギンガ, 銀河, *n.* The milky-way.

GIN-SHU, ギンシユ, 銀主, *n.* A capitalist, or one who advances the money.

GIN-SZ, ギンス, 銀子, *n.* Silver money.

GIN-ZA, ギンザ, 銀座, *n.* The mint where silver money is coined.

GIN-ZAIKU, ギンザイク, 銀細工, *n.* Silver ware.

GIRI, ギリ, 義理, *n.* Right, just, that which is proper, just, reasonable; meaning, signification. — *aru haha*, rightful mother. — *wo shiranu h'to da.* — *ni kanau. Kono ji no* — *wa nani*, what is the meaning of this word? Syn. DŌRI.

GIRI-DATE, ギリダテ, 義理立, *n.* Doing justly, or acting kindly to others. — *wo szru.*

GIRI-GIRI, ギリギリ, 旋毛, *n.* The crown of the head. The very lowest price. — *ikura made make-nasaru*, what is the very lowest you will take? Syn. TSZMOJI.

GIRO-GIRO, ギロギロ, or GIRO-TSZKI,*–ku, –ita*, ギロツク, *adv.* Bright, shining.

†GIRŌ, ギロウ, 妓樓, *n.* A prostitute house.

†GIRON, ギロン, 議論, *n.* Debate, discussion, reasoning, argument.

GI-SHIKI, ギシキ, 儀式, *n.* Etiquette, forms of ceremony. Syn. HŌSHIKI.

GI-SHIN, ギシン, 疑心, *(utagau kokoro,) n.* Doubt, suspicion.

GITCHŌ, ギツチヤウ, 毬杖, *n.* A toy shaped like a wooden mallet.

GIU-TŌ, ギウトウ, 牛痘, *(uye bōso,)* Vaccine disease.

GI-WAKU, ギワク, 疑惑, *(utagai.) n.* Doubt, suspicion. *Shin chiu — wo shōdzru*, to beget suspicion.

GIYAKU, ギヤク, 瘧, *(okori,) n.* Intermittent fever.

GIYAKU, ギヤク, 逆, Contrary, adverse, opposite, — *na koto*, a matter the reverse of what it should be, — *ni kazoyeru*, to count backwards. — *ni nagareru*, to flow backwards. Syn. SAKASAMA.

GIYAKU-FŪ, ギヤクフウ, 逆風, *n.* A contrary wind. Syn. MUKAI-KAZE.

GIYAKU-I, ギヤクイ, 逆意, *n.* Treason, treachery, rebelliousness, perfidy.

GIYAKU-JŌ, ギヤクジヤウ, 逆上, *(nobose,) n.* Congestion or rush of blood to the head.

GIYAKU-SHIN, ギヤクシン, 逆臣, *n.* A treacherous or disloyal servant.

GIYAKU-ZAN, ギヤクザン, 逆產, *n.* An unnatural labor.

GIYAKU-ZOKU, ギヤクゾク, 逆賊, *n.* A traitor, rebel.

GIYAMAN, ギヤマン, 玻璃, *n.* Glass. Syn. BIDORO.

†GIYO, ギヨ, 魚, *(uwo), n.* Fish. *Taigiyo*, 大魚, a large fish. Syn. SAKANA.

GIYO, ギヨ, 御, An epithet applied to the Mikado, Imperial. — *i* 御衣, Emperor's clothes. — *ken*, 御劍, Emperor's sword.

GIYŌ, ギヤウ, 行, Religious austerities, or discipline. The numeral for rows. *Go* —, 五行, the five elements. *San* —, three rows. — *wo szru*, to practice religious austerities, (as fasting, pilgrimages.) *Giyō-i*, 行衣, the white clothes worn by pilgrims.

GIYŌ-DZI, ギヤウズイ, 行水, *n*, Bathing with warm water.

†GIYO-FU, ギヨフ, 漁夫, *n.* A fisherman. Syn. RIYŌSHI.

GIYŌ-GI, ギヤウギ, 行儀, Correct, conformed to propriety and decorum; deportment, manner. — *ga warui*, rude, illmannered. — *yoku narabu*, arranged in proper order. Syn. TADASHII.

GIYŌ-GIYŌSHI, ギヤウギヤウシ, 鸖鵲, *n.* The name of a noisy bird.

GIYŌ-GIYŌSHII,–KI, ギヨウギヨウシイ, 囂囂, *a.* Shrieking in sudden fright or anger; noisy, clamerous.

GIYO-I, ギヨイ, 御意, *(o kokoro.)* Imperial mind, (used also to any honorable person.) — *no tōri*, as your excellency pleases.

GIYŌ-JA, ギヤウジヤ, 行者, *n.* One who practices religious austerities, or goes on a pilgrimage; a hermit.

GIYŌ-JI, ギヤウジ, 行事, *n.* An umpire, or judge, (of wrestlers).

GIYŌ-JŌ, ギヤウジヤウ, 行狀, *n.* Actions, conduct. Syn. OKONAI.

GIYO-RUI, ギヨルイ, 魚類, *n.* The fish class of living things.

GIYŌ-SAN, ギヤウサン, 仰山, Very many, amazingly great. — *aru*, there are a great many. — *na koto wo iu*, to exaggerate. Syn TAISŌ.

GIYŌ-SEKI, ギヤウセキ, 行跡, *n.* Conduct, actions, doings.

GIYO-SHIN, ギヨシン, 御寢, Sleep, (only used in addressing a superior.)

GIYŌ-RETSZ, ギヤウレツ, 行列, *n.* Procession, ranks.

GIYŌ-TEN,*–szru*, ギヤウテン, 仰天, To be amazed, astonished, surprised. Syn. BIKKURI.

GIYO-TŌ, ギヨトウ, 魚油, *n.* Fish-oil.

GIYOTTO, ギヨツト, 愕, *adv.* In an astonished surprised manner.

GI-ZETSZ, ギゼツ, 義絕, *n.* Breaking off friendly relations or intimacy. Syn. ZEKKŌ.

GO, ゴ, 御, A term of respect or politeness used in addressing a superior,=honorable, excellent, but frequently only equivalent in English to, you, your. *Go-yō*, 御用, government service. *Go-hatto*, government prohibition. *Gokanai*, your (honor's) wife. *Go-shisoku*, your son. *Go-chisō*, your entertainment. *Go-kigen yoroshii ka*, are you in good health? *Go-men nasare*, I beg your pardon. *Okini go-kurō*, I am much obliged to you. (for your trouble). *Ari-*

gatō go-zarimasz, I thank you. *Go-shinsetsz*, your kindness. *Go-sznka de go-zarimasz ka*, are you at leisure? *Go-setsz wa go mottomo de gozarimasz*, what you say, Sir, is quite true.
Syn. GIYO, ON, O.

GO, ゴ, *n.* Beans mashed into paste. *Mame no* —.

GO, ゴ, 五, Five. *Jū-go*, fifteen. *Go-jū* fifty. *Go bu*, five parts, half an inch. *Gobu ichi*, one fifth. *Go-nin*, five persons. *Go-tabi*, five times. Syn. ITSZTSZ.

GO, ゴ, 碁, *n.* Checkers. *Go-ishi*, (idem.) (white are called *Shiro-ishi*; black *Kuro-ishi*). *Go wo utsz*, to play checkers.

GO, ゴ, 期, *n.* The time, proper time, fixed time. *Sono go ni ittatte yakujō wo somuku*, when the time came he broke his promise. *Rin-jū no go ni nozomu*, to be near the time of death. Syn. TOKI, NICHIGEN.

GŌ, ガウ, 强, (*tszyoi,)* Strong, powerful, stout, brave, intrepid. — *teki*, 强敵, a powerful enemy

GŌ, ゴウ, 劫, *n.* A measure of time used by the Buddhists, Williams' Dict. says 500 years. Kanghi Dict. says, one generation.

GO, ゴ, 後, *(nochi,).* After in time, behind. *Sono go wa otodzre ga nai*, after that there were no tidings. *San nen go*, after three years. *Zen go*, before and behind.

GŌ, ガフ, 合, *n.* A box for measuring grain, or liquids, 4 $\frac{62}{100}$ inches square, and 2.$\frac{50}{100}$ inches deep, containing 53.$\frac{475}{1000}$ cub. inches.

GŌ, ゴフ, 業, *n.* The deeds, actions, or conduct of man in this life or in a previous state. *Aku* —, 悪業, evil deeds. *Zen* —, 善業, good deeds. *Shiku* —, 宿業, deeds done in a previous state of existence. *Hi-gō*.非業, guiltless, having done neither good or evil. — *biyō*, 業病, sickness, supposed to be a punishment of deeds done in a previous state. *Midzkara no gō nite midzkara k'wa wo uru*, each one is rewarded according to his own doings. — *no hakari*, 業秤, a pair of scales in hades, in which the deeds of men are weighed.
Syn. OKONAI.

GOBAI-SHI, ゴバイシ, 五倍子, *(fushi,) n.* Gall-nuts.

GOBAN, ゴバン, 棊盤, *n.* A checker-board. — *no me*, the squares on a checker-board.

†GŌ-BATSZ, ガウバツ, 毫髮, A hair's breadth. — *mo chigai ga nai*, not the difference of a hair's breadth.

GO-BŌ, ゴバウ, 牛房, *n.* The dock (vegetable.)

GŌ-BUKU,*-szru*, ゴウブク, 降伏, *t. v.* To bring into subjection *Akuma wo* —, to exorcise evil spirits.

GODZME, ゴツメ, 後拒, *n.* A rear body of troops.

GODZMEDZ, ゴツメツ, 牛頭馬頭, *n.* Demons, having heads like the ox and horse, said to execute the office of gaolers in Hades. (Bud,)

GO-FŪ, ゴフウ, 護符, *n.* A charm, or small piece of paper on which a sentence from the Buddhist sacred books is written by a priest, it is sometimes rolled up, thrown into water, and drunk, in order to cure disease, Syn. MAMORI.

GO-FUKU, ゴフク, 呉服, *n.* Dry goods.

GO-FUKUYA, ゴフクヤ, 呉服屋, *n.* A dry-goods store.

GOFUKU-ZASHI, ゴフクザシ, 呉服尺, *n.* A measure of 2½ feet long used by mercer's; a yard-stick.

GOFUN, ゴフン, 五分, *n.* Half a momme, =29.165 grs. Troy.

GOFUN, ゴフン, 胡粉, *n.* Chalk.

GŌ-GI, ガウギ, *a.* Used as a coll. superlative, applied to any thing great or extraordinary. — *na h'to*, a great man ; — *ni kane wo mōketa.*

GŌGI-NI, ガウギニ, 剛氣, *adv.* Daring, boldly, insolently.

GŌ-GŌ, ゴウゴウ, *adv.* The sound of snoring. — *to naru.*

GO-HAN, ゴハン, 御飯, *(o-meshi,) n.* Boiled rice, a meal. *Asa gohan*, breakfast. *Hirugohan*, dinner. *Yu-gohan*, supper.
Syn. GOZEN.

GO-HATTO, ゴハット, 御法度, *n.* An imperial law or prohibition.

GOHEI, ゴヘイ, 御幣, *n.* The cut paper placed in *Miya's* to represent the *Kami.*

GOHEI-KATSZGI, ゴヘイカツギ, 御幣擔, Superstitious, observant of lucky or unlucky signs. —*no h'to.*

GO-HEN, ゴヘン, 御邊, pro. You (to equals.)

GŌ-IN, ガウイン, 强淫, To ravish, to violate.

GO-IN, ゴイン, 五音, *n.* The five kinds of articulate sounds.

GO-JIN, ゴヂン, 後陣, *n.* The rear ranks of an army, the rear part of a camp.

GŌ-JŌ, ガウジヤウ, 强情, *n.* Obstinate, headstrong, strong self-will.

GO-JŪ, ゴジフ, 五十, *a.* Fifty. — *ichi*, fifty one.

GO-JŌ-MOKU, ゴゼウモク, 御條目, *n.* An imperial edict or proclamation published and hung up for the public.

GŌ-KA, ガウカ, 豪家, *n.* A wealthy house or family, (applied only to lower classes.)

GO-KAI, ゴカイ, 五戒, *n.* The five Buddhist commandments, against stealing, lying, intemperance, murder, and adultery.

GO-KAKU, ゴカク, 互格, *n.* Even, undecided, (as a battle.) a drawn game. — *no tatakai*, a drawn battle. *shōbu ga — da*, victory was undecided.

GOKE, ゴケ, 後家, *n.* A widow. Syn. YAMOME.

GŌ-KETSZ, ガウケツ, 豪傑, *n.* A person preëminent for learning, or ability of any kind, a hero.

GŌ-KI, ガウキ, 强氣, *n.* Stout hearted, bravery, courage, bold. — *ga nai h'to.*

GO-KIYŌ, ゴキヤウ, 五經, *n.* The five Chinese classics.

GO-KOKU, ゴコク, 後刻, By and by, in a few minutes. Syn. NOCH'HODO.

GO-KOKU, ゴコク, 五穀, The five cereals, wheat, rice, millet, beans, and *kibi.*

GOKU, ゴク, 極, *adv.* In a superlative degree, extremely, eminently. — *warui*, extremely bad. — *yoi*, the best. — *atszi*, extremely hot. Syn. ICHI, HANAHADA, ITO.

GOKU-DŌ, ゴクダウ, *n.* A dissolute, profligate person.

GOKU-GETSZ, ゴクゲツ, 極月, *n.* The last month of the year. Syn. SHIWASZ, JŪ-NI-G'WATSZ.

GOKU-HIN, ゴクヒン, 極品, *n.* An article of the very best quality.

GOKU-I, ゴクイ, 極意, *n.* The essential principle, chief point, ultimate end, or object. Syn. Ō-GI.

GOKU-JŌ, ゴクジヤウ, 極上, *n.* The very best, or highest kind. — *no shina.*

GOKU-MON, ゴクモン, 獄門, *n.* The scaffold on which the head of a criminal is exposed to the public.

GOKU-RAKU, ゴクラク, 極樂, *n.* The place of highest happiness; Paradise of the Buddhists. — *sekai*, Paradise. — *sekai ni umaruru*, to enter Paradise. — *no shujō*, the inhabitants of Paradise.

GOKU-SOTSZ, ゴクソツ, 獄卒, *n.* A goaler, the persons who looks after prisoners in a gaol.

GOKU-YA, ゴクヤ, 獄舍, *n.* A gaol, prison. Syn. RŌYA.

GOKU-TSZBUSHI, ゴクツブシ, 穀潰, *n.* A drone, idler.

GOMA, ゴマ, 胡麻, *n.* The sesamum orientalis. — *no abura*, the oil of the s. o. used for cooking. *Goma no hai*, a highway robber. *Goma wo szru*, to court, or curry favor by speaking evil of others, to slander.

GOMA, ゴマ, 護摩, *n.* A Buddhist rite; of saying prayers while fire is burning in a brazier. — *wo taku*, performing the above ceremony.

GOMAKASHI,*-sz,-sh'ta*, ゴマカス, *t.v.* To hoodwink, blind, to conceal, or turn off by a devise.

GO-MEN, ゴメン, 御免, *(o yurushi nasare).* Your honor's permission; excused, pardoned by a superior. — *kudasare*, excuse me, pardon me. — *wo negau*, to ask permission of a superior. *Oyaku gomen ni natta*, excused from public service.

GOMI, ゴミ, 塵, *n.* Dirt, dust, litter. — *wo haku*, to sweep up dirt. — *wo harau*, to brush off dust. *Gomi-tori*, a dust pan.

GOMI, ゴミ, *n.* The Eleagnus.

GO-MI-SHI, ゴミシ, 五味子, *n.* A kind of medicine.

GOMOKU, ゴモク, 塵芥, *n.* Litter, dirt, rubbish. — *ba*, a dirt heap, place where dirt and rubbish is thrown.

GOMOKU-MESHI, ゴモクメシ, 五目飯, *n.* A kind of food made by mixing several kinds of vegetables with rice.

GŌ-MON, ガウモン, 拷問, *n.* Examination by torture, torture to extort confession.

GON, ゴン, 權, Written with a title to show that it is a brevet, or honorary title merely, as, *Musashi gon no kami*, honorary *Musashi no kami*. *Gon dai na gon*, honorary *Dai na gon.*

GON, ゴン, 言, *(kotoba,) n.* A word. *Ichi gon mo nai*, had not a word to say.

GŌNA, ガウナ, *n.* A small kind of mollusca.

†GON-GIYŌ, ゴンギヤウ, 勤行, Industrious in the performance of religious austerities.

GON-GO, ゴンゴ, 言語, *n.* Words, speech, language. — *no oyobu tokoro ni aradz*, that which no words can express. — *dō dan*, inexpressible, unutterable. — *ni zesszru*, exceeding the power of language.

GON-JŌ,*-szru*, ゴンジヤウ, 言上, To tell or report to a superior. Syn. MOSHI-AGERU.

†GON-KU, ゴンク, 言句, *n.* A word or sentence. — *mo demasen*, did not utter a word.

GO-NICHI, ゴニチ, 後日, *n.* A future day.

GO-ON, ゴオン, 呉音, *n.* The name given to those sounds of the Chinese characters, brought to Japan in the reign of the 16th

Emperor, and taught by *Wani*, a Corean. The Buddhist use these sound only.

GO-RAN, ゴラン, 御覽, Look, (respectful and used only in speaking to another,) — *nasare*, look here. — *ni ireru*, show you, let you see. *Chō-ren wo goranjita ka*, did you see the parade?

†GŌ-REI, ガウレイ, 號令, *n*. The word of command, order. — *wo kudasz*, to give an order.

GŌRIKI, ガウリキ, 强力, *n*. A strong man.

†GO-RIN, ゴリン, 五輪, Five different layers of sculpture, one on the top of the other. — *no tō*, a monument made of 5 styles of sculpture.

†GO-RIN, ゴリン, 五倫, *n*. The five human relations, of father and son; master and servant; husband and wife; of friends; and of brothers.

GORO, ゴロ, 語路, *n*. The combination of syllables in a word, or of words in a line of poetry in respect of euphony, or measure. Syn. SHIRABE.

GORO, ゴロ, 呉羅, *n*. Camlet.

GORO-GORO, ゴロゴロ, *adv*. The sound of rumbling, or rolling as of thunder, or a waggon. *Kami nari ga — to naru*, the thunder rolls.

GOROJI, ゴラウジ, (Yed. coll. for *Goran*). — *nasare*, look!

GORO-JŪ, ゴラウヂウ, 御老中, *n*. The council of State at Yedo.

GOROTSZKI, ゴロツキ, *n*. An idle vagabond, or bully, who extorts money by intimidation.

GOROTSZKI,*-ku,-ita*, ゴロツク, *i.v*. To lead an idle vagabond life, loafing; to make a rumbling noise.

GO-SAI, ゴサイ, 後妻, *n*. A second wife. — *wo ireru*, to marry a second wife.

GO-SAN-NARE, ゴサンナレ, 御參成, Come on. Syn. IZA.

GO-SE, ゴセ, 後世, (*nochi no yo*.) *n*. The world to come, future state. (Bud.)

GŌ-SEI, ガウセイ, 强勢, *adv*. Mighty, great, important, very. — *atszi*, mighty (very) hot. — *na koto wo sh'ta*.

GO-SHA, ゴシャ, 御赦, Imperial pardon, amnesty.

GO-SHI,*-sz,-sh'ta*, ゴス, 期, *t.v*. To fix, appoint a time. *Hi wo gosz*, to appoint a day. *Toki wo —*, to set a time, fix an hour. Syn. SADAMERU.

†GŌ-SHI,*-sz,-sh'ta*, ガウス, 號, *t.v*. To name, to call. *Na wo sadajiro to gōsz*, called his name, *Sadajiro*. Syn. NATZKERU, MŌ-Z.

GO-SHIN-ZŌ, ゴシンザウ, 御新造, *n*. Your honor's wife.

GO-SHŌ, ゴシヤウ, 後生, *n*. Future life of happiness. (Bud.)

GOSHO, ゴショ, 御所, *n*. The imperial residence, the court.

GO-SHUDEN, ゴシュデン, 御朱殿, *n*. The residence of the females of a noble's family, the harem.

GO-SHU-IN, ゴシユイン, 御朱印, *n* The seal of the *Shōgun*, (*Tykun*.) — *chi*, land granted by the *Shōgun*, to which his seal is affixed.

†GOSZI, ゴスイ, 午睡, *n*. Sleeping in the day time.

†GO-SZI, ゴスイ, 五衰, The five decays in the condition of the *Tennin*, when their period of happiness is completed.

GOTA-GOTA, ゴタゴタ, *adv*. Confused, mixed, jumbled together, mingled. — *shte iru*.

GO-TAI, ゴタイ, 五躰, *n*. The five members of the body as the head, arms, and legs; the whole body.

GO-TAI-RŌ, ゴタイラウ, 御太老, *n*. The prince regent.

GOTAMAZE, ゴタマゼ, *n*. Jumbled together, mixed together in confusion. — *ni naru*,

GOTA-NI, ゴタニ, *n*. A hodge-podge; medley of different kinds of food boiled together.

GOTATSKI,*-ku,-ita*, ゴタツク, *i.v*. To be jumbled, confused, mixed together.

GŌ-TŌ, ガウタウ, 豪盜, *n* Bandit, robber, highway man.

GOTO-GOTO TO, ゴトゴトト, *adv*. The sound of water flowing from a bottle; gurgling. — *oto ga szru*, to make a gurgling noise.

GOTOKI,-KU,-SHI, ゴトク, 如, Like to, as, same manner. *Kono gotoku*, thus, in this manner. *H'to no gotoshi*, like a man. *Moshi mōsz tokoro no gotokumba*, if it be as you have said. Syn TŌRI, YŌ.

GO-TOKU, ゴトク, 五德, *n*. A three legged iron stand, used in boiling a tea kettle.

GOTO-NI, ゴトニ, 毎, *a*. Every, each. *H'to gotoni*, every body. *Kuni gotoni*, every country.

GOTSZ-GOTSZ, ゴツゴツ, *adv*. The sound of hard things striking together. — *to tataku*.

GŌ-YOKU, ガウヨク, 强欲, Strong lust, exceedingly covetous, greedy, or avaricious.

GOZA, ゴザ, 御座, *n*. A mat, Chinese matting.

GO-ZANOMA, ゴザノマ, 御座之間, *n*.

The room in which a Lord or master generally sits.

GOZAFUNE, ゴザフ子, 御座舩, *n.* An imperial yacht.

GOZARI,*-ru,-tta*, ゴザル, 御座, *i.v.* To be, to have; to come, (respectful for *Aru.*) *Gozarimasz,* I have, there is. *Gozarimasen,* have not, there is not. *Gozarimasz ka,* have you? is there? *Gozarimashō,* I think there is, or I think I have.

GOZE, ゴゼ, 瞽女, *n.* Blind women, who go about singing and playing on the guitar.

GOZEN, ゴゼン, 御膳, *n.* Boiled rice, or food generally. Syn. MESHI, GOHAN.

GO-ZEN, ゴゼン, 御前, *n.* The presence of the Emperor, also, "your excellency," in speaking to a *Daimio.*

†GU, グ, 愚, Foolish, stupid, (used often as an humble word for one's-self.) *Gu-nah'to,* a dunce. *Gunakoto wo iu,* to talk nonsense. *Gu-sai,* my (stupid) wife, *Gusoku,* my (stupid) son, *Gu an,* my (humble) opinion, *Gui,* my (stupid) mind. Syn. BAKA.

†GŪ, グウ, 偶, Even number. *Ki-gu,* odd and even. Syn. CHŌ.

GUAI, グアヒ, 工合, *n.* The state, condition; the fit, working, or movement of things which are adjusted to one another, as, *Kono hiki-dashi no guai ga yoi,* this drawer works neatly and smoothly. *Shōji no guai ga warui,* the screen does not work smoothly. *Guai wa dō da,* how are you? Syn. AMBAI, CHŌ-SHI.

GUBUNIN, グブニン, 供奉人, *n.* The attendents of the Emperor in going out; or of a *Kami* when carried out in procession.

GU-CHI, グチ, 愚癡, *n.* Nonsense, foolishness, silliness. *—wo kobosz,* to talk nonsense, *onna wa — na mono.*

GUDO-GUDO, グドグド, *adv.* The sound of complaining, grumbling. — *iu,* to grumble.

GUDON, グドン, 愚鈍, *n.* Foolish and dull.

GUDO-TSZKI,*-ku,-ita*, グドツク, *i. v.* To loiter, to dilly-dally, to be slow and dilatory. *Nani wo gudotszite iru, yuku nara, hayaku ike,* what are you dilly-dallying about, if you are going, go quick.

GUDZ-GUDZ, グヅグヅ, *adv.* Sound of grumbling, foolish and idle complaining; dilly-dallying, loitering, idling, lazily. *— to sh'te,* to be idle and without any fixed purpose.

GUDZ-TSZKI,*-ku,-ita*, グヅツク, *i. v.* (idem.)

GUDZRI,*-ru,-tta*, グヅル, 哄, *t. v.* To tease by unreasonable demands, to vex, annoy. Syn. NEDARU.

†GU-HŌ, グハフ, 弘法, (*hō wo hiromeru,*) To disseminate, or propagate religious doctrines (Bud.)

†GUMAI, グマイ, 愚昧, Ignorant, stupid.

GUMBAI, グンバイ, 軍配, *n.* A fan used in giving a command by military officers.

GUM-BIYŌ, グンビヤウ, 軍兵, *n.* An army. Syn. GUNZEI.

GUMI, グミ, *n.* A small red berry.

†GU-MŌ, グモウ, 愚蒙, Ignorant, stupid.

†GUM-PŌ, グンポウ, 群蜂, A swarm of bees.

GUM-PŌ, グンパフ, 軍法, *n.* Military tactics.

†GUN, グン, 軍, (*ikusa,*) *n.* An army, war. — *chiu,* in the army. *Ta-gun,* a large army.

GUN-DAI, グンダイ, 郡代, *n.* The superintendant of a county.

GUN-DAN, グンダン, 軍談, (*ikusa no hanashi,*) *n.* Talking about war, war-stories.

GUN-GAKU, グンガク, 軍學, *n.* The art of war.

GUN'YA-GUN'YA, グニヤグニヤ, *adv.* Limber, soft, plaiant, flabby.

GUN'YARI, グニヤリ, (idem.)

GUN-JIN, グンジン, 軍神, (*ikusa no kami,*) *n.* The god of war. (*Hachi-man sama.*)

GUN-JIN, グンギン, 軍陣, *n.* An encampment.

GUN-KAN, グンカン, 軍艦, *n.* A ship of war.

GUN-REI, グンレイ, 軍令, *n.* An order, or command given to an army.

GUN-SAN, グンサン, 群參, (*muragari mairu.*) To flock together, assemble in droves.

GUN-SHI, グンシ, 軍師, *n.* An army officer.

GUN-SHIN, グンシン, 群臣, *n.* The whole crowd of servants.

GUN-SHO, グンショ, 軍書, *n.* A history of wars.

GUN-SOTSZ, グンソツ, 軍卒, *n.* Common soldiers.

GUN-ZEI, グンゼイ, 軍勢, *n.* An army.

GUN-YŌ-KIN, グンヨウキン, 軍用金, *n.* Army or war expenses.

GURA-GURA, グラグラ, *adv.* A rocking motion. *Fune ga — szru,* the boat rocks. *Iye jishin de — szru,* the house is rocked by the earthquake. *Ha ga — szru,* the tooth is loose.

GURE,*-ru,-ta*, グレル, *i. v.* To slip off; to

fail to perform (as a promise.) *Yak'soku ga gureta*, the engagement has failed. *Ki ga* — to be out of one's mind.

GU-RŌ, グロウ, 愚弄, *n.* Ridicule, derision, joking, making sport. — *szru.* Syn. AZAKERU, NABURU.

GUSA TO, グサ, (coll.) The sound of stabbing a hollow place. *Abara wo gusa to tszku*, stabbed him in the chest. *Nodo wo — irareru*, shot him in the neck.

GUSHI, グシ, 髮, *n.* The hair, (only used with *o* or *mi* preceeding), as, *Migushi*, your (honor's) hair. *Ogushi agemashō*, let me do up your hair. Syn. KAMI.

GUSHI,*-szru,-sh'ta*, グスル, 倶, *i.v.* To accompany, go along with. *Gush'te yuku.*

GUSOKU, グソク, 具足, *n.* A coat of mail, complete armor. Syn. KATCHIU, YOROI-KABUTO.

GUSOKU,*-szru*, グソク, 具足, *i. v.* To be complete, perfect, entire, completely furnished, to have. Syn. SONAWARU.

GUTA-GUTA TO, グタグタ, *adv.* In a flabby limber manner.

GUTARI TO, グタリ, (idem.)

GUTATSZKI,*-ku,-ita*, グタツク, To be limber.

GUTTO, グツト, *adv.* In a flash, in an instant. — *nomi-komu*, swallowed it in one gulp, or understood it at once.

G'WAI-BUN, グワイブン, 外聞, *(hoka ye kikoyeru). n.* The hearing by others, or the publishing of anything which one would keep secret, or is ashamed of; publicly known, notoriety, reputation. — *ga warui*, ashamed to have others know. *Yose — ga warui*, stop, don't let others hear you. *Iye no — ni kakawaru*, to be injurious to the reputation of a family.

†G'WAISOFU, グワイソフ, 外祖父, *n.* Maternal grandfather.

G'WAN, グワン, 願, *(negai), n.* Desire, or request, made to the *kami;* prayer, supplication, vow. — *wo tateru*, to make supplication, or offer up a prayer. — *wo kakeru*, idem. — *wo hatasz*, to perform one's vow. — *hodoki wo szru*, idem. — *ga kanōta*, the prayer has been heard.

G'WAN-JITSZ, グワンジツ, 元日, *n.* New year's day, the first day of the year.

G'WAN-NIN, グワンニン, 願人, *n.* A begging priest.

G'WANRAI, グワンライ, 元來, *(moto yori), adv.* Originally, anciently, from the first, always before this. *Kono h'to — yowai*, this man has always been weak. — *tszyoi kuni naredomo ima wa yowaku-natta*, it was originally a powerful state, but it is now weak. Syn. ZEN-TAI, HON-RAI.

G'WAN-RI, グワンリ, 元利, *n.* Principal and interest.

G'WAN-SHO, グワンシヨ, 願書, *(negai-sho), n.* A petition in writing. — *wo sashi-ageru.*

G'WANYAKU, グワンヤク, 丸藥, *n.* A pill.

G'WATSZ, グワツ, 月, *(tszki), n.* Moon, month. *Shō-g'watsz*, the first month. *Ni* —, the second month. Syn. GETSZ.

H.

HA, ハ, 派, *n.* Sect, denomination, party. *Nani ha*, what sect? Syn. SHŪ-SHI, RUI.

HA, ハ, 齒, *n.* A tooth; the cutting edge, — *wo kui-shibaru*, to bite the teeth together; gnash the teeth. — *ga uku*, to set the teeth on edge. — *ga kawaru*, cutting the permanent teeth. — *ga hayeru*, to cut teeth. — *ga tatsz mono nai*, too hard for the teeth. (fig.) invincible. *Maye-ba*, incisors. *Kiba*, tusks. or canine teeth; *Okuba*, molars. *Mushi-ba*, a carious tooth. *Ireba*, a false tooth. *Nokojiri no ha*, the teeth of a saw. *Katana no ha*, the edge of a sword, or knife. *Ha wo nuku*, to extract a tooth. — *wo migaku*, to clean the teeth.

HA, ハ, 葉, *n.* A leaf. *Ki no* —, leaf of a tree. *Kono-ha*, (idem.)

HA-ARI, ハアリ, 羽蟻, *n.* A winged ant

HABA, ハバ, 幅, *n.* The breadth. — *wa ni shaku*, the breadth is two feet. *Haba wo szru*, to take up all the room, to crowd others out. *Maye-haba*. the breadth in front. *Yoko-haba*, breadth.

HABAKARI,*-ru,-tta*, ハバカル, 憚, *i. v.* To fear, dread, to be backward in. *Ayamatte aratamuru ni habakaru koto nakare*, having committed an error don't be afraid to reform it. *Habakari nagara*, while dreading, (a respectful phrase, used in apologizing for what one is about to say, or do,)= allow me, excuse me, beg pardon for. *Habakari de gozraimasz*, much obliged to you, thank you. *Habakari ni yuku*, to go to the privy. Syn. YENRIYO SZRU.

HABAKI, ハバキ, 刃卷, *n.* The metal ring which fastens the sword-blade to the handle.

HABAKI, ハバキ, 脛巾, *n.* Cloth-leggings. Syn. K'YAHAN.

||HABAMI,-*mu*,-*nda*, ハバム, 沮, *t. v.* To oppose, resist. Syn. KOBAMU.

HABARI, ハバリ, 刃針, *n.* A lancet.

||HABATTAI, ハバツタイ, Filled full, too large for the mouth. *Kuchi ni* —, the mouth stuffed full.

†HABERI,-*ru*,-*nu*, ハベル, 侍, *i. v.* Used only in books, and as a substantive verb, to be, to have, same as *sōrō*. *Ware seijin no soba ni haberite*, I being at the side of the sage. *Haberinu*, pret. *Haberan*, fut.

HABIKORI,-*ru*-*otta*, ハビコル, 蔓延, *i. v.* To spread, to multiply, increase, extend, disseminate, (fig.) to be arrogant, conceited. *Kusa ga habikotta*, the grass has spread all about. *Deki-mono ga habikotta*, the eruption has spread. *Ano h'to habikotte oru*, that man is puffed up, or, makes a swell. *Shūshi ga* —, the sect spreads. Syn. FUYERU, SHIGERU, HIROGARU,

HA-ŌKI, ハバウキ, 羽箒, *n.* A feather-brush.

HABUKARE,-*ru*,-*ta*, ハブク, 除, (pass. of *Habuku.*) *Ano h'to wa nakama wo habukareta*, that man has been left out of the company.

HABUKI,-*ku*,-*ita*, ハブク, 省, *t. v.* To lessen, diminish, curtail, to shorten, to reduce in number or quantity, to deduct, subtract, to abbreviate, to elide, (as a syllable) *Kadz wo habuku*, to lessen the number. *Tsziye wo* —, to reduce expenses. *Ji no kaku wo* —, to abbreviate a word, (in writing). *Ogori wo* —, to curtail extravagance in living. Syn. HERASZ, GENDZRU, GEN-SHŌ SZRU.

HABURI, ハブリ, 羽振, *n.* The flapping of wings, (fig.) power, influence, authority. — *ga yokunatta*.

HABUTAYE, ハブタヘ, 羽二重, *n.* A kind of silk fabric.

HACHI, ハチ, 八, *a.* Eight. *Hachi-jū*, eighty. *Jū-hachi*, eighteen. Syn. YATSZ.

HACHI, ハチ, 鉢, *n.* A bowl, pot, basin. *Atama no* —, the skull. *Wiyeki no* —, a flower-pot. *Hibachi*, a brazier. *Kibachi*, a wooden bowl.

HACHI, ハチ, 蜂, *n.* A bee. *Mitsz-bachi*, the honey-bee. *Kuma-bachi*, a humble-bee. — *no sz*, a bee-hive.

HA-CHIKU, ハチク, 淡竹, *n.* A kind of bamboo.

†HA-CHIKU, ハチク, 破竹, The splitting of a bamboo. *Ikioi, ha-chiku no gotoku*, a force, or power which breaks whatever opposes it, as easy as splitting a bamboo.

HACHI-MAKI, ハチマキ, *n.* A handkercehif tied around the head.

HACHI-MAN, ハチマン, 八幡, *n.* An Emperor of Japan, of the 16th dynasty, (about A. D. 275) in whose reign the Chinese classics, and art of weaving, were introduced into Japan. He is now worshiped as the god of war.

HACHI-MITSZ, ハチミツ, 蜂蜜, *n.* Honey.

HACHI-NIN-GEI, ハチニンゲイ, 八人藝, *n.* A ventriloquist.

HACHISZ, ハチス, 蓮, *n.* The Althea. Syn. MOKUGE.

HACHI-TATAKI, ハチタタキ, 鉢扣, *n.* A begging priest who goes about beating an iron bowl.

HADA, ハダ, 肌; *n.* Bare, naked; the skin, the body. *Kata-hada nuide shigoto wo szru*, baring one shoulder to work. *Moro-hada*, both shoulders bare. *Katana no hada*, the naked blade of a sword. *Ki no hada*, the body of a tree (the bark removed.) *Hada no kuroi h'to*, a man with a black skin. *Moto yori otoko no* — *wo furenai*, never had carnal intercourse with a man. Syn. HADAYE, KAWA.

HADA-GI, ハダギ, 肌著, *n.* A shirt, or garment worn next the skin. Syn. JIBAN.

HADAKA, ハダカ, 裸, Naked, bare. *Kimono wo nuide* — *ni naru*, to take off the clothes and become naked. *Ano h'to* — *de iru*, that man is naked.

HADAKARI,-*ru*,-*tta*, ハダカル, *i. v.* To straddle; to part the legs wide, or stretch the arms out. *Hadakari-tatsz*, to stand with the legs wide apart. Syn. FUMBARU.

HADAKE,-*ru*,-*ta*, ハダケル, 哆, *t. v.* To make bare, to uncover, to stretch apart, stretch open. *Futokoro wo* —, to bare the breast. *Me wo* —, to open the eyes. *Kuchi wo* —, to stretch open the mouth. Syn. HIRAKU.

HAĎANKIYŌ, ハダンキヤウ, 巴旦杏, *n.* An almond.

HADANUGI,-*gu*,-*ita*, ハダヌグ, 袒, *i. v.* To be bare or naked to the waist. *Hadanuite oru*, to be naked to the waist.

HADASHI, ハダシ, 徒跣, *n.* Bare-footed.

HADATSZKE, ハダツケ, 韉, *n.* The pad beneath the saddle.

HADAYE, ハダヘ, 膚, *n.* The bare skin, the surface, the body, (same as *Hada*). *Kin no hadaye*, a golden body.

HADE, ハデ, 葉手, Gay, fine, gaudy. showy. *Hadena kimono*, gay clothing. *Hadesha*, a person fond of dress, a fop, *Hade-ni kiru*, to dress gaily. Syn. HANAYAKA, DATE.

HADZ, ハツ, 巴豆, *n.* The Croton seeds. — *no abura*, Croton-oil.

HADZ, ハツ, *n.* The groove in an arrow, in which the bow-string fits. Should, ought, proper, must, obligation, duty, right. *Yahadz*, the groove of an arrow. *Kuru-hadz*, should come. *Szru-hadz no mono*, a thing that should be done. *Sō szru hadz ga nai*, he ought not to do so; it is what ought not to be done; not obliged to do so. *Hadz ga chigôta*, has failed to do what should have been done. *Sō iu hadz ga nai*, it cannot be so. Syn. DŌRI, BEKI, SUJI.

HADZKASHIGARI,*-ru,-tta*, ハツカシガル, 羞, *i.v.* To be bashful, modest, shy, ashamed. *Muszme ga hadzkashigarite sekimen szru*, the girl being bashful blushes.

HADZKASHII,-KI,-SHI, ハツカシイ, 耻, *a.* Ashamed, mortified, abashed. *Hadzkashikii koto*, a thing to be ashamed of.

HADZKASHIKU, ハツカシク, 耻, *adv.* — *omō*, to feel ashamed. Syn. MEMBOKUNAI.

HADZKASHIMI, ハツカシメ, 辱, *n.* Shame, insult.

HADZKASHIME,*-ru,-ta*, ハツカシメル, 辱, *t v.* To cause another to feel shame, to make ashamed.

HADZKASHISA, ハツカシサ, 耻, *n.* Shame.

HADZKI, ハツキ, 八月, *(hachi g'watsz)*, *n.* The eighth month.

HADZMI, ハツミ, *n.* Spring, bound, recoil, rebound, reaction, impulse. *Teppō wo hanasz hadzmi ni korolu*, to fall by the recoil of a gun. — *ni tobu*, to jump with a spring. *Dō-yu hadzmi de taorimash'ta rō*, how did you happen to fall? *Tachi-agaru hadzmi ni ashi wo fumi-szberashi aomukesama ni taoreta*, in rising up her foot slipped and she fell backwards.

HADZMI,*-mu,-nda*, ハツム, *i.v.* To rebound, to recoil, react, to spring. *Iki ya hadzmu*, to catch the breath.

HADZNA, ハツナ, 絆綱, *n.* A halter, or rope passed through the nose.

HADZRE, ハツレ, 端, *n.* The end. *Michi no* —, the end of a road. *Shiku no* —, the end of the town. Syn. TSZMARI, OWARI.

HADZRE,*-ru,-ta*, ハツレル, 外, *i.v.* To be out of the place in which it fits, to bè unfastened, unfixed, dislocated, disjointed, separated from, to fail, miss. *Shōji ga* —, the screen has slipped out of the groove. *To ga* —, the door is unhinged. *Ine ga* —, the crop has failed. *Kondo shibai ga* —, this time the theatre has been a failure. *Michi ni* —, to be out of the right way. *Mato wo ya ga* —, the arrow has missed the mark. *O hadzre*, a great failure.

HADZSHI,*-sz,-sh'ta*. ハツス, 外, *t.v.* To undo, to take out of the place in which it fits, to unfasten, unfix, disconnect, to avoid, to miss. *Shōji wo* —, to take a screen out of its place. *To wo* —, to unhinge a door. *Toki wo* —, to miss the time. *H'to wo* —, to avoid a person, to slip out of his way. *Yumi no tszru wo* —, to unbend a bow. *Mato wo* —, to miss the mark.

HA-FU, ハフ, 破風, *n.* The gable of a house.

HAGAI, ハガイ, 翼, *n.* The wings of a bird. Syn. HANE, TSZBASA.

HA-GAKI, ハガキ, 端書, *n.* A memorandum, a note.

HAGAMI, ハガミ, 咬牙, *n.* Gnashing the teeth. — *wo szru*, to gnash the teeth.

HAGANE, ハガネ, 鋼, *n.* Steel.

HAGARE,*-ru,-ta*, ハガレル, 被剝. Pass, of *Hagu*. To be stripped of one's clothes, &c., by another. *Tōzoku ni kimono wo hagareta*, to be stripped of clothes by thieves.

HAGASHI,*-sz,-sh'ta*, ハガス, 令剝, *t. v.* To strip off, flay, denude.

HAGATAME, ハガタメ, 歯固, *n.* Hardening the teeth as, by eating *mochi* on new year's day. — *no kuszri*, medicine for hardening the teeth.

HAGAYU,-KI,-SHI, ハガユイ, 歯癢, *a.* Itching of the teeth, setting the teeth on edge; the excitement felt in beholding a contest of any kind, and desire to help the weaker party; the desire to try one's hand at what others are doing; itching to interfere. *Hagayuku, adv.* Syn. MODOKASHIKU OMŌ,

HAGE, *-ru,-ta*, ハゲル, *i.v.* To be bald, bare, denuded, stripped, divested of covering. *Atama ga hageta*, head has become bald. *Nete iru futon ga hageta*, while sleeping the cover got off. *Uso ga hageta*, the lie is exposed. *Urushi ga hageta*, the varnish has peeled off. *Kabe ga hageta*, the plaster has fallen off. *Hage-atama*, a bald head. *Hage-yama*, a mountain bared of vegetation.

HAGEMASHI,*-sz,-sh'ta*, ハゲマス, 勵, *t. v.* To urge on, incite, stimulate, quicken, rouse up, to animate. *Ki wo hagemasz*, to rouse the spirits. *Koye wo* —, to speak with a low and stern voice.

HAGEMI,*-mu,-nda*, ハゲム, 勵, *i.v.* To be diligent, assiduous, ardent, zealous in doing, to exert one's-self, to strive at. *Shigoto wo hagemu*, to be diligent in business.

Hagende gakumon wo szru, to study with zeal. Syn. FUMPATSZ SZRU, SEI WO DASZ.

HAGEMI-AI,-*au*,-*atta*, ハゲミアヒ, 勵合, *i. v.* To strive together for, to vie with each other, to contend for.

HAGESHII,-KI, ハゲシイ, 烈, *a.* Violent, vehement, furious, severe, (of wind, rain, fire, waves, &c) Syn. TSZYOI, KIBISHII, ARAI.

HAGESHIKU,-U, ハゲシク, 烈, *adv.* idem.

HAGI, ハギ, 荻, *n.* The Lespedeza.

HAGI, ハギ, 脛, *n.* The shin. *Fukura-hagi*, calf of the leg. — *no hone*, the tibia, shin-bone.

HAGI,-*gu*,-*ida*, ハグ, 剝, *t. v.* To skin, flay, denude, to strip off the skin or clothes. *Kawa wo* —, to skin. *Kimono wo* —. *Oi-hagi ni au*, to get stripped of clothes (as by robbers.) Syn. MUKU, NUGU

HAGI,-*gu*,-*ida*, ハグ, *t. v.* To patch, splice, join together, to veneer. *Ita wo* —, to patch, or join boards together. *Hagi-hagi no kimono*, clothes made of patch-work. *Tate wo* —, to make a shield. Syn. TSZGU.

HAGI,-*gu*,-*ida*, ハグ, 矧, *t. v.* To feather an arrow. *Ya wo* —.

HA-GIRI, ハギリ, 切歯, *n.* Gritting, or gnashing the teeth. *Nete* — *wo szru*, to grit the teeth in sleep

HAGISHIRI, ハギシリ, 切歯, *n.* Gritting, or gnashing the teeth.

HAGO, ハゴ, 羽子, *n.* A kind of trap for catching birds. — *wo kakeru*, to set a trap.

HAGO, ハゴ, 羽子, *n.* A shuttle-cock. — *wo tszku*, to strike the shuttle-cock.

HAGOITA, ハゴイタ 羽子板, *n.* A battle-dore.

HAGOKUMI,-*mu*,-*nda*, ハゴクム, 育, *t. v.* To rear, to bring up (by feeding,) to support. *Shō-ni wo* —, to rear up a child. Syn. SODATERU, YASHINŌ.

HAGOROMO, ハゴロモ, 羽衣, *n.* The feather garments worn by Tennin.

HA-GOTAYE, ハゴタエ, 歯應, *n.* Hard to the teeth, hard to chew. *Tōfu wa* — *ga nai*, *Tōfu* is easy to chew.

HAGUKI, ハグキ, 齦, *n.* The gums.

HAGUMA, ハグマ, 白熊, *n.* A white bear, a white tassel fixed on the head of a spear.

HAGURE,-*ru*,-*ta*, ハグレル, 逸, *i v.* To be stripped off, made bare, denuded, uncovered, separated. *Kimono ga* —, to be stripped of one's clothes. *Tszre ni hagurete h'tori de kita*, losing my companion by the way, I have come alone. *F'ton ga* —, the quilt is off. Syn. SORERU.

HAGURI,-*ru*,-*tta*, ハグル, 撥, *t. v.* To turn over a covering, to turn up, or uncover. *Hon wo haguru*, to turn over the leaves of a book. *Futon wo hagutte miru*, to turn down the bedquilt and look. Syn. MAKU.

HAGURO, ハグロ, 鐵醤, *n.* The black dye used by Japanese women in staining the teeth. Syn. KANE.

HAGUSA, ハグサ, 歯瘡, *n.* Tares, weeds. *Ine no* — *aru ga gotoku*, like tares mixed with rice.

HAHA, ハハ, 母, *n.* Mother. *Haha-bun*, like a mother, the part of a mother. *Haha-kata no shinrui*, relations on the mother's side. Syn. OKKA SAN, O-FUKURO

HA-HON, ハホン, 零本, *n.* An imperfect book; a broken set of books.

HAI, ハヘ, 蠅, *n.* A fly.

HAI, ハイ, 唯, Exclam. used in answering, same as *He*.

HAI, ハイ, 灰, *n.* Ashes. *Ishi-bai*, (stone ashes,) lime. *Hai wo kaki-narasz*, to level the ashes (in a brazier.)

HAI, ハイ, 肺, *n.* The lungs. *Hai no zō*, the lungs. *Hai no kin-shō*, inflammation of lungs.

HAI, ハイ, 盃. The numeral for full, a wine cup. *Ippai*, once full. *Ni hai*, twice full. *Sambai*, three times full. *Cha wan shi-hai no midz*, four tea cups full of water. — *wo fukumu*, to drink wine. *Tai-hai*, a large cup.

HAI, ハイ, 拜, (*ogamu.*) To bow, worship, (used in compound words meant to convey respect.) — *wo szru*, to bow, worship.

HAI,-*au*,-*atta*, ハフ, 匍匐, *i. v.* To creep crawl. *Hatte kuru*, to creep and come.

HAI-AGARI,-*ru*,-*tta*, ハヒアガル, 這上, *t. v.* To ascend by creeping, creep up.

HAI-BOKU, ハイクボ, 敗北, (*make-nigeru.*) Routed, put to flight, dispersed.

†HAI-BŌ, ハイバウ, 敗亡, (*make-horobiru.*) Routed, scattered and destroyed.

†HAI BUKI, ハイブキ, 灰吹, *n.* Silver ingots.

HAI-BUN, ハイブン, 配分, (*kubari-wakeru*) To distribute, apportion, divide.

HAI-CHŌ, ハイチヤウ, 蠅帳, *n.* A safe to protect food from insects.

HAI-DATE, ハイダテ, 佩楯, *n.* Armor for the thighs.

HAI-DEN, ハイデン, 拜殿, *n.* A hall for worship in front of a *Miya*.

†HAI-DOKU, ハイドク, 拜讀, (*itadaki-yomu.*) To reverently read.

HAI-DOKU, ハイドク, 蠅毒, *n.* A fly-poison.

HAI-DZMI, ハイズミ, 掃墨, *n.* Black paint made of powdered charcoal.

HAI-FUKI, ハイフキ, 灰吹, *n.* A section of bamboo used for blowing the tobacco ashes into.

†HAI-GA, ハイガ, 拜賀, (*go shū-gi moshi-ageru.*) Felicitation, or congratulation to superiors.

†HAI-GAKU, ハイガク, 廢學, (*Gakumon wo yameru.*) To abandon study, cease learning. *Hisashiku — itashimash'ta,* I have long ago ceased to study.

†HAI-GAN, ハイガン, 拜顔, To meet, see.

HAI-GUN, ハイグン, 敗軍, (*make-ikusa.*) Routed, defeated. — *ni naru*; — *szru.*

†HAI-GŪ,*–szru,* ハイグウ, 配偶, To unite, as in marriage.

†HAI-JIN, ハイジン, 廢人, *n.* An invalided or disabled person.

HAI-JIN, ハイジン, 俳人, *n.* A teacher, or professor of Haikai.

†HAI-JU, ハイジユ, 拜受, (*itadaku*) To respectfully receive (from a superior.)

HAI-KA, ハイカ, 配下, *n.* The body of troops, or of persons, under the command of another, a command, subjects. *Waga haika,* my command.

HAI-KAI, ハイカイ, 俳諧, *n.* A kind of verse or poetry of 17 syllables.

HAI-KAN, ハイカン, 肺肝, (lit. lungs and liver,) fig. — *wo kudaku,* to do with great labor, or pains. — *wo mi-nuku,* to see through a person.

†HAI-K'WAI,*–szru,* ハイクワイ, 徘徊, (*tachi-motōru*) To go about, wander about, going hither and thither, prowling about. *Kono goro wa tō-zoku hai-k'wai sh'te oru,* at present robbers are prowling about. Syn. BURA-TSZKU, URO-TSZKU.

HAI-KEN, ハイケン, 拜見, To look, see, (respectful to be used only in speaking of one's self.) — *itashitō gozarimasz.* I would like to see it, if you please. *O-zashiki wo — sh'tai,* I wish to see your parlor.

HAI-KOMI,*–mu,–nda,* ハイコム, 這込, *t.v.* To creep into.

HAI-MATOI,*–ō,–otta,* ハイマトフ, 蔓絡, *t.v.* To creep around wind around, (as a vine.)

†HAI-MEN, ハイメン, 拜面, (*o me ni kakaru.*) To see, or meet.

†HAI-MIYŌ, ハイミヤウ, 俳名, *n.* The fictitious name subscribed to a *Hai-kai.*

HAI-NOBORI,*–ru,–tta,* ハイノボル, 這登, To creep up, ascend by creeping (as a snake.)

†HAI-RAN, ハイラン, 拜覽, Same as Haiken.

HAI-REI, ハイレイ, 拜禮, *a.* The worship of a divine being. *Kami wo — szru,* to worship God.

HAIRI,*–ru,–tta,* ハイル, 入, *i.v.* To enter, go into. *Yu ni —,* to take a hot bath. *Iye ni —,* to go into the house. *Hebi ga ana ye haitta,* the snake has gone into the hole. *Nakama ye, —* to enter a company. *Me ni gomi ga haitta,* has got dust in his eye. Syn. IRU.

HAI-RIYŌ,*–szru,* ハイリヤウ, 拜領, To receive as a present from a master, or lord. Syn. KIMI YORI CHŌ-DAI SZRU KOTO, ITADAKI, MORAU KOTO.

†HAI-RU, ハイル, 配流, To banish, exile. *Kimi ni hairuserareta,* banished by his Prince. Syn. SHIMA NAGASHI.

HAISATSZ, ハイサツ, 配札, (*fuda wo kubaru,*) *n.* A charm distributed to the worshipers of a temple.

HA-ISHA, ハイシヤ, 齒醫, *n.* A dentist.

HAI-SHAKU, ハイシヤク, 拜借, (*o kari mōsz,*) Borrowing. *Hon wo — szru,* to borrow a book. *Kane wo — szru,* to borrow money. *Haishaku kin,* borrowed money. Syn. KARIRU, SHAKU YŌ SZRU.

†HAI-SHI,*–szru,–sh'ta,* ハイシ, 配, To compare, to pair, to match, to equal; to exile, transport a criminal. *Sono toku hi no hikari ni haisz,* his virtue was like the light of the sun. Syn. NARABU, AWASERU, NAGASZ.

†HAI-SHI,*–sz,–sh'ta,* ハイス, 廢, *t.v.* To leave off, abandon, give up doing, desert; to put away a wife. (only of Tenshi,) to dethrone. *Gakumon wo haiszru,* to give up study. *Kurai wo —,* to depose from rank. Syn. STERU, YAMERU.

†HAI-SHI,*–sz,–sh'ta,* ハイス, 敗, *i.v.* To be defeated, routed, lose the game. *Teki no gunzei ga haish'ta,* the army of the enemy was defeated. Syn. MAKERU, YABURERU.

†HAI-SHI,*–sz,–sh'ta,* ハイス, 拜, *t.v.* To bow, to worship. *Kami wo, —* to worship God. Syn. OGAMU, OJIGI SZRU.

HAI-SHO, ハイシヨ, 配所, *n.* A place of banishment, (for nobles,) — *de yonda uta,* poetry composed while in banishment. Syn. NAGASARETE ORU TOKORO.

†HAI-SŌ,*–szru,* ハイソウ, 敗走, To flee away defeated. Syn. MAKETE NIGERU.

HAI-TŌ,*–szru,* ハイタウ, 配當, (*kubari-ateru.*) *t.v.* To distribute, apportion, allot. Syn. HAIBUN.

†HAI-YETSZ, ハイエツ, 拜謁, To look, to see.

HAI-YŌ, ハイヨウ. 肺癰, *n.* Pulmonary consumption.

HAI-ZAI, ハイザイ, 配劑, *n.* A consultation of physicians, — *szru*, to consult. *Isha atszmatte haizai sh'ta*, the doctors met and consulted together.

HAJI, ハヂ, 耻, *n.* Shame, disgrace, reproach, — *wo kaku*, to be put to shame, to be disgraced. *Tō-zoku wo haji to szru*, considered thieving to be disgraceful, — *wo szszgu*, to wipe away a reproach. *Haji wo kakusz*, to hide one's shame. *H'to ni — wo kakaseru*, to insult, or put another to shame. Syn. CHIJOKU.

HAJI,*-ru,-ta*, ハヂル, 耻, *i. v.* To be ashamed, to feel ashamed. *Ano h'to ga hajita*, he is ashamed. *Hajite kuni wo chikutensh'ta*, ashamed he absconded from his country. Syn. CHIJOKU NI OMŌ.

HAJIKAMI, ハジカミ, 生姜, *n.* Ginger. Syn. SHŌGA.

HAJIKE,*-ru,-ta*, ハジケル, *i. v.* To burst open (from inside pressure.) *Meshi wo tanto kutte wa hara ga hajikeru zo*, I have eaten so much I feel ready to burst. *Tawara ga hajiketa*, the bag has burst. Syn. HAZERU, SABAKERU.

HAJIKI, ハジキ, *n.* A spring.

HAJIKI,*-ku,-ita*, ハジキ, 彈, *t. v.* To jerk, to snap, to cause to move with a sudden spring. *Yubi wo* —, to fillip; to snap tho finger. *Soroban wo* —, to move the balls of the abacus with a quick motion. *Midz wo hajiku yō ni abura wo hiku*, grease it so that it will turn off water. *Ito wo* —, to twang a string.

HAJIKI-GANE, ハジキガネ, 彈金, *n.* The hammer of a gun-lock, a spring.

HAJIMARI, ハジマリ, 始, *n.* Beginning, commencement of a course of action or being, origin. *Toshi no* —, beginning of the year. *Fushin no* —. *Nin-gen no* —.

HAJIMARI,*-ru,-tta*, ハジマル, 始, *i. v.* To be begun, commenced, originated. *Fushin ga* —, the building is commenced. *Ima yomi hajimatta*, has now commenced reading.

HAJIME, ハジメ, 始, *n.* The beginning, the first of anything, the origin, the commencement, *Toshi nō hajime wo gan-jitsz to iu*, The beginning of the year is called *ganjitsz*. *Kore wo hajime to szru*, begin here, or do this first. *Hajime-owari*, the beginning and ending, first and last. Syn. SHOTE.

HAJIME,*-ru,-ta*, ハジメル, 始, *t. v.* To begin, to commence. *Fushin wo hajimeta*, have commenced to build. *Yomi hajimeta*, has begun to read. *Kore kara hajimete miyo*, begin at this place to look.

HAJIMETE, ハジメテ, 初, *adv.* For the first time. — *o me ni kakaru*, I see you for the first time. — *yokohama ye kita*, this is my first visit to *Yokohama*. Syn. HATSZ NI.

†HAJIRAI,*-ō,-ōta*, ハヂラフ, 含羞, *i.v.* To feel ashamed, bashful. Syn. HADZKASHIGARU.

HAJISHIME,*-ru,-ta*, ハヂシメル, 辱, *t. v.* To make another feel ashamed, to disgrace. Syn. HADZKASHIMERU, HAJI WO KAKASZRU.

HAKA, ハカ, 墓, *n.* A grave, tomb. — *wo horu*, to dig a grave.

HAKA, ハカ, *n.* The amount, or quantity of work done, the result accomplished. — *ga szkunai*, have accomplished but little. — *ga ōi*, the amount of work done is large. — *ga yuku*, to accomplish a great deal. *H'tori shigoto wa — ga yukanu*, the work of one person does not accomplish much.

HAKABA, ハカバ, 墓場, *n.* A cemetery.

HAKABAKASHII,-KI, ハカバカシイ, *a.* That which accomplishes much. — *tegara mo nai*, a skill that accomplishes but little.

HAKABAKASHIKU, ハカバカシク, *adv.* idem.

HAKACHI, ハカチ, 墓地, *n.* A cemetery, grave yard.

HAKADORI,*-ru,-otta*, ハカドル, *i. v.* To accomplish much. *Shigoto ga taisō hakadorimash'ta*, you have done a great deal of work. Syn. KACHI GA AKU.

HAKAI, ハカイ, 破戒, Breaking the commandments of Buddha. — *no sō*, a priest who transgresses the five commandments.

HAKA-JIRUSHI, ハカジルシ, 墓標, *n.* A tombstone.

HAKAMA, ハカマ, 袴, *n.* The loose trowsers worn by *Samurai*, — *wo haku*, to wear trowsers. — *no machi*, the crotch of the trowsers; — *no koshi*, the board on the back of the trowsers.

HAKAMAGI, ハカマギ, 著袴, *n.* The ceremony of putting on the *hakama* for the first time, at the age of 5 years, always on the 15th day of the 11th month.

HAKAMA-JI, ハカマヂ, 袴地, *n.* The cloth of which *Hakama* are made.

HAKA-MORI, ハカモリ, 墓守, *n.* The sexton of a cemetery.

HAKANAI,-KI,-SHI, ハカナイ, 墓無, *a.* Very small, fleeting, evanescent. *Hakanaki koye*, almost inaudible voice. *Natsz mushi no hi ni iru yori hakanaki waza nari*, it was more evanescent than the life of a summer insect burnt in the fire. — *inochi*, fleeting life.

HAKANAKU, ハカナク, 無墓, *adv.* id. — *naru*, to die, pass away. — *kiyuru*, to vanish quickly away. Syn. MOROI.

HAKARADZ, ハカラズ, 不圖, *(futo)*, *adv.* Suddenly, unexpectedly. Syn. OMOWADZ.

HAKARAI,*–au,–atta*, ハカラフ, 計, *t. v.* To transact, manage, to do. Syn. TORI-HAKARAU, ATSZKAU.

HAKAREI, ハカラヒ, 計, *n.* Management, administration, transacting. *Watakushi no — ni dekimasen*, I cannot do it.

HAKARI, ハカリ, 秤, *n.* A weighing beam, scales, steelyard — *no fundō*, the weight of a steelyard. — *no tembin*, the beam of a steelyard. — *no o*, the cord by which scales are suspended. — *no mi*, the marks on a steelyard. — *ni kakete miru*, to weigh and see how much.

HAKARI,*–ru,–tta*, ハカル, 量, or 度, *t. v.* To weigh, to measure, to estimate, to reckon, to plot, contrive, to consult, to deceive. *Umi no fukasa wo hakaru*, to measure the depth of the sea. *Hoshi no kadz wa hakari-shirarenai*, the stars cannot be numbered. *Kome wo masz de hakaru*, to measure rice. *Tszmori-hakaru*, to estimate, reckon. *Teki wo —*, to deceive the enemy. *Tszma ni —*, consult with one's wife. Syn. TSZMORU.

HAKARIGOTO, ハカリゴト, 謀, *n.* A plan, scheme, artifice, stratagem. — *wo megurasz*, to devise a plan. Syn. BŌKEI.

HAKARI-KIRI,*–ru,–tta*, ハカリキル, 量盡, To level off the top of any thing measured, to make it even with the measure.

HAKARI-MUSHI, ハカリムシ, 尺蠖, *n.* A caterpillar. Syn. SHAKUTORI-MUSHI.

HAKASE,*–ru,–ta*, ハカセル, *t. v.* (The caust. of *Haki.*) To cause to vomit, or spit out; to make flow out, to discharge, sell off. To make put on, to make to sweep. *Ike no midz wo —*, to let out the water from a pond. *Kuszri wo nomasete hakaseru*, to vomit a person with medicine. *Nimotsz wo hakaseru*, to clear out goods (by selling off.) *Tabi wo —*, to make one put on his stocking.

HAKASE, ハカセ, 博士, *n.* The title of a learned man, a professor. Syn. MONO-SHIRI.

HAKAWARA, ハカハラ, 墓原, *n.* A cemetery.

HAKE,*–ru,–ta*, ハケル, 吐, The pass. or potential mood of *Haki.* Can spit, or vomit. *Tozai wo nonde mo hake-masen*, although I have taken an emetic I cannot vomit.

HAKE,*–ru,–ta*, ハケル, 穿, Pot. mood of *Haki.* Can wear, or put on. *Kono tabi wa chīsai kara hake-masen*, I can't wear these socks, they are too small. *Kono momohiki wa hakeru ka*, can you wear these trowsers?

HAKE,*–ru,–ta*, ハケル, 掃, Poten. mood of *Haki.* Can sweep. *Yoku hakeru hōki*, a broom that can sweep well.

HAKE, ハケ, 刷毛, *n.* A brush, (made of bristles,) the Japanese cue, (from its resemblance to a brush.) *Nori-bake*, a paste-brush. *Hake-saki wo chirasz*, to spread the end of the cue (in disorder.)

HAKE,*–ru,–ta*, ハケル, 消售, *i. v.* To be sold off, cleared out, (as goods.) *Ito ga haketa*, the silk is all sold.

HAKE, ハケ, *n.* The sale, or demand of goods. *Kono shina wa — ga yoi*, this article is in great demand, or sells well.

HAKEKUCHI, ハケクチ, 售口, *n.* Demand, sale. — *ga yoi*, good demand, or sale. *Kono setsz ito wa hagekuchi ga nai*, there is now no demand for silk.

HAKI,*–ku,–ita*, ハク, 吐, *t.v.* To spit, vomit. *Tszbaki wo —*, to spit. *Chi wo —*, to vomit, or spit blood. *Haki-dasz*, to spit out. *Haki-kakeru*, to spit on.

HAKI,*–ku,–ita*, ハク, 穿, *t. v.* To wear, put any thing on the feet or legs, as, *Hakama*, *Kiyahan*, *Momo-hiki*, *Tabi*, *Zōri*, *Geta*, *Ashida*, *Kutsz*, *&c.*

HAKI,*–ku,–ita*, ハク, 佩, *t. v.* To hang from the belt. *Tachi wo —* to gird on the sword.

HAKI,*–ku,–ita*, ハク, 掃, *t. v.* To sweep, brush. *Hōki de tatami wo —*, to sweep the mat with a broom. *Gomi wo haki-dasz*, to sweep out the dirt. *Szmi ye haki-yoseru*, to sweep into a corner.

HAKI-DAME, ハキダメ, 掃溜, *n.* A place where dirt and rubbish are thrown.

HAKI-HAKI, ハキハキ, *adv.* Smart, quick, active in doing, plain, distinct. — *to sh'te miyeru*, distinctly seen. Syn. SADAKA-NI, RACHI GA AKU.

HAKIKI, ハキキ, 羽利, Influential, having authority, weight of character. powerful. *Ano h'to Yokohama de hakiki da*, he is an influential man in Yokohama. *Kane ga dekitareba ha ga kīte kita*, when a person becomes rich he becomes powerful. *Ha ga kikanu Daimio*, a prince of no power. Syn. IKIOI NO TSZYOI.

HAKI-MONO, ハキモノ, 履, *n.* Shoes, articles worn on the feet.

†HA-KIYAKU,*–szru*, ハキヤク, 破却, To break, destroy.

HAKKA, ハクカ, 薄荷, *n.* Peppermint.

HAKKAN, ハクカン, 白鷴, *n.* The silver pheasant.

HAKKE, ハツケ, 八卦, *n.* The eight diagrams.

HAKKEI, ハツケイ, 八景, *n.* The eight celebrated views in Japan.

HAKKIRI, ハツキリ, *adv.* Clear, plain, distinct, clean, perfectly. *Kono han wa — to sh'te iru,* the type are very distinct. *— to sh'te miyeru,* clearly seen. *— to sh'ta tenki,* clear weather. *Mada — to naorimasen,* not yet perfectly well. Syn. FUM-MIYŌ.

†HAKKIYŌ, ハツキヤウ, 發狂, To become insane.

HAKKŌ, ハツカウ, 發向, (*Yuku.*) Going. *Yedo ye itsz — itashimas'ka,* when are you going to Yedo?

HAKKŌ,-*szru*, ハツカウ, 發行, *t v.* To be prevalent, most general, fashionable. *Korori ga — shimasz,* Cholera is prevalent. *Hadena nari ga — szru,* Gay clothing is fashionable. Syn. HAYARU.

HAKO, ハコ, 箱, *n.* A box. *— wo sasz,* to make a box. *— ni tszmeru,* to pack in a box. *— ni ireru,* to put into a box. *Hakoiri muszme,* a young girl who is carefully kept at home.

HAKOBASE,-*ru*,-*ta*, ハコバセル, 令運, caust. of *Hakobi.* To make or order another to convey, to transport. *Nimotsz wo h'to ni hakobaseru,* to get a person to transport goods.

HAKOBE, ハコベ, 蘩縷, *n.* A kind of medicinal plant.

HAKOBI,-*bu*,-*nda*, ハコブ, 運, *t. v.* To transport, to convey, to move from one place to another. *Nimotsz wo fune de —,* to transport goods by ship. *Ashi wo —,* to walk. Syn. OKURU, UTSZSZ.

HAKOBI, ハコビ, 運, *n.* Transportation, conveyance, moving. *Ashi no — ga warui,* walking is difficult. *Ichi nin de ichi nichi hakobi wa dono kurai,* how much can one man carry in a day. *Chi no — ga nibui,* the circulation of the blood is languid.

HAKU, ハク, see *Haki.*

†HAKU, ハク, 白, (*shiroi.*) White, clear, shining. *Haku-hatsz,* grey hair. *Hakumai,* cleaned rice. *Hakuye,* white clothes. *Hakuchō,* 白鳥, a white bird. *Haku-jitsz,* 白日, shining sun.

HAKU, ハク, 箔, *n.* Foil, leaf, as, *Kimpaku,* gold-leaf. *Gimpaku,* silver foil. *Szdz-haku,* tin foil. *Kin wo haku ni utsz,* to beat gold into leaf. *— wo osz,* to plate.

†HAKUBO, ハクボ, 薄暮, *n.* The evening. Syn. TAZOKARE.

†HAKUBO, ハクボ, 伯母, *n.* Aunt. Syn O-BA.

HAKUCHIU, ハクチウ, 白晝, *n.* Noon, middle of the day. Syn. HIRU.

HAKU-CHŌ, ハクチヤウ, 白張, *n.* White clothes, such as are worn by the servants of a Kuge, or at festivals.

†HAKU-GAKU, ハクガク, 博學, (*hiroku manabu,*) *n.* Learned, versed in literature. Syn. MONOSHIRI.

HAKU-HIYŌ, ハクヒヤウ, 薄冰, (*uszki kōri,*) *n.* Thin ice. *— wo fumu no gotoku,* like walking on thin ice, dangerous.

†HAKU-JIN, ハクジン, 白刃, *n.* A glittering sword. *— wo hiramekasz,* to brandish a sword.

HAKU-JŌ, ハクジヤウ, 薄情, Without natural affections, unfeeling, callous, cruel, insincere, false-hearted. Syn. NASAKE-NAI.

HAKUJŌ,-*szru*, ハクジヤウ, 白狀, *t. v.* To confess, acknowledge. *Tsmi wo —,* to confess a crime. Syn. ZANGE SZRU.

†HAKU-MAKU, ハクマク, 白膜, *n.* The conjunctiva.

†HAKU-NAISHŌ, ハクナイシヤウ, 白內障, *n.* Cataract of the eye.

HAKU-RAI, ハクライ, 舶來, *n.* Foreign productions, articles brought from foreign countries. *Kore wa — de gozarimas.*

HAKU-RAKU, ハクラク 伯樂, *n.* A horse doctor.

HAKUSEKKŌ, ハクセツカウ, 白雪糕, *n.* A kind of confectionary.

†HAKU-SHIKI, ハクシキ, 博識, (*hiroku shiru.*) *n.* Learned.

†HAKU-TAI, ハクタイ, 白苔, *n.* A white fur on the tongue. *Sh'tani — ga aru,* the tongue is furred.

HAKU-YA, ハクヤ, 箔匠, *n.* A gold beater,

HAMA, ハマ, 濱, *n.* The sea beach, or coast.

HAMA-BE, ハマベ, 濱, *n.* idem.

HAMA-GURI, ハマグリ, 蛤, *n.* A clam. Syn. UMUGI.

HAMARI,-*ru*,-*tta*, ハマル, *i. v.* To be put, fitted, or entered into anything, to be in, immersed in, addicted to. *Wa ga yubi ni hamatta,* the ring is on the finger. *Shōji ga shikii ni —,* the sash is in the groove. *Midz ni —,* to enter the water. *Nedzmi ga midz-game ni —,* a rat has got into the water-jar. *Bakuchi ni —,* to be addicted to gambling. Syn. HAIRU, OBORERU.

HAMATE, ハマテ, 濱手, *n.* Near the sea beach.

HAMBERU, ハンベル, see *Haberi.*

HAMBITSZ, ハンビツ, 半 櫃, *n.* A small trunk.

HAMBUN, ハンブン, 半 分, *n.* Half. — *ni kiru,* cut into halves, cut in two. — *wo chōdai,* give me half. Syn. NAKABA.

HAME, ハメ, 板 壁, *n.* A weather-board, clapboard. — *wo utsz,* to weather-board.

HAMERI,-*ru*,-*ta*, ハメル, *t. v.* To fit anything in its place, to put into, (as a screen, door, drawer, &c.) To immerse, or plunge into; to cheat, take in. *Shōji wo hameru,* to put a screen into its place. *Yubi ni wa wo* —, to put a ring on the finger. *H'to wo* —, to cheat a person. *Inu wo kawa ye* —, to put a dog into the river.

†HAMETSZ, ハメツ, 破 滅, Broken and destroyed.

‖HAMI,-*mu*,-*nda*, ハム, 食, *t. v.* To eat. *Meshi wo* —, to eat rice. *Sakana ga ye wo* —, the fish takes the bait. *Uwabami h'to wo* —, the anaconda swallows men. Syn. KURŌ, TABERU.

HAMI-DASHI,-*sz*,-*sh'ta*, ハミダス, 喰 出, *t. v.* To project, or be forced out from between two surfaces, or from inward pressure.

HAM-MAI, ハンマイ, 飯 米, *(meshi gome,) n.* Rice used for eating. 半 枚, half a sheet.

HAM-MEN, ハンメン, 半 面, *(katadzra.) n.* Half the face. — *no yedz,* a profile likeness.

HAM-MIYŌ, ハンメウ, 斑 猫, *n.* The spanish fly, Cantharidis.

†HAM-MO, ハンモ, 繁 茂, *(shiyeru,)* Luxuriant, exuberant.

HAMO, ハモ, 鱧, *n.* A kind of eel.

†HA-MON,-*szru*, ハモン, 破 門, To expel from school, dismiss a scholar; to break off the relation of teacher and pupil.

HA-MONO, ハモノ, 刃 物, *n.* Edgéd tools; cutting instruments.

HAM-PA, ハンパ, 半 端, *n.* A part, fragment, fraction. Syn. HASH'TA.

†HAM-PAKU, ハンパク, 頒 白, Grizzled, a mixture of white and black hair. Syn. SHIRAGA-MAJIRI.

†HAMPI, ハンピ, 半 臂, *n.* A kind of coat with short sleeves.

†HAM-PON, ハンポン, 版 本, *n.* A printed book.

†HAM-PUKU, ハンプク, 半 腹, *n.* Half way up a mountain. — *ni noboru.*

HAMU, ハム, See *Hami.*

HAMUSHA, ハムシヤ, 端 武 者, *n.* Common soldiers.

HAN, ハン, 判, *n.* A seal; stamp, (板,) a block for printing. — *wo szru,* to print. — *wo osz,* to stamp, seal. — *ni okosz,* to cut in blocks for publishing. — *wo horu,* to cut a seal or stamp, to cut characters on blocks. Syn. IN.

HAN, ハン, 奇, Odd. — *no kadz,* an odd number. *Chō-han,* even and odd. Syn. KI.

HAN, ハン, 半, Half. *Ichi ri han,* a mile and a half. *Han-michi,* half a mile. *Han-ya,* half the night. *Hanshi hanshō,* half dead and alive.

HANA, ハナ, 初, *(hajime,) n.* The first, beginning. *Kono nasz wa hana da,* this is the first pear of the season.

HANA, ハナ, 鼻, *n.* The nose. — *no ana,* the nostrils. — *no saki,* the tip of the nose; — *szji,* the contour of the nose; — *wo kamu,* to blow the nose; — *wo szszru,* to snuff up the nose; — *wo kujiru,* to pick the nose; — *wo nejiru,* to pull the nose; — *wo tszmamu,* to hold the nose; — *wo sogu,* to cut off the nose; — *wo tszku,* to strike the nose against; — *ni kakeru,* to put on the nose, to vaunt one's self. — *ga tareru,* to run at the nose; — *ga takai h'to,* a proud, haughty person; — *no mizo,* the raphe under the nose. *Hana-shiru,* mucous of the nose; — *ga fusagaru,* the nose is stopped up. *Yama no* —, a bluff or spur of a mountain.

HANA, ハナ, 花, *n.* A flower, blossom. — *no utena,* the calix of a flower; — *no tszbomi,* a flower bud; — *no kuki,* the germ of a flower; — *no jiku,* the stem of a flower; — *wo tszmu,* to pluck a flower; — *wo kazaru,* adorn with flowers; — *no fu,* a botanical work. — *wo ikeru,* to keep flowers alive in water. *Hana no,* adj, beautiful. —*szgata,* a beautiful form; — *kambase,* beautiful face.

HANA, ハナ, 纏 頭, *n.* A present of money, clothes &c., made to a wrestler, play-actor, musician, dancing girl &c., in admiration of their performances. — *wo yaru.*

HANABANASHII,-KI, ハナバナシイ, 花 花, *a.* Beautiful, handsome, glorious, splendid, admirable, (mostly of actions) — *ikusa,* a glorious battle. Syn. RIPPA, KIREI, MIGOTO.

HANABANASHIKU,-*u*, バナバナシク, 花 花 *adv.* idem.

HANA-BASAMI, ハナバサミ, 花鋏, *n.* Flower scissors.

HANABI, ハナビ, 花 火, *n.* Fireworks. — *wo ageru,* to set off fireworks.

HANABIRA, ハナビラ, 葩, *n.* The petals of a flower.

HANACHI,*–tsz,–tta*, ハナツ, 放, *t. v.* To let go, set free, liberate, same as *Hanashi.*

HANADZRA, ハナヅラ, 鼻面, *n.* Tip of the nose.

HANA-GAMI-BUKURO, ハナガミブクロ, 鼻紙袋, *n.* The wallet in which paper for wiping the nose is carried. Syn. KAMI-IRE.

HANA-GAI, ハナガイ, 鼻拳, *n.* The nose ring for oxen.

HANA-GAWA, ハナガハ, 紲革, *n.* The part of the bridle which crosses the nose; the nose-strap.

HANA-GE, ハナゲ, 鼻毛, *n.* The hair in the nostrils.

HANA-HADA, ハナハダ, 甚, *adv.* Very, extremely. — *katai*, very hard. — *yoi*, good. — *ilukashii*, exceeding strange. Syn. ITO, ITATTE.

HANAHADASHII,*–KI*, ハナハダシイ, 甚敷, *a.* Extreme, utmost, greatest, most. *Jadō kore yori hanahadashiki wa nashi*, there is no more pernicious way than this. *Itami wa* —, the pain is extreme. Syn. GOKU, SHIGOKU, HIDOKU.

HANAHADASHIKU,*–U*, ハナハダシク, 甚敷, *adv.* id.

HANAHIYU, ハナヒユ, 五色莧, *n.* Portulacca.

HANAIKE, ハナイケ, 花瓶, *n* A vessel for holding water and flowers to keep the latter in bloom; a flower vase.

HANA-IKI, ハナイキ, 鼻息, *n.* Nose-breathing. — *ga arai*, breathes loud through the nose.

HANAIRO, ハナイロ, 縹色, *n.* A blue color.

HANAJI, ハナヂ, 血鼻, *n.* Bleeding at the nose.

HANA-KAGO, ハナカゴ, 花籠, *n.* A flower basket.

HANA-KUSO, ハナクソ, 鼻垢, *n.* The hard mucous which collects in the nose.

HA-NAMI, ハナミ, 歯并, *n.* The order or arrangement of the teeth. — *ga warui*, the teeth are irregular.

HANA-MI, ハナミ, 花見, *n.* Looking at flowers. — *ni mairimash'ta*, gone on an excursion to see the flowers.

HANA-MORI, ハナモリ, 花守, *n.* The keeper of a flower garden.

HANA-MUKE, ハナムケ, 餞別, *n.* A present to a bride leaving her father's house, to a person setting out on a journey, or to one who has returned to his home. Syn. SEMBETSZ.

HANAMUKO, ハナムコ, 花婿, *n.* A bridegroom.

HANA-O, ハナヲ, 鼻緒, *n.* The thong, or strap by which sandals are fastened to the feet. — *wo szgeru*, to fix the thong in the sandal. — *ga kireta*, the strap is broken.

HANAODZRE, ハナヲズレ, 鼻緒摺, *n.* Chafed by the thong of the sandal.

HANARE,*–ru,–ta*, ハナレル, 離, *i.v.* Separated, parted, sundered, loose, opened, (*t.v.*) To leave, to separate from, to part. *Uma ga hanareta*, the horse is loose. *Tszgime ga* —, the joint is parted. *Oya ni hanareta*, to be left by one's parents. *Oya wo hanarete hōkō wo szru*, to leave one's parents and go out to service. *Iye wo hanarete hi wo take yo*, kindle the fire away from the house. *Hanare-gatashi*, hard to part. *Hanarenu-naka*, indissoluble relation. Syn. HEDATERU, WAKARERU.

HANARE-BANARE, ハナレバナレ, 離離, *adv.* Separated, apart, scattered, — *ni natte oru*, to live apart, or separately.

HANARE-JIMA, ハナレジマ, 孤島, *n.* A solitary island.

HANARE-YA, ハナレヤ, 離屋, *n.* A house apart or distant from others.

HANASHI,*–sz,–sh'ta*, ハナス, 放, *t.v.* To let go, to set free, to loosen, liberate, let off, to discharge, let fly. *Teppō wo* —, to fire a gun. *Ya wo* —, to let fly an arrow. *Te wo* —, to let go the hand. *Me wo hanasadz miru*, to look without taking off the eyes.

HANASHI,*–sz,–sh'ta*, ハナス, 談, *t.v.* To say, to utter, speak. talk, tell. *Mukashi no koto wo* —, to tell an old story. *Biyōnin no yōdai wo hanashi nasare*, tell me how the sick man is. *Haha ye itte hanase*, go and tell your mother. Syn. KATARU, IU.

HANASHI, ハナシ, 話, *n.* A saying, talk, story, a tale. *Mukashi no* —, an ancient story. *Okashii hanashi*, a funny story. *Usobanashi*, a lie, a fiction. *Otoshi-banashi*, a comical story, an anecdote.

HANASHI-AI,*–au,–atta*, ハナシアフ, 談合, *i.v.* To talk together, to converse.

HANASH'KA, ハナシカ, *n.* A story-teller. Syn. KŌSHAKUSHI.

HANASHIRU, ハナシル, 鼻洟, *n.* Thin mucous from the nose.

HANA-TAKE, ハナタケ 鼻茸, *n.* A nasal polypus.

HANATARE, ハナタレ, 鼻垂, *n.* Snotty nose.

HANATSZ, ハナツ, See *Hanachi.*

HANA-TSZKURI, ハナツクリ, 花匠, *n.* A maker of artificial flowers; a flower gardener.

HANA-UTA, ハナウタ, 鼻歌, *n.* Singing in a low voice, humming a tune. — *wo utau,* to hum a tune.

HANAYAKA, ハナヤカ, 華美, Beautiful, handsome, elegant, gay, showy, — *na shōzoku,* gay clothing. Syn. RIPPA, KIREI, HADE.

HANA-YOME, ハナヨメ, 花婦, *n.* A bride.

HANA-ZAKARI, ハナザカリ, 花盛, Full-bloom, — *ni natta,* to be in full-bloom. *Jū-roku sh'chi no muszme wo — to iu,* a young lady of 16 or 17 is said to be in her full-bloom.

HANDA, ハンダ, 盤陀, *n.* Tin (in block.)

HAN-DAI, ハンダイ, 飯臺, *n.* A dining table.

HAN-DAN, ハンダン, 半端, *n.* Half a piece of cloth.

HANDAN,*-szru,* ハンダン, 判斷, *t.v.* To explain, solve, interpret,. *Kikkiyō wo —,* to determine whether any event is lucky or unlucky. *Yume wo —,* to interpret a dream. *Nazo wo —,* to solve a riddle. Syn. TOKU, KANGAYERU, HANJIRU.

HANDŌ, ハンダウ, 飯桶, *n.* A bucket for carrying boiled rice.

HANE, ハネ, 羽, *n.* A wing, a feather, the paddles of a paddle-wheel. — *wo hirogeru,* to expand the wings.

HANE, ハネ, 撇, *n.* The right or left oblique down stroke of a Chinese character..

HANE, ハネ, 跳, *n.* Particles of mud spattered about, — *ga agaru,* the mud spatters.

HANE,*-ru,-ta,* ハネル, 駻, *i.v.* To prance, as a horse, (驋), to flounce, flounder, leap, spring, bounce (跳), To spatter, splash about, (as mud.) *M'ma ga haneru,* the horse prances. *Sakana ga —,* the fish leaps. *Doro ga haneru,* the mud spatters. Syn. ODORI-AGARU, TOBU.

HANE,*-ru,-ta,* ハネル, 撥, 跳, *t.v.* To splash, to spatter, to cut off (the head.) *Doro wo —,* to spatter mud. *Kubi wo —,* to cut off the head. *Ni wo —,* to throw goods overboard.

HANE-AGARI,*-ru,-tta,* ハネアガル, 撥揚, *i.v.* To spring, leap, or bound up. *Mari ga —,* the ball bounces. *Uwo midz kara —,* the fish leaps out of the water.

HANE-DZKUROI, ハネヅクロイ, *n.* Preparing to fly, the position of a bird about to fly.

HANEGUKI, ハネグキ, 翅管, *n.* A quill.

HANE-KAKE,*-ru,-ta,* ハネカケル, 撥掛, *t. v.* To splash, to spatter.

HANE-KAYE,*-ru,-ta,* ハネカヘル, 跳反, *i. v.* To spring, bounce, or leap back, rebound. *Hane-kayesz,* to make rebound, &c.

HANE-MAWARI,*-ru,-tta,* ハネマワル, 跳廻, *i. v.* To prance, leap, bound, or dance around.

HANE-NOKE,*-ru,-ta,* ハネノケル, 撥除, *t. v.* To throw out, or jerk out.

HANE-OKI,*-ru,-ta,* ハネオキル, 撥起, *i.v.* To jump or spring up, (from lying down.)

HANE-TSZRUBE, ハネツルベ, 桔槹, *n.* A well bucket swung on the end of a pole.

HAN-GETSZ, ハンゲツ, 半月, *n.* Half a month, half-moon, or semicircular in shape.

HANGI, ハンギ, 版木, *n.* A block for printing.

HANGIYA, ハンギヤ, 板木屋, *n.* A block-cutter.

HAN-GIYŌ, ハンギヤウ, 判形, *n.* A seal mark, the impression left by a seal.

HANJI,*-ru,-ta,* ハンジル, 判, *t. v.* To solve, interpret, (a dream.) *Yume wo —.*

HANJIMONO, ハンジモノ, *n.* Anything represented by emblems or symbols, or concealed under the names of natural objects, an emblem.

HAN-JŌ, ハンデフ, 半疊, *n.* Half a mat, half a quire.

HAN-JŌ, ハンジヤウ, 繁昌, Prosperous, thriving, flourishing, increasing in wealth and trade. — *szru,* to be prosperous, &c. — *na tochi* a busy, thriving place. Syn. NIGIYAKA.

†HANJUKU, ハンジユク, 半熟, *(nama niye.)* Half cooked.

HAN-KA, ハンカ, 繁華, see *Hank'wa.*

HANKA, ハンカ, 半可, Affecting, or putting on the appearance of learning,

HAN-KAN, ハンカン, 反間, By stratagem to produce discord, or ill-feeling between a prince and his ministers, or parties who are allied together. — *no hakarigoto,* a stratagem planned for such a purpose.

HANKI, ハンキ, 半期, *n.* Half a year.

HANKIN, ハンキン, 半金, *n.* Half the money or price of anything.

HAN-KIRI, ハンキリ, 半切, *n.* A kind of letter paper.

HANKIU, ハンキウ, 半弓, *n.* A small bow.

HAN-KŌ, ハンカウ, 版行, *n.* A block used in printing.

HAN-KU, ハンク, 半工, *n.* Half a day's

work. — *kakarimash'ta*, has required half a day's work.

HANKW'A, ハンクワ, 繁華, Prosperous, thriving, bustling, (of places.) — *na tochi*.

HAN-NIN, ハンニン, 半人, *n*. Half a day's work, a pimp, procurer.=*zegen*. — *hodo kakatta*, have done half a day's work.

HAN-NIN, ハンニン, 判人, *n*. An indorser, surety, bondsman, security. Syn. UKEAI NIN, SHŌNIN.

HAN-NIYA, ハンニヤ, 般若, *n*. The canonical books of the Buddhists.

HAN-NOKI, ハンノキ, 榛, *n*. A kind of tree, black alder? The Alnus Japonica.

HANSAN, ハンサン, 半產, *n*. An abortion, miscarriage.

HANSHI, ハンシ, 半紙, *n*. A kind of paper.

†HAN-SHIN, ハンシン, 反臣, *n*. A rebel, revolted servant. Syn. MUHON NO KERAI.

HANSHŌ, ハンシヤウ, 半鐘, *n*. A small bell, a fire-bell.

HAN-SH'TA, ハンシタ, 版下, *n*. The copy used in cutting blocks.

HAN-SH'TA-KAKI, ハンシタカキ, 版下書, *n*. The person who writes the copy by which blocks are cut.

HAN-SZRI, ハンスリ, 版摺, *n*. A printer.

HAN-TA, ハンタ, 繁多, Busy, actively employed, hard at work, full of business. — *ni tori-magereru*, to be distracted with a press of business. *Hanta ni tszki hata to shitsznen itashimashta*, I have so much to do that I quite forgot it. Syn. ISOGASHII, SEWASHII, YŌ-JI ŌI.

HAN-TEN, ハンテン, 半體衣, *n*. A kind of coat.

HAN-TO, ハント, 半途, *adv*. Half-way, half-done, half-through. *Ikusa wa hanto de yameru*, to stop fighting while only half through. *Shigoto wa hanto de yameru*, to stop work when only half done.
Syn. CHIUTO.

†HAN-TAI, ハンタイ, 反對, Opposite, contrary, antithesis, contrast. *Kitsz to kiyō wa hantai nari*, lucky and unlucky are the opposites of each other. Syn. URA-OMOTE, URAHARA.

HANUKE, ハヌケ, 齒脫, *n*. A person who has lost his teeth.

HANUKEDORI, ハヌケドリ, 羽脫鳥, *n*. A moulting bird.

HANUKI, ハヌキ, 齒抜, *n*. Tooth forceps, a person who extracts teeth.

HAN-YŌ, ハンヨウ 繁用, Busy, full of business. Syn. HANTA.

HAORI, ハオリ, 羽織, *n*. A coat. — *wo kiru*, to put on a coat. — *no yeri*, the collar of a coat. — *no sode*, the sleeve of a coat. — *no machi*, the gore of a coat. — *no himo*, the cord which fastens a coat

HAPPA, ハツパ, Eight times eight; sixty four.

HAPPI, ハツピ, 法被, *n*. A kind of coat worn by the followers of Nobles.

†HAPPIYŌZAI, ハツペウザイ, 發表劑, *n*. A diaphoretic medicine.

HAPPŌ, ハツパウ, 八方, Eight sides, all about. *Shi hō happō*, on all sides.

†HAPPU, ハツプ 髮膚, (*kami to hadaye*). Hair and skin. *Shin-tai happu kore wo fubo ni uku*, our whole body is gotten from our parents.

HARA, ハラ, 原, *n*. A moor, prairie, a wild uncultivated region.

HARA, ハラ, 腹, The belly, abdomen. (fig.) Mind, conscience, heart. — *no uchi*, in the belly; (fig.) in the heart, mind. — *ga tatsz*, to be angry. — *wo kiru*, to commit suicide, by cutting the belly. — *ga heru*, to be hungry. *Hara wo szyete kakaru*, to be determined. *Hara ni aru*, have it in mind. *Hara ga naru*, to have a rumbling in the belly. — *ga kudaru*, the bowels are loose. *Sh'ta hara*, the hypogastric region. *Yoko-hara*, the side of the belly. — *wo mesaruru*, to commit suicide. *Hara no warui h'to*, a bad hearted man. *Hara ga au*, to be of the same mind. *Hara no nai*, pusillanimous. *Hara no ōki h'to*, magnanimous.

HARA-ATE, ハラアテ, 腹當, *n*. A cloth worn over the chest and belly; armor for covering the abdomen.

HARABAI,-*au*,-*atta*, ハラバフ, 匍, 匐, *i.v.* To lie on the belly. *Harabatte neru*, or, *Harabai ni neru*, to sleep lying on the belly.

HARA-DACHI, ハラダチ, 腹立, *n*. Anger.

HARA-GAWARI, ハラガハリ, 異腹, Different mother, but the same father. — *no kiyōdai*, half-brothers.

HARA-GOMORI, ハラゴモリ. 腹籠, *n*. *Kono ko ga* — *no toki ni*, while pregnant with this child.

HARA-GONASHI ハラゴナシ, 消食, *n*. Promoting digestion, assisting digestion. — *ni achi-kochi aruku*, to walk about to promote digestion. — *ni shigoto wo szru*, to work in order to assist digestion.

HARA-HARA TO, ハラハラ, *adv*. The sound of rustling, as of silk, or of leaves blown by the wind, the sound of tears dropping, of or crying. *Namida wo* — *nagasz*.

HARAI,-*au*,-*atta*, ハラフ, 拂, *t.v.* To clear away, drive away, expel, to pay.

Kane wo —, to pay money. *Kanjō wo* —, to settle an account. *Gomi wo* —, to dust, clear away dirt. *Akuma wo* —, to expel evil spirits. *Wazawai wo* —, to clear off misfortune. *Harai-mono*, an article not wanted, and for sale. *Harai-gwa no warui h'to*, a person slow in paying debts. *Atari wo* —, to clear away all about him. *Temaye wo* —, to clear all before him. *Harai-dasz*, to drive out, expel. *Harai-komu*, to sweep into (as a pan.)

HARAI, ハラヒ, 拂, *n.* A payment. — *wo szru*, to make a settlement of a bill.

HARAI, ハラヒ, 祓, *n*, Sintoo prayers. — *wo yomu.*

HARA-ITAMI, ハライタミ, 腹痛, *(fuku-ts'ū)*, *n.* Colic, belly-ache.

HARA-KAKE, ハラカケ, 掛腹, *n.* A cloth covering tied over the chest and abdomen.

†HARA-KARA, ハラカラ, 同腹, *n.* Brethren.

HARAKUDARI, ハラクダリ, 泄瀉, *n.* A diarrhæa, bowel-complaint.

HARA-MAKI, ハラマキ, 腹卷, *n.* Armor for the abdomen.

HARAMASE,*-ru,-ta*, ハラマセル, 令孕, Caust of *Harami.*

HARAMI,*-mu,-nda*, ハラム, 孕, *i.v.* To be pregnant, to conceive, to be with child. *Onna ga haranda*, the woman is pregnant. *Harami onna*,a pregnant woman. *Haramanu kuszri*, medicine to prevent conception. *Harami-dzki*, month of conception. Syn. MIGOMORU, NINSHIN SZRU, KWAININ, KWAI-TAI SZRU.

HARAMI, ハラミ, 孕, *n.* Pregnancy, conception.

HARA-OBI, ハラオビ, 孕帶, *n.* A belly-band.

HARARAGO ハララゴ, 魚子, *n.* Fish-roe, (of salmon.)

HARASE,*-ru,-ta*, ハラセル, 令張, Caust. of *Hari.* To cause or order to spread, &c.

HARASHI,*-sz,-sh'ta*, ハラス, 霽, *t.v.* To clear away, drive away, dispel; to swell. *Ikidōri wo* —, to dispel anger.

||HARASZJINA, ハラスジナ, 腹筋, *a.* Laughable, ridiculous.

HARAU, or HARŌ, ハラウ, See *Harai.*

HARAWATA, ハラワタ, 腸, *n.* The bowels, intestines.

†HARAYA, ハラヤ, 輕粉, *n.* A preparation of mercury used as a medicine.

HARE,*-ru,-ta*, ハレル, 晴, *i.v.* To be cleared away, dispelled; clear, open, without concealment, public. *Ame ga* —, the rain has cleared off. *Tenki ga hareta*, the weather has cleared off. *Utagai ga* —, doubts are dispelled. *Tenka harete no shōbai*, a business publicly carried on. *Tenka harete omaye no niyōbo*, publicly known to be your wife.

HARE,*-ru,-ta*, ハレル, 腫, *i.v.* Swollen. *Me ga* —, eye is swollen. *Hare agaru*, to swell up.

HARE, ハレ, 腫, *n.* The swelling. *Hare ga h'ita*, the swelling is gone done.

HARE-BARE, ハレバレ, 晴晴, *adv.* Clear, bright, open, unclouded, easy in mind. *Ki wo kitta* — *sh'ta*, when the trees are cut away it becomes clear. *Yō wo szmash'te* — *sh'ta*, by doing up one's business to feel free and easy.

HAREBARESHII,-KI, ハレバレシイ, 晴晴, *a.* Fine, splendid. — *hataraki da*, a splendid action.

HAREBARESHIKU,*-u*, ハレバレシク, 晴晴, *adv.* id.

HAREGI, ハレギ, 公服, *n.* Dress-clothes worn on going out, or on special occasions.

HARE-MONO, ハレモノ, 腫物, *n.* A swelling, boil.

HARE-NA, ハレナ, 晴, *a.* Fine, grand, illustrious, eminent, heroic (used in praising.) — *waza*, a daring, heroic feat.

HAREYAKANA, ハレヤカナ, *a.* Clear, unclouded, bright; cleared, open. — *tenki*, clear weather; — *tokoro*, an open place cleared of trees.

HARI, ハリ, 針, *n.* A needle; pin. — *no me*, the eye of a needle. — *no saki*, the point of a needle. — *wo utsz*, or — *wo hineru*, to insert the needle in acupuncture.

HARI, ハリ, 莿, *n.* A thorn. Syn. TOGE.

HARI, ハリ, 梁, *n.* The heavy beams in a roof. Syn. UTSZBARI.

†HARI, ハリ, 玻璃, *n.* Crystal, glass.

HARI,*-ru,-tta*, ハル, 貼, *t. v.* To paste over, nail over. spread over. *Kami wo* —, to paper (a wall.) *Ita wo* —, to board over, weather-board. *Atama wo* —, to slap the head (of another,) (fig.) to take a certain percentage from the wages of those whom one has aided in finding employment, to squeeze. *Shōji wo haru*, to paper a screen. *Kara-kasa wo* —, to make an umbrella.

HARI,*-ru,-tta*, ハル, 張, *t. v.* To stretch, to extend. to display, exhibit, (*i.v.*) To be swollen, distended. *Yumi wo* —, to bend a bow. *Nawa wo* —, to stretch out a line. *Ami wo* —, to spread a net. *Mise wo* —, to display the wares of a shop. *Omote wo* —, to endeavour to keep up appearances. *Iji wo* —, to be obstinate. *Ki wo* —, to strain every nerve. *Seken wo* —, to strive to make a good show in the world. *Me wo* —, to stare. *Chichi ga* —, the breasts are distended. (with milk.)

HARI-AI,*-au,-atta*, ハリアフ, 張合, *i. v.* To rival, to vie with each other, emulate.

HARI-AI, ハリアヒ, 張合, *n.* Emulation, rivalry, a striving together.

HARI-BAKO, ハリバコ, 針箱, *n.* A needle-box.

HARI-DASHI,*-sz,-sh'ta*, ハリダス, 張出, *t.v.* To jut out, protrude, swell out, stretch out.

HARI-GANE, ハリガネ, 銅線, *n.* Wire.

HARI-I, ハリイ, 針醫, *n.* A needle doctor, one who performs acupuncture.

HARI-IRE, ハリイレ, 針入, *n.* A needle case.

HARI-ITA, ハリイタ, 張板, *n.* The board on which clothes are starched and dried after washing.

HARI-KO, ハリコ, 張籠, *n.* A box made of paper.

HARI-KOMI,*-mu,-nda*, ハリコム, 張込, *i. v.* To stretch a point, to do what requires some effort. *Hari-konde kau*, to buy when the price is rather more than one can afford.

HARI-ME, ハリメ, 貼目, *n.* The edge or seam formed by joining paper together.

HARINUKI, ハリヌキ, 張拔, *n.* Articles made of a kind of papier-mache.

HARI-SAKE,*-ru,-ta*, ハリサケル, 張裂, *i. v.* To tear by stretching. *Atama ga hari-sakeru yō ni itai*, head aches ready to burst.

HARI-TSZKE, ハリツケ, 磔, *n.* Punishment by crucifixion and spearing.

HARI-TSZKE,*-ru,-ta*, ハリツケル, 貼附, *t. v.* To paper, to paste over with paper.

HARI-YABURI,*-ru,-tta*, ハリヤブル, 張破, *t. v.* To tear by stretching.

HARU, ハル, See *Hari*.

HARU, ハル, 春, *n.* The spring.

HARU-BARU, ハルバル, 遙遙, *adv.* Far, distant. — *to kuru*, to come from afar.

HARUBI, ハルビ, 鞁, *n.* A saddle-girth.

HARUKA, ハルカ, 遙, Far, distant, remote, very, much. — *ni miyeru*, seen from a distance. — *ni masaru*, much better, far better. — *ni hedatsz*, widely separated. — *mukashi*, romote antiquity.

HARUMEKI,*-ku,-ita*, ハルメク, Spring like, having the appearance of spring. *Atataka de harameite mairi-mash'ta*, owing to the warmth it begins to look like spring.

HARUSAME, ハルサメ, 春雨, *n.* Spring rains.

HASAMARI,*-ru,-tta*, ハサマル, 夾, *i.v.* To be between two other things. *Ha no aida uwo no hone ga hasamatta*, a fish bone has got between the teeth.

HASAMI, ハサミ, 剪刀, *n.* Scissors, — *de kiru*, to cut with scissors.

HASAMI,*-mu,-nda*, ハサム, 插, *t.v.* To take, place, or hold between two other things. *Hashi de uwo wo* —, to take fish with chop-sticks. *Hana wo hon no aida hasande oku*, to place a flower between the leaves of a book. *Hibashi de hi wo hasamu*, to take up fire with tongs. *Hon wo waki no sh'ta ni* —, to hold a book under the arm.

HASAMI-BAKO, ハサミバコ, 挾箱, *n.* A black box fixed to each end of a pole, and carried over the shoulder; (fig.) the mumps.

HASAMI-IRE,*-ru,-ta*, ハサミイレル, 插入, *t.v.* To take up with sticks and put in; to interleaf, interline.

HASAMI-KIRI,*-ru,-tta*, ハサミキル, 挾切, *t.v.* To cut with scissors.

HASAMI-UCHI, ハサミウチ, 挾伐, *n.* An attack on each flank at the same time. — *ni szru*, to attack on each flank.

HASE,*-ru,-ta*, ハセル, 馳, *t.v.* To ride fast, to run. *m'ma wo* —, to gallop a horse. *Hase-atszmaru*, 馳集, to run together. *Hase-kayesz*, 馳返, to cause to ride back. *Hase-kayeru*, 馳返, to ride back. *Hase-kitaru*, 馳來, to come fast on horse-back. *Hase-mawaru*, 馳廻, to ride around. *Hase-mukau*, 馳向, to ride to meet. *Hase-tszku*, 馳付, to ride and overtake.

HASEN, ハセン, 破舩, *n.* A shipwreck. — *sh'ta*, shipwrecked.

HASHI, ハシ, 橋, *n.* A bridge. — *wo kakeru*, to throw a bridge across. *Hashi-bushin szru*, to build or repair a bridge. — *wo wataru*, to cross a bridge. — *no ran-kan*, the rail of a bridge. *Ipponbashi*, a bridge made of one stick. *Hashi-dzme*, end of a bridge.

HASHI, ハシ, 箸, *n.* Chop-sticks. — *de hasamu*, to take up with chop-sticks. — *wo toru*, to take the chop-sticks.

HASHI, ハシ, 咮, *n.* The bill of a bird. Syn. KUCHIBASHI.

HASHI, ハシ, 端, The edge, margin, brink, side. A small piece, fragment. *Ito no* — the end of a thread. *Michi no* —, side of a road. *Tszkuye no* —, the edge of a table. *Hashijika* near the edge. *Arasoi no hashi wo hiki-dasz*, to commence a dispute. Syn. FUCHI.

HASHI-BASHI, ハシバシ, 四陲, *n*. Four sides.

HASHIGO, ハシゴ, 梯, *n*. A ladder. — *no ko*, the rungs of ladder.

HASHI-GUI, ハシグイ, 橋杭, *n*. The wooden piles which support a bridge.

HASHI-ITA, ハシイタ, 橋板, *n*. Floor of a bridge.

HASH'KA, ハシカ, *n*. The beard of wheat. Syn. NOGI.

HASH'KA, ハシカ, 痲疹, *n*. The measles, — *wo szru*, to have the measles. Syn. MASHIN.

HASHI-KAKE, ハシカケ, 橋掛, *n*. A mediator. — *szru*, to mediate.

HASHIKE,*-ru,-ta*, ハシケル, *t.v.* To unload, or distribute cargo from a ship. *Ni wo* —, to unload goods.

HASH'KE-BUNE, ハシケブネ, *n*. A cargo-boat.

HASH'KOI,-KI,-SHI, ハシコイ, *a*. Shrewd, active, smart, cunning. Syn. KASH'KOI, RIKŌ.

HASH'KOKU, ハシコク, *adv*. idem.

HASHIRA, ハシラ, 柱, *n*. A post, pillar, column. — *wo tateru*, to set up a post. *Hashira kakushi*, pictures or inscriptions hung against the pillars of a house to hide them. *Hashiradate wo szru*, to set up the frame work of a house.

HASHIRASHI,*-sz,-sh'ta*, ハシラス, 令走, caust. of *Hashiri*. To make to run, sail, &c.

HASHIRI,*-ru,-tta*, ハシル, 走, *i.v.* To run, to move fast, to flee. To flow, or sail fast. *M'ma ga* —, the horse runs. *Fune ga* —, the ship sails. *Midz ga* —, the water flows. *H'to ga* —, the man runs. *Chi ga* —, the blood flows. *Katana ga hashitta*, the sword has dropped out of the sheath. *Hashiri-agaru*, 走上, to run up. *Hashiri-kayeru*, 走返, to run back. *Hashiri-ideru*, 走出, to run out. *Hashiri-koyeru*, 走越, to run across. *Hashiri-kudaru*, 走下, to run down. *Hashiri-mawaru*, 走廻, to run around. *Hashiri-mukau*, 走向, to run to meet. *Hashiri-tobu*, 走飛, to run. *Hashiri-yoru*, 走倚, to run near. Syn. KAKERU, TOBU.

HASHIRI, ハシリ, 走, *n*. The first fruits, or first caught fish of the season, first goods. The running, flow, movement. *Kono to no — ga yoi*, this door moves easily.

HASHIRI-GAKI, ハシリガキ, 走書, *n*. Fast writing, a running hand.

HASHIRI-KURABE, ハシリクラベ, 走競, *n*. A race.

HASH'TA, ハシタ, 半, *n*. A fraction, fragment, an imperfect part. — *ni naru*, to be imperfect, broken, insufficient. — *ga deru*, there is a little over, a fragment too much. Syn. FU-SOKU, HANTA.

HASH'TAME, ハシタメ, 婢女, *n*. A female servant.

‖HASH'TANAI,-KI,-SHI, ハシタナイ, *a*. Low, mean, of humble condition.

‖HASH'TANAKU, ハシタナク, *adv*. idem.

HASHIYAGASHI,*-sz,-sh'ta*, ハシヤガス, 令燥, caust. of *Hashiyagi*. To cause to dry. Syn. KAWAKASZ.

HASHIYAGI,*-gu,-ida*, ハシヤグ, 乾, *i.v.* To be dry, arid, parched. *Tszchi ga* —, the ground is dry. *Kuchi ga* —, the mouth is dry. Syn. KAWAKU.

HASHIYAGI, ハシヤギ, 燥, *n*. Dryness, aridity.

HA-SHŌFU, ハシヤウフ, 破傷風, *n*. Lock-jaw, Tetanus.

HASHORI,*-ru,-tta*, ハシヲル, 端折, *t.v.* To shorten, to reduce in length, abbreviate. *Shiri wo* —, to tuck up the skirt of the long coat, by sticking it under the girdle. *Bun wo* —, to shorten a writing. Syn. HABUKU, MIJIKAKU SZRU.

HASON, ハソン, 破損, *n*. Broken, damaged, injured. — *szru*, to damage, injure. — *wo tszkurō*, to repair a damaged place.

†HAS-SAKU, ハツサク, 八朔, *n*. The first day of the eighth month.

HAS-SAN, ハツサン, 八算, *n*. The rule of division, in arithmetic.

HASSHI,*-sz,-sh'ta*, ハツス, 發, *t. v.* To cause to go out or issue forth, to rouse, to open out, (as a flower) manifest, to display, appear. *Gunzei wo* —, to send forth an army. *Toki no koye wo* —, to raise a shout. *Netsz wo* —, to have a fever. *Ikari wo* —, to get angry. Syn. OKOSZ, HIRAKU.

HASSHI-TO, ハツシト, *adv*. The sound made by the mouth in striking, chopping, &c. — *utsz*.

HASSHŪ, ハツシウ, 八宗, The eight Buddhist sects, viz., *Ritsz*, 律, *Gusha*, 俱舍. *Jō-jitsz*, 成實. *Hossō*, 法相. *San-ron*, 三論. *Ten-dai*, 天台. *Ke-gon*, 花嚴. *Shin-gon*, 眞言, of these only *Ten-dai*, and *Shin-gon* remain at the present day. Besides these there are now. *Zen-shū*, 禪宗, *Jō-do* 淨土, *Mon-to* 門徒, *Hokke*, 法華, *Ji-shū* 時宗, some of which are again subdivided.

HASZ, ハス, 蓮, *n.* The lotus plant. — *no hana*, the lotus-flower. — *no utena*, the calyx of the lotus flower. — *no ike*, a lotus pond. Syn. RENGE.

HASZRU, ハスル, Same as *Hashiru*.

HATA, ハタ, 畑, *n.* A field. (of upland.) *Hatamono*, a thing grown in the upland fields.

HATA, ハタ, 旗, *n.* A flag, ensign. — *wo ageru*, to hoist a flag. — *no sao*, a flag-staff. *Hata sh'ta*, under the flag, under the command of.

HATA, ハタ, 機, *n.* A loom. — *wo heru*, to arrange the yarn in a loom. — *wo oru*, to weave. *Kinu-bata*, a silk-loom; *Hata-mono*, a weaving machine.

HATA, ハタ, 傍, *n.* The side, near by. *I-do no hata ye*, to the side of the well, or near to the well. *Hata no h'to*, by-standers. *Hata kara kuchi wo dasz-na*, by-standers must not put in a word. *Kawa no* —, the bank of a river.
Syn. KATAWARA, SOBA, HOTORI.

HATACHI, ハタチ, 廿歳, Twenty years old.

HATAGASHIRA, ハタガシラ, 旗頭, *n.* The name of a military officer.

HATAGO, ハタゴ, 旅籠, *n.* Stopping to rest and lunch while traveling, the fare charged for lodging. *Hiru-hatago*, stopping to lunch at noon. *Hatago wa yaszi*, the fare is cheap.

HATAGOYA, ハタゴヤ, 旅籠屋, *n.* An inn, hotel.

HATA-HATA, ハタハタ, 蟆螋, *n.* A grasshopper.

HATA-HIRO, ハタヒロ, 機尋, *n.* Seven fathoms = 28 feet.

HATA-JIRUSHI, ヘタジルシ, 旗號, *n.* A flag, ensign.

HATAKARI, *-ru, -tta*, ハタカル, See *Hadakari*.

HATAKE, *-ru, -ta*, ハタケル, See *Hadake*.

HATAKE, ハタケ, 圃, *n.* A field, vegetable garden.

HATA-KEGASA, ハタケガサ, 疥癩, *n.* A kind of skin disease.

HATAKI, *-ku, -ita*, ハタク, 拂, *t. v.* To beat with a stick, to strike. *Gomi wo* —, to beat out the dust. *Tatami wo* —, to beat a mat, to clean it. Syn. TATAKU, UTSZ,

†HATA-MATA, ハタマタ, 將又, *conj.* A word used in letters when commencing another subject, = again, moreover.
Syn. KATSZ-MATA.

HATAMEKI, *-ku, -ita*, ハタメク, 硍, *i. v.* To thunder, to make a loud noise, as thunder. *Rai ga hatameki-wataru*, the thunder rolls. Syn. NARU, HIBIKU, TODOROKU.

HATA-MOTO, ハタモト, 旗下, *n.* A feudatory of the *Shōgun*.

HATARAKASHI, *-sz, -sh'ta*, ハタラカス, 令働, Caust of *Hataraki*. To make to work, set to work, to employ, to conjugate.

HATARAKI, *-ku, -ita*, ハタラク, 働, *t. v.* To work, to labor, to do, commit, to move, to act, perform. *Kagiyō wo* —, to work at one's business. *Nogiyō wo* —, to work at farming. *Motto hataraki nasare*, (to a merchant,) cheapen it. *Yoku hataraite ikura*, what is the lowest you can sell it at? *Htotsz hataraite mimashō*, I will try and see what I can do. *Buma wo* —, to commit a blunder.

HATARAKI, ハタラキ, 働, *n* Action, movement, working, operation, deed, function. — *no aru h'to*, a clever, intelligent person. *Sode nagakute te no hataraki ga warui*, if the sleeve is long it impedes the motion of the arm.

HATARAKI-KOTOBA, ハタラキコトバ, 動詞, *n.* A verb.

HATARI, *-ru, -tta*, ハタル, *t. v.* To demand payment, to dun. *Kane wo hataru*, to demand the payment of money. *Mishin wo* —, to ask for the payment of a debt. *Waruku* —, to dun immoderately.
Syn. SAI-SOKU SZRU, SEMERU.

HATASADZ, ハタサズ, 不果, neg. of *Hatashi*.

HATA-SAKU, ハタサク, 畑作, *n.* The products of the farm, the crop. *Ko-toshi no* —, this year's crop.

HATASHI, *-sz, -sh'ta* ハタス, 果, *t. v,* To finish, to end, complete, fulfill, perform. *Gwan wo* —, to fulfill a vow. *Nen-rai no kokoro-gake aihatashi mōshi soro.*
Syn. SZMASZ, OWARU.

HATASH'TE, ハタシテ, 果, *adv.* To result, turn out, in the end, ultimately. — *iu tōri ni natta*, it turned out just as I said. — *oboshi-meshi no tōri*, it resulted just as I said. Syn. AN-NO-GOTOKU.

HATASHI-AI, *-au, -atta*, ハタシアヒ, 果合, *t. v.* To kill each other.

HATATAKI, ハタタキ, 鼓翅, *n.* Clapping the wings. *Niwatori* — *wo sh'te toki wo tszkuru*, the cock claps his wings and crows.

HATA-TO, ハタト, 礑, *adv.* The sound of clapping the hands, or of a sudden blow. *Ima sara kayō ni on kotowari kudasarete wa hata-to tō-waku tszkamatszri soro*, owing to your having made known your refusal at this late moment I am suddenly put to great inconvenience. — *te wo utsz*, striking the hands together in sudden perplexity. — *waszreru*, there! I forget all about it.

HATAYE, ハタヘ, 二十重, Twenty fold.

HATE, ハテ, 果, *n.* The end, termination, result, conclusion, extremity. *Michi no* —, end of a road. — *wa dō naru ka shire nai*, I don't know what the result may be. *Hate nashi*, without end. *Hate wo omoi-yaru*, to consider the end.
Syn. OWARI, SHIMAI.

HATE,*-ru,-ta*, ハテル, 果, *i. v.* To end, terminate, conclude, to die. *Hi wa kurehateta*, the sun is set. *Biyō-nin ga hateta*, the sick man is dead. *Tszki-hateta*, entirely used up. Syn. OWARU, SHIMAU.

HATESHI, ハテシ, *n.* The end, termination, conclusion, limit. — *ga nai*, no end, no limit. Syn. KAGIRI.

†HATŌ, ハトウ, 波濤, (*nami,*) *n.* The waves. *Ban ri no hatō wo koyete kuru*, to come across the wide ocean.

HATO, ハト, 鳩, *n.* A dove, pigeon. *Yamabato*, a wild-pigeon.

HATOBA, ハトバ, 埠頭, *n.* A pier, wharf, a landing.

HATO-MUNE, ハトムネ, 鳩胸, *n.* Chicken-breasted.

HATSZ, or HATSZRU, ハツ, Same as *Hateru.*

HATSZ, ハツ, 初, The first, the beginning. *O me ni kakaru wa kon-nichi hatsz da*, to day is the first of my seeing you. *Hatszharu*, the beginning of spring. *Hatsz-dori*, the first crowing of a cock on the new year. *Hatsz-gōri*, *Hatsz-shimo*, *Hatszyuki*, the first ice, frost, or snow, of the season. *Hatsz mono*, the first things of the season. *Hatsz yama*, first visit to a sacred mountain.

HATSZBŌ, ハツバウ, 發泡, *n.* A blistering plaster. — *wo haru*, to apply a blister.

†HATSZ-DATSZ,*-szru*, ハツダツ, 發達, To improve. *Kenjutsz ni* —, improve in fencing. *Gakumon ni* —. Syn. SHŌDATSZ SZRU, JŌDZ NI NARU.

HATSZKA, ハツカ, 廿日, Twentieth day of the month. Twenty days.

HATSZKA-NEDZMI, ハツカネヅミ, 小鼠, *n.* A mouse.

HATSZ-MEI, ハツメイ, 發明, *n.* Intelligent, ingenious, clever; an invention. — *na mono*, an intelligent person. — *szru*, to invent, discover. *Shin* —, a new invention. Syn. KASH'KOI, RIKŌ.

HATSZMEIRASHII,-KI,-KU, ハツメイラシイ, 發明敷, Having an intelligent look, *ganshoku* —, intelligent looking countenance.

HATSZ-O, ハツホ, 初穗, *n.* The first fruits offered to the gods, applied also to small offerings of money. — *wo ageru*, to offer up money.

HATZRI,*-ru,-tta*, ハツル, 斫, *t.v.* To hew, cut with a broad-axe or adze, to chip off, clip off. *Ki wo* —, to hew timber.

HATSZ-TAKE, ハツタケ 初茸, *n.* A kind of edible mushroom.

HATTANGAKE, ハツタンガケ, 八端掛, *n.* Cloth containing enough for eight suits of clothing.

HATTO, ハツト, 法度, *n.* Law, ordinance, a prohibition. — *wo tateru*, to pass a law. — *wo somuku*, to disobey a law. — *wo yameru*, to annul a law. — *wo okasz*, to offend against the laws. — *wo yaburu*, to break a law. *Go-hatto*, it is contrary to law. Syn. OKITE.

HATTO, ハツト, *adv.* Same as *Hatato.*

HAU, ハフ, To creep, see *Hai.*

HA-UCHIWA, ハウチハ, 羽扇, *n.* A feather-fan.

HAWASHI,*-sz,-sh'ta*, ハワス, 令這, Caust. of *Hai*, to make to creep or crawl. *Ko wo* —, to make a child creep.

HAYA, ハヤ, 鰷魚, *n.* A kind of small river fish.

HAYA, ハヤ, 早, Exclam. of surprise, apprehension, or disappointment,=alas! oh. *Ima wa haya nogaruru michi nashi*, alas! there is now no way of escape. *Haya itte shimatta*, alas! he has gone. *Haya kita ka*, has he already come? *haya dekita*, is it already done?

HAYA, ハヤ, 駅, *n.* An express, a postman, a courier. — *ga kita*, an express has come.

HAYA, ハヤ, 早 Fast, quick, swift, soon, early. (used only in comp. words.)

HAYA-ASHI, ハヤアシ, 早足, Swift-footed.

HAYA-BAYA-TO, ハヤバヤト, *adv.* Quickly, soon, early.

HAYA-BIKIYAKU, ハヤビキヤク, 早飛脚, *n.* An express post.

HAYABUSA, ハヤブサ, 隼, *n.* A kind of small hawk.

HAYA-DAYORI, ハヤダヨリ, 早便, *n.* Quick mode of communication, quick or early opportunity.

HAYA-FUNE, ハヤフネ, 早舩, *n.* A fast-boat, a clipper ship.

HAYA-GAKI, ハヤガキ, 早書, *n.* Fast writing. — *ni kaku,* to write fast.

HAYA-GANE, ハヤガネ, 早鐘, *n.* An alarm-bell, fire-bell.

HAYAI,-KI,-SHI, ハヤイ, 早, *a.* Fast, quick, swift, early, soon. *Ano fune ga hayai,* that ship is swift. *Ki ga hayai,* to be quick witted, of quick perception. *Haya-ki koto ya no gotoku,* as swift as an arrow. *Shigoto ga hayai,* quick at working. *Mi-mi ga* —, quick to hear. *Dochira ga hayai,* which are the earliest or fastest?

HAYAKU, or HAYŌ, ハヤク, 早, *adv.* id. — *szru,* to do quickly. *Asa — okiru,* to rise early in the morning. *Tszki hi wa — tatsz,* the time passes swiftly. —*koi,* come quickly. Syn. JIKI-NI, SZGU-NI, SASSOKU, SZMIYAKA-NI.

HAYA-KUSA, ハヤクサ, 丹毒, *n.* A kind of skin disease.

HAYAMARI,-*ru,*-*tta,* ハヤマル, 早謬, *i.v.* To mistake by being quick or fast; too fast, over hasty, precipitate. *Hayamatta koto wo sh'ta,* he has done wrong in being so hasty.

HAYAME, ハヤメ, 催產, *n.* Hastening parturition. — *no kuszri,* medicines which hasten labor. — *no gō-fū,* a charm swallowed to hasten labor.

HAYAME,-*ru,*-*ta,* ハヤメル, 令早, *t.v.* To hasten, quicken, accelerate. *Ashi wo hayamete aruku,* to walk faster. *Toki wo hayamete kane wo tszku,* to be in a hurry to ring the bell. *M'ma wo* —, to urge on a horse.

HAYA-MICHI, ハヤミチ 捷徑, *n.* A near way.

HAYA-NAWA, ハヤナハ, 徽纒, *n.* A cord carried by policemen to bind criminals with.

HAYA-O, ハヤヲ, 早緒, *n.* The rope used in sculling a boat, the band of a wheel.

HAYA-OKE, ハヤヲケ, 早桶, *n.* A ready made tub in which paupers are buried.

HAYA-OKI, ハヤオキ, 早起, *n.* An early riser.

HAYARASE,-*ru,*-*ta,* ハヤラセル, 令流行, Caust. of *Hayari.* To make popular, fashionable, or prevalent.

HAYARI,-*ru,*-*tta,* ハヤル, 流行, *i.v.* To be prevalent, popular, fashionable. *Ha-sh'ka ga* —, the measles are prevalent. *Goro ga* —, camlets are fashionable. *Ki no hayaru mono,* a person of a quick and impetuous temper. *Hayari-yamai,* a prevalent disease, epidemic. *Hayari-gami,* a popular god. *Hayari-kotoba,* a popular word. Syn. RIU-KŌ SZRU.

HAYARI-O, ハヤリヲ, 逸雄, *n.* Impetuous, daring, heroic.

HAYASA, ハヤサ, 早, *n.* Quickness, swiftness, earliness, celerity.

HAYASE, ハヤセ, 急瀬, *n.* A swift current, rapids.

HAYASHI, ハヤシ, 林, *n.* A wood, forest.

HAYASHI, ハヤシ, See *Hayai.*

HAYASHI, ハヤシ, 囃子, *n.* A band of music, an orchestra. — *mono,* musical instruments. — *wo szru,* to make music. — *kata,* musicians.

HAYASHI,-*sz,*-*sh'ta,* ハヤス, 囃子, *t.v.* To play on musical instruments, to praise, flatter. *Uta wo hayasz,* to assist a person singing with an instrument, or chorus.

HAYASHI,-*sz,*-*sh'ta,* ハヤス, 令生, *t.v.* To let, or make to grow. *Kami wo* —, to let the hair grow. *Hige wo hayash'te iko-ku no mane wo szru,* to let the beard grow in imitation of foreigners *Ki wo* —, to grow trees.

HAYASHI,-*sz,*-*sh'ta,* ハヤス, 割, *t.v.* To To cut, to slice. *Mochi wo* —. *Daikon wo* —, to slice a radish.

HAYASHI-TATE,-*ru,*-*ta,* ハヤシタテル, 囃立, *t.v.* To play on musical instruments, to make music, to rouse up, excite. Syn. ODATERU.

HAYATE, ハヤテ, 暴風, *n.* A tempest, storm of wind.

HAYA-WAZA, ハヤワザ, 早業, *n.* Sleight of hand, adroit, dexterous. — *wo szru,* to perform sleight of hand tricks, or legerdemain. — *na h'to,* an adroit person.

HAYE, ハエ, 榮, *n.* Splendor, brilliant, glorious. *Asa-baye,* splendor of the sky at sunrise. *Yū-baye,* the splendor of the setting sun. *Haye nai waza da,* not an honorable employment. *Oi-naru wo motte haye to sz,* pride themselves in having it large.

HAYE,-*ru,*-*ta,* ハヘル, 生, *i.v.* To grow, sprout up, shoot up. *Kusa ga hayeta,* the grass has sprouted up. *Hiyoko ga hayeta,* the chick has burst the shell. *Kami ga hayeta,* the hair has grown out, (where once shaved off). *Kabi ga hayeta,* it has moulded. *Ha ga hayeta ka,* has it cut its teeth? Syn. OIRU.

HAYE,-*ru,*-*ta,* ハヘル, 拼, *t.v.* To pile up, to arrange in a pile. *Tawara wo* —, to pile up bags, (of rice, &c.) *Nimotsz wo* —, to pile up goods.

HAYE-GIWA, ハヘギハ, 髮際, *n.* The edge, or border of the hair.

HAYE-SAGARI,-*ru,*-*tta,* ハヘサガル, 生垂, *i. v.* Growing downward.

HAYŌ, ハヤウ, 早, See *Hayaku*. *O hayō gozarimasz*, you are early; this is contracted to, *O hayo*, good morning.

HAYURO, ハユル, Same as *Hayeru*.

HAZAMA, ハザマ, 挾間, *n*. Port holes, embrasures. *Shiro no* —, embrasures in a castle. Syn. HŌ-MON.

HAZE, ハゼ, 沙魚, *n*. The name of a fish.

HAZE,-*ru*,-*ta*, ハゼル, *i.v*. To burst open, as ripe fruit, or as parched corn. Syn. YEBIBU.

HAZE, ハゼ, *n*. Rice bursted by roasting.

HE, へ, 屁, *n*. A fart. — *wo hiru*, to break wind, to fart.

HE,-*ru*,-*ta*, ヘル, 經, or 歴, *t.v*. To pass, to spend, to live through. To pass from one place to another, move along. *Yo, toshi, tszki, hi, toki nado wo heru. Michi wo* —, to pass along the several stages of a road. *Kanagawa wo hete Yedo ye yuku*, passing through Kanagawa to go to Yedo. *Ito wo heru*, to arrange yarn for the loom. *Dan-dan yaku wo hete agaru*, to be gradually promoted from one official grade to another. Syn. FURU, TŌRU, SZGIRU, KOSZ.

HE-AGARI,-*ru*,-*tta*, ヘアガル, 經上, *i. v*. To pass from a lower rank or condition to a higher; to rise, advance. *Karui yaku kara omoi yaku ye he-agaru*, to advance from an inferior to a more important office.

HEBARI-TSZKI,-*ku*,-*ita*, ヘバリツク, 粘著, *i.v*. To stick, adhere. *Urushi ga hebaritszite hanare nai*, the varnish sticks and it can't be separated. *Uchi ni bakari hebaritszite iru h'to da*, a person who does nothing but stay in the house.

HEBI, ヘビ, 蛇, *n*. A snake, serpent. — *no uroko*, the scales of a snake. — *no nukegara*, the cast-off skin of a snake. — *ni kui-tszkareru*, to be bitten by a snake. Syn. JA, KUCHINAWA.

HEBI-ICHIGO, ヘビイチゴ, 蛇苺, *n*. A tasteless kind of strawberry.

HEBI-TSZKAI, ヘビツカヒ, 弄蛇者, *n*. A serpent-charmer.

HECHIMA, ヘチマ, 絲瓜, *n*. The snake gourd.

HEDATARI,-*ru*,-*tta*, ヘダタル, 隔, *i. v*. To be separated, apart, asunder, distant. *Roku ri hodo hedatatte oru*, they are six miles apart. *Oya ko no naka ga hedataru*, the parent and child are distant (indifferent,) to one another. Syn. HANARERU

HEDATE,-*ru*,-*ta*, ヘダテル, 隔, *t. v*. To leave, separate from, part from. To interpose, place between; separated by, severed. *Iye wo hedatete tabi ni oru*, he has left home on a journey. *Amerika to Nippon to umi wo hedatete oru*, America and Japan are separated by the ocean. *Yama wo hedateru*, to be separated by a mountain. *Hedate-gokoro*, estranged, alienated. *Hedateru kokoro wa nashi*, makes no distinction, no respect for persons, impartial. Syn. HANARERU, BETSZNI SZRU, TŌZAKARU.

HEDATE, ヘダテ, 隔, *n*. A partition, distinction, separation. — *ga aru*. — *wo szru*, to make a partition, make a distinction.

HEDATSZRU, ヘダツル, Same as, *Hedateru*.

HEDO, ヘド, 反吐, *n*. Eructation of food. — *wo haku*, to eject food from the stomach. *Hedo wo tszku*, (idem.)

HEDZRI,-*ru*,-*tta*, ヘヅル, 斫, *t.v*. To cut or chip off a part, to clip off, to dock. *Dai wo hedztte shō ni tassz*, to clip off from the big and add to the small. *Hedzri-toru*, (idem.) Syn. HATSZRU.

HEGASHI,-*sz*,-*sh'ta*, ヘガス, 令剝, Caust. of *Hegi*, to tear off, strip off. *Kara kami wo hegash'te hari-kayeru*, tear off the wall-paper and put on new.

HEGI,-*gu*,-*ida*, ヘグ, 剝, *t.v*. To strip off, peel off, split off. *Ki no kawa wo* —, to peel off the bark of a tree. *Yane-ita wo* —, to split shingles. Syn. HAGI MUKU.

HEGI, ヘギ, *n*. A strip of wood split off. *Hegi-bon*, a kind of tray made of strips of bamboo; *Shōga h'to hegi*, one slice of ginger.

HEI, ヘイ, exclam. used in answering, same as *Hai*, = yes.

HEI, ヘイ, 屛, *n*. A fence, wall. *Do-bei*, a mud wall. *Ita-bei*, a board fence. *Ishi-bei*, a stone fence. *Neri-bei*, a fence made of bricks and mortar.

HEI, ヘイ, 平, *n*. Even, level, plain, common, ordinary, usual, peaceful, tranquil, used only in compound words. *Tai-hei*, 大平, long peace.

HEI, ヘイ 幣, *n*. The cut paper placed in a *Miya* to represent the *Kami*.

HEI, ヘイ, 兵, *n*. An army. — *wo okosz*, to raise an army, to begin a war. — *wo neru*, to drill an army.

HEI-AN, ヘイアン, 平安, *n*. Peace, tranquility, freedom from sickness calamity or trouble. Syn. BUJI.

HEI-AN-JŌ, ヘイアンジヤウ, 平安城, *n*. The Mikado's palace.

HEI-CHI, ヘイチ, 平地, (*tairakana tszchi.*) Level ground or country, a plain.

†HEI-CHŌ,-*szru*, ヘイチヤウ, 閉帳, To conceal or veil an idol from sight.

HEIDA, ヘイダ, *n*. A bamboo withe.

†HEI-DON,-*szru*, ヘイドン, 幷呑, (*awase nomu.*) To despise, look down on; to subjugate, conquer. *Tenka wo —*,

HEI-FUKU, ヘイフク, 平服, (*tszne no kimono,*) *n.* Common usual or every-day clothes, (not a dress of ceremony.)

HEI-FUKU,-*szru*, ヘイフク, 平伏, To bow low, to prostrate one's self.

†HEI-G'WA,-*szru*, ヘイグワ, 平臥, To lie down. *Biyōki de — sh'te oru.*

†HEI-JI, ヘイジ, 瓶子, *n.* A pitcher, bottle. Syn. TOKKURI, BIN.

HEI-JI,-*szru*, ヘイヂ, 平治, (*tairage osameru.*) *i.v.* To quell, subdue, to tranquilize, to quiet. *Tenka —*, to quiet and restore peace to the empire. *Ran wo —*. to quell a riot.

HEI-JITSZ, ヘイジツ, 平日, Common, usual, ordinary, customary, habitual, every-day; always, constantly. *— no kimono*, every-day clothes. *— to wa chigau*, different from what is usual. *— no tōri ni*, in the usual manner. Syn. FUDAN, TSZNE-DZNE.

†HEIKA, ヘイカ, 陛下, *n.* The Emperor, Mikado.

HEIKEGANI, ヘイケガニ, 車蟹, *n.* A kind of crab.

HEI-KI, ヘイキ, 兵器, *n.* Weapons of war.

HEI-KIN,-*szru*, ヘイキン, 平均, (*tairakani h'toshii.*) *t.v.* To make equal or even, equalize; to balance, to average *Nedan wo hei-kin sh'te ikura*, what is the average price. NARASZ, BIYŌDŌ.

HEI-KI, ヘイキ, 平氣, *n.* Calm, tranquil, or undisturbed in mind, equanimity, composure, coolness. *Iye ga yaketemo — de iru.* He is calm even if his house should burn.

HEI-KŌ,-*szru*, ヘイコウ, 閉口, (*kuchi wo tojiru.*) To shut the mouth, to be silenced, or defeated in argument.

†HEI-MIN, ヘイミン, 平民, *n.* The common people, (not the gentry.)

HEI-MIYAKU, ヘイミヤク, 平脉, *n.* The usual or healthy pulse.

HEI-MON,-*szru*, ヘイモン, 閉門, (*mon wo tojiru.*) To imprison in one's own house.

†HEI-MOTSZ, ヘイモツ, 聘物, *n.* Presents of congratulation; marriage presents.

HEI-NIN, ヘイニン, 平人, (*tszne-bito,*) *n.* A common or ordinary person.

†HEI-REI, ヘイレイ, 聘禮, *n.* Presents made on espousal, or on visits of ceremony.

HEI-SAN, ヘイサン, 平產, An ordinary or natural parturition.

HEI-SHA, ヘイシヤ, 兵車, *n.* A war chariot.

†HEI-SHI, ヘイシ, 兵士, *n.* A soldier.

HEI-SOKU, ヘイソク, 幣束, *n.* Paper fixed to the end of a stick and placed before the *Kami. — wo tateru.*

†HEI-SOKU,-*szru*, ヘイソク, 閉塞, (*toji fusagaru.*) To shut up, stop up, close, obstruct, *Jōki wo —*, to check perspiration.

HEI-SOTSZ, ヘイソツ, 兵卒, *n.* Common soldiers.

HEI-WA, ヘイワ, 平和, *n.* Peace, tranquility, freedom from disturbance.

†HEI-WA, ヘイワ, 平話, *n.* Common colloquial, the language of the common people. Syn. ZOKUDAN.

HEI-YU, ヘイユ, 平愈, *n.* Restoration to health, cured. *Biyōki ga — sh'ta.* Syn. ZENK'WAI, HOMBUKU.

HEI-ZEI, ヘイゼイ, 平生, Common, usual, ordinary, customary, habitual, every-day.

HEKI, ヘキ, 僻, or 癖, *n.* A bent, propensity, peculiar habit, way or eccentricity. *Heki no aru h'to*, an eccentric person. *Heki wo iu*, to say odd things. Syn. KUSE, HENKUTSZ.

†HEKI-GIYOKU, ヘキギヨク, 璧玉, *n.* A kind of precious stone of green color; jade.

†HEKI-REKI, ヘキレキ, 霹靂, *n.* Flashing, (of lightning, of sword, &c.)

†HEKI-YEKI,-*szru*, ヘキエキ, 辟易, To shrink back in fear, to recoil. *Sono ikioi ni —*.

HEKOMASHI,-*sz*,-*sh'ta*, ヘコマス, 令陥, *t.v.* To indent, to pit, hollow. *Yubi de —*, to indent with the finger.

HEKOMI,-*mu*,-*nda*, ヘコム, 陥, *i.v.* To be indented, pitted, hollowed, (fig.) to be defeated, to give in. *Kana dzchi de tataita ka hekonde oru.* I suspect it was indented by the blow of a hammer. *Hen-tō dekinakute hekonde shimatta*, not being able to reply he was defeated. Syn. KUBOMU.

HEKOMI, ヘコミ, 陥, *n.* An indentation, a loss in measure or weight, a falling short. *Hekomi ga dekita*, it has fallen short (in measure, &c.) it is indented. *— ni natta*, to be short in measure.

†HEM-BEN,-*szru*, ヘンベン, 返辨, *t.v.* To repay, pay back, refund, make restitution. Syn. KAYESZ.

HEM-BUTSZ, ヘンブツ, 偏物, *n.* An eccentric person, an obstinate bigoted person.

HE-MEGURI,-*ru*,-*tta*, ヘメグル, 歴廻, *t.v.* To travel about. *Kuni-guni wo —*, to travel from country to country.

†HEM-PA, ヘンパ, 偏頗, (*katayori.*) *n.*

Partiality, favoritism. *Hiki hempa nashi ni*, without favor or partiality. *Hempa no h'to nite wa mina-mina komari iru.* Syn. HIKI, KATADZMU.

HEM-PAI, ヘンパイ, 返杯, Returning the wine-glass. — *itashimasz*, I return you the glass.

†HEM-PEN-TO, ヘンペン, 翩翩, *adv.* In a fluttering manner, wavering. *Hata — nabiku*, the flag waves (in the wind.) *Yuki — furu.* Syn. HIRA-HIRA TO.

HEM-PI, ヘンピ, 偏鄙, A remote country, retired, rural. — *na tokoro.*

HEM-PŌ, ヘンパウ, 返報, *n.* Answer, reply, requital, revenge, vengeance. *Teki ni — wo szru*, to take vengeance on an enemy. *Tegami de — wo szru*, to answer by letter.

HEM-PON-TO, ヘンポン, 翩翻, *adv.* In a waving fluttering manner. *Hata hempon to kaze ni nabiku*, the flag waves in the wind. — *szru*, to flutter, or fly.

†HEM-PUKU, ヘンプク, 蝙蝠, *n.* A bat. Syn. KŌMORI.

HEN, ヘン, 邊, *n.* Part, region, place, side. *Kono-hen*, this side, neighborhood, or region. *Ano hen*, that side, that place. Syn. HOTORI. ATARI.

HEN, ヘン, 篇, *n.* A section, or book, a set of books under one cover. *Ippen, ni-hen, sam-ben*, first second and third books, or sets of books. *Ni hen me*, the second book.

HEN, ヘン, 變, An unusual or strange affair. *Nan no hen mo nai*, nothing unusual. *Hen-na koto*, a strange or extraordinary affair. *Tai-hen*, a great or dreadful affair.

HEN, ヘン, 遍, *(tabi,)* Numeral for times. *Ippen*, once. *Nihen*, twice. *Sam-ben*, three times.

HEN, ヘン, 偏, *n.* The left side radicals of a character, as. *Ki-hen, nim-ben, kane-hen.*

HEN-DO, ヘンド, 邊土, A remote country region. KATA INAKA, HEM-PI.

HEN-GAI, ヘンガイ, 變改, To change, alter *Yak'soku wo — szru*, to change an agreement.

HEN-GE, ヘンゲ, 變化, To transform, metamorphose. *Kitszne ga henge sh'te h'to to naru*, the fox is changed into a man. *Henge-mono*, metamorphosed things. Syn. BAKERU.

†HEN-I, ヘンイ, 變異, A wonder, prodigy, a strange or unusual phenomenon. — *ga aru.*

HEN-JI, ヘンジ, 返事, *n.* An answer, reply. — *suru*, to return answer, to reply. — *ga nai*, no answer. Syn. HEN-TO, KOTAYE.

HENJI, *-ru, -ta*, ヘンジル, 變, *t. v.* To change, alter, transform, to metamorphose. *Ishi wo henjite kin to szru*, to change stones into gold.

HEN-JI, ヘンジ, 變事, *(kawatta koto,) n.* An unusual or strange event, a wonder.

HEN-JŌ, *-szru*, ヘンジヤウ, 返上, To return, send back, repay. Syn. KAYESHI-TATEMATSURU.

†HEN-KAI, ヘンカイ, 遍界, The whole world. Syn. AMANEKI-SEKAI.

†HEN-KAKU, *-szru*, ヘンカク, 變革, *t.v.* To alter, reform, to change. *Okite wo —*, to alter the laws.

†HEN-K'YAKU, *-szru*, ヘンキヤク, 返却, *t. v.* To pay-back, return, restore. Syn. HEMBEN, HEYESZ.

HEN-KUTSZ, ヘンクツ, 偏屈, Set in one's opinions or ways, bigoted, dogmatic, obstinate. — *na h'to.* Syn. KATAKURUSHII, KATAKUNA.

HEN-K'WA, ヘンクワ, 變化, *n.* Change, alteration, transformation, variation, vicissitude, metamorphosis — *szru*, to change, vary. *Shiki no—*, the changes of the four seasons. Syn. KAWARU, BAKERU.

HEN-NŌ, ヘンナウ, 片腦, *n.* Camphor.

†HEN-NŌ, *-szru*, ヘンナフ, 返納, To return, send-back, restore, pay-back, (as a borrowed thing.) Syn. KAYESZ HENJŌ SZRU.

HENOKO, ヘノコ, 陰莖, *n.* Membrum virile. Syn. INKIYŌ, NANKON, MARA, CHIMPŌ, SHIJI.

HEN-REI, *-szru*, ヘンレイ, 返禮, To return a compliment, make a present in return.

†HEN-REKI, *-szru*, ヘンレキ, 遍歷, To travel about. Syn. HEMEGURI, YUREKI.

HEN-SAI, ヘンサイ, 返濟, To return, repay, restore.

HEN-SHI, ヘンシ, 片時, *n.* A short time, a moment. — *mo waszredz*, not to forget for a moment. Syn. KATA-TOKI.

HEN-SHI, ヘンシ, 變死, *n.* A strange, unusual, or unnatural death.

†HEN-SHIN, ヘンシン 偏身, *n.* The whole body.

||HEN-SHIN, ヘンシン, 返進, *(kayeshi mairaszru.)* To return, send back, (to a superior. Syn. HENJŌ.

†HEN-SHŪ, ヘンシフ, 偏執, Obstinate, stubborn, fixed in opinion, pertinacious. — *wa kayete waga mi no gai ni ai-nari*, obstinacy may become injurious to one's-self. Syn. KATAI.

HEN-TETSZ, ヘンテツ, Effect, result, utility, virtue, taste, good quality, always followed by *mo nai*. *Kono karashi nan no — mo nai*, this mustard has not the least taste. *Kuszri wa nan no — mo nai*, the medicine has no taste, or, has no effect. *Omoshiroku mo — mo nai*, not the least pleasant.

HEN-TŌ, ヘンタフ, 返答, Answer, reply. — *szru*, to answer, reply. — *ga nai*, no answer. Syn. HENJI, HEMPŌ, KOTAYE.

HENU, ヘヌ, neg. of *Heru*.

HEO, ヘヲ, 足組, *n*. The cord attached to a falcon's foot.

HEPPIRIMUSHI, ヘッピリムシ, 氣蠜, *n*. A kind of stinking bug.

HERA, ヘラ, 鎞, A paddle, spatula, a trowel. *Kanebera*, a metal spatula, a trowel.

HERADZ, ヘラズ, 不減, Neg. of *Heru*. — *guchi wo iu*, to continue to talk after being defeated in argument.

HERASHI,*–sz,–sh'ta*, ヘラス, 減, *t.v.* To lessen, diminish, reduce in number, or bulk. *H'to wo* —, to reduce the number of persons. *Iriyō wo* —, to lessen expenses. *Kui-herasz*, to lessen by eating. *Tszkai-herasz*, to lessen by using. Syn. GENSHŌ SZRU, SZKUNAKU SZRU, HABUKU.

HERI, ヘリ, 緣, *n*. A border, binding, edging of a garment, mat &c. — *wo toru*, to make a border. *Heri-tori-goza*, a mat with a binding.

HERI,*–ru,–tta*, ヘル, 減, *i.v.* Lessened in bulk, diminished in number, to wear away. *Kadz ga hetta*, the number is diminished. *Hara ga heru*, to be hungry. *To-ishi ga* —, the whet-stone wears away. Syn. GENSHŌ SH'TA, SZKUNAKU NATTA.

HERI, ヘリ, 減, *n*. A diminution, loss, waste. *Heri ga tatsz*, there is a loss, or waste, (in goods, &c., as from handling.) Syn. HEKOMI.

HERI-KUDARI,*–ru,–tta*, ヘリクダル, 謙, *i.v.* To humble one's self. *Me wiye no h'to ni heri-kudaru*, to humble one's self before a superior. Syn. KEN-TAI, KEN-SON, HIGE SZRU, S'HTA NI DERU.

HESAKI, ヘサキ, 艗, *n*. The bow of a ship. Syn. MIOSHI.

||HESHI,*–sz,–sh'ta*, ヘス, 著壓, *t.v.* To press down, force down, to crush, to repress, subdue. *H'to wo hesz*, to treat another with arrogance. *Kuchi wo* —, to force to be silent. Syn. OSZ.

||HESHI-ORI,*–ru,–tta*, ヘシオル, 拗折, *t.v.* To break by pressing down, (as across the knee).

||HESHI-TSZKE,*–ru,–ta*, ヘシツケル, 壓著, Same as *Hesz*.

HESO, ヘソ, 巻子, *n*. A ball of thread.

HESO, ヘソ, 臍, *n*. The navel. — *no wo*, the navel string. Syn. HOZO.

HESO-KURI-GANE, ヘソクリガネ, 私房銀, *n*. Pin money, the small private earnings of the wife.

HETA, ヘタ, 蔕, *n*. The calyx of the blossom which remains attached to the fruit.

HETA, ヘタ, 下手, Unskillful, inexperienced, unused to, clumsy, bungling, awkward. — *wo sh'ta*, to bungle. — *no isha*, an unskillful doctor. *Sake wa heta de gozarimas*, excuse me, I am not used to *sake*. *Saiku ga — da*, the work is badly done. Syn. BUCHŌHŌ, JŌDZ NAI.

HETABARI,*–ru,–tta*, ヘタバル, *i.v.* To bend down, to bow low. *Hetabari-tszku*, (idem).

||HETA-HETA TO, ヘタヘタト, *adv*. Limber, pliant, flexible. *Hetarito*, (idem).

HETTSZI, ヘッツイ, 竈, *n*. A cooking range. Syn. KAMADO.

HETSZRAI,*–au,–atta*, ヘツラフ, 諂諛, *t.v.* To flatter, to fawn upon, pay court to, to play the sycophant, to endeavour to please. *H'to ni hetszrau*, to flatter others. *Hetszrai mono*, a flatterer, a sycophant. *Me wiye no h'to ni hetszratte shusse wo szru*, to flatter a superior and get promotion. Syn. KOBIRU, TSZISHŌ-SZRU.

HETSZRAI, ヘツラヒ, 諂, *n*. Flattery, adulation, sycophancy. Syn. TSZISHŌ, KOBI.

HETSZRU, ヘツル, See *Hedzri*.

HEYA, ヘヤ, 部室, *n*. A room, apartment.

HEYADZMI, ヘヤズミ, 房住, *n*. A son who still lives with his parents.

HI, ヒ, 日, *n*. The sun. — *no hikari*, the light of the sun. — *no de*, the rising of the sun. — *no iri*, the setting of the sun. — *no tōru michi (sekidō)*, the equinoctial, or, the orbit of the sun. — *ga teru*, sun shines. — *ga utszru*, the sun shines on, or, is reflected in. *Hi ga takeru*, the sun is getting high. — *ni sarasz*, to expose to the sun. Syn. NICHI-RIN, TENTOSAMA, TAIYŌ.

HI, ヒ, 日, *n*. Day. — *ga nagai*. — *ga mijikai*. — *wo heru*, to spend the time, — *wo nobasz*, to postpone the day. — *wo sadameru*, to fix the day. — *wo kurasz*, to spend the day. — *wo szgosz*, (idem). *Hi wo tateru*, (idem). *Hi wo okuru*, (idem). Syn. NICHI, JITSZ.

HI, ヒ, 火, *n*. Fire. — *ga moyeru*, the fire burns. — *ga kieru*, the fire is going out. — *ga tszku*, to catch fire. — *wo taku*, to make a fire. — *wo mosz*, (idem). — *wo kesz*, to put out fire. — *wo utsz*, to strike fire, (with a flint). — *wo ikeru*, to keep fire in, (by covering it with ashes). — *no te*, the flame of a conflagration. — *no miban*, a fire watch. — *no yō-jin*, preparation, or care against a fire. — *ni ataru*, to warm at the fire.

HI, ヒ, 血漕, *n*. The longitudinal groove in a sword blade.

†HI, ヒ, 脾, *n*. The spleen. *Hi no zō*, (idem).

HI, ヒ, 緋, *n*. Vermilion color. *Mi no koromo*, a crimson robe.

†HI, ヒ, 冰, *(kōri)*, *n*. Ice. *Usz-hi*, thin ice.

HI, ヒ, 非, *n*. Bad, wrong, not so. — *wo utsz*, to criticise, point out the defects. — *ni ochiru*, to be convicted of wrong; to be cast in a suit, proven guilty. *Ze to hi no wakaranu mono*, a person who does not know the difference between right and wrong. *H'to no hi wo ī-tateru*, to speak of the evil doings of others. Syn. ASHI.

HI, ヒ, 樋, *n*. A water pipe, spout, trough, a faucet. *Hi no kuchi*, the mouth of a faucet, or drain. — *wo udzmeru*, to lay a a water-pipe under ground. Syn. TOI.

HI, ヒ, 梭, *n*. A weaver's shuttle. *Hata no hi*.

HI, ヒ, 碑, *n*. A monument, a stone tablet, a stone cut for lithographing. *Hi wo tateru*, to erect a monument. *Seki hi*, a stone monument. *Hi no mei*, the inscriptions on a monument.

HI,*-ru,-ta*, ヒル, 干, *i.v.* Dried in the sun; dry. *Urushi ga hita*, the lacquer is dry. *Daikon ga hita*, the radish is dry. *Shiwo ga* —, the tide has ebbed. *Hi-kata*, the dry beach. *Hi-agaru*, fully dried. *Hi-mono*, articles of food dried in the sun, particularly dried fish. *Ron ga hi-nai*, the discussion is not ended. Syn. KAWAKU, HASHIYAGU.

HI,*-ru,-ta*, ヒル, 簸, *t.v.* To winnow or clean grain by throwing it up in the air and catching it in a basket. *Mi de kome wo hiru*, to winnow rice with a basket.

HI,*-ru,-tta*, ヒル, 放, *t.v.* Used in the phrase. *Hana wo* —, to sneeze. *He wo* —.

HI-ABURI, ヒアブリ, 火刑, *n*. Punishment by burning at the stake. — *ni szru*, to burn at the stake

HI-AI, ヒアヒ, 日間, *n*. Many days, a number of days. — *ga tatta*, many days have elapsed.

†HI-AI, ヒアイ, 悲哀, *(kanashimi-kanashimu.)* Grief, sorrow.

HI-AGARI,*-ru,-tta*, ヒアガル, 干上, *i.v.* Dried, arid, parched. Syn. KAWAKU.

HI-ASHI, ヒアシ, 日脚, *n*. The rays of the sun. *Mado kara hi-ashi ga sasz*, the sun's rays enter by the window.

†HI-AYAUSHI, ヒアヤウシ, Exclam. = "Be careful of fire," the call of a watchman at night.

HI-BA, ヒバ, 乾葉, *n*. Dried radish leaves.

HIBA, ヒバ, 杜松, *n*. A kind of evergreen, The Thujopsis delabrata.

HIBABA, ヒイババ, 曾祖母, *n*. Great-grand mother.

HĪBABA, ヒババ, 高祖母, *n*. Great-great grand mother.

HIBACHI, ヒバチ, 火鉢, *n*. A brazier.

HIBAN, ヒバン, 非番, Not on duty, off-duty. *Konnichi hiban de gozarimas*, am off-duty to day. *Hi-ban tō-ban naku tszmekiri*, to be always on duty, without a division of watch.

HIBANA, ヒバナ, 火花, *n*. A spark. — *wo chirash'te tatakau*, to fight until the sparks fly.

HI-BARI, ヒバリ, 雲雀, *n*. A sky-lark.

HIBASAMI, ヒバサミ, 火挾, *n*. The cock of a gun, or the place where the match is held in a match-lock.

HI-BASHI, ヒバシ 火箸, *n*. Two iron rods used for taking up fire; tongs.

HIBI, ヒビ, 胼, *n*. Chaps, or cracks in the hands produced by cold. *Te ni — ga kireta*, the hands are chapped. *Hibi-akagire*, chapped and cracked.

HIBI, ヒビ, 璺, *n*. The cracked appearance of porcelain. — *ga itta setomono. Hibi-yaki*, a kind of porcelain made to look as if cracked.

HI-BI-NI, ヒビニ, 日日, *adv*. Daily, every day.

HIBI-HIBI-NI, ヒビヒビ, (idem.) Syn. NICHI-NICHI NI, MAI-NICHI.

HIBIKASE,*-ru,-ta*, ヒビカセル, 令響, Caust. of *Hibiki*, to cause to reverberate, or echo.

HIBIKI,*-ku,-ita*, ヒビク, 響, *i.v.* To echo, resound, reverberate, to extend, as, an impulse, shock, or concussion. *Toki no koye ten ni hibiku*, the shout resounded to the heavens. *Teppō ga natte shōji ni hibiku*, the sound of the guns reverberates against the windows. *Hibiki-wataru*, to reverberate on every side. *Ashi no itami ga atama ye* —, the pain of the foot reaches to the head.

HIBIKI, ヒビキ 響, *n*. Sound, noise, report,

echo; shock, concussion; a crack. *Teppō ni hibiki*, the report of a gun. *Jishin no —*, the shock of an earthquake. *— ga iru*, to be cracked.

HIBISO, ヒビソ, *n.* An inferior kind of raw silk from the outside fibres of a cocoon.

HIBO, or HIMO, ヒボ, 紐, *n.* Cord, braid, a plaited string.

HIBOSHI, ヒボシ, 暴乾, Dried in the sun, (fig.) emaciated by starvation. *Hiboshigaki*, dried persimmons. *— ni sareru*, to be starved, shrivelled by starvation.

HI-BUKURE, ヒブクレ, 火腫, *n.* The blister from a burn. *Yakedo sh'te — ni natta*, to be burnt and blistered.

HI-BUN, ヒブン, 非分, Unbecoming one's station, wrong, improper, unjust, unreasonable. *— no furumai*, improper conduct. *— no sata*, an unjust sentence. *— no tszmi ni ochiru*, to receive an undue degree of punishment. Syn. ATARIMAI WO HADZRERU.

HI-BURUI, ヒブルイ, 日戰, *n.* Daily shake of the ague.

HI-BUTA, ヒブタ, 火門蓋, *n.* The trigger of a gun.

HICHI, ヒチ, 質, see *Shichi.*

HICHI, ヒチ, 七, Seven, same as *Shichi.*

HIHCIRIKI, ヒチリキ, 篳篥, *n.* A small pipe, or flageolette. *— no sh'ta*, the reed of a flageolette.

HIDA, ヒダ, 積, *n.* Plaits, folds. *— wo toru*, to plait.

†HIDAI, ヒダイ, 肥大, Corpulent, fat.

HIDACHI,*-tsz,-tta*, ヒダツ, 日足, *i.v.* To gradually imı rove, or grow better in health or size, (said of a sick person, or infant.) *Akambo ga dan-dan hidatsz*, the infant gradually grows in size.

HIDACHI, ヒダチ, 日足, *n.* The daily improvement, or convalescence of a sick person, the daily growth of an infant. *— ga hai.*

HIDAMA, ヒダマ, 火玉, *n.* Will of the wisp, ignis fatuus, a ball of fire.

HIDARI, ヒダリ, 左, *n.* The left. *— no te*, the left arm. *— no hō*, the left side.

HIDARI-GAMAYE, ヒダリガマヘ, 左搆, *n.* A left position, or left guard, (as in fencing.)

HIDARI-GIKI, ヒダリギキ, 左利, or HIDARI-GITCHŌ, ヒダリギッチヨ, *n.* Left-handed.

HIDARI-MAKI, ヒダリマキ, 左捲, *n.* Turning towards the left in winding.

HIDARI-MAYE, ヒダリマヘ, 左衽, *n.* Buttoning on the left side, the right breast of the coat being folded over the left. *Shinshō — ni natta*, to suffer a reverse of fortune.

HIDARI-NAWA, ヒダリナハ, 左繩, *n.* A rope made by twisting to the left.

HIDARUI,-KI,-SHI, ヒダルイ, 空腹, *a.* Hungry. Syn. HARAHERU, HIMOJII, KŪFUKU, WIYERU.

HIDARUGARI,*-ru,-tta*, ヒダルガル, *i.v.* To feel hungry, to talk of being hungry.

HIDARUKU, or HIDARŪ, ヒダルク, 飢, *adv.* Hungry.

HIDARUSA, ヒダルサ, 飢, *n.* Hunger.

HI-DASHI,*-sz,-sh'ta*, ヒダス, 簸出, *t. v.* To winnow, or clean by throwing up the grain with a shallow basket called a *mi.*

HĪDE,*-ru,-ta*, ヒイデル, 秀, *i. v.* To grow up to full size as a plant, to excel, surpass, to be preëminent, beautiful. *Hīdete minorazaru mono*, a plant that has attained its full size but produces no fruit. *Gaku ni hīderu*, to excel in learning. *Mayu ga —*, her eyebrows are surpassingly beautiful. *Hīdetaru kō wo tateru*, to perform a work of surpassing merit. Syn. SZGURERU, NUKINDERU.

HIDEN, ヒデン, 秘傳, *n.* A secret, or private formula, art, or instruction which one has been taught by others, or which has come down in one's family. *— wo oshiyeru, sadzkeru, ukeru, yurusz.*

HIDERI, ヒデリ, 旱, *n.* A drought, long continuance of clear weather. *— doshi*, a year of drought. Syn. KAMPATSZ.

HI-DŌ, ヒダウ, 非道, *(michi ni aradz.)* Cruel, unjust, outrageous. *— na koto. — wo szru*, to behave tyranically.

HI-DŌGU, ヒダウグ, 火道具, *n.* Tools for striking fire, (as flint, steel, tinder, &c.)

HIDOI,-KI,-SHI, ヒドイ, 酷, *a.* Cruel, severe, grievous, inhuman, hard, outrageous, excessive, atrocious. *Hidoi me ni au*, to meet with cruel or hard treatment. *Hidoi h'to da*, a cruel, hard man. *Hidoi nedan*, an exorbitant price. *Hidoi atszi da*, it is exceedingly hot. Syn. NASAKE-NAI, MUGOI.

HIDOKEI, ヒドケイ, 日時計, *n.* A sundial.

HIDOKO, ヒドコ, 火所, *n.* A fire-place.

HIDOKU, ヒドク, 酷, *adv.* see *Hidoi.*

HIDORI,*-ru,-tta*, ヒドル, 焙, *t. v.* To dry by heating in a pan, to roast. *Cha wo —*, to fire tea.

HIDORI, ヒドリ, 日取, *n.* Selecting or fixing on a day. *— wo szru*, to fix on a day.

HIDOSA, ヒドサ, *n.* Severity, atrocity, &c., see *Hidoi.*

HIDZME, ヒヅメ, 蹄, *n.* The hoof of an animal.

HIDZMI,-*mu*,-*nda*, ヒヅム, 歪, *i. v.* Deviating from a straight line, inclined, oblique, aslant, awry, askew, crooked. *Shōji ga hidznde tatemasen*, the sash is askew and will not shut. Syn. SZJIKAU, MAGARU.

HIFU, ヒフ, 披風, *n.* A kind of coat, worn by doctors, priests, or gentlemen who have retired from business.

†HIFU, ヒフ, 皮膚, (*kawa, hadaye.*) The skin, texture and color of the skin.

HIFUKI, ヒフキ, 火吹, *n.* A vessel into which tobacco ashes are blown from the pipe. — *dake*, a piece of bamboo used for blowing the fire.

HIGAKE, ヒガケ, 日掛, *n.* Daily payments or contributions. *Tana-chin wo — ni sh'te toru*, to receive the house rent in daily payments.

HIGA-KOTO, ヒガコト, 僻事, *n.* Anything incorrect, false, untrue, improper or absurd.

HIGAMBANA, ヒガンバナ, 彼岸花, *n.* The ornithoglum.

HIGA-ME, ヒガメ, 僻目, *n.* Seeing incorrectly, eyes mistaken or deceived. *Tai-shō to miru wa — ka*, are my eyes mistaken in thinking I see the general?

HIGAMI,-*mu*,-*nda*, ヒガム, 僻, *i.v.* Crooked, warped, depraved, perverse, prejudiced, partial. *Kokoro wa higande oru*, his mind is depraved. *Higami kon-jō*, perverse disposition. *To ga* —, the door is warped. Syn. KATAYORU, MAGARU, NEJIKERU.

HIGAN, ヒガン, 彼岸, *n.* A period of 7 days in the 2nd and 8th months, appropriated to the worship of Buddha.

HIGANA-ICHI-NICHI, ヒガナイチニチ, 日一日, The whole day. Syn. HINEMOSZ, SHŪJITSZ.

HIGANZAKURA, ヒガンザクラ, 彼岸櫻, *n.* A kind ot cherry tree.

HI-GARA, ヒガラ, 日柄, The kind of day, as to lucky or unluky; or simply, day. — *ga yoi*, a lucky day. — *ga warui*, a bad, or unlucky day. — *tachite nochi*, after some days.

HIGARAME, ヒガラメ, *n.* Squint-eyed. Syn. SZGAME.

HIGASA, ヒガサ, 日傘, *n.* A parasol, sun-shade.

HIGASHI, ヒガシ, 東, *n.* The east. — *no hō*. — *no kata*, eastern side. — *muki*, facing the east. — *uke*, (idem).

HI-GASHI, ヒガシ乾,菓子,*n.* See *Hig'washi.*

HI-GAYERI, ヒガヘリ, 日歸, Going and returning on the same day. — *ni szru*, to go and return on the same day.

HIGE, ヒゲ, 髭, The beard. *Uwa-hige*, a mustache. *Hō-hige*, whiskers. *Sh'ta-hige*, the beard on the chin.

HIGE, ヒゲ, 卑下, Behaving in an humble manner, taking a low place; depreciating one's self. *Hige sh'te mono wo iu*, to speak humbly. *Dzi-bun hige itasz ni shikadz*, there is nothing better than an humble deportment. *Hige szgiru*, to be over modest or humble. Syn. KEN-SON, KEN-TAI, HERI-KUDARU.

†HIGI, ヒギ, 非義, (*gi ni aradz*). Unjust, unreasonable.

HI-GIRI, ヒギリ, 日限, *n.* A fixed time, a set time in which to do anything. — *wo szru*, to set a time. Syn. NICHI-GEN.

†HI-GIYŌ, ヒギヤウ, 飛行, (*tobi yuku*). Flying. *Sennin higiyō jizai*, the Sennin fly whenever they please.

HIGO, ヒゴ, 籤, *n.* A long and slender slip of bamboo, used in making baskets.

HI-GŌ, ヒゴフ, 非業, Innocent, guiltless, not having done anything in the previous state of existence to bring down retribution in this life, (Bud). *Higō na shi wo awaremu*, to deplore the death of one cut off (apparently) without cause.

HI-GORO, ヒゴロ, 日來, Common, usual, for years past, habitual. — *no negai ga kanōta*, have gained what I have for years been wanting. — *no yūriki*, his usual power.

HI-GOTAI, ヒゴタヘ, 火堪, *n.* The property of enduring fire. — *ga yoi*, incombustible, fire proof. — *ga warui*, easily consumed.

HI-GOTO-NI, ヒゴトニ, 毎日, (*mainichi*), *adv.* Daily, every day. Syn. NICHI-NICHI.

HI-GUCHI, ヒグチ, 火口, *n.* The touch-hole of a gun. Syn. K'WAMON.

HI-GURASHI, ヒグラシ, 蜩, *n.* A kind of Cicada.

HI-GURE, ヒグレ, 日晩, *n.* Sunset, evening.

HIG'WASHI, ヒグワシ, 乾菓子, *n.* A kind of confectionary-

HI-HAN,-*szru*, ヒハン, 批判, *t. v.* To criticise, to point out the defects, animadvert upon. *Bun wo* —, to criticise a writing. *Shimo to sh'te o kami no koto wo — szbekaradz*, an inferior should not criticise the acts of his superior. *Hihan szru tokoro nashi*, there is no room for criticism. Syn. HI WO UTSZ.

HIHARA, ヒハラ, *n*, The side of the abdomen.

HI-HI, ヒヒ, 狒狒, *n.* The orang-outang.

†HI-HŌ, *-szru,* ヒハウ, 誹謗, *t.v.* To speak evil of, slander, calumniate. *H'to wo —.* Syn. SOSHIRU, WARUKU-IU.

HIJI, ヒヂ, 臂, The elbow. *— wo haru,* to stretch out the elbows, (as in a dispute). *— wo magete makura to szru,* to make a pillow of the arm.

HI-JI, ヒジ, 非時, *n.* A feast on the eve of the anniversary of a death.

†HIJI, ヒヂ, 泥, *(doro), n.* Mud.

HIJI, ヒジ, 秘事, *n.* A secret.

HIJI-JI, ヒヂヂ, 曾祖父, *n.* Great-grand father.

HĪJIJI, ヒイヂヂ, 高祖父, *n.* Great-great grand father.

HIJIKI, ヒヂキ, 臂木, *n.* A wooden elbow, brace, a wooden knee.

HIJIKI, ヒジキ, 鹿角菜, *n.* A kind of edible seaweed.

HI-JINI, ヒジニ, 餓死, *(wiyejini,)* To starve to death.

HIJIRI, ヒジリ, 聖, *n.* A sage, one intuitively wise and good, a Buddhist priest. *Kōya-hijiri,* a Buddhist saint. Syn. SEI-JIN.

HI-JIRIMEN, ヒヂリメン, 緋縐緬, *n.* Red crape.

HIJITSZBO, ヒヂツボ, 肘鈕, *n.* A hook and staple hinge.

†HIJŌ, ヒジヤウ, 非常, *(tszno ni aradz,)* Uncommon, unusual, strange, extraordinary, an unexpected event, emergency.

†HI-JŌ, ヒジヤウ, 非情, *(kokoro aradz,)* Without feeling, inanimate, (as trees &c.) *U-jō hi-jō,* animate and inanimate.

HIJŌGI, ヒジヤウギ, 日定木, *n.* A post used for showing the hour by its shadow.

†HI-JUTSZ, ヒジユツ, 秘術, *n.* Secret art, or skill.

HIKAGE, ヒカゲ, 晷, *n.* Sunlight, sunshine. *Hikage wo midz ni shinda,* died without seeing the light. *Hikage atataka ni natta,* the sun is warm. *Hikage mono,* one who, for some offence, is compelled to live in privacy.

HIKAKI, ヒカキ, 火斗, *n.* A fire-poker.

HIKAN, ヒカン, 脾疳, *n.* Marasmus,

HIKARABI, *-ru,-ta,* ヒカラビル, 枯乾, *i. v.* Dried and shriveled.

HIKARAKASHI, *-sz,-sh'ta,* ヒカラカス, 令光, or, HIKARASE, *-ru,-ta,* Caust. of *Hikari,* to cause to shine, to make bright.

HIKARE, *-ru,-ta,* ヒカレル, 被引, Pass. of *Hiku,* to be led, &c.

HIKARI, ヒカリ, 光, *n.* Light, lustre, radiance, refulgence, brightness, gloss, brilliance, glitter, (fig.) influence, power, virtue. *Hi no —,* light of the sun. *— wo tsztszmu,* to hide one's light. *— ga sasz,* the light shines.

HIKARI, *-ru,-tta,* ヒカル, 光, *i. v.* To shine, to glitter, sparkle, glisten, glossy, bright, to flash, gleam. *Hoshi ga hikaru,* the stars shine. *Hikari-wataru,* to flash or glisten on all sides. *Inadzma ga —,* the lightning flashes. Syn. KAGAYAKU.

HIKASARE, *-ru,-ta,* ヒカサレル, 被引, Pass. of *Hiku,* same as *Hikareru,* to be tempted, enticed, led astray. *Sake ni hikasarete michi wo somuku,* to be led astray by *sake* and forsake the right way.

HIKASE, *-ru,-ta,* ヒカセル, or HIKASHI, *-sz,-sh'ta,* ヒカス, The caust. of *Hiku.*

HIKATA, ヒカタ, 干潟, *n.* A dry sandy beach,

HIKAYE, *-ru,-ta,* ヒカヘル, 控, *t. v.* To pull back, to draw back, to restrain one's self, refrain, to hold-back, to check, stop, to forbear. *Uma wo —,* to rein back a horse. *Sode wo hikayete tō,* to pull the sleeve (of any one going) and inquire. *Sake wo —,* to diminish the amount of wine a person drinks. *Yenriyō sh'te hikayeru,* to refrain on account of diffidence. *Chō-men ni —,* to make a memorandum, or note of anything, in a note book. *Hon wo hikayete kōshaku wo kiku,* to listen to a lecture following it out of the book. *O hikaye nasare,* please restrain yourself. *Kuchi wo —,* to refrain from speaking. *Kikayete h'to wo tōsz,* to step back and let another pass. *Iye no maye ni ido wo —,* to make a well near the front of a house.

HIKAYE, ヒカヘ, 控, *n.* An entry, or memorandum made as a voucher, anything kept as a pattern. *Chō-men ni — ga aru,* there is a memorandum in the ledger.

‖HIKAYE-BASHIRA, ヒカヘバシラ, 支柱, *n.* A prop. Syn. TSZKKAIBŌ.

HIKAYE-GAKI, ヒカヘガキ, 控書, *n.* A memorandum, a note, minute, or voucher.

HIKAYEME, ヒカヘメ, 控目, *n.* Forbearance, self-restraint, modesty, moderation, temperance. *— ni szru,* to exercise moderation. *Kuchi wo — ni szru,* to be moderate in talking. *Ban-ji — ni nasare,* be temperate in all things. Syn. UCIBA, YENRIYO.

HIKAYESASE, *-ru,-ta,* ヒカヘサセル, 令控, Caust. of *Hikayeru.*

HIKE, ヒケ, 引, *n.* Only used in phrase, *— wo toru,* to be defeated.

HIKE, *-ru,-ta,* ヒケル, 引, *i. v.* To withdraw, retire, to cheapen. *Ban-sho ga hiketa,* the officers have left the guard house. *Nedan wa hike-masen,* I cannot cheapen it. *Asa ban ni dete yūgata hikeru,* to go out on duty in the morning, and leave in the evening. *Hike-kuchi,* about to retire.

†HIKEN, *-szru,* ヒケン, 披見, (*hiraki miru,*) To open and read (a letter.)

HIKESHI, ヒケシ, 火消, *n.* A fire-man. — *gumi,* a fire company.

HIKETSZ, ヒケツ, 秘結, *n.* Constipation of bowels.

HIKI, ヒキ, 匹, Numeral for animals; for a piece of silk of 52 feet long; for ten cash. *Uma nampiki,* how many horses? *Ushi sambiki,* three head of oxen. *Kinu ippiki,* one piece of silk. *Zeni jippiki,* a hundred cash. *H'yappiki,* one ichibu.

HĪKI, ヒイキ, 贔屓, *n.* Partiality, favoritism, patronage. — *wo szru,* to favor, to act with partiality. —*ni omō,* to feel partial, to favor. — *no hiki-daoshi,* injured by partiality. — *ni sareru,* to be regarded with favor or partiality, to be patronized.

HIKI, ヒキ, 蟇, *n.* A frog. Syn. KAWADZ.

HIKI, *-ku, -īta,* ヒク, 引, *t.v.* To pull, draw, haul, drag, lead, tow; To retire, withdraw from, retreat; to stretch, prolong, extend, spread; to deduct, subtract; to quote, cite, to look for a word in a dictionary; to distribute; to saw, to grind, to play on a stringed instrument. *Uma wo* —, to lead a horse. *Dai-kon wo* —. to pull up a radish. *Haha no te wo hīte aruku,* to walk holding a mother's hand. *Chimba wo hīte aruku,* to walk dragging a lame leg. *Fune wo* —, to tow a boat. *Iki wo* —, to draw a breath. *Yumi wo* —, to draw a bow. *Yedz wo* —, to draw a picture. *Jin wo* —, to remove a camp. *Mise wo* —, to retire from a shop, (for the day.) *Ban wo* —, to leave off a watch. *Ami wo* —, to drag a net. *Koye wo* —, to utter a long sound. *Ato wo* —, to hold on, or prolong the doing of anything. *Sakadzki wo* —, to prolong a drink of wine. *Ito wo* —, to pull a string, or lay a rope. *Kaze wo* —, to catch a cold. *Kiu-kin wo* —, to cut one's wages. *Nedan wo* —, to cheapen the price. *Ji wo* —, to look for a word. *Uta wo* —, to quote poetry. *Tatoye wo* —, to cite an illustration. *K'washi wo* —, to pass round a dessert. *Rō wo* —, to spread wax. *Mi wo* —, to retire. *Kokoro wo* —, to draw out one's opinion, to try, tempt. *Ita wo* —, to saw boards. *Usz wo* —, to grind a mill. *Kushi wo* —, to make a comb, (by sawing.) *Samisen wo* —, to play the guitar. *Koto wo* —, to play a harp. *Tō no uchi nanatsz hīte mitsz nokoru,* subtract seven from ten and three remains.

HIKI-AGE, *-ru, -ta,* ヒキアゲル, 引上, *t.v.* To draw up, to go up in price, to be promoted. *Sōba dai-bun hiki-ageta,* the market price has gone up considerably.

HIKI-AI, *-au, -atta,* ヒキアフ, 引合, *t.v.* To pull in opposite directions, or against each other; to be profitable, to consult together. *Te wo hikiatte aruku,* to walk hand in hand. *Hiki-au mono,* a profitable article of sale. *Hiki-awanu,* unprofitable article or business.

HIKI-AI, ヒキアヒ, 引合, *n.* A summons to appear before a magistrate to certify to some fact; implicated or involved along with others; a mercantile arrangement. — *wo kū,* to receive a summons, or to be implicated with others.

HIKI-AKE, *-ru, -ta,* ヒキアケル, 引明, *t.v.* To draw or pull open. *Shōji wo* —, to draw open a screen.

HIKI-AKE, ヒキアケ, 黎明, *n.* Day break, dawn.
Syn. YO-AKE.

HIKI-AMI, ヒキアミ, 引網, *n.* A seine.

HIKI-ATE, ヒキアテ, 引當, *n.* Security, pledge. — *ni szru,* to give security. *Iye wo — ni szru,* to give a house as security.
Syn. SHICHI.

HIKI-ATE, *-ru, -ta,* ヒキアテル, 引當, *t.v.* To place together, in order to compare, match, or value; to pit against.

HIKI-AWASE, *-ru, -ta,* ヒキアハセル, 引合, *t.v.* To introduce, make acquainted, to to draw together. To compare together, to collect. *Kono h'to wo ano h'to ni* —, to introduce this man to that one. *Ingiyō wo hiki-awash'te mo awanai,* having compared the seals together found they did not agree. *Yoroi no hiki-awase,* the joints of armor where it is fastened together.

HIKI-CHA, ヒキチャ, 末茶, *n.* Powdered tea.

HIKI-CHIGAYE, *-ru, -ta,* ヒキチガヘル, 引違, *t.v.* To dislocate, to succeed one who has just left. *Hone wo* —, to dislocate a bone. *Hiki-chigayete kuru,* to come in the place of one who has just retired.

HIKI-DASHI, *-sz, -sh'ta,* ヒキダス, 引出, *t.v.* To draw or pull out, to find a word in the dictionary, to quote, cite.

HIKI-DASHI, ヒキダシ, 引出, *n.* A drawer.

HIKI-DEMONO, ヒキデモノ, 引出物, *n.* A present.

HIKI-DO, ヒキド, 引戸, *n.* A sliding door.

HIKI-DZRI, *-ru, -tta,* ヒキズル, 引摺, *t.v.* To drag along the ground.

HIKI-FUDA, ヒキフダ, 引札, *n.* A circular, a handbill, notice. — *wo mawasz,* to circulate a notice. — *wo kubaru,* to distribute a notice.

HIKI-FUNE, ヒキフ子, 引舟, *n.* A towboat, a tug.

HIKI-GANE, ヒキガ子, 引金, *n.* The trigger of a gun.

HIKI-HADA, ヒキハダ, 引肌, *n.* A leather sword case.

HIKI-HADZSHI, *-sz, -sh'ta,* (coll. *Hippadzshi,*) ヒキハヅス, 引外, *t.v.* To pull out of its place, or from its fastenings, (as a door, or screen.)

HIKI-HAGI, *-gu, -ida,* ヒキハグ, (coll. *Hippagi,*) 引剝, *t.v.* To pull or strip off a covering, clothes, skin, &c.

HIKI-HANASHI, *-sz, -sh'ta,* (coll. *Hippanashi,*) ヒキハナス, 引放, *t.v.* To pull apart, to separate by pulling, as two persons, a branch, &c.

HIKI-HARI, *-ru, -tta,* (coll. *Hippari,*) ヒキハル, 引張, *t. v.* To pull, to stretch, to make taught, make tense.

HIKI-HASAMI, *-mu, -nda,* (coll. *Hippasami*) ヒキハサム, 引挾, *t. v.* To take up with two sticks, to place between two things.

HIKI-HATAKE, *-ru, -ta,* (coll. *Hippatake,*) ヒキハタケル, 引刷, *t. v.* To pull open, or apart, as the eye-lids, mouth, &c.

HIKI-HATAKI, *-ku, -ita,* (coll. *Hippataki,*) ヒキハタク, 引韃, *t. v.* To beat, (as in dusting a mat.)

HIKI-I, *-iru, -īta,* ヒキ井ル, 率, *t. v.* To lead, conduct, to bring. *Gunzei wo hikīte teki no shiro wo semeru,* to lead an army and attack an enemy's castle.

‖HIKII, -KI, -SHI, ヒキイ, 低, Low, same as *Hikui.*

HIKI-IRE, *-ru, -ta,* ヒキイレル, 引入, *t. v.* To pull in, to lead in; seduce, entice, persuade to enter.

HIKI-IRO, ヒキイロ, 引色, *n.* Appearance of retreating, to look like giving way.

HIKI-KABURI, *-ru, -tta,* (coll. *Hikkaburi,*) ヒキカブル, 引被, *t. v.* To draw over the head.

HIKI-KADZKI, *-ku, -ita,* (coll. *Hikkadzki,*) ヒキカヅク, 引被, *t.v.* To throw over the head.

HIKI-KAYE, *-ru, -ta,* ヒキカヘル, 引替, *t. v.* To exchange, to turn back, to repent.

HIKI-KAYESHI, *-sz, -sh'ta,* (coll. *Hikkayeshi,*) ヒキカヘス, 引返, *t. v.* To draw or pull back, to turn over, to lead back, to retract.

HIKI-KAZE, ヒキカゼ, 引風, *n.* A cold. — *wo sh'ta,* have caught a cold.

HIKI-KOMI, *-mu, -nda,* ヒキコム, 引込, *t. v.* To draw, or put into; to persuade, induce, or entice to enter; to draw in, contract, to embezzle.

HIKI-KOMORI, *-ru, -tta,* ヒモキコル, 引籠, *i. v.* To be confined, shut up, immured.

HIKI-KOSHI, *-sz, -sh'ta,* (coll. *Hikkosh.*) ヒキコス, 引越, *t.v.* To remove one's dwelling, to move from one house to another, change one's residence.

HIKI-KOTO, ヒキコト, 引事, *n.* A quotation, citation.

HIKI-KUDAKI, *-ku, -ita,* ヒキクダク, 引碎, *t. v.* To break, or grind to pieces.

HIKI-KUMI, *-mu, -nda,* (coll. *Hikkumi,*) ヒキクム, 引組, *i.v.* Clasped together (as wrestlers.

HIKI-KURABE, *-ru, -ta,* ヒキクラベル, 引競, *t. v.* To compare.

HIKI-MADO, ヒキコド, 牽窓, *n.* A sliding window in the roof.

HIKI-MATOME, *-ru, -ta,* ヒキマトメル, 引全, *t. v.* To collect in a pile, to gather, to assemble.

HIKI-MAWASHI, *-sz, -sh'ta,* ヒキマワス, 引廻, *t. v.* To lead about, to pull around.

HIKI-ME, ヒキメ, 蟇目, *n.* A kind of conjuration, by means of a bow and arrow, for the purpose of nullifying evil influences.

‖HIKI-MI, *-ru, -ta,* ヒキミル, 引見, *t. v.* To try, prove, tempt.

HIKI-MODOSHI, *-sz, -sh'ta,* ヒキモドス, 引戾, *t. v.* To lead, draw, or pull back.

HIKI-MOGI, *-gu, -ida,* ヒキモグ, 引捩, *t. v.* To twist off, to wrench off.

HIKI-MONO, ヒキモノ, 引物, *n.* Articles turned in a lathe. A dessert of fruit, or confectionary.

HIKI-MUKE, *-ru, -ta,* ヒキムケル, 引向, *t. v.* To pull in front of, pull opposite.

HIKI-MUSHIRI, *-ru, -ta,* ヒキムシル, 引招, *t. v.* To pluck off, (as grass, without eradicating.)

HIKI-MUSZBI, *-bu, -nda,* ヒキムスブ, 引結, *t. v.* To draw and tie in a knot.

HIKI-MUSZBI, ヒキムスビ, *n.* A bow-knot.

HIKI-NARASHI, *-sz, -sh'ta,* ヒキナラス, 彈

鳴, *t.v.* To twang, or play. (as a guitar). (引平), To level, make even.

HIKI-NOBASHI,*-sz,-sh'ta,* ヒキノバス, 引延, *t.v.* To pull and lengthen, to stretch.

HIKI-NOBE,*-ru,-ta,* ヒキノベル, 引延, *t.v.* (Idem).

HIKI-NOKE,*-ru,-ta,* ヒキノケル, 引退, *t.v.* To pull to one side, or out of the way, to pull out from amongst others, to subtract.

HIKI-NOKORI, ヒキノコリ, 引殘, *n.* The balance of an account; the remainder after deducting a part.

HIKI-NUKI,*-ku,-ita,* ヒキヌク, 引拔, *t.v.* To pull up by the roots, to extract, eradicate; to pick out, select.

HIKI-OI, ヒキオヒ, 引負, *n.* A debt, loss, obligation, or liability incurred in trade. — *ga dekita,* have incurred a debt.

HIKI-OKOSHI,*-sz,-sh'ta,* ヒキオコス, 引起, *i.v.* To pull and make to stand up, to raise up.

HIKI-OROSHI,*-sz,-sh'ta,* ヒキオロス, 引卸, *t.v.* To help down, to pull or drag down from a high place.

HIKI-OTOSHI,*-zs,-sh'ta,* ヒキオトス, 引落, *t.v.* To pull down, pull off, so as to fall. 准除, to subtract, (on the *soroban*).

HIKI-SABAKI,*-ku,-ita,* (coll. *Hissabaki,*) ヒキサバク, 引捌, *t.v.* To tear.

HIKI-SAGE,*-ru,-ta,* (coll. *Hissage,*) ヒキサゲル, 引提, *i.v.* To fall in price.

HIKISAKI,*-ku,-ita,* ヒキサク, 引裂, *t.v.* To tear.

HIKI-SHIBARI,*-ru,-tta,* (coll. *Hitchibari,*) ヒキシバル, 引縛, To tie, bind, (as a criminal).

HIKI-SHIBORI,*-ru,-tta,* ヒキシボル, 引絞, *t.v.* To draw (a bow).

†HIKI-SHIRAI,*-au,-atta,* ヒキシロフ, *i.v.* To be long, protracted, delayed, lingering, slow. *Zenkwai to miyetemo tokaku hiki-shirō,* although I am convalescing it is very slow. Syn. HAKADORANU.

HIKI-SHIRIZOKI,*-ku,-ita,* ヒキシリゾク, 引退, *i.v.* To retreat, retire, withdraw, leave.

HIKI-SHIWO, ヒキシホ, 引汐, *n.* Ebb-tide.

HIKI-SOYE,*-ru,-ta,* ヒキソヘル, 引添, *t.v.* To draw near, bring close, hold close to.

HIKI-TAOSHI,*-sz,-sh'ta,* ヒキタフス, 引倒, *t.v.* To pull over, (anything standing), pull down.

HIKI-TATE,*-ru,-ta,* ヒキタテル, 引立, *t.v.* To pull up, to pull and make erect; to favor, to promote.

HIKI-TAWAME,*-ru,-ta,* ヒキタワメル, 引撓, *t.v* To pull and bend down (as the branch of a tree).

HIKITE, ヒキテ, 引手, *n.* A knob, a catch in a screen to pull it by.

HIKI-TODOME,*-ru,-ta,* ヒキトドメル, 引留, *t.v.* To pull and stop, to detain, to stay.

HIKI-TOME,*-ru,-ta,* ヒキトメル, 引留, *t.v.* (Idem).

HIKI-TORI,*-ru,-tta,* ヒキトル, 引取, *t.v.* To take or bring away, to take back, to remove, to withdraw, to draw (as money from a bank).

HIKI-TSZDZKI,*-ku,-ita,* ヒキツヅク 引續, *i.v.* To continue a length of time, to succeed in a long series.

HIKI-TSZKE,*-ru,-ta,* ヒキツケル, 引著, *t.v.* To draw close to, to have a fit, to be convulsed, to faint.

HIKI-TSZKUROI,*-ō,-ōtta,* ヒキツクロフ, 引繕, *t.v.* To pull and adjust one's clothes, to mend.

HIKI-TSZME,*ru,-ta,* ヒキツメル, 引詰, *t.v.* To spread out, extend to its utmost, (as a bow).

HIKI-TSZRE,*-ru,-ta,* ヒキツレル, 引連, *t.v.* To lead, to take along with, accompany.

HIKI-TSZRI,*-ru,-tta,* ヒキツル, 拘攣, *i.v.* To be cramped, contracted, drawn together, (as by cramp.) *Yakedo no ato ga hikitszttе oru,* the cicatrice of the burn is contracted.

HIKI-UKE,*-ru,-ta,* ヒキウケル, 引受, *i.v.* To engage, to undertake, to contract, to be responsible for, to take, receive. *Mi no wiye ni —,* to take upon one's self.

HIKI-USZ, ヒキウス, 挽磨, *n.* A mill stone.

HIKI-WAKE,*-ru,-ta,* ヒキワケル, 引分, *t.v.* To pull apart, separate, (as two men fighting,) to part.

HIKI-WARI,*-ru,-tta,* ヒキワル, 挽割, *t.v.* To saw in two.

HIKI-WARI, ヒキワリ, 挽割, *n.* A kind of coarsely ground barley.

HIKI-WATASHI,*-sz,-sh'ta,* ヒキワタス, 引渡, *t.v.* To pass over, hand over, deliver up.

HIKI-YABURI,*-ru,-tta,* ヒキヤブル, 引破, *t.v.* To pull and tear.

HI-K'YAKU, ヒキヤク, 飛脚, *n.* A postman, courier.

†HI-K'YOKU, ヒキヨク, 祕曲, *n.* Secret art, or accomplishment.

HI-K'YŌ, ヒキヤウ, 卑怯, Craven-hearted, cowardly, weak-hearted, timid. — *na yatsz da*, a cowardly fellow.
Syn. OKBUIYŌ, KOSHINUKE.

HIKI-YOSE,*-ru,-ta*, ヒキヨセル, 引寄, *t. v.* To pull or lead near; to draw near, approach.

HIKIYURU, ヒキウル, 率, same as *Hikii.* To lead, command, conduct. *Gunzei wo* —, to lead an army.

HIKKA, ヒツカ, 筆架, *n.* A pen-rest, pen-rack.

HIKKAGAMI, ヒツカガミ, 膕, *n.* The hollow behind the knee.

HIKKAKARI,*-ru,-tta*, (*Hiki-kakari,*) ヒキカカル, 引掛, *i. v.* To be caught, hooked, hitched or entangled in any thing.

HIKKAKE,*-ru,-ta*, (*Hiki-kake,*) ヒキカケル, 引掛, *t. v.* To hitch, hook, catch, or fasten on to any thing.

HIKKAKAYE,*-ru,-ta*, (*Hiki-kakaye,*) ヒキカカヘル, 引抱, *t. v.* To take, embrace, or carry in the arms.

HIKKARAGE,*-ru,-ta*, (*Hikikarage,*) ヒキカラゲル, *t. v.* same as *Karage.*

HIKKATSZGI,*-gu,-ita*, (*Hiki-katszgi,*) ヒツカツグ, 引擔, *t. v.* same as *Katszgi.*

HIKKI, ヒツキ, 筆記, *n.* A journal, note-book, a note, or memorandum.

HIKKIYŌ, ヒツキヤウ, 畢竟, *adv.* In fine, at last, the sum of it, the long and short of it, after all. *Sei to jō to wakete wa iyedo, hikkiyō kokoro no koto ja*, although divided into what is called *sei* and *jō*, it is after all the mind only. Syn. SHOSEN, TSZMARI.

HIKKŌ, ヒツカウ, 筆耕, *n.* Making a business of copying, or a living by writing. *Hikkō-kaki*, a copyist.

HIKKOKASHI,*-sz,-sh'ta*, ヒツコカス, 引轉, *t. v.* To pull over, to pull down anything.

HIKKOMI,*-mu,-nda*, ヒツコム, see *Hikikomi*, 引込, *i. v.* To draw back, to be sunk in or hollowed, to be confined to the house.

HIKKUKURI,*-ru,-ta*, ヒツククル, 引縛, *t. v.* To bind, tie, to choke.

HIKKURIKAYE,*-ru,-ta*, ヒツクリカヘル, 翻顛, *i. v.* To be upset, capsized, over turned, over-set; to turn about.

HIKKURIKAESHI,*-sz,-sh'ta*, ヒツクリカヘス, 顛倒, *t, v.* To upset, capsize, overset, overturn.

HIKO, ヒコ, 曾孫, *n.* Great grandson.

HIKOBAYE, ヒコバヘ, 蘖, *n.* The sprouts which shoot up from the stump of a tree.

HIKOBOSHI, ヒコボシ, 彥星, *n.* The name of a star worshiped on the 7th day of the 7th month.

HIKUI,*-KI,-SHI*, ヒクイ, 卑, or, 低, *a.* Low, not high. *Sei ga* —, low in stature. *Koye ga* —, the voice is low. *Yaku ga* —, low in office. *Hikui yama*, a low hill. *Hikui ki*, a low tree.

HIKUKU, or, HIKŪ, ヒクヒク, *adv.* idem. *Hi ga — natta*, the sun is low. *H'to ni — deru*, to take a low place before others. — *szru*, to make low.

‖HIKUMEKI,*-ku,-ita*, ヒクメク, *i. v.* To jerk, twitch, or start, as in sleep.
Syn. BIKUTSZKU.

HIKUSA, ヒクサ, 低, *n.* The lowness, shortness, the height, as of stature.

HIMA, ヒマ, 隙, or, 間, *n.* An interval, or space between things. Spare or unoccupied time, leisure, time, opportunity. Breach of friendship, discord. — *ga nai*, have no time, no leisure. — *ga kakaru*, takes time. *Hima kara kaze ga tōsz*, the wind blows through the crack. *Hima na toki*, a time of leisure. *Hima na h'to*, a man out of employment, or who has not much to do. *Hima no aki shidai yukimashyō*, I will go as soon as I have time. *Hima wo dasz*, to dismiss, (as a servant.) *Hima wo yaru*, (idem.) — *wo negau*, to ask for dismission, (from employment.) — *wo morau*, to get a dismission. — *wo oshimu*, to grudge the time. — *wo nuszmu*. to steal time. — *wo ukagō*, to watch for an opportunity. — *ga iru*, to require time. — *wo tsziyasz*, to waste time. — *no koma*, (time's horse,) the flight of time.
Syn. SZKI, ITOMA.

HIMACHI, ヒマチ, 日祭, *n.* The worship of the rising sun.

HIMADORI,*-ru,-tta*, ヒマドル, 隙取, *i. v.* To be slow, tardy, dilatory, late, to delay. *Michi de himadotte osoku kita*, by delaying on the way he was late in coming.
Syn. TEMA WO TORU, HIMA-IRU.

HĪMAGO, ヒイマゴ 曾孫, *n.* Great-great-grand son.

HIMA-IRI,*-ru,-tta*, ヒマイル, 隙入, *i. v.* same as *Himadoru.*

†HI-MAN, ヒマン, 肥滿, *n.* Corpulent, fat. — *na h'to.* — *szru.*

HIMASHI, ヒマシ, 卑麻子, *n.* Castor bean. — *no abura*, Castor oil.

HIMAWARI, ヒマハリ, 向日葵, *n.* The sunflower.

HIMASHI-NI, ヒマシニ, 日増, *adv.* Daily more and more, increasing day by day. —

ambai ga yoku naru, he is getting better daily.

HIME, ヒメ, 姫, *n.* A princess. The daughter of the *Shōgun*, of a *Daimiyō*, or *Kuge*.

HIME,–*ru*,–*ta*, ヒメル, 秘, *t. v.* To hide, conceal, to keep private. *Hime-oku*, to hide away. Syn. HISZRU, KAKUSZ.

HIME-GIMI, ヒメギミ, 姫君, *u.* A princess.

HIME-HAJIME, ヒメハジメ, *n.* The first needle work of a new year.

†HI-MEI, ヒメイ, 非命, (*temmei ni aradz,*) Ill-fated, untimely. — *no shi wo nasz*, to die an untimely death,

HIME-MIYA, ヒメミヤ, 姫宮, *n.* A princess, only applied to the daughter of the *Mikado*.

HIME-MOSZ, ヒメモス, 終日, *adv.* The whole day. Syn. SHŪJITSZ.

HIME-NORI, ヒメノリ, 米糊, *n.* A kind of starch.

HIME-URI, ヒメウリ, 姫瓜, *n.* A kind of melon.

HIME-YURI, ヒメユリ, 姫百合, *n.* A kind of lily. The lilium callosum.

HI-MITSZ, ヒミツ, 秘密, *n.* A secret, mystery. — *wo iu*, to tell a secret. — *wo arawasz*, to reveal a secret.

†HIM-MIN, ヒンミン, 貧民, *n.* Poor people.

HIMO, ヒモ, 紐, *n.* A cord, braid, ribbon, — *wo muszbu.* — *wo toku.*

HI-MOCHI, ヒモチ, 火持, *n.* Not quickly consumed. *Kono szmi wa — ga ī*, this charcoal does not burn away rapidly.

HI-MŌDE, ヒモウデ, 日詣, *n.* Daily visiting the temples for devotion. — *wo szru.* Syn. NISSAN.

HIMOJII,–KI, ヒモジイ, *a.* Hungry. — *ga aru*, to be hungry. Syn. HIDARUI, WIYERU, HARA GA HERU.

HIMOJIKU, ヒモジク, *adv.* — *nai*, Not hungry.

HIMOJISA, ヒモジサ, *n.* Hunger.

HIMON, ヒモン, 秘文, *n.* A secret sentence used by conjurers, an incantation. — *wo tonayete ame wo furaseru*, to use incantations and bring rain.

HIMONO, ヒモノ, 干物, *n.* Dried fish.

HIMONO, ヒモノ, 檜物, *n.* Articles made of the *Henoki*, such as pill-boxes, &c.

HIMONOSHI, ヒモノシ, 檜物師, *n.* The maker of the above articles.

†HIMOROGI, ヒモロギ, 膰, *n.* Flesh offered to idols.

HIMOTO, ヒモト, 火元, *n.* The place where a conflagration commences.

†HIMOTSZ, ヒモツ, 被物, (*katszge mono,*) *n.* A reward, present. Syn. HŌBI.

†HIM-PU, ヒンプ, 貧富, Rich and poor.

HI-MURO, ヒムロ, 氷室, *n.* An ice house.

HIN, ヒン, 貧, (*madzshii,*) Poor, poverty. — *jin*, a poor man. — *ni semaru*, to be straitened with poverty. *Hin szreba don szru* = "A poor man is despised of his neighbour".

HIN, ヒン, 品, (*shina,*) *n.* Kind, sort, quality. *Jō-hin*, superior quality. *Ge-hin*, inferior quality. *Hin no yoi h'to*, a fine looking man. Syn. KURAI.

HINA, or, HĪNA ヒナ, 雛, *n.* Small images made of clay, or toys, set out on the festival of the 3rd day of the 3rd month, called *Hina no sekku*, or, *Hina no matszri.* also a young bird.

†HINA, ヒナ, 鄙, (*inaka,*) *n.* The country, rural, rustic.

†HINA-BITARU, ヒナビタル, 鄙, Rustic, clownish, awkward. Syn. INAKAMEKU, IYASHII.

†HINA-BITO, ヒナビト, 鄙人, *n.* (*inakamono*) A country-man, villager.

†HINADZRU, ヒナヅル, 雛鶴, *n.* A young crane.

HINA-GATA, ヒナガタ, 雛形, *n.* A miniature, plan, design, model. *Iye no — wo hiku*, to draw a plan of a house.

HI-NAKA, ヒナカ, 日中, During the day, in day-light, day-time. *Hiru hinaka*, id. Syn. HIRU, HAKUCHIU.

HINAMI, ヒナミ, 日並, Daily, every day, day after day, ordinarily. *Hinami ni kin jū riyō dztsz ri wo yete tszki ni ikura*, if a person gains ten *riyō* a day, how much will he gain in a month? Syn. NICHI-NICHI, MAI-NICHI.

HINAN, ヒナン, 誹難, *n.* Criticism, censure, fault-finding. — *szru*, to criticise, censure. — *wo iu.*

HI-NASHI, ヒナシ, 日済, *n.* Money borrowed to be repaid with interest by daily instalments. — *wo karu.*

HINATA, ヒナタ, 日向, *n.* Sunshine, a sunny place. — *ni iru to doku da*, it is hurtful to be in the sun. *Hinata-kusai*, stinking from exposure to the sun.

HINATABOKKO, ヒナタボクコ, 負暄, Basking in the sun. — *szru*, to bask in the sun.

HINAYE,–*ru*,–*ta*, ヒナエル, 乾萎, *i.v.* To be wilted, or flaccid by drying (as a fresh leaf). Syn. SHINABIRU.

HINAWA, ヒナハ, 火縄, *n.* A match, (for powder)

†HIN-CHI, ヒンチ, 貧地, *n.* A poor temple, poor soil, barren country.

HINE, ヒネ, 老, *(furu,)* Old, not of last crop. *Hine-gome*, old rice. *Tane ga hine de hayenu*, the seed is old and will not grow.

‖HINE,*-ru,-ta*, ヒネル, *i. v.* To be old, musty, or mildewed.

HINE-KURI,*-ru,-tta*, ヒネクル, *t. v.* To twist, or roll in the fingers, to turn, to screw. *Kō-jō wo* —, to use high-flown language.

HINE-KURI-MAWASHI,*-sz,-sh'ta*, ヒネクリマワス, 把玩, *t. v.* To twirl in the fingers, to play with, or turn about in the hands.

HINERI,*-ru,-tta*, ヒネル, 捻, *t. v.* To twist, roll in the fingers, to screw, turn, to knead. *Koyori wo* —. to twist paper. *Nomi wo* —, to roll a flea (in the fingers.) *Mi wo* —, to twist the body around. *Hineri-te* one who uses difficult language. Syn. NEJIRU.

HINERI-BUMI, ヒネリブミ, 捻書, *n.* A note fastened by being twisted or folded instead of being sealed.

HINICHI, ヒニチ, 比日, *n.* Day, same as *Hi.*

†HI-NIKU, ヒニク, 皮肉, *n.* Skin and flesh.

HI-NIN, ヒニン, 非人, *(h'to ni aradz.)* One so low as not to be regarded as a man. A beggar, a leather dresser. Syn. YETA.

HI-N'YAKU, ヒニヤク, 悼弱, Weak, feeble, not strong in body. Syn. JŪJAKU.

†HIN-KA, ヒンカ, 貧家, *(madzshiki ye)* A poor family.

HIN-KIU, ヒンキウ, 貧窮, Poor to the last degree, miserably poor. — *na mono.* — *ni kurasz.* — *de komaru.*

HIN-KU, ヒンク, 貧苦, *(madzshiki kurushimi.)* Poor and distressed.

†HIN-NIYO, ヒンニヨ, 貧女, *(madzshiki onna.)* A poor woman. *Chō-ja no man-dō yori hinniyo no-ittō*, the one light (offered to the *kami)* of a poor woman is better than ten thousand offered by a rich man.

HI-NOBE, ヒノベ, 日延, *n.* Extension of time, postponement. —*wo szru*, to extend the time, to postpone. — *wo negau*, to ask for an extension of time.

HI-NO-DE, ヒノデ, 日出, *n.* Sunrise.

HI-NO-IRI, ヒノイリ, 日入, *n.* Sunset.

HI-NO-IN, ヒノイン, 火印, *n.* A kind of conjuration, in which, by folding the fingers together in a certain way, and repeating incantations, fire is kindled; used by *Yama-bushi.*

HI-NO-KI, ヒノキ, 檜, *n.* A kind of pine. The retinispora obtusa.

HI-NO-KO, ヒノコ, 火粉, *n.* Sparks.

HI-NO-KOROMO, ヒノコロモ, 緋衣, *n.* A crimson garment worn by a priest.

HI-NO-MARU, ヒノマル, 日丸, *n.* The Japanese flag of a red ball on a white ground.

HI-NO-MIYAGURA, ヒノミヤグラ, 望火櫓, *n.* A fire tower, or look-out.

HI-NO-MOTO, ヒノモト, 日本, *n.* Japan, 火元, A fire-place. — *go yō-jin nasare*, be careful of your fire-places.

HI-NO-MONO-DACHI, ヒノモノダチ, 火物絕, *n.* Abstinence from all cooked food in performance of a vow.

HINOSHI, ヒノシ, 熨斗, *n.* A smoothing iron. — *wo kakeru*, to iron clothes.

HI-NO-TE, ヒノテ, 火手, *n.* The flame of a conflagration.

HI-NO-TO, ヒノト, 丁, *n.* One of the ten calender signs, used in designating years, months, days, hours, points of compass, &c.

HI-NO-YE, ヒノエ, 丙, *n.* One of the ten signs, see *Hinoto.*

HI-NO-ZŌ, ヒノザウ, 脾, *n.* The spleen.

†HIN-SEN, ヒンセン, 貧賤, *(madzshiki, iyashii.)* Poor and mean.

HI-OBA, ヒヲバ, 祖叔母, *n.* Grand-father's aunt.

HI-ODOSHI, ヒオドシ, 緋絨, *n.* Armor, the plates of which are bound together by red thread.

HI-ŌGI, ヒアフギ, 檜扇, *n.* A fan made of *Hinoki.*

HIŌGI, ヒアフギ, 射干, *n.* The Ixia Chinensis.

HI-ŌI, ヒオホイ, 日覆, *n.* A sun screen.

HI-OKORI, ヒオコリ, 日瘧, *n.* A quotidian ague.

HIPPAKU, ヒクパク, 逼,迫, *n.* Destitution, want, scarcity. *Ano h'to wa hippaku no yōsz da*, he appears to be very destitute. *Kome ga* —, the rice is out. *Ito ga — ni natta*, silk has become very scarce. Syn. SASHI-TSZMARU, HIN-KIU.

HIPPARI,*-ru,-tta*, ヒツパル, See *Hikihari.*

HIPPASAMI,*-mu,-nda*, ヒツパサム, 引挾, *t.v.* The same as *Hasami.*

HIPPATAKI,*-ku,-ita*, ヒツパタク, 引鞋, *t.v.* The same as *Hataki.*

HIP-PŌ, ヒツパフ, 筆法, *n.* The rules of penmanship, mode of writing, or forming characters. — *ga yoi*, — *ga warui.* Syn. FUDE NO TSZKAI-KATA.

†HIP-PU, ヒツプ, 匹夫, *n.* A low, vulgar

person, a person of low rank, or station. — *no yū*. brute courage.

HIRA, ヒラ, 平, *n*. Flat, level, plain, common, surface. *Te no hira*, the palm of the hand. *Hira-samurai*, common soldier. *Katana no* —, the flat of a sword. *Hira uchi ni szru*, to strike with the flat of the sword. *San no hira*, the third leaf of a book. *Hira ichi men*, the whole, universal. *Omote no* —, the front surface. *Ura no* —, the inside.

HIRA, ヒラ, *n*. A lacquered bowl with a cover.

HIRA-BARI, ヒラバリ, 平針, *n*. A lancet.

HIRA-BITO, ヒラビト, 平人, *(hei nin.) n*. A common person. Syn. TADABITO.

HIRA-CHI, ヒラチ, 平地, *(heichi.) n*. Level ground.

HIRADA, ヒラダ, 艜, *n*. A flat-boat.

HIRA-HIRA-TO, ヒラヒラト, 片片, *adv*. With a fluttering, waving, or undulating motion. *Cho ga — to tobu*, the butterfly flies with a fluttering motion.

HIRA-GAMA, ヒラガマ, 平釜, *n*. A kind of flat pot for cooking.

HIRAGI, ヒラギ, 柊, *n*. A kind of evergreen tree with thorny leaves. The Olea aquifolium.

HIRA-KANA, ヒラカナ, 平假名, *n*. The Japanese grass characters.

HIRAKE,-*ru*,-*ta*, ヒラケル, 開, *i. v*. To open, unfold, to be civilized. *Ame-tszchi hirakete kara*, from the beginning of creation. *Hana ga* —, the flower opens. *Yoku hiraketa kuni da*, a highly civilized country.

HIRAKI,-*ku*,-*ita*, ヒラク, 開, *t. v*. or *i. v*. To open, to unclose, unseal, uncover, unfold, spread out, to begin, to lay out, to explain, to reveal, to clear from obstruction. *To, hon, me, te, f'tokoro, tegami nado wo* —, to open a door, book, the eye, hand, bosom, or a letter. *Michi wo* —, to open a road. *Mise wo* —, to open a shop; to set up shop. *Hata wo* —, to clear land, lay out new fields. *Dō-ri wo* —, to explain the reason. *Tera wo* —, to leave the charge of a temple. *Seki wo* —, to dismiss a meeting. *Fune ga iwa wo hiraite hashiru*, the ship gives the rock a wide berth. *Hana ga hiraita*, the flower has opened. Syn. AKERU.

HIRAKI, ヒラキ, *n*. The opening, beginning, blooming. A door. *Mise-biraki wo szru*, to open a new store. *Hiraki wo akete miyo*, open the door and look. *Hiraki wo noru*, to sail close to the wind. *Hana no — ga hayai*, the flowers bloom early.

HIRAKI-DO, ヒラキド, 開戸, *n*. A door which turns on hinges.

HIRAME, ヒラメ, 比目魚, *n*. The sole fish.

HIRAME,-*ru*,-*ta*, ヒラメル, 匾, *t. v*. To flatten. *Mochi wo* —.

HIRAMEKASHI,-*sz*,-*sh'ta*, ヒラメカス, 閃, *t. v*. To wave, brandish, flourish, flash, glisten. *Katana wo* —, to brandish a sword. *Hata wo* —, to wave a flag.

HIRAMEKI,-*ku*,-*ita*, ヒラメク, 閃, *i. v*. To wave, undulate, to flash, glisten, glitter. *Hata ga* —, the flag waves. *Inadzma ga* —, the lightning flashes.

HIRAMI, ヒラミ, *n*. Flat in shape, flattish. — *wo tszkeru*, to flatten.

HIRAMI,-*mu*,-*nda*, ヒラム, *i. v*. To be flat (in shape.) *Pan ga hiranda*, the bread is flat.

HIRA-NI, ヒラニ, 平, *adv*. Earnestly, importunately, urgently, pressingly. — *negō*, to earnestly implore. — *fusz*, to bow humbly. — *tanomu*, to ask urgently. Syn. HITASZRA-NI.

HIRA-OSHI-NI, ヒラオシニ, 平推, *adv*. Violently, forcibly. Syn. MURI-NI, SHITE.

HIRARI-KURURI-TO, ヒラリクルリト, 旋轉, *adv*. Turning, or brandishing; a flashing, glittering appearance. *Katana wo — mawash'te teki ni kakatta*, brandishing his sword rapidly he fell upon the enemy.

HIRARI-TO, ヒラリト, 閃, *adv*. In a quick, nimble manner, like the flutter or turn of a leaf, like a flash. — *mi wo kawashi*, quickly to turn the body; nimbly to dodge. *Uma yori — tobi-oriru*, to jump nimbly from off a horse.

HIRATAGUMO, ヒラタグモ, 壁錢, *n*. A kind of spider.

HIRATTAI,-KI,-SHI, ヒラツタイ, 匾, *a*. Flat. — *ishi*, a flat stone.

HIRATTAKU, or HIRATTŌ, ヒラツタク, 匾, *adv*. idem. — *szru*, to flatten. — *naru*, to become flat.

HIRATTASA, ヒラツタサ, *n*. Flatness.

HIRAUCHI-NO-HIMO, ヒラウチノヒモ, 平打紐, *n*. Flat-braid.

HIRA-YA, ヒラヤ, 平屋, *n*. A one storied house, a low or flat house.

HIRE, ヒレ, 魚翅, *n*. The fins of a fish.

HIRE-FUSHI,-*sz*,-*sh'ta*, ヒレフス, 平伏, *i. v*. To bow low with the face to the earth. *Gozen ni hire-fush'te aisatsz szru*, bowing down low before the prince to salute him. Syn. HEI-FUKU SZRU.

†HI-REI, ヒレイ, 非禮, Impolite, ill-mannerd, rude, contrary to etiquette. Syn. BUREI, SHITSZ-REI.

†HI-RETSZ, ヒレツ, 卑劣, Mean, base, vulgar, low. *Hiretsz-na h'to*, a low-minded person. Syn. IYASHII.

†HI-RI, ヒリ, 非理, (*Dōri de nai.*) Unreasonable.

HIRI-HIRI, ヒリヒリ, *adv*. With a smarting or burning pain. — *itamu*, to smart, burn.

†HI-RIKI, ヒリキ, 非力, (*chikara nashi.*) Weak, feeble, without strength.

HIRI-TSZKI, *-ku,-ita*, ヒリツク, *t. v.* To smart, to burn.

HIRIŌDZ, ヒリヨウヅ, *n.* A kind of foo d.

HIRO, ヒロ, 尋, *n.* A fathom, of about 5 feet English, the distance between the hands when the arms are out-stretched. *H'to hiro ya-biki*, one length and a half of the out-stretched arms. *Umi no fukasa wa iku hiro tatsz*, how many fathoms deep is the sea? *Nana-hiro*, 7 fathoms=35 feet.

HIRŌ, ヒロウ, 披露, *n.* Introduction, ushering, publishing. — *wo szru*, to usher, introduce, to tell, to publish, make known, to herald, proclaim, make public, to report to a superior. *Yome-iri no — wo szru*, to conduct a bride around and introduce her to the neighbours. *On tszide no migiri yoroshiku go hirō negai age soro*, when you have a convenient time please make it known to your superior.

†HI-RŌ, ヒラウ, 疲労, *i.v.* Faint, or exhausted by sickness.

HIRŌ, ヒロフ, To pick up, see *Hiroi*.

HIRO-BA, ヒロバ, 廣場, *n.* A wide, spacious place.

HIRO-BIRO-TO, ヒロビロト, 廣廣, *adv.* Wide, spacious, large, roomy. — *sh'ta hara*, a wide plain.

HIRO-BUTA, ヒロブタ, 廣蓋, *n.* A large tray, or waiter.

HIROGARI, *-ru,-tta*, ヒロガル, 廣, *i.v.* To spread, extend over; enlarged, propagated, published, diffused, *H'yōban ga* —, the report spreads

HIROGE, *-ru,-ta*, ヒロゲル, 擴, *t.v.* To open out, extend, widen, unfold.

†HIROI, *-ō,-ōta*, ヒロフ, 拾步, *i.v.* To walk. Syn. ARUKU.

HIROI, -KI,-SHI, ヒロイ, 廣, *a.* Wide, broad, spacious, roomy, extensive. — *iye*, a spacious house. — *kokoro*, magnanimous.

HIROI, *-ō,-ōta*, ヒロフ, 拾, *t.v.* To pick up. *Tori ga ye wo hirō*, the bird picks up its food. *Hiroi-mono wo sh'ta*, to pick up something which has been dropped.

HIROI-ATSZME, *-ru,-ta*, ヒロヒアツメル, 拾集, *t.v.* To pick up and put together, to gather into a pile.

HIROKU, or HIRŌ, ヒロク, 廣, *adv*, See *Hiroi*. — *szru*, to widen, to make spacious.

HIRO-MA, ヒロマ, 廣間, *n.* A large room in a prince's house, a parlour.

HIROMARI, *-ru,-tta*, ヒロマル, 弘, *i.v.* Spread abroad, made known widely, published, advertised. *Na ga* —, his name is spread abroad.

HIROME, *-ru,-ta*, ヒロメル, 弘, *t. v.* To spread abroad, publish, make known, promulgate, to advertise. *H'yōban wo* —, to spread a report.

HIROME, ヒロメ, 弘, *n.* Introduction, publishing, promulgation, advertisement. *Yome no — wo szru*, to lead a bride around and introduce her to the neighbours. *Nabirome*, a publishing, or advertisement of one's name, (when changed).

HIROMI, ヒロミ, *n.* A large, spacious place.

HIRO-NIWA, ヒロニハ, 廣庭, *n.* A spacious yard.

HIRO-YEN, ヒロエン, 廣椽, *n.* A wide verandah.

HIRU, ヒル, 蒜, *n.* Garlic. Syn. NIN-NIKU.

HIRU, ヒル, See *Hi*.

HIRU, ヒル, 蛭, *n.* A leech, blood-sucker.

HIRU, ヒル, 晝, *n.* Noon, day-time. *Yoru hiru*, day and night. *Hiru no nanatsz*, 4 o'clock in the day. *Hiru-ne*, sleeping in the day time. *Hiru-gohan*, dinner. *Hiru-meshi*, (idem).

HĪRU, ヒヒル, 蠶蛾, *n.* The moth of a silkworm.

HIRU-DOKI, ヒルドキ, 正午, *n.* 12 o'clock M.

HIRU-GAO, ヒルガホ, 鼓子花, *n.* The Ipomœa filicaulis.

HIRU-GAYE, *-ru,-ta*, ヒルガヘル, 飜, *i.v.* To turn over and over, as a leaf or flag blown by the wind; to wave, to turn, change about. *Hata ga* —. *Mikata ga hirugayette teki ni natta*, the friend has turned to be an enemy. *Aku nin hirugay ette zen-nin to natta*, the bad man has turned to be good. Syn. HIKURI-KAYERU, URAGAYERU.

HIRU-GAYESHI, *-sz,-sh'ta*, ヒルガヘス, 飜, *t.v.* To turn over, change-round, shift about. *Yak'soku wo* —, to break a promise.

†HIRUI, ヒルイ, 比類, Anything to compare with. — *nashi*, incomparable.

HIRUMAKI, ヒルマキ, 蛭纏, *n.* The iron rings around the end of a spear.

HIRU-MA, ヒルマ, 晝間, *n.* The middle of the day, noon.

HIRU-MAYE, ヒルマヘ, 晝前, *n.* Forenoon.

HIRUMESHI, ヒルメシ, 晝飯, *n.* Noon-meal, dinner.

HIRUMI,,*-mu,-nda*, ヒルム, *i.v.* To draw back in fear, to flinch, to be disheartened, lose courage. *Mikata no taigun wo mite teki wa szkoshiku hirumitari*, the enemy seeing our large army began to lose courage. Syn. CHIJIMU, IJIKERU.

HIRUNE, ヒル子, 晝寐, *n.* Sleeping in the day time.

HIRU-SZGI, ヒルスギ, 晝過, *n.* Afternoon.

HISA-BISA, ヒサビサ, 久久, *adv.* A long time. — *o me ni kakarimasen*, have not seen you for a long time.

HISAGE, ヒサゲ, 提子, *n.* A kind of kettle for holding *sake*. Syn. CHŌSHI.

HISAGI,*-gu,-ida*, ヒサグ, 販, or 鬻, *t.v.* To hawk goods; to sell in the streets; to peddle.

HISAGO, ヒサゴ, 瓢, *n.* A calabash, gourd. Syn. H'YŌTAN.

HISA-KATA, ヒサカタ, 久堅, A word without meaning (called *makura-kotoba*,) used only in poetry in connection with heavenly objects, as. — *no sora*; — *no hi*; — *no tszki*; — *no ame*; — *no hikari*.

HISAO, ヒサヲ, 槲杖, *n.* A ramrod.

HISASHII,-KI, ヒサシイ, 久, *a.* A long time, ancient. *Hisashii-yamai*, an old complaint. *Hisashii-hanashi*, an ancient story. *Hisashii ato*, a long time ago.

HISASHI, ヒサシ 庇, *n.* A penthouse, or small roof projecting over a door or window.

HISASHI-BURI, ヒサシブリ, 久振, Long time since, a long time has elapsed since. — *de aimash'ta*, it is a long time since I met him.

HISASHIKU, or HISASHŪ, ヒサシク, 久, *adv.* A long time, anciently. —*o me ni kakarimasen*, have not seen you for a long time.

HISASHISA, ヒサシサ, *n.* The length of time since.

†HI-SATSZ, ヒサツ, 飛札, *n.* A letter by post.

†HI-SEKI, ヒセキ, 砒石, *n.* Arsenic.

†HI-SEN, ヒセン, 卑賤, *(iyashii.)* Low, mean, vulgar. *Hisen-na h'to.*

HI-SHI,*-szru,-sh'ta*, ヒスル 秘, *t.v.* To keep secret, to conceal. Syn. KAKUSZ.

HISHI, ヒシ, 菱, *u.* A kind of water plant, water caltrops. The Trapa incisa.

HISHI, ヒシ, *n.* Diamond-shaped.

†HI-SHI,*-szru,-sh'ta*, ヒスル, 比, *(kuraberu.)* To compare.

HISHI-BISHI-TO, ヒシビシト, *adv.* Severely, harshly, violently. — *shibaru*, to tie tightly. — *utsz*, to beat severely. — *iu beki koto wo iu*, to say what ought to be said in a harsh manner.

HISHIGE,*-ru,-ta*, ヒシゲル, *i.v.* To be crushed, mashed, to be flattened.

HISHIGE-BANA, ヒシゲバナ, 凹鼻, *n.* A flat nose; or a nose broken and flattened by disease.

HISHIGI,*-gu,-ida*, ヒシグ, 挫, *t.v.* To crush, mash, to flatten; break into pieces, to bruise. *Take wo —. Te wo —. Ikioi wo —.* Syn. TSZBUSZ.

HISHIGO, ヒシゴ, 鯷, *n* A kind of fish.

HISHIKUI, ヒシクヒ, 鴻, *n.* A swan.

HISHIMEKI,*-ku,-ita*, ヒシメク, 鬩, *i.v.* To make a noise, clamor, tumult, or uproar. Syn. SAWAGI-TATSZ, SŌDŌ SZRU.

HISHI-TO, ヒシト, 必至, *adv.* Firmly, strictly, severely, earnestly. — *kokoro ni kakeru* to fix in the mind. — *tanomu*, earnestly to ask. (2.) The sound of slamming, or dashing. *Fuszma, to nado wo — sasz*, to shut the screen, or door with a slam.

HISHIWO, ヒシホ, 醢, *n.* A kind of food made of pickled minced meat. *Ume bishiwo*, plum-jelly.

HI-SHIWO, ヒシホ, 干汐, *n.* The ebb-tide.

†HI-SHO, ヒシヨ, 秘書, *n.* Books on secret subjects.

†HI-SHŌ, ヒシヤウ, 悲傷, *(kanashimi itamu.)* Sad and afflictive.

†HISHU, ヒシユ, 匕首, *(himo gatana.) n.* A dirk.

HISO-HISO, ヒソヒソ, 蜜蜜, *adv.* Secretly, privately, softly, stealthily. — *mono wo iu*, to speak secretly. Syn. NAISHŌ, KOSSORI.

HISOKA-NA, ヒソカナ, 密, *a.* Secret, private, hidden. — *tokoro*, a secret place.

HISOKA-NI, ヒソカニ, 私, *adv.* Secretly, privately, softly, stealthily. — *mono wo iu*, to speak privately.

HISOME,*-ru,-ta*, ヒソメル, 潜, *t. v.* To hide, conceal. 顰, To wrinkle, contract, pucker up. *Koye wo —*, to speak in a low voice, to whisper. *Mi wo —*, to hide one's self. *Mayu wo —*, to wrinkle or contract the brow, (as in pain, anger,) to frown. *Kuchi wo —*, to pucker the mouth.

HISOMEKI,*-ku,-ita*, ヒソメク, *t.v.* To tell secretly, to whisper. *Uwasa wo —*, to tell secretly a report. Syn. SASAYAKU.

HISOMI,*-mu,-nda*, ヒソム, 潜, *i.v.* To hide, conceal, lie hid, lurk, 顰, To contract, wrinkle, to fall in, (as the mouth of an old person.) *Hibari wa kusa no naka ni hi-*

sonde iru, the lark hides in the grass. *Sakana ga iwa no aida ni* —, the fish hides among the rocks. Syn. KAKURURU, SHINOBU.

HISŌSEKI, ヒサウセキ, 砒霜石, *n.* Arsenic.

HISSAGE,—*ru,–ta,* ヒツサゲル, 引提, *t. v.* To carry anything hanging from the hand.

HISSABAKI,*-ku,–ita,* ヒツサバク, See *Hiki-sabaki.*

†HISSEKI, ヒツセキ, 筆跡, *n.* A writing, manuscript, record.

HISSHI, ヒツシ, 必死, *(kanaradz shisz,)* Must certainly die. — *ni natte tatakau,* to fight with desperation. *Ima wa — to kokoro wo sadame,* made up his mind that now he must die.

HISSOKU, ヒクソク, 逼促, To be reduced in circumstances, diminished or impoverished.

HISSORI-TO, ヒツソリト, 寂莫, *adv.* Quiet, still, silent. — *sh'te iru,* to be still. — *sh'ta tokoro,* a still, quiet place.

HISSO-TO, ヒツソト, Same as *Hissori to.*

†HISZI, ヒスイ 翡翠, *n.* A king-fisher. Syn, KAWASEMI.

HISZRU, ヒスル, 比, See *Hi-shi.*

HITA, ヒタ, 引板, *n.* A thing for scaring birds from a rice field. Syn. NARUKO.

HITA-HITA, ヒタヒタ, *adv.* The sound of water splashing. *Midz ga — to funa-bata ni utsz,* the water splashes against the sides of the boat. — *to uchi-noru,* to ride splashing through the water.

HITAI, ヒタイ, 額, *n.* The forehead. — *no shiwa,* the wrinkles in the forehead. — *no ao-szji,* the blue veins in the forehead.

HITAKI, ヒタキ, 火燒, *n.* A fireman, stoker.

HITAKI, ヒタキ ,鶲, *n.* A kind of bird.

HITAMONO, ヒタモノ, *adv.* Bent on, earnestly, intently, importunately, constantly. Syn. HITASZRA, MOPPARA.

†HI-TAN, ヒタン, 悲歎, *(kanashimi nageku,)* To mourn, weep, lament. — *no namida ni kureru,* blinded by tears of sorrow.

HITASHI,*-sz,–sh'ta,* ヒタス, 浸, *i. v.* To soak, steep, moisten, macerate. *Midz ni* —, to steep in water. Syn. TSZKERU.

HITASZRANI, ヒタスラニ, 只管, *adv.* Earnestly, wholly taken up with, vehemently, importunately. — *tanomu,* to ask importunately. *Gaku mon wo — ssszmeru,* to earnestly urge another to learn. — *iken wo kuwayeru,* to earnestly caution. Syn. HITAMONO, MOPPARA, ICHIDZ-NI, SHIKIRI-NI.

HITATARE, ヒタタレ, 直垂, *n.* A kind of robe worn by nobles.

HITA-TO, ヒタト, 渾, *adv.* Closely, tightly, the sound made by striking a thing against another. — *tszku,* to put close against, to stick tightly. — *narabete oku,* to arrange closely together.

H'TO, ヒト, 人, *n.* A man, a person (male, or female.) people, mankind, others. — *to naru,* to become a man, to be full grown. — *wo h'to ni omowadz,* to despise others, caring not for men. — *ni kakaru,* to be dependent on others. — *ni szgiru,* to excel others.

H'TO, ヒト, 一, One; same as *H'totsz.* (used only in compound words.) as, *H'to-tabi,* once, one time. *H'to-toshi,* a year. *H'to-tszki,* a month. *H'to-toki,* an hour. *H'to-hi,* one day. *H'to-yo,* a night. *H'to mawari,* one revolution, one week, (only in taking medicine).

H'TO-AI, ヒトアヒ, 人合, *n.* Popular, friendly. — *no yoi h'to,* a person friendly, companionable.

H'TO-BANARE, ヒトバナレ, 人離, *n.* Apart from men, separate from the society of others.

H'TO-BARAI, ヒトバラヒ, 人拂, *n.* Clearing the room or place of people. — *de mitszdan szru,* to clear the room and talk in secret.

H'TO-BASHIRA, ヒトバシラ, 人柱, *n.* Burying a man alive, on laying the foundation of a castle, (an ancient custom). — *wo ireru.*

H'TO-BITO, ヒトビト, (plural.) Men, people.

H'TO-DAKARI, ヒトダカリ, 人簇, *n.* A crowd, of people. — *szru,* to crowd together,

H'TO-DAMA, ヒトダマ, 人魂, *n.* A phosphorescent ball which flies from one place to another, supposed to be the spirit of a dead person.

H'TO-GARA, ヒトガラ, 人柄, *(jim-pin,) n.* Kind, or quality of man. — *no yoi h'to,* a fine man, (in personal appearance). — *no warui h'to,* a vulgar looking fellow.

H'TO-GATA, ヒトガタ, 人形, *n.* A statue, or image of a man.

H'TOGOMI, ヒトゴミ, *n.* A crowd.

H'TO-GOROSHI, ヒトゴロシ, 人殺, *n.* Manslaughter, murder.

H'TO-GOTO, ヒトゴト, 人言, *n.* Talking about others. — *wo iu na,* don't talk about others.

H'TO-GOTO-NI, ヒトゴト, 毎人, Every body, each person.

H'TO-JICHI, ヒトジチ, 人質, *n.* A hostage. — *wo toru,* take a hostage. — *wo yaru,* to give a hostage.

H'TO-JINI, ヒトジニ, 人死, *n.* A person dead, somebody killed. — *ga atta*, there was a person killed. — *wa nakatta*, there was nobody killed.

H'TO-KADZ, ヒトカズ, 人數, *n.* The number of persons, the population.
Syn. NIN-DZU.

H'TO-KIWA, ヒトキハ, 一際, *adv.* Especially, particularly, preëminently.

H'TO-MADZ, ヒトマヅ, 一先, *adv.* In the first place.

H'TO-MANE, ヒトマ子, 人眞似, *n.* Mimicking, or imitating others. — *wo szru*, to mimick, or imitate others.

H'TO-ME, ヒトメ, 人目, The eyes of others, the public, the world. — *wo habakaru*, to fear, or shun the notice of others. — *wo hajiru*, to be bashful, or ashamed before others. — *ni kakaru*, to expose to the world.

H'TOMI, ヒトミ, 瞳子, *n.* The pupil of the eye.

H'TO-MI-GOKŪ, ヒトミゴクウ, 人身牲, *n.* Human sacrifices offered to the Kami.

H'TOMOJI, ヒトモジ, 葱, *n.* An onion.
Syn. NEGI.

H'TOMUKI-NI, ヒトムキニ, 一向, *adv.* With the whole heart strength or care; earnestly, attentively; with one turn. — *mono wo szru*, to do any thing with the whole heart. *H'tomuki na h'to*, one who engages earnestly in any thing.

H'TO-NAMI, ヒトナミ, 人並, Like men generally, like other people, or the common run of mankind. — *ni haori wo kiru*, to wear the coat as people generally do. — *na h'to*, a person not different from others.

H'TORASHII,-KI, ヒトラシイ, *a.* Looking, or acting like a man, or human being.

H'TORASHIKU, ヒトラシク, *n.* idem.

H'TORI, ヒトリ, 一人, One person, alone, single. *Nin-soku wa h'tori yonde koi*, call a coolie. *H'tori de yuku*, to go alone, or by one's self. *H'tori-muszko*, an only son. *H'tori-mono*, a single person, without relatives, or a person who lives alone. *H'tori-ne wo szru*, to sleep alone.

H'TORIDACHI, ヒトリダチ, 獨立, *n.* Independent, free of others, standing alone, (as a child learning to walk.) — *no kuni* a country independent of any other.
Syn. DOKU-RIU.

H'TORI-DZMI, ヒトリズミ, 獨居, *n.* Living alone.

H'TORI-GO, ヒトリゴ, 獨子, *n.* An only child.

H'TORI-GOTO, ヒトリゴト, 獨語, *n.* Talking to one's self. — *wo iu*, to talk to one's self.

H'TORI-MI, ヒトリミ, 獨身, (*doku shin.*) Alone, solitary, single, without kindred.

HI-TORI-MUSHI, ヒトリムシ, 火取蟲, Insects which in summer fly into a light, and sometimes extinguish it.

H'TO-SASHI-YUBI, ヒトサシユビ, 食指, *n.* The index-finger.

H'TOSHII,-KI, ヒトシイ, 齊, *a.* Same, equal, like, same time, together. — *kokoro*, like minded. Syn. DŌZEN, ONAJI.

H'TOSHIKU, ヒトシク, 齊, *adv.* idem. *Haru no yo no yume ni* —, like the dream of a spring night. Syn. GOTOKU.

H'TO-SHIKIRI, ヒトシキリ, 一頻, One sharp or violent effort, one paroxysm. — *wa ayaukatta*, at one awful moment he was in great danger. *Ame ga — futte hareru*, it rained violently for a while and then cleared off.

H'TOSHINAMI-NI, ヒトシナミニ, 等並, *adv.* In the same manner, like. Syn. DŌYŌ-NI.

H'TOSHIWO, ヒトシホ, 一入, *adv.* Still more. — *yoroshii*, better still.
Syn. NAO.

H'TO-SZJI-NI, ヒトスヂニ, 一筋, *adv.* Directly, exclusively.

H'TO-TO-NARI, ヒトトナリ, 爲人, *n.* Character, disposition, nature. *Sono — jihi fukashi*, he was a man of an exceeding kind disposition.

H'TOTSZ, ヒトツ, 一, (*ichi,*) *a.* One, same. — *to sh'te yoi koto mo nai*, there is nothing good, or, not a single good thing.

H'TOYA, ヒトヤ, 牢獄, *n.* A gaol, prison.
Syn. RŌYA.

H'TOYA, ヒトヤ, 人家, *n.* A human habitation.

H'TOYE, ヒトヘ, 單, One thickness, single, not double.

H'TOYE-NI, ヒトヘニ, 偏, *adv.* Earnestly, wholly, entirely, only, to the exclusion of every thing else. — *tanomu*, to earnestly request. Syn. HITASZRA-NI, NANIBUN.

HITOYOGIRI, ヒトヨギリ, 一節截, *n.* A kind of pipe, or flute, open at the top.
Syn. SHAKUHACHI.

HITSZ, ヒツ, 櫃, *n.* A trunk, a chest for clothes

HITSZ, ヒツ, 筆, (*fude,*) *n.* A pencil, pen. *Ippitsz*, one pen. *Ippitsz kei-jō itashi soro*, I respectfully write you these few lines, (in commencing a letter.)

HITSZ-DAN, ヒツダン, 筆談, Communicating by letter, or by writing.

HITSZGI, ヒツギ, 柩, n. A coffin. *Hitszgi-guruma*, a hearse. Syn. K'WAN.

HITSZ-I, ヒツイ, 筆意, n. Penmanship, mode of writing.

HITSZJI, ヒツジ, 羊, n. A goat, one of the 12 signs. — *no ayumi*, (fig.,) the leading of a criminal to punishment. — *no kata*, the s.s.w. point of the compass. — *no toki*, 2 o'clock P.M. (8 of Japanese.) *Hitszji-saru*, the s.w.

HITSZJI-BO, ヒツヂボ, 穭, n. The rice that sprouts up after the first crop is cut.

HITSZ-JŌ, ヒツヂヤウ, 必定, (*kanaradz sadamaru.*) Certain, sure, fixed, settled, decided, determined. Syn. TASH'KANI, KITTO, ZEHI.

HI-TSZKE, ヒツケ, 火付, n. An incendiary.

†HITSZ-METSZ, ヒツメツ, 必滅, (*kanaradz shinuru*), (Bud). Must surely die. *Shō-ja hitsz-metsz*, death is the doom of every living thing.

HITTACHI,*-tsz,-tta*, ヒツタツ, 引立, i. v. Greatly improved in appearance. *Mon wo nuttareba ōkini hittatte-kita*, if the door is painted it will look much better.

HITTAKURI,*-ru,-tta*, ヒツタクル, t.v. To snatch.

HITTATE,*-ru,-ta*, ヒツタテル, See *Hiki-tate.*

HITTARI-TO, (coll. *Pittarito*), ヒツタリト, *adv.* Closely, tightly. — *tszku*, to stick tight. — *yoru*, crowd close together.

HITTEKI,*-szru*, ヒツテキ, 匹敵, To match, to oppose as equal. *Ware to hitteki subeki mono ni aradz*, there is no one able to contend with me.

HITTSZKAMAE,*-ru,-ta*, ヒツツカマヘル, 引抓, t.v. To seize, lay hold of, catch hold of, to grasp.

HITTSZKAMI,*-mu,-nda*, ヒツカツム, (Id.)

HITSZ-ZEN, ヒツゼン, 必然, (*kanaradz shikaru*), *adv.* Must certainly be so, necessarily so, by necessity.

HI-UCHI, ヒウチ, 燧, n. A steel for striking fire.

HI-UCHI-BUKURO, ヒウチブクロ, 燧袋, n. A bag for holding the instruments for striking fire.

HI-UCHI-GANA, ヒウチガマ, 打火刀, n. A steel for striking fire.

HI-UCHI-ISHI, ヒウチイシ, 打火石, n. A flint.

HI-UCHI-KADO, ヒウチカド 打火角 n. (Idem).

HI-UWO, ヒウヲ, 干魚, n. Dried fish.

HIWA, ヒワ, 鶸, n. A kind of small bird.

HIWADA, ヒハダ, 檜皮, n. The bark of the *Hi* tree used for roofing. *Hiwada-buki*, a roof of the above bark, used only for *Miya* and *Mikado's* palace.

HI-WARE,*-ru,-ta*, ヒワレル, 干裂, i. v. Dry and cracked.

HI-YA, ヒヤ, 火箭, n. A fire-arrow, a rocket.

HI-YA, ヒヤ, 火屋, n. A place where the bodies of the dead are burned. Syn. KASŌBA, DABI.

HIYA, ヒヤ, 冷, Cool, cold. *Hiya-midz*, cool water. *Hiya-ase*, cold sweat- *Hiya-meshi*, cold rice. *O hiya motte-oide*, bring some cold water. — *de nomu*, to drink anything cool.

HIYAKASHI,*-sz,-sh'ta*, ヒヤカス, 冷却, t.v. To cool, to divert, or amuse one's self by merely looking at and not buying, (as goods. *Uri-mono wo hiyakashte aruku*, to go about the shops looking at goods and not buying. Syn. REI-K'YAKU, SZKEN.

HIYAKK'WAN, ヒヤククワン, 百官, n. All the government officers of every rank.

HIYAKOI,-KI, ヒヤコイ, 冷, a. Cool, cold. *Midz ga* —, the water is cold.

HIYAKOKU, or HIYAKŌ, ヒヤコク, 冷, *adv.* (Idem). — *naru*, to become cool. — *szru*, to make cool. Syn. TSZMITAI.

HIYAK'SHŌ, ヒヤクシヤウ, 百姓, n. A farmer, husbandman.

HIYAKU, ヒヤク, 百, A hundred, (in composition frequently used as a plural prefix = the many). *Ni-hiyaku*, two hundred. *Sam-biyaku*, three hundred. *Roppiyaku*, Six hundred.

HI-YAKU, ヒヤク, 秘藥, n. Secret medicine.

HIYAKU-GAI, ヒヤクガイ, 百骸, n. The bones of the body.

HIYAKUJIKKŌ, ヒヤクジツコウ, 百日紅, n, The lagerstramia indica.

HIYAKU-HIRO, ヒヤクヒロ, 百尋, n. The intestines.

HIYAKU-MAN, ヒヤクマン, 百萬, One million.

HIYAKU-ME, ヒヤクメ, 百目, A hundred momme, or one picul, = 133 lbs. avoirdupois.

HIYAKUSŌ-SŌ, ヒヤクサウサウ, 百艸霜, n. A kind of medicine made of a hundred different kind of plants dried and reduced to charcoal.

HIYAKU-YAKU, ヒヤクヤク, 百藥, n. All medicines. *Sake wa* — *no chō*, wine is the best of all medicines.

HIYAKU-YE, ヒヤクヱ, 百會, *n.* The crown of the head. Syn. NŌTEN.

HIYASHI,*–sz,–sh'ta*, ヒヤス, 冷, *t. v.* To cool. *Hitai wo midz de hiyasz*, to cool the forehead with water. *Hiyash'te oku*, to put away to cool. Syn. SAMASZ.

HIYAYAKA, ヒヤヤカ, 冷, *a.* Cool, —*na midz*, cool water. Syn. TSZMETAI.

HIYE,*–ru,–ta*, ヒヘル, 冷, *i.v.* To be cool, cold. *Meshi ga hiyeta*, the rice is cold. *Ashi ga* —, the feet are cool.

HIYE-ATARI, ヒヘアタリ, 冷病, *n.* Sick from exposure to cold.

HIYŌ, ヘウ, 表, *n.* A letter to the Mikado. — *wo aguru.*

HIYŌ, ヘウ, 豹, A leopard.

HIYŌ, ヘウ, 雹, *n.* Hail. — *ga furu*, it hails.

HI-YŌ, ヒヨウ, 日雇, *n.* Day-labor, wages, hire. *Kon-nichi — ni kite okure*, come and work for me to-day. — *wo toru*, to work by the day. Syn. YATOI.

H'YŌ, ヘウ, 俵, *n.* A straw bag. *Ippiyō*, one bag. *Ni-h'yō*, two bags. *Samb'yō*, three bags. *H'to-hiyō*, one bag full, = about 2½ bushels.

H'YŌ-BAN, ヒヤウバン, 評判, *n.* Repute, reputation, fame, report, rumor. — *ga yoi*, of good repute. — *ga warui h'to*, a man of bad reputation. — *szru*, to be publicly talked about, to be a matter of common talk.

HIYODORI, ヒヨドリ, 鵯, *n.* The name of a bird.

HIYŌGE,*–ru,–ta*, ヘウゲル, 剽戯, *i.v.* To sport, play frolic, jest. *Hiyōgeta h'to*, a witty person. Syn. TAWAMURERU.

H'YŌGI,*–szru*, ヒヤウギ, 評議, *i. v.* To discuss, and deliberate on, to consult about. Syn. H'YŌ-JŌ, SŌDAN.

H'YŌGU, ヘウグ, 裱工, *n.* The mountings of a picture.

H'YŌGU, ヒヤウグ, 兵具, *n.* Weapons of war.

H'YŌGU-YA, ヘウグヤ, 裱工屋, *n.* A paper-hanger. Syn. KIYŌJIYA.

†H'YŌ-HAKU,*–szru*, ヘウハク, 漂泊, *i. v.* To wander about, to float about. Syn. RURŌ, TADAYŌ.

H'YOI-TO, ヒヨイト, *adv.* In a sudden manner, unexpectedly, accidentally. — *sh'ta koto.* Syn. FUTO, OMOWADZ-NI.

H'YŌ-JŌ,*–szru*, ヒヤウヂヤウ, 評定, *i. v.* To diliberate and decide on.

H'YŌ-JŌ-SHO, ヒヤウヂヤウシヨ, 評定所, *n.* Supreme court house.

H'YŌ-JŌ-SHU, ヒヤウヂヤウシユ, 評定衆, Members of the supreme court.

HI-YOKE, ヒヨケ, 日除, *n.* An awning, (火除,) a vacant space about a house as protection against fire.

H'YŌKIN, ヘウキン, Facetious, merry. — *na h'to.*

H'YOKKURI-TO, ヒヨククリト, 慓然, *adv.* Sudden and unexpectedly.

HIYOKO, ヒヨコ 㲉, *n.* A young bird.

HIYOKO-HIYOKO, ヒヨコヒヨコ, *adv.* Hopping (as a frog), leaping. — *tobu*, to hop and jump.

HIYOKU-NO-TORI, ヒヨクノトリ, 比翼鳥, *n.* A fabulous bird, the male and female said to be joined together in one body.

HIYOMEKI, ヒヨメキ, 顖門, *n.* The fontanel in a child's head.

HIYON-NA, ヒヨンナ, *(Hen-naru,)* Strange, unusual, odd, wonderful. — *koto.* — *mono.* Syn. KOTONARU, KAWATTA.

HIYON-NOKI, ヒヨンノキ, 蚊子木, *n.* Name of a tree. The distylium racemosum.

HIYŌRAN, ヒヤウラン, 兵亂, *n.* The disturbance and commotion caused by war.

HIYŌ-RI, ヘウリ, 表裏, *(ura omote,)* Outside and inside, (fig.) False hearted, hypocritical, double-dealing, also force, impulse, effort. — *ga yoi*, fortunate, a good chance. — *no aru mono*, a false, deceitful person. *Tatsz hiyōri ni atama wo utta*, struck his head in the act of rising.

HIYŌ-RIU, ヘウリウ, 漂流, Floating, or carried about by the waves, *Fune ga — sh'te shima ye tszku*, the ship floating about stranded on an island.

HIYŌ-RŌ, ヒヤウロウ, 兵粮, *n.* Food for soldiers, provisions. — *ni tszmaru*, distressed for provisions. — *ga tszkita*, provisions are exhausted.

HIYORO-HIYORO-TO, ヒヨロヒヨロト, 踉蹌, *adv.* In a limping staggering manner.

HIYŌRŌ-KATA, ヒヤウラウカタ, 兵粮方, *n.* Commissary.

HIYŌ-RŌN,*–szru*, ヒヤウロン, 評論, *i.v.* To diliberate on, to discuss.

HIYOROTSZKI,*–ku,–ita*, ヒヨロツク, *i.v.* To limp, stagger.

HIYŌRŌZEME, ヒヤウラウゼメ, 兵粮攻, *n.* Starving out a garrison.

HIYŌSATSZ, ヘウサツ, 標札, *n.* A tablet with the name of the person residing hung at the door of a house, a door plate.

HIYŌ-SHI, ヘウシ, 表紙, *n.* The paper cover, or binding of a book. *Ita-biyōshi.* board-covers. *Kawa no* —, leather binding.

HIYŌ-SHI, ヒヤウシ, 拍子, *n*, Beating time to music. — *wo toru*, to beat time. *A-shi-biyōshi*, drumming with the foot. *Te-biyōshi*, beating time with the hand. *Ko-robu hiyōshi ni*, by the force of the fall, or act of falling.

†HIYŌ-SHI, *-szru, -sh'ta*, ヒヤウスル, 評, *t. v.* To discuss the merits of, to criticise, to judge of. *H'to no yoshi ashi wo hiyō-szru*, to criticise the merits or demerits of others.

†HIYŌ-SHI, *-szru, -sh'ta*, ヘウスル, 表, To signify, be a sign of, represent, to show, be emblematic of. *Go-gatsz no sekku ni nobo-ri wo tatszru wa kachi-ikusa wo hiyo-seshi mono nari*, the raising of flags on the festi-val of the fifth month is in memory of a victory.

HIYŌSŌ, ヘウサウ, 裱装, *n.* The mount-ings of a picture.

HIYŌSO, ヘウソ, 瘭疽, *n.* A Whitlow.

HIYŌ-SOKU, ヒヤウソク, 秉燭, *n.* A kind of lamp.

HIYŌ-TAN, ヘウタン, 瓢簞, *n.* A gourd, calabash. Syn. FUKUBE, HISAGO.

HIYŌ-TO, ヒヤウト, *adv.* The sound of an arrow flying. *Ya wo — hanatsz.*

HI-YŌ-TORI, ヒヨウトリ, 日雇取, *n.* A day-laborer. Syn. YATOI-NIN.

HIYOTTO, ヒヨツト, 慓, *adv.* If, supposing that. — *shiretara dō nasaru*, if he should know, what should you do? *Hiyotto-szre-ba*, perhaps, it may be. *Hiyotto shitara.* idem. Syn. MOSHI.

HIYOTTOKO, ヒヨツトコ, *n.* A kind of mask,

HIYOWAI, -KI, -SHI, ヒヨワイ, *a.* Weak, feeble, not strong, delicate. Syn. KAYO-WAI.

HIYOWAKU, ヒヨワク, *adv.* idem.

HIZA, ヒザ, 膝, *n.* The knee. — *no sara*, the knee-pan. — *wo oru*, to bend the knee. — *wo kumu*, to sit tailor fashion.

HIZA-GASHIRA, ヒザガシラ, 膝頭, *n.* The knee.

HI-ZAKARI, ヒザカリ, 日盛, *(nitchiu,) n.* Noon, the hottest period of the day in summer.

HI-ZAKURA, ヒザクラ, 緋櫻, *n.* A scarlet blossom cherry tree.

HIZAMADZKI, *-ku, -ita*, ヒザマヅク, 跪, *i. v.* To kneel. *Hizamadzite kami wo ogamu*, to kneel down and worship God.

HIZA-MOTO, ヒザモト, 膝下, *n.* By the knees, near to. *Oya no —*, at the parent's knee.

HI-ZARA, ヒザラ, 火皿, *n.* The pan of a gun-lock, the bowl of a pipe.

HI-ZASHI, ヒザシ, 日刺, *n.* Sunlight, the sun's rays.

HIZEN, ヒゼン, 疥癬, *n.* A cutaneous dis-ease, the itch?

HIZŌ, ヒザウ, 秘藏, Kept with great care, — *muszme*, a daughter kept with great care. *Sho-motsz wo — szru*, to prize and keep books carefully.

HI-ZORI, *-ru, -tta*, ヒゾル, 乾反, *i. v.* Warped, bent by the heat.

HO, ホ, 帆, *n.* A sail. — *wo ageru*, to hoist a sail. — *wo sageru*, to lower a sail; — *wo kakeru*, to hoist a sail. — *wo go-gō bakari ageru*, to half reef a sail.

HO, ホ, 穗, *n.* The ear, or head of rice wheat &c. *Ine no —*, an ear of rice. *Mugi no ho*, a head of wheat.

HŌ, ホホ, 頬, *n.* The cheek. *Hō-bone*, the cheek-bone, (malar.)

HŌ, ハフ, 法, *n.* Rule, law, usage, doctrine, maxim, religious rites or practices; in-cantation. *Kuni no hō*, the laws of a country. *Butsz no —*, *(Buppō,)* the doc-trines, or religion of the Buddhist. *Ame wo furazeru hō*, the incantations used to bring rain. *Soroban no hō*, the rules of the abacus. — *wo tateru*, to make a law, or rule.

HŌ, ハウ, 方, *(kata) n.* Side, region, place, direction, part, person, thing, a re-cipe. *Kono-hō*, here, I. *Sono-hō*, or *Ano-hō*, there; you. *Shiroi-hō*, the white. *Chīsai-hō ga yoi*, the small one is the best. *Kuszri no hō*, a medical recipe. *Nishi no hō*, the west. *Yedo no hō ye nigeta*, has fled towards *Yedo.*

†HŌ, ハウ, 報, *n.* Answer, reply to a letter. *Go hō ni makase*, according to your an-swer. Syn. HEN-TO.

HO-ASHI, ホアシ, 帆脚, *n.* The foot, or lower part of a sail.

HŌ-ATE, ホホアテ, 頬當, *n.* The visor of a helmet.

HŌ-BAI, ホウバイ, 朋輩, *n.* A friend, com-panion, comrade.
Syn. HŌYU, TOMODACHI.

HŌ-BARI, *-ru, -tta*, ホウバル, *t. v.* To fill the mouth, to cram the mouth full. *Mochi wo —*, to fill the mouth with rice-cake. *Saru ga kuri wo —*, the monkey fills his cheeks with chesnuts.

HO-BASHIRA, ホバシラ, 檣, *n.* A mast.

HŌ-BEN, ハウベン, 方便, *n.* A device, art, invention, plan, or expedient used to convert people to Buddhism, or to lead a virtuous life; (it is now not restricted to the Bud. meaning.) — *wo iu*, to mention an expedient. — *wo megurasz.* — *wo motte h'to wo michibiku.* *Go — na mono.* Syn. TEDATE, JUTSZ.

HŌ-BETA, ホホベタ, *n.* The cheeks.

HŌBI, ハウビ, 褒美, *n.* A reward. — *wo yaru,* to give a reward. — *to sh'te kane wo kudasaru,* gave money as a reward.

HOBO, ホボ, 粗, or 略, *adv.* For the most part, nearly, almost. — *nite iru,* almost alike. — *deki-agatta,* nearly done. Syn. ŌKATA, ARAMASHI, Ō-MUNE, TAI-GAI.

HŌ-BŌ, ハウバウ, 方方, *adv.* Here and there, all about, on all sides, every direction, every where, every-place. — *sagash'te mo sappari gozaimasen,* I have searched in every direction but can find none. Syn. SHO-SHO; SHO HŌ;

HŌ-BŌ, ホウボウ, *n.* A kind of fish.

†HŌCHIKU, ハウチク, 放逐, Driving out, expelling. — *szru.*

HŌ-CHŌ, ハウチヤウ, 庖丁, *n.* A table or kitchen knife.

HŌDAI, ハウダイ, 放題, (Used only in combination with other words,) at will, according to one's pleasure, without restraint, at liberty. *H'to no mi-hōdai ni sh'te oku,* to let people look at it as much as they please. *Uri-hōdai,* selling without restraint, anything one pleases. *Shi-hōdai,* doing as one pleases. See *Dehōdai, Tori-hōdai.*

HŌ-DAI, ハウダイ, 炮臺, *n.* A fort, battery.

HŌ-DAN, ハフダン, 法談, *n.* Preaching, a discourse on religious subjects; sermon. (Bud.) — *szru,* to preach. — *wo kiku,* to listen to a sermon. Syn. SEPPŌ, DANGI.

HO-DANA, ホダナ, 帆棚, *n.* The place on which a sail rests when furled.

HODASARE,,*-ru,-ta,* ホダサレル, 被絆, Pass. of *Hodashi.* To be shackled, fettered, hampered, encumbered, embarrassed, bound. *Ko ni hodasarete deraremasen,* hindered by the child I cannot go out. *Mi ni* —, encumbered by the body. *On mi no nasake ni hodasareta,* bound by your kindness.

HADASHI,*-sz,-sh'ta,* ホダス, 絆, *t. v.* To shackle, to fetter. *Uma no ashi wo* —, to shackle a horse. Syn. TSZNAGU.

HODASHI, ホダシ, 覊, *n.* A clog, hindrance, encumbrance. *Sai shi ga hodashi to naru,* wife and child became an encumbrance.

†HŌDO, ハウド, 報土, *(mukuyuru kuni.) n.* Heaven, (as being the place where the believers in *Amida* are rewarded.)

HODO, ホド, 程, *n.* Quantity, of space or time; time; quality, kind; as, since. *Hodo no yoi h'to,* a man of good manners, or a pleasant man. — *wo hedateru,* to separate, put an interval between; or, after some time. *Kore-hodo,* so much, or, this much. *Sore-hodo,* so much, or, that quantity. *Yohodo,* a good deal. *Dore-hodo,* how much? *Nani-hodo,* how much? *Hodo-naku,* very soon, a short time. *Kono-hodo,* lately; short time ago. *Kesa-hodo,* in the morning. *Ban-hodo,* evening. *Dekiru hodo,* as much as you can. *Fum-betsz szru hodo jama ni naru,* the more you think about it the worse it is. *Anata hodo no h'to ga kayō na koto wa shi sō mo nai mono da,* I did not suppose that such a man as you would do such a thing. *Mi no hodo,* one's position in life; proper place. *Go men no hodo negai tatematszri soro,* I pray you to excuse me. *Mo nai hodo ni agemasen,* as I have no more I cannot give you.

HODO-AI, ホドアイ, 程間, *n.* Interval of space, or time. *Mo — wa gozarimasen.*

HODOBASHIRASHI,*-sz,-sh'ta,* ホドバシラス, 令迸, *t.v.* To spatter, to splash.

HODOBASHIRI,*-ru,-tta,* ホドバシル, 迸, *i.v.* To fly, splash about, spatter about, as water. *Yu-dama takaku* —, the drops of hot water spattered high.

HODO-CHIKAI, ホドチカイ, 程近, Soon, short time, near, short distance.

HODOHE,*-ru,-ta,* ホドヘル, 程經, *i. v.* Lapse of time, after some time has passed. *Hodohete yuku,* to go after a while. *Hodohete kore wo shiru naraba,* if hereafter they should know.

†HODO-HODO, ホドホド, 程程, (plural.) Positions, ranks, or places in life; very much, greatly. — *hana wo chirashitszru kana,* how much have the flowers fallen! — *gi-shin wo kandzru,* he greatly admired his honesty.

HODOKE,*-ru,-ta,* ホドケル, 解, *i. v.* Untied, loosed, (fig.) to relax, remit, give up. *Muszbi-me ga hodoketa,* the knot is untied. *Obi ga* —, the belt is loose. *Ki no hodokenai h'to,* a person of a hard unyielding spirit. Syn. TOKERU.

HODOKI,*-ku,-ita,* ホドク, 解, *t. v.* To untie, loose. *Ito no muszbore wo* —, to untie the knot in a thread. *G'wan wo* —, to perform a vow. Syn. TOKU.

HODOKOSHI,*-sz,-sh'ta,* ホドコス, 施, *t. v.* To give alms, to bestow, confer, impart. *Hōbi wo* —, to confer a reward. *Kome wo* —, to give rice in charity. *Hakarigoto wo* —, to practise a stratagem. *Memboku wo* —, to feel elated, or proud. Syn. SE-GIYŌ SZRU, SADZKI-ATAYERU.

HODOKOSHI, ホドコシ, 施, *n.* Bestowment of alms, or charitable gifts.

HODORAI, ホドライ, *n.* The capacity, size, or quality of things; the station, or position in life or society.

HŌDZ, ハウヅ, *n.* End, limit. — *ga nai*, no end, or limit.

HŌ-DZKI, ホホヅキ, 酸醬, *n.* A kind of plant.

HO-DZNA, ホヅナ, 帆緈, *n.* A halyard.

HŌDZRU, ハウズル, *n.* see *Hōji.*

HOFURI,-*ru*,-*tta*, ホフル, 屠, *t. v.* To kill, butcher, slaughter. *Ushi wo* —, to butcher an ox.

HŌGA, ホウガ, 奉加, *n.* Contributions for religious purposes. — *kin*, money contributed to temples. — *wo szru*, to contribute, &c. Syn. KI-SHIN, KAN-KE.

HŌGA-CHŌ, ホウガチヤウ, 奉加帳, *n.* A subscription book, in which contributions for religious purposes are written.

HŌ-GAI, ハフガイ, 法外, see *Hog'wai.*

HŌ-GAKU, ハウガク, 方角, *n.* Direction, point of the compass, quarter, bearing, locality. *Yedo no — wa dochira*, in what direction is Yedo? *Doṅo — ni ataru*, in what direction?

†HOGAMI, ホガミ, 肚腹, *n.* Pit of the stomach, epigastric region.

†HOGARAKA, ホガラカ, 朗, *a.* Bright, clear. *Tszki ga* —, the moon is bright. — *na iye*, a spacious house.

†HOGE, ホゲ, 炎氣, *n.* Heat. Syn. HŌNO, KAYEN.

HOGETA, ホゲタ, 帆架, *n.* The yard, or spar to which a sail is fastened.

HŌ-GIYO, ホウギヨ, 崩御, *n.* The death of the Mikado.

†HŌ-GŌ, ハフガウ, 法號, *n.* Name given by the Buddhists to a deceased person. Syn. KAI-MIYO, HŌ-MIYŌ.

HŌGU, ホウグ, 反故, *n.* Waste-paper, paper scraps.

HOGURE,-*ru*,-*ta*, ホグレル, *i. v.* Untied, loosed, unwoven, unlaced, unraveled, frayed, untwisted. *Furoshiki ga* —, the wrapper is frayed.

HOGUSHI, -*sz*,-*sh'ta*, ホグス, *t.v.* To unravel, to fray, untwist.

HOGUSHI, ホグシ, 火串, *n.* A pine torch, used by hunters to decoy deer.

HŌ-G'WAI, ハフグワイ, 法外, (*hō no hoka.*) Contrary to rule or usage, anomalous, outrageous, exorbitant, excessive. — *no ne wo tszkeru*, to ask an exorbitant price. — *ni chigau*, exceedingly different. — *na koto wo iu.* — *na mono.*

HO-HEI, ホヘイ, 步兵, *n.* Common foot-soldiers, infantry.

HŌ-HEI, ホウヘイ, 奉幣, *n.* Offerings to the *Kami.*

HŌ-HIGE, ホホヒゲ, 頰毛, *n.* Whiskers.

HŌ-HŌ, ハフハフ, 這這, *adv.* In a creeping manner. — *no tei de nigeru*, to creep, or slink away.

HOHOYEMI,-*mu*,-*nda*, ホホヱム, 微笑, *i.v.* To smile.

HOI, ホイ, 布衣, *n.* A kind of court dress worn by inferior Government officers.

HOI, ホイ, 本意, Same as *Honi.* — *nai*, not according to one's mind or desire.

HŌI, ハフイ, 法衣, *n.* A garment worn by Buddhist priests.

HŌ-IN, ハフイン, 法印, *n.* The name of a rank among the Buddhists and *Yamabushi.*

HOIRO, ホイロ, 焙爐, *n.* A utensil made of paper, used for heating tea-leaves.

HŌITSZ, ハウイツ, 放逸, Dissolute, vicious, profligate. Syn. HŌ-TO, BURAI.

HŌ-JI, ハフジ, 法事, *n.* Prayers and religious ceremonies of the Buddhists, generally those performed on the anniversary of a death. Syn. TSZIZEN.

†HŌJI,-*dzru*, or *ru*,-*ta*, ハウジル, 報, (*muku.*) To repay, requite, to recompense, to avenge; to answer; to report, tell, proclaim. *On wo* —, to repay a kindness. *Ada wo*, — to take vengeance on an enemy. *Kachi wo* —, to proclaim a victory. Syn. KOTAYERU, KAYESZ.

HŌJI,-*dzru*,-*ta*, ホウズル, 崩, *i.v.* To die, (used only of the *Mikado.*)

HŌJI,-*ru*,-*ta*, ホウズル, 焙, *t.v.* To roast, parch, or fire, as tea. *Cha wo hōjiru*, to fire tea.

HŌJIGUI, ハウジグヒ, 牓示杭, *n.* Posts set up to mark the boundaries of a country.

HOJIRI,-*ru*,-*tta*, ホジル, 掊, *t.v.* To dig up, grub up, to pick out. *Imo wo* —, to dig up potatoes. *Buta ga tszchi wo* —, the hog roots up the ground. *Toge wo* —, to pick out a thorn.

HŌJIRO, ホホジロ, 畫眉鳥, *n.* A kind of bird.

†HŌJISHI, ホジシ, 脯, *n.* Dried flesh.

HŌ-JŌ, ハウヂヤウ, 方丈, *n.* A monastery; also, a Buddhist priest.

HŌ-JŌ, ハウジヤウ, 放生, (*ikeru wo hanatsz.*) Setting free live things that have been confined, (as birds, &c.)

†HOJO,-*szru*, ホジヨ, 補助, *t.v.* To aid, help, assist. Syn. TETSZDAI.

Hōjutsz, ハウジユツ, 砲術, *n.* Musket exercise.
Ho-jutsz, ハフジユツ, 法術, *n.* Magical arts.
Hoka, ホカ, 外, Different, another, besides, except; outside, external. *Kono hoka ni fude ga nai,* I have no pencil except this. *Hoka no h'to,* a different person. *Hoka ye deta,* he has gone out. *Sono hoka,* besides that, moreover. Syn. yoso, betsz.
Ho-kake-bune, ホカケブネ, 帆掛舩, *n.* A sail-boat, a ship with sails.
Ḥō-kamuri, ホホカムリ, 頬冠, Covering the head with the handkerchief. — *wo szru.*
Hōke,*-ru,-ta,* ホホケル, *i. v.* Frayed, abraded, (as cloth.)
Hōke-dachi,*-tsz,-tta,* ホホケダツ, *i.v.* To be frayed, rubbed out, abraded. Syn. kebadatsz.
Hōki, ハハキ, 箒, *n.* A broom.
†Hō-ki, ホウキ, 蜂起, *(hachi no gotoku okoru.) n.* An insurrection, rebellion. — *szru,* to raise an insurrection. Syn. ikki.
†Hō-ki, ハウキ, 寳器, *(takara mono.)* A valuable article.
Hōki-boshi, ハハキボシ, 彗星, *n.* A comet. Syn. szisei.
†Hō-kiyō, ホウキヨウ, 豐凶, Fruitful and unfruitful.
Hōkiyō, ハウキヤウ, 包莖, *n.* Phymosis.
†Hokka, ホツカ, 發駕, Setting out on a journey. Syn. hossoku.
Hokkai, ホクカイ, 北海, *(kita no umi.) n.* Arctic ocean. North sea.
Hokke, ホツケ, 法華, *n.* The name of a sect of Buddhists. — *kiyo,* the sacred books of this sect.
†Hokki, ホツキ, 發起, To arise, or spring up, set a going, to start, set on foot, originate. — *nin,* originator.
Hokkiyoku, ホクキヨク, 北極, *n.* The north-pole.
Hokkoku, ホクコク, 北國, *(kita no kuni,) n.* Northern country.
Hokku, ホツク, 發句, A verse of poetry, consisting of 17 syllables.
Hoko, ホコ, 鉾, *n.* A kind of spear. *Hokosaki,* the point of a spear.
Ho-kō, ホカウ, 歩行, *n.* Walking. — *szru,* to walk. Syn. aruku.
Hō-kō, ホウコウ, 奉公, *n.* Service, duty done to a master, the labor, business, or duty of a servant. — *szru,* to perform the duties of a servant.
Hoko-hoko, ホコホコ, 燠燠, *adv.* Warm, comfortable. *Kimono wo kitaraba — szru,* by wearing clothes I become warm.
Hōkō-nin, ホウコウニン, 奉公人, *n.* A servant.
Hokora, ホコラ, 祠, *n.* A small Sintoo shrine.
Hokori, ホコリ, 埃, *n.* Fine-dust, (fig.,) a very small fraction. — *ga tatsz,* the dust rises. — *wo harau,* to dust. — *harai,* a duster. — *ga deru,* there is a very small fraction over. Syn. chiri, gomi.
Hokori,*-ru,-tta,* ホコル, 誇, *i. v.* To be vain, proud, conceited, puffed up, to vaunt, *Chikara ni hokoru,* to be vain of one's strength. *Ken-i ni hokotte h'to wo mi-sageru,* to be vain of one's authority and despise others. Syn. ji-man szru.
Hokorobi,*-bu,-nda,* ホコロブ, 綻, *i. v.* Ripped open, (as a seam,) torn. To open, (as flowers.) *Nui-me ga —,* the seam is ripped. *Hana ga —,* the flower is open. Syn. hodokeru, tokeru.
Hoku, ホク, 北, *(kita.)* North. *Hokufū,* north-wind.
Ho-kuchi, ホクチ, 火口, *n.* Tinder.
Hokuro, ホクロ, 黒痣, *n.* A mole, freckle.
Hoku-shin, ホクシン, 北辰, *n.* The north star.
Hokusoyemi,*-mu,-nda,* ホクソヱム, 微笑, *i.v.* To smile. Syn. hohoyemu.
Hoku-to, ホクト, 北斗, *n.* Ursa major.
†Hō-k'wa, ハウクワ, 放火, Setting on fire. — *szru,* to set on fire.
Homachi, ホマチ, *n.* Perquisite. *Kore wa yaku-nin no — da,* this is the officer's perquisite.
Homare, ホマレ, 譽, *n.* Praise, eulogy, fame, renown, celebrity. — *wo arawasz,* to get renown. — *wo toru,* to get praise. Syn. meiyo.
Hom-buku, ホンブク, 本復, *n.* Restoration to health, recovery from sickness. — *sh'ta,* restored to health. Syn. zen-k'wai, k'wai-ki, naoru, iyuru, hei-yu.
Home,*-ru,-ta,* ホメル 譽, *t.v.* To praise, eulogize, commend. *H'to wo —,* to praise another.
‖Homeki,*-ku,-ita,* ホメク, 燠, *i.v.* To be like fire, hot, to have a fever. *Mi ga homeku,* the body is hot. Syn. atszi.
Homerare,*-ru,-ta,* ホメラレル, 被譽, Pass. of *Homeru,* to be praised. *H'to ni —,*
Home-soyashi,*-sz,-sh'ta,* ホメソヤス, 褒奨, *t. v.* To praise and encourage, to inspirit, animate by praising.

Hōmiyō, ハフミヤウ, 法名, *n.* Name given to a deceased person by the Buddhists. Syn. KAI-MIYŌ, HŌ-GŌ.

‖Homma, ホンマ, 本眞, True. — *de gozarimas,* it is true. Syn. HON-TŌ, MAKOTO, SHIN-JITSZ.

Hommaru, ホンマル, 本丸, *n,* The principal part of a castle

†Hom-matsz, ホンマツ, 本末, (*moto to sz-ye,*) Root and branches, (fig.) Beginning and end, first and last.

Hom-miyō, ホンミヤウ, 實名, *n.* True or real name. Syn. JITSZMIYŌ, NANORI.

Hom-mō, ホンマウ, 本望, *n.* One's great desire, or principal object. — *wo togeru,* to obtain one's desire.

Hom-mon, ホンモン, 本文, *n.* The text of a commentary, or of a book as distinguished from the notes.

Hō-motsz, ハウモツ, 寳物, (*takara,*) *n.* Things valued, prized and rare.

‖Homura, ホムラ, 炎, *n.* The flame of fire. — *wo moyasz,* to be inflamed with anger. Syn. HONŌ.

Hōmuri,*–ru,–tta,* ハウムル, 葬, *t. v.* To bury a dead person. *Haka ni* —, to bury in a grave. Syn- UDZMERU.

Hon, ホン, 本, *n.* A book. — *wo arawasz,* to publish a book. — *wo kaku, tszkuru, utszsz, tojiru, yomu.* Sny. SHOMOTSZ, SHO-JAKU.

Hon, ホン, 本, Original, principal, true, real, genuine, fixed, settled, numeral for pencils, posts, sticks, masts, &c. *Hon-nedan,* fixed price. *Hashira ippon,* one mast. *Fude ni hon,* two pencils.

Ho-nami, ホナミ, 穂並, *n.* The even rows of the ears of rice, or any grain.

Hon-chō, ホンテウ, 本朝, *n.* One's native country. Syn. WAGA-KUNI.

Hon-chōshi, ホンテウシ, 本調子, *n.* The key note.

Hon-dana, ホンダナ, 本棚, *n.* A bookcase.

Hon-dana, ホンダナ, 本店, *n.* The original, or principal store.

Hon-dō, ホンダウ, 本堂, *n.* The main, or principal part of a temple.

Hon-dō, ホンダウ, 本道, *n.* A physician (not a surgeon.) Syn. NAI-KA.

Hone ,ホネ, 骨, *n.* A bone. — *no tszgai,* the articulation of a bone. — *wo tateru,* to get a bone in the throat. — *wo oru,* to break a bone ; (fig.) to be industrious, laborious. — *wo chigai,* to dislocate a bone. — *kujiku,* to sprain a bone. — *wo tszgu,* to set a dislocated bone. — *mi ni tesszru.* (fig.) to pierce through the flesh and bones, feel deeply. — *wo oshimu,* to spare the bones, dislike labor. *Chō-chin no hone,* the bamboo ribs of a lantern. *Shō-ji no hone,* the frame of a screen. *Ōgi no hone,* the sticks of a fan.

Hone-chigai, ホネチガヒ, 骨違, *n.* Dislocation of a bone.

Hone-garami, ホネガラミ, 結毒, *n.* Syphilitic pains in the bones.

Hone-gumi, ホネグミ, 骨格, *n.* The bony frame; the frame work. — *no takumashī h'to,* a strong brawny man.

Hō-nen ホウネン, 豐年, (*yutakana toshi*) A fruitful year,

Hone-ori, ホネヲリ, 勞力, *n.* Labor, toil, industry, activity, exertion. — *shigoto,* hard work. Syn. TAIGI.

Hone-ori,*–ru,–tta,* ホネヲル, 勞力, *i. v.* To be laborious, to toil, work hard, to be industrious. *Honeotte shigoto wo szru,* to labor diligently at one's work.

Honeppoi, ホネツポイ, Full of bones, (as a fish,) bony, thin, emaciated.

Hone-tszgi, ホネツギ, 接骨, *n.* Bone setting. — *isha,* a bone setter.

Hon-giyaku, ホンギヤク, 叛逆, Rebellion, revolt, sedition. — *wo kuwadatszru,* to plan rebellion.

Hon-goku, ホンゴク, 本國, (*moto no kuni,*) Native country,

Hon-i, ホンイ, 本意, *n.* Desire, mind, intention, object, inclination, purpose. — *ni kanau,* to accord with one's mind. — *wo somuku,* to be contrary to one's inclination.

Hon-ji, ホンジ, 本寺, *n* The original, or first temple, from which others have branched off.

Hon-jin, ホンヂン, 本陣, *n.* The headquarters of an encampment. The hotel where a Daimiyo stops in travelling.

Hon-ke, ホンケ, 本家, (*moto no iye*). The homestead, the principal family.

Hon-ni, ホンニ, 本, *adv.* Truly, indeed, really. Syn. MAKOTO-NI, JITSZ-NI.

Hon-nin, ホンニン, 本人, *n.* The principal, chief-man, ringleader. Syn. TŌ-NIN, HOTTŌ-NIN.

Honnori-to, ホンノリ, *adv.* With a slight blush of redness, lightly shaded. — *yo ga aketa.*

Ho-nō, ホノホ, 炎, *n.* The flame of fire, — *ga agaru.* Syn. K'WA-YEN.

Hō-nō, ホウナウ, 奉納, (*osame tatematszru*). Offered to the *Kami.* — *szru,* to offer, or present to the *Kami.*

†HONO-BONO, ホノボノ, Dimly, like the dawning of the day. — *idzru tō-yama no tszki*, the rising of the moon above the distant mountains. — *miyeru*, dimly seen. *Yo no — ake ni mairō*, I will come when the morning begins to dawn.

HONO-GURAI, ホノグライ, Dim, or grey twilight, obscure. — *uchi ni*, while it is yet twilight.

HONOKA-NI, ホノカニ, 髣髴, Dimly, indistinctly, obscurely. — *ni kiku*, to hear indistinctly. — *ni miru*, to see dimly. Syn. KASZKA-NI, BONYARI.

HONOMEKASHI,-sz,-sh'ta, ホノメカス, *t. v.* To allude to, mention incidentally, to hint. *Maye-motte honomekash'te oku*, to allude to a matter before hand.

HONOMEKI,-ku,-ita, ホノメク, *i. v.* To shine with a dim light. *Kumo-ma kara tszki ga honomeku*, the moon shines dimly between the clouds.

HON-RAI, ホンライ, 本來, (*motoyori*). Originally, in the beginning, at first. Syn. G'WAN-RAI.

HON-SAI, ホンサイ, 本妻, *n.* Real wife, the wife as distinguished from the concubine.

HON-SHIN, ホンシン, 本心, *n.* The right mind, the mind in the original state free from evil and uncorrupted. — *ni tachikayeru*, to return to one's right mind; to reform the life. — *ni sh'tagau*, to act according to right reason. — *wo ushinau*, to lose one's mind; to act like one destitute of reason.

HON-SHŌ, ホンシヤウ, 本性, *n* One's original, or natural disposition. *Namayoi hon-shō tagawadz*, a drunken man acts true to his nature. — *ga tszita*, has come to his senses.

†HONSŌ,-szru, ホンソウ, 奔走, (*hashiru*). To go about here and there. *Isha ga riyōji ni achi-kochi — szru*, the doctor goes about here and there prescribing medicines.

HON-TAKU, ホンタク, 本宅, *n.* The homestead, the mansion, or place of residence.

HON-TŌ, ホンタウ, 本當, True, real, genuine. — *ka uso ka* is it true or false? — *de gozarimas*, it is true. — *ni shirimasen*, indeed I don't know. Syn. MAKOTO, JITSZ.

HON-YA, ホンヤ, 書肆, *n.* A book store. Syn. SHORIN.

HON-YAKU,-szru, ホンヤク, 飜譯, To translate, to interpret, render into another language. *Yei-go wo wa-go ni* —, to translate from the English language into the Japanese. Syn. NAOSZ.

HON-ZEN, ホンゼン, 本膳, *n.* The principal table at an entertainment.

HON-ZON, ホンゾン, 本尊, *n.* The principal idol in a Buddhist temple.

†HOPPŌ, ホクパウ, 北方, (*kito no hō*), *n.* The north.

HORA, ホラ, 洞, *n.* A cave, cavern.

HORA, or, HORAGAI, ホラ, 法螺, *n.* A conch-shell, used for blowing. — *wo fuku*, to blow a conch, to exaggerate.

HORA-FUKI, ホラフキ, 法螺吹, *n.* One who exaggerates; a blower.

HŌ-RAI ホウライ, 蓬萊, *n.* The name of a fabulous mountain in the sea where the Sen-nin reside in immortal youth and happiness; Elysium; also, a representation of the above in miniature, often presented to a newly married couple. *Hōrai-san* the Elysian mountain. Syn. SHIMA-DAI.

HŌRAKU, ハフラク, 法樂, *n.* Religious entertainments, or theatrical exhibitions, in the presence of idols, which they are supposed to take pleasure in. — *shi-tatematszru*, to please the gods with &c.

HORASE,-ru,-ta, ホラセル, 令掘, Caust. of *Horu*.

HŌ-RATSZ, ハウラツ, 放埒, Profligate, dissolute, abandoned. — *na mono*, a dissolute profligate person. Syn. BURAI, HŌTŌ, DŌRAKU.

HORE,-ru,-ta, ホレル, 鑿, To be carved, engraved, sculptured, dug out, excavated, worn into hollows. *Kono ishi ama-dare de horeta*, this stone is hollowed by the raindrops. *Kono ji wo horeru ka*, can you engrave this letter? *Katakute horenai*, it is too hard to be engraved, &c.

HORE,-ru,-ta, ホレル, 耄, *i.v.* To dote, to be silly from age; to be old and childish. Same as *Boreru*. Syn. OI-BORERU, BOKERU.

HORE,-ru,-ta, ホレル, *t.v.* To love, (between the sexes only). ● *Watakushi ano onna ni horeta*, I love that woman. *Onna ni horerareta*, to be loved by a woman. *Unu-bore*, (*onobore*), self-esteem. Syn. REM-BO, KOISHITAU, OKKOCHIRU.

HORE-GUSZRI, ホレグスリ, 媚藥, *n.* Aphrodisiac medicine.

HŌ-REI, ハフレイ, 法例, *n.* Common custom, customary usage, ordinance. Syn. HŌSHIKI.

†HŌ-REN, ホウレン, 鳳輦, *n.* Mikado's chariot.

HŌRENSŌ, ハウレンサウ, 菠薐草, *n.* A kind of spinach.

HORI,*-ru,-tta*, ホル, 掘, *t.v.* To dig, excavate, to quarry, to carve, engrave, sculpture, to tatoo. *Tszchi wo* —, to dig the ground. *Ido wo* —, to dig a well. *Ki wo* —, to carve wood. *Ishi wo* —, to engrave a stone, to sculpture. *Nomi de* —, to cut with a chisel. Syn. UGATSZ.

HŌRI,*-ru,-tta*, ハフル, *t.v.* To throw, fling, cast. Syn. NAGERU.

HORI, ホリ, 掘, *n.* A canal. —*wo horu*, to dig a canal. — *wo umeru*, to fill up a canal.

HORI-DASHI,*-sz,-sh'ta*, ホリダス, 掘出, *t.v.* To dig-out, dig-up. *Sek'tan wo* —, to dig out coal.

HŌRI-DASHI,*-sz,-sh'ta*, ハフリダス, *t.v.* To throw out.

HORI-KOMI,*-mu,-nda*, ホリコム, 掘込, *t.v.* To dig into, enter by digging.

HORI-MONO, ホリモノ, 彫物, *n.* A carving, engraving.

HORI-MONO-SHI, ホリモノシ, 雕物師, *n.* A carver, engraver, sculptor.

HORO, ホロ, 縨, *n.* A kind of cushion stuffed with cotton worn by cavalry to protect the back.

HOROBI,*-bu,-ta*, ホロブ, 亡, *i.v.* Destroyed, overthrown, ruined. *Kuni, iye, shiro, mi, shindai nado ga horobiru*, a country, house, castle, self, or property is destroyed. Syn. TSZBURERU, METSZBŌ SZRU.

HOROBOSHI,*-sz,-sh'ta*, ホロボス, 亡, *t.v.* To destroy, overthrow, ruin. *Teki no kuni wo* —, to destroy an enemy's country. Syn. TSZBUSZ.

HORO-HORO TO, ホロホロト, *adv.* Appearance of fruit, leaves, or drops of rain falling, or, the sound of crying. — *to naku. Namida* — *kobore-ochiru*, the tears fell in drops.

HŌROKU, ホウロク, 沙鍋, *n.* An earthen dish used in baking.

HŌRON, ハフロン, 法論, A debate or discussion on religious subjects. — *szru*, to argue on religious subjects.

HORORI-TO, ホロリト, *adv.* The manner of tears falling. — *namida wo nagasz*, to shed tears.

HOROYOI, or, HOROYEI, ホロヨヒ, 微酔, Half drunk. — *ni natta.*

HORUTOGARU, ホルトガル, 波爾杜瓦爾, Portugal.

†HOSA,*-szru*, ホサ, 補佐, (*taszkeru,*) To aid, assist, to act as guardian. — *no shin*, the minister of a prince. Syn. KŌKEN SZRU.

HŌ-SAKU, ホウサク, 豐作, *n.* A fine crop.

HŌ-SENKWA, ホウセンクワ, 鳳仙花, *n.* The Balsam, or Lady's slipper.

HŌ-SHA, ホウシヤ, 硼砂, *n.* Borax.

†HŌ-SHA, ハウシヤ, 報謝, *n.* Alms, charity. — *wo negau*, to ask alms.

HŌ-SHI, ホウシ, 法師, *n.* A bonze.

†HŌ-SHI, ハウシ, 芳志, Your agreeable intention, (in letters,) *Go* — *no dan arigataku*, thank you for your kind wishes.

HOSHI, ホシ, 星; *n.* A star. 翳, A white speck on the cornea. The centre of a target.

HOSHI,*-sz,-sh'ta*, ホス, 乾, *t. v.* To dry. *Hi ni* —, to dry in the sun. *Hi de* —, to dry at the fire. Syn. KAWAKASZ.

HOSHI-BUDŌ, ホシブダウ 乹蒲萄, *n.* Raisins, dried grapes.

HOSHI-GARI,*-ru,-tta*, ホシガル, 欲, *i. v.* To desire, want, long after, covetous. *Kono yedz wo h'to ga* —, people are desirous of having this picture.

HOSHII,*-KI,-SHI*, ホシイ, 欲, *a.* Wanting, desiring, wishing for. *Sake ga* —, want *sake. Kore ga hoshii ka*, do you want this? *Yoi tszma wo hoshii mon da*, I want a good wife.

HOSHI-I, ホシイヒ, 糒, *n.* Rice boiled and dried.

HOSHI-KA, ホシカ, 干鰯, *n.* A kind of dried fish.

HŌSHIKI, ハフシキ, 法式, *n.* Established rule, usage, law, or custom. Syn. JŌREI.

HOSHIKU, or HOSHŪ, ホシク 欲, *adv.* Desirous of, wishing for, wanting. *Nani mo* — *nai*, I don't want anything. *Kane ga hoshikuba akindo ni nare*, if you want money be a merchant.

HOSHĪ-MAMA, ホシイママ, 恣, Having one's own way, doing as one pleases. — *ni szru*, to do as one pleases. *Kodomo wo* — *ni sasete okeba hōratz ni naru*, if you let a child have its own way it will become a profligate.

HOSHI-MATSZRI, ホシマツリ, 星祭, *n.* Star-festival, held on the 7th day of the 7th month, also, a festival held to counteract the evil influences of the ruling star.

HOSHI-MISE, ホシミセ, 干店, *n.* Selling in the open air, where the wares are spread out on a mat.

HŌ-SHO, ホウシヨ, 奉書, *n.* A kind of fine paper, also, a letter from the *Shōgun.*

†HŌSHO, ハウシヨ, 芳書, *n.* Your delightful letter.

†HŌ-SHŌ, ホウシヤウ, 褒賞, *t.v.* To praise, to reward.

HŌ-SŌ, ハウサウ, 疱瘡, *n.* Small pox. —

wo szru, to have the small-pox. — *gami*, the god of small-pox. *Wiye-bōsō*, vaccination. — *ga hayaru*, the small-pox is prevalent.

HOSO, or HOZO, ホソ, 臍, *n.* The navel. — *no o*, navel string, umbilical cord. — *wo kamu*, to bite the navel, (fig.) to repent, feel regret, remorse. Syn. HESO.

HOSO, ホソ, 細, Fine (same as *Hosoi.*) used only in compound words.

HOSO-BIKI, ホソビキ, 細引, *n.* A kind of rope, or cord made of hemp.

†HOSO-DONO, ホソドノ, 廊, *n.* A corridor, or gallery leading from one building to another. Syn. RŌKA.

HOSOI,-KI,-SHI, ホソイ, 細, *a.* Fine, (as thread,) slender, narrow, delicate, thin, small. — *ito*, fine thread. *Michi ga* —, the road is narrow. *Te ashi ga hosoi*, the limbs are slender, or thin. — *koye*, a shrill voice. *Shin-sho ga* —, his property is small. — *f'toi*, fine and coarse.

HOSOKU, or HOSŌ, ホソク, 細, *adv.* idem. — *naru*, to become slender. — *szru*, to make fine. *Me wo* — *szru*, to nearly close the eyes.

HOSO-MAYU, ホソマユ, 細眉, *n.* Delicate eyebrows.

HOSOME,-*ru*,-*ta*, ホソメル, 細, *t. v.* To make fine, thin, slender, or delicate. *Koye wo hosomete iu*, to speak in a shrill voice.

HOSOME, ホソメ, 細目, *n.* Eyes slightly open, a narrow crack. *To wo hosome ni akete yuki wo miru*, to open the door a little and look out at the snow. — *de miru*, to look with the eyes partly closed.

HOSO-MICHI, ホソミチ, 細道, *n.* A narrow road, path.

HOSONAGAI, ホソナガイ, 細長, Long and slender.

HOSO-NE, ホソネ, 細音, *n.* A fine, shrill voice, or sound.

HOSO-NUNO, ホソヌノ, 細布, *n.* Fine muslin.

HO-SOTSZ, ホソツ, 步卒, *n.* Foot soldier, infantry. Syn. HO-HEI, ASHIGARU.

†HOSOWATA, ホソワタ, 胞, *n.* The placenta. Syn. YENA, NOCHI-ZAN.

†HOSSHI,-*szru*,-*sh'ta*, ホツスル, 欲, *i. v.* To wish, desire, want. Syn. NEGAU, NOZOMU.

HOSSHIN, ホツシン, 發心, *n.* Conversion, or turning from vicious habits to a moral life. (Bud.) — *sh'te bōdz ni naru*, to be converted and become a priest.

HOSSOKU, ホツソク, 發足, Starting or setting out on a journey. Syn. DETACHI.

HOSSŌSHŪ, ホツサウシウ, 法相宗, *n.* The name of a Buddhist sect; (now extinct.)

HOSSZRU, ホツスル, See *Hosshi.*

HOSZ, ホス, See *Hoshi.*

HOSSZ, ホツス, 拂子, *n.* A brush of long white hair carried by Bud. priests.

†HŌ-SZN, ハウスン, 方寸, *n.* The heart, mind. — *no uchi ni*, in the mind.

HOTA, ホタ, 杻械, *n.* The stocks. Syn. ASHI-KASE.

†HŌ-TAI, ホウタイ, 帮帶, *n.* A bandage, (for a wound.)

HOTARU, ホタル, 螢, *n.* A fire-fly,

HOTARUBI, ホタルビ, 螢火, *n.* The light of the fire-fly.

HO-TATE-GAI, ホタテガイ, 帆立貝, *n.* A kind of shell-fish, the nautilus.

‖HOTAYE,-*ru*,-*ta*, ホタエル, 挑, *i. v.* To play, sport, to romp. Syn. TAWAMURERU, JARERU.

HOTE-HOTE, ホテホテ, *adv.* Large, corpulent, big-bellied. — *f'totte iru*, to be big and corpulent.

HOTEPPARA, ホテツパラ, *n.* The belly. *Yari de* — *wo tszki-nuku*, to run the belly through with a spear.

HOTERI,-*ru*,-*ta*, ホテル, 熱, *i. v.* To be hot, burning, to smart. *Kao ga* —, the face burns. *Mimi ga* —, the ears burn. Syn. NESSZRU.

HOTERI, ホテリ, 熱, *n.* Heat, burning, a smarting or burning pain. *Hiru no* — *de yoru mo atszi*, owing to the heat of the day the night is also hot.

†HŌ-TO, ハウタウ, 放蕩, Profligate, dissolute. Syn. HŌRATSZ.

HŌ-TO, ホウトウ, 奉燈, *n.* Lights placed before idols.

HOTOBAKASHI, or HOTOBASHI,-*sz*,-*sh'ta*, ホトバス, *t.v.* To soften by steeping in water. *Nikawa wo* —, to soften glue in water.

HOTOBASHIRI,-*ru*,-*tta*, ホトバシル, 迸, See *Hodobashiri.*

HOTOBI,-*ru*,-*ta*, ホトビル, *i.v.* To be softened by steeping in water.

HOTOBORI, ホトボリ, *n.* Heat. *Hets'i no* —, the heat of a furnace.

HOTO-HOTO-TO, ホトホトト, *adv.* The sound made by beating a door, rapping. *To wo* — *uchi-tataku*, to rap at the door. Syn. HATA-HATA.

HOTOKE, ホトケ, 佛, *n.* The general name for the divinities worshiped by the Buddhists, who were all originally human. The soul of the dead. — *no zō*, an idol. — *no mei-nichi*, the anniversary of a death.

Iki-botoke, one who by his virtue resembles the gods.

HOTOKE-NO-ZA, ホトケノザ, 佛座, *n.* Name of a plant.

HOTONDO, ホトンド, 殆, *adv.* Almost, well nigh, nearly, greatly, very much. — *midz ni ochiru*, came near falling into the water. — *komaru*, greatly troubled. Syn. SZDE-NI, YOPPODO.

HOTORI, ホトリ, 邊, *n.* Neighborhood vicinity. *Kawa no* —, near the river. *Shiro no* —, vicinity of the castle. SOBA, HEN, ATARI, HATA, KIMPEN.

†HOTORI,*-ru*,*-tta*, ホトル, 熱, *i.v.* To be hot, feverish. *Atama ga* —, head is hot.

†HOTORI, ホトリ, 熱, *n.* Fever, heat. — *wo samasz*, to cool the fever. Syn. NETSZ.

HOTOTOGISZ, ホトトギス, 杜鵑, *n.* The name of a bird. The cuckoo?

†HOTSZGO, or HOTS-GON, ホツゴ, 發語, 發言, Speaking first, or beginning to speak. — *szru.*

HOTSZKI,*-ku*,*-ita*, ホツク, 撒, *t.v.* To fray, ravel, to tear lint.

†HOTSZ-NETSZ, ホツネツ, 發熱, *n.* The springing up of fever. — *szru.*

HOTSZRE,*-ru*,*-ta*, ホツレル, *i.v.* Frayed, rubbed, worn, (as cloth.) *Kimono ga* —.

†HOTTAI, ホツタイ, 法體, *n.* Shaven headed, as a Bud. priest. — *szru*, to shave the head.

†HOTTAN, ホツタン, 發端, *n.* The beginning, commencement. Syn. HAJIMARI.

HOTTO, ホツト, *adv.* The sound of sighing, or drawing a long breath. *Hot o tame-iki wo tszku*, to draw a long breath.

HOTTŌ-NIN, ホツトウニン, 發頭人, *n.* Originator, first mover, or doer, ringleader. Syn. HOKKI-NIN, CHŌBON-NIN.

HŌWŌ, ハフワウ, 法皇, *n.* A Mikado who has abdicated the throne, shaven his head, and devoted himself to a religious life.

HŌWŌ, ホウワウ, 鳳凰, *n.* The name of a fabulous bird, the phœnix.

HOYA, ホヤ, 寄生, *n.* A parasitic plant, misletoe.

†HOYAKU, ホヤク, 補藥, *(oginai guszri.) n.* Tonic medicines, medicines which strengthen the body, or keep off disease.

HOYE,*-ru*,*-ta*, ホエル, 吠, *i.v.* To bark, to bellow, roar, (the cry of any animal.) *Inu ga* —, the dog barks. *Ushi ga* —, the cow bellows.

†HŌ-YE, ハフヱ, 法會, *n.* An assembly of Bud. priests, for the performance of religious ceremonies.

†HŌ-YE, ハフエ, 法衣, *n.* The peculiar dress of a Bud. priest.

†HŌ-YE, ハウエ, 胞衣, *n.* The afterbirth; placenta and membranes. Syn. YENA.

HOYE-DZRA, ホエヅラ, 哭顔, *(nakigao.) n.* The face of one crying.

†HO-YEKI,*-szru*, ホエキ, 補益, *(oginai masz,)* To repair a defect, to complete, to strengthen, recruit. *Kekki no fu-soku wo — szru*, to strengthen the vital powers. Syn. TASZ.

†HO-YEN, ホエン, 步欄, *n.* A long corridor.

HŌ-YEN, ハウエン, 方圓, *(shikaku maru.)* Square and round.

HO-YŌ ホヤウ, 保養, *(tamochi yashinau.)* Preserving the health, strengthening the body. — *wo szru*, to attend to one's health. Syn. YŌJŌ.

HŌYŪ, ホウイウ, 朋友, *n.* A friend, companion. Syn. TOMODACHI, HŌBAI.

HOZAKI,*-ku*,*-ita*, ホザク, *i.v.* To say, to speak, (a contemptuous word used in anger to an inferior.)

†HŌ-ZAI, ハウザイ, 方劑, *n.* A compounded medicine. Syn. AWASE-GUSZRI.

HŌ-ZEN, ハウゼン, 寶前, Before a *Miya*, or *Kami*. — *ni gaku wo kakeru*, to hang up a picture before a *miya* as an offering.

†HŌ-ZŌ, ハウザウ, 寶藏, *(takara kura.) n.* A store house in which valuable things are kept.

I

I, イ, 膽, *n.* Gall, bile. *Kuma no i*, bear's gall. *Ushi no i*, ox-gall.

I, 井, 猪, *n.* A wild hog, and (亥,) one of the 12 signs. *I no toki*, 10 o'clock at night. *I no kata*, N. N. west. *I no ko*, or *I no hi*, a festival on the "hog-day" of the 10th month. *I-naka no tszki*, the moon on the 20th day of the month.

I, 井, 胃, *n.* The stomach. *I chiu*, in the stomach. *I no fu*, the stomach. *I no jō-kō*, the cardiac orifice. *I no ge-kō*, the pyloric orifice.

I, イ, 意, *(kokoro-base,) n.* The mind, thoughts, intention, will, feeling, meaning, — *ni kanau*, to agree with one's ideas, or mind. — *ni somuku*, to be contrary to one's mind. *Kono i wo ajiwau*, to perceive the meaning of. *Ichi i ni naru*, to be of one mind.

I, 井, 藺, *n*, The rush of which matting is made. *I-goza*, or *I-mushin*, a mat.

I, イ, 異, (*kotonari*,) Different, strange, unusual. *I fu dō bo*, a different father, but the same mother. *I-koku*, foreign country. *I-ku-dō-on*, 異口同音, all together with one voice. *I na h'to*, an eccentric person.

I, 井, 位, (*kurai*,) *n*. Rank, dignity. *Mu i mu k'wan*, without rank or office. *I no takai h'to*, a man of high rank. *I wo otosz*, to be degraded. *I ni szszmu*, to be promoted in rank. *Ichi i*, the first or highest rank of nobility.

I, 井, 威, (*ikioi*,) *n*. Dignity, majesty, power, authority, influence. — *no aru h'to*, one having authority. — *furū*, to show one's power. — *wo otosz*, to loose one's power. Syn. ISEI, KEN.

I, 井, 井, *n*. A well. — *no midz*, well water. *I no naka no kawadz no gotoku*, like a frog in a well. *I wo sarayeru*, to clean a well. Syn. IDO.

I, イ, 醫, *n*. A doctor, physician, medicine, — *wo manabu*, to study medicine. — *wo giyō to szru*, to follow the business of a physician. *Mei-i*, a celebrated doctor. *Tai-i*, a great doctor.

I, *–ru*, *–ta*, イル, 射, *t. v*. To shoot, (a bow,) *yumi wo iru*, to shoot a bow. *Ite hadzsz*, to shoot and miss.

I, *–ru*, *–ta*, イル, 鑄, *t. v*. To cast, to found, to run metal in moulds. *Kane wo iru*, to cast money. *Zeni wo* —, to cast iron cash. *Nabe wo* —, to cast pots.

I, *–ru*, *–ta*, 井ル, 居, *i. v*. To be, to dwell, sit. *Doko ni i-nasaru*, where do you live? *Kanagawa ni imasz*, I live in *Kanagawa*. *Daidokoro ni imasz*, he is in the kitchen. *Nani wo sh'te iru*, what are you doing? *Hataraite-iru*, he is working.

Ī, イイ, 好, *a*. Good, right, fine, pretty. *Īkeshiki*, a beautiful landscape. *Itte mo ī*, had better go. *Ī-midz*, good water. *Ī-kimono*, nice clothes. *Dōdemo ī*, anyhow will do. Syn. YOI, YOROSHII.

†Ī, イヒ, 飯, (*meshi*,) *n*. Boiled rice.

Ī, *iu*, *iuta*, イフ, 言, *t. v*. To say, speak, tell. *Mono wo iu*, to talk. *Nan to iuta*, what did you say? *Wiye wo ten to iu*, that which is above is called heaven. *Na wa kichi to iu*, his name is called *Kichi*. *Achi ye ite sō iye*, go there and say so. *Sada ni sakana wo katte-koi to iye*, tell *Sada* to buy some fish. Syn. MŌSZ.

†I, *iru*, *ita*, 井ル, 率, *t. v*. To take along with, to lead, conduct. Syn. HIKI-IRU, TSZRERU.

I-AI, 井アヒ, 居合, *n*. The drawing of a long sword while sitting; (a difficult act in fencing.) — *wo nuku*, to draw a sword while sitting. *I-ai goski ni naru*, to put one's self in the posture of drawing the sword &c.

†IAKU, 井アク, 帷幄, *n*. A curtain.

†I-AN, イアン, 醫案, *n*. Medical directions. — *wo kaku*, to write down the history of a case with the proper medicines to be used.

I-ATE, *–ru*, *–ta*, イアテル, 射中, *t. v*. To shoot and hit. *Ya wo mato ni i-ateru*, to shoot an arrow and hit the mark.

Ī-ATE, *–ru*, *–ta*, イヒアテル, 言中, *t. v*. To guess, conjecture, find out, to say and hit.

I-AWASE, *–ru*, *–ta*, 井アハセル, 居合, *i. v*. To happen to be present. *Sono za ni i-awasete, hanashi wo kīta*, I happened to be present at the meeting and heard what was said.

ĪAWASE, *–ru*, *–ta*, イヒアハセル, 言合, *i. v*. To agree in saying; to say in concert, or by collusion, to consult together.

Ī-AYAMARI, *–ru*, *–tta*, イヒアヤマル, 言誤, *i. v*. To mistake in saying, or say by mistake, blunder, mis-state.

I-BA, イバ, 射場, *n*. A place for shooting the bow, shooting ground.

IBAI, *–ō*, *–atta*, イバフ, 嘶, *i. v*. To neigh. *Uma ga ibō*. the horse neighs. Syn. INANAKU.

†I-BAKU, 井バク, 帷幕, *n*. A curtain. Syn. MAKU.

I-BARA, イバラ, 荊棘, *n*. The name of a thorny tree. Syn. ODORO.

IBARA-GAKI, イバラガキ, 荊棘垣, *n*. A hedge of thorns.

||IBARI, 井バリ, 尿, *n*. Urine. — *bukuro*, the bladder. — *wo szru*, to urinate. Syn. SHŌ-BEN, SHIKO.

IBARI *–ru*, *–tta*, イバル, 威張, *i. v*. To boast, to vaunt, make a swell, act pompously. *Ibatte aruku*, to swagger, strut. *Ibatte h'tori haba wo szru*, to act pompously and crowd others away. *Ibatte h'to wo mi-sageru*. Syn. HOKORU, RIKIMU, TAI-HEIRAKU.

IBIKI, イビキ, 睡息, *n*. Snoring. — *wo kaku*, to snore.

||IBIRI, *–ru*, *–tta*, イビル, *t.v*. To parboil, to scald, (as vegetables,) to roast slightly in ashes. *Hai ni* —, to heat in ashes. *Yu de* —, to scald in hot water. *Ibiri korosz*, to afflict or torment to death.

IBITSZ, イビツ, *n*. Oval. — *nari*, an oval form.

†Ī-BITSZ, イヒビツ, 飯櫃, *n*. A box for carrying boiled rice. Syn. BENTŌ.

IBO, イボ, 肬, *n.* A wart, small tumor. — *ga dekita,* to have a wart.

†I-BŌ,–*szru,* 井バウ, 遺忘, (*waszreru.*) To forget.

IBŌ, イバフ, 嘶, To neigh, see *Ibai.*

IBOI,–ō,–*otta,* イボフ, 火傷, *i.v.* To suppurate, to matter, only used of the moxa. *Kiu ga ibotta,* the moxa has suppurated.

IBOI, イボヒ, *n.* The pus of a moxa.

IBUKARI,–*ru,–tta,* イブカル, 訝, *i.v.* To wonder at, consider strange or dubious, to suspect. Syn. AYASHIMU, FUSHIN SZRU.

IBUKASHII,–KI, イブカシイ, 不審, *a.* Strange, mysterious, unintelligible, doubtful, suspicious.

IBUKASHIKU,–Ū, イブカシク, 不審, *adv.* *Ibukashiku omō,* to feel dubious about, to wonder at. *Ikaga to — zonji-soro,* wondering what I should do. Syn. FU-SHIN, UTAGAWASHII, AYASHII.

IBUKASHISA, イブカシサ, *n.* Doubtfulness, dubiousness, mysteriousness.

IBUKI, イブキ, 伊吹木, *n.* The Juniper tree. Syn. BIYAKU-SHIN.

IBUKURO, 井ブクロ, 胃腑, *n.* The stomach.

Ī-BUN, イヒブン, 言分, *n.* Something to be said against, some fault to find. *Omaye ni — ga aru,* I have some fault to find with you. — *ga nai,* nothing to be said against it.

IBURI,–*ru,–tta,* イブル, 燻, *i.v.* To smoke. *Hi ga ibutta,* the fire smokes. Syn. FUSZBORU, KUYORU.

||IBURI, イブリ, 安忍, Cruel, unfeeling, unmerciful. — *na h'to,* a cruel person.

IBUSARE,–*ru,–ta,* イブサレル, 被燻, Pass. of *Iburi,* to be smoked, (fig.) annoyed, tormented.

†IBUSEI,–KI,–SHI, イブセイ, 鬱悒, *a.* Gloomy, dismal, disagreeable. Syn. UTTŌSHI, URUSAI, KEMUTTAI.

†IBUSEKU, イブセク, 鬱悒, *adv.* idem. — *omō,* to feel gloomy.

IBUSHI,–*sz,–sh'ta,* イブス, 燻, *t.v.* To smoke, fumigate, (fig.) to annoy, vex, torment. *Katsz-bushi wo ibusz,* to smoke the flesh of the *Katszo.* *Ka wo —,* to smoke out musquitoes. Syn. FUSZBERU, KUYORASZ.

IBUSHI-GUSZRI, イブシグスリ, 燻薬, *n.* Fumigating medicines.

||ICHATSZKI,–*ku,–ita,* イチャツク, 狎戯, *i.v.* To flirt, to sport with girls. Syn. TAWAMURERU.

ICHI, イチ, 一, (*h'totsz.*) One; first, prime, whole. *Ichi-ichi,* each one, every one, every particular, one by one. *Ichi-yō,* alike, same. *Ichi-do,* once. *Ichi gi ni mo oyobadz,* without a single objection. *Ichi-men,* the whole surface. *Ichi no h'to,* the first of men in rank, (viz. a *dai-jōdaijin.*) — *dai-ji,* of prime importance. — *no miya,* eldest daughter of the Mikado.

ICHI, イチ, 位置, *n.* The order, arrangement, or method in which things are placed. — *ga yoi.* — *ga warui.*

ICHI, イチ, 市, *n.* A market, a fair. *Ichi-ba,* market place. *Asa-ichi,* morning market. *Ichi ni itte katte koi,* go to the market and buy. *Sakana-ichi ga tatsz,* the fish market is open. *Ichi-bito,* market people.

ICHI-ASHI, イチアシ, 一足, (As in the phrase.) — *wo dash'te nigeru,* ran away as fast as his legs could carry him. — *ni nigeru,* id.

ICHI-BAN, イチバン, 一番, Number one, the first, the best. — *me,* the first one, the very best.

ICHI-BU, イチブ, 一分, *n.* A silver coin = about 33 cents; one part.

ICHI-BU-SHI-JŪ, イチブシジウ, 一部始終, From beginning to end. every thing. — *wo kataru,* to tell all from beginning to end.

ICHI-DŌ, イチドウ, 一同, *adv.* All, every one, the whole.

ICHI-DZ, イチヅ, 一途, (*h'to szji*), *adv.* Only, alone, nothing else, obstinately, persistently. *Chiu-gi ishidz ni omoi-tszmeru,* thinking of nothing but loyalty. *Ichi-dz no riyō-ken,* possessed with one idea, or feeling. — *ni sō omō,* persist in thinking so.

ICHI-GAI, イチガイ, 一槩, *adv.* Wholly, without exception or distinction; entirely, indiscriminate. *Ano h'to warui to ichigai ni mo iuwaremai, mata yoki koto mo aru de arō.* it should not be said that he is wholly bad, for I think he has some good qualities. *Ichi-gai na mono,* one who is indiscriminate in what he says or does.

Ī-CHIGAI,–*au,–atta,* イヒチガフ, 言違, *i.v.* To mistake in saying or telling, to say by mistake, to blunder.

ICHIGO, イチゴ, 苺, *n.* A raspberry.

ICHI-GO, イチゴ, 一期, *n.* Whole life. Syn. ISSHŌGAI.

ICHI-JI, イチジ, 一時, *adv.* At one time, same time, together; once on a time.

ICHIJIKU, イチヂク, 無花果, *n.* The fig.

ICHIJIRUSHI, イチジルシ, 著明, Plain, clear, manifest, obvious, evident, apparent. *Sei-jin no michi —,* the doctrine of the sages is clear. *Kami no ri-yaku —,* the help of the *Kami* is plainly seen. Syn. AKIRAKA, MEI-HAKU, FUM-MIYŌ.

ICHI-JUN, イチジユン, 一旬, *n.* One decade.

ICHIKO, イチコ, 降巫, *n.* A fortune-teller, or spiritualist. Syn. ADZSAMIKO.

ICHI-MEI, イチメイ, 一命, *n.* One's life.

ICHI-MI, イチミ, 一味, One ingredient. *Daiwō ichi-mi no g'wanyaku*, a pill made of rhubarb alone. — *ni naru*, to become one of the same party, or army.

†ICHI-MOTSZ, イチモツ, 逸物, *n.* A good horse.

ICHI-RAKU, イチラク, *n.* A fine kind of ratan-work.

Ī-CHIRASHI,*–sz,–sh'ta*, イヒチラス, 言散, *t.v.* To scatter, spread, or disseminate by talking.

ICHI-RI-DZKA, イチリツカ, 一里塚, *n.* Mile-stones.

ICHI-YEN, イチエン, 一圓, *adv.* Positively, peremptorily; (with a negative), by no means.

ICHI-YŌ, イチヤウ, 一様, Alike, same.

ICHŌ, イテウ, 銀杏, *n.* Name of a tree, the Salisburia adiamtifolia. Syn. GINNAN.

I-DAKE-TAKA-NI, 井ダケタカニ, 居尺高, *adv.* Drawing one's self up, sitting erect. — *natte nonoshiru*, drawing one's self up to scold.

IDAKI,*–ku,–ita*, イダク, 抱, *t.v.* To embrace, to hold in the arms, (fig.) to hold in the heart, to harbor in the mind, cherish. *Kodomo wo* —, to carry a child in the arms, *Urami wo* —, cherish hatred. Syn. DAKU, KAKAYERU.

IDAKI-TSZKI,*–ku,–ita*, イダキツク, 抱附, *t.v* To embrace, hug.

IDASHI,*–sz,–sh'ta*, イダス, 出, *t. v.* To cause to go out, to send forth Syn. DASZ.

Ī-DASHI,*–sz,–sh'ta*, イヒダス, 言出, *t.v.* To pronounce, to utter, to tell, to begin to speak.

IDE, or, IDE-YA, イデ, Exclam. used to an antagonist in bantering, come on, now then, well. *Ide o aite ni narimashō*, come on, I will be your antagonist, Syn. DORE, SA.

IDE,*–ru,–ta*, イデル, 出, To go out, issue forth. *Uchi yori ideru*, to go out of the house. Syn. DERU.

†IDE-AI,*–au,–atta*, イデアフ, 出逢, *i.v.* To meet in the street or while out.

†IDE-IRI, イデイリ, 出入, Going out and coming in, expenses and receipts. — *mono*, one who frequents a place. Syn. DE-IRI.

IDE-TACHI, イデタチ, 出立, *n.* The style or manner in which a person is dressed, the costume, equipment, accoutrement. — *wo szru*, to dress, or equip one's self. *Sono hi no — ni wa*, his dress on that day was, &c. Syn. GIYŌ-SŌ, YOSO-OI.

IDE-TACHI,*–tsz,–tta*, イデタツ, 出立, *i.v.* To be dressed up, accoutred, equiped. Syn. YOSOŌ.

†IDEYU, イデユ, 温泉, *n.* A hot-spring. Syn. ONSEN.

IDO, 井ド, 井, *n.* A well —*wo horu*, to dig a well. — *wo umeru*, to fill up a well. — *wo kayeru*, to clean a well.

†I-DŌ, イダウ, 醫道, (*isha no michi*). *n.* The science of medicine. Syn. I-JUTSZ.

IDOBATA, or, IDO-NO-HATA, 井ドバタ, 井傍, Near the well, vicinity of the well.

IDO-GAWA, 井ドガハ, 井側, *n.* A well-crib.

IDO-GAYE, 井ドガヘ, 井浚, *n.* Cleaning a well. — *wo szru*, to clean a well.

IDO-HORI, 井ドホリ, 井掘, *n.* A well digger.

I-DOKORO, 井ドコロ, 居所, *n.* A dwelling place.

†IDOMI,*–mu,–nda*, イドム, 挑, *t.v.* To excite,stir up. *Tatakai wo idomu*, to stir up war.

†IDOMI-AI,*–au,–atta*, イドミアフ, 挑合, *i.v.* To contend, or strive together. Syn. TATAKAU.

†IDOMI-ARASOI,*–ō,–ōta*, イドミアラソフ, 挑爭, *i.v.* To contend, or strive together.

IDOMI-TATAKAI,*–au,–atta*, イドミタタカフ, 挑戰, *i. v.* To battle, make war.

IDZ, イズ, neg. of *Iru*.

†IDZCHI, イツチ, 何地, (*Doko*,) *adv.* Where, what place. — *to mo naku*, any where, wheresoever. — *yuki ken*, I wonder where he has gone.

†IDZKATA, イツカタ, 何方, (*Doko, dochira.*) *adv.* Where.

†IDZKO, or IDZKU, イツク, 何處, (*Doko.*) Where. — *ni mo*, every-where. — *nite mo*, in every place, every where. — *to mo naku*, wheresoever, every place whatever. — *yori to mo naku kitaru*, come from some place no difference where, or what place soever he comes from. *Idzku mo onaji aki no yūgure*, autumnal evenings are the same every where. *Idzku-zo ya*, where?

IDZKUMARI,*–ru,–tta*, 井ズクマル, 坐縮, *i. v.* To sit cramped with cold. *Samui kara idzkumatte oru.*

†IDZKUN-ZO, イツクンゾ, 焉, (*dōsh'te*,) Exclam. how! why? — *kakusan ya*, how can he hide it?

IDZMI, イツミ, 泉, *n.* A spring of water.

IDZMŌ, 井ズマフ, 居角力, *n.* Wrestling

in a sitting posture. — *wo toru*, to wrestle while sitting. Syn. SZWARI-DZMŌ.

†IDZNA, イヅナ, 飯繩, *n.* A kind of sorcery or magic. — *wo tszkau*, to practice sorcery.

†IDZNA-TSZKAI, イヅナツカヒ, 役鬼者, *n.* A sorcerer, a magician.

IDZRE, イヅレ, 何, *adv.* Where, what, which, who, still, yet, however, at all events. *Idzre mo*, every where, every one, any one. *Idzre demo yoi*, any way will do. *Idzre ni mo*, in every place. *Idzre nite mo*, in any place whatever, or any one whatever, both, either. *Idzre sono uchi o mi ni kakarimashō*, however, or at all events I shall see you again. — *ni sh'te mo yoi mono de wa nai*, at all events he is a bad fellow.

IDZRU, イヅル, same as *Ideru*. *Idzru hi*, the rising sun.

I-DZTSZ, 井ヅツ, 筒, *n.* A well-crib.

I-FŪ, イフウ, 異風, *(kawatta nari.)* Strange appearance or style of dress.

I-FUKU, イフク, 衣服, *n.* Clothing, apparel. Syn. KIMONO, MESHI-MONO, I-SHŌ.

Ī-FUKUME,-*ru*,-*ta*, イヒフクメル, 言含, *t. v.* To tell, explain, or make known so as fully to understand.

Ī-FURASHI,-*sz*,-*sh'ta*, イヒフラス, 流言, *t. v.* To publish, proclaim, or tell all about.

Ī-FUSE,-*ru*,-*ta*, イヒフセル, 言伏, *t.v.* To defeat in an argument, to vanquish by talking, to talk down.

Ī-FUSEGI,-*gu*,-*ida*, イヒフセグ, 言防, *t.v.* To talk and defend one's self, to deny, contradict.

IGA, イガ, 刺, *n.* A bur, prickly shell. *Kuri no* —, a chesnut-bur. *Iga-guri atama*, a head covered with short stiff hair, like a chesnut bur.

Ī-GAI-NAKI,-SHI, イヒガイナキ, 無云甲斐, *a.* Not worth speaking to, or no use in speaking to. — *mono domo.*

†IGAKI, イガキ, 笊, *n.* A kind of bamboo basket. Syn. ZARU.

†I-GAKI, イガキ, 瑞籬, *n.* A picket-fence around a *Miya*. Syn. MIDZ-KAKI.

||IGAMASE,-*ru*,-*ta*, イガマセル, 令曲, caust. of *Igami*. To bend, to crook, to make crooked. *Hari wo* —, to bend a pin. Syn. MAGERU.

||IGAMI,-*mu*,-*nda*, イガム, 曲, *i.v.* Crooked, bent, (of what should be straight), (fig.) depraved. *Hari ga iganda*, the pin is bent. *Ki no iganda h'to*, a perverse fellow Syn. MAGARU.

IGAMI,-*mu*,-*nda*, イガム, 啤, *i. v.* To snarl, growl, (as a dog,) to caterwaul.

IGAMI-AI,-*au*,-*atta*, イガミアフ, 啤合, *i. v.* To snarl, or growl at each other, to quarrel.

IGATA, イガタ, 鎔, *n.* A mould for casting. *Tama no* —, a bullet mould.

Ī-GATAI,-KI,-SHI, イヒガタイ, 難言, *a.* Hard, or difficult to say or tell, hard to utter or pronounce.

Ī-GATAKU, or Ī-GATŌ, イヒガタク, 難言, *adv.* id.

I-GE, イゲ, 飯氣, *n*, The steam from boiling rice.

I-GE, イゲ, 以下, Below, inferior. *Kore yori ige*, below this, or after this (in books.) *Samurai ige no mono*, persons below the rank of gentry. Syn. SHIMOTSZKATA, IKA,

IGETA, 井ゲタ, 井桁, *n.* A well-crib. Syn. IDOGAWA.

†I-GI, 井ギ, 威儀, Imposing, commanding or authoritative appearance, majestic, august, princely. — *wo tori-tszkurō*, to adjust, or put one's self in a dignified posture. — *tō-tō*, great majesty. Syn. MOTTAI.

I-GI, イギ, 異儀, Strange, unusual, different. *Igi-nashi*, nothing unusual, nothing particular.

IGIRISZ, イギリス, 伊幾里須, *n.* England, — *no*, English.

†IGITANAI,-KI,-SHI, イギタナイ, *a.* Sleepy, drowsy. *Igitanakute nebokeru*, to be drowsy and stupid. Syn. NEMUGARU.

I-GIYŌ, イギヤウ, 異形, *(kawatta katachi,)* Strange, unnatural, or monstrous in form, (as a person with one eye.)

I-GO, イゴ, 以後, After this, hereafter, henceforth. *Kore yori igo*, or *Kono igo*, henceforth. Syn. KONO NOCHI, SONO NOCHI, KONO-KATA.

†I-GO, 井ゴ, 圍碁, *n.* The game of checkers.

||I-GUCHI, イグチ, 缺脣, *n.* Hare-lip. Syn. MITSZ-GUCHI.

Ī-GUSA, イヒグサ, 言種, *(hanashi no tane,) n.* A matter or subject of talk, an occasion for talk, excuse, pretext. *Ano h'to no īgusa ga warui kara hara ga tatsz*, I am angry because what he said was bad. *Ī-gusa no tane ni naru*, to become a subject for talk. — *ga nai*, nothing to be said, no fault to find. — *ni szru*, to make as a pretext.

IHAI, 井ハイ, 位牌, *n.* A wooden tablet, (of the dead.)

IHAI, 井ハイ, 違背, To disobey. *Shu-jin no ī-tszke wo — szru*, to disobey the orders of a master. Syn. SOMUKU.

I-HADZSHI,*–sz–sh'ta*, イハヅス, 射外, *t. v.*. To miss the target.

Ī-HADZSHI,*–sz,–sh'ta*, イヒハヅス, 言外, *t. v.* To fail, or miss to tell, fail to guess.

Ī-HAGURAKASHI,*–sz,–sh'ta*,イヒハグラカス, *t. v.* To turn the conversation to something else, to change the subject.

Ī-HARI,*–ru,–tta*, イヒハル, 言張, *i.v.* To persist in saying, positive, dogmatic and unyielding.

IHEN, 井ヘン, 違變, Failure, breach of promise. *Yak'soku wo — szru*, to fail in fulfilling an agreement. — *naku* without fail. Syn. TAGŌ, HEN-GAYERU, SOMUKE, CHIGAYERU.

†IHEN, イヘン, 異變, Uncommon, unusual, strange, extraordinary. — *na koto*. Syn. K'WAI-I.

†IHŌ, イハウ, 醫方, *n.* A medical prescription, or recipe,

Ī-HODOKI,*–ku,–ita*, イヒホドク 言解, *t. v.* To explain, solve, interpret, analyze.

Ī-IRE,*–ru,–ta*, イヒイレル, 言入, *t. v.* To propose, to offer, to put in an offer or petition.

†I-JI, イジ, 異事, *(kawatta koto,)* Any thing strange, unusual, uncommon, or extraordinary.

IJI, イヂ, 意地, *n.* Spirit, temper. — *no warui h'to*, a bad tempered person, cross. — *wo haru.* to be obstinate, cross-grained. Syn. KI, KOKORO.

IJI-BARI,*–ru,–tta*, イヂバル, 意地張, *i.v.* To be obstinate, head-strong, unyielding.

IJI-DZKU, イヂヅク, 意地盡, Excited, roused to obstinacy. — *ni naru*, to become excited and unyielding, (as in a dispute.) Syn. HARI-AI.

IJI-IJI,*–szru*, イヂイヂ, *i. v.* To fret, to be irritated, peevish. *Kodomo ga —*, the child frets, or is peevish.

IJIKE,*–ru,–ta*, イヂケル, *i. v.* To shrink, contract into a smaller compass. *Samukute ijikeru*, to shrug up with the cold. *Kono ji wa ijikete dekita*, this letter is written very small.

IJIME,*–ru,–ta*, イヂメル, *t. v.* To bully, hector, to treat with insolence, to vex, tease, to annoy, to chafe. *H'to wo ijimeru. Inu wo —*,

I-JIN, イジン, 異人, *n.* A foreigner, a strange person.

IJIRASHII,–KI, イヂラシイ, *a.* That which causes fretting, worry, grief, sorrow, or vexation.

IJIRASHIKU, イヂラシク *adv.* id. — *omou*, to feel vexed.

IJIRI,*–ru,–tta*, イヂル, 弄, *t.v.* To handle, to feel, meddle with, also to oppress, vex, tease, to insult. *Tanto ijiri-nasan-na*, don't handle it much. Syn. SAINAMU.

IJIRI-DASHI,*–sz,–sh'ta*, イヂリダス, *t.v.* To drive away by persecuting, vexing, or oppressing.

I-JŌ, イジヤウ, 以上, Above, before. *Roku-jū i-jō*, above 60 years. At the end of a letter, = this is the end, or conclusion, = finis. *Chiu yori — no mono*, persons above the middle class

I-JŪ, 井ジユウ, 居住, Dwelling, residing, living. — *szru.*

I-JUTSZ, イジユツ, 醫術, *n.* The medical art.

I-KA, イカ, 以下, Below this, from this on, henceforth, after this. *Chiu i-ka no mono*, persons below the middle class.

IKA, イカ, 烏賊, *n.* The cuttle-fish.

IKABAKARI, イカバカリ, 如何計, *(nani hodo ka.) adv.* How much? how great? very great. — *ka ureshi karō*, how great was his joy!

Ī-KACHI,*–tsz,–tta*, イヒカツ, 云勝, *t. v.* To defeat by talking, to vanquish, beat, overcome in argument.

IKADA, イカダ, 筏, *n.* A raft of timber.

IKADA-SHI, イカダシ, 筏師, *n.* A raftsman.

IKADEKA, イカデカ, 爭, *(dōsh'te.) adv.* How, why. — *kore ni masaru beki*, how can it be better than this? — *saru koto no aran*, how could such a thing be? Syn. NANISH'TE.

IKADZCHI, イカヅチ, 雷, *n.* Thunder. Syn. KAMI-NARI, RAI.

IKAGA, イカガ, 如何, *adv.* How, why, what; doubt, hesitation. — *shen*, or — *itasō*, what shall I do? *Yo ni iri kayeru mo ikaga nareba*, being doubtful about returning in the night. *Kore wa ikaga de gozaru*, how is this? *Michi wa ikaga de gozarimasz*, how is the road? *Biyō-nin no yōdai wa ikaga*, how is the sick-man? Syn. DŌ, NANI.

IKAGASHII,–KI, イカガシイ, 如何敷, *a.* Doubtful, dubious, uncertain. *Amari ikagashii kara itashimasen*, as it is very doubtful, I shall not do it. Syn. OBOTSZKANAI, UTAGAWASHII.

IKAGASHIKU, or IKAGASHŪ, イカガシク, 何如敷, *adv.* idem.

IKAHODO, イカホド, 何程, How much. — *aru*, how much is there? — *mo nai*, have not much. — *hone wo otte mo dekinai*, how much soever I labor, I can't do it. Syn. DORE-HODO, NANI-HODO, DONO KURAI.

‖IKAI, イカイ, 大, *a.* Great, big; much. — *koto aru*, have a great many. — *tawake mon da*, a great dunce. — *o sewa ni nari-mash'ta.* I have given you much trouble. Syn. ŌKI, TAK'SAN.

†I-KAI, 井カイ, 位階, *n.* Rank, grades. — *wo szszmu*, to rise in rank. — *wo sada-meru*, to fix the number and order of ranks. Syn. KURAI.

IKAKE,*-ru,-ta*, イカケル, 鑄掛, *t. v.* To repair castings. *Nabe wo* —, to mend a kettle.

Ī-KAKE,*-ru,-ta*, イヒカケル, 言掛, *t.v.* To charge with, to blame, or accuse falsely, to begin to say and suddenly leave off.

IKAKEYA, イカケヤ, 釦屋, *n.* A tinker, a repairer of utensils made of cast metal.

Ī-KAKUSHI,*-sz,-sh'ta*, イヒカクス, 言隱, *t. v.* To conceal, or cover over by talking, to palliate.

‖IKAMESHII,-KI, イカメシイ, 稜威, *a.* Having a stern, severe, or austere appearance. — *ide-tachi*, clothed in armor and having a savage appearance. Syn. IKATSZI, ARAI.

IKAMESHIKU, or IKAMESHŪ, イカメシク, 稜威, *adv.* idem.

IKAMONOGUI, イカモノグイ, 何物吃, *n.* One who dares eat any thing, poison or not. Syn. AKU-JIKI.

†IKAN, イカン, 如何, *adv.* of interrogation, or doubt,═How, what. — *to szru*, what shall I do? — *to mo szru koto nashi*, do as I may, nothing could be done. *Ko-re wo ikan to mo szbekaradz*, I cannot possibly do this; cannot in any way do this. *Ikan to nareba*, for what reason, why, whereof. *Ikan zo yuku beken*, how can I go? Syn. NAZE, DŌSH'TE, DŌMO.

IKANARU, イカナル, 如何, *a.* What kind, what manner. *Kore wa — furumai zo ya*, what kind of conduct is this? — *h'to ja*, what kind of a man? *Kiyō wa — kichi ni-chi zo*, why should this be such a lucky day? Syn. DONO-YO NA, DONNA.

IKANAREBA, イカナレバ, same as *Ikan to nareba.* Why, for what purpose, wherefore, for what reason, how is it that.

Ī-KANE,*-ru,-ta*, イヒカヌル, 言兼, *i. v.* Don't like to say, dislike to tell, hard to say.

IKANI, イカニ, 如何, *pro.* or *adv.* of interrogation, or doubt. How, what. — *shen*, what shall I do? *Kimi wo ikani tabakari nasan*, how can I deceive my master? *Ika-ni mo yoi*, any way will do. *Ikaniya*, how is it? Syn. DOSH'TE.

IKANOBORI, イカノボリ, 紙鳶, *n.* A kite. — *wo ageru*, to fly a kite. Syn. TAKO.

IKARASE,*-ru,-ta*, イカラセル, 令怒, caust. of *Ikari.* To make angry

IKARERU, イカレル, 怒, *a.* Angry. — *gan-shoku*, angry countenance.

IKARE,*-ru,-ta*, イカレル, 行, poten. of *Iku.* To go. — *nai*, can't go, can't be done.

IKARI, イカリ, 碇, *n.* An anchor. — *wo orosz*, to cast anchor. — *wo ageru*, to heave up the anchor.

‖IKARI,*-ru,-atta*, イカル, 怒, *i. v.* To be angry. *Ikatte mono wo iu*, to talk in anger. Syn. OKORU, HARATATSZ, RIPPUKU.

IKARI,*-ru,-atta*, イカル, 活, *i. v.* To be put in water and kept alive (as a flower.) *Kono hana wa yoku ikari-mash'ta*, this flower (in water,) has kept well.

IKARI, イカリ, 怒, *n.* Anger. — *wo okose*, to excite anger. — *wo fukumu*, to look angry. — *wo nadameru*, to soothe anger. Syn. HARADACHI.

IKASAMA, イカサマ, 何樣, *adv.* How, in what way, but in coll. used in expressing surprise or assent to what another says. ═ Indeed, truly. — *sō de gorzarimashō*, yes! it is so. Syn. GENI, NARU-HODO.

IKASE,*-ru,-ta*, イカセル, 令行, caust. of *Iku*, used in com. coll. for *Yukaseru.* To make to go, let go, to send. *Ikasate kudasare*, let me go. *H'to wo Yedo ye* —, to send a man to Yedo.

IKASHI,*-sz,-sh'ta*, イカス, 活, *t. v.* To restore to life, revive, to let live. *Shini kakatta h'to wo kuszri de ikasz*, to revive one almost dead with medicine. *Ishi wo ika-shite tszkau*, to use stones (in a garden) so as to add to its beauty. *Kane wo ikash'te tszkau*, to spend money usefully. *Tori wo ikash'te oku*, let the bird live.

Ī-KASZME,*-ru,-ta*, イヒカスメル, 言掠, *t. v.* To hide, or conceal, to obfuscate, or obscure by telling.

Ī-KATA, イヒカタ, 言方, *n.* Any thing said, — *ga nai*, nothing can be said. *Nan to demo — ga aru*, something may be said, no matter what.

Ī-KATAME,*-ru,-ta*, イヒカタメル, 云堅, *t. v.* To confirm, to strengthen, to promise. *Chikatte yakujō wo* —, to confirm a promise with an oath.

Ī-KATSZ, イヒカツ, See *I-kachi.*

IKATSZI,-KI,-SHI, イカツイ, *a.* Violent, fierce, angry, rough in manner, severe, — *h'to*, a person rough in manner. Syn. ARAI, HAGESHII.

IKATSZGAMASHII,-KI, イカツガマシイ, *a*, In an angry, violent, or boisterous manner.

IKATSZGAMASHIKU, イカツガマシク, *adv.* id.

IKATSZKU, イカツク, *adv.* See *Ikatszi.* — *mono wo iu.*

Ī-KAWASHI,–*sz*,–*sh'ta*, イヒカハス, 言交, *t. v.* To speak with, or make a verbal agreement.

Ī-KAYE,–*ru*,–*ta*, イヒカヘル, 言替, *i.v.* To take back what one has said, retract, disavow.

I-KAYESHI,–*sz*,–*sh'ta*, イカヘス, 射反, *t. v.* To shoot back. *Ya wo* —, to shoot an arrow back.

Ī-KAYESHI,–*sz*,–*sh'ta*, イヒカヘス, 言反, *t. v.* To say back, to retort,

IKA-YŌ, イカヤウ, 如何様, *adv.* How, in what way. — *de mo yoroshī*, anyhow will do. — *na koto nite mo*, in any affair whatever. Syn. DONOYŌ.

IKE, イケ, 池, *n.* A pond.

IKE,–*ru*,–*ta*, イケル, 活, or 生, *t. v.* To keep alive. *Hana wo* —, to put flowers in water so as to keep them alive, *Sakana wo* —, to keep fish alive by putting them in a basket in the water.

IKE,–*ru*,–*ta*, イケル, 埋, *t. v.* To bury in the ground, to plant. *Gomi wo tszchi ni* —, to bury litter in the ground. *Hashira wo* —, to set up, or plant a post. *Haka ni* —, to bury in the grave. *Hi wo* —, to cover fire with ashes. Syn. UDZMERU.

IKE,–*ru*,–*ta*, イケル, 可行, Potent. of *Iku*, (com. coll. for *Yukeru.*) can go. *Kono michi wa ikeru ka*, is this road passable? *Kon-nichi Yedo ye ikeru ka*, can you go to *Yedo* to day?

IKE-BANA, イケバナ, 插花, *n.* A flower kept alive by putting in water.

IKEDORI,–*ru*,–*tta*, イケドル, 生捕, *t. v.* To take alive, take prisoner. *H'to wo* —, to take a man prisoner. *Sh'ka wo* —, to catch deer alive.

IKE-GAKI, イケガキ, 生垣, *n.* A live hedge.

IKE-MORI, イケモリ, 活盛, *n.* A kind of food made of raw fish.

I-KEN, イケン, 異見, *n*, Counsel, advice, opinion, judgment, admonition, reproof. — *wo szru*, to counsel, admonish. — *wo kuwayeru.* to give one's opinion, or advice. — *wo mochīdz*, not to follow advice. Syn. ISAME.

IKENAI, イケナイ, 不可行, *(neg. of Iku,* to go.) Cannot go, used in com. coll. in the sense of, of no use, bad, won't do, can't do. *Kono fude* —, this pen is bad, of no use. — *kara sztete-okure*, as it will not do, throw it away. — *koto wo sh'ta*, I have committed a great blunder. *Otenki ga warukutte ikenai*, the weather is bad and unfavorable. *Ambai ga warukutte ikemasen*, I am so unwell I can't do my work. *Kono uchiwa ikenakunatta*, this fan is done for, or no longer fit to use.

IKENGAMASHII,–KI,–KU, イケンガマシイ, 異見敷, In the manner of advice, or admonition. *Amari* — *koto wo iu na*, don't be always speaking your advice, or I want none of your advice.

IKENIYE, イケニヘ, 牲, *n.* Animal sacrifices. — *wo ageru*, to offer an animal in sacrifice. *H'to wo* — *ni ageru*, to offer a human sacrifice. *H'to no kawari ni* — *wo ageru*, to offer an animal in sacrifice instead of a man. *Hto no tame ni* — *ni naru*, to be a sacrifice for man.

IKESZ, イケス, 生巣, *n.* A basket in which fish are kept alive.

Ī-KESHI,–*sz*,–*sh'ta*, イヒケス, 言消, *t. v.* To deny, contradict. *H'to no hanashi wo* —, to contradict what another has said.

IKI, イキ, 息, *n.* The breath. — *wo szru*, to breathe. — *wo hiku*, to draw in the breath. — *wo fuki-dasz*, to blow out the breath. — *wo fuki-kayesz*, to begin to breathe again (after suspended animation.) — *wo nonde naku*, to cry holding the breath. — *wo tszku*, to sigh. — *wo kitte kuru*, to come out of breath. — *ga tayeru*, stopped breathing. — *ga kireru*, to be out of breath, short winded. — *wo tszmeru*, to hold the breath. — *no ne wo tomeru*, (fig.) to cut off the head. — *ga hadzmu*, to catch the breath.

IKI, イキ, *n.* Elegant, stylish, genteel, refined. *Ano onna* — *da.* — *ni natta.* — *demo yabo demo kamawa nai.*

IKI,–*ru*,–*ta*, イキル, 生, *i.v.* To be alive, to live. *Ikiteoru*, living. *Ikita sakana*, live fish. *Naga-iki*, long life. *Iki nagara jigoku ye ochiru*, to go to hell alive. *Senjō kara ikite kayeru*, to return alive from battle.

IKI,–*ku*,–*tta*, イク, 行, *i.v.* (Com. coll. for *yuku.)* to go. *Itte mo ī*, you had better go. *Kanagawa ye itte kuru*, to go and come back from Kanagawa. *Itte totte koi*, go and bring. *Yedo ye itta toki*, when I went to Yedo. *Itte miru*, to go and see. *H'tori iki-mashō*, I will go alone. *Omaye Yedo ye ikeba tanomitai*, if you go to Yedo I have a favor to ask. *Iku ka ikanu ka shirimasen*, I dont know whether I shall go or not. Syn. MAIRU.

IKIDAWASHI,–KI, イキダワシイ, *a.* Having a difficulty in breaking.

IKIDAWASHIKU, イキダワシク, *adv.* id.

†IKIDŌRI,*-ru,-tta*, イキドホル, 憤, *i. v.* To be angry, to be in a passion, exasperated, enraged, incensed, irritated. Syn. HARA-TATSZ, IKARU, RIPPUKU.

IKIDŌRI, イキドホリ, 憤, *n.* Anger, resentment. — *wo fukumu*, to feel angry.

IKI-DZKAI, イキヅカイ, 氣調, *n.* Respiration, breathing. — *ga arai*, breathing is hard, or loud. — *wo sh'te kikase-nasare*, let me listen to your breathing.

IKI-DZYE, イキヅヱ, 息杖, *n.* The staff carried by chair bearers to rest the chair on when stopping.

IKIGAKE-NI, イキガケニ, 行掛, *adv.* While going, while on the way. — *yotte kudasare*, call while you are going. *Kanagawa ye ikigake ni unjō-shō ye yoru*, when you are going to Kanagawa stop at the Custom-house.

IKI-GIRE, イキギレ, 息切, Hard breathing, short-breathing, out of breath. — *ga szru*, to breathe with difficulty.

IKI-JI, イキヂ, 意氣地, *n.* Passion, irritation, excitement, temper, (same as *Iji.*) — *wo haru*, to show bad temper, or obstinacy. — *ni naru*, to become irritated, in a passion.

Ī-KIKASHI,*-sz,-sh'ta*, イヒキカス, 言聞, *t.v.* To tell, inform.

IKI-KAYE,*-ru,-ta*, イキカヘル, 甦, *i.v.* To revive, come to life again. Syn. YOMI-GAYERU.

IKI-KUSAI,-KI, イキクサイ, 息臭, *a.* Having a foul breath. — *h'to*, a person with a foul breath.

IKIKUSAKU, イキクサク, *adv.* idem.

IKIMAKI,*-ku,-ita*, イキマク, 息巻, *i. v.* To be out of breath, to breathe hard, or pant, (as an angry person). *Ikimakite araku nonoshiru*, breathing hard he scolded violently.

IKIMI, イキミ, 裏急, *n.* Straining, urgent desire to go to stool or to urinate, tenesmus; bearing down pains of labor. — *ga kuru*, the pains have come on.

IKIMI,*-mu,-nda*, イキム, 裏急, *i.v.* To strain, press, or bear down, (at stool, or in labor). *Ko wo umu ni ikimu. Ikinde daiben wo szru.*

†IKIMITAMA, イキミタマ, 生御魂, *n.* The Bon festival.

IKI-NA, イキナ, 意氣, *a.* Lively, gay, stylish, tasty, elegant, refined. — *koye*, lively voice. — *onna*, a stylish woman. Syn. FŪRIU, SZINA.

IKI-NAGARAYE,*-ru,-ta*, イキナガラヘル, 存命, *i.v.* Living, whilst living, during life. — *te oru uchi ni nozomi ga togetai*, as long as one lives he has hope. Syn. ZON-MEI.

IKIOI, イキホヒ, 勢, *n.* Power, force, momentum, strength, authority, might, influence, business, trade. — *no tszyoi h'to*, a man of great power, or authority. *Ya no* —, the force of an arrow. *Tama no* —, the force of a ball. *Ito no — ga yoi*, the trade in silk is active. Syn. KENI, KENSHIKI, ISEI.

IKIRE,*-ru,-ta*, イキレル, 熅, *i.v.* To be very hot and close, sultry. *Hidoi ikire de gozarimas*, it is very hot. *Kusa-ikire*, the odor of hot grass. Syn. MUSHI-ATSZI.

IKI-RIYŌ, イキリヤウ, 生靈, *n.* The ghost of a living person. — *ga tori-tszita*, bewitched, or smitten by some one living. The opposite of *Shi-riyō*.

IKI-SEKI-TO, イキセキト, *adv.* Hurried breathing, panting, blowing. — *tachikayeru*, come panting back.

IKI-SZGI, イキスギ, 行過, *n.* One who makes a show of knowing or doing what he knows nothing about, a pretender, braggart. Syn. DE-SZGI MONO, NAMA-IKI, KITAFŪ.

IKI-UTSZSHI, イキウツシ, 生寫, *n.* Life like, or exact resemblance.

Ī-KIWAME,*-ru,-ta*, イヒキハメル, 言究, *t.v.* To settle, decide.

‖IKIYAKU,*-szru*, 井キヤク, 畏却, To be troubled, annoyed.

IKI-ZASHI, イキザシ, 氣調, *n.* The breathing, respiration.

IKKA, イクカ, 幾日, (contraction of *Iku-ka*). What day? *Kon-nichi wa ikka*, what day of the month is this? *Ikka me ni kayerimasz ka*, on what day will you return? *Mo ikka tatte kimashō ka*, in how many days will you come?

IKKA, イツカ, 一荷, One load, (for a man). — *no ni*, one load of goods. — *no hakobi-chin wa ikura*, what is the charge for carrying one load?

IKKADO, イツカド, 一廉, *adv.* Especial, particular, chiefest, most eminent. — *ho-neotte koshirayeru*, I have taken particular pains to make this. — *no h'to*, the most eminent person. Syn. H'TO-KIWA.

IKKI, イツキ, 一揆, *n.* A revolt, mob, insurrection. — *wo okosz*, to excite a revolt. —*ga okoru*, there is a mob. Syn. TOTŌ, HŌKI.

†IKKIYO, イツキヨ, 一擧, *adv.* One effort, one blow, one charge. *Tada — ni seme-yaburu*, to defeat with only one charge. *Kuni no anki kono — ni ari*, the safety of the country depends on this effort.

†IKKIYŌ, イツキヨウ, 一 興, *n.* A pleasant time, frolic, diversion. — *wo moyōsz,* to get up a frolic.

IKKŌ, イツカウ, 一 向, *adv.* With a negative verb, =not at all. —*zonjimasen,* don't know. *Ano h'to — miyenai,* he is not to be seen. Syn. SAPPARI.

IKŌ, イカウ, 欲 往, (dubitative form of *Iku),* = I think, or desire to go. — *to omōtemo hima ga nai,* I thought of going but had no time.

IKŌ, イコフ, 休, See *Ikoi.*

IKŌ, イカウ, 衣 桁, *n.* A rack or stand for hanging clothes on.

I-KŌ, 井クワウ, 威 光, *n.* Power, authority. Syn. O-KAGE, HIKARI, I-SEI.

†IKOI,-ō,-ōta, イコフ, 休, *i.v.* To rest. *Ikō koto atawadz,* cannot rest.
Syn. YASZMU, KIU-SOKU SZRU.

Ī-KOME,-ru,-ta, イヒコメル, 言 籠, *t.v.* To put to silence, to shut the mouth of another, to defeat by talking.

I-KON, 井コン, 遺 恨, *(nokoru urami).* Malice, resentment, or ill-will. — *wo fukumu,* to feel malice.

I-KOROSHI,-sz,-sh'ta, イコロス, 射殺, *i.v.* To shoot and kill, to kill with an arrow.

†IKOWASHIMU, イコハシム, 令 休, caust. of *Ikoi,* cause or let rest.

IKU, イク, see *Iki,* to go.

IKU, イク, 幾, *adv.* How many. — *do,* how often? — *tabi,* how often? — *tari,* or — *nin,* how many persons? — *ye,* how many folds, how often? — *ka,* or *nichi,* how many days? —*tszki,* — *toshi,* — *yo,* — *asa.* — *ri,* how many miles? — *man,* how many myriads? *Iku-hodo mo naku,* in a very short time. Syn. NANI.

†IKUBAKU, イクバク, 幾 許, *(nanihodo),* How much, how many. — *mo-nashi,* not much, or a little while. Syn. IKURA.

Ī-KUBI, 井クビ, 猪 頸, *n.* (pig-neck). Short-necked.

IKU-HISASHIKU, イクヒサシク, 幾 久, *adv.* A long time, a long time to come.— *medetaku soi-toge nasare,* I wish you much happiness for many years.

IKUJINAI,-KI,-SHI, イクヂナイ, *a.* Devoid of spirit, or courage; weak or craven hearted.

IKURA, イクラ, 幾 等, *adv.* How much, How many. — *de gozarimasz ka,* how much is it? *Nedan wa —,* what is the price? *Kono hon wa mada ikura mo arù,* have still many of these books. — *de mo yoi,* as many as you please.
Syn. DORE-HODO, NANI-HODO.

Ī-KURASHI,-sz,-sh'ta, イヒクラス, 言 暮, *t.v.* To spend the whole day in talking. *Oya no koto wo —,* to spend the whole day in talking about one's parents.

Ī-KUROME,-ru,-ta, イヒクロメル, 言 黒, *t.v.* To dupe, impose on, deceive by talking. *Sagi wo karasz ni īkuromeru,* (prov.) to talk so as to make white appear to be black.

IKUSA, イクサ, 軍, *n.* War, an army. — *szru,* to war, to fight. — *wo idomu,* to make war. — *wo idasz,* to march out an army. — *wo hikiyu,* to command an army. — *no dōgu,* weapons of war.
Syn. GUN-ZEI, TATAKAI, KASSEN.

IKUTSZ, イクツ, 幾 個, How many. *Kadz wa —,* what is the number? how many? *Omaye no otoshi wa —,* how old are you?
Syn. IKURA, NAMBŌ

I-K'WAN, 井クワン, 位 官, *n.* Rank, and office.

†I-K'WAN, イクワン, 胃 脘, *n.* The stomach.

IKU-YE-NI-MO, イクヘニモ, In beseeching, imploring, requesting, earnestly, urgently. — *yoroshiku o tanomi-mōshimas,* I urgently request you.

I-MA, 井マ, 居 閒, *n.* A sitting room.

IMA, イマ, 今, *adv.* Now, at present, modern, — *no yo,* the present age or generation. — *yori,* or *kara,* henceforth, after this. — *goro,* or — *jibun,* now at present (indefinite), made, until now to this time. *Ima ya ima ya to matsz,* to wait in momentary expectation. —*Imani,* now, presently. *Ima-deki,* of modern make.

I-MACHI-NO-TSZKI, 井マチノツキ, 居待月, The moon on the 17th day of each month, which rises immediately on the setting of the sun.

IMADA, イマダ, 未, *adv.* Yet, still. —*konu,* not yet come. — *konu maye ni,* before he comes. *Watakushi mo imada Yokohama ni orimasz,* I am still living in Yokohama.
Syn. MADA.

Ī-MAGIRASHI,-sz,-sh'ta, イヒマギラス, 言 紛, *t.v.* To speak confusedly so as to conceal the truth, to blind or mystify by talking.

IMA-IMASHII,-KI, イマイマシイ, 忌忌敷, *a.* Unlucky, disagreeable, annoying, provoking. — *koto wo iu na,* don't speak of any thing disagreeable, or unlucky.
Syne. IYA-NA, FU-KITSZ-NA.

IMAIMASHIKU, イマイマシク, *adv.* id.

Ī-MAKE,-ru,-ta, イヒマケル, 言 負, *t. v.* To be defeated, or vanquished in talking.

IMAMEKASHII,-KI,-KU, イマメカシイ, 今様, Being in modern style, or like present custom. Syn. IMAYŌ, TŌ-SEI.

IMASARA, イマサラ, 今更, *adv.* Now at last, now after so long a time. — *sō wa ī-ware-nai*, it is too late to say it now. — *kō-k'wai sh'te mo oyobanai*, it is now too late to confess. — *riyō-ji sh'te naorimasen*, no treatment will now be of any use.

†IMASHI,-*sz*,-*sh'ta*, イマス, 在, *t.v.* To be, to dwell, (used only of gods, or superior beings.) *Kami wa ten ni imasz*, God is in heaven. Syn. OWASHIMAS.

I-MASHI,-*sz*,-*sh'ta*, 井マシ, 居, *i.v.* (*I*, to be, dwell, and *masz* honorific). *Danna wa uchi ni imasz ka*, is your master at home? *Namban ni i-masz ka*, what is the number of your house? *I-masen*, is not at home. Syn. ORU.

†IMASHI, イマシ, 汝, *pro.* You.

IMASHIGATA, イマシガタ, 今方, *adv.* Just now, a moment ago. Syn. SENKOKU.

IMASHIME,-*ru*,-*ta*, イマシメル, 戒, *t.v.* To admonish, caution, counsel, to warn; to threaten, to reprove, to punish, to correct, chastise. *Kodomo wo* —, to instruct a child in the right way. *Toga-nin wo* —, to punish a criminal.

IMASHIME, イマシメ, 戒, *n.* Instruction, admonition, caution, counsel, warning, correction, punishment, reproof, prohibition. *Kami hotoke no* —, the correction or chastisement of the gods. — *no nawa*, the cord with which criminals are bound. *Hidoi* — *ni au*, to get severely punished. Syn. SHI-OKI, KORASHIME.

†IMASHIWA, イマシハ, 今, Now, (poet. word.)

IMAWA, イマハ, 末期, (*matsz go.*) The end of life, the time of death. — *no kiwa*, article of death. — *no toki.* idem. Syn. RIN-JŪ.

†IMAWASHII,-KI, イマハシイ, Disagreeable, odious, dreadful, unlucky.

†IMAWASHIKU, イマハシク, *adv.* idem.

Ī-MAWASHI,-*sz*,-*sh'ta*, イヒマハス, 言廻, *t.v.* To handle a subject skilfully; to use circumlocution so as to soften an unpleasant subject.

†IMA-YŌ, イマヤウ, 今様, *n.* A song current at any particular age, also, the present style. — *wo utau.* — *szgata*, the present style of dress.

IM-BAN, インバン, 印判, *n.* A seal, stamp. Syn. HAN-KŌ, IN-GIYŌ.

†IM-BO, インボウ, 隠謀, *n.* Secret intrigue, secret conspiracy. — *wo kuwadateru.*

†IM-BON, インボン, 婬犯, To commit adultery, (used generally of Bud. priests.)

IME, イメ, 夢, *n.* A dream, same as *Yume.*

IMI,-*mu*,-*nda*, イム, 忌, *t.v.* To have a superstitious dread of, to fear, shun, dislike. *Shinda mono wo miru wo imu*, to have a superstitious dread of seeing a dead body. *Kegare wo* —, to shun any unclean thing. *Kono kuszri wa harami-onna ni imu beshi.* Syn. KIRAU.

IMI, イミ, 忌, *n.* The mourning on the death of a relative. — *ga kakaru*, to be in mourning. — *ga aketa*, the period of mourning is ended. *Chichi no imi*, mourning on the death of a father. — *no uchi*, during the time of mourning.

IMI, イミ, 意味, *n.* Meaning, sentiment, sense, significance. — *no f'kai koto*, an affair of deep significance. *Nani ka imi no aru koto*, a matter which has some meaning.

IMI-AKE, イミアケ, 忌明, *n.* The end of mourning. — *ni naru.*

IMI-BUKU, イミブク, 忌服, *n.* The period of mourning. — *ga kakari kami ye mairarenu*, during the period of mourning we must not visit the *miya.*

||IMI-GOMEN, イミゴメン, 忌御免, *n.* Excused from mourning (by a prince, in order to attend. to one's duty.) — *wo ōsetszkerareru*, to be excused from, &c.

†IMIJII,-KI,-KU,-Ū, イミジイ, (Used as a superlative,) very, in a high degree. *Imijū mizore furu yo*, a very sleety night. *Imijū ureshī*, very sad. *On keshiki no imijiki wo mi-tatematszreba*, when he sees your excellency's sternness. *Onna mo ito imiji to mi-tatematszrite*, the woman also appeared exceedingly beautiful.

IMI-KIRAI,-*au*,-*atta*, イミキラフ, 忌嫌, *t.v.* To dislike, regard with aversion or disgust.

||IMI-MONO, イミモノ, 忌物, *n.* Things which one avoids or abstains from, forbidden things. Syn. KIM-MOTSZ.

IMINA, イミナ, 諱, *n.* The name of a person, the mention of which is avoided.

†I-MIYŌ, イミヤウ, 異名, Another or different name for any thing.

†IM-MON, インモン, 陰門, *n.* The vulva. Syn. OMANKO.

IM-MOTSZ, インモツ, 音物, *n.* A present.

IMO, イモ, 芋, *n.* An edible root, potato. *Satsz-ma imo*, sweet potato. *Jangatara-imo*, common potato. *Sato-imo*, the Taro. *Yama no imo*, or *Nagai-imo*, a kind of long edible root.

IMO-GARA, イモガラ, 芋莖, *n.* The stems of the Taro plant. Syn. DZIKI.

IMOJI, イモジ, 裩, (coll. for *Yumoji,*) *n.* The cloth worn around the waist, *(Fundoshi.)*

IMOJI, イモジ, same as *Imonoshi.*

IMOMUSHI, イモムシ, 芋蠋, *n.* The large green caterpillars found on the Taro plant.

IMONO, イモノ, 鑄物, *n.* Articles made by casting,

IMONOSHI, イモノシ, 鑄物師, *n.* A founder, caster of metal utensils

IMORI, イモリ, 守宮, *n.* A kind of water lizard.

†IMOSE, イモセ, 妹兄, *(fūfu)* Husband and wife. — *no katame.*

IMŌTO, イモウト, 妹, *n.* Younger sister. — *muko,* the husband of a younger sister.

†IM-PON, インポン, 印本, *n.* A printed book. Syn. HAM-PON.

IM-PU, インプ, 婬婦, *n.* An adulterous woman. Syn. INRAN NO ONNA.

†IN, 井ン, 韻, *n.* A rhyming syllable. — *wo fumu,* to rhyme. — *wo tszgu,* to match a word so as to rhyme.

†IN, イン, 印, *n.* A stamp, seal. — *wo osz,* to fix a seal, to stamp. Syn. HAN.

†IN, イン, 婬, *n.* Licentiousness, lewdness. — *wo konomu.*

†IN, 井ン, 院, *n.* A Buddhist temple, applied also to the residence of the Kuge and of a retired Emperor, to a school house, court house, or government office.

IN, イン, 印, *n.* A kind of magic ceremony performed by folding the hands in various ways and praying, used by the sect of Shingon, and Yama-bushi. — *wo muszbu,* to perform the above incantation.

IN, イン, 陰, *n.* The female principle of Chinese philosophy.

INA, イナ, 撥尾魚, *n.* A kind of river fish, said to be the young of the Bora.

†INA, イナ, 否, *adv.* No, not so, a negative particle. — *to iu,* said no. Syn. ĪYE, INIYA, IYA.

I-NA, or I-NARU, イナ, 異, *a.* Different, strange, extraordinary, wonderful. — *koto wo iu,* to tell of something extraordinary. Syn. KOTONARU, AYASHII, MEDZRASHI.

INABIKARI, イナビカリ, 電, *n.* Lightning. Syn. INADZMA, DENK'WA.

INADA, イナダ, 鰍, *n.* A kind of mackerel.

Ī-NADAME,-*ru*,-*ta*, イヒナダメル, 言宥, *t. v.* To soothe, pacify.

Ī-NADZKE, イヒナヅケ, 許嫁, *n.* Betrothing, espousing. — *wo szru,* to betroth.

Ī-NADZKE,-*ru*,-*ta*, イヒナヅケル, 許嫁, *t. v.* To betroth, to promise in marriage.

INADMZA, イナヅマ, 稲妻, *n.* Lightning.

INAGO, イナゴ, 蝗, *n.* A locust.

INAJIMI,-*mu*,-*nda*, 井ナジム, 居馴染, *i. v.* To become used to living in, to be at home in, or accustomed to a place. Syn. INARERU.

INAKA, 井ナカ, 田舍, *n.* Any place away from the capital, country. — *ni oru,* to live in the country. — *mono,* a countryman. — *fū,* country style, (of dress, or manner.) — *kusai,* boorish, rustic. Syn. DEN-SHA.

†INAMI,-*mu*,-*nda*, イナム, 辭, *t.v.* To decline, refuse. *Kimi no ōse inami-gataku,* I cannot refuse to do as my lord says. *Kataku inamu,* firmly decline. Syn. JI-TAI SZRU.

INA-MURA, イナムラ, 稲邑, *n.* Stacks of rice-straw.

INANAKI,-*ku*,-*ita*, イナナク, 嘶, *i. v.* To neigh. *M'ma ga* —, the horse neighs. Syn. IBŌ.

I-NAORI,-*ru*,-*tta*, 井ナホル, 居直, *t. v.* To change one's seat, or adjust one's self in a seat.

I-NARABI,-*bu*,-*nda*, 井ナラブ, 坐列, *i.v.* To sit in a row.

Ī-NARAI,-*ō*,-*ōta*, イヒナラフ, 言慣, *i. v.* To learn to talk.

I-NARE,-*ru*,-*ta*, 井ナレル, 居馴, *t. v.* To be used to a place, become familiar, or accustomed to living in a place.

‖INARE,-*ru*,-*ta*, イナレル, 去, *t. v.* To go, leave. *K'yaku ga inareta,* the guest has left. Syn. YUKU, SARU.

INARI-SAMA, イナリサマ, 稲荷樣, *n.* The god of rice, who employs the fox as his servant.

Ī-NASHI,-*sz*,-*sh'ta*, イヒナス, 言成, *t.v.* To say and make anything different from what it is; to show, represent. *Uso wo makoto ni* —, to make a lie appear to be the truth. *Aru-koto wo nai ni* —, to represent a thing that is, as if it were not.

INAYA, イナヤ, 否, *adv.* Whether or not; how. *Yedo ye yuku ya inaya,* going to Yedo or not. *Inaya wo kiku,* to inquire how he is. — *wo mōsz,* to say whether or not. *Kiku ya inaya kayetta,* scarcely waiting to hear, he returned, or he returned as soon as he heard it.

INCHIN, インチン, 茵蔯, *n.* A kind of medicine.

†INCHI, インチ, 因地, Same as *Ini.* (Bud.)

INDŌ, インダウ, 引導, (*michibiku,*) *n.* Guiding, showing the way; but commonly, spoken of funeral ceremonies in a temple, performed to guide the soul to the other world. — *wo watasz,* to perform funeral services for a deceased person.

†INE, *-ru, -ta,* イネル, 寐, *i.v.* To sleep, to be in bed. Syn. NERU.

INE, イネ, 稻, *n.* Rice in the stalk,—while growing; paddy. — *wo haru,* to cut, or harvest rice. — *wo koku,* to thresh rice, by drawing it through iron teeth.

I-NEMURI, 井ネムリ, 坐睡, *n.* Dozing, drowsy, or sleeping while sitting. — *wo szru,* to sit dozing.

IN-GIN, インギン, 慇懃, Polite, courteous, civil, kind. — *no aisatsz,* a polite, or kind welcome. *H'to wo — ni motenasz,* to entertain a person handsomely. Syn. NENGORO, SHIN-SETSZ, TEI-NEI.

IN-G'YŌ, インギヤウ, 印形, *n.* A seal, stamp. Syn. HAN, IM-BAN.

†IN-GO, インゴ, 隱語, (*kakushi kotoba*), *n.* Disguised, secret, or concealed language, an enigma.

IN-GŌ, インガウ, 院號, *n.* The name of a temple attached to the name of a deceased person.

IN-G'WA, イングワ, 因果, *n.* A Bud. word, *In,* the deeds of one in a previous state, *K'wa,* his retribution in this life; also, his deeds in this life, and his retribution in the next world, commonly used for punishment in this life. — *no mukui,* retribution, or punishment for one's deeds in a previous state. — *no me ni au,* to be punished as above. *Nan no — de konna kurō wo szru,* what evil have I done that I should suffer such trouble?

†INI, *-nu, -nda,* イヌ, 行, *i.v.* To go, to leave. Syn. YUKU.

†INI, イン井, 因位, (Bud.) The existence of Buddhist deities in an inferior state previous to their deification. — *no toki.*

Ī-NIKUI, *-KI, -KU,* イヒニクイ, 言惡, Hard, difficult, or disagreeable to say.

†INISHI, ppt. of *Ini,* イニシ, 往, = *yukishi.* Gone, past. — *toshi,* a past year.

INISHIYE, イニシヘ, 古, Ancient time, antiquity. — *no h'to,* an ancient. — *no michi,* ancient doctrines. — *yoru tsztawaru,* come down from antiquity. Syn. MUKASHI.

†IN-JA, インジヤ, 隱者, *n.* A hermit, recluse.

†IN-JI, インジ, 隱事, (*kakureta koto*). *n.* A concealed, or hidden affair, a secret, mystery. — *wo abaku,* to divulge a secret. Syn. MITSZJI, NAISHŌGOTO.

INJI, インヂ, 印地, *n.* Marbles. — *wo utsz,* to play marbles.

†IN-JI, インジ, 韻字, *n.* The last, or rhyming syllable in Chinese poetry.

IN-JU, インジユ, 院主, *n.* The superior of a monastery, Abbot.

†INJU, インジユ, 員數, (*kadz*). Number. *Tawara no —,* the number of bags.

†IN-KA, インカ, 印可, *n.* A graduation, or diploma given to a pupil on becoming proficient. (Bud.) Syn. MEN-KIYŌ.

IN-KAN, インカン, 印鑑, *n.* The facsimile of a seal shown as a passport, or in proof of anything.

IN-KI, インキ, 陰氣, Gloomy, dull, sombre. — *no uchi,* a gloomy house. — *na h'to,* a gloomy person.

IN-K'YO, インキヨ, 隱居, *n.* Living in retirement or seclusion, retired from business. *Ka-giyō wo yudztte — wo szru,* to resign business and retire into private life.

IN-K'YŌ, インキヤウ, 陰莖, *n.* Membrum virile. Syn. HENOKO, MARA, CHIMBŌ.

INKO, インコ, 鸚哥, *n.* A parrot. Syn. Ō-MU.

†IN-K'WA, インクワ, 陰火, *n.* A kind of phosphorescent light, ignis fatuus.

IN-NEN, インネン, 因緣, *n.* (Bud.) Affinity in a previous state, according to which men are supposed to be punished in this life.) = Cause, reason, secret affinity, relation, or connection. *Nan no — de nangi shimasz,* what is the cause of this affliction? *Dō-iu — de kō natta,* what is the reason of my being in this condition? Syn. ING'WA.

IN-NIKU, インニク, 印肉, *n.* The ink used for seals.

†IN-NŌ, インノウ, 陰囊, *n.* The scrotum. Syn. KIN.

‖INNOKO, インノコ, Coll. for *Inugo.*

INNOKO-INNOKO, インノコインノコ, The name of a song used in hushing children.

Ī-NOBE, *-ru, -ta,* イヒノベル, 云延, *t.v.* To postpone, to put off, to defer; to tell, to inform. *Asatte made to —.* To postpone it until day after to-morrow.

INOCHI, イノチ, 命, *n.* Life. — *wo taszkeru,* to save life. — *wo nobasz,* to prolong life. — *wo tamotsz,* to sustain, or preserve life. — *wo oshimu,* to be afraid of losing one's life. — *shiradz,* regardless of life, reckless. — *wo szteru,* to throw away one's life, desperate. — *no kagiri*, the end of life. — *ga chijimaru*, life is shortened. — *wo nagarayeru*, to pass the life, live. — *wo kakeru*, to risk the life. — *ni kakaru*, to be at the risk of life. Syn. JU-MIYŌ.

INOCHI-GAKE, イノチガケ, 懸命, Hazardous, dangerous, perilous. — *no shigoto*, dangerous work.

INOCHI-GOI, イノチゴイ, 乞命, *n.* Asking, or praying for life. *Korosō to szreba* — *wo szru*, when they were about to kill him, he prayed for his life.

I-NOGARE,-*ru*,-*ta*, イヒノガレル, 言遁, *t.v.* To evade, avoid, or escape by saying. *Nangi wo.* —

†INOKO, 井ノコ, 豕子, *n.* A pig. Syn. BUTA.

INORI,-*ru*,-*tta*, イノル, 祈, *i.v.* To pray. *Kami ni* —, to pray to God. *Tszmi wo yurushi-tamaye to inoru.* Syn. KI-TŌ SZRU, KI-SEI WO KAKERU.

INORI, イノリ, 祈, *n.* Prayer. — *wo szru*, to pray. — *ga kīta*, the prayer is answered.

INORI-KOROSHI,-*sz*,-*sh'ta*, イノリコロス, 呪殺, *t.v.* To kill by prayer, to pray the gods to kill.

INOSHISHI, 井ノシシ, 猪, *n.* A wild hog. — *musha*, a ferocious soldier.

†IN-RAKU, インラク, 婬樂, *n.* Carnal pleasures, sensuality.

†IN-RAN, インラン, 婬亂, *n.* Adultery, fornication, lasciviousness — *wo konomu*, fond of venery. — *na h'to*, a lascivious person. Syn. SZKEBE.

†IN-RITSZ, インリツ, 韻律, *n.* Musical tone. — *wo tadasz.* — *wo shiraberu.*

INRŌ, インロウ, 印籠, *n.* A nest of small boxes carried suspended from the belt, used for carrying medicines in.

†IN-SHIN, インシン, 音信, *n.* Tidings, word, communication, account, message. — *ga nai*, there are no tidings. — *wo ts'udzru*, to send word. Syn. OTODZRE, TAYORI.

†IN-SHŌ, インシヤウ, 陰証, *n.* Internal congestion.

†IN-SHŌ, インシヤウ, 印章, *n.* A seal, stamp. Syn. IN-GIYŌ, HAN.

IN-SHOKU, インシヨク, 飲食, (*nomi kui.*) Drink and food. — *szru*, to eat and drink. — *wo tsztszshimu*, to be careful about what one eats and drinks.

†IN-SHU, インシユ, 飲酒, (*sake wo nomu.*) Drinking wine.

†IN-S'U, インスウ, 陰數, *n.* Even numbers. Syn. CHŌ.

†IN-SZI, インスイ, 婬水, *n.* The semen.

†IN-TOKU, イントク, 陰德, Charity, or meritorious deeds done in secret. — *wo tszmu.* Syn. ZEN-GON.

†IN-TON, イントン, 隱遁, To retire from the world, become a recluse.

INU, 井ヌ, 不居, neg. of *Iru*, not in. *Inu ka*, is he in?

INU, イヌ, 犬, *n.* A dog. Also, 戌, one of the 12 calender signs. — *no ko*, a pup. — *ga hoyeru*, the dog barks. — *no toki*, 8 o'clk at night. — *no kata*, the W.N.W. — *ga kami-au*, the dogs fight. — *wo keshi-kakeru*, to set a dog on.

†IN-U, インウ, 陰雨, Dull and rainy.

INUGO, イヌゴ, 路歧痛, *n.* Swelling of the lymphatic glands in the armpit, or groin.

INU-I, イヌ井, 乾, *n.* The N.W.

Ī-NUKE,-*ru*,-*ta*, イヒヌケル, 言拔, *i. v.* To get out of, slip out of, or escape by talking.

I-NUKI,-*ku*,-*ita*, イヌク, 射貫, *t. v.* To shoot an arrow through, pierce by shooting.

INUKORO, イヌコロ, 狗子, *n.* A pup.

INURU, イヌル, See *Ineru.*

IN-YEN, インエン, See *Innen.*

IN-YŌ, インヤウ, 陰陽, The male and female, or active and passive principles of nature, (according to Chinese philosophy.)

†IN-YOKU, インヨク, 婬欲, *n.* Lascivious desires, lust, lewdness.

IN-ZEN, インゼン, 院宣, *n.* A writing from a Mikado who has retired from the throne.

Ī-OKI,-*ku*,-*ita*, イヒオク, 言置, *t. v.* To leave word. *Kuwashiku īoite kayeru*, leaving particular directions he returned.

†IORI, イホリ, 庵, *n.* A hut. Syn. AN.

Ī-ŌSE,-*ru*,-*ta*, イヒオホセル, 言負, *t.v.* To impute, lay to the charge of another, to blame with.

IPPAI, イツパイ, 一杯, (See *Hai.*) Once full. *Midz ga ippai ni natta*, it has become full of water. — *ni tszgu*, pour it full.

IPPEN, イツペン, See *Hen.*

IPPIKI, イツピキ, See *Hiki.*

IPP'YŌ, イツペウ, See *H'yō.*

IPPITSZ, イツピツ, See *Hitz.*

IPPON, イツポン, See *Hon.*

IPPONDACHI, イツポンダチ, 一本立, Standing alone; alone, by one's self; independent of others. — *de szru*, to do anything alone, without the help of others.

IPPUKU, イツプク, See *Fuku.*

IRA, イラ, 刺蟲, *n.* The Nettle. — *ni sasareta*, stung by nettles.

IRACHI,–*tsz*,–*tta*, イラツ, 苛, *t.v.* To irritate, fret, or vex one's self. *Ki wo iratsz*, to be impatient, and fretful.

IRADACHI,–*tsz*,–*tta*, イラダツ, 苛立, *t. v.* Idem. *Ki wo* ——.

IRADZ, イラズ, 不入, Neg. of *Iri*.

IRAI, イライ, 以來, *adv.* After in time; since. *Kugatsz irai*, since the 9th month. *Kore yori irai*, from this time, henceforth.

IRA-IRA, イライラ, 苛苛, *adv.* Pricking, irritating, (fig.) peevish, irritable. — *szru*, to prick, irritate, smart.
Syn. KUSHA-KUSHA.

IRA-IRASHII,-KI,-KU, イライラシイ, 苛苛, Having an irritable, peevish, passionate, or impatient manner.

IRAKA, イラカ, 甍, *n.* A tiled roof. — *wo narabete tachi-tsdzku*, the continuous row of tiled roofs.

IRAMUSHI, イラムシ, 蛅蟖, *n.* A kind of caterpillar covered with sharp hairs.

†IRAN, 井ラン, 違亂, *(chigai midaruru,)* Disputing the validity of a claim or title. — *wo iu*, to dispute, &c. — *wa nai*, no flaw in the title, no one to dispute or lay in a claim. — *wo mōsz mono ichi nin mo kore naku soro*, there is nobody to dispute the claim.

IRA-NAI, イラナイ, Coll. for *Iranu*, neg. of *Iru*. — *mono*, useless things. — *kotoba*, useless words. *Kore wa — ka*, do you want this?

IRANEBA, イラネバ, neg. cond. of *Iru*, if you do not go in, if you don't want. — *naranu*, must go in. — *kayeshi-nasare*, if you don't want it, bring it back.

IRARE,–*ru*,–*ta*, 井ラレル, 被居, pass. or pot. of *Iru*. *Sen-koku aszko no uchi ni iraremashta*, he was in yonder house a few minutes ago. *Kono atszi tokoro ni irarenu*, I connot live in such a hot place as this.

IRASSHARI,–*ru*,–*tta*, イラツシヤル, 被爲入, Polite coll. in speaking to another, either in coming, going, entering, or being. (In Yedo coll. this is prononced *Irasshaimas*.) *Achira ye irassharimasz*, go there. *Kochira ye irassharimasz*, come here, or come in here. *Danna ni kai ni* —, master is up stairs. *Doko ye irasshaimasz*, where are you going? Syn. OIDE.

†IRATAKA, イラタカ, 平高, *n.* A kind of flat shaped rosary.

IRATSZKI,–*ku*,–*ita*, イラツク, 苛着, *i. v.* Excited, irritated, impatient, peevish.

†IRAYE, イラヘ, 應, *n.* Answer, reply, response. — *wo szru*, to answer, reply. — *nashi*, no answer.

†IRAYE,–*ru*,–*ta*, イラヘル, 應, *i. v.* To answer, to reply. Syn. KOTAYERU.

IRE,–*ru*,–*ta*, イレル, 入, *t. v.* To put into, to place in, take in. *Te wo futokoro ni* —, put the hand in the bosom. *Hako ni* —, put into a box. *Isame wo* —, to admonish, or acquiesce, consent. *Muko wo* —, to bring a son in law into one's family by marrying the daughter. *Fune wo minato ni* —, to bring a ship into harbor. *Nen wo* —, to pay attention to. *Hima wo* —, to take time.

IRE,–*ru*,–*ta*, イレル, 熬, *i. v.* To be parched, toasted. *Kono mame yoku ire-mash'ta*, these beans are well parched. *Ki no ireta h'to*, an impatient person.

IREBA, イレバ, 入齒, *n.* Artificial tooth. — *wo szru*, to put in an artificial tooth.

IREBA-SHI, イレバシ, 入齒師, *n.* A dentist.

IRE-BOKURO, イレボクロ, *n.* Small spots tattooed in the skin.

IRE-CHIGAI,–*ō*,–*ōta*, イレチガフ, 入違 *t. v.* To put in by mistake.

IRE-DZMI, イレズミ, 黥, *n.* Marks tattooed in the skin of criminals with ink.

IRE-FUDA, イレフダ, 入札, *n.* A written bid at an auction, a written proposal, a ballot. — *wo szru*, to put in a written bid.
Syn. NIU-SATSZ.

IRE-GAMI, イレガミ, 髢, *n.* False-hair.

IREGOMI, イレゴミ, 入込, *n.* Mixed, jumbled together. — *ni szru*, to be jumbled together.

†I-REI, 井レイ, 違例, Contrary to custom, or usage. Indisposed, unwell. *Irei mo naku sh'te iki tayetari*, died without appearing to be different from his usual state.

IRE-KAYE,–*ru*,–*ta*, イレカヘル, 入反, *t.v.* To take out and put in, to change the contents of any thing.

IRE-KO, イレコ, 入子, A nest, or set of boxes, where one fits into another. — *bashi*, a nest of bowls.

IRE-KOMI,–*mu*,–*nda*, イレコム, 入籠, *t. v.* To invest, to contribute, as capital in trade, to put into. *Akinai ni kane yohodo ire-konda*, invested a great deal of money in trade.

IRE-ME, イレメ, 假瞳, *n.* Artificial eye.

IRE-MONO, イレモノ, 入物, *n.* A vessel for holding any thing.

IRE-OKI,–*ku*,–*ita*, イレオク, 入置, *t.v.* To put into, place in and leave.

IRI,–*ru*,–*tta*, イル, 入, *i. v.* To go into,

enter. To use, to want, to need. *Iye ni iru*, to enter the house. *Hi ga iru*, the sun is setting. *Tszki ga itta*, the moon has set. *Kore wa iru-mono da*, I need this. *Kore wa nan ni iru no da*, of what use is this? *Kore wa irimasen ka*, do you want this? *Iri-mas*, I want it.
Syn. HAIRU, MOCHIIRU.

IRI,*–ru,–tta*, イル, 煎, *t. v.* To parch, roast *Mame wo* —, to parch peas. *Cha wo* —, to fire tea.

IRI-AI, イリアヒ, 入相, *n.* Sundown. — *no kane*, the bell rung at sundown in Buddhist temples. Syn. KURE-GATA.

IRI-CHIGAI,*–au,–tta*, イリチガフ, 入違, *i. v.* To enter and pass each other, to be athwart, to pass in entering. *Sao ga iri-chigatte oru*, the poles are crossed. *Yubi wo* —, to place the fingers of one hand between those of the other.

IRI-GOME, イリゴメ, 熬米, *n.* Parched rice.

IRI-HI, イリヒ, 入日, *n.* The setting sun.

IRIKA, イリカ, 入費, *n.* Expenses, expenditures, disbursements. — *wa nani-hodo*, what is the amount of expenses? — *ga ōi*, the expenses are great.
Syn. IRIYŌ, IRI-ME, NIU-YŌ, ZAPPI.

IRI-KAWARI,*–ru,–tta*, イリカハル, 入代, *i.v.* To enter in the place of one gone out, to take turns in doing.

IRIKO, イリコ, 煎海參, *n.* Bich-de-mer.

IRI-KOMI,*–mu,–nda*, イリコム, 入込, *i.v.* To enter in. *Fune ga minato ni iri-konda*, the ship has entered the harbor.

IRI-KUCHI, イリクチ, 入口, *n.* Entrance, door. Syn. HAIRI-GUCHI.

IRI-KUMI,*–mu,–nda*, イリクム, 入組, *t. v.* To be confused, mixed together, jumbled. *Machi no iye irikunde oru*, the houses of the town are irregular, or jumbled together. *Iri-kunda hanashi da*, a confused story.

IRI-MAJIRI,*–ru,–tta*, イリマジル, 入交, *i.v.* Mixed, blended, mingled together, intermingled.

IRI-MAME, イリマメ, 炒豆, *n.* Parched peas.

IRI-ME, イリメ, 入目, *n.* Expense, cost, disbursement. *Kono fushin no irime wa ikura de gozarimasz ka*, what was the cost of this building?
Syn. IRI-KA, IRI-YŌ.

IRI-MIDARI,*–ru,–tta*, イリミダル, 入亂, *i.v.* To be confused, mixed, jumbled together.

IRIMUKO, イリムコ, 入壻, *n.* A son in law who lives in his wife's family.

†IRIN, イリン, 彝倫, *n.* The five relations of master and servant, parent and child, brethren, husband and wife, and friends.

IRINABE, イリナベ, 熬鍋, *n.* A pan for parching.

IRI-TSZKE,*–ru,–ta*, イリツケル, 熬著, *i.v.* To fry, or roast in a pan, until the oil or sauce in which a thing is fried is dried up, and it sticks to the pan. *Sakana wo* —.

IRI-TSZKI,*–ku,–ita*, イリツク, 熬著, *i.v.* To be fried or roasted until dry or browned. *Sakana ga iritszita.*

IRI-UMI, イリウミ, 入海, *n.* A bay, gulf, inlet, arm of the sea.

IRI-YE, イリエ, 入江, *n.* A bay, inlet, or recess in the shore of a river.

IRI-YŌ, イリヨウ, 入用, *n.* Expense, outlay, use. — *wa ikura kakari-mash'ta*, what was the expense? *Toki-doki* — *no mono*, an article in frequent use. *Kore wa nan no* — *ni szru*, of what use is this?

IRO, イロ, (coll. imp. of *Iru*). *Hon wo yonde iro*, read your book. *Meshi wo tabete iro*, eat your rice.

IRO, イロ, 倚廬, *n.* White clothes worn by women at funerals.

IRO, イロ, 色, *n.* Color, (fig.) Appearance, sign or semblance, tone, variety. *Iro ni go shiki ari*, there are five kinds of color, (viz white, black, red, yellow, green.) — *ga kawaru*, to fade, change color. *Koi iro*, a deep color. *Uszi iro*, a light color. — *wo tszkeru*, to color. — *wo otosz*, or — *wo nuku*, to extract the color. — *ga sameru*, to become lighter in color, to fade. *Iro wo ageru*, to restore the color. *Akai iro ni someta*, dyed in red. *Kao no iro*, the complexion. *Me no iro*, color of the eyes. — *wo ushinō*, to lose color, (fig.) to be afraid. *Osoruru iro naku*, no appearance of fear. *Teki wa make iro ni natta*, the enemy showed signs of giving way. *Iro wo tadashiku*, to compose or settle the expression of the face. *Kane no ne-iro*, the tone of a bell. *H'to no kowa-iro wo tszkau*, to imitate the voice of another.

†IRŌ, イラフ, Same as *Irayeru.*

IRO, イロ, 色, *n.* Love, lewdness, venery, a mistress, paramour, lover. — *wo szru*, to have sexual intercourse. — *ni naru*, to be in love; lust after. — *ni fukeru*, given up to lust. — *wo konomu*, fond of venery. — *ni motsz*, to keep as a mistress. — *ga aru*, to have a lover.

IRO-AGE, イロアゲ, 色揚, *n.* Restoring a color to its original lustre. — *wo szru*,

IRO-AI, イロアヒ, 色相, *n.* The colors,

coloring, appearance. — *ga yoi*, the coloring is good. *Teki no* — *wo miru*, to see the state, or appearance of the enemy.

IRO-BANASHI, イロバナシ, 色話, *n.* An obscene story, a love story.

IRODORI,-*ru*,-*tta*, イロドル, 彩, *t. v.* To paint with a variety of colors. *Ye wo* —, to paint a picture with many colors.
Syn. SAI-SHIKI SZRU, YEDORU.

IRODORI, イロドリ, 彩, *n.* Painting, coloring. — *ga yoi.* — *wo szru.*

IRO-DZKI,-*ku*,-*ita*, イロヅク, 色附, *i. v.* To become ripe or mature, to put on a ripe color. *Kaki wa irodzita*, the persimmons have turned yellow.

IRO-GOTO, イロゴト, 色事, *n.* A love intrigue, a love affair.

IRO-GURUI, イログルイ, 色狂, *n.* Abandoned to debauchery, or lewdness. — *wo sh'te kandō wo ukeru.*

I-RO-HA, イロハ, *n.* The first three syllables of the Japanese syllabary, the A B C, the alphabet, the name of a verse composed of the syllables of the alphabet.

IRO-IRO, イロイロ, 色, Various, many, different kinds, diverse. *Hon ga* — *aru*, have various kinds of books. — *na koto wo iu*, to speak of many things.
Syn. SHINA-JINA, SHU-JU, SAMA-ZAMA.

IROKA, イロカ, 色香, *n.* Color and fragrance, beauty and loveliness of women. *Hana no* —, the color and fragrance of a flower. *Tayenaru* —, exquisite loveliness. — *ni mayō*, to be fascinated by female beauty.

IROKEDZKI,-*ku*,-*ita*, イロケヅク, 色氣附, *i.v.* To arrive at the age of puberty. *Muszme ga* —,

IRO-KICHIGAI, イロキチガヒ, 色氣違, *n.* Insanity accompanied with lasciviousness.

IROKO, イロコ, 鱗, *n.* Dandruff, the scales of a fish. Syn. FUKE.

IRO-MACHI, イロマチ, 色町, *n.* Prostitute quarter.

IROMEKASHII,-KI,-KU,-Ū, イロメカシイ, 好色, Having a lascivious appearance, having lewd thoughts, or feelings. — *miyeru.*

IROMEKI,-*ku*,-*ita*, イロメク, *i.v.* To have the appearance of defeat (of an army). *Iromeite miyeru*, to appear to give way, or to suffer defeat.

†IRON, イロン, 異論, *n.* A different opinion or argument. — *wo tateru*, to advance a different opinion.

IRO-NAOSHI, イロナホシ, 色直, *n.* An entertainment some two or three days after a wedding.

IRO-NAI, or IRO-NO-NAI, イロナイ, 無色, without a paramour; cold, not cordial, rough in manner, not courteous.

IRONE, イロネ, 色音, *n.* The tone, sound. *Fuye no* —, the tone of a flute.

†IRONE, イロネ, 兄, or 姊, *n.* Elder brother or sister, (Poet.)

IRO-ONNA, イロヲンナ, 色女, *n.* A mistress.

IRO-OTOKO, イロヲトコ, 色男, *n.* A paramour.

IRORI, 井ロリ, 地爐, *n.* A hearth, or fireplace sunk in the middle of a floor.
Syn. RO, YURURI.

†IROTO, イロト, 妹, *n.* Younger sister, (Poet.)

IRO-TSZYA, イロツヤ, 色艶, *n.* The gloss, lustre, brightness, complexion of anything. *Kao no* — *ga warui*, your complexion is bad.

IRU, イル, See *Iri*, and *I*, *iru.*

I-RUI, イルイ, 衣類, Clothing.
Syn. KIMONO.

IRUKA, イルカ, 江豚, *n.* The tunny-fish.

†IRUKASE, イルカセ, 忽, Careless, negligent, inattentive. — *ni naru.*

IRUMAJIKI,-KU, イルマジキ, 入間敷, Will not need, will not expend. *Kotoba ni mono wa irumajiki ni naze ichi gon mo ī-dasanai*, since in speaking you incur no expense, why will you not utter a word?

IRURU, イルル, See *Ireru.*

Ī-SABAKI,-*ku*,-*ita*, イヒサバク, 言捌, *t.v.* To unfold, explain, clear up what is obscure, or difficult.

ISAGIYOI,-KI,-KU,-SHI, イサギヨイ, 潔, Pure, clean, undefiled. — *kokoro*, a pure heart. Syn. KIYORAKA, KEPPAKU, SHŌJŌ.

ISAGO, イサゴ, 沙, *n.* Sand. Syn. SZNA.

ISAI, イサイ, 委細, *n.* The particulars, minutiæ, minute detail. — *wo iu*, to tell the particulars. — *wo kiku*, to hear, &c.

ISAI-NI, イサイニ, 委細, *adv.* Particularly, minutely, circumstantially.
Syn. TSZBUSANI, KUWASHIKU, KOMAKANI.

ISAKAI,-*au*,-*atta*, イサカフ, 鬪諍, *i. v.* To quarrel, dispute, wrangle, contend. *F'tari tomo ni isakau koto wa naranu zo yo*, cease your quarreling.
Syn. KŌ-RON, ARASOI, KEN-K'WA.

ISAKAI, イサカヒ, 鬪諍, *n.* A quarrel, dispute, contention. *F'tari tomo ni* — *mu yō*, don't quarrel with each other. *Kiyōdai* — *wo szru*, the brothers quarrel.

ISAKUSA, イサクサ, *n.* Contention, row, brawl. — *wo iu*, to quarrel.

Ī-SAMASHI,-sz,-sh'ta, イヒサマス, 言冷, *t v.* To dissuade from; to cool, or abate the desire for any thing.

ISAMASHII,-KI, イサマシイ, 勇, *a.* Courageous, brave, manly, bold, intrepid; brisk, lively, noisy. Syn. YU-YUSHII, TAKESHII.

ISAMASHIKU, or ISAMASHŪ, イサマシク, 勇, *adv.* idem. — *miyeru.*

ISAMASHISA, イサマシサ, 勇, *n.* Bravery courage.

Ī-SAMATAGE,-ru,-ta, イヒサマタゲル, 言妨, *t.v.* To hinder, obstruct, interfere, or prevent by speaking.

ISAME,-ru,-ta, イサメル, 諫, *t.v.* To caution, remonstrate, or plead with a superior; *Kimi oya nado wo isameru,* to remonstrate with one's master or parents.
Syn. KANGEN SZRU.

ISAME,-ru,-ta, イサメル, 慰, *t.v.* To soothe, appease, tranquilize, please, (of the gods.) *Kami wo* —, to please the gods. *Kami wo isameru szdz no oto,* the sound of the bell which is pleasing to the gods.

ISAME, イサメ, 諫, *n.* Remonstrance, caution warning, or advice to a superior. — *wo iru.* — *wo kiku.*

ISAMI,-mu-nda, イサム, 勇, *i.v.* To be bold, courageous, intrepid, fearless. *Isande teki ni mukō,* he boldly faced the enemy.

ISAMI, イサミ, 俠者, *n.* A bold, intrepid person. Syn. OTOKODATE.

ISAŌ, or ISAŌSHI, イサホシ, 功, *n.* Merit; great, eminent, or distinguished deeds. — *no aru h'to,* a distinguished man. — *wo tateru.* Syn. KŌ.

†ISARAI, イサライ, 臀, *n.* The buttocks. Syn. SHIRI.

†ISARI, イサリ; 漁, *n.* Fishing. — *wo szru,* to fish.

†ISARIBI, イサリビ, 漁火, *n.* A torch used in fishing at night.

†ISARI-BUNE, イサリブネ, 漁舩, *n.* A fishing-boat. Syn. RIYŌ-SEN.

ISASAKA, イササカ, 聊, Small, little, trifling. — *na koto ni hara wo tatsz,* to get angry for a trifling thing. — *mo nai,* not the least, by no means. Syn. CHITTO, SZKOSHI, WADZKA.

†ISASAME, イササメ 假初, *adv.* Slightly, little, temporary. (Poet.)
Syn. KARISOME.

Ī-SASHI,-sz,-sh'ta, イヒサス, 言差, To leave off talking before one is done, owing to some interruption.

†ISE,-ru,-ta, イセル, 縝, To sew and gather when sewing a long edge to a shorter. *Iseru tokoro wa nai,* sewed even and smooth without a wrinkle. *Isenui shi-nai demo yoi,* better sew so as not to wrinkle.

I-SEI, 井セイ, 威勢, *a.* Power, authority, might. — *no aru h'to,* a powerful man. — — *wo katte ibaru,* to act arrogantly on an assumed authority. Syn. I-KŌ, IKIOI.

†I-SEI, イセイ, 遺精, Nocturnal emissions. — *szru.* Syn. MŌ-ZŌ.

I-SHA, イシャ, 醫者, *n.* A physician, doctor. — *wo yobu.* — *wo tanomu.* — *ni kakaru,* to employ a doctor. *Yabu* —, a quack doctor.

ISHI, イシ, 醫師, *n.* idem.

ISHI, イシ, 石, *n.* A stone. — *wo kiru,* to cut a stone. — *wo horu,* to quarry stone. — *wo migaku,* to polish a stone. — *wo nageru,* to throw a stone.

ISHIBAI, イシバイ, 石灰, *n.* Lime made of limestone.

ISHI-BASHI, イシバシ, 石橋, *n.* Stone-bridge.

ISHI-BIYA, イシビヤ, 銅發熕, *n.* A cannon.

ISHI-BOTOKE, イシボトケ, 石佛, *n.* A stone idol.

ISHI-BUMI, イシブミ, 石碑, (*seki-hi,*) *n.* A stone tablet, or monument bearing an inscription.

ISHI-DAN, イシダン, 石壇, *a.* A stone platform.

ISHI-DŌRŌ, イシドウロウ, 石燈籠, *u.* A stone lamp post.

ISHI-DZKI, イシヅキ, 鐏, *n.* The but end of a spear.

Ī-SHIDZME,-ru,-ta, イヒシヅメル, 言鎮, *t. v.* To hush, quiet, still by speaking.

ISHI-DZMI, イシズミ, 石炭, *n.* Stone-coal, Syn. SEKITAN.

ISHI-DZRI, イシズリ, 石摺, *n.* A lithograph, a print from stone.

ISHI-DZYE, イシヅヱ, 礎, *n.* A stone pedestal, a stone foundation. Syn. DODAI.

ISHI-GAKI, イシガキ, 石垣, *n.* Stone wall.

ISHI-GAKI, イシガキ, 石磴, *n.* Stone steps.

ISHI-GURUMA, イシグルマ, 石車, *n.* (lit. a stone waggon) fig. treading on a round stone. — *ni nori korobu,* to fall by treading on a round stone.

ISHIKI, 井シキ, 居鋪, *n.* The buttocks. Syn. SHIRI.

ISHI-KIRI, イシキリ, 石工, *n.* A stonecutter.

ISHIKO, イシコ, 石子, *n.* Stone chips.

†ISHIKI,–KU,–Ū, イシク, 善, Good, well. (Poet.) *Nanji ishiku mairitari*, you have done well in coming, it is good that you have come. *Ishiku mo kokoro-dzkitaru mono kana* what a mindful person you are! Syn. YOKU-KOSO, UMAKU.

ISHIKODZME, イシコヅメ, 石子瘞, *n.* Killing and burying under a pile of stones. — *ni szru.*

ISHI-MOCHI, イシモチ, 石首魚, *n.* A kind of fish, (said to have a stone in its head.)

I-SHIRAMASARE,–*ru*,–*ta*, イシラマサレル, 被射煞, pass. To be overwhelmed with arrows and made to give way.

I-SHIRAMASHI,–*sz*,–*sh'ta*, イシラマス, 射煞, *t. v.* To overwhelm with arrows, and cause the enemy to give way.

ISHITATAKI, イシタタキ, 鶺鴒, *n.* A kind of bird. Syn. SEKI-REI, NIWA-NABURI.

ISHI-USZ, イシウス, 石磨, *n.* A stone mill, also 石臼, a stone mortar.

ISHIYA, イシヤ, 石工, *n.* A stone cutter, stone mason.

ISHI-YUMI, イシユミ, 弩, *n.* A bow for throwing stones, catapult.

I-SHO, イシヨ, 醫書, *n.* Medical books.

ISHŌ, イシヤウ, 衣裳, *n* Clothes. Syn. KIMONO, MESHI-MONO, I-FUKU.

I-SHOKU, イシヨク, 衣食, *n.* Clothes, and food. — *ni fujiyū wa nai*, not easy to procure food and clothing.

I-SHU, イシユ, 意趣, *n.* Hatred, malice, enmity, meaning, mind, intention, object, — *gayeshi wo szru*, to take vengeance. — *wo mōshi-noberu*, to state one's intention or mind. Syn. SHUI, OMOMUKI, IMI, URAMI.

†ISO, イソ, 五十, Fifty. (Poet.) *Isoji*, fifty years.

ISO, イソ, 磯, *n.* Sea-shore, sea coast. Syn. UMI-BATA.

†ISŌ, イソウ, 異相, *n.* A strange, or uncommon physigonomy.

I-SŌ, ヰサウ, 居相, Appears to be, looks as if there is. *Aszko ye — de gozarimasz*, I think it is yonder; looks as if it might be there. *Kiyō wa uchi — na mon da*, it is probable he is at home to day.

ISO-BATA, イソバタ, 磯端, *n.* The seacoast.

ISO-BE, イソベ, 磯邊, *n.* Idem.

ISOGASHII,–KI, イソガシイ, 忙, *a.* Busy, actively engaged, doing with haste, hurry, bustling, urgent. *Kiyō wa* —, I am busy to-day. — *shigoto*, urgent business. *Ki no — h'to*, a person always in a hurry, a driving person. Syn. SEWASHII, HANTA.

ISOGASHIKU, or, ISOGASHŪ, イソガシク, 忙, *adv.* Idem. — *iu*, to hurry up another. — *nai*, not busy.

ISOGASHISA, イソガシサ, 忙, *n.* The hurry, press of business, bustle. *Amari — ni meshi mo kuwanai*, not able to eat food on account of the exceeding press of business.

ISOGAWASHII,–KI, イソガハイシ, Same as *Isogashii.*

ISOGI,–*gu*,–*ida*, イソグ, 急, *i.v.* To hasten, to hurry, urgent, pressing. *Isoide kuru*, come in haste. *Isoide szru*, to do in haste. *Isogimashō*. I will hurry. Syn. KIU-NI, SZMIYAKA, HAYAKU.

ISO-ISO, イソイソ, *adv.* In a quick, hurried manner, blithesome, gay. *Ki no — sh'ta h'to.*

Ī-SOME,–*ru*,–*ta*, イヒソメル, 言初, *i.v.* Derived, or coined, (as a word), first spoken, to begin to talk. *Mono wo* —, to begin to talk, (as a child).

Ī-SONJIRI,–*ru*,–*ta*, イヒソンジル, 言損, *t.v.* To mistake in saying, to speak incorrectly.

ISŌRŌ, イサフラフ, 寄食兒, *n.* A hanger-on, a dependant. Syn. KAKARIUDO.

ISSAI, イツサイ, 一切, All, whole. — *shu-jō*, all living things. *Iye no dōgu issai*, all the household furniture. Syn. SZBETE, MINA, NOKORADZ.

ISSAKUJITSZ, イツサクジツ 一昨日, Day before yesterday. Syn. OTOTOI.

ISSAKUNEN, イツサクネン, 一昨年, Year before last. Syn. OTODOSHI.

ISSAN, イツサン, 駃參, With the utmost speed, with a bound. *Uchi kara — ni kakedasz*, he bounded out of the house.

†ISSHI,–*szru*,–*ta*, イツスル, 揖, *i.v.* To bow. Syn. YESHAKU SZRU.

ISSHIN, イツシン, 一心, Whole heart. — *furan ni ka-giyō wo hagemu*, to be entirely taken up with one's business. — *furan ni kami wo ogamu*. — *wo korash'te inoru*, to pray with the whole heart

†ISSHIN, イツシン, 一身, Alone, one person. — *de dekinu koto*, a thing which cannot be done alone.

ISSHO-KEMMEI, イツシヨケンメイ, 一處懸命, *adv.* In desperation, disregarding safety or danger. — *ni tatakau.*

ISSHO-NI, イツシヨニ, 一所, *adv.* Together, along with, in concert, in company with. — *yuku*, to go together. *Are to kore to — szru*, do this and that at the same time.

ISSHŌ, イッシヤウ, 一生, The whole life. — *fu-jiyū*, whole life miserable. — *no aida*, during one's life.

ISSO, イッソ, 寧, (in comparison). Better, rather. *Fuchiu na mono wo yashinō yori wa isso inu wo yashinau hō ga yoi*, better nourish a dog than an unfaithful servant.

ISZ, イス, 柞, *n.* A kind of hard wood, of which combs are made, also called *Yusz.*

ISZ, イス, 椅子, *n.* A chair.

Ī-SZGI,*–ru*,*–ta*, イヒスギル, 言過, *i.v*, To say too much, to blackguard, revile.
Syn. K'WA-GON.

ISZKA, イスカ, 鶍, *n.* A kind of bird, a crossbill. *Omō-koto — no hashi hodo chigau.*

Ī-SZTE,*–ru*,*–ta*, イヒステル, 言捨, *i. v.* To say and go away, without waiting for a reply. *Īsztete yuku.*

I-SZWARI,*–ru*,*–tta*, イスハル, 䲶, *i.v.* To run aground, to ground. *Fune ga iszwatta*, the ship has grounded.

ITA, イタ, 板, *n.* A board. — *wo hiku*, to saw boards, (make them). — *wo kedzru*, to plane boards. — *wo haru*, to lay boards, to board. *Tetsz no ita*, sheet iron.

ITA-BAME, イタバメ, 板壁, *n.* Weather board, clapboard.

ITABASHI, イタバシ, 板橋, *n.* A bridge of a single board.

ITABEI, イタベイ, 板屏, *n.* A board-fence.

ITA-BISASHI, イタビサシ, 板庇, *n.* A board roof over a door, or window.

ITA-BUKI, イタブキ, 板葺, *n.* A board or shingle roof.

ITABURI,*–ru*,*–tta*, イタブル, *t.v* To oppress, maltreat, or wrong, by filching money, to squeeze for money.

ITACHI, イタチ, 田鼠, *n.* A weasel.

ITADAKI,*–ku*,*–ita*, イタダク, 戴, *t. v.* To put on the head. To receive respectfully. *Dzkin wo* —, to put on a cap. *Kane wo* —, to receive money. *Chichi no ada ni wa tomoni ten wo itadakadz*, should not live under the same sky with a father's murderer. Syn. NOSERU, SASAGU, CHŌDAI.

ITADAKI, イタダキ, 頂, *n.* The top of the head, top, summit. — *wo naderu*, to smooth or pat the head. *Yama no* —, the top of a mountain.
Syn. CHŌ-JŌ, ZETCHŌ.

ITA-DATAME, イタダタミ, 板疊, *n.* A board mat, a board floor.

ITADE, イタデ, 傷手, *n.* A wound. — *wo ukeru*, to receive. — *wo ō*, (idem.)
Syn. TEOI.

ITA-DO, イタド, 板戸, *n.* A door made of boards.

ITADORI, イタドリ, 虎杖, *n.* A kind of plant.

ITADZGAWASHII,–KI,–KU,–U,–SA, イタヅガハシイ, 勞, Troublesome, laborious, hard, afflictive.
Syne. WADZRAWASHI, KURŌ, HONE-ORI.

ITADZKI, イタヅキ, 勞, *n.* Sickness, affliction, labor, hardship, trouble. *Niwaka no — nite mimakaru*, to die with sudden sickness. Syn. WADZRAI.

ITADZRA, イタヅラ, 徒, Idle, vain, useless, unprofitable, mischievous, indecent, immodest, lewd. — *wo szru*, to do mischief. — *mono*, a mischievous fellow. — *goto*, a useless, or indecent matter.
Syn. MUDA, MUNASHII.

ITADZRA-NI, イタヅラニ, 徒, *adv.* Uselessly, vainly, idly, unprofitably.
Syd. MUDA-NI, MUNASHIKU.

ITA-GAKOI, イタガコイ, 板圍, *n.* A fence, board enclosure.

ITA-GAMI, イタガミ, 板紙, *n.* Paste-board.

ITA-GANE, イタガネ, 板金, *n.* Sheet-metal.

ITAGARI,*–ru*,*–tta*, イタガル, 疼, *i. v.* To suffer pain, to be in pain. *Maiban itagatte nemasen*, he is in such pain every night he cannot sleep.

ITAGO, イタゴ, 板子, The deck of a ship.

ĪTAI,–KI,–KU,–SHI, イヒタイ, Wish to say. *Ano hto ni ītai koto yama-yama aru*, I have many things I wish to say to him. *Ītaku nai*, don't wish to speak.

ITAI,–KI,–SHI, イタイ, 痛, *a.* Painful; a superlative, very, excessive, exceedingly great. *Kidz ga itai*, the wound is painful. *Me ga* —, my eye pains.

ITAIKE, イタイケ, 最愛氣, Pretty, darling, lovely. — *sakari no ko*, a darling child. Syn. KAWAIRASHI.

‖ITA-ITASHII,–KI,–KU,–Ū,–SA, イタイタシイ, 痛痛敷, Distressing, sad, pitiful.

ITA-JIKI, イタジキ, 板敷, *n.* Board-floor.

ITAKU, イタク, *adv.* Painful, severe, (see *Itai*). — *nai*, it is not painful. — *shikarareta*, severely scolded. *Itakute tamaranai*, it is so painful I cannot bear it.

I-TAKU, 井タク, 居宅, *n.* A dwelling house.

ITAMASHII,–KI,–KU,–Ū,–SA, イタマシイ, 傷敷, Distressing, sad, pitiful, mournful. Syn. KANASHII.

†ITAMASHIME,*–ru*,*–ta*, イタマシメル, 痛, *t.v.* To afflict, cause pain, or trouble.

ITAME,*–ru*,*–ta*, イタメル, 痛, *t.v.* To pain, afflict, hurt, injure. *Mune wo* —, to trouble, grieve. *Kimono wo* —, to spoil one's clothes.

ITAME, イタメ, 板目, *n.* The curved grain, or veins of wood. Syn. MASAME.

ITAMEGAMI, イタメガミ, 合紙, *n.* Pasteboard.

ITAMI,*-mu,-nda*, イタム, 痛, *t.v.* To pain, hurt; also, 傷, To injure, damage, hurt, spoil, to grieve for. *Kidz ga itamu*, the wound pains. *Mune ga* —, heart is pained. *Shinda h'to wo* —, to grieve for a dead person· *Kono daikon ga itanda*, this radish is spoiled. *Chawan ga itanda*, the teacup is injured,
Syn. YAMERU, KIDZ-TSZKU, KANASHIMU.

ITAMI, イタミ, 痛, *n.* Pain, hurt, injury, 傷, grief, sadness. *Kuszri wo tszketareba itami ga sarimash'ta*, when I applied the medicine the pain left. *Itami no aru chawan*, a damaged tea cup. *Itami no shi*, mournful poetry, elegy. *Mune no itami wo naosz kuszri ga nai*, there is no medicine for a wounded heart.

ITAMI-IRI,*-ru,-tta*, イタミイル, 痛入, *i.v.* To feel distressed or pained with a sense of obligation. *Go shinsetsz no oboshimeshi itami-iri tatematszri soro*, I feel greatly obliged to you for your kindness.

Ī-TAOSHI,*-sz,-sh'ta*, イヒタフス, 言倒, *t.v.* To knock-down by argument, to vanquish, defeat by speaking.

I-TAOSHI,*-sz,-sh'ta*, イタフス, 射斃, *t. v.* To shoot down, kill with an arrow.

ITARAGAI, イタラガイ, 海扇, *n.* A kind of shell-fish.

ITARASHIME,*-ru,-ta*, イタラシメル, 令至, Caust. of *Itaru*, to send, cause to go, or arrive at.

ITARI,*-ru,-tta*, イタル, 至, *i.v.* To arrive at, to reach, to attain, extend to. *Yedo ni* —, to arrive at Yedo. *Ten ni* —, to reach to heaven. *Mukashi kara ima ni itaru made*, from ancient times even until now. *Kami yori shimo ni itaru made*, from the highest to the lowest, *Gaku-mon ni itatta h'to*, a man perfect in literary attainments.
Syn. TODOKU.

ITARI, イタリ, 至, *n.* The utmost extent. *Yorokobi no* —, the utmost joy. *Hirei no* —, exceedingly impolite.

ITASA, イタサ, *n.* Pain. — *wo shinobu*, to endure pain.

ITASHI,*-sz,-sh'ta*, イタス, 致, *t.v.* To do. *Shigoto wo itashimash'ta*, I have done my work. *Itash'kata ga nai*, there is no help for it. *Dō itashimash'ta* what have I done, used in depreciating one's services when thanked by another. Syn. SZRU, NASZ.

Ī-TATE,*-ru,-ta*, イヒタテル, 言立, *t.v.* To set-a-going, to get up, to originate, to raise (as a report.)

I-TATE,*-ru,-ta*, イタテル, 射立, *t. v.* To shoot often and in rapid succession.

ITATTE, イタッテ, 至, *adv.* Superlatively, very, exceedingly. — *yoroshii*, exceedingly good. — *samui*, very cold. Syn. SHIGOKU, HANAHADA.

ITAWARI,*-ru,-tta*, イタハル, 勞, *t. v.* To pity, to feel a tender concern for, to compassionate, to care for, to love. *Haha oya wa ko wo itawarite yoru mo nemuradz*, the mother out of love for her child does not sleep at night. Syn. AWAREMU, FU-BIN NI OMŌ, ITŌSHIMU.

ITAWASHII,-KI,-KU,-Ū,-SA, イタハシイ, 悼敷, Tender concern, careful love, pitiful, compassionating. *Itawashiku omō.*

ITA-YA, イタヤ, 板屋, *n.* A house with a shingle-roof. A board yard.

IT-CHI, イッチ, 一致, Together, at the same time, with one accord. Syn. ICHIYŌ, ICHIDO.

IT-CHI, イッチ, 最, *adv.* Superlatively. — *yoi*, the best. — *warui*, the worst.
Syn. ICHI-BAN, ITATTE, SAI-JŌ, GOKU.

||ITE,*-ru,-ta*, イテル, 凍, *i. v.* Frozen-hardened, congealed. *Chawan ga itete wareru*, the tea cup is cracked by the cold *Kōri itete tszrugi yori mo szrudoshi.*

ITE, イテ, 射手, *n* An archer, bowman.

†I-TEI, イテイ, 異體, *(kotonaru katachi.)* Strange or extraordinary in form, or appearance.

†I-TEKI, イテキ, 夷狄, *n.* Barbarian, foreigner. — *no h'to*, a barbarian.
Syn. YEBISZ, YEMISHI.

ITŌ, イタフ, Same as *Itaku*, painful. — *gozarimas*, it is painful, Sir.

ITO, イト, 絲, *n,* Thread, a string, twine. *Kinu-ito*, silk thread. *Momen-ito*, cotton thread. *Asa-ito*, linen-thread. *Ki-ito*, raw-silk. *Ito no fushi*, knots, or uneven places in thread. — *wo toru*, to spin thread. — *wo hiku*, (idem.) — *wo kuru*, to reel thread. — *wo yoru*, to twist thread. *Samisen no* —, the strings of a guitar.

†ITO, イト, 最, *adv.* Superlatively, exceedingly, very. — *sewashii*, very busy. — *yasashii*, very amiable. *Ito karui*, very light.
Syn. HANAHADA, ITCHI.

†ITODO, イトド, 彌, *adv.* More, more and more, still more. *Biyō-ki naoradz itodo omoku naru*, disease uncured becomes still more severe. Syn. IYO IYO, NAO, MASZ-MASZ.

ITODOSHII,–KI,–KU,–Ū,–SA, イトドシイ, 彌敷, Very, exceeding.
Syn. HANAHADASHI.

I-TOGE,*–ru,–ta*, 井トゲル, 居遂, *t. v.* To complete the whole of one's time of service, to live through and finish one's time, serve out one's time. *Hōkō-nin jū nen i-togeta*, the servant has completed his ten years. *Shūto ga warukute yomi ga i-togeye-nai*, the father in law was so bad, the daughter in law could not live with him.

ITO-GUCHI, イトグチ, 緒, *n.* The end of a thread.

ITO-GURUMA, イトグルマ, 紡車, *n.* A spinning-wheel.

ITOI,*–ō,–ōta*, イトフ, 厭, *t. v.* To be tired of, weary of, to dislike, to mind, or care for. *Yo wo itō*, to be weary of the world. *Oya no tame ni shinku wo itowadz*, for her parent's sake she cared for no trouble. *On itoi nasaru-beku soro*, be careful about yourself, (health, &c.) *Kaze wo itō*, to dislike the wind. *Inochi wo ushinō wo itowadz*, did not mind losing his life.
Syn. KIRAU, AKU, TAIKUTSZ.

ITOKENAI,–KI,–KU,–SHI,–SA, イトケナイ, 幼, Youthful, young, tender.
Syn. OSANASHI, WAKAI.

ITOKO, イトコ, 從兄弟, *n.* A cousin.

ITOKO-DŌSHI, イトコドウシ, 從兄弟同士, *n.* Cousins to each other.

ITOKONI, イトコニ, 最濃煮, *n.* A kind of food.

†I-TOKU, 井トク, 威德, *n.* Majesty, dignity, power, authority. — *wo motte h'to fukuseshimu.*

ITO-KURI, イトクリ, 絡柅, *n.* A reel.

ITOMA, イトマ, 暇, *n.* Leisure, freedom from occupation or business, time, liberty from service. *O — mōshimasz*, (said in leaving the presence of any one,) I will take my leave. — *wo negō*, to ask for dismissal from service. — *wo yaru*, to grant a dismissal. — *wo dasz*, to dismiss from service. *Han-nichi no — mo nai*, not even a half day's leisure. — *ga nai*, have no time. Syn. HIMA, TESZKI.

ITOMAGOI, イトマゴヒ, 暇乞, *n.* Taking leave. — *wo szru*, to take leave.

ITO-MAKI イトマキ, 絲絡, *n.* A spool for winding thread on.

‖ITO-ME, イトメ, 絲目, *n.* The strings of a kite.

ITO-MO, イトモ, 最, *n.* see *Ito.*

ITONAMI, *–mu,–nda*, イトナム, 營, *t. v.* To do, make, build, perform. *Kagiyō wo* — to labor at one's calling. *Ikusa wo* —, to plan a campaign. *Iye wo* —, to build a house. *Butsz-ji wo* —, to perform religious services for the dead. *Yo wo* —, to make a living. TSZKURU, SZRU.

†ITONAMI, イトナミ, 營, *n.* Business, occupation.

Ī-TORI,*–ru,–tta*, イヒトル, 言取, *t. v.* To explain, say, tell, express in words. *Kokoro ni wakarite wa iyedomo ītorukoto ga mudzkashii*, although I understand it clearly it is difficult to explain it.

Ī-TŌSHI,*–sz,–sh'ta*, イヒトホス, 言透, *i.v.* To persist in saying, continue to say, to say constantly. *Kakunogotoku -ītōshi shi-jū ichi gon mo aratame mōsadz soro*, she persists in saying so and will not alter a single word.

I-TŌSHI,*–sz,–sh'ta*, イトホス, 射透, *t. v.* To shoot an arrow through any thing.

ITŌSHII-KI,–KU,–Ū,–SA, イトホシイ, 最愛, Very dear, darling, beloved, exciting pity or compassion. — *koto*, a thing exciting pity. *H'to no nangi wo itōshiku omō*, to pity the afflictions of men.
Syn. KAWAI, FUBIN, AWAREMI.

†ITOSHIGO, イトシゴ, 愛子, *n.* A beloved child.

ITŌSHIMI,*–mu,–nda*, イトホシム, 愛惜, *t.v.* To pity, compassionate.
Syn. AWAREMU.

ITO-SZJI, イトスヂ, 線, *n.* A thread.

ITO-TAKE, イトタケ, 絲竹, *n.* Stringed and wind instruments of music.

†ITOYŪ, イトユフ, 遊絲, *n.* The undulatory appearance of the atmosphere in a hot day.

ITO-ZAKURA, イトザクラ, 絲櫻, *n.* A kind of cherry-tree with long hanging branches.

ITOZOKO, イトゾコ, 絲底, *n.* The raised edge on the bottom of a cup.

ITSZ, イツ, contrac. of *Itsztsz*, five. *Itsz tose*, five years.

ITSZ, イツ, 何時, *(nandoki). adv.* When, usual, ordinary, common. — *kimashita*, when did you come? — *kairi-nasaru*, *(kairashsharu)*, when will you return? *Itsz no ma*, when. *Itsz yori mo okureru*, later than usual.

ITSZ, イツ, 一, One, used only in compound words.

ITSZDEMO, イツデモ, 何時, *(maido). adv.* Always, continually, constanly, anytime whatever. *Matsz no ki — aoi*, the pine is always green. — *sake ni yotte kuru*, he always comes drunk. — *yoroshii*, any time will do. — *yoi*, id.

Ī-TSZGI,*–gu,–ida*, イヒツグ, 言接, *t.v.* To

pass a word or message from one to another. Syn. DENGON.

ITSZ-GORO, イツゴロ, 何頃, *adv.* When, at what time.

ITSZ-JIBUN, イツジブン, 何時分, *adv.* (idem).

ITSZ-KA, イツカ, *adv.* (*Itsz* when, and *ka* of doubt). Some time not known, as, *H'to wa itszka ichido wa shinuru mono da*, every body will die sometime or other. — *kaita no da*, wrote it sometime or other — *wa jōjū sen*, I wonder when it will be done.

ITSZKA, イツカ, 五日, The fifth day of the month; also, five days.

ITSZ-KARA, イツカラ, 從何時, From what time, how long since, (of time past). —*Yedo ni szmi nasaru*, how long have you lived in Yedo? *Omaye* — *waruku natta*, how long have you been sick?

Ī-TSZKE, *-ru, -ta*, イヒツケル, 言附, *t. v.* To give orders, to command, to tell, inform.

Ī-TSZKE, イヒツケ, 言附, *n.* A command, order.

I-TSZKI, *-ku, -ita*, 井ツク, 居著, *t.v.* To be stuck fast, fixed, settled in a place. *Fune ga itszita*, the ship has stuck fast. *Hōkō-nin ga i-tszita*, the servant is settled in a place.

Ī-TSZKURAI, *-ō, -atta*, イヒツクラフ, 言繕, *t.v.* To adjust, mend, repair by talking.

Ī-TSZKUSHI, *-sz, -sh'ta*, イヒツクス, 言盡, *t.v.* To exhaust a subject, to say all that can be said.

†ITSZKUSHII, -KI, -KU, -Ū, -SA, イツクシイ, 儼然, Austere, grave, dignified. Also, 美, beautiful. Syn. GENJŪ, OGOSOKA.

†ITSZKUSHIMI, *-mu, -nda*, イツクシム, 慈愛, *t.v.* To love, to regard with tenderness, pity, compassion, or kindness.
Syn. MEGUMU, AWAREMU, JIHI, ITŌSHIMU.

ITSZKUSHIMI, イツクシミ, 愛, Love, pity, compassion, tenderness.

ITSZ-MADE, イツマデ, 何時迄, *adv.* When, to what time, how long, (of time future.) — *Yedo ni irassharu*, how long will you be in Yedo? *Itszmademo orimasz*, I shall live there always.

Ī-TSZME, *-ru, -ta*, イヒツメル, 言詰, *t. v.* To convince, convict, confute, to corner, (by talking.)

ITSZ-MO, イツモ, *adv.* Usual, common, customary, always, constantly. — *no tōri*, or — *no gotoku*, as you always do, in the usual, customary way. — *no tokoro*, the usual place. *Itszmo nagara hon wo haishaku itashitai*, pardon me for so oftēn troubling you, I wish again to borrow a book. *Itszmo yori omoshiroi*, more agreeable than common. — *kawaradz*, never changing.

Ī-TSZMORI, *-ru, -tta*, イヒツノル, 言募, *i.v.* Aggravated by talking, to grow more and more excited or determined in an argument.

†ITSZSHIKA, イツシカ, 何時, Same as *Itszka*. — *kuru de arō*, I wonder when he will come.

Ī-TSZTAYE, *-ru, -ta*, イヒツタヘル, 言傳, *i.v.* Handed down by word, told from one to another, from mouth to mouth.

ITSZ-TO-NAKU, or, ITSZ-TO-NŌ, イツトナク, 無何時, *adv.* Gradually, the commencement or time not being known. — *yoku natta*, he gradually became better. — *yami-tszita*, he gradually became sick.

ITSZ-TOTEMO, イツトテモ, 雖何時, *adv.* Always; or never, (with a negative verb.) — *kawara-nai*, will never change.

ITSZTSZ, イツツ, 五, Five. — *no toki*, at five years of age. Syn. GO.

ITSZWARI, *-ru-tta*, イツハル, 僞, *t.v.* To deceive, lie, mislead, cheat, beguile, delude. Syn. DAMASZ, AZAMUKU.

ITSZWARI, イツハリ, 僞, *n.* A lie, deception. — *wo iu*, to tell a lie. Syn. USO.

ITSZZOYA, イツゾヤ, 日外, *adv.* Some time before, (but uncertain when). — *yori gambiyō wo wadzrau*, suffering for sometime with sore eyes.

ITTAI, イツタイ, 一體, *n.* One person, one being; (adv.) usually, commonly, = *Zentai*. — *ni sh'te san-tai nari*, one substance, but three persons.

†ITTAN, イツタン, 一旦, *adv.* Once, one time.

IU, イフ, 言, See Ī, *iu*, to speak.

IU-FUKU, イウフク, 有福, Wealthy, rich, prosperous, fortunate. — *ni kurasz*. — *na h'to*.

IU-HITSZ, イウヒツ, 祐筆, *n.* A secretary, amanuensis.

IUWABA, イハバ, 言則, conj. mo. of Ī, *iu*. If I should say; for instance.

IU-WARE, イハレ, 謂, *n.* See *Iware*.

IU-YŌ, イフヤウ, 言樣, Way of speaking, = he said. *Ano h'to no* — *ni wa kayō de gosaru*, as to that which he said, it was so and so. *Omaye no* — *ni mo dekinai*, I cannot do as you said. *Asa yū kanashiki koto wo nomi* — *ni nari*, it became so that from morning to night she did nothing but complain.

IWA, イハ, 岩, *n.* A rock, a reef. — *no hazama,* a cleft in the rocks.

IWADE, or, IWADZ, イハデ, 不 言, neg. of Ī, *iu,* Not to say.

IWAI,*-au,-atta,* イハフ, 祝, *t.v.* To congratulate, to celebrate; felicitate. compliment; to worship. *H'to wo kami ni iwau,* to worship a man as if he were God. *Gan-jitsz wo* —, to celebrate new year's day. *Toshi wo totta h'to wo* —, to congratulate a man who has reached old age. Syn. SHUKU SZRU, MATSZRU.

IWAI, イハヒ, 祝, *n.* Congratulation, felicitation, celebration; a feast, festive occasion. — *wo szru,* to celebrate a festive occasion. *Sagare no* —, a celebration on account of a son. *Gan-jitsz no* —. *Sh'chijū no* —.

IWAIBI, イハヒビ, 祝 日, *n.* A holiday.

Ī-WAKE, イヒワケ, 言 譯, *n.* Explanation, apology, excuse, extenuation. — *wo szru,* to offer an explanation or apology. — *ga nai,* have nothing to say in extenuation.

Ī-WAKE,*-ru,-ta,* イヒワケル, 言 譯, *t. v.* To explain, to exculpate.

†IWAKU, イハク, 曰, To say. *Kōshi no* —: Confucius said.

IWAN, イハン, fut. of Ī, *iu. Ureshisa — kata mo nashi,* impossible to say how happy she was. *Masani — to szru,* was just about to speak.

IWANU, イハヌ, (Coll. *Iwanai),* neg. of Ī, *iu.* Not say.

IWANYA, イハンヤ, 况, *adv.* Much more, how much more. Syn. MASH'TE YA.

IWAO, イハホ, 巖, *n.* Rocks, a cliff, reef.

IWA-OKOSHI, イハオコシ, 岩 興, *n.* A kind of hard cake made of rice.

I-WARE, イハレ, 謂, *n.* Reason, cause, history, explanation. — *wo iu.*

ĪWARE,*-ru,-ta,* イハレル, pass. or pot. of Ī, *iu, itta,* to be said or can say. *H'to ni waruku iwareru,* to be evil spoken of by others. *Hadzkashikute iwarenai,* so ashamed she could not speak.

IWARENGE, イハレンゲ, 佛 甲 草, (*Hotoke no tszme*) *n.* A kind of rock-moss.

IWASE,*-ru,-ta,* イハセル, 令 言, Caust. of *I, iu,* To make, or let another tell. *Watakushi ni iwasete kudasare,* I pray you, let me speak.

IWASHI, イワシ, 海鰮 or 鰯, *n.* A kind of fish, the sardine. — *no kashira mo shinkō kara,* it is all of faith, though you worship the head of the *iwashi.*

IWASHIME,*-ru,-ta,* イハシメル 使 言, Same as *Iwaseru.*

IWA-TAKE, イハタケ, 岩 茸, *n.* A kind of mushroom that grows on rocks.

IWATA-OBI, イワタオビ, 纈 帶, *n.* The bandage worn by pregnant women, from the 6th month.

Ī-WATASHI,*-sz,-sh'ta,* イヒワタス, 言 渡, *t.v.* To give orders, to pass a word or order from one to another.

IWATSZTSZJI, イハツツジ, 羊 躑 躅, *n.* A kind of flowering shrub.

†IWAYURU, イハユル, 所 謂, The above mentioned, aforesaid, the said.

IWŌ, イハウ, (dubit. of Ī, *iu,*) Would say. — *to omō koto,* that which I thought to say.

IWO, イヲ, 魚, *n.* A fish. — *no wata,* fish-guts. Syn. SAKANA.

IWŌ, イワウ, 硫 黄, *n.* Sulphur, brimstone, (also pronouued *yuwō.*)

IWONOME, イヲノメ, 胈 目, *n.* A corn (on the foot.)

†IWO-TSZRI, イヲツリ, 漁 人, *n.* An angler, fisherman. Syn. RIYŌSHI, SZNADORI, ISARI.

IYA, イヤ, 否, *adv.* No, don't want, will not. — *da,* I won't, will not. — *da yo,* id. — *wo no henji,* an answer in the negative.

Ī-YABURI,*-ru,-tta,* イヒヤブル, 言 傷, *t.v.* To divulge, to confute, convince. *Kakush'ta koto wo* —, to divulge a secret. Syn. SEPPA SZRU.

IYAGARI,*-ru,-tta,* イヤガル, *i.v.* To dislike, have an aversion or repugnance to, to be unwilling. Syn. KIRAU, ITŌ.

IYAGAWIYE, イヤガウヘ, 彌 上, *adv.* One on top of another. *Jimba — ni kasanari,* men and horses were piled up one &c.

IYAITOKO, イヤイトコ, 再 從 兄 弟, *n.* A second cousin.

†IYAKU, イヤク, 醫 藥, *n.* Medicine. Syn. KUSZRI.

†IYAKU,*-szru,* 井ヤク, 違約, (*yaku wo tagayeru,*) *t.v.* To break a promise, or agreement.

IYA-MASARI,*-ru,-tta,* イヤマサル, 彌 勝, *i.v.* To become more and more, greater and greater.

IYAMASHI-NI, イヤマシニ, 彌 増, *adv.* More and more, increasing more and more.

IYAMI, イヤミ, *n.* Gay and showy in order to attract notice tawdry, affected. — *no nai ye* a picture not too highly colored. — *no nai h'to,* a man who does not dress, or behave so as to attract.

IYA-NA, イヤナ, 否, *a.* Disagreeable, unpleasant, offensive, odious, disgusting.

IYASHII,*-KI,* イヤシイ, 賤, *a.* Low in rank, base, vulgar, ignoble, vile, mean. *Kurai* *iyashiki h'to*, a person of low rank. — *kotoba*, vulgar language. Syn. GESEN, HIKUI.

†IYASHI,*–sz,–sh'ta*, イヤス, 愈, *t. v.* To cure, heal. *Yamai wo —. Kidz wo —.* Syn. NAOSZ, JISZRU.

IYASHIKU, or IYASHŪ, イヤシク, 賤, *adv.* See *Iyashii.*

†IYASHIKUMO, イヤシクモ, 苟, *conj.* If, if indeed, but, nevertheless, however.

IYASHIME,*–ru,–ta*, イヤシメル, 卑, *t.v.* To despise, contemn, to look down on. Syn. KARONDZRU, KEI-SOTSZ, ANADORU.

†IYATOYO, イヤトヨ, = *Sō de wa nai*, it is not so.

IYE, イヘ, 家, *n.* A house, a family. — *wo tateru*, to erect a house. — *wo fushin szru*, to build a house. — *wo osameru*, to govern a family. *Tszburetaru iye wo tateru*, to raise up a fallen house, or family. Syn. UCHI, TAKU.

ĪYE, イイエ, 否, *adv.* No, (in replying.)

IYE,*–ru,–ta*, イエル, 愈, *i.v.* To be healed, cured. *Yamai ga iyeta*, the disease is cured. *Kidz ga iyete*, the wound is healed. Syn. NAORU, ZEN-K'WAI, HOM-BUKU, JI-SZ.

IYE-BATO, イヘバト, 鴿, *n.* A house pigeon.

IYEDOMO, イヘドモ, 雖, *adv.* Although, yet, but. *Kuszri wo mochīyu to iyedomo yamai jisedz*, although medicine is taken the disease is not cured.

†IYE-DZTO, イヘヅト, 家苞, *n.* Presents to one's household on returning from a journey. — *ni szru.* Syn. UCHI-MIAGE.

IYE-GAMAYE, イヘガマヘ, 家構, *n.* The structure of a house, or plan on which it is built. — *ga yoi*, this house is well planned.

IYE-GARA, イヘガラ, 家柄, *n.* The kind of family, family line or rank. — *ga yoi*, of good family. Syn. IYESZJI.

IYE-KANE,*–ru,–ta*, イエカネル, 愈兼, *i.v.* Hard to heal, difficult to cure.

†IYEKI, 井エキ, 胃液, *n.* The gastric-juice.

IYE-NAMI, イヘナミ, 家並, *n.* Row of houses. — *no yoi machi*, a street with fine rows of houses. — *ni go yō-kin wo ateru*, to assess a tax, house by house.

IYE-NUSHI, イヘヌシ, 家主, *n.* Owner of a house, landlord.

IYE-SZJI, イヘスヂ, 家系, *n.* Family line, lineage, pedigree. — *ga yoi*, of good family.

†I-YETSZ,*–szru*, イエツ, 怡悦, (*yorokobu.*) To rejoice.

IYE-TSZDZKI, イヘツヅキ, 家續, A continuous line of houses, or houses all along the way.

IYE-TSZGI, イヘツギ, 家嗣, *n.* An heir. Syn. KATOKU.

Ī-YŌ, イヒヤウ, 言様, Same as *Iuyō.*

I-YŌ, 井ヤウ, 居様, *n.* Manner of sitting.

IYO-IYO, イヨイヨ, 彌彌, *adv.* More and more, gradually, certainly, positively. Syn. MAZS-MASZ, IYAMASHI-NI, NAO, KITTO.

Ī-YORI,*–ru,–tta*, イヒヨル, 言寄, *t. v.* To woo, court, to approach and say.

†IYOYAKA, イヨヤカ, 矗, Luxuriant, and straight.

IYURU, イユル, 愈, See *Iyeru.*

†IZA, イザ, 去來, Exclam. of inciting, encouraging or daring. — *tachi wo awasen*, come on let us cross swords. — *yukimashō*, come let's go. — *tamaye*, come on. Syn. IDE, SA.

I-ZAISOKU,*–szru*, 井ザイソク, 居催促, *t. v.* To sit and dun for the payment of money. *Kane wo* —, to dun for money.

IZA-KOZA, イザコザ, *adv.* Saying this and that, asserting and contradicting, as persons in anger, or quarreling. — *itte kenk'wa wo szru.*

Ī-ZAMA, イヒザマ, 言様, *n.* Way of speaking. — *no warui h'to*, one accustomed to speak in an angry, ill-tempered way.

IZANAI,*–au,–atta*, イザナフ, 誘, *t. v.* To persuade, to urge, to tempt, to induce, to draw, lead, entice. Syn. SASOI, YŪ IN, SO-SONOKASZ.

IZARI, イザリ, 蹇, *n.* A cripple, one who cannot walk.

IZARI,*–ru–atta*, イザル, 膝行, *i. v.* To move as a cripple, to shuffle, or push one's self along.

†IZAYOI, イザヨイ, 十六夜, *n.* The 16th night of the month, when the moon rises quickly after the sun is set. — *no tszki.*

IZEN, イゼン, 以前, Before, previous, former. — *no tōri*, the previous manner. *Kono* —, before this, previously to this. — *yori*, from former times. Syn. MAYE-KADO.

J

JA, ジヤ, 蛇, *n.* A large snake. — the figure of a circle within a circle.

†JA, ジヤ, 邪, (*Yokoshima.*) Evil, bad, wicked, vile, corrupt, erroneous. — *wa tadashiki wo gai-szru koto atzwadz*, the evil cannot hurt the good. — *wo imashimeru*, to reprove evil. Syn. MAGARU, AKU.

JA, ヂャ, A coll. particle. = *de wa.* Ī *h'to ja nai ka,* what a fine man he is. *Sō ja nai,* it is not so.

†JA-CHI, ジャチ, 邪智, *(yokoshima no chiye,) n.* Corrupt talents, wisdom used for vicious purposes, subtilty, cunning. — *ga fukai.*

†JA-DŌ, ジャダウ, 邪道, *(yokoshima no michi,) n.* Evil way.

JAGATARA, ジャガタラ, 咬𠺕吧, *n.* Batavia. — *imo,* the common potato.

JA-HŌ, ジャハフ, 邪法, *(yokoshima no michi.)* Vicious doctrines, or a corrupt religion.

†JA-IN, ジャイン, 邪婬, *n.* Adultery. — *szru,* to commit adultery.

JA-JA-UMA, ジャジャウマ, 跳跳馬, *n.* A vicious horse.

JA-KAGO, ジャカゴ, 蛇籠, *n.* A long basket made of bamboo, filled with stones and used for damming up water.

JAKAN-SEKI, ジャカンセキ, 蛇含石, *n.* Bismuth.

JA-KEN, ジャケン, 邪見, Distitute of kindness or pity, cruel, hard-hearted. — *na h'to. Osoroshiku — ni szru.*

JAKI, ジャキ, 邪氣, *n.* An influenza, pestilential vapor or disease. — *wo fusegu,* to keep off disease. Syn. AKKI.

JA-KŌ, ジャカウ, 麝香, *n.* Musk.

†JAKU, *-szru,* ジャク, 寂, *i.v.* To die, (only of a Bud. priest.)

†JAKU, *-szru,* ヂャク, 著, To be carried away with, bewitched, charmed, fascinated, captivated. *Ri-yoku ni* —, smitten with avarice.
Syn. SHŪ-JAKU, TSZKU.

JAKU-HAI, ジャクハイ, 若輩, *(wakaki tomogara).* Young, immature in knowledge or experience, (used also in humbling one's self.) *—na mono.*

†JAKU-JAKU, ジャクジャク, 寂寂, *adv.* Quiet, still, free from noise or bustle.
Syn. SAMISHII, SHIDZKA.

†JAKU-MAKU, ジャクマク, 寂莫, *adv.* (idem.)

†JAKU-METSZ, ジャクメツ, 寂滅, *n.* Death, (Bud.) — *iraku,* or, — *wo tanoshimi to szru,* glad to die.

JAKU-NEN, ジャクネン, 若年, *(wakaki toshi.)* Young, youthful, time of youth. — *no toki ni,* when young.

JAKURO, ジャクロ, 石榴, *n.* Pomegranate.

JAMA, ジャマ, 邪魔, *n.* Obstruction, hindrance, impediment. — *wo szru,* to obstruct, hinder, impede. — *ni naru,* to be in the way. *O — de gozarimasz,* excuse me for being in your way. — *wo harau,* to clear away an obstruction.
Syn. SAMATAGE, KOSHŌ.

†JA-NEN, ジャネン, 邪念, *n. (yokoshima gokoro.)* Evil thoughts.

JANKO, ジャンコ, 痘痕, *n.* Pock marks.
Syn. ABATA.

JARA-JARA, ジャラジャラ, *adv.* Sporting, wanton, lewd jesting, or badinage. — *ī nasaru na,* abstain from lewd jesting.

JARASHI, *-sz, -sh'ta,* ジャラス, Caust. of *Jareru.* To make to play, romp, or sport. *Neko wo* —, to play with a cat.

JARA-TSZKI, *-ku, -ita,* ジャラツク, To be playful, sportive, romping, frolicsome.

JARE, *-ru, -ta,* ジャレル, *i.v.* To play, frolic, sport, romp. *Neko ga* —, the cat plays. *Kodomo ga* —, the children romp.
Syn. TAWAMURERU.

JARI, ジャリ, 沙礫, *n.* Gravel. — *wo shiku,* to spread gravel.

†JA-SHIN, ジャシン, 邪心, *(yokoshima na kokoro.) n.* An evil, perverse mind.

†JA-SHŌ, ジャシヤウ, 邪正, Crooked and straight, vicious and virtuous.

JA-SHŪ, ジャシウ, 邪宗, *(yokoshima na shūshi.)* A corrupt or wicked religion, Christianity.

JA-SHŪ-MON, ジャジウモン, 邪宗門, *n.* Depraved, or corrupt sect, Christianity. *Go hatto no — nite wa gozanaku soro,* does not belong to the forbidden sect of christians.

JA-SZI, ジャスイ, 邪推, *n.* Evil, or suspicious thoughts of others. — *wo mawasz,* to think evil of others.

JE, ゼ, Of Nagasaki dialect, see *Ze.*

JI, ジ, 字, *n.* A chinese character; a word. *wo kaku,* to write a chinese character. — *wo shiru h'to,* a person who reads the chinese character well. — *wo hiku,* to look for a word in a dictionary.

JI, ジ, 寺, *(tera.) n.* A Buddhist monastery or temple.

†JI, ヂ, 路, *n.* A road, way, journey. *Kayeri ji wo unagasz,* to prepare to return.

JI, ヂ, 痔, *n.* Disease of the Anus.

JI, ヂ, 地, *(tszchi.) n.* The ground, earth, place, region, texture, material; the ground, (on which figures are painted) natural habit, usual custom. *Tszmaranai koto wo iu no ga ano h'to no ji da,* he is in the habit of saying foolish things. *Momen no ji,* the texture of cloth.

JI, ジ, 不, A future negative affix to verbs, expressing doubt or uncertainty, = *maszmai,* of the colloquial. *Kitaru maji,* will not come I think. *Ware ni oyobaji*, will not come up to me. *H'to ni mirareji*, that he might not be seen by others.

JI, シ, 時, *(toki.)* n. Time, hour, season. *Shi-ji*, the four seasons. *Hiru roku ji*, the six hours of the day. *Jū-ni ji*, 12 o'clock.

†JI, シ, 事, *(koto.)* n. An affair, matter, act, transaction, only used in composition, as *Buji*, *Daiji*.

JĪ, ヂイ, 祖父, n. Grandfather. *O jī san*, in addressing a grandfather, or any old man.

JI, ヂ, 柱, n. The bridge over which the strings of a harp pass.

†JI-AI, シアイ, 自愛, *(midzkara aiszru.)* Self-love, care for one's own person, happiness, or health. — *szru.*

JI-AI, ヂアヒ, 地合, n. Texture, material. *Tam-mono no* —, the texture of cloth. — *ga warui.* — *ga yoi.*

JI-BAN, シバン, (coll. for *Juban*,) n. A shirt.

JIBIKI, シビキ, 字引, n. A dictionary, lexicon.

‖JI-BIN, シビン, 自鬢, n. Dressing one's own hair. — *wo szru*, to dress &c.

JI-BIYŌ, ヂビヤウ, 持病, n. A disease with which one is often sick.

JI-BO, シボ, 字母, n. The five vowel sounds.

JIBŌ-JIMETSZ, シバウシメツ, 自亡自滅, Self-destruction, ruin which is the natural fruit of one's evil ways.

JI-BOSO, ヂボソ, 地細, Fine in texture. — *no momen.*

JI-BUN, シブン, 自分, n. Self, one's self, — *de kaita*, wrote it myself. *Omaye go — de oide nasare*, come by yourself. Syn. JI-SHIN, MIDZKARA, ONORE.

JIBUN, シブン, 時分, n. The time, proper time. — *ga kita*, the time has come. — *tōrai szru*, (idem.) — *ga itatta*, (idem.) — *wo ukagō*, to watch for a proper time. — *wo hadzreru*, to miss the right time. *Ikusa no* —, time of war. *Itsz-ji-bun*, at what time? *Hiru jibun*, noon. *Yatsz jibun*, 2 o'clock P.M. Syn. JI-SETSZ, KOKUGEN, JI-KOKU, TOKI, JIKŌ.

JIBUN-GARA, シブンガラ, 時分柄, Although it is in season, or that which is suited to the season. — *kanki tszyoku*, the cold is severe for the season.

JI-BUTO, ヂブト, 地太, Coarse in texture. — *no momen.*

JIBUTSZ, ヂブツ, 持佛, n. The idol which one especially worships above all others.

JIDAI, シダイ, 時代, n. Age, period of time. *Nobunaga no* —, in the time of *Nobunaga*. — *mono*, antique thing.

JI-DAI, ヂダイ, 地代, n. Ground-rent. — *wo harau*, to pay ground-rent.

JIDANDA, ヂダンダ, 頓足, n. Stamping with the feet, (as in anger.) — *wo funde ikaru*, to stamp the feet in rage. — *wo funde naku.* Syn. ASHIDZRI.

JIDARAKU, シダラク, 自墮落, Slovenly, wanting in neatness and order, careless in manner. — *na h'to*, a sloven. — *na fu*, a slovenly appearance. — *ni sh'te oku*, to place in a disordered way.

†JI-DŌ, シドウ, 兒童, n. A child under 15 years. Syn. KODOMO, WARAMBE, CHIGO.

JIDORI, ヂドリ, 地取, n. Wrestling in sport, or in training. — *wo szru*, to wrestle.

†JI-FU, シフ, 慈父, n. A kind or loving father; father.

†JI-FU, シフ, 自負, Vain-glorious, self-praise, vaunting one's self, boastful. *Ame ga sh'ta ni ware ni masaru mono araji to jifu szru*, he boasted that there was no body in the world that could excel him. Syn. JI-MAN, UNUBORE.

†JI-FUKU, シフク, 時服, n. Clothes suitable to the season.

JIGABACHI, シガバチ, 似我蜂, n. A kind of bee.

JI-GAI, シガイ, 自害, *(midzkara sokonau.)* Suicide, (by cutting the throat.) — *szru*, to commit suicide.

JI-GAMI, ヂガミ, 地紙, n. Fan-paper.

JIGE, ヂゲ, 地下, n. Inferior servant of a Kuge.

†JIGEN, シゲン, 示現, n. Divine manifestation, or revelation from a divine being. *Hotoke no — wo kōmuru*, to have a revelation from Hotoke.

JIGI, シギ, 辭宜, n. A bow, declining, excusing one's self. *O jigi wo szru*, to bow, salute by bowing. — *nashi*, without making any excuse, or without ceremony. Syn. AISATSZ, YESHAKU.

†JIGI, シギ, 時宜, n. Times, season. — *ni sh'tagau*, to comply with the times, to suit the age. — *ni kanawanai*, not to suit the times. — *ni yotte kawaru*, to change with the times.

JI-GIYŌ, ヂギヤウ, 地形, n. The ground on which a house is built. — *wo narasz*, to level the ground for a house.

JI-GŌ, シガウ, 寺號, n. The name of a temple. *Kono tera no — wa nan to mōshimas*, what is the name of this temple?

JI-GŌ, シゴフ, 自業, One's works or actions, according to which reward, or punishment is allotted in a future state. (Bud.) *Ji-gō ji-toku*, to receive according to one's deeds; (what a man soweth that shall he also reap.)

JI-GOKU, ヂゴク, 地獄, *n.* Hades, hell or place of punishment of the Buddhist, of which there are eight principal one's, these are each subdivided into 16, making in all 128. — *ni ochiru*, to go to hell.

JI-GOYE, ヂゴヱ, 地聲, *n.* One's natural voice.

JI-GUCHI, ヂグチ, 地口, *n.* A pun, playing on words. — *wo iu.*

†JI-G'WA, ジグワ, 自畫, *(midzkara yegaku).* Drawn, or sketched by one's self.

JIHI, ジヒ, 慈悲, *n.* Pity, compassion, parental love, mercy, benevolence, kindness. — *wo hodokosz*, to show pity, bestow love. — *wo taretamaye*, have pity, (in supplicating a superior). — *wo kō*, to ask for mercy. — *wo ukeru*, to find mercy. — *ga fukai*, of great mercy.
Syn. ITSZKUSHIMI, NASAKE, MEGUMI, AWAREMI.

†JIJAKU, ジジヤク, 自若, *adv.* As before, previously. — *to sh'te oru*, to be as before. — *to sh'te kawaru koto nashi*, just the same as before.

†JI-JI, ジジ, 時時, *(toki-doki)*, *adv.* Every hour, hourly, often, frequently.
Syn. ORI-ORI.

†JI-JI, ジジ, 事事, *(koto goto)*, *adv.* Every affair.

JI-JĪ, ヂヂイ, 老翁, *n.* An old man.

JIJIMUSAI,-KI, ヂヂムサイ, *a.* Dirty, filthy.

JI-JIN, ヂジン, 地神, *(tszchi no kami)*, *n.* Gods that protect the soil; the earthly-gods of Japanese fable of whom there where five dynasties.

†JI-JITSZ, ジジツ, 事實, *n.* The truth of the matter, the facts. — *wo tadasz*, to examine the facts.

†JI-JITSZ, ジジツ, 時日, *(toki hi)*, *n.* An hour or day. — *wo utszsadsz*, without waiting a moment.

†JI-JŌ, ヂヂヤウ, 治定, Fixed, settled, determined. — *szru.* Syn. SADAMARU, KESSZRU.

JI-JŌ, ジジヤウ, 辭讓, Declining, or excusing one's self through politeness, or modesty. — *sedz sh'te kotayuru wa rei ni arazaru nari*, to answer without excusing one's self is not polite. — *no kokoro rei no hashi nari*, modesty is the beginning of politeness. Syn. JITAI, JIGI.

JI-JŪ, ジジウ, 侍從, *n.* A title of rank.

JIKA-NI, ヂカニ, 直, *adv.* Immediately, without the intervention of a second person or thing. *H'to ni — hanasz*, to speak to one personally. *Hatszbō — tszkeru*, to apply a blister next the skin, without anything intervening.

JIKI, ヂキ, 直, *adv.* Immediately, instantly, quickly; also, immediate, close, next, without anything or person intervening. — *hashi no soba*, next to the bridge. *Ima — ni yuku*, go at once. *H'to ni — ni iu*, to speak personally to another. — *ni kayeru*, to return quickly. Syn. SZGUNI, HAYAKU.

JIKI, ジキ, 食, *n.* A meal, food. — *ni komaru*, in want of food. *Chiu — wo kū*, to eat dinner. *Hi ni ni — szru*, to eat twice a day. Syn. TABE-MONO, KUI-MONO, SHOKU, YE-JIKI.

JIKI-DAN, ヂキダン, 直談, Private, or personal conversation, without the intervention of another. — *szru.*

JIKI-DEN, ヂキデン, 直傳, Received immediately from another, handed down without intervention.

JIKI-HITSZ, ヂキヒツ, 直筆, *n.* The very hand writing, autograph. *Mukashi no h'to no —*, the very hand writing of an ancient person.

JIKI-RŌ, ジキロウ, 食籠, *n.* A box for carrying food in.

JIKI-SŌ, ヂキサウ, 直訴, *n.* A complaint made to an official in person, without the intervention of another. — *szru.*

†JIKKAN, ジツカン, 十幹, *n.* The ten stems or characters used in designating hours, days, months, years points of compass, &c.

†JIKKAI, ジツカイ, 十界, *n.* The ten places of abode of the Buddhists, viz. Jigoku, Gaki, Chikushō, Shura, Ningen, Tenjō, Shōmon, Yengaku, Bosatsz, Butsz.

†JIKKEI, ジツケイ, 實景, *n.* A real picture or sketch, not one of fancy.

JIKKEN, ジツケン, 實檢, Verifying by inspection, inspection. *Kubi wo — szru*, to inspect and verify the head of a slain enemy.

†JIKKIN, ジツキン, 昵近, *n.* A near attendant on a noble. Syn. O-SOBA, KINJU.

†JIKŌ, ジコ, 自己, pro. I myself.
Syn. ONORE, MIDZKARA.

JIKŌ, ジコウ, 時候, *n.* The weather, or temperature of the season, climate. *Natsz no — wa atszi*, the weather is hot in summer. *Fuyu no — wa samui.* — *sōō ni natta*, the weather is seasonable. — *wa fu sō-ō* the weather is unseasonable. —

no sei, influence of the climate.
Syn. YŌKI, KIKŌ.

JI-KOKU, ジコク, 時刻, *n.* Time, the hour, or moment. — *ga utszru*, time passes. — *tōrai szru*, the time or hour has come. *Neru — ga kita* the time for going to bed has come. *Kuru — wa itsztsz doki de gozarimas*, the hour for coming is eight o'clock.

†JI-KOKU, ジコク, 自國, *n.* One's own country.

†JIKON, ジコン, 自今, *(imakara). adv.* Henceforth, after this. — *igo*, id.

JIKU, ヂク, 軸, *n.* The stick, stem, stalk, *Fude no* —, the stick of a pencil. *Kuruma no* —, the axletree, or shaft of a wheel. *Kakemono no* —, the stick on which a picture is rolled.

JIKU-JIKU, ヂクヂク, *adv.* Wet, moist. — *sh'te iru.*

‖JIKURI, or JIKKURI, ジックリ, 熟, *adv.* Maturely, fully thoroughly, wholly, perfectly. — *kagayeru*, to consider well. — *aimash'ta*, fit tightly.

JI-MAN, ジマン, 自慢, Vain-glorious, vain, proud, vaunting, boasting, self-praise, self-conceit. — *wa h'to ni nikumaruru*, self-praise is hateful to others. — *szru*, to boast, or vaunt one's self.
Syn. JIFU, UNUBORE, HOKORU.

JIMAN-KUSAI, ジマンクサイ, 自慢臭, Vaunting, or boastful.

JI-MATSZRI, ヂマツリ, 地祭, *n.* A celebration on building a house, (to propitiate the gods of the soil.)

JI-MAWARI, ヂマハリ, 地廻, *n.* Neighbourhood, region, surrounding country. — *no wakai-shu*, the young people of the neighbourhood. — *nite wa sabake mōsadz*, no demand for it in this region.

JIMAYE, ジマヘ, 自前, *n.* A harlot whose earnings are all her own.

†JIMBA, ヂンバ, 陣場, *n.* Camping ground.

JIMBAORI, ヂンバオリ, 陣羽織, *n.* A kind of coat without sleeves, worn over armour.

JIMBASŌ, ジンバサウ, 神馬藻, *n.* A kind of sea-weed. Syn. HONDAWARA, NANORISO.

†JIMBEN, ジンベン, 神變, *n.* A strange, miraculous, wonderful thing. — *wo gendzru*, to work a miracle.

JIMBURE, ヂンブレ, 陣觸, *n.* An order issued to an army.

JIMBUTSZ, ジンブツ, 人物, *n.* Kind, or quality of man, a man. — *ya yoi*, an excellent man. — *ni ni-awanu koto wo szru*, to do something improper for a man to do. — *no ye wo kaku*, to draw pictures of men. *Ano — yudan ga naranu*, must be suspicious of that kind of person.
Syn. H'TOGARA, GIM-PIN.

JI-MEN, ヂメン, 地面, *n.* Lot of ground, land, farm, plantation. *Omaye no — wa nani hodo aru*, how much land have you? *Hiroi* —, a large farm.
Syn. JISHO, DENJI.

JI-METSZ, ジメツ, 自滅, *n.* Self-ruin, self-destruction. — *szru*, to destroy one's self. — *wo maneku*, to hasten one's ruin.

JIMI, ヂミ, 地味, Plain, not ornamented, not gay, simple, unaffected, frank. — *na kimono*, plain clothes. — *no h'to*, an honest, unaffected man. — *na moyō*, a small figure (on cloth.)
Syn. SHITSZBOKU.

JI-MICHI, ヂミチ, 地道, *n.* An easy gait, easy, gentle, or moderate manner. — *ni aruku*, to go at an easy gait. — *no saisoku de wa torenu*, it will not be got by moderate urging.

JIMI-JIMI, ジミジミ, *adv.* Moist, damp, wet. — *ase ga deru* wet with sweat. — *sh'ta tokoro*, a wet place.

†JIM-MI-RAI-SAI, ジンミライサイ, 盡未來際, Eternity to come.

†JIM-MŌ, ジンマウ, 人望, *n. (H'to no nozomi.)* Human desires or hopes.

†JI-MON, ジモン, 自問, Stating a question to one's self for solution. — *jitō szru*, to state a question and answer it.

JIM-PIN, ジンピン, 人品, *(h'togara)*, *n.* The kind, or quality of man. — *no yoi h'to*, a fine man, (in looks.)
Syn. JIMBUTSZ.

JIN, ジン, 人, *(h'to)*, *n.* A man, person, human. — *shin*, the human heart. — *tai*, human form.

JIN, ジン, 仁, *n.* Love, benevolence humanity, kindness. — *wa banmin wo aiszru no michi.* — *wa watakushi no kokoro naki wo iu.*
Syn. MEGUMI, ITSZKUSHIMI, JIHI.

†JIN, ヂン 塵, *(chiri, hokori)*, *n.* Dust, dirt; fig, the world. *Shutsz jin*, to leave the world and enter on a religious life.

JIN, ヂン, 陣, *n.* An army, troops arranged in ranks. — *wo sonayeru*, or — *wo kamayeru*, to arrange troops in order of battle. — *wo haru*, (idem.) — *wo toru*, to pitch a camp. — *wo harau*, to break up a camp. *Senjin*, the van of an army. *Gojin*, the rear. *Nijin*, the second division of an army.

JIN, ジン, 腎, *n.* The kidneys. — *no zō*, (idem.)

JI-NARI, ヂナリ, 地鳴, *n.* Noise, or rumbling of an earthquake.

JIN-CHŌKE, ヂンチヤウケ, 沈丁花, *n.* The Daphne odora.

†JIN-DO, ヂンド, 塵土, (*chiri, tszchi*), Dust and dirt, used by the Buddhist for the fashion, pleasures, honors, &c. of the world. — *ni kegareru*, polluted by the world.

JIN-DORI, ヂンドリ, 陣取, *n.* Forming a camp, or pitching tents. — *szru.*

†JIN-DZU, ジンヅウ, 神通, *n.* Divine knowledge of past, present and future events, divine power. (Bud.) *Sen-nin — wo yeta*, the sennin possess superhuman power.

JINEN-BAYE, ジチンバヘ, 自然生, Growing of itself, wild, or without cultivation.

JINENGO, ジチンガウ, 自然秔, *n.* The fruit of the bamboo.

JINEN-JŌ, ジチンジヨ, 自然薯, *n.* A kind of long root growing wild, much prized for eating. Syn. YAMA-NO-IMO, NAGA-IMO.

JI-NEN, ジチン, 自然, *adv.* Spontaneously, of itself. — *to dekiru*, produced spontaneously. Syn. ONODZKARA, SHIZEN, H'TORI-DE-NI.

JIN-GASA, ヂンガサ, 陣笠, *n.* A kind of hat worn by soldiers.

†JIN-GO, ジンゴ, 盡期, *n.* End, time when done, finished, or exhausted. *Kai-nen no g'yo-kei — arubekaradz*, the new year's holiday will never cease. Syn. KAGIRI, KIWAMARI, TSZKURU, SAIGEN, HATESHI.

JINGOYA, ヂンゴヤ, 陣小屋, *n.* An encampment, barracks.

†JIN-JA, ジンジヤ, 神社, (*kami no yashiro,*) *n.* A Miya, or Sintoo temple.

†JIN-JI, ジンジ, 神事, (*kami no koto,*) *n.* A Sintoo festival.

†JIN-JI, ジンジ, 仁慈, *n.* Love, benevolence, kindness. Syn. JIHI.

JIN-JŌ, ジンジヤウ, 尋常, (*yo no tszne.*) Common, usual, ordinary, of no superior excellence; delicate, genteel in form, gentle, calm, amiable. — *na h'to*, an ordinary person, an amiable person. — *ni shōbu shiro*, contend in a calm and self-possessed way. Syn. NAMI-NAMI.

JIN-KI, ジンキ, 人氣, (*H'to no ki,*) *n.* The mind, heart, or temper of people generally, the public mind. — *ga tatsz*, the public are roused.

JIN-K'YO, ジンキヨ, 腎虚, Impotent, or worn out by excessive venery. — *sh'te shinda.*

JINKŌ, ヂンカウ, 沈香, *n.* Aloes-wood.

†JIN-ON, ジンオン, 仁恩, *n.* Benevolence and favor, grace, clemency, (of superiors.)

JI-NORI, ヂノリ, 地乗, Horsemanship, leaning to ride. — *wo szru*, to practice horsemanship.

JIN-RIKI, ジンリキ, 神力, (*kami no chikara,*) *n.* Divine power.

†JIN-RIN, ジンリン, 人倫, *n.* The five human relations, viz., parent and child, master and servant, husband and wife, elder and younger brothers, and friends.

JIN-SEI, ジンセイ, 仁政, *n.* A humane government.

†JIN-SAKU, ジンサク, 神策, A wonderful stratagem or plan.

JIN-SEN, ヂンセン, 陣扇, *n.* A fan with iron stays used by an officer in war.

†JIN-SHA, ジンシヤ, 仁者, *n.* A benevolent man.

JIN-SOKU, ジンソク, 迅速, Quick, fast, in haste. Syn. HAYAI, TOKU, SZMIYAKA.

†JIN-SZI, ジンスイ, 腎水, *n.* The semen. Syn. INSZI, REI.

JIN-TAI, ジンタイ, 人體, (*h'to no karada.*) Kind of person. — *no yoi h'to*, a person of good character, or appearance. — *ni ni-awanu koto wo iu*, to talk inconsistently with one's position, or character. Syn. JIMPIN, H'TOGARA.

JIN-YA, ヂンヤ, 陣屋, *n.* A camp. The castle of a Hatamoto, or Daik'wan.

JIN-YAKU, ジンヤク, 腎藥, *n.* Medicines used to strengthen the virile power.

JIPPU, ジツプ, 實否, *n.* True or false, true or not. — *wo tadasz*, to ascertain whether it is true or not. Syn. ZE-HI.

JIPPU, ジツプ, 實父, *n.* Real father.

JI-RAI-K'WA, ヂライクワ, 地雷火, *n.* A mine of powder. — *wo shi-kakeru*, to lay a mine.

JIRASHI,-*sz*,-*sh'ta*, ジラス, *t.v.* To chafe, to provoke, vex, irritate, tease, annoy. *H'to wo jirashi nasaruna*, must not tease others. Syn. MODAYESASZ, KI WO MOMASERU.

JIRE,-*ru*,-*ta*, ジレル, *i.v.* To be fretful, irritable, impatient, vexed, annoyed. *Ki ga jireru*, to be in a bad humor. *Jirete naku*, to cry from vexation. Syn. MODAYERU, IJIMERU.

JIRE, ジレ, *n.* Bad-humor, irritation, crossness. — *ga kita.*

JIRETTAI,-KI,-KU, ジレツタイ, Provoking,

vexatious, causing bad-humor, or impatience. — *koto da, nani wo sh'te iru*, it is provoking, what are you about? — *nei, hayaku sh'te okure*, be quick, don't keep me waiting.

†JI-RI, ジリ, 事理, (*koto no dōri.*) *n.* The truth, or principle of anything.

JIRI-JIRI-TO, ヂリヂリト, *adv.* The sound of water beginning to boil, or of anything heavy scraping over a floor. — *atoshizari szru*, to move back with a grating noise.

†JI-RIKI, ジリキ, 自力, (*midzkara no chikara.*) One's own strength, or means. *Taibiyō — ni oyobadz, jin-riki wo tanomu beshi.*

†JI-RITSZ, or JI-RIU, ジリフ, 自立, Of one's self, without the help or permission of others, independent. — *sh'te koto wo szru.* Syn. H'TORI-DACHI, DOKURIU.

†JI-RIYŌ, ヂレウ, 治療, *n.* The treatment of disease.

JI-RIYO, ジリヤウ, 寺領, (*tera-chi.*) *n.* Land belonging to a temple, a glebe.

JIRŌ, ヂロウ, 痔瘻, *n.* Fistula in Ano.

JIRO-JIRO-TO, ジロジロト, *adv.* In a fixed, staring manner. — *miru*, to look fixedly at, stare at.

JIRORITO, ジロリト, *adv.* (idem.)

†JI-SAKAI, ヂサカイ, 地境, *n.* Boundary of land.

†JI-SAKU, ジサク, 自作, (*midzkara tszkuru.*) Made by one's self. — *no uta*, a song composed by one's self. — *no hotoke*, gods made by one's self.

†JI-SAN, ジサン, 自讚, (*midzkara homeru.*) Poetry, or a song written in one's own praise, self praise. Syn. JI-MAN.

JI-SAN, ヂサン, 持參, (*mochi mairu.*) To take away, or bring. — *itashimashō*, I will take it away.

JI-SAN-KIN, ヂサンキン, 持參金, *n.* A bridal present of money.

†JI-SEI, ジセイ, 辭世, *n.* Poetry composed by a person about to die. — *wo yomu.* — *wo nokosz.*

JI-SEI, ヂセイ, 治世, (*osamareru yo.*) A time of peace, tranquil and peaceful age.

JI-SEI, ジセイ, 時勢, (*toki no ikioi.*) *n.* Present power, the power of the country at the time. — *wa otoroyeta*, the power has declined. — *ni makaseru*, to comply with the force or circumstances of the times.

JI-SETSZ, ジセツ, 時節, *n.* The time, season, times. — *ga warui*, the times are bad. *Hana no hiraku — ni natta*, the time of the blooming of flowers has come. — *no shina de naki mono*, a thing out of its proper season. — *tōrai*, the time has come. *Warui koto bakari ni atte, — to akirameru*, meeting with nothing but bad luck, he resigned himself to his fate. *Ima no — ni awanu*, unsuitable to present times.

JI-SHA, ジシャ, 寺社, (*tera, yashiro.*) Buddhist and Sintoo temples. — *bugiyō*, superintendant of Buddhist and Sintoo temples.

†JI-SHA, ジジャ, 侍者, *n.* An attendant, servant, minister. Syn. O-SOBA.

JI-SHAKU, ジシャク, 磁石, *n.* A loadstone, magnet, a mariner's compass.

†JI-SHI, *-szru, -sh'ta*, ジスル, 辭, *t. v.* To decline, excuse one's self from, refuse. — *Okuri-mono wo jiszru*, to decline a present. Syn. INAMU, JITAI SZRU, KOTOWARU.

†JI-SHI, *-szru, -sh'ta*, ヂスル, 治, *t. v.* To cure, heal. *Yamai wo* —, to cure disease. *Jishi-gatai*, difficult to cure. Syn. NAOSZ. IYASZ.

†JI-SHI-IS-SHŌ, or JISSHI-ISSHŌ, ジッシイッシャウ, 十死一生, Ten chances for dying and only one for living, at great risk of life, dangerous, hazardous. — *no tatakai wo nasz*, to fight where there was every probability of being killed. Syn. KIU, SHI ISSHŌ.

JI-SHIN, ヂシン, 地震, *n.* An earthquake. — *ga yoru*, — there is an earthquake. Syn. NAI.

JI-SHIN, ジシン, 自身, *n.* One's self, self. — *de koshirayeru*, made it myself. — *wo homeru*, to praise one's self. Syn. JI-BUN, MIDZKARA.

JI-SHIN-BAN, ジシンバン, 自身番, *n.* A watch supported by the citizens of the ward.

†JISHISEN, ヂシセン, 地子錢, *n.* Rent paid for land, ground rent.

JI-SHŌ, ヂシャウ, 地性, *n.* Quality, or nature of the soil. — *ga yoi.* — *ga warui.*

JISHSHI, ジッジ, 實子, *n.* True or real child, own child.

||JISHSHŌ, ジッシャウ, 實正, Sound in mind. *Shinu-toki — de atta*, was sound in mind at the hour of death. *Kin-sz shakuyō tszkamatszri sōrō tokoro — nari.*

†JI-TA, ジタ, 自他, Self and others. *Hataraki kotoba ni — no shabetsz ga aru*, verbs are divided into transitive and intransitive.

†JITA-BIYŌ-DŌ, ジタビヤウドウ, 自他平等, Self and others alike. — *ni mono wo waritszkeru* to divide equally, giving to others as to one's self.

JI-TAI, ジタイ, 辭退, Declining, refusing, excusing one's self. — *szru.*
Syn. JISZRU, JI-GI, INAMU.

||JITA-JITA-TO, ジタジタト, *adv.* In a wet, moist, manner. *Midz ga iwa kara — ochiru,* the water trickles from the rocks.

JI-TŌ, ヂトウ, 地頭, *n.* The lord of the estate or manor. Syn. RIŌSHU.

†JI-TOKU, ジトク, 自得, (*midzkara yeru*), To know naturally; to receive according to one's deeds. *Sei-jin wa umare nagara — sh'te oru,* the sages naturally comprehend all things.

JITSZ, ジツ, 日, (*hi*) *n.* The sun, day. — *getsz imada chi ni ochidz.*
Syn. NICHI.

JITSZ, ジツ, 實, (*makoto*), True, real, not false. *Sono hanashi wa — ka,* is that story true? — *wo motte majiwaru,* to be sincere in one's intercourse with others. — *ga aru,* sincere. — *ga nai,* false, insincere.

JITSZ-BO, ジツボ, 實毋, *n.* Real, or true mother.

JITSZI, ジツイ, 實意, *n.* Sincerity.

JITSZ-JI, ジツジ, 實事, *n.* A true or real affair.

JI-TSZKI,-*ku*,-*ita*, ヂツク, 地著, *i.v.* To be a permanent resident, or fixed to a place by owning a house, or land. *Yokohama ni jitszita mono de wa nai,* he is not a fixed resident of Yokohama.

JI-TSZKI, ヂツキ, 地搗, *n.* Pounding the ground to render it compact before building. — *wo szru.*

JITSZ-MIYŌ, ジツミヤウ, 實名, *n.* Real name.

JITSZ-NI, ジツニ, 實, *adv.* Really, truly, indeed. Syn. MAKOTO-NI, HON-NI.

JITSZRASHII,-KI,-SHI,-KU, ジツラシイ, *a.* Having an appearance of truth, sincerity, reality, or honesty. — *hanashi,* a story that has the semblance of truth.

JITTEI, ヂツテイ, 鐵梃, *n.* A metal mace carried by policemen. — *wo furū,* to brandish a mace.

JITTEI, ジツテイ, 實體, Honest, upright, sincere. — *na h'to.*

JITTO, ジツト, *adv.* Fixedly, firmly, steadily, without motion. — *sh'te ire,* hold still. — *miru,* to look steadfastly at any thing. — *te wo shimeru,* to squeeze the hand hard.

JITTOKU, ジツトク, 直裰, *n.* A kind of coat worn by priests, and old men.

JIYAKU, ジヤク, 持藥, *n.* Medicine which one is in the constant habit of taking, mostly as a tonic. — *ni szru,* to doctor one's self.

†JI-YO, ジヨ, 自余, Other, not one's own. — *no koto,* another thing. — *no h'to-bito,* other people.

JIYŪ, ジユウ, 自由, Freely, at one's own pleasure, without constraint, voluntarily, convenient. — *ni szru* to do as one pleases. — *ni nara nai,* cannot do as I please, or not to one's mind. — *ni saseru,* to let another do as he pleases. — *jizai ni,* freely and easily. *Shin-sho ga — de nai,* to be hampered in one's circumstances. — *ni ugoku,* to move freely without obstruction.

JI-ZAI, ジザイ, 自在, Freely, easily, at one's own pleasure, without obstruction.

JIZAI-KAGI, ジザイカギ, 自在鈎, *n.* A hook, used for hanging pots over a fire, which can be raised or lowered to suit the occasion.

||JI-ZORI, ジゾリ, 自剃, *n.* Shaving one's-self. — *wo szru.*

JO, ジヨ, 序, *n.* The preface of a book. — *wo kaku.* Syn. HASHIGAKI.

JO, ヂヨ, 女, (*onna*), *n.* A woman.
Syn. NIYO, ME.

JŌ, ジヤウ, 情, (*kokoro*), *n.* Emotion, passion, feeling, love, affection, obstinacy. *Sh'chi jō* the seven passions, viz., joy, anger, sorrow. pleasure, love, hatred, desire. — *wo haru,* to be stubborn, obstinate. *Gō jō na mono,* or *jō no kowai mono,* an obstinate person. — *ga nai,* no feeling of kindness, or pity.

JŌ, ジヤウ, 城, (*shiro*), *n.* A castle, the residence of a nobleman, or prince. — *shu,* the lord of a castle. — *chiu,* inside of a castle. — *nai,* (idem.) — *g'wai,* outside of a castle. — *shi,* a messenger from the Shōgun to a Daimio.

JŌ, ヂヤウ, 錠, *n.* A lock. — *to kagi,* lock and key. — *wo orosz,* to lock. — *wo akeru,* to unlock.

JŌ, ジヤウ, 上, (*wiye*). Superior, best, to go up, ascend. — *chiu ge,* three qualities of superior, middling, and inferior. — *hin,* superior quality. *Goku-jō,* the very best. *Miyako ye jō-ge szru,* to go and return from Miyako. Syn. KAMI, AGARU, NOBORU.

JŌ, デフ, 帖, *n.* A quire of paper, (of some kinds, 20 sheets make a quire, of others 40 sheets,) a book that folds up like a fan. *Kami ichi jō,* one quire of paper.

JŌ, デウ, 條, *n.* Article, item, particular. *San jō no okite,* three separate laws. *Mōsz-jō sō-i naku soro,* no mistake in what you said, just as you said. *Migi no jō-jō*, the above items.

Jō, ジヤウ, 狀, *(fumi)*, *n.* A letter. — *wo yaru*, to send a letter. Syn. TEGAMI.

†Jō, ジヨウ, 丞, *n.* An old man, (only used in the Drama). — *to uba*, old man and old woman.

Jō, ヂヤウ, 丈, Mister, appended to names, not so respectful as *Sama. Kikujirō jō ye yaru*, give it to Mister Kikujirō.

Jō, ヂヤウ, 娘, Used in calling, or respectfully addressing young ladies. *O jō san.*

Jō, デフ, 疊, Used in counting mats. *Tatami ichi jō*, one mat. *Tatami ni jō*, two mats.

Jō, ヂヤウ, 丈, *(take)*, *n.* A measure of ten feet in length. *Isshaku tō ichi jō*, ten feet make one pole. *Tammono no — ga mijikai*, this piece of cloth is short in measure.

Jō-AI, ジヤウアヒ, 情合, *n.* Mutual affection, or love, civility, courteousness. *Fūfu no — ga utszranu*, there is no love between the husband and wife. — *no nai h'to da*, he is an uncivil person.

†Jō-BA, ジヨウバ, 乘馬, *(nori uma)*. *n.* A saddle horse.

Jō-BAN, ヂヤウバン, 定番, *n.* A watch or guard placed to protect a place.

JōBITA, ジヤウビタ, 上品, Superior, excellent, fine. — *h'to*, an excellent man.

†Jō-BOKU, ジヤウボク, 上木, To print, (as a book).

†Jō-BOKU, ジヨウボク, 繩墨, *(szmi nawa)*, *n.* The blackened line used by carpenters.

Jō-BU, ヂヤウブ, 丈夫, Strong, firm, solid, hale, in good health, courageous, safe. — *na h'to*, a robust man. — *na hashira*, a strong pillar. — *de gozarimas*, he is well.
Syn. TASH'KA, TSZYOI.

Jō-BUN, ジヤウブン, 上聞, *(kami no kiku)*. To tell to a superior. — *ni tasszru*, to report to a superior.

Jō-BUTSZ, ジヤウブツ, 成佛, *(Hotoke ni naru)*. To become a god, — to enter paradise.

†Jō-CHIU, デウチウ, 絛虫, *n.* A tapeworm. Syn. SANADA-MUSHI.

Jō-DAI, ジヤウダイ, 城代, *n.* A person who has the charge of a castle in the absence of the lord.

Jō-DAN, ジヤウダン, 情斷, *n.* Sport, play, jest, joke, fun. — *wo iu*, to jest, joke. — *szru*, to sport, frolic, to make fun. Syn. TAWAMURE.

Jō-DAN, ジヤウダン, 上段, *n.* A raised floor in temples or houses; upper row, or grade.

Jō-DO, ジヤウド, 淨土, *(kiyoki kuni)*. The clean country, holy land, or paradise of the Buddhists.

JōDō, ジヤウダウ, 成道, To become perfect, ro a god, said of *Shaka Niurai*, after passing through his 12 years of discipline; which is now commemorated on the 8th day of the 12th month.

Jō-DZ, ジヤウヅ, 上手, Skilful, expert dexterous, adept. — *na h'to*. — *ni dekita*, well done. — *ka heta ka shirenu*, don't know whether he is skilful or not.
Syn. TAKUMI.

Jō-FU, ヂヤウフ, 定府, *n.* A prince who resides all the time at Yedo.

Jō-FU, ジヤウフ, 上布, *n.* Grass cloth of the finest quality.

Jō-FUKU, ジヤウフク, 常服, *n.* *(tszne no kimono)*. Common clothes, such as are usually worn.

†Jō-GEN, ジヤウゲン, 上元, *n.* The 15th day of 1st month.

Jō-GI, ヂヤウギ, 定規, *n.* A ruler for drawing lines.

Jō-GO, ジヤウゴ, 上戸, *n.* A funnel, (fig.) a sot, drunkard.

†Jō-Gō, ヂヤウゴフ, 定業, Fixed fate, doom, or retribution decreed for deeds done in a previous state. (Bud.)

JO-GON, ジヨゴン, 助言, *(taszkeru kotoba)* To prompt, or assist another by speaking, to dictate. *Shōbugoto ni — wo szru koto nakare*, don't prompt one in playing games.

Jō-HAI, ジヤウハイ, 上輩, *(wiye no tomogara.)* Superiors, the great, the upper class of people. — *wa ge-hai wo awaremu*, the great feel compassion for the lower classes.

Jō-HARI-NO-KAGAMI, ジヤウハリノカガミ, 淨波梨鏡, *n.* A mirror in Hades, which reflects the good or evil deeds, which those that look into it, have done while in the world.

Jō-HIN, ジヤウヒン, 上品, Superior in quality.

Jō-Hō, ヂヤウハフ, 定法, Fixed rules, stipulated articles of a treaty, laws.

Jō-I,-*szru*, ジヤウヰ, 讓位, *(kurai wo yudzru.)* To abdicate the throne.

Jō-I, ジヤウイ, 上意, *n.* The mind, or wish of a lord.

JōJI,-*dzru*,-*ta*, ジヨウズル, 乘, *t. v.* To ride: fig. to avail one's self of an opportunity. *M'ma ni jōdzru*, to ride a horse. *Hen ni jōjite ikusa wo okosz,* took advantage of the event to declare war. *Yei ni* —, carried away with intoxication, under the influence of wine. Syn. NORU, TSZKE-KOMU.

JŌ-JITSZ, ヂヤウジツ, 定日, (*sadamareru hi.*) Fixed day, set day. *Sam-pachi wa kenjutsz no jō-jitsz,* the fixed days for fencing are the days of the month which have a 3 and 8 in them.

JŌ-JŌ, ジヤウジヤウ, 上上, Best, highest in quality. *Goku* —, the very best. — *kichi,* (idem.)

JŌ-JU, ジヤウジユ, 成就, To complete finish, perfect. *Iye no fushin — itash'ta,* have finished building the house. *Mada — senu,* not yet completed. *Negai ga — sh'ta,* my petition has been granted.
Syn. TOGERU, DEKI-AGARU.

JŌ-JUN, ジヤウジユン, 上旬, *n.* The first ten days of the month.

JŌ-KA, ジヤウカ, 城下, *n.* The town in the vicinity of a castle.

†JŌ-KAI, ジヤウカイ, 上界, *n.* The upper-world, paradise. (Bud.)

JŌ-KAKU, ヂヤウカク, 定格, *n.* The established rules.

JŌ-KI, ジヤウキ, 上氣, *n.* A rush of blood to the head. — *szru.* Syn. NOBOSE, JŌ-SHŌ.

JŌ-KI, ジヨウキ, 蒸氣, *n.* Steam. — *ga tatsz,* she steam begins to rise.
Syn. YU-GE.

JŌK'SHA, ジヨウキシヤ, 蒸氣車, *n.* A steam car, locomotive. — *michi,* a rail-road.

JŌK'SEN, ジヨウキセン, 蒸氣船, *n.* A steam-boat.

JŌ-KO, ジヤウコ, 上古, *n.* Remote antiquity. Syn. INISHIYE, MUKASHI.

†JŌ-KŌ, ジヤウカウ, 常香, *n.* Perpetual incense.

JŌ-KŌ-BAN, ジヤウカウバン, 常香盤, *n.* An incense dish, a censer,

JŌ-MAYE, ヂヤウマヘ, 錠, *n.* A lock.

†JŌ-ME, ジヨウメ, 乗馬, (*nori m'ma.*) *n.* A horse for riding.

JŌ-MI, ジヤウミ, 上巳, *n.* A holiday on the 3rd day of the 3rd month.

JŌ-MIYAKU, ジヤウミヤク, 靜脈, *n.* A vein.

†JŌ-MIYŌ, ヂヤウミヤウ, 定命, (*sadamatta inochi.*) *n.* The fixed period, or duration of life.

JŌ-MOKU, デウモク, 條目, *n.* Edict, proclamation, notice. Syn. KA-JŌ.

JŌPPARI, ジヤウツパリ, 情張, Obstinate, stubborn. — *na mono.*

JŌ-RAKU, ジヤウラク, 上洛, Going up to the Capital.

JO-RIKI, ジヨリキ, 助力, (*chikara wo taszkeru.*) *n.* Aid, help, assistance.

JŌ-RIKU, ジヤウリク, 上陸, Disembarking, landing from a ship, going ashore.
Syn. KUGA YE AGARU.

†JŌ-RIYAKU,–*szru,* ジヤウリヤク, 上略, To abridge by cutting off the beginning, or first and complimentary part of a letter.

JŌ-RŌ, ジヤウラフ, 上臈, *n.* A female officer in the house of a noble.

JŌ-RO, ヂヨラウ, 女郎, *n.* A prostitute, harlot. In ancient books pronounced *Jo-rō,* meaning a woman.

JŌRO, ジヨウロ, 噴壺, *n.* A kind of watering-pot.

JORO-JORO TO, ヂヨロヂヨロト, *adv.* Rippling of flowing water. — *nagareru,* to flow in a rippling current.

JŌRO-YA, ヂヨラウヤ, 女郎屋, *n.* A house of ill-fame.

JŌRURI, ジヤウルリ, 淨瑠璃, *n.* A kind of musical drama or song. — *wo kataru.*

JOSAINAI,–KI,–SHI,–KU, ジヨサイナイ, 無如在, Active, smart, careful, industrious. — *h'to.* Syn. YUDAN-NAI.

†JŌ-SEI, ジヤウセイ, 上世, *n.* Remote times, the fabulous age.

JŌ-SEI,–*szru,* ジヨセイ, 助成, (*taszkenasz.*) To aid, help, assist, to contribute.

JŌ-SEN, ジヨウセン, 乗舩, (*fune ni noru.*) To embark in a ship, to sail in a ship.

JŌ-SHIKI, ヂヤウシキ, 定式, *n.* Established rule, or custom.

JŌ-SHOKU, ヂヨジヨク, 女色, Beauty of women. — *ni mayō,* fascinated by a pretty woman.

†JO-SHI,–*szru,*–*sh'ta,* ジヨズル, 叙, *t.v.* To promote to a rank, to confer a brevet, or title upon.

†JO-SHI,–*szru,*–*sh'ta,* ヂヨスル, 恕, To excuse, to pardon, to bear patiently, to be indulgent to.

JŌ-SHŌ-JIN, ジヤウシヤウジン, 常精進, Perpetual abstinence from fish, or flesh of any kind.

JO-TAN, ジヨタン, 助炭, *n.* A screen, or fender placed over a brazier.

JO-YA, ヂヨヤ, 除夜, *n.* The last night of the old year, new year's eve.
Syn. ŌMISOKA NO YO.

JŌ-YAKU, ヂヤウヤク, 定約, *n.* A covenant, agreement, treaty, alliance. — *wo muszbu,* to make a treaty. — *wo tagau,* to break a treaty.
YAKU-SOKU.

†Jō-YE, ジヤウエ, 淨衣, *n.* Official robes worn by Buddhist priests.

†Jo-YO, ジヨヨ, 薯蕷, (*yama no imo.*) *n.* A long edible root growing wild.

JŌZA, ジヤウザ, 上坐, An upper, or high seat. A word affixed to the name of a deceased person by the Buddhists signifying his rank.

JŪ, ジフ, 十, (*tō.*) Ten. — *bu ichi*, one tenth. — *nin-nami*, an average kind of person.

JŪ, ヂユウ, 重, (*kasane.*) The numeral for things placed one above another, as boxes, stories of a tower, folds of cloth, the same also as *Jūbako*. *Ku jūno tō*, a nine storied pagoda.

JŪ-AKU, ジフアク, 十惡, *n.* The ten sins of the Buddhists. viz., *Seshohō*, killing any thing that has life. *Chūtō*, stealing. *Tonyoku*, covetousness. *Gu-chi*, foolishness. *Ja-in*, adultery. *Mōgo*, lying. *Kigo*, scoffing. *Akkō*, cursing. *Riyōzetsz*, double-tongued. *Shini*, anger.

JŪ-BAKO, ヂユウバコ, 重箱, *n.* A nest of boxes connected together by a handle.

JU-BAN, ジユバン, 襦袢, *n.* A shirt. Syn. HADAGI.

JŪ-BIN, ヂユウビン, 重便, (*kasanete no tayori.*) Another opportunity. — *ni mōshi-ageru*,. KŌ-BIN.

JŪ-BIYŌ, ヂユウビヤウ, 重病, (*omoki yamui*,) *n.* A severe sickness. Syn. TAI-BIYŌ.

JŪ-BUN, ジフブン, 十分, Full, as much as any thing will hold, abundant, plenty, enough. — *ni tabemash'ta*, have eaten to the full. — *nareba kobore yaszi*, when a thing is full it is easily spilt. — *ni aru*, have plenty, or enough. — *de wa nai*, it is not full. Syn. TAK'SAN, TAPPURI.

JŪ-DAI, ヂユウダイ, 重代, Many generations. — *no katana*, a sword come down from one's ancestors for several generations.

†JU-DAI, ジフダイ, 入內, To enter the Mikado's harem. — *wo nasz.*

JU-DŌ, ジユダウ, 儒道, (*kōshi no michi.*) The doctrines of Confucius, Confucianism.

JU-DZ, ジユズ, 數珠, *n.* A rosary. — *wo tszmaguru*, to tell the rosary.

JU-GAKU, ジユガク, 儒學, Studying the works of Confucius.

†JŪ-GI, ジフギ, 十義, *n.* The ten relative virtues of the Confucianists, viz., benevolence in the master, fidelity of servants, parental love, filial-piety, brotherly love, conjugal affection, kindness of the elder and submission of the younger.

†JU-GIYO, ジフギヨ, 入御, To go in, enter (used only of the Mikado.)

†JŪ-JAKU, ジウジヤク, 柔弱, Weak, feeble, unfit for service, invalid. Syn. NIUJAKU, YOAI.

JŪ-JI, ヂユウヂ, 住持, *n.* The superior, or rector of a Buddhist temple. Syn. OSHŌ.

JŪ-JŪ, ヂユウヂユウ, 重重, (*kasane gasane*) Repeated, over and over, again and again, time and again. Syn. DAN-DAN.

†JŪ-JUN, ジウジユン, 柔順, Gentle, mild, amiable.

JŪ-JUTSZ, ジウジユツ, 柔術, *n.* The art of wrestling, or of throwing others by sleight. Syn. YAWARA.

JŪ-KIYO, ヂユウキヨ, 住居, (*szmai*), *n.* Residence, dwelling.

†JUKKAI, ジユツクワイ, 述懷, (*omoi wo noberu*), Telling the thoughts. — *szru.*

†JUKKEI, ジユツケイ, 術計, (*tedate hakarigoto*), *n.* Plan, device, stratagem. — *wo tszkusz*, to exhaust every plan. Syn. BŌKEI, KEI-RIYAKU, SAKU.

JUKKON, ジユクコン, 熟懇, Intimate, friendly. — *no majiwari*, intimate friendship. Syn. NENGORO.

JUKU, ジユク, 塾, *n.* A private school, a study-room. *Dare no — ni itta deshi da*, whose school do you go to?

JUKU-DAN, ジユクダン, 熟談, To talk over fully or thoroughly.

JUKUSHI, *-sz*, *-sh'ta*, ジユクス, 熟, *i.v.* To be ripe, mature, mellow, thorough, perfect. *Kaki ga jukush'ta*, the persimmon is ripe. *Gakumon ga —*, ripe in learning. *Mada jukushimasen*, not yet ripe. Syn. UMU.

JUKU-SHI, ジユクシ, 熟柿, *n.* A ripe-persimmon.

†JUKU-SZI, ジユクスイ, 熟睡, *n.* A sound sleep.

†JŪ-MAN, ジユウマン, 充滿, (*michi-mitszru*), Full, abounding. — *szru*, to fill, abound. *Gunzei ga no yama ni — szru*, the army covered the plains and hills.

JUM-BAN, ジユンバン, 順番, Regular order, regular succession or turn, according to the number. — *ni tsztomeru*, to serve in regular order. — *de kuru*, to come in regular succession.

JU-MIYŌ, ジユミヤウ, 壽命, *n.* Life. *Nagai —*, long life. — *ga nobiru*, life is lengthened out. — *ga mijikai*, his life was short. Syn. INOCHI.

†JU-MOKU, ジユモク, 樹木, (*ki*), *n.* A tree.

JU-MON, ジユモン, 咒文, *n.* A written prayer, charm, spell or incantation. — *wo tonayeru*, to say over an incantation.

JŪ-MON-JI, ジフモンジ, 十文字, *n.* The character for ten, shape of a cross. — *ni kiru*, to cut into quarters, or crosswise. — *no yari*, a spear with a head in the shape of a cross.

†JUM-PITSZ, ジユンピツ, 潤筆, *n.* Money paid for writing.

JUM-PŪ, ジユンプウ, 順風, *n.* A favorable wind.

JUN, ジユン, 順, Regular, in order, in proper succession. — *ni yuku*, to go one after the other in regular order. — *wo midasz*, to derange the order. Syn. SHIDAI.

JUN-DATSZ,-*szru*, ジユンダツ, 順達, *t. v.* To pass from one to another in order. *O-fure wo* —, to pass around a government order.

†JUN-DŌ, ジユンダウ, 順道, *n.* The proper road, right way.

†JUN-GIYAKU, ジユンギヤク, 順逆, Fair and foul, favorable and unfavorable, forwards and backwards, right and left, direct and reverse. *Kuruma wo — ni mawasz*, to turn a wheel in a direct and reverse way.

JUN-GURI, ジユングリ, 順操, Regular order or turn, one after the other. — *ni h'to wo tszkau*, to employ men in regular turn.

†JŪ-NIN, ヂユウニン, 住人, (*szmu-h'to*), *n.* Inhabitant, resident.

JUNJI,-*ru*, or *dzru*,-*ta*, ジユンズル 準, To resemble, to compare, to liken. *Ano koto wa kore ni junjite shiru beshi*, that may be known by comparing it with this. Syn. NAZORŌ, KURABERU, YOSOYERU.

†JUN-JŌ, ジユンジヨウ, 準繩, *n.* A line and level, the laws.

JUN-JUN-NI, ジユンジユン, 順順, *adv.* In order, regular turn, regular succession, by turns, consecutively.

†JUN-KŌ,-*szru*, ジユンカウ, 巡行, (*meguri-aruku*), To go around. *Sho-sho wo* —, to go about in every place.

†JUN-K'WAN, ジユンクワン, 循環, *n.* Revolution, circulation. — *szru*, to revolve, circulate. *Tszki no* —, the revolution of the moon. *Chi no* —, circulation of the blood.

JŪ-NŌ, ジフノウ, 火斗, *n.* A fire-shovel.

JUNŌ, ジユナウ, 受納, To receive. *Okuri mono wo — tszkamatszri soro*, have received the present. *Go — kudasaru beku soro*, please receive it. Syn. UKERU, OSAMERU.

JUN-REI, ジユンレイ, 巡禮, (*meguri ogamu*), One who goes about from temple to temple to worship. — *szru*, to go about, &c. *Jin-ja bukkaku wo — szru.*

JUN-SAI, ジユンサイ, 蓴菜, *n.* A kind of water plant. Limnanthemum peltatum. Syn. NUNAWA.

JUN-SHI, ジユンシ, 殉死, Accompanying to Hades, as servants who commit suicide on the death of a master. *Chiu-shin wo sh'te — seshimuru oshimubeki kana.*

†JUN-SHOKU, ジユンシヨク, 潤色, Restoring a color to its original brightness. Syn. IRO-AGE.

†JUN-SZI, ジユンスイ, 純粋, Pure, unadulterated, unmixed.

JUN-TAKU, ジユンタク, 潤澤, (*uruoi uruosz*). To enrich, to promote prosperity, to benefit. *Jin-sei tami wo — sz.*

†JUNTŌ, ジユントウ, 順痘, *n.* Small-pox, that is uncomplicated, and goes through its regular stages.

JUNTŌ, ジユンタウ, 順當, Regular order or turn, regular succession.

JUN-YŌSHI, ジユンヤウシ, 順養子, *n.* A younger brother adopted as a son and heir.

JŪ-Ō, ジフワウ, 十王, *n.* The ten kings of Hades.

JU-RAI, ジフライ, 入來, To come, visit. *Go — kudasaru beku soro*, please make me a visit. Syn. KŌRAI, OIDE.

†JŪ-RAI, ジユウライ, 從來, *adv.* Originally, previously, hitherto, from the first. Syn. MOTOYORI, MAYE-KARA, ZENTAI.

†JŪ-RIN,-*szru*, ジウリン, 蹂躙, (*fumi nijiru*). To grind, or crush with the foot.

†JURIYO,-*szru*, ジユリヤウ, 受領, Giving the title of sovereign of a country to any one, as, *Hizen no kami wo — szru*, to give the title of Hizen no kami.

JU-RŌ, ジフラウ, 入牢, (*rōya ni ireru*), To send to gaol. *Zainin wo — szru.* — *mōshi-tszkeru*, to condemn to imprisonment.

JU-SHA, ジユシヤ, 儒者, *n.* A Confucianist, one who teaches and explains the writings of Confucius.

†JŪ-SHA, ジユウシヤ, 從者, *n.* Attendant, follower. — *no indz sono bungen ni szgubekaradz*, must not have a larger number of attendants than comports with his station. Syn. TOMO.

JŪSHI,-*sz*,-*sh'ta*, ヂユウス, 住, *i.v.* To reside, dwell. Syn. SZMU, ORU.

JŪ-SHO, ヂユウシヨ, 住所, *n.* A dwelling place, residence. Syn. SZMIKA.

JŪSHOKU,–szru, ヂユウシヨク, 住職, To reside in a monastery.

JŪ-SHOKU,–szru, ジユウソク, 充塞, (*michi fusagaru*). To obstruct, hinder, block up a way. *Ja-dō sei-jin no michi wo — szru.*

JŪ-TAKU, ヂユウタク, 住宅, (*szmika*), *n.* Dwelling, residence. Syn. JŪ-KIYO.

JUTSZ, ジユツ, 術, *n.* Art, science, rules, principles, artifice, trick. *Uma ni noru ni — ga aru,* there are rules to be observed in riding a horse. *Teki no — ni ochiru,* to fall into a trap laid by the enemy.

†JUYO, ジフヨ, 入輿, (*koshi wo ireru*). To place a daughter in a norimon to go to the bridegroom's house, (used only of the Emperor). *Muszme dairi ni — shimash'ta.*

†JUYO,–szru, ジユヨ, 授.與, (*sadzke atayeru*). To give.

K

KA, カ, 蚊, *n.* A musquito. — *ga sasz,* the musquito bites. — *wo ibusz,* to smoke off musquitoes. — *ni kuwareta,* bitten by musquitoes.

KA, カ, 香, *n.* Smell, odor, scent, perfume. — *wo kagu,* to smell a perfume. *Ī ka,* a delightful odor. *Kono cha-wan sake no ka ga aru,* this tea cup smells of *sake.* — *wo tomeru,* to perfume, scent. *Ka ga kikoyeru,* to perceive an odor. *Mitsz-bachi — wo sh'tō,* the bee scents the perfume. Syn. NIOI, KAORI, KŌBASHI.

KA, カ, 荷, *n.* A load for a man. *Midz ikka,* a load of water. *Szmi go-jikka,* fifty loads of charcoal. Syn. NINAI, NI.

KA, カ, 個, A classifier for periods of time, countries. *Ikka tszki,* one month. *Ni ka tszki,* two months. *San ga koku,* three provinces.

KA カ, 乎, An interrogative particle, = to the interrogation mark, ? *Atta ka,* have you found it? *Omaye Yedo ye oide nasaru ka,* are you going to Yedo? With a negative it expresses a strong affirmative. *Yoi h'to ja nai ka,* what a fine man he is. *Ammari no fushingi-na yume ja nai ka,* what an exceedingly strange dream.

A particle expressing doubt, if, whether, or. *Danna san kita ka miyo,* see if the master has come. *Ame furu ka furanu ka shire-nai,* I don't know whether it will rain or not. *Aru ka to omō,* I think there are. *Aru ka mo shirenai,* I don't know whether there are. *Itsz-ka watakushi no toko ye kita h'to da,* he came to my house some time ago. *Don-na yume da ka hanash'te kikase-na,* tell me what kind of a dream it was. Syn. YA.

KA-AI, or KAWAI, カアイ, 可愛, Darling, beloved, dear. *Ka-aikute nara-nai,* exceedingly dear. *Kore wa ichiban kawai ko da,* this is the child I love best. Syn. ITŌSHII.

KA-AIRASHII, or KAWAIRASHII,–KI,–KU,–U,–SA, カアイラシイ, 可愛敷, Darling, beautiful, pretty, lovely. — *kodomo,* a darling, or pretty child.

KA-AI-SŌ, or KAWAISŌ, カアイサウ, 可愛相, Pitiable, a condition to be pitied, cruel. — *na koto da,* it is a cruel thing, or a thing to be pitied.

KABA, カバ, 樺, A kind of flowering cherry.

KABAI,–*au*,–*atta*, カバフ, *t.v.* To cover or shield from danger or injury, to keep in safety, to protect, to screen, defend, guard, preserve. *Niwatori ko wo kabau,* the hen protects her chickens. *Daikon wo tszchi ni kabatte oku,* to put radishes in the ground to preserve them. Syn. ABAU, FUSEGU, MAMORU, KAKŌ.

KA-BAKARI, カバカリ, 斯許, This much, so much, such as this. — *no kane,* so much money. — *no daiji,* such an important matter as this. Syn KOREHODO.

KA-BAN, カバン, 加番, *n.* A reinforcement to the number of a guard or watch. — *szru,* to increase a guard.

KABANE, カバネ, 尸, *n.* A dead body, the carcass of a man. Syn. SHIGAI, SHIKABANE, NAKIGARA.

†KABANE, カバネ, 姓, *n.* The clan name, same as *Sei,* which see.

KABE, カベ, 壁, *n.* Plaster, a plastered wall. — *wo nuru,* to plaster. — *ni mimi ari, h'to no uwasa wo szru koto nakare,* there are ears in the wall, so don't tattle about others. — *goshi mono wo iu,* to talk to another through a wall.

KABE-NURI, カベヌリ, 壁塗, *n.* A plasterer, plastering. — *wo szru,* to be engaged in plastering. Syn. SAKANYA.

KABE-SH'TAJI, カベシタヂ, 壁下地, *n.* The lathing on which plaster is daubed. Syn. KOMAI.

KA-BI, カビ, 蚊火, *n.* Fire made to smoke away musquitoes.

KABI, カビ, 黴, *n.* Mould, mildew. *Pan ni — ga hayeta,* the bread is mouldy. — *ga dekita* it is mouldy.

KABI,–*ru*,–*ta*, カビル, 殕, *i.v.* To mould,

mildew. *Pan`ga kabimash'ta*, the bread has moulded.

KABI-KUSAI, カビクサイ, 黴臭, Mouldy and stinking.

KABI-TSZKI, *-ku, -ita*, カビツク, 黴著, To be mouldy.

KABOCHA, カボチャ, 番南瓜, *n.* A pumpkin, named after the country Cambojia, from which it was first brought. Syn. TŌNASZ.

†KA-BU, カブ, 歌舞, *(utai-mai.)* Singing and dancing, as in an opera.

KABU, カブ, 株, *n.* The stump of a tree. A government license, a guild, or fraternity of persons engaged in the same kind of business; a habit or custom to which one is addicted. *Ki no* —, stump of a tree. — *wo morau*, to get a license. — *wo uru*, to sell one's license. *Toiya no* — *ni hairu*, to enter the guild of commission merchants. *O* — *wo iu*, to say something that one is in the habit of saying.

KABU, カブ, 蕪菁, *n.* A turnip.

KABUKI, カブキ, 歌舞伎, *n.* A kind of opera.

KABUKI, カブキ, 冠木, *n.* A horizontal piece of timber over a gate, a lintel.

KABUKI-MON, カブキモン, 冠木門, *n.* A gate with a lintel over it.

†KA-BUN, カブン, 下問, *(shimo ni tō.)* Inquiring of a low person. *Kunshi wa* — *wo hajidz*, the superior man is not ashamed to inquire of his inferiors.

KABURA, カブラ, Same as *Kabu.* A turnip.

KABURAYA, カブラヤ, 鏑箭, *n.* An arrow with a head shaped like a turnip having a hole in it, which causes it to sing as it flies.

KABURE, *-ru, -ta*, カブレル, *i.v.* To be infected, to have an eruption from coming in contact with others or with something poisonous. *Urushi ni* —, poisoned with lacquer. *Kōyaku ni* —, to have an eruption on the skin after using a plaster. *Omaye gin-san ni* —, you have caught that habit from *Gin-san.* Syn. MAKERU, UTSZRU.

KABURI, *-ru, -tta*, カブル, 冠, *t.v.* To put on the head, to cover over with, to cap. *Kasa wo* —, to put on a hat. *Men wo* —, to put on a mask. *Ō ame de ine ga midz wo* —, the rice is covered with water from the heavy rain. *H'to no tszmi wo kaburanu yō ni kokoro wo tszku beshi*, take care that you be not involved in the crimes of others. *Yama ga kumo wo* —, the mountain is covered with a cloud. Syn. KADZKU.

KABURI-FURI, *-ru, -tta*, カブリフル, 掉頭, *i.v.* To shake the head in dissent.

KABURI-MONO, カブリモノ, 冠物, *n.* A covering for the head, bonnet, cap.

KABURO, カブロ, 禿, *n.* A young girl who wears her hair long.

KABUSARI, *-ru, -tta*, カブサル, 被, *i. v.* To have the head or top covered, to be overspread, capped, sheltered, protected, screened. *Kumo ga yama ni kabusaru*, the the mountain is capped with a cloud. *Oya ga ko wo sh'kareba baba ga* —, when the parent scolds the child he is screened by the grandmother.

KABUSE, *-ru, -ta*, カブセル, 覆, Caust. of *Kaburi.* To cover, or spread over the head of another, to impute, charge, blame. *H'to ni te-nugui wo* —, to cover a person's head with a handkerchief. *H'to ni tszmi wo* —, to lay one's crimes to the charge of another. Syn. Ō-Ō, KISERU, KADZKERU.

KABUTA, カブタ, Same as *Kabu*, a stump.

KABUTO, カブト 鍪, or 兜, *n.* A helmet.

KABUTO-GANE, カブトガネ, 兜金, *n.* The metal cap on the end of a sword handle.

KACHI, カチ, 徒, On foot, walking. — *de yuku*, to go on foot. — *samurai*, the guards that walk on each side of the *norimon* of the *Shōgun. Kachi-metszke*, a kind of censor or spy. — *de kawa wo wataru*, to ford a river on foot.

KACHI, *-tsz, -tta*, カツ, 勝, *t.v.* (governing the dative.) To conquer, win, defeat, overcome, gain the victory, to control. *H'to ni katsz*, to defeat another. *Onore ni* —, to conquer self, deny one's self. *Ri ni katte hi ni ochiru*, having the right on one's side, yet succumb to another. *Katsz ni noru*, taking advantage of victory.

KACHI, カチ, 勝, *n.* A victory, advantage, superiority. — *wo toru*, to gain a victory.

KACHI-KACHI, カチカチ, *adv.* The sound of hard things striking together, clashing, clacking, clicking.

KACHI-DOKI, カチドキ, 勝鬨, *n.* The shout of victory. — *wo ageru.* Syn. TOKI NO KOYE.

KACHI-HADASHI, カチハダシ, 徒跣, Without a horse and barefoot. — *ni naru*, to be horseless and barefoot.

KACHI-HOKORI, *-ru, -tta*, カチホコル, 勝誇, *i.v.* To be puffed up by victory.

KACHI-GURI, カチグリ, 搗栗, *n.* Dried chesnut kernels.

KACHI-JI, カチヂ, 歩路, By land. *Fune de yuku ka* — *wo yuku ka*, are you going by sea or by land? Syn. KUGA, RIKU.

KACHI-MAKE, カチマケ, 勝負, *n.* Lose and win, victory and defeat. — *wo arasō*, to dispute about who is the winner.

†KACHI-MŌDE, カチマウデ, 徒詣, *n.* Visiting the temples on foot.

KACHI-MUSHA, カチムシャ, 徒武者, *n.* A foot soldier.

KACHIN, カチン, 餠, *n.* Bread made of pounded rice, same as *Mochi.*

KACHI-NIGE, カチニゲ, 勝逃, *n.* Having won to run away, (as a gambler.)

KACHI-WATARI, カチワタリ, 徒渉, *n.* Wading across, crossing on foot. — *wo szru.*

KACHŌ, カチヤウ, 蚊帳, *n.* Musquito-net. Syn. KAYA.

‖KADAMI,-*mu*,-*nda*, カダム, *t. v.* To screen, or protect from injury, fend off. *Kidz wo* —, to protect a sore, (from being hurt.)

KADEN, カデン, 家傳, *n.* Any thing transmitted in a family from one generation to another. *Kono kuszri wa* — *de gozarimasz.*

KADO, カド, 角, *n.* A corner, angle, a flint. *Shi-hō no* —, the angles of a square. — *wo tatete mono wo iu*, to speak sharply. — *ga toreta h'to*, a good natured person. *Kado-ishi*, a flint. Syn. SZMI.

KADO, カド, 門, *n.* The outside entrance or door of a house. — *wo hiraku*, to open the door. — *no to wo shimeru*, to shut the outside door. — *chigai szru*, to mistake the door. — *okuri szru*, to accompany a guest to the door, to take leave. — *ye deru*, to go to the gate, also to go out into the yard. Syn. MON.

‖KADO, カド, 鯟, *n.* (*kadz no ko.*) A kind of fishroe.

KADO, カド, 廉, *n.* An item, particular. *Kono* — *ni yotte toga wo mōshi-tszkeru*, we judge him guilty on account of this one charge. *Jō-moku no kado-kado ni kokorodzki mōszbeku*, should give good heed to the various articles of the edict.

†KA-DŌ, カダウ, 歌道, (*uta no michi.*) Rules of poetry.

KADO-BI, カドビ, 門火, *n.* A fire kindled at the door, after the death of a person, to light the way of the soul to the next world.

KADO-DE, or KADO-IDE, カドデ, 首途, Leaving home, setting out on a journey. — *wo szru.*
Syn. SHUTTATSZ.

KADO-GUCHI, カドグチ, 門口, *n.* Entrance, or door of a house.

KADO-KADOSHII,-KI,-KU, カドカドシイ, 稜稜, Crabbed, rough, peevish.

†KADOMO, カドモ, Contract. of *Keredomo*, Although.

KADO-MUKAI, カドムカヒ, 門迎, *n.* Meeting a guest at the door. — *ni deru*, to go to the door to meet a guest.

KADO-NAMI, カドナミ, 門並, Each house in order, house by house, from door to door. *Kojiki* — *ni moratte aruku*, the beggar goes from door to door begging.

KADOWAKASHI,-*sz*,-*sh'ta*, カドハカス, 勾引, *t.v.* To kidnap. *Kodomo wo kadowasz*, to kidnap a child.

KADZ, カズ, 數, *n.* Number. — *wo mite okure*, see how many. — *kagiri nashi*, infinite in number. — *naranu*, unimportant, of little consequence. *Kadz-kadz*, many, numerous. — *ni ireru*, to include in the number.

KADZKE,-*ru*,-*ta*, カヅケル, 被, *t. v.* To lay over the head of another, lay to the charge of another, impute. *Waga toga wo h'to ni kadzkeru*, to lay one's crimes to the charge of another. *Koromo wo* —, to spread a coat over the head of another. Syn. KABUSERU, OWASERU.

KADZKE-MOMO, カヅケモノ, 被物, *n.* A reward, or present of flowers, &c., in acknowledgment of merit. Syn. HIMOTSZ, HŌBI.

KADZKI,-*ku*,-*ita*, カヅク, 被, *t.v.* To cover the head. *Kinu wo* —, to veil the face. Syn. KABURU.

KADZRA, カヅラ, 葛, *n.* A creeping vine.

KADZRA, カヅラ, 鬘, *n.* A wig. — *wo kaburu*, to put on a wig.

†KA-FŪ, カフウ, 家風, (*Iye no narawashi.*) The customs, or rules of a family.

KAGAMARI,-*ru*,-*tta*, カガマル, 屈, *i.v.* To be bent, crooked. *Toshi-yotte se ga kagamatta*, the back is bent with age. *Yubi ga kagamaranu*, the finger is stiff.
Syn. MAGARU.

KAGAME,-*ru*,-*ta*, カガメル, 屈, *t. v.* To bend, to crook, stoop, bow. *Koshi wo* —, to bend the back. *Yubi wo* —, to bend the finger. *Bō wo* —, to bend a pole. *Kakande mon wo kuguru*, to stoop and pass through a gate. Syn. MAGERU, YUGAMERU.

KAGAMI,-*mu*,-*nda*, カガム, 屈, *i. v.* To bend, to crook, to stoop, to bow. *Koshi ga kaganda*, back is bent. *Kusa no aida ni kakande oru*, hiding amongst the grass. *Yubi ga kagande nobi-masen*, the finger is bent and cannot be extended.

KAGAMI, カガミ, 鏡, *n.* A mirror, looking-glass; fig. the head of a barrel, an example, or pattern. — *ni utszru*, to look at one's self in a mirror. — *ga kumotta*, the mirror is dim. — *ni kage wo utszsz*, to reflect the image of any thing in a mirror. — *no saya*, the case of a mirror. — *no dai*, stand for a mirror. *Taru no — wo nuku*, to take out the head of a barrel. *H'to no — to naru*, to be an example for others. *Kagami-do*, a shining door, clean and bright door. *Kagami-ita*, a clean bright board. — *wo togu*, to polish a mirror.

KAGAMI-MOCHI, カガミモチ, 鏡餅, *n.* A cake of rice bread, (large and round like a mirror.)

KAGAMI-SHI, カガミシ, 鏡師, *n.* A maker of mirrors.

KAGARI,-*ru*,-*ita*, カガル, 絓, *t. v.* To embroider with long stitches, to lace together by sewing, to darn, cross-stitch. *Mari ni ume no hana wo kagaru*, to work the figure of a plum-blossom on a ball. *Ho wo —*, to lace the edges of a sail together.

KAGARI, カガリ, 篝, *n.* A kind of iron brazier for burning torches in.

KAGARIBI, カガリビ, 篝火, *n.* A torch-light.

KAGASHI, カガシ, 案山子, *n.* A scare-crow made in the shape of a man.

KAGAYAKI,-*ku*,-*ita*, カガヤク, 輝, *i.v.* To be bright, glisten, glitter, sparkle, shine, to be brilliant, effulgent. *Hi ga kagayaku*, the sun is bright. *Asa hi ni kagayaku tszrugi no inadzma*, the lightning of their swords flashed in the morning sun.
Syn. HIKARU, TERU.

KAGAYAKI, カガヤキ, 輝, *n.* Lustre, brilliancy, glory, effulgence, brightness. *Hi, tszki, hoshi nado no —*, the glitter of the sun, moon, or stars. Syn. HIKARI.

KAGAYAKI-WATARI,-*ru*,-*tta*, カガヤキワタル, 輝渡, *i. v.* To shine all around, to shine across.

KA-GE, カゲ, 鹿毛, (*sh'ka no ke.*) Deer-color, chestnut color. — *no m'ma*, a horse of the color of a deer.

KAGE,-*ru*,-*ta*, カゲル, 毀, see *Kake, ru.* Nicked, notched, flawed.

KAGE, カゲ, 景, *n.* Shade, shadow, reflection, light; (fig.) secret, unseen; influence, power, beneficence, help. *Hi, tszki, hoshi, tomoshibi nado no —*, the light of the sun, moon, stars, lamp, &c. *Yama, ki iye, h'to nado no —*, the shade of a mountain, &c. — *ni naru*, to be in one's light. — *wo utszsz*, to reflect the image of anything. *Kage de kiku*, to hear in secret. — *nagara uketamawaru*, to hear any thing privately, or whilst not seen. *O kage de naorimash'ta*, cured by your kind influence, or power. *Tenshi no o-kage*, the beneficent influence of the Mikado.

KAGE-BOSHI, カゲボシ, 陰乾, *n.* Dried in the shade.

KAGE-BŌSHI, カゲボウシ, 影法師, *n.* The shadow of a person.

KAGE-GOTO, カゲゴト, 陰言, *n.* Talking of one behind his back. — *wo iu*, to talk of any one in secret.

KAGEMA, カゲマ, 男娼, *n.* A boy used by sodomists.

KAGEN, カゲン, 加減, (*mash'tari herash'tari*), *n.* Adding medicines to, or taking them from, a prescription to suit the condition of a patient; the proportion of the ingredients in any compound; the seasoning, flavoring, taste; the feelings or condition of body. *O-isha sama — no o-kuszri*, the carefully prepared medicine of the doctor. *Kuszri wo — sh'te tszkawasz*, to send medicine that has been carefully compounded so as to suit the patient's condition. *Danna sama — warukute fusete oru*, master not feeling well is lying down. *Kono meshi midz — ga warui*, there is too little (or too much) water in this rice.
Syn. AMBAI, SASHI-HIKI.

KAGERI,-*ru*,-*tta*, カゲル, 陰, *i.v.* To be obscured, shaded. *Hi ga kumo de kagetta*, the sun is obscured by a cloud.

KAGERŌ, カゲロフ, 陽焰, *n.* The waving or flickering appearance of the air rising from a hot surface in the summer.

KAGERŌ, カゲロフ, 蜉蝣, *n.* A kind of insect, said to begin to live in the morning and to die at night.

KAGEZEN, カゲゼン, 陰膳, *n.* Food set away for an absent one. — *wo szyeru*, to put food away for one who is absent.

KAGI, カギ, 鍵, *n.* A key.

KAGI, カギ, 鉤, *n.* A hook. *Ago wo — ye kakeru*, (to hang the chin on a hook) neglecting business, leading a dissolute life, and coming to poverty.

KAGI,-*gu*,-*ida*, カグ, 齅, *t.v.* To smell. *Hana wo —*, to smell a flower.

KAGI-BANA, カギバナ, 齅鼻, *n.* Smelling, scenting. *Inu ga — wo sh'te oru*, the dog is scenting something.

KAGI-DASHI,-*sz*,-*sh'ta*, カギダス, 齅出, *t.v.* To scent, to find out by smelling.

KAGI-GUSZRI, カギグスリ, 薫藥, *n.* Fumigating medicines. Errhine.
Syn. IBUSHI-GUSZRI, KUN-YAKU.

KAGI-NARE,-*ru*,-*ta*, カギナレル, *t.v.* Accustomed to the smell of any thing.

KAGIRI,-*ru*,-*tta*, カギル, 限, *i.v.* To be limited, ended, bounded, confined, restricted. *Inochi kagiritatakau*, to fight till death. *Kore ni kagitte*, this only, this alone. *Ano h'to ni kagitte uso wo iwanai*, that man only will not lie. *Iki wo kagiri ni hashiru*, to run until out of breath. *Omaye ni* —, you alone can do it.
Syn. SADAMARU, KIMARU.

KAGIRI, カギリ, 限, *n.* The limit, end, utmost extent. *Koye no — ni naki-sakebu*, cried out at the top of his voice. *Kadz — wa nai*, innumerable. *Inochi no* —, the end of life. *Kami no chikara ni — wa nai*, there is no limit to the power of God. Syn. SAIGEN, KIWA, HATESHI.

KAGI-TABAKO, カギタバコ, *n.* Snuff.

KAGI-TSZKE,-*ru*,-*ta*, カギツケル, 鼻着, *t.v.* Accustomed to the smell, to perceive by the smell. *Niyoi wo kagitszkete kuru*, to come attracted by the smell.

KA-GIYŌ, カギヤウ, 家業, *n.* Business, occupation, or calling of a family.
Syn. SHŌBAI, SHOKU-BUN, SZGIWAI, TOSEI.

KAGO, カゴ, 駕籠, *n.* A sedan chair, or basket made of bamboo for riding in. — *ni noru*, to ride in a sedan-chair. — *wo katszgu*, or — *wo kaku*, to carry a sedan chair. — *wo yatoi*, to hire a sedan chair. Syn. NORIMONO.

KAGO, カゴ, 籠, *n.* A basket, a cage. *Tori no* —, a bird cage.

†KA-GO, カゴ, 加護, *n.* Care, providence, protection (of the gods.) *Kami no — de taszkaru.* Syn. MAMORU.

KAGOJI, カゴジ, 雙鈎, *n.* A character, or word written in outline.

KAGO-KAKI, カゴカキ, 舁夫, *n.* Chair-bearers.

†KA-GOTO, カゴト, 假言, A pretext, excuse, same as *Kakotszke.*

KAGOYA, カゴヤ, 駕籠屋, *n.* A place where norimons are kept for hire.

KA-GU, カグ, 家具, *n.* House furniture. Syn. JŪ-MOTSZ.

KAGURA, カグラ, 神樂, (*kami wo nagasameru*), *n.* A theatrical exhibition in front of a temple to entertain the Kami; also persons wearing the head of a lion as a mask, who go about the streets dancing and begging. *Benten sama ye o kagura wo ageru. Kado nami — wo mawasz.*

KA-HAN,-*szru*, カハン, 加判, To endorse, to fix one's seal to a paper and go security.

KAHAN-NIN, カハンニン, 加判人, *n.* An endorser, security.

†KA-HI, カヒ, 可否, Good or bad, good or not, should or not. — *wo tszmabiraka ni sedz*, whether it is good or not is not fully known. Syn. ZEHI, YOSHI-ASHI, ZEN-AKU, KIKKIYŌ.

†KAHITSZ, カヒツ, 加筆, (*fude wo kuwayeru*). To correct a manuscript.

KA-HŌ, カハフ, 家法, (*Iye no narawashi*), *n.* The customs, or rules of a house; a secret medicine or medical prescription.

KAHODO, カホド, 斯程, (*kore hodo*). This much, so much, so much as this.

KAI, カヒ, 甲斐, *n.* Profit, advantage, use, benefit. — *ga nai*, no advantage. *Kuszri nonda — ga nai*, no benefit from having taken the medicine. *Shimbō sh'ta — ga aru*, I enjoy now the benefit of patience. Syn. YEKI.

KAI, カイ, 櫂, *n.* An oar, paddle. — *wo tszkau*, to work an oar.

KAI, カイ, (com. coll for *Kayu*). *n.* Gruel.

KAI, カヒ, 貝, *n.* A clam, any small bivalve.

KAI, カイ, 蓋, The numeral used in counting hats. *Kasa-ikkai, nikai, sangai, &c.*

KAI, カイ, 階, The numeral used in counting the stories of a house. *Ni-kai, sangai dzkuri no iye.*

KAI, カイ, 戒, (*Imashime*), *n*- The prohibitions, or commandments of the Buddhists. *Go-kai wo tamotsz*, to keep the five Buddhist commandments. *Ha-kai no sō*, a priest who breaks the commandments. *Kaigiyō szru*, to practice the commandments. — *wo yaburu*, to break &c.,

KAI, カイ, 海, (*umi*), *n.* The ocean, sea. *Tō-kai*. The eastern ocean.

KAI,-*au*,-*atta*, カフ, 買, *t.v.* To buy. *Katte koi*, go and buy. *Kau h'to ga nai*, nobody will buy it. *Sakana wo kai ni itta*, has gone to buy fish. *Omaye uru nara kaimashō*, if you will sell I shall buy it. *Kai-masen*, I will not buy. *Yaszku katta*, bought it cheap.

KAI,-*au*,-*atta*, カフ, 飼, *t.v.* To keep animals. *Ushi, m'ma, inu, neko, niwatori nado wo* —. *Ano h'to m'ma sampiki katte oru*, that man keeps three horses. *Kore wa omaye no katte oku inu ka*, is this your dog? *Tora wo katte urei wo nokosz*, (prov.) if you keep a tiger you will have nothing but trouble.

KAI,-*au*,-*atta*, カフ, *t.v.* To put anything under, against, or between something else in order to support, brace, prop, level, or stay it. *To ni shimbari wo kau,* to put a brace against a door to keep it shut.

KAI-AWASE, カヒアハセ, 鬪貝, *n.* A kind of game played with shells.

KAI-BA, カイバ, 海馬, *n.* The sea-horse; Hippocampus.

KAI-BA, カヒバ, 飼葉, *n.* Horse feed.

KAI-BIYAKU, カイビヤク, 開闢, *n.* Creation, the first organization of the visible universe, supposed to be spontaneous. *Ten chi kaibiyaku i-rai,* from the creation of heaven and earth. — *kono kata,* since the beginning of the world.

†KAI-BŌ, カイバウ, 解剖, *n.* Anatomical dissection. *H'to no karada wo — szru,* to dissect the human body, in order to study its anatomy.

†KAI-BŌ, カイバウ, 海防, *n.* Defence of the sea-coast. — *wo gen-jū ni szru,* to strengthen the sea-coast defences,

KA-IBUSHI, カイブシ, 蚊薫, *n.* A smoke made to keep off musquitoes. — *wo szru.* Syn. KAYARI.

KAI-CHIU, カイチウ, 海中, (*umi no naka*). In the sea or ocean. — *ni aru mono,* the things that are in the sea.

KAI-CHŌ, カイチヤウ, 開帳, (*Tobari wo hiraku*). The ceremony of opening the shrine in which idols are kept, for the public to see and worship. *Kon-nichi kara — de gozarimasz.*

†KAI-DAI, カイダイ, 海内, *n.* All within the four seas, the whole empire of Japan.

†KAI-DASHI, *-sz, -sh'ta,* カヒダス, 買出, *t.v.* To buy up goods or produce from the producer or manufacturer. Syn. SHI-IRERU, SHI-KOMU.

KAI-DARUI, -KI, -KU, -SHI, -Ū, -SA, カイダルイ, Torpid, dull, dead, heavy, languid, sluggish. *Kaidarukute nobi wo szru,* to feel sluggish and stretch one's self. Syn. DARUI.

KAI-DATE, カイダテ, 搔楯, *n.* A parapet or breast-work made by joining large wooden shields together.

KAIDE, カヘデ, 楓, *n.* A kind of maple.

KAI-DŌ, カイダウ, 海棠, *n.* The Pyrus spectabilis.

KAI-DŌ, カイダウ, 海道, *n.* A road near the sea coast.

KAIGAI-SHII, -KI, -KU, -Ū, -SA, カビガヒシイ, 甲斐甲斐敷, Spoken in admiration or praise of something bold, heroic or useful, done by one of whom it could hardly be expected.

KAI-GAN, カイガン, 海岸, *n.* Sea-shore, sea-coast. — *dōri,* a street along the sea-shore. Syn. UMIBATA.

KAI-GARA, カヒガラ, 貝殼, *n.* Empty sea-shells.

KAI-GEN, カイゲン, 改元, Altering the name of the year or era. *Nengō wo — szru.*

KAI-GEN, カイゲン, 開眼, (*me wo hiraku*). The ceremony of consecrating an idol, when the god is supposed to take possession of it. *Mokuzō wo — szru.*

†KAI-GIYŌ, カイギヤウ, 戒行, Practising the five Buddhist commandments.

†KAI-GIYŌ, カイゲフ, 開業, Setting up, or commencing business, opening shop.

KAI-GURI, *-ru, -tta,* カイグル, 搔操, *t. v.* To haul in hand over hand. *Tako wo —,* to haul in a kite. *Ikari wo —,* to haul in an anchor. *Tadzna kaiguri,* hauling tight the reins. Syn. TAGURU.

KAI-HAMARI, *-ru, -tta,* カヒハマル, 買陷, *i.v.* To buy goods at a losing or extravagant price, to make a bad purchase.

KAI-HAN, *-szru,* カイハン, 開版, To cut on blocks, to publish by cutting on blocks. *Shomotsz wo — szru.*

KAI-HEN, カイヘン, 海邊, (*umi no hotori*). *n.* Near the sea, sea-coast.

KAI-HŌ, カイハウ, 介抱, (*taszke idaku.*) Nursing the sick, waiting, or attending on as a nurse. — *szru,* to nurse. *Ichi ni —, ni ni kuszri,* nursing is of more importance than physic. Syn. KAM-BIYŌ.

KAI-HŌ-NIN, カイハウニン, 介抱人, *n.* A nurse, one who attends on a sick person.

KAI-HOTSZ, カイホツ, 開發, Opening, or clearing new ground for cultivation. *Denji wo —.*

KAII, -KI, -KU, カイイ, (coll. for *Kayui,*) 癢, Itching. *Kaii tokoro wo kaku.* to scratch an itching place. *Kaikute ike-nai,* I can't endure the itching.

KAI-IDAKI, *-ku, -ita,* カイイダク, 搔抱, *t.v.* To take in the arms, embrace.

KAI-IRE, *-ru, -ta,* カヒイレル, 買入, *t.v.* To buy up, and lay in goods.

†KAI-JIN, カイヂン, 凱陣, The return of an army.

†KAI-KA, カイカ, 改嫁, To marry into another family, (said of a woman whose husband is dead, or of one divorced.)

KAI-KABURI, *-ru, -tta,* カヒカブル, 買被, *i.v.* To buy at an extravagant price, to be taken-in in the purchase of any thing.

KAI-KAKU, カイカク, 改革, (*aratame*). To change, reform, alter. *Sei-dō wo — szru,* to reform the administration of government.

KAI-KI, カイキ, 開基, (*motoi wo hiraku.*) *n.* The founder, originator, (of a temple or sect). *Kono tera no — wa nan to iu sō da,* what priest founded this temple?

KAI-KI, カイキ, 改機, *n.* A kind of glossy silk, lustring.

KAIKO, カヒコ, 蠶, *n.* A silk-worm.

†KAI-KŌ, カイコウ, 開港, (*Minato wo hiraku.*) To open a port to trade. *Yokohama wo — szru.*

†KAI-KOKU, カイコク, 開國, (*Kuni wo hiraku,*) To open a country to foreign incourse.

KAI-KOMI,-*mu*,-*nda*, カヒコム, 買込, *t.v.* To buy up and lay in goods.

KAI-KOMI,-*mu*,-*nda*, カイコム 掻込, *t.v.* To hold the spear in position for charging. *Yari wo kowaki ni —,* to hold the spear close to the side as in charging.

†KAI-KU, カイク, 海狗, (*ottosei*), *n,* The seal.

KAIMAMI, イイマミ, 垣間見, *n.* Looking through a crack. — *wo szru..*

†KAI-MEI, カイメイ, 改名, (*na wo kayeru*). Changing the name.

†KAI-MEN, カイメン, 海面, (*umi no omote*). *n.* The surface of the sea.

KAI-MIYŌ, カイミヤウ, 戒名, *n.* The name given by the Buddhists to a deceased person.

KAI-MOKU, カイモク, 皆目, *adv.* All, entirely, wholly, (with a negative). — *yaku-ni-tatanu,* wholly useless.
Syn. MINA.

KAI-MOTOME,-*ru*,-*ta*, カヒモトメル, 買求, *t. v.* To get by purchase.

KAI-MU, カイム, 皆無, (*mina nashi*). Not the least, not any. *Ko-toshi ine ga kai-mu de wa komaru,* in trouble because this year the rice has failed.

KAI-NA, カイナ, 臑, *n.* The arm from the shoulder to the elbow.

KAI-NAI,-KI,-KU,-Ō, カヒナイ, 無甲斐, Weak, feeble, unprofitable, useless.

KAI-NEN, カイネン, 改年, (*aratamatta toshi*). *n.* The new year.

KAI-NOKOSHI,-*sz*,-*sh'ta*, カヒノコス, 買殘, *i.v.* To leave a part unbought; to forget to buy.

KAI-NUSHI, カヒヌシ, 買主, *n.* The buyer, purchaser. Syn. KAI-TE.

KAI-OKI,-*ku*,-*ita*, カヒヲク, 買置, *t. v.* To buy and keep, or lay-by.

KAI-OKI,-*ku*,-*ita*, カヒヲク, 畜置, *t. v.* To keep, as domestic animals. *Uma nihiki wo —,* to keep two horses.

KAIRAGI, カイラキ, 鰄, *n.* A kind of fish.

KAI-RIKU, カイリク, 海陸, (*umi to kuga*). Sea and land.

†KAI-RIYŌ-MAN-ZOKU, カイリヤウマンゾク, 皆令滿足, (*mina michitarashime tamaye*) Used at the conclusion of a prayer Grant all my request. (Bud).

†KAI-RŌ, カイラウ, 偕老, (*tomoni oiru*). Growing old together, (of husband and wife). — *dō-ketsz no chigiri,* a union last ing down to old age and unbroken in the grave.

KAI-SAN, カイサン, 開山, (*yama wo hiraku*). *n.* The founder of a temple, or sect. Syn. KAI-KI.

†KAI-SEI,-*szru*, カイセイ, 改正, (*aratame tadasz*). To correct.

KAI-SHAKU,-*szru*, カイシヤク, 介錯, To cut off the head of one who is in the act of committing *harakiri.* — *nin,* the person who aids one who is committing *harakiri* by cutting off his head.

†KAI-SHAKU,-*szru*, カイシヤク, 妎妁, To act as an assistant, or attendant.

KAI-SHIKI, カイシキ, 皆式, *adv.* All, wholly, entirely. — *muda na mono.*
Syn. MINA.

KAI-SHIME,-*ru*,-*ta*, カヒシメル, 買占, *t.v.* To buy up goods and keep them, in order to raise the price. *Ni wo kaishimete sōba wo ageru.*

KAISŌ, カイサウ, 海葱, *n.* Squills.

KAITA, カヒタ, Pret. of *Kaki.*

KAI-TAI,-KI,-KU,-Ō,-SHI, カヒタイ, 買度, Wish to buy. *Kaitaku omō,* to feel like buying. *Kaitaku nai,* do not wish to buy.

KAITE, カヒテ, The gerund of *Kaku.*

KAITE, カヒテ, 買人, *n.* A buyer, customer. *Kono mise — ga ōi,* this shop has many customers.

KAITSZBURI, カヒツブリ, 鸊鷉, *n.* The widgeon.
Syn. NIWO.

KAI-TSKAMI,-*mu*,-*nda*, カイツカム, 掻抓, *t. v.* To seize hold of, to catch up in the hand.

KAI-TSZKURAI,-*ō*,-*ōta*, カイツクロフ, 掻繕, *t. v.* To arrange the clothes, to pick and adjust the feathers, as a bird.

KAI-TSZMAMI,-*mu*,-*nda*, カイツマム, 掻撮, *t. v.* To make extracts, to select passages from a book, to epitomize, abridge.

KAI-UN, カイウン, 開運, (*un wo hiraku.*) A change of fortune for the better, a change from bad luck to good.

†KAI-YEKI, カイエキ, 改易, (*aratame kayeru.*) To change, alter.

KAI-ZOKU, カイゾク, 海賊, *n.* A pirate.

KAI-ZOYE, カイゾヘ, 介副, *n.* An assistant, attendant, a bridesmaid.

KA-JI, カジ, 家事, *n.* Household matters, family affairs.

KAJI, カヂ, 楫, *n.* A rudder, the helm. — *wo toru,* to steer. — *wo hineru,* to turn the helm. *Omo-kaji,* helm to the starboard. *Torikaji,* helm to the port side.

KAJI, カヂ, 梶, *n.* The paper mulberry.

KAJI, カヂ, 鍜冶, *n.* A smith, blacksmith. *Katana-kaji,* a swordsmith.

KAJI, カヂ, 加持, *n.* Prayers said by a priest for the sick. — *wo szru.*

KAJIKA, カジカ, 川鹿, *n.* A kind of small river fish, said to sing.

KAJIKE,*–ru,–ta,* カジケル, 憔悴, *t. v.* To be cold, benumbed, to be lean, gaunt emaciated.

KAJIME, カヂメ, 搗布, *n.* Kind of sea weed. Syn. SAGARAME.

KA-JIN, カジン, 歌人, (*Uta yomi,*) *n.* A poet.

†KAJIN, カジン, 佳人, *n.* A handsome person.

KIJIRI.*–ru,–tta,* カジル, 耗, To gnaw, or bite any thing hard.

KAJI-TORI, カヂトリ, 揖取, *n.* A helmsman, steersman.

†KA-JITSZ, カジツ, 夏日, (*natsz no hi.*) *n.* A summer day.

†KA-JITSZ, カジツ, 暇日, (*itoma no hi.*) A holiday, or day of leisure.

KAJIYA, カヂヤ, 鍜冶, *n.* A blacksmith.

KĀ-KĀ, カアカア, *n.* Caw, the cry of a crow. *Karasz ga — to naku.*

KAKA, カカ, *n.* Mother, (used by children,) also, wife. *Kochi no — san,* my wife.

KAKADŻ, KAKANU, or KAKANAI, カカズ, The neg. of *Kaki.*

†KAKADZRAI,*–au,–atta,* カカヅラフ, 拘, *i. v.* same as *Kakawari.*

KAKAGE,*–ru,–ta,* カカゲル, 揭, (cont. of *Kaki* and *Ageru,*) *t. v.* To raise up, hoist, lift up. *Hata, misz, maku, szdare, szso nado wo —,* to hoist a flag, blind, curtain, shade, the skirts, &c.

KAKAGE-IDASHI,*–sz,–sh'ta,* カカゲイダス, 揭出, *t. v.* To hang out, to set forth, produce, bring up, record. *Kam-ban wo —,* to hang out a sign.

KAKARI,*–ru,–tta,* カカル, 懸, *i. v.* To be suspended, hung up, hooked to, fixed on, or laid over some thing. *Fune ga kakatta,* the ship has anchored. *Kagi ni —,* hung on a hook. *Sao ni kimono ga kakatte iru,* the clothes are hanging on a pole. *Me ni —,* to be seen, meet with. *Ko ga oya ni —,* the child is dependent on its parents. *H'to no te ni —,* killed by some person. *Isha ni —,* to consult a physician. *Watakushi no mi ni kakatta koto de wa nai,* it is nothing that concerns me. *Nawa ni —,* bound with a rope. *Sakana ga ami ni —,* fish are caught in a net. *Kokoro,* or *ki ni —,* to be concerned about. *Fushin ni kakatte iru,* engaged in building. *Nani hodo kakari-mashta,* how much did it cost? *Ame ni kakatte kita,* came in the rain. *Midz ga kakaru,* it is getting wet. *Ta-nin no te ni —,* it belongs to others to do it. *Shigoto ni —,* to go at his work. *Teki ni —,* to attack the enemy. *Tszye ni —,* to hold to a cane. *H'to no kuchi ni —,* to be a subject of talk. *Tōri-kakatte,* happening to pass. *Shi ni kakatte oru,* to be dying, about to die. *Kiri-kakaru,* about to cut, or ready to cut. *Ī-kakaru,* about to speak. *Koye ga hana ni —,* he speaks through his nose. *Kagami ni kumori ga —,* the mirror is cloudy.

KAKARI, カカリ, 懸, *n.* The cost, expense, duty, department of business, or labor. — *ga tszyoi,* the cost is great. *Omaye no — wa nani,* what is the duty assigned to you?

KAKARI-AI,*–au,–atta,* カカリアフ, 懸合, *i.v.* To be concerned in, mixed up with, to meddle with.

KAKARI-BITO, カカリビト, 食客, *n.* A dependent, a hanger on. Syn. SHOKKAKU, KAKARI-UDO, ISŌRO.

KAKARI-MAKE, カカリマケ, 懸負, *n.* Expenses larger than the profits.

KAKARIUDO, カカリウド, Same as *Kakaribito.*

KAKARI,–RU, カカル, 斯在,(comp. of *Kaku,* thus, and *aru,* is.) Like this, (before mentioned); so, thus, such, this manner, (of something said before.) *Kakarishi hodo ni,* after this, so then, (in continuing a narrative.) Syn. KAYŌ, KAKUNOGOTOKU.

KAKASE,*–ru,–ta,* カカセル, 令舁, Caust. of *Kaku.* To make, or let another ride, (in a sedan chair.) *Watakushi ni kakasete okure,* let me ride. *H'to ni kago wo —,* to make one ride in a chair.

KAKASE, *–ru,–ta,* カカセル, 令書, Caust. of *Kaku.* To let, or cause another to write. *Watakushi ni kakasete kudasare,* let me write. *Tegami wo —,* to cause another to write a letter.

KAKATO, カカト, 踵, *n.* The heel. Syn. KIBISZ.

KAKAWARI,*–ru,–tta,* カカハル, 拘, *i.v.* To be of interest, importance; to concern, affect, to be at the risk of, to relate, or belong to, to interfere, meddle. *Mi ni* —, to affect one's self, be injurious to one's self. *Iye ni* —, to be injurious to one's family. *Inochi ni* —, at the risk of life. *Shin-shō ni — hodo no son de wa nai*, it is not a loss sufficient to affect his fortune. Syn. KAMAU, ADZKARU.

KAKAYE, *-ru, -ta*, カカヘル, 抱, *t. v.* To hold in the arms, embrace; to employ in one's service. *Ko wo* —, to hold a child in the arms. *Hara wo kakayete warau*, to laugh holding one's sides. *Kodzkai ichi nin kakaye-mash'ta*, have employed one servant. *Hō-kō-nin wo* —, to engage a servant.

KAKE, *-ru, -ta*, カケル, 驅, *i. v.* To run. *Iye ye kakete-kuru*, came running home. *Kakete mukai ni deru*, to run out to meet. Syn. HASHIRU.

KAKE, *-ru, -ta*, カケル, 缺, *i.v.* To be flawed, nicked, broken, defective, missing, wanting, omitted. *Katana no ha ga kaketa*, the edge of the sword is nicked. *Tszki ga kaketa*, the moon has begun to wane. *Go nin no kiyōdai h'tori kaketa*, one of the five brothers is missing. *Maye no hō ga kaketa*, the first part is wanting.

KAKE, *-ru, -ta*, カケル, 懸, or 掛, *t. v.* To hang up, or on; to hook on; to lay over; to place across, to place, or put on. *Yedz wo* —, to hang up a picture. *Kimono wo sao ni* —, to hang clothes over a pole. *Megane wo* —, to put on spectacles. *Hashigo wo* —, to put up a ladder. *Hashi wo* —, to lay a bridge across. *Kagi wo* —, to hook any thing. *Koshi wo* —, to sit on a bench. *Kumo ga sz wo* —, the spider weaves its net, (lit. hangs its nest.) *Koyashi wo* —, to manure. *Midz wo* —, to water. *Shiwo wo* —, to salt. *Sato wo* —, to sugar. *Ho wo* —, to hoist sail. *Mekata wo* —, to weigh. *Nasake wo* —, to do kindness to one, to feel kindly to. *Kō wo kokoro ni* —, to be filial. *Inochi wo* —, to risk life. *Kane wo* —, to stake money, to bet. *Tanomi wo* —, to make a request. *Koye wo* —, to lift up the voice. *Kokoro ni* — to fix in the mind, bear in mind. *Ki ni* —, to brood over. *Go-ku-rō wo* —, to give trouble. *Shiro ni hi wo* —, to set fire to a castle. *Kane wo kakete koshirayeta*, to expend a great deal of money in making. Suffixed to other verbs in comp. words, it signifies, to begin to do and soon leave off, as *Shigoto wo shi-kakete asonde iru*, having commenced his work he leaves to go a pleasuring. *Mikan no kui-kake*, an orange which one began to eat and has left.

KAKE, カケ, Imp. mood of *Kaki*.

KAKE, カケ, 掛, *n.* A debt, or money owed for goods bought on credit. — *wo toru*, to collect a debt. — *wo szmasz*, to discharge a debt. — *wo hataru*, to dun for a debt.

KAKE-AGARI, *-ru, -tta*, カケアガル, 驅上, *i.v.* To run up. *Yama ni* —, to run up a hill.

KAKE-AI, *-au, -atta*, カケアフ, 掛合, *i.v.* To consult together, to talk over, to refer, to attack, or butt against each other, to be matched, or equal (as antagonists.) Syn. DAN-KŌ, SŌDAN, HANASHI-AI.

KAKE-AI-NI, カケアヒニ, 掛合, *adv.* Alternately, only used of dramatic performances. — *kataru*, to recite alternately as in a drama

KAKE-AWASE, *-ru, -ta*, カケアハセル, 驅合, *t.v.* To ride to encounter each other, to charge on each other.

KAKEBERI, カケベリ, 量減, *n.* Deficiency in weight. — *ga tatsz*, there is a deficiency in weight. — *ga ikura*, what is the deficiency in weight?

KAKE-DASHI, *-sz, -sh'ta*, カケダス, 驅出, *t.v.* To run out. (量出), to make a thing weighed to be overweight. *Inaka kara kakedash'te kuru*, to come from the country to Yedo. *Mekata wo* —, to make the weight too much.

KAKE-DZKURI, カケヅクリ, 懸作, *n.* A house built on piles on a slope.

KAKEGANE, カケガネ, 鐉, *n.* A ring and staple for fastening a door.

KAKEGO, カケゴ, 掛子, *n.* A small box that fits into a larger.

KAKE-GOTO, カケゴト, 賭事, *n.* Betting, staking money. — *wo szru*, to bet, gamble by betting.

KAKE-GOYE, カケゴヱ, 掛聲, *n.* The sound made by persons straining at their work, as coolies when pushing a cart, chopping wood, &c.

KAKE-HASHI, カケハシ, 棧道, *n.* A bridge over a mountain gorge, or along the side of a precipice, a ladder. *Kumo ni* —, a ladder to the clouds (a proverb).

KAKE-HI, カケヒ, 筧, *n.* A pipe for conducting water. Syn. TOI.

KAKE-HIKI, カケヒキ, 駈引, *n.* Advance and retreat, (fig.) of adventuring, or declining in any transaction. — *ga jōdz*, said of a merchant who is clever in knowing when, and when not, to buy.

†KA-KEI, カケイ, 家系, *(Iye no szji)* *n.* Family line, pedigree. Syn. CHISZJI.

†KA-KEI, カケイ, 嘉慶, (*Yoki yorokobi*). Congratulation, felicitation. *Kai-nen no — medetaku mōshi osame soro.*

†KA-KEI, カケイ, 佳景, (*Yoki keshiki.*) A fine landscape.

KAKE-JI, カケヂ, 懸地, *n.* A hanging picture. Syn. KAKE-MONO.

KAKE-KŌ, カケカウ, 掛香, *n.* A bag of perfume.

KAKE-MAWARI,-*ru*,-*tta*, カケマハル, 駆廻, *t.v.* To run about, or around.

KAKE-MAKUMO, カケマクモ, 懸巻茂, used only reverentially in prayers to the *Kami*, = *kotoba ni kakeru mo. — kashikoshi. — katajikenashi.*

KAKEME, カケメ, 量目, *n.* The weight. — *wa nani hodo* how much does it weigh? Syn. MEKATA.

KAKE-MOCHI, カケモチ, 兼帶, (*kentai*). *n.* Carrying on business at two different places. — *ni szru.*

KAKE-MONO, カケモノ, 掛物, *n.* Hanging pictures.

KAKE-MONO, カケモノ, 賭, *n.* Any thing laid as a bet or wager.

KAKE-MUKAI, カケムカヒ, 懸向, *n.* A husband and wife who live alone and childless.

KAKE-NE, カケネ, 掛値, *n.* Selling for more than the fixed price, two prices. *Gen-kin — nashi,* no credit and but one price.

KAKE-NUKE,-*ru*,-*ta*, カケヌケル, 駈拔, *t.v.* To ride through, to run-past.

KAKE-OCHI, カケオチ, 欠落, *n.* Running away by stealth, absconding, decamping, escaping. — *wo szru.*
Syn. SHUPPON, CHIKU-TEN, NIGERU.

KAKE-SEN, カケセン, 掛錢, *n.* Money staked in a bet, lottery, or in gambling; also instalments of money paid.

KAKE-TORI, カケトリ, 掛取, *n.* A collector of debts, or of merchants bills.

KAKE-URI, カケウリ, 掛賣, *n.* Selling on credit.

KAKEYA, カケヤ, 懸屋, *n.* A large wooden mallet.

KAKE-YORI,-*ru*,-*tta*, カケヨル, 駈寄, *t.v.* To ride up to, to run near to.

KAKE-ZAN, カケザン, 掛算, *n* Multiplication.

KAKI, カキ, 柿, *n.* The persimmon.

KAKI, カキ, 牡蠣, *n.* An oyster.

KAKI, カキ, 垣, *n.* A fence, hedge. Syn. HEI.

KAKI,-*ku*,-*ita*, カク, 書, *t.v.* To write, to sketch, to draw. *Hon, ji, tegami nado wo kaku. Ye wo* —, to sketch a picture. *Fude de kaita hon,* a book written with a pen. *Kaite shimatta,* have finished writing.

KAKI,-*ku*,-*ita*, カク, 搔, *t.v.* To scratch, to rake, to bind strips of anything together in rows, to slice. *Atama wo* —, to scratch the head, (fig.) to feel ashamed. *Kayui tokoro wo* —, to scratch an itchy place. *Haji wo* —, to feel ashamed. *Shitsz wo* —, to get the itch. *Kasa wo* —, to contract syphilis. *Ibiki wo* —, to snore. *Kubi wo* —, to cut off the head by seizing hold with one hand, and drawing the knife towards one. *Sz-noko wo* —, to make a floor of split bamboo by tying them together. *Komai wo* —, to tie lathing together, (for plastering).

KAKI,-*ku*,-*ita*, カク, 舁, *t.v.* To carry on the shoulders, (only used of a norimon). *Kago wo* —, to carry a chair.

KAKI,-*ku*,-*ita*, カク, 闕, *t.v.* To nick, to make a flaw in, to break off a small piece, to omit. *Katana no ha wo* —, to nick the edge of a sword. *Sara wo* —, to nick a plate. *Koto wo* —, to be short handed. *Ishi wo* —, to knock a piece off a stone. *Utagawashiki wo kaku,* to omit that which is doubtful.

KAKI-ARAWASHI,-*sz*,-*sh'ta* カキアラハス, 書著, *t.v.* To publish.

KAKI-ATSZME,-*ru*,-*ta*, カキアツメル, 書集, *t.v.* To collect and write down, also, 搔集, *t.v.* To rake or scrape together.

KAKI-AYAMARI,-*ru*,-*tta*, カキアヤマル, 書誤, *i.v.* To make a mistake in writing.

KAKI-BAI, カキバヒ, 牡蠣灰, *n.* Lime made of shells.

KAKI-DASHI, カキダシ, 書出, *n.* A bill, an account of things bought on credit.

KAKI-DASHI,-*sz*-*sh'ta*, カキダス, *t.v.* To copy out of a book, or ledger, to begin to write, to rake or scratch out.

KAKI-HAN, カキハン, 花押, *n.* A seal made with a pen.

KAKI-IRE,-*ru*,-*ta*, カキイレル, 書入, *t. v.* To write in, insert by writing, interline. *Iye wo kaki-irete kane wo karu,* to borrow money by mortgaging a house. *Hon ni* — to write in a book.

KAKI-KAYE,-*ru*,-*ta*, カキカヘル, 書替, *t.v.* To write over again, to alter what is written; rewrite.

KAKI-KESHI,-*sz*,-*sh'ta*, カキケス, 搔消, *t. v.* To scratch, or rub out, obliterate. *Kakikesz gotoku use ni keri,* to disappear as if rubbed out.

KAKI-KIRI,-ru-tta, カキキル, 搔切, t.v. To cut off by holding the thing to be cut with one hand, and cutting with the other. *Kusa wo* —.

KAKI-KUMORI,-ru,-tta, カキクモル, 搔陰, i.v. To be clouded over, darkened. *Sora ga* —.

KAKI-KURE,-ru,-ta, カキクレル, 搔暮, i.v. To be blinded, as, *Namida ni* —, blinded with tears.

KAKI-MAWASHI,-sz,-sh'ta, カキマハス, 搔廻, t.a. To stir-round. *Saji de* —, to stir with a spoon.

KAKI-MAZE,-ru,-ta, カキマゼル, 攪和, t.v. To mix together, stir and mix.

KAKI-MIDASHI,-sz,-sh'ta, カキミダス, 攪亂, t. v. To mix, jumble together, confuse, derange.

KAKI-MORASHI,-sz,-sh'ta, カキモラス, 書漏, t. v. To omit in writing, forget to write.

KAKI-MUSHIRI,-ru,-tta, カキムシル, 搔毟, t. v. To scratch and tear off, strip off.

KAKIN, カキン, 瑕瑾, n. Injury, shame, dishonor, disgrace. *Iye no* —, disgrace to a family. Syn. KIDZ.

KAKI-NADE,-ru,-ta, カキナデル, 搔撫, t. v. To smooth, or caress with the hand.

KAKI-NAOSHI,-sz,-sh'ta, カキナホス, 書直, t. v. To write and correct, to write over again.

KAKI-NARASHI,-sz,-sh'ta, カキナラス, 搔平, t. v. To scrape and level, also, 搔鳴, To twang, (as the string of a guitar.)

KAKI-NARE,-ru,-ta, カキナレル, 書習, i. v. To learn to write, to become used to writing.

KAKINE, カキネ, 垣根, n. A fence, hedge. Syn. HEI.

KAKI-NIKUI,-KI,-KU,-SHI, カキニクイ, 書悪, Bad for writing, hard to write with, hard to write.

KAKI-NOBORI,-ru,-tta, カキノボル, 搔登, t.v. To climb up, scramble up.

KAKI-NOKE,-ru,-ta, カキノケル, 搔除, t. v. To push to one side so as to pass through, (as a crowd.)

KAKI-NOSE,-ru,-ta, カキノセル, 書載, t. v. To record, to write down, register.

KARI-NUKI,-ku,-ita, カキヌク, 鈔書, To make written extracts, (from a book.)

KAKI-OKI, カキオキ, 遺書, n. A will, any writing left by a person going away.

KAKI-ŌSE,-ru,-ta, カキオホセル, 書果, t. v. To finish writing, to do up a large amount of writing.

KAKI-OTOSHI,-sz-,sh'ta, カキオトス, 搔落, t. v. To cut off by holding any thing in one hand, and cutting towords one's self with the other, to scratch off, also 書落. To omit, or forget to write.

KAKI-OWARI,-ru,-tta, カキヲハル, 書終, To finish writing.

KAKI-SAGASHI,-sz,-sh'ta, カキサガス, 搔捜, t. v. To search for, to scratch and search for, (as a fowl.)

KAKI-SAKI,-ku,-ita, カキサク, 搔裂, t. v. To scratch and tear.

KAKI-SHIRUSHI,-sz,-sh'ta, カキシルス, 書記, t. v. To write down, record, make a memorandum.

KAKI-SHITATAME,-ru,-ta, カキシタタメル, 書認, t. v. To write, compose and write. to engross.

KAKI-SOKONAI,-au,-ta, カキソコナフ, 書損, t. v. To write wrong, mistake in writing.

KAKI-SOYE,-ru, カキソヘル, 書添, t. v. To add to a writing, to write a postcript.

KAKI-SZYE,-ru,-ta, カキスヱル, 舁居, t. v. To set down a sedan chair when carrying it

KAKI-TAI,-KI,-KU,-SHI, カキタイ, 書度, Wish to write. *Kakitaku nai*, do not wish to write.

KAKI-TASHI,-sz,-sh'ta, カキタス, 書足, t.v. To write what is necessary to make complete.

KAKI-TATE,-ru,-ta, カキタテル, 書立, t.v. To write down many items, to write up (as a list,) also, 搔立. To pick up (as the wick of a lamp.) 攪和. To stir and mix together.

KAKI-TORI,-ru,-tta, カキトル, 書取, t. v. To copy, transcribe.

KAKI-TSZDZKE,-ru,-ta, カキツヅケル, 書續, t.v. To write down in succession, to connect by writing, to continue to write.

KAKI-TSZKE, カキツケ, 書附, n. A writing, note, memorandum.

KAKI-TSZKE,-ru,-ta, カキツケル, 書附, t.v. To note down, make a memorandum of.

KAKI-TSZKUSHI,-sz,-sh'ta, カキツクス, 書盡, t. v. To exhaust a subject by writing, to finish writing.

KAKI-TOME,-ru,-ta, カキトメル, 書留, t.v. To record, register, make a note of.

KAKI-TSZTAYE,-ru,-ta, カキツタヘル, 書傳, t.v. To write and hand down to others.

KAKI-UTSZSHI,-sz,-sh'ta, カキウツス, 書寫, t.v. To copy, transcribe.

KAKI-YABURI,-*ru*,-*tta*, カキヤブル, 搔破, *t.v.* To scratch and tear.

†KA-K'YOKU, カキヨク, 歌曲, *n.* Song, sonnet.

KAKI-YOSE,-*ru*,-*ta*, カキヨセル, 搔寄, *t.v.* To rake, or scratch any thing towards one's self with the fingers, 舁寄. To bring near in a norimon.

KAKI-ZOME, カキゾメ, 書初, *n.* The first writing of the new year.

KAKKE, カクケ, 脚氣, *n.* Dropsy of the legs.

KAKKŌ, カツコウ, 恰好, (*adakamo yoshi.*) *n.* Shape, proportions, just right. — *ga yoi.* — *ga warui.* — *wo konomu*, to be particular about the looks of any thing. *Nedan* — *ni sh'te agemasz*, to sell at a reasonable price. Syn. NARI, KATACHI, HODOYOI.

KAKKO, カツコ, 羯鼓, *n.* A kind of drum.

KAKKON, カツコン, 葛根, *n* A kind of medicine.

KAKO, カコ, 水手, *n.* A common sailor. Syn. SZI-SHU, SENDŌ.

†KAKOCHI,-*tsz*, カコツ, *i.v.* Troubled, worried, sad, gloomy. (poet.) *Kakochi-gao*, troubled countenance. *Kakochi-namida ni kure ni keru*, blinded with anxious tears. Syn. WABIRU, KOMARU, TSZRAI.

KAKOI,-*ō*,-*ōta* カコフ, 圍, *t.v.* To inclose, to fence, to shut in, to surround, to cover in order to preserve, as fruits, &c. *Iye wo ita-bei de* —, to inclose a house with a fence. *Imo wo* —, to preserve potatoes in the ground. *Mikan wo* —, to preserve oranges (in fine leaves.)

KAKOI, カコヒ, 圍, *n.* An inclosure, fence, barrier. — *wo szru*, to make a fence.

KAKOI-ME, カコヒメ, 外妾, *n.* A mistress, or concubine kept in private.

KAKOI-MONO, カコヒモノ, *n.* idem.

KAKOMARE,-*ru*,-*ta*, カコマレル, 被圍, Pass. of *Kakomu.*

KAKOMI,-*mu*,-*nda*, カコム, 圍, *t. v.* To surround, inclose, confine on all sides, encompass. *Teki wo* —, to surround the enemy. *Shiro wo kakonde semeru.* Syn. TORI-MAKU.

KAKOMI, カコミ, 圍, *n.* The inclosure, that which surrounds or shuts in, a siege, blockade, circumvallation. — *wo tszite kake-nukeru*, to pass through a besieging army and escape. — *wo toku*, to raise a siege.

KAKOTSZKE,-*ru*,-*ta*, カコツケル, 託, *t. v*, To make as a pretext, pretence, excuse. make believe. *Sankei wo kakotszkete asobi-ni yuku*, under the pretence of going to the temple he went a pleasuring. Syn. DASHI NI SZRU, I-GUSA NI SZRU, KOTOYOSERU.

KAKOTSZKE, カコツケ, 託, *n.* Pretext, pretence, excuse. *Nanni mo* — *ga nai*, no pretence whatever. *Go-yō wo* — *ni szru*, to make public service a pretext.

KAKU, カク, See *Kaki.*

KAKU, カク, 角, *n.* A musket target.

KAKU, カク, 格, *n.* Rank, grade, degree of elevation or dignity, station, pattern, rule. *Kaku ga yoi h'to*, a man of high rank. *Kono kaku de koshiraye*, make after this pattern. — *wo hadzreru*, to depart from a rule, make an exception. Syn. KURAI.

KAKU, カク, 客, (*marōto*). *n.* A guest, visitor, stranger. Syn. KIYAKU.

KAKU, カク, 角, *n.* Corner, angle, a horn, square. *Shi-kaku*, square. *San-kaku*, three cornered. *Kaku-bashira*, a square post. *Kaku no bon*, a square tray. — *ni kiru*, to cut anything square. — *na moji*, the square form of the Chinese character.

||KAKU, カク, *n.* A blow with both heels given to a horse while riding. *H'to* — *wo utsz*, or *kaku wo ireru.*

KAKU, カク, 斯, *a.* This. — *no tōri*, this way, this manner. *Nanji ga* — *szru wa ikanaru kokoro zo ye*, what was your intention in doing this? *Kaku no h'togara*, this kind of a person. Syn. KONO, KŌ, KORE.

KAKU, カク, 膈, *n.* A disease of stomach characterized by vomiting of what has just been eaten.

†KAKU-BAKARI, カクバカリ, 斯計, *adv.* Thus, so, or this much.

KAKU-BAN, カクバン, 隔番, Alternate watches, watch and watch. — *ni tsztomeru.* Syn. KAWARI-BAN.

KAKU-BETSZ, カクベツ, 格別, *a.* Particular, special, different from ordinary, important. — *kawatta koto mo gozaimasen*, there is no particular change. — *itamimasen*, it is not particularly painful. *Kore wa* — *ni yoroshi*, this is particularly good. — *no yamai de wa nai*, it is not a serious sickness. Syn. TORI-WAKETE, BETSZDAN.

KAKU-DAN, カクダン, 格段, Different from ordinary, particular, special, important. — *no chigai wa nai*, no especial difference. Syn. BETSZDAN.

KAKU-GWAI, カクグワイ, 格外, Extraordinary, contrary to the rule, an exception, particular, special. — *no iriyō*, extraordinary expenses. *Onna wa* — *ni szru*, women are an exception. — *ni yaszi*, extraordinarily cheap.

KAKU-GETSZ, カクゲツ, 隔月, *n.* Alternate months, month about, every other month.

KAKUGO, カクゴ, 覺悟, *n.* The conclusion or decision of the mind in view of some future event; having one's mind made up, or prepared for some thing anticipated; preparation, resignation, readiness. *Ame furu no — de amagu wo mottekita*, concluding that it was going to rain I brought my rain clothes. *Nureru — de kita*, I determined to come even should I get wet. *Omō koto ga kanawanu toki wa shinō to no* —, when matters do not go as I wish I have made up my mind to die. — *no maye*, conclusion of mind. — *wa yoi ka* are you ready? *Shinuru — se yo*, prepare to die.

KAKUI, カクイ, 隔意, (*hedate-gokoro*) Separation of heart, unfriendliness. — *naku*. Syn. K'YAKU-SHIN.

KAKU-JITSZ, カクジツ, 隔日, *n.* Alternate days, day about, every other day.
Syn. ICHI-NICHI-OKI.

†KAKU-KAKU, カクカク, 赫赫, *adv.* Bright, shining, refulgent, glittering. *Riyō gan — to sh'te nichirin no narabi idetaru gotoku.*
Syn. KAGAYAKU, PIKA-PIKA, TEKA-TEKA, KIRA-KIRA.

KAKUMAI,-*au*,-*atta*, カクマフ, 匿, *t.v.* To conceal, hide. *Toganin wo kakumōte taszkeru*, to save a criminal by concealing him. Syn. KAKUSZ.

†KAKU-MAKU, カクマク, 膈膜, *n.* The cornea.

†KA-KUN, カクン, 家訓, (*Iye no oshiye*). Home education, rules of a family.

KAKU-NEN, カクネン, 隔年, *n.* Alternate years, year about, every other year.

KAKU-NO-GOTOKI,-KU,-SHI, カクノゴトキ, 如是, Thus, in this way, so, such, referring to something said before.
Syn. KONO-YŌ, KONO-TŌRI, KA-YŌ.

KAKURE,-*ru*,-*ta*, カクレル, 隱, *i.v.* To be hid, concealed, secret, to die. *Tszki kumo ni kakureta*, the moon is hid by the cloud. *Iye no kage ni* —, hid in the shade of the house. *Kakuretaru yori arawaretaru wa nashi*, there is nothing more manifest than what is concealed.
Syn. HISOMU.

†KAKURE-GA, カクレガ, 隱家, *n.* A secluded or retired house.

KAKUREMBŌ, カクレンボウ, *n.* The game of blind-man's buff.

||KAKURE-MI, カクレミ, 隱身, *n.* One living in seclusion, or concealment.

†KAKU-SEI, カクセイ, 客星, *n.* A new, or strange star.

KAKUSHI,-*sz*,-*sh'ta*, カクス, 藏, *t.v.* To hide, conceal, to secrete. *Mi wo* —, to hide one's self, or live in seclusion. *Toganin wo* —, to conceal a criminal. *Chiye wo* —, to hide one's talents. *Nedzmi wo toru neko wa tszme wo* —, (prov.)

KAKUSHI-BAIJO, カクシバイヂヨ, 私賣女, *n.* A secret prostitute, who does not live in the prescribed place.

KAKUSHIKI, カクシキ, 格式, *n.* Rank grade, degree of elevation or dignity, station in society. Syn. KURAI, BUN-GEN, HŌSHIKI, REISHIKI.

†KAKU-SHIN, カクシン, 隔心, *n.* Estranged, distant, cool, unfriendly.

KAKUTE, カクテ, 然而, *adv.* Then, after that, and, so then. Syn. SŌSH'TE.

KAKU-UCHI, カクウチ, 角打, *n.* Target-shooting.

KAKU-YA, カクヤ, 角夜, *n.* Alternate nights, night about, every other night,

KAKU-YAKU, カクヤク, *adv.* Bright, shining, glittering.

KAMA, カマ, 鎌, *n.* A sickle. — *de ine wo karu*, to cut rice with a sickle. — *wo kakeru*, to apply the sickle, (fig.) to elicit the truth by pretending to know all about it.

KAMA, カマ, 釜, *n.* An iron pot.

KAMABISZSHI,-KI,-KU,U-, カマビスシ, 喧, Tumultuous, noisy. Syn. SAWAGASHII, YAKAMASHII.

KAMABOKO, カマボコ, 蒲鉾, *n.* A kind of food made of fish cut up fine rolled into a ball and baked.

KAMA-BUTA, カマブタ, 釜蓋, *n.* A pot lid.

KAMACHI カマチ, 框, *n.* The frame of a door, or window.

KAMADO, カマド, 竈, *n.* A furnace, kitchen range.

KAMAI,-*au*, or *ō*,-*atta*, カマフ, 搆, *i. v*, To meddle with, interfere, to be concerned about, to mind, care for. *O kamai nasaru na*, don't trouble your self about it, let it alone. *Watakushi no kamō koto de wa ṅai*, it is an affair in which I have no business to meddle. *Dare wa omaiye wo kamatta*, who hurt you? *Dōdemo kamai-masen*, it don't matter how. *Sonna koto ni kamatte wa irarenu*, I can't be bothered with such a matter as that. *Kamō koto wa nai*, it is not worth caring for.

KAMA-ITACHI, カマイタチ, 鎌鼬, *n.* An invisible animal supposed to inflict wounds on people: thus if a person should fall, and without any apparent cause, receive a cut, they say he is, *kamaitachi ni kirareta.*

KAMA-KIRI, カマキリ, 蟷螂, *n.* A mantis. Syn. TŌRŌ, IBOJIRI.

KAMARE,-*ru*,-*ta*, カマレル, 被噬, (pass. or pot. of *Kami*, *mu*). To be bitten, can bite. *Inu ni kamareta*, bitten by a dog. *Ha nashi de kamarenai*, he has no teeth and cannot bite.

KAMASE,-*ru*,-*ta*, カマセル, 令噬, (caus. of *Kamu*). To cause, or let bite. *Inu ni h'to wo kamaseru koto nakare*, don't set the dog on people. *Uma ni kutszwa wo* —, to put a bit in the horse's mouth.

KAMASZ, カマス, 褁子, *n.* A straw bag.

KAMASZ, カマス, 梭魚, *n.* A kind of fish.

KAMAWADZ, KAMAWANU, or KAMAWANAI, カマハズ, (neg. of *Kamai.*)

KAMAWARE,-*ru*,-*ta*, カマハレル, (pass. of of *Kamai*, *au*.

KAMAYE,-*ru*,-*ta*, カマヘル, 構, *t.v.* To enclose, to prepare, to assume an attitude, posture, or position; to build, frame, construct, to concoct, devise. *Shiro wo* —, to construct a castle. *Uma wo noran to* —, to be in the attitude of mounting a horse. *Tedate wo* —, to devise a plan. *Chinzen wo* —, to prepare a sumptuous feast. Syn. SONAYERU.

KAMAYE, カマヘ, 構, *n.* The external arrangement, form, and appearance of a building, manner, attitude, posture, position, an enclosure. *Kono iye no — ga ī*, the structure and arrangement of this house is fine. *Mi-gamaye wo szru*, to put one's self in the proper posture. *Yumi-gamaye wo szru*, to put one's self in the proper attitude for shooting the bow.

KAM-BAN, カンバン, 記號, *n.* A coat worn by a servant having the master's coat of arms on the back.

KAM-BAN, カンバン, 看版, *n.* A signboard. — *wo kakeru*, to hang up a sign.

†KAM-BASE, カンバセ, 顔, *n.* The face, countenance. Syn. KAO, TSZRA.

KAM-BATSZ, カンバツ, 旱魃, *n.* A drought, want of rain. Syn. HIDERI.

KAM-BEN, カンベン, 勘辨, To consider, think over, reflect, deliberate on, to weigh in the mind, to pardon. — *sh'te kudasare*, have patience with me, or pardon me. *Yoku — sh'te mi-mashō*, I will consider well about it. — *naranu*, unpardonable. Syn. KANGAYERU, RIYŌ-KEN, KAN-KŌ.

KAM-BIYŌ, カンビヤウ, 看病, Nursing, or attending on the sick. — *nin*, a sick-nurse. Syn. KAI-HŌ.

†KAM-BŌ, カンボウ, 感冒, (*kaze wo hiku.*) To catch cold.

KAM-BUTSZ, カンブツ, 乾物, *n.* Vegetables dried for food.

KAME, カメ, 龜, *n.* A tortoise. — *no kō*, the shell of a tortoise.

KAME, カメ, 瓶, *n.* A jar.

KAME-BARA, カメバラ, *n.* Kind of disease.

KAME-NO-O, カメノヲ, 龜尾, *n.* The Coccyx. Syn. BITEIKOTSZ.

KAMI, カミ, 神, *n.* God. This word is applied only to the deities worshiped by the *Sintoo.*

KAMI, カミ, 守, *n.* A title of rank.

KAMI, カミ, 上, (*wiye.*) Superior, above, high, upper in rank or place, ruler, wife. — *ni tatsz h'to*, superiors. *Kawa-kami*, up the river. — *ye noboru*, to go up a river, or to the capital. *Kami tō-ka*, the first ten days of a month. *Kami no okite*, the laws of the government. *O kami san*, your wife, also a title used in addressing any married woman, = Mrs.

KAMI, カミ, 紙, *n.* Paper. — *wo szku*, to make paper.

KAMI, カミ, 髮, *n.* The hair of the head. — *wo yū*, to dress the hair. — *wo kaku*, to scratch the head. — *wo tokasz*, to comb the head. — *wo szku*, to scrape the dandruff off with a fine comb. — *wo hayasz*, to let the hair grow long. — *wo soru*, to shave off the hair. — *wo orosz*, to enter the priesthood.

†KA-MI, カミ, 加味, Adding medicines in extemporaneous prescriptions. — *szru.* Syn. KAGEN.

KAMI,-*mu*,-*nda*, カム, 嚙, *t.v.* To bite, chew, gnaw. *Kande fukumeru*, to chew the food and feed it to the young, (fig.) to nourish and rear up with care, to instruct. *Inu ga* —, the dog bites.

KAMI-AI,-*ō*-*atta*, カミアフ, 嚙合, *i.v.* To bite each other, to fight, as dogs. *Inu ga* —,

KAMI-GATA, カミガタ, 上方, *n.* The capital, the region about *Kiyoto.*

KAMI-IRE, カミイレ, 紙入, *n.* A wallet for holding paper.

KAMI-KIRI, カミキリ, 紙切, *n.* A papercutter.

KAMI-KIRI, カミキリ, 天牛, *n.* A kind of beetle.

KAMI-KIRI,-*ru*,-*tta*, カミキル, 嚙斷, *t.v.* To bite off.

KAMI-KONASHI,-sz,-sh'ta, カミコナス, 嚙化, t.v. To masticate.

KAMI-KUDAKI,-ku,-ita, カミクダク 嚙碎, t.v. To break, or crush with the teeth, to craunch.

KAKI-MUKI, カミムキ, 上向, n. Used in speaking of a master, or the government.

KAMI-NARI, カミナリ, 雷, n. Thunder. — *ga goro-goro to naru*, the thunder rolls. — *ga ochiru*, the lightning strikes. — *yoke*, a charm against lightning, a lightning rod. Syn. RAI, IKADZCHI.

KAMI-OKI, カミヲキ, 髮署, n. The ceremony on the occasion of first letting a child's hair grow, at about 5 years of age.

KAMI-SAKAYAKI, カミサカヤキ, 髮月代, n. Dressing the hair in Japanese style. — *wo szru.*

KAMI-SHIME,-ru,-ta, カミシメル, 嚙緊, t. v. To gnash the teeth.

KAMI-SHIMO, カミシモ, 上下, Above and below, superiors and inferiors; also, a peculiar dress worn on occasions of ceremony.

KAMI-SORI, カミソリ, 剃刀, n. A razor.

KAMI-SZKI, カミスキ, 紙漉, n. A paper maker.

KAMI-SZKI-BA, カミスキバ, 紙漉場, n. A paper mill.

KAMI-TSZKI,-ku,-ita, カミツク, 嚙着, t. v. To bite, lay hold of with the teeth.

KAMI-YA, カミヤ, 紙屋, n. A paper store.

KAMI-YUI, カミユヒ, 髮結, n. A barber, hair-dresser.

†KAM-MON, カンモン, 勘文, n. A written opinion sent to the *Tenshi.*

KAMMURI, カンムリ, 冠, n. A kind of black cap worn by nobles.

KAMMURI, カンムリ, see *Kaburi*,

KAMO, カモ, 鴨, n. A wild duck.

KAMOI, カモ井, 鴨居, n. The upper beam, in the groove of which a door, or screen slides; the lower is called *Shikii.*

KAMOJI, カジヂ, 髢, n. False hair.

KAMOME, カモメ, 鷗, n. A kind of sea-gull.

†KA-MON, カモン, 家門, n. The family, house, clan, tribe.

KAMOSHI,-sz,-sh'ta, カモス, 釀, t, v. To brew. — *sake wo*, to brew *sake. Nemuri wo* —, to compose one's self to sleep. *Urami wo* —, to produce hatred.

KAMOSHIKA, カモシカ, 羚羊, n. A kind of wild stag.

KAMPAN, カンバン, 艦板, n. The deck of a ship.

†KAMPASHI,-szru,-sh'ta, カンパスル, 看破, *(mi-yaburu,)* t. v. To discover, understand, to see into, or perceive something that does not lie on the surface.

KAMPIYŌ, カンペウ, 乾瓢, n. A kind of dried melon.

KAM-PŌ, カンパウ, 漢方, *(kara no hō,)* n. Chinese system of medicine.

†KAM-PŪ, カンプウ, 寒風, n. A cold wind.

KAMPUKU, カンプク, 感服, Admiration, commendation, approval. — *szru.* Syn. KAN-SHIN.

KAN, カン, 欠, n. Deficiency in weight or number, loss, waste. — *ga tastz*, there is a deficiency. Syn. HERI, MERI.

KAN, カン, 寒, *(Samui.)* Cold. — *ga hidoi*, the cold is severe. *Shō-kan*, the period of moderate cold, 15 days about the beginning of the 12th month. *Dai-kan*, the period of severe cold, in the 12th month.

†KAN, カン, 漢, n. China. *Wa-kan*, Japan and China. *Kango*, the Chinese language. *Kan-ji*, Chinese characters.

KAN, カン, 肝, *(Kimo.)* n The liver. *Kan no zō*, (idem.)

KAN, カン, 疳, n. Marasmus. — *no yamai*, idem.

KAN, カン, 癇, n. Epilepsy. Syn. TEN-KAN.

KAN, カン, 勘, n. Quick of perception, clever, or quick witted. — *no yoi zatō*, a blind person who is clever in finding his way. — *wo tszkeru*, to be quick to perceive, guess, or suspect.

KAN, カン, 感, n. Admiration. — *ni tayetari*, affected to admiration. — *no amari ni hōbi wo yatta.*

KAN, カン, 燗, *(atatameru.)* Used as follows. *Sake no* — *wo szru*, or — *wo tszkeru*, to warm *sake* by setting the bottle in hot water.

†KANA, カナ, 哉, Exclam. used at the end of a sentence, = to the interjection sign! *Fushingi naru kana*, how wonderful!

KANA, カナ, 假字, n. The 46 characters of the Japanese alphabet, so called from their having been *borrowed* from the Chinese. — *de kaku*, to use the Japanese characters in writing. *Katakana, Hirakana.*

‖KANA, カナ, 紺絲, n. Violet colored thread.

KANA-AMI, カナアミ, 銅網, n. A wire netting, wire gauze.

KANA-BASAMI, カナバサミ, 鉸刀, n. Shears for cutting metal.

KANA-BASHI, カナバシ, 火鉗, *n.* A blacksmith's tongs.

KANA-BERA, カナベラ, 鐵匙, *n.* An iron spatula.

KANA-BŌ, カナボウ, 銕棒, *n.* An iron rod, or staff.

KANA-BUTSZ, カナブツ, 金佛, *n.* A metal image of Buddha.

KANA-DARAI, カナダライ, 銅盥, *n.* A copper basin.

†KANADE,*-ru*, カナデル, 奏, *i.v.* To dance to music.

KANA-DOYU, カナドユ, 銅樋, *n.* A copper pipe.

KANA-DZCHI, カナヅチ, 銕鎚, *n.* An iron hammer.

KANA-DZKAI, カナヅカヒ, 假字遣, Spelling with the Japanese syllables. — *ga warui.* — *ga yoi.*

†KANADZRU, カナヅル, 奏, Same as *Kanaderu.*

KANAGAI, カナガヒ, *n.* Lead or tin foil.

KANA-GAI, カナガヒ, 銅匕, *n.* A metal spoon made in the shape of a shell.

KANA-GAKI, カナガキ, 假名書, Written in the Japanese characters.

KANAGASHIRA, カナガシラ, 鯠, *n.* A kind of fish. Syn. HŌBŌ.

KANAGU, カナグ, 金具, *n.* The ornamental metal work on bureaus, boxes, &c., A metal ring, clasp lock.

||KANAGURI,*-ru,-tta*, カナグル, 捸, *t.v.* To coil, (as a rope) to wrench off, to scratch. *Nawa wo* —, to coil a rope. *Yajiri wo* —, to wrench off an arrow head. Syn. TAGURU, SAGURU.

KANA-GUSARI, カナグサリ, 鏁, *n.* A chain.

KANA-GUTSZ, カナグツ, 銕靴, *n.* Horseshoe.

KANA-HIBASHI, カナヒバシ, 銕火箸, *n.* Iron-tongs.

KANAI, カナイ, 家内, *n.* Family, house, wife. *Go* — *no nindz iku tari,* how many persons are there in your family? *Go* — *sama,* your wife.

KANAI,*-au,* or *ō,-atta*, カナフ, 叶, *i.v.* To agree with, to suit, accord. *Kokoro,* or *ki ni* —, to like, to suit one's mind. *Michi ni* —, to be reasonable. *Negai ga* —, to obtain a request.

KANA-KIN, カナキン, 洋布, *n.* Muslin, long-cloth of foreign make.

KANA-KUGI, カナクギ, 鐵釘, *n.* An iron nail.

KANA-KUSO, カナクソ, 鐵屑, *n.* Metal cinders.

KANAME, カナメ, 要, *n* The rivet or pin of a fan, (fig,) the important, or governing principle, the cardinal point. Syn. KIKIME, KANYŌ.

KANARADZ, カナラズ, 必, *adv.* Positively, certainly, necessarily, must. *Kore,* — *kurō ni szru na yo,* you must not feel troubled. — *iu na,* must not speak of it. *Nochi ni* — *wazawai aran,* afterwards misfortune will certainly befall you. Syn. KESSH'TE, ZEHI, KITTO.

KANARI, カナリ, 可也, Tolerably, middling well, passibly, can or may do. *Kono hōchō* — *ni kirimashō,* this knife cuts tolerably well. Syn. MAYOI.

KANARIYA, カナリヤ, *n.* A canary bird.

KANASHII,*-KI*, カナシイ, 悲哀, *a.* Sad lamentable, sorrowful, afflictive. Syn. UREI.

KANA-SHIKI カナシキ, 鐕, *n.* An anvil.

KANASHIMI, カナシミ, 悲, *n.* Sorrow, sadness, grief.

KANASHIKU, カナシク, 悲, *adv.* See *Kanashii.*

KANASHIMI,*-mu,-nda*, カナシム, 悲, *t. v* To grieve, to lament, mourn, to sorrow. *Oya no shinda koto wo* —, to mourn the death of a parent.

KANASHISA, カナシサ, 哀, *n.* Sorrow, sadness. — *wo kakusz,* to conceal one's sorrow.

KANATA, カナタ, 彼方, (cont. of *Kano kata.*) There, that place. — *konata,* here and there, place to place, all about. — *konata mi wo kawasz,* to move here and there. Syn. ANATA, ANO-HO, ACHIRA, AS'KO.

KANA-TEKO, カナテコ, 鉄梃, *n.* An iron crowbar.

KANA-TOKO, カナトコ, 鐵牀, *n.* An anvil. Syn. KANASHIKI.

KANATSZMPŌ, カナツンポウ, *n.* A deaf-person.

KANAWADZ, KANAWANU, KANAWANAI, カナハズ, 不叶, The neg. of *Kanai, au.* Cannot, impossible. *Futa-tabi shō-ten szru koto* —, cannot ascend to heaven again.

†KANAYE, カナヘ, 鼎, *n.* A three legged kettle, used in ancient times.

†KAN-CHI, カンチ, 奸智, *(yokoshima no chiye,) n.* Wicked, cunning, subtlilty, wiliness.

KAN-CHIKU, カンチク, 漢竹, *n.* A kind of bamboo.

†KAN-DAN, カンダン, 寒暖, *(Samui-atszi.)* Cold and hot, temperature. — *wo hakaru,* to observe the temperature.

†KAN-DAN, カンダン, 閑談, (*Shidzkana hanashi.*) A quiet talk, conversing while at leisure.

KAN-DAN-KE, カンダンケ, 寒暖計, *n.* A thermometer.

KAN-DŌ, カンダウ, 勘當, *n.* Disinheriting, discarding, or turning a disobedient son out of the family. — *szru*, to disinherit a child. — *wo ukeru*, to be turned out of the family.

†KAN-DŌ, カンダウ, 間道, (*nuki michi,*) *n.* A by-way, a secret way.

KANDZRU, カンズル, 感, see *Kanji, ru,*

KANE, カ子, 金, *n.* Metal, ore, money. — *wo horu*, to dig ore. — *wo fuku*, to smelt ore. — *wo mōkeru*, to earn money. — *no ri*, interest of money. — *no tszru*, a vein of metal-ore. — *wo dasz ki ga nai*, not disposed to spend money.

KANE, カ子, 鐘, *n.* A bell. — *wo narasz*, to ring a bell. — *wo tszku*, to strike a bell. — *no ne*, the sound of a bell.

KANE, カ子, 鉄漿, *n.* The stuff used by Japanese women for staining the teeth. — *wo tszkeru*, or — *wo fukumu*, to apply the black-stain.

KANE,*-ru,-ta*, カ子ル, 兼, *t. v.* To discharge the duties of two, or more offices at the same time; to use a thing for two purposes; to comprehend, or include two or more things in one; to have a feeling of dread, and consequent effort to please. Difficult, or hard, cannot. *H'tori de futatsz wo —. Kerai wa shu-jin no ki wo kaneru*, the servant fears and tries to please his master. *Isogashikute yuki-kaneru*, I am so busy I cannot go. *Chi yū wo kane-sonayeru*, possessing both wisdom and valor. *F'ta yaku kaneru*, holding two offices.
Syn. KENTAI.

KANE-BAKO, カ子バコ, 金箱, *n.* A money-box.

KANE-FUDE, カ子フデ, 鉄漿筆, *n.* A brush used in staining the teeth.

KANE-FUKI, カ子フキ, 金吹, *n.* A metallurgist.

KANE-GANE, カ子ガ子, 兼兼, *adv.* Previously, before. — *o shirase mōsz tori*, in the way you told me before.
Syn. KANETE, MAYEMOTTE.

†KANE-GOTO, カ子ゴト, 兼言, *n.* A secret or previous promise, (as of marriage.)

KANE-GURA, カ子グラ, 金藏, *n.* A money-vault, a money-safe, a treasury.

KANE-HORI, カ子ホリ, 礦夫, *n.* A miner.

KANE-IRE, カ子イレ, 金入, *n.* A purse.

KANEKASHI, カ子カシ, 金貸, *n.* A money-lender, a bank.

KANE-MOCHI, カ子モチ, 金持, *n.* A rich-man.

KANE-MOCHI-RASHII,*-KI,-KU*, カ子モチラシイ, Having the appearance of a rich-man, like a rich-man.

KANETE, カ子テ, 兼, *adv.* Previously, before, beforehand. — *mōshi tszketa tōri*, as it was ordered before. — *yōri*, before. — *yaku-jō sh'ta tōri ni nasare*, do it in the way you before promised. Syn. KATSZTE, SENDATTE, MAYEMOTTE.

KANE-TSZBO, カ子ツボ, 鉄漿壺, *n.* A jar for holding tooth-dye.

KANE-TSZKE-ISHI, カ子ツケイシ, 試金石, *n.* A touch-stone.

KANE-ZASHI, カ子ザシ, 曲尺, *n.* A carpenter's square.

KANGAMI,*-ru,-ta*, カンガミル, 鑑, (*Kangami-miru,*) *t. v.* To look at as in a mirror, to regard as an example, (for immitation, or warning.) *Midz ni* —, to look into water as in a mirror. *Inishiye ni* —, to look upon the ancients as examples.

KANGAYE,*-ru,-ta*, カンガヘル, 考, *i.v.* To think on, to reflect, consider, to ponder. *Dōsh'te yoi ka kangayte mi-nasai*, think over how it had better be done. *Kangayete mo wakaranu*, think over it as I may I can't understand it. Syn. OMŌ, KAMBEN SZRU, ANDZRU.

KANGAYE, カンガヘ, 考, *n.* Thought, consideration, reflection. — *ga tszkanu*, I can't make it out. Syn. OMOI.

KAN-GEN, カンゲン, 諫言, *n.* Expostulation, or remonstrance with a superior. *Kimi wo — szru*, to expostulate with a master, id.
Syn. ISAME, IKEN.

KANI, カニ 蟹, *n.* A crab. — *no hasami*, a crabs claws.

KANI-BABA, カニババ, or KANI-KUSO, カニクソ, 胎屎, *n.* The meconium.

†KA-NI-KAKU, カニカク, Various, this and that. Syn. TONIKAKU.

†KAN-IN, カンイン, 奸婬, *n.* Rape. — *szru*, to commit a rape. Syn. GŌ-IN.

†KA-NIU,*-szru*, カニウ, 加入, (*kuwaye-ireru.*) To join, to become one of the same company, to go along with.

KAN-JA, カンジヤ, 間者, *n.* A spy. — *wo irete teki no kiyo-jitsz wo saguru*, to send a spy and find out the affairs of the enemy.
Syn. SAI-SAKU, SHINOBI.

†KAN-JA, カンジヤ, 寒邪, *n.* Sickness from severe cold weather — *ni ataru*

†KAN-JA, カンジヤ, 奸邪, Unprincipled, villainous, depraved.

KAN-JI,-*dzru*,-*ta*, カンズル, 感, *i. v.* To admire; to regard with approbation, esteem, or admiration; to be moved, affected. *Kanjite raku-rui szru*, to be affected to tears. *Kaze ni* —, affected by the wind. Syn. KAN-SHIN SZRU.

KANJI,-*dzru*,-*ta*, カンズル, 寒, *i.v.* To be cold. *Hidoku kandzru*, to be extremely cold.

KANJI, カンジ, 寒, *n.* The cold. — *ga tszyoi.*

KANJIKI, カンジキ, 橇, *n.* Snow-shoes. Syn. SORI.

†KAN-JIN, カンジン, 奸人, *n.* A villian, traitor, a depraved unprincipled man.

KAN-JIN, カンジン, 肝腎, (lit. bowels and kidneys.) *n.* Important, essential, principal part. — *no yō waszreta*, have forgotten the most important business. Syn. KAN-YŌ, KANAME, TAI-SETSZ, SENICHI.

||KAN-JO, カンジヨ, 閑所, *n.* A privy. Syn. SETSZIN, CHŌDZBA.

†KAN-JŌ, カンジヤウ, 感狀, *n.* A letter of praise for meritorious services, from a *Kimi*.

KAN-JŌ, カンヂヤウ, 勘定, *n.* An account, reckoning, calculation, a bill, the amount. — *szru*, to count up, to reckon, number, to settle an account, to pay a bill. — *wo shimeru*, to find the sum. — *wo awaseru*, to add up an account. — *chigai*, the account is wrong. — *no shime*, the sum of an account. *Fukanjō*, careless of accounts. — *wa ikura*, what is my bill, or what is the amount? — *ga warui*, your reckoning will not suit. *Chōdo sono — da*, you are right, or it is just as you make it. Syn. SANTŌ.

†KAN-KA, カンカ, 閑暇, *n.* Leisure. Syn. HIMA, ITOMA.

†KAN-KEI, カンケイ, 奸計, *n.* Nefarious plan, or scheme, a conspiracy, treason. Syn. WARUDAKUMI.

KAN-KI, カンキ, 寒氣, *n.* Cold. Syn. SAMUSA,

KAN-KI, カンキ, 勘氣, *n.* The discharge of a servant for some offence, disgrace, *Kimi no — wo kōmuru*, to be disgraced by a master. Syn. SHIKUJIRI.

†KAN-KIYO, カンキヨ, 閑居, Living retired from business. — *szru.*

KANKODORI, カンコドリ, 寒子鳥, *n.* A kind of bird.

†KAN-KU, カンク, 難苦, Hard and bitter circumstances, difficult and painful.

†KAN-K'WA, カンクワ 干戈, (*tate hoko.*) Shield and spear. — *wo ugokasz*, to excite war.

KANNA, カンナ, 鉋, *n.* A plane. — *no dai*, the wooden part of a plane. — *kudz*, shavings. *Ita wo — de kedzru*, to plane boards.

KAN-NABE, カンナベ, 燗鍋, *n.* A pot for warming *sake*.

†KANNAGI, カンナギ, 巫, *n.* A dancer in a *Kagura*. Syn. MIKO.

KANNAN, カンナン, 艱難, *n.* Trouble, difficulty, adversity, calamity, affliction. Syn. NAN-GI, KAN-KU, KURŌ.

†KAN-NEI, カンネイ, 奸佞, Subtle, cunning, treacherous, crafty.

KANNIN, カンニン, 勘忍, (*koraye shinobu*), *n.* Patience, forbearance, self-restraint. — *szru*, to be patient, to restrain one's self, to bear patiently. — *sh'te o kun-nasai*, please be patient with me, pardon me. *Naru — wa dare mo szru, naramu — szru ga kannin*, (prov.)

†KAN-NŌ, カンオウ, 感應, *n.* Answer to prayer. — *ga aru.*

KAN-NŌ, カンノウ, 堪能, Skilful, expert,

KAN-NUSHI, カンヌシ, 神主, *n.* The priest of a Sintoo miya. Syn. NEGI.

KANO, カノ, 彼, *pro.* That. — *h'to*, that man. — *tokoro*, that place. Syn. ANO, KŌ.

KANŌ, カナフ, See *Kanai*, *ō*.

KANOKO, カノコ 鹿子, *n.* A fawn, spotted like a fawn.

KANOSHISHI, カノシシ, 鹿, *n.* A deer, stag.

KAN-RAN, カンラン, 橄欖, *n.* The Chinese olive.

†KAN-REI, カンレイ, 寒冷, (*samuku hiyayaka*). Cold and chilly.

KAN-RIYAKU, カンリヤク, 簡略, To be economical, saving, frugal. — *wa fu-ka nitemo dai ichi ni okonō beki koto*, economy should be observed even in wealthy families. Syn. KENYAKU, TSZDZMAYAKA.

†KAN-RO, カンロ, 甘露, *n.* Manna, a sweet dew said to fall from the sky. — *ga furu.*

†KAN-RUI, カンルイ, 感淚, *n.* Tears of joy, or admiration. — *wo nagasz*, to weep for joy.

KAN-SATSZ, カンサツ, 鑑札, *n.* A wooden ticket, or pass.

†KAN-SHA, カンシヤ, 甘蔗, *n.* Sugar cane. Syn. SATŌ-KIBI.

KAN-SHAKU, カンシヤク, 肝積, *n.* Quick temper, passion, petulance. — *wo okosz*, to rouse up anger. Syn. TANKI.

KAN-SHIN, カンシン, 感心, *n.* Admiration, wonder. — *szru,* to be affected to admiration.

†KAN-SHŌ,*-szru,* カンシヤウ, 感賞, To admire and praise.

KAN-SHŌ, カンシヨウ 甘松, *n.* A kind of fragrant wood.

KAN-SHO, カンシヨ, 諫書, *n.* A letter of remonstrance, or expostulation to a superior.

KAN-SZ, カンス, 監司, *n.* The purveying priest of a Buddhist monastery of the Fuke sect.

†KAN-TAN,*-szru,* カンタン, 感嘆, To admire, applaud, to cry or sigh in admiration, or applause.

†KAǸ-TAN, カンタン, 肝膽, *n.* Liver and gall-bladder. *Kantan wo kudaku,* (fig.) with great pains, with great care and anxiety.

†KAN-TEI, カンテイ, 鑒定, Inspecting and judging of the qualities of works of art. — *sha,* a connoisseur, critic, judge. Syn. MEKIKI.

KAN-TEN, カンテン, 乾心太, *n.* A kind of food made of dried sea-weed.

†KAN-WA, カンワ, 閑話, *n.* Leisure talk.

KAN-YETSZ, カンエツ, 感悦, *n.* Admiration and joy.

KAN-ZAKE, カンザケ, 燗酒, *n.* Warm *sake.*

KAN-ZASHI, カンザシ, 簪, *n.* Ornamental hair pins worn by women.

KAN-ZŌ, カンザウ, 甘草, *n.* Liquorice.

KAO, カホ, 顔, *n.* The face, countenance. — *wo szru,* to shave the face. — *wo tszbusz,* to put out of countenance, to abash. *Waga mono-gao ni,* acting or looking as if it was one's own. *Shiranai kao wo sh'te iru,* looking as if he did not know, dissembling. Syn. TSZRA, OMOTE, KAMBASE.

KAO-IRO, カホイロ, 顔色, *n.* The complexion.

KAORASHI,*-sz,-sh'ta,* カヲラス, 令薫, Caust. of *Kaori.* To perfume.

KAORI,*-ru,-tta,* カヲル, 薫, *i.v.* To emit a perfume. *Hana ga kaoru.* Syn. NIŌ.

KAORI, カヲリ, 薫, *n,* A perfume, odor. Syn. NIOI.

KAPPA, カツバ, 合羽, (derived from the Spanish Capa). *n.* A rain coat.

KAPPA, カツパ, 河童, *n.* A fabulous animal, something like a monkey, said to inhabit rivers. Syn. KAWATARŌ.

‖KAPPA-TO, カツパト, *adv.* The sound of falling or of throwing one's self down as, — *fusz.* — *taoreru.*

KAPPOKO, or KAPPUKU, カツプク, *n.* The shape, or proportions. — *ga yoi h'to,* a man of fine proportions.

KARA, カラ, 唐, *n.* China. Syn. MOROKOSHI.

KARA, カラ, 空, *a.* Empty, void, vacant — *ni naru,* to become empty. *Kara-bako,* an empty box. *Kara ido,* a dry well. *Kara hori,* a dry canal. *Kara seki,* a dry cough. *Kara naki,* crying without tears. *Karadeppō,* an unloaded gun. *Hako wo — ni szru,* to empty a box. Syn. AKI.

KARA, カラ 殼, *n.* An empty shell. *Kuri no —,* a chesnut shell. *Kaigara,* clam-shells. *Naki-gara,* empty shell, (fig.) of a lifeless body. *Tamago no —,* an egg shell. *Semi no —,* the cast off shell of a locust.

KARA, カラ, *post pos.* and *adv.* (1.) 自, or 從, From, since. (2.) 故, Because, since, as. (3.) 由, Than. (1.) *Yedo — kita* came from Yedo. *Higashi — nishi made,* from East to West. *Doko —,* from whence? *Itszkara,* when? from what time? *Ima —,* from now, henceforth. *Wiye —,* from above. *Sh'ta kara,* from below. *Sakunen —,* since last year. *Uchi —,* from within. *Soto —,* from without. *Kore —,* then, after this. (2.) *Rusz da kara shiranai,* as I was absent I don't know. *Kaze ga fuku kara yuki-masen,* since the wind blows I will not go. (3.) *Ano hon kara miru to kono hon ōki,* this book looks larger than that. *Kore kara mireba ano hō wa rippa da,* that is more splendid than this. Syn. YORI.

KARA-AYA, カラアヤ, 唐綾, *n.* A kind of silk stuff.

KARABI,*-ru-ta,* カラビル, 乾枯, *i.v.* To be dry, arid, parched. Syn. KAWAKU,

KARADA, カラダ, 體, *n.* The body. Syn. TAI, DŌ.

KARADZ, カラズ, Neg. suffix. contracted of final *ku* and *aradz,* as *Yokaradz,* from *Yoku-aradz.*

KARA-GARA, カラガラ, 辛辛, *adv.* In great danger, or hardly. *Inochi — nigete kuru,* barely escaped with his life.

KARAGE,*-ru,-ta,* カラゲル, 絡, *t.v.* To tie up, to bind with a cord, (as a bundle). *Ni wo —,* to tie up goods. *Nawa de —,* to bind with a rope. *Shiri wo —,* to gird up the skirt of the dress,—gird up the loins. Syn. SHIBARU, KUKURU.

KARAI,*-KI,* カライ, 辛, *a.* Acrid, pungent, sharp in taste, (fig.), severe, harsh. *Koshō ga —,* pepper is pungent. *Ajiwai ga karai,* the taste is acrid. *Karai me ni atta,* met with harsh treatment.

KARAKAI,-*ō*,-*tta*, カラカフ, 哶, *t. v.* To tease, vex, chafe. *Inu ni* —, to tease a dog. *Amari karakō to kui-tszkareru,* if you tease him much you will be bitten. *Kodomo wo* —, to tease a child. Syn. ARASŌ, KAMAU.

KARA-KAMI, カラカミ, 唐紙, *n.* Wall-paper.

KARA-KANE, カラカネ, 鎕, *n.* Bronze.

KAKA-KARA TO, カラカラ, 呵呵, *adv.* The sound of laughter, of rattling. — *uchi warau,* burst out laughing.

KARA-KARA, カラカラ, *adv.* Dry, empty. *Szdzri ga — sh'te iru,* the ink stand is dry.

KARA-KASA, カラカサ, 傘, *n.* An umbrella.

KARAKŌ, カラカフ, See *Karakai.*

KARAKU, カラク, 辛, *adv.* See *Karai.*

KARAKURI, カラクリ, 關捩, *n.* Machinery. Syn. SHIKAKE.

KARAKURI,-*ru*,-*tta*, カラクル, 關捩, *t. v.* To set in motion as a machine, used only figuratively as. *Shinshō wo* —, to trade largely on a small capital.

KARAKUSA, カラクサ, 唐艸, *n.* The ornamental figure of a vine, in cloth, pictures, &c.

KARAMARI,-*ru*,-*tta*, カラマル, 絡, *i. v.* Twined around, coiled; wound round in a spiral form, like a vine, twisted round. *Matsz no ki ni kadzra ga karamatta,* the vine has twined itself around the pine. Syn. MATŌ, MOTSZRERU.

KARAME,-*ru*,-*ta*, カラメル, 縛, *t. v.* To bind. *H'to wo* —, to bind a man. *Ni wo* —, to bind up goods. Syn. SHIBARU.

KARAMETE, カラメテ, 搦手, *n.* The back gate of a castle.

KARAME-TORI,-*ru*,-*tta*, カラメトル, 搦捕, *t.v.* To seize and bind, (as a thief).

KARAMI,-*mu*,-*nda*, カラム, 縛, *t. v.* To coil, twine, or wind round. *Tszta ga ki ni* —, the ivy twines around the tree. *Hebi ga ki ni karande noboru,* the snake climbs a tree by winding around it. Syn. MATOI.

KARAMI, カラミ, 辛味, *n.* Acrid, or pungent, in taste, also a kind of pungent food. — *wo tszkeru.* — *ga aru.*

KARAMI-AI,-*au*,-*atta*, カラミアフ, 相絡, *t.v.* To be coiled, or twined together.

KARAMI-TSZKI,-*ku*,-*ita*, カラミツク, 絡著, *t.v.* To wind, coil, twine round and cleave to anything. *Hebi ga ki ni* —. *Ki no ne ga ishi ni* —,

KARAPPŌ, カラツポウ, 空虛, Empty, dry. — *ni natta.*

KARARI-TO, カラリト, 鏗爾, *adv.* The sound of rattling, in falling. *Yumi wo — nage-szteru.*

KARARI-TO, カラリト, 朗然, *adv.* Clear, free from shade, bright, not gloomy, light. — *yo ga aketa,* the morning has fully dawned.

KARASA, カラサ, 辛, *n.* Acridity pungency, sharpness.

KARA-SAO, カラサホ, 連耞, *n.* A flail. Syn. KURURI.

KARASHI, カラシ, 芥子, *n.* Mustard.

KARASHI, カラシ, 辛, *a.* Acrid, pungent.

KARASHI,-*sz*,-*sh'ta*, カラス, 殺, *t.v.* To make, or let wither, or dry. *Kusa wo kitte karasz.* to cut grass and let it dry.

KARASHI-NA, カラシナ, 芥菜, *n.* The mustard plant.

KARASZ, カラス, 鴉, *n.* A crow.

KARASZ-HEBI, カラスヘビ, 烏蛇, *n.* A black-snake.

KARASZKI, カラスキ, 犂, *n.* A plough.

KARASZMI, カラスミ, 鰤脯, *n.* Dried Salmon's-roe.

KARASZ-URI, カラスウリ, 天瓜, *n.* A kind of melon, used only as a medicine.

KARA-TACHI, カラタチ, 枳, *n.* A kind of thorny bush. Ægle sepiaria. Syn. KIKOKU.

KARA-USZ, カラウス, 碓, *n.* A mortar for cleaning rice, (the pestle is worked by the foot).

KARE, カレ, 彼, *pro.* That thing, that person, he. *Kare ga tame ni,* for his sake. — *wo nikumu mono ga ōi,* there are many who hate him. Syn. K'YATSZ

KARE,-*ru*,-*ta*, カレル, 枯, *i.v.* Withered, dried, dead, (as a tree, grass), 涸, dried up (as water), 嗄, hoarse, husky, (of the voice). *Ki ya kusa nado ga kareta,* the tree or grass is withered. *Kaze wo hīte koye ga* —, the voice is hoarse from a cold. *Te ga* —, to be a good penman. *Midz ga* —, the water is dried-up,

KAREBA, カレバ, 枯葉, *n.* Withered leaves.

KARE-GARE, カレガレ, 枯枯, Withered, dried, empty.

†KAREI, カレイ, 嘉例, A celebration or usage founded on some lucky event.

KAREI, カレイ, 鰈, *n.* A kind of fish.

KARE-KI, カレキ, 枯木, *n.* A withered, or dead tree-

KARE-KORE, カレコレ, 彼此, This and that, one thing or another, about. — *tori-soroyeru,* to pick out and put various things

in a lump. — *szru uchi hi ga tatsz*, while doing this and that the days passed. — *jū nen*, about ten years.

KARERA, カレラ, 等彼, plural of *Kare*. Those.

KARI,-*ru*,-*tta*, or *rita*, カル, 刈, *t. v.* To cut, (as grain, hay,) to harvest, reap. *Ine wo* —, to cut rice. *Mugi wo* —, to reap wheat.

KARI,-*ru*,-*tta*, カル, 獵, *t. v.* To hunt, (animals,) to chase game. *Kuma wo* —, to hunt the bear. *Yama wo* —, to hunt in the mountains.

KARI-*ru*, or *riru*,-*ita*, カル, 借, *t.v.* To borrow, to rent. *Kane wo karu*, to borrow money. *Iye wo karita*, have rented a house. *H'to no te wo* —, to get another to lend a hand.

KARI,-*ru*,-*tta*, カル, 驅, *t. v.* To drive, urge onward, to hurry. *Uma wo katte hashiru.*

KARI, カリ, 獵, *n.* The chase, a hunt. — *wo szru*, to hunt. — *ni yuku*, to go a hunting.

KARI, カリ, 鴈, *n.* A wild goose. Syn. GAN.

KARI, カリ, *n.* The corrona glandis.

KARI, カリ, 假, Temporary, for a short time. — *no yadori*, a temporary lodging. — *no yo*, this world which is only temporary (Bud.) — *no hashi*, a temporary bridge.

KARI, カリ, 借, *n.* Borrowing, a debt incurred from borrowing money. *Ano akindo taisō* — *ga dekita*, that merchant has borrowed much, or is a great deal in debt.

KARI-ATSZME,-*ru*,-*ta*, カリアツメル, 駈集, *t.v.* To drive together, to urge to assemble.

KARIBA, カリバ, 獵場, *n.* Hunting ground.

KARI-DZMAI, カリズマ井, 借住居, *n.* A temporary residence.

KARI-GANE, カリガ子, 鴈, *n.* A wild goose, the cry of the wild goose. Syn. GAN.

KARI-GI, カリギ, 借著, *n.* Borrowed clothes.

KARIGINU, カリギヌ, 狩衣, *n.* A kind of coat worn by nobles.

KARI-IYE, カリイヘ, 借家, *n.* A rented house.

KARI-KABU, カリカブ, 刈株, *n.* Stubble, after the grain is cut.

KARI-KATA, カリカタ, 借方, *n.* The borrower, a lessee.

KARI-KURA, カリクラ, 狩倉, *n.* Hunting ground.

KARI-KURASHI,-*sz*,-*sh'ta*, カリクラス, 狩暮, *i.v.* To live by hunting, to spend the day hunting.

KARI-MATA, カリマタ, 鴈股, *n.* An arrow with two heads.

KARI-MONO, カリモノ, 借物, *n.* Borrowed things.

KARI-MOYŌSHI,-*sz*,-*sh'ta*, カリモヨホス, 駈催, *t.v.* To drive or hurry to do. *Hanami ni h'to wo kari-moyōsz*, to hurry persons to get ready to go to see the flowers.

KARI-NE, カリ子, 假寐, *n.* A transient sleep. Syn. UTATANE.

KARI-NI, カリニ, 假, *adv.* Temporarily, for a short time only, lightly. — *hashi wo kakeru*, to throw over a temporary bridge. — *mo warui koto woba yuwanu ga yoi*, it is better not to speak evil even in sport. — *sō sh'te oku*, let it be so for the present.

KARI-NUI, カリヌヒ, 假縫, *n.* Temporary sewing, basting.

‖KARI-SHUN, カリシュン, 芟時節, *n.* Harvest time.

KARISOME, カリソメ, 假初, Small in degree, trivial, trifling, little, slight. — *kara koto ga okoru*, great events arise from trifling causes. — *ni mo uso wo tszkanu ga yoi*, it is better not to tell even a trifling lie.

KARI-UDO, カリウド, 狩人, *n.* A hunter.

KARI-YA, カリヤ, 借居, A rented house.

KARI-YASZ, カリヤス, 藎草, *n.* A kind of plant.

KARIYŌBINGA, カリヨウビンガ, 迦陵頻伽, *n.* A bird in the Buddhist paradise, having a human face, and a charming voice.

KARI-YOSE,-*ru*,-*ta*, カリヨセル, 駈寄, *t.v.* To drive near.

KARŌ, カラウ, 家老, *n.* The ministers, or council of a *Daimio*. Syn RŌ-SHIN.

KARŌ, カラウ, A dubitative suffix to adjectives, contracted from the terminal syllable, *ku*, and *arō*. As *yokarō*, contracted from *Yoku arō*, I think it will do. *Ashikarō*, from *Ashiku arō*, I think it is bad. *Kurokarō*, I think it is black. *Amakarō*, I think it is sweet.

KARŌ, カラウ, 辛, *adv.* Acrid, pungent, harsh.

KARO-GAROSHII,-KI,-KU, カロガロシイ, 輕輕敷, Lightly, inconsiderately, heedlessly, undignified light or trifling in manner.

KAROI,-KI, カロイ 輕, Light not heavy, same as *Karui*.

†KARŌJITE, カラウジテ, 辛, *adv.* With much difficulty, hardly, barely. — *deru*, to get out with difficulty.

KARON-JI,-*dzru*,-*ta*, カロンズル, 輕, *t.v.*

To make light of, to despise, contemn, to esteem of little value, disregard, slight. *Hokotte h'to wo karondzru koto nakare*, must not arrogantly despise others. *Inochi wo* — to disregard life.
Syn. KEI-BETSZ, NAIGASHIRO, ANADORU.

KAROSHIME,-*ru*,-*ta*, カロシメル, 輕, *t. v.* To make light of, despise, contemn, disregard, slight. *H'to wo* —.

KARŪ, カルウ, 輕, *adv.* same as *Karuku.*

KARU, カル, see *Kari.*

KARUGARUSHII, カルガルシイ, same as *Karogaroshii.*

KARU-GAYUYE-NI, カルガユヱニ, 故, *adv.* Therefore, on this account, for this reason.
Syn. YUYENI, KONOYUYENI.

KARU-HADZMI, カルハヅミ, 輕逸, Careless, heedless, reckless. — *na h'to*, a reckless person.

KARUI,-KI, カルイ, 輕, *a.* Light, not heavy, mean, low in social position. *Mekata ga karui*, the weight is light. *Karui h'to*, person of low position.

KARU-ISHI, カルイシ, 浮石, *n.* Pumice stone. Syn. FUSEKI.

KARUKO, カルコ, 輕籠, *n.* A basket carried by coolies, a coolie, porter.
Syn. NINSOKU.

KARUKU, カルク, 輕, *adv.* Light, see *Karui.*

KARU-KUCHI, カルクチ, 輕口, *n.* Fluent in talking, voluble, flippant.

KARUME,-*ru*,-*ta*, カルメル, 輕, *t. v.* To make light, to lighten. *Karumete yarō*, will lighten it.

KARUMERU, カルメル, *n.* Calomel.

KARU-NI, カルニ, 輕荷, *n.* Ballast.

KARUSA, カルサ, 輕, *n.* Lightness.

KARUSHI, カルシ, 輕, *a.* Light, not heavy, low in social position.

KARUTA, カルタ, 骨牌, *n.* Playing cards. — *wo hiku*, to play cards.

KARU-WASA, カルワザ, 輕態, *n.* Acrobatic feats.

KASA, カサ, 笠, *n.* A broad rimmed hat, generally made of split bamboo. — *wo kaburu*, to put on a hat. *Kasa ikkai*, one hat.

KASA, カサ, 瘡, *n.* An eruption on the skin, but now mostly used of syphilis. — *wo kaku*, to get syphilis.

KASA, カサ, 傘, *n.* An umbrella. — *wo hirogeru*, to open an umbrella. — *mo szbomeru*, to shut an umbrella. — *no hajiki gane*, the spring of an umbrella. — *no hone*, the stays of an umbrella. — *no rokuro*, the ring into which the stays converge. — *wo haru*, to make an umbrella. *Kasa ippon*, one umbrella. *Hi-gasa*, a parasol, *Sashigasa*, umbrella.

KASA, カサ, 蓋, *n.* The wooden lid of a cup, or bowl.

KASA, カサ, 暈, *n.* The ring round the sun, or moon in hazy weather. *Tszki ga — wo totta ame ga furu de arō*, when the moon has a ring around it, it will probably rain.

KASA, カサ, 嵩, *n.* A heap, pile, or bulk made by laying one thing on another. — *wa dorehodo aru*, how high is the pile. *Midz no kasa*, the heap of waters. *Kasa no nai mono*, things of small bulk.

KASA, カサ, 梂, *n.* The hull of some kinds of nuts.

KASABARI,-*ru*,-*tta*, カサバル, 嵩張, *i. v.* To be large and bulky. *Karukute mo kasabatte iru kara semai michi torarenu*, they are light, but being bulky they cannot be carried through a narrow way. *Kasabaru nimotsz wa funadzmi ni komaru*, bulky goods are troublesome to stow in a ship.

KASA-BUKURO, カサブクロ, 傘袋, *n.* An umbrella-case.

KASABUTA, カサブタ, 痂, *n.* A scab.

KASADAKA, カサダカ, 嵩高, Bulky, occupying a large space, making a large pile. — *ni naru*, to be bulky. *Mekata wadzka naredomo — nite komaru*, the weight is small, but it is so bulky I am inconvenienced.

KASAHARI, カサハリ, 傘張, *n.* An umbrella maker.

KASA-KAKI, カサカキ, 患瘡人, *n.* A person who has the syphilis.

KASAMI,-*mu*,-*nda*, カサム, 嵩, *i. v.* To accumulate, to increase. *Shakkin ga nennen ni* —, his debts increased year by year.

KASANARI,-*ru*,-*tta*, カサナル, 重, *i. v.* To be piled up, heaped up by laying one on another, placed one on another, to increase in number by adding one to another. *Hi ga kasanatte futoru* as the days increase in number it grows larger. *Ochiba ga* —, the falling leaves are piled on one another.

KASANE,-*ru*,-*ta*, カサネル, 重, *t. v.* To pile, or lay one thing on another. *Te wo* —, to lay one hand on another. *Hon wo* —, to pile books or lay one on another. *Hi wo kasanete jō-ju szru*, to take many days to complete anything. *Kame wo kasenete tsztszmu*, wrap it in several sheets of paper.

KASANE, カサネ, 襲, *n.* A pile, consisting of two or three things of the same kind laid one on the other. *Kosode h'to* —, a pair of garments, (outside and inside.)

KASANE-AGE,*-ru,-ta*, カサネアゲル, 重上, *t.v.* To pile up by placing one on another.

KASANE-GASANE, カサネガサネ, 重重, *adv.* Over and over, repeatedly, many times, often. Syn. TABI-TABI, SAI-SAI, SHIBA-SHIBA, JŪJŪ.

KASANETE, カサネテ, 重, *adv.* Again. — *agari-mashō*, I will come again. — *kuru ni wa oyobanu*, it is unnecessary to come again.

KASASAGI, カササギ, 鵲, *n.* A kind of bird.

KASE, カセ, 械, *n.* Shackles, fetters. *Te-kase*, hand-cuffs. *Kubikase*, the cangue, yoke. *Ashi-kase*, fetters, stocks.

KASE, カセ, 桛, *n.* A reel. *Ito h'to kase*, a hank, or skein of yarn. *Ito wo — ni kakeru*, to reel thread into a skein.

KASE,*-ru,-ta*, カセル, *i.v.* To form a scab, to scab. *Hōzō ga kaseta*, the pock has scabbed.

KASEGI,*-gu,-ida*, カセグ, 稼, *t.v.* To do or work with diligence, industry or zeal. *Kagigō wo —*, to work diligently at one's business. *Kasegu ni oi-tszku bimbō nashi*, poverty cannot overtake diligence.
Syn. HATARAKU.

KASEI, カセイ, 加勢, *(kuwayeru hei). n*, Auxiliary troops, reinforcement, joining an army. — *szru*, to unite forces, to join an army, to reinforce, to help, second.

†KASEI, カセイ, 苛政, Tyranical government.

†KASHAKU, カシャク, 呵責, *(shikari semeru)*. Punishment, torture, torment, (Bud). *Zainin wo — szru*, to punish a criminal.

KASHI, カシ, 橿, *n.* The oak.

KASHI, カシ, 川岸, *n.* River bank.
Syn. KISHI.

KASHI, カシ, An exclam. used at the end of a sentence of exhortation, entreaty or request, = O that, I pray that, I hope that, request that. *Sono mi wo tsztszshimi, oyago ni kō-kō shi-tamaye kashi*, I beseech you to be watchful of yourselves, and be obedient to your parents. As an expletive, perhaps giving emphasis to the preceding sentiment, as. *Sa mo ari-ken kashi*, I think it is so.

KASHI,*-sz,-sh'ta*, カス, 貸, *t.v.* To lend, to rent. *Kash'te okure*, lend me. *Kane wo kash'te ri wo toru*, to lend money on interest. *Iye wo —*, to rent a house. *Choito mimi wo kash'te kudasare*, please listen to me a moment. Syn. YŌDATERU.

†KA-SHI,*-szru,-sh'ta*, カスル, 嫁, *t.v.* To marry a husband, to go as a bride to her husbands house.
Syn. TOTSZGU, YOME-IRI WO SZRU.

||KASHI,*-sz,-sh'ta*, カス, 淅, *t.v.* To soak in water before boiling. *Kome wo kasz.*
Syn. HITASZ.

KASHIBATA, カシバタ, 川岸端, *n.* River-bank.

†KASHIDZKI,-KU,-ITA, カシヅク, *t.v.* To attend, wait on, to take care of, to nurse, to bring up, to treat respectfully.
Syn. MORI WO SZRU.

KASHIDZKI, カシヅキ, *n.* A nurse, waiting maid, attendant, a servant. — *ra*, the attendants.

KASHIGI,*-gu,-ida*, カシグ, 傾, *i.v.* To incline, lean to one side, to careen. *Fune ga —*, the boat careens over.
Syn. KATAMUKU.

†KASHIKAMASHII,-KI,-KU,-U, カシカマシク, 聒, Loud and noisy, deafening, stunning. *Taki no oto wa mimi ni kashikamashiu todoroki-hibiku.*
Syn. KAMABISZSHII, YAKAMASHII.

KASHIKATA, カシカタ, 貸方, *n.* A lender, creditor. Syn. KASHI-NUSHI.

†KASHIKI,*-ku,-ita*, カシク, 炊, *t.v.* To cook rice. — *meshi wo —*.
Syn. TAKU.

KASH'KO, カシコ, 彼處, *adv.* There, yonder, that place. *Koko kash'ko*, here and there. Syn. ANATA, ASZKO, ACHIRA.

KASH'KOI,-KI,-KU,-Ō,-SA, カシコイ, 賢, Feeling awe, dread, or fear; intelligent, clever, sagacious. *Kaso'koku mo mōshi idashi*, have said it though feeling great awe. *Kash'koi h'to*, a clever man.
Syn. RIKŌ, HATSZMEI.

KASH'KOMARI,*-ru,-tta*, カシコマル, 畏, *i. v.* To sit in the Japanese mode, respectfully and humbly to consider, or promise obedience to what one is told to do. *Ōse-kudasare sōro omomuki kash'komari tatematszrisoro*, I will most respectfully obey your instructions.

†KASH'KOMI, カシコミ, 畏, *(Kash'kosa ni.)* With awe, dread, or profound veneration. *Kash'komi-kash'komi mo haruka ni ogami-tatematszru*, worship afar off with awe.

KASHIKU, カシク, 賢, The closing word of a letter, meaning respectfully.

†KASHIMASHII,-KI,-KU,-U,-SA, カシマシイ, 聒, Loud and noisy, boisterous, tumultuous. Syn. YAKAMASHII.

KA-SHIN, カシン, 家臣, *n.* Retainer, serf.

KASHIRA, カシラ, 頭, *n.* The head, the

chief, headman. — *no h'to*, the headman. *Uma no* —, the head of a horse.
Syn. ATAMA.

KASHIWA, カシハ, 槲, *n.* A kind of oak. — *ni neru*, to sleep with the under quilt folded over for a covering.

KASHIWADE, カシハデ, 栢手, *n.* Clapping the hands together when praying. — *wo utte ogamu.*

KASHIWA-MOCHI, カシハモチ, 槲葉餅, *n.* A kind of rice food boiled in the leaves of the Kashiwa.

†KA-SHOKU, カショク, 家職, *n.* Family business, occupation, calling.
Syn. KA-GIYŌ, SHŌBAI, SHOKU-BUN.

KA-SŌ, カサウ, 家相, *n.* The form, or position of a house, in respect of its being lucky or unlucky.

KASSEN, カッセン, 合戰, *n*, A battle. — *szru*, to fight a battle. *Kassemba*, the place where a battle is fought.

KASSZI, カッスイ, *n.* Dry, deficient in water, as, a river, paddy-field, &c. — *de fune ga agaremasen.*

KASZ, カス, 貸, see *Kashi.*.

KASZ, カス, 粕, *n.* Dregs, sediment, grounds, lees, settlings, residuum.

KASZ-DZKE, カスヅケ, 粕漬, *n.* Pickled in *sake* lees.

KASZGAI, カスガヒ, 鎹, *n.* An iron clamp.

KASZGE, カスゲ, 糟毛, *n.* An iron grey horse.

†KA-SZI, カスイ, 河水, *(kawa no midz,)* *n.* River water.

KASZKA-NARU, カスカナル, 微, *a.* Faint, indistinct, dim, obscure. — *koye*, a faint sound.

KASZKA-NI, カスカニ, 微, *adv.* Slightly, faintly, indistinctly, obscurely, dimly. *Fuye no ne kaszka-ni kikoyeru*, the sound of the flute was faintly heard. — *miyeru*, dimly seen.

KASZME,*-ru,-ta*, カスメル, 掠, *t. v.* To rob, take by force, to seize; to make hazy. *Shu-jin no mono wo* —, to rob one's master. *H'to no me wo* —, to rob a person secretly. *Kuni wo* —, to take possession of a country. *Kuro kemuri tenchi wo* —, the black smoke made the sky and earth hazy.
Syn. UBAU, NUSZMU.

KASZMI,*-mu,-nda*, カスム, 霞, or 眊, *i. v.* To be hazy, dim, clouded. *Sora ga* —, the weather is hazy. *Me ga* — eyes are hazy, dim.

KASZMI, カスミ, 霞, *n.* Haze, mist. *Harugaszmi*, the spring-haze. — *ga tanabiku.*

KASZMI-WATARI, *-ru,-tta*, カスミワタル, 霞渡, *i. v.* To be hazy all over.

†KASZMO, カスモ, 雀斑, *n.* Freckles on the face. Syn. SOBAKASZ.

KASZRE,*-ru,-ta*, カスレル, 渴, *i. v.* To be unevenly colored, having spots where the ink or color has left no mark. *Ji ga kaszreta*, the character is written so that in places the ink has made no trace.

KASZRI,*-ru,-tta*, カスル, *t. v.* To graze, to wound slightly in passsing, to fling an indirect sarcasm at another. *Ki wo kasztte tōru*, to graze a tree in passing. *Kaszrikidz*, a slight wound, made by the grazing of a ball, arrow, &c.

KASZRI, カスリ, *n.* Money taken as percentage, or commission, or cabbage, squeeze money, black mail. — *wo toru*, to levy black mail, to squeeze. *Kashira ga ninsoku no atama wo hatte* — *wo toru*, the coolie master levies a small squeeze on each of the coolies. Syn. UWAMAYE.

KASZTERA, カステラ, *n.* Castile in Spain, also, sponge-cake.

KATA, カタ, 肩, *n.* The shoulder. *Kata wo haru*, to shrug the shoulders. *Kata wo nuku*, to get out of a bad scrape. — *wo naraberu mono wa nai*, has no equal.

KATA, カタ, 方, *(hō)*, *n.* Side, part, region, party, person, mark, trace. *Migi, hidari, kita, minami nado no kata*, the right or left side, northern or southern region. *Ano o kata*, that person. *Anatagata*, you, (plural). *Itash'kata*, or *shi-kata ga nai*, there is no resourse, no help. *Shikata ga warui*, what he does is bad. *Hiyō-rō kata*, the commissariat department. *Ōdztsz kata*, the artillery. *Mi kata. Tekikata. Yuki-gata shiradz*, don't know where he has gone. *Yorokobi h'to* — *naradz*, was greatly rejoiced. — *ga tszku*, to be decided, settled. — *wo tszkeru*, to fix on, or decide on the way of doing.

KATA, カタ, 型, *n.* A mould, matrice. 形, pattern form, figure, shape, copy, model. *Imono no* —, the mould for castings. *Some mono no* —, the pattern of any dyed article. — *wo tszkeru*, to adorn with figures. *Kono* — *wo totte koshirayeru*, make it after this pattern.

KATA, カタ, 片, *n.* One of a pair, used mostly in compound words.

KATA, カタ, 當, *n.* A pledge, pawn. — *ni adzke-oku*, to give as a pledge.
Syn. HIKI-ATE.

KATA-AGE, カタアゲ, 肩上, Tucking the sleeve at the shoulder,—as in childhood to allow for growing. — *no kimono.*

KATA-ASHI, カタアシ, 片足, *n.* One leg. — *de tatsz,* to stand on one leg.

KATA-ATE, カタアテ, 肩當, *n.* A shoulder pad.

KATA-BAMI, カタバミ, 酸漿, *n.* Sheep's sorrel.

KATA-BĪKI, カタビイキ, 片贔屓, *n.* Favoritism, partiality, preference of one over another. — *wo szru,* to be partial, to favor one side. Syn. YEKO.

KATA-BINGI, カタビンギ, 片便宜, *n.* Communication only in one direction,—having no return. — *de am-pi ga shirenu,* as there is only an opportunity for sending a letter and none for receiving, I don't know how they are. Syn. KATADAYORI.

KATABIRA, カタビラ, 帷子, *n.* A very thin kind of summer garment.

KATABUKE,*-ru,-ta,* カタブケル, 傾, See *Katamuke, ru.*

KATABUKE,*-ku,* カタブク, See *Katamuki, ku.*

KATACHI, カタチ, 形, *n.* Figure, form, shape, likeness. *H'to no* —, form of a man. *Kami wa — no nai mono,* God is without shape. *Kage mo — mo nai koto wo iu,* to say what has neither shadow or substance—a lie. — *wo tszkuru,* to adorn the person. Syn. SZGATA, NARI.

KATA-CHIMBA, カタチンバ, 片跛, *n.* Lame in one leg. Syn. BIKKŌ.

KATA-DAYORI, カタダヨリ, 片便, *n.* Same as *Katabingi.*

KATADORI,*-ru,-tta,* カタドル, 像, *t.v.* To make in the likeness of, to imitate, resemble. *Fuji-san wo kotadotte yama wo tszkuru,* to make a mountain in imitation of Fuji-yama. *H'to no na wo katadotte tszkeru,* to name after another person. Syn. MANERU, NISERU.

†KATADORI,*-ru,-tta,* カタドル, 片取, *t.v.* To place near to for defence, or support, to rest against. *Yama wo katadotte jin wo toru,* resting the flank of the army against a hill to put it in order of battle. Syn. HIKAYERU.

KATADZ, カタズ, 不勝, neg. of *Kachi, tsz.*

KATADZ, カタヅ, 乾津, *n.* Spittle, saliva, used only in the phrase, *Katadz wo nomu,* to swallow the spittle, a fig. expression for anxiety, or solicitude, with attention. Syn. TSZBAKI.

KATADZKE,*-ru,-ta,* カタヅケル 片附, *t.v.* To lay to one side; put away, set away, fig. to place a daughter in the house of a husband. *Tori midaretaru mono wo katadzkete oku,* to collect and put away things that are laying about in confusion. *Shigoto wo* —, to do up or finish one's work. *Muszme wo* —, to marry off a daughter.

KATADZKI,-KU,-ITA, カタヅク, 片附, *i.v.* Put away, set aside; finished, done; married off.

KATADZMI,*-mu,-nda,* カタズム 僻, *i.v.* To incline to one side, biased, prejudiced, warped; rustic.

KATADZRI,*-ru,-tta,* カタズル, 片重, Lopsided, heavier on one side than the other.

KATA-GATA, カタガタ, 旁, Doing anything by the way, or whilst attending to the principal matter to take the opportunity to do something else; whilst, besides. *San-kei kata-gata Kamakura ye yuku,* whilst going to the temple to worship to take the opportunity of visiting Kamakura. *Kai-mono katagata asobi ni yuku,* whilst going out to make some purchases to take a walk. Syn. GATERA, NAGARA.

KATAGATA, カタガタ, 方方, Plur. of *Kata,* persons. *Hanayakanaru on katagata.*

KATAGE,*-ru,-ta,* カタゲル, 擔, *t.v.* To lay, or carry on the shoulder. (傾) To incline, turn on the side, careen. *Chawan wo katagereba midz ga koboreru,* if you incline the cup the water will spill. *Ni wo* —, to carry a burden on the shoulder. Syn. KATSZGU, KATAMUKERU.

KATAGI, カタギ, 樫, *n.* Hard wood, especially oak.

KATAGINU, カタギヌ, 肩衣, *n.* That part of the dress of ceremony worn on the shoulders.

KATA-HASHI, カタハシ, 片端, *n.* One edge, one side. *Michi no — yotte aruku,* to walk along one side of a road.

KATA-HIJI, カタヒヂ, 片臂, *n.* One elbow.

KATAI,-KI,-SHI, カタイ, 堅, *a.* Hard, solid, compact, firm, tight, close, strict, moral, severe, (難) hard to do, difficult. *Katai ki,* hard wood. *Ishi ga* —, a stone is hard. — *h'to,* a moral man. *Deki-gatai,* hard to do. *Katai koto da,* a difficult thing. *Ji-shi-gatai,* hard to cure.

KATAI, カタ井, 乞食, *n.* A beggar. Syn. HI-NIN, KOJIKI.

KATA-IJI, カタイヂ, 偏意地, *n.* Obstinate, stubborn, churlish. — *na h'to.* — *wo haru.* Syn. HEN-KUTSZ.

KATA-IKI, カタイキ, 肩息, Gasping for breath, out of breath. *Ino wo tataite — ni sh'ta,* the dog has been beaten and lies gasping. — *ni natte kaketa kita,* came running out of breath.

KATA-INAKA, カタヰナカ, 片田舍, *n.* Remote country, far away inland.
Syn. HEM-PI.

KATAIPPŌ, or KATAPPŌ, カタイツパウ, 片一方, One of a pair, one side. *Te ga — kikanai*, one of my hands is useless. *Zōri ga — miyenu*, one of my sandals is lost. *Michi no* —, one side of a road. — *no ashi*, one foot.

KATA-JI, カタヂ, 堅地, *n.* Hard ground, hard or solid in texture.

KATAJIKENAI,-KI,-KU,-Ō, カタジケナイ, 辱, Thankful, much obliged,—in acknowledgment of a favor. *Katajikenaku zonji-tatematszri soro*, or *katajikenō gozaimasz*, I am obliged to you. *Kore wa katajikenai*, I am obliged to you for this.
Syn. ARIGATAI.

KATA-KANA, カタカナ, 片假名, *n.* A kind of Japanese character,—the sharp contracted form such as are here used.

KATA-KATA, カタカタ, 片方, One of a pair, one side. *Zōri — naku-natta*, have lost one of my sandals.

KATA-KATTA, カタカツタ, Coll. for *Kata-kuatta*, was hard or difficult.

KATA-KAWA, カタカハ, 片側, *n.* One side, *Michi no* —, side of the road. *Michi no — ni mise ga aru*, there are shops on one side of the street.

KATAKI, カタキ, 敵, *n.* Enemy, adversary, foe. — *wo utsz*, to kill an enemy. — *wo toru* (idem.) Syn. ADA, TEKI, AITE.

KATAKI-UCHI, カタキウチ, 敵討, *n.* Slaying an enemy in revenge.

KATA-KOTO, カタコト, 方言, *n.* Provincialism, or vulgar pronunciation.

KATAKU, カタク, 堅, *adv.* Hard, rigid, solid, compact, firm, tight, strict, moral, severe, difficult. — *szru*, to harden, &c. — *mōshi-tszkeru*, to rigidly command. — *mamoru*, to keep strictly. *Michi wo mamoru koto — nai*, it is not difficult to do right. — *shiboru*, to tie tightly.

KATAKU-NA, カタクナ, 頑, Obstinate, stubborn, head-strong. Syn. HEN-KUTSZ.

KATA-KURUSHII,-KI,-KU,-Ū, カタクルシイ, 佶屈, Painfully strict in manner, rigid or severe in temper, severely exact.

KATAMARI,-*ru*,-*tta*, カタマル, 固, *i.v.* To become hardened, solidified, coagulated, condensed, (fig.) to be obdurate, confirmed in, fixed in, obstinately bent on, bigoted. *Tszchi, chi, chi-chi, nori nado ga* —, earth, blood, milk and paste become hard. *Buppō ni* —, bigoted in Buddhism. *Gaku-mon ni kori-katamaru*, engrossed in study.
Syn. KORU, SHŪ-JAKU.

KATAMARI, カタマリ, 塊, *n.* A hard lump. *Tszchi no* —, a clod of earth. *Hara ni — aru*, has a tumor in the abdomen. *Chi no* —, a clot of blood.

†KATAMASHII,-KI,-KU,-U, カタマシイ, 姦, Depraved, abandoned, unprincipled.
Syn. YOKOSHIMA, KAN-JA.

KATAME,-*ru*,-*ta*, カタメル, 固, *t. v.* To harden, to make solid, strong, firm, or secure, to strengthen, to defend, to guard, to congeal, solidify. *Mame no gō wo katamete tōfu ni szru*. *Shiro wo* —, to fortify a castle with troops.

KATAME, カタメ, 約, *n.* Promise, agreement, word of honor, pledge, vow.
Syn. YAK'SOKU.

KATAME, カタメ, 固, *n.* A guard.
Syn. KEI-GO.

KATAME, カタメ, 片目, One eye. — *de teppō wo tameru*, to level a gun with one eye. — *de miru*, to look with one eye.

†KATAMI, カタミ, 筐, *n.* A basket.
Syn. KAGO.

KATAMI, カタミ, 記念, *n.* A memento, or present made to a friend on taking a journey, or dying. — *wo yaru*. — *wo oku*. — *wo nokosz*.
Syn. YUI-MOTSZ, YUDZRI-MONO.

†KATAMI-NI, カタミニ, 各自, *adv.* Together, mutually. — *sode wo shiboritsztsz*, whilst they both were wringing their sleeves. Syn. TAGAI-NI, AI-TOMO-NI.

KATAMI, カタミ, 偏身, *n.* One side of the body, half of the body. — *ga shibireru*, one side is paralized.

KATA-MI, カタミ, 肩身, *n.* Shoulders and body, (fig.) of one's bearing, carriage, as. — *ga semai*, to appear abashed, sheepish. — *ga hiroi*, to be bold, manly.

KATA-MICHI, カタミチ, 片路, One way, of either going or returning. — *kachi de yuki*, — *fune de kayeru*, to go on foot and return by ship.

KATAMUKE,-*ru*,-*ta*, カタムケル, 傾, *t.v.* To incline, to bend to the side, to make lean over, to overthrow, subvert. *Atama wo* —, to incline the head. *Kuni wo* —, to ruin a country. *Sake wo* —, to drink wine. *Kokoro wo* —, to feel inclined to.

KATAMUKI,-*ku*,-*ita*, カタムク, 傾, *i.v.* To be inclined, bent over, to lean over, to careen, to decline. *Hi ga* —, the sun is declining. *Aku ni* —, inclined to evil. *Kuni ga* —, the country is tending to ruin.

KATANA, カタナ, 刀, *n.* A sword, knife.

Ko-gatana, a small knife, penknife. — *wo sasz*, to wear a sword. — *wo nuku*, to draw a sword. — *wo saya ni osameru*, to put a sword into the scabbard. — *wo utsz*, to forge a sword. — *wo togu*, to sharpen a sword. — *wo koshirayeru*, to fit out a sword. — *no ha*, the edge of a sword. — *no mune*, the back of a sword. — *no mi*, the blade of a sword. — *no kisaki*, the point of a sword. — *no tszka*, the hilt of a sword. — *no tszba*, the guard of sword. — *no saya*, the scabbard of a sword. — *ni hon*, two swords.

KATANA-KAKE, カタナカケ, 刀架, *n.* A sword-rack.

KATANA-KIDZ, カタナキヅ, 刀瘢, *n.* A sword-cut.

KATANA-TOGI, カタナトギ, 刀研, *n.* A sword sharpener.

†KATA-NO-GOTOKI,-KU,-SHI, カタノゴトキ, ク, 如形, *adv.* According to the pattern, example, or usage. Syn. REI NO TŌRI.

†KA-TAN,-SZRU, カタン, 荷擔, To take part with, to side with, to confederate with, to join, help. *Karera ni katan itasz-beki szji wa gozanaku soro.* Syn. SATAN.

‖KATANUGI,-*gu*,-*ida*, カタヌグ, 袒, *i. v.* To bear the shoulder. Syn. HADANUGU.

‖KATA-OCHI, カタオチ, 偏貶, *n.* One side or party unjustly blamed through partiality for the other. — *ni naru.* — *ni szru.*

KATA-OMOI, カタオモヒ, 片思, *n.* One sided, love on one side, and not reciprocated. *Iso no awabi no* —.

KATA-OMOTE, カタオモテ, 半面, (*hammen,*) *n.* One face, or surface, of any thing that has two; half the face.

KATA-OYA, カタオヤ, 片親, *n.* One parent, the other being dead.

KATAPPIRA, カタツピラ, 片平, *n.* One side, surface, or page.

KATARAI,-*ō*,-*atta*, カタラフ, 語合, *i. v.* To converse together, to consult together; to talk with in order to gain over. Syn. DAN-KŌ, SŌ-DAN, HANASHIAI.

KATARAI, カタラヒ, 語合, *n.* Conversation, consultation.

KATARI,-*ru*,-*tta*, カタル, 語, *t. v.* To talk, tell, to sing in a recitative manner, to chant. *Mukashi wo* —, to talk about old times. *Jōruri wo* —, to sing an operatic song. Syn. HANASZ, DAN-DZRU.

KATARI,-*ru*,-*tta*, カタル, 騙, *t. v.* To impose on by false representations, to dupe, to say fraudulently, to defraud, *H'to wo katatte kane wo toru*, to impose upon a person and get his money. *H'to no namaye wo* —, to assume the name of another, (in order to defraud.) Syn. ITSZWARU, DAMASZ, AZAMUKU.

KATARI, カタリ, 騙, *n.* False representation, imposition, fraud. — *wo szru.*

KATARI-MONO, カタリモノ, 騙者, *n.* An impostor, swindler, knave

KATA-SAGARI, カタサガリ, 偏低, *n.* The slope of one side of a hill; hanging down on one side.

†KATASHIKI,-*ku*, カタシキ, 片敷, *t.v.* To spread out one side of a garment, or sleeve. *Koromo katashiki h'tori ka mo nen.*

KATASHIME,-*ru*,-*ta*, カタシメル, 令勝, caust. of *Kachi*. To make to conquer.

†KATASHIRO, カタシロ, 尸, *n.* An effigy, image, or likeness. — *wo koshirayeru*, to make an effigy. Syn. H'TO-GATA.

KATA-SZMI, カタスミ, 偏隅, *n.* One corner, or angle. — *ye yoru*, gathered into one corner.

KATA-TE, カタテ, 隻手, *n.* One hand. — *ni motsz*, to carry in one hand.

KATA-TOKI, カタトキ, 片時, (*hen shi.*) Short time, little while. — *mo waszrenai*, did not forget it even for a little while.

KATATSZMURI, カタツムリ, 蝸牛, *n.* A snail. Syn. DEDEMUSHI, MAIMAITSZBURI.

KATAWA, カタハ, 支離, *n.* Maimed, crippled, deformed, not sound in body. Syn. FUGU.

KATAWARA, カタハラ, 傍, *n.* Side. *Michi no* —, side of the road. — *ni*, by the way, besides. Syn. WAKI.

KATA-WARE, カタワレ, 偏破, *n.* Divided into halves, half of any whole thing, as an orange, &c. — *dzki*, half moon. *Sōdan — ga sh'ta*, the council was equally divided.

KATAYE, カタヘ, 傍, *n.* Side. *Michi no* —, side of the road. — *ni oru h'to*, the person at one's side. Syn. KATAWARA.

KATAYORI,-*ru*,-*tta*, カタヨル, 倚, *t. v.* To go to one side, incline or lean to one side, biased, partial.

KATAYUKI, カタユキ, 肩行, *n.* The measure of a coat from the central seam on the back to the end of the sleeve.

KATAZARU, カタザル, 不勝, neg. of *Kachi*.

KATCHIU, カツチウ, 甲冑, (*yoroi kabuto,*) *n.* Helmet and coat of mail, armor. Syn. GU-SOKU.

KATE, カテ, 粮, *n.* Provisions, food. — *wo tszmu*, to store up provision. — *ni tszmaru*, straitened for provisions. Syn. SHOKURIYŌ.

KATE,-*ru*,-*ta*, カテル, 勝, pot. mood. of *Kachi*. Can conquer, overcome.

KATEBA, カテバ, sub. mood. of *Kachi*.

KATENU, カテヌ, 不可勝, neg. potent. of *Kachi*. *Tszyoi kara* —.

KATŌ, カタウ, See *Katai*.

KATŌDO, カタウド, 方人, *n*. A second, abettor, confederate, partisan. Syn. KATAN-NIN.

KA-TOKU, カトク, 家督, *n*. Inheritance, heritage, estate, patrimony. — *no shisoku*, the heir of an estate. — *szru*, to inherit, succeed to an inheritence. — *wo tszgu*, (idem). — *wo yudzru*, to cede, or transfer an estate to the heir, and retire into privacy.

KATSZ, ガツ, 勝, See *Kachi*.

KATSZ, カツ, 擣, *n*. A mallet, or pestle for pounding in a large wooden mortar. Syn. KINE.

KATSZ, カツ, 渴, *n*. Thirst. — *ga aru*, is thirsty. — *ni semaru*, tortured with thirst. Syn. KAWAKI.

KATSZ, カツ, 且, *adv*. Moreover, besides, furthermore, again. *Katsz tatakai katsz shirizoku*, now fighting then retreating. *Katsz odoroki katsz kandzru*, one while alarmed, and then wondering: *Katsz wa yorokobi soro*, besides I am rejoiced. Syn. MATA. SONO WIYE.

KATSZGARE,–*ru*,–*ta*, カツガレル, Pass. of *Katszgu*. To be carried on the shoulder, to be made a fool of, hoaxed.

KATSZGASE,–*ru*,–*ta*, カツガセル, Caust. of *Katszgu*, to make or let carry on the shoulder.

KATSZGI,–*gu*,–*ida*, カツグ, 擔, *t. v*. To carry on the shoulder (as coolies do), to befool, hoax. *Nimotsz wo* —, to carry goods, *H'to wo katszide yatta*, to hoax a person. Syn. NINAU.

KATSZGI, カツギ, *n*. (an abbreviation of *Gohei katszji*), Superstitious.

KATSZGI, カツギ, *n*. A hawker.

KATSZGI, カツギ, *n*. A veil worn by women.

KATSZ-MATA, カツマタ, 且 又, *adv*. Again, besides, moreover, also, (at the beginning of a sentence.)

KATSZ-MEI, ケツメイ, 渴 命, (*Wiye jini*) *n*. Death from thirst, or starvation. — *ni oyobu*.

KATS'O, カツヲ, 鰹 *n*. A kind of fish.

†KATS'OBUSHI, カツヲブシ, 鰹 節, *n*. Smoked *katszo*.

KATSZRA, カツラ, See *Kadzra*.

KATSZRA-OTOKO, カツラヲトコ, 桂男, *n*. The man in the moon.

KATSZTE, カツテ, 嘗, *adv*. (of past time,) Before, previously, formerly, once. — *kayō ni omoi-dashi mōshi-soro*, I thought so before. *Katszte nashi* never (of time previous). — *shiranu koto*, a thing before unknown. Syn. KANETE, MAYE-DO, MOTO.

KATSZYAKASHI,–*sz*,–*sh'ta*, カツヤカス, Caust. of *Katszyeru*. To starve, cause to hunger.

KATSZYE,–*ru*,–*ta*, カツエル, 渴 飢, *i.v*. To starve, to suffer for want of food, to be hungry. *Midsz ni* —, to perish with thirst. *Tabe-mono ni* —, starving for want of food. *Katszye-jini*, starved to death. *Onna ni* —, hungry after women. Syn. WIYERU.

KATTA, カツタ, Pret. of *Kachi*, 勝.

KATTA, カツタ Pret. of *Kai, au, tta*, 買.

KATTAI, カツタイ, 癩 病, *n*. The leprosy. Syn. RAI-BIYŌ.

KATTE, カツテ, Gerund of *Kachi*, 勝, and *Kai*, 買.

KATTE, カツテ, 勝 手, *n*. Convenience, agreeable. *Jibun no* — *shidai*, at your own convenience. — *no ī yō-ni nasare*, do whatever will suit you best. *Go* — *ga yoi*, you have every thing very convenient. Syn. BENRI, TSZGŌ.

KATTE, カツテ, 勝 手, *n*. A kitchen. — *guchi*, kitchen-door. Syn. DAIDOKORO.

KAU, カフ, 買, See *Kai*,

KAWA, カハ, 側, *n*. Side, row. *Michi no riyō kawa*, both sides of a road. *Migi kawa*, right side. *Kita-gawa*, north-side (of a street.) *Tszwamono futa kawa ni narabu*, solders arranged in two rows. Syn. KATA.

KAWA, カハ, 皮, *n*. Skin, peel, rind, bark, leather, hide. *Ki no* —, the bark of a tree. *Tszra no* — *no atszi yatsz*, an impudent fellow. *Mikan no* —, orange peel. — *wo muku*, to skin, to peel.

KAWA, カハ, 川, *n*. A river. — *no nagare*, the current of a river. — *no hata*, the bank of a river. — *no fuchi*, an eddy or deep place in a river.

KAWA-BAKAMA, カハバカマ, 皮 袴, *n*. Leather-breeches.

KAWA-BAORI, カハバヲリ, 皮 羽 織, *n*. Leather or fur coat.

KAWA-BATA, カハバタ, 川 端, *n*. River-bank. Syn. KASHI.

KAWABE, カハベ, 川 邊, *n*. River-bank.

KAWA-BŌ, カハバウ, 皮, 坊, *n*. A leather dresser, *Yeta*.

KAWA-BUKURO, カハブクロ, 皮 袋, *n*. A leather-bag.

KAWADZ, カハヅ, 蛙, *n*. A frog. Syn. KAYERU.

KAWA-DZKIN, カハヅキン, 皮頭巾, *n.* Leather-cap.

KAWA FUNE, カハフネ, 川舩, *n.* A river-boat.

KAWA-GARI, カハガリ, 川狩, *n.* Fishing in a river.

KAWA-GISHI, カハギシ, 川岸, *n.* Bank of a river.

KAWAGO, カハゴ, 皮籠, *n.* A box, or trunk made of bamboo, or of leather

KAWA-GOROMO, カハゴロモ, 裘, *n.* Fur or leather coat.

KAWAGUCHI, カハグチ, 川口, *n.* The mouth of a river.

KAWA-GUTSZ, カハグツ, 革靴, *n.* Leather shoes.

KAWAI, カワイ, 可愛, See *Ka-ai.*

KAWAIRASHII, カワイラシイ, See *Ka-airashi.*

KAWAISŌ, カワイサウ, See *Ka-aisō.*

KAWA-KABURI, カハカブリ, 蒙混, *n.* Phimosis.

KAWA-KAMI, カハカミ, 川上, Up the river, upper part of the river. — *ni noboru,* to go up the river.

KAWAKASHI,-*sz*,-*sh'ta*, カハカス, 乾, *t.v.* To dry, to exsiccate, desiccate. *Kimono wo* —, to dry clothes.

KAWAKI,-*ku*,-*ita*, カハク, 乾, *i.v.* To be dry, arid. 渇, thirsty. *Kawate midz wo nomitagaru,* thirsty and wishing to drink.

KAWA-OSO, セハオソ, 河獺, *n.* An otter.

KAWARA, カハラ, 瓦, *n.* A tile. — *wo fuku,* to roof with tiles.

KAWARA, カハラ, 川原, *n.* That part of the stony bed of a river which is dry, except in high water.

KAWARA-BUKI, カハラブキ, 瓦葺, *n.* Roofed with tiles.

KAWARA-GAMA, カハラガマ, 瓦竈, *n.* A tile kiln.

KAWARAKE, カハラケ, 土器, *n.* A wine cup of unglazed earthenware.

KAWARASE,-*ru*,-*ta*, カハラセル, 令代, (caust. of *Kawaru*). To change, to put one in the place of another, to exchange, to substitute. *Ban-nin wo* —, to change a guard.

KAWARASHI, カハラシ, 瓦師, *n.* A tile-maker.

KAWARAYA, カハラヤ, 瓦屋, *n.* A shop where tiles are sold.

KAWARA-YANE, カハラヤネ, 瓦屋根, *n.* A tile roof.

KAWARI,-*ru*,-*ta*, カハル, 代, or 變, *i.v.* Changed, exchanged, substituted; one thing put in the place of another; altered, transformed into something else; new, strange. *Iro ga* —, the color is changed. *Ban ga* —, the watch is changed. *Yedo ni kawatta koto arimasz ka,* is there anything new in Yedo? *Ko ga chi-chi ni kawatte tszmi-serareru,* the son was executed in the place of the father. *Kase ga kawatta,* the wind has changed. *Kokoro-gawari szru,* to change one's mind.

KAWARI, カハリ, 代, *n.* A substitute, in the place of, instead of. *H'to no* — *ni tatsz,* to stand as a substitute for another. — *no h'to,* a substitute. *Sake no* — *ni cha wo nomu* to drink tea instead of wine. Syn. DAI.

KAWARU-GAWARU, カハルガハル, 更, *adv.* By turns, alternately. — *ban wo szru,* to watch turn about. Syn. KOMO-GOMO, TAGAI-NI.

KAWASE, カハセ, 爲替, *n.* Exchange, Drawing money on a note, drawing a bill of exchange. — *tegata.* a bill of exchange. — *kata,* a banker, exchanger. — *wo szru,* to draw a bill of exchange. — *wo kumu,* idem.

KAWASE, カハセ, 川瀬, *n.* The rapids of a river, a swift current.

KAWASEMI, セハセミ, 翡翠, *n.* A kingfisher. Syn. HI-SZI, SONI.

KAWASHI,-*sz*,-*sh'ta*, カハス, 交, *t.v.* To exchange, to give and receive reciprocally, to shift one's place. *Kotoba wo* —, to exchange words, to promise. *Mi wo* —, to to turn one's self, to dodge.

KAWA-SHIMO, カハシモ, 川下, *n.* Down the river, the lower part of the river.

KAWA-SHIRI, カハシリ, 川尻, *n.* The lower part of a river.

KAWA-SZJI, カハスヂ, 川筋, *n.* The course of a river.

KAWATA, カハタ 屠, 兒, *n.* A tanner, leather-dresser. Syn. YETA, KAWABŌ, KAWAYA.

KAWATARŌ, カハタラウ, 河童, *n.* Same as *Kappa.*

KAWA-YA, カハヤ, 皮屋, *n.* A leather dresser.

†KAWAYA, カハヤ, 厠, *n.* A privy. Syn. CHŌDZBA, SETSZIN.

KAWA-YANAGI, カハヤナギ, 檉, *n.* River-willow.

KAWAYOKE, ケハヨケ, 川除, *n.* A break-water, to protect the banks of a river from the current.

KAWAYUI,-KI,-KU,-SHI, カワユイ, 可愛, Beloved, dear, lovely, darling.

KAYA, カヤ, 茅, *n.* A kind of rush.

KAYA, カヤ, 蚊幮, *n.* Musquito net.

KAYA, カヤ, Comp. of *Ka*, and *Ya*, a particle of interrogation, and doubt. *Nan to kaya mōshimash'ta ga waszreta*, I have forgotten what he said. *H'yaku nen zen yori hajimarishi to kaya*, I think it began about a hundred years ago.

KAYA-BUKI, カヤブキ, 芽葺, *n.* Thatched with rush.

KAYA-JI, カヤヂ, 幃羅, *n.* The stuff of which musquito nets are made.

KA-YARI-BI, カヤリビ, 蚊遣火, *n.* A smoke made to keep off musquitoes.

KAYE,*–ru,–ta*, カヘル, 替, *t.v.* To exchange, change one thing for another, to change, alter, to substitute. *Kimono wo*—, to change the clothes. *Szgata wo* —, to change one's appearance. *Kane wo* —, to change money. *Te wo* —, to do in another way, or change one's tactics. *Mi ni kayete h'to wo omō*, disregarding one's self to think of others. *Sen tabi kuyuredomo kayeradz*, although you repent a thousand times it will make no difference. *Ido wo* —, to draw off the water of a well, and let fresh water flow in; to clean a well.

KAYE-BUTA, カヘブタ, 替蓋, *n.* An inside cover, or lid.

KAYE-DASHI,*–sz,–sh'ta*, カヘダス, *t. v.* To dip out, bale out. *Fune no aka wo* —, to bale out a boat.

KAYEDE, カヘデ, 楓, A species of maple.

KAYERI, カヘリ, 反, *n.* The barb of a hook or arrow.

KAYERI,*–ru,–tta*, カヘル, 歸, *i. v.* To return, to come or go back, often joined to the roots of other verbs to intensify their meaning. *Uchi ye* —, to return home. *Kuyande mo kayeranu*, repentance will be of no avail. *Shidzmari kayeru*, to be perfectly still. *Niye-kayeru*, to boil hard. Sgn. MODORU.

KAYERI,*–ru,–tta*, カヘル, 孚, *i.v.* To be hatched as an egg. *Hatszka tatsz to tamago ga* —, an egg is hatched in twenty one days.

KAYERI-CHIU, カヘリチウ, 歸忠, *n.* Return to loyalty or fidelity and turning informer. — *wo szru.*

KAYERI-GAKE-NI, カヘリガケニ, 歸次, *adv.* On returning, on the way back. — *sh'tateya ni yotte okure*, call at the tailors on your way back.

KAYERI-GOTO, カヘリゴト, 返事, *(henji.) n.* An answer, reply.

KAYERI-MI,*–ru,–ta*, カヘリミル, 顧, *t. v.* To look back, to reflect on, consider; to regard, mind, care for. *Onore wo* —, to examine one's self. *Ushiro wo* —, to turn and look back, to reflect on past conduct. *Kayeri-midz*, neg. disregard, not caring for.

†KAYERI-MŌDE, カヘリマウデ, 賽, *n.* Returning thanks to the *Kami*, for favors received. — *wo szru.*

KAYERI-UCHI, カヘリウチ, 返伐, *n.* The killing also of the avenger of one previously slain by the same person. — *ni au.*

KAYERU, カヘル, 蛙, *n.* A frog. Syn. KAWADZ.

KAYESHI,*–sz,–sh'ta*, カヘス, 返, *t. v.* To return, to send back, restore, repay, requite, recompence, to revenge. *Kane wo* —, to repay money. *Ada wo* —, to kill an enemy. *On wo* —, to requite a kindness. *Kotoba wo* —, to answer back, to retort. *Hon wo kayesh'te kudasare*, please return the book. *Kash'ta mono wo kayese*, return what you borrowed.

KAYESHI,*–sz,–sh'ta*, カヘス, 孚, *t. v.* To hatch eggs. *Tamago wo* —.

KAYESHI,*–sz,–sh'ta*, カヘス, 切, *t. v.* To spell, to form one syllable by syncope from the first and last sounds of two others. *Moji wo* —.

KAYESZ-GAYESZ, カヘスガヘス, 返返, *adv.* Again and again, repeatedly, over and over again. — *mo nen wo ireru*, to apply the mind over and over again. Syn. KURE-GURE.

KAYETTE, カヘツテ, 却, *adv.* On the contrary, on the other hand, vice-versa, rather, better. — *sen yori waruku sh'ta*, it is, on the contrary, worse than before. — *toku*, it is rather an advantage. *Ato ye* —, returning to the previous subject. Syn. KEKKU.

KAYŌ, カヤウ, 斯樣, (cont. of *Kono* and *yō*,) *adv.* Thus, so, in this way.

KAYOI,*–ō,–ōta*, カヨフ, 通, *i. v.* To go and come, to pass to and fro, to pass along or through, to circulate, to frequent, *Michi ni* —, to go to and fro through a road. *Sakaya ni* —, to frequent the dram-shop. Syn. TŌRU, Ō-RAI SZRU.

KAYOI, カヨヒ, 通, *n.* A pass-book, passing to and fro, intercommunication, circulation. — *no gin*, the account in a passbook. *Kono toyu midz no* — *ga warui*, the water does not flow freely through this pipe. — *ga tayetta*, the communication is stopped. *Chi no* — *ga tomeru*, the circulation of blood is stopped. Syn. YUKIKI, Ō-RAI, TŌRI.

KAYOI-BITZ, カヨヒビツ, 通櫃, *n.* A box used for sending things to and fro.

KAYOI-CHŌ, カヨヒチヤウ, 通帳, *n.* A pass-book.

KAYOI-GUCHI, カヨヒグチ, 通口, *n.* A door for passing in and out.

KAYOWAI,-KI,-KU,-SHI, カヨワイ, Weak, feeble, delicate. Syn. YOWAI.

KAYOWASHI,-*sz*,-*sh'ta*, セヨハス, 通, *i. v.* To send backwards and forwards, to interchange, exchange, reciprocate. *Tegami wo* —, to communicate with each other by letter. *Yoshimi wo* — reciprocate friendship.

KAYU, カユ, 粥, *n.* Rice gruel, congee.

KAYUI,-KI,-KU,-Ū,-SHI,-SA, カユイ, 痒, Itching, the sensation in the skin which inclines one to scratch. *Kayui tokoro wo kaku*, to scratch an itching place. *Kayu-ku nai*, it does not itch. *Kayui tokoro ye te ga todokanu*, (prov.) unable to do what one itches to do.

KAYU-GARI,-*ru*,-*tta*, カユガル, 癢, *i. v.* To be in the habit of scratching, given to itching.

KAZA, カザ, 氣, *n.* Smell, odor. Syn. NIOI.

KAZA-ANA, カザアナ, 風穴, *n.* Air-hole.

KAZA-GOYE, カザゴヱ, 風聲, *n.* A voice altered by a cold in the head.

KAZA-GUSZRI, カザグスリ, 風薬, *n.* Medicine for a cold.

KAZA-GURUMA, カザグルマ, 風車, *n.* A toy made of a paper wheel turned by the wind; a wind-mill.

KAZAI, カザイ, 家財, *n.* Household furniture.

KAZAKAMI, カザカミ, 風上, *n.* Windward.

KAZAKIRIBA, カザキリバ, 風切羽, *n.* The long feathers in the wing of a bird.

KAZAMI, カザミ, 風見, *n.* A wind vane.

KAZA-NAMI, カザナミ, 風候, *n.* The state of the wind. — *wa ikaga*, how is the wind? — *ga yoi*, the wind is fair.

KAZARI,-*ru*,-*tta*, カザル, 装, *t. v.* To ornament, embellish, adorn, deck. *Kado-guchi wo* —, to adorn the door of a house, (as on new year's day.) *Atama wo* —, to adorn the head. *Ayamachi wo* —, to gloss over a fault. Syn. YOSOŌI.

KAZARI, カザリ, 飾, *n.* An ornament, decoration, embellishment.

KAZARI-SHI, カザリシ, 錺師, *n.* A jeweller.

KAZARI-TSZKE,-*ru*,-*ta*, カザリツケル, 飾置, *t. v.* To ornament, embellish, adorn, deck, to gloss over.

KAZARI-YA, カザリヤ, 飾屋, *n.* Jeweller's shop.

KAZASHI,-*sz*,-*sh'ta*, カザス, 簪, *t. v.* To stick in the hair, (翳.) To hold over the eyes so as to screen off the sun. *Hitai ni te wo kazasz*, to screen the eyes by putting the hand to the forehead. *Ōgi wo* —, to screen with a fan. *Hana wo* —, to stick flowers in the hair.

KAZA-SHIMO, カザシモ 風下, *n.* Leeward. —, *ni mukō*, facing to the leeward.

KAZA-YOKE, カザヨケ, 風除, *n.* A wind screen.

KAZE, カゼ, 風, *n.* The wind. — *ga fuku*, the wind blows. — *wo hiku*, to catch cold. — *ga kawatta*, the wind has changed. — *ga deru*, the wind begins to blow. — *ga shidzmaru*, the wind lulls.

KAZE-JIRUSHI, カゼジルシ, 風標, *n.* A flag for showing the direction of the wind, a vane.

KAZE-SH'TA, カゼシタ, 風下, *n.* Leeward.

KAZŌ, カザウ, 家藏, *n.* Property, any thing which a person owns. *Kore wa anata no — de gozarimasz ka*, is this your property? *Watakushi no — no hon.*

KAZŌ, カザウ, 加增, Increasing the pay, or adding to the income of an officer.

†KAZO-IRO, カゾイロ, 父母, *n*, Father and mother, (poet) Syn. CHICHI-HAHA.

KA-ZOKU, カゾク, 家族, *n.* Family.

KAZOYE,-*ru*,-*ta*, カゾヘル, 算, *t. v.* To count, number, to reckon, enumerate. *Kadz wo* —, to count the number. *Kazo-yete mi-yo*, count how many. *Agete kazoye-gatashi*, cannot be numbered. Syn. SHIRABERU, KAN-JŌ-SZRU.

KAZOYE-KIRI,-*ru*,-*tta*, カゾヘキル, 算切, *t.v.* To finish counting. — *kiranu*, innumerable.

KAZOYE-TATE,-*ru*,-*ta*, カゾヘタテル, 算立, *t.v.* To count off, to enumerate, reckon up. *H'to no tszmi wo* —.

KE, ケ 毛, *n.* Hair, fur, the small feathers of a bird.

KE, ケ, 氣, *n.* Same as *Ki*, used mostly as a suffix, = feeling, nature, like, disposition. *Nani ge naku miru*, to look at without showing any particular emotion *Samu-ke ga szru*, to feel chilly. *Abura-ke*, oily. *Abuna-ge*, appearance of danger.

KE-AGE,-*ru*,-*ta*, ケアゲル, 蹴上, *t.v.* To send up with a kick, to kick up.

KE-AI, ケアヒ, 蹴合, *n.* A cock-fight.

KE-ANA, ケアナ, 毛孔, *n.* The pores of the skin.

KE-AWASE,-*ru*,-*ta*, ケアハセル, 蹴合, *t.v.* To fight cocks.

KEBADACHI,-*tsz*,-*tta*, ケバダツ, 毛起, *i.v.* To be rough and nappy, frizzed, (as cloth or paper.)

KE-BIKI, ケビキ, 界行, *n.* The fine lines on paper for writing.

KEBIKI-GAMI, ケビキガミ, 界行紙, *n.* Ruled paper.

KE-BIYŌ, ケビヤウ, 假病, *n.* Feigned, sickness. — *wo tszkau*, to feign sickness.

KE-BORI, ケボリ, 毛彫, *n.* Fine hair lines in engraving.

‖KEBUNA, ケブナ, 怪異, *a.* Strange, odd, eccentric. — *h'to*, a strange man.
Syn. AYASHII.

KEBURI, ケブリ, 煙, *n.* Smoke, same as *Kemuri.*

KEBURIDASHI, ケブリダシ, See *Kemuridashi.*

KEBUTAI, ケブタイ, See *Kemutai.*

KECHI, ケチ, Mean, low, contemptible, stingy; unlucky. — *na yatsz*, a mean fellow. — *na koto wo iu*, to speak in a penurious manner. — *wo tszkeru*, to give a bad or unlucky name to a house.
Syn. GEBI, SHIWAI, FUKITSZ.

†KECHI-G'WAN, ケチグワン, 結願, *(negai wo muszbu).* The end of a fast, or vow. (Bud).

KECHI-KECHI, ケチケチ, *adv.* Stingy, miserly, mean.

KECHI-MIYAKU, ケチミヤク, 血脉, *(chiszji). n.* Lineage, family line. — *ga tayeru*, the family line is extinct.

KE-CHIRASHI,-*sz*,-*sh'ta*, ケチラス, 蹴散, *t.v.* To kick and scatter.

†KECHI-YEN, ケチエン, 結緣, *(yen wo muszbu), n.* Union or fellowship with Hotoke by faith and worship. (Bud.)
— *wo szru.*

†KE-DAI, ケダイ, 懈怠, Negligent, idle, lazy, careless, indolent. — *szru*, to be idle. Syn. BUSHŌ, OKOTARU.

KE-DAKAI,-KI,-KU,-Ō,-SHI, ケダカイ, 氣高, Noble, high-minded, dignified. — *h'to.* Syn. ATEYAKA.

KEDAMONO, ケダモノ, 獸, *n.* Animal, quadruped.

†KEDASHI, ケダシ, 蓋, *conj.* A continuative particle, introducing something probably explanatory of what goes before, = it is probable, it is likely, perhaps.
Syn. ŌKATA.

KEDATAMASHII,-KI,-KU, ケダタマシイ, Crying out in alarm, screaming in sudden fright. Syn. GIYO-GIYOSHII.

KEDŌ,-*szru*, ケド, 化度, *t.v.* To convert, to bring into the way of salvation. (Bud.) *Issai shu-jō wo* —, to save the whole world.
Syn. SAI-DOSZRU, DOSZRU, KIYŌ-KUNSZRU.

†KEDŌ, ケダウ, 化導, *(michi ni hiki-ireru.)* To convert and lead into the right way. (Bud.)
Syn. MICHI-BIKU, ANNAI-SZRU.

KEDORI,-*ru*,-*tta*, ケドル, 暗會, *t. v.* To suspect, to mistrust, to conjecture. *Dorobō to kedoru*, to suspect one to be a robber. Syn. AYASHIMU, SZI-SZRU.

KEDZME, ケヅメ, 蹴爪, *n.* The small horny projection above a horse's hoof. The spur of a cock.

KEDZRI,-*ru*,-*tta*, ケヅル, 削, *t.v.* To plane, shave, cut, scrape, to comb. *Ita wo kanna de* —, to plane a board. *Ke wo kushi-kedzri szru*, to comb the hair. *Seki-hitsz wo* —, to sharpen a lead pencil. *Daimiyō no chi-giyō wo* —, to cut down the revenue of a *Daimio.*

KEGA, ケガ, 傷, *n.* A wound, hurt, injury, damage, accident. — *wo szru.* — *wo ukeru.* — *no kō-miyō*, a fortunate accident, an injury that turns out to be a blessing.
Syn. AYAMACHI, SO-SŌ, KIDZ.

KAGARAWASHII,-KI,-KU,-U,-SA, ケガラハシイ, 穢敷, Dirty, polluted, unclean, obscene. *Kegarawashii mono*, an unclean person. Syn. FUJŌ, OYE.

KEGARE,-*ru*,-*ta*, ケガレル, 穢, *i. v.* To be defiled, unclean, polluted, foul. *Kokoro ga* —, the heart is defiled. Syn. BIRŌ, KITANAI, YOGORERU, FU-JŌ.

KEGARE, ケガレ, 穢, *n.* Impurity, defilement, pollution, uncleanness.

KEGASHI,-*sz*,-*sh'ta*, ケガス, 令穢, *t. v.* To pollute, to corrupt, vitiate, defile, make foul or unclean. deprave. *Mi wo* —, to defile one's self. *Chi wo ayash'te miya wo* —, to defile a temple by spilling blood in it. Syn. KITANAKU SZRU, YOGOSZ.

†KEGI, ケギ, 常衣, *n.* Common clothes, every day clothes. Syn. FUDANGI.

KEGIWA, ケギハ, 毛際, *n.* The edge or border of the hair.

KEGOROMO, ケゴロモ, 毛衣, *n.* Fur-coat.

‖KE-GUSAI,-KI,-KU,-Ō, ケグサイ, 毛臭, *n.* Smelling of burnt hair.

KEGUTSZ, ケグツ, 毛靴, *n.* Fur-shoes.

KE-HANASHI,-*sz*,-*sh'ta*, ケハナス, 蹴放, *t.v.* To kick open, or apart.

KE-HAWAKI, ケハハキ, 毛掃, *n.* A hair brush.

†KE-I, ケイ, 怪異, Strange, suspicious. Syn. AYASHII.

KEI, ケイ, 磬, *n.* A kind of gong, used in Buddhist temples.

KEI, ケイ, 景, *n.* Landscape, view, scenery. — *ga yoi,* the scenery is fine.

KEI-BA, ケイバ, 競馬, *n.* A horse race. — *ga aru.* — *wo mi ni yuku,* to go to see the horse race.

KEI-BATSZ, ケイバツ, 刑罰, *n.* Punishment. — *szru,* to punish (a criminal.) — *wo okonō,* (idem.) Syn. SHI-OKI.

†KEI-BETSZ, ケイベツ, 輕蔑, To despise, contemn, Syn. ANADORU.

†KEI-BI, ケイビ, 輕微, Small, little, of little worth. — *no itari ni sōrayedomo,* although it is very little. Syn. SZKOSHI.

†KEI-BO, ケイボ, 繼母, *n.* Step mother. Syn. MAMA-HAHA.

†KEI-BŌ, ケイバウ, 閨房, *n.* Bed-chamber. Syn. NEYA.

KEI-BUTSZ, ケイブツ, 景物, *n.* Articles appropriate to the season, presents made to customers on opening a new store.

KEI-DZ, ケイヅ, 系圖, *n.* Genealogical record.

†KEI-FU, ケイフ, 繼父, *n.* Step-father. Syn. MAMA-CHICHI.

KEI-FUN, ケイフン, 輕粉, *n.* Calomel.

†KEI-GA, ケイガ, 慶賀, *(yorokobi iwau.)* *n.* Congratulation, felicitation. *Hassaku no — mōshi-iresoro,* I wish you much joy on the 1st of the 8th month.

†KEI-GI, ケイギ, 計議, *(hakari-goto.)* *n.* A plan, scheme, device. — *szru,* to plan.

KEI-GO, ケイゴ, 警固, *n.* A guard, watch, sentry. — *no kei,* a guard of soldiers. *Roji wo — szru,* to guard the roads. — *wo soyeru,* to accompany with a guard.

KEI-HAKU, ケイハク, 輕薄, False-hearted, perfidious, double-faced, insincere, inhuman, — *naru h'to.* Syn. FUJITSZ, HAKUJŌ.

KEI-HEI, ケイヘイ, 經閉, *n.* Amenorrhœa.

†KEI-JŌ, ケイジヤウ, 啟上, *(mōshi ageru).* Used in commencing a letter, as *Ippitsz — tszkamatszri soro,* I take up my pen to write to you.

†KEI-JŪ, ケイヂユウ, 輕重, *(omoi karui).* Light and heavy. *Tszmi no — wo tadasz,* to examine into the heinousness of a crime. — *wo hakaru,* to find out the weight.

†KEI-KEN, ケイケン, 經驗, To prove, try or experiment with medicine. *Yamai wo —,* to experiment with medicine in the cure of disease. — *sh'ta kuszri,* a medicine whose efficacy has been well proved.

KEI-KI, ケイキ, 景氣, *n.* Appearance of business, trade, activity, or strength. *Yedo no — ga yoi,* business is brisk at Yedo. *Fu-keiki,* dull, no business doing. *Kono setz no — ikaga,* how is business now? — *no yoi h'to,* an active person. *Ito no — ga warui,* the trade in silk is dull. Syn. IKIYOI.

KEI-KO, ケイコ, 稽古, Practising, drilling, exercising,—in order to learn. *Kenjutsz no —,* practice of fencing. — *szru,* to practise, exercise, learn. Syn. MANABI.

†KEI-KŌ, ケイカウ, 經候, *n.* The menses. Syn. MEGURI.

KEIKO-BA, ケイコバ, 稽古場, *n.* A fencing school.

†KEI-KOTSZ, ケイコツ, 輕忽, Light, trifling, careless. Syn. KARU-GARUSHII.

†KEI-K'WANSŌ, ケイクワンサウ, 鷄冠草, *n.* Cockscomb (flower.) Celosia cristata.

†KEI-MEI, ケイメイ, 鷄鳴, *n.* Cock-crowing, early dawn. — *goro,* time of cock-crowing. Syn. YO-AKE.

†KEI-RAN, ケイラン, 鷄卵, *(Niwatori no tamago).* *n.* Hen's-egg.

†KEI-REKI,-*szru,* ケイレキ, 經歷, To travel about, to pass, as time.

†KEI-RIKU, ケイリク, 刑戮, *n.* Capital punishment. — *wo kuwayeru,* to inflict capital punishment, to execute.

†KEI-RIYAKU, ケイリヤク, 計略, *n.* A plan, device, scheme. — *wo megurasz,* to contrive or invent a plan. Syn. HAKARIGOTO.

†KEI-SAKU, ケイサク, 計策, *n.* A stratagem. Syn. HAKARIGOTO.

†KEI-SEI, ケイセイ, 傾城, *(shiro wo katamuku).* *n.* A mistress, harlot.

KEI-SHI, ケイシ, 桂枝, *n.* Cinnamon, Cassia.

†KEI-SHI, ケイシ, 京師, *n.* Miyako.

KEI-SHIN, ケイシン, 桂心, *n.* Cassia buds.

†KEI-SHITSZ, ケイシツ, 繼室, *n.* A second wife. Syn. NOCHIZOYE, GO-SAI.

†KEI-SHŌ, ケイセウ, 輕少, Little, small, trifling in quantity, or value. *Itatte — ni gozarimasz.* Syn. SZKUNAI, WADZKA, ISASAKA.

KEI-SHO, ケイシヨ, 經書, *n.* The Chinese classics.

†KEI-SHOKU, ケイシヨク, 景色, *n.* View scenery, prospect. Syn. KEI-SHIKI, FŪKEI

†KEI-SHŪ, ケイシウ, 競舟, *(funa-gisoi).* *n.* A boat-race.

†KEI-SOTSZ, ケイソツ, 輕率, Careless, trifling, unimportant, of little account. — *na h'to.*

KEISZI, ケイスイ, 經水, *n.* Menses.

KEI-TEI, ケイテイ, 兄弟, *(kiyōdai). n.* Brethren.

KEI-TŌ, ケイトウ, 鷄頭, *n.* Cock's-comb, (flower.) Celosia cristata.

†KEI-TŌ, ケイトウ, 惠投, *(megumi-atayeru).* To bestow, give.

KEI-YAKU, ケイヤク, 契約, *n.* A covenant, an agreement, promise. — *szru.*
Syn. YAKU-JŌ.

KEI-YEI, *-szru*, ケイヱイ, 警衛, To guard, defend, protect.
Syn. KATAMERU, MAMORU.

KEI-YEI, *-szru*, ケイエイ, 經營, To build, construct,
Syn. KOSHIRAYURU, TSZKURU, ITONAMU.

†KEI-YŌ, ケイヨウ, 形容, *n.* Form, figure, appearance, looks.
Syn. KATACHI, SZGATA.

†KEI-YŌ-SHI, ケイヨウシ, 形容詞, *n.* An adjective.

KEI-ZAI, ケイザイ, 經濟, *n.* Economy, judicious use of money or property, in order to increase wealth. — *gaku*, political economy.

†KEJIME, ケジメ, 結目, *n.* Difference, distinction. *Teki mikata no — mo naku*, there was no distinguishing friend from foe. Syn. WAKACHI, SHABETSZ, WAIDAME.

KEJIRAMI, ケジラミ, 毛虱, *n.* A louse.

KE-KAKE, *-ru, -ta*, ケカケル, 蹴掛, *t. v.* To kick, or splash about with the feet, *Uma ga doro wo —.*

KE-KAYESHI, *-sz, -sh'ta*, ケカヘス, 蹴返, *t. v.* To kick back.

KEKKAFUZA, ケツカフザ, 結跏趺坐, *n.* Sitting in silent contemplation, (as the Buddhists.)

†KEKKI, ケツキ, 血氣, *n.* The glow, vehemence, or ardor of youth. — *no sakannaru mama*, like the vehemence of youth. — *no yū ni makaseru*, trusting in the vigor of youth.

KEKKŌ, ケツカウ, 結搆, A word of admiration, or commendation,=Fine, splendid, excellent, beautiful, grand, delicious, delightful. — *na kimono.* — *na otenki.* — *na iye.* — *na shina.* — *na kurashi.*
Syn. RIPPA, YOI.

KEKKU, ケツク, 結句, *conj.* On the contrary, rather, better. The last word of a sentence, or stanza of poetry.
Syn. KAYETTE.

KE-KOMI, *-mu, -nda*, ケコム, 蹴込, *t. v.* To kick into.

KE-MAN, ケマン, 花鬘, *n.* An ornament placed on the head of idols. A kind of figure made of braid. The name of a flower, Eucapnos spectabilis.

KE-MARI, ケマリ, 蹴鞠, *n.* A foot-ball.

KEM-BEKI, ケンビキ, 痃癖, *n.* A place on the back of the shoulder above the spine of the scapula.

KEM-BETSZ-NI, ケンベツニ, 軒別, *adv.* House by house, to each house. *Kane wo — wari-tskeru*, to divide the money in proportion to the number of houses.

†KEM-BI, ケンビ, 兼備, *(kane-sonawaru.)* Doubly furnished. *Bum-bu — no taisho*, a prince perfect both in military art and in literature.

KEMBIKIYŌ, ケンビキヤウ, 顯微鏡, *n.* A microscope.

KEM-BIYŌ, ケンビヤウ, 硯屛, *n.* A small ornamental screen.

†KEM-BŌ, ケンバウ, 健忘, *n.* A disease characterized by loss of memory.

KEM-BUN, ケンブン, 見分, *(mi-wakeru.) n.* Official examination, or inspection. — *szru*, to examine, inspect.

KEMBUTSZ, ケンブツ, 見物, *n.* Seeing, looking at for recreation or curiosity, sight-seeing. *Szmō wo — ni yuku*, to go to see the wrestlers. — *szru*, to look at for recreation, or curiosity.

†KEMI, *-szru*, ケミ, 閱, To revise, inspect, examine, critise. *Hon wo —*, to review, or inspect a book so as to correct it.

KE-MIYŌ, ケミヤウ, 假名, *(kari no na,) n.* An assumed name, false name.

KEM-MI, ケンミ, 撿見, *n.* Inspection, examination, especially of the rice crop. — *no yakunin*, rice inspector.

†KEM-MON, *-szru*, ケンモン, 見聞, *(Mikiki szru.)* To see and hear. *Kem-mon-roku*, book in which what one sees and hears is noted down.

KE-MONO, ケモノ, 獸, *n.* Animal, beast. Syn. KEDAMONO.

†KEM-PŌ, ケンパフ, 劍法, *n.* The rules of fencing.

†KEM-PŌ, ケンパフ, 憲法, *n.* Law, edict. Syn. OKITE.

KEMPONASHI, ケンポナシ, 枳椇, *n.* A kind of fruit. Hovenia dulcis.

KEM-PU, ケンプ, 絹布, *n.* Silk and cotton cloth.

†KEM-PU, ケンプ, 賢婦, *n.* An intelligent woman.

†KEM-PU, ケンプ, 賢父, *n.* Your honorable father.

KEMURI, ケムリ, 煙, *n.* Smoke.

KEMURI-DASHI, ケムリダシ, 煙出, *n.* A chimney, stove pipe.

KE-MUSHI, ケムシ, 毛蟲, *n.* A kind of caterpillar.

KE-MUSHIRO, ケムシロ, 毛席, *n.* A rug, or mat made of wool.

KEMUTAI,-KI,-KU,-Ō,-SHI, ケムタイ, 煙度, Smoky, disagreeable on account of smoke.

KEN, ケン, A particle expressing doubt or uncertainty of something past. *Iku tose ka furi ni hen,* I wonder how many years old it is! *Idzku ye ka tachi-sariken,* I wonder where he has gone.

KEN, ケン, 劍, *n.* A sword, a bayonet. Syn. KATANA, TSZRUGI.

†KEN, ケン, 嶮, *(kewashii).* A precipice, steep.

KEN, ケン, 間, *n.* A measure of length of six Japanese feet, = 71½ inches English.

KEN, ケン, 軒, Numeral in counting houses. *Iye ikken,* one house. *Iye ni ken,* two houses.

KEN, ケン, 權, *n.* Power, authority, influence. — *wo furū,* to show one's power. — *wo toru,* to hold the power, to have the authority. — *wo katte mono wo iu,* to talk assuming an air of authority. Syn. IKIYOI.

†KEN, ケン, 賢, Intelligent, clever, wise, prudent. — *naru h'to,* an intelligent man. — *jin,* (idem). — *sha,* (idem). Syn. KASH'KOKI, RIKŌ.

KEN, ケン, 拳, *n.* A game played with the hands, *Ken wo utsz.*

KENAGE, ケナゲ, 健氣, Gallant, spirited, heroic, bold, brave, noble. — *na yatsz,* a noble fellow. *Samade — no hataraki,* such a heroic deed. — *ni iu,* to speak boldly.

‖KENARII,-KI,-KU, ケナリイ, Enviable, that which one would like to be, or be like. Syn. URAYAMASHII.

KENASHI,-*sz*,-*shta*, ケナス, *t.v.* To speak lightly, or contemptuously of, to depreciate. *Shina wo kenash'te yaszku kau,* to cry down the price of anything and buy it cheaply, *H'to wo —,* to run down a person.

KENCHI, ケンチ, 撿地, *n.* Measuring, or surveying land. — *wo utsz,* to survey land.

KEN-DAI, ケンダイ, 見臺, *n.* A book rest, or stand, a desk for resting a book on.

†KEN-DON, ケンドン, 慳貪, Close, stingy, miserly, covetous, cruel, inhuman, hard-hearted. — *naru h'to.* (Bud.) Syn. MUSABORU, NASAKENAI, FU-JITSZ.

KENDZRU, ケンズル, 獻, See *Kenji.*

†KE-NEN, ケネン, 懸念, *(kokoro ni kakeru).* To be concerned about, have on the mind. — *szru.*

†KEN-GAKU, ケンガク, 兼學, Learned in two or many subjects.

†KENGA-NO-BEN, ケンガノベン, 懸河之辨, Fluent in speaking.

†KEN-GEKI ケンゲキ, 劍戟, *(Tszrugi hoko).* Sword and halberd. — *wo ugokasz,* to stir up war.

†KEN-GIU, ケンギウ, 牽牛, *n.* The name of a constellation near the milky way. — *shoku-jo no k'waigo,* a festival on the 7th of the 7th month. Syn. TANABATA.

†KEN-GIU-K'WA, ケンギウクワ, 牽牛花, *n.* The morning-glory. Syn. ASAGAO.

KEN-GIYŌ, ケンギヤウ, 撿挍, *n.* Formerly an official title, now the name of the highest rank of the blind.

KEN-GO, ケンゴ, 堅固, *(katai-kataku).* Strong, firm, secure, safe, well-fortified, strict, rigid, severe, correct, firm in principle. Syn. KIBISHII, GENJŪ.

†KEN-GU, ケング, 賢愚, Clever and stupid.

KENJI,-*dzru*,-*ta*, ケンズル, 獻, To present, offer or give to a superior. Syn. TEI-SZRU, AGERU.

†KEN-JŌ, ケンジヤウ, 獻上, (idem). — *mono,* a present to a superior.

†KEN-JŌ, ケンジヤウ, 謙讓, *(yudzri yudzru).* Humbly to decline, or excuse one's self.

KEN-JUTSZ, ケンジユツ, 劍術, *n.* The art of fencing.

†KEN-KAKU, ケンカク, 懸隔, *(kake-hedateru).* Separated, far apart, far removed. *Ten-chi — no chigai,* as different as heaven and earth.

†KEN-KON, ケンコン, 乾坤, Heaven and earth. Syn. TENCHI.

KEN-K'WA, ケンクワ, 喧嘩, *n.* A quarrel, fight. — *szru,* to quarrel, or fight.

KEN-NAN, ケンナン, 劍難, *n.* A sword wound.

†KEN-NUN, ケンヌン, 眩暈, *n.* Dizziness, vertigo. — *szru,* to become dizzy. Syn. KURUMEKU, MEMAI.

†KEN-RAN, ケンラン, 賢覽, To see (in speaking of another).

KEN-RIYO, ケンリヨ, 賢慮, *(oboshimeshi).* Your intelligent opinion.

†KEN-SAI, ケンサイ, 賢才, *(rikona chi-*

ye). Clever, intelligent, ingenious, sagacious.

KEN-SHI, ケンシ, 撿屍, *(kabane wo miru), n.* Coroner, one who makes an official inquest.

KEN-SHIKI, ケンシキ, 見識, *n.* Intelligence, discernment, judgment. — *wo toru,* to affect pomp, or make a display of one's authority.

KENSO, ケンソ, 嶮岨, *n.* Steep, precipitous. Syn. KEWASHII.

KEN-SON, ケンソン, 謙遜, Humble; to humbly excuse one's self. — *szru,* to humble one's self. — *naru h'to,* an humble person. Syn. HERI-KUDARU, KENTAI, JITAI.

KEN-SZU, ケンスウ, 軒數, *n.* Number of houses, or of *ken* in length. — *nani hodo,* how many houses.

†KEN-TAI, ケンタイ, 兼帶, *(kane tsztomuru).* Discharging the duties of two different offices. *Futa yaku wo — szru.*

†KEN-TAI, ケンタイ, 謙退, To be humble. — *naru h'to,* an humble man. Syn. KENSON, HERI-KUDARU, HIGE.

KEN-TŌ, ケンタウ, 見當, *n.* Aim. — *szru,* to take aim at, to take sight. — *chigai,* to miss the aim. — *ga hadzreta,* to be disappointed in one's object. *Mato wo — szru,* to aim at a target. Syn. ME-ATE.

KE-NUKI, ケヌキ, 毛拔, *n.* Tweezers.

KEN-YAKU, ケンヤク, 儉約, *n.* Economy, saving in expenses. — *naru,* economical, saving, frugal. — *wo szru,* to be economical in the use of anything. — *ni kane wo tszkau,* to spend money economically. Syn. SHIMATSZ, TSZDZMAYAKA, SEKKEN.

KEN-YAKU, ケンヤク, 兼約, A previous agreement, covenant, or promise. — *dōri kane wo watasz,* to pay over money according to a previous agreement.

KEN-YŌ, ケンヨウ, 兼用, *n.* Using anything for two purposes; using anything in addition to something else.

†KEN-YŌ, ケンヨウ, 懸癰, *n.* A boil on the perineum.

†KEN-YO, ケンヨ, 權輿, *n.* The beginning, origin, or first discovery of anything. Syn. HAJIMARI, OKORI.

KEN-ZAO, ケンザヲ, 間棹, *n.* A measuring pole.

†KEN-ZEN, ケンゼン, 現然, *adv.* Manifestly, clearly. Syn. MA-NO-ATARI.

KEN-ZOKU, ケンゾク, 眷屬, *n.* Family, household, including servants or retainers.

KEORI, ケオリ, 毛織, *n.* Hair-cloth.

KEPPAKU-NA, ケツパク, 潔白, Clean, free from defilement or impurity, honest, upright. — *utzwa mono,* a clean vessel. — *h'to,* an honest man. Syn SEI-CHOKU, ISAGIYOI.

KEPPAN, ケツパン, 血判, Sealed with blood. — *szru,* to seal with blood.

KERA, ケラ, 螻, *n.* A cricket.

KERAI, ケライ, 家來, *n.* Servant, retainer.

KERAKU, ケラク, 快樂, Happy, joyful, light-hearted. Syn. KOKOROYOI, TANOSHIMI.

KEREBA, ケレバ, A conjuctive word formed from *Keri,* and affixed to the root of verbs, or adjectives, as *Na-kereba,* if there is not. *Hori-kereba,* when I dug. *Yomi-kereba,* when I read. *Samu-kereba,* if you are cold, *Kuro-kereba,* if it is black.

KEREDOMO, ケレドモ, (formed from *Keri* and *domo),* conj. Although, but, still, notwithstanding. Syn. IEDOMO.

KERI, KERU, ケリ, An auxilliary verb, of no intrinsic meaning, whose forms are used as suffixes to form the moods and tenses of other verbs. Final and pret. *Keri.* Pret. and adj. *Keru.* Conj. *Kereba* and *Keredomo,* Fut. and dubit. *Ken.*

KERI,*–ru,–tta,* ケル, 蹴, *t. v.* To kick. *Uma ga h'to wo ketta,* the horse kicked the man.

KESA, ケサ, 今朝, *adv.* This morning. Syn. KON-CHŌ.

KESA, ケサ, 袈裟, *n.* A scarf worn by Buddhist priests across the shoulder.

KESAN, ケサン, 卦算, *n.* A paper-weight.

KESHI,*–sz,–sh'ta,* ケス, 消, *t. v.* To extinguish, efface, put out, erase. *Hi wo —,* to extinguish a fire. *Ji wo —,* to erase a word. *Doku wo —,* to counteract a poison.

KESHI, ケシ, 罌粟, *n.* The poppy.

KESHI-BŌDZ, ケシバウズ, 芥子坊主, *n.* One who has the hair all shaved, except a circular patch behind, like children, or Chinamen.

KESHI-DZMI, ケシズミ, 消炭, *n.* The cinders of wood.

KESHI-KAKE,*–ru,–ta,* ケシカケル, *t. v.* To set on, incite, instigate. *Inu wo keshi-kakete kami-awaseru,* to set dogs to fight. Syn. ODATERU.

KESHIKARANU, ケシカラヌ, *a.* Extraordinary, uncommon; strange, outrageous. — *sawagi,* extraordinary tumult. — *sama,* strange appearance. — *ō ame da,* a very heavy rain. Syn. HANAHADASHIKU.

KESHIKI, ケシキ, 景色, *n.* Landscape, scenery, view, 氣色, appearanee, show, sign, expression of face. — *ga yoi,* the scenery is fine. *Makeru — mo nai*, no sign of defeat. *Yorokobu — mo nai*, no appearance of joy. Syn. KEI-SHOKU, YŌSZ, IRO.

†KESHIN, ケシン, 化身, (*baketaru mi.*) *n.* Transformation, transfiguration, incarnation, (of a god or devil. (Bud.) *Kami no —*, an incarnation of a god. *Mida no —*, incarnation of *Amida*.

KESHI-NINGIYŌ, ケシニンギヤウ, 芥子人形, *n.* Very small figures of men.

KESHIRAI, ケシラヒ, *n.* Appearance, sign, indication, symptom. *— mo nai*, no indication. Syn. KIZASHI.

KESHŌ, ケシヤウ, 化粧, Adorning the face with white powder and rouge. *— wo szru. Keshōbeya*, a dressing-room.

KESHŌ-NO-MONO, ケシヤウノモノ, 化生者, *n.* A hideous or unnatural form, monstrosity. Syn. HENGE.

†KESŌ, *-szru*, ケサウ, 懸想, (*omoi wo kakeru.*) To lust after, to love. *Onna ni —*, to lust after a woman. Syn. HORERU.

†KESŌ-BUMI, ケサウブミ, 懸想書, *n.* A love-letter. Syn. TSZKE-BUMI.

KESOKUDAI, ケソクダイ 花束臺, *n.* A flower stand in temples.

†KESSAI, ケツサイ, 潔齋, Abstaining from flesh or fish, in devotional purification. *Shōjin — szru.* (idem).

KESSEKI, ケツセキ, 闕席, Failing to take one's seat in an assembly, absent from one's seat.

KESSHI-*szru*, *-sh'ta*, ケツスル, 決, *t.v.* To settle, decide, determine. *Shō-bu wo kesszru*, to decide which is victorious. *Kokoro wo —*, to decide. Syn. KIMERU, SADAMERU.

KESSHI, *-szru*, *-sh'ta*, ケツスル, 結, *t. v.* To be constipated. *Dai-ben ga kesszru*, the bowels are constipated.

KESSH'TE, ケツシテ, 決, *adv.* Positively, certainly, decidedly. *— sō de wa nai*, it is positively not so. *— o kamai nasaru na*, you must not trouble yourself about it. Syn. KIWAMETE, KITTO, ZEHI.

KESZ, ケス, See *Keshi*.

KESSHO, *-szru*, ケツシヨ, 闕所, To confiscate, or seize the property of a person for crime committed.

KETA, ケタ, 桁, *n.* The cross-beams of a roof. *Hogeta*, the yards of a sail.

KETABŌ, ケタボウ, 桁棒, *n.* The yards of a sail.

KETADE, ケタデ, 毛蓼, *n.* A kind of plant.

‖KETAI, ケタイ, 卦體, *n.* Luck. *— ga warui*, unlucky.

KE-TAOSHI, *-sz*, *-sh'ta*, ケタフス, 蹴倒, *t.v.* To kick over, kick down any thing standing.

KE-TATE, *-ru*, *-ta*, ケタテル, 蹴立, *t.v.* To kick up. *Hokori wo —*, to kick up a dust.

KETCHAKU, *-szru*, ケツチヤク, 決着, To decide, fix, settle, determine, (adv.), positively. *Hiyō-gi ga ketchaku sh'ta*, the council has come to a decision.

KE-TOBASHI, *-sz*, *-sh'ta*, ケトバス, 蹴飛, *t.v.* To cause to fly up by kicking. *Kemari wo —*, to kick a football up into the air.

KETSZ-DAN, ケツダン, 決斷, Decision, determination, final judgment. *— szru*, to decide, determine, judge.

KETSZ-JI, ケツジ, 闕字, *n.* The space left blank in writing, before the names of the great and venerated.

KETSZ-JŌ, ケツヂヤウ, 決定, Fixed, settled, determined, sure. *— szru*, Syn. SADAMARU, KIWAMARU.

KE-TSZMADZKI, *-ku*, *-ita*, ケツマヅク, *i. v.* To stumble, trip, or strike the foot against any thing. Syn. FUMI-ATERU.

†KETSZ-NIKU, ケツニク, 血肉, *n.* Flesh and blood. *— no kiyōdai.*

†KETSZ-RIN, ケツリン, 血淋, *n.* Hæmaturia, bloody urine.

KETTŌ, ケツトウ, 血統, Family-line, lineage, natural descent, consanguinity.

KE-U, ケウ, 希有, Rare, strange, wonderful. *— na koto*, a strange affair. Syn. HENNA, MIYŌNA.

†KEWAI, *-szru*, ケハイ, 粧, To dress, adorn one's self adjust one's dress. Syn. YOSŌ-Ō.

KEWAI, ケハイ, *n.* Manner, sign, indication, appearance. Syn. YŌSZ, KESHIRAI, KESHIKI.

KEWAI-JO, ケハイジヨ, 粧所, *n.* A dressing-room. Syn. KESHŌBEYA.

KEWASHII, -KI, -KU, -Ū, ケハシイ, 嶮, Steep, precipitous, hasty, hurried, urgent. Syn. KENSO, SEWASHII, ISOGAWASHII.

KEYAKI, ケヤキ, *n.* A kind of tree.

KE-YAKI, ケヤキ, 毛燒, *n.* Singing the feathers of a fowl. *— szru.*

KI, キ, 木, *n.* A tree, wood. *— no ha*, leaf of a tree. *— no me*, fruit of a tree. *— no ne*, root of a tree. *— no miki*, trunk of a tree. *— no kabu*, stump of a tree. *— no yani*, gum. *— no shiru*, sap of a tree. *— no me*, the buds of a tree. *— no hana*, blossoms. *— no mata*, crotch of a tree, *— no shin*, the pith of a tree. *— no fushi*, knot of a tree. *— no mokume*, the grain of wood. — *de koshirayeru,* made of wood. — *wo kiru,* to cut wood.

KI, キ, 氣, *n.* The spirit, temper, feeling, mind, heart, disposition; vapor, exhalation. — *ni iru,* to accord with one's mind, to like. — *ni iranu,* to dislike, does not suit. — *ni kakeru,* to be concerned about, to lay to heart. — *ni szru,* to keep in mind, to take to heart. — *ga tōku naru,* to lose consciousness. — *wo ushinau,* idem. — *ga mijikai,* impatient, irritable. — *no kīta h'to,* a sharp, quick witted person. — *ni kanau,* to suit one's fancy, to be agreeable. — *no nagai h'to* a deliberate person, not hasty. — *w osandzru,* to enliven the spirits, dispel vapors. — *wo momu,* to fret or vex the mind, — *ga muszboreru,* to be gloomy, moody. — *wo fusagu,* to lose heart, become melancholy. — *ga semai,* pusillaminous. — *wo tszkeru,* to take care, heed, mind. — *no mudzkashii h'to,* a person hard to please. *H'to no ki ni sakaru,* to offend a person. — *ga tatsz,* to be excited, or aroused, the vapor rises.

KI, キ, 黃, *n.* Yellow.

†KI, キ, 奇, Odd number. *Kigū,* odd and even. Syn. HAN.

†KI, キ, 奇, Strange. *Ki-naru,* strange. *Kore wa ki-na mono da,* this is a strange thing. Syn. MEDSZRASHI, MIYŌ.

†KI, キ, 機, *n.* Circumstances, opportunity. — *ni ōdzru,* to avail one's self of circumstances. — *wo ushinau,* to lose the opportunity.

†KI, キ, 紀, *n.* A space of twelve years. *Ikki,* one period of 12 years.

KI, キ, 騎, Numeral for horse-men. *Ikki,* one horseman. *Ikkigaki wo szru,* to ride out alone. *Ikki tō-sen no tszwamono,* a daring soldier, who is not afraid alone to face ten thousand.

KI, KURU, KITA, キ, 來, *i.v.* To come. *Kiteoru,* is coming. *Nandoki kita ka,* what o'clock did you come? *Yedo kara kita,* came from Yedo. neg. *Konu,* not come. Imp. *Koi,* come. *Koko ni koi,* come here. Neg. imp. *Kuna,* don't come. *Koko ni kuna,* don't come here. *Ame ga futtekita,* it has begun to rain. *Kaze ga futte-kita,* the wind has begun to blow. *Kite mi nasai,* come and see. *Cha wo katte-koi,* go and buy some tea. *Cha wo katte-kita,* he has bought the tea.

KI, KIRU, KITA, キ, 著, *t.v.* To wear, put on clothes, to dress. *Kimono wo kiru,* to put on one's clothes. *On wo kiru,* to receive favors. *Haori wo kite yuku,* put on one's coat and go. Syn. CHAKU-YŌ.

†KI, キ, 記, *n.* History, record, chronicle. *Ni-hon-ki,* the history of Japan.

KI-AI, キアヒ, 氣合, *(kibun,) n.* The spirits, feelings. — *ga warui,* to feel bad. Syn. KOKORO-MOCHI.

KIBA, キバ, 牙, *n.* A tusk, the canine teeth.

†KIBA, キバ, 騎馬, *n.* A horseman, trooper. *Kibamusha,* (idem.)

KI-BACHI, キバチ, 木盤, *n.* A large wooden bowl.

KI-BAMI, *-mu, -nda,* キバミ, 黃, *i. v.* To become yellowish. *Kao ga kibande oru,* his face is yellow. *Ki no ha ga* —, the leaves are turned yellow.

KIBARASHI, キバラシ, 氣晴, *n.* Pastime, amusement, driving off gloom, or melancholy. — *wo szru.*

KIBARI, *-ru, -tta,* キバル, 氣張, *i. v.* To force one's self to do a liberal act.

KI-BASAMI, キバサミ, 木鋏子, *n.* Shears for pruning trees.

KIBAYAI, -KI, -KU, -Ō, -SHI, キバヤイ, 氣早, Quick of apprehension; prompt, excitable, or easily roused, quick tempered.

KIBI, キビ, 黍, *n.* A kind of millet, sorghum.

KIBI, キビ, 氣味, same as *Kimi.*

KIBISHII, -KI, -KU, -Ū, キビシイ, 嚴, Severe, strict, stringent, rigid, stern. *Samusa ga* —, the cold is severe. *Oya no shitszke ga* —, parent's rules are strict. *Kibishiku katameru,* strictly guarded. *Kibishiku imashimeru,* to severely reprimand. Syn. GEN-JŪ, KATAI.

‖KIBISHO, キビシヨ, *n.* A small tea pot, same as *Kiusz.*

‖KIBISZ, キビス, 跟, *n.* The heel. Syn. KAKATO, KUBISZ.

KIBO, キボ, 規模, *n.* Example worthy of imitation, precedent, pattern; renown, illustrious deed. — *wo nokosz,* to leave behind a good example. — *wo tateru,* to set an example. *Matsz dai no* —, a glorious example to the latest generations. Syn. TEHON, KATA, HŌ, ISAO.

†KI-BŌ, キボウ, 奇謀, *(medzrashi hakarigoto,) n.* A strange scheme, wonderful plan.

†KI-BOKU, キボク, 貴墨, *(tattoki szmi.)* Precious ink, a phrase used for a letter.

KI-BONEORI, *-ru, -tta,* キボチオル, 氣骨折, *i. v.* To be full of care, concern, or anxiety, usually written *Kibone wo oru.*

‖KIBUI-KI, -KU, -SHI, -Ū, -SA, キブイ, 釀, Sharp, strong, or harsh to the taste. *Sake ga kibui.* Syn. TSZYOI.

KI-BUN, キブン, 氣分, *n.* The spirits, state of the body. — *ga warui*, to feel unwell. *O — wa ikaga*, how are you? Syn. KOKORO-MOCHI.

KI-BURI, キブリ, 木振, *n.* The shape, or trim of a tree. — *wo naosz*, to improve the shape of a tree.

KI-BURUSHI, キブルシ, 著古, *n.* Old and worn out clothing. *Danna no — wo moratte kiru*, to wear master's old clothes.

KIBUSAI,-KI,-KU,-SHI,-Ō, キブサイ, 氣塞, Disagreeable, hard to bear, causing dejection or depression of spirits. Syn. UTTŌSHII.

KI-BUSHŌ, キブシヤウ, 氣無性, Idle, indolent, lazy.

KI-BUTSZ, キブツ, 奇物, (*medzrashi mono,*) *n.* A strange, or wonderful thing.

KI-BUTSZ, キブツ, 器物, *n.* A vessel, utensil, furniture, implement. Syn. UTSZWA, KIKAI.

KI-CHAKU,-*szru*, キチヤク, 歸著, To return home, come back.

KICHI, キチ, 吉, *a.* Lucky, fortunate. — *nichi*, a lucky day. — *dzi*, a lucky sign. — *jō*, lucky. — *ji*, lucky affair, good luck. Syn. YOI.

KI-CHIGAI, キチガイ, 狂氣, Crazy, insane, mad, out of one's mind. — *na h'to*, a crazy man, lunatic. Syn. RAN-SHIN, HAKKIYO, MONO-GURUI.

KICHI-REI, キチレイ, 吉例, *n.* The anniversary of a fortunate event.

KI-CHIU, キチウ, 忌中, (*imi no uchi.*) The period of mourning. Syn. MO-CHIU.

KICHŌ, キチヤウ, 几帳, *n.* Silk-curtain.

KICHŌMEN, キチヤウメン, Exact, accurate, precise, punctual.

KI-DACHI, キダチ, 木太刀, *n.* A wooden long-sword.

KI-DATE, キダテ, 氣立, *n.* Disposition, temper. — *no warui h'to*, a person of bad disposition. Syn. SHŌNE.

KIDEN, キデン, 貴殿, (*tattoki tono.*) Honorable lord, a phrase used for, You.

†KI-DEN, キデン, 記傳, (*shirushi tsztaye.*) *n.* Records, history.

KIDO, キド, 木戶, *n.* A gate.

†KI-DO, キド, 喜怒, (*yorokobi ikaru.*) Joy and anger.

KIDOKU, キドク, 奇特, Strange, wonderful, rare, admirable, (used in praise only.) — *na h'to*. — *na koto*. Syn. SHIMBIYŌ.

KI-DŌSHI, キドホシ, 著通, Always wearing the same clothes. — *ni szru*.

KIDZ, キズ, 不着, (Neg. of *Kiru.*) not wear.

KIDZ, キツ, 木兎, *n.* A kind of owl. Syn. MIMIDZKU.

KIDZ, キズ, 疵, *n.* A wound, hurt, a scar, cicatrice; 玷, a blemish, defect. — *wo ukeru*, to receive a wound, or hurt. — *wo tszkeru*, to wound, hurt. Syn. KEGA.

KI-DZI, キズヰ, 氣隨, Selfish, serving one's own pleasure or convenience. — *na h'to*. Syn. KI-MAMA.

KI-DZI, キズヰ, 奇瑞, *n.* A strange sign, a wonder, unusual phenomenon, — *ga arawareru*. Syn. FUSHIGI.

KI-DZKAI, キツカヒ, 氣遣, *n.* Concern, anxiety, fear. — *wo szru*, to feel anxious. — *wa nai*, there is no fear. Syn. SHIMPAI, ANJIRU.

KIDZKAWASHII,-KI,-KU, キツカハシイ, 氣遣敷, Anxious, concerned, fearful.

KIDZKI,-*ku*,-*ita*, キツク, 築, *t.v.* To build with stones or earth. *Odaiba wo* —, to build a fort. *Dote wo* —, to build an embankment.

KIDZKIGAMI, キズキガミ, 生漉紙, *n.* A kind of unglazed paper.

KIDZMARI,-*ru*,-*tta*, キツマル, 氣迫, *i.v.* To be dejected, oppressed in spirits, to be gloomy.

†KIDZNA, キツナ, 絏, *n.* Bonds, only used figuratively. *On ai no — ni hikaruru*, drawn by the cords of kindness and love.

KIDZTSZKI,-*ku*,-*ita*, キズツク, 傷, *t. v.* To wound, hurt. *H'to ni* —, to wound another.

KI-DZYOI,-KI,-KU,-Ō,-SHI, キツヨイ, 氣强, Resolute, stout-hearted, of great fortitude, nerve, or endurance. — *h'to*.

KI-FU, キフ, 寄附, Contributions for building, or repairing a temple. — *szru*, to contribute, &c.

KI-FUDA, キフダ, 木札, *n.* A wooden ticket, or pass.

KI-FUKU,-*szru*, カフク, 歸服, *i. v.* To obey, submit, be in subjection. Syn. S'HTAGAU.

KIGA, キガ, 木臭, *n.* Tasting of wood. *Kono sake — kusai*, this wine tastes of the cask.

KI-GANE, キガネ, 氣兼, *n.* Care, anxiety, or solicitude not to offend. — *wo szru*, to be careful to please. Syn. SHIMPAI, KIDZKAI.

KI-GARUI,-KI,-KU, キガルイ, 氣輕, Lighthearted, sprightly.

KI-GAYE, キガヘ, 著替, *n.* Changing the clothes, a change of clothing. — *wo szru*, to change one's dress. — *no kimono*, a change of clothes.

KIGEN, キゲン, 機嫌, *n.* Feeling, spirits,

temper. — *ga warui*, to feel unwell, out of temper. *Go — yoroshii ka*, how do you do? are you well? (in saluting.) — *wo sonjiru*, to offend, hurt the feelings. — *wo toru*, to please, to gratify, to conciliate.

KI-GIKU, キギク, 黄菊, *n.* A yellow crysanthimum.

KIGOMI, キゴミ, 着込, *n.* A kind of padded garment worn in winter under armor.

KI-GU, ケグ, 木具, *n.* Wooden ware.

KI-GUSHI, キグシ, 木梳, *n.* A wooden comb.

†KI-G'WAN, キグワン, 祈願, (*Inori negau.*) *n.* Prayer, supplication. — *wo kakeru*, to offer up prayers.

KIGU-YA, キグヤ, 木器舗, *n.* A seller of wooden ware.

KIHADA, キハダ, *n.* Oakum.

†KI-HAN, キハン, 歸帆, (*kayeru fune*). Sailing of a ship on her return. — *szru.*

†KI-HEI, キヘイ, 奇兵, (*ayashiki tszwamono*). Soldiers used to decoy, or surprise an enemy.

†KI-HEN, キヘン, 貴邊, (*tattokihō*), = Your honor, in respectfully addressing another.

†KI-HŌ, キハウ, 貴報, (*tattoki kotaye*),= Your honorable answer.

†KI-I, キイ, 貴意, (*anata no oboshimeshi*). =Your honor's meaning or mind.

†KI-I, キイ, 奇異, (*ayashii*). Strange, wonderful.

KI-IRO, キイロ, 黄色, *n.* Yellow.

KIJI, キジ, 雉子, *n.* A pheasant.

†KI-JI, キジ, 記事, *n.* History.

KI-JI, キヂ, 木地, *n.* The nature or quality of wood. *Kono hako wa — ga warui kara yowai*, the box is not strong because of the bad quality of the wood.

KI-JITSZ, キジツ, 枳實, *n.* A kind of medicine.

KI-JŌ-NA, キジヤウナ, 氣情, Resolute, firm, determined.
Syn. KIDZYOI.

†KIKA, キカ, 貴家, (*anata*). = You, in addressing equals.

KIKADSZ, KIKANU, KIKANAI, キカズ, 不聞, Neg. of *Kiki*.

KIKADZMBA, キカズンバ, Neg. conj. of *Kiki*, = if he don't hear, the not hearing. — *aru bekaradz*, must hear.

KIKAI, キカイ, 器械, *n.* Any instrument, tool, utensil, furniture or machine used by man to aid him in his labor.

†KIKAI, キカイ, 機械, *n.* A machine, engine.

†KIKAMAHOSHIKU, キカマホシク, 欲聞, Wish to hear. Syn. KIKI-TAI.

†KI-KAN, キカン, 飢寒, (*wiye samui*). Hunger and cold. — *wo shinogu*, to endure hunger and cold.

†KIKAN, キカン, 龜鑑, *n.* Example for imitation.

KI-KASANE,-*ru*,-*ta*, キカサヌル, 着重, *t.v.* To wear many clothes one over the other.

KIKASE,-*ru*,-*ta*, キカセル, 令聞, Caust. of *Kiki*. To inform, tell. *O kikase nasare*, tell me. *H'to ni kikasete wa warui*, don't tell any body. Syn. HANASZ.

KI-KATSZ, キカツ, 飢渴, *n.* Hunger and thirst. — *ni kurushimu.*

KIKAYE,-*ru*,-*ta*, キカヘル, 著替, *t.v.* To change the clothes. *Kimono ga nureta kara* —, to change one's clothes because they are wet.

KI-KAZARI,-*ru*,-*tta*, キカザル, 著飾, *t.v.* To adorn with fine clothing.

†KI-KENJŌ, キケンジヤウ, 喜見城, *n.* Heaven. (Bud.)

†KI-KETSZ, キケツ, 氣血, *n.* Vital spirits and blood.

KIKI,-*ku*,-*ita*, キク, 聞, *t.v.* or *i.v.* To hear, listen; to inquire, to perceive, to grant, or permit; to be efficacious, to have effect, power, strength, virtue, or influence; to be clever, acute, or expert. *Mimi de* —, to hear with the ears. *Hanashi wo* —, to listen to what is said. *Mono no nedan wo* —, to inquire the price of anything. *Danna ga kikimasen*, master will not grant it. *Kīte mimashō*, I will inquire about it. *Kuszri wa yoku kīta*, the medicine has had a good effect. *Ikura shikatte mo kikimasen*, scold as much as I may it has no effect. *Imashime ga kīta*, the reproof was efficacious. *Kuji ga kikanu*, the nail took no hold. *Te no kīta h'to*, a person handy or skilful at doing any thing. *Me no kīta h'to*, a sharp sighted person. *Sz ga yoku kiku*, the vinegar is sharp. *Nioi wo* —, to perceive an odor.

KIKI, キキ, 聞, *n.* The effect, efficacy, influence, virtue, strength. *Imashime no — ga yoi*, the reproof had a good effect.

KIKI-ATE,-*ru*,-*ta*, キキアテル, 聞當, *t.v.* To guess by hearing, to find out by hearing.

KIKI-AWASE,-*ru*,-*ta*, キキアハセル, 聞合, *t.v.* To inquire and find out.

KIKI-AYAMARI,-*ru*,-*tta*, キキアヤマル, 聞誤, *i.v.* To make a mistake in hearing, not to hear correctly.

KIKI-CHIGAI, *-au,-atta*, キキチガフ, 聞違, *i.v.* (Idem).

KIKI-DASHI, *-sz,-sh'ta*, キキダス, 聞出, *t.v.* To find out by hearing.

KIKI-GAKARI, キキガカリ, 聞掛, *n.* The one entrusted with the hearing, the person who happened to hear. — *wo dare da*, who was it that heard it?

KIKI-GAKI, キキガキ, 聞書, *n.* A memorandum, or note. — *wo szru*, to note down what one hears.

KIKI-GAKU, キキガク, 耳學, *n.* Learning got by hearing, learning by the ear.

KIKI-HADZSHI, *-sz,-sh'ta*, キキハヅス, 聞迯, *t.v.* To miss in hearing, to fail to hear. *Osoku kite seppō kiki-hadzsh'ta*, by being late I missed hearing the sermon.

KIKI-IRE, *-ru,-ta*, キキイレル, 聞入, *t.v.* To consent to, allow, listen to, to heed. *Tanomu koto kiki-iremasen*, would not listen to the request.

KIKI-KANE, *-ru,-ta*, キキカヌル, 聞難, Disagreeable or hard to hear; hard to consent to.

KIKIME, キキメ, 驗, *n.* Virtue, strength, efficacy. *Kono kuszri wa — ga miyenu*, this medicine has no strength.

KI-KIN, キキン, 飢饉, *n.* Famine.

KIKI-NAGASHI, *-sz,-sh'ta*, キキナガス, 聞流, *t.v.* To hear but not to mind, to take no notice of what is heard.

KIKI-NAOSHI, *-sz,-sh'ta*, キキナホス, 聽直, *t.v.* To hear and correct, listen to so as to correct.

KIKI-NARAI, *-ō,-ōta*, キキナラフ, 聞習, *i.v.* To learn by hearing.

KIKI-NARE, *-ru,-ta*, キキナレル, 聽熟, *t.v.* To be accustomed to the hearing of anything, used to hearing.

KIKI-NIKUI, -KI, -KU, -Ū, -SHI, キキニクイ, 聞惡, Disagreeable to hear, offensive to the ear.

KIKI-NOKOSHI, *-sz,-sh'ta*, キキノコス, 聞殘, *t.v.* To omit the hearing of anything, to put off hearing.

KIKI-OBOYE, *-ru,-ta*, キキオボエル, 聞覺, *t.v.* To learn, or remember anything by hearing it.

KIKI-OTOSHI, *-sz,-sh'ta*, キキオトス, 聞落, To miss hearing, to fail to hear what is said, to fail or forget to inquire about.

KIKI-OYOBI, *-bu,-nda*, キキオヨブ, 聞及, *t.v.* To get or attain to the hearing of anything, to be apprised of.

KIKI-SADAME, *-ru,-ta*, キキサダメル, 聞定, *t.v.* To hear or inquire and determine, to be confirmed in what one hears.

KIKI-SHIRI, *-ru,-tta*, キキシル, 聞知, *t.v.* To know by hearing, or inquiry.

KIKI-SOKONAI, *-ō,-atta*, キキソコナフ, 聞損, *i.v.* To hear incorrectly, mistake what one hears.

KIKI-SONJI, *-ru,-ta*, キキソンジル, 聞損, (Idem).

KIKI-SZMASHI, *-sz,-sh'ta*, キキスマス, 聞濟, *t.v.* To finish hearing, to hear and grant.

KIKI-SZTE, *-ru,-ta*, キキステル, 聞捨, *t.v.* To hear and take no notice of, not to mind.

KIKI-TADASHI, *-sz,-sh'ta*, キキタダス, 聞糺, *t.v.* To hear and judge of, to inquire and find out the truth of anything.
Syn. SENSAKU SZRU, GIMMI SZRU.

KIKITAGARI, *-ru,-tta*, キキタガル, Fond of hearing.

KIKI-TAGAYE, *-ru,-ta*, キキタガヘル, 聞違, *t.v.* To hear incorrectly, mistake what is heard.

KIKI-TATE, *-ru,-ta*, キキタテル, 聞立, *t.v.* To hear and determine the truth, to hear and find out.

KIKI-TODOKI, *-ku,-ita*, キキトドク, 聞屆, *t.v.* To hear fully, finish hearing.

KIKI-TODOKE, *-ru,-ta*, キキトドケル, 聞屆, *t.v.* To permit, grant.

KIKI-TOGAME, *-ru,-ta*, キキトガメル, 聞咎, *t.v.* To hear and reprimand, to censure what one hears.

KIKI-TORI, *-ru,-tta*, キキトル, 聞取, *t.v.* To understand or distinguish what is heard, to get or find out by inquiring, or listening.

KIKI-TSZKE, *-ru,-ta*, キキツケル, 聞付, *t.v.* To hear accidentally, to happen to hear.

KIKI-TSZKURAI, *-ō,-tta*, キキツクロフ, 聞補, *t.v.* To inquire and adjust, or rectify a mistake.

KIKI-TSZKUSHI, *-sz,-sh'ta*, キキツクス, 聞盡, *t.v.* To inquire about or hear any thing fully.

KIKI-TSZTAYE, *-ru,-ta*, キキツタヘル, 聞傳, To hear from others, or by tradition.

†KI-KIU, キキフ, 危急, Danger, peril. — *na*, dangerous, perilous. — *ni nozomu*, to be in imminent peril. Syn. AYAUI.

†KI-KIU, キキウ, 氣球, *n.* A balloon. Syn. KŪSEN.

KIKI-WAKE, *-ru,-ta*, キキワケル, 聞分,

t.v. To hear and understand; to inquire and distinguish.

†KI-KIYO, キキヨ, 起居, (*tachi i.*) *n.* Standing or sitting, deportment, behaviour, manners. Syn. TACHI-FURUMAI.

†KI-KIYŌ, キキヤウ, 歸鄉, Returning to one's country. Syn. FURUSATO YE KAYERU.

KIKIYŌ, キキヨウ, 桔梗, *n.* A kind of flower. Platycodon grandiflorum.

KIKKIYŌ, キツキヤウ 吉凶, *n.* Lucky, or unlucky. *Mono wo — wa sadamari-gatashi*, it is hard to decide when a thing is lucky or unlucky.

KI-KŌ, キコウ, 貴公, = You, to an equal.

†KI-KŌ, キコウ, 季侯, *n.* Climate. Syn. JIKŌ, YŌ KI.

KI-KOKU, キコク, 歸國, (*kuni ye kayeru.*) Returning to one's country.

KI-KOKU, キコク, 枳殼, *n.* A kind of medicine.

KI-KON, キコン, 氣根, *n.* Energy, or vigor of body, strength. *— ga tszyoi*, great vigor. *— shigoto*, a work requiring a strong constitution.

KIKONASHI,*-sz,-sh'ta*, キコナス, 穿得好, *t.v.* To dress with neatness, or taste.

KIKORI, キコリ 樵夫, *n.* A wood-chopper, woodman.

†KIKOSHIMESHI,*-sz,-sh'ta*, キコシメス, 聞召, *t.v.* To hear, (used only to superiors.)

KIKOYE,*-ru,-ta*, キコエル, 聞, Pass. and pot. of *Kiku.* To be heard, to be known, celebrated. *Kikoyenu koto wo iu*, to say something senseless and absurd. *Kikoyeta h'to*, a celebrated person.

KIKOYE, キコエ, 聞, *n.* Fame, celebrity, notoriety. *— wo habakaru*, to shun notoriety. *— ga yoi*, of good reputation. Syn. FŪBUN, HIYŌBAN, TORI-SATA.

KIKU, キク, See *Kiki.*

KIKU, キク, 菊, *n.* The Chrysanthimum.

KI-KU, キク, 規矩, (*Bunmawashi to kanezashi*, — Compass and square.) *n.* A rule, established custom, to which any thing is to be conformed, or by which it is to be regulated. *— ga tatanu*, the rule is useless. *— ni hadzreru*, contrary to rule. *— wo hadzsz*, to break the rule. Syn. SA-HŌ, HŌ SHIKI, TE-HON, KAKU.

KIKU-DZKI, キクヅキ, 菊月, *n.* The 9th month.

KI-KUGI, キクギ, 木釘, *n.* A wooden nail.

KI-KUI-MUSHI, キクヒムシ, 木蠹, *n.* A kind of insect that bores in wood.

KIKUITADAKI, キクイタダキ, *n.* A kind of small bird.

†KIKU-MON,*-szru*, キクモン, 鞠問, To judge, to examine (a prisoner). *Tszmibito wo —*, to examine a prisoner. Syn. GIMMISZRU, SAIBANSZRU, TADASZ.

†KI-KUN, キクン, 貴君, = You, (respectful.)

KI-KURAGE, キクラゲ, 木耳, *n.* A kind of fungus which grows from the bark of trees.

KI-K'WA, キクワ, 歸化, Becoming a citizen or subject of another country; changing one's allegiance. *— Nippun ni — szru*, to become a subject of the Japanese Government.

KI-K'WAI-NA, キクワイナ, 奇怪, *n.* Abominable, disagreeable. *— yatsz.* Syn. IMAIMASHII.

KI-MAKURA, キマクラ, 木枕, *n.* A wooden pillow.

KI-MAMA, キママ, 氣儘, Selfish, self-willed, having one's own way, following one's own convenience or pleasure. Syn. KI-DZI, WAGA-MAMA.

KI-MAMORI, キマモリ, 殘果, *n.* Fruit left on a tree after the fruit is gathered.

KIMARI,*-ru,-tta*, キマル, 極, *t. v.* To be fixed, settled, determined, definite, sure, certain. neg. *Kimara-nai*, not sure, not fixed. *Yakujō ga kimatta*, the treaty is settled. *Kimari ga nai*, not fixed, uncertain. Syn. SADAMARU.

KIM-BAN, キンバン, 勤番, Leaving one's family at home to be engaged in official duty in another place. *— szru.* *— mono.*

KIME, キメ, 理, *n.* The texture. *Kawa no —*, the texture of the skin. *— ga komakai*, the texture is fine. *— hosoi*, (idem.) *— arai*, coarse in texture. Syn. JI-AI, HADA.

KIME,*-ru,-ta*, キメル, 極, *t. v.* To fix, settle, establish, set, determine, to make sure. *Nedan wo —*, to fix a price. *Hidori wo —*, to set a day. SADAMERU.

KIME,*-ru,-ta*, キメル, 嚇殺, *t.v.* To reprimand, scold, censure, reproach. *H'to wo —.* Syn. TOGAMERU, NONOSHIRU, SHIKARU.

KI-MEI, キメイ, 忌明, *n.* End of mourning. *— no on rei ni demash'ta.*

†KI-MEN, キメン, 貴面, = You, respectful.

KIME-TSZKE,*-ru,-ta*, キメツケル, 嚇著, *t. v.* To reprimand, scold, censure, reproach.

KIMI, キミ, 君, *n.* Lord, master.

KIMI, キミ, 氣味, *n.* The state of one's mind, or feelings. *Kimi waruku mono wo kū*, to eat any thing with a feeling of

doubt, or dread. — *waruku fune wo noru*, to sail in a boat with feelings of alarm, or dread. — *ga yoi*, to feel easy, comfortable, and free from alarm.
Syn. KOKORO-MOCHI.

KIMI, キミ, *n.* The yolk of an egg.

KI-MIJIKAI,-KI,-KU, キミジカイ, 短氣, Quick-tempered, irascible, easily provoked. Syn. TAN-KI.

†KI-MITSZ, キミツ, 機密, *n.* A secret. — *wo morasz*, to divulge a secret.
Syn. MITSZ-JI.

KI-MIYŌ, キミヤウ, 奇妙, Marvellous, wonderful, strange, admirable, remarkable, curious. — *na mono*, a marvellous thing. — *ni*, wonderfully.
Syn. MEDZRASHII, FUSHIGI, AYASHII.

KIMMOTSZ, キンモツ, 禁物, *n.* Prohibited things, things forbidden to be eaten, (as in sickness.)

KIM-MUKU, キンムク, 純金, *n.* Pure gold.

KIMO, キモ, 膽, *n.* Liver, (met.) courage, bravery. — *no f'toi h'to*, a man of courage. — *no hosoi*, cowardly. — *wo tszbusz*, (met.) astonished, thunderstruck. — *wo hiyasz*. — *mo kesz*, (idem.)

KIMO-IRI, キモイリ, 肝煎, *n.* Assistance, aid; one to whom especially the care, or superintendence of any thing belongs. *H'to ni* — *wo szru*, to render aid, or assistance to another. Syn. SEWA.

KI-MON, キモン, 鬼門, *n.* The north east, from which an evil influence is supposed to come. — *ni ataru*, to face towards the N.E. — *yoke ni kami wo matszru.*

KIMONO, キモノ, 著物, *n.* The long robe worn by the Japanese; clothing.

KIM-PAKU, キンパク, 金箔, *n.* Gold-leaf.

KIM-PEI, キンペイ, 金幣, *(kin no go hei.)* *n.* Gold-leaf, or gilt paper hung in Miyas to represent the Kami.

KIM-PEN, キンペン, 近邊, *n.* Neighborhood, vicinity. *Kono* —, this neighborhood. *Yedo no* —, the vicinity of Yedo.

KIM-PUN, キンプン, 金粉, *n.* Gold-dust.

‖KIMUSAI,-KI,-KU, キムサイ, 氣碍, Disagreeable, offensive, disgusting.

KIMUDZKASHII,-KI,-KU, キムツカシイ, Trying to the temper, tedious.

KIMUSZME, キムスメ, 處女, A chaste woman.

KIN, キン, 金, *n.* Gold. — *de koshirayeru*, made of gold. — *no*, golden.
Syn. KOGANE.

KIN, キン, 斤, *n.* A catty = 1⅓ lb. avoirdupois.

†KIN, キン, 琴, *(koto).* *n.* A harp. — *wo dandzru*, to play on a harp.

KIN, キン, 陰囊, *n.* The scrotum, also testicles. Syn. INNŌ, KINTAMA.

KIN, キン, 磬, *n* A kind of gong or timbrel, used in Bud. temples. Syn. KEI.

KI-NAGAI,-KI,-KU, キナガイ, 性慢, Easy, and calm in temper, deliberate.

KINAI, or GO-KINAI, キナイ, 畿內, The five provinces of Yamashiro, Yamato, Kawachi, Idzmi, Settsz. — *hen*, the region of Miyako.

KINAKA, キナカ, 半文, *n.* Half a *zeni.*

KINAKINA, キナキナ, *n.* Quinine.

KINA-KO, キナコ, 黄粉, *n.* A kind of food made of beans.

KI-NAN, キナン, 危難, *n.* Danger, peril, disaster. — *ni au*, to be in great jeopardy.
Syn. AYAUI.

KINCHAKKIRI, キンチヤクキリ; 巾著切, *n.* A cut-purse, a pickpocket.
Syn. SZRI, CHIBO.

KINCHAKU, キンチヤク, 巾著, *n.* A purse.

KIN-CHIU, キンチウ, 禁中, *n.* In the Mikado's palace.

†KIN-CHŌ, キンチヤウ, 錦帳, *n.* Curtains of embroidered work.

†KIN-CHŌ, キンチヤウ, 金打, Swearing or confirming a promise by striking swords; or where one party is a woman, by striking the sword across the back of a mirror. — *szru.*

KINDACHI, キンダチ, 公達, A prince, the son of a Daimio.

KIN-DAN, キンダン, 禁斷, *n.* Prohibition, interdict.

KIN-DEI, キンデイ, 金泥, *n.* A kind of gilt paint.

KINDZRU, キンズル, See *Kinji.*

KINDZKURI, キンヅクリ, 金飾, *n.* Gold mounted, wrought of gold, (as a scabbard.)

KINE, キネ, 杵, *n.* The mallet used in pounding rice, a pestle.

KI-NEN, キネン, 祈念, *n.* Prayer, petition. — *wo kakeru*, to offer up a prayer.

†KIN-GAKU,-*szru*, カンガク, 勤學, *(tsztomete manabu).* To study, to learn diligently.

†KIN-GEN, キンゲン, 謹言, *(tsztszshinde mōsz).* Respectfully said, (at the close of a letter), = respectfully your, &c.

KIN-GEN, キンゲン, 金言, *n.* Golden saying, wise maxim, or precept. — *wo iu.*

KINGIN, キンギン, 金銀, *n.* Gold and silver; money.

KIN-GIYO, キンギヨ, 金魚, *n.* Gold-fish.

†KIN-GIYOKU, キンギヨク, 金玉, *n.* Gold and pearls. — *no kotoba*, wise maxims or precepts.

KIN-GŌ, キンガウ, 近鄕, (*chikaki sato*). *n.* Neighboring village.

KIN-GOKU, キンゴク, 近國, (*chikaki kuni*). *n.* Neighboring states or provinces.

KI-NICHI, キニチ, 忌日, *n.* The day of the month on which a person has died.

†KI-NIN, キニン, 貴人, (*tattoki h'to*). Honorable person, of high rank.

KINJI,–*dzru*,–*ta*, キンズル, 禁, *t.v.* To prohibit, forbid, interdict. *Bakuyeki wo* —, to prohibit gambling.
Syn. IMASHIMERU.

KINJITZ, キンジツ, 近日, (*chikai hi*). Soon, in a few days, a few days past.

KIN-JO, キンジヨ, 近所, (*chikaki tokoro*). *n.* Neighborhood, vicinity.

KIN-JŌ-KŌ-TEI, キンジヤウクワウテイ, 今上皇帝, *n.* The present Emperor.

†KIN-JŪ, キンジウ, 禽獸, (*Tori kedamono*). *n.* Birds and beasts.

KIN-JU, キンジユ, 近習, *n.* An attendant of a Noble.

KIN-KAN, キンカン, 金柑, *n.* The kumkwat. Citrus japonica.

KIN-KEI, キンケイ, 錦鷄, *n.* The golden pheasant.

KIN-KIN, キンキン, 近近, *adv.* Soon, in a short time.

†KIN-KO, キンコ, 金皷, *n.* Gong and drum.

KIN-KO, キンコ, 海參, *n.* Bich-de-mer.

KIN-KON, キンコン, 筋根, *n.* A tendon.

KIN-KOTSZ, キンコツ, 筋骨, Bone and sinew. — *szkoyaka.*

KIN-KU, キンク, 禁句, *n.* Anything said which is offensive, insulting, or wounding to the feelings. — *wo iu na*, don't say offensive things.

KIN-NEN, キンネン, 近年, (*chikaki toshi*,) *n.* Few years past, late years, recent time.

KINŌ, キノフ, 昨日, *n.* Yesterday.
SAKUJITSZ.

KINODOKU, キノドク, 氣之毒, *n.* Sorrow, or concern for others. — *ni omō*, to feel sorry for another. — *no koto*, something concerning another for which one feels sorry. — *nagara o tanomi-mōshimas*, I am sorry to trouble you, but I have a request to make.

KINOKO, キノコ, 菌, *n.* A kind of mushroom, or fungus which grows from the bark of trees

KINOKOMORI,–*ru*,–*tta*, キノコモル, 陰鬱, *i. v.* Confined, close, unventilated. *Kinokomoru tokoro*, a close place.

KINOME, キノメ, 木芽, *n.* The bud of a tree.

KINOMI, キノミ, 木實, *n.* The fruit of a tree.

KIN-RAI, キンライ, 近來, *adv.* Of late, recently. Syn. CHIKAGORO.

KIN-RAN, キンラン, 金襴, *n.* A kind of gold brocade.

KIN-RI, キンリ, 禁裏, *n.* The palace of the Mikado. *Kinri-sama*, the Mikado.
Syn. DAIRI.

†KIN-RIN, キンリン, 近隣, (*chikaki tonari*,) *n.* Neighborhood, vicinity.
Syn. TONARI.

KIN-SATSZ, キンサツ, 禁札, *n.* A prohibitory edict, (written on a board.)

KIN-SEI, キンセイ, 近世, *n.* The present age, recent or modern times.

†KIN-SEI, キンセイ, 金星, *n.* The planet Venus.

KIN-SEN, キンセン, 金錢, (*kin to zeni.*) Gold and copper coin; money.

†KIN-SHA, キンシヤ, 金砂, *n.* Gold dust.

KIN-SHI, キンシ, 金絲, *n.* Gold-thread.

†KIN-SHI, キンシ, 勤仕, *n.* Duty, official employment, service.
Syn. TSZTOME.

†KIN-SHI, キンシ, 禁止, *n.* Prohibiting, stopping, forbidding, interdicting. — *szru*, to prohibit.

KIN-SHITSZ, キンシツ, 琴瑟, *n.* The harp and harpsicord.

KIN-SHŌ, キンシヤウ, 焮衝, *n.* Inflammation. — *szru*, to be inflamed. *Hai no* —, inflammation of lungs.

KIN-SHOKU, キンシヨク, 金色, *n.* Golden color.

KIN-SHU, キンシユ, 金主, *n.* The person who supplies the capital in any business.

KIN-SHU, キンシユ, 禁酒, *n.* Leaving off the use of ardent spirits. — *szru*, to leave off, &c.

KIN-SŌ, キンサウ, 金瘡, *n.* An incised wound. Syn. KIRI-KIDZ.

KIN-SOKU, キンソク, 禁足, (*ashi wo imashimeru.*) Forbidden to leave the house, confined to the house, (as a punishment. — *wo mōshi-tszkeru.*

†KIN-SON, キンソン, 近村, (*chikaki mura.*) A neighboring town, or village.

KINSZ, キンス, 金子, *n.* Money.

KIN-SZNA-GO, キンスナゴ, 金砂子, *n.* A kind of wall paper spotted with gold.

KIN-TAMA, キンタマ, 睾丸, *n.* Testicles. Syn. INNŌ.

KIN-TEI, キンテイ, 禁庭, *n.* The inclosure of the Mikado's palace.

KINTŌ, キントウ, 均等, Used only in the phrase, *Go-kin-tō*, in complimenting another for promptness, or exactness in paying money, or returning a borrowed thing.

KIN-TON, キントン, 經飩, *n.* A kind of confectionary.

KINU, キヌ, 不着, neg. of *Ki, kiru*, not wear.

†KIN-U, キンウ, 金烏, *(kane no tori.)* The golden bird, a name given to the sun. Syn. NICHI-RIN.

KINU, キヌ, 絹, *n.* Silk-goods.

KINU-B'ARI, キヌバリ, 絹張, *n.* Glazed or spread with silk, (as screens, lanterns, &c.)

KINU-CHIJIMI, キヌチヂミ, 絹縮, *n.* A kind of silk stuff.

KINUKE, キヌケ, 氣拔, Idiotic, foolish, wanting intelligence. *Kinuke na h'to*, an idiotic person.

KINUTA, キヌタ, 碪, *n.* A mallet for fulling cloth.

KIN-ZAI, キンザイ, 近在, *n.* Neighborhood, vicinity, or the country near any place.

KIN-ZEI, キンゼイ, 禁制, *n.* Forbidden, prohibited, interdicted. — *szru.* Syn. KINDAN, KINSHI.

†KIN-ZEN-TO, キンゼント, 欣然, *adv.* Joyfully.

KI-OCHI, キオチ, 氣落, *n.* Despondency, loss of hope or courage, dejection. —*ga szru*, to despond.

KIOI,–*ō*,–*ōta*, キオフ, 競, *i. v.* To strive to excel, to emulate, to rival. Syn KISOI, HAGEMU.

†KI-OKU, キオク, 記憶, *n.* Memory, remembrance. — *no yoi h'to*, a person of good memory. — *szru*, to commit to memory. Syn. OBOYE.

KI-OKURE, キオクレ, 氣後, *n.* Losing one's presence of mind, forgetting one's self. *Bikkuri sh'te — ga sh'ta*, to be alarmed and lose one's presence of mind.

†KIPPAN,–*szru*, キツパン, 吃飯, *(meshi wo kū.)* To eat food.

KIRA, キラ, 綺羅, *n.* Gorgeous or splendid clothing. — *wo kazaru*, to adorn with gorgeous clothing.

KIRABIYAKA, キラビヤカ, 美麗, Gorgeous, splendid. — *ni ifuku wo aratame.*

KIRADZ, キラヅ, 雪花菜, *n.* The refuse left in making *tōfu.*

KIRADZ, KIRANU, or KIRANAI, キラズ, 不切, Neg. of *Kiru*, not cut.

KIRAI,–*ō* or *au*,–*atta*, キラフ, 嫌, *t.v.* To dislike, to regard with aversion, disrelish, or disgust. *Tabako wo* —, to dislike tobacco. *Kaiko wa kemuri wo* —, smoke is disagreeable to silkworms. *Sake wa kirai de gozarimas*, I do not like ardent spirits.

KIRA-KIRA-TO, キラキラ, 煌煌, *adv.* Glitteringly, sparklingly, brilliantly. *Hoshi ga — hikaru*, the stars sparkle. Syn. KAGAYAKU, HIKARU.

KIRA-KIRASHII,–KI,–KU, キラキラジイ, 煌煌, Having a glittering, or sparkling appearance.

KIRAKU-NA, キラクナ, 氣樂, *a.* Merry, light-hearted, free from care.

†KIRAKU, キラク 歸洛, Returning to Miyako.

KIRAMEKI,–*ku*,–*ita*, キラクメ, 暉, *i.v.* To glitter, sparkle, shine, flash. *Inabikari ga kirameki wataru*, the lightning flashed across (the sky.) Syn. HIKARU, TERASZ, KAGAYAKA.

KIRARA, キララ, 雲母, *n.* Talc, mica.

KIRARA-GAMI, キララガミ, 雲母紙, *n.* A kind of paper.

KIRARE,–*ru*,–*ta*, キラレル, 被著, Pass. or pot. of *Kiru*. To wear, to be worn, can wear, or can be worn. *Kirarenu*, cannot wear.

KIRARE,–*ru*,–*ta*, キラレル, 被切, Pass. or pot. of *Kiru*. To be cut by another; can cut. *Kirarenu*, cannot be cut.

KIRATSZKI,–*ku*,–*ita*, キラツク, *i. v.* Glittering, shining, sparkling.

KIRAWARE,–*ru*,–*ta*, キラハレル, 被嫌, Pass. of *Kirai*. To be disliked, or shunned by others.

KIRAWASHII,–KI,–KU, キラハシイ, 嫌, Disagreeable, unpleasant, odious. Syn. IYARASHII.

KIRE, キレ, *n.* A piece, bit, scrap (of cloth or paper.) *Momen, kami nado no kire.*

KIRE,–*ru*,–*ta*, キレル, 斷, *i.v.* To be broken, severed, stopped, spent, frayed, parted; can cut. *Ito ga kireru*, the yarn, or thread is broken. *Ori-me ga kireru*, the edge of the fold is frayed. *Nawa ga* —, the rope has parted. *Yen ga* —, the relationship is broken off. *Kono katana yoku* — this sword is sharp. *Sono katana de ki ga kireru ka*, can you cut wood with that knife? *Iki ga kireru*, he has stopped breathing. *Kawa ni midz ga kireta*, the river is dry. *H'to-dōri ga kireta*, people have ceased passing along. *Abura ga kirete hi ga kiyeru*, the lamp has gone out for want of oil.

KIRE-GIRE, キレギレ, 斷續, *n.* Pieces.

KIREI, キレイ, 奇麗, *a.* Clean, clear, pure, beautiful, neat. *Kirei-na midz,* clean water. *Kirei-na kimono,* clean, or beautiful clothes. *Kirei-na hana,* a beautiful flower. *Kirei-ni sōji wo szru,* sweep it clean. Syn. ISAGIYOI, KEPPAKU, UTSZKUSHII.

KIREME, キレメ, 切目, *n.* The indentations in the edge of a leaf, saw, file, &c. *Ha no —.*

KIRE-MONO, キレモノ, 切物, *n.* Cutting instruments, edged tools.

KIREPPASH', キレッパシ, *n.* A piece, bit, scrap, (of paper cloth, board &c.) *Ningen no —,* only a piece of a man, (in contempt.)

KIRI, キリ, 錐, *n.* A gimlet, an awl, a drill. *— wo momu,* to turn a gimlet.

KIRI, キリ, 霧, A fog. *— ga furu,* it is foggy. *— ga tatsz,* idem. *— ga tanabiku,* a fog spreads over.

KIRI, キリ, *n.* The circles in a target. *Ichi no —,* the centre ring of a target.

KIRI, キリ, 切, *n.* A stop, period, end; only; an act of a play. *— ga nai,* unlimited, endless. *Kori kiri,* this is all I have, or only this and no more. *Hon ni — wo tszkeru,* to make punctuations or stops in a book. *Tanomi kiri no h'to,* the only person one depends on. *Nenkiri hōkō,* a fixed period of service. *Sore kiri yame ni sh'ta,* he stopped after that, *Shibai wo h'to kiri miru,* to see one act of a play. Syn. KAGIRI.

KIRI, キリ, 桐, *n.* A kind of tree. Paullownia imperialis.

KIRI, KIRU, KITTA, キル, 切, *t.v.* To cut, to sever, divide; affixed to the roots of verbs signifies that the action expressed by the verb is finished, or ended. *Kubi wo kiru,* to cut off the head. *Katana de —,* to cut with a sword. Imp. *Kire.* Subj. *Kiraba. Kono hon wo yomi-kitta,* I have finished reading this book, *Ī-kiru,* to finish saying. *Yen wo —,* to sever a connection.

KIRI-AI, *-au, -atta,* キリアフ, 切合, *i.v.* To fight together with swords, to cut each other.

KIRE-AKE, *-ru, -ta,* キリアケル, 切開, *t.v.* To cut open.

KIRI-AME, キリアメ, 霧雨, *n.* A mist, fine rain drizzling rain.

KIRI-AWASE, *-ru, -ta,* キリアハセル, 切合, *v.* To cut and fit together, to fight together with swords.

KIRI-CHIRASHI, *-sz, -sh'ta,* キリチラス 切散, *t.v.* To cut and scatter.

KIRI-DORI, キリドリ, 切捕, *n.* Killing and robbing. *— szru,* to kill and rob. *— gōdō,* a murdering robber.

KIRI-DŌSHI, キリドホシ, 切通, *n.* A deep road cut through a mountain.

KIRIFU, キリフ, 翦斑, *n.* Spotted with black and white. Syn. MADARA.

KIRI-FUSE, *-ru, -ta,* キリフセル, 切伏, *t.v.* To cut down.

KIRI-GIRISZ, キリギリス, 蛬, *n.* A cricket.

KIRI-HANASHI, *-tsz, -sh'ta,* キリハナツ, 切放, *t. v.* To cut apart, separate by cutting.

KIRI-HARAI, *-au, -atta,* キリハラフ, 切拂, *t. v.* To cut and clear away, (as an obstruction.)

KIRI-HIRAKI, *-ku, -ita,* キリヒラク, 切開, *t.v.* To cut open, to clear off by cutting down trees, &c.

KIRI-IRI, *-ru, -tta,* キリイル, 切入, *t. v.* To cut and enter, to cut a way into.

KIRI-ISHI, キリイシ, 切石, *n.* Cut-stone, hewn-stone.

KIRI-KATA, キリカタ, 切形, *n.* A mark made by cutting.

KIRI-KIDZ, キリキズ, 切疵, *n.* An incised wound, a cut.

KIRI-KIRI, キリキリ, 切切, *adv.* Quickly, speedily; in a cutting manner. *— itte koi,* go quickly. *— tate,* clear out quickly. *— itamu,* to pain, or smart severely. *Koma ga — mau,* the top spins round.

KIRI-KIRI TO, キリキリト, *adv.* The creaking sound of a bow when drawn to its utmost. *Yumi wo — hiki-shiboru.*

KIRI-KISHI, キリキシ, 截岸, *n.* A bank cut and walled up.

KIRI-KIZAMI, *-mu, -nda,* キリキザム, 割刻, *t.v.* To cut fine.

KIRI-KAKARI, *-ru, -tta,* キリカカル, 切掛, *i.v.* To begin to cut, to be about to cut.

KIRIKO, キリコ, 切籠, *n.* A figure with the corners squared, cutglass.

KIRIKŌJŌ, キリコウジヤウ, 切口上, *n.* A formal, or precise way of speaking. *— de mono wo iu.*

KIRI-KOMI, *-mu, -nda,* キリコム, 切込, *t.v.* To cut into, to cut and fit (as timber for building.)

KIRI-KOROSHI, *-sz, -sh'ta,* キリコロス, 切殺, *t.v.* To slay, to kill by cutting.

KIRI-KUCHI, キリクチ, 切口, *n.* The mouth of a wound, the place where any thing is cut.

KIRI-KUDAKI,-*ku*,-*ita*, キリクダク, 切碎, *t.v.* To cut something hard into fine pieces, chop fine.

KIRI-KUDZSHI,-*sz*,-*sh'ta* キリクヅス, 切崩, *t v:* To hew down, to cut and destroy.

KIRI-MAI, キリマイ, 切米, *n.* Rice-rations paid to inferior officers, or soldiers. Syn. FUCHIMAI

KIRI-ME, キリメ, 割目, *n.* A cut, the mark of a cut.

KIRI-MOMI, キリモミ, 錐揉, *n.* Boring with a gimlet, or drill. — *wo szru*, to bore with a gimlet.

KIRIN, キリン, 麒麟, *n.* A fabulous animal, said not to tramp on live insects, or to eat live grass.

KIRIN-KETSZ, キリンケツ, 麒麟血, *n.* Dragon's blood.

KIRI-NABIKE,-*ru*,-*ta*, キリナビケル, 斬靡, *t.v.* To bring into subjection with the sword.

KIRI-NOKE,-*ru*,-*ta*, キリノケル, 切退, To cut and make one's escape.

KIRI-OTOSHI,-*sz*,-*sh'ta*, キリオトス 切落, *t.v.* To cut down, of anything suspended.

KIRI-SAKI,-*ku*,-*ita*, キリサク, 開剖, *t.v.* To rip, or cut open, (as the abdomen,)

KIRISH'TAN, キリシタン, 切支丹, *n.* Christian.

KIRI-SOGI,-*gu*,-*ita*, キリソグ, *t.v.* To cut, to shave, or whittle, to cut across obliquely.

KIRI-SZTE,-*ru*,-*ta*, キリステル, 切捨, *t.v.* To cut and throw away, to kill and leave.

KIRI-TAOSHI,-*sz*,-*sh'ta*, キリタフス, 切倒, *t.v.* To cut down anything standing.

KIRITE, キリテ, 切手, *n.* The slayer, killer, murderer.

KIRI-TSZKE,-*ru*,-*ta*, キリツケル, 切付, *t.v.* To engrave on, to cut into (as letters on a stone), to cut.

KIRI-TSZKUSHI,-*sz*,-*sh'ta*, キリツクス 切盡, *t.v.* To kill and exterminate.

KIRITSZ-KIRARETSZ, キリツキラレツ, *adv.* To cut and get cut, in fighting; to kill and be killed.

KIRIYŌ, キリヤウ, 器量, *n.* Capacity, ability, talent, genius. — *no nai h'to*, a person of no talent. Syn. CHIYE, SAI.

KIRIYŌ, キリヤウ, 容色, *n.* Countenance, — *no yoi onna*, a beautiful woman. Syn. YŌBŌ, MIME.

KIRIYOKU, キリヨク, 氣力, *n.* Natural vigor, force, strength, or energy of mind or body. — *ga tszyoi*.

KIRO, キロ, 生羅, *n.* A kind of light silk stuff.

†KI-RO, キロ, 歸路, (*kayeri michi*), *n.* The road back, the way home.

†KI-RŌ, キラウ, 貴老, (*tattoki rōjin*). = you, in speaking to an elder.

KIRŌ, or KIRAU, キラフ, 嫌, See *Kirai.*

KI-ROKU, キロク, 記錄, *n.* A record, history, chronicle, journal. — *ni noseru*, to record in a journal. Syn. KIU-KI.

KIRU, キル, 着, To wear, see *Ki.*

KIRU, キル, 切, To cut, see *Kiri.*

†KIRUI, キル井, 衣類, *n.* Clothing. Syn. KIMONO.

†KI-SAI, キサイ, 奇才, *n.* Extraordinary ability. — *na h'to*, a man of uncommon talents.

KISAKI, キサキ, 后, *n.* Empress.

KISAMA, キサマ, 貴樣, You, in addressing an inferior.

KI-SAN, キサン, 歸山, To come back, return. *Hōkōnin yōyaku — ga dekita*, the servant was at last received back again, (into his place).

KI-SANJI, キサンジ, 氣散, *n.* Recreation, diversion, amusement. Syn. NAGUSAMI, KIBARASHI.

KISARAGI, キサラギ, 如月, *n.* The second month. Syn. NIGATSZ.

†KI-SATSZ, キサツ, 貴札, (*o tegami*). = your letter.

KISE,-*ru*,-*ta*, キセル, 著, *t.v.* To put on, (as clothes), dress up, to overlay, to plate. *Kimono wo h'to ni kiseru*, to put clothing on another. *Kin wo* —, to plate with gold. *Yosegi nite* —, to veneer with different kinds of wood. *On wo* —, to bestow kindness. *Kin-kise*, gold-plated. *Gin kise*, silver-plated.

†KI-SEI キセイ, 稀世, Rare, strange, uncommon. KITAI, MARE, MEDZRASHII.

KI-SEI, キセイ, 祈誓, (*inori chikau*), *n.* A vow. — *szru*, to vow.

KISE-KAKE,-*ru*,-*ta*, キセカケル, 著掛, *t.v.* To lay over, cover over, to impute, charge with, attribute. *H'to ni tszmi wo* —, to charge another with crime.

KI-SEN, キセン, 貴賤, (*tatoki, iyashiki*). High and low, noble and plebian, honorable and mean.

KISERU, キセル, 烟筒, *n.* A tobacco-pipe. — *no gankubi*, the bowl of a tobacco-pipe. — *no rao*, the bamboo tube of a tobacco-pipe.

KISHI, キシ, 岸, *n.* A bank, a wall, a cliff. — *no kiwa*, the edge of a bank.

KISHIMI,-*mu*,-*nda*, キシム, *i. v.* To stick

or rub in moving, not to move or work easily or freely, to move with much friction, to creak. *To ga kishimu*, the door sticks. *Hikidashi ga kishinde hairanu*, the drawer sticks and will not go in. *Abura wo tszkereba kishima nai*, if you lubricate it with oil, it will not stick.

KI-SHIN, キシン, 寄進, *n.* Contributions, or offerings to temples. — *szru.* — *no seshu*, one who makes an offering. Syn. KIFU.

KI-SHIRI,–*ru*,–*tta*, キシル, 輾, *n.* To rub, or grate against, to creak. *Funabata wo* —, to grate against each other, as two ships lying along side, and moved with the waves.

KI-SHITSZ, キシツ, 氣質, *n.* Natural temperament, nature, constitution, disposition. — *no warui h'to.* Syn. UMARETSZKI, TACHI.

†KI-SHO, キシヨ, 貴所, = Your house, also you. — *sama*, you.

KI-SHŌ, キシヤウ, 氣象, *n.* Natural disposition, character, temper. *Oni demo totte kui-sō na — da.*

KI-SHOKU, キシヨク, 氣色, *n.* Feelings, spirits, health. — *ga warui*, to feel unwell. — *ga yoi*, to be cheerful.
Syn. AMBAI, KOKOROMOCHI.

KI-SHŌMON, キシヤウモン, 起請文, *n.* An indenture, a written contract, bond.
Syn. SEISHI.

KI-SHUKU,–*szru*, キシユク, 寄宿, To lodge, sojourn, board, or dwell for a short time.

KI-SHUKU-NIN, キシユクニン, 寄宿人, *n.* A lodger, boarder, sojourner.

KISOI,–*ō*,–*ōta*, キソフ, 競, *i.v.* To emulate, compete, strive to excel, contend for mastery. *Tagai-ni bugei wo* —.
Syn. KIOI, ARASOI.

KI-SOKU, キソク, 規則, *n.* A rule, precept, maxim, law. — *wo tateru*, to make a rule.

KISSAKI, キツサキ, 鋒, *n.* The point of a sword.

†KISSHIN, キツシン, 吉辰, *n.* A lucky day.
Syn. KICHI-NICHI.

KISSHIRI TO, キツシリト, *adv.* Tightly, closely. *Hako ni — tszme-komu*, to pack tightly in a box. Syn. KATAKU, SHIKKARI.

KISSŌ, キツサウ, 氣相, *n.* The expression of the face, countenance. — *wo kayeru*, to change countenance.
Syn. KESHIKI.

KISSŌ, キツサウ, 吉相, *n.* Good news, joyful tidings.

KISZ, キス, *n.* A kind of fish.

KISZGO, キスゴ, *n.* A kind of small fish.

KI-SZRU, キスル, 歸, *n.* To obey, become subject to.

†KI-SZRU, キスル, 記, (*shirusz,*) *t.v.* To record, write down.

†KI-SZRU, キスル, 著, *t.v.* To put on, clothe, dress, overlay, cover.
Syn. KISERU.

KITA, キタ, 北, *n.* North. *Kita no hō*, north side or region. *Kita kaze*, north wind. *Kita ga fuku*, (idem.) Syn. HOKU, NE NO HŌ.

KĪTA, キイタ, pret. of *Kiki.*

KITA, キタ, pret. of *Ki, kuru.*

KITA-GOCHI, キタゴチ, 北東風, *n.* Northeast wind.

KĪTAFŪ, キイタフウ, *n.* One who makes a show, or pretends to know or be what he is not, a boaster, braggadocio.

KI-TAI, キタイ, 稀代, (*Yo ni marenakoto.*) Strange, rare, uncommon, wonderful. *Kitai na koto*, a strange thing.
Syn MEDZRASHI.

KITAI,–*ō*,–*atta*, キタフ, 鍜, *t. v* To forge iron, to temper iron by pounding it.

KITAI-GANE, キタヒガ子, 熟鐵, *n.* Tempered, or wrought iron.

KI-TAKU, キタク, 歸宅, (*Iye ni kayeru.*) To return home.

KITANABIRE,–*ru*,–*ta*, キタナビレル, *i. v.* To be dirty, foul, mean, base, or low.
Syn. GESZBARU.

KITANAI,–KI,–KU,–Ō,–SHI, キタナイ, 穢, Dirty, foul, filthy, (fig.) mean, base, despicable. Syn. BIRŌ, KEGARE, YOGORE.

KITA-NO-KATA, キタノカタ, 北之方, *n.* Northern direction; also the wife of a noble.

KITARI,–*ru*,–*tta*, キタル, 來, *i.v.* To come. *Kitaru toshi*, the coming year, next year. *Kitaru jū-go nichi*, the coming fifteenth day of the month. Syn. KURU.

KITCHŌ, キツテウ, 吉兆, (*yoi shirase*). A lucky omen.

KĪTE, キイテ, ppr. of *Kiki.*

KI-TEN, キテン, 機轉, Intelligent, quick to perceive. — *no kīta h'to*, a person of quick perception.

KI-TŌ, キタウ, 祈禱, *n.* Prayer, supplication to the *Kami.* — *wo szru*, to pray to the *Kami.* Syn. INORI.

†KI-TŌ, キタフ, 貴答, (*anata ni henji wo szru*). Replying to you.

KITŌ, キタフ, 鍜, See *Kitai.*

KITSZI,–KI,–KU,–Ū,–SHI, キツイ, Strong,

severe, intense, harsh, hardy, stouthearted, manly; tired. — *kaze*, a strong wind. — *ame*, a hard rain. — *sake*, strong liquor. — *h'to*, a strong man, also a man of nerve. *Atszsa ga* —, the heat is intense.
Syn. TSZYOI, HAGESHII.

KI-TSZKE, キツケ, 氣付, *n.* A cordial. — *no kuszri*, a cordial medicine.

KITSZKU キツク, *adv.* See *Kitszi.*

†KTSZ-MON, キツモン, 詰問, *n.* Cross-examination, rigid inquiry, as of a criminal. — *szru*, to examine closely.
Syn. TOI-TSZMERU.

KITSZ-MU, キツム, 吉夢, *(yoi yume). n.* A lucky dream.

KITSZNE, キツ子, 狐, *n.* A fox.

KITSZNE-BI, キツ子ビ, 狐火, *n.* Jack with a lantern.

KITSZNE-DO, キツ子ド, 狐戸, *n.* A lattice door.

KITSZSHI, キツシ, *a.* Sěe *Kitszi.*

KITSZTSZKI, キツツキ, *n.* A wood-pecker.

†KITTAN, キツタン, 吉旦, *n.* A lucky day. Syn. KICHINICHI.

KITTACHI,*-tsz,-tta*, キツタツ, 屹立, *i. v.* To be precipitous, steep. *Kono yama kittatte iru*, this mountain is steep.

KITTE, キツテ, 切手, *n.* A passport, a pass, a ticket sold by a merchant, allowing the holder to draw on him for goods to the amount written on it; a certificate.
Syn. TEGATA.

KITTO, キツト, 急度, *adv.* Surely, certainly, positively, without fail, attentively, fixedly. — *kayeshimasz*, will certainly return it. — *sō ka*, is it positively so? — *oboyete iyo*, mind and don't forget it. — *miru*, to look attentively at. — *shian szru*, to fix one's thoughts on.
Syn. SH'KATO, TASH'KANI.

KIU, キフ, 急, *n.* An emergency, exigency, urgency, pressing necessity. — *wo tszgeru*, to inform of an emergency, and need of haste. — *no ma ni awanu*, not suitable to the pressing need.

†KIU, キウ, 弓, *(yumi). n.* A bow.

†KIU, キウ, 九, *(kokonotsz). a.* Nine.
Syn. KU.

KIU, キウ, 灸, *n.* The moxa. — *wo szyeru*, to apply the moxa. — *wo orosz*, to mark the place where the moxa is to be applied. — *no f'ta*, the scab of a moxa. — *no iboi*, the pus of a moxa. — *h'to-hi*, or *f'ta hi*, one moxa, two moxas. Syn. YAITO.

†KIU, キウ, 救, *(taszkeru).* To save, aid, assist, help. Syn. SZKU.

†KIU, キフ, 舊, *(furui).* Old, ancient, former. — *ni yotte tszkoyaka nari*, as stout as he used to be.

†KIU-AKU, キフアク, 舊惡, *n.* An old offence. — *ga arawareta.*

KIU-BA, キウバ, 弓場, *n.* A place for practising archery.

KIU-BA, キフバ, 急塲, *n.* A sudden emergency.

†KIU-BI, キウビ, 鳩尾, *n.* The pit of the stomach, epigastrium. Syn. MIDZOCHI.

KIU-BIN, キフビン, 急便, *(Isogino tayori). n.* Quick communication, despatch, express messenger.

KIU-BIYŌ, キフビヤウ 急病, *n.* Sudden and rapid sickness.

†KIU-CHIU, キウチウ, 宮中, *n.* Within the Mikado's residence.

†KIUDEN, キウデン, 宮殿, *n.* The Mikado's palace.

KIU-HEN, キフヘン, 急變, *n.* A sudden event or calamity.

†KIU-I, キウイ, 休意, *(kokoro yaszmuru). n.* Freedom from care, easy in mind, happy. Syn. ANSHIN.

†KIU-IU, キフイウ, 舊友, *(furuki tomo).* An old friend.

KIU-JI, キフジ, 給仕, *n.* Waiting, or serving at table; also, a waiter, table servant. — *wo szru*, to wait at table.

KIU-JI, キウヂ, 灸治, Applying the moxa. — *szru.*

KIU JITSZ, キウジツ, 休日, *(yaszmibi.) n.* Day of rest, holiday.

†KIU-JO, キウヂヨ, 宮女, *n.* Female servants connected with the Mikado's court.

KIU-JUTSZ, キウジユツ, 弓術, *n.* The rules of archery.

KIU-KA, キフカ, 舊家, *n.* An old family.

†KIU-KAN, キウカン, 鳩灌, *n.* A parrot.

KIU-KETSZ, キウケツ, 灸穴, *n.* The places for applying the moxa.

KIU-KETSZ, キウケツ, 九穴, The nine holes of the body.—The eyes, ears, nostrils, mouth, urinary and fecal.

KIU-KI, キフキ, 舊記, *n.* Ancient history.

KIU-KIN, キフキン, 給金, *(atayuru kane.) n.* Wages, hire.

KIU-KUTSZ, キウクツ, 窮屈, *n.* Crowded, confined, strictness, rigor. — *de komaru*, distressed by the rigorous rules. — *na me ni au*, to be greatly crowded.

KIU-MEI, キウメイ, 糺明, Judging or examining minutely into anything.
Syn. GIMMI, GŌMON, TADASZ.

†KI-UN, キウン, 氣運, *n.* Changes, fluctuations. *Sabake kata no*, —, fluctuations of the market.

KIU-NA, キフナ 急, *a.* Pressing, urgent, requiring haste, hasty, rapid, steep, sudden. — *yō ga dekite kayeru*, having urgent business to return. — *saka*, a steep slope. — *se*, a rapid current. Syn. ISOGI.

KIU-NEN, キフネン, 舊年, *n.* Last year, the old year. Syn. KIYO-NEN.

KIU-NI, キフニ, 急, *adv.* Urgently, pressingly, quickly, hastily, rapidly, steeply, suddenly. — *kayeru*, to return quickly.

KIU-REI, キフレイ, 舊例, *n.* An old custom.

KIU-RI, キフリ, 舊里, *(furusato.)* Native village, native place. Syn. KO KIYO.

KI-URI, キウリ, 胡瓜, *n.* Cucumber.

KIURI, キウリ, 久離, *(hisashiku hanareru.) n.* Cutting off a child from the family, disinheriting. — *kiru.* (idem.) Syn. KANDŌ.

KIU-RŌ, キフラフ, 舊臘, *n.* Last winter, or the twelfth month of last year.

KIU-SEKI, キフセキ, 舊跡, *n.* Ancient ruins, remains of old places.

†KIU-SEN, キウセン, 弓箭, *(yumi ya.)* Bow and arrow.

†KIU-*shi*,–*szru*,–*sh'ta*, キウスル, 窮, *i.v.* To be poor, distressed.

KIU-SHI, キフシ, 急死, *(tachimachi shinuru.) n.* Sudden death.

†KIU-SHIKI, キフシキ, 舊識, *(furuki tomodachi.) n.* An old acquaintance.

KIU-SOKU, キウソク, 休息, *(iki wo yaszmu.)* Resting, ceasing from labor or motion. — *szru*, to rest. Syn. IKŌ, YASZMU.

KIU-SOKU, キフソク, 急速, Quick, hasty, urgent, pressing. Syn. HAYAKU, SZMIYAKA.

KIUSZ, キウス, 球子, *n.* A small teapot.

KIU-TAKU, キフタク, 舊宅, *(furuki iye.) n.* An old house.

KIU-TEN, キウテン, 灸點, *n.* The mark made with ink to show where the moxa should be placed. — *wo orosz*, to make the above mark.

†KI-UTSZ, キウツ, 氣鬱, *n.* Melancholy, gloom, lowspirits.

†KIU-U, キフウ, 急雨, *(niwaka-ame.) n.* Sudden rain, shower.

†KIU-WA, キフワ, 舊話, *(furuki hanashi.) n.* An old story.

KIU-YŌ, キフヨウ, 急用, *n.* Urgent business.

†KIU-ZOKU, キウゾク, 九族, The nine generations of great great grandfather, great grandfather, grandfather, father, self, son, grandson, great grandson, great great grandson.

KIWA, キハ, 際, *n.* Margin, brink, edge, verge, border; the point of time when anything is done. *Midz no* —, the edge of the water. *Ido no kiwa*, margin of the well. *Kabe no* —, the place where a wall joins the floor or ground. *Hashi no* —, adjoining the bridge. *Shinigiwa ni natta*, to be at the point of death. *Sono — ni natte nanjū szru* when that time comes you will have trouble. *Tachigiwa*, point of starting. — *ga tatsz*, to be separate, or distinct.

KIWADA, キハダ, 黃檗, *(ōbaku)*, *n.* A kind of bark used in dyeing yellow.

KIWADACHI,–*tsz*,–*tta*, キハダツ, 際立, *i.v.* To be distinct, separate, or different. *Midz to abura ga* —, the oil and the water are separated. *Szmu to nigoru ga kiwadatte miyeru*, the clear and the muddy are seen to be distinct.

KIWADOI, キハドイ, *a.* The last moment, or nick of time. — *tokoro ni ki-awaseru*, he came at the last moment (after which it would have been too late). — *tokoro de atta*, I was just in the nick of time.

KIWADZKI,–*ku*,–*ita*, キハヅク, 際附, *i.v.* To show the line of junction, to appear distinct, or separate. *Kono kabe wa ato kara nutta no ga kiwadzite miyeru*, as this plaster was put on after, the line of junction appears.

KIWAMARI,–*ru*,–*tta*, キハマル, 極, *i.v.* To be determined, settled, fixed, established, finished, ended, come to the last extremity, utmost point. *Toki ga* —, the time is fixed. *Nai ni* —, it is settled that there is none. *Tō-ka ni* — it is fixed on the tenth day. *H'to no inochi wa kiwamarinashi*, the life of man is not fixed (to any certain time). Syn. SADAMARU, KIMARU.

KIWAME,–*ru*,–*ta*, キハメル, 極, *t.v.* To determine, decide, fix, establish, settle; to end, finish, exhaust, to carry to the utmost. *Nichigen wo kiwameru*, to fix a day. *Hō wo* —, to establish a rule. *Nedan wo* —, to fix the price. *Kotoba wo kiwamete toku*, to exhaust language in explaining. Syn. SADAMERU, TSZKUSZ.

KIWAME, キハメ, 極, *n.* The time when anything was made, and the maker. *Katana no — wo tszkeru*, to fix the date when a sword was made, also the maker.

KIWAMETE, キハメテ, 極, *adv*, Positively, assuredly must, certainly. Syn. KANARADZ, SADAMETE.

KIWATA, キワタ, 木綿, *n.* A kind of tree. Gossypium herbaceum.

KIWATAGURI, キワタグリ, 攪車, *n.* A machine for cleaning cotton of its seeds.

‖KIYAFU, キヤフ, 脚布, *n.* A cloth worn by women around the loins. Syn. YUMAKI, F'TANO.

KIYAHAN, キヤハン, 脚絆, *n.* Leggins.

KIYAKARABA, キヤカラバ, 迦可羅婆, *n.* The (Sanscrit?) character written at the top of a *Sotoba.*

KIYA-KIYA, キヤキヤ, *adv.* — *itamu,* to have a pricking pain.

KIAKU, キヤク, 客, *n.* A guest, visitor, a passenger, customer. *Kiyaku-jin,* (idem).

KIYAKU-BUN, キヤクブン, 客分, *n.* The part of a guest, the same as a guest, or visitor. — *ni sh'te oku,* to make it appear that he is a guest, or visitor only, (though secretly he may be his son in law).

KIYAKUDEN, キヤクデン, 客殿, *n.* A house close to a monastery for the reception of visitors.

KIYAKU-RAI, キヤクライ, 客來, *n.* (*kiyaku ga kitaru*). *Kon-nichi wa — ga aru,* the guests are coming to-day.

KIYAKURO, キヤクロ, 脚爐, *n.* A foot-stove.

†KIYAKU-SŌ, キヤクソウ, 客僧, *n.* A priest who is a guest.

KI-YAMI, キヤミ, 氣病, (*kokoro no wadzrai,*) *n.* Distress, trouble of mind, depression of spirits.

KIYARA, キヤラ, 伽羅, *n.* Aloes-wood, or Agallochum.

KIYARI, キヤリ, *n.* The song of persons uniting their strength to do any thing, as lifting, pulling. — *wo iu.* — *wo utau. Kiyariondō.*

KIYASHA, キヤシヤ, 花奢, Genteel, delicate. — *na h'to,* a delicate, slender person.

KI-YASZME, キヤスメ, 氣安, *n.* Consolation, comfort. — *wo iu,* to console with, to alleviate grief.

KIYATATSZ, キヤタツ, 脚榻, *n.* A step-ladder, a high bench for standing on. Syn. FUMI-DAI.

KIYATSZ, ナヤツ, 渠, That fellow, that rascal, (a contemptuous word.

KIYE,-*ru*,-*ta*, キエル, 消, *i. v.* To be extinguished, quenched, put out, effaced, to vanish, disappear, (fig.) to die. *Hi ga kiyeru,* the fire is out. *Akari ga —,* the light is out. *Yūrei ga —,* the ghost has vanished. *Yuki ga —,* the snow has disappeared. *Kumo ga —,* the cloud has disappeared. *Ato ga —,* the mark is gone.

KIYE,-*szru*, キエ, 皈依, (*Shitagau,*) (Budd.) To respect and follow as a master or priest, look up to as a religious teacher. *Ano oshō ni kiye szru h'to ga nai,* nobody respects that priest.

†KI-YEN, キエン, 奇緣, *n.* A strange friendship, or connection.

KI-YEN, キエン, 棄捐, *n.* Letting off, or forgiving, (as a debt) — *ni szru.*

†KI-YETSZ, キエツ, 喜悅, (*Yorokobi.*) *n.* Joy, gladness, pleasure.

KIYO, キヨ, 虛, (*munashii.*) False, weak, weakness, unguarded places. *Teki no — ni jōjite,* taking advantage of the enemy's weak points, or carelessness. *Kiyo sh'ta h'to,* an impotent person. — *wo ukagau,* to spy out the weak points of an enemy.

KIYŌ, ケフ, 今日, *adv.* To-day. Syn. KON-NICHI.

KIYŌ, キヨウ, 凶, Unlucky.

KIYŌ, キヤウ, 經, *n.* Canonical, or sacred books, especially of the Buddhists; the Chinese classics. — *wo yomu,* to recite from the sacred books, in praying.

KIYŌ, キヨウ, 興, *n.* Sport diversion, amusement, pleasure, fun, entertainment. — *ni iru tokoro,* when he had begun to feel jolly, or merry. — *no sametaru kao de,* with a countenance expressive of spoiled pleasure. — *ga sameru,* the pleasure is spoiled. — *szru,* to make merry, to frolic.

KI-YŌ-NA, キヨウナ, 器用, *a.* Ingenious, expert, clever, having genius, adroit. Syn. HATSZMEI, SAISHI.

KIYŌDOKU, ケウボク, 梟木, *n.* The gibbet on which the heads of executed criminals are exposed.

†KIYO-BIYŌ, キヨビヤウ, 虛病, *n.* Disease characterized by weakness and emaciation. Syn. JIN-K'YO.

†KIYŌCHIU, キヨウチウ, 胸中, (*mune no uchi.*) In the breast, (fig.) mind, heart.

KIYŌDAI, キヤウダイ, 兄弟, *n.* Brother. — *bun,* the part of, or the same as a brother. Syn. KEITEI.

KIYŌ-DAI, キヤウダイ, 鏡臺, *n.* A mirror stand. Syn. KAGAMI NO DAI.

†KIYODAKU,-*szru*, キヨダク, 許諾, To assent, consent. Syn. SHŌ-CHI, GA-TEN.

KIYO-DAN, キヨダン, 虛談, (*uso no hanashi,*) A lie, falsehood, a fiction, story.

KIYŌDAN, キヤウダン, 卿談, (*Inaka kotoba,*) *n.* Provincialism, country dialect. Syn. NAMARI.

†KIYŌ-FŪ, キヤウフウ, 驚風, *n.* Convulsions, fits. *Kikkiyōfū,* severe convulsions. *Man kiyōfū,* mild convulsions.

†KIYŌ-FU, キヨウフ, 恐怖, *n.* Fear — *szru,* to be afraid.

KIYŌ-GAI, キヤウガイ, 境界, *n.* Condition,

circumstances, worldly state, mode oflife. *Isshō no* —, life long condition.
Syn. TOSEI, MINOWYE.

KIYOGAKI, キヨガキ, 清書, *n.* A clean copy. — *wo szru.* Syn. SEI-SHO.

KIYO-GANNA, キヨガンナ, 清鉋, *n.* A smoothing or finishing plane.

KIYŌ-GEN, キヤウゲン, 狂言, *n.* A play, drama, farce.
Syn. SHIBAI.

KIYO-GETS, キヨゲツ 去月, *n.* Last month.

KIYŌ-GŌ,, キヤウガフ, 校合, Correcting a writing, correcting a proof. Syn. SANTEI.

KIYO-GON, キヨゴン, 虛言, *n.* A falsehood, lie. — *wo iu,* to tell a lie.
Syn. USO, ITSZWARI.

KIYOI,-KI,-SHI, キヨイ, 清, *a.* Clean, clear, pure, free from defilement. *Kiyoki nagare,* a clear stream. — *kokoro,* a clean heart. Syn. ISAGIYOKI, KIREI.

†KIYO-JAKU, キヨジヤク, 虛弱, Feeble, weak in body, without natural vigor. — *na h'to.* Syn. YOWAI, HIYOWAI.

KIYŌ-JAKU, キヤウジヤク, 强弱, *n.* Strength or weakness.

KIYŌJI, キヨウジ, 凶事, *n.* Unlucky affair.

KIYŌJI, キヤウジ, 經師, A maker of wall-paper, paper hangings, or pictures.

†KIYŌJI,-*ru*,-*ta*, キヨウジル, 興, *i.v.* To be delighted, pleased, diverted by any thing. *Shibai wo k'yōjite miru,* to be diverted in loooking at a play.
Syn. OMOSHIROGARU.

KIYŌ-JIN, キヤウジン, 狂人, *n.* A madman, lunatic. Syn. KICHIGAI.

KIYŌ-JITSZ, キヨジツ, 虛實, *n.* True and false. — *wo tadasz,* to ascertain the truth or falsity of any thing. *Kuni no* —, the real condition of a country.

KIYŌ-JI-YA, キヤウジヤ, 經師屋, *n.* A maker of wall-paper, paper hangings, screens, &c.

HIYO-JŌ, キヨジヤウ, 居城, *(iru shiro). n.* The castle in which one resides.

KIYŌ-JŌ, キヤウジヤウ, 刑狀, *n.* The sentence, judgment, or judicial decision passed on a criminal. — *ga sadamaru.*

KIYO-JŪ,-*szru*, キヨジユウ, 居住, To dwell, reside. Syn. SZMAI.

KIYŌ-JU, キヤウジユ, 敎授, *(oshiye sadzkeru). n.* Teaching, instruction, education. *Deshi ni* — *szru.*

KIYO-JŪ-KATA, キヤウジユカタ, 敎授方, *n.* A teacher.

KIYŌ-KA, キヤウカ, 狂哥, *(Tawamureru uta). n.* Comic poetry.

†KIYŌ-KAKU, キヨウカク, 胸膈, *(mune), n.* The breast, the chest.

KIYŌKATABIRA, キヤウカタビラ, 經帷, *n.* Grave clothes, a shroud, winding-sheet.

†KIYŌ-KI, キヤウキ, 狂氣, *n.* Insanity, madness.

KIYŌKŌ, キヤウコウ, 向後, *(kono nochi). adv.* Henceforth, after this, hereafter.
Syn. I-GO.

†KIYŌKOTSZ, キヤウコツ, 鮫骨, Rough, rude, harsh, violent, boisterous. — *na h'to,* a violent, boisterous man.

KIYOKU, キヨク, 曲, *n.* Entertaining performances, or diversions, such as circus-riding, rope-dancing, top-spinning, theatrical exhibitions, music, dancing, &c. — *wo szru,* to perform entertaining feats. *Uta ikkiyoku,* one song. *Koma no* —, top-spinning. *Uma nori no* —, circus riding.

KIYOKU, キヨク, 清, *adv.* Clear, clean, pure. — *szru,* to cleanse.

KIYOKUBA, キヨクバ, 曲馬, *n.* Equestrian feats, circus-riding. — *wo szru.*

†KIYOKU-JI, キヨクジ, 曲事, *n.* Guiltiness, guilty of having committed a crime, condemnation. (Legal). — *mōshi-tszkeru,* to pronounce guilty, to condemn.

KIYOKU-MOCHI, キヨクモチ, 曲持, *n.* Feats of strength or dexterity. — *wo szru,* to perform feats of strength or dexterity, (as of lifting weights, &c.)

KIYŌ-KUN, キヤウクン, 敎訓, *n.* Instruction, teaching of the principles of morality and religion, education. — *szru,* to educate in morals, behaviour, social and religious duties.
Syn. OSHIYERU.

KIYOKU-NORI, キヨクノリ, 曲騎, *n.* Equestrian feats.

KIYOKU-ROKU, キヨクロク, 曲彔, *n.* A large chair used by priests in temples.
Syn. KOSHIKAKE.

KIYŌ-K'WAN, ケウクワン, 呌喚, *(sakebi sakebu).* Lamentation and wailing. — *szru,* to lament and wail. *Dai* —, loud crying and wailing. *Kiyō k'wan-jigoku,* one of the eight Buddhist hells.

†KIYŌ-MAN, ケウマン, 驕漫, *n.* Pride, arrogance. — *szru,* to be arrogant.
Syn. JIMAN, KŌ-MAN, TAKA-BURU.

KIYOMARI,-*ru*,-*tta*, キヨマル, 清, *i.v.* To be clean, pure, free from defilement.

KIYŌ-MON, キヤウモン, 經文, *n.* A writing or sentence from a Buddhist sacred book.

KIYOME,-*ru*,-*ta*, キヨメル, 清, *t. v.* To

cleanse, purify, free from defilement, *Te wo* —, to cleanse the hands. *Shiwo wo futte mi wo* —, to free one's self from defilement by sprinkling salt. *Fujō wo* — cleanse from defilement. *Kokoro wo kiyomete kami wo haisz*, having cleansed the heart to worship the gods. Syn. SHŌJŌ NI SZRU, SZSZGU.

KIYOME, キヨメ, 清, *n.* Cleansing, purification.

KIYO-NEN, キヨネン, 去年, *n.* Last year. Syn. SAKU-NEN.

KIYŌ-NEN, キヨウネン, 凶年, *n.* An unlucky year, an unfruitful year.

KIYŌ-NIN, キヤウニン, 杏仁, *n.* The kernel of an apricot stone, an almond.

KIYŌ-Ō,*-szru*, キヤウオウ, 饗應, *t.v.* To treat, entertain guests, to feast. Syn. MOTENASZ, TORIMOTSZ.

KIYORAKA-NA, キヨラカナ, 清, *a.* Clean, pure, free from defilement. — *kaze*, pure air. — *h'to*, a man free from guile.

KIYORAKA-NI, キヨラカニ, 清,*adv.* Cleanly.

KIYŌ-RAN, キヤウラン, 狂亂, *n.* Crazy, deranged, mad, insane.

KIYORŌ, キヨラウ, 虛癆,*n.* Atrophy.

KIYORO-K'YORO-TO, キヨロキヨロト, Looking about in a staring manner, peering about. — *to miru*, idem.

KIYORORI-TO, キヨロリト, *adv.* Staringly, gazing about. — *szru.*

KIYORO-TSZKI,*-ku,-ita*, キヨロツク, *i.v.* To stare, gape about, to peer, or gaze around indecently.

†KIYOSA, キヨサ, 清, *n.* Cleanliness, purity.

KIYŌ-SAKU, キヨウサク, 凶作, *n.* Bad crops.

KIYO-SETSZ, キヨセツ, 虛說,*(usobanashi)*, *n.* A lie, falsehood, a story.

†KIYŌ-SHA, ケウシヤ, 驕奢, *n.* Vain-glory, pride and pomp. Syn. OGORI.

†KIYO-SHO, キヨシヨ, 居所, *(idokoro)*, *n.* Dwelling place.

KIYO-SHOKU, キヨシヨク, 虛飾, *n.* False show, affectation. Syn. MEKASZ.

KIYŌ-SOKU, ケウソク, 脇息, *n.* A kind of padded stool for leaning against in sitting.

KIYO-TAKU, キヨタク, 居宅, *(iru tokoro)*, *n.* Dwelling, home.

†KIYŌ-TEN, ケウテン, 曉天, *n.* Dawn, day-break. Syn. YOAKE.

KIYŌ-TO, キヤウト, 京都, *n.* The capital, residence of the Mikado, metropolis.

KIYO-YŌ,*-szru*, キヨヨウ, 許容, To grant, permit, allow.
Syn. YURUSZ, SŌCHI SZRU.

KIZA, キザ, 象, *n.* An elephant. Syn. ZŌ.

KIZA, キザ, 氣障, *(ki ni sawaru)*. Disagreeable, unpleasant, odious. — *na h'to*, a person of uncongenial temper. — *na koto wo iu.* Syn. IYARASHII.

KIZAHASHI, キザハシ, 階, *n.* Stairs, a flight of steps.

KI-ZAI, キザイ, 器財, *n.* Household furniture.

KIZAMI,*-mu,-nda*, キザム, 刻, *t. v.* To cut into small pieces, to chop, to carve, (as an image), to sculpture. *Tabako wo* —, to cut tobacco fine. *Butsz-zō wo* —, to carve an image of Buddha. *Ji wo* —, to carve letters. Syn. KIRU, HORU.

KIZAMI, キザミ, 刻, *n.* Time, period of time. *O me ni kakatta kizami ni*, at the time when I saw you. Syn. TOKI, KORO, MIGIRI.

KIZASHI,*-sz,-sh'ta*, キザス, 萌, *t. v.* or *i. v.* To bud, to sprout, to shoot, germinate, begin to appear. *Ki no me ga kizash'ta*, the trees have budded. *Itami ga kizasz*, the pain begins. *Shakkiga ki zash'te kita*, the cramp in the stomach has commenced again. *Muhon wo kizasz*, to conceive rebellion.

KIZASHI, キザシ, 萌, *n.* The first beginning, shooting up, or first feeling of anything; sign, omen. *Ben no — ga aru*, begin to feel like going to stool. *Kono itami wa dekimono no — de arō*, I think this pain is the commencement of a sore. — *ga nai*, there is no sign of.

KIZAWASHI, キザワシ, *n.* A kind of persimmon that ripens on the tree.

KIZETSZ, キゼツ, 氣絕, *(iki ga tomaru.)* *n.* Stoppage of the breath, faintness, choking. — *szru*, to stop the breath, choke.

KO, コ, 子, *n.* A child, the young of anything. — *wo haramu*, to be pregnant. — *wo umu*, to bring forth a child. — *wo orosz*, to produce abortion. — *wo mōkeru*, to beget a child — *wo nagasz*, to miscarry.

KO, コ, 糸, *n.* A numeral for threads, or strands, as, *H'to ko*, one strand, *Futa ko*, two strands, *Mi ko*, three strands.

KO, コ, 小, A particle prefixed to words to give them a diminutive sense, as, *Koyumi*, a little bow, *Kobune*, a small boat, *Ko-nuszbito*, a pilferer, *Ko-ushi*, a small cow; sometimes it does not affect the meaning, as *Ko-gitanai*, dirty, *Ko-girei*, clean, *Kobayaku*, fast.

KO, コ, 粉, *n.* Fine powder of anything. *Mugi-no-ko*, flour. *Soba-no-ko*, buck-wheat meal. *Kome-no-ko*, rice flour. *Ko ni szru*, to pulverize. *Kome wo ko ni hiku*, to grind rice. Syn. KONA, SAI-MATSZ.

Ko, コ, 蠶, *(kaiko.) n.* A silk-worm. — *wo kau*, to feed silk-worms.

†Ko, コ, 木, *n.* A tree. *Ko no sh'ta kage*, the shade of a tree. *Ko no moto*, at the foot of a tree. *Ko no ma*, between the trees.

†Ko, コ, 古, Ancient, (used only in comp. words.) *Kojin*, a man of ancient times. *Kosei*, ancient sage.
Syn. MUKASHI, INISHIYE.

Ko, コ, 孤, *(minashigo.) n.* An orphan, solitary, alone. *Toku ko naradz, kanaradz tonari ari*, virtue is not solitary, it must have neighbours.

†Kō, コウ, 候, *n.* A period of five days, of which there are seventy-two in a year.

†Kō, カウ, 更, *n.* A watch of the night, of which there are five, commencing at sundown, or six o'clock. *Sho-kō*, the first watch, (until 8 o'clock;) *ni-kō, san-kō, shi-kō, go-kō*, until 4 o'clock, A. M. *Kō ga takeru*, it is growing late.

Kō, コフ, 乞, (see *koi.*) To beg, ask for, request. *Itoma wo* —, to ask leave to go, = take leave; to ask for dismission from service. *Shoku wo* —, to beg for food.
Syn. MOTOMERU.

†Kō, コウ, 公, *(kimi.) n.* Lord, master, a title of nobility and respect.

Kō, カウ, 孝, *n.* Filial piety, obedience to parents. *Oya ni kō wo tszkusz*, to obey one's parents in all things, and to the utmost of one's power. *Fu-kō*, disobedient.

Kō, コウ, 功, *n.* Actions of merit, worth, or excellence; actions worthy of praise; talent, ability, virtue. *Kō wo nasz*, to perform meritorious actions. — *wo tateru*, (id.) *Kō wo tszmu*, to multiply worthy deeds, to become more skilful, to improve. *Kō no nai h'to*, one that has never done anything worthy of praise. *Rō sh'te kō nashi*, much labor for nothing. Syn. TEGARA, ISAO, HATARAKI.

Kō, カウ, 香, *n.* Incense, fragrant or aromatic substances, perfume. — *wo taku*, to burn incense, to perfume, to fumigate. — *wo tomeru*, to carry perfumery about one's person. — *wo kuyurasz*, to fumigate with an aromatic.

Kō, コウ, 濃, *adv.* Same as *Koku;* see *Koi.*

Kō, コウ, 鸛, *n.* A kind of crane.

Kō, カウ, (contract of *Kaku.*) *adv.* So, thus, this manner. *Kō shi nasare*, do it so. *Kō-sh'te kō-szriya kō naru koto to shiritsztsz kō-sh'te kō-natta*, (prov.) while I knew that by so doing such would be the case, by so doing have come to it.

Ko-AGE, コアゲ, 小舉, *n.* A coolie, a porter. Syn. KARUKO, NINSOKU.

Kō-BAI, コウバイ, 紅梅, *(akai ume,) n.* A species of plum bearing red blossoms.

Kō-BAI, コウバイ, *n.* The slope or inclination of a roof. — *ga hayai*, the roof is steep. — *ga osoi*, the slope of the roof is gentle.

Ko-BAKAMA, コバカマ, 小袴, *n.* A kind of trowsers.

KOBAMI, *-mu, -nda*, コバム, 拒, *t. v.* To oppose, withstand, hinder, prevent, to object, to contradict, to deny.
Syn. SAKARAU, KODAWARU, FUSEGU, SASAYERU.

Ko-BAN, コバン, 小判, *n.* The name of a gold coin, = four ichibus.

KOBAN-NARI, コバンナリ, *n.* Elliptical in shape.

KōBASHII, -KI, -KU, -U, -SA, カウバシイ, 香, Fragrant, odorous, aromatic.

†Kō-BATSZ, コウバツ, 攻伐, *(seme utsz.)* To attack, or assault in war.

KōBE, カウベ, 首, The head. — *wo tareru*, to bow the head. Syn. ATAMA, KASHIRA.

KOBERITSZKI, *-ku, -ita*, コベリツク, 粘著, *i. v.* To stick, to adhere, to harden and stick to any thing, as gum. *Nori ga te ni koberitszita*, the paste sticks to the hand.
Syn. BETATSZKU.

KOBI, *-ru, -ta*, コビル, 媚, *i. v.* To court favor, to pay court to, to endeavour to please, or ingratiate one's self with another, to fawn, to flatter. *H'to ni* —, to court the favor of another. Syn. HETSZRAU.

KOBI, コビ, 媚, *n.* Flattery, courting favor, blandishment.

KOBI-HETSZRAI, *-au, -tta*, コビヘツラフ, 阿諂, *t. v.* To flatter, pay court to, to fawn, to use blandishments. *H'to ni* —, to flatter others.

Ko-BIKI, コビキ, 木挽, *n.* A sawyer.

Kō-BIN, カウビン, 幸便, *(saiwai no tayori,) n.* A good opportunity.

KOBOCHI, *-tsz, -tta*, コボツ, 毀, *t. v.* To break, destroy. *Iye wo uchi-kobotsz*, to tear down a house.

Kō-BON, カウボン, 香盆, *n.* A tray for putting perfume on.

KOBORE, *-ru, -ta*, コボレル, 毀, *i. v.* To be notched, nicked, broken on the edge. *Katana no ha ga* —, the edge of the sword is nicked. Syn. KAKERU.

KOBORE, *-ru, -ta*, コボレル, *i. v.* To spill,

to run over, to shed, (as tears,) to drop from being too full. *Midz ga koboreru*, the water spills out. *Fude no szmi ga* —, the ink drops from the pen. *Namida ga* —. Syn. AFURERU.

KOBORE-ZAIWAI, コボレザイハイ, 僥倖, (*Gyō-kō*,) *n.* The turning out to be fortunate, of what at first appeared only a misfortune. — *to naru.*

KOBOSHI,-*sz*,-*sh'ta*, コボス, *t. v.* To spill, shed, to make run-over, to pour out. *Midz wo* —, to spill, or pour out water. *Namida wo* —, to shed tears. *Szmi wo kobosz na*, don't spill the ink.

KOBOTSZ, コボツ, 毀, see *Kobochi*.

KOBU, コブ, 瘤, *n.* A wen, fleshy tumor, excrescence, lump. — *ga dekita*, has a wen. *Ki no* —, an excrescence growing on a tree.

KOBU, コブ, 昆布, *n.* Edible sea-weed.

KO-BUKAI,-KI,-KU,-Ō, コブカイ, 木深, Densely wooded and shady.

KO-BUKURO, コブクロ, 子宮, *n.* The womb. Syn. SHI-KIU.

†KO-BUN, コブン, 古文, (*furui fumi*). Ancient writings.

KO-BUN, コブン, 子分, *n.* The part, or place of a child, an apprentice, protege; a person belonging to a laborer's guild, the chief of which is called *Oya-bun*, or *Oya-kata*.

KOBURA, コブラ, See *Komura*.

KOBURI, コブリ, 小振, *n.* Small size. *Kono tokkuri yori koburi na ga yoi*, a bottle of a smaller size than this is better.

KOBURI, コブリ, 小降, *n.* A little shower of rain. *Ame ga — ni natta.*

KO-BUSHI, コブシ, 拳, *n.* The fist. — *de butsz*, to strike with the fist. — *wo nigiru*, to make a fist.

KŌBUSHI, カウブシ 香附子, *n.* Kind of medicine.

KO-BUTSZ, コブツ, 古物, (*furuki mono*). *n.* An ancient thing, antique. — *ka*, an antiquarian.

KŌ-BUTSZ カウブツ, 好物, (*konomu mono*). A thing one is fond of. *Watakushi wa mikan ga dai kōbutsz de gozaru*, I am exceedingly fond of oranges.

†KŌ-BUTSZ, クワウブツ, 礦物, *n.* Minerals.

KO-CHA, コチャ, 古茶, *n.* Old tea, last year's tea.

KOCHA, コチャ, 粉茶, *n.* Broken tea-leaves, tea-dust.

KOCHI, or KOTCHI, コチ, 此方, (*kono hō*). *adv.* Here, this place. I, me. *Achi kochi*, here and there. — *ye koi*, come here. — *ni oke*, put it here. — *no koto de wa nai*, it is none of my business.

KOCHI, コチ, 鯒, *n.* A kind of fish.

KOCHI, コチ, 東風, (*higashi kaze*), *n.* East wind.

KOCHIRA, コチラ, Same a *Kochi*. Here, this place.

†KOCHITAKI,-KU, コチタク, 言痛, Tedious, uninteresting, prosy. — *made ni*, until it becomes tedious. *Kochitaku iu*, to talk until one is tired of it.

KOCHŌ, コテフ, 胡蝶, *n.* A kind of butterfly.

†KOCHŌ, コチヤウ, 鼓脹, *n.* Dropsy of the abdomen, ascites. Syn. CHŌ-MAN.

KODACHI, コダチ, 木立, *n.* Trees, in relation to the manner of planting, or standing. — *ga yoi*, the trees are planted in beautiful order. — *no hima*, the space between trees. — *no kage*, the shade of trees.

KO-DACHI, コダチ, 小刀, *n.* A small sword.

KŌDAI, クワウダイ, 廣大, See *K'wōdai*.

KŌ-DAI, カウダイ, 香臺, *n.* The dish of an incense cup.

KODAMA, コダマ, 木靈, *n.* An echo. — *ga hibiku*, there is an echo.

KODAMAGIN, コダマギン, 小玉銀, *n.* A kind of bullet-shaped coin.

†KŌ-DAN, カウダン, 講談, *n.* Discourse, lecture. — *szru*, to discourse, lecture, preach. Syn. KŌSHAKU.

KODATE, コダテ, 木楯, *n.* Making a shield of a tree, screening one's self by getting behind a tree. *Kata-ye no matsz wo — ni toru.*

KŌ-DATSZ, コウダツ, 口達, *n.* Verbal message. — *szru*, to send a verbal message.

KODAWARI,-*ru*,-*atta*, コダハル, *i. v.* To hinder, prevent, to be jammed, or wedged in, so as to obstruct. *Toyu no naka ni kodawaru mono ga aru*, there is something obstructing the pipe.
Syn. KOBAMU, JAMA WO SZRU.

KŌDŌ, コウダウ, 公道, (*oyake no michi*). Just, right, proper. Syn. TADASHII.

KŌDŌ, カウダウ, 講堂, *n.* A house or temple for preaching, or discoursing in, a church. (Bud.)

†KODOKU, コドク, 孤獨, *n.* An orphan. Syn. MINASHIGO.

KODOMO, コドモ, 子供, *n.* A child. *Kodomora*, children. Syn. WARAMBE.

KODOMORASHII,-KI,-KU,-U, コドモラシイ, Like a child.

Kōdz, カウズ, 楮, *n.* The paper mulberry. Broussonetia papyrifera.

†Kōdz, or Kōdzru, コウズル, 薨, To die, (only of a person of the highest rank).

Kō-dszi, コウズ井, 洪水, *n.* An inundation, flood.

Kodzka, コヅカ, 小柄, *n.* A knife carried in the scabbard of the small sword.

Kodzkai, コヅカヒ, 小使, *n.* A servant.

Kodzkai, コヅカヒ, 小遣, *n.* Cash or money spent in daily petty expenses, pocket money.

†Kodzmi,*-mu,-nda*, コヅム, *t.v.* To pile up, to store away; to incline to one side. to be partial. *Nimotsz wo kura ni kodzmu*, to pile up goods in a store house.
Syn. tszmu.

Kōdzru, カウズル, 講, See *Kōji.*

Ko-dzye, コズヱ, 梢, *n.* The small branches of a tree.

Ko-fū, コフウ, 古風, *(mukashi no fū.) n.* Ancient custom, old fashions, antiquated, antique.

Kōgai, カウガイ, 笄, *n.* An ornament made of shell, worn by married women in the hair; also, two iron rods carried in the scabbard of the short sword, used as chopsticks.

Kogai, コガヒ, 子飼, *n.* An indentured servant boy, or girl, about 7 or 8 years old.

Kogane, コガネ, 金, *(kin.) n.* Gold.

Kogare,*-ru,-ta*, コガレル, 焦, *i.v.* To be charred, scorched, burnt, blackened with fire; (fig.) to long, or pine for, to be troubled about. *Meshi ga kogareta*, the rice is burnt. *Ko ga haha ni* —, the child pines after its mother.

Kogare-kusai,-ki,-ku,-ō, コガレクサイ, 焦臭, Charred and stinking.

Kogare-tszki,*-ku,-ita*, コガレツク, 焦付, *i.v.* To burn and stick to the pot, or pan.

Kogashi,*-sz,-sh'ta*, コガス, 焦, *t.v.* To char, scorch, burn, or blacken with fire. *Kuro kẹmuri ten wo kogash'te ōi kakaru*, the black smoke spread over the heavens.
Syn. yaku.

Kogashi, コガシ, *n.* A kind of food made of parched meal.

Kogatana, コガタナ, 小刀, *n.* A small knife, pocket knife.

Koge,*-ru,-ta*, コゲル, 焦, *i.v.* To be charred, to burn, to scorch, toasted. *Meshi ga* —, the rice is burnt. *Pan ga kogeta*, the bread is burnt. *Hinoshi de kimono ga kogeta*, the clothes are scorched with the smoothing iron.

Kō-ge, カウゲ, 高下, *(takai hikui.)* High or low, good or bad. — *aru*, there are high priced and low priced.

†Kō-gei, コウゲイ, 虹蜺, *n.* *(niji.)* Rainbow.

†Kō-geki,*-szru*, コウゲキ, 攻撃, *(seme utsz.)* To attack, assault, invade in war.

Kō-gen, クワウゲン, 廣言, *n.* Boasting, vaunting. — *wo haku*, to speak boastingly.

Kogi,*-gu,-ida*, コグ, 漕, *t.v.* To scull, row. *Fune wo* —, to scull a boat.

‖Kogi,*-gu,-ida*, コグ, *t.v.* To pull up by the root, root up. *Kusa no ne wo kogu.*

Kogi,*-gu,-ida*, コグ, 扱, *t.v.* To thresh grain by drawing through iron teeth, to hackle, to strip. *Ine wo kogu*, to thresh rice. *Ha wo kogi-otosz*, to strip off leaves.
Syn. shigoku.

Kōgi, コウギ, 公儀, *n.* The court, the government. Syn. seifu, kōhen.

†Kogi, コギ, 狐疑, Doubt, hesitation, indecision. — *szru*, to hesitate, be in doubt.
Syn. tamerai.

Koginoko, コギノコ, *n.* A shuttlecock.

Ko-gire, コギレ, 小切, *n.* A small piece of cloth, patch.

‖Kogiri,*-ru,-tta*, コギル, *i.v.* To chaffer, or higgle in buying, to beat down the price. Syn. negiru.

Kogi-modoshi,*-sz,-sh'ta*, コギモドス, 漕戻, *t.v.* To scull back.

‖Kogi-tori,*-ru,-tta*, コギトル, *t.v.* To pluck up by the roots; to strip off, (as leaves.)

Kogi-watari,*-ru,-tta*, コギワタル, 漕渡, *t.v.* To scull across.

†Kō-giyō, カウゲフ, 耕業, *n.* Husbandry, farming. — *wo szru.*

Kōgiyō, コウギヤウ, 興行, Making or getting up an entertaining performance, or exhibition. *Shibai wo kō-giyō szru*, to get up theatrical performances.

Ko-go, コゴ, 古語, *(furui kotoba), n.* An ancient or obsolete word, ancient language.

Kō-gō, カウガフ, 交合, *(majiwari au), n.* Sexual intercourse or commerce, coition. *Nan niyo no* —.

Kogome, コゴメ, 小米, *n.* Broken rice.

Kogori,*-ru,-tta*, コゴル, 凝, *i.v.* To congeal, coagulate, curdle. Syn. katamaru.

Kogoshi, コゴシ, 小腰, *n.* A slight bow to a superior. — *wo kagamu*, to stand in a bowing posture.

Kogoto, コゴト, 小言, *n.* Grumbling,

fault finding, complaining, censuring. — *wo iu*, to find fault.

KOGOYAKASHI,*-sz,-sh'ta*, コゴヤカス 令凍, (caust. of *Kogoyeru*) To cause to be chilled, or benumbed; to freeze.

KOGOYE,*-ru,-ta*, コゴエル, 凍, *i.v.* Benumbed, chilled, stiff with cold, frozen. *Te ga kogoyeta*, hands are numb with cold.

KOGOYE-JINI, コゴエジニ, 凍死, *n.* Frozen to death. — *szru.*

KOGU, コグ, See *Kogi.*

KŌ-GU, カウグ, 香具, *n.* Utensils used in burning incense, or in fumigating with aromatics.

KOGUCHI, コグチ, 木口, *n.* The cut end of a tree, or cut end of anything.

KOGUCHI-GAKI, コグチガキ, 小口書, *n.* The title of a book written on the outside, across the edges of the leaves.

KO-GUSZRI, コグスリ, 粉藥, (*sanyaku*), *n.* Medicinal powder, powdered medicine.

†KŌ-HAI, クワウハイ, 荒廢, (*are-hateru*). Dilapidated, going to ruin, decayed, (as a temple, or house).

†KŌ-HAI, コウハイ, 興廢, (*sakannaru otoroyeru*). Rise and fall, flourish and decay.

KOHAKU, コハク, 琥珀, *n.* Amber.

KOHAN, コハン, 枯礬, (*yaki miyoban*) *n.* Burnt alum.

KŌHAN, コウハン, 皓礬, *n.* Sulphate of zinc.

KO-HAN-TOKI, コハントキ, 小半時, *n.* A quarter of a Japanese hour, = half an hour English.

KOHARU, コハル, 小春, *n.* Little spring, the tenth month of the Japanese year ; it is so called, from the weather so much resembling spring weather.

KOHAZE, コハゼ, *n.* A clasp, or locket.

KŌHI, カウヒ, *n.* Coffee, (a word recently introduced from the English.)

KO-HIYŌ, コヒヤウ, 小兵, *n.* Small in stature.

KŌ-HEN, コウヘン, 公邊, *n.* Court, government, the place where public affairs and justice is administered. *Kono koto wa — ni itashimashō*, I will carry this matter to a court of justice.

KŌ-HONE, カウホネ, 川骨, *n.* A kind of water-plant. Nuphar japonica.

†KŌ-I, コウイ, 厚意, (*atszki kokorozashi*) *n.* Great kindness, or benevolence.

KOI, コヒ, 鯉, *n.* A kind of river fish.

KOI,*-KI,-SHI*, コイ, 濃, *a.* Thick, or dense in consistence ; deep in color, strong in taste. *Iro ga koi*, the color is deep. *Koi szmi*, thick, or black ink. *Kono cha ga koku natta*, this tea has become too strong. *Koi-kami*, a thick head of hair. Syn. ATSZI.

KOI, コヒ, 戀, *n.* Love, (between the sexes); also, brotherly love. — *wo shikakeru*, to make love. — *wo szru*, to love. — *no uta*, a love song. Syn. JŌAI,

KOI, KŌ, KŌTA, コフ, 請, or 乞, *t.v.* To request, ask courteously, to beg. Syn. NEGŌ.

KOI-BITO, コヒビト, 戀人, *n.* A person loved, a loved one.

KOI-CHA, コイチヤ, 濃茶, *n.* Powdered tea.

KOIGUCHI, コヒグチ, *n.* The joint, or place where the sword handle meets the scabbard. — *wo kutszrogeru*, to draw the sword a little from the scabbard, so as to ease the tightness, and be ready for instant use.

KOI-KA, コヒカ, 戀歌, *n.* A love song.

KOI-KOGARE,*-ru,-ta*, コヒコガレル, 戀焦, To be inflamed with love.

KOI-MANEKI,*-ku,-ita*, コヒマネク, 請招, *t.v.* To call, invite, bid. Syn. SHŌDAI SZRU.

KOI-MOTOME,*-ru,-ta*, コヒモトメル, 乞求, To get by asking.

†KŌIN, コウイン, 後胤, *n.* Descendant, posterity. Syn. SHI-SON.

KŌ-IN, クワウイン, 光陰, *n.* Time. See *K'wōin.*

†KŌIN, コウイン, 後音, (*nochi no tayori,*) *n.* Future opportunity, (in writing,) at another time. *Nao — wo goshisoro*, I will write you again.

KOI-NEGAWAKUBA, コヒネガハクバ, 希, *adv.* That which I earnestly request, beg, or particularly desire.

KOI-NEGAI,*-ō,-ōta*, コヒネガフ, 希, *t.v.* To beg for, earnestly request, or desire, to pray for.

KO-INU, コイヌ, 小狗, *n.* A young dog, pup.

KOI-OTOKO, コヒオトコ, 戀男, *n.* A lover.

KOISHIGARI,*-ru,-tta*, コヒシガル, 戀, *i.v.* To long for, to desire earnestly to see, to think fondly of.

KOISHII,-KI, コヒシイ, 戀, *a.* That which is absent and thought of with love, desire, or fondness. *Oya ga* —, longing to see one's parents. *Furusato ga* —, thinking fondly of one's native place. *Koishiki mukashi wo omoi-dasz*, to think fondly of old times. Syn. NATSZKASHII, YUKASHII, SH'TAU.

KOISHIKU, コヒシク, 戀, *adv.* idem.

KOISHISA, コヒシサ, 戀, *n.* Longing desire to see, love for an absent one.

KOI-SH'TAI,-ō,-ōta, コヒシタフ, 戀慕, *t. v.* To long after, pine for, or desire to see. *Ko wo* —.

KOITSZ, コイツ, 這奴, vulg.=you blackguard, you rascal.

KOI-UKE,-ru,-ta, コヒウケル, 請受, *t. v.* To ask and get, to obtain by request. *Muszme wo niyobō ni koi-ukeru.*

KOI-WADZRAI,-ō,-ōta, コヒワヅラフ, 戀煩, *i. v.* To be love sick. *Onna wo omōte koi-wadzrō.*

KOI-WADZRAI, コヒワヅラヒ, 戀煩, *n.* Love-sickness.

KO-JI, コジ, 故事, (*furuki koto.*) Ancient customs and things, antiquities. — *wo shiru h'to*, an antiquarian.

KO-JI, コジ, 居士, *n.* A title given by Buddhists to deceased believers.

†KOJI,-*szru*, コジ, 固辭, (*kataku jitai szru.*) Firmly to decline, refuse stoutly.

KOJI,-ru,-tta, コジル, *t. v.* To pry with a lever. *Kuwa de ishi wo* —, to pry up a stone with a hoe.

KŌ-JI, コウジ, 柑子, *n.* A kind of orange.

KŌJI,-ru,-ta, カウジル, *i. v.* To become chronic, confirmed, or inveterate, as disease. *Yamai ga* —, the disease has become chronic.

KŌJI, コウヂ, 小路, *n.* Small, or narrow streets.

KŌJI, カウヂ, 麴, *n.* Malt made by fermenting rice or barley, in the process of making *sake*, and *soy*.

KOJI-AGE,-ru,-ta, コジアゲル, *t. v.* To pry up, to lift with a lever.

KOJI-AKE,-ru,-ta, コジアケル, *t. v.* To pry open.

KŌJI-BUTA, カウヂブタ, 麴蓋, *n.* A shallow box for holding malt.

KOJI-HANASHI,-sz,-sh'ta, コジハナス, *t. v.* To pry apart.

KOJIKI, コジキ, 乞食, *n.* A beggar. Syn. HI-NIN.

KŌ-JIKI, カウヂキ, 高直, *n.* High price.

KO-JIN, コジン, 古人, (*mukashi no h'to,*) *n.* An ancient, a man of ancient times, a deceased person,=the late.

KOJIRI, コジリ, 鐺, *n.* The metal, or horn tip on the end of a scabbard.

KOJIRU, コジル, see *Koji.*

†KŌ-JITSZ, コウジツ, 口實, *n.* A plea, excuse, a reason given in justification. — *ni szru*, to plead in justification of one's self. Syn. Ī-GUSA.

KO-JITSZ, コジツ, 故實, *n.* Antiquities. — *ni kuwashii h'to*, a person skilled in ancient customs, an antiquary.

KOJITSZKE,-ru,-ta, コジツケル, 牽强, *t. v.* To force, strain, or wrest the meaning of words, drawing forced resemblances, or analogies. Syn. FUK'WAI SZRU.

KOJITZKE, コジツケ, 附會, *n.* Forcing, or wresting the meaning of words, a forced analogy, resemblance, or inference. — *wo kaku.* — *wo iu.* Syn. FUK'WAI.

KŌ-JŌ, コウジヤウ, 口上, (*kuchi de iu*). *n.* Word of mouth, verbal report, or message. — *de shiraseru.* — *wo noberu.*

KŌ-JŪ, コウヂウ, 講中, *n.* A company of persons assembled at a temple to chant prayers. — *atszmatte kiyō wo yomu.*

‖KO-JŪ-HAN, コヂウハン, 小晝飯, *n.* A lunch taken between dinner and supper.

†KŌ-JUN, カウジユン, 孝順, *n.* Obedient and compliant. — *na h'to.*

KOJŪTO, コジウト, *n.* Brother-in-law.

KO-JŪ-TOME, コジウトメ, *n.* Sister-in-law.

KŌ-KA, コウカ, 後架, *n.* Back-house, privy. Syn. CHŌDZBA.

KO-KAGE, コカゲ, 木陰, *n.* Shade of a tree.

KOKE, コケ, 鱗, *n.* Scales, (of a fish.) Syn. UROKO.

KOKE, コケ, 苔, *n.* Moss. — *ni udzmoru*, covered with moss.

‖KOKE,-ru,-ta, コケル, 倒, *i.v.* To fall over, fall down. Syn. TAORERU.

KŌ-KE, カウケ, 高家, (*Takai iye*). *n.* High family, noble house.

KŌ-KEN, コウケン, 後見, (*ushiromi*) *n.* A guardian. — *szru*, to act as guardian to a child. — *ni naru.*

KO-KEN-JŌ, コケンジヤウ, 沽券狀, *n.* A deed of sale.

KOKERA-BUKI, コケラブキ, 柿葺, *n.* A kind of roofing with shingles, where the shingles are several layers deep.

‖KOKETSZ-MAROBITSZ, コケツマロビツ, *adv.* Stumbling and falling.

†KŌ-KI, カウキ, 高貴, (*takaki tattoshi*). High and noble. — *na h'to.*

KŌ-KI, コウキ, 紅木, *n.* A kind of red wood.

†KŌ-KI, カウキ 香氣, *n.* Fragrance, perfume, odor, smell, aroma. Syn. KAORI.

KOKI, コキ 濃, See *Koi.*

KO-KIU, コキウ, 鼓弓, *n.* A violin, or fiddle of three strings. — *no tszru*, fiddle strings. — *wo szru*, to play on the violin.

†KO-KIU, コキフ, 呼吸, *n.* Expiration and

inspiration, the breathing. — *ga kurū*, the breathing is deranged.

KO-KIYŌ, コキヤウ, 故鄉, *(furu-sato)* n. Native village, birth-place. — *ye kayeru*, to return to one's birth-place. — *waszregatashi*, it is impossible to forget the place of one's birth. Syn. KIURI.

KOKKA, コクカ, 國家, *(kuni iye).* n. Country and family; the Emperor. — *no tame ni inochi wo szteru*, to die for one's country.

KOKKEI, コツケイ, 滑稽, n. Comical talk, any thing exciting laughter. — *wo iu*, to talk comically. Syn. SHARE, TAWAMURE.

†KOKKIN, コクキン, 國禁, n. The laws, or prohibitions of a country, or state. — *wo okasz*, to violate the laws of a country.

KŌ-KŌ, カウカウ, 香香, n. Any thing pickled in salt. *Dai-kon no* —, pickled radishes.

KOKO, ココ, 爰, (contr. of *kono tokoro*). *adv.* Here, this place. *Koko kashiko*, here and there, all about, every where. Syn. KOCHI.

†KO-KŌ, ココウ, 餬口, *(kuchiszgi)*. n. A living, livelihood.

†KO-KŌ, コカウ, 股肱, *(momo hiji).* n. Used only in the phrase; — *no shin*, a faithful servant,—one who is to his master like legs and arms.

KŌ-KŌ, カウカウ 孝行, n. Obedience to parents, filial piety. *Oya ni — wo szru*, to obey one's parents.

KO-KŌ, ココウ, 虎口, *(tora no kuchi).* n. A place, or condition of extreme danger. — *no nan wo nogareru.*

†KŌ-KŌ, クワウクワウ, 煌煌, *adv.* Bright, shiny, clear. — *to sh'ta ten-ki*, a bright, sunny day.

KOKOCHI, ココチ, 心地, (contr. of *kokoro mochi*). n. The feelings, sensations, spirits. — *ga warui*, to feel unwell. Syn. KI-BUN, KI-SHOKU, KI-AI, AMBAI.

†KOKODA, or KOKODAKU, ココダク, 許多, Many. — *no tszmi*, many sins.

KOKOMOTO, ココモト, 此元, This place, here; I, me.

KO-KON, ココン, 古今, *(mukashi to ima).* n. Ancient and modern times. — *ni maremaru h'to.*

KOKONOKA, ココノカ, 九日, Ninth day of the month.

KOKONOTSZ, ココノツ, 九, Nine. — *doki*, twelve o'clock, M.

†KOKONOYE, ココノヘ, 九重, n. The Mikado's palace. (From its nine inclosures.)

†KOKORA, ココラ, 許多, Many. — *no toshi*, many years.

KOKORO, ココロ, 心, n. Heart, mind, will, thought, affection, reason, meaning, signification. — *ni kakaru*, to be anxious, concerned. — *ni kakeru*, to bear in mind, charge the mind with. — *wo tszkush'te*, with the whole heart. — *ni kanō*, to suit one's mind. — *no nai h'to*, one without natural affection; a careless, thoughtless person. *Ji no* —, the meaning of a character. *Nan no — de ikatta ka wakaranai*, I don't know why he became angry. — *ni makasz*, to suit one's pleasure.

KOKORO-ATE, ココロアテ, 心當, n. That on which one depends, trusts, calculates on, or looks to, as a support or encouragement in doing anything. — *ga nai*, have no one to look to. — *ni naranu h'to*, a person not to be depended on. — *ga hadzreru*, to fail in one's hope. Syn. ATE, TANOMI.

KORORO-BASE, ココロバセ, 意, n. The thoughts.

KOKORO-BAYE, ココロバヘ, 情, n. The natural disposition, heart. — *no yoki onna*, a good hearted woman. Syn. SHINTEI.

KOKORO-BOSOI, ココロボソイ, 心細, n. Sad and anxious, pensive, gloomy, lonely in feeling.

KOKORO-DATE, ココロダテ, 心立, n. Temper, disposition, heart. Syn. KOKORODAYE.

KOKORO-DZKAI, ココロヅカヒ, 心遣, n. Trouble of mind, solicitude, anxiety, perplexity, care. — *wo szru*, to be troubled about. Syn. SHIMPAI, KIDZKAI.

KOKORO-DZKI, *-ku, -ita*, ココロヅク, 心附, *i.v.* To suddenly recollect, or think of, to strike one's mind, or attention. *Kokorodzite sagasz*, suddenly recollecting to search for any thing.

KOKORO-DZMORI, ココロヅモリ, 意匠, n. Thinking over, planning, reckoning, or estimating in the mind. — *wo szru.*

KOKORO-GAKARI, ココロガカリ, 心懸, n. Any thing on one's mind, care, concern.

KOKORO-GAKE, *-ru, -ta*, ココロガケル, 心懸, *i.v.* To keep in mind, fix in the mind, to have a care about, to think about. *Heizei kokorogakete iru.*

KOKORO-GAKE, ココロガケ, 心懸, n. Thought, care, caution. — *ga yoi*, thoughtful, careful, mindful.

KOKORO-GAMAYE, ココロガマヘ, 心構, n. Previous preparation, or readiness of mind, mind made up before hand for a future contingency. — *wo sh'te matsz*, to wait for anything with one's mind ready to meet it.

KOKORO-GAWARI, ココロガハリ, 心替, *n.* Changing one's mind, renouncing former views. — *ga sh'te teki ni naru,* to be a turncoat and become an enemy.

KOKORO-GOKORO, ココロゴコロ, 心心, Various minds, diverse opinions. — *no yo no naka,* a world of various opinions. — *ni mono wo szru,* to do things, each according to his own notion, or pleasure.

KOKORO-KUBARI, ココロクバリ, 心配, *n.* Distraction, or perplexity of mind from various engagements.

KOKORO-MADOI, ココロマドヒ, 心惑, *n.* Perplexity, bewilderment.

KOKORO-MAKASE-NI, ココロマカセニ, 隨意, *(dzi-i.) adv.* As one pleases, just as one likes, to his own mind.

KOKORO-MI, *-ru, -ta,* ココロミル, 試, *t. v.* To try, prove, test, examine. Syn. TAMESZ.

KOKORO-MOCHI, ココロモチ, 心氣, *n.* The feelings, spirits. — *ga warui,* to feel bad or unwell. *Yoi — da,* how pleasant it is, (to one's feelings.)

KOKORO-MOTO-NAI, -KI, -KU, ココロモトナイ, 無心元, That which one is uneasy about, uncertain and anxious, doubtful, apprehensive. *Yo no ma no kaze mo* —, am apprehensive the wind may blow to night. *Kokoro motonaku omō,* to feel doubtful about. Syn. OBOTSZKANAI FU-ANSHIN.

||KOKORO-MUKE, ココロムケ, 氣質, *n.* Disposition, temper. Syn. KI-SHITSZ, KOKORO-BAYE.

KOKORO-NARADZ, ココロナラズ, 不成心, Contrary to one's will, or desire; without wishing. — *dete kayeru,* contrary to his wishes he returned. Syn. HOI NAKU, FU-HON-I.

||KOKORO-NE, ココロ子, 心根, *n.* Heart, disposition, temper. Syn. SHIN-TEI.

KOKORO-OKI-NAKU, ココロオキナク, 無心置, *adv.* Without backwardness, without fear, or hesitation. Syn. HABAKARI NAKU, YENRIYO NAKU.

KOKORO-YASZI, -KI, -KU, ココロヤスイ, 心安, Easy, not difficult, intimate, friendly, easy, free from care. *Kokoro-yaszi h'to,* a friend.

KOKOROYE, *-ru, -ta,* ココロエル, 心得, *t. v.* To know, perceive, to notice, understand, comprehend, to assent to.

KOKORO-YOI, -KI, -KU, -Ō, -SHI, ココロヨイ, 快, Well, easy, comfortable. *Kokoro-yoku kurash'te oru,* living comfortably, at ease.

KOKORO-ZASHI, *-sz, -sh'ta,* ココロザス, 志, *t. v.* To purpose, intend, design, to aim at, to desire. *Osaka ye kokorozash'te yuku,* to purpose going to Osaka.

KOKORO-ZASHI, ココロザシ, 志, *n.* The purpose, intention, design, aim, desire, hope. — *wo tageru,* to succeed in one's aim. — *no ōki h'to,* a person of great aims, an ambitious man.

KOKU, コク, 斛, or 石, *n.* A grain measure of ten *to,* equal to 5.13 bushels, or 7.551 cub. feet.

KOKU, コク, 國, *(Kuni,) n.* Kingdom, state, country. *Ikkoku,* one state.

KOKU, コク 濃, *adv.* Thick, or dense in consistence, deep in color, strong in taste. see *Koi.*

†KOKU, コク, 黒, *(Kuroi.)* Black.

KOKU, コク, 刻, *n.* The fourth of a Japanese hour,=half an hour English.

KOKU, コク, 穀, *n.* Cereals, grain. *Gokoku,* the five cereals.

KO-KŪ, コクウ, 虛空, *n.* Empty space. *Kurushinde — wo tszkamu,* in agony to grasp at empty air. — *ni agaru,* to ascend into space.

KO-KUBI, コクビ, 小首, Used in the phrase; *Kokubi wo katamukuru,* to incline the head to one side for a little while, (as in deep thought.)

†KOKU-BIYAKU, コクビヤク, 黒白, *(kuro shiro.)* White and black.

†KOKU-BO, コクボ, 國母, *(kuni no haha,) n.* The Emperor's mother, the Queen-mother.

KOKUCHIU, コクチウ, 國中, *(kuni no uchi.)* The whole state. — *ni fure-watasz,* to proclaim through the whole state.

KOKU-DO, コクド, 國土, *(kuni tszchi.) n.* Country, state.

KOKU-DZKE, コクヅケ, 刻付, *n.* Marking the time on a letter, or circular, when it was received and transmitted, to insure despatch. — *wo sh'te tegami wo yaru.*

KOKU-FŪ, コクフウ, 國風, *(kuni no fūzoku.) n.* Customs of a country.

KOKU-GEN, コクゲン, 刻限, *(toki wo kagiru,) n.* The fixed time, appointed time, the time, hour. — *dōri ni kuru,* to come punctually to the time. — *wo kimeru,* to set a time.

KOKU-HŌ, コクハフ, 國法, *n.* Laws of a state.

KOKU-IN, コクイン, 刻印, *n.* The stamp, or private chop on a coin. — *wo utsz.*

KOKU-MOTSZ, コクモツ, 穀物, *n.* Grain, cereals.

KOKU-Ō, コクワウ, 國王, *n.* The King, ruler of a state.

KO-KURAGARI, コクラガリ, 小暗, Little dark, twilight, dusky, gloomy.

KOKU-SAN, コクサン, 國產, *n.* The productions of a country.

KOKU-SEI, コクセイ, 國政, *(kuni no matsz-rigoto,) n.* The government of a state.

||KOKU-SEI, コクセイ, 國製, *n.* The manufactures of a country.

KO-KUSHI, コクシ, 國司, *(kuni no tsz-kasa,) n.* The title of the eighteen principal Daimios of Japan.

†KOKU-SHŌGAN, コクシヤウガン, 黑障眼, *n.* Amaurosis. Syn. SOKOHI, NAI-SHŌ, SEIMŌ.

†KOKU-SHOKU, コクシヨク, 黑色, *(Koroi iro,) n.* Black color.

†KOKU-SHOKU, コクシヨク, 國色, *n.* A most beautiful woman.

KOKU-SHOKU, コクシユ, 國守, *n.* The lord, or ruler of a state, same as *Koku-shi.*

KOKU-SO, コクソ, *n.* A kind of stuff used for staining wood.

†KOKU-SZ, コクス, 哭, *(naku.)* To cry.

KOKU-TAN, コクタン, 黑檀, *n.* Ebony.

KŌ-K'WAI, コウクワイ, 後悔, *(nochi ni kuyamu,) n.* Sorrow, or regret for something done, repentance, remorse, compunction. — *szru,* to repent. — *saki ni tatadz,* repentance cannot mend it.

†KŌ-K'WATSZ, カウクワツ, 狡猾, Cunning, knavish. Syn. WARUGASHIKOI, SARUJIYE.

KOKU-YAKU, コクヤク, 國役, *n.* Public service, work done for the government by farmers, for which no pay is received; tax in money paid to defray public expenses. — *wo tsztomuru.* — *wo dasz.* Syn. KUYAKU, YAKU.

KOKU-YE, コクエ, 黑衣, *(kuroi kimono), n.* The black robe worn by Buddhist priests, on first entering the priesthood.

†KOMA, コマ, 高麗, *n.* The ancient name of Corea.

KOMA, コマ, *n.* A top. — *wo mawasz,* to spin a top.

KOMA コマ, 棊馬, *n.* Chessmen, a pawn. — *wo sasz,* to move a chessman.

KOMA, コマ, 駒, *n.* A colt.

KO-MA, コマ, 小間, *n.* A small room.

KOMA, コマ, 柱, *n.* The bridge of a guitar.

KOMADORI, コマドリ, 駒鳥, *n.* A small bird.

KOMADSZKAI, コマヅカヒ, 小間使, *n.* A small servant girl.

KOMA-GOMA-TO, コマゴマト, 細細, *adv.* Minutely, particularly. — *iu.* — *kaku.* Syn. KUWASHIKU, NENGORONI.

||KOMAGOTO, コマゴト, 小言, *n.* Same as *Kogoto.*

KO-MAI, コマイ, 古米, *(furugome), n.* Old rice.

KOMA-INU, コマイヌ, 駒犬, *n.* The stone image of a dog before Sintoo temples.

KOMAKA-NA, コマカナ, 細, *a.* Fine, small, minute, stingy. Syn. HOSOI, CHISAI.

KOMAKA-NI, コマカニ, 細, *adv.* Minutely, particularly, fine, small. — *kaku,* to write particularly. — *kiru,* to cut fine.

KO-MAKURA, コマクラ, 小枕, *n.* A small pad, or cushion, fixed on a wooden pillow to make it softer.

KOMAMONO, コマモノ, 小間物, *n.* Toilet articles, such as, mirror, comb, rouge, toothbrush, powder, &c. *Komamonoya,* a shop where ladies toilet articles are sold.

KŌ-MAN, カウマン, 高慢, *n.* Pride, haughtiness, arrogance, boasting. — *naru,* proud, haughty, arrogant, consequential. — *szru,* to be proud, to boast, brag. TAKA-BURU, HOKORU, JI-MAN.

KO-MANAKA, コマナカ, 小間中, *n.* The quarter of a mat.

KO-MANEKI,*-ku,-ita,* コマネク, 小招, *t.v.* To beckon with the hand.

KOMANUKI,*-ku,-ita,* コマヌク, 拱, *t. v.* To fold the arms. *Te wo komanuite tatsz,* to stand with folded arms.

KOMARASE,*-ru,-ta,* コマラセル, 令困, (caust. of *Komaru*). To trouble, afflict, vex, annoy, molest, distress. *H'to wo —,* to cause trouble to others.

KOMARI,*-ru,-tta,* コマル, 困, *i.v.* Troubled, annoyed, vexed, afflicted, distressed. *Kane ga nakute komaru,* troubled because one has no money. *Samukute —,* distressed by the cold. Syn. MEIWAKU SZRU.

KOMATA, コマタ, 小股, *n.* The crotch between the legs, short steps. — *ni aruku,* to walk with short steps.

KOMAYAKA, コマヤカ, 細, Fine, small, minute, delicate, (same as *Komaka*). — *na g'wan-yaku,* small pills. — *ni kiku,* to listen attentively.

KOMAYE, コマヘ, 小前, *n.* Lowest classes of people.

KOMAYE, コマヘ, 壁骨, *n.* The bamboo strips used as lathing for plastered walls. — *wo kaku,* to lath.

KOMAYOSE, コマヨセ, 駒寄, *n.* A low picket fence, pale-fence.

KOM-BAN, コンバン, 今晩, *adv.* To night, this evening. Syn. KON-YA.

KOM-BU, コンブ, 昆布, *n.* A kind of seaweed, (same as *Kobu*).

KOME, コメ, 米, *n.* Rice, (the grain unboiled. — *no ko*, rice flour. — *h'to tszbu*, a grain of rice.

KOME,*-ru,-ta*, コメル, 籠, *t.v.* To put into. *Teppō ni tama wo* —, to load a gun with a ball. *Kokoro wo komete hon wo yomu*, to read with attention. *Yo wo komete tori no sora ne wo hakaru*, rising before dawn to imitate the crowing of a cock. (poet). *Shiro ni tszwamono wo* —, to place troops in a fortress. Syn. IRERU.

KOME-BITSZ, コメビツ, 米櫃, *n.* A rice-box.

KOME-BUKURO, コメブクロ, 米袋, *n.* A rice-bag or sack.

KOME-BURUI, コメブルヒ 米篩, *n.* A rice seive.

KOME-DAWARA, コメダハラ, 米俵, *n.* A straw rice-bag.

KOMEGURA, コメグラ, 米藏, *n.* A storehouse for rice, rice granary.

KŌ MEI, カウメイ, 高名, (*nadakai*). *n.* Famous, celebrated, great reputation.

KOME-KAMI, コメカミ, 蜂谷, *n.* The temples, or articulation of the lower jaw.

KOME-MUSHI, コメムシ, 米虫, *n.* A rice weevil.

KOME-OKI,*-ku,-ita*, コメオク, 籠置, *t.v.* To place in, to garrison.

KOMERŌ, コメラウ, 小女郎, *n.* A young female servant.

KOMERU, コメル, See *Kome*.

KOMETSZKI, コメツキ, 米搗, *n.* A person who cleans rice by pounding it in a mortar.

KOMEYA, コメヤ, 米屋, *n.* A rice-store, grain merchant.

†KŌ-MI, カウミ, 好味, (*yoki ajiwai*). *n.* Good flavor, sweet taste. Syn. UMAI.

KOMI,*-mu,-nda*, コム, 込, *t.v.* To put into; mostly used affixed to the roots of verbs, with the meaning of, into, or in. *Teppō ni tama wo* —, to put a ball into a gun. *Nage-komu*, to throw into. *Buchi-komu*, to hammer into, &c.

KOMI, コミ, 込, *n.* In the lump; several things of different kinds, or values, at once. *Komi ni kau*, to buy in the lump, or gross. *Komi de ikura*, how much for the lot? or in the lump?

KOMI-AGE,*-ru,-ta*, コミアゲル, 嘔逆, *t.v.* To retch, heave, or strain in vomiting. *Tabeta mono wo komiageru*, to retch, and vomit what has been eaten.

KOMI-AI,*-au,-atta*, コミアフ, 込合, *i.v.* Crowded together.

KOMI-IRI,*-ru,-tta*, コミイル, 込入, *i.v.* To enter pell-mell. *Teki shiro ni komi-itta.*

KO-MIJIN, コミヂン, 微塵, *n.* Fine pieces. — *ni kudaku*, to break into powder.

KOMI-YA, コミヤ, 槊杖, *n.* A ramrod.

KŌ-MIYŌ, コウミヤウ, 功名, *n.* Famous, celebrated, or illustrious deeds.

†KŌ-MIYŌ, クワウミヤウ, 光明, *n.* Glory, splendor, halo of light. *Hi no* —, the glory of the sun. *Butsz no* —, the glory around the head of Buddha.

†KOMMŌ, コンマウ, 懇望, (*shikirini nozomu*). Earnest desire. — *szru.*

KOMMORI-TO, コンモリト, *adv.* Dark. — *sh'ta yama*, a dark, wooded, mountain detached from others, as seen from a distance.

KOMO, コモ, 薦, *n.* Straw matting, used for making bags.

†KO-MOCHI-DZKI, コモチヅキ, 小望月, *n*- The fourteenth day of the month.

KOMO-DARE, コモダレ, 薦垂, *n.* A straw mat hung before the door of the poor.

†KOMOGOMO, コモゴモ, 交, *adv.* Mutually. *Jō ge — ri wo totte kuni ayaukaran*, when superiors and inferiors try to snatch the profit one from the other the country is endangered. Syn. TAGAI NI.

KOMO-KABURI, コモカブリ, 薦冠, *n.* Covered with straw matting, (as a *sake* tub.)

KO-MON, コモン, 小紋, *n.* Small figures on cloth.

KŌ-MON, コウモン, 肛門, *n.* The anus.

KO-MONO, コモノ, 小者, (*meshitszkai*). *n.* A young servant boy.

KOMARASE,*-ru,-ta*, コモラセル, 令籠, (caust. of *Komoru.*) To order to, or let, others be confined, or shut up in quarters.

KOMORI,*-ru,-tta*, コモル, 籠, *i. v.* To be shut up in, confined in, immured, included, contained, comprised. *Tszwamono shiro ni komotte teki wo matsz*, the troops shut up in the castle wait for the enemy. *Fuyu-gomori*, confined to the house by the cold, to go into winter quarters. *Heya ni kuki ga* —, the air of this room is close.

KO-MORI, コモリ, 小守, *n.* A young female nurse.

KŌMORI, カウモリ, 蝙蝠, (*hempuku.*) *n.* A bat.

KOMORI-DŌ, コモリダウ, 籠堂, *n.* A place near a *Miya*, where the worshiper remains shut up for several days, without sleep or food, to supplicate the *Kami* for some favor.

KOMOSŌ, コモソウ, 虚無僧, *n.* A kind of Buddhist religionist, who, when he goes out begging, dresses in white, wears a basket over his head and face, and plays on a flute.

†KOMPAKU, コンパク, 魂魄, *n.* The spirit of the dead, the soul. Syn. TAMASHII.

KOM-PAN, コンパン, 今般, *adv.* This time. Syn. KONDO, KONO-TABI.

KOMPEITŌ, コンペイタウ, 金平糖, *n.* A kind of candy.

KOM-PON, コンポン, 根本, *n.* The origin, beginning; the place or cause from which any thing originates. Syn. MOTO, HAJIMARI, SHO-HOTSZ, KON-GEN.

KOMUGI, コムギ, 小麦, *n.* Wheat. — *no-ko*, wheat flour.

KOMURA, コムラ, 腨, *n.* The ankle bone; maleolus.

KOMURAGAYERI, コムラガヘリ, *n.* Cramp in the calf of the leg.

KŌMURI,*-ru,-tta*, カウムル, 蒙, *i. v.* To receive from a superior. *Go-men wo* —, to receive permission from government. *On wo* —, to receive kindness, (from superiors.) Syn. UKETAMAWARU, MORAU, UKERU.

KŌMURI, カウブリ, 冠, *n.* A kind of cap worn by nobles.

KON, コン, 献, Numeral for glasses of wine, as, *Sake ikkon*, one wine-glass full of *sake ; ni-kon ; san-gon.*

†KON, コン, 金, (*kin.*) *n.* Gold, golden.

†KON, コン, 今, (*ima.*) Now, this; used only in comp. words.

KON, コン, 紺, *n.* A dark blue color. *Kon no iro.*

KONA, コナ, 粉, *n.* Flour, meal, fine powder of any thing. — *ni szru*, to pulverize.

KONAIDA, コナイダ, 此間, (cont. of *Kono aida.*) *adv.* Lately, recently, within a few days.

†KŌ-NAN, コウナン, 後難, (*nochi no nangi.*) Future calamity, future trouble.

KONARE,*-ru,-ta*, コナレル, 熟, *i. v.* Reduced to powder, digested. *Shokumotsz ga* —, food is digested. Syn. SHŌ-K'WA SZRU.

KONASHI,*-sz,-sh'ta*, コナス, *t. v.* To reduce to powder, or make fine; to digest, to thresh, to deride, to treat with ridicule. *Tszchi wo* —, to break fine the hard soil. *Shokumotsz wo* —, to digest food. *Ine wo* —, to thresh rice. *H'to wo* —, to ridicule another.

KONATA, コナタ, 此方, (contr. of *Kono-kata.*) *adv.* Here, this side; I, you, (to inferiors.) *Kawa no* —, this side of the river. *Konata wa doko ye itta*, where have you been? *Anata-konata*, here and there, both sides, both persons.

KON-CHŌ, コンテウ, 今朝, *adv.* This morning. Syn. KESA.

KON-DO, コンド, 今度, *adv.* This time, now, at the present time. Syn. KONO-TABI.

†KON-DZRU, コンズル, 混, (*majiru.*) *t. v.* To mix, mingle.

KONE,*-ru,-ta*, コネル, 捏, *t. v.* To knead, to work. *Pan wo* —, to knead bread. *Tszchi wo* —, to work mortar.

KŌNEN, コウネン, 後年, (*nochi no toshi,*) *n.* Future year, years to come.

†KON-GEN, コンゲン, 根元, *n.* Beginning, origin. Syn. KOMPON.

KON-GETSZ, コンゲツ, 今月, (*ima no tszki,*) *n.* This month, present month.

†KON-GI, or KON-TENGI, コンギ, 渾儀, *n.* A celestial globe.

†KON-GI, コンギ, 婚儀, *n.* Marriage contract. — *wo tori-muszbu*, to contract a marriage.

†KON-GŌ, コンガウ, 金剛, *n.* Adamant, hard, invincible.

KON-GŌ-RIKI-SHI, コンガウリキ, 金剛力士, *n.* The monster idols, which guard the gates of Buddhist temples. Also called, *Ni-ō*, the two Kings.

KON-GŌ-SEKI, コンガウセキ, 金剛石, *n.* The diamond.

KON-GŌ-SHA, ゴンカウシヤ, 金剛沙, *n.* Diamond sand, or emery.

KONGŌTSZYE, コンガウツヱ, 金剛杖, *n.* A staff with metal rings on the top, carried by Buddhist priests.

KON-I, コンイ, 懇意, (*nengoro no kokoro.*) Intimate, familiar, friendly. — *no h'to*, a friend.

KONIDA, コニダ, 小荷駄, *n.* A pack-horse.

KŌ-NIN, コウニン, 降人, *n.* One who surrenders, and sides with the victorious party.

KON-IN, コンイン, 婚姻, *n.* A marriage, wedding. Syn. KON-REI.

†KON-JIKI, コンジキ, 金色, (*kogane no iro.*) Golden color. — *no hikari*, golden brightness.

KON-JŌ, コンジヤウ, 今生, (*ima no inochi.*) This life. — *no itomagoi wo szru*, to take leave of life, or of friends, when about to die.

KON-JŌ, コンジヤウ, 根性, *n.* Natural disposition, temper. Syn. KOKORODATE.

KON-KI, コンキ, 根氣, *n.* Natural vigor, nervous power, energy.

KON-KIU, コンキウ, 困窮, *n.* Poverty, want. Syn. BIMBŌ.

†KON-KIYŌ, コンケウ, 今曉, Early this morning, to-day's dawn.
Syn. KESA NO ASAKE.

†KON-KU, コンク, 困苦, *n.* Distress and hardship.

KONNA, コンナ, 此樣, (contr. of *Kono-yōna.*) This way, this manner, so, thus, such. *Konna koto wa nai*, there never was any thing like this. *Kono ko wa dōsh'te konna koto wo iu darō*, why does this child talk in this way? *Konna muszme*, such a daughter as this.

KON-NEN, コンネン, 今年, (*ima no toshi.*) This year. Syn. KO-TOSHI, TŌ-NEN.

KON-NICHI, コンニチ, 今日, To-day, this day. *He kon-nichi*, a salutation,=good day. Syn. KIYŌ, TŌ-JITSZ.

KON-NIYAKU, コンニヤク, 祸腐, *n.* A kind of edible root.

KONO, コノ, 此, (Comp. of *Ko*, this, and gen. part. *No.*) *n.* This. *Kono h'to*, this man. *Kono hon*, this book. *Yorokobi kono wiye wa nashi*, no greater joy than this.

KŌ-NŌ, コウノウ, 功能, *n.* Virtue, efficacy, power, (only of medicine.) *Kono kuszri wa kō-nō ga nai*, this medicine has no virtue. Syn. KIKIME.

KONO-AIDA, コノアイダ, 此間, *adv.* Lately, recently, within a few days past.
Syn. KONO-GORO, SEN-JITSZ, ITSZZŌYA, SENDATTE.

KONO-BUN, コノブン, 此分, *n.* This way, this manner, this condition. — *ni sh'te szmasz ka*, shall I let it stop here? or end in this manner? Syn. KONO-MAMA, KONO-NARI.

†KONO-CHI, コノチ, 此地, *n.* This place, or region.

KŌNŌ-GAKI, コウノウガキ, 功能書, *n.* A paper containing an account of the virtues of a medicine.

KONO-GO, コノゴ, 此後, *adv.* After this, hereafter, henceforth.
Syn. KONO-NOCHI.

KONO-GORO, コノゴロ, 此頃, *adv.* Lately, recently. Syn. KONO-AIDA.

KO-NO-HA, コノハ, 木葉, *n.* A leaf of a tree.

KONO-HEN, コノヘン, 此邊, *n.* This neighborhood.

KONO-HŌ, コノハウ, 此方, *n.* This side, this one; I, me. — *ga yoi*, this is the best.

KONO-HODO, コノホド, 此程, *adv.* Lately, recently.

KONO-HOKA, コノホカ, 此外, Besides this, excepting this, besides, moreover yet. — *ni mada aru ka*, have you any besides this?

†KONO-KAMI, コノカミ, 兄, *n.* Elder brother. Syn. ANI.

KONO-KATA, コノカタ, 此方, *adv.* From that time until now, since that time, since then, ever since. *Kai-biyaku* —, since the beginning of the world. *Ano h'to Yedo ye itte kara kono-kata wadzratte imasz*, he has been sick ever since he went to Yedo. Syn. IMA-MADE, I-RAI.

||KONOMASHII,-KI,-KU,-U, コノマシイ, 好敷, Agreeable, pleasant, desirable.

KONOME, コノメ, 木芽, *n.* Bud of a tree.

KONOMI, コノミ, 木實, *n.* Fruit of a tree.

KONOMI,*-mu,-nda*, コノム, 好, *t.v.* To like, be fond of, to relish, to be pleased with, to desire. *Mikan wo* —, like oranges. *Tabako wo konomanu*, do not like tobacco. *Yedo wo konomi-masen*, don't like Yedo. *Hon wo konomu*, fond of books. Syn. SZKU, NOZOMU, NEGAU.

KŌ-NO-MONO, カウノモノ, 香物, *n.* Radishes pickled in salt and bran, very offensive to the smell.

KONO-NOCHI, コノノチ, 以後, *(irai), adv.* Hereafter, henceforth, after this.
Syn. KONOGO.

KONO-OKATA, コノオカタ, 此御方, This man, this person, (polite).

KONORI, コノリ, 鷙, *n.* A small kind of hawk.

KONOSHIRO, コノシロ, 鰶, *n.* A kind of fish.

KONO-TABI, コノタビ, 此度, *adv.* This time, Syn. KONDO.

KONO-YUYE-NI, コノユヱニ, 此故, On this account, therefore. Syn. KORE-DE.

†KON-RAN, コンラン, 混亂, Confused, mixed, blended together in disorder.
Syn. MUCHA-MUCHA.

KON-REI, コンレイ, 婚禮, A wedding, marriage ceremonies. — *wo szru*, to celebrate a wedding. Syn. KON-IN.

KON-RIU,*-szru*, コンリフ, 建立, To build, erect. Syn. TATERU.

KON-RO, コンロ, 涼爐, *n.* An earthenware furnace.

†KON-SEI, コンセイ, 懇情, *(nengoro-na nasake).* Kindness, friendship, benevolence. Syn. SHIN-JITSZ, SHIN-SETSZ.

KON-SEKI, コンセキ, 今夕, This evening. Syn. KOMBAN.

†KON-SHI, コンシ, 懇志, (*nengoro naru kokorozashi*). Kindness, goodwill, benevolence. Syn. SHIN-SETSZ.

†KON-TŌ, コンタウ, 昏倒, Falling, from dizziness, or faintness.

†KON-TON, コントン, 渾沌, *n.* Chaos, the condition of the earth before it was reduced to form and order.

KONU, コヌ, 不來, (neg. of *Ki, kuru, kita*). Not come. *Mada konu*, not yet come. *Ano h'to konu maye ni yuki-nasare*, go before he comes.

KONUKA, コヌカ, 糠, *n.* Rice-bran.

KONUKA-AME, コヌカアメ, *n.* A fine, drizzling rain.

KON-YA, コンヤ, 今夜, To-night, this night.

KON-YA, コンヤ, 紺屋, *n.* A dye-house, dyer.

KON-ZATSZ, コンザツ, 混雜, *n.* Confusion, disorder; mixed, or jumbled together. — *szru.* Syn. TORI-KOMI.

KŌ-OTSZ, カフオツ, 甲乙, (*tari dari*). These and those persons, good or bad, superior or inferior. — *nashi*, they are all alike. — *wo tszkeru*, to say which is best.

KOPPA, コッパ, 木片, *n.* A chip of wood. *Koppayaro*, a block-head.

†KOPPAI, カッパイ, 項背, *n.* Back of the head, occiput.

†KOPPŌ, コッパフ, 骨法, (*hone gumi*) *n.* The frame of the body.

KOPPU, コップ, 酒鍾, (derived from the Dutch), *n.* A wine glass.

KŌRAI, カウライ, 高麗, *n.* Corea.

†KORAI, コライ, 古來, (*mukashi yori*). From ancient times.

†KŌ-RAI, コウライ, 後來, *adv.* Henceforth, in future, hereafter.

†KŌRAI, クワウライ, 光來, = *Oide nasaru;* your coming, used in letters only, as, *Go kōrai kudasare sōrayedomo o me ni kakaradz.*

KŌ-KAN, コウラン, 勾欄, *n.* A balustrade around the top of a building. Syn. RAN-KAN.

KORARE,*-ru,-ta*, ゴラレル, 被來, Poten. mood of *Ki, Kuru, Kita*, can come. Neg. *Korarenu*, cannot come. Neg. conj. *Koraredzmba*, if he cannot come. *Ash'ta korareruka*, can you come to-morrow?

KŌRASE,*-ru,-ta*, コホラセル, 令凝, (caust. of *Kōru.*) To cause to freeze. *Midz wo* —, to freeze water.

KORASHI,*-sz,-sh'ta*, コラス, 懲, *t. v.* To correct, punish, chastise, or reprove for one's good, to chasten. 凝, To give one's whole mind to, or concentrate one's powers on anything. *Aku wo* —, to punish wickedness. *Kokoro wo korash'te gakumon wo szru*, to concentrate one's mind on study. Syn. SEKKAN SZRU, SEMERU.

KORASHIME, コラシメ, 懲, *n.* Reproof, punishment, chastisement, correction. — *no tameni kandō wo szru*, to punish a son by disinheriting him. Syn. IMASHIME.

KORASHIME,*-ru,-ta*, コラシメル, 懲, *t.v.* To correct, reprove, to punish, chastise.

KORAYE,*-ru,-ta*, コラエル, 堪, *t. v.* To bear, endure, suffer patiently, to forbear. *Itami wo* —, to bear pain. *Ikari wo* —, to forbear anger. Syn. KAN-NIN SZRU, SHINOBU, SHIM-BŌ SZRU, GA-MAN SZRU.

KORAYE-KANE,*-ru,-ta*, コラエカネル, 堪兼, *t.v.* Impossible to bear, or hard to bear.

KORAYERARE,*-ru,-ta*, コラエラレル, Pass. or poten. mood of *Koraye.* Can bear. *Korayerarenu*, neg. cannot be borne.

KORE, コレ, 是, or 此, *pro.* This. *Korekara*, or *Koreyori*, after this, henceforth. *Kore giri*, this is all. *Kore nomi*, this only. *Kore hodo*, so much. *Kore bakari*, this only. *Kore ni yotte*, on this account. *Kore wa nani*, what is this?

KORE, コレ, Exclam. in vulg. coll. in ordering, or commanding an inferior, as, *Kore sa koko ye konai ka*, are you not coming here?

KORERA, コレラ, 此等, (plural of *Kore.*) These.

KORE-SHIKI, コレシキ, 此敷, This kind. — *no koto.* — *no h to.* Syn. KONO-KURAI.

KŌ-RI, カウリ, 高利, *n.* High rate of interest, usury. — *wo toru.*

KŌRI, カウリ, 箇, *n.* A bale, package, generally of 100 catties. *Ito h'to kōri*, one bale of silk.

KŌRI, コホリ, 氷, *n.* Ice. — *ga haru*, the ice forms, it freezes. — *ga tokeru*, the ice thaws.

KŌRI,*-ru,-tta*, コホル, 凍, *i.v.* To freeze, congeal. *Samusa nite midz ga kōtta*, it is so cold the water has frozen.

KŌRI, コホリ, 郡, *n.* The subdivision of a *Kuni*, a county.

KŌRI, カウリ, 行李, *n* A trunk, or box made of cane, used in travelling.

KŌRI, コホリ, 艙, *n.* The hold of a junk, where goods are stored.

KORI, コリ, 垢離, *n.* Dirt of the body, uncleanness. *Kori wo torite kami wo inoru*, having cleansed one's self to worship.

KORI,*-ru,-ta*, コリル, 懲, *i.v.* To be punished, corrected, reproved, chastised; to feel the painful, or troublesome effects of any course. *Korite sake wo yameru*, to feel the baneful effects of wine and to leave it off. *Yake-dzra hi ni koridz*, (prov.) a burnt face will not shun the fire.

KORI,*-ru,-tta*, コル, 凝, *i. v.* To freeze, congeal, crystalize; to be wholly given up to, abandoned to, engrossed in. *Midz ga* —, the water freezes. *Chi ga* —, blood congeals. *Baku-chi ni* —, abandoned to gambling. *Gaku-mon ni* —, engrossed in study. Syn KATAMARU.

KORI,*-ru,-tta*, コル, 樵, *i. v.* To cut timber. *Ki wo* —,

KORI-KATAMARI,*-ru,-tta*, コリカタマル, 凝固, *i.v.* To be engrossed in, absorbed, taken up with, wholly given up to.

KO-RIKŌ, コリコウ, 小利口, Handy, smart, clever. — *na h'to.* — *ni tachimawaru*, to move about at one's business briskly.

KORI-KORI,*-szru*, コリコリ, 懲懲, To leave off any thing from disgust, or experience of its hurtful effects. *Tabi-tabi son wo sh'te mō — sh'ta*, I have suffered loss so often, I shall have nothing more to do with it.

†KŌRIN, クワウリン, 光臨, See *K'wōrin*,

KŌ-RIYOKU, カフリヨク, 合力, *n.* Benefactions, charitable donations, contributions, help, assistance to the poor. — *wo szru*, to make charitable donations. — *ni adzkaru*, to receive &c. *Go — wo tanomimasz*, I ask your assistance.
Syn. MEGUMI, TASZKE, JOSEI.

KŌRIZATO, コホリザタウ, 冰糖, *n.* Crystalized sugar, rock-candy.

†KORŌ, コラウ, 古老, *n.* An old man, or woman. Syn. RŌJIN.

KORO, コロ, 頃, *n.* Time, period of time. — *wa iku nen ato*, how many years since? *Nandokigoro*, what o'clock? *Itszgoro*, when? Syn. TOKI, JIBUN, AIDA.

KŌ-RO, カウロ, 香爐, *n.* A censer, for burning incense.

†KŌ-RŌ, カウロウ, 高樓, *n (Taka nikai).* The second or third story of a house.
Syn. TAKADONO.

KOROBASHI,*-sz,-sh'ta*, コロバス, 轉, *t. v.* To roll. *Ishi wo* —, to roll a stone.
Syn. MAROBASZ.

KOROBI,*-bu,-nda*, コロブ, 轉, *i. v.* To roll, to fall and roll over. *Mari ga* —, the ball rolls.
Syn. MAROBU.

KOROGARI,*-ru,-tta*, コロガル, 轉, *i.v.* To roll about.

KOROGASHI,*-sz,-sh'ta*, コロガス, Same as *Korobashi.*

KORO-KORO-TO, コロコロト, *adv.* The sound, or appearance of any thing rolling. — *korobu.*

†KŌ-ROKU, カウロク, 高祿, *n.* High salary. — *wo toru*, to receive high wages.

KOROMO, コロモ, 衣, *n.* The outside robe worn by Buddhist priests.

KOROMO-GAYE, コロモガヘ, 更衣, *n.* Changing the clothes, from the wadded clothes of winter, to the lighter clothes of summer, on the 2nd day of the 4th month. —*wo szru*, to change the clothes.

KŌRON, コウロン, 口論 *n.* Quarrel, angry contention, brawl, dispute. —*wo szru*, to quarrel, wrangle, squabble.
Syn. ARASOI, Ī-AU, ISAKAI.

KORO-OI, コロホヒ, 頃, *n.* Time, period of time. *Itsz no* —, at what time? *Mō kayeru — da*, it is time to return.
Syn. JIBUN.

KORORI, コロリ, *n.* Asiatic cholera. This word is the Japanese pronunciation of cholera.

KORORI-TO, コロリ, *adv.* In a rolling manner, or sound; suddenly. — *shinuru*, to die suddenly.

KOROSHI,*-sz,-sh'ta*, コロス, 殺, *t. v.* To kill, slay, murder; com. coll. = to die. *H'to wo* —, to kill a man. *Koroshitaku nai monda*, I should be sorry to have him die. Syn. GAI-SZRU, SHI-SZRU.

KOROTSZKI,*-ku,-ita*, コロツク, 轉付, *i.v.* To roll about.

KŌRU, コホル, 冰, See *Kōri.*

KOSA, コサ, 濃, *n.* The thickness, consistence.

KŌ-SAI, コウサイ, 後妻, *(nochi no tszma). n.* Second wife, (the first being dead.)

‖KOSAI-NI, コサイニ, 巨細, *adv.* Minutely, particularly. — *iu*, to tell particularly.
Syn. KOMAYAKANI, KUWASHIKU, TSZBUSA-NI.

KŌSAKU, カウサク, 耕作, *(tagayeshi tszkuru.)* Cultivation of the land, farming. — *szru.*

KO-SAN, コサン, 古參, *(furuku mairu.) n.* Oldest come, longest come, as. *Ko-san no deshi*, a pupil who has been in the school the longest,

KŌ-SAN, コウサン, 降參, *(kudari mairu.)* Submission, surrender, capitulation. — *szru*, to surrender, capitulate. — *wo kō*, to offer to surrender.

KOSAME, コサメ, 小雨, *n.* A shower.

KŌ-SATSZ, カウサツ, 高札, *n.* The board containing the Imperial edicts, hung up under a shed for public instruction.

‖KOSEBITSZ, or KOSEGASA, コセビツ, *n.* An eruption on the skin.

KŌ-SEI, カウセイ, 行星, *n.* A planet.

KŌ-SEI, コウセイ, 後世, *(nochi no yo,) n.* Future generations, future times. Syn. MATSZ-DAI.

†KŌ-SEI, カウセイ, 厚情, *(atszi nasake.)* Great kindness. *Go — no dan katajikenaku zonji soro.*

†KŌ-SEKI, カウセキ, 講席, *n.* A hall where stories are told, or discourses delivered; an auditory.

KO-SEKI, コセキ, 古跡, *n.* Ruins, or remains of ancient places.

KOSE-KOSE, コセコセ, *adv.* Busy, and active in small matters. *Yoku — hataraku h'to da.*

KŌ-SEN, コウセン, 口錢, *n.* Commission for selling goods, percentage. *— wo toru,* to charge percentage.

†KŌ-SEN, クワウセン, 光線, *n.* The light. Syn. AKARI.

KŌ-SEN, カウセン, 香煎, *n.* An infusion of *Shiso* and parched rice, used instead of tea.

KŌ-SEN, クワウセン, 黄泉, see *K'wōsen.*

KOSETSZKI,*-ku,-ita,* コセツク, *i. v.* To be busy, and active in trifling matters.

†KO-SHA, コシヤ, 瞽者, *n.* A blind person. Syn. MEKURA.

KŌ-SHA, カウシヤ, 巧者, *n.* An ingenious person.

KOSHAKU-NA, コシヤクナ, *a.* Having a smattering of knowledge, pedantic. Syn. CHOKOSAI-NA, NAMAIKI.

KŌ-SHAKU, コウシヤク, 講譯, *n.* Exposition, discourse, lecture, disquisition, sermon. *— szru,* to lecture, discourse.

KŌSHAKU-SHI, コウシヤクシ, 講譯師, *n.* A public story-teller, or lecturer on ancient history.

†KŌ-SHI, コウシ, 公私, Public and private. *— no oime,* public and private debts.

KŌ-SHI, カウシ, 講師, *n.* One who lectures, or delivers an exposition on the Buddhist sacred books.

KŌSHI, コウシ, 孔子, *n.* Confucius.

KŌSHI, カウシ, 格子, *n.* Lattice work. *— mado,* a latticed window. *— do,* a door made of latticed bars. *Ko-gōshi,* fine lattice work. *Ara-gōshi,* coarse lattice work.

KOSHI, コシ, 柩, *n.* A coffin. Syn. K'WAN, HITSZJI, HAYA-OKE.

KOSHI, コシ, 輿, *n.* A sedan chair, only used by the Mikado, or Kuge; also, the chair, or shrine in which the Kami are carried at festivals.

KOSHI, コシ, 濃, *a.* Thick in consistence, see *Koi.*

KOSHI, コシ, 腰, *n.* The loins. *— no kakanda baba,* an old woman bent with age. *— wo nosz,* to straighten one's self, stand erect.

KOSHI,*-sz,-sh'ta,* コス, 越, *t. v.* To cross over. *Yama, kawa, hashi nado wo kosz,* to cross a mountain, river, or bridge. Syn. KOYERU, WATARU.

KOSHI,*-sz,-sh'ta,* コス, 漉, *t. v.* To strain, to filter. *Szna koshi midz,* water filtered through sand. *Midz wo —,* to filter water. *Momen de —,* to strain through muslin.

KOSHI-ATE, コシアテ, 腰當, *n.* A kind of shield over the loins, to protect it from the quiver.

KOSHI-BARI, コシバリ, 腰張, *n.* Wall paper, spread on a wall some two feet high from the floor, to protect the clothes from the plaster.

KOSHI-BIYŌBU, コシビヤウブ, 腰屏風, *n.* A low kind of screen.

KOSHI-BONE, コシボ子, 腰骨, *n.* The os sacrum.

KOSHI-BOSO, コシボソ, 細腰蜂, *n.* A kind of wasp.

KOSHI-ITA, コシイタ, 腰板, *n.* The board worn in the back of the Hakama, to make them stick out.

KOSHI-IRE, コシイレ, 輿入, *n.* The putting the bride into the norimon to convey her to the house of her husband.

KOSHI-KAKI, コシカキ, 輿舁, *n.* The bearers of the *Koshi.*

KOSHI-KAKE, コシカケ, 腰掛, *n.* A raised seat, a chair.

KOSHI-KATA, コシカタ, 來方, *n.* The past, the time past of one's life. *— yukuszye no kotodomo mono-gatari tsztsz,* while talking over the past and the future. Syn. IZEN, K'WA-KO.

KOSHIKE, コシケ, 帶下, *n.* Fluor-albus.

KOSHIKI, コシキ, 甑, A vessel for steaming food in; (轂,) the hub of a wheel.

KOSHI-MAKI, コシマキ, 腰纒, *n.* A kind of petticoat, or shirt worn by women.

KOSHI-MINO, コシミノ, 腰簑, *n.* A kind of covering made of straw, tied around the waist, to protect the hips and thighs from rain, worn by fishermen.

KOSHI-MOTO, コシモト, 侍女, *n.* A maidservant, a chamber-maid.

KOSHINO-MONO, コシノモノ, 腰物, *n.* The sword.

KOSHI-NUKE, コシヌケ, 腰抜, *n.* A cripple; a coward. — *bushi,* a cowardly soldier.

KOSHIORE, コシオレ, 蜂腰, *n.* Poetry defective in melody. — *uta.*

KOSHIRAYE,-*ru*,-*ta*, コシラヘル, 拵, *t.v.* To make, to form, fashion, prepare, make ready. *Iye wo* —, to build a house. *Fude wo* —, to make a pen. *Kane wo* —, to make money. *Go-chisō wo* —, to make a feast. *Uma wo* —, to make ready a horse, (to saddle or harness.) *Kimono wo* —, to make clothes. *Nai koto wo koshirayete hanasz,* to tell a story which one has made up of himself. Syn. TSZKURU, SEISZRU.

KOSHIRAYE-GOTO, コシラヘゴト, 拵事, *n.* A fiction, a made-up story.

KOSHI-SAGE, コシサゲ, 腰提, *n.* Articles worn suspended from the belt.

†KOSHITSZ, コシツ, 痼疾, *n.* An inveterate, or chronic disease.

KŌ-SHITSZ, コウシツ, 後室, *n.* The second wife, (the first being dead,) only used of nobles.

KOSHU, コシユ, 古酒, *(furui sake)* *n.* Old *sake.*

KOSHŪ コセウ, 胡椒, *n.* Black pepper.

KOSHŌ, コシヤウ, 故障, *n.* Objection; adverse reason, or circumstances; hindrance, impediment, (legal). — *wo iu,* to object. — *ga aru,* there are objections. Syn. SAWARI, JAMA.

KO-SHŌ, コシヤウ, 小性, *n.* A boy servant who waits upon a noble, or the head priest of a Buddhist temple; a page.

KŌ-SHO, コウシヨ, 口書, *n.* A written confession, a deposition, written declaration. — *ni tszme-in wo szru,* to seal a deposition with the mark of the nail. — *wo toru,* to take down a confession.

†KŌ-SHŌ, コウシヤウ, 工匠, *(daiku.)* *n.* A carpenter.

†KŌ-SHŌ, コウシヤウ, 工商, *n.* Mechanic and merchant.

KŌSHOKU, カウシヨク, 好色, *(iro wo konomu.)* Lewd, lecherous, lascivious. —*na h'to.*

†KŌSO, コウソ, 公訴, A complaint made to an official. Syn. UTTAYERU.

†KŌSO, カウソ, 高祖, *n.* The founder of a family, or sect.

KOSO, コソ, 古曾, (1). A particle which serves to particularize, or give emphasis to the word, or phrase preceeding, as, *Watakushi yori mo anata koso jōdz da,* you (especially) are more skilful than me. *Kono yuye ni koso kunshi wa moto wo tsztomuru mono nare,* it is for this reason (especially) that the good man attends to the fundamental duties. (2). With an imperative, as a particle of desire, or wishing; = O that! I wish that! let me! *Ware ni tszge koso,* O that! he would tell me. *Sakurano hana wa chiradz are koso,* I wish that the cherry blossoms would never fall.

‖KOSOBAI, コソバイ, 酸澁, (a contr. of *Kosobayui.*) The sensation of tickling. *Karada ga* —, the body tickles.

KOSOBAIGARI,-*ru*, コソバイガル, 酸澁, To be ticklish. *Te wo saye daseba kosobaigaru,* he feels ticklish if even a finger is pointed at him.

‖KOSOBAISA, コソバイサ, *n.* Ticklishness.

†KOSOBAYUI,-KI,-KU,-SHI,-Ū, コソバユイ, 酸澁, Having the sensation of tickling. Syn. KUSZGUTTAI.

KOSODE, コソデ, 小袖, *n.* The short sleeved coat usually worn by the Japanese.

KOSOGE,-*ru*,-*ta*, コソゲル, 刮去, *t.v.* To scrape. *Kutsz no doro wo kosoge-otosz,* to scrape the mud off the shoes. *Urushi wo kosogeru,* to scrape the lacquer off of any thing.

KOSOGURI,-*ru*,-*tta*, コソグル, 格指, *t.v.* To tickle. *H'to wo* —,

KOSO-KOSO, コソコソ, *adv.* Secretly, clandestinely, stealthily. — *to hanasz,* to talk secretly. — *to nigeru,* to run away clandestinely. Syn. NAI-NAI, HISOKA-NI.

†KOSOKU, コソク, 姑息, Temporizing, procrastinating, easy and complying. — *no hakarigoto,* a temporary scheme. Syn. YEN-NIN, GUDZ-GUDZ.

KOSSORI-TO, コツソリ, *adv.* Secretly, clandestinely, stealthily.

KOSZ, コス, 小簾, *n.* A hanging shade, or screen made of bamboo.

KOSZ, コス, See *Koshi.*

KOSZI, コスイ, 湖水, *n.* A lake. Syn. MIDZUMI.

KOSZRI,-*ru*,-*tta*, コスル, 擦, *t.v.* To rub, to use friction to any thing. *Me wo* —, to rub the eyes. Syn. SZRU.

KOSZRI-KOMI,-*mu*,-*nda*, コスリコム, 擦入, *t.v.* To rub into. *Kuszri wo kawa ni,* —, to rub medicine into the skin.

KOSZRI-OTOSHI,-*sz*,-*sh'ta*, コスリオトス, 擦落, *t.v.* To rub out. *Ji wo* —, to rub out a word.

KOSZRI-TSZKE,-*ru*,-*ta*, コスリツケル, 擦付, *t.v.* To rub on.

KOTACHI, コタチ, 兒等, *n.* Children, same as, *Kodomo-ra, Kodomotachi.*

KŌ-TAI, カウタイ, 交代, Alternation, to do by turns. — *szru,* to do by turns, alternate. *Daimiyō ga Yedo ye — szru,* the Daimios reside in Yedo alternately. Syn. KAWARI-GAWARI.

KŌ-TAKE, カウタケ, 香菌, *n.* A kind of fragrant mushroom.

†KO-TAKU, コタク, 古宅, *(furui iye).* Old house.

†KŌ-TAN, コウタン, 降誕, *n.* Born, birth. *Shaka Niyorai shi gatsz yōka ni — arasetamō,* Shaka was born on the 8th day of the 4th month. — *no hi,* birth day.

KOTATSZ, コタツ, 火閣, A hearth or fireplace.

KOTAYE,*–ru,–ta,* コタヘル, 答, *t.v.* To answer, to reply, to respond; fig. 徹, to feel, to penetrate, or reach to, (as pain). 耐, to suffer, endure, bear. *Kotayete iwaku,* replying said. *Tōi ni kotayeru,* reply to a question. *Hone mi ni —,* to feel in the flesh and bones, (as pain, shame, cold). *Itami ga kotayerarenu,* the pain cannot be endured.
Syn. HENJI SZRU, TESSZRU, KORAYERU.

KOTE, コテ, 小手, *n.* Defensive armor for the arm and hand; a bracelet.

KOTE, コテ, 鏝, *n.* A trowel.

†KŌ-TEI, カウテイ, 行程, *(michi-nori). n.* The road, way, length of the way.

KOTE-ITA, コテイタ, 鏝板, *n.* A paddle used by masons, and plasterers,

KOTE-KOTE, コテコテ, *adv.* Much, abundantly, a good deal. *Meshi wo — moru,* to heap up the rice in the bowl.
Syn. TAPPURI, TANTO, DONTO.

KŌ-TŌ, コウトウ, Plain, simple, void of ornament, not showy, artless. — *na umaretszki,* an artless person.
Syn. JIMI, SHITSZBOKU.

KŌ-TŌ, コウタウ, 勾當, Anciently an official title, now the name of the second rank of the blind.

KOTO, コト, 琴, *n.* A harp. — *no o,* the strings of a harp. — *no tszme,* the ivory finger shield used in playing the harp. — *no ji,* the bridge over which the strings pass. — *wo hiku,* to play a harp.

KOTO, コト, 事, 言, *n.* Affair, event, transaction, occurence, fact, business, concern, circumstance, accident, thing, matters, word. *Koto to mo sedz,* made nothing of it, did not mind. — *ga okoru,* trouble will come of it. *Koto mo nai yōsz,* unconcerned manner, making light of it. *Koto mo nage naru tei,* (idem). *Koto no ha,* word, language. *Koto ga kakeru,* lacking in something necessary, troubled for lack of something. *Koto ni yoru,* according to circumstances, complyng with the occasion.

KOTO, コト, 異, Different, changed. *Tszne no idokoro wo koto ni szru,* to change his usual place of sitting, *Koto-gokoro wo idaku,* to have a treacherous heart.

KOTOBA, コトバ, 言, *n.* A word, language, speech. — *wo kawasz,* to make a verbal promise, or mutual agreement. *Nippon no* — the Japanese language.

KOTOBA-DZKAI, コトバヅカヒ, 言遣, *n.* Use of words, way of talking, manner of pronouncing. — *ga yoi h'to,* one who uses good language.

KOTOBA-JICHI, コトバジチ, 言質, *n.* A promise, the pledge of one's word, or veracity. — *wo toru,* to take a promise.

KOTOBA-UTSZSHI NI, コトバウツシ, 言寫, *adv.* Word for word, verbatim. — *szru,* to tell, or report word for word.

KOTOBUKI, コトブキ, 祝壽, *n.* Complimentary language, a toast in honor or in praise. — *wo nasz,* to wish well to any one.

KOTODZKARI,*–ru,–tta,* コトヅカル, 傳言, *i.v.* To be entrusted with a message, or commission to another.

KOTODZKE, コトヅケ, or, KOTODZTE, コトヅテ, 傳言, *n.* A verbal message. — *wo yaru,* to deliver a message. — *wo tanomu,* to request one to take a message.

KOTODZKE,*–ru,–ta,* コトヅケル, 囑托, *t.v.* To deliver a message, or entrust anything to be conveyed to another. *Tegami wo kotodzkete Yedo ye yaru,* to send a letter to *Yedo* by another.

KOTO-FURE, コトフレ, 託者, *n.* A strolling foreteller of the weather, crops, sickness, &c.

KOTO-GARA, コトガラ, 事柄, *n.* Kind, or nature of affair; as, — *mo wakimayedz,* does not discriminate different cases. — *ni yotte,* according to the merits of the case.

KOTO-GOTOKU, コトゴトク, 盡, *adv.* All, every one. Syn. MINA, NOKORADZ, SZBETE.

KOTO-GOTO-NI, コトゴトニ, 毎事, *adv.* Everything, everymatter or circumstance. *Kōshi tai-biyō ni irite — tō,* when Confucius entered the great temple he inquired about everything.

KOTO-GOTOSHII,*–KI,–KU,* コトゴトシイ, 事事, Making much of an affair, exaggerating. — *mōshitateru*, to give an exaggerated report of a matter.

†KOTOI, コトイ, 犢, *n.* A bull.

KOTOKAGI,*–gu,–ta*, コトカグ, 事缺, *t. v.* Embarrassed for the want, or lack of something. *Kodzkai ambai warukute koto kagu*, I am embarrassed y the sickness of my servant.

KOTO-KAWARI,*–ru,–tta*, コトカハル, 事換, *i.v.* To differ, to be dissimilar, distinct, unlike. *Ima wa mukashi ni* —, the present is unlike former times.

KOTO-KIRE,*–ru,–ta*, コトキレル, 事切, *i.v.* To die.

KOTO-KOMAYAKA-NI, コトコマヤカニ, 仔細, *adv.* Minutely, particularly.

KOTONARI,*–ru*, コトナル, 異, *i.v.* To be different, unlike, unusual. *Tszne ni* —, extraordinary, unlike what is common. Syn. CHIGAU, TAGAU.

KOTO-NI, コトニ, 殊, *adv.* Especially, particularly. Syn. BESSH'TE, KAKUBETSZ-NI.

KOTO-NO-HOKA, コトノホカ, 殊外, *adv.* Unusually, extraordinarily, uncommonly, different from what was anticipated. — *samuku natta.*

†KOTO-OSOI, コトオソイ, 訥, Slow of speech, stammering.

KO-TORI, コトリ, 小鳥, *n.* A small bird.

KOTOSARA-NI, コトサラ, 殊更, *ada.* Purposely, intentionally. Syn. WAZA-TO, TOBOKETE.

KOTO-SHI, コトシ, 琴工, *n.* Harp-maker.

KO-TOSHI, コトシ, 今年, *(konnen.) n.* This year.

†KOTOSHIGEKI,*–KU*, コトシゲク, 事繁, Busy, hurried with business Syn. ISOGASHII, SEWASHII.

KOTOTARI,*–ru*, コトタル, 事足, To answer the purpose, will do, to be content, satisfied. *Sofuku naredomo kototaru beshi*, although the clothes are coarse I am content. *Hin-kiu naredomo koto-taru nari*, I am poor, but contented with my lot.

KOTOWARI,*–ru,–tta*, コトワル, 斷, *i. v.* To refuse, decline; to state, mention. *Kane wo kasz kato wo kotowaru*, refused to lend money. *Mayemotte kotowatte oku*, to mention before hand. *Kotowari nashi ni uchi ye hairu koto wa naranu*, entering the house without asking (or without permission) is forbidden. *O kotowari mōsz*, I will decline, or please excuse me.

KOTOWARI, コトワリ, 理, *n.* Reason, principal, cause, nature, excuse, plea. — *wo iu*, to plead an excuse. Syn. DŌ-RI, SZJI-MICHI.

KOTOWAZA, コトワザ, 俚諺, *n.* An adage, common-saying, proverb.

KOTOYOSE,*–ru,–ta*, コトヨセル, 事寄, To make a pretext of, to pretend, to do as an excuse. *Shu-yen ni kotoyosete h'to wo korosz*, under the pretext of making a wine party to plan the murder of a man. Syn. KAKOTSZKERU, DASHI NI TSZKAU.

†KOTSZ, コツ, 骨, *(Hone,) n.* Bone.

KO-TSZBO, コツボ, 子宮, *n.* The womb. Syn. SHI-KIU.

KOTSZ-DZI, コツズ井, 骨髓, *n.* The marrow. — *ni tesszru*, to pierce to the very marrow

KO-TSZ-DSZMI, コツツミ, 小鼓, *n.* A small kind of drum.

†KOTSZGAI, コツガイ, 乞丐, *n.* A beggar. Syn. KOJIKI.

KOTSZ-GARA, コツガラ, 骨柄, *n.* The bony condition, or frame, figure, or make of body. — *no yoi h'to*, a finely formed person, of fine figure. Syn. HONE-GUMI.

KOTSZJIKI, コツジキ, 乞食, *n.* A beggar, pronounced in com. coll. *Kojiki.*

KOTSZ-NIKU, コツニク, 骨肉, *n.* (Flesh and bones,) only fig. for relation, kindred. — *no aidagara*, (idem.) — *yori mo shitashi*, to love another more than one's relations.

†KOTSZ-RIU, コツリウ, 骨瘤, *n*, A bony tumor.

†KOTSZ-ZEN-TO, コツゼント, 忽然, *adv.* Suddenly. Syn. TACHI-MACHI.

KOTTA, コツタ, pret. of *Kori.*

KO-URI, コウリ, 小賣, *n.* A retail-merchant.

KO-USHI, コウシ, 小牛, *n.* A calf.

KO-UTA, コウタ, 小歌, *n.* A sonnet, ditty.

KOWA, コハ, 是, (contr. of *Kore wa.*) This; also an exclamation of surprise, as, *Kowa! ikani sh'te yokaran*, O! what shall we do.

KOWABARI,,*–ru,–tta*, コハバル, 勁直, *i. v.* To be hard and stiff. *Kimono ga nori de kowabaru*, the clothes are stiffened with starch. *Shigai ga* —, the corpse is stiff. Syn. KATAKU NARU.

KOWADAKA, コワダカ, 高聲, *n.* Loud voice. — *ni mono wo iu*, to speak with a loud voice.

KOWADZKURI, or KOWADZKUROI, コワヅクリ, 欬, *n.* Clearing the throat, to hem. — *wo szru*, to hem, to clear the throat. Syn. SEKI-BARAI, SHIWABUKI.

KOWAGARI,*–ru,–tta*, コハガル, 怖畏, *i.v.* To be timid, afraid, to be frightened.

Kowagaru na, don't be afraid. Syn. OSORERU.

KOWAGOWA, コハゴハ, 慄慄, Fearful, afraid, dreadful. — *wataru marukibashi,* what a fearful crossing, is a bridge of one round log. Syn. BIKU-BIKU SZRU.

KOWAI,-KI,-KU,-SHI, コハイ, 恐怖, Fearful, afraid, dreadful, dangerous, alarming. *Kowaku nai,* not afraid. *Kowai h'to,* a fearful looking person. *Kowa ya,* be careful, (in case of danger), or, how dreadful!

KOWAI,-KI,-KU,-SHI, コハイ 强, Stiff, hard, rigid, unyielding. *Kowakute kuwarenu,* so hard it cannot be chewed. *Fude no ke ga kowai,* the hairs of the pencil are stiff. Syn. KATAI.

KOWAIRO, コワイロ, 聲色, *n.* The tone of voice. — *wo tszkau,* to imitate the voices of different persons, (as in theatres).

KOWAKU, コハク, *adv.* See *Kowai.*

KOWAMESHI, コハメシ, 强飯, *n.* A kind of food made of rice and beans.

KOWANE, コワ子, 聲音, *n.* The tone of voice.

KO-WARABE, or KOWARAMBE, コワラベ, 小童, *n.* A little boy.

KOWARE,*-ru,-ta,* コワレル, 破, *i. v.* To break, (as of hard, compact substances). *Koware-yaszi,* easily broken. *Koware-gatai,* hard to break. *Fune ga kowareta,* the ship is wrecked. *Iye ga* —, the house is dilapidated. *Bīdoro ga* —, the glass is broken. *Kuchi ga* —, the mouth is sore. Syn. YABURERU, KUDAKERU.

KOWARI,*-ru,-tta,* コハル, 硬, *t.v.* Hard, and painful, (only of the abdomen.) *Kowari-hara.*

KOWASA, コハサ, 强, *n.* Stiffness hardness, rigidity; (恐), fearfulness, dreadfulness. See *Kowai.*

KOWASARE,*-ru,-ta,* コワサレル, 被破, Pass. of *Kowasz.* to get broken.

KOWASHI,*-sz,-sh'ta,* コワス, 壞, *t.v.* To break, crush, dash in pieces, destroy. *Ishi wo* —, to break a stone. *Iye wo* —, to tear down a house. *Kowash'te wa warui,* you must not break it. *Shinsho wo* —, to destroy one's property.

KOWASHI, コハシ, *a.* See *Kowai.*

KOWŌ, コハウ, Same as *Kowaku.*

KŌ-YA, コウヤ, 紺屋, *n.* A dye-house, dyer. Syn. KONYA.

KOYA, コヤ, 小屋, *n.* A small house, hut, pen. *Kojikigoya,* a beggar's hut. — *no mono,* a beggar. *Butagoya,* a pigsty.

KO-YAKAMASHII,-KI,-KU, コヤカマシイ, 小喧, Noisy, making a disturbance, fault finding, captious.

KŌ-YAKU, カウヤク, 膏藥, *n.* A medical plaster, ointment, cerate. — *wo noberu,* to spread a plaster. — *wo haru,* to apply a plaster.

KOYASHI, コヤシ, 糞, *n.* Manure. — *wo kakeru,* to manure. Syn. KOYE.

KOYASHI,*-sz,-sh'ta,* コヤス, 糞, *t.v.* To fertilize, to enrich, to manure. *Tszchi wo* —, to manure the ground.

KOYASHI-TSZBO, コヤシツボ, 糞壺, *n.* A large jar used for holding manure.

KOYASZ-GAI, コヤスガヒ, 子安貝, *n.* A species of cowry.

KOYATSZ, コヤツ, 這奴, (Contr. of *Kono yatsz.*) A vulgar epithet, same as *Koitsz.*

KOYE, コヱ, 聲, *n.* The voice. *Takai koye,* a loud voice. *Ōki-na* —, (idem). *Hikui* —, a low voice, *Chīsai* —, (idem). — *ga kareru,* voice is hoarse. — *wo ageru,* to cry out. — *wo hasszru,* to utter a sound. *Toki no* — *wo ageru,* to give a shout (of many persons at once). — *ga kawatta,* voice has changed, (as at puberty). — *wo kakeru,* to call out.

KOYE, コエ, 糞, *n.* Manure, (same as *Koyashi).* — *wo ireru,* or — *wo kakeru* to manure.

KOYE,*-ru,-ta,* コエル, 肥, *i.v.* To grow fat, plump, or fleshy; to be fertile, rich, productive. *Ushi ga koyeru,* the ox is fat *Koyeta h'to,* a corpulent man. *Ta hatake ga koyeru,* to fields are fertile. Syn. FUTORU.

KOYE,*-ru,-ta,* コエル, 越, *t.v.* To cross, pass over, to excel, surpass; to trangress. *Umi yama wo* —, to cross over seas and mountains. *Gei nō h'to ni koyetari,* excelling others in polite accomplishments and talents. *Hatto wo koyeru,* to transgress the laws. *Toshi wo* —, to pass the year. *Midz ga hiza wo* —, the water was above his knees.

KOYEDA, コエダ, 小枝, *n.* A twig, small branch, shoot.

KOYE-FUTORI,*-ru,-tta,* コエフトル, 肥太, *i.v.* To grow fat and large.

KŌYEKI, カウエキ, 交易, *n.* Barter, exchange of commodities.

†KŌ-YEN, コウエン, 後園, *n.* A back garden.

KŌ-YŌ, コウヨウ, 公用, *n.* Public service, public business. Syn. GO-YŌ.

†KŌ-YŌ, コウエフ, 紅葉, *(momijiba) n.* The change of the leaf in autumn to red. *Kō-yō sh'ta,* the leaves have changed to red.

Koyoi, コヨヒ, 今宵, *adv.* This evening. Syn. kom-ban.

Koyomi, コヨミ, 暦, *n.* Almanac, calendar, — *hakase*, almanac maker.

†Koyonaki, コヨナキ, 無此上, (contr. of, *Kono wiye naki*). Lit. nothing above this, = highest, greatest. — *sai-wai*, greatest good fortune.

Koyori, コヨリ, 紙撚, *n.* A string made of twisted paper. — *wo yoru*, to make a string.

Ko-yubi, コユビ, 小指, *n.* The little finger.

Koyumaki, コユマキ, 裩褡, *n.* An under garment worn by women from the waist to the knee.

Koyuru, コユル, See *Koye.*

Kō-za, カウザ, 高座, *n.* A rostrum, or high platform from which speakers address an audience, a pulpit.

Kozakashii,-ki,-ku, コザカシイ, 黠智, Having a shallow smartness, or low cunning; adroit.

†Ko-zen-to, コウゼン, 公然, *adv.* Publicly, openly. Syn. omotemuki.

Kō-zo, カウゾ, 楮, *n.* The paper mulberry. Syn. kaji.

†Kozo, コゾ, 去年, *(kiyo nen).* Last year.

Ko-zō, コザウ, 小僧, *n.* A young Buddhist priest, a small servant boy.

Kozō-kozō, コザウコザウ, Exclam. the sound made in calling a dog, or cat.

Kozori-atszmari,*-ru,-tta*, コゾリアツマル, 舉集, *i.v.* To be assembled together.

Kozotte, コゾツテ, 舉, *adv.* Including every one. *Fune wo — odoroku*, all in the ship were alarmed. *Yo wo — mina nigoreri ware h'tori szmeri*, the whole world is unclean, I alone am pure.

Ku, ク, 九, Nine. Syn. kokonotsz.

†Ku, ク, 句, *n.* A verse, or stanza of poetry; a sentence. — *wo yomu*, to compose a verse of poetry. *Ikku*, one sentence.

Ku, ク, 苦, *n.* Trouble, pain, labor, hard work, toil, solicitude, anxiety, uneasiness of mind. *Ku ni yamu*, to be sick with anxiety. — *wo sh'te nochi wo raku ni kurase-yo*, by taking pains at first afterwards all will be easy. Syn. shimpai, kurushimi.

Kū, クフ, 吃, To eat. See *Kui.*

Kū, クウ, 空, *n.* Empty space, the air, the sky. — *ni agaru*, to rise into the air.

Kubari,*-ru,-tta*, クバル, 配, *t. v.* To distribute, to deal out, divide. *Kinjo ye mochi wo —*, to distribute rice-cakes amongst the neighbors. *Sōbadzke wo —*, to distribute price-currents. *Kokoro wo —*, to distract the mind with many cares. *Ji-kubari*, the order, or arrangement of characters. Syn. wakeru, wari-tszkeru.

Kubari,*-ru,-tta*, クバル, 爇, *i. v.* To fall into the fire. *Kodomo ga hi ni kubatte shinda*, the child died by falling into the fire.

Kube,*-ru,-ta*, クベル, 爇, *t.v.* To put into the fire. *Maki wo hi ni kuberu*, to put wood on the fire.

Kubi, クビ, 首, *n.* The neck, the head. — *no hone*, the cervical vertebra. — *wo kiru*, to behead, decapitate. — *wo haneru*, or *kubi wo utsz*. (idem). — *wo sarasz*, to expose the head of a criminal after execution. — *ni kukeru*, to hang around the neck.

Kubi-biki, クビビキ, 首引, *n.* Trying the strength of the neck, by two persons putting their necks through a loop in a rope, and pulling in opposite directions; (fig.) to bid against each other in buying.

Kubi-dai, クビダイ, 首代, *n.* Money paid as commutation for one's life.

Kubi-gase, クビガセ, 枷, *n.* The cangue.

Kubiki, クビキ, 首木, *n.* A yoke.

Kubikiri,*-ru,-tta*, クビキル, 斬首, *t. v.* To cut off the head, to behead, decapitate. *Tszmibito wo kubikiru*, to behead a criminal.

Kubi-kukuri,*-ru,-tta*, クビククル, 縊, *i.v.* To hang one's self. *Kubi wo kukutte shinuru*, to die by hanging one's self. Syn. kubireru.

Kubi-maki, クビマキ, 領巻, *n.* A cravat, tippet.

Kubire,*-ru,-ta*, クビレル, 縊, *i. v.* To hang one's self. *Kubirete shinuru. Midzkara kubireru.*

Kubire-jini, クビレジニ, 縊死, *n.* Suicide by hanging.

Kubiri,*-ru,-tta* クビル, 縊, *t.v.* To choke, strangle. *H'to wo kubitte korosz*, to kill a person by strangling.

Kubiri-koroshi,*-sz,-sh'ta*, クビリコロス, 縊殺, *t.v.* To strangle, to kill by strangling.

Kubisz, クビス, 踵, *n.* The heel. — *wo megurasz bekaradz*, in less time than one could turn on his heel. Syn. kakato, kibisz.

Kubi-szji, クビスヂ, 首筋, *n.* The muscles on the back of the neck.

Kubi-tama, クビタマ, 首環, *n.* A collar for the neck. *Inu ni — wo kakeru*, to put a collar on a dog.

Kubō, クバウ, 公方, *n.* The highest executive officer in Japan; he now resides at

Yedo, and is erroneously called by foreigners, Taikun; also called *Shōgun*. *Kubō sama.* (idem.)

KUBŌ, クボウ, Same as *Kuboku*.

KUBOI,-KI,-SHI, クボイ, 窪, *a.* Concave, depressed, hollowed, indented, sunken. *Kuboi tokoro ni midz ga tamaru*, the water settles in hollow places.

KUBOKU, クボク, 窪, *adv.* idem. — *szru*, to hollow out. — *naru*, to become hollowed, or concave.

KUBOMI,-*mu*,-*nda*, クボム, 窪, *i. v.* To be concave, depressed, hollowed, sunken, indented. *Me ga kubonda*, his eye's are sunken.

KUBOMI, クボミ, 窪, *n.* A concavity, a hollow place, a depression, indentation.

KU-BU, クブ, 九分, Nine parts. — *ichi.* one ninth. *Kubu-kurin*, ninety nine parts in a hundred.

†KU-BUTSZ,-*szru*, クブツ, 供佛, (*Hotoke ni sonayeru.*) To make offerings to Buddha.

KŪ-CHI, クウチ, 空地, *n.* Vacant ground, waste-land.

KUCHI, クチ, 口, *n*, The mouth, orifice, aperture, entrance, door, opening; in mercantile language,=demand, request; kind, language. — *wo aku*, or — *wo hiraku*, to open the mouth. — *wo tojiru*, *fusagu*, or *tszgumu*, to shut the mouth. — *ga chigau*, his story does not agree. *Ito no* — *ga aita*, there is a demand for silk. — *wo tataku*, to prate, babble. — *wo kiku*, to talk to the purpose. *Hōkō no* — *ga nai*, there is no demand for servants. *Kono* — *wa mo arimasen*, I have no more of this kind. *Waru* — *wo iu*, to calumniate, speak evil of. — *ga szberu*, to make a slip of the tongue. *Tokkuri ni kuchi wo szru*, to cork a bottle. — *ga omoi*, slow of speech. — *ga karui*, rapid in talking, talkative. — *ni makasz*, to talk at random. — *de uru*, to sell by the quantity. *H'to* — *ni uru*, to sell in the lump. *Mōke* — *ga nai*, no chance to make money. *Taru ni* — *wo szru*, to put a spile into the hole of a cask.

KUCHI,-*ru*,-*ta*, クチル, 朽, *i. v.* To decay, to rot, decompose. *Ki, niku nado ga kuchiru.* Syn. KUSARU.

KUCHI-AKE, クチアケ, 口開, *n.* Opening of a sale, commencement of sale. *Mada kiyō wa* — *ga nai*, have made no sales yet to-day.

KUCHI-BA, クチバ, 朽葉, *n.* Withered leaves.

KUCHI-BASHI, クチバシ, 嘴, *n.* The bill, or beak of a bird.

‖KUCHI-BASHIRI,-*ru*,-*tta*, クチバシル, 口走, *t. v.* To be possessed by the spirit of one dead, and utter his mind; to rave like a madman,

KUCHIBIRU, クチビル, 脣, *n.* The lips.

KUCHIBUYE, クチブエ, 口笛, *n.* Whistling. — *wo fuku*, to whistle.

†KŪCHIU, クウチウ, 空中, In the air, in empty space. — *ni agaru.*

KUCHI-DOME, クチドメ, 口止, *n.* Hushing, or silencing another from saying what he knows, the telling of which would be to one's disadvantage. *Kuchi-dome wo sh'te oku*, to bribe one to secrecy. — *ni gochisō szru*, to give one a feast in order to secure secrecy.

KUCHI-DZKARA, クチヅカラ, 口, With one's own mouth. — *waga gei wo hokoru*, boasting of one's acquirements with his own mouth.

KUCHI-DZSAMI, クチズサミ, 口號, *n.* Humming, or singing to one's self.

KUCHI-GAKI, クチガキ, 口書, *n.* A deposition, written confession.

KUCHI-GITANAI,-KI,-KU,-SHI, クチギタナイ, 口汚, Foul mouthed, black-guard.

KUCHI-GOMORI,-*ru*,-*tta*, クチゴモル, 口澁, *i. v.* To stutter, stammer, hesitate or falter in speaking *Hen-ji ga kuchi-gomoru*, to hesitate in replying.

KUCHI-GŌ-SHA, クチゴウシャ, 口功者, *n.* A person clever at talking, eloquent.

KUCHI-GOTAYE, クチゴタヘ, 口答, *n.* Answering back in a surly manner to a superior.

†KUCHI-GOWA, クチゴハ, 口硬, *n.* Rigid, or inflexible vocal organs.

KUCHI-GUSE, クチグセ, 口癖, *n.* Peculiarity in talking, habit of saying; cant word. *Sate to iu koto ga ano h'to no* — *da*, *sate* is a cant word with him.

KUCHI-GUSZRI, クチグスリ, 口藥, *n.* Powder used only for priming.

KUCHI-HATE,-*ru*,-*ta*, クチハテル, 朽果, *i.v.* Completely decayed.

KUCHI-KI, クチキ, 朽木, *n.* A decayed tree, rotten wood.

KUCHI-KIKI, クチキキ, 口利, *n.* Clever at talking or persuading, eloquent.

†KUCHIKU, クチク, 苦竹, *n.* A kind of bamboo.

KUCHI-MAI, クチマイ, 口米, *n.* Rice extracted from a bag as a sample, which becomes the perquisite of the inspector.

KUCHI-MANE, クチマネ, 口眞似, *n.* Repeating what another says, mimicking another's way of talking, mocking. *H'to no* — *wo szru.*

KUCHI-MOTO, クチモト, 口本, *n.* The form or expression of the mouth.

KUCHI-NAGUSAMI, クチナグサミ, 口慰, *n.* Talking for amusement, or pastime.

KUCHI-NAMEDZRI, クチナメズリ, *n.* Licking the mouth, or chops, (as a dog after eating.)

KUCHINASHI, クチナシ, 梔子, *n.* The Cape Jasmine. Gardenia floribunda.

KUCHINAWA, クチナハ, 蛇 *n.* A snake. Syn. HEBI.

KUCHI-OSHII,-KI,-KU,-SA,-U, クチオシイ, 口惜, A thing to be regretted, deplored, or sorry for, or which excites disappointment. Syn. KUYASHII, MU-NEN, ZAN-NEN.

KUCHIRU, クチル, 朽, See *Kuchi.*

KUCHI-RIKŌ, クチリコウ, 巧言, *n.* Clever at talking.

KUCHISAGANAI,-KI,-KU, クチサガナイ, 囂, Babbling, tattling, given to idle and indiscreet talking.

KUCHI-SAGASHII,-KI,-KU, クチサガシイ, Plausible, specious in talking.

KUCHI-SOSOGI, クチソソグ, 漱, *n.* Cleansing the mouth, gargling. *Te-arai kuchi-sosogi sh'te kami wo hai-szru,* having washed the hands and cleansed the mouth to worship the Kami. Syn. UGAI WO SZRU.

KUCHISZGI, クチスギ, 餬口, *n.* A living, livelihood, means of getting food. — *no tame ni hōkō szru,* to go out to service in order to get the means of living. — *ga deki-kaneru,* difficult to make a living. Syn. KURASHI, TOSEI, NARIWAI, K'WAKKEI, KOKŌ.

KUCHI-TORI, クチトリ, 點心, *n.* Fruits, or confectionary taken between meals.

KUCHI-YAKAMASHII,-KI,-KU, クチヤカマシイ, Noisy, or troublesome from much talking.

KUDA, クダ, 管, *n.* A section of bamboo, a pipe stem, a tube, the spindle of a spinning wheel. *Kuda wo maku,* (fig.) to talk long and confusedly, to spin out a yarn.

KUDAKE,-*ru*,-*ta*, クダケル, 碎, *i.v.* Broken into pieces, shivered, crushed. *Nami ga iwa ni atatte kudakeru,* the waves are broken against the rocks. Syn. KOWARERU.

KUDAKI,-*ku*,-*ita*, クダク, 碎, *t.v.* To break, shiver, crush. *Kan-tan wo kudaku,* to do with great care and diligence. *Mi-jin ni* —, to break into pieces,—smash to atoms. Syn. KOWASZ.

KUDA-KUDASHII,-KI,-KU, クダクダシイ, Prolix and confused, or full of digressions, tediously spun out.

KUDAMONO, クダモノ, 果, *n.* Fruit.

KUDAN, クダン, 件, Before mentioned, the said, aforesaid, above mentioned. — *no gotoshi,* as it was said above. — *no sho-men hisokani o me ni kake soro,* I will privately show you the said letter. Syn. KANO,

KUDARI,-*ru*,-*tta*, クダル, 下, *i.v.* To go down, get down, descend, to purge, to depreciate in quality. 降, To surrender, yield. *Yama kawa nado wo* —, to descend a mountain or river. *Chi ga* —, to pass blood from the bowels. *Shina ga* —, the article has fallen off in quality. *Kiyoto kara* — to go, or come from Kiyoto. *Teki ga* —, the enemy surrenders. *Ame-kudaru,* to descend from heaven. Syn. ORIRU, SAGARU.

KUDARI, クダリ, 行, *n.* A row from top to bottom. *Bun h'to* —, one line of writing. *Bun mi* — *han,* three lines and a half of writing. Syn. GIYO.

KUDASAI-MASHI,-*sz*,-*sh'ta*, クダサイマス, Yedo coll. for *Kudasari.*

KUDASARE,-*ru*,-*ta*, クダサレ, 被下, To let descend, to receive from a superior. *Kite kudasareru ka,* can you come? *Kane wo kudasareta,* I have received the money. *Misete kudasare,* let me see it. *Iūte kudasare,* please tell me.

KUDASARI,-*ru*,-*tta*, クダサル, 被下, *t.v.* To give, spoken of a superior, to receive from a superior. *Kimi yori kudasatta,* received from the lord.

KUDASHI,-*sz*,-*sh'ta*, クダス 下, *t.v.* To cause to go down, or descend, to send down, to purge, to cause to surrender, or yield. *Ikada wo* —, to send down a raft. *Hara wo* —, to purge. *Yomi-kudasz,* to read down a line. *Shiro wo* —, to take a castle, (cause it to surrender). *Teki wo* —, to cause an enemy to capitulate.

KUDASHI-GUSZRI, クダシグスリ, 下藥, *(ge-zai), n.* Cathartic medicine.

KU-DEN, クデン, 口傳, *(kuchidztaye) n.* Oral tradition, learning or teaching by oral instruction. — *wo szru,* to teach orally, to lecture.

||KUDO, クド, 曲突, *n.* A kitchen range, furnace. Syn. HETSZI, KAMADO.

KUDOI,-KI,-KU,-SHI,-Ō,-SA, クドイ, Tedious, or troublesome reiteration, tediously going over and over an unimportant matter. *Sonna ni kudoku iwadz to mo wakaru,* I understand you very well without telling me over and over again. Syn. SHITSZKOI, AKUDOI.

KUDOKARE,-*ru*,-*ta*, クドカレル, pass. of *Kudoki.*

KUDOKI,*-ku,-ita*, クドク, 口説, *t.v.* To importune, to solicit over and over again, to entreat, persuade, to coax.

KUDOKI-OTOSHI,*-sz,-sh'ta*, クドキオトス, 口説落, *t.v.* To overcome by importunity, or frequent solicitation.

KUDOKU, クドク, 功德, *n.* Merit, good works, virtuous and meritorious actions. — *wo tszmu,* to accumulate merit. — *wo tsznde gokuraku ni yuku,* to accumulate merit and go to heaven. Syn. KURIKI.

KUDZ, クズ, 屑, *n.* Rubbish, waste and useless scraps, worthless articles. *Oga-kudz,* sawdust. *Kanna-kudz,* shavings. *Tachi-kudz,* waste scraps left after cutting out a garment, also paper shavings. *Kono fude no naka — ga deru,* among these pens there are some worthless one's.

KUDZ, クズ, 葛, *n.* The Pachyrrhizus thunbergianus.

KUDZ-ORE,*-ru,-ta*, クヅオレル, 頽折, *i.v.* Decrepit, broken down, or infirm with age. *Naki-kudzoreru,* worn out with crying. *Oi-kudzoreru,* infirm with age.

KUDZRE,*-ru,-ta*, クヅレル, 崩, *i. v.* To break and give way, of anything built up or arranged; to slip, or slide, (as earth from a hill); to cave in, to crumble, to fall to pieces; to break in confusion and run, (as troops); to open, or break, (as an abscess); to be depraved, vitiated, corrupted; to go to decay, or neglect, (as laws, usages). *Pan ga kawaki-szgite kudzreta,* the bread by becoming too dry has crumbled.

KUDZSARE,*-ru,-ta*, クヅサレル, 被崩, Pass. of *Kudzsz.*

KUDZSHI,*-sz,-sh'ta*, クヅス, 崩, *t. v.* To break down, tear down, throw down, (as a hill, house); to infringe, violate, (as laws, rank); to deprave, vitiate, demoralize. *Ki wo kudzsedz,* not to lose courage. *Teki no sonaye wo —,* to break the enemy's ranks. *Fūsoku wo —,* to deprave the manners.

KUDZSHI-GAKI, クヅシガキ, 省筆, *n.* A running hand.

KUDZ-YA, クズヤ, 茅屋, *n.* A thatched house.

KUFŪ, クフウ, 工夫, *n.* Contrivance, plan, scheme, invention. — *szru,* to devise, contrive, plan. *Yoi — da,* it is a fine contrivance. — *wo megurasz,* to devise, to turn over in the mind. Syn. HAKARIGOTO, KAGAYE, SHIAN, SHUKŌ.

KŪ-FUKU, クウフク, 空腹, *(hara ga heru.) n.* Hungry, stomach empty. — *ni naru,* to become hungry. Syn. HIDARUI, WIYERU.

KUGA, クガ, 陸, *n.* Land, (as distinct from water). — *dōri de yuku,* to go by land. Syn. RIKU, OKA.

KU-GAI, クガイ, 苦界, *(kurushiki tokoro.)* Bitter, disagreeable. — *no tsztome,* disagreeable service. (of a harlot.)

KUGAJI, クガヂ, 陸路, *n.* Land route. — *wo yuku,* to go by land.

KUGE, クゲ, 公家, *n.* The name of the ancient nobility of Japan, residing at Kiyoto, and attached to the court of the Mikado.

†KU-GEN, クゲン, 苦患, *(kurushimi urei.)* Afflictions, hardships, oppression.

KUGI, クギ, 釘, *n.* A nail. — *wo utsz,* to drive a nail, also to make a nail.

KUGI-KAKUSHI, クギカクシ, 釘隱, *n.* An ornamental covering for concealing the head of a nail.

KUGI-NUKI, クギヌキ, 釘拔, *n.* (nail extractors). Pincers.

KU-GIRI, クギリ, 句截, *n.* Marks of punctuation. — *wo tszkeru,* to punctuate.

‖KUGUMARI,*-ru,-tta*, クグマル, 僂, *i. v.* Bent in the back, with age or disease, to stoop, to be humpbacked.

KUGUMORI,*-ru,-tta*, クグモル, 溟涬, *i.v.* To be in a state of chaos; without form and void. *Ame tszchi imada wakarezarishi toki kugumorite kizashi wo fukumeri.* The heavens and the earth before they were separated, were blended together in a confused mass, and contained a germ, (like an egg). Syn. KON-TON NARU.

KUGURI,*-ru,-tta*, クグル, 俛出, *t. v.* To stoop and pass under or through, to worm through, to dive. *Ko mon wo —,* to pass through a low gate. *Midz wo —,* to dive under the water. *Saki wo —,* (fig.) to anticipate, or forestall, in buying or selling.

KUGURI, クグリ, 扈, *n.* A small low door in a gate.

†KUGUSE, クグセ, 傴僂, *n.* Humpbacked. Syn. SEMUSHI.

†KUGUTSZME, クグツメ, *n.* Waiting girls at an inn, a harlot.

KUI, クヒ, 杭, *n.* A pile, stake, post. — *wo utsz,* to drive a pile.

KUI, KŪ, KŪTA, クフ, 食, *t.v.* To eat, to bite. *Meshi wo kūte oru,* is eating his food. Syn. KURAU, HAMU, TABERU.

KUI-AWASE,*-ru,-ta*, クヒアハセル, 合食, *t. v.* To mix together and eat.

KUI-CHIGAI,*-au,-tta*, クヒチガフ, 齟齬, *i. v.* Cross-billed, thwarted in one's hopes, to be disappointed.

KUI-IRI,*-ru,-tta*, クヒイル, 食入, *t.v.* To

eat into, to eat its way into, to corrode. *Mushi ga ita ni* —, the insects eat into the board.

KUI-KIRI,*–ru,–tta*, クヒキル, 噬切, *t. v.* To bite off, to cut off with the teeth.

KUI-MONO, クヒモノ, 食物, *n.* Food, eatables, provisions. Syn. SHOKU-MOTSZ.

KUINA, クイナ, 秧雞, *n.* A kind of snipe.

KUI-SHIBARI,*–ru,–tta*, クヒシバル, 咬緊, *t. v.* To clinch the teeth. *Ha wo* —, id.

KUI-SHIMERI,*–ru,–ta*, クヒシメル, *t.v.* To crush, or hold fast in the teeth.

KUI-SHIMESHI,*–sz,–sh'ta*, クヒシメス, *t. v.* To wet, or moisten with the mouth.

KUI-SOME, クヒソメ, 百祿兒, *n.* The first feeding of an infant.

KUI-TOME,*–ru,–ta*, クヒトメル, 吃止, *t. v.* To oppose, hold in check, to stop. Syn. TOMERU.

KUI-TSZKI,*–ku,–ita*, クヒツク, 吃着, *t. v.* To bite, to seize with the teeth.

KUI-TSZME,*–ru,–ta*, クヒツメル, 口禁, *i. v.* Straitened for food, to clinch the teeth. *Ha wo* —, id. *Yedo no — mono*, one who can't make a living in Yedo.

KUI-TSZMI, クヒツミ, 食積, *n.* A small stand on which nuts, oranges, rice, and a pine-branch are arranged, on new years day. — *wo koshirayeru.*

KUI-WAKE,*–ru,–ta*, クヒワケル, 吃分, *t.v.* To discern by chewing, to taste.

KUJAKU, クジヤク, 孔雀, *n.* A peacock.

KUJI, クジ, 公事, *(ōyake goto,) n.* An action at law, a suit, prosecution, dispute. — *wo szru*, to bring suit; enter a complaint. Syn. SO-SHŌ, UTTAYE, DE-IRI.

KUJI, クジ, 鬮, *n.* The lot. — *wo toru*, to draw lots. — *wo hiku*, (idem).

KUJI, クジ, 九字, *n.* A diagram, used as a charm against evil spirits. — *wo kitte akuma wo harō.*

KUJI-BA, クジバ, 訟庭, *n.* A court-room, a bar.

KUJI-DORI, クジドリ, 鬮取, *n.* Drawing lots. — *wo szru*, to draw lots.

KUJIKA, クジカ, 麕, *n.* A kind of stag.

KUJIKI,*–ku,–ita*, クジク, 挫, *t.v.* To dislocate, sprain. *Te wo kujita*, have sprained the hand. *Ikioi wo* —, to discourage, to cool the courage. *Gun-zei wo* —, to discourage an army.

KUJIRA, クヂラ, 鯨, *n.* A whale.

KUJIRA-JAKU, or KUJIRAZASHI, クヂラジヤク, 鯨尺, *n.* A cloth measure, equal to 1 foot 2 inches of the *Kanazashi*, or 15 inches English.

KUJIRI,*–ru,–tta*, クジル, 抉, *n.* To pick, bore, or gouge. *Hana mimi nado wo* —, to pick the nose, or ear. *Me wo kujitte toru*, to gouge out the eye.

KUJIRI, クジリ, 鱐, *n.* A small curved knife, a gouge.

KUJISHI, クジシ, 公事師, *n.* A lawyer, one who advocates the cause of another before a judge, (in Japan a despised class.)

KUJI-YADO, クジヤド, 公事宿, *n.* An inn where only persons who have lawsuits lodge.

KU-JŪ, クジフ, 九十, Ninety.

KUKE,*–ru,–ta*, クケル, 縴, *t. v.* To sew the edges of two pieces together, so that the thread cannot be seen.

†KU-KETSZ, クケツ, 口訣, *n.* Oral instruction. Syn. KUDEN.

KŪ-KI, クウキ, 空氣, *n.* The atmosphere, air.

KUKI, クキ, 岫, *n.* A mountain gorge, glen.

KUKI, クキ, 莖, *n.* A stem. *Hana ha nado no* —, the stem of a flower, or leaf.

†KU-KIYŌ, クキヤウ, 恭敬, *n.* Reverence. Syn. WIYAMAI.

KŪ-K'YO, クウキヨ, 空虛, Empty, vacant, void, a vacuum. — *ni naru*, to become empty. Syn. KARA.

KUKKIRI-TO, クツキリ, *adv.* Tall and slim. — *sh'ta onna.* Syn. SZRARI-TO.

KUKKIYŌ, クツキヤウ, 究竟, Excellent, eminent, distinguished, illustrious. — *no waka-mono domo*, young men surpassing in strength and courage. — *no iyegara*, of illustrious family. — *na uma*, a fine horse. Syn. TAKUMASHII.

KUKU, クク, 九九, Nine times nine, the multiplication table.

KUKUME,*–ru,–ta*, ククメル, 哺, *t.v.* To feed, to put into the mouth of another. Syn. FUKUMERU.

KUKUMI,*–mu,–nda*, ククム, 哺, *i.v.* To hold in one's mouth. Syn. FUKUMU.

KUKUNAKI, ククナキ, *n.* The clucking of a hen.

KUKURI,*–ru,–tta*, ククル 縛, *t.v.* To bind, tie. *Nawa de* —, to bind with a rope. Syn. SHIBARU, YUWAYERU.

KUKURI, ククリ, 括, *n.* Bound, limit, proper restraint. *Mono ni taitei — wo tszkeru*, to set proper bounds in our use of every thing. Syn. SHIMAKI, KIKU.

KUKURI-HAKAMA, ククリバカマ, 括袴, *n.* A kind of trowsers full and tied at the knee.

Kukuri-makura, ククリマクラ, 括枕, *n.* A pillow made of muslin stuffed and tied at the ends.

†**Kukuzen**, ククゼン, 栩栩然, *adv.* At pleasure, at will. — *to sh'te tobu*, to fly about wherever it pleases.

Kuma, クマ, 熊, *n.* A bear. — *no i*, bear's gall.

†**Kuma**, クマ, 隈, *n.* Border, edge. *Umi no* —, sea shore. *Yama no* —, edge or foot of a mountain. Syn. HOTORI, KIWA.

Kuma-bachi, クマバチ, 熊蜂, *n.* A large kind of bee.

Kumade, クマデ, 熊手, *n.* A rake.

Kumadori,*-ru,-tta*, クマドル, 暈, *t.v.* To edge with colors. *Kuni-yedz no sakai wo* —, to color the boundary lines of a map.

Kumashi,*-sz,-sh'ta*, クマス, 令汲, Caust. of *Kumi*. To cause or let draw water. *Midz wo kumash'te okure*, allow me to draw some water.

Kumashi,*-sz,-sh'ta*, クマス, 令組, Caust. of *Kumi*. To cause, or let join, braid &c. *Ito wo kumash'te kudasare*, let me braid the thread.

Kuma-taka, クマタカ, 鵰, *n.* A kind of falcon.

Ku-men, クメン, 工面, *n.* Pecuniary ability, means, able to afford or raise money. — *ga yoi*, to be well off. — *ga warui*, to be bad off, without means. — *wa dekimu*, cannot raise the money. — *wa dekinai ka*, can't you raise the money? — *sh'te kudasai*, try and afford it. *Ash'ta made ni* — *sh'te okō*, I will try and lend you to-morrow. Syn. SAN-DAN, SAI-KAKU.

Kumi,*-mu,-nda*, クム, 組, *t.v.* To braid, plait, weave, twist, or knit together; to interlace, intertwine, to lay hold of, or grapple as a wrestler, (*i v.*) To join together in one company, to club or league together. *Ito wo kumu*, to braid thread. *Hiza wo* —, to sit tailor fashion. *Te wo* —, to fold the arms. *San nin kunde akinai wo szru*, three men went partners in trade.

Kumi,*-mu,-nda*, クム, 汲, *t.v.* To draw, or dip up, as water; to lade. *Tszrube de midsz wo* —, to draw water with a bucket. *Shaku de sake wo* —, to dip up *sake* with a dipper. *Kumi-tate no midz*, water just drawn. Syn. SHAKŪ.

Kumi, クミ, 組, *n.* A company, band, partnership, league, firm, club. — *wo tateru*, to form a company. *Go-nin-gumi*, a company of five persons or families, into which the Japanese are subdivided.

Kumi-ai,*-au,-tta*, クミアフ, 組合, *i.v.* Joined together in one company, band, or firm; to have hold of each other, as wrestlers; knit together, linked together.

Kumi-fuse,*-ru,-ta*, クミフセル, 組伏, *t.v.* To throw, as wrestlers.

Kumi-gashira, クミガシラ, 組頭, *n.* The head of a company, a captain.

Kumi-himo, クミヒモ, 組紐, *n.* Braid, plaited cord.

Kumi-ito, クミイト, 組絲, *n.* Silk-braid.

Kumi-jū, クミヂウ, 組重, *n.* A nest of boxes, one fitting on top of another, for holding food.

Kumi-kawashi,*-sz,-sh'ta*, クミカハス, 交酌, *t.v.* To drink wine together, to pass the cup from one to another.

Kumi-ko, クミコ, 組子, *n.* The members of a company, or club.

Kumi-shiki,*-ku,-ita*, クミシク, 組敷, *t.v.* To throw in wrestling.

Kumi-tori,*-ru,-tta*, クミトル, 酌取, *t. v.* To guess, conjecture, divine. *H'to no kokoro wo* —, to conjecture what the mind of another is. Syn. SZIRIYŌ SZRU, OSHI-HAKARU, SHIN-SHAKU.

Kumi-tszki,*-ku,-ita*, クミツク, 組附, *t.v.* To seize hold of each other, as wrestlers.

†**Kummei**, クンメイ, 君命, *n.* The commands of the lord, or master.

Kumo, クモ, 雲, *n.* A cloud. — *ga deru*, it is clouding over. *Kumo ga hareta*, the clouds are cleared away. — *no ashi*, the appearance of rain falling in the distance. — *no kakehashi*, a high tower for scaling walls in warfare. — *no wiyebito*, an epithet applied to the Mikado and Kuge.

Kumo, クモ, 蜘蛛, *n.* A spider. — *no sz*, a spider's web.

Kumoi, クモ井, 雲居, *n.* The dim cloudy distance, the horizon. The dwelling of the Mikado. — *no hoka ni*, beyond the horizon. — *ni chikaki no h'to*, one who is high in rank near the Emperor.

Kumorase,*-ru,-ta*, クモラセル, 令曇, (caust of *kumori.*) To cause the clouds to rise, to make dim.

Kumori,*-ru,-tta*, クモル, 陰, *i.v.* To be cloudy, dim. *Kumotte mo furimasen*, it is cloudy, but it will not rain. *Kagami wa* —, the mirror is clouded, or dim. *Me ga* —, eyes are dim.

Kumoszke, クモスケ, 雲輔, *n.* A low kind of coolie who frequents the great highways.

Kumo-szki, クモスキ, 雲透, *n.* Projected against the clouds, or horizon. *Fune ga* — *ni miyeru*, the ship is visible in the horizon.

KU-MOTSZ, クモツ, 供物, *n.* Things offered to idols, such as rice, fruits, cakes, &c.

†KUM-PU, クンプ, 君夫, *n.* Lord and father.

KUMU, クム, 組, and 汲, See *Kumi.*

†KUN, クン, 訓, (*yomi.*) The signification of a Chinese character, or its equivilent in Japanese.

KUN, クン, 君, (*kimi.*) Lord, master, prince; also a respectful title,=Mister.

KUNA, クナ, 勿來, (imp. neg. of *kuru.*) Don't come.

†KU-NAN, クナン, 苦難, Pain, trouble, hardship, affliction. — *wo ukeru,* to suffer affliction.

†KUN-DOKU, クンドク, 訓讀, (*yomu.*) To read by translating the Chinese characters into Japanese. — *szru,* to read.

†KUNDZRU, クンズル, 訓, To give the Japanese equivalent of a Chinese character.

KUNDZRU, クンズル, 薫, See *Kunji.*

KUNE, クネ, *n.* A wattled bamboo fence.

†KUNE,*–ru,–ta,* クネル, *i.v.* To be spiteful, jealous, to hate. *Kuneru namida,* tears of spite.

†KUNE-GUNESHII,–KI,–KU, クネグネシイ, Spiteful, jealous.

KUNEMBŌ, クネンボウ, 香橙, *n.* A kind of large, thick-skinned orange.

KUNI, クニ, 國, (*koku*), *n.* Country, state, kingdom.

KUNITSZ-KAMI, クニツカミ, 地祇, *n.* Earthborn gods, (the syllable *tsz,* being an ancient and obsolete genitive particle).

KU-NIU, クニウ, 口入, Acting as a go-between, agent, or broker.

KU-NIU-NIN, クニウニン, 口入人 *n.* A middleman, broker, agent.

KUNI-YEDZ, クニヱヅ, 輿地圖, *n.* A map.

KUNI-ZAKAI, クニザカイ, 國界, *n.* Boundary of a state.

KUNJI,*–ru,–ta,* クンジル, 薫, *i.v.* To send forth a perfume. *Kunji-wataru,* to perfume all about. Syn. KAORU.

KUNJI,*–dzru,–ta,* クンズル, 訓, *t.v.* See *Kundzru.*

KUN-JU,*–szru,* クンジュ, 群集, To crowd together, to flock together, assemble. Syn. ATSZMARU.

KUN-KUN-TO, クンクン, 薫薫, *adv.* Sending forth a smell, or perfume. — *niō.*

†KU-NŌ, クナウ, 苦惱, (*kurushimi nayamu*). Afflicted, suffering. — *wo szku,* to help the sick and afflicted.

KUN-SHI, クンシ, 君子, *n.* The superior man, the good man. — *wa ayauki ni chikayoradz,* the good man does not expose himself to danger; or does not expose himself to temptation.

KUN-SHIN, クンシン, 君臣, (*kimi to kerai*). Lord and minister, master and servant.

KUN-SZ, クンス, 裙子, *n.* A garment worn by priests around the loins.

KUN-TEN, クンテン, 訓點, *n.* The marks made in reading a Chinese composition, to show the order in which the characters must be rendered to suit the Japanese idiom. — *wo tszkeru.*

†KUPPUKU,*–szru,* クツプク, 屈伏, To submit, yield. *Ri ni* —, to submit to reason.

KURA, クラ, 藏, A fire-proof store-house.

KURA, クラ, 鞍, *n.* A saddle.

KURABE,*–ru,–ta,* クラベル, 比, *t.v.* To compare, to measure anything with something else. *Chikara wo* —, to measure strength. *Nagasa wo* —, to compare lengths.

KURA-BONE, クラボネ, 鞍橋, *n.* A saddle-tree.

KURAGARI, クラガリ, 暗, *n.* A dark-place, darkness.

KURAGE, クラゲ, 水母, *n.* A species of medusa.

KURAI,–KI,–KU, クライ, 暗, Dark. *Kurai ban,* a dark night. *Kuraku naru,* to become dark. *Kurō gozarimas,* it is dark. *Kuraku szru,* to darken. *Kurakute ikenai,* it is too dark.

KURAI, クラ井, 位, *n.* Rank, dignity, grade, the Imperial throne, kind, sort, manner, way, quantity. — *naki h'to,* a person without rank. — *ni tszku,* to ascend the throne. — *wo yudzru,* to abdicate the throne. *Kono kurai,* this kind, this way. *Dono kurai,* how much? in what way? *San riyō gurai,* about three *riyō.* Syn. KAKUSHIKI, HODO.

KURAI,*–au,–tta,* クラフ, 食, *t.v.* To eat, to munch, (vulgar). Syn. TABERU, KŪ, HAMU.

KURAKU, クラク, See *Kurai.*

KURA-KURA, クラクラ, *adv.* Dizzy, giddy, having a sensation of whirling in the head. *Me ga — szru,* eyes are dizzy. — *niyetatz,* to boil (the water having a whirling motion).

KURA-MAGIRE, クラマギレ, 暗紛, Bewildered owing to the darkness; dark and not able to distinguish any thing; under cover of the darkness. — *ni nigeta,* fled away in the darkness. — *ni ashi wo yogosh'ta,* muddied my feet in the dark.

KURAMI,*-mu,-nda*, クラム, 暗, *i. v.* To grow, or become dark, to be dizzy. *Me ga kuramu*, eyes grow dizzy.

KURAMASHI,*-sz,-sh'ta*, クラマス, 令暗, *t.v.* To darken, cause to become dark, to blind. *Manako wo* —, to blind the eyes. *Ato wo kuramash'te nigeru*, to flee away and destroy all trace.

KURA-ŌI, クラオホヒ, 鞍覆, *n.* A saddle-cloth.

KURASA, クラサ, 暗, *n.* The state, or degree of darkness.

KURASHI,*-sz,-sh'ta*, クラス, 暮, *t. v.* To spend one's time, to live. *Hi, tszki, toshi nado wo* —, to spend one's days, months, or years. *Naite kurasz*, to spend the time crying. *Asonde* —, to spend one's time in pleasure.

KURASHI, クラシ, 暗, *a.* Dark.

KURASHI, クラシ, 暮, *n.* The means, or manner of living. — *ni komaru*, distressed for the means of living. — *ga yoi*, to live well. *Hitori-gurashi*, to live alone. *Sono hi-gurashi no h'to*, one who lives from hand to mouth.

KURASHI-KATA, クラシカタ, 暮方, *n.* idem.

KURASHIKI, クラジキ, 倉敷, *n.* Money paid for the storage of goods.

KURA-TSZBO, クラツボ, 鞍局, *n.* The seat of a saddle.

KURAU, クラフ, 食, see *Kurai.*

KURAWARE,*-ru,-ta*, クラハレル, 被食, pass. of *Kurai.*

KURAWASE,*-ru,-ta*, クラハセル, 令喫, *t.v.* To make, or let another eat; to strike, hit. *H'to no atama ni bō wo* —, to strike a person on the head with a club.

KURAWASHI,*-sz,-sh'ta*, クラハシ, (idem.)

KURAYAMI, クラヤミ, 闇夜, *n.* Dark. — *ni naru*, to become dark. — *ni aruku*, to walk in the dark.

KURE, クレ, 榑, *n.* A stave.

KURE,*-ru,-ta*, クレル, 暮, *i. v.* To set, go down, (as the sun.) To darken, grow dim, be bewildered. *Hi ga kureta*, the sun is set. *Toshi ga kureta*, the year is ended. *Namida ni kure ni keru*, to be blinded with tears. *Tohō ni kureru*, to be in a quandary.

KURE, クレ, 暮, *n.* The setting, end, close. *Hi no kure*, the setting of the sun. *Kure maye*, before sunset. *Kure szgi*, after sunset. *Toshi no* —, end of the year. *Kure no haru*, end of spring, third month.

KURE,*-ru,-ta*, クレル, 與, *t. v.* To give, (used mostly as an auxilliary verb, and perhaps a contract. of *Kudasaru.*) *Mite kure*, or *mite o kure*, let me see it. *Hanash'te o kure*, tell it to me. *Kash'te kure nai ka*, will you lend it to me? *Dare ga kureta*, who gave it to you? *Kite kureta*, he has come. *Mite kureta*, he has seen. *Kuredz*, (neg.)

KURE-GURE, クレグレ, 呉呉, *adv.* Over and over, again and again, repeatedly. — *mo o negai mōshimasz*, excuse me for again and again asking you.
Syn. KAYESZ-GAYESZ.

KURE-KATA, クレカタ, 暮方, *n.* The evening, sunset.

†KURENAI, クレナ井, 紅, *n.* Pink, or scarlet color.

KURE-TAKE, クレタケ, 呉竹, *n.* A kind of bamboo.

KURI, クリ, 栗, *n.* A chesnut. — *no ki*, chesnut tree. — *no iga*, a chesnut bur.

KURI,*-ru,-tta*, クル, 繰, *t. v.* To reel. *Ito wo* —, to reel thread. *Wata wo* —, to drive cotton between two rollers in order to press out the seed, to gin.

KURI,*-ru,-tta*, クル, 刳, *t.v.* To scoop out, hollow, to excavate, to bore, (as a canoe, pump, cannon). *Ki wo* —, to bore a log.

KURI-AGE,*-ru,-ta*, クリアゲル, 繰上, *t.v.* To finish reeling, to wheel round, to withdraw, or retreat, (as an army).

KURI-AWASE,*-ru,-ta*, クリアハセル, 繰合, *t.v.* To slacken, or lengthen the strans of a hoop so as to make it fit. (fig.) to take time from business, or adjust one's business, so as to get time for something else.

KURI-BIKI,*-ku,-īta*, クリビク, 繰引, *t.v.* To wheel round and withdraw, retire, or retreat.

KURI-DASHI,*-sz,-sh'ta*, クリダス, 繰出, *t.v.* To file out, to wheel out in long files.

KURIGE-UMA, クリゲウマ, 騂騮, *n.* A chesnut colored horse.

KURI-GOTO, クリゴト, 操言, *n.* Repeating the same story; dwelling much, and talking often on one subject. — *wo iu.*

KURI-IRE,*-ru,-ta*, クリイレル, 操入, *t.v.* To turn, or wheeland go in, to file into, (a castle, as an army.)

KURI-IRO, クリイロ, 栗色, *n.* Chesnut color.

‖KURI-ISHI, クリイシ, 栗石, *n.* Pebble-stones, gravel. Syn. JARI.

KURI-KANNA, クリカンナ, 刳鉋, *n.* A plane for grooving.

KURI-KAYE,*-ru,-ta*, クリカヘル, 繰替,

i.v. To turn back, or wheel around and go over again; to unreel.

KURI-KAYESHI,*–sz,–sh'ta*, クリカヘス, 繰返 *t.v.* To turn and go over again, to reverse the turn. *Hon wo kuri-kayesh'te miru*, to review a book.

KU-RIKI, クリキ, 功力, *n.* Virtue, power, efficacy. *Nembutsz no — de yamai ga naotta*, diseases are cured by the efficacy of repeating the prayer, "*Namu amida butsz.*"

KURIN, クリン, 九輪, *n.* A spire on the top of a tower, having nine circular wheels.

KURIWATA, クリワタ, 繰綿, *n.* Ginned cotton.

†KURI-YA, クリヤ, 廚, *n.* A kitchen. Syn. DAIDOKORO.

KURO, クロ, 畔, *n.* The banks, or dikes between rice fields; a mound of earth. Syn. AZE.

KURO, クロ, 黒, Black, (used only in comp. words.)

KURŌ, クラフ, 食, See *Kurai*.

KURŌ, クラウ, Black, or dark. See *Kuroi* and *Kurai*.

KU-RŌ, クラウ, 苦勞, *n.* Trouble, difficulty, care, concern, anxiety, toil. — *mo naku*, without trouble, without difficulty. — *ni szru nai yo*. don't trouble yourself about it. Syn. SHIMPAI, KOKORO-DZKAI.

KURO-BIKARI, クロビカリ, 黒光, Black and shining.

KURO-BOKU, クロボク, 黒石, *n.* A kind of black stone.

KURO-DAI, クロダイ, 黒鯛, *n.* A kind of black fish.

KURO-GANE, クロガ子, 鐵, *n.* Iron. Syn. TETSZ.

KURO-GOME, クロゴメ, 玄米, *n.* Unhulled rice.

KUROI,–KI, クロイ, 黒, *a.* Black. *Iro ga kuroi*, the color is black. *Kuroi kumo*, a black cloud. *Kuroku naru*, to become black. *Kuroku szru*, to blacken. *Kuroku to minikui*, black and ugly. *Kuroku-nai*, or *Kurokaradz*, it is not black. *Kurō-gozarimas*, it is black.

KUROKU, クロク, 黒, *adv.* idem.

KUROKUWA, クロクハ, 黒鍬, *n.* A common laborer, those only in government employ.

KURO-MADARA, クロマダラ, 黒斑, *n.* Spotted with black, piebald. Syn. BUCHI.

KUROMASHI,*–sz,–sh'ta*, クロマス, 令涅, *t.v.* To blacken.

KUROMATSZ, クロマツ, 黒松, *n.* The pinus densifloris.

KUROMBŌ, クロンボウ, 黒人, *n.* A black man, a negro.

KUROME,*–ru,–ta*, クロメル, 令涅, *t.v.* To blacken. fig. to conceal, hide.

KUROMI,*–mu,–nda*, クロム, 黒, *i. v.* To become black. *Ano h'to no kao hi ni yakete kuronda*, his face is sunburnt and blackened.

KURORO, クロロ, 黒羅, *n.* Black silk gauze.

KUROSA, クロサ, 黒, *n.* Blackness.

KUROSHI, クロシ, 黒, *a.* Black, see *Kuroi.*

KURO-TAMA, クロタマ, 睛, *n.* The iris and pupil of the eye.

KURŌTO, クロウト, *n.* A word of extensive application, meaning; one belonging to, or skilled in, the profession, business, or trade spoken of; in distinction from, *Shirōto*, one not belonging to, or skilled in the profession, business, or trade.

KUROYAKI, クロヤキ, 黒燒, *n.* Anything reduced to a cinder, or burnt to a coal. *Hebi wo — ni sh'te kuszri ni szru*, a snake burnt to a cinder is good for medicine.

KUROZATŌ, クロザタウ, 黒砂糖, *n.* Brown sugar.

KURU, クル, 來, See *Ki*, *Kuru*, *Kita*.

KURU, クル, 繰, See *Kuri.*

KURU, クル, 刮, See *Kuri.*

KURŪ, クルフ, 狂, See *Kurui*.

KURUBUSHI, クルブシ, 腂, *n.* The ankle bone, malleolus. *Uchi* —, internal malleolus. *Soto* —, external malleolus.

KURUI,*–ū,–ūta*, or *utta*, クルフ, 狂, *i.v.* To be wild, frenzied, mad, disordered in mind; to act irregularly; twisted, turned, or warped from the true direction. *Ano h'to wa chō-shi ga kurutte iru*, that man is not in his right mind. *Kurui ideru*, to rush madly out. *Kan-jō ga* —, the account is not right.

KURUI, クルヒ, 歪, *n.* Bent, warped, crooked; derangement, *Kono hashira wa — ga deta*, this pillar is warped.

KURU-KURU-TO, クルクルト, 旋旋, *adv.* Round and round, around. — *mawaru*, to go round and round. *Szdare wo — maki-ageru*, to roll up a window shade. *Koma ga — mawaru*, the top spins round.

KURUMA, クルマ, 車, *n.* A wheel, a cart, waggon. — *no wa*, the wheel of a cart. — *no ya*. the spoke of a wheel. — *no shingi*, axletree of a waggon. — *no koshiki*, the hub of a wheel. — *no nagaye*, the shaft of a waggon. — *wo hiku*, to draw a waggon. — *ni noru*, to ride in a waggon.

KURU-MAKI, クルマキ, 絞車, *n.* A screw-press.

KURUMA-ZA, クルマザ, 團坐, *n.* Sitting in a circle. — *ni natte sake wo nomu,* to sit in a circle and drink *sake.*

||KURUMA-ZAKI, クルマザキ, 車裂, *n.* Punishment of being broken on the wheel.

KURUMEKI,-*ku*,-*ita*, クルメク, 眩暉, *i.v.* To become dizzy. *Me ga kurumeite taoreta,* becoming dizzy he fell down..
Syn. KENNUN, TACHI-GURAMI.

KURUMI, クルミ, 胡桃, *n.* A walnut.

KURURI, クルリ, 連枷, *(kara sao.) n.* A flail.

KURURI-TO, クルリト, 旋, *adv.* Around. — *mawaru,* to turn around, revolve.

KURURU, クルル, 樞, *n.* The pivot on which a door turns, or hinges.

KURUSHII,-KI, クルシイ, 苦, *a.* Painful, distressing, difficult; causing concern, or anxiety; toilsome.

KURUSHIKU, クルシク, 苦, *adv.* idem.

KURUSHIME,-*ru*,-*ta*, クルシメル, 令苦, *t.v.* To afflict, distress, trouble, torment, persecute, grieve, worry, vex.
Syn. HIDOIME NI AWASERU, IJIMERU, KOMARASERU, SHIYETAGERU.

KURUSHIMI,-*mu*,-*nda*, クルシム, 苦, *i.v.* To suffer pain, affliction, distress, torment, to grieve, worry; to toil, labor. *Biyōki de* —, afflicted with sickness.

KURUSHIMI, クルシミ, 苦, *n.* Suffering, affliction, distress, pain, toil, hard labor.

KURUSHISA, クルシサ, 苦, *n.* The state, or degree of suffering.

KURUSHIU, クルシウ, 苦, same as *Kurushiku.*

KURUWA, クルワ, 廓, *n.* An inclosure, area separated by an inclosure. Prostitute quarters.

KURUWASE,-*ru*,-*ta*, クルハセル, 令狂, *t.v.* (caust. of *Kurui).*

KUSA, クサ, 頭瘡, *n.* Crustea lactea.

KUSA, クサ, 艸, *n.* Grass, a plant. — *wo karu,* to cut grass.

KUSABA, クサバ, 艸葉, *n.* Leaf of grass. — *no kage,* the grave.

KUSABI, クサビ, 楔, *n.* A wedge driven in to tighten a joint.

KUSABIRA, クサビラ, 菌, *n.* A mushroom, toadstool. Syn. TAKE, KINOKO.

KUSA-DZRI, クサズリ, 艸摺, *n.* The skirt of a coat of mail.

KUSA-GUSA, クサグサ, 種種, Many kinds, various subjects. Syn. SHU-JU, IRO-IRO, SHINA-JINA.

KUSA-GIRI, クサギリ, 耘, *n.* Grass-cutting, weeding.

KUSAI,-KI, クサイ, 臭, *a.* Stinking, offensive to the smell, fetid, rancid, putrid. Used in comp. in the same sense as, *rashii*; = manner, appearance, as, *Jiman-kusai, Furu-kusai. Inaka kusai. Nioi ga kusai,* the smell is offensive. *Niku ga* —, the meat is putrid.

KUSAKU, クサク, 臭, *adv.* Idem. — *naru,* to become putrid.

KUSAME, クサメ, 嚏, *n.* Sneeze. — *wo szru,* to sneeze.

KUSAMI, クサミ, 臭, *n.* Stinking smell, offensive smell. *Kono niku wa — ga aru,* this meat begins to stink.

KUSA-MURA, クサムラ, 叢, *n.* A spot of luxuriant grass.

KUSARAKASHI,-*sz*,-*sh'ta*, クサラカス, 腐, caust. of *Kusaru.* To cause to putrify, to corrode, to make to slough, to cauterize.

KUSARAKASHI, クサラカシ, 腐藥, *n.* Caustic, escharotic, or corrosive medicine.

KUSARI, クサリ, 鎖, *n.* A chain.

KUSARI,-*ru*,-*tta*, クサル, 腐 *i. v.* To putrify, rot, to be fetid, to stink. *Niku ga kusatta,* the meat stinks.

KUSARI-KATABIRA, クサリカタビラ, 鎖帷子, *n.* A shirt of mail, made of rings interlaced.

KUSASA, クササ, 臭, *n.* Stink, putridity, fetor, rottenness.

KUSASHI, クサシ, 臭, *a.* Stinking, see *Kusai.*

KUSASHI,-*sz*,-*sh'ta*, クサス, *t.v.* To speak evil of, depreciate, run down, detract, calumniate. *Shina wo kusash'te yaszku kau,* to depreciate an article and buy it cheap. *H'to wo 'kusash'te wa warui,* it is wrong to speak evil of others. Syn. KENASZ, SOSHIRU.

KKSAWARA, クサハラ, 草原, *n.* A moor, prairie.

KUSA-YA, クサヤ, 草屋, *n.* A thatched house.

KUSAZŌSHI, クサザウシ, 草雙紙, *n.* Story books for children, the name of a kind of light, fictitious literature, a novel.

KUSE, クセ, 癖, *n,* Habit, peculiarity of manner, or of like or dislike, eccentricity, propensity, inclination, fondness for. *Ōse wa m'ma no kuse ari,* Ōse had a fondness for horses. *Kōrochoku kō no — ari,* Kōrochoku was fond of perfumery. *Ano kodzkai wa teguse ga warui,* that servant has a bad habit of pilfering. *Uta ga kuchikuse ni naru,* to be in the habit of singing, or humming tunes. *Ke ni kuse ga tszku,* the hair has a twist, curl, or tendency to lay in one position. *De-kuse ga tszku,* has a propensity to be out of the house. —

wo naosz, to correct a bad habit. *H'to ni h'to kuse*, every one has some peculiar habit. *Kodomo wa amayakasz to — ni naru*, if a child is petted he will be spoiled.

†KUSE-GOTO, クセゴト, 曲事, (*kiyoku ji*), *n.* Criminal act, offense. *Kono okite wo okasz ni oite wa — taru beshi*, the transgression of this law is a criminal act.

KUSE-MONO, クセモノ, 曲物, n. A suspicious looking person, a thief, robber.

KŪ-SEN, クウセン, 空舩, *n.* A balloon. Syn. KIKIU.

KUSHA-KUSHA, クシャクシャ, 苛苛, *adv.* Irritating, pricking. — *szru*, to irritate, prick, to vex. Syn. IRA-IRA.

KUSHATSZKI,*-ku,-ita*, クシャツク, 苛刻, *i,v.* To prick, irritate.

KUSHI, クシ, 櫛, *n.* A comb. — *no ha*, the teeth of a comb, — *wo hiku*, to make a comb. — *de kami wo toku*, to comb the hair with a comb.

KUSHI, クシ, 串, *n.* A skewer, or stick of bamboo, on which fish or fruit are strung to dry, a spit.

KUSHIBI, クシビ, 靈, Strange, wonderful, miraculous.

KUSHI-GAKI, クシガキ, 串柿, *n.* Persimmons strung, and dried on a stick.

KUSHI-HARAI, クシハラヒ, 刷子, *n.* A brush for cleaning a comb.

KUSHIKO, クシコ, 串海鼠, *n.* Bich-de mer strung on a stick and dried.

†KU-SHIN, クシン, 苦辛, *n.* Hard labor, toil. Syn. KUKŌ.

KUSO, クソ, 糞, *n.* Feces, dung, excrements. Syn. FUN.

KUSO-BAYE, クソバヘ, 青蠅, *n.* A greenbottle fly.

‖KUSO-BUKURO, クソブクロ, 大腸, *n.* The large intestine.

KUSSHI,*-szru,-sh'ta*, クツスル, 屈, To yield, submit, to succumb, to give up. *Shibaraku kussh'te ji-setsz wo matsz*, to yield for a while and wait for a propitious time. *Szkoshi mo kusszru keshiki naku*, did not show the least sign of yielding. *Ki wo kussedz*, did not feel discouraged.

KUSZ, クス, 楠, *n.* The camphor tree.

KUSZBE,*-ru,-ta*, クスベル, 燻, *t. v.* To smoke, to fumigate. *Ka wo* —, to smoke out musquitoes. Syn. FUSZBERU.

KUSZBORI,*-ru*, クスボル, 燻, *i. v.* To be smoked, smoky. Syn. FUSZBORI.

KUSZGURI,*-ru,-tta*, クスグル, *t. v.* To tickle. *H'to wo kuszgutte warawaseru*, to tickle a person and make him laugh.

KUSZGUTTAI,-KI,-KU,-Ō, クスグツタイ, Ticklish. — *kara o yoshi*, I am ticklish, stop. Syn. KOSOBAYUI.

KUSZMI,*-mu,-nda*, クスム, 口默, *i. v.* Quiet, sedate, sober grave.

KUSZNE,*-ru,-ta*, クスネル, *t. v.* To pilfer, steal. Syn. NUSZMU.

KUSZRI, クスリ, 藥, *n.* Medicine, drug; gunpowder; the material used in glazing porcelain, enamel. — *no kōnō*, the virtues of medicine. — *ga yoku kikimash'ta*, the medicine has been very efficacious. — *ga kikimasen*. the medicine has had no effect. — *wo fuku szru*, to administer medicine. — *wo mochīru*, to use medicine. — *wo nomu*, to take medicine. *Teppō no* — unpowder.

KUSZRI-BAKO, クスリバコ, 藥箱, *u.* A medicine chest.

KUSRI-KIZAMI, クスリキザミ, 藥刀, *n.* A knife and block used in cutting medicines.

KUSZRI-NABE, クスリナベ, 藥鐺, *n.* A pot for making medicinal decoctions.

†KUSZSHII,-KI,-KU, クスシイ, 奇, Extraordinary, wonderful. Syn. AYASHII.

KUTABARI,*-ru,-tta*, クタバル, 斃, *i. v.* To die, (vulgar.) Syn. SHINURU.

KUTABIRE,*-ru,-ta*, クタビレル, 草臥, *i. v.* Tired, fatigued, to become weary. *Shigoto de kutabireta*, fatigued with work. Syn. TSZKARERU.

KUTABIRE, クタビレ, 草臥, *n.* Fatigue, weariness. — *ga deru*, to begin to feel tired.

KU-TŌ, クトウ, 句讀, *n.* Reading and punctuating. — *wo kiru*, to point, or punctuate sentences.

†KU-TŌSHI, クトウシ, 句讀師, *n.* A teacher. Syn. SHISHŌ.

KUTSZ, クツ, 履, *n.* A leather shoe.

KUTSZ-BAMI, クツバミ, 馬銜, *n.* The bit of a bridle.

KUTSZGAYE,*-ru,-ta*, クツガヘル, 覆, *i. v.* To upset, capsize, overturn; subverted, overthrown. *Fune ga kutszgayeta*, the boat is capsized. Syn. HIKURI-KAYERU.

KUTSZGAYESHI,*-sz,-sh'ta*, クツガヘス, 覆, *t.v.* To upset, capsize, overturn; to subvert, overthrow. Syn. HIKURIKAYESZ.

KUTSZ-KUTSZ-WARAU, クツクツワラフ, 竊笑, *i.v.* To laugh secretly, or in a suppressed manner, to giggle.

KUTSZ-MAKI, クツマキ, 履卷, *n.*. The wrapping near the head of an arrow, to fix it in its place.

KUTSZ-NUGI, クツヌギ, 履脱, *n.* The place where shoes are taken off, in entering a house.

KUTSZROGE,*-ru,-ta*, クツロゲル, 放寛, *t.v.* To slacken, loosen, free from tightness, to relax, to ease. *Koiguchi wo kutszrogeru*, to loosen the sword, (so as to be ready for use.) *Tszchi wo* —, to loosen the earth, (by digging.) *Obi wo* —, to loosen the belt. Syn. YURUMERU.

KUTSZROGI,*-gu,-ida*, クツログ, 寛, *i.v.* To be loose, slack, to relax, remit effort or attention, to be at ease, free from anxiety. Syn. YURUMU, AN-SHIN SZRU.

KUTSZRU, クツル, 朽, See *Kuchi*.

KU-TS'Ū, クツウ, 苦痛, *n.* Trouble and pain, suffering.

KUTSZWA, クツワ, 馬銜, *n.* A bridle-bit. Syn. KUCHI-BAMI.

‖KUTSZWA, クツワ, 忘八, *n.* A prostitute house.

KUTSZWA-DZRA, クツワヅラ, 轡, *n.* The rein of a bridle. Syn. TADZNA.

KUTSZWA-MUSHI, クツワムシ, 紡績娘, *n.* A kind of cricket.

KUWA, クハ, 鍬, *n.* A hoe, mattock.

KUWA, クハ, 桑, *n.* The mulberry, on which silk-worms feed.

†K'WABI, クワビ, 花美, *(hanayakani utszkushii)*. *n.* Gorgeousness, splendor. — *wo tszkusz.*

K'WA-BIN, クワビン, 花瓶, *n.* A flower vase.

K'WA-BOKU, クワボク, 花木, *(hana no ki)*. *n.* A flowering tree.

K'WA-BUN, クワブン, 過分, *(bun ni szgiru)*. Beyond one's deserts, more than one is worthy of, undeserving, unworthy. *Yempō on tadzne kudasare — no itari ni zonji soro*, I feel that I am quite unworthy that you should have come so far to inquire about me. — *na koto*, a thing above one's desert. Syn. MI NI AMARU, K'WA-TŌ.

K'WA-DAN, クワダン, 花壇, *n.* A flower bed, or mound.

KUWADATE,*-ru,-ta*, クワダテル, 企, *t.v.* To plot, to devise, to scheme, to plan, contrive, to conspire. *Muhon wo* —, to plot rebellion. *Kane-mōke wo* —, to contrive how to make money.
Syn. MŌYOSZ, HAKARU.

KUWADATE, クワダテ, 企, *n.* A plot, plan, device, scheme. *Muhon no* —, a plot of insurrection.

KUWADATSZRU, クワダツル, Same as *Kuwadateru*.

†K'WA-DOKU, クワドク, 花牘, *(hanayakanaru fumi)*. Letter, epistle. — *haiken tszkamatszrisoro.*

†K'WA-FUKU, クワフク, 禍福, *n.* Fortune and misfortune. — *mon nashi.*

†K'WA-FUSOKU, クワフソク, 過不足, Too much or too little, excess or deficiency. — *no nai yōni*, so that there may be neither too much or too little.

K'WAGON, クワゴン, 過言, *(kot oba wo szgosz)*. Language that violates propriety, intemperate, violent, or abusive language. — *wo iu* to speak abusive words.
Syn. AK-KŌ

K'WAHAN, クワハン, 過半, *(hambun szgi.)* *n.* More than half, the greater part, the majority, the most. *Gunzei — nige-usetari*, most of the army ran away.

K'WA-HŌ, クワハウ, 果報, *n.* Retribution, the recompense, or reward of one's deeds. (Bud). — *no yoi h'to*, or — *mono*, a fortunate person. Syn. IN-G'WA, UN.

†K'WAI, クワイ, 回, *n.* A chapter, section. *Ikk'wai*, one chapter. *Ni k'wai me*, the second chapter.

K'WAI, クワイ, 會, *n.* A meeting, assembly. *Hana no — wo moyōsz*, to get up a meeting to show flowers. *Go no* —, a meeting to play checkers.

K'WAI-BUN, クワイブン, 回文, *n.* A sentence, or verse in which the words are the same, read either forwards or backwards.

K'WAI-CHIU, クワイチウ, 懷中, *n.* Inside of the clothing covering the breast; the bosom. — *ni ireru*, to put in the bosom. — *szru*, (idem). — *mono*, things usually carried in the bosom, especially the the paper wallet. Syn. FUTOKORO.

K'WAI-CHIU, クワイチウ, 蚘蟲, *n.* Worms in the stomach.

K'WAI-DAN, クワイダン, 怪談, *n.* A strange story, a ghost story.

†K'WAI-DOKU, クワイドク, 會讀, *(atszmatte yomu.)* *n.* Assembling together to read. — *szru.*

K'WAI-FUKU, クワイフク, 快復, *n.* Recovery from sickness, restoration to health. Syn. HOM-BUKU, ZEN-K'WAI.

K'WAI-GŌ,*-szru*, クワイガフ, 會合, *(atszmari au.)* To assemble, to meet together.

K'WAI-HŌ, クワイハウ, 快方, Convalescing, growing better in sickness. *Konnichi — de gozarimas*, he is better to day.

†K'WAI-I, クワイイ, 怪異, Strange, wonderful, surprising. Syn. AYASHII.

K'WAI-JŌ, クワイジヤウ, 回狀, *n.* A circular, a letter circulated. — *wo mawasz.*

K'WAI-KEN, クワイケン, 懷劍, *n.* A small sword, or dirk carried in the bosom.

K'WAI-KI, クワイキ, 快氣, *n.* Convalescence, restoration to health. — *iwai*, a feast made to friends on recovery from sickness.

†K'WAI-KIU, クワイキフ, 懷舊, (*furuki wo omō.*) Thinking upon old times, remembering past events.

K'WAI-KOKU,-*szru*, クワイコク, 回國, (*kuni wo meguru.*) To travel, or go round the different provinces of the empire.

K'WAI NIN, クワイニン, 懷妊, Being with child. — *szru*, to be pregnant.
Syn. HARAMU, NIN-SHIN, MIMOCHI.

K'WAIRŌ, クワイラウ, 廻廊, *n.* A corridor, or gallery built round a house.

K'WAIRO, クワイロ, 懷爐, *n.* A small metal box for holding fire, carried in the bosom to warm the chest.

K'WAI-SEI, クワイセイ, 快晴, *n.* Pleasant and clear weather.

K'WAI-SEN, クワイセン, 廻船, (*mawaru fune.*) *n.* A packet ship, a ship that trades from port to port. — *dayori ni nimotsz wo okuru*, to send goods by a packet.

†K'WAI-SHA, クワイシヤ, 膾炙, (lit. raw and cooked fish). used fig. as, *Jin-kō ni — sz*, to be in every body's mouth, much talked of.

K'WAI-SHI,-*szru*,-*sh'ta*, クワイスル, 會, *i.v.* To assemble, to meet together.
Syn. ATSZMARU, YORI-AU.

K'WAI-SHO, クワイシヨ, 會所, *n.* A place for assembling to transact public business; a public hall, town-house.

K'WAI-SHU, クワイシユ, 會主, *n.* The head man of an assembly, meeting, or party of pleasure; a chairman.

†K'WAI-TAI, クワイタイ, 懷胎, *n.* Pregnant, with child. Syn. K'WAI-NIN.

†'KWAI-TŌ, クワイタフ, 回答, Returning an answer. Syn. HENJI.

†K'WAI-YEN, クワイエン, 會宴, *n.* Wine party, a convival meeting. — *szru*, to make an entertainment. Syn SHUYEN.

K'WAI-YEN, クワイエン, 囘緣, *n.* A distant relation.

†K'WAI-ZEN, クワイゼン, 快然, Pleasant, cheerful, joyful. — *no keshiki*, cheerful manner. Syn. KOKOROYOI.

K'WA-JI, クワジ, 火事, *n.* A fire, conflagration. — *shōzoku*, a fireman's uniform. — *ga aru*, there is a fire.

K'WA-KI, クワキ, 火氣, *n.* Heat, caloric. Syn. HONOKE.

K'WA-KIU, クワキフ, 火急, (*ō isogi*). Great haste, urgent, or pressing.

†K'WAKKEI, クワツケイ, 活計, *n.* Livelihood, way or expedients used for getting a living. — *ga tsztanai*, inexpert at making a living.
Syn. KUCHISZGI, KURASH'KATA.

K'WAKKŌ, クワツカウ, 霍香, *n.* A kind of medicinal plant.

K'WA-KO, クワコ, 過去, (*szgisaru*). *n.* The previous state of existence. (Bud.); the past.

K'WAKU, クワク, 畫, *n.* The strokes of a character. *Kono ji wa jūsan — de gozarimas*, this character has 13 strokes. *Iku —*, how many strokes?

K'WAKU, クワク, 槨, *n.* A vault in which a coffin is placed.

†'K'WAKU-GEN, クワクゲン, 確言, (*katai kotoba*). *n.* Firm, certain, or sure saying.

K'WAKU-RAN, クワクラン, 霍亂, *n.* Cholera morbus.

K'WAKU-SHIPPŪ, クワクシツプウ, 鶴膝風, *n.* Name of a scrofulous disease of the joints.

K'WAKU-SHITSZ, クワクシツ, 確執, *n.* Ill-will, spite, enmity, malice. *Isasaka no machigai yori — ni nari*,
Syn. MU-JUN, URAMI, MOME.

K'WAKU-YOKU, クワクヨク, 鶴翼, *n.* An order of battle, in shape like a crane with wings extended.

K'WAM-BAKU, クワンバク, 關白, *n.* An officer who acts as the Prime Minister of the Mikado.

K'WAM-BUTSZ-YE, クワンブツヱ, 灌佛會, *n.* The festival of the 8th day of the 4th month, being the birth day of Shaka.

K'WAM-MIYŌ, クワンミヤウ, 官名, (*Yaku no na*). *n.* Official title.

K'WAM-MON, クワンモン, 關門, (*Seki no to*). *n.* A gate on a public road, near a police station house, where persons and goods are inspected, passports demanded, &c. Syn. SEKI-SHO.

K'WAN, クワン, 官, (*Yaku*). Office, official. — *ni aru mono*, those who hold public office.

K'WAN, クワン, 棺, *n.* A coffin.
Syn. HITSZGI.

K'WAN, クワン, 環, *n.* A ring.
Syn. WA.

K'WAN, クワン, 館, (*yakata*). *n.* A large house. *Shō-k'wan*, a merchant's house.

K'WA-NAN, クワナン, 火難, (*hi no wazawai*). *n.* Calamity, or misfortune caused by a fire.

K'WAN-I, クワン井, 官位, *n.* Office, and rank.

†K'WANJI-TO, クワンジ, 莞爾, *adv.*

Smilingly. — *sh'te uchi-warau*, to smile. Syn. NIKO-NIKO.

K'WAN-JŌ, クワンジヤウ, 勸請, Erecting a temple for the worship of a god of another country.

K'WAN-KE, クワンケ, 勸化, *n.* Contributions for temple, or religious purposes. — *szru*, to make contributions. — *wo tanomu*, to solicit contributions. Syn. HŌGA.

†KW'AN-KEI, クワンケイ, 關係, Concern, meddling with, interfering in, mixing up with, endangering, involving, a person in trouble. *Ayaui koto ni — senu ga yoi*, it is better to have nothing to do with a dangerous business. *Watakushi wa — wa nai*, I will have nothing to do with it,— will not meddle with it. Syn. KAKARI-AI.

†K'WAN-KI, クワンキ, 歡喜, *n.* Joy, delight, pleasure. — *yōyaku*, to dance for joy. Syn. YOROKOBI.

K'WAN-NEN, クワンネン, 觀念, *n.* Concluding, or making up one's mind to anything, resignation. (Bud.) *Yo no naka wo hakanaki mono to — szru.*

†K'WAN-NIN, クワンニン, 寬仁, Clement, lenient, benignant generous.

K'WAN-NO-KI, クワンノキ, 關木, *n.* A bar, or bolt, for fastening a gate.

†K'WAN-RAKU, クワンラク, 歡樂, *n.* Happiness, pleasure. — *wo kiwamuru*, to enjoy the highest degree of happiness.

K'WAN-ROKU, クワンロク, 官祿, *n.* Salary, or income of nobles and officials. Syn. TAKA, ROKU.

K'WAN-SHOKU, クワンショク, 官職, *n.* Office. Syn. YAKUME.

K'WAN-SŌ, クワンサウ, 觀想, *n.* A Buddhist word, the same as *K'wan-nen.*

K'WAN-SZ, クワンス, 鑵子, *n.* An iron tea-kettle.

†K'WAN-TAI, クワンタイ, 緩怠, (*yuruku okotaru.*) Slow, dilatory, procrastinating.

†K'WANTARU, クワンタル, 冠, (cont. of *Kwan to aru.*) The principal, chief, most important. *K'wan to szru*, to regard as the principal. — *mono.*

K'WAN-TŌ, クワントウ, 關東, The eight departments of Musashi, Awa, Kadzsa, Shimōsa, Kōdzke, Shimotszke, Hitachi, and Sagami.

K'WAN-ZŌ, クワンザウ, 萱草, (*waszre gusa.*) A kind of flowering plant.

K'WARARI-TO, クワラリト, 豁然, *adv.* Fully, thoroughly, clearly. *Yo ga — aketa*, it has become broad day-light. Syn. K'WATSZ-ZEN.

†K'WA-REI, クワレイ, 花麗, Beautiful, splendid. Syn. UTSZKUSHII, HANAYAKA.

K'WARIN, クワリン, 花梨, *n.* A kind of tree, quince?

K'WA-RIYŌ, クワレウ, 過料, *n.* A fine, mulct, penalty, forfeit. — *wo toru*, to impose a fine.

K'WA-SAI, クワサイ, 火災, *n.* Calamity, or loss from a fire. Syn. K'WA-NAN.

KUWASE,-*ru*,-*ta*, クハセル, 令喫, Causative of *Kui*. To cause, or let another eat, to feed. *Kuwaseru koto deki-nai*, cannot get anything for them to eat, cannot support them.

†K'WA-SEI, クワセイ, 火星, *n.* The planet Mars.

†K'WASEI, クワセイ, 化生, (*kawari umareru.*) Transformation, or change of a living thing. *Kaiko ga chō ni — sh'ta*, the silk worm is changed into a butterfly.

K'WA-SEKI, クワセキ, 化石, (*ishi ni kawaru,*) *n.* Petrifaction. *Hamaguri no —*, a petrified clam.

K'WA-SHA, クワシヤ, 花車, *n.* A maid servant in a prostitute house. Syn. YARITE.

K'WASHI, クワシ, 菓子, *n.* Confectionary, sweetmeats, fruit.

K'WA,-*shi*,-*szru*,-*sh'ta*, クワスル, 化, *t.v.* To transform, change, metamorphose. *Ki ga ishi ni k'wash'ta*, wood is changed into a stone. Syn. HENDZRU, KAWARU.

KUWASHI,-*sz*,-*sh'ta*, クハス, 令喫, caust. of *Kui*. To give, or let another eat. *Kuwash'te kudasare*, let me eat it, or give me to eat.

†K'WA-SHI,-*szru*,-*sh'ta*, クワスル, 和, *t. v.* To unite, mix, blend. Syn. MAZERU.

KUWASHII,-KI, クハシイ, 精, *a.* Minute, particular, intimately. *Kuwashiku shiranu.* do not know particularly. *Buppō ni kuwashii*, intimately acquainted with Buddhist doctrines. Syn. KOMAYAKA.

K'WASHI-BON, クワシボン, 菓子盆, *n.* A small tray.

KUWASHIKU, or KUWASHIU, クハシク, *adv.* see *Kuwashii.*

K'WASHI-YA, クワシヤ, 菓子屋, *n.* A confectionary shop.

†K'WA-SHOKU,-*szru*, クワショク, 貨殖, (*takara wo fuyasz.*) To increase in riches, to grow rich. Syn. KANE WO NOBASZ.

K'WA-SŌ,-*szru*, クワサウ, 火葬, To burn the bodies of the dead. Syn. DABI.

K'WASZRU, クワスル, See *K'washi.*

†K'WA-TŌ, クワタウ, 過當, Beyond one's

desert, above what one's position entitles him to. — *no itari zonji soro*, feel it to be far above my desert. Syn. K'WABUN.

K'WATSZ, クワツ, 活, *n.* Life. — *wo ireru*, to resuscitate, (as a person apparently dead).

†K'WATSZ-BUTSZ, クワツブツ, 活物, (*ikimono*), *n.* Living things, things having life.

K'WATSZ-JI, クワツジ, 活字, *n.* A movable type. — *ban*, printed by movable type.

†K'WATSZ-ZEN TO, クワツゼン, 豁然, *adv.* Clearly, luminously. *Me ga — hiraku*, eyes suddenly and completely opened.

K'WATTO, クワツト, 豁, *adv.* In a sudden flash, or blaze. — *moyetatsz*, to blaze up suddenly. — *seki-men szru*, to grow suddenly red in the face. Syn. TACHI-MACHI.

K'WA-YAKU, クワヤク, 火藥, *n.* Gunpowder. Syn. YEN-SHŌ.

K'WA-YEN, クワエン, 火焔, *n.* A flame, blaze. Syn. HO-NŌ.

KUWAYE,-*ru*,-*ta*, クハヘル, 啣, *t. v.* To bite, to hold in the mouth, or between the teeth. *Kiseru wo* —, to hold a pipe in the mouth. *Fude wo* —, to hold a pen in the mouth.

KUWAYE,-*ru*,-*ta*, クハヘル, 加, *t.v.* To add something to another, to join, combine, unite, to augment. *Chikara wo* —, to help, assist. *Gun-zei wo* —, to join an army. *Fude wo* —, to make additional corrections with the pen. Syn. SOYERU, MASZ.

†K'WA-ZAI, クワザイ, 過罪, *n.* Crime, transgression. Syn. TSZMI, TOGA,

†K'WŌDAI, クワウダイ, 廣大, (*hiroku ōinaru*). Great, extensive, vast. — *no go on arigataku zonji soro*, thankful for your great kindness. — *mu-hen*, great and boundless. Syn. TAK'SAN.

K'WŌGŌ, クワウゴウ, 皇后, *n.* Empress, queen.

K'WŌ-IN, クワウイン, 光陰, *n*, Time, — *ya no gotoku*, time flies like an arrow. — *wo tsziyasz*, the waste time. *Itadzrani — wo okuru*, to spend time uselessly. Syn. TOKI, TSZKI-HI.

†K'WŌ-KOTSZ, クワウコツ, 恍惚, Entranced, enraptured; indistinctly, confusedly, (to remember).

†K'WŌ-RIN, クワウリン, 光臨, Coming. *Go — no hodo machi tatematszri soro*, I shall wait for your coming.

‖K'WŌ-SEN, クワウセン, 黃泉, *n.* Hades, the place of the dead. Syn. YOMI-NO-KUNI.

K'WŌTEI, クワウテイ, 皇帝, *n.* Emperor.

KU-YAKU, クヤク, 公役, *n.* Labor exacted by the government from farmers, for which no pay is received, public service. — *ga ataru*, to be pressed into public service. Syn. YAKU.

KUYAMI,-*mu*,-*nda*, クヤム, 悔, *t.v.* To repent, to be sorry for, regret, deplore, to feel compunction. *Tszmi wo* —, to feel sorrow for one's crimes, or sins. *Kuyande mo kayeranu*, repentance will be of no avail. Syn. KŌK'WAI, ZAN-NEN.

KUYAMI, クヤミ, 悔, *n.* Regret, repentance, sorrow, remorse, compunction. — *wo iu*, to express regret.

KUYASHII,-KI, クヤシイ, 悔, *a.* Producing sorrow, repentance, or regret, lamentable. *Kuyashii koto*, a thing exciting regret, or disappointment.

KUYASHIGARI,-*ru*,-*tta*, クヤシガル, 悔, To be always feeling regret, sorrow, or penitence, to be disappointed.

KUYASHIKU, or KUYASHIU, クヤシク, 悔, *adv.* Sorrowful, repentantly, remorseful. — *omō*, to regret.

KUYASHISA, クヤシサ, 悔, *n.* Repentance, regret, remorse, sorrow, compunction.

KU-YŌ,-*szru*, クヤウ, 供養, To make offerings to the gods, or to the spirits of the dead.

KUYOKU, クヨク, 苦薏, *n.* Camomile flowers.

KUYO-KUYO, クヨクヨ, *adv.* Having the mind anxiously brooding over anything, thinking long and anxiously about. — *omō.*

KUYORI,-*ru*,-*tta*, クヨル, 燻, *i.v.* To burn slowly without blaze, to moulder, to smoke. *Kō no kuyoru gotoku*, like the burning of incense. Syn. IBURU, SHITAMOYERU.

KUYORASHI,-*sz*,-*sh'ta*, クヨラス, 燻, *t.v.* To burn slowly and emit smoke, to smoke. *Kō wo* —, to burn incense.

KUZETSZ, クゼツ, 口舌, *n.* A dispute, or quarrel between husband and wife, or brothers. — *goto tayedz.*

M

MA, マ, 間, *n.* A room; interval of time or space, leisure, opportunity. *Tszgi no ma*, the next room. — *nashi*, or — *mo naku*, but a short time; in a little while. *Yoi ma ga attaraba ki-mashō*, if I should have leisure I will come. *Ma wo mi-awasete hanashi wo szru,* to watch one's opportunity and speak. Syn. AIDA, HEYA.

MA, マ, 目, *n.* The eye, only used in compound words.

MA, マ, 魔, A demon, evil spirit. *Akuma,* (idem.)

MA, マ, 眞, Just, true, perfectly, exactly. *Ma ni ukeru,* to take to be true,—to believe. *Massakasama,* exactly upside down, —exactly reversed. *Ma-aomuke,* face turned exactly upward.

MA, マ, *adv.* Yet, still, more. *Ma h'totsz,* one more. *Ma szkoshi,* a little more. *Ma ichido,* once more. *Ma chitto,* a little more. Syn. MO, IMA.

MĀ, マア, Exclam. of entreaty, satisfaction, wonder, surprise, admiration. *Mā, watakushi no iu koto kiki nasare. Mā, yoroshii,* well, that will do. *Mā, tōbun kōsh'te okimashō,* well, I'll let it be so for the present. *Mā utszkushii hana de wa nai ka,* is it not a beautiful flower? *Mā komaru ja nai ka,* how troublesome it is!

MABARA, マバラ, 疏, Apart, separated, scattered, not close together, at intervals. — *ni naru,* to become separated, one here and one there. — *ni szru,* to place apart, or scatter about. *Ame ga — ni furu,* the rain fell in scattered drops. Syn. ARAI.

MABAYUI,-KI,-KU,-SHI, マバユイ, 眩, Dazzled, overpowered by too strong a light. *Mabayukute mirarenu,* so dazzling I cannot see. Syn. MABUSHII.

MA-BI, マビ, 間日, (*aida no hi*). *n.* Intervening, or intercurrent day.

MABIKI,-*ku,*-*ita,* マビク, 間曳, *t.v.* To thin out, to make less close, as plants or trees. *Na wo mabiku,* to thin the rape-seed plant, (when too close together.)

MABISASHI, マビサシ, 眼庇, *n.* Eye-shade, frontlet of a helmet. *Te de — wo szru,* to shade the eyes with the hand.

MABOROSHI, マボロシ, 幻, *n.* A vision, optical illusion, unreal. *Yume maboroshi no yo no naka,* the world (is) like a dream, or vision.

MABU, マブ, 坑, *n.* A mine from which ore is dug.

MABU, マブ, 私夫, *n.* A paramour, lover.

MABUCHI, マブチ, 眼眶, *n.* Eye-lid.

MABUKA-NI, マブカニ, 目深, *adv.* Eyes deeply shaded, or set deep in the head. — *kaburu.*

MABURE,-*ru,*-*ta,* マブレル, 塗, *n.* Smeared, or daubed with any thing, dusted over. *Hai-mabure,* covered with ashes. *Chi-mabure,* smeared with blood. *Doro ni mabureru,* smeared with mud.
Syn. DARAKE, MAMIRE, MIDORO.

MABURI,-*ru,*-*tta,* マブル, 塗, *t. v.* To smear, or daub with. *Dango ni satō wo maburu,* to cover the outside of a dumpling with sugar. *Szmi wo —,* to daub with ink. Syn. NURU.

MABUSHI,-*sz,*-*sh'ta,* マブス, 塗, *t.v.* idem.

MABUSHII,-KI,-KU,-U, マブシイ, Dazzled, overpowered by the light. *Mabushikute me ga akerare nai,* my eyes are so dazzled I cannot open them.
Syn. MABAYUI.

MABUTA, マブタ, 瞼, *n.* The upper eyelid.

MACHI, マチ, 町, *n.* A street, a town. — *no hadzre,* end of a street. Syn CHŌ.

MACHI, マチ, 襠, *n.* The gore which connects the legs of trowsers.

MACHI, *matsz,*-*tta,* マツ, 待, *t. v.* To wait, to stay, to expect, look for. *Mate,* (imp.) wait. *O machi nasare,* or *matte kudasare,* idem. *Hisashiku matta,* have waited long. *Mateba yoroshii,* you had better wait. *Mataneba naran,* must wait. *Matō ka,* or *machimashō ka,* shall I wait? *Matte mo yoi ka,* will it do if I wait? *Matanai hō ga yoi,* it is better not to wait. *Matadz ni yukimash'ta,* he went without waiting. *Mataba matte mo yoi,* if you wait, very well. *Matte-iru,* is waiting.

MACHI-AI,-*au,*-*atta,* マチアフ, 待合, *i. v.* To wait for each other, to wait by appointment, or for the coming of another.

MACHI-AKASHI,-*sz,*-*sh'ta,* マチアカス, 待明, *t. v.* To wait the whole night.

MACHI-AWASE,-*ru,*-*ta,* マチアハセル, 待合, *t. v.* same as *Machiai.*

MACHI-BUGIYŌ, マチブギヤウ, 町奉行, *n.* Mayor of a city.

MACHI-BUSE, マチブセ, 待伏, *n.* Lying in wait, or in ambush. *Monokage ni — wo szru.*

MACHI-DŌI,-KI,-KU, マチドホイ, 待遠, Long in coming, long delayed, seeming long deferred. *Yo no akeru no ga machidōi,* the day seems so long in breaking. *Omaye no kuru no ga machidōkatta,* you seemed so long in coming.

MACHIGAI,-*au,*-*tta,* マチガフ, 間違, *i. v.* To mistake, to miss, to err, to be different. *Michi ga machigatta,* have missed the road. Syn. CHIGAU, TAGAU.

MACHIGAI, マチガヒ, 間違, *n.* Mistake, error, miss. — *ga dekita,* have made a mistake. — *ga nai,* there is no mistake.

MACHI-GAI-SHO, マチグワイショ, 町會所, *n.* A town hall, a justice's office, or court room.

MACHIGAYE,*-ru,-ta*, マチガヘル, 間違, *t. v.* To mistake, miss. *Michi wo* —, to mistake the road. *H'to wo* —, to mistake a person.

MACHI-KAKE,*-ru,-ta*, マチカケル, 待掛, *t. v.* To wait for, expecting every moment.

MACHI-KANE,*-ru,-ta*, マチカヌル, 待兼, *t. v.* To wait impatiently for, hard to wait for. *Hana no saku wo* —.

MACHI-KURASHI,*-sz,-sh'ta*, マチクラス, 待暮, *t. v.* To wait the whole day, or any indefinite time.

MACHI-MACHI, マチマチ, 區區, Many and different, various, diverse. — *no h'to kokoro*, various are the minds of men. Syn. IRO-IRO, SAMA-ZAMA.

MACHI-MŌKE,*-ru,-ta*, マチマウケル, 待設, *t.v.* To get ready in expectation of, to be prepared for and wait. *Go-chisō wo sh'te kiyaku wo* —, to make ready a feast and wait for the guests.

MACHIN, マチン, 馬陳, *n.* Nux-vomica.

MACHI-TSZKE,*-ru,-ta*, マチツケル, 待着, *t.v.* Having waited, at length to meet, or find.

MACHITTO, マチツト, 今少, Just a little, but a little. — *machinasare*, wait but a moment.

MACHI-UKE,*-ru,-ta*, マチウケル, 待受, *t.v.* To wait and receive, to wait for the coming of any one, (as guests.)

MACHI-WABI,*-ru,-ta*, マチワビル, 待侘, To wait anxiously for, or in suspense, to long for the coming. *Yo no akeru wo* —, to long for the day to break.

MACHI-YA, マチヤ, 町屋, *n.* The houses in a street, or town. Syn. CHŌKA.

MADA, マダ, 未, *adv.* Still, yet. *Mada konu*, not yet come. *Mada kayeranai*, not yet returned. *Mada hayai*, yet early, too early. *Mada yoroshii*, it will still do.

†MADAKI, マダキ, 未明, (*imada akezaru.*) *n.* Early, before daylight, beforehand, previously. *Niwatori no — ni nakite. Waga na wa — tachi ni keri*, my name is already blazed abroad. *Madaki ni iu*, to speak of something still future.

MADARA, マダラ, 斑, Spotted, dappled, marked with different colors. — *ni naru.*

MADARUI,-KI,-KU,-SHI,-Ū,-SA, マダルイ, 目倦, Tardy, slow, taking time. Syn. HIMADORU, TEMA GA IRU.

MADASHIMO, マダシモ, Still, yet, after all, better, or preferable. *Dorobō yori wa — bakuchi no hō tszmi ga karui*, the crime of gambling is lighter than that of robbery. *Dōgu naku sh'te mo inochi ga areba — no koto*, if one should lose all his furniture (by fire) and yet save his life, he is well off.

MADE, マデ, 迄, *post-pos.* To, until, till, even to, as far as to. *Yedo kara Yokohama made*, from Yedo to Yokohama. *Itsz made kakattara dekimashō ka*, how long will it take you to do this? *Ima made*, until now. *Iu made mo nai koto*, a thing of which there is no need to speak. *Dekinakereba sore made no koto*, if you cannot do it, so let it rest. *Omaye made ga sonna koto wo iu*, I tell that matter even to you. *Doko made*, to what place, how far? *Koko made*, to this place, so far. Syn. OYOBU.

MADO, マド, 窓, *n.* A window. — *no ko*, the bars of a window.

MA-DŌ マダウ, 魔道, *n.* (*akuma no michi.*) *n.* Devilish, or infernal doctrines.

MADŌ, マドフ, 惑, See *Madoi.*

MADOI,*-ō,-otta*, マドフ, 惑, *i.v.* To stray, to wander from the right way, to err, to be deluded, misled, beguiled. *Onna ni madōte michi ni somuku*, beguiled by women he forsook the right way. Syn. MAYŌ, OBORERU, AZAMUKARERU, DAMASARERU.

MADOI, マドヒ, 惑, *n.* Delusion, error. — *wo toku*, set free from error.

MADOI,*-ō,-otta*, マドフ, 賠, *t.v.* To make up a loss, to indemnify, to make good, to pay, as a surety. *H'to no shakkin wo* —, to pay, as a surety, money that another has borrowed. Syn. TSZGUNAU, AGANAU.

MADŌI,-KI,-KU,-SHI, マドホイ, 間遠, Long intervals, distant intervals, seldom.

†MADOI, マド井, 圓居, Sitting in a circle, or ring. *Madoish'te mono-gatari wo szru.* KURUMAZA.

†MADOKA, マドカ, 圓, *n.* Round, circular. — *naru tszki*, the round moon. Syn. MARUI.

MADORI, マドリ, 間取, *n.* The arrangement of rooms in a house, plan of a house. *Iye no — ga warui*, the house is badly arranged.

MADOROI,-KI,-KU,-SHI,-Ō,-SA, マドロイ, Slow, tardy, inactive, dilatory, tedious. Syn. MADARUI.

MADOROMI,*-mu*, マドロム, 間眠, *i.v.* To doze, to drowse, fall into a short nap. *Madoromitaru yume*, a dream seen in a short doze. Syn. INEMURI.

MADOWASHI,*-sz,-sh'ta*, マドハス, 令惑, *t.v.* To lead astray, cause to err, or wander from the right way, to delude, beguile. *Ayashiki hō nite yo wo madowasz*, to delude the world with strange doctrines. Syn. AZAMUKU, TABURAKASZ, MAYOWASZ, DAMASZ.

MADZ, マヅ, 先, *adv.* First, in the first place; however, still, yet, upon the whole. *Madz sono mi wo osameneba iye wa osamaranu*, if a person does not first govern himself, he cannot govern his family. *Madz yoroshii*, however, it will do. *Madz sonna mon da*, upon the whole, it is about so. Syn. SAKI NI, MAYE MOTTE, MĀ.

MADZI,-KI,-KU,-SHI,-Ū,-SA, マヅイ, Unpleasant to the taste, nasty. *Kono sake wa madzi*, this wine is nasty.
Syn. UMAKUNAI.

†MADZMOTTE, マヅモツテ, 先以, *adv.* First, in the first place, (epistolary word).

MADZSHII,-KI,-KU,-SHI,-Ū,-SA, マヅシイ, 貧, Poor, destitute, needy. Syn. BIMBŌ, HIN-KIU, KON-KIU.

†MAGA, マガ, 禍, *(wazawai).* Misfortune, unfortunate.

MAGAI,-au,-ōta, マガフ, 紛, *i.v.* To imitate, or resemble, to be confounded with. *Kumoi ni magō okitsz shira-nami*, the large white waves blended with the clouds.

MAGAI, マガヒ, 紛, *n.* Imitation, resemblance. *Kin-magai*, imitation of gold. *Bekkō-magai*, imitation of tortoise shell.

MAGAKI, マガキ, 籬, *n.* A fence made of bamboo.

†MAGA-MAGASHII,-KI,-KU, マガマガシイ, Unfortunate, unlucky.
Syn. FUKITSZ, IMAIMASHII.

†MAGANE, マガネ, 鐵, *n.* Iron.
Syn. TETSZ.

MAGAO, マガホ, 眞顔, *(makoto no kao), n.* A sincere countenance, a straight face. *— ni natte uso wo iu*, to tell a lie with a straight face.

MAGARI,-ru,-tta, マガル, 曲, *i.v.* Bent, crooked, not straight; morally crooked, perverse, depraved. *Hari ga magatta*, the needle is crooked. *Konjō no magatta yatsz*, a fellow of perverse temper.
Syn. KAGAMU.

MAGARI-GANE, マガリガネ, 矩, *n.* A carpenter's square.

MAGARI-KADO, マガリカド, 曲角, *n.* The bend, or corner of a road.

MAGARI-MICHI, マガリミチ, 曲路, *n.* A crooked road.

MAGASHIRA, マガシラ, 内眥, *n.* Inner canthus of the eye.

MAGAWASE,-ru,-ta, マガハセル, 令紛, *t.v.* To imitate, counterfeit, or cause to resemble.

MAGAYE,-ru,-ta, マガヘル, 紛, *t. v.* To make in imitation, to counterfeit. *Bīdoro wo szishō ni magayeru*, to make glass in imitation of crystal.

MAGE, マゲ, 髷, *n.* The cue worn by Japanese men on the top of the head; also the hair gathered and tied into a bunch, as is done by the women. — *wo yū*, to dress the hair. Syn. WAGE.

MAGE,-ru,-ta, マゲル, 曲, *t.v.* To bend, to crook; also 枉, to force, compel; used also in entreaty. *Yubi wo mageru*, to bend the finger. *Ri wo hi ni magete mo watakushi no negai wo kite kudasare.* I pray you most earnestly to grant my request, let the consequences be what they may. *Ga wo —*, force or turn your carriage this way, (used in polite and pressing invitation to make a visit.) Syn. KAGAMERU, TAWAMERU.

MAGE-MONO, マゲモノ, 曲物, *n.* Round boxes, such as pill-boxes, made by bending wood.

MAGETE, マゲテ, (*pp.* of *Mageru*). *adv.* Used in entreaty, when there is some unwillingness in the person entreated. = I pray you, please try and to accede to my request. *Magete o-tanomi-mōsz*, idem. *Magete h'to no kokoro ni sh'tagau*, try and submit to his will.

MAGIRAKASHI,-sz,-sh'ta, マギラカス, 紛, *t.v.* To cause to be undistinguishable, or discernable, to obscure, confuse, to confound, mystify. *Uta wo utatte shimpai wo —*, to sing a song, and forget one's troubles. *Ōkina koye wo sh'te h'to no hanashi wo —*, to make a loud noise, in order to prevent one from hearing what others are saying.

MAGIRAWASHII,-KI,-KU,-Ū, マギラハシイ, 紛敷, That which imitates, counterfeits, or resembles the appearance, form, or manner of something else. *I-fū no nari wo itashi, rō-nin ni magirawashiku, hanahada furachi no koto ni soro.*

MAGIRE,-ru,-ta, マギレル, 紛, *i.v.* To be undiscernable, or undistinguishable because of being like, or resembling each other; to be confounded with, blended with. *Yo ni magirete tachi-noku*, to escape under cover of the night. *Teki no gun-zei ni migirete shinobi-iru*, confounded with the army of the enemy he remained concealed.

MAGIRE, マキレ, 紛, *n.* Confusion, mistake, error, perplexity. — *nashi*, no mistake.

MAGIRE-KOMI,*–mu,–nda*, マギレコム, 紛, 込, *i.v.* Mingled with other things in confusion so as to be undistinguishable.

MAGIRE-MONO, マギレモノ, 紛物, *n.* A thing made in imitation of a genuine article, a counterfeit. Syn. MAGAI-MONO,

MAGIRI,*–ru,–tta*, マギル, 間遮, *t.v.* To brace a sail to the wind. *Ho wo magitte hashiru*, to sail with the sails braced to the wind.

MAGIWA, マギハ, 眞際, *n.* The time near, or bordering on any event. *Shuttatsz no* —, the time near to the moment of starting.

MAGO, マゴ, 孫, *n.* Grandchild.

MAGO, マゴ, 馬子, *n.* One who leads, or attends on a pack-horse.

MAGŌ, マガフ, See *Magai*.

†MAGOKORO, マゴコロ, 眞心, True, sincere, without deception or hypocrisy.

MAGO-MAGO,*–szru*, マゴマゴ, Confused, perplexed what to do, in a quandary. — *sh'te iru.* Syn. URO-URO.

MAGO-NO-TE, マゴノテ, 瓜杖, *n.* An instrument made of wood to scratch the back with.

MAGOTSZKI,*–ku,–ita*, マゴツク, *i.v.* To be confused, uncertain, or perplexed what to do, to be in a quandary.

MAGUCHI, マグチ, 間口, *n.* The front dimensions of a house. — *wa jikken, oku-yuki wa jūgo ken*, the front, is 60 feet, depth 90 feet.

MAGURE,*–ru,–ta*, マグレル, *i.v.* To be deranged, confused. *Ki ga magureta*, to be deranged in mind, to become desperate or careless from misfortune.

MAGURE-ATARI, マグレアタリ, 偶中, *n.* Hit at random, hit by a chance shot, to guess by chance.

MAGURE-KOMI,*–mu,–nda*, マグレコム, same as *Magire-komu.*

MAGURO, マグロ, 鮥, *n.* The tunny fish.

MAGURU, マグル, see *Mage.*

MA-GUSA, マグサ, 馬艸, *n.* Grass, such as is fed to horses.

MA-GUSO, マグソ, 馬糞, *n.* Horse dung.

MA-GUWA, マグハ, 馬把, *n.* A harrow.

†MAHI,*–szru*, マヒ, 麻痺, *(shibireru.)* To be numb, palzied, devoid of sensation.

MAHIRU, マヒル, 正晝, *n.* Noon, midday.

MAHO, マホ, 眞帆, *n.* A sail squared to the wind. — *kakete hashiru.*

MA-HŌ, マハフ, 魔法, *n.* Devilish, or infernal rites, magic arts, conjuration. — *tszkai*, a conjurer, sorcerer, magician.— *wo tszkau*, topractise sorcery, or enchant.

†MAHOSHII,–KI,–KU,–Ū,–SA, マホシイ, An affix to verbal roots, compounded of *ma*, (the same as *mu*, or *n*, future), and *hoshi*, to wish, desire, thus; *Kika-mashoshi*, = *Kikan to hosszru*, wish to hear. *Mi-mahoshii*, = *Min to hosszru*, wish to see.

MAI, マイ, 毎, *a.* Every, each. *Mai nichi*, every day. *Maichō*, every morning. *Maiban*, every evening. *Mai ji*, every business. *Mainen*, *Mai getsz.* Syn. GOTO-NI.

MAI,*–au*, or *ō,–tta*, or *ōta*, マフ, 舞, *t.v.* To dance to music. Syn. ODORU.

MAI, マイ, A coll. fut. neg. affix to verbs; having also a dubitative meaning, as, *Yuki-maszmai*, or *Yuku-mai*, will not go, or, I think will not go. *Aru mai*, or *Ari-maszmai*, there are not, or, I think there are not.

MAIBA, マヒバ, 撥柎, *n.* A reel.

MAI-BITO, マヒビト, 伶人, *n.* A dancer.

MA-ICHIDO, マイチド, 今一度, Once more, again.

MAI-DO, マイド, 毎度, *adv.* Often, frequently. Syn. TABI-TABI.

†MAIFUKU, マイフク, 埋伏, *n.* An ambush. — *szru*, to lay in ambush. Syn. FUSEZEI.

MAI-GIRI, マヒギリ, 牽鑽, *n.* A drill.

MAI-HADA, マイハダ, 捲絮, *n.* A kind of oakum used for caulking boats. — *wo tszmeru*, to caulk. — *wo kau*, id. — *wo ireru*, id. Syn. MAKIHADA.

MAIKAI, マイクワイ, 玫瑰, *n.* A kind of flower. Rosa rugosa.

MAI-KAZE, マヒカゼ, 旋風, *n.* A whirlwind. Syn. TSZMUJI-KAZE.

†MAI-K'YO, マイキヨ, 枚擧, To specify, enumerate. — *ni itoma aradz*, have not time to enumerate.

MAI-KO, マヒコ, 舞妓, *n.* A dancing-girl.

MAI-MAI, マイマイ, 毎毎, *adv.* Often, frequently. Syn. TABI-TABI.

MAI-MAI-MUSHI, マヒマヒムシ, 豉虫, *n.* A kind of small bug which floats on water. Syn MIDZSZMASHI.

MAI-MAI-TSZBURA, マヒマヒツブラ, 蝸牛, *n.* A snail.

MAI-NAI, マヒナヒ, 賄賂, *n.* A bribe. — *wo tszkau*, to bribe. Syn. WAIRO.

†MAIRASHI,*–sz,–sh'ta*, マヰラス, 進, *t. v.* To present, to give, to send to a superior, to offer to the *Kami*. *Oshiye-mairaszbeshi*, will teach (to a superior). *Shisha wo* —, to send a messenger. Syn. SHINJŌ, AGEMASZ.

MAIRADO, マヒラド, 眞平戸, *n.* A door with cross-pieces of wood at narrow intervals,

MAIRI,*-ru,-tta,* マヰル, 參, *i.* or *t. v.* To go, to come, to go to a temple for worship. To take, (as food, but only when speaking of others), also an auxilliary verb, same as *Yuku,* = can, or neg. cannot. *Itsz yedo ye mairimasz,* when are you going to Yedo? *Itsz yedo kara mairimash'ta,* when did you come from Yedo? *Tera ye mairu,* to visit the temple. *Meshi wo mairu,* to take food. *Dōmo gaten ga mairi-masen,* I can't understant it, all I can do.
Syn. YUKU, KURU, MŌDZRU, SANKEI, AGARU.

MAISZ, マヒス, 賣僧, *n.* A hypocritical priest, an avaricious priest who applies temple funds to his private purposes.

MAJI, マヂ, 間風, *n.* A south-west wind.

MAJI,-KI,-KU, マジ, 間敷, A neg. affix to verbs, having a future, or dubitative meaning. *Iumajiki koto,* a thing that should not be said. *Mōszmajiku soro,* will not say.

MAJIKAI,-KI,-KU,-SHI,-Ō, マヂカイ, 間近, Close by, near in space or time. *Teki no toki no koye majikaku kikoye,* the shouts of the enemy were heard close by.

||MAJI-MAJI-SH'TE, マジマジシテ, *adv.* Grave, sober in manner, dull, listless.

MAJIME, マジメ, 馬自物, Grave, sober, serious in manner. — *na kao de uso wo iu,* to tell a lie with a straight face.
Syn. MAGAO.

MAJINAI,*-au,-tta,* マジナフ, 咒, *t.v.* To charm, to bind by a spell, or magic influence, to exorcise, bewitch. *Mushiba wo* —, to charm the toothache.

MAJINAI, マジナヒ, 咒, *n.* A charm, spell, enchantment. — *wo szru.*

†MAJIRAI, マジラヒ, 交, *n.* Friendship, fellowship, intimacy. Syn. TSZKIAI.

MAJIRI,*-ru,-tta,* マジル, 雜, *t.v.* To mix, mingle, to alloy, to blend. *Kono sake ni wa midz ga majitte iru,* there is water mixed with this *sake.* *Kana majiri ni kaku,* to write with both Chinese and Japanese characters intermixed.
Syn. KONDZRU.

MAJIRI, マジリ, 外眥, *n.* External canthus of the eye.

MAJIROKI,*-ku,-ita,* マジロク, 瞷, *i.v.* To wink, (as with a strong light, or when a sudden motion is made towards one's face), to blink. *Hadaye tayumadz me majirokadz,* his body did not flinch, nor his eyes blink, (at a sudden thrust.) Syn. MATATAKI.

MAJIWARI,*-ru,-tta,* マジハル, 交, *i.v.* To associate, to be intimate, keep company with, to be friendly with, 雜, mixed, mingled together. *Ashiki tomo ni majiwaru bekaradz,* should not associate with bad companions.
Syn. TSZKI-AU, NAJIMU.

MAJIWARI, マジハリ, 交, *n.* Intimacy, friendship. — *wo muszbu,* to contract a friendship. — *wo tatsz,* to sunder a friendship.

MAJIYE,*-ru,-ta,* マジヘル, 雜, To mix, mingle, blend together.

MA-JUTSZ, マジユツ, 魔術, *n.* Sorcery, magic, witchcraft.

MAKAGE, マカゲ, 目陰, *n.* Eye-shade. *Te nite* — *wo szru,* to shade the eyes with the hand. Syn. MABISASHI.

†MA-KAI, マカイ, 魔界, *n,* The region inhabited by evil spirits.

MAKANAI,*-au,-tta,* マカナフ, 賄, *t.v.* To furnish provisions, provide food, to board, to purvey. *Hitori maye ichibu nite makanau,* to furnish board at an ichibu a head.
Syn. YASHINAU, MOTENASZ.

MAKANAI, マカナヒ, 賄, *n.* Board, entertainment, food. — *wo szru,* to furnish food. — *kata,* the person who boards, or furnishes food to others. — *riyō,* expense of board.

MAKANU, MAKADZ, or MAKANAI, マカヌ, The neg. of *Maki.*

MAKARI,*-ru,* マカル, 罷, To go, return, take leave, to die; now used in combination with other words, without appearing to affect their meaning, except to give an air of sternness, or severity to what is said, and thus much used by officials. *Makari-naranu,* cannot allow it. *Sessha sassoku makari-kosō,* I will go immediately. *Buji ni makari-ari soro,* we are all well no change in our affairs.

MAKASE,*-ru,-ta,* マカセル, 任, *t.v.* To commit to the will of another, to leave to, trust to. *Un wo ten ni makasete h'to ikusa szru,* to go to war leaving one's fate at the disposal of heaven. *Kokoro ni makaseru,* to leave one to do as he likes. *Fude ni makasete kaku,* to write anything that comes uppermost. *Mise wo bantō ni makaseru,* to leave a shop to the management of a clerk. *Ashi ni makasete yuku,* to go not knowing where. Syn. YUDANERU.

MAKASHI,*-sz,-sh'ta,* マカス, 令負, *t. v.* To cause to lose, (in a game or contest), to defeat, conquer, beat, vanquish. *Shōji de h'to wo makasz,* to defeat another in a a game of drafts.

MAKASHI,-*sz*,-*sh'ta*, マカス, 令蒔, Caust. of *Maki*. To cause or let sow, or sprinkle. *Watakushi ni tane wo makash'te kudasare*, let me sow the seed.

MAKASAI,-*sz*,-*sh'ta*, マカス, 令巻, Caust. of*Maki*. To cause or let wind, or bind, &c.

MAKE,-*ru*,-*ta*, マケル, 負, *i v.* To lose in a game or contest, to be defeated, conquered, vanquished, to cheapen, to lessen the price, to be easily affected by, susceptible of. *Ikusa ni makeru*, to be defeated in battle. *Mo szkoshi make-nasare* cheapen it a little. *Szkoshi mo makerare-masen*, I cannot cheapen it in the least. *Nomi ni* —, to suffer from flea-bites. *Urushi ni* —, to be easily poisoned by lacquer.

MAKE-IRO, マケイロ, 負色, The appearance of defeat, signs of giving way. *Teki no ikusa — ni natta*, the army of the enemy showed signs of defeat.

MAKEJI-DAMASHII, マケジダマシヒ, 不負魂, *n.* A person of an unyielding spirit.

MAKE-KACHI, マケカチ, 負勝, *n.* Lose and win. *Mada — wa wakaranu*, do not yet know which will be victorious. Syn. SHŌBU.

MAKE-OSHIMI, マケオシミ, 負惜, *n.* Sorrow, or chagrin on account of being defeated. — *wo iu.*

MAKI, マキ 薪, *n.* Firewood. Syn. TAKIGI.

MAKI, マキ, 槇, *n.* A kind of fir tree.

MAKI, マキ, 巻, *n.* The numeral for volumes of a book. *Jō chiu ge no maki*, the first, middle, and last volume of a book. Syn. KWAN, SATSZ.

MAKI, マキ, 牧, (contr. of *Uma*, and *Oki*). *n*, Pasture ground for horses.

MAKI,-*ku*,-*ita*, マク, 播, *t.v.* To sow, to sprinkle, scatter. *Tane wo maku*, to sow seed. *Midz wo* —, to sprinkle water.

MAKI,-*ku*,-*ita*, マク, 絡, *t.v.* To wind, to turn round some fixed object, to bind, to roll up, to curl. *Ho wo maku*, to furl a sail. *Ito wo* —, to wind thread on a spool. *Ikari wo* —, to heave up an anchor.

MAKI-AGE,-*ru*,-*ta*, マキアゲル, 捲上, *t.v.* To roll up. *Szdare wo* —, to roll up a blind.

MAKI-AMI, マキアミ, 巻網, *n.* A seine. Syn. JIBIKIAMI.

MAKI-CHIRASHI,-*sz*,-*sh'ta*, マキチラス, 撒, *t. v.* To scatter about, to squander. *Kane wo* —,

MAKI-FUDE, マキフデ, 巻筆, *n.* A pencil having the hair secured to the handle with thread.

MAKI-GAMI, マキガミ, 巻紙, *n.* Paper used for letters, kept in long rolls.

MAKI-GARI, マキガリ, 巻狩, *n.* Hunting by surrounding a large district, and gradually driving the animals to the centre.

MAKI-HADA, マキハダ, The same as *Maihada.*

MAKI-JIKU, マキヂク, 巻軸, *n.* The round stick, on which pictures are rolled.

MAKI-KAYESHI,-*sz*,-*sh'ta*, マキカヘス, 巻返, *t.v.* To roll, or wind in an opposite direction, or by reversed turns.

MAKI-KOMI,-*mu*,-*nda*, マキコム, 巻込, *t.v.* To roll, or wind one thing within another.

MAKI-MODOSHI,-*sz*,-*sh'ta*, マキモドス, 巻戻, Same as *Maki-kayeshi.*

MAKI-MONO, マキモノ, 巻物, *n.* Pictures, that are kept rolled up, not hung up.

MAKI-ROKURO, マキロクロ, 捲轆轤, *n.* A capstan, windlass.

MAKI-TABAKO, マキタバコ, 捲煙艸, *n.* A cigar.

MAKI-TSZKE,-*ru*,-*ta*, マキツケル, 巻着, *t.v.* To bind on thing to another by winding many turns of thread &c., around them.

MAKI-WARA, マキワラ, 草把, *n.* A bundle of straw, used as a target.

MAKI-WARI, マキワリ, 槇割, *n.* An axe, used for splitting firewood.

MAKIYE, マキヱ, 巻繪, *n.* Gold lacquered. — *no tansz*, gold lacquered cabinet. — *shi*, a person who paints gold lacquer.

MAKI-ZOYE, マキゾヘ, 連累, *n.* Implicated, or involved in trouble through the offence of another. — *ni au*, to be involved, &c. Syn. REN-RUI.

MAKKAI, or MAKKA-NA, マツカナ, 眞赤, Deep red.

MAKKAKU, マツカク, 眞角, True, or perfectly square. — *na*, *adj.* — *ni*, *adv.*

MAKKŌ, マツカフ, 眞甲, Directly over the head. *Tachi — ni nuki-kazashi*, to hold the sword directly over the head, for a downward blow.

MAKKŌ, マツカウ, 抹香, *n.* A kind of incense.

MAKKURA, マツクラ, 眞暗, Very dark.

MAKKURO, マツクロ, 眞黒, Deep black.

MAKOMO, マコモ, 眞菰, *n.* A kind of rush, used in making coarse bags, and mats.

MAKOTO, マコト, 眞, *n.* Truth. — *wo iu*, to speak the truth. — *wa ten no michi nari*, truth is the way of heaven. *Makoto no*, *adj.* True, real, genuine. *Makoto to szru*, or *Makoto to omō*, to regard as true, to believe. *Makoto to sedz*, to disbelieve.

MAKOTO-NI, マコトニ, 誠, *adv*. Truly, really, indeed.

MAKOTORASHII,-KI,-KU,-Ū, マコトラシイ, Truth-like, having the appearance of truth. *Makotorashii uso wo iu*, to tell a lie which has the semblance of truth. *Makotorashiku hanasz*, to speak with an appearance of truth.

MAKOTOSHIYAKANI, マコトシヤカニ, *adv*. Making a show of truth, having the appearance of being true.

MAKU, マク, 卷, or 播, See *Maki*.

MAKU, マク, 負, See *Make*.

MAKU, マク, 幕, *n*. A curtain, such as are hung before the government stations, around encampments, or before theatres. — *no chi*, the loops in a curtain. *Maku no kushi*, the hooks on which a curtain is hung. — *no monomi*, the hole in a curtain for looking out. — *wo tareru*, to hang up, or let down a curtain. — *wo shiboru*, to gather a curtain up at intervals and let it hang in festoons.

MAKU, or MASHI, マシ, An ancient, and now obsolete affix to verbs, for which the final *n* is now substituted, as. *Mi-maku no hoshiki*, = *min to hosszru*, or coll. *mitai*, desire to see.

MAKUHAI, マクハイ, 交合, *n*. Coition.

MAKURA, マクラ, 枕, *n*. A pillow. — *wo szru*, to lay the head on a pillow. — *wo sh'te neru*. *Shiro wo — ni uchi-jini szru*, to die defending his castle.

MAKURA-BIYŌBU, マクラビヤウブ, 枕屏, *n*. A small screen placed near the bed.

MAKURA-KOTOBA, マクラコトバ, 枕詞, *n*. Words without meaning, used in poetry merely for ornament, or to preserve the proper accent, and number of feet.

MAKURA-YE, マクラヱ, 春畫, *n*. Obscene pictures.

MAKURI,-*ru*,-*tta*, マクル, 捲, *t,v*. To roll up. *Ude wo* —, to roll up the sleeve. *Szdare wo* —, to roll up a shade. *Szso wo* —, to tuck up the skirts.

MAKURI, マクリ, 海仁艸, (*Kainnisō*). *n*. A purgative medicine much used in children's complaints.

MAKUWAURI, マクハウリ, 甜瓜, *n*. Muskmelon.

MAMA, ママ, 儘, State condition, manner way. *Konomama ni sh'te oku*, let it be just as it is. *Sono mama ni wa szte okarenu*, it cannot be left in that state. *Miru mama ni utszsz*, to copy any thing just as one sees it. *Kiku mama ni kaku*, to write down just as one hears. *Mama yo*, let it be as it is. *Kokoro no mama*, just as one thinks, or likes. *Mama naranu uki-yo*, a world fullof disappointments, — where people have not every thing to their mind.

MAMA, ママ, 間間, *adv*. Sometimes. occasionally, from time to time. *Mama kore ari soro*, this occasionally happens. Syn. ORI-ORI, ORIFUSHI. TAMA-TAMA.

MAMA, ママ, 飯, *n*. Boiled rice. Vulg. *o mamma*. Syn. MESHI, GOZEN, HAN.

||MAMA, ママ, 乳母, *n*. A wetnurse. Syn. UBA.

MAMA-CHI-CHI, ママチチ, 繼父, *n*. Stepfather.

MAMAGOTO, ママゴト, *n*. Children's teaparty, played with wooden cups and saucers.

MAMA-HAHA, ママハハ, 繼母, *n*. Stepmother.

MAMA-KO, ママコ, 繼子, *n*. Stepchild.

MAM-BEN, マンペン, 滿遍, (*michi amaneshi*). Extending over every place, every where, all over. — *ni satō wo tszkeru*, sprinkle sugar all over it. *Hi ga — ni terasz*, the sun shines every where.

MAMBIKI, マンビキ, 扒手, *n*. A shoplifter, thief.

MAME, マメ, 豆, *n*. Bean, pea. — *no saya*, bean-pod. — *no ko*, bean flour.

MAME, マメ, 肉刺, *n*. The hard callus, or corns formed on the hands, or feet, by hard work.

MAME, マメ, 健, Strong, robust, hale, active, busy. *Mame na h'to*, active, or industrious person. *Mame de iru ka*, are you well? (to inferiors). *Mame de kurash'te orimasz*, we are all well. Syn. SZKOYAKA.

MAMEGARA, マメガラ, 豆萁, *n*. The shell of beans.

†MAMETSZ, マメツ, 磨滅, Defaced, marred, obliterated. — *sh'te ji ga yomenu*, the letters are defaced and cannot be read.

MAMEYAKA, マメヤカ, Robust, hale, active, prompt, quick in doing, faithful, constant.

MAMIGE, マミゲ, 眉毛, *n*. The eyebrow. Syn. MAYU.

MAMIRE,-*ru*,-*ta*, マミレル, 塗, *i.v.* Smeared, daubed, bedaubed. *Chi-mamire*, besmeared with blood. *Doro-mamire*, bedaubed with mud. Syn. DARAKE, MABURE.

MAMIYE,-*yuru*, マミユル, 見, To go to see

or visit, only used of persons of high rank. Syn. YESSZRU.

†MAMIYESHIMI,-*mu*, マミエシム, 令見, Caust. of *Mamiye*. To introduce.

MAMMAKU, マンマク, 幔幕, *n*. A kind of curtain.

MAMMAN, マンマン, 漫漫, *adv*. Spreading far and wide, (as the ocean).

MAMMARU, マンマル, 眞圓, Perfectly round. — *na tszki*, a full moon.

MAMORASE,-*ru*-*ta*, マモラセル, 令守, Caust. of *Mamoru*, To order, or cause another to protect. *Yakunin ni mamorasete oku*, to give in charge to an officer to protect.

MAMORI,-*ru*,-*tta*, マモル, 守, *t. v.* To guard, to watch, keep, defend, protect, preserve, take care of; to rule over. *Kuni wo* —, to rule over and protect a country. *Mi wo* —, to preserve one's self, (from any kind of harm). Syn. SHUGO SZRU, BAN WO SZRU.

MAMORI, マモリ, 神符, *n*. A charm, amulet. — *wo motsz*, to wear a charm.

MOMORI-BUKURO, マモリブクロ, 符袋, *n*. A bag in which charms are kept, worn around the neck.

MAMORI-KATANA, マモリガタナ, 護身刀, *n*. A small sword, or dirk, carried secretly to defend one's self. Syn. K'WAI-KEN.

MAMPACHI, マンパチ, 萬八, *n*. A lie. Syn. USO.

†MAMPITSZ, マンピツ 漫筆, *n*. Miscellaneous writings.

MAMPUKU, マンプク, 満腹, (*hara ni mitszru*). Full stomach. — *itashi mash'ta*, have eaten to the full, have made a hearty meal.

†MAMPUKU, マンプク, 萬福, (*yorodz no sai-wai*). Ten thousand blessings. *Fuki mampuku to on iwai mōshi age soro.*

MAMUKI, マムキ, 眞向, Directly opposite.

MAMUSHI, マムシ, 蝮, *n*. A viper.

MAN, マン, 萬, Ten-thousand, myriad, all, every. — *ni h'totsz*, ten-thousand to one, if, peradventure.

MANA, マナ, 正字, *n*. The true, or real characters,—applied to the Chinese characters, from which the *kana*, or Japanese characters are borrowed,

MANABASHI, マナバシ, 生箸, *n*. The chop-sticks used in dressing fish.

MANABI,-*bu*,-*nda*, マナブ, 學, *t. v.* To learn, to imitate. *Sho wo* —, to learn to write. *Ken wo* —, to learn fencing. Syn. NARAU.

†MANAI,-KI,-KU,-SHI, マナイ, 無間, Without interval, constantly, incessantly, uninterruptedly.

MANAITA, マナイタ, 生板, *n*. A board for cutting fish on.

MANAJIRI, マナジリ, 外眥, *n*. The external canthus of the eye.

MANAKATSZWO, マナカツホ, 鯧, *n*. The name of a fish.

MANAKO, マナコ, 眼, *n*. The eye. Syn. ME.

MANDARA, マンダラ, 曼荼羅, *n*. A picture of Buddhist deities.

MANDOKORO, マンドコロ, 政所, *n*. The office for transacting government business at Kiyoto. *Kita no madokoro*, the wife of the most noble of the Kuge.

MANE,-*ru*,-*ta*, マネル, 眞似, *t v.*. To imitate, mimic, to mock. *Seiyō no fū wo* —, to imitate European customs. *H'to no koye wo* —. to imitate the voice of another.

MANE, マネ, 眞似, *n*. Imitation, mimicry. *H'to mane wo szru*, to imitate others,—to do as others do. *U no — wo szru karasz*, (prov.), like the crow who imitated the cormorant.

MANEBI,-*bu*,-*ta*, マネブ, 學, *t. v.* To imitate.

MANEKI,-*ku*,-*ita*, マネク, 招, *t. v.* To beckon, to call, invite. *Te de maneku*, to beckon with the hand. *Tegami wo motte maneku*, to invite by means of a letter. Syn. YOBU.

MANEKI, マネキ, 招, *n*. Beckoning, invitation. *Konnichi wa on — kudasare katajikenaku zonjisoro*, (epist.) am obliged to you for your invitation to day.

MANEKI, マネキ, 機躡, *n*. The lever by which the reeds of a loom are raised and lowered.

MANEKI-ATSZME,-*ru*,-*ta*, マネキアツメル, 招集, *t.v.* To call together, to invite to assemble

MANGACHI, マンガチ, 目勝, Greedy and selfish, wanting to take all regardless of others.

MANGETSZ, マンゲツ, 満月, *n*. The full-moon, the 10th month, or full-time of uterogestation.

MANG'WAN, マングワン, 満願, *n*. The last day of a vow, or prayer. *Konnichi wa — de gozarimasz.*

MANI-AI,-*au*,-*tta*, マニアフ, 間合, *i. v.* To suit, to do, to answer the purpose. *Osokute maniawanu*, if you are late it will not do. *Miyōnichi made ni maniau ka*, will it do until to-morrow?

MANI-AI, マニアヒ, 間合, *n*. A kind of plain wall-paper.

MA-NI-AWASE,*-ru,-ta*,マニアハセル,合間, *t. v.* To cause to suit, to make do, or answer the purpose. *Kore de maniawasete oku*, I will make this do. *Miyō-nichi made ni maniawasemashō*, I will make it do until to-morrow.

MAN-ICHI, マンイチ, 萬一, *adv.* Ten-thousand to one, if, providing that, supposing. Syn. MOSHI.

MANIHŌJU, マニハウジユ, 摩尼寶珠, *n.* A gem held in the hand of idols, supposed to protect them against evil spirits.

†MANI-MANI, マニマニ, 隨意, Pleasure, will. Syn. MAMA-NI.

MANJI, マンジ, *n.* The name of a figure, or diagram, of this shape, 卐

MAN-JŪ, マンヂウ, 饅頭, *n.* A kind of round cake, a dumpling.

†MAN-KI, マンキ, 慢氣, *n.* Arrogance, pride. — *szru*, to be arrogant, proud. Syn. MAN-SHIN, JI-MAN.

MAN-KIN-TAN, マンキンタン, 萬金丹, *n.* The name of an anodyne pill, much used by the Japanese.

MAN-KIYŌ-FU, マンキヤウフ, 漫驚風, *n.* A convulsive disease of children.

MAN-NAKA, マンナカ, 眞中, The centre, middle. *Mato no* — *ni ateru*, to hit the centre of a target.

MAN-NEN-GAMI, マンネンガミ, 萬年紙, *n.* A thick kind of paper varnished, and used as a slate.

MA-NO-ATARI, マノアタリ, 眼前, (*ganzen.*) *adv.* Before one's eyes. — *mita koto*, a thing seen with my own eyes.

MAN-RIKI, マンリキ, 萬力, *n.* A windlass, capstan. Syn. MAKIROKURO.

MANROKU, マンロク, 眞正, Level, even, horizontal. — *na tokoro*, a level place. Syn. TAIRA.

MAN-SAKU, マンサク, 滿作, *n.* Full crop, abundant crop. Syn. HŌNEN.

MAN-SHIN, マンシン, 慢心, *n.* Arrogance, pride, haughtiness. Syn. MAN-KI, UNUBORE.

†MAN-SŌ, マンサウ, 蔓艸, (*tszru kusa.*) *n.* A vine, a climbing plant.

MANUKARE,*-ru,-ta*, マヌカレル, 免, *t. v.* To escape, avoid, evade, to be pardoned. *Tszmi wo* —, to escape the punishment of one's crimes. Syn. NOGARERU, YURUSARERU, GOMEN.

MANUKE, マヌケ, 間脫, *n.* Stupid, foolish. — *me*, stupid fellow, dunce. Syn. TONCHIKI, BAKA.

MANUKI,*-ku,-ita*, マヌク, 間拔, *t.v.* To take anything from between others, where there are too many, to thin out. *Ki wo manuku*, to thin out trees.

MANURUI,-KI,-KU,-SHI, マヌルイ, 間温, Sluggish, dull, inactive, stupid. *Manurui koto de kane ga mōkaranu*, money cannot be earned by laziness.

†MAN-YETSZ, マンエツ, 滿悅, Full of joy. — *ni zonjitatematszru.*

†MAN-ZA, マンザ, 滿座, *n.* Whole or full assembly. — *no uchi nite ukeau*, to promise before the whole assembly.

MANZAI, マンザイ, 萬歲, (*yorodz no toshi*), *n.* Strolling ballet singers and dancers, who go about at the beginning of the new year.

MANZAIRAKU, マンザイラク, 萬歲樂,) *n.* idem.

MANZARA, マンザラ, 眞更, *adv.* Wholly, entirely, very. — *waruku mo nai*, not as bad as might be.

MANZOKU, マンゾク, 滿足, (*michitaru.*) Fully, or completely satisfied, having nothing more to be desired, complete, perfect. — *ni omō*, to feel that one's happiness is full, or that one has enough. — *senu*, not complete.

MAO, マヲ, 麻苧, *n.* A kind of flax from which grass cloth is made.

MA-OTOKO, マヲトコ, 密夫, *n.* A paramour, lover. Syn. MIPPU.

MAPPADAKA, マツパダカ, 赤裸, Stark-naked.

MAPPIRA, マツピラ, 眞平, *adv.* Earnestly, importunately. — *gomen kudasare*, earnestly beg you to excuse me. Syn. HIRA-NI.

MARA, マラ, 陰莖, *n.* The membrum virile. Syn. INKIYŌ.

MARE, マレ, 稀, Rare, strange, uncommon, scarce, extraordinary. *Mare-mono*, a rare thing, rarity. *Mare-naru tegara*, uncommon skill. Syn. MEDZRASHII, SZKUNAI, KITAI.

†MARE, マレ, (cont. of *mo*, and *are*). A conjunctive particle, = *demo*, or *mo*. *Nani ni mare*, any kind whatever. *H'to ni mare, oni ni mare*, whether man or devil. *Mi-mare midz-mare*, whether I see or not. *To-mare kaku-mare*, = *To-mo kakumo*, however the case may be, whether this way, or that way; nevertheless, or notwithstanding.

MARE-MARE, マレマレ, 稀稀, *adv.* Seldom, rarely, not often, infrequently. Syn. TAMA-TAMA.

MARE-NI, マレニ, 稀, *adv.* Idem. — *sonna koto ga aru*, such a thing is rare.

MARI, マリ, 鞠, *n.* A ball, foot-ball. *Te-*

mari, hand-ball. — *wo tszku*, to strike a ball. — *wo keru*, to kick a ball.

†MARO, マロ, 麻呂, *pers. pro.* I, used by the Mikado, or Kuge, when speaking of themselves; also, a common name. Syn. CHIN.

†MAROBI,*-bu,-nda*, マロブ, 轉, *i.v.* To fall and roll over. Syn. KOROBU.

†MAROI,-KI,-SHI, マロイ, 圓, *a.* Round; the ancient and obsolete form of *Marui*.

MAROKASE, マロカセ, 丸, *n.* A ball. *Tetsz no* —, a ball of iron.

MAROKU, マロク, See *Maroi*.

MAROME,*-ru,-ta*, マロメル, 令圓, *t.v.* To make round. Syn. MARUKU SZRU.

MARŌTO, マラウト, 賓客, *n.* A guest, visitor. Syn KIYAKU.

MARU, マル, 丸, *n.* A circle; the name given to the different divisions of a castle, as, *Hommaru, Nino Maru, San no maru.* Used also as a title, or name for ships of war, as, *Shin-soku maru*; or for swords, as, *Hige-kiri-maru*; or the Japanese flag, as, *Hi no maru.* — *wo kaku*, to draw a circle.

MARU-BACHI, マルバチ, 丸蜂, *n.* A kind of bee.

MARUBON, マルボン, 圓盆, *n.* A round tray.

MARU-DE, マルデ, 全, *adv.* Wholly, entirely, altogether. — *chigau*, entirely different. — *nomu*, to swallow it whole.

MARU-HADAKA, マルハダカ, 赤裸, *n.* Stark-naked. Syn. MAPPADAKA.

MARU-GOSHI, マルゴシ, 丸腰, *n.* Going without one's sword, unarmed. Syn. MUTŌ.

MARUI,-KI, マルイ, 圓, or 丸, *a.* Round, circular, globular. *Sekai wa marui mono*, the earth is round.

MARUKI, マルキ, 丸木, *n.* A round log.

MARUKI-BASHI, マルキバシ, 獨木橋, *n.* A bridge made with a round log.

MARUKI-BUNE, or MARUTABUNE, マルキブ子, 刳木船, *n.* A canoe.

MARUKU, マルク, 圓, *adv.* Round. — *szru*, to make round. — *naru*, to become round.

MARUME,*-ru,-ta*, マルメル, 令丸, *t. v.* To make round. *Gwanyaku wo* —, to make a pill round.

MARUMERO, マルメロ, 榲桲, *n.* A kind of fruit. Cydonia vulgaris.

MARUNE, マル子, 假寐, *n.* Sleeping in one's clothes. — *wo szru.*

MARUNOMI, マルノミ, 捲鑿, *n.* A round chisel, or gouge.

MARU-NOMI, マルノミ, 丸呑, *n.* Swallowing whole. — *ni szru.*

MARUSHI マルシ, 圓, *a.* Round.

MARUSA, マルサ, 圓, *n.* Roundness.

MARUTA, マルタ, 丸太, *n.* A round log

MARU-TOSHI, マルトシ, 周歳, A whole year. Coll. *Maru ichi nen.*

†MASAGO, マサゴ, 眞砂, *n.* Sand. Syn. SZNA.

MASAKA, マサカ, 正歟, *adv.* Just at the time when any thing is about to take place, as, *Masaka kassen ni naru to okobiyōgami ga tszku*, just as the battle was about to commence he was seized with cowardice. *Masaka sono ba ni naru to sō mo nara nai*, when it came to the point I could not do it. *Masaka no toki*, the critical time, juncture. (2). with a negative verb, = not likely, improbable. *Masaka sono yō na koto shimasz mai*, it is not probable that he did such a thing. *Masaka sō demo arumai.* I think it is very unlikely. Syn. YOMOYA.

MASAKARI, マサカリ, 鉄, *n.* A broad axe. Syn. YOKI.

MASAKI, マサキ, 杜仲, *n.* The Evonymus. japonicus.

†MASAKIKU, マサキク, 眞幸, (obs.) Fortunate, free from accident. *Masakiku araba mata kayeri min*, if nothing prevents I shall again return to see you. Syn. ANZEN, BUJI.

MASAME, マサメ, 緑豆, *n.* A kind of small green bean. Syn. YAYENARI.

MASAME, マサメ, 正理, *n.* The grain of wood.

†MASAME, マサメ, 正眼, *n.* Before one's eyes. — *ni miru*, to be an eye witness.

†MASANAI,-KI,-KU,-SHI, マサナイ, 無正, Improper, wrong, unbecoming. *Masanaku mo teki ni ushiro wo misetamō kana*, how unbecoming is it to show your back to the enemy. Syn. TSZMARANU.

MASA-NI, マサニ, 正, or 將, *adv.* Near in time or action, just, almost, about, exactly, should, ought. — *ima*, just now. — *yoshi*, just right. — *ochin to szru*, just about to fall. — *yukan to szru*, just ready to go. — *tsztomu beki no kiu tari*, the most important of that which should be attended to.

MASARI,*-ru,-tta*, マサル, 勝, *i.v.* To excel, surpass, outdo; to be superior, more excellent, better; to increase, become greater. *Ame ga sh'ta ni ware ni masaru mono araji*, no one under the heavens better than himself. *Kono ni nin idzre ka masaritaru ni ya*, which of these two persons is the best? *Onore ni masaru koto wo imu*, to dislike to be excelled by others. *Midz ga masaru*, the water increases. Syn. SZGURERU, KATSZ, MASZ.

MASASHII,-KU,-KI,-U, マサシイ, 正敷, True, real, certain, sure. *Masashiki shōko*, certain proof. Syn. TASH'KA.

MASATSZCHI, マサツチ, 正土, *n.* Soil that has not yet been worked, virgin-soil. Syn. TOKOTSZCHI.

MASAYUME, マサユメ, 正夢, *n.* A true dream, a dream which comes to pass.

MASEGAKI, マセガキ, 笆籬, *n.* A fence made of bamboo placed upright.

MASHI, *masz*, *mash'ta*, マス, 申, A respectful colloquial suffix to the roots of verbs, altered from *Mōshi*, *mōsz*, *mōsh'ta*. It does not change the meaning of the verb to which it is joined, and passes through all the moods and tenses. Thus *Mi*, to see, becomes, *Mi-masz;* pret. *Mi-mash'ta;* fut. *Mi-mashō;* neg. *Mi-masenu;* conj. *Mi-maszreba;* neg. conj. *Mi-masene-ba;* neg. fut. *Mi-maszmai*.

MASHI,-*sz*,-*sh'ta*, マス, 增, *t. v.* To increase, to augment, to add to, make greater. *Midz wo* —, to add more water. *Kiukin wo* —, to increase the wages. Syn. KUWAYERU, FUYERU.

†MASHI, or MASHIRA, マシ, 猿, *n.* A monkey. Syn. SARU.

MASHI, マシ, *adv.* Better, preferable. *Shiranu ga mashi da*, it is better not to know. *Shinda hō ga mashi de arō*, I think it is better to die.

MASHI-MASHI,-*sz*, マシマス, 在坐, *i. v.* To dwell, (used only of the Mikado and Kami.) *Kami wa ten ni mashimasz*, God dwells in heaven.

†MASHI-MIDZ, マシミヅ, 眞淸水, *n.* Pure water.

†MASHIN, マシン, 麻疹, *n.* Measles. Syn. HASH'KA.

†MASHI-NARAME, = MASHI-NARAN, マシナラメ, Better, preferable.

MASH'TE, マシテ, 况, *adv.* Much more, still more. *Tori kedamono mo ko wo awaremu — h'to ni oite wo ya*, even birds and beasts love their young, how much more should men! *Mash'te ya*, or *Mash'te iwan ya*, how much more! Syn. NAO.

MASSAKA-SAMA, マツサカサマ, 眞倒, *adv.* Up-side-down, headlong. — *ni ochiru*, to fall head foremost.

MASSAKI, マツサキ, 眞先, *adv.* The very first, the foremost. — *ni szszmu*, to take the lead.

MASSAO, マツサヲ, 眞靑, Deep blue, livid. — *na umi*. — *na kao*.

†MASSE, マツセ, 末世, (*szye no yo,*) *n.* Last times, or ages. (Bud.) — *ni itareba h'to no inochi ga mijikaku naru*, in the last ages, the life of man will become short.

MASSHA, マツシヤ, 末社, *n.* The small shrines near a Miya..

†MASSHIKURA-NI, マツシクラニ, 驀地, *adv.* Riding furiously regardless of danger. — *kakete yuku*.

MASSHŌMEN, マツシヤウメン, 眞正面, Directly in front.

MASSZGU-NA, マツスグナ, 眞直, *a.* Perfectly straight, not crooked, direct.

MASSZGU-NI, マツスグニ, 眞直, *adv.* idem. — *kiru*, to cut straight.

MASZ, マス, see *Mashi*.

MASZ, マス, 升, *n.* A measure of capacity for liquids, grain, &c. *Ichi-go masz*, *Go-go masz*, *To-masz*. — *de kakaru*, to measure.

MASZ, マス, 鱒, *n.* A salmon?

MASZGATA, マスガタ, 升形, *n.* The space between the outer and inner gates of a castle.

MASZI, マスイ, 麻醉, Anodyne, narcotic, anasthetic. — *szru*, to be narcotized, or in a state of anasthesia.

MASZI-ZAI, マスイザイ, 麻醉劑, *n.* Narcotic medicine.

MASZKAGAMI, マスカガミ, 眞澄鏡, *n.* The mirror in a Miya, which is worshiped as a Kami.

MASZKAKI, マスカキ, 斗格, *n.* A stick used in leveling the top of a measure.

MASZ-MASZ, マスマス, 益, *adv.* More and more, still more, increasingly. *Yokohama — hanjō itashimasz*, Yokohama is growing more and more flourishing. Syn. IYO-IYO.

†MASZRAO, マスラヲ, 丈夫, *n.* A strong and fearless man, a hero.

†MASZRATAKEO, マスラタケヲ, 大丈夫, *n.* idem.

MATA, マタ, 又, *adv.* Again, likewise, moreover, also. — *oide nasare*, come again. — *furisō ni natta*, it looks like rain again. *Kore mo mata yoroshii*, this too is good.

MATA, マタ, 股, *n.* The crotch of the legs, a crotch, fork. *Kawa no* —, the forks of a river. *Ki no* —, the crotch of a tree. *Michi no* —, the forks of a road.

MATABURI, マタブリ, *n.* A kind of fork used at fires, or to catch thieves with. Syn. SASZMATA.

MATA-DONARI, マタドナリ, 又隣, *n.* Next neighbour but one.

MATADZ, MATANU, MATANAI, マタズ, 不待, neg. of *Machi.*

MATA-GAI, マタガヒ, 轉買, *n.* Buying second-handed, or from one who previously bought it. — *wo szru.*

MATA-GARI, マタガリ, 轉借, *n.* Borrowing what has before been borrowed, or at second hand.

MATAGARI,*-ru,-tta,* マタガル, 跨, *i.v.* To sit, or stand astride of any thing, straddling, bestriding. *Ita-bei ni matagaru,* sitting astride of a fence.

MATAGE,*-ru,-ta,* マタゲル, 跨, *t. v.* To step over, to straddle. *Kawa wo matageru,* to step over a rivulet.

MATAGI,*-gu,-ida,* マタグ, 跨, *n.* To straddle, to step over. *Shikii wo mataide hairu,* to step across the threshold and enter.

MATAGURA, マタグラ, 胯, *n.* The crotch, groin.

||MATAI,-KI,-KU,-SHI, マタイ, Gentle, tame, amiable. Syn. OTONASHI, SZNAO.

MATA-ITOKO, マタイトコ, 三從兄弟, *n.* Second cousin.

MATA-MATA, マタマタ, 又又, *adv.* A Again and again, repeatedly.

MATA-MONO, マタモノ, 陪臣, *n.* The servant of one who is himself the servant of another; a rear vassal.

MATASE,*-ru,-ta,* マタセル, 令待, caust. of *Machi.* To cause another to wait. *Nagaku matasete wa kinodoku da,* I am sorry I kept you waiting so long.

MATATABI, マタタビ, 天蓼, *u.* A kind of tree. Trochostigma polygama.

MATATAKI,-KU, マタタク, 瞬, *t. v.* To wink, to flicker, (as a candle,) to twinkle. *Tomoshibi ga matataku,* the lamp flickers. *Matataku-ma,* in a twinkling, in an instant. *Matataki wo szru,* to wink.

MATA-UKE, マタウケ, 又受, *n.* A second security or bondsman,—one who is surety for a surety. — *wo tateru,* to give a second security. — *ni tatsz,* to stand as second security.

MATA-WA, マタハ, 又, *conj.* Again, besides, moreover, furthermore, likewise.

MATAZORO, マタゾロ, 又候, *adv.* Again, besides, furthermore.

MATE, マテ, 蟶, *n.* The solenensis.

MATE, マテ, imp. mood. of *Machi,* wait.

MATO, マト, 的, *n.* A target. — *no kuroboshi,* the black spot in the centre of a target. — *ni ateru,* to hit the mark.

MATŌ, マトフ, 綢, see *Matoi.*

MATOBA, マトバ, 的塲, *n.* A place for target shooting.

MATOI, マトヒ, 纒, *n.* A kind of ensign carried at fires.

MATOI,*-ō,-ōtta,* マトフ, 纒, *t. v.* To twine around, to wind around, (as a vine.) Syn. MOTZRERU, KARAMU.

MATOI-TSZKI,*-ku,-ita,* マトヒツク, 纒着, *t. v.* To twine around, wind around, coil round. *Hebi ga take ni* —, the snake winds around the bamboo.

MATOMARI,*-ru,-tta,* マトマル, 圓集, *i.v.* Assembled together, collected, gathered. Syn. ATSZMARU, YORU.

MATOME,*-ru,-ta,* マトメル, 令圓, *t. v.* To collect, to gather together, to assemble, bring together. Syn. ATSZMERU, YOSERU,

MATOMO, マトモ, 眞艫, *adv.* Right aft, directly astern. *Kaze — de fune ga hayai,* the wind being directly aft the ship sails fast.

MATOWARE,*-ru,-ta,* マトハレル, 被纒, pass. of *Matoi.* Twined around, encircled, as by a vine.

MATOWARI,*-ru,-tta,* マトハル, 纒, *i. v.* Twined around, wound around, encircle. *Tszru ga ki ni* —, the vine is twined around the tree.

MATSZ, マツ, 待, See *Machi.*

MATSZ, マツ, 松, *n.* Pine. — *no ki,* a pine tree. — *no yani,* pitch.

MATSZ, マツ, 末, *n.* Fine powder. *Kuszri wo — ni szru,* to reduce a medicine to powder. Syn. KONA.

MATSZ-CHI, マツチ, 眞土, *n.* New or fresh soil, clay.

MATSZ-DAI, マツダイ, 末代, *n.* Future ages, latest generations. *Hto wa ichi dai, na wa matszdai,* man lives one generation, but his name to distant ages. Syn. KŌ-DAI.

MATSZGE, マツゲ, 睫毛, *n.* Eye-lash. *Saka-matsege,* entropium.

MATSZ-GO, マツゴ, 末期, *n.* The end of life, the time just before death. — *no yui-gen,* the last words, or verbal will of a dying person. — *no midz,* the water put into the lips of a dying man. Syn. IMAWA NO KIWA.

MATZHODO, マツホド, 伏苓, *n.* China-root. Syn. BUKURIYŌ.

MATSZ-JI, マツジ, 末寺, *n.* A branch temple, a temple which is an offshoot from a *honji,* or main temple.

MATSZKASA, マツカサ, 松球, *n.* A pine-bur.

MATSZMARI,*-ru,-tta,* マツマル, Same as *Matomari.*

MATSZME,–*ru*,–*ta*, マツメル, Same *Matome*.

MATSZMUSHI, マツムシ, 松虫, *n*. A kind of cricket.

MATSZRI,–*ru*,–*tta*, マツル, 祭, *t.v.* To offer sacrifices, to worship. *Shimbutsz wo* —, to worship the gods. *Kō hana wo tamukete senzo wo matszru*, to worship one's ancestors by offering incense and flowers. Syn. SAIREI SZRU.

MATSZRI, マツリ, 祭, A religious festival, or celebration.

MATSZRIGOTO, マツリゴト, 政事, *n*. Administration of public affairs, government. — *wo szru*, to govern, to administer public affairs. — *wo motte tami wo michibiku*, by good government to guide the people. Syn. SEIJI.

MATSZ-RIU, マツリウ, 末流, *n*. Latest descendants, or followers.

†MATSZRAI,–*au*, マツラフ, 歸順, To submit, become subject, yield to authority. *Matszrawanu*, neg.

MATSZTAKE, マツタケ, 松蕈, *n*. A kind of mushroom.

MATSZWARI,–*ru*,–*tta*, マツハル, 纏, *i. v.* Same as *Matowari*.

MATSZ-YANI, マツヤニ, 松脂, *n*. Pitch, turpentine. Syn. SHŌSHI, CHAN.

MATSZYOI, マツヨヒ, 待宵, *n*. The 14th night of the 8th month.

†MATTADANAKA, マツタダナカ, 眞正中, The centre. *Mato no* — *wo i-nuku*, to pierce the centre of a target. Syn. MANAKA.

MATTAI,–KI, マツタイ, 全, *a*. Whole, complete, entire, perfect.

MATTAKU, マツタク, 全, *adv*. Idem. *Kono hon issatsz nite mattaku gozarimasz*, this book is complete in one volume. *Mattaku shirimasen*, I am entirely ignorant of it. *Mattaku szru*, to complete, make perfect.

MATTASHI, マツタシ, 全, *a*. Idem.

MATTŌ, マツタウ, Same as *Mattaku*.

MAU, マフ, 舞, See *Mai*.

MA-UTSZMUKE, マウツムケ, 眞俯, Face directly downward. — *ni taoreru*, to fall with the face to the earth.

MAWARI,–*ru*,–*tta*, マハル, 廻, *t.* or *i. v.* To go round, to turn round, to revolve, circulate, rotate, spin round, whirl. *Kuruma ga* —, the wheel turns round. *Tszki wa chi-kiu wo* —, the moon revolves around the earth. Syn. MEGURU.

MAWARI, マハリ, 廻, *n*. A turn, revolution; a period of seven days, (in taking medicine.) *H'to mawari*, one turn. *Kuszri wo h'to mawari nomu*, to take medicine one turn of seven days. *Mi no* —, the clothing. *Onna no* — *wo toru*, to abuse a woman by turns, (of several persons.)

MAWARI-BAN, マハリバン, 輪番, A watch, in which each one takes his turn. — *szru*, to keep watch by turns. Syn. JUMBAN.

MAWARI-DŌI,–KI,–SHI, マハリドホイ, 迂遠, *a*. Round about, circuitous, not direct, prolix, lengthy, tedious, dilatory, slow. Syn. UYEN, KUDOI, RACHI-GA-AKANU.

MAWARI-DŌKU, マハリドホク, 迂遠, *adv*. idem.

MAWARI-DŌRŌ, マハリドウロウ, 影燈, *n*. A lantern with a revolving shade.

MAWARI-G'WAI, マハリグワイ, 輪會, *n*. A meeting, or party which meets at different places in turn.

MAWARI-MAWARI-NI, マハリマハリ, 巡巡, *adv*. By turns. — *ban wo szru*, to keep watch by turns. Syn. JUN-JUN-NI.

MAWARI-MICHI, マハリミチ, 廻道, *n*. A round about, or circuitous road.

MAWASHI,–*sz*,–*sh'ta*, マハス, 廻, *t.v.* To turn, to turn round, to wheel, whirl, spin, to circulate. *Kuruma wo* —, to turn a wheel. *Koma wo* —, to spin a top. *Te wo mawasz*, to turn the hand to this and that work, in order to facilitate something else. *Masz-me wo mawash'te miru*, to find out the average measure. *Me wo mawasz*, to swoon, or faint. *Sakadzki wo* —, to circulate the wine-cup. Syn. MEGURASZ.

MAWASHI–*sz*,–*sh'ta*, マハス, 令舞, (caust. of *Mai*.) To make dance. *Saru wo* —, to make a monkey dance. *Nin-giyō wo* —, to make puppits dance. Syn. ODORASERU.

MA-WATA, マワタ, 眞綿, *n*. Floss silk.

MAWATASHI, マワタシ, 壁帯, *n*. The cross strips on which lathes are tied for plastering.

MAYAKU, マヤク, 麻藥, (*shibire guszri.*) *n*. Narcotic medicines, anasthetics. Syn. MASZIZAI.

MAYABUNIN, マヤブニン, 摩耶夫人, *n*. The mother of *Shaka Niyorai*.

MAYAKASHI,–*sz*,–*sh'ta*, マヤカス, 衒, *t.v.* To cheat, deceive, to hoax, to gull. Syn. TABURAKASZ, AZAMUKU, DAMASZ.

MAYASHI, マヤシ, 衒人, *n*. One who obtains money by cheating, or trickery, a juggler, cheat, swindler. Syn. KATARI.

MAYE, マヘ, 前, (*zen.*) Before, front, former, previous. *Iye no maye*, the front of the house. *Maye no yo*, previous state of existence, or former generation. — *no otto*, former husband. *Me no* —, before one's eyes. *Sono maye ni*, previous to that.

Maye-toshi, year before. (2.) = Proper quantity, portion, or share. *Chawan jūnin maye*, tea cups for ten men. *Meshi go nin maye*, rice for five men. *Ichi nin maye kome go go*, five measures of rice to one man. *Ni nin maye ichibu dztsz*, one ichibu to every two persons. *Ikken maye kin go riyō dztsz daseba, jikken go-jūriyō*, if each house gives five *riyō* a piece, ten houses will give fifty *riyō*. *Ichi nin maye no shigoto*, the work of one man.
Syn. SAKI, BUN..

MAYE-BA, マヘバ, 前歯, *n*. The front, or incisor teeth, a foretooth.

MAYE-BI, マヘビ, 前日, *n*. Day before, previous day. Syn. ZEN-JITSZ.

MAYE-BIRO-NI, マヘビロニ, 前廣, *adv*. Beforehand, some time before.
Syn. MAYE-MOTTE.

MAYE-DARE, マヘダレ, 前垂, *n*. An apron.

MAYE-GAMI, マヘガミ, 前髪, *n*. Fore-lock of hair.

MAYE-GARI, マヘガリ, 前借, *n*. Drawing money before it is fully due. *Kiu-kin wo — ni sh'te nigeta*, he drew his wages before and ran away.

MAYE-KADO, マヘカド, 前廉, Former, or previous thing. — *no negai*, a former request.

MAYE-KAKE, マヘカケ, 蔽膝, *n*. An apron. Syn. MAYEDARE.

MAYE-KAKI, マヘカキ, 耨, *n*. A kind of hoe.

MAYE-KATA, マヘカタ, 前方, *adv*. Before, previously. Syn. SEN-JITSZ, SEN-DATTE.

MAYE-KIN, マヘキン, 前金, *n*. Advance money, earnest-money.

MAYE-MOTTE, マヘモツテ, 前以, *adv*. Beforehand previously. — *hanash'te oku*, left word before hand. — *shitte oru*, knew it before.
Syn. ARAKAJIME, KANETE.

MAYE-OKI, マヘオキ, 前置, *n*. Any thing said as an introduction, prelude, or preface to the main subject. — *wo iu*.

MAYE-USHIRO, マヘウシロ, 前後, (*zengo*). Before and after, before and behind, front and rear.

MAYE-WATASHI, マヘワタシ, 前渡, *n*. Money paid before hand, earnest money, bargain money.
Syn. ZENKIN, MAYE-KIN.

MAYŌ, マヨフ, 迷, See *Mayoi*.

MAYOI,-ō,-tta, マヨフ, 迷, *i.v.* To be bewildered, confused, perplexed, infatuated, lost in, given up to. *Michi ni mayō*, to miss, or loose the way. *Onna ni —*, infatuated by women. *Kororo ga —*, his mind is confused.
Syn. MADOI.

MAYOI, マヨヒ, 迷, *n*. Perplexity, bewilderment, maze. — *wo toku*.

MA-YOKE, マヨケ, 魔除, *n*. Any thing that will keep off evil spirits. — *no mamori mi ni kakeru*, to wear a charm to keep off evil spirits.

MA-YORI, マヨリ, 眵涙, *n*. The hard mucous which collects about sore eyes.
Syn. ME-YANI.

MAYORU, マヨル, 中夜, *n*. Midnight.
Syn. YONAKA.

MAYOWASHI,-sz,-sh'ta, マヨハス, 迷, *t.v.* To delude, mislead, beguile, to lead astray, to charm.
Syn. MADOWASZ, AZAMUKU.

MAYU, マユ, 眉, *n*. The eyebrows. — *wo soru*, to shave the eyebrows.

MAYU, マユ, 繭, *n*. Silkworm.

MAYU-AI, マユアヒ, 眉間, *n*. The space between the eyebrows.

MAYU-DZMI, マユズミ, 黛, *n*. Ink used for blacking the eyebrows.

MAYUGASHIRA, マユガシラ, 眉頭, *n*. The end of the eyebrow near the nose.

MAYU-GE, マユゲ, 眉毛, *n*. The hairs of the eyebrows.

MAYU-HAKE, マユハケ, 眉刷, *n*. A brush used in powdering the face.

MAYUMI, マユミ, 衛矛, *n*. A kind of tree. Evonymus thunbergianus.

MAYU-SHIRI, マユジリ, 眉尾, *n*. The outer end of the eyebrow.

MAZERI,-ru,-tta, マゼル, 雑, *t.v.* (cont. of *Majiyeru*). To mix, mingle, blend, to adulterate. *Midz wo sake ni —*, to mix water with spirits. *Kuszri wo midz ni mazete nomu*, take the medicine in water.

MAZE-KAYESHI,-sz,-sh'ta, マゼカヘス, 雑返, *t.v.* To make a disturbance, or to throw into confusion. *Kodomo ga —*, the children make a noise.

ME, メ, 目, or 眼, *n*. The eye. — *no tama*, the ball of the eye. — *no fuchi*, the lower eyelid. — *wo hiraku*, to open the eye. — *wo akeru*, idem. — *wo awasz*, to shut the eye. — *wo tojiru*, idem. — *wo fusagu*, idem. — *wo samasz*, to awake from sleep. — *wo tszkeru*, to look at. — *ni kakaru*, to lay eyes on, to see. — *wo kakeru*, to look at with pity. — *wo kuramasz*, to cheat, deceive. — *wo odorokasz*, to frighten with a sudden motion. — *ni kado wo tatsz*, to look angrily at.

(2.) A tooth. *Nokogiri, oroshi, yaszri, nado no me*, the teeth of a saw, grater, or file. *Hiki-usz no me*, the furrows cut on a mill-stone.

(3.) A joint, or place where two things, as paper, or boards are united, as, *Awashi-me*, *Tszgime*, *Szki-me*.

(4.) The meshes of a net, as, *Ami no me;* the space between the threads of any thing woven, as, *Ori-me;* or between the sticks of a basket, as, *Zaru no me*.

(5.) The grain, or veins of wood, as, *Moku-me*.

(6.) The graduated marks on a weighing beam, as, *Hakari no me;* on a measure, as, *Monosashi no me;* on a thermometer, as, *Kandanke no me;* the marks on dice, as, *Sai no me;* the squares of a checker-board, as, *Go-ban no me*.

(7.) Used to specify or particularize, as, *Ichi-ban-me*, the first one. *Nidome*, the second time. *Mikka-me*, the third day. *Yodai-me*, the fourth reign, or generation.

(8.) After contemptuous epithets, as, *Yatsz-me*, *Nikui-yatsz-me*, *Koitsz me*.

(9.) Affair, accident. *Hidoi-me ni atta*, met with hard, or cruel treatment. *Kurushiime ni atta*.

ME, メ, 妻, *n.* A female, woman, wife. *Me wo metoru*, to marry a woman. *H'to no me to naru*, to become a wife. (2.) 牝, the female of animals, as, *Me-ushi*, a cow, *me-inu*, a bitch. (3.) 雌, the female of birds, as, *Mendori*, a female bird. Syn. MESZ.

ME, メ, 芽, *n.* A bud, (of a leaf,) a sprout. *Ki no me ga deru*, the trees are budding.

ME, メ, 和布, *n.* A kind of sea-weed.

ME, *meru*, *meta*, メル, An affix to the root form of adjectives forming a causative, or transative verb, as *Hayameru*, to cause to be fast, to quicken. *Kubomeru*, to hollow out. *Kuromeru*, to blacken. *Fukameru*, to deepen, &c.

ME-AKASHI, メアカシ, 眼明, *n.* A spy, secret policeman. Syn. OKKAPIKI.

ME-ATE, メアテ, 目的, *n.* The object at which one aims, or to which one looks for help, or direction. — *ga hadzreta*, missed his object, or disappointed in one's hopes. *Nani wo — ni sono yō na koto wo szru*, what induced you to do so? *Ano ki wo — ni sh'te yuku*, go making a landmark of that tree. Syn. ATE.

ME-AWASE, *-sz*, *-ta* メアハス, 妻, *t. v.* To give in marriage. *Muszme wo h'to ni me-awasz*, to give a daughter in marriage. Syn. YOME NI YARU.

ME-BARI, メバリ, 目張, *n.* Pasting paper over a crack or joint. — *wo szru*.

ME-BATAKI, メバタキ, 瞬, *n.* Winking flickering. — *wo szru*, to wink. Syn. MATATAKI.

ME-BAYAI, -KI, -KU, -SHI, -Ō, メバヤイ, 目早, Sharpsighted, quicksighted.

ME-BAYE, メバヘ, 芽生, *n.* A sprout.

MEBUKI, *-ku*, *-ita*, メブク, 芽, *i. v.* To bud, sprout. *Yanagi ga mebuita*, the willow has budded.

ME-BUN-RIYŌ, メブンリヤウ, 目分量, *n.* Judging of the weight, or measure of anything with the eye.

ME-DACHI, *-tsz*, *-tta*, メダツ, 芽立, *i.v.* To bud, to sprout. *Ki ga medatta*, the tree had budded.

ME-DACHI, *-tsz*, *-tta*, メダツ, 目立, *i. v.* To attract attention, to be conspicuous, to be showy, gay. *Amari medatsz nari wo senu ga yoi*, better dress so as not to attract attention.

MEDAKA, メダカ, 丁班魚, *n.* A very small kind of fresh water fish.

MEDAKE, メダケ, 女竹, *n.* A kind of bamboo.

ME-DAMA, メダマ, 睛, *n.* The ball of the eye, also, the crystaline lens.

ME-DARUI, -KI, -KU, -SHI, メダルイ, 目倦, Eyes tired, or fatigued by looking.

ME-DASHI, メダシ, 萌芽, *n.* Sprouting, germinating.

MEDATAWASHII, -KI, -KU, メダタハシイ, 目立敷, Anything which attracts observation, or the eyes of others.

MEDATŌSHII, -KI, -KU, メダタウシイ, Coll. contr. of the above.

†MEDE, *medzru*, メデ, 愛, *t.v.* To love, admire, to be fond of. *Tszki hana wo medetsztsz asobu yo ni wa aradz*, this is not a time to go about admiring the moon and flowers. *Nanjira ga kenagenaru kokoro ni mede*, I admire your courage. Syn. KANDZRU, AISZRU.

MEDETAI, -KI, -SHI, メデタイ, 目出度, *a.* A matter for congratulation, joyful, happy, fortunate. *Medetai toki*, a time for congratulation. *O medetō gozarimasz*, I wish you joy, I congratulate you. *Medetaku nai koto*, an unlucky event.

MEDETAKU, or MEDETŌ, メデタク, 目出度, *adv.* Idem.

MEDOGI, メドギ, 筮竹, *n.* Divining sticks.

MEDŌRI, メドホリ, 目通, *n.* Admission into the presence of a superior officer. *O medōri wo negai mōshimas*.

MEDZRASHII, -KI, -SHI, メヅラシ, 珍敷, *a.* Rare, unfrequent, unusual, singular, strange, extraordinary, remarkable, curious, odd. *Medzrashii mise-mono*, a rare

show. —*hanashi*, a singular story. *Medzrashıkaradz*, it is not strange. *Ito medzrashii*, very unfrequent.
Syn. MARE NARU, KI-MIYŌNA.

MEDZRASHIKU, or MEDZRASHIU, メヅラシク, 珍敷, *adv.* idem. —*nai*, not strange.

MEDZRASHISA, メヅラシサ, 珍敷, *n.* Rareness, singularity, strangeness.

†MEDZRU, メヅル, 愛, See *Mede.*

MEGA, メガ, 牝鹿, *n.* A female deer, a doe. Syn. MEJIKA.

MEGAKE,*-ru,-ta*, メガケル, 目掛, *t.v.* To single out, to keep the eye on. *Ichi nin wo megakete kitte kakaru*, to single out a man and cut him down.

MEGAMI, メガミ, 女神, *n.* A female divinity, a goddess.

MEGANE, メガネ, 眼鏡, *n.* Spectacles. — *wo kakeru*, to put on spectacles.

†MEGARENU, or MEGARESEDZ, メガレヌ, 目不離, Cannot keep the eyes off. — *nagameru.*

||MEGE,*-ru,-ta*, メゲル, 破, *i.v.* To break, crush. *Chawan ga megeta*, the cup is broken. Syn. KOWARERU.

MEGUMI,*-mu,-nda*, メグム, 惠, *i. v.* To show kindness, or mercy, to pity and aid. *Kon-kiu no h'to wo megumu*, to show kindness to the poor. *Tami wo megumu wa jin-sha no matszrigoto*, to show kindness to his people will be the effort of a good-ruler. Syn. AWAREMU.

MEGUMI, メグミ, 惠, *n.* Kindness, beneficence, grace, benevolence, good-will, favor. *H'to wa kami no megumi nite ikiteiru*, men live on the mercies of God. *Kekkō naru shina on megumi ni adzkari arigataku zonji soro.* I thank you for the the beautiful thing you have kindly bestowed on me. Syn. AWAREMI, ONTAKU.

MEGUMI,*-mu,-nda*, メグム, 萌芽, *i.v.* To bud, to sprout. Syn. MABUKU, MEDATSZ.

MEGURASHI,*-sz,-sh'ta* メグラス, 令旋, (caust. of *meguri.*) To make go round, to turn, to cause to circulate, revolve, to revolve in the mind, to set a going. *Hakarigoto wo* —, to contrive a plan; to put plans in execution. *Chiye wo* —, to set one's ingenuity to work. Syn. MAWASZ

MEGURI,*-ru,-tta*, メグル, 巡, *t.v.* To go round, to revolve, circulate, to rotate. *Kuni-guni wo* —, to travel about various countries. *Chi ga* —, the blood circulates. Syn. MAWARU.

MEGURI, メグリ, 巡, *n.* Turn, round, revolution, circuit, rotation, vicinity, catamenia. *Chi no* —, circulation of the blood. *Kuruma no — ga hayai*, the wheel turns rapidly. *Yedo no* —, the country about Yedo.

MEGUWASE, メグハセル, 目合, *n.* Hinting or giving a signal by winking. *Shiba-shiba meguwase szre-domo satoradz*, he frequently winked at him but he did not understand.

MEI, メイ, 名, Name; only used in comp. words, signifying having a great name, famous, celebrated renowned, eminent, illustrious.

†MEI, メイ, 命, *n.* Life, fate, destiny; command, order, decree. *Mei naru kana*, alas! it is so ordained of heaven. *Shi sei mei ari*, life and death are decreed (by God). *Mei no gotoku*, as you commanded, (of a superior.) *Mei wo kōmuru*, to receive commands. — *wo ukeru.* idem.
Syn. INOCHI, ŌSE, I-TSZKE.

MEI, メイ, 銘, *n.* The name of the maker inscribed on a sword blade, &c. — *kiru*, to inscribe the name.

MEI, メヒ, 姪, *n.* A niece.

MEI-BA, メイバ, 名馬, *n.* A celebrated house.

MEI-BUTSZ, メイブツ, 名物, *n.* A celebrated thing.

MEI-DO, メイド, 冥途, *n.* Hades, the invisible world, region of the dead. (Bud.) — *ni yuku*, to die, to go to hades.
Syn. YOMIJI.

†MEI-DŌ,*-szru*, メイドウ, 鳴動, (*nari ugoku.*) To send forth a sound and shake. *Yama ga* —, the mountain groaned and trembled (by an earthquake).

MEIDZRU, メイズル, 命, See *Meiji.*

†MEI-FU, メイフ, 冥府, *n.* The tribunal of Yemma the king of Hades.

MEI-FUKU, メイフク, 冥福, *n.* Good fortune, or happiness sent from the unseen world. *Ten no — wo kōmuru.*

MEI-GETSZ, メイゲツ, 明月, *n.* Clear or bright moon.

MEI-HAKU, メイハク, 明白, (*akiraka-ni shiroshi.*) Clear, open; free from doubt, suspicion, or guile; above-board, without concealment, frank, candid, fair. *Banji — ni szru ga yoi*, it is always better to be open and above-board. — *na h'to*, a fair, frank man. Syn. ARITEI, ARINOMAMA NI, MUKIDASHI.

MEI-I, メイイ, 名醫, *n.* A celebrated doctor.

ME-ISHA, メイシヤ, 眼科, *n.* An oculist.

MEIJI,*-JIRU*, or DZRU,*-JITA*, メイズル, 命, *t.v.* To command, order, give instructions to a servant. Syn. ITSZKERU.

MEIJI,*-JIRU*, or DZRU,*-JITA*, メイズル, 銘,

To engrave, or inscribe. *Oya no iken wo kimo ni meijite waszredz*, to inscribe parental advice on one's liver (heart) and not forget it.

MEI-JITSZ, メイジツ, 明日, *(miyō-nichi)*, *adv.* To-morrow. Syn. AKURUHI, ASZ, ASH'TA.

MEI-KA, メイカ, 名家, *n.* A celebrated or illustrious family.

†MEI-KAN, メイカン, 明鑒, *(akirakanaru kagami)*, *n.* The clear mirror, (= just balance), in which the actions of men are truly reflected, just judgment. *Ten no — makoto ni osoru-beshi.*

MEI-KEN, メイケン, 名劍, *n.* A famous sword.

MEI-MEI, メイメイ, 名名, *adv.* Separately, each by himself, each and all, every one. *Gozen — ni taberu*, to dine each by himself. *Mei-mei sama*, every one of you. Syn. ONO-ONO, BETSZ-BETSZ.

†MEI-MEI, メイメイ, 冥冥, Dark, obscure, — *taru anya*, a dark night. *Ten fuku wo — no uchi yori tamō*, heaven from the midst of darkness gives prosperity.

MEI-MUKO, メヒムコ, 姪壻, *n.* A neice's husband.

MEI-NEN, メイネン, 明年, Next year. Syn. RAI-NEN, MIYŌ-NEN, AKURU-TOSHI.

MEI-NICHI, メイニチ, 命日, *n.* The day of the month, or year in which a person's death is commemorated. *Chichi haha no —.*

MEI-REI, メイレイ, 命令, *n.* Command, order. Syn. GE-JI, Ī-TSZKE.

‖MEIRI, *-ru, -tta*, メイル, 沈湎, *i.v.* To be given up to drink.

MEI-SAKU, メイサク 名作, *n.* An article made by a celebrated maker.

MEI-SAN, メイサン, 名産, *n.* A celebrated article of production, or manufacture.

†MEI-SATSZ, メイサツ, 明察, *n.* Clear discernment.

MEI-HITSZ, メイヒツ, 名筆, *n.* A famous penman.

†MEI-SHŌ, メイシヨウ, 明證, *n.* Clear proof.

MEI-SHO, メイシヨ, 名所, *n.* A celebrated place.

†MEI-SZ, メイス, 命數, *n.* The length of life. *Taitei h'to no — wa rokujū nen*, the length of man's life is about sixty years.

†MEI-TEI, メイテイ, 酩酊, Very drunk. *Saku-ban hanahada — itashi-mash'ta*, I was very drunk last night.

†MEI-TOKU, メイトク, 明德, *n.* Illustrious virtue.

MEI-WAKU, メイワク, 迷惑, *n.* Trouble, calamity, annoyance. Syn. NAN-JŪ, KOMARU.

†MEI-YAKU, メイヤク, 盟約, *n.* Covenant, agreement, promise, treaty. — *wo somuku*, to break an agreement. Syn. YAK'SOKU.

MEJIKA, メジカ, 牝鹿, *n.* A doe.

ME-JIRUSHI, メジルシ, 目標, *n.* A sign, mark, signal, beacon.

MEKADO, メカド, 目稜, Sight, perception. — *yoki h'to* a sharp sighted person, or a person who having seen another once, will after a long time recognise him again. Syn. GAN-RIKI.

MEKAGO, メカゴ, 目籠, *n.* An open-worked basket.

MEKAKE, メカケ, 妾, *n.* A concubine. S. TEKAKE, SHŌ.

ME-KAKUSHI, メカクシ, 目隱, *n.* Blind man's buff, a board-screen.

ME-KAO, メカホ, 目顏, *n.* Grimace, or signs made by the eye or face. — *de shiraseru*, to inform by a wink, or motion of the face.

ME-KARI, メカリ, 和布刈, *n.* A gatherer of sea-weed.

MEKASHI, *-sz, -sh'ta*, メカス, To dress in fine clothing, to adorn or deck one's self. *Ano h'to wa mekash'te iru h'to da*, he is richly dressed. Syn. YATSZSZ.

MEKATA, メカタ, 目方, *n.* Weight. — *wo hakaru*, to find the weight. Syn. KAKEME, BUNRIYŌ.

†MEKI, *-ku, -ita*, メク, A verb affix, having the meaning of, *like, appearance of*, found in the words; *Haru-meku*, spring-like. *Iromeku*, lascivious. *Homeku*, like fire, hot.

MEKIKI, メキキ, 目利, *n.* Expert in judging of the qualities of any work of art, as a sword, painting, &c.; or of the qualities of silk, tea, &c. *Mekiki-sha*, a connoisseur, an inspector. Syn. KAN-TEI.

MEKKACHI, メツカチ, 偏盲, *n.* Blind of one eye.

MEKKI, メツキ, 滅金, *n.* Plated with gold. — *wo szru*, to plate with gold.

MEKKIRI, メツキリ, *adv.* Exceedingly, very, — *samukunatta*, has become very cold. Syn. HIDOKU, HANAHADA.

†MEKK'YAKU, メツキヤク, 滅卻, Destroyed, broken.

MEKU, メク, See *Meki.*

MEKUBARI, メクバリ, 目配, *n.* Overseeing, superintending, or watching many things; attention directed to many things, looking about. *Kadz ga ōkute — ga yukitodokanu,* there are so many it is impossible to over see them all. *Me ga kubarikirenu,* cannot all be watched.

MEKUGI, メクギ, 目釘, *n.* *n.* A rivet.

MEKURA, メクラ, 盲, *n.* A blind person. Syn. MŌ-MOKU, MESHII.

MEKURA-MASHI, メクラマシ, 術人, *n.* A juggler, one who performs sleight of hand tricks. Syn. HAYAWAZA.

MEKURA-UCHI, メクラウチ, 泿打, *n.* Striking, or shooting at random.

MEKURI, メクリ, 打馬, *n.* A kind of game played with cards. — *wo szru,* to play cards.

MEKURI,-*ru*,-*tta*, メクル 捲, *t.v.* To roll up, same as *Makuri.*

MEKURI-FUDA, メクリフダ, 骨牌, *n.* Playing cards.

ME-KURUMEKI,-*ku*, メクルメク, 瞑眩, To be lightheaded, dizzy, vertiginous, giddy.

ME-KUSO, メクソ, 眵, *n.* Gummy discharge from the eyes. Syn. MAYORI, MEYANI.

ME-MAI, メマヒ, 眩暈, *n.* Dizziness, vertigo, giddiness. — *ga szru,* to be dizzy. Syn. KEN-NUN.

ME-MAGIRE,-*ru*,-*ta*, メマギレル, 目眩, *i.v.* To have the sight confused, (as by too strong a light).

†MEMBAKU,-*szru*, メンバク, 面縛, To bind, tie. *Toga nin wo —,* to bind a criminal. Syn. SHIBARU.

MEM-BIRŌDO, メンビロウド, 綿絨, *n.* Cotton velvet. Syn. MENTEN.

MEM-BŌ, メンバウ, 面帽, *n.* A woman's bonnet.

MEM-BŌ, メンボウ, 麪棒, *n.* A wooden rolling-pin.

†MEM-BŌ, メンボウ, 面貌, *(kao katachi), n.* The face and figure.

MEMBOKU, メンボク, 面目, *n.* (fig.) Face, countenance; confidence, boldness. — *ga nai,* to be out of countenance ashamed, crestfallen. — *wo ushinau,* to lose face, to be humiliated, mortified, out of countenance. — *wo hodokosz,* to put in countenance, to encourage.
Syn. MEMPI.

†MEM-BU, メンブ, 面部, *n.* The face.

MEMESHII,-KI,-KU,-SHI,-Ū, メメシイ 女, 女敷, Womanish, feminine, weak, timid.

MEMMA, メウマ, 牝馬, *n.* A mare.

MEM-MEN, メンメン, 面面, *adv.* Each and every one, every one, each one. Syn. MEI-MEI, ONO-ONO.

MEM-MITSZ, メンミツ, 綿密, Attentive, heedful, careful. — *ni shigoto wo szru,* to do one's work carefully. — *na h'to.* Syn. NEN WO IRERU, TEI-NEI.

ME-MOTO, メモト, 目本, *n.* The expression of the eye. — *ga kawairashii,* a pretty eye.

†MEMPAI, メンパイ, 面拜, *n.* Meeting, seeing face to face. — *no wiye mōshi-age soro,* after I have seen you I will tell you. Syn. HAI-GAN, TAI-MEN.

MEMPI, メンピ, 面皮, *(tszra no kawa.) n.* Fig. the face, countenance. — *wo kaku,* to cause shame, to put out of countenance. — *ni kakawaru,* idem. Syn. MEMBOKU.

MEMPUKU, メンプク, 綿服, *n.* Clothing made of cotton.

MEN, メン, 假面, *n.* A mask. — *wo kaburu,* to put on a mask.

MEN, メン, 面, *n.* The face, surface. *Nin men ni sh'te jū-shin no mimochi nari,* having a human face but acting like a beast. *Men wo toru,* to shave slightly the sharp edge of a board.

MEN, メン, 税則, *(nengu,) n.* Tax on the products of the farm. — *wo ageru,* to pay tax.

ME-NARE,-*ru*,-*ta*, メナレル, 目馴, *i. v.* Used to, or accustomed to seeing any thing.

MEN-CHI, メンチ, 免地, *n.* Land exempted from taxes.

†MEN-DAN, メンダン, 面談, Speaking face to face. — *szru.*

MENDŌ, メンダウ, 面倒, Troublesome, tedious, irksome, requiring time and care. — *na koto,* a troublesome affair.
Syn. URUSAI, MUDZKASHII, MODOKASHII.

MENDORI, ハンドリ, 雌, *n.* A female bird, a hen.

MENDZRU, メンズル, 面, see *Menji.*

†MEN-GIYŌ, メンギヤウ, 面形, *n.* Form of the face, physiognomy.

MENJI,-*ru*, or *dzru*,-*ta*, メンズル, 面, *t. v.* To allow, excuse, forgive, to spare, to remit, dispense with, mitigate, (as punishment.) *Watakushi ni menjite yurush'te kudasare,* extend pardon to him as if to myself. Syn. YURUSZ, SHŌ-CHI SZRU.

MEN-JŌ, メンジヤウ, 免狀, *n.* A written permit, a license, diploma, commission. Syn. YURUSHI-BUMI.

†MENJO,-*szru*, メンジヨ, 免除, To remit taxes.

MEN-KEN,-*szru*, メンケン, 瞑眩, To be dizzy, giddy, light headed. *Kuszri no tame-ni — sh'ta,* to be made dizzy by medicine. Syn. MEKURUMEKI, MEMAI.

MEN-K'YO, メンキヨ, 免許, *n.* Permission. — *szru*, to permit. — *wo ukeru*, to receive permission. Syn. YURUSHI.

†MEN-K'WAI, *-szru*, メンクワイ, 面會, To meet. Syn. AU.

MENŌ, メナウ, 碼碯, *n.* Agate.

MENO-KO-ZAN, メノコザン, 女子算, *n.* The way of reckoning used by those ignorant of the abacus, as counting on the fingers.

†MENOTO, メノト, 乳母, *n.* A wet-nurse. Syn. UBA.

MENOTO-GO, メノトゴ, 乳母子, *n.* The child of a wet-nurse.

MEN-RUI, メンルイ, 麪類, *n.* Food made of wheat flour.

†MEN-REN-TO, メンレント, 綿聯, *adv.* In continuous succession, one after the other. *Gan ga — sh'tė tobu. Kettō — sh'te tayedz.* Syn. TSZDZKU.

MEN-SEN, メンセン, 綿氈, *n.* A cotton rug.

MEN-SŌ, メンサウ, 面相, *n.* The physiognomy, expression of the face. — *wo kayete mono wo iu*, changing countenance to speak.

MEN-TEI, メンテイ, 面體, *n.* The form, or features of the face, looks.

MEN-TEN, メンテン, 綿天, *n.* Cotton-velvet. Syn. MEMBIRŌDO.

MEN-TS'Ū, メンツウ, 麪桶, *n.* A wooden box carried by beggars, for keeping food in.

†MEN-YETSZ, メンエツ, 面謁, Meeting face to face. — *nite kuwashiku mōshi age soro*, I will tell you more particularly when I meet you.
Syn. HAI-YETSZ, MEN-K'WAI.

MEN-YŌ-NA, メンヤウナ, *a.* Strange, bewildering, astonishing, surprising.

†MEN-ZŌ, メンザウ, 眠藏, *n.* A chamber. Syn. NANDO, NEDOKORO.

†ME-O, メヲ, 女男, Male and female. Syn. NAN NIYO.

ME-OBOYE, メオボヘ, 目覺, *n.* Memory of something which the eye has seen. — *no aru hitai no hokuro*, a mole on the forehead which one remembers to have seen. — *ga nai*, no recollection of seeing.

‖ME-OI, メオヒ, 醵錢, *n.* An entertainment, the expenses of which are defrayed by joint contribution.

ME-ONI, メオニ, 目鬼, *n.* The person who is blindfolded in blindman's buff.

ME-OTO, メヲト, 妻夫, *(fūfu). n.* Husband and wife.

MEPPŌ, メツパフ, 滅法, Rash, desperate extravagant. — *na yatsz*, a desperado. — *na nedan*, an extravagant price.
Syn. MUKŌ-MIDZ, MESSŌ.

MERI, メリ, *n.* Deficiency or loss in weight, or quantity, — *ga tatsz*, there is a deficiency. — *ga deru*, idem.

MERI-KOMI, *-mu, -nda*, メリコム, *i.v.* To be deficient in weight, or quantity.

MERI, MERU, MERE, メル, are auxilliary verbal suffixes same as, *Naru*, but having a dubitative sense, = *beshi*, or coll. *darō.*

MERIYASZ, メリヤス, 目利安, *n.* Any knit work; gloves; name of a tune.

ME-RŌ, メラウ, 女郎, *n.* A contemptuous epithet for a woman.

ME-SAME, *-ru, -ta*, メサメル, 目覺, *i. v.* To awake from sleep.

MESARE, *-ru, -ta*, メサレル, 被召, Pass. and honorific of *Meshi.* To be called, sent for, ordered, (used only of persons in high rank). *Kiu no goyō nite Kiyoto ye mesareta*, called to *Kiyoto* on important business. *Ichi mei wo —*, to punish with death. Syn. YOBARERU, MANEKARERU.

MESARE, *-ru, -ta*, メサレル, 被著, Pass. of *Meshi*, but used in a honorific and active sense. To wear, to put on, to dress. *Katabira wo mesareta*, dessed in thin summer clothes. Syn. KINASARERU.

MESARU, メサル, Same as *Mesareru.*

MESEKI-AMI, メセキアミ, 密網, *n.* A net with fine meshes.

MESHI, メシ, 飯, *n.* Boiled rice. — *wo taku*, to cook rice. — *wo taberu*, to eat food.

MESHI, *-sz, -sh'ta*, メス, 召, *t.v.* To call, send for, summon, cite, to order, (used of those in authority). *Danna sama ga meshimasz*, the master calls for you. Syn. YOBU.

MESHI, *-sz, -sh'ta*, メス, 著, *t.v.* To wear, put on, dress, (only of those high in rank.) Syn. KIRU.

MESHI-AGARI, *-ru, -tta*, メシアガル, 召上, *i.v.* To take food, to eat, (polite). *Nanzo meshi agari-mash'ta ka*, have you eaten any thing?

MESHI-AGE, *-ru, -ta*, メシアゲル, 召上, *t.v.* To take away, take possession of, seize, to levy. *Chigiyō wo —*, to take away an estate (from a noble for some offense). *Go-yō-kin wo —*, to levy a tax to defray government expenses.

MESHI-ATSZME, *-ru, -ta*, メシアツメル, 召集, *t.v.* To call or summon together.

MESHI-BITSZ, メシビツ, 飯匱, *n.* A tub, or pail for carrying boiled rice in.
Syn. MESHI-TSZGI, HAN-DŌ.

MESHI-BUMI, メシブミ, 召文, *n.* A letter

sent to summon attendance, a subpena, a written summons, or citation.
Syn. GEKI-BUN.

MESHI-DASHI,*-sz,-sh'ta*, メシダス, 召出, *t. v.* To call out into public service, to appoint to office.

MESHI-GUSHI,*-sz*, メシグス, 召具, *t. v.* To take along with, or in company.

MESHI-HANASARE,*-ru,-ta*, メシハナサレル, 召離, *i.v.* To be turned out or expelled from office, to have one's estate or salary taken away.

MESHII, メシヒ, 瞽者, *n.* A blind person. Syn. MEKURA.

MESHI-JŌ, メシジヤウ, 召状, *n.* A written summons to court, a subpena.
Syn. MESHI-BUMI.

MESHI-KAKAYE,*-ru,-ta*, メシカカヘル, 召抱, *t.v.* To appoint to office, to take into service.

MESHI-MONO, メシモノ, 衣服, *n.* Clothes. Syn. KIMONO.

MESHI-MORI, メシモリ, 驛妓, *n.* Hotel servant girls, who are also prostitutes.

MESHI-SOME, メシソメ, 召初, *n.* The first dressing in the *Kamishimo.*

ME-SH'TA, メシタ, 卑行, *n.* Inferiors, persons of low rank. — *no mono.*

MESHI-TAKI, メシタキ, 飯焚, *n.* A cook.

MESHI-TORI,*-ru,-tta*, メシトル, 召捕, *t.v.* To arrest, to seize (a criminal), apprehend. *Toga nin wo meshitoru,* to arrest a malefactor.

MESHI-TSZGI, メシツギ, 飯斗, *n.* A tub for holding boiled rice.

MESHI-TSZKAI, メシツカヒ, 召使, *n.* A servant. Syn. KODZKAI.

MESHI-TSZRE,*-ru,-ta*, メシツレル, 召連, *t.v.* To take along with.

MESHI-UDO, メシウド, 罪囚, *n.* A prisoner, criminal. Syn. TOGANIN, TSZMI-BITO.

MESHI-YOSE,*-ru,-ta*, メシヨセル, 召寄, *t.v.* To summon or call together, to call near.

MESOKAKI,*-ku,-ita*, メソカク, *i. v.* To prepare to cry, to be on the point of crying, (as a child). *Kodomo ga mesokaite iru,* the child looks as if it would cry.

MESSŌ, メツサウ, 滅相, Outrageous, extravagant, exorbitant. — *na yatsz,* an outrageous fellow. — *na nedan,* exorbitant price. Syn. MEPPŌ.

†MESSHI,*-sz,* or*-szru,-sh'ta*, メツスル, 滅, *(horobiru.) i.v.* To die, to finish, to destroy, exterminate.

MESZ, メス, 召, See *Meshi.*

MESZ, メス, 牝, *n.* Female of birds, animals, &c.

MESZ-OSZ, メスヲス, 牝牡, *n.* Male and female; gender. Syn. SHI-YŪ.

ME-TADARE, メタダレ, 目爛, *n.* Soreness of the eyelids, bleareyed.

ME-TATE, メタテ, 目立, *n.* A saw-sharpener, a repairer of the teeth of a grater, or of millstones.

METE, メテ, 右手, *(migi no te.) n.* The right-hand.

METEZASHI, メテザシ, 鮮手, *n.* A dagger worn in the belt on the right side.

METORI,*-ru,-tta*, メトル, 娶, *t.v.* To marry a wife. *Tszma wo* —, to marry a wife.

ME-TSZBO, メツボ, 目局, *n.* The orbit of the eye.

METSZBŌ, メツバウ, 滅亡, *n.* Destruction, ruin. *Mi, kuni, iye, nado no* —.
Syn. HOROBIRU.

ME-TSZBURE-DAKE, メツブレダケ, 目潰菌, *n.* A kind of puff-ball the dust of which is poisonous to the eyes.

ME-TSZBUSHI, メツブシ, 目潰, *n.* Any thing thrown into the eyes to cause blindness.

ME-TSZKE, メツケ, 目附, *n.* The name of a class of government officers of different ranks, whose duty it is to keep an eye on other officials and report to government. A public censor, or spy.

ME-TSZKI, メツキ, 目貌, *n.* The expression of the eye. — *ga yoi.*
Syn. MEMOTO.

†METSZMON, メツモン, 滅門, *n.* An unlucky day.

METTA, メツタ, Reckless, careless, indiscriminate, desperate, thoughtless. *Metta-na koto wo iuware-nai,* a person should not speak heedlessly *Metta-yatara ni kiri-tateru,* to cut about right and left without aim. *Metta-mushō ni okkakete yuku,* to pursue regardless of place, or obstacles. *Metta-banashi,* reckless talk, talking at random. *Metta-gaki,* careless writing. *Metta-uchi,* random firing.
Syn, MUYAMI, MUKŌMIDZ, BU-YEN-RIYO, YATARA,

METTA-NI, メツタニ, *adv.* Carelessly, heedlessly, thoughtlessly; always used in a negative sentence, with the meaning of, seldom, infrequent. — *nai,* not often, seldom. — *konai,* seldom comes. — *aru mono de wa nai,* it is a rare thing, a thing not often met with. — *haitte wa warui,* must not enter just when you please.
Syn. MIDARI-NI.

ME-YAMI, メヤミ, 目病, *n.* Sore eye.

MEYANI, メヤニ, 眵, *n.* Gummy, or mucous discharge from the eyes.

MEYASZ, メヤス, 目安, *n.* A written complaint, or petition. — *wo ageru,* to hand up a petition. Syn. MOKU-AN, NEGAI-SHO.

MEYASZ, メヤス, 目安, *n.* A number set down on the abacus or slate, merely that it may be remembered. — *wo oku.*

MEYASZ-BAKO, メヤスバコ, 目安箱, *n.* A box placed before the gate of a Daimio, into which petitions are thrown by any one.

MEZAMASHII,-KI,-KU,-U, メザマシイ, 目冷, Awaking the attention, terrible, tremendous, awful, horrible. *Mezamashiki h'to ikusa sh'te uchi jini sen tote ide-tachi keri.* Syn. HANABANASHII.

MEZASHI, メザシ, 目刺, *n.* A kind of small fish dried by stringing them on a stick passed through the eyes.

MEZASHI,-*sz*,-*sh'ta*, メザス, 目差, *t. v.* To fix the eyes on, to aim for, to direct the attention to. *Ni-hon-bashi wo meza-sh'te yuku,* to set out to go to the Nihon-bashi. Syn. MEATE.

MEZATOI,-KI,-KU,-SHI,-Ō, メザトイ, 目敏, Easily awakened.

MEZAWARI, メザハリ, 目障, *n.* In the way of the eyes, obstructing the sight, offensive to sight. — *ni naru ki wo kiru,* to cut down a tree that obstructs the view.

MI, ミ, 箕, *n.* A kind of shallow basket used for cleaning rice. *Kome wo mi de hiru.*

MI, ミ, 實, *n.* Fruit, seed, nut; anything produced from a tree, grass, &c. *Ki no mi,* the fruit of a tree. — *wo muszbu,* to bear fruit.

MI, ミ, 身, *n.* The body, person, self. — *ni amaru,* unworthy, above one's desert. — *wo sageru,* to humble one's self. — *ni naradz,* to be of no benefit to a person. — *no furumai,* one's behaviour, conduct. — *no hodo,* one's station in life, position in society. — *no wiye,* concerning one's self, relating to one's self. — *no mama ni szru,* to do as one likes. *Mi no ke,* the hair on the body. — *no nari-yuki,* the end of one's life. *On mi ga nasake,* your kindness.

MI, ミ, 刃, *n.* The blade of a sword. *Katana no mi,* idem.

MI, ミ, 底, *n.* The body of a box or cup, in distinction from the lid. *Mi to f'ta,* the box and lid.

MI, ミ, 肉, *n.* Flesh, meat. *Sakana no mi,* the flesh of fish. Syn. NIKU.

MI, ミ, 三, Three, more frequently, *Mitsz.*

MI, ミ, 身, *Per. pron.* I, (only used by superiors in speaking to inferiors). *Mi-domo,* we. *Mi ga wakai toki ni,* when I was young. Syn. WARE.

MI, ミ, 巳, *n.* The snake, one of the twelve signs. *Mi no toki,* 10 o'clock A.M. *Mi no tszki,* the 4th month.

MI, ミ, 御, A term of honor or respect prefixed to words relating to the *Kami* or *Mikado,* as, *Mi akashi, Mi-koshi, Miyuki, Mi-kuruma.*

†MI, ミ, 眞, A prefix, adding the idea of eminence, excellence, or greatness to the word with which it is joined, similar to the prefex *ma,* as, *Mi yama, Mi-yuki, Mi-kusa.*

†MI, ミ, A particle affixed to words, in poetry or prose composition, equivalent to *sa ni,* as, *Kaze hayami,* = *Kaze no hayasa ni,* on account of the swiftness of the wind. *No no natszkashi mi,* = *No no natszkashisa ni,* because of my fondness for the moors. *Yama takami,* = *Yama no takasa ni,* because of the height of the mountain.

†MI, ミ, A particle affixed to verbs in composition, equivalent to, *tari,* as, *naki-mi warai-mi* = *naki tari warai-tari* crying and laughing. *Furi-mi furadz-mi,* = *futta-ri yandari,* sometimes raining, sometimes not. *Hari-mi kumori-mi,* = *hari-tari kumot-tari,* sometimes clear, sometimes cloudy.

MI, ミ, A particle affixed to adjectives, equivalent to *tokoro,* as, *Takami,* — *takaki tokoro,* a high place. *Fukami,* = *fukaki tokoro,* a deep place. *Kubomi,* a hollow place. *Hiromi,* a wide place &c.

MI, ミ, 味, Taste, flavor; a numeral for medicine. *Bimi,* pleasant taste. *Sammi,* sour. *Kuszri sammi,* three kinds of medicine. *Kono sake wa nigami ga aru,* this wine has a bitter taste. *Kono satō ama mi ya uszi,* this sugar has but little sweetness. *Ichi mi no mono,* a friend, one of the same mind or party.

MI,-*ru*,-*ta*, ミル, 見, *t.v.* To see, look at, perceive. *Me de miru,* to see with the eyes. *Miyo,* or *minasare,* imp. look, see. *Tabete mite kudasare,* taste and see what it is like. *Isha ni mite morau,* let a doctor see it. *Miyaku wo miru,* to feel the pulse. *Aru ka nai ka kīte miru,* inquire whether there are any or not.

MI-AGE,-*ru*,-*ta*, ミアゲル, 見上, *t.v.* To look up at. *Tszki wo* — to look up at the moon.

MI-AKASHI, ミアカシ, 御燈, *n.* Lights set before the *Kami,* or used at festivals.

MI-AKI,-*ku*,-*ita*, ミアク, 見飽, *i.v.* To

be tired of looking at, to loathe the sight of.

MI-AWASE,*-ru*,*-ta*, ミアハセル, 見合, *t.v.* To look out for, to search and find, to look and ascertain, to look at each other. *Basho wo miawasete szmai wo szru*, to look out a suitable place and live there. *San nin kao wo* —, the three men looked each other in the face. *Hiori wo miawasete iru*, to be waiting, or looking for good weather.

MI-AWASHI,*-sz*,*-sh'ta*, ミアハス, 配偶, *t.v.* To join in body, marry.
Syn. MEAWASERU.

MI-AYAMACHI,*-tsz*,*-tta*, ミアヤマツ, 見過, *t.v.* To mistake in seeing, to mistake one thing for another. Syn. MI-CHIGAI, MI-SOKONAI.

MIBA ミバ, 見塲, *n.* The looks, appearance. — *ga yoi*, it looks well, or makes a good show.
Syn. MIDATE.

MI-BAYE, ミバヘ, 子生, *n.* Growing wild, (as a plant), or growing from the seed, not ingrafted.

MI-BĪKI, ミビイキ, 身引, *n.* Partiality, favoritism. — *wo szru*, to be partial, to favor one more than another.

MI-BUN, ミブン, 身分, *n.* One's proper place, or social position, condition, rank, or station in life. — *sō-ō*, suitable to one's social position. — *no yoi h'to*, a respectable person. Syn. BUN-GEN.

MI-BURI, ミブリ, 身振, *n.* Gesture, gesticulation, motion of the body. *Okashii mi-buri wo szru h'to*, a person of queer carriage.

MI-BURUI, ミブルヒ, 戰慄, *n.* Shaking, trembling or shivering of the body. — *wo szru*, to tremble.

MICHI, ミチ, 道, *n.* A road, way, (fig.) the right way or course of conduct, truth, principles, doctrine, teaching, duty, art. — *no hotori*, side of a road. — *no hadzre*, end of a road. — *wo kiru*, to cross a road. — *wo tszmeru*, to shorten a journey. — *ni mayō*, to lose the way. — *wo somuku*, to act contrary to what is right. — *ni hadzreru*, to miss the way.

MICHI,*-tszru*, or *ru*,*-ta*, ミチル, 滿, *i.v.* To be full, fill up or occupy the whole extent. *Shiwo ga michita*, the tide is full. *Tszki ga mitszru*, the moon is full, or the time of utero-gestation is full. *Sake ga sakadzki ni michita*, the cup is full of *sake*. *Gunzei ga no yama ni michite iru*, the army fills the plains and the mountain. *Urami ga kokoro ni mitszru*, his heart is full of malice.

MICHI-BATA, ミチバタ, 道傍, *n.* The side of a road.

MICHI-DZRE, ミチヅレ, 道連, *n.* Fellow traveler, companion on a journey. — *ni szru*, to join a person on the road.

MI-CHIGAYE,*-ru*,*-ta*, ミチガヘル, 誤認, *i.v.* To see and mistake, or not know. *Ano muszme wa michigayeru hodo utszkushiku natta*, that girl has become so pretty I did not know her.

MICHI-GUSA, ミチクサ, 演路, *n.* Sporting or playing by the way. — *wo szru*, to play or trifle while in the way.

MICHI-HI, ミチヒ, 滿干, *n.* Ebb and flow of the tide.

MICHI-KAKE, ミチカケ, 滿缺, *n.* The waxing and waning of the moon.

MICHI-MICHITARI, ミチミチタリ, 滿滿, Filling up, or occupying every place. *Gunzei ga no yama ni michi-michitari.*

MICHI-MICHI, ミチミチ, 道道, *adv.* While in the way, or on the road. *Uta wo utatte — yuku*, to go along the road singing songs. Syn. MICHI SZGARA.

†MICHI-NO-BE, ミチノベ, 道邊, *n.* Side of the road. Syn. MICHI-BATA.

MICHI-NOKI, ミチノキ, 紀行, *n.* A journal kept while traveling. Syn. KIKŌ, TABI-NIKKI.

MICHINORI, ミチノリ, 道程, *n.* Length of a road, distance in miles.

MICHI-SHIKI,*-KU*, ミチシク, 滿敷, Full, filled, as, *Ume no hana michishiki-taru tokoro*, a place filled with plum blossoms.

MICHI-SHIRUBE, ミチシルベ, 道標, *n.* A sign-board, or stone to show the way.

MICHI-SHIWO, ミチシホ, 滿潮, *n.* Flood tide.

MICHI-SZGARA, ミチスガラ, 道中, *adv.* In the road, while in the way, the whole journey. — *hanashi wo sh'te aruku*, to talk while walking along the road.
Syn. MICHI-MICHI.

MICHI-SZJI, ミチスヂ, 道條, *n.* A road, public ways. — *wa jin-ka ga ōi*, dwelling houses are mostly found near roads.

MICHI-WATARI,*-ru*,*-tta*, ミチワタル, 滿亘, Filling every place, spreading over.

MIDA, ミダ, 彌陀, Contract. of *Amida*, Buddha.

MI-DAIDOKORO, ミダイドコロ, 御臺所, *n.* The kitchen of the Emperor, Kubō, or Kuge; the dwelling of the wives of the Kubō, or Kuge.

MI-DAISAMA, ミダイサマ, 御臺樣, *n.* The wife of the Kubō or Kuge.

MIDAME, ミダメ, 自爲, cont. of *Mi no ta-*

me. One's own interest, self-interest. — *ni naranu koto wa senu,* doing nothing that will not be for one's own good, or interest.

MIDANUKI, ミダヌキ, 貒, *n.* A kind of animal.

MIDARA-NA, ミダラナ, 淫, *n,* Licentious, lewd, adulterous. — *onna.*

MIDARE,*-ru,-ta,* ミダレル, 亂, *i. v.* Disturbed, disordered, thrown into confusion, excited to tumult, agitated. *Yo, kuni, iye, kokoro nado ga midareru. Midaregami,* dishevelled hair. *Midare ikusa,* an army thrown into confusion.

MIDARE, ミダレ, 亂, *n.* Disturbance, excitement, disorder, confusion, tumult. — *no hashi,* the origin of a disturbance. — *wo shidzmeru,* to quell a tumult.

MIDARE-IRI,*-ru,-tta,* ミダレイル, 亂入, *i. v.* To enter in confusion, to go in helter-skelter,

MIDARI-NI, ミダリニ, 妄, *adv.* Disorderly, carelessly, irregularly, not in accordance with law, order, propriety, or custom. — *kane wo tszkau,* to squander money. — *iru bekaradz,* must not enter without permission.

MIDASHI,*-sz,-sh'ta,* ミダス, 亂, *t. v.* To derange, throw into disorder, to disturb the regular order, to break down, confuse, to deprave, corrupt. *Retsz wo* —, to derange the ranks.

MI-DASHI,*-sz,-sh'ta,* ミダス, 見出, *t. v.* To find by looking for, to discover, descry.

MIDATE, ミダテ, 見立, *n.* Appearance calculated to strike the eye, or arrest attention, show, display. — *no nai mono,* a thing which makes no show.
Syn. MIBA, MIKAKE.

MI-DOKORO, ミドコロ, 見所, *n.* Something noticeable, or worthy of observation. — *no nai h'to,* one who has nothing about him worth noticing.

MIDORI, ミドリ, 綠, *n.* Green colour.

†MIDORIGO, ミドリゴ, 嬰兒, *n.* An infant.
Syn. AKAMBŌ.

MIDORO, ミドロ, 塗, Smeared over with; as, *Chi-midoro,* smeared with blood. *Ase-midoro,* covered with sweat.
Syn. DARAKE, MABURE.

MIDZ, ミズ, 不見, neg. of *Miru.*

MIDZ, ミヅ, 水, *n.* Water.

MIDZ-ABI, ミヅアビ, 水浴, *n.* Bathing with cold water.

MIDZ-AGE, ミヅアゲ, 水揚, *n.* Unloading goods from a ship or boat, discharging cargo. — *wo szru,* to unload a ship.

MIDZ-AI, ミヅアヒ, 滖, *n.* The junction of two streams of water.

MIDZ-AME, ミヅアメ, 水飴, *n.* A kind of syrup made of malt.

MIDZASAGI, ミヅアサギ, 水淺黃, *n.* A light green color.

MIDZ-BANA, ミヅバナ, 清涕, *n.* Mucous discharge from the nose, as in catarrh.

MIDZ-BARE, ミヅバレ, 水腫, *n.* A watery swelling, dropsical swelling.

MIDZBUKI, ミヅブキ, 芡, *n.* The name of an aquatic plant. Euryale ferox.

MIDZ-BUKURE, ミヅブクレ, 水脹, *n.* A waterblister.

MIDZ-BUKURO, ミヅブクロ, 脬, *n.* The air bladder of fishes.

MIDZ-BUNE, ミヅブネ, 水槽, *n.* A vat, trough, or box for holding water.

MIDZCHŌ, ミヅチヤウ, 御圖帳, *n.* A land register, or record containing charts and plans of all the land of the empire.

MIDZ-DEPPŌ, ミヅデツパウ, 唧筒, *n.* A squirt, syringe.

MIDZ-DOKEI, ミヅドケイ, 漏刻, *n.* A clepsydra.

MIDZ-DORI, ミヅドリ, 水鳥, *n.* A water fowl.

MIDZ-FUKI, ミヅフキ, 噴壺, *n,* A utensil for watering plants.

MIDZ-GAKI, ミヅガキ, 瑞籬, *n.* A picket fence around a Miya.

MIDZ-GIWA, ミヅギハ, 水際, *n.* Edge of the water.

MIDZ-GURUMA, ミヅグルマ, 水車, *n.* A water-wheel.

MIDZ-GUSA, ミヅグサ, 水艸, *n.* Grass, or weeds growing in the water.

MIDZ-G'WASHI, ミヅグワシ, 水果子, *n.* Fruit.
Syn. KUDAMONO.

MIDZ-HIKI, ミヅヒキ, 水引, *n.* A fine cord of white and red colour, made of paper, and used for tying up presents; a curtain before the stage of a theatre; letting out water from a channel for irrigation, by opening an embankment.

MIDZ-IMO, ミヅイモ, 水痘, *n.* Chicken pox.

MIDZ-IRE, ミヅイレ, 水滴, *n.* A vessel for holding the water used in rubbing ink.

MIDZ-IRO, ミヅイロ, 水色, *n.* A light blue color.

MIDZ-JAKU, ミヅジヤク, 水尺, *n.* A rod, or line for measuring the depth of water.

MIDZ-KAGAMI, ミヅカガミ, 水鑑, *n.* Water used as a mirror.

MIDZ-KAGE, ミヅカゲ, 水影, *n.* The

shadow of anything in water, or reflection of water.

MIDZKAI,-*au*, ミツカフ, 水飼, *t.v.* To water animals. *Uma wo midzkau*, to water a horse.

MIDZKAKE-RON, ミヅカケロン, 堅白論, *n.* A dispute in which each charges the other with blame.

MIDZ-KAME, ミヅカメ, 水瓶, *n.* A water-jar.

MIDZ-KANE, ミヅカネ, 水銀, *n.* Quick-silver. Syn. SZIGIN.

MIDZKARA, ミヅカラ, 自, *pers. pron.* Of one's self, it may mean myself, yourself, himself, herself, according to its connection. — *naseru wazawai wa nogaru bekaradz*, misfortune which one has brought on himself cannot be avoided.

MIDZKIN, ミヅキン, 水金, *n.* The capital, or funds employed in business. — *wo kakeru*, to employ capital. Syn. MOTODE,

MIDZ-KASA, ミヅカサ, 水勢, *n.* The body, or quantity of water. — *ga masaru*, the water increases.

MIDZ-KEMURI, ミヅケムリ, 水煙, *n.* The mist which rises from water.

MIDZKO, ミヅコ, 稚子, *n.* A new born infant.

MIDZ-KOSHI, ミヅコシ, 水漉, *n.* A strainer, a filter.

MIDZ-KUGURI,-*ru*,-*tta*, ミヅクグル, 泳, *i.v.* To dive under water.

MI-DZKUROI, ミヅクロヒ, 身繕, *n.* Adjusting one's clothes.

MIDZ-KUSA, ミヅクサ, 水瘡, *n.* An eruption about the mouth of children.

MIDZ-KUSAI, ミヅクサイ, 水臭, Raw or fresh taste, insipid, luke warm, unfeeling, false hearted, insincere, not to be depended on.

MIDZ-MIDZ-TO, ミヅミヅト, 稚稚, *adv.* Fresh and beautiful, having a fresh, lively, and unfaded look. — *sh'ta kodomo.*

MIDZ-MONO, ミヅモノ, 水物, *n.* A fluid, liquid.

MIDZ-MORI, ミヅモリ, 水盈, *n.* A water-level. — *wo szru*, to level.

MIDZNA, ミヅナ, 水菜, *n.* A kind of greens.

MIDZ-NAWA, ミヅナハ, 準繩, *n.* A line used in leveling ground. — *wo hiku*, to stretch a line.

MIDZ-NO-DEBANA, ミヅノデバナ, 水出花, *n.* The highest point of a rise of water, or inundation; fig. of the time when young love is the strongest.

MIDZ-NOMI, ミヅノミ, 蠡器, *n.* A cup for drinking water. — *h'yak'shō*, a poor farmer, who can't afford to drink *sake* or tea.

MIDZ-NO-TARU, ミヅノタル, 水之垂, Smooth, shining, and beautiful, like the surface of water. — *yō na* id.

MIDZ-NO-TE, ミヅノテ, 水手, *n.* The supply of water. — *wo kiru*, to cut off the supply of water (from a place.)

MIDZNOTO, ミヅノト, 癸, *n.* One of the ten calender signs.

MIDZNOYE, ミヅノエ, 壬, *n.* One of the ten calender signs.

MIDZ-NUKI, ミヅヌキ, 水拔, *n.* A drain for draining off standing water.

MIDZOCHI, ミヅオチ, 鳩尾, *n.* The pit of the stomach.

MIDZ-SAKI, ミヅサキ, 水衛, *n.* A ship's pilot.

MIDZ-SASHI, ミヅサシ, 水注, *n.* A pitcher, or pot for pouring water.

MIDZ-SEKI, ミヅセキ, 水堰, *n.* A dam for obstructing a current of water.

†MI-DZ-SHI-DOKORO, ミヅシドコロ, 御厨子所, *n.* The Mikado's library.

†MIDZSHIME, ミヅシメ, 下婢, *n.* A female servant. Syn. GE-JO.

MIDZ-SZJI, ミヅスヂ, 水脈, *n.* A vein of water, as in digging for a well; currents in the ocean.

MIDZ-SZMASHI, ミヅスマシ, 豉虫, *n.* A kind of bug which moves about on the surface of water.

MIDZ-TA, ミヅタ, 水田, *n.* Rice-fields which are alway wet and boggy, and which cannot be drained.

MIDZTADE, ミヅタデ, 水蓼, *n.* Water-cress.

MIDZTAMA, ミヅタマ, 水晶, *n.* Crystal, or quartz, also, drops of water, or spray. Syn. SZISHO.

MIDZ-TAME, ミヅタメ, 水溜, *n.* A rain-tub, cistern for holding rain-water.

†MIDZTORUTAMA, ミヅトルタマ, 水精, *n.* Crystal, quartz. Syn. SZISHO.

MIDZ-UMI, ミヅウミ, 湖, *n.* A lake.

MIDZUMI, ミヅウミ, 水膿, *n.* The pustules of small-pox.

MIDZ-YOKE, ミジヨケ, 水除, *n.* A break-water.

MIDZ-ZEME, ミヅゼメ, 水責, *n.* Torture by water.

MIGAKI,-*ku*,-*ita*, ミガク, 磨, *t.v.* To make to shine, to polish, burnish, to rub-up; (fig.) to refine, purify, make more elegant. *Ha wo* —, to clean the teeth. *Gaku-mon wo* —, to improve one's literary knowledge. *Kokoro wo* —, to purify the heart. *Kutsz wo* —, to black shoes. *Kagami wo* —, to polish a metal mirror.

MIGAKI, ミガキ, 磨, *n.* Polishing, burnishing.

MIGAKI-KO, ミガキコ, 磨粉, *n.* Polishing-powder.

MI-GAMAYE, ミガマヘ, 身構, *n.* Posture, or position of the body, (as in fencing.) — *wo szru*, to put one's self into position, (for attack, or defence).

MI-GARA, ミガラ, 身柄, *n.* The kind or quality of person, either physically, or socially. — *ga yoi h'to.* Syn. MIBUN.

MI-GATERA, ミガテラ, 見且, While looking at, or at the same time that one is looking at. *Shibai wo mi-gatera mono wo kai ni yuku*, to go out a shopping, and at the same time to look in at the theatre.

MI-GATTE, ミガツテ, 身勝手, *n.* One's own convenience, or pleasure. — *wo szru*, to seek one's own convenience.
Syn. TEMAYE-GATTE.

MI-GAWARI, ミガハリ, 身代, *n.* Giving one's self as a substitute for another. *Shujin no — ni kerai ga shinuru*, the servant died in place of his master.

MIGI, ミギ, 右, *n.* Right. — *hidari*, right and left. — *no te*, right hand. — *no hō*, right side, or region. — *no tōri*, as said or written above; as aforesaid. *Sono — ni idzru mono wa nai*, there was no one could match him.

MIGIRI, ミギリ, 砌, *n.* A stone pavement, or wall, (2.) 右, right, (3.) 刻, time, period of time. *On tszide no — ni*, when you have a convenient time.

MI-GIWA, ミギハ, 汀, *n.* Edge of the water, shore.

MI-GIYŌSHO, ミギヤウシヨ, 御教書, *n.* A letter of instruction, or order from the *Shōgun*, or *Kuge*.

MIGO, ミゴ, *n.* The stem on which the grains of rice grow.

MI-GOMORI, ミゴモリ, 身籠, *n.* Pregnant, with child. Syn. K'WAI-TAI.

MI-GOROSHI, ミゴロシ, 見殺, *n.* Beholding a person dying. — *ni szru.*

MIGOTO, ミゴト, 美観, Beautiful, handsome. — *na hana*, a beautiful flower.
Syn. UTSZKUSHII.

MIGURUSHII,-KI,-KU,-Ū, ミグルシイ, 見苦敷, Ugly, offensive to the eyes, homely. Syn. MINIKUI.

MIGUSHI, ミグシ, 髪, *n.* The hair of the head. — *oroshi*, one who shaves the head and retires from public life, (only of high personages). Syn. OGUSHI, KAMI.

MIHABA, ミハバ, 身幅, *n.* The width of a dress. *Kono haori wa — ga semai*, this coat is too tight. — *ga hiroi*, it is large.

MI-HADZSHI,-*sz*,-*sh'ta*, ミハヅス, 見外, *t.v.* To overlook, miss seeing.

†MI-HAKASHI, ミハカシ, 御刀, *n.* The sword of the Mikado.

MI-HAKARAI,-*au*,-*tta*, ミハカラフ, 見計, *i.v.* To judge of, or estimate by the eye.

MI-HARASHI-*sz*,-*sh'ta*, ミハラス, 見晴, *t.v.* To look at a prospect or distant objects from a height.

MI-HARASHI, ミハラシ, 見晴, *n.* A wide or extensive view.
Syn. MI-WATASHI, CHŌBO.

MI-HARI,-*ru*,-*tta*, ミハル, 見張, *i.v.* To look out and watch what is passing. *Bansho no yaku-nin ga mi-hatte iru*, the officers at the station sit watching. *Me wo* —, to stare.

MI-HARI, ミハリ, 見張, *n.* A look-out, or station house, where policemen sit watching.

MI-HASHI, ミハシ, 御階, *n.* The steps before the door of the Mikado's palace.

MI-HIRAKI,-*ku*,-*ita*, ミヒラク, 看破, *t.v.* To discover, lay open, or disclose something before concealed.

MI-IRI, ミイリ, 實入, *n.* The fruiting, the bearing of fruit, the quality of the fruit, the crop. *Ko-toshi ine no — ga yoi*, this year the rice is of fine quality.
Syn. MINORI.

MI-ITOKO, ミイトコ, 三從兄弟, *n.* The grandchild of a cousin, a third cousin.

†MIJI, ミジ, Comp. of *Mi*, to see, and *Ji*, fut. neg suffix, = will not see. *Kono haru wa — to omoishi hana*, a flower which I did not expect to see this spring.

MIJIKAI,-KI,-SHI, ミジカイ, 短, Short, not long. *Hi ga* —, the days are short. *Ki ga* —, quick tempered.

MIJIKAKU, ミジカク, 短, *adv.* id. — *szru*, to shorten. — *naru*, to become short. — *nai*, not short.

MIJIKASA, ミジカサ, 短, *n.* Shortness, the length.

MIJIKŌ, ミジカウ, 短, Same as *Mijikaku*.

MIJIMAI, ミジマヒ, *n.* Dressing, attiring, adorning. — *wo szru.*
Syn. KESHŌ, YOSŌI.

MI-JIN, ミヂン, 微塵, *n.* Fine dust, smallest particle, a mite. — *ni kudaku*, to break into powder. — *mo gozarimasen*, there is not a mite. — *mo nomimasen*, I did not drink a particle.

MIJIROKI,-*ku*, ミジロク, 身退, *i.v.* To

shrink back in fear, to drawback, to flinch, to start in alarm. *Mijiroki mo sedz kotaye keru.* Syn. BIKU-BIKU, ATOSHIZARI.

MIJŌ, ミジヤウ, 身性, *n.* Natural constitution, temperament, disposition.
Syn. UMARETSZKI.

MI-JUKU, ミジユク, 未熟, Not yet ripe, fig. not yet fully attained, imperfect in learning, or skill, green, inexperienced.

MI-KADO, ミカド, 御門, *n.* The Emperor. Syn. KINRI, TENSHI, K'WŌ-TEI, HEI-KA.

MIKA-DZKI, ミカヅキ, 朏, *n.* New-moon, the moon as seen on the third day.

MI-KAGAMI, ミカガミ, 神鏡, *n.* The mirror placed in a *Miya*, and worshiped as a representation of the *Kami.*

MI-KAGIRI,*-ru,-tta*, ミカギル, 見限, *i.v.* To be able no longer to endure the sight of, no longer willing to see.
Syn. MIKUBIRU.

MI-KAGURA, ミカグラ, See *Kagura.*

MI-KAKE, ミカケ, 見掛, *n.* Appearance, looks. — *ni wa yoranu mono*, a person who is different from what he appears,— who cannot be judged by his appearance. — *yori umai mono*, sweeter than it looks. Syn. MI-DATE, MIBA.

MI-KAKE,*-ru,-ta*, ミカケル, 見掛, *t. v.* To lay eyes on, to see, to meet. *Hisashiku mikakemasenanda*, I have not seen you for a long time.

MI-KAKE-DAOSHI, ミカケダフシ, 見掛倒, *n.* Any thing different from what it appears, false or deceptive in appearance.

MIKAN, ミカン, 蜜柑, *n.* An orange.

MIKATA, ミカタ, 御方, *n.* A friend, one of the same army, side, or party. *Teki mikata*, enemy and friend.

MI-KAYE,*-ru,-ta*, ミカヘル, 見返, *i.v.* To look back, look behind. 見換, To change the object of one's admiration for something else.

MI-KAWASHI,*-sz,-sh'ta*, ミカハス, 見交, *t.v.* To exchange glances, to look at and recognise. *Tagai ni — kao to kao*, to look at each other face to face.

†MIKE, ミケ, 御饌, *n.* The food of the *Mikado.* *Asa-mike*, breakfast of the *Mikado.*

MIKEN, ミケン, 眉間, *n.* The space between the eyebrows,

MI-KE-NEKO, ミケネコ, 三毛猫, *n.* A cat of three colors.

MIKI, ミキ, 神酒, *n.* *Sake* offered to the *Kami.*

MIKI, ミキ, 幹, *n.* The trunk of a tree.

MI-KIKI, ミキキ, 見聞, *n.* Seeing and hearing. — *sh'ta koto wo kaki-tszkete oku*, to write down that which one sees and hears.

MI-KIRENU, ミキレヌ, 不見切, Cannot be wholly seen, too much for the eye to see at once. *Umi ga hirokute me ni mikirenu*, the ocean is so wide it cannot be all seen at once.

MI-KIRI,*-ru,-tta*, ミキル, 見切, *i.v.* To settle in one's mind, decide on. *Mikitte uru*, to decide on selling. *Mi-kiri ga tszkanu*, cannot make up one's mind, cannot decide. Syn. KETCHAKU, OMOI-KIRU.

MI-KIWAME,*-ru,-ta*, ミキハメル, 見極, *t.v.* To decide on, settle in one's mind, take good aim at.

MIKKA, ミツカ, 三日, The third day of the month, three days. — *miban nemurimasen*, have not slept for three days and three nights. *Mikka me ni*, on the third day.

†MIKKAN,*-szru*, ミツカン, 密諫, (*hisokani isameru*). To privately caution, or reprimand.

†MIKKEI, ミツケイ, 密計, (*hisokana hakarigoto*). A secret plot, conspiracy. — *wo morasz* to divulge a conspiracy.

†MIKK'WAI, ミツクワイ, 密會, (*hisokani atszmaru*). A secret meeting.

MIKO, ミコ, 皇子, *n.* A prince, or son of the *Mikado.* *Hime miko*, a princess.
Syn. SHIN-NŌ, MIYA.

MIKO, ミコ, 巫女, *n.* A female dancer or performer in a *kagura.*
Syn. KANNAGI.

MIKO, ミコ, 三糸, Three strands. — *ito*, thread of three strands.

MIKO, ミコ, 三子, *n.* Triplets.

MI-KOMI,*-mu,-nda*, ミコム, 見込, *t. v.* To see through, or perceive clearly the nature or qualities of anything.

MIKOSHI, ミコシ, 神輿, *n.* The sacred car in which the mirror, which represents the *Kami*, is taken out in processions, and festivals.

MIKOTO, ミコト, 尊, *n.* A respectful title affixed to the name of a *Kami*, also, 命, a command of a *Kami*, or of the *Mikado.*

MIKOTO-NORI, ミコトノリ, 勅, *n.* An order, or command of the *Mikado.* — *szru*, to command. Syn. CHOKU-MEI, SENJI.

MI-KUBIRI,*-ru,-tta*, ミクビル, *t.v.* No longer able to bear the sight of.
Syn. MI-KAGIRU.

MI-KUDASHI,*-sz,-sh'ta*, ミクダス, 見下, *t.v.* To look down; to despise, look down on.

MIKUDZ, ミクズ, 水屑, *n.* Rubbish floating in water.

MI-KUJI, ミクヂ, 神籤, *n.* Divining sticks, used in temples to know the mind of the *Kami*.

MI-KUSA, ミクサ, 水草, *n.* Sea-weed; any grass growing in water.

MI-MAGAI,*-au*, or*-ō*, ミマガフ, 見紛, *t.v.* To mistake one thing for another, to confound different things. *Mikata wo teki to mimagō*, he mistook his friends for the enemy.

†MIMAHOSHII,-KI,-KU, ミマホシイ, 欲見, Desirous of seeing, wishing to see.

MIMAI,*-au*,*-atta*, ミマフ, 見舞, *t.v.* To condole with, to make a visit of sympathy to one in trouble. *Biyōnin wo* —, to condole with a sick person. Syn. TOMORAU.

MIMAI, ミマヒ, 見舞, *n.* A visit of friendship, condolence, or sympathy. — *ni yuku*, to go on such a visit. — *wo iu*, to visit and inquire after another's health, or condole with the sick. — *no jō*, a letter of condolence, or friendly inquiry after another's health. Syn. TOMORAI.

†MIMAKARI,*-ru*, ミマカル, 死, *i. v.* To die. Syn. SHINURU.

MIMASHI, ミマシ, 見増, Best looking. *Dochira ga — da*, which is the best looking, or the prettiest? — *na hō wo toru ga ī*, better take the prettiest.

MI-MAWARI,*-ru*,*-tta*, ミマハル, 見廻, *t.v.* To go about looking, to go around on watch.

MI-MAWARI, ミマハリ, 見廻, *n.* Looking around, going around as a watchman. — *no yakunin*. — *ni yuku*.

MI-MAWASHI,*-sz*,*-sh'ta*, ミマハス, 見廻, *t.v.* To look around.

†MIM-BU, ミンブ, 民部, *n.* That department of the government at *Kiyoto* which superintends the census, boundary lines, maps, and charts.

MIME, ミメ, 眉目, *n.* The countenance, face. — *yoki onna*, a woman of a beautiful countenance. *Mime-katachi*, personal appearance. Syn. YŌBŌ, KIRIYŌ.

MI-MEGURI,*-ru*,*-tta*, ミメグル, 巡見, *i.v.* To go about looking (as in curiosity.)

†MI-MEI, ミメイ, 未明, (*imada akedz*), *n.* Before the dawn of day. — *ni shuttatsz szru*, to start before the dawn of day.

MIMI, ミミ, 耳, *n.* The ear, the selvedge of cloth, list. — *no ana*, the hole of the ear. — *no aka*, ear-wax. — *ga tōi*, hard of hearing. — *ga naru*, ears ring. — *ga tszbureru*, to be deaf. — *ni sakarau*, to offend the ears. — *ni tomaru*, to stick in the ear, to remember. *Midz-oto ga — ni tszite nerarenu*, I could not sleep for the noise of the water. — *ni tatsz*, to strike the ear, arrest the attention. *Nabe no* —, the ears of a pot. *Orimono no* —, the selvedge, or list of cloth.

MIMI-DARAI, ミミダライ, 耳盥, *n.* A bason with ears.

MIMI-DARE, ミミダレ, 聤, *n.* A discharge from the ears.

MIMIDZ, ミミズ, 蚯蚓, *n.* A red earthworm.

MIMIDZKA, ミミヅカ, 耳塚, *n.* A tomb, where the ears cut from those killed of the enemy are buried.

MIMIDZKU, ミミヅク, 木兎, *n.* A kind of owl.

MIMI-GAKUMON, ミミガクモン, 耳學, *n.* Learning acquired by the ear.

MIMI-GANE, ミミガネ, 耳鐶, *n.* Ear ring, ornaments worn in the ear.

MIMI-HARAI, ミミハラヒ, *n.* An ear-pick.

MIMI-KAKI, ミミカキ, *n.* An ear-pick.

MIMI-KOSZRI, ミミコスリ, 耳語, *n.* Whispering, back-biting, secret slander. — *wo szru*.

MIMI-KUSO, ミミクソ, 盯聹, *n.* Ear-wax.

MIMI-SHII, ミミシヒ, 聾者, *n.* A deaf person.

MIMI-TABU, ミミタブ, 耳捶, *n.* The lobe of the ear.

MIMITAKE, ミミタケ, 木耳, *n.* A mushroom which grows from the trunk of a dead tree. Syn. KIKURAGE.

MIMITCHII, ミミツチイ, vulg. col. Stingy, penurious, miserly. Syn. SHIWAI.

MIMITCHIKU, ミミツチク, *adv.* idem.

†MI-MIYŌ, ミミヤウ, 微眇, Exceeding small.

MIMŌ, ミマフ, 見舞, see *Mimai*.

MIMOCHI, ミチモ, 有身, *n.* Conduct, behavior, deportment. — *ga warui*, (2.) Pregnant, with child. — *ni naru*, to become pregnant. Syn. (1) GIYŌ-JŌ, (2) K'WAI-NIN.

MIMOCHI, ミモチ, *n.* A small insect destructive to rice, called by some *Imochi*.

MI-MUKI, ミムキ, 見向, *n.* Looking towards. — *mo sedz*, would not even look towards him.

†MIN, ミン, 見, fut. of *Miru*,= col. *Miyō*. — *to hosszru*, desire to see. *Mata mo min*, will see [you] again.

†MIN, ミン, 民, (*tami.*) *n.* People; the unofficial part of the people.

MINA, ミナ, 蝸蠃, *n.* A kind of river shell, like the Eulima.

MINA, ミナ, 皆, *a.* (Also pronounced *Min-na*). All, every, the whole. Syn. NOKORADZ, SZBETE, KOTOGOTOKU.

MINADZKI, ミナヅキ, 六月, *n.* The sixth month.

MI-NAGASHI, ミナガシ, 見流, *n.* Letting any thing pass without noticing, seeing but taking no notice of it. — *ni szru.*

MI-NAGE, ミナゲ, 身投, *n.* Drowning one's self. — *wo szru,* to commit suicide by drowning.

MINAGI, ミナギ, 水葱, *n.* A kind of water plant.

MINAGIRI, *-ru,* ミナギル, 漲, *i. v.* To rise and swell, as waves; to surge. *Taka nami ten ni minagiru,* the big waves rose to the heavens. *Midz wa waite ten ni —,* the water boiling rose up to the sky, [of Buddhist hades.]

†MINAGIWA, ミナギハ, 水際, *(Midz no kiwa,) n.* Water's edge.

MINA-GOROSHI, ミナゴロシ, 鏖, *n.* Putting all to death, extermination by the sword. — *ni szru,* to exterminate with the sword.

MINAKAMI, ミナカミ, 水上, *n.* The head-waters, fountain-head, source, origin. *Kawa no —,* the head-waters of a river. Syn. MINAMOTO.

†MINAKUCHI, ミナクチ, 水口, *(midz no kuchi,) n.* The openings made for water to flow out of, as in the banks of rice-fields, or ponds.

MINAMI, ミナミ, 南, *n.* The south. — *no hō,* on the southern side.

MINA-MINA, ミナミナ, 皆皆, *adv.* All, every, the whole. — *sama,* the whole family, or every one addressed.

MINAMOTO, ミナモト, 源, *n.* The fountain-head, the head or source of a river, the name of an ancient, noble and powerful family, of which the families of *Kishū. Owari* and *Mito* are branches.

MI-NAOSHI, *-sz, -sh'ta,* ミナホス, 見直, *t. v.* To look over again, in order to find, correct, &c.

MI-NARAI, *-au, -atta,* ミナラフ, 見習, *t. v.* To look on and learn, learn by seeing.

MI-NARE, *-ru, -ta,* ミナレル, 見馴, *i. v.* To get used to seeing, to be accustomed to any thing by often seeing it.

MINARI, ミナリ, 身形, *n.* The dress, clothing. — *ga warui,* to be slovenly, or ragged in dress. — *wo kudzsanu,* to be always fully and neatly dressed. Syn. MI NO MAWARI, NARIFURI.

MINA-SAMA, ミナサマ, 皆様, *n.* All of you. — *ohaiyo,* good morning to you all.

MINASHI, ミナシ, 見成, *n.* Fancy, whim, freak, caprice of the sight. — *ni yotte chigau,* differs merely according to one's fancy. *Anata no — da,* merely a fancy of yours.

MINASHIGO, ミナシゴ, 孤兒, *n.* An orphan.

MINASOKO, ミナソコ, 水底, *n.* The bottom of water, (sea, river, &c.)

MINATO, ミナト 港, *n.* Harbor, port, or mart, where ships anchor and trade.

†MINAWA, ミナハ, 水泡, *(midz no awa,) n.* The foam of water.

MINAYO, ミナヨ, coll. imp. of *Miru.*=*Miyo,* or *Minasai.*

MINE, ミネ, 峯, *n.* Mountain peak.

MINEBA, ミネバ, neg. conj. of *Miru.* — *wakarimasen,* I don't know without seeing it.

MI-NIKUI, *-KI, -KU, -SHI, -SA,* ミニクイ, 醜, Ugly, homely. 見惡, hard to see.

†MIN-KA, ミンカ, 民家, *n.* The houses of the common people.

MINO, ミノ, 蓑, *n.* A rain-coat made of hemp.

MI-NOGASHI, *-sz, -sh'ta,* ミノガス, 見遁, *t. v.* To see but let pass, (as an offence,) to overlook, to take no notice of.

MI-NOKORI, *-ru, -tta,* ミノコル, 見殘, *i. v.* Remaining over unseen, passed by unseen, overlooked.

MI-NOKOSHI, *-sz, -sh'ta,* ミノコス, 見殘, *t.v.* To leave unseen, to overlook.

MINOMUSHI, ミノムシ, 蓑虫, *n.* A small kind of worm.

MINORI, *-ru, -tta,* ミノル, 實, *i.v.* To bear fruit; to head, or ear as grain.

MINORI, ミノリ, 實, *n.* The bearing of fruit, the heading, earing of grain. *Kotoshi wa ine no — ya yoi,* the rice has headed well this year. Syn. MI-IRI.

MINOWATA, ミノワタ, 三膲, *n.* The internal organs, of the thorax and abdomen.

MINU, ミヌ, 不見, Neg. of *Miru.*

MI-NUKI, *-ku, -ita,* ミヌク, 見徹, *i.v.* To see through the future and comprehend coming events, foresee.

MINUSA, ミヌサ, 大麻, *n.* Paper hung up in a *Miya.* Same as *Gohei.*

MI-O, ミヲ, 水路, *n.* A channel, through which a boat or ship may pass.

MI-OKURI, *-ru, -tta,* メオクル, 見送, *t.v.* To see off, to accompany one who is leaving to the door.

MIOGUI, ミヲグヒ, 澪標, *n.* A graduated post planted in the water to show the height of the tide.

MIOJIRUSHI, ミヲジルシ, idem.

MIOTSZKUSHI, ミヲツクシ, idem.

MIOSHI, ミオシ, *n.* The bow of a ship.

MI-OTOSHI,*-sz,-sh'ta*, ミオトス, 見落, *t.v.* To overlook, miss seeing.

MIPPU, ミツプ, 密夫, (*hisoka no otoko*). *n.* A paramour, secret lover. Syn. MAOTOKO.

MIPPŪ, ミツプウ, 密封, Tightly sealed.

MI-RAI, ミライ, 未來, (*kitaradz*). Not yet come, future time, the future state. — *no yo*, the world to come.

MIRARE,*-ru,-ta*, ミラレル, 被見, Pass. of *Mi.* *H'to ni mirareru*, to be seen of men.

MI-REN, ミレン, 未練, (*imada neredz*). Not yet inured, matured, hardened, or trained; undisciplined, inexperienced; not yet hardened into stoicism, indifference or insensibility, raw, green, having qualms, or scruples. *Sonna — na koto de wa bu-shi ni wa narenu*, if you are so raw you will never make a soldier. — *ga nokoru*, to have some feeling of regret, or tenderness of mind after having done some wrong act.

MIRENRASHII,-KI,-KU, ミレンラシイ, 未練敷, Tenderhearted, not hardened, or stoical like a green, inexperienced person.

MI-RIN-SHU, ミリンシユ, 美輪酒, *n.* A kind of sweet *sake.*

MIRO, ミロ, Coll. imp. of *Miru*, = *Miyo.*

MIROKUBUTSZ, ミロクブツ, 彌勒佛, *n.* The third and last Buddha,—not yet come.

MIRU, ミル, 見, See *Mi.*

MIRU, ミル, 水松, *n.* A kind of sea weed, something like Iceland moss.

MIRUCHA, ミルチヤ, 水松茶, *n.* A yellowish-green color.

MIRUGAI, or MIRUKUI, ミルガヒ, 西施舌, *n.* A large kind of clam.

MIRU-ME, KAGU-HANA, ミルメカグハナ, 善部童惡部童, Two beings in the Buddhist hades who try the conduct of men, and witness against them.

MISAGO, ミサゴ, 鵙, *n.* A fish-hawk.

MI-SAI, ミサイ, 微細, Minute, particular. Syn. KOMAYAKA.

†MI-SAI, ミサイ, 未濟, (*imada szmadz*). *n.* Not yet paid. *Nengu no —*, unpaid taxes.

MISAKI, ミサキ, 岬, *n.* A cape, point of land.

MISAO, ミサホ, 操, *n.* Chastity, virtue or fidelity of a widow to her deceased husband. — *wo mamoru*, to preserve chastity. — *wo kudszsz*, to fall from chastity, by marrying again Syn. SESSŌ.

MISAO, ミサホ, 棹, *n.* A boat pole.

MISASAGI, ミササギ, 御陵, *n.* The tomb of a *Mikado.*

MISE,*-ru,-ta*, ミセル, 令見, *t.v.* To make, or let see, to show, exhibit, to expose, to cause to suffer. *Yorodz no kurushimi wo* —, to make one suffer tenthousand pains. *Misete kudasare*, please let me see it. *Kono kagami wa ōkiku miseru*, this mirror magnifies.

MISE, ミセ, 店, *n.* A shop, where anything is exposed for sale, a prostitute-house. — *wo haru*, to arrange goods in order and expose them for sale; also spoken of harlots. — *wo hiraku*, to set up or open a shop. — *wo dasz*, to open another shop in some other place. Syn. TANA.

MISE-BIRAKI, ミセビラキ, 店開, *n.* Opening or setting up a store, or shop.

MISE-BIRAKASHI,*-sz,-sh'ta*, ミセビラカス, *t.v.* To show, or make a display of anything in order to excite desire, or tease; to tantalize. *Mikan wo kodomo ni* —, to tease a child by showing it an orange.

MISE-MONO, ミセモノ, 觀物, *n.* A show, exhibition, anything exhibited for money. — *wo dasz*, to open an exhibition.

†MISESHIME,*-ru,-ta*, ミセシメル, 令視, *t.v.* To cause or order to be shown to another.

MISESHIME, ミセシメ, *n.* Warning, reproof.

MI-SHIN, ミシン, 未進, *n.* Deficiency in the payment of taxes, unpaid taxes. *Nengu no —ga aru.* Syn. MI-SAI.

MI-SHIRI,*-ru,-tta*, ミシル, 見識, *t.v.* To know by sight, having seen to know anything.

MI-SHIRIZOKI,*-ku,-ita*, ミシリゾク, 身退, *i.v.* To retire, to withdraw, to quit a company or place.

†MISHŌ, ミセウ, 微笑, *n.* A smile. Syn. NIKO-NIKO.

†MI-SHŌ, ミシヤウ, 未生, Not yet born. — *i-zen*, before birth.

MISO, ミソ, 味噌, *n.* A kind of sauce made of beans.

MISOJI, ミソジ, 三十歲, Thirtieth year of age.

MISOKA, ミソカ, 三十日, *n.* The thirtieth day of the month; last day of the month.

MI-SOKONAI,*-au,-tta*, ミソコナフ, 見誤, *i.v.* To mistake in seeing.

MISOME,*-ru,-ta*, ミソメル, 見初, *t.v.* To see for the first time and fall in love with. *Onna wo misomeru*, to see and be smitten with a woman.

†MISONAWASHI,*-sz*, ミソナハス, 御覽, *t.v.*

To sec, (used only of the Mikado and Kami.)

†MISORA, ミソラ, 御空, *n.* The sky.

MISORE,*-ru,-ta*, ミソレル, 見反, To have an indistinct recollection of having seen a person, but unable to say who he is, to forget having seen a person. *H'to wo —. O misore mōshi-mash'ta*, pardon me, I cannot recall your name, or I do not recollect meeting you.

MISOSAZAI, ミソサザイ, 鷦鷯, *n.* The wren.

†MISSAKU, ミツサク, 密策, *n.* A secret scheme, or plan.

†MISSHO, ミツシヨ, 密書, *n.* A secret letter.

MISZ, ミス, 御簾, *n.* A window or door shade made of fine strips of bamboo. *— goshi mono wo iu*, to talk to another through a shade.

MISZBORASHII,-KI,-KU, ミスボラシイ, 憔悴, Poor and dirty in appearance, abject.

MISZDZ, ミスズ, 水篶, *n.* A small kind of bamboo, like stiff grass. Syn. SZDZ.

MISZGI, ミスギ, 活業, *n.* Business, employment. Syn. YOWATARI, KUCHI-SZGI, TOSEI.

MI-SZGOSHI,*-sz,-sh'ta*, ミスゴス, 見過, *t.v.* To glance at in passing. *Mi-szgoshi gataku omō*, hard to pass without stopping to look.

MI-SZKASHI,*-sz,-sh'ta*, ミスカス, 見透, *t.v.* To look though anything at something else, to foresee, foreknow. *Ko-no-ma yori tszki wo —*, to look at the moon through the trees. *Giyaman de tszki wo —*, to look at the moon through the glass. *Mirai no koto wo —*, to foresee future events. Syn. MI-TŌSHI.

MI-SZMASHI,*-sz,-sh'ta*, ミスマス, 見澄, *t.v.* To mark, to notice, to see and make sure of. *Teki no make iro wo mi-szmash'te utte idzru*, observing that the enemy were about to give way he went out to attack them.

MISZ-MISZ, ミスミス, 看看, *adv.* While looking at, before one's eyes. *— korosh'te shimau wa kawai sō da*, what a pity to see him die. Syn. MITSZTSZ, MI-NAGARA.

MI-SZRU, ミスル, Same as *Miseru.*

MI-SZTE,*-ru,-ta*, ミステル, 見捨, *t.v.* To look at and let alone, to see and not mind, turn away from.

MITA, ミタ, pret. of *Miru.* Have seen. *Watakushi — koto wa nai*, I have never seen it. *— h'to ga arimaszka*, did any body see it?

MITAI,-KI,-KU,-Ō, ミタイ, 見度, Wish to see, desirous of seeing. *Mitaku wa nai ka*, do you wish to see? *Mitai h'to wa ōku*, many were desirous of seeing.

MI-TAKARA, ミタカラ, 御寳, *n.* The precious things belonging to a *Miya*, or to the Mikado; these last are a mirror, a sword, and a jewel, the insignia of his rank.

†MI-TAMA, ミタマ, 靈魂, *n.* The soul, spirit. Syn. REIKON, TAMASHII.

MITARASHI, ミタラシ, 御手洗, *n.* A place where worshipers at a Miya wash their hands before worshiping.

MITASHIME,*-ru,-ta*, ミタシメル, 令満 caust of *Michi.* To order, or cause another to fill, to cause to abound. *Midz wo ike ni mitashimeru*, to order the pond to be filled with water.

MITATE,*-ru,-ta*, ミタテル, 見立, To see one off on a journey, to choose, select, to diagnosticate disease. *Tabidachi no h'to wo mitateru. Doredemo ki ni itta shina wo o mitate nasare*, select anything that you please. *Biyōki wo —*, to diagnosticate disease. *Mitate ga warui*, the diagnosis is wrong.

MITCHA, ミツチヤ, 痳面, Marked with small-pox. Syn ABATA.

MITE, ミテ, pp. of *Miru.*

MITE,*-ru,-ta*, ミテル, 満, *t.v.* To fill.

†MITEGURA, ミテグラ, 幣, *n.* The cut paper hung up in a Miya. Syn GOHEI, NUSA.

MITŌ, ミタウ, Same as *Mitaku*, see *Mitai.*

MITOCHŌ, ミトチヤウ, 御戸帳, *n.* A curtain hung before the altar in a Miya.

MI-TODOKE,*-ru,-ta*, ミトドケル, 見届, *t.v.* To ascertain or find out by seeing, to certify by seeing, detect, discover. *Dorobō wo —*, to detect a thief.

MI-TOME,*-ru,-ta*, ミトメル, 認, *t.v.* To see and fix in the memory, to mark, to take particular notice of in order to remember.

MITOMONAI,-KI,-KU, ミトモナイ, 醜, Disagreeable to look at, unfit to be seen, ugly, unseemly, indecent. Syn. MINIKUI, MIGURUSHII.

MI-TORE,*-ru,-ta*, ミトレル, 見蕩, *i.v.* Captivated, charmed with, or smitten by anything beautiful.

MI-TŌSHI,*-sz,-sh'ta*, ミトホス, 見通, *t.v.* To look through, to see through the future, foresee, anticipate. *Ima yori szye wo mitōsz*, to foresee the end from the present time. MI SZKASHI.

MITSZ, ミツ, 三, Three. Syn. SAN.

MITSZ, ミツ, 蜜, *n*. Honey.

†MITSZ, ミツ, 密, Secret. — *na koto*.

MITSZBACHI, ミツバチ, 蜜蜂, *n*. A honey-bee.

MITSZBAZERI, ミツバゼリ, 三葉芹, *n*. A kind of plant.

MITSZCHI, ミツチ, 蛟, *n*. A boa-constrictor.

†MITSZ-DAN, ミツダン, 密談, (*hisokani hanasz*). Talking secretly.

MI-TSZGI,-*gu*,-*ida*, ミツグ, 見績, *t.v.* To give money to assist a poor person, to support. *Kane wo mitszide yaru*, to give money in order to aid another.

MITSZGI, ミツギ, 租調, *n*. Tribute. — *wo osameru*, to pay tribute.

MITSZGO, ミツゴ, 品胎, *n*. Triplets, also, a child of three years old.

†MITSZJI, ミツジ, 密事, *n*. A secret.

MI-TSZKE,-*ru*,-*ta*, ミツケル, 見附, *t.v* To detect, to discover, to find out, to watch, descry.

MITSZKE, ミツケ, 見附, *n*. The gate of the *Shōgun's* castle.

MITSZ-KUCHI, ミツクチ, 缺脣, *n*. Hare-lip.

MI-TSZKURAI,-*ō*,-*tta*, ミツクラフ, 見繕, *t.v.* Try and make do, or answer the purpose.

MITSZ-MATA, ミツマタ, 密蒙花, *n*. A kind of tree from which paper is made. Edgeworthia papyrifera.

MI-TSZME,-*ru*,-*ta*, ミツメル, 直視, *t. v.* To fix the eye, stare, gaze. *Me wo* —, to fix the eyes, (as in a fit.)

MITSZMEGIRI, ミツメギリ, 三目錐, *n*. A triangular shaped drill.

†MITSZ-MITSZ, ミツミツ, 密密, *adv*. Secretly. Syn. NAI-NAI.

MITSZRŌ, ミツラフ, 密蠟, *n*. Bee's wax.

MITSZRU, ミツル, 滿, To be full, abound with. See *Michi*.

†MITS'Ū, ミツツウ, 密通, Secret, or illicit connection, adultery. — *szru*.

MI-UCHI, ミウチ, 親內, *n*. Kindred, relations. Syn. SHINRUI.

MIUCHI, ミウチ, 周身, *n*. The whole body. — *ga itai*, whole body is in pain.

MI-UGOKI, ミウゴキ, 身動, *n*. Movement of body. — *mo sedz*, without moving the body.

MI-UKE, ミウケ, 贖身, *n*. Redeeming a harlot, and delivering her from her engagement to her employer. — *tegata*, a document certifying the redemption of one from whoredom.

MI-WAKE,-*ru*,-*ta*, ミワケル, 見分, *t. v.* To discriminate, to discern, distinguish between. *Zen aku wo* —, to discern between right and wrong.

MI-WASZRE,-*ru*,-*ta*, ミワスレル, 見忘, *t.v.* To forget having seen.

MI-WATASHI,-*sz*,-*sh'ta*, ミワタス, 見渡, *t.v.* To look across, look over.

MIYA, ミヤ, 宮, *n*. The temple of the *Kami*, the dwelling of the *Mikado*, the title of the children of the *Mikado*. *Hime-miya*, a princess. *Nino miya*, the second son. *San no miya*, the third son. *Miya-sama*, in speaking of a child of the *Mikado*.

†MIYABI, ミヤビ, 風流, Refined in taste or manner, polite, polished, elegant, classical, genteel. Syn. FŪRIU.

MI-YABITO, ミヤビト, 宮人, *n*. Persons who live near the *Mikado*,—the Kuge.

†MIYABIYAKA, ミヤビヤカ, 閑雅, Genteel, refined, polite, polished, elegant. Syn. FŪRIU-NA.

MI-YABURI,-*ru*,-*tta*, ミヤブル 看破 *t. v.* To see and lay open, as something hidden; to explain, reveal, disclose.

MIYA-DZKAYE, ミヤヅカヘ, 宦, *n*. Servants, mostly female, employed in the service of the Mikado.

MIYAGE, ミヤゲ, 土產, *n*. A present made by one returning home from a journey, or by one coming from another place, generally of some rare, or curious production of another place. — *ni szru*.

MIYAKO, ミヤコ, 都, *n*. The place in which the Mikado resides, the Imperial-city. Capital.

MIYAKODORI, ミヤコドリ, 都鳥, *n*. A kind of water-fowl, same as *Kamome*.

MIYAKU, ミヤク, 脈, *n*. Blood-vessel. — *wo miru*, to feel the pulse.

MI-YAMA, ミヤマ, 深山, *n*. A great mountain.

MIYA-MORI, ミヤモリ, 宮守, *n*. The keeper of a Miya.

MIYASZDOKORO, ミヤスドコロ, 御息所, *n*. A concubine of the Mikado, or the wife of the hier-apparent.

MIYE,-*ru*-*ta*, ミヘル, 見, Pass. or pot. mood of *Miru*. Can see, to appear, be visible. *Koko kara Yedo ga miyeru ka*, can Yedo be seen from this place? *Mekura wa me no miyenu h'to*, a blind man is one who cannot see. *Miye-gatashi*, hard to be seen.

MIYE, ミエ, 虛飾, *n*. Display, ostentation,

vain show, affectation. *Kiyōdai no naka ni — wa iranu koto,* there is no need of affectation amongst brethren.

MIYE-KAZARI, ミエカザリ, 虛飾, *n.* (id.)

MIYO, ミヨ, Impf. of *Miru.*

MIYŌ, メウ, 妙, Admirable, excellent, fine, remarkable, wonderful. — *naru.*

MIYŌBAN, ミヤウバン, 明礬, *n.* Alum.

MIYŌ-BAN, ミヤウバン, 明晚, *n.* To-morrow evening. Syn. ASZ NO BAN.

MIYŌ-CHŌ, ミヤウテウ, 明朝, *n.* To-morrow morning. Syn. ASZ NO ASA.

MIYŌ-DAI, ミヤウダイ, 名代, *n.* A substitute. — *szru; — wo tateru.*
Syn. KAWARI.

MIYŌGA, メウガ, 蘘荷, *n.* A kind of plant. Zingiber mioga.

MIYŌGA, ミヤウガ, 冥加, The help or benefactions of an unseen providence, favor, grace; the benefactions of superiors, thanks for favors. *Ten-dō no —,* the blessings of heaven. *Miyōga kin,* money presented to the *Kubō sama* in acknowledgement of some favor. *Inochi-miyōga no h'to,* one whose life is saved from great danger. — *shiranu,* ungrateful.

MIYŌGŌ, ミヤウガウ, 名號, *n.* Name, only applied to Buddha. *Rokuji no —,* the name composed of six characters, viz, *Na-mu-a-mi-da-buts.*

MIYOJI, ミヤウジ, 名字, *n.* One of the five kinds of names, answering to the surname.

†MIYŌ-JŪ, ミヤウジウ, 命終, *(inochi no owari.) n.* The end of life.

MIYŌ-JŌ, ミヤウジヤウ, 明星, *n.* The planet Venus.

†MIYŌ-JO, ミヤウジヨ, 冥助, *n.* Providential aid.

†MIYŌ-K'WA, メウクワ, 猛火, *n.* Devouring, or raging fire.

†MIYŌ-K'WAN, ミヤウクワン, 冥官, *n.* Officers who have the management of Hades. (Bud.)

MIYŌ-MIYŌ-GO-NICHI, ミヤウミヤウゴニチ, 明明後日, *adv.* Two days after to-morrow.
Syn. SHIASATTE.

†MIYŌ-MOKU, ミヤウモク, 名目, *n.* Name. — *wo karu,* to borrow the name of another, to transact any business under his protection, sanction, or authority.
Syn. NAMAYE.

†MIYŌ-MON, ミヤウモン, 名聞, *(na wo kikoyeru,) n.* Fame, or reputation only. — *no tame ni szru,* to do any thing merely to get a name.

MIYŌ-NEN, ミヤウネン, 明年, *n.* Next year. Syn. RAI-NEN.

MIYORI, ミヨリ, 親族, *n.* Relations.
Syn. SHIN-RUI.

MIYŌ-RI, ミヤウリ, 名利, *(na to ri,) n.* Reputation and gain. — *no tame ni kokoro ga kuramu,* his mind is debased for the sake of reputation and gain.

MIYŌ-RI, ミヤウリ, 冥理, *n.* The hidden or secret principle, providence; or retribution.

MIYŌ-SEKI, ミヤウセキ, 明夕, *n.* To-morrow evening.

MIYŌ-SEKI, ミヤウセキ, 名跡, *n.* The name and estate of a family. — *wo tszgu,* to inherit the name and estate of a family.

†MIYŌ-SHUN, ミヤウシユン, 明春, *n.* Next spring.

†MIYŌ-TAN, ミヤウタン, 明旦, *n.* To-morrow morning.

†MI-YUKI, ミユキ, 深雪, A deep snow.

MIYUKI, ミユキ, 御行, *n.* Traveling, going, only of the Mikado. *Mikado shokoku ni — mashi-masz,* the Mikado visited every province.

MI-ZAME, ミザメ, 見冷, *n.* Losing one's ardor, or interest in any thing by seeing it, to become stale, to lose its novelty, or power to please. *Kono ye wa — ga sh'ta,* this picture has grown stale.

MIZARU, ミザル, 不見, neg. of *Mi, miru.*

†MI-ZEN, ミゼン, 未然, *(imada shikaradz,) n.* The future, that which has not yet come to pass. Syn. MIRAI.

MIZO, ミゾ, 溝, *n.* A ditch, drain, furrow.
Syn. DOBU.

MIZO, ミゾ, 人中, *n.* The furrow under the nose.

†MI-ZŌ, ミゾウ, 未曾有, *(imada katszte aradz.)* Never was so before. *Ko kon mizō,* never was so, either in ancient or modern times.

†MIZO, ミゾ, 御衣, *n.* The Mikado's clothes.

MIZORE, ミゾレ, 霙, *n.* Sleet. — *ga furu.*

†MO, モ, 裳, *n.* A kind of skirt, or loose trowsers.

MO, モ, 喪, *n.* The time of mourning. *Mo chiu,* during the time of mourning.

MO, モ, 藻, *n.* A kind of grass growing in water.

MO, モ, A particle of extensive use, = and, also, too, more, yet; any, soever. *Are mo kore mo watakushi no,* that is mine and so is this. *Kore mo irimaszka,* do you want this too? *Mushi mo, uwo mo, tori mo, kedamono mo mina kami no tszkuritaru mono,* insects, fish, birds and beasts, were all made by God. *Mo chitto* or *mo szkoshi*, a little more, just a little. *Mo h'totsz*, one more, another. *Mo jū nen kakarimashō*, it will yet require ten years. *H'totsz mo nai*, have not one. *Itte mo yoi ka*, had I better go? or may I go? *Nandemo*, any. *Dokodemo*, any place.

MŌ, モオ, An exclam. of doubt, perplexity, anxiety, = alas. *Mō dō shiyō ka shirimasen*, I don't know what I shall do!

MŌ, モウ, An exclam. of relief of mind, or satisfaction, at something done or past. *Mō yoroshi*, that will do. *Mō shimai*, there! I have done. *Mō nai*, they are all gone, or, there are no more. *Mō irimasen*, don't want any more. *Mō kayetta*, he has returned. Syn. MŌ-HAYA.

MŌ, モウ, 牟, The bellowing of a cow, mooing, a child's name for a cow.

MOCHI, or MOCHII, モチ, 餅, *n.* A kind of bread made of rice.

MOCHI, モチ, 黏黐, *n.* Bird-lime.

†MOCHI, モチ, 望, *n.* The full-moon. — *dzki.*

MOCHI,*-tsz,-tta*, モツ, 持, *t.v.* To hold in the hand, to carry, to have, own, possess; to last, endure. *Kane wo motte-oru h'to*, a person who has money. *Kono sakana miyōnichi made mochimashō ka*, will this fish keep until to-morrow? *Kono hon wo mochinasare*, please hold this book.

MOCHI, モチ, 持, *n.* The property of lasting durability. —*ga yoi*, durable. — *ga warui*, not durable, quickly wearing out or perishing.

MOCHI-AGUMI,*-mu,-nda*, モチアグム, 持倦, *i.v.* Tired of having, or of owning, desirous of getting rid of something which one owns.

MOCHI-ASOBI, モチアソビ, 玩物, *n.* Toy, play-thing. Syn. OMOCHA.

MOCHI-ATSZKAI,*-ō,-tta*, モチアツカフ, 持扱, *i.v* To be perplexed or troubled to know what to do with something which one owns.

MOCHI-BA, モチバ, 持塲, *n.* Property, possession in land; the place one's duty requires him to keep, or hold.

MOCHI-GOME, モチゴメ, 糯, *n.* A kind of glutinous rice, of which rice bread is made.

MOCHI-HAKOBI,*-bu,-nda*, モチハコブ, 持運, *t.v.* To convey, transport, to carry.

MOCHII, モチヒ, 餅, *n.* Same as *Mochi.*

MOCHII,*-u*, or *-ru,-ta*, モチウル, 用, *t. v.* To use, employ, to follow, obey. *Isha no mochiiru dōgu*, an instrument used by physicians. *Kono kuszri no muchii-kata shirimasen*, I don't know how this medicine is to be used. *Iken wo* —, to follow advice.

MOCHI-KITARI, モチキタリ, 持來, *n.* Any property which has come down from one's ancestors; heirloom. *Senzo yori — no takara.*

MOCHI-KITARI,*-ru,-tta*, モチキタル, 持來, *t.v.* To carry and come, to bring.

MOCHI-KOSHI,*-sz,-sh'ta*, モチコス, 持越, *i.v.* To last over, to keep over, as from one year to another, to carry over. *Kanjō wo rai-nen ye* —, to carry an account over to the next year.

MOCHI-KOTAYE,*-ru,-ta*, モチコタヘル, 持堪, *i.v.* To last, endure, hold out.

MOCHI-KUCHI, モチクチ, 持口, *n.* A place one is to superintend, keep, or defend; a post, station.

MOCHI-MAYE, モチマヘ, 本色, Proper, peculiar, appropriate, natural, that which naturally belongs to, inherent. — *no shōbai*, one's appropriate business. *Hi wa atszi no ga — da*, it is natural for fire to be hot. Syn. ATARIMAYE.

MOCHI-MONO, モチモノ, 持物, *n.* Property, possession. *Kono fude wa watakushi no* —, this pencil belongs to me.

MOCHI-RON, モチロン, 勿論, *adv.* Without dispute, indisputable, unquestionable, self-evident.

MOCHI-TSZYE,*-ru,-ta*, モチツタヘル, 持傳, *t.v.* To inherit, receive by inheritance, to be hereditary. Syn. OYAYUDZRI.

MOCHIYURU, モチユル, Same as *Mochii, ru.*

†MODASHI,*-sz,-ta*, モダス, 默止, *i.v.* To refrain from speaking, to bear in silence. *Modashi-gataku*, hard to remain silent. Syn. DAMARU, MOKUNEN.

MODAYE,*-ru,-ta*, モダエル, 悶, *i. v.* To feel pain or sorrow, to suffer, to writhe in pain or anguish.

†MŌDE,*-ru*, or *-dzru*, マウデル, 詣, *i.v.* To go to a temple for worship. Syn. MAIRU, SANKEI SZRU.

†MODOKASHI,*-KI,-KU*, モドカシ, 戻敷, Tedious, slow and difficult, tiresome. Syn. MENDO, MUDZKASHII.

†MODOKI,*-ku*, モドク, 戻, *t.v.* To criticise, to pass judgment on, to find fault with, to censure. *H'to no ī-modokan koto mo hadzkashii.* Syn. TOGAMERU.

†MODOKI, モドキ, 戻, *n.* Criticism, judgment, censure. *Yo no* —, the criticism of the world. Syn. SOSHIRI.

‖MODORI,*-ru,-tta*, モドル, 返, *i.v.* To return. *Yedo kara* —, to return from Yedo. Syn. KAYERU.

MODOSHI,*-sz,-sh'ta*, モドス, 返, *t. v.* To return, restore, give or send back. *Tabemono wo* —, to vomit one's food. Syn. KAYESZ.

MODZ, モズ, 鵙, *n.* The shrike, or butcher bird.

MODSKU, モヅク, 海雲, *n.* A kind of seaweed.

MŌDZRU, マウヅル, 詣, See *Mōde.*

†MŌ-FŪ, マウフウ, 猛風, (*tszyoi kaze.*) A violent wind.

MO-FUKU, モフク, 喪服, *n.* Mourning clothes.

MOGAKI,*-ku,-ita*, モガク, *t.v.* To writhe, or contort the body in pain, or effort. *Koye wo taten to mogakedomo atawadz.*

†MOGA, or MOGANA, モガ, Exclam. of desire, or hope; comp. of *mo* and *ga*, = wish that, desire that, hope that. *Yoki hima mogana to kore wo ukagai*, have watched him hoping to have a good opportunity, (to kill him). *Kokoro-gaye szru mono ni moga*, I wish that I could exchange hearts with him.

MOGARI, モガリ, *n.* Strips of bamboo used by dyers for stretching cloth while drying.

†MOGASA, モガサ, 疱瘡, *n.* Small-pox. Syn. HŌSŌ.

||MOGI,*-gu,-ida*, モグ, To pluck off, pull off, as fruit. *Kani no ashi wo mogu*, to pull off the legs of a crab. Syn. TORU.

†MOGIDŌ, モギダウ, 沒義道, Cruel, inhuman. Syn. MUGOI.

†MŌGO, マウゴ, 妄語, *n.* Falsehood, fabrication.

MOGURA, モグラ, See *Mugura.*

MOGURAMOCHI, モグラモチ, See *Muguramochi.*

MOGURI,*-ru,-tta*, モグル, 潜, *t. v.* See *Muguri*,

MOGUSA, ,モグサ 熟艾, *n.* The leaves of a species of Artimesia used as a moxa.

†MOHARA, モハラ, See *Moppara.*

MOHAYA, モハヤ, 最早, *adv.* Already, with a pret. verb; soon, in a little while, presently. — *yo ga akemash'ta*, the day has already dawned. — *yo ga akemashō*, the day will soon dawn. Syn. MO.

†MŌ-JA, マウジヤ, 亡者, (*shinda h'to*). A dead person.

MOJI, モジ, 字, *n.* A character, word, a letter.

MOJI, モヂ, 綟, *n.* A kind of thin, light stuff; cotton gauze.

†MŌ-JIN, マウジン, 盲人, *n.* A blind-man. Syn. MEKURA.

MOJIRI,*-ru,-tta*, モヂル, 戾, *t.v.* To twist, to knit in loops. Syn. NEJIRU.

MOJIRI, モヂリ, 狼牙棒, *n.* An iron intrument kept at police stations to seize offenders with. Syn. SODEGARAMI.

†MŌ-JŪ, マウジウ, 猛獸, *n.* Ferocious animals, a wild beast.

MŌKE,*-ru,-ta*, マウケル, 設, *t.v.* To gain, earn, to acquire, to get, beget, to prepare, to make. *Kane wo* —, to make money. *Ko wo* —, to beget a child. *Shu-yen wo* — to make a feast. *Oshiye wo* —, to construct a system of doctrine. Syn. YERU, TSZKURU.

MOKKE-NO-SAIWAI, モツケノサイハイ, 沒計之福, *n.* Unexpectedly fortunate; what at first seems to be a calamity, or a misfortune, but which turns out to be fortunate. Syn. KOBORE-SAIWAI.

MOKKIN, モツキン, 木琴, *n.* A kind of musical instrument.

†MOKKIYAKU, モツキヤク, 沒却, *n.* The confiscation of a Daimiyo's estate by the SHŌGUN.

MOKKO, モツコ, 簣, *n.* A kind of basket made of rope, for carrying earth, &c.

MOKKŌ, モツカウ, 木香, *n.* A kind of medicinal plant. Rosa Banksiœ.

MOKKO-FUNDOSHI, モツコフンドシ, *n.* A cloth worn over the secrets, which is fastened to a string around the waist.

MŌKŌ, モウコウ, 孟汞, *n.* Corrosive sublimate.

†MŌ-KO, マウコ, 猛虎, (*takeki tora*). A ferocious tiger.

MŌ-KO, モウコ, 蒙古, *n.* Mongolia.

MOKU, モク, 木, (*ki*), *n.* A tree, wood.

†MOKU, モク, 默, Silent. — *szru*, to be silent. Syn. DAMARU.

MOKU-BA, モクバ, 木馬, *n.* A wooden horse.

MOKU-BUTSZ, モクブツ, 木佛, *n.* A wooden image of Buddha.

MOKUDAI, モクダイ, 目代, (*meshiro*), *n.* The name of an inferior officer in the times of Yori-tomo.

MOKUDZ, モクズ, 藻屑, *n.* Rubbish floating in water. Syn. MIKUDZ.

MOKU-GIYO, モクギヨ, 木魚, *n.* A hollow wooden block, which priests strike in praying.

MOKU-JIKI, モクジキ, 木食, *n.* Eating the fruit of trees only, as certain Buddhist priests.

MOKU-ME, モクメ, 木理, *n.* The veins, or grain of wood.

†MOKU-MOKU, モクモク, 默默, *adv.* Silent.

MOKU-NEN, モクチン, 默然, Silent. — *to sh'te oru.* Syn. DAMARU.

MOKURANJI, モクランジ, 木欒子, *n.* A glossy black color, name of a fruit.

MOKU-REI, モクレイ, 默禮, *n.* A silent salutation. — *wo sh'te yuki-szgiru.*

†MOKU-REN, モクレン, 木蓮, *n.* The purple magnolia. Burgeria obovata.

MOKUROKU, モクロク, 目錄, *n.* An index, list, table of contents, bill, catalogue.

MOKUROMI,*-mu,-nda,* モクロム, 目論, *i.v.* To plan, to consider or turn over in the mind, to speculate.
Syn. TAKUNAMU, KUWADATERU.

MOKUROMI, モクロミ, 目論, *n.* Plan, device.

†MOKU-SAN, モクサン, 默算, (*damatte hakaru.*) Mental arithmetic. — *szru*, to calculate in the mind.

MOKUSEI, モクセイ, 木犀, *n.* The Osmanthus fragrans.

MOKU-SEI, モクセイ, 木星, *n.* The planet Jupiter.

†MOKU-YŌ, モクエフ, 木葉, (*ki no ha.*) *n.* Leaf of a tree.

†MOKU-YOKU, モクヨク, 沐浴, *n.* Bathing in hot or cold water. — *szru.*

†MOKU-ZA, モクザ, 默坐, *n.* Sitting in silence.

MOKU-ZEN, モクゼン, 目前, (*me no maye.*) Before one's eyes, immediately.
Syn. GAN-ZEN.

MOKU-ZŌ, モクザウ, 木像, *n.* A wooden image.

MOMARE,*-ru,-ta,* モマレル, 被揉, Pass. of *Momu.*

MOMASE,*-ru,-ta,* モマセル, 令揉, (caust. of *Momu*). To cause or let rub, shampoo.

MOM-BAN, モンバン, 門番, *n.* A porter, gate keeper.

MOME,*-ru,-ta,* モメル, 揉, *i.v.* To be rubbed, chafed, fretted, frayed, to quarrel. *Nimotsz ga mometa*, the goods are rubbed, or chafed. *Ki ga momeru*, to be anxious, troubled. *Uchiwa ga* —, the family is in a constant fret.

MOME, モメ, 揉, *n.* Contention, quarreling, dissension.

MOMEN, モメン, 木綿, *n.* Cotton cloth.

MOMI,*-mu,-nda,* モム, 揉, *t.v.* To rub and roll between the hands, to shampoo, to struggle, or make violent efforts, (as in a contest.) *Kiri wo momu*, to turn a drill. *Kami wo* —, to rub and soften paper. *Mi wo* —, to rub and knead the body, as a shampooer. *Ki wo* —, to fret or trouble one's self with anxiety. *Momi ni monde semeru*, to contend against with continued and vigorous efforts.

MOMI, モミ, 絳絹, *n.* A kind of red silk.

MOMI, モミ, 籾, *n.* Unhulled rice.

MOMI-AI,*-au,-tta,* モミアフ, 揉合, *i.v.* To contend or struggle vigorously together, as wrestlers.

MOMI-DANE, モミダチ, 籾種, *n.* Seed rice.

MOMI-DASHI,*-sz,-sh'ta,* モミダス, 揉出, *t.v.* To rub and press out, to get by hard labor or diligence. *Te kara momi-dash'ta shinsho.*

MOMI-GARA, モミガラ, 籾殼, *n.* Rice-hulls. Syn. SZKUMU.

MOMI-GURA, モミグラ, 穀藏, *n.* A rice granary, or store-house for unhulled rice.

MOMI-HOGUSHI,*-sz,-sh'ta,* モミホグス, 揉解, *t. v.* To loosen the texture, or soften anything by rubbing in the hands.

MOMIJI, モミヂ, 紅葉, *n.* The red leaves of autumn. — *szru*, to turn red, as leaves in autumn.

MOMI-KESHI,*-sz,-sh'ta,* モミケス, 揉消, *t.v.* To rub out, extinguish by rubbing, to utterly destroy in battle.

MOMI-KOMI,*-mu,-nda,* モミコム, 揉込, *t.v.* To rub in, as a color, to scatter by rubbing as a tumor.

MOMI-KUDAKI,*-ku,-ita,* モミクダク, 揉碎, *t.v.* To break by rubbing in the hands, to crumble.

MOMI-OTOSHI,*-sz,-sh'ta,* モミオトス, 揉落, *t.v.* To rub off between the hands, as dry mud from a garment.

MOMI-SZRI-USZ, モミスリウス, 礱磨, *n.* A mill for hulling rice.

MOMI-YAWARAGE,*-ru,-ta,* モミヤハラゲル, 揉和, *t.v.* To soften by rubbing in the hands.

MOMME, モンメ, 匁, *n.* A measure of weight, = 58-33 grains troy.

MOMMŌ, モンマウ, 文盲, Unlearned, unable to read, ignorant.
Syn. MUGAKU.

MŌ-MŌ, モウモウ, 濛濛, *adv.* Dull, stupid, obscure, foggy.

†MOMO, モモ, 百, Hundred. *Momotose*, a hundred years.

MOMO, モモ, 桃, *n.* Peach. — *no ki*, peach-tree. — *no hana*, peach-blossom. — *no shekku*, the third day of the 3rd month.

MOMO, モモ, 股, *n.* The thigh.

MOMOCHIDORI, モモチドリ, 百千鳥,

(*h'yakusen-tori*). A multitude of little birds.

MOMODACHI, モモダチ, 股立, Hitching up the trowsers. — *wo toru.*

MOMOHIKI, モモヒキ, 股引, *n.* Trowsers, pantaloons, drawers.

MOMO-IRO, モモイロ, 桃色, *n.* Peach-color.

†MŌ-MOKU, マウモク, 盲目, *n.* Blind. Syn. MEKURA.

MOMONE, モモ子, *n.* The groin.

MOMPA, モンパ, 文派, *n.* Cotton flannel.

MOMPUKU, モンプク, 紋服, *n.* Clothes which have the family badge on them.

MOMU, モム, 揉, See *Momi.*

MON, モン, 門, *n.* A gate, outside entrance to a house or inclosure. — *no tobera,* the door of a gateway. Syn. KADO.

MON, モン, 紋, *n.* Badge, coat of arms, crest. — *wo tszkeru.*

MONAKA, モナカ, 最中, *n.* The middle, midst of. *Aki no* —, the middle of autumn. Syn. SAI-CHIU, MANAKA, NAKABA.

MON-CHAKU, モンチヤク, 悶著, *n.* Quarrel, dispute, contention. Syn. MOME,

MON-CHŌ, モンチヤウ, 紋帳, *n.* A book in which the different coat of arms are registered.

MON-DAN, モンダン, 文段, *n,* The composition, or construction, as of a letter.

MON-DŌ, モンダフ, 問答, (*toi kotaye*). *n.* Question and answer. — *szru,* to question and answer, discuss, catechise.

MON-DOKORO, モンドコロ, 紋所, *n.* Badge, coat of arms, insignia, crest.

MONDORI-UCHI, *-tsz,-tta,* モンドリウツ, To throw, or trip one up, so as to fall on his head.

MŌ-NEN, マウ子ン, 妄念, *n.* Evil thoughts; a depraved mind; the curse, or evil influence of one dead. — *ga toritszita,* smitten by the curse of one dead.

MONGAMACHI, モンガマチ, 門檣, *n.* The lintel and sill of a door.

MONGON, モンゴン, 文言, The composition, or words of a letter.

†MON-G'WAI, モングワイ, 門外, (*kado no soto*). Outside of the gate.

MON-JI, モンジ, 文字, *n.* Character, letter, word. Syn. MOJI, JI.

MON-JIN, クンジン, 門人, *n.* A disciple, pupil, follower. Syn. DESHI.

†MON-JIN, *-szru,* モンジン, 問訊, To question, to interrogate.

†MON-KA, クンカ, 門下, *n.* Disciple pupil.

MON-KAKU, モンカク, 門客, *n.* A pupil, or disciple who lives with his teacher.

†MON-KO, モンコ, 門戶, (*kado to*). *n.* The gate and door of the house.

MON-KU, モンク, 文句, *n.* The sentences of a composition.

MONO, モノ, 物, *n.* Thing, article, matter; used also in the formation of many compound words. *Kore wa nan to iu mono da,* what is this thing called? — *wo iu,* to speak. — *no kadz to mo sedz,* to make light of; consider of no account. *Ame wo furase-taku nai mono da,* I hope it will not rain. *Komatta mono da,* a sad affair!

MONO, モノ, 者, *n.* Person. *Kami ni tatsz mono,* superiors. *Kotaru mono,* children. *Iyashiki mono,* vulgar fellow. *Watakushi wa Nippon kotoba wo naraitai mono da,* I wish to learn the Japanese language.

†MONO-DŌI,-KI,-KU,-O, モノドホイ, 物遠, Distant, seldom seen, seldom visiting, stranger. *Kono goro wa on mono-dō ni zonjisoro,* you have lately become a great stranger. Syn. SOYEN.

MONO-DOMO, モノドモ, 物等, Plural of *Mono,* things, persons. *Kanai no* —, the members of a family. *Tszdzke ya* —, follow me, soldiers!

MONO-DZKI, モノズキ, 好事, *n.* Strange, odd, or eccentric in taste, or manner. — *na h'to.* Syn. KŌDZ.

MONO-GAMASHII,-KI,-KU,-U, モノガマシイ, 物間敷, Making much of a little, exaggerating. *Monogamashiku iu.* Syn. KOTOGOTOSHII.

MONO-GANASHII,-KI,-KU, モノガナシイ, 物悲, Sad, gloomy.

MONO-GASHIRA, モノガシラ, 隊長, *n.* The chief or captain of a company.

MONO-GATAI,-KI,-KU, モノガタイ, 謹厚, Strict, temperate, exact in conduct.

MONO-GATARI, *-ru,-tta,* モノガタル, 物語, *t.v.* To relate, narrate, tell.

MONO-GATARI, モノガタリ, 物語, *n.* History, story, narration.

MONO-GONOMI, モノゴノミ, 物好, *n.* Particular in taste, and fond of good eating, fine clothes, or rare things.

MONOGOSHI, モノゴシ, 擧止, *n.* Deportment, behaviour, manner. Syn. TACHII-FURU-MAI.

MONO-GOSHI-NI, モノゴシニ, 物越, *adv.* Through or over something intervening, as, — *kiku,* to hear through a partition. — *miru,* to look across a fence.

†MONO-GURUI, モノグルヒ, 發狂, *n.* Madness, lunacy, frenzy. Syn. KICHIGAI, KANSHIN.

†MONO-GURUWASHI,-KI,-KU, モノグルハ

シイ, 物狂, Like a crazy or mad person, frenzied frantic.

MONO-GUSAI,-KI,-KU, モノグサイ, 懶惰, Lazy, indolent, slovenly. Syn. BUSHŌ, RANDA.

MONO-II, モノイヒ, 物言, *n.* Language, style or way of speaking, talking. — *ga yoi*, his language is good. — *ga aru*, to have a dispute. — *goye*, the sound of talking.

MONO-IMI, モノイミ, 物忌, *n.* Abstinence from certain articles of food for a certain time, in order to religious purification. — *wo szru.*

MONO-IRI, モノイリ, 費耗, Expense, outlay. — *ga ōi*, expenses are great. Syn. NIU-YŌ, IRIYŌ.

MONO-IWAI, モノイハヒ, 物祝, *n.* Felicitation, celebration of some happy event. — *wo szru.*

MONO-KAKI, モノカキ, 物書, *n.* Secretary, clerk. Syn. YŪ-HITSZ.

MONO-KUI, モノクヒ, 物食, *n.* Eating, feeding. — *no warui uma*, a horse that is a bad feeder.

MONO-MANABI, モノマナビ, 物學, *n.* Learning, gaining instruction.

MONO-MANE, モノマ子, 物眞似, *n.* Gesture, gesticulation. — *wo szru*, to make gestures.

MONO-MI, モノミ, 物見, *n.* Sight seeing; a lookout-place. — *ni yuku*, to go to see a show.

MONOMI, モノミ, 斥候, *n.* A spy. Syn. SHINOBI.

MONO-MŌ, モノモウ, An exclamation used in calling at the gate of a noble, by a person seeking admission, the answer by a person inside is *ō*, or *dōre.*

MONO-MŌDE, モノマウデ, 物詣, *n.* Visiting a temple for worship, pilgrimage. — *wo szru.*

†MONO-MONOSHII,-KI,-KU, モノモノシイ, 物物敷, Affecting undue importance; making much of one's self. *Mono-mono-shiki teki no kō gen kana.*

MONO-MORAI, モノモラヒ, 乞丐, *n.* A beggar. Syn. KOJIKI.

MONO-MORAI, モノモラヒ, *n.* A sty on the eyelid.

MONO-NARI, モノナリ, 物成, *n.* Rice tax; the salary of officials received in rice. Syn. FUCHI.

MONO-NETAMI, モノ子タミ, 嫉妬, *n.* Jealousy. — *wo szru.*

MONONOFU, モノノフ, 武士, *n.* A soldier. Syn. BUSHI.

MONONOGU, モノノグ, 物具, *n.* Military arms, and armor. Syn. BUKI.

†MONO-NOKE, モノノケ, 物怪, *n.* Bewitched, smitten by some evil influence. — *nite yami-fusz.*

MONO-NUI, モノヌヒ, 執針, *n.* A seamstress. Syn. OHARI.

MONO-OBOYE, モノオボエ, 記憶, *n.* The memory. — *ga yoi*; — *ga warui.*

MONO-OKI, モノオキ, 物置, *n.* A pantry, store-room.

MONO-OMOI, モノオモヒ, 物思, *n.* Thinking, reflecting, cogitating. — *wo sh'te iru*, he is thinking about something.

MONO-OSHIMI, モノオシミ, 吝嗇, *n.* Stingy, grudging.

MONO-SABISHII,-KI,-KU, モノサビシイ, 寂寥, Lonely, solitary.

MONOSASHI, モノサシ, 裁尺, *n.* Any instrument for measuring length; a foot measure.

MONO-SAWAGASHII,-KI,-KU, モノサワガシイ, 物騷, Making a disturbance, commotion, or noise.

MONO-SHIDZKA, モノシヅカ, 物靜, Quiet, still, free from noise, or bustle.

MONO-SHIRI, モノシリ, 識者, *n.* A philosopher, a learned man.

MONO-SZGOI,-KI,-KU,-SHI, モノスゴイ, 物凄, Exciting fear, dread, or alarm, startling. *Mono-szgoki ori*, a time when one is full of dread, or easily startled. *Oto mono-szgoku kikoye*, heard a startling noise.

MONO-SZSAMAJII,-KI,-KU, モノスサマジイ, 物凄, idem.

MONO-TACHI, モノタチ, 裁刀, *n.* A knife used in cutting cloth.

MONO-TOGAME, モノトガメ, 物咎, *n.* Scolding, fault-finding. — *wo szru.*

MONO-UI,-KI,-KU,-SHI, モノウイ, 懶, Lazy, indolent. Syn. TAIGI.

MONO-WARAI, モノワラヒ, 物笑, Laughable, ridiculous.

MONO-WASZRE, モノワスレ, 物忘, Forgetful.

†MON-SAI, モンサイ, 文才, *n.* Knowledge of letters.

MON-SHA, モンシヤ, 文紗, *n.* A kind of silk gauze.

MON-TEI, モンテイ, 門弟, *n.* A disciple, pupil. Syn. DESHI.

MON-TO, モント, 門徒, *n.* A disciple of a Buddhist priest. *Monto-shū*, a sect of Buddhists.

MONUKE, モヌケ, 蛻, *n.* The cast-off skin of a snake, or insect. Syn. NUKEGARA.

MON-ZETSZ, モンゼツ, 悶絶, Fainting with anguish, or pain.

MOPPARA, モツパラ, 專, *ad.* Only, alone, exclusively, mostly, chiefly, principally, most important, best, earnestly, diligently. *Gakumon wo — ni szru,* applied himself principally to study. *Kono goro wo — to szru,* consider this the best time.
Syn. DAI-ICHI, H'TOYE-NI.

MORAI,-*au*,-*tta*, モラフ, *t. v.* To receive, to accept, to get. *Okurimono wo* —, to receive a present. *Miyaku wo mite moraitai,* I want you to feel my pulse. *Satō anata ni kite moraitai, Satō* wants you to come to his house.
Syn. ITADAKU, CHŌ-DAI.

MORAI-GUI, モラヒグヒ, *n.* Asking for something to eat. —*wo szru.*

MORAI-NAKI, モラヒナキ, *n.* Affected to tears by seeing others cry. — *wo szru.*

MORASHI,-*sz*,-*sh'ta*, モラス, 洩, caust. of *Mori.* To cause or let leak, to let escape, to make known, divulge. *H'tori wo morasz na,* don't let one person escape. *Mitszji wo* —, to let a secret leak out.

MORE,-*ru*,-*ta*, モレル, 洩, *i.v.* To leak, to leak out, escape, to be left out, omitted. *Hakarigoto ga moreta,* the scheme has leaked out. *Oshiye ni moredz,* not left uninstructed. *More-kikoyeru,* to leak out and be heard. *Moredz yō ai-fure,* promulgate it, so that every one shall hear.

†MŌ-REI, マウレイ, 亡靈, *n.* The spirit of one dead, a ghost. Syn. NAKI-TAMA.

†MŌ-RETSZ, マウレツ, 猛烈, Fierce, ferocious, violent. Syn. TAKEKI, HAGESHII.

MORI, モリ, 傅婢, *n.* A child's nurse.

MORI, モリ, 森, *n.* A grove, or clump of trees.

MORI, モリ, 銛, *n.* A harpoon.

MORI, モリ, 守, *n.* A guard, watch, keeper. *Miya-mori,* the keeper of a *Miya.*

MORI,-*ru*,-*tta*, モル, 洩, *i. v.* To leak. *Yane ga moru,* the roof leaks. *Fune ga moru,* the ship leaks.

MORI,-*ru*,-*tta*, モル, 盛, *t.v.* To put into a cup, plate, &c., to pour into. *Meshi wo wan ni moru,* to put rice into a cup. *Midz wo* —, to pour water (into a cup.)
Syn. TSZGU, YOSŌ.

MORI, モリ, 洩, *n.* A leak. — *ga kakatta,* got wet by water leaking on it. — *wo ukeru,* to place a vessel to catch leaking water. *Fune no — wo tomeru,* to stop a leak in a ship.

MORI-AGE,-*ru*,-*ta*, モリアゲル, 盛上, *t.v.* To heap up. *Meshi wo* —.

MORI-KOROSHI,-*sz*,-*sh'ta*, モリコロス, 盛殺, *t.v.* To kill by putting poison in the food.

MORI-MONO, モリモノ, 盛物, *n.* Food offered to idols. Syn. KUMOTSZ.

MORI-SODATE,-*ru*,-*ta*, モリソダテル, 守育, *t.v.* To nurse and bring up, as an orphan.

MORI-TATE,-*ru*,-*ta*, モリタテル, 守立, *v.t.* To bring, or rear up a child, (as a guardian).

MORI-YAKU, モリヤク, 守役, *n.* An officer who has the charge of the child of a Noble.

MORŌ, モラフ, 貰, Same as *Morau.*

MORŌ, モロウ, 脆, See *Moroi.*

MORO-ASHI, モロアシ, 兩足, *n.* Both feet or both legs.

†MORO-BITO, モロビト, 諸人, *n.* All men. Syn. SHO-NIN.

MORO-HA, モロハ, 兩刃, *n.* Two-edged. — *no katana,* a two-edged sword.

MOROHADA-NUGI, モロハダヌギ, 兩袒, Both shoulders bare.

MORO-HIZA, モロヒザ, 兩膝, *n.* Both knees.

MOROI,-KI, モロイ, 脆, *a.* Brittle, friable, fragile, frail. *Moroi mono,* a brittle thing.

MOROKO, モロコ, *n.* A kind of river fish, two or three inches long.

MOROKOSHI, モロコシ, 唐土, *n.* China, broom-corn.

MŌROKU, モウロク, (vulg. coll.) Old and foolish, decrepit, childish with age. — *szru.*

MOROKU, モロク, 脆, *adv.* Brittle, friable, frail. — *nai,* not brittle.

MOROMI-ZAKE, モロミザケ, 濁醪, *n.* A kind of *sake,* in which the rice-grounds are not separated from the liquid.

MORO-MORO, モロモロ, 諸, All, every. — *no h'to,* all men, every-body.

MOROSA, モロサ, 脆, *n.* Brittleness.

MOKOSHI, モロシ, 脆, *a.* See *Moroi.*

MORO-SHIRAGA, モロシラガ, 偕老, Both (husband and wife) growing gray together.

MOROTE, モロテ, 兩手, *n.* Both hands.

MOROTOMO-NI, モロトモニ, 諸共, *adv.* All together.

MORU, モル, See *Mori.*

MŌSADZ, マウサズ, 不申, neg. of *Mōshi.*

†MŌSAKU, マウサク, Obsolete, same as *Mōsz.*

MŌSARE,-*ru*,-*ta*, マウサレル, 被申, pass. of *Mōshi.*

†Mōsei, マウセイ, 猛勢, *(takeki ikioi)*. Valiant, intrepid.

Mōsen, モウセン, 毛氈, *n.* A rug, drugget.

†Mō-setsz, マウセツ, 妄説, *n.* Falsehood, fiction, fable.

Moshi, モシ, 若, *adv.* If, provided that, whether. Syn. hiyotto, man-ichi.

Moshi, モシ, Exclam. used in addressing, or calling one whose name is not known.

†Mōshi, マウシ, 孟子, *n.* Mencius, a Chinese sage.

Mōshi,*-sz,-sh'ta*, マウス, 申, *i. v.* To speak, say, tell, call *Rei wo mōsz*, to salute. *Na wo Gin to* —, his name is called Gin.

(2.) The substantive verb, to be, to do; as, *On tomo mōshi-taku zonji soro*, I would like to be your companion, or, would like to go with you. *Bu-sata mōsh'ta*, I have been remiss in coming, or sending to inquire about you. *Deki-mōshi soro*, have finished. *Itashi mōshi soro*, have done, or will do. *O tanomi mōshi masz*, I have a request to make of you. This word is much used in epistolary writings, and in respectful address. As the compound words formed by adding another verb to to root of this, do not differ in meaning, from the compounds formed by the same words with Ī, the root of *Iu*, to speak, the scholar is refered to them, as *Mōshi-ageru* =*Ī-ageru*, *Mōshi-bun*=*Ī-bun*, *&c.* This word also seems to be the primitive, from which the colloquial suffix, *Mashi*, *masz*, *mash'ta* has been altered.

Mōshi-go, マウシゴ, 申子, *n.* A child born in answer to prayer.

Moshikuba, モシクバ, 儻, *adv.* If, supposing that, if perchance, in case.

Moshi-mata, モシマタ, 若又, *adv.* If, supposing that.

Moshi-ya, モシヤ, 若哉, *adv.* If, lest, for fear that. — *fu-kiyo naru koto mo aran ka*, lest there should be something unclean in it.

Mōsō, マウソウ, 孟宗, *n.* A kind of large bamboo.

Mosshu,*-szru*, モツシユ, 沒收, To confiscate the estate of a noble.
Syn. mokkiyaku szru.

Mosso, モツソ, 盛裝, *n.* The day's rations of a common soldier in cooked rice,— about a quart of uncooked rice.

Mōsz, マウス, 申, see *Moshi*.

Moszso, モスソ, 裔, *n.* The skirt of a robe.

†Motage,*-ru,-ta*, モタゲル, 擡, *t. v.* *(Mochi ageru.)* To lift up, raise up.

†Motarashi,*-sz,-sh'ta*, モタラス, 齎, *t. v.* To carry in the hand.
Syn. tadzsayeru.

Motare,*-ru,-ta*, モタレル, 凭, *i. v.* To lean on, rest against. *Tszkuye ni motareru*, to lean on the table.
Syn. yori-kakaru.

Motase,*-ru,-ta*, モタセル, 凭, *t. v.* To lean, or rest against. *Tszye wo kabe ni motaseru*, to rest a cane against the wall.

Motase,*-ru,-ta;* モタセル, 令持, caust. of *Motsz*. To make or let carry, to cause to have or own, to make to last or endure. *Motasete agemashō*, I will get it carried for you. *Ni tomo ni* —, to give one's luggage to a servant to carry.

Mote-amashi,*-sz,-sh'ta*, モテアマス, 持餘, *i. v.* Troubled, or perplexed about something which one owns, and would like to get rid of.
Syn. mochi agumu, mochi-atszkau.

Mote-asobi,*-bu,-nda*, モテアソブ 弄 *t.v.* To divert or amuse one's self with, to sport, or toy with.

Mote-asobi, モテアソビ, 玩物, *n.* Any thing used for diversion or amusement, a toy. Syn. omocha.

Mote-atszkai,*-au,-tta*, モテアツカフ, 持扱, *t.v.* To use, to manage, to deal in.
Syn. tori-atszkai.

Mote-hayashi,*-sz,-sh'ta*, モテハヤス, *t.v.* To celebrate far and wide, to spread or make known. *Yo ni medzrashiki mono to motehayasz.*
Syn. chin-chō szru, hiyō-ban szru.

Mote-ki,*-kuru,-kita*, モテクル, 持來, *t.v.* To bring. *Akari wo mote-koi*, bring a light. *Cha wo mote-k'ta ka*, have you brought the tea? *Mada mote-kimasen*, have not yet brought it.

Mote-nashi,*-sz,-sh'ta*, モテナス, 欵待, *t.v.* To treat, to entertain kindly or with civility. *K'yaku wo* —, to entertain a guest.

Mō-tō, モウトウ, 毛頭, *(ke no kashira)*. *adv.* As much as the end of a hair. — *mōshi-bun gozanaku soro.*

†Mō-tō, マウトウ, 孟冬, *n.* The tenth-month.

Moto, モト, 元, *n.* The origin, beginning, the first, source, fountain-head, cause. 許, house, home; you, in addressing another. —*yori*, from the first. —*no tōri*, like as at first, or like the first. *Sono-moto*, you. *On-moto*, you. *On yado-moto*, your house.
Syn. g'wan-rai, hajime.

Moto-date, モトダテ, 根本, *n.* Beginning, origin, root, first.
Syn. okori, hajimari.

Motode, モトデ, 本錢, *n.* Capital in trade. — *ga nai kara shōbai ya dekinu*, as I have no capital I cannot do business. — *wo koshirayeru*, to raise capital, (in order to commence business.)

†**Motodori**, モトドリ, 髻, *n.* The cue or tuft of hair, such as is worn by the Japanese. Syn. mage.

Moto-dzki,*-ku,-ita*, モトヅク, 本附, *i.v.* To make as a basis or foundation, to found. *Kono shibai wa nani ni motodzite tszkutta ka*, on what is this play founded?

Motoi, モトヰ, 基, *n.* Foundation, basis, beginning, origin, cause.

Moto-jime, モトジメ, 元締, *n.* A steward, treasurer, or one who controls the finances of any business. — *wo szru.*

Moto-kata, モトカタ, 本方, *n.* The producer, or maker of any kind of goods, first seller, or holder. — *ga takai kara mōkarimasen*, as the first holder sold the goods high, I can make no profit.

Motome,*-ru,-ta*, モトメル, 求, *t.v.* To search for, to seek, to get, obtain, acquire, to buy. *Sho-sho hō-bō ai-motome sōrayedo-mo imada mi-atari mōsadz*, although I have sought for it all over, I have not yet found it. *O tanomi mōsh'ta mono motomete kudasari-mash'ta ka*, have you got the article you ordered?
Syn. sagasz, yeru, kau.

Moto-ne, モトネ, 元直, *n.* First cost.

†**Motori**,*-ru,-tta*, モトル, 悖, *i.v.* To oppose perversely, to act with contumacy or insubordination, to rebel against.
Syn. sakarau.

Moto-yui, モトユヒ, 髻結, *n.* The cord with which the cue is tied.

Motsz, モツ, 持, See *Mochi.*

†**Motsz**, モツ, 物, *(mono.) n.* Thing. *Ban-motsz*, all things.

Motszre,*-ru,-ta*, モツレル, 縺, *i.v.* To be entangled; (fig.) confused, intricate, involved, embarrassed. *Ito ga motszreta*, the thread is tangled. Syn. muszboreru.

Motszyaku, モツヤク, 沒藥, *n.* Myrrh.

Mottai, モッタイ, 物體, *n.* Affectation of state above one's station, airs, haughtiness. — *wo tszkeru*, to put on airs.

Mottainai,*-ki,-ku,-shi,-ō,-sa*, モッタイナイ, 無物體, Profane, irreverent, impious, sacriligious, ungrateful. This word is used also in the opposite sense, of, sacred, entitled to reverence. *Go-koku wo tsziyasz koto wa* —, it is profane to waste grain.

Motte, モッテ, 以, With, by, by means of; (2.) used also to intensify the word to which it is added, without affecting the meaning. *Tegami wo motte mōshi-ageru*, to inform by means of a letter. *Fude wo motte kaku*, to write with a pen. (2.) *Makoto-ni-motte. Hanahada-motte. Madz-motte.*
Syn. nite, de.

Motte-no-hoka, モッテノホカ, 以外, *adv.* Unusual, extraordinary, beyond what was previously supposed or imagined.
Syn. zonjinohoka.

Mottoi, モットヒ, A coll. contract of *Motoyui.*

Mottomo, モットモ, 最, *adv.* Reasonable, just, right, proper, (2.) used as a superlative, = most, in the highest degree. *Go mottomo de gozarimasz*, you are certainly right, or most reasonable in what you say. — *yoroshii*, the best
Syn. dōri, (2.) wakete.

Moya, モヤ, 霧, *n.* Fog. Syn. kiri.

Mo-ya, モヤ, Exclam; = coll. *Mā.*

Moyai,*-au,-tta*, モヤフ, 舫, *t.v.* To lash boats, or ships together. *Fune wo* —,

Moyai-bune, モヤヒブ子, 舫舩, *n.* Boats lashed together.

Moyai-nawa, モヤヒナハ, 舫繩, *n.* A rope for lashing boats together.

Moya-moya, モヤモヤ, 鬱鬱, Melancholy, gloomy. Syn. utsz-utsz.

Moyashi, モヤシ, 糵牙, *n.* Malt. *Mugi no* —, malt made of barley.

Moyashi,*-sz,-sh'ta*, モヤス, 令燃, caust. of *Moye.* To burn. *Hi wo moyasz*, to make a fire burn. *Kami wo hi ni moyasz*, to burn paper in the fire. Syn. taku.

Moyashi,*-sz,-sh'ta*, モヤス, 令萌, caust. of *Moye.* To cause to sprout or germinate, to malt. *Mugi wo moyasz*, to malt barley.

Moye,*-ru,-ta*, モエル, 燃, *i.v.* To burn. *Hi ga moyeru*, the fire burns.
Syn. yakeru.

Moye,*-ru,-ta*, モエル, 萌, *i.v.* To sprout, germinate. *Mugi ga* —, the wheat sprouts.
Syn. hayeru.

Moye-agari,*-ru,-tta*, モエアガル, 燃上, *i.v.* To burn up in a flame, to blaze up.

Moyegi, モエギ, 萌黃, *n.* A light green color.

Moye-kui, モエクヒ, 燼, *n.* A fire-brand, ember.

Moye-kudz, モエクヅ, *n.* Embers, cinders.

Moye-kusa, モエクサ, 燒草, *n.* Combustible matter. — *ga nai kara yake-masen*, as there is no more combustible matter the fire will go out.

MOYE-SASHI, モエサシ, *n.* A firebrand.

MOYE-TACHI,-*tsz*,-*tta*, モエタツ, 燃立, *i. v.* To blaze, burn up.

MOYE-TSZKI,-*ku*,-*ita*, モエツク, 燃著, *i. v.* To take, or catch fire, to ignite. *Hi ga nama maki ni moye-tszkanu*, green wood does not easily ignite.

MOYŌ, モヤウ, 摸様, *n.* The figures dyed, embroidered, or woven in cloth. (2) condition, state, circumstances. *Some-moyō*, *Nui-moyō*, *Ori-dashi-moyō*. (2) *Biyō-nin no moyō ga kawatta*, the state of the patient is different. *Yedo no — wa ikaga*, how are matters at Yedo?
Syn. (1) KATA, (2) YŌDAI, YŌSZ.

MOYORI, モヨリ, *u.* Vicinity, neighborhood. *Kono — ni sakaya wa nai ka*, is there a grog-shop in this neighborhood? *Moyori-moyori no samurai*, the soldiers of the various places in the vicinity.
Syn. KIMPEN.

MOYŌSHI,-*sz*,-*sh'ta*, モヨホス, 催, *t.v.* To prepare, make ready, to stir up, excite. *Shu-yen wo —*, to make an entertainment. *Ame wo —*, to gather up for rain. *Namida wo —*, to bring tears. *Gunzei wo —*, to raise an army. *Ikari wo —*, to excite anger.

MOYŌSHI, モヨホシ, 催, *n.* Making ready, preparation. *Ikusa no —*, preparing for war. *Shu-yen no —*, preparing for a feast.

MOYURU, モユル, see *Moye*.

MŌ-ZŌ, マウザウ, 妄想, *n.* Wicked or disorderly thoughts, lascivious desires. — *wo miru*, (fig.) to have nocturnal emissions.

MU, ム, 六, Contraction of *Mutsz*, six.

MU, ム, 無, *(nashi.)* A negative prefix. — *ni naru*, to be in vain.

MU, ム, Is frequently used at the end of a word for *n*, the future ending of verbs, thus, *Min* is written *mimu*; *kikan, kikamu*, &c.

MUBE, ムベ, see *Ube*.

MUBE-KADZRA, ムベカヅラ, 郁子, *n.* The clematis. Stauntonia hexaphylla.

MU-BIYŌ, ムビヤウ, 無病, *(yamai-nashi.)* Not sick, well, healthy.

MUCHA-KUCHA, ムチヤクチヤ, or MUCHA-MUCHA, ムチヤムチヤ, Mixed, confused, jumbled together so as to be unintelligible.

†MU-CHI, ムチ, 無智, *(chiye-nashi.)* Unwise, foolish, stupid.

MUCHI, ムチ, 鞭, *n.* A whip. — *wo utsz*, to whip. — *no himo*, the cord on the handle of a whip, to fasten it on the hand.

MUCHI-DZWAE, ムチズハヘ, *n.* A switch, rod.

MU-CHIU, ムチウ, 夢中, *(yume no uchi.)* In a dream, absent minded, dreamy, visionary, in an unreal condition, crazy, fascinated, or absorbed in any thing.
Syn. UCHŌTEN.

MUCHI-UCHI,-*tsz*,-*tta*, ムチウツ, 鞭撻, *t. v.* To whip, to flog, to lash. *Uma ni —*, to whip a horse. Syn. BUTSZ.

MUDA, ムダ, 徒, Useless, vain, without advantage, or profit. *Muda-na koto*, useless affair. *Muda-bone wo oru*, to labor in vain. *Muda-bito*, one who has nothing to do.

MUDA-DZIYE, ムダツヒエ, 徒費, *n.* Useless expense, waste. — *ga ōi*, much useless expense.

MUDA-DZKAI, ムダツカヒ, 徒遣, *n.* Useless, or unprofitable expense.

MUDA-NI, ムダニ, 徒, *adv.* Uselessly, vainly, unprofitably.

MUDZ-TO, ムツト, 無手, *adv.* As in the phrase, *Mudz-to kumu*, to seize each other suddenly and violently, as wrestlers.

MUDZKARI,-*ru*,-*tta*, ムツカル, 憤, *i. v.* To be impatient, cross, to fret (as a child). *Kodomo ga —*, the child frets.

MUDZKASHII,-KI,-SHI, ムツカシイ, 六敷, *a.* Difficult, hard to be done; troublesome. *Biyōki ga —*, the disease is hard to cure, or incurable. — *h'to*, a person hard to deal with, or please. Syn. KATAI, MENDŌ.

MUDZKASHIKU, or MUDZKASHIU, ムツカシク, 六敷, *adv.* Idem. — *nai*, not hard.

MUDZKASHISA, ムツカシサ, 六敷, *n.* The difficulty, hardness.

MUDZ-MUDZ, ムツムツ, *adv.* In an idle, lazy manner, without object; tickling, itching. — *sh'te iru*; — *kaii*. Syn. GUDZ-GUDZ.

MU-FUMBETSZ, ムフンベツ, 無分別, Without judgment or discrimination, unintelligent.

†MU-GA, ムガ, 無我, *(watakushi nashi).* Unselfish, impartial.

MU-GAKU, ムガク, 無學, *(gakumon nashi).* Ignorant, unlearned, illiterate.

MUGE-NI, ムゲニ, 無下, *(kore yori shimo nashi), adv.* Very lowest, most vulgar, worst. — *iyashiki h'to ni wa aradz*, he is not the most vulgar of men.

MUGEI, ムゲイ, 無藝, Without polite accomplishments.

MUGI, ムギ, 麥, *n.* Barley, wheat. *Ōmugi*,

barley. *Ko-mugi*, wheat. — *no nogi*, the beard of wheat.

MUGI-AKI, ムギアキ, 麥秋, *n.* The fourth month, or wheat harvest.

MUGI-BATAKE, ムギバタケ, 麥畠, *n.* Wheat-field.

MUGI-MESHI, ムギメシ, 麥飯, *n.* Boiled barley.

MUGI-WARA, ムギワラ, 麥稈, *n.* Wheat straw. — *zaiku*, articles made of straw.

MUGI-WARI-MESHI, ムギワリメシ, 麥割飯, *n.* Food made of cracked barley boiled.

MUGOI,-KI,-SHI, ムゴイ, *a.* Unmerciful, without compassion or pity, barbarous, cruel. *Mugoi me ni au*, to meet with cruel treatment.

MUGOKU, or MUGŌ. ムゴク, *adv.* Idem.

MUGOSA, ムゴサ, *n.* Cruelty, barbarity.

MU-GON, ムゴン, 無言, (*kotoba nashi*). Silent, having nothing to say. — *de iru.* Syn. DAMARU.

MUGURA, ムグラ, 葎, *n.* The Humulus lupulus.

MU-GURAMOCHI, ムグラモチ, 土龍, *n.* A mole.

MUGURI,-*ru*,-*tta*, モグル, 潛, *t.v.* To dive under, to stoop and pass under. *Midz wo* —, to dive in water. Syn. KUGURU.

MU-HEN, ムヘン, 無邊, (*kagiri nashi*). Illimitable, infinite, boundless.

MU-HITSZ, ムヒツ, 無筆, *n.* Unable to write.

MU-HŌ, ムハフ, 無法, (*nori nashi*). Not conforming to rule, lawless, improper, rude, insolent.

MU-HON, ムホン, 謀叛, (*hakatte somuku*). Rebellion, sedition, treason, conspiracy. — *wo okosz*, to excite rebellion.

MU-I, ムヰ, 無位, (*kurai nashi*). Without rank, untitled.

MU-ICHI-MOTSZ, ムイチモツ, 無一物, Not one thing, nothing. *Honrai* —, at first there was nothing (in existence).

MUIKA, ムイカ, 六日, *n.* The sixth day of the month; six days.

MU-IN, ムイン, 無印, Unstamped, unsealed.

MUJI, ムヂ, 無地, Plain, unfigured, (as cloth).

MU-JIHI, ムジヒ, 無慈悲, (*awaremi-nashi*). Without pity, compassion, or love.

MU-JIN, ムジン, 無盡, (*tszkiru koto nashi*). Inexhaustible; a kind of lottery.

MUJINA, ムジナ, 貉, *n.* An animal something like a badger.

MU-JIN-TŌ, ムジントウ, 無盡燈, *n.* A kind of lamp.

MU-JITSZ, ムジツ, 無實, (*makoto nashi.*) Untrue, false, not real.

MU-JŪ, ムジウ 無住, (*juji nashi*). Without a resident priest, priestless.

MU-JŌ, ムジヤウ, 無常, (*tszne nashi*). Inconstant, mutable, changing, not lasting, evanescent, fleeting, passing away, death. (Bud.)

†MU-JŌ, ムジヤウ, 無上, (*wiye nashi*) Highest, most excellent, supreme.

MU-JŌ-SON, ムジヤウソン, 無上尊, Supremely honorable, a title of *Shaka-niyo-rai.*

†MU-JUN, ムジユン, 鉾楯, *n.* Enmity, malice. Syn. K'WAKU-SHITSZ.

MUKA-BA, ムカバ, 板齒, *n.* The front, or incisor teeth.

MUKABAKI, ムカバキ, 行縢, *n.* A kind of leather armor worn on the front of the thigh.

MUKABARATATSZ, ムカバラタツ, To flash up in sudden anger. Syn. MUTTO SZRU.

MUKADE, ムカデ, 蜈蚣, *n.* A centipede.

MUKADZKI,-*ku*,-*ita*, ムカツク, 煩嘔, *i.v.*. To loathe, to feel nausea, or sick at the stomach.

MUKAGO, ムカゴ, 零餘子, *n.* The fruit of the *Yamaimo.*

MUKAI,-*au*, or *ō*,-*tta*, ムカフ, 向, *i.v.* To face, to stand with the face towards, to front, to be opposite any thing, to go to meet, to confront, to oppose, to be near to (in time). *Teki ni mukau*, to go to meet or face the enemy. *Ten ni mokatte tszba haku ga gotoshi*, like spitting against the wind. *Haru ni* —, the spring is drawing near. *Hashi no mukō no iye*, the house opposite the bridge. *Kawa mukō*, fronting the river.

MUKAI, ムカヒ, 迎, *n.* Calling, inviting; a messenger sent to call a person. *Isha wo — ni yuku*, to go to call a doctor. *Tegami de — ni yokosh'ta*, have sent a letter to call him. — *wo yokoshite kudasare*, send a messenger for me. — *wo age mashō*, I will send a person to call you.

MUKAI-BARA, ムカヒバラ, 迎腹, *n.* The pains preceding labor.

MUKAI-BUNE, ムカヒブネ, 迎舩, *n.* A boat or ship sent to bring a person.

MUKAI-IRE,-*ru*,-*ta*, ムカヒイレル, 迎入, *t.v.* To go to meet and bring in, (as an honored guest.)

MUKA-MUKA, ムカムカ, 煩嘔, *adv.* Sick at the stomach, to feel nausea, to loathe. *Mune ga — szru.*

MUKASHI, ムカシ, 昔, *n.* Ancient times,

former ages, antiquity, old, a period of 10 years. — *yori mōshi-tsztayeta*, handed down from ancient times. — *mo ima mo onajikoto*, same now as in old times. — *no h'to*, men of ancient times. — *banashi*, ancient story, talking of old times. *H'to mukashi*, ten years. *F'ta* —, twenty years. Syn. INISHIYE, FURUKI, KOSHIKATA.

MUKASHI-GATARI, ムカシガタリ, 昔話, *n.* A story of ancient times.

MUKASHI-KATAGI, ムカシカタギ, 古頑, *n.* Prejudiced in favor of old times. — *na o-jisan.*

MUKAWARI, ムカハリ, 周歳, *n.* The first anniversary of a death.

MUKAYE,-*ru*,-*ta*, ムカヘル, 迎, *t. v.* To go to the door to welcome, to receive, or bring in (as a visitor,) to call, to invite to one's house. *Yome wo* —, to bring a daughter in law into the family, marry a wife. *Haru wo* —, to welcome the spring. *K'yaku wo* —, to meet and welcome a guest.

MUKAYEBI, ムカヘビ, 迎火, *n*, A fire kindled on the 13th day of the 7th month, as part of ancestral worship.

MUKE,-*ru*,-*ta*, ムケル, 向, *t. v.* To turn any thing towards, to direct towards, to cause to front, or point towards. *H'to wo Yedo ye mukete yaru*, to direct a person to go to Yedo. *Iye wo dochira ye mukete tatemashō ka*, in what direction will you make your house to front? *Yama ye mukete teppō wo hanasz*, to shoot a gun in the direction of the hill.

MUKE,-*ru*,-*ta*, ムケル, 剝, *i. v.* To peel off, to lose the skin, bark, or rind. *Kawa ga muketa*, the skin has peeled off. Syn. HAGERU.

MUKE-KAYE,-*ru*,-*ta*, ムケカヘル, 向替, *t. v.* To face any thing about, turn any thing in a different direction. *Tszkuye wo* —, to change the position of a desk.

MUKE-NAOSHI,-*sz*,-*sh'ta*, ムケナホス, 向直, *t. v.* To alter the direction of any thing.

MU-KEN-JIGOKU, ムケンヂゴク, 無間地獄, *n.* The severest place of torment in the Buddhist infernum.

MUKI,-*ku*,-*ita*, ムク, 剝, *t. v.* To skin, to peel, to strip off the bark. *Mikan wo* —, to peel an orange. *Ushi wo* —, to skin an ox. Syn. HAGU.

MUKI,-*ku*,-*ita*, ムク, 向, *i. v.* To turn the face towards, to front, to incline towards. In mercantile language, to be in request, or demand. *Higashi ye muku*, to face towards the east. *Gai-koku no akindo ye kami ga muki-mashō ka*, do you think paper would be saleable to foreign merchants? *Muki-maszmai*, I think it is not in request. Syn. MUKAU.

MUKI, ムキ, 向, *n.* The direction, frontage, aspect, exposure; request, demand. *Kono iye no — ga warui*, the frontage of this house is bad. *Minami-muki*, a southern aspect. *Ito no — ga yoi*, silk is in great request. *Muki ni natte hara wo tateru*, to get angry at what was said in jest. *Shina no h'to ni — ga yoi*, it is saleable to the Chinese.

MUKI-AI,-*au*,-*tta*, ムキアフ, 向合, *i. v.* To be opposite each other.

MUKI-DASHI,-*sz*,-*sh'ta*, ムキダス, 剝出, *t. v.* To peel off the skin and take out. *Me wo* —, to stare.

MUKI-DASHI-NI ムキダシニ, 剝出, *adv.* Without concealment, in a straight-forward, open manner.

MUKI-KUCHI, ムキクチ, 向口, *n.* Demand, request. — *ga nai*, not in demand.

MUKI-MUKI, ムキムキ, 向向, Every direction. — *ye tszkai wo dasz* to send messengers in every direction.

†MU-KIU, ムキウ, 無窮, (*kiwamari nashi.*) Endless, inexhaustible. *Kō mei wo — ni tsztayeru.*

MUKKURI, ムックリ, *adv.* Round and projecting above the surrounding parts, as a swelling, protuberance, hill or knoll. — *okiru*, to jump up or rise up suddenly.

MUKO, ムコ, 婿, *n.* Son in law. — *wo toru*, to take a husband for one's daughter.

MUKŌ, ムカフ, 向, See *Mukai.*

||MUKŌBA, ムカフバ, 向歯, *n.* The front teeth.

MUKŌ-DŌSHI, ムカフドウシ, 向同士, *n.* Opposite house.

MUKŌDZNE, ムカフズネ, 胻骨, *n.* The shin.

MUKŌ-DZRA, ムカフヅラ, 向頬, *n.* An adversary, enemy. Syn. TEKI.

MUKŌ-GASHI, ムカフガシ, 向河岸, *n.* Opposite bank.

MUKŌ-KAZE, ムカフカゼ, 向風, *n.* Head wind. Syn. G'YAKUFŪ.

MUKŌ-MIDZ, ムカフミズ, 向不見, Regardless of what is before, rash, reckless, incautious, fool-hardy. Spn. MUTEPPŌ. MUYAMI.

MUKU, ムク, 剝 or 向, See *Muki.*

MU-KU, ムク, 無垢, *n.* Pure, unalloyed. *Kin no — de koshirayeru*, made of pure gold. *Shiro-muku*, pure white clothes, lined also with the same material.

MUKU, ムク, 椋, *n.* A kind of tree, the leaves of which are used by carpenters for polishing wood. Celtis muku.

MUKŪ, ムクウ, 報, Same as *Mukuyuru*, see *Mukui*.

MU-KUCHI, ムクチ, 無口, Silent, taciturn, not given to much talking.

MUKU-GE, ムクゲ, 柔毛, *n.* The soft down beneath the long hair of animals.

MUKUGE, ムクゲ, 木槿, *n.* The Hibiscus syriacus.

MUKUI,-YU, or -YURU,-TA, ムクユル, 報, To requite, recompense, compensate, to repay, to retaliate, take vengeance on. *On wo* —, to requite a kindness. *Ada wo* —, to take vengeance on an enemy.
Syn. HŌDZRU, KAYESZ.

MUKUI, ムクヒ, 報, *n.* Recompense, requital, retribution, compensation. — *wo ukeru*, to receive a recompense, or compensation.

MUKU-INU, ムクイヌ, 尨, *n.* A shaggy dog.

MUKUMEKI,-*ku*, ムクメク, 蠢, *t. v.* To crawl as a worm, to move up and down like the crawling of a caterpillar.

MUKUMI,-*mu*,-*nda*, ムクム, *i.v.* To be bloated, swollen, puffed up. *Ne szgite kao ga mukunda*, his face is bloated with too much sleep. Syn. HAREBU.

MUKU-MUKU,-*szru*, ムクムク, 蠢蠢, *i.v.* To be moved by something moving underneath, as a quilt when a person sleeping under it moves.

MUKURE,-*ru*,-*ta*, ムクレル, 剝, *i.v.* Peeled, skinned, flayed, bare. *Kawa ga mukureta*, the skin is off. *Yogi ga mukurete kaze wo hikimash'ta*, my night clothes got off and I caught a cold.

MUKURENJI, ムクレンジ, Same as *Mukuranji*.

MUKURI,-*ru*,-*tta*, ムクル, 剝, *t.v.* To strip off, take off a covering. *Futon wo* —, to strip off a quilt.

MUKURI, ムクリ, 蒙古, *n.* The ancient name for Mongolia, same as *Mōko*.

†MUKURO, ムクロ, 軀, *n.* The body.

†MUKUTSZKE,-KI,-KU,-SHI, ムクツケ, Low, vulgar, and dirty.
Syn. BUKOTSZ.

MU-K'WAN, ムクワン, 無官, Without office.

MU-KUYE, ムクヱ, 無垢衣, *n.* Pure white clothes lined with the same material as the outside.

MUKUYURU, ムクユル, see *Mukui*

M'MA, ムマ, 馬, (more correctly written *uma*). *n.* A horse.

M'MARE,-*ru*,-*ta*, ムマレル, 生, See *Umare*.

M'MARETSZKI, ムマレツキ, 性質, See *Umaretszki*.

M'ME, ムメ, 梅, See *Ume*.

MU-MEI, ムメイ, 無名, (*na nashi*). Without the maker's name inscribed on it, without cause or reason. — *no katana*. — *no ikusa*.

†MU-MI, ムミ, 無味, (*ajiwai nashi*). Insipid, dull, flat, wanting in pleasing qualities.

†MU-MIYŌ, ムミヤウ, 無明, (*akiraka nashi*). Not clear, obscure. — *no yami*, stygian darkness.

MU-MON, ムモン, 無文, Without coat of arms. — *no kami-shimo kite haka ye mairu*.

MUNA-ATE, ムナアテ, 胸當, *n.* A breastplate.

MUNA-BONE, ムナボネ, 胸骨, *n.* The breast-bone, sternum.

MUNA-DZKAI, ムナヅカヒ, 胸塞, *n.* An uneasiness or stoppage in the chest; care, anxiety, trouble.

MUNA-DZMORI, ムナヅモリ, 臆算, *n.* Mental arithmetic, reckoning in the mind.

MUNA-FUDA, ムナフダ, 棟牌, *n.* A writing fixed to the ridge pole of a house, telling when and by whom the house was built.

MUNA-GAWARA, ムナガハラ, 棟瓦, *n.* The tiles laid over the ridge of a roof.

MUNA-GI, ムナギ, 棟, *n.* The ridge-pole of a roof.

MUNAGURA, ムナグラ, 胸倉, *n.* The breast of a coat. — *wo toru*, to seize a person by the breast of his coat; to collar.

MUNA-HIGE, ムナヒゲ, 胸毛, *n.* The hair on the breast.

MUNA-ITA, ムナイタ, 胸板, *n.* The front of the chest.

MUNA-SAKI, ムナサキ, 胸先, *n.* The pit of the stomach.

MUNA-SAWAGI, ムナサワギ, 胸騷, *n.* Perturbation, agitation, or commotion of mind.

MUNASHII,-KI, ムナシイ, 空, *a.* Empty, vacant, void, vain, naught, useless. *Munashiki kara*, a dead body. — *fune*, an empty boat.
Syn. AKI, KARA, MUDA.

MUNASHIKU, or MUNASHIU, ムナシク, 空, *adv.* Vacantly, vainly, for naught, uselessly. — *hi wo okuru*, to spend one's time for naught. — *kayeru*, to return without having accomplished any thing. — *naru*, to die. *Munashikaradz*, neg. is not vain, not useless. Syn. MUDA-NI, ITADZRA-NI.

MUNASHISA, ムナシサ, 空, *n.* Uselessness.

MUNA-ZAN-YŌ, ムナザンヨウ, 臆算用, *n.* Mental calculation, plan.

MUNE, ムネ, 胸, *n.* The breast, front of the chest, pit of the stomach. 心, The breast as the seat of the affections, = heart, or mind. 旨, The important or principal point, or meaning; the design, object, intention, reasons. — *ga itai*, the breast pains. — *ga warui*, to feel sick at the stomach. — *ga yakeru*, to feel a burning in the pit of the stomach. — *wo kogasz*, to fret or pine with care, or sorrow. — *wo hiyasz*, to be terrified. — *to szru*, to make it the principal object. — *ga hiraku*, mind is relieved of anxiety.

MUNE, ムネ, 棟, *n.* The ridge of a roof.

MUNE, ムネ, 背, *n.* The back of a sword, knife, comb, &c. *Katana no* —.

MUNE-AGE, ムネアゲ, 棟上, *n.* The celebration on completing the setting up of the frame of a house.

MUNE-ATE, ムネアテ, See *Muna-ate.*

MU-NEN, ムネン, 無念, Regret, sorrow, repentance, disappointment, dislike, aversion. — *ni omō*, to feel regret.
Syn. ZAN-NEN, KUYASHII.

†MUNETO, ムネト, 宗徒, *n.* The principal, or chief among vassals. — *no mono.*

MUNI, ムニ, 無二, (*f'tatsz nashi.*) Not the second, the first. — *no tomodachi*, most intimate friend. — *mu zan ni*, pell-mell, confusedly and violently, regardless of order.

†MU-NŌ, ムノウ, 無能, Without ability, or talent.

MURA, ムラ, 村, *n.* A small district of country, the subdivision of a *Kōri*, or county.

MURA, ムラ, *n.* Clustered, or in spots; not even, irregular. *Iro wa — ga dekita*, the color is not even, — here deep, there light. *Ki ni — no nai h'to*, a person of even temper. *Shoku ni — ga aru*, to have an irregular appetite. — *no nai yō-ni somete kudasare*, dye it so that the color will be even.

MURA-DACHI, ムラダチ, 群立, *n.* Standing in a cluster. *Matsz no* —, a cluster of pines.

†MURADO, ムラド, 腎, *n.* The kidneys. Syn. JIN.

MURA-GARASZ, ムラガラス, 群鴉, *n.* A flock of crows.

MURAGARI,*-ru,-tta*, ムラガル, 群, *i.v.* To flock together, to be clustered together, to herd. *Tori ga muragaru*, the birds flock together. Syn. ATSZMARU.

MURAGARI, ムラガリ, 群, *n.* A flock, herd, drove, cluster, clump, crowd, group.

MURA-KUMO, ムラクモ, 簇雲, *n.* Clusters of clouds. — *ga dete tszki ga miyenu.*

MURA-MURA, ムラムラ, 村村, *n.* Townships. 群群, *adv.* Broken into groups, clusters, &c.

MURA-OSA, ムラオサ, 村長, *n.* The headman of a township. Syn. NANUSHI, SHŌYA.

MURASAKI, ムラサキ, 紫, *n.* Purple color.

MURA-SAME, ムラサメ, 村雨, *n.* Rain falling in showers here and there.

MURA-SHIGURE, ムラシグレ, 村時雨, *n.* idem.

MURE,*-ru,-ta*, ムレル, *i. v.* To become musty, to mould, to heat by fermenting. Syn. MUSERU.

MURE, ムレ, 群, *n.* Flock, drove, herd, crowd, band, group, company, cluster, clump, class. *H'to mure no kuro-qumo*, a black cloud.

MURE,*-ru,-ta*, ムレル, 群, *i.v.* To flock, herd, crowd, swarm together.

MURE-ATSZMARI,*-ru,-tta*, ムレアツマル, 集群, *i.v.* To flock together, crowd together, to collect in swarms, or herds.

MURE-I,*-ru,-tta*, ムレ井ル, 群居, *i.v.* To be in a flock, herd, crowd, &c.

MU-RI, ムリ, 無理, (*kotowari nashi.*) Without reason, right, or principle; unjust, unreasonable; oppression, violence. — *wo iu.* — to speak unjustly, or injuriously.

MURÍ-NI, ムリニ, 無理, *adv.* By force, or compulsion, by violence, unjustly, unreasonably. *Muri-mutai-ni.* idem.

MU-RISOKU, ムリソク, 無利息, Without interest, (of money).

†MU-RIYŌ, ムリヤウ, 無量, Innumerable, immeasurable, infinite.

MURO, ムロ, 室, *n.* A room, an oven, cave, cellar, a chamber dug in the ground for preserving vegetables. *Hi-muro*, ice house.

MU-ROKU, ムロク, 無祿, Without wages, salary, or support from government. — *no rō-nin.*

MU-RUI, ムルイ, 無類, (*tagui nashi*). Without an equal, or the like; without comparison.

MUSABORI,*-ru,-tta*, ムサボル, 貪, *t.v.* To covet, to desire inordinately, to be greedy of; lust after. *Ri wo* —, to thirst after gain. Syn. YOKUBARU.

†MU-SAI, ムサイ, 無妻, (*tszma nashi*). Wifeless, celibacy.

MUSAI,-KI,-SHI, ムサイ, 陋, *a.* Dirty, mean, vile, applied generally to a house; slovenly. Syn. KITANARASHII.

MUSAKU, or MUSŌ, ムサク, 陋, *adv.* idem.

MUSA-KURUSHI,-KI,-KU, ムサクルシイ, 陋苦, Dirty and mean, slovenly.

MUSA-KUSA-SH'TE, ムサクサシテ, *adv.* Perplexed, distracted, vexed. *Ki ga — tama-ra-nai,* he was perplexed beyond endurance.

MUSA-MUSA-SH'TE, ムサムサシテ, *adv.* idem. *kokoro — mune ga ippai ni naru.*

†MU-SAN, ムサン, 無算, Ignorant of arithmetic.

MUSANKO-NI, ムサンコニ, *adv.* In a hurried and confused manner, without reflection or discrimination. *Gunzei ga — nigeru,* the army fled helter-skelter. Syn. YATARA, YAMIKUMO.

MUSASABI, ムササビ, 鼯鼠, *n.* A kind of large bat.

MUSASHI, ムサシ, 格戯, *n.* A kind of game, in which checkers are used.

MUSE,-*ru*,-*ta*, ムセル, 蒸, *i.v.* To mould, to be musty, to heat by fermenting, to ferment.

MUSE,-*ru*,-*ta*, ムセル, 噎, *i.v.* To choke, to strangle and cough by something getting into the larynx. *Kemuri ni museru,* to be choked with smoke.

MUSEBI,-*bu*,-*nda*, ムセブ, 咽, *i.v.* idem.

MUSE-KAYE,-*ru*,-*ta*, ムセカヘル, 咽返, *i.v.* To choke or strangle very much.

MU-SHA, ムシヤ, 武者, *n.* A soldier. Syn. TSZWAMONO.

†MU-SHABETSZ, ムシヤベツ, 無差別, No difference, the same, alike.

MUSHI, ムシ, 蟲, *n.* Insects, worms, bugs.

MUSHI,-*sz*,-*sh'ta*, ムス, 蒸, *t. v.* To cook by steaming, to steam, to foment. *Kome wo musz,* to steam rice. *Haremono wo —,* to foment a boil. Syn. FUKASZ, ATATAMERU.

†MU-SHI, ムシ, 無始, (*hajime nashi*). Without beginning.

MUSHI-ATSZI, ムシアツイ, 蒸暑, *n.* Damp and hot, sultry.

MUSHI-BA, ムシバ, 蟲歯, *n.* A decayed, or carious tooth. 蟲葉, A worm eaten leaf. — *wo nuku,* to extract a carious tooth.

MUSHI-BAMI, ムシバミ, 蠹蝕, *n.* Worm eaten.

MUSHI-BOSHI, ムシボシ, 蟲曝, *n.* Drying so as not to be injured by insects.

MUSHIBOTARU, ムシボタル, *n.* A glowworm.

MUSHIDZ, ムシズ, 蟲酢, *n.* Acidity of stomach, waterbrash, pyrosis. — *ga deru,* to have the waterbrash. Syn. RIUIN.

MUSHI-KE, ムシケ, 蟲氣, *n.* The appearance of having worms, (as children). — *dzku,* sick with worms.

MUSHI-KUI, ムシクヒ, 蠹蝕, *n.* Worm eaten. — *ba,* a decayed tooth.

MUSHI-KUSO, ムシクソ, 蟲糞, *n.* Insect dirt.

MUSHI-MEGANE, ムシメガネ 顯微鏡, *n.* A microscope. Syn. KEMBIKIYŌ.

MUSHI-MONO, ムシモノ, 蒸物, *n.* Articles cooked with steam.

MU-SHIN, ムシン, 無心, (*kokoro nashi*). *n.* Reluctant request for something, begging with reluctance for something which one wants of another. — *wo iu,* to make a request for something. *Kono hon wo go — mōshi-tai,* I want you to give me this book. — *wo kikadz,* not to grant the thing asked for. *Go — nagara kane wo kash'te kudasare,* I feel very reluctant to request you to lend me some money.

MUSHIRI,-*ru*,-*tta*, ムシル, *t.v.* To pluck, or strip off, (as feathers, hair). *Tori no hane wo —,* to pluck off the feathers of a bird. *Kusa wo —,* to pluck off grass. *Hige wo —,* to pluck off the beard.

MUSHIRO, ムシロ, 席, *n.* A mat.

†MUSHIRO, ムシロ, 寧, *adv.* Better, or least of two evils, rather. *Bakuchi utsz yori wa — sake wo nomu,* better to drink than to gamble,

MU-SHITSZ, ムシツ, 無失, (*tszmi nashi*). Not guilty, innocent, — *no togame wo kōmuru,* to be involved in a crime of which one is innocent.

†MU-SHO, ムシヨ, 墓所, *n.* A cemetery. Syn. HAKASHO.

MU-SHŌ-NI, ムシヤウ, 無正, *adv.* Recklessly, rashly, regardless of consequences.

†MU-SŌ, ムサウ, 無雙, (*narabi nashi*). Without an equal, second to none.

†MU-SŌ, ムサウ, 夢想, (*yume ni omo*). Revealed in a dream. *Go musō no kuszri,* a medicine discovered to one in a dream.

MU-SŌ, ムサウ, 無操, *n.* Dovetailed, or interlaced. — *makura,* a kind of camp-pillow. — *mado,* a window made with moveable slats.

†MUSOJI, ムソヂ, 六十歳, (*roku-jissai*). Sixty years old.

†MU-SOKU, ムソク, 無息, Without interest, (of money). Syn. MURISOKU.

MUSZ, ムス, 蒸, See *Mushi.*

MUSZBI,-*bu*,-*nda*, ムスブ, 結, *t.v.* To tie, to knot; (fig.) to produce, form, make. *Nawa wo* —, to tie a rope. *Mi wo* —, to produce fruit. *Yakujō wo* —, to make a compact. *Yen wo* — to form a marriage relation. *Iori wo* —, to build a hut by tying the timbers together. *Midz wo* —, to dip up water in the hollow of the hand. *Tszyu wo* —, to form dew. *In wo* —, to make various motions with the hands in conjurations, as done by the Yamabushi. *Yume wo* —, to have a dream. Syn. YŪ.

MUSZBI-BUMI, ムスビブミ, 結文, *n.* A letter closed with a knot.

MUSZBI-ME, ムスビメ, 結目, *n.* A knot.

MUSZBI-TSZKE,-*ru*,-*ta*, ムスビツケル, 結著, *t. v.* To tie anything on something else. Syn. YUITSZKERU.

MUSZBORE,-*ru*,-*ta*, ムスボレル, 結, *t.v.* To be tied together, knotted, tangled; perplexed, distracted, embarrassed. *Ito ga muszborete tokenu*, the thread is so tangled it cannot be loosened. *Ki ga* —, to be perplexed.

MUSZKO, ムスコ, 男, *n.* A son, boy. Syn. SEGARE.

MUSZME, ムヌメ, 女, *n.* Daughter, girl, miss, young lady.

MU-TAI, ムタイ, 無體, Wrong, improper, unjust. Syn. ARUMAJIKI, MURI.

MU-TEN, ムテン, 無點, Without side marks to the characters to show in what order they are to be read.

MUTEPPŌ, ムテツパフ, 無手法, Regardless of anybody or anything, rash, reckless. Syn. MUKŌMIDZ.

MU-TOKUSHIN, ムトクシン, 無得心, Not to consent, not allow, not permit; not to perceive or understand.

†MU-TOSE, ムトセ, 六年, *(roku-nen)*. Six years.

MUTSZ, ムツ, 六, Six. — *doki*, six o'clock. *Kure-mutsz*, six o'clock in the evening. *Ake-mutsz*, six in the morning. Syn. ROKU.

MUTSZ, ムツ, 鯥, *n.* A kind of river fish, about 6 inches long, of a red color.

MUTZBI, ムツビ, 睦, *n.* The bond, or relation of love or friendship. *Fubo no* — *wo hiki hanatsz*, to tear asunder the parental relation.

†MUTSZ-GOTO, ムツゴト, 睦言, *n.* Affectionate conversation, as betweeu husband and wife.

†MUTSZKI, ムツキ, 正月, *n.* The first month. Syn. SHŌG'WATSZ.

†MUTSZKI, ムツキ, *n.* A diaper worn by infants. Syn. SHIMESHI.

MU-TSZKI, ムツキ, 六月, Six months.

MUTSZMAJII,-KI, ムツマジイ, 睦, *a.* Friendly, amicable, harmonious, on good terms. Syn. SHITASHII, NAKA GA YOI.

MUTSZMAJIKU, or MUTSZMAJŪ, ムツマジク, 睦, *adv.* Idem. — *nai*, not friendly

†MUTSZMAYAKA, ムツマヤカ, Idem.

MUTTO,-*szru*, ムツト, 憤然, To flash up with sudden anger. Syn. MUKABARA.

MU-YAKU, ムヤク, 無益, *(yeki nashi)*. Useless, unprofitable, unserviceable. — *na koto*, Syn. MUDA, MUYŌ.

MU-YAKU, ムヤク, 無役, Out of service, or official employment. *Ano h'to ima wa* — *da*, he is now out of official employment.

MUYAMI, ムヤミ, Head-strong, obstinate, violent, rash, regardless of everything. *Muyami na koto*, rash affair. — *ni tatakau*, to fight recklessly. Syn. MUKŌMIDZ, MUTEPPŌ.

MU-YEKI, ムエキ, 無益, Useless, of no profit or advantage, unserviceable.

MU-YEN, ムエン, 無緣, Without kindred, or relations, having no affinity, or connection. *Mu-yen no shu-jō wa doshigatashi*, those who have no affinity (with the Buddhist faith) cannot be saved. *Mu-yen ni hodokosz*, to bestow without any obligation to do so.

MU-YŌ, ムヨウ, 無用, *(mochiiru koto nashi)*. Useless, not needed, not necessary. Used also as an imperative, do not, cannot, must not. — *na mono*, a useless thing. *Kono tokoro gomi szteru koto* —, don't throw rubbish here.

†MU-YOKU, ムクヨ, 無慾, Not covetous, without irregular desires.

†MU-ZAI, ムザイ, 無罪, *(tszmi nashi)*, Without crime, without sin; not guilty, innocent. Syn. MUSHITSZ.

†MU-ZAN, ムザン, 無慙, Cruel, without pity or compassion, barbarous. *Mu zan ya*, how cruel! what a pity! Syn. MUGOI.

MUZA-MUZA-TO, ムザムザト, *adv.* Cruelly, inhumanly.

MU-ZŌSA, ムザウサ, 無造作, Not difficult, easy.

N

NA, ナ, 名, *n.* Name, renown, fame, reputation. — *wo tszkeru*, to name. — *wo kayeru*, to change the name. — *wo toru*, to get a name, become famous. — *wo ushinau*, to become in bad repute. — *wo ageru*, to get renown.

NA, ナ, 菜, *n.* Leaves of various plants, as rape, turnip, radish, cabbage, &c., boiled and used for food; greens.

NA, ナ, 勿, A particle either prefixed, or affixed to a verb, forming the negative imperative mood,= do not, don't. *Waszreru na*, or *na-waszre-tamai so*, = don't forget. *Yuku na*, or *Na-yuki so*, don't go Syn. NAKARE.

NA, ナ, A particle affixed to the root of a verb, forming an affirmative imperative, as *Kiki-na*, listen. *Kochi-kina*, come here. *Sō shina*, do so. *O machi na*, wait.

NA, or NĀ, ナ, An exclam. *Kikitai-nā Sore wa na.*

NA, ナ, A contraction of *Naru*, affixed to words to form an attributive adjective, as, *Kon-kiu-na h'to*, a poor man. *Fū ki na iye*, a rich house. *Ōki-na koye*, a loud voice. *Chīsa-na ishi*, a small stone.

NABA, ナバ, A suffix to the root of verbs, forming a conditional word, used only in composition. *Kiki-naba*, if you hear. *Hana ya chiri-naba*, if the flowers fall,

NABE, ナベ, 鍋, *n.* A pot, kettle. — *no tszru*, the handle of a pot.

NABE-BUTA, ナベブタ, 鍋 蓋, *n.* A pot-lid.

NABETE, ナベテ, 並, General, common, usual, ordinary. — *no yo no h'to ni szguretaru mono*, one who is superior to the common run of men.
Syn. SŌTAI, TS'Ū-REI.

NABE-ZENI, ナベゼニ, 鏂, *n.* Small iron cash.

NABIKASHI,*-sz,-sh'ta*, ナビカス, 令 靡, Caust. of *Nabiku*. To cause to bend, lean, incline, yield, or comply to some power or influence. *Kaze ga ine wo nabikasz. Hata wo kaze ni nabikasz. H'to no kokoro wo —.*

NABIKE,*-ru,-ta*, ナビケル, 靡, *t. v.* To bend, lean, or incline in the direction of something moving; to make to yield, or comply. *Kaze ni nabikeru kemuri*, the smoke inclining to the wind.

NABIKI,*-ku,-ita*, ナビク, 靡, *i.v.* To bend, lean, incline, or yield to some power or motion, to follow, or comply with. *Kusa ki ga kaze ni nabiku*, grass and trees bend with the wind.

NABURI,*-ru,-tta*, ナブル, 調 弄, *t.v.* To jest with, banter, to hoax, make a fool of, to play tricks on, make sport with, to chafe, tease. *Kō-jin wo — koto nakare*, don't play tricks on old people.
Syn. GURŌ SZRU, CHŌRO-SZRU.

NABURI-KOROSHI,*-sz,-sh'ta*, ナブリコロス, 弄 殺, *t.v.* To kill by a slow death,—inflicting various cruelties.

NADA, ナダ, 洋, *n.* Ocean. *ō-nada*, idem, *Soto-nada*, idem. *Uchi-nada*, inland sea.
Syn. UMI.

NADA, ナダ, 灘, *n.* Coast, shore.
Syn. ISO.

NA-DAI, ナダイ, 名 代, *n.* Celebrated, famous. *Yedo no — mono*. a famous production of Yedo.

NA-DAKAI,-KI,-KU,-SHI,-Ō,-SA, ナダカイ, 高 名, Celebrated, famous, distinguished, having a great name. *Nadakai gakusha*, a celebrated scholar.

NADAME,*-ru,-ta*, ナダメル, 寛, *t. v.* To soothe, assuage, allay, appease, pacify, quiet, tranquilize, console. 宥, To mitigate or lessen, (a punishment.) *Ikari wo —*, to appease anger, *Tszmi wo —*, to mitigate the punishment of a crime.
Syn. NAGUSAMERU.

†NADARAKA-NA, ナダラカナ, *a.* Smooth, even, level, not rough.

NADARE, ナダレ, *n.* An avalanche, snow-slip. *Yuki-nadare.*

†NADARE, ナダレ, Gentle declivity or slope. — *no chi.*

NADE,*-ru,-ta*, ナデル, 撫, *t.v.* To stroke, to rub gently with the hand, to smooth, fig. To compassionate, pity, to comfort. *Kodomo no atama wo —*, to stroke a child's head.

NADE-AGE,*-ru,-ta*, ナデアゲル, 撫 上, *t.v.* To stroke, rub, or smooth up. *Kami wo —.*

NADESHIKO, ナデシコ, 撫 兒, *n.* A pink, (flower.) Syn. TOKONATSZ, SEKI-CHIKU.

NADE-TSZKE,*-ru,-ta*, ナデツケル, 撫 著, *t.v.* To comb, rub, stroke, smooth. *Kami wo —.*

NADO, ナド, 等, And so on, et cetera, or such like, or others of the kind; often, a plural particle. *Ki kusa nado ga kareta*, the trees, grass and such like things are withered. *Watakushi nado ga shitta koto de wa nai*, we know nothing about it.

NADO, ナド, Obs. for *Nato*, a contraction of *Natote*, why.

†NADOKORO, ナドコロ, 名 所, A celebrated place. Syn. MEI-SHO.

NADZKE,*-ru,-ta*, ナヅケル, 名, *t. v.* To give a name, to name, to call. *Takaki wo* *yama to* —, a high place is called a mountain. Syn. SHŌSZ, IU.

†NADZKI, ナヅキ, 腦, *n.* The head. Syn. ATAMA.

NADZMI,*-mu,-nda*, ナヅム, 拘泥, *i. v.* To be attached to anything from long custom, obstinately or bigotedly attached to. *Sono narawashi ni nadznde aratameru koto dekinu*, being bigotedly attached to that custom he cannot alter it.

NADZNA, ナヅナ, 薺, *n.* A kind of wild plant. Capsella burs pastoris.

NADZRAYE,*-ru,-ta*, ナズラヘル, 準, Obs. form of *Nazoraye.*

†NADZSAI,*-au*, ナヅサフ, 馴傍, *i.v.* To be intimate, or on friendly terms.

NAGA-AME, ナガアメ, 霖, *n.* A long-rain.

NAGA-BAKAMA, ナガバカマ, 長袴, *n.* The long trowsers worn at court.

NAGA-BANASHI, ナガバナシ, 長話, *n.* A long story.

NAGACHI, ナガチ, 帶下, *n.* Menorrhagia.

NAGA-DACHI, ナガダチ, 長太刀, *n.* A long sword.

NAGA-I, ナガ井, 長居, *n.* Remaining long in any place. — *wo sh'te h'to ga komaru*, if you stay long people will be annoyed. Syn CHŌZA.

NAGAI,-KI, ナガイ, 長, *a.* Long (in space or time). *Nagai tszki hi*, a long time. — *michi*, a long road. — *inochi*, long life. *Hi ga* —, the days are long. — *tegami*, a long letter.

NAGA-IKI, ナガイキ, 長壽, *n.* Long life.

NAGA-IMO, ナガイモ, 長芋, *n.* The long root of a wild plant much esteemed by the Japanese.

NAGA-JIRI, ナガジリ, 長尻, *n.* A long sitter, a tedious visitor.

NAGAKU, ナガク, 長, *adv*, Long. — *szru*, to make long, lengthen. *Hi ga — natta*, the days have become long. *H'to no inochi wa — nai*, the life of man is not long. *Nagaku-te ikenai*, it is so long I cannot stand it.

NAGAME,*-ru,-ta*, ナガメル, 眺, *t. v.* To direct the eyes towards any thing without any special intention, to look long at, to gaze at fondly, to contemplate. *Tszki wo* —, to gaze at the moon.

NAGAME, ナガメ, 眺望, *n.* Viewing, looking; a view, prospect. — *ni akunu keshiki*, a prospect one is never tired of looking at. Syn. KESHIKI, CHŌBO.

NAGA-MOCHI, ナガモチ, 長持, *n.* A long chest, or box; lasting or enduring a long time.

NAGA-NAGA, ナガナガ, 長長, *adv.* Very long. — *no biyōki*, a very long sickness.

NAGARA, ナガラ, 乍, *adv.* While, during, at the same time that; although, notwithstanding; together. *Hana wo mi nagara aruku*, to walk while looking at the flowers. *Ame wa furi nagara hi ga teru*, while it was raining the sun shone. *Habakari nagara*, while feeling backward &c. *Shikashi-nagara*, while it is so, but, nevertheless. *F'tari nagara*, both together. *Umare nagara no katawa mono*, a cripple from his birth. *Kaze tai boku wo ne nagara ni fuki-nuki*, the wind blew the big trees out by the roots. Syn. TSZTSZ.

NAGARAKU, ナガラク, *adv.* A long time. — *wadzraimash'ta*, have been a long time sick.

NAGARAYE,*-ru-ta*, ナガラヘル, 長生, *i. v.* To live, to be living, continue in life. *Oya mada nagarayete oru*, parents are still living. Syn. ZOMMEI.

NAGARE,*-ru,-ta*, ナガレル, 流, *i. v.* To flow; to move, pass, or run as a fluid; to float, to drift with the stream. *Midz ga* —, the water flows. *Shichi ga* —, the article pledged at a pawn-brokers can no longer be redeemed. *Fune ga* —, the boat is adrift.

NAGARE, ナガレ, 流, *n.* A current, a stream; (fig.) lineage, race; numeral for flags, streamers. *Midz no* —, a stream of water. *Shichi no — ga deta*, the time for taking up a pawned article is past. *Hata h'to* —, one flag. *Nagare no mi*, a prostitute. — *ni natta*, to let fall through, to let go, or let be.

NAGARE-BUNE, ナガレブ子, 流舩, *n.* A boat or ship drifting about without any one in it.

NAGARE-WATARI,*-ru,-ta*, ナガレワタル, 流渡, *i. v.* To float or drift across.

NAGARE-YA, ナガレヤ, 流矢, *n.* A random shot, (of an arrow).

NAGARE-ZAN, ナガレザン, 流産, *n.* Miscarriage, abortion.

NAGASA, ナガサ, 長, *n.* The length. — *wa iku shaku*, how many feet long?

NAGASARE,*-ru,-ta*, ナガサレル, 被流, Pass. of *Nagashi*, to be floated, or drifted by a current. 配流, To be transported, or exiled. *Shima ni* —, exiled to some island for crime.

NAGASHI,*-sz,-sh'ta*, ナガス, 流, *t. v.* To cause to, or let flow, float, or drift; to set adrift, to exile. *Tamari midz wo* —, to let out water that is dammed up. *Iranu mono wo kawa ye* —, to throw a useless thing into a stream (to be carried away.) *Chi wo* —, to let blood. *Shima ye* —, to transport to an island, (for crime). *Ko wo* —, to produce abortion. *Shichi wo* —, to let a pawned article go unredeemed. *Na wo* —, to spread abroad one's name.

NAGASHI, ナガシ, 浄槽, *n.* A sink.

NAGASHI, ナガシ, 長, *a.* Long. see *Nagai.*

NAGASHI-MONO, ナガシモノ, 流人, *n.* An exile. Syn. RU-NIN.

||NAGASZ, ナガス, A large whale. Syn. KUJIRA.

NAGATARASHII,-KI, ナガタラシイ, *a.* Long and tedious; prolix.

NAGATARASHIKU, ナガタラシク, *adv.* idem.

†NAGA-TSZKI, ナガツキ, 九月, *n.* The ninth month.

NAGAYE, ナガエ, 轅, *n.* The shaft of a carriage. 長柄, The shaft of a spear, handle of an umbrella.

NAGA-ZASHIKI, ナガザシキ, 長坐, *n.* A long visit from a guest; staying long at an entertainment. — *wo szru.*

NAGE,*-ru,-ta*, ナゲル, 投, *t.v.* To throw, cast, fling. *Ishi wo* —, to throw a stone. *Mi wo* —, to cast one's self into the water, to commit suicide. Syn. HŌRU, TŌDZRU.

NAGE-AGE,*-ru,-ta*, ナゲアゲル, 投上, *t.v.* To throw up.

NAGE-DASHI,*-sz,-sh'ta*, ナゲダス, 投出, *t.v.* To throw out.

NAGE-IRE,*-ru,-ta*, ナゲイレル, 投入, *t.v.* To throw into.

NAGE-KAWASHII,-KI, ナゲカハシイ, 歎敷, *a.* Lamentable, sad.

NAGEKAWASHIKU, ナゲカハシク, 歎敷, *adv.* idem.

NAGEKI,*-ku,-ita*, ナゲク, 歎, *t.v.* To draw a long breath, or sigh from any strong emotion, whether of joy, grief, love, admiration, pain, &c.; mostly, however, to grieve, lament, mourn, to complain. *Yo wo* —, to sigh over the wickedness of the world, or over the times. *Seifu ye* —, to complain to the government about one's wrongs. Syn. TANSOKU.

NAGE-KOMI,*-mu,-nda*, ナゲコム, 投込, *t.v.* To throw into.

NAGE-KOSHI,*-sz,-sh'ta*, ナゲコス, 投越, *t.v.* To throw across, or over.

NAGE-OROSHI,*-sz,-sh'ta*, ナゲオロス, 投下, *t.v.* To throw down, (from a height).

NAGESHI, ナゲシ, 長押, *n.* A horizontal piece of timber in the frame of a house.

NAGE-SZTE,*-ru,-ta*, ナゲステル, 投棄, *i.v.* To cast away.

NAGE-TSZKE,*-ru,-ta*, ナゲツケル, 投著, *t.v.* To throw against.

NAGE-UCHI,*-tsz,-tta*, ナゲウツ, 投打, *t.v.* To throw and hit, to hit, beat, to throw away.

NAGE-YARI, ナゲヤリ, 投遣, *n.* Let alone, neglect, cast aside, give up. — *ni szru*, or — *sh'te oku.*

NAGI,*-gu,-ida*, ナグ, 薙, *t.v.* To mow, to cut with a sweep. *Kusa, ine, mugi nado wo nagu.*

NAGI,*-gu,-ida*, ナグ, 和, *i.v.* To be calm, still, quiet, (as the waves, or wind). *Umi ga* —, the sea is calm. Syn. ODAYAKA, SHIDZKA.

NAGI, ナギ, 和, *n.* A calm. *Asa-nagi*, the morning calm.

NAGI, ナギ, 水葱, *n.* A kind of water plant. Syn. MIDZ-AOI.

NAGI, ナギ, 竹柏, A kind of tree. The podocarpus nageia.

NAGI-FUSE,*-ru,-ta*, ナギフセル, 薙伏, *t.v.* To mow down, to cut down.

NAGI-HARAI,*-au,-tta*, ナギハラフ, 薙佛, *t.v.* To clear away by mowing.

NAGI-NATA, ナギナタ, 長刀, *n.* A halberd.

†NAGISA, ナギサ, 渚, *n.* A beach, shore. Syn. ISO.

NAGI-TAOSHI,*-sz,-sh'ta*, ナギタフス, 薙倒, *t.v.* To mow down.

NAGI-TATE,*-ru,-ta*, ナギタテル, 薙立, *t.v.* To mow, to cut with a sword with a mowing motion.

NAGŌ, ナガウ, 長, Same as *Nagaku.*

NAGO, ナゴ, 海市, *n.* A mirage. Syn. SHINKIRŌ.

NAGORI, ナゴリ, 餘波, *n.* Relics, remains, vestige, ruins. That portion of time which remains before separation, or parting. *Mukashi no* —, the vestiges of antiquity. — *wo oshimu*, to feel sorry that the time before parting is passing away.

NAGU, ナグ, See *Nagi.*

NAGURE,*-ru,-ta*, ナグレル, *i.v.* To glance off, slip off, (as an arrow). *Ya ga nagureta*, the arrow has glanced off. Syn. SORERU.

NAGURI,*-ru,-tta*, ナグル, 擲, *t.v.* To beat, strike. *H'to wo* —, to strike a man. *Naguri-taosz*, to knock down. Syn. BUTSZ, CHOCHAKU SZRU.

NAGUSAME,*-ru,-ta*, ナグサメル, 慰, *t.v.* To cheer, amuse, divert; to console, to comfort, to soothe, pacify, appease, to calm. *Hana wo mite ki wo* —, to amuse one's self looking at flowers.

NAGUSAMI,*-mu,-nda*, ナグサム, 慰, *i. v.* To amuse, divert one's self.

NAGUSAMI, ナグサミ, 慰, *n.* Amusement, diversion, recreation.

NAI,*-au,-tta*, ナフ, 綯, *t.v.* To twist a rope. *Nawa wo nau*, to make a rope.

NAI,-KI,-SHI, ナイ, 無, *a.* Not, is not, have not; dead. *Shiranai*, don't know. *Wakaranai*, don't understand. *Sō de wa nai*, it is not so. *Nai de wa nai*, it is not that there is none, or it is not that I have none. *Nai nara nakute mo yoi*, if there is none, we can do without it. *Nai nara nai de ī*, (idem.) *Nai mono hoshii*, wanting something which one has not. *Nai mono wa nai*, have every thing, or destitute of nothing. *Aru ka nai ka shira nai*, don't know whether there are any or not. *Naki ni shi mo naku*, it is not that there are none. *Naku-te kanawanu mono*, a thing one can't do without, necessary. *Naku-te ike-nai*, must have, indispensable, can't do without.

†NAI, ナヰ, 地震, *n.* Earthquake. Syn. JI-SHIN.

NAI-BUN, ナイブン, 内分, Secret, private, not public. — *de szmasz*, to settle a matter privately. — *ni szru*, to do privately. Syn. NAISHŌ, HISOKA.

NAI-DAI-JIN, ナイダイジン, 内大臣, *n.* The name of a rank, the third below the *Ten-shi*,

NAI-DAN, ナイダン, 内談, (*hisokani hanasz*). Private talk.

†NAI-DEN, ナイデン, 内典, *n.* The Buddhist sacred books are so called.

NAIGASHIRO-NI, ナイガシロ, 輕蔑, *adv.* Treating as of no consequence, making light of, slightingly, disregarding, insultingly. *H'to wo — szru*, to treat a person as unworthy of notice. Syn. KEI-BETSZ, KARONDZRU, MIKUDASZ.

NAI-GI, ナイギ, 内儀, *n.* Wife; only used in speaking of another's wife.

NAI-G'WAI, ナイグワイ, 内外, (*uchi soto*), Inside and outside, within and without, private and public, domestic and foreign.

†NAI-HŌ, ナイハウ, 内方, (*uchi kata*). Wife. See *Naigi*.

NAI-I, ナイイ, 内意, *n.* Private opinion, design, or intention.

NAI-JAKURI, ナイジャクリ, 咲哏, *n.* A sob, (in crying). — *wo szru*, to sob.

NAI-KEN, ナイケン, 内見, Looking over privately before-hand, reading or examining privately. *Ash'ta no kōshaku no tame ni — sh'te oku*, to read over the lecture to be delivered to-morrow. Syn. SH'TAMI.

NAI-KŌ, ナイカウ, 内攻, Receding, or striking in of an eruption. *Shitsz ga — sh'ta* the itch has struck in.

NAI-NAI, ナイナイ, 内内, (*uchi-uchi*). *adv.* Secretly, privately, not publicly or openly. Syn. NAI-SHŌ, MITSZ-MITSZ, HISOKANI.

NAIRA, ナイラ, 内爛, *n.* A disease of horses.

†NAI-RAN, ナイラン, 内覽, *n.* Looking at privately.

NAI-RAN, ナイラン, 内亂, *n.* Civil broil, intestine commotion, domestic trouble, (of a country or family). — *ga okoru*.

NAIRI, ナイリ, 奈利, *n.* One of the Buddhist infernums. — *no soko ni otosz.*

NAI-SEKI, ナイセキ, 内戚, *n.* The blood relations of the *Mikado*.

†NAI-SHI, ナイシ, 乃至, (*sznawachi itaru made*). *conj.* Or, even to. Syn. ARUIWA.

†NAI-SHI, ナイシ, 内侍, *n.* Female servants of the *Mikado*.

†NAI-SHI-DOKORO, ナイシドコロ, 内侍所, *n.* The place where the mirror of the *Mikado* is kept.

NAI-SHIN, ナイシン, 内心, (*sh'ta gokoro*). Secret mind or desires, real state of mind, private opinion.

NAI-SHITSZ, ナイシツ, 内室, *n.* Wife. Syn NAIGI.

NAI-SHŌ, ナイシヨウ, 内證, Secret, private, not public, not apparent. Syn. NAINAI, HISOKANI.

†NAISŌ, ナイサウ, 内奏, *n.* Speaking privately to the Emperor.

†NAI-SON, ナイソン, 内損, (*uchi wo sokonai*), *n.* Internal injury, or disease.

NAITA, ナイタ, pret. of *Naki.* To cry.

NAITE, ナイテ, pp. of *Naki.*

NAI-TS'Ū, ナイツウ, 内通, *n.* Secret communication with an enemy. — *szru.*

†NAI-YAKU, ナイヤク, 内藥, *n.* Medicines given internally.

NAI-YEN, ナイエン, 内緣, (*hisokana chigiri*). Secret alliance, secret marriage.

†NAJIKAWA, ナジカハ, obsol. for *Nanikawa.* Why? for what reason? — *kore wo yorokobizaran*, why should they not rejoice?

NAJIMI,*-mu,-nda*, ナジム, 馴染, *i.v.* To be familiar, friendly, domesticated, tame, to feel at home. Syn. NATSZKU.

NAJIMI, ナジミ, 熟客, *n.* A familiar, or intimate acquaintance.

NAJIRI,–*ru*,–*tta*, ナジル, 詰, *t.v.* To inquire in a peremptory manner.

NAJIRI-TŌ, ナジリトフ, 詰問, To demand, or inquire in a peremptory manner.

†NAJŌ, ナデウ, 何條, (contr. of *Nani-jō*). What, what kind. — *on koto ka sōrō ya*, what reason you may have, &c.

NAKA, ナカ, 中, *n.* Inside, within, in, middle, midst, among, between; the state of feeling between persons, relations. *Iye no* —, in the house, inside of the house. *Kono hon no — ni wa nai*, it is not in this book. *Fū-fu no — ga warui*, the husband and wife are on bad terms. — *wo naosz*, to restore amicable relations. — *wo tagō*, to break off friendly relations. Syn. UCHI.

NAKABA, ナカバ, 半, *n.* Middle, centre, half, midst. *Roku-gatsz* —, middle of the sixth month. — *torimash'ta*, have taken the half. *Shu-yen* —, midst of a feast. Syn. HAMBUN, CHIU-Ō.

NAKA-BIKU, ナカビク, 中低, *n.* Concave, hollow, or depressed in the centre.

NAKA-DACHI, ナカダチ, 媒妁, *n.* A go-between, middleman in marriages. Syn. NAKŌDO, CHŪNIN, BAISHAKU.

NAKADAKA, ナカダカ, 凸, *n.* High in the centre, convex, bulging in the middle, arched.

NAKADAYE,–*ru*,–*ta*, ナカダエル, 中絶, *i.v.* To become estranged, distant, alienated in feeling, to cease friendly relations, break off an intimacy. Syn. CHIU-ZETSZ.

NAKAGAI, ナカガヒ, 仲買, *n.* A wholesale dealer. Syn. TOI-YA.

NAKAGO, ナカゴ, 中心, *n.* That part of the sword blade which runs into the handle.

NAKA-GORO, ナカゴロ, 中頃, Middle ages, or middle of a month.

NAKA-HODO, ナカホド, 中程, *n.* The middle, half, centre.

NAKA-ICHI-NEN, ナカイチネン, 隔年, The third year from now, after one full year has intervened.

NAKA-ICHI-NICHI, ナカイチニチ, 隔日, After one day has intervened, or on the third day counting the first and last. — *oite kuru.*

NAKA-IRI, ナカイリ, 中入, *n.* The recess, or interval in play, when the actors rest and eat.

NAKA-KUBO, ナカクボ, 凹, *n.* Concave, hollowed in the middle. Syn. NAKABIKU.

NAKAMA, ナカマ, 仲間, *n.* A company, firm, class, society, party, fraternity. Syn. KUMI, SHACHIU.

NAKA-MUKASHI, ナカムカシ, 中古, *n.* Middle ages.

NAKA-NAKA, ナカナカ, 中中, *adv.* Really, truly, indeed, in fact, (referring to some change in the subject). Syn. KAYETE, NAMA-NAKA, JITSZ-NI.

†NAKANDZKU, ナカンヅク, 就中, *adv.* Especially, particularly, in comparison with others, above all the others, in the mean while. — *kono h'to ga hatarakimash'ta*, this person has been more diligent than all the others. — *kono shina migoto ni soro*, this one is especially beautiful. Syn. NAKA-NI-MO, BETSZ-DAN, TORI-WAKI, MOTTOMO.

NAKANIMO, ナカニモ, *adv.* In comparison with others, especially, particularly. *Kedamono ōku aru nakanimo inu ga yoku h'to ni najimu*, of all the animals the dog is the most attached to man.

NAKARA, ナカラ, 半, *n.* The middle, half. *Tszki no* —, middle of the month. Syn. NAKABA, HAMBUN.

†NAKARAN, ナカラン, fut. of *Nakari*. Will not be, as, *Sono kai* —, it will be of no advantage.

†NAKARE, ナカレ, neg. imper. from *Nakari*. Do not, have not. *H'to wo korosz koto nakare*, thou shall not kill.

NAKARI,–*ru*,–*tta*, ナカル, (formed from *Naku*, not, and *ari*, is, or have). *i.v.* Is not, have not. *Omōta yori itaku nakatta*, it did not hurt as much as I expected. *Waga nakaran nochi*, after I am dead. *Nochi no urei nakaru beshi*, will not be a matter of future trouble.

†NAKARISEBA, ナカリセバ, Same as *Nakereba.*

NAKATE, ナカテ, 中稲, *n.* Middling rice, that ripens neither early or late, the early is called *Wase*, the late *Okute*.

NAKATSZKAMI, ナカツカミ, 豹, *n.* A leopard. Syn. HIYŌ.

NAKA-ZASHI, ナカザシ, 中刺, *n.* An ornament worn in the hair by women.

NAKA-ZORA, ナカゾラ, 中天, *n.* Mid-heaven.

NAKA-ZORI, ナカゾリ, 中剃, *n.* Shaving the middle, or top of the head, as the Japanese do.

NAKEREBA, ナケレバ, subj. mood of *Nakari*. If there is not, or if—have not, *Sake ga — cha demo yoi*, if you have no wine, tea will do.

NAKEREDOMO, ナケレドモ, conj. mood of *Nakari*. Although there is not.

NAKI, ナキ, 無, *a*. Same as *Nai*, which see; much used with the character 亡, for dead, death, as *Naki-ato*, after death. — *haha*, dead mother. — *gara*, dead body. *Nakidama*, the spirit of one dead. *Naki-bito*, a dead man.

NAKI,-*ku*,-*ita*, ナク, 啼, *i. v*. To cry, to weep, to bawl, squall; used also in a general sense for the loud cry or noise made by birds, animals, or insects. *Kodomo ga* —, the child cries. *Tori ga*—, the bird sings. *Inu ga* —, the dog barks.

NAKI-AKASHI,-*sz*,-*sh'ta*, ナキアカス, 啼明, *t. v*. To spend the night in crying. *Yo wo* —, id.

†NAKI-DOYOMI,-*mu*,-*nda*, ナキドヨム, 啼哄, *i. v*. To make a loud noise, as when many persons are crying out together.

NAKI-DZRA, ナキヅラ, 泣面, *n*. Crying face, tearful countenance.

NAKI-FUSHI,-*sz*,-*sh'ta*, ナキフス, 泣伏, *t. v*. To cry lying down.

NAKI-GOTO, ナキゴト, 啼言, *n*. Complaining, whining, whimpering.

NAKI-GOYE, ナキゴヱ, 啼聲, *n*. A cry, the voice of one crying.

NAKI-HARASHI,-*sz*,-*sh'ta*, ナキハラス, 啼腫, *t.v*. To swell the eyelids with crying, *Me wo* —.

NAKI-MODAYE,-*ru*,-*ta*, ナキモダエル, 哭悶, *t. v*. To cry and writhe, or throw one's self about.

NAKI-SAKEBI,-*bu*,-*nda*, ナキサケブ, 號泣, *i. v*. To shriek and cry, or cry with a loud voice.

NAKI-SAWAGI,-*gu*,-*ida*, ナキサワグ, 啼騷, *i. v*. To cry in great agitation, or excitement; to make a disturbance by crying.

NAKI-SHIORE,-*ru*,-*ta*, ナキシホレル, 啼萎, *i.v*. To become weak, or faint with crying.

NAKI-SH'TAI,-*au*,-*tta*, ナキシタフ, 啼慕, *t. v*. To cry and long for a loved one who is absent.

NAKŌDO, ナカウド, 仲人, *n*. A go-between, middleman in marriages. Syn. CHIU-NIN.

NAKU, ナク, 啼, see *Naki*.

NAKU, ナク, 無, see *Nai*.

NAKUMBA, ナクンバ, same as *Nakereba*.

NAKUNARI,-*ru*,-*tta*, ナクナル, 無成, *i. v*. Lost, missing, no longer in existence, come to naught, done, used up, all gone, dead. *Hon ga nakunatta*, the book is lost. *Kane ga* —, the money is all gone. *H'to ga* —, the man is dead. *Tanoshimi ga* —, there is no longer any pleasure.

NAMA, ナマ, 生, *a*. Raw, crude, uncooked, green, unseasoned, fresh; inexperienced, immature, imperfectly acquainted, unskilled; imperfectly, superficially. *Nama-mono*, raw or uncooked things. *Nama-samurai*, an inexperienced soldier. *Nama uwo*, raw-fish. *Nama-gai*, raw clams. *Te wo — arai ni szru*, to wash the hands imperfectly, or half washed.

NAMABI, ナマビ, 生干, *n*. Only partially dried, half dried, *Kimono ga — da*, the clothes are only half dried.

NAMADZ, ナマヅ, 鯰魚, *n*. A kind of cat-fish.

NAMADZ, ナマヅ, 癜風, *n*. A species of macula, (disease of the skin).

NAMAGATEN, ナマガテン, 生合點, Comprehending imperfectly, inattentive.

NAMA-GIKI, ナマギキ, 生利, *n*. One who pretends to, or affects a skill or knowledge which he does not possess.

NAMA-GOROSHI, ナマゴロシ, 生殺, *n*. not quite killed, half dead.

NAMA-GUSAI,-KI,-KU,-SHI, ナマグサイ, 腥, Smell of raw flesh, or of raw fish.

NAMA-HIYŌHŌ, ナマヒヤウハフ, 生兵法, Vain boasting of one's skill in fencing.

NA-MAIKI-NA, ナマイキナ, *a*. Affecting, or pretending to a refinement or cleverness which one does not possess. — *koto wo iu*, talking with an affectation of knowledge. — *h'to*, an affected person, a charlatan.

NAMAJII, ナマジヒ, 慭, *adv*. On the contrary, better, rather. — *me de mite, ki wo momu yori mo, issō mekura ga mashide arō* it is better to be blind, than by seeing to be unhappy.

NAMAJIKKA, ナマジッカ, *adv*. On the contrary; better.

†NAMAJĪ-NARU, ナマジヒナル, 慭, *a*. Imperfect, half done. — *ikusa*, a war imperfectly prepared for and feebly carried on.

NAMAKE,-*ru*,-*ta*, ナマケル, 懶惰, *i.v*. To be weak, languid, lazy, indisposed to exertion. — *mono*, a lazy fellow.
Syn. BUSHŌ, YURUMU.

NAMA-KI, ナマキ, 生木, *n*. Unseasoned or green wood.

NAMAKO, ナマコ, 海鼠, *n*. A kind of mollusk.

NAMAKURA, ナマクラ, 鈍刀, *n*. A bad tempered blade, a dull sword.

†NAMAMEKI,-*ku*,-*ita*, ナマメク, 媚, *v. i*. To affect a fascinating manner; to adorn one's self, and act with the desire to please, or captivate; to flirt, coquet.

NAMA-MONO-JIRI, ナマモノジリ, 生物知, *n.* One who has only a superficial knowledge of things, but who affects the philosopher.

NAMA-NAKA, ナマナカ, 生中, *adv.* On the contrary, better, rather. — *shiranu hō ga yoi*, it is better not to know. — *ī-dash'te komatta*, speaking only led to trouble. Syn. NAKA-NAKA, KAYETE.

NAMA-NAMA, ナマナマ, 生生, Raw, green, &c. see *Nama.*

NAMA-NIYE, ナマニヘ, 生煮, *n.* Half cooked, imperfectly cooked. *Kono imo wa mada — da*, these potatoes are only half-done.

NAMARI, ナマリ, 鉛, *n.* Lead.

NAMARI, ナマリ, 方言, *n.* Dialect, manner of speaking, provincialism.

NAMARI,-*ru*,-*tta*, ナマル, 訛, *i.v.* To speak with a provincial accent, or manner. *Ano h'to wa kotoba ga namaru.*

NAMASZ, ナマス, 膾, *n.* A kind of food made of raw fish.

NAMA-WAKAI,-KI,-KU,-SHI, ナマワカイ, 生弱, Still tolerably young, not past maturity.

NAMA-YAKE, ナマヤケ, 生燒, Half baked, or roasted.

NAMAYE, ナマヘ, 名, *n.* Name. *Anata no onamaye wa nan to mōshimasz*, what is your name? Syn. NA.

NAMA-YEI, ナマヱヒ, 酔客, *n.* Half-drunk, fuddled.

NAMBA, ナンバ, *n.* A kind of wooden boots worn by farmers in working in deep rice fields; also maize.

NAM-BAI, ナンバイ, 何杯, How many times full? *Midz wo — iremashō.*

NAM-BAN, ナンバン, 南蠻, (*minami no yebisz*). Southern barbarians; formerly applied to the Portuguese, Dutch and other Europeans.

NAM-BIYŌ, ナンビヤウ, 難病, (*naori gataki yamai*). An incurable disease.

NAM-BŌ, ナンバウ, 南方, (*minami no hō*). Southern side, southern countries.

‖NAM-BŌ, ナンバウ, 何程, (*nani hodo*). How much? How many? Syn. IKURA.

NAM-BU, ナンブ, 何分, How many tenths of an inch?

NAM-BUN, ナンブン, 何分, Same as *Nanibun.*

NAME,-*ru*,-*ta*, ナメル, 舐, *t.v.* To lick, to taste, to moisten by applying the tongue. Syn. NEBURU.

NAMEDZRI,-*ru*, ナメズル, *i.v.* To lick the mouth, (as an animal after eating).

†NAMEGENARU, ナメゲナル, 無禮, Rude, impolite. Syn. BUREI.

NAMEHARA, ナメハラ, 白痢, *n.* Mucous diarrhœa.

NAMEKUJI, ナメクジ, 蛞蝓, *n.* A slug.

NAMERAKA, ナメラカ, 滑, *n.* Slippery, smooth, glib, oily, unctious, (fig.) bland, flattering. — *na ishi*, a slippery stone.

NAMESHI,-*sz*,-*sh'ta*, ナメス, 究, *t.v.* To tan, to dress and soften skins. *Kawa wo* — to tan leather.

NAMESHI-GAWA, ナメシガハ, 韋, *n.* Leather.

NAMI, ナミ, 波, *n.* Waves. *ōnami*, big waves. — *no une*, the ridges of the waves. *Nami-uchi-giwa*, wave beaten shore.

NAMI, ナミ, 並, Common, ordinary, usual, average quality, in general. — *no h'to*, a man of ordinary abilities. — *yori ōki*, larger than is usual. — *no shina de gozarimasz*. it is an article of the average quality. *H'to nami ni aradz*, not like other men. *Toshi-nami*, yearly. *Tszki-nami*, monthly. *Hi-nami*, daily, day by day. Syn. TS'Ū-REI, TSZNE, ATARI-MAYE.

NAMIDA, ナミダ, 涙, *n.* Tears. — *wo kobosz.* — *wo nagasz.* —*wo tareru*, to shed tears. — *wo harau*, to wipe away the tears.

NAMIDA-GUMI,-*mu*,-*nda*, ナミダグム, 涙含, *i.v.* Eyes filling with tears, to have the appearance of one about to cry.

NAMI-I,-*iru*,-*ita*, ナミイル, 並入, *i.v.* To be in a row, sit in a row.

NAMI-KI, ナミキ, 列樹, Trees planted in a row, generally along the side of a road, or before a *Miya.*

NAMI-MA, ナミマ, 波間, (*nami no aida*). Between, or amongst the waves. — *ni miyuru fune.*

NAMI-NAMI, ナミナミ, 並並, *adv.* Ordinary, usual. — *naranu*, extraordinary.

NAMI-YOKE, ナミヨケ, 波除, *n.* A breakwater, any thing used for breaking the force of the waves.

NAMMON, ナンモン, 難問, A difficult question. — *szru*, to propose a difficult question.

†NAMMERI, ナンメリ, Comp. of *Nan*, the fut. of *Naru*, and *Meri;* same as *Narubeshi*, = coll. *darō*, should be.

NAMOMI ナモミ, *n.* A kind of weed.

NAMPŪ, ナンプウ, 難風, *n.* Adverse wind.

NAMU, or NAMURU, ナム, Same as *Nameru.*

NAMU, ナム, 南無, A word derived from the *Pali* prefixed to the name of Buddha and other divinities in praying. *Namu amida butsz.*

NA-MUSHI, ナムシ, 蠋, A kind of caterpillar which feeds on the leaves of the rape-seed plant.

NAN, ナン 難, *(katai)*. Hard, difficult; adversity, calamity, misfortune, objection. *— ni nozomite shi wo damo osoredz,* when [one's country] is in danger [a patriot] will not fear death. *Ichi — ari,* there is one difficulty, or objection. *— ni au,* to meet with adversity. *— wo tszkeru,* to raise an objection. *— nashi,* without difficulty. *— wo szkū,* to deliver from evil.

†NAN, ナン, A particle affixed to verbs, giving them, (1.) a future meaning, as, *Hakanaku narinan nochinimo omoi-dashi-tamaye,* after I shall have passed away think of me. *Yoki tokoro ni utszrinan,* I will remove into a good place. (2.) of desiring, wishing, imploring, as, *Haya yo mo akenan,* I would it were morning. *Waga nageku kokoro wo h'to mo shiranan,* I would not that others should know my sadness.

†NAN, ナン, An emphatic particle. = *zo,* as, *Kono koto ima mo ari to nan,* there are such things even at the present time. *Midz ni nan utszri keru,* it is reflected in the water. *Kaze no oto ni nan ari keru,* it is the sound of the wind.

†NAN, ナン, 南, *(minami)*. *n.* South.

†NAN, ナン, 男, *(otoko)*. A male, man, only used in comp. words. *Nan-niyo.*

NAN, ナン, 何, A contracted form of *Nani.* What. *Nan doki,* what o'clock? *Nan nen,* what year? *Nan getsz,* what month? *Omaye no na wa nan to mōshimasz,* what is your name? *Kore wa nan to iu mono,* what do you call this?

NANA, ナナ, Cont. of *Nanatsz,* seven.

NANAKO, ナナコ, 七子, *n.* A kind of silk goods.

NANA-KUSA, ナナクサ, 七草, *n.* Seven kinds of greens, (viz, *seri, nadzna gogiyō, hakobera, hahako, szdzna, szdzshiro*), cooked and eaten on the 7th day of the 1st month.

NANAME, ナナメ, 斜, Inclined, slanting, oblique, diagonal. *— ni kiru,* to cut diagonally. Syn. SZJIKAI.

†NANAME-NARADZ, ナナメナラズ, 不斜, *adv.* Very great, not a little. *Kiyetsz —,* my joy is very great.

†NANASOJI, ナナソヂ, 七十, Seventy years of age.

NANATSZ, ナナツ, 七, *n.* Seven. Syn. SH'CHI.

†NANDA, ナンダ, 涙, Same as *Namida.*

NANDA, ナンダ, Coll. cont. of *Nani de aru,* what is it? what is the matter? *Ano sawagi wa nanda,* what disturbance is that?

NAN-DAI, ナンダイ, 難題, *n.* A hard theme; a difficult subject; a hard, unjust or cruel matter. *— wo ī-kakeru,* to propose a hard theme.

NANDEMO, ナンデモ, Same as *Nanidemo.*

NANDO, ナンド, 納戸, *n.* A private room, closet.

NANDO, ナンド, 等, Same as *Nado.*

NANDO, ナンド, 何度, How often. = *ikutabi.*

NANDOMO, ナンドモ, *conj.* How often so-ever; many times.

†NANDZ, ナンズ, A future suffix, = *nan to szru,* or coll. *mashō,* as, *Shinandz,* = *shinan to szru,* about to die. *Ushinainandz* = *ushinainan to szru,* will lose.

NANDZRU, ナンズル, 難, See *Nanji.*

NAN-GI, ナンギ, 難儀, *n.* Affliction, trouble, misery, calamity, disaster. Syn. NANJŪ, KON-KU.

†NAN-GIYŌ, ナンギヤウ, 難行, *n.* Hard and painful religious works, as fasting, self-inflicted torture; penance.

NANI, ナニ, 何, *pro.* What. *Kore wa nani,* what is this? *Nani wo sh'te iru ka,* what are you doing? *Nani wo ka makoto to iu ya,* what do you call truth? *Nani h'totsz to sh'te,* in every particular. *Nani ni ka sen,* what will be the use?

NANI-BITO, ナニビト, 何人, What man? who. *— no,* whose.

NANI-BUN, ナニブン, 何分, Some way or other, any-how, any-way whatever. *— yoroshiku otanomi-mōshimas,* I request you to do it in any way you think best. Syn. DŌZO, DŌMO.

NANI-DE, ナニデ, With, by, from or out of what? *Kore wa — koshiraye-mash'ta ka,* what is this made of? *— gozarimasz,* what is it?

NANI-DEMO, ナニデモ, Anything whatever. *— yoroshii,* anything will do.

NANI-GANA, ナニガナ, See *Gana.*

NANIGASATE, ナニガサテ, Exclam. *— o yaszi go yō de gozarimasz,* it is a very easy business.

NANI-GASHI, ナニガシ, 何某, *n.* A certain person, somebody, some one whose name is forgotten. *Mukashi no —,* some one of the ancients.

NANI-GE-NAI,-KI,-KU,-SHI,-O, ナニゲナイ, 無何氣, Without any appearance whatever of minding, caring about, or knowing; with a careless, or indifferent manner; without letting on. *Nanigenaki tei ni* id.

NANI-GOKORO-NAKU, ナニゴコロナク, 無何心, Not thinking, not intending, without minding.

NANI-GOTO, ナニゴト, 何事, Why, what reason; what news, matter or business. *Kano haori wa — zo*, why are you wearing this coat? *— mo nai*, nothing the matter whatever. *— ka aru to miyeru*, something appears to be the matter. *— ga aru no da*, what is the matter? *— ni yoradz*, no matter what.

NANI-KA, ナニカ, *adv.* What *— shirimasen*, what it is, I don't know. *— yō ga aru ka*, what is your business? or have you any business? (with me). *— yoi mono ga ari-sō na mono da*, I think there must be something that will do, or answer the purpose. *— to sewashii*, busy with many and various things. *Nani-ka wa motte*, how, in what way. *Nani-ka no sewa wo szru*, render every kind of aid. *— no koto made ki wo tszkeru*, give attention to every thing (no matter what it is.)

NANI-KURE, ナニクレ, 何是, Any and every thing. *— to isogashii*, busy in various ways.

NANI-MO, ナニモ, *adv.* Everything. With a neg. Nothing. *— ka mo shitte-iru*, knows every thing, (no matter what). *— nai*, nothing. *Kimono mo — doro darake ni sh'ta*, his clothes and every thing else were covered with mud. *— miyemasen*, there is nothing to be seen.

NANI-MONO, ナニモノ, 何物, What thing? what person? *— da*, who is that? or what thing is that? *— no shitaru waza ni ya ariken*, I wonder who did this.

NANI-NI, ナニニ, *adv.* Anything whatever. *— yoradz*, no matter what. *— mo naranu*, of no use, good for nothing. *— mo seyo*, be it as it may; however it may be. *— shiro kawai-sō na koto da*, be it as it may, it is a cruel thing.

NANI-NO, ナニノ, see *Nan-no.*

†NANI-Ō, ナニオフ, 名負, *a.* Celebrated, famous.

NANI-SAMA, ナニサマ, 何様, *adv.* Some how, some way or other. *— makoto to wa omowaredz*, some how it cannot be considered as true.

†NANI-SHI-NI, or NANI-SHI-KA, ナニシニ, Why, for what reason.

NANI-TO, ナニト, see *Nan to. — iwarete mo kamai-masen*, don't mind anything he says. *— naku*, without any special reason. *— sen*, or *— shō*, what shall I do?

†NANI-TO-KAYA, ナニトカヤ, What, of doubt, or uncertainty, = I wonder what.

NANI-TOMO, ナニトモ, *adv.* Anything whatever. *— nai*, not at all. *— omowanu*, not thinking of anything.

†NANI-TOTE, ナニトテ, *adv.* Why, for what reason. *— kakaru tokoro ni wa owashimasz zo*, why are you living in such a place?

NANI-TO-ZO, ナニトゾ, Exclam. in requesting, beseeching; I pray you, please. Syn. DŌZO.

NANI-YARA, or NANI-YARAN, ナニヤラ, What, (don't certainly know) something or other. *Kono-hodo nani-yara kurō-naru kokoro-gakari ga, kiyami to nari*, she lately became gloomy, from some care or other, (which was not known).

NANI-YORI, ナニヨリ, Than anything whatever. *— kekkō na mono*, more splendid than anything else.

†NANJI, ナンヂ, 汝, *pro.* You. *Nanji-ra*, plur. you. Syn. ANATA, OMAYE.

†NANJI, *-dzru*, *-ta*, ナンズル, 難, *i.v.* To object to, to state a difficulty.

NAN-JŪ, ナンジウ, 難澁, *(katai shibui) n* Affliction, hardship, misery, trouble.

†NAN-JO, ナンジヨ, 難所, A difficult place.

NAN-KIN, ナンキン, 南京, *n.* Nankin in China, vulg. for, China.

†NAN-KIYOKU, ナンキヨク, 南極, *n.* South star.

NAN-KO, ナンコ, 藏鉤, *n.* The game of odd and even.

†NAN-KON, ナンコン, 男根, *n.* Membrum virile.

†NAN-NAN, ナンナン, 向, [from *Nari nan*]. *adv.* Almost, nearly, about to, approaching to. *Shi ni — to sz*, almost dead. *H'yaku nen ni — to sz*, almost a hundred years. Syn. NARI-KAKARU.

NAN-NIYO, ナンニヨ, 男女, *(otoko onna). n.* Man and woman, male and female.

NAN-NO, ナンノ, *(nani no).* Of what. *— iriyō da*, of what use is it? *— yakuni mo tatanu mono*, a thing of no use at all. *Nan-no ka-no to iute osoku-natta*, owing to one thing or another, I was late.

†NANORI, *-ru*, *-tta*, ナノル, 名告, *t.v.* To tell one's name.

NANORI, ナノリ, 名, *n.* Name. *On — wa nan to mōshimasz zo*, what is your name? Syn. NA, JITSZ-MIYŌ.

NANORI-AI, *-au*, *-atta*, ナノリアフ, 名告合, *t.v.* To tell each other their names.

†NANORI-SO, ナノリソ, 神馬藻, *n.* A kind of seaweed.

NAN-RA, ナンラ, 何等, What? of several. *— no yuye ni*, why? for what reasons?

NAN-SEN, ナンセン, 難舩, *n.* Shipwreck. *— szru.*

NAN-SHI, ナンシ, 男子, (*otoko no ko*). *n.* A male child, boy.

NAN-SHOKU, ナンショク, 男色, *n.* Sodomy. *— szru.*

†NAN-SZRE-ZO, ナンスレゾ, 何為, Why? for what reason?

†NAN-TACHI, ナンタチ, 汝等, You, [plur.] Syn. NANJIRA, TEMAYERA.

NAN-TO, ナント, See *Nani-to.*

NANUKA, ナヌカ, 七日, *n.* The seventh day of the mouth, seven days.

NANUSHI, ナヌシ, 名主, *n.* The head-man of a village, or street.
Syn. SHŌYA.

NAN-ZAN, ナンザン, 難產, *n.* Difficult parturition. *— szru.*

NAN-ZO, ナンゾ, 何, Any thing, something, how, why. *—torare wa shinai ka*, has he not taken something? *— yakunitatsz darō*, thinking it might be of some use. *— umai mono wa nai ka*, have you not something good to eat? *Ware — oyoban ya*, how can I come up to him?

NAO, ナホ, 尙, *adv.* Still, yet, more. *— yoi*, better. *— warui*, worse. *Sono hikari tszki yori mo nao akiraka nari*, its light was brighter than the moon. Syn. MADA, SONO WIYE.

†NAOI,-KI,-SHI, ナホイ, 直, *a.* Straight, correct, upright, just, honest.
Syn. SZGUI.

NAOKU, ナホク, 直, *adv.* Idem.

†NAO-MATA, ナホマタ, 尙又, *conj.* Moreover, again, furthermore.

NAO-MOTTE, ナホモツテ, 尙以, *adv.* Still more.

†NAO-NAO, ナホナホ, 尙尙, *adv.* More and more, still more.

NA-ORE, ナヲレ, 名折, *n.* [lit. name breaking]. Disgrace, infamy, reproach. *Iye no —*, disgrace of a house. Syn. HAJI, KAKIN.

NAORI,*-ru,-tta*, ナホル, 瘉, *i. v.* To be cured, healed. 直, To mend, repair, fig. to restore friendship, translated from one language into another. *Yamai ga naotta*, the disease is cured. *Naka ga naotta*, the quarrel, or breach of friendship is healed. *Nippon no kotoba ni naoru ka*, is it translated into Japanese? *Michi ga naotta*, the road is mended. *Kaze ga —*, the wind has become favorable. *Za ni —*, to resume one's seat.

†NAO-SARA, ナホサラ, 尙更, *adv.* Still more.

NAOSHI,*-sz,-sh'ta*, ナホス, 瘉, *t. v.* To cure, heal. 直, To mend, repair; to correct, to rectify, reform, to straighten, to restore friendship; to translate. *Yamai wo —*, to heal disease. *Michi wo —*, to repair a road. *Naka wo —*, to restore friendship. *Kugi wo —*, to straighten a nail. *Ki-gen wo —*, to restore the spirits. *Za wo —*, to adjust one's self in sitting. *Shin-sho wo* to retrieve a fortune. *Nippon no kotoba ni —*, to translate into Japanese.

NAOSHI, ナホシ, 直衣, *n.* The clothes usually worn by Kuge.

NAOSHI, ナホシ, *n.* A cobbler

NAOZARI, ナホザリ, 等閑, Careless and indifferent, slighting, disregarding, of no importance. *Go hatto wa — no koto de wa nai*, the laws are not to be disregarded. *— ni sh'te oku*, to treat with indifference. Syn. NAGEYARI, KI WO TSZKENU.

NARA, ナラ, 楢, *n.* The name of a tree, a species of oak?

NARA, ナラ, (cont. of *Naraba*). If. *Yedo ye yuku-nara*, if you go to Yedo, &c. *Mata kuru-nara motekoi*, if you come again, bring it.

NARABA, ナラバ, *adv.* If. *Aru naraba kudasare*, if you have any give it to me.

NARABE,*-ru,-ta*, ナラベル, 並, *t.v.* To place in order, arrange in a row, to match. *H'to wo retsz ni —*, to place men in ranks. *Narabete kaku*, to write in a row. *Narabete oku*, to place in a row. *Tōji Yedo ni oite kata wo naraberu mono nashi*, there is now none in Yedo equal to him.
Syn. TZRANARU.

NARABI,*-bu,-nda*, ナラブ, 並, *i.v.* To be in a row, to be arranged in order, matched. *Hon ga narandeiru*, the books are arranged in a row. Syn. TSZRANARU.

NARABI, ナラビ, 並, A row, rank, series. Syn. RETSZ, TSZRA.

NARABI-NI, ナラビニ, 幷, *conj.* Together with, and, also. Syn. OYOBI, TSZGI-NI.

NARADE, ナラデ, (cont. of *Naradz sh'te*). Not being, without it is, unless, excepting. *Hoshi wa yoru narade wa miye-masen*, stars cannot be seen excepting at night. *Kore — hoka ni wa nai*, have none except this. Syn. NAKEREBA.

NARADZ, ナラズ, 不成, neg. of *Nari.*

NARADZMONO, ナラズモノ, 無頼者, *n.* A good for nothing fellow.

NARAI,*-au,-atta*, ナラフ, 習, *t. v.* To study, to learn, to acquire skill. 倣, To imitate. *Nippon no kotoba wo —*, to study the Japanese language. *Fuye wo fuki-narau*, to learn to play on the flute. *Gaikoku no ifuku ni narōte koshirayeru*, made in imitation of foreign clothes.
Syn. MANABU.

NARAI, ナラヒ, 俗習, *n.* Custom, usage, fashion, manner, way, practice. *Yo no —*, custom of the times. Syn. FŪSOKU, NARAWASHI.

NARAI, ナライ, *n.* North-east wind.

†NARAKU, ナラク, 奈落, *n.* Infernum. (Bud.) Syn. JIGOKU.

†NARAME, ナラメ, Same as *Naran*.

†NARAN, ナラン, The future tense of *Nari*.

NARAN, ナラン, a coll. contr. of the neg. *Naranu*, also used by officials as an imper. Forbidding. *Tōru koto —*, you must not pass through.

NARA-NAI, ナラナイ, same as *Naranu*, the neg. of *Nari*. *Samukute naranai*, it is so cold I can't stand it. *Nakute nara-nai*, can't do without. *Itakute naranai*, it pains so that I cannot endure it.

NARASHI,*-sz,-sh'ta*, ナラス, 鳴, caust. of *Nari*. To cause to sound, to sound, to ring, to play on. *Kane wo —*, to ring a bell. *Taiko wo —*, to play the drum.

NARASHI,*-sz,-sh'ta*, ナラス, 平, *t.v.* To level, make even; to average. *Tszchi wo —*, to level the ground. *Narash'te h'totsz ga ikura ni ataru*, how much would they average?

NARASHI,*-sz,-sh'ta*, ナラス, 令熟, *t.v.* To train, drill, or exercise so as to be perfect in, or familiar with, to familiarize. *Hiyak'shō wo bugei ni —*, to familiarize the farmers with the art of war.

NARASHI, ナラシ, *n.* Training, drilling, or exercising so as to be familiar with. *Shibai no —*, training for the theatre.

†NARASHIME,*-ru,-ta*, ナラシメル, 令成, *t.v.* To cause to be, or become.

NARAU, ナラフ, 習, See *Narai*.

NARAWASE,*-ru,-ta*, ナラハセル, 令習, caust. of *Narai*. To cause to learn, order to be taught.

NARAWASHI, ナラハシ, 風俗, *n.* Custom, fashion, manner, practice, way.
Syn. FŪSOKU.

NARE,*-ru,-ta*, ナレル, 慣, *i.v.* To be accustomed to, used, habituated, familiar, inured to, well acquainted with. *Tochi ni —*, to be familiar with a place. *Tszkai-nareru*, familiar with the use of. *Mi-na-renu h'to*, a person one is not used to seeing.

NARE-AI, ナレアヒ, 馴合, *n.* Collusion, a secret agreement, or understanding for fraudulent purposes.

NAREBA, ナレバ, subj. mood of *Nari*. If it be, if he has.

†NAREBA-NARI, ナレバナリ, [always final]. It is because, because.

NARE-DOMO, ナレドモ, conj mood of *Nari*. Although it is.

†NAREGINU, ナレギヌ, 馴衣, *n.* Clothes which one is accustomed to from long use.

NARE-NARESHII,*-KI,-KU*, ナレナレシイ, 馴馴, Familiar, intimate, not formal or distant, free or easy in manner.

NARE-SOME,*-ru,-ta*, ナレソメル, 馴初, *i.v.* To commence, to be intimate, or acquainted.

NARI,*-ru,-tta*, ナル, 成, *i.v.* To be, become. *Midz ga kōri ni naru*, water becomes ice. *Samuku naru*, to become cold. *Atszku natta*, it has become hot. *Kome ga takaku natte tami ga komaru*, the people are distressed by the high price of rice.

NARI,*-ru,-tta*, ナル, 鳴, *i.v.* To sound, to make a noise, to ring. *Kane ga —*, the bell rings. *Mimi ga —*, the ears ring. *Kaze ga —*, the wind sounds.

NARI,*-ru,-tta*, ナル, 生, *i. v.* To form fruit, to grow, or appear as fruit. *Mi ga naru*, the fruit grows. *Uri no tszru ni wa naszbi wa naranu*, (prov.) the egg-plant does not grow on a melon-vine.

†NARI, ナリ, 也, A final word in writing, = coll. *da*, *de aru*, or *de gozarimas*. It is. Sometimes used only for elegance.

†NARI, ナリ, 癩病, *n.* Leprosy.
Syn. RAI-BIYŌ.

NARI, ナリ, 形, *n.* Form, figure, shape, manner, appearance, style, air.

NARI, ナリ, 鳴, *n.* Sound, noise. *— no yoi kane ja nai ka*, is not that a fine toned bell?

NARI-AGARI,*-ru,-tta*, ナリアガル, 成上, *i.v.* To rise in rank or fortune from a low grade.

NARI-AGARI,*-ru,-tta*, ナリアガル, 鳴上, *i.v.* To sound upwards. *Toki no koye ten ni —*.

NARI-DOYOMI,*-mu,-nda*, ナリドヨム, 鳴哄, *i.v.* To sound loud.

NARI-FURI, ナリフリ, 形振, *n.* Manner, deportment, appearance, mode of dress.
Syn. SZGATA, NARI.

NARI-GATAI,*-KI,-KU,-SHI*, ナリガタイ, 難成, Difficult to be, or to do, hard to obtain. *Kan-nin ga nari-gatai*, hard to be patient.

†NARI-HATE,-*ru*,-*ta*, ナリハテル, 成果, *i.v.* To end, finish, conclude one's course, to come to. *Nari-haten sama wo min to omō*, thought to see what condition they were come to.

†NARI-HATE, ナリハテ, 成果, *n.* The end of one's course, final condition of life.

NARI-HIBIKI,-*ku*,-*ita*, ナリヒビク, 鳴響, *i.v.* To resound, reverberate.

NARI-KAKARI,-*ru*,-*tta*, ナリカカル, 成掛, *i.v.* To begin to be, to commence. *Akaku nari-kakaru*, to begin to turn red. *Kuraku nari-kakaru*, to begin to be dark.

NARI-KATAÇHI, ナリカタチ, 容貌, *n.* The form, figure, shape, appearance.

NARI-KAWARI,-*ru*,-*tta*, ナリカハル, 成變, *i.v.* To change into, transform.

NARI-KUDARI,-*ru*,-*tta*, ナリクダル, 成下, *i.v.* To descend from a high to a low station in life, to fall to a low estate.

NARI-MONO, ナリモノ, 鳴物, *n.* Musical instruments, any thing used for producing sound.

NARI-MONO, ナリモノ, 生物, *n.* Fruit.

NARI-SAGARI,-*ru*,-*tta*, ナリサガル, 成下, *i.v.* Same as *Nari kudari*.

NARI-SŌ, ナリサウ, 成相, Appears as if it would be, seems as if. *ōkiku nari-sō na mono*, it looks as if it would become large. *Kayeri-taku — na mono*, he seems as if he would like to return.

NARI-TACHI, ナリタチ, 成立, *n.* Bringing up, education.
Syn. SODACHI.

NARI-TOMO, ナリトモ, subj. mood of *Nari*. Although, even if. *Shō-shō ne-age nasarete nari-tomo*, even if the price should have risen a little, &c.

NARI-WAI, ナリハヒ, 業, *n.* Employment, occupation, business; cultivating or tilling the earth. Syn. TOSEI, KAG'YŌ, SHŌBAI.

NARI-WATARI,-*ru*,-*tta*, ナリワタル, 鳴渡, *t.v.* To reverberate, or resound far and wide.

NARI-YUKI, ナリユキ, 成行, *n.* The series or train of events, history, circumstances.

NARŌ, ナラフ, Same as *Narau*.

NARŌ, ナラウ, Coll. for *Naru* *Narō koto nara kash'te kudasare*, if you can, lend it to me.

NARU, ナル, 成, See *Nari*

NARU-HODO, ナルホド, 成程, Exclam. used in expressing one's understanding, assent or approbation, = I understand, very true, indeed!

†NARU-KAMI, ナルカミ, 雷, *n.* Thunder.
Syn. KAMI-NARI, RAI.

NARU-KO, ナルコ, 鳴子, *n.* A kind of scare-crow.

NARURU, ナルル, 馴, See *Nare*.

NARU-TAKE, ナルタケ, 成丈, *adv.* As much as possible, as much, or as good as you can. — *hone otte kudasare*, do it as well as you can. — *yoi no ga hoshii*, I want one as good as possible. — *shimbō shi-nasare*, be as patient as you can.

NASAI, ナサイ, Yedo coll. for *Nasare*.

NASAKE, ナサケ, 情, *n.* Kindness, pity, humanity, benevolence, favor. — *no nai h'to*, an unkind person. — *wo kakeru*, to pity. — *nai*, cruel, unfeeling, unkind.
Syn. JŌ-AI, AWAREMI FUBIN.

NASARE,-*ru*,-*ta*, ナサレル, 被成, (Pass. of *Nashi*, used respectfully). To do. *Kono hon wa anatta no nasareta no de gozarimasz ka*, did you make this book? *O kaki nasare*, please write. *Kō nasare*, do it this way.

NASARI,-*ru*,-*tta*, ナサル, 被成, *t.v.* *Ano koto wa dō nasaru*, what are you going to do about that matter? *Nani wo* —, what are you doing? *Nani ni* —, what are you going to do with it?
Syn. SZRU, ITASZ, NASZ.

NASASHIME,-*ru*,-*ta*, ナサシメル, 令成, or

NASASHIMU, ナサシム, Caust of *Nasz*. To cause, order, make, or let do. *Yōi wo* — to order to get ready.

NASE, ナセ, Imp. of *Nashi*, do.

NASHI,-*sz*,-*sh'ta*, ナス, 爲, *t.v.* To do, to, make, to beget. *Aku wo* —, to do evil. *Zen wo* —, to do good. *Rei wo* —, to salute. *Kari wo nasz*, to return that which one has borrowed. *Ko wo* —, to beget a child. Syn. SZRU, ITASZ.

NASHI, ナシ, 無, *a.* See *Nai*.

NASHI, ナシ, 梨, *n.* A pear. — *no ki*, a pear tree.

NASHIJI, ナシヂ, 梨地, *n.* A kind of lacquer, having a pear colored ground sprinkled with gold leaf.

NASHI-KUDZSHI, ナシクヅシ, 濟崩, *n.* Paying by instalments. *Shak'kin wo — ni szru*, to pay off a debt by instalments.
Syn. HIGAKE, NEMPU.

NASSHO, ナツシヨ, 納所, *n.* The room in a monastery where all business is transacted.

NASZ, ナス, see *Nashi*.

NASZ, ナス, or NASZBI, ナスビ, 茄子, *n.* The egg-plant.

NASZRI,-*ru*,-*tta*, ナスル, 擦, *i. v.* To daub

smear, (fig) to lay the blame on others, to impute, or charge to others. *H'to no tszra ni doro wo naszru*, to daub a person's face with mud; (fig.) to bring shame or disgrace on others.
Syn. KURU.

NATA, ナタ, 鉈, *n.* A hatchet.

NATAMAME, ナタマメ, 刀豆, *n.* A kind of bean.

NA-TANE, ナタ子, 菜種, *n.* Rape-seed.

NATOKA, or NADOKA, ナトカ, (contr. of *Nani to ka*,) Why.

†NATOTE, or NADOTE, ナトテ, (cont. of *Nani to te*,) Why.

NATSZ, ナツ, 夏, *n.* Summer.

NATSZGE, ナツゲ, 夏毛, *n.* The brown hair of which pencils are made.

NATSZ-GI, ナツギ, 夏衣, *n.* Summer clothes.

NATSZGO, ナツゴ, 夏蠶, *n.* A kind of silk-worm that makes a cocoon twice a year.

NATSZKASHII,-KI, ナツカシイ, 懐敷, *a.* That which is absent and thought of with love, or longed after. *Oya ga natszkashii*, I long to see my parents. *Uchi ga natszkashii ka*, are you home sick?
Syn. KOISHII, SH'TAU, YUKASHII.

NATSZKASHIGARI,-*ru*,-*tta*, ナツカシガル, *i.v.* To long after, to think affectionately of something absent.

NATSZKASHIKU, or NATSZKASHIU, ナツカシク, *adv.* Affectionately thinking of, or longing after something absent. *O natszkashiu gozarimash'ta*, I have often thought of you, or I have longed to see you.

NATSZKE,-*ru*,-*ta*, ナツケル, 馴着, *t.v.* To tame, to make gentle or docile; to domesticate; to soften, mollify, to gain the friendship of a person. *Inu wo* —, to attach a dog to one's self.

NATSZKI,-*ku*,-*ita*, ナツク, 懐, *i.v.* To be friendly, to be fond of, or attached to; tame, domesticated. Syn. NAJIMU.

NATSZME, ナツメ, 棗, *n.* The date fruit.

NATSZMI,-*mu*,-*nda*, ナツム, see *Nadzmi.*

NATTŌ, ナツトウ, 納豆, *n.* A kind of food made of beans.

NATTOKU,-*szru*, ナツトク, 納得, To assent, to consent, to admit, approve, allow.
Syn. SHŌ-CHI SZRU, GATTEN SZRU.

NAU, ナフ, 綯, see *Nai.*

NA-UTE, ナウテ, Celebrated, famous, well-known. — *no szmōtori*, a famous wrestler.
Syn. NANIŌ, NADAI.

NAWA, ナハ, 繩, *n.* A rope, line. — *wo nau*, to make a rope. — *ni kakaru*, to be bound with a rope. — *ga kireru*, the rope is broken.

NAWA-BARI, ナハバリ, 繩張, *n.* Laying out, or measuring ground with a line.

NAWA-HASHIGO, ナハハシゴ, 繩梯子, *n.* A rope ladder.

NAWAME, ナハメ, 縲絏, *n.* Bonds. — *ni au*, to be bound, (as a criminal).

NAWASHIRO, ナハシロ, 苗代, *n.* A hotbed.

NAWATE, ナハテ, 畷, *n.* A road through rice-fields.

NAWA-TSZKI, ナハツキ, 繩付, *n.* A person in bonds, a criminal.

NAYA, ナヤ, 納屋, *n.* A store room.

†NAYAMASHI,-*sz*,-*sh'ta*, ナヤマス, 惱, *t.v.* To afflict, to trouble, distress, to persecute, harass. *Tami wo* —, to oppress the people. *Teki wo* —, to harass the enemy.
Syn. KURUSHIMERU.

†NAYAMASHII,-KI,-KU,-U,-SA, ナヤマシイ, 惱敷, Afflictive, distressing, bitter, painful.

NAYAMI,-*mu*,-*nda*, ナヤム 惱, *i.v.* To be distressed, afflicted, tormented, harassed, to suffer. Syn. KURUSHIMU.

NAYAMI, ナヤミ, 惱, *n.* Affliction, suffering, malady, pain.

NAYARAI, ナヤラヒ, 追儺, *n.* The ceremony of expelling evil spirits, or sickness.
Syn. TSZINA.

NAYASHI,-*sz*,-*sh'ta*, ナヤス, 痿, *t.v.* To make limber, pliant, or soft.

NAYE, ナヘ, 苗, *n.* The young shoots, or sprouts of any tree, grass, grain, or vegetable, especially of rice; spawn of fish.

†NAYE, ナヱ, 地震, *n.* same as *Nai.* Earthquake.

NAYE,-*ru*,-*ta*, ナエル, 痿, *i. v.* To be limber, pliant, soft, paralysed; dead, or deficient in power. *Te ga* —, the hand is paralyzed.

NAYE, ナエ, 陰痿, *n.* Impotence.

†NAYORAKA-NA, ナヨラカナ, Delicate in form, or graceful in motion.

NAYOSHI, ナヨシ, 鯔, *n.* A kind of fish, same as the *Bora.*

NAYURU, ナユル, 痿, see *Nayeru.*

NAZO, ナゾ, (contr. of *Nanzo*,) Why?

NAZO, ナゾ, 謎, *n.* A riddle, enigma. — *wo kakeru*, to propound a riddle. — *wo toku*, to interpret a riddle.

NAZORAYE,-*ru*,-*ta*, ナゾラヘル, 準, *t.v.* To do in imitation of, to use figuratively, to compare, liken, to illustrate, to give as an example, to learn. *Midz wo sake ni nazorayete nomu*, to drink water in imitation of wine. *Moku-zō wo oya ni nazorayete tszkayeru*, to serve a wooden image as if it were a parent. Syn. YOSOYERU. NISERU, JUNJIRU, KURABERU.

NAZOYE, ナゾヘ, Inclined, slanting, sloping, oblique. — *na michi*, an inclined road. — *ni sh'te ageru*, to raise it up in an inclined direction.

NE, 子, 根, *n.* The root. *Ki no ne*, root of a tree. *Ne-agari no matsz*, a pine some of the roots of which are above the ground. — *wo hotte kiku*, to search down to the root of a matter.

NE, 子, 直, *n.* Price, cost. — *wo tszkeru*, to fix the price. — *ga takai*, the price is high. — *ga yaszi*, the price is low. — *wo kīte miru*, to inquire the price.
Ryn. NEDAN, ATAI

NE, 子, 音, *n.* The sound, tone; noise. *Tori no ne*, singing of birds. Syn. OTO.

NE, 子, 子, (contr. of *Nedzmi, rat*). One of the twelve calender signs. *Ne no toki*, 12 o'clock at night. *Ne no hō*, the north.

NE, 子, 鏃, *n.* The head of an arrow. *Ya no* —, idem.

NE, 子, 嶺, *n.* The peak of a mountain. *Yama no takane*, idem. Syn. MINE.

NE, 子, An exclam. much used in the Yedo coll. difficult to define, as, *Sore kara ne. Watakushi ga ne. Sō shitara ne.*
(2.) It is also used as an imperative particle both in coll. and in books, as, *Iki ne*, = *iki nasare. Kiki ne*, = *kiki-nasare.*
(3.) Used in Yedo coll. for *nu, nai*, as, *Abune*, for *Abunai*, *Kikane*, for *Kikanu* or *Kikanai*, &c.

NE,*-ru,-ta*, 子ル,-寢, *i.v.* To sleep; to lie down, to go to bed. *Nete iru*, is sleeping, is lying down. (imp.) *Ne-yo*, go to bed. (neg.) *Nenu, nedz, nenai. Nete mitemo nemurare-masen*, he tried to sleep but could not. *Mo nemashō*, I will go to bed. *Nemash'ta*, has gone to bed. *Ne nai ka*, will you not go to bed? *Biyōki de nete iru*, confined to bed by sickness.
Syn. NEMURU.

NE-AGE, 子アゲ, 直上, *n.* Rise in price. — *wo szru*, to raise the price.

NE-ASE, 子アセ, 盗汗, *n.* Night-sweat. — *ga deru*, to have night-sweats.

NEBAI,-KI,-SHI, 子バイ, 粘, *a.* Sticky, adhesive, gluey, viscous, glutinous, tenacious, cohesive. *Nikawa ga* —, glue is sticky.

NEBAKU, 子バク, 粘, *adv.* idem. — *szru*, to make sticky. — *naru*, to become sticky. — *nai*, not sticky.

NEBA-NEBA, 子バ子バ, 粘粘, *adv.* Sticky, adhesive, tenacious, glutinous.

NEBARI,*-ru,-tta*, 子バル, 粘, *i.v.* To be sticky, adhesive, gummy, viscous, tenacious or cohesive.

NEBARI-KE, 子バリケ, 粘氣, *n.* Gummy, of an adhesive, glutinous, sticky, tenacious nature or quality.

NEBARI-TSZKI,*-ku,-ita*, 子バリツク, 粘著, *i.v.* To stick, to adhere, to cohere.

NEBASA, 子バサ, 粘, *n.* Adhesiveness, viscidity, tenacity, cohesiveness.

NEBASHI, 子バシ, 粘, *a.* See *Nebai.*

NEBA-TSZCHI, 子バツチ, 粘土, *n.* Sticky earth, clay.

NE-BIKI, 子ビキ, 直引, *n.* Reduction of price. — *wo szru*, to reduce the price.

NE-BIYE, 子ビエ, 寢冷, *n.* Catching cold in sleep.

NE-BŌ, 子バウ, 寢防, *n.* A sleepy head.

NEBŌ, 子バウ, 粘, Same as *Nebaku.*

NEBOKE,*-ru,-ta*, or NEBORE,*-ru,-ta*, 子ボケル, 寐惚, *i.v.* To be stupid or bewildered, as when suddenly roused from sleep, to walk in sleep.

NEBUKA, 子ブカ, 葱, *n.* A kind of garlic.

NEBURI,*-ru,-tta*, 子ブル, 眠, Same as *Nemuri.*

||NEBURI-*ru,-tta*, 子ブル, 舐, *t.v.* To lick, to taste, to apply the tongue to.
Syn. NAMERU.

NEBUTAI, 子ブタイ, See *Nemutai.*

NEBUTO, 子ブト, 癤, *n.* A boil.
Syn HAREMONO.

NEDA, 子ダ, 牘, *n.* The lower sill of a building on which the upright timbers rest.

NEDAN, 子ダン, 直段, *n.* Price, cost. — *wa ikura*, what is the price? — *ga takai*, the price is high. — *ga yaszi*, the price is low. Syn. NE, ATAI.

NEDARI,*-ru,-tta*, 子ダル, *t.v.* To extort, or wrest by threat or violence, (as money). To demand importunately, to tease by asking for. Syn. YUSZRU.

NE-DŌGU, 子ダウグ, 寢道具, *n.* Articles used in sleeping, as bedding and night clothes.

NEDOKO, 子ドコ, 臥床, *n.* A bedstead, a sleeping place.

||NEDOI, 子ドヒ, 敢問, Asking a person to repeat what he has said. — *wo sh'te kiku.*

NEDZ, 子ズ, 不寢, (Neg. of *Ne,-ru*). Not sleeping.

NEDZMI, 子ズミ, 鼠, *n.* A rat.

NEDZMI-IRO, 子ズミイロ, 鼠色, *n.* Mouse color, a lead color.

NEDZMI-KOROSHI, 子ズミコロシ, 鼠殺, *n.* Rats-bane.

NEDZMI-NAKI, ネズミナキ, 鼠鳴, *n.* The noise made with the lips, like the squeaking of a rat, as in calling a dog. — *wo szru.*

NEDZMI-OTOSHI, ネズミオトシ, 鼠機, *n.* A kind of rat trap.

NEDZMI-WANA, ネズミワナ, 鼠機, *n.* (idem).

NE-DZYOI,-KI,-KU,-SHI,-Ō, ネヅヨイ, 根強, Strongly rooted, firm, of good stamina, resolute, confident.

NEGAI,*-au* or*-ō,-atta* or*-ōta*, ネガフ, 願, *t.v.* To desire, to request, entreat, beseech, to pray for, supplicate, to petition. *Go-shō wo* —, to desire salvation. *O jihi wo* —, pray you to have mercy.
Syn. HOSSZRU, NOZOMU, KŌ.

NEGAI, ネガヒ, 願, *n.* Desire, request, entreaty, petition, prayer. *Isshō no* — *wa gakusha ni nari-tai*, I have all my life long desired to be a learned man. — *to sh'te mitazaru wa nashi*, every desire was gratified. Syn. NOZOMI.

NEGAI-SHO, ネガヒシヨ, 願書, *n.* A written petition.

NEGAWAKUBA, ネガハクバ, Conj. same as *Negau wa*, I desire that &c.

NEGAWANU,*-dz,-nai,-zaru*, ネガハヌ, 不願, Neg. of *Negai*, desire not.

NEGAWASHII,-KI, ネガハシイ, 願, *a.* Desirable, that which is prayed for.

NEGAWASHIKU, or NEGAWASHIU, ネカハシク, 願, *adv.* id.

NE-GAYERI, ネガヘリ, 寢反, *n.* Changing one's position in sleep. — *wo szru*, to turn in bed.

NEGI, ネギ, 葱, *n.* Onion.

NEGI, ネギ, 禰宜, *n.* A Sintoo priest.
Syn. KANNUSHI.

NEGIRAI,-Ō, ネギラフ, 犒, *t.v.* To salute and congratulate, or refresh another after some toilsome, difficult or dangerous work. *Chō to no tszkare wo negirai*, to refresh and congratulate one after the fatigue of a long journey.

NEGIRI,*-ru,-tta*, ネギル, 直切, *t.v.* To cheapen, to reduce the price. *Ne wo* —.

NEGŌ, ネガフ, See *Negai*.

NE-GOTO, ネゴト, 寢言, *n.* Talking in sleep. — *wo iu.*

NEGURA, ネグラ, 塒, *n.* A roost, perch.

NEHAN, ネハン, 涅槃, *n.* The death of *Shaka*, the state of absorption,—neither life nor death. — *ni iru*, to die. — *no zō*, pictures of the death of *Shaka*.

†NEI,*-szru*, ネイ, 佞, *(hetszrau)*. To flatter, to fawn.

†NEI-BEN, ネイベン, 佞辨, *(hetszrau kotoba)*. *n.* Flattery, adulation.

†NEI-JIN, ネイジン, 佞人, *n.* A flatterer, sycophant.

†NEI-KAN, ネイカン, 佞姦, Flattery. — *naru h'to.*

NE-IKI, ネイキ, 寐息, *n.* The breathing of one asleep. *Dorobō ga* — *wo ukagau*, a robber watches the breathing of one asleep.

NE-IRI,*-ru,-tta*, ネイル, 寐入, *i.v.* To sleep.

NE-IRIBANA, ネイリバナ, 寐入花, *n.* The time of deepest sleep.

NEIRO, ネイロ, 音色, *n.* The tone of voice, or of an instrument of music.

†NEI-SHA, ネイシヤ, 佞者, *n.* A flatterer, sycophant.

NEI-YU, ネイユ, 佞諛, *n.* Flattery.

NEJI, ネヂ, 螺釘, *n.* A screw.

NEJI,*-ru,-ta*, ネヂル, 捩, *t.v.* To screw, to twist, to wring, to contort, distort.

NEJI-AI,*-au,-atta*, ネヂアフ, 捩合, *i.v.* To wrestle together. Syn. KUMI-AU.

NEJI-AKE,*-ru,-ta*, ネヂアケル, 捩開, *t.v.* To open by twisting, or screwing.

NEJI-HANASHI,*-sz,-sh'ta*, ネヂハナス, 捩離, *t.v.* To separate by twisting, twist apart.

NEJIKE,*-ru,-ta*, ネヂケル, 佞, *i.v.* To be unprincipled, perverse.

NEJIKE-BITO, ネヂケビト, 佞人, *n.* An unprincipled, crooked, or perverse person.

NEJI-KIRI,*-ru,-tta*, ネヂキル, 捩切, *t.v.* To twist, or wring off.

NEJI-KOMI,*-mu,-nda*, ネヂコム, 捩込, *t.v.* To screw, or twist into.

NEJI-MAWASHI,*-sz,-sh'ta*, ネヂマハス, 捩廻, *t.v.* To screw, twist, or turn round.

NE-JIME, ネジメ, 根締, *n.* Planting firmly, making the earth about the roots compact.

NEJIRE,*-ru,-ta*, ネヂレル, 捩, *t.v.* To be twisted, warped, distorted, to be askew, contorted.

NE-JIRO, ネジロ, 根城, *n.* The principal castle.

NEJI-ORI,*-ru,-tta*, ネヂオル, 捩折, *t.v.* To break off by twisting.

NEJI-SHIBORI,*-ru,-tta*, ネヂシボル, 捩絞, *t.v.* To press out by twisting, to wring.

NEJI-TAOSHI,*-sz,-sh'ta*, ネヂタフス, 捩倒, *t.v.* To throw down in wrestling by a twisting motion.

NEKASHI,*-sz,-sh'ta*, ネカス, 令臥, *t.v.* To make, or let go to sleep, to lay down any thing standing, to let rest. *Kodomo wo* —, to put a child to sleep. *Tszye wo nekash'te oku,* to lay a cane down horizontally. *Kane wo nekash'te oku,* to let one's money lie not employing it in trade. *Pan wo nekash'te oku,* to set bread away to raise.

NEKKARA, 子ツカラ, *adv.* (with a neg. verb makes a strong negative), Not at all. — *mimasen,* I never see him. — *kimasen,* he never comes here. Syn. IKKŌ, SARA-NI.

†NEKKI, 子ツキ, 熱氣, *n.* Fever. Syn. NETSZ.

NEKO, 子コ, 猫, *n.* A cat.

NEKODA, 子コダ, *n.* A kind of coarse mat made of straw.

†NEKOMA, 子コマ, *n.* A cat.

NEKO-NADEGOYE, 子コナデゴヱ, 絮語, *n.* The coaxing sound made in fondling or talking to a cat, or in talking to children.

NE-KOROBI,-*bu*,-*nda*, 子コロブ, 寢轉, *i.v*, To lie down any where, to throw one's self down any where to sleep, as a person very much exhausted.

NEKOSOGE, 子コソゲ, *adv.* All, everything, (down to the very roots). — *totte shimatta,* took every thing.

NE-KUBI, 子クビ, 寢首, *n.* Cutting off the head of a person asleep. — *wo sasz,* to cut off, &c.

NE-MA, 子マ, 寢間, *n.* A chamber. Syn. NANDO.

NE-MAKI, 子マキ, 被, *n.* Night gown.

NE-MAROBU, 子マロブ, Same as *Nekorobu.*

NEMASHI, 子マシ, 直増, *n.* Raising the price. — *wo szru.*

NEMBAN, 子ンバン, 年番, *n.* A year's watch, doing duty for a year, at any one place. — *wo szru.*

NEMBARASHI, 子ンバラシ, 念晴, *n.* Driving away care, or unpleasant thoughts.

NEMBUTSZ, 子ンブツ, 念佛, *n.* Praying by repeating the words; *Namu amida butsz.* — *wo iu;* — *szru;* — *wo mōsz.*

NEME-MAWASHI,-*sz*,-*sh'ta*, 子メマハス, *i.v.* To look around fiercely.

NEME-TSZKE,-*ru*,-*ta*, 子メツケル, *t.v.* To look fiercely at, to glare at. Syn. NIRAMU.

†NEMPAI, 子ンパイ, 年輩, *n.* Age. *Onaji* — *no tomodachi,* companions of the same age. — *wa ikutsz gurai de gozarimasz,* how old are you? Syn. YOWAI, NENREI, TOSHIKORO.

NEMPU, 子ンプ, 年賦, Yearly instalments, annual payments. — *ni sh'te harau,* to pay by yearly instalments.

NEMUI,-KI,-SHI, 子ムイ, 睡, *a.* Sleepy, drowsy. Syn. NEMUTAI..

NEMUKU, 子ムク, 睡, *adv,* id. — *naru,* to become sleepy. — *nai,* not sleepy.

NEMUNOKI, 子ムノキ, 夜合花, *n.* The magnolia.

NEMURI,-*ru*,-*tta*, 子ムル, 眠, *i. v.* To sleep. *Nemutte iru,* to be asleep. *Mada nemuri-masen,* is not yet asleep, or not yet gone to bed. Syn. NE-IRU, NERU.

NEMURI, 子ムリ, 眠, *n.* Sleep. — *wo samasz,* to wake from sleep. — *wo moyōsz,* to become sleepy.

NEMUSA, 子ムサ, 眠, *n.* Sleepiness.

NEMUTAI,-KI,-SHI, 子ムタイ, 眠度, *a.* Sleepy, drowsy.

NEMUTAKU, or NEMUTŌ, 子ムタク, 眠度, *adv.* — *natta,* have become sleepy.

NEN, 子ン, 年, *(toshi). n.* Year. *Iku nen ato,* how many years ago? *Nan nen,* how many years?

NEN, 子ン, 念, *n,* Care, heed, notice, attention, regard. — *wo irete szru,* to do carefully. — *ni oyobanu,* no need of special care. — *wo harasz,* to drive away care. Syn. OMOI.

NENDAIKI, 子ンダイキ, 年代記, *n.* Chronology.

NENDZRU, 子ンズル, See *Nenji.*

†NENGA, 子ンガ, 年賀, *(toshi no iwai). n.* Compliments or congratulations at the beginning of a new year.

NEN-GEN, 子ンゲン, 年限, *(toshi no kagiri). n.* A term of years, limited number of years, an appointed year.

NEN-GIYŌ-JI, 子ンギヤウジ, 年行事, *n.* One year's term of public service.

NENGIYOKU, 子ンギヨク, 年玉, *(toshidama). n.* New year's gift. — *wo yaru,* to present a new year's gift.

NEN-GŌ, 子ンガウ, 年號, *n.* Name of the year, or epoch. — *wo aratameru,* to change the name of the year.

NENGORO, 子ンゴロ, 懇, Friendly, kind, courteous, polite, affable. — *na h'to,* a courteous person. — *ni k'yaku wo motenasz,* to treat a guest kindly. Syn. SHIN-SETSZ, INGIN, TEI-NEI.

NEN-GU, 子ング, 年貢, *n.* Tax on land paid to government. — *wo osameru,* to pay tax.

NEN-GW'AN, 子ングワン, 念願, *n.* Desire, wish. Syn. NEGAI, NOZOMI.

NENJI,-*ru* or-*dzru*,-*ta*, 子ンズル, 念, *t. v.* To repeat prayers, to pray. *Hotoke wo* —, to supplicate Buddha. Syn. INORU, OGAMU.

NEN-JŪ, 子ンヂウ, 年中, The whole year.

NEN-JU, 子ンジユ, 念珠, *n.* A rosary. Syn. JUDZ.

†NEN-JU, 子ンジユ, 念誦, *n.* Reciting the sacred books of the Buddhists. — *szru.*

NENKI, 子ンキ, 年季, *n.* The term of service of a servant. *Ichi* —, one year's service. *Jū* —, ten years service. — *ga nagai,* the term of service is long. A half year's service is called *hanki.* — *jō mon,* an indenture.

NEN-KI, 子ンキ, 年忌, *n.* The day celebrated in commemoration of the death of a relative, viz., on the 1st, 2nd, 3rd, 7th, 13th, 33rd, 50th, and 100th year after death.

NEN-KIRI, 子ンキリ, 年限, *n.* A limited number of years, term of years. Syn. NEN-GEN.

NEN-NAI, 子ンナイ, 年內, (*toshi no uchi*). *adv.* Within this year.

NENNE, 子ン子, 嬰兒, *n.* An infant, child. — *ga dekita,* have begotten a child.

NEN-NEN, 子ン子ン, 年年, (*toshi-doshi*). *adv.* Yearly, every year. Syn. MAI-NEN.

NEN-RAI, 子ンライ, 年來, Some years past, for many years past. — *no nozomi ga kanōta,* have obtained the desire of many years.

NEN-REI, 子ンレイ, 年齡, *n.* Age. — *shi-jū kurai na h'to,* a man about forty years old. Syn. NEMPAI, YOWAI.

NEN-REI, 子ンレイ, 年禮, *n.* The congratulations of the new-year. — *ni mawaru.* to go about wishing a happy new year. Syn. NENGA.

†NEN-REKI, 子ンレキ, 年歷, *n.* Years, number of years.

NENRIKI, 子ンリキ, 念力, (*omou chikara*). The power of attention, resolution, fixedness of purpose, determination. — *iwa wo mo tōsz,* determination will pierce even the rocks.

†NEN-RIYO, 子ンリヨ, 念慮, *n.* Thought, attention, careful consideration.

NEN-SHA, 子ンシヤ, 念者, *n.* A careful, thoughtful, provident person.

NEN-SHI, 子ンシ, 年始, (*toshi no hajime*). *n.* Beginning of the year.

†NENSHŌ, 子ンセウ, 年少, (*toshi waka*). *n.* A person young in years, youth.

NEN-SZU, 子ンスウ, 年數, (*toshi no kadz*). *n.* The number of years. — *wo heru,* to pass many years. *Yedo ni oru — wa ikura,* how many years have you lived in Yedo?

NEN-TO, 子ントウ, 年頭, (*toshi no hajime*). *n.* First of the year. — *no go shūgi wo mōshi-agemas,* I wish you the compliments of the season.

NEO, 子ヲ, 根緒, *n.* Round silken cord.

NE-OBIRE,-*ru*,-*ta*, 子オビレル, *i. v.* To wake from sleep bewildered. *Kodomo ga neobirete naku.* Syn. NEBOKERU.

NE-OKI, 子オキ, 寢起, *n.* Rising from sleep. — *ga osoi,* you are late in rising.

†NEPPŪ, 子ツプウ, 熱風, (*atszi kaze*). *n.* A hot wind.

NERAI,-*au*,-*atta*, 子ラフ, 覘, *t.v.* To aim at, to fix the eye on, to look steadily at, to watch, lie in wait for, to glare at. *Neko ga nedzmi wo nerau,* the cat watches the rat. *Teppō de tori wo* —, to aim a gun at a bird. *Hima wo* —, to watch one's opportunity.

NERAI, 子ラヒ, 覘, *n.* Aim. — *ga hadzreta,* missed his aim. — *wo sadameru,* to make sure the aim.

NERAI-YORI,-*ru*,-*tta*, 子ラヒヨル, 覘倚, *t.v.* To aim at, or watch anything and approach.

NERE,-*ru*,-*ta*, 子レル, 練, *i.v.* To be softened, well worked into proper consistence, tempered, trained. *Kō-yaku ga nereta,* the medical plaster is well worked.

NERE,-*ru*,-*ta*, 子ル, 練, *t.v.* To work into proper consistence, of softness or hardness, to temper, to harden, to train. *Pan wo* —, to knead bread. *Hei wo* —, to drill troops. *Tetsz wo* —, to temper iron.

NERI, 子リ, 練, *n.* A kind of white silk.

NERI,-*ru*,-*tta*, 子ル, 邌, *i.v.* To walk at a slow pace.

NERI-ARUKI,-*ku*,-*ita*, 子リアルク, 練步, *i.v.* To walk slowly

NERI-BEI, 子リベイ, 錬屏, *n.* A wall built of tiles and mortar.

NERI-KITAI,-*au*,-*tta*, 子リキタフ, 鍛錬, *t.v.* To harden, to temper, (as metals), Syn. TANREN.

NERI-MONO, 子リモノ, 練物, *n.* A car drawn at festivals, filled with dancers.

NERI-MONO, 子リモノ, 錬物, *n.* Ornaments made of wax, &c., in imitation of coral, or precious stones.

NERI-YAKU, 子リヤク, 煉藥, A medical paste, or conserve.

NERI-ZAKE, 子リザケ, 煉酒, *n.* A kind of white *sake.*

NERU, 子ル, 寢, See *Ne.*

NERU, 子ル, 練, See *Neri.*

NESARE,-*ru*,-*ta*, 子サセル, 令寢, *t.v.* To

make, or let go to sleep, or lie down. *Kodomo wo* —, to make a child lie down.

NE-SHIDZMARI,*–ru,–tta*, 子シヅマル, 寢沈, *i.v.* To sink into quiet sleep.

NE-SZGI,*–ru,–ta*, 子スギル, 寢過, *i.v.* To oversleep, sleep too long.

†NE-SZRIGOTO, 子スリゴト, 佞言, *n.* Flattery, or currying favor by traducing others. Syn. ZAN-GEN.

NETA, 子タ, pret. of *Neru.*

NETAMASHII,–KI, 子タマシイ, 妬, *a.* That of which one is envious, or jealous; hateful, odious.

NETAMASHIKU, or NETAMASHIU, 子タマシク, 妬, *adv.* Idem.

NETAMI,*–mu,–nda*, 子タム, 妬, *t. v.* To be jealous of, to envy, to hate. *Kami san wa mekake wo* —, the wife is jealous of the concubine. *H'to no fūki wo netamu koto nakare*, don't envy the rich. Syn. SONEMU.

NETAMI, 子タミ, 妬, *n.* Jealousy, envy. — *wa onno no tszne*, women are mostly jealous. *H'to no* — *wo ukeru*, to be envied by others. Syn. SHITTO, SONEMI.

NE-TARANU, 子タラヌ, 寢不足, Not sleep enough. *Mada* —, not yet slept enough.

NETE, 子テ, *pp.* of *Ne.*

NETOBOKE,*–ru,–ta*, 子トボケル, 寢惚, Same as *Neboke.*

NETSZ, 子ツ, 熱, *n.* Fever. — *ga deta*, has fever. — *ga demaszka*, have you any fever? — *no sashi-hiki*, the rise and fall of fever.

NETSZ-BIYŌ, 子ツビヤウ, 熱病, *n.* A fever, or febrile disease.

NE-TSZGI, 子ツギ, 根續, *n.* Splicing the decayed end of posts, especially those which serve to support a house.

NETSZI,–KI,–KU, 子ツイ, 涅, Slow, dull, stolid, prosy. *Kotoba ga* —, prosy in talking.

NETSZKE, 子ツケ, 根付, *n.* A kind of carved button, used for suspending the tobacco pouch to the belt.

NE-TSZKI,*–ku,–ita*, 子ツク, 寢著, *i.v.* To fall asleep.

NETSZ-SAMASHI, 子ツサマシ, 熱醒, *n.* A medicine that cures a fever, febrifuge.

†NETTŌ, 子ツタウ, 熱湯, *n.* Boiling-water.

NE-UCHI, 子ウチ, 直打, *n.* Setting the price, fixing the price. — *ga shirenu*, don't know the price. — *wo fumu*, to appraise. Syn. NE-DAN

NE-WASZRE-*ru,–ta*, 子ワスレル, 寢忘, *i. v.* To forget by oversleeping.

NEYA, 子ヤ, 閨, *n.* A chamber.

NEYASHI,*–sz,–sh'ta*, 子ヤス, 挻, *t. v.* To work or stir into proper consistence, to knead *Ishi-bai wo* —, to work lime, for plastering.

NE-YASZ, 子ヤス, 直安, Cheap.

NE-ZAME, 子ザメ, 寢覺, *n.* Awake. *O* — *ni nattaka*, is your master awake? *Tabitabi wo* — *szru*, to wake up often.

NE-ZAME,*–ru,–ta*, 子ザメル, 寢覺, *i.v.* To awake, to wake from sleep.

NE-ZASHI,*–sz,–sh'ta*, 子ザス, 根刺, *i.v.* To take root; fig. to originate.

NEZATOI,–KI,–KU, 子ザトイ, 寢聰, Easily waking from sleep, sleeping lightly. *Nezatoii h'to*, a light sleeper.

NEZERI, 子ゼリ, 根芹, *n.* A kind of celery.

NEZŌ, 子ザウ, 寢相, *n.* The way of sleeping, the position in sleep. — *ga warui*, his manner of sleeping is bad.

NI, ニ, *(f'tatsz).* Two. *Nido*, twice.

NI, ニ, 荷, *n.* Anything packed, or tied up, to be carried by man, horse, or ship; a package or bale of goods; baggage, luggage, a burden, load, cargo. — *wo katsgu*, or — *wo ninau*, to carry goods.

NI, ニ, *post-pos.* In, into, to, on, at, by. *Yedo ni oru*, to live in *Yedo*. *Umi ni aru mono* things in the sea. *Hako ni ireru*, to put into the box. *Ame no furu ni kita*, came in the rain. *Unjōsho ni yuku*, to go to the Custom house. *Ten ni mukau*, to look up to the sky. *Dai ni oku*, to place on the table. *Sake wo nomi ni kita*, came to drink wine. *Hanashi wo kiki ni ita*, has gone to hear what is said. *H'to ni iute wa warui*, you must not tell it to any one. *Gakumon ni wa gozarimasen*, as to learning he has none. *Nasake ni hodasareta*, constrained by kindness. *H'to no te ni shinuru*, to die by the hand of man.

(2.) Adverbial ending, as *Makoto-ni*, truly. *Szde ni*, already. *Daiji-ni*, carefully.

(3.) Conjunctive particle, in enumerating several things,= and. *Sake ni budō ni mikan ni sono hoka iro iro aru* ,there were wine, grapes and oranges beside many other things.

NI, *niru, nita*, ニル, 煮, *t. v.* To cook in boiling water, to boil. *Meshi wo niru*, to boil rice. *Imo wa nineba kuyemasen*, if potatoes are not boiled they cannot be eaten. Syn. TAKU.

NI, *niru, nita*, ニル, 似, *i. v.* To resemble, to be similar, alike. *Yoku nite oru*, they are very much alike. *Nita koto ga aru*, have some resemblance. *Kodomo ga haha ni nite iru*, the child resembles its mother.

NIAI,*-au,-tta*, ニアフ, 似合, *i.v.* To suit, to fit, to accord, adapt, to become. *Yoku niatta fūfu*, a husband and wife well suited to each other. *Ni-awanu*, not suited, not becoming.

NIBE, ニベ, 鰾, *n.* A fish's air bladder, isinglass.

†NI-BEN, ニベン, 二便, *n.* The two calls of nature. (urine and feces).

NI-BŪ, ニブウ, 鈍, same as *Nibuku.*

NIBUI,-KI, ニブイ, 鈍, *a.* Dull, blunt; stupid, sluggish, slow, inactive, awkward. *Katana ga nibui*, the sword is dull. Syn. DON.

NIBUKU, ニブク, 鈍, *adv.* idem.

NI-BUNE, ニブネ, 貨舩, *n.* A merchant ship.

NIBUSA, ニブサ, 鈍, *n.* Dullness.

NIBUSHI, ニブシ, 鈍, *a.* see *Nibui.*

NICHI, ニチ, 日, *n.* Day. *Iku nichi*, how many days? Syn. HI.

NICHI-GEN, ニチゲン, 日限, *n.* A fixed, or set day, a limited number of days. — *wo sadameru*, to set a day. Syn. HIGIRI.

NICHI-NICHI, ニチニチ, 日日, *adv.* Daily, every day.
Syn. HIBI.

NICHI-RIN, ニチリン, 日輪, *n.* The sun. — *no hikari*, light of the sun. — *wo ogamu*, to worship the sun. Syn. HI, HINO-KAMI.

NICHI-YA, ニチヤ, 日夜, *n.* Day and night. Syn. HIRU-YORU.

NICHI-YŌ, ニチヨウ, 日用, *n.* Daily, or constant use. — *no kotoba*, language in daily use.

NIDŌ, ニダウ, 二道, The two sciences, which a soldier should know, viz. Literature and military.

NIDO, ニド, 二度, *adv.* Twice.
Syn. F'TA-TABI.

NI-DZKURI, ニヅクリ, 荷作, *n.* Making up into bales, or packages, for transportation. — *wo szru*, to make &c.

NIGAI,-KI, ニガイ, 苦, *a.* Bitter, (fig.) severe, sarcastic. *Ajiwai ga nigai*, the taste is bitter. *Nigai kotoba*, sarcastic language.

NIGAKU, ニガク, 苦, *adv.* idem.

†NIGAMI,*-mu,-nda*, ニガム, 苦, *i. v*, To have an angry look.

NIGAMI, ニガミ, 苦味, *n.* Somewhat bitter in taste, bitterishness. *Kono mikan wa — ga aru*, this orange has a slightly bitter taste.

NIGA-NIGASHII,-KI, ニガニガシイ, 苦苦, *a.* Disagreeable, painful to one's feelings, distasteful, provoking, bitter.

NIGA-NIGASHIKU, ニガニガシク, *adv.* id.

NIGAO, ニガホ, 似顔, *n.* A likeness, portrait. — *wo kaku*, to draw a likeness. *Ya-k'sha no* —, the portrait of an actor.

NIGARI,*-ru,-tta*, ニガル, 苦, *i. v.* To feel bitterly, to be provoked, or angry. *Nigarikitte mono wo iu*, to speak sarcastically or with anger.

NIGARI, ニガリ, *n.* The brine formed by the deliquescence of salt

NIGASA, ニガサ, 苦, *n.* Bitterness.

NIGASHI, ニガシ, 苦, *a.* Bitter, see *Nigai.*

NIGASHI,*-sz,-sh'ta*, ニガス, 令逃, caust of *Nigeru.* To make, or let escape.

NIGA-WARAI, ニガワラヒ, 冷笑, *n.* A sardonic laugh.

NIGE,*-ru,-ta*, ニゲル, 逃, *i. v.* To run away, to flee away, to escape. *Dorobō ga nigeta*, the thief has escaped. *Gunzei wa makete nigeru*, the army broke and fled. Syn. CHIKUTEN, SHUPPON.

NIGE-CHIRI,*-ru,-tta*, ニゲチル, 逃散, *i. v.* To flee and scatter. *Gunzei ga hōbō ye* —, the army scattered and fled in all directions.

NIGE-HASHIRI,*-ru,-tta*, ニゲハシル, 逃走, *i.v.* To run away, escape by running.

NIGE-KAKURE,*-ru,-ta*, ニゲカクレル, 逃隱, *i. v.* To escape and conceal one's self.

NIGENAI,-KI, ニゲナイ, 無似氣, *a.* Unlike, not appearing to be like. *Onago ni nigenaki k'wai riki*, a wonderful strength unlike that of a woman.

NIGENAKU, ニゲナク, 無似氣, *adv.* Idem.

NIGI-NIGISHII,-KI, ニギニギシイ, 賑賑, *a.* Bustling, thronged, crowded and lively.

NIGINIGISHIKU, ニギニギシク, *adv.* Idem.

NIGIRI,*-ru,-tta*, ニギル, 握, *t.v.* To grasp or hold in the hand, to clutch, clinch, to gripe. *Ten ga wo tanagokoro ni nigiru*, to seize the government of the whole empire. *Kane wo nigittara mo hanashimasen*, when he gets hold of money he does not let go of it. Syn. TSZKAMAYERU.

NIGIRI, ニギリ, 握, *n.* The place where the hand grasps the bow.

NIGIRI-KOBUSHI, ニキリコブシ, 握拳, *n.* The fist.

NIGIRI-MESHI, ニギリメシ, 握飯, *n.* Cold rice eaten by making it into a ball.

NIGIRI-SHIME,*-ru,-ta*, ニギリシメル, 握緊,

t.v. To squeeze tight in the hand, to grasp tightly.

NIGIRU, ニギル, 握, See *Nigiri.*

†NIGITE, ニギテ, *n.* The cut paper hung up before the *Kami*. Syn. GO-HEI.

NIGIWAI,*-au,-tta*, ニギハフ, 賑, *i.v.* To be crowded and busy, bustling, thronged and lively. *Matszri de machi ga* —, the street is thronged because of a festival.

NIGIWASHII,-KI, ニギハシイ, 賑, *a.* Bustling, thronged and lively, crowded with busy people.

NIGIWASHIKU, ニギハシク, 賑, *adv.* idem. *Yokohama ga — natta*, Yokohama has become a very bustling place.

NIGIWASHISA, ニギハシサ, 賑, *n.* Bustle, stir.

NIGIWASHI,*-sz,-sh'ta*, ニギハス, 賑, *t. v.* To make busy, active, or lively. To relieve the sufferings of the people by giving supplies. *Tami wo* —, idem.

NIGIYAKA, ニギヤカ, 賑, Bustling, lively, active, thronged with busy people. — *na tokoro*, a bustling place. — *ni naru*, to become bustling.

NIGŌ, ニガウ, 苦, *adv.* Bitter.

†NIGOKE, ニゴケ, 毳, *n.* The soft short hair of the body.

NIGON, ニゴン, 二言, *n.* Contradicting, or denying what one has said or promised previously, breaking or retracting one's word. *Bushi ni — wa nai*, a soldier never breaks his word. — *wo iu*, to contradict one's self. — *wo tszkau*, idem.

NIGORI,*-ru,-tta*, ニゴル, 濁, *i.v.* To be muddy, turbid, not clean, impure. *Midz ga nigoru*, the water is turbid. *Nigoru koye*, the impure, or soft sound of a consonant, as the impure sound of *ha* is *ba*, of *sa* is *za* &c.

NIGORI, ニゴリ, 濁, *n.* Turbid, impure. *Kono sake wa ga — aru*, this *sake* is turbid.

NIGOSHI,*-sz,-sh'ta*, ニゴス, 令濁, caust. of *Nigoru*. To make turbid, to muddy. *Midz wo* —, to muddy the water. *Sagi wa tatte mo ato wo nigosadz.* (prov).

NI-GURA, ニグラ, 荷鞍, *n.* A pack-saddle.

NIGUROME, ニグロメ, 烏銅, *n.* Bronzed copper.

NIGURU, ニグル, Same as *Nigeru.*

†NII, ニヒ, 新, (*atarashi.*) (only used in compound words). New, as, *Nimakura*, a new pillow.

NIJI, ニヂ, 虹, *n.* A rainbow. — *ga deru*, there is a rainbow. — *ga tatsz*, (idem). — *ga kiyeru*, the rainbow has disappeared.

NIJIKI, ニキジ, 二食, *n.* Two meals a day.

NIJIMI,*-mu,-nda*, ニジム, *i.v.* To spread (as a blot of thin ink, or oil). *Abura ga* —, the oil spreads.

NIJIRI,*-ru,-tta*, ニジル, 躙, *i.v.* To shove one's self along on the buttocks, to wriggle. *Soba ye nigiri-yoru.*

NIJIRI-GAKI, ニジリガキ, *n.* Uneven, awkward hand-writing.

NI-JŪ, ニジフ, 二十, *a.* Twenty. — *ichi*, twenty one.

NIJŪ, ニヂウ, 二重, Twice, over again. — *ni kaku*, to write over again. *Koto — ni naru*, the business had all to be gone over again. Syn. F'TA-YE.

NIKAI, ニカイ, 二階, *n.* Second story of a house. — *ni agaru.*

NIKATA, ニカタ, 煮方, *n.* A cook.

NIKAWA, ニカハ, 膠, *n.* Glue. — *de tszkeru*, to join together with glue.

NIKAWADZKE, ニカハヅケ, 膠付, *n.* Gluing together. — *wo szru*, to glue together.

NIKAWA-NABE, ニカハナベ, 膠鍋, *n.* A glue-pot.

NIKI, ニキ, 二氣, *n.* The two principles, or powers of nature, viz, male and female. Syn. IN-YŌ.

NIKI, ニキ, 二季, *n.* The two periods of time, viz, last day of 6th and 12th months. — *no harai*, payments of money at these periods.

NIKIBI, ニキビ, 面胞, *n.* Pimples on the face, acne.

NIKKEI, ニクケイ, 肉桂, *n.* Cinnamon,

NIKKI, ニツキ, 日記, *n.* A diary, journal.

NIKKIN, ニツキン, 日勤, (*hidztome*). *n.* Daily service, or official duty.

NIKKO-TO-WARAI,*-au,-tta*, ニツコトワラフ, 莞爾, *i.v.* To smile.

†NIKK'WA, ニツクワ, 日課, *n.* Daily work, daily task.

NI-KOMI,*-mu,-nda*, ニコム, 煮込, *t.v.* To boil into, to boil and incorporate one thing with another. *Shiwo wo niku ni* —, to incorporate salt with flesh by boiling.

NIKO-NIKO-TO, ニコニコト, 莞爾, *adv.* Smilingly, pleasantly. — *warau*, to smile.

NI-KOROSHI,*-sz,-sh'ta*, ニコロス, 煮殺, *t.v.* To boil to death, to kill by putting into boiling water.

NIKOYAKA, ニコヤカ, 堆笑, *a.* Smiling, pleasant, cheerful, merry. — *na kao*, a smiling face.

NIKŪ, ニクウ, 悪, *adv.* Same as *Nikuku.*

NIKU, ニク, 肉, *n.* Flesh, meat. The coloring stuff used for sealing, or stamping. *Ushi no* —, beef. *Buta no* —, pork. Syn. MI.

NIKUDZKU, ニクヅク, 肉荳蔻, *n.* Nutmeg.

NIKUI,-KI, ニクイ, 悪, *a.* Hateful, odious, detestable, abominable. Affixed to the root of verbs it means, hard, difficult. *Nikui-yatsz*, a detestable fellow. *Yomi-nikui*, hard to read. *Kiki-nikui*, difficult or disagreeable to hear.

NIKU-IRO, ニクイロ, 肉色, *n.* Flesh-color.

NIKU-JIKI, ニクジキ, 肉食, *n.* Flesh-eater, carniverous.

NIKUKU, ニクク, 悪, *adv.* Hateful, odious, detestable, see *Nikui.*

NIKUMI,-*mu*,-*nda*, ニクム, 憎, *t. v.* To hate, dislike, detest, abominate. *Sono tszmi wo nikude h'to wo nikumadz*, to hate the sin but not the man.
Syn. URAMU.

NIKUMI, ニクミ, 憎, *n.* Hatred, dislike.

NIKU-NIKUSHII,-KI,-KU, ニクニクシイ, 可悪, *a.* Hateful, odious, abominable.

NIKURASHII,-KI,-KU,-Ū, ニクラシイ, Having a somewhat hateful, or odious appearance.

†NIKU-RIU, ニクリウ, 肉瘤, *n.* A fleshy tumor. Syn. KOBU.

NIKU-SŌ-NA, ニクサウナ, *a.* Same as *Nikurashii.*

NIKU-TEI, ニクテイ, 悪體, *n.* A hateful or disgusting appearance, or form.

NIM-BA, ニンバ, 人馬, (*h'to to ma*). *n.* Man and horse.

NIMBEN, ニンベン, 人偏, (*h'to ji hen.*) *n.* The radical for man (イ) written on the left side of a character.

NIMBETSZ, ニンベツ, 人別, *n.* Registered as a citizen, or registry of citizenship, census. *Doko no — de gozarimas*, where are you registered as a citizen? *Yedo no — ni naru*, to be registered as a citizen of Yedo. — *wo aratameru*, to examine and correct the census, (of any place).

NIMBETSZ-CHŌ, ニンベツチヤウ, 戸籍, *n.* The book in which the names of citizens are registered, census-roll.

NIMBU, ニンブ, 人夫, *n* Farmers called out for any public service.

†NIM-MEN, ニンメン, 人面, (*h'to no kao*). *n.* Man's face. —*jū shin*, human face and a beast's heart.

NI-MOCHI, ニモチ, 荷持, *n.* A coolie who carries one's luggage in travelling.

NIMOTSZ, ニモツ, 荷物, *n.* Baggage, luggage, goods in packages.

†NIMPININ, ニンピニン, 人非人, (*h'to ni sh'te h'to ni aradz*). A man in appearance but not in heart, a beast of a man.

NIN, ニン, 人, (*h'to*). *n.* Man, person. *Iku nin*, how many persons? *Jū nin*, ten men. *Nin wo mite hō wo toku*, to adapt the preaching to the hearer, (prov.)

‖NIN, ニン, 任, *n.* Trust, office, duty. *Waga — ni aradz*, it is not my duty.

†NIN, ニン, 仁, *n.* The kernel of a peach-stone, plumstone, &c. Syn. SANE.

NINA, ニナ, 蜷, *n.* Same as *Mina*, the name of an insect.

NINAI,-*au*,-*tta*, ニナフ, 擔, *t.v.* To carry with a pole across the shoulder. *Ni ka no nimotsz wo ikka ni awasete ninau*, to carry at one load the loads of two men.
Syn. KATZSGU.

NINAI, ニナヒ, 擔桶, *n.* A bucket for carrying water.

NINAI-BŌ, ニナヒボウ, 棬, *n.* A pole used for carrying burdens across the shoulder.

NINAWASE,-*ru*,-*ta*, ニナハセル, 令擔, caust. of *Ninau.* To cause, or let another carry a load.

NINDŌ, ニンドウ, 忍冬, *n.* The honey-suckle, the Lonicera japonica.

NINDZU, ニンズウ, 人數, (*h'to no kadz*). *n.* The number of persons, population, census. *Gunzei no — wa iku nin*, what is the number of men in the army? *Yedo no — wa dono kurai aru*, what is the population of Yedo? Syn. NIMBETSZ.

NINDZRU, ニンズル, 任, See *Ninji.*

†NIN-GARA, ニンガラ, 人柄, (seldom used). Same as *H'togara.*

NIN-GEN, ニンゲン, 人間, *n.* Mankind, man, a human being, the world. Syn. H'TO.

NIN-GIYŌ, ニンギヤウ, 人形, (*h'to no katachi*). *n.* A statue of a man, a doll, a puppet.

NIN-G'YO, ニンギヨ, 人魚, *n.* A mermaid.

NINJI,-*ru* or -*dzru*,-*ta*, ニンズル, 任, *t.v.* To appoint to, or invest with an office. (coll). To commit or leave to the will of another, to confide to. *Dainagon ni nindzru*. to invest with the office of *Dainagon*. *Watakushi ni ninjite oki-nasare* leave it to me.
Syn. MŌSHI-TSZKERU.

NINJIN, ニンジン, 人參, *n.* Ginseng.

NIN-JIN, ニンジン, 胡蘿蔔, *n.* The carrot

NINJŌ, ニンジヤウ, 人情, (*h'to no kokoro*). *n.* The heart. feelings, or affections common to man, humanity, kindness. — *wo shiranu h'to.* Syn. NASAKE.

NIN-JŌ, ニンジヤウ, 刃傷, *n.* Fighting,

or cutting with a sword (in a private quarrel), a duel. — *ni oyobu*, to end in a sword-fight.

NIN-JU, ニンジユ, 人數, Same as *Nindz*.

NIN-K'WAN, ニンクワン, 任官, Investing with office, or title. — *szru*.

NIN-NIKU, ニンニク, 大蒜, *n.* Garlic.

NINŌ, ニナフ, See *Ninai*.

NI-NO-ASHI-WO-FUMU, ニノアシヲフム, To take two steps backwards, to hesitate, to pause in doubt. Syn, TAMERAU.

NI-NOMARU, ニノマル, 二之丸, *n.* The second or inner castle.

NIN-SHIN, ニンシン, 妊娠, *n.* Pregnant, with child. Syn. HARAMU, K'WAI-NIN.

NIN-SŌ, ニンサウ, 人相, *n.* The physiognomy. — *ga yoi*. — *ya warui*.

NINSŌJA, ニンサウジヤ, 人相者, *n.* A physiognomist.

NIN-SOKU, ニンソク, 人足, *n.* A coolie. Syn. KARUKO.

NIN-TAI, ニンタイ, 人體, *(h'to no karada)*. *n.* Human body.

NI-NUSHI, ニヌシ, 荷主, *n.* The owner of goods, or luggage.

†NIN-YŌ, ニンヨウ, 妊孕, Pregnant. Syn. K'WAI-NIN.

NIO, ニホ, 鸊鷉, *n.* The widgeon. Syn. KAITSZBURI.

NIŌ, ニホフ, See *Nioi*.

NIOI,-*ō*-*ōta*, ニホフ, 香, *i.v.* To emit an odor, to smell. *Hana go niō*, the flower is fragrant, Syn. KAORU.

NIOI, ニホヒ, 香, *n.* An odor, scent, smell, fragrance, an exhalation. *Nioi no yoi hana*, a fragrant flower. *Haka kara — ga tatsz*, an exhalation rises from the grave.

NIOI-BUKURO, ニホヒブクロ, 香囊, *n.* A scent-bag.

NIOI-WATARI,-*ru*,-*tta*, ニホヒワタル, 香渡, *i.v.* To spread all about, as an odor.

†NIOYAKA, ニホヤカ, 芬芳, New and fresh in color, bright. — *na iro*.

NIPPON, ニツポン, 日本, *n.* Japan.

NIRA, ニラ, 韮, *n.* Kind of garlic.

NIRAMI,-*mu*,-*nda*, ニラム, 白眼, *t.v.* To look fiercely at, to glare at.

NIRAMI-AI,-*au*,-*atta*, ニラミアフ, *i.v.* To look fiercely at each other.

NIRAMI-TSZKE,-*ru*,-*ta*, ニラミツケル, *t.v.* To look fiercely at.

NIRAMI-TSZME,-*ru*,-*ta*, ニラミツメル, *t.v.* To look at fiercely for some time.

NIRE, ニレ, 楡, *n.* The name of a small tree, Microptelea parviflora.

NIRU, ニル, 煮, See *Ni*.

NIRU, ニル, 似, See *Ni*.

NISAMASHI,-*sz*,-*sh'ta*, ニサマス, 煎冷, *t v.* To set aside to cool after boiling.

NĪSAN, ニイサン, 兄様, *n.* Elder brother, same as *Anisan*.

NISE,-*ru*,-*ta*, ニセル, 倣, *t.v.* To counterfeit, to forge, to imitate, falsify. *Kane wo* —, to counterfeit money. *H'to no te wo* —, to imitate a person's handwriting.

NISE-GANE, ニセガネ, 假金, *n.* Counterfeit money.

NISE-KICHIGAI, ニセキチガヒ, 佯狂, *n.* Feigned madness.

NISE-MONO, ニセモノ, 贋物, *n.* A counterfeit, imitation, not genuine.

NISHI, ニシ, 西, *n.* The west.

NISHI, ニシ, 螺, *n.* The name of a shell of the Buccinida genus.

NISHIKI, ニシキ, 錦, *n.* A kind of silk, rich and woven in flowers, brocade.

NISHIKIGAI, ニシキガヒ, 錦貝, *n* A kind of cowry.

NISHIKIGI, ニシキギ, *n.* The name of a tree, the same as *Mayumi*.

NISHIME, ニシメ, 烹染, *n.* A kind of food, made by boiling together various kinds of vegetables.

†NI-SHIN, ニシン, 二親, *n.* Parents. Syn. FUTA-OYA.

NISHIN, ニシン, 鯡, *n.* A kind of fish.

NISHU, ニシユ, 二朱, *n.* Half an ichibu.

NISŌBAI, ニサウバイ, 二相倍, *adv.* Twice as much. *Nedan ga — ni natta*, the price has become twice as high.

NISSAN, ニツサン, 日參, *(mai nichi mairu)*, *n.* Daily worshiping at the temples. — *szru*.

NISSHOKU, ニツショク, 日蝕, *n.* Eclipse of the sun.

NITA, ニタ, pret. of *Niru*, see *Ni*.

NITARI,-*ru*, ニタル, 似, (cont. of *Nitearu*). To be like, resemble, similar. *Nitaru mono*, a similar thing.

NITCHIU, ニツチウ, 日中, *n.* Middle of the day, meridian.

NITE, ニテ, *post-posit.* With, by, (as cause, instrument, or means), in; = being, as it is, since it is. *Te — butsz*, to strike with the hand. *Kama — yu wo wakasz*, to boil water in a pot. *Yedo — katta*, bought in Yedo. *Fune — Yedo ye yuku*, to go to Yedo by ship. *H'tori nite yomu*, to read by one's self. *Kago — yuku*, to go in a sedan-chair. *Kodomo — waszreta*, being a child he forgot. *Dokuna mono nite taberaremasen*, as it is poisonous it is not eatable. Syn. DE.

NITEMO, ニ テ モ, Same as *Demo*. Ever, so ever. *Doko* —, where-ever. *Dare* —, who-soever.

NI-TSZME,*-ru,-ta*, ニツメル, 煎 詰, *t. v.* To boil down, to thicken by boiling. *Umi no midz wo nitszmete shiwo wo toru*, to make salt by boiling down sea water.

NIU, ニフ, 入, *(iru)*. To enter, (used only in comp. words).

NIU, (coll.) ニウ, *n.* A crack, (or rather) the appearance of a crack, in porcelain, or ivory. — *ga dekita*, it is cracked,

NIU-BAI, ニフバイ, 入 梅, *n.* The rainy season (in the 5th month).

NIUBIK'WAN, ニウビクワン, 乳 糜 管, *n.* The thoracic duct.

NIU-BŌ, ニウボウ, 乳 棒, *n.* A pestle.

†NIU-BU, ニフブ, 入 部, *n.* Entering one's domain, (of a Daimiyo).

NIU-BUTSZ, ニフブツ, 入 佛, *n.* Placing an idol in a temple. Syn. ANCHI.

NIU-DŌ, ニフダウ, 入 道, *(michi ni iru)*. To forsake the world and enter upon a religious life, signified by shaving the head; this word was used anciently as a title.

†NIU-FU, ニフフ, 入 夫, *(iri muko)*. *n.* A son in law.

NIUHACHI, ニウハチ, 乳 鉢, *n.* A mortar for pulverizing medicines.

NIU-GAKU, ニフガク, 入 學, *n.* Entering school.

NIU-JAKU, ニウジヤク, 柔 弱, Weak, feeble, delicate in constitution. — *no h'to*. Syn. YOWAI.

NIU-JŌ, ニフジヤウ, 入 城, *(shiro no iru)*, *n.* Entering a castle.

†NIU-JŌ, ニフヂヤウ ,入 定, Burying one's self alive, as a religionist.

NIUKŌ, ニウカウ, 乳 香, *n.* Olibanum.

NIU-KŌ, ニフコウ, 入 港, *(minato ni iru)*. Entering a port. — *szru*.

NIU-KOKU, ニフコク, 入 國, *(kuni ni iru)*, *n.* Entering one's state, or country.

†NIU-METSZ, ニフメツ, 入 滅, To die, (only used of Shaka.

NIU-MON, ニフモン, 入 門, Becoming a pupil, or disciple. Syn. DESHI-IRI.

NI-URI-MISE, ニウリミセ, 烹 賣 店, *n.* A small refectory, or eating house.

NIU-SATSZ, ニフサツ, 入 札, *(ire-fuda)*, *n.* Buying at auction, or handing in a bid, (by writing the bids on a card, and handing them in), a ballot. — *szru*.

NIU-SEN, ニフセン, 入 舩, *(irifune)*, *n.* Coming into port.

†NIU-SHU, ニフシユ, 入 手, *(te ni iru)*. To come to hand, to be received. *On nimotsz tash'kani — itashi soro*, your goods have come to hand.

NIU-TŌ, ニフタウ, 入 湯, *(yu ni iru)*. Taking a hot bath. — *sh'te kuru*.

NIU-TSZ, ニフツ, 入 津, *(minato ni iru)*, *n.* Entering a harbor, coming into port. Syn. NIUKŌ.

NIU-WA, ニウワ, 柔 和, Amiable, gentle, meek, not easily provoked. — *na h'to*.

NIU-YŌ, ニフヨウ, 入 用, *n.* Expense, outlay, expenditure, cost. Syn. ZAPPI, IRI-YŌ.

NIU-YŌ, ニウヨウ, 乳 癰, *n.* Cancer of the breast.

NIWA, ニハ, 庭, *n.* A flower garden, a yard, a court-yard, compound.

NIWABI, ニハビ, 燎, *n.* The fire kindled in front of a house after a corpse has been taken out, after a bride has left, or to give light for night-theatricals in the Mikado s compound.

NIWAKA, ニハカ, 俄, Sudden, unexpected. — *omoi-tachi*, sudden determination. — *ame*, a sudden shower. — *jini*, a sudden death. — *kaze*, a sudden blow. Syn. TACHI-MACHI, KIU, F'TO.

NIWAKA, ニハカ, 俄, *n.* A buffoon, clown.

NIWAKA-NI, ニハカニ, 俄, *adv.* Suddenly, unexpectedly.

†NIWATADZMI, ニハタヅミ, 潦, *n.* A puddle of water.

NIWATATAKI, ニハタタキ, 鶺 鴒, *n.* The wagtail. Syn. SEKI-REI.

NIWATOKO, ニハトコ, 接 骨 木, *n.* The Sambucus ebuloides.

NIWATORI, ニハトリ, 鶏, *n.* The domestic fowl, chicken.

NIWA-TSZKURI, ニハツクリ, 庭 作, *n.* A gardener.

NIYAKE,*-ru,-ta*, ニヤケル, *i.v.* To be effeminate, womanish in manners, or appearance.

NIYĀ-NIYĀ, ニヤアニヤア, *adv.* The mewing of a cat.

NIYAWASHII,-KI,-KU, ニヤハシイ, 似 合 敷, Alike, resembling, similar.

NIYAWANU, ニヤワヌ, 不似合, See *Niai*.

NIYE,*-ru,-ta*, ニエル, 煎, *i. v.* Boiled, cooked by boiling.

NIYE, ニヘ, 贄, *n.* Offerings made to the Kami, or Tenshi.

NIYE-KAYE,*-ru,-tta*, ニエカヘル, 沸 却, *i.v.* To boil fiercely.

NIYE-KOBORE,*-ru,-ta*, ニエコボレル, 沸 溢, *i.v.* To boil over.

NIYE-TAGIRI,*-ru,-tta*, ニエタギル, 沸激, *i.v.* To boil.

NIYE-TACHI,*-tsz,-tta*, ニエタツ, 沸立, *i.v.* To bubble and boil. Syn. TAGIRU.

†N'YO, ニヨ, 女, *(onna). n.* A woman, female. *Nan-n'yo*, male and female.

N'YŌBŌ, ニヨウバウ, 女房, *n.* Wife. Syn. TSZMA, NAIGI, KANAI, KAMI-SAN.

N'YŌ-GO, ニヨウゴ, 女御, *n.* A concubine of the Tenshi.

N'YŌ-HACHI, ニヤウハチ, 鐃鉢, *n.* Cymbals, (used in Bud. temples).

N'YOI, ニヨイ, 如意, *n.* A kind of baton carried by priests.

N'YOKI-N'YOKI-TO, ニヨキニヨキト, *adv.* Undulating, rising and falling, (as the outlines of mountains, or as the motion of waves).

N'YOKO-N'YOKO-TO, ニヨコニヨコト, *adv.* idem.

N'YOKKORI, ニヨツコリ, *adv.* The appearance of a single mountain standing alone.

†N'YO-NIN, ニヨニン, 女人, *n.* A female, woman.

N'YO-RAI, ニヨライ, 如來, *n.* The title of the highest Buddhist divinities, of Amida, Shaka, &c.

N'YORO-N'YORO TO, ニヨロニヨロト, *adv.* With a slow zigzag, or undulating motion.

N'YO-SHI, ニヨシ, 女子, *(onna no ko). n.* A girl.

†N'YO-TEI, ニヨテイ, 女帝, *n.* A queen, empress, said only of one who governs.

NO, ノ, 之, *postpos.* Of. *Tszki no hikari*, light of the moon. *Hana no iro*, color of a flower.

(2). used as an adjective particle, as, *Muda no koto*, useless thing. *Makoto-no kokoro*, a sincere heart. *Hiya-no sake*, cold *sake*. *Matsz-no ki*, a pinetree.

(3). used to form a present, or perfect participle. as, *O-masz no naku no wo shikaru*, scolded *O-masz's* crying. *Yuki no futta no de*, on account of its having snowed. *Ama-zake to mōsz no ni*, in respect to what is called *Ama-zake*, &c.

NO, ノ, 野, *n.* A wild uncultivated level region, a moor, prairie, desert, wilds.

NO, ノ, 幅, *n.* Breadth, or width of cloth, muslin, silk, &c. *H'to no*, one breadth. *F'ta no*, two breadths. *Mi no*, three breadths *Itsz no buton*, a quilt made of five breadths of cloth.

NO, ノ, 箆, *n.* The bamboo of which arrows are made, the shaft of an arrow.

NŌ, ノオ, Exclam. used much in familiar talk, similar to *ne*, but untranslatable.

†NŌ, ノウ, 農, *(ta wo tszkuru)*. Husbandry farming, agriculture. — *wo motte giyō to sz*, to follow the occupation of farming. — *no toki tagō koto nakare*, make no mistake in the times for farming.

†NŌ, ノウ, 能, *n.* Skill, ability, cleverness, genius, talent; virtue, strength, or power, (as of medicines). *Ta nō na h'to*, a person of varied accomplishments, or clever at many things. *Nō nashi*, a dunce. Syn. GEI, KIRIYŌ.

NŌ, ノウ, 能, *n.* A kind of operatic performance, consisting of music and dancing.

NŌ, ナウ, 無, Same as *Naku. adv.* Not, not having, without. *Shin nō-sh'te wa tatsz-bekaradz*, without truth there is no success. *Oya wa nō-te mo ko wa sodatsz*, a child will grow even without parents.

NŌ-BAKAMA, ノバカマ, 野袴, *n.* A kind of trowsers gathered and tied at the knee.

NO-BARA, ノバラ, 野原, *n* A moor, uncultivated and level tract of country.

NOBASHI,*-sz,-sh'ta*, ノバス, 令伸, *t. v.* To stretch, to lengthen, to extend, to reach out, to continue, or prolong the time, to postpone, to spread, or smooth out, (the wrinkles or inequalities of any thing). *Tetsz wo* —, to stretch iron, (by hammering). *Te, ashi wo* —, to extend the arm or leg. *Shin-sho wo* —, to enlarge one's fortune. *Nichi-gen wo* —, to extend the time. *Kō-yaku wo* —, to spread a plaster. *Shiwa wo* —, to smooth out the wrinkles. *Nori wo* —, to thin paste. *Nawa wo* —, to pay out a rope.

NOBE, ノベ, 野邊, *n.* Moor.

NOBE,*-ru,-ta*, ノベル, 述, *t.v.* To tell, narrate, to state the particulars, to record. *Kōjō wo* —, to deliver a message. *Ikusa no yōsz wo* —, to give an account of the war.

NOBE,*-ru,-ta*, ノベル, 伸, or 延, *t.v.* To stretch, extend, lengthen out, reach out, to postpone, or prolong to some future time, to give credit or to trust, to spread out, to expand, to dilute.

NOBE-GANE, ノベガネ, 伸金, *n.* Metal stretched by hammering, the money for goods bought on credit.

NOBI, ノビ, 野火, *n.* A prairie-fire.

NOBI,*-ru,-ta*, ノビル, 伸, *i.v.* To stretch, to extend, to reach, to grow, to expand, to enlarge, to spread. to be prolonged, or lengthened in time. *Sei ga* —, has grown tall. *Ki ga* —, the spirits expand, to be relieved of gloom.

NOBI, ノビ, 伸, *n.* Stretching, lengthening. — *wo szru,* to stretch, (as when tired).

NOBI-AGARI,*-ru,-tta,* ノビアガル, 伸上, *i.v.* To stretch up one's self (as if to look).

NOBI CHIJIMI, ノビチヂミ, 伸縮, *n.* Expanding and contracting.

NOBIKI, ノビキ, 野引, *n.* One who goes into the streets to draw guests into hotels, theatres, &c., a runner.

NOBIRU, ノビル, 野蒜, *n.* A kind of wild garlic.

||NOBIYAKA, ノビヤカ, 舒, Expanded, free from care or gloom. — *na.*

NOBORASHI,*-sz,-sh'ta,* ノボラス, 令登, Caust. of *Noboru.* To make, or let ascend, or go up.

NOBORI,*-ru,-tta,* ノボル, 登, *t.v.* To go up, ascend. *Yama wo* —, to ascend a mountain. *Hashigo wo* —, to go up a ladder. Syn. AGARU.

NOBORI, ノボリ, 幟, *n.* Flags raised at festivals.

NOBORI-TSZME,*-ru,-ta,* ノボリツメル, 登詰, *t.v.* To ascend to the highest point.

NOBOSE,*-ru,-ta,* ノボセル, 上氣, *i.v.* To be lightheaded, to have a feeling of fulness in the head, to be wild, enthusiastic, or extravagant in opinions or ways. *Ano h'to ga nobosete-iru,* he is a light headed man.

NOBOSE, ノボセ, 上氣, *n.* Rush of blood to the head, light-headed, enthusiasm, wildness, or extravagance.

NOBOSHI,*-sz,-sh'ta,* ノボス, 令登, *t. v.* To make or let ascend, to send up.

NO-BUDŌ, ノブダウ, 野葡萄, *n.* A kind of wild grape, Ampelopsis heterophilla.

NOBURU, ノブル, see *Noberu.*

NOBUSERI, ノブセリ, 野伏, *n.* A vagabond, beggar.

NO-BUSHI, ノブシ, 野武士, *n.* An outlawed *Samurai,* a bandit.

NOCHI, ノチ, 後, After in time. — *no yo,* the next world. — *no tszma,* a second wife. *Sono-nochi,* after that. *Kono-nochi,* after this, hereafter.

NOCHI, ノチ, 後, *n.* Descendant, lineage. *Dono h'to no — da,* whose descendant is he? Syn. SHISON.

NOCHI-NI, ノチニ, 後, *adv.* By and by, in a little while, afterwards. Syn. ATO-DE.

NOCHIDZRE, ノチヅレ, 後夫, *n.* Second husband.

NOCHI-HODO, ノチホド, 後程, *adv.* By and by, after a little while.

NOCHIKATA, ノチカタ, 後刻, *(gokoku,) adv.* (idem).

NOCHIZOYE, ノチゾヘ, 後妻, *(gosai,) n.* Second wife.

NODACHI,*-tsz,-tta,* ノダツ, 伸立, *i. v.* To grow up. *Ki ga* —.

NODACHI, ノダチ, 野刀, *n.* A short sword worn in hunting.

NODO, ノド, 咽, *n.* The throat. — *ni hone ga kakatta,* has a bone in his throat.

NODO-BONE, ノドボネ, 結喉, *n.* The hyoid bone.

NODO-BUYE, ノドブエ, 咽吭, *n.* The windpipe. — *wo tatsz,* to cut the windpipe, or throat.

NODOKA, ノドカ, 長閑, Clear, pleasant spring weather. — *naru haru no kaze,* the zephyr of a soft, and pleasant spring day. *Yo wo — ni kurasz,* to pass one's life pleasantly.

NŌ-DOKU, ノウドク, 能毒, *n.* Efficacious or poisonous, properties, (of medicines). — *shiraneba kuszri wa tszkawarenu,* medicines should not be used without knowing their properties.

†NODOYAKA, ノドヤカ, *n.* same as *Nodokai.*

NODZCHI, ノヅチ, 野槌, *n.* A kind of po sonous snake.

NODZRA, ノヅラ, 野面, *n.* Brazen-faced. — *na yatsz.*

†NŌFU, ノウフ, 農夫, *n.* A farmer. Syn. HIYAK'SHŌ.

NŌGAKI, ノウガキ, 能書, *n.* An advertisement of the efficacy of a medicine.

NOGARE,*-ru,-ta,* ノガレル, 脫, *t. v.* To avoid, escape, to shun. *Wazawai wo* —, to escape misfortune. *Nogare-gataki yōji,* unavoidable business. Syn. MANUKARERU, SAKERU, YOKERU.

NOGASHI,*-sz,-sh'ta,* ノガス, 令脫, caust of *Nogeru.* To make, or let escape.

NOGI, ノギ, 芒, *n.* The beard of grain, as of wheat, rice.

NŌGIYŌ, ノウゲフ, 農業, *n.* Husbandry, farming.

NOGOI,*-ō,-ōta,* ノゴフ, 拭, same as *Nugui.*

NŌ-HITSZ, ノウヒツ, 能筆, *n.* An expert penman.

NO-JI, ノヂ, 野路, *n.* A road through a moor.

NŌJU, ナフジユ, 納受, *n.* Hearing prayer. *Kami ga — mashimas.*

NOJUKU, ノジユク, 野宿, Sleeping in the moor.

†NŌKA, ノウカ, 農家, *n.* Farm house.

NOKARE,-ru,-ta, ノカレル, 退, pot. or pass. of *Noki*.

NOKE,-ru,-ta, ノケル, 退, *t. v.* To take away, to remove, (as anything in the way), to take or leave out of the number, to exclude, except. *Iye wo tori-nokeru*, to take down and remove a house. *Futa wo nokete miru*, to take off the lid and look. *H'tori wo nokereba hoka wa mina sake-nomi da*, they all drink *sake*, except one person. *Nokete oku*, to take anything from a number and lay it aside. *Noke*, (imp.) get out of the way.

NOKE-SAMA-NI, ノケサマニ, 仰様, *adv.* Face upwards. — *uma yori dō-to ochiru*, he fell backwards from the horse slap on the ground.

NOKEZORI,-ru,-tta, ノケゾル, 仰反, *i. v.* To bend backwards, to fall backwards. *Nokezori-kayette shinda*, fell back and died.

NOKI,-ku,-ita, ノク, 退, *i.v.* To withdraw, retire, to leave, go aside, depart from. *Nakama wo* —, to withdraw from a company. Syn. YOKERU.

NOKI, ノキ, 檐, *n.* The eaves of a house.

NOKIBA, ノキバ, 檐端, *n.* idem.

NOKKE, ノツケ, *adv.* Beginning, first. — *ni*, at first. Syn. HAJIME.

NOKOGIRI, ノコギリ, 鋸, *n.* A saw. — *no ha*, the teeth of a saw. — *kudz*, saw-dust.

NOKORADZ, ノコラズ, 不殘, *neg.* of *Nokoru*. Not left, none remaining, all, every one. *H'tori mo* —, not a man left. — *utte-shimatta*, have sold them all.

NOKORI,-ru,-tta, ノコル, 殘, *i.v.* To remain over, to be left. *Mada szkoshi nokotte oru*, there is still a little left. *Tada ishi-dzye ga nokotte iru*, the foundation stone only remains. *Kokoro ga* —, to leave one's heart behind, or feel regret at leaving anything. Syn. AMARU.

NOKORI, ノコリ, 殘, *n.* The remainder, residue, remnant, anything left over. — *naku totte shimau*, to take all not leaving a scrap. Syn. AMARI, YO.

NOKOSHI,-sz,-sh'ta, ノコス, 殘, *t.v.* To let remain over, to leave, to keep back. *H'totsz nokosh'te hoka wa mina motte-yuke*, take all but one. *Kokoro wo nokosh'te kayeru*, to return leaving one's heart behind. *Haji wo* —, to leave a bad reputation. *Nokosadz ni mina toru*, take all without leaving one.

NOKU, ノク, See *Noki*.

NOMARE,-ru,-ta, ノマレル, 被呑, Pass. or pot. of *Nomu*. To be drunk, or swallowed. *Kayeru ga hebi ni nomareta*, the frog was swallowed by the snake. *Atszku-te nomare-masen*, it is so hot I cannot drink it.

NOMASE,-ru,-ta, ノマセル, 令飲, caust. of *Nomu*. Make or let drink. *O nomase nasare*, let me drink. *Nomasete mite kudasare*, let me drink and see (if it is so and so). *H'to ni kuszri wo* —, to give a person medicine.

NOME-NOME-TO, ノメノメト, *adv.* In an insensible, unconcerned, indifferent, careless or apathetic manner, with effrontery.

NOMERI,-ru,-tta, ノメル, (coll.) *i. v.* To slip and fall. *Michi ga warui kara nometta*, the road was so bad I slipped and fell. Syn. SZBERU.

NOMI, ノミ, 狗虱, *n.* A flea.

NOMI, ノミ, 鑿, *n.* A chisel.

NOMI, ノミ, 而已, *adv.* Only, nothing more. *Sore* — *naradz*, not only that. *Kore* — *ni aradz*, not only so. *Tada sore* — *ka*, is it that only? Syn. BAKARI.

NOMI,-mu,-nda, ノム, 飲, *t.v.* To drink, to swallow. *Tabako wo* —, to smoke tobacco. *Sake wo* —, to drink ardent spirits. *G'wanyaku wo* —, to take a pill.

NO-MICHI, ノミチ, 野道, *n.* A road through a moor.

NOMI-GUCHI, ノミグチ, 鑿口, *n.* A faucet. — *wo sasz*, to put in a faucet.

NOMI-HOSHI,-sz,-sh'ta, ノミホス, 飲乾, *t. v.* To drink dry.

NOMI-KOMI,-mu,-nda, ノミコム, 呑込, *t.v.* To swallow; fig. to perfectly understand, or comprehend, to consent. Syn. SHŌCHI SZRU.

NOMI-KUI, ノミクヒ, 飲食, *n.* Eat and drink, food, victuals.

†NŌ-MIN, ノウミン, 農民, *n.* Farmers. Syn. H'YAK'SHŌ.

NOMI-SASHI-NI, ノミサシニ, *adv.* To stop drinking before one has finished to attend to something else. *Cha wo* — *sh'te deru*.

NOMITE, ノミテ, 飲客, *n.* A hard drinker.

NOMU, ノム, 飲, See *Nomi*.

NONDA, ノンダ, *pret.* of *Nomi*.

NONDAKURE, ノンダクレ, *n.* A drunkard.

NONDO, ノンド, 咽, *n.* The throat, same as *Nodo*.

NONKI, ノンキ, 延氣, Same as *Nodoka*.

‖NONOMEKI,-ku,-ita, ノノメク, *i.v.* To be noised abroad, reported or talked of with much noise.

NONOSHIRI,-ru,-tta, ノノシル, 罵詈, *t.v.* To revile, to reproach, to rail at, to abuse, to curse, to speak loudly, angrily, or contemptuously Syn. AKKO SZRU.

NOPPERAPŌ, ノッペラポウ, *n.* A bald head, a smooth, round club.

NOPPERI, ノッペリ, *adv.* Even, or smooth in outline, without irregularities, or roughness. — *to sh'ta kao*, a flat face. — *to sh'ta yama*, a smooth, even mountain.

NOPPIKI, ノッピキ, 退引, Flee from, shun, escape, only used with a negative, as, — *naradz*, impossible to escape. — *sasenu tedzme no saisoku.*

NOPPŌ, ノッパウ, *n.* A giant.

NORA, ノラ, 野, *n.* A moor.

NORA-KURA, ノラクラ, Wandering idly about, loafing. — *sh'te iru*, to pass the time wandering about idly. — *mono*, an idler, vagrant, loafer.

NORARI-KURARI-TO, ノラリクラリト, *adv.* (Idem.)

†NŌRAN, ナウラン, 惱亂, (*nayami-midareru*). Tormented and crazed with suffering or sickness.

NŌREN, or NOREN, ノレン, 暖簾, *n.* A curtain.

NORI, ノリ, 糊, *n.* Paste made of flour, starch, cement. *Katana no* —, the blood sticking to a sword

†NORI, ノリ, 法, *n.* Law, rule, doctrine, precept. Syn. HŌ, KISOKU.

NORI, ノリ, 海苔, *n.* A kind of edible sea-weed.

NORI, ノリ, 乘, *n.* Measurement. dimensions. *Hako no uchi-nori*, the inside dimensions of a box. *Soto-nori*, the outside dimensions.

NORI,-*ru*,-*tta*, ノル, 乘, *i.v.* To ride on any thing. *Uma ni* —, to ride on a horse. *Fune ni* —, to ride in a boat. *Fune ni notte Osaka ye yuku*, to go to Osaka by ship. *Kago ni* —, to ride in a chair. *Katsz ni* —, emboldened, or encouraged by victory.

NORI,-*ru*,-*tta*, ノル, 登, *i.v.* To bear fruit. *Mi ga noru* (idem.)

NORI-AI, ノリアヒ, 乘合, *n.* Riding together, going in company. — *bune*, a passenger boat, (in which many persons ride together). — *de akinai wo szru*, to do business in partnership.

NORI-BAKE, ノリバケ, 糊刷毛, *n.* A paste-brush.

NORI-GAYE, ノリガヘ, 乘替, *n.* A relay of horses. — *wo hiku*, to bring up a fresh horse.

NORI-KAKE,-*ru*,-*ta*, ノリカケル, 乘掛, *t.v.* To ride over or upon any thing.

NORI-KAYE,-*ru*,-*ta*, ノリカヘル, 乘替, *t.v.* To change in riding (from one horse to another, or from one boat to another). *Ushi wo uma ni* —.

NORI-KOMI,-*mu*,-*nda*, ノリコム, 乘込, *t.v.* To ride into. *Ta no naka ye uma wo norikonda*, rode the horse into a rice field.

NORI-KOYE,-*ru*,-*tta*, ノリコエル, 乘越, *t.v.* To ride across or over.

NORI-MAWASHI,-*sz*,-*sh'ta*, ノリマハス, 乘迴, *t.v.* To ride around.

NORI-MODOSHI,-*sz*,-*sh'ta*, ノリモドス, 乘戻, *i.v.* To ride back.

NORI-MONO, ノリモノ, 乘物, *n.* A sedan chair.

NORI-SZTE,-*ru*,-*ta*, ノリステル, 乘捨, *t.v.* To stop and leave the horse or boat on which one has been riding. *Kash'ko ni uma wo* —, left his horse there.

NORI-TAMAI,-*au*,-*atta*, Same as *Notamai.*

NORITO, ノリト, 祝詞, *n.* A written prayer to the *Kami.*

NORI-TORI,-*ru*,-*tta*, ノリトル, 乘取, *t.v.* To seize, gain possession of, (as a castle.)

NORI-TSZKE,-*ru*,-*ta*, ノリツケル, 乘附, *t.v.* To ride up to.

NORI-UTSZRI,-*ru*,-*tta*, ノリウツル, 乘移, *t.v.* To change from one boat, horse, or chair, to another. To possess, or influence, (as a spirit), to inspire, bewitch. *Kami wa h'to ni nori-utsztte mono wo iu. Kitszne ga h'to ni* —.

NŌRIYŌ, ナフリヤウ, 納涼, (*szdzmi*). Cool and refreshing in hot weather. — *no tame ni fune ni noru*, to take a boat ride in order to cool and refresh one's self in hot weather.

NORI-ZOME, ノリゾメ, 納初, *n.* The first ride of the new year.

NORŌ, ノロウ, *adv.* Same as *Noroku.*

NOROI,-*ō*,-*ōta* ノロフ, 呪咀, *t v.* To invoke evil or curses on any one, to imprecate, curse. *Kami ni inotte h'to wo* —, to bring evil on one by invoking the *Kami.* Syn. TOKOBU, SHUSO SZRU.

NOROI, ノロヒ, 呪咀, *n.* A curse, imprecation.

NOROI,-KI, ノロイ, *a.* Slow, not fast, dull, sluggish in mind. *Uma wa hayai ushi wa noroi.* Syn. OSOI.

NOROKE,-*ru*,-*ta*, ノロケル, *i.v.* To be infatuated, captivated, or fascinated by love. *Onna ni noroketa.*

NOROKE, ノロケ, *n.* Love, passion. — *wo iu*, to speak of one's passion, or love for a woman. — *wo ukeru*, to listen to, &c.

NOROMA, ノロマ, 癡漢, *n.* A dolt, blockhead.

NOROKU, ノロク, *adv.* Slow, sluggish, dull.

NORO-NORO-TO, ノロノロト, *adv.* Slowly. — *aruku*, to walk slowly.
Syn. SORO-SORO-TO.

NORORI-TO, ノロリト, *adv.* Dull, stupid, sluggish, slow. — *sh'te iru.*

NOROSA, ノロサ, *n.* Sluggishness, slowness.

NOROSHI, ノロシ, 烽火, *n.* A signal rocket.

NOROSHI, ノロシ, *a.* See *Noroi.*

NORU, ノル, 乘, See *Nori.*

NOSABARI,*-ru,-tta,* ノサバル, *i. v.* To stretch one's self back, (as from ennui).

†NŌ-SAI, ノウサイ, 能才, *n.* Ingenuity, skill, talents.

†NŌ-SAKU, ノウサク, 農作, *n.* Farming.

NOSA-NOSA-TO, ノサノサト, *adv.* With an erect, or strutting air.

NŌ-SHO, ノウシヨ, 能書, *n.* Skillful penman.

NOSE,*-ru,-ta,* ノセル, 載, *t.v.* To make, or let ride, to place, to record, to write in a book. *Uma ni noseru,* to ride another on a horse, or to put anything on a horse. *Tszkuye ni* —, to place anything on the table. *Hon ni nosete aru,* is contained in a book.

NOSHI, ノシ, *n.* The piece of dried *awabi* which is always attached to a present; it now also includes the colored paper in which it is folded.

NOSHI, ノシ, 熨斗, *n.* A smoothing iron. — *de kimono wo nobasz,* to iron clothes.

NOSHI, ノシ, 紫苑, *n.* A flowering plant.

NOSHI,*-sz,-sh'ta,* ノス, 伸, *t.v.* To stretch, to extend. *Shiwa wo* —, to smooth out the wrinkles. *Koshi wo* —, to stretch one's self after stooping. Syn. NOBASHI.

NOSHI-ITO, ノシイト, 伸絲, *n.* The coarse silk reeled from the outside of the cocoon.

NOSHIME, ノシメ, 熨斗目, *n.* A kind of clothes, only worn by Samurai on particular occasions.

NOSZ, ノス, See *Noshi.*

NOSZRU, ノスル, Same as *Noseru.*

NOTAKURI,*-ru,-tta,* ノタクル, *i. v.* To writhe, to twist about, (as a wounded snake).

NOTAMAI,*-au,,* ノタマフ 宣, *i.v.* To speak, to say, (only used of high personages).

NOTAMAWAKU, ノタマハク, Same as *Notamau.*

NOTA-UCHI-MAWARI,*-ru,-tta,* ノタウチマハル, *i.v.* To writhe about, to wallow.

NOTTO, ノット, 祝詞, *n.* Same as *Norito.* A written Sintoo prayer.

NOTTO, ノット, Same as *Niyokkori.*

NOTTORI,*-ru,-tta,* ノットル, Same as *Noritori.*

NOTTORI,*-ru,* ノットル, 法, (comp. of *nori* and *toru*). To set as an example, to imitate. *Bun-ō wa — ni tarazaruka,* is not king Bun a sufficient object for imitation?

†NOWAKI, ノワキ, 暴風, *n.* A violent autumnal wind.

NŌYAKUSHA, ノウヤクシヤ, 能役者, *n.* An opera dancer.

NOZARASHI, ノザラシ, 野曝, *n.* Bones or carcass left bleaching on the moor.

NOZOKE,*-ru,-ta,* ノゾケル, 覗, *t. v.* To hold out; put forth or out; hang out; to stretch out, or forth; extend. *Mado kara kao wo* —, to put one's head out of a window. *Kodomo wo ido no wiye ni nozokeru na,* don't hold the child over the well.

NOZOKI,*-ku,-ita,* ノゾク, 覗, *t.v.* To bend the head and look down, to look into, (as a hole), to peep through. *Mado kara nozoite miru,* to look down from a window. *Mimi wo nozoku,* to look into the ear. *To no szkima kara* —, to peep through the crack of a door.

NOZOKI,*-ku,-ita,* ノゾク, 除, *t.v.* To remove, to take away, to subtract, leave out, to except. *Wazawai wo* —, to remove calamity. *H'totsz nozoite ato mina agemashō,* I will give all but one. *Fuku chiu no doku wo* —, to remove injurious matters from the stomach. Syn. NOKERU.

NOZOKI, ノゾキ, *n.* A camera-obscura.

NOZOKI, ノゾキ, *n.* A light-blue color.

NOZOMI,*-mu,-nda,* ノゾム, 望, *t. v.* To desire, to hope for. *Fūki wo nozomu wa nin-jō no tszne,* the desire of riches is common to men.
Syn. NEGAU, HOSSZRU.

NOZOMI,*-mu,-nda,* ノゾム, 臨, *i. v.* To approach to, to be near to, to be at the point of, to look down upon, to behold. *Inochi owaru no toki ni nozomite,* drawing near to the end of life. *Oi ni nozomu,* approaching old age. *Nan ni nozomite shu wo szte nige-kakaruru mono ni aradz,* he is not the one to run away and hide when his lord is in difficulty. *Kawa ni* —, to look into the water.

NOZOMI, ノゾミ, 望, *n.* Desire, hope, wish. — *to sh'te tarazaru wa naku,* every desire was satisfied. — *wo ushinau,* to be disappointed. Syn. NEGAI.

NU, ヌ, 不, A negative affix of verbs, always preceded by a syllable ending in *a*, or *e.* *Kikanu, Kikarenu, Wakaranu Wakarenu.*

†NU, ヌ, An affix of verbs, forming the preterite tense, following a syllable ending in *i.* or *e.* *Kikinu,* have heard. *Wakarinu,* have separated.

NŪ, ヌフ, 縫, See *Nui.*

†NU, NURU, ヌ, 寢, (obs. poetical word), To sleep.

†NUBATAMA, ヌバタマ, 野干玉, *n.* (*numa,* and *tama*). The name of a black root growing in a swamp, used only in poetry as a *Makura kotoba,* with *Yami, Kuroi,* or *Yoru.* — *no yami,* = pitch darkness.

†NUBI, ヌビ, 奴婢, (*shimobe*). *n.* Male and female servant.

†NUBOKU, ヌボク, 奴僕, Manservant.

NUGASE,*-ru,-ta,* ヌガセル, caust. of *Nugu.* To strip off the clothes of another, to bare, denude.

NUGE,*-ru,-ta,* ヌゲル, 脫, *i.v.* To be bare of clothes, to be off, (of clothing). *Kaze ga fuite yeboshi ga nugeta,* his cap is blown off by the wind. *Futon ga nugeta,* the quilt is off.

NUGI,*-gu,-ida,* ヌグ 脫, *t.v.* To take off, (the clothes or covering), to strip off, to bare, denude. *Kimono, dzkin, tabi, momohiki nado wo nugu,* to take off the coat, cap, stockings, or trowsers. *Nuide oku,* to take off and lay down.

NUGI-KAKE,*-ru,-ta,* ヌギカケル, 脫掛, *t.v.* To take off and hang up (as a coat &c).

NUGI-SZTE,*-ru,-ta,* ヌギステル, 脫捨, *t.v.* To take off and cast way. *Kabuto mo yoroi mo nugi-sztete nigeru,* taking off his helmet and armor he threw them away and fled.

NUGU, ヌグ, See *Nugi.*

NUGUI,-Ū,-ŪTA, ヌグウ, 拭, *t.v.* To wipe. *Te wo* —, to wipe the hands. *Katana wo* —, to wipe a sword.
Syn. FUKU.

NUI,-Ū,-ŪTA, ヌウ, 縫, *t. v.* To sew, to stitch, to embroider. *Hari de kimono wo* —, to sew clothes with a needle. *Hana wo* —, to embroider a flower.

NUI, ヌヒ, 繡, *n.* Embroidery. — *no mon,* the figure of an embroidery.

NUI-AWASE,*-ru,-ta,* ヌヒアハセル, 縫合, *t.v.* To sew together.

NUI-HAKU-YA, ヌヒハクヤ, 縫箔屋, *n.* An embroiderer.

NUI-ME, ヌヒメ, 縫目, *n.* A seam.

NUI-MON, ヌヒモン, 繡文, *n.* An embroidered coat of arms.

NUI-MONO, ヌヒモノ, 繡物, *n.* Embroidery.

NUI-TORI, ヌヒトリ, 繡鳥, *n.* Idem. — *no fukuro,* and embroidered bag.

NUI-TSZGI,*-gu,-ida,* ヌヒツグ, 縫接, *t.v.* To splice, or lengthen by sewing.

NUI-TSZKE,*-ru,-ta,* ヌイツケル, 縫付, *t.v.* To sew one thing on, or to another, (as a patch).

NUI-ZARASA, ヌヒザラサ, 繡花, *n.* Embroidery.

NUKA, ヌカ, 糠, *n.* Rice-bran.

†NUKA, ヌカ, 額, *n.* The forehead.
Syn. KITAI.

NUKADZKI,*-ku,-ita,* ヌカツク, 叩頭, *i.v.* To bow touching the forehead to the ground.

NUKAGO, ヌカゴ, See *Mukago.*

NUKA-KUGI, ヌカクギ, 糠釘, *n.* A small tack.

NUKA-MISO, ヌカミソ, 糠味噌, A kind of pickle for vegetables.

NUKARI,*-ru,-atta,* ヌカル, 泥濘, *i.v.* To be muddy. *Michi ya nukaru,* the road is muddy.

NUKARI,*-ru,-tta,* ヌカル, *i.v.* To be remiss, inattentive, negligent, heedless, careless, stupid. *Nukatta koto wo sh'ta,* have done a stupid thing. *Nukaranu kao de,* with a straight face, or unconscious of his mistake.

NUKARUMI, ヌカルミ, 泥濘, *n.* A muddy place. *Tai-hen no — da,* what a mud hole! — *ye hamaru,* to fall into the mud.

NUKASHI,*-sz,-sh'ta,* ヌカス, *t.v.* To say, speak, (a low word). *Nani wo nukasz no da,* what are you saying?

NUKE,*-ru,-ta,* ヌケル, 拔, *i. v.* To be drawn out, extracted, to lose. *t.v.* To pass through a narrow way, to escape, flee away. *Ha ga nuketa,* the tooth is out. *Ke ga* —, hair has fallen out. *Nioi ga* —, it has lost its odor. *Aji ga* —, it has lost its taste. *Iro ga* —, has lost its color. *Ki ga* —, has lost his mind. *Ana wo nukeru,* to pass through a hole. *H'to-gomi wo tōri-nukeru,* to wind one's way through a crowd. *Rōya wo* —, to escape from goal. *Tori ga kago wo nuketa,* the bird has escaped from the cage.

NUKE-AKINAI, ヌケアキナヒ, 密買, *n.* Clandestine trade, smuggling.
Syn. BAHAN.

NUKE-ANA, ヌケアナ, 拔穴, *n.* A tunnel, a passage way through a hill or under ground, &c.

NUKE-GAKE, ヌケガケ, 拔掛, *n.* Stealing

away clandestinely and attacking, forestalling others in the market.

NUKE-GARA, ヌケガラ, 蛻, *n.* The cast off skin of a snake, or shell of an insect.

NUKE-ME, ヌケメ, 拔目, *n.* Way or place for money to slip out. — *ga ōi kara kane-mochi ni narimasen,* his expenses are so many he cannot become rich. — *no nai h'to,* a vigilant and prudent person.

NUKE-MICHI, ヌケミチ, 拔道, *n.* A byway.

NUKE-MONO, ヌケモノ, 拔物, *n.* Stolen goods, especially such as are offered for sale. — *wa katte hikiai ni tszku,* to be hauled up before a magistrate for buying stolen goods.

NUKE-NI, ヌケニ, 拔荷, *n.* Smuggled goods.

NUKE-NUKE, ヌケヌケト, *adv.* Clandestinely, stealthily, sheepish. — *to sh'ta kao,* sheepish countenance. — *ni nigeru,* to flee away stealthily.

NUKI, ヌキ, 緯, *n.* The woof. Those syllables which end with the same vowel sound, and which are arranged cross-wise in the table of 50 sounds.

NUKI, ヌキ, *n.* The stick that is passed through morticed holes in upright pieces of timber to keep them together, a brace.

NUKI,*-ku,-ilu,* ヌク, 拔, *t.v.* To draw out, to take out, to extract, to root up, pluck out. *Ha wo* —, to extract a tooth. *Katana wo* —, to draw a sword. *Kugi wo* —, to draw out a nail. *Te wo* —, to slight over, do carelessly. *Kata wo* —, to shift from one's shoulders to another's. *Iro wo* —, to take out a color. *Shimi wo* —, to take out a stain. *Hon kara* —, to extract from a book.

NUKI, ヌキ, 拔, *n.* An extractor, forceps, (used only in comp. words).

NUKI-ASHI, ヌキアシ, 蹐, *n.* Noiseless steps. — *de aruku.*

NUKI-ATSZME,*-ru,-ta,* ヌキアツメル, 抄集, *t.v.* To collect extracts from books; to pluck up and collect.

NUKI-AWASE,*-ru,-ta,* ヌキアハセル, 拔合, *t. v.* To draw and cross swords as in the commencement of a combat. *Tagai ni katana wo* —.

NUKI-DASHI,*-sz,-sh'ta,* ヌキダス, 拔出, *t.v.* To draw out.

NUKI-DE-WATA, ヌキデワタ, 拔出綿, *n.* Old cotton, that has been used for wadding.

NUKI-HANASHI,*-sz,-sh'ta,* ナキハナス, 拔放, *t. v.* To draw a sword out of the sheath.

NUKI-GAKI, ヌキガキ, 抄書, *n.* Extracts from books, an epitome, or abridgment of a book or writing.

NUKINDE,*-dzru,-ta,* ヌキンズル, 抽, *i.v.* To excel, surpass, to out do, to be distinguished, or eminent above others. *Shū ni nukindetaru kō-miyō,* merit surpassing all the others. Syn. HIDERU, BAKKUN.

NUKI-NUKI, ヌキヌキ, 拔拔, *adv.* Extracting here and there from a book, or writing. — *utszsz.*

NUKI-SASHI, ヌキサシ, 拔刺, *n.* Taking out, and putting in.

NOKI-TŌSHI,*-sz,-sh'ta,* ヌキトホス, 貫通, *t. v.* To pass through, to thread, to string.

NUKI-TSZRE,*-ru,-ta,* ヌキツレル, 貫連, *t.v.* To draw swords together, (of several persons).

NUKI-UCHI, ヌキウチ, 貫撃, *n.* Drawing and striking with a sword.

NUKI-UTSZSHI, ヌキウツシ, 拔寫, *n.* A brief summary or abstract of a book or writing, and epitome, abridgment.

NUKU, ヌク, 拔, See *Nuki.*

||NUKUMORI,*-ru,-tta,* ヌクモル, 温, *i. v.* To be warm, comfortable.

NUMA, ヌマ, 沼, *n.* A marsh, swamp.

NUME, ヌメ, 光綾, *n.* White satin.

NUME-NUME, ヌメヌメ, 滑滑, *adv.* Slippery, smooth, oily. Syn. NAMERAKA.

NUMERI,*-ru,-tta,* ヌメル, 滑, *i.v.* To be slippery. *Michi ga* —, the road is slippery. Syn. SZBERU.

NUMERINDZ, ヌメリンヅ, Same as *Nume.*

NUNO, ヌノ, 布, *n.* Linen, grasscloth.

NUNOKO, ヌノコ, 布子, *n.* Padded winter clothes.

NUNOME, ヌノメ, 布目, *n.* The figure or impression like the meshes of cloth, on paper, porcelain &c. — *wo utsz.*

NUNOMEGAMI, ヌノメガミ, 布目紙, *n.* A kind of paper used for book covers.

NURAKURA, ヌラクラ, *n.* same as *Norakura.*

NURA-NURA, ヌラヌラ, same as *Nume-nume.*

NURASE,,*-ru,-ta,* ヌラセル, 令塗, caust. of *Nuru.* To cause or let another paint, lacquer, or plaster.

NURASHI,*-sz,-sh'ta,* ヌラス, 濡, caust. of *Nureru.* To wet, to dampen, moisten. *Fukin wo nurash'te fuku,* to wet the towel and wipe. *Namida de sode wo* —, to wet the sleeve with tears.

NURATSZKI,,-*ku*,-*ita*, ヌラツク, 滑著, *i. v.* To be slippery, smooth, oily.

NUNAWA, ヌナハ, 蓴菜, *n.* A kind of water plant, marsh mallow? Syn. JUNSAI.

NURE,-*ru*,-*ta*, ヌレル, 濡, *i. v.* To be wet. damp, moist. *Ame ni* —, to be wet with rain. *Kimono ga nureta.* the clothes are wet. Syn. SHIMERU.

NURE-TŌRI,-*ru*,-*tta*, ヌレトホル, 濡透, *i. v.* Wet through.

NURI,-*ru*,-*tta*, ヌル, 塗, *t. v.* To cover, besmear, or daub with any thing, to paint, to lacquer, to varnish, to plaster. *Urushi wo* — to lacquer. *Kabe wo* —, to plaster. *Szmi wo* —, to cover with ink. *Abura wo* —, to smear with oil. *H'to ni tszmi wo* —, to blame a crime on another.

NURI, ヌリ, 塗, *n.* Lacquering, painting. *Kono hako wa — ga warui*, this box is badly lacquered.

NURI-AI,-*au*,-*atta*, ヌリアフ, 塗合, *i. v.* (fig.) To blame each other. *Tagai ni tszmi wo* —.

NURIBON, ヌリボン, 塗盆, *n.* A lacquered tray.

NUKI-FUSAGI,-*gu*,-*ida*, ヌリフサク, 塗塞, *t. v.* To close, or shut up with plaster, to varnish or paint over, (to hide defects &c.)

†NURI-GOME, ヌリゴメ, 塗籠, *n.* A fire-proof store-house. Syn. DOZŌ.

NURI-MONO, ヌリモノ, 塗物, *n.* Lacquered ware.

NURI-TSZKE,-*ru*,-*ta*, ヌリツケル, 塗付, *t. v.* To paint, lacquer, varnish or plaster; to daub, smear with anything adhesive or unctuous, to blame, or impute a fault. *H'to ni tszmi wo nuri-tszkeru*, to lay the blame on another.

NURI-TSZKURAI,-*au*,-*atta*, ヌリツクラフ, 塗繕, *t. v.* To repair by varnishing, painting, plastering &c. (fig.) To varnish over (as errors), to palliate, gloss over.

NURI-YA, ヌリヤ, 塗屋, *n.* A plastered house.

NURU, ヌル, 塗, see *Nuri.*

†NURU, ヌル, A pret. affix, same as *Nu*; = the coll. *ta*, or *taru*, as. *Tō ni amari-nuru h'to*, a person more than ten years old. *Furi-nuru*, = *futta.*

NURU, ヌル, 寝, see *Nu.*

NURŪ, ヌルウ, same as *Nuruku.*

NURUDE, ヌルデ, 白膠木, *n.* The Rhus semialata, the tree which produces the *fushi*, or Japanese Galls.

NURUI,-KI, ヌルイ, 温, *a.* Luke-warm, moderately warm, slow, dilatory, lazy, stupid, dull. *Nurui-yatsz*, a lazy, stupid fellow. *Nurui yu*, luke-warm water.

NURUKU, ヌルク, 温, *adv.* idem.

NURURU, ヌルル, same as *Nureru.*

NURUMI,-*mu*,-*nda*, ヌルム, 温, *i.v.* To be tepid, luke-warm. *Midz ga nurunda*, the water is tepid.

NURU-NURU-TO, ヌルヌルト, *adv.* Slippery, smooth.

NURUSA, ヌルサ, *n.* Tepidness.

NURUSHI, ヌルシ, *a.* See *Nurui.*

†NUSA, ヌサ, 奴佐, *n.* Cut paper, hung up in a *Miya* before the *Kami.* Syn. GOHEI, NIGITE.

NUSHI, ヌシ, 主, *n.* Lord, master, owner, also used by vulgar persons in addressing another, = you. *Ame no mi-naka nushi no mikoto*, (the name of a *Kami*). *Iye no* —, the master, or owner of a house. *Ji-men no* —, owner of land.

NUSHI-YA, ヌシヤ, 塗師, *n.* A lacquerer, varnisher, painter.

NUSZBITO, ヌスビト, 盗, *n.* A thief, robber. Syn. DOROBŌ, TŌZOKU.

NUSZMI,-*mu*,-*nda*, ヌスム, 盗, *t. v.* To steal. *Kane wo* —, to steal money. *Hima wo nusznde asobi ni yuku*, to steal time and go a pleasuring.

NUSZMI, ヌスミ, 盗, *n.* Theft, stealing, robbery.

NUSZMI-DASHI,-*sz*,-*sh'ta*, ヌスミダス, 盗出, *t.v.* To take out by stealth, to go out clandestinely.

NUSZMI-TORI,-*ru*,-*ta*, ヌスミトル, 盗取, *t.v.* To steal, to take by stealth.

NUTA ヌタ, *n.* A kind of sauce.

NUTAKURI,-*ru*,-*ta*, ヌタクル, Same as *Notakuri.*

NUTTO-DE,-*ru*,-*ta*, ヌツトデル, *i. v.* To slip out, to spring out suddenly.

NUWASE,-*ru*,-*ta*, ヌハセル, 令縫, caust. of *Nui.* To make or let another sew. *Watakushi ni nuwasete kudasare*, allow me to sew it. *Shitateya ni kimono wo* —, to give the garment to the tailor to sew.

NUYE,-*ru*,-*ta*, ヌヘル, 縫, pass. or pot. of *Nui.* To be sewed, can sew. *Magatta hari de nuyeru ka*, can you sew with a crooked needle? *Kimono ga nuyeta*, the garment is sewed.

NUYE, ヌエ, 鵼, *n.* A kind of night bird.

O

O, ヲ, 苧, *n.* Hemp.

O, ヲ, 尾, The tail. *O no saki*, tip of the tail. *Inu ga o wo furu*, the dog wags his tail. Syn. SHIPPO.

O, ヲ, 緒, *n.* The string or cord with which any part of the dress is fastened. *Kamuri no o*, cap-strings *Zōri no o*, the strings of a sandal. *Tachi no o*, strap or cords of a sword.

O, ヲ, 牡, A male. *Me o*, female and male. *O-tori*, a male bird. *O-inu*, a he-dog.

O, オ, 御, An honorable prefix in addressing, or in speaking respectfully of another, as, *O kami-san*, in speaking to, or of the wife of another. *O-isha san*, the doctor. *O-yaku-nin*, the officer. *O tera*, a temple. *O-tento san*, the sun.

O, ヲ, 小, A diminutive prefix. *Obune*, a little boat. *Oguruma*, a little waggon. *Ogushi*, a little-comb.

†O, ヲ, 男, A man. *Shidz no o*, a low person.

O, ヲ, The objective particle. See *wo*.

O, オウ, 應, Used as a numeral in letters. *Ichi ō*, once. *Sai ō*, twice. *Ichi ō go gimmi nitewa yuki-todoki-kane soro*, by one examination it is impossible to complete it.

Ō, ヲヲ, 唯唯, Exclam. in answering a call, an affirmative = yes. *Ō to hengi wo szru*, he answered saying "Ō." *Iya ka ō ka*, (lit. no or yes), yes, or no?

Ō, ワウ, 王, *n.* A king. *Kuni no ō*, the king of a country.

Ō, オホ, 大, *a.* Great, large, only used in compound words.

Ō, オフ, 生, 負, 追, See *Oi*.

Ō-AME, オホアメ, 大雨, *n.* A heavy-rain, hard shower.

Ō-ARASHI, オホアラシ, 大嵐, *n.* A gale, hurricane.

Ō-ARE, オホアレ, 大荒, *n.* A violent storm of wind and rain.

O-ASHI, オアシ, *n.* The small copper coin, same as *Zeni*.

Ō-AZAMI, オホアザミ, 大薊, *n.* A thistle.

OBA, ヲバ, 伯母, *n.* Aunt.

Ō-BA, オホバ, 祖母, *n.* Grandmother.

Ō-BAKO, オホバコ, 車前草, *n.* The common plantain, plantago major.

Ō-BAKU, ワウバク, 黄柏, *n.* The name of a medicine, and dyestuff.

Ō-BAN, オホバン, 大判, *n.* A large gold coin.

OBANA, ヲバナ, 尾花, *n.* A kind of tall grass.

OBĀ-SAN, オバアサン, 御婆樣, *n.* An old woman (used in respectfully addressing an old woman, or in speaking to others.)

OBASHIMA, ヲバシマ, 欄干, *n.* Balustrade, Syn. RANKAN.

OBI,-*ru*,-*ta*, オビル, 帶, *t. v.* To carry in the belt, to gird on, to wear, (fig.) to have, to include, to carry, to contain, to exhibit. *Katana wo* —, to carry a sword in the belt. *Yama ga kumo wo* —, the mountain is girded with a cloud. *Hana ga tszyu wo* —, the flower holds the dew. *Urei wo obitaru kao*, a face wearing an expression of sorrow. *Kono sake wa szkoshi nigami wo obite iru*, this *sake* has a slightly bitter taste. *Akami wo obite iru*, to be tinged with red. *Ya wa nageki no kokoro wo obi*, The word *Ya* has an interjectional, or emotional meaning.

OBI, オビ, 帶, *n.* A belt, girdle, sash worn around the waist. — *wo szru*, to put on the belt. — *wo muszbu*, to tie the belt. — *wo toku*, to loosen the belt.

OBIKI,-*ku*,-*ita*, ヲビク, 誘引, *t. v.* To decoy, to lure, to entice, or lead by artifice. *Teki wo shiro yori obiki-dasz*, to decoy the enemy from his castle. *Obiki-ireru*, to entice, take in, to inveigle. *Obiki-komu*, idem.

OBISHIME, オビシメ, 帶締, *n.* A narrow belt.

OBI-SH'TA, オビシタ, 帶下, *n.* The part of the body under the belt, the waist.

OBITADASHII,-KI,-KU,-Ū,-SA, オビタダシイ, 夥敷, Great many, numerous, great in quantity, or violence. *Obitadashiku kane wo mōketa*, have earned a great deal of money. *Obitadashiki ame, kaze, jishin, kaminari*, a violent rain, wind, earthquake, or thunder.

OBIYAKASHI,-*sz*,-*sh'ta* オビヤカス, 刧, *t.v.* To frighten, to scare, to alarm, terrify. *H'to wo obiyakash'te kane wo toru*, to frighten a person and take his money. Syn. ODOROKASZ.

OBIYE,-*ru*,-*ta*, オビエル, 愶, *i.v.* To start in alarm or surprise.
Syn. BIKKURI SZRU.

OBIYU, オビユ, Same as *Obiyeru*.

OBOKO, ヲボコ, 鯔魚, *n.* The young of the fish called *Bora*.

OBOKO, ヲボコ, *n.* A young girl. — *muszme no adokenaku*, the simplicity of a young girl.

OBORAKASHI, -*sz*,-*sh'ta*, オボラカス 令,

溺, Caust. of *Oboreru*. To drown, to submerge.

OBORE,-*ru*,-*ta*, オボレル, 溺, *i.v.* To be drowned, submerged, immersed, to sink. *Midz ni* —, submerged in water. *Midz ni oborete shinda*, drowned in water. *Sake, iro, ai nado ni* —, to be drowned in wine, lust, or love. Syn. SHIDZMU, HAMARU.

OBORE-JINI, オボレジニ, 溺死, *n.* Drowned. Syn. DEKISHI.

OBORO, オボロ, 朧, Moonlight being clouded, or obscured. *H'to gao — nite tare to mo shiradz*, not to know whose face it was the moon being clouded. *Oboro yo*, a clouded moonlight night.

OBORO-DZKI, オボロヅキ, 朧月, *n.* A clouded moon.

†OBOROGE-NA, オボロゲナ, 朧月, Obscure, cloudy.

OBOSHII,-KI, オボシイ, 思敷, *a.* Appearing like, thinking or supposing to be, take to be. *Taki no kan-ja to ob^oshiki mono*, a person taken to be a spy of the enemy.

OBOSHIKU, オボシク, *adv.* Idem.

OBOSHIMESHI,-*sz*,-*sh'ta*, オボシメス, 思召, *t.v.* To think, suppose, (only used to honorable persons).

OBOSHIMESHI, オボシメシ, 思召, *n.* Thought, opinion, sentiment.

OBOSZ, オボス, cont. of *Oboshimesz. Ikani obosz ya*, what think you?

OBOTSZKANAI,-KI, オボツカナイ, 無覺束, *a.* Doubtful, uncertain, not sure. *Miyōnichi no tenki wa obotszkanai*, to-morrow's weather is uncertain.

OBOTSZKANAKU, オボツカナク, 無覺束, *adv.* Idem. — *omō*, to consider as doubtful.

OBOTSZKANASA, オボツカナサ, 無覺束, *n.* Doubtfulness, uncertainty.

OBOYE,-*ru*,-*ta*, オボエル, 覺, *t. v.* To remember, to perceive, to feel, to learn. *Sake ni yotte nani wo iuta ka oboye-masen*, he was so drunk he does not remember what he said. *Itami wo oboyeru ka*, do you feel the pain? *Ichi do yonde oboyeta*, remember it by once reading.

OBOYE, オボエ, 覺, *n.* Memory. — *ga yoi*, good memory.

OBOYE-CHIGAI,-*au*,-*tta*, オボエチガウ, 覺違, *t.v.* To mistake in remembering.

†OBU,-*ru*, オブル, 帶, Same as *Obi-ru*.

OBUI,-*ū*,-*ūta*, オブウ, 負, *t.v.* To carry on the back (as as child). *Muszme ga kodomo wo obūte hane wo tszku*, the girl plays battledoor with a child on her back.

Syn. SEŌU.

OBUNE, ヲブネ, 小舟, *n.* A little boat.

Ō-BUNE, オホブネ, 大舟, *n.* A big ship, or boat.

Ō-CHAKU, ワウチヤク, 横着, Unprincipled, dishonest, knavish. *Ōchaku-mono*, a knave. Syn. DZRUI.

†OCHI, ヲチ, 彼地, *adv.* There, yonder, otherside. *Yama no — ye tobu tori.*

ŌCHI, アフチ, 楝, *n.* The pride of India, a species of Melia.

OCHI,-*ru*,-*ta*, オチ, ル, 落, *i.v.* To fall, or drop down from a height, to run away, to flee, to fall away, to fall off, decline. *Ki no ha ga ochita*, the leaves have fallen. *Kami-nari ga* —, the lightning (Jap. thunder) has struck. *Tori ga* —, the bird is dead. *Kaze ga* —, the wind has lulled. *Kitszne ga* —, the fox has left (one who was supposed to be bewitched.) *Okori ga* —, the ague has left. *Chikara ga* —, lost all hope, or courage. *Shukke ga* —, the priest has apostatized, or fallen from his faith. *Shina ga* —, the quality of the goods is inferior. *Iro ga* —, the color has faded. *Ire-fuda ga* —, the goods are knocked off. *Hana ga* —, his nose has fallen in. *Ji ga* —, the word is left out. *Tszki ga* —, the moon has set. *Kakushiki ga* —, has fallen in rank. *Jigoku ni ochiru*, to go to hell. *Tszmi ni ochiru*, to fall into sin. *Shō-jin wo ochiru*, to cease to abstain from vegetable food, *Shiro ga* —, the castle has fallen (into the enemy's hands.) *Shiro wo* —, to escape from a castle. *Ochiru beki iro nashi*, no signs of falling, or of running away. *Kiyaku ga* —, customers are falling off.

OCHI, オチ, 落, *n.* A fall, omission. — *ga aru*, there is an omission. — *naku kiku*, to listen without losing a word.

OCHI-AI, オチアヒ, 落合, *n.* The confluence, or junction of two rivers.

OCHI-AI,-*au*,-*atta*, オチアフ, 落合, *i.v.* To meet together without previous concert.

OCHI-ATSZMARI,-*ru*,-*tta*, オチアツマル, 落集, *i.v.* To escape, and afterwards come together.

OCHIBA, オチバ, 落葉, *n.* A fallen leaf. *Ki ga — szru*, the leaves are falling from the trees.

OCHI-BURE,-*ru*,-*ta*, オチブレル, 落魄, *i.v.* To fall from prosperity into deep poverty. Syn. REIRAKU SZRU.

OCHI-CHIRI,-*ru*,-*tta*, オチチル, 落散, *i. v.* To fall and scatter. To escape and scatter.

OCHIDO, ヲチド, 越度, *n.* Error, fault, mistake. Syn. AYAMACHI.

OCHI-FUDA, オチフダ, 落札, *n.* Successful bid. *Watakushi ga — ni natta*, my bid was the successful one, or the goods were knocked off to me.

OCHI-IRI,*-ru,-tta*, オチイル, 陷, *i.v.* To fall into. *Midz ni —. Teki no hakarigoto ni —.*

OCHI-KAKARI,*-ru,-tta*, オチカカル, 落掛, *i.v.* To be on the point of falling, ready to fall. To fall and strike.

OCHI-KASANARI,*-ru,-tta*, オチカサナル, 落重, *i.v.* To fall and pile up one on the other.

†OCHI-KATA, ヲチカタ, 彼方, *n.* There, yonder, the other side, far side. *Yama no —*, other side of the mountain. Syn. ACHI.

†OCHI-KOCHI, ヲチコチ, 彼此, *adv.* Here and there, far and near. Syn. ACHI KOCHI.

OCHI-KUBOMI,*-mu,-nda*, オチクボム, 落坳, *i.v.* To sink, cave, or fall in, (as the earth).

OCHI-KOMI,*-mu,-nda*, オチコム, 落込, *i.v.* To fall into.

OCHI-MUSHA, オチムシャ, 落武者, *n.* A runaway, or an escaped soldier, deserter.

OCHI-TSZKE,*-ru-ta*, オチツケル, 落著, *t. v.* To calm, quiet, settle, tranquilize, still. *Kokoro wo —.*

OCHI-TSZKI,*-ku,-ita*, オチツク, 落著, *i.v.* To become quiet, calm, settled, tranquil, composed. To stop, settle down in a place, to become still. *Ki ga ochi-tszita*, mind has become calm. *Sawagi ga —*, the tumult is stilled. *Koko ni —*, have settled down in this place. Syn. RAKU-CHAKU, SHIDZMARU.

OCHI-TSZKI, オチツキ, 落著, *n.* Calmness, composure, tranquility.

OCHI-UDO, オチウド, 落人, *n.* One who has fled, or escaped from war, a deserter.

OCHI-USE,*-ru,-ta*, オチウセル, 落失, *i.v.* To flee, escape.

ODAMAKI, ヲダマキ, *n.* Name of a flower.

ODAMAKI, ヲダマキ, 小手卷, *n.* A spool of yarn.

ŌDAN, ワウダン, 黃疸, *n.* Jaundice.

ODATE,*-ru,-ta*, オダテル, *t.v.* To stir up, instigate, agitate, to excite, to disturb, disquiet. *Gomi wo —*, to raise a dust. *Nigori wo —*, to disturb a sediment. *H'yaku-shō wo odatete sōdō wo okosz*, to stir up the farmers and excite rebellion. Syn. UGOKASZ, SAWAGASZ.

ŌDATSZ, ワウダツ, 橫奪, *(yoko-dori)*. Trespassing, or encroaching upon the rights or possessions of another.

ODAYAKA, オダヤカ, 穩, Calm, quiet, tranquil, still, serene; free from agitation. *Nami ga — ni natta*, the sea has become calm. *Odayaka-na yoi ten ki*, a serene day.

Ō-DE, オホデ, 大手, (only used in the phrase). *— wo hirogeru*, to spread out the arms.

Ō-DO, ワウド, 黃土, *n.* A kind of yellow paint.

Ō-DŌ, ワウダウ, 橫道, Unprincipled, wicked, knavish, dishonest. *— mono*, a dishonest fellow, knave. Syn. Ō-CHAKU.

ODOKE,*-ru,-ta*, ヲドケル, *i. v.* To sport, play, romp, frolic, to joke, jest; to be witty, facetious, or humerous. *Kodomo wo aite ni sh'te odokeru*, to romp with a child. *Odoke-banashi*, a facetious story.

ODOKE, ヲドケ, *n.* Sport, fun, frolic, wit, jest, facetiousness. *— wo iu.* Syn. SHARE.

ODOMI,*-mu,-nda*,, オドム, *i.v.* To settle, to fall to the bottom of liquids. *Kasz ga soko ni —*, the dregs fall to the bottom.

ODORI,*-ru,-tta*, ヲドル, 踊, *i.v.* To dance, to jump up and down, to leap and frisk about. *H'to ga —*, the man dances.

ODORI, ヲドリ, 踊, *n.* A dance.

ODORI-AGARI,*-ru,-tta*, ヲドリアガル, 踊上, *i.v.* To jump up.

ODORI-KOYE,*-ru,-ta*, ヲドリコエル, 踊超, *t.v.* To jump across.

ODORO, オドロ, 荆棘, *n.* A place overgrown with brambles, a thicket. *— no kami*, dishevelled hair.

ODOROKASHI,*-sz,-sh'ta*, オドロカス, 令驚, caust. of *Odoroku.* To astonish, to surprise, to amaze; to scare, to frighten, to startle.

ODOROKI,*-ku,-ita*, オドロク, 驚, *i.v.* To be astonished, surprised, amazed; startled with fright, or alarm. Syn. BIKKURI SZRU, OBIYERU.

ODORO-ODOROSHII,-KI,-KU, オドロオドロシイ, Startling, alarming, fearful. *Kaminari ito — ku naru.*

ODOSHI,*-sz,-sh'ta*, オドス, 令威, *t.v.* To make afraid, frighten, to scare, alarm, to terrify by threat, or menace, intimidate.

ODOSHI, オドシ, 嚇, *n.* Fright, fear, consternation.

ODOSHI,*-sz,-sh'ta*, オドス, 縅, *t. v.* To sew together the metal plates of a coat of mail. *Yoroi wo odosz.*

ODOSHI, オドシ, 縅, *n.* The thread used for connecting the plates of armor together.

Hi odoshi no yoroi, armor the plates of which are sewed together with red thread.

†Ō-DZME, オホツメ, 大詰, *n.* The end, time of completion. Syn. TAI-BI.

ŌDZNA, オホツナ, 大綱, *n.* A cable, hawser.

ODZ-ODZ-TO, オツオツト, 怖怖, *adv.* With fear, alarm, or apprehension. — *shirasz ye deru,* to come before the judgment bar with fear. Syn. KOWA-GOWA.

ODZRU, オヅル, See *Oji.*

Ō-DZTSZ, オホツツ, 大砲, *n.* A cannon, great-gun.

ŌFŪ, オホフウ, 尊大, Haughty, arrogant, supercilious, proud, insolent. — *na yatsz da,* an arrogant fellow. — *na kotoba wo tszkau,* to use supercilious language. Syn. TAKABURU, Ō-HEI.

Ō-FUDE, オホフデ, 大筆, *n.* A large pencil.

O-FUKURO, オフクロ, 阿母, *n.* Mother. Syn. HAHA.

ŌGA, オホガ, 大鋸, *n.* A large saw. — *kudz,* saw-dust.

ŌGA, オホガ, 繰車, *n.* A kind of reel for reeling silk.

OGAMI,*-mu,-nda,* ヲガム, 拜, *t.v.* To worship, to adore: to behold or see, (only used in this sense of beholding the sun, or the face of the *Tenshi*). *Te wo awasete kami wo —,* to fold the hands and worship God. *Tenshi no kao wo —,* to see the face of the *Mikado.* Syn. HAI-SZRU.

OGAMI-UCHI, ヲガミウチ, 拜打, *n.* A downward blow with a sword, with the body bending forwards like one worshiping.

OGARA, ヲガラ, 麻柄, *n.* The sticks of hemp, after the bark has been stripped off.

OGAWA, ヲガハ, 小川, *n.* A rivulet, or small stream of water.

Ō-GI, アフギ, 扇, *n.* A fan, (one that opens and shuts.) — *no hone,* the stays of a fan.

†Ō-GI, アウギ, 奥義, *n.* The profound, or most difficult parts of an art, or science, the mysteries. *Heigaku no — wo kiwameru,* to know perfectly the deepest principles of military science.

ŌGI, ワウギ, 黄耆, *n.* Name of a medicine.

OGI, オギ, 荻, *n.* A kind of reed.

OGINAI,*-au,-atta,* オギナフ, 補, *t.v.* To make up a deficiency or loss, to repair, to restore, to mend. *Fusoku wo —,* to make up a deficiency. *Chikara wo —,* to restore the strength. Syn. SOYERU, TASZ, TSZKURAU.

OGINAI, オギナヒ, 補, *n.* Repairing, restoring, recuperation. *Niku wo tabete karada no — ni szru,* to restore the strength by eating flesh. Syn. TASHI.

OGINAI-GUSZRI, オギナヒグスリ, 補藥, *(hoyaku), n.* Tonic medicines.

†OGINORI,*-ru,-tta,* オギノル, 賒, *t.v.* To buy on credit, (seldom used).

Ō-GIYŌ, ワウギヤウ, 横行, Audacious, impudent, or daring transgression of law and order. — *na koto wo sh'te wa warui.*

†Ō-GO, オウゴ, 擁護, *n.* Protection, (of Kami) providence. *Kami no — wo kōmuru,* to be under divine protection. Syn. MAMORU.

Ō-GO, ワウコ, 往古, *n.* Ancient times. — *kara ī-tsztayeta koto,* a tradition of ancient times. Syn. INISHIYE, MUKASHI.

OGO, ヲゴ, 海髪, *n.* A kind of sea-weed.

ŌGON, ワウゴン, 黄金, *(kogane), n.* Gold. Syn. KIN.

ŌGON, ワウゴン, 黄芩, *n.* Name of a medicine.

OGORI,*-ru,-tta,* オゴル, 奢, *t.v.* Given to extravagance, luxury, sumptuousness, or grandeur in living, to live in splendor. *Ogoru mono hisashikaradz,* an extravagant person cannot last long.

OGORI, オゴリ, 奢, *n.* Extravagance, luxury or splendor in living. — *ni kurasz,* to live in luxury. — *ga szgitte shinshō wo tszbusz,* ruined his fortune by extravagance. Syn. SHASHI.

OGOSOKA, オゴソカ, 嚴, Strict, severe, rigid, firm, grave. Syn. GENJŪ.

Ō-GOYE, オホゴヱ, 大聲, *n.* Loud voice.

Ō-GURAI, オホグラヒ, 大食, *n.* A great eater, a glutton.

OGURAI,-KI,-KU,-SHI, ヲグライ, 小暗, (Little dark), dull, dusky, shady, gloomy.

OGURUMA, ヲグルマ, 小車, *n.* The sunflower, Inula-Japonica.

OGUSHI, オグシ, *n.* The hair, (a word peculiar to women). Syn. KAMI.

O-HARI, オハリ, 阿針, *n.* A seamstress.

ŌHEI, アフヘイ, 押柄, Arrogant, proud, haughty, insolent. Syn. ŌFU.

Ō-HEN, ワウヘン, 往返, *(yuki kayeri).* Going and coming. *Yedo ye — no niuyō wa ikura,* what is the expense of going to Yedo and back? Syn. YUKIKI, ŌRAI.

Ō-HIDERI, オホヒデリ, 大旱, *n.* A long drought.

OHIYA, オヒヤ, *n.* Cool water, (for drinking). — *motte-koi,* bring me a glass of water.

OHIYE, オヒエ, *n.* A padded coat.

OI, ヲヒ, 甥, *n*. Nephew.

OI, オヒ, 笈, *n*. A kind of box with feet used for carrying burdens on the back.

OI, *oiru*, *oita*, オイル, 老, *i. v.* To grow old. *Oite futatabi chigo ni naru*, to grow old and become a child again. Syn. TOSHI GA YORU.

OI, オイ, 老, *n*. Old age. *Shi-jū wa — no hajime*, forty years is the beginning of old age. — *wo yashinau*, to support the aged. Syn. TOSHI-YORI.

†ŌI, *ōu*, or *ōru*, *ōita*, オフル, 生, *i.v.* To grow or shoot up, (as grass.) *Kusa ga ōru*, the grass sprouts up. Syn. HAYERU.

ŌI, *ōu*, *ōta*, オホフ, 掩, *t. v.* To cover, to screen, to hide, conceal. *Te de me wo* —, to cover the eyes with the hand. *Tszmi wo* —, to hide one's sins. Syn. KAKUSZ.

OI, オイ, Exclam. used in calling to attract the persons attention, = hollo.

OI, *ō*, *ōta*, オフ, 負, *t. v.* To carry on the back, to owe. *Senaka ni ni wo ō*, to carry goods on the back; *Shaku-sen wo* —, to owe borrowed money. *Te wo* —, to receive a wound. Syn. SEŌ, OBŪ.

OI, *ō*, *ōta*, オフ, 追, *t. v.* To pursue, to chase, to drive, to follow, to imitate. *Teki wo* —, to pursue an enemy. *Hi wo ōte*, daily, or day by day, gradually. *Seijin no ato wo* —, to follow in the steps of the sages. *Ushi wo ō*, to drive a cow.

OI, オヒ, 負, *n*. Something given to boot. *Ichi-bu — wo utsz*, to give an *ichi-bu* to boot.

ŌI, -KI, オホイ, 多, *a*. Many, numerous. *Kotoshi ame no furu hi ga ōi*, there were a great many rainy days this year. Syn. TANTO, TAK'SAN.

OI-ATSZME, *-ru*, *-tta*, オヒアツメル, 追集, *t.v.* To drive together, to collect together by driving.

OI-BARA, オヒバラ, 追腹, as in the phrase, — *wo kiru*, to commit suicide in order to follow a deceased master.

OI-BORE, *-ru*, *-ta*, オイボレル, 耄, *i. v.* To become childish with age, to be in one's dotage, decrepit. *Oi-bore-me*, a dotard. Syn. RŌMŌ SZRU.

OI-CHIRASHI, *-sz*, *-sh'ta*, オヒチラス, 追散, *t. v.* To drive and scatter.

OI-DASHI, *-sz*, *-sh'ta*, オヒダス, 追出, *t. v.* To drive out.

OI-DE, オイデ, 御出, (This word seems to be composed of *o* polite, and *ide*, the root form of *ideru;* used only as an imperative, or joined to the sub. verb.) Come, go. *Doko ye oide-nasaru*, where are you going? *Yedo ye oide nasaimash'ta ka*, have you been to *Yedo? Miyō-nichi oide*, or *oide-nasai*, Come to-morrow.

(2.) 御居, To be. *Damatte oide*, be silent, or don't tell. *Doko ni oide nasaru*, where do you live?

OIDO, オ井ド, 尻, *n*. (A polite word used by women). The buttock, posteriors. Syn SHIRI.

OI-HAGI, オヒハギ, 追褫, *n*. A highwayman, robber. Syn. DOROBŌ.

OI-HANACHI, *-tsz*, *-tta*, オヒハナツ 追放, *t.v.* To drive away so as not to return, to expel. *Kuni yori tszmibito wo* —, to exile a criminal.

OI-HARAI, *-au*, *-tta*, オヒハラフ, 追拂, *t.v.* To drive off, drive away, or expel, (as something annoying, or hurtful). *Aku-ma*, *tōzoku*, *teki nado wo* —, to drive away evil spirits, robbers, the enemy &c.

OI-HASHIRASHI, *-sz*, *-sh'ta*, オヒハシラス, 追走, *t. v.* To pursue and cause another to run.

OI-IDASHI, *-sz*, *-shta*, オヒイダス, same as *Oidashi*.

OI-KAKE, *-ru*, *-ta*, オヒカケル, 追掛, *t.v.* To drive on, to set on. *Inu wo h'to ni* —, to set a dog on a man. *Sakana wo ami ni* —, to drive fish into a net.

OI-KAYESHI, *-sz*, *-sh'ta*, オヒカヘス, 追返, *t v.* To drive back, to pursue and make return.

OI-KAZE, オヒカゼ, 追風, *n*. A fair wind. Syn. OITE, JUMPŪ.

OI-KOMI, *-mu*, *-nda*, オヒコム, 追込, *t.v.* To drive into. *Teki wo kawa ni* —, to drive the enemy into the river. *Shitsz wo* —, to drive in the itch.

OI-KOSHI, *-sz*, *-sh'ta*, オヒコス, 追越, *i.v.* To drive across, (as a mountain). To pursue and pass.

OI-KUDASHI, *-sz*, *-sh'ta*, オヒクダス, 追下, *t.v.* To drive down.

OI-MAKURI, *-ru*, *-tta*, オヒマクル, 追捲, *t.v.* To drive with violence, to roll up or back (the enemy's column.)

OI-MAWARI, *-ru*, *-tta*, オヒマワル, 追廻, *t.v.* To pursue all about, to follow around.

OI-MAWASHI, *-sz*, *-sh'ta*, オヒマワス, 追廻, *t.v.* To drive round, or about.

OI-ME, オヒメ, 負目, *n*. A debt, (little used), — *wo nugu*, to discharge a debt. Syn. SHAKKIN.

OI-MUKE, *-ru*, *-ta*, オヒムケル 追向 *t. v.* To drive opposite to.

†ŌI-NARU, オホイナル, 大, *a*. Large, great,

big. — *kana kami no megumi*, how great are the mercies of God!

OI-NOKE,-*ru*,-*ta*, オヒノケル, 追退, *t. v.* To drive away, to drive and cause to leave.

OI-OI, オヒオヒ, 追追, *adv.* Gradually, by degrees. Syn. SHIDAI, DAN-DAN.

OI-OTOSHI, オヒオトシ, 追落, *n.* A highwayman, robber. Syn. OI-HAGI.

OIRA, オイラ, 我等, *pro.* I, (Yedo vulg. coll). — *wa iya da*, I wont. Syn. WATAKUSHI.

†OIRAKU, オイラク, 老, *n.* Old-age. Syn. RŌ.

OIRAN, ホイラン, 花魁, *n.* The belle of harlots.

OIRU, オイル, 老, See *Oi*.

OISHIGERI,-*ru*,-*ta*, オヒシゲル, 生繁, *i. v.* To grow up luxuriantly. *Kusa, ki ga* —.

OISHII,-KI, オイシイ, 旨, *a.* Pleasant to the taste, delicious. Syn. UMAI.

OISHIKU, オイシク, 旨, *adv.* idem. — *nai*, not pleasant to the taste. *Shokumotsz wa* — *nai*, have no appetite.

OI-SHIRIZOKI,-*ku*,-*ita*, オヒシリゾク, 追退, *t.v.* To drive away.

OISHISA, オイシサ, 旨, *n.* Deliciousness, or pleasantness of taste.

OISHIU, オイシウ, 旨, *adv.* Same as *Oishiku*.

OI-TACHI, オヒタチ, 生立, *n.* Bringing up, growing up, growth. *Kodomo no* — *ga yoi*, the child grows finely.

OI-TATE,-*ru*,-*ta*, オヒタテル, 追立, *t. v.* To drive away, or expel from a place, not allow to dwell in a place.

OITE, オヒテ, 追風, *n.* A fair wind. Syn. JUMPŪ.

OITE, オヒテ, 追手, Same as *Otte*.

OITE, オイテ, 於, *post-posit.* (always preceded by *ni*). In, in respect of, in the case of, as to, in regard to. *Chō-jū nao rei ari, iwanya h'to ni oite wo ya*, beasts and birds even have manners, how much more then should men. *Kono tokoro ni* —, in this place.

OI-TSZKI,-*ku*,-*ita*, オヒツク, 追着, *t. v.* To overtake. *Hashitte h'to wo* —, to run and overtake a person.

OI-TSZME,-*ru*,-*ta*, オヒツメル, 追詰, *t.v.* To drive into a confined place, to drive and straiten, to corner. *Teki wo nan-jo ni* —, to drive the enemy into a strait place.

OI-UCHI, オヒウチ, 追討, *n.* Pursuing and killing. *H'to wo* — *ni szru*, to overtake and kill a person.

OI-USHINAI,-*au*,-*tta*, オヒウシナフ, 追失, *t.v.* To pursue after and lose or miss the object.

OI-WAKE, オヒワケ, 岐, *n.* A forked road.

OI-YARI,-*ru*,-*tta*, オヒヤル, 追遣, *t. v.* To drive off, to drive away.

OI-YOME, ヲヒヨメ, 姪婦, *n.* Nephew's wife.

†Ō-JAKU, ワウジヤク, 尫弱, Deformed and feeble.

OJI, ヲヂ, 伯父, *n.* Uncle.

ŌJI, オオヂ, 祖父, *n.* Grandfather.

ŌJI,-*jiru*, or -*dzu*,-*ta*, オウズル, 應, *i.v.* To accord with, agree, suit; to be proper, meet, appropriate, becoming; to respond to, to comply with, to obey. *Mi-bun ni ōdzru*, suitable to one's station in life. *Aidz ni ōjite*, conforming to the signal, &c. *Mei ni ōdzru mono nashi*, no one obeyed the command. Syn. AWASERU, KOTAYERU.

OJI,-*ru*,-*ta*, オヂル, 畏, *i. v.* To fear. *Sono ikioi ni ojite somuku mono nashi*, fearing his power all obeyed him, Syn. OSORERU.

OJIKE,-*ru*,-*ta*, オヂケル, 畏悸, *i. v.* To be afraid. *Ojikete mono mo iyenu*, so afraid he could not speak. Syn. KOWAGARU.

OJIKE, オヂケ, *n.* Fear. — *ga tszku*, smitten with fear.

OJIME, ヲジメ, 紐占, *n.* A slide on the strings of a bag or pouch to fasten it.

OJI-ONONOKI,-*ku*,-*ita*, オヂヲノノク, 戰慄, *i.v.* To tremble with fear.

OJI-OSORE,-*ru*,-*ta*, オヂオソレル, 恐怖, *i.v.* To fear.

†ŌJITSZ, ワウジツ, 往日, *n.* Past days, days gone by.

OJI-WANANAKI,-*ku*,-*ita*, オヂワナナク, Same as *Ojiononoki*.

ŌJŌ, ワウジヤウ, 王城, *n.* The capital, residence of the Emperor.

Ō-JŌ, ワウジヤウ, 往生, (*yuki umareru*). *n.* Going from this world and born into the next, — entering into life. (Bud). — *wo togeru*, to attain to life beyond the grave.

OKA, ヲカ, 岡, *n.* A hill.

OKA, ヲカ, 陸, *n.* Land. *Ōsaka ye — wo yuku*, to go by land to Osaka. Syn. KUGA, RIKU.

OKABO, ヲカボ, 陸穗, *n.* Hill-rice.

OKADZ, オカズ, *n.* Any thing eaten with rice. *Sakana wo — ni szru*, to eat fish as a relish with rice.

OKAGE, オカゲ, 御蔭, (lit. honorable shade). *n.* Kindness, help, influence, favor, grace. — *de naorimash'ta*, healed by your kind help. *Kami no — wo kōmuru*, to receive help from God.

OKA-ME, ヲカメ, 陸眼, *n.* (Lit, land-eyes), used only fig. of the judgment of a by-stander, or disinterested person. — *de mite wa wakaranu*, if you regard it from your stand point you cannot understand it. Syn. YOSOME.

ŌKAMI, オホカミ, 狼, *n.* A wolf.

†OKAN, ヲカン, 悪寒, *n.* The chill, the cold stage of fever. — *hotsz netsz*, chill and fever.

OKAPPIKI, ヲカツピキ, 岡引, *n.* A secret policeman, a spy.

OKASARE,*–ru,–ta*, オカサレル, 被侵, pass. of *Okasz.* To be invaded, or attacked. *Yamai ni* —, to be attacked by disease.

OKASHI,*–sz,–sh'ta*, オカス, 犯, *t.v.* To attack and invade, to make an incursion, to offend against, transgress, to usurp. *Hatto wo* —, to transgress the laws. *Tszmi wo* —, to commit a crime. *Kami wo* —, to offend against superiors. *Kuni wo* —, to invade a country. *Tekichi wo* —, to invade an enemy's country.

OKASHII,–KI, ヲカシイ, 可咲, *a.* Laughable, ludicrous, funny, odd, singular; delightful. — *banashi*, a laughable story. — *kao*, an odd face.

OKASHIKU, or OKASHIU, ヲカシク, 可咲, *adv.* . — *te tamaranu*, so ludicrous I could not help laughing.

OKASHISA, ヲカシサ, 可笑, *n.* Ludicrousness, oddity.

ŌKATA, オホカタ, 大方, *adv.* For the most part, chiefly, perhaps, probably, most likely. — *dekimash'ta*, it is for the most part done. — *naradz*, was not a little (*i.e.* very great). — *sō darō*, perhaps it is so. — *machigai wa arumai*, there is probably no mistake. Syn. TAI-TEI, KEDASAI, TABUN.

Ō-KAWA, オホカハ, 大川, *n.* A big-river.

Ō-KAZE, オホカゼ, 大風, *n.* A gale, tempest.

OKE, ヲケ, 桶, *n.* A bucket, tub.

OKE, オケ, imper. of *Oki.* Put down.

†ŌKENAI,–KI,–KU,–SHI, オホケナイ, 無負氣, Impossible, impracticable.

OKERA, ヲケラ, 蒼朮, *n.* A kind of medicinal plant. Syn. SŌJUTSZ.

†OKERU, オケル, 於, *post-pos.* same as *Oite.* In respect of, in regard to, in the case of, as to. *Kunshi no tenga ni* —, in regard to the good man in the world, &c. Syn. TSZITE.

†OKETSZ, ヲケツ, 悪血, *n.* Bad-blood.

OKI, オキ, 瀛, *n.* The wide sea, (in opposition to land). *Fune wo — ye kogi-dasz*, rowed the boat sea ward, or out to sea.

OKI, オキ, *n.* Coals of fire, live coals. — *ga dekitara okure*, when it (the wood) becomes coals bring them.

OKI,*–ku,–ita*, オク, 置, *t. v.* To place, to put, to lay, to set, to fix, settle, to let be. *Hon wo tszkuye ni* —, to lay a book on the table. *Tszyu ga oita*, the dew has fallen. *Shimo ga* —, frost has fallen. *Hōkōnin wo* —, to hire a servant. *Omaye wo oite hoka ni tanomu h'to wa nai*, there is no one to call on for assistance but yourself. *Tada oku mono ka*, do you think I will let it rest? *Tada wa okanu*, not to let a matter rest. *Kaite oku*, to write down, to make an entry, (in a book, &c.) *Mite oita*, have seen it. *Yaku-soku sh'te oita*, have made an agreement. *Atszraite oita*, have given the order for them to be made. *Shimatte oku*, to put away. *Sztete oku*, to let alone. *Shichi wo* —, to give a pledge. *Kokoro wo* —, to be reserved, to restrain one's self from being familiar, or open.

OKI,*–ku* or *–ru,–ta*, オキル, 起, *i.v.* To rise up from a recumbent position, to awake, to arise from sleep, to get up. *Yo ga akete mo mada okinu.* he is not awake, (or up) although it is morning. *Osoku okite wa warui*, late rising is bad. *Taorete okiru.* to fall down and get up. *Akambō ga okita*, the baby is awake.

OKI-AGARI,*–ru,–tta*, オキアガル, 起上, *i.v.* To rise up from sleep.

OKI-AGARI-KOBOSHI, オキアガリコボシ, 起上小法師, *n.* A toy which always turns head up.

OKI-AGE, オキアゲ, 置上, *n.* Low relief of figure in painting, sculpture, &c.

OKI-AI,*–au,–atta*, オキアフ, 置合, *t.v.* To be mutually reserved, or restrained. *Tagai-ni kokoro wo okiau*, idem.

OKI-BURUSHI, オキブルシ, 置古, *n.* Old and spoiled from being kept too long (as goods).
Syn. TANAZARASHI.

OKI-DOKORO, オキドコロ, 置所, *n.* A resting or stopping place, a place for putting anything. *Mi no — ga nai*, no place where he could stop.

OKI-FUSHI, オキフシ, 起臥, *n.* Awake or asleep, lying down or rising up.

OKI-GOTATSZ, オキゴタツ, 置火閣, *n.* A kind of movable fire-place.

ŌKII,–KI, オホキイ, 大, *a.* Large, big, great. — *yama*, a large mountain. *Ano fune yori kono fune ga okii*, this ship is larger than that.

ŌKIKU, オホキク, 大, *adv.* Idem. — *naru*, to become large. — *szru*, to make large. — *nai*, not large.

Ō-KIMI, オホキミ, 大君, *n.* The Emperor.

OKI-MIAGE, オキミヤゲ, 置土產, *n.* A present made on leaving, of something which one cannot take with him.

OKINA, オキナ, 翁, *n.* An old man, (respectful).

ŌKI-NA, オホキナ, 大, *a.* Large, big, great. — *koye*, a loud voice. — *shinsho*, a large fortune.

†OKINAGUSA, オキナグサ, 菊, *n.* The Chrysanthimum.

ŌKI-NI, オホキニ, 大, *adv.* Greatly, much. — *arigatō*, am much obliged. — *goshisō ni narimas'ta*, thank you for your delightful entertainment.

ŌKISA, オホキサ, 大, *n.* The bigness, size. — *wa dono kurai*, how large is it?

ŌKISHI, オホキシ, 大, *a.* See Ōkii.

OKITE, オキテ, 掟, *n.* Law, enactment, decree, statute, ordinance. *Kuni no — wo sadameru*, to enact the laws of a country. Syn. GO-HATTO, KISOKU.

OKITE-DŌRI, オキテドホリ, 掟通, Lawful, according to law. — *no akinai*, lawful trade. — *ni szru*, to do according to law.

OKI-TSZKE, オキツケ, 置付, *n.* Fixture, anything belonging to, or part of a house.

OKI-ZARI, オキザリ, 置去, *n.* Desertion of one's family, forsaking. *Kanai wo — ni szru*, to desert one's family.

OKKĀ, オクカア, 阿母, *n.* Mother. *Okkā-san*, (idem).
Syn. HAHA.

OKKAKE,*-ru,-ta*, オツカケル, 追驅, To pursue, to chase. *Koma wo hayamete okkake-kitaru*, urging on his horse he came in pursuit.

OKKANAI,-KI,-KU,-Ō,-SA, オクカナイ, 無奥, Afraid, fearful. Ō *okkanai*, take care! or you are in danger. *Okkanaku nai*, is not afraid. Syn. KOWAI.

OKKAYESHI,*-sz,-sh'ta*, オツカヘス, 追返, *t.v.* To drive back.

OKKOCHI,*-ru,-ta*, オツコチル, 落, *i.v.* (Yed. coll.) Same as *Ochiru*. To fall, to fall in love with. *Onna ni okkochita*, fell in love with a woman.
Syn. HORERU, REMBO.

OKKOCHI, オツコチ, *n.* A lover.

OKKŪ, オツクウ, *n.* Difficult, tedious. — *ni omō*, to consider difficult. — *ni szru*, to magnify the difficulties of any thing, to make a thing appear difficult when it is not.

†ŌKO, アフコ, 檜杖, *n.* A pole for carrying burdens. Syn. TEMBIMBŌ.

†OKO, ヲコ, 尾籠, Foolish, silly, ridiculous, laughable. — *no mono*, a silly person. — *no waza*. *Oko-naru kuse-mono kana*, what a silly fellow!

OKOGAMASHII,-KI,-KU, ヲコガマシイ, 尾籠敷, Ridiculous, or silly in manner or appearance.

OKONAI,*-au,-atta*, オコナフ, 行, *t.v.* To perform, to do, to execute, to practice. *Matszrigoto wo* —, to manage public affairs. *Michi wo* —, to practice the moral duties. *Zen wo* —, to act virtuously. *Tszmi wo* —, to execute punishment.

OKONAI, オコナヒ, 行, *n.* Actions, conduct, doings. *Mi no — ga warui*, his conduct is bad. Syn. GIYŌJO.

OKORI,*-ru,-tta*, オコル, 起, or 發, *i.v.* To arise, to originate, begin, to break out, to be excited, provoked, angry. *Hi ga* —, the fire begins to burn. *Yamai ga* —, sickness has broken out. *H'to ga* —, the man is angry. *Nani kara okotte dearō*, what could have been the cause? *Itsz no toki kara okotta*, when did it originate?
Syn. HAJIMARU, HASSZRU.

OKORI, オコリ, 起, *n.* The rise, origin, cause; anger, passion.
Syn. HAJIMARI, YUYE, KENYO, SHO-HOTSZ.

OKORI, オコリ, 瘧, *n.* Intermittent-fever, ague. Syn. G'YAKU.

OKOSHI,*-sz,-sh'ta*, オコス, 起, *t.v.* To excite, rouse up, stir up, cause to begin, raise up, to cause. *Neta h'to wo* —, to rouse a person sleeping. *Hi wo* —, to kindle a charcoal fire. *Sōdō wo* —, to excite a disturbance. *Ikari wo* —, to stir up anger. *Yamai wo* —, to cause sickness *Ikusa wo* —, to stir up war, or raise an army. *Shin-jin wo* —, to excite devotion. *Yama wo* —, to break up uncultivated ground. *Taoreta ki wo* —, to raise up a fallen tree. *Horobitaru kuni wo* —, to raise up a kingdom that has once been overthrown. *Hiki-okosz*, to pull up.
Syn. HAJIMERU, HASSZRU.

OKOSHI,*-sz,-sh'ta*, オコス, 遣, *t.v.* To send. *Onna ga okosh'ta fumi*, a letter received from a woman.
Syn. YOKOSZ, OKURU.

OKOSHI, オコシ, 粔籹, *n.* A kind of confectionary made of parched rice and sugar.

OKOTARI,*-ru,-tta*, オコタル, 怠, *t.v.* To neglect, to be careless, or lazy in doing.

Tsztome wo —, to neglect one's duty. *Kagiyō wo* —, to neglect business.

OKOTARI, オコタリ, 怠, *n.* Negligence, laziness, remissness.
Syn. BUSHŌ, TAIDA, RANDA.

†OKOTO, or OKOTORA, オコト, 汝, *pro.* You. Syn. OMAYE, NANJI.

OKU, オク, 置, See *Oki.*

ŌKU, オホク, 多, *adv.* Many, numerous. — *naru*, to become numerous.

OKU, オク, 億, *n.* A million.
Syn. HYAKU-MAN.

OKU, オク, 奥, *n.* The back, or the innermost part of any thing, or most remote from the front. *Iye no* —, the back or the most inner part of a house. *Yama no* —, the deepest parts of mountains. *Kuchi no* —, the back of the mouth. — *no hō*, the back or innermost part. — *no ma*, the back room. *Kokoro no* —, the inmost recesses of the heart. *Hon no* —, the back part of a book.

OKUBA, オクバ, 奥歯, *n.* The back teeth, molars.

OKUBI, オクビ, 噯氣, *n.* Belching, eructation. — *wo szru*, to belch.

OKUBI, オクビ, 衽, *n*, The gore sewed into the front of Japanese *Kimono.*

OKUBIYŌ, オクビヤウ, 臆病, *n.* Cowardice, — *na h'to*, or — *mono*, a coward.
Syn. HIKIYŌ.

OKU-BUKAI,-KI,-KU,-SHI,-Ō,-SA, オクブカイ, 奥深, Far back, deep, profound, obscure. *Okubukai zashiki*, a room extending far back, a deep room. *Yama ye okubukaku hairu*, to go deep into the mountains,

ŌKUCHI, ヲホクチ, 大口, *n.* A wide kind of trowsers.

OKUGAKI, オクガキ, 跋, *n.* The writing at the end of a Japanese or Chinese book, a seal or signature at the end of a writing to authenticate it.

OKU-GATA, オクガタ, 奥方, *n.* Wife (of honorable persons.)

OKUGI, オクギ, 奥義, Same as *Ōgi.*

OKU-I, オクイ, 奥意, *n.* The most abstruse, recondite, or profound parts of a subject. Syn. ŌGI.

OKURE,-*ru*,-*ta*, オクレル, 後, *i.v.* To be behind, to be left, or fall behind, to flag, to be late, slow, or tardy in comparison with others. *Ashi ga yowai kara okureta*, being weak in the legs he fell behind. *Riu-kō ni okureru*, to be behind the fashion. *Haha ni* —, left behind by the mother (as a child, the mother dying.)

OKURE, オクレ, The imp. of *Okuri,-ru*, to send.

OKURE, オクレ, Imp. of *Kure,-ru*, to give, with *O* polite. *Mite okure*, let me see. *Tempo okure*, give me a *tempo. Midz wo nonde okure*, give me a drink of water.

OKURE, オクレ, 後, *n.* Backwardness, fear, cowardice, faint-hearted. —*wo toru*, to be seized with cowardice. See *Ki-okure, Te-okure.*

OKURE-BASE, オクレバセ, 後走, *n.* Being late, or behind-hand to hurry after. —*ni kita*, being late have come in a hurry.

OKURI,-*ru*,-*tta*, オクル, 送, *t.v.* To send, to accompany, or attend, (as a guest). To pass the time, to live, to recompence. *Tegami wo* —, to send a letter. *Ni wo Ōsaka ye* —, to send goods to Osaka. *Yo, tszki, hi, toshi wo* —, to pass one's life, months, days or years. *Kiyaku wo hashi made* —, to accompany a guest as far as the bridge. *On wo* —, to recompense kindness.

OKURI, オクリ, 送, *n* Sending, accompanying; a funeral.

OKURI-DASHI,-*sz*,-*sh'ta*, オクリダス, 送出, *t.v.* To send out, or away; to go along with, (as a guest.)

OKURI-JŌ, オクリジヤウ, 送状, *n.* A memorandum, or list of articles, sent along with the articles, an invoice.

OKURI-MONO, オクリモノ, 贈, *n.* A present.

OKURI-MUKAI, オクリムカヒ, 送迎, *n.* Accompanying a guest to the gate, or going out to meet him.

OKURI-NA, オクリナ, 諡, *n.* A posthumous title, or name given after death.

OKURI-TEGATA, オクリテガタ, 送手形, *n.* A letter of introduction.

OKUSAMA, オクサマ, 奥様, *n.* Wife.

†OKUSETSZ, オクセツ, 臆説, *n.* Original thought, or a story of one's own conception.

OKU,-*shi*,-*sz*,-*sh'ta*, オクスル, 臆, *i. v.* To be afraid, cowardly, ashamed. *Okush'taru iro naku*, no signs of fear, or cowardice.

OKU-SHO, オクシヨ, 奥書, *n.* A writing added to certify to, or authenticate, an indorsement.

OKU-SOKO-NAI,-KI,-KU, オクソコナイ, 無奥底, fig. of a person who is open, frank, without concealment, or disguise.

OKUTE, オクテ, 晩稲, *n.* Late rice.

OKUYUKASHII,-KI,-KU, オクユカシイ, 奥床敷, Profound or erudite but unaffected and simple.

OKU-YUKI, オクユキ, 奥行, *n.* The depth,

or dimension from front to rear. *Iye no — wa jū-san gen*, the house is seventy-eight feet deep.

OMAHAN, オマハン, *pro.* You, (same as *Omayesan*, only used by low women).

ŌMAKA-NA, オホマカ, *a.* Magnanimous, honorable, liberal. — *na h'to.*
Syn. TAIRIYŌ.

OMAMMA, オマンマ, 飯, *n.* Boiled rice.

†OMANDOKORO, オホマンドコロ, (*obs.*) The steward of the *Shōgun* in the times of *Ashi-kaga.*

OMANKO, オマンコ, 陰門, *n.* The vulva.
Syn. IMMON, TSZBI.

OMAYE, or OMAI, オマヘ, 御前, *pro.* You. Syn. ANATA, NANJI,

OMBA, オムバ, 乳母, *n.* A wet-nurse.
Syn. UBA.

†OMBEN, オンベン, 音便, (*koye no taori*). Contracting or altering the pronunciation of words, in order to easy utterance, as, *Gozarimas*, into *Gozaimas*, or *Gozas*, *Riyokuhan* into *Rōha.*

OM-BIN, オンビン, 隱便, Secret, concealed, hushed up. — *ni szru*, to suppress, or hush up a matter so as not to become public.
Syn. HISOKA, NAIBUN.

OME,–*ru*,–*ta*, オメル, *i. v.* To be bashful, timid, diffident, ashamed. *Ometaru iro naku*, without any appearance of diffidenee. *Omedz-okusedz*, without diffidence or fear.
Syn. HADZKASHIGARU, WAROBIRERU.

†O-MEI, ヲメイ, 汚名, (*kegaretaru na.*) *n.* Bad name, foul reputation. — *wo ukeru*, to get a bad name.

OMEKI,–*ku*,–*ita*, ヲメク, 叫, *i. v.* To make a great outcry or confused noise, as of many persons shouting at once, to clamor, to shout, halloo.
Syn. WAMEKU, SAKEBU.

OMEKI-SAKEBI,–*bu*,–*nda*, ヲメキサケブ, *i. v.* To make a great clamor and noise.

OME-MUSHI, オメムシ, 地虱, *n.* The wood-louse.

OME-OME-TO, オメオメト, *adv.* In a sheepish, bashful, or abashed manner, in a confused manner. — *kayette kuru*, come back crestfallen.

ŌMIDZ, オホミヅ, 大水, *n*, An inundation.
Syn. KŌDZI.

†Ō-MIKE, オホミケ, 大御食, *n.* The boiled rice offered to the *kami*, or eaten by the *Tenshi.*

†OMINA, ヲミナ, 女, (*obs.*) A woman, female.

OMINAMESHI, ヲミナメシ, 女郎花, *n.* The name of a flower.

Ō-MISOKA, オホミソカ, 大晦日, *n.* The last day of the 12th month.

OMŌ, オモフ, 思, see *Omoi.*

OMŌ, オモウ, 重, *adv.* same as *Omoku.*

†OMO, オモ, 面, *n.* The face, the surface. *Umi no* —, the surface of the sea. *Midz no* —, the face of the waters.
Syn. TSZRA, MEN.

OMOCHA, オモチヤ, 玩物, *n.* Toy, plaything. Syn. G'WAMBUTSZ, MOTEASOBI.

†OMO-DACHI, オモダチ, 面貌, *n.* The form of the face, the features.

OMODACHI,–*tsz*,–*tta*, オモダツ, 重立, *i.v.* To be chief in authority, to be high or principal. *Omodatta yaku-nin wa mada konai*, the chief officer has not yet come.

OMODAKA, オモダカ, 澤瀉, *n.* A kind of water plant.

OMODE, オモデ, 重手, *n.* A severe wound. — *wo ō*, to receive a severe wound.

‖OMŌDOCHI, オモフドチ, 思同士, *n.* Persons of the same mind.

OMOGAI, オモガヒ, 鞴, *n.* A bridle.

OMOGAWARI, オモガワリ, 面變, *n.* Alteration or change in the face, (as by age)

OMOHAYUI,–KI,–KU, オモハユイ, 面羞, *a.* and *adv.* Bashful, diffident, timid.
Syn. HADZKASHII.

†OMOHOYE,–*ru*, オモホエル, 所思, (*obs*). To think, perceive, to regard. Same as *Omoi*,–*ō*.

OMOI,–KI, オモイ, 重, *a.* Heavy, weighty, severe, important. *Mekata ga*—, the weight is heavy. *Kurai ga* —, high in rank. *Tszmi ga* —, the crime is great. *Ki ga* —, spirits are dull. *Yamai ga* —, disease is severe. — *yakume wo tsztomeru* ,to discharge important duties.

OMOI,–*ō*,–*ōta*, オモフ, 思, *t.v.* To think, suppose, consider, regard, to think about, long after. *Nan to omō*, what do you think? *Nan to mo omowanu*, to think nothing of, to disregard, or make light of. *Oya wo* —, to think about one's parents. *Yoi to omō*, think well of it.
Syn. SHIYUI SZRU, KANGAYERU.

OMOI, オモヒ, 思, *n.* Thought, expectation. — *no hoka*, unexpected or different from what was expected, disappointment. — *no mama*, as one expects, or wishes. — *wo noberu*, to express one's thoughts.
Syn. SHINEN, KOKOROBASE.

OMOI-AI,–*au*,–*atta*, オモヒアフ, 思合, *i.v.* To regard each other with affection, to think of each other.

OMOI-AMARI,–*ru*,–*tta*, オモヒアマル, 思餘, *i.v.* Unable to restrain one's feelings of love, anger, hatred, &c., overcome by feeling.

OMOI-ATARI,-*ru*,-*tta*, オモヒアタル, 思當, *i.v.* To be struck with the thought, to call to mind, to be think one's self.

OMOI-AYAMARI,-*ru*,-*tta*, オモヒアヤマル, 思誤, *i. v.* To mistake in thinking of any thing, to misconceive.

OMOI-BA, オモヒバ, 思羽, *n.* The beautiful feathers on the back of certain wild-fowls, as the duck, pheasant, &c.

OMOI-BITO, オモヒビト, 思人, *n.* One much thought of, one loved.
Syn. KOIBITO.

OMOI-CHIGAI,-*au*,-*tta*, オモヒチガフ, 思違, *i. v.* To differ, or mistake, in what one thinks or supposes, to misapprehend.

OMOI-DASHI,-*sz*,-*sh'ta*, オモヒダス, 思出, *t. v.* To recollect, to bring to mind, to remember.

OMOI-GAKE-NAI,-KI,-KU, オモヒガケナイ, 無思掛, Unexpected, unthought of, unlooked for, incidental.

OMOI-GO, オモヒゴ, 思子, *n.* Much thought of child, a beloved child.

OMOI-GOTO, オモヒゴト, 思事, *n.* Care, anxiety, trouble.
Syn. SHIMPAI, KURŌ.

OMOI-GUSA, オモヒグサ, 思草, *n.* A loved plant; subject, or matter for thought, care, or anxiety.

OMOI-KAMAYE,-*ru*,-*ta*, オモヒカマヘル, 思構, *t.v.* To think of and be prepared for, to anticipate.

OMOI-KAYESHI,-*sz*,-*sh'ta* オモヒカヘス, 思返, *t. v.* To think over again, to reconsider.

OMOI-KIRI,-*ru*,-*tta*, オモヒキル, 思切, *t.v.* To cease thinking about, to make up one's mind, to resolve.

OMOI-KOMI,-*mu*,-*nda*, オモヒコム, 思込, *i.v.* To entertain the opinion, to be under the impression, or for some time to be thinking. *Tash'kani aru to omoikonde ita ga nakatta*, I thought it was certainly so, but find it is not.

OMOI-MAWASHI,-*sz*,-*sh'ta*, オモヒマハス, 思回, *t.v.* To revolve in the mind, to reflect on.

OMOI-MEGURASHI,-*sz*,-*sh'ta*, オモヒメグラス, 思回, *t.v.* (idem).

OMOMI, オモミ, 重, *n.* Weight, heaviness, importance, dignity or rank.

OMOI-MIDARE,-*ru*,-*ta*, オモヒミダレル, 思亂, *t.v.* To be perplexed, confused, distracted.

OMOI-MŌKE,-*ru*,-*ta*, オモヒモウケル, 思設, *i.v.* To think of before hand and be prepared for.

OMOI-NAOSHI,-*sz*,-*sh'ta*, オモヒナホス, 思直, *t.v.* To reconsider, to think better of, to alter one's opinion about.

OMOI-NASHI, オモヒナシ, 思成, *n.* Fancy, conceit, imagination, opinion, theory. *Omaye no* — *da*, that is a fancy of yours.

OMOI-NOKOSHI,-*sz*,-*sh'ta*, オモヒノコス, 思殘, *t.v.* To feel sorrow, or regret at leaving.

OMOI-OKI,-*ku*,-*ita*, オモヒオク, 思置, *i.v.* To have anything on the mind which one wishes to say.

OMOI-SADAME,-*ru*,-*ta*, オモヒサダメル, 思定, *t.v.* To make up one's mind, to resolve, or determine on.

OMO-IRE, オモイレ, *adv.* As much as one wishes, opinion, supposition, according to one's mind. Syn. ZOMBUN.

OMOI-SAGE,-*ru*,-*ta*, オモヒサゲル, 思下, *t.v.* To think meanly of, to despise, contemn.

OMOI-SOME,-*ru*,-*ta*, オモヒソメル, 思始, *t.v.* To begin to love.

OMOI-SZGOSHI,-*sz*,-*sh'ta*, オモヒスゴス, 思過, *t.v.* To think too much about, to be too anxious or solicitous about, to love too much.

OMOI-SZTE,-*ru*,-*ta*, オモヒステル, 思捨, *t.v.* To cease thinking about, banish from one's mind.

OMOI-TACHI,-*tsz*,-*tta*, オモヒタツ, 思立, *i.v.* To resolve in one's mind, to suddenly think about.

OMOI-TAGAYE,-*ru*,-*ta*, オモヒタガヘル 思違, Same as *Omoichigai*.

OMOI-TORI, オモヒトリ, 思取, *n.* Understanding, or comprehension.

OMOI-TSZKI,-*ku*,-*ita*, オモヒツク, 思著, *t.v.* To think of, to recollect; call to mind, to be attached to, to cleave to in heart.

OMOI-TSZME,-*ru*,-*ta*, オモヒツメル, 思詰, *t.v.* To dwell upon in thought, to think upon constantly, to be absorbed in, wrapped up in.

OMOI-TSZMORI,-*ru*,-*tta*, オモヒツモル, 思積, *i.v.* To think more and more about, to grow more concerned about.

OMOI-WABI,-*ru*,-*ta*, オモヒワビル, 思侘, *i.v.* To think and fret about.

OMOI-WADZRAI,-*au*,-*atta*, オモヒワヅラフ, 思煩, *i.v.* Idem.

OMOI-WAKE, オモヒワケ, 思分 *n.* Judgment, discernment, discrimination. — *no nai h'to*, a man of no judgment.

OMOI-WASZRE, *-ru, -ta*, オモヒワスレル, 思忘, *t.v.* To forget, not to think of.

OMOI-YARI, *-ru, -tta*, オモヒヤル, 思遣, *t.v.* To banish out of one's thoughts. 想像, To imagine, or think how others feel and do, to sympathize with, have a fellow feeling for.

OMOI-YORANU, オモヒヨラヌ, 不思依, Unexpected, unthought of, not anticipated, incidental. *Omoi mo yorazarikereba*, being taken by surprise, or unawares. — *saiwai*, unexpected good fortune.

OMO-KAGE, オモカゲ, 面影, *n.* The likeness of another pictured in the imagination, or in vision. *Oya no szgata ga — ni miyeru*, the likeness of his parent appeared to his fancy.

OMOKAJI, オモカヂ, 面梶, *n.* The helm to the starboard. — *wo toru*, to starboard the helm.

OMOKU, オモク, 重, *adv.* Heavy. — *naru*, to become heavy.

OMOKUSA, オモクサ, 面瘡, *n.* An eruption on the face.

OMŌ-MAMA-NI, オモフママ, 思儘, *adv.* At one's pleasure, according to one's own mind, or choice. Syn. KOKORO SHIDAI.

†OMOMMIRU, *-mireba*, オモンミル, 以, *conj.* On reflection.

OMOMOCHI, オモモチ, 面持, *n.* Countenance, expression of face. *Kikitaru — sedz*, did not let on that he heard.

†OMOMPAKARI, *-ru, -tta*, オモンパカル, 慮, *i.v.* To consider, reflect, deliberate, ponder.

OMOMUKI, *-ku, -ita*, オモムク, 趣, *i.v.* To go. *Fune nite ōsaka ye omomukimash'ta*, has gone by ship to Osaka. Syn. YUKU.

OMOMUKI, オモムキ, 趣, *n.* Subject, meaning, purport, tenor, fashion, form. *Tegami no —*, the purport of a letter. *Hon no —*, the subject of a book. Syn. WAKE, YŌSZ.

†OMOMURO-NI, オモムロニ, 舒, *adv.* Softly, gently, (as of zephyrs). *Sei fū — kitaru.*

OMO-NAGA, オモナガ, 面長, *n.* Long-face.

†OMONAKI, -KU, -SHI, オモナキ; 無面, *a.* Ashamed. Syn. HADZKASHII, OMOHAYUI.

†OMONERI, *-ru, -ta*, オモネル, 阿諛, *i.v.* To flatter, to be obsequious, compliant. Syn. HETSZRAU, RAIDŌ, KOBIRU.

OMO-NI, オモニ, 重荷, *n.* Heavy burden or load. *H'to no isshō wa — wo ōte tōki michi wo yuku ga gotoshi*, the life of man is like going a long road carrying a heavy load.

OMO-NI, オモニ, *adv.* Generally, principally, for the most part, chiefly, mainly. *Nippon no h'to — kome wo kū*, the Japanese principally eat rice. Syn. MOPPARA.

OMONJI, *-ru*, or *-dzru, -ta*, オモンズル, 重, *t.v.* To esteem, value, prize, to regard with respect, to dignify, honor. *Inochi wo karonji gi wo omondzru*, to prize right more than life. Syn. TATTOBU.

OMO-OMOSHII, -KI, -KU, -U-, SA, オモオモシイ, 重重, Grave, sober, dignified, consequential, imposing, momentous, important, serious.

OMORI, オモリ, 錘, *n.* A weight, (used in weighing).

OMORI, *-ru, -tta*, オモル, 重, *i.v.* To be grave, weighty, serious, important, of consequence. *Yamai ga —*, the disease is dangerous.

O-MORI, オモリ, 御守, *n.* The attendant, or guard of the children of nobles.

OMŌSAMA, オモフサマ, 思樣, *adv.* As much as one pleases, or wills. — *ni shikaru*, to scold severely. Syn. OMOIRE, ZOMBUN.

OMOSHI, オモシ, 重, *a.* Heavy, weighty, important.

OMOSHI, オモシ, 壓石, (cont. of *Omoi*, heavy, and *Ishi*, stone). *n.* A weight, (for pressing or weighing). — *ga kikanu yakunin*, an officer of no influence.

OMOSHIRŌ, オモシロウ, Same as *Omoshiroku.*

OMOSHIROGARI, *-ru, -tta*, オモシロガル, 面白, *i*, or *t.v.* To be pleased, delighted, glad, to enjoy. *Shibai wo —*, to be delighted with the theatre.

OMOSHIROI, -KI, -SHI, オモシロイ, 面白, *a.* Pleasant, delightful, agreeable, amusing, curious. Syn. TANOSHII.

OMOSHIROKU, オモシロク, 面白, *adv.* Id. — *nai*, not pleasant.

OMOSHIROSA, オモシロサ, 面白, *n.* Agreeableness, enjoyment, pleasure.

OMOTAI, -KI, -SHI, オモタイ, 重, *a.* Heavy, weighty, same as *Omoi*. *Nimotsz ga —*, the goods are heavy.

OMOTAKU, オモタク, 重, *adv.* Idem.

OMOTE, オモテ, 表 or 面, *n.* The face, front, surface, outside. After the name of a place it has no meaning. *Tatami no —*, the outside cover of a mat. *Iye no —*, front of a house. *Kimono no —*, outside of a garment. *Umi no —*, surface of the sea. *Yedo — ye yuku*, to go to Yedo. — *wo furū*, to shake the head (in dissent). — *wo akameru*, to blush. *Ya-omote ni szszmu*, to advance within range of arrows. Syn. MEN, HIYŌ.

OMOTE-BUSE, オモテブセ, 面伏, *n.* Hanging the head for shame, downcast.

OMOTE-DACHI, *-tsz*, *-tta*, オモテダツ, 表立, *i.v.* To be public, open, not private.

OMOTE-MON, オモテモン, 表門, *n.* Front-door.

OMOTE-MUKI, オモテムキ, 表向, *adv.* Openly, publicly, apparently, in appearance, seemingly. Syn. Ō-YAKE.

OMOTE-OKOSHI, オモテオコシ, 面起, *n.* Lifting up the head on account of merit, or honor.

OMOTO, オモト, 萬年青, *n.* The name of a plant.

OMŌ-TSZBO, オモフツボ, 思所, *n.* The place intended or aimed at. — *wo i-nuku*, to hit the mark with an arrow.

OMOWABA, オモハバ, subj. mood of *Omoi*.

OMOWAKU, オモハク, 思, *n.* (Same as *Omō*). Mind, opinion, sentiment. *H'to no — wa wakaranu*, don't know the opinions of others.

OMOWASE, *-ru*, *-ta*, オモハセル, 令思, caust. of *Omoi*. To cause, or induce another to think. *H'to ni waruku omowaseru*, to cause others to think ill of.

OMOWASHII, -KI, -KU, オモハシイ, 令敷, That which is to one's mind, desirable; thoughtful, or full of care. *Mono omowashii kao-tszki* a careworn countenance. *Omowashiku naï*, not to one's mind.

OMOYA, オモヤ, 正屋, *n.* The main building, or the house, as distinguished from the out-houses.

OMOYASE, *-ru*, *-ta*, オモヤセル, 面瘦, *t.v.* To be thin or lean in the face, cadaverous.

OMOYATSZRE, *-ru*, オモヤツレル, Idem.

†OMOYERAKU, オモヘラク, 以爲, To think, be of the opinion. *Ware — shikaradz*, in my judgment it is not so.

OMOYU, オモユ, 稀粥, *n.* A thin gruel made of rice.

OMOZASHI, オモザシ, 面刺, *n.* The countenance, the appearance of the face, the features. *Ko no — chichi ni niteoru*, the countenance of the child resembles his father's. — *no yoi h'to*, a person of fine countenance. Syn. KAO-TSZKI.

ŌMU, アウム, 鸚鵡, *n.* A parrot.

Ō-MUGI, オホムギ, 大麥, *n.* Barley.

ŌMUKASHI, オホムカシ, 大古, *n.* Remote antiquity.

Ō-MUNE, オホムネ, 大概, *adv.* Generally, in the main, without detail, without particularity. Syn. TAIGAI, TAI-TEI, TAI-RIYAKU.

ON, オン, 恩, *n.* Favor, kindness, grace, benefits, mercy. — *wo kōmuru*, or — *wo ukeru*, to receive kindness. — *wo mukū*, to requite favors. — *wo kiseru*, to bestow kindness. — *wo shiranu h'to*, an ungrateful person. Syn. MEGUMI.

ON, オン, 音, *n.* Sound, voice. *Ji no —*, the sonnd of a character. *Dai on*, loud voice.

ON, オン, 御, An honorable or respectful prefix, same as *Go*, and *O*. There seems to be no rule, but custom or euphony, to determine which of these prefixes should be used in any particular case, in preference to the others.

ON-AI, オンアイ, 恩愛, *n.* Parental, filial or conjugal love.

O-NAGA-MUSHI, ヲナガムシ, 尾長虫, *n.* A maggot.

ONAGO, ヲナゴ, 女子, *n.* A woman, female. Syn. ONNA.

ONAGORASHII, ヲナゴラシイ, *a.* Having the appearance or manner of a woman, like a woman.

ONAJI, -KI, オナジ, 同, *a.* Same, like. *Onaji na*, same name. *Onaji yō ni*, in the same way. *Onaji-koto*, same thing, alike. *Onaji-tokoro*, same place. Syn. DŌ, HITOSHII.

ONAJIKU, オナジク, 同, *adv.* Id. Ditto, aforesaid. — *nai*, not alike. — *naru*, to become like.

ONAJIKUBA, オナジクバ, (cont. of *Onajiku* and *Naraba*). If it is all one, if it makes no difference.

ONAKA, オナカ, 腹, *n.* Belly, abdomen, (used by women). Syn. HARA.

‖ONAME, ヲナメ, 牝牛, *n.* A cow.

O-NARI, オナリ, 御成, *n.* Going, (used only of the Kubō, or officers of the same rank). *Kubō-sama — de gozarimas* the Kubō is going out.

ONDO, オンド, 音頭, Raising the tune, or leading in singing. — *wo toru*, to lead in singing.

ONDOTORI, オンドトリ, 音頭取, *n.* The person who raises the tune, or leads in singing.

†ONDOKU, オンドク, 音讀, *n.* Reading the characters according to their sounds, without rendering into Japanese. — *szru*.

ONDORI, ヲンドリ, 雄鳥, *n.* A male bird, a cock.

†ONETSZ, ヲネツ, 悪熱, *n.* A bad fever.

ONGAKU, オンガク, 音樂, *n.* An entertainment of vocal and instrumental music, accompanied with dancing. — *wo sō szru.*

ON-GAYESHI, オンガヘシ, 恩返, *n.* Repayment of a kindness.

ON-G'YOKU, オンギヨク, 音曲, *n.* Same as *Ongaku.*

ONGOKU, ヲンゴク, 遠國, (*tōi kuni*), *n.* Distant country.

ONI, オニ, 鬼, *n.* A devil, demon. Syn. MA.

ONI-AZAMI, オニアザミ, 鬼薊, *n.* A kind of thistle.

ONIBI, オニビ, 鬼火, *n.* Ignis-fatuus, jack with a lantern.

ONI-MUSHI, オニムシ, 鬼蟲, *n.* A species of horned beetle.

ONI-YARAI, オニヤラヒ, 儺, *n.* The ceremony of driving out evil spirits, at the close of the year.

ON-JAKU, ヲンジヤク, 温石, *n.* A stone heated, plunged into water and applied to a painful part.

ON-JŌ, オンジヤウ, 音聲, *n.* The voice. *Dai — ni yobitateru,* to call out with a loud voice.

ON-JUN, ヲンジユン, 温順, *n.* Meek, amiable, gentle. — *na h'to,* an amiable person. Syn. ONTŌ.

†ON-K'WA, ヲンクワ, 温和, Idem.

ONNA, ヲンナ, 女, *n.* or *a.* A female, woman. — *no ko,* a girl, female child. — *isha,* a female physician. — *kiyōdai,* sisters. Syn. JO, FUJIN.

ONNAGAMI, ヲンナガミ, 女神, *n.* A goddess.

ONNA-GATA, ヲンナガタ, 女方, *n.* A play-actor who represents the female part.

ONNARASHII,-KI,-KU, ヲンナラシイ, 女敷, Having the manner or appearance of a woman, feminine.

ONNEN, ヲンネン, 怨念, (*urami no omoi*). *n.* Resentment, hatred for wrongs inflicted, spite, enmity.

ONO, ヲノ, 斧, *n.* A broad-axe.

ONODZKARA, オノヅラカ, 自, *adv.* Of itself, of its own accord, spontaneously, naturally, fortuitous. Syn. SHIZEN.

ONODZTO, オノヅト, 自, (Idem.)

ONOGA, オノガ, 己, *poss. pro.* Own, either my own, or his own, according to its connection. Syn. WAGA, ONOREGA.

†ONOKO, ヲノコ, 男, *n.* A male, man. — *go,* a male child, boy. Syn. NANSHI, OTOKO.

ONONOKI,-*ku,*-*ita,* ヲノノク, 戰慄, *i.v.* To tremble with fear. Syn. WANANAKU.

ONO-ONO, オノオノ, 各, *a.* Each, every one. — *gata yoku kikinasare,* let each one of you listen attentively. Syn. ICHI-ICHI.

ONORE, オノレ, 己, *per. pro.* I, you, myself, yourself, himself, one's self. *Onore ni katsz,* to conquer one's self, = deny thyself. *Onorega,* my, your, my own, your own, one's own. *Onore-ra,* plur. we, you. *Onore-ra ga yō na warui mono wa nai,* there are no persons as bad as you. *Onore-me,* you, (addressing a contemptible person.)

†ONOYE, ヲノヘ, 丘上, *n.* A low hill, a high-place. — *no matsz.*

ON-RIYŌ ヲンリヤウ, 怨靈, (*urami no tamashii*). *n.* The manes of a deceased enemy, supposed still to retain enmity.

ON-ROKU, オンロク, 恩祿, *n.* Salary, or pension in rice paid by a lord to his vassal.

ON-RU, ヲンル, 遠流, (*tōku nagasz*). *n.* Exile, or banishment to a distant place. Syn. SHIMA-NAGASHI, RUZAI, YENTŌ.

†ON-SEI, オンセイ, 音聲, *n.* The voice. Syn. KOYE.

ON-SEN, ヲンセン, 温泉, *n.* A hot spring. Syn. IDE-YU.

†ON-SHA, オンシヤ, 恩謝, *n.* Gratitude, thanks for kindness received.

†ON-SHAKU, オンシヤク, 恩借, To borrow. — *itash'ta kane,* money which you kindly lent me.

ON-SHŌ, オンシヤウ, 恩賞, *n.* Reward, conferred for services, by a superior.

ON-TAKU, オンタク, 恩澤, (*megumi no uruoi*). *n.* Grace, favor, kindness, benefactions. *Kami no — wo kōmuru,* to receive blessings from God.

†ON-TŌ, ヲンタウ, 穩當, Amiable, gentle, meek, mild. Syn. ONJUN.

†ON-TOKU, オントク, 恩德, *n.* Same as *On-taku.*

ONYŌSHI, オンヤウシ, 陰陽師, *n.* The soothsayer, or oracle of the *Tenshi.*

†Ō-Ō-TO, アウアウト, 快快, *adv.* Gloomy, melancholy, dejected in spirits. *Kokoro — sh'te tanoshimadz,* he was gloomy and unhappy. Syn. UTSZ-UTSZ.

Ō-Ō, ワウワウ, 往往, *adv.* Sometimes, now and then, here and there, some places, eventually, in process of time. — *miru h'to ari,* now and then there are persons who see it. *Yokohama — wa ōkina minato ni narimashō,* Y. will in process of time become a great mart of trade. Syn. MAMA, ORI-ORI, YUKU-YUKU.

OPPANASHI,-*sz,*-*sh'ta,* オツパナス, 追放, Same as *Oi-hanachi.*

OPPARAI,*-au,-atta*, オツパラフ, 追拂, Same as *Oi-harai*.

OPPUSE,*-ru,-ta*, オツプセル, 壓伏, *t. v.* (cont. of *Oshi-fuseru*). To seize and force down to the ground.

ŌRAI, ワウライ, 往來, *(yukiki)*. *n.* Passing to and fro, going and coming, communication, intercourse; a road, title of a book. *Yo ga fukete — ga tayeru*, when it is late at night the passing to and fro of people ceases. Syn. ŌHEN, MICHI.

ORANDA, オランダ, 荷蘭陀, *n.* Holland. *— no h'to*, a Hollander.

†ORANDZRAN, ヲランヅラン, (obs.) Same as coll. *Orimashō*.

ORASE,*-ru,-ta*, ヲラセル, 令居, Caust. of *Ori*. To cause to be, or dwell.

ORE, ワレ, 予, *per. pro.* I, (vulgar). *Orega*, my own, my. Syn. WARE.

ORE,*-ru,-ta*, ヲレル, 折, *i.v.* Broken, (of a stick, or any thing long). *Hone ga oreta*, the bone is broken; fig. hard worked.

ORE, ヲレ, 居, The *imp.* of *Ori*. *Damatte ore*, be still.

ORE, ヲレ, 折, *n.* A broken piece, or fragment of any thing long. *Kugi no —*, a piece of nail.

OREKUCHI, ヲレクチ, 折口, *n.* A death, or a funeral; used by persons who have a superstitious dread of using the plain word for death, *(h'to ga shinda)*. *— ga aru*, there is a person dead.

ŌREN, ワウレン, 黄連, *n.* Gentian.

ORI, ヲリ, 折, *n.* Time, occasion, opportunity. *Imada — wo yedz*, could not get an opportunity. *Kono — kara*, after this time. Syn. TOKI, KORO.

ORI, *oru, otta*, ヲル, 折, *t. v.* To break any thing long and slender, as a stick; to fold any thing stiff. *Hone wo —*, to break a bone, (fig.) to toil, labour industriously. *Kami wo —*, to fold paper. *Hiza wo —*, to bend the knees.

ORI, *oru, otta*, オル, 織, *t.v.* To weave, to work a loom. *Hata wo —*, to work a loom. *Momen wo —*, to weave cotton cloth.

ORI, *oru, otta*, ヲル, 居, *i.v.* To be, to dwell, live. *Nete oru*, is asleep. *Hi ga moyete oru*, the fire is burning. *Doko ni oru*, when is it? or, where do you live? *Danna orimaska*, is the master of the house at home? *Ori-masen*, he is not in.

ORI, *oriru, orita*, オリル, 下, *t.v.* To descend, to go down, to light from, to alight. *Yama wo oriru*, to descend a mountain. *Uma wo —*, or *Uma kara —*, to alight from a horse. Syn. KUDARU, SAGARU.

ORI, ヲリ, 檻, *n*, A pen, a cage, coop. *Buta no —*, a hog-pen. *Tori no —*, a chicken coop. *Tora no —*, a tiger's cage.

ORI, ヲリ, 牢, *n.* Goal, prison.

ORI, ヲリ 折, *n.* A small box made of thin board by folding the corners, used for holding confectionary, &c.

ORI, オリ, *n.* The fine sediment, lees, or settlings from tea, wine, or any liquid; deposit. Syn. KASZ.

ORI-AI,*-au,-tta*, ヲリアフ, 居合, *i. v.* To be composed, settled; to subside, abate. *Jinki ga ori-atta*, people's minds have become composed. Syn. SHIDZMARU.

ORI-ASHIKU, or ORI-ASHŪ, ヲリアシイ, 折惡, *adv.* In a bad time, in an unfortunate time. *Ori-ashiku rusz ye kita*, I have unfortunately come when he is absent.

ORI-DO, ヲリド, 折戸, *n.* A folding door.

ORI-DOKORO, ヲリドコロ, 居所, *n.* A dwelling place, room or space to live, sit, stand, or lie in.

ORI-FUSHI, ヲリフシ, 折節, *adv.* Sometimes, now and then, occasionally; just then, at that time, instant, or conjuncture. Syn. TOKI-DOKI, YORI-YORI.

ORIHA, ヲリハ, 折羽, *n.* A kind of game played with dice.

ORI-HIME, オリヒメ, 織女, *n.* The name of a star.

ORI-HON, ヲリホン, 折本, *n.* A folding-book.

ORI-ITTE, ヲリイツテ, 折入, *adv.* Earnestly, urgently, importunately. *— otanomi mōshi tai koto ga aru*, I have a matter in which I am very anxious to get your assistance. Syn. HITASZRA.

ORI-KAMI, ヲリカミ, 折紙, *n.* A document accompanying any curiosity stating its history &c. a certificate.

ORIKARA, ヲリカラ, 折柄, *adv*, Just then, at that time, instant, or conjuncture. *Sono —*, at that time. Syn. ORI-FUSHI, TOKI.

ORI-KATA, ヲリカタ, 折形, *n.* A crease, or mark made by folding.

ORI-KU, ヲリク, 折句, *n.* An acrostic.

ORI-KUGI, ヲリクギ, 折釘, *n.* A hook for hanging anything on.

ORI-MAGE,*-ru,-ta*, ヲリマゲル, 折枉, *t. v.* To break and bend.

ORI-ME, ヲリメ, 折目, *n.* The crease, or place where any thing is folded.

ORI-MONO, オリモノ, 織物, *n* Woven goods, cloth.

ORI-ORI, ヲリヲリ, 折折, *adv.* Sometimes,

occasionally, now and then.
Syn. TOKIDOKI.

ORIRU, オリル, 下, see *Ori*.

ORI-SHIMO, ヲリシモ, *adv*. Time, occasion; just then, at that time.
Syn. ORI, TOKI, KORO.

Ō-RIYŌ, アフリヤウ, 押領, Taking violent or unjust possession, trespassing or encroaching on the rights of another. — *szru*, to encroach on the territory or rights of another.

ORI-YOI,-KI,-KU, ヲリヨイ, 折能, Good time, fortunate, or opportune time.

†OROCHI, ヲロチ, 蛇, *n*. A large snake.

OROKA, オロカ, 愚, Foolish, silly, simple, ignorant. — *naru h'to*, and ignorant person. *Mōsz mo naka-naka — nari*, it would be foolish to try to speak of it, impossible to do justice to it.

†OROKASA, オロカサ, *n*. Folly, foolishness.

†ORO-ORO, オロオロ, *adv*. A little, few. — *to naku*, to cry a little. — *namida*, to shed a few tears.

OROSHA, オロシヤ, 魯西亞, Russia.

OROSHI,-*sz*,-*sh'ta*, オロス, 卸, *t. v*. To take down from a height, to put down on the ground, to let down; to sell at wholesale. *Ikari wo* —, to drop the anchor. *Ho wo* —, to unfurl a sail. *Maku wo* —, to let down a curtain. *Uma no ni wo* —, to unload a horse. *Kura wo* —, to take off a saddle. *Kashira wo* —, to shave the head, and become a priest. *Yeda wo* —, to cut off a branch of a tree. *Ko wo* —, to produce abortion. *Hon wo orosh'te kudasare*, take down the book. *Oi-orosz*, to drive down. *Mi-orosz*, to look down. *Zōri wo* —, to break in a new pair of sandals. *Fune wo* —, to launch a ship. *Ito wo yaszku orosz*, to sell silk cheap by the quantity.

OROSHI,-*sz*,-*sh'ta*, オロス, *t. v*. To reduce to a fine state, by cutting, grating, triturating or filing. *Daikon wo* —, to grate radishes. *Uwo wo* —, to cut a fish into thin slices. *Kuszri wo* —, to triturate medicines. *Yaszri de tetsz wo* —, to reduce iron by filing.

OROSHI, オロシ, 薑研, *n*. A grater.

OROSHI, オロシ, *n*. Selling by the quantity, and at small profit, to merchants; wholesale. — *to ko uri wa nedan ga chigau*, in selling by wholesale or retail the price is different.

OROSOKA, オロソカ, 疎, Careless, remiss, or negligent, especially in showing due respect to others. *H'to wo — ni szru*, to treat others disrespectfully.
Syn- SORIYAKU, SOMATSZ.

ORU, ヲル, 居 or 折 or 織, see *Ori*.

OSA, ヲサ, 筬, *n*. The reed of a loom.

OSA, ヲサ, 長, *n*. The chief, head, or principal man. *Mura no* —, the head man of a township. *Fune no* —, the captain of a ship. Syn. KASHIRA.

ŌSA, オホサ, 多, *n*. Numerousness, the number.

OSAMARI,-*ru*,-*tta*, ヲサマル, 治, *i. v*. To be regulated, governed; tranquilized, quieted; paid up or collected (as taxes).

OSAME,-*ru*,-*ta*, ヲサメル, 治 or 納, *t.v*. To regulate, to govern, to quiet, tranquilize, allay; to pay in (taxes); to lay up, to store away; to bury, inter; put away. *Kuni, i ye, mi, yo wo* —, to govern the state, the family, one's-self, the world. *Sōdō, ki, kororo wo* —, to tranquilize sedition, the spirits, or mind. *Nengu wo* —, to pay in taxes. *Kome wo* —, to store up rice. *Shigai wo* —, to bury a corpse. *Bumbu no michi wo* —, to store up literary and military knowledge. *Katana wo saya ni* —, to put a sword into in its scabbard. *Hon wo tana ni* —, to put a book in the book case. *Kome wo kura ni* —, to store rice in a store house. Syn. SHIDZMERU, IRERU.

OSANAGO, ヲサナゴ, 小兒, *n*. A young person. child.

OSANAI,-KI,-SHI, ヲサナイ, 幼, Young, youthful, Syn. ITOKENAI.

OSANAKU, ヲサナク, 幼, *adv*. idem.

OSA-OSA, ヲサヲサ, 頗, *adv*. Much, great deal. *Watakushi mo ano h'to ni — otoranu*, I am not much inferior to him.
Syn. YOPPODO.

OSARABA, オサラバ, Exclam. used at parting or taking leave, = farewell, good-bye.
Syn. SAYŌNARA.

OSARE,-*ru*,-*ta*, オサレル, 被壓, Pass. of *Oshi*, *osz*. To be pushed, pressed, forced; thrust aside, &c ,

OSAYE,-*ru*,-*ta*, オサヘル, 抑, *t.v*. To press upon or against, to push against, to repress, restrain, to keep down, keep back, to stop, to stay, to check. *Ikari wo* —, to restrain anger. *Namida wo* —, to repress the tears. *Atama wo* —, to humble a person.

OSAYE, オサヘ, 壓, *n*. A stop, check, restraint, stay. *Ishi wo — ni oku*, to put a stone against anything to hold it.

OSAYE, オサヘ, 押後, *n*. The rear column of an army.

ŌSE,-*ru*,-*ta*, オフセル, 負, *t.v*. used only in connection with *Te*, as, *Te wo ōseru*, to wound.

Ōse, オフセ, 仰, The root of an imperfect verb. To say, speak, only used of honorable persons, as rulers, teachers, or masters, and combined with other verbs.

Ōse, オフセ, 仰, *n.* The word, command, or instruction of an honorable person; charge, order. *Kami no — wo uketamawaru*, to receive the commands of a lord. Syn. mei.

Ōserare, *-ru, -ta*, オフセラレル, 被仰, *i.v.* To speak, to say, command, charge, used only of honorable persons.

Ōsetsz, オウセツ, 應接, *n.* A meeting, interview. — *szru*, to meet. Syn. au, tai-men szru.

Ōshi, or Oshi, オフシ, 瘂, *n.* Deaf and dumb, a mute.

Oshi, オシ, 壓石, *n.* A weight, for pressing upon anything. (fig.) influence, authority. — *wo kakeru*, to put on a weight. — *ga kikanu yaku-nin*, an officer who has but little influence. — *no tszyoi h'to*, a persistent person.

Oshi, *-sz, -sh'ta*, オス, 推, *t.v.* To push, to shove, to thurst, to press, to squeeze, to force, compel, constrain, to drive, to infer, deduce. *Fune wo* —, to push a boat. *Han wo* —, to stamp, or seal. *Ro wo* —, to scull (a boat). *Ne wo* —, to search out the origin, or cause of anything. *Sono yo wa oshite shiru beshi* the rest may be inferred. *Kami no chiye wa kore ni yotte oshite shiru beshi*, from this we may infer how great is the wisdom of God.

Oshi-age, *-ru, -ta*, オシアゲル, 推上, *t.v.* To push up.

Oshi-ai, *-au, -atta*, オシアフ, 推合, *i.v.* To push one another.

Oshi-ake, *-ru, -ta*, オシアケル, 推開, *t.v.* To push, or force open.

Oshi-ate, *-ru, -ta*, オシアテル, 推當, *t.v.* To push anything against something else. *Kuchi ni tamoto wo* —, to hold one's sleeve to the mouth.

Oshi-buchi, オシブチ, 押緣, *n.* Small strips of wood fastened against the edges of wall-paper. Syn. shibuichi.

Oshi-dashi, *-sz, -sh'ta*, オシダス, 推出, *t.v.* To push, thrust or force out.

Oshi-dori, ヲシドリ, 鴛鴦, *n.* The mandarin duck.

Oshi-dori, オシドリ, 推取, *n.* Taking by force. — *wo szru.*

Oshi-dzyoi, *-ki, -ku*, オシツヨイ, 押强, Obstinate, pertinacious, persisting. *Oshidzyoku tanomu*, to persevere in asking.

Oshi-fuse, *-ru, -ta*, オシフセル, 抑伏, *t.v.* To push down, to force down with the face to the ground.

Oshige-mo-naku, ヲシゲモナク, 無惜氣, *adv.* Without appearing to grudge, not seeming to mind, or regret. *Kane wo — tszkau*; to spend money ungrudgingly.

Oshi-hakari, *-ru, -tta*, オシハカル, 推量, *t.v.* To guess, conjecture, suppose, to infer. Syn. sziriyō.

Oshi-hedate, *-ru, -ta*, オシヘダテル, 推隔, *t.v.* To separate by force, as by getting between two persons fighting, to push apart.

Oshi-hiraki, *-ku, -ita*, オシヒラク, 推開, *t.v.* To push or force open,

Oshi-hirame, *-ru, -ta*, オシヒラメル, 推匾, *t.v.* To press and flatten any thing round.

Oshi-hiroge, *-ru, -ta*, オシヒロゲル, 擴, *t.v.* To force open, as any thing folded up, to spread out.

Oshii, *-ki*, ヲシイ, 惜, *a.* That which is deplored or regretted, grudged, or highly prized and unwillingly parted with, lamentable. *Oshii koto wo sh'ta*, I have met with a sad accident. — *h'to ga shinda*, a person greatly deplored has died. *Kane ga oshiute tszkawarenu*, grudging the money I can not spend it. *Oshii inochi*, precious life.

Oshi-ire, *-ru, -ta*, オシイレル, 推入, *t.v.* To force into, to put into by force, or violence.

Oshi-ire, オシイレ, 押入, *n.* A closet.

Oshi-iri, *-ru, -itta*, オシイル, 推入, *i.v.* To force, or push one's way into, to enter violently.

Oshi-kake, *-ru, -ta*, オシカケル, 推掛, *t.v.* To attack, assault, with force and numbers.

Oshi-katame, *-ru, -ta*, オシカタメル, 推固, *t.v.* To press together into a hard mass.

Oshi-kayeshi, *-sz, -sh'ta*, オシカヘス, 推返, *t.v.* To push, or force back, to force another to take back, or do over again. *Oshi-kayesh'te tadzneru*, to question over and over again.

†Ōshiki, *-ku*, ヲヲシキ, 雄雄敷, Manly, bold, or daring in appearance.

Oshi-kiri, *-ru, -tta*, オシキル, 推切, *t.v.* To press and cut, (as any thing hard), to break by pushing forcibly against (as a rope.)

Oshi-kome, *-ru, -ta*, オシコム, 推籠, *i.v.* To be forced, or compelled to remain shut inside, (as an offender, in his own house), to confine.

OSHI-KOMI,*–mu,–nda*, オシコム, 推籠, *t.v.* To push, press, or force one thing into another.

OSHI-KOROSHI,*–sz,–sh'ta*, オシコロス, 推殺, *t.v.* To press, or squeeze to death.

OSHIKU, ヲシク, 惜, *adv.* See *Oshii.*

OSHI-KUDAKI,*–ku,–ita*, オシクダク, 推碎, *t.v.* To press on and break into pieces, to crush.

OSHI-KUDASHI,*–sz,–sh'ta*, オシクダス, 推下, *t.v.* To push, or force down, depress.

OSHIMADZ, ヲシマズ, 不惜, Neg of *Oshimu.* Without grudging, without regret.

OSHI-MADZKI, オシマヅキ, 几, *n.* A stand for resting against while sitting.
Syn. K'YŌSOKU.

OSHI-MAGE,*–ru,–ta*, オシマゲル, 推曲, *t.v.* To bend by force.

OSHI-MAKI,*–ku,–ita*, オシマク, 推捲, *t.v.* To push and roll up.

OSHI-MAROME,*–ru,–ta*, オシマロメル, 推團, *t. v.* To press and make round.

OSHIMI,*–mu,–nda*, ヲシム, 惜, *t. v.* To feel sorrow at the loss of anything prized, to regret to lose or spend; to spare, to grudge, to value, prize. *Na wo* —, to regret the loss of one's good name. *Inochi wo oshimadz tatakau,* to fight regardless of one's life. *Kane wo oshinde tszkau,* to spend money grudgingly. *Koye wo oshimadz naku,* to cry out at the top of the voice.

OSHI-NABETE, オシナベテ, 推並, *adv.* All, universally. *Tattoki iyashiki wo* —, all whether high or low.

OSHI-NAGASHI,*–sz,–sh'ta*, オシナガス, 推流, *t.v.* To carry, or float away by a current.

OSHI-NAOSHI,*–sz,–sh'ta*, オシナホス, 推直, *t.v.* To press on and mend (as anything bent).

OSHI-NOKE,*–ru,–ta*, オシノケル, 推退, *t.v.* To push aside, or out of the way.

OSHI-NUGI,*–gu,–ida*, オシヌグ, 推脫, To strip off.

OSHIROI, オシロイ, 白粉, *n.* The white powder used by women for powdering the face.

OSHIROI-BANA, オシロイバナ, 紫茉莉, *n.* Mirabilis jalapa.

OSHISA, ヲシサ, 惜, *n.* Unwillingness to lose or part with, preciousness. *Inochi ga — ni nigeru,* he ran way, because he was unwilling to lose his life.

OSHI-SAGE,*–ru,–ta*, オシサゲル, 推下, *t.v.* To push or force down.

OSHI-SHIDZME,*–ru,–ta*, オシシヅメル, 推沈, *t.v.* To push, or force under water; to quiet, hush, pacify, restrain, (as an uproar, anger).

OSHISŌ-NI, ヲシサウニ, 惜相, *adv.* Grudgingly, with an appearance of regret. — *kane wo tszkau,* to spend money grudgingly.

OSHI-TAOSHI,*–sz,–sh'ta*, オシタフス, 壓倒, *t.v.* To push, or force over, so as to fall.

OSHI-TATE,*–ru,–ta*, オシタテル, 推立, To push, or force to stand up.

OSHI-TAWAME,*–ru,–ta*, オシタワメル, 推撓, *t.v.* To bend by force, to press on and bend.

OSHITE, オシテ, 推, *adv.* By force, by violence, by compulsion, presumptuously, pertinaciously. *Iye ni — hairu,* to enter a house by force.
Syn. SHITE, MURI-NI.

OSHI-TODOME,*–ru,–ta*, オシトドメル, 抑留, *t.v.* To stop by force, to push and stop.

OSHI-TŌSHI,*–sz,–sh'ta*, オシトホス, 押通, *t.v.* To push, or force through.

OSHI-TSZBUSHI,*–sz,–sh'ta*, オシツブス, 壓潰, *t.v.* To crush, or break with violence, to press on and crush.

OSHI-TSZKE,*–ru,–ta*, オシツケル, 推付, *t.v.* To push, or force one thing against another.

OSHI-TSZME,*–ru,–ta*, オシツメル, 推詰, *t.v.* To push, or force into a narrow, or strait place, to straiten, confine.

OSHI-TSZTSZMI,*–mu,–nda*, オシツツム, 推包, *t.v.* To wrap up, to fold up.

OSHI-UGOKASHI,*–sz,–sh'ta*, オシウゴカス, 推動, *t.v.* To push and shake.

OSHI-URI, オシウリ, 推賣, *n.* Pressing the purchase of something which one wishes to sell, importunately desirous of selling.

OSHI-WAKE,*–ru,–ta*, オシワケル, 推分, *t.v.* To push, or force apart, separate forcibly.

OSHI-WATASHI,*–sz,–sh'ta*, オシワタス, 推渡, *t.v.* To push across, (as a boat).

OSHI-YABURI,*–ru,–tta*, オシヤブル, 推破, *t.v.* To push and break, to attack and break.

OSHIYE,*–ru,–ta*, ヲシヘル, 敎, *t. v.* To teach, instruct, to educate, to caution, warn. *Shishō ga deshi ni* —, the teacher instructs the pupil. Syn. KIYŌ KUN SZRU, NARAWASERU.

OSHIYE, ヲシヘ, 敎, *n.* Teaching, instruction; precept, doctrine, sect, religion. *Yesz no* —, christianity.

OSHI-YOSE,*–ru,–ta*, オシヨセル, 推寄,

t.v. To push, or force near to, to attack, or forcibly approach to.

OSHŌ, ヲシヤウ, 和尙, *n.* A Buddhist priest. Syn. BŌDZ.

†OSO, ヲソ, 悪阻, *n.* The bodily disorders caused by pregnancy. Syn. TSZWARI.

OSOBA, オソバ, 近習, *n.* The pages, or immediate attendants of nobles. Syn. KIN-JŪ.

OSOI,-ō,-ōta, オソフ, 襲, *t.v.* To attack, invade, to make a foray, to spread or cover over. *Teki no shiro wo* —, to attack an enemy's castle. Syn. SEMERU.

OSOI,-KI, オソイ, 遲, *a.* Late, slow, tardy, dull. *Omaye kiyō ga osoi*, you are late in coming. *Henji ga* —, the answer is late. *Naori ga* —, the cure is slow. *Ashi ga* —, slow of foot.

OSOIBA, オソイバ, 齵, *n.* The wisdom teeth.

OSOI-GAKI, オソイガキ, 襲書, *n.* Writing, or drawing by placing the paper over the thing to be drawn, and tracing the lines.

OSOKU, オソク, 遲, *adv.* Late, tardy, slow. — *natta*, you are late. — *okiru*, to get up late.

OSOMAKI, オソマキ, 晩種, *n.* Grain, or any seed sown late in the season.

‖OSONAWARI,-*ru*,-*tta*, オソナハル, 遲, *i.v.* To be late, slow, or tardy.

OSORAKUBA, オソラクバ, 恐, *adv.* I am afraid that, &c , I fear that, &c., I doubt whether, &c., perhaps. — *nochi no wazawai wo okosan*, I fear it may cause future calamity.

OSORE,-*ru*,-*ta*, オソレル, 恐, *t.v.* To be afraid of, to fear, to dread. *H'to wo* —, to be afraid of a man. Syn. KOWAGARU.

OSORE, オソレ, 恐, *n.* Fear, dread. — *wo idaku*, to fear. *K'waji no osore ari*, am in dread of fire.

OSORE-AI,-*au*,-*atta*, オソレアフ, 恐合, *i.v.* To fear each other, to be afraid, (spoken of many persons).

OSORE-IRI,-*ru*,-*tta*, オソレイル, 恐入, *i.v.* To be filled with fear, (used mostly in respectful address to officials). *Osore-ittaru yōsz mo naku*, no appearance of fear. *Osore-irimash'ta*, (used apologetically in acknowledging one's error).

OSORE-NAGARA, オソレナガラ, 乍恐, *adv.* Although, or whilst I am afraid, &c. (used in prefacing an address to officials). — *kakitszke wo motte negai-age tatematszri soro*, I humbly beg to hand up this communication.

OSORE-ŌI,-KI,-KU, オソレオホイ, 恐多, Fearful, dreadful, (used only to officials.)

OSORE-ONONOKI,-*ku*,-*ita*, オソレヲノノク, 恐怖, *i.v.* To tremble with fear, to do with fear and trembling.

OSORESHIME,-*ru*,-*ta*, オソレシメル, 令恐, caust. of *Osore*. To make afraid, frighten.

OSOROSHII,-KI, オソロシイ, 恐敷, *a.* Fearful, dreadful, awful, surprising, used much in vulg. coll. as a superlative, = extremely, very.

OSOROSHIKU, or OSOROSHŪ, オソロシク, 恐敷, *adv.* Idem.

OSOROSHISA, オソロシサ, 恐敷, *n.* Dreadfulness, fearfulness.

OSOSA, オソサ, 遲, *n.* Lateness, slowness.

OSO-UMA, オソウマ, 駑馬, *n.* A slow horse. Syn. DOBA.

OSOWARE,-*ru*,-*ta*, オソハレル, *t.v.* To have the nightmare, or incubus. Syn. UNASARERU.

OSSO, ヲツソ, 越訴, *n.* A petition or complaint made immediately to a high official without passing through those below him. — *wo szru*. Syn. UTTAYE.

OSZ, ヲス, 牡, *n.* The male of birds and animals.

OSZ, オス, 推, See *Oshi*.

Ō-TAI, オウタイ, 應對, *n.* A meeting, interview. — *szru*, to meet.

OTAMAYA, オタマヤ, 御靈屋, *n.* The cemetery of the *Kubō sama*.

ŌTE, オフテ, 追手, *n.* The front of a castle.

OTEDAMA, オテダマ, 阿手玉, *n.* Jackstones, or marbles used by children for playing with.

ŌTEKI, ワウテキ, 橫笛, *n.* A flute.

OTEMBA, オテンバ, *a.* Immodest, bold, impudent, (only of females.) — *muszme*, a bold, forward girl.

OTO, オト, 音, *n.* Sound. *Kane, teppō, fuye, nami, kuruma kaze nado no* —, the sound of a bell, gun, flute, waves, waggon, wind, &c. Syn. NE, KOYE.

†OTO, オト, 於菟, *n.* A tiger, (not used.) Syn. TORA.

‖OTO, オト, 乙, *n.* The youngest child. — *no ko*, idem.

OTODO, オトド, 大臣, *n.* The title of a *Kuge* of high rank, same as *Daijin*.

†OTODOI, オトドイ, 兄弟, *n.* Brothers, or sisters. Syn. K'YŌ-DAI.

OTODOSHI, オトドシ, 去去年, *n.* Year-before-last. Syn. ISSAKUNEN, KIYO-KIYO-NEN.

OTODZKI, オドツキ, 十二月, *n.* The twelfth month.

OTODZRE, オトヅレ, 音信, *n.* Message, word, communication, tidings, account, information. — *wo szru*, to send word. — *mo nai*, no tidings.
Syn. TAYORI, INSHIN, SHŌSOKU.

OTOGAI, オトガヒ, 頤, *n.* The chin.
Syn. AGO.

OTOGO, オトゴ, 末子, *n.* The youngest child.

OTOKO, ヲトコ 男, *n.* A male, man. — *no ko*, a manchild, boy. — *wo tatzru mono*, a manly, brave person. Syn. ONOKO.

OTOKO-BURI, ヲトコブリ, 男振, *n.* Manly appearance, or bearing. — *ga yoi*, idem. — *ga warui*, not to behave in a manly way.

OTOKO-DATE, ヲトコダテ, 男立, *n.* A manly, noble minded person, manful person.

OTOKOGI, ヲトコギ, 男氣, *n.* Manly, spirited, bold, courageous. — *na h'to.*

OTOKO-MASARI, ヲトコマサリ, 男勝, *n.* Masculine in appearance, or strength, spoken only of a woman.

OTOKORASHII,-KI, ヲトコラシイ, 男敷, Manlike, manly, noble, brave.

OTOKORASHIKU, ヲトコラシク, 男敷, *adv.* Idem.

OTOKO-TSZKI, ヲトコツキ, 男付, *n.* Manly bearing, or appearance.

†OTOME, ヲトメ, 少女, *n.* A young woman, girl. Syn. MUSZME.

OTOMUSZME, オトムスメ, 末女, *n.* Youngest daughter.

OTONA, オトナ, 長者, *n.* A grown-up person, adult, full-grown.

OTONAGENAI,-KI,-KU,-SHI,-Ō, オトナゲナイ, 無長者氣, Childish, puerile, foolish, silly.

OTONASHII,-KI, オトナシク, 長敷, *a.* Quiet, mild, gentle, tame, not turbulent, or refractory.

OTONASHIKU, オトナシイ, 長敷, *adv.* Idem. *Otonashiku sh'te ore*, be quiet.

OTONASHISA, オトナシサ, *n.* Gentleness, tameness.

OTONASHIYAKA, オトナシヤカ, Quiet, gentle, mild.

OTORI,-*ru*,-*ta*, オトル, 劣, *i.v.* To be inferior or less in size, degree, excellence, quality, &c., worse than, not so good as. *Shiru wa shiranu ni otoru*, to know it is worse than not to know it. *Gin wa kin ni* —, silver is inferior to gold.
Syn. MAKERU.

OTORI, オトリ, 劣, *n.* Inferiority, worse. *Masari otori nashi*, neither better nor worse.

OTORI, ヲトリ, 媒鳥, *n.* A bird used to decoy others.

OTORŌ, オトロフ, 衰, Same as *Otoroyeru.*

OTOROYE,-*ru*,-*ta*, オトロヘル, 衰, *t.v.* To grow worse, to be impaired, to decline, decay, to fail in strength or power, to deteriorate. *Toshi ga yotte chikara ga* —, as one grows old the strength fails.
Syn. SZIBI SZRU.

OTOSHI,-*sz*,-*sh'ta* オトス, 落, *i.v.* To drop, to let fall, to omit, leave out, to lose, to debase, degrade. *Inochi wo* —, to take life. *Chikara wo* —, to lose heart, to be discouraged. *Namida wo* —, to shed tears. *Okori wo* —, to get rid of the ague. *Kitszne wo* —, to drive out a fox, (that has bewitched a person). *Ki-no-mi wo* —, to knock off fruit. *Kimo wo* —, to be greatly alarmed. *Kubi wo* —, to take off the head. *Shimi wo* —, to take out a stain. *Iro wo* —, to remove a color. *Shiro wo* —, to take a castle by storm. *Kaki-otosz*, to omit something in writing. *Mi-otosz*, to overlook. *Kurai wo* —, to degrade in rank. *Tszmi ni* —, to cause to sin. *Tenugui wo* —, to lose a handkerchief. *Yakume wo* —, to degrade from office. *Ki wo* —, to deject, dishearten.

OTOSHI, オトシ, *n.* A kind of trap for catching birds.

OTOSHI-ANA, オトシアナ, 阱, *n.* A pitfall.

OTOSHI-BANASHI, オトシバナシ, 落語, *n.* A witticism.

OTOSHI-DANE, オトシダ子, 落種, *n.* The bastard child of a person of rank.

OTOSHI-IRE,-*ru*,-*ta*, オトシイレル, 陷, *t.v.* To drop into, to decoy, to entrap, insnare. *Tszmi ni* —, to entrap into sin.

†OTOSHIMI,-*mu*,-*nda*, オトシム, 落見, *t.v.* To look down on, to despise.
Syn. SAGESHIMI.

OTOSHI-TSZKE,-*ru*,-*ta*, オトシツケル, 落著, *t.v.* To settle, calm. quiet, tranquilize. *Kokoro wo* —, to calm the mind.
Syn. OSHI-TSZKERU, SHIDZMERU.

OTO-OTO, or OTŌTO, オトウト, 弟, *n.* Younger brother.

OTOTOI, or OTOTSZI, オトトヒ, 一昨日, *n.* Day before yesterday.

OTOTSAN, オトツサン, 阿爺, *n.* (Contraction of *O-toto-san*). Father.
Syn. CHICHI.

OTSZ-NA, ヲツナ, *a.* Strange, odd, unusual,

singular. — *kao*, a strange looking face. — *koye*, a strange voice.
Syn. HENNA, OKASHII-NA.

†OTSZNEN, ヲツネン, 越年, *(toshi wo koyeru)*. Passing the time, living. — *szru*.

OTSZRU, オツル, 落, Same as *Ochiru*.

O-TSZTSZ, ヲツツ, 尾筒, *n.* The bag for a horse's tail.

OTTA, ヲツタ, *pret.* of *Ori*.

OTTE, ヲツテ, *pp.* of *Ori*.

OTTE, オツテ, 追而, *adv.* By and by, presently, soon, after a little.
Syn. NOCH'HODO, ATOKARA.

OTTE, オツテ, 追手, *n.* The pursuing party, a pursuer.

OTTO, ヲツト, 良人, *n.* Husband.
Syn. TEISHU.

OTTO, オツト, Exclam. of sudden surprise, or hesitation, = oh! hold on! stop!

OTTORI,*-ru,-tta*, オツトル, 押取, *t.v.* To take or seize in a hurry, to snatch. *Katana wo ottori tachi-agatta*, seizing his sword he sprang up.

OTTORI, オツトリ, *adv.* Immediately, at once. — *henji wa dekinu*, cannot at once give an answer.

OTTORI-KOME,*-ru,-ta*, オツトリコメル, *t.v.* To surround, environ, encompass. *Shiro wo ottori-komete semeru*, to surround a castle and beseige it.

OTTORI-MAKI,*-ku,-ita*, オツトリマク, *t. v.* idem.

OTTOSEI, オツトセイ, 膃肭, *n.* The seal.
Syn. ASH'KA.

OTTSZ-KAYESHITSZ, オツツカヘシツ, *adv.* Advancing and retreating, pursuing and being pursued. — *takakau*.

OTTSZKE,*-ru,-tta*, オツケル, 推付, *t.v.* Same as *Oshitszkeru*.

OTTSZKE, オツツケ, 追付, *adv.* By and by, soon, presently. Syn. NOCH HODO, YAGATE.

ŌU, オホフ, 掩, See *Ōi*.

Ō-UCHI, オホウチ, 大裏, *(dairi)*. *n.* The Mikado's palace.

O-UMA, ヲウマ, 牡馬, *n.* A stallion.

O-USHI, ヲウシ, 特牛, *n.* A bull.

OWARE,*-ru,-ta*, オハレル, 被負, pass. of *Oi*. To be borne or carried. *H'to no senaka ni* —, to be carried on a man's back.

OWARE,*-ru,-ta*, オハレル, 被追, pass. or pot. of *Oi*. To be pursued, driven, chased. *Shigoto ni* —, driven, or hurried with work. *Inu ni* —, pursued by a dog.

OWARI,*-ru,-tta*, ヲハル, 終, *i.* or *t.v.* To end, finish, complete, terminate; to die. *Toshi ga owatta*, the year is ended. *Hon wo yomi-owaru*, to finish reading a book.
Syn. SHIMAU, SZMU.

OWARI, ヲハリ, 終, *n.* The end, termination. *Inochi no* —, end of life.

OWASE,*-ru,-ta*, オハセル, 令負, caust. of *Oi*. To place on the back of another, to load, to impute, charge with. *Uma ni ni wo* —, to load a horse with a burden. *Na wo* —, to give a name. *H'to ni tszmi wo* —, to charge another with crime.

OWASE,*-ru,-ta*, オハセル, 令追, caust. of *Oi*. To cause or let anything pursue or chase another. *H'to wo inu ni* —, to set a dog after a man.

OWASHI,*-sz,-sh'ta*, or OWASHI-MASHI,*-sz,-sh'ta*, オハス, 在, *i. v.* To be, to dwell, (used only of honorable persons). *Kami wa ten ni owashimasz*, God dwells in heaven. *Kami wa doko ni demo owashimasz*, God is in every place.

OYA, オヤ, 親, *n.* Parents.
Syn. RIYŌ SHIN.

OYA, オヤ, Exclam. of surprise.

OYA-BUN, オヤブン, 親分, *n.* One who acts a parent's part; a head-man, master, boss.

OYA-GO, オヤゴ, 親御, *n.* Your parents, (respectful).

OYA-JI, オヤヂ, 親父, *n.* Father.
Syn. CHI-CHI.

OYA-KATA, オヤカタ, 親方, *n.* Same as *Oya-bun*.

ŌYAKE, オホヤケ, 官, *n.* The government, the rulers. — *no sata*, a government order.
Syn. SEIFU.

ŌYAKE, オホヤケ, 公, Public, open, not private, just, fair, equitable, disinterested. — *ni szru*, to do publicly. — *naru koto*, a just thing. Syn. OMOTE-MUKI.

OYA-KO, オヤコ, 親子, *n.* Parent and child.

‖OYAMA, オヤマ, 阿娼, *n.* A harlot, the female character in a theatre.
Syn. JŌRO, ONNA-GATA.

OYA-YUDZRI, オヤユヅリ, 親譲, *n.* Anything received by inheritance from one's parents.

‖OYE,*-ru,-ta*, ヲヘル, 終, *i. v.* To be ended, terminated, finished, completed.

OYE, ヲヱ, 汚穢, Unclean, polluted, dirty, foul. Syn. KEGARE, YOGORE.

ŌYŌ, オホヤウ, 大様, Amiable, generous, liberal. Syn. ONTO.

ŌYŌ-NI, オホヤウニ, 大様, *adv.* Generally, mostly.

OYOBADZ, or OYOBANU, オヨバズ, 不及,

neg. of *Oyobi*. Cannot reach, extend, or attain to, inferior, impracticable, unnecessary. *Ano h'to ni wa* —, inferor to him. *Iu ni wa* —, unnecessary to speak of. *Chikara ni* —, impossible to do.

OYOBI,*-bu,-nda*, オヨブ, 及, *i.v.* To reach to, attain to, extend to, to terminate in, result in, issue in; until, till. *Takasa ten ni* —, its height reached to heaven. *Ken-k'wa ni* —, to result in a fight. *Ikusa ni* —, to result in a war. *Sono hi ni* —, until that day. *Chikara no oyobu take*, to the full extent of one's power. *Waga chikara oyobu tokoro ni aradz*, it is beyond my power.
Syn. TODOKU, ITARU, MADE.

OYOBI, オヨビ, 及, *conj.* And, together with. *Kami* — *fude szmi nado kau*, to buy paper, pen and ink.
Syn TO, ARUIWA.

OYOBOSHI,*-sz,-sh'ta*, オヨボス, 及, caust. of *Oyobi*. To extend, cause to reach, to impart. *Megumi wo h'to ni* —, to extend blessings to men.

OYOGI,*-gu,-ida*, オヨグ, 游, *t.v.* To swim. *Midz wo* —, to swim in the water. *Oyogu koto wo shiranu*, don't know how to swim. *Yoku oyogu h'to*, a good swimmer. *Kawa oyoide wataru*, to cross a river by swimming. *Szbete midz ni oyogu mono*, all that swim in the water.

OYOGI-AGARI,*-ru,-ta*, オヨギアガル, 游上, *t. v.* To swim up. *Kawa wo* —.

OYOGI-DE,*-ru,-ta*, オヨギデル, 游出, *t. v.* To swim out of.

OYOGI-KOSHI,*-sz,-sh'ta*, オヨギコス, 游越, *t.v.* To pass another in swimming, to swim across.

OYOGI-WATARI,*-ru,-tta*, オヨギワタル, 游渡, *t.v.* To swim across. *Kawa wo* —.

OYORI,*-ru,-tta*, オヨル, *i.v.* To sleep, (respectful). *Oyotte gozarimas*, master is asleep.

OYOSO, オヨソ, 凡, *adv.* For the most part, generally, mostly, in general, about. — *go h'yaku gurai*, about five hundred. — *ikito shi ikeru mono*, almost all living things, or living things generally.
Syn. Ō-KATA.

ŌYUBI, オホユビ, 大指, *n.* The thumb.

Ō-ZAKE-NOMI, オホザケノミ, 大酒飲, *n.* A drunkard.

ŌZAPPAI, オホザツパイ, Prodigal, lavish, profuse or liberal in giving or using. — *na h'to*. — *ni kane wo tszkau*, to spend money lavishly or without stint.

ŌZOKKOKU, アウゾクコク, 罌粟殼, *n.* Poppy-capsules.

‖OZOMASHII,-KI,-KU, オゾマシイ, *a.* Foolish, silly.

Ō-ZORA, オホゾラ, 大空, *n.* The sky.

P

PAN, パン, 麵包, *n.* Bread. (This word is derived from the Italian, or Portugese).

PANYA, パンヤ, *n.* A species of Asclepias, or milk weed, also the silky material obtained from it.

PARA-PARA-TO, パラパラト, *adv.* The sound, or manner of rain, hail, tears, &c., falling in big and scattered drops. *Arare ga* — *furu*.

PARARI-TO, パラリト, *adv.* In a scattered, dispersed, or sprinkled manner. *Hōsō ga* — *dekita*, the small pox pustules are distinct (not confluent). *Hoshi ga* — *deta*.

PATA-PATA, パタパタ, *adv.* The sound of repeated slaps, flaps, or clapping. *Niwatori ga — to habataki wo szru.*

PATCHI, パツチ, *n.* Trowsers, pantaloons, such as are worn by the lower classes. — *wo haku*, to wear breeches.

PATCHIRI, パツチリ, *adv.* The sharp, sudden sound of any thing cracking, snapping, splitting, as of splitting a bamboo, bursting the air-bladder of a fish, &c.

PATCHI-PATCHI, パツチパツチ, *adv.* Sounding in a sudden sharp manner, clapping, snapping, cracking, popping. *Te wo* — *to tataku*, to clap the hands.

PATTARI, パツタリ, *adv.* The sound made by any thing falling, slapping, slamming. — *to taoreru*, to fall with a bang.

PATTO, パツト, *adv.* In the manner of any thing suddenly bursting out, spreading. *Hiyōban ga* — *hirogatta*. the report suddenly spread.

PIRI-PIRI, ピリピリ, *adv.* In a pricking, burning or smarting manner, (as the taste of pepper).

PISSHARI, ピスシヤリ, *adv.* Like the sound of the crushing of egg-shells, shutting a screen, slamming a door. *To wo* — *to shimeru*, to slam the door.

PIYOI-TO, ピヨイト, *adv.* Hopping like a frog, bird &c. skipping. *Kogawa wo* — *tobikosz*, to hop, or skip across a narrow rivulet.

PIYOKO-PIYOKO-TO, ピヨコピヨコト, *adv.* Same as *Hiyoko-hiyoko*.

PIYŌ-TO, ピヤウト, *adv.* The whizzing sound made by an arrow. *Ya ga* — *hibiku*.

POKI-POKI, ポキポキ, *adv.* The sound of cracking. *Yubi wo — oru,* to crack the fingers.

POKU-POKU, ポクポク, *adv.* Like the sound of striking pieces of wood together. *Moku-giyo wo — to tataku.*

PON-PON, ポンポン, *adv.* The sound of successive reports, as of guns. *Teppō wo — to hanasz.*

POPPO, ポツポ, *n.* The bosom of the dress, (used by children).

POPPO-TO, ポツポト, *adv.* Hot, heated appearance. *— atszi.*

POTCHARI, ポツチヤリ, *adv.* Same as *Botteri.*

POTCHIRI, ポツチリ, 一點, *adv.* or *n.* A drop, jot, dot, the least quantity, *Tszyu ga — to ochitta,* a drop of dew fell. *— mo nai,* not a drop. *— de yoi,* the least quantity will do.

POTSZ-POTSZ, ポツポツ, *adv.* A little spot here and there, or in a scattered manner. *Hōsō ga — to dekita.*

PUN–PUN, プンプン, *adv.* In the manner of a delicious perfume. *Hana ga — to kaoru,* the flowers send forth a sweet perfume.

PURI-PURI, プリプリ, *adv.* Shaking or moving like jelly. *— sh'ta mono.*

R.

RA, ラ, 等, A plural suffix, as *Ware-ra,* we, *On-mi-ra,* you, but sometimes of no meaning, as *Achira, Kokora, Nanra.*
Syn. DOMO, TACHI, NADO.

‖RA, ラ 陰莖, *n.* The membrum virile.
Syn. INK'YŌ.

RACHI, ラチ, 埒, *n.* A picket fence. *— no soto,* outside of the fence. *— mo naki,* without order, confused. *— ga akanu,* slow, tedious, undetermined, unsettled. *— wo akeru,* to decide, conclude on, settle (something about which one has been long in suspense.

RACHI-AKI,*-ku,-ita,* ラチアク, 埒明, *i. v.* To finish, conclude. settle, dispatch, or expedite a tedious matter. *Nani-bun hayaku rachi-aku yō ni sh'te kudasare,* please finish the matter as expeditiously as possible.

RA-DEN, ラデン, 螺鈿, *n.* Mosaic work of mother of pearl.

RAI, ライ, 雷, *(kaminari.) n.* Thunder. *— ga ochita,* the lightning has struck.

†RAI,*-szru,* ライ, 禮, To worship.
Syn. OGAMU, HAI.

RAI-BIN, ライビン, 來便, *(kitaru taori.) n.* The next opportunity.

RAI-BIYŌ, ライビヤウ, 癩病, *n.* Leprosy.
Syn. KATTAI.

†RAI-BON, ライボン, 雷盆, *(szri bachi.) n.* A bowl used for washing rice in before boiling.

RAI-CHŌ, ライチヤウ, 來朝, *n.* To morrow morning. *— szru,* to come to Japan.
Syn. MIYŌ-ASA.

†RAI-DEN, ライデン, 雷電, *(kaminari, inabikari). n.* Thunder and lightning.

RAI-DŌ, ライドウ, 雷同, To be obsequious, compliant, to flatter. Syn. OMONERU.

†RAI-GA, ライガ, 來駕, *n.* Coming (respectful.) *Go — machi-tatematszri soro,* I will await your coming.

RAI-GETSZ, ライゲツ, 來月, *(kitaru tszki.)* Next month.

†RAI-GI, ライギ, 來儀, (Same as *Raiga*).

RAI-GŌ, ライガウ, 來迎, *(kitari mukayeru). n.* Coming to meet, (Bud. said of *Amida* coming in the clouds to receive the soul of a dying man who trusts in him). *Amida no —.*

†RAI-HAI, ライハイ, 禮拜, *(wiyamai-ogamu).* To worship.

RAI-HARU, ライハル, 來春, *n.* The coming spring, next spring. Syn. RAISHUN, RAIYŌ.

†RAI-I, ライイ, 來意, *n.* The intention, or meaning (of your letter which has been) received. *— no gotoku,* as you have writter.

RAI-JIN, ライジン, 雷神, *n.* God of thunder.

RAI-JITSZ, ライジツ, 來日, *(kitaru hi.) n.* Next day, to-morrow.

RAIJŪ, ライジウ, 雷獸, *n.* An animal which is supposed to fall when the lightning strikes. *— ga ochita.*

RAI-KIYAKU, ライキヤク, 來客, *n.* A guest who has just come.

RAI-MEI, ライメイ, 雷鳴, *(ikadzchi naru). n.* The sound of thunder. *Fuku chiu — szru,* to have a rumbling in one's belly.

RAI-NEN, ライネン, 來年, *(kitaru toshi). n.* Next year. the coming year.

RAI-REKI, ライレキ, 來歷, *n.* The history, annals. Syn. YURAI.

†RAI-RIN, ライリン, 來臨, *n.* The coming of a noble person.

RAI-SE, ライセ, 來世, *(kitaru yo.) n.* The next world, Syn. GO-SE.

RAI-SHUN, ライシユン, 來春, *(kitaru haru). n.* The next spring.

†RAI-U, ライウ, 雷雨, *(kaminari, ame). n.* Thunder and rain.

†RAI-YŌ, ライヤウ, 來陽, *n.* Next spring. Syn. RAI HARU.

RAI-YOKE, ライヨケ, 雷除, *n.* A lightning rod.

†RAI-YU, ライユ, 來由, *n.* History. — *wo kataru*, to narrate the history. Syn. RAI-REKI.

RAKAN, ラカン, 羅漢, *n.* The sixteen disciples of *Shaka*.

RAKAN, ラカン, *n.* Bacon.

†RAKANSHŌ, ラカンシヨウ, 羅漢松, *n.* A kind of fir-tree, Same as *Maki*.

RAKKAN, ラクカン, 落欵, *n.* Affixing one's seal to a drawing.

RAKKIYŌ, ラツキヤウ, 薤, *n.* A vegetable of the garlic class.

†RAKKIYO, ラクキヨ, 落居, To be settled, concluded, finished. Syn. SZMU.

†RAKK'WA, ラククワ, 落花, *n.* Fall of the flowers. — *yeda ni kayeradz*, the fallen flower does not return to the branch. (prov).

RAKK'WASHŌ, ラククワシヤウ, 落花生, *n.* A groundnut

RAKU, ラク, 樂, (*tanoshimi*). *n.* Comfort, ease, freedom from pain, toil, or hard labor. — *ni kurasz*, to live in ease. — *na koto*, easy, or pleasant thing. *Itami ga — ni natta*, the pain has become easy. *Isogashiku te — ga dekinu*, am so busy I can't find any ease.

†RAKU, ラク, A suffix to verbs, the same as *ru*, (used only in poetry), as, *Miraku*, = *Miru*, *Omoyeraku* = *omoyeru*, *Kōraku*, = *kōru*.

RAKU-BA, ラクバ, 落馬, (*uma yori otszru.*) *n.* Fall from a horse. — *sh'te kega wo sh'ta*, fell from the horse and was hurt.

RAKU-CHIU, ラクチウ, 洛中, *n.* Miako,

RAKUDA, ラクダ, 駱駝, *n* A camel.

RAKU-GAKI, ラクガキ, 樂書, *n.* Writing at will, upon walls, stones, trees, &c. — *mu yō*, do no writing here.

RAKUGAN, ラクガン, 落鴈, *n.* A kind of confectionary.

RAKU-G'WAI, ラクグワイ, 洛外, *n.* Suburbs of Miako.

†RAKU-HATSZ, ラクハツ, 落髮, (*kami wo otosz*). *n.* Shaving the head.

RAKU-JAKU, ラクチヤク, 落着, (*ochi-tszku*). To settle, finish, conclude. Syn. SZMU, RACHIAKU, KATADZKU.

RAKU-JI, ラクジ, 落字, (*otszru moji*). *n.* A word omitted. — *ga aru*, a word is omitted.

RAKU-JIN, ラクジン, 樂人, *n.* One who lives in ease, free from care or labor.

RAKU-JITSZ, ラクジツ, 落日, (*iri hi*). *n.* Setting sun.

RAKU-JŌ, ラクジヤウ, 落城, (*ochiru shiro*). *n.* A fallen castle, a castle taken and destroyed.

RAKU-MEI, ラクメイ, 落命, (*inochi wo otosz*). *n.* Losing life. *Gun chiu ni — sh'ta*, lost his life in battle.

RAKU-RAKU-TO, ラクラクト, 樂樂, *adv.* Easily, pleasantly, comfortably, free from care or labor. Syn. YASZ-YASZ-TO, YŌI-NI.

RAKU-RUI, ラクルイ, 落涙, (*namida wo otosz*). *n.* Shedding tears. — *szru.*

†RAKU-SHO, ラクシヨ, 落書, (*otoshi bumi*). *n.* Anonymous writing.

RAKU-SHU, ラクシユ, 落首, *n.* A lampoon, any satirical or cutting writing. — *wo kaku*, to write a lampoon.

RAKU-SHU, ラクシユ, 落手, (*te ni iru*). Come to hand, receive. *Tash'kani — itashimash'ta.*

†RAKU-YEKI, ラクエキ, 絡繹, Uninterrupted stream, or succession. — *to sh'te tszdzku.*

RAKU-YŌ, ラクエフ, 落葉, (*ochiba*). *n.* Fallen leaves.

†RAKUYŌ, ラクヤウ, 洛陽, *n.* Miako.

RAMBIKI, ランビキ, *n.* A still.

RAMBŌ, ランバウ, 亂妨, *n.* Disorder, riot, tumult, violent and unlawful conduct. — *nin*, a rioter, a violent and turbulent person. — *szru*, to act in a violent and disorderly manner. Syn. ABARERU.

RAMMA, ランマ, 欄間, *n.* The ornamental work over the screens of a house.

†RAMMAN, ランマン, 爛熳, Scattered, (as flowers).

‖RAMPATSZ, ランパツ, 亂髮, (*midare gami*). *n.* Disheveled hair.

RAMPITSZ, ランピツ, 亂筆, *n.* A bad hand, or slovenly penmanship.

RAN, ラン, 覽, (*miru*). To look, to see. *Ichi ran szru*, having one look. *Go ran nasare*, look here.

RAN, ラン, 亂, *n.* Disorder, confusion, tumult, riot, disturbance. — *wo okosz*, to raise a tumult. Syn. MIDARE.

RAN, ラン, 蘭, *n.* The name of a flower.

RAN, ラン, 鸞, *n.* The phœnix.

†RAN, ラン, A verbal suffix, having a dubitative, or conjectural meaning, as, *Tare naru-ran*, who is it! or I wonder who it is! *Naniya-ran*, something, (which is only conjectural). = *Naniyara*, or *Nandearō*.

RAN-DA, ランダ, 懶惰, Lazy, idle.
Syn. BUSHŌ.

RAN-GAKU, ランガク, 蘭學, The study of the Dutch language or books.

†RAN-GIYŌ, ランギヤウ, 亂行, (*midari no okonai*). *n.* Riotous conduct.

RAN-GOKU, ランゴク, 亂國, *n.* A country disturbed with war.

RAN-GUI, ラングヒ, 亂杭, *n.* Posts or stakes driven into the ground to molest or hinder the enemy.

RAN-GUN, ラングン, 亂軍, (*midare ikusa*). *n.* An army thrown into confusion, or disorder.

RANJATAI, ランジヤタイ, 蘭奢待, *n.* A kind of aromatic wood.

RAN-KAN, ランカン, 欄干, *n.* A balustrade. Syn. TESZRI.

RAN-KI, ランキ, 亂氣, (*midare kokoro*). *n.* Crazy, deranged in mind.
Syn. KICHIGAI, MONO-GURUI.

RAN-SEI, ランセイ, 亂世, (*midaretaru yo*). *n.* A time, or age disturbed with war.

RAN-SHIN, ランシン, 亂心, (*midaretaru kokoro*). Crazy, deranged in mind.
Syn. KICHIGAI, KIYŌKI.

†RANSHO, ランショ, 蘭書, (*oranda no hon*). *n.* Dutch books.

†RAN-SHŌ, ランシヤウ, 濫觴, *n.* The origin rise, commencement.
Syn. HAJIMARI.

†RAN-SHŌ, ランシヤウ, 卵生, *n.* Oviparous.

RAN-SHU, ランシユ, 亂酒, Violent and disorderly from drinking ardent spirits. — *da kara nomase-nai ga yoi*, better not give him drink as he becomes violent.

RANSŌ, ランソウ, 卵叢, *n.* The ovaries.

RAN-TŌ, ランタフ, 卵塔, *n.* A kind of monument over a grave.

RANYO, ランヨ, 鑾輿, *n.* The car in which the Tenshi rides.

RAO, ラウ, 喇管, *u.* A bamboo pipe-stem.

RAPPA, ラツパ, 喇叭, *n.* A trumpet.

RAPPAK'WAN, ラツパクワン, 喇叭管, *n.* The fallopian tubes.

RASEITA, ラセイタ, 羅脊板, *n.* Flannel.

RASETSZ, ラセツ, 羅刹, *n.* A demon of the Buddhist hades.

RASHA, ラシヤ, 羅紗, *n.* Woollen cloth.

RASHII,-KI,-KU, ラシイ, A suffix, adding the idea of, like, appearance, or manner to the root word, as, *Onna-rashii*, like a woman. *Kodomo-rashii*, child-like. *Ame ga fururashii*, it looks like rain. *Fuyu-rashii*, it looks like winter.
Syn. SŌNA.

RASSHI, ラツシ, 薾次, *n.* Order, arrangement, always used with a negative, as, — *mo nai*, disordered, confused, without order, or arrangement. *Rasshi naku*, id. *Heya no uchi wo — mo naku sh'te aru*, the room is all in disorder.

RASSOKU, ラツソク, *n.* A kind of candle, having a stick projecting from the end of it for carrying in the hand.

REI, レイ, 禮, *u.* Politeness, decorum, etiquette; salutation, a thank offering, or present in acknowledgment of a favor. — *wo shiranu h'to*, impolite person. — *wo szru*, to show respect, to bow, to make a present out of thankfulness; to pay a doctor's fee, to pay a teacher. — *wo iu*, to express one's thanks. *Nippon no —*, Japanese etiquette.

REI, レイ, 令, *n.* A command, order. — *wo idasz*, to issue an order. — *wo kudasz*, idem. Syn. GEJI, MEI, Ī-TSZKE.

REI, レイ, 例, (*tameshi*), *n.* Rule, custom, usage practice, example, precedent, instance, usual, common. — *ni yotte okonau*, to act according to established rule. — *no nai koto*, not customary. — *naradz*, unusual.

REI, レイ, 靈, (*tamashii*), *n.* The soul, spirit, manes, or ghost of a dead person. *H'to no — wo matszru*, to worship the manes of the dead. — *wo shidzmeru*, to pacify the spirits of the dead.
Syn. KOMPAKU.

REI, レイ, 鈴, *n.* A small bell.
Syn. RIN.

REI, レイ, 零, This word is used as a cipher, or to show that one denomination is omitted, as, *San zen rei hachi-jū*, = 3080.

REI-BOKU, レイボク, 靈木, *n.* A tree in which a spirit, or a Kami is supposed to dwell.

†REI-BUTSZ, レイブツ, 靈佛, *n.* An idol of great virtue, in which a spirit or Hotoke dwells.

REI-CHI, レイチ, 靈地, *n.* A sacred place.

REI-FŪ, レイフウ, 冷風, *n.* A cold wind.

REI-FUKU, レイフク, 禮服, *n.* Dress of ceremony.

REI-GAKU, レイガク, 禮樂, *n.* Etiquette and music.

REI-GEN, レイゲン, 靈驗, *n.* A wonderful exhibition of divine power, either in answering prayer, or punishing offenders.

REI-GI, レイギ, 禮義, *n.* Propriety, etiquette, decorum, ceremony. — *wo mamoru*, to observe the rules of propriety.

†REI-HAI, レイハイ, 靈牌, *n.* The tablet on which the name of the dead is inscribed. Syn. IHAI.

REI-HŌ, レイホウ, 靈寶, *(takara mono). n.* The precious things treasured up in temples or Miyas.

REI-JIN, レイジン, 伶人, *n.* An opera dancer. Syn. GAKUNIN.

REI-JITSZ, レイジツ, 例日, *n.* Anniversary day.

†REI-JŌ, レイジヤウ, 禮讓, *(herikudaru), n.* Humility, modesty.

REI-JŌ, レイジヤウ, 禮狀, *n.* A letter of thanks.

REI-JŌ, レイジヤウ, 靈場, *n.* A sacred place.

REI-KI, レイキ, 冷氣, *n.* Cold, cool. *Asa ban wa yohodo — ni natta,* the mornings and evenings are become quite cool.

REI-KIN, レイキン, 禮金, *n.* A fee, money given in acknowledgment of a favor.

REI-KON, レイコン, 靈魂, *(tamashii), n.* The soul, spirit, ghost, manes of the dead.

||REI-K'YAKU, レイキヤク, 冷却, *(kiyakasz).* Cooling anything. — *szru,* to cool.

†REI-MEI, レイメイ, 令名, *(yoki na), n.* Excellent name.

†REI-MIN, レイミン, 黎民, *(tada-bito), n.* The common people, farmers, laborers.

REI-MOTSZ, レイモツ, 禮物, *n.* Any thing given as an expression of gratitude.

REI-MU, レイム, 靈夢, *n.* A dream in which a divine revelation is received.

REI-NEN, レイネン, 例年, *(itszmo), n.* Ordinary years. — *no tōri,* in the usual yearly manner.

REI-RAKU, レイラク, 零落, *(ochi-bure-ru). n.* Falling from a prosperous condition into want, ruin. Syn. KURŌ.

||REI-REI, レイレイ, 麗麗, Plain, bold; as, — *to kaku,* to write in large, bold characters, (as on a signboard).

†REI-RI, レイリ, 伶俐, Ingenious, clever, smart, shrewd. Syn. RIKŌ, KASH'KOI.

†REI-RO, レイロウ, 玲瓏, Clear, transparent and bright, (as a gem).

REI-ROKU, レイロク, 禮祿, *n.* Any thing given as an expression of gratitude.

†REI-SHA, レイシヤ, 禮謝, *n.* Thanks, ackowledgment. — *wo szru.*

REI-SHI, レイシ, 靈芝, *n.* A species of hard mushroom, also called, *Man-nentake.*

REI-SHI, レイシ, 苦瓜, *n.* The balsam-apple.

REI-SHI, レイシ. 茘枝, *n.* The Lichi.

REI-SHI, レイシ, 令子, *(yoki ko), n.* Son, (in letters). *Go — sama.*

REI-SHIKI, レイシキ, 禮式, *n.* Etiquette, propriety, decorum, ceremony.

REI-SHITSZ, レイシツ, 令室, *(yoki tszma), n.* Wife. *Go rei-shitz,* your wife.

†REI-SHU, レイシユ, 冷酒, *(hiyazake) n.* Cold *sake.*

†REI-SZI, レイスイ 冷水, *(hiya midz) n.* Cold water.

†REI-YAKU, レイヤク, 靈藥, A wonderful medicine, (either because of its virtues, or of its origin, being revealed by the gods.)

REIYŌKAKU, レイヤウカク, 靈羊角, *n.* A kind of hartshorn, used as a medicine.

REIZEN, レイゼン, 靈前, *(ihai no maye).* Before the ancestral tablet. — *ye sonaye-ru,* to place, &c.

†RE-KI, レキ, 曆, *n.* A calendar year, an almanac. Syn. TOSHI, KOYOMI.

REKI-DAI, レキダイ, 歴代, *(yo-yo), n.* Successive generations, or dynasties. Syn. DAI-DAI.

†REKI-GAKU, レキガク, 曆學, *n.* Study or learning pertaining to the almanac, or calendar. — *wo szru,* to make astronomical calculations for the almanac.

REKI-REKI, レキレキ, 歴歴, Standing out conspicuous from amongst others, prominent, illustrious, eminent, clear, plain, evident, distinct. — *no iye-gara,* the most illustrious families. — *no gaku sha,* the most eminent scholars. — *to sh'te kazō beshi,* so distinct as to be counted.

REKISHI, レキシ, 歴史, *n.* A history, chronicle.

†REKISZU, レウスキ, 歴數, *(toshi no kadz), n.* Number of years. Syn. NENSZU.

†REKIZEN, レキゼン, 歴然, *adv.* Clear, plain, manifest, distinct. Syn. MEIHAKU.

†REKK'WA, レツクワ, 烈火, *n.* A raging fire.

REM-BAN, レンバン, 連署, *n.* Several seals affixed in succession to the same document.

REM-BO, レンボ, 戀慕, *(koi sh'tau), n.* Love, (sexual). — *szru,* to love. Syn. HORERU.

†REMMA, レンマ, 錬摩, *(neri migaku). n.* To exercise, train, or drill one's self in any thing. — *no kō,* skill obtained by much practice. Syn. TANREN.

REM-MEN, レンメン, 聯綿, Uninterrupted succession, line, or series. — *to sh'te tayedz.* Syn. RAKUYEKI.

REM-MIN, レンミン, 憐愍, *(awaremi)*. *n.* Pity, compassion, mercy.
Syn. JIHI, NASAKE.

REM-MIYŌ, レンミヤウ, 連名, *n.* A series, row, string, or list of names.

REN, レン, 聯, *n.* A pair of boards on which stanzas of poetry, &c., are written and hung up for ornament.

REN, レン, 連, *n.* A row, series, used in counting things strung together. *Nenjū ichi ren,* one string of rosary. *Tama ichi* —, a string of beads.

†REN-CHI, レンチ, 廉耻, Pure and susceptible of shame, upright. — *ga nai,* shameless, extortionate, corrupt.

REN-CHIU, レンチウ, 連中, *(misz no uchi)*. *n.* Inside of the blinds, (fig.) the wife of a *Kuge,* or *Shōgun.*

REN-CHIU, レンチウ, 簾中, *n.* Companion, company, club. *Shibai no* —, theatrical company. Syn. SHACHIU.

†REN-CHOKU, レンチヨク, 廉直, Honest, upright, exact, precise, accurate.
Syn. SHŌJIKI.

REN-DAI, レンダイ, 蓮臺, *(hasz no utena)*. *n.* The lotus-flower seat on which *Amida* is represented as sitting.

†REN-DAI, レンダイ, 輦臺, *n.* A hand barrow, a bier.

REN-GA, レンガ, 連歌, *n.* A pastime in which one extemporizes the first half of a stanza of poetry, and another finishes it.

REN-GE, レンゲ, 蓮華, *(hachisz bana)*. *n.* The lotus flower.

RENGE, レンゲ, *n.* The liver of a fowl, or ox.

RENGESŌ, レンゲサウ, 蓮華草, *n.* The name of a small flower, Sedum.

RENGIYŌ, レンギヤウ, 連翹, *n.* A flowering shrub.

REN-IN, レンイン, 連印, *n.* A row of seals affixed to the same paper. Syn. REMBAN.

REN-JAKU, レンジヤク, 鍊雀, *n.* The name of a beautiful bird.

REN-JAKU, レンジヤク, 連尺, *n.* A wooden frame slung over the back, used for carrying bulky articles, as straw, &c.

REN-JI, レンジ, 檽子, *n.* The frame work of upright wooded bars before windows.

REN-JITSZ, レンジツ, 連日, *n.* A succession of days. — *no uten,* a succession of rainy days.

†REN-JŌ, レンジヤウ, 戀情, *(shitau kokoro)*. *n.* Love, (between sexes.)

REN-JŌ, レンジヤウ, 連狀, *n.* A writing subscribed by a row of names.

†REN-JU, レンジユ, 鍊脩, *(neri osameru)*. To exercise, or drill one's self in.

†REN-JUKU, レンジユク, 鍊熟, To become proficient, or adept in by practice.

†REN-NEN, レンネン, 連年, *n.* A series or succession of years. — *no hōsaku,* a succession of fruitful years.

REN-NIKU, レンニク, 蓮肉, *(hasz no mi)*. *n.* The fruit or seeds of the Lotus.

REN-RI, レンリ, 連理, *n.* United by growing together. — *no yeda,* the branches of a tree united by growing together.

†REN-RUI, レンルイ, 連累, *n.* Involved in trouble through the crimes of another.
Syn. MAKIZOYE.

†REN-SHI, レンシ, 連枝, *n.* (fig.) Brethren.

†REN-YA, レンヤ, 連夜, *n.* A succession of nights.

REN-YŌ, レンエフ, 蓮葉, *(hasz no ha)*. *n.* The lotus leaves.

REN-ZOKU, レンゾク, 連續, *(tszdzku)*. To continue without interruption, to endure. — *szru.*

†REPPŪ, レツプウ, 烈風, *(hageshik kaze)*. *n.* A violent wind, storm.

†RERU, レル, 被, The adjective termination of the passive verb, as, *H'to ni aiserareru,* to be loved by men.

†RESSHI, *-szru, -sh'ta,* レツスル, 列, *i.v.* To rank with, stand with, or take one's place amongst. *Daimiyō ni* —, to rank with a Daimiyo.

†RESSHUKU, レツシユク, 列宿, *n.* The constellations, (of which the Japanese reckon twenty-eight.)

†RETEIGU, レテイグ, 釐等, *n.* A *rin* weight. Syn. RIN-DAME.

RETSZ, レツ, 列, *(tszra)*. *n.* The order, or arrangement of men in ranks, files, lines, &c. — *wo tadasz,* to dress the ranks. — *wo midasz,* to derange the ranks.

†RETSZ-JO, レツジヨ, 烈女, *n.* A chaste woman, a faithful widow.

RETSZ-ZA, レツザ, 列坐, *n.* Sitting in a row.

RI, リ, 里, *n.* A mile, = 4320 yds., or nearly $2\frac{1}{2}$ miles Eng. *Yedo made iku ri,* how many miles to Yedo?

RI, リ, 理, *n.* The natural laws, or inherent principles of things, reason, principle, that which is right, just, proper. — *arazaru koto nashi,* there is reason in every thing.

RI, リ, 利, *n.* Profit, gain, interest, advantage, victory. — *wo yeru,* to get profit. *Kono shina-mono utte ikura no ri ga aru,* what profit have you on the sale of these goods? *Ri wo toru*, to make a profit. *Ri wo tszkete kayesz*, to pay back the principal and interest. *Ri wo ushinau*, to lose the victory.

RI-AI, リアヒ, 利合, *n.* Interest on money.

RI-BETSZ, リベツ, 離別, *(hanare wakare). n.* Parting, separation, divorce. — *no kanashimi* the sorrow of parting. *Niyōbō wo — szru*, to divorce a wife.

RI-BIYŌ, リビヤウ, 痢病, *n.* Dysentery. Syn. SHIBURI-HARA.

RI-BUN, リブン, 利分, *n.* Profit, gain. — *ga uszi*, the profit is small. Syn. MŌKE, RIJUN.

RICHI-GI, リチギ, 律義, Just upright, honest, moral. — *na h'to.*

†RI-DON, リドン, 利鈍, *(toki nibuki.)* Sharp and dull, clever and stupid.

RIDZME, リツメ, 理詰, Convinced by the reasons given. — *ni makeru*, to yield to the force of reasons.

RI-FU-JIN, リフジン, 理不盡, *(kotowari wo tszkusadz.)* Contrary to right, or reason; unjust, unreasonable, violently, forcibly. Syn. MUTAI, MURINI.

RI-GAI, リガイ, 利害, Profit or loss, advantage or disadvantage. — *wo toku*, to show the advantage of doing anything.

†RIGAK'SHA, リガクシヤ, 理學者, *n.* A rationalist, infidel.

RI-GIN, リギン 理銀, *n.* Interest money.

RI-HATSZ, リハツ, 理發, *n.* Acuteness of mind, sagacity, cleverness. Syn. RIKŌ, KASH'KOI, REIRI.

RI-HI, リヒ, 理非, *n.* The right or wrong, justice or injustice, reasonable or unreasonable. — *wo tadasz*, to ascertain the right or wrong of any thing.

RI-JUN, リジユン, 利潤, *n.* Profit, gain. — *ga ōi akinai*, a trade which brings large profit. Syn. MŌKE.

RI-KAI, リカイ, 理解, *(kotowari wo toku.)* Explaining or unfolding the reason or principles. — *wo szru.*

RI-KATA, リカタ, 利方, Most profitable, advantageous, or convenient way. *Nimotsz wo okuru ni wa fune no hō ga — da*, it will be the most profitable to send the goods by ship. Syn. TOKUYŌ.

RIKI, リキ, 力, *(chikara). n.* Strength, power, force. Syn. RIYOKU.

RIKIMI, *-mu, -nda*, リキム, *i.v.* To make a show of one's strength, or authority, to swagger, bully, to strain, to exert one's self. *Rikinde aruku*, to walk in a swaggering manner, to strut. *Rikinde mono wo iu*, to talk in a bullying manner. Syn. IBARU.

RIKIMI, リキミ, *n.* Vigor, power, strength, authority. — *no aru kao*, an intrepid countenance. — *no aru koye*, powerful voice.

RIKIMI-AI, *-au, -atta*, リキミアフ, *i.v.* To make a show of each others strength, (as wrestlers before contending).

RIKIMI-CHIRASHI, *-sz, -sh'ta*, リキミチラス, *t.v.* To strut, swagger, or make a display of one's authority all about.

RIKIMI-KAYE, *-ru, -ta*, リキミカヘル, *i. v.* To strut, swagger, bully or boast immoderately.

RIKIMI-KI, *-ru, -tta*, リキミキル, (idem).

RIKIRIYŌ, リキリヤウ, 力量, *(chikara no hakari). n.* Strength, power; ability, talent.

RIKI-SHA, リキシヤ, 力者, *n.* A strong man.

RIKI-SHI, キリシ, 力士, *n.* A strong man; a wrestler.

RIKIU, リキウ, 離宮, *n.* A pleasure house of the *Tenshi.*

RIKKA, リツカ, 立夏, *n.* The first day of summer.

RIKK'WA, リツクワ, 立花, *(tate-bana).* Flowers arranged in a vase.

RIKŌ, リコウ, 利口, *n.* Acuteness of mind, shrewdness, cleverness, ingenuity, expertness. *Rikō na mono*, smart person (either in a good or bad sense.) Syn. KASH'KOI, RIHATSZ.

RIKŌ-DATE, リコウダテ, 利口立, *n.* Displaying one's smartness; affectation of cleverness. — *wo szru.*

RI-KON, リコン 利根, *n.* Sagacity, cleverness, ingenuity, acuteness.

RIKŌRASHII, -KI, リコウラシイ, 利口敷, *a.* Having the appearance of cleverness, acuteness, &c.

†RIKU, クリ, 六, Six: only used in comp. words.

RIKU, リク, 陸, *n.* The land (as opposed to water or sea). *Ōsaka ye — wo yuku*, to go to *Osaka* by land. Syn. OKA, KUGA.

†RIKU-CHIN, リクチン, 陸沈, To be fallen, ruined, (as a person once prosperous). — *szru.* Syn. REIRAKU.

†RIKU-GEI, リクゲイ, 六藝, *n.* The six acquirements, viz. Reading, arithmetic, etiquette, archery, horsemanship and music

†RIKU-GŌ, リクガフ, 六合, *n.* The six sides of the universe, viz, the heaven, earth, and four cardinal points.

RIKU-GUN, リクグン, 陸軍, A land force or army.

RIKUJI, リクヂ, 陸路, (*oka no michi*). *n.* By land. — *wo yuku*, to go by land.

RIKUTSZ, リクツ, 理屈, *n.* Reason, cause, false reasoning, caviling, captious objections, quibble, sophistry. — *wo iu*, to quibble, or cavil. *Kaminari no naru — wa nani*, what is the reason of the sound of thunder?

RIKUTSZRASHII,–KI, リクツラシイ, 理屈敷, *a.* Having the manner of a captious person.

RIKUTSZ-SHA, リクツシヤ, 理屈者, *n.* A caviler, captious reasoner.

†RIM-BAN, リンバン, 輪番, *n.* By turns, in turn, one after another. — *ni szru*, to take turns. Syn. MAWARI-BAN.

RIM-BIYŌ, リンビヤウ, 淋病, *n.* Gonorrhœa. Syn. RINSHITSZ.

†RIMIN, リミン, 里民, (*satobito*). *n.* A country-man, villager, farmer.

RIN, リン, 鈴, A small bell. — *wo furu*, to ring the bell.

RIN, リン, 釐, *n.* A weight, the tenth part of a *fun*, = 0.583 of a grain troy.

RIN, リン, 麟, *n.* The name of a fabulous animal, unicorn.

RIN, リン, 輪, *n.* The corolla (of a flower).

RIN-CHŌ, リンチヤウ, 隣町, (*tonari machi.*) *n.* The next ward of a street.

RIN-DAME, リンダメ, 釐等, *n.* A copper rin weight. Syn. RETEIGU.

RIN-DEN, リンデン, 輪轉, *n.* The transmigration of souls (Budd.) Syn. RINYE.

RIN-DŌ, リンダウ, 龍膽, *n.* Gentian. Syn. RIUTAN.

RINDZ, リンズ, 花綾, *n.* A kind of figured satin.

†RIN-GEN, リンゲン, 綸言, (*mikotonori*). The words of the *Tenshi*.

RIN-GETSZ, リンゲツ, 臨月, (*umidzki.*) *n.* The month of parturition, (the 10th month according to Japanese reckoning).

RINGO, リンゴ, 林檎, *n.* An apple.

RIN-GOKU, リンゴク, 隣國, (*tonari kuni*). *n.* The neigbouring country.

RIN-JI, リンジ, 臨時, Accidental, casual, contingent, happening out of the regular order. — *no yō*, casual business. — *no kiyaku*, accidental visitor. — *g'wa-yaku*, casual public service, (on extraordinary occasions.) — *no niu-yō*, contingent expenses. Syn. OMOIGAKE-NAI, FUI.

RIN-JŪ, リンジウ, 臨終, (*owari ni nozomu*). *n.* The moment of death, drawing near to death. — *no toki* Syn. SAIGO.

RIN-KA, リンカ, 隣家, (*tonari no iye*) *n.* The next or neighbouring house or family.

RINKI, リンキ, 吝氣, *n.* Jealousy. — *wo szru*, to feel jealous. Syn. SHITTO, NETAMI, YAKIMOCHI.

RIN-KI-Ō-HEN, リンキオウヘン, 臨機應變, *n.* Acting according to the occasion, changing to suit the circumstances. — *wa akindo no kanyō nari*, the important thing for a merchant is to suit himself to the changes (in the market). — *ni tori-hakarau*, to act according to circumstances.

†RIN-KŌ, リンカウ, 臨幸, (*miyuki*). *n.* The going of the *Tenshi* to any place.

†RIN-KŌ, リンコウ, 輪講, *n.* Reciting by turns.

†RIN-RIN, リンリン, 凛凛, *adv.* Very cold, (fig.) awe-inspiring, awful, grand, imposing. *Yuki — to szru.*

RIN-SHI, リンシ, 綸旨, *n.* A warrant, commission, or written order from the *Tenshi*.

RIN-SHITSZ, リンシツ, 淋疾, *n.* Gonorrhœa. Syn. RIMBIYŌ.

†RIN-SHŌ, リンシヨウ, 林鍾, *n.* The sixth month.

RIN-SHOKU, リンシヨク, 吝嗇, (*oshimi oshimu*). *n.* Stingy, miserly, niggardly, parsimonious. — *na h'to*, a parsimonious person. —*ni szru*, to be miserly. Syn. SHIWAI.

RIN-SON, リンソン, 隣村, (*tonari mura*). *n.* The next or neighbouring village.

RIN-TŌ, リントウ, 輪燈, *n.* A lamp suspended by large brass rings in front of an idol.

†RIN-U, リンウ, 霖雨, (*naga ame*). *n.* A long rain.

RIN-YE, リンヱ, 輪回, *n.* Transmigrations of the soul. (Bud.) — *ni mayō*, lost in endless transmigrations. Syn. RINDEN.

RIN-YEN, リンエン, 林園, *n.* A park, garden.

RIN-ZAN, リンザン 臨產, *n.* The approach of parturition. — *no toki.*

RIN-ZŌ, リンザウ, 輪藏, *n.* A circular book-case, made to revolve round a vertical axis.

RIPPA, リツパ, 立派, *a.* Splendid, fine magnificent. — *na otoko-buri*, a splendid looking man. — *na otenki*, splendid weather. Syn. KEKKŌ, UTSZKUSHII.

RIPPUKU, リツプク, 立腹, (*hara wo tateru*). *n.* Angry. — *szru*, to be angry. Syn. IKARU, OKORU.

RIRISHII,-KI,-KU,-U,-SA, リリシイ, 凜凜 Grand, imposing, severe. striking with awe, or fear. *Ririshiku shitaku totonoye,* dressed himself in the most imposing manner. Syn. RIN-RIN.

RI-SAN, リサン, 離散, (*hanare chiru*). Separated and scattered. *Shi hō ni — sh'ta.* Syn. CHIRI-JIRI.

RISHI,*-szru,-sh'ta,* リスル, 利, To gain, make a profit. Syn. MŌKERU.

RI-SHŌ, リシヤウ, 利生, *n.* Favor, aid, grace, (only of Kami). *Kami no — wo kōmuru.* Syn. OKAGE, MEGUMI.

RI-SOKU, リソク, 利息, *n.* Interest on money. *— wa ichi wari,* the interest is one per cent a month. Syn. RI, RIGIN.

RISSHIN, リツシン, 立身, (*mi wo tatszru*). *n.* Rising in rank, wealth, honor; promotion, advancement. Syn. SHUSSEI.

RISSHŪ, リツシウ, 立秋, *n.* The first day of autumn.

RISSHUN, リツシユン, 立春, The first day of spring.

RISSŌ, リツソウ, 律僧, *n.* An order of Buddhist priests.

RISZ, リス, 栗鼠, *n.* A squirrel.

RITTŌ, リツトウ, 立冬, *n.* The first day of winter.

RIU, リウ, 龍, (*tatsz*), *n.* A dragon, the emblem of Imperial power.

RIU, リウ, 流, (*nagare*), *n.* A current; style, or manner, sect, either of religion, or philosophy; line, or succession of family. *Seiyō — no gumpō,* European style of military tatics.
Syn. RIUGI, FŪ, HA.

RIU-BETSZ, リウベツ, 留別, *n.* A parting, leaving, separation. *— no k'wai,* a party given by one about to leave.

†RIU-DŌ-BUTSZ, リウドウブツ, 流動物, *n.* A fluid, liquid.

RIUDZ, リウヅ, 龍頭, (*tatsz-gashira*). *n.* Dragon's head, the place on the top of a large bell by which it is suspended.

†RIU-GAN, リウガン, 龍顔, (*tatsz no kao*), *n.* The dragon's face,—Imperial presence.

RIU-GAN-NIKU, リウガンニク, 龍眼肉, *n.* The lungyen, (a Chinese fruit).

RIU-GAWARI, リウガハリ, 流替, *n.* Difference of style, or of sect.

†RIU-GEN, リウゲン, 流言, (*nagashi kotoba*), *n.* A false report, a story fabricated and made current.

RIU-GI, リウギ, 流義, *n.* Style, manner, or method of wr iting, drawing, singing, fencing, of medical practice, or of any work of art; a sect, creed, system, order. *— wo tateru,* to introduce a new style. Syn. RIU, HA.

RIU-GO, リウゴ, 輪鼓, *n,* A small wheel on the spindle of a spinning-wheel, over which the band passes.

RIU-GO-SHA, リウゴシヤ, 龍骨車 *n.* A kind of water-wheel, used for irrigating.

RIU-GŪ-JŌ, リウグウジヤウ, 龍宮城, *n.* The castle of the king of the dragons, supposed to be at the bottom of the ocean.

RIU-G'WAN, リウグワン, 立願, (*negai wo tatszru*), *n.* Offering up of prayers, or desires (to the Kami).
— wo szru. — wo kakeru.

RIU-IN, リウイン, 留飲, *n.* Pyrosis, water-brash.

RIU-JIN, リウジン, 龍神, (*tatsz no kami*), *n.* The dragon god.

RIU-JŌ, リウジヨ, 柳絮, (*yanage no wata*), *n.* The catkins of the willow.

RIU-KIU, リウキウ, 琉球, *n.* The Lew Chew islands.

RIU-KŌ, リウカウ, 流行, (*nagare yuku*). *n.* Prevailing, current, predominant, or fashionable way, style, fashion. *— szru,* to prevail (as disease), to be fashionable, (as dress). *— okure na h'to,* a person behind the fashion. *Yo no — to iu mono wa miyō-ni utszri-kawaru mono da,* the fashions of the world are wonderfully changeable. Syn. HAYARU.

RIU-KOTSZ, リウコツ, 龍骨, (*tatsz no hone*). *n.* Dragons-bone, a species of cactus.

RIU-ME, リウメ, 龍馬, *n.* A splendid horse.

RIU-MON, リウモン, 素紬, *n.* A kind of white-silk.

†RIU-NEN, リウネン, 流年, (*nagaruru toshi*). *n.* The rapidly passing years.

RIU-NŌ, リウナウ, 龍腦, *n.* Refined camphor.

RIU-RAKU, リウラク, 流落, Reduced from honour or wealth to poverty and misery. Syn. OCHI-BUKERU, REI-RAKU, RURŌ.

†RIU-REN, リウレン, 流連, Continuing long away from home absorbed in anything.

RIU-RIU, リウリウ, 劉劉, *adv.* The whizzing sound of a ball, arrow, or spear in its flight. *Tama — to naru,* the ball whizzes. *— hasshi to tszku.*

RIU-SEI, リウセイ, 流星, *n.* A meteor. Syn. YOBAIBOSHI.

RIU-SZI, リウスイ, 流水, (*nagareru midz*). *n.* A current of water, a stream.

†RIU-TAI, リウタイ, 留滯, (*todomari todokōri*). Detained, hindered, stopped, obstructed.

RIU-TAN, リウタン, 龍膽, *n.* Gentian.
Syn. RINDŌ, SASARINDO.

RIU-TEI, リウテイ, 流涕, (*namida wo nagasz*). Shedding tears.
Syn. RAKU-RUI.

RIU-TO-SZI, リウトスイ, 龍吐水, *n.* A fire engine.

RIU-WŌ, リウワウ, 龍王, *n.* The king of the dragons, (supposed to govern the rain).

RIU-YEI, リウエイ, 柳營, *n.* The castle of the Shōgun.

RIU-YŌ, リウヨウ, 立用, (*yō wo tateru*). To lend, to use temporarily as a convenience, to make do, to make answer the purpose. *Kane wo — szru*, to lend money. *Kore wo — itashimashō*, I will make this do. *Kore wa — itashimasen*, this will not answer. Syn. KASZ, MA NI AWASERU.

RIU-ZAN, リウザン, 流產, *a.* Abortion, miscarriage at the 3d month.

RIU-ZŌ, リウザウ, 立像, (*tateru kata*). *n.* A standing image.

†RIU-ZOKU, リウゾク, 流俗, *n.* Current customs, (customs come down from antiquity and which have deteriorated).

RI-YAKU, リヤク, 利益, *n.* Help, aid or favor of a divine being. *Kami no go — de buji ni kayetta*, through the favor of God I have got back without accident.
Syn. OKAGE, RISHŌ.

RIYAKU, リヤク, 畧, *n.* Abridgment, abbreviation, summary, epitome. — *szru*, to abridge, to abbreviate, to curtail, to shorten, to slight, to omit. Syn. HABUKU.

RIYAKU-BUN, リヤクブン, 畧文, *n.* An abbreviated letter.

RIYAKU-GI, リヤクギ, 畧儀, *n.* An abridging or omitting of proper, or customary forms.

RIYAKU-JI, リヤクジ, 畧字, *n.* An abbreviated word, contracted character.

RIYAKU-SHIKI, リヤクシキ, 畧式, *n.* An abridgment of the proper form, mode, or rule.

RI-YEKI, リエキ, 利益, *n.* Profit, gain, advantage. *Akinai no — wa szkunai*, the profit from trading is small. — *ni naranu*, unprofitable.

RI-YEN, リエン, 離緣, *n.* Separation, sundering of a relationship, divorce. — *szru*, to separate (as husband and wife), to divorce. Syn. RI-BETSZ.

RIYEN-JŌ, リエンジヤウ, 離緣狀, *n.* A writing of divorcement. Syn. SARI-JŌ.

RIYŌ, リヨウ, 龍, (*tatsz*). *n.* A dragon.

RIYŌ, リヤウ, 兩, *n.* The value of four ichibus, represented by a *Koban.* Two, both. — *san nin*, two or three men. *Ichi — nichi*, one or two days. — *ashi*, both feet. — *mimi*, both ears.

RIYŌ, リヤウ, 輛, *n.* The numeral used in counting waggons. *Kuruma san riyō*, three waggons.

†RIYŌ, リヤウ, 靈, (*tamashii*). A spirit, (see *Iki-riyō*, *Shi-riyō*).

RIYŌ, レフ, 獵, *n.* Hunting, fishing. — *wo szru*, to fish, to hunt. Syn. KARI.

RIYŌ, レウ, 寮, *n.* A cottage.
Syn. BESSŌ.

RIYŌ, レウ, 料, *n.* Value, price, cost, material. *Kimono no — ni kane wo yatta*, gave him money enough to buy clothes with. *Kimono no — ni momen wo yaru*, to give cotton cloth as material for clothes. *Sake no —*, the price of *sake*.
Syn. SHIRO, KAWARI.

RIYŌ, リヤウ, 領, *n.* The dominion, territory or estate belonging to a lord, or ruler, jurisdiction. — *szru*, to rule, govern.

RIYŌ, リヤウ, 量, *n.* Ability, talent, capacity. — *no hiroi h'to*, a man of great ability. Syn. KI-RIYŌ.

RI-YŌ, リヨウ, 利用, *n.* Utility, usefulness. — *wo moppara to szru*, to make utility of the first importance.

RIYŌ, リヤウ, 良, Used only as an adjective of praise, = good, excellent, skilful, as, *Riyō-ba*, 良馬, a good horse. *Riyō-i*, 良醫, a good physician. *Riyō-shō*, 良將, a good general. *Riyō-yaku*, 良藥, excellent medicine.

RIYŌ-AN, リヤウアン, 諒闇, *n.* The three years of mourning on the death of the Tenshi.

RIYŌ-BU, リヤウブ, 兩部, Both religions (of Sintoo and Buddhism).

RIYŌ-BUN, リヤウブン, 領分, *n.* Dominion, territory, or estate belonging to a king a lord, or monastery; jurisdiction. — *no h'yak'shō*, the farmers or serfs belonging to an estate.

RIYŌ-CHI, リヤウチ, 領地, *n.* The territory, or estate belonging to a lord, or temple.

RIYŌ-DO, リヤウド, 兩度, *adv.* Two times, twice, both times.
Syn. FUTA-TABI.

†RIYŌ-FŪ, リヤウフウ, 涼風, (*szdzshiki kaze*). *n.* A cool and pleasant wind.

RIYŌ-GAKE, リヤウガケ, 兩懸, *n.* The two black boxes carried in the train of officials. Syn. HASAMI-BAKO.

RIYŌ-GAN, リヤウガン, 兩眼, *n.* Both eyes.

RIYŌ-GAYE, リヤウガヘ, 兩替, *n.* Changing money. — *wo szru*, to change money.

RIYŌ-GAYE-YA, リヤウガヘヤ, 兩替屋, *n.* A money changer.

†RIYŌGE, リヤウゲ, 領解, *n.* Comprehension or thorough understanding.

†RIYŌ-GI, リヤウギ, 兩儀, The dual principles of nature,—the *In* and *Yō*.

RIYO-G'WAI, リヨグワイ, 慮外, (*omoi no hoka*), *n.* Impolite, rude, ill-mannered, rough. — *na mono*, an ill-mannered person. — *wo szru*, to do rough, or rude things. — *nagara*, excuse my impoliteness. Syn. SHITSZREI, BUSHITSZKE, BUREI.

RIYO-HAKU, リヨハク, 旅泊, (*tabi no tomari*), *n.* Lodging at an inn while on a journey. — *szru*.

RIYŌ-HŌ, リヤウハウ, 兩方, *n.* Two sides, both persons, both. *Ano iye wa — ni mon ga aru*, that house has a gate on both sides. — *tomo rikōna mono*, they are both clever persons. — *ye wakareta*, have separated into two parties. Syn. FUTA-KATA.

RIYŌ-JI, レウヂ, 療治, *n.* Treatment of disease medical attendance. — *szru*, to treat disease, to prescribe for the sick.

RIYO-JIN, リヨジン, 旅人, (*tabi-bito*), *n.* A traveller.

RIYŌ-JŌ, リヤウジヤウ, 領掌, To assent to, to receive, to comply with. *Mei wo — szru*, to comply with an order. Syn. SHŌCHI.

RIYO-KAKU, リヨカク, 旅客, (*tabi-bito*), *n.* A traveller, or guest at an inn.

RIYŌ-KEN, リヤウケン, 量見, *n.* Sentiment, thought, opinion, notion, mind, judgment, pardon, excuse, intention. *Watakushi no — ni wa naranu*, it does not rest with me to say. *Omaye no — shidai*, act according to your own judgment. — *chigai*, mistaken in judgment. *Go — kudasare*, I beg your pardon. — *naranu*, inexcusable. *Kon ya dō szru — da*, what do you intend to do to-night? Syn. OMOI, KANGAYE, KOKORO.

RIYO-KŌ, リヨカウ, 旅行, (*tabi yuku*) To go on a journey, to travel.

†RIYO-KŌ, リヨコウ, 閭巷, *n.* A town. — *no setsz*, an idle report, a town talk.

RI-YOKU, リヨク, 利欲, Desire of gain, avarice, covetousness, love of money. — *no tame ni szru*, to do anything from the love of gain. — *na h'to*, an avaricious man. — *mayō*, to be led astray by the love of money. Syn. MUSABORU.

†RIYOKU, リヨク, 綠, (*midori*), *a.* Green-color. — *sō*, 綠草, green grass. — *chiku*, 綠竹, green bamboo. — *szi*, 綠水, green or deep water.

RIYOKU-BAN, リヨクバン, 綠礬, *n.* Sulphate of Iron. Spn. RŌHA.

RIYO-K'WAN, リヨクワン, 旅館, (*tabi no yadori*), *n.* An inn, a lodging house, hotel.

RIYŌ-ME, リヤウメ, 量目, *n.* The weight. Syn. BUN-RIYŌ, KAKEME.

RIYŌ-MEN, リヤウメン, 兩面, (*futa omote*). Two faces, both sides, or surfaces, (as of paper), double faced. — *no kagami*, a mirror which reflects from both sides.

RIYŌ-NAI, リヤウナイ, 領內, (*riyōbun no uchi*), *n.* In the territory, or dominion. *Ōsaka wa doko no — da*, in whose territory is Osaka?

RIYŌ-RA, リヨウラ, 綾羅, *n.* A kind of rich silk stuff.

‖RIYŌRI,-*ru*,-*tta*, レウル, 料理, *t.v.* To cook. *Sakana wo —*, to cook a fish.

RIYŌ-RI, レウリ, 料理, *n.* Preparing, dressing, or cooking food. — *szru*, to prepare, or cook food.

RIYŌRI-YA, レウリヤ, 兩料理, *n.* An eating house, restaurant, a person who keeps an eating house.

RIYŌ-SEN, リヤウセン, 漁舟, *n.* A fishing boat, a whaling ship.

RIYŌ-SETSZ, リヤウセツ, 兩說, *n.* Two different reports, versions, or stories about the same thing. — *ga aru*.

RIYŌ-SHI, レフシ, 獵師, *n.* A hunter.

RIYŌ-SHI, レフシ, 漁者, *n.* A fisherman.

RIYŌ-SHIN, リヤウシン, 兩親, (*futa oya*), *n.* Both parents.

RIYŌ-SHU, リヤウシユ, 領主, *n.* The lord of a district of country, or state.

RIYO-SHUKU, リヨシユク, 旅宿, (*tabi no yadori*), *n.* Stopping at an inn, or hotel, sojourning, at an inn, lodging place. — *szru*, to stop at an inn, to sojourn.

RIYŌ-SOKU, リヤウソク, 兩足, *n.* Both feet.

RIYŌ-TAN, リヤウタン, 兩端, Double-sided. — *no hakarigoto*, two plans which if one fails the other may be successful. *Koto wo — ni szru*, to manage a matter in a double or underhanded way.

RIYŌ-TE, リヤウテ, 兩手, *n.* Two, or both hands.

RIYŌ-TEN, リヤウテン, 兩天, *n.* Both clear and rainy weather.

RIYOTEN, リヨテン, 旅店, *n.* An inn, hotel, lodging-house.

RIYŌ-TŌ, リヤウトウ, 兩刀, *n.* Two swords.

RIYŌ-YŌ, リヨヨウ, 旅用, *n.* Travelling expenses.

RIYŌ-YŌ, リヤウヤウ, 兩様, *(futa tōri)*, *n.* Two, or both ways, both kinds.

RIYŌ-ZEKI, リヤウゼキ, 兩關, *n.* The two champions amongst wrestlers.

RIYŌ-ZETSZ, リヤウゼツ, 兩舌, *n.* Double-tongued.

RO, ロ, 艣, A scull, (of a boat). — *wo osz*, to work a scull.

RO, ロ, 爐, *n.* A hearth, or fire-place in the floor. — *wo kakomu*, to sit round the fire place. — *ni ataru*, to warm one's self at the hearth.

RO, ロ, 羅, *n.* A kind of gauze silk, used for dresses.

RO, ロ, 驢, *(usagi uma)*, *n.* A mule, donkey.

†RO, ロ, 露, *(tszyu)*, *n.* Dew. *Chō ro*, morning dew.

RO, ロ, 路, *(michi)*. A road. *Chō ro*, a long road. *Yen ro*, a distant journey.

RO, ロ, *a.* vulgar coll. imp. suffix, peculiar to the neighbourhood of Yedo. *Miro*, look. *Shi-ro*, do it. *Totte kurero*, bring it here.

RŌ, ラフ, 蠟, *n.* Wax, also enamel.

RŌ, ロウ, 樓, *(takadono)*, *n.* The second, or upper floor of a house, a brothel. — *ni noboru*, to ascend to the second-story.

RŌ, ラウ, 牢, *(h'to-ya)*, *n.* A gaol. Syn. RŌYA.

RŌ, ロウ, 櫳, *(ori)* *n.* A pen, cage.

RŌ, ラウ, 老, *(oi)*, *n.* Old-age, old, aged. — *wo waszrete tawamureru*, to forget old-age and engage in play.

RŌ, ラウ, 勞, *(tszkaruru)*, *n.* Toil, labor, trouble, fatigue, weariness.

RŌ, ラウ, *n.* Consumption, phthisis.

RŌ, ラウ, 癆, A future, or dubitative suffix. *Arō mo shiredz nakarō mo shiredz*, whether there are or not I know not. *Ame ga furō ka to omō*, I think it will rain. *Sore de yokarō*, I think that will do. *Dekita-rō*, I think it is done. *Yuku de atta-rō*, he might have gone. *Uru de atta-rō*, I might have sold. *Atarō mo shire-nakatta*, I might have hit him.

ROBA, ロバ, 驢馬, *n.* A mule, donkey.

†RŌ-BA, ラウバ, 老馬, *n.* An old horse.

†RŌ-BA, ラウバ, 老婆, *n.* An old woman.

†RŌ-BAI, ラウバイ, 狼狽, *(awateru)*. Alarm, consternation, fright. Syn. UROTAYERU.

RŌ-BAN, ラウバン, 牢番, *n.* A gaoler.

RO-BAN, ロバン, 露盤, *n.* A steeple, spire.

RŌBA-SHIN, ラウバシン, 老婆心, An old woman's heart, kind and thoughtful, tender solicitude, anxious care.

ROBESO, ロベソ, 艣枘, *n.* The wooden pin on which a scull works.

RŌ-BO, ラウボ, 老母, *n.* Old mother.

†RO-BŌ, ロバウ, 路傍, *(michi no hotori)*. *n.* Wayside.

RŌ-BUGIYŌ, ラウブギヤウ, 牢奉行, *n.* The superintendant of a prison.

RŌDŌ, ラウドウ, 郎等, *n.* The servants or followers of a lord.

†RODON, ロドン, 魯鈍, Stupid, dull. Syn. BAKA.

RŌDZ, ラウズ, 滯貨, *n.* The unsalable goods in a store, old goods. Syn. TANAZARASHI.

†RŌ-FU, ラウフ, 老父, *(oitaru chichi)* *n.* Old father.

†RŌ-FU, ラウフ, 老婦, *(oitaru onna)*. *n.* Old woman.

RŌ-GAI, ラウガイ, 癆咳, *n.* Consumption, phthisis.

RŌGETSZ, ラフゲツ, 臘月, *(shiwasz)*. *n.* The twelfth month.

RŌ-GI, ロウギ, 螻蟻, *(kera ari)*. *n.* Crickets and ants.

RO-GIN, ロギン, 路銀, *n.* Road money, money for travelling.

RŌ-GO, ラウゴ, 老後, *(oite nochi)*. *n.* After one is old, in one's old age.

†RŌ-GOKU, ラウゴク, 牢獄, *n.* A gaol, prison. Syn. RŌYA.

RŌ-GOSHI, ラウゴシ, 囚車, *n.* A coarse basket for conveying prisoners.

RŌHA, ラウハ, 綠礬, *n.* Sulphate of iron. Syn. RIYOKUBAN.

RO-IRO, ロイロ, 蠟色, *n.* A glossy greenish black color.

RŌ-JAKU, ラウジヤク, 老弱, *n.* Old and young.

ROJI, ロジ, 路次, *n.* An alley, court.

RŌ-JIN, ラウジン, 老人, *(oitaru h'to)*. *n.* An old man.

RŌ-JŌ, ロウジヤウ, 籠城, *(shiro ni komoru)*. Shut up or besieged in a castle. — *szru*, to shut themselves up in a castle for its defence.

RŌ-JO, ラウヂヨ, 老女, *n.* An official title applied to the matrons who superintend the *Shōgun's* harem.

RŌ-JŪ, ラウヂウ, 老中, See *Gorōju*.

RŌ-JŪ, ラウジウ, 郎從, Same as *Rōdō*.

RŌKA, ラウカ, 廊架, *n.* A corridor, gallery, covered way. Syn. WATARI-DONO.

RŌ-KAKU, ロウカク, 樓閣, *n.* A large two storied house.

ROKEN, ロケン, 露顯, To be known, revealed, disclosed, made public, (as of any thing concealed.) Syn. ARAWARERU.

†ROKITSZ, ロキツ, 盧橘, *n.* The loquat. Syn. BIWA.

RŌ-KIYO, ロウキヨ, 籠居, (*uchi ni komoru*). Confining one's self to the house, living in retirement, or seclusion.

ROKKAKU, ロクカク, 六角, *n.* Six-angled, hexagon.

ROKKAKU, ロクカク, 鹿角, (*shika no tszno*). *n.* Hatshorn.

†ROKKON, ロクコン, 六根, *n.* The six senses, according to the Japanese, viz., the eyes, ears, nose, tongue, body, and heart.

†RŌ-KŌ, ロウコウ, 陋巷, *n.* An ugly, or mean town.

RŌ-KŌ, ラウコウ, 老功, *n.* Veteran skill. — *no bushi*, a veteran soldier.

†RŌ-KOKU, ロウコク, 漏刻, *n.* A clepsydra.

ROKU, ロク, 六, (*mutsz*). Six. *Jū-roku*, sixteen. *Roku-roku*, six times six. *Roku-jū*, sixty. *Roku-bu ichi*, one sixth. *Roku-ban*, the sixth. *Roku-bam-me*, the sixth one. *Roku-nin*, six persons. *Roku-do*, six times.

ROKU, ロク, 錄, *n.* A record, account. — *szru*, to record, to write an account of, make a note of. *Fu-roku*, an appendix to a book. Syn. KI

ROKU, ロク, 祿, *n.* The salary, pay, or rations of an officer, the income of a lord.

ROKU, ロク, 圓, Even, level, good, well. — *na tokoro ni oki-nasare*, put it on an even place. — *na aisatsz wa shinai*, did not give a satisfactory answer. — *na koto de wa nakarō*, I do not think well of it. — *ni shiranu*, do not know it well. — *ni iru*, to sit at ease, or in a comfortable position. — *na yatsz de wa nai*, he is not a good man. Syn. TAIRAKA.

ROKUBISŌ, ロクビサウ, 鹿尾草, (*hijiki*). *n.* A kind of sea-weed.

ROKU-CHIKU, ロクチク, 六畜, *n.* The six domestic animals, viz., the fowl, dog, cow, goat, horse, and hog.

ROKU-DŌ, ロクダウ, 六道, (*mutsz no michi*). *n.* The six roads of the Buddhist hades, into which the souls of the dead after they are judged are sent, viz., *Jigoku*, *Gaki*, *Chikushō*, *Shura*, *Ningen*, *Tenjō*.

ROKUJŌ, ロクジヨウ, 鹿茸, *n.* Hartshorn.

ROKURO, ロクロ, 轆轤, *n.* A pulley, windlass, capstan, a lathe, a potters wheel, the rings in which the frame of an umbrella works.

ROKURO-GIRI, ロクロギリ, 牽鑽, *n.* A drill worked by a lathe.

ROKU-ROKU, ロクロク, *adv.* Well. — *shiranu*, do not know it well. — *kamawanai*, did not treat him well. Syn. YOKU.

†ROKU-ROKU, ロクロク, 碌碌, *adv.* Triflingly, frivolously. — *to sh'te yo wo okuru*, to live a useless life. Syn. GUDZ GUDZ.

ROKURO-KUBI, ロクロクビ, 飛頭蠻, *n.* The name of a disease, in which the neck is supposed to lengthen to an enormous extent.

ROKUSAI, ロクサイ, 六齋, *n.* The sixth days of the month, being every fifth day, on which religious services are held at a temple, or lectures, &c., are given, thus *ichi-roku*, are the 1st, 6th, 11th, 16th, 21st, 26th days. *Sam-pachi*, are the 3rd, 8th, 13th, 18th, 23rd, 28th, &c.

ROKU-SHAKU, ロクシヤク, 力者, (a corruption of *Riyoku sha*). A Daimio's chair-bearer.

ROKU-SHIN, ロクシン, 六親, (*mutsz no shitashimi*). *n.* The six relations, viz., father, mother, older-brother, younger-brother, wife, and child.

ROKU-SHŌ, ロクシヤウ, 銅綠, *n.* Verdigris.

ROKU-YOKU, ロクヨク, 六欲, *n.* The six desires or lusts, which come by the six senses.

ROK'WAI, ロクワイ, 蘆薈, *n.* Aloes.

ROMEI, ロメイ, 露命, (*tszyu no inochi*). *n.* Life evanescent as the dew. — *wo tsznagu*.

RŌMŌ, ラウマウ, 老耄, To be childish from age, decrepit, infirm. Syn. BOKERU, OIBORE.

RŌ-MUSHA, ラウムシヤ, 老武者, *n.* A veteran soldier.

RON, ロン, 論, (*kataru.*) *n.* Dispute, debate, argument, discourse, discussion. *Gu-nin ni* — *wa muyaku nari*, it is useless to dispute with a fool. — *wo szru* to dispute.

†RON-DAN, ロンダン, 論談, Disputation.

RŌ-NEN, ラウネン, 老年, (*oitaru toshi*). *n.* Old-age.

RON-GI, ロンギ, 論議, *n.* Discourse, discussion, disputation.

RON-GO, ロンゴ, 論語, *n.* The Confucian analects.

RONJI, -*ru*, or *dzru*, -*ta*, ロンズル, 論, *t.v.* To discuss, to discourse on, debate, argue, dispute.

RŌ-NIN, ラウニン, 浪人, *n.* A samurai,

who for some offence to his superior has been dispossessed of his estate, revenue, or pay, and dismissed from service, an outcast, vagrant.

ROPPAI, ロクパイ, 六杯, Six times full. *Chawan ni — no midz*, six teacups full of water.

ROPPIKI,, ロクヒキ, 六匹, Six tails (head) of animals, or six pieces of cloth. *Ushi* —, six head of oxen.

ROPPIYAKU, ロクヒヤク, 六百, Six hundred. — *man*, six millions.

ROPPIYŌ, ロクペウ, 六俵, Six bags of any thing. *Kome* —, six bags of rice.

ROPPŌN, ロクポン, 六本, Six sticks; used in counting sticks, timber, posts, pencils &c.

ROPPU, ロクプ, 六腑, *n.* The six viscera, viz. Lungs, heart, liver, spleen, kidneys, and ovaries.

ROPPUKU, ロクプク, 六服, Six doses of medicine. *Kuszri* —, id.

RŌRŌ, ラウラウ, 浪浪, Wandering, outcast, homeless. *Shū no — mi-szte-gataku*, hard to see one's master an outcast.

RŌSEKI, ラフセキ, 蠟石, *n.* Marble.

RŌSEN, ロウセン, 樓舩, (*yakata bune*) *n.* A boat with a saloon built on it, for pleasure excursions.

RŌSHA, ラウシヤ, 牢舍, *n.* Imprisonment. — *wo mōshi-tszkeru*, to send to prison. Syn. JURŌ.

RŌSHI, ラウシ, 牢死, *n.* Dying in gaol.

RŌ*shi*,–*szru*,–*sh'ta*, ロウスル, 弄, *t.v.* To deride, make sport of. Syn. AZAKERU.

RŌ*shi*,–*szru*,–*sh'ta*, ラウスル, 勞, *i.v.* To toil, labor, to be oppressed with trouble, or care. *Rōsh'te kō nashi*, to take much trouble for nothing. *Chikara wo* —, to labor with the hands. *Kokoro wo* —, to labor with the head.
Syn. HONEORI.

RŌSHIN, ラウシン, 老親, (*oitaru oya*). *n.* Old parents.

†RŌSHITSZ, ロウシツ, 陋室, (*iyashiki iye*). My mean house, (humble).

†ROSHITSZ, ロシツ, 漏失, *n.* Nocturnal emissions. Syn. ISEI, MŌZŌ.

RŌSHO, ラウシヤウ, 癆証, *n.* Consumption, phthisis. Syn. RŌGAI.

RŌSHŌ, ラウセウ, 老少, (*oitaru wakaki.*) Old and young. — *fujō*, the length of one's life is uncertain.

RŌSOKU, ラフソク, 蠟燭, *n.* A candle. — *tate*, a candlestick.

RŌSZI, ラウスイ, 老衰, (*oi-otoroyeru*). *n.* Old and decrepit.

ROTAI, ロタイ, 露臺, *n.* A platform built on the roof of a house.

RŌTŌ, ラウタウ, 莨菪, *n.* Belladonna.

ROTŌ, ロトウ, 路頭, (*michi no hotori*). *n.* Road-side. — *ni tatsz*, to stand by the wayside, as a beggar. — *ni mayō*, to be friendless and reduced to beggary.

RŌYA, ラウヤ, 牢屋, *n.* A gaol, prison. Syn. H'TO-YA.

†RŌYEI, ラウエイ, 朗詠, *n.* Singing with a loud voice.

†RŌYEN, ラウエン, 狼烟, (*noroshi*) *n.* A signal rocket.

ROYŌ, ロヨウ, 路用, *n.* Travelling expenses.

RŌZEKI, ラウゼキ, 狼籍, Brutal and violent, savage, cruel. — *mono*, a ruffian. *Hone niku — to midari nari*, the bones and flesh were mingled in disorder.
Syn. RAMBŌ, ABARERU.

RU, ル, The terminal syllable of the adjective, or attributive form of the verb; as, *Miru h'to*, the seeing man, or the man who is looking, or will look. *Miyeru hana* the being seen flower, or flower that is seen. *Kikitaru h'to*, the person who heard. *Kaitaru mono*, the thing which was purchased.

RUFU,–*szru*, ルフ, 流布, *i.v.* To spread, extend over. *Hiyōban ga seken ni* —, the report spread over the world. *Buppō tenga ni* —, Buddhism has spread over the empire. Syn. HIROMARU.

RUI, ルイ, 類, (*tagui*). *n.* Kind, sort, class, race, genus. *Watakushi ichi rui no mono*, persons of the same family name as myself. — *wo motte atszmeru*, to arrange in classes. — *szru*, to be alike, of the same kind.

RUI, ルイ, 壘, *n.* A parapet, wall, or rampart, intrenchment, embankment. — *wo kataku szru*, to strengthen the rampart. *Kabane wa tsznde rui-rui tari*, the dead bodies lay in heaps.

RUI DAI, ルイダイ, 累代, Several successive generations, or reigns. Syn. FUDAI.

†RUI-GAN, ルイガン, 涙眼, (*namida no me*). *n.* Tearful eyes.

†RUI-GETSZ, ルイゲツ, 累月, (*kasanaru tszki*). *n.* Several months in succession, a number of months.

†RUI-JITSZ, ルイジツ, 累日, (*kasanaru nichi*). *n.* Several days in succession, a number of days.

†RUI-KON, ルイコン, 涙痕, (*namida no ato*). *n.* The mark, or trace left by tears.

†RUI-K'WAN, ルイクワン, 涙管, *n.* The lachrymal duct.

†Rui-nen, ルイネン, 累年, (*kasanaru toshi.*) *n*, Several years in succession, a series or number of years. Syn. RENNEN.

†Rui-ran, ルイラン, 累卵, (*kasaneru tamago*). *n*. Eggs laid one on top of another, a pile of eggs. — *yori mo ayaushi*, more dangerous than a pile of eggs.

Rui-reki, ルイレキ, 瘰癧, *n*. Scrofula.

†Rui-rei, ルイレイ, 類例, (*nitaru tameshi.*) *n*. A similar instance, an example of the same kind.

Rui-rui, ルイルイ, 累累, (*kasanari kasanaru*). *adv*. Piled up one on top of another, (of any thing round). — *to sh'te tama no gotoshi*, piled up on one another like balls.

†Rui-se, ルイセ, 累世, (*kasanaru yo*). *n*. Several successive generations, a number of generations.

†Rui-setsz, ルイセツ, 縲絏; *n*. Bonds, fetters. Syn. NAWAME.

Rui-shō, ルイセウ, 類燒, *n*. Consumed in the same conflagration. — *ni au*.

Rui-yaku, ルイヤク, 類藥, (*nitaru kuszri*) *n*. Same kind of medicine.

Rui-yen, ルイエン, 類緣, *n*. Related, connected by birth.

†Rui-yō, ルイエフ, 累葉, *n*. Several branches or members of a family in succession.

†Rui-zoku, ルイゾク, 類族, Related, connected by birth, same family.

Ru-kei, ルケイ, 流刑, *n*. Transportation, or exile for crime. Syn. RUZAI, YENTŌ.

Ru-nin, ルニン, 流人, (*nagashibito*) *n*. An exile, or one transported for crime.

Ruri, ルリ, 瑠璃, *n*. The name of a precious stone of a green color, emerald?

Ruri, ルリ, 翠鳥, *n*. The name of a bird, the variegated kingfisher?

Ru-rō, ルラウ, 流浪, Wandering about without any settled home, as an outcast. — *no mi ni naru*, to become a wanderer or exile. — *szru*, to wander.
Syn. SAMAYOI.

Ruru, ルル, 被, Same as *reru*, a terminal word used only in books.

Rusz, ルス, 留守, (*todomari mamoru*). *n*. Keeping watch, or taking care of a house during the absence of the master; absent, not at home. — *wo szru*, to keep a house, &c. *Mina — da*, they are all out, or there is nobody at home.

Rusz-ban, ルスバン, 留守番, *n*. Keeping watch during the absence of the master. — *szru*.

Rusz-chiu, ルスチウ, 留守中, During one's absence. — *shime-kiri*, to lock the house up during one's absence.

Rusz-i, ルス井, 留守居, *n*. The name of an officer of a Daimio, who has the care of the family in his master's absence, and who is also the agent for transacting all outside business.

Rusz-mori, ルスモリ, 留守, Same as *Ruszban*.

†Ru-ten, ルテン, 流轉, *n*. The transmigrations of the soul (Budd.)
Syn RIN-YE, RINDEN

†Ru-ts'u, ルツウ, 流通, (*nagare kayō*). *n*. Passing, or circulating from one to another, current. Syn. TSZYŌ.

Rutszbo, ルツボ, 鑪缸, *n*. A crucible.

Ru-zai, ルザイ, 流罪, *n*. Transported or exiled for crime. — *ni okonawareru*, punished with transportation.
Syn. SHIMA-NAGASHI, YENTŌ, RU-KEI.

S

†Sa サ, 左, (*hidari*). *n*. The left. — *ni mōshi age sōrō shina*, the thing mentioned below. *Sa no tōri*, as follows, — in the manner following.

Sa, サ, A syllable affixed to the root form of adjectives, denoting their abstract quality, state, or condition, as, *Shirosa*, the whiteness. *Nagasa*, the length. *Itasa*, the painfulness. *Omosa*, the heaviness. *Hana wo mitasa ni yuku*, to go with the desire of seeing the flowers.

Sa, サ, 然, (contract. of *Shika*). *adv*. So, thus. — *ni aradz*, it is not so. — *wa iyedomo*, although it is so, still, however, nevertheless. — *wa omoyedomo*, although I think so, &c. — *wa shiradzsh'te*, without knowing it was so. — *wa naku*, not so.
Syn. SO.

Sa, サ, Exclam. peculiar to Yedo, used at the end of a sentence, to give force, or positiveness. *Gozarimasen no sa*, it is no such thing. *Sō sa*, just so, yes.

Sā, サア, Exclam. of defying, urging. *Sā koi*, come on! Syn. IZA.

Saba, サバ, 青魚, *n*. Mackerel. *Sashi saba*, salt mackerel.

Saba, サバ, 左波, *n*. An offering of a small portion of food, made to the Kami before eating. — *wo toru*, to offer, &c.

Sabakari, サバカリ, *adv*. Such, like this, this kind. Syn. SAHODO.

SABAKE,*-ru,-ta*, サバケル, 捌, *i.v.* To be disentangled, unraveled, loose; to be sold off; to be yielding, compliant. *Ito ga sabaketa*, the thread is disentangled. *Kuji ga* —, the law-suit is settled. *Ni ga* —, the goods are sold off. *Sabaketa h'to*, a person of a free, open, or yielding temper. Syn. HODOKERU.

SABAKE, サバケ, 捌, *n.* The sale of goods, market. *Ito no — ga yoi*, the market for silk is good. Syn. HAKE, URE.

SABAKE-KATA, サバケカタ, *n.* The sale, market.

SABAKE-KUCHI, サバケクチ, *n.* idem.

SABAKI,*-ku,-ita*, サバク, 捌, *t. v.* To disentangle, unravel, loose; to sell off; to judge, to examine and decide a matter. *Motszre wo* —, to disentangle. *Kuji wo* —, to try a law suit. *Ni wo* —, to sell off goods.
Syn. HODOKU, SAIBAN SZRU.

SABAKI, サバキ, *n.* The unraveling of anything perplexing, or intricate, as a law-suit. The selling of goods.

†SA-BAKU, サバク, 沙漠, *n.* A desert. Syn. SZNA-BARA.

SABI,*-ru,-ta*, サビル, 鏽, *i.v.* To rust. *Tetsz ga sabita*, the iron is rusted. *Kin wa sabinu mono*, gold will not rust.

SABI,*-ru,-ta*, サビル, *i. v.* To be hoarse, rough, or harsh in voice. *Sabita koye*, a hoarse voice.

SABI, サビ, 鏽, *n.* Rust. — *ga tszku*, to be rusty. — *ga deru*, idem. *Tetsz no* —, iron rust.

SABI-IRO, サビイロ, 鏽色, *n.* Rust-color.

SABISHII,-KI, サビシイ, 寂寥, *a.* Lonely, solitary, desolate, still, quiet, dull, destitute of stir, or bustle. — *tokoro*, a still or lonely place.

SABISHIKU, サビシク, 寂寥, *adv.* Idem. — *naru*, to become lonely, or dull.

SABISHISA, サビシサ, *n.* Loneliness, solitude, stillness, dullness.

SABI-TSZKI-GE, サビツキゲ, 桃華馬, *n.* Rust colored horse.

SABOSHI,*-sz,-sh'ta*, サボス, *t. v.* To dry or air anything damp. *Kimono wo* —, to air or dry clothes.

SABOTEN, サボテン, 仙人掌, *n.* The prickly-pear.

SABURAI, サブラヒ, See *Samurai*.

†SACHI, サチ, 幸, (*saiwai*). *n.* Fortunate. — *naki mono*, an unfortunate person.

†SADA, サダ, 蹉跎, *adv.* Missing the opportunity.

SADAKA, サダカ, 定, Certain, sure, distinct, plain. — *naru koto*. — *naradz*. Syn. TASH'KA.

SADAKA-NI, サダカニ, 定, *adv.* Certainly, surely, distinctly, plainly.
Syn. TASH'KA NI.

SADAMARI,*-ru,-tta*, サダマル, 定, *i. v.* To be determined, decided, settled, fixed, certain, sure, confirmed, resolved. *Nichigen ga* —, the day is fixed. *Mada sadamarimasen*, it is not yet determined. *Kokoro ga* —, his mind is made up.
Syn. KIWAMARU.

SADAME,*-ru,-ta*, サダメル, 定, *t.v.* To determine, decide, fix, settle, conclude, to confirm, to resolve. *Yakujō wo* —, to make an agreement. *Kiu-kin wo* —, to fix the wages. *Sadame-naki yo no naka*, the world, in which things are so uncertain. *Kokoro wo* —, to make up one's mind. Syn. KIWAMERU, KETSZ-JŌ SZRU.

SADAME, サダメ, 定, *n.* That which is fixed, settled, or agreed on, the conclusion, decision. Syn. KIWAME.

SADAMETE, サダメテ, 定而, *adv.* In all probability, perhaps, likely, positively. — *sō de arō*, I think it must be so.
Syn. TABUN, ŌKATA.

SADE, サデ, 扠網, *n.* A kind of net for catching fish.

SADŌ, サダウ, 茶道, *n.* An inferior servant of a Daimio.

SADZKARI,*-ru,-tta*, サヅカル, 授, *i.v.* To receive from a superior, imparted, bestowed. *Ten yori sadzkatta inochi* a life received from heaven. *Oshiye wo shishō yori sadzkaru*, to receive instruction from a teacher. Syn. UKERU.

SADZKE,*-ru,-ta*, サヅケル, 授, *t.v.* To bestow, impart, to give, to communicate, (only used of a superior). *Oshiye, michi hō, hi-den, kurai, nado wo* —,
Syn. DEN-JŪ SZRU.

†SAGA, サガ, 祥, *n.* An omen, sign, prognostic. *Yoki saga*, a good omen.
Syn. ZEMPIYŌ, KIZASHI.

†SAGA, サガ, 質, *n.* Disposition, temper. *Gaman no* —, obstinate disposition. — *nikuki h'to*, a person of a hateful disposition. Syn. SHŌ, SHITSZ, SEI-SHITSZ.

SAGANAI,-KI, サガナイ, *a.* Mean, low, vulgar. Syn. IYASHII.

SAGANAKU, サガナク, *adv.* idem.

SAGARI*-ru,-tta*, サガル, 下, *i.v.* To go down, to hang down, to decline, to sink down, to fall in value or rank. *Te ga* —, to become less expert in doing. *Goten kara* —, to return from the palace. *Ni ga* —, the price declines. *Ato ni* —, to take a lower place in rank. *Kurai ga* —, to fall in rank. Syn. KUDARU, ORIRU.

SAGASHI,-*sz*,-*sh'ta*, サガス, 搜, *t.v.* To search, seek, look for, inquire for. *Sagash'te mo miyemasen*, I have searched for it but cannot find it. Syn. TADZNERU.

SAGASHII,-KI, サガシイ, 險阻, *a.* Steep, precipitous. *Michi ga* —, the road is steep. Syn. KEWASHII.

SAGASHI-DASHI,-*sz*,-*sh'ta*, サガシダス, 搜出, To search and find.

SAGASHIKU, or SAGASHŪ, サガシク, *adv.* Steep, precipitous.

SAGASHISA, サガシサ, *n.* Steepness.

SAGE,-*ru*,-*ta*, サゲル, 下, or 提, *t. v.* To hang down, to suspend, to let down, to lower, to take down, to send down, to abase. *Ne wo* —, to lower the price. *Atama wo* —, to bend the head. *Mi wo* —, to abase, or humble one's self. *Koshi ni* —, to hang in the belt. *Te ni* —, to carry suspended from the hand. Syn. KUDASZ, OROSZ.

SAGE-GAMI, サゲガミ, 墮髻, *n.* The hair worn hanging down the back, as the ladies of a Kuge's family.

SAGE-GATANA, サゲガタナ, 提刀, *n.* A sword carried in the hand.

SAGE-JŪ, サゲヂウ, 提重, *n.* A nest of boxes set in a handle for carrying.

SAGE-MONO, サゲモノ, 提物, *n.* The articles which the Japanese carry suspended from the belt, as the tobacco pouch and pipe, inkstand and pen.

SAGEO, サゲヲ, 下緒, *n.* The cord around the sword handle.

SAGE-SHIMI,-*mu*,-*nda*, サゲシム, 下視, *t.v.* To despise, disdain, to regard with contempt. Syn. KARONDZRU, NAIGASHIRO NI SZRU.

SAGE-SZMI,-*mu*,-*nda*, サゲスム, Idem.

SAGE-SZMI, サゲスミ, 垂準, *n.* A plumbline, or plummet made of a carpenter's ink-box and line.

SAGI, サギ, 鷺, *n.* The snowy heron, (Egretta candidissima).

†SA-GŌ, サゴフ, 作業, *n.* Deeds, works. (Bud.) — *ni yorite mukui wo ukeru*, to be rewarded according to one's works.

SAGO-BEI, サゴベイ, 西國米, *n.* Sago.

†SAGOROMO, サゴロモ, 狹衣, *n.* The long coat, same as *Koromo*, (only used in poetry).

SAGURI,-*ru*,-*tta*, サグル, 探, *t.v.* To search for by feeling, to feel after, to grope for, to probe, to sound. *Sagutte aruku*, to walk groping one's way. *Sagutte miru*, to examine by touch, by feeling, or probing. *H'to no kokoro wo* —, to feel out one's opinions. Syn. SAGASZ, TADZNERU.

SAGURI, サグリ, 探, *n.* A mark or notch on anything to be noticed by feeling, (as that on the bow, or seal), a probe.

SAGURI-ASHI, サグリアシ, 探足, *n.* Feeling one's way with the feet. — *de aruku.*

SAGURI-DASHI,-*sz*,-*sh'ta*, サグリダス, 探出, *t.v.* To feel after and take out, to extract with forceps (when the thing is not visible).

SAGURI-KIKI,-*ku*,-*ta*, サグリキク, 探聞, *t.v.* To inquire, or endeavour to ascertain anything indirectly.

SAGURI-MOTOME,-*ru*,-*ta*, サグリモトメル, 探索, To search for and find. Syn. TANSAKU SZRU, SAGASZ.

SAGURU, サグル, 下, see *Sage*, 探, or *Saguri*.

SAHACHI, サハチ, 沙鉢, *n.* A platter, or large dish.

SA-HAI, サハイ, 差配, Superintending, directing, managing. — *szru*. Syn. SASHI-KUBARU, KIMOIRI, SAIRIYŌ.

SAHARI, サハリ, 白銅, *n.* A kind of metalic composition, white copper.

SAHŌ, サハフ, 作法, Law, rule, custom, usage. — *wo somuku*, to transgress the laws. — *wo shiranu*, ignorant of the rules of politeness. Syn. OKITE, HŌSHIKI, KISOKU, REI.

SAHODO, サホド, 左程, *a.* Such, so much, thus much. — *itaku wa naze riyōji wo senu*, if it hurts you so much, why don't you do something for it? — *ni mo nai*, not much, not so much as you think. Syn. SABAKARI.

SAI, サイ, 妻, *n.* Wife. — *wo metoru*, to to marry a wife. Syn. TSZMA.

SAI, サイ, 菜, *n.* Anything eaten along with rice. Syn. OKADZ, SOYE-MONO.

SAI, サイ, 犀, *n.* A rhinoceros.

SAI, サイ, 骰子, *n.* A dice. — *no me*, the marks on a dice. — *wo furu*, to shake the dice. — *wo nageru*, to throw the dice.

SAI, サイ, 才, *n.* Ability, capacity, talent, sagacity. — *no aru h'to*, a man of talent. Syn. CHIYE, CHIKARA.

†SAI, サイ, 材, *n.* Material, stuff. *Go sai*, the five elements, of fire, water, wood, metal and earth.

SAI, サイ, 歳, *n.* Year of age. *Iku sai*, how old? *Gojissai*, fifty years old.

SAI, サイ, 寨, *n.* Encampment, a stockaded camp. — *wo kidzku,* to construct an encampment.

†SAI-AI, サイアイ, 最愛, (*mottomo aiszru.*) Most beloved, well beloved. — *no ko,* dearly beloved child.

SAI-BAN,-*szru,* サイバン, 裁判, *t.v.* To examine and decide on the case of a criminal, to judge, to try. *Kuji wo* —, to try a law-suit. Syn. SABAKU, SAI-KIYO, SAIDAN.

†SAI-BARA, サイバラ, 催馬樂, *n.* The name of a kind of ancient song sung only at a Kagura.

SAI-BASHI, サイバシ, 菜箸, *n.* The chop-sticks used for helping fish or vegetables.

SAI-BO, サイボ, 歳暮, (*toshi no kure*). *n.* The close of the year, the last ten days of the year.

SAI-CHI, サイチ, 才智, *n.* Wisdom, sagacity, intelligence, skill. Syn. CHIYE.

SAI-CHIU, サイチウ, 最中, (*monaka*). *n.* The very middle, the time when anything is at its height, acme, climax, perfection, the very midst. *Hana no* —, when flowers are in the highest bloom. *Haru no* —, the most delightful time of spring.
Syn. MANNAKA.

†SAI-DAI, サイダイ, 最大, (*mottomo ōki.*) The largest.

SAI-DAN,-*szru,* サイダン, 裁斷, To judge, to examine and decide.
Syn. SABAKU, SAI-BAN.

SAIDE, サイデ, 段布, *n.* Scraps of silk left after cutting out a garment; also imperfect cocoons.

SAI-DO,-*szru,* サイド, 濟度, *t.v.* To save from destruction after death (Bud). *Muyen no shu-jō wa saido shi-gatashi,* he that believeth not in Buddhism cannot be saved. *H'to wo* —, to save the soul.
Syn. TASZKERU, SZKŪ.

†SAIDO, サイド, 再度, (*nido.*) Twice.
Syn. RIYŌ-DO.

SAI-DZCHI, サイヅチ, 木推, *n.* A small wooden mallet.

SAI-FU, サイフ, 財布, *n.* A money bag, a purse. Syn. ZENE-IRE.

†SAI-GAI, サイガイ, 災害, (*wazawai*), *n.* Calamity, misfortune, evil.

†SAI-GEN, サイゲン, 際限, (*kagiri*) *n.* Bound, limit. — *wa nai,* boundless.

†SAI-GETSZ, サイゲツ, 歳月, (*toshi tszki*), *n.* The years and months, time. *Munashiku* — *wo okuru,* to pass the time uselessly.

SAI-GO, サイゴ, 最後, (*mottomo nochi,*) *n.* The last period of life, death. — *no kassen,* the last battle, (in which one is slain). Syn. RINJU.

SAI-HAI,-*szru,* サイハイ, 再拜, (*futatabi ogamu*). To bow down twice.

SAI-HAI, サイハイ, *n.* A baton carried by the general in chief of an army, and used in giving orders.

SAI-HAN, サイハン, 再板, (*f'tatabi han ni okosz*). *n.* A reprint. — *szru,* to reprint, republish.

†SAI-HATZ, サイハツ, 才發, Manifesting ability, talent, genius. — *na mono.*
Syn. HATSZMEI, RIKŌ.

†SAI-HITZ, サイヒツ, 細筆, (*komayakana fude*). Written in small letters, small hand.

SAI-HŌ, サイハウ, 西方, (*nishi no kata.*) *n.* The west, western region.

SAI-HOTZ,-*szru,* サイホツ, 再發, (*f'tatabi okoru.*) To break out again, (as disease or sedition), to recur, relapse.
Syn. SAI-KAN.

†SAI-JI, サイジ, 細字, *n.* Small characters or letters.

†SAI-JI, サイジ, 歳時, (*toshi toki.*) *n.* The year and the seasons, time.

SAI-JITSZ, サイジツ, 祭日, (*matszribi*). *n.* The day on which a festival is celebrated.

†SAI-JO, サイヂヨ, 妻女, *n.* Wife.
Syn. TSZMA.

SAI-JŌ, サイジヤウ, 最上, (*mottomo wiye*). *n.* Most excellent, best, highest.

SAI-KACHI, サイカチ, 皂角子, *n.* The name of a tree.

†SAI-KAI, サイカイ, 西海, (*nishi no umi.*) *n.* The western sea.

SAI-KAKU, サイカク, 犀角, (*sai no tszno*). *n.* Rhinoceros horn, (used as a medicine.)

SAI-KAKU,-*szru,* サイカク, 才角, To plan or scheme in order to raise a sum of money. Syn. CHŌDATSZ SZRU, SANDAN.

SAI-KAN,-*szru,* サイカン, 再感, To be taken or affected the second time with disease. *Hash'ka ga saikan sh'ta,* have a second attack of measles.
Syn. BURI-KAYESZ, SAI-HOTSZ.

SAI-KAYERI,-*ru,*-*tta,* サイカヘル, 再廻, *i.v.* To return again. *Samusa ga sai-kayetta,* it has become cold again.

SAI-KIN,-*szru,* サイキン, 再勤, (*f'tatabi tsztomeru*). To fill an office the second time, reappointed to office.

SAI-KIN, サイキン, 細瑾, (*komaka-naru kidz*). *n.* A slight failing, defect, or fault.

Tai kō wa — wo kayeri-midz, in one who has great merit overlook a slight failing.

SAI-K'YO,*–szru*, サイキヨ, 裁許, To examine and decide on, to judge. *Tszmi wo* —, to judge crime.
Syn. SABAKU, SAI-BAN, SAI-DAN.

SAI-KO, サイコ, 柴胡, *n.* The name of a medicine.

SAI-KŌ,*–szru*, サイカウ, 再興, (*f'tatabi okosz.*) To raise up again, to rebuild, to restore, reconstruct, to begin again after an interruption, to resume.

SAI-KOKU, サイコク, 西國, (*nishi no kuni.*) *n.* Western provinces. — *kiu-shū.*

SAI-KON,*–szru*, サイコン, 再建, (*f'tatabi tateru*). To rebuild, re-erect, reconstruct.

SAI-KU, サイク, 細工, *n.* Fine work, workmanship, manufacture, fabric, ware. — *szru*, to manufacture, to fabricate. *Kin-zaiku*, gold-ware, any thing manufactured of gold, also, *Gin-zaiku*, silver-ware. *Bīdoro-zaiku*, glass-ware. *Tazaiku*, any thing made by one's self,—home made.

SAI-KU-NIN, サイクニン, 細工人, *n.* A mechanic, artisan, workman.

†SAI-K'WAI,*–szru*, サイクワイ, 再會, (*f'tatabi au*). To meet again, to reassemble.

SAI-MATSZ, サイマツ, 細末, (*komayaka*). *n.* Fine powder. — *ni szru*, to reduce to a powder. *Dai-yō no* —, powdered rhubarb. Syn. KO, KONA.

SAI-MATSZ, サイマツ, 歳末, (*toshi no szye*). *n.* End of the year.

SAI-MI, サイミ, 柴布, cont. of *Sayomi.* *n.* A coarse kind of hemp cloth.

SAI-MITSZ-NI, サイミツニ, 細密, (*komaka ni.*) *adv.* Particularly, minutely, carefully. Syn. KUWASHIKU, KOMAKANI.

‖SAINAMI,*–mu,–nda*, サイナム, *t. v.* To handle, to vex, torture. *H'to wo kiri-sainamu*, to torture a person by cutting. Syn. IJIRU.

SAI-NAN, サイナン, 災難, (*wazawai*). *n.* Calamity, misfortune, evil. Syn. FUKŌ.

SAI-NICHI, サイニチ, 祭日, *n.* See *Saijitsz.*

†SAI-NŌ, サイノウ, 才能, *n.* Talent, ability.

SAI-NO-KAMI, サイノカミ, 道祖神, *n.* The god of roads, protector of travelers.

SAI-Ō, サイオウ, 再應, (*nido.*) *adv.* Twice, two times. Syn. FUTA-TABI,

†SAI-RAI, サイライ, 再來, Coming again into the world, the second coming. (only of *Amida*, or the soul of the dead), transmigration or metempsychosis.

SAI-REI, サイレイ, 祭禮, (*matszri.*) *n.* A religious festival, or celebration.

SAI-RIYŌ, サイリヤウ, 宰領, To superintend, to manage, supervise, control. — *nin*, a supervisor, superintendent.
Syn. SAHAI SZRU, KIMO-IRI.

†SAI-RŌ, サイラウ, 豺狼, *n.* A wolf. — *no kokoro*, wolfish heart, cruel.

SAI-RŌ, サイラウ, 菜籠, *n.* A box for carrying food.

‖SAI-SAI, サイサイ, 再再, (*tabi-tabi.*) *adv.* Again and again, often, repeatedly.
Syn. DODO.

SAI-SAN, サイサン, 再三, (*ni san do*). *adv.* Two or three times, repeatedly.

SAI-SEI, サイセイ, 再生, (*f'tatabi ikiru*). To return to life, to revive. — *no omoi wo nasz*, to feel as if one had come to life again.

SAI-SEN, サイセン, 賽錢, *n.* Offerings of copper cash in temples, (either cast into a box, or on the floor.)

SAI-SHI, サイシ, 妻子, (*tszma ko*). *n.* Wife and child.

†SAI-SHI, サイシ, 才子, (*rikō na h'to*). *n.* A wise, sagacious, intelligent person.

SAI-SHIKI, サイシキ, 彩色, (*irodoru*). *n.* Coloring, painting in various colors. — *wo szru.* Syn, YEDORI.

SAI-SHIN, サイシン, 細辛, *n.* The name of a medicine.

SAI-SHO, サイシヨ, 最初, (*ichiban hajime*). *adv.* The very first, at the beginning, commencement.
Syn. SHOTE, HAJIME.

†SAI-SHO, サイシヨ, 細書, (*kuwashiki fumi.*) A writing or letter full of details, or particulars.

SAI-SHŌ, サイシヤウ, 宰相, *n.* A ruler one that exercises supreme power.

†SAI-SHŌ, サイセフ, 妻妾, (*tszma mekake.*) *n.* Wife and concubine.

SAISOKU,*–szru*, サイソク, 催促, To hasten or hurry the performance or doing of any thing, to dun, to demand. *Kash'ta kane wo* —, to dun for a debt.

SAITADZMA, サイタヅマ, 虎杖, *n.* The name of a plant.

SAI-TAI, サイタイ, 妻帶, (*tszma wo obiru*). *n.* Having a wife, (said only of the *Montoshu* priests). — *Montoshū no bōdz wa — szru.*

†SAI-TAN, サイタン, 歳旦, *n.* The first day of the year.

SAI-TORI, サイトリ, 經紀人, *n.* A middleman between seller and buyer, a broker.

SAI-TORI-SASHI, サイトリサシ, 刺鳥,

n. One who catches birds with a pole armed with bird-lime.

SAI-TORI-ZAO, サイトリザホ, 刺鳥竿, *n.* A pole armed with bird-lime for catching birds.

SAITSZKORO, サイツコロ, 先頃, *adv.* Before, previously, sometime ago. Syn. SENJITSZ, SENDATTE.

SAIWAI, サイハイ, 幸, *n.* or *adv.* Fortunate, opportune, lucky, happy, favorable. 福, Good fortune, blessings, prosperity, happiness, good. — *no ori*, fortunate time. — *yoi tenki de gozarimas*, fortunately the weather is fine. *Chōdo yoi* —, how very opportune. *Ten yori — wo kudasz*, to receive blessings from heaven. Syn. FUKU.

†SAI-YAKU, サイヤク, 災厄, *n.* Calamity, misfortune.

†SAI-YAKU, サイヤク, 採藥, *n.* Searching for medicinal herbs, or plants. *Yama ye — ni yuku.*

SAI-YEN, サイエン, 再緣, *n.* A second marriage. — *szru*, to marry again.

SAI-YŌ, サイヤウ, 西洋, *n.* Western countries, European. Syn. SEIYŌ.

SAI-ZEN, サイゼン, 最前, *adv.* Before, previously, for some time before this. — *yori matte iru*, waiting for some time. Syn. SAKI-HODO, SENKOKU.

SAJI, サジ, 匙, *n.* A spoon.

SAJIKI, サジキ, 棧敷, *n.* The box, or gallery in a theatre.

SAKA, サカ, 阪, *n.* A road up a mountain, a steep road. — *wo noboru.* — *wo oriru. Nobori-saka* an ascent. *Kudari saka*, the road down a mountain.

SAKA, サカ, 逆, Upside down. — *tateru*, to stand anything upside down. — *ni motsz*, to hold upside down. Syn. G'YAKU.

SAKA-BARI-TSZKE, サカバリツケ, 逆磔, Crucifixion with the head downward. — *ni okonau.*

SAKA-BAYASHI, サカバヤシ, 酒帘, *n.* A green bamboo, or flag erected in front of a *sake* brewery, as a sign.

SAKA-BITARI, サカビタリ, 酒浸, *n.* A sot, drunkard.

SAKA-BUKURO, サカブクロ, 酒袋, *n.* A bag used for straining *sake* in breweries.

SAKA-BUNE, サカブネ, 酒槽, *n.* A large vat used in making *sake.*

SAKA-DACHI, *-tsz*, *-tta*, サカダツ, 逆立, *i. v.* The hair to stand erect, (as in anger.)

SAKA-DACHI, サカダチ, 逆立, *n.* Standing on the head. — *wo szru.*

SAKA-DAI, サカダイ, 酒代, *n.* The price of, or money due for *sake.*

SAKA-DARU, サカダル, 酒樽, *n.* A wine cask.

SAKADE, サカデ, 逆手, *n.* Grasping the handle of a sword or knife, so that the point is downwards. *Katana wo — ni motsz.*

SAKADZKI, サカヅキ, 盃, *n.* A winecup. *Fūfu no — wo szru*, to drink wine and thus celebrate the marriage ceremony.

SAKADZKI-DAI, サカヅキダイ, 盃臺, *n.* The stand of a wine cup.

SAKA GAME, サカガメ, 酒甕, *n.* A large wine-jar.

SAKA-GO, サカゴ, 逆產, *n.* A foot or breech presentation. Syn. G'YAKUZAN.

SAKA-GOMO, サカゴモ, 酒薦, *n.* The mat which is wrapped round a wine-cask.

SAKA-GOTO, サカゴト, 反語, *n.* Pronouncing a word backwards.

SAKA-GURA, サカグラ, 酒藏, *n.* A house in which wine is stored.

SAKAHA, サカハ, 鐖, *n.* A barb, (of a hook).

SAKA-HADZRE, サカハヅレ, 酒外, *n.* One who in a wine party avoids drinking.

SAKAI, サカヒ, 境, *n.* A boundary, border, confines, frontier, limit. *Kuni no* —, boundary of a state. *Iki shini no* —, the confines of life and death. — *ron*, a dispute about a boundary. Syn. KIWA.

SAKAI, *-ō*, *-ōta*, サカフ, 忤, *t. v.* To go against or contrary to, to oppose, disobey, to contradict. *Nagare kaze nado ni* —, to go against the current, or wind. *Oya ni* —, to disobey parents. Syn. MOTORU.

SAKAI-ME, サカヒメ, 堺目, *n.* A boundary line, border.

SAKA-KABU, サカカブ, 酒株, *n.* A license from government to manufacture *sake.*

SAKAKI, サカキ, 榊, *n.* The name of a tree.

SAKA-KIGEN, サカキゲン, 酒興, *n.* The spirits, or excitement produced by wine. Syn. SHUKIYŌ.

||SAKA-KUBE, サカクレ, 逆臚, *n.* A hang nail. — *ga dekita.* Syn. SAKA-MUKE.

SAKA-MAKU-MIDZ, サカマクミヅ, 逆捲水, *n.* Water whirling in a circle, an eddy.

SAKA-MASZGE, or SAKA-MATSZGE, サカマスゲ, 倒睫, *n.* Entropium.

SAKA-ME, サカメ, 逆目, *n.* Against the grain of wood. — *ni ita wo kedzru*, to plane a board against the grain.

SAKAMOGI, サカモギ, 鹿柴, *n.* Trees and brush wood, placed around a fortification to keep off or hamper the approach of an enemy.

SAKA-MORI, サカモリ, 酒宴, *n.* A wine

party, entertainment, feast, banquet. Syn. SHUYEN.

SAKA-MUKAI, サカムカヒ, 坂迎, *n.* The going out of a company of friends to meet one returning from a journey, and giving him an entertainment.

SAKAMUKE, サカムケ, *n.* A hangnail, same as *Sakakure.*

SAKAN, サカン, 盛, *n.* A state of prosperity, full bloom, or vigor; flourishing, exuberant. — *no h'to,* a person in full vigor or prime of life. *Kekki — no waka mono,* young men in the full bloom of strength.

SAKANA, サカナ, 肴, *n.* Any kind of food taken with *sake;* fish.

SAKANA-ICHI, サカナイチ, 魚市, *n.* A fish-market.

SAKA-NAMI, サカナミ, 逆浪, *n.* Adverse or opposing waves or current, a head-sea.

SAKANA-YA, サカナヤ, 魚屋, *n.* A shop where fish are sold, a fish-monger.

SAKA-NEJI, サカネヂ, 逆憀, *n.* The reverting of an attack on another upon one's self. — *ni au.*

SAKA-NOBORI,*-ru,-tta,* サカノボル, 溯, *i.v.* To go against a current, to go up stream. *Kawa ni —,* to go up a river.

SAKANNARU, サカンナル, 盛, *a.* Prosperous, flourishing, blooming, in full vigor, or prime. — *toki,* time of full bloom, or vigor.

SAKARAI,*-au,* or ō,*-ōtta,* サカラフ, 逆, *t.v.* To go against, or contrary to, to oppose, to disobey. *Kaze nagare ni —,* to go against wind and current. *H'to no kokoro ni —,* to act contrary to the wishes of others. *Oya ni —,* to disobey one's parents. Syn, MOTORU, SAKŌ.

SAKARE,*-ru,-ta,* サカレル, 被裂, pass. or pot. of *Saki.* To be torn, rent, ripped. *Watakushi no kimono wo h'to ni sakareta,* my clothes were torn by a man. *Yoku no kumataka ga mata wo sakareru,* (prov.)

SAKARI,*-ru,-tta,* サカル, 盛, *i. v.* To be flourishing, to be at its height, or acme. *Shibai ga —,* the theatre is flourishing. *Saki-sakaru,* height of blooming. *Hi ga moye-sakaru toki,* when the fire is burning at its height.

SAKARI,*-ru,-tta,* サカル, 交尾, *i.v.* To be in heat, to rut. *Inu ga —,* the dog is in heat. Syn. TSZRUMU.

SAKARI, サカリ, *n.* The heat of animals. — *ga tszku,* to be in heat.

SAKARI, サカリ, 盛, *n.* The bloom, prime, time of highest vigor, acme, height, culminating point. Syn. DEBANA, TŌGE.

SAKARŌ, サカラフ, See *Sakarai.*

SAKASAMA, サカサマ, 逆, Upside down, head-foremost, in a contrary direction, topsy-turvy. *Ki kara — ni ochita,* fell head foremost from the tree. *Hon wo — ni motsz,* to hold a book upside down. *Midz ga — ni nagareru,* the water flows up stream. Syn. G'YAKU NI, SAKASHIMA.

SAKASHII,*-KI,* サカシイ, 伶俐, *a.* Clever, smart, intelligent, shrewd. — *koto wo iu,* to say something clever. Syn. RIKŌRASHII.

SAKASHIKU, サカシク, *adv.* Idem.

†SAKASHIMA, サカシマ, 倒, *adv.* Upside-down, head-foremost, in a contrary direction.

†SAKASHIRA, サカシラ, 謬, *n.* A smart, or ingenious story, an interpolation, or spurious story.

†SAKASHIRAGOTO, サカシラゴト, 謬言, *n.* A smart, or cleverly invented story, a spurious story, an intepolation. Syn. HIGAGOTO.

SAKATE, サカテ, 酒錢, *n.* Money for buying *sake.*

SAKATŌJI, サカトウジ, 酒刀自, *n.* One acquainted with the art of brewing *sake,* a brewer.

SAKA-TSZBO, サカツボ, 酒壺, *n.* A *sake* jar.

SAKA-UNJŌ, サカウンジヤウ, 酒税, *n.* The tax or duty levied by government on the manufacturers of *sake.*

SAKAYA, サカヤ, 酒屋, *n.* A brewery, a shop where *sake* is sold,—grog-shop.

SAKAYAKI, サカヤキ, 月題, *n.* The shaven part of the Japanese head. — *wo szru,* to shave the top of the head.

SAKA-YAMAI, サカヤマヒ, 酲, *n.* The indisposition felt after a debauch.

SAKAYE,*-ru,-ta,* サカエル, 榮, *i. v.* To flourish, to prosper, bloom. *Tomi-sakayeru,* to be rich and flourishing. *Ine ga ta ni —,* rice flourishes best in wet soil.

SAKA-YOMI, サカヨミ, 逆讀, *n.* Reading backwards. — *wo szru.*

SAKA-YOSE,*-ru,-ta,* サカヨセル, 逆寄, *t.v.* To drive back an attacking party and in return invest his stronghold.

SAKA-ZAKASHII,*-KI,-KU,* サカザカシイ, Same as *Sakashii.*

SAKE サケ, 酒, *n.* A fermented liquor made from rice. — *wo kamosz,* to brew *sake.* — *ni yō,* to be drunk. — *no wiye ga warui h'to,* one who behaves disorderly because of drink.

SAKE, サケ, 鮭, *n.* A salmon.

SAKE,-*ru*,-*ta*, サケル, 避, *t. v.* To flee from, to escape, avoid, shun, to elude. *Ayauki wo* —, to flee from danger. *Utagai wo* —, to avoid suspicion.
Syn. YOKERU, NOGARERU.

SAKE,-*ru*,-*ta*, サケル, 裂, *i.v.* To be torn, ripped, rent, sundered. *Kimono ga* —, the clothes are ripped.

SAKEBI,-*bu*,-*nda*, サケブ, 叫, *i.v.* To cry out with a loud voice, to shout, to clamor, vociferate, halloo, scream, to bawl.
Syn OMEKU.

SAKEBI, サケビ, 叫, *n.* A loud cry, clamor, shout. *Ya — no koye*, the sharp or shrill sound of an arrow.

SAKEDZKI, サケズキ, 酒好, *n.* One fond of *sake*.

SAKE-NOMI, サケノミ, 酒客, *n.* A drunkard, a wine-bibber.

SAKI, サキ, 先, *n.* Front, foremost part of anything, the van, before, the future, the other party, or person. *Saki ye yuku*, to go to the front, or go in advance, to go ahead. — *ni aruku*, to walk in front, or ahead. *Gunzei no* —, the van of an army. — *wo arasō*, to contend who shall be first. — *ni iutta koto*, the subject spoken of before. — *wo kagayeru*, to reflect upon the future, or what is before. — *ga nagai*, the future is long. — *no hi*, a previous day. *Saki no yo*, the future state; also, the previous state, (of existence). — *ga shōchi semu*, the opposite part does not consent. — *to szru*, to be first, or principal.
Syn. SEN.

SAKI, サキ, 鋒, *n.* The point, or end of anything long. *Fude no* —, point of a pen or pencil. *Katana no* —, point of a sword. *Tszye, sao, hana, yubi, hari nado no* —, the end or point of a cane, pole, nose, finger, or needle.

SAKI, サキ, 碕, *n.* A cape, promontory.

SAKI,-*ku*,-*ita*, サク, 咲, *i.v.* To open or bloom, as a flower; to blossom, to flower. *Hana ga saita*, the flower has opened.
Syn. HIRAKU.

SAKI,-*ku*,-*ita*, サク, 裂, *t. v.* To tear, to rip, rend asunder, to rend open, to split off. *Kami wo* —, to tear paper. *Ki no yeda wo* —, to tear off the branch of a tree. *Kimono wo* —, to rend the clothes.

SAKI-AGARI, サキアガリ, 前上, *n.* A gentle ascent. — *no michi*, a road having a gradual rise.

SAKI-BARAI, サキバラヒ, 先拂, *n.* Clearing the way before a high official, by making people squat down. — *wo szru.*

SAKI-BASHIRI,-*ru*,-*tta*, サキバシル, 先走, *i.v.* To forestall, anticipate others, to get ahead of others. *Sakibashitte mono wo kau.*

SAKI-BŌ, サキボウ, 前棒, *n.* The front, or forward coolie, where two are carrying with the same pole.

SAKI-BURE, サキブレ, 前觸, *n.* A notice sent in advance advising of the coming of any one, harbinger, forerunner.

SAKI-DACHI,-*tsz*,-*tta*, サキダツ, 前立, *i.v.* To be first in importance, or to be thought of before anything else. To die before others. *Nani wo szru ni mo kane ga* —, in doing anything the first thing is the money. *Sakidatsz mono wa namida nari-keri*, tears always come first, (in sorrow). *Ko ga oya ni* —, the child died before its parents.

SAKI-DACHI, サキダチ, 先立, *n.* The officers who go in the front of a Daimiyo's train.

SAKI-DATE,-*ru*,-*ta*, サキダテル, 先立, *t.v.* To make, or let another go before, to die before.

SAKI-DATTE, サキダッテ, *adv.* Before (in time), previously, lately, short-time ago.
Syn. SENDATTE, KONAIDA, ITSZZOYA.

SAKI-GAKE, サキガケ, 先登, *n.* The first to make an attack on the enemy.

SAKI-GANE, サキガヲ, 前金, *n.* Earnest money, money paid in advance.
Syn, MAYE-KIN.

SAKI-GARI, サキガリ, 前借, *n.* Borrowing or drawing money in advance.
Syn. ZENSHAKU.

SAKI-GASHI, サキガシ, 前借, *n.* Lending, or paying money in advance.

SAKI-HODO, サキホド, 先程, *adv.* Before, previously, a few minutes, hours, or days before. Syn. SEN-KOKU.

SAKI-KATA, サキカタ, 先方, *n* The other party, or person in any affair, the opposite party. Syn. SEMPŌ, AITE.

SAKI-KUGURI, サキクグリ, 先泳, *n.* Anticipating others in an underhanded way, forestalling.

†SAKI-KUSA, サキクサ, 萬年松, *n.* Lycopodium, a kind of moss.

SAKI-MICHI,-*ru*,-*ta*, サキミチル, 滿開, *i.v.* To be full of flowers, to bloom luxuriantly.

SAKI-MOTO, サキモト, 先許, *n.* The other, or opposite party in any affair.
Syn. SAKIKATA, SEMPŌ.

†SAKINJI,-*dzru*,-*ta*, サキンズル, 先, *t. v.* To regard as the first or the principal thing, to do first. *Kunshi wa gi wo sakindz*, the superior man regards justice as of first importance.

SAKI-NORI, サキノリ, 前乘, *n.* The person who rides first in a train.

SAKI-OTODOSHI, サキヲトドシ, *n.* Two years before last.

SAKI-OTOTOI, or SAKI-OTOTSZI, サキヲトツヒ, *n.* Two days before yesterday.

SAKI-SAMA, サキサマ, 先樣, *n.* The other or opposite party or person in any affair.

SAKI-SOME,-*ru*,-*ta*, サキソメル, 咲初, *i.v.* To begin to flower.

SAKITE, サキテ, 先手, *n.* The advance guard, or van of an army.

SAKI-WAKE, サキワケ, 咲分, *n.* Blooming with flowers of different colors.

SAKI-ZAKI, サキザキ, 前前, *n.* The different places ahead.

SAKI-ZONAYE, サキゾナヘ, 先備, *n.* The front rank of an army.

†SAKKAN, サクカン, 錯簡, *n.* Confusion, derangement, in the leaves of a book.

SAKKON, サクコン, 昨今, (*kinō kiyo*). Yesterday and to-day, a few days past, lately. — *no chikadzki*, only a few days acquaintance.

SAKKURI, サツクリ, *adv.* Crisp, brittle, crumbling, or friable (fig.) prompt, ready, not slow or hesitating.

SA-KŌ,-*szru*, サカウ, 鎖港, (*minato wo tozasz*). To close a port to trade, to blockade a port. *Yokohama wo — sh'te Ōsaka wo kaikō szru*, to close the port of Yokohama and open Osaka.

SAKŌ, サカウ, See *Sakai*.

SA-KOKU, サコク, 鎖國, (*kuni wo tozasz*). To close a country against foreigners.

†SAKOSO, サコソ, (comp. of *Sa*, so, thus, and *koso*, emphatic). Just so. — *aru-beki koto nare*, I thought it would be so. — *arame*, (idem).

SAKU, サク, See *Saki*.

SAKU, サク, 策, *n.* A stratagem, plan, scheme, expedient. *Nanzo yoi — ga ari-sō na mono da*, I wish I could think of some good plan. — *wo megurasz*, to use a scheme. Syn. HAKARIGOTO, FUMBETSZ.

SAKU, サク, 作, *n.* The crop, harvest, farming, work, make, manufacture, author. *Ko-toshi no — wa yoi*, this year's crop is good. *Nani hodo — wo nasaru*, how much ground do you cultivate? *Jō-saku*, a fine crop. *Man-saku*, an abundant harvest. *Kono katana wa dare no — da*, who is the maker of this sword? *Hon no —*, author of a book.
Syn. DEKI, TSZKURI.

SAKU, サク, *n.* A furrow.

SAKU, サク, 柵, *n.* A stockade, a fence of high-posts. — *wo iu*, or — *wo tateru*, to erect a stockade. Syn. YARAI.

SAKU-BAN, サクバン, 昨晚, *n.* Last-night.

SAKU-BIYŌ, サクビヤウ, 詐病, *n.* A feigned sickness.

†SAKU-BŌ, サクボウ, 朔望, *n.* The first and fifteenth days of the month, which are observed as days of rest, or holidays.

†SAKU-BUN, サクブン, 作文, *n.* Composition, writing.

SAKU-CHŌ, サクチヤウ, 昨朝, *n.* Yesterday morning. Syn. KINŌ NO ASA.

†SAKUGO, サクゴ, 錯誤, (*ayamari*). *n.* Mistake, error. *Kono hon wa — ga ōi*, this book has many mistakes.
Syn. MACHIGAI, GODATSZ.

†SAKU-I, サクイ, 作意, *n.* A fiction, conceit, invention, or fancy of an author. — *yori idzru*, produced from his own fancy.

SAKUI,-KI, サクイ, 脆, *a.* Easily broken or torn, brittle, not tough, crumbling, prompt, ready. — *h'to*, one prompt or quick in deciding. Syn. MOROI.

SAKU-JI, サクジ, 作事, *n.* The work of building, repairing. — *kata*, superintendent of buildings, (an official.)

SAKU-JITSZ, サクジツ, 昨日, *n.* Yesterday. Syn. KINŌ.

SAKUKE, or SAKUMŌ, サクケ, 作毛, *n.* The crop as it appears before it is cut.

SAKUKU, サクク, 脆, *adv.* Brittle, easily torn, crumbling.

SAKU-MONO, サクモノ, 作物, *n.* The work or manufacture of a celebrated maker.

SAKU-MONO-GATARI, サクモノガタリ, 作物語, *n.* A fiction, novel.

SAKU-MOTSZ, サクモツ, 作物, *n.* Anything grown by farming, the productions of the soil.

SAKU-NEN, サクネン, 昨年, *n.* Last year. Syn. KIYO-NEN.

SAKU-NIN, サクニン, 作人, (*tszkuru h'to*). *n.* A laborer on a farm, a farmer, gardener.

SAKURA, サクラ, 櫻, *n.* A cherry-tree. The prunus pseudo-cerasus, cultivated only for the beauty of its blossoms

†SAKURAN, サクラン, 錯亂, *n.* Confusion, mistaking one thing for another. — *szru*, to confound, mistake.

SAKURASŌ, サクラサウ, 櫻草, *n.* The name of a flower.

†SAKU-RIYAKU, サクリヤク, 策略, *n.* A stratagem, scheme, plan, device.

SAKU-RIYŌ, サクリヤウ, 作料, *n.* The wages of workmen. Syn. TEMACHIN.

SAKURU, サクル, same as Sakeru, see *Sake.*

SAKU-SAKU-TO, サクサクト, *adv.* The sound of cutting any thing crisp and friable. — *kiru.*

SAKU-SHA, サクシヤ, 作者, *n.* Author, writer of a book, maker.

SAKU-SEKI, サクセキ, 昨夕, *n.* Last evening.

SAKUSHI, サクシ, 脆, *a.* See *Sakui.*

SAKU-TOKU, サクトク, 作得, *n.* The farmer's share of the crops after the tax is paid.

SAKUWAN, サクワン, 左官, *n.* A plasterer, same as *Shak'wan.*

SAKU-YA, サクヤ, 昨夜, *n.* Last night.

SAKU-YŪ, サクユフ, 昨夕, *n.* Last evening.

SAMA, サマ, 樣, *n.* Form, shape, appearance, manner, fashion, condition. — *wo kayeru,* to change one's appearance. *Utsz-beki sama,* appearing as if he would strike.
Syn. KATACHI, NARI, YŌSZ, YŌDAI, FUZEI.

SAMA, サマ, 樣, *n.* A respectful title appended to the names of persons, and sometimes of things, as, *Kami-sama, Hotoke sama, Kubō sama, Tono sama, Anata sama, Omaye sama, O-isha sama, O-tento sama, Otszki-sama, Ginko-sama.*

SAMA, サマ, 懸眼, *n.* A loop-hole in the wall of a castle, porthole. — *no futa,* the cover of a loop-hole.

SAMADE, サマデ, To that extent, so much, such, (referring to something said before). — *shimpai ni wa oyobanu,* it is needless to feel so much anxiety. — *fukaki hakarigoto wa araji,* it is not such a deep laid stratagem. — *kenage no hataraki,* such a heroic deed.

SAMASHI,*-sz,-sh'ta,* サマス, 覺, *t. v.* To wake up from sleep, to arouse. *Me wo* —, to wake up. *Yume wo* —, to wake up from a dream. *Yoi wo* —, to make sober after intoxication.

SAMASHI,*-sz,-sh'ta,* サマス, 冷, *t. v.* To cool any thing hot. *Yu wo* —, to cool hot water. *Netsz wo* —, to cool a fever.
Syn. HIYASZ.

SAMATAGE,*-ru,-ta,* サマタゲル, 妨, *t.v.* To obstruct, hinder, impede, to interrupt. *Uma wo yokotayete michi wo* —, to put one's horse across and obstruct the road. *H'to no shigoto wo* —, to interrupt a person at work. Syn. JAMA SZRU, SASAYERU, SAYEGIRU.

SAMATAGE, サマタゲ, 妨, *n.* Obstruction, hindrance, impediment, interruption.
Syn. JAMA, GAI, KOSHŌ, SASHIAI, SAWARI.

SAMATSZ, サマツ, 早蕈, *n.* An early kind of edible mushroom.

||SAMAYOI,*-ō,-ōta,* サマヨフ, 吟行, *i.v.* To wander about bewildered, (as an outcast, or one in great trouble). *Soko koko to tadzne samayō,* to wander about inquiring here and there. *Samayoi-aruku,* to ramble about. Syn. RURŌ.

SAMA-ZAMA, サマザマ, 樣樣, *adv.* Many and various forms, appearances, or conditions.

SAMBASHI, サンバシ, 棧, *n.* A plank laid from a boat or ship for crossing, also a wooden jetty at which boats land.

†SAMBI,*-szru,* サンビ, 讃美, To praise, commend, extol. Syn. SHŌBI, HOMERU.

SAM-BIYŌ, サンビヤウ, 三病, *n.* The three incurable diseases, viz. leprosy consumption, and syphilis.

†SAM-BŌ, サンボウ, 三寶, *(mitsz no takara) n.* The three precious thing, viz. Buddha, the doctrines or rites of Buddhism, and the priests.

SAMBŌ, サンボウ, 三方, *n.* A kind of stand on which offerings are presented to the *Kami.*

SAMBUTSZ, サンブツ, 產物, *n.* A product, production, or staple commodity of a country.

SAME, サメ, 鮫, *n.* A shark, shark-skin.

SAME,*-ru,-ta,* サメル, 醒, *i.v.* To awake, to fade, to become sober. *Me ga* —, to be awake. *Iro ga* —, the color is faded. *Yoi ga* —, to become sober (from intoxication). *Mayoi ga* —, his maze has passed off.

SAME,*-ru,-ta,* サメル, 冷, *i. v.* To become cool; fig. to become calm, allayed. *Yu ga* —, the hot water is cool. *Kokoro ga* —, the excitement or pleasure has cooled.

†SAME-ZAME, サメザメ, 潸然 *adv.* The manner, or appearance of tears flowing down the face, or dropping from the eyes. — *to naku.*

SAMIDARE, サミダレ, 梅雨, *n.* The rainy season in the 5th month.

SAMISEN, サミセン, 三絃, *n.* A guitar. — *wo hiku,* to play the guitar.

SAMISHII, サミシイ, Same as *Sabishii.*

SAMISHI,*-szru,-sh'ta,* サミスル, To revile, to abuse, to speak evil of, to treat contemptuously, to despise.
Syn. ANADORU, KAROSHIMERU.

SAMMAI, サンマイ, 三昧, *n.* A cemetery. *Is-sammai ni,* with the whole heart. *Goshō is-sammai ni negau*, to seek salvation with the whole heart. Syn. ICHIDZNI.

SAMMI, サンミ, 酸味, *n.* Sour taste.

SAMMON, サンモン, 山門, *n.* The outside gate of a Buddhist temple, or monastery.

†SA-MO, サモ, *adv.* So, thus. *Samo are*, so be it, let it be so. *Somo araba are*, let it be as it is, it will do as it is. *Samo nakute*, if it be not so. *Samo aru beshi*, it should be so.

SAMO, サモ, Exclam, how! just, truly. — *nitari*, how much alike! or just alike. — *osoroshiki oni no gotoku naru mono*, something just like a terrible demon. *Samo ureshi sō*, appearing truly pleased, or just as if she were pleased. Syn. SAZO.

†SAMPAI, サンパイ, 三拜, *n.* Worshiping by bowing three times.

SAMPAIYEKI, サンパイエキ, 酸敗液, *n.* The waterbrash, pyrosis.

SAMPAKU, サンパク, 三白, *n.* The Jasminum sambac.

SAMPEI, サンペイ, 散兵, *n.* Skirmishers.

SAM-PITSZ, サンピツ, 算筆, *n.* Arithmetic and penmanship.

SAM-PŌ, サンパフ, 算法, *n.* The rules of arithmetic, mathematics.

SAM-PU, サンプ, 產婦, *n.* A woman in child-bed. — *ni imu mono*, things to be avoided by a woman in child-bed.

†SAM-PUKU, サンプク, 山腹, *n.* Half way up a mountain, the side of a mountain. — *made yoji-noboru.*

SAM-PUKU-NICHI, サンプクニチ, 三伏日, *n.* Three days in the 6th month, the hottest period of summer.

SAMŪ, サムウ, Same as *Samuku*. *O samū gozarimas*, it is cold, (in saluting another).

SAMUGARI,-*ru*,-*ta*, サムガル, 寒, *i.v.* To be sensitive to, or afraid of the cold, to be chilly.

SAMUI,-KI, サムイ, 寒, *a.* Cold, chilly, (spoken only of the weather, or of one's feelings). *Samui hi*, a cold day. — *kaze*, a cold wind. *Kesa wa* —, the morning is cold. — *ban*, a cold night.

SAMUKU, サムク, 寒, *adv.* Cold. — *naru*, to become cold. — *nai*, it is not cold. *Samuku te komaru*, in pain with the cold, or annoyed with the cold weather. *Kesa wa samukatta*, the morning was cold.

SAMURAI, サムラヒ, 士, *n.* A general name for all persons privileged to wear two swords, from the Shōgun, and Daimiyo down to the lowest grade; the military class. Syn. BUSHI, BUKE.

†SAMURAI,-*ō*,-*ōta*, サムラフ, 侍, *i.v.* (obs.) To be, same as *Sōrō*.

SAMURU, サムル, Same as *Sameru.*

SAMUSA, サムサ, 寒, *n.* The coldness.

SAMUSHI, サムシ, 寒, *a.* See *Samui.*

SAMUSHII,-KI, サムシイ, 寂寥, *a.* Lonely, solitary, quiet, desolate, (same as *Sabishii*).

SAMUSHIKU, サムシク, *adv.* Idem.

SAN, サン, 三, *(mitsz)*, *a.* Three. *San san ga ku*, three times three are nine.

SAN, サン, 產, *n.* Parturition, birth. — *wo szru*, to be in labor. — *ga karui*, the labor was easy. — *ga omoi*, the labor was difficult. — *no ke ga tszku*, to have the appearance of being confined. *Watakushi wa Kiushū no — de gozarimas*, I was born in Kiushu.

SAN, サン, 算, *n.* Reckoning on the abacus, ciphering, calculating; arithmetic, mathematics. — *wo szru*, to calculate, reckon, cipher. — *ga tassha da*, he is expert in arithmetic.

†SAN, サン, 讚, *(homeru)*, *n.* A verse written on a picture in praise of it. — *wo szru.*

SAN, サン, 棧, *n.* The sash, or frame which supports a panel; the stick or cleat under a shelf.

SAN, サン, 山, *n.* A mountain. *Fuji-san*, Fuji mountain. Often used for a Buddhist temple, from the fact of these temple being generally built on a hill or mountain.

†SAN, サン, 散, *n.* Medicinal powder. *Daiyō san*, powdered rhubarb.
Syn. KOGUSZRI.

SAN, サン, (a contraction of *Sama*). A familiar title to names.

†SAN, サン, 參, *(mairi)*, *n.* Going, (Epist.) — *wo motte mōshi agu-beku soro*, I will go and tell you.

†SANA, サナ, *a.* So, that kind, (obs. same as, *Sō-na*, or *Sayō-na*).

SANADA, サナダ, 狹機, *n.* Flat braid, tape.

SANADA-MUSHI, サナダムシ, 絛蟲, *n.* A tape-worm.

SANAGARA, サナガラ, *adv.* Just, exactly, precisely. — *jigoku no seme no gotoku*, just like the torments of hell.
Syn. ADAKAMO, CHŌDO.

SANAGI, サナギ, *n.* The silk-worm during its cocoon life, a chrysalis.

SANAKI,-KU, サナキ, Not so. *Sanaki dani*, if not so, if otherwise.

SANAYE, サナエ, 早苗, *n.* Young rice sprouts.

SAN-CHAKU, サンチヤク, 參著, (*mairi tszku*). Arrival. *Buji ni — itasz*, to arrive in safety.

SAN-CHIU, サンチウ, 山中, (*yamanonaka*), Amongst the mountains.

†SAN-CHŌ, サンチヤウ, 山頂, (*yama no itadaki*), *n.* The top of a mountain.

†SAN-DAI, サンダイ, 參內, (*uchi ye mairu*). Going to the palace of the Mikado. — *szru.*

SAN-DAN, サンダン, 參談, *n.* Consultation, deliberation, scheming, devising, planning. — *ga tszkanu*, the consultation resulted in nothing. *Kane no — wo szru*, to scheme how to raise money. Syn. SAI-KAKU, KUMEN.

SANDAWARA, サンダハラ, 棧俵, *n.* The round straw lid of a straw-bag.

†SAN-DŌ, サンダウ, 棧道, (*kake hashi*), *n.* A plank-road constructed on the face of a precipice.

SANDZGAWA, サンヅガハ, 三途川, *n.* The river which the souls of the dead cross in going to Hades, the river Styx.

SANDZI, サンズイ, *n.* The radical, (氵), for water written at the side of a character.

SANE, サネ, 核, *n.* The seeds of fruit, melons, &c., the plates or scales of armor. *Nashi no —*, pear seeds.

SANEKADZRA, サネカヅラ, 五味子 *n.* The Kadzra Japonica.

SAN-GAI, サンガイ, 三階, *n.* Three storied, third story.

SAN-GAI, サンガイ, 三界, *n.* The three worlds, or states of existence,—the past, present, and future.

SAN-GAKU, サンガク, 算學, *n.* Arithmetic, mathematical study, or learning. — *wo szru*, to learn arithmetic.

†SAN-GAKU, サンガク, 山嶽, *n.* A high mountain or peak.

SAN-GA-NICHI, サンガニチ, 三賀日, *n.* The first three days of the new year, (given up to complimentary visiting).

SAN-GE, *-szru*, サンゲ, 懺悔, To confess one's sins. *Kami ni tszmi wo —*, to confess one's sins to God.

SAN-GI, サンギ, 算木, *n.* Sticks used in divining, or in calculating. — *wo naraberu.*

†SAN-GIYŌ, サンゲフ, 產業, *n.* Occupation, business, livelihood. Syn. KAGIYŌ, SHŌBAI.

†SAN-GO, サンゴ, 產後, After parturition.

SANGOJU, サンゴジユ, 珊瑚珠, *n.* Coral.

SAN-G'WATSZ, サングワツ, 三月, *n.* The third month.

SANHICHI, サンヒチ, 山七, *n.* The name of a flower.

†SAN-IN, サンイン, 山陰, *n.* The northern or shady side of a mountain.

SAN-JAKU-OBI, サンジヤクオビ, 三尺帶, *n.* A belt made of a piece of common muslin passing once around, worn by low people.

SAN-JI, サンジ, 山寺, (*yamadera*). *n.* A Buddhist temple on a mountain.

†SANJI, *-ru*, or *-dzru*, *-ta*, サンズル, 散, (*chiru*). *i.v.* To scatter; dispersed, dissipated.

SANJI, *-ru*, or *-dzru*, *-ta*, サンズル, 參, (*mairu*). *i.v.* To come, to go. *Tadaima sanjimash'ta*, has just come. *Yedo ye sanjita*, has gone to Yedo.

SANJIKI, サンジキ, Same as *Sajiki*.

†SAN-JIN, サンジン, 山人, (*yamabito*). *n.* One who retires from the world, and lives amongst the mountains.

SAN-JO, サンヂヨ, 產女, *n.* Same as *Sampu.*

†SAN-JŌ, サンジヤウ, 山上, (*yama no wiye*). On the top of the mountain.

SAN-JŪ, サンジフ, 三十, Thirty. — *san*, thirty three.

†SAN-JŪ, サンジユウ, 三從, *n.* The three great duties of a woman; viz. when unmarried, obedience to parents; when a wife, obedience to her husband; when a widow, obedience to her son, (who inherits the estate). — *no michi.*

SAN-JUTSZ, サンジユツ, 算術, *n.* Arithmetic.

†SAN-KA, サンカ, 山下, (*yama no sh'ta*). *n.* At the foot of a mountain.

†SAN-KA, サンカ, 山家, (*yama no iye*). *n.* A house on or amongst the mountains.

†SAN-KAI, サンカイ, 山海, (*yama umi*). *n.* Mountain and sea.

SAN-KAN, サンカン, 三韓, *n.* Corea, formerly divided into three states. Syn. CHŌSEN.

SAN-KAKU, サンカク, 三角, *n.* A triangle.

SAN-KEI, サンケイ, 參詣, (*mōdzru*). Going to a temple for worship. — *szru*, to go, &c.

SAN-KI, サンキ, 山氣, Fond of speculating or commercial ventures. — *no aru h'to*, a person fond, &c. Syn. YAMA-GOKORO.

SAN-KIN, サンキン, 參勤, The going to, and residence in Yedo, of a Daimiyo for a certain portion of his time.

SANKIRAI, サンキライ, 山歸來, *n.* Sarsaparilla, — Smilax pseudo-china.

†SAN-K'YO, サンキヨ, 山居, (*yamadzmi*). *n.* Dwelling among the mountains.

†SAN-K'YOKU, サンキヨク, 三曲, *n.* The three musical instruments; viz. drum, guitar, and flute.

†SAN-KO, サンコ, 三鈷, *n.* A small brass instrument with three prongs on each end, held by some Buddhist priests in praying.

†SAN-KŌ, サンコウ, 三公, *n.* The three highest ministers of the Mikado, viz., Dajōdaijin, Sadaijin, and Udaijin.

†SAN-KŌ,-*szru*, サンカウ, 參考, To collate the text of various editions of the same book and correct it.

†SAN-KŌ, サンコウ, 參候, To come, (only in epist.) as, *otte — itasz beku soro*, I will come by and by.

†SAN-KŌ, サンカウ, 參向, idem.

†SAN-KOKU, サンコク, 山谷, (*yama tani*). *n.* Mountains and valleys.

SAN-K'WAI, サンクワイ, 參會, (*mairi au*). To come and meet together, to assemble.

†SAN-K'WŌ, サンクワウ, 三光, (*mitsz no hikari*). The three luminaries; viz. sun, moon, and stars.

SAN-K'WŌ-DORI, サンクワウドリ, 三光鳥, *n.* The name of a bird, whose cry is supposed to resemble the sound of "*Tszki hi hoshi.*"

SAN-NAN, サンナン, 三男, *n.* The third son.

†SAN-NIU, サンニフ, 參入, (*mairi iru*). To come.

SANNURU サンヌル, 去, *a.* Past, gone by, last. — *uma no toshi hachi g'watsz*, the 8th month of the last horse-year.

SANOMI, サノミ, 然耳, *adv.* So much, such. — *kurushiku mo nai*, not much pain, — *midokoro nashi*, nothing much to see, nothing worth looking at.
Syn. SAHODO.

†SAN-RAN, サンラン, 散亂, (*chiri midareru*). Scattered in disorder.

SAN-RI, サンリ, 三里, *n.* The space just below the head of the fibula, a good place for applying the moxa!

†SAN-RIN, サンリン, 山林, (*yama hayashi*). *n.* Mountain and forest.

†SAN-RO, サンロ, 山路, (*yama michi*). *n.* A mountain road.

†SAN-SAI, サンサイ, 三才, *n.* The three powers that rule all things; viz. heaven, earth, and man.

SANSHISHI, サンシシ, 山梔子, *n.* The seed-capsule of the white Jasmine, used for dying yellow.

†SAN-SHITSZ, サンシツ, 散失, (*chiri nakunaru*). Scattered and lost, dissipated.

SAN-SHŌ, サンセウ, 山椒, The Zanthoxylon piperitum, an aromatic shrub, the leaves and seeds of which are used as a condiment.

SANSHŌ-UWO, サンシヤウウヲ, 鯢魚, *n.* A kind of lizard.

SAN-SHUN, サンシユン, 三春, *n.* The three spring months.

†SAN-SO, サンソ, 酸素, *n.* Oxygen gas.

†SANSŌRO, サンサフラウ, Exclam. used in replying, or assenting to what is said; So, yes, indeed. = col, *sayō de gozarimas.*

†SAN-TAN, サンタン, 讃歎, (*home nageku*). To praise, to extol, admire.
Syn. SAMBI.

SAN-TEI,-*szru*, サンテイ, 參訂, To examine and collate the text of books, to correct a writing.
Syn. SANKŌ, KIYŌ-GŌ.

SAN-TŌ, サンタウ, 算當, *n.* Calculation, computation, account. — *wa hadzreta*, to mistake in one's calculation.
Syn. KANJŌ, TSZMORI, SAN-YŌ.

SANTOME, サントメ, 聖多默, *n.* Taffachillas.

†SAN-YAKU, サンヤク, 散藥, A powdered medicine. Syn. KOGUSZRI.

†SAN-YAKU, サンヤク, 山藥, *n.* The same as *Yamaimo.*

†SAN-YETZ, サンエツ, 參謁, To come to see, (epist.)

SAN-YŌ, サンヨウ, 算用, *n.* Account, calculation, reckoning. — *szru*, to calculate.
Syn. KAN-JŌ.

SAN-ZAI, サンザイ, 散財, Spending money, squandering money.

SAN-ZAN, サンザン, 山山, A superlative, generally used in a bad sense. — *na koto*, a very bad affair. — *waruku naru*, to become exceedingly bad.

SANZASHI, サンザシ, 山查子, *n.* The Cratagus cuneata.

†SAN-ZE, サンゼ, 三世, *n.* The three worlds, or states of existence, past, present, and future.

SAN-ZŌ-BAI, サンザウバイ, 三相倍, *adv.* Three times as much.

†SAN-ZOKU, サンゾク, 山賊, *n.* A highway robber, bandit, brigand.
Syn. YAMADACHI, DOROBŌ.

SAO, サヲ, 竿, *n.* A pole.

SA-OSHIKA, サヲシカ, 牡鹿, *n.* A male deer, a buck.

SA-OTOME, サヲトメ, 插秧女, *n.* A girl who plants young rice shoots.

SAO-TORI, サヲトリ, 竿取, *n.* A boatman who pushes with a pole.

SAPPARI, サツパリ, *adv.* Neat and free from any thing unpleasant or unclean, thoroughly, quite, perfectly, entirely, wholly, fully. *Ki ga — sh'ta*, his spirits are quite relieved. *Biyōki ga mada — to senu*, not entirely recovered from sickness. *— to sh'ta tenki*, a clear day. *— shirimasen*, I am entirely ignorant of it. *— sh'ta h'to*, a manly well bred man. Syn. SARA-NI, ISAGIYOI.

SAPPŪKEI, サツプウケイ, 殺風景, (lit.) Any thing that spoils the prospect, uncongenial, disagreeable, incongruous. *— na mono*, anything that is an eye-sore.

SARA, サラ, 碟, *n.* A plate, saucer, dish. *Hiza no —*, the kneepan.

†**SARABA**, サラバ, (cont. of *Sa*, and *araba*). *adv.* So then, well then, after that.

SARADZ, サラズ, 不去, Neg. of *Sari.*

SARAI, サラヒ, 筢, *n.* A rake. Syn. KUMADE.

SA-RAI-NEN, サライネン, 再來年, *n.* Year after next,

SARAKEDASHI,*–sz*,*–sh'ta*, サラケダシ, *t.v.* To haul out any thing carelessly. *Kodomo ga tansz no kimono wo —*, the child has pulled the clothes out of the bureau.

SARA-NI, サラニ, 更, *adv.* Quite, wholly, clean, altogether, entirely, totally, anew. *— nashi*, there is not a particle. *Kuyu to mo — kai arumaji*, should you even repent it would be quite useless. *— shikayeru*, make it all over. Syn. MATTAKU, SAPPARI, ARATA-NI.

†**SARA-NARI**, サラナリ, 更也, *adv.* Of course, needless, unnecessary. *Iu mo —*, needless to speak of it. Syn. MOCHRON.

†**SARANU**, サラヌ, (comp. of *Sa* and *aranu*). Not so. *— dani samui fuyu ni*, even in a winter that is not so very cold, &c. *— tei*, appearing as if nothing was the matter.

SARARE,*–ru*,*–ta*, サラレル, 被去, *pass.* or *pot.* of *Sari.* To be divorced.

SARARI-TO, サラリト, *adv.* Like the noise or in the manner of sliding, rolling, or rustling.

SARASA, サラサ, 印花布, *n.* Calico, chintz.

SARA-SARA-TO, サラサラト, *adv.* Like the sound, or in the manner of rolling beads, or pebbles between the hands with a slipping, rattling, or rustling noise. *Amado no aku oto — kikoye*, heard the rattling sound of the outside doors opening. *Judz wo — momu*, to roll the rosary in the hands with a rattling noise.

SARASHI,*–sz*,*–sh'ta*, サラス, 晒, *t.v.* To expose to the sun or weather, to expose to public view, to bleach, to sun. *Haji wo —*, to expose another's shame. *Kubi wo —*, to expose the head of a criminal. *Kabane wo —*, to leave a dead body exposed without burial. *Kome wo —*, to bleach rice by washing.

SARASHI, サラシ, 晒布, *n.* White, or bleached muslin.

SARAYE,*–ru*,*–ta*, サラヘル, 浚, *t. v.* To clean out or deepen by scooping or dredging, as a well, the channel of a stream, &c. *Ido wo —*, to clean out a well. *Kawa wo sarayete fukaku szru*, to deepen a river by dredging.

SARAYE,*–ru*,*–ta*, サラヘル, *t.v.* To review, revise, to go over again, as a lesson. *Hon wo —*, to review a book.

SARAYE, サラヘ, *n.* A review, revision, (of a book, lesson.)

SARAYE-DASHI,*–sz*,*–sh'ta*, サラヘダス, *t.v.* To scrape out, scoop out.

SARAYE-KOMI,*–mu*,*–nda*, サラヘコム, *t.v.* To scrape into, to fill up by scraping into.

SARE,*–ru*,*–ta*, サレル, 曝, *i.v.* To be exposed or bleached in the sun. *Sare-kōbe*, a skull left bleaching on the ground.

†**SAREBA**, サレバ, (comp. of *Sa*, and *areba*). *adv.* So then, well then, used in resuming a narative.

†**SAREDOMO**, サレドモ, *conj.* But, however, although it was so, nevertheless, notwithstanding. Syn. SH'KASHI-NAGARA.

SARI,*–ru*,*–tta*, サル, 去, *i*, or *t.v.* To leave, go away from, depart, to reject, to forsake. *Yo wo —*, to leave the world, to die. *Ima wo saru koto jū nen*, it was ten years ago. *Tszma wo —*, to desert a wife. *Itami ga satta*, the pain has gone. Syn. SZTERU, NOZOKU.

SARI-GATAI,*–KI*,*–KU*, サリガタイ, 難去, *a.*, and *adv.* Impossible to leave. *Sarigataki yōji*, business which one cannot leave.

SARIGENAI,*–KI*,*–KU*, サリゲナイ, 無然氣, Not appearing to know any thing about it, without letting on, not appearing as if it were so.

SARI-JŌ, サリジヤウ, 去狀, *n.* A bill of divorcement. Syn. RI-YEN-JŌ.

SARI-NAGARA, サリナガラ, 乍去, *conj.* Yet, however, but, still, nevertheless. Syn. SH'KASHI-NAGARA, SAREDOMO, KEREDOMO.

†SARI-NI-SHI, サリニシ, *a.* Past, gone, departed, deceased. — *toshi*, the year or years that are past. — *h'to*, the deceased person. Syn. SANNURU, SZGINISHI.

†SARINU-BEKI, サリヌベキ, 可然, (*comp.* of *Sa, aru*, and *beki.*) Appearing to be right or good, looking as if it were good. — *katana*, a sword which appears to be a good one, but which one does not certainly know.

†SARI-TOMO, サリトモ, (comp. of *Sa, ari*, and *tomo.*) *conj.* Although it be so, but still, however, nevertheless.

†SARITOTE, サリトテ, (comp. of *Sa, ari*, and *to-iu-te.*) *conj.* Even if it be so, but still, nevertheless, however, notwithstanding.

SA-RIYAKU, サリヤク, 作略, *n.* Services, assistance, exertions. Syn. SHŪSEN.

SARU, サル, 猿, *n.* A monkey, ape. — *no toki*, four o'clock P.M. — *no kata*, the south-west.

SARU, サル, 去, See *Sari.*

SARU, サル, 然, (comp. of *Sa*, and *aru*). *a.* A certain, so, such, same, as mentioned. — *h'to*, a certain man. — *tokoro*, a certain place. — *iye ni*, in a certain house. *Saru-koto*, such a thing. — *ni yotte*, on account of its being so, therefore. — *nite mo*, although it was so, still, nevertheless. — *yū-shi naredomo*, although he was such a brave man. — *koro*, on a certain time. Syn. ARU.

SARU-BŌ, サルボウ, 朗光, *n.* The name of a bivalve shell.

SARU-GAKU, サルガク, 散樂, *n.* A kind of operatic performance.

SARU-GASH'KOI,-KI,-KU, サルガシコイ, 獪, *a.*, and *adv.* Artful, cunning, clever, or smart in a trifling way. Syn. SARURIKŌ.

SARUGI, サルギ, 猿木, *n.* The posts to which a horse is tied in a stable.

SARU-GUTSZWA, サルグツワ, 猿轡, *n.* A gag.

†SARUHODO-NI, サルホドニ, 去程, (comp. of *Sa, aru*, and *hodoni.*) Used in continuing a narrative that had been interrupted, or in introducing a new subject connected with what was said, = So then, accordingly, thus.

SARU-JIYE, サルヂヱ, 猿智慧, *n.* Cunning, artfulness.

SARUKO, サルコ, 猿子, *n.* A wadded coat with sleeves, worn outside of the other clothes in cold weather.

SARU-KORO, サルコロ, 去頃, *adv.* Some time ago, some time since. Syn. SENDATTE.

SARU-MAWASHI, サルマハシ, 狙公, *n.* One who leads a monkey about to show his tricks for a livelihood.

SARU-MONO, サルモノ, 然物, Such a person (as was mentioned), a celebrated person, a clever person.

SARU-NO-KOSHI-KAKE, サルノコシカケ, *a.* (monkey's stool). A kind of large fungus growing from decayed trees.

SARU-RIKŌ, サルリコウ, 猿利根, *n.* Artful, cunning, trickish. Syn. SARUCHIYE.

SARU-SZBERI, サルスベリ, 紫薇樹, *n.* The lagerstramia indica. Syn. HIYAKUJIK'KŌ.

SASA, ササ, 小竹, *n.* A kind of small bamboo grass.

SASA, ササ, 酒, *n.* Same as *sake*, (the language of women.)

SASAGANI, ササガニ, 小蟹, *n.* A small kind of land crab.

SASAGE,-*ru*,-*ta*, ササゲル, 捧, (*cont.* of *Sashi*, and *ageru*,) *t.v.* To present to a superior, to offer up. *Kami ni miki wo* —, to make an offering of wine to the *Kami*. *Mitszgi wo* —, to offer tribute. Syn. TATEMATSZRU.

SASAGE, ササゲ, 角荳, *n.* A long bean.

SASAHERI, ササヘリ, 細緣, *n.* Braid used for edging. — *wo toru*, to edge with braid.

SASAI, ササイ, 瑣細, Small, little, few, fine, trifling, trivial. — *naru shina*, a little thing. Syn. CHĪSAI, KOMAKA, WADZKA.

†SASAMEGOTO, ササメゴト, 私語, *n.* Talking in a whisper or low voice.

SASAMEKI,-*ku*,-*ita*, ササメク, 耳語, *i. v.* To talk in a low voice, to whisper, to murmur, to grumble. Syn. SASAYAKU.

SASARA, ササラ, 竹籔, *n.* A small brush made of split bamboo.

†SASARAGATA, ササラガタ, 印華, *n.* Calico. Syn. SARASA.

†SASARAYE-OTOKO, ササラヱヲトコ, 陰魄, *n.* The moon.

SASARE,-*ru*,-*ta*, ササレル, 被刺, Pass and pot, of *Sashi*.

SASARINDŌ, ササリンダウ, Same as *Rindō*; Common gentian.

SASAWARI,-*ru*,-*tta*, ササハル, 障, *i. v.* To be obstructed, hindered, impeded, interrupted, stopped, checked. *Michi ni* —, to be obstructed in the way. *Yubi ni kega wo sh'te tenarai ni* —, to be hindered in learning to write by a hurt on the finger. *Kagiyō ni* —, hindered in one's business. Syn. SAMATAGERU, JAMA NI NARU, SASHIAI.

SASAWARI, ササハリ, 障, *n.* A hindrance,

obstruction, impediment, interruption, stoppage. — *ga dekita*.
Syn. JAMA, KOSHŌ, SAMATAGE, SAWARI, SASHIAI.

SASAYAKA, ササヤカ, 瑣小, *a*. Small, little, fine, few, trivial. — *naru*, id.
Syn. CHISAI, KOMAKA, WADZKA.

SASAYAKI, *-ku,-ita*, ササヤク, 密語, *t. v.* To whisper, to talk in a low voice. *F'tari de nani ka sasayaite otta*, what are they whispering about? Syn. SASAMEKI.

SASAYE, *-ru,-ta*, ササヘル, 支, *t. v.* To obstruct, block-up, hinder, impede, interrupt; to stop, check, prevent, restrain, intercept. *Michi wo* —, to obstruct a road. *H'to sasaye mo sasayedz*, did not once check (the enemy).
Syn. SAYEGIRU, SAMATAGERU.

SASAYE, ササエ, 小竹筒, *n*. A vessel for carrying *sake*, made of a section of bamboo.

SASE, *-ru,-ta*, サセル, 令為, *t. v.* The caust. form of *szru*. To make or let do, to cause, to give, to induce, bring. *Ji-shin de szru yori wa h'to ni saseru ga yoi*, it would be better to let others do it, than do it yourself. *Fukō na ko wa oya ni nangi wo saseru*, a disobedient child brings sorrow to his parents. *Watakushi ni mo sase-nasare*, let me also do it.

SASEMOGUSA, サセモグサ, 艾草, *n*. The artemisia, or mugwort, of which moxa is made. Syn. YOMOGI.

†SASEN, サセン, 左遷, Degraded and banished from the court or captial, (spoken of the Kuge). — *szru*. Syn. RUZAI.

SASHI, サシ, 尺, *n*. A foot measure. *Naga-zashi*, a cloth measure. — *de sasz*, to measure with a foot measure.

SASHI, サシ, 索子, *n*. The string used for stringing cash.

SASHI, サシ, 探筒, *n*. A stick of bamboo shaved off obliquely at the end, for pushing into a bag of grain and drawing out a muster.

SASHI, ザシ, *n*. The bag or case of a tobacco pipe.

SASHI, *-sz,-sh'ta*, サス, 刺, 差, 指, 螫, *t.v.* To stick, pierce, stab, thrust, prick; to sting, to point, to measure. *Katana wo* —, to stick the sword in the belt. *Katana de*—, to stab with a sword. *Hachi ga* —, the bee stings. *Sakadzki wo* —, to pass the wine cup to another. *Kuszri wo me ni* —, to drop medicine into the eye. *Ki wo* —, to plant a branch of a tree by sticking it into the ground. *Hako wo* —, to join or make a box. *Tori wo* —, to catch a bird with bird-lime. *To wo* —, to bolt a door. *Ishi wo* —, to lift a heavy stone on the hand above the head. *Shiwo ga* —, the tide rises. *Nuno wo* —, to quilt muslin. *Tatami wo* —, to sew a mat. *Momen wo* —, to measure cloth. *Hi ga mado ni* —, the sun shines into the window. *Tszki ga midz ni* —, the moon shines into the water. *Sake wo midz ni* —, to pour a little *sake* into water. *Shōyu wo* —, to season with soy. *Nishi wo* —, to point to the west. *Nishi wo sash'te yuku*, to go towards the west. *Yubi wo* —, to point the finger. *Kasa wo* —, to hold up an umbrella. *Todome wo* —, to give the coup de grace. *Zeni wo* —, to string cash. *Na wo sashite wa imasen*, would not mention him by name. *Nani wo sash'te iu*, what do you allude to? *Yedo ye sash'te yuku h'to*, a man bound for Yedo. *Doko ye sash'te yuku*, where are you bound for?

SASHI, *-sz,-sh'ta*, or *-ita*, サス, 殘, *t.v.* To leave anything unfinished or partly done, used only as second of a comp. word, as, *Shigoto wo shi-sash'te asobi ni yuku*, to leave one's work undone and go to play. *Sake wo nomi-sashi ni sh'te deru*, to go out leaving his wine unfinished. *Meshi no kui-sashi*, the rice one has left without eating.

SASHI-AGE, *-ru,-ta*, サシアゲル, 差上, *t.v.* Same as *Ageru*.

SASHI-AI, *-au,-atta*, サシアフ, 差合, *i.v.* To be prevented, obstructed, hindered.

SASHI-AI, サシアイ, 差合, *n*. Something that acts as a hindrance, obstruction, or embarrassment. *Kon-nichi — ga atte yukimasen*, I am so engaged to-day I cannot go.

SASHI-ASHI, サシアシ, 刺足, *n*. Soft, or stealthy steps. — *de aruku*.

SASHI-ATARI, *-ru,-tta*, サシアタル, 差當, *i.v.* To be of pressing, or urgent necessity, happening unexpectedly and requiring instant attention. *Sashi-atatta nangi*, a calamity happening unexpectedly and calling for immediate action. *Sashi-atatte komaru. Sashi-atatte yōji mo nai*, no business requiring immediate attention.

SASHI-ATARI, サシアタリ, 差當, *n*. An emergency, exigence, a matter of pressing necessity.

SASHI-DASHI, *-sz,-sh'ta*, サシダス, 差出, *t.v.* To hand up, to give.

SASHIDE, サシデ, *adv*. Spoken of two persons doing anything together, as, — *sake wo nomu*, to drink wine together. — *ni wo katszgu*. to carry a burden together.

SASHI-DE, *-ru,-ta*, サシデル, 差出, *i. v.*

To put one's self forward, to be forward, bold, confident, or presumptuous in speaking.

SASHI-DE-GUCHI, サシデグチ, 差出口, *n.* Interrupting others by putting in a word. — *wo szru*, to interrupt by speaking.

SASHIDZ, サシヅ, 指揮, *n.* Command, order, instruction, direction. — *wo szru.* — *wo ukeru.* Syn. SAHAI, SHIKI.

SASHI-DZME, サシヅメ, 差詰, *adv.* Just now, at present.

SASHI-GAMI, サシガミ, 指紙, *n.* A summons.

SASHI-GANE, サシガネ, 規, *n.* A carpenter's metal square.

SASHI-GASA, サシガサ, 雨傘, *n* An umbrella.

SASHI-GUMI, *-mu, -nda*, サシグム, 指汲, *i.v.* The eyes to fill with tears. *Namida ga —.*

SASHI-GUSHI, サシグシ, 刺櫛, *n.* A comb worn in the hair for ornament.

SASHI-GUSZRI, サシグスリ, 刺藥, *n.* Medicine for dropping into the eye.

SASHI-HASAMI, *-mu, -nda*, サシハサム, 挾, *t.v.* To stick between two things, to press between two things. *I-kon wo —*, to harbor malice.

SASHI-HIKAYE, *-ru, -ta*, サシヒカヘル, 差控, Same as *Hikayeru.*

SESHI-HIKAYE, サシヒカヘ, 差控, *n.* Punishment by confinment to one's house. — *wo zzru.*

SASHI-HIKI, サシヒキ, 差引, *n.* To deduct from an account money previously advanced, or to balance an account by adding or deducting previous transactions. *Saki gashi wo kiukin de — ni szru.*

SASHI-HIKI, サシヒキ, 差引, *n.* The ebb and flow, (of the tide); rise and fall, (of fever); adding to, or subtracting from, (an account.)

SASHI-JIYE, サシヂヱ, 刺智, *n.* A lesson or trick which one has learned from another, without understanding it himself.

SASHI-KAKARI, *-ru, -tta*, サシカカル, 差掛, *t.v.* The be near to, on the eve of, approaching to. *Haru ni —*, to be near spring. *Ganjitsz ni sashi-kakatte tabi ye tattarenu*, as it is near new-year's day I cannot set out on the journey. Syn. NOZOMU.

SASHI-KAKE, サシカケ, 差掛, *n.* An extension built to a house. — *wo szru*, to build an extension.

SASHI-KAMAYE, *-ru, -ta*, サシカマヘル, 差搆, Same as *Kamayeru.*

SASHI-KAMAYE, サシカマヘ, 差搆, *n.* Concern, importance, moment, matter. *Watakushi ni — wa nai*, it makes no matter to me.

SASHI-KI, サシキ, 揷, *n.* A branch without a root planted by sticking into the ground.

SASHI-KO. サシコ, 刺著, *n.* A quilted coat.

SASHI-KOMI, *-mu, -nda*, サシコム, 差込, *t.v.* To stick into; to have severe pain or cramp in the stomach, to be convulsed.

SASHI-KOROSHI, *-sz, -sh'ta*, サシコロス, 刺殺, *t.v.* To stab and kill.

SASHI-KOSHI, *-sz, -sh'ta*, サシコス, 差越, *t.v.* To come, to send, hand over.

SASHI-MANEKI, *-ku, -ita*, サシマネク, 麾, *t.v.* To beckon.

SASHI-MI, サシミ, 膾, *n.* Raw fish cut in thin slices, and eaten with soy. — *bōchō*, a long slender knife for slicing fish.

SASHI-MO, サシモ, (comp. of *Sa*, so, *shi*, euphonic, and *mo*, even). *a.* So, such a kind or degree, referring to something said or known before. — *samui to mo omoi-masen*, I do not think it so cold, (as you think). — *gō-naru taishō saye*, even such a daring general. — *no ōzei mo*, even such a large army. Syn. SASZGA, SAMO.

SASHI-MONO, サシモノ, 拴物, *n.* Cabinet-ware.

SASHI-MONO, サシモノ, 背旗, *n.* A small flag, or banner.

SASHI-MONO-SHI, サシモノシ, 拴物師, *n.* A cabinet-maker.

SASHI-MUKAI, *-au, -atta*, サシムカウ, 差向, *t.v.* To be face to face, to be together alone, spoken of two persons.

SASHI-MUKE, *-ru, -ta*, サシムケル, 差向, *t.v.* To send. Syn. YARU, OKURU.

SASHI-NABE, サシナベ, 銚子, *n.* A pot with a long spout, used for warming *sake.*

SASHI-NAWA, サシナハ, 差繩, *n.* The cord with which criminals are bound. Spn. IMASHIME NAWA.

SASHI-NINAI, *-au, -atta*, サシニナウ, 差荷, *t.v.* To carry on the shoulder between two.

SASHI-NUKI, サシヌキ, 刺貫, *n.* A kind of long trowsers, worn by nobles.

SASHI-OKI, *-ku, -ita*, サシオク, 差置, *t.v.* To let be, let rest, to leave, quit, forbear. *Sono mama ni —*, to let it be as it is.

SASHI-OKURI, *-ru, -tta*, サシオクル, 差送, *t.v.* Same as *Okuri.*

SASHI-RIYŌ, サシリヤウ, 指料, *n.* The long sword one is accustomed to wear.

SASHI-SHIWO, サシシホ, 刺潮, *n.* The rising tide.

SASHITARU, サシタル, 爲差, *a.* Special, particular, important. — *koto mo nai,* nothing of any special importance.
Syn. BETSZDAN, KAKUBETSZ.

SASHITE, サシテ, 指而, *adv.* Particularly, especially. — *kawaru koto mo nai,* there is no change worth mentioning.
Syn. BESH'TE, KOTO-NI.

SASHI-TOME,*-ru,-ta,* サシトメル, 差止, *t.v.* To stop, forbid, to intercept, obstruct.

SASHI-TŌSHI,*-sz,-sh'ta,* サシトホス, 刺透, *t.v.* To pierce through, transfix, to run through, with any pointed instrument.

SASHI-TSZKAYE,*-ru,-ta,* サシツカヘル, 差支, *i.v.* To be hindered, interrupted, embarassed, obstructed. *Kane ni,* —, embarrassed for want of money.

SASHI-TSZKAYE, サシツカヘ, *n.* Hindrance, obstruction, difficulty, impediment, engagement, embarrassment. — *ga atte yukaremasen,* as I have an engagement I cannot go. *Kurashi ni — wa nai,* not embarassed in circumstances.
Syn. KOSHŌ, TODOKŌRI, SASAWARI.

SASHI-TSZKE,*-ru,-ta,* サシツケル, 差付, *t.v.* To thrust against.

SASHI-TSZMARI,*-ru,-tta,* サシツマル, 差詰, *i.v.* See *Tszmari.*

†SASHITSZME-SASHITSZME, サシツメ, *adv.* — *iru,* to shoot (with the bow) rapidly, in quick succession.

SASHI-WATASHI, サシワタシ, 直徑, *n.* The distance across, distance in a straight line, diameter. *Kawa no — wa han-michi,* the river was half a mile across.

SASHI-YAME,*-ru,-ta,* サシヤメル, 差止, *t.v.* To stop, frustrate, balk.

SASHI-ZOYE, サシゾヘ, 差添, *n.* The small sword.

SA-SHŌ, マセウ, 瑣少, Little, few, trifling. — *nagara,* although few, or of little worth. — *no shina,* a trifling thing.
Syn. SZKOSHI, WADZKA.

SASOI,*-ō,-ōta,* サソフ, 誘, *t.v.* To invite, or persuade to go with, to urge another to accompany, to entice.
Syn. IZANAU, YŪ-IN, SOSONOKASZ.

SASOI-DASHI,*-sz,-sh'ta,* サソヒダス, 誘出, *t.v.* To lead along with, to entice out.

†SA-SOKU, サソク, 左足, *n.* The left foot.

SASOKU, サソク, Quick, ready, or prompt. — *no chiye,* quick witted. — *no hentō,* a ready answer. Syn. SOKUZA.

SASORI, サソリ, 蠍, *n.* A scorpion.

SASOWARE,*-ru,-ta,* サソハレル, 被誘, *pass.* and *pot.* of *Sasoi.* To be invited to go with, to be enticed or led away.

SASSA-TO, サツサト, *adv.* Fast, quick, briskly. — *aruku,* to walk fast. — *shigoto wo szru,* to work fast.

†SASSATSZ-TO, サツサツト, 颯颯, *adv.* The sound made by the wind, or the sleeves in dancing.

SASSHI,*-szru,-sh'ta,* セツスル, 察, *t.v.* To conjecture, to form an opinion of, to judge of, consider. Syn SZRIYŌ, OSHIHAKARU.

SASSOKU, サツソク, 早速, *adv.* Quick, hastily, speedily, soon. — *mairimashō,* I will come soon. Syn. HAYAKU, KIU-NI.

SASZ, サス, See *Sashi.*

SASZ, サス, 擡梁, *n.* A pole sharp at the ends used by farmers in carrying sheaves of grain. Syn. ŌKO.

SASZGA, サスガ, 裁刀, *n.* A pocket knife.

SASZGA, サスガ, 流石, *adv.* (comp. of *Shika,* or *sa,* so, *szru,* being, and *nagara,* whilst). While it was so, such being the case, so, therefore, still, really, indeed. — *nai to mo iwarenu,* so, I could not say I had none. — *ni shiranu kao mo serarenu,* so, I could not appear not to know.
Syn. MASAKA.

SASZGA-NO, サスガノ, *a.* (same word as the above). Although such, (as was mentioned or referred to), even such a person or thing as. — *O Tama mo,* even such a person as Tama. — *yū-shi mo odoroita,* even such a brave soldier was alarmed, or brave soldier as he was yet he was alarmed. Syn. SASHIMO.

SASZ-MATA, サスマタ, 刺杈, *n.* A weapon in shape something like a pitch-fork used sometimes by policemen.

SASZ-NOMI, サスノミ, 刺鑿, *n.* A tool used by carpenters for making holes by driving it into the wood.

SASZRAI,*-ō,-ōta,* サスラウ, 左遷, *i.v.* To be degraded in rank and banished from the capital, to wander about as a *rōnin.*
Syn. SASEN, RUZAI.

†SASZRAYE,*-ru,-ta,* サスラヘル, Same as above.

†SASZREBA, サスレバ, *adv.* So then, since it is so, then, (commencing a sentence and referring to something before.)

SASZRI,*-ru,-tta,* サスル, 擦, *t.v.* To rub the body with the hand. *Senaka wo —,* to rub the back. Syn. KOSZRU, NADERU.

SATA, サタ, 沙汰, *n.* Report, rumor, word, tidings, communication, account, talk, conversation, order, command, message. — *wo szru,* to send word. — *nashi ni szru,* don't let it be known. *Shin-jin no —,* a talk about faith. *Seifu no —,* government communication or message. — *no*

kagiru, inexpressibly, exceedingly.
Syn. H'YŌBAN, OTODZRE.

SATAN,*-szru*, サタン, 左 祖, To be a friend, ally, or confederate.
Syn. MIKATA SZRU.

SATE, サテ, 扠, (cont. of *Shika*, or *sa*, so, and *atte*). It being so, so then, (used in resuming a narrative, or commencing a new subject.)
(2). as an exclam. of admiration, salutation.

SATE-KOSO, サテコソ, Exclam. of admiration. So indeed! just so! referring to something before. — *yuki ga futta*, So! it has snowed! (just as I expected.)
Syn. HATASH'TE.

SATE-MATA, サテマタ, *adv.* Again, used in commencing another subject.

SATEMO, サテモ, Exclam. of admiration, surprise.

SATEMO-SATEMO, サテモサテモ, Exclam. (idem.)

†SA-TEN, サテン, 茶 店, *n.* A tea-house.
Syn. CHA-MISE.

SATE-SATE, サテサテ, Exclam. of admiration or surprise.

SATE-WA, セテハ, Exclam. So then!

SATŌ, サトウ, *adv.* Same as *Satoku.*

SATO, サト, 里, *n.* A village, a district of cultivated country smaller than a county; a country place, a brothel.

SATŌ, サタウ, 砂 糖, *n.* Sugar. *Kuro-zatō*, brown sugar. *Shiro-zatō*, white sugar.

SATO-BANARE, サトバナレ, 里 離, *n.* The wild country on the outskirts of a village.

†SATOBI-KOTOBA, サトビコトバ, 俚 語, *n.* The common colloquial language.
Syn. ZOKU-GO.

SATO-BIRAKI, サトビラキ, 歸 寧, *n.* The first visit of a bride to her father's house after marriage.

SATO-DAIRI, サトダイリ, 行 在 所, *n.* The stopping place of the *Tenshi* when away from his home.

SATO-GAYERI, サトガヘリ, 里 歸, *n.* Same as *Sato-biraki.*

SATO-GO, サトゴ, 里 兒, *n.* A child sent away from home to be brought up.

SATOI,-KI, サトイ, 聰, *a.* Intelligent, knowing, clear sighted, quick in discerning or perceiving. Syn. HATSZMEI.

SATO-KATA, サトカタ, 里 方, *n.* The wife's family or relations.

SATŌ-KIBI, サタウキビ, 甘 蔗, *n.* The sorghum, or sugar-cane.

SATOKU, サトク, 聰, *adv.* See *Satoi.*

SATORI,*-ru,-tta*, サトル, 悟, *t.v.* To discern or understand the truth, or nature of any thing; to discover, distinguish, perceive; to quickly divine or see through any thing intricate or obscure. *Mayoi wo satoru*, to see through that in which one was before bewildered. *Yo wo hakanashi to* —, to know that the world is evanescent.

SATORI, サトリ, 悟, *n.* Perception, discernment, understanding of the truth or nature of any thing. — *ga hayai*, of quick discernment. — *ga warui*, slow to perceive. — *wo hiraku*, to enlighten the understanding.

SATOSHI,*-sz,-sh'ta*, サトス, 諭, *t. v.* To make to know, to instruct, teach, to enlighten.
Syn. OSHIYERU, NOMI-KOMASERU.

SATOSHI, セトシ, *a.* Same as *Satoi.*

†SATSZ, サツ, 札, *n.* A bank-note.
Syn. TEGATA.

SATSZ-BATSZ, サツバツ, 殺 伐, Violent, fierce, ferocious, cruel, tyrannical. — *na h'to.*

†SATSZ-H'TO, サツヒト, 薩 人, *n.* A hunter. Syn. KARIUDO.

†SATSZKI, サツキ, 五月, *n.* The fifth month.

SATSZMA-IMO, サツマイモ, 薩 摩 芋, *n.* Sweet potato.

†SATSZ-O, サツヲ, 薩 男, *n.* A hunter.

†SATSZ-RIKU, サツリク, 殺戮, *n.* Slaughter, slaying.

†SATSZ-YA, サツヤ, 薩 箭, *u.* A hunting arrow.

SATTA, サツタ, *pret.* of *Sari.*

SATTE, サツテ, *pp.* of *Sari.*

SATTO, サツト, *adv.* Suddenly, quickly, with a quick motion. — *deru*, to slip out. *Kaze ga — fuku*, a sudden blast of wind.

SATTŌ, サツトウ, 察 當, *n.* Censure, reprimand, reproof, (spoken mostly of government). — *wo kōmuru*, to be reprimanded by government.
Syn. TOGAME.

SAWA, サハ, 澤, *n.* A marsh, swamp.
Syn. NUMA.

†SAWA, サハ, 多, (obs.) Many, numerous.
Syn. TAK'SAN.

SAWA-DACHI,*-tsz,-tta*, サワダツ, 騷 立, *i.v.* To be excited, agitated, to be in a tumult, ferment, commotion; disturbed. *Jin-ki ga sawadatsz*, people's minds were much agitated.

SAWA-GASHI,*-sz,-sh'ta*, サワガス, 騷, caust. of *Sawagu.* To excite, agitate, disturb, throw into tumult or commotion.

Tami wo —, to cause a tumult among the people.

SAWAGASHII,-KI,-SHI, サワガシイ, 騷, *a.* Turbulent, boisterous, tumultuous, noisy, uproarious, disturbed. *Seken ga* —, the world is in an uproar.

SAWAGASHIKU, サワガシク, 騷, *adv.* Idem.

SAWAGASHISA, サワガシサ, 騷, *n.* The noise, disturbance, tumultuousness.

SAWAGI,-*gu*,-*ida*, サワグ, 躁, *i.v.* To be agitated, excited, to make a noise, tumult, disturbance, commotion, or uproar. *Szkoshi mo sawagadz*, without the least agitation.

SAWAGI, サワギ, 躁, *n.* Excitement, commotion, disturbance, uproar, tumult, clamor. — *wo okosz*, to excite a tumult. Syn. SŌDŌ.

SAWAIYE, サハイヘ, (comp. of *Sa*, *wa* and *iye*). *adv.* Nevertheless, still, notwithstanding. Syn. SHIKASHI.

SAWARA, サハラ, 鰆, *n.* The name of a fish.

SAWARA, サハラ, 弱 檜, *n.* A species of fir-tree, the Thujopsis Dolabrata.

SAWARI,-*ru*,-*tta*, サハル, 障, *i.v.* To be hindered, impeded, obstructed, embarrassed; to oppose. *Sawaru koto ga atte kimasen*, being hindered I did not come. Syn. SASAWARU, SAMATAGERU.

SAWARI, サハリ, 障, *n.* Hindrance, impediment, obstruction, interruption, opposition, interference. *Jikō no* —, sickness induced by the climate. — *naku*, without hindrance. Syn. KOSHŌ.

SAWARI,-*ru*,-*tta*, サハル, 觸, *i.v.* To hit, or strike against anything, to clash against, to meddle, to touch, handle. *Te ga* —, to hit the hand against anything. *H'to no ki ni* —, to hurt the feelings of others. Syn. FURERU, ATARU.

SAWARI, セハリ, 月 水, *n.* The menses.

SAWA-SAWA-TO, サワサワト, 爽 爽, *adv.* Clear, pure, the sound of rippling water. — *sh'ta koye*, a clear voice. *Midz ga — nagareru.*

SAWASHI-GAKI, サワシガキ, 醂 柿, *n.* Persimmons treated with *sake* to remove astringency. Syn. TARUGAKI.

SAWATE, サハテ, 澤 手, *n.* Damaged, or stained with water. *Kono ni wa — ga aru*, these goods are damaged with water. — *mono*, damaged goods.

SAWAYAKA, サワヤカ, 爽, Clear, pure, serene, clean, cheerful. — *naru tenki*, clear sky. — *na kokoro*, a cheerful mind. Syn. KIYORAKA, HAKKIRI, SAPPARI.

SAYA, サヤ, 鞘, *n.* A sheath, case, scabbard, husk. *Mame no* —, a bean pod. *Fude no* —, the bamboo case which covers the end of a pencil, a pencil case.

SAYA, サヤ, 綾, *n.* Damask.

SAYA-BASHIRI,-*ru*,-*tta*, サヤバシル, 鞘 走, *i.v.* To fall from the scabbard.

†SAYAGI,-*gu*, サヤグ, 戰, *i.v.* To rustle as the leaves of a tree when shaken by the wind.

SAYAKA-NA, サヤカナ, *a.* Clear, bright, distinct, plain. Syn. HAKKIRI, FUMMIYO.

SAYAKA-NI, サヤカニ, *adv.* Clearly, distinctly, plainly.

SAYAKEKI,-SHI サヤケキ, *a.* Clear, bright, distinct.

SAYAKEKU, サヤケク, *adv.* Clearly, distinctly.

SAYAKESA, サヤケシ, *n.* Clearness, brightness.

†SAYAKU, サヤク, 鎖 鑰, *n.* The out-posts, or defences of a country.

SAYA-MAME, サヤマメ, 莢 豆, *n.* String-beans.

||SAYASHI, サヤシ, *n.* An auction. Syn. SERI.

SAYE, サヘ, *adv.* Even, so much as. *Kuchi de iu saye kirai*, dislike even to speak of it. *Ichi mon — oshimu*, he grudges even a penny. Syn. DANI, DEMO, SZRA.

SAYE,-*ru*,-*ta*, サエル, 沍, *i.v.* To be cold, chilly, to have a clear, cold, or frosty appearance. *Kaze ga* —, the wind is cold. *Shimo ga* —, the frost looks cold. *Sayeta tszki*, a cold moon light.

SAYE,-*ru*,-*ta*, サヘル, 塞, *t.v.* To obstruct, intercept, to stop, hinder, oppose, prevent. Syn. FUSEGU, SASEYERU, SAMATAGERU.

SAYE,-*ru*,-*ta*, サエル, *i.v.* To be clear. bright. *Iro ga* —, the color is bright.

†SAYEDA, サエダ, 小 枝, *n.* The end of a branch, twig.

SAYEDSZRI,-*ru*,-*tta*, サヘヅル, 囀, *i.v.* To twitter, chirp as a flock of birds, to chatter, to prate. Syn. SHABERU.

SAYEGIRI,-*ru*,-*tta*, サヘギル, 遮, *t.v.* To block-up, obstruct, intercept, to hinder, prevent; to be constrained. Syn. HEDATERU, SASAYERU.

SAYE-KAYE,-*ru*,-*ta*, サエカヘル, 沍 返, *i.v.* To become cold again in spring.

†SAYEN, サエン, 菜 園, *n.* A vegetable garden. Syn. HATAKE.

SAYERARE,-*ru*,-*ta*, サヘラレル, 被 塞, Pass. and pot. of *Sayeru*, to be hindered, &c.

SAYE-WATARI,-*ru*,-*tta*, サエワタル, *i. v.* To be clear and free from haze.

†SAYE-ZAYESHII,-KI,-KU, サエザエシイ, *a.* and *adv.* Strong, hale, hearty, well. *On saye-zayeshiku kurashi nasare medetaku zonjisoro.* Syn. SZKOYAKA.

SAYŌ, サヤウ, 左様, (comp. of *sa*, such, and *yō*, like; such like, that kind). *adv.* Yes, just so. — *de gozarimas*, just so, just as you say. — *kana*, indeed! is it possible!

†SAYO-FUKE,-*ru*, サヨフケル, 夜深, *i.v.* Late in the night.

SAYOMI, サヨミ, 柴布, *n.* A coarse kind of hemp cloth.

†SAYONAKA, ザヨナカ, 夜中, *n.* Midnight. Syn. YACHIU.

SAYŌNARA, サヤウナラ, *interj.* A salutation at parting, farewell, good-bye. Syn. SHIKARABA, O-SARABA.

SAYŌ-NARABA, サヤウナラバ, Same as *Sayōnara.*

SAYORI, サヨリ, 細魚, *n.* Belone Gigantea.

SAYU, サユ, 白湯, *n.* Hot water for drinking.

SA-YŪ, ザユウ, 左右, *n.* Left and right.

SAZAN, サザン, *a.* (cont. of *San-zan*), Three times three. — *ga ku*, three times three are nine.

†SAZANAMI, サザナミ, 小浪, *n.* Small waves, ripple.

SAZANK'WA, サザンクワ, 山茶花, *n.* A species of Camelia.

†SAZAREISHI, サザレイシ, 小石, *n.* Gravel, small pebbles. Syn. JARI.

SAZAYE, サザエ, 栄螺, *n.* A shell, species of Murex.

SAZEN, サゼン, 作善, *(zen wo nasz). n.* Doing good. — *no mukui*, the reward of good works. Bud.

SAZO, サゾ, 嘸, *adv.* (comp. of *sa*, so, and *zo*, emphatic), The case being so, then, referring to something before. *Sazo ureshikarō*, how happy he must be! — *samishi karō*, you must be very lonely. — *kurō darō*, she must be in great trouble. — *itakarō*, it must be very painful. Syn. SAMO.

SAZOYA, サゾヤ, *adv.* idem.

SE, セ, 瀬, *n.* Rapids, a swift-current

SE, セ, 畝, *n.* A land measure, = thirty *tszbo*, = 1,080 sq. feet. *To-se ittan*, ten *se* make one *tan.*

SE, セ, 背, *n.* The back. — *ga kagamu*, back is bent. Syn. SENAKA.

SE, セ, 世, *n.* cont. of *Sei.* The world, present state of existence. *Kon se*, this world. *Rai se*, next world. Syn. YO.

†SE, セ, 兄, *n.* Elder-brother. Syn. ANI.

SE, セ, 為, imp. of *Szru.* Do. *Hayaku se yo*, do it quick. *Sō se*, do so. Syn. ITASE, NASARE.

SEBA, セバ, cont. of *Szreba*, subj. mood of *szru.*

SEBAI,-KI,-KU, セバイ, *a.* See *Semai.*

SEBAME,-*ru*,-*ta*, セバメル, 狭, *t. v.* To make narrow, to reduce in extent or size, to contract the dimensions of any thing. Syn. SEMAKU SZRU, TSZMERU.

SEBONE, セボネ, 背骨, *n.* The back-bone, spine. Syn. SEKIDZI.

SE-BUMI, セブミ, 瀬踏, *n.* Wading into a current to try its depth; fig. trying anything in order to find out. — *wo szru.*

SEBURI,-*ru*,-*tta*, セブル, *t.v.* To tease and extort by frequent demands. *Dōraku muszko ga haha wo sebutte kane wo toru*, a dissolute son teases and extorts money from his mother.

†SECHI, セチ, 切, Earnest, deep, vehement. — *naru kokoro*, a heart bent on, or feeling intensely about, anything. — *ni omō*, to think deeply about.

SECHI-GASH'KOI,-KI,-KU, セチガシコイ, 狡獪, *a.* Cunning, artful, crafty. Syn. SARUGASH'KOI.

†SECHIYE, セチヱ, 節會, *n.* A banquet, or entertainment given by the *Tenshi* to the *Kuge*, when they assemble to congratulate him on certain feast days. — *wo szru.*

SEDEWA, セデハ, cont. of *Sedzte wa*, same as *Seneba*, the neg. sub. of *Szru. Sedewa naranu*, must do.

SEGAKI, セガキ, 施餓鬼, *n.* The ceremony of feeding the hungry spirits. — *wo szru.*

‖SEGAMI,-*mu*,-*nda*, セガム, *t.v.* To tease, worry, vex. Syn. IJIMERU.

SEGARE, ヨガレ, 賤息, *n.* Son, (in speaking of one's own son to others, humble language).

†SE-GIYŌ, セギヤウ, 施行, *(hodokoshi okonō). n.* Giving alms. — *wo szru*, to give alms.

†SEI, セイ, 星, *(hoshi). n.* A star.

SEI, セイ, 姓, *(kabane). n.* This word originally designated the name of the rank, or social station, into which Japanese society was anciently divided; it has now lost this peculiarity owing to changes made by time; it differs from

Uji in that those who bear the same *Sei* have not necessarily any blood relation. It is sometimes erroneously used for *Uji*, family name.

†SEI, セイ, 生, *(ikiru)*. *n*. Life. *Shi sei mei-ari*, death and life are fixed by providence.

SEI, セイ, 丈, *(take)*. *n*. Stature. — *no ta-kai h'to*, a tall man. — *no hikui h'to*, a person of short stature.

SEI, セイ, 聲, *(koye)*. *n*. Voice; numeral for sounds. *Tai sei*, a loud voice. *Issei no teppō*, one report of a gun.

SEI, セイ, 勢, *(ikioi)*. *n*. Strength, force, energy, vigor, ability; power, authority, influence; an army. *Kuszri no sei ga tszyoi*, the medicine is strong. — *ga tszki-ru*, strength is exhausted. — *wo dasz*, to put forth one's strength. *Teki no* —, the enemy's army. — *ga tszku*, to be invigorated. — *ippai ni*, with all one's ability. — *no yowai h'to*, a person of no vigor.

SEI, セイ, 精, *n*, The semen. — *wo mora-sz*, to have seminal emissions.

†SEI, セイ, 性, *(umaretszki)*. *n*. Natural disposition; nature, essential quality of any thing. *H'to no — wa zen nari*, man's natural disposition is good. — *wo kayeru*, to change one's nature.
Syn. SHŌ.

†SEI, セイ, 制, *n*. Command, order, instructions. *Yokokama no bugiyō wa gorojū no sei wo ukeru*, the governor of *Yokohama* receives his instructions from the *Gorujū*.
Syn. SASHIDZ, GEJI.

†SEI, セイ, 製, *(koshiraye)*. *n*. The form, fashion, or mode in which any thing is made. *Kimono no* —, the fashion of clothes.

†SEI, セイ, 政, *(matszrigoto)*. *n*. Rule, government, administration of the laws. *Zen sei*, good government. *G'yaku* —, bad government.

†SEI, セイ, 正, *(tadashiki)*. *n*. Correct, straight, right; just. *Ja sei*, wrong and right.

SEI, セヰ, 所爲, *(nasz tokoro)*. *n*. Cause, reason, effect, consequence. *Ame no futta sei de michi ga warui*, the roads are bad by reason of the rain. *Nan no sei de kaze wo hikimash'ta*, what is the cause of your cold? *Cha wo nonda sei nemurarenu*, your not being able to sleep was the effect of drinking tea. *Sake no sei de bimbō sh'ta*, became poor through drink. Syn. YUYE, WAZA, WAKE.

SEI-BAI, セイバイ, 成敗, *n*. Punishment of crime. — *szru*, to punish crime. *Sei-bai-shiki-moku*, criminal code.
Syn, KEI-BATSZ.

SEI-BATSZ, セイバツ, 征伐, *n*. Punishment of the rebellion or disobedience of a tributary by war. — *szru*.

SEI-BO, セイボ, 歳暮, *(toshi no kure)*. *n*. End of the year. Syn. SAI-MATSZ.

SEI-BUN, セイブン, 精分, *n*. Strength, vigor of body. — *ga nuketa*, lost his strength. — *no tszku kuszri*, strengthening medicine. Syn. CHIKARA.

†SEI-CHIU, セイチウ, 誠忠, *n*. True loyalty, pure patriotism, or fidelity to a master.

SEI-CHŌ, セイチヤウ, 成長, *(okiku naru)*. *n*. Full grown, full size. — *szru*, to be full grown.

†SEI-CHOKU, セイチヨク, 正直, Honest, upright, just.

†SEI-DAKU, セイダク, 清濁, *(szmu nigo-ru)*. Pure and impure, clear or turbid, clean or foul.

SEI-DASHI,-*sz*,-*sh'ta*, セイダス, 出精, *i.v*. To put forth strength, to exert one's self. *Seidash'te shigoto wo szru*, to work with all the might.

SEI-DŌ, セイダウ, 政道, *(matszrigoto no michi)*. *n*. System, or form of government, the government.

SEI-DO, セイド, 政度, *n*. Idem.

SEI-DŌ, セイダウ, 聖堂, *n*. A temple of Confucius.

SEI-DŌ, セイダウ, 青銅, *(aoki akagane)*. *n*. Green copper,—copper that has turned green from rust.

SEI-FU, セイフ, 政府, *n*. The place where the Council of State meets,—the Council chamber, (per met.) the council of state itself, or the *Shōgun's* government.

SEIGIRI, セイギリ, *adv*. The extreme price. — *ichi riyō made kaimashō*, I will not give more than one *riyō* for it. — *ichi riyō made ni makemashō*, I will not take less than one *riyō*. — *ikura made ni makemas*, what is the very lowest you will take for it?

SEIGŌ, セイガウ, 精好, *n*. A kind of silk stuff.

SEI-GON, セイゴン, 誓言, *n*. An oath. — *wo tateru*, to take an oath. Syn. CHIKAI.

SEI-G'WAN, セイグワン, 誓願, *n*. Swearing to accomplish one's desire, a vow, (spoken generally of *Hotoke*).

†SEI-HEI, セイヘイ, 精兵, *n*. Picked soldiers.

†SEI-HITSZ, セイヒツ, 靜謐, *n*. A state of peace, freedom from war.

SEI-HŌ, セイハウ, 製法, *(koshiraye kata)*.

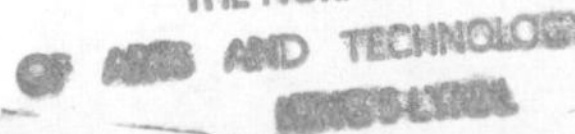

n. The way of making any thing, the composition, recipe, formula. *Kono kuszri no — ga shirenu*, I don't know how this medicine was made. *Seihō-sho*, a receipt book.

†SEI-HŌ, セイハウ, 西方, *n.* The west.

SEI-HON-YA, セイホンヤ, 製本屋, *n.* A book-bindery, a book-binder.

SEI-IKU, セイイク, 生育, *n.* Bringing up a child, including feeding, clothing, instruction, &c. *Kodomo wo — szru*, to bring up a child. Syn. SODATERU.

SEI-JI, セイジ, 政事, (*matszrigoto*). *n.* The government, administration of public affairs, constitution or system of government.

SEI-JI, セイジ, 青磁, *n.* Green porcelain.

SEI-JIN, セイジン, 聖人, *n.* A sage, spoken generally of Confucius, or of Giyō and Sun, the ancient emperors of China.

SEI-JIN, セイジン, 成人, (*h'to to naru*). *n.* A full grown person. *— szru*, to be grown up.

†SEI-JITSZ, セイジツ, 誠實, *n.* True, not false.

†SEI-JITSZ, セイジツ, 生日, (*umarebi*). *n.* Birth day. Syn. TANJŌBI.

†SEI-KEN, セイケン, 聖賢, *n.* Sage and philosopher, used generally of Confucius and Mencius.

SEI-KETSZ, セイケツ, 清潔, (*kiyoku isagiyoki*). Clean, pure, free from all impurity, just, upright, honest. *— na midz*, pure water.

†SEI-KETSZ, セイケツ, 精血, *n.* Pure, or healthy blood. *— wo toru*, to bleed, take blood.

SEI-KI, セイキ, 精氣, *n.* Essence, active principle, the strength. *Sake no — wo shō-chiu to iu*, the active principle of *sake* is called alcohol.

†SEI-KI, セイキ, 旌旗, *n.* A flag. Syn. HATA.

SEI-KIN, セイキン, 精勤, Attending diligently to one's official duties. *— szru*, actively to discharge one's duties.

SEI-KIN, セイキン, 制禁, *n.* Prohibition, interdict. *— szru*, to prohibit, forbid. Syn. GOHATTO, KINZEI.

SEI-KIU, セイキフ, 性急, Impetuous temper, hasty in disposition; impatient. *— na h'to.*

SEI-KIYO, セイキヨ, 逝去, Leaving the world, decease. *— szru*, to die.

†SEI-KON, セイコン, 精魂, *n.* The soul, spirit, ghost. Syn. TAMASHII.

†SEI-KON, セイコン, 精根, *n.* Strength, vigor, energy either of body or mind. Syn. KONKI.

SEI-MEI, セイメイ, 姓名, *n.* Name, including the family and surname. *Go seimei wa nan to mōshimas*, what is your surname?

†SEI-MEI, セイメイ, 性命, (*inochi*). *n.* Life.

†SEI-MEI, セイメイ, 清明, *n.* The name of one of the periods into which spring is divided, commencing with the third month.

†SEI-MITSZ, セイミツ, 細密, Same as *Saimitsz.*

SEI-MIYŌ, セイメウ, 精妙, Exquisite, most excellent, remarkably fine. *— na saiku*, exquisite workmanship.

SEI-MON, セイモン, 誓文, *n.* A writing confirmed with an oath, written agreement sealed with blood.

SEI-MU, セイム, 政務, *n.* Official or government duties. *— ga isogashii*, hurried with government business.

SEI-RIKI, セイリキ, 勢力, *n.* Strength, power, force. *Uma no —*, the strength of the horse. Syn. CHIKARA.

†SEI-RIU, セイリウ, 清流, (*kiyoki nagare*). *n.* A clear stream.

†SEI-RIYAKU,*–szru*, セイリヤク, 省略, To abridge, to lessen, diminish, curtail. Syn. HABUKU.

†SEI-RIYOKU, セイリヨク, 精力, *n.* Strength, vigor.

SEI-RIYŌ-ZAI, セイリヤウザイ, 清涼劑, *n.* A medicine used in the treatment of fever, a febrifuge. Syn. NETSZ-SAMASHI.

SEIRŌ, セイロウ, 蒸籠, *n.* A vessel for cooking with steam.

SEI-RŌ, セイロウ, 井樓, *n.* A fortress constructed with timbers laid one over the other; a block-house.

†SEI-RŌ, セイロウ, 青樓, *n.* A prostitute house. Syn. JŌRO-YA.

†SEI-RO, セイロ, 世路, (*yo no michi*). *n.* The world, its pleasures and honors. *Ash'ta ni kō-gan atte sei-ro ni hokoru, yube ni hakkotsz to natte ya gwai ni kutszru*, in the morning beautiful and puffed up with the world; in the evening bones rotting on the moor.

†SEI-ROKU, セイロク, 世祿, *n.* An annual income, or stipend received from government and continued to a family from generation to generation.

SEI-SAI, セイサイ, 正載, *adv.* At the most, at the highest, farthest. *— hiyaku riyō gurai na mono*, at the most not worth over a hundred *riyō*. *— hachi ri gurai*, at

the farthest about eight miles.
Syn. TSZMARI.

SEI-SAKU, セイサク, 製作, *n.* Construction, make, structure, way of making. *Kono iye no — ga warui*, this house is badly built. — *szru*, to construct, build, make. Syn. TSZKURI.

†SEISAN, セイサン, 生產, *n.* Occupation, means.

†SEI-SAN, セイサン, 清算, Accurately calculated, fully summed up.

SEI-SATSZ, セイサツ, 制札, *n.* The boards on which the laws are written and hung up. Syn. KŌ-SATSZ.

SEI-SHI, セイシ, 制止, To stop, prevent, forbid, prohibit. — *szru.*
Syn. KINDZRU.

SEI-SHI, セイシ, 誓紙, *n.* A paper or writing sworn to; a written promise, or agreement sealed with one's blood.

†SEI-SHI, セイシ, 世子, *n.* The heir of a noble.

SEI-SHI,*-szru,-sh'ta*, セイスル, 製, *t.v.* To make, manufacture. *Hon, hako, katana, fude, szmi, tansz nado wo —*, to make a book, box, sword, pencil, ink, bureau, &c. *Momen wo sei-sh'te kami wo koshiraye*, to work up muslin and make it into paper.
Syn. KOSHIRAYERU, TSZKURU.

SEI-SHI,*-szru,-sh'ta*, セイスル, 征, *t.v.* To reduce to obedience, to punish rebellion.
Syn. SEIBATSZ SZRU.

SEI-SHI,*-szru,-sh'ta*, セイスル, 制, *t.v.* To stop, forbid, prevent prohibit to control, govern.
Syn. KINDZRU, SEISHI SZRU.

†SEI-SHIN, セイシン, 星辰, *n.* A star.
Syn. HOSHI.

SEI-SHIN, セイシン, 精神, *n.* Mental or physical power, vigor, energy, life, vital power. — *ga otoroyeru*, vital power is failing. — *wo korasz*, to concentrate the mind on anything. Syn. KIRIYOKU, KONKI, SEIKON.

SEI-SHITSZ, セイシツ, 青漆, *(ao urushi)*, *n.* Green lacquer.

SEI-SHITSZ, セイシツ, 性質, *(umare-tszki)*, *n.* Nature, constitution, temperament, natural disposition, temper. *Ano h'to no — wa tanki.* he is of an irascible nature.
Syn. SHŌ.

SEI-SHO, セイショ, 清書, *(kiyogaki)*, *n.* A clean writing, or finished copy.

†SEI-SHOKU, セイショク, 聲色, Behavior, manners, deportment.

†SEI-SHUKU, セイシュク, 星宿, *n.* Stars, constellations.

†SEI-SŌ, セイサウ, 星霜, *n.* Time. — *wo hetaru iye*, an old house.
Syn. TOSHI-TSZKI.

†SEI-SŌ, セイソウ, 清僧, *n.* A pure or holy priest.

†SEI-SZI, セイスイ, 清水, *(kiyoki midz)*. *n.* Pure or clear water.

SEI-SZI, セイスイ, 盛衰, *(sakan-naru otoroyeru)*. *n.* Flourish and decay, rise and fall, prosperity and adversity. *Yo no —*, the vicissitudes of life.

SEITA, セイタ, pret. of *Seki.*

†SEI-TAI, セイタイ, 世態, *(yo no arisama)*. *n.* The world, — its fashions and manners.

SEITE, セイテ, *pp.* of *Seki.*

SEI-TEN, セイテン, 晴天, *n.* Clear weather, unclouded sky.

SEI-TŌ, セイトウ, 青銅, *n.* A name given to copper cash. Syn. ZENI.

SEI-YAKU, セイヤク, 製藥, *(kuszri wo koshirayeru)*. *n.* Manufacturing, or compounding medicines. — *szru*, to make medicines.

†SEI-YŌ, セイヤウ, 西洋, *n.* Western countries.

†SEI-YŌ, セイヤウ, 青陽, *n.* Spring.
Syn. HARU.

SEI-ZŌ,*-szru*, セイザウ, 製造, *t. v.* To make, manufacture.
Syn. KOSHIRAYERU, SEI-SZRU.

SEI-ZOROYE, セイゾロへ, 勢揃, *n.* Mustering or parading an army. — *wo szru.*

SEJI, セジ, 世事, *(yo no koto)*. *n.* The world, — its business, customs, cares, &c. Civility, courtesy, politeness. — *wo mendōgaru*, to be tired of the world. — *ni karamaru*, to be absorbed in the world. — *wo iu*, to talk courteously. — *no yoi h'to*, an affable, courteous man. Syn. AISŌ.

†SEJIN, セジン, 世人, *(yo no h'to)*. *n.* People, men, mankind. — *mina kane wo konomu*, everybody loves money.

†SE-JŌ, セジヤウ, 世上, *n.* The world, same as *Seken.*

SE-KAI, セカイ, 世界, *n.* The earth, the world, the globe.

SEKASE,*-ru,-ta*, セカセル, 令急, caust. of *Seki.* To hurry another, to get another to hurry.

SEKA-SEKA, セカセカ, 急急, *adv.* Impetuous, driving, pushing, hasty. *Ki no — sh'ta h'to.*

SEKATSZKI,*-ku,-ita*, セカツク, *i. v.* To be impetuous, driving, or always in a hurry.

SEKEN, セケン, 世間, *(yo no naka)*. *n.*

The world, — its people, pleasures, manners, &c.; secular life. —*no h'to*, mankind, people. — *wo hanareru*, to leave the world, to enter on a religious life. — *ga sawagashiku*, the whole country is in an uproar. — *ni oru*, to live in the world, or in secular life. — *ittō*, the whole world, *i.e.* all countries. — *shiradz*, ignorant of the world. — *de hiyōban szru*, to be a public report. — *wo haru*, to make a show, or ostentatious display. — *wo itowadz*, not caring for the world.

SEKEN-TEI, セケンテイ, 世間體, *n.* The light or estimation in which anything is regarded by the world. *Sore de wa — ga warui*, if you do so people will laugh at you.

SEKI, セキ, 咳, *n.* A cough. — *ga deru*, to cough. — *ga demasz ka*, have you a cough?

SEKI,-*ku*,-*ita*, セク, 咳, *t.v.* To cough. *Seite nerare masen*, I could not sleep for coughing. *Seki wo* —, to cough. *Tan wo seki-dasz*, to cough up phlegm. *Tan wo seki-kiru*, to hawk up phlegm.

SEKI,-*ku*,-*ita*, セク, 急, *t. v.* To hurry, to make haste, to urge, drive. *Shigoto wo seku*, to hurry on work. *Michi wo* —, to make haste in traveling. *Seite aruku*, to walk in a hurry. *Shokunin wo* —, to hurry up workmen.
Syn. ISOGU, SAISOKU SZRU, SERI.

SEKI, セキ, 席, *n.* A mat, a seat or place where one sits; a room; a place of meeting; an assembly or meeting, rank. — *wo shiku*, to spread a mat. — *wo mōkeru*, to arrange the seats. — *wo tatsz*, to rise up from one's seat. *Daimiyō no kakushiki wa — de sadamaru*, a daimiyo's rank is determined by the room (in the palace) in which he sits.

SEKI, セキ, 關, *n.* A guard house and gate, or barrier, where travelers are stopped and passports examined, a pass.

SEKI, セキ, 夕, *n.* Evening, night. *Kon seki*, this night. *Chō* —, morning and evening.
Syn. YŪBE.

SEKI,-*ku*,-*ita*, セク, 堰, *t. v.* To stop a stream of water by a bank of earth, &c., to dam. *Kawa wo* —, to dam up a river. *Namida wo seki-ayenu*, could not restrain the tears.

†SEKI-AKU, セキアク, 積惡, Accumulated wickedness, one wickedness added to another. — *no tszmi nogare-gataku*.

†SEKI-BAKU, セキバク, 寂莫, Lonely, solitary, retired. Syn. SAMUSHII.

SEKI-BAN, セキバン, 石版, *n.* The stone used for lithographing.

SEKI-BARAI, セキバライ, 咳掃, *n.* Clearing the throat. — *wo szru*, to cough and clear the throat.

SEKI-CHIKU, セキチク, 石竹, *n.* The pink (flower). Syn. NADE-SHIKO.

SEKIDA, セキダ, 雪踏, *n.* Sandals with iron heels fastened to the sole.

SEKI-DAI, セキダイ, 石臺, *n.* A flower-pot.

SEKI-DAN, セキダン, 石壇, *n.* Stone-step.

SEKI-DŌ, セキダウ, 赤道, *n.* The equator.

†SEKI-DOKU, セキドク, 尺牘, *n.* A letter, epistle. Syn. TEGAMI.

†SEKIDZI, セキズイ, 脊髓, *n.* The spinal marrow.

SEKI-FUDA, セキフダ, *n.* The sign-board placed before the door of the hotel where a Daimiyo is stopping.

SEKI-GAKI, セキガキ, 席書, *n.* Specimens of penmanship written by pupils for examination.

†SEKI-GAKU, セキガク, 碩學, *n.* Great learning. — *no h'to*, a man of great learning.

SEKI-HAN, セキハン, 赤飯, *n.* A kind of food made of red-beans and rice, eaten on fete days.

SEKI-HI, セキヒ, 石碑, *n.* A stone monument. Syn. SEKITŌ.

SEKI-HITSZ, セキヒツ, 石筆, *n.* A lead-pencil.

†SEKI-IN, セキイン, 石印, *n.* A stone seal.

SEKI-IRE,-*ru*,-*ta*, セキイレル, 堰入, *t. v.* To dam-up a stream and conduct it into another channel. *Midz wo hori ni seki-ireru*, to dam-up water and conduct it into a channel.

†SEKI-JITSZ, セキジツ, 昔日, (*mukashi no hi*), *n.* Former, past, ancient.

SEKI-JŌ, セキジヤウ, 席上, In the room, or hall where a meeting for any purpose is held; during, or in the meeting, or assembly.

SEKI-JUN, セキジユン, 席順, Order of sitting. — *ni sakadzki wo mawasz*, to pass the wine-cup around in the order of the seats.

SEKI-KAYESHI,-*sz*,-*sh'ta*, セキカヘス, 堰反, *t.v.* To dam, or obstruct a stream and cause the the water to set back.

SEKI-KOMI,-*mu*,-*nda*, セキコム, 急込, *t.v.* To be out of breath with haste.

SEKI-KOMI,-*mu*,-*nda*, セキコム, 堰込, To confine by damming up.

SEKI-MEN, セキメン, 赤面, *n.* Reddening of the face from shame, diffidence, &c. blushing. — *szru,* to blush.

SEKI-MORI, セキモリ, 關守, *n.* The guard, or officers who are stationed at a barrier.

†SEKI-NEN, セキネン, 昔年, *n.* Former years, years gone by.
Syn. MUKASHI.

†SEKI-NEN, セキネン, 積念, (*tszmoru omoi*), *n.* Brooding over, or thinking about anything for a long time. — *wo sandzru,* to dispel such feelings.

SEKI-REI, セキレイ, 鶺鴒, A species of wagtail.

†SEKI-RIN, セキリン, 石淋, *n.* Stone in the bladder, calculus.

†SEKI-RIYŌ, セキレウ, 寂寥, Lonely, solitary, retired. Syn. SEKI-BAKU.

SEKI-SAI, セキサイ, 釋菜, *n.* Sacrificing to Confucius, festival in honor of Confucius.

†SEKI-SHI, セキシ, 赤子, (*akago*), *n.* An infant, newly born child. Syn. AKAMBŌ.

†SEKI-SHIN, セキシン, 赤心, *n.* True, sincere, honest. — *de kami wo haiszru,* to worship God with a sincere heart.

†SEKI-SHITSZ, セキシツ, 石室, (*iwa muro*), *n.* A cave.

SEKI-SHO, セキシヨ, 關所, *n.* Same as *Seki.* A barrier, pass. — *yaburi,* passing a barrier without a passport.

SEKI-SHŌ, セキシヤウ, 石菖, *n.* A kind of flag, (Acorus).

SEKI-SHO-FUDA, セキシヨフダ, 關所札, *n.* A passport.

SEKI-SHOKU, セキシヨク, 赤色, (*akai iro*), *n.* Red color.

†SEKI-SO, セキソ, 尺素, *n.* A letter, epistle. Syn. TEGAMI.

†SEKI-SZN, セキスン, 尺寸, *n.* (Foot, or inch). — *mo tagawadz,* not the least difference.

†SEKI-TEN, セキテン, 釋奠, Same as *Sekisai.*

SEKI-TŌ, セキタフ, 石塔, *n.* A tomb-stone, monument over a grave.

SEKI-TOME, *-ru, -ta,* セキトメル, 堰止, *t.v.* To dam, bar, obstruct, hinder, or prevent the passing, or flow of any thing. *Kawa no midz wo* —, to dam up the water of a river. *Michi ni h'to wo* —, to stop people from passing through a road.

SEKI-TORI, セキトリ, 關取, *n.* The champion, or best of wrestlers.

†SEKI-UTSZ, セキウツ, 積鬱, *n.* Long continued melancholy, despondency, or gloom. — *wo sandzru.* to dispel a settled gloom.

†SEKI-YŌ, セキヤウ, 夕陽, *n.* Setting sun. Syn. IRI-HI.

†SEKI-ZEN, セキゼン, 積善, *n.* Accumulation of virtuous deeds.

SEKI-ZŌ, セキザウ, 石像, *n.* A stone image of a man, a stone idol.

SEKI-ZORO, セキゾロ, 節季, *n.* The singing and dancing of common beggars, at the end of the year, from house to house for money.

SEKKACHI, セツカチ, An impetuous, hasty, hurrying person.

SEKKAI, セツカイ, 刷匙, *n.* A kind of wooden paddle straight on one edge.

SEKKAKU, セツカク, 折角, *adv.* (*tszno wo oru,* to break the horns) Especial pains, much care, much trouble, (but in vain). — *kita no ni riyōji wo sh'te morawanu koto ga zannen,* having taken so much trouble to come, I am disappointed in not receiving medical treatment. — *no honeori ga muda ni natta,* all my trouble has been for nothing. — *oide no tokoro rusz nite okinodoku,* I am very sorry that I was absent, after you took so much trouble to come. — *on itoi nazaru beku soro,* be careful of yourself.

SEKKAN, *-szru,* セツカン, 折檻, *t.v.* To punish, chastise, correct, reprimand.
Syn. SEMERU, KORASZ.

†SEKKAN, *-szru,* セツカン, 切諫, To reprove one's lord with severity.
Syn. ISAMERU.

†SEKKEN, セツケン, 節儉, Economy. — *na h'to,* economical person.
Syn. KENYAKU, TSZDZMAYAKA.

SEKKEN, セツケン, 石鹼, *n.* Soap.
Syn. SHABON.

SEKKI, セツキ, 節季, (*toshi no kure*), *n.* The end of the year.

SEKKŌ, セキカウ, 石膏, *n.* Gypsum, or Sulphate of Lime.

SEKKOKU, セキコク, 石斛, *n.* An orchis.

SEKKU, セツク, 節供, *n.* Certain holidays, as, the 7th day of the 1st month; the 3rd day of the 3rd month; 5th day of the 5th month; 7th day of the 7th month; and 9th day of the 9th month.

SEKK'WAISZI, セツクワイスイ, 石灰水, *n.* Lime-water.

SEKO, セコ, 列卒, *n.* Persons who beat the bush in hunting.

SEKU, セク, See *Seki.*

†SEMAHOSHII, -KI, -KU, セマホシク, (comp. of *Sen,* to do, and *hoshii.*) Desire to do.

SEMAI, -KI, セマイ, 狹, *a.* Narrow, not wide or broad, of little extent, contracted, small. *Semai michi*, a narrow road. — *iye*, a small house. — *kokoro*, narrow minded.

SEMAI, セマイ, (cont. of *Szru-mai*). Will not do, will not be.

SEMAJI,–KI,–KU, セマジ, The same as above.

SEMAKU, セマク, 狹, *adv.* Narrow, not wide, not extensive or large.

SEMARI,–*ru*,–*tta*, セマル, 迫, *i.v.* To be pressed, straitened, confined, constricted, to be ill used, persecuted. *Mune ga semaru*, to have constriction of chest. *H'to ni* —, to be ill used by others. *Shin ni* —, to be almost like the genuine article.

SEMASHI, セマシ, 狹, *a.* See *Semai.*

SEM-BAN, センバン, 千萬, (lit. a thousand myriads). *adv.* Exceedingly, very much, (used only in expressing thanks). — *katajikenai*, exceedingly obliged. *Kinodoku* —, very sorry. *Go-kurō* —, many thanks for your trouble.

SEM-BAN, センバン, 前晚, (*maye no yo*). Former, or previous evening.

†SEM-BATSZ,–*szru*, センバツ, 戰伐, To make war with and punish.
Syn. SEIBATSZ.

SEM-BEI, センベイ, 煎餅, *n.* A kind of cracknel.

†SEM-BEN-BAN-K'WA, センベンバンクワ, 千變萬化, A thousand myriads, or, a great many ways, forms, or changes.

SEM-BETSZ, センベツ, 餞別, *n.* A parting present. — *szru*, to give a farewell dinner.
Syn. HANA MUKE

SEM-BŌ, センボウ, 先鋒, *n.* The van of an army. Syn. SAKITE.

SEMBURI, センブリ, 胡黃連, *n.* The pleurogyne rotata.

SEME,–*ru*,–*ta*, セメル, 攻, *t.v.* To attack, assault, to fight with, to charge. *Teki wo* —, to attack the enemy. *Shiro wo* —, to besiege a castle.
Syn. UTSZ.

SAME,–*ru*,–*ta*, セメル, 責, *t.v.* To torture, torment, to punish, to harass, vex, to persecute, scold, to afflict. *Tszmi-bito wo semete hakujō saseru*, to torture a criminal and make him confess. *Kokoro no oni ga mi wo* —, the devil in the heart torments a person.

SEME, セメ, 攻, *n.* An attack, assault, a charge.

SEME, セメ, 責, *n.* Torture, punishment, torment. *Midz-zeme*, water torture. — *wo ukeru*, to be tortured. *Jigoku no* —, the torments of hell.

SEME, セメ, 頭緒, *n.* A clasp, a band, (as for a fan, umbrella.)

SEME-AGUMI,–*mu*,–*nda*, セメアグム, 攻倦, *i.v.* To be tired, or disgusted with attacking, besieging, or torturing.

SEME-AI,–*au*,–*atta*, セメアフ, 攻合, *i.v.* To attack each other.

SEME-DASHI,–*sz*,–*sh'ta*, セメダス, 責出, *t.v.* To afflict and expel. *Mamako wo* —, to drive away a stepchild by cruel treatment.

SEME-DŌGU, セメダウグ, 責道具, *n.* Instruments of torture or punishment.

SEME-FUSE,–*ru*,–*ta*, セメフセル, 攻伏, *t.v.* To attack and reduce, or bring into subjection.

SEME-GI, セメギ, 責木, *n.* A wedge.

†SEMEGI,–*gu*,–*ida*, セメグ, 鬩, *t.v.* To quarrel, wrangle, dispute.
Syn. ISAKAI, ARASOI.

SEME-GUCHI, セメグチ, 攻口, *n.* The point of attack, a breach.

SEME-HATARI,–*ru*,–*tta*, セメハタル, 責虐, *t.v.* To treat cruelly, oppress, harass, vex.

SEME-IRI,–*ru*,–*tta*, セメイル, 攻入, *i.v.* To attack and enter.

SEME-NOBORI,–*ru*,–*tta*, セメノボル, 攻上, *t.v.* To go up to attack, (spec. of *Kiyoto.*)

SEMENSHĪNA, セメンシイナ, *n.* The cemencinæ, or wormseed.

SEME-OTOSHI,–*sz*,–*sh'ta*, セメオトス, 攻落, *t.v.* To take by storm, take by assault.

SEMETE, セメテ, *adv.* At least. *Mina dekineba semete ham-bun demo kayese*, if you can't pay it all, pay at least a half. — *moto-dake demo tori-tai mono*, I would like to get back at least the original outlay.

SEME-TOI,–*ō*,–*ōta*, セメトフ, 責問, *t.v.* To examine by torture, to annoy by persistent inquiry.

SEME-TORI,–*ru*,–*tta*, セメトル, 攻取, *t.v.* To attack and seize, to take by assault.

SEME-YOSE,–*ru*,–*ta*, セメヨセル, 攻寄, *t.v.* To approach in order to attack, to charge.

SEMI, セミ, 蟬, *n.* Cicada, or locusts. — *no nukegara*, the cast off shell of a locust.

SEMMEN, センメン, 扇面, *n.* The surface of a fan.

†SEM-MIYŌ, センミヤウ, 宣命, *n.* Command of the *Tenshi.* — *wo kudasz.*

SEMMON, センモン, 專門, *n.* Special or particular object of pursuit or study, speciality. *Ano h'to no semmon wa temmon*, astronomy is his speciality. — *no giyo*, special object of pursuit.

SEMŌ, セマウ, 狹, *adv.* Same as *Semaku.*

SE-MOTSZ, セモツ, 施物, *n.* Alms, or contributions to Bud. priests.

†SEM-PAI, センパイ, 先輩, *n.* Those who came before, or preceded, predecessors.

SEM-PAN, センパン, 先般, *adv.* Before, previously, some time ago. — *ohanashi mōsh'ta koto wa ikaga,* how about the matter I spoke to you of some time ago. Syn. SENDATTE.

SEM-PI, センピ, 先非, (*maye no ashiki koto*). Former errors or transgressions. — *wo kuyuru,* to repent of former errors. — *wo kō-k'wai szru,* idem.

SEM-PŌ, センポウ, 先方, (*saki kata*). *n.* The other party or person.

SEMPUKUGE, センプクゲ, 旋覆花, *n.* The Inula japonica.

SEMURU, セムル, See *Seme.*

SEMUSHI, セムシ, 瘻, *n.* Humpback. also 傴人, a humpbacked person.

SEN, セン, 千, *n.* A thousand. *Issen,* one thousand.

SEN, セン, 栓, *n.* A wooden or metal pin passed through a hole, to fasten anything. — *wo sasz.* — *de tomeru.*

SEN, セン, 先, First, previous, former, before. — *no tszma,* former wife. — *ni hanashita koto,* the subject mentioned before. *Omaye yori watakushi ga sen da,* I am before you. — *wo toru,* to draw the first move (as in playing chess). Syn. SAKI.

SEN, セン, 詮, *n.* Profit, advantage, use. — *mo nai,* useless. — *naki-koto,* useless thing. Syn. KAI, YEKI.

SEN, セン, 錢, (*zeni*). *n.* Small copper coin.

SEN, セン, 仙, *n.* A sort of imaginary beings, who live amongst the mountains; genii, fairy. — *ni naru,* to become a genius.

SEN, ヤン, 專, (*moppara*). Chief, principal, most important. — *to szru,* to regard as the chief thing.

SEN, セン, 鏟, *n.* A drawing-knife, used by coopers.

SEN, セン, 爲, (the fut. or dubitative form of *shi, szru,* same as *shō,* of the coll). *Ikani sen,* what shall I do? *Nani to sen,* idem. *Sen kata nashi,* nothing can be done, no resource, no help for it.

SEN, セン, 令, a cont. of *Shimen,* the fut. of *Shimeru,* suffixed to the roots of verbs; a future causative. *Misen,* from *Mishimeru,* or *Miseru,* will show. *Kikasen,* from *Kikashimeru,* or *Kikaseru,* will cause to hear, will inform.

SEN, セン, a cont. of *senu,* a neg. suffix, as, *Shirimasen,* don't know. *Wakari-masen,* don't understand.

SENA, セナ, A contraction of *Senaka,* the back.

SENAKA, セナカ, 脊, *n.* The back. — *bone,* the spine, back-bone. Syn. SOBIRA.

SEN-CHA, センチヤ, 煎茶, *n.* Infusion of tea-leaves, tea.

†SEN-CHI, センチ, 淺智, (*asai chiye*). *n.* Shallow ability, little intelligence.

SEN-CHIU, センチウ, 舩中, (*fune no naka*). In a ship, or boat.

SEN-DACHI, センダチ, 先達, *n.* The headman of the *Yamabushi,* who acts as guide to worshipers at their miyas.

SEN-DAI, センダイ, 先代, *n.* The previous, or last generation. — *no jūji,* the previous head of a monastery. — *no tono sama,* the last chief.

SENDAN, センダン, 苦楝, *n.* The Melia azedarach. Syn. ŌJI.

SEN-DATTE, センダツテ, 先立, *adv.* Before, recently, lately, a few day ago. — *wa arigatō,* thanks for your recent kindness. Syn. SENJITSZ, SAKI, KONAIDA, ITSZZOYA.

SENDO, センド, 先度, (*saki no tabi*). Before, former or previous time, lately, past occasion.

SENDO, センド, 前途, (*maye no michi*) *n.* Future course, until death. *Kimi no sendo wo mitodokeru,* to follow one's master to the last. *Chichi no — wo mizarishi kō-k'wai szru,* regretted that he was not with his father until the last.

SENDO, センド, 專度, *adv.* Most important time; used only in *Koko wo sendo to tatakau,* to fight as if all depended on this battle, — to fight with desperation.

SENDŌ, センドウ, 舩頭, (*fune no kashira*) *n.* Captain of a ship; This word is now commonly used for boatman, sailor.

SENDZRI, センズリ, *n.* Masturbation. — *wo kaku,* to practice m.

SENDZRU, センズル, 煎, See *Senji.*

SENDZRU-TOKORO, センズルトコロ, 所詮, *adv.* In fine, the sum of it, the upshot of the matter, conclusion. Syn. HIKKIYŌ, TSZMARI.

SENGE, センゲ, 宣下, (*mikotonori wo kudasz*). Imperial order or command.

†SENGE, センゲ, 遷化, *n.* Spoken of the death of Buddhist priests. — *szru,* to die.

SEN-GETSZ, センゲツ, 先月, (*maye no tszki*). *n.* The last month.

SEN-GI, センギ, 僉議, Examining, or in-

quiring into the truth, or facts. — *szru*, to judge, scrutinize, or inquire into.
Syn. SENSAKU.

†SENGIYO, センギヨ, 鮮魚, *n.* Fresh fish.

†SEN-GIYŌ, センゲフ, 專業, (*moppara no waza*). *a.* Chief, or special occupation.

†SEN-GO, センゴ, 譫語, (*uwa koto*). *n.* Delirious, raving or wild talk (as of a sick person). — *wo iu*, to rave, or talk deliriously.

†SEN-GOKU, センゴク, 戰國, (*ikusa no kuni*). *n.* A country disturbed by war.

SENGOKU-BUNE, センゴクブネ, 千斛舩, *n.* A junk of one thousand *koku* burden, now the name of any large junk.

SEN-GOKU-DŌSHI, センゴクドホシ, 千斛簁, *n.* The name of a machine for cleaning rice, a wind-mill.

SEN-GURI-NI, セングリニ, 先繰, *adv.* According to priority or precedence, one after another. — *shussei szru*, to be promoted according to priority.

SEN-ICHI, センイチ, 專一, *adv.* Most important, principal, chief. Syn. KEN-JIN, MOPPARA.

SEN-JA, センジヤ, 撰者, *n.* Author, writer of a book.

SEN-JA-MAN-BETSZ, センジヤマンベツ, 千差萬別, Very many and different, great variety. — *no h'to-gokoro*.

SENJI,-*ru*, or -*dzru*,-*ta*, センズル 煎, *t.v.* To boil, to make a decoction. *Kuszri wo* —, to make a medical decoction.

†SEN-JI, センジ, 宣旨, (*mikotonori*). *n.* Command of the *Mikado*.

SENJI-DASHI,-*sz*,-*sh'ta*, センジダス, 煎出, *t.v.* To extract by boiling.

SENJI-GARA, センジガラ, 煎滓, *n.* The grounds or refuse left after boiling or making a decoction. *Cha no* —, tea-grounds.

SEN-JIN, センヂン, 先陣, *n.* The van or front column of an army.
Syn. SAKITE, SEMBŌ.

SEN-JITSZ, センジツ, 先日, *adv.* A few days ago, a previous or former day.
Syn. SENDATTE.

SENJI-TSZME,-*ru*,-*ta*, センジツメル, 煎詰, *t.v.* To boil down to greater consistence.

†SEN-JO, センヂヨ, 仙女, *n.* Female genii, a fairy.

SEN-JŌ, センジヤウ, 戰場, (*tatakai ba*). *n.* The field of battle. Syn. KASSEMBA.

SEN-JUTSZ, センジユツ, 仙術, *n.* Magic-arts, or miraculous performances of *Sennin*, as riding on the clouds, making it rain, &c.

SEN-JUTSZ,-*szru*, センジユツ, 選述, To compose, to compile a book.
Syn. ARAWASZ.

†SEN-KA, センカ, 泉下, *n.* Under the ground, in the grave, dead. — *no h'to*, a deceased person.

SEN-KAKU, センカク, 先格, *n.* Former or established custom, or use; precedent.
Syn. SENREI.

SEN-KATA, センカタ, 爲方, *n.* Resource, remedy, means, expedient. — *nashi*, no resource. — *tszkite kōsan sh'ta*, having exhausted every means he surrendered.
Syn. SHIKATA.

†SEN-KEN, センケン, 先見, *n.* Opinion or judgment of future events, fore-sight, foreknowledge. — *szru*, to foresee.

†SEN-KEN, センケン, 先賢, *n.* Ancient, or former philosophers.

†SEN-KEN, センケン, 嬋娟, Beautiful, elegant. — *taru onna*.
Syn. UTSZKUSHII, ADAYAKA.

SEN-KI, センキ, 疝氣, *n.* A general term for pains, or complaints in the loins, pelvis, or testicles.

SEN-KI, センキ, 先規, *n.* Former example, established custom, or use.
Syn. SEN-KAKU.

SEN-KIU, センキウ, 川芎, *n.* The name of a bitter medicine.

SEN-KIYAKU, センキヤク, 先客, The guest or visitor that precedes or comes before a person.

†SEN-KIYŌ, センキヤウ, 仙境, *n.* The place where *sennin* are supposed to dwell. — *ni iru ga gotoshi*, like living in fairy-land.

SEN-KŌ, センカウ, 線香, *n.* Joss-sticks, incense sticks.

SEN-KŌ, センカウ, 戰功, *n.* Valor, or prowess in battle.

SEN-KŌ, センコウ, 先公, *n.* The previous or late lord or duke.

SEN-KOKU, センコク, 先刻, *n.* A few minutes ago, a short time before.
Syn. SAKIHODO, SENDATTE.

SEN-KUDZ, センクヅ, 鏇屑, *n.* Metal shavings, or filings.

SEN-KUN, センクン, 先君, *n.* Same as *Senkō*.

SEN-NEN, センネン, 先年, (*saki no toshi*). *n.* A former year, some years before.

†SEN-NEN, センネン, 專念, (*moppara ni nendzru*). Making it one's chief business to recite the Buddhist prayer, "*Namu amida butsz.*"

SEN-NIN, センニン, 仙人, *n.* Same as *Sen.*

SEN-REI, センレイ, 先例, *n.* Former example or custom, previous rule, precedent, ancient use. Syn. SEN-KAKU, SEN-KI, KIU-REI.

†SEN-RITSZ, センリツ, 戰慄, (*wananaku*). *n.* Trembling with fear or cold, shivering, quaking. — *szru.*

SENROPPU, センロツプ, 纎蘿葍, *n.* Radishes cut up very fine, and eaten with fish.

SEN-SAI, センサイ, 先妻, (*saki no tszma*). *n.* Former wife, late wife.

SEN-SAKU, センサク, 穿鑿, *n.* Examination, inquiry, search, inquisition. — *szru,* to examine into, to inquire.
Syn. SAGASZ, SHIRABERU, GIM-MI, TADASZ.

SEN-SEI, センセイ, 先生, *n.* (lit. first born). A polite name used in addressing an elderly man, a physician, or a scholar.

†SEN-SEN-KIYŌ-KIYŌ, センセンキヤウキヤウ, 戰戰兢兢, *adv.* Trembling with fear, quaking. — *to sh'te uszki kōri wo fumu ga gotoshi.*

SENSHAKU, センシヤク, 疝癪, *n.* Colic.

†SEN-SHI, センシ, 先師, *n.* Teacher.
Syn. SHISHŌ.

SEN-SHIN-BAN-KU, センシンバンク, 千辛萬苦, Many and various difficulties and hardships, or great labor and suffering.

SEN-SHU, センシュ, 先主, Former, late, or deceased lord or master.

†SEN-SHŪ-BAN-ZEI, センシウバンゼイ, 千秋萬歳, (lit. A thousand autumns and ten thousand years). A great many, used only in complimentary letters.

SEN-SŌ, センソウ, 戰爭, *n.* A battle. — *szru,* to fight.
Syn. TATAKAI, KASSEN.

SEN-SOKU, センソク, 洗足, (*ashi wo arau*). *n.* Washing the feet.

SENSZ, センス, 扇子, *n.* A fan, that opens and shuts. Syn. ŌGI.

SEN-SZI, センスイ, 泉水, *n.* An artificial pond.

SEN-TAKU, センタク, 洗濯, *n.* Washing, used only of clothing. — *szru,* to wash clothes.

SEN-TATSZ, センタツ, 先達, *n.* Former, or ancient philosophers or wise men.

SEN-TE, センテ, 先手, *n.* The person who comes first, or has the first turn, or comes before another. *Atszraye-mono wo — kara jun ni yaru,* to do work for persons in the order of their ordering it.

†SEN-TEI, センテイ, 先帝, *n.* The last emperor.

SEN-TEN-BIYŌ, センテンビヤウ, 先天病, *n.* A congenital or hereditary disease.

†SEN-TETSZ, センテツ, 先哲, *n.* Same as *Sentatsz.*

†SEN-TO, セント, 遷都, (*miyako wo utszsz*). *n.* To change the seat of government, or Capital.

†SEN-TŌ, セントウ, 先登, *n.* The first man to scale the walls, or enter a besieged fortress. Syn, SAKIGAKE.

†SEN-TŌ, セントウ, 仙洞, (*Tenshi no inkiyo*). The residence of an emperor who has abdicated the throne.

†SEN-TŌ, セントウ, 戰鬭, *n.* A battle.
Syn. SENSŌ.

SEN-TŌ, センタウ, 錢湯, *n.* A public bathhouse.

SEN-YA, センヤ, 先夜, *n.* A previous night.

SEN-YAKU, センヤク, 煎藥, *n.* A medical decoction.

SEN-YAKU, センヤク, 先約, *n.* A previous engagement, promise, or contract.

SEN-YŌ, センエフ, 千葉, *n.* Many leaved. — *no hana,* a flower with many petals.

†SEN-YŌ, センエウ, 專要, Most important, necessary.
Syn. KANYŌ, MOPPARA.

†SEN-ZA, センザ, 遷座, (*za wo utszsz*). To change or remove one's seat.

SEN-ZAI, センザイ, 前栽, *n.* A garden or yard about a house.

SEN-ZAN-KŌ, センザンカフ, 穿山甲, *n.* The skin or scales of the manis, or pangolin, used as a medicine.

SEN-ZEN, センゼン, 前前, Former, previous.

SEN-ZO, センゾ, 先祖, *n.* Ancestor, forefather, progenitor.

†SEN-ZŌ-KU-YŌ, センゾウクヤウ, 千僧供養, *n.* An assembly of a thousand priests to chant the Bud. sacred books.

SEOI,-ō,-*ōta*, セオフ, 背負, *t.v.* (in com. coll. pronounced *Shōi, ō, ōta*). To carry on the back. Syn. Ō.

SEPPA,-*szru*, セツパ, 說破, (*toki yaburu*) To confute, to show to be false or defective, disprove. Syn. Ī-YABURU.

SEPPA, セツパ, 切羽, *n.* A metal plate or ring round the sword blade near the hilt.

SEPPAKU, セツパク, 節迫, (*setsz no shimari*). *n.* The close of the year.

†SEPPAKU, セツパク, 雪白, (*yuki-jiro*). *n.* White as snow.

†SEPPŌ, セツパフ, 說法, (*hō wo toku*). *n.* Explaining, expounding, or discoursing on the doctrines of Buddhism. — *szru,* to preach. Syn. HŌDAN.

†SEPPU, セップ, 節婦, *n.* A chaste, or virtuous womau. Syn. RETSZ-JO.

SEPPUKU, セップク, 切腹, *(hara kiri)*, *n.* Cutting open the abdomen in suicide. —*szru.*

SERAI,*–au,–atta*, セラフ, 迫合, *t.v.* To be envious of, jealous of. *Otōto ga ani wo* —, the younger brother is envious of the older. Syn. YAKKAMU.

SERARE,*–ru,–ta*, セラレル, 被爲, pass. or pot. of *Shi, szru.* To be the object of something done by another. *Watakushi wa h'to ni jama wo serareta*, I have been hindered by him. *Bōdz ni serareta*, to have one's head shaved by force.

SERI, セリ, 芹, A kind of cress.

SERI,*–ru,–tta*, セル, 出投, *t.v.* To sell at auction. *Nimotsz wo* —, to sell goods at auction.

SERI,*–ru,–tta*, セル, *t.v* To hasten, hurry, quicken. Syn. SEKU, ISOGU.

SERI, セリ, *n.* Auction. — *ga aru*, there is an auction. — *no hiki-fuda*, auction advertisement.

†SERI, セリ, The imperfect tense of *Shi, szru*, used only in books. *Raku-rui seri*, shed tears.

SERI-AGE,*–ru,–ta*, セリアゲル, (coll.) *i. v.* To rise-up in the chest and choke. *Mune ye* —, to have a feeling of choking or suffocation.

SERI-AI,*–au,–atta*, セリアフ, *i. v.* To struggle, rush, or strive together who shall be first, spoken of a crowd. *Kuwaji ga atte shibai yori h'to ga seriatte deru*, when there is fire, people struggle to get out of the theatre.

SERI-AKINDO, セリアキンド, *n.* A peddler.

SERI-DASHI,*–sz,–sh'ta*, セリダス, *t. v.* To force or squeeze out, (as anything through a hole). *Sen-kō wo* —, to force the composition of which joss-sticks are made, through small holes, thus forming it into long sticks. *Yakusha wo* —, to bring an actor on the stage.

SERIFU, セリフ, *n.* A dispute, altercation, wrangle. — *wo iu*, to dispute. Syn. KŌRON.

SERIURI, セリウリ, 投賣, *n.* Peddling.

SERU, セル, See *Seri*.

†SESAI, セサイ, 世才, Shrewdness, cleverness, discretion, prudence, common sense.

SESERAWARAI,*–au,–atta*, セセラワラフ, 冷笑, *t.v.* To laugh scornfully at, or in derision. Syn. AZAWARAU.

SESERAKI, セセラキ, 磧礫, *n.* Shallow, or shoal water.

SESERI,*–ru,–tta*, セセル, *t. v.* To pick, to to peck at. (as a fowl in eating, or a fly, mosquito, flea. &c.) *Ha wo seseru*, to pick the teeth. *Kusa wo sesete hebi wo dasz*, to pick at the grass (with a stick), and drive out a snake, (a proverb). *Tori ga mi wo* —, the fowl picks its feathers.

SESHI, セシ, a pret. particle, = *sh'ta.* Have done, as *Waga* — *koto ni aradz*, it is none of my doing. *Nani mono no* — *waza naran*, I wonder who did this.

SESHIME,*–ru,–ta*, セシメル, 令爲, causat. of *Shi, szru,* To cause another to be or do. *H'to ni kanshin seshimeru*, to cause a person to admire. *Kurō seshimeru*, to give trouble.

SESHIME-URUSHI, セシメウルシ, *n.* A kind of cement or paste made of lacquer.

SESHIMURU, セシムル, Same as *Seshime.*

SE-SHU, セシユ, 施主, *(hodokosz nushi)*, *n.* One who makes an offering or contribution to a temple.

SESSHA, セッシヤ, 拙者, *pers. pro.* I. (used only by Samurai). Syn. WARE.

†SESSEI, セッセイ, 攝生, *n.* Health. Syn. YŌJŌ.

†SESSEN, セッセン, 接戰, *(tatakai wo majiyeru)*. Joining battle. — *szru.* Syn. KASSEN.

SESSETSZ, セッセツ, 切切, *adv.* Often, frequently, many times. Syn. SHIBA-SHIBA, TABI-TABI.

†SES-SHI,*–szru,–sh'ta*, セッスル, 攝, To hold more than one office at the same time. *Matszrigoto wo sesszru*, to act as regent, the emperor being still on the throne. Syn. KANERU.

†SESSHI,*–szru,–sh'ta*, セッスル, 接, *t. v.* To join, connect, to continue. Syn. TSZDZKU.

SESSHO, セッショ, 切所, *n.* A difficult pass or defile. *Teki wo* — *ni sasayeru*, to oppose the enemy at a defile. Syn. NANJO.

SESSHŌ, セッシヤウ, 殺生, *n.* Taking life, killing anything. (Bud). — *wo szru*, to kill, or take life. — *kai*, the commandment against taking life.

SESSHŌ, セッシヤウ, 攝政, *n.* Regent, or acting emperor, same as K'wambaku.

†SESSŌ, セッサウ, 節操, *n.* Virtue, fidelity, integrity.

SE-SZJI, セスヂ, 脊筋, *n.* The line down the back over the back-bone.

SETAGE,*–ru,–ta*, セタゲル, 虐, (cont. of *Shiyetageru*). *t. v.* To oppress, maltreat.

H'yak'shō wo —, to oppress the farmers. Syn. KURUSHIMERU.

SETAI, セタイ, 世帯, *n.* No longer dependent on one's parents to set up for one's self, keeping house, or going to housekeeping. — *wo motsz*, to keep house, to be a house-holder. — *dōgu*, house-keeping utensils, mainly kitchen furniture.

SETAKE, セタケ, 脊丈, *n.* Full-growth or stature. — *ga nobita*, has grown to his full height.

SETCHIN, セツチン, 青椿, *n.* A privy, water-closet.
Syn. SETSZIN, CHŌDZBA.

SETCHIU,-*szru*, セツチウ, 折衷, To compile, to select and arrange from different authors.

SETCHIU, セツチウ, 雪中, (*yuki no naka*). In the snow. — *ni yuku*, to go in the snow, or while snowing.

SETO, セト, 狹門, *n.* A strait, a narrow channel of water.

SETO-GIWA, セトギハ, 狹門際, *n.* The border of a strait; fig., a difficult, or important part of one's life.

SETOMONO, セトモノ, 瀬戸物, *n.* Porcelain ware, crockery, (so called from *Seto*, a place in *Owari*, where most of the porcelain is manufactured).

SETSZ, セツ, 節, *n.* Virtue, fidelity, or constancy of a widow to her deceased husband, fidelity, patriotism, or constancy of one in the midst of trial or sufferings to his lord or country. — *wo mamoru*, to preserve one's constancy.
Syn. MISAO.

SETSZ, セツ, 節, *n.* Time, period, season, opportunity; a term of about 15 days, of which there are 24 in a year. *Kono setsz*, at this time, or season. — *ga okureru*, the season is backward. *Hana ga — ni okureru*, the flower is backward in blooming. *Setsz wo ukagau*, to watch for a good opportunity, to bide one's time.
Syn. TOKI, KOKO, JIBUN.

SETSZ, セツ, 說, (*hanashi*). *n.* Saying, teaching, discourse, doctrine; common talk, report, rumor. *Kōshi no* —, teachings of Confucius. *Iro iro no — ga aru*, there are various reports. *Bussetsz*, a doctrine of the Buddhists. *Atarashii — wo tateru*, to set up a new dogma, or set a going a new report.

SETTA, セツタ, 雪踏, *n.* Sandals armed with iron heels, same as *Sekida*.

SETTAI, セツタイ, 接待, *n.* Gratuitously dealing out food to poor people, or worshipers at a temple. — *wo szru*.

†SETTAKU, セツタク, 拙宅, (*watakushi no iye*). My house.

†SATSZ, セツ, 拙, (*tsztanai*). *n.* Stupidity, unskilfulness, ignorance, I (humbly). — *wo ō*, to hide one's ignorance.

SETSZ-BUN, セツブン, 節分, *n.* The time which marks the passing of the old into the true lunar year, when the sun enters the 15° of Aquarius, about the 5th of February.

SETSZ-DAN, セツダン, 截斷, (*kiri-tatsz*). *n.* An amputation. *Ude wo — szru*, to amputate the arm.

SETSZ-GAI, セツガイ, 切害, To kill, slay, to murder. Syn. KIRI-KOROSZ.

SETSZ-GAWARI, セツガハリ, 節替, *n.* The change of season, or term.

†SETSZ-GI, セツギ, 節義, *n.* Virtue, fidelity, constancy. See *Setsz*.

SETSZ-IN, セツイン, 雪隱, *n.* A privy.
Syn. CHŌDZBA, KŌKA.

SETSZ-NA, セツナ, 刹那, *n.* Moment, instant, the shortest interval of time. — *no aida mo waszreru koto nashi*, have not forgotten it for a moment.

SETSZNAI,-KI, セツナイ, 切, *a.* Painful, distressing, oppressive, causing extreme suffering. — *me ni atta*, met with an occasion of extreme suffering. *Mune ga* —, have great distress in the chest.

SETSZNAKU, セツナク, 切, *adv.* Idem.

SETSZNARU, セツナル, *a.* Distressing, painful, afflicting.

SETSZNASA, セツサ, *n.* Suffering, distress, difficulty, extremity.

SETSZNASHI, セツナシ, *a.* See *Setsznai*.

†SETSZWA, セツワ, 說話, *n.* Same as *Setsz*.

SEWA, セワ, 世話, *n.* Help, aid, assistance, patronage, kind offices, agency, intervention. — *wo szru*, to befriend, aid, or assist. — *wo yaku*, idem. — *ni naru*, to reeeive help. — *wo sh'te yaru*, to render assistance. *H'to no — ni wa naranu*, not to be dependent on others. *Yome no — wo szru*, to aid a person in getting a wife for his son. Syn. TASZKE, SHŪSEN.

SEWANIN, セワニン, 世話人, *n.* One who aids, renders assistance, or acts as a gobetween for others, an agent.
Syn. KIMOIRI, SEWAYAKI.

SEWARI, セワリ, 脊割, *n.* Cutting open a fish along the back. *Sakana no — wo szru.*

SEWA-RIYŌ, セワリヤウ, 世話料, *n.* Money presented to any one as an acknowledgment for kind serv ices.
Syn. REIGIN.

SEWA-SEWASHII,-KI,-KU, セワセワシキ, Bustling stirring, or active.

SEWASHII,-KI, セワシイ, 忙, *a.* Busy, hurried, distracted with business, or cares. Syn. ISOGASHII.

SEWASHIKU, セワシク, 忙, *adv.* Idem. — *naru*, to become busy.

SEWASHINAI,-KI, セワシナイ, *a.* Busy, hurried, or distracted with business.

SEWASHINAKU,-NŌ, セワシナク, *adv.* Idem.

SEWASHISA, セワシサ, *n.* The state of being busy or actively engaged.

SEWAYAKI, or SEWAYAKU, セワヤキ, Same as *Sewanin.*

SE-YAKU, セヤク, 施藥, *n.* Medicines dispensed gratuitously.

†SEZARE, セザレ, (cont. of *Sedz*, and *are*). Neg. imper. of *Shi*, *szru*, do not, don't do. *Aku wo* —, do no evil.

||SEZENAGI, セゼナギ, *n.* A drain, ditch, or sink to carry off filthy water.

SHA, シヤ, 紗, *n.* Silk gauze.

SHA, シヤ, 者, (*mono, h'to*), (only used in compound words). Person, man. *Gak'sha*, a learned man or scholar. *Isha*, a healing man, or physician.

†SHA, シヤ, 赦, *n.* Amnesty, pardon. — *wo okonau*, to grant a general amnesty or pardon to criminals.

†SHA, シヤ, 射, (*iru*). *n.* Archery. — *wo manabu*, to practice archery.

†SHA, シヤ, 社, (*nakama*). *n.* A club, association, clique, society. — *wo muszbu*, to form a society.

SHABA, or SHABA-SEKAI, シヤバ, 娑婆, *n.* This world. (Bud). *Shaba-fusagi*, a useless fellow. Syn. SEKAI.

SHABERI,-*ru*,-*tta*, シヤベル, *t.v.* To talk much and annoyingly, to prate, tattle, chatter. Syn. SAYEDZRU.

SHA-BETSZ, シヤベツ, 差別, *n.* Difference, distinction.
Syn. WAKACHI, KEJIME, WAIDAME.

SHABON, シヤボン, 石鹼, *n.* (from the Spanish jabon). Soap. Syn. SEKKEN.

SHABOTEN, シヤボテン, Same as *Saboten.*

SHABURI,-*ru*,-*tta*, シヤブル, *t.v.* To suck. *Mikan wo* —, to suck an orange.
Syn. SZU.

SHACHI, シヤチ, 車地, *n.* A capstan used for dragging heavy weights.
Syn. ROKURO.

†SHA-CHI, シヤチ, 社地, *n.* The area, or place where a *Miya* or *Yashiro* is built, a "high-place."

SHACHIHOKO, シヤチホコ, 鯱, *n.* The name of a fish, the ornament like a fish on the end of the roofs of temples, &c.

SHA-CHIU, シヤチウ, 社中, (*nakama uchi*). *n.* Society, club, clique, party. *Waga — no mono*, a member of my club.

SHA-DAN, シヤダン, 社壇, *n.* The raised ground on which a *Miya* or *Yashiro* is built.

SHAGA, シヤガ, 蝴蝶花, *n.* The iris, or fleur de lis.

SHAGAMI,-*mu*,-*nda*, シヤガム, *i.v.* To squat, or sit down on the heels, to crouch.
Syn. UDZKUMARU.

†SHA-GEI, シヤゲイ, 射藝, *n.* Archery.

SHA-GI, シヤギ, 謝儀, *n.* A present made out of gratitude for a favor, a thank offering. Syn. REI-MOTSZ.

SHAGIRI, シヤギリ, 鈸, *n.* A small kind of cymbal.

SHA-HON, シヤホン, 寫本, (*utszshi hon*). *n.* A book written with a pen, not printed, a manuscript.

†SHA-JIKU, シヤヂク, 車軸, *n.* The hub of a wheel. Syn. KURUMA NO SHINGI.

†SHA JUTSZ, シヤジユツ, 射術, *n.* Archery.

SHAKA, シヤカ, 釋迦, *n.* The son of Jōbon king of Makada and founder of Buddhism, lived in the time of Xerxes, and died about 475 B.C. He is worshipped by the Buddhists, also called Shaka-Niyorai.

SHAKE, シヤケ, Same as *Sake.* A salmon.

SHAKE, シヤケ, 社家, *n.* A Sintoo priest.
Syn. KANNAGI, KANNUSHI.

†SHA-KIN, シヤキン, 沙金, *n.* Gold-dust.

SHA-KIN-SEKI, シヤキンセキ, 沙金石, *n.* Glass with small pieces of gold foil sprinkled through it.

†SHAKIYŌ, シヤキヤウ, 舍兄, (*ani.*) *n.* Elder brother.

SHAKKI, シヤクキ, 癪氣, *n.* Same as *Shaku.*

SHAKKIN, シヤクキン, 借金, (*karita kane*). Borrowing money, debt accruing from borrowing money, a loan. — *ga aru*, to be in debt. — *szru*, to borrow money. — *wo harau*, to pay back money borrowed.
Syn. KARI, SHAKUSEN, SHAKUGIN.

SHAKKIRI, シヤツキリ, *adv.* Stiff, hard. — *to szru*, to become hard or stiff.

SHAKKIYŌ, シヤクキヤウ, 釋教, (*Shaka no oshiye*). *n.* Buddhism, the teaching of Shaka.
Syn. BUPPŌ, BUTSZDŌ.

SHAKO, シヤコ, 硨磲, *n.* Mother of pearl, or coral?

SHAKO, シヤコ, *n.* The squilla mantis, a species of crustacea.

SHAKO, シヤコ, 鷓鴣, *n.* The name of a bird, the quail?

SHAKU, シヤク, 尺, *n.* A foot of ten inches; (same length as the English foot). *Issha-ku*, one foot. *Tammono no — ga mijikai*, the piece of cloth is deficient in length.

SHAKU, シヤク, 笏, *n.* A wooden tablet carried by nobles when in the presence of the emperor, formerly used for noting memoranda on, but now merely a part of court etiquette.

†SHAKU, シヤク, 爵, *n.* Rank, degree of nobility. Syn. KURAI, KAKUSHIKI.

†SHAKU, シヤク, 釋, *n.* The title of a Buddhist priest. *Shaku no chijō*, the Rev. Mr. Chijō. — *szru*, to explain, comment on.

SHAKU, シヤク, 勺, *n.* A measure of capacity, the tenth part of a *gō*.

SHAKU, シヤク, 杓, *n.* A dipper, ladle.

SHAKŪ, シヤクウ, See *Shakui.*

SHAKU, シヤク, 酌, *n.* Pouring wine into the cup. — *wo szru*, to pour out wine.

SHAKU, シヤク, 癪, *n.* A disease said by Japanese physicians to be, "cramp of the Uterus," perhaps Hysteria?

SHAKU-BA, シヤクバ, 借馬, *(kari uma).* A hired horse.

SHAKU-DŌ, シヤクドウ, 赤銅, *n.* A kind of red metal made by mixing copper and silver.

SHAKU-GIN, シヤクギン, 借銀, *n.* Borrowing money, debt accruing from borrowing money, a loan; same as *Shakkin.* — *wo szru*, to borrow money.

SHAKU-HACHI, シヤクハチ, 尺八, *n.* A kind of flute, or pipe blown at the end.

SHAKUI, *-kū, -kūta*, シヤクウ, 杓, *t.v.* To dip up, to lade. *Midz wo shakū*, to dip water. Syn. KUMU.

SHAKU-JŌ, シヤクヂヤウ, 錫杖, *n.* A staff, the top of which is armed with metal rings, carried by begging priests.

SHAKUMI, *-mu, -nda*, シヤクム, *i.v.* To be bent, curved, or warped so as to be concave. *Shakunda kao*, a face in which the nose sinks in. *Ita ga shakunda*, the board is warped.

†SHAKU-MON, シヤクモン, 釋門, *n.* Buddhism, Shamanism. — *ni iru*, to become a Buddhist.

SHAKU-NAGE, シヤクナゲ, 石楠花, *n.* The rhododendron.

SHAKU-NIN, シヤクニン, 酌人, *n.* A waiter who serves out the wine.
Syn. SHAKUTORI.

SHAKURI, シヤクリ, 噦, *n.* Hiccough. — *ga tszku*, to hiccough.

SHAKURI, *-ru, -tta*, シヤクル, *t.v.* To pull with a sudden jerk, to twitch, to snap (as a whip). *Nawa wo* —, to jerk a rope. *Muchi wo* —, to crack a whip.

SHAKU-SEN, シヤクセン, 借錢, *n.* Same as *Shakkin*, or *Shakugin.*

SHAKUSHI, シヤクシ, 杓子, *n.* A wooden ladle.

SHAKUSHI, シヤクシ, 釋氏, *n.* Shaka, the founder of Buddhism. — *no setsz*, the sayings of *Shaka.*

SHAKU-TORI, シヤクトリ, 酌取, *n.* A waiter who serves out the wine.

SHAKU-TORI-MUSHI, シヤクトリムシ, 尺蠖, *n.* A caterpillar.

SHAK'WAN, シヤクワン, 左官, *n.* A plasterer, same as *Sak'wan.*

SHAKU-YA, シヤクヤ, 借屋, *(kari-iye). n.* A hired house.

SHAKU-YAKU, シヤクヤク, 芍藥, *n.* The herbaceous peony.

SHAKU-YŌ, シヤクヨウ, 借用, To borrow. — *sh'ta kane*, borrowed money.
Syn. KARU.

SHAKU-ZAI, シヤクザイ, 借財, *n.* Borrowed money, same as *Shakkin.*

SHAMEN, シヤメン, 赦免, *n.* Pardon, forgiveness. — *szru*, to pardon. — *ni au*, to be pardoned. *Go — nasare*, pardon me, excuse me. Syn. YURUSHI.

SHAMI, シヤミ, 沙彌, *n.* One who is preparing to be a Buddhist priest, a novice.

SHAMI-SEN, シヤミセン, Better *Samisen*, which see.

SHAMO, シヤモ, *n.* A large kind of fowl, introduced originally from Siam.

SHAMON, シヤモン, 沙門, *n.* Buddhist, a Budd. priest.
Syn. BŌDZ, SHUKKE.

†SHAMON, *-szru*, シヤモン, 借問, To briefly inquire. Syn. TŌ, TADZNERU.

†SHA-MU, シヤム, 社務, *(miya no tsztome). n.* Duties connected with a *miya.*

SHAMURO, シヤムロ, 暹羅, *n.* Siam.

SHANIN, シヤニン, 社人, *n.* A Sintoo priest, same as, *Shake.*

SHANSHI, *-sz, -sh'ta*, シヤンス, Much used in dramatical works, as an auxilliary verb, same as *szru, nasaru*, to be, to do. *Shi-na-shansh'ta*, has died. *Iwa-shansh'ta*, has said.

SHAN-TO, シヤント, Same as *Chan-to.*

SHARADOKE, シャラドケ, *n* Untied, loose, undone. *Obi ga — szru.* belt is loose.

†SHARAKU, シャラク, 洒落, Refined, genteel, chaste; humorous, witty. — *na h'to,* Syn. FŪRIU, MIYABIYAKA.

SHARAKUSAI, シャラクサイ, Dissembling, hypocritical. — *koto wo iu,* to speak hypocritically. — *yatsz,* a hypocrite.

SHARE, シャレ, 洒落, *n.* A witticism, a humorous or comical saying. — *wo iu,* to say anything ludicrous.
Syn. KOKKEI, TAWAMURE.

SHARE,*-ru,-ta,* シャレル, 洒落, *i. v.* To be elegant, refined, stylish. *Shareta h'to,* a stylish person. Syn. FŪRIU NI SZRU.

SHA-REI, シャレイ, 謝禮, *n.* Acknowledgment of a favor, expressing thanks.
Syn. SHAGI.

SHARI, シャリ, 舍利, *n.* A small hard substance like a gem, supposed to be left in the ashes after burning the dead body of a Buddhist saint; this is preserved as a relic, held in great veneration and worshiped; a relic.

SHA-RIKI, シャリキ, 車力, *n.* A laborer who pushes, or pulls a cart.

SHARI-KŌBE, シャリカウベ, 髑髏, *n.* A skull.

†SHA-RIN, シャリン, 車輪, *n.* The rim of a wheel.

SHARI-SHARI-TO, シャリシャリト, *adv.* The sound made by crushing anything hard and brittle, as an egg-shell.

SHARI-YEN, シャリエン, 舍利鹽, *n.* Epsom-salts.

†SHA-SAN, シャサン, 社參, *(miya ye mairu). n.* Going to a Sintoo temple.

†SHA-SEI, シャセイ, 寫生, *n.* A correct, or life-like picture of anything, a fac-smile. — *no ye.*

SHĀ-SHĀ, シャアシャア, *adv.* Shamelessly, brazen-faced, impudently. — *sh'te oru,* to be impudent.

†SHA-SHI, シャシ, 奢侈, *(ogori). n.* Extravagance, prodigality, luxury, pomp. — *mo kiwameru.*

†SHASHI,*-szru,-sh'ta,* シャスル, 謝, *t v.* To thank, to acknowledge a kindness.

†SHASHI,*-sz,-sh'ta,* シャスル, 瀉, *t. v.* To purge, to be loose in the bowels, have a diarrhœa.

SHA-SHIN, シャシン, 寫眞, A life-like likeness, true picture of any thing. — *no ye.*

SHA-SHIN-KIYŌ, シャシンキヤウ, 寫眞鏡, *n.* A camera-obscura, a photographic instrument. — *de utszsz,* taken by photography.

SHA-TEI, シャテイ, 舍弟, *(otōto). n.* Young brother.

†SHA-TŌ, シャトウ, 社頭, *n.* The ground where a Sintoo temple is built.
Syn. SHACHI.

SHĀTSZKU, シャアツク, coll. *n.* An impudent fellow, shameless person. — *da.*

SHATTSZRA, シャツツラ, *n.* The face, (used only in contempt or anger). — *ye tatakitszkeru,* to strike one in the face.

SHI, シ, 四, *(yotsz). a.* Four.

SHI, シ, 詩, *(uta). n.* Chinese poetry, an ode, poem. — *wo tszkuru,* to write poetry.

†SHI, シ, 士, *(samurai). n.* A person belonging to the military class, or gentry.

SHI, シ, 死, *n.* Death, the dead. — *wa yaszku shō wa katashi,* death is easy, and life is hard (in such circumstances). — *wo arasō,* to strive who shall die first.

SHI, シ, 師, *(shishō), n.* Teacher. *Dare wo — to sh'te manabu,* with what teacher are you learning.

SHI, シ, 蒒, *n.* The name of a plant. The Oxalis acetosella.

†SHI, シ, A suffix to the root of verbs, forming the pret. tense, same as *ta* of the coll. *Mi-shi h'to,* the person who has seen. *Kayeri-shi hi,* the day on which he returned. *Yeda yore chiri ni shi hana,* the flowers that have fallen from the branches.

(2). A particle without meaning, used in poetry, or ancient composition, for the sake of euphony, or to complete the required number of feet. *Matsz to shi kikaba,* if you hear it said "wait." *Taiyete shi nakuba.* also, in *Ori shi mo, Koro shi mo.*

(3). A predicative or final adjective suffix, as *Takashi,* it is high. *Omoshi,* it is heavy. *Karushi,* it is light.

SHI, *sz* or *szru, sh'ta,* スル, 爲, *t. v.* To do, to be, to make; (2) used as a verbalizing affix or substantive verb to words derived from the Chinese. *Shigoto wo szru,* to do one's work. *Ikusa wo szru,* to make war. (2) *Ai-szru,* to love. *Hai-szru,* to worship. *Anshin szru,* to be well and free from evil. Syn. NASZ, ITASZ.

SHĪ,-RU,-TA, シヒル, 强, *t. v.* To urge, to press, to importune unreasonably. *Sake wo —,* to press a person to drink wine. *Shīte sake wo nomu,* to force one's self to drink wine. Syn. OSZ.

SHĪ, シヒ, 椎, *n.* The live-oak. *Shīnoki,* idem.

†SHĪ, シヒ, 瞽, *(mekura).* Blind. *Riyō gan — taru h'to,* a man blind of both eyes.

SHI-AGE,-*ru*,-*ta*, シアゲル, 仕上, *t.v.* To do up, to finish doing, get through. *Shigoto wo* —, to finish one's work. *Hōsō wo* —, to get through with the small pox. *Shi-age ni natta*, to be finished.

SHI-AI, シアヒ, 試合, *n.* A single combat with wooden swords, as a trial of skill. — *wo szru.*

SHI-AI,-*au*,-*atta*, シアフ, 仕合, *t.v.* To do mutually, do to or for each other. *Tagai ni sewa wo* —, to render assistance to each other.

SHI-AKI,-*ku*,-*ita*, シアク, 仕飽, *i.v.* To tire of doing anything, disgusted with doing.

SHI-AN, シアン, 思案, *(kangaye)*, *n.* Thought, consideration, reflection. — *wo szru*, to think over, consider. — *wo megurasz*, to revolve in the mind, ponder. — *no hoka*, different from what one supposes, or thinks. *Iro wa shian no hoka*, love is not subject to one's judgment. Syn. FUMBETSZ.

SHI-ASATTE, シアサツテ, 大後日, *adv.* Two days after to-morrow.

SHIAWASE, シアハセ, 仕合, *n.* Fortune, luck. — *no yoi h'to*, a fortunate man. — *ga warui*, my luck is bad. Syn. UN.

SHIBA, シバ, 柴, *n.* Brushwood. — *wo karu*, to cut brushwood.

SHIBA, シバ, 芝, *n.* Sod, turf, grass-plot. — *wō skiku*, to sod.

SHIBA-GAKI, シバガキ, 柴垣, *n.* A hedge or fence made of brushwood.

SHIBAI, シバ井, 劇場, *n.* Theatrical performances, drama. — *wo szru*, to play in a theatre. — *ye yuku*, to go to a theatre.

SHIBAIGOYA, シバ井ゴヤ, *n.* A theatre.

SHIBARAKU, シバラク, 暫時, *adv.* For a short time, a little while. — *o machi nasare*, wait a few minutes. — *no aida*, a little while, short time. Syn. ZANJI, CHOTTO, SZKOSHI.

SHIBARARE,-*ru*,-*ta*, シバラレル, 被縛, pass. and pot. of *Shibaru.* To be bound, tied, confined, restrained. *Ai ni* —, restrained by love.

SHIBARI,-*ru*,-*tta*, シバル, 縛, *t.v.* To bind, tie, to fasten by encircling with a cord. *Tszmi-bito wo* —, to bind a criminal. *Ni wo* —, to bind up packages of goods. *Te wo* —, to tie the hands. Syn. KUKURU, YUWAYERU.

SHIBASHI, シバシ, Same as *Shibaraku.*

SHIBA-SHIBA, シバシバ, 數, *adv.* Often, frequently. Syn. TABI-TABI.

SHIBA-TATAKI,-*ku*,-*ita*, シバタタク, *i. v.* To wink frequently.

SHIBE, シベ, *n.* The nerves of a leaf, the pistil of a flower, the stalk to which the grains of rice are attached.

†SHI-BETSZ, シベツ, 死別, (*shi ni wakare*) *n.* Separated by death. — *ni naru.*

SHIBI, シビ, 鮪, *n.* Tunny fish.

SHIBIN, シビン, 溺器, *n.* A urinal, chamber pot.

SHIBIRE,-*ru*,-*ta*, シビレル, 痺, *i.v.* To be numb, devoid of feeling, palsied, dead. *Te ga* —, hand is numb, or asleep. Syn. MAHI SZRU.

SHIBIRE-GUSZRI, シビレグスリ, 麻藥, *n.* Narcotic, or anœsthetic medicines. Syn. MAYAKU.

SHI-BITO, シビト, 死人, *n.* A dead man. Syn. SHININ.

SHIBOMI,-*mu*,-*nda*, シボム, 萎, *i. v.* To close, or shut, as a flower. *Hana ga shibonda*, the flower has closed.

SHIBORI,-*ru*,-*tta*, シボル, 絞, *t.v.* To press or squeeze out, to express, to wring. *Ushi no chichi wo* —, to milk a cow. *Kimono wo* —, to wring clothes. *Abura wo* —, to express oil, (out of seeds). *Maku wo* —, to pull up a curtain.

SHIBU, シブ, 澁, *n.* The sap of a tree; the thin skin round the kernel of a chesnut. The juice expressed fro n unripe persimmons, used as a stain or varnish. — *wo hiku*, to varnish with the above.

SHIBŪ, シブウ, *adv.* Same as *Shibuku.*

SHIBU-GAKI, シブガキ, 澁柿, *n.* An astringent kind of persimmon.

SHIBUI,-KI, シブイ, 澁, *a.* Astringent in taste. *Ajiwai ga shibui.*

SHI-BU-ICHI, シブイチ, 四分一, One-fourth; the thin moulding used by paper-hangers; the name of a composite-metal, made of copper three parts and silver one part.

SHIBU-IRO, シブイロ, 澁色, *n.* A reddish brown color.

SHIBU-ITA, シブイタ, 四分板, *n.* A board four-tenths of an inch in thickness.

SHIBU-KAMI, シブカミ, 澁紙, *n.* A kind of tough paper, used for wrapping.

SHIBU-KAWA, シブカハ, 澁皮, *n.* The inner bark of a tree.

SHIBUKI, シブキ, 斜雨, *n.* A driving rain.

SHIBUKU, シブク, 澁, *adv.* Astringent.

†SHI-BUN, シブン, 詩文, *n.* Poetry and prose.

SHIBURI,-*ru*,-*tta*, シブル, 澁, *i.v.* To be obstructed or impeded in flowing, not passing easily or freely. *Shōben ga* —, to have difficulty in passing urine. *Hara ga* —, to have an inclination to stool with tenesmus. *Kuchi ga* —, to have an impediment in the speech.

SHIBUSA, シブサ, *n.* Astringency.

SHIBUSHI, シブシ, *a.* See *Shibui.*

SHIBU-SHIBU, シブシブ, 澁澁, *adv.* Slowly and reluctantly. — *shōchi szru,* to consent reluctantly. — *tenki ni natta,* has cleared off slowly.

SHIBUTOI,-KI,-KU,-SHI,-Ō,-SA, シブトイ, Lazy and obstinate, slow in doing, not prompt.

SH'CHI, シチ, 七, (*nanatsz*). *a.* Seven.

SH'CHI, シチ, 質, *n.* A pawn, pledge, or deposit given as security for money borrowed. — *wo oku,* to give in pawn. — *ga nagareru,* the pawn is forfeited, or not redeemed. — *wo ukeru,* to redeem, or receive a deposited article, by paying the money borrowed. — *wo toru,* to take things on deposit. Syn. TEMBUTSZ.

†SH'CHI-JŌ, シチジヤウ, 七情, *n.* The seven passions; viz., anger, joy, sadness, happiness, love, hatred, and desire.

SHI'CHI-JŌ, シチゼウ, 七條, The scarf worn by Buddhist priests, same as *Kesa.*

SHICHIKU, シチク, 紫竹, *n.* A purple kind of bamboo.

†SHI-CHIKU, シチク, 絲竹, (*ito take*). *n.* String, and reed instruments of music.

SH'CHI-KUSA, シチクサ, *n.* Articles that can be pawned. — *ga nai,* having nothing I can pawn.

SH'CHI-MOTSZ, シチモツ, *n.* Articles placed in pawn.

SH'CHI-YA, シチヤ, 質屋, *n.* A pawnbroker's shop, a pawnbroker.

SHI-CHŌ, シチヤウ, 紙帳, (*kami no kaya*). *n.* A mosquito net made of paper.

SHI-CHIU, シチウ, 市中, (*ichi no naka*) *n.* In the market; the market town. — *ga fukeiki,* the town, or the market is dull. — *no mono,* the market people.

SHIDA, シダ, 齒朶, *n.* A fern.

SHIDAI, シダイ, 次第, *n.* Order, arrangement, reason, account, consideration, in proportion to, according to, as soon as. — *ushinau,* to lose the proper order. — *wo midasz,* to disarrange. — *ga warui.* — *ga yoi. Migi no — de,* for the above reasons. *Sono — ni yotte,* on that account. — *wo kiki-tadasz,* to inquire into the reasons. *Kokoro-shidai,* according to one's mind, or just as one pleases. *Mekata-shidai,* according to the weight. *Deki-shidai,* as soon as it is done. *Tegami no tszki-shidai,* as soon as the letter is received. *Ame no yami-shidai,* as soon as it stops.
Syn. JUN, WAKE, MAKASE, MAMA.

†SHI-DAI, シダイ, 四大, *n.* The four elements according to the Buddhists; viz., earth, water, fire, and wind.

SHIDAI-NI, シダイニ, 次第, *adv.* Gradually, by degrees, by little and little. — *samuku-naru,* gradually becomes colder.
Syn. DAN-DAN.

SHIDAI-SHIDAI-NI, シダイシダイニ, idem.

SHIDARA, シダラ, *n.* Order, system, method, reason, (always with a negative). — — *mo nai h'to,* a person without system or method. — *naki,* disordered, confused.

SHIDARE,-*ru*,-*ta*, シダレル, 絲垂, *i.v.* To curve and bend downwards, (as the branch of a willow). *Niwatori no o ga shidareru,* the cock's tail curves downwards.

SHIDARI-YANAGI, シダリヤナギ, 垂柳, *n.* The weeping willow.

SHI-DASHI,-*sz*,-*sh'ta*, シダス, 仕出, *t. v.* To begin to make or do, to enlarge. — *Iye wo* —, to enlarge a house.

SHI-DASHI, シダシ, 仕出, *n.* Food cooked and supplied to order. — *wo tanomu.*

SHI-DASHI-YA, シダシヤ, *n.* A restaurant where food is prepared and supplied to order.

SHIDE-NO-YAMA, シデノヤマ, 死出山, *n.* A mountain in Hades, over which passes the road, which the souls of the dead must travel to reach Yemmachō, the place of judgment, see *Yomiji.* (Bud).

SHIDOKENAI,-KI, シドケナイ, *a.* Slovenly, disorderly, loose, not neat or methodical.

SHIDOKENAKU, シドケナク, *adv.* idem. — *kaku,* to write in a slovenly way.

SHI-DŌ-KIN, シダウキン, 祠堂金, *n.* Money paid to temples to provide for the saying of prayers for the dead.

SHIDOME, シドメ, coll. The Pirus Japonicus. Syn. BOKE.

SHIDONE, シドネ, 褥, *n.* A rug for sitting on.

SHIDORO-MODORO-NI, シドロモドロニ, *adv.* In a confused manner, disorderly. — *aruku,* to stagger like a drunken man. — *nige-hashiru,* to run in confusion and disorder, (as a routed army).

SHIDORO-NI, シドロニ, idem.

†SHIDZ, シヅ, 賤, (*iyashii*). Mean, low, poor, humble. — *no waraya,* a mean thatched hut. — *no mono,* a person in

humble life. — *no me*, a woman in low station.

SHIDZKA, シヅカ, 靜, Quiet, still, calm, tranquil, peaceful, free from commotion, disturbance or noise, slow. — *naru yo*, a peaceful age. — *ni seyo*, be still. — *ni aruku*, to walk slowly. Syn. ODAYAKA.

SHIDZKU, シヅク, 滴, *n.* A drop. *Ame no* —, rain drops. — *wo tarasz*, to let the drops fall, to drop. Syn. TEKI, SHITATARI.

SHIDZMARI,*-ru,-tta*, シヅマル, 靜, *i.v.* To be stilled, quieted, lulled, tranquilized, calmed, pacified, subsided. *Sawagi ga* —, the tumult is quieted. *Itami ga* —, the pain is easy. *Nami ga* —, the waves are stilled. *Kaze ga* —, the wind has lulled. *K'waji ga* —, the fire has subsided. Syn. OSAMARU.

SHIDZMARI,*-ru,-tta*, シヅマル, 沈, *i.v.* To be immersed, sunk, or covered over in water. *Midz ni* —, immersed in water. *Shu-shoku ni* —, immersed in wine and lust. Syn. OBORERU, HAMARU.

SHIDZME,*-ru,-ta*, シヅメル 靜, *t.v.* To quiet, still, calm, tranquilize, to settle. *Sawagi sōdō nado wo* —, to still a noise or tumult. Syn. OSAMERU.

SHIDZME,*-ru,-ta*, シヅメル, 沈, *t. v.* To immerse, to sink, put under water, submerge; fig. to drown, overwhelm, immerse, or sink in (as lust, or wine), *Shu-shoku ni mi wo* —, to drown one's self in wine and lust. *Midz ni* —, to immerse in water. Syn. HAMERU.

SHIDZMI,*-mu,-nda*, シヅム, 沈, *i. v.* To sink, to be submerged, or immersed in water; fig. to be overwhelmed, drowned, or sunk in wine, lust, &c. *Midz ni* —, sunk in the water. *Shu-shoku ni* —, immersed in wine and lust. *Omoi ni* —, lost in thought.

SHIDZ-SHIDZ-TO, シヅシヅト, 靜靜, *adv.* Quietly, still, without noise or excitement, softly, slowly.

SHI-FU, シフ, 紙布, *n.* Cloth made by weaving threads made of twisted paper, paper-cloth.

SHIFU, シフ, 師父, (*shishō chichi*). *n.* Teacher and father.

†SHIFU, シフ, 詩賦, *n.* Chinese poetry, poem, verse.

†SHI-FŪ, シフウ, 士風, (*samurai no narawashi*). *n.* The manner or customs of the gentry.

SHIGAI, シガイ, 死骸, *n.* A corpse, dead body. Syn. SHIKABANE.

SHI-GAKU, シガク, 思覺, *n.* Contriving, planning, devising. — *wo szru*, to plan, contrive, devise. Syn. KUFŪ, SANDAN.

SHIGAMI-TSZKI,*-ku,-ita*, シガミツク, *i.v.* To clasp, shut, or fasten on, to twine around, (as a vine), to throw the arms around. *Yoroi no szso ni shigamitszki koye oshimadz naki-sakebu*, clasping the skirt of his armor she cried aloud.

†SHIGARAMI, シガラミ, 篰. *n.* Piles driven along the banks of a stream, and interwoven with bamboo, to protect the bank from the current. Syn. SAKU.

SHI-GATAI,-KI,-KU,-SHI,-Ō,-SA, シガタイ, 仕難, Difficult to do.

SHI-GATSZ, シグワツ, 四月, *n.* The fourth month. Syn. UDZKI.

†SHIGE, シゲ, 齒牙, *n.* The teeth, (front and back teeth). — *ni kakeru*, to talk about, speak of.

SHIGEI,-KI, シゲキ, 繁, *a.* Thick, close together, dense, (as grass, or leaves); many, numerous, much. *Sigeki kono ha*, the thick leaves of a tree. *Shigeki ga yuye ni habuku*, to omit them because they are so numerous.

SHIGEDŌ, シゲドウ, 重藤, *n.* A bow wrapped round with rattan.

SHIGEKI, シゲキ, 刺撃, *n.* A pricking, sharp pain, irritation. — *ni yotte kinshō ga okoru*, inflammation is caused by pain.

SHIGEKU, シゲク, 繁, *adv.* See *Shigei*. *Ame yori — ya ga tobu*, the arrows fell thicker than rain.

SHIGERI,*-ru,-ta*, シゲル, 稠, *i.v.* To be thick, dense, close together, (as leaves, or grass). *Kusa ga* —, the grass is thick.

SHGERI-AI,*-au,-atta*, シゲリアフ, 稠合, To be close, or thick and matted together, (as bushes, &c.)

SHIGESA, シゲサ, *n.* Density, closeness, thickness.

SHIGESHI, シゲシ, *a.* See *Shigei*.

SHIGE-SHIGE, シゲシゲ, 繁繁, *adv.* Often, frequently. Syn. SHIBA-SHIBA, TABI-TABI.

SHIGI, シギ, 鷸, *n.* A species of snipe.

SHIGI, シギ, 仕義, *n.* Circumstance, account, reason, fact of the case. *Kono — ni yotte*, on this account. Syn. SHIDAI, ARISAMA.

†SHĪ-G'YAKU,*-szru*, シイギヤク, 弑逆, To murder one's master, or parent.

SHIGO, シゴ, 死期, (*shini giwa*), *n.* The time of death. — *ni nozomu*, to be near death.

SHI-GO, シゴ, 死後, (*shinda nochi*), *n.* After death.

SHIGOKI,*-ku,-ita*, シゴク, 扱, *t. v.* To

draw anything through the hand. *Nawa wo* —, to draw a rope through the hand (in order to smooth it). *Yari wo* —, to move, or work a spear through the left hand. *Ha wo* —, to strip off leaves (by drawing a branch through the hand). Syn. KOKU.

SHIGOKU, シゴク, 至極, *adv.* A superlative, = very, extremely, exceedingly, most. — *yoi*, extremely good. *Mendō* —, extremely difficult. Syn. HANAHADA.

†SHĪGOTO, シヒゴト, 誣, *n.* False accusation, calumny, slander. Syn. ZANGEN.

SHIGOTO, シゴト, 仕事, *n.* Work, labor, employment, manual labor, needle work. — *wo szru*, to do one's work. — *ga nai*, have no work, or nothing to do. *Ano onna wa — ga heta da*, that woman is a poor seamstress.

SHIGOTOSHI, シゴトシ, 仕事師, *n.* A laborer, coolie.

SHIGUMA, シグマ, 羆, *n.* A white bear.

†SHIGURE,*-ru,-ta*, シグレル, *i.v.* To rain in showers, to drizzle, only spoken of rain in the 10th month. *Tenki ga shigureta.*

SHIGURE, シグレ, *n.* A drizzling shower of rain in the 10th month.

SHI-HAI, シハイ, 支配, *n.* Rule, superintendence, management, government, administration of affairs, control, direction. — *szru*, to rule, govern, direct. *Yokohama no — wa dare ga shimas*, who has the government of Yokohama?

SHI-HAININ, シハイニン, 支配人, *n.* A superintendent, factor, or agent in a mercantile house.

SHI-HAMBUN, シハンブン, 四半分, *n.* One fourth, a quarter.

†SHIHAN, シハン, 師範, *n.* A teacher, instructor. Syn. SHISHŌ.

SHI-HAN-GIN, シハンギン, 四半斤, *n.* A quarter of a catty.

SHI-HŌ, シハウ, 四方, *n.* The four quarters, or cardinal points, the four sides, all sides. *Iye no* —, the four sides of the house. — *ni teki wo ukeru*, to be attacked on all sides. *Shihō-happō*, on every side, in every direction.

SHI-HŌ, シハフ, 仕法, The way, manner of doing, or making anything; a way, method, course of procedure. — *wo tszkeru*, to direct as to what is to be done. *Kono — wa shiremu*, I don't know how this is done. Syn. SHIKATA.

†SHII,*-yuru,-ta*, シフル, 誣, *t.v.* To backbite, vilify, slander. Syn. ZANSZRU.

SHI-IRE,*-ru,-ta*, シイレル, 仕入, *t.v.* To buy, or lay in a quantity of anything in order to sell. *Yaszku shi-irete takaku uru*, to lay in goods when they are cheap, and sell at high prices. Syn. SHI-KOMU.

SHI-IRE, シイレ, 仕入, *n.* Buying or laying in goods by the quantity. — *ga takai kara yaszku urenu*, as I had to buy at a high price, I cannot sell cheap. — *ni yuku*, to go to lay in goods.

SHI-IRE-KATA, シイレカタ, 仕入方, *n.* The purchasing clerk or agent in a mercantile house; also, the way in which goods have been purchased.

SHI-IRE-MONO, シイレモノ, 仕入物 *n.* Articles, or goods laid in or purchased by the quantity.

SHĪ-JI, シイジ, 四時, *n.* The four-seasons, viz. spring, summer, autumn, winter.

SHIJIMI, シジミ, 蜆, *n.* A kind of small shell-fish.

SHIJIMI,*-mu,-nda*, シジム, Same as *Chijimu.*

†SHI-JIN ジジン, 詩人, *n.* A poet.

SHIJIRA, シジラ, 縮羅, *n.* A kind of crape.

SHIJIRERU, シジレル, Same as *Chijireru.*

SHI-JŪ, シジウ, 始終, *(hajime owari)*, *n.* From beginning to end, the whole, the end; at the last, the result; always, constantly. — *no yōsz wo kīte-oru*, I hear the whole affair. — *ga komari-mashō*, it will result in trouble. — *hon wo yonde-oru* he is always reading. — *itamimas*, pains constantly. Syn. MATTAKU, SZYE, TŌSHI.

SHI-JŪ, シジウ, 四十, *n.* Forty. — *ni* forty two.

SHI-JŪ-GARA, シジフガラ, 四十雀, *n.* The name of a small bird.

†SHĪ-KA, シイカ, 詩歌, *n.* Chinese and Japanese poetry.

SH'KA, シカ, 鹿, *n.* A deer, stag. — *no tszno*, a deer's horns. — *wo ō*, to chase a deer. — *wo karu*, to hunt a deer.

†SHIKA, シカ, 疵瑕, *n.* Disgrace, cause of shame. *Iye no* —, disgrace to one's family. Syn. KAKIN.

†SHIKA, シカ, 然, *adv.* So, thus, in this manner. — *nadzkuru narubeshi*, (for the fore-mentioned reasons), it is so named. — *wa aredomo*, although it is so. — *nomi naradz*, no only so, moreover. — *bakari de wa nai*, it is not only so. — *iu*, so it is said. Syn SA, SŌ.

SHIKABANE, シカバネ, 屍, *n.* A corpse, dead body, carcass. Syn. SHIGAI.

SHI-KAI, シカイ, 四海, *n.* The four seas around Japan, the whole world.

†SHIKADZ, シカズ, 不若, Not so, is not like, is not so good, not equal to. *Waga gaku wo konomu ni wa shikadz*, is not so fond of learning as I.

†SHIKAJI, シカジ, 不如, I think it is not, or I doubt if it is so good, or equal to, &c. *Kore ni wa shikaji*, I think it is not so good as this.

SHI-KAKE,*-ru,-ta*, シカケル, 仕掛, *t.v.* To begin to do, to set about doing. *Shigoto wo* —, to set about one's work. *H'to ni ken-k'wa wo* —, to force a quarrel upon another. Syn. HAJIMERU.

SHI-KAKE, シカケ, 仕掛, *n.* A work commenced and left partly done.

SHIKAKE, シカケ, 仕掛, *n.* Machinery, a machine. *Jōki no* —, steam machinery. *Zemmai* —, machinery moved by a spring. *Midz no* —, machinery moved by water. — *de mugi wo hiku*, to grind wheat by machinery. Syn. KARAKURI.

SHIKAKE, シカケ, 袿, *n.* A long loose robe worn by women over their other garments.

†SHIKAKU, シカク, 刺客, *n.* An assassin.

SHI-KAKU, シカク, 四角, *n.* Four cornered, square. — *na tszkuye*, a square table. — *na moji*, the square characters (*kaisho*). — *na hashira*, a square post.

†SHIKAKU, シカク, 然, *adv.* So, thus, in such a way. — *nageku koto nakare*, don't grieve so.

SHIKAKUBARI,*-ru,-tta*, シカクバル, 四角張, *i. v.* To be formal, precise, exact, or punctilious in manner, or language. *Shikakubatte mono wo iu.*

SHIKAME*-ru,-ta*, シカメル, 蹙, *t. v.* To wrinkle or contort the face, to make a wry-face, to frown. *Kao wo* —.

SHIKAMI,*-mu,-nda*, シカム, 蹙, *i.v.* To have a wrinkled, contorted or wry-face, to frown.

SHIKAMI-DZRA, シカミヅラ, 蹙面, *n.* A wry-face, wrinkled, or frowning face.

SHIKA-MO, シカモ, *adv.* Besides, moreover, further-more, more than that. *Szde ni tezei tszkarete shikamo kozei nareba*, your army is already tired besides being small, &c. Syn. SONO WIYE.

†SHIKAN, シカン, 如, Fut. or dubit. of *Shiku. Idzre ka kore ni* —, what can be better than this.

SHI-KANE,*-ru,-ta*, シカネル, 仕兼, *t. v.* To do with difficulty, hard to do, or make. *Kuchi-szgi wo* —, hard to make a living. Syn. SHIGATAI.

†SHIKARADZ, シカラズ, 不然, Neg. of *Shikaru.* It is not so, = *sō de nai.*

SHIKARARE,*-ru,-ta*, シカラレル, 被呵, Pass of *Shikaru.* To get a scolding.

†SHIKARASHIMURU, シカラシムル, 令然, Caust. of *Shikaru.* To make or cause to be so, to decree it should be so. *Ten ri no* — *tokoro*, providence caused it to be so.

†SHIKARAZAREBA, シカラザレバ, Neg. sub. of *Shikaru*, = *sō de nakereba*, if it be not so.

†SHIKARAZARU, シカラザル, 不然, Neg. adj. form of *Shikaru*, = *sō de nai*, not being so. — *toki*, when it is not so.

SHIKARE,*-ru,-ta*, シカレル, 被壓, Pass. or pot. of *Shiku.* To be pressed under any thing, or overlaid, as by a stone, waggon, &c. *Kuruma ni shikareru*, crushed under a waggon.

†SHIKAREBA, シカレバ, Conj. mood of *Shikaru.* If so, then, if it be so, therefore, thus. Syn. SAREBA.

†SHIKAREDOMO, シカレドモ, Conj. mood of *Shikaru.* Although it be so, nevertheless, still, but, however, yet.
Syn. SAREDOMO, NAREDOMO.

SHIKARI,*-ru,-tta*, シカル, 呵, *t. v.* To scold, to chide, rate, censure. *Kodomo wo* —, to scold a child. Syn. TOGAMERU.

†SHIKARI,*-ru,-shi*, シカル, 然, *i. v.* (cont. of *Shika*, so, and *aru*, to be). To be so, thus, in this way.

†SHIKARI-TO-IYEDOMO, シカリトイヘドモ, 雖然, Although it be so.

†SHIKARUBEKI,*-KŪ,-SHI*, シカルベキ, 可然, Ought, should, or must be so, proper, fitting, suitable. — *h'to*, a proper person. — *koto*, a proper, right thing.
Syn. SARUBEKI.

SHIKARU-NI, シカルニ, *conj.* But, yet, however, still, notwithstanding, nevertheless.

SHIKARU-TOKORO, シカルトコロ, *conj.* But, yet, however, still, nevertheless.

†SHIKARU-WO, シカルヲ, *conj.* But, yet, however, still.

SHIKASE,*-ru,-ta*, シカセル, 令敷, *t. v.* Caust. of *Shiku.* To make, or let another spread anything. *Zashiki ni goza wo* —, to cause a mat to be spread in the parlor.

SHIKASHI, シカシ, (cont. of *Shikarishi*, the pret. of *Shikaru*). *conj.* But still, however, yet, nevertheless, notwithstanding.

†SHIKA-SHIKA, シカシカ, *adv.* So and so, and so on, (used in the place of something omitted) — *to kataru*, he said so and so.

SHIKASHI-NAGARA, シカシナガラ, 乍然, *conj.* But, however, yet, nevertheless. Syn. KEREDOMO, SAREDOMO, TADASHI.

†SHIKASH'TE, シカシテ, 然而, *adv.* Then, afterward, in that case.

SHI-KATA, シカタ, 仕方, *n.* Way of doing, treatment, conduct toward others; way of making, how any thing is made; resource; gesture, or sign. *Mama-haha no — ga warui kara kodomo wa uchi ni oranu,* the step-mother treats the child so bad he cannot live at home. *Kono shikake no — ga wakaranu,* I don't understand how this machine is made. *Shikata ga nai,* no resource. *— de shiraseru,* tell him by signs. Syn. SHIYŌ, SHI-HŌ, SHI-UCHI.

SHIKATA-BANASHI, シカタバナシ, Talking or narrating a story with much gesticulation. *— wo szru.*

SHIKA-TO, シカト, *adv.* Well, fully, certainly, firmly. *— sō-dan itashimashō,* I will certainly consult well about it. *— wakaranai,* I don't fully understand it. *— miyemasen,* I cannot see it clearly. Syn. TASH'KA-NI.

SHIKATSZBERASHII,-KI, シカツベラシイ, (cont. of *Shikaru,* so, *beki,* should be, and *rashii,* manner). Extremely precise, exact, or formal in talking.

SHIKATSZBERASHIKU, シカツベラシク, *adv.* id.

SHI-KAYE,*-ru,-ta,* シカヘル, 仕替, *t.v.* To do, or make over again, to mend by replacing the injured part with a new one. *Tsz-kuye no ashi wo —,* to repair a table by making a new leg. Syn. NAOSZ.

SHIKE, シケ, 連陰, *n.* A long rain, or continued damp water; a scarcity of fish in the market. *Shike biyori,* a continuation of rainy weather..

SHIKEITO, シケイト, 絓, *n.* The silk reeled from the outside of a cocoon, and of an inferior quality, same as *Noshi.*

SHIKI, シキ, 四季, *(yotsz no toki). n.* The four seasons. Syn. SHIJI.

†SHIKI, シキ, 色, *(iro). n.* Color, lewdness. *Go shiki,* the five colors; viz. green, red, white, black, and yellow.

SHIKI, シキ, 式, *n.* Law, rule, custom, usage. *— wo tateru. — wo sadameru,* to enact a law. *— wo somuku,* to break a law. Syn. REI, HŌSHIKI, KAKU.

†SHI-KI, シキ 指揮, *(sashidz). n.* Command, order. *— szru,* to give orders. *— wo ukeru,* to receive an order. Syn. GEJI.

†SHIKI, シキ, 識, *(chiye). n.* Knowledge, experience of men and things.

SHIKI, シキ, 士氣, *n.* Military spirit. *— ga otoroyeta,* martial spirit has degenerated.

SHIKI,*-ku,-ita,* シク, 敷, *t. v.* To spread; to pass over, overlay. *Goza, futon, nado wo —,* to spread a mat, or quilt. *Shiba wo —,* to lay sod. *Ishi wo —,* to pave with stones. *Kusa wo shīte zasz,* to sit down upon the grass. *Shiri ni —,* to sit upon. *Kuruma ga inu wo shiku,* a waggon has gone over the dog.

SHIKI-BUTON, シキブトン, 臥褥, *n.* A mattrass.

SHIKI-DAI,*-szru,* シキダイ, 色代, To bow respectfully, or apologetically, to excuse one's self, or beg pardon. Syn. YESHAKU.

SHIKI-DAI, シキダイ, 式臺, *n.* The stoop or pavement before the main entrance of a house.

SHIKI-GAMI, シキガミ, 敷紙, *n.* A kind of thick paper used for spreading over a floor.

SHIKI-GAWA, シキガハ, 敷皮, *n.* A fur-skin used for sitting on.

SHIKI-GAWARA, シキガハラ, 敷瓦, *n.* Tiles or bricks used for paving.

SHIKI-HŌ, シキハフ, 式法, *n.* Law, rule, custom, usage. Syn. HŌSHIKI.

SHIKII, シキ井, 敷居, *n.* The threshold, or lower beam in which a screen or door slides. Syn. TOJIKIMI.

SHIKI-ISHI, シキイシ, 敷石, *n.* Flat paving stones, a pavement.

SHIKI-JITSZ, シキジツ, 式日, *n.* A day set apart for any purpose by custom, or usage.

SHIKI-KIN, シキキン, 敷金, *n.* A deposit of money as security, made by a tenant to the landlord, which is returned when the tenant moves away.

SHIKIMI, シキミ, 閾, *n.* Same as *Shikii.*

SHIKIMI, シキミ, 莽草, *a.* The name of a tree.

SHIKI-MONO, シキモノ, 敷物, *n.* Anything used for spreading, as a carpet, rug table-cloth, mat, &c.; a spread.

SHIKI-REI, シキレイ, 式例, *n.* A law, rule, custom, usage. Syn. HŌSHIKI, REI.

SHIKIRI, シキリ, 仕切, *n.* A closing up account rendered of the sale of goods and expenses accruing. *— kin,* the balance paid on closing an account.

SHIKIRI, シキリ, *n.* A partition; a dividing line. *— wo szru. — wo ireru.* Syn. HEDATE.

SHIKIRI,*-ru,-tta,* シキル, 仕切, *t. v.* To divide or cut off, by a partition, fence, or line; to cut down the price of anything. *Heya futatsz ni —,* to divide a room by a partition. *Ame ga furi-shikiru*, the rain pours incessantly. Syn. HEDATERU.

SHIKIRI-NI, シキリニ, 頻, *adv.* Constantly, incessantly. — *ame ga furu*, it rains incessantly. — *saisoku*, to dun incessantly.
Syn. TSZDZKETE, TABI-TABI, TŌSHI.

SHIKI-SA-HŌ, シキサハフ, 式作法, *n.* Law rule, custom, usage. Syn. HŌSHIKI.

SHI-KI-SE, コキセ, 四季施, *n.* Clothes given to a servant at the change of the season.

†SHIKI-SHA, シキシヤ, 識者, *n.* A learned man.

SHIKI-SHI, シキシ, 色紙, *n.* Tinted or watered paper for writing verses on.

SHI-KITARI,*–ru,–tta,* シキタル, 仕來, *i. v.* To be practiced, or observed, from ancient times. *Nen-nen shi-kitatta rei*, a usage observed and come down for many years.

SHI-KIYO,*–szru,* シキヨ, 死去, *(shinuru).* To die.

†SHI-KIYOKU, シキヨク, 私曲, *(watakushi no magari). n.* Any wrong or corruption committed for private ends.

†SHIKI-YOKU, シキヨク, 色慾, *n.* Lust, lasciviousness, lewdness. Syn. IRO.

SHIKKAI, シツカイ, 悉皆, *(koto-gotoku). adv.* All, every thing. Syn. NOKORADZ, MARUDE, SZKKARI, MINA.

SHIKKARI, シツカリ, *adv.* Strong, stanch; firmly, tightly; certainly, not doubtful. — *to sh'ta h'to*, a trustworthy person. — *shibari-tszkeru*, to tie tightly.
Syn. TASH'KA, KATAKU.

SHIKKE, シツケ, or SHIKKI, シツキ, 濕氣, *n.* Moist, or damp air, humidity, dampness, moisture. — *ga agaru* the damp air rises.

SHIKKEI, シツケイ, 失敬, Disrespectful, uncivil, impolite. — *na mono.* — *itashimash'ta*, I beg pardon.
Syn. BUREI, SHITSZREI.

†SHIKKEN, シツケン, 執權, *n.* A primeminister.

SHIKKI, シツキ, See *Shikke.*

SHIKKUI, シツクイ, 石灰, (pronounced *Shikk'wi*). *n.* A white plaster, or cement made by mixing lime in the water in which *nori* has been boiled.

SHIKKURI-TO, シツクリト, *adv.* Exactly, accurately, nicely, snugly. — *au*, to fit accurately. Syn. SHIKKARI.

†SHIKK'WA, シツクワ, 失火, *n.* A fire, conflagration. Syn. K'WAJI.

SHIKO, シコ, *n.* The name of a small sea fish.

†SHIKŌ, シコウ, 伺候, Coming to see, (epist.) — *no wiye on hanashi mōshi soro*, after I come I will tell you.
Syn. SAN-YETSZ.

SHIKŌ, or SHIKOGUSA, シコヲ, Same as *Shion.*

SHĪKO, シイコ, *n.* Urine, (only used to children). — *se yo*, (imper).
Syn. SHŌBEN.

‖SHIKODZRI,*–ru,–tta,* シコヅル, 譖, *t.v.* To calumniate, slander.

SHI-KOMI,*–mu,–nda,* シコム, 仕込, *t. v.* To make and fix any thing inside of something else, (as the lead inside of a leadpencil, or a sword inside of a cane). To buy up, or lay in, a quantity of goods; to teach, to educate. *Tszye ni katana wo —.* to fit a sword in a cane. *Ito wo —*, to lay in a quantity of silk. *Gei wo —*, to teach accomplishments to a child.
Syn. SHI-IRE.

SHI-KOMI, シコミ, 仕込, *n.* Buying, or laying in goods; instruction.

SHIKON, シコン, 紫根, *n.* The root of the Lythospermum erythrorhizon, used as a dye-stuff.

SHIKORI, シコリ, 塊, *n.* An induration, or tumor. — *ga dekita*, have got a tumor.

SHIKORO, シコロ, 錏, *n.* The back part or cape of a helmet, which protects the neck.

SHI-KOSHI,*–sz,–sh'ta,* シコス, 仕越, *t.v.* To beat another at work, to do more than is required. *Shigoto wo —*, to exceed the required amount of work, or work later than the fixed time.

†SHIKŌSH'TE, シカウシテ, 而, *conj.* And, but, yet.

SHIKU, シク, 若, To be as, to be like, as good as, or equal to, better than. *Kannin ni shiku wa nashi*, there is nothing like patience. *Kore ni shiku mono nashi*, nothing so good as this. (This word seems to be a defect. verb. of which, *Shikadz*, and *Shikan*, are the only other form used.)

SHIKU, シク, 敷, See *Shiki.*

SHIKUJIRI,*–ru,–tta,* シクジル, *t.v.* In doing or making any thing to spoil it, to mismanage, to commit a mistake, to blunder, to lose, or be turned out of office, or place. *Saiku wo —*, to spoil a piece of work. *Akinai wo —*, to lose in trading. *Bantō ga o-tana wo shikujitta*, the clerk has been turned out of his place. *Yakunin ga yaku wo —*, the officer has lost his place.
Syn. FU-SHUBI, SHISOKONAU, YARI-SOKONAU.

SHIKUJIRI, シクジリ, *n.* A blunder, mistake, mismanagement, turned out of office or place. Ō — *wo sh'ta*, have committed a great blunder. — *ni natta*, has been dismissed from office.

SHIKUMI,-*mu*,-*nda*, シクム, 仕組, *i.v.* To do together, to be partners in doing, to conspire to do. *San nin shikunde akinai wo szru*, the three men are partners in business. *Go nin shikunde muhon wo kuwadateru*, the five men conspired together and plotted rebellion.

SHIKU-SHIKU, シクシク, *adv.* In a low voice, or slight degree. — *to naku*, to cry in a low voice. — *itai*, to pain slightly, to prick.

SHI-K'WAN, シクワン, 仕官, Filling a public office, acting as an officer. — *szru*, to engage in official employment.

SHIMA, シマ, 嶋, *n.* An island.

SHIMA, シマ, 縞, *n.* The striped figure in cloth.

SHIMADA, シマダ, 嶋田, *n.* The manner in which the hair of unmarried females is worn. *Kami wo — ni yu.*

SHIMADAI, シマダイ, 嶋臺, *n.* A stand on which branches of bamboo, pine, and plum, together with figures of the crane tortoise, of an old man and woman are arranged, and set out on marriage occasions, being emblematic of virtue, happiness, and long life.

SHIMAI,-*au*,-*atta*, シマフ, 仕舞, *t.v.* To do, end, finish; to set or put away, (as anything not in use). *Shigoto wo* —, to finish one's work. *Hon wo yonde shimatta*, have done reading the book. *Cha-wan wo shimaye*, or *shimatte oke*, put the tea-cups away. Syn. OWARU, SZMU, OSAMERU.

SHIMAI, シマヒ, 仕舞, *n.* End, conclusion, termination. — *ni natta*, is finished. *Shimai-mono*, anything remaining over, after selling all the rest; unsold goods.

||SHIMAKI, シマキ, *n.* A shower of rain. Syn. SHIGURE.

SHIMARI,-*ru*,-*tta*, シマル, 締, *i. v.* To be tight, tense, pressed together, close, compact, shut, closed, to be strict, or careful in conduct. *Nawa ga* —, the rope is taught. *Obi ga* —, belt is tight. *To ga* —, the door is shut. *Shimatta h'to*, a temperate, discreet person.

SHIMARI, シマリ, 締, *n.* Tightness, tenseness, compactness, firmness, solidity, closeness, strictness, discipline, order. *Kono nawa no — ga warui*, this rope is not tight, or it is loose in texture. *Kokoro ni — ga nai*, no firmness or stability of mind. *Gunzei no — ga nai*, the army is without discipline. *Iye no* —, the order or discipline of a family. — *wo szru*, to maintain order, or discipline. Syn. TORI-SHIMARI.

SHI-MASHI,-*sz*,-*sh'ta*, シマス, (comp. of *Shi*, and *masz*, respectful). *t v.* To do, to make. *Nani wo shimasz*, what are you doing?

SHI-MATSZ, シマツ, 始末, (*moto szye*). *n.* The origin and end, all the circumstances, the whole state or condition of anything, economy. *Sōdō no — wo tadasz*, to investigate the origin and all the circumstances of a rebellion. — *na h'to*, an economical or judicious person. — *wo szru*, to be economical, careful.

SHIMBARI, シンバリ, *n.* A brace, fastening, or prop, as a stick placed against a door to keep it shut. — *wo kau.* — *wo szru*, to brace with a stick.

SHIM-BATSZ, シンバツ, 神罰, *n.* Punishment inflicted by the *Kami*, divine punishment. — *wo kōmuru.* Syn. BACHI.

†SHIMBEN, シンベン, 神變, Miraculous, supernatural. — *fushigi no jutsz*, supernatural or miraculous acts. Syn. KIMIYŌ, FUSHIGI.

SHIM-BIYŌ, シンビヤウ, 神妙, Wonderful, marvellous, grand, glorious, (used in praising another.) Syn. KIDOKU.

SHIMBŌ, シンバウ, 辛抱, *n.* Perseverance, diligent or patient continuance in any thing, patience, patient endurance, or bearing with, self-denial. — *szru*, to persevere, to bear patiently, to patiently continue, to hold on. — *shete kane wo tameru*, to lay up money by denying one's self the pleasures procured by spending it. *Mō — dekimasen*, I cannot endure it any longer. — *dekiru hodo no atszsa*, as hot as can be borne. — *ni oi-tszku bim-bō nashi*, poverty cannot overtake diligence. *Shimbō szru yori dorobō shansei, kubi no nai no mo ikina mono*, better be a thief than a drudge, a fellow without a head is stylish too. Syn. BENKIYŌ, GAMAN.

SIMBOCHI, シンボチ, 新發意, *n.* One who experiences a change of heart and enters a convent; a novice.

SHIM-BOKU, シンボク, 神木, *n.* A sacred tree, a tree the Kami is supposed to delight in.

SHIMBŌ-NIN, シンバウニン, *n.* One who is diligent in business, and denies himself useless pleasures.

SHIM-BUN, シンブン, 新聞, (*atarashiku kiku*), *n.* News. — *wo noberu*, to tell the news. Syn. CHINDAN.

SHIM-BUN-SHI, シンブンシ, 新聞紙, *n.* A newspaper.

SHIME, シメ, 緘, *n.* The mark (メ) made on the back of a letter, intended as a seal.

SHIME, シメ, *n.* The same as *Seme.* A clasp, or band, (as for a fan or umbrella).

SHIME, シメ, *n.* Same as *Shime-nawa.* — *wo haru.* — *wo hiku.*

SHIME, シメ, *n.* The name of a small bird.

SHIME, シメ, *n.* Same as *Shimedaka.* The amount, sum, total. — *wa ikura ni narimas,* what is the amount?

SHIME,-*ru*,-*ta*, シメル, 締, *t.v.* To tighten, to press, squeeze, to fasten, to make firm, compact, or hard. 閉, To shut, close. 計, To sum up, add together. 占, To take or get possession of. *Nawa wo* —, to tighten a rope. *Nodo wo* —, to choke. *Obi wo* —, to tighten a belt. *Tszchi wo* —, to make the earth compact, or hard. *Abura wo* —, to express oil. *To wo* —, to shut the door. *Hikidashi wo* —, to shut a drawer. *Kanedaka wo* —, to add together various sums, to find the amount. *Za wo* —, to take a seat. *Hiki-shimeru,* to draw taught. *Daki-shimeru,* to hug tightly. *Nigiri-shimeru,* to squeeze tightly in the hand. *Kui-shimeru,* to hold tightly in the teeth. *Kanjō wo* —, to sum up an account.

SHIME-DAKA, シメダカ, *n.* The amount, sum, total. — *wa ikura,* what is the amount? Syn. TSZGŌ.

SHIME-GI, シメギ, *n.* A press.

SHIMEJI, シメジ, *n.* A kind of mushroom.

SHIME-KAZARI, シメカザリ, 注連飾, *n.* The decorations of straw-rope, pine, bamboo, charcoal, crab, fern, &c., hung over the door, at the beginning of the new year.

SHIME-KOROSHI,-*sz*,-*sh'ta*, シメコロス, 絞殺, *t.v.* To choke to death.

SHI-MEN, シメン, 四面, *(yotsz no omote)*, *n.* The four sides of anything. *San-gen* —, 18 feet square. *Iye no — ni niwa ga aru,* a yard around the house.

SHIMEN, シメン, 紙面, *(kami no omote)*, *n.* A letter. *Go — no omomuki,* the contents of your letter. Syn. TEGAMI.

SHIME-NAWA, シメナハ, 注連繩, *n.* The straw rope hung before Miyas, or, before houses on the beginning of the new year.

SHIMERI,-*ru*,-*tta*, シメル, 沾, *i.v.* To be wet, damp, or moist. 鎮, To be extinguished, go out. *Tszchi ga ame de* —, the ground is wet with rain. *Tomoshibi ga shimetta,* the lamp has gone out. *Kwaji ga* —, the fire is extinguished. Syn. URUŌ, NURERU, SHITORU, KIYERU.

SHIMERI, シメリ, 濕, *n.* Dampness, slightly wet, moisture. — *wo utsz,* to dampen, sprinkle with water. *Kimono wa — ga aru,* the clothes are damp. Syn. SHITORI.

SHIMESHI,-*sz*,-*sh'ta*, シメス, 令沾, *t. v.* To wet, moisten, dampen; to extinguish, put out, quench. *Midz de* —, to wet, or moisten with water. *Hi wo* —, to extinguish fire. *Tomoshibi wo* —, to blow out, or extinguish a lamp. Syn. NURASZ, URUOSZ.

SHIMESHI,-*sz*,-*sh'ta*, シメス, 示, *t.v.* To show, to make known, to declare, inform, to publish, show forth, indicate. *Shimbun wo* —, to publish the news. *I wo* —, to show one's power. *Magokoro wo* —, to show sincerity. *Yuyake wa miyōnichi no ame wo* —, a red sky in the evening indicates rain to-morrow. *Haku-tai wa i-chiu no yamai wo* —, a furred tongue indicates a disordered stomach. Syn. MISERU, KIKASERU.

SHIMESHI, シメシ, *n.* A diaper, napkin, or clout, used to receive the excrements of infants.

SHIMETA, シメタ, the pret. of *Shimeru.* Have got! have found it! Syn. YETARI.

SHIMETE, シメテ, 總計, *pp.* of *Shimeru.* In all, the sum, amount. — *h'yaku riyō,* amounting to one hundred *riyō.* Syn. SZBETE, AWASETE, TSZGŌ.

SHIME-TSZKE,-*ru*,-*ta*, シメツケル, 締著, *t.v.* To tighten, fasten.

SHIMEYAKA, シメヤカ, Quiet, still, free from noise, or commotion. — *naru yo,* a still night. — *naru haru no ame,* a spring rain. Syn. SHIDZKA, ODAYAKA, SHIN-CHIN.

SHIME-YOSE,-*ru*,-*tta*, シメヨセル, 締寄, *t.v.* To press, or force together.

SHIMI,-*u*,-*ita*, シム, *t.v.* To pierce, penetrate, or affect deeply; to smart, or cause a sharp, piercing pain; to stain, to spot, discolor. *Kaze ga mi ni* —, the wind penetrates the body. *Kimo ni* —, to pierce the liver, affect deeply. *Kuszri ga me ni* —, the medicine smarts the eye. *Abura ga kimono ni* —, oil stains the clothes. *Shimi-wataru,* to pierce through, (as cold).

SHIMI, シミ, *n.* A stain. — *ga dekita,* it is stained. — *wo nuku,* or, — *wo otosz,* to take out a stain.

SHIMI, シミ, 蠹魚, *n.* A moth, book-worm.

SHIMIDZ, シミヅ, 清水, (*kiyoki midz*), *n.* Pure or clear water.

SHIMI-JIMI-TO, シミジミト, *adv.* In a penetrating, or deeply affecting manner. — *kanashikatta*, pierced with grief.

SHIMI-KOMI,–*mu*,–*nda*, シミコム, To eat into, to corrode, penetrate into, as an acid, stain, &c.

SHI-MIN, シミン, 四民, (*yotsz no tami*), *n.* The four classes of people; viz. the nobility, farmers, mechanics, and merchants.

SHIMIRU, シミル, Same as *Shimu*, see *Shimi.*

SHIMITARE, or SHIMITTARE,–*ru*,–*ta*, シミタレル, *i.v.* To be lazy and slovenly, indolent, and dirty. Syn. BUSHŌ.

†SHIM-MAI, シンマイ, 新米, (*atarashii kome*). *n.* New rice, this year's rice.

†SHIMME, シンメ, 新芽, *n.* New-sprouts, (as from a stump).

†SHIM-MEI, シンメイ, 神明, *n.* Same as *Kami.* The deities worshiped at *Sintoo* temples. — *no bachi wo kōmuru.* — *no waza.*

SHIMMI, シンミ, 親身, *n.* Kindred, relation. — *no mono*, a relation.
Syn. SHINRUI.

SHIM-MIYŌ, シンミヤウ, Same as *Shimbiyō.*

SHIMMOTSZ, シンモツ, 進物, *n.* A present, — *wo szru*, to make a present.
Syn. SHINJŌ-MONO.

SHIMO, シモ, 霜, *n.* Hoar-frost. — *ga futta*, the frost has fallen. — *ga oku*, (idem).

SHIMO, シモ, 下, Below, down, inferiors. *Kawa no* —, down the river. — *no tō ka*, the last ten days of a month. *Shimo no h'to*, an inferior, common people. *Kami, naka, shimo*, superior, middle and inferior.
Syn. SH'TA.

†SHIMO, シモ, See under *Shi*, an euphonic particle.

SHIMO-BASHIRA, シモバシラ, 霜柱, *n.* The small icy columns observed in frozen, wet ground, frost.

SHIMOBE, シモベ, 下部, *n.* A servant.
Syn. GEJO, GENAN.

SHIMOGARE, シモガレ, 霜枯, Withered by the frost, frosty, wintry. — *no keshiki*, a wintry landscape.

SHIMOGOYE, シモゴヱ, 下糞, *n.* Night-soil.

SHIMO-JIMO, シモジモ, 下下, *n.* Lower classes, common people. Syn. SH'TA-JITA.

SHIMOKU, シモク, 橦木, *n.* The hammer, or stick used for striking a bell.

SHIMO-KUDZRE, シモクヅレ, 霜崩, *n.* Crumbled, or disintegrated by frost.

SHIMOKUDZYE, シモクヅヱ, 丁杖, *n.* A cane with a handle in the shape of a cross given by the *Shōgun*, as a reward of merit or mark of favor, and carried in a woollen case by a servant of its owner.

SHI-MON-SEN, シモンセン, 四文錢, *n.* The name of an iron coin, of which 24 make one *tempō*.

SHIMO-ONNA, シモヲンナ, 下女, (*ge-jo*). *n.* A female servant, maid-servant.

SHIMO-OTOKO, シモヲトコ, 下男, (*ge nan*). *n.* A man-servant.

SHIMOTO, シモト, 笞, *n.* A stick or rod used for flogging.

SHIMOTSZKE, シモツケ, 下野花, *n.* A species of Spiræa.

SHIMO-TSZKI, シモツキ, 十一月, *n.* The eleventh month. Syn. JŪ-ICHI GATSZ.

SHIMO-YAKE, シモヤケ, 寒瘡, *n.* Frost-bitten. — *ga dekita.*

SHIMO-YASHIKI, シモヤシキ, 別莊, (*bessō*). *n.* A house belonging to a noble used only as a temporary residence.

SHIMO-ZAMA, シモザマ, 下樣, *n.* The lower classes, common people.
Syn. SHIMO-JIMO.

SHIMPAI, シンパイ, 心配, *n.* Concern, anxiety, care, solicitude, trouble. — *szru*, to be concerned or troubled about.
Syn. KIDZKAI, KURŌ, ANJI.

SHIM-PAN, シンパン, 新板, (*atarashii ita*). *n.* A new book, a new edition, a reprint.

SHIMPATSZ,–*szru*, シンパツ, 進發, To invade an enemy's country, to march an army, or go on a military expedition.

†SHIMPI, シンピ, 深秘, (*fukaku kakusz*). *n.* A profound secret.

SHIM-PITSZ, シンピツ, 眞筆, *n.* A genuine writing, the autograph.
Syn. SHINSEKI.

SHIM-PŌ, シンパフ, 新法, (*atarashii hatto*). *n*, A new law, a new edict.

SHIM-PUKU, シンプク, 心服, Hearty, or sincere obedience.

SHIMU, or SHIMURU, シム, See *Shimi.*

SHIMUKE, シムケ, 仕向, *n.* Treatment or behavior toward any one. — *ga warui.* — *ga yoi.* Syn. SHIUCHI.

SHIN, シン, 神, *n.* The ancient deities of Japan, as distinguished from *Hotoke* the divinity of the Buddhists, worshiped at the *Miya*; God.

SHIN, シン, 新, (*atarashii*). New. *Furudemo shin demo yoi*, either old or new will do.

SHIN, シン, 臣, (*kerai*). The retainer, vassal, serf or servant of a noble; minister of a prince; officer, a subject.

SHIN, シン, 心, (*kokoro*). *n.* The heart, the wick of a candle, the pith of a tree, the small paper cone which support the hairs of a pencil, the heart of fruit. — *kara kawai*, love from the heart.

†SHIN, シン, 眞, (*makotò*). Real, genuine, true. — *ni semaru*, like the real article. — *ni*, indeed, really, truly.

SHIN, シン, 信, (*makoto, otodzre*). *n.* Truth, faith, sincerity; word, tidings, communication. *H'to ni majiwaru ni — wo motte sz*, in intercourse with men be sincere. — *no nai h'to*, a person without faith, or truth. — *wo toru*, to believe, to be devout. — *wo ts'udzru*, to send word.

SHĪNA, シヒナ, 秕, *n.* Imperfect or immature ear of corn.

SHI-NA, シナ, Coll. imp. of *Shi*, *szru*, = *seyo*. *Hayaku shi-na*, do it quick.

SHINA, シナ, 品, *n.* A thing, kind or quality of a thing, events or circumstances. *Kono shina wa nan to mōsz mono*, what do you call this thing? *Onaji mono nagara shina ga warui*, although it is the same thing the quality is bad. — *ni yotte yukimashō*, my going depends on circumstances. Syn. MONO, HIN, GARA.

SHINA, シナ, 支那, *n.* China. Syn. KARA, MOROKOSHI, KANDO.

SHINA, シナ, A suffix to verbs, = whilst, when. *Yuki-shina ni* while going. *Yama wo koye-shina ni*, when crossing the mountain. *Kayeri-shina*, while returning. Syn. GAKE, TSZIDE-NI

SHINABI,*-ru,-ta*, シナビル, *i.v.* To wilt, to begin to wither, to become soft or flaccid. *Nashi ga shinabita*, the pear has begun to wither. Syn. HINAYERU.

SHINA-DAMA, シナダマ, 品玉, *n.* The balls and articles used in sleight-of-hand tricks. — *wo tszkau*, to perform sleight-of hand tricks. *Shina-dama-tszkai*, a juggler.

SHINADARE,*-ru,-ta*, シナダレル, *i.v.* To act in a soft, sweet, or loving manner to one of another sex. *Onna ni shinadare-kakaru.*

SHINA-GIRE, シナギレ, 品切, *n.* To be out, or deficient of any article of merchandise (having sold all). — *de gozarimasen*, I have not got it, having sold all I had.

SHI-NAI, シナイ, 不爲, Coll. neg. of *szru*, = *senu*, or *sedz*. Not do. — *hō ga yoi*, better not do it. — *naraba buchimashō*, if you don't do it I will whip you.

SHINA-JINA, シナジナ, 品品, Many or various things, different articles, or kinds, Syn. IRO-IRO.

SHINA-KATACHI, シナカタチ, 品形, *n.* Form, figure, shape.

SHINA-MONO, シナモノ, 品物, *n.* A thing, article, kind or quality of anything. — *ga chigau*, the quality is different.

SHINAN, シナン, 指南, *n.* Teaching, instruction. — *szru*, to teach, to show how. — *wo ukeru*, to receive instruction. Syn. OSHIYE.

†SHINAN, シナン, fut. of *Shinuru*. — *to szru*, to be dying, or about to die.

SHI-NAOSHI,*-sz,-sh'ta*, シナホス, 仕直, *t.v.* To mend, repair, to alter, to make over.

SHI-NARE,*-ru,-ta*, シナレル, 仕馴, *i.v.* To be used or accustomed to do or make, to be skilful in doing or making. *Pan wo shinareta*, have become used to making bread. *Shinareneba dekinu*, if you don't get used to doing it you won't succeed.

SHI-NASARE,*-ru,-ta*, シナサレル, 仕被成, *t.v.* (Respectful), same as, *Shi*, *szru*, to do, to make.

SHI-NASHI, シナシ, 仕爲, *n.* Treatment behavior, way of acting or doing. Syn. SHIMUKE, SHIUCHI.

SHINAYAKA, シナヤカ, *a.* Soft and flexible, pliant, delicate, limber, graceful. Syn. TAOYAKA.

SHINAYE, シヘエ, 竹刀, *n.* A bamboo-sword used for fencing.

SHINAYE,*-ru,-ta*, シナヘル, *i.v.* To bend downward, as the branch of a tree. *Yuki de take ga —*, the bamboo bends with the weight of the snow. *Ine ga —*, the rice stalk bends. Syn. TAWAMU.

SHIN-CHA, シンチャ, 新茶, (*atarashii cha*). *n.* New tea, or this year's tea.

SHIN-CHI, シンチ, 新地, *n.* A new estate, or fief received by a vassal from his lord; new made ground.

†SHIN-CHIN, シンチン, 深沉, Quiet, still; free from noise or excitement. Syn. SHIMEYAKA, SHIDZKA.

SHIN-CHIU, シンチユウ, 眞鍮, *n.* Brass.

SHIN-CHIU, シンチウ, 心中, (*kokoro no uchi*). In the heart or mind. *H'to no — wo sziriyō szru*, to guess what is in one's mind.

SHINDA, シンダ, pret. of *Shini*. Dead. — *h'to*, a dead person.

SHIN-DAI, シンダイ, 身代, *n.* Property, possessions, estate. Syn. SHINSHO.

†SHINDAN, シンダン, 震旦, *n.* China.

SHINDE, シンデ, pp. of *Shini*.

SHIN-DEN, シンデン, 新田, (*atarashii ta*) *n.* Newly reclaimed rice fields.

†SHINDEN, シンデン, 寢殿, *n.* The common sitting room or chamber in the house of a noble.

SHINDŌ,–*szru*, シンドウ, 震動, (*furui ugoku*). To shake, tremble. *Yama kawa ga* —, the hills and rivers shake.

SHINDZRU,シンヅル,信, See *Shinji.*

SHINE, シネ, imp. of *Shini.* = *Shine yo,* die.

SHI-NEN, シネン, 思念, (*omoi omō*). *n.* Thinking, thought. *Shinen szru,* to think. *Nan no — mo nai,* not thinking of anything.

SHINGAKU, シンガク, 心學, *n.* Moral essays or discourses.

SHINGARI, シンガリ, 殿, *n.* The rear-guard of a retreating army.

SHINGATA, シンガタ, 新形, *n.* A new figure, design, or style, (of manufactured articles).

SHINGI, シンギ, 眞僞, *n.* True or false, genuine or spurious. — *wo tadasz,* to ascertain whether anything is genuine or spurious, &c.

SHINGI, シンギ, 心木, *n.* The centre-pin about which anything turns, axle-tree, axis.

SHIN-GIYŌ-SŌ, シンギヤウサウ, 眞行草, *n.* The three modes of writing Chinese characters; viz., the genuine or square, the running hand, and grass character.

SHNIG'WAI, シングワイ, 心外, (*kokoro no hoka*). *adv.* Different from one's mind, expectation or intention. — *go busato itashimash'ta,* I did not think I should be so long without paying my compliments to you.

SHIN-G'WAN, シングワン, 心願, (*kokoro no negai*). *n.* Heart's desire,

SHIN-I, シンイ, 瞋恚, (*ikari*). *n.* Anger, wrath. — *no kambashi,* angry countenance. Syn. IKIDŌRI, HARADACHI.

SHINI,–*uru*,–*da*,, シヌル 死, *i.v.* To die. *Biyōki de* —, to die of disease. *Hara wo kitte* —, he died by cutting his belly open. *Kubi wo kukutte* —, he hung himself. *Shinde hana mi ga saku mono ka,* when a flower is dead can it bear fruit? (prov).

SHINI, シニ, 死, *n.* Death. *Aware-na — wo sh'ta,* died a pitiful death.

SHINI-GAO, シニガホ, 死面, The face of one dead.

SHINI-HATE,–*ru*,–*ta*, シニハテル, 死果, *i.v.* To die out, to be all cut off by death, (as a family).

SHINI-IRI,–*ru*,–*tta*, シニイル, 死入, *i.v.* To be like one dead, (as from fright).

SHINI-KAKARI,–*ru*,–*tta*, シニカカル, 死掛, *i.v.* To be at the point of death, about to die.

SHINI-ME, シニメ, 死目, *n.* The time of death, the article of death. *Oya no — ni awanu,* was not present at his parent's death.

SHINI-MONO-GURUI, シニモノグルイ, 死物狂, (lit. death-fury), Desperation. — *wo szru,* to fight with desperation. — *ni tatakau.* (idem).

SHI-NIN, シニン, 死人, *n.* A dead person.

SHINI-NOKORI,–*ru*,–*tta*, シニノコル, 死殘, *i.v.* To be left alive, to escape death, all the others having died.

SHINI-TAYE,–*ru*,–*ta*, シニタエル, 死絶, *i.v.* Cut off by death, to die out. *Shison ga shinitayeta,* his posterity have become extinct.

SHINI-WAKARE,–*ru*,–*ta*, シニワカレル, 死別, *i.v.* To be separated by death. *Oya ko* —.

SHINI-YAMAI, シニヤマイ, 死病, *n.* A mortal disease.

SHINJA, シンジヤ, 信者, *n.* A devout, religious person, a believer, a saint.

SHINJI,–*dzru* or –*ru*,–*ta*, シンズル, 信, *t.v.* To believe, to regard as true, to believe in. to confide in, to trust in. *Zan-gen wo shindzru koto nakare,* don't believe a slander. *Shinjirarenu hanashi,* an incredible story. *Shinji-gatai,* hard to believe. *Kami wo* —, to believe in God, or to believe there is a God.

SHIN-JI, シンジ, 信士, *n.* A devout person, a believer, a saint.

SHIN-JIN, シンジン, 信心, *n.* Devotion, piety, faith. — *wo szru,* to be devout or much engaged in religious worship. — *na h'to* a devout person. — *wo okosz,* to excite devotion.

SHIN-JITSZ, シンジツ, 眞實, True, sincere, faithful, honest, real. — *ni,* truly, sincerely, indeed. — *na h'to,* a sincere person.
Syn. MAKOTO, JITSZ.

SHIN-JŌ, シンジヤウ, 進上, (*szszme ageru*). — *szru.* To give as a present, to present. *Kono hon wo shin-jō itashimasz,* I make you a present of this book. — *mono,* a present.
Syn. YARU, AGERU.

SHIN-JO, シンジヨ, 寢所, *n.* A bed-chamber.

SHIN-JŌ, シンヂウ, 情死, (*aitaijini*). Committing suicide together. — *szru.*

SHIN-JU, シンジユ, 眞珠, (*madama*). *n.* A pearl.

SHIN-JUTSZ, シンジユツ, 心術, (*kodorodate*). *n.* The thoughts or motions of the mind, the heart and its objects. — *no warui h'to,* a bad hearted man.

SHIN-KA, シンカ, 臣下, *n.* A retainer, serf, servant.

SHIN-KARA, シンカラ, 心肝, *adv.* Truly, indeed, heartily. — *kirai,* heartily dislike. — *kawai kodomo,* a truly lovely child. Syn. JITSZ-NI.

SHIN-KEI, シンケイ, 神經, *n.* A nerve.

SHIN-KEN, シンケン, 眞劍, (*makoto no tszrugi*). *n.* Real sword, (not a wooden one). — *no shō-bu,* a duel, or combat with real swords.

SHIN-KI, シンキ, 神氣, *n.* The natural force, vigor, strength, or energy of the body. *Biyōki de — ga otoroyeta,* owing to sickness he has grown weak.

SHIN-KI, シンキ, 新規, (*arata*). New. — *na iye,* a new house. — *ni koshirayeru,* newly made.

SHIN-KI, シンキ, *n.* Melancholy, gloom, depression of spirits. — *de komaru,* affected with low spirits. Syn. UTSZ UTSZ.

SHIN-KIKU, シンキク, 神菊, *n.* The name of a flowering plant.

†SHIN-KIN, シンキン, 宸襟, *n.* The heart of the *Tenshi.* — *wo nayamase tamō,* to afflict, or give trouble to the Emperor.

SHIN-KIRI, シンキリ, 燭剪, *n.* Snuffers.

SHIN-KIRŌ, シンキロウ, 蜃氣樓, *n.* A mirage. — *ga tatsz.*

SHINKO, シンコ, 眞粉, *n.* A kind of confectionary made of rice flour.

SHIN-KŌ, シンカウ, 深更, (*yofuke*). *n.* Late watch of the night.

SHIN-KŌ, シンカウ, 信仰, Faith, belief, trust, confidence. — *szru,* to believe, credit, trust, confide in. *Kami wo —,* to believe in God. Syn. SHINJI.

SHIN-KOKU, シンコク, 神國, (*kami no kuni*), *n.* The country of the gods, viz. Japan.

SHIN-KON, シンコン, 心魂, *n.* The heart, only used in the phrase. — *tesszru,* to pierce to one's heart, to feel deeply.

SHIN-KU, シンク, 辛苦, (*kurō*). *n.* Toil, labor, hardship, pain, difficulty; trouble. — *szru.* Syn. KANNAN.

SHIN-NEN, シンネン, 新年, (*atarashii toshi*). *n.* The new year.

SHIN-NIYO, シンニヨ, 信女, *n.* A devout woman.

SHIN-NŌ, シンワウ, 親王, *n.* A son of the *Tenshi,* a prince. *Naishinnō,* a princess. Syn. MI-KO, MIYA-SAMA.

SHIN-NO-ZŌ, シンノザウ, 心臟, *n.* The viscus called the heart.

SHINŌ, シナウ, Coll. fut. or dub. of *Shinuru,* same as *shinan.* — *to omōta,* thought I would die.

SHINO, or SHINODAKE, シノ, 小竹, *n.* A small kind of bamboo.

SHINOBI,*-bu,-nda,* シノブ, 忍, *t.v.* To bear with patience, to endure, to conceal one's self from, to avoid, shun, to disguise one's self, to think of, or long after. *Miru ni shinobidz,* could not bear to see it. *Haji wo —,* to put up with an insult. *H'to no me wo —,* to conceal one's self from the eyes of others. *Yo wo —,* to live in concealment. *Onna wo —,* to think about a woman. Syn. KANNIN SZRU, KORAYERU, SHINOGU, KAKUSZ, SH'TAU.

SHINOBI, シノビ, *n.* Disguise, concealment, a spy, or disguised person. — *wo ireru,* to send a spy. — *ni sode wo shiboru,* to wring the tears from one's sleeve unperceived by others. — *de aruku,* to walk in disguise or incognito. — *no mono,* a spy. Syn. HISOKA-NI.

SHINOBI-TSZMA, シノビツマ, *n.* A mistress kept secretly.

SHINOBI-GAYESHI, シノビガヘシ, 遮欄, *n.* Sharp sticks fixed on the top of a fence to prevent persons from climbing over.

SHINOBI-NAKI, シノビナキ, *n.* Weeping in secret.

SHINOBIYAKA-NI, シノビヤカニ, *adv.* Secretly, privately, stealthily, incognito, in disguise, clandestinely. Syn. HISOKANI.

SHINOBU, or SHINOBUGUSA, シノブグサ, 垣衣, *n.* The name of a vine.

SHINOGI,*-gu,-ida,* シノグ, 凌, *t.v.* To bear up under, or get through with, as hardship, or suffering; to have fortitude, to support, stand, sustain, endure, to bear, to keep off, to rise, ascend, or pass above. *Samusa wo —,* to stand the cold. *Nangi wo —,* to endure hardship. *Nemuri wo —,* keep off sleep. *Bim-bō de shinogi-kaneru,* being poor finds it hard to get along. *Wata-iri nashi de wa fuyu ga shinogarenu,* cannot get through the winter without a padded coat. *Kurai wo —,* to get above another in rank. *Kumo wo shinoide noboru,* to ascend above the clouds. Syn. SHIMBŌ SZRU, SHINOBU, TAYERU, TŌSZ.

SHINOGI, シノギ, 刃稜, *n.* The raised line along the blade of a sword. — *wo kedzru,* to clash swords in fighting.

SHI-NOKOSHI,-sz,-sh'ta, シノコス, 仕殘, *t. v.* To leave over the doing of any thing to another time, to put off to do, to postpone.

SHINONDA, シノンダ, *pret.* of *Shinobu.*

SHINONDE, シノンデ, *pp.* of *Shinobu.*

SHINONOME, シノノメ, *n.* The dawn of day. Syn. AKATSZKI.

†SHIN-RA, シンラ, 新羅, *n.* One of the four ancient divisions of Corea.

†SHIN-RA-BAN-SHŌ, シンラバンシヤウ, 森羅萬象, *n.* All things. *Kami wa — wo tszkuri-tamō,* God created all things.

SHIN-RAN, シンラン, 進覧, To give as a present to an honorable person.

†SHIN-REI, シンレイ, 神靈, (lit. divine spirit). Same as *Kami;* supernatural, miraculous.

SHIN-RIKI, シンリキ, 神力, *(kami no chikara). n.* The power of the Kami, divine power.

†SHIN-RIKI, シンリキ, 信力, *n.* The power or efficacy of faith or devotion. Bud.

SHIN-RIYŌ, シンリヤウ, 神領, *(kami no riyōbun). n.* The estate or glebe belonging to a Miya.

†SHIN-RIYO, シンリヨ, 神慮, *(kami no oboshimeshi). n.* The mind or will of the Kami.

†SHIN-RIYOKU, シンリヨク, 心力, *(kokoro chikara). n.* The heart and strength. — *wo tszkusz,* to do with all the heart and strength.

SHIN-RUI, シンルイ, 親類, *n.* Kindred, relations either by birth or marriage.

†SHIN-SATSZ, シンサツ, 診察, *n.* Examination of a patient by a physician. *Biyōnin wo — szru,* to examine a sick person.

†SHINSEI, シンセイ, 辰星, *n.* A star, same as, *Seishin.* Syn. HOSHI.

SHIN-SEKI, シンセキ, 親戚, *n.* Kindred, relations, connection. Syn. SHINRUI.

SHIN-SEKI, シンセキ, 眞蹟, *(makoto no ato). n.* A genuine writing, real handwriting, autograph. Syn. SHIMPITSZ.

†SHIN-SEN, シンセン, 深淺, *(fukai, asai). n.* Deep or shallow.

SHIN-SETSZ, シンセツ, 深切, *n.* Kindness, benevolence. — *na h to,* a kind person. — *ni,* kindly. Syn. NENGORO.

SHIN-SETSZ, シンセツ, 新説, *(atarashii hanashi). n.* News. Syn. SHINBUN.

SHIN-SHA, シンシヤ, 眞砂, *n.* Cinnabar.

SHIN-SHAKU, シンシヤク, 斟酌, *n.* Complimentary excuse, apology, backwardness. — *szru,* to politely excuse one's self, or decline. Syn. YENRIYŌ.

SHIN-SHI, シンシ, 親子, *(oya ko). n.* Parent and child.

SHIN-SHIN-TO, シンシント, *adv.* In a tingling, or thrilling manner, as, *Itami ga — mi ni kotayeru,* the pain tingled through the whole body.

SHIN-SHIN-TO, シンシント, 深深, *adv.* Quiet, retired, solitary, lonely. — *sh'ta tokoro,* a retired, or lonely place. Syn. SAMUSHII.

SHIN-SHO, シンシヨ, 身上, *(mi no wiye). n.* Property, means, substance, possessions, estate, finances. Syn. SHINDAI.

SHIN-SHOKU, シンシヨク, 神職, *n.* One who has the charge and direction of a Miya, and Sintoo worship. Syn. KANNUSHI, SHANIN.

†SHIN-SŌ, シンサウ, 心想, *n.* Fancy, conception, imagination. — *szru,* to fancy or picture in the mind. Syn. OMOI-NASHI.

SHIN-SOKU, シンソク, 神速, *n.* Great quickness or rapidity. — *na,* exceeding quick or rapid. — *ni,* very quick. Syn. SASSOKU.

†SHIN-SON, シンソン, 神孫, *n.* The descendent of the Kami, viz., the Mikado.

†SHIN-SOTSZ, シンソツ, 眞率, Prompt, direct, straight-forward in conduct. — *na h'to.* Syn. SAKU-I.

SHIN-SHU, シンシユ, 新酒, *(atarashii sake). n.* New wine.

SHIN-TAI, シンタイ, 身體, *n.* The body. — *szkoyaka na h'to,* a person of a vigorous body.

SHIN-TAI, シンタイ, 進退, *(szszmu, shirizoku). n.* Advancing and retreating. *Gunzei no —,* the advance and retreat of an army.

SHIN-TAKU, シンタク, 新宅, *(atarashii iye). n.* A new house.

†SHIN-TAKU, シンタク, 神託, *n.* Divine communication or inspiration. — *wo kōmuru,* to be inspired.

SHIN-TEI, シンテイ, 心底, *(kokoro no soko). n.* The bottom of the heart; the heart, mind.

SHIN-TŌ, シンタウ, 神道, *(kami no michi.) n.* The religion or worship of the Kami, "Sintooism,"—the most ancient religion of the Japanese.

SHIN-TŌ, シンタウ, 新到, *(atarashiku itaru).* New or lately imported goods. — *no shina.* idem.

†SHIN-TOKU, シントク, 神德, *n.* The virtues of the Kami.

†SHIN-TS'U, シンツウ, 神通, *n.* Divine power, miraculous power.

†SHIN-TS'U, シンツウ, 心痛, *n.* Care, anxiety, trouble. Syn. SHIMPAI, KURŌ.

SHINURU, シヌル, 死, See *Shini.*

†SHIN-YA, シンヤ, 深夜, Late at night.

†SHINYEKI, シンエキ, 津液, *n.* The saliva. Syn. TSZBAKE.

SHIN-YO, シンヨ, 神輿, *(kami no koshi).* The shrine or box carried in processions performed in honor of a Kami.

SHIN-YŪ, シンユウ, 親友, *n.* An intimate or familiar friend. Syn. HŌYU, TOMODACHI.

SHIN-ZAN, シンザン, 新參, *(ima mairi).* Lately or newly arrived, a new-comer.

SHIN-ZEN, シンゼン, 神前, *(kami no maye).* In front of a Miya, before a Kami.

SHIN-ZŌ, ンシザウ, 新造, *(atarashii fune). n.* A new ship.

SHIN-ZŌ, シンザウ, *n.* A young lady. *Go-shin-zō,* your wife.

SHIN-ZOKU, シンゾク, 親族, *n.* Kindred, relations, connections on both sides. Syn. SHINRUI.

SHIO, シホ, 鹽, *n.* Salt. — *wo yaku,* to make salt. — *wo dasz,* to soak in water in order to deprive of saltness. — *ni tszkeru,* to salt, or pickle. — *wo szru,* to sprinkle with salt.

SHIŌ, シワウ, 雌黃, *n.* Gamboge.

SHIO, シホ, 潮, *n.* The water of the ocean, the tide. — *ga michiru,* the tide is full. — *ga sasz,* the tide is rising. — *ga hiku,* the tide is falling. — *ga hiru,* the tide is down. — *ai yoki goro,* a fortunate time. — *ai wo machi-awaseru,* to wait for a favourable time. *Sore wo shio ni dete-yuku,* took that opportunity, or favourable moment to go out. — *ni mukō,* to go against the tide.

SHIO-BIKI, シホビキ, 鹽引, *n.* Salted, or pickled salmon.

SHIO-BURO, シホブロ, 鹽風爐, *n.* A salt-water bath.

SHI-OCHI, シオチ, 仕落, *n.* Mistake, omission, oversight. Syn. OCHIDO, AYAMACHI.

SHIO-DZKE, シホヅケ, 鹽漬, *n.* Pickled, or salted food.

SHIO-HAMA, シホハマ, 鹽濱, *n.* The salt-beach where salt is made.

SHIO-HAYUI,-KI,-KU,-SHI, シホハユシ, 鹹, Salt in taste, salty.

SHIO-HI, シホヒ, 潮乾, *n.* The beach over which the tide ebbs and flows.

SHIO-KARA, シホカラ, 鹽辛, *n.* A kind of food made by salting fish.

SHIO-KARAI,-KI,-KU,-SHI, シホカライ, 鹹 Over salted, disagreeably salt.

SHI-OKI,*-ku,-ita,* シオク, 仕置, *t.v.* To do and leave for others; to enact. *Sen-zō no skioita okite,* a law enacted by ancestors and left to their descendents.

SHI-OKI, シオキ, 仕置, *n.* Punishment of crime. — *wo szru,* to punish a criminal. *Omoi* —, severe punishment. Syn. KEIBATSZ.

SHIO-MIDZ, シホミヅ, 鹽水, *n.* Salt water, brine.

SHION, シオン, 紫苑, *n.* The name of a flower.

SHIOPPAI, シホツパイ, *a.* Salt in taste, salty, briny.

SHIOPPAKU, シホツパク, *adv.* Idem.

SHIORASHII,-KI,-KU, シホラシイ, Pleasant, agreeable, delightful. — *onna.*

SHIORE,*-ru,-ta,* シヲレル, 萎, *i. v.* To droop, to languish, to lose heart, to be dispirited. *Hana ga* —, the flower droops. *Chikara wo otosh'te shiorete iru,* to become disheartened and droop.

SHIORI, シヲリ, 栞, *n.* A book-mark.

SHIORIDO, シヲリド, 栞戶, *n.* A door that swings on hinges, same as *Hirakido.*

SHI-ŌSE,*-ru,-ta,* シオホセル, 仕果, *t. v.* To finish, complete, to do, perform, accomplish. Syn. SHITOGERU, HATASZ.

SHIO-SHIO-TO, シヲシヲト, 萎萎, *adv.* In a sad, dispirited manner, drooping, languishing.

†SHIOSZ, シホス, 鹽酢, *n.* Muriatic acid.

SHIO-TARE,*-ru,-ta,* シホタレル, 鹽垂, *i.v.* To be dirty and greasy. *Shiotareta kimono.* Syn. YOGORERU.

SHIO-YA, シホヤ, 鹽屋, *n.* A salt merchant

SHIO-ZE, シホゼ, 潮瀨, *n.* A current in the ocean.

SHIPPARAI, シツパライ, 後殿, *n.* The rear-guard of an army. — *sh'te shiro ni hiki-kayesz.* Syn. SHINGARI.

SHIPPEI, シツペイ, 竹篦, *n.* A piece of broken bow, used as a ferule.

SHIPPŌ, シツパウ, 七寶, *(nanatsz no takara).* The seven precious things, viz. gold, silver, emerald, coral, agate crystal, and pearl.

†SHIPPŪ, シツプウ, 疾風, *n.* A hurricane.

SHIRABAKURE,*-ru,-ta,* シラバクレル, *i.v.* To appear not to know; to pretend, or feign ignorance; to dissemble, to connive at. Syn. TOBOKERU.

SHIRABE,-*ru*,-*ta*, シラベル, 調, *t.v.* To examine, investigate, inquire into, to judge, to search into, to tune, to play on a musical instrument. *Tszmi wo* —, to judge a crime. Syn. SENSAKU SZRU, TADASZ, GIMMI SZRU.

SHIRABE, シラベ, 調, *n.* The harmony, or concord of different chords of a guitar, or of different instruments. *Kotoba no* —, the quantity, measure, or euphony of words.

SHIRABE-YAKU, シラベヤク, 調役, *n.* A judge.

SHIRA-BIYŌSHI, シラビヤウシ, 白柏子, *n.* A female dancer.

SHIRADZ, シラズ, 不知, neg. of *Shiru*. Not knowing.

SHIRAGA, シラガ, 白髮, *n.* Gray hair.

SHIRA-GAYU, シラガユ, 白粥, *t.v.* Rice-gruel, congee.

SHIRAGE,-*ru*,-*ta*, シラゲル, 精, *t. v,* To whiten, (used only of whitening rice, by pounding it in a mortar, or of a board by planing). *Kome ita nado wo* —.

SHIRAHA, シラハ, 白歯, *n.* White teeth. — *no muszme*, a young unmarried woman. Also 白刃, a naked sword. — *wo nukiawaseru*, to draw swords and fight. Also 白羽, white feather, as, — *no ya*, a white feathered arrow.

SHIRA-HADA, シラハダ, 白癜, *n.* Vitiligo.

SHIRA-HATA, シラハタ, 白旗, *n.* A white flag.

SHIRA-JIRASHII,-KI,-KU, シラジラシイ, Having a doubtful, or false appearance. — *koto wo iu.*

SHIRA-KABE, シラカベ, 白壁, *n.* White plaster.

SHIRAKE,-*ru*,-*ta*, シラケル, *i.v.* To become white, only used figuratively, as. *Kiyō ga* —, the fun began to moderate. *Gunzei ga shirakete miyeru*, the army showed signs of giving way.

SHIRAKI, シラキ, 白木, Plain, unvarnished, unpainted. — *no tansz*, an unlacquered bureau.

†SHI-RAKU, シラク, 刺絡, *n.* Blood-letting, venesection. — *wo szru*, to bleed.

SHIRAKUMO, シラクモ, 白雲, *n.* An eruption on the scalp of children; Pityriasis?

SHIRAMI, シラミ, 虱, *n.* A louse. — *ga dekita*, to have lice. — *takari*, a lousy person.

SHIRAMI,-*mu*,-*nda*, シラム, 白, *i.v.* To become white, or grey; to break as the morning; to break or show less courage. *Yo ga* —, the day dawns. *Teki ga* —, the enemy begins to give way. *Kiyō ga* —, the sport moderates.

SHIRAN, シラン, 紫蘭, *n.* The Bletia hyacinthina.

SHIRA-NAMI, シラナミ, 白波, *n.* White waves,—waves capped with foam.

SHIRANU, シラヌ, 不知, Neg. of *Shiru.* Not knowing. *Shiranu kao*, appearing as if he did not know, pretending not to know.

SHIRARE,-*ru*,-*ta*, シラレル, 被知, Pass. and pot. of *Shiru.* To be known.

SHIRASE,-*ru*,-*ta*, シラセル, 令知, Caust. of *Shiru.* To make or cause to know; to tell, inform, acquaint. *H'to ni shirasete wa warui*, it will be wrong to tell any one.

SHIRASE, シラセ, 兆, *n.* A sign, omen, prognostic.

SHIRASZ, シラス, 白沙, *n.* The place spread with white sand, where criminals are placed to be judged; the bar.

SHIRA-TSZYU, シラツユ, 白露, *n.* Dew.

SHIRE,-*ru*,-*ta*, シレル, 知, Poten. of *Shiru.* May or can know, to get the knowing of. *Hon wo yomeba shireru*, if you read the book you can know.

†SHIRE-MONO, シレモノ, 白痴, *n.* A fool, dunce. Syn. BAKA, GUNIN.

SHIRI, シリ, 尻, *n.* The buttock, posteriors. — *ga wareru*, his lie is known. — *ga nagai*, sitting, or staying long (as a visitor). — *wo hashoru*, to tuck up the skirts of the long coat.

SHIRI,-*ru*,-*tta*, シル, 知, *t.v.* To know, to understand. *Nan demo shitte-iru*, knows every thing. *Narawadz ni* —, to know without learning. *Mite shiru*, to know by seeing. Syn. WAKARU.

SIHRI-AI, シリアヒ, 知合, *n.* An acquaintance, mutually acquainted.

SHIRIASHI, シリアシ, *n.* Hesitation, pausing in doubt, or standing ready to go back. — *wo fumu*, to recede, or go back.

SHIRI-BITO, シリビト, 知人, *n.* An acquaintance. Syn. CHIKADZKI, SHIRUBE.

SHIRIGAI, シリガイ, 鞦, *n.* A crupper.

SHIRI-KIWAME,-*ru*,-*ta*, シリキハメル, 知極, *t.v.* To know perfectly.

SHIRIME, シリメ, 流眄, Used only in the phrase, *Shirime ni miru*, to look askant, or out of the corner of the eye.

†SHIRIN, シリン, 四隣, *n.* The neighbors on the four sides of one's dwelling.

†SHI-RIN-SHA, シリンシヤ, 四輪車, *n.* A four wheeled carriage.

SHI-RIYŌ, シリヤウ, 死靈, (*shinda h'to no tamashii*). *n.* The spirit of a dead person.

— *no tatari*, some evil supposed to be inflicted by the spirit of one who while living was an enemy.

SHIRIYO, シリヨ, 思慮, *n.* Thought, consideration, reflection, judgment. — *wo megurasz*, to think, consider, or ponder over.

SHI-RIU, シリウ, 支流, *(yeda ha). n.* A branch, division, or off-shoot of a sect.

SHIRI-UMA, シリウマ, Only used in the phrase, *shiriuma ni noru*, to ride behind another on horseback; fig. to slavishly imitate another.

SHIRIYE, シリヘ, 後, *n.* Behind. — *ni tatsz*, to stand behind. Syn. ATO.

SHIRIZOKE,*-ru,-ta*, シリゾケル, 退, *t. v.* To cause to retire, retreat or leave, to drive back, to cause to withdraw. *Teki wo* —, to cause the enemy to retreat.

SHIRIZOKI,*-ku,-ita*, シリゾク, 退, *i.v.* To retreat, retire, leave, withdraw. *Teki ga* —, the enemy retreats.

SHIRO, シロ, 城, *n.* A castle, the fortified residence of a feudal chief, a fortress, citadel.

†SHIRO, シロ, 代, *(kawari). n.* Price, money given in exchange. *Mi no shiro*, the money paid to the parents for prostituting their daughter. Syn. DAI.

SHIRO, シロ, A Yed. coll. imp. of *Szru*, = *seyo*, do it. *Nan ni shiro kawaisō-na koto da*, it is a cruel thing be it as it may. *Hayaku shiro*, do it quickly.
Syn. SHI-NA, SHI NASARE.

SHIRŌ, シロウ, 白, *adv.* Same as *Shiroku.*

SHIRO-ATO, シロアト, 城蹟, *n.* The ruins or vestiges of an ancient castle.

SHIROI,-KI, シロイ, 白, *a.* White. — *kuroi ga wakaranu*, can't distinguish between white and black. — *hana*, a white flower.

SHIRO-KANE, シロカネ, 銀, *n.* Silver.
Syn. GIN.

SHIROKO, シロコ, 白子, *n.* An albino.

SHIROKU, シロク, 白, *adv.* White. — *szru*, to whiten. — *naru*, to become white.

SHIROME, シロメ, 白眼, *n.* The white of the eye, sclerotic.

SHIROMI,*-mu,-nda*, シロム, 白, *i.v.* To become white, whiten. *Ke ga shironda*, the hair has become gray.

SHIROMI, シロミ, *n.* A tinge of white, white of an egg, the enamel inside of a copper pot. — *ga aru*, it has a white tinge, or shade of whiteness.

SHIRO-MONO, シロモノ, 貨, *n.* Goods, any article exchanged for money. — *nakute wa kane wo haraimasen*, I shall not pay the money without I receive the goods.
Syn. SHINA-MONO.

SHIROMUKU, シロムク, 白無垢, *n.* White garments, such as are worn by women at funerals and weddings.

SHIRO-NAMADZ, シロナマヅ, 白瘢, *n.* Vitiligo. Syn. SHIRAHADA.

SHIROSA, シロサ, 白, *n.* Whiteness.

SHIROSHI, シロシ, 白, *a.* See *Shiroi.*

SHIROSHIMESHI,*-sz,-sh'ta*, シロシメス, 知召, *t.v.* To govern, rule, to know, only used of a noble person. *Tenshi wa tenka wo* —, the Mikado governs the empire.
Syn. SHI-HAI SZRU.

†SHIROTAYE, シロタヘ, 白妙, (poet.). White. — *no yuki*, white snow.

SHIRŌTO, シロウト, 白人, *n.* One who does not properly belong to the trade or profession spoken of, an outsider. — *wa daiku no shigoto wo dekinu*, one who is not a carpenter cannot do a carpenter's work: (the opposite is *kurōto*). Syn. HETA.

SHIRŌTORASHII,-KI,-KU, シロウトラシイ, Having the look or manner of an unskilful, bungling, or uninitiated person.

SHIROZAKE, シロザケ, 白酒, *n.* A kind of drink made of rice.

SHIRU, シル, 知, See *Shiri.*

SHIRU, シル, 汁, *n.* Juice, the fluid part of any substance, sap, gravy. — *wo shiboru*, to press out the juice.

SHĪRU, シヒル, See *Shī.*

SHIRUBE, シルベ, 知音, *n.* Acquaintance, a guide, a sign or mark to show the way. — *wo szru*, to guide or point out the way. *Ishi wo — ni tateru*, to set up a stone as a way mark. *Yedo ni — ga nai*, have no acquaintance in Yedo.
Syn. SHIRIBITO, TAYORI.

SHIRUKE, シルケ 汁氣, *n.* Juicy, succulent.

SHIRUKO, シルコ, 汁粉, *n.* A kind of sauce made of red-beans and sugar, eaten with rice-cake.

SHIRUSHI,*-sz,-sh'ta*, シルス, 誌, *t. v.* To write down, to enter in a book, to record, to mark. *Hon ni* —, to write in a book.
Syn, KAKU, TSZKERU.

SHIRUSHI, シルシ, 標, *n.* A mark or sign by which any thing is known, a token, symptom, emblem, a badge, crest; signal; proof, evidence. *Shirushi wo tszkeru*, to mark. *Kuszri wo nonde mo — ga nai*, I have taken medicine but without effect, or good results. *Rōshō no* —, a symptom of consumption. *Iye no* —, a family crest.
Syn. SHŌKO, MON.

SHISAI, シサイ, 子細, *n.* Reason, cause, motive; matter, particulars, circumstances. — *wo iu,* to tell the reason or circumstances. *Nan no — de,* for what reason? *Kotonaru — mo nashi,* there were no more remarkable phenomenon. — *wa nai,* there is no difficulty. Syn. WAKE.

†SHI-SAKU, シサク, 詩作, Making verses, or poetry. — *szru,* to write poetry.

SHISAI-NI, シサイニ, 仔細, *adv.* Minutely, particularly, attentively.
Syn. KOMAYAKA-NI.

SHISAIRASHII,-KI,-KU, シサイラシイ, Having a consequential, important, or conceited manner. Syn. JIMANRASHII.

SHI-SASHI,*-sz,-sh'ta,* シサス, 仕刺, *t. v.* To leave a thing partly done. *Shigoto wo shisash'te shibai wo mi ni yuku,* to leave one's work partly done and go to the theatre. Syn. SHIKAKERU.

†SHISEI, シセイ, 四聲, *n.* The four tones of Chinese characters.

SHISEKI, シセキ, 咫尺, *n.* The distance of about a foot, used only fig. for a very short distance. — *no uchi mo miyedz,* could not see even a foot before him.

†SHI-SEKI-YEI, シセキエイ, 紫石英, *n.* An amethyst.

†SHI-SEN, シセン, 詩箋, *n.* Paper used for writing verses on.

†SHISERI,*-ru,* シセル, 死, *i. v.* To die.

†SHI-SETSZ, シセツ, 使節, *n.* An ambassador, commissioner, envoy. Syn. TSZKAI.

SHI-SHA, シシヤ, 使者, *n.* A messenger. Syn. TSZKAI.

SHISHI, シシ, 獅子, *n.* A lion. — *wa kedamono no ō nari,* the lion is the king of beasts.

SHISHI, シジ, 猪, *n.* A wild-hog. Also 鹿, a deer, (derived from *Shishi,* flesh, because anciently the flesh of the wild hog and deer was the only flesh eaten.)

†SHISHI, シシ, 肉, *(niku). n.* Flesh.

||SHISHI, シシ, 私私, *(shōben). n.* Urine; used only to children. — *wo szru.*

†SHISHI, シシ, 四肢, *(yotsz no yeda). n.* The four limbs or extremities of the body; viz. legs and arms.

†SHISHI,*-szru,-sh'ta,* シスル, 死, *(shinuru). i. v.* To die.

†SHISHIBISHIO, シシビシホ, 醢, *n.* Salted mince meat. *Mi wo — ni nasz,* to chop a person into mince meat.

SHISHI-BUYE, シシブエ, 鹿笛, *n.* A kind of whistle used by hunters to decoy deer.

SHISHI-GARI, シシガリ, 鹿狩, *n.* A deer hunter.

SHISHI-GASHIRA, シシガシラ, 獅子頭, *n.* A mask like a lion's head, used by *Daikagura,* to scare away evil spirits from a house.

SHISHIMAI, シシマヒ, 獅子舞, *n.* The dance performed by the *Daikagura* from house to house.

†SHISHIMURA, シシムラ, *n.* The flesh on the ham and thigh.

†SHISHIN, シシン, 私心, *(watakushi gokoro). n.* Selfishness, private interest, partiality.

†SHI-SHO, シシヨ, 四書, *n.* The four books, or Chinese classics.

SHI-SHŌ, シシヤウ, 師匠, *n.* A teacher, master.

SHI-SHUKU, シシユク, 止宿, *(tomari yadoru). n.* Lodging, stopping, or sojourning. — *szru,* to lodge, stop, or sojourn.

SHI-SO, シソ, 紫蘇, *n.* Name of a plant.

SHI-SO, シソ, 始祖, *n.* The first ancestor. Syn. G'WANSO.

SHI-SOKU, シソク, 子息, *n.* Son. *Go shisoku,* your son. Syn. KO, SEGARE, MUSZKO.

†SHI-SOKU, シソク, 四足, *(yotsz ashi). n.* Quadruped.

SHI-SOKONAI,*-au,-atta,* シソコナウ, 仕損, *t.v.* To mar, hurt, injure, or spoil in doing, or making anything.

SHI-SOME,*-ru,-ta,* シソメル, 仕始, *t. v.* To begin to do.

SHI-SON, シソン, 子孫, *n.* Posterity, descendent.

SHI-SONJI,*-ru* or *-dzru,-ta,* シソンズル, 仕損, To hurt, mar, injure or spoil in doing, or making anything.

SHI-SOTS, シソツ, 士卒, *n.* Common soldiers. Syn. TSZWAMONO.

†SHISSO, シツソ, 質素, *n.* Economy, frugality, plainness, or simplicity in dress, &c. Syn. KENYAKU.

SHISZ, or SHISZRU, シス, 死, See *Shishi.*

SHI-SZMASHI,*-sz,-sh'ta,* シスマス, 仕濟, *t.v.* To finish doing, or making anything, to accomplish.

SH'TA, シタ, 舌, *n.* The tongue. — *wo maku,* or — *wo furū,* to be struck with fear or awe. *Kage ye muite — wo dasz,* to turn the head and stick out the tongue, as in derision or jesting. — *wo tareru,* to let the tongue hang out (as a dog). — *wo utsz,* to make a clicking sound with the tongue, to chirrup.

SH'TA, シタ, 下, *(shimo), post-posit.* Below, beneath, under, down. *Ame no —,* under the heavens, the Japanese empire. *Iye no —,* under the house. — *ni oru,* to squat down as a Japanese to a great man. — *ni naru*, to become lower, inferior. — *kara deru*, to humble one's self, or speak humbly of one's self before others.

SH'TA, シタ, *n.* Any thing given to boot, or to make up the difference in value of things bartered. — *ni toru*, to take boot. — *ni yaru*, to give to boot. Syn. OI.

SH'TA, シタ, The pret. of *Shi, szru, sh'ta*, Have done.

SH'TA-BA, シタバ, 下葉, *n.* The lowermost leaves of a tree, &c.

SH'TA-BI, シタビ, 下火, *n.* A conflagration on the decline. — *ni natta*, the fire is going out.

SH'TAGAI,*-au,-atta*, シタガウ, 從, *i.v.* To follow, to go after, to obey, to comply with, according with, agree to, to submit, yield, conform to. *H'to ni sh'tagatte aruku*, to walk after another. *Oya ni* —, to obey one's parents. *Kuni no okite ni* —, to obey the laws of the country. *Iro ni sh'tagatte nedan ga chigau*, the price differs according to the color.

SH'TA-GAKI, シタガキ, 下書, *n.* The copy, or original writing to be copied; a first draught.

SHITAGANE-YA, シタガネヤ, 下金屋, *n.* A person who buys old metal.

SHITAGARI,*-ru,-tta*, シタガル, *i. v.* To desire to do, anxious to do.

SH'TAGAYE,*-ru,-ta*, シタガヘル, 從, *t. v.* To cause to follow, to cause to obey or submit, bring into subjection. — *Teki wo* —, to bring an enemy into subjection.

SH'TA-GI, シタギ, 下著, *n.* An under coat.

SH'TAGŌ, シタガフ, Same as *Sh'tagau.*

SH'TA-GOKORO, シタゴコロ, 下情, *n.* Inclined, minded or disposed to anything.

SH'TA-GUTSZ, シタグツ, 韈子, *n.* A sock, or stocking worn inside of a shoe.

SIHTAI,-KI, シタイ, 仕度, *a.* Wish to do or make. *Kono hon wo han ni sh'tai*, I wish to print this book. *I-jutsz no keiko wo sh'tai*, I wish to study medicine.

SH'TAI,*-au,-ōta*, シタフ, 慕, *t.v.* To love and long for, to yearn after, to pine for, to desire, to feel home sick. *Ko ga oya wo* —, the child longs for its parent. *Kuni wo* —, to feel homesick. *Ato wo sh'taite yuku*, to go longing after some one left behind, to feel sorry to leave. Syn. KOISHII, HOSSZRU, NATSZKASHII.

†SHI-TAI, シタイ, 四體, *n.* The four limbs.

SH'TAGI, シタヂ, 下地, *n.* The first coat of plaster or paint, &c., a priming.

SH'TAJI, シタヂ, *n.* Soy, (used only by women). Syn. SHŌYU.

SH'TA-JITA, シタジタ, 下下, Inferior, or lower classes of people. Syn. SHIMO-JIMO

SH'TAKU, シタク, 支度, *n.* Preparation, readiness. — *wo szru*, to make preparation, to get ready. *Mada — ga dekinu*, I am not yet ready. *Gochisō no — wo szru*, to make preparations for a feast. Syn. YŌI.

SHITAKU, シタク, *adv.* Wish to do, or make. *Shigoto wo — nai*, do not wish to work.

†SHITAKU, シタク, 私宅, *(watakushi no iye)*, *n.* My house.

SH'TA-KUCHIBIRU, シタクチビル, 下脣, *n.* The lower lip.

SH'TA-MABUCHI, シタマブタ, 下眶, *n.* The lower eyelid.

SHITAMAI,*-au*, or *ō,-ōta*, シタマフ, 仕給, *t.v.* To do, spoken only of honorable persons.

SHITA-ME, シタメ, 下目, *n.* Contempt. — *ni miru*, to look down on, to despise.

SH'TAMI,*-mu,-nda*, シタム, 湑, *t.v.* To let a fluid drain from anything. *Tokkuri no midz wo* —, to drain the water from a bottle.

SH'TAMI, シタミ, 板壁, *n.* Clapboarding, weatherboarding. — *wo utsz*, to clapboard.

SH'TA-MOTSZRE, シタモツレ, 舌縺, *n.* An impediment in the speech, lisping.

SH'TAN, シタン, 紫檀, *n.* A kind of hard wood imported from China.

SH'TA-OBI, シタオビ, 下帶, *n.* The cloth worn around the loins and over the privates. Syn. FUNDOSHI.

SH'TARIGAO, シタリガホ, *n.* The face of one who has done something for which he feels elated, a vainglorious countenance.

SH'TASHII,-KI, シタシイ, 親, *a.* Friendly, amicable, intimate, harmonious. *Sh'tashii naka*, friendly or amicable terms.

SH'TASHIKU, シタシク, 親, *adv.* idem. — *szru*, to be friendly. *Watakushi sh'tashiku mita koto*, I was an eye-witness of it, or a thing which I saw with my own eyes. Syn. MUTSZMAJII.

SH'TASHIMI,*-mu,-nda*, シタシム, 親, *i.v.* To be friendly, amicable, or harmonious with.

SH'TASHIMI, シタシミ, 親, *n.* Friendship, amity, harmony, concord. Syn. KON-I.

SH'TASHIMONO, シタシモノ, *n.* Boiled greens.

SH'TASHŪ, シタシウ, Same as *Shitashiku.*

SH'TATAKA-NI, シタタカニ, *adv.* Severely, much. — *tszku*, to stab severely, or deeply.

SH'TATAME,*–ru,–ta*, シタタメル, 認, *t. v.* To write. *Tegami wo* —, to write a letter. Syn. KAKU.

SH'TATARI,*–ru,–tta*, シタタル, 滴, *i.v.* To drop, or drain from, to drip. *Yane kara ame ga* —, the rain drops from the roof.

SH'TA-TARADZ, シタタラズ, *n.* Tongue-tied, one who lisps.

SHI-TATE,*–ru,–ta*, シタテル, 仕立, *t.v.* To make up, (as clothes), to make ready, prepare, to get up, to bring up, educate, to put on, or assume (as a garb.) *Kimono wo* —, to make clothes. *Uma wo* —, to get a horse ready. *Kodomo wo* —, to bring up a child in the right way. Syn. KOSHIRAYERU.

SH'TA-TE, シタテ, 下手, *n.* Under the control of, or subject to another, as, *H'to no — ni tszku.*

SHI-TATE-KATA, シタテカタ, 仕立方, *n.* The manner in which anything is got up, or prepared. — *ga wakaranu*, don't know how it is made, or put together.

SHITATE-YA, シタテヤ, 仕立屋, *n.* A tailor.

SH'TA-UCHI, シタウチ, 咜, *n.* A clicking, or smacking sound made with the tongue.

SH'TAWASHII,–KI, シタハシイ, 慕, *a.* Longed for, desired, yearned after.

SH'TAWASHIKU, シタハシク, 慕, *adv.* idem.

SH'TA-YE, シタヱ, 粉本, *n.* The first draught of a picture, first copy of a drawing.

SHITCHI, シツチ, 濕地, *n.* Wet or moist ground.

SH'TE, シテ, *pp.* or *ppr.* of *Shi, szru.* Being, doing; sometimes it seems redundant. *Nani wo — iru*, what are you doing? *Shigoto wo — shimau*, to finish doing one's work. *H'totsz to — warui mono wa nai*, there is not a single bad one. *Kiku to — obeyezaru wa nashi*, have not forgotten anything I heard. *H'to to — tori ni shikazaru beken ya*, should a human being be inferior to the birds? *Fubō wo sh'te anshin seshimu*, to make parents happy. *H'to wo sh'te yorokobashimu*, to cause joy to others. *Kotszzen to — miyedz*, it suddenly vanished out of sight.

†SH'TE, シテ, *n.* The principal performer in an opera.

SH'TE, シテ, 爲者, *n.* The doer, maker. *Kono shigoto no — wa dare*, who did this work?

SHĪTE, シヒテ, 强, *adv.* (the *pp.* of *Shī.*) By force, by compulsion, by constraint, against the will; obstinately, wilfully, stubbornly. Syn. MURI-NI.

†SHI-TEI, シテイ, 師弟, *n.* Teacher, and pupil.

SH'TŌ, シタウ, See *Sh'tai.*

SHI-TOGE,*–ru,–ta*, シトゲル, 仕遂, *t.v.* To succeed in doing, finish doing, accomplish. Syn. SHIŌSERU.

SHI-TOME,*–ru,–ta*, シトメル, 仕留, *t.v.* To finish by slaying, to give the finishing blow.

SH'TOMI, シトミ, 𥈄, *n.* A kind of moveable lattice window frame.

SH'TONE, シトネ, 褥, *n.* A mattrass. Syn. FUTON.

SH'TORI,*–ru,–tta*, シトル, 濕, *i.v.* To be damp. Syn. SHIMERU.

SH'TO-SHTO, シトシト, *adv.* In a damp manner, or appearance.

SH'TOYAKA, シトヤカ, Dignified in manner, easy, graceful, genteel. Syn. KŌTO.

SHITSZ, シツ, 質, *n.* Nature, substance, material. *Kono ki no — wa arai*, this wood is of a coarse nature. Syn. UMARETSZKI.

SHITSZ, シツ, *n.* The itch, scabies. Syn. HIZEN.

SHITSZ, シツ, 室, *n.* A room, a wife. Syn. HEGA.

SHITSZ-BŌ,*–szru*, シツバウ, 失望, To be disappointed, fail to get one's desire.

SHITSZ-BOKU, シツボク, 質樸, Plain, rustic, unsophisticated, simple-minded, honest. Syn. JIMI-NA.

†SHITSZ-JI, シツジ, 執事, *n.* One who directs, or manages any matter for others, same as *Sewa-nin.*

SHI-TSZKE,*–ru,–ta*, シツケル, 仕付, *t. v.* To cultivate, to till, to produce by tillage; to refine, or improve by teaching; to educate; accustomed, or used to doing. *Ine ta wo* —, to cultivate rice, or rice-fields. *Kodomo wo* —, to educate a child (in polite accomplishmentc).

SHĪ-TSZKE,*–ru,–ta*, シヒツケル, 强著, *t.v.* To insist on, to urge, to press, importune, to compel. *H'to ni shī-tszkete sake wo nomaseru*, to compel a person to drink wine.

SHITSZKE, シツケ, 仕付, *n.* Cultivation, bringing-up, or care of parents to improve their children in manners, &c. The basting-threads in a new garment. — *no yoi h'to*, a well bred person.

SHITSZKE-GATA, シツケガタ, 仕付方, *n.* Politeness, etiquette, rules of good breeding, or way of bringing up.

SHITSZKOI,-KI, シツコイ, *a.* Gross, or indelicate in taste, nauseous, rude, unrefined, coarse in manners, rudely persistent, importunate, prolix. Syn. AKUDOI.

SHITSKOKU, シツコク, *adv.* Idem.

SHITSZ-NEN, シツネン, 失念, Forgetfulness. — *szru*, to forget. Syn. WASZRERU.

SHITSZRAI,*-au,-ōta*, シツラフ, 經營, *t.v.* To build, to erect, spoken only of a house. *Iye wo* —, to erect a house. Syn. TSZKURU, ITONAMU.

SHITSZ-REI, シツレイ, 失禮, Rude, impolite, ill-mannered. — *na h'to.* Syn. BUREI.

†SHI-TS'U-ZAI, シツウザイ, 止痛藥 *n.* Anodyne medicines. Syn. YURUME-GUSZRI.

SHITTA, シツタ, *pret.* of *Shiru.*

SHITTAN, シツタン, 悉曇, *n.* The Pali characters, or the language in which the Buddhist canonical books were originally written.

SHITTE, シツテ, *pp.* of *Shiru.*

SHITTEMBATTŌ, シツテンバツタウ, 七顚, 八倒, Writhing, or throwing one's self about in pain.

SHITTO, シツト, 嫉妬, *(netami). n.* Envy, jealousy. —*wo okosz*, to excite jealousy. — *szru*, to be jealous.

SHITTORI-TO, シツトリト, *adv.* In a damp manner, or appearance.

SHITTSZI, シツツ井, 失墜, *n.* Loss, waste, or sinking of money from useless expenditure. —*ga oi.* Syn. ZAPPI, NIUYŌ.

SHI-UCHI, シウチ, 仕打, *n.* Treatment, conduct towards any one. Syn. SHIMUKE, MOTENASHI.

SHIWA, シワ, 皺, *n.* Wrinkles, folds, rumples, a crease. — *ga yoru*, to be wrinkled. — *wo nobasz*, to smooth out the wrinkles. — *wo yoseru*, to wrinkle, corrugate. Syn. HIDA.

SHIWABUKI, シワブキ, 嗽, *n.* Clearing the throat, hemming. — *wo szru.* Syn. SHEKIBARAI.

SHIWAGARE-GOYE, シワガレゴヱ, *n.* A hoarse voice. Syn. KARETARU KOYE.

SHIWAI,-KI, シワイ, 吝, *a.* Stingy, close, parsimonious, miserly. *Shiwai h'to*, a stingy person. Syn. RINSHOKU-NA.

SHI-WAKE,*-ru,-ta*, シワケル, 仕分, *t.v,* To make in a different way, to distinguish by making, to divide.

SHIWAKU, シワク, *adv.* Stingy, parsimonious, miserly, niggardly.

SHIWAKUCHA, or SHIWAKUTA, シワクチヤ, Rumpled, wrinkled. —*ni szru*, to rumple.

SHIWAMBŌ, シワンボウ, *n.* A miser, a stingy fellow.

SHIWAMI,*-mu,-nda*, シワム, 皺, *i.v.* To be wrinkled, rumpled. *Kao ga shiwanda*, his face is wrinkled.

SHIWA-NOSHI, シワノシ, 皺伸, *n.* Taking out the wrinkles. — *wo szru*, to smooth.

SHIWARI,*-ru,-tta*, シワル, *i.v.* To bend, (as a pole by a weight). Syn. SHINAYERU.

SHIWASHI, シワシ, *a.* See *Shiwai.*

SHI-WAZA, シワザ, 仕業, *n.* Work, doing, deed. *Dare no —ka shiranu*, I know not whose work this is. Syn. GŌ.

SHIYEN, シエン, 紫圓, *n.* The croton bean.

SHIYETAGE,*-ru,-ta*, シヘタゲル, 虐, *t. v.* To oppress, treat with cruelty or tyranny. *Tami wo* —, to oppress the people. Syn. SETAGERU, GIYAK'U SZRU.

†SHI-YŌ, シヨウ, 私用, *n.* Private business. — *de Yedo ye yuku*, to go to Yedo on private business.

SHI-YŌ, シヤウ, 仕樣, *n.* The way or manner of doing or making any thing, how to do, resource, expedient. — *ga wakaranu*, don't know how it is done. — *ga nai*, no resource. Syn. SHI-KATA.

SHI-YOI,-KI, シヨイ, 仕好, *a.* Easy, or pleasant to do, or make. *Shi yoi shigoto*, easy, or pleasant work.

†SHI-YOKU, シヨク, 私慾, One's own lusts or pleasures, selfish desires, self-interest.

†SHI-YŪ, シユウ, 雌雄, *(mesz osz). n.* Female and male; (fig.) lose or win, conquer or get defeated. — *wo kesszru*, to decide a contest. Syn. SHŌBU.

†SHI-YUI,*-szru*, シユ井, 思惟, *(kagayeru).* To reflect, think about.

SHIYURU, シフル, 誣, See *Shii.*

SHI-ZAI, シザイ, 死罪, *n.* Capital punishment. — *ni okonō*, to punish capitally. — *wo moshi-tszkeru*, to condemn to death.

SHIZARI,*-ru,-tta*, シザル, *i.v.* To take a few steps backwards, to move backwards, (as a servant who hands his master any thing). Syn. ATO YE YORU.

SHIZEN, シゼン, 自然, Spontaneously, of itself, of its own accord, naturally, of course. Syn. ONODZKARA.

†SHIZOKU, シゾク, 支族, *n.* Family, clan, all who bear the same surname.

†SHO, シヨ, 書, *(fumi, kaku). n.* A book, writing. — *szru*, to write. — *wo yomu*, to

read books. — *wo manabu,* to learn to write.

†SHO, シヨ, 諸, (*moro-moro*). *a.* Many; used in an indefinite sense as a plural prefix; as, *Shonin,* the people of any place; *Sho-koku,* the states, or many states; *Sho-shin,* the lords, or ministers.

†SHO, シヨ, 所, (*tokoro*). Place; used only in comp. words, as, *Ba-sho, Yaku-sho, Unjō-sho, K'wai-sho.*

†SHŌ, シヤウ, 賞, (*home*). *n.* Praise, reward. — *ni adzkaru,* to receive a reward. — *wo okonau,* to confer a reward.
Syn. HŌBI.

†SHŌ, シヤウ, 將, *n.* A general, a chief, commander. *Kai-gun no* —, the commander of a ship of war, admiral.

SHŌ, シヤウ, 笙, *n.* A kind of wind instrument.

SHŌ, セウ, The fut. or dubit. of *Shi, szru,*= *sen. Nani to* —, what shall I do? — *to omōte waszreta,* I intended to do it but forgot. — *koto nashi,* nothing I could do, or nothing to do.

SHŌ, シヤウ, 性, *n.* Nature, character, natural disposition, constitution, temperament, temper, quality, kind. *H'to no* —, a man's natural temper.
Syn. SEISHITSZ, UMARETSZKI, SHŌ-AI.

SHŌ, シヤウ, 症, *n.* Nature or kind of disease, diathesis. *Biyōki no* —.

SHŌ, シヤウ, 鉦, *n.* A kind of gong, or cymbal. — *wo utsz.*

†SHŌ, シヤウ, 正, (*makoto*). True, real, genuine. — *no mono,* a genuine article.

†SHŌ, シヤウ, 牀, *n.* A couch, bed, sofa, divan. — *ni fusz,* to recline on a couch.
Syn. TOKO.

†SHŌ, シヤウ, 庄, *n.* A village, or township. Syn. MURA, SATO.

†SHŌ, シヤウ, 章, *n.* A chapter, section. *Shi isshō,* one piece of poetry.

†SHŌ, シヤウ, 上, (*wiye*). *n.* Above, upon. A title of the *Tenshi,*= your highness, his majesty.

†SHŌ, シヤウ, 祥, (*kizashi*). *n.* Omen, sign, prognostic. *Ki-kin no* —, sign of a famine.
Syn. ZEMPIYŌ.

†SHŌ, シヤウ, 匠, *n.* A workman, mechanic, artisan. Syn. SHOKUNIN.

†SHŌ, シヤウ, 商, (*akindo*). *n.* A merchant, traffic. *Yeishō,* an English merchant.

SHŌ, シヨウ, 證, (*akashi.*) Proof, testimony, witness, evidence.
Syn. SHŌKO.

SHŌ, シヨウ, 升, *n.* A measure, either dry or liquid, equal to ten *go,* or 109.752 cub. inches, = a little more than 1qt. 1pt. ½ gill imperial measure.

SHŌ, セフ, 妾, (*mekake*). *n.* A concubine, = pers. pron. I, by women in speaking humbly of themselves.

SHŌ, セウ, 小, (*chīsai*). Small, little in size; or 少, (*szkoshi,*) a little in quantity. *Shō no tszki,* a short month of 29 days. *Dai-shō ga aru,* there are large and small.

SHŌ-AI, シヤウアヒ, 性合, *n.* Nature, quality. — *warui kane,* metal of bad quality.
Syn. SHITSZ, UMARETSZKI.

SHŌ-AI, シヨウアイ, 鍾愛, *n.* Love, affection. — *szru,* to love. Syn. AISZRU.

†SHŌ-AKU,-*szru,* シヤウアク, 掌握, (*tanagokoro ni nigiru*). To possess or reign over, to govern.

SHŌ-BAI, シヤウバイ, 商買, *n.* Mercantile business; also any business, or occupation. — *szru,* to trade, traffic. *Omaye no* — *wa nani,* what is your occupation?
Syn. AKINAI, KAGIYŌ.

SHŌ-BAN,-*szru,* シヤウバン, 陪膳, To make one of a company at an entertainment, to dine with and assist in entertaining guests.

†SHŌ-BATSZ, シヤウバツ, 賞罰, *a.* Reward and punishment.

SHŌ-BEN, セウベン, 小便, *n.* Urine. — *wo szru,* to urinate.
Syn. IBARI, SHŌYŌ, SHISHI.

SHŌ-BI, シヤウビ, 賞美, *n.* Praise, applause, commendation. — *szru,* to praise.
Syn. HOMERU.

SHŌ-BI, セウビ, 薔薇, *n.* A rose.
Syn. BARA.

SHO-BIYŌ, シヨビヤウ, 諸病, (*moro-moro no yamai*) *n.*. All kinds of diseases, diseases generally.

†SHŌ-BŌ,-*szru,* セウバウ, 燒亡, To be burnt up, consumed with fire.

SHOBO-SHOBO, シヨボシヨボ, *adv.* The sound of rain falling. *Ame ga* — *furu.*

SHŌ-BU, シヨウブ, 勝負, (*kachi make*), *n.* Win or lose, victory or defeat, gaming. — *wo kesszru,* to decide a contest. — *ga tszkanu,* the issue is not decided.
Syn. SHIYŪ.

SHŌBU, シヤウブ, 菖蒲, *n.* The sweet flag, Acorus Calamus.
Syn. AYAME.

SHŌBU-GOTO, シヨウブゴト, 勝負事, *n.* Any kind of game. — *wo szru,* to game.

SHŌ-BUN, シヤウブン, 性分, *n.* Nature, natural disposition, temper, temperament. *Ki no mijikai* —, irritable temper.
Syn. SHŌ-AI, SEISHITSZ.

SHŌ-BUTSZ, シヤウブツ, 正物, (*makoto no*

mono), n. Real, or genuine article, (not spurious). Syn. HOMMONO.

SHŌ-CHI, シヤウチ, 承知, *n.* Consent, permission, assent. — *szru*, to consent, assent to, accede, grant. Syn. NATTOKU, K'YŌ-YŌ, YURUSZ, SHŌ-IN.

SHO-CHI, シヨチ, 處置, *n.* Management, or conduct of business. — *szru.*
Syn. HAKARAI, ATSZKAI.

SHŌ-CHIU, セウチユウ, 燒酎, *n.* Alcohol, or distilled spirits.

SHO-CHIU, シヨチウ, 書中, *(fumi no uchi), n.* In the book, letter, or writing.

SHO-CHIU, シヨチウ, 暑中, *(atsza no uchi),* During the heat of summer.

SHŌ-DAI,*-szru*, シヤウダイ, 請待, *(koi matsz),* To invite, call. Syn. MANEKU, YOBU.

SHŌ-DAKU,*-szru*, シヤウダク, 承諾, To consent, assent to, allow, permit.
Syn SHŌCHI, UKE-HIKU.

†SHŌ-DAN, セウダン, 笑談, *(warai kataru), n.* Talking and laughing together, (as a company of friends).

†SHŌ-DEN, シヤウデン, 上殿, *(tono ni noboru), n.* The privilege of admission into the Tenshi's palace. — *wo yurusz.*

SHŌDZRU, シヤウズル, See *Shōji.*

SHŌ-FU, シヤウフ, 生麩, *n.* A starch made of wheat flour.

SHŌ-GA, シヤウガ, 生姜, *n.* Ginger.

SHŌ-GA, シヤウガ, 唱歌, *(utau uta), n.* A song, ballad, song singing.

SHŌ-GAI, シヤウガイ, 生涯, *(iki no kagiri), n.* Life, period or duration of life, life long. *Isshō-gai,* the whole life.
Syn. ISSHŌ.

SHŌ-GAI, シヤウガイ, 生害, *n.* Suicide. — *szru,* to commit suicide.

SHŌGAKUBŌ, セウガクバウ, *n.* A large kind of Turtle.

SHŌ-GATSZ, シヤウグワツ, 正月, *n.* The first month.

†SHŌ-GE, シヤウゲ, 障礙, *(jama), n.* Hindrance, obstruction, impediment.
Syn. SAWARI, SAMATAGE.

SHŌ-GI, シヤウギ, 床机, *n.* A camp stool.

SHŌ-GI, シヤウギ, 象棋, *n.* The game of chess. — *wo sasz,* to play chess. — *ni ban,* two games of chess.

SHO-GIYŌ, シヨギヤウ, 所行, *(okonau tokoro), n.* Actions, conduct, deeds, doing. Syn. OKONAI, GIYŌ-JŌ.

SHŌ-GUN, シヤウグン, 將軍, *n.* A general, commander. This word is now only used of the Kubōsama, or Taikun.

†SHŌ-HAI, シヨウハイ, 勝敗, *(kachi yaburi), n.* Victory or defeat.
Syn. SHŌBU.

SHO-HOTSZ, シヨホツ, 初發, *(hajime). n.* The beginning, origin.

†SHO-I, シヨ井, 所爲, *(nasz tokoro). n.* The deed, doing, work; cause, reason; effect, consequence, result.
Syn. SHI-WAZA, SEI, YUYE.

SHO-IN, シヨ井ン, 書院, *n.* The parlor, drawing room. Syn. HIROMA.

SHŌ-IN,*-szru*, シヤウイン, 承引, *(ukehiki).* To consent, assent, agree to, yield, concede. Syn. SHŌCHI, NATTOKU, UKEGAU.

SHO-JAKU, シヨジヤク, 書籍, *(shomotsz). n.* A book. Syn. HON.

SHO-JI, シヨヂ, 所持, *(motsz tokoro). n.* Property, possession, that which one owns. — *szru,* to own, possess. — *no hon,* a book which is one's own property.

SHŌ-JI, シヤウジ, 障子, *n.* Window or door sash covered with thin paper. *Giyaman* —, a glass window.

SHŌJI,*-jiru* or *-dzru,-jita*, シヤウズル, 生, *(umareru). t.* or *i. v.* To produce, beget, bring-forth, bear, to create, make, to cause to exist or arise, develop, to be manifested. *Ki ga mi wo* —, the tree bears fruit. *Akushin wo* —, to beget a wicked heart. *Kami wa ban-motsz wo* —, God created all things. *Kabi wo* —, to rust, or mildew. Syn. HAYERU, DEKIRU.

SHŌ-JIKI, シヤウヂキ, 正直, Honest, upright, frank, sincere, faithful. — *na mono,* an honest person. Syn. SZGUI, SEI CHOKU, NAOI.

SHŌ-JIN, シヤウジン, 精進, Abstaining from everything that defiles and unfits one for the worship of Amida, as flesh and fish. — *szru.*

†SHŌ-JIN, セウジン, 小人, *n.* The mean man, *i.e.*, the ignorant and immoral.

SHŌ-JIN, シヤウジン, 正身, True, real, genuine. — *no kuma no i,* genuine bear's-gall. Syn. SHŌBUTSZ, HONTO.

†SHOJO, シヨヂヨ, 處女, *n.* A young girl, a young lady.

SHŌJO, セウヂヨ, 小女, *n.* idem.

SHO-JŌ, シヨジヤウ, 書狀, *n.* A letter, epistle. Syn. TEGAMI, FUMI.

†SHŌ-JŌ, シヤウジヤウ, 清淨, *(isagiyoi).* Clean, free from defilement.
Syn. KEPPAKU.

SHŌ-JŌ, シヤウジヤウ, 猩猩, *n.* The orang outang. Syn. HI-HI.

SHŌ-JŌ-HI, シヤウジヤウヒ, 猩猩緋, *n.* Red woolen cloth.

SHO-KA, シヨカ, 初夏, (*natsz no hajime*) *n.* Beginning of summer.

SHŌ-KACHI シヤウカチ, *n.* Female gonorrhœa.

SHŌ-KAI, シヤウカイ, 紹介, *n.* An introduction. — *szru*, to introduce one person to another.

SHŌ-KAN, シヤウカン, 傷寒, *n.* Acute febrile disease.

†SHO-KAN, シヨカン, 書翰, *n.* A letter, epistle. Syn. TEGAMI.

SHŌ-KATSZ-BIYŌ, シヤウカツビヤウ, 消渇病, *n.* Diabetes.

SHO-KE, シヨケ, 所化, *n.* A young novice or pupil of a Bud. priest.

SHŌ-KI, シヤウキ, 正氣, *n.* Right mind or senses. — *wo ushinau*, to lose one's right mind, to become delirious.

SHO-KI, シヨキ, 暑氣, *n.* Heat or hot weather. — *ga tszyoi.*

SHŌ-KIN, シヤウキン, 正金, *n.* Money or cash; (not barter). — *de kau*, to buy with money.

SHŌ-KŌ, セウカウ, 燒香, Burning incense. — *szru*, to burn incense.

SHŌ-KO, シヨウコ, 證據, *n.* Proof, testimony, evidence. — *szru*, or — *tatsz*, to bear witness. Syn. AKASHI.

†SHŌ-KO, シヤウコ, 商賈, *n.* A merchant. Syn. AKINDO.

†SHO-KŌ, シヨコウ, 諸侯, *n.* The nobles or barons.

†SHO-KŌ, シヨカウ, 初更, *n.* The first watch of the night,—from 8 to 10 o'clock.

SHŌ-KOKU, シヤウコク, 生國, (*umare guni*). *n.* Native country.

SHŌ-KO-NIN, シヨウコニン, 證據人, *n.* A witness.

SHOKU, シヨク, 職, *n.* Trade, mechanical employment, business. *Ano h'to no — wa nani*, what is his trade? *Daiku wo — to szru*, he is a carpenter by trade.

SHOKU, シヨク, 食, (*kurau*). Eating, taking food, appetite. — *szru*, to eat. — *wa ikaga*, how is your appetite? Syn. TABERU, KŪ.

SHOKU, シヨク, 燭, (*tomoshibi*). *n.* A light, lamp. — *wo mottekoi*, bring a light. Syn. AKARI.

SHOKU-BA, シヨクバ, 職場, *n.* The place where a workman does his work.

SHOKU-BUN, シヨクブン, 職分, *n.* Branch of work, a part of one's business, employment, or duty. *Watakushi no — de wa nai*, it is not my work or duty.

SHOKU-DAI, シヨクダイ, 燭臺, *n.* A candle stick, lamp-stand.

SHOKU-DŌ, シヨクダウ, 食道, *n.* The gullet, esophagus.

SHOKU-JI, シヨクジ, 食事, (*kūkoto*). *n.* Eating, taking food, appetite. — *wa ikaga*, how is your appetite? — *ga warui*, have no appetite.

SHOKU-JO, シヨクヂヨ, 織女, *n.* Name of a star near the milky-way, same as *Tanabata.*

SHOKU-MOTSZ, シヨクモツ, 食物, (*kui mono*). *n.* Food, articles of food, victuals, provisions. Syn. TABE-MONO.

SHOKU-NIN, シヨクニン, 職人, *n.* A mechanic, artisan.

SHOKU-RIYŌ, シヨクリヤウ, 食糧, *n.* Provisions, supply of food. *Buta wo katte gunzei no — ni szru*, to buy pork for provisioning an army. Syn. SHOKUMOTSZ.

SHOKU-SEN, シヨクセン, 卓氈, *n.* A woollen table cover.

SHOKU-SHŌ, シヨクシヤウ, 食傷, *n.* Pain, or sickness produced by something eaten, indigestion. Syn. MONO-ATARI.

†SHOKU-SHŌ, シヨクシヤウ, 職掌, *n.* The duties of one's office, duty. — *wo tszkusz*, to discharge one's duty.

SHOKU-TAI, シヨクタイ, 食滯, *n.* Indigestion. — *szru.* Syn. SHOKU-SHŌ.

†SHŌ-K'WA, -*szru*, セウクワ, 消化, *n.* Digestion. — *no warui mono*, an indigestible thing. — *senu mono*, (idem.) Syn. KONARERU.

SHŌ-K'WAN, -*szru*, シヤウクワン, 賞玩, (*home moteasobu*). To admire, praise, or express delight for a present received.

SHOKU-YE, シヨクヱ, 觸穢, (*kegare ni fureru*). Ceremonial uncleanness, contracted by entering a house where there is a dead body, or where a woman has had an abortion, or by eating rice prepared by a menstruating woman, &c. — *ni yotte kami ye mairarenu.*

SHOMBORI-TO, シヨンボリ, *adv.* The appearance of one sitting alone and gloomy.

SHŌ-MEI, シヤウメイ, 正銘, *n.* Genuine name or mark, (affixed to a knife blade, &c.).

SHŌ-MEN, シヤウメン, 正面, *n.* The exact front. — *ni mawatte miru*, to turn and look at it directly in front.

SHO-MEN, シヨメン, 書面, *n.* A letter. Syn. TEGAMI.

†SHŌ-METSZ, -*szru*, セウメツ, 消滅, (*kiye horoburu*). To put an end to, to blot out, expunge, (Bud.) *Zai-shō —*, to blot out sins.

SHŌ-MI, シヤウミ, 正味, *n.* The real or

exact weight, the real substance or essence separated from adventitious matter. — *no nedan wa ikura,* what is the true price? — *wa ikura,* what is the weight of the article freed from all foreign substances?

SHŌ-MIYŌ, シヤウミヤウ, 聲明, *n.* A song of praise to *Hotoke,* celebrating the praise of *Hotoke* by singing. — *szru.* — *wo tonayeru.*

SHO-MŌ, シヨマウ, 所望, (*nozomi*). *n.* That which one desires or hopes for. — *no mono,* idem. — *szru,* to desire.

SHŌ-MON, シヨウモン, 證文, *n.* A bond, certificate, debenture, any writing made as evidence or in proof of a transaction. — *wo kaku.*

SHO-MOTSZ, シヨモツ, 書物, *n.* A book. Syn. HON.

SHŌ-NE, シヤウ子, 性根, *n.* Perception, sense, feeling, disposition, temper. — *wo ushinau,* to lose one's senses, (as in fainting). — *wo ireru,* to give close attention; to endow with sense, (as an idol). — *no warui h'to,* a bad tempered man. — *nashi,* forgetful, heedless. *Te ga shibirete — ga nai,* the hand is numb, and without feeling. — *no nuketa h'to,* an idiot. — *ga tszku,* to to come to one's senses. Syn. SHŌ, KI, KOKORO.

SHŌ-NEN, セウ子ン, 少年, *n.* A young man.

†SHŌ-NETSZ-JIGOKU, セウ子ツヂゴク, 焦熱地獄, One of the Buddhist hells.

†SHŌ-NI, セウニ, 小兒, *n.* A child. Syn. KODOMO, DŌJI.

SHO-NICHI, シヨニチ, 初日, (*hajime no hi*). *n.* The first day, (of an exhibition.)

SHŌ-NIN, シヤウニン, 商人, *n.* A merchant.

SHŌ-NIN, シヨウニン, 證人, *n.* A witness. Syn. SHŌKONIN.

SHŌ-NIN, シヤウニン, 上人, *n.* The title affixed to the name of a priest, = highness or Revd., as *Tokujō shōnin.* Syn. SHAKU.

SHŌ-NŌ, シヤウナウ, 樟腦, *n.* Crude camphor. Syn. RIUNŌ, HENNŌ.

†SHŌ-RAI, シヤウライ, 生來, *n.* Nature, essential quality of any thing. Syn. SHŌ-AI.

SHŌ-RAKU, シヤウラク, 上洛, (*miyako ye noboru*). Going to the capital.

†SHŌ-RAN, シヤウラン, 上覽, Sending any thing for the *Tenshi* to look at. *Mono wo — ni sonayeru.*

†SHŌ-REI-DOKU, シヤウレイドク, 瘴癘毒, *n.* Malaria, pestilential vapors.

SHŌ-RI, シヨウリ, 勝利, *n.* Victory or advantage in a contest. — *wo yeru,* to get the victory.

†SHO-RIN, シヨリン, 書林, *n.* A bookstore. Syn. HONYA.

SHO-RIYŌ, シヨリヤウ, 所領, *n.* Estate, territory, dominion. Syn. RIYŌBUN.

SHŌ-RIYŌ, シヤウリヤウ, 生靈, *n.* The spirits of the deceased, or of one's ancestors. — *wo matszru,* to worship the spirits of the deceased.

SHŌ-RIYŌ, セウリヤウ, 小量, Small mental capacity, little ability, narrow minded, illiberal, pusillanimous.

SHŌ-RO, シヨウロ, 松露, *n.* A kind of mushroom.

SHŌ-RŌ, シヨウロウ, 鐘樓, *n.* A bell-tower.

SHŌ-RO, シヤウロ, 正路, *n.* Honesty, uprightness, rectitude, artlessness. Syn. SHŌJIKI

†SHŌ-RUI, シヤウルイ, 生類, (*ikeru tagui*). *n.* Things that have animal life.

SHO-SA, シヨサ, 所作, *n.* Conduct, actions, deeds, behavior, doings. Syn. FURUMAI.

†SHO-SAI, シヨサイ, 書齋, *n.* A library, study, or reading room.

SHŌ-SAN, セウサン, 小產, *n.* A premature birth. — *szru.*

SHŌ-SAN-GIN, セウサンギン, 消酸銀, *n.* Nitrate of silver, or lunar caustic.

†SHŌSEI, セウセイ, 小生, I, (in letters speaking humbly of one's self.)

SHO-SEI, シヨセイ, 書生, *n.* A pupil, scholar, student.

SHŌ-SEKI, シヤウセキ, 上席, *n.* High seat, high rank.

SHŌ-SEKI, セウセキ, 消石, *n.* Nitrate of Potash, saltpetre.

SHO-SEKI, シヨセキ, 書跡, *n.* Writing, penmanship.

SHŌ-SEKI-SAN, セウセキサン, 消石酸, *n.* Nitric Acid.

SHO-SEN, シヨセン, 所詮, *adv.* In the end, at last, after all; the conclusion or sum of the whole matter; the result. Syn. HIKKIYŌ, TSZMARI.

SHŌ-SEN, シヤウセン, 商舩, (*akinai bune*). *n.* A merchant ship.

SHŌ-SEN, セウセン, 小錢, *n.* A small iron coin.

SHŌ-SETSZ, セウセツ, 小說, *n.* A story book, novel, fiction.

†SHO-SHA, *-szru,* シヨシヤ, 書寫, (*hon wo kaku*). To write a book.

SHŌ-SHI, セウシ, 笑止, Pitiful, sad, to be

commiserated, (used in an insincere or jocular manner). — *na koto*, a sad business. Syn. KINODOKU.

SHŌ-SHI,-*szru*,-*sh'ta*, シヤウスル, 稱, *t.v.* To name, to call, designate. *Midzkara ō to* —, called himself a king. *Na wo Ginkō to* —, called his name *Ginkō*.
Syn. NADZKERU, GŌ-SZRU.

†SHO-SHI, シヨシ, 書肆, *n.* A book-store. Syn. SHO-RIN.

†SHO-SHI, シヨシ, 庶子, *n.* A younger son of the Tenshi, or of a noble, who does not inherit the throne or estate.

†SHO-SHI,-*szru*,-*sh'ta*, シヨスル, 書, (*kaku*). To write.

†SHO-SHI,-*szru*,-*sh'ta*, シヨスル, 處, *t.v.* To assign, to allot, to appoint each to his proper place, to manage, direct. *Shizai ni shoszru*, to condemn to death.

†SHŌ-SHI,-*szru*,-*sh'ta*, セウスル, 消, To digest. *Shoku-motsz wo* —, to digest food. Syn. KONARERU, SHŌ-K'WA SZRU.

SHO-SHI-DAI, シヨシダイ, 所司代, *n.* The minister of the Shōgun or Yedo government, who resides in Kiyoto.

SHO-SHIKI, シヨシキ, 諸色, *n.* All kinds of things, things generally. — *ga kōjiki ni natta*, every thing has risen in price.

SHO-SHIN, シヨシン, 初心, *n.* (*hajime no kokoro*). A novice, or beginner in anything, inexperienced.

SHŌ-SHIN, シヨウシン, 昇進, *n.* Promotion, advancement in rank, or office. — *szru.* Syn. SHUSSEI.

SHŌ-SHIN, セウシン, 小身, A person of small property or income. — *mono.*

†SHŌ-SHITSZ, セウシツ, 燒失, (*yake useru*). Consumed, or burnt up. Syn. SHŌBŌ.

SHŌ-SHŌ, セウセウ, 少少, *adv.* A little in quantity or degree.
Syn. SZKOSHI, CHITTO.

†SHO-SHŪ, シヨシウ, 初秋, (*aki no hajime*). *n.* The beginning of autumn.

SHŌ-SHUN, セウシユン, 小春, (*koharu*). Little spring,—the springlike weather in the 10th month.

SHO-SON, シヨソン, 書損, (*kaki-sokonai*). *n.* A mistake, or error in writing.

SHŌ-SOKU, セウソク, 消息, *n.* Word, tidings, message, account. — *wo szru*, to send word. Syn. OTODZRE, TAYORI, SATA, SŌ.

†SHŌ-SZI,-*szru*, セウスヰ, 憔悴, (*yase otoroyeru*). To become emaciated, or cadaverous.

SHŌ-SZI, セウスイ, 小水, *n.* Urine.
Syn. SHŌBEN.

SHO-TAI, シヨタイ, 所帶, *n.* Holding property, keeping house. — *wo motsz*, to be a householder, or to keep house. — *dōgu*, house-keeping articles. Syn. SHINSHŌ.

SHŌ-TAI, シヤウタイ, 正體, (*makoto no karada*). *n.* True or real person, or character, natural condition of mind or body. *Bake mono — wo arawasz*, the apparition revealed its true character. *Sake ni yōte — wo ushinau*, he was so drunk he was not himself.

SHO-TAI-MEN, シヨタイメン, 初對面, To meet for the first time.

SHŌ-TAN, セウタン, 小胆, (small liver). Little courage, cowardice. — *na mono*, a person of little courage.

SHŌ-TATSZ,-*szru*, シヤウタツ, 上達, To become proficient, or adept in, completely versed in. Syn. JŌDZ NI NARU.

SHO-TE, シヨテ, 初手, (*hajime*). *n.* The first, beginning, commencement. — *kara*, from the first or beginning.

SHŌ-TEN, シヨウテン, 昇天, (*ten ni noboru*). To ascend to heaven.

†SHO-TŌ, シヨトウ, 初冬, (*fuyu no hajime*) *n.* The beginning of winter, the tenth month.

SHŌ-TOKU, シヤウトク, 生得, (*umaretszki*). *adv.* Naturally, by force of one's nature, inborn, constitutionally. — *sake wa kirai da*, have a natural dislike of ardent spirits.

†SHO-YA, シヨヤ, 初夜, (*yoi*). The beginning of night, 8 o'clock.

SHŌ-YA, シヤウヤ, 庄屋, *n.* The head man of a village, same as *Nanushi.*

SHO-YAKU, シヨヤク, 書役, *n.* A clerk, book-keeper, writer.

SHOYEN, シヨエン, 所縁, *n.* Relationship, connection; acquaintance, friend, or helper in time of need. Syn. YOSZGA, TAYORI.

SHO-YŌ, シヨヨウ, 所用, (*mochiiru tokoro*). *n.* Anything which one uses. *Kore wa watakushi no — da*, this is a thing which I use.

SHŌ-YŌ, セウヨウ, 小用, *n.* Urine. — *szru*, to urinate. Syn. SHŌBEN, SHŌSZI.

†SHŌ-YŌ, セウエウ, 逍遙, Rambling, or sauntering about for pleasure. — *wo konomu.* — *szru.* Syn. ASOBI-ARUKU.

SHŌYU, シヤウユ, 醬油, *n.* Soy, a kind of sauce made of fermented wheat and beans.

SHŌ-ZA, シヤウザ, 上座, (*kami za*). *n.* The upper or highest seat in a room, or assembly.

SHOZAI, シヨザイ, coll. always with a negative, as, — *ga nai*, nothing to do.

†SHO-ZŌ, シヨザウ, 所藏, (*osamuru tokoro*). *n.* Anything kept stored or treasured up.

†SHŌ-ZŌ, セウザウ, 肖像, (*nitaru katachi*). *n.* A likeness, portrait.

SHŌ-ZOKU, シヤウゾク, 裝束, *n.* Dress, garb, clothes, uniform, livery. *Tszwamono no* —, the uniform of a soldier. *K'wa-ji no* —, fire uniform. Syn. IFUKU, KIMONO.

†SHO-ZOKU, シヨゾク, 所屬, Subject to, under the dominion or power of, as. *Riu-kiu wa Nippon no — nari*, the Loochoo islands are subject to Japan.

SHO-ZON, シヨゾン, 所存, (*omō tokoro*), *n.* The thoughts, what one is thinking about, mind, opinion. *I kaga no — de h'to no mono wo nuszmu zo*, what do you mean by stealing? *— no hoka*, different from what was expected.
Syn. ZONNEN, KOKORO.

SHU, シユ, 朱, *n.* Vermilion, cinnabar, red-ink. — *de kaku*, to write with red-ink. — *wo szru*, to rub red-ink on an inkstone.

SHU, シユ, 主. (*nushi*), *n.* Lord, master. — *to kerai*, master and servant. — *to szru*, to make it the prime object, or of most importance.

SHŪ, シユウ, 衆, The many, the multitude, the people; a plural particle. *K'wa wa — ni teki sedz*, a few cannot contend with many. — *wo ushinayeba kuni wo ushinau*, by losing the people the kingdom is lost. *Yakunin-shū*, the officers. *H'yakushō-shū*, the farmers. Syn. MORO-MORO, ŌI, SHO, RA.

SHU, シユ, 酒, (*sake*), *n.* Wine, ardent spirits.

SHŪ, シユウ, 宗, A sect. *Nani — de gozarimas*, what sect do you belong to? *Tendai shū*, the sect called Tendai.

SHŪ, シウ, 州, (*kuni*), *n.* A state, province. *Chō-shū*, the province of Nagato.

†SHŪ, シウ, 秋, (*aki*), *n.* Autumn, fall.

SHU-BI, シユビ, 首尾, (*hajime owari*), *adv.* or *n.* (lit. head, and tail), from beginning to end. — *yoku*, all has passed off well, favourably, or satisfactorily; all right. — *ga warui*, the matter or case looks bad or unfavourable. — *wa ikaga*, how does the matter look? or, how does the case stand?

†SHU-BIKI, シユビキ, 朱引, *n.* Drawing a red line along words.

SHŪBUN, シウブン, 秋分, *n.* The autumnal equinox.

SHU-DAN, シユダン, 手段, (*tedate*), *n.* Plan, scheme, way, device. — *ga tszkanu*, can't devise any plan.
Syn. HAKARIGOTO.

†SHU-DZMI, シユズミ, 朱墨, *n.* Red ink.

SHU-FUKU, -*szru*, シユフク, 修復, To repair by building. Syn. ZŌSAKU SZRU.

SHŪ-GEN, シフゲン, 祝言, *n.* The marriage ceremony, a wedding, nuptials. — *szru*, to perform the, &c. Syn. KONREI.

SHUGEN, or SHUGENJA, シユゲン, 修驗, *n.* The same as *Yamabushi*.

SHŪGI, シユウギ, 衆議, *n.* An assembly of a number of persons for consultation, or deliberation; the whole council.

SHŪ-GI, シフギ, 祝儀, (*iwai*) *n.* Congratulation, felicitation, compliment, a present made on a holiday. *Nenshi no go — wo mōshiageru.*

SHU-GIYŌ, シユギヤウ, 修行, (*okonai wo osameru*), *n,* Regulating the conduct, self discipline, the practice, study, or cultivation of virtue, science, or accomplishments. — *szru. Gaku-mon* —, the study of letters.

SHU-GO, -*szru*, シユゴ, 守護, (*mamoru*), *t.v.* To guard, protect, keep, preserve, watch over. *Kami wa ban-min wo shu-go sh'tamō*, God is the preserver of all men. *Ware wo buji ni shu-go sh'tamaye*, keep me from all evil.

SHU-I, シユイ, 主意, *n.* The principal purpose, main object, chief design, intention, point, or subject of a matter, the motive. Syn. HON-I.

SHŪ-I, -*szru*, シフイ, 拾遺, (*otosz wo hirō*.) To collect things forgotten, or left out. *Uta wo — szru*, to collect scattered poems.

†SHU-IN, シユイン, 朱印, *n.* A red seal, or stamp.

†SHŪ-ITSZ, シウイツ, 秀逸, (*hīde szgureru*), Most excellent, surpassing all others.

SHU-JIN, シユジン, 主人, (*nushi aruji*), *n.* Lord, master.

SHŪ-JIN, シユウジン, 衆人, (*moro moro no h'to*), *n.* The people, men.

SHŪ-JITSZ, シユウジツ, 終日, *n.* The whole day, from morning to night.
Syn. HIMEMOSZ, ICHI-NICHI.

†SHU-JŌ, シユジヤウ, 主上, *n.* A title of the Tenshi, = supreme lord.

SHU-JŌ, シユジヤウ, 衆生, (*moro-h'to*), *n.* *n.* All men, men, mankind. (Bud.) — *wo saido szru*, to save men.

SHU-JŪ, シユジウ, 主從, *n.* Master and servant, Lord and retainer.

SHU-JU, シユジユ, 種種, (*kusa gusa*), Many kinds, various kinds. — *na mono*,

many kinds of things.
Syn. IRO-IRO, SAMA-ZAMA.

†SHU-KA, シユカ, 首夏, *n.* The fourth month, or beginning of summer.

SHU-KAIDŌ, シウカイダウ, 秋海棠, *n.* The name of a flower.

SHU-KAKU, シユカク, 主客, *n.* Host and guest, landlord and guest.

SHU-KAKU, シユカク, 酒客, *n.* A drunkard, one fond of wine.

†SHU-KI, シユキ, 酒氣, (*sake no ki*), *n.* The taste, or smell of *sake*. *Ano h'to — ga aru,* he smells of *sake.*

†SHU-KI, シユキ, 酒旗, (*saka-bayashi*), *n.* The flag used as a sign of a brewery.

†SHU-KIKU, シフキク, 蹴鞠, (*mari wo keru*), *n.* Playing at floot-ball.

†SHU-KIN, シユキン, 手巾, (*tenugui*). *n.* A handkerchief.

†SHU-KIU, シユキフ, 首級, *n.* The head of a decapitated person.

†SHU-KIYŌ, シユキヨウ, 酒興, *n.* Exhilarated with wine.

SHUKKAKU, シユツカク, 出格, (*kaku wo idzru*). Extraordinary, different from the usual method, rule, or order; exception, as. — *no shōshin,* promotion not gradual step by step, but by leaping over several intervening grades.

SHUKKE, シユツケ, 出家, (*iye wo idzru*). *n.* Forsaking home, surname, and the world to enter a Buddhist monastery; a Bonze, or Buddhist priest. — *szru.* — *ni naru,* to become a priest.

SHUKKIN, シユツキン, 出勤, (*ide-tsztomeru*). Attending to one's official duties away from home. *Unjōsho ye — szru,* to do duty at the Custom house.

SHUKK'WAI, シユツクワイ, 出會, (*de-ai*). *n.* Meeting any one while out. *Tochiu ni — sh'ta,* meet him in the road.

SHU-KŌ, シユカウ, 趣向, (*omomuki*). *n.* Plan, contrivance; design, style. — *szru,* to plan, design. Syn. KUFŪ.

SHUKU, シユク, 宿, *n.* A lodging place, a post-station; or place where relays of horses and coolies are kept. — *szru,* to stop, to lodge at a hotel or inn.
Syn. YEKI.

SHUKU, シユク, 祝, (*iwau*). Congratulation, felicitation, celebration. *Shinnen wo — szru,* to celebrate the new year. *Gochisō sh'te tanjōbi wo — szru,* to celebrate a birthday by making a feast. Syn. SHŪGI'

SHUKUBA, シユクバ, 驛, *n.* A post-station, or halting place, a lodging place.

SHUKU-BO, シユクボ, 叔母, (*oba*). *n.* An aunt, spoken only of father's younger sister, or father's younger brother's wife.

SHUKU-BŌ, シユクバウ, 宿房, *n.* A temple in which travelers may rest, or lodge.

SHUKU-GŌ, シユクゴフ, 宿業, *n.* Deeds done in a previous state of existence, for which retributions are received in this.

†SHUKU-G'WAN, シユクグワン, 宿願, *n.* An old or long cherished desire.

†SHUKU-HŌ, シユクホウ, 祝砲, *n.* Guns fired in honor of any one, or to celebrate any occasion. — *wo szru,* to fire guns &c.,

†SHUKU-I, シユクイ, 宿意, *n.* Malice, enmity or grudge of long standing. *Toshitszki no — wo toge-baya to omō.*

†SHUKUIN, シユクイン, 宿因, *n.* Same as *Shukugō.*

SHU-KUN, シユクン, 主君, *n.* Lord, master.

†SHUKU-RŌ, シユクラウ, 宿老, (*toshi yori*). *n.* A aged person, one who still lives, his generation having passed away.

†SHUKU-SEI, シユクセイ, 宿世, (*maye no yo*). *n.* A previous state of existence.
Syn. ZENSEI

†SHUKU-SHI, シユクシ, 宿紙, (*uszdzmi*). *n.* A kind of paper, used by the *Tenshi* for writing edicts &c.

†SHUKU-SZI, シユクスイ, 宿醉, *n.* Drunkenness continued for several days.
Syn. FUTSZ KA YOI,

SHUM-BUN, シユンブン, 春分, *n.* The vernal equinox.

SHUMISEN, シユミセン, 須彌山, *n.* The name of a fabulous mountain of the Buddhist, on the top of which *Tai-shaku-tenwo,* the ruler of the universe, is supposed to dwell.

†SHUMME, シユンメ, 駿馬, (*haya uma*). *n.* A fast horse.

SHUMOKU, シユモク, 橦木, *n.* Same as *Shimoku.*

SHŪ-MON, シユウモン, 宗門, *n.* Religious sect.

†SHU-MOTSZ, シユモツ, 腫物, (*dekimono*). *n.* A sore, ulcer, or boil on the skin.

†SHUN, シユン, 春, (*haru*), *n.* Spring; time when any article of food is in season. *Kaki wa ima ga — da,* persimmons are now in season. — *hadzre,* to be out of season.

†SHUN-DAN, シユンダン, 春暖, (*haru no atatakasa*). *n.* A warm time in spring.

†SHUN-KAN, シユンカン, 春寒, (*haru no samusa*). *n.* A cold time in spring.

†SHŪ-NEN, シフネン, 執念, *n.* Unceasing enmity, jealousy, or malice.

†SHŪ-NEN, シウネン, 終年, *n.* The whole year. Syn. NENJŪ.

SHU-NŌ, シユナフ, 收納, (*osameru*). *n.* The receipts or payments of taxes, or of money collections. *Nen-gu wo — szru,* to collect taxes, or to pay in taxes. *Ko-toshi no — ga warui,* this year's receipts are small. *Shu-nō-chō,* a book in which the sums paid in, or collected, are registered.

†SHUN-SOKU, シユンソク, 駿足, (*haya ashi*). Swift footed, fleet.

SHUPPAN, シユツパン, 出帆, Sailing out, setting sail. — *szru,* to sail, or set out on a voyage.

SHUPPAN, シユツパン, 出版, To publish, or edit a book.

SHUPPON, シユツポン, 出奔, (*idete hashiru*). Running away. — *szru,* to run or flee away, to abscond. Syn. NIGERU, CHIKUTEN, KAKE-OCHI.

SHURA, or SHURA-DŌ, シユラ, 修羅, *n.* One of the hells of the Buddhists, filled with fighting and slaughter.

SHU-RAN, シユラン, 酒亂, *n.* Frenzied or delirious from drinking ardent spirits. Syn. SZIKIYŌ.

†SHU-REN, シユレン, 習練, (*narai-neru*). *n.* Skill or dexterity acquired by long practice. Syn. TANREN.

SHŪ-REN, シウレン, 收斂, Astringent. — *szru,* to be astringent; (fig.) to be penurious.

†SHŪ-REN-ZAI, シウレンザイ, 收斂劑, *n.* Astringent medicines.

†SHURI,–*szru,* シユリ, 修理, To repair a building. Syn. SHUFUKU, ZO-SAKU.

SHURIKEN, シユリケン, 手裡劍, *n.* A dirk, used by throwing.

SHŪ-RO, シユウロ, 手爐, *n.* A small brazier for warming the hands.

SHU-RO, シユロ, 棕櫚, *n.* A species of palm-tree common in Japan.

†SHU-RŌ, シユロウ, 酒樓, *n.* A kind of restaurant. Syn. RIYŌRI-YA.

SHU-RŌ, シユロウ, 鐘樓, *n.* Same as, *Shōrō,* A bell-tower.

SHŪ-RON, シユウロン, 宗論, *n.* A dispute between religious sects. — *szru,* to dispute about sects.

SHU-RUI, シユルイ, 種類, *n.* Kind, class, species, varieties. Syn. TAGUI, RUI.

SHU-SEKI, シユセキ, 手跡, *n.* Hand-writing, penmanship.

SHU-SEKI-SAN, シユセキサン, 酒石酸, *n.* Tartaric Acid.

SHŪ-SEN, シウセン, 周旋, (*sewa wo yaku*). *n.* Services or kind assistance rendered to others, patronage, help.

†SHU-SHI,–*szru,*–*sh'ta,* シユスル, 修, *t.v.* To practice, cultivate, to perfect one's self in anything.

SHU-SHŌ, シユシヨウ, 殊勝, (*kotoni szgureru*). Excellent, eminent for worth, or virtue, admirable — *ni omō,* Syn. KIDOKU.

†SHŪ-SHŌ,–*szru,* シウシヤウ, 周章, (*awateru*). To be astonished, stupefied, bewildered. *Ikaga wa sen to —,* bewildered not knowing what to do.

†SHŪ-SHŌ,–*szru,* シウシヤウ, 愁傷, (*urei itamu*). To be in great sorrow, or distress.

†SHU-SO, シユソ, 呪咀, (*norō*). Imprecating or invoking evil upon an enemy. — *szru,* to invoke evil, &c.

†SHŪ-SO,–*szru,* シウソ, 愁訴, (*ureye utayeru*). To petition government for mercy or help in distress, to make a complaint. Syn. TANG, WAN.

†SHU-SOKU, シユソク, 手足, (*te ashi*). *n.* Hands and feet.

SHUS-SAN, シユツサン, 出產, *n.* Parturition. — *szru,* to bear, to beget, bring-forth a child. Syn. SAN.

SHUS-SEI, シユツセイ, 出世, (*yo ni deru*). Rising in the world, rising in rank, dignity, or fortune; leaving the world to enter a monastery. — *szru.*

SHUS-SEI, シユツセイ, 出情, (*sei wo dasz.*) Putting forth strength, striving or exerting one's self to do anything. — *szru.*

SHUS-SEKI, シユツセキ, 出席, (*seki ye deru*). Going to an assembly, or meeting.

SHUSSEN, シユツセン, 出舩, (*defune*). The sailing or departure of a ship. *Nan doki no — da,* what o'clock does the boat leave?

SHUS-SHI,–*szru,* シユツシ, 出仕, To attend to official duties. Syn. SHUKKIN.

SHUS-SHŌ,–*szru,* シユツシヤウ, 出生, (*umare deru*). To be born, to beget. *Sakuban kodomo ga — sh'ta,* a child was born last night.

SHUSZ, シユス, 繻子, *n.* Satin.

SHU-SZDZRI, シユスズリ, 朱硯, *n.* A red-ink stone.

†SHŪ-TA, シユウタ, 衆多, (*ōi*). Many in number. — *na h'to,*

†SHŪ-TAN,–*szru,* シウタン, 愁歎, (*urei nageku*). To lament, to sorrow, grieve.

SHUT-CHŌ,–*szru,* シユツチヤウ, 出張, (*debari*). To leave home and open shop, to do business in another place, to go forth and commence military operations.

SHU-TŌ, シユトウ, 種痘, (*wiye-bōso*). *n.* Vaccine, disease, vaccination. — *szru*, to vaccinate.

SHŪTO, シウト, 舅, *n.* Father in law.

SHŪTO-ME, シウトメ, 姑, *n.* Mother in law.

†SHUTSZ-GEN, シユツゲン, 出現, (*arawareru*). The appearing or manifestation of an invisible being. *Kami ga — sh'tamau.*

†SHUTSZ-GIYO, シユツギヨ, 出御, The going out or appearing in public of the *Tenshi*, or of any other very high personage.

†SHUTSZ-NIU, シユツニフ, 出入, (*de iri*). *n.* Going out, and coming in.

†SHUTSZ-NŌ, シユツナフ, 出納, (*dashi ire*). *n.* Paying out, and taking in money. — *szru*, to pay out, and receive money.

†SHUTSZ-RI,–*szru*, シユツリ, 出離, (*de hanareru*). To leave and be separated from, as, *Shō-shi — szru*, to leave this world where men live and die, and to go to heaven ; or no longer to concern one's self about the things of this world. (Bud.)

SHUTSZ-ZA,–*szru*, シユツザ, 出座, (*za ye deru*). To go out to take one's seat in an assembly or meeting. Syn. SHUSSEKI.

SHUTTAI,–*szru*, シユツタイ, 出來, (*dekiru*). To be done, made, to finish. *Chū-mon no shina ga — sh'ta*, the article ordered is finished.

SHŪ-YA, シユウヤ, 終夜, The whole night. Syn. YOMOSZGARA, YO-JŪ.

SHU-YEN, シユエン, 酒宴, *n.* (*sakamori*). A banquet, feast, or entertainment, where wine is a principal article. — *wo moyōsz*, to prepare a banquet.

†SHŪ-YEN, シユウエン, 終焉, (*owari*). *n.* The end of life. — *wo togeru*, to arrive at the end of one's life. — *no kokorozashi*, a desire lasting as long as life.

†SHU-YU, シユユ, 須臾, (*szkoshi no aida*). A short time, an instant, moment. *Michi wa — mo hanareru bekaradz*, the way must not be left for a moment. Syn. SHIBARAKU, ZANJI.

†SHU-YU, シユユ, 茱萸, *n.* The name of a seed used as a medicine.

SO, ソ, 粗, Coarse, rude, rough, unpolished, inelegant. (疎), Thin, not close together. *So na mono*, a coarse thing. Syn. ZATSZ, ARAI.

†SO, ソ, 祖, (*senzo*). *n.* Ancestor, progenitor. *Waga so*, my ancestor.

†SO, ソ, 祚, (*kurai*). *n.* Office or dignity, (spoken only of *Tenshi*). *Tenshi no so wo fumu*, to occupy the imperial dignity —the throne.

SO, ソ, *adv.* Coll. contraction of *Sore.* There. Used also as an exclamation, as in giving, or showing anything.

SŌ, ソウ, 僧, *n.* A Buddhist priest. Syn. BŌDZ, HŌ-SHI, OSHŌ.

SŌ, サウ, 相, *n.* The physiognomy. *H'to no — wo miru*, to examine the physiognomy.

SŌ, ソウ, 奏, *n.* A report, or memorial to the *Tenshi*, to do, perform. — *szru*, to memorialize or exhibit to the emperor. *On-gaku wo — szru*, to make music.

†SŌ, ソウ 叟, (*okina*). *n.* A respectful appellation, in speaking to, or of an old man, = venerable sir.

SŌ, サウ, 然, (derived from *Shika*). *adv.* So, thus, this way, this manner. — *shi-na yo*, don't do so, — *ka*, so ? or indeed ! — *de wa nai;* it is not so. — *sh'te oku*, let it be as it is. — *iu koto de wa nai*. it is no such thing. — *sh'te mo yoi*, it will do as it is. Syn SAYŌ.

SŌ, ソウ, 總, (*szbete*). *a.* The whole. — *taka wa ikura*, what is the whole amount? — *shime*, whole sum, total. — *nin-jū*, the whole number of persons. Syn. MINA.

SŌ, サウ, 草, (*kusa*). *n.* Grass, herb; a running hand, or grass character. — *de kaku*, to write in a running hand.

SŌ, ソウ, 艘, *n.* The numeral in counting ships, or boats. *Fune issō*, one ship. *San-sō*, three sail.

SŌ, サウ, 左右, (*otodzre*). *n.* Message, tidings, word, account, news. — *ga nai*, no news, no word. — *wo szru*, to send word. Syn. TAYORI.

SŌ, サウ, *n.* Look, appearance of, likelihood, probability, used frequently as a suffix to verbs. *Yedo ni ari-sō na mono*, a thing which is likely to be in Yedo. *Hare-mono ga tszbure-sō da*, the boil looks as if it would break. *Ochi-sō na mono*, a thing which looks as if it would fall. *Kire-sō ni natte kirenu*, it looks as if it would break, but does not. *Ame ga furi-sō-da*, it has the appearance of rain, or looks like rain. *Ano h'to atszi sō da*, that man appears to be hot. Syn. YŌ, RASHII.

SŌ, ソウ, *adv.* Softly, gently, without disturbing or shaking. — *to sh'te oku*, don't disturb them. — *to ite miru*, go softly and look. Syn. SORORI.

SŌ, ソフ, 添, See *Sōi.*

SŌAI, サウアイ, 草鞋, *n.* Chinese grass slippers.

†Sō-AN, サウアン, 草庵, *(kusa no iori)*. *n.* A thatched hut or cottage.

SOBA, ソバ, 側, *n.* Side, the place near, adjoining, or contiguous. *H'to no — ye yoru*, to approach near to a person. Syn. HOTORI, KIWA, ATARI.

SOBA, ソバ, 岨, *n.* A steep-side of a mountain, precipice, cliff. *Yama no — ga kudzreta*, the side of the mountain has slidden. Syn. GAKE.

SOBA, ソバ, 蕎麥, *n.* Buckwheat. *— no ko*, buckwheat meal. *Ki-soba*, pure buckwheat.

SŌBA, サウバ, 相庭, *n.* The current, or market price. *Kome no —*, the current price of rice. *Kome ippiyō no — wa ikura*, what is the market price of a bag of rice? *Ito no — ga yaszi*, the market price of silk is low. Syn. NEDAN.

SOBA-DZKAYE, ソバヅカヘ, 侍兒, *n.* A page, waiter, attendant.

SŌBA-DZKE, サウバヅケ, 相庭付, *n.* A price current.

SOBADACHI, *-tsz, -tta*, ソバダツ, 峙, *i.v.* To be steep, precipitous. *Yama ga —*, the mountain is steep. Syn. SOBIYERU.

SOBADATE, *-ru, -ta*, ソバダテル, 攲, *t.v.* To erect or stretch out. *Mimi wo —*, to erect the ears (as an animal) or to incline the head to listen (as man). *Ashi wo —*, to stand on tiptoe. *Makura wo —*, to raise the head from the pillow (to listen). *Kasa wo sobadatete ame wo fusegu*, to incline the umbrella so as to keep off the rain.

SOBA-GARA, ソバガラ, 蕎麥殻, *n.* The chaff, or shells of buckwheat.

SOBAGAKI, ソバガキ, 河漏, *n.* Porridge, or mush made of buckwheat.

SŌ-BAI, サウバイ, 相倍, The same quantity added, as, *Nisōbai*, two fold, or twice as much. *San sōbai*, three fold, or three times as much.

SOBAKASZ, ソバカス, 雀斑, *n.* Freckles.

SOBAKIRI, ソバキリ, 蕎麥麵, *n.* A kind of food made of buckwheat.

SOBAME, *-ru, -ta*, ソバメル, 仄, *t.v.* To turn side ways. *Mi wo sobamete tōru*, to go through side ways, (as a narrow passage). *Me wo sobamete miru*, to look askant at another.

†SOBAME, ソバメ, 妾, *n.* A concubine. Syn. MEKAKE.

SOBAMU, ソバム, Same as *Sobameru*.

SOBAYA, ソバヤ, 蕎麥屋, *n.* A shop or eating house, where food made of buckwheat is sold.

SOBAYERU, ソバヘル, Same as *Sobiyeru*.

SŌ-BETSZ, ソウベツ, 總別, *adv.* All or singly, all together or separately, in any way they are taken. Syn. SZBETE, SŌJITE.

SOBIKI, *-ku, -ta*, ソビク, *t.v.* To pull, or drag by force. *Sobiki-dasz*, to drag out. Syn. HIKU.

†SOBIRA, ソビラ, 背, *n.* The back. Syn. SENAKA.

SOBIYAKASHI, *-sz, -sh'ta*, ソビヤカス, 聳, *t.v.* To elevate, stretch up. *Kata wo —*, to elevate or shrug the shoulders.

SOBIYE, *-ru, -ta*, ソビエル, 聳, *i.v.* To be erect, to stretch up high. *Yama ga kumo no wiye ni sobiyeru*, the mountain reaches above the clouds.

†SO-BIYŌ, ソベウ, 祖廟, *n.* An ancestral temple.

SO-BŌ, ソバウ, 粗暴, Coarse, careless, vulgar; unrefined in manners. *— na h'to*, a careless person. Syn. SOSŌ.

†SOBO, ソボ, 祖母, *n.* Grand mother. Syn. OBĀSAN.

†SŌ-BŌ, ソウバウ, 僧房, *n.* A Buddhist monastery or temple.

†SŌ-BOKU, サウボク, 草木, *(kusa, ki)*. *n.* Grass, or herbs and trees.

SOBURI, ソブリ, *n.* Manner, deportment, behavior, appearance. *— de shireru*, known by his manner. *Ureshiki —*, joyful manner. Syn. KEWAI, FURI, YŌSZ.

SO-BUTSZ, ソブツ, 粗物, *(somatsz na mono)*. *n.* Anything coarse in texture make or manner, rude, unpolished.

SOCHA, ソチャ, 粗茶, Coarse or inferior tea.

SOCHI, ソチ, (coll. *sotchi*). 其地, *adv.* That place, there, that thing, (pointing to it). You. *Sochi ye ikimashō*, I will go there. Syn. SOKO.

SOCHIRA, ソチラ, idem.

SODA, ソダ, *n.* Branches of trees or brushwood used for lighting fires.

SODACHI, *-tsz, -tta*, ソダツ, 育, *i. v.* To grow, to enlarge in bulk or stature. *Kodomo ga yoku sodatta*, the child has grown finely. Syn. OI-TATSZ.

SODACHI, ソダチ, 育, *n.* Growth, bringing up, rearing, education, cultivation. *— ga warui*, badly brought up, or badly educated.

SŌ-DAI, ソウダイ, 總代, *(szbete no kawari.)* *n.* The agent, deputy, substitute or representative of a body or number of persons. A committee. *— wo tateru*, to send a committee.

SŌ-DAN, サウダン, 相談, *(aikatari)*. *n.* Consultation, conference. *— szru*, to con-

sult or confer together.
Syn. HIYŌGI, DANKŌ.

SODATE,-ru,-ta, ソダテル, 育, t. v. To raise, to bring up, rear up, to cause to grow, cultivate. *Ko wo* —, to rear up a child. *Ine wo* —, to raise rice.
Syn. YASHINAU.

SODE, ソデ, 袖, n. The sleeve of a garment.
Syn. TAMOTO.

SODEGAKI, ソデガキ, 袖垣, n. A short fence adjoining a house.

SODE-GŌRO, ソデガウロ, 袖香爐, n. A small censer used by carrying in the sleeve.

SODE-JIRUSHI, ソデジルシ, 袖標, n. The badge worn on the sleeve.

SODE-KUCHI, ソデクチ, 袖口, n. The end or hole of a sleeve, the cuff.

SODE-MAKURA, ソデマクラ, 袖枕, n. A pillow made of the arm and sleeve. — *wo sh'te neru*, sleeping with his arm for a pillow.

SODE-NASHI, ソデナシ, 無袖, n. A vest or jacket without sleeves.

SŌ-DEN, サウデン, 相傳, (*ai-tsztaye*). n. Handed-down or transmitted from former generations, inherited. — *no yaku-hō*, a medical recipe handed, &c.

SODENAI,-KI,-KU, ソデナイ, a. Different from what it should be; not true, insincere, false. — *mono*, a counterfeit article. — *kokoro*, false hearted.

SODE-TOME, ソデトメ, 袖止, n. The sewing up of a part of the opening of the sleeve, when a child becomes about five years old, so as to make a pocket.

SODE-UTSZSHI, ソデウツシ, 袖移, n. Handing anything secretly to another through the sleeve. — *ni mono wo yaru*.

SŌ-DŌ, サウドウ, 騷動, n. Disturbance, riot, tumult, uproar, row, war. — *wo okosz*, to excite a riot, raise a disturbance. — *wo szru*, to make a disturbance.
Syn. SAWAGI, RAN.

SŌDOKU, サウドク, 瘡毒, n. Syphilis.
Syn. KASA.

SODOKU, ソドク, 素讀, n. Reciting the names of the Chinese characters without learning their meaning; as children in first learning to read. — *szru*, to recite, &c.

SŌDZ, ソホヅ, 案山子, n. The effigy of a man, used to scare animals or birds from a grain-field, a scarecrow.
Syn. KAGASHI.

†SŌ-DZ, ソウヅ, 僧都, n. The name of a rank in the Buddhist priesthood.

†SO-FU, ソフ, 祖父, n. Grandfather on the father's side.

SO-FUKU, ソフク, 粗服, n. Coarse clothing.

SŌ-GAMI, ソウガミ, 總髪, n. Unshaven head, long hair.

SOGARE,-ru,-ta, ソガレル, 被斫, pass. and pot. of *Sogi*. To be sliced off.

SOGE,-ru,-ta, ソゲル, 殺, i. v. To be cut, pared, or sliced obliquely, to be splintered. *Hana ga sogeta*, his nose is cut off.

SOGI,-gu,-ida, ソグ, 殺, t.v. To cut or pare off obliquely, (as in pointing a pencil or stake), to slice off, to chip off. *Sekihitsz wo* —, to point a lead-pencil.

†SOGO,-szru, ソゴ, 齟齬, (*kui-chigau*). To mistake. Syn. MACHIGAI, SŌI.

SO-GON, ソゴン, 粗言, (*somatsz na kotoba*). n. Coarse or blackguard language. — *wo haku*.

SOGU, ソグ, 殺, See *Sogi*.

SŌ-HATSZ, ソウハツ, 鬆髪, n. The hair unshaven, long hair. — *no h'to*, a person who does not shave his head. — *ni naru*.
Syn. SŌGAMI.

SŌ-HŌ, ソウハウ, 雙方, (*riyō-hō*). n. Both sides, both parties, both persons.

†SOI, ソイ, 素意, (*hon-i*). n. One's desire, wish, or hope.

†SOI, ソイ, 疎意, (*utoki kokoro*). n. Distant, strange, cold, or unfriendly in feeling, treating with neglect; mostly connected with a negative; as, *Soi-naku*, without reserve or neglect, intimate, friendly. *Soi ni wa kesshite mōsadz soro*.

SŌI, サウ井, 相違, (*ai-tagō*). n. Mistake, error, failure. — *szru*. to make a mistake. — *naku*, without fail. *Ano h'to ga totta ni — wa nai*, there is no mistake about his taking it. Syn. MACHIGAI.

SOI,-ō,-ōta, ソフ, 添, i.v. To be at the side of, near to, along with, added, joined, united, annexed, or associated with, appended. *Kawa ni sōte yuku*, to go along, or follow the course of the river. *Ko wa haha ni sōte szwaru*, the child sits by the side of the mother. *Tszma wa otto ni sō*, the wife is joined to her husband. *Tszki wa chikiu ni sōta mono*, the moon is a satellite of the earth. *Kokoro mo mi ni sowadz*, to lose one's presence of mind.
Syn. TSZKU.

SOIDA, ソイダ, *pret*. of *Sogi*.

SOIDE, ソイデ, *pp*. of *Sogi*.

SOI-BUSHI, ソヒブシ, 添臥, n. Sleeping together.

SOI-NE, ソヒネ, 添寢, n. Idem.

SOI-MONO, ソヒモノ, 添物, *n.* Anything that appertains, belongs to, or is always associated with something else, an appendage; as. *Ya wa yumi ni* —, the arrow belongs to the bow. *Kura wa uma ni* —, the saddle belongs to the horse.

SOITSZ, ソイツ, (cont. of *Sono yatsz*), *n.* A word of contempt, that rascal.

SŌ-IU, サウイフ, (cont. of *Shika iu*, so said). That kind, such. — *koto de wa nai*, there is no such thing.

SŌJI, サウヂ, 掃除, *n.* Cleaning, or putting in order by sweeping or dusting. *Zashiki no — wo szru*, to sweep and dust the parlor, to put the room to rights.

SO-JIKI, ソジキ, 粗食, *n.* Eating coarse, or mean food. — *wo szru.*

SŌJITE, ソウジテ, 總, *adv.* Generally, for the most part, commonly.
Syn, SZBETE, Ō-MUNE.

†SO-JŌ, ソジヤウ, 訴狀, (*uttaye gaki*), *n.* A written petition, memorial, or complaint to officials. — *wo ageru.*

SŌ-JUTSZ, サウジユツ, 槍術, *n.* The art of using the spear, the spear exercise. — *no keiko.*

SŌ-JUTSZ, サウジユツ, 蒼朮, (*okera*), *n.* The name of a plant.

†SŌ-KAI, サウカイ, 滄海, (*au unabara*), *n.* The blue sea, ocean.

†SOKEN, ソケン, 素絹, *n.* The white garment worn by a priest, a surplice.

SŌ-KEN, サウケン, 壯健, (*szkoyaka*), Strong, robust, hale, healthy. *Go — de omedetō gozarimas*, I congratulate you on your good health.

†SOKKA, ソクカ, 足下, You, (used in addressing another respectfully).
Syn. KIDEN, NANJI.

SOKKIN, ソクキン, 即金, *n.* Ready money, cash paid down. — *de kau*, to buy for cash, (not on credit).
Syn. GEN-KIN.

†SOKKIYO,–*szru*, ソツキヨ, 卒去, To die, spoken of a noble.

†SOKKIYŌ, ソクキヨウ, 即興, *n.* Immediate merriment, quick fun.

SOKKŌ, ソクコウ, 即功, *n.* Immediate action, or quick operation (of medicines). *Kono kuszri wa — ga aru*, this medicine gives prompt relief.

SOKKOKU, ソクコク, 即刻, *adv.* In a moment, promptly, immediately, at once.
Syn. SZGU-TO, TACHI-DOKORO-NI.

SOKKON, ソクコン, 即今, *adv.* Now, at once, this moment, immediately.
Syn. TADAIMA.

SOKKŌSHI, ソクカウシ, 即, 功紙, *n.* The name of a medicinal plaster.

SOKKUBI, ソツクビ, (coll. contemptuous word, cont. of *Sono kubi*). His head. — *wo hikinuke*, pull his head off.

SOKKURI, ソツクリ, coll. *adv.* All just as they are without disturbing or moving, entirely, wholly.

SOKO, ソコ, 其處, (cont. of *Sono tokoro*), That place, there. — *ye yuku.* — *wo noke*, clear out from there. *Koko kara — made*, from here to there.

SOKO, ソコ, 底, *n.* The bottom, the lowest part of anything. — *wo tataku*, to empty to the last particle, as by striking the bottom of a measure when turned up. *Kokoro no* —, the bottom of the heart. *Midz no* —, the bottom of water. *Taru no* —, the bottom of a cask.

SOKO, ソコ, 壘, *n.* The wall, or rampart of a castle, the earth thrown out of a ditch or intrenchment and used as a defence.

SŌ-KŌ, サウカウ, 艸冠, (*kusa kamuri*), *n.* The radical for grass, (艹), over a Chinese character.

†SŌ-KŌ, サウカウ, 草稿, *n.* The first, or rough copy, or draught.
Syn. SH'TAGAKI, GESHO.

SŌ-KŌ, サウカウ, coll. *adv.* That and this. — *szru uchi ni toshi ga kureta*, while doing this and that the year ended.

SOKOBAKU, ソコバク, 許多, *adv.* A good deal, much, many. Syn. IKUBAKU.

SOKODE, ソコデ, 乃, An illative conjunction, = then, after that, whereupon.

SOKO-DZMI, ソコヅミ, 底積, *n.* Packed, or stowed away in the bottom (of a ship, box, &c.)

†SOKOHAKA TO NAKU, ソコハカトナク, *adv.* Without object, or special reason. — *aruki-mawaru*, to walk about without any special object.

SOKOHI, ソコヒ, 内障, *n.* Amaurosis.
Syn. NAISHŌ.

SOKO-I, ソコイ, 底意, *n.* Secret, concealed, or latent thoughts, or intention; reservation. — *naku*, without concealment, or reservation.

SOKO-KIMI, ソコキミ, 底氣味, *n.* The deep, or latent feeling, or emotion which is felt but not manifested, the shudder which is felt in looking over a precipice, &c.

SOKO-MAME, ソコマメ, 底豆, *n.* Corns on the sole of the foot.

SOKO-MOTO, ソコモト, 足下, *pro.* You.
Syn. SOKA, OMAYE, KIDEN.

SOKONAI,*-au,-atta*, ソコナフ, 害, *t.v.* To injure, hurt, damage, harm, to spoil, to mistake. *Ki wo* —, to offend, hurt the feelings. *Kiki-sokonau*, to mistake in hearing. *Deki-sokonau*, to spoil anything in making. Syn. SONDZRU.

SOKONE,*-ru,-ta*, ソコネル, 毀, Same as *Sokonai*.

SOKO-NUKE, ソコヌケ, 底抜, *n.* Without a bottom, a great drinker of wine. — *no oke*, a bucket without a bottom.

SOKORA, ソコラ, *adv.* There, more indefinite than *soko*.

SOKO-SOKO-NI, ソコソコニ, *adv.* In a hasty, rough, or half-finished manner. *Shitaku — totonoi*, got ready in a hurried and incomplete manner. Syn ZATTO.

SOKOTSZ, ソコツ, 粗忽, Rude, coarse, vulgar in manners, rough, unpolished, gross. — *na furu mai*, rude behavior. — *ni*, roughly, rudely, coarsely.

SOKO-TSZKI, ソコツキ, 底付, *n.* Sticking to the bottom, as any thing cooking in a pan or pot, and therefore, burnt, charred. *Meshi no — wo kū*, to eat that which sticks to the pot.

SOKU, ソク, 足, *n.* A pair of any thing worn on the feet or legs. *Tabi issoku*, a pair of stockings. *Zōri ni soku*, two pairs of sandals.

SOKU, ソク, 束, *n.* A bundle, used in counting paper, straw, wood. &c.; a hand's breadth, in measuring the length of an arrow. *Kami issoku*, one ream of paper. *Wara ni soku*, two sheaves of straw. *Jūgo soku mitsz-buse*, the breadth of fifteen hands and three fingers long.

SOKUI,*-ū,-ūta*, ソクフ, 束, *t. v.* To bind several things into a bundle, or sheaf. Syn. TABANERU, TSZGANERU.

SOKUĪ, ソクイヒ, 續飯, *n.* Paste made of boiled rice.

†SOKUI, ソク井, 即位, (*kurai ni tszku*) *n.* The coronation, inauguration or investing a prince with the insignia of royalty. — *no rei wo okonau*.

†SOKU-IN, ソクイン, 惻隱, *n.* Pity, commiseration, a fellow-feeling. — *no kokoro jin no hashi nari*, pity is a small scrap of benevolence. Syn. JIHI, AWAREMI.

SOKU-JI, ソクジ, 即時, *adv.* At once, this moment, immediately, the same hour, or instant. — *ni dekiru*, to do at once.

SOKU-JITSZ, ソクジツ, 即日, *adv.* Same day, that very day, immediately. Syn. SONO HI.

†SOKU-JO, ソクギヨ, 息女, Your daughter (respectful).

†SOKU-NAN, ソクナン, 息男, Your son, (respectful).

SOKU-RIYŌ,*-szru*, ソクリヤウ, 測量, To measure the depth of water, take soundings. *Umi wo — szru*, to sound the depth of the sea.

SOKU-SAI, ソクサイ, 息災, Free from sickness, misfortune or evil. — *ni kurash'te oru*, to live free from all calamity. — *ni on-mamori kudasare*, preserve me from evil (in praying). Syn. BUJI.

SOKU-SEKI, ソクセキ, 即席, Same assembly, or meeting, while at the meeting, prompt, at once, immediately, on the spot. — *ni shi wo tszkuru*, to compose verses while at the meeting.

†SOKU-SEN, ソクセン, 燭剪, *n.* Snuffers. Syn. SHINKIRI.

SOKU-SHI, ソクシ, 即死, *n.* Sudden death, dying on the spot.

†SOKU-SHŪ, ソクシユウ, 束脩, *n.* A present made to a teacher on entering school.

†SOKU-TAI, ソクタイ, 束帶, *n.* The court costume.

†SOKU-TŌ, ソクタフ, 即答, *n.* Immediate or instant answer; replying at once.

†SŌ-KUTSZ, ソウクツ, 巣窟, *n.* The den of a wild beast.

†SO-K'WAI, ソクワイ, 素懷, *n.* A hope or desire long entertained. Syn. SHUKU-G'WAN, HOMMŌ.

SOKU-ZA, ソクザ, 即座, *adv.* On the spot, immediately, while sitting.

†SOMA-BITO, ソマビト, 樵, *n.* A woodman, wood chopper. Syn. KIKORI.

SOMADZ, or SOMANU, ソマズ, 不染, *neg.* of *Somari. Kokoro ni — koto*, a thing for which one has no taste.

†SŌMAI, サウマイ, 草昧, Early or dark ages. — *no yo*.

SOMARI,*-ru,-tta*, ソマル, 染, *i. v.* Dyed, colored, tinged, stained. *Akaku somaru*, dyed red. *Chi ni* —, stained with blood. *Aku ni* —, corrupted with wickedness.

SOMATSZ, ソマツ, 粗末, Coarse, rough, rude, careless, badly made, vulgar. — *na mono*, a thing coarsely made. *Oya wo — ni szru*, to behave disrespectfully to parents. *Hon wo — ni szru*, to treat a book roughly. Syn. ZATSZ, SORIYAKU.

†SOM-BŌ, ソンバウ, 存亡, Existence or destruction; life or death. *Kuni no — ni kakawaru ikusa*, a war upon which the existence of a state depends.

SOME,*-ru,-ta*, ソメル, 染, *t. r.* To dye. *Kinu wo someru*, to dye silk. *Akazome*, dyed red. *Kurozome*, dyed black.

SOME,*-ru,-ta*, ソメル, 初, To begin, or do anything for the first time, only used in comp. with other verbs; as, *Aruki-someru*, to begin to walk. *Hana ga saki-someru*, the flower begins to bloom. *Kiki-someru*, to hear for the first time.

†SŌ-MEI, ソウメイ, 聰明, Acute in perceiving, clever, sagacious.

†SŌ-MEI, サウメイ, 滄溟, *n.* The wide blue ocean. Syn. AOUNABARA.

SOME-IRO, ソメイロ; 染色, *n.* The color of which anything is dyed.

SOMEIRO-NO-YAMA, ソメイロノヤマ, 蘇迷盧山, *n.* The same as *Shumisen.*

SOME-KAYESHI,*-sz,-sh'ta*, ソメカヘス, 染反, *t.v.* To dye anything in a different color.

SOME-KUSA, ソメクサ, 染草, *n.* Dye-stuff. *Mushi wo — ni szru*, to make a dye-stuff of insects.

SOME-MONO, ソメモノ, 染物, *n.* Anything undergoing the process of dyeing.

SOME-MONO-YA, ソメモノヤ, 染物屋, *n.* A dye house, or dyer. Syn. KŌYA.

SŌMEN, サウメン, 索麵, *u.* Vermicelli.

SOME-TSZKE, ソメツケ, 染付, *n.* Figured, either by the pencil, as porcelain, or by dyeing.

SŌMI, ソウミ, 總身, *n.* The whole body.

SOMI,*-mu,-nda*, ソム, 染, *t.v.* (Contracted form of *Somari*,) To be dyed. *Yamai ni somita*, to be infected with disease.

SŌ-MIYŌ, ソウミヤウ, 總名, A general name, name of a class.

SŌ-MIYŌ-DAI, ソウミヤウダイ, 總名代, *n.* An agent, deputy, substitute, or representative of a body, or number of persons. Syn. SŌDAI.

†SO-MITSZ, ソミツ, 疏密, (*arai komayaka*). Fine or coarse, close together or separated.

†SOM-MEI, ソンメイ, 尊命, (*tattoki ōse*). *n.* Honorable commands, or instructions; used in speaking to, or of an honorable person.

SOM-MŌ, ソンマウ, 損亡, *n.* Loss of money. *Yama ga hadszrete — wo sh'ta*, the speculation has failed and I have lost. Syn. SON.

†SOMO, ソモ, 抑, Same as, *Somosomo.*

†SŌMŌ, サウマウ, 草莽, (Lit. thick grass, jungle, used only in humble address to honorable persons),= I, a vulgar clownish person.

SŌ-MOKU, サウモク, 草木, (*kusa ki*). *n.* Herbs and tress, the vegetable kingdom.

†SŌ-MON,*-szru*, ソウモン, 奏聞, To address, or report to the *Tenshi.*

SŌ-MON, ソウモン, 總門, *n.* The principal gate or entrance into a castle.

†SOMOSAN, ソモサン, 作麼生, *adv.* of interrogation. = *ikaga*, how is it? used only by the *zen* sect of Buddhist in discussions, &c.

†SOMO-SOMO, ソモソモ, 抑抑, *conj.* Used in commencing a narrative or introducing a new subject, = Now, things being so, after this. Syn. SATEMATA.

†SOMPI, ソンピ, 尊卑, (*tattoki iyashii*). *n.* Honorable and base, noble and ignoble.

SOMU, ソム, 染, See *Somi.*

SOMUKE,*-ru,-ta*, ソムケル, 背, *t.v.* To cause, or make turn the back to, to turn away. *Kao wo —*, to turn the face away.

SOMUKI,*-ku,-ita*, ソムク, 背, *t.v.* To turn the back on, to act contrary to, to oppose, disobey, rebel against, to transgress, break. *Akari ni somuite tatsz*, to stand with the back turned to a light. *Yo wo —*, to turn one's back on the world. *Michi ni —*, to forsake the right way. *Okite wo —*, to break the laws. *Yak'soku wo —*, to break an agreement. *Shujin ni —*, to rebel against one's lord. Syn TAGAU.

SOMURU, ソムル, Same as *Someru.*

SON, ソン, 損, *n.* Loss. *— wo szru*, to lose. *Watakushi no — da*, it is my loss. Syn. SOMMŌ, SONSHITZ.

SON, ソン, 孫, *n.* Descendent, posterity. *Tenshi no —*, a descendent of the Mikado. Syn. SHISON.

SON, ソン, 罇, *n.* A numeral in counting tubs, barrels, casks, &c. *Sake isson*, one barrel of wine. *Abura ni son*, two tubs of oil.

†SON, ソン, 尊, (*tattoki*). Honorable, respected, holy, noble, a term of great respect used in addressing or speaking of high, or divine persons. *Son-gan*, honorable face, or your face. *Sontaijin*, your honorable father. *Shakuson*, Shaka.

SONATA, ソナタ, 其方, (Cont. of *sono kata*). That side, you, spoken to inferiors.

SONAWARI,*-ru,-tta*, ソナハル, 備, *i.v.* To have or to be endowed with, to be fully furnished, to be perfect, or complete in. *Toku ga mi ni —*, to be endowed with all virtue.

SONAYE,*-ru,-ta*, ソナヘル, 備, *t.v.* To set before an honorable person, to offer, to set in order, arrange, to provide against, to furnish. *Miki wo kami ni —*, to set wine as an offering before the *Kami*. *Goran ni —*, to lay before an honorable person to look at. *H'to wo kurai ni —*, to set a person on the throne. *Gunzei wo —*, to

set an army in order of battle.
Syn. TAMUKERU, AGERU.

SONAYE, ソナヘ, 備, *n.* Provision, preparation; disposition, order, or arrangement of troops. *Fui no — wo szru*, to make provision against an accident. *Gunzei no* —, the disposition of an army.

SONDZRU, ソンヅル, See *Sonjiru.*

SONEMI,*-mu,-nda*, ソネム, 猜, *t.v.* To envy, to be jealous of and hate. *H'to wo* —, to envy another. Syn. NETAMU, URAYAMU.

SONEMI, ソネミ, 猜, *n.* Envy, jealousy.

†SŌNEN, サウネン, 壯 年, *(sakannaru toshi). n.* The flower of one's age, (about the 20th year.)

SONIN, ソニン, 訴 人, *n.* An informer.

SONJI,*-dzru* or *-ru,-ta*, ソンヅル, 損, *t.v.* To injure, hurt, damage, spoil, to mistake, to do erroneously. *Hon ga sonjita*, the book is damaged. *Mi-sonjiru*, the mistake in seeing. *Kaki-sonjiru*, to commit an error in writing. Syn. SOKONAU.

†SON-KA, ソンカ, 村 家, (*mura no iye*). *n.* A farm house, village house.

SON-KIN, ソンキン, 損 金, *n.* Money sunk or lost in business. — *wa issen riyō.*

†SON-KIYO, ソンキヨ, 村 居, (*mura ni oru*). *n.* Residing in the country.

SON-KIYŌ,*-szru*, ソンキヤウ, 尊 敬, (*tattobi wiyamau*). To honor and respect, to reverence, venerate, to hallow. *Kami wo — szru*, to reverence the *Kami.*

†SON-KŌ, ソンコウ, 尊 公, Honorable lord, or sir, = you, in espistles.

SONNA, ソンナ, (cont. of *Sono yōna.*) *a.* That kind, such, so much. — *koto de wa nai*, it is not that kind of thing. — *ni naku na*, don't cry so much. — *ni samuku mo nai*, it is not so very cold. — *ni itaku mo nai*, it don't hurt so very much.
Syn. SAHODO.

SONNARA, ソンナラ, *adv.* If so, so then. — *sō shō*, if so, I will do so. — *kayerō*, so then I will return.

SONŌ, ソナフ, 備, Same as *Sonayeru.*

SONO, ソノ, 園, *n.* A flower garden.

SONO, ソノ, 其, *pro.* That, those, his, her's, its. *Sono h'to*, that man, or those men. *Sono mono*, that thing or those things. — *toki ni*, at that time. — *on chi ni*, in your country

SONO-HŌ, ソノハウ, 其 方, That side, that country, that person or thing; you, (contemptuously. = *Temaye.*)

SONO-HOKA, ソノホカ, 其 外, *adv.* Besides that, moreover, also.
Syn. NAOMATA.

SONO-KAMI, ソノカミ, 當 時, *adv.* Formerly, anciently. Syn. MUKASHI.

SONO-KATA, ソノカタ, 其 方, Same as *Sonohō.*

SONO-MAMA, ソノママ, 其 儘, *adv.* That way or manner. — *ni sh'te oku*, let it be as it is.

SONO-MI, ソノミ, 其 身, He, himself, itself.

SONO-MOTO, ソノモト, 其 許, *pro.* You. (polite). Syn. OMAYE.

SONO-NAKA, ソノナカ, 其 中, *adv.* Amongst them.

SONO-NOCHI, ソノノチ, 其 後, *adv.* After that, afterwards.

SONO-UCHI, ソノウチ, 其 中, *adv.* During that time, in the mean time, amongst them, soon, in a few days.

SONO-WIYE, ソノウヘ, 其 上, *adv.* Besides that, in addition to that, moreover, stillmore, on top of that, furthermore.

SONO-YUYE, ソノユヱ, 其 故, *adv.* On that account, for that reason, because of that, therefore.

SON-RIYŌ, ソンリヤウ, 損 料, *n.* The hire, price paid for things hired, such as clothes, furniture, utensils.

†SON-RIYO, ソンリヨ, 尊 慮, *n.* Your honorable opinion or will, used only in letters.

SON-SHITSZ, ソンシツ, 損 失, *n.* Loss.
Syn. SOMMŌ, SON.

†SON-SŌ,*-szru*, ソンソウ, 尊 崇, *(tattomiagameru).* To honor, to adore, worship.

SON-TOKU, ソントク, 損 得, *n.* Loss and gain, profit and loss.

SON-YEKI, ソンエキ, 損 益, *n.* Loss and gain, increase or diminish, advantage or disadvantage.

SŌ-Ō, サウオウ, 相 應, Suitable, fitting, becoming. *Mi no bun-gen ni — szru*, to be suitable to one's position or circumstances. — *na yakume*, a suitable office. — *ni kurasz*, to be in tolerably good circumstances. Syn. TEKITŌ, KANAU.

SOPPA, ソツパ, 反 歯, *n.* Projecting front teeth. — *no h'to*, a person who has projecting teeth.

SORA, ソラ, 空, *n.* The sky, the heavens; the space between heaven and earth; time, or season; false, fictitious, feigned, pretended; flighty. — *de oboyeru*, to learn by ear. — *de yomu*, to recite from memory. *Aki no* —, time of autumn, *Kokoro ga sora ni naru*, the mind to become flighty. *Ashi mo — ni naru*, not to know whether one is walking on earth, or air, (from emotion). *Tachi-i no — mo obo-*

yenu, did not know whether he was standing or sitting. *Nani wo szru — mo nai*, not appearing to know what he was doing. *Miru sora mo nai arisama*, a condition not fit to be seen. *Sora-toboke*, feigned ignorance. — *warai*, feigned laughter. — *ne* feigned sleep. — *yoi*, pretended intoxication. — *mimi*, pretending not to hear. — *yamai*, feigned sickness. — *tszmpo*, feigned deafness. — *usofuku*, whistling in affected ignorance.

SORA-GOTO, ソラゴト, 虚言, *n.* A falsehood, a lie. Syn. USO.

SORA-IRO, ソライロ, 空色, *n.* A sky-blue color.

†SORAKU,-*szru*, ソラク, 殂落, To die; spoken only, of the death of foreign emperors or kings.

SORA-MAME, ソラマメ, 蠶豆, *n.* A kind of bean.

†SŌ-RAN, サウラン, 騒亂, *n.* Disturbance, commotion, war.

SORANDZRU, or SORANJI,-*ru*,-*ta*, ソランズル, 諳, *t. v.* To recite from memory, to commit to memory. *Hon wo* —, to recite a book from memory.

SORASANU, ソラサヌ, 不外, *neg.* of *Sorashi.*

SORASE,-*ru*,-*ta*, or SORASHI,-*sz*,-*sh'ta*, ソラス, 反, *t.v.* To cause to bend backwards or outwards. *Mi wo* —, to bend one's self backwards. *Te wo* —, to bend the hand back.

SORASHI,-*sz*,-*sh'ta*, ソラス, 外, *t. v.* To cause to glance or fly off, to turn off; to offend. *Ya wo* —, to turn off an arrow. *Kiyaku wo* —, to offend a guest, and cause him to leave. *H'to no ki wo* —, to offend another.

SORASHI,-*sz*,-*sh'ta*, or SORASE,-*ru*,-*ta*, ソラス, 令剃, Caust of *Sori*. To cause or let shave. *Kamiyui ni hige wo* —, to get a barber to shave one's beard.

SŌRAWABA, サフラハバ, Sub. mo. of *Sōrō.*

SŌRAWADZ, サフラハズ, Neg. of *Sōrō.*

SŌRAWAN, サフラハン, Fut. tense of *Sōrō.*

SŌRAYEDOMO, サフラヘドモ, *conj.* form of *Sōrō.*

SORE, ソレ, 夫, *pro.* That, so; used also as an initial particle, = now. — *de wa nai*, it is not that. — *demo yoi*, that will do. — *kara*, after that, then. — *yuye*, on that account, therefore. — *kore*, this and that. here and there, about. — *dake*, that much. — *de yoi*, that will do.

SORE,-*ru*,-*ta*, ソレル, 外, *i. v.* To glance, or fly-off obliquely, to be offended or turned away; to deviate from the right way, deflected. *Ya ga soreta*, the arrow glanced off. *Teppō no tama ga* —, the ball glanced. *Ki ga* —, to be offended.

SORE,-*ru*,-*ta*, ソレル, 剃, *i. v.* To be shaved. *Kami-sori de hige ga soreta*, the beard has been shaved with a razor. *Hige wa yoku soreta*, the beard is well shaved.

SOREGASHI, ソレガシ, 某, A certain person, used when the name is unknown; also I. — *no muszme*, a certain young lady. — *ra*, we.

SŌ-REI, サウレイ, 葬禮, *n.* Funeral ceremonies, a funeral.

SORE-SORE, ソレソレ, 某某, Each and every one.

SORE-YA, ソレヤ, 外矢, *n.* An arrow that has glanced.

†SŌRI, ソウリ, 腠理, *n.* The pores of the skin. Syn. KEANA.

SORI,-*ru*,-*tta*, ソル, 剃, *t. v.* To shave. *Hige wo* —, to shave the beard.

SORI,-*ru*,-*tta*, ソル, 反, *i. v.* To bend backwards, or outwards, to warp. *Te ga* —, the hand is bent back. *Sotte aruku*, to walk bending back. *Hon no hiyoshi ga sotta*, the cover of the book is warped.

SORI, ソリ, 反, *n.* The curved back of a sword. — *wo utsz*, to turn the back of the sword upwards in the belt preparatory to drawing.

SORI, ソリ, 橇, *n.* Skates, also a sled, or sleigh.

SORI-HASHI, ソリハシ, 反橋, *n.* An arched bridge.

SORI-KAYE,-*ru*,-*ta*, ソリカヘル, 反却, *i.v.* To bend backwards, to warp.

SORI-KE, ソリケ, 剃毛, *n.* The refuse hair that has been shaved off.

†SŌRIN, ソウリン, 叢林, *n.* The name of a *Zenshu* monastery.

SORI-YA, ソリヤ, Same as *Sorewa*, exclam.

SO-RIYAKU, ソリヤク, 疏略, Careless, neglectful, treating with slight, indifference, inattention, or disrespect. — *ni omō*, to disregard. — *ni szru*, to treat with neglect, to slight, to do carelessly, or coarsely. — *naru itash'kata*, rude, or coarse treatment. Syn. OROSOKA, NAIGASHIRO.

SŌ-RIYŌ, ソウリヤウ, 總領, *n.* Eldest son. Syn. CHAKUSHI

†SORIYU, ソリウ, 庶流, *n.* The line of descent by a younger son, not by primogeniture.

†SŌRŌ, サフラフ, 候, A substantive verb, much used in epistolary writings, formed from the ancient form of *Samurō;* To be.

†SORO, ソロ, A contracted form of *Sōrō*, often used also as a final particle without meaning.

SOROBAN, ソロバン, 算盤, *n.* Abacus. — *szru*, to calculate, or reckon on the abacus. — *sh'te miru*, reckon how much. — *ni ataranu*, not to come up to one's calculations.

SOROI,-ō,-ōta, ソロフ, 揃, *i.v.* To be equal, even, uniform, alike; to agree, to accord, to be in union; to match, to have the full number, to be complete. *Ashi ga sorowanu*, they do not keep step, or his legs are not of the same length. *Chōshi ga* —, to be in unison, or accord in music. *Hana ga saki-sorōta*, the blossoms are all in complete bloom. *Nin-jū ga sorōta*, the number of persons is complete. *Fū-fu no sei ga sorowanu*, the height of the man and his wife is unequal. *Ki ga* —, to be of one mind.

SŌ-RON, サウロン, 論爭, *(arasoi rondzru)*. *n*, A dispute, contention, quarrel, altercation.

SORORI-TO, ソロリト, *adv.* Slowly, softly, gently.

SORO-SORO-TO, ソロソロト, 徐徐, *adv.* Slowly, softly, gently.

SOROWADZ, or SOROWANU, ソロハヌ, 不揃, Neg. of *Soroi*. Unequal, not uniform.

SOROYE,-*ru*,-*ta*, ソロヘル, 揃, *t. v.* To equalize, make even, uniform or alike; to make to accord or be in unison, to match, to complete the full number, to furnish or supply with any thing requisite. *Kuchi wo soroyete mōsz*, to say unanimously. *Ashi wo soroyete aruku*, to keep step in walking. *Koye wo soroyete tonayeru*, to recite prayers in unison. *Gunzei wo* —, to draw up an army. *Kadz wo* —, to complete the number. *Tszbu wo* —, to make the pellets of the same size. *Katte-dōgu wo* —, to furnish a kitchen with utensils.

SORU, ソル, See *Sori*.

†SO-SEI,-*szru*, ソセイ, 蘇生, To come to life again, to revive. Syn. YOMI-GAYERU.

†SŌ-SEI, サウセイ, 早世, *(yo wo hayaku sz)*, *n.* Dying in youth, or childhood, early death. Syn. WAKA-JINI.

†SO-SHI, ソシ, 祖師, *n.* The first teacher, or founder of a sect.

†SOSHI, ソシ, 素志, *n.* Constant desire. SOK'WAI.

†SOSHI-I, ソシイ, 疏食, *n.* Coarse rice.

SŌ-SHIKI, サウシキ, 葬式, *n.* Funeral rites. Syn. SŌREI.

SŌ-SHIME, サウシメ, 總計, *n.* The sum total, whole amount.
Syn. TSZGŌ, SHIMETE.

SOSHIRI,-*ru*,-*tta*, ソシル, 誹, *t.v.* To speak evil of, to run-down, decry vilify, backbite, slander, calumniate. *H'to no gakumon wo* —, to depreciate another's learning. Syn. HIHŌ SZRU, ZANGEN.

SOSH'TE, ソシテ, *adv.* Then, after that. *Sono shigoto wo shimatte sosh'te o yu ni haitte koi*, when you have finished that work, then go and take a bath.

SŌ-SHŌ, ソウシヤウ, 宗匠, *n.* A teacher of polite accomplishments such as music, singing, making-tea, setting flowers, &c.

SO-SHŌ,-*szru*, ソショウ, 訴訟, To make a complaint, (to officials), to accuse, to bring suit against. Syn. UTTAYERU.

†SO-SHOKU, ソショク, 疏食, *n.* Coarse food.

†SO-SHU, ソシユ, 疏酒, *n.* Poor, or bad wine.

SO-SŌ, ソサウ, 粗相, Coarse, vulgar, rude, ill-mannered, heedless. — *naru h'to*, an ill-mannered person.
Syn. BUSAHŌ, SOBŌ, SORIYAKU.

SŌ-SŌ, サウサウ, 早早, *adv.* Quickly, with haste, expeditiously. — *kayette koi*, come back quickly. Syn. HAYAKU.

SŌ-SŌ, サウソウ, 葬送, *(hōmuri)*, *n.* A funeral. — *szru*, to inter, to bury.
Syn. NOBE NO OKURI. TOMURAI.

SOSOGASE,-*ru*,-*ta*, ソソガセル, 令灑, caust. of *Sosogu*. To make, or let sprinkle. *Chikai-bumi ni chi wo* —.

SOSOGI,-*gu*,-*ida*, ソソグ, 灑, *t.v.* To sprinkle; used often for *Szszgu*, to wash. *Midz wo hana ni* —, to sprinkle water upon flowers. *Midz wo sosoide michi wo haku*, to sprinkle and sweep the street. *Te wo* —, to wash the hands. Syn. KAKERU, UTSZ.

SOSOKASHII,-KI, ソソカシイ, 粗粗, *a.* Hasty, impetuous, or precipitate in manner, heedless, careless, rude, coarse.

SOSOKASHIKU, ソソカシク, *adv.* Idem.

SOSOKE,-*ru*,-*ta*, ソソケル, *i.v.* To be loose, or dishevelled (as the hair). *Bin ga sosoketa.*

SŌ-SON, ソウソン, 曾孫, *(mago no ko)*. Great-grand-child. Syn. HIMAGO.

SOSONOKASHI,-*sz*,-*sh'ta*, ソソノカス, 唆, *t.v.* To tempt, beguile, entice, seduce. *H'to wo sosonokash'te bakuchi wo utz*, to entice another to gamble. *Muszme wo* —, to seduce a young woman.
Syn. IZANAU, HIKIDASZ, SASŌ.

SOSORI,-*ru*,-*tta*, ソソル, Same as *Szszru*.

†SŌ-SOTSZ, サウソツ, 倉卒, *adv.* Suddenly, unexpectedly.
Syn. NIWAKA-NI, FUTO.

†SOSSHI,-*szru*,-*sh'ta*, ソツスル, 率, (*hiki-iru*), *t.v.* To lead, command, or head an army.

SŌ-TAI, ソウタイ, 總體, (*subete*), *adv.* All, generally, the most part, the majority. Syn. TAITEI.

SŌ-TAI-SHŌ, ソウタイシヤウ, 總大將, *n.* General in chief.

SOTCHIU, ソツチウ, 卒中, *n.* Falling down dead, a sudden death.

SŌ-TEN, サウテン, 早天, *adv.* Early in the morning, dawn of day. — *okiru*, to rise early. Syn. ASAHAYAKU.

SOTETSZ, ソテツ, 蘇鐵, *n.* The sago-palm.

SŌ-TŌ, サウタウ, 相當, Suitable, proper, fitting, becoming, proper. *Ano h'to ni — na yaku*, an office suitable to the man. — *szru*, to be suitable.
Syn. SŌ-Ō KANAU.

†SŌ-TŌ, ソウトウ, 雙刀, (*futatsz no katana*), *n.* Two swords. — *wo obiru*, to carry two swords in the belt.
Syn. NI-HON.

SOTO, ソト, 外, *n.* Outside, out, outer, external, abroad. *Iye no* —, out of the house. — *ye deru*, to go outside. — *kuru bushi*, the external maleolus.

SŌTO, ソウト, *adv.* Same as *Sotto*,

†SOTOBA, ソトバ, 卒堵婆, *n.* A long narrow wooden tablet set up near a grave, inscribed with Sanscrit characters, a sentence from the Buddhist sacred books, and the name of the deceased; supposed to facilitate the entrance of the soul into paradise. Syn. TŌ-BA.

SOTO-BORI, ソトボリ, 外濠, *n.* The ditch around a castle.

SOTO-GAMAYE, ソトガマヘ, 外搆, *n.* The outside inclosure of a castle.

SOTO-GAWA, ソトガハ, 外側, *n.* The outside.

†SOTOMO, ソトモ, 外面, *n.* The outside.

SOTO-NORI, ソトノリ, 外法, *n.* The outside dimensions, or measurement; the inside is called *uchinori*.

†SOTSZ, ソツ, 卒, *n.* A foot-soldier.
Syn. HOHEI, ASHIGARU.

SOTSZ, ソツ, coll., *n.* The waste, refuse, imperfect, or damaged goods usually found in a large lot; also waste, or useless work. — *ga deru*, there is some waste. — *ga aru*, idem. Syn. KUDZ.

†SOTSZJI, ソツジ, 率爾, *adv.* Hastily, abruptly and rudely; lightly, without proper respect or diffidence.

†SOTSZ-ZEN, ソツゼン, 卒然, Idem.

SOTTO, ソツト, *adv.* Quietly, gently, softly, secretly, stealthily.
Syn. SHIDZKANI, HISOKANI.

SOWA, ソハ, The same as *Soba*.

SOWADZ, ソハズ, 不添, neg of *Soi*.

SOWA-SOWA SH'TE, ソハソハ, *adv.* Restless, unquiet, uneasy, not calm or deliberate.

SOYE,-*ru*,-*ta*, ソヘル, 添, *t.v.* To annex, to add, unite, or join a smaller to a greater or principal, to append. *Onna ni kodzkai wo soyete yaru*, to send a servant along with the woman. *Kotoba wo* —, to put a word in, or add a word to what is said. *Kokoro wo* —, to give heed, or attend to. Syn. TSZKERU.

†SOYE-BUMI, ソヘブミ, 添書, (*tensho*). *n.* A letter of recommendation or introduction.

SOYE-GAKI, ソヘガキ, 添書, *n.* A postscript.

SOYE-GAMI, ソヘガミ, 添髮, *n.* Artificial hair worn by one whose hair is thin.

SOYEJI, ソヘヂ, 添乳, *n.* Suckling a child. — *wo szru.*

SOYE-JŌ, ソヘジヤウ, 添狀, Same as *Soyebumi*.

SOYEN, ソエン, 疎遠, (*utoku tōshi*). Without communication or friendly intercourse. — *ni uchi szgiru*, to live without hearing from, or visiting one another.
Syn. BUSATA, TŌDŌSHI, TŌZAKARU.

SOYOGI,-*gu*,-*ida*, ソヨグ, 戰, *i. v.* To shake or flutter in the wind, to blow gently. *Ki no ha ga kaze ni* —, the leaves of the tree flutter in the wind — *Kaze ga* —.

SOYO-SOYO-TO, ソヨソヨト, 習習, *adv.* In a gentle, soft manner, only of the blowing of the wind. *Kaze ga — fuku*, the wind blows gently. *Soyo-to mo oto ga senu*, softly and without noise.

SŌ-ZOKU, サウゾク, 相續, (*ai-tszgu*). *n.* Succeeding to, or inheriting an estate. — *szru*, to inherit. — *nin*, an heir. *Ka-toku wo — szru*, to inherit the estate.

SŌ-ZOKU, ソウゾク, 僧俗, *n.* Priest and people, clergy and laity, religious and secular.

†SOZORO, ソゾロ, 坐, Unintentional, involuntary, instinctive, unwitting, without design or reflection, spontaneous. — — *naru adashi-gokoro*, involuntarily falling in love. — *namida*, tears that flow

spontaneously. — *ni aware ni oboyeru*, could not help but feel pity.

Sōzōshii,-ki,-ku,-ū,-sa, サウザウシイ, 騒騒敷, Noisy, tumultuous, turbulent, uproarious, Syn. sawagashii.

Sz, ス, 巣, *n.* A nest, of birds or insects. *Tori no sz*, a bird's nest. *Hachi no* —, a bee's nest. *Kumo no* —, a spider's web. — *wo kakeru*, to build a nest on anything. — *wo kū*, to build a nest (with the bill, as a bird). — *wo hanareru*, to leave the nest (as a young bird). — *wo tatsz*, (id).

Sz, ス, 醋, *n.* Vinegar, acid.

Sz, ス, 洲, *n.* A sand bank in a stream, a bar. *Kawa no* —.

Sz, ス, 簀, *n.* A mat made of bamboo, or reeds woven together.

Sz, ス, 為, See *Shi*, same as *Szru*.

†Szai, スアイ, 市儈, *n.* A peddler, broker.

Szashi, スアシ 跣, *n.* Bare-feet. — *de aruku*.

Szbako, スバコ, 寸白, (cont. of *Szmpaku*). which see.

Szbakuri-nuke,-ru,-ta, スバクリヌケル, *i.v.* To slip away, (as an eel or anything slippery).

Szbanashi, スバナシ, 素談, *n.* Conversation only without wine or refreshments. — *de omoshiroku nai*, as there was nothing but talk, it was not agreeable.

Szbarashii,-ki,-ku, スバラシイ, coll. A superlative, = very, extremely, splendid, grand, magnificent. — *ōkina koye*, a very loud noise. — *rippa na iye*, a very grand house. Syn. hanahada.

Szbashiri, スバシリ, 鯔魚, *n.* The name of a fish, same as *Bora*.

Szbayai,-ki,-ku, スバヤイ, 素早, Quick, fast, acute, sharp, keen in wit.

Szbe, スベ, (cont. of *sz-beki*,) *n.* Way, manner, how. *Mono wo iu* — *mo shiranu*, did not know the proper way of talking, did not know what to say. — *ga nai* or, — *naku*, nothing more can be done, no resource. Syn. shi-kata.

†Szbe,-ru, スベル, 統, *i.v.* To include in one, taking the whole. *Szbe awasete iwaba*, to speak uniting them in a whole to speak generally. *Ten-ga wo szbe-osameru*, to govern the whole empire.

†Szbekaraku, スベカラク, 須, *adv.* Well, or proper to do, necessary, requisite.

Szbeki,-shi, スベキ, 可為, *a.* Should or ought to do, proper to do. *Oya ni kō-kō wa ko no* — *koto*, children should be obedient to their parents.

Szbeku, スベク, 可為, *adv.*

†Szberagi, スベラギ, 天皇, *n.* Emperor, or Tenshi.

Szberakashi,-sz,-sh'ta, スベラカス, 令滑, caust. of *Szberi*. To cause to or let slide or slip. *Kami wo szberakash'te oku*, to let the hair hang down the back.

Szberi,-ru,-tta, スベル, 滑, *i.v.* To slide, slip, to be slippery. *Michi ga* —, the road is slippery. *Kōri wo* —, to slide on the ice. *Kurai wo* —, to abdicate the throne. *Kuchi ga* —, to make a slip of the tongue.

Szberibiyu, スベリビユ, 馬歯莧, *n.* A species of Portulaca.

Szbeta, スベタ, coll. *n.* A slattern.

Szbete, スベテ, 總, *adv.* All, wholly, totally, also commonly.
Syn. mina, sōjite, oyoso, sōtai.

Szbiki, スビキ, 素引, *n.* Drawing an empty bow, *i.e.*, without an arrow. — *wo szru.*

Szboke,-ru,-ta, スボケル, Coll. same as *Szbomi*.

Szbome,-ru,-ta, スボメル, *t.v.* To contract or draw together the end of any thing, to pucker. *Kuchi wo* —, to pucker the lips. *Kasa wo* —, to shut an umbrella.

Szbomi,-mu,-nda, スボム, *i.v.* To be contracted or drawn together at the end, gathered, puckered. *Kuchi no szbonda tokkuri*, a bottle which gradually narrows to the mouth.

Szburu, スブル, 統, Same as *Szberu*.

Szdachi, スダチ, 巣立, *n.* Leaving the nest, (as a young bird able to fly). — *wo szru*.

Szdaki,-ku,-ita, スダク, *i.v.* To sing as an insect. *Kiri-girisz ga* —, the cricket sings.

Szdare, スダレ, 簾, *n.* A blind or shade made of split bamboos or reeds.

Szdate, スダテ, 素立, *n.* The frame of a building, not including the clap-boarding, plastering, &c.

Szde, スデ, 素手, *n.* Empty-handed. — *de kayeru*, to come back empty-handed.

Szde-ni, ケデニ, 既, or 已, *adv.* (Referring either to past or future time). Already, almost, about to. *H'to ga* — *saru*, the man has gone. *Shigoto wa* — *szuda*, the work is finished. — *shinan to sz*, was almost dead. — *ayaui tokoro ni taszkatta*, was saved from the midst of danger.
Syn. mo-haya, yoppodo, hotondo.

Szdo, スド, 簀戸, *n.* A door made of split bamboos.

Sz-do, スド, 數度, *adv.* Several times.

Szdz, スズ, 鈴, *n.* A kind of bell, such as

are hung upon pack-horses; or a gong, such as is suspended before *Miyas* or temples.

SZDZ, スズ, 錫, *n.* Tin.

SZDZ, スズ, 篶, *n.* A small kind of bamboo.

SZ-DZKE, スヅケ, 酢漬, *n.* Any thing pickled in vinegar.

SZDZKI, スズキ, 鱸, *n.* The Labrax Japonicus.

SZDZME, スズメ, 雀, *n.* A sparrow.

SZDZMI,-*mu*,-*nda*, スズム, 涼, *i. v.* To cool, or refresh one's self in hot weather. *Fune ni notte szdzmu* to take a boat ride in order to cool one's self. *Hi kage de* —, to cool off in the shade. *Szdzmi ni deru*, to go out to get cool.

SZDZMI-DAI, スズミダイ, 涼臺, *n.* A bench set before the door in summer evenings.

SZDZMUSHI, スズムシ, 鈴蟲, *n.* The name of an insect that sings like the sound of a bell.

SZDZNARI, スズナリ, 鈴成, *n.* Growing thick or in great luxuriance, used only of fruit. *Budō ga — ni natta.*

SZDZRI, スズリ, 硯, *n.* An ink-stone.

SZDZRI-BAKO, スズリバコ, 硯箱, *n.* The box in which an inkstone and pencils are kept.

SZDZRI-BUTA, スズリブタ, 硯蓋, *n.* A large lacquered tray or waiter.

SZDZRO, スズロ, Same as *Sozoro.*

SZDZSHII,-KI, スズシイ, 涼, Cool, refreshing, or airy, in hot weather. *Szdzshii tokoro*, a cool place.

SZDZSHIKU, スズシク, 涼, *adv.* Idem. *Kinō no ame de szdzshiku natta*, it is cool and pleasant after yesterday's rain.

SZDZSHISA, スズシサ, 涼, *n.* Coolness.

SZGAI,-ō,-ōta, スガフ, 過合, *i.v.* (Cont. of *Szgi-ai*). To pass each other.

SZGAITO, スガイト, *n.* Raw silk.

SZGAKI, スガキ, *n.* A mat work of bamboo.

SZGAME,-*ru*,-*ta*, スガメル, 眇, *t. v.* To look at with one eye, to draw up the eyes or slightly close them as when the light is too strong. *Me wo szgamete miru.*

SZGAME, スガメ, 眇, *n.* Near-sighted or half closed eyes.

SZGAO, スガホ, 素顔, *n.* A face unpowdered or unrouged.

SZGARA, スガラ, Used only as an affix, meaning, the whole. *Michi-szgara*, the whole way. *Yomo-szgara*, the whole night.

SZGARI,-*ru*,-*tta*, スガル, 縋, *i.v.* To cling to, to hold fast to, to stay by catching hold of, to lean upon, to rely on, depend on. *Tszye ni* —, to lean upon a staff. *Nawa ni szgatte oriru*, to let one's self down by a rope. *Sode ni* —, to cling to another's sleeve. *Okotoba ni szgatte mairimash'ta*, relying upon your word I have come. Syn. TORITSZKU.

SZGARI-TSZKI,-*ku*,-*ita*, スガリツク, 縋付, *t.v.* To cling fast to. *Chichi no hiza ye* —, to cling to the father's knee. *Yoroi no sode ni* —, to cling to the skirt of his armor. Syn. SHIGAMI-TSZKU.

†SZGA-SZGASHII,-KI,-KU, スガスガシク, 清清, (obs.) Clear, pure, free from impurity. *Kokoro — ku omō.* Syn. ISAGIYOI.

SZGATA, スガタ, 姿, *n.* Form, figure, looks, shape, appearance, manner, method, likeness, image, condition. *Ima no — to mukashi no — to chigau*, the appearance of things is different now from what it was formerly. *Yoi* —, a fine form. Syn. KATACHI, OMOMUKI, YŌSZ.

SZGATAMI, スガタミ, 姿見, *n.* A large mirror, in which the whole figure may be seen.

SZ-GATARI, スガタリ, 素語, *n.* A song, or dramatical performance, unaccompanied with music.

SZGE,-*ru*,-*ta*, スゲル, 着, *t.v.* To fasten by passing into, or through a hole; as, *Hari ni ito wo* —, to thread a needle. *Geta no o wo* —, to fasten the strap on a sandal. *Nomi no ye wo* —, to fasten a handle on a chisel. Syn. TSZKERU.

SZGE, スゲ, 菅, *n.* A kind of rush, used for making mats, raincoats, and hats.

SZGENAI,-KI, スゲナイ, 無素氣, *a.* Destitute of affection, or feeling; unkind. Syn. NASAKE-NAI.

SZGENAKU, スゲナク, *adv.* Idem.

SZ-GETSZ, スゲツ, 數月, *n.* Several months, or a few months.

SZGI,-*ru*,-*ta*, スギル, 過, *i.v.* and *t.v.* To exceed, to pass, or go beyond; to pass over, to go too far, pass the proper bounds; to be in excess, too much; to surpass, excel. *Szgitaru wa oyobazaru ga gotoshi*, going too far is as bad as not going far enough. *Tszki hi wo* —, to pass time, or live. *Tszki hi wa hayaku* —, time passes rapidly. *Ano h'to ni wa szgita kimono da*, the clothes are too fine for him. *Biyōki wa sake ga szgiru kara dekita*, the sickness comes from drinking too much liquor. *Kono sake wa midz ga* —, there is too much water in this liquor. *Kuchi ga* —, he talks too much. *Hashi wo* —, to cross a bridge. *Nomi-szgiru*, to drink too much. *Yuki* —, to go too far, go beyond.

SZGI, スギ, 杉, *n.* The cedar, or Chriptomiria Japonica.

SZGI-HARA, スギハラ, 杉原, *n.* The name of a kind of paper.

SZGI-NARI, スギナリ, 杉形, *n.* A pyramidal shape. *Tawara wo — ni tszmu*, to pile bags up one over the other, in the shape of a cedar tree, or pyramid,

SZGI-NISHI, スギニシ, 過西, *a.* Past. — *toki*, past time.

SZGIRU, スギル, See *Szgi.*

SZGI-SARI, *-ru,-tta*, スギサル, 過去, *i.v.* To be past, gone. *Fuyu ga szgisatta*, the winter is past.

SZGIWAI, スギハイ, 活業, *n.* A living, livelihood, occupation. *Daiku wo — ni szru*, to follow carpentering for a livelihood. Syn. NARIWAI, KAGIYŌ, TOSEI.

SZGI-YUKI, *-ku,-ita*, スギユク, 過行, To pass, to go by. *Tszki hi ga* —, the time passes.

SZGOI, -KI, スゴイ, *a.* Inspiring fear, faintheartedness or shuddering; lonely, solitary, chilly, dreary. — *yama michi*, a lonely road which makes a traveller feel timid. — *kaze*, a chilly wind.
Syn. SZZAMASHII, KIMI-WARUI.

SZGOKI, *-ku,-ita*, スゴク, 扱, *t. v.* To draw through the hand, to strip by drawing through the hand. *Nawa wo* —, to draw a rope through the hand, in order to smooth or straighten. *Yari wo* —, to push a spear moving it through the left hand. *Ki no ha wo szgoki-otosz*, to strip off the leaves from a branch. Syn. KAGU.

SZGOKU, スゴク, *adv.* See *Szgoi.*

SZGOMORI, スゴモリ, 巣籠, *n.* A young bird still confined to the nest, a nestling.

SZGOROKU, スゴロク, 雙六, *n.* A game played with dice, backgammon.

SZGOSHI, *-sz,-sh'ta*, スゴス, 過, *t. v.* To pass by, to exceed or do anything in excess, to pass the time, to live. *Ano h'to wa nani wo sh'te tszki-hi wo szgosz de arō*, I wonder what that man does for a living. *Sake wo* —, to drink too much wine. *Ne szgosz*, to sleep too much. *Ire* —, to put in too much. Syn. UTSZSZ.

SZGOSHI, スゴシ, *a.* See *Szgoi.*

SZGO-SZGO, スゴスゴ, *adv.* In a forlorn destitute or solitary manner.

SZGU, スグ, Same as *Szgiru.*

SZGUI, -KI, スグイ, 直, *a.* Straight, not crooked; direct, upright, honest.
Syn. NAOI, MATSZGU.

SZGUKU, スグク, 直, *adv.* idem.

SZGU-NARU, スグナル, *a.* Straight, direct, upright, honest.

SZGU-NI, or SZGU-TO, スグニ, 直, *adv.* Directly, immediately, at once.
Syn. JIKI-NI.

SZGURE, *-ru,-ta*, スグレル, 勝, *i. v.* To be select, choice; to excel, to be superior, better. *Yo ni szgureta kō wo tateru*, to excel others in merit. *Szgureta gakusha*, an excellent scholar.
Syn. HIDERU, NUKINDERU, BAKKUN.

SZGURI, *-ru,-tta*, スグル, *t. v.* To choose, select, pick out. *Sei-hei wo* —, to select good soldiers. Syn. YERAMU, YORU.

SZGUSAMA, スグサマ, 直樣, *adv.* Immediately, at once, directly.

SZGUSHI, スグシ, *a.* See *Szgui.*

SZHADA, スハダ, 素肌, *n.* Bare or naked body. — *de neru*, to sleep in a state of nudity.

†SZHAMA, スハマ, 洲濱, *n.* obs. The same as *Shimadai.*

SZHEN, スヘン, 數遍, *adv.* Several times, a few times.

SZI, -KI, スイ, 酸, *a.* Sour. *Szi kinomi*, sour fruit. Syn. SZPPAI.

†SZI, スイ, 水, *(midz). n.* Water.

SZI, *-u,-ta*, スフ, 吸, *t.v.* To suck, to sip. *Hiru ga chi wo* —, the leech sucks blood. *Shiru wo* —, to sip soup.

SZI-AGE, *-ru,-ta*, スヒアゲル, 吸上, *t. v.* To suck up.

SZI-BI, ス井ビ, 衰微, *(otoroyeru). n.* Decaying, declining, failing, unprosperous, fading, impaired. — *szru*, to fail, decline, deteriorate.

SZI-DŌ, スイダウ, 水道, *(midz no michi). n.* A conduit or channel for conducting water, an aqueduct.

SZI-FUKUBE, スヒフクベ, 吸胡盧, *n.* Cups for drawing blood.

SZI-GAKI, スイガキ, 透垣, *n.* A fence made of bamboo set upright at short intervals.

†SZI-GAN, ス井ガン, 衰顏, *(otoroyeru kao). n.* A face faded with age.

†SZI-GAN, ス井ガン, 衰眼, *(otoroyeru me). n.* Failing sight.

SZI-GARA, スヒガラ, 吸唐, *n.* The ashes of tobacco.

†SZI-GEN, スイゲン, 水源, *(minamoto) n.* The head-waters, origin, or source of a stream.

SZI-GIN, スイギン, 水銀, *(midzkane), n.* Quicksilver.

SZI-GIU, スイギウ, 水牛, (*midz no ushi*), *n.* The buffalo.

†SZI-HEN, スイヘン, 水邊, (*midz no hotori*), *n,* Near the water.

SZI-HI, *-szru*, スイヒ, 水飛, To wash any pulverulent substance in water, to elutriate.

†SZI-JAKU, *-szru*, ス井ジヤク, 衰弱, (*otoroye yowaru*). To decline and grow weak.

SZI-JIN, スイジン, 水神, (*midz no kami*), *n.* The god of water, called *Midzhanome no mikoto.*

SZIKADZRA, スヒカヅラ, 忍冬, *n.* The honey-suckle. Syn. NINDŌ.

SZIKI, スイキ, 水氣, *n.* Vapor.

SZI-KIYO, ス井キヨ, 推擧, *n.* Influence, aid, or assistance used to advance or promote one to office.

SZI-KIYŌ, ス井キヨウ, 醉狂, (*yoi kurū*). Drunk or intoxicated and violent. Syn. SHURAN.

SZI-KŌ, *-szru*, ス井カウ, 推敲, To correct, (as a manuscript).

SZI-KOMI, *-mu*, *-nda*, スヒコム, 吸込, *t.v.* To suck in, draw into by suction, to imbibe, to inhale, to snuff up. *Iki wo* —, to take an inspiration.

SZI-K'WA, スイクワ, 西瓜, *n.* A water-melon.

SZI-K'WA, スイクワ, 水火, (*hi midz*). *n.* Fire and water.

†SZIMIN, ス井ミン, 睡眠, *n.* Sleep. — *wo moyosz.*

SZI-MIYAKU, スイミヤク, 水脈, *n.* The veins of water under ground struck in digging a well.

SZI-MON, スイモン, 水門, *n.* A water-gate, a lock, floodgate.

SZI-MONO, スヒモノ, 吸物, *n.* Soup.

‖SZINA, ス井ナ, 粹, *a.* Genteel, elegant, tasty. Syn. FŪRIU, IKINA.

SZI-NAN, スイナン, 水難, *n.* Calamity, or loss occasioned by water, as an inundation, shipwreck, drowning.

SZI-NŌ, スイナウ, 水囊, *n.* A strainer.

†SZI-RAN, ス井ラン, 醉亂, (*yoi midareru*), *n.* Drunk and violent.

SZI-REN, スイレン, 水練, (*oyogi*), *n.* The art of swimming. — *wo narau*, to learn to swim.

SZIRI, スイリ, 素入, *n.* Diving in water. — *wo szru*, to dive.

SZI-RIYŌ, ス井リヤウ, 推量, (*oshi-hakaru*), *n.* Conjecture, surmise, guess, supposition, inference. *Omaye no — ni tagawadz*, it is just as you conjectured. *Go — no tōri*, idem. — *szru*, to conjecture. Syn. SZISATSZ, SASSZRU.

†SZI-SAI, スイサイ, 水災, (*midz no wazawai*), *n.* Calamity or loss occasioned by an inundation. Syn. SZINAN.

SZI-SAI, スイサイ, 水塞, *n.* A water battery, or fort built near the water.

†SZI-SAN, ス井サン, 推參, (*oshite mairu*), Coming without being invited, rudely pushing one's way in, (used often in speaking humbly of one's self).

SZI-SATSZ, ス井サツ, 推察, *n.* Conjecture, surmise, supposition, guess, suspicion. — *szru*, to conjecture to infer.

SZI-SEI, ス井セイ, 衰世, (*otoroyetaru yo*), *n.* A degenerated age, times that have deteriorated.

†SZI-SEI, ス井セイ, 彗星, *n.* A comet. Syn. HŌKIBOSHI.

SZI-SEI, スイセイ, 水勢, (*midz no ikioi*), *n.* The force of a current of water.

†SZI-SEN, スイセン, 水戰, *n.* A battle upon the water, a sea-fight.

SZISENK'WA, スイセンクワ, 水仙花, *n.* The Nayacinth, Narcissus tazetta.

SZI-SHA, スイシヤ, 水瀉, *n.* A watery diarrhœa.

SZI-SHA, スイシヤ, 水車, (*midz guruma*), *n.* A water wheel.

SZI-SHAKU, *-szru*, ス井シヤク, 垂跡, (*ato wo tareru*). To make himself known, or dwell as a god in a temple. *Kono tokoro ni — shitumō kami*, the god who reveals himself or dwells in this place.

†SZI-SHI, スイシ, 水死, *n.* Drowning. Syn. DEKISHI, OBOREJINI.

SZI-SHI, *-szru*, *-sh'ta*, ス井スル, 推, *t. v.* To conjecture, guess, surmise. Syn. OSHI-HAKARU.

SZI-SHŌ, スイシヤウ, 水晶, *n.* Crystal, quartz.

SZI-SHU, スイシユ, 水手, (*midz no te*), *n.* A sailor, waterman. Syn. KAKO, SENDŌ.

SZI-SŌ, スイサウ, 水葬, (*midz ni hōmuru*), *n.* Burying by casting into the water, or throwing overboard.

SZI-SON, スイソン, 水損, (*midz ni sokonau*), *n.* Loss, or injury caused by water.

SZITA, スイタ, The pret. of *Szki.*

SZITE, スイテ, *pp.* of *Szki.*

SZITA-DŌSHI, スイタドウシ, Being in love with each other, liking each other. — —*fū-fu ni natta.*

†SZI-TEI, スイテイ, 水亭, *n.* A house built over or near the water.

†SZI-TETSZ, スイテツ, 水蛭, *n.* A leech, bloodsucker.

SZI-TON, スヰトン, 水團, *n.* A kind of food.

SZI-TORI,*-ru,-tta*, スヒトル, 吸取, *t.v.* To suck out, draw out by suction.

SZI-TSZKI,*-ku,-ita*, スヒツク, 吸著, To stick fast by suction, (as a leech).

SZJI, スヂ, 筋, A tendon, sinew; a vein, a line, streak or long mark; lineage, family line; reason, right, business. — *wo hiku,* to draw a line. — *wo tzkeru,* to make a mark. *Ki no ha no* —, the nerves of a leaf. *Iye no* —, a family line. *Chi* —, blood relation. *Michi* —, a road. *Nan no szji de koko ye kita,* what business, or right, have you to come here? *Omaye no szru — de wa nai,* it is none of your business, or you have no right to do so. — *ga wakaranu,* I don't understand the reason. — *naki mono,* a person not of good lineage. *Te no* —, the lines in the palm of the hand.

SZJI-AI, スヂアイ, 理合, *n.* Reason, right, business. *Nan no — de,* by what right, &c.?

SZJI-GAKI, スヂガキ, 筋書, *n.* An outline sketch or drawing.

SZJIKAI,*-au,-atta*, タヂカフ, 筋違, *i. v.* To be oblique, slanting, diagonal.

SZJIKAI, スヂカヒ, 筋違, (cont. of *szji* and *chigai*). Oblique, slanting, diagonal. — *ni yuku,* to cross obliquely, or take a near cut. — *michi,* an oblique road.

SZJI-ME, スヂメ, 筋目, *n.* Lineage, pedigree, family, blood. — *ga tadashii,* of good family.

SZJI-MICHI, スヂミチ, 道理, *(dōri). n.* Reason, right, meaning.

SZJI-MUKAI, スヂムカヒ, 筋向, Obliquely, opposite.

SZ-JIN, スジン, 數人, *n.* Several men, a few persons.

SZJIRI,*-ru,-tta*, スヂル, *t.v.* To twist or bend from a straight line, distort.

SZJIRI-MOJIRI, スヂリモヂリ, *adv.* Zigzag. — *aruku,* to walk in a zigzag manner.

SZJŌ, スシヤウ, 素性, *n.* Family line, blood, lineage. Syn. SZJIME.

SZ-JŪ-NIN, スジフニン, 數十人, Several tens of men.

SZ-KADO, スカド, 數個度, *adv.* Several times.

SZKA-JŌ, スカゼウ, 數個條, Several articles, items, or sections.

SZKAMBŌ, スカンボウ, 酸模, *n.* Oxalis acetosella.

SZKANU, or SZKADZ, スカヌ, 不透, neg. of *Szki.* Impervious.

SZKANU, スカヌ, 不愛, neg. of *Szku.* Do not like, am not fond of.

SZKARE,*-ru,-ta*, スカレル, 被愛, pass. of *Szku.* To be liked, to be loved.

SZKARI-TO, スカリト, *adv.* — *kiru,* to cut off at a blow, to clip off.

SZKASADZ, スカサズ, 不透, neg. of *Szkashi.* Immediately, at once.

SZKASHI,*-sz,-sh'ta*, スカス, 透, *t. v.* To make openings in or to separate things that are dense, close, or crowded; to thin, to open. *Kami wo szkash'te miru,* to hold paper up to the light to examine its texture, or to see any indistinct lines on it. *Kinu no ji wo szkash'te miru,* to examine the texture of silk by holding it before the light. *Ko no ma wo szkasz,* to look through a thick grove of trees. *Ki no yeda wo* —, to thin out the branches of a tree. *Aida wo szkash'te naraberu,* to arrange by placing a little apart.

SZKASHI,*-sz,-sh'ta*, スカス, 賺, *t. v.* To coax, to wheedle, or persuade by soft words; to soothe, to trick, hoax, to inveigle. *Naku ko wo* —, to coax a crying child. *H'to wo szkash'te kane wo toru,* to hoax a person and take his money.
Syn. NADAMERU, AZAMUKU.

SZKASHI, スカシ, 透, *n.* The water lines, or figures in the texture of paper, a transparency.

SZKASHI-BORI, スカシボリ, 透彫, *n.* Ornamental carved open-work.

SZKE,*-ru,-ta*, スケル, 助, *t. v.* To help, assist, aid, lend a hand. *Szkete kudasare,* help me. *Szkete yarō,* I will help you.
Syn. TETSZDAI.

SZKEBEI, スケベイ, *n.* (vul. coll). Lewd, lascivious, wanton. — *na otoko,* a lewd man. — *dzra,* a wanton face.
Syn. SZKIMONO.

SZKEDACHI, スケダチ, 助刀, *n.* A second in a duel.

SZ-KEN, スケン, 素見, *(tada miru).* Merely looking at anything without buying.
Syn. HIYAKASHI.

SZKI,*-ku,-ita*, スク, 透, *i.v.* To be open or separated, as of things dense or crowded; to be thinned out, scattered, dissipated; to be transparent, pervious. *Awaseme ga* —, the joint is open, or separated. *Midz soko no ishi ga szite miyeru,* the stones under the water are seen through it. *Giyaman wa yoku szkitaru mono,* glass is a very transparent thing. *Te ga szita,* have an interval of rest from work. *Midz ga szite deru,* the water oozes through. *Mune ga szku,* my stomach is empty. *Hara ga* —, to be hungry. *Umiwata ga midz no szku mono*, sponge is pervious to water. *Midz no szkanu mono*, a thing impervious to water.

SZKI,*-ku,-ita*, スク, 疏, *t.v.* To comb with a fine comb. *Kami wo —*, to comb the hair.

(2). 漉, to make paper. *Kami wo —*, to make paper.

(3). 耡, to dig with a spade. *Ta wo —*, to dig a rice-field.

(4). 結, to net, or make a net. *Ami wo —*. id.

SZKI,*-ku,-ita*, スク, 好, *t.v.* To like, to be fond of. *Sake wo —*, to be fond of wine. *Hon wo szite yomu*, to be fond of reading. *Bakuchi ga szki*, fond of gambling. Syn. KONOMU, AISZRU.

SZKI, スキ, 酸, *a.* Sour, see *Szi.*

SZKI, スキ, 耡, *n.* A kind of spade.

SZKI, スキ, 透, *n.* An opening, interval, a crack; chance, opportunity, leisure. *— wo mitszkete nige-dasz*, he watched for an opportunity and escaped. *To no — kara kaze ga hairu*, the wind enters through a crack in the door. Syn. HIMA, SZKIMA.

SZKI, スキ, 好, *n.* One who likes, or is fond of, a lover. *Sake ga szki da*, he is a lover of wine.

SZKI-HARA, スキハラ, 空腹, *n.* Empty stomach, hungry. *— ye kuszri wo nomu*, to take medicine on an empty stomach.

SZKI-KAYESHI,*-sz,-sh'ta*, スキカヘス, 漉反, *t.v.* To work old paper over again into new. This kind of paper is called *Szkikayeshi.*

SZKI-KIRAI, スキキライ, 好嫌, *n.* Like and dislike. *Mono ni — ga aru*, people have their likes and dislikes.

SZKI-MA, スキマ, 透間, *n.* Opening, interval, crack, time, chance, opportunity, leisure. Syn. SZKI, HIMA.

SZKI-MI, スキミ, 透見, *n.* Peeping, or looking through a crack. *— wo srzu.*

SZ-KIN, スキン, 素金, *n.* Money only. *— de kau*, to buy with money—not to exchange for goods.

SZKI-TŌRI,*-ru,-ta*, スキトホル, 透通, *t.v.* To pass through, to be transparent. *Midz ga futon wo —*, the water has wet through the quilt. *Mushi ga szishō wo szki-tōte miyeru*, the insect is visible through a crystal.

SZKI-UTSZSHI,*-sz,-sh'ta*, スキウツス, 透寫, *t.v.* To trace, or copy by placing the paper over the figure to be copied.

SZKIYA, スキヤ, 茶寮, *n.* A tea-room.

SZKKARI, スクカリ, *adv.* All, entirely. *Kane ga — nakunatta*, his money is clean gone. Syn. SAPPARI.

SZKKIRI, スクキリ, *adv.* Idem.

SZKKOMI,*-mu,-nda*, スツコム, (vul. coll.) *t.v.* To draw in, (as a tortoise its head), go in, hide. *Kitszne ga ana ye szkkonda*, the fox has drawn its head back into its hole.
Syn. HIKKOMU.

SZKKU, スツク, *adv.* Straight, erect. — to stand erect. Syn. MATSZGU.

SZKOBURU, スコブル, 頗, *adv.* Considerable, a good deal, very. *— ōi*, very many. Syn. YOHODO.

SZ-KON, スコン, 數獻, *n.* Several wine glasses full.

SZKOSHI,-KI, スコシ, 少, *a.* or *adv.* Little, few. *Szkoshi mate*, wait a little. *— no aida*, a little while. Syn. CHITTO.

†SZKOSHIKU, スコシク, 少, *adv.* idem. *— kotonari*, a little different.

SZKOYAKA, スコヤカ, 健, Strong, hale, hearty, well, robust, healthy. *— na h'to*, a hale person. Syn. TASSHA, JŌBU.

SZKU, スク, See *Szki.*

SZKŪ, スクフ, See *Szkui.*

SZKU, スク, 酸, *adv.* Sour. *Kono sake wa — natta*, the wine has become sour.

SZKUI,*-ū,-ūta*, スクフ, 救, *t. v.* To save, rescue, deliver; to aid, help. *Hin-ku wo —*, to help the poor. *H'to no inochi wo —*, to save a man's life. Syn. TASZKERU.

SZKUI,*-ū,-ūta*, スクフ, 掬, *t.v.* To scoop, to dip, or lade out, to take up with a dipper, spoon &c., *Meshi wo —*, to dip out rice. *Ami de uwo wo —*, to catch fish with with a dip-net.

SZKUI-AMI, スクヒアミ, 掬網, *n.* A hand net.

SZKUME,*-ru,-ta*, スクメル, 縮, *t. v.* To contract, constringe, to draw into a smaller compass, to restrain, curb. *Kata wo —*, to shrug the shoulders. Syn. CHIJIMERU.

SZKUMI,*-mu,-nda*, スクム, 縮, *i.v.* To be drawn up, contracted, cramped; to shrink. *Ashi ga szkunda*, the leg is cramped. Syn. CHIJIMU.

SZKUMO, スクモ, *n.* Rice-hulls; peat, or turf used for burning.

†SZKUMO-ISHI, スクモイシ, 石炭, (*obs.*) *n.* Stone-coal. Syn. SEKITAN, ISHIDZMI.

SZKUMOMUSHI, スクモムシ, 蠐螬, *n.* A grub-worn.

SZKUNAI,-KI, スクナイ, 少, *a.* A little, few, small in quantity. *H'to ga —*, there are but few people. Syn. SZKOSHI.

SZKUNAKU, or SZKUNŌ, スクナク, *adv.* idem. — *naru*, to become few.

SZKUNASA, スクナサ, *n.* Fewness.

SZKUNASHI, スクナシ, *a.* See *Szkunai.*

†SZKU-SE, スクセ, 宿世, *n.* The previous state of existence. Bud.
Syn. SHUKUSE, ZEN-SE.

SZMA, スマ, 隅, *n.* An inside corner or angle. Syn. SZMI.

SZMAI, *-au* or *-ō*, *-atta* or *-ōta*, スマウ, 住, *i. v.* To reside, dwell, live. *Yedo ni* —, to reside in *Yedo.* Syn. JŪKIYO SZRU.

SZMAI, スマ井, 住居, *n.* A residence, a dwelling place.

SZMAKI, スマキ, 簀捲, *n.* A mode of punishment; viz. tying the criminal in a bamboo mat, and casting him into the water. — *ni szru.*

SZMAN, スマン, 數萬, *n.* Several tens of thousands, several myriads.

SZMANU, or SZMASZ, スマヌ, 不濟, *neg.* of *Szmi.*

SZMASHI, *-sz*, *-sh'ta*, スマス, 濟, *t. v.* To finish, to end, to settle, (澄), To cleanse, purify. *Shigoto wo szmash'ta*, have finished work. *Midz wo* —, to purify water by letting it stand and settle. *Ken-k'wa wo* —, to settle a quarrel. *Kokoro wo* —, to purify the heart, *Mi-szmasz*, to see and be certain of. *Kiki-szmasz*, to hear and be sure of. Syn. SHIMAU.

SZM-BUN, スンブン, 寸分, (lit. inch, grain.) — *tagawadz*, not the least difference.

†SZMERAMIKOTO, スメラミコト, 皇帝, *n.* The *Mikado.*

SZMERU, スメル, 住, *a.* Dwelling. — *tokoro*, a dwelling place.

SZMERU, スメル, 淸, *a.* Pure, clear. — *midz*, water that has been settled.

SZMEN, スメン, 素面, *n.* The face unprotected by the mask used in sword exercise; a face free from the influence of wine; sober or straight face.

SZMI, *-mu*, *-nda*, スム, 住, *i. v.* Same as *Szmai.* To dwell, reside, live. *Yedo ni szmu*, to live in Yedo.

SZMI, *-mu*, *-nda*, スム, 濟, *i. v.* To end, finish, conclude, settle. (澄), To be clear, pure, without sediment. *Ikusa ga sznda*, the war is ended. *Midz ga szmu*, the water is clear. *Ki ga sznda*, my mind is now easy, or at rest. *Szmanu koto*, any thing for which one reproaches himself, or feels uneasy. *Anata ni taish'te szmi-masen*, I feel conscience stricken in regard to you.
Syn. SHIMAU.

SZMI, スミ, 墨, *n.* Ink. — *wo szru*, to rub ink on the stone. — *wo hiku*, to make an ink line. — *wo utsz*, to make a mark by snapping a line that has been inked.

SZMI, スミ, 炭, *n.* Charcoal. — *wo okosz*, to kindle charcoal. — *wo tszgu*, to put charcoal on a fire.

SZMI, スミ, 隅, *n.* An inside corner, or angle.

SZMIBI, スミビ, 炭火, *n.* A charcoal fire.

SZMI-CHIGAI, スミチガヒ, 隅違, *n.* The figure of lines drawn diagonally from the opposite angles of a square and cutting each other in the centre. — *ni szji wo hiku.*

SZMI-GAMA, スミガマ, 墨竈, *n.* A kiln in which charcoal is made.

SZMI-IRE, スミイレ, 墨池, *(bocuchi). n.* An inkstand.

SZMI-IRO, スミイロ, 墨色, *n.* The quality of the color of ink. — *ga yoi*, ink of a beautiful black.

SZMI-KA, スミカ, 住家, *n.* A dwelling house, residence.

SZMI-KAKI, スミカキ, 炭鈎, *n.* A scraper used for cleaning out a furnace.

SZMI-KESHI, スミケシ, 墨消, *n.* Blotting out, erasing with ink.

SZMI-NAGASHI, スミナガシ, 墨流, *n.* Marbling, or variegating like marble, as paper. — *no kami*, marble paper.

SZMI-NARE, *-ru*, *-ta*, スミナレル, 住馴, *i.v.* To be used or accustomed to living in.

SZMI-NAWA, スミナハ, 墨縄, *n.* The inked line used by carpenters.

†SZMINOYAMA, スミノヤマ, 須彌山, *n.* Same as *Shumisen.*

SZMIRE, スミレ, 菫, *n.* The violet.

SZMI-SASHI, スミサシ, 墨刺, *n.* The inked stick used by carpenters for drawing lines.

SZMI-TORI, スミトリ, 炭斗, *n.* A coal-scuttle.

SZMI-TSZBO, スミツボ, 墨斗, *n.* The ink pot used by carpenters.

SZMI-YA, スミヤ, 墨店, *n.* A shop where ink or charcoal is sold.

SZMIYAKA, スミヤカ, 速, Quick, fast, swift, soon. — *naru koto ya no gotoshi*, swift as an arrow. Syn. HAYAI, SASSOKU.

SZMI-YE, スミヱ, 墨畫, *n.* A picture drawn with ink.

SZMŌ, スマフ, 相撲, *n.* Wrestling. — *wo toru*, to wrestle.

SZMOMO, スモモ, 李, *n.* A kind of plum.

SZMŌTORI, スマフトリ, 相撲, *n.* A wrestler.

SZMŌ-TORI-GUSA, スマフトリグサ, *n.* The violet. Syn. SZMIRE.

SZMPAKU, スンパク, 寸白, *n.* The name of a class of disorders peculiar to women, characterized by pain in the back and loins.

SZMPŌ, スンパフ, 寸法, *n.* The dimensions. *Hako no — wa ikura,* what are the dimensions of the box?

SZMU, スム, See *Szmi.*

SZN, スン, 寸, *n.* An inch,—the tenth part of a foot. — *wo toru,* to measure the length.

SZNA, スナ, 砂, *n.* Sand.

SZNA-BACHI, スナバチ, 砂盆, *n.* A shallow flower pot.

†SZNADORI, *-ru,* スナドル, 漁, *i.v.* To fish. *Sznadoru fune,* a fishing boat. *Sznadori ni yuku,* to go a fishing. Syn. RIYŌ.

SZNADORI, スナドリ, 漁, *n.* A fishing, fisherman. Syn. RIYŌ-SHI.

SZNA-DOKEI, スナドケイ, 沙漏, *n.* An hour-glass.

SZNA-GO, スナゴ, 砂子, *n.* Gold or silver dust, used to ornament lacquer, or paper.

SZNA-GOSHI, スナゴシ, 沙漉, *n.* Any thing strained or filtered through sand. — *no midz,* filtered water.

SZNAO, スナホ, 質直, Simple, plain guileless, artless, honest, gentle, amiable. — *na h'to.* Syn. SHITSZBOKU, OTONASHII.

SZNAPPA, スナツパ, 沙場, *n.* A sandy place, desert. Syn. SABAKU.

†SZNAWACHI, スナハチ, 則, *conj.* Then, that is, namely. *O tadzne nasaru h'to wa — kore nite soro,* this is he about whom you inquired. Syn. SOKODE.

SZNA-WARA, スナハラ, 砂原, *n.* A sandy plain, a desert.

†SZN-CHIU, スンチウ, 寸忠, A little fidelity or patriotism, used in humble language.

SZNDA, スンダ, *pret.* of *Szmi.*

SZNDE, スンデ, *pp.* of *Szmi.*

SZNE, スネ, 脐脛, *n.* The shin, or leg between the knee and ankle. Syn. HAGI.

SZNE, *-ru, -ta,* スネル, *i,v.* To be cross, ill-humored, sulky. *Kodomo ga sznete mono wo iuwanu,* the child is sulky and won't speak.

SZNE-ÀTE, スネアテ, 脛當, *n.* Armor for the front of the leg, or shin.

SZNE-MONO, スネモノ, *n.* A sullen, morose person, eccentric person.

SZ-NEN, スネン, 數年, *n.* Several years, a few years.

†SZN-IN, スンイン, 寸陰, (lit. an inch of sunshade). The smallest portion of time. — *wo oshimu,* to grudge a moment.

†SZN-KA, スンカ, 寸暇, *n.* A moment of leisure. — *mo nai,* have not a moment of leisure.

SZN-KŌ, スンカウ, 寸功, *n.* A small degree of merit, a few praise-worthy actions. — *nakush'te tai roku wo ukeru.*

SZNOKO, スノコ, 簀子, *n.* A floor made of bamboo.

SZN-SHAKU, スンシヤク, 寸尺, (lit. inch, foot). Dimensions, size. — *ga shirenu,* don't know the size.
Syn. SZMPŌ.

†SZN-SHI, スンシ, 寸志, (lit. an inch of intention). A small token of one's kind wishes, (humbly). — *bakari nite soro.*

SZN-SZN, スンスン, 寸寸, *adv.* Into inches, or small pieces. — *ni kiru,* to cut to pieces.

SZŌ, スオウ, 蘇木, *n.* Sapan-wood.

SZŌ, スハウ, 素袍, *n.* A kind of coat.

SZPPA, スツパ, *adv.* The sound of a cut with a sword. — *to kiru.*

SZPPADAKA, スツパダカ, 素裸, Stark naked. Syn. MAPPADAKA.

SZPPARI-TO, or SZPPERI, スツパリト, Same as *Sappari.*

SZPPON, スツポン, 鼈, *n.* A kind of turtle.

SZPPON-TO, スツポン, *adv.* The sound of drawing a cork from a bottle. — *naru.*

SZRA, スラ, *adv.* Even, in like manner. *Tori kemono szra ko wo aiszru,* even birds and beasts love their young. *Korori nite wa isha szra shinimas,* even the doctors die of cholera. *Sei-jin szra,* even the sages. Syn. SAYE, DANI, DEMO.

†SZ-RAN, スラン, (comp. of *Sz,* to do, and *ran,* dubitative suffix.) *Ame ga furi mo ya szran,* I wonder if it will rain.

SZRARI-TO, スラリト, *adv.* In an even, smooth manner; without obstructions, sleek and easy, glibly. — *dekita,* to do anything easily without obstructions. *Sei no — sh'ta onna,* a tall and slender woman. *Katana wo — nuku,* to draw a sword with one even sweep.

SZRA-SZRA-TO, スラスラト, *adv.* Smoothly, sleekly, glibly, without obstructions.

SZRE, *-ru, -ta,* スレル, 摺, pot. mood of *Szri.* Can print. *Ichi nichi ni iku mai szreru,* how many sheets can you print in a day?

SZRE, *-ru, -ta,* スレル, 摺, *i.v.* To be rubbed, chafed, galled, worn by friction, (fig.) to have one's rough points rubbed off, or to become keen or sharp by contact with the world. *Ishi ga szrete maruku natta,* the stone by friction has become round.

SZRE-AI,*–au,–atta*, スレアフ, 摺合, *i.v.* To rub against each other.

SZRE-AI, スレアヒ, *n.* Friction.

SZREBA, スレバ, sub. mo. of *Szri*, or of *Shi.*

SZREKKARASHI, スレツカラシ, (yed. coll). Keen, sharp, cunning, artful from contact with the world.

SZRI,*–ru,–tta*, スル, 摺, *t.v.* To rub, to file, to print, to chafe. *Szmi wo —*, to rub ink on the stone. *Yaszri de —*, to file. *Hankō wo —*, to print on a block. *Te wo —*, to rub the hands. *Kuszri wo yagen de —*, to pulverize medicine by rubbing in a mortar. Syn. KOSZRU.

SZRI, スリ, *n.* A pilferer, thief. Syn. MAMBIKI, KONUSZBITO.

SZRI-BACHI, スリバチ, 雷盆, *n.* An earthenware bowl, used for washing rice before boiling.

SZRI-CHIGAI,*–ō,–tta*, スリチガウ, 摺違, *t.v.* To rub past, to strike against each other in passing. *Fune ga —.*

SZRI-HAGASHI,*–sz,–sh'ta*, スリハガス, 摺剝, *t.v.* To rub off the skin, bark, lacquer, or outside of anything.

SZRI-KIRI,*–ru,–tta*, スリキル, 摺切, *t. v.* To cut off anything by rubbing, to file off, to cut by chafing. *Yaszri de kane wo —*, to cut off metal by filing.

SZRI-KOGI, スリコギ, 雷木, *n.* The stick used in washing rice in a *Szribachi.*

SZRI-KOMI,*–mu,–nda*, スリコム, 摺込, *t. v.* To rub in. *Kuszri wo szri-konde shitsz wo naosz*, to cure itch by rubbing in medicine.

SZRI-KUDAKI,*–ku,–ita*, スリクダク, 摺碎, *t.v.* To pulverize by rubbing.

SZRI-KUDZ, スリクヅ, 摺屑, *n.* Filings.

SZRI-MIGAKI,*–ku,–ita*, スリミガク, 摺磨, *t.v.* To polish by rubbing.

SZRI-MUKI,*–ku,–ita*, スリムク, 摺剝, *t.v.* To rub off or abrade the skin.

SZRI-NUKE,*–ru,–ta*, スリヌケル, 摺拔, *t.v.* To rub or squeeze through a crowd.

SZRI-OTOSHI,*–sz,–sh'ta*, スリオトス, 摺落, *t.v.* To rub off.

SZRI-TSZBUSHI,*–sz,–sh'ta*, スリツスブ, 摺潰, *t.v.* To break, or crush by rubbing, to efface by rubbing.

SZRI-TSZKE,*–ru,–ta*, スリツケル, 摺付, *t.v.* To apply anything by rubbing, to rub anything on another.

SZRI-TSZKEGI, スリツケギ, 摺付木, *n.* A friction match.

SZRIYA, スリヤ, (coll.) Same as *Szreba.* So then.

SZRI-YABURI,*–ru,–tta*, スリヤブル, 摺破, *t.v.* To tear or wear by rubbing or friction, to chafe.

SZRU, スル, 摺, See *Szri.*

SZRU, スル, 爲, See *Shi.*

SZRUDOI,–KI,–SHI, スルドイ, 鋭, *a.* Sharp, acute, keen, penetrating, piercing, quick of discernment. *Szrudoi me-iro*, piercing eyes. *— katana*, a sharp sword. Syn. TOI.

SZRU-DOKU, スルドク, 鋭, *adv.* Idem.

SZRUME, スルメ, 瑣管, *n.* The Onychoteuthis Banksii.

SZRURI-TO, スルリト, *adv.* Same as *Szrarito.*

SZRU-SZRU-TO, スルスルト, *adv.* In a slippery manner, smoothly.

SZSA, スサ, 寸莎, *n.* Anything like hair, or straw mixed with plaster to make it stick.

SZSAMASHII,–KI, スサマシイ, 冷, *a.* Fearful, frightful, producing dread, or shuddering. *— yamaji wo itowadz*, did not mind the frightful mountain road. *— ōkaze*, a fearful storm. Syn. OSOROSHII.

SZSAMASHIKU, スサマシク, *adv.* Idem.

†SZSAMI,*–mu,–nda*, スサム, 荒, *i.v.* To be taken up with, absorbed in, infatuated. *Tanoshimi ni —*, absorbed in pleasure. Syn. FUKERU, HAMARU, OBORERU.

SZSHI, スシ, 鮓 *n.* A kind of food.

SZSHI, スシ, 酸, *a.* Sour.

SZSO, スソ, 裾, *n.* The skirt of a coat. *Yama no —*, the base or foot of a mountain. *Uma no —*, the feet of a horse.

SZSO-WAKE, スソワケ, 裾分, *n.* Dividing anything which one has received with others. *— wo szru.*

SZSO-YU, スソユ, 裾湯, *n.* Warm water used for washing a horse's feet

SZSZ, スス, 煤, *n.* Soot.

SZSZDAKE, ススダケ, 煤竹, *n.* Bamboo that has been stained with smoke.

SZSZDOI, ススドイ, Same as *Szrudoi.*

SZSZGI,*–gu,–ida*, ススグ, 淸, *t.v.* To cleanse, to rinse, wash. *Haji wo —*, to cleanse, or wipe away a reproach. *Kuchi wo —*, to rinse the mouth. *Kimono wo —*, to rinse clothes. Syn. KIYOMERU, ARAU, YUSZGU.

SZSZHAKI, ススハキ, 煤掃, or SZSZHARAI, ススハラヒ, *n.* House cleaning. *— wo szru.*

SZSZKE,*–ru,–ta*, ススケル, *i.v.* To be fouled with smoke or soot.

SZSZKI, ススキ, 薄, *n.* A kind of long grass.

SZSZMANU, ススマヌ, 不進, neg. of *Szszmu.* Not to advance or go forward, not inclined to do, disinclined.

SZSZME,*-ru,-ta*, ススメル, 前, *t. v.* To press, urge, solicit, persuade, exhort. *Zen wo* —, to exhort to the practice of virtue. *Sake wo* —, to press another to drink wine. *Uma wo* —, to urge on a horse. *Za wo* —, to move forward in one's seat.

SZSZME, ススメ, 勸, *n,* Persuasion.

SZSZMI,*-mu,-nda*, ススム, 進, *i. v.* To advance, go forward; to be eager for, ardent, or zealous in the pursuit of. *Ki ga* —, to be eager or zealous. *Shokumotsz ga* —, to have a good appetite. *Gakumon ni* —, to be fond of study. *Saki ni* —, to advance to the front. *Gakumon ga* —, to advance in learning.

SZSZMI, ススミ, 進, *n.* Advancement, improvement, ardor or eagerness for anything.

SZSZRI,*-ru,-tta*, ススル, 啜, *t. v.* To sip, sup, to snuff, sniff. *Kayu wo* —, to sip up gruel. *Hana wo*, —, to snuff a flower.

SZSZRI-GUSZRI, ススリグスリ, 啜藥, *n.* Errhine medicines.

SZTARE,*-ru,-ta*, スタレル, 廢, *i. v.* Thrown away, discarded, abandoned rejected; forsaken. *Sztaretaru tszdzre wo atszmete kiru*, to collect and wear cast off rags.

SZTARI,*-ru,-tta*, スタル, 棄, *i. v.* To be left, left over, cast away, abandoned, forsaken. *Michi ni sztatte iru mono wo hirō*, to pick up something left lying in the road.

SZTARI, スタリ, 棄, *n.* A remnant, waste, that which is rejected or useless.

SZTA-SZTA, スタスタ, *adv.* The sound made by sandals in walking. — *aruku.*

SZTE,*-ru,-ta*, ステル, 捨, *t. v.* To throw away, to reject, discard, to leave, abandon, forsake, to let be, let alone, to desert. *Gomi wo* —, to throw away rubbish. *Tszma ko wo sztete nigeru*, leaving his wife and child he fled away. *Inochi wo sztete tatakau*, to fight regardless of his life. *Yo wo* —, to forsake the world. *Aku wo sztete zen wo toru*, to forsake evil and cleave to that which is good. *Sztete oku*, to let alone. Syn. UTCHARU.

SZTE-BUCHI, ステブチ, 捨扶持, *n.* A pension, or daily ration of rice given by government to disabled, or helpless servants.

SZTE-FUDA, ステフダ, 捨榜, *n.* A public notice of the crime and execution of a criminal.

SZTE-GO, ステゴ, 捨子, *n,* A foundling.

SZTEKI-NI, ステキニ, *adv.* Exceedingly, very. — *samui*, very cold.
Syn. HANAHADA, GŌGI-NI.

SZTE-OKI,*-ku-ita*, ステオク, 捨置, *t. v.* To let alone, let be as it is. *Kono biōki wa szte-oite mo naoru*, if this sickness be left to itself it will get well.

SZTSZRU, スツル. Same as *Szteru.*

SZU, スウ, 數, *(kadz). n.* Number, several, an indefinite number from three to eight. — *ga shireru*, the number is unknown. — *wo shirusz*, to set down the number. — *jū nin*, several tens of men. — *h'yaku*, several hundred. — *nen*, several years. — *dai*, several generations, or dynasties.

SZU, スフ, 吸, To sip, suck, see *Szi.*

SZWA, or SZWAYA, スハ, Exclam. of surprise, or sudden start. There! *Szwa to iwaba hashiri ide.* Syn. SORIYA.

SZWARI,*-ru,-tta*, スワル, 居, *i. v.* To sit, to be set, placed, fixed. *Tatami ni* —, to sit on the mat. *Fune ga szwatta*, the ship is aground. *Monji ga yoku szwatta*, the letters are neatly placed. Syn. ZASZRU.

SZYA-SZYA-TO-NERU, スヤスヤト子ル, To sleep in a quiet, easy manner after great toil or pain.

SZYE,*-ru,-ta*, スヱル, 居, *t. v.* To place, lay, set, fix, to settle, to apply. *Kiu wo* —, to set the moxa. *Ishidzye wo* —, to lay a stone foundation. *Ki wo* —, to settle or compose one's mind. *Han wo* —, to fix a seal. *Zen wo* —, to set a table (before any one). Syn. OKU.

SZYE, スヱ, 末, *n.* The end, termination, the ultimate branch; a descendant; the future. *Ki no* —, the top of a tree, or ultimate branches of a tree. — *no yo*, the last ages of the world; or the world since the death of *Shaka.* — *wo anjiru*, to be anxious about the future. — *no yak'soku*, an agreement about something future. *Yo ga — ni natta*, the world has deteriorated. *Toshi no* —, the end of the year. — *no ko*, the youngest child. *Yori-Tomo no* —, a descendant of *Yori-Tomo.*

SZYE,*-ru,-ta*, スエル, 餧, *i.v.* To be spoiled, unfit to eat. *Kono niku ga szyeta*, this meat is spoiled. Syn. AZARERU, KUSARU.

SZYE-DZYE, スヱズヱ, 末末, *(shimo-jimo). n.* The lower or inferior classes of people. — *no samurai*, inferior class of soldiers.

SZYE-FURO, スヱフロ, 居風爐, *n.* A moveable bath tub.

SZYEHIRO, スヱヒロ, 末間, *n.* A fan.

†SZYEMONO, スヱモノ, 陶, *n.* Ornamental porcelain.

SZYENARI, スヱナリ, 末成, *n.* The latest fruits, of those kinds that ripen through a considerable period of time.

SZYE-TSZKATA, スヱツカタ, 末方, *n.* The end of the month. Syn. TSZKIDZYE.

SZYE-ZEN, スヱゼン, 居膳, *n.* A table with food set out before a guest; used fig. of any thing which comes unexpectedly to hand just as one was wishing for it.

†SZYURU, タユル, Same as *Szyeru.*

SZZARU, タザル, Same as *Shizaru.*

SZZAMASHI, スザマシ, Same as *Szsamashi.*

T

TA, タ, 田, *n.* A rice-field. — *wo tszkuru,* to cultivate rice-fields.

TA, タ, 他, *n.* Others, other persons, things, or places. (*a.*) Other. *Sono ta wa oshite shiru beshi,* (knowing a part) to form an opinion of the rest. Syn. YO, HOKA.

†TA, タ, 多, *(ōi).* *a.* Many. *Ta nen,* many years.

TA, タ, 誰, *pro.* Who. *Ta ga tame ni,* for whose sake? *Ta ga tszma,* whose wife? Syn. TARE.

TA, タ, coll. pret. suffix; perhaps, an abbreviation of *tari.* *Mita,* have seen. *Kīta,* have heard. *Yukimash'ta,* have gone.

TABA, タバ, 束, *n.* A bundle, (as of straw, wood, bamboo, &c.) *Wara h'to taba,* a bundle of straw- — *ni szru,* to make into a bundle. Syn. WA, TABANE.

TABAI,–ō,–ōta, タバウ, *t.v.* To preserve, save. *Inochi wo* —, to save one's life. Syn. MAMORU, KABAU.

TABAKARARE,–ru–ta, タバカラレル, 被誑, *pass.* of *Tabakaru.* To be cheated, or imposed on.

TABAKARI,–ru,–tta, タバカル, 誑, *t.v.* To cheat, deceive, impose on, to hoax, to gull. Syn. DAMASZ, ITSZWARU, AZAMUKU, TABURAKASZ.

TABAKO, タバコ, 烟艸, *n.* Tobacco. — *wo nomu,* to smoke tobacco.

TOBAKO-BON, タバコボン, 烟艸盆, *n.* A box in which fire is kept for lighting pipes.

TABAKO-IRE, タバコイレ, 烟囊, *n.* A tobacco-pouch.

TABANE,–ru,–ta, タバネル, 束, *t.v.* To tie or make into a bundle, to bundle. *Ine wo* —, to bind rice into sheaves. *Kami wo* —, to tie up the hair. Syn. TSZGANERU.

TABANE, タバネ, 束, *n.* A bundle. Syn. WA, TABA.

TABASAMI,–mu,–nda, タバサム, 挾, *t. v.* (comp. of *te,* and *hasamu*). To hold under the arm, or by putting between anything. *Ya wo* —, to hold arrows under the arm. *Dai-shō wo koshi ni* —, to carry the long and short swords in the belt. Syn. HASAMU.

TABE,–ru,–ta, タベル, 食, *t. v.* To eat. *Meshi wo* —, to eat rice. Syn. KŪ, KURŌ.

TABE-MONO, タベモノ, 食物, *n.* Food, provisions, victuals. Syn. KUIMONO.

†TA-BEN, タベン, 多辯, Much talking. — *na h'to,* a great talker. Syn. KUCHI-MAME.

TABI, タビ, 短韈, *n.* Stockings, socks. — *wo haku,* to wear stockings.

TABI, タビ, 旅, *n.* A journey, traveling, a stranger. — *ye yuku,* to go on a journey. — *no h'to,* a traveler. — *no szmai,* a place of sojourn.

TABI, タビ, 度, *n.* Time, or repetitions. *H'to tabi,* once. *F'ta tabi,* twice. *Mi-tabi,* three times. *Iku tabi,* how often? Syn. DO.

†TABI,–bu, タブ, 賜, Same as *Tamai,* -*ō.* To receive from a superior.

TABI-BITO, タビビト, 旅人, *n.* A traveler.

TABI-DACHI, タビダチ, 旅立, *n.* Setting out on a journey. — *ni yoi hi,* a lucky day for setting out on a journey.

TABI-DSZKARE, タビヅカレ, 旅疲, *n.* Fatigue from traveling.

TABI-JI, タビヂ, 旅路, *n.* A journey, the road in which one travels.

TABI-NE, タビネ, 旅寢, *n.* Sleeping while on a journey, or in a strange place.

TABI-TABI, タビタビ, 度度, *adv.* Often, frequently. Syn. DO-DO, SHIBA-SHIBA.

TA-BIYŌ, タビヤウ, 多病, Often sick, sickly. — *no h'to,* a sickly person.

TABO, タボ, *n.* The puff, or swell made in dressing the hair on the back of the head. — *wo dasz.*

TABU, タブ, *n.* The lobe of the ear.

†TABU, タブ, Same as *Tamō,* see *Tabi.*

TA-BUN, タブン, 多分, *n.* The most part, majority, chief-part. (*adv.*) Perhaps, probably, likely, much, a great deal. — *ni sh'tagau,* to follow the majority. — *kinsz,* much money. Syn. ŌKATA, ŌKU, TAI-HAN.

TABURAKASHI,–sz,–sh'ta, タブラカス, 誑,

t.v. To deceive, cheat, impose on, hoax, gull. Syn. DAMASZ, AZAMUKU, TABAKARU.

TABUSA, タブサ, 髻, *n.* The Japanese cue. Syn. MAGE, MODOTORI.

TABU-TABU, タブタブ, *adv.* Shaking with a quivering motion, like jelly, or like oil in a cask, when shaken. *— to ugoku.*

TACHI, *-tsz, -tta*, タツ, 立起, *i. v.* To stand up, rise up, to erect one's self; to start, set out, or leave; to begin, to pass, (as time), to stick into, fit for, useful; to evaporate. *Tatte yo*, or, *o tachi-nasare*, stand up. *Yaku ni tatanu*, useless, good for nothing. *Yō ni tatsz*, useful. *Ki ga —*, to be angry. *Hara ga —*, idem. *Me ni tatsz*, striking, or attracting the attention. *Ki no me ga —*, the tree is budding. *Tszki hi ga —*, time passes. *Mika tatte mata koi*, come again after three days. *Haru ga —*, spring has commenced. *Osaka ye itsz tachimas*, when do you start for Osaka? *Hari ga ashi ni tatta*, have run a needle into my foot. *Ya ga —*, the arrow sticks. *Na ga —*, name is famous. *Ashi ga tatanu*, lame in the feet. *Ichi ga —*, the market is open. *Yu ga —*, the water is boiled. *Tori ga —*, the bird has flown. *Kemuri ga —* it smokes. *Hokori ga —*, the dust rises, or it is dusty. *Za wo —*, to leave one's set. *Nami ga —*, the waves rise. *Shōchiu ga tatsz*, the alcohol evaporates. *Sziki ga —*, the vapor rises, or evaporates.

TACHI, *-tsz, -tta*, タツ, 裁斷, *t.v.* To cut out, to cut off, to leave off, to stop. *Kimono wo —*, to cut out clothes. *Momen wo tatte kimono ni szru*, to cut cotton cloth and make it into a coat. *Sake wo —*, to leave off drinking wine. *Cha wo —*, to stop drinking tea. *Inochi wo —*, to take life.
Syn. KIRU.

TACHI, タチ, 太刀, *n.* A long sword. *— wo haku*, to wear a sword.

TACHI, タチ, 立, The nature, character, quality. *Kane no — ga warui*, this metal is of bad quality. *— no yoi h'to*, a person of good character, Syn. SHŌ.

TACHI, タチ, 等, a plural suffix; as, *Omaye-tachi*, you. *Kodomo-tachi*, children. *Yakunin-tachi*, officers.
Syn. RA, DOMO, GATA.

†TACHI, タチ, 館, *(yakata)*, *n.* A mansion, the house of a noble.

TACHI-AGARI, *-ru, -tta*, タチアガル, 立上, *i.v.* To rise up, to arise.

TACHI-AI, *-au, -atta*, タチアフ, 立合, *i.v.* To meet together, assemble, to meet in combat. Syn. ATSZMARU.

TACHIBANA, タチバナ, 橘, *n.* The general name for fruits of the orange kind.

TACHIDO, or TACHI-DOKORO, タチドコロ, 立所, *n.* A standing place, a place to live in. *— wo saradz tatakau*, to fight without leaving one's place. *Mi no — mo nai*, having not even a standing place.

TACHI-DOKORO-NI, タチドコロニ, *adv.* Immediately, at once.
Syn. TACHIMACHI, NIWAKA-NI.

TACHI-FURUMAI, タチフルマヒ, 擧動, *n.* Actions, conduct, behavior.
Syn. OKONAI.

TACHI-GATAI, *-KI, -SHI*, タチガタイ, 難立, *a.* Useless. *Mono no yō ni wa tachigatashi*, not good for anything.

TACHI-GIKI, タチギキ, 立聞, *n.* Standing to listen, listening stealthily. *— wo szru*, to stand listening.

TACHI-GIYE, タチギエ, 立消, *n.* Quickly extinguished.

TACHI-GURAMI, タチグラミ, 眩暉, *n.* Sudden vertigo, or dizziness on rising up.
Syn. KENNUN.

TACHI-I, タチ井, 起居, Standing or sitting. *— ga jiyū ni dekinu*, cannot stand or sit with comfort.

TACHI-IDE, *-ru, -ta*, タチイデル, 立出, *i.v.* To arise and go out.

TACHI-IRI, *-ru, -tta*, タチイル, 立入, *i. v.* To enter, go in. *Kenk'wa no naka ni tachi-itte naka wo naosz*, to go in amongst persons fighting and make peace.

TACHI-KAYERI, *-ru, -tta*, タチカヘル, 立歸, *t.v.* To return, go back.

TACHI-KOYE, *-ru, -ta*, タチコエル, 立超, *t.v.* To surpass, be superior to, exceed.

TACHIMACHI, タチマチ, 忽, *adv.* Immediately, suddenly, at once.
Syn. NIWAKA-NI, KOTSZZEN.

TACHI-MAJIRI, *-ru, -tta*, タチマジル, 立交, *t.v.* To associate, consort with.

TACHI-MAWARI, *-ru, -tta*, タチマハル, 立回, *i.v.* To move about, to act, conduct one's self.

TACHI-MOTŌRI, *-ru-ta*, タチモトホル, 躑躅, *i. v.* To walk backward and forward, as in suspense, or deep thought.

TACHI-MUKAI, *-au, -atta*, タチムカウ, 立向, *i.v.* To stand opposite to, to rise and meet, to confront, face.

TACHI-NOKI, *-ku, -ita*, タチノク, 立退, *t.v.* To leave, depart from.

TACHI-NUI, タチヌヒ, 裁縫, *n.* Cutting out and sewing, tailoring.

TACHI-SAWAGI,*-gu,-ida*, タチサワグ, 立騒, *i.v.* To rise with tumult, or noise.

TACHI-TOMARI,*-ru,-tta*, タチトマル 立止, *i.v.* To stop, to stand still.

TACHI-URI, タチウリ, 裁賣, *n.* Selling by slices, (as watermelon, fish, &c). *Szik'a no* —.

TADA, タダ, 只, *adv.* Only, merely, just, alone, simply, but, gratis, gratuitously. Also an adj. Usual, common, ordinary. *Tada miru bakari*, merely looking. — *morau*, to receive gratuitously or without paying. — *yaru*, a free gift. — *kuru*, to come only, without business. — *h'tori*, alone, or only one person. — *sō iyeba yoi*, better say nothing but that. — *mono ni aradz*, not a common person. — *no h'to*, a common person. — *naranu*, not usual, uncommon, strange. *Kokoro-mochi tada naradz*, feeling different from usual.
Syn. NOMI, BAKARI, TSZNE, REI.

TADA-BITO, タダビト, 凡人, *n.* A common or ordinary person. Syn. BON-NIN.

TADACHI-NI, タダチニ, 直, *adv.* Immediately, directly, straight. — *kayeru*, to return directly. Syn. SZGU-NI, JIKI-NI.

†TADADZMI,*-mu,-nda*, タダズム, 彳, *i. v.* To stand still, stop while walking. *Hashi no wiye ni* —, to stop on the bridge.
Syn. TACHI-TOMARU.

TADAIMA, タダイマ, 唯今, *adv.* Now, just now, at present. Syn. IMA, SOKKON.

TADAKKO, タダツコ, *adv.* Gratis, gratuitously.

†TADAMUKI, タダムキ, 腕, (obs.) *n.* The arm. Syn. UDE.

TADANAKA, タダナカ, 正中, *n.* The centre, middle. *Mattadanaka wo iru*, to hit directly in the centre (of a target).
Syn. MANNAKA.

TADARAKASHI,*-sz,-sh'ta*, タダラカス, 令爛, caust. of *Tadare*. To cause to be sore, irritated, or inflamed.

TADARE,*-ru,-ta*, タダレル, 糜爛, (*bi-ran*). *i.v.* To be inflamed, sore and irritated. *Me no fuchi ga* —, the eyelids are sore. *Kidz-guchi ga* —, the wound is inflamed.

TADAREME, タダレメ, *n.* Blear-eyed.

TADASHI, タダシ, 但, *conj.* But, however, or. Syn. SHIKASHI, MATAWA.

TADASHI,*-sz,-sh'ta*, タダス, 糾, *t. v.* To examine into, to inquire into, to judge, to ascertain, to adjust, rectify. *Tszmi wo* —, to judge crime. *Yeri wo* —, to adjust the collar of one's coat.
Syn. SHIRABERU, GIMMI SZRU.

TADASHII,*-KI*, タダシイ, 正, *a.* Correct, right, just, upright, honest. — *h'to*, an honest person. *Okonai ga tadashii*, his conduct is correct.

TADASHIKU, タダシク, 正, *adv.* idem. *Tadashiku minami ye mukau*, to face directly to the south. — *nai*, not right.

TADASHISA, タダシサ, 正, *n.* Correctness, rectitude.

TADAYOI,*-ō,-ōta*, タダヨフ, 漂, *i. v.* To float or drift about, to be adrift. *Fune ga nami ni* —, the ship drifts about on the waves. Syn. UKU.

TADAYOWASHI,*-sz,-sh'ta*, タダヨハス, 令漂, caust. of *Tadayoi*. To cause to float or drift about. *Kaze ga kumo wo* —, the wind drives the clouds about.

TADE, タデ, 蓼, *n.* A species of Polygonum, the water-pepper, or smart-weed.

TADE,*-ru,-ta*, タデル, *t. v.* To foment, to stupe. *Fune wo* —, to clean the bottom of a junk with fire. *Yu nite* —, to foment with warm-water. Syn. MUSZ.

TADON, タドン, 炭團, *n.* A ball made of charcoal and seaweed, for burning in braziers.

TADORI,*-ru,-tta*, タドル, *t.v.* To walk by feeling or groping the way. *Yamiji wo* —, to grope one's way at night. *Tadoru tadoru to ayumu*, to walk groping one's way.

†TADO-TADO-TO, タドタドト, *adv.* Walking in a groping manner, or with uncertain steps.

†TADO-TADOSHII,*-KI,-KU*, タドタドシイ, Going along groping one's way.

†TADZ, カツ, 鶴, *n.* A crane.
Syn. TSZRU.

†TADZKI, タツキ, 手著, *n.* (comp. of *Te*, and *tszdzki*). A helper, one to lean or depend on. Syn. TAYORI.

TADZNA, タツナ, 手綱, (comp. of *Te*, and *tszna*). *n.* A rein, or strap of a bridle. — *wo motsz*, to hold the rein.

TADZNE,*-ru,-ta*, タツヌル, 尋, *t. v.* To inquire, ask, to search for, hunt after. *Hisashiku o tadzne-mōshimasen*, I have not heard from you for a long time. *H'to ni* —, to inquire of another. *Dorobō wo* —, to search for a thief. Syn. TŌ, SAGASZ.

TADZNE, タツヌ, 尋, *n.* Inquiry, search.

TADZNE-AI,*-au,-atta*, タツヌアフ, 尋合, *t.v.* To inquire of each other, to search after each other.

TADZNE-DASHI,*-sz,-sh'ta*, タツヌダス, 尋出, *t.v.* To inquire or search out, to find out.

TADZSAWARI,*-ru,-tta*, タツサハル, 黨, *t.v.* To join with, club, or league with, to take part in, to participate in. *Muhon ni* —, to take part in a conspiracy.

TADZSAYE,*-ru,-ta*, タヅサヘル, 携, *t. v.* To carry hanging in the hand, (as a basket), to carry. *Tszye wo* —, to carry a cane. *Kago wo* —, to carry a basket. Syn. MOTSZ, SAGERU.

TAFU, タフ, 太布, *n.* Cotton damask.

†TA-FUKU, タフク, 多福, (*ōi saiwai*). *n.* Much happiness, many blessings. — *wo shūku szru*, to wish another much happiness.

TAGA, タガ, *n.* A hoop. — *wo hameru*, to to put on a hoop. — *wo kakeru*, idem. Syn. WA.

TAGAI,*-au* or*-ō,-atta* or*-ōta*, タガフ, 違, *t. v.* To differ, disagree; not to conform to or accord with; to miss, err from, mistake. *Naka wo* —, to be at variance. *H'to no kokoro ni* —, to differ in opinion from another. *Yak'soku ni* —, not to conform to a promise. *Michi ni* —, not according to the truth. *Ashi wo* —, to put the foot out of joint. Syn. CHIGAU.

TAGAI, タガヒ, 互, Mutual, reciprocal. *O tagai de gozarimas*, I may ask a favor of you in return.

TAGAI-CHIGAI-NI, タガヒチガヒニ, 參差, *adv.* Alternately missing each other.

TAGAI-NI, タガヒニ, 互, *adv.* Mutually, reciprocally, each other, one another. — *horeru*, to love each other. — *sashi-chigaye-te shinuru*, each stabbed and killed the other. — *yen-riyo naku tszki-au*, to associate with each other without formality. Syn. TOMONI, KATAMI-NI.

TAGANE, タガネ, 鏨, *n.* A chisel or graver used for engraving on metal.

TAGAWASE,*-ru,-ta*, タガハセル, 令違, caust. of *Tagai*. To cause to differ or disagree.

TAGAYE,*-ru,-ta*, タガヘル, 違, *t. v.* Not to conform to, to act contrary to. *Yak'soku wo* —, to break a promise. *Dōri wo* —, not to conform to reason.

TAGAYESHI,*-sz,-sh'ta*, タガヘス, 耕, *t. v.* To cultivate the fields, to labor as a farmer. *Ta wo* —.

†TA-GEI, タゲイ, 多藝, Many polite accomplishments. — *na h'to*, an accomplished man.

†TA-GEN, タゲン, 多言, Many words, much talking. Syn. KUCHIMAME, TA-BEN.

TAGIRI,*-ru,-tta*, タギル, 激, *i.v.* To boil. *Yu ga* —, the water boils. *Tagiri-koboreru*, to boil over. Syn. NIYETATSZ.

TAGIRASE,*-ru,-ta*, タギラセル, 令激, caust. of *Tagiri*. To cause or let boil.

TA-GIYŌ,*-szru*, タギヤウ, 他行, (*yoso ye yuku*). To go some where, to be absent from home.

TAGŌ, タガフ Same as *Tagau*, see *Tagai*.

TAGO, タゴ, 桶子, *n.* A bucket. Syn, TE-OKE,

TA-GON, タゴン, 他言, Telling to others, divulging, blabbing. — *wo sh'te kudasaru na*, don't tell it to any one. — *wa go mu-yō*. idem.

TAGUI, タグイ, 類, (*rui*). *n.* Kind, sort. *Ano tagui no h'to*, that kind of man. *Sono — ni aradz*, Nothing equal to it. *Tagui nashi*, uncommon, extraordinary. Syn. SHURUI.

TAGURI,*-ru,-tta*, タグル, 手繰, *t. v.* To haul in a rope hand over hand. *Nawa wo* —, idem. *Fune wo taguri-yoseru*, to haul in a boat by pulling the rope.

TAGURI-DASHI,*-sz,-ta*, タグリダス, 捲出, *t.v.* To pay out (as a rope). *Nawa wo* —, to pay out a rope.

TAGURI-KOMI,*-mu,-nda*, タグリコム, 捲込, *t. v.* To haul in hand over hand.

TAI, タヒ, 鯛, *n.* The Serranus marginalis.

TAI, タイ, 體, *n.* Body, substance. *Kami wa itta*, there is only one God.

TAI, タ井, 田居, *n.* A house in the rice-fields, a farm-house.

TAI, タイ, 胎, *n.* The pregnant womb. — *wo ukeru*, to be pregnant.

TAI,-KI,-KU,-Ō,-SHI,-SA, タイ, 度, To desire, wish, want; used only as a suffix to verbs; as, *Mi-tai*, wish to see. *Kiki-tai*, wish to hear, *Kai-tai*, want to buy. *Yu-ki-taku-nai*, do not wish to go. *Hanashi-tō gozarimas*, I wish to speak.

TAI, タイ, 大, (*ōkii.*) *a.* Great, large, chief, illustrious, distinguished, severe; used mostly in compounds.

TAI-BIYŌ, タイビヤウ, 大病, (*omoi yamai*). *n.* A severe or malignant disease.

TAI-BŌ, タイボウ, 大鵬, *n.* A fabulous bird of immense size. whose wings are supposed to be several thousand miles long.

†TAI-DA, タイダ, 怠惰, (*okotari*). *n.* Negligence, carelessness, inattention to duty. Syn. RANDA, KEDAI.

TAI-DAN, タイダン, 對談, (*mukai kataru*). *n.* Meeting and conversing together. — *no wiye de sadameru*.

†TAI-DO, タイド, 大度, Magnanimous, great of mind. Syn. K'WAN-NIN.

TAI-DOKU, タイドク, 胎毒, *n.* Congenital disease.

TAI-FŪ, タイフウ, 大風, (*ō kaze*). *n.* A typhoon, hurricane, tempest.

TAI-FUKU-HI, タイフクヒ, 大腹皮, *n.* The shell of the Areca nut.

TAI-FŪ-SHI, タイフウシ, 大風子, *n.* Name of a medicine.

TAI-GAI, タイガイ, 大概, (*ōmune*). *adv.* The most part, generally; about, more or less. Syn. TAITEI.

TAI-GI, タイギ, 大儀, Tired, weary; faint from exertion, or indisposed to exertion; used often in expressing thanks, as. *Go tai-gi da*, I have given you great trouble, or I am much obliged. *— da kara yaszmu*, as I am tired I will rest. Syn. KURŌ.

†TAI-GO, タイゴ, 隊伍, *n.* A company, or corps of an army.

TAI-HA, タイハ, 大破, Greatly dilapidated or broken; irremediably ruined, or injured; spoken of any structure.

†TAI-HAKU-SEI, タイハクセイ, 大白星, *n.* The planet Venus.

TAI-HAN, タイハン, 大半, More than half, the greater part, most part.
Syn. ŌKATA, K'WA-HAN.

TAI-HEI, タイヘイ, 大平, *n.* Profound peace, or freedom from war.

TAI-HEI-RAKU, タイヘイラク, 大平樂, *n.* Speaking in an arrogant, overbearing, or insolent manner; boasting. *— wo iu*, id.

TAI-HEN, タイヘン, 大變, (lit. great change). A great, important, or serious affair; a fearful or terrible event; very.

TAI-HŌ, タイハウ, 大砲, (*ō-dztsz*). *n.* A cannon, artillery.

TAI-HŌ, タイハウ, 大方, (*ōkata*). The most part, generally; perhaps, probably.
Syn. TAI-RIYAKU.

†TAI-HŌ-TAI, タイハウタイ, 大砲隊, *n.* Artillery company or corps.

TAI-I, タイイ, 大醫, *n.* A great physician.

TAI-I, タイイ, 大意, The principal meaning, the substance, in the main, chiefly. *— wa shitte oru*, in the main I understand the meaning. Syn. ŌMUNE.

†TAI-IN, タイイン, 大陰, *n.* The moon.
Syn. TSZKI.

TAIJI, *-szru*, タイヂ, 退治, (*shirizoke osameru*). To suppress, subdue, destroy. *Akuma wo —*, to subdue evil spirits.
Syn. TAIRAGERU.

†TAI-JIN, タイジン, 大人, *n.* A great man, one eminent for virtue.

TAI-JIN, *-szru*, タイヂン, 退陣, To withdraw an army

TAI-KE, タイケ, 大家, *n.* A great house, illustrious family.

TAI-KEI, タイケイ, 大慶, (*ōini yorokobu.*) To rejoice greatly, great joy.

TAI-KEN, タイケン, 帶劍, (*katana wo obiru*). Carrying a sword in the belt.

TAI-KETSZ, *-szru*, タイケツ, 對决, To judge of a matter at law, by having the plaintiff and defendant confront each other.

†TAI-KI, タイキ, 大器, Great talents, noble, magnanimous.

TAI-KIN, タイキン, 大金, (*ōgane*). *n.* Great wealth, a great deal of money.

†TAI-KIYO, タイキヨ, 大虚, (*ōsora*). *n.* The sky.

TAI-KIYO, *-szru*, タイキヨ, 退去, (*shirizoki saru*). To leave, depart, go away.

†TAI-KIYOKU, タイキヨク, 大極, *n.* The first principle, or germ of all things in Chinese philosophy.

TAI-KO, タイコ, 大古, (*ōmukashi*). *n.* Remote antiquity, earliest ages.

TAIKO, タイコ, 大鼓, *n.* A drum.

TAI-KŌ, タイカウ, 大功, *n.* Great merit, very eminent or praise-worthy deeds.

TAIKOMOCHI, タイコモチ, 帮漢, *n.* A jester, or one who, on account of his wit or comic talents, is called to assist at entertainments.

TAI-KUTSZ, タイクツ, 退屈, *n.* Ennui, tired, disgusted, or wearied with any thing tedious, or for want of occupation. *Matte ite mo — da kara kayetta*, he wanted me to wait for him but getting tired I returned. *— sh'te asobini deru*, being tired (of having nothing to do), went out to take a walk.
Syn. AGUMU, TOZEN.

TAI-MAI, タイマイ, 玳瑁, *n.* A kind of tortoise-shell.

TAI-MAI, タイマイ, coll. Much, a great deal, only spoken of money. *— no kane.*

TAI-MAN, *-szru*, タイマン, 怠慢, (*okotaru*). To be negligent or careless.
Syn. TAIDA, KEDAI.

TAI-MATSZ, タイマツ, 燒松, *n.* A pine torch, flambeau.

TAI-MEI, タイメイ, 台命, *n.* An order, or command from the *Shōgun*.

†TAI-MEI, タイメイ, 大名, (*ōinaru na*). *n.* Great name, fame, celebrity.

TAI-MEN, タイメン, 對面, *n.* Meeting face to face. *— no wiye nita ohanashi itashimashō*, I will tell you when we meet.

TAI-MŌ, タイマウ, 大望, (*ōinaru nozomi*). *n.* Great desires, or ambition. *— no aru h'to*, a man of great ambition.

TAI-NAI, タイナイ, 胎內, (*hara no uchi.*)

In the womb, during uterine life. — *ni oru toki*, when in the womb.

TAIRA, タヒラ, 平, Level, plain, even. — *naru tokoro*, a level place. — *ni szru*, to make level.
Syn. HIRATTAI.

TAIRAGE,-*ru*,-*ta*, タヒラゲル, 平, *t.v.* To level, make plain or even; to quell, subdue; to quiet, tranquilize. *Ran wo* —, to quell a disturbance.
Syn. OSAMERU, TAIJI SZRU.

TAIRAGI, タヒラギ, 江瑤, *n.* A species of shell.

TAIRAKA, タヒラカ, 平, Level, plain, even, quiet, calm, tranquil, — *naru tokoro*, a level place. *Nami ga — ni natta*, the waves have become still.
Syn. YASZRAKA, ODAYAKA.

TAI-RAN, タイラン, 大亂, (*ōini midareru*). Great commotion or disturbance, as from war.

TAI-RIYAKU, タイリヤク, 大略, For the most part, generally, about, more or less, probably. Syn. TAIGAI, Ō-MUNE, Ō-KATA.

TAI-RIYŌ, タイリヤウ, 大量, Magnanimous, generous, liberal, honorable.
Syn. ŌMAKA-NA.

†TAI-RIYU,-*szru*, タイリウ, 滯留, (*todomaru*). To stop, stay, remain.
Syn. TŌRIU.

TAISAN, タイサン, *adv.* Very much, a great many, very, (a corrupt coll. word peculiar to Yokohama.)

†TAI-SAN,-*szru*, タイサン, 退散, (*shirizoki chiru*). To leave, or retreat and scatter.

TAI-SETSZ, タイセツ, 大切, Important, of great consequence, highly valued or esteemed. — *na mono*, a thing which is set great store by. — *ni szru*, to regard as of great importance, to value, care for.
Syn. DAIJI.

TAI-SHA, タイシヤ, 大赦, (*ōyurushi*). *n.* General amnesty, or pardon. — *wo okonau.*

TAISHASEKI, タイシヤセキ, 代赭石, *n.* Red ochre.

TAI-SHI, タイシ, 大子, *n.* The prince royal, eldest son of the *Tenshi*.

TAI-SHI,-*sz*,-*sh'ta*, タイス, 對, *i.v.* To front, to be opposite to, in the presence of, towards, with respect to, to. *Yama ni taish'ta iye*, the house fronting the hill. *Shu-jin ye taish'te shitszrei*, rude to one's lord. *Oya ni taish'te fukō*, disobedient to parents. Syn. MUKAU.

†TAI-SHI,-*sz*,-*sh'ta* タイス, 帶, (*obiru*). *t.v.* To carry in the belt, to carry. *Dai-shō wo taisz*, to carry a long and short sword.

TAI-SHIN, タイシン, 退身, (*mi wo shirizokeru*). — *szru*, to resign a service, to withdraw from a place.

TAI-SHIN, タイシン, 大身, *n.* Large property, wealthy. — *na h'to*, a man of large possessions.

TAISH'TA, タイシタ, 大, *a.* coll. Great, important, serious, severe. — *biyōki de wa nai*, not a serious sickness.
Syn. KAKUBETSZ-NA.

TAISH'TE, タイシテ, *pp.* of *Taishi*.

TAI-SHO, タイシヨ, 大暑, *n.* The period of greatest heat in summer.

TAI-SHŌ, タイシヤウ, 大將, *n.* General in chief, chief: also in com. coll. for *Danna*, master, mister,

†TAI-SHŌ, タイシヤウ, 胎生, *n.* Viviparous.

TAI-SHŌGUN, タイシヤウグン, 大將軍, *n.* Generalissimo, commander in chief, specially applied to the *Kubō sama*.

TAI-SHOKU, タイシヨク, 大食, (*ō-gui*). — *szru*, to eat much. — *na mono*, a gormandizer.

TAI-SHU, タイシユ, 大守, *n.* The chief ruler, or lord of a state.

TAI-SHU, タイシユ, 大酒, (*ōzake*). *n.* Drinking much wine, a great drinker.

TAI-SHUTSZ,-*szru*, タイシユツ, 退出, (*shirizoki-idzru*). To leave, withdraw, depart. Syn. SARU.

TAI-SO, タイソ, 大祖, *n.* First progenitor, earliest ancestor.

TAI-SŌ, タイサウ, 大壯, Great many, great deal, much, very, exceeding. — *kane ga iru*, cost a great deal of money. — *fukai*, very deep. — *ōkina koye*, a very loud voice,
Syn. ŌKI, HANAHADA.

TAI-SOKU, タイソク, 大息, *n.* A long breath. — *szru*, to draw a long breath.

TAISZ, タイス, See *Taishi*.

TAISZU, タイスウ, 大數, *n.* The average number.

TAI-TEI, タイテイ, 大抵, For the most part, generally, in the main; about, nearly, on an average. — *no shina*, a thing of ordinary or average quality. — *ni sh'te oku*, need not be very particular about how it is done. — *h'yaku nin gurai*, about one hundred persons.
Syn. TAI-GAI, OYOSO.

TAI-TEKI, タイテキ, 大敵, *n.* A powerful enemy. *Yudan* —, negligence is a powerful enemy.

TAI-TŌ, タイトウ, 帶刀, *(katana wo obiru)*. Wearing a sword.

†TAI-WA, タイワ, 對話, *n.* Talking face to face, conversation. Syn. TAIDAN.

TAI-YA, タイヤ, 逮夜, *n.* The night before the anniversary of a death.

†TAI-YAKU, タイヤク, 對譯, A word for for word translation.

TAI-YAKU,-*szru*, タイヤク, 退役, *(yaku wo shirizoku)*, To resign an office.

TAI-YAKU, タイヤク, 大役, *n.* Great, or important office.

†TAI-YŌ, タイヤウ, 大陽, *n.* The sun. Syn. HI, NICHIRIN.

†TAI-YŌ, タイヤウ, 對揚, Matched, equal, — *sedz*, not matched, unequal, (as antagonists).

TAI-YŪ, タイユウ, Generous, magnanimous, liberal.

TAI-ZA,-*szru*, タイザ, 對座, Sitting opposite each other.

TAI-ZA,-*szru*, タイザ, 退座, (*za wo shirizoku*). To leave one's seat, withdraw.

TAI-ZAI, タイザイ, 大罪, *(ōinaru tszmi)*. *n.* A great crime. — *wo okasz*, commit a great crime.

†TA-JIN, タジン, 他人, (*yoso no h'to*). *n.* Other persons, or persons not related, not kindred. Syn. TANIN.

TAJIRE,-*ru*,-*ta*, タジレル, coll. *i.v.* To be childish from age, to dote. Syn. BOKERU.

TAJIROKI,-*ku*,-*ita*, タジロク, coll. *i.v.* To stagger, start, or to become weak from sudden surprise, shock, or fright.

TAJI-TAJI, タジタジ, coll. *adv.* In a staggering, unsteady manner. *Kodomo ga — aruku.*

†TA-JITSZ, タツジ, 他日, (*hoka no hi)*. *adv.* Another day.

TAKA, タカ, 鷹, *n.* A falcon, hawk. — *wo tszkau*, to hunt with a falcon.

TAKA, タカ, 高, *n.* Income, produce from a farm, revenue; also the size of a farm, the amount, sum. — *ga szkunai*, the income is small. *Ichi nen no mōke-daka*, the amount of one year's earnings. *Kan-jō-daka*, the sum of an account. *Daimiyō no* —, the revenue or income of a noble.

TAKABURI,-*ru*,-*tta*, タカブル, 傲, *i.v.* To be haughty, proud arrogant, pompous. *Samurai ga takabutte h'to wo mikudasz*, the gentry are haughty and despise others. Syn. JIMAN SZRU.

TAKA-DAKA, タカダカ, 高高, *adv.* High, loud. — *to nobi-agaru*, to ascend high. — *to yomu*, to read with a loud voice.

TAKADEKODE, タカデコデ, Only used in the phrase. — *ni shibaru*, to tie the hands behind the back.

†TAKADONO, タカドノ, 樓, *n.* The second story of a house. Syn. RŌ.

TAKADŌRO, タカドウロ, 高燈, *n.* A light house.

TAKA-FUDA, タカフダ, 高札, *(kō-satsz)*. *n.* The boards on which the imperial edicts are published.

TAKA-GARI, タカガリ, 鷹狩, *n.* Hunting with a hawk, hawking.

TAKA-GOYE, タカゴヱ, 高聲, *n.* A loud voice.

TAKAI,-KI,-KU,-SHI,-Ō, タカイ, 高, High, loud, dear in price, expensive, exalted, honorable. *Takai yama*, a high mountain. *Nedan ga takaku natta*, the price has become high. *Kurai takaki h'to*, a person of high rank. *Ki ga takai*, haughty, proud. *Hana ga takai*, the nose is long, also proud. *Koye ga takai*, the voice is loud. *Takō-natta*, has become high. *Takaku szru*, to make high, heighten. *Takakutszku*, costly, expensive.

TAKAJŌ, タカゼウ, 鷹尉, *n.* A falconer.

TAKAMA-NO-HARA, タカマノハラ, 高天原, *n.* The place in which the *Kami* dwell.

TAKAMAKIYE, タカマキヱ, 高蒔繪, *n.* Embossed gilt lacquer.

TAKAME,-*ru*,-*ta*, タカメル, 高, *t.v.* To make high, heighten.

TAKAMI, タカミ, *n.* A high place.

TAKAMURA, タカムラ, 竹叢, *n.* A bamboo grove. Syn. YABU.

TAKANA, タカナ, 菘, *n.* A kind of greens.

TAKANE, タカネ, 高嶺, *n.* A high mountain peak. Syn. MINE, ZETCHŌ.

TAKARA, タカラ, 寶, *n.* Precious thing, anything valued, wealth. — *to szru*, to esteem, value. — *wo tsziyasz*, to squander one's wealth. Syn. ZAIHŌ, HŌMOTSZ.

TAKARAGAI, タカラガイ, 貝, *n.* A cowry.

TAKARAKA, タカラカ, 高, High, loud. — *na koye*, a loud voice.

TAKARI,-*ru*,-*tta*, タカル, 集 *i.v.* To collect in a crowd, to swarm together. *Hai ga* —, the flies swarm. *Mimidz ni ari ga* —, the ants swarm about an earth-worm. Syn. ATSZMARU.

TAKASA, タカサ, *n.* The height. elevation, altitude. — *wa dono kurai*, how high is it?

TAKASE, タカセ, 高瀬, *n.* A river boat.

TAKASE,-*ru*,-*ta*, タカセル, 令燒, caust. of *Taku*. To cause or let a fire be kindled, &c.

TAKASHI, タカシ, *a.* See *Takai.*

TAKA-TSZKI, タカツキ, 高杯, *n.* A wooden bowl, or tray for holding fruit.

TAKA-WARAI, タカワラヒ, 高笑, *n.* A loud laugh.

TAKE, タケ, 竹, *n.* Bamboo. — *no fushi,* the joints of bamboo. — *no ko,* bamboo sprouts. —*na kawa,* the sheath of young bamboo. —*bashi,* bamboo chopsticks. —*zao,* a bamboo pole. — *dzye,* a bamboo cane.

TAKE, タケ, 菌, *n.* Mushroom. Syn. KI-NO-KO, KUSABIRA.

TAKE, タケ, 長, *n.* The length, measure. — *ga nagai.* — *ga mijikai. Mi no* —, the height of the body, the stature. *Midz no — wa roku shaku,* the depth of the water is six feet. — *ga tatanu,* too deep, over one's head. — *ni amaru,* longer than one's body, (as clothing). — *no takai h'to,* a tall man. Syn. NAGASA.

†TAKE, タケ, 嶽, *n.* A high mountain. Syn. ŌYAMA.

†TA-KE, タケ, 他家, (*hoka no iye*). *n.* Another family, no connexion, not related.

TAKE, タク, *imp.* of *Taki.*

TAKE,-*ru*,-*ta*, タケル, *i.v.* To be high, well advanced, eminent. *Hi ga taketa,* the sun is high. *Toshi ga taketa h'to,* a person well advanced in age. *Chiye ga* —, eminent in wisdom. Syn. FUKERU.

†TAKEBI,-*bu*,-*nda*, タケブ, *i.v.* To be fierce, furious, savage.

TAKE-GARI, タケガリ, 菌狩, *n.* Hunting for mushrooms. — *ni yuku.*

TAKEKI,-KU,-SHI, タケキ, 猛, Valiant, brave, courageous, fearless, fierce, strong. — *mononofu,* a brave soldier. — *honō,* a hot fire. Syn. TSZYOI.

TA-KEN, タケン, 他見, Seen by others. — *wo yurusadz,* will not allow others to see it. — *wa go muyō,* don't let others see it.

†TAKENAWA, タケナワ, 闌, Past the height, beginning to decline or fail. *Yo ga — ni natta,* to be past midnight. *Sake ga — ni oyobu,* the drinking had begun to flag. *Kassen szde-ni — naran toki,* when the battle would begin to flag.

TAKERI,-*ru*,-*tta*, タケル, *i.v.* To be fierce, ferocious, savage, to growl. *Tora ga h'to ni takeri-kakatta,* the tiger ferociously sprang on the man.

TAKE-TABA, タケタバ, 竹束, *n.* Bundles of bamboo, fascines.

TAKE-TAKA-YUBI, タケタカユビ, 長指, *n.* The long, or middle finger.

TAKE-UMA, タケウマ, 竹馬, *n.* A wooden horse, or stilts used by boys.

TAKI, タキ, 瀑, *n.* A waterfall, cataract.

TAKI,-*ku*,-*ita*, タク, 燒, *t. v.* To burn, kindle, to boil. *Maki wo* —, to burn wood. *Kō wo* —, to burn incense. *Hi wo* —, to make a fire. *Meshi wo* —, to boil rice. Syn. YAKU, MOYASZ, NIRU.

TAKIBI, タキビ, 燒火, *n.* A fire.

TAKIGI, タキギ, 薪木, *n.* Firewood. Syn. MAKI.

TAKI-MONO, タキモノ, 燒物, *n.* Fuel, incense. Syn. KŌ.

TAKI-TATE, タキタテ, 燒立, Just boiled. — *no meshi,* rice that has just been boiled.

TAKI-TSZBO, タキツボ, 瀑壺, *n.* The deep hollow place excavated by the water of a cataract.

TAKI-TSZKE,-*ku*,-*ta*, タキツケル, 燒付, *t.v.* To kindle a fire; fig. to make angry. *Hi wo* —.

TAKI-TSZKE, タキツケ, 燒付, *n.* Kindling-wood.

TAKITSZSE, タキツセ, 激湍, *n.* The rapids in a river.

TAKO, タコ, 紙鳶, *n.* A kite. — *wo ageru,* to fly a kite. Syn. IKANOBORI.

TAKO, タコ, 章魚, *n.* The cuttle-fish.

TAKO, タコ, 䐁, *n.* The callosity on the hands produced by work.

TAKŌ, タカウ, 高, *adv.* Same as *Takaku.*

TA-KOKU, タコク, 他國, (*yoso no kuni*). *n.* Another state, other countries.

TAKU, タク, See *Taki.*

TAKU, タク, 宅, *n.* A house. Syn. IYE.

TAKUBOKU, タクボク, 啄木, *n.* The cord used for tying up a picture mounted on a roller.

TAKU-HATSZ, タクハツ, 托鉢, *n.* Begging from house to house, as Buddhist priests. — *wo szru,* to beg, &c.

†TAKUMA, タクマ, 琢磨, Cutting and polishing, as gems. — *szru,* to polish. Syn. MIGAKU.

TAKUMASHII,-KI,-KU,-U, タクマシイ, 逞, Large and strong, robust, lusty, and powerful; frowardly, recklessly, skilfully, ingeniously, adroitly. — *uma,* a large and powerful horse. — *kodomo,* a robust child.

TAKUMI,-*mu*,-*nda*, タクム, 巧, *t. v.* To devise, plan, contrive, invent. *Muhon wo* —, to plan a rebellion. Syn. KUFŪ SZRU.

†TAKUMI, タクミ, 匠, *n.* A carpenter. Syn. DAIKU.

TAKUMI, タクミ, 巧, Skilful, clever, adroit,

ingenious, artful. *Kotoba wo — ni szru*, to be clever at talking. — *na saiku*, an ingenious machine. Syn. JŌDZ.

TAKUNAMI,*-mu,-nda*, タクナム, 巧, *t.v.* To devise, contrive, invent.

†TAKURABE,*-ru,-ta*, タクラベル, 較, *t.v.* To compare. Syn. KURABERU.

TAKURE,*-ru,-ta*, タクレル, *i. v.* To be rumpled, wrinkled, kinked, corrugated. *Ito ga* —, the thread is kinked. *Kimono ga* —, the clothes are rumpled. *Kawa ga* —, skin is excoriated.

TAKURI,*-ru,-tta*, タクル手, 繰, *t.v.* same as *Taguri*. To haul in hand over hand, as a rope, to snatch, to embezzle, defraud.

TAKURI-KOMI,*-mu,-nda*, タクリコム, *t.v.* To embezzle.

TAKUSAN, or TAK'SAN, タクサン, 澤山, Many, plenty, abundant. Syn. TANTO, ŌI.

†TAKU-SEN, タクセン, 託宣, *n.* A communication, or revelation from a Kami, made through human organs of speech, an oracle. *Kami no — ni yotte miya wo tateru*, to erect a temple according to a revelation from the Kami.

†TAKUSHI,*-szru,-sh'ta*, タクスル, 託, *t.v.* To intrust to, charge with, commit, to depend on, engage to do, ask to do, make an excuse of, to use as a pretext.
Syn. ATSZRAYERU, ADZKERU, KAKOTSZKERU.

†TAKUSHIKI, タクシキ, 卓識, Quick of discernment.

TAKUWANDZKE, タクアンヅケ, 澤庵漬, *n.* Radishes pickled in salt and bran.

TAKUWAYE,*-ru,-ta*, タクハヘル, 貯, *t.v.* To store up, to lay up, to keep, preserve, to hoard, accumulate, to amass. *Hiyōrō wo* —, to store up provisions. *Kane wo* —, to accumulate money.
Syn. OSAMERU, TAMERU.

TAKUWAYE, タクハヘ, 蓄, *n.* A supply, provision. *Kuszri no — mo nai*, not even a supply of medicines.

TAMA, タマ, 玉, or 丸, *n.* A ball, precious stone, a bead: (fig). spirit, soul; precious, valuable. *Teppō no* —, a musket, or a cannon ball. *Me no* —, the eyeball. *Muszbi* —, a knot tied on a string. *Ki no* —, a wooden ball. *Hi no* —, a ball of fire. — *wo migaku*, to polish a precious stone; or fig. to cultivate the mind. *H'to no* —, a man's soul.

†TAMADZSA, タマヅサ, 玉章, Your precious letter.

TAMA-GAKI, タマガキ, 玉垣, *n.* The picket fence around a Miya.

TAMAGE,*-ru,-ta*, タマゲル, 魂銷, (cont. of *Tama*, the mind and *kiye*, extinguished). *i. v.* To be surprised, astonished, startled. *Hatto tamageru onna no naki koye*,he was startled, hearing the cry of a woman. Syn. BIKKURI SZRU, ODOROKU.

TAMAGO, タマゴ, 卵, *n.* An egg. — *wo umu*, to lay an egg. — *no shiromi*, the white of an egg. — *no kimi*, the yolk of an egg.

TAMAGO-IRO, タマゴイロ, 卵色, *n.* The color of the yolk of an egg, — yellow.

TAMAGO-NARI, タマゴナリ, 卵形, *n.* Egg-shape, elliptical.

TAMA-GUSZRI, タマグスリ, 玉藥, *n.* Powder and ball.

TAMAI,*-ō,-ōta*, タマフ, 賜, *t.v.* To give to inferiors, used only when speaking of the most honorable persons; as, *Kami*, *Tenshi*, or *Shujin*, and affixed to other verb roots. *Kami wa tenchi wo tszkuritamp̄*, God made heaven and earth. *Waga mi wo yaszku arashime-tamaye*, grant me freedom from evil. *Mi-tamau*, to see *Kiki-tamau*, to hear.
Syn. NASARU, KUDASARU.

TAMAKI, タマキ, 環, *n.* A bracelet.
Syn. KUSHIRO.

TAMAKA, タマカ, coll. Economical, saving, frugal, not wasteful. — *na h'to*, an economical person. — *ni szru*, to be economical. Syn. KENYAKU.

TAMAKURA, タマクラ, Same as *Temakura*.

TAMA-MATSZRI, タマヽツリ, 魂祭, *n.* The festival for the dead, observed on the 15th day of the 7th month, same as Bon.

TAMA-MONO, タマモノ, 賜物, *n.* A gift, anything received from an honorable person. *Inochi wa sznawachi kami no mi — nari*, life is the gift of God.

TAMA-MUSHI, タマムシ, 玉蟲, *n.* A kind of beetle.

TAMA-NI, タマニ, *adv.* Seldom, occasionally. — *kuru*, seldom comes.
Syn. MARE-NI.

†TAMA-NO-O, タマノヲ, 玉緒, *n.* The string on which beads are strung; (fig.) life. — *no taye yo kashi*, I would that I might die. Syn. INOCHI.

TAMARANU, or TAMARANAI タマラヌ, 不堪, neg. of *Tamari*. Cannot bear, cannot endure, insufferable. *Samukute tamaranai*, it is so cold I can't stand it.

TAMARI,*-ru,-tta*, タマル, 溜, *i. v.* To collect, accumulate, stand. (堪,) To endure, bear, suffer, *Midz ga kubomi ni* —, the water stands in hollow places. *Gomi* *ga* —, the dust collects. *Kane ga* —, money accumulates. *Uma ni tamaradz*, could not keep on the horse. *Tamaru mono ka*, is it right to endure it? Syn. TOMARU, TSZMORU.

TAMARI-NO-MA, タマリノマ, 溜間, *n.* An ante-chamber. *Musha-damari*, an open place within the walls of a castle where the soldiers assemble.

TAMASAKA, タマサカ, Seldom, rare, occasional. — *na*, idem. — *ni, adv.* rarely, occasionally. Syn. TAMA-TAMA.

TAMASHII, タマシヒ, 靈, *n.* The soul, spirit, ghost. — *mo mi ni sowadz*, the soul left the body (said of one greatly alarmed.) Syn. KOMPAKU, REI.

TAMA-TAMA, タマタマ, 偶, Occasional, rare, seldom, sometimes. — *ni kuru*, seldom comes. Syn. ORIFUSHI, MARE-NI.

TAMAWARI,*-ru-tta*, タマハル, 賜, *t.v.* To give, (spoken only of most honorable persons), also to receive from a superior.

TAMAYA, タマヤ, 靈屋, *n.* A tomb, sepulchre. Syn. HAKA.

TOMAYOBAI, タマヨバヒ, 招魂, *n.* Calling from the roof, to the spirit of one just dead to return, (as is the custom in some parts of Japan).

TAM-BETSZ, タンベツ, 段別, *n.* The quantity of land held by a farmer; the registry of land.

TAMBO, タンボ, 段畝, *n.* Rice-fields. Syn. DENJI.

TAME, タメ, 爲, *n.* Sake, account, purpose, reason. motive, for; by, denoting the agent, or means; to, or relation. *Kimi ga tame*, for master's sake. *Oya ga kodomo no tame ni kurō szru*, the parent is anxious on account of his children. *Tame ni naranu*, good for nothing, useless. *Omaye no tame ni shūto*, your father in law. *Omaye no tame ni nanda*, what relation is he to you? *Sono ko no tame ni korosareta*, he was slain by his son.

TAME,*-ru,-ta*, タメル, 溜, *t.v.* To collect, to put together in one place anything scattered about. *Amamidz wo* —, to catch rain water. *Kane wo* —, to lay up money. Syn. ATSZMERU, TAKUWAYERU.

TAME,*-ru,-ta*, タメル, 矯, *t.v.* To straighten, make straight, to correct what is wrong. *Ya wo* —, to straighten an arrow. *Teppō wo tamete tori wo utsz*, to level a gun and shoot a bird. *Ki wo tame-naosz*, to alter one's mind, or overcome one's disinclination to anything. Syn. NERAU.

TAME-IKI, タメイキ, 大息, *n.* A long breath, a gasp. — *wo tszku*, to take a long breath.

TAMENURI, タメヌリ, 溜塗, *n.* Black lacquer.

TAMERAI,*-au* or*-ō,-ōta*, タメラフ, 狐疑, *i.v.* To hesitate, to be undecided, to be in doubt, quandary, or suspense. *Ikaga sen to tamerō*, was at a loss what to do. Syn. YŪYO SZRU, KOGI SZRU.

TAMERU, タメル, See *Tame*.

TAMESARE,*-ru,-ta*, タメサレル, 被試, pass. of *Tamesz*. To be proved, tried.

TAMESHI,*-sz,-sh'ta*, タメズ, 試, *t.v.* To try, prove, experiment, examine. *Katana wo* —, try a sword. *Uma wo* —, to try a horse. *Kuszri wo tameshite miru*, to try or experiment with a medicine. Syn. KOKOROMIRU.

TAMESHI, タメシ, 例, *n.* A case, example, precedent, former instance. — *ni hiku*, to give as an example or instance. *H'totsz no* — *mo nai*, not a single instance. Syn. REI.

TAMI, タミ, 民, (from *Ta*, field and *mi*, person). *n.* People.

TAM-MEI, タンメイ, 短命, (*mijikai inochi*). *n.* Short life. — *ni sh'te shidz*, to die in youth.

TAMMONO, タンモノ, 端物, *n.* Cloth, or peice goods.

TAMŌ, タマフ, See *Tamai*.

TAMOCHI,*-tsz,-tta*, タモツ, 保, *t. v.* (from *Te*, hand and *motsz*, hold). To keep, guard, protect, preserve, to watch over and defend from evil; to sustain, support; to last, endure; to have, hold. *Kuni wo* —, to protect, or defend a country. *Iye wo* —, to keep one's family, to protect it. *Mi wo* —, to take good care of one's self. *Niku ga nagaku tamota-nai*, flesh does not keep long. *Inochi wo* —, to sustain life. Syn. MOTSZ,

TAMOCHI, タモチ, 保, *n.* Enduring, keeping or lasting long. *Fuyu wa niku no* — *ga yoi*, flesh keeps well in winter.

†TA-MON, タモン, 他聞, The hearing of others, publ city, as. — *habakaru*, to dread that others should hear. Syn. G'WAI BUN.

TAMOTO, タモト, 袂, *n.* The pocket in the sleeve.

TAMOTO-OTOSHI, タモトオトシ, *n.* A small purse or wallet carried in the sleeve.

TAMOTSZ, タモツ, See *Tamochi*.

TAMPAKU, タンパク, 淡泊, Delicate in taste or color; fresh, tasteless; fig. unambitious, devoid of strong desires or lusts. *Ajiwai wa* — *na mono*. Syn. USZI.

TAMPAN, タンパン, 膽礬, *n.* Sulphate of Copper.

TAMPEI, タンパイ, 短兵, *n.* A short sword. — *wo motte semeru*, to fight at close quarters. — *kiu ni*, fig. in a great hurry, with intense activity.

TAMPO, タンポ, A soft pad affixed to the point of a spear in the spear exercise.

TAMPO, or TAMPOPO, タンポポ, 蒲公英, *n.* The dandelion.

†TAMU, or TAMURU, タムル, Same as *Tameru.*

TAMUKE,*-ru,-ta*, タムケル, 手向, *t.v.* To place before an idol, to make as an offering. *Hana wo* —, to offer a flower.
Syn. SONAYERU, AGERU.

TAMUKE, タムケ, *n.* An offering made to idols or at the graves.

†TAMURO, タムロ, 屯, (Derived from *Te* and *mure*). *n.* An encampment, or station for troops; barracks, a garrison. — *szru*, to station troops. — *wo haru*, to encamp. Syn. JIN; YEI.

TAMUSHI, タムシ, 頑癬, *n.* A ring-worm.

TAN, タン, 痰, *n.* Mucous, phlegm, expectoration in coughing, — *ga deru*, to expectorate. — *Tan-kiri-kuszri*, expectorant medicines.

TAN, タン, 丹, *n.* Redoxide of lead.

TAN, タン, 端, *n.* A piece of cloth, the half of a *hiki*, = 28 feet in length. *Momen ittan*, one piece of long cloth, of 28 feet in length. *Ni tan*, two pieces.

TAN, タン, 段, *n.* A plot of ground, = ten *se*, or 300 tszbo, = 10,800 sq. feet or about ¼ of an acre.

†TAN, タン, 膽, *n.* The gall-bladder. *Tan-no-zō*, idem. Syn. I.

TANA, タナ, 棚, *n.* A shelf. *Kami-dana*, the shelf in houses on which the household gods stand. *Tana ye agete oku*, to place on a shelf.

TANA, タナ, 店, *n.* A shop. Syn. MISE.

TANABATA, タナバタ, 織女, *n.* The name of a star near the Milky way, worshiped on the 7th day of the 7th month.
Syn. SHOKUJO.

TANABIKI,*-ku,-ita*, タナビク, 棚引, *i.v.* To be spread abroad in the air, as clouds, fog, haze, or smoke. *Kumo ga tanabīte fuji-no-yama wo kakusz*, the clouds have spread over and concealed mount Fuji.

TANA-CHIN, タナチン, 店賃, *n.* House-rent.

TANA-DATE, タナダテ, 店立, *n.* Ejection of a tenant. — *wo szru.*

TANA-GARI, タナガリ, 店借, *n.* One who rents a house, or shop; a tenant.

TANA-GAYE, タナガヘ, 店替, *n.* Removal from one shop to another.

TANAGO, タナゴ, *n.* The name of a small fresh water fish.

TANAGOKORO, タナゴゴロ, 掌, *n.* The hollow or palm of the hand.
Syn. TE NO HIRA.

TANAKO, タナコ, 店子, *n.* Persons living in rented houses, a tenant.

TANA-MONO, タナモノ, 店者, *n.* The persons belonging to a shop, clerks.

TANDZRU, タンズル, See *Tanji.*

TANE, タネ, 種, *n.* A seed: (fig.) the occasion, cause, or origin from which any thing springs; yeast, or ferment. — *wo maku*, to sow seed. — *wo wiyeru*, to plant seed. — *wa onaji hara ga chigau*, the same father but different mother. *Uri no* — *ni naszbi wa hayenu*, an eggplant does not grow from a melon seed (prov.) *Kenk'wa no* — *ni naru*, to become the cause of a quarrel. *Ī-wake no* —, the grounds of an excuse. *Hakarigoto no* —, the grounds of a stratagem. *Pan no* —, yeast.

TA-NEDZMI, タネヅミ, 田鼠, *n.* A field-rat.

TANE-GAMI, タネガミ, 蠶紙, *n.* The paper on which the eggs of silk-worms are deposited.

TANEGASHIMA, タネガシマ, 種嶋, *n.* A pistol; (derived from a province of that name in the province of Kiushū where they were first introduced).

TANE-GAWARI, タネガハリ, *n.* Having a different father, but the same mother. — *no kiyōdai*, step-brothers.

TANE-HON, タネホン, 種本, *n.* The original copy of a book or picture.
Syn. GEMPON.

TA-NEN, タネン, 多年, (*ōi toshi*). *n.* Many years.

TA-NEN, タネン, 他年, (*hoka no toshi*) *n.* Some future year, another year.

TA-NEN, タネン, 他念, (*hoka no omoi*). *n.* Another mind. — *naku*, minding or thinking of nothing else, without distraction.

TANGO, タンゴ, 端午, *n* The 5th day of the 5th month, a holiday.

TANG'WAN,*-szru*, タングワン, 歎願, To complain in tears, to plead, to supplicate earnestly.

TANI, タニ, 谷, *n.* A valley. *Tani-guchi*, the entrance to a valley. *Tanigawa*, a stream running through a valley, rivulet.

TA-NIN, タニン, 他人, *(yoso no h'to)*. *n.* Persons who are not related, strangers.

TA-NIN-JU, タニンジユ, 多人數, *n.* A great many people. Syn. ŌZEI.

TANISHI, タニシ, 田螺, *n.* A snail.

TAN-JAKU, タンジヤク, 短尺, *n.* Paper cut into long and narrow strips used for writing poetry.

†TAN-KEI, タンケイ, 短檠, *n.* A lamp. Syn. ANDON.

TAN-KI, タンキ, 短氣, *(mijikai ki)*. *n.* Quick to get angry, passionate, irascible. — *na h'to*, a quick tempered man.

†TANJI,*-ru*, or*-dzru,-ta*, タンズル, 歎, *(nageku)*. *t.v.* To sigh, to lament, mourn. *Tanjite iwaku*, sighing he said. *Yo wo —*, to lament on account of the times. Syn. TANSOKU SZRU.

TANJI,*-ru*, or*-dzru,-ta*, タンジル, 彈, *(hiku)*. *t.v.* To play on a stringed instrument, as the harp. *Koto wo —*, to play on the harp. *Biwa wo —*, to play the banjo.

†TAN-JITSZ, タンジツ, 短日, *(mijikai hi)*, *n.* A short day.

TAN-JŌ, タンジヤウ, 誕生, *(umare)*, *n.* Birth, nativity. — *szru*, to bear, beget. — *wo iwau*, to celebrate a birth.

TANJŌ-BI, タンジヤウビ, 誕生日, *n.* Birth-day.

†TANKATSZ, タンカツ, 短褐, *n.* (obs.) A kind of short coat worn only by low people.

TANNŌ,*-szru*, タンノウ, coll. To be satiated, filled, satisfied (as with seeing, hearing or eating). *Ichi nichi shibai wo mite — sh'ta*, have been looking at the play all day and have had quite enough. Syn. AKU, TARU.

†TA-NŌ, タノウ, 多能, Many abilities, or talents. — *na h'to*.

TANOMI,*-mu,-nda*, タノム, 頼, *t. v.* To call, ask, or apply to for aid, or assistance; to request, solicit; to trust to, depend on, confide in. *Ninsoku wo —*, to call a coolie. *Kami wo —*, to call upon the Kami for help. *Isha wo —*, to call in a doctor. *Ikō wo —*, to confide in one's power. *Chikara wo tanonde*, relying on one's strength. *Otanomi-mōshi mas*, I beg or request you to do me a favor Syn. NEGAU.

TANOMI, タノミ, 頼, *n.* Request, solicitation, petition; trust, reliance, dependence. *H'to no — ni yotte szru*, to do anything at the request of another. — *ni naranu mono*, a person not to be depended on. — *szkunai*, none to depend on. *Chikara wo — ni sh'te h'to wo anadoru*, relying upon his strength he despised others. Syn. NEGAI, TAYORI.

TANOMOSHII,*-KI,-KU,-Ū,-SA*, タノモシイ 頼, Reliable, to be depended on, hopeful, promising, giving ground to expect aid, or help from. *Tanomoshiku omō*, to regard as promising, or to be relied on.

TANOSHII,*-KI*, タノシイ, 樂, *a.* Pleasant, delightful, agreeable, happy. Syn. OMOSHIROI.

TANOSHIKU, タノシク, 樂, *adv.* idem.

TANOSHISA, タノシサ, 樂, *n.* Happiness, delight, pleasantness. *Gokuraku no — wa kono sekai ni tagui nashi*, there is nothing in this world like the happiness of heaven. Syn. OMOSHIROSA.

TANOSHIMI,*-mu,-nda*, タノシム, 樂, *v. t.* To take pleasure in, to be happy in, to delight in, rejoice in, to enjoy, to anticipate with pleasure. *Hana wo mite —*, to delight in looking at the flowers. *Tanoshinde matsz*, joyfully to wait for. *Szye wo —* to look forward to a happy future. Syn. OMOSHIROGARU.

TANOSHIMI, タノシミ, 樂, *n.* Pleasure, happiness, delight. Syn. KIYŌ.

†TAN-REN,*-szru*, タンレン, 鍛錬, *(kitai neru)*. To exercise one's self in any art in order to be perfect, to drill. *Kenjutsz wo —*, to practice the art of fencing. Syn. REMMA, KEIKO, SHUGIYŌ.

TAN-RIYAKU, タンリヤク, 膽畧, Bold or ingenious in planning.

†TAN-RIYO, タンリヨ, 短慮, Quick tempered, hasty, irritable. — *na h'to*. Syn. TANKI.

TAN-SAI, タンサイ, 短才, *(uszi chiye)*. *n.* Little wit, small ability.

†TAN-SAKU,*-szru*, タンサク, 探索, *(sagashi motomeru)*. To search for, look for, inquire after.

TAN-SAN, タンサン, 炭酸, *n.* Carbonic acid.

TAN-SEI, タンセイ, 丹誠, *n.* Labor, exertion, pains, diligence. — *sh'te koshirayeru*, to make with much pains. — *wo nukindzru*, to exert one's self to the utmost. Syn. HONEORI, NEN-IRI.

†TAN-SEKI, タンセキ, 旦夕, *(asa ban)*. *n.* Morning and evening. Syn. CHŌ-SEKI.

†TAN-SHIN, タンシン, 丹心, *(akaki kokoro)*. *n.* A pure, or sincere heart. Syn. MAGOKORO, SEKI-SHIN.

†TAN-SO, タンソ, 炭素, *n.* Carbonic acid gas.

TAN-SOKU,*-szru*, タンソク, 歎息, To sigh, to lament, grieve. Syn. NAGEKU.

TAN-SOKU, タンソク, 短束, *n.* A fuse, or match of a fire-cracker or rocket.

TANSZ, タンス, 簞子, *n.* A chest of drawers, bureau.

TAN-TEKI-NI, タンテキニ, 短的, *adv.* At once, immediately, suddenly. Syn. KIU-NI, TACHI-MACHI-NI.

TAN-TO, タント, *adv.* coll. (this word is probably derived from the Spanish). Much, many. Syn. ŌKU. TAK'SAN.

TAN-TŌ, タントウ, 短刀, (*mijikai katana*). *n.* A short sword.

TANUKI, タヌキ, 狸, *n.* A badger.

†TAN-YA, タンヤ, 短夜, (*mijikai yo*). *n.* A short night.

TAORE,*-ru,-ta*, タフレル, 倒, *i. v.* To fall down, (of any thing erect or standing). *Iye ga* —, the house has fallen. *Ki ga* —, the tree has fallen. *Namayoi ga taorete okimasen*, the drunken man has fallen down and cannot rise.

†TAORI,*-ru,-tta*, タヲル, 手折, *t. v.* To break off, pluck off with the hand. *Ki no yeda wo* —, to break off a branch. *Hana wo* —, to pluck a flower. Syn. ORU.

TAOSARE,*-ru,-ta*, タフサレル, pass. or pot. of *Taoshi*. To be thrown down, to be defrauded.

TAOSHI,*-sz,-sh'ta*, タフス, 倒, *t. v.* To throw down any thing standing, to prostrate, to throw over; to defraud. *Ki wo kiri-taosz*, to cut down a tree. *H'to wo oshi-taosz*, to push a man over. *H'to wo* —, to defraud a person of his dues.

†TAOYAKA, タヲヤカ, 窈窕, Graceful, genteel. Syn. SHINAYAKA, ADANA.

†TAOYAME, タヲヤメ, 手弱女, *n.* A graceful woman.

TAPPITSZ, タツピツ, *n.* coll. Characters written with a pen full of ink, and in large size. — *ni kaku.*

TAPPURI, タツプリ, *adv.* coll. Much, a great deal, plenty. *Goshaku — aru*, there is a little over five feet. *Fude ni szmi wo — tszkeru*, take plenty of ink on your pen. Syn. TAK'SAN, TANTO.

TARA, タラ, 雪魚, *n.* Cod-fish.

TARA, タラ, 楤木, *n.* The name of a thorny tree.

TARA, タラ, cont. of *te araba*, used as a suffix to verbs; = When, if. *Hana ga saitara mi ni ikō*, when the flowers have bloomed I will go to see them. *Samuku nattara hi wo taita*, when it became cold I made a fire. *Sakana ga attara motte koi*, if there are any fish bring them.

†TARACHINE, タラチネ, 垂乳根 *n.* Mother. Syn. HAHA.

TARADZ, or TARANU, タラズ, 不足, neg. of *Tari*. Not enough, insufficient, wanting, deficient, unworthy, not competent. *Osoru ni* —, not worth fearing. *Toru ni* —, not worth counting.

TARAI, タラヒ, 盥, (from *te* hands, and *arai* to wash). *n.* A wash-bason, a tub.

TARAI,*-ō,-ōta*, タラフ, 足, *i. v.* To be enough, sufficient, adequate, competent, complete, qualified. *Nandemo tarai kitte oru*, have enough of every thing.

TARARI-TO, タラリト, *adv.* The manner of any thing hanging down, or sound of drops falling. *Inu ga sh'ta wo — sageru*, the dog hangs his tongue out.

TARA-TARA-TO, タラタラト, *adv.* Idem.

TARASHI,*-sz,-sh'ta*, タラス, 滴, *t. v.* To drop, let fall, or run down as a liquid, to let hang down, as a tassel. *Namida wo* —, to let tears fall. *Zashiki ye midz wo tarashite wa warui*, you should not have let the water drop in the parlor. *Hana wo* —, to let mucous run from the nose. Syn. OTOSZ.

TARASHI, タラシ, 滴, (*teki*). *n.* A drop. *Midz h'to* —, one drop of water. *Mi* —, three drops. Syn. SHIDZKU.

TARASHI-KOMI,*-mu,-nda*, タラシコム, 滴込, *t.v.* To drop, or let a liquid fall or run into anything.

TARASHIME,*-mu*, タラシム, (from the particle *to*, and *arashimu*, cause to be). To cause to be, to make. *Monjin wo sh'te shin* —, to make a servant of one who was a pupil.

TARAWANU, タラハヌ, 不足, neg. of *Tarai*. Not enough, insufficient. — *koto nashi*, deficient in nothing.

TARAYŌ, タラエフ, 多羅葉, The Holly, Ilex latifolia.

TARE, タレ, 誰, *pro.* Who, (in com. coll. *dare*). *Tare-mo-ka-mo*, every body. *Tare ka shiranu mono wa nai*, there is no body that did not know.

TARE,*-ru,-ta*, タレル, 垂, *i.v.* or *t.v.* To drop, or run down, as a liquid; to hang down, as any thing suspended; to bestow or give to an inferior. *Midz ga* —, the water drops. *Namida ga* —, the tears run down. *Kōbe wo* —, to hang down the head. *Te wo* —, to let the hands hang down. *Awaremi wo tare-tamaye*, have pity upon me. *Shōben wo* —, to urinate. *Szdare wo* —, to let the window shade hang down. Syn. SAGERU.

TARE-KASZ, タレカス, 垂糟, *n.* The sedi

ment or grounds left after straining or filtering.

Tare-kome,-ru,-ta, タレコメル, 垂籠, t.v. To shut in, or screen with hanging curtains.

Tari,-ru,-ta or -tta, タル, 足, i.v. To be enough, sufficient, adequate, competent, qualified. *Taishō to naru ni* —, competent to be a general. *Taru koto wo shiranu*, to be discontented,—never to have enough. *Ne ga tatta*, has enough sleep. *Tari-nai* or *Tari-masen*, not enough. *Niju ni taradz*, do not amount to twenty.

Tari,-ru, タル, An auxiliary verbal suffix formed from *to*, and *ari*. *Ko-taru mono*,= *ko to aru mono*, one who is a child. *Shintaru no michi*, the duty of a minister. *Mitari kitari sh'ta koto wo kaite oku*, to write down things which one sees and hears. *Netari okitari sh'te iru*, to be sometimes lying down, and sometimes sitting up,—to be up and down.

†Ta-riki, タリキ, 他力, n. The strength or power of another. — *no taszke*, salvation through the merit or power of another. (Bud.)

Ta-riyō, タリヤウ, 他領, n. The territory, or estate of another person.

Ta-riyu, タリウ, 他流, n. The style, method, practice, or system of another.

Taru, タル, 足, See *Tari*.

Taru, タル, 樽, n. A barrel, cask.

Tarui,-ki, タルイ, a. Slack, not tense. *Nawa ga* —, the rope is slack.
Syn. yurui.

†Taruhi, タルヒ, 垂冰, n. An icicle.
Syn tszrara.

Taruki, タルキ, 椽, n. The timbers of a roof, a rafter.

Taruku, タルク, adv. Slack, not tense.

Tarume,-ru,-ta, タルメル, t.v. To slacken, to loosen; to remit care or attention. *Nawa wo* —, to slacken a rope.
Syn. yurumeru.

Tarumi,-mu,-nda, タルム, coll. i.v. To be slack, loose, to become remiss. *Nawa ga tarunda*, the rope has become slack.
Syn. yurumu.

Tarushi, ニルシ, a. Slack, not tense.

Tashi,-sz,-sh'ta, タス, 足, t.v. To make up a deficiency, to complete; to add to, so as to make up the full number or quantity, to fill up. *Fusoku wo* —, to make up what is wanting. *Tegami wo kaki tasz*, to fill up an unfinished letter. *Tszgitasz*, to fill out by splicing.
Syn. soyeru.

Tashi, タシ, 足, n. The full number or quantity, complement. — *ni szru.*

Tash'ka-na, タシカナ, 慥, a. Certain, true, sure, safe. — *shōko*, certain proof. — *h'to*, a safe person.
Syn. katai, shikkari to sh'ta.

Tash'ka-ni, タシカニ, 慥, adv. Certainly, surely, truly, positively. — *uketoru*, certainly received. — *oboyete oru*, surely remember.

Tashimaye, タシマヘ, n. Boot, anything given to make the exchange equal. — *wo toru*, to take boot. — *wo yaru*, to give boot. Syn. oi, sh'ta.

†Tashimi,-mu,-nda, タシム, 嗜, t.v. To be fond of, like have pleasure in. *Sake wo* —, to be fond of *sake*.
Syn. szku, konomu.

Tashinami,-mu,-nda, タシナム, 謹, t. v. To be circumspect, cautious, careful watchful, prudent, provident. *Mi wo* —,, to conduct one's self with propriety.
Syn. tsztszshimu, yō-jin szru.

Tashinami, タシナミ, 謹, n. Circumspection, caution, prudence. — *no ī h'to*, a person of great prudence, or one who is well provided with acquirements for a future contingency.
Syn. tsztszshimi, yōjin.

Ta-sho タショ, 他所, (*yoso*), n. Another or strange place. — *no mono*, a stranger. — *ye deru*, to go to a strange place.

Ta-shō, タセウ, 多少, (*ōi, szkunai*), Many or few. — *ni kakawaradz*, no matter whether many or few.

Ta-shū, タシウ, 他宗, n. Another or different sect.

Ta-soku, タソク, 多足, That which serves to make up a deficiency, or to make a sufficiency. — *ni naru*, to make up the deficiency, or full measure. Syn. tashi.

Tassha, タッシャ, 達者, Vigorous, well, healthy, robust, strong. *Anata no otots'-san* — *de gozarimas ka*, is your father well? — *na h'to*, a sound man.
Syn. szkoyaka. jōbu.

Tassha-ni, タッシャニ, adv. Vigorously, in a strong, robust or active manner. *Michi wo* — *aruku*, to walk along actively without fatigue. — *kurash'te iru*, to live in vigorous health.

Tasshi,-sz,-sh'ta, タッス, 達, i.v. To be thoroughly versed in, proficient in, to reach, attain to. *Bumbu ni tassh'ta h'to*, a person perfect in literature and military art. *Jō-bun ni* —, to reach the ears of the Mikado. Syn. todoku, oyobu.

TASSHI-GAKI, タッシガキ, 達書, *n.* A government circular or proclamation.

TASZ, タス, See *Tashi.*

TASZKARANU, タスカラヌ, 不可助, neg. of *Taszkaru.* Cannot be saved.

TASZKARI, *-ru,-tta,* タスカル, 助, *i.v.* To be saved, preserved, delivered, helped, aided. *Inochi ga taszkatta,* his life was saved.

TASZKE, *-ru,-ta,* タスケル, 助, *t.v.* To save, deliver, preserve, rescue; to aid, assist. *H'to no inochi wo —,* to save the life of another. *Ware wo tatszke-tamaye,* save me. Syn. SZKŪ.

TASZKE, タスケ, 助, *n.* Salvation, preservation, deliverance, succor, help, aid. *Kami no — wo kōmuru,* to receive help from *Kami.* *— no hei,* succoring troops. *— bune,* a boat which saves from drowning or shipwreck.

TASZKE-AI, *-au,-atta,* タスケアフ, 助合, *i.v.* To aid, help or assist each other.

TASZKEDZ, クスケズ, 不助, neg. of *Taszkeru.* Cannot or will not save or help; without helping or saving.

TASZKERARE, *-ru,-ta,* タスケラレル, 被助, pass. or pot. of *Taszkeru.* To be saved or helped by another.

TASZKERARENU, タスケラレヌ, 不可助, neg. of *Taszkeraru.* Cannot be saved.

TASZKI, タスキ, 襷, *n.* A cord used for girding up the sleeves, while working. *— wo kakeru,* to put on the cord, &c.

TATAKAI, *-au,-atta,* タタカフ, 戰, *t. v.* (deriv. from *Tataki,* to beat, and *au* each-other). To fight, to war, to contend or engage in battle. *Teppō de —,* to fight with guns. *Mikata ga teki to —,* we engaged the enemy. Syn. KASSEN SZRU.

TATAKAI, タタカヒ, 戰, *n.* War, battle, contention. *— wo szru,* to make war. *— ni shinda,* died in battle.

TATAKAWASE, *-ru,-ta,* タタカハセル, 令戰 caust. of *Tatakai.* To cause to, or let war, to make fight.

TATAKI, *-ku,-ita,* タタク, 叩, *t. v.* To strike, beat, knock, rap, to pound, to chop fine. *To wo —,* to knock at the door. *Taiko wo —,* to beat a drum. *Kuchi wo* to talk much, babble. *Niku wo —,* to chop meat.
Syn. UTSZ, BUTSZ.

TATAKI, タタキ, A hard floor made by pounding small stones and mortar together.

TATAKI-AI, *-au,-atta,* タタキアフ, 叩合, *t.v.* To fight or beat each other.

TATAKI-KOROSHI, *-sz,-sh'ta,* タタキコロス, 打殺, *t.v.* To beat to death.

TATAMARI, *-ru,-tta,* タタマル, 疊, *i.v.* To be folded, shut. *Hon ga —,* the book is shut.

TATAMI, *-mu,-nda,* タタム, 疊, *t v.* To fold, or double up. *Kimono wo —,* to fold clothes. *Hon wo —,* to shut a book. *Iye wo —,* to take down a house and pile the timbers together, in order to put it up again in another place. *Kami wo —,* to fold paper. Syn. ORU.

TATAMI, タタミ, 疊, *n.* A floor mat. *— wo sasz,* to make a mat. *— wo shiku,* to lay down a mat.

TATAMI-BARI, タタミバリ, 疊針, *n.* A long needle used for sewing mats.

TATAMI-KAKETE, タタミカケテ, 疊掛, Repeatedly, over and over again. *— kiru,* to cut repeatedly. Syn. TSZDZKETE.

TATAMI-SASHI, タタミサシ, 疊刺, *n.* A maker of floor-mats.

TATAMI-YA, タタミヤ, 疊屋, *n.* Idem.

TATAMI-ZAN, タタミザン, 疊算, *n.* A way of divining, or settling a doubt, by casting anything on a mat, and counting the square on which it falls.

†TA-TAN, タタン, 多端, Many or numerous items of business.

TATARA, タタラ, 蹈鞴, *n.* A large bellows used in founderies, worked by treading. *— wo fumu.*

TATARI, タタリ, 祟, *n.* Curse, evil, or calamity inflicted by a Kami, evil spirit, or ghost of a dead person. *Kami no —.* Syn. BACHI.

TATARI, *-ru,-tta,* タタル, 祟, *t.v.* To inflict evil or calamity, to smite with a curse. *Kami ga h'to ni —,* the gods inflict evil upon men. Syn. BACHI WO ATERU.

TATASE, *-ru,-ta,* タタセル, 令立, caust. of *Tatsz.* To help up, cause to get up, to set free, to help off on a journey.

TATAYE, *-ru,-ta,* タタヘル, 湛, *t.v.* or *i.v.* To fill up to the brim, to be brimful, full to overflowing. *Midz wo oke ni —,* to fill the tub full of water. *Umi ni tatayetaru midz,* the water which fills the sea.
Syn. MICHIRU.

TATE, タテ, 經, *n.* The warp or threads which are extended lengthwise in a loom.

TATE, タテ, 楯, *n.* A shield. *— ni toru,* to use as a shield.

TATE, タテ, 立, *n.* The height or length, used only in measuring. 行, A row from top to bottom. *— wa roku shaku, yoko wa san jaku,* it is 6 feet high and 3 feet wide.

TATE,-*ru*,-*ta*, タテル, 立, *t.v.* To set up, to erect, raise, fix, establish. *To wo* —, to shut a door. *Koye wo* —, to raise the voice. *Iye wo* —, to erect a house. *Kado wo* —, to sharpen the corners of anything. *Nokogiri no me wo* —, to sharpen a saw. *Kokorozashi wo* —, to form a resolution. *Hara wo* —, to get angry. *Negai wo* —, to offer up a petition or request. *Chikai wo* —, to make an oath. *Shōko wo* —, to bring proof. *Na wo* —, to make famous. *Okite wo* —, to enact laws. *Kami wo* —, to let the hair grow. *Hari wo* —, to stick with a needle. *Yu wo* —, to boil. *Cha wo* —, to stir powdered tea and hot water together until it foams. *Uma wo* —, to stop a horse. *Hi wo* —, to pass the time. *Szji wo* —, to make a line or mark. *Ichi wo* —, to hold a fair, or market. *Kago wo* —, to stop or rest a sedan chair. *Shōchiu wo* —, to evaporate alcohol.

TATE, タテ, 立, *adv.* Just now. *Kumi-tate no midz*, water just drawn. *Ki-tate no k'yaku*, a guest who is just come. *Deki-tate*, just finished, or just made. *Watakushi ki-tate da kara yōsz wo shiranu*, as I have just come I don't know how it is.

TATE-BA, タテバ, 立場, *n.* Stopping places on a road for chair bearers, or horses.

TATE-GAMI, タテガミ, 鬣, *n.* A horse's mane.

TATE-GU, タテグ, 立具, *n.* Articles used in building a house, as screens, doors, &c. kept ready made for sale.

TATEGU-YA, タテグヤ, 立具屋, *n.* The shop in which the above articles are sold.

TATE-KOMORI,-*ru*,-*tta*, タテコモル, 楯籠, *i.v.* To be shut up in a fortress, or inclosed with defences, to be intrenched, to to be garrisoned. *Yama ni* —. *Shiro ni* —. Syn. RŌJŌ SZRU.

TATEMATSZRI,-*ru*,-*tta*, タテマツル, 奉, *t.v.* To give or offer to a superior: used in epistles as a very respectful adjunct to other verbs. *Miki wo kami ni* —, to offer up wine to the Kami. *Mōshi-age-tate-matszri soro*, = *mōshimas*, to say. *Zonji-tatematszri-soro*, = *zonjimas*, to think, or feel.

TATE-MONO, タテモノ, 立物, *n.* The horns or plume on a helmet, a crest.

‖TATERA, タテラ, A word only found in combination with a few words, as, *Onna*, *otoko*, *kodomo*, having the idea of not being suitable, proper or becoming, = *nagara;* as, *Onna-tatera ikusa ni detagaru*, woman as she is, or unwomanlike she wishes to go to the war. *Kodomo-tatera ōfu na koto wo iu*, being only a child he talks arrogantly.

TATE-TSZKE, タテツケ, 立著, *n.* The crack of a door or window, where the sashes meet.

TATE-TSZKETE, タテツケテ, 立著, *adv.* In quick succession, one after the other. *Sake wo sambai — nonda*, drank three glasses of wine one after the other.
Syn. TSZDZKETE.

TATE-YEBOSHI, タテヱボシ, 立帽, *n.* A kind of long hat worn by *Buke*.

TATE-YOKO, タテヨコ, *n.* Length and breadth, or lengthwise and crosswise.

TATŌGAMI, タタウガミ, 疊紙, *n.* A portfolio.

TATOI, タトヒ, 假令, *adv.* If, although, even if. — *shindemo haku-jō wa senu*, will not confess though he die for it. — *nan to ittemo yurushimasen*, let him say what he will I will not pardon. Syn. MOSHI.

TATOYE,-*ru*,-*ta*, タトヘル, 譬, *t. v.* To compare, liken for the purpose of illustration, to elucidate. *Tatoyete yuwaba*, to illustrate by saying. *Tatoyen mono mo nashi*, nothing to which it can be compared. Syn. HISZRU, KURABERU.

TATOYE, タトヘ, 譬, *n.* Comparison, illustration. — *wo motte*, to use a comparison.

TATOYEBA, タトヘバ, 譬, *adv.* For instance, by way of illustration, for example.

TATOYE-BANASHI, タトヘバナシ, 譬話, *n.* An illustration, a parable.

TATSZ, タツ, 龍, *n.* A dragon. 辰, One of the twelve signs. — *no koku*, 8 o'clock A.M. — *no hō*, E. S. E.

TATSZ, タツ, See *Tachi*.

†TATSZ-BEN, タツベン, 達辨, Eloquent, proficient in talking. — *na h'to*.
Syn. KUCHIMAME.

TATSZKI, タツキ, 手著, *n.* (from *Te*, hand, and *tszki*, to hold). Something for the hand to lay hold of, a hold, expedient, way. *Yo wo wataru* — *ga nai*, no way of making a living.
Syn. TEDATE, YOSZGA.

TATSZMI, タツミ, 辰巳, *n.* — *no hō*, S. east. — *no toki*, from 8 to 10 A.M.

TATTA, タツタ, pret. of *Tachi*

TATTA, タツタ, coll. same as *Tada. adv.* Only, merely. — *kore dake*, only so much.

TATTA-IMA, タツタイマ, Same as *Tadaima.* Now, presently.

TATTE, タツテ, *adv.* Urgently, importunately, right or wrong. — *negau*, urgently to request. Syn. ZEHI, OSHITE.

TATTE, タッテ, pp. of *Tachi*.

TATTŌ, タットウ, *adv*. Same as *Tattoku*.

TATTOBI,–*bu*,–*nda*, タットブ, 尊, *t.v.* To honor, respect, reverence, esteem, to value, prize. *Kami wo* —, to reverence the gods. *Kimi wo* —, to honor a lord. *Kin yori tattobu mono nashi*, there is nothing more prized than gold.
Syn. WIYAMAU, OMONDZRU.

TATTOI,–KI,–SHI, タットイ, 貴, *a*. Exalted, honorable, noble; precious, valuable, esteemed, excellent. *Kami yori tattoki mono wa nai*, there is nothing more exalted than the Kami. Syn. OMOI.

TATTOKU, タットク, 貴, *adv*. idem.

TATTOMARE,–*ru*,–*ta*, タットマレル, 被貴, pass. of *Tattomu*. To be honored, or esteemed.

TATTOMI,–*mu*,–*nda*, タットム, Same as *Tattobi*.

TATTOSA, タットサ, *n*. Honorableness, eminence, preciousness.

TAWAI, タワイ, coll. always with a negative; as, *Tawai mo nai*. Stupid, dull, senseless, powerless. — *naku nete-iru*, to be in a heavy sleep. *Sake ni yotte — ga nai*, to be drunk and stupid. *Kusatta ito wa — ga nai*, rotten thread has no strength.

TAWAKE, タワケ, 呆, *n*. A dunce, fool, (used in scolding). — *me*, or — *mono*, idem. *ō-dawake*, a great dunce.
Syn. BAKA, AHŌ.

TAWAKE,–*ru*,–*ta*, タワケル, 奸, *i. v.* To commit fornication; to be silly, foolish. *Onna ni* —. *Tawaketa koto wo iu*, to talk foolishness. Syn. INRAN SZRU.

TAWA-KOTO, タワコト, 戯言, *n*. Foolishness, nonsense, (used in scolding). — *wo iu na*.

TAWAME,–*ru*,–*ta*, タワメル, 撓, *t. v.* To bend, to curve. *Yeda wo tawamete mi wo toru*, to bend the limb of a tree and pluck the fruit. Syn. KAGAMERU, MAGERU.

TAWAMI,–*mu*,–*nda*, タワム, 撓, *i.v.* To bend, to sag. *Ni ga omokute bō ga tawanda*, the load being heavy the pole bends.
Syn. SHINAYERU, MAGARU.

TAWAMURE,–*ru*,–*ta*, タワムレル, 戯, *i.v.* To play, sport, to frolic, make merry, romp, make fun, joke, dally. *Chō hana ni* —, the butterfly plays with the flowers.
Syn. JŌDAN SZRU.

TAWARA, タハラ, 俵, *n*. A bag made of straw, for holding grain, &c.

†TAWAREME, タワレメ, 遊女, *n*. A prostitute.

TAWAYAKA, タワヤカ, Bending, flexible.

TAYASHI,–*sz*–,*sh'ta*, タヤス, 令絶, *t.v.* To cause to cease, to cut off, to put an end to, exterminate. *Shison wo* —, to cut off the posterity. *Tayasadz*, without ceasing.

TAYASHI,–KI,–SHI, タヤズイ, 容易, *a*. Easy, not difficult. — *koto*, an easy thing.

TAYASZKU, タヤスク, *adv*. idem. — *dekiru*, easily done.

TAYE,–*ru*,–*ta*, タエル, 絶, *i. v.* To come to an end, cease, not to continue, to fail, to be extinct, exhausted, cut off. *Chi-szji ga* —, family line is extinct. *Kawa no midz ga* —, the water of the river has failed. *Inochi ga* —, life is extinct. *Naka ga* —, friendship has ceased.
Syn. KIRERU, DANZETSZ SZRU.

TAYE,–*ru*,–*ta*, タヘル, 堪, *i.v.* To bear, endure, suffer, support, sustain; to hold out. *Atszsa ni* —, to bear heat. *Tayegatai*, hard to bear. *Taye-kaneru*, idem. *Owari made* —, to hold out to the end.
Syn. KORAYERU, SHINOBU.

TAYEDZ, タエズ, 不絶, neg. of *Taye*. Unending, unceasing, unfailing, everlasting, perpetual.

TAYEDZ, タヘズ, 不堪, neg. of *Taye*. Unbearable, insufferable, intolerable, insupportable.

TAYE-HATE,–*ru*,–*ta*, タエハテル, 絶果, *i. v.* To be extinct, cut off, ended.

TAYE-IRI,–*ru*,–*tta*, タエイル, 絶入, *i. v.* To die. *Taye-iru hodo no kurushimi*, suffering enough to take one's life.
Syd. SHINURU.

TAYEMA, タエマ, 絶間, *n*. Interruption, interval of space or time. *Kumo no — kara tszki ga sasz*. the moon shines from between the clouds. Syn. SZKIMA, AIDA.

†TAYENARU, タヘナル, 妙, *a*. Marvelous, most wonderful, most excellent, indescribable. — *szgata*, exceedingly beautiful.
Syn. MIYŌ-NARU.

TAYE-SHINOBI,–*bu*,–*nda*, タヘシノブ, 堪忍, *t. v.* To bear patiently.

TA-YŌ, タヨウ, 多用, Much business, very busy. — *de ikaremasen*, so busy I cannot go.

TA-YOKU, タヨク, 多慾, Covetous, avaricious; lewd, sensual.

TAYORI, –*ru*,–*tta*, タヨル, 便, *t.v.* To have one's hope or expectation fixed on; to look to for aid, or help; to lean upon for support, to depend on, rely on, to trust in, to befriend. *Tayoru tokoro mo nai*, none to look to for assistance or to depend on. *Tayotte kita h'to ga shinda*, the person I looked to for aid when I came is dead. Syn. TANOMU.

TAYORI, タヨリ, 便, *n.* Support, reliance, dependence, trust, any thing to look to, or lean upon for help; word, tidings news; information. *Kane wo — ni szru*, to trust in wealth. *— no nai mono*, a person who has none to look to for help, or support. *Nani wo — ni kurashimas*, what does he depend on for a living? *Yedo kara — ga nai*, there is no word from *Yedo*. *H'to no kotoba wo — ni szru*, fo rely upon the word of another. *— ni naranu muszko*, a son to whom one cannot look for help.
Syn. TANOMI, OTODZRE, BINGI.

TAYOWAI,-KI,-SHI, タヨワイ, 手弱, *a.* Weak, feeble.

TAYOWAKU, タヨワク, *adv.* idem.

†TAYUME,-*ru*,-*ta*, タユメル, 弛, *t. v.* To slacken, relax, unbend.
Syn. YURUMERU.

TAYUMI,-*mu*,-*nda*, タユム, 弛, *i. v.* To be slack, to relax, or remit exertion, to be come careless, or inattentive. *Ki ga —*, to become careless. *Yūki ga —*, to relax in ardor, or courage. Syn YURUMU.

†TAYURU, タユル, Same as *Tayeru*.

TAYUTAI,-*au*,-*atta*, タユタフ, *i. v.* To be tossed about on the waves; to hesitate, to waver in doubt, to falter. *Fune ga nami ni —*, the ship is tossed about on the waves. *Kokoro ga —*, his mind wavers.
Syn. TADAYŌ, TAMERŌ.

TA-ZAI, タザイ, 多罪, (*ōki tszmi*). *n.* Many crimes, or sins.

TA-ZEI, タゼイ, 多勢, (*ōzei*). *n.* A large army, or crowd of men.

TAZOKARE, タゾカレ, 黄昏, *n.* Dusk, twilight. *— ni kayetta*, returned in the dusk of the evening. Syn. HAKUBO.

TE, テ, 手, *n.* The hand, the arm: (fig). a body or division of troops; a path, or road; a tune; skill, plan, tactics, art, device; manner of performing, or doing; style of penmanship; handle; a person. *Migino —*, right hand. *Hidari no —*, left hand. *Tszru no —*, the tendril of a vine. *Kago no —*, the handle of a basket. *Midz no —*, water-courses. *Yama no —*, roads in a mountain. *Hi no —*, flames of a fire. *Saki-te*, the van, or front division of an army. *F'ta te ni wakaru*, to divide into two divisions. *Kai-te* the buyer. *Uri-te*, the seller. *— no kīta h'to*, a skilful person, a good hand. *— no nagai h'to*, a thief, a long fingered fellow. *— wo wakeru*, to divide into companies. *— wo karu*, to borrow a hand to help. *— wo kash'te kudasare*, lend us a hand. *— wo dasz*, to take hold, to help to do. *— wo tszganeru*, to fold the arms, to give up effort. *— wo kumu*, or *— wo komanuku*, idem. *— wo szru*, or *— wo momu*, to rub the hands. *— wo hiku*, to lead by the hand; to withdraw the hand, or stop doing. *— wo kudasz*, to reach down the hand, to condescend to do. *— wo ō*, to be wounded. *— wo kiru*, to break off connection or relationship. *— wo tszkeru*, to apply the hand to, to touch, to set a tune to words. *— wo utsz*, to clap the hands, to strike a bargain. *— wo tataku*, idem. *— wo awaseru*, to join the hands together, as in prayer. *— wo toru*, to take or hold the hand. *— wo tszkusz*, to exhaust one's skill or art. *— wo kayeru*, to change the tactics or plan. *— wo komeru*, to do with great care, or attention. *— wo ushinau*, to fail in one's plan, miss one's aim. *— wo tszku*, to place the hand on the floor, in a polite posture, like a toad. *— ni sawaru*, to feel with the hand. *— ni fureru*, idem. *— ga tatsz*, skilful, dexterous. *— ga agaru*, to improve in penmanship. *— ga fusagaru*, to have one's hands full, busy. *Kondo watakushi no — da*, it is now my hand, or turn at a game. *Damasz ni — nashi*, (prov). no art against deception. *— ni amaru*, too much for the hands, more than one is able to do. *Sono — wa kuwanu*, that device won't do.

TE, テ, 而, A suffix to the root of verbs, forming the *pp.* or *ppr.* as, *Mite*, having seen or by seeing. *Kite*, having heard, or by hearing. *Utte*, sold, or by selling.

TE, テ, coll. *n.* Way, mode, manner. *Kono te ni itashimashō*, I will do it in this way.
Syn. TŌRI.

TEAI, テアヒ, 徒, *plural noun.* Persons, fellows. *Ano teai*, those persons.
Syn. TOMOGARA.

TE-AKI, テアキ, 手明, Nothing to do, hands unoccupied. *— no nai*, no leisure, hands full.

TE-ARAI,-KI,-KU,-SHI, テアライ, 手荒, Rough, rude, violent in doing, coarse in manner.

TE-ASOBI, テアソビ, *n.* A toy.
Syn. OMOCHA.

TE-ATARI, テアタリ, 手當, *n.* The feel, or state of any thing as perceived by the touch; any thing within one's reach, or near at hand. *— no yoi kinu*, silk pleasant to the touch. *— shidai ni totte nageru*, seizing whatever was within reach he flung it. Syn. TEZAWARI.

TE-ATE, テアテ, 手當, *n.* Preparation, outfit, provision, supplies, equipment.

Ikusa no — wo szru, to make preparations for a war. *Fune no — wo szru*, to equip a ship. *Tabi no — wo szru*, to make preparation for a journey. Syn. SHITAKU, YŌI.

TE-ATSZI,-KI,-KU,-SHI, テアツイ, 手厚, Liberal, generous, magnificent, well.

TE-AWASE, テアハセ, 手合, *n.* First encounter, or meeting of hostile armies.

TE-AYAMACHI, テアヤマチ, 手過, *n.* A mistake or blunder occasioned by the hands.

TE-BAKO, テバコ, 手箱, *n.* A small box.

TE-BANA, テバナ, 手鼻, Hand and nose, used only in the phrase. — *wo kamu*, to blow the nose with the fingers.

TE-BANASHI,-*sz*,-*sh'ta*, テバナス, 手放, *t.v.* To let go the hold, remove the hands, let go. *Ko wo tebanash'te yoso ye yaru*, to let a child go and send him amongst strangers.

TE-BARI,-*ru*,-*tta*, テバル, 手張, *i.v.* To be more than one can attend to, too much for one to do. *Ichi nichi no shigoto ni wa tebaru*, too much for one to do in a day.

TE-BASH'KOI,-KI,-KU, テバシコイ, Ready and expert with the hands, dexterous, adroit.

TE-BATAKI, テバタキ, 手拍, *n.* Clapping the hands, (in mercantile lang.) just clearing one's expenses. — *wo szru*, to clap the hands; to sell any thing for just enough to clear one's expenses.

TE-BAYAI,-KI,-KU,-SHI, テバヤイ, 手早, Expert with the hands, dexterous, adroit, nimble, quick.

TE-BI, テビ, 手火, *n.* A torch-light, flambeau.

TE-BIKI, テビキ, 手引, *n.* One who leads another by the hand to show the way, a guide, an introduction. — *wo szru*. — *ga nai*. Syn. ANNAI, NAKADACHI.

TE-BIROI,-KI,-KU,-SHI, テビロイ, 手廣, Wide, extensive, widely extended. *Tebiroku akinai wo szru*, to do an extensive business.

TE-BIYŌSHI, テビヤウシ, 手拍子, *n.* Beating with the hands, in music; drumming with the fingers. — *wo toru*. — *wo utsz.*

TE-BŌ, テバウ, 手棒, *n.* A person who has lost his hand.

TE-BŌKI, テボウキ, 手箒, *n.* A small broom.

TE-BUKURO, テブクロ, 手袋, *n.* A glove.

TE-BURI, テブリ, 手振, *n.* Empty handed, behavior, manner, customs. — *de kuru*, to come empty handed. *Miyako no — narau.* — *ga yoi.* Syn. KARATE, FŪZOKU.

TE-CHIGAI, テチガイ, 手違, *n.* A mistake, blunder, error. Syn. MACHIGAI.

TE-CHŌ, テチヤウ, 手帳, *n.* A small account or note book.

TE-DAI, テダイ, 手代, *n.* An agent, factor, a substitute.

TEDARI, テダリ, 手垂, *n.* A skilful archer, good bowman.

TEDATE, テダテ, 術, *n.* Plan, device, stratagem, scheme, trick, way. — *wo szru*, to devise a plan.
Syn. KUFŪ, HAKARIGOTO, JUTSZ.

TEDŌ, テドホ, 手遠, Distant, long way. — *na tokoro*, a distant place.

TEDZKAMI, テヅカミ, 手掴, *n.* Seizing hold of, taking with the hand. *Meshi wo — ni sh'te kū*, to eat with the fingers.

TE-DZKARA, テヅカラ, 手自, *adv.* With one's own hand. — *koshirayeta*, made it myself.

TE-DZKAYE, テヅカヘ, 手支, *n.* Hands full of business, busy. — *ni naru*, to be busy. Syn. SASHITSZKAYE.

TE-DZKURI, テヅクリ, 手作, *n.* Any thing made by one's self, not by a regular manufacturer, home-made. — *no pan*, home made bread. — *no nuno*, home-made cloth.

TE-DZMA, テヅマ, 手妻, *n.* Sleight of hand tricks, legerdemain.
Syn. TEJINA, SHINADAMA.

TE-DZMASHI, テヅマシ, 手妻師, *n.* A juggler.

TE-DZME, テヅメ, 手詰, *n.* Extremity, extremely pressing or urgent. — *no saisoku*, the last demand for payment, when grace will no longer be extended.

TE-DZMORI, テヅモリ, 手量, *n.* Measuring with the hands. — *wo szru*, to measure with the hand.

TE-DZRU, テヅル, 手蔓, *n.* A go-between, or a series of mutual acquaintances serving to introduce two persons who are strangers.

TE-DZSAMI, テヅサミ, 隨手, *n.* Doing any thing merely to relieve tedium, as a pastime, or diversion. — *ni ye wo kaku*, to draw pictures of any thing to relieve tedium.

TE-DZYOI,-KI,-KU,-SHI, テヅヨイ, 手强, Firm, resolute, unyielding, decided.

TEEBA, テヘバ, 云者, (cont of *to iyeba*). A particle serving to give emphasis to what is said, = I say, as, *Nai-teeba*, I say there is not. *Aru-teeba*, there are, I tell you.

TE-FUDA, テフダ, 手札, *n.* A visiting card. NAFUDA.

TE-GAI, テガイ, 手飼, Fed by the hand, reared by one's self, tame, domestic, used only of animals. *Tegai no inu*, a dog kept by one's self. *Neko wa — no tora*, a cat is a domestic tiger.

TE-GAKARI, テガカリ, 手掛, *n.* A hold, or any thing to lay the hand on; a clew, trace.

TEGAMI, テガミ, 手紙, *n.* A letter, epistle. — *wo kaku*, to write a letter. — *wo yaru*, to send a letter. — *ga kita*, a letter has come. Syn. JŌ, SHOKAN, FUMI.

TE-GANE, テガネ, 手鎖, *n.* Manacle, handcuff.

TEGARA, テガラ, 手柄, *n.* A daring, bold, or heroic deed. — *wo szru*, to do a heroic deed. — *na*, heroic, daring, venturesome. Syn. KŌMIYŌ.

TE-GARUI,-KI,-KU,-SHI, テガルイ, 手輕, Easy to do, without difficulty. *Tegaruku dekita*, easily done. Syn. TAYASZI.

TE-GASA, テガサ, 手傘, *n.* A parasol, sunshade.

TE-GASE, テガセ, 手杻, *n.* Handcuffs.

TE-GATA, テガタ, 手形, *n.* A certificate, receipt, voucher, passport, a ticket, banknote.

TE-GATAI,-KI,-KU,-SHI, テガタイ, 手堅, Firm, strong, durable, safe, secure.

TE-GINE, テギネ, 手杵, *n.* A pestle, or small pounder.

TE-GIRE, テギレ, 手切, *n.* Cut off, broken off, dissolved, (as relationship). — *ni naru*.

TE-GIREI, テギレイ, 手綺麗, Doing in a clean, neat way. — *ni szru*.

TE-GIWA, テギハ, 手際, *n.* Workmanship, skill in doing or making. *Kono yedz wa — ga warui*, this picture is badly done. — *no yoi daiku*, a skilful carpenter.

TE-GOME, or TEGOMI, テゴメ, 手籠, *n.* Taking by force, or against the will of another. *Kane wo — ni toru*, taking money from another by force.

TE-GORO, テゴロ, 手頃, *n.* Suited to the size or strength of the hand, handy, convenient in size. — *na tszye*, a cane suiting the hand. — *na bō*, a club just fitting the hand.

TE-GOTAYE, テゴタヘ, 手答, *n.* The sensation felt in the hand, when striking against something with anything held in it. — *ga szru*.

TE-GOWAI, テゴハイ, 手剛, Rough, rude, violent, or coarse in manner; exact, strict.

TE-GUMI, テグミ, 手組, *n.* Folding the arms; a plan, scheme, trick. — *wo szru*, to fold the arms. — *ga hadzreta*, my scheme has failed. Syn. MOKUROMI.

TE-GURI, テグリ, 手操, *n.* Adjusting one's business so as to get leisure, or time for something else. — *wo sh'te yuku*. Syn. KURIAWASE.

TEGURUMA, テグルマ, 輦, *n.* A kind of sedan, used only by the Tenshi's family.

TEGUSZ, テグス, 天蠶絲, *n.* A kind of fishing line.

TE-HADZ, テハヅ, 手筈, *n.* Plan, arrangement, scheme, project. — *ga hadzreru*.

TE-HAJIME, テハジメ, 手始, *n.* The commencement, or first part of any work.

TE-HIDOI,-KI,-KU,-SHI, テヒドイ, Severe, violent, cruel.

TE-HODOKI, テホドキ, 手解, *n.* The commencement or beginning of any work.

TE-HON, テホン, 手本, *n.* A copy for imitation, a sample, pattern, model, specimen, example. *H'to no — ni naru*, to be an example to others. Syn. MIHON, KIKAN.

TEI, テイ, 亭, *n.* A roof supported by pillars, a pavilion, shed, summer house. Syn. CHIN.

TEI, テイ, 體, *n.* Form, appearance, looks, fashion, manner. — *wo kayeru*, to change one's appearance. *H'yakushō no — ni naru*, to look like a farmer. Syn. KATACHI, SZGATA.

†TEI, テイ, 帝, *n.* The Mikado.

TEI-HATSZ,-*szru*, テイハツ, 剃髮, To shave the head, to become a Bonze. Syn. RAK'SHOKU.

†TEI-HEI, テイヘイ, 逞兵, *n.* A daring soldier.

†TEI-JO, テイヂヨ, 貞女, *n.* A virtuous woman.

†TEI-JŌ,-*szru*, テイジヤウ, 呈上, To give a present, to present. Syn. SHINJŌ.

TEIKA-KADZRA, テイカカヅラ, 絡石, *n.* The name of a vine, Malouetia Asiatica.

TEI-NEI, テイネイ, 丁寧, Neat, nice, exact, scrupulous, careful, particular, delicate, genteel, courteous, polite. — *na*, adj. — *ni*, adv. — *ni oshiyeru*, to teach carefully. — *ni mono wo tsztszmu*, to wrap up any thing neatly. Syn. INGIN, MEMMITSZ NENGORO.

TE-IPPAI, テイツパイ, 手一盃, *n.* A handful. *Akinai wo — ni szru*, to trade with one's own capital;—without a partner; also, to invest one's whole property in business.

TE-IRADZ, テイラズ, 手不入, New, not yet used. — *no mono*, a thing that has not yet been used.

TE-IRE, テイレ, 手入, *n.* Repairing, mending. — *wo szru*, to mend, repair. Syn. NAOSZ.

†TEI-SETSZ, テイセツ, 貞節, *n.* Female virtue. — *wo mamoru.*

†TEI-SHIN, テイシン, 貞心, Virtuous. — *na onna.*

TEI-SHI, *-sz* or *-szru,-sh'ta*, テイスル, 呈, *t.v.* To present to a superior, to petition, memorialize.
Syn. AGERU.

TEI-SHU, テイシユ, 亭主, *n.* The master of a house, head of a family, a husband.
Syn. ARUJI, OTTO.

TE-ITA, テイタ, 手版, *n.* A wooden tablet carried by a *Kuge*, same as *Shaku.*

TE-ITAI,-KI,-KU,-SHI,-Ō, テイタイ, 手痛, Severe, vehement, violent, until the hand is tired. *Teitaku semeru*, to torture severely. — *tatakau*, to fight hard.

†TEI-TAI, テイタイ, 停滯, *n.* Indigestion, dyspepsia. — *szru*, to have indigestion.

†TEI-TARAKU, テイタラク, 爲體, *n.* The condition, manner, circumstances.
Syn. ARISAMA.

†TEITO, テイト, 帝都, *n.* The capital, or residence of the Emperor. Syn. MIYAKO.

†TEI-TŌ, テイトウ, 低頭, *(kashira wo tareru).* Bowing the head low in saluting. — *szru.*

†TEI-ZEN, テイゼン, 庭前, *n.* A flower garden. Syn. SONO.

TE-JIKA, テヂカ, 手近, Near at hand, within reach. — *na tokoro*, a place near at at hand. — *no mono*, any thing within reach. Syn. TE-MOTO.

TE-JINA, テジナ, 手品, *n.* Motions, or gestures of the hand, movement of the hands in dancing.

TE-JŌ, テジヤウ, 手鎖, *n.* Handcuffs, manacles. Syn. TEGASE.

TE-JŌBU, テヂヤウブ, 手丈夫, Strongly made, durable, firm.

TE-JUN, テジユン, 手順, *n.* The order, or method of doing. *Shigoto no — ga warui*, the work is not done in the proper order.

TE-KADZ, テカズ, 手數, *n.* Number of hands or workmen, much labor, frequent services. — *ga ōi kara hayaku dekiru*, as there are many hands at work it will soon be done. — *ga kakaru*, to require much labor. *Iro-iro o — wo kakemash'ta*, I have troubled you many times, many thanks.

TEKAKE, テカケ, 妾, *n.* A concubine.
Syn. MEKAKE.

TEKAKI, テカキ, 手書, *n.* A good penman.

TEKI, テキ, 敵, *n.* The enemy, an adversary, foe, antagonist.
Syn. KATAKI, AITE.

TE-KIBISHII,-KI,-KU, テキビシイ, 手嚴, Severe, rigorous, strict.

†TEKI-CHI, テキチ, 敵地, The enemy's country, a hostile country.

TEKI-CHIU, *-szru*, テキチウ, 的中, *(mato ni ataru)*, To hit the mark, to suit precisely, to agree, accord. *Ano h'to no itta koto ga — sh'ta*, it has turned out just as he said.

TEKI-HAKI, テキハキ, *adv.* Soon, quickly. — *to tenki ni naranu*, it will not clear off very soon. Syn. HAYAKU.

†TEKI-I, テキイ, 適意, *(kokoro makase.)* According to one's will or pleasure. — *ni se yo*, do just as you please, use your own pleasure. — *ni nomu*, drink as much as you please.

TE-KIKI, テキキ, 手利, *n.* Smart, active, or expert in doing anything.

TEKI-MEN, テキメン, 覿面, *adv.* Quick and manifest, immediate and obvious, in a striking manner. — *ni kuszri ga kīta*, the effects of the medicine were quickly manifest. — *ni bachi ga atatta*, he was quickly smitten with unmistakable punishment.
Syn. ICHI-JIRUSHI, MEIHAKU, FUMMIYŌ.

TE-KIN, テキン, 手金, *n.* Earnest money, advance money.

TEKI-SHI, *-sz* or *-szru,-sh'ta*, テキスル, 敵, *t.v.* To oppose, resist, to act against, as an enemy, antagonist, or competitor. *Tekiszru mono ga nai*, there was no one that could oppose him. *H'to ni teki szru*, to oppose a person. Syn. AITE NI NARU.

TEKITAI, *-au,-atta*, テキタフ, 敵對, *t.v.* To be hostile, inimical, unfriendly, to meet as an enemy, or antagonist; to oppose. *Tekitō kokoro nashi*, have no desire to oppose. Syn. AITEDORU.

†TEKI-TŌ, テキタウ, 的當, *(mato ni ataru.)* Suitable, proper, just, adequate. — *no homo kata*, praise just suitable to one's merit. — *sh'taru reigi*, suitable ceremonies. Syn. SŌ-Ō, CHŌDO YOI.

TEKI-YAKU, テキヤク, 敵藥, *n.* An incompatible medicine.

TEKKIU, テツキウ, 鐵橋, *n.* A gridiron.
Syn. ABURIKO.

TEKKŌ, テツカフ, 手甲, *n.* A kind of long mitten covering only the back of the hand and arm.

TEKKOKU, テキコク, 敵國, (*teki no kuni.*) *n.* The enemy's country.

TEKO, テコ, 木梃, *n.* A lever.

TE-KUBARI, テクバリ, 手配, *n.* Distribution of troops, or hands for any kind of work, division of labor. — *wo szru.* Syn. TEWAKE.

TE-KUBI, テクビ, 手首, *n.* The wrist.

TE-KUDA, テクダ, 手管, *n.* Artifice, deception, trick. — *ni kakaru,* to be the subject of a deception.

TE-KUSE, テクセ, 手癖, *n.* Habit, or style of penmanship; also, a habit of pilfering.

TEMA, テマ, 手間, (*te no ima*), *n.* The time spent in work or doing anything. *Tanto — no iru shigoto,* a work which will take a long time to do. *Mo szkoshi — ga iru,* it will take a little more time yet. — *wo ireru,* to spend a long time in doing. — *no kakaru shigoto,* work requiring time to do. Syn. HIMA.

TEMA-CHIN, テマチン, 手間賃, *n.* The price of labor, wages of workmen, reckoned according to the time spent on the work.
Syn. SAKURIYŌ.

TEMA-DAI, テマダイ, 手間代, Idem.

TEMA-DORI,*-ru,-tta*, テマドル, 手間取, *i.v.* To spend or take time, to be tardy, slow, to delay, procrastinate.
Syn. HIMADORU.

TE-MAKURA, テマクラ, 手枕, *n.* The arm used as a pillow. — *wo sh'te neru,* to sleep with the head on the arm.

TE-MANE, テマ子, 手眞似, *n.* Gesture, or motions of the hands. — *wo sh'te hanashi wo szru,* to talk and gesticulate.

TE-MANEKI, テマ子キ, 手招, *n.* Beckoning with the hand.

TE-MARI, テマリ, 手毬, *n.* A small ball, hand-ball. — *wo tszku,* to strike a ball.

TEMARI-BANA, テマリバナ, 繡球花, *n.* Hoya carnosa.

TEMA-TORI, テマトリ, 手間取, *n.* An assistant to a workman, an under workman.
Syn. YATOIDO, HIYŌ.

TE-MAWARI, テマハリ, 手廻, *n.* Any place near one's hand, close by; also, one's business in respect to paying out or taking in money; or the money passing through one's hand.

TE-MAWASHI, テマハシ, 手廻, *n.* Doing this and that in anticipation, or in providing for something to come. *Shō-g'watsz no — wo szru,* to get ready, by doing this and that, for the new year's holidays.

TE-MAYE, テマヘ, 手前, *pro.* I, (in speaking humbly of one's self); or you, (in speaking contemptuously to another); this side. *Temaye domo,* we or you, (plur.) *Kawa no —,* this side of the river. *H'to no — ga hadzkashii,* ashamed in the presence of others. *Temaye-gatte,* selfish, seeking mainly one's own pleasure.
Syn. WARE, OMAYE, KOCHI.

†TEMBATSZ, テンバツ, 天罰, *n.* The punishment of heaven.

TEMBIN, テンビン, 天秤, *n.* Scales for weighing, a balance. — *ni kaketa mekata wo hakaru,* to place in the scales and weigh.

TEMBIN-BŌ, テンビンボウ, 擔梁, *n.* The pole used by coolies for carrying burdens across the shoulder.

TEMBU, テンブ, 天部, *n.* The general name for the 33 Buddhist divinities.

†TEMBUTSZ, テンブツ, 典物, *n.* Anything pawned at a pawnbroker's shop, a pledge. — *szru,* to pawn. — *wo ukeru,* to redeem anything pawned. Syn. SHICHI-GUSA.

TE-MIJIKA, テミジカ, 手短, Short, brief, concise. — *na oshiye,* short lessons, or instructions easily comprehended. — *ni mono wo iu,* to tell anything in a few words. — *ni szru,* to do up expeditiously.
Syn. KAMBEN-NI.

TEMMA, テンマ, 天魔, *n.* A devil, demon.

TEMMA, テンマ, 天麻, *n.* The name of a plant, the root of which is used as a medicine.

TEMMA, テンマ, 哨船, *n.* A small boat, used for plying between a ship and the land.

TEMMA, テンマ, 傳馬, *n.* The relay of pack-horses kept at a post-station.

TEMMAKU, テンマク, 天幕, *n.* Curtains hanging around a room from the ceiling, in theatres, temples, &c.

TEMMEI, テンメイ, 天命, *n.* Heaven, the will or decree of heaven, fate, providence, destiny.

TEMMOKU, テンモク, 天目, *n.* A large tea cup.

TEMMON, テンモン, 天文, *n.* Astronomy, astrology.

TEMMON-DAI, テンモンダイ, 天文臺, *n.* An observatory.

TEMMON-DŌ, テンモンドウ, 天門冬, *n.* Asparagus.

TEMMON-SHA, テンモンシヤ, 天文者, *n.* An astrologer, astronomer.

TE-MODORI, テモドリ, 手戻, *n.* A relapse, (as in disease), turning back in order to do over again. — *ga sh'ta.*

TE-MOTO, テモト, 手許, Near, at hand, convenient, within reach. *Ima — ni kane ga nai,* I have no money by me just now. — *ni aru mono wo totte nageru,* threw anything he could lay his hands on.

TE-MOTSZRE, テモツレ, 手纒, *n.* Entanglement, perplexity; difficult and tedious.

†TEMPEN, テンペン, 天變, *n.* A sign in the heavens. — *ga arawareru,* a sign appeared in the heavens.

TEMPO, テンポ, 天保, *n.* The name of a brass coin, of which 16 and a small fraction make an Ichibu.

†TEM-PŌ,–*szru,* テンパウ, 轉方, *n.* To change a prescription, or mode of treatment.

TEMPURA, テンプラ, 天麩羅, *n.* Fish dipped in batter and fried, fish-cutlets.

TE-MUKAI, テムカイ, 手向, *n.* Opposition, resistance. — *wo szru.*

TEN, テン, 天, *(ame). n.* The sky, the heavens; heaven, the supreme power, providence, or nature. — *ye noboru,* to ascend to heaven. — *kara ochiru,* to fall from heaven. — *wo ogamu,* to worship heaven. Syn. SORA.

TEN, テン, 點, *n.* A dot, point. — *wo utsz,* to make a dot.

TEN, テン, 貂, *n.* A marten. — *no kawa,* the skin of a marten.

TENAGAZARU, テナガザル, 猿猴, *n.* A long-armed ape.

TE-NAMI, テナミ, 手波, *n.* Hand, or skill in fencing. — *no hodo wo miyo,* let us see your skill.

TE-NARAI, テナライ, 猿習, *n.* Learning to write, penmanship. — *wo szru,* to practice penmanship, to learn to write.

TENARASHI,–*sz,*–*sh'ta,* テナラス, 令手馴, *t. v.* To break in, to accustom to one's use, to train. *Uma wo —,* to break in a horse.

TENARE,–*ru,*–*ta,* テナレル, 手馴, *i.v.* To be accustomed to the use of anything, to be in the habit of using, used to. *Watakushi no tenareta ōgi,* a fan I am in the habit of using.

TEN-CHI, テンチ, 天地, *(ame tszchi). n.* Heaven and earth.

†TEN-CHIU, テンチウ, 天誅, *n.* The punishment of heaven. — *wo kōmuru.*

†TEN-CHŌ, テンテウ, 天朝, *n.* The court of the Mikado; the country of Japan.

†TEN-CHŌ, テンチヤウ, 天聽, *(tenshi no kiku koto). n.* The hearing of the Mikado. — *ni tasszru.*

TEN-DAI-SHŪ, テンダイシウ, 天台宗, *n.* The name of a sect of Buddhists.

TEN-DEN, テンデン, *adv.* Each one, every one, all. Syn. ONO-ONO, MEI-MEI, MEN-MEN.

†TEN-DŌ, テンダウ, 天堂, *n.* Paradise, heaven, a Budd. word. — *ni umareru,* to enter paradise. Syn. GOKURAKU, JŌDO.

TEN-DŌ, テンダウ, 天道, *(shizen no michi). n.* The laws or ordinances of heaven, laws of nature. — *ni somuku,* to break the laws of nature. Syn. DŌRI.

†TEN-DŌ, テンダウ, 顛倒, *(kutszgayeri taoru).* Turning upside down. *Ki ga — szru,* to be surprised and bewildered.

†TEN-DOKU, テンドク, 轉讀, The manner in which the Buddhist priests recite the sacred books, reading a little here and there, and skipping over many leaves. — *szru,* to recite the sacred books in the above manner.

TENDZRU, テンズル, 轉, See *Tenji.*

TEN-GA, テンガ, 天河, *(ame no kawa). n.* The milky-way.

†TEN-GAI, テンガイ, 天涯, *n.* The horizon, the utmost verge of the heavens.

TENGAI, テンガイ, 天蓋, *n.* A kind of canopy or dome of wood, carried over the coffin at funerals.

TEN-GAN, テンガン, 天顔, *n.* The face of the Mikado.

TEN-GAN-KIYŌ, テンガンキヤウ, 天眼鏡, *n.* A mirror which magnifies the face.

TENGŌ, テンガウ, *n.* Playing with anything in the hands. — *szru.*

TEN-GU, テング, 天狗, *(ten no inu). n.* An imaginary being supposed to inhabit mountains and unfrequented places, represented in pictures with a long nose, wings, and two claws on each foot and hand; an elf, or hobgoblin, devil. — *ni naru,* to become proud or vain.

TENGUJŌ, テングジヤウ, 天郡上, *n.* A kind of fine thin paper.

TE-NI-WO-HA, テニヲハ, *n.* The particles used by the Japanese to show the relations of words to each others; the rules of grammar. *Kono bun wa — ga totonowanu,* this composition does not accord with the rules of grammar.

†TENJI,–*ru,* or–*dzru,*–*ta,* テンズル, 轉, *t.v.* To change, to vary, alter. *Hō wo —,* to change a prescription, mode of treatment, or of making anything. *Ikari wo*

—, to change from anger to merriment. *Ki wo* —, to change the spirits, (as by a change of place.) Syn. KAYERU.

TENJIKU, テンヂク, 天竺, *n.* India.

TENJO, テンヂヨ, 天女, *n.* Same as *Tennin.*

TENJŌ, テンジヤウ, 天井, *n.* The ceiling of a room.

TEN-JŌ, テンジヤウ, 天上, (*ten no wiye*). *n.* Heaven, paradise. — *szru*, to ascend to heaven, to mount up into the air. — *ni umareru*, to go to heaven.

†TEN-JŌ-BITO, テンジヤウビト, 殿上人, *n.* The persons belonging to the Mikado's court, the Kuge.

TEN-JŪ,–*szru*, テンジユウ, 轉住, To change from one monastery to another.

TEN-KA, テンカ, 天下, (*ame no sh'ta*). *n.* The world, but especially the empire of Japan. — *ni nai*, nothing like it in the world. — *ittō*, the whole world, or the whole empire. — *bu-sō*, not another like it in the world, &c.

TEN-KAN, テンカン, 癲癇, Epilepsy.

TENKARA, テンカラ, coll. *adv.* From the first, from the beginning.

†TEN-KEI-BIYŌ, テンケイビヤウ, 天刑病, *n.* The disease inflicted by heaven, viz., the leprosy. Syn. RAI-BIYŌ, KATAI.

TEN-KI, テンキ, 天氣, *n.* The weather. — *ga yoi*, the weather is pleasant. — *ga warui*, the weather is unpleasant. — *ni natta*, it has become pleasant weather. Syn. HIYORI.

†TEN-KOKU,–*szru*, テンコク, 篆刻, To engrave letters on a seal.

TENNANSHŌ, テンナンシヤウ, 天南星, *n.* The arum tryphillum, dragon-root, or Indian turnip.

TENNEN, テンネン, 天然, Natural, produced or effected by nature, of itself, spontaneous. Syn. SHIZEN.

†TEN-NEN, テンネン, 天年, The natural term of life as fixed by heaven.

TEN-NIN, テンニン, 天人, *n.* Imaginary beings, represented by the Buddhists as beautiful females, enjoying perpetual youth, clothed in feather robes, with wings, skilled in music and singing, and dwelling in heaven. An angel.

†TEN-NIN,–*szru*, テンニン, 轉任, To promote to a higher rank, to change the office, or service.

TEN-ON, テンヲン, 天恩, *n.* Blessings, benefactions, or favors conferred by heaven.

†TEN-RAN, テンラン, 天覽, (*Tenshi no miru koto*). The eyes, or sight of the *Mikado.* — *ni sonayeru*, to show to the *Mikado.*

†TEN-RAN-K'WAI, テンランクワイ, 展覽會, *n.* An exhibition or collection of rare things for show.

TEN-SAI, テンサイ, 天災, *n.* A calamity caused by the great powers of nature, as by an earthquake, tempest, inundation &c.

TEN-SAKU,–*szru*, テンサク, 添削, (*soyeru kedsru*). To correct by adding to or erasing. *Bunshō wo* —. Syn. KAHITSZ, NAOSZ.

TEN-SEI, テンセイ, 天性, *n.* Natural disposition, or temperament. — *ni*, naturally, constitutionally. Syn. UMARETSZKI.

TEN-SHI, テンシ, 天子, *n.* The son of heaven; viz. the *Mikado*, or so called "spiritual emperor," residing at *Kiyoto*, but in fact the real emperor of Japan, "descended in an unbroken line from the gods," and after death supposed to become a Kami.

†TEN-SHO, テンシヨ, 篆書, *n.* That form of Chinese writing, called, "seal character."

TEN-SHO, テンシヨ, 添書, (*soye-bumi*). *n.* A letter of introduction.

TEN-SHU, テンシユ, 天守, *n.* A tower of several stories within the walls of a castle.

TEN-SHU-KIYŌ, テンシユキヤウ, 天主教, *n.* The Roman Catholic religion.

TEN-SZI-OKE, テンスイヲケ, 天水桶, *n.* A rain tub.

TEN-TAKU,–*szru*, テンタク, 轉宅, *n.* To change a residence, move to another house.

†TEN-TEKI, テンテキ, 點滴, *n.* The rain drops from the eaves of a house. Syn. AMADARE.

TEN-TŌ, テンタウ, 天道, *n.* The ruling power of nature, the Deity, heaven. — *wo osorezaru mono*, one who has no fear of Heaven. *Tentō-sama*, Heaven; this word is much used by the people of *Yedo* for the sun, which is worshiped.

TEN-TŌBOSHI, テンタウボシ, 日曝, *n.* In the open air; without a covering. — *de akinai wo szru*, to sell goods spread out on a mat on the ground without a covering.

TEN-TOKU, テントク, 天得, *n.* A mattress made of thick paper stuffed with straw &c,

TE-NUGUI, テヌグイ, 手拭, *n.* A handkerchief, a towel, napkin.

TE-NUKE, テヌケ, 手拔, *n.* An unintentional omission, or failure to do something which should have been done. Syn. OCHIDO.

TE-NUKI, テヌキ, 手抜, *n.* An intentional omission, neglect, or slighting of any work. — *wo szru.*

TE-NURUI,-KI,-KU, テヌルイ 手鈍, Slow, dull, inactive in doing; easy, or gentle,

TENYA,, テンヤ, coll. *n.* A shop where boiled fish and vegetables are sold.

TEN-YAKU,*-szru,* テンヤク, 轉役, *(yakugaye).* To be changed from one official position to another. Syn. TENNIN.

TENYAKU-NO-KAMI, テンヤクノカミ, 典藥頭, The title of the physician to the *Mikado.*

†TEN-YU,*-szru,* テンユ, 諂諛, *(omoneri hetszrau).* To flatter, to wheedle.

TE-OBOYE, テオボエ, 手覺, *n.* A mark, or anything used to aid one to remember. — *ni kaite oku,* to write down in order to remember.

TE-OCHI, テオチ, 手落, *n.* An omission, neglect.

TEOI, テオヒ, 手負, *n.* A wound. — *ni naru,* to be wounded. — *ni szru,* to wound.

TE-ŌI, テオホヒ, 手覆, *n.* A kind of mitten covering the arm and back of the hand, same as *Tekkō.*

TE-OKI, テオキ, 手置, *n.* The manner of putting away for keeping. *Katana no — ga warui kara sabita,* because the sword was badly put away it has rusted.

TE-OKURE, テオクレ, 手後, *n.* Late in doing. *Riyōji ga — ni natte mō naoranu,* the treatment was commenced too late and (the disease), could not be cured.

TE-OMOI,-KI,-KU,-SHI, テオモイ, 手重, Difficult to do, tedious, slow; important. *Teomoi riyōji,* tedious to cure. *Teomoi koto,* an important matter.

TE-ONO, テオノ, 手斧, *n.* A hatchet, or small axe.

TE-ORI, テオリ, 手織, *n.* Woven by one's self, or at home, not by a regular manufacturer. — *momen,* cotton cloth of domestic manufacture.

TEPPATSZ, テツパツ, 鐵鉢, *n.* An iron bowl carried by begging priests.

TEPPŌ, テツパウ, 鐵砲, *n.* A gun, cannon, or fire arms of any kind. — *wo hanasz,* or — *wo utsz,* to fire a gun. — *ni tama wo komu,* to load a gun with a ball. *Tamagome no* —, a loaded gun.

TEPPŌ-DAI, テツパウダイ, 鐵砲臺, *n.* A gun carriage, gun-stock.

TEPPŌ-KAJI, テツパウカヂ, 鐵砲鍛冶, *n.* A gun-smith.

TEPPUN, テツプン, 鐵粉, *n.* Iron filings, powdered iron.

TERA, テラ, 寺, *n.* A Buddhist temple, or monastery.

TERAI,*-au,-atta,* テラフ, 衒, *t.v.* To make a display of anything (as beauty, learning, wares) in order to deceive, or allure. *Iro wo* —, to make a meretricious display.

TERA-IRI, テライリ, 寺入, *n.* Entering school. — *wo szru.*

TERAKOYA, テラコヤ, 寺子屋, *n.* A school-house.

TERA-TERA, テラテラ, 耀耀, *adv.* Shiny, glossy, oily in appearance.

TERASHI,*-sz,-sh'ta,* テラス, 照, *t. v.* To cause to shine, to give light, to illuminate, lighten, enlighten. *Hi ga sekai wo* —, the sun gives light to the world. *Tszki ga* —, the moon shines.

TERATSZ-TSZKI, テラツツキ, *n.* A wood pecker.

TERAU, テラフ, See *Terai.*

TERA-UKEJŌ, テラウケジヤウ, 寺受狀, *n.* A certificate or letter of dismission from one Buddhist temple to another. Syn. SHŪSHI-TEGATA.

‖TEREN, テレン, coll. *n.* Artifice, deception, fraud. — *ni noru,* to be imposed upon. Syn. TEKUDA.

TERI,*-ru,-tta,* テル, 照, *i. v.* To shine, give light. *Hi ga* —, the sun shines. *Tszki no teranu yo,* a moonless night. Syn. HIKARU.

TERI-TERI-BŌDZ, テリテリボウズ, 掃晴娘, *n.* A piece of paper cut in the shape of a man, and hung on the door by children, to bring clear weather.

TERU, テル, See *Teri.*

TE-SAKI, テサキ, 手先, *n.* A secret policeman, a spy, the end of the fingers. Syn. OKAPPIKI.

TE-SAKU, テサク, 手作, *n.* Produced, or grown by one's self, home product, domestic manufactory. — *daikon,* radishes grown by one's self.

TE-SEI, テセイ, 手製, *n.* Made by one's self, manufactured at home. — *no sake,* home made wine.

TE-SHIWO-ZARA, テシホザラ, 手鹽皿, *n.* A small plate.

TE-SHIMA-ISHI, テシマイシ, 手嶋石, *n.* A kind of soft stone used in building.

TE-SHOKU, テショク, 手燭, *n.* A hand-lamp.

TE-SŌ, テサウ, 手相, *n.* The lines on the palm of the hand examined in palmistry. — *wo miru,* to tell fortunes by the palm of the hand.

TESŌ-MI, テサウミ, 手相見, *n.* Palmistry.

†TESSEKI, テツセキ, 鐵石, *n.* Iron and stone, adamantine. — *shin*, firm, immovable, or unyielding of heart.

TESSEN, テツセン, 銕扇, *n.* A fan, the frame of which is made of iron, carried only by officials.

TESSEN, テツセン, 鉄錢, *n.* A small iron coin, 96 of which make one *tempo*.

TESSHA, テツシヤ, 鐵砂, *n.* Iron filings.

†TESSHŌ, テツシヤウ, 銕醬, *n.* The fluid made of iron and gall-nuts, used by women for blacking the teeth.
Syn. OHAGURO, KANE.

†TESSHI,-*szru*,-*sh'ta*, テツスル, 徹, (*tōru*). To penetrate, pierce through, to affect deeply. *Kimo ni* —, to pierce through the liver,—to feel deeply.

TE-SZU, テスウ, 手數, Same as *Tekadz*.

TE-SZKI, テスキ, 手透, *n.* Intervals of leisure from work. — *ni hon wo yomu*, to study in the intervals of work.
Syn. HIMA.

TE-SZRI, テスリ, 手摺, *n.* A rail, extending from post to post, or over balusters for the hand to rest on. Syn. RANKAN.

TETE, or TETEOYA, テテ, 爺, (*chichi*). *n.* Father.

TETE-NASHI-GO, テテナシゴ, 無父兒, *n.* A child without a father, viz., a bastard.

TETSZ, テツ, 鐵, *n.* Iron.
Syn. KUROGANE.

†TETSZ-BEN, テツベン, 鐵鞭, *n.* An iron cane.

TETSZ-BIN, トツビン, 鐵瓶, *n.* An iron pot used for boiling water.

TE-TSZDAI,-*au*,-*atta*, テツダフ, 手傳, *t.v.* To lend a hand, help, or assist in doing. *Shigoto wo* —, to help another at work. *Kono tszkuye wo ageru wo tetszdatte kudasare*, please help me lift this desk.
Syn. TASZKERU.

TETSZDAI, テツダヒ, 手傳, *n.* A helper, assistant at any work.

TETSZDZKI, テツヅキ, 手續, *n.* A mutual friend, or acquaintance, to serve as go-between, or to introduce two parties who are strangers. Syn. TEDZRU, TSZTE.

TE-TSZIDE, テツイデ, 手次, *n.* A convenient time, when engaged in doing; as, *Sentaku no — ni kore wo araye*, when you wash the clothes, wash this too. *Kiyō ga — nai kara mata araimashō*, as I am not engaged in doing so to day, I will wash it at another time.

TETSZ-IRO, テツイロ, 鐵色, *n.* Iron color.

TETSZ-JŌ, テツヂヤウ, 鐵杖, *n.* An iron cane.

TE-TSZKE-KIN, テツケキン, 手付金, *n.* Money paid in advance to confirm a bargain, earnest money. — *wo utsz*, to pay earnest money, to make a deposit.
Syn. UCHI-KIN.

†TETSZ-MEM-PI, テツメンピ, 鐵面皮, *n.* A brazen-faced person, impudent.
Syn. ATSZKAWADZRA.

†TETSZYA, テツヤ, 徹夜, *n.* Passing the night without going to bed. — *wo sh'te hon wo yomu*, to spend the whole night in reading. Syn YODŌSHI.

†TETTEI, テツテイ, 徹底, (*soko ni tōru*). *adv.* Until the end or last, always; with a negative verb, = never.

TETTŌ, テツトウ, 鐵刀, *n.* An iron sword.

TE-WAKE, トワケ, 手分, *n.* Division of labor, hands, or company, in doing any thing; division of a body of troops. — *wo sh'te sagasz*, to separate and make search. Syn. TEKUBARI.

TE-WATASHI,-*sz*,-*sh'ta*, テワタス, 手渡, *t.v.* To hand over, to pass over to another.

TE-WAZA, テワザ, 手業, *n.* Work, anything for the hands to do.

TE-YARI, テヤリ, 手鎗, *n.* A short spear, a javelin.

TE-YOKI, テヨキ, 手鉞, *n.* A hand axe, hatchet.

TE-YOWAI,-KI,-KU,-SHI, テヨワイ, 手弱, Weak, not strong, without nerve, cowardly.

TE-ZAIKU, テザイク, 手細工, *n.* Any small or ingenious work made by one's self, or at home. Syn. TESEI.

TE-ZAWARI, テザハリ, *n.* The feel of any thing. — *ga arai*, it feels rough.
Syn. TEATARI.

TE-ZEI, トゼイ, 手勢, *n.* One's company, or division of troops.

TE-ZEMA, テゼマ, 手狹, Narrow, close, confined.

TE-ZOROI, テゾロヒ, 手揃, *n.* Full complement or number of hands. — *de shigoto ga hayai*, when there is a full number of hands work is done rapidly.

To, ト, 戶, *n.* A door. — *wo akeru*, to open a door. — *wo tateru*, or — *wo shimeru*, to shut a door.

To, ト, 砥, *n.* A whetstone.

To, ト, 與, *conj.* And, that: used to mark a quotation, or to indicate some thing said, or thought. *Ame to tszchi*, heaven and earth. *Szmi to fude to kami to wo mottekoi*, bring the ink, pencil and paper. *Mō nai to mōshimash'ta*, he said there was no more. *Na wa Ginko to iu*, his name is called Ginko. *Muszme no na wo O Tomi to tszketa*, they called the girl's name *O Tomi*. *Moku-zō wo kami to szru*, he made a wooden image his god. *Tatakawan to yōi wo szru*, to make preparations for war, (lit. "I will go to war" (thinking) he made preparations). *Kore wa nan to iu mono*, what do you call this thing? *H'to ga kuru to nigeru*, when, or as soon as any body comes it runs away. *To wo akeru to kaze ga hairu*, open the door and the wind enters. *Kore de yoi to omō*, that will do, I think.

To, ト, 籐, *n*, Ratan.

Tō, タウ, 餹, *n*. Candy, used only in compound words; as, *Kompeitō*. *Hakkatō*, peppermint candy. *Shōgatō*, ginger candy.

Tō, トヲ, 十, Ten. Syn. JŪ.

Tō, トウ, 等, A plural particle; as, *Kami szmi fude tō wa nichi-yō no mono da*, paper, ink and pencil are things of daily use. Syn. NADO, SHO, RA, DOMO.

Tō, タウ, 湯, An infusion, or decoction; only used in comp. words; as, *Keishi-tō* infusion of cinnamon.

To, ト, 斗, A grain or fluid measure, equal to ten *shō*, and the tenth part of a *koku*, = 1097.520 cub. in, or a little less than half an imperial bushel.

Tō, タフ, 塔, *n*. A tower, pagoda.

Tō, タウ, 黨, *n*. A club, party, band, junto, faction, league. —*wo muszbu*, to band together. Syn. NAKAMA, MURE.

To, ト, 徒, *n*. Club, party, company. *Waga to ni aradz*, does not belong to my company.

Tō, タウ, 當, *a*. This. *Tō koku*, this country. *Tō nen*, this year. *Tō getsz*, this month. *Tō haru*, this spring. *Tō-chi*, this place. Syn. KONO.

Tō, トウ, 東, *(higashi)*, *n*. East.

Tō, トウ, cont. of *Toku*, see *Toi*.

Tō, トフ, See *Toi*, 問.

Tō, トホ, 遠, Same as *Toku*. Far, see *Toi*.

Tō, トタ, 薹, *n*. The stem of vegetables which have gone to seed. *Chisha ni — ga tatte taberarenu*, the salad has gone to seed and cannot be eaten.

TOAMI, トアミ, 鳥網, *n*. A net for catching birds.

Tō-AMI, タウアミ, 唐網, *n*. A net for catching fish, used by throwing.

†TO-ARITE, トアリテ, (*To*, conj. and *arite*), *adv*. In a little while, soon after. Syn. SHIBARAKU SH'TE.

TO-ARU, トアル, (*To*, conj. and *aru*), *a*. A certain, same as *Aru*. — *yama ni*, on a certain mountain.

TŌBA, タフバ, 塔婆, *n*. Same as *Sotoba*.

TŌBAN, タウバン, 當番, *n*. On duty, on guard or watch, the opposite is *Hi-ban*. *Konnichi wa watakushi no — de gozarimas*, this is my day to be on guard. — *da kara ikaremasen*, as I am on duty I cannot go.

TOBARI, トバリ, 帷, *n*. A curtain over a window or door.

TOBASE,-*ru*,-*ta*, トバセル, 令飛, caust. of *Tobu*. To cause to or let fly, jump or run. *Ishi wo nagete tori wo tobaseru*, to throw a stone at a bird and make it fly.

TOBASHI,-*sz*,-*sh'ta*, トバス, Idem.

TOBASHIRI,-*ru*,-*tta*, トバシル, 迸, *i.v.* To splash, to spatter about, as water falling upon anything. *Midz ga* —.

TOBASHIRI, トバシリ, 沫, *n*. The drops of water spattering about. — *ga kakaru*.

TOBI, トビ, 鳶, *n*. A hawk.

TOBI,-*bu*,-*nda*, トブ, 飛, *n*. To fly, to jump, to spring, to move rapidly. *Tori ga* —, the bird flies. *Ya ga* —, the arrow flies. *Tonde nigeru*, to flee away.

TOBI-AGARI,-*ru*,-*tta*, トビアガル, 飛上, *i.v.* To fly up, to jump up.

TOBI-CHI, トビチ, 飛地, *n*. Territory isolated and lying in a distant region, not continuous with the main country.

TOBI-CHIGAI,-*au*,-*atta*, トビチガウ, 飛違, *i.v.* To fly, or jump past each other, to be far apart or very different. *Nedan ga tobichigatte iru*, there is a great difference in the price.

TOBI-GUCHI, トビグチ, 鳶口, *n*. A fire-hook, or hook for hauling timber.

TOBI-HANARE,-*ru*,-*ta*, トビハナレル, 飛離, *i. v.* To fly apart, to fly away; to jump suddenly from one subject to another.

TOBI-HI, トビヒ, 飛火, *n*. Sparks, or flakes of fire flying from a conflagration.

TOBI-IRI,-*ru*,-*tta*, トビイル, 飛入, *t. v.* To fly or jump into, to enter suddenly.

TOBI-IRO, トビイロ, 鳶色, *n*. Hawk's color, a light brown.

TOBI-KAKARI,-*ru*,-*ta*, トビカカル, 飛掛, *i.v.* To fly upon, to rush upon, spring on. *Inu ga h'to ni* —, the dog flew upon the man.

TOBI-KAYERI,-*ru*,-*tta*, トビカヘル, 飛反, *i.v.* To fly-back.

TOBI-KIRI, トビキリ, 飛切, Superfine, extra good. — *no shina*. Syn. GOKUJŌ.

TOBIKŌ, トビカフ, 飛交, def. verb. To

fly about as insects in the sun. *Niwa ni chō ga* —, the butterflies flutter about the garden.

TOBI-KOMI,*–mu,–nda*, トビコム, 飛込, *t.v.* To fly into, jump or spring into. *Midz ni* —, to jump into the water.

TOBI-KOSHI, トビコシ, *n.* The game of leapfrog.

TOBI-KOYE,*–ru,–ta*, トビコエル, 飛越, *t.v.* To fly across, or over; jump or spring over. *Dobu wo* —, to jump across a ditch.

TOBI-KUDARI,*–ru,–tta*, トビクダル, 飛下, *t.v.* To fiy, jump, or spring down.

TOBI-NOKI,*–ku,–ita*, トビノク, 飛退, *t.v.* To fly, jump, or spring aside and avoid, to flee away.

TOBI-NO-MONO, トビノモノ, 鳶者, *n.* Firemen, persons who carry firehooks.

TOBI-ORI,*–riru,–rita*, トビオリル, 飛下, *t.v.* To fly, or jump down from a height.

TOBIRA, トビラ, 扉, *n.* The leaf of a door.

TOBI-SARI,*–ru,–tta*, トビサル, 飛去, *t.v.* To fly away, to flee away.

TOBI-TACHI,*–tsz,–tta*, トビタツ, 飛立, *i.v.* To start and fly, or flee away. *Tobitatsz yōni omō*, felt like flying away.

TOBI-TSZKI,*–ku,–ita*, トビツク, 飛著, *t.v.* To spring upon and seize, or bite.

TOBI-UWO, トビウヲ, 飛魚, *n.* A flying-fish.

TOBI-WATARI,*–ru,–tta*, トビワタル, 飛渡, *t.v.* To fly, jump or spring across.

TOBOKE,*–ru,–ta*, トボケル, 惚, *i.v.* To be stupid, unconcious; to feign, to pretend, dissemble; to be silly with age. *Tobokete waga ko no kao mo shiranu*, to be so stupid as not to know the face of his own child. *Tobokete shiranu kao wo szru*, in pretence he put on an air of not knowing. Syn. RŌMŌ, SHIRABAKKURERU.

TOBORI,*–ru,–tta*, トボル, *i. v.* To burn, to flame, or blaze as oil, a lamp or candle. *Kono abura wa yoku toboru* this oil burns brightly.
Syn. MOYERU.

TOBOSHI,*–sz,–sh'ta*, トボス, *t.v.* To cause to burn or flame, to light. *Andon wo* —, to light a lamp. *Tomoshibi wo* —, idem. *Hi wo* —, to make a light.

TOBOSHII,–KI,–KU, トボシイ, 乏, Deficient, wanting, scarce; poor, destitute. *Midz ni toboshii*, deficient in water. *Kate hibi ni toboshiku naru*, the provisions daily become scarce. *Toboshiki wo ureyedz*, not minding poverty.
Syn. FUSOKU, HIN, BIMBŌ.

TOBOSO, トボソ, 扉, *n.* The leaf of a door. Syn. TOBIRA.

TOBO-TOBO, トボトボ, *adv.* In a hobbling or halting manner. — *to aruku*, to hobble along.

TOBU, トブ, 飛, See *Tobi*.

TO-BUKURO, トブクロ, 戸袋, *n.* The place into which doors slide, and are kept during the day.

TŌ-BUN, タウブン, 當分, *adv.* At present, for the present, just now, temporarily. — *sono yōsz mo nai*, there is no appearance of it at present. — *yoroshii*, it will do for the present. Syn. TŌJI.

TŌ-BUN, トウブン, 等分, Same weight, equal quantity or proportion. *Kuszri sammi — ni awasete g'wan-yaku ni szru*, mix three kinds of medicine together in equal quantities, and make into pills.

†TOBURAI,*–au,–atta*, トブラフ, 訪, *t. v.* To make a visit of condolence, to inquire after the health: also, 吊, to visit a tomb, or ruins. Syn. MIMAI.

TŌ-CHAKU, タウチヤク, 到着, (*itari tszku*). *n.* Arrival. — *wo tszkeru*, to enter the arrival in a book. — *szru*, to arrive.

TO-CHAKU, トチヤク, 土着, Belonging to the soil, or country. — *no tami*, the farmers belonging to any place. — *no hei*, the farmers organized into militia.

TOCHI, トチ, 土地, *n.* Country, place, region, soil. Syn. TOKORO.

TOCHINOKI, トチノキ, 七葉樹, *n.* Horse chesnut, Aesculus turbinata.

TO-CHIU, トチウ, 途中, (*michi no naka*). In the road, while in the way. — *de ame ni au*, to meet with rain while on the road.

TO-CHŌ, トチヤウ, 戸帳, *n.* A curtain. Syn. TOBARI.

TŌ-DAI, トウダイ, 燈臺, *n.* A lamp. Syn. TOMOSHIBI.

TŌ-DAI, タウダイ, 當代, *n.* The present dynasty, the present age, or time; that age. — *no jūji*, the present incumbent, (priest).

TODANA, トダナ, 戸棚, *n.* A cupboard, closet, wardrobe.

TO-DAYE, トダエ, 時絶, *n.* Ceasing for a while, interruption. *Yukiki no h'to mo — ga szru*, the people also ceased to pass to and fro.

TŌDO, タウド, 唐土, *n.* China.

TODOKE,*–ru,–ta*, トドケル, 屆, *t. v.* To make to reach, or arrive at; to send, or deliver a letter; to report, to inform. *Hikiyaku wo tanonde tegami wo todokeru*, to send a letter by a postman *Todokete*

agemashō, I will deliver it for you. *Tegami de* —, to inform by letter.
Syn. TASSZRU.

TODOKE-SHO, トドケシヨ, 屆書, *n.* A report in writing.

TODOKI,*-ku,-ita*, トドク, 屆, *i. v.* To reach, extend, attain to, arrive. *Te ga tenjō ni* —, his hand reaches to the ceiling. *Nen ga* —, to obtain one's wishes. *Me ga todokanu*, the eye cannot reach it. *Tegami ga todoita*, the letter has arrived. *Te ni todoku*, to come to hand.
Syn. OYOBU.

TODOKŌRI,*-ru,-tta*, トドコホル, 滯, *t. v.* To be obstructed, impeded, retarded, delayed, kept back, stopped, clogged. *Midz ga szna de* —, the water is prevented from flowing by the sand. *Mune ni shokumotsz ga* —, the food is stopped in the gullet from passing into the stomach. *Shakkin ga* —, the payment of one's debts is stopped, or delayed. *Todokōri naku*, without stoppage, or delay. *Omoku nigoru mono todokōrite tszchi to naru*, the heavy dirty part impeded in its motion became earth.
Syn. TAMARU.

TODOMARI,*-ru,-tta*, トドマル, 止, *i.v.* To stop, to cease from motion, to remain, continue. Syn. TOMARU.

TODOME,*-ru,-ta*, トドメル, 止, *t. v.* To stop, to arrest motion. *Uma wo todomete hana wo miru*, to stop the horse and look at the flowers. Syn. TOMERU.

TODOMERARE,*-ru,-ta*, トドメラレル, 被留, pass. of *Todomeru*. To be stopped, or arrested.

TODOME WO SASZ, トドメヲサス, To give the coup de grace.

TODO NO TSZMARI, トドノツマリ, *n.* The end, ultimate point, highest degree; at the last.

TŌDORI, トウドリ, 頭取, *n.* A headman, chief, a commandant.

TODOROKASHI,*-sz,-sh'ta*, トドロカス, 轟, caust. of *Todoroku*. To cause to resound, or reverberate. *Na wo* —, to cause one's name to be heard.

TODOROKI,*-ku,-ita*, トドロク, 轟, *i.v.* To sound with a rolling or rumbling noise, like thunder, or a waggon going over stones. *Kaminari ga* —, the thunder rolls. *Kuruma ga* —, the waggon rumbles.

†TODZ, or TODZRU, トヅル, 閉, See *Toji*.

†TŌDZ, or TŌDZRU, トウズル, 投, See *Tōji*.

TŌFU, トウフ, 豆腐, *n.* A kind of food made of beans.

TŌ-FŪ, トウフウ, 東風, *(higashi kaze)*. *n.* An east wind. Syn. KOCHI.

TOGA, トガ, 科, or 咎, *n.* A crime, offence, fault. — *wo okasz*, to commit a crime. — *ni otosz*, to convict of crime. — *nai*, without crime, innocent Syn. TSZMI.

TOGA, トガ, 栂, *n.* Name of a tree, the Abies tszga.

TOGAME,*-ru,-ta*, トガメル, 咎, *t.v.* To find fault with, to censure, reprove, to blame, reprehend, rebuke, to scold; to be fretted, irritated, as a sore. *H'to no ayamachi wo* —, to censure a person for a fault. *Kidz ga togameru*, the sore is irritated. Syn. SHIKARU.

TOGAME, トガメ, 咎, *n*: Censure, reproof, blame, reprehension. — *wo ukeru*, to be censured.

TŌGAN, トウガン, 冬瓜, *n.* Same as *Tōg'wa*.

TOGA-NIN, トガニン, 科人, *n.* A criminal, offender Syn. TSZMIBITO, ZAININ.

TOGARAKASHI,*-sz,-sh'ta*, トガラカス, 尖, caust. of *Togaru*. To make into a sharp point, to point, sharpen, pucker to a point. *Ki wo kedztte* —, to cut a stick to a point. *Kuchi wo* —, to pucker the mouth. *Koye wo togarakash'te shikaru*, to scold with a sharp voice.

TŌGARASHI, ダウガラシ, 辣椒, *n.* Cayenne pepper.

TOGARI,*-ru,-tta*, トガル, 尖, *i.v.* To be pointed, sharp, peaked. *Atama no togatta yama*, a peaked mountain. *Saki no togatta bō*, a sharp pointed pole. *Togari-goye*, a sharp voice.

TŌGE, ダウゲ, 嶺, *n.* A high pass between two mountains; a climax, acme, summit.

TOGE,*-ru,-ta*, トゲル, 逐, *t.v.* To accomplish, achieve, succeed in, to effect, to perform, to make good, to obtain, to execute, complete. *Nozomi wo* —, to obtain one's desire. *Fushin wo* —, to complete a building. *Negai wo togedz ni shinda*, died without obtaining his wish. *Yak'soku wo* —, to make good a promise.
Syn. SZMU, JŌJU SZRU, OWARU.

TOGE, トゲ, 刺, *n.* A thorn, splinter. *Yubi ni — ga tatsz* to run a splinter into the finger.

TOGE,*-ru,-ta*, トゲル, 磨, *i.v.* To be rubbed smooth, polished by friction, to be whetted, honed, sharpened. *Toishi de togeba yoku togeru*, if it is rubbed on a whetstone it will become sharp.
Syn. SZRERU, MIGAKERU.

TOGI, トギ, 伽, *n.* A nurse to a sick person. — *wo szru*. Syn. KAIHŌ, MORI.

TOGI,*-gu,-ida*, トグ, 磨, *t.v.* To rub, to make smooth, to polish, to whet, to sharpen; to refine, or improve. *Kagami wo* —, to polish a (metal), mirror. *Katana wo* —, to whet a sword. *Kome wo* —, to wash rice. Syn. MIGAKU.

TOGI-KAWA, トギカハ, 磨皮, *n.* A razor-strop.

TOGIRE, *-ru, -ta,* トギレル, 時絶, *i.v.* To cease for a while, to be interrupted. *Yuki ga futte ōrai ga* —, the passing to and fro is interrupted by the snow.
Syn. TODAYE.

TOGI-OTOSHI, *-sz, -sh'ta,* トギオトス, 磨落, *t.v.* To take out by rubbing, as a flaw, or nick.

TOGI-SHI, or TOGIYA, トギシ, 硎師, *n.* A person whose business it is to sharpen swords.

†TOGIYO, *-szru,* トギヨ, 渡御, To go, or visit, spoken only of nobles.
Syn. YUKU, KURU.

TOGU, トグ, See *Togi.*

TO-GUCHI, トグチ, 戸口, *n.* A door, entrance.

†TOGURA, トグラ, 塒, *n.* A chicken coop, or roost. Syn. TOYA.

TOGURO, トグロ, *n.* A coil, (as of a snake). *Nawa wo — ni maku,* to coil a rope.

†TOGURU, トグル, Same as *Togeru.*

TOGURUMA, トグルマ, 戸車, *n.* A small wheel on which doors or sashes are rolled, a caster.

TŌG'WA, トウグワ, 冬瓜, *(fuyu no uri).* *n.* A pumpkin.

TŌHIU, トウヒユ, 橙皮油, *n.* Oil of lemon.

TOHŌ, トハウ, 途方, *n.* *(michi no hōgaku mo miyenu).* Used only in the following phrases. *Tohō wo ushinau,* to lose one's presence of mind. — *ni kureta,* to be in doubt, or perplexity what to do; to be in a quandary, or dilemma; to be at a stand, bewildered, puzzled. *Tohō mo nai, a.* Outrageous, exceeding reason or decency, extravagant; as, — *koto wo iu.* — *yatsz da.*

TŌHŌ, タウハウ, 當方, *(kono kata).* This side, this person; = I, we.
Syn. KOCHIRA.

TOI, トイ, *n.* A pipe for conducting water.
Syn. HI, TOYU.

TOI, *-KI, -SHI, -KU,* トイ, 早, *a.* and *adv.* Quick, fast, early, soon. *Toku hashiru,* to run fast. *Toku okiru,* to rise early. *Tō ni shinda,* died long ago. *Toku okita,* was up long ago, or early. *Toki uma,* a fast horse. *Toku yori shitte oru,* I knew it before.
Syn. HAYAI.

TOI, *tō, tōta,* トフ, 問, *t.v.* To inquire, to ask, to question. *Ampi wo* —, to inquire after the health of any one. *Michi wo* —, to inquire about the way.
Syn. TADZNERU, KIKU.

TOI, トヒ, 問, *n.* A question, inquiry. — *ni kotayeru,* to reply to an inquiry.
Syn. TADZNE.

TŌI, *-KI, -KU, -SHI, -Ō,* トホイ, 遠, Far. distant. *Fune ga tōku natta,* the ship has got far away. *Tōi tokoro,* a distant place. *Tōkute miyemasen,* cannot be seen afar off. *Tō gozarimas,* it is far, sir.
Syn. HARUKA, YEMPŌ.

TOI-AWASE, *-ru, -ta,* トヒアハセル, 問合, *t.v.* To make inquiry about. *Toi-awasete agemashō,* I will see about it and tell you.
Syn. KIKI-AWASERU.

TOIKI, トイキ, 大息, *n.* A long breath, sigh. — *wo tszku,* to sigh, draw a long breath. Syn. TAMEIKI.

TOISHI, トイシ, 砥, *n.* A whetstone, hone.

TO-ITA, トイタ, 戸板, *n.* A sliding door.

TOI-TSZME, *-ru, -ta,* トヒツメル, 問詰, *t.v.* To question closely, inquire strictly, to scrutinize.

TOIYA, トヒヤ, 問屋, *n.* A wholesale commercial house, or wholesale merchant; one who receives merchandize directly from the producer, or manufacturer, and sells to retailers.

TŌJI, トウヂ, 杜氏, *n.* A brewer of *sake.*

TŌ-JI, トウジ, 冬至, *n.* The winter solstice.

TŌ-JI, タウヂ, 湯治, *n.* Hot-springs. — *ni yuku,* to visit the hot-springs.

TŌ-JI, ダウジ, 當時, *(tadaima). adv.* At present, for the present. Syn. TŌBUN.

TOJI, *-ru, -ta,* トヂル, 閉, *t. v.* To close, shut, to fasten. *To wo* —, to shut or lock a door. *Me kuchi nado wo* —, to shut the eyes or mouth. *Kōri ga* —, the ice has closed up (the water).
Syn. TOZASZ, SHIMERU.

TOJI, *-ru, -ta,* トヂル, 緘, *t. v.* To sew or tack together, to fasten together with a thread, to bind as a book. *Hon wo* —, to sew the leaves of a book together, to bind a book. *Futon wo* —, to quilt or stitch a mattress. *Toji-hon,* a bound book.

†TŌJI, *-dzru, -ta,* トウズル, 投, *(nageru).* *t.v.* To throw, cast, toss. *Ishi wo* —, to cast a stone.

TOJIKIMI, トジキミ, 戸道, *(to no michi).* *n.* The groove in which a door slides.
Syn. SHIKII.

TOJI-KOMORI, *-ru, -tta,* トヂコモル, 閉籠,

i.v. To shut, or lock one's self in. *Toji-komotte hon wo yomu*, to lock one's self in and read a book. *H'to wo toji-komeru*, to lock a person in.

TOJI-KOMI, *-mu,-nda*, トヂコム, 緘込, *t.v.* To sew in, or amongst the leaves of a book, bind up with. *Yedz wo hon ni —*, to bind a map, or picture in a book.

TO-JIMARI, トジマリ, 戸緘, *n.* Closing, fastening, or locking a door. *— wo sh'te neru*, to lock the door and go to bed.

TOJIME, *-ru,-ta*, トヂメル, 緘, *t.v.* To conclude, to end, terminate.
Syn. SZMU, OWARU.

TOJIME, トヂメ, 緘, *n.* The binding, or knot that fastens the thread with which a book is bound, the fastening of a door, the conclusion. *Uta no —*, the conclusion of a poem.

TŌ-JIN, タウジン, 唐人, *(kara no k'to). n.* A Chinaman; now used as a contemptuous name for all foreigners. *Onna —*, a foreign woman.

TŌ-JITSZ, トウジツ, 當日, *adv.* At that time, or day, at this time or this day, the proper time or proper day.

TOJI-TSZKE, *-ru,-ta*, トヂツケル, 緘付, *t.v.* To sew or tack any thing to another.

TO-JŌ, トジヤウ, 登城, *(shiro ye noboru).* Going to the castle, or court. *— szru.*

TOKA, トカ, 都下, *n.* Kiyoto.

TŌ-KA, トヲカ, 十日, *n.* The tenth day; also, ten days.

TOKAGE, トカゲ, *n.* A lizard.

TO-KAI, トカイ, 渡海, *(umi wo wataru).* To cross the ocean. *— szru*, idem. *To-kai-fune*, a ship from across the ocean.

TŌ-KAI, トウカイ, 東海, *(higashi no umi).* The eastern sea. *Tō-kai-dō, n.* The road extending from Yedo to Kiyoto along the eastern coast.

TOKAKI, トカキ, 斗槩, *n.* A stick used for leveling a measure of grain, &c. a strike.

TOKAKU, トカク, 兎角, *adv.* The characters used for this word are merely phonetic. According to Japanese etymologists, it is derived from *To*, outside, = that, and *kaku*, this manner; = in that way and this way; in various ways, in one way and another, some how or other. *— szru uchi ni hi ga kureru*, while busy about this and that the sun set. *— ni yo no naka ga osamaranu*, from one cause and another the times are unsettled. *— mada yoku narimasen*, for one cause and another he has not yet recovered.

TOKASHI, *-sz,-sh'ta*, トカス, 鮮, *t.v.* To dissolve, to melt, to untie, unravel. *Kuszri wo midz ni —*, to dissolve medicine in water. *Kōri wo —*, to melt ice.

TOKE, *-ru,-ta*, トケル, 解, *i.v.* To be dissolved, melted, untied, unraveled, loosed, cleared off, explained, ended. *Rō, kōri, kane nado ga —*, the wax, ice, or metal is melted. *Obi ga —*, the belt is loose. *Utagai ga —*, the doubt is dispelled. *Kakomi ga —*, the siege is ended. *Namari wayoku tokeru*, lead is easily melted.

TOKE-AI, *-au,-atta*, トケアウ, 鮮合, *i.v.* To be reconciled to each other, or restored again to friendship, to be mutually free from restraint or backwardness.

TOKEI, トケイ, 時辰錶, *n.* A watch, clock.

†TŌ-KEI, トウケイ, 鬪鷄, *n.* Cock-fighting. *— wo szru.* Syn. TORI-AWASE.

TOKEI-BANA, トケイバナ, *n.* The Passion flower.

†TOKEN, トケン, 杜鵑, *n.* The *Hototogisz.*

†TŌ-KEN, タウケン, 搪犬, *n.* A large dog.

TO-KETSZ, トケツ, 吐血, *(chi wo haku).* Vomiting, or spitting of blood.

TOKI, トキ, 時, *n.* Hour, time, season; any period of time; the times; a favorable time or opportunity; occasion, the time when. *Nan doki*, what o'clock? *— ga warui*, the times are bad. *— waruku rusz da*, unfortunately happens to be out. *— ga szgitta*, the time is past. *— ga itaru*, the time is come. *— ga utszru*, the time passes. *— ni shitagau*, to adapt one's self to the times or occasion. *— ni au*, to suit the times. *— ni okureru*, behind the times. *— ni yoru*, to accord with the time, or occasion. *— ni totte no saiwai*, a timely good fortune. *— wo utszsz*, to pass the time. *— wo ushinau*, to lose the favorable time, or opportunity. *— wo yeru*, or *uru*, to get a favorable time. *— wo hadzsz*, to miss the opportunity. *— wo matsz*, to wait for a favorable time. *— wo tszkuru*, to crow, (as a cock), to shout. *— ni jōdzru*, to improve the occasion. *Toki to sh'te*, sometimes. *Toki no kane*, a bell on which the hours are struck. *Gozen taberu toki*, when eating dinner. *Kodomo no umareta toki*, when the child was born.
Syn. SETSZ, KORO, JIBUN, JISETS.

TOKI, トキ, 齋, *n.* Dinner: so called only by priests of the *Zenshū* sect. *— wo sonayeru.*

TOKI, *-ku,-ita*, トク, 解, *t. v.* To melt, dissolve; to unite, loosen, disentangle, to unravel, rip open; to explain; undo; to comb. *Kane kōri rō nado wo —*, to melt metal, ice or wax. *Satō wo midz ni —*, to dissolve sugar in water. *Ikari wo* —, to allay anger. *Kakomi wo* —, to raise a siege. *Obi wo* — to loosen the belt. *Muszbime wo* —, to untie a knot. *Kimono wo* —, to rip up a garment. *Wake wo* —, to explain, or give the reason. *Kami wo* —, to comb the hair. Syn. HODOKU.

TOKI, トキ, 桃花鳥, *n.* The ibis.

TOKI-DOKI, トキドキ, 時時, *adv.* Sometimes, now and then, occasionally.
Syn. ORI-ORI, TOKI-YORI, ORIFUSHI.

TOKIHIJI, トキヒジ, 齋非時, *n.* A feast made on the anniversary of a death, accompanied with religious ceremonies. — *ni h'to wo shōdzru*, to invite persons to the above feast.

†TOKIJIKU, トキジク, *adv.* Always, continually. Syn. SHIJŪ, TŌSHI.

TOKI-MAI, トキマイ, 齋米, *n.* The rice received by a Buddhist priest by begging.

†TOKIMEKI,*-ku,-ita*, トキメク, *i.v.* To be at the most flourishing, or prosperous period. *Tokimeitaru h'to*, the most prosperous or famous man of his time.

TOKI-MORI, トキモリ, 時守, *n.* One who strikes the hours on a bell.

TOKIN, トキン, 頭巾, *n.* A kind of cap worn by a *Yamabushi*.

TOKI-NARANU, トキナラヌ, 不時, *n.* Out of season. — *mono wo kū na*, don't eat any thing that is out of season.

TOKI-NI, トキニ, 時, *adv.* Used in introducing another subject; or in interrupting a conversation to speak of something which suddenly comes to mind.
Syn. SATE, SOMO-SOMO.

TOKI-NO-KE, トキノケ, 時氣, *n.* The noxious influences peculiar to the season.

TOKI-NO-KOYE, トキノコヱ, 時聲, *n.* A loud shout, as that raised by an army on making an onset. — *wo ageru*, to shout, cheer.

†TOKIWA, トキハ, 常磐, (contracted from *Toko*, unchangeable, and *iwa*, stone). Permanent as a stone, lasting, perpetual.

TOKIWA-GI, トキハギ, 常葉木, *n.* An evergreen tree.

TOKKO, トクコ, 獨鈷, *n.* A kind of brass mace held by a Buddhist priest in praying.

TOKKUMI,*-mu,-nda*, トツクム, 取組, *t.v.* (comp. of *Tori*, and *kumu*). To seize and embrace, as wrestlers.

TOKKURI, トツクリ, Same as *Tokuri*.

TOKKURI-TO, トツクリト, *adv.* Attentively, carefully, well. — *miru*, to look at closely. — *kangayeru*, to consider well.
Syn. TOKU-TO.

TOKO, トコ, 牀, *n.* A bed, bed-stead.

TOKO, トコ, *n.* A hot-bed.

TOKŌ, トカウ, 兎角, (contracted from *Tokaku*). This or that. — *mōsz ni oyobadz*, no use in saying anything more.

TOKO, トコ, 底, *n.* The lower piece of wood or bottom of a plough.

†TOKOBI,*-bu,-nda*, トコブ, 詛, *t. v.* To imprecate, or invoke evil upon, curse.
Syn. NORŌ, SHUSO.

TOKODZRE, トコズレ, 牀瘡, *n.* A bedsore.

TOKON, トコン, 吐根, *n.* Ipecacuanha.

TOKONATSZ, トコナツ, 瞿麥, *n.* The pink.
Syn. SEKICHIKU.

TOKO-NOMA, トコノマ, 牀間, *n.* That part of a Japanese room which is raised a few inches above the floor, anciently used for spreading a bed on.

TOKORO, トコロ, 所, or 處, *n.* A place; when, that which. *Kono* —, this place. *Szmau* —, the place where one lives. — *no h'to*, a resident of the place. *Kanete mita* — *no mono to chigai*, different from the thing I saw before. *Iu* — *ni tagawadz*, just as was said. *Waga shiru* — *ni aradz*, it is something which I don't know. *Ikō to omō* — *kita*, he came just as I was thinking I would go.
Syn. SHO, BASHO, TOCHI, TOKI.

TOKORO, トコロ, 薢, *n.* The name of a bulbous root.

TOKORO-BARAI, トコロバライ, 所拂, *n.* Banishment, or expulsion from a place as a punishment. — *ni szru*, — *ni naru*.
Syn. TSZIHŌ.

TOKORO-DOKORO, トコロドコロ, 處處, Various places, here and there.
Syn. SHOSHO, ACHI-KOCHI.

TOKORO-GAKI, トコロガキ, 處書, *n.* The written directions of a place, as the name of the place, street &c.

TOKORO-GARA, トコロガラ, 處柄, *n.* The kind or character of a place. — *ga warui*, a bad place.

TOKORO-GAYE, トコロガヘ, 處替, *n.* A change of place, removal from one place to another. — *wo szru.*

TOKOROTEN, トコロテン, 心太, *n.* A kind of jelly made of seaweed.

†TOKOSHINAYE-NI, トコシナヘニ, 長, *adv.* Always, constantly, perpetually, eternally. — *yaki-yamadz*, will never cease to burn, — *kakunogotoku*, always so.
Syn. ITSZMADEMO, NAGAKU, TSZNENI.

TOKO-YAMI, トコヤミ, 長闇, *n.* Utter darkness, such as the earth was involved in, when the sun god in anger shut himself up in a cave.

TOKU, トク, 解, See *Toki*.

TŌKU, トホク, 遠, *adv.* Far, see *Tōi*.

TOKU, トク, 早, *adv.* Early, soon, see *Tōi*.

TOKU, トク, 德, *n.* Virtue, moral excellence, honor. — *wo tszmu*, to perform meritorious acts. — *no aru h'to*, a person whose presence commands respect. Syn. KUDOKU, KŌ.

TOKU, トク, 得, *n.* Profit, gain, or pecuniary advantage. — *ga nai*, no profit. *Son mo — mo nai*, neither loss nor gain. Syn. MŌKE, YEKI.

†TOKU-BIKON, トクビコン, 犢鼻褌, *n.* A cloth worn about the loins. Syn. FUNDOSHI.

TOKU-BUN, トクブン, 得分, *n.* The profit, the part, or share which one has gained. Syn. MŌKE.

†TOKU-DATSZ, トクダツ, 得脫, *n.* Deliverance or salvation from evil in this world, or from future punishment. (Budd.) — *szru.*

†TOKU-DO, トクド, 得度, Obtaining salvation, or passage into paradise. (Budd.) — *szru*, to obtain salvation.

†TOKU-DŌ, トクダウ, 得道, (*michi wo yeru*). Entering a monastery, or priesthood. — *szru*, to enter a monastery. Syn. SHUKKE SZRU.

†TOKU-HITSZ, トクヒツ, 禿筆, *n.* A spoiled and useless pen.

TOKU-I, トクイ, 得意, *n.* A customer; any thing with which one is well acquainted, experienced, or is skilful in; forte, speciality. *Tokui na kao*, pleased countenance. *Ano h'to wa watakushi no — de gozarimas*, he is a customer of mine. — *na koto*, a thing in which one excels, or is an adept in. Syn. YETE.

TOKU-JITSZ, トクジツ, 篤實, Sincere, honest. — *na h'to.* Syn. SHŌJIKI.

TOKURI, トクリ, 德利, *n.* A bottle, phial, jug, decanter. Syn. BIN

TOKUSA, トクサ, 木賊, *n.* Equisetum, or scouring rush.

TOKU-SHIN, トクシン, 得心, *n.* Assent, consent, to agree, concede, or yield. Syn. SHŌCHI SZRU, YURUSZ.

TOKU-SHITSZ, トクシツ, 得失, *n.* Profit and loss. Syn. SON YEKI.

TOKU-SHO, *-szru*, トクシヨ, 讀書, (*hon wo yomu*). To read books. — *jin*, a learned man.

TOKU-TO, トクト, 篤, *adv.* Attentively, carefully, minutely, well. — *miru*, to look closely at. Syn. YOKU, KOMAKA-NI.

†TOKU-TOKU, トクドク, 早早, *adv.* Quickly. Syn. HAYAKU.

TOK'WAI, トクワイ, 都會, *n.* A large city.

TOKU-YŌ, トクヨウ, 德用, Good, or serviceable, useful, profitable, advantageous. *Ishi no iye — da*, a stone house is most serviceable. Syn. RIKATA.

TOMA, トマ, 篷, *n.* A mat used for covering the cargo in junks, or for roofing. — *wa fuku*, to roof with the above.

TO-MADOI, トマドヒ, 戸迷, *n.* Rising from sleep bewildered and unable to find the door. — *wo szru.*

TOMARI, *-ru, -tta*, トマル, 止, *i.v.* To stop, to cease from motion; to light, as a bird, to roost. *Kuruma ga —*, the wheel has stopped. *Itami ga —*, the pain has ceased. *Yadoya ni —*, to stop at an inn. *Me ni tomatta mono*, any thing which has particularly attracted one's notice. *Koye ga —*, to lose the voice. *Tori ga —*, the bird has lit. *Seki-sho ga —*, the gate (at a pass) is closed. Syn. YAMU, TODOMARU.

TOMARI, トマリ, 止, *n.* A stop, cessation, stoppage, a stopping place. *Kon ban no — ga doko da*, where will you stop to night? — *ga nai*, no cessation.

TOMARI-BUNE, トマリブネ, 泊舟, *n.* A ship lying at anchor in a harbor.

TOMARI-GAKE, トマリガケ, 泊掛, *n.* — *ni yuku*, to go to any place with the intention of stopping a night or two.

TOMARI-GI, トマリギ, 止木, *n.* The pole on which fowls roost, a perch.

TŌMARU, トウマル, 東鷄, *n.* A large kind of fowl.

†TOMASHI, *-sz, -sh'ta*, トマス, 富, *t.v.* To enrich, to make wealthy. *Kuni wo —*, to enrich a nation.

TOMASZ, トマス, 斗, *n.* The same as *To*, a measure of grain.

TŌ-MAWASHI-NI, トホマハシ, 遠回, Indirectly, in a roundabout way.

TOMAYA, トマヤ, 苫屋, *n.* A small hut, thatched with *toma.*

TOMBI, トンビ, 鳶, *n.* Same as *Tobi*, a hawk.

TOMBŌ, トンボウ, 蜻蛉, *n.* A dragon fly.

TOME, *-ru, -ta*, トメル, 留, *t.v.* To stop, cause to cease, or put an end to any motion, to hold, to check, to detain, to harbor. *Uma wo —*, to hold a horse. *Kuruma wo —*, to stop a wheel, or waggon. *Itami wo —*, to stop the pain. *Chi wo —*, to stop the flow of blood. *Uwasa wo* —, to stop a report. *Me wo tomete miru*, to look fixedly at. *Tszmi-bito wo* —, to harbor a criminal. Syn. TODOMERU.

TOME-BA, トメバ, 止場, *n.* A region of country in which hunting is prohibited except to the lord of the soil.

TOME-BARI, トメバリ, 止釘, *n.* A pin.

TOME-CHŌ, トメチヤウ, 止帳, *n.* A memorandum book.

TOME-DO, トメド, 止所, *n.* A stop, end, cessation, a stopping place.
Syn. TOMARI, KIRI, KAGIRI, SAI-GEN.

TŌ-MEGANE, トホメガネ, 遠鏡, *n.* A spy-glass, telescope.

†TOMERI,*-ru*, トメル, *i. v.* To be rich, wealthy. *Tomeru h'to*, a rich man.

TOME-YAMA, トメヤマ, 止山, *n.* Hills or forests reserved as the hunting ground of a noble.

TOMI,*-mu,-nda*, トム, 富, *i.v.* To be rich, wealthy, prosperous. *Kuni ga* —, the country is wealthy.

TOMI, トミ, 富, *n.* Riches, wealth, prosperity. A kind of lottery. *Tomi to tattoki to wa h'to no hos-szru tokoro nari*, wealth and honor are that which men desire.
Syn. FŪKI.

TŌ-MI, トホミ, 遠見, *n.* A scout, a look-out. — *no hei*, (idem). — *wo dasz.*

TŌ-MI, タウミ, 唐箕, *n.* A wind-mill for cleaning grain.

†TOMI-KŌMI, トミカウミ, (derived from *Tokō*, a cont. of *Tokaku*, and *mi*, to see). Looking here and there. — *sh'te szszmanu*, looking here and there hesitating to go forward.

†TOMI-NI, トミニ, 頓, *adv.* Quickly, hastily, suddenly. Syn. KIU-NI.

TŌ-MIYŌ, トウミヤウ, 燈明, *n.* A light burnt before a god. Syn. MIAKASHI.

TOMMA, トンマ, Stupid, silly, dull, foolish. — *na yatsz*, a blockhead, an ass. — *na kao wo sh'te iru*, to have a stupid face.
Syn. MANUKE.

TOMO, トモ, 友, *n.* A friend, companion.
Syn. HŌYU, YŪJIN.

TOMO, トモ, 艫, *n.* The stern of a boat, or ship.

TOMO, トモ, 從者, *n.* An attendant, servant. — *wo szru*, to go along with. — *wo tszreru*, to take an attendant. *O — wo itashimashō* I will go with you.
Syn. JŪSHA, TOMOBITO.

TOMO, トモ, 鞆, *n.* A leather shield worn around the wrist by archers.

TOMO, トモ, (a conjunctive particle, comp. of *to* and *mo*). Though, even if, whether, even. *Szru tomo shinai tomo kokoro makase*, do it or not just as you please. *Naku tomo yoi*, if there are none, very well. *Nan tomo nai*, nothing at all. *Itsz tomo shirenu*, don't know when.

TOMO-ARE, トモアレ, (a contraction of *Tomo-kaku-mo*, and *are*, the imper. of *ari*). Let it be as it may; however it is, so be it; never mind. *H'to ni mo ashiku omowaruru wa tomoare*, if people do think evil of you, never mind. *Sore wa tomoare*, let that be as it is.

TOMO-BITO, トモビト, 從人, *n.* Attendants, followers, servants. Syn. JŪSHA.

TOMO-DACHI, トモダチ, 朋友, *n.* A friend, companion. Syn. HŌYU, HŌBAI.

TOMO-DOMO NI, トモドモニ, 共共, *adv.* Together, altogether, in company.

TOMO-DZNA, トモヅナ, 纜, *n.* A rope, or hawser from the stern of a ship.

TOMO-GARA, トモガラ, 徒, A collective noun designating the whole class of persons to which it is joined; a plural word. *Yakunin no tomogara*, officials, or the official class. *Kodomo onago no* —, children and women. Syn. YAGARA.

TOMO-KAKUMO, トモカクモ, *adv.* (comp. of *Tokaku*, and *mo*). In what manner soever, howsoever, however it may be. — *nanji yoki-ni hakarau beshi*, manage the matter, in whatever way you may think best.

TOMO-KŌMO, トモカウモ, Idem.

TOMO-MAWARI, トモマハリ, 供廻, *n.* The attendants, or servants around a person of rank.

TOMONAI,*-au,-atta*, トモナフ, 伴, *i. v.* To accompany, to go along with, to attend. Syn. TSZRERU.

TOMO-NI, トモニ, 共, *adv.* Together, in company with, along with. *Watakushi to — Yedo ye yuku*, to go with me to Yedo. Syn. ISSHO-NI.

TOMORI,*-ru,-tta*, トモル, 燃, *i.v.* To burn so as to give light, see *Tobori.*

TŌMOROKOSHI, タウモロコシ, 玉黍, *n.* Maize, or Indian corn.

TOMOSHI,*-sz,-sh'ta*, トモス, 燃, *t.v.* To light, (spoken only of a light, lamp, or candle), see *Toboshi*. *Akari wo* —, to strike a light. *Andon wo* —, to light a lamp. *Tomoshi-abura*, lamp oil.

TOMOSHIBI, トモシビ, 燈火, *n.* A light.

TOMOSHII,-KI,-KU, トモシイ, See *Toboshii.*

TOMOYE, トモヱ, 巴, A figure like this ◐, is so called *Mitszdomoye*, is like ✪,

TOMU, トム, 富, See *Tomi.*
TOMU, トム, 止, contracted from of *Tomuru*, or *Tomeru*, to stop, cease, end.
†TOMURAI,–*au*,–*atta*, トムラフ, 訪, or 吊, The same as *Toburai.*
TOMURAI, トムラヒ, 送葬, *n.* A funeral. Syn. SŌREI, SŌSHIKI, OKURI.
TO-MUSHIRO, トムシロ, 籐席, *n.* A mat made of ratan.
†TŌ-NAN, タウナン, 盗難, *n.* Calamity or loss from robbers. — *ni au.*
TONARI, トナリ, 隣, Neighboring, adjoining ; a neighbor. — *no iye.* — *no h'to.* — *no kuni.*
TŌNASZ, タウナス, 南瓜, *n.* A squash. Syn. KABOCHA.
TONAYE,–*ru*,–*ta*, トナヘル, 唱, *t. v.* To say, to recite, to call or name, to sing. *Nembutsz wo* —, to recite prayers. *Uta wo* —, to sing a song. *Na wo Sodajiro to* —, called his name Sodajiro.
Syn. SHŌ-SZRU.
TON-CHI, トンチ, 頓智, Quick of perception, ready or quick witted. — *no yoi h'to.*
‖TONCHIKI, トンチキ, *n.* A stupid fellow, a dunce, dolt, ass. Syn. TOMMA.
TONDA, トンダ, 飛, *pret.* of *Tobi.* Has flown; this word is much used in the Yedo coll, as a superlative. — *koto ga dekita*, or — *me ni atta*, have met with a shocking affair.
TONDE, トンデ, *pp.* of *Tobi* or *Tomi.*
†TONERI, トネリ, 舍人, *n.* A servant of the Tenshi.
†TONIU, トニウ, 吐乳, (*chichi wo haku*). Throwing up milk, as infants.
TONJAKU, トンヂヤク, 貪著, To meddle, to intrude to take an interest in, concern one's self about; intermeddle. — *senu*, indifferent, unconcerned. *Yo ni* — *szru*, to be concerned about, or meddle with the affairs of the world. *Namayoi ni* — *szru na*, have nothing to do with a drunken man. *Sonna koto wa* — *shimasen*, I will not meddle in such business.
Syn. KAMAU, TORIAU.
TO-NI-KAKU-NI, トニカクニ, (comp. of *To-kaku*, and *ni*), *adv.* In any manner soever, in any way whatever.
TŌ-NIN, タウニン, 當人, *n.* The principal person, or chief party, the person most interested in any business. — *ga fushōchi da*, the chief person will not consent. Syn. HONNIN.
TŌ-NIN, タウニン, 桃仁, *n* A peach kernel.
†TON-NI, トンニ, 頓, (*niwakani*), *adv.* Suddenly, hastily.
TONO, トノ, 殿, *n.* A seigneurial residence, or palace; also the occupant, a lord, seignior. *Tono-sama*, the lord. *Tono-bara*, the lords.
†TONŌ, トナフ, 唱, See *Tonaye.*
‖TONOGO, トノゴ, 殿子, A respectful, or affectionate title, used by a wife in speaking of her husband.
†TONOI, トノ井, 宿直, *n.* Keeping watch, or guard in the palace of the Tenshi at night. — *wo szru.*
TONOKO, トノコ, 礪粉, *n.* The fine powder of a whetstone, used for polishing. — *szru.*
TON-SEI, トンセイ, 遁世, (*yo wo nogareru*). To shave the head and forsake the world, to retire from business.
TON-SHI, トンシ, 頓死, (*niwakani shinuru*). A sudden death.
TONTO, トント, *adv.* Entirely, quite, wholly, at all. — *shirimasen*, know nothing at all about it. — *nite i-nai*, wholly unlike. Syn IKKŌ, SARA-NI.
TON-TON, トントン, *adv.* The sound of beating a drum. All, the whole, (Yokohama coll.) *Taiko wo* — *tataku.* — *ikura*, how much for the whole lot?
TON-YOKU, トンヨク, 貪慾, *n.* Covetousness, avarice. —*no fukai h'to*, a very avaricious man. Syn. MUSABORI.
TORA, トラ, 虎, *n.* A tiger: also 寅, one of the 12 signs. — *no tszki*, the first month. —*no toki*, 4 o'clock A,M. — *no hō*, the E.N.E.
TŌ-RAI,–*szru*, タウライ, 到來, (*itari kitaru*). To arrive, come. *Mada jikoku ga tōrai senu*, the time has not yet come. *Tegami ga tōrai sh'ta*, the letter has arrived. *Tōrai-mono*, a present.
†TORAKASHI,–*sz*,–*sh'ta*, トラカス, 蕩, *t.v.* To shake, to unsettle, to corrupt or debauch. *Fune wo* — to rock a boat. *Shushoku ni kokoro wo* —, to debauch the heart with wine and lust.
Syn. UGOKASZ, TADAYOWASZ.
TORARE,–*ru*,–*ta*, トラレル, 被取, pass. of *Tori.* To be taken or seized.
TORASE,–*ru*,–*ta*, トラセル, 令取, caust. of *Tori.* To cause to, or let take, seize,
TORAWARE, トラワレ, 囚, *n.* A prisoner. Syn. MESHIUDO, TORIKO.
TORAWARE,–*ru*,–*ta*, トラハレル, 被捕, pass. of *Torayeru.* To be taken, seized, or arrested.
TORAYE,–*ru*,–*ta*, トラヘル, 捕, *t. v.* To

take, to seize, to catch, arrest. *Dorobō wo* —, to arrest a thief. *Nuszbito wo torayete mireba waga ko nari,* (prov.)

TORE,*-ru,-ta,* トレル, 取, pass. or pot. of *Toru.* To be taken, seized, plucked off, &c. *Kono kobu wa toremashō ka,* can you take this lump off? *Toreru,* I can, or it can be taken off. *Tenki ga yokute sakana ga tanto toreru,* if the weather is fine fish can be caught in abundance. *Dobin no te ga toreta,* the handle of the kettle is off.

TORI, トリ, 鳥, *n.* A bird: also, 酉, one of the 12 signs. — *no toki,* 6 o'clock P.M., or sunset. — *no hō,* west.

TŌRI, トホリ, 通, *n.* Manner, way, mode; kind, sort; like. *Migi no* — *ni,* in the way mentioned above. *Kono* — *ni shi nasare,* do it in this way, or make it like this. *Mita* —, like that I saw before.
Syn. GOTOKU, YŌ, MAMA.

TŌRI, トホリ, 通, *n.* A street, avenue, thoroughfare; the line, direction or course in which anything points, faces, or moves; the passing of anything through, along, or from one to another. *Kai-gan-dōri,* the street next the sea. *Nishi no* —, west street. *Yubi no* — *ni miyeru fune,* the ship seen in a line with my finger. *Mado wa mon no* — *ni ataru,* the window is in a line with the door. *H'to no* — *ga ōi,* a great many people pass through. *Kono kiseru wo* — *ga yoi,* the air passes easily through this pipe. *Hajime no na ga* — *ga yoi,* his first name is the most current,

TŌRI,*-ru,-tta,* トホル, 通, *t.v.* or *i.v.* To pass through, or to be current, pervious. *Michi wo* —, to pass along a road. *Iki ga tōranu kiseru,* a pipe through which the smoke cannot pass. *Kono kane wa tōrimasen,* this money will not pass.
Syn. KAYŌ.

TORI,*-ru,-tta,* トル, 取, *t.v.* To take, to catch, seize, to pluck off; to receive, to get, obtain; to steal; to admit, or receive as true; to select. *Te ni mono wo* —, to take anything in the hand. *Sakana wo* —, to catch fish. *Ki no mi wo* —, to pluck fruit off a tree. *Kane wo* —, to steal money, to take or receive money. *Tenga wo* —, to seize the government. *Ano h'to no setsz wo* —, to take what he says to be true. *Chi wo* —, to take blood. *Shichi wo* —, to take a pawn. *Yome wo* —, to take a wife. *Kubi wo* —, to take off the head. *Te wo* —, to take the hand. *Shishō wo* —, to get a teacher. *Inochi wo* —, to take life. *Na wo* —, to get a name. *Toi de midz wo* —, to catch water by a spout. *Shaku wo* —, to help to wine. *Yado wo* —, to take lodgings at an inn. *Szmpō wo* —, to take the dimensions. *Hiyōshi wo* —, to beat time. *Szmō wo* —, to wrestle. *Itoma wo* —, to take leave. *Toshi wo* —, to get old. *Sh'ta ni* —, to take something to boot. *Za wo* —, to take a seat. *Kuji wo* —, to draw lots. *Szishō de hi wo* —, to converge the sun's rays with a lens. *Mado wo akete hikari wo* —, to cut a window in order to get light. *Kasa wo* —, to take off the hat. *Kadz wo* —, to mark the number. *Toru ni taradz,* worthless, or of no account. *Tori mo naosadz,* without alteration, without change. *Kado wo* —, to round off the angles. *Hike wo* —, to get the worst of it. *Haji wo* —, to be put to shame. *Kachi wo* —, to win, get the victory. *Kigen wo* —, to please, humor.

TORI-AGE,*-ru,-ta,* トリアゲル, 取上, *t.v.* To take up, take and lift up, receive and hand up, to confiscate. *Nengu wo* —, to take and pay in taxes, (as an inferior officer).

TORI-AGE-BABA, トリアゲババ, 穏婆, *n.* A midwife.

TORI-AI,*-au,-atta,* トリアフ, 取合, *t. v.* To take hold of each other, to mind, concern one's self about, or take notice of. *Te wo toriatte aruku,* to walk holding each others hand. *Nama-yoi ni toriau na,* don't meddle with a drunken man.
Syn. KAMAU, TONJAKU.

TORI-AMI, トリアミ, 鳥網, *n.* A net for catching birds.

TORI-ATSZKAI,*-au,-atta,* トリアツカフ, 取扱, *t.v.* To negotiate between others, to manage, to treat; to handle, use. *Kuji wo* —, to manage a law suit, or settle a dispute. *Atszku* —, to treat handsomely. *Katana wo* —, to handle a sword.
Syn. ATSZKAU, MOTENASZ.

TORI-ATSZME,*-ru,-ta,* トリアツメル, 取集, *t.v.* The same as *Atszmeru.*

TORI-AWASE, トリアハセ, 闘鶏, *n.* A cock-fight. — *wo szru.*
Syn. TŌKE.

TORI-AWASE,*-ru,-ta,* トリアハセル, 取合, *t.v.* To take and put many things together, to mix together.

TORI-AYEDZ, トリアヘズ, 不取敢, *adv.* Immediately, forthwith, at once without waiting to take or do anything.
Syn. SZGU-TO, TACHI MACHI, JIKI-NI.

TORI-CHIGAYE,*-ru,-ta,* トリチガヘル, 取違, *t.v.* To take anything in the place of another, to take by mistake; exchange. *Kaza wo* —, to take an umbrella belonging to another and leave one's own, (either intentionally or by mistake).

TORI-CHIRASHI,-*sz*,-*sh'ta*, トリチラス, 取散 *t.v.* Same as *Chirashi.*

TORI-DASHI,-*sz*,-*sh'ta*, トリダス, 取出, *t.v.* To take out.

TORIDE, トリデ, 砦, *n.* A fort.

TORI-DOKORO, トリドコロ, 取所, *n.* A place for catching hold of: used only fig. as, — *mo nai h'to*, a worthless person, one of no account.

TORI-DORI, トリドリ, 取取, Various, diverse, sundry, different. — *no hiyōban*, various reports. — *ni*, in various ways. Syn. MACHI-MACHI, SAMA-SAMA.

TORI-HADA, トリハダ, 鳥膚, *n.* The corrugation of skin produced by cold, goose-flesh.

TORI-HADZSHI,-*sz*,-*sh'ta*, トリハヅス, 取外, *t.v.* To let anything slip from the hand, or let go accidentally, to take apart, to remove.

TORI-HADZSHI, トリハヅシ, 取外, *n.* Anything made so as to be taken apart, and put together. — *no dekiru tszkuye*, a table like the above.

TORI-HAKARAI,-*au*,-*atta*, トリハカラフ, 取計, *t.v.* To manage, to conduct, direct, control, to transact, to do, negotiate. Syn. TORI-ATSZKAU.

TORI-HAKARAI, トリハカラヒ, 取計, *n.* Management, direction, negotiation, conduct.

TORI-HANASHI,-*sz*,-*sh'ta*, トリハナス, 取放, *t.v.* To separate, to take away, to take from.

TORI-HARAI,-*au*,-*atta*, トリハラフ, 取拂, *t.v.* To tear away and remove, to clear away. *Iye wo* —, to tear down and clear away a house.

TORI-HARAI, トリハラヒ, 取拂, *n.* Clearing away, removal.

TORI-HIKI, トリヒキ, 取引, *n.* Business, trade, mercantile transactions. *Ano h'to to — wo senu*, to have no trade with him. Syn. URI-KAI.

TORI-HISHIGI,-*gu*,-*ita*, トリヒシグ, 取挫, *t. v.* To abase, humble, bring down, to crush, or destroy.

TORI-HŌDAI, トリハウダイ, 取放題, *n.* Taking without restraint, or at pleasure. *Michi-bata no hana wa h'to no — da*, any one is at liberty to take the flowers on the road-side.

TORI-I, トリ井, 鳥居, *n.* A portal, or a structure of stone or wood, something like the frame of a gate, erected in front of *Sintoo* temples.

TORI-IRI, -*ru*,-*tta*, トリイル, 取入, *i. v.* To get into the good graces of any one, to curry favor with. *Bugiyō ni* —, to curry favor with the governor.

TORI-KA, トリカ, 取個, *n.* Gain, income, revenue. *Kiu-kin no hoka ni — ga nai*, besides the wages there is nothing to be got from it. *Kuni no* —, the revenue of a country. Syn. TOKUBUN.

TORI-KABUTO, トリカブト, 烏頭, (*udz*). *n.* Aconite.

TORI-KABUTO, トリカブト, 鳥兜, *n.* A kind of cap worn by dancers.

TORI-KAGO, トリカゴ, 鳥籠, *n.* A bird cage.

TORI-KAJI, トリカヂ, 取楫, *n.* Helm to the larboard. — *wo szru*, to port the helm.

TORI-KAKARI,-*ru*,-*tta*, トリカカル, 取掛, *i. v.* To commence to do. *Shigoto ni* —, to commence work. Syn. HAJIMERU.

TORI-KATADZKE,-*ru*,-*ta*, トリカタヅケル, 取方付, *t. v.* To put to oneside, to put away.

TORI-KAWASHI,-*sz*,-*sh'ta*, トリカハス, 取交, *t. v.* To exchange reciprocally, as a treaty, or agreement. *Kakitszke wo* —, to exchange writings.

TORI-KAWASHI, トリカハシ, 取交, *n.* Exchange, giving and receiving reciprocally. *Yakujō no — ga sznda*, the treaty has been exchanged.

TORI-KAYE,-*ru*,-*ta*, トリカヘル, 取替, *t.v.* To exchange one thing for another, to give and take, to reciprocate. *Szmi wo fude to* —, to exchange ink for a pen.

TORI-KAYESHI,-*sz*,-*sh'ta*, トリカヘス, 取返, *t. v.* To take back, retake, recapture, to reclaim. *Yatta mono wo* —, to take back something given to another. Syn. TORIMODOSZ.

TORI-KAYESHI, トリカヘシ, 取返, *n.* Taking back, retaking, recapture, reclamation. — *ga tszkanu*, cannot be reclaimed.

TORI-KI, トリキ, 取木, *n.* Propagating trees by layers, or by binding together two branches of different trees partially cut.

TORI-KIRI,-*ru*,-*tta*, トリキル, 取切, *t. v* To take all. *Hana wo tori-kitta*, has plucked off all the flowers. *Nashi ga tori-kiri ni natta*, the pears have all been taken.

TORI-KO, トリコ, 俘, *n.* A prisoner of war, a captive. — *ni szru*, to take prisoner. Syn. TORAWARE.

TORI-KOMI,-*mu*,-*nda*, トリコム, 取込, *t. v.* To take up and put in, to take into, to bring in; to be busy and perplexed; to extort. *Mainai wo* —, to take bribes.

TORI-KOSHI,*-sz,-sh'ta*, トリコス, 取越, *t. v.* To anticipate the doing of any thing, to do before the fixed time. *Matszri wo* —, to celebrate a festival before the proper time.

TORI-KUDZSHI, トリクヅス, 取崩, *t. v.* To dismantle, to take apart, take down.

TORI-MAGIRE,*-ru,-ta*, トリマギレル, 取紛, *t. v.* To be distracted, perplexed, or occupied with much business.

TORI-MAKI,*-ku,-ita*, トリマク, 取捲, *t. v.* To surround, encompass, environ.

TORI-MAWASHI, トリマハシ, 取廻, *n.* A person's movements, the moving of any thing. — *ga warui*, to be awkward, clumsy. *Tszkuye ga omoku te — ni komaru*, the table is so heavy it is hard to move about.

TORI-ME, トリメ, 酉眼, *n.* Night blindness.

TORI-MOCHI, トリモチ, 鳥黏, *n.* Bird-lime.

TORI-MOCHI,*-tsz,-tta*, トリモツ, 取持, *t. v.* To recommend, to offer, or commend to another's notice. *H'to ni yome wo* —, to recommend a wife to another. *Torimotte hōkō wo saseru*, to recommend and get a place for another as a servant.

TORI-MOCHI, トリモチ, 取持, *n.* Recommendation. — *wo szru.*

TORI-MODOSHI,*-sz,-sh'ta*, トリモドス, 取戻, *t. v.* To take back, retake, reclaim, recapture.

TORI-MUSZBI,*-bu,-nda*, トリムスブ, 取結, *t. v.* To unite or join together. *Konrei wo* —, to unite in marriage, *Jōyaku wo* —, to make an agreement.

TORI-NAOSHI,*-sz,-sh'ta*, トリナホス, 取直, *t.v.* To alter, change for the better, to mend. *Kokoro wo* —.

TORI-NASHI,*-sz,-sh'ta*, トリナス, 取成, *t. v.* To intercede, to mediate, to advocate the cause of another, to manage in behalf of another. *Muszko no tame-ni oya ni* —, to intercede with the parent for a son.

TORI-NASHI, トリナシ, 取成, *n.* Mediation, intercession, advocacy.

TORI-NAWA, トリナハ, 捕繩, *n.* A rope used for binding criminals.
Syn. HAYA-NAWA.

TORI-NIGASHI,*-sz,-sh'ta*, トリニガス, 捕逃, *t. v.* To let anything escape which one has almost had in his power. *Dorobō wo tori-nigash'te zan-nen da.* I regret that I let the thief get away.

TORI-NIGE, トリニゲ, 取走, *n.* Stealing and running away. — *wo szru.*

TORI-NOKE,*-ru,-ta*, トリノケル, 取退, *t. v.* To take and put out of the way.

TORI-NOKI,*-ku,-ita*, トリノク, 取退, *i.v.* To take and withdraw.

TORI-NOKO, トリノコ, 鳥子, *n.* A kind of thick paper.

TORI-NOKOSHI,*-sz,-sh'ta*, トリノコス, 取殘, *t. v.* To leave some having taken a part.

TORI-NOKOSHI, トリノコシ, 取殘, *n.* The remainder after a part has been taken.

TORI-ODOSHI, トリオドシ, 鳥威, *n.* A scarecrow.
Syn. KAGASHI.

TORI-OI, トリオヒ, 鳥追, *n.* Females who go from house to house on the beginning of a new-year, playing on the guitar and singing for money.

TORI-OKI,*-ku,-ita*, トリオク, 取置, *t. v.* To take and put away.

TORI-OKONAI,*-au,-atta*, トリオコナフ, 執行, To conduct, perform, to do. *Matszrigoto wo* —, to administer the government. *Hōji wo* —, to celebrate religious services.
Syn. OKONAU, SZRU.

TORI-OTOSHI,*-sz,-sh'ta*, トリオトス, 取落, *t. v.* To let fall, or let slip from the hand any thing taken up.

TORI-SABAKI,*-ku,-ita*, トリサバク, 取捌, *t. v.* To judge, to hear and determine a a case, to adjudicate. *Kuji wo* —, to try a law suit.

TORI-SASHI, トリサシ, 鳥刺, *n.* A person who catches birds with a pole armed with bird-lime.

TORI-SATA, トリサタ, 取沙汰, *n.* Current report. — *szru*, to be common talk.
Syn. HIYŌBAN, FŪSETSZ.

TORI-SAYE,*-ru,-ta*, トリサヘル, 取遮, *i. v.* To part, separate, as person's fighting.

TORI-SHIMARI, トリシマリ, 取締, *n.* Exactness, regularity, strictness, carefulness in managing, order, discipline, method. — *no nai h'to*, a person immethodical, irregular, careless, or loose in his way of doing. — *no yoi iye*, a well ordered family. *Gunzei no — ga warui*, the army is under bad discipline. — *wo szru*, to preserve order or discipline.
Syn. SHIMARI.

TORI-SHIME,*-ru,-ta*, トリシメル, 取締, *t.v.* To extort, to exact, or gain by oppression.

TORI-TATE,*-ru,-ta*, トリタテル, 取立, *t.v.* To collect, to promote, or advance in office. *Nengu wo* —, to collect taxes. *Tana-chin wo* —, to collect rent.

TORI-TE, トリテ, 捕手, *n.* An officer who arrests offenders, a policeman.

TŌRITEN, トウリテン, 忉利天, *n.* The name of one of the Buddhist heavens.

TORI-TOME,*-ru,-ta*, トリトメル, 取留, *i.v.* To adopt, or receive as certain, sure, undoubted, or reliable. *Iro-iro hiyōban szredomo tori-tometa hanashi mo nai*, there are various reports but nothing reliable.

TORI-TOME, トリトメ, 取留, *n.* Bound, limit, cessation, end, certainty. — *mo nai koto wo iu*, to say any thing which is uncertain, Syn. SAIGEN, KAGIRI.

TORI-TSZGI,*-gu,-ida*, トリツグ, 取次, *t.v.* To take any thing and hand it over to another. *Tegami wo* —.

TORI-TSZGI, トリツギ, 取次, *n.* An officer whose duty it is to attend to the door of a noble's house, an usher.

TORI-TSZKI,*-ku,-ita*, トリツク, 取著, *t.v.* To take, catch, or seize hold of, to bewitch. *Nawa ni* —, to catch hold of a rope. *Kitszne ga h'to ni* —, the fox bewitches men.

TORI-TSZKI, トリツキ, 取着, *n.* Taking hold to do any thing, the commencement.

TORI-TSZKURAI,*-au,-atta*, トリツクロフ, 取繕, *t.v.* To mend, repair, to smooth over, palliate, or excuse, as a fault, *H'to no ayamachi wo* —, to smooth over another's fault.

TŌRIU,*-szru*, トウリウ, 逗留, (*tomaru*). To stop, stay, or remain for an indefinite time in a place, to sojourn, to board. *Dochira ni — nasaru*, where are you staying? *Nagaku — sh'ta*, have sojourned a long time.

TORI-WAKE, or TORI-WAKETE, トリワケ, 取分, *adv.* Particularly, especially, above all. Syn. BETSZDAN, KOTO-SARA-NI.

TORI-WAKE,*-ru,-ta*, トリワケル, 取分, *t.v.* To distribute, divide.

TORIYA, トリヤ, 鳥屋, *n.* A shop where fowls or birds are sold.

TORIYE, トリエ, Coll. *n.* Worth or useful quality. — *mo nai h'to*, a worthless person. Syn. TORI-DOKORO.

TŌ-RIYŌ, トウリヤウ, 棟梁, *n.* A head-carpenter, foreman.

TORI-YOSE,*-ru,-ta*, トリヨセル, 取寄, *t.v.* To bring, fetch, import, draw. *Nippon kara cha wo* —, to import tea from Japan.

TŌRŌ, トウロウ, 燈籠, *n.* A lantern, or stationary lamp.

TŌRŌ, タウラウ, 螳螂, *n.* A mantis. Syn. KAMAKIRI.

TOROI,*-KI,-SHI*, トロイ, 鈍, *a.* Dull, sluggish, slow of motion, stupid. *Hi ga toroi*, the fire is dull. Syn. NOROI.

TOROKE,*-ru,-ta*, トロケル, *i.v.* To dissolve, to soften, liquify, to be debased. Syn. TOKERU.

TOROKU, トロク, *adv.* See *Toroi.*

TORORO, トロロ, *n.* A kind of gruel made of *Yamaimo.*

TORO-TORO-TO, トロトロト, *adv.* In a slight or short manner. — *neru*, to doze, to have short naps.

TORU, トル, 取, See *Tori.*

TŌRU, トホル, 通, See *Tōri.*

TOSAKA, トサカ, 鷄冠, *n.* A cock's comb.

TOSAN, トサン, 土產, *n.* Any article for the production or manufacturing of which a place is noted; domestic manufactory, a present made on returning from a journey. Syn. SAMBUTSZ.

†TOSE, トセ, 年, *n.* The same as *Toshi*, a year.

TOSEI, トセイ, 渡世, (*yo watari*). *n.* Business, occupation, employment. Syn. KAGIYŌ, SHŌBAI.

TŌ-SEI, タウセイ, 當世, *n.* The present age, the present time. —*fu*, present customs.

TO-SEN, トセン, 渡舩, (*watashi-bune*). *n.* A ferry-boat, a packet-ship. *Tosemba*, a jetty.

†TŌ-SEN, タウセン, 當千, (*sen ni ataru*). *n.* A match for a thousand. *Ichi nin — no mono naru*, one man is a match for a thousand.

†TŌSEN,*-szru*, トウセン, 鬪戰, (*tatakau*). To war, fight.

TŌ-SEN-GUSA, トウシングサ, 燈心草, *n.* The grass of which matting is made.

†TO-SEN-KAKU-SEN, トセンカクセン, (comp. of *Tokaku*, and *sen*, the fut. of *Shi*, to do). Shall I do this or shall I do that, or how shall I do, (in doubt or perplexity.)

TŌ-SETSZ, タウセツ, 當節, (*konotoki*). *adv.* Now, at the present time. Syn. IMA.

†TO-SHA, トシヤ, 吐瀉, (*haki kudashi*). *n.* Vomiting and purging.

TŌSHI,*-sz,-sh'ta*, トホス, 通, *t.v.* To cause to pass through, let through. Comp. with other verbs, = through, from one side to the other, from beginning to end, or constantly, always. *Michi wo akete h'to wo* —, to remove obstructions from a road to let people through. *Tōsh'te kīta*, have heard it through. *Hari ni ito wo* —, to thread a needle. *Kaze wo* —, to let the air pass through. *Yu wo* —, to strain hot water through any thing. *Tōshi itai ka*, does it pain constantly? *Tōsh'te itamimas*, it pains constantly.

TŌSHI, トホシ, 篩箕, *n.* A sieve.

TŌSHI, トホシ, 遠, *a.* Far, see *Tōi.*

TOSHI, トシ, 利, *adv.* Soon, early, see *Toi.*

TŌSHI, タウシ, 唐紙, (*kara no kami.*) *n.* Chinese paper.

†TOSHI, *-sz, -sh'ta*, トス, 吐, *t.v.* or *i.v.* To vomit. Syn. HAKU.

TOSHI, トシ, 年, *n.* Year. — *no kure*, close of the year. — *no hajime*, the beginning of the year. — *wo kurasz*, to live or pass one's life. — *ga tszmoru*, to grow old. — *ga yoru*, to become old. — *wa ikutsz*, how old are you? *Ore yori* — *ga wiye*, older than me. Syn. NEN.

TOSHIBAYE, トシバエ, *n.* Age. — *ga wakai h'to*, a person young in years. — *wa ikutsz gurai na h'to*, a person of about what age was he? Syn. YOWAI, NEN-REI.

TOSHI-DAMA, トシダマ, 年玉, A new-year's gift.

TOSHI-DOSHI, トシドシ, 年年, *adv.* Yearly, every year. Syn. NEN-NEN.

TOSHI-GO, トシゴ, 年子, *n.* Bearing a child every year. — *wo umu*, to bear a child yearly.

TOSHI-GORO, トシゴロ, 年來, *n.* Age, time of life, some years duration. — *no urami*, an enmity of some years duration.

TOSHI-GOTO-NI, トシゴトニ, 毎年, *adv.* Every year, yearly. Syn. MAI-NEN, NEN-NEN.

TOSHI-HA, トシハ, *n.* Age, used generally in the phrase. — *ga yukanu*, not advanced in years, still young.

TOSHI-KASA, トシカサ, 年重, *n.* Age, number of years old, elder in years. — *ga ōi*, very old. *Watakushi yori* — *da*, older than me.

TOSHI-KOSHI, トシコシ, 年越, *n.* The passing of the old year into the new year.

†TO-SHIN, トシン, 妬心, (*netamu kokoro*). Jealousy, envy. — *wo okosz.*

TŌ-SHIN, トウシン, 燈心, *n.* The wick of a lamp, or candle.

TOSHI-NAMI, トシナミ, 年次, *adv.* Yearly, each year, year by year. Syn. MAINEN.

TOSHISHI, トシシ, 兎絲子, *n.* The name of a parasitic vine, the Cuscuta major.

TOSHI-WAKA, トシワカ, 年少, *n.* Young in years, youthful.

TOSHI-WASZRE, トシワスレ, 年忘, *n.* An entertainment made at the close of the year, to forget its toils and troubles.

TOSHI-YORI, トシヨリ, 年寄, *n.* An old man; an elder of a street, or village, who ranks next below a *nanushi*; the council of state same as *Gorōjū.*

TOSHIYORI, *-ru, -tta*, トシヨル, 年寄, *i.v.* To be old, aged.

†TOSHUSEKI, トシユセキ, 吐酒石, *n.* Tartar emetic.

TOSO, トソ, 屠蘇, *n.* A kind of spiced *sake.*

TOTAN, トタン, 白鉛, *n.* Spelter, or zinc.

TOTAN, トタン, *n.* The act, or effort of doing. *Uma wo yokeru* — *ni dobu ni hamaru*, in the act of dodging the horse he fell into a ditch.

†TO-TAN, トタン, 塗炭, (*doro szmi*). *n.* Mire and charcoal, or dust and ashes; used only to convey the idea of extreme misery. — *ni kurushimu.*

TOTE, トテ, (contraction of *to*, pointing to what is said immediately before, and *iute*, having said, or *sh'te*, doing, or *omōte*, having thought). *Tszno wo naosz tote ushi wo korosz*, in mending the horn he killed the ox, (lit. "I will mend the horn" which doing, he, &c.) *Hanami ni tote demash'ta*, he went out, saying he "was going to see the flowers." *Tenjiku ni dachō tote ōkina tori ga iru*, in India there is a large bird called a *Dachō.*

†TOTEI, トテイ, 徒弟, *n.* Disciples, followers. Syn. MONTO.

TOTEMO, トテモ, *adv.* (comp. of *Tote* and *mo*). Following the verb. Although, even if, notwithstanding; as, *Yama dake no kuszri wo nomu totemo, naorimasen*, although you should take a mountain of medicine you cannot be cured. *Sen-ki ga ikki ni naru totemo kono seme-guchi wo yaburadzmba, h'to ashi mo hikaji*, although a thousand men should be reduced to one man, we will not retreat a step until we have taken this place.

(2). It is used as if the first part of the sentence was understood, = notwithstanding every way; or with a negative verb, in no way whatever, by no means. *Totemo-no-koto-ni*, = better, rather, by all means.

TOTO, トト, coll. Father. — *sama*, idem. Syn. CHICHI, OTOTSZ SAN.

TŌ-TŌ, トウトウ, *adv.* Onomato. In imitation of the sound of the wind. *Kaze ga* — *to todomeki wataru.*.

TŌ-TŌ, トウトウ, *adv.* coll. At length, at last; in the end, after all. — *szmi-mash'ta*, have finished at last. Syn. TSZI-NI.

TO-TŌ, トタウ, 徒黨, A band, league, confederacy, faction, conspiracy. — *szru*, to band or league together.

TŌTOI,-KI,-SHI, タフトイ, 貴, *a.* Honorable, noble, precious, valuable.
Syn. TATTOI.

TŌTOKU, タフトク, *adv.* idem.

TŌTOMI,*-mu,-nda*, タフトム, 貴, *t.v.* To honor, venerate, to esteem, prize.
Syn. TATTOMI, WIYAMAU, AGAMERU.

TOTONOI,*-ō,-ōta*, トトノフ, 調, *i.v.* To be in harmony, to accord, to be in tune. *Samisen no chōshi ga totonōta*, the strings of the guitar are in tune. *Iye ga —*, the family is harmonious.

TOTONOYE,*-ru,-ta*, トトノヘル, 調, *t.v.* To regulate, harmonize, adjust, to own, to get, obtain, buy, to make, to prepare. *Iye wo —*, to regulate a family. *Chōshi wo —*, to tune. *Kuszri wo —*, to prepare medicine. Syn. KOSHIRAYERU, MOTOMERU.

†TOTSZBEN, トツベン, 訥辨, Slow of speech. — *na h'to.*

‖TOTSZGI,*-gu,-ida*, トツグ, 嫁, *t. v.* To marry a wife, to be given in marriage.

TOTSZKAWA, トツカハ, *adv.* coll. Unexpectedly, suddenly.
Syn. FUTO.

†TOTSZ-KUNI, トツクニ, 外國, *n.* A foreign country. Syn. G'WAI-KOKU.

†TOTSZ-OITSZ, トツオイツ, *adv.* In doubt what to do, this way or that way. — *anjiwadzrō*, anxiously reflecting what to do.

†TŌTSZOYA, トホツオヤ, 遠祖, *n.* Ancestor. Syn. SENZO.

†TOTSZ-ZEN, トツゼン, 突然, *adv.* Abruptly, suddenly. Syn. FUTO, TOTSZKAWA.

TOTTA, トツタ, pret. of *Tori.*

TOTTE, トツテ, *pp.* of *Tori.*

TOTTE, トツテ, *n.* A knob, or catch to take hold of.

TOTTOKI, トツトキ, 取置, (cont. of *Torite* and *oki*). coll. That which is laid up, or reserved for a time of need or future use. — *no kane wo dash'te tszkau*, to use money which had been kept in reserve.

TOWADZ, トハズ, 不問, neg. of *Toi.* Without asking, or inquiring. — *gatari*, a story told without being prompted to it.

TŌWAKU, タウワク, 當惑, Doubt, perplexity, trouble, dilemma. — *szru*, to be in doubt and perplexity.
Syn. TOHŌ NI KURERU.

TOWARE,*-ru,-ta*, トハレル, 被問, pass. of *Toi.*

TOWASE,*-ru,-ta*, トハセル, 令問, caust. of *Toi.* To cause another to ask, or to get for one's self permission to ask or inquire.

TOWATARI, トワタリ, 會陰, *n.* The perineum.

TŌ-WŌ, トウワウ, 藤黄, *n.* Gamboge.

TŌYA, トホヤ, 遠失, *n.* A long shot with a bow.

TOYA, トヤ, 鳥屋, *n.* A chicken coop.
Syn. TOGURA.

TOYA, トヤ, *n.* Moulting of birds. — *wo szru*, to moult.

TO-YA-KAKU-TO, or TOYAKŌTO, トヤカクト, Derived from *Tokaku.* That way or this, various ways.

TOYE, トヘ, imp. of *Toi.* Ask, inquire. — *yo*, idem.

TO-YE, トヘ, 十重, Ten folds, or ten-layers.

TOYU, トユ, *n.* A pipe for conducting water. Syn. TOI, HI.

TŌYU, ドウユ, 桐油, *n.* Oiled paper, a rain-coat made of oiled paper.

TŌZA, タウザ, 當坐, For this time only, temporary, for the time being. — *no hōbi*, a reward intended only for the time being, until something better can be obtained.

TŌ-ZAI, ドウザイ, 東西, *(higashi nishi).* East and west.

TO-ZAI, ドザイ, 吐劑, *(haku guszri). n.* An emetic.

TŌZAKARI,*-ru,-tta*, トホザカル, 遠, *i. v.* To keep at a distance from, not to be familiar with, estranged.

TŌZAKE,*-ru,-ta*, ドホザケル, 遠, *t.v.* To keep at a distance, keep away. *Aku-nin wo —. Teki wo —.*

TOZAMA, ドザマ, 外樣, *n.* A noble or baron who is not a vassal of the *Shōgun.*

TŌZAN, タウザン, 唐棧, *n.* Taffachelles.
Syn. SANTOME.

TOZASHI,*-sz,-sh'ta*, ドザス, 鎖, *t.v.* To shut, close. *To wo —*, to shut the door.
Syn. TOJIRU, SHIMERU.

TOZEN, トゼン, 徒然, *n.* Leisure and ennui, when one has nothing to do and time hangs heavy. — *de komaru.* — *wo nagusameru.* Syn. TAIKUTSZ, TSZREDZRE.

TŌ-ZEN, タウゼン, 當然, *(shikaru beki).* Proper, right, that which ought to be; natural, or according to the stated course of things, of course. Syn. ATARI-MAYE.

TŌZOKU, タウゾク, 盜賊, *n.* A robber, thief. Syn. DOROBŌ, NUSZBITO.

TSZ, ツ, 津, *(minato). n.* A harbor, a port for ships.

†TSZ, ツ, An obs. pret. suffix, = *ta*, or *tari*. *Mitsz* = *mita* : *Kikitsz* = *kīta* : *Ame ga furitsz yamitsz*, = *ame ga futtari yandari*, it rains by fits and starts.

†TSZ, ツ, An obs. gen. suffix to nouns, = *no*, of. *Amatsz*, of heaven. *Kunitsz*, of the state.

TSZBA, ツバ, 鐔, *n.* The guard on the hilt of a sword.

TSZBA, or TSZBAKI, ツバキ, 唾, *n.* Saliva. — *wo haku*, to spit.

TSZBAKI, ツバキ, 椿, *n.* The Camelia Japonica.

TSZBAKURA, ツバクラ, 燕, *n.* The swallow, or martin.

TSZBAME, ツバメ, 燕, *n.* Idem.

TSZBANA, ツバナ, 茅花, *n.* The flower of a kind of grass.

TSZBARA, or TSZBARAKA, ツバラカ, Contracted form of *Tszmabiraka.*

TSZBASA, ツバサ, 翼, *n.* The wings of a bird. Syn. HANE, HAGAI.

‖TSZBI, ツビ, 陰戸, (*immon*). *n.* The vulva.

TSZBO, ツボ, 坪, *n.* A land measure of six feet square, or 36 sq. feet.

TSZBO, ツボ, 壺, *n.* A jar.

TSZBOMARI,-*ru*,-*tta*, ツボマル, *i.v.* To be puckered up, drawn together, or contracted, same as *Szbomaru*. *Fukuro no kuchi ga* —, the mouth of the bag is drawn together.

TSZBOME,-*ru*,-*ta*, ツボメル, *t.v.* To pucker, draw together, or contract. *Kuchi wo* —, to pucker the mouth. Syn. SZBOMERU.

TSZBOMI,-*mu*,-*nda*, ツボム, *i. v.* To be puckered, drawn together, contracted, to be closed or shut as a flower.
Syn. SZBOMU, SHIBOMU.

TSZBOMI, ツボミ, 蕾, *n.* A flower-bud.

TSZBONE, ツボネ, 局, *n.* A room, generally used of the rooms occupied by female servants in the house of a noble, also the women who occupy them.

TSZBOYANAGUI, ツボヤナグヒ, 壺籙籙, *n.* A quiver of the shape of a long jar.

TSZBU, ツブ, 粒, *n.* A grain; the numeral in counting grains, seeds, pills, or any thing small and roundish. *Kome h'to* —, one grain of rice. *G'wanyaku mi tszbu*, three pills.

TSZBURE,-*ru*,-*ta*, ツブレル, 潰, *i. v.* To be broken; said of things like an egg, bubble, the eye, gall-bladder, &c. to be burst, mashed, worn off or effaced, as by friction; stopped up or closed up, as a hole; to be bankrupt and ruined. *Tamago ga* —, the egg is broken. *Me ga* —, the eye is spoiled. *Deki-mono ga* —, the boil is broken. *Hari no ana ga* —, the eye of the needle is closed up. *Yaszri no me ga* —, the teeth of the file are worn off. *Kabu ga* —, his license is broken, or taken away. *Iye ga* —, his house is bankrupt. *Kimo ga* —, gall-bladder is mashed, *i.e.* to be greatly astonished. *Mimi ga* —, to be deaf. *Koye ga* —, to lose the voice.
Syn. KOWARERU, YABURERU, KUDZRERU.

TSZBURI, ツブリ, See *Tszmuri*.

TSZBUSA-NI, ツブサニ, 具, *adv.* Minutely, particularly, in detail.
Syn. KUWASHIKU, ISAI, KOMAYAKA-NI, TSZMABIRAKA-NI.

TSZBUSHI,-*sz*,-*sh'ta*, ツブス, 潰, *t.v.* To break, to mash, burst, to crush, to spoil, or destroy; to fill up, as a hole; to rub off, or wear off by friction. *Tamago wo* —, to break an egg. *Kimo wo* —, to be astonished. *Ji wo* —, to erase a letter.
Syn. KOWASZ, YABURU, KUDZSZ.

TSZBUTE, ツブテ, 礫, *n.* A small stone, a pebble. — *wo utsz*, to throw stones. *H to wo* — *ni utsz*, to fling a man, as if he were a stone.

TSZBU-TSZBU, ツブツブ, 粒粒, *n.* Grains, any small lumps, granulations. *Kono nori wa* — *ga dekita*, this paste is lumpy, not smooth.

TSZBUYAKI,-*ku*,-*ita*, ツブヤク, *i. v.* To grumble, murmur, or complain or mutter to one's self.

TSZCHI, ツチ, 土, *n.* Earth, clay, soil, ground, mortar. 地, The earth.

TSZCHI, ツチ, 槌, *n.* A hammer, mallet.

TSZCHIBETA, ツチベタ, *n.* The ground. — *ni neru*, to lie on the ground. — *ni oku*, to set it on the ground.

TSZCHI-BOTOKE, ツチボトケ, 土佛, *n.* A clay idol. Syn. DOBUTSZ.

TSZCHI-DO, ツチド, 土戸, *n.* A door made of plaster, as in fire-proof store-houses.

TSZCHI-GUMO, ツチグモ, 土蜘蛛, *n.* A species of spider.

TSZCHI-HOTARU, ツチホタル, 土螢, *n.* A glow-worm.

TSZCHIKAI,-*ō*,-*ōta*, ツチカフ, 培, *t.v.* To hoe and draw the earth around the stems of grain, &c. *Mugi ni* —.

TSZCHI-KAWADZ, ツチカハヅ, 土蛙, *n.* A toad.

TSZCHI-KAZE, ツチカゼ, 土風, *n.* A sand storm, or wind accompanied with dust.

TSZCHIKURE, ツチクレ, 塊, *n.* A clod of earth.

TSZCHI-NINGIYŌ, ツチニンギヤウ, 土人形, *n.* Clay figures of men.

TSZCHINOYE, ツチノエ, 戊, and TSZCHI-NOTO, ツチノト, 巳, *n.* Two of the ten signs used in numbering years, months, days, hours, &c.

†TSZDOI,-ō,-ōta, ツドフ, 聚, *i.v.* To assemble, to collect together, gather. Syn. ATSZMARU.

TSZDO-TSZDO, ツドツド, 度度, *adv.* Each time, every time. Syn. GOTO-NI.

TSZDOYE,-*ru*,-*ta*, ツドヘル, 度, *t.v.* To assemble, collect, gather. Syn. ATSZMERU.

‖TSZDZ, ツヅ, 十, *n.* Ten years old. — *ya hatachi*, ten or twenty years old.

TSZDZKANAI,-KI,-SHI, ツヅカナイ, 無恙, Well, free from sickness, safe, free from harm, or accident. Syn. MUBIYŌ, BUJI.

TSZDZKANAKU, ツヅカナク, *adv.* Idem. — *o kurashi nasaru ka*, are you in good health?

TSZDZKE,-*ru*,-*ta*, ツヅケル, 續, *t.v.* To do without interruption, to do continuously, in succession, or consecutively; to lengthen or splice, to connect. *Kuszri wo tszdzkete nomu*, to persevere in taking medicine, or to take it regularly. *Hiyōrō wo* —, to keep up a regular supply of provisions. *Sake wo tszdzkete jippai nonda*, have drunk ten glasses of wine one after the other. *Nawa wo* —, to splice and lengthen a rope. *Tomoshibi ni abura wo* —, to supply oil regularly to a lamp. Syn. TAYEDZ.

TSZDZKI,-*ku*,-*ita*, ツヅク, 續, *i. v.* To continue uninterrupted, or unbroken; to be continued in regular succession. *Tenki ga* —, the weather continues fine. *Ame ga tszdzite furu*, to rain several days in succession. *Chi-szji ga tszdzite oru*, the family line continues unbroken.

TSZDZMARI,-*ru*,-*tta*, ツヅマル, 約, *i.v.* To contract, to become smaller, to be abridged, to conclude, end, (as a story). Syn. CHIJIMARU.

TSZDZMAYAKA, ツヅマヤカ, 約, Economical, frugal, saving. Syn. KENYAKU.

TSZDZME,-*ru*,-*ta*, ツヅメル, 約, *t.v.* To diminish, reduce in length, or size; to contract, abridge, to end, conclude. *Jissatsz wo go satsz ni* —, to abridge a book of ten volumes to five. Syn. CHIJIMERU.

TSZDZMI, ツヅミ, 鼓, *n.* A drum. — *no oto*, the sound of a drum.

TSZDZRA, ツヅラ, 葛, *n.* The name of a vine used in making baskets, &c.

TSZDZRA, ツヅラ, 葛籠, *n.* A basket, or box made of Tszdzra, or bamboo.

TSZDZRA-ORI, ツヅラオリ, 羊腸, *n.* Zigzag. — *no michi.* a zig-zag road.

TZSDZRE, ツヅレ, 襤褸, *n.* Ragged clothes, rags. Syn. BORO.

TSZDZRI,-*ru*,-*tta*, ツヅル, 綴, To sew patches together, to patch; to compose a work of fiction. *Kogire wo tszdztte f'ton ni szru*, to make a quilt by sewing patches together.

TSZGAI,-*au*,-*atta*, ツガフ, 番, (contr. of *Tszgi* and *ai*), *t.v.* To join one thing to another by a joint, or hinge. *Yumi ni ya wo* —, to fix the arrow to the bow string. Syn. HAMERU.

TSZGAI, ツガヒ, 番, *n.* A pair consisting of male and female; a joint, hinge, or place where two things hinge on each other, as a screen. *Niwatori h'to* —, a pair of fowls. *Biyōbu no — ga kireta*, the joint of the screen is broken.

TSZGAI-ME, ツガヒメ, 番目, *n.* A joint, hinge. *Hone no* —, the joint of a bone.

TSZGANE,-*ru*,-*ta*, ツガネル, 束, *t.v.* To bind into a bundle, as straw, sticks. *Wara wo* —, to bind straw into a sheaf. Syn. TABANERU, SOKŪ.

TSZGASE,-*ru*,-*ta*, ツガセル, 令續, caust. of *Tszgi.* To cause, or let splice, &c. *Nawa wo* —, to order another to splice a rope.

TSZGASHI,-*sz*,-*sh'ta*, ツガス, Idem.

TSZGE,-*ru*,-*ta*, ツゲル, 告, *t.v.* To tell, inform, to announce, relate. *Shu-jin ni* —, to tell the master. Syn. KIKASERU.

TSZGE, ツゲ, 黄楊, *n.* Boxwood.

TSZGE-GUCHI, ツゲグチ, 告口, *n.* Telling tales or informing on others. — *wo szru.*

TSZGI,-*gu*,-*ida*, ツグ, 繼, *t. v.* To join or connect one thing to another, so as to lengthen, repair, or supply a deficiency; to splice, to graft, to mend; to inherit, to succeed another; to pour into, to cement. *Chawan wo* —, to join together the pieces of a broken tea cup. *Hone wo* —, to set a broken bone. *Ki wo* —, to graft a tree. *Nawa wo* —, to splice a rope. *Iye* or *yo wo* —, to succeed to a family estate, or name. *Ato wo* —, idem. *Cha, midz, abura, sake nado wo* —, to pour tea, water, oil, or wine into a cup. *Kimono wo* —, to patch or lengthen a garment. *Yo wo hi ni tszide yuku*, to go constantly day and night. *Setomono wo* —, to cement porcelain.

TSZGI, ツギ, 繼, *n.* Enlarging, lengthening, or repairing, by joining one thing to another; splicing; a patch. — *wo szru*, to splice, to patch.

TSZGI, ツギ, 次, *n.* The next, succeeding, adjacent, contiguous, adjoining, inferior. *Sono — wa dare*, who comes next to him? *Kono shina mono wa — da*, this article is inferior in quality. — *no heya*, the next room.

TSZGI-AWASE, *-ru, -ta*, ツギアハセル, 繼合, *t.v.* To join together, connect, splice together.

TSZGIHO, ツギホ, 椄穗, *n.* The branch that is ingrafted into a tree, a graft.

TSZGIKI, ツギキ, 椄木, *n.* A grafted tree.

TSZGIME, ツギメ, 續目, *n.* The place where two things are joined, a joint, seam.

TSZGI-MONO, ツギモノ, 繼物, *n.* Mending, or patching garments. — *wo szru.*

TSZGI-NI, ツギニ, 次, *adv.* Next in time, order, or place; adjoining to, contiguous to, adjacent to; after. *Hon wo yonde — tenarai wo szru*, after reading to practice writing.

TSZGI-NO-MA, ツギノマ, 次之間, *n.* The next room.

TSZGI-TASHI, *-sz, -sh'ta*, ツギタス, 續足, *t.v.* To lengthen, to enlarge, to splice. *Iye wo —* to enlarge a house. *Nawa wo —*, splice a rope.

TSZGI-TSZGI-NI, ツギツギニ, 續續, *adv.* One after the other, in succession, consecutively. — *riyōji wo szru*, to prescribe for patients one after another.
Syn, JUN-JUN-NI.

TSZGŌ, ツガフ, 都合, *(szbete awaseru)*, *n.* The sum total, amount, aggregate. — *ikura*, what is the amount? — *ga warui*, inconvenient. — *ga yoi*, convenient. — *shidai ni szru*, to act according to circumstances. Syn. SHIMETE.

TSZGŌ, ツガフ, 番, See *Tszgai*.

†TSZGOMORI, ツゴモリ, 晦日, *n.* The last day of a month. Syn. MISOKA.

TSZGU, ツグ, 繼, See *Tszgi.*

TSZGUMI, ツグミ, 鶫, *n.* The name of a bird.

TSZGUMI, *-mu, -nda*, ツグム, 咁, *t.v.* To shut, spoken only of the mouth. *Kuchi wo —*, to shut the mouth, to keep silence.

TSZGUNAI, *-au, -atta*, ツグナフ, 償, *t. v.* To make good, to indemnify, to make satisfaction or compensation, to commute, to make amends, to atone for, answer for, to expiate. *Tomodachi no shakkin wo —*, to pay the debts of a friend. *Kō wo tatete tszmi wo —*, to atone for one's crimes by good conduct.
Syn. AGANAU, MADŌ.

TSZGUNAI, ツグナヒ, 償, *n.* Compensation. reparation, indemnification, restitution, atonement, commutation.

TSZGUNAI-KIN, ツグナヒキン, 償金, *n.* Money paid as indemnity, satisfaction money, ransom.

TSZGURU, ツグル, 告, Same as *Tszgeru.*

TSZI, ツイ, *adv.* Quickly, soon, promptly. — *dekimas*, I will do it soon.
Syn. JIKI-NI, SZGU-NI.

TSZI, ツ井, 對, *n.* A couple, or two of like things, a pair; alike, same. *Ittszi no kake-mono*, a pair of hanging pictures. — *no kimono*, clothes that are alike, or match. — *no nari*, same style. *Ittszi no hanaike*, a pair of flower vases.
Syn. SOROI.

TSZI, ツヒ, An exclam. of regret, sorrow, or disappointment in making a mistake, committing a blunder, or on forgetting anything; as. *Tszi waszremash'ta*, there! I have forgotten. *Tszi otosh'ta. Tszi ayamatta.*

TSZIBAMI, *-mu, -nda*, ツイバム, 啄, (comp. of *Tszki*, to pick, and *hamu*, to eat), *t.v.* To pick-up and eat, as a bird. *Tori ga ye wo —*, the bird picks up its food.

TSZIDE, ツイデ, 序, *n.* Regular order, turn, occasion, convenience, opportunity. — *wo midasz*, to disturb the order. — *ni yotte kuru*, to come in regular order. — *ga attara yorimashō*, when I have an opportunity I shall call. — *nagara mōshi age soro*, I take this opportunity to say. — *wo matsz*, to wait for a convenient time. *On — no setsz* when you have a convenient time. *Tōru — ni yoru*, to call as one is passing. *Sentaku no — ni kore wo araye*, wash this when you are washing clothes.

TSZI-FUKU, ツイフク, 對幅, *n.* A pair of hanging pictures.

TSZIGASANE, ツイガサネ, 衝重, *n.* A set of boxes, either wood or porcelain, fitting one on the other.

TSZI-HŌ, ツ井ハウ, 追放, *(oi-hanatsz)*, *n.* Banishment or expulsion from a place, as a punishment for crime. — *szru.*
Syn. TOKORO-BARAI.

TSZIJI, ツイヂ, 墻, *n.* A fence, or wall made of earth, or clay. Syn. NERIBEI.

TSZIKA, ツ井カ, 追加, *n.* An appendix.

†TSZIMATSZ, ツイマツ, 續松, *n.* A torch made of pine, flambeau. Syn. TAIMATSZ.

TSZI-NI, ツヒニ, 終, *adv.* At least, at length,

finally, after all: with a negative verb, = never. *Riyō-ji wo sh'te mo — shinimashō,* do all you can for him he will die after all. *— mita koto mo nai,* have never seen it. Syn. TŌ-TŌ.

TSZI-SHŌ, ツ井シヨウ, 追従, Flattery. — *szru,* to flatter. — *wo iu,* idem. Syn. HETSZRAU.

TSZI-SHU, ツ井シユ, 堆朱, *n.* Red lacquer carved or embossed.

TSZITA, ツイタ, 付, pret. of *Tszki.*

TSZITACHI, ツイタチ, 朔日, *n.* The first day of a month.

TSZI-TATE, ツイタテ, 衝立, *n.* A screen set on a stand.

TSZITE, ツイテ, 付, *pp.* of *Tszki.*

†TSZITŌ,*–szru,* ツ井タウ, 追討, *(oiutsz).* To drive and smite with the sword, to destroy, as a body of rebels.

TSZIYASHI,*–sz,–sh'ta,* ツヒヤス, 費, *t.v.* To waste, squander, to spend uselessly. *Kingin wo —,* to waste money. *Munashiku toki wo —,* to spend time uselessly. *Chikara wo —,* to waste the strength.

TSZIYE,*–ru,–ta,* ツヒエル, 費, *i. v.* To be wasted, squandered, consumed or spent uselessly. *Kane no tsziyeru koto wo szru na,* don't waste money.

TSZIYE, ツヒエ, 費, *n.* Waste, useless consumption.

TSZIZEN, ツ井ゼン, 追善, *n.* Mass said or offerings made for the dead. *— wo szru,* to perform mass. Syn. HŌJI.

TSZJI, ツジ, 辻, *n.* The place where two streets cross, or where a street forks. Syn. CHIMATA.

TSZJI-BAN, ツジバン, 辻番, *n.* A guard house at a cross-street.

TSZJI-DŌ, ツジダウ, 辻堂, *n.* A small shed with an idol in it erected at a crossing, or at the fork of a road.

TSZJI-GIRI, ツジギリ, 辻切, *n.* Killed or murdered in the streets.

TSZJITSZMA, ツジツマ, Always used with *awanu;* as, *— ga awanu koto,* something contradictory, or incompatible with what was said before.

TSZJI-URI, ツジウリ, 辻賣, *n.* Selling in the streets.

TSZKA, ツカ, *n.* A prop, brace. *— wo kau,* to brace.

TSZKA, ツカ, 塚, *n.* A tomb, a mound of earth. *Ichi ri tszka,* mounds along a road for marking the miles. Syn. HAKA.

TSZKA, ツカ, 欛, *n.* The hilt of a sword; handle of a knife,

TSZKA, ツカ, 束, *n.* A hand breadth. *Tō — no tszrugi,* a sword ten hands long.

TSZKA-BUKURO, ツカブクロ, 欛袋, *n.* The covering of a sword hilt.

TSZKADZ, ツカズ, 不付, *neg.* of *Tszki.*

TSZKAI, ツカヒ, 使, *n.* A messenger. Syn. SHISHA.

TSZKAI,*–au,–atta,* ツカフ, 使, *t.v.* To use, employ, to send (a messenger). *Kane wo —,* to spend money. *H'to wo —,* to employ a man. *Ki wo —* to be anxious, or worried. *Kokoro wo —,* idem. Syn. MOCHIRU.

TSZKAI-HATASHI,*–sz,–sh'ta,* ツカヒハタス, 使果, *t. v.* To use up, to spend all.

TSZKAI-KATA, ツカヒカタ, 使方, *n.* The way of using, or how to use anything. *— wo shiranu,* don't know how to use it. *— ga nai,* of no use.

TSZKAI-MICHI, ツカヒミチ, 使道, *n.* idem.

TSZKAI-MONO, ツカヒモノ, 遣物, *n.* A present. Syn. REIMOTSZ, SHINJŌ-MONO.

TSZKAI-NIKUI,*–KI,–KU,* ツカヒニクイ, 使難, Difficult, or disagreeable to use or employ; unhandy.

TSZKAI-SZGI, ツカヒスギ, 使過, *n.* Using or spending to excess, wastefulness, prodigality, extravagance.

TSZKAI-TE, ツカヒテ, 使手, *n.* A user, an employer.

TSZKA-ITO, ツカイト, 欛絲, *n.* The thread used for winding round the hilt of a sword.

TSZKAI-YŌ, ツカヒヤウ, 遣様, *n.* The way of using, how to use. Syn. TSZKAI-KATA.

TSZKAMARE,*–ru,–ta,* ツカマレル, 被扼, pass. of *Tszkami.* To be grasped in the hand. to be caught, seized.

TSZKAMATSZRI,*–ru,–tta,* ツカマツル, 仕, To do; a respectful word used to superiors or honorable persons; the same as *Szru, Itasz, Nasz. O tomo tszkamatszri-mashō,* = *O tomo shi-mashō,* I shall go with you.

TSZKAMAYE,*–ru,–ta,* ツカマヘル, 扼, *t. v.* To grasp, lay hold of, to seize, to catch, to arrest, capture. *Dorobō wo —,* to catch a thief. *Hashiri uma wo —,* to catch a run away horse. *Nawa wo tszkamayete noboru,* to climb up by a rope. Syn. TORAYERU, NIGIRU.

TSZKAMI,*–mu,–nda,* ツカム, 扼, *t. v.* To grasp, to lay hold of, to seize, to catch, to clutch. *Washi wa hebi wo —,* the eagle seizes the snake. *Ki no ne wo tszkande yama ye noboru,* to climb the mountain by catching hold of the roots of trees. Syn. NIGIRU.

TSZKAMI, ツカミ, 抓, *n.* A handful. *Kome h'to* —, a handful of rice.

TSZKAMI-AI,–*au*,–*atta*, ツカミアヒ, 抓合, *t. v.* To grasp each other. *Kami wo tszkamiatte kenk'wa szru*, to seize hold of each others hair aud fight.

TSZKAMI-DASHI,–*sz*,–*sh'ta*, ツカミダス, 抓出, *t. v.* To seize hold of and put out, or take out.

TSZKAMI-DORI, ツカミドリ, 抓取, *n.* Seizing or clutching all one can get, snatching.

TSZKAMI-KAKARI,–*ru*,–*tta*, ツカミカカル, 抓掛, About to lay hold, or seize.

TSZKAMI-KOROSHI,–*sz*,–*sh'ta*, ツカミコロス, 抓殺, *t.v.* To squeeze, or choke to death, with the hand.

TSZKAMI-KOWASHI,–*sz*,–*sh'ta*, ツカミコハス, 摑破, *t.v.* To break by squeezing in the hand, to crush with the hand.

TSZKAMI-KUDAKI,–*ku*,–*ita*, ツカミクダク, 握摧, To crush with the hand.

TSZKANU, or TSZKADZ, ツカヌ, 不付, neg. of *Tszku*. *Ki ga tszkananda*, did not take notice.

TSZKARAKASHI,–*sz*,–*sh'ta*, ツカラカス, 疲, caust. of *Tszkareru*. To cause to be tired, or fatigued. *Umo wo* — to tire a horse.

TSZKARE,–*ru*,–*ta*, ツカレル, 被著, pass. of *Tszku*. To be fastened on, bewitched, fixed to, &c.

TSZKARE,–*ru*,–*ta*, ツカレル, 疲, *i.v.* To be tired, fatigued, wearied, faint, exhausted, worn out, enfeebled. *Nagamichi wo aruite ashi ga tszkareta*, my feet are tired by walking so far. *Ara shigoto de tszkareta*, worn out by hard work.
Syn. KUTABIRERU.

TSZKARE,–*ru*,–*ta*, ツカレル, 被, pass. or pot. of *Tszki*. To be stabbed, &c. *Yari de tszkareru*, stabbed by a spear.

TSZKARE, ツカレ, 疲, *n.* Fatigue, weariness, exhaustion. *Tabi no* —, the fatigue of traveling. *Biyō-go no* —, the weakness produced by sickness. — *ga deru*, to become tired.

TSZKARI,–*ru*,–*tta*, ツカル, 浸, *i. v.* Used only in the phrase. *Midz ni* —, to be in the water. *Nagaku midz ni tszkatte ita kara omoku natta*, it is heavy from being long in the water.

TSZKASA, ツカサ, 司, *n.* Ruler, superintendent, director. Syn. CHŌ, KASHIRA.

TSZKASADORI,–*ru*,–*tta*, ツカサドル, 司, *t.v.* To govern, direct, rule, superintend. *Kuni no seiji wo* —, to rule over a country. *Fushin wo* —, to superintend a building. Syn. SHI-HAI SZRU.

TSZKA-TSZKA, ツカツカ, coll. *adv.* Suddenly, abruptly. Syn. SOTSZ-ZEN.

TSZKAU, ツカフ, 使, See *Tskai*.

TSZKAWARE,–*ru*,–*ta*, ツカハレル, 被使, pass. of *Tszkai*. To be used or employed.

TSZKAWASHI,–*sz*,–*sh'ta*, ツカハス, 遣, *t.v.* To send, to give, only spoken to an inferior. *Tszkai wo* —, to send a messenger. *Tegami wo Yedo ye* —, to send a letter to Yedo. *Kore wa sono-hō ye tszkawasz*, I give this to you. Syn. YARU.

TSZKAYE,–*ru*,–*ta*, ツカヘル, 事 or 仕, *t.v.* To serve, to wait upon, minister to, to perform official duties, to obey. *Fubo ni* —, to obey one's parents. Syn. TSZTOMERU.

TSZKAYE,–*ru*,–*ta*, ツカヘル, 支, *i. v.* To obstruct, block up, impede, stop, hinder, clogged. *Mune ga* —, to have an obstruction in the stomach.
Syn. TODOKŌRU, FUSAGARU.

TSZKAYE, ツカヘ, 支, *n.* Obstruction, impediment, stoppage.
Syn. JAMA, TODORŌRI, SAWARI.

TSZKE,–*ru*,–*ta*, ツケル, 付, *t.v.* To apply, fix, or fasten one thing to another, to put on, set. *Na wo* —, to give a name. *Kidz ni kuszri wo* —, to apply medicine to a wound. *Iro wo* —, to color, or dye. *Kabe wo* —, to put on plaster, to plaster. *Oshiroi wo* —, to powder the face. *Hi wo* —, to kindle, or set on fire. *Chōmen ni* —, to write any thing in an account book or register. *Ban wo* —, to set a watch. *Me wo* —, to fix the eye on. *Hari ni ito wo* —, to thread a needle. *Ne wo* —, to fix a price. *Shirushi wo* —, to mark, fix a mark on. *Kane wo* —, to blacken the teeth. *Ki wo* —, to give heed to, be careful of. *Nan wo* —, to fasten trouble upon any one, as by a false report. *Tegami wo* —, to send a letter. *Midz ni* —, to put into water, to soak. *Shio wo tszkete kū*, eat it seasoned with salt. *Fude wo szmi ni* —, to dip the pen into ink.

TSZKE-BANA, ツケバナ, 付鼻, *n.* Artificial nose.

TSZKEBI, ツケビ, 付火, *n.* A conflagration caused by an incendiary.

TSZKE-GAMI, ツケカミ, 付髮, *n.* False hair. — *wo szru*, to put on false hair.

TSZKEGI, ツケギ, 火奴, *n.* A match, made of sticks tipped with sulphur.

TSKE-GUSZRI, ツケグスリ, 傅藥, *n.* Medicines used by external application.

TSZKE-KAKE, ツケカケ, 付掛, *n.* Overcharging, charging in a day book more than the price for which anything was bought.

TSZKE-ISHI, ツケイシ, 試石, *n.* A touchstone.

TSZKE-KOMI,*–mu,–nda*, ツケコム, 付込, Observing the condition of anything in order to take advantage of it; to mark, take notice of. *H'to no yowami wo tszkekonde komaraseru*, to take advantage of the weak points of another to vex him.

TSZKE-MONO, ツケモノ, 漬物, *n.* Anything pickled in brine.

TSZKERU, ツケル, 付, See *Tszke.*

TSZKETARI, ツケタリ, 附, *n.* Any thing added as a note, or addendum.

TSZKETE, ツケテ, *pp.* of *Tszke.*

TSZKE-YAKI-BA, ツケヤキバ, 附焼刃, *n.* An edge put on a sword by roasting, so as to resemble a good edge; fig. spoken of a person who pretends to a knowledge or skill which is not real.

TSZKI, ツキ, 月, (*getsz*). *n.* The moon, month. — *ga deru*, the moon rises. — *ga iru*, the moon sets. — *ga mitszru*, the moon is full. — *ga kakeru*, the moon wanes. *Kono* —, this month. *Ato no* —, last month. Syn. G'WATSZ,

TSZKI, ツキ, 槻, *n.* The name of a tree, same as *Keyaki.*

TSZKI, ツキ, The name of a bird, same as *Toki.*

TSZKI, ツキ, *n.* Form, manner, used only in compound words; as, *Kao-tszki*, expression of face. *Me-tszki*, the expression of the eye. *Te-tszki*, the form of the hand, or way of using it. *Ashi-tszki*, way of walking. *Kotoba-tszki*, manner of speaking, or voice. Syn. NARI, FURI.

TSZKI,*–ku,–ita*, ツク, 付, *i.v.* To stick, cleave or adhere to, to be fixed or fastened to; to arrive; to follow, join or side with; to belong to; to bewitch, spell, (as a fox). *Szmi ga te ni* —, the ink sticks to the hand. *Kutsz ni doro ga* —, the mud sticks to the shoes. *Shōne ga* —, to come to one's senses. *Kitszne ga* —, possessed by a fox. *Biyōki ga* —, infected with disease. *Fune ga tszita*, the ship has arrived. *Wiyeki ga* —, the shrub has taken root. *Kurai ni* —, to ascend the throne. *Za ni* —, to take a seat. *Waga te ni* —, to join my command, or party. *Kerai ga shujin ni* —, the servant adheres to, or sides with his lord. *Fune ni ro ga* —, the oar belongs to, or is a part of the boat. *Migi ni tszite*, on account of the foregoing reasons. *Katte ni tszki tentaku szru*, to move one's residence for the sake of convenience. *Iro ga* —, to be stained or colored. *Ato kara tszite koi*, follow me, or come after me. *Hi ga tszita*, the fire begins to burn. *Kono sekitan wa hi ga tszkanu*, this coal will not burn.

TSZKI,*–ku,–ita*, ツク, 突, *t.v.* To thrust, or strike with anything pointed; to stab; to pound as with a pestle. *Kane wo* —, to ring a large bell, (by thrusting a stick of wood against it). *Tszye wo tszite aruku*, to walk with a cane. *Mochi wo* —, to beat rice bread in a mortar. *Yari de* —, to stab with a spear. *Iki wo* —, to make a forcible expiration.

TSZKI,*–ku,–ita*, ツク, 築, *t. v.* To build with stones, or earth. *Shiro wo* —, to build a castle. *Ishigaki, toride, odaiba, hettszi nado wo* —, to build a stonewall, intrenchment, fort, or furnace.
Syn. KIDZKU.

TSZKI,*–ru,–ta*, ツキル, 盡, *i.v.* To be used up, to be exhausted, consumed, spent, finished, ended. *Kane ga tszkita*, the money is all gone. *Chikara ga* —, strength is exhausted. *Toshi ga* —, the year is ended. Syn. NAKUNARU.

TSZKI-AGE*–ru,–ta*, ツキアゲル, 突上, *t.v.* To thrust upward at anything. 築上, To finish building as a wall, &c.

TSZKI-AI,*–au,–atta*, ツキアフ, 著合, *i.v.* To associate, keep company, to have intercourse, or communion. 突合, To thrust, push at, or gore each other. *Aku nin ni tszki-au na*, keep no company with a wicked man. Syn. MAJIWARU.

TSZKI-AI, ツキアヒ, 著合, *n.* Associating, keeping company, intercourse, communion, acquaintance.
Syn. MAJIWARI.

TSZKI-AKARI, ツキアカリ, 月明, *n.* Moonlight. — *de hon wo yomu*, to read a book by moonlight.

TSZKI-ATARI,*–ru,–tta*, ツキアタル, 突當, *t.v.* To strike against, to collide.

TSZKI-BAN, ツキバン, 月番, *n.* Monthly duty as guard or watchman.

TSZKI-BARAI, ツキバラヒ, 月掃, *n.* Monthly payments, paying by the month.

TSZKI-DASHI,*–sz,–sh'ta*, ツキダス, 突出, *t.v.* To drive or push out.

TSZKIDEPPŌ, ツキデツポウ, *n.* A popgun.

TSZKI-DZKI, ツキヅキ, 月月, *adv.* Monthly, each month.

TSZKI-DZYE, ツキズヱ, 月末, *n.* The last ten days of a month. Syn. GE-JUN.

TSZKI-FU, ツキフ, 月賦, *n.* Monthly instalments, or payments of a debt. — *ni sh'te kane wo harau*, to pay money by monthly instalments.

TSZKI-FUSE,*–ru,–ta*, ツキフセル, 突伏,

t.v. To stab or thrust and cause to fall with the face downwards.

TSZKI-GAKE, ツキガケ, 月掛, *n.* Monthly dues, or payments of money. — *ni sh'te kane wo atszmeru,* to collect money by monthly collections.

TSZKI-GANE, ツキガネ, 鍾, *n.* A large bell rung by thrusting a stick of wood against it.

TSZKI-HATE,*-ru,-ta,* ツキハテル, 盡果, *i.v.* To be exhausted, used up, finished.

TSZKI-IRE,*-ru,-ta,* ツキイレル, 突入, *t.v.* To thrust in, to push or pound in with any thing pointed.

TSZKI-JI, ツキヂ, 築地, *n.* Land made by filling in, as a swamp; reclaimed land. Syn. UMECHI.

TSZKI-KAGE, ツキカゲ, 月影, *n.* Moon-light.

TSZKI-KAKARI,*-ru,-tta,* ツキカカル, 突掛, *i.v.* To be about to thrust or stab.

TSZKI-KAYESHI,*-sz,-sh'ta,* ツキカヘス, 突返, *t.v.* To thrust back, to stab back or in return.

TSZKI-KOMI,*-mu,-nda,* ツキコム, 突込, *t.v.* To thrust into.

TSZKI-KOROSHI,*-sz,-sh'ta,* ツキコロス, 突殺, *t.v.* To kill by stabbing, or thrusting with the point of any thing.

TSZKI-KUDAKI,*-ku,-ita,* ツキクダク, 搗摧, *t.v.* To break and pulverize by pounding in a mortar. or with the point of any thing.

TSZKI-KUDZSHI,*-sz,-sh'ta,* ツキクヅス, 突崩, *t.v.* To throw down any thing piled up, by thrusting, battering, or pushing.

TSZKI-MACHI, ツキマチ, 月祭, *n.* A religious celebration in honor of the moon.

TSZKI-MATAGE, ツキマタゲ, 月跨, *n.* Straddling, or stretching across from one month to another, as an unfinished work, &c. *Tōriu sh'te — ni naru,* continued to stay on from month to month.

TSZKI-MATOI,*-ō,-ōta,* ツキマトフ, 著纒, *t.v.* To cleave to, adhere to and follow.

TSZKI-MAWARI, ツキマハリ, 月廻, *n.* Month about, alternate months. — *ni ban wo szru.* to watch month about.

TSZKI-MI, ツキミ, 月見, *n.* The 5th day of the 8th moon; set apart especially to conviviality, or paying homage to the moon.

TSZKI-MODOSHI,*-sz,-sh'ta,* ツキモドス, 突戻, *t.v.* To thrust back, to stab back.

TSZKI-MONO, ツキモノ, 付物, *n.* Any thing which is attached to, or is an indispensable part or accompaniment of another, as an oar to the boat, a cork to a bottle, &c. *Ro wa fune no —,* the oar is a part of a boat. *Jō ni kagi wa — da,* the key is a part of the lock.

TSZKI-NAMI, ツキナミ, 月並, Each month, monthly, month by month. *Jū go nichi wa — no yaszmi da,* the 15th day is a monthly rest. Syn. MAI-TSZKI, TSZKI-DZKI.

TSZKI-NO-MONO, ツキノモノ, 月經, *n.* The menses. Syn. SAWARI, KEISZI.

TSZKI-NUKI,*-ku,-ita,* ツキヌク, 衝拔, *t.v.* To thrust through, stick through.

TSZKI-OTOSHI,*-sz,-sh'ta,* ツキオトス, 突落, *t.v.* To thrust down, to knock down.

TSZKI-SASHI,*-sz,-sh'ta,* ツキサス, 衝刺, *t.v.* To stick, or thrust into.

TSZKI-SOI,*-ō,-ōta,* ツキソフ, 付添, *i.v.* To cleave to, or be joined together, as a wife to her husband. *Isshō tszkisō teishu.*

TSZKI-SOI, ツキソヒ, 付添, *n.* An escort, a guard.

TSZKI-TAOSHI,*-sz,-sh'ta,* ツキタフス, 突倒, *t.v.* To thrust over any thing standing, to stab and cause to fall.

TSZKI-TATE,*-ru,-ta,* ツキタテル, 突立, *t.v.* To thrust in, and cause to stand, as a stick into the ground.

TSZKI-TŌSHI,*-sz,-sh'ta,* ツキトホス, 突通, *t.v.* To thrust through. *H'to ni yari wo —,* to run a spear through a man.

TSZKI-YA, ツキヤ, 舂屋, *n.* A person who cleans rice by pounding it in a mortar.

TSZKI-YABURI,*-ru,-tta,* ツキヤブル, 突破, *t.v.* To break or tear by thrusting.

TSZKI-YAMA, ツキヤマ, 築山, *n.* An artificial mountain, or hillock; rock-work.

TSZKI-YATOI, ツキヤトヒ, 月雇, *n.* Hired by the month.

TSZKIYO, ツキヨ, 月夜, *n.* A moon-light night.

TSZKKAIBŌ, ツツカヒボウ, coll. *n.* A prop. — *wo szru.*

TSZKKAKARI, ツツカカリ, coll. cont. of *Tszkikakari.*

TSZKKOMI, ツツコミ, coll. cont. of *Tszkikomi.* — *nedan,* the price of any thing in the lump without assorting.

TSZKŌ, ツカフ, 使, See *Tszkai.*

TSZKU, ツク, See *Tszki.*

TSZKUBAI,*-au,-atta,* ツクバフ, coll. *i.v.* To sit down on the heels, to squat down.

TSZKUBŌ, ツクバウ, 鐵把, *n.* A weapon in the shape of a cross, armed with sharp teeth, kept standing in a frame before guard houses.

TSZKU-DZKU, ツクヅク, 熟, *adv.* Attentively, carefully, thoroughly. — *to kangayeru*, to consider thoroughly. — *to miru*, to look at attentively. Syn. TSZRA-TSZRA.

TSZKU-DZKU-BŌSHI, ツクヅクボウシ, *n.* A kind of locust.

TSZKUIMO, ツクイモ, *n.* The name of an edible root.

TSZKUNEN, ツクネン, *adv.* Sitting alone, alone and quiet. — *to sh'te hi wo kurasz*, to pass the time alone and without employment.

TSZKURAI,–*au*,–*atta*, ツクラフ, Same as *Tszkuroi*.

TSZKURASE,–*ru*,–*ta*, ツクラセル, 令作, caust. of *Tszkuri*. To cause to, or let make or produce.

TSZKURI,–*ru*,–*tta*, ツクル, 作, *t. v*, To make; to form, fashion; to produce, cultivate; compose. *Iye wo* —, to build a house. *Katachi wo* —, to adorn one's person. *Ta wo* —, to cultivate ricefields. *Ine wo* —, to grow rice. *Uta wo* —, to compose a song. *Hon wo* —, to make a book. *Tszmi wo* —, to commit a crime. *Toki wo* —, to crow as a cock.
Syn. SAKU, KOSHIRAYERU SZRU, NASZ.

TSZKURI, ツクリ, 作, *n.* Production, crop. *Ko-toshi no — wa yō gozarimas*, this year's crop is good.

TSZKURI-AGE,–*ru*,–*ta*, ツクリアゲル, 作上, *t.v.* To build up, to erect; to finish making.

TSZKURI-AWASE,–*ru*,–*ta*, ツクリアハセル, 作合, *t.v.* To make so as to fit. *Toki wo* —, to shout, in answer to the shout of the opposite party.

TSZKURI-BANA, ツクリバナ, 作花, *n.* Artificial flowers.

TSZKURI-GOTO, ツクリゴト, 作言, *n.* A fiction, a made up story, a myth.

TSZKURI-GOYE, ツクリゴヱ, 作聲, *n.* A fictitious, or counterfeit voice.

TSZKURI-KAWA, ツクリカハ, 作革, *n.* Leather.

TSZKURI-MONO, ツクリモノ, 作物, *n.* Anything made, or produced; crop, production. *Mugi wa h'yak'shō no — da*, wheat is raised by farmers.

TSKURI-MONO-GATARI, ツクリモノガタリ, 作物語, *n.* A novel, fictitious story, romance.

TSZKURI-TSZKE, ツクリツケ 作付, *n.* Made of one piece, or put on when made; not made separately and afterwards joined together.

TSZKURI-WARAI, ツクリワラヒ, 作笑, *n.* A forced, or feigned laugh.
Syn. AZAWARAI.

TSZKURI-YAMAI, ツクリヤマヒ, 作病, *n.* A feigned sickness.

TSZKUROI,–*ō*,–*ōta*, ツクロフ, 繕, *t.v.* To repair, to mend; to remedy, to adjust, or put in order. *Yane wo* —, to repair a roof. *Mi wo* —, to adjust one's clothes.
Syn. OGINAU; NAOSZ.

TSZKUROI, ツクロヒ, 繕, *n.* Repair, mending, remedy.

TSZKUSHI,–*sz*,–*sh'ta*, ツクス, 盡, *t. v.* To use up, to exhaust, consume, to do to the utmost, to spend the whole, to finish, end. *Te wo* —, to exhaust one's art, or skill. *Chikara wo tszkush'te kimi ni tsztomeru*, to serve one's lord to the utmost of his ability. *Kokoro wo tszkush'te oya ni tszkayeru*, to serve one's parents with the whole heart.

TSZKUYE, ツクヱ, 几, *n.* A writing table, desk.

TSZMA, ツマ, 妻, *n.* A wife; also 夫, husband, but now obsolete.
Syn. KANAI, NIYŌBO.

TSZMA, ツマ, 裾, *n.* The skirt of a garment. *Noki no* —, the eaves of a house.
Syn. SZSO.

TSZMABIRAKA, ツマビラカ, 詳, Particular, minute, clear. — *ni*, particularly, minutely, fully. Syn. ISAI, KOMAYAKA.

TSZMADACHI,–*tsz*,–*tta*, ツマダツ, 爪立, *t.v.* To stand on tiptoe. *Ashi wo* —, idem.

TSZMADORI,–*ru*,–*tta*, ツマドル, 褄, *t. v.* To hold up the skirts of the dress.

TSZMADZ, or TSZMANU, ツマズ, 不摘, or 不積, *neg.* of *Tszmi*.

TSZMADZKI,–*ku*,–*ita*, ツマヅク, 躓, *t. v.* To strike the foot against anything in walking, to stumble. *Ishi ni tszmadzite korobu*, to stumble against a stone and fall.
Syn. KE-TSZMADZKU.

TSZMAGI, ツマギ, 妻木, *n.* Brush-wood, branches collected for firewood.

TSZMAGURI,–*ru*,–*tta*, ツマグル, 爪繰, *t. v.* To roll between the thumb and finger, to turn with the nail, to feel with the fingers, to finger. *Judz wo* —, to tell the rosary. *Hige wo* —, the feel the beard.

TSZMA-HAJIKI, ツマハジキ, 爪彈, *n.* A fillip, or snapping with the finger and thumb.

TSZMA-JIRO, ツマジロ, 下白, *n.* A horse with four white legs.

TSZMA-JIRUSHI, ツマジルシ, 爪印, *n.* A mark made with the nail.

TSZMAMI,–*mu*,–*nda*, ツマム, 撮, *t. v.* To take between the ends of the fingers, to take a pinch. *Shio wo* —, to take a pinch of salt

TSZMAMI, ツマミ, 撮, *n.* A pinch of anything; a knob, as of a drawer. *H'to — no cha wo ireru,* to put in one pinch of tea.

TSZMAORIGASA, ツマオリガサ, *n.* A hat with the rim bent.

TSZMARANU, ツマラヌ, 不満, *neg.* of *Tszmaru.* Not clogged, or filled up: much used in vul. coll. to express disapprobation, = stupid, useless, foolish, absurd. — *koto wo iu na,* don't say any thing so absurd. — *yatsz da,* a stupid, useless fellow.

TSZMARI,-*ru*,-*ta*, ツマル, 塞, *i. v.* To be stopped up, obstructed, clogged, stuffed up, filled up, choked. *Hana ga* —, the nose is stopped up (as by a cold). *Nodo ga* —, the throat is obstructed. *Kiseru ga* —, the pipe is clogged up. *Kotoba ga* —, no words with which to reply. *Ri ni* —, convinced by reason. Syn. FUSAGARU.

TSZMARI,-*ru*,-*tta*, ツマル, *i. v.* To become short, or less in size, to shrink. *Take ga tszmatta,* to be diminished in length. *Hi ga* —, the days have become short.

TSZMARI, ツマリ, 詰, *n.* A corner, a place beyond which there is no passing, a closure, stoppage.

TSZMARI, ツマリ, *adv.* After all, in the end. at last. Syn. HIKKIYŌ, SHOSEN.

TSZMBŌ, ツンボ, 聾, *n.* Deaf. — *ni naru,* to become deaf. *Kata* —, deaf in one ear. Syn. MIMISHII.

TSZME, ツメ, 爪, *n.* The nail of the finger, or toe; a hoof, claw, talon. *Yubi no* —, a finger nail. *Ashi no* —, toe nail. *Uma no* —, horse's hoof. *Neko no* —, a cat's claw. *Washi no* —, an eagle's talons.

TSZME,-*ru*,-*ta*, ツメル 捻, *t. v.* To pinch. *Waga mi wo tszmete h'to no itaki wo shire,* (prov.) pinch yourself and know how others feel.

TSZME,-*ru*,-*ta*, ツメル, *t. v.* To shorten, to to make smaller, to abridge, to contract, reduce in size, to crowd together, to restrain, to corner, to fill; to stuff, to pack tight, to make close; to serve, to perform official duty; to do constantly, or without ceasing. *Kimono no take wo* —, to shorten a coat. *Nagai mono wo* —, to shorten any thing long. *Fukuro ni wata wo* —, to stuff cotton in a bag. *Iki wo* —, to suppress the breathing, breathe softly. *Tszmete itamu,* to pain incessantly. *Nimots wo hako ni* —, to pack goods in a box. *Yakusho ye* —, confined closely to one's office.
Syn. TSZDZMERU, KOMERU, TŌSZ.

TSZME, ツメ 塞, *n.* Anything used for filling, stuffing, or packing a hole, crack, or waste place; a block, or wedge used to prevent anything from moving, or shaking. — *wo ireru.* — *wo szru.* or — *wo kō.*

TSZME-AI,-*au*,-*atta*, ツメアフ, 詰合, *i.v.* To press each other closely, or violently, as in fighting or in argument.

TSZME-KOMI,-*mu*,-*nda*, ツメコム, 詰込, *t.v.* To stuff, press, or pack into. *Nimotsz wo fune ni* —, to pack goods in a ship.

TSZMERARE,-*ru*,-*ta*, ツメラレル, pass. or pot. of *Tszme.*

TSZME-SHO, ツメシヨ, 詰所, *n.* The place of service, or duty.

TSZMETAI,-KI,-SHI, ツメタイ, 冷, *a.* (*Tszme,* nails and *itai,* painful). Cold, spoken only of things; as. *Te ashi ga* —, hands and feet are cold. — *midz,* cold water. Syn. HIYAYAKA.

TSZMETAKU, or TSZMETŌ, ツメタク, *adv.* Idem.

TSZMETASA, ツメタサ, *n.* Coldness, chilliness.

TSZME-YORI,-*ru*,-*tta*, ツメヨル, 詰寄, *t.v.* To approach close to, close with.

TSZMI, ツミ, 罪, *n.* Crime, trespass. guilt, sin : also the punishment of crime. — *wo okosz,* to commit a crime, or sin. — *wo tszkuru,* or — *wo nasz,* idem. — *wo yurusz,* to pardon sin, or crime. — *szru,* to punish a criminal. — *wo okonau,* idem. — *wo sange szru,* to confess one's sins. — *wo horobosz,* to wipe out sin, (by sacrifice, or alms). — *wo manukareru,* to escape punishment for one's crimes. — *ni otosz,* to condemn. Syn. TOGA.

TSZMI,-*mu*,-*nda*, ツム, 積, *t.v.* To pile, heap up, to pack; to accumulate, increase, amass, to deposit. *Fune ni ni wo* —, to put cargo into a ship. *Ishi wo* —, to pile stones. *Toshi wo* —, to add year to year. *Kō wo* —, to accumulate merit.
Syn. KASANERU.

TSZMI,-*mu*,-*nda*, ツム, 摘, *t.v.* To pinch off with the nails, or scissors. *Cha no ha wo* —, to pluck off tea-leaves.

TSZMI, ツミ, 野桑, *n.* A kind of mulberry-tree.

TSZMI-AGE,-*ru*,-*ta*, ツミアゲル, 積上, *t.v.* To pile up, heap up.

TSZMI-BITO, ツミビト, 罪人, (*zai-nin*), *n.* A criminal, a transgressor, sinner.
Syn. TOGANIN.

TSZMI-HOROBOSHI, ツミホロボシ, 罪滅, *n.* Anything done to blot out sin, penance. — *ni hodokoshi wo szru,* to give alms in order to wipe away one's sins.

TSZMI-KASANE,-*ru*,-*ta*, ツミカサネル, 積重 To pile up one on another.

TSZMI-KAYESHI,-*sz*,-*sh'ta*, ツミカヘス, 積返, *t.v.* To reship, to load and send back.

TSZMI-KOMI,-*mu*,-*nda*, ツミコム, 積込, *t.v.* To pile up anything inside of something else, as cargo in a ship ; or 摘込, to pluck off, (as leaves), and put into (as a basket).

TSZMI-KIRI,-*ru*,-*tta*, ツミキル, 摘切, *t.v.* To pinch or pluck off, as a leaf.

†TSZMINAI,-*au*,-*atta*, ツミナフ, 罪, *t. v.* To punish for crime. *H'to wo* —, to punish a person for crime. Syn. BASSZRU.

TSZMOGORI, ツモゴリ, incorrect for *Tszgomori.*

TSZMORI,-*ru*,-*tta*, ツモル, 積, *i.v.* To be piled or heaped ; to accumulate, to increase in number. *Chiri tszmotte yama to naru*, (prov.) dust heaped up becomes a mountain. *Yuki ga* —, the snow is deep. Syn. KASANARU.

TSZMORI,-*ru*,-*tta*, ツモル, 計, *t. v.* To reckon, estimate, compute, calculate. *Kono fushin ikura de dekiru ka tszmotte minasare*, estimate how much you can do this work for. Syn. HAKARU.

TSZMORI-GAKI, ツモリガキ, 計書, *n.* A written estimate.

TSZMORI, ツモリ, 計, *n.* Calculation, reckoning, supposition, presumption, meaning, design, intention. — *ga hadzreru*, to mistake in one's reckoning. *Dō szru — de koko ni kita*, what was his intention in coming here? *Nai — da*, I think not, or I reckon there is not. *Kono tana wa nani ni szru — darō ka*, what do you intend doing with this shelf?
Syn. HAKIRI, RIYŌKEN.

TSZMU, ツム, 紡錘, *n.* The spindle of a spinning-wheel.

TSZMU, ツム, See *Tszmi.*

TSZMUGI, ツムギ, 紬, *n.* Pongee.

TSZMUGI,-*gu*,-*ida*, ツムグ, 紡, *t.v.* To spin. *Ito wo* —, to spin thread, or yarn.

TSZMUJI, ツムジ, 旋毛, *n.* The whirl of hair on the crown of the head.

TSZMUJI-KAZE, ツムジカゼ, 旋風, *n.* A whirlwind.

TSZMURI, ツムリ, 頭, *n.* The head.
Syn. ATAMA.

TSZNA, ツナ, 綱, *n.* A rope, cable, hawser. — *wo utsz*, to make a rope.
Syn. NAWA.

TSZNAGARE,-*ru*,-*ta*, ツナガレル, 被繫, pass. or pot. of *Tsznagi.*

TSZNAGI,-*gu*,-*ida*, ツナグ, 繫, *t.v.* To tie with a rope or halter, to hitch, to tether ; support, or lengthen, (as life). *Uma wo ki ni* —, to hitch a horse to a tree. *Fune wo* —, to moor a ship or boat. *Inochi wo* —, to support life.

TSZNAGI, ツナギ, *n.* Straw, or any other fibre, mixed with plaster, to make it stick together. Syn. SZSA, TSZTA.

TSZNAMI, ツナミ, 海嘯, *n.* A large wave which rolls over and inundates the land.

TSNASHI, ツナシ, *n.* The name of a fish.

TSZNA-WATARI, ツナワタリ, 綱渡, *n.* Walking the rope.

TSZNE, ツネ, 常, Usual, common, ordinary. — *no koto*, a common occurrence. — *no tōri*, the usual way. — *no kimono*, every day clothes. Syn. FUDAN, ITSZMO, HEIZEI.

TSZNE-DZNE, ツネヅネ, 常常, *adv.* Always, constantly, habitually, commonly.
Syn. JŌ-JŪ, MAI-MAI.

TSZNE-NARADZ, or TSZNE-NARANU, ツネナラヌ, 不常, Unusual, strange, uncommon, not habitual, not constant or enduring. *Kokochi* —, feel different from one's ordinary state.

TSZNE-NI, ツネニ, 常, *adv.* Always, constantly, commonly, ordinarily.
Syn. ITSZMO. HEIZEI.

TSZNO, ツノ, 角, *n.* A horn. *Ushi shika nado no* —, a cow, or deer's horns.

TSZNO-GAMI, ツノガミ, 角髪, *n.* The two locks of hair left after shaving a child's head.

TSZNO-MATA, ツノマタ, 角菜, *n.* A kind of seaweed.

TSZNORI,-*ru*,-*tta*, ツノル, 募, *t.v.* To raise, collect, gather ; (*i.v.*) To increase, or grow more severe, or violent. *Hei wo* —, to levy troops. *Kin wo* —, to collect money. *Kaze, biyōki, samusa, atszsa nado ga* —, the wind, sickness, cold, or heat increases in severity. *Ī-tsznoru*, to become more violent, or obstinate in talking.
Syn. ATSZMERU, TSZYORU.

TSZPPARI,-*ru*,-*tta*, ツツパル, 突張, *t.v.* (*Tszki* and *haru*). To prop up. *Iye wo* —, to prop a house.

TSZPPARI, ツツパリ, 突張, *n.* A prop.
Syn. TSZKKAIBŌ.

TSZRA, ツラ, 頰, *n.* The cheeks, the face.
Syn. KAO, OMOTE.

TSZRA, ツラ, 連, *n.* A row, rank, file, series. *Gan h'to* —, a row of wild geese.

TSZRA-BONE, ツラボネ, 輔骨, *n*, The cheek bones.

TSZRA-BUCHI, ツラブチ, 面扶持, *n.* One ration apiece, according to the number in the family. Syn. MEMBUCHI.

TSZRA-DZYE, ツラヅヱ, 頬杖, *n.* Resting the face on the hand and elbow. — *wo tszku.*

TSZRA-GAMAYE, ツラガマヘ, 顔搆, *n.* The features, expression of countenance.

TSZRAI,-KI,-SHI, ツライ, *a.* Cruel, hard, unfeeling; painful, disagreeable, grievous, miserable. *Tszraki shujin,* a cruel master. *Tszrai koto da,* hard lot, a cruel thing. Syn. HAKUJŌ-NA.

TSZRAKEN, ツラケン, *n.* A kind of sport in which the players make grimaces, and the person who first laughs pays a forfeit.

TSZRAKU, ツラク, *adv.* idem.

TSZRANARI,-*ru*,-*tta*, ツラナル, 連, *i. v.* To be arranged in a row, file, or rank; to be connected, continued. *Gan ga tszranatte tobu,* wild geese fly in rows. *Retsz ni* —, arranged in ranks. Syn. NARABU, TSZDZKU.

TSZRANE,-*ru*,-*ta*, ツラヌル, 連, *t.v.* To arrange in a row, rank, or file; to place in order. Syn. NARABERU.

TSZRA-NIKUI,-KI,-KU, ツラニクイ, 頬憎, Of a homely or ugly countenance.

TSZRANUKI,-*ku*,-*ita*, ツラヌク, 貫, *t. v.* To run or pierce through; to string together. *Ito ni tama wo* —, to string beads. *Tszranuite yomu,* to read through a succession of volumes. Syn. TŌSZ.

TSZRARA, ツララ, 冰柱, *n.* An icicle. Syn. TARUHI.

TSZRARE,-*ru*,-*ta*, ツラレル, 被鈎, pass. or pot. of *Tszri.*

TSZRASE,-*ru*,-*ta*, ツラセル, 令鈎, caust. of *Tszri.*

TSZRA-TSZRA, ツラツラ, 熟, *adv.* Thoroughly, maturely, attentively, carefully. — *to miru,* to look attentively at. — *kangayeru,* to consider carefully. Syn. TSZKU-DZKU.

TSZRA-YOGOSHI, ツラヨゴシ, 面汚, *n.* (lit. dirtying the face). Shame, disgrace. *Oya no — wo szru,* causing shame to a parent.

TSZRE, ツレ, 伴, *n.* A companion, or company in going or traveling. — *ga nai kara yukimasen,* as I have no companion I shall not go. — *wo sasōte yuku,* to invite another to go along with.

TSZRE,-*ru*,-*ta*, ツレル, 連, *t.v.* To lead, or take in company, to conduct, go along with, together with. *Tomo wo* —, to take a servant along in going to any place. *Asate tszrete kuru,* bring him with you tomorrow. *Ji-kō ni tszrete biyōki ga okoru,* diseases vary with the climate. *Toki yo ni tszrete fūzoku ga kawaru,* customs change with the times.

TSZRE,-*ru*,-*ta*, ツレル, 鈎, *i. v.* To be caught with a hook and line, as a fish.

TSZRE-AI,-*au*,-*atta*, ツレアフ, 連合, *i.v.* To go together, or in company.

TSZRE-AI, ツレアヒ, 連合, *n.* Companion, husband.

TSZRE-DACHI,-*tsz*,-*tta*, ツレダツ, 連立, *i.v.* To go together, or in company. *Tszredatte yuku.*

†TSZRE-DZRE, ツレヅレ, 徒然, In an irksome manner, as when one has nothing to do and time hangs heavy, ennui. Syn. TOZEN, TAIKUTSZ.

TSZRE-KO, ツレコ, 連兒, *n.* A stepchild, or a child by a former marriage which the mother takes with her when she marries another husband.

TSZRENAI,-KI,-SHI, ツレナイ, *a.* Hard, unfeeling, heartless, cruel, severe. — *h'to,* a man void of feeling, or pity. — *inochi,* a hard, or painful life. Syn. TSZRAI, HAKU-JŌ-NA.

TSZRERU, ツレル, See *Tszre.*

TSZRE-SOI,-*ō*,-*ōta*, ツレソフ, 連添, *i.v.* To go together, or in company.

TSZRETE, ツレテ, *pp.* of *Tszreru.*

TSZRI, ツリ, 鈎, *n.* Fishing with a hook and line, angling. — *ni yuku,* to go a fishing. — *wo szru,* to fish with a hook and line.

TSZRI, ツリ, *n* Change, or the balance of money paid beyond the price of goods purchased. — *wo toru,* to receive the change.

TSZRI, ツリ, *n.* A line with the upper end fixed, and used to brace or support anything from falling. — *wo kakeru,* to attach or support with a line.

TSZRI,-*ru*,-*tta*, ツル, 鈎, *t v.* To suspend, or hang by a line; to fish with hook and line, to allure or catch by artifice, decoy. *Sakana wo* —, to fish with a hook and line. *Tana wo* —, to hang up a shelf by ropes. *Jōro ga kiyaku wo* —, the harlot allures visitors.

TSZRI,-*ru*,-*tta*, ツル, 攣, *i.v.* To be contracted by disease, cramped. *Szji ga* —, the muscles are cramped or contracted.

TSZRI-AGE,-*ru*,-*ta*, ツリアゲル, 鈎上, *t.v.* To fish up, to climb up on a dangling rope, hang up.

TSZRI-AI,-*au*,-*atta*, ツリアフ, 鈎合, *i.v* To balance, to be in equipoise, as of weights suspended from each end of a weighing-beam, equilibrium. *Tszri-awanu,* do not balance.

TSZRI-BARI, ツリバリ, 鈎, *n.* A fish-hook.

TSZRI-BASHI, ツリハシ, 鈎橋, *n.* A suspension bridge.

TSZRI-BUNE, ツリブ子, 鈎舟, *n.* A fishing-boat, used in angling.

TSZRI-DAI, ツリダイ, 鈎臺, *n.* A box, or frame used by coolies suspended from a pole.

TSZRI-DASHI, *-sz, -sh'ta*, ツリダス, 鈎出, *t.v.* To draw out with a hook and line, to lure out, draw or entice out of the house, to decoy.

TSZRI-DŌRO, ツリドウロ, 鈎燈龍, *n.* A hanging lantern.

TSZRI-GANE, ツリガ子, 鐘, *n.* A large hanging bell.

TSZRI-HASHIGO, ツリハシゴ, 鈎梯, *n.* A hanging rope ladder.

TSZRI-ITO, ツリイト, 鈎絲, *n.* A fishing line.

TSZRI-KOMI, *-mu, -nda*, ツリコム, 鈎込, *t.v.* To allure, entice, or draw into. Syn. HIKI-IRERU.

TSZRI-SAGE, *-ru, -ta*, ツリサゲル, 鈎下, *t.v.* To hang, or suspend so as to swing, to dangle. Syn. TSZRUSZ.

TSZRI-SEN, ツリセン, *n.* Change, same as *Tszri.*

TSZRI-TE, ツリテ, 鈎手, *n.* A cord, or rope by which anything is suspended.

TSZRI-YOSE, *-ru, -ta*, ツリヨセル, 鈎寄, *t.v.* To allure, entice, attract, to draw near or close to.

TSZRI-ZAO, ツリサヲ, 鈎竿, *n.* A fishing rod.

TSZRU, ツル, 鈎, or 攣, See *Tszri.*

TSZRU, ツル, 鶴, *n.* A crane, stork; an emblem of long life, said to live a thousand years.

TSZRU, ツル, 蔓, *n.* A vine. *Budō no* —, a grape-vine. — *ga nobiru.* — *ga hau.*

TSZRU, ツル, 弦, *n.* A bow-string. — *wo kakeru,* to fix the string to the bow. — *wo hadzsz,* to loose the bowstring. *Nabe no* —, the bow like handle of a pot. *Masz no* —, the diagonal iron bar across the top of a grain measure.

†TSZRU, ツル, A pret. suffix to verbs, = *taru. Yume ni h'to wo mitszru yo,* the night when she saw a man in a dream.

TSZRUBASHI, ツルハシ, *n.* A pick.

TSZRUBE, ツルベ, 鈎瓶, *n.* A well-bucket.

TSZRUGI, ツルギ, 劍, *(kane). n.* A long double edged sword used in ancient times.

TSZRUMI, *-mu, -nda*, ツルム, *i.v.* To copulate, to cover, or tread, as animals, or fowls. *Tori, kedamono, mushi nado ga* —.

TSZRUSHI, *-sz, -sh'ta*, ツルス, 鈎, *t.v.* To let hang by a rope, to suspend, hang. *Tōrō wo* —, to hang a lantern or lamp. Syn. SAGERU.

TSZRU-TSZRU, ツルツル, *adv.* In a gliding manner, glibly, smoothly. — *to szberu,* to slide glibly. — *sh'ta mono,* a smooth thing.

TSZTA, ツタ, 蔦, *n.* Ivy, Cissus Thunburgii.

TSZTAI, *-au, -atta*, ツタフ, 傳, *t.v.* To walk or climb along any thing narrow and extended, as a rope, limb of a tree, a rail, pole, &c. *Kumo ga ito wo* —, the spider climbs its thread. *Ishi wo* —, to walk over a line of stone's. *Midz ga kakehi wo* —, the water runs along the (outside of) pipe.

†TSZTANAI, -KI, ツタナイ, 拙, *a.* Unskillful, unhandy, inexpert, awkward, clumsy, ignorant, rude, rough, or badly done. *Saiku wa* —, the work is clumsily done. Syn. HETA, BUSAIKU, BUKIYŌ.

†TSZTANAKU, ツタナク, 拙, *adv.* Idem.

TSZTAWARI, *-ru, -tta*, ツタハル, 傳, *i.v.* To be transmitted, delivered, or passed along from one to another, or from age to age. *Senzo yori tszwatta mono,* a thing handed down from one's ancestors.

TSZTAYE, *-ru, -ta*, ツタヘル, 傳, *t. v.* To transmit or pass along from one to another, hand down by tradition. *Shison ni mono wo* —, to transmit any thing to posterity. Syn. SADZKERU.

TSZTAYE, ツタヘ, 傳, *n.* Tradition, transmission, handing from one to another.

TSZTAYE-KIKI, *-ku, -īta*, ツタヘキク, 傳聞, *t. v.* To hear by tradition, to hear through others.

TSZTE, ツテ, 傳, *n.* An introducer, go-between, or mediator between two parties who are strangers to each other. Syn. TETSZDZKI.

†TSZTO, ツト, 晨, *n.* Early in the morning. — *ni okiru,* to rise early.

TSZTO, ツト, 苞苴, *n.* A wrapper of straw, such as that in which eggs are carried.

†TSZTO, ツト, *n.* A present brought from another place. Syn. MIYAGE.

TSZ-TO, ツト, *adv.* In a sudden, or quick manner, hastily, abruptly. — *tatte deru,* got up hastily and went out.

TSZTŌ, ツタフ, 傳, See *Tsztai.*

TSZTOMARI, *-ru, -tta*, ツトマル, 勤, *i.v.* To be served, attended to; done, discharged, as service, or official duty. *Yaku no tsztomaranu h'to,* a person who does not discharge the duties of his office.

TSTOME, *-ru, -ta*, ツトメル, 勤, *t. v.* To

serve, attend, wait on, to perform official duty; to do, as a servant, or official; to do diligently, to constrain one's self to do. *Yaku wo* —, to attend to one's official business. *Hōkō wo* —, to do the work of a servant.

TSZTOME, ツトメ, 勤, *n.* Service, office, ministry; the labor or duty which one owes to a master, or lord.
Syn. HŌKŌ, YAKU.

TSZTSZ, ツツ, 筒, *n.* A pipe, tube. *Teppō no* —, a gun-barrel.

TSZTSZ, ツツ, A suffix to verbs, = while, or every now and then; as, *Ame ga furi-tsztsz hi ga teru*, while it was raining the sun shone. *Oya no koto wo ī-tsztsz hi wo okuru*, spent the time in talking about his parents. Syn. NAGARA.

TSZTSZGANAI, ツツガナイ, See *Tsztszkanai*.

TSZTSZ-GUCHI, ツツグチ, 筒口, *n.* The muzzle of a gun.

TSZTSZJI, ツツジ, 杜鵑花, *n.* Azalea, Rododendron indicum.

TSZTSZKI,-*ku*,-*ita*, ツツク, *t.v.* (contr. of *Tszki-tszki*). To punch, stick, or thrust at repeatedly, to pick, peck. *Bō de nedzmi no ana wo* —, to punch into a rat hole with a stick. *Ana wo* —, to peck a hole.

TSZTSMASHII,-KI,-KU, ツツマシキ, 包敷, That which one wishes to conceal or cover up, causing shame. *Tsztszmashiku omō*, to feel ashamed.
Syn. HADZKASHII, OMOTEBUSE.

TSZTSZMI,-*mu*,-*nda*, ツツム, 包, *t.v.* To wrap up, to cover, to conceal, to hide, envelope. *Kami ni* —, to wrap in paper. *Kumo ga tszki wo* —, a cloud covers the moon. *Haji wo* —, to conceal a shame. *Kin de akagane wo* —, to cover copper with gold. *Hon wo* —, to cover a book.
Syn. KAKUSZ, Ō.

TSZTSZMI, ツツミ, 包, *n.* A covering, wrapper, a packet, package, or bundle. *H'to — no kuszri*, one paper of medicine.

TSZTSZMI, ツツミ, 堤, *n.* A bank or dike around a pool of water.

TSZTSZSHIMI,-*mu*,-*nda*, ツツシム, 謹, *t.v.* To keep a watch over one's self so as not to offend against decorum or propriety; to restrain one's self, to be careful, reverential; to confine one's self to the house. *Mi wo* —, idem. *Hitori wo* —, to be watchful of self even when alone. *Tsztsz-shinde mōshi-ageru*, respectfully to say (to a superior). *Tszmi atte uchi tsztszshinde iru*, to keep in the house on account of crime.

TSZTSZSHIMI, ツツシミ, 謹, *n.* Care, watchfulness, or circumspection over self, self restraint, confinement to one's house for some offence. — *wo mōshi-tszkeru*, to order a person to confine himself to the house.

TSZTTACHI,-*tsz*,-*tta*, ツツタツ, 突立, (cont. of *Tszki* and *tatsz*). *i.v.* To rise up.

TSZTTO, ツツト, *adv.* In the manner of any thing passing along quickly. — *deru*, to slip out.

TSZŪJI,-*ru*, or -*dzru*,-*ta*, ツウズル, 通, To have communication or intercourse, to pass through freely or without obstruction. *Teki ni* —, to have secret communication with the enemy. *Onna ni* —, to have illicit intercourse with a woman. *Kokoro wo* —, to communicate one's mind. *Daiben ga* —, to have a free or unconstipated condition of bowels. Syn. KAYŌ.

T'SŪJI, ツウジ, 通詞, *n*, An interpreter, translator.

TS'ŪJI, ツウジ, 通, *n.* A free, an unobstructed passage. *Dai-ben no — wa ikaga*, how are your bowels?

TS'Ū-REI, ツウレイ, 通例, *n.* Common usage, customary or current mode or example.

TS'Ū-RIKI, ツウリキ, 通力, *n.* Supernatural power; as, of becoming invisible, of seeing, hearing or knowing all things.

TS'Ū-RO, ツウロ, 通路, *n.* An open road, or thoroughfare, communication. — *wo tatsz*, to cut off the communication.

TS'Ū-SHŌ, ツウシヤウ, 通稱, *(zoku miyō)*. *n.* The name by which one is generally known.

TS'ŪYA, ツウヤ, 通夜, *n.* Passing the whole night in a temple on the occasion of a vow. — *wo szru*.

TS'Ū-YŌ, ツウヨウ, 通用, Current, passing freely from one to another, freely used. *Nippon de wa doru ga — senu*, the dollar is not current in Japan.

TSZWABUKI, ツハブキ, 石蕗, *n.* Name of a flowering plant, Ligularia Kampferi.

TSZWAMONO, ツハモノ, 兵, *n.* A common soldier.
Syn. HEI SHI.

TSZWARI, ツハリ, 紐, *n.* The bodily disorders caused by pregnancy. — *yami*, the indisposition attending quickening.

TSZYA, ツヤ, 光澤, *n.* Gloss, shine, lustre, polish. — *ga aru*, to be glossy. — *wo dasz*, to make to glisten.

†TSZYA-TSZYA, ツヤツヤ, *adv.* Well, satisfactorily. — *gugo wo meshi-tamawadz*, did not eat his food with relish.

TSZYE, ツヱ, 杖, A cane. — *wo tszku*, to carry a cane.

TSZYŌ, ツヨウ, The same as *Tszyoku*.

TSZYOI,-KI,-SHI, ツヨイ, 強, *a*. Strong, powerful, violent, mighty, severe, firm. *Tszyoi kaze*, a violent wind. *Ikiyoi ga* —, of great power. *Tszyoi h'to*, a mighty man.

TSZYOKU, ツヨク, 強, *adv*. Idem. — *naru*, to become strong or powerful.

TSZYOME,-*ru*,-*ta*, ツヨメル, 強, *t.v.* To make strong, to strengthen, encourage, invigorate. *Hi wo* —, to make a fire burn more intensely. *Kokoro wo* —, to encourage, or animate. *Karada wo yōjo sh'te tszyomeru*, by taking care of one's health to invigorate the body.

TSZYOMI, ツヨミ, 強, *n*. Strength, support, a stay. Syn. CHIKARA.

TSZYORI,-*ru*,-*tta*, ツヨル, 強, *i.v.* To grow stronger, severe, or more violent. *Zen ga tszyoreba aku ga yowaru*, as virtue becomes stronger vice grows weaker. *Kaze ga* —, the wind increases in violence.

TSZYOSA, ツヨサ, 強, *n*. Power, might.

TSZYU, ツユ, 梅雨, *n*. The rainy season, commencing about the 1st of June.

TSZYU, ツユ, 露, *n*. Dew: fig for the smallest particle, brief. — *ga oku*, the dew falls. — *no inochi*, life as evanescent as the dew. — *utagau beki tokoro mo nashi*, not the least reason for doubt. — *hodo mo shiradz*, don't know the least.

TSZYU-HARAI, ツユハラヒ, 露拂, *n*. The person who goes before a noble to clear the way, and to make people squat down; also, an inferior actor, who amuses people assembling in a theatre until the principal actor makes his appearance.

TSZYUKEI,-KI,-KU,-SHI, ツユケイ, Wet with dew, dewy. *Tszyukeki michi*, a road wet with dew.

U

U, ウ, 鸕鷀, *n*. A cormorant. — *wo tszkau*, to fish with a cormorant.

U, ウ, 卯, *n*. (The first syllable of *usagi*, a hare). One of the twelve signs. — *no toki*, 6 o'clock A.M. — *no hō*, the east.

†U, ウ, 有, (*Go-on*. The *kan-on* pronunciation of *Yu*, is preferred by the Japanese). *n*. Possession, property. *Mina kare ga u to naru beshi*, all will become his property.

†U,-*ru*, ウル, 得, *t.v.* To get, obtain. Syn. YERU, UKERU.

UBA, ウバ, 乳母, *n*. A wet-nurse.

†UBA, ウバ, 老婆, *n*. An old woman. Syn. ŌBA.

UBAI,-*au*,-*atta*, ウバフ, 奪, *t.v.* To take by force, or violence; to seize, to rob, steal. *Kane wo ubau mono wa korosare, kuni wo ubau mono wa ō to naru*, (prov.) he that steals money is killed, but he that steals a country becomes a king. Syn. NUSZMU.

UBAI, ウバイ, 優婆夷, *n*. The name of an order of female religionists among the Buddhists.

UBAI, ウバイ, 烏梅, *n*. A kind of dried plum, used as a medicine.

UBASOKU, ウバソク, 優婆塞, *n*. The name of an order of religionists, same as *Shugenja*, and *Yamabushi*.

UBAWARE,-*ru*,-*ta*, ウバハレル, 被奪, pass. or pot. of *Ubai*. To be taken by force, seized, robbed.

†UBE, ウベ, 宜, Right, proper, that which ought or should be. Syn. MOTTOMO.

UBENAI,-*au*,-*atta*, ウベナイ, 諾, *t.v.* To assent, consent, acquiesce. *Ubenawadz*, neg. would not consent. Syn. SHŌCHI SZRU, YURUSZ.

UBŌ, ウバフ, Same as *Ubau* 奪, see *Ubai*.

UBU, ウブ, 生, Natural state, simple, unwrought, unadorned. — *na ishi*, a stone unpolished. — *na muszme* an unsophisticated young lady. — *no mama*, natural state. Syn. SHIZEN.

UBUGOYE, ウブゴヱ, 産聲, *n*. The first cry of an infant just born.

UBUKE, ウブケ, 産毛, *n*. The hair of a newly born infant.

UBUKI, ウブキ, 産衣, *n*. The first clothes worn by an infant.

U-BUNE, ウブネ, 鵜舩, *n*. A boat used in fishing with a cormorant.

UBUSZNA, ウブスナ, 産土, *n*. The tutelary god of a place. Syn. UJIGAMI.

UBUYA, ウブヤ, 産屋, *n*. A lying-in chamber.

UBUYU, ウブユ, 産湯, *n*. The warm water in which an infant is first washed.

UCHI, ウチ, 内, or 中, *n*. Inside, within, whilst, among, in, into; a house. *Omaye no — wa doko*, where do you live? — *ye hairu*, to enter the house. *Iye no* —, inside of a house. *Hako no — ni ireta*, have put it in the box. *Ni san nichi no — ni yukimashō*, I shall go within two or three days. *Gakusha no — ni kono h'to ga dai ichi da*, this person is the first among the learned. *Kurenu — ni kayere*, come back before sun-set. *Nippon ye konu uchi ni*, before I came to Japan. *Hiru no —*, in the day time. Syn. NAKA, AIDA.

UCHI,*-tsz,-tta*, ウツ, 打, *t.v.* To strike, knock, beat, smite, shoot; often used prefixed to other words to add force to them, or for elegance. *Taiko wo —*, to beat, or play a drum. *Kane wo —*, to strike, or ring a bell. *Toki wo —*, to strike the hour. *Hi wo —*, to strike fire. *Kataki wo —*, to kill an enemy. *Shiro wo —*, to destroy a castle. *Kubi wo —*, to cut off the head. *Katana wo —*, to forge a sword. *Kugi wo —*, to hammer a nail, or drive a nail. *Te wo —*, to clap the hands. *Go wo —*, to play checkers. *Bakuchi wo —*, to gamble. *Momen wo —*, to mull cloth. *Teppō de tori wo —*, to shoot a bird with a gun. *Ishi wo —*, to throw a stone. *Midz wo —*, to sprinkle water. *Himo wo —*, to make braid. *Ami wo —*, to cast a net.
Syn. BUTSZ, TATAKU.

UCHI-AGE,*-ru,-ta*, ウチアゲル, 打上, *t.v.* To strike up. *Nami ga iso ye —*, the waves beat up against the beach.

UCHI-AI,*-au,-tta*, ウチアフ, 打合, *t.v.* To strike, beat, smite. kill, or shoot each other.

UCHI-BA, ウチバ, 内場, *n.* Moderation, a proper medium, temperance. *Naniqoto mo — ni szru ga yoi*, it is well to exercise moderation in all things.
Syn. HIKAYEME.

UCHI-BAN, ウチバン, 打盤, *n.* A block on which any thing is beaten, or for ringing coin.

UCHI-DASHI,*-sz,-sh'ta*, ウチダス, 打出, *t. v.* To begin to shoot, or play draughts; to raise by beating, as letters, or figures.

UCHI-FUSE,*-ru,-ta*, ウチフセル, 打伏, *t. v.* To knock down with the face to the ground.

UCHI-GIRI, ウチギリ, 打錐, *n.* A punch.

UCHI-HARAI,*-au,-atta*, ウチハラフ, 打拂, *t. v.* To clear away by beating, or shooting; to beat off or away, as dust, an enemy &c.

UCHI-HATASHI,*-sz,-sh'ta*, ウチハタス, 打果, *t. v.* To destroy by killing or shooting.

UCHI-HIMO, ウチヒモ, 打緒, *n.* Braid, silk-cord.

UCHI-HIRAME,*-ru,-ta*, ウチヒラメル, 打平, *t. v.* To beat flat, to flatten by beating.

UCHI-JINI, ウチジニ, 戰死, (*senshi*). Killed in battle.

UCHI-KAKE,*-ru,-ta*, ウチカケル, 打掛, *t. v.* To throw over or upon. To be about to strike or shoot, play, throw &c.

UCHI-KATA, ウチカタ, 内方, (*nai-hō*), *n.* Wife. Syn. KANAI, OKAMI-SAN.

UCHI-KATAME,*-ru,-ta*, ウチカタメル, 打固, *t. v.* To harden by beating.

UCHI-KAYESHI,*-sz,-sh'ta*, ウチカヘス, 打反, *t. v.* To strike back, return a blow.

UCHI-KI, ウチキ, 内氣, Retiring, diffident, modest, bashful. *— na onna*, a modest woman. Syn. HADZKASHIGARU.

UCHI-KIDZ, ウチキズ, 打疵, *n.* A wound made by a blow, contused wound.

UCHI-KIRI,*-ru,-tta*, ウチキル, 打切, *t. v.* To strike and cut, as with a sword, axe &c.

UCHI-KOMI,*-mu,-nda*, ウチコム, 打込, *t. v.* To throw or shoot into.

UCHI-KOROSHI,*-sz,-sh'ta*, ウチコロス, 打殺, *t. v.* To kill by striking, beating or shooting.

UCHI-KOWASHI,*-sz,-sh'ta*, ウチコハス, *t. v.* To break by striking; to break down, as a building; demolish.

UCHI-KUDAKI,*-ku,-ita*, ウチクダク, 打碎, *t. v.* To smash or crush by beating.

UCHI-KURUBUSHI, ウチクルブシ, 内踝, *n.* The internal ankle bone.

UCHI-MI, ウチミ, 内肉, *n.* A bruise, contusion.

UCHI-MONO, ウチモノ, 内物, *n.* Anything made on an anvil, or by forging.

UCHI-MORASHI,*-sz,-sh'ta*, ウチモラス, 内洩, *t. v.* To let escape from slaughter.

UCHI-NARASHI,*-sz,-sh'ta*, ウチナラス, 内鳴, *t. v.* To sound by striking or beating.

UCHI-NIWA, ウチニハ, 内庭, *n.* A small court yard or area inclosed by a house.

UCHI-NORI, ウチノリ, 内規, *n.* Inside measurement or dimensions.

UCHI-SHIKI, ウチシキ. 打敷, *n*, A spread for a table or stand.

UCHI-SZYE,*-ru,-ta*, ウチスヱル, 打居, *t. v*, To beat one into a sitting posture.

UCHI-TAOSHI,*-sz,-sh'ta*, ウチタフズ, 打倒, *t. v.* To beat or knock down any thing standing.

UCHI-TOKE,*-ru,-ta*, ウチトケル, 打解, *i. v.* To be free from doubt, or suspicion; to feel at ease, or free from restraint.

UCHI-UMI, ウチウミ, 内海, *n*, An inland sea.

UCHI-UCHI, ウチウチ, 内内, Private, or that which concerns one's family only. — *no koto*, a private or family affair.

UCHI-TOME,*-ru,-ta*, ウチトメル, 内留, *t. v.* To shoot, and give a quietus to.

U-CHIU, ウチウ, 宇宙, *n.* All under the canopy, the world.

U-CHIU, ウチウ, 雨中, (*ameno uchi*). In the rain. — *no tabi*, traveling in the rain.

UCHI-WA, ウチハ, 團扇, *n.* A fan, such as do not fold.

UCHI-WA, ウチハ, 內, *n.* A family, household. Syn. KANAI.

UCHI-YABURI,*–ru,–tta*, ウチヤブル, 打破, *t. v.* To break, or tear by a blow.

UCHŌTEN, ウチヤウテン, 有頂天, *n.* Absent minded, or absorbed in one thing and oblivious of every thing else. — *ni naru.* Syn. MUCHIU, UWANOSORA.

UDE, ウデ, 腕, *n.* The arm.

UDE,*–ru,–ta*, ウデル, *t. v.* To cook by boiling, to boil; same as *Yuderu.*

UDE-KUBI, ウデクビ, 腕首, *n.* The wrist. Syn. TEKUBI.

UDE-MAKURI, ウデマクリ, 腕捲, *n.* Rolling up the sleeve.

UDE-OSHI, ウデオシ, 腕押, *n.* Pushing each other by taking hold of the arms, as a trial of strength.

UDO, ウド, 獨活, *n.* The name of a vegetable, Aralia edulis.

UDON, ウドン, 溫飩, *n.* Macaroni.

UDONGE, ウドンゲ, 優曇華, *n.* The name of a fabulous flower, said to bloom but once in a thousand years.

UDONKO, ウドンコ, 麪粉, *n.* Wheat flour. Syn. KOMUGI NO-KO.

UDZ, ウヅ, 渦, *n.* A whirlpool, eddy.

UDZ, ウヅ, 烏頭, *n.* Aconite root. Syn. TORIKABUTO.

†UDZI, ウヅ井, 踞, *n.* Sitting cross-legged. Syn. AGURA.

UDZKI, ウヅキ, 四月, (*shigatsz*). *n.* The fourth month.

‖UDZKI,*–ku,–ita*, ウヅク, 疼, *i.v.* To pain severely, to ache. *Hone ga* —, to have pain in the bones. *Ha ga* —, to have tooth ache. Syn. ITAMU.

†UDZKUMARI,*–ru,–tta*, ウヅクマル, 踠, *i. v.* To sit on the heels, to squat down, to crouch down. Syn. SHAGAMU.

UDZMAKI,*–ku,–ita*, ウヅマク, 渦卷, *t. v.* To whirl around, to gyrate. *Kuro-kemuri udzmaki-kitaru*, the black smoke came whirling over.

UDZMARI,*–ru,–tta*, ウツマル, 埋, *i. v.* Buried under, or covered with any thing; filled up, to be buried. *Michi ga yuki de* —, the road is covered with snow. *Tszchi ni* —, buried in the earth.

UDZME,*–ru,–ta*, ウヅメル, 埋, *t.v.* To bury, to cover over, as with earth, leaves, snow, &c. to fill up, to inter. *Kiri ga tani wo* —, the fog covered the valley. *Ido wo* —, to fill up a well. *Haka ni* —, to bury in the grave. *Numa wo* —, to fill up a swamp.

UDZMI,*–mu,–nda*, ウヅム, 埋, *i.v.* To be buried under, covered, filled up. *Udzmibi*, a fire covered with ashes.

UDZRA, ウヅラ, 鶉, *n.* A quail.

UGACHI,*–tsz,–tta*, ウガツ, 穿, *t.v.* To dig, to penetrate, pierce. *Ko-no-ha wo fuji no ito-mote ugachi*, strung leaves together with a thread of wisteria. *Ana wo* —, to make a hole. Syn. HORU.

UGAI, ウガイ, 嗽, *n.* Washing, or rinsing the mouth, gargling. — *wo szru.* Syn. KUCHI-SOSOGI.

U-GIYŌ-TAI, ウギヤウタイ, 有形體, *n.* Things having shape or body, material.

†U-GO, ウゴ, 雨後, (*ame no nochi*). After a rain.

UGOKASHI,*–sz,–sh'ta*, ウゴカス, 動, *t.v.* To move, shake, to agitate, excite, persuade, affect. *Kaze ga ki-no-ha wo* —, the wind shakes the leaves. *Kokoro wo* —, to move, or affect the mind.

UGOKI,*–ku,–ita*, ウゴク, 動, *i.v.* To move, shake; to be affected, agitated, excited. *Ha ga* —, the tooth is loose. *Jishin de yama ga* —, the mountains shake with an earthquake. *Kaze de ki ga* —, the tree is shaken by the wind. Syn. YURUGU.

†UGOMEKI,*–ku,–ita*, ウゴメク, 蠕, *i.v.* To move slightly, to have the appearance of moving, to creep.

UGOMOCHI,*–tsz,–ta*, ウゴモツ, *i. v.* To crumble, disintegrate, to become loose in texture, and friable. *Kabe ga* —, the plaster crumbles.

UGUI, ウグヒ, *n.* The name of a small fish.

UGUISZ, ウグヒズ, 鶯, *n.* The name of a small singing bird.

†UI, ウヒ, 初, *a.* The first. — *zan*, a first labor, or parturition. — *go*, a first child. — *jin*, first battle. — *manabi no tame ni*, for the sake of those commencing to learn.

UI,*–KI*, ウイ, 憂, *a.* Sad, sorrowful, miserable, dreary, cheerless. *Yo wo uki-mono ni omō*, regarded the world as a miserable place. *Oya ni wakaruru uki koto*, the sad thing of being separated from her parents. *Uki-me ni au*, to meet with trouble or hardship. Syn. KANASHII.

UKI-KUMO, ウキクモ, 浮雲, *n.* A flying cloud.

UIKIYŌ, ウイキヤウ, 茴香, *n.* Anise-seed.

UITA, ウイタ, *pret.* of *Uki.*

UITE, ウイテ, *pp.* of *Uki.*

†UITEMBEN, ウ井テンベン, 有爲轉變, Full of changes, or vicissitudes. (Bud.) — *no yo no naka.*

†UI-UISHII,-KI,-KU,-U,-SA, ウヒウヒシイ, 初初敷, Youthful, inexperienced, a novice, or tyro in appearance or manner. Syn. WAKA-WAKASHII.

UJI, ウジ, 蛆, *n.* A maggot. — *ga waku,* to breed maggots.

UJI, ウヂ, 氏, *n.* Family name.

UJIGAMI, ウヂガミ, 氏神, *n.* The penates, or tutelary god of a house, or place. Syn. UBUSZNA.

UJIKO, ウヂコ, 氏子, *n.* The persons living in a place under the protection of an *Ubuszna;* the parishoners of a Miya.

UJI-UJI,-*szru,* ウジウジ, To loiter, idle, or waste time by procrastinating. Syn. GUDZ-GUDZ SZRU.

UJŪKITSZ, ウジユキツ, 雲州橘, *n.* A kind of orange without seeds.

UKABASE,-*ru,*-*ta,* ウカバセル, 令泛, caust. of *Ukabe.* To cause to float.

UKABE,-*ru,*-*ta,* ウカベル, 泛, *t. v.* To float, or ride upon the water, to swim. *Fune wo* —, to float, or launch a ship. *Midz ni ukaboru fune,* the ship floating on the water. *Namida wo* —, eyes filling with tears. *Ki wo* —, to rouse the spirits. Syn. UKERU.

UKABI,-*bu,*-*nda,* ウカブ, 浮, *s. v.* To float, swim, or to be supported on the water, to rise to the surface. *Fune ga* —, the ship floats.

UKAGAI,-*au,*-*atta,* ウカガフ, 窺, *t.v.* To inquire, ask after; to find out, or ascertain, descry, to spy out, to explore, to watch secretly, to peep at, look at secretly, to reconnoitre. *Ampi wo* —, to inquire after one's health. *Miyaku wo* —, to feel the pulse. *Hima wo* —, to seek for an opportunity. *Teki no yōsz wo* —, to reconnoitre the state ef the enemy. Syn. TADZNERU, NERAU.

U-KAI, ウカヒ, 鵜飼, *n.* A person who fishes with cormorants.

UKAME,-*ru,*-*ta,* ウカメル, 泛, *t. v.* The same as *Ukabe.*

UKAMI,-*mu,*-*nda,* ウカム, 泛, *i.v.* Same as *Ukabi.*

UKARE,-*ru,*-*ta,* ウカレル, 浮, *i.v.* To be carried away, transported, or fascinated with anything, as music, flowers. *Ongiyoku ni ukarete odoru,* carried away with the music he danced.

†UKAREBITO, ウカレビト, 浮人, *n.* A wanderer, one who has no settled dwelling place. Syn. RŌNIN.

UKAREME, ウカレメ, 遊女, *n.* A prostitute. Syn. JŌRO.

UKASARE,-*ru,*-*ta,* ウカサレル, 被浮, pass. of *Ukashi.* To cause to be floated, to be carried away, transported fascinated; to be made delirious. *Netsz ni ukasarete uwakoto wo iu,* made delirious by the fever he talked foolishly.

UKASHI,-*sz,*-*sh'ta,* ウカス, 浮, *t. v.* To cause to swim, to float. *Midz ga fune wo* —, the water floats the ship.

UKA-UKA, ウカウカ, *adv.* Heedlessly, inattentively, forgetfully, vacantly. — *to yomu,* to read inattentively. — *to yo kurasz,* to live in a dreamy or absent minded way.

UKE,-*ru,*-*ta,* ウケル, 浮, *t. v.* To float, make to swim on the surface. *Fune wo* —, to float a ship.

UKE, ウケ, 筌, *n.* A weir, or bamboo basket fixed in a stream for catching fish.

UKE, ウケ, 泛子, *n.* The float of a net, or fishing line, a buoy.

UKE,-*ru,*-*ta,* ウケル, 受, *t.v.* To receive, to get, to hold, take; to be the subject of, to parry. *Ame wo* —, to get wet with rain. *Kidz wo* —, to receive a wound, or to be wounded. *Utagai wo* —, to be suspected. *Shimo wo* —, to be frosted. *Tszyu wo* —, to be wet with dew. *Sewa wo* —, to receive assistance. *Kakomi wo* —, to be surrounded. *Katana wo tszye de* —, to parry a sword cut with a cane. *Kono fune wa iku nin ukeru,* how many men will this boat hold? *On wo* —, to receive kindness. Syn. YERU.

UKE, ウケ, 有氣, *n.* A period of good luck. — *ni iru,* to enter a lucky period.

UKE, ウケ, 承, or 受, *n.* A reply, answer; the position, exposure, or situation of a place in regard to points of the compass. — *wo szru,* to answer. *Nishi-uke,* a western exposure, or facing the west. *Kaze-uke ni kaki wo szru,* to erect a fence to keep off the wind.

UKE-AI,-*au,*-*atta,* ウケアフ, 受合, *t. v.* To warrant, to guarantee, to insure, to engage one's self for the performance of or truth of anything, to certify, to pledge one's self for, go security for, to contract, bargain, promise. *Fushin wo* —, to contract to build. Syn. YAK'SOKU SZRU.

UKE-AI-NIN, ウケアヒニン, 受合人, *n.* A surety, insurer, contractor.

UKEBORI, ウケボリ, 浮彫, *n.* Raised or embossed carving.

†UKEBUMI, ウケブミ, 受文, *n.* A letter sent in reply to a government order.

UKEDACHI, ウケダチ, 受刀, *n.* The sword placed in guard, or to fend off, in fencing.

UKE-DASHI,*-sz,-sh'ta*, ウケダス, 受出, *t. v.* To take out, to redeem, as any thing pawned, or a prostitute, before her time of service is up.

UKEGAI,*-au,-atta*, ウケガフ, 信, *t.v.* To assent to, receive as true, to believe. *Ukegai-gataki*, hard to believe.
Syn. UBENAI, SHŌCHI, YURUSZ, SHINJIRU.

UKE-HIKI,*-ku,-ita*, ウケヒク, 承引, *i.v.* To concede, consent, yield, give in, agree to, accede to. Syn. YURUSZ, SHŌCHI SZRU.

UKE-JŌ, ウケジヤウ, 受狀, *n.* An indenture or written contract binding a person to service.

UKE-KAYESHI,*-sz,-sh'ta*, ウケカヘス, 受返, *t.v.* To redeem, or get out of pawn.

UKE-KOTAYE, ウケコタヘ, 承答, *n.* Answer, reply. — *wo szru.*

UKE-KOMI,*-mu,-nda*, ウケコム, 受込, *i.v.* To undertake, engage, take in hand, to take the charge of. *Gunzei no makanai kata wo* —, to undertake to furnish an army with provisions. Syn. HIKI-UKERU.

UKEMI, ウケミ, 受身, *n.* Acting on the defensive, in fencing.

UKE-NIN, ウケニン, 受人, *n.* A surety, bail, bondsman. Syn. UKEAININ.

UKEOI, ウケオヒ, 請負, *n.* A contract. — *shigoto*, work done by contract. — *nin*, a contractor.

UKEORI, ウケオリ, 浮織, *n.* Woven with raised figures.

UKETAMAWARI,*-ru,-tta*, ウケタマハル, 承, To hear, to be told, or receive by report; used in respectfully speaking to another. Syn. KIKU.

UKE-TORI,*-ru,-tta*, ウケトル, 受取, *t.v.* To receive certainly or without fail. *Kane wo* —, to receive money.

UKE-TORI, ウケトリ, 受取, *n.* A receipt.

UKE-URI, ウケウリ, 受賣, *n.* Selling as one gets, or doing a retail business.

UKI,*-ku,-ita*, ウク, 浮, *i.v.* To float, swim on the surface, to be buoyant, light, fickle. *Fune ga* —, the boat floats. *Ki no uita h'to*, a fickle person. *Ki ga* —, to be light-hearted, or merry.

UKI, ウキ, 憂, See *Ui.*

UKI-AGARI,*-ru,-tta*, ウキアガル, 浮上, *i.v.* To rise and float.

UKI-GUSA, ウキグサ, 萍, *n.* A plant that floats upon the water.

UKIKI, ウキキ, 翻車魚, *n.* The sunfish. (Orthragoriscus mola.)

UKI-NA, ウキナ, 浮名, *n.* A bad name, or reputation. — *wo nagasz*, to spread an evil report of any one.

UKI-UKI-TO, ウキウキト, 泛泛, *adv.* In a buoyant floating manner, in a buoyant light-hearted manner, a drift, drifting.

UKI-YO, ウキヨ, 浮世, *n.* This fleeting or miserable world, — so full of vicissitudes, and unsettled.

UKKARI, ウツカリ, *adv.* Vacantly, listlessly, carelessly, without attention. — *miru*, to look at in a vacant or abstracted manner.

UKKI, ウツキ, 鬱氣, *n.* Vapors, gloom, melancholy. — *wo harau*, to dispel gloom.

UKU, ウク, 憂, *adv.* See *Ui.*

UKU, ウク, 浮, See *Uki.*

†UKURU, ウクル, 受, Same as *Ukeru*, see *Uke.*

UK'WATSZ, ウクワツ, 迂闊, Dull, stupid, slow. — *na h'to.*

UMA, ウマ, 馬, *n.* A horse: also, 午, one of the 12 signs. — *no toki*, 12 o'clock M. — *no hō*, the south. — *ni noru*, to ride on a horse. — *wo koshirayero*, get the horse ready.

UMADZ, ウマズ, 不生, neg. of *Umi;* also a barren woman.

UMAGOYASHI, ウマゴヤシ, 苜蓿, *n.* Trefoil, or clover.

UMAGUWA, ウマグハ, 馬把, *n.* A rake drawn by a horse, or harrow.

UMAI,*-KI*, ウマイ, 甘, or 旨, *a.* Sweet, pleasant to the taste, agreeable, good, mild, savory. *Niku ga* —, flesh is pleasant to the taste. *Umaku nai*, unpleasant, not good to eat. *Umaku iu*, to talk smoothly, or blandly. Syn. OISHII.

†UMAI, ウマイ, 熟睡, Sound sleep. — *szru*, to sleep soundly.

UMA-JIRUSHI, ウマジルシ, 馬幟, *n.* A flag, or banner, used for distinguishing the commander of an army.

UMA-KATA, ウマカタ, 馬方, *n.* The person who attends and leads a pack-horse.

UMA-KEMURI, ウマケムリ, 馬烟, *n.* The dust raised by horses traveling.

UMAKU, ウマク, 甘, *adv.* Sweet, pleasant to the taste. — *szru*, to sweeten. — *nai*, not sweet.

UMANORI, ウマノリ, 馬乘, *n.* A horse

rider, a teacher of horsemanship, a horse-race.

UMARE, *-ru,-ta*, ウマレル, 生, *i.v.* To be born, brought forth. *Akambō ga umareta*, a child was born. *Watakushi no umareta kuni*, the country where I was born. Syn. SHUSSHŌ SZRU, SHŌDZRU.

UMARE, ウマレ, 生, *n.* The condition, or place in which one is born; birth, extraction. — *ga warui.* — *ga yoi.*

UMAREBI, ウマレビ, 生日, *n.* Birth-day. Syn. TANJŌBI.

UMAREGO, ウマレゴ, 生子, *n.* An infant. Syn. AKAMBŌ, MIDORIGO.

UMARE-KAWARI, *-ru,-tta*, ウマレカハル, 生變, *i.v.* To pass by birth from one thing into another, to transmigrate, as the soul of the dead (Budd). *H'to ga inu ni* —, the soul of a man passes into the body of a dog.

UMARE-KAWARI, ウマレカハリ, 生變, *n.* Transmigration of the soul, metempsychosis.

UMARE-MASARI, *-ru,-tta*, ウマレマサル, 生增, *i.v.* To rise above the condition or station in which one was born.

UMARE-OTORI, *-ru,-tta*, ウマレオトル, 生劣, *i.v.* To fall below the condition, or station in which one was born.

UMARE-TATE, ウマレタテ, 生立, Just born. — *no ko.*

UMARE-TSZKI, ウマレツキ, 生付, *n.* Nature, inborn or natural constitution, disposition, or temperament. — *no yoi h'to*, a person of a naturally good disposition. — *no katawa*, a cripple from birth. Syn. SHŌ-TOKU.

UMARE-TSZKI, *-ku,-ita*, ウマレツク, 生著, *i.v.* To be natural, inborn, innate, congenital. *Rikō ni* —, to be naturally clever. *Umaretszkanu katawa*, a cripple but not from birth.

UMARI, *-ru,-tta*, ウマル, 埋, *i. v.* A contraction of *Udzmari.*

UMASA, ウマサ, 甘, *n.* Sweetness.

UMASHI, ウマシ, 旨, See *Umai.*

UMA-TSZGI, ウマツギ, 驛, *n.* A post-station, or relay station on a public road. Syn. SHUKUBA.

UMA-UMA-TO, ウマウマト, *adv.* Cleverly, adroitly, skillfully, artfully. — *damash'ta.*

UMAYA, ウマヤ, 厩, *n.* A horse stable.

UMAYAJI, ウマヤヂ, 驛路, (*yekiro*). *n.* A public road.

UME, ウメ, 梅, (*bai*). *n.* The plum tree. — *no hana*, the blossoms of plum trees.

UME, *-ru,-ta*, ウメル, 埋, *t.v.* (contract. of *Udzmeru*). To bury, to cover, fill up, to pour in in order to reduce the temperature, or strength; to dilute. *Ido wo* —, to fill up a well. *Sake ni midz wo* —, to dilute wine with water. *Yu ni midz wo* —, to cool boiling water by pouring in water.

UME-AGE, *-ru,-ta*, ウメアゲル, 埋上, *t.v.* To bury, cover, or fill up.

UME-AWASE, *-ru,-ta*, ウメアハセル, 埋合, *t.v.* To fill up and make even. (as a hollow); to square or make even one's losses by his gains.

UME-BOSHI, ウメボシ, 白梅, (*hakubai*). *n.* Dried plums.

UME-CHI, ウメチ, 埋地, *n.* Ground or land made by filling in a swamp or shoal water. Syn. TSZKIJI.

UME-DOYU, ウメドユ, 埋樋, *n.* A water pipe laid under the ground.

UME-DZ, ウメズ, 梅酢, *n.* Vinegar made of plum juice.

UME-DZKE, ウメヅケ, 梅漬, *n.* Pickled plums.

UMEKI, *-ku,-ita*, ウメク, 呻, *t.v.* To groan in pain or sorrow, to moan. Syn. UNARU.

UME-KUSA, ウメクサ, 埋草, *n.* Any material used for filling up. *Ido no* — *ga nai*, have nothing with which to fill up the well.

UME-ZONO, ウソゾノ, 梅園, *n.* A plum garden.

UMI, ウミ, 海, (*kai*). *n.* The sea, ocean.

UMI, ウミ, 膿, *n.* Pus, matter. — *ga dekiru*, to suppurate. — *wo motsz*, to contain matter. — *ga deru.* Syn. NŌ.

UMI, *-mu,-nda*, ウム, 生, *t. v.* To bear, give birth to, bring forth, to lay, (as a fowl). *Ko wo* —, to bring forth a child. *Tamago wo* —, to lay an egg. Syn. SAN SZRU.

UMI, *-mu,-nda*, ウム, 熟, *i.v.* To ripen, to soften, or come to maturity, (as fruit); to suppurate. *Ume ga mada umimasen*, the plums are not yet ripe. *Hari-mono ga unda*, the boil has suppurated. Syn. JUKUSZ.

UMI, *-mu,-nda*, ウム, 倦, *i.v.* To be tired, or weary of, fatigued. *Gakumon ni unda*, tired of study. Syn. TAIKUTSZ.

UMI, *-mu,-nda*, ウム, 紡, *t.v.* To twist and join the threads of hemp together in order to lengthen, preparatory to twisting into a cord. *O wo* —.

UMIBATA, ウミバタ, }
UMIBE, ウミベ, } 海邊, *n.* The sea-shore, sea-coast.
UMIBETA, ウミベタ, }

UMI-DASHI, *-sz,-sh'ta*, ウミダス, 產出, *t.v.* To bring forth, to lay (as an egg); fig.

to save a little, as out of one's expenses, or in cutting out a garment.

UMI-DZKI, ウミヅキ, 生月, *n.* The last month of gestation. Syn. RINGETSZ.

UMI-DZRA, ウミヅラ, 海面, *n.* The surface of the ocean.

UMI-HECHIMA, ウミヘチマ, 海絲, *n.* Sponge. Syn. UMI-WATA.

UMIJI, ウミヂ, 海路, (*kairo*). *n.* A journey by sea, a voyage.

UMI-MATSZ, ウミマツ, 海松, *n.* Coral.

UMI-OTOSHI,*–sz,–sh'ta*, ウミオトス, 生落, *t.v.* To give birth to, bring forth.

UMI-TSZKARE,*–ru,–ta*, ウミツカレル, 倦疲, *i.v.* To be tired, or disgusted with.

UMI-UMA, ウミウマ, 海馬, *n.* The sea-horse, Hippocampus.

UMI-TSZKE,*–ru,–ta*, ウミツケル, 生附, *t.v.* To deposit eggs on anything, as silk worms on paper.

UMI-WATA, ウシワタ, 海綿, *n.* Sponge.

UMI-YANAGI, ウミヤナギ, 海柳, *n.* A species of coral.

†UMMEI, ウンメイ, 運命, *n.* Good fortune, good luck.

UMMO, ウンモ, 雲母, *n.* Talc or mika used in making the figures on wall-paper. Syn. KIRARA.

UMORE,*–ru,–ta* ウモレル, 埋, *i.v.* To be buried, or covered up, to be filled up. *Ishi ga tszchi ni* —, the stone is buried in the earth. Syn. UDZMARU, UMARU.

UMOREGI, ウモレギ, 埋木, *n.* Fossil wood.

UMORI,*–ru,–tta*, ウモル, 埋, *i.v.* The same as *Umore*.

UMU, ウム, 生, 倦, 熟, 紡, See *Umi*.

U-MU, ウム, 有無, (*aru nashi*). Are or are not, have or have not. — *no ron ni mo oyobadz*, unnecessary to dispute whether there is, or is not. *Tszmi no umu ni kakawaradz mina rōya ni ireru*, without respect to guilt or innocence he put them all in gaol.

†UMUGI, ウムギ, 蛤, *n.* A clam.

UN, ウン, 運, *n.* Fortune, luck, chance, turn, time, vicissitude. — *no yoi h'to*, a lucky person. *Kodomo ni — ga warui*, unfortunate in one's children, (all dying). — *ga nai*, to have no luck. — *ni makaseru*, to leave it to chance. — *wo ten ni makaseru*, to commit one's fortune to heaven. — *ga naotta*, fortune has changed for the better.

UN, ウン, 雲, (*kumo*). A cloud. *Unsho*, above the clouds. *Unchiu*, in the clouds.

UN, ウン, Exclam. of assent. — *to iu.*

†UNABARA, ウナバラ, 海原, (*umi no hara*). The wide sea.

UNADARE,*–ru,–ta*, ウナダレル, 項垂, (*unaji wo tareru*). *i.v.* To hang the head, (as in shame or trouble). *Unadarete mono mo iwadz ni oru*, hung his head and remained silent.

UNADZKI,*–ku,–ita*, ウナヅク, 點頭, *i.v.* To nod the head in assent, or to beckon with a nod.

†UNAGASHI,*–sz,–sh'ta*, ウナガス, 促, *t.v.* To press, urge, to hurry, to order to make ready. *Kamakura ye ga wo* —, to order the norimon and go to *Kamakura*.

UNAGI, ウナギ, 鰻鱺, *n.* An eel.

UNAI,*–au,–atta*, ウナフ, 耡, *t.v.* To cultivate, plough, farm. *Ta wo* —, to cultivate the rice fields.

†UNAIGO, ウナヒゴ, *n.* A little girl.

UNAJI, ウナジ, 項, *n.* The nape of the neck.

UNARI,*–ru,–tta*, ウナル, 吁鳴, *i.v.* (*u to naru*, sounding u----u). To resound in a prolonged manner, as a bell for some time after it is struck; to hum, as a humming kite or top; to groan, to moan. *Tako ga* —, the kite hums. *Hara ga itakute unatte iru*, groaning with pain in the stomach. *Tszrigane ga nagaku unaru*, the bell resounds for a long time. Syn. UMEKU.

UNASARE,*–ru,–ta*, ウナサレル, 魘, *i.v.* To have the night-mare, to have a horrible dream. *Unasareru no wo kiki-tszkeru*, to hear some one crying out in the night-mare. Syn. OSOWARERU.

UNAU, ウナフ, See *Unai*.

UNAWA, ウナハ, 鵜縄, *n.* A line used in fishing with a cormorant.

UNCHIN, ウンチン, 運賃, *n.* The money or hire paid for carrying, or transporting goods either by horse, coolie, ship, or waggon; freight, fare. Syn. DACHIN.

UN-DEI, ウンデイ, 雲泥, (*kumo doro*). *n.* Clouds and mud, used only in the phrase. — *no chigai*, different as clouds and mud.

UNDŌ, ウンドウ, 運動, *n.* Motion, circular movement, exercise. — *szru*, to move, to take exercise. *Chi no* —, circulation of the blood. — *shi-nikui mono*, a thing difficult to move. Syn UGOKU, MEGURU.

UNDON, ウンドン, Same as *Udon*.

UNE, ウネ, 畝, *n.* The ridges of a ploughed field, a furrow.

UNEKUNE, ウネクネ, *adv.* Convoluted, or zig-zag, winding and turning in form or manner. *Hebi ga — to hau.*

UNEKURI,*–ru,–tta*, ウネクル, *i.v.* To

twist and turn, to coil in and out, to be convoluted.

UNEME, ウネメ, 采女, *n.* Female servant of the Tenshi.

UNERI, *-ru, -tta*, ウネル, *i.v.* To be wavy, or up and down like the ridges of a ploughed field, serpentine, anfractuous, or winding and turning.

UNI, ウニ, 海膽, *n.* A kind of food made of clams.

UNIKŌRU, ウニコオル, 犀, *n.* A rhinoceros

UNJŌ, ウンジヤウ, 運上, *n.* Duty, customs or toll paid on goods. — *wo harau*, to pay duty. — *wo toru*, to take duty.

UNJŌ-SHO, ウンジヤウシヨ, 運上所, *n.* Custom house.

UN-KA, ウンカ, 雲霞, *(kumo kaszmi). n.* Clouds and haze. — *no gotoku.*

†UNKI, ウンキ, 雲氣, *n.* The motions, or influence of the clouds.

UNKO, ウンコ, *n.* The feces, used by children.

†UN-NUN, ウンウン, 云云, At the end of a sentence, = it is said, or so it is said; also used in reference to something said before to save repetition, = mentioned above, afore-mentioned, afore-said, et cetera, and so on. Syn. SHIKA-SHIKA.

UNSAI, ウンサイ, 雲紗, *n.* A kind of thick cotton cloth, used for making the soles of stockings.

UN-SEI, ウンセイ, 運勢, *n.* Fortune, luck, the changes, or turns in human life.

UNSŌ, ウンサウ, 運送, *(hakobi okuru). n.* Transportation, or carrying of goods. — *szru*, to transport.

UNSZI, ウンスイ, 雲水, *(kumo midz). n.* A wandering priest. — *no sō*, idem.

UNU, ウヌ, (vul. coll. for *onore*). *pro.* You; own. — *ga ko*, your child; one's own child. — *ra*, you fellows, (used to contemptible persons). Syn. TEMAYE, NANJI.

UNUBORE, ウヌボレ, 自信, *n.* Self-love, self-esteem, vanity, egotism. — *no fukai onna*, a woman of great vanity.

†UNYEKI, ウンエキ, 瘟疫, *n.* A plague, pestilence, severe epidemic disease.

UNYEN, ウンエン, 雲煙, *n.* Haze.

UPPUN, ウツプン, 鬱憤, *n.* Hatred, malice, or enmity treasured up in the heart. — *wo harasz.*

URA, ウラ, 浦, *n.* Sea-coast, or country near the coast, a village on the sea-coast.

URA, ウラ, 梢, *n.* The topmost part of a tree. Syn. KODZYE.

URA, ウラ, 裡, *n.* The inside surface, (as of cloth, paper); the rear, back. *Te no* —, palm of the hand. *Ashi no* —, the sole of the foot. *Iye no* —, the rear of a house. — *no mon*, the back gate. — *wo iu*, to speak ironically. — *ni satoru*, to understand it ironically. — *wo utsz*, to paste paper on the back of anything to strengthen it. *Kimono no* —, the inside of a coat. Syn. USHIRO.

URA-BITO, ウラビト, 浦人, *n.* A person living on the sea-coast.

URABON, ウラボン, 于蘭盆, *n.* The 15th day of the 7th month, when the festival for the dead is celebrated.

†URABURE, *-ru, -ta*, ウラブレル, *i.v.* To be exhausted, languid, weary.
Syn. KUTABURERU, TSZKARERU.

URA-DANA, ウラダナ, 裡店, *n.* A rear house.

URA-GAKI, ウラガキ, 裡書, *n.* An indorsement, or writing on the back of a letter.

URA-GAYE, *-ru, -ta*, ウラガヘル, 裡反, *i.v.* To become inside out, or turned about in an opposite direction. *Mikata ga uragayette teki ni naru*, our allies are turned and become our enemy.

URA-GAYESHI, *-sz, -sh'ta*, ウラガヘス, 裡反, *t. v.* To turn the inside out. *Kimono wo* —, to turn a garment.

URA-GIRI, ウラギリ, 裡切, *n.* Treacherously attacking and slaying the army to which one belongs.

URA-GUCHI, ウラグチ, 裡口, *n.* The back door of a house.

URA-HAN, ウラハン, 裡判, *n.* The seal affixed to an indorsement.

URA-HARA, ウラハラ, 裡原, *n.* Contrary to each other, the reverse, or opposites of each other, contrast, antithesis. *Kun-shi to shō-jin to itszmo — nari*, the good man and bad man are always the reverse of each other. *Aru to nai to wa — da*, *aru* and *nai* are the opposites of each other.
Syn. HIYŌ-RI, HANTAI.

URA-IN, ウライン, 裡印, *n.* The seal affixed to an indorsement.

†URA-KATA, ウラカタ, 卜方, *n.* The fortune, or future events, as told by a fortune-teller.

URAMESHII, -KI, -KU, ウラメシイ, 恨敷, Exciting displeasure, or resentment. *Urameshiku omō*, to feel displeased or offended.

URAMI, *-mu, -nda*, ウラム, 恨, or 怨, *t.v.* To be displeased with, offended at, to feel spite, ill-will, enmity or resentment, to hate. *Ten wo* —, to be displeased or angry at heaven. *Mi wo* —, to be vexed with one's self. *H'to wo* —, to feel offended at another. Syn. NIKUMU.

URAMI, ウラミ, 恨, *n.* Resentment, enmity, malice, malevolence, spite, ill-will.

URAMI,*-ru,-ta*, ウラミル, 恨, *t.v.* The same as *Uramu.*

URA-MICHI, ウラミチ, 裏路, *n.* A back road.

URAMIRARE,*-ru,-ta*, ウラミラレル, 被恨, pass. of *Uramu.* To be regarded with enmity, or malice.

URANAI,*-au,-atta*, ウラナフ, 占, *t.v.* To foretell, prognosticate by divination, to divine, to augur. *Mi no wiye wo* —, to tell one's fortune. Syn BOKU SZRU.

URANAI, or URANU, ウラヌ, 不要賣, neg. of *Uri.* Will not sell.

URANAI, ウラナヒ, 卜, Divination, prognostication, augury, fortune telling.

URANAIJA, ウラナヒジヤ, 卜者, *n.* A diviner, fortune-telling.

URARAKA, ウララカ, 麗, Clear, bright, serene. — *na tenki.* Syn. NODOKA.

URARE,*-ru,-ta*, ウラレル, 被賣, pass. or pot. of *Uri.* To be sold.

URASE,*-ru,-ta*, ウラセル, 令賣, caust. of *Uri.* To cause to sell or let sell.

URA-UCHI, ウラウチ, 裡打, *n.* Pasting paper on the back of a picture, &c., in order to strengthen it. — *wo szru.*

URA-WIYE, ウラウヘ, 裡上, *n.* The contrary, opposite, or reverse.
Syn URAHARA.

URAYAMASHII,-KI,-KU, ウラヤマシイ, 羨, That which one would like to be, or resemble, enviable. *Urayamashiku omō*, to desire to resemble, to envy.
Syn. AYAKARI TAI, KENARII.

URAYAMI,*-mu,-nda*, ウラヤム, 羨, *t.v.* To desire to be like, or in the place of anything which one admires; to envy, to be jealous of. *Tori wo* —, to desire to be a bird. *H'to no hanjō wo* —, to desire to be as prosperous as some one else.

URE,*-ru,-ta*, ウレル, 賣, Sold, can be sold. *Sono ne de wa uremasen*, it cannot be sold at that price. *Ito ga ureru ka*, is raw silk saleable? or in demand? *Hon ga ureta*, the book is sold. *Kao no ureta h'to*, a well known person.

URE, ウレ, 賣, The sale. *Ito no — ga yoi*, silk is in great demand. — *ga tōi mono*, an unsaleable article.

URE, ウレ, 梢, Same as *Ura.*

URE-KUCHI, ウレクチ, 售口, *n.* Sale, demand, buyers. *Ito no — ga nai*, no demand for silk; same as *Urikuchi.*

UREI, ウレヒ, 患, *n.* Distress, sorrow, grief, sadness; anxiety, trouble. — *wo moyōsz*, to excite sorrow. — *wo fukumu*, to be sorrowful. *Ishi no iye wa kw'aji no — ga nai*, a stone house is in no danger of being burnt.
Syn. KURŌ, SHIMPAI, ANJI.

†UREI,*-iō,-eita*, ウレフ, 憂, *i.v.* To be distressed, sad, to sorrow; to be anxious, to fret about. *Chichi no yamai wo ureite kami wo inoru*, anxious about her father's sickness she prayed to the Kami.
Syn. KANASHIMU.

URENAI, or URENU, ウレナイ, 不售, neg. of *Ureru.* Unsaleable. *Urenai mono*, an unsaleable article. *Urenakute mo kamaimasen*, no matter if it is unsaleable.

URE-NOKORI, ウレノコリ, 賣殘, *n* A remnant, or anything remaining after a sale.

URESHIGARI,*-ru,-tta*, ウレシガル, 喜, To be joyful, pleased, delighted.

URESHIGE, ウレシゲ, 喜氣, *n.* Pleased, or delighted appearance. — *na kao*, joyful countenance.

URESHII,-KI, ウレシイ, 喜, Delightful, pleasant, joyful, happy. *Kon-na ureshii koto wa nai*, there is nothing so delightful as this. *Ureshikute tamara-nai*, so happy he could not contain himself.
Syn. YOROKOBU.

URESHISA, ウレシサ, 喜, *n.* Joy, delight, pleasure, happiness.

URI, ウリ, 瓜, *n.* A melon. *Uri-batake*, a melon patch.

URI,*-ru,-tta*, ウル, 賣, *t.v.* To sell. *Na wo* —, to sell one's name, to use artifice in order to gain notoriety. *Ikura de urinasaru* what do you sell this at? *H'yaku riyō de urimashō*, I will sell it for one hundred *riyō*. Syn. SABAKU.

URI-AGE,*-ru,-ta*, ウリアゲル, 賣上, *t. v.* To finish selling.

URI-DASHI,*-sz,-sh'ta*, ウリダス, 賣出, *t.v.* To sell, to commence, or open the sale of anything; to come out with something over, after having sold all the rest.

URI-DORI, ウリドリ, 賣取, *n.* Selling something belonging to another, and keeping the money. — *ni szru.*

URI-HARAI,*-au,-atta*, ウリハラフ, 賣拂, *t.v.* To clear off by selling, to sell off.

URI-HIROME,*-ru,-ta*, ウリヒロメル, 賣弘, *t.v.* To sell all about, to sell extensively; or spread about by selling.

URI-KAI, ウリカヒ, 賣買, *n.* Buying and selling, trade, traffic. — *wo szru.*

URI-KIRI,-*ru*,-*tta*, ウリキル, 賣切, *t.v.* To sell all, so that none is left.

URI-KOMI,-*mu*,-*nda*, ウリコム, 賣込, *t.v.* To sell into; in selling anything to fall short of the original quantity; to be used to selling anything.

URI-KUCHI, ウリクチ, 賣口, *n.* An outlet for the sale of anything, demand. — *ga nai*, = no demand, or no buyer. Syn. SABAKI-KUCHI.

URI-MOMI, ウリモミ, 瓜揉, *n.* A dish made of cucumbers sliced and seasoned with vinegar.

URI-MONO, ウリモノ, 賣物, (*bai-butsz*). *n.* Articles for sale, merchandise.

URI-NUSHI, ウリヌシ, 賣主, *n.* The seller.

URIŌ, ウレフ, 患, See *Urei*.

URI-SABAKI,-*ku*,-*ita*, ウリサバク, 消售, *t.v.* To sell off.

URI-SAKI, ウリサキ, 賣先, *n.* The buyer, or person to whom anything is sold. Syn. KAITE.

URI-SHIRO, ウリシロ, 賣代, *n.* The price or money received in exchange for goods. Syn. DAIKIN.

URI-SZYE, ウリスヱ, 賣居, *n.* A house that is for sale. — *ga deta*, there is a house for sale.

URITE, ウリテ, 賣手, *n.* The seller. Syn. URI-NUSHI.

URI-WATASHI,-*sz*,-*sh'ta*, ウリワタス, 賣渡, *t.v.* To sell and deliver the goods.

URI-ZANE, ウリザネ, 瓜核, *n.* A melon seed. — *gao*, a long face.

URŌ, ウラウ, fut. or dub. of *Uru*. Will sell, would like to sell, or think of selling. — *to iute mo kaite ga nai*, I wanted to sell but no body would buy.

URO, ウロ, 空, *n.* A hollow. *Uro no ki*, a hollow tree. — *no tama*, a hollow ball. Syn. KARA.

†U-RO, ウロ, 雨露, (*ame tszyu*), *n.* The rain and dew. — *no on*, kindness like rain and dew.

UROKO, ウロコ, 鱗, The scales of a fish or snake. Syn. KOKE.

UROKUDZ, ウロクズ, 鱗類, (*giyo rui*), *n.* A general term for fishes. Syn. UWO.

URON, ウロン, 胡亂, Admitting of doubt, doubtful, questionable, suspicious. — *na h'to*, a suspicious person. Spn. USAN, UTAGAWASHII, GATEN-YUKADZ.

UROTAYE,-*ru*,-*ta*, ウロタヘル, 狼狽, *i.v.* To be confused, bewildered, agitated, perplexed, flurried. *Urotayete yuki-dokoro mo shiranu*, so bewildered he did not know where to go. Syn. RŌBAI SZRU.

URO-TSZKI,-*ku*,-*ita*, ウロツク, coll. *i. v.* Same as *Urotaye*.

URO-URO, ウロウロ, *adv.* In a wandering, confused, bewildered, or perplexed manner. — *to sh'te iru*.

URU, ウル, 賣, See *Uri*, to sell.

URU, ウル, 得, See *U*, to get.

URŪDZKI, ウルフヅキ, 閏月, *n.* Intercallary month.

URUI,-*ū*,-*ūta*, ウルフ, 潤, coll. contr. of *Uruoi*.

URUKA, ウルカ, 江豚, *n.* The name of a fish.

URUMI,-*mu*,-*nda*, ウルム, 痕, *i. v.* To become black and blue, as a bruise; or discolored as a cicatrice. *Kidz ga urumu.*

URUMI,-*mu*,-*nda*, ウルム, coll. *i. v*, To be moist. damp. *Me ga* —, eyes are moist with tears. *Koye ga* —, voice to be tremulous as in weeping.

URUOI, ウルホヒ, 潤, *n.* Moisture, wetness; wealth, prosperity, Syn. SHIMERI, NURE.

URUOI,-*ō*,-*ōta*, ウルホフ, 潤, *i.v.* To be moist, wet; irrigated; to be rich, prosperous, wealthy. *Ame de tszchi ga* —, the ground is wet with rain. *Kuni ga* —, the country is rich. Syn. SHIMERU, NURERU.

URUOSHI,-*sz*,-*sh'ta*, ウルホス, 潤, *i. v.* To moisten, to wet; irrigate; to enrich to make wealthy. *Ame ga tszchi wo* —, the rain moistens the ground. *Kin-gin wa kuni wo* —, gold and silver enrich a country. Syn. SHIMESZ, NURASZ.

URUSAI,-KI,-SHI, ウルサイ, *a.* Troublesome, annoying, disagreeble, irksome, tiresome. *Urusai h'to*, a bore, troublesome person. Syn. MENDŌ.

URUSAKU, ウルサク, *adv.* id.

URUSHI, ウルシ, 漆, *n.* Lacquer, varnish. —, *no ki*, the tree from which lacquer is obtained. — *wo kaku*, to box the lacquer tree. — *de nuru*, to lacquer. — *de tszgu*, to glue, or cement with lacquer. — *ni kabureru*, to be poisoned with lacquer.

URUSHI-KABURE, ウルシカブレ, 漆瘡, *n.* Lacquer poison.

URUSHI-MAKE, ウルシマケ, 漆瘡, *n.* idem.

URUSHINE, ウルシネ, 粳, *n.* Rice. Syn. KOME, TADAGOME.

URUSHIYA, ウルシヤ, 漆屋, *n.* A lacquerer, varnisher.

†URUWASHII,-KI,-KU,-U,-SA, ウルハシイ, 美, Beautiful, elegant, graceful lovely, good. Syn. UTSZKUSHII.

USA, ウサ, See *Ui*. *n.* Sadness, sorrow; gloom, melancholy. — *wo harasz*, to dispel gloom.

USAGI, ウサギ, 兎, *n.* A hare.

USAGI-AMI, ウサギアミ, 兎網, *n.* A net for catching hares.

USAGI-UMA, ウサギウマ, 驢, *n.* An ass.

USAN, ウサン, 胡散, *n.* Doubt, suspicion, distrust. — *ga kakaru*, to entertain suspicion of any one. — *ni omō*, to regard with suspicion. Syn. URON, UTAGAI.

USANRASHII,-KI,-KU, ウサンラシイ, Doubtful, suspicious. Syn. UTAGAWASHII.

USE,-*ru*,-*ta*, ウセル, 失, *i.v.* To be lost, to disappear, vanish, to die. *Fude ga* —, the pen is lost. Syn. NAKU-NAKU.

USE-MONO, ウセモノ, 失物, *n.* A lost thing, a stolen article. — *ga deta*, the lost thing is found. — *wo uranau*, to consult a fortune teller about any thing lost.

USHI, ウシ, 牛, *n.* A cow, ox; also 丑 one of the 12 horary characters. — *no toki*, 2 o'clock A.M. — *no hō*, the N.N.E.

USHI, ウシ, See *Ui. a.* Sad, gloomy, melancholy.

USHI-KAI, ウシカヒ, 牛飼, *n.* A cowherd.

USHINAI,-*au*,-*atta*, ウシナフ, 失, *t.v.* To lose. *Ki wo* —, to lose one's senses, become insensible. *Inochi wo* —, to lose life. *Mi wo* —, to ruin one's self by dissipation. *Mi chi wo* —, to lose the way.
Syn. NAKUNARU.

USHIO, ウシホ, 潮, *n.* The water of the ocean.

USHIRO, ウシロ, 後, *n.* The back, or part opposite the front, the rear; behind. *Iye no* — the back part of a house. *Iye no* — *ni*, behind the house. *Teki ni* — *wo miseru*, to show the back to the enemy, to flee. Syn. URA.

USHIRO-ASHI, ウシロアシ, 後足, *n.* Taking a few steps backward, as in hesitation or doubt. — *wo fumu.*

USHIRO-DATE, ウシロダテ, 後楯, *n.* A shield, or defence to the back. *Ki wo* — *ni totte tataku*, to fight with the back against a tree.

USHIRO-DE, ウシロデ, 後手, *n.* The hands behind the back, only in the phrase. — *ni shibaru*, to tie the hands &c.

USHIRO-GURAI,-KI,-KU, ウシログライ, 後暗, Conscious of guilt. *Ushiro-gurai koto wo shite wa h'to ni tszki-awarenu*, conscious of having done something criminal he cannot associate with others. *Ushiroguraku omō*, to feel conscious of guilt.

USHIRO-KAGE, ウシロカゲ, 後影, *n.* The image of the back, = back; used in, — *no miyeru made mi-okuru*, to look at a person as far as he can be seen.

†USHIRO-METAI,-KI,-KU,-SHI, ウシロメタイ, Regarding with care, or anxiety, troubled about. *Ushiro-metaku omō*, id.

USHIRO-MI, ウシロミ, 後見, (*kōken*). *n.* A guardian, one who has the charge of an orphan or minor. — *wo szru*, to act as guardian.
Syn. HOSA.

USHIRO-MUKI, ウシロムキ, 後向, *n.* Having the back towards any thing; as, — *ni szwaru*, to sit with the back towards a person.

USHIRO-YUBI, ウシロユビ, 後指, *n.* as. — *wo sasz*, to point the finger at any one behind his back, to ridicule, or backbite.

USHI-TORA, ウシトラ, 丑寅, — *no kata*, the N.E.

USHI-SAKI, ウシサキ, 牛裂, *n.* The punishment of being drawn by oxen.

USO, ウソ, 虚言, *n.* A lie, falsehood. — *wo tszku*, to tell a lie.
Syn. ITSZWARI, KIYO-GON, SORAGOTO.

†USOBUKI,-*ku*,-*ita*, ウソブク, 嘯, *t.*. To whistle, to roar; only of the tiger.
Syn. KUCHI-FUYE WO FUKU.

USORASHII,-KI,-KU,-Ū,-SA, ウソラシイ, Having the appearance of not being true: looking as if false.

USOTSZKI, ウソツキ, *n.* A liar.

†USSAN, ウツサン, 鬱散, Dispersing gloom, enlivening the spirits. — *szru.* — *no tame ni.* Syn. KIBARASHI.

USSZRI-TO, ウススリト, *adv.* Thinly, not close together, scattered, not deep in color. — *someru.*

USZ, ウス, 臼, *n.* A large wooden or stone mortar for pounding rice; also the gizzard of a fowl.

USZ, ウス, 薄, 淡, Thin, rare, not dense; not close, or crowded together; light, not deep in color, (used only in compound words.)

USZ-AKAI,-KI,-KU, ウスアカイ, 薄赤, Light red.

USZ-AKARI, ウスアカリ, 薄明, *n.* Dim-light.

USZBA, ウスバ, 薄刃, *n.* A thin-bladed knife used in the kitchen.

USZBERI, ウスベリ, 薄縁, *n.* A mat made by lining good matting with a coarser kind, and binding the edges with cloth.

USZ-CHA, ウスチヤ, 薄茶, *n.* Weak tea.

USZ-DE, ウスデ, 薄手, *n.* Slight wound; thin in make. — *no chawan*, a thin tea cup.

USZ-DZMI, ウスズミ, 淡墨, *n.* Thin ink.

USZGESHŌ, ウスゲシヤウ, 淡粧, *n.* Powdering the face thinly with white powder. — *wo szru.*

USZ-GURAI,-KI,-KU, ウスグライ, 淡闇, Slightly dark.

USZ-GUROI,-KI,-KU, ウスグロイ, 淡黒, Light black.

USZI, ウスイ, 薄 or 淡, *a.* Thin, rare, not dense, not close or crowded together, light, not deep in color, slight, not profound. *Uszi kōri,* thin ice. *Iro ga uszi,* the color is of a light shade. *Nasake ga* —, of little kindness.

USZ-KAWA, ウスカハ, 膜, *n.* A membrane, thin pellicle, or film.

USZKKURAI, ウスツクライ, coll. same as *Uszgurai.*

USZKU, ウスク, 薄, *adv.* Thin; see *Uszi.* — *szru,* to make thin. — *kiru,* to cut in thin slices. — *naru,* to become thin. — *someru,* to dye of a light shade. *Itami ga — naru,* the pain becomes light.

USZROGI,-*gu*,-*ida*, ウスログ, 薄, *i. v.* To gradually become thin, rare, less dense, or lighter in color, to fade, to remit, to abate in intensity, diminish in severity. *Iro ga* —, the color fades. *Kōri ga* —, the ice becomes thin. *Kiri ga* —, the fog clears away. *Samusa ga* —, the cold abates. *Itami ga* —, the pain abates.

†USZRU, ウスル, Same as *Useru.* 失, to lose.

USZSA, ウスサ, See *Uszi. n.* Thinness, rareness, density.

USZSHI, ウスシ, See *Uszi.*

USZ-TSZKI,-*ku*,-*ita*, ウスツク, 舂, *t.v.* To pound in a mortar.

USZ-USZ, ウスウス, 淡淡, *adv.* Slightly, a little. — *shitte iru,* to know but little, or imperfectly about any thing.
Syn. SHŌ-SHŌ.

UTA, ウタ, 歌, *n.* A song, a ballad, a poem, — *wo utau,* to sing a song. — *wo yomu,* to make poetry.

UTA-BITO, ウタビト, 歌人, *n.* A poet, a ballad maker.

UTAGAI,-*au*,-*atta*, ウタガフ, 疑, *t.v.* To doubt, to be uncertain about, to suspect, distrust. *H'to wo* —, to distrust, or suspect another. *Dorobō ka to utagau,* suspect him to be a thief.
Syn. AYASHIMU, FUSHIN NI OMŌ.

UTAGAI, ウタガヒ, 疑, *n.* Doubt, suspicion, distrust. — *ga tokeru,* doubt is dispelled. — *wo ukeru,* to be suspected. — *nashi,* without doubt. — *wo tadasz,* to settle a doubt. Syn. FUSHIN, GIWAKU.

UTAGARUTA, ウタガルタ, 歌牌, *n.* Cards on which a part of a verse is written, used in playing.

UTAGAU, ウタガフ, See *Utagai.*

UTAGAWARE,-*ru*,-*ta*, ウタガハレル, 被疑, pass. or pot. of *Utagai.*

UTAGAWASHII,-KI,-KU-Ū,-SA, ウタガハシイ, Doubtful, uncertain, suspicious.
Syn. FUSHIN NA, GATEN-YUKANU.

UTAGŌRAKUBA, ウタガフラクバ, *adv.* I suspect that.

UTAU,-*au*,-*atta*, ウタフ, 謡, *t.v.* To sing. *Uta wo* —, to sing a song.
Syn. GINDZRU, YEIDZRU.

UTAI, ウタヒ, 謡, *n.* A song.

†UTATA, ウタタ, 轉, *adv.* Greatly.

UTATANE, ウタタ子, 轉寐, *n.* Lying down any place to sleep. — *wo szru,* to lie down any place and sleep.

†UTATE, ウタテ, Cruel, inhuman, grievous. — *aru yo,* an age full of cruelty, or inhumanity.

†UTATEI,-KI,-SHI, ウタテイ, Idem.

UTAWASE,-*ru*,-*ta*, ウタハセル, 令歌, caust. of *Utai.* To cause or let sing. *H'to ni utawasete kiku,* to get another to sing that we may hear.

UTAYOMI, ウタヨミ, 歌人, *(kajin). n.* A poet.

UTCHARI,-*ru*,-*tta*, ウチヤル, 打遣, *t. v.* To throw away (as a useless thing), to reject. *Gomi wo* —, to throw away dirt. *Utchatte oku,* to let alone, let be.
Syn. SZTERU.

UTE,-*ru*,-*ta*, ウテル, 打, Can hit, shoot, or play. *Oshi ni uteru,* to be struck down by any thing heavy.

†U-TEN, ウテン, 雨天, *n.* Rainy weather
Syn. AMEFURI.

UTENA, ウテナ, 臺, *n.* The calyx of a flower, a high terrace, balcony, or gallery without a roof.

UTŌ, ウタウ, Same as *Utau,* see *Utai,* 歌.

UTŌ, ウタウ, The coll. fut. of *Uchi,* 打.

UTŌ, ウトウ, See *Utoi,* 疏.

UTOI,-KI,-KU,-SHI, ウトイ, 疏, Unacquainted, not familiar, not intimate, distant, cold, strange. *Nin-jō ni utoi,* to be cold, unfeeling. *Se-ji ni* —, unacquainted with the world. *Kane-mōke ni* —, slow or dull in making money. *Chiye ga* —, to be dull of comprehension.
Syn. SOYEN, TSZTANAI, HETA.

UTOMARE,-*ru*,-*ta*, ウトマレル, 被疏, pass. or pot. of *Utomi.* To be disliked or treated with coldness.

UTOMASHII,-KI,-KU, ウトマシイ, 疏, Cold, distant, strange, no longer intimate or familiar, estranged.

UTOMASHI,–*sz*,–*sh'ta*, ウトマス, 令疏, caust. of *Utomi*. To cause to dislike.

UTOMI,–*mu*,–*nda*, ウトム, 疏, *t.v.* To dislike, to be cool, distant or unfriendly, not to be intimate, or familiar with. *Aku-nin wo* —, not to be familiar with wicked men. Syn. TŌZAKERU.

†UTONJI,–*dzru*,–*ta*, ウトンズル, 疏, *t. v.* Idem.

UTO-UTO-NEMURU, ウトウトネムル, To doze.

UTO-UTOSHII,–KI,–KU,–U, ウトウトシイ, 疏疏, No longer familiar, or intimate, estranged, alienated.

UTSZ, ウツ, 打, See *Uchi*.

UTSZ, ウツ, 鬱, *n*. Gloom, melancholy, low spirits. — *wo harau*, to dispel gloom.

UTSZBARI, ウツバリ, 梁, *n*. The timbers of a roof, rafters.

UTSZBO, ウツボ, 靫, *n*. A quiver. Syn. YUGI, YEBIRA.

UTSZBUSHI, ウツブシ, 俯伏, Lying with the face downwards, prone. — *ni taoreru*, to fall with the face downwards.

UTSZDAKAI,–KI,–KU,–SHI, ウツダカイ, 堆, Piled up high.

UTSZGI, ウツギ, 卯木, *n*. The name of a flowering shrub, Deutzia scabra.

U-TSZKAI, ウツカイ, 鵜遣, *n*, A person who fishes with a cormorant.

UTSZKE, ウツケ, 癡人, *n*. A fool, ignoramus. —*mono*, idem. Syn. BAKA.

UTSZKUSHII,–KI, ウツクシイ, 美, *a*. Beautiful, handsome, pretty, elegant, good. — *hana*, a beautiful flower. Syn. KIREI-NA.

UTSZKUSHIKU, ウツクシク, 美, *adv*. Idem. — *naru*, to become beautiful.

UTSZKUSHIMI,–*mu*,–*nda*, ウツクシム, 愛, *t.v.* To love. *Ko wo* —, to love a child. Syn. AISZRU.

UTSZKUSHISA, ウツクシサ, *n*. Beauty, elegance.

UTSZMUKE,–*ru*,–*ta*, ウツムケル, 俯, *t. v.* To turn the face downwards, to turn bottom up, to turn upside down. *Fune wo* —, to turn a boat bottom up. Syn. FUSERU.

UTSZMUKI,–*ku*,–*ita*, ウツムク, 俯, *i. v.* To look, or bend the face downwards, to be turned upside down.

UTSZRAI,–*au*,–*atta*, ウツラフ, 映, *i.v.* See *Utszroi*.

UTSZRA-UTSZRA, ウツラウツラ, *adv*. In a dozing manner. — *to sh'te iru*, to be dozing. *Sake ni yotte — to sh'te aruku*, to be drunk and walk along in a half conscious state.

UTSZRI, ウツリ, *n*. Any thing sent back to express thanks in the vessel in which a present has been received.

UTSZRI,–*ru*,–*tta*, ウツル, 遷, or 移, *i.v.* To pass, or move from one place, or person, to another; to emigrate; to change from one to another; to be derived, as a word; to tinge or fade, as color; to be reflected as in a mirror; to be catching or infectious, as disease; to agree, suit, accord. *Toki, hi, tszki, toshi nado ga* —, the hours, days, months and years pass or are spent. *Yamai ga* —, the disease is contagious, or passes from one to another. *Kuse ga* —, evil habits are catching. *Yedo ye* —, to move to Yedo. *Kage ga kagami ni* —, the image is reflected in the mirror. *Iro ga* —, the color fades, or tinges something which is in contact with it. *Bōdz ga kami-shimo wo kitte mo utszranai*, even if a priest should wear the dress called *Kamishimo*, it would be unbecoming. *Peke wa malayu no pergi to iu kotoba yori utsztta, peke* is derived from the Malay word *purgi*. Syn. KOSZ.

UTSZRI, ウツリ, 遷, *n*. Fitness, congruity. — *ga warui*, unbecoming.

UTSZRI-GA, ウツリガ, 移香, *n*. The odor perceived in anything which has been in contact with a perfume.

UTSZRI-KAWARI,–*ru*,–*tta*, ウツリカハル, 遷變, *i.v.* To change with the lapse of time, or by removals. *Yo ga* —, the times change.

UTSZRIGI-NA, ウツリギナ, 遷氣, *a*. Changeable, fickle, inconstant. — *h'to*, a fickle person.

UTSZRO, ウツロ, 空, *n*. A hollow in a tree. Syn. URO, UTSZWO.

UTSZROI,–*ō*,–*ōta*, ウツロフ, 映, *i.v.* To be reflected, as in a mirror; to change or fade, as a color. *Ki no kage ga midz ni* —, the shadow of the tree is reflected in the water.

UTSZSHI,–*sz*,–*sh'ta*, ウツス, 寫, or 移, *t.v.* To transfer, change or convey from one place to another, to move; to transplant, transpose, to copy; to pass, or spend time; to reflect as in a mirror; to communicate as disease. *Hon wo* —, to copy a book. *Yedz wo* —, to copy a picture. *Iye wo* —, to move a house, or a family to another place. *Kagami ni kage wo* —, to reflect an image in a mirror. *Yamai wo* —, to communicate disease.

Tszki-hi wo —, to pass the time. *Naye wo* —, to transplant young shoots.

UTSZSHI, ウツシ, 寫, *n.* A copy.

UTSZSHI-YE, ウツシヱ, 影戯, *n.* A magic lantern; or a picture made by reflection.

UTSZTSZ, ウツツ, 現, *n.* This visible and real state of existence; real, actual, substantial, not dreamy, or ideal. *Ima no — ni,* in this world. — *no yo,* this present world. *Yume ka — ka to utagau,* doubted whether it was a dream or reality. Syn. GENZAI.

UTSZ-UTSZ, ウツウツ, *adv.* In a dozing manner, a dejected manner, cast-down or melancholy.

UTSZWA, ウツハ, 器, *n.* Utensil, vessel, implement. Syn. DŌGU, KIKAI.

UTSZWO, ウツホ, 空, *n.* A hollow in a decayed tree. Syn. URO.

UTSZWO-BASHIRA, ウツホバシラ, 空柱, *n.* The verticle pipe for conducting off rain-water.

UTSZWO-BUNE, ウツホブネ, 空舟, *n.* A canoe. Syn. MARUTABUNE.

UTTA, ウツタ, the pret. of *Uri,* 賣,

UTTA, ウツタ, the pret. of *Uchi,* 打.

UTTAYE,*-ru,-ta,* ウツタヘル, 訟, *t. v.* To refer, or appeal to a civil officer, or court; to inform against, to enter a complaint, or bring accusation or suit against any one; to confess. *Tszmi wo* — to confess one's guilt. *Yakusho ye* —, to appeal to a civil court. *H'to wo bugiyō ye* —, to accuse a person to the governor. Syn. SOSHŌ SZRU.

UTTAYE, ウツタヘ, 訟, *n.* A complaint, or appeal to a civil officer, or judge; an accusation, petition.

UTTE, ツツテ, the *pp.* of *Uri,* 賣, or of *Uchi,* 打.

UTTE, ウツテ, 討手, *n.* A force sent to put down rebellion.

UTTORI-TŌ, ウツトリト, *adv.* In a dull, heavy, absent-minded manner. — *sh'te iru,* to be in a revery.

UTTŌSHII,-KI, ウツタウシイ, 鬱陶, *a.* Cloudy, dark, dull, gloomy, dismal, dejected, disagreeable, annoying. *Uttōshii otenki,* gloomy weather. Syn. KIBUSAI.

UTTŌSHIKU, ウツタウシク, 鬱陶, *adv.* idem. — *omō,* to feel gloomy, or dejected.

UTTSZBUSHI,*-sz,-sh'ta,* ウチツブス, Same as *Uchi-tszbushi.*

UWABA, ウハバ, 上牙, *n.* The upper teeth.

UWABAMI, ウハバミ, 蟒, *n.* The anaconda, or boa constrictor.

UWABE, ウハベ, 上邊, *n.* The outside, the external, and visible. — *wo kazaru,* to adorn the outside. Syn. OMOTE.

UWA-DZMI, ウハズミ, 上澂, The clear liquor from which the sediment has settled.

UWA-DZTSZMI, ウハヅツミ, 上包, *n.* The outside wrapper, or covering.

UWA-GAKI, ウハガキ, 上書, *n.* The direction on the back of a letter, or outside of a packet.

UWA-GAMI, ウハガミ, 上紙, *n.* The outside cover of a book, paper cover.

UWA-GI, ウハギ, 上衣, *n.* The outside garment, overcoat.

UWA-GUSZRI, ウハグスリ, 上藥, *n.* Medicines applied, or used externally.

UWA-JIKI, ウハジキ, 上敷, *n.* A carpet, mat, or anything covering the floor.

UWA-KAWA, ウハカハ, 表皮, *n.* The outside skin, the cuticle, scum. *Chi-chi no* —, the cream which forms on the surface of milk.

UWAKI, ウハキ, 浮氣, *n.* Lewdness, lust. — *na,* lewd, licentious. — *mono,* a lewd person, rake.

UWA-KOTO, ウハコト, 譫語, *(sengo). n.* The talk of one in delirium. — *wo iu,* to talk deliriously.

UWA-MAYE, ウハマヘ, 上前, *n.* The outside breast of a coat. Money secretly retained, or filched as a perquisite, or squeeze, same as *Kaszri.*

UWA-MIDZ, ウハミヅ, 上水, *n.* The clear water standing above settlings.

UWA-MUKI, ウハムキ, 上向, *n.* Outside, external, outward. Syn. UWABE, OMOTE-MUKI.

†UWANARI, ウハナリ, 後妻, *n.* A second wife. Syn. GOSAI, NOCHI-ZOI.

UWA-NORI, ウハノリ, 上乘, *n.* A person who goes with a cargo as a guard, a supercargo.

UWA-NO-SORA, ウハノソラ, 上空, *n.* Absence of mind, abstraction, or inattention. — *ni kiku,* to hear in an abstracted manner. Syn. UCHŌTEN, MUCHIU.

UWA-NURI, ウハヌリ, 上塗, *n.* The outside coat of plaster, varnish, or paint.

UWA-OSOI, ウハオソヒ, 上襲, *n.* Covering anything so as to screen or protect. *Naye ni — wo szru,* to cover plants.

UWARI,*-ru,-tta,* ウワル, 植, *i. v.* To be planted. *Ta ni naye ga uwatta,* the rice plants are planted in the paddyfield.

UWASA, ウハサ, 噂, *n.* Talking about another who is not present; gossip, report, rumor. *Sadajiro no — wo sh'te oru,* we are talking about Sodajiro. — *wo szreba kage ga sasz*, (prov.) talk about another and he is sure to come. — *wo kiku*, to hear a report. — *wo szru*, to talk gossip. Syn. HIYŌBAN, FŪ-BUN.

UWA-TE, ウハテ, 上手, *n.* The best hand in doing, making, or in writing; up the river. *Kono h'to wa — da*, this person is the best. — *ni noboru fune*, a boat going up the river.

UWATSZKI,–*ku*,–*ita*, ウハツク, *t.v.* To be fickle, capricious, whimsical, notional, irresolute.

UWA-UWA, ウハウハ, *adv.* In a fickle, flighty manner, capriciously, whimsically. *Ki ga — sh'te iru*, to be fickle, irresolute.

UWAYE, ウハヱ, 上繪, *n.* Touching over with a pencil figures that have been marred in dyeing. — *wo kaku.*

UWO, ウヲ, 魚, *n.* Fish. Syn. GIYO, SAKANA.

U-WŌ-SA-WŌ, ウワウサワウ, 右往左往, To the right and left. — *nige-hashiru*, fleeing right and left.

†UYOKU, ウヨク, 羽翼, *n.* Wings. Syn. TSZBASA.

†UZAI, ウザイ, 有罪, (*tszmi aru*). Guilty. — *muzai*, guilty or not.

†UZAI-GAKI, ウザイガキ, 有財餓鬼, *n.* A miser; one who has money but starves himself rather than spend it. Syn. SHIWAMBŌ.

UZA-UZA, ウザウザ, 蠕蠕, *adv.* Swarming like insects. *Ki no yeda ni kemushi ga — sh'te iru*, the caterpillars swarm on the trees.

UZŌ-MUZŌ, ウザウムザウ, 有象無象, All things material or immaterial, visible or invisible. — *no mono*, idem. Used in com. coll. for all, = *mina*. Syn. SHINRABANSHŌ.

W.

WA, ワ, 輪, *n.* A ring, wheel, circle. *Kuruma no —*, the wheel of a waggon. *Yubi no —*, a finger ring. *Oke no —*, the hoop of a bucket. — *wo kaku*, to draw a circle.

†WA, ワ, 我, (obs.) *pro.* I, me, my. *Wa iye*, my house. *Nani sen ni wa meszrame ya*, why did you call me? *Wa woba omowadz*, they don't think of me.

(2). It is often used for, you, your, or as an affectionate prefix to names; as, *Wa ko-sama*, your children. *Wa-onore*, you. *Wa-dono*, master. *Wa-onna*, you women.

WA, ワ, 和, (*yamato*), *n.* Japan.

†WA, ワ, 和, (*tairagu*), *n.* Peace. — *wo muszbu*, to make a treaty of peace.

WA, ハ, 者, A particle which is placed after, and serves to designate, the subject of a sentence; as, *Kore wa nani*, what is this? *Sore wa ishi da*, that is a stone. *Koko ye kite wa warui*, lit. the coming here is bad, = you must not come here. *Sore ni wa oyobanu*, that is unnecessary.

WA, ハ, 把, or 羽, *n.* The numeral in counting bundles and fowls. *Maki ichi wa*, one bundle of wood. *Tori ichi wa*, one fowl. *Wara sam ba*, three bundles of straw. *Hatto jippa*, ten doves.

WĀ, ワア, Exclaim. in shouting, or crying. *Wā-wā to naku.*

WABI,–*ru*,–*ta*, ワビル, 侘, *t.v.* To implore pardon, ask forgiveness, to pray for mercy; to be distressed, miserable, forlorn; affixed to other verb roots it means, to do with difficulty or trouble what the other verb signifies; as, *Machi-wabiru*, to be troubled about or find it hard to wait. *Szmi-wabiru*, to feel it hard to dwell. *Tszmi wo kami ni —*, to implore the pardon of one's sins of God. *Ayamachi wo danna ni —*, to ask forgiveness of a master for one's faults. Syn. AYAMARU, KANERU.

WABI, ワビ, 侘, *n.* Asking for pardon or mercy, — *wo szru.*

WABI-BITO, ワビビト, *n.* A poor genteel person.

WABI-DZMAI, ワビズマヒ, 侘住, *n.* A poor looking house in a lonely place.

WABI-KOTO, ワビコト, 侘言, *n.* Supplication, or petition for mercy, or forgiveness.

WABISHII,–KI,–KU, ワビシイ, 侘敷, Poor, miserable, distressed, wretched. Syn. NANGI-NA.

WA-BOKU, ワボク, 和睦, *n.* Peace, friendship, harmony. — *szru*, to make a treaty of peace.

WA-BUN, ワブン, 和文, (*yamato bumi*), Japanese writing, or books written in Japanese character.

WA-CHIGAYE, ワチガヘ, 輪違, *n.* The figure of rings linked together.

‖WACHIKI, ワチキ, 我, vul. coll. for *Watakushi*. I, me.

WADAKAMARI,–*ru*,–*tta*, ワダカマル, 蟠, *i.v.* To be coiled up, as a snake; to be convoluted, tortuous, winding.

WA-DAN, ワダン, 和談, *n.* A conference for the purpose of restoring peace, friendship, or harmony, where before there was war, or variance. — *ni naru.*

WADONO, ワドノ, 我殿, *n.* You.
Syn. OMAYE.

WADZKA, ハツカ, 僅, Little, few, slight; small in degree quantity, or importance. — *na kane*, only a little money. — *mikka no aida*, in the slight space of three days. Syn. SZKOSHI, CHITTO.

WADZRAI,*-au,-atta*, ワヅラフ, 煩, *t.v.* To be sick, ill, diseased; to be troubled, perplexed. *Me wo* —, to be diseased in the eyes. *Shō-kan wo* —, to be sick with fever. *Omoi-wadzrō*, to be perplexed about. Syn. YAMU.

WADZRAWSHI,*-sz,-sh'ta*, ワヅラハス, 煩, *t.v.* To make sick, to afflict, to trouble, to distress. *Kokoro wo* —, to distress one's self. Syn. KURUSHIMERU.

WADZRAWASHII,-KI,-KU,-Ū,-SA, ワツラハシイ, 煩, Troublesome, perplexing, vexatious.

WAGA, ワガ, 我, *pro.* One's own; either my own, or your own; self. — *mi*, one's self, myself, yourself, himself. — *kuni*, one's own country. — *mono*, one's own thing, either my own, or his own. — *mono-gao ni*, as if it was his own.

WA-GAKU, ワガク, 和學, *n.* Japanese literature, or science.

WAGA-MAMA, ワガママ, 我儘, *n.* Self-will, obstinate, stubborn. — *na kodomo*, a self-willed child. — *ni sasete oku*, to let one have his own way. Syn. KIMAMA.

WAGANE,*-ru,-ta*, ワガヌル, 綰, *t. v.* To bend into a ring, to coil. *Take wo* —, to bend a bamboo into a ring, or hoop. *Nawa wo* — to coil a rope.

†WAGA-SEKO, ワガセコ, 吾兄子, *n.* (obs) My husband, (in affectionate language).

WA-GE, ワゲ, 和解, Rendered or translated into the Japanese language. — *szru.*

WAGE,*-ru,-ta*, ワゲル, 曲, *t.v.* To bend. *Ki wo* —, to bend wood. Syn. MAGERU.

†WA-GI, ワギ, 和議, *n.* Peace, amity, friendship, harmony, concord.

†WAGIMOKO, ワギモコ, 吾妹子, *(obs).* My wife (in the language of endearment.)

†WA-GO, ワゴ, 和語, *n. (yamato kotoba).* Japanese language.

WA-GŌ, ソガフ, 和合, Peace, friendship, or harmony. — *szru*, to be at peace with one another.

†WA-HEI, ワヘイ, 和平, *n.* Peace, tranquility, harmony. — *szru.*

WAIDAME, ワイダメ, 差別, *n.* Difference, distinction. *Kami shimo* — *nashi*, no distinction of high and low.
Syn. SHABETSZ, KEJIME, WAKACHI.

WAIRO, ワイロ, 賄賂, *n.* A bribe. — *wo toru*, to take a bribe.
Syn. MAINAI.

WAI-WAI, ワイワイ, exclam. The noise of one crying, or of many shouting. — *to sawagu.*

WAIZATSZ, ワイザツ, 猥褻, Obscene, indecent. — *na hanashi*, obscene language.

†WA-JUKU, ワジユク, 和熟, Perfect harmony, peace, or friendship. — *szru.*

WA-JUN, ワジユン, 和順, Amicable, harmonious, propitious.

†WA-KA, ワカ, 和歌, *(yamato uta). n.* Japanese poetry, or song.

WAKA, ワカ, 若, Young, used only in compound words.

WAKA-BA, ワカバ, 若葉, *n.* Young leaves.

WAKACHI,*-tsz,-tta*, ワカツ, 別 or 分, *t.v.* To divide, distinguish, discriminate, understand. *Zehi wo* —, to distinguish between right and wrong. *Futatsz ni* —, to divide into two. Syn. WAKERU.

WAKACHI, ワカチ, 別, *n.* Difference, distinction, division.
Syn. SHABETSZ, WAIDAME, KEJIME.

WAKA-DANNA, ワカダンナ, 若檀那, *n.* Young master.

†WAKADZ, or WAKANU, ワカズ, 不分, contr. of *Wakatadz*, neg. of *Wakachi.*

WAKAGE, ワカゲ, 若氣, *n.* Youthful spirits, or temper. — *no ayamachi.*

WAKAGIMI, ワカギミ, 小君, *n.* Young prince.

WAKAI,-KI, ワカイ, 弱, *a.* Young, youthful. *Wakai h'to.* a young man. *Ki no wakai h'to*, a person of youthful spirits. *Wakaku miyeru*, to look young.

WAKA-JINI, ワカジニ, 早世, *(sōsei). n.* Early death, dying while young.

WAKA-KI, ワカキ, 若木, *n.* A young tree.

WAKAKI, ワカキ, *a.* See *Wakai.*

WAKAKU, ワカク, *adv.* See *Wakai.* — *naru*, to become young.

WAKAME, ワカメ, 若海布, *n.* A kind of sea weed.

WAKA-MIYA, ワカミヤ, 若宮, *n.* Young prince, only of a son of the *Mikado.*

†WA-KAN, ワカン, 和漢, *n.* Japan and China.

WAKARE,*-ru,-ta*, ワカレル, 別, pass. of *Wake.* To be divided, separated, parted. *Tszma ga otto ni wakareta*, the wife is divorced from her husband. *Michi ga f'tatsz*

ni —, the road is divided into two.
Syn. HANARERU.

WAKARE, ワカレ, 別, *n.* Separation, parting, a branch, division. — *wo oshimu*, to be sorry to part. *Michi no* —, the forks of a road.

WAKARE-MICHI, ワカレミチ, 岐路, *n.* A branch-road.

WAKARE-SZJI, ワカレスヂ, 分筋, *n.* A branch line of a family.

WAKARI,*-ru,-tta*, ワカル, 分 or 別, *i.v.* To separate, divide, to part; to distinguish, understand, comprehend. *Riyō hō ni* —, to be divided into two parties or parts. *Futatsz ni* —, idem. *Buppō wa ha-shū ni* —, Buddhists are divided into eight sects. *Dōri ga wakatta*, I understand the reason. *Wakaranu*, I don't understand.
Syn. HANARERU, SHIRU.

WAKASA, ワカサ, 弱, *n.* Youthfulness, youthful condition.

WAKASHI, ワカシ, 弱, See *Wakai.*

WAKASHI,*-sz,-sh'ta*, ワカス, 沸, caust. of *Waki.* To cause to boil, to boil. *Midz wo* —, to boil water. *Yu wo* —, idem.

WAKA-SHIRAGA, ワカシラガ, 若白髪, *n.* Becoming grey headed while young.

WAKA-SHŪ, ワカシウ, 少年, *n.* A young man, or youth of about 16 years.

WAKA-TŌ, ワカタウ, 若黨, *n.* The persons who attend a noble when he goes abroad.

WAKA-TONO, ワカトノ, 若殿, *n.* A young lord, or son of a noble.

WAKATSZ, ワカツ, 分, See *Wakachi.*

WAKA-WAKASHII,-KI,-KU,-Ū,-SA, ワカワカシイ, Youthful, young in appearance, manner, or feeling.

WAKAYAGI,*-gu,-ida*, ワカヤグ, *i.v.* To become youthful, or young in looks, or feeling.

WAKAYAKA, ワカヤカ, *a.* Young, youthful.

WAKAYE,*-ru,-ta*, ワカヘル, 若回, *i.v.* To turn young, or youthful. *Ano h'to wa wakayeta*, he has become young again.

WAKA-ZAKARI, ワカザカリ, 若盛, *n.* The vigor of youth.

WAKE,*-ru,-ta*, ワケル, 分 or 別, *t.v.* To divide, to separate, part, to distinguish, understand. *F'tatsz ni* —, to divide into two parts. *Szkoshi wakete kudasare*, part with a little and give to me. *Kiki-wakeru*, to hear and understand. *Mi-wakeru*, to distinguish by looking at.

WAKE, ワケ, 訣, *n.* The meaning, reason, signification, cause, effect.
Syn. RIKUTSZ, DŌRI.

WAKE-AI, ワケアヒ, 訣合, *n.* Idem.

WAKE-GI, ワケギ, 葱, *n.* A kind of garlic.

WAKE-MAYE, ワケマヘ, 分前, *n.* Each one's share, or portion.

WAKEME, ワケメ, 分目, *n.* The dividing line; only figurative for the critical, or important event on which a cause depends. *Tenga* — *no ikusa*, a battle which decides the fate of an empire.

WAKETE, ワケテ, coll. for *Wakite.*

WAKI, ワキ, 脇, *n.* The side of the chest, the place bordering on, or at the side of any thing. — *no sh'ta*, the armpit. *Michi no* —, the side of a road. — *ni oku*, to place to one side. — *ye yore*, stand aside, make way. Syn. KATAWARA, SOBA.

WAKI,*-ku,-ita*, ワク, 涌, *i.v.* To boil, to gush forth, or bubble up, (as water in a spring); to ferment, to swarm, as insects. *Yu ga* —, the water boils. *Mushi ga* —, the insects swarm.

WAKI-AGARI,*-ru-tta*, ワキアガル, 涌上, *i.v.* To boil up, to ferment.

WAKIAKE, ワキアケ, 脇明, *n.* A coat with a slit in the sleeve, such as is worn by children.

WAKI-BARA, ワキバラ, 脇腹, *n.* The side of the abdomen. — *no ko*, the child of a concubine.

WAKI-BASAMI,*-mu,-nda*, ワキバサム, 挾, *t.v.* To hold between the arm and the side; to hold under the arm. *Tszye wo* —, to hold the cane under the arm.
Syn. TABASAMU.

WAKI-DACHI, ワキダチ, 脇立, *n.* The smaller idols that stand on each side of the principal one.

WAKI-DE,*-ru,-ta*, ワキデル, 涌出, *t.v.* To gush forth, as water from a fountain; to swarm forth, as insects.

WAKI-IDZRU, ワキイヅル, id.

WAKI-GA, ワキガ, 脇臭, *n.* The offensive smell of the armpit.

WAKI-GE, ワキゲ, 脇毛, *n.* The hair in the armpit.

WAKI-KAYE,*-ru,-ta*, ワキカヘル, 涌却, *i.v.* To boil and surge round, (as boiling water), to boil with rage.

WAKI-MAYE,*-ru,-ta*, ワキマヘル, 辨, *t.v.* To discriminate, distinguish, discern. *Zen aku wo* —, to distinguish between good and bad. Syn. WAKATSZ, BEMBETSZ.

WAKI-MAYE, ワキマヘ, 辨, *n.* Discrimination, judgment, discernment. *Kodomo wa* — *ga nai*, children have no judgment.
Syn. FUMBETSZ, KAMBEN.

WAKI-ME, ワキメ, 脇目, *n.* Looking to

one side. — *mo furadz ni miru*, to look straight forward, or intently looking at. — *yori miru*, looking at anything, as a by-stander, or from another's stand point. Syn. OKAME.

WAKI-MICHI, ワキミチ, 脇道, *n.* A side, or branch road.

WAKI-TACHI,*-tsz,-tta*, ワキタツ, 涌立, *i.v.* To commence boiling, or swarming.

WAKI-TE, ワキテ, 別, *adv.* Especially, particularly. Syn. BESHITE, KOTONI

WAKI-WAKI, ワキワキ, 脇脇, Other places or other persons. — *de wa dekinu*, it cannot be done in other places. Syn. HOKA-HOKA.

WAKI-ZASHI, ワキザシ, 脇刺, *n.* The short-sword worn in the belt.

†WA-KOKU, ワコク, 和國, *n.* Japan.

WAKU, ワク, See *Waki.*

WAKU, ワク, 籰, *n.* A reel: also 幀, a frame, (as of a picture).

†WAKUN, ワクン, 和訓, *n.* Rendering Chinese characters into their equivalent Japanese words. — *de yomu*, to read Chinese by construing into Japanese, and not by giving the sound of the characters.

†WAKURAN,*-szru*, ワクラン, 惑亂, *(madoi midareru).* To be bewildered, fascinated, intoxicated.

†WAKURAWA, ワクラハ, 病葉, Rare, seldom, like a withered leaf on a green tree. Syn. TAMASAKA.

WAMBAKU, ワンパク, coll. *n.* A self willed, spoiled child, obstinate. — *mono.* — *na kodomo.*

WAMEKI,*-ku,-ita*, ワメク, 喚, *i.v.* To cry out, to vociferate, scream; to clamor. Syn. OMEKU, SAKEBU.

WAN, ワン, 盌, *n.* A cup, bowl.

WANA, ワナ, 羂, *n.* A trap, snare, loop. — *wo haru*, to set a trap. — *ni kakaru*, to be caught in a trap.

WANÁ-NAKI,*-ku,-ita*, ワナナク, 戰慄, *i.v.* To tremble, shake with fear, or cold, to shiver. Syn. ONONOKU, FURŪ.

WANAMI, ワナミ, 吾儕, *pro.* I, me. Syn. WARE.

WANA-WANA, ワナワナ, *adv.* In a trembling manner. — *furū*, to tremble. Syn. BURU-BURU.

WANI, ワニ, 鰐, *n.* Alligator, or Crocodile.

WANI-GUCHI, ワニグチ, 鰐口, *n.* A kind of gong suspended before Miyas.

†WANUSHI, ワヌシ, 吾主, *pro.* You.

‖WAPPA, ワツパ, coll. *n.* A boy, used in scolding.

WAPPU, ワツプ, 割賦, *n.* A share, part, portion, or division. — *szru*, to apportion, or distribute to each his share. — *no tegata*, the ticket on which the share apportioned is written. Syn. WARI-TSZKE.

WARA, ワラ, 稿, *n.* Straw.

WARABE, ワラベ, 童, *n.* A child.

WARABI, ワラビ, 蕨, *n.* Fern.

WARABIDE, ワラビデ, 蕨手, *n.* The shape of fern sprouts, (ᘓᘓ), scroll.

WARABI-NAWA, ワラビナハ, 蕨繩, *n.* A rope made of fern-stalks.

WARA-DZTO, ワラヅト, 稿苞, *n.* Same as *Tszto.*

WARAI,*-au,-atta*, ワラフ, 笑, *i.v.* To laugh: or *t.v.* To laugh at, ridicule; to open, as a joint or seam. *H'to ga* —, people laugh. *H'to wo* —, to laugh at another. *Waratte son wo sh'ta yōna kao wo sh'te iru*, his face looks as if he would suffer loss by laughing, = as if he were afraid to laugh.

WARAI, ワラヒ, 笑, *n.* Laughter, ridicule. *H'to no — wo ukeru*, to be laughed at by others.

WARAI-GUSA, ワラヒグサ, 笑種, *n.* A cause, subject, or occasion for laughter, something to laugh at. — *ni naru.*

WARAJI, ワラジ, 草鞋, *n.* Straw-sandal.

WARAMBE, ワランベ, 童, *n.* Same as *Warabe.*

WARANJI, ワランジ, Same as *Waraji.*

†WARAWA, ワラハ, 妾, *pro.* I, me; used only by women in speaking of themselves.

†WARAWA, ワラハ, 童, *m.* A child. *Me no* —, a girl.

WARAWADZ, ワラハズ, 不笑, *neg.* of *Warai.*

WARAWAKASHI,*-sz,-sh'ta*, ワラハカス, coll. for *warawaseru.* To make a person laugh.

WARAWARE,*-ru,-ta*, ワラハレル, 被笑, pass. of *Warai.* To be laughed at.

WARAWASE,*-ru,-ta*, ワラハセル, 令笑, caust. of *Warai.* To cause, or let laugh.

WARAYA, ワラヤ, 草屋, *n.* A thatched house.

WARE, ワレ, 予, 吾, 我, *pro.* I, me, himself; you, in speaking contemptuously to another. *Ware saki ni* "I first," or best fellow foremost. *Ware mo waremo,* "I too," "I too," of several persons striving together for something. Syn. WATAKUSHI, ORE.

WARE,*-ru,-ta*, ワレル, 破, or 割, pass. of *Wari*). To be split, rent asunder, divided, broken, cracked. *Take ga* —, the bamboo is split. *Chawan ga* —, the tea cup is broken. *Uchiwa ga* —, the family is divided.

WARE, ワレ, 破, *n.* A split, rent, crack, fissure. — *ga deta*, it is split.

WAREME, ワレメ, 破目, *n.* A crack, split, rent, or fissure.

WARERA, ワレラ, 吾等, plural of *Ware.* We: also you, in speaking contemptuously to others.

WARE-WARE, ワレワレ, 吾吾, plural of *Ware.* We.

WARI,*–ru,–tta*, ワル, 割, 破, *t.v.* To split, rend asunder, to part, divide, to crack. *Maki wo* —, to split firewood. *Mitsz ni* —, to divide into three parts. *Hiki-waru*, to draw asunder.

WARI, ワリ, 和利, *n.* A share, portion, dividend, proportion, profit, lot, percentage, or rate of interest. — *ga warui.* — *ga yoi. Ichi* —, one per cent. *Ichi* — *go bu*, one and a half per cent. *Risoku wa iku wari*, what per cent is the interest?

WARI-AI, ワリアヒ, 割合, *n.* The dividing or partitioning of any thing amongst several; dividing into proper shares, parts, or proportions; proportion, allowance, parcel, share, portion, profit. *Ichi nin no* — *ga ikura*, how much is the share of one person? *Tammo no* — *ga warui*, the cloth does not cut to advantage.

WARI-AWASE,*–ru,–ta*, ワリアハセル, 割合, *t.v.* To apportion, to allot shares. Syn. WARITSZKERU.

WARI-FU, ワリフ, 割符, *n.* A block containing a part of a seal, corresponding to the part on another block,—a tally.

WARI-FURI,*–ru,–tta*, ワリフル, 割振, *t.v.* To apportion, divide into shares.

WARI-GAKI, ワリガキ, 割書, *n.* The small letters in double column, in which notes on the text are written.

WARIGO, ワリゴ, 破籠, *n.* A kind of box for holding rice. Syn. BENTŌ.

WARI-HAN, ワリハン, 破判, *n.* The part of a seal on a document, which corresponds to the part on its duplicate.

WARI-KOMI,*–mu,–nda*, ワリコム, 割込, *t.v.* To force into and divide or split, as with a wedge; to crowd in between others.

WARI-MAYE, ワリマヘ, 割前, *n.* The share or portion allotted to each, each one's share.

†WARINAI,–KI,–KU,–SHI, ワリナイ, 無理, Compulsory, irresistible, that cannot be restrained, or prevented, unavoidable. Syn. MURINI, ANAGACHINI.

WARI-TSZKE,*–ru,–ta*, ワリツケル, 害付, *t.v.* To distribute, apportion, allot, to partition, divide into shares, to parcel. *H'yaku riyō wo go nin ni* —, to divide a hundred *riyo* amongst five men.

WARI-ZAN, ワリザン, 割算, *n.* The rule of division, in arithmetic.

WARŌ, ワラフ, 笑, same as *Warau.*

WAROBIRE,*–ru,–ta*, ワロビレル, *i.v.* To appear ashamed, crestfallen, confused, or disconcerted. *Warobire mo sedz*, did not appear the least confused. Syn. OMERU, OKU SZRU.

WAROKI,–KU,–SHI, ワロシ, 悪, same as *Waruki, ku, shi*,—see *Warui.*

WARU, ワル, 割, see *Wari.*

WARU, ワル, 悪, Bad, used only in compound words.

WARUBIRE,*–ru,–ta*, ワルビレル, *i.v.* The same as *Warobire.*

WARU-DAKUMI, ワルダクミ, 奸計, (*kankei*). *n.* A wicked, fraudulent, or treacherous artifice, or trick.

WARUI,–KI, ワルイ, 悪, Bad, not good, wrong, evil, wicked, depraved. *Warui h'to*, a bad man. *Kokoro mochi ga warui*, to feel bad or unwell. *Warui to omō*, to regard as bad. *Taisō warui*, very bad. *H'to wo waratte wa warui*, it is not right to laugh at others.

WARU-JIYE, ワルヂヱ, 悪智, *n.* Artfulness, cunning, craftiness.

WARUKU, ワルク, 悪, *adv.* Bad, evil; see *Warui. H'to wo* — *iu*, to speak evil of others. — *omō*, to think evil of, — *nai*, is not bad. — *naru*, to become bad.

WARUKU-CHI, ワルクチ, 悪口, *n.* Evil or contemptuous speaking, detraction, sarcasm. — *wo iu.*

WARU-MONO, ワルモノ, 悪者, *n.* A bad fellow, a rascal, knave. Syn. AKU-NIN.

WARUSA, ワルサ, *n.* Bad state, or condition; badness, evil, mischief.

WARUSHI, ワルシ, see *Warui.*

WASA, ワサ, *n.* A loop.

WASABI, ワサビ, 山葵, *n.* Horseradish. — *oroshi*, a horseradish grater.

WASAN, ワサン, 和讃, *n.* Buddhist hymns or psalms translated into the Japanese.

WASE, ワセ, 早稲, *n.* Early rice.

†WA-SEI, ワセイ, 和製, *n.* Anything made by Japanese; Japanese manufacture.

WASHI, ワシ, 鷲, *n.* An eagle.

WASHI, ワシ, 吾, pro. cont. of *Watakushi*, I, me.

WA-SHI,–*szru*,–*sh'ta*, ワスル, 和, *i.v.* To make peace; to mix, blend, harmonize. Syn. K'WASHI, WABOKU.

WA-SHIN, ワシン, 和親, *(yawaragi shitashimu)*. *n.* Amity, friendship, harmony. — *wo muszbu*, to make a treaty of amity, or friendship.

WASHIRI,–*ru*,–*ta*, ワシル, 走, *i.v.* The same as *Hashiru*, to run.

WASSARI, ワッサリ, Incorrectly for *Assari*.

WASZRARE,–*ru*,–*ta*, ワスラレル, 被忘, pass. or pot, of *Waszre*. To be forgotten.

WASZRE,–*ru*,–*ta*, ワスレル, 忘, *t. v.* To forget, not to remember. *Na wo waszreta*, have forgotten the name. *Bentō wo waszrete kita*, I came forgetting my rice-box. Syn. BŌ-KIYAKU SZRU.

WASZRE, ワスレ, 忘, *n.* Forgetfulness.

WASZRE-GACHI, ワスレガチ, 忘勝, *n.* Inclined to forget, a poor memory, forgetful.

WASZRE-GAO, ワスレガホ, 忘顔, *n.* The countenance of one who pretends not to know.

WASZRE-GUSA, ワスレグサ, 萱艸, *n.* The iris, or fleur-de-lis.

WASZREPPOI,–KI,–KU,–SHI, ワスレツポイ, *a.* yed. coll. Forgetful, heedless, inattentive.

WATA, ワタ, 綿, *n.* Cotton, floss-silk: also, 腸, Intestines. *Sakana no* —, intestines of a fish. *Hara-wata*, intestines. *Umi-wata*, sponge.

WATA-BŌSHI ワタバウシ, 綿帽子, *n.* A bonnet made of floss-silk, worn by women.

WATA-GAMI, ワタガミ, 綿嚙, *n.* A cotton pad attached to a coat of mail, and worn across the shoulders.

WATA-IRE, ワタイレ, 綿入, *n.* A padded coat.

WATA-KURI, ワタクリ, 綿操, *n.* A machine for cleaning cotton of its seeds.

WATAKUSHI, ワタクシ, 私, *pro.* I, me; private interest, private, selfish. — *domo*, or — *ra*, we. — *no nai h'to*, an unselfish person. — *no kokoro*, my heart, or selfish mind.

WATAMASHI, ワタマシ 徙家, *(ya utszri)*. *n.* Moving into a new house. — *wo szru*. — *no iwai*, the compliments passed on moving into a new house.

†WATARAI,–ō, ワタラフ, 渡, *t. v.* To live. *Yo watarai-kaneru*, difficult to get along in the world.

WATARASE,–*ru*,–*ta*, ワタラセル, 令渡, caust. of *Watari*. To make, or let cross over; to live, to go or come, used only of honorable persons. *Ikaga watarase-tamō ya*, how are you getting on? *Koko ye watarase tamaye*, come here.

WATARI,–*ru*,–*tta*, ワタル, 渡, *t. v.* To pass from side to side, to cross over, as a river, ocean. *Yo wo* —, to pass through the world, to live. *Shanghai ye* —, to cross over to Shanghai. *Kawa umi hashi tszna nado wo* —, to cross over a river, sea, bridge, or rope. *Tobi-wataru*, to jump across. *Hibiki-wataru*, to sound across.

WATARI, ワタリ, 渡, *n.* The distance across, the passage; a thing from a foreign country; as, — *no shina*.

WATARI-AI,–*au*,–*atta*, ワタリアフ, 渡合, *i.v.* To cross over and meet together.

WATARI-MONO, ワタリモノ, 渡物, *(tōbutsz)*, *n.* A foreign article, a thing from across the sea.

WATASHI,–*sz*,–*sh'ta*, ワタス, 渡, *t. v.* To carry, place, send, or ferry across: to pass anything over to another; to deliver up, to give, to send, to pay. *Hashi wo* — to place a bridge across a river. *Fune de h'to wo* —, to carry a person across by a boat. *Kane wo* —, to pay over money. *Tszna wo* —, to stretch a rope across. *Miwatasz*, to look across.

WATASHI, or WATASHIBA, ワタシ, 渡, *n.* A crossing place, a ferry.

WATASHI, ワタシ, 私, *pro.* coll. contr. of *Watakushi*. I, me.

WATASHI-BUNE, ワタシブネ, 渡舟, *n.* A ferry-boat.

WATASHI-MORI, ワタシモリ, 渡守, *n.* A ferry man.

WATA-UCHI, ワタウチ, 綿打, *n.* A person who whips cotton with a bow string.

WATTO, ワット, *adv.* The sound of a sudden burst of noise. — *naki dasz*, burst out crying. — *amata no h'to goye*.

WAYAKU, ワヤク, *n.* Jesting, sport, play, joking. — *wo szru*, play tricks. — *wo iu*, to jest, joke.

WA-YAKU, ワヤク, 和藥, *n.* Japanese medicine.

WAYA-WAYA-TO, ワヤワヤト, coll. *adv.* The confused noise of many persons talking. — *to sawagu*.

WAZA, ワザ, 業, *n.* Work, act, deed. art, cause, reason. *Kuchi hodo wa — ga dekinu*, his performance is not as good as his word. *Ta wo tszkuru* —, the art of husbandry. *Nan no — de*, by what cause? in what way? Syn. SHIGOTO, SHOI, GIYŌ, GEI.

WAZAOKI, ワザオキ, 俳優, *n.* A play actor. Syn. YAKUSHA.

WAZA-TO, ワザト, 態, *adv.* Intentionally, purposely, by design. — *kita*, came on purpose. — *kowash'ta*, broke it intentionally.
Syn. KOTO-NI, WAZA-WASA.

WAZAWAI, ワザハイ, 禍災, *n.* Misfortune, calamity, adversity, evil, trouble.
Syn. MAGA-KOTO, SAI-NAN.

WAZA-WAZA, ワザワザ, *adv.* Intentionally, on purpose, by design.

WIYAMAI, *-au, -atta*, ウヤマフ, 敬, *t. v.* To reverence, respect, to honor, to adore. *Kami wo* —, to reverence, or adore God. *Oya wo* —, to respect one's parents.
Syn. KEI SZRU.

WIYAMAI, ウヤマヒ, 敬, *n.* Reverence, respect, veneration, honor.

†WIYA-WIYASHII, -KI, -KU, ウヤウヤシイ, 恭, Reverential in deportment, humble in manner, modest.

WIYE, ウヘ, 上, *n.* The top, higher, or upper part; above, superior; outside, exterior; more than, beyond, besides; used in speaking to the Tenshi, = your highness. *Yama no — ni agaru*, to ascend to the top of the mountain. — *no hō*, the upper side. — *no h'to*, upper classes of men, superiors. *Tszkuye no — ni oku*, to place it on the table. *Kono — wa ikaga sen*, what can I do more than this, or besides this? *On mi no — wo anji-wadzrai*, anxious about you. *Kono — wa nai*, there is nothing superior to this. Syn. JŌ, KAMI.

WIYE, *-ru, -ta*, ウヱル, 飢, *i. v.* To be hungry. Syn. HIMOJII, HIDARUI, HARA-HERU.

WIYE, *-ru, -ta*, ウヱル, 殖, *t.v.* To plant, to colonize. *Tane ki nado wo* —, to plant seeds, or a tree. *Hōsō wo* —, to vaccinate. *H'to wo shima ni* —, to colonize an island with men.

WIYE-BŌSŌ, ウヱバウサウ, 殖疱瘡, *n.* Vaccination.

WIYE-GOMI, ウヱゴミ, 殖込, *n.* A flower garden. Syn. SONO.

WIYE-JINI, ウヱジニ, 飢死, *n.* Death by starvation. — *wo sh'ta*, died of starvation. Syn. GASHI.

WIYE-KAYE, *-ru, -ta*, ウヱカヘル, 殖替, *t.v.* To transplant. *Naye wo* —, to transplant young shoots.

WIYEKI, ウヱキ, 殖木, An ornamental garden plant.

WIYEKI-YA, ウヱキヤ, 殖木屋, *n.* A gardener, florist, or one who raises ornamental plants and trees for sale.

WIYE-MONO-GAKU, ウヱモノガク, 殖物學, *n.* Botany.

†WIYEN, ウヱン, 迂遠, (*mawari dōi*). Slow, tedious, prolix, round-about. — *na hakarigoto.*

WO, ヲ, 袁, A particle which comes after, and designates, the object of a transitive verb,—the sign of the objective case; as, *Inu wo butsz*, to strike a dog. *Nani wo sh'te iru*, what are you doing? *Haha ga musko wo anjite-iru*, the mother is anxious about her son. *Kiyaku wo matte iru*, waiting for a guest, or customer.

(2). The subject of a passive and intransitive verb; as, *Watakushi no ashi wo inu ni kui-tszkareta*, my foot was bitten by a dog. *Ano h'to no iye wo tszkebi de yakareta*. that man's house was burnt by an incendiary.

(3). Following *mono*, at the end of a sentence, it expresses a feeling of regret or sorrow; as, *Anata ga itara shini wa senu mono wo*, if you had been here he would not have died. *Hayaku kayereba yokatta mono mo*, it would have been better if I had returned earlier. *Dase to ittemo nai mono wo*, you want me to give it to you but I have not got it.

WOBA, ヲバ, Same as *Wo*.

Y.

YA, ヤ, 矢, *n.* An arrow. *Yumi ni — wo tszgau*, to fix the arrow to the bow. — *wo iru*, to shoot an arrow.

YA, ヤ, 屋, *n.* A house, or shop; also for the person who does business in the place to which it is affixed; used generally as a suffix. *Kuszri-ya*, a drug store, also a druggist. *Waga ya*, my house.

YA, ヤ, 柯, *n.* A wedge. — *wo utsz*, to drive a wedge. Syn. KUSABI.

YA, ヤ, 輻, *n.* The spoke of a wheel. *Kuruma no* —.

YA, ヤ, 谷, (*tani*). *n.* A valley; used only suffixed to names; as, *Sh'ta-ya*, the valley called Sh'ta.

YA, ヤ, 八, *n.* Eight, same as *Yatsz.*

YA, ヤ, 夜, (*yoru*). *n.* Night.

YA, ヤ, 耶, A particle of interrogation, or doubt, having the same meaning as, *ka*, but weaker and more gentle; as, *Ikaga sen ya*, what shall I do? *Yukan ya kayeran ya*, shall I go or shall I return? *Ari ya nashi ya to tō*, to inquire whether he has or not.

(2). Used also as a simple exclâmation, or pause, in enumerating several things; or as an accent, similar to *yo*; as, *Hana ya chō ya*, the flowers and butterflies, &c. *Kowai ya*, or *osoroshi ya*, how dreadful! *Oira ja nai ya*, it was not me.

(3). As an imperative particle; as *Szsz-me ya*, advance. *Koko ye ki ya*, come here. *Itte kikase ya*, tell me.

YĀ, ヤア, Exclamation of surprise.

YA-BA, ヤバ, 矢場, *n.* A place for practising archery.

YA-BAN, ヤバン, 夜番, *n.* A night watch.

YA-BANE, ヤバネ, 矢羽, *n.* The feather of an arrow.

YABO, ヤボ, 野父, *n.* A boor, clown, rustic. — *na h'to*, a boorish person.
Syn. BUKOTSZ, BUIKI.

YABU, ヤブ, 竹叢, *n.* A bamboo grove, or cane-break. — *wo tsztszite hebi wo dasz*, poke a cane break and you will drive out a snake. (prov.)

YA-BUDŌ, ヤブダウ, 野葡萄, *n.* Wild grapes.

YABUI, or YABUISHA, ヤブイ, 庸醫, *n.* A charlatan, empiric, or quack doctor.

YABUIRI, ヤブイリ, *n.* The 16th days of the first, and seventh months, which persons out at service have as holidays to visit their homes.

YABU-KA, ヤブカ, *n.* A large kind of musquito which infests cane-breaks.

YA-BUMI, ヤブミ, 矢文, *n.* A letter fixed to an arrow, and sent by shooting from a bow.

YABUN, ヤブン, 夜分, *n.* Night.
Syn. YORU.

YABUNIRAMI, ヤブニラミ, *n.* Squint-eyed.

YABURARE,*-ru,-ta*, ヤブラレル, 被破, pass. or pot. of *Yaburi*. To be torn, broken.

YABURASE,*-ru,-ta*, ヤブラセル, 令破, caust. of *Yaburi*. To cause, or let break.

YABURE,*-ru,-ta*, ヤブレル, 破, *i.v.* To be torn, broken, rent; to be defeated, routed; to be infringed, or violated; to be divulged. *Kimono ga* —, the coat is torn. *Shiro ga* —, the castle is taken. *Haremono ga* —, the abscess is broken.

YABURI,*-ru,-tta*, ヤブル, 破, *t.v.* To tear, break, rend; to defeat, rout, to infringe, violate; to divulge, disclose; to ruin. *Kimono wo* —, to tear one's clothes. *Teki no shiro wo* —, to assault and take an enemy's castle. *Gohatto wo* —, to break the laws. *Yakujō wo* —, to break an agreement. *Iye wo* —, to bring ruin on a family. *Seki-sho wo* —, to pass by force through a pass, or guarded station. *Mitsz-ji wo* —, to divulge a secret.
Syn. KOWASZ, KUDAKU.

†YABUSAKA, ヤブサカ, 吝, Stingy, niggardly, avaricious, miserly.
Syn. SHIWAI, RINSHOKU.

YABUSAME, ヤブサメ, 騎射, *n.* Shooting with a bow at a target from horseback, while the horse is running. — *wo szru.*

YABUSZMA, ヤブスマ, 矢衾, *n.* A line or column of archers, or a volley of arrows.

†YACHI, ヤチ, 八千, Eight-thousand; used only for an indefinite number, = very many, a multitude. — *tose*, = a great many years.

YA-CHIN, ヤチン, 家賃, *n.* House-rent.

YA-CHIU, ヤチウ, 夜中, *n.* In the night, during the night.

YA-DANE, ヤダネ, 矢種, *n.* The supply of arrows in a quiver. — *ga tszkiru*, the arrows are all spent.

YADO, ヤド, 家所, or 宿, *n.* House, home, dwelling place, a shelter, a sojourn, temporary residence, a lodging. — *ye kayeru*, to return home. — *wo szru*, to afford a temporary residence to any one. — *wo toru*, to sojourn, or make a temporary home with another.

YADO-GAYE, ヤドガヘ, 宿替, *n.* Change of residence. — *wo szru.*

YADO-HIKI, ヤドヒキ, 宿引, *n.* Persons at inns, who watch for travelers and invite them to stop.

YADO-NASHI, ヤドナシ, 無宿, *(mu-shuku)*. Homeless, houseless.

YADORI,*-ru,-tta*, ヤドル, 宿, *i.v.* To sojourn, to stop, or lodge, as at an inn; to roost. *Tai nai ni* —, to be in the womb, as a fetus. *Tori ga ki ni* —, the bird roosts in the tree. *Yadoya ni* —, to lodge at an inn. Syn. SHUKU SZRU.

YADORI, ヤドリ, 宿, *n.* A lodging place.

YADŌRI, ヤドオリ, 宿下, *n.* Returning home from service.

YADORI-GI, ヤドリギ, 寄生, *n.* A parasitic plant.

||YADOROKU, ヤドロク, *n.* A vulgar title applied to a husband, or head of a family.

YADO-SEN, ヤドセン, 宿錢, *n.* The money paid for lodging at a hotel, fare.

YADOSHI,*-sz,-sh'ta*, ヤドス, 宿, *t. v.* To lodge, to deposit. *Tszki ga kage wo midz ni* —, the moon lodges her image in the water.

YADOYA, ヤドヤ, 宿屋, *n.* A hotel, inn, tavern. Syn. HATAGOYA.

YADZKA, ヤヅカ, 矢束, *n.* A bundle of arrows.

YA-DZKURI, ヤヅクリ, 屋形, *n.* The form or construction of a house.

YA-DZTSZ, ヤヅツ, 矢筒, *n.* A quiver.

YAGAKARI, ヤガカリ, 矢掛, *n.* Bow-shot. — *no yoi tokoro*, a place where the bow can be used to advantage.

YAGARA, ヤガラ, 族, *n.* A plural noun, = persons, fellows. *Anna — ni aite ni naru na*, don't keep company with such persons. *Ichi mon no —*, all the persons of the family. Syn. TOMOGARA.

YAGARA ヤガラ, 戴帽魚, *n.* The tobacco pipe fish, Fistularia tabaccaria. Syn. TAIHŌGIYO.

YAGATE, ヤガテ, *adv.* Soon, presently, forthwith, then, directly; that is, to wit, alias. Syn. JIKINI, HODONAKU, SZNAWACHI.

YAGEN, ヤゲン, 藥研, *n.* A machine made like a trough with a wheel playing in it, used for pulverizing medicines.

YAGI, ヤギ, 羊, *n.* A goat. Syn. HITSZJI.

YAGORO, ヤゴロ, 矢頃, *n.* Bow-shot. *Tōi —*, a long bow-shot. — *chikaku natte ya wo hanasz*, to shoot when within short range.

YAGOTO, ヤゴト, same as *Yangoto.*

YAGU, ヤグ, 夜具, *n.* Articles used in sleeping; as, bed-clothes, mattress, and pillow.

YAGURA, ヤグラ, 櫓, *n.* A tower within the walls of a castle.

YAHADZ, ヤハズ, 矢筈, *n.* The notch in the end of an arrow for receiving the bow-string, or similar notch in any stick.

YA-HAN, ヤハン, 夜半, *n.* Midnight. Syn. YONAKA.

YAHARI, ヤハリ, 仍, *adv.* Still, yet, also, too, likewise. — *moto no tōri*, still the same as it was. Syn. NAO, MOMATA.

YAIBA, ヤイバ, 刃, *n.* Edge of the sword. — *ni kakatte shinda*, died by the edge of the sword.

YAINO, ヤイノ, Exclam. in calling.

||YAITO, ヤイト, 灸, (*kiu*). *n*, The moxa. — *wo szyeru*, to apply the moxa.

YAJIMMA, ヤジンマ, *n.* Yed. coll. One that interferes in things which do not concern him, a meddler.

†YAJIN, ヤジン 野人, *n.* A rustic, a clown.

YAJIRI, ヤジリ, 鏃, *n.* The head or barb of an arrow.

YAJIRIKIRI, ヤジリキリ, 穿偷, *n.* A house breaker, thief.

YAKAMASHII,-KI,-KU,-Ū,-SA, ヤカマシイ, 喧, Noisy, tumultuous; causing a disturbance, or uproar; annoying, or giving trouble. *Yakamashiku iu*, to scold, or forbid with anger and loud talking. *O yakamashū gozarimash'tarō*, I fear it has been troublesome (by its noise) to you. Syn. KAMABISZSHI, SAWAGASHII.

YAKAN, ヤクワン, 藥罐, *n.* A tea kettle. Syn. DŌBIN.

YAKARA, ヤカラ, see *Yagara.*

YAKARE,-*ru*,-*ta*, ヤカレル, 被燒, pass. of *Yaki.* To be burnt.

YAKASE,-*ru*,-*ta*, ヤカセル, 令燒, caust. of *Yaki.* To cause to, or let burn, or bake.

YAKATA, ヤカタ, 舘, *n.* A large house, or palace, the residence of a noble.

YAKATABUNE, ヤカタブネ, 樓舟, *n.* A boat with a roof and handsome cabin for pleasuring.

YAKE,-*ru*,-*ta*, ヤケル, 燒, *i. v.* To burn, to be on fire; to bake; roasted; to be tanned, sun burnt, tarnished, to have the sensation of burning. *Pan ga yaketa*, the bread is baked. *Iye ga yakete shimau*, the house is burnt up. *Yama ga —*, the mountain is burning. *Sewa ga —*, to have a great deal to do; to be kept very busy. *Hi ni —*, to be sunburnt. *Kimpaku ga —*, the gilding is tarnished. Syn. MOYERU.

YAKE, ヤケ, *n.* Desperation, a giving up of hope, and yielding to despair. — *ni naru*, to become desperate. — *wo okosz*, id. *Yake-zake no yei*, intoxication gone into from desperation.

YAKE-AGARI,-*ru*,-*tta*, ヤケアガル, 燒上, *i. v.* To flame up; to be all baked.

YAKE-ATO, ヤケアト, 燒跡, *n.* The place where there has been a conflagration.

YAKE-DO, ヤケド, 火傷, *n.* A burn. — *wo sh'ta*, to have a burn.

YAKE-ISHI, ヤケイシ, 燒石, *n.* Pumice stone, lava.

YAKE-JINI, ヤケジニ, 燒死, *n.* Burned to death.

YAKE-KUSA, ヤケクサ, 燒草, *n.* Materials or matter for burning; anything to feed a fire.

YAKE-NOKORI,-*ru*,-*tta*, ヤケノコル, 燒殘, *i. v.* To remain, or be left unburnt, or unbaked.

YAKE-SHIDZMARI,-*ru*,-*tta*, ヤケシヅマル, 燒鎮, *i. v.* To stop burning.

YAKE-TADARE,-*ru*,-*ta*, ヤケタダレル, 燒

爛, *i.v.* To be burnt, sore and inflamed.

YAKE-WARA, ヤケハラ, 燒原, *n.* An area, or district from which the houses have been burnt off.

YAKI,*–ku,–ita*, ヤク, 燒, *t. v.* To burn, to roast, to bake, to toast. *Pan wo* —, to bake bread. *Niku wo* —, to roast meat. *Sh'ta wo* —, to burn one's tongue. *Te wo* —, to burn the finger. *Sewa wo* —, to busy one's self in doing anything for others. Syn. MOYASZ.

YAKI-BA, ヤキバ, 燒刃, *n.* The edge of a sword hardened by fire, a tempered edge.

YAKI-BA, ヤキバ, 燒塲, *n.* The place where dead bodies are burnt.

YAKI-BAN, ヤキバン, 燒判, *n.* A hot iron used for branding, or stamping.
Syn. YAKI-IN.

YA-KIDZ, ヤキヅ, 箭瘢, *n.* A wound made by an arrow.

YAKI-FUDE, ヤキフデ, 燒筆, *n.* A pencil made of charcoal.

YAKI-HARAI,*–au,–atta*, ヤキハラフ, 燒拂, *t. v.* To clear off by burning.

YAKI-IN, ヤキイン, 燒印, *n.* same as *Yakiban.*

YAKI-KOROSHI,*–sz,–sh'ta*, ヤキコロス, 燒殺, *t.v.* To kill by burning.

YAKIKK'WA, ヤキククワ, 野菊花, *n.* Camomile flowers.

YAKI-MOCHI, ヤキモチ, 燒餅, *n.* Baked rice bread; jealousy. — *wo yaku*, to be jealous.
Syn. RINKI, NETAMI, SHITTO.

YAKI-MONO, ヤキモノ, 燒物, *n.* Any kind of earthen ware, as crockery, or tiles.

YAKI-MONOSHI, ヤキモノシ, 燒物師, *n.* A general term for a maker of any kind of earthen ware that is burnt in a kiln, a potter.

YAKI-TE, ヤキテ, *n.* A jealous, or envious person.

YAKI-UCHI, ヤキウチ, 燒打, *n.* Attacking and burning, as a castle, or town, in war.

YAKKAI, ヤクカイ, 厄介, *n.* Assistance, or help rendered to persons in need. — *wo szru*, to aid, help, assist. — *ni naru*, to receive aid. — *ni adzkaru*, id.
Syn. SEWA.

YAKKAI-NIN, ヤクカイニン, 厄介人, *n.* A person who is dependant on another for support, a hanger on.
Syn. ISŌRŌ; SHOKKAKU.

YAKKAMI,*–mu,–nda*, ヤツカム, *i.v.* To be jealous, envious, to have heart burnings, or secret enmity. *Ani wo aiszreba otōto ga* —, if you love the eldest son the younger will be jealous.

YAKKI, ヤツキ, *adv.* Suddenly flushed, as with anger. — *to naru.*

YAKKO, ヤツコ, 奴, A servant boy.
Syn. KOZŌ.

YAKO, ヤコ, 野狐, *(nogitszne). n.* A fox.

YAKU, ヤク, 燒, see *Yaki.*

YAKU, ヤク, 藥, *(kuszri). n.* Medicine, only used in comp. words.

YAKU, ヤク, 役, *n.* Office, duty, service, or employment performed for the government. — *wo tsztomeru*, to attend to one's official duty. *Ikken yaku*, the public service, or its equivalent in money exacted from each house. *Kō-yaku*, public service. — *wo motsz*, to hold office. — *wo ageru*, to remove from office. — *wo yameru*, to retire from office. — *ga agaru*, to be turned out of office.
Syn. K'WAN-SHOKU, TSZTOME.

YAKU, ヤク, 約, An agreement, covenant, promise. — *wo muszbu*, to make an agreement. — *wo somuku*, to break an agreement. Syn. YAKUSOKU, YAKUJŌ.

YAKU, ヤク, 厄, *n.* A critical year of one's life, used for *Yuku-doshi.*

YAKU-BIYŌ, ヤクビヤウ, 病疾, *n.* A pestilence, plague, contagion.

YAKU-DAI, ヤクダイ, 藥代, *n*, The price of medicine.

YAKU-DAKU, ヤクダク, 約諾, *n.* Agreement, promise, covenant. — *nō tori*, according to agreement. Syn. YAKU-SOKU.

YAKU-DOSHI, ヤクドシ, 厄年, *n.* The critical years of life, supposed to be the 7th; 25th, 42nd, and 61st of a man's; and the 7th, 8th, 33rd, 42nd, and 61st of a woman's.

YAKU-CHI, ヤクチ, 益智, *n.* Cardamon seed.

YAKU-HARAI, ヤクハラヒ, 厄拂, *n.* Driving away evil, or misfortune from the critical years.

YAKU-HIN, ヤクヒン, 藥品, *(kuszri no shina). n.* The quality of a medicine.

YAKU-JŌ, ヤクヂヤウ, 約定, *n.* An agreement, covenant, promise.

YAKU-ME, ヤクメ, 役目, *n.* Office, official duty; duty, business. — *wo tsztomeru*, to attend to the duties of one's office, or place. *Watakushi no* — *de wa nai*, it is not a part of my duty, or none of my business. *Nengu wo harau no wa h'yak'shō no* — *da*, it is the duty of farmers to pay their tax.
Syn. SHOKUBUN.

YAKU-MAYE, ヤクマヘ, 役前, *n.* idem.

YAKUMI, ヤクミ, 味藥, *n.* Any thing spicy, or pungent added to food to give it a relish, seasoning. — *wo ireru.*

YAKU-MUKI, ヤクムキ, 役向, *n.* The particular duties of one's office.

YAKU-NAN, ヤクナン, 厄難, *n.* Evils which happen on a critical year.

YAKU-NIN, ヤクニン, 役人, *n.* A government officer; applied to any employe of government who receives regular pay or rations.

YAKUNITACHI, *-tsz, -tta*, ヤクニタツ, 益立, *i.v.* To be useful, serviceable. *Yakunitatanu*, useless, of no use.
Syn. YŌNITACHI.

YAKU-NŌ, ヤクノウ, 藥能, *n.* The virtues or powers of a medicine, medical virtues.

YAKU-REI, ヤクレイ, 藥禮, *n.* A present made to a physician for services rendered, (Japanese physicians receive no regular fee; only such presents as the gratitude of his patients may prompt them to give).

YAKU-RIKI, ヤクリキ, 藥力, *n.* The strength or virtue of medicine.
Syn. KŌNŌ.

YAKU-RIYŌ, ヤクリヤウ, 役料, *n.* The pay or salary of an officer of government.

YAKU-RŌ, ヤクロウ, 藥籠, *(kuszri bako). n.* A medicine chest.

YAKUSHA, ヤクシヤ, 俳優, *n.* A play actor.

YAKU-SHO, ヤクシヨ, 役所, *n.* An office or house where public business is transacted.

YAKU-SHU, ヤクシユ, 藥種, *(kuszri no rui). n.* A medicine, or drug; (in the raw state). — *ya*, a drug-store.

YAKU-SŌ, ヤクサウ, 藥草, *n.* A medicinal plant.

YAK'SOKU, ヤクソク, 約束, *n.* An agreement, covenant, promise, bargain; decree of heaven; fate or destiny appointed to each before his birth into this life, (Budd). — *wo szru*, to make an agreement. — *wo somuku*, to break a promise. — *wo tagayeru*, or — *wo chigayeru*, idem.
Syn. YAKU-JŌ.

YAKUTAI-NASHI, ヤクタイナシ, Confused, jumbled together; absurd, nonsensical.
Syn. MUCHA KUCHA.

YAKU-TAISHI, ヤクタイシ, 藥袋紙, *n.* A kind of paper used for wrapping medicine in.

YAKU-TOKU, ヤクトク, 役得, *n.* Emoluments of office.

YAK'WAN, ヤクワン, see *Yakan*.

YAKU-YEN, ヤクエン, 藥園, *n.* A garden where medicinal plants are cultivated.

YAKU-YŌ, ヤクヨウ, 役用, *n.* Government service.

YAKUZA, ヤクザ, Coarse, mean, poor, badly made, useless. — *na mono*, a thing coarsely made and of little value.

YAKU-ZAI, ヤクザイ, 藥劑, *n.* A medical compound, a medicine prepared for use.

YAKU-ZAI-SHO, ヤクザイシヨ, 藥劑書, *n.* A pharmacopœia.

YAMA, ヤマ, 山, *n.* A mountain, hill, a heap or pile. — *ni noboru*, to ascend a mountain. — *ni agaru*, id. — *wo kudaru*, to descend a mountain. — *no itadaki*, the top of a mountain. *H'to yama ikura*, how much for one heap? (of goods).

YAMA, ヤマ, *n.* A mercantile speculation, an enterprise or adventure having pecuniary gain for its object. — *wo szru*, to speculate. — *ga hadzreta*, speculation has failed. — *ga atatta*, the speculation has been fortunate.

YAMA-AI, ヤマアヒ, 山間, *n.* Between the mountains. — *no michi.* — *no kawa.*

YAMA-BATO, ヤマバト, 山鳩, *n.* A wild pigeon, or dove.

YAMABE, ヤマベ, 山邊, *n.* Near, or at the foot of a mountain.

YAMA-BITO, ヤマビト, 山人, *n.* A mountaineer; also, 仙, the same as *Sen-nin*, a genius, or fairy.

YAMABUKI, ヤマブキ, 山吹, *n.* The Kerria japonica.

YAMA-BUSHI, ヤマブシ, 山臥, *n.* A low sect of religionists, an offshoot from the Budd. sect of *Shingon*, who practise divination, and fortune telling.
Syn. SHUGENJA.

YAMA-DA, ヤマダ, 山田, *n.* Rice-fields amongst the mountains.

YAMADACHI, ヤマダチ, 山賊, *n.* A mountain robber, brigand. Syn. SANZOKU.

YAMA-DASHI, ヤマダシ, 山出, *n.* A rustic, one fresh from the country.

YAMA-DORI, ヤマドリ, 山鷄, *n.* A kind of pheasant.

YAMA-GA, ヤマガ, 山家, *n.* A house, or village among the mountains.

†YAMAGATSZ, ヤマガツ, 山夫, *n.* A mountaineer, a woodman.

YAMAGONNIYAKU, ヤマゴンニヤク, 天南星, *n.* The same as *Tennanshō*.

YAMAHIKO, ヤマヒコ, 山彥, *n.* An echo.

YAMAI, ヤマヒ, 病, *n.* Sickness, disease. — *wo naosz*, to cure disease. — *no riyōji wo szru*, to treat a sickness. — *ga na-*

oranu, the disease is incurable.
Syn. BIYŌKI.

YAMAI-KE, ヤマヒケ, 病氣, *n.* A sickly condition, or feeling. — *ga nai, jōbu na h'to*, he is not sickly, he is a healthy man.

YAMA-INU, ヤマイヌ, 豺, *n.* A wild dog, or wolf.

YAMAJI, ヤマヂ, 山路, *n.* A mountain road.

YAMAME, ヤマメ, 鰀, *n.* Trout.

YAMAMICHI, ヤマミチ, 山道, *n.* A mountain road.

YAMA-MORI, ヤマモリ, 山盛, *n.* Heaping up anything in measuring, heaping full.

YAMA-MOTO, ヤマモト, 山下, *n.* Base, or foot of a mountain.

YAMA-NO-HA, ヤマノハ, 山端, *n.* The mountains, or land that bounds the horizon. — *ni tszki ga kakureru*, the moon is hid behind the distant mountains.

YAMA-NOTE, ヤマノテ, 山手, *n.* A region of country near the mountains.

YAMA-OROSHI, ヤマオロシ, 山下風, *n.* A storm of wind blowing down from the mountains.

YAMA-SHI, ヤマシ, 山師, *n.* A mercantile speculator, or adventurer.

†YAMASHII,-KI,-KU, ヤマシイ, 痛, Uneasy, troubled, distressed.

†YAMASHIME,-*ru*,-*ta*, ヤマシメル, 疾, *t.v.* To cause pain, or sickness. *Kōbe wo* —, to make the head ache.

YAMA-TACHIDANA, ヤマタチバナ, 平地木, *n.* The name of a plant.

YAMATO, ヤマト, 大和, *n.* Japan. — *kotoba*, Japanese language.

YAMATO-DAMASHII, ヤマトダマシヒ, 大和靈, *n.* Japanese spirit, or temper; viz., courage. fearlessness, and disregard of death.

YAMA-WAKE, ヤマワケ, 山分, *n.* An equal division of profits.

YAMA-YAMA, ヤマヤマ, 山山, *adv.* Mountains; only used figuratively for, a great deal. — *katajikenaku*, greatly obliged.

YAMA-ZATO, ヤマザト, 山里, *n.* A village among the mountains.

YAME,-*ru*,-*ta*, ヤメル, 止, *t.v.* To cease from, stop, leave off, give up, abandon. *Shigoto wo* —, to cease from work. *Sake wo* —, to leave off drink. *Sendō wo yamete akindo ni natta*, he has stopped being a sailor and become a merchant. *Gakumon wo* —, to abandon study. Syn. HAISZRU.

‖YAME,-*ru*,-*ta*, ヤメル, 病, *i.v.* To pain, ache. *Atama ga* —, head aches.
Syn. ITAMU.

YAME, ヤメ, 止, *n.* A stop, cessation. *Ikusa — ni natta*, the war is ended. *Mo — ni shimashō*, I will stop, or cease to do. *Mo — da*, idem.

YAMERARE,-*ru*,-*ta*, ヤメラレル, 被止, pass. or pot. of *Yami*. To be left, or abandoned, or given up.

YAMESASE,-*ru*,-*ta*, ヤメサセル, 令止, caust. of *Yami*. To cause or let cease from.

YAMI, ヤミ, 闇, *n.* A night without moonlight, darkness. — *no yo*, a dark night.

YAMI,-*mu*,-*nda*, ヤム, 止, *i.v.* To cease, stop. *Ame ga yanda*, the rain has stopped. *Itami ga* —, the pain has stopped. *Yamu koto nashi*, without ceasing, incessant. *Yamu koto wo yedz*, must of necessity could not help but, no alternative, obliged.

YAMI,-*mu*,-*nda*, ヤム, 病, *t.v.* or *i.v.* To be diseased, to be sick with. *Shō-kan wo* —, to be sick with a fever. *Rōgai wo* —, sick with consumption. Syn. WADZRAU.

YAMI-AGARI, ヤミアガリ, 病後, (*biyō-go*). Convalescing or getting up from sickness.

YAMI-HŌKE,-*ru*,-*ta*, ヤミハウケル, *i.v.* To become imbecile from disease.

YAMI-JI, ヤミヂ, 闇路, *n.* A dark road, or travelling in a dark night.

YAMIKUMO, ヤミクモ, *adv.* In a confused hurried manner, recklessly, indiscriminately, thoughtlessly.

YAMI-TSZKARE,-*ru*,-*ta*, ヤミツカレル, 病疲, *t.v.* To be weakened, or exhausted by disease.

YAMI-TSZKI,-*ku*,-*ita*, ヤミツク, 病付, *i-v.* To be taken sick. *Itsz-kara yami-tszita*, how long have you been sick?

YAMI-UCHI, ヤミウチ, 闇討, *n.* Killing in the dark. *H'to wo — ni szru*, to kill a man at night.

YAMI-YAMI, ヤミヤミ, *adv.* Uselessly, for naught. — *to korosz*.
Syn. MUNASHIKU, MUDA-NI.

YAMOME, ヤモメ, 孀, *n.* A widow, or widower.

YA-MORI, ヤモリ, 屋守, *n.* One placed in a house to keep it, a watchman, also a species of lizard that frequents houses.

YAMU, ヤム, see *Yami*.

YAMURU, ヤムル, same as *Yameru*.

YANA, ヤナ, 梁, *n.* A weir, and basket to take fish.

YANAGI, ヤナギ, 柳, *n.* A willow.

YANAGUI, ヤナグヒ, 胡籙, *n.* A quiver.
Syn. YEBIRA, YADZTSZ.

YANDA, ヤンダ, *pret.* of *Yami*.

YANDE, ヤンデ, *pp.* of *Yami*.

YANE, ヤネ, 屋根, *n.* A roof. — *wo fuku*, to cover a roof with shingles, tiles, &c.

YANE-ITA, ヤネイタ, 屋根板, *n.* Shingles.

YANE-YA, ヤネヤ, 屋根屋, *n.* A person whose occupation is to roof houses.

YANGOTONAKI, ヤンゴトナキ, 無止事, *a.* Ineffable, indescribable. — *mi hotoke.*

YANI, ヤニ, 脂, *n.* The pitch, or gum that exudes from certain kinds of trees. *Me-yani*, a gummy discharge from the eyes.

YANIWA-NI, ヤニハニ, 矢庭, *adv.* Immediately, instantly, quickly.
Syn. KIU-NI, NIWAKA NI.

YANOMUNE, ヤノムネ, 屋上, *n.* The ridge of a house, or top of the roof.

YANONE, ヤノネ, 鏃, *n.* An arrow head.
Syn. YAJIRI.

YANYA, ヤンヤ, (a reduplication of the exclam. *Ya*), exclam. of admiration, or praise, uttered by a crowd of persons. — *to hayasz.*

†YAOKA, ヤヲカ, 八日, *n.* The eight day of the month, also eight days. Syn. YŌKA.

YA-OMOTE, ヤオモテ, 矢面, *n.* The range of an arrow, or ball, bowshot. — *ni szszn-de teki wo nonoshiru*, advancing within range of the arrows he reviled the enemy.

YAORA, ヤヲラ, *adv.* Softly, quietly, gently. — *mi wo okosz*, softly raised himself up. — *daki okosz*, to raise up gently.
Syn. SOTTO.

YAORE, ヤヲレ, Exclam. same as *Yare.*

YAOYA, ヤホヤ, 八百屋, *n.* A seller of vegetables, a green-grocer.

YAOYORODZ, ヤホヨロヅ, 百萬, (lit. eight hundred myriads). = All, the whole multitude of. — *no kami*, all the gods.

YAPPARI, ヤッパリ, *adv.* same as *Yahari.*

YARA, ヤラ, (derived from *Ya*, and *ra*, contr. of *ran*). A conjunctive particle, or a particle expressing doubt, or uncertainty, = And, or, whether, I wonder. *Sake wo nomu yara odoru yara*, drinking wine and dancing. *Doko ye itta yara*, I wonder where he has gone. *Dō sh'te yara*, I wonder what he is doing, (of one sent on an errand and who is slow to return.) *Dare yara kita sō da*, I think some body has come. *Hana ga chiru yara*, I wonder if the flowers are falling.

YARAI, ヤラヒ, 柵, *n,* A picket fence, a stockade.

‖YARAKASHI,*-sz,-sh'ta*, ヤラカス, *t.v.* To do, to work, (vulgar coll). *Shigoto wo* —, to do one's work. Syn. SZRU.

YARAN, ヤラン, same as *Yara. Ikanaru koto yaran*, what kind of an affair can it be? *Ikaga — to o anji mōshimash'ta*, I felt anxious about you, or wondered how you were doing.

YARADZ, or YARANU, ヤラズ, 不遣, neg. of *Yari.*

YARARE*-ru,-ta*, ヤラレル, 被遣, pass. or pot. of *Yari.*

YARASE,*-ru,-ta*, ヤラセル, 令遣, caust. of *Yari.* To cause, or order another to send, or give. *Tszkai wo* —, to order a messenger to be sent.

YARE, ヤレ, Exclam. of surprise, fear, pain, &c.

YARI, ヤリ, 鎗, *n.* A spear, lance. — *no mi*, the head of a spear. — *no ye*, handle of a spear. — *de tszku*, to thrust with a spear.

YARI,*-ru,-tta*, ヤル, 遣, *t.v.* To give, bestow, to send, transmit, to do, to let, allow, permit. *H'to ni kane wo* —, to give money to another. *Yedo ye* —, to send to Yedo. *Mo yatte shimatta*, I have finished. *Midz wo niwa ye* —, to conduct a stream of water into the yard. *Mite yaru*, let me see. *Sh'te yaru*, let me do. *Tegami wo* —, to send a letter. *Butte yaru*, to give a blow. *Omoi wo* —, to get rid of or dismiss the thought.
Syn. TSZKAWASZ, OKURU.

YARIDO, ヤリド, 遣戸, *n.* A sliding door.

YARIHA, ヤリハ, 遣場, *n.* A place to send, or put away anything. — *ga nai*, have no place to send it. — *de komaru*, troubled about a place to put it.

YARI-JIAI, ヤリジアヒ, 鎗仕合, *n.* A combat with spears.

YARI-JIRUSHI, ヤリジルシ, 鎗幟, *n.* A small flag attached to a lance.

YARIKAKE, ヤリカケ, 槍掛, *n.* A spear rack.

YARI-KOMI,*-mu,-nda*, ヤリコム, *t.v.* To put to silence, refute, convict. *Giron wo sh'te h'to wo yari-konda.*

YARI-KURI,*-ru,-tta*, ヤリクル, 遣操, *t.v.* To plan, or devise how to raise money, to turn over one's money. *Shinshō wo* —.

YARI-MIDZ, ヤリミヅ, 遣水, *n.* A stream of water brought from a distance.

YARI-MOCHI, ヤリモチ, 槍持, *n.* Spearmen, lancers.

YARIPPANASHI, ヤリッパナシ, 遣放, Leaving one's work in disorder, without putting things in their proper places, slovenly, careless, neglecting order and neatness. — *na h'to.* — *ni szru.* — *ni sh'te oku.*

YARI-SOKONAI, *-au,-atta*, ヤリソコナフ, 遣損, *t.v.* To injure in making, to spoil; to lose one's place, or employment.
Syn. SHIKUJIRU, SHI-SOKONAU.

YARITE, ヤリテ, 遣手, *n.* The sender, or giver. The female keeper of a brothel.

YARŌ, ヤラウ, 野老, *n.* (A contemptuous epithet). = Low fellow. Syn. YATSZ.

YARU, ヤル, 遣, see *Yari.*

YARU-KATA, ヤルカタ, 遣方, used in the phrase; — *naku*, cannot help, or cannot get rid of, unavoidable.

YARUSE, ヤルセ, (same as *Yaru-kata*). — *ga nai*, cannot help, or get rid of, cannot restrain. — *namida*, tears that one cannot keep back.

YA-SAGASHI, ヤサガシ, 屋探, *n.* Searching a house. — *wo szru*, to search a house.

YASA-GATACHI, ヤサガタチ, 瘦形, *n.* Thin, slim, or lean in body.

YASAI, ヤサイ, 野菜, *n.* Vegetables.

YA-SAKEBI, ヤサケビ, 矢叫, *n.* The sound made by an arrow in flying.

YA-SAKI, ヤサキ, 矢先, *n.* The point of an arrow.

YASASHII,-KI,-KU,-Ū,-SA, ヤサシイ, 優, Amiable, gentle, tender, soft; easy, not difficult. *Yasashii h'to*, an amiable person. *Yasashiku mono wo iu*, to speak gently. Syn. KAWAIRASHII.

†YASHA, ヤシヤ, 夜叉, *n.* A demon, or devil. Syn. ONI.

YASE,*-ru,-ta*, ヤセル, 瘦, *i.v.* To be emaciated, thin, wasted in flesh; to pine, to be poor, sterile, as soil. *Yamai de yaseta*, wasted by sickness. *Tszchi ga* —, the soil is poor.

YASECHI, ヤセチ, 瘠地, *n.* Poor or sterile soil.

YASE-GAMAN, ヤセガマン, *n.* Putting on an appearance the reverse of one's real feelings, so as to conceal them. *Hara ga hete mo — wo szru*, although a person is hungry to make believe he is not.

†YA-SEI, ヤセイ, 野生, An humble word used in speaking of one's self, = I.

YASEN, ヤセン, 野戰, *n.* A field battle, a battle on land.

YASE-OTOROYE, *-ru, -ta*, ヤセオトロヘル, 瘦衰, *i v.* To become emaciated and feeble.

YASE-TSZCHI, ヤセツチ, *n.* Same as *Yasechi.*

YASHI, ヤシ, 野師, *n.* A class of persons, who by various tricks of jugglery attract persons in the street to buy secret medicines, charms, &c., it includes dentists, conjurers, street-showmen, sword-swallowers, serpent-charmers, top-spinners, pedlers, &c. a mountebank.

YASHI, ヤシ, 椰子, *n.* A cocoanut.

YASHIKI, ヤシキ, 屋敷, *n.* The lot of ground on which a house stands; the house of a noble.

YASHIMA, ヤシマ, 八洲, *n.* The eight islands, *i.e.*, Japan.

YASHIN, ヤシン, 野心, *n.* Treason, treachery. — *wo kuwadatsz*, to devise treason. — *no mono*, a traitor. Syn. F'TAGOKORO.

YASHINAI,*-au,-atta*, ヤシナフ, 養, *t. v.* To nourish, foster, to support, maintain, sustain; to rear, bring up. *Ko wo* —, to nourish a child. *Ki wo* —, to support the spirits. Syn. SODATERU, BUIKU SZRU.

YASHINAIGO, ヤシナヒゴ, 養子, (*yōshi*). *n.* A foster child.

YASHIRO, ヤシロ, 祠, *n.* A Sintoo temple, or shrine.

YASHŌBI, ヤセウビ, 野薔薇, *n.* A white rose.

YASHOKU, ヤシヨク, 夜食, *n.* Supper. Syn. YUMESHI.

YASO, ヤソ, 八十, Eighty. Syn. HACHIJŪ.

YASOJI, ヤソヂ, 八十歲, *n.* Eighty years of age.

YASZ, ヤス, *n.* A fish-gig.

YASZU, ヤスウ, contr. from *Yaszku*, see *Yaszi.*

YASZDE, ヤスデ, *n.* The julus, or gally worm.

YASZI,-KI,-SHI, ヤズイ, 安, *a.* Easy, not difficult; cheap, low in price, peaceful, free from trouble. *San ga yaszi*, the labor was easy. *Hōsō ga* —, the small-pox was light, not dangerous. *Nedan ga* —, the price is cheap. *Yaszi shigoto*, easy work. *Kokoro yaszi h'to*, an intimate acquaintance. *Kodzkai no kiukin ga yaszi*, the wages of servants are low.

YASZKU, ヤスク, *adv.* see *Yaszi.* — *nai*, not easy, or not cheap. — *omō*, to consider easy, cheap, &c. — *szru*, to cheapen, or make easy.

YASZME,*-ru,-ta*, ヤスメル, 休, *t. v.* To rest, to repose, to ease; to set at rest, to make tranquil, or free from uneasiness. *Me wo* —, to rest the eyes. *Te wo* —, to rest the hand. *Oya no kokoro wo* —, to set the mind of a parent at ease.

YASZMEJI, ヤスメチ, 休地, *n.* Fallow ground, ground suffered to lie without tillage.

YASZMI,*-mu,-nda*, ヤスム, 休, *i. v.* To rest from labor, or fatigue; to repose, to cease from work, to be quiet, tranquil, or at ease. *Shigoto wo* —, to cease from work. *O yaszmi nasare*, take a rest, or I wish you good night (on leaving). Syn. IKŌ, KIU-SOKU SZRU.

YASZMI, ヤスミ, 休, *n.* Rest, repose, cessation from work.

YASZMI-BI, ヤスミビ, 休日, (*kiu-jitsz*). *n.* Day of rest, a holiday. Syn. ANSOKU-NICHI.

YASZMONO, ヤスモノ, 安物, *n.* Low priced things.

YASZNJI,*-dzru,-ta*, ヤスンズル, 安, *t.v.* To make peaceful, happy, or contented; to tranquilize, to govern, to preserve peace. *Kuni wo* —, to tranquilize a state. *Kokoro wo* —.

YASZ-NE, ヤスネ, 安直, *n.* Cheap, low price.

YASZPPOI,-KI,-KU,-Ō, ヤズッポイ, coll. Cheap, low-priced, coarse. — *mono*, low-priced things.

†YASZRAI,*-au,-atta*, ヤスラフ, 休, *i.v.* To rest.

YASZRAKA, ヤズラカ, 安, Easy, not difficult; free from trouble, tranquil, gentle, mild. — *naru*. — *ni*.

YASZRI, ヤスリ, 鉎, *n.* A file. — *de orosz*, to reduce by filing. — *de szru*, to file. — *me*, the marks left by filing. — *no me*, the teeth of a file.

†YASZRU, ヤスル, the same as *Yaseru*.

YASZSA, ヤスサ, 安, *n.* Easiness, facility.

YASZ-YASZ-TO, ヤスヤスト, 安安, *adv.* Easily, without difficulty, tranquilly, gently.

YATAI, ヤタイ, 屋臺, *n.* A kind of car drawn through the streets in festivals.

YATAKE, ヤタケ, 彌武, Courageous, spirited, heroic, fierce, savage. — *gokoro*. Syn. TAKEKI.

YATARA-NI, ヤタラニ, *adv.* In a hurried or confused manner, indiscriminately, without thought or care. *Mono wo hako ni — ireru*, to put things into a box in confusion and without care.

YATATE, ヤタテ, 墨斗, *n.* A portable ink-stand, such as is carried suspended from the belt.

YATŌ, ヤタウ, 夜盗, *n.* A thief who steals at night.

†YATOI,*-ō,-ōta*, ヤトフ, 倩, *t.v.* To hire temporarily, to call, as a coolie. *Ninsoku wo* —, to call a coolie. Syn. TANOMU.

YATOI, or YATOIDO, ヤトヒ, 倩, *n.* A person hired temporarily.

YATOWARE,*-ru,-ta*, ヤトハレル, 被倩, pass. of *Yatoi*.

YATSZ, ヤツ, 八, Eight. Syn. HACHI.

YATSZ, ヤツ, 奴, *n.* A low fellow, rascal.

YATSZBARA, ヤツバラ, 奴等, *plu.* Fellows, rascals.

YATSZBO, ヤツボ, 矢壺, *n.* A target, or any object an arrow is aimed at.

†YATSZGARE, ヤツガレ, 僕, *pro.* I.

YATSZ-ME, ヤツメ, 奴目, *n.* Rascal, villain.

YATSZME-UNAGI, ヤツメウナギ, 八目鰻, *n.* A lamprey, Petromyzon fluviatilis.

YATSZRE,*-ru,-ta*, ヤツレル, 憔悴, *i.v.* To become thin, emaciated, or debilitated; to be ragged, filthy and poor in appearance. Syn. YASE-OTOROYERU, SHŌSZI.

YATSZSHI,*-sz,-sh'ta*, ヤツス, *t.v.* To dress-up, to deck, adorn one's self; to alter one's appearance, to disguise one's self. *Mi wo yatszash'te shinobi ni yuku*, to disguise one's self and go incognito. *Szgata wo* —, to disguise one's appearance. Syn. MEKASZ.

YATSZ-YATSZSHII,-KI,-KU, ヤツヤツシイ, 窶, Poor, miserable, dirty and ragged.

YATTO, ヤツト, *adv.* At length, at last, barely, scarcely, hardly. Syn. YŌYAKU.

YATTOKO, ヤツトコ, *n.* A smith's tongs, used in handling hot metal.

YA-UTSZRI, ヤウツリ, 家移, *n.* Moving from one house to another. — *wo szru*. Syn. WATAMASHI.

YAWAKA, ヤハカ, *adv*, It is doubtful whether, I doubt if, I rather think. *Kumotte wa iru ga — furi mo szmai*, although it is cloudy I rather think it will not rain. — *yuruszmaji*, I doubt if he will permit it. Syn. YOMOYA.

YAWARA, ヤハラ, 拳法, *n.* Wrestling. — *wo toru*. Syn. JŪ-JUTSZ.

YAWARAGE,*-ru,-ta*, ヤハラゲル, 和, *t. v.* To soften, to mollify, mellow, to compose, appease, pacify. *Koye wo* —, to soften the voice. *Nite* —, to soften by boiling. *Kokoro wo* —, to soften the heart. *Ikari wo* —, to appease anger.

YAWARAGI,*-gu,-ida*, ヤハラグ, 和, *i.v.* To become soft, to be mellowed, mollified, to be easy, composed.

YAWARAKA, ヤハラカ, 和, Soft, not hard; gentle, mild, delicate, tender. — *ni szru*, to make soft. — *na kokoro*, soft hearted, amiable.

YAYA, ヤヤ, *n.* An infant, (yed. coll.). Syn. AKAMBO.

YAYA, ヤヤ, 稍, *adv.* Considerably, tolerably, pretty, good, rather. — *hisashiku*, a good while ago. — *nitari*, pretty much alike. — *samukunatta*, it has become tolerably cold. — *atte*, after a good while, or after some time.

YAYA-MO-SZREBA, ヤヤモスレバ, 動, *adv.* Sometimes, or occasionally and contrary to the usual practice, or in spite of efforts to the contrary. — *kana wo machigayeru h'to ga ōi*, most persons will sometimes make mistakes in spelling. *Shibai wa — hadzreru*, theatres sometimes prove a failure.

YAYE, ヤヘ, 八重, Eight fold, many fold. *Hana ga — ni saku*, the flower blooms with many petals, (or double). — *no sakura*, a cherry tree that bears a double blossom.

YAYENARI, ヤヘナリ, 緑豆, *n.* A kind of pea, or bean.

YAYO, ヤヨ, Exclam. used in calling to another, = Hollo. — *matte*, Hollo! wait a little.

†YAYOI, ヤヨヒ, 三月, *(san g'watsz)*, *n.* The third month.

YAZAMA, ヤザマ, 矢間, *n.* A port hole, or embrasure for shooting arrows.

YAZEN, ヤゼン, 夜前, *n.* Last night. Syn. SAKUBAN.

YE, エ, 柄, *n.* A handle. *Kuwa no —*, the handle of a hoe.

YE, ヱ, 繪, *n.* A picture, drawing. — *wo kaku*, to draw a picture. Syn. G'WA, YEDZ.

YE, エ, 江, *n.* A river, or an arm or inlet of the sea; a sound, frith, fiord. *Hori ye*, a canal.

YE, ヱ, 餌, *n.* The food of birds, or fishes; a bait. *Tori ni ye wo yaru*, to feed the birds.

YE, エ, 榎, *n.* The name of a tree. *Ye-no-ki*, the Celtis Willdenawiana.

YE, エ, 荏, *n.* The name of a plant, from the seeds of which oil is obtained.

YE, ヱ, 穢, *(kegare)*, *n.* Defilement, pollution, or ceremonial uncleanness. — *ni fureru*, to be defiled.

†YE, ヱ, 會, *(k'wai) n.* A meeting, assembly. *Nem-butsz ye. Busshō ye.*

YE, ヘ, 重, *n.* A fold, layer, ply, sheet, or thickness. *H'to ye*, a single thickness, fold, or layer. *F'ta ye*, double thickness. *Iku ye*, how many fold?

YE, ヘ, 方, *post-posit.* Noting motion toward or into; = To, toward, in, into; sign of the dative. *Dōko ye yuku*, where are you going? *Yedo ye itte oru*, going to Yedo. *Hon ye kaku*, to write in a book *Cha-wan ye tszgu*, pour it into a tea-cup. *Sh'ta ye oriru*, to go down. Syn. NI.

YE, エ, coll. Exclam. of interrogation, or doubt. *Doko no ye*, where? or which? *Sō ka ye*, is it so? or indeed? *Shitte iru ka ye*, do you know?

YE, エ, Exclam. of grief, repentance, anger, dislike, &c. — *kuyashii.*

YE,*-ru,-ta*, エル, 得, *t.v.* To get, obtain, to receive; can, able. *Ri wo —*, to get profit. *Saiwai wo —*, to be fortunate. *Miru koto wo —*, to get to see. *Shiru koto wo yedz*, could not find out, or, obtain the knowledge of. *Me atte miru koto wo yeru*, having eyes we are able to see. Syn. URU, MOTOMERU.

YE, エ, 枝, *n.* A branch, or limb of a tree. *Ume ga ye*, the branch of a plum tree. Syn. YEDA.

YEBA, エバ, 餌, *n.* The food of birds, or fishes.

YEBAMI,*-mu,-nda*, ヱバム, 啄, *t.v.* To eat, or feed; used only of birds or fishes. *Tori ga yebande iru*, the birds are feeding.

YEBI,*-ru,-ta*, エビル, *i.v.* To burst open as ripe fruit. *Kuri ga yebita.* Syn. HAZERU.

YEBI, エビ, 鰕, *n* A shrimp, prawn.

†YEBI, エビ, 葡萄, *n.* The grape. — *dzru*, grape-vine. Syn. BUDŌ.

YEBI-IRO, エビイロ, *n.* Grape color, purple.

YEBI-JŌ, エビジヤウ, 魚鑰, *n.* A kind of padlock, shaped like a fish.

YEBIRA, エビラ, 蠶簿, *n.* A mat made of bamboo on which silkworms are fed.

YEBIRA, エビラ, *n.* A kind of quiver. Syn. YANAGUI.

YEBISZ, エビス, 夷, *n.* A barbarian, savage.

YEBISZ, エビス, 蛭子, *n.* The god of wealth, and guardian of markets. He was the third son of *Izanagi-no mikoto.*

YEBIWARE,*-ru,-ta*, エビワレル, pass. of *Yebiru.* To be burst or split open as ripe fruit.

YEBOSHI, エボシ, 烏帽子, *n.* A kind of black cap worn on the crown of the head by nobles, also by *Manzai* and *Kannushi.*

YEBUKURO, ヱブクロ, 餌袋, *n.* The crop, or craw of fowls; the first stomach of some animals.

YEBURI, エブリ, 杁, *n.* An instrument like a scraper used by farmers for breaking hard clods and leveling the ground,

YEDÀ, エダ, 枝, *n.* A branch, bough, or limb of a tree; a limb, or extremity of the body, a branch of a river, or of a family, of a sect, &c.

YEDA-HA, エダハ, 枝葉, *n.* Branches and leaves; subdivision, or branches of a sect.

YEDA-MICHI, エダミチ, 枝道, *n.* A branch road.

YEDO, ヱド, 穢土, (*kegare kuni*). *n.* This unclean, or sinful world, (Budd).
Syn. SHABASEKAI.

YEDORI, -*ru*, -*tta*, ヱドル 彩, *t. v.* To paint in various colors. *Kao wo* —, to paint the face, as play actors.
Syn. IRODORU, SAISHIKI WO SZRU.

YEDZ, ヱヅ, 繪圖, *n.* A picture, drawing; a map; a plan of a building. — *wo hiku*, or, — *wo kaku*, to draw a picture, plan, or map.

YEDZ, エズ, 不得, *neg.* of *Ye;* Cannot get, unable to do. *Yamu koto wo* —, cannot stop, no alternative.

YEDZ-HIKI, ヱヅヒキ, 繪圖引, *n.* An architect.

YEDZKI, -*ku*, -*ita*, ヱヅク, 嘔, *i.v.* To gag, reach, or make an effort to vomit.

YE-FU, ヱフ, 衛符, *n.* A sign-board attached to the baggage of officials, or persons on public business.

YE-FUDE, ヱフデ, 畫筆, *n.* A drawing pencil, or paint brush.

YEGAKI, -*ku*, -*ita*, ヱガク, 畫, *t. v.* To draw, delineate, to picture. *Hana wo* —, to draw a flower.

YE-GAO, ヱガホ, 笑顔, *n.* A laughing, or smiling face.

YE-GATAI, -KI, -KU, -SHI, エガタイ, 難得, Difficult to obtain, hard to get.

YEGO-MATA, エゴマタ, *n.* Bandy-legged.

YEGO-YEGO, エゴエゴ, *adv.* In a waddling manner, (as a goose). — *sh'te aruku*, to waddle.

YEGUI, -KI, ヱグシ, 醶, *a.* The taste or tingling sensation produced in the throat by eating raw *satoimo.*

YEGUKU, ヱグク, 醶, *adv.* id.

YEGURI, -*ru*, -*tta*, エグル, 剜, *t. v.* To cut with a twisting motion, to scoop. *Ana wo* —, to scoop out a hole.

YEGUSA, ヱグサ, *n.* Tingling sensation in the throat.

YEHŌ, エハウ, 吉方, *n.* The point of the compass corresponding to the name of the year; as, *u no toshi*, corresponds to, *u no hō*, or the east.

YEHON, ヱホン, 繪本, *n.* A drawing book, or picture book.

YEI, エヒ, 醉, *n.* Intoxication, drunkenness. *Fune no* —, sea-sickness. Syn. YOI.

YEI, エイ, 纓, *n.* The strings of a cap.

†YEI-BUN, エイブン, 叡聞, The hearing of the *Mikado.*

†YEI-CHI, エイチ, 叡智, *n.* Divine or superior intelligence, such as the sages possess.

YEIDZRU, エイズル, 詠, or 映, see *Yeiji.*

YEI-FUSHI, -*sz*, -*sh'ta*, エヒフス, 醉臥, *i. v.* To be drunk and lie down.

YEI-GO, エイゴ, 英語, *n.* The English language.

YEI-GURUI, -*ū*, -*ūta* エヒグルフ, 醉狂, *i. v.* To be raving drunk, crazed with drink.

YEI-G'WA, エイグワ, 榮華, *n.* Splendor. magnificence, luxury, sumptuousness. — *ni kurasz*, to live sumptuously.
Syn. YEIYŌ.

YEIJI, -*dzru*, -*ta*, エイズル, 詠, *t. v.* To sing. *Uta wo* —. Syn. UTAU, GINDZRU.

YEIJI, -*dzru*, -*ta*, エイズル, 映, (*utszru*). *i. v.* To reflect, as a mirror; to shine.

†YEI-JI, エイジ, 嬰兒, *n.* An infant, babe.

†YEI-JITSZ, エイジツ, 永日, (*nagaki hi*). *n.* A long day.

†YEI-JŪ, エイヂユウ, 永住, (*nagaku szmu*). A long residence. — *szru*, to live long in a place.

YEI-KAN, エイカン, 叡感, *n.* The admiration of the *Mikado.* — *asakaradz.*

YEI-KIYO, エイキヨ, 盈虚, (*michi kake*). Waxing and waning, increase and decrease, ebb and flow.

†YEI-KIU, エイキウ, 永久, (*nagaku hisashi*). Long, lasting, enduring. — *no majiwari*, long intimacy.

YEI-KO, エイコ, 榮枯, (*sakayeru kareru*). Flourishing and decaying; blooming and withering, rise and fall.

YEI-KOKU, エイコク, 英國, *n.* England.

†YEI-MEI, エイメイ, 英名, (*szguretaru na*) Illustrious name.

YEI-RAN, エイラン, 叡覽, *n.* The eyes, notice, or seeing of the *Mikado.*

YEI-RIYO, エイリヨ, 叡慮, *n.* The mind, opinion, or thought of the *Mikado.*

YEI-SAME, -*ru*, -*ta*, エイサメル, 醉醒, *i.v.* To recover from intoxication, become sober.

YEI-SHIRE, -*ru*, -*ta*, エイシレル, 醉愚, *i.v.* To become foolish, or silly from intoxication.

YEI-TAI, エイタイ, 永代, (*nagaki yo*). Long ages, forever, always.
Syn. YEIYEI.

YEI-TAORE, -*ru*, -*ta*, エイタフレル, 醉倒, *i. v.* To fall down from intoxication.

YEI-YA, エイヤ, Exclam. used by a number of persons in exerting their strength all together.

YEI-YEI, エイエイ, Exclam. id.

YEI-YEI, エイエイ, 永永, (*naga naga*). *adv.* Forever, ever, perpetually, always. Syn. ITSZMADEMO, NAGAKU.

YEI-YŌ, エイエフ, 榮耀, (*sakaye kakayaku*). Glory, magnificence, splendor, pomp. *Nin-gen no — fū zen no chiri*, human glory is like the dust before the wind. Syn. YEIG'WA OGORI.

YEI-YŪ, エイユウ, 英雄, *n.* A hero, an eminent man. Syn. GŌKETSZ.

YEJIKI, エジキ, 餌食, *n.* The food of birds, fishes, or animals.

YEKAKI, エカキ, 畫師, *n.* A painter, sketcher, or drawer of pictures.

YEKI, エキ, 益, *n.* Profit, advantage, benefit. — *mo nai*, unprofitable. Syn. KAI.

YEKI, エキ, 易, *n.* The art of divining by means of diagrams, sticks, &c. — *wo miru*, to divine. Syn. URANAI.

YEKI, エキ, 驛, *n.* A post station. Syn. SHUKU.

YEKI, エキ, 役, *n.* A pestilence, contagion, epidemic. Syn. YAKUBIYŌ.

†YEKI, エキ, 疫, *n.* A campaign, the time of a war. *Chōsen no — ni*, in the war with Corea. Syn. IKUSA.

†YEKI-BA, エキバ, 驛馬, *n.* A post horse. Syn. SHUKUBA.

YEKI-REI, エキレイ, 疫癘, *n.* A pestilence, plague.

†YEKI-RO, エキロ, 驛路, *n.* A post road.

†YEKI-TEI, エキテイ, 驛亭, *n.* An inn, or tea house on a post road. Syn. YADOYA.

†YEKKI, エツキ, 悦喜, *n.* Joy, delight. Syn. YOROKOBI.

YEKO, エコ, 依怙, *n.* Partiality, bias, favoring one more than another. — *hīki szru*, to show partiality. Syn. HIKI.

YEKŌ, エカウ, 回向, *n.* Repeating prayers as Buddhist priests. — *szru*.

YEKUBO, エクボ, 靨, *n.* A dimple in the cheek when laughing.

YEMA, エマ, 繪馬, *n.* The pictures, (especially of a horse) hung up in *Sintoo* temples as thank offerings.

†YEMAI,-ō,-ōta, エマフ, 笑, *i.v.* To laugh. Syn. WARAU.

†YEMBU, or YEMBUDAI, エンブ, 閻浮, *n.* This world. — *no chiri*, (Bud.).

YEMI,-*mu*, エム, 笑, *i. v.* To laugh, to smile.

YEMI, エミ, 笑, *n.* Laughter. — *wo fukumu*, to smile.

YEMISHI, エミシ, 夷, same as *Yebisz.*

YEMMA, エウマ, coll. for *Yema*, which see.

YEMMA, or YEMMA-Ō, エンマ, 閻魔王, *n.* The king of Hades, who judges the souls of the dead, and according to their conduct in this life sends them to heaven, or to hell. — *no chō*, the judgment seat or court of *Yemma.*

YEMMAN, エンマン, 圓滿, (*madoka ni mitszru*). Lit. Round and full. Perfect, complete, deficient in nothing; only used by the Buddhists in speaking of *Hotoke* who is said to be; *Man-toku yem-man*, all perfect.

YE-MO-IWADZ, エモイハズ, 不得言, Unspeakable, inexpressible, ineffable. — *utszkushiki tokoro*, a place of ineffable beauty.

YEMON, エモン, 衣紋, *n.* The wrinkles, or folds in the dress. — *wo tszkurō*, to adjust, or smooth one's dress.

YE-MONO, エモノ, 獲物, *n.* Game taken in hunting, or fishing.

YE-MORI, エモリ, 柄漏, *n.* The leaking along the handle of an umbrella.

YEM-PEI, エンペイ, 援兵, *n.* Auxiliary troops. Syn. KASEI.

†YEM-PEN, エンペン, 緣邊, *n.* Relations, connections. Syn, SHINRUI.

YEM-PŌ, エンパウ, 遠方, (*tōitokoro*). *n.* A distant place, far, distant. — *kara kita*, came from a distant place.

YEMU, エム, see *Yemi.*

YEN, エン, 緣, *n.* Relation, affinity, connection; secret cause, influence, or combination of circumstances. *Fū-fu no —*, the relation of husband and wife. — *wo muszbu*, to form a connection. *Mu-yen no h'to*, a person who has no relations, or friends. — *wo kiru*, to sever a connection, or relationship. *Nan no — de koko ni kite iru*, what strange concatenation of causes has brought you here? *Fushigi na — de fū-fu ni natta*, became husband and wife by a strange providence. Syn. CHINAMI.

YEN, エン, 緣, *n.* A verandah, porch, balcony. *Ochi-yen*, a low porch close to the ground. *Age-yen*, a porch which can be raised, or let down.

YENA, エナ, 胞, *n.* The placenta.

YEN-DŌ, エンドウ, 豌豆, *n.* A kind of pea.

YEN-DŌI,-KI,-KU,-SHI, エンドホイ, 緣遠, Late in forming a marriage relation, used only of a woman. *Yendōi onna*, an old maid. *Yendōi mono*, an article for which there is no demand.

YEN-DZKI,*–ku,–ita*, エンヅク, 緣著, *i.v.* To be affianced or contracted in marriage; in mercantile language, to meet with a buyer, or be in demand. *Muszme ga mada yendzkimasen*, my daughter is not yet betrothed.

YENDZKI, エンヅキ, 緣着, *n.* Betrothment, demand for goods.

YENGAWA エンガハ, 緣側, *n.* A portico, verandah, porch, balcony.

YENGI, エンギ, 緣起, *n.* The origin, or historical record of the origin of a *Miya*, or *Tera*.

YENGI, エンギ, 延喜, *n.* Omen, sign, prognostic. — *ga yoi*, a good sign. — *ga warui*, a bad sign. Syn. ZEMPIYO.

YEN-GUMI, エングミ, 緣組, *n.* Marriage relation, matrimony. — *wo szru*, to contract a marriage.

YENIN, エンイン, 延引, see *Yennin*.

†YENISHI, エニシ, 緣, *n.* The same as *Yen*, relation, affinity.

YEN-JA, エンジヤ, 緣者, *n.* Relations, connections. Syn. SHINRUI, AIDAGARA.

YEN-KIN, エンキン, 遠近, (*tōi chikai*). Far and near.

YEN-KIRI, エンキリ, 緣切, *n.* Breaking off the conjugal relation, divorce.

YENKŌ, エンコウ, 猿猴, *n.* A long armed ape.

†YEN-KŌ, エンカウ, 遠行, Going far away, or to a distant place. — *szru.*

†YEN-NETSZ, エンネツ, 炎熱, *n.* Extreme heat of weather.

YEN-NICHI, エンニチ, 緣日, *n.* A fixed day of the month, when the god is supposed to be especially propitious to worshipers visiting his temple.

YEN-NIN, エンニン, 延引, Delay, tardiness, lateness, dilatory, slow. — *szru*, to be late, slow. Syn. OSOKU-NARU.

YE-NOGU, エノグ, 顏料, *n.* Paints used in drawing. — *zara*, the cups in which paints are mixed.

YENOKI, エノキ, see *Ye*.

YENOKORO, エノコロ, 狗兒, *n*, A young dog, a pup.

YEN-RAI, エンライ, 遠來, (*tōku kitaru*). Come from a distant place. — *no chimbutsz.*

YEN-RI, エンリ, 厭離, (*itoi hanareru*). Disgusted with the world and separating one's self from it. (Budd.) — *no kokoro wo okosz.*

YENRIYO, エンリヨ, 遠慮, (*tōki omompakari*). *n.* Thinking of and providing against future contingencies, provident; reserve, self-restraint, backwardness, diffidence, *H'to — naki toki wa kanaradz kin yu ari*, when a person does not look well to the future, trouble is near. — *naku mōsare yo*, speak without restraint. Syn. YŌ-JIN, HABAKARI.

YEN-RO, エンロ, 遠路, (*tōi michi*). *n.* A long road, or journey.

YEN-SHO, エンシヨ, 炎暑, *n.* Hot weather, the heat. Syn. ATSZSA.

YEN-SHŌ, エンセウ, 焰硝, *n.* Gunpowder. Syn. K'WA-YAKU.

YEN-TEN, エンテン, 炎天, (*atszi sora*). *n.* Hot weather, — *ni midz ga kareta.*

YEN-TŌ, エンタウ, 遠嶋, (*tōi shima*). Exile, or banishment to a penal island. Syn. RUZAI, SHIMA NAGASHI.

YEN-TŌ, エンタウ, 鉛糖, *n.* Sugar of lead.

YENU, エヌ, 不得, neg. of *Ye,–ru.*

†YEN-YEN, エンエン, 餤餤, *adv.* In a flaming manner. — *to moye-agaru.*

YEN-ZA, エンザ, 圓座, *n.* A round cushion for sitting on.

YEN-ZAI, エンザイ, 寃罪, (*mushitsz no tszmi*). Punishment inflicted on an innocent person. — *wo kōmuru*, to be punished for a crime which one has not committed.

†YEN-ZETSZ, エンゼツ, 演說, To tell, to speak of, talk of. — *ni oyobu*, no need of speaking about.

†YEPPUKU,*–szru*, エツプク, 悅服, (*yorokobi sh'tagau*). To render cheerful obedience.

YERA, エラ, 鰓, *n.* The gills of a fish.

YERABARE,*–ru,–ta*, エラバレル, 被選, pass. or pot. of *Yerabu*. To be chosen, can be chosen.

YERABI,*–bu,–nda*, エラブ, 選, *t.v.* same as *Yerami*.

YERAI,–KI,–KU, エライ, *a.* Extraordinary, wonderful, remarkable; very. — *h'to da*, a remarkable man. — *ō ame futta*, a very great rain has fallan. Syn. OSOROSHII, TAISŌ.

YERAMARE,*–ru,–ta*, エラマレル, 被選, same as *Yebarareru*.

YERAMI,*–mu,–nda*, エラム, 選, *t. v.* To choose, select, pick out, to elect. *Yoi no wo —*, select a good one. *Yoki wo yerande ashiki wo szteru*, choose the good and reject the bad. Syn. YORU, YERU.

YERAMI, エラミ, 選, *n.* Choice, selection, election.

YERAMI-DASHI,–*sz*,–*sh'ta*, エラミダス, 選出, *t.v.* To pick out, select. Syn. YORI-DASZ.

YERAMI-TORI,–*ru*,–*tta*, エラミトル, 選取, *t.v.* Idem. Syn. YORI-TORU.

YERARE,–*ru*,–*ta*, エラレル, 被得, pass. or pot. of *Yeru*. To be obtained, can be obtained.

YERARENU, エラレヌ, 不被得, neg. of *Yerareru*. Cannot be obtained.

YEREKITER, エレキテル, 電氣, *n.* Electricity, (this word is derived from the Dutch but now currently used).

YERI,–*ru*,–*tta*, エル, 擇, *t.v.* To choose, select, pick-out, to elect. Syn. YORU, YERABU.

YERI,–*ru*,–*tta*, エル, 彫, *t,v.* To engrave, carve. *Ji wo ishi ni* —, to engrave letters on stone. Syn. CHIRIBAMU, HORU.

YERI, エリ, 襟, *n.* The collar of a coat.

YERI-ASHI, エリアシ, *n.* The loose hairs on the back of the neck.

YERI-DASHI,–*sz*,–*sh'ta*, エリダス, 擇出, *t. v.* To pick out,, choose, select, to elect. Syn. YORIDASZ.

YERI-KUBI, エリクビ, 領, *n.* The nape of the neck.

YERI-MAKI, エリマキ, 領巾, *n.* A tippet, or comforter worn around the neck.

YERI-WAKE,–*ru*,–*ta*, エリワケル, 擇分, *t. v.* To pick out and separate, (as the good from the bad).

YERU, エル, The adjective form of *Ye*, 得, which see.

YERU, エル, 擇, or 彫, see *Yeri*.

YESASE,–*ru*,–*ta*, エサセル, 令得, caust. of *Ye*. To cause to get, or receive; to let have, to give.

YESASHIZAO, エサシザホ, 黏竿, *n.* A pole armed at the end with bird-lime for catching birds.

†YESE, エセ, (obs). *a.* Mean, vile, infamous, wicked. — *mono*, a vile fellow.

YESHAKU, エシヤク, 會釋, *n.* A courteous excuse, or apology for a seeming rudeness, as in passing in front of another, or drinking before another, = excuse me, beg pardon. *Yenriyo* — *mo nai*, without reserve or apology. Syn. SHIKIDAI.

YE-SHI, エシ, 畫師, *n.* A painter, or drawer of pictures.

†YESSHI,–*szru*,–*sh'ta*, エツスル, 謁, *t. v.* To visit a superior.

YETA, ヱタ, 穢多, *n.* A class of persons occupying the lowest social position, said to be descendants of Corean prisoners. They follow the occupation of leather-dressers, or buriers of dead animals; they are compelled to live separate from others and not allowed to enter a house, to sit, or cook at the same fire with persons out of their own class.

YETA, エタ, pret. of *Ye*, 得. Have got, have obtained. *Kiki-yeta*, have succeeded in hearing.

YETE, エテ, *pp.* of *Ye*, 得.

YETE, エテ, 得手, *n.* Experienced in doing, skilled, well versed, an adept, expert. *Teppō ga* — *da*, an adept in the use of a gun. *Nan-zo* — *ga aru ka*, what are you most expert at? — *katte wo szru*, to do according to one's own interest, to follow one's own inclination. Syn. TOKUI.

YETE,–*ru*,–*ta*, エテル, 得手, *i.v.* To be skilled or versed in, to be an adept at, expert in, experienced in. *Yeteta koto da kara shiyaszi*, as it is a thing I have experience in, it is easy to do.

YETO, エト, 甲乙, The ten stems, used in naming years, days, &c.

YETOKI, ヱトキ, 繪說, *n.* Explanation, illustration. — *wo szru*, to illustrate, or explain.

YETOKU,–*szru*, ヱトク, 會得, To comprehend, understand. Syn. NOMI-KOMU, GATEN SZRU.

†YETORI, ヱトリ, 穢取, *n.* (obs). The same as *Yeta*.

†YETSZ, エツ, 悅, (*yorokobi*). *n.* Joy, gladness. *Tai yetsz ni zonji soro*, shall be greatly delighted.

YETSZBO, エツボ, 笑壺, *n.* Used only in the phrase; — *ni iru*, to laugh.

YEYŌ, エエウ, 榮曜, *n.* Luxury, grandeur, magnificence, splendor. *Waga mi no* — *wo koto to nashi*, made luxury in living his only object. Syn. YEIG'WA, OGORI.

YEZŌ, ヱザウ, 繪像, *n.* A portrait, likeness.

YEZO, エゾ, 蝦夷, *n.* The island of Jesso.

YO, ヨ, 世, *n.* The world, age, generation; life; the times. *Kono* —, this world, this life. — *ni deru*, to become known, or famous. — *wo saru*, to leave the world, to die. — *wo szgiru*, to die. — *wo wataru*, to live. — *wo tszgu*, to inherit an estate. — *ga warui*, the times are bad. — *ga yo nara*, if times were as they used to be with me. — *no tszne no mono ni kawaru*, different from the generality of men. Syn. DAI, SEKEN, JISETSZ, SHABA.

YO, ヨ, 四, *a.* Four. Syn. SHI, YOTSZ.

†YO, ヨ, 予, (*ware*), *pro.* I. *Yo ga*, my.

YO, ヨ, 餘, (*amari*). More than, above; other, different, besides. *Ni jū yo nin*,

more than twenty men, twenty men or more. *Sen yo nen*, above a thousand years. — *no h'to*, another person. *Sono yo*, besides that, moreover.
Syn. HOKA, TA.

YO, ヨ, *n.* The part of a bamboo between the joints. *Take no yo*, a joint of bamboo. *F'ta yo*, two joints of bamboo.

YO, ヨ, An imperative or emphatic particle; as, *Mi yo*, look. *Kike yo*, listen. *Mate yo*, wait. *Yō-jin se yo*, be careful. *Iya da yo*, I won't. *Mo nai yo*, there is no more. *Shiranai yo*, I don't know, I tell you. *Abunai yo*, take care.

YO, ヨ, 夜, *n.* Night. — *ga aketa*, it is day light, or the morning has dawned. *Hon wo yonde yo wo akasz*, to spend the whole night in reading. — *wo hi ni tszide aruku*, to walk without stopping night and day.
Syn. YORU, YABUN, YA.

YŌ, ヨウ, 癰, *n.* A carbuncle.

YŌ, ヨウ, 用, *n.* Business, something to do, use. — *ga atte kimash'ta*, have come on business. *Omaye nan no — da*, what do you want? *Kiyō wa mō — wa nai*, have nothing more to do to-day. *Kono hako wa nan no — ni moshiiru no da*, what do you use this box for?

YŌ, ヤウ, 樣, Way, manner, mode; kind, sort; form, fashion, appearance, in order to, to the end that, for the purpose of, so as. *Kono — ni sh'te kudasare*, do it in this way. *Sono — na mono wa nai*, have nothing like it. *Aru — ni miyeru*, looks as if there was. *Nai — ni omō*, I think there is no appearance of it. *Koroba-nai — ni ki wo tszke-nasare*, take care that you don't fall. *Moredz —*, so as not to miss. *Ochi-nai — ni*, so as not to fall. *H'to no inochi wo taszkeru — ni*, in order to save life. *Ichi yō*, alike.
Syn. SAMA, TŌRI.

†YŌ, ヤウ, 陽, *n.* The male principal of nature in Chinese philosophy.

YŌ, エウ, 要, *(kaname)*, *n.* The principal thing, important subject, that which is essential. *Okotari naki wo — to sz*, make diligence the principal thing.
Syn. DAI ICHI, KANJIN.

†YŌ, エウ, 幼, *(itokenai)*, *n.* The young, youth.

YŌ, ヨウ, 好, (contr. of *Yoku*,) *adv.* Good, well. *Kore de — gozarimas*, this will do.

YŌ, ヨフ, 醉, see *Yoi*. Drunk.

YO-AKE, ヨアケ, 夜明, *n.* Dawn of day.
Syn. AKATSZKI, AKEBONO.

YO-AKINAI, ヨアキナイ, 夜商, *n.* A traffic carried on at night. — *wo szru*

YO-ARUKI, ヨアルキ, 夜行, *n.* Walking in the night. — *wo szru.*

YO-ASOBI, ヨアソビ, 夜遊, *n.* Night amusement. — *wo sh'te warui.*

†YOBAI, *-au, -atta*, ヨバフ, 喚, *i.v.* To cry out, call aloud. 婚, To marry a wife.
Syn. SAKEBU.

†YOBAI, ヨバヒ, 婚, *n.* Marrying a wife. (obs.), its present meaning is, illicit intercourse.

YOBAIBOSHI, ヨバヒボシ, 流星, *n.* A meteor, shooting star.

YŌBAISŌ, ヤウバイサウ, 楊梅瘡, *n.* A venereal eruption.

YO-BAN, ヨバン, 夜番, *n.* A night watch. — *wo szru.*

YOBARE, *-ru, -ta*, ヨバレル, 被呼, pass. of *Yobi.* To be called, invited, summoned.

YO-BATARAKI, ヨバタラキ, 夜動, *n.* Work done by night.

YOBAWARI, *-ru, -tta*, ヨバハル, 喚, *i. v.* To cry out, call aloud.

†YOBE, ヨベ, *n.* Last night; same as *Yūbe.*
Syn. SAKUBAN.

YOBE, ヨベ, *imp.* or *Yobi.*

YOBI, *-bu, -nda*, ヨブ, 呼, *t.v.* To call, to invite, to summon, to name; to marry a wife. *Te wo tataite yobu*, to call by clapping the hands. *Kiyaku wo —*, to invite a guest. *Kodzkai wo yonde koi*, call the servant. *Isha wo —*, to call a physician.
Syn. MANEKU.

YOBI, ヨビ, 呼, *n.* Call, invitation. — *ni yuku*, go to call. — *ni adzkaru*, to be invited. — *ni kita*, have come to call.

YOBI-ATSZME, *-ru, -ta*, ヨビアツメル, 呼集, *t. v.* To call together, to convoke, summon together.

YOBI-DASHI, *-sz, -sh'ta*, ヨビダス, 呼出, *t.v.* To call out, invite to come out, to challenge, banter.

YOBI-IKE, *-ru, -ta*, ヨビイケル, 呼生, *t. v.* To call to life; to revive by calling, (as a person in coma, or fainting).

YOBI-KAYESHI, *-sz, -sh'ta*, ヨビカヘス, 呼返, *t. v.* To call back, invite to return

YOBI-KOMI, *-mu, -nda*, ヨビコム, 呼込, *t.v.* To call in, invite to come in.

YOBI-KOYE, ヨビコヱ, 呼聲, *n.* The cry of street hucksters.

YOBI-MUKAYE, *-ru, -ta*, ヨビムカヘル, 呼迎, *t.v.* To call, or send for, to summon.

YOBINA, ヨビナ, 呼名, *n.* The name by which a person is generally known.
Syn. TS'USHŌ.

YOBI-YOSE,-ru,-ta, ヨビヨセル, 呼寄, *t.v.* To call near, to invite to approach.

YOBŌ, ヨバフ, same as *Yobau*, see *Yobai*.

YŌBŌ, エウバウ, 容貌, (*kaokatachi*), *n.* The countenance, form, features or expression of face.

YŌ-BO, ヤウボ, 養母, *n.* Foster-mother.

YOBU, ヨブ, 呼, see *Yobi*.

YOBUKO-NO-FUYE, ヨブコノフエ, 喚子笛, *n.* A whistle used for calling, or giving signals.

YO-BUN, ヨブン, 餘分, *n.* More than enough, more than one wants, needs, or deserves; too much, a superfluity, redundancy. — *ga aru nara kudasare*, if you have more than you want give it to me. — *ni wa irimasen*, I want no more than enough. Syn. YOKEI.

†YOCHI, ヨチ, 輿地, *n.* The earth, world. — *no dz*, a map of the world.
Syn. CHIKIU.

†YŌ-CHI, エウチ, 幼稚, *n.* A youth, child.
Syn. ITOKENAI, OSANAI.

YOCHI-YOCHI TO, ヨチヨチト, *adv.* The unsteady and tottering walk of a child. — *aruku.*

†YŌ-CHŌ, エウテウ, 窈窕, (*miyabiyaka*). Genteel, elegant, graceful, (of a lady's form).

YŌDACHI,-tsz,-tta, ヨウダツ, 用立, *i.v.* To be of use, useful.

YODACHI,-tsz,-tta, ヨダツ, *i.v.* To stand on end, (as the hair when one is cold, or frightened). *Mi no ke ga* —, his hair stood on end.

YŌ-DAI, ヨウダイ, 容體, *n.* Condition, state, circumstances. *Biyō-nin no — wo kiku*, to inquire after the state of a sick person. Syn. YŌSZ, ARISAMA.

YŌ-DAN, ヨウダン, 用談, *n.* Talking on business. — *ga atte kita*, have come to talk on business.

YODARE, ヨダレ, 涎, *n.* The saliva, (especially that flowing from the mouth of a child or animal), slaver, drivel. — *wo tareru*, idem.

YODARE-KAKE, ヨダレカケ, 涎掛, *n.* A small apron worn under the chin over armor, or under the chin of infants to catch the saliva.

YŌDATE,-ru,-ta, ヨウダテル, 用立, *t. v.* To lend. *Kane wo* —, to lend money.
Syn. KASZ.

YODO, ヨド, 淀, *n.* An eddy or sluggish place in a stream. Syn. FUCHI.

†YŌ-DŌ, エウドウ, 幼童, *n.* A child.
Syn. KODOMO.

YODOME,-ru,-ta, ヨドメル, 淀, *t.v.* To arrest the flow, to make stagnant, or dam a current of water. *Yodomeru midz*, stagnant water.

YODOMI,-mu,-nda, ヨドム, 淀, *i.v.* To be stagnant, or sluggish in its flow, as water; to be slow, or to hesitate in speaking, to falter. *Nagare ga* —, the current is stagnant. *Kotoba ga* —, to falter in speaking.

YODOMI, ヨドミ, 淀, *n.* Stagnation, or sluggishness in a current; torpor, hesitation in speaking.

YO-DŌSHI, ヨドホシ, 夜通, *n.* The whole night. — *aruku.* — *hanashi wo sh'ta.*
Syn. YOMOSZGARA.

YŌ-FU, ヤウフ, 養父, *n.* Foster-father.

YO-FUKAI,-KI,-KU,-SHI,-Ō,-SA, ヨフカイ, 夜深, Late at night. *Yofukaku kayetta*, came back late at night.

YO-FUKASHI, ヨフカシ, 夜深, *n.* Up late at night. *Mai ban no — de nemui*, by being up so late every night I am sleepy.

YO-FUNE, ヨフネ, 夜舟, *n.* A night boat. — *ni noru*, to travel in a boat by night.

YŌ-GAI, エウガイ, 要害, *n.* A place strong by nature, or well fortified, a fortress, stronghold. — *wo kamayeru*, to build a fortress.

†YŌ-GAKU, エウガク, 幼學, *n.* Literature for children.

†YŌ-GAN, ヨウガン, 容顔, *n.* The countenance, physiognomy.

YO-GARA, ヨガラ, 世柄, *n.* The state of the times. — *ga warui.*

YO-GATARI, ヨガタリ, 世語, *n.* Conversing about current subjects of the times.

YO-GEN, ヨゲン, 豫言, (*arakajime iu*). *n.* A prophecy, prediction, foretelling.

YO-GI, ヨギ, 夜衣, *n.* Night clothes.

†YŌ-GI, ヨウギ, 容儀, *n.* The countenance, or form of the body.

YŌ-GIN, ヤウギン, 洋銀, *n.* European coin, especially the dollar.

YOGINAI,-KI,-KU,-SHI,-Ō, ヨギナイ, 無餘義, That which must be done, than which there is no other way, necessary, indispensable, obligatory, unavoidable.
Syn. YONDOKORONAI, YAMUKOTO WO YEDZ.

YOGIRI,-ru,-tta, ヨギル, 過, *t.v.* To stop in passing. *Tomodachi no iye ni* —.

†YŌ-GŌ, ヤウガウ, 永劫, *n.* Eternity, (Budd.) Syn. YEI-YEI.

YO-GOMORI, ヨゴモリ, 夜籠, *n.* Passing the night in a temple for worshiping.

YOGORE,-ru,-ta, ヨゴレル, 汚, *i.v.* To be dirty, foul, filthy, to be unclean, defiled,

polluted. *Te ga* —, the hands are dirty. *Kimono ga* —, the clothes are dirty.
Syn. KEGARERU.

YOGORE, ヨゴレ, 汚, *n.* Dirt, filthiness, defilement. *Shiroi kimono wa — ga hayai,* white clothes are easily soiled.

YOGOREME, ヨゴレメ, 汚目, *n.* A dirty spot, stain.

YOGOSHI,–*sz,–sh'ta*, ヨゴス, 汚, *t. v.* To dirty, soil, foul, to make unclean, to defile, pollute. *Te wo* —, to soil the hands. *Kao wo* —, to make ashamed. Syn. KEGASZ.

YO-GOTO-NI, ヨゴトニ, 毎夜, Every night. Syn. MAIBAN.

YOHODO, ヨホド, 餘程, *adv.* A great deal, good many; almost, nearly; for the most part; very. — *dekita,* nearly done, best part is done. — *yoku dekimash'ta,* it is done very well. — *midz ni ochi-kakatta,* almost fell into the water. Syn. HOTONDO.

†YOHORO, ヨホロ, 丁, *n.* A laborer, a coolie. (obs.) Syn. NINSOKU.

YŌI, ヨウイ, 用意, *n.* Preparation, provision, readiness. *Ikusa no — wo szru,* to make preparation for war. *Tabi no — wo szru,* to get ready for a journey.
Syn. SHITAKU.

†YŌ-I, ヨウイ, 庸醫, *n.* A quack doctor, an unskilful physician.
Syn. YABU-ISHA.

YŌI, ヨウイ, 容易, Easy, not difficult. — *na koto,* an easy thing. — *ni,* easily. — *narazaru jisetsz,* difficult or troublous times. Syn. TAYASZI, ZŌSAMONAI.

YOI,–KI, ヨイ, 好, *a.* Good, right, well. *Yoi h'to,* a good man. *Sore de yoi,* that will do. *Mo yoi ka,* will that do? *Chōdo yoi,* just right. *Yoi toki ni kita,* came in a good time. *Yuku hō ga yoi,* it would be better to go. *Itte mo yoi,* you had better go.

YOI,–Ō,–*ōta*, ヨフ, 酔, *i.v.* To be drunk, intoxicated. *Sake ni yōta,* drunk. *Fune ni yō,* sea sick. *Kago ni* —, sick from riding in a chair. *H'to ni* —, sick from being in a crowd. Syn. YEI.

YOI, ヨヒ, 酔, *n.* Intoxication. — *ga sameru,* to become sober.

YOI, ヨヒ, 宵, *n.* Evening. Syn. YŪBE.

YO-ICHI, ヨイチ, 夜市, *n,* A market open at night.

YOI-DZKI, ヨヒヅキ, 宵月, *n.* An evening moon.

YOI-FUSHI,–*sz,–sh'ta*, ヨヒフス, 酔臥, *i.v.* To lie in a state of intoxication.
Syn. YEIFUSZ.

YOI-GOSHI, ヨヒゴシ, 宵越, *n.* Left over from the evening before. — *no mono wo taberu na,* don't eat any thing left &c.

YOI-GURUI, ヨヒグルヒ, 酔狂, Drunk and crazy. Syn. SZIKIYŌ, YEI-GURUI.

YŌ-IKU, ヤウイク, 養育, *(yashinai sodateru).* Nourishing and bringing up a child. *Kodomo wo — szru.*

YO-IKUSA, ヨイクサ, 夜戰, *n.* A battle in the night.

YOI-NE, ヨヒネ, 宵寐, (lit. evening sleep). Going to bed early. — *ga tszki,* likes to go early to bed.

YOIPPARI, ヨヒツパリ, 宵張, *n.* Sitting up late, (lit. spreading out the evening). — *no asane-dzki,* one late to bed and late to rise.

YOI-YAMI, ヨヒヤミ, 宵闇, *n.* The evenings in the month when there is no moon.

YOI-YOI, ヨイヨイ, *n.* yed. coll. Palsy of one side. Syn. CHIU-KI.

YŌ-JI, ヨウジ, 用事, *n.* Business, something to be done.
Nan no — de kita, what business have you come on? — *ga nai,* have nothing to do.

YŌJI, ヤウジ, 楊枝, *n.* The stick with which the Japanese clean their teeth, a tooth-brush. — *de ha wo migaku,* to clean the teeth with a tooth-brush. — *wo tszkau,* to use a tooth-brush.

YO-JI, ヨジ, 餘事, *(hoka no koto). n.* Another thing, anything else.

YOJI,–*ru,–ta*, ヨヂル, 攀, *t. v.* To climb up, (as a mountain) by laying hold of bushes and pulling one's self up. *Yama wo yoji-noboru.*

YŌ-JIN, ヨウジン, 用心, *n.* Caution, heed, care, or prudence in regard to danger; circumspection, watchfulness. — *ni shiku wa nashi,* there is nothing like cautiousness. *Hi no* —, careful about fire.

YOJIRE,–*ru,–ta*, ヨヂレル, *i. v.* To be twisted. *Obi ga yojirete iru,* your belt is twisted.

YOJIRI,–*ru,–tta*, ヨヂル, *t. v.* To twist. *Nawa wo* —, to twist a rope.

YO-JITSZ, ヨジツ, 餘日, *(amaru hi). n.* Remaining days, time yet remaining. — *ga nai kara isogashii,* as only a few days remain I am very busy.

YŌ-JO, ヤウヂヨ, 養女, *n.* A foster-child (female). adopted daughter.

†YŌ-JO, エウヂヨ, 幼女, *(osanaki onna).* A young girl.

YŌ-JŌ, ヤウジヤウ, 養生, *(sei wo yashinau).* Fostering, or preserving health, the care of one's health, (by attending to diet, apparel &c.) — *wo szru,* to take care of

one's health. — *no yoi h'to*, a person careful of his health. — *no hō*, the rules of hygiene. — *no tame ni undō szru*, to take exercise for the sake of health. — *ni naru*, healthful, good for one's health. — *ni naranu yō-ki*, an unhealthy climate.
Syn. HOYŌ.

†YŌ-JUTSZ, エウジユツ, 妖術, *n.* Magical arts.

YŌKA, ヤウカ, 八日, *n.* The eighth day of the month, or eight days.

‖YOKAMBEI, ヨカンベイ, 可好, (Yed. coll. cont. of *Yoku, aru, beshi.*) Will be good, or right, will do. *Kore de — ka*, do you think this will do? *Itte mo* —, I think you had better go. Syn. YOKARŌ.

YŌKAN, ヤウカン, 羊羹, *n.* A kind of confectionary made of sugar and beans.

†YOKAN, ヨカン, 餘寒, *n.* Cold weather continuing into the spring.

YOKARI,*-ru,-tta*, ヨカル, 好, *i.v.* (derived from *Yoku*, and *aru*), To be good, right, proper, well. *Yokaran*, or *Yokarō*, I think it will do. *Yokaranu*, not good. *Yokare-ash'kare*, whether good or bad no matter. *Ame ga furanai de yokatta*, it was well it did not rain.

YOKE,*-ru,-ta*, ヨケル, 避, *t. v.* To get out of the way of, to avoid, shun, evade, elude, to pass by; to keep off, fend off, protect from, to avert, to dodge. *Wazawai wo* —, to avert misfortune. *Kuruma wo* —, to get out of the way of a waggon. *Kaze, hi, nami, shimo nado wo* —, to protect any thing from the wind, sun, waves, or frost. *Michi wo* —, to give the way.
Syn. SAKERU, FUSEGU.

YOKE,*-ru,-ta*, ヨケル, 除, *t. v.* To take, or leave out of the number, to put aside, to except, to exclude, to omit, pass by. *Warui no wo yokete yoi no wo toru*, to reject the bad and take the good.
Syn. NOZOKU, NOKERU.

YOKEI, ヨケイ, 餘計, (*amaru bakari.*) More than the proper quantity, or than is necessary, too much, excess, a great deal, overmuch, superfluous. — *na kurō wo sh'ta*, have had unnecessary trouble. — *na koto wo iu na*, don't speak when you are not wanted.
Syn. YOBUN.

YOKERARE,*-ru-ta*, ヨケラレル, 被避, pass. or pot. of *Yoke*.

YOKI, ヨキ, *a.* Good, see *Yoi.*

YOKI, ヨキ, 斧, *n.* A broad axe.

YŌKI, ヤウキ, 陽氣, *n.* Climate; also, cheerful, lively. — *no warui tokoro*, a place the climate of which is bad. — *no sei*, the influence or effect of climate. — *na h'to*, a cheerful, lively person.
Syn. JIKŌ.

YŌ-KIN, ヨウキン, 用金, *n.* An extraordinary levy, or exaction of money from the people by government.

YŌ-KIU, ヤウキウ, 楊弓, *n.* A small bow, used as a toy.

†YŌKIYŌ, ヤウキヤウ, 佯狂, (*nise kichigai*). Feigned insanity.

YOKKA, ヨツカ, 四日, *n.* The fourth day of the month, or four days.

†YOKKAI, ヨクカイ, 欲界, *n.* This world. (Budd.)

YŌKŌ, ヤウコウ, 洋紅, *n.* Cochineal.

YOKO, ヨコ, 横, Across, crosswise, from side to side, athwart, transverse, horizontal, side ways. — *ga sanjaku*, three feet across. — *ye nagai*, long from side to side, or broad. *Kani ga — ni hau*, the crab goes sideways. — *ni kaku*, to write from side to side. — *ni kiru*, to cut transversely. — *ni naru*, to lie down.

YOKO-AI, ヨコアヒ, 横合, *n.* The side, or flank of an army.

YOKO-AME, ヨコアメ, 横雨, *n.* A driving rain.

YOKO-BUYE, ヨコブエ, 横笛, *n.* A flute.

YOKO-CHŌ, ヨコチヤウ, 横町, *n.* A cross-street.

YOKO-DE, ヨコデ, 横手, *n.* Used in the phrase; — *wo hatta to utsz*, to clap the hands.

YOKODORI, ヨコドリ, 横取, *n.* Seizing anything while passing along from one to another; trespassing, or encroaching on others. — *wo szru*, to trespass.

YOKOGI, ヨコギ, 横木, *n.* A cross-bar.

YOKO-GIRI,*-ru,-tta*, ヨコギル, 横切, *t. v.* To go across, transversely, or horizontally; to cut across, intersect. *Michi wo* —, to go across a road, also to block up and cut off a road. *Ame ga yokogitte furu*, the rains falls obliquely.

YOKO-GUMO, ヨコグモ, 横雲, *n.* A cloud spread out in horizontal strata.

YOKO-MACHI, ヨコマチ, 横町, *n.* A cross street.

YOKO-ME, ヨコメ, 横目, *n.* A secret police, a spy; askant. — *de miru*, to look askant. Syn. OKKAPPIKI.

YOKO-MICHI, ヨコミチ, 横道, *n.* A cross-road.

YOKO-MOJI, ヨコモジ, 横字, *n.* A word written cross wise.

YOKO-NAGA, ヨコナガ, 横長, Broad, wide, or greater in breadth than length.

YOKO-NAMARI,*-ru,-tta*, ヨコナマル, 訛, *t. v.* To corrupt or change the spelling, or pronunciation of a word.

YOKO-NE, ヨコネ, 便毒, *n.* A bubo, or enlarged inguinal gland.
Syn. BENDOKU.

YOKO-SAMA, ヨコサマ, 橫 樣, Crosswise, athwart, across, side ways. — *ni kiru*, to cut it crosswise.

YOKOSHI,*-sz,-sh'ta*, ヨコス, *t.v.* To give, hand over, to send; to receive, spoken only by the person to whom the article is given, or sent. *Kane wo yokoseba shiromono wo yaru*, if you pay me the money I will give you the goods. Syn. KURERU.

YOKOSHIMA, ヨコシマ, 邪, *(ja).* Wicked, vicious, malignant, depraved, corrupt. — *na kokoro.* — *na h'to.*

YOKOTAWARI,*-ru,-tta*, ヨコタハル, 橫, *i.v.* To be or lie across, or athwart. *Hebi ga michi ni yokotawatte tōraremasen* a snake is lying across the road and I cannot pass.

YOKOTAYE,*-ru,-ta*, ヨコタヘル, 橫, *t. v.* To place across, athwart, or horizontally. *Katana wo yokotayette aruku*, to walk with the sword sticking horizontally in the belt.

YOKO-TOJI, ヨコトヂ, 橫 綴, *n.* A book broader than it is long.

YOKO-TSZJIKAI, ヨコスヂカヒ, 橫 筋 違, Oblique, slanting, diagonal.

YOKO-YA, ヨコヤ, 橫 矢, *n.* An arrow coming crossways to one's direction.

YOKU, ヨク, 好, *adv.* see *Yoi.* Good, right, well. — *dekita*, it is well done. — *nai*, it is not good, bad.

YOKU, ヨク, 慾, *n.* Lust, inordinate desire, concupiscence, covetous. — *no fukai h'to*, an avaricious, or covetous person.
Syn. MUSABORI.

YOKU, ヨク, 翌, *a.* Next, ensuing, following. *Sono* —, the next day, mostly used in comp. words.

†YOKU, ヨク, 翼, *(tszbasa). n.* Wings. *Sa-yū* —, left and right wings, (of an army).

YOKUBARI,*-ru,-tta*, ヨクバル, 欲 張, *i.v.* To be covetous, avaricious, greedy.
Spn. MUSABORU.

YOKUBUKAI,-KI,-KU,-SHI,-Ō, ヨクブカイ, 欲 深, Covetous, avaricious, greedy.

YOKU-CHŌ, ヨクテウ, 翌 朝, *(akuru asa). n.* The next morning, the morning after.

YOKUININ, ヨクイニン, 薏 苡 仁, *n.* The fruit of the Coix lacryma.

YOKU-JITSZ, ヨクジツ, 翌 日, *(akuru hi). n.* The next day, succeeding day, or day after.

YOKU-NEN, ヨクネン, 翌 年, *(akuru toshi).* The next year, succeeding year.

†YOKURIU,*-szru*, ヨクリウ, 抑 留, *(oshitomeru).* To force to stop, or remain; to detain by force, to cause to desist.

†YOKUSHI,*-sz,-sh'ta*, ヨクスル, 浴, *i. v.* To bathe. Syn. ABIRU.

YOKU-SHIN, ヨクシン, 欲 心, Covetousness, avariciousness, cupidity.

†YOKU-SHITSZ, ヨクシツ, 浴 室, *n.* A bath room.
Syn. YUDONO.

YOKU-TOKU, ヨクトク, 欲 得, Greedy of gain, avaricious.

YOKU-TSZKI, ヨクツキ, 翌 月, *(akuru tszki).* The next month, month after.

YOKU-YOKU, ヨクヨク, 好 好, *adv.* Well, carefully, attentively.

YOMADZ, or YOMANU, ヨマズ, 不 讀, neg. of *Yomi.*

YOMARE,*-ru,-ta*, ヨマレル, 被 讀, pass. or pot. of *Yomi.* To be read. *Ji ga kiyete yomarenai*, the words are erased and cannot be read.

YOMASE,*-ru,-ta*, ヨマセル, 令 讀, caust. of *Yomi.* To cause, or let read, to order to read. *Kodomo wo* —, to make a child read.

YO-MAWARI, ヨマハリ, 夜 廻, *n.* A night watch, or patrol.

YOME, ヨメ, 媳, *n.* A daughter in law. — *wo toru*, to take a wife for a son. — *wo mukayeru*, idem.

YOME,*-ru,-ta*, ヨメル, 讀, poten. of *Yomi.* Can be read, or can read, legible. *Kono hon wa yomeru h'to ga nai*, no person can read this book. *Ano h'to no te wa yoku yomeru*, his hand writing is very legible.

YO-MEI, ヨメイ, 餘 命, *(amaru inochi).* The remnant, or residue of life, only spoken of aged persons. — *wa ikahodo mo nai.*

YOME-IRI, ヨメイリ, 嫁, *n.* The going of the bride to the house of her husband. — *wo szru.*

YOMENA, ヨメナ, 嫁 菜, *n.* A kind of greens.

YOMI,*-mu,-nda*, ヨム, 讀, *t.v.* To read. *Hon wo* —, to read a book. *Uta wo* —, to compose poetry. *Kadz wo* —, to count.

YOMI, ヨミ, 訓, *n.* The Japanese equivalent of a Chinese character.

†YOMI, ヨミ, 黄 泉, *n.* The place of departed spirits, hades of the *Sintoo.* — *no kuni*, idem.

YOMI-AGE,-*ru*,-*ta*, ヨミアグル, 讀上, *t.v.* To finish reading.

YOMI-AKIRAME,-*ru*,-*ta*, ヨミアキラメル, 讀明, *t.v.* To understand clearly any subject by reading.

YOMI-ATARI,-*ru*,-*tta*, ヨミアタル, 讀當, By reading to hit upon something one wants to find,

YOMI-AWASE,-*ru*,-*ta*, ヨミアハセル, 讀合, *t.v.* To read and compare, to collate.

YOMI-AYAMARI,-*ru*,-*tta*, ヨミアヤマル, 讀誤, *i.v.* To make a mistake in reading.

YO-MICHI, ヨミチ, 夜道, *n.* Going by night. — *yuku*, idem.

†YOMI-DZTO, ヨミヅト, *n.* A present, or offering sent to hades.

YOMI-GAYE,-*ru*,-*ta*, ヨミガヘル, 蘇, *i.v.* (lit. returning from hades). To return to life again, to revive.

YOMI-GATAI,-KI,-KU, ヨミガタイ, 讀難, Hard, or difficult to read. *Yomigataku nai*, not hard to read.

YOMIJI, ヨミヂ, 黄泉路, *n.* A road in Hades, by which, the souls of the dead, crossing, the *Shide* mountain and the *Sandz* river, travel to reach *Yemma shō*, the place of judgment. From this place two roads branch off, one to *Gokuraku*, (paradise), the other to *Jigoku*, (hell). Before crossing the river they are stripped of their clothes by an old woman, called *Sandz gawa no obāsan*. Budd.

YOMI-KAKE,-*ru*,-*ta*, ヨミカケル, 讀掛, *t.v.* To commence reading, or to be about to read.

YOMI-KAKI, ヨミカキ, 讀書, *n.* Reading and writing.

YOMI-KIKASE,-*ru*,-*ta*, ヨミキカセル, 讀聞, *t.v.* To read anything to another.

YOMI-KIRI, ヨミキリ, 讀切, *n*, Points or marks used in reading, punctuation. — *wo tszkeru*, to punctuate.

YOMI-KUCHI, ヨミクチ, 讀口, *n.* The place to commence reading.

YOMI-MONO, ヨミモノ, 讀物, *n.* Reading. — *wo szru*, to read.

YOMI-NARE,-*ru*,-*ta*, ヨミナレル, 讀馴, *t.v.* To be accustomed to read, to be familiar, or used to reading anything.

YOMI-NASHI,-*sz*-,*sh'ta*, ヨミナス, 讀成, *t.v.* To pretend to read, to read off something different from that which is written.

YOMI-NIKUI,-KI,-KU,-SHI, ヨミニクイ, 難讀, Difficult, or hard to read.

YO-MISE, ヨミセ, 夜店, *n.* A shop open for trade at night.

†YOMISHI,-*szru*,-*sh'ta*, ヨミズル, 好, *t.v.* To love. Syn. AISZRU.

YOMI-SOKONAI,-*au*,-*atta*, ヨミソコナフ, 讀損, *t. v.* To mistake in reading, to read wrong.

YŌ-MIYŌ, エウミヤウ, 幼名, (*osana na*). *n.* The name given to a child.

YOMO, ヨモ, 四方, Four sides, four quarters of the compass, all parts. Syn. SHI-HŌ.

YOMOGI, ヨモギ, 艾, *n.* Artemisia.

YOMOSZGARA, ヨモスガラ, 終夜, (*tetsz ya*). The whole night. Syn. YODŌSHI.

YOMOYA, ヨモヤ, *adv.* of conjecture, or surmise, = I rather think, am inclined to think, perhaps. — *uso de wa arumai*, I am inclined to think it is not false. Syn. YAWAKA.

YOMU, ヨム, 讀, see *Yomi.*

YŌMUKI, ヨウムキ, 用向, *n.* Business. Syn. YŌJI.

YŌ-NA, ヤウナ, 樣成, *a.* Like, similar, resembling. See *Yō*. *Ishi no — mono*, a thing like a stone. *Mita — h'to da*, like some one I have seen, or, think I have seen him before.

YO-NABE ヨナベ, 夜鍋, *n.* Any work done at night. — *wo szru*, to work, &c.

YO-NAKA, ヨナカ, 夜半, (*yahan*). *n.* Midnight.

YO-NAKI, ヨナキ, 夜啼, *n.* Crying at night (as an infant.)

YONA-YONA, ヨナヨナ, 夜夜, (*yo-yo*). *adv.* Every night. Syn. MAI-BAN.

YONDA, ヨンダ, *pret.* of *Yomi.* Have read.

YONDA, ヨンダ, *pret.* of *Yobu.* Has called.

YONDE, ヨンデ, *pp.* of *Yomi*, or *Yobu.*

YONDOKORONAI,-KI,-KU,-SHI,-Ō, ヨンドコロナイ, 無據, That must be done, necessary, unavoidable, obliged to be done. — *yō-ji ga atte Yedo ye yukimasz*, having unavoidable business I am going to Yedo. Syn. YAMU-KOTO-WO YEDZ, YOGINAI.

†YONE, ヨネ, 米, *n.* Rice. Syn. KOME.

YŌ-NEN, エウネン, 幼年, *n.* Youth, time of youth.

YŌ-NI, ヤウニ, 樣, *adv.* See *Yō.*

YO-NEN-NAKI,-KU,-SHI,-Ō, ヨネンナキ, 無餘念, Not minding or thinking about any thing, not having any thing on the mind, free from care, light hearted. — *tei*, a light hearted manner.

YŌ-NIN, ヨウニン, 用人, *n.* A chamberlain, or officers in a *Daimio's* court.

YŌ-NI-TACHI,-*tsz*,-*tta*, ヤウニタツ 益立, *i.v.* Fit, or good for use, useful, helpful, serviceable, Syn. YAKUNITATSZ.

YOPPARAI, *-au,-atta*, ヨツパラフ, Yed. coll. To be drunk, intoxicated. Syn. YO.

YOPPIKI, *-ku,-ita*, ヨクヒク, 能引, *i.v.* To draw a bow powerfully to the full length of the arrow. *Yoppite piyō to hanatsz.*

YOPPITEE, ヨツピテエ, 夜一夜, Yed. coll. The whole night. — *okite ita*, was up all night. YOJŪ, YOMOSZGARA.

YOPPODO, ヨツポド, 餘程, same as *Yohodo. adv.* A great deal, good many, much, for the most part, almost, nearly, very. — *dekita*, have done a great deal, or, almost done. — *ochi sō ni natta*, came near falling.

YORADZ, or YORANU, ヨラズ, 不依, neg. of *Yori. Nani ni yoradz*, no matter what. *Ikusa wa sei no ta sho ni* —, a battle does not depend on the size of an army.

YŌRAKU, エウラク, 瓔珞, *n.* A necklace worn by women, a fringe.

YORARE, *-ru,-ta*, ヨラレル, 被依, pass. of *Yori.*

YORASE, *-ru,-ta*, ヨラセル, 令依, caust. of *Yori.*

YORE, *-ru,-ta*, ヨレル, 搓, *i.v.* To be twisted. *Ito ga* —, the thread is twisted.

YORE, ヨレ, 搓, *n.* A twist, kink. *Nawa ni — ga aru*, the rope has a kink in it.

YORI, ヨリ, 自, or 從, *post-posit.* From, a sign of the ablative case: also 與, than, in comparing. *Yedo* —, from Yedo. *Ima* —, from this time, henceforth. *Neko — inu ga ōki*, a dog is larger than a cat. *Sore — mo kore ga yoi*, this is better than that. *Omōta — itakatta*, it hurt more than I thought it would. *Watakushi yori tanto motteoru*, he has more than I. Syn. KARA.

YORI, ヨリ, *n.* A sore, or gathering, so called from the supposition that an eruption, or the virus is collected into one spot.

YORI, *-ru,-tta*, ヨル, 搓, *t.v.* To twist, used only of twisting a single strand. *Kami wo* —, to twist paper. *Ito wo* —, to twist thread.

YORI, ヨリ, 搓, *n.* The twist of a cord or thread. — *no tszyoi ito*, a cord closely twisted. — *ga amai*, the twist is loose. — *wo kakeru*, to twist a cord still tighter.

YORI, *-ru,-tta*, ヨル, 擇, *t.v.* To choose, select, pick out. *Warui no wo yotte szteru*, to pick out the bad and throw them away. Syn. YERU, YERABU.

YORI, *-ru,-tta*, ヨル, 依, 集, 寄, 凭, 因, *i.v.* To approach, draw near; to call, or stop in passing; to assemble, or collect together; to lean upon, to depend on, rely on, to be according to, on account of, owing to. *Kaze ga fuite fune ga iso ni yoru*, the boat by the blowing of the wind nears the shore. *H'to no soba ye* —, to draw near to a person. *Tōri-gake ni yorimashō*, I will call as I pass by. *Kayeri-gake ni yori-nasare*, call as you come back. *Ōzei h'to tokoro ye* —, the crowd collected in one place. *Ran-kan ni yotte yaszmu*, to rest by leaning on the railing. *Tszye ni yotte tatsz*, stood leaning on his staff. *Shōbu wa toki no un ni yoru*, victory depends on the turn of fortune. *Watakushi no riyō-ji wa ano shomotsz ni yorimasen*, in my treatment of disease I do not go according to that book. *Mono no na wa tokoro ni yotte chigau*, the names of things vary with the place. *Koto ni yoru*, according to circumstances, or depends on circumstances. *Omaye no hone-ori ni yotte dekita*, finished through your industry. *Okage ni yotte naorimash'ta*, have got well through your kind assistance.

YORI-AI, *-au,-atta*, ヨリアフ, 集會, *i.v.* To assemble, or collect together. Syn. ATSZMARU.

YORI-AWASE, *-ru,-ta*, ヨリアハセル, 搓合, *t.v.* To twist together.

YORI-BITO, ヨリビト, 擇人, *n.* The person chosen, or elected.

YORI-BŌ, ヨリボウ, 捍棒, *n.* An oak pole or club six feet long used by policemen.

YORI-DASHI, *-sz,-sh'ta*, ヨリダス, 擇出, *t.v.* To select, choose, elect, pick out. Syn. YERAMI-DASZ.

YORI-DOKORO, ヨリドコロ, 據, *n.* Something to rest, or depend on; a basis, foundation, proof, used only of statements, doctrines, opinions, &c. — *mo nai setsz*, a saying that has nothing to substantiate it. Syn. SHŌKO.

YORI-ITO, ヨリイト, 搓絲, *n.* Thread.

YORI-KAKARI, *-ru,-tta*, ヨリカカル, 凭掛, *i.v.* To lean upon. Syn. MOTARERU.

YORIKI, ヨリキ, 與力, *n.* A policeman, or constable, a grade higher than *Dōshin.*

YORI-KOMI, *-mu,-nda*, ヨリコム, 搓込, *t.v.* To twist into, as a string into a hole.

YORI-KOZORI, *-ru,-tta*, ヨリコゾル, 集舉, *i.v.* To assemble. Syn. ATSZMARU.

YORI-KUDZ, ヨリクヅ, 擇屑, *n.* The refuse left after picking out the best.

YORI-ME, ヨリメ, 搓目, *n.* The mark, or crease in a string made by twisting it.

YORI-NUKI, *-ku,-ita*, ヨリヌク, 擇拔, *t.v.* To select, choose out.

YORI-NUKI, ヨリヌキ, 擇拔, *n.* Anything choice, select, or highly approved.

YORI-SOI,-*ō*,-*ōta*, ヨリソフ, 依添, *i. v.* To be near the side of another.

YORI-TSZGI,-*gu*,-*ida*, ヨリツグ, 搓續, *t. v.* To join to, splice or lengthen by twisting the ends together.

†YO-RIU, ヨリウ, 餘流, *n.* A branch, or off-shoot, as a sect.

YO-RIYOKU, ヨリヨク, 餘力, *n.* Spare time, leisure. — *aru toki.* Syn. HIMA.

YORI-YORI, ヨリヨリ, 折折, same as *Ori-ori.* Sometimes, occasionally.
Syn. TOKI-DOKI.

YOROBOI,-*ō*,-*ōta*, ヨロボフ, *i.v.* To stagger, to reel. *Sake ni yotte yorobōta*, he staggered from intoxication.
Syn. HIYORO-HIYORO SZRU.

YORODZ, ヨロヅ, 萬, *n.* Ten thousand. — *no mono*, all things. Syn. BAN, or MAN.

YOROI,-*ō*,-*ōta*, ヨロフ, 鎧, *t.v.* To wear a coat of mail, or armor. *Yorōtaru musha*, a soldier clothed in armor.

YOROI, ヨロヒ, 鎧, *n.* A coat of mail.

YOROKOBASHI,-*sz*,-*sh'ta*, ヨロコバス, 令悅, caust. of *Yorokobu.* To cause to rejoice.

YOROKOBASHII,-KI,-KU,-Ū, ヨロコバシイ, 悅, Joyful, glad.

YOROKOBI,-*bu*,-*nda*, ヨロコブ, 悅, *i. v.* To rejoice, to be glad, joyful, pleased. *Sei-ji ga yoi kara tami ga* —, the people rejoice because of good government.
Syn. URESHIGARU.

YOROKOBI, ヨロコビ, 悅, Joy, gladness, pleasure. — *wo iu*, to congratulate, to express one's joy. Syn. URESHISA.

YOROMEKI,-*ku*,-*ita*, ヨロメク, *i. v.* To stagger, reel. Syn. YOROBOI.

YOROSHII,-KI,-KU,-Ū,-SA, ヨロシイ, 宜, That which is good, right, proper; well. *Kore de yoroshii*, this will do. *Sakana wa yoroshiu gozarimas'ka*, do you want to buy any fish? *Mina sama ye yoroshiku iute kudasare*, present my compliments to your family. *Mo yoroshii*, that will do. *Yoroshiku o tanomi mōshimas*, please do the best you can for me. *Yoroshiku nai*, it is not right. Syn. YOI.

YORO-YORO, ヨロヨロ, *adv.* In a staggering, reeling manner. *Namayoi ga — to aruku.*

YORU, ヨル, see *Yori.*

YORU, ヨル, 夜, *n.* Night. — *no mono*, bed clothes. Syn. YA.

YORUBE, ヨルベ, *n.* One to depend on, or look to for aid; a friend helper. — *naki mi wo nani to sen*, what will become of me who have no helper? Syn. TAYORI.

YO-RIU, ヨルイ, 餘類, *n.* The remnant of a gang, or company.

YORUSE, ヨルセ, same as *Yorube.*

YOSA, ヨサ, 好, *n.* The goodness, excellence, see *Yoi.*

YŌ-SAKI, ヨウサキ, 用先, *n.* The place where one has business, or something to do.

YOSAMU, ヨサム, 夜寒, *n.* Cold nights. The period of the year when the nights are cold.

YOSASŌ-NA, ヨサヽウナ, *a.* Having the appearance of being good. *Aji no — sakana*, a fish that looks as if it might taste good.

†YŌSATSZ, エウサツ, 夭札, Dying when young. — *szru*,

YOSE, ヨセ, imp. of *Yoshi.* Stop.

YOSE, ヨセ, *n.* A house where public entertainments are given, such as story-telling, singing, dancing, topspinning, &c. — *no teishu*, the proprietor of a *Yose.*

YOSE,-*ru*,-*ta*, ヨセル, 寄, 集, *t.v.* To bring near, cause to approach; to cause or order to call, or stop in passing; to gather, collect, assemble; to bring close together. *H'to wo yosete kōshaku wo kikaseru*, to assemble people and lecture to them. *Soba ye* —, to cause to come near.
Syn. ATSZMERU.

YOSE-ATSZME,-*ru*,-*ta*, ヨセアツメル, 寄集, *t. v.* To gather, collect, or assemble together.

YOSEKI, ヨセキ, 輿石, *n.* Arsenic.

YOSERU, ヨセル, see *Yose.*

YOSE-TE, ヨセテ, 寄手, *n.* The attacking force, storming party.

YOSE-TSZGI, ヨセツギ, 寄接, *n.* A mode of grafting, done by binding together two branches of different trees that have been slightly pared, and after they have knit together, detaching one of them.

YŌ-SHA, ヨウシヤ, 用捨, *n.* Regard, or attention to circumstances, consideration. — *wo sh'te hanashi wo szru*, to speak considering well the persons to whom one is talking. — *mo naku*, without regard to any one; irrespectively, regardless of persons.

YŌ-SHA, ヨウシヤ, 容赦, *n.* Pardon. — *kudasare*, pardon me, excuse me.
Syn. KAN-NIN.

YOSHI, ヨシ, 由, *n.* Subject, matter, affair, event, thing, fact, case, circumstance; reason, cause. *Kono — wo kuwashiku chiu-*

shin se-yo, give a particular report of this matter. *Yoshi nashi*, useless. — *aru h'to*, a person of good family.
Syn. KOTO, OMOMUKI.

YOSHI, ヨシ, 好 or 吉, see *Yoi*. It is good, right, or well. — *ashi*, good or bad.

YOSHI, ヨシ, 葦, *n*. Rush, same as *Ashi*.

YOSHI, ヨシ, 縱, *adv*. Very well, never mind, all right, it is enough.

YŌSHI, ヤウシ, 養子, *n*. A foster-child, an adopted son.

YOSHI,*-sz,-sh'ta*, ヨス, 止, *t.v.* To stop, quit, to leave off, give up, to cease. *Mo yoshimashō*, I will stop. *Shigoto wo yosh'te kayetta*, he has stopped work and gone home. Syn. YAMERU, OKU.

YOSHIDZ, ヨシズ, 葦簾, *n*. A mat made of rushes. — *bari*, a booth in the street for selling small wares.

YOSHIGO, ヨシゴ, 蘆芽, *n*. The young sprouts of the *Yoshi*.

YOSHI-KA, ヨシカ, (*yoshi*, well, and *ka* interrogative), Used in calling attention, in explaining or narrating anything. = do you understand? do you perceive? well?

YOSHI-KIRI, ヨシキリ, 葦切, *n*. The name of a small bird.

YOSHIMBA, ヨシンバ, If, supposing that. — *atta tote shikata ga nai*, even supposing you had it, it would be of no avail.
Syn. TATOI, MOSHI.

YOSHIMI, ヨシミ, 好, *n*. Friendship, friendly relations, intimacy, good will. *Kingoku no* —, the friendship of a neighboring state. — *wo muszbu*, to contract friendly relations. Syn. NASAKE, SHITASHIMI.

YOSHINA-NI, ヨシナニ, same as *Yoroshiku*. — *o negai mōshimas*, I beg your kind assistance. — *otorimashi kudasari-mase*.

YOSHI-YA, ヨシヤ, *adv*. If, but if, but supposing that.
Syn. TATOI, MOSHI.

YOSHI-YOSHI, ヨシヨシ, 好好, Exclam. of consent, or permission; = very well, all right, very good. Syn. YOROSHII.

YŌ-SHŌ, エウセウ, 幼少, Youth, time of childhood. — *no toki kara*, from one's youth. Syn. ITOKENAI, OSANAI.

YOSO, ヨソ, 餘所, (*hoka no tokoro*). Another or different place, abroad, away, elsewhere, foreign. — *ye ita*, has gone out. — *no koto wa kamaimasen*, I will not meddle with other people's business. — *ni mite tōru*, to pass by without noticing. — *no h'to*, a stranger, or a person of another place, or family. — *no kuni*, another country. — *nagara*, although a stranger, or, one whom it don't concern.
Syn. TASHO.

YOSŌ, ヨサウ, fut. of *Yoshi*. I think I will stop? — *to omō tokoro ni*, just as I was thinking of stopping.

YOSŌ, ヨソフ, see *Yosoi*.

YŌ-SO, ヨウソ, 癰疽, *n*. Cancer.

YOSOGAMASHII,-KI,-KU,-U, ヨソガマシイ, Like, or in the manner of a stranger, distant, reserved, cold or disinterested in behavior.

YOSO-GOTO, ヨソゴト, 外事, *a*. Something belonging to another, that which does not concern one's self, something foreign.

YOSOI,*-ō,-ōta*, ヨソフ, *t.v.* To put rice into a cup, to help one to rice. *Meshi wo* —.
Syn. TSZGU, MORU.

†YOSOJI, ヨソヂ, 四十, *n*. Forty years of age. Syn. SHIJISSAI.

YOSOME, ヨソメ, 餘所目, *n*. The eyes of another, or of one disinterested, the eyes or notice of others. — *ni miru*, to look at with the eyes of one whom the matter don't concern. — *wo habakaru*, to shrink from, or avoid the notice of others. — *hadzkashii*, to feel ashamed of the notice of others. Syn. OKAME.

YOSOMI, ヨソミ, 餘所見, *n*. Looking off from what one is doing. — *sedz ni hon wo yome*, read, and don't look off your book.

YOSOOI,*-ō-,ōta*, ヨソホフ, 粧, *t. v.* To adorn, ornament, to dress up. *Mi wo* —, to adorn one's self.
Syn. KAZARU, YATSZSZ.

YOSOYE,*-ru,-ta*, ヨソヘル, 準, *t.v.* To liken to, to represent, compare to, resemble, to personify. *Mokuzō wo kami ni yosoyete ogamu*, to worship a wooden image supposing it to represent the deity.
Syn. NAZORAYERU.

YOSO-YOSOSHII,-KI,-KU, ヨソヨソシイ, Like a stranger in manner, cold, distant, indifferent, unconcerned, or disinterested in manner.

YOSZ, ヨス, 止, see *Yoshi*.

YŌSZ, ヤウス, 様子, *n*. State, condition, circumstances. *Teki no* — *wo ukagau*, to spy out the state of the enemy. *Fune no* — *wo ukagau*, to examine into the condition of the ship. *Biyō-nin no* —, the state of a patient. Syn. YŌ-DAI, ARISAMA.

YŌSZAI, ヤウスアヒ, 様子合, *n*. The same as *Yōsz*, the state, condition.

YOSZGA, ヨスガ, 緣, *n*. Connection, affinity; opportunity, or convenient way; something to depend on. *Chikaki* —, near relation. *Tegami wo yaru* — *mo nai*, no opportunity for sending a letter. *O masz wo tomeru — no ame*, a rain which came most opportunely to keep *O masz* from going. Syn. TAYORI, CHINAMI, YEN.

YOSZGARA, ヨスガラ, 終夜, The whole night. Syn. YOJŪ.

YO-SZGI, ヨスギ, 世過, *n.* A living, support, livelihood. *— ga deki-kaneru*, hard to make a living.

YŌSZI, ヨウスイ, 用水, *n.* Water used or kept ready for irrigation, fires, &c.

YŌ-SZJI, ヨウスヂ, 用筋, *n.* Business, some thing to be done. Syn. YŌJI.

YŌ-SZKI, ヨウスキ, 用透, *n.* Interval of rest, or leisure between work or business. *— ni ikimashō*, I will go between working hours. Syn. TESZKI.

YŌ-SZMI, ヨウスミ, 用濟, *n.* Completion, or finishing of any business. *Kon nichi wa mō — da*, the business is finished to day.

YO-SZMI, ヨスミ, 四隅, *n.* The four inside corners.

YO-SZTE-BITO, ヨステビト, 世捨人, *n.* One who forsakes the world, — a wandering bonze. Syn. UNSZI.

YŌSZU, ヤウスウ, 陽數, *n.* Odd numbers. Syn. HAN.

YŌTA, エフタ, pret. of *Yoi*. Drunk.

YOTAKA, ヨダカ, 夜發, *n.* A low prostitute.

YOTARI, ヨタリ, 四人, *(yonin)*. Four persons.

YOTŌ, ヨダウ, 夜盜, *n.* A night robber. Syn. DOROBŌ.

YO-TŌ, ヨタウ, 餘黨, *(amari no tomogara)*. The remnant of a company, or gang. Syn. YO-RUI, ZANTŌ.

YOTOGI, ヨトギ, 夜伽, *n.* Sitting up at night with a sick-person. *— wo szru.*

YOTSZ, ヨツ, 四, *n.* Four. Syn. YO, SHI.

YOTSZ-ASHI, ヨツアシ, 四足, *n.* A four footed-animal.

YOTSZ-DAKE, ヨツダケ, 四竹, *n.* Castanets. *— wo utsz*, to play with castanets.

YOTSZDE, or YOTSZDEAMI, ヨツデ, 四手, *n.* A net for catching fish, let down by the four corners.

YOTSZDE-KAGO, ヨツデカゴ, 四手籠, *n.* An inferior kind of sedan chair, suspended by the four corners to the pole.

YO-TSZGI, ヨツギ, 世續, *n.* An heir. Syn. ATOTSZGI.

YOTSZJIRO, ヨツジロ, 四白, *n.* A horse with four white feet.

YOTSZME, ヨツメ, 四目, *n.* A figure of this shape 囲.

YOTSZ-MEGIRI, ヨツメギリ, 四稜錐, *n.* A drill with four faces.

YOTSZ-TSZJI, ヨツツヂ, 四辻, *n.* Cross-roads.

YOTTA, ヨツタ, pret. of *Yori*.

YOTTA, ヨツタ, coll. pret of *Yoi*. Incorrectly used for *Yōta*,

YOTTARI, ヨツタリ, coll. for *Yotari*.

YOTTE, ヨツテ, *pp.* of *Yoi*. Drunk, also *pp.* of *Yori*.

YO-UCHI, ヨウチ, 夜打, A night attack. *— wo szru*, to make an attack at night.

†YOWA, ヨハ, 夜, *n.* Night.

YOWAGE, ヨワゲ, 弱氣, *n.* Appearing to be feeble or weak. *— na h'to.*

YOWA-GOSHI, ヨワゴシ, 弱腰, *n.* Weak in the loins.

YOWAGI, ヨワギ, 弱氣, *n.* Dispirited, discouraged. *— wo dasz*, to become discouraged.

†YOWAI, ヨハヒ, 齡, *n.* Age. *Tszru wa sen nen no —*, the age of a crane is a thousand years. Syn. TOSHI.

YOWAI,-KI,-KU,-SHI, ヨワイ, 弱, Weak, not strong, feeble, infirm. *Yowai h'to*, a weak man. *Yowai nawa*, a weak rope. *— shōchiu*, weak alcohol. *Kuni ga —*, the state is weak. Syn. JŪJAKU, HINIYAKU.

YOWAKU, ヨワク, 弱, *adv.* Idem. *— naru*, to become weak. *— nai*, not weak. *Nawa ga — te kireru*, the rope is weak and will break.

YOWAME,*-ru,-ta*, ヨワメル, 弱, *t. v.* To weaken, to enfeeble, debilitate, enervate.

YOWAMI, ヨワミ, 弱, *n.* Weakness, feebleness, weak place, or time of weakness. *Teki no — wo tszke-konde semeru*, to discover the enemy's weakness and attack him.

YOWARASE,*-ru,-ta*, ヨワラセル, 令弱, caust. of *Yowari*. To cause to become weak, to weaken.

YOWARI,*-ru,-tta* ヨワル, 弱, *i.v.* To be weak, feeble, debilitated.

YOWATARI, ヨワタリ, 世渡, *(tosei)*. *n.* Passing through the world, a living, subsistence. *— wo shi-kaneru*, hard to make a living. Syn. KUCHI-SZGI.

YOWASA, ヨワサ, 弱, *n.* Weakness, feebleness. *Chikara ga — ni maketa*, was defeated on account of weakness.

YOWASHI, ヨワシ, 弱, see *Yowai*.

YOWA-YOWASHII,-KI,-KU,-Ū, ヨワヨワシイ, Having the appearance of weakness.

YŌYAKU, ヤウヤク, 漸, *adv.* At last, at length, after long waiting, or great difficulty, scarcely, hardly, barely. *— o ten-*

ki ni natta, it has at last become pleasant weather. Syn. YATTO, YOYO.

YŌ-YŌ, ヤウヤウ, 漸, *adv.* Contraction of *Yōyaku.*

YOYO, ヨヨ, *adv.* The sound, or voice of one crying. —*to naku.*

‖YOYO, ヨヨ, *n.* A calf.

YU, ユ, 湯, *n.* Hot water. —*wo wakasz*, to boil water. —*ga watta*, the water has boiled. —*ni hairu*, to bathe in hot water.

YU, or YUDZ, ユ, 柚, *n.* A pumelo.

YŪ, ユフ, 結, see *Yui.*

YŪ, ユフ, 木綿, *n.* A kind of cloth made of the bark of the mulberry, worn in ancient times.

YUABI, ユアビ, same as *Yuami.*

YU-AGARI, ユアガリ, 湯上, *n.* Coming out of a hot bath.

YU-AMI, ユアミ, 浴, *n.* Bathing in hot water. —*wo szru*

YU-BA, ユバ, 湯場, *n.* A place where there are hot springs. Syn. TŌJIBA.

YUBA, ユバ, 湯葉, *n.* A kind of food made of beans.

YŪBE, ユフベ, 夕, *n.* The evening; also, last night. Syn. BAN, SAKUBAN.

YUBESHI, ユベシ, 柚醬, *n.* A kind of confectionary made of the rind of the pumelo.

†YŪ-BI, ユウビ, 優美, Genteel, refined, graceful, gentle. —*no szgata.* —*no koye.* Syn. JŌHIN, MIYABIYAKA.

YUBI, ユビ, 指, *n.* A finger. *H'to ni — wo sasz*, to point the finger at a person. *Oya-yubi*, the thumb. *H'to sashi* —, the index finger. *Naka* —, the middle finger. *Beni-sashi* —, the ring finger. *Ko* —, the little finger — *wo otte kazoyeru*, to count with the fingers. —*no saki*, the tip of the finger.

YU-BIKI, ユビキ, 湯引, *n.* Sponging certain kinds of new cloth, in order to take out the starch.

YUBI-MAKI, ユビマキ, 指環, *n.* A finger ring. Syn. YUBIWA.

YUBI-NUKI, ユビヌキ, 指貫, *n.* A thimble.

YUBI-ORI, ユビオリ, 屈指, *n.* Counting upon the fingers. —*wo szru*, to count on the fingers. —*no h'to*, a few persons, whose number may be counted on the fingers.

YUBI-WA, ユビワ, 指環, *n.* A finger-ring.

YUBI-ZASHI, ユビザシ, 指, *n.* Pointing the finger. *H'to ni — wo sh'te warau*, to point the finger at a person and laugh. —*wo sh'te oshiyeru*, to inform by pointing with the finger.

†YŪ-CHŌ, ユウチヤウ, 優長, Sedate, calm, composed, magnanimous.

YŪ-DACHI, ユフダチ, 夕立, *n.* A shower, a thunder storm, squall.

YU-DAMA, ユダマ, 湯玉, *n.* The bubbles in boiling water.

YU-DAN, ユダン, 油斷, *n.* Negligence, inattention, slothfulness, heedlessness, carelessness, remissness. —*tai-teki*, negligence is a great enemy, (prov.) —*wo szru*, to be negligent. —*naku kagiyō wo hagemu*, to attend industriously to one's calling. Syn. OKOTARI.

YUDANE,-*ru*,-*ta*, ユダヌル, 委, *t. v.* To commit to the will, or control of another, to leave to another, to intrust, to delegate, to confide. *Matszrigoto wo shin ni* —, to commit the government to the ministers. Syn. MAKASERU, NINDZRU.

YUDARI,-*ru*,-*tta*, ユダル, 煠, *i.v.* To be cooked by boiling. *Tamago wa mada yudari-masen*, the eggs are not yet done, (by boiling). *Imo ga yudatta*, the potatoes are boiled. Syn. NIYERU.

YUDATE, ユダテ, 湯立, *n.* The ceremony of boiling water before the *Kami* and sprinkling it around with a bunch of bamboo, for purification.

YUDE,-*ru*,-*ta*, ユデル, 煠, *t.v.* To cook by boiling. *Tamago wo* —, to boil eggs. Syn. NIRU.

YU-DŌFU, ユドウフ, 湯豆腐, *n.* Boiled *tōfu.*

YUDONO, ユドノ, 浴室, *n.* A bath room. Syn. FUROBA, YOKUSHITSZ.

YUDZ, ユズ, 柚子, A pumelo, same as *Yu.*

YUDZKE, ユヅケ, 湯漬, *n.* Rice eaten with hot water poured on it.

YŪ-DZKI-YO, ユフヅキヨ, 夕月夜, *n.* A moonlight evening.

YUDZRI,-*ru*,-*tta*, ユヅル, 讓, *t.v.* To cede, yield, resign, give up, to give place to, relinquish. *Kurai wo* —, to resign the throne. *Za wo* —, to give up a seat to another. *Kagiyō wo* —, to relinquish business in favor of another.

YUDZRI, ユヅリ, 讓, *n.* Resignation, cession, yielding, or giving up. —*wo ukeru.*

YUDZRIJŌ, ユヅリジヤウ, 讓狀, *n.* A deed of conveyance, a grant in writing.

YŪDZU, ユウヅウ, 融通, *n.* The circulation of money from one to another; trade, business. —*ga warui*, trade is dull. *Fu* —, idem.

YŪFUKU, ユウフク, 有福, Wealthy, rich. —*na h'to*, a rich man.

YUGAKE, ユガケ, 韘, *n.* A glove worn by archers to protect the hand.

YUGAKI, *-ku, -ita*, ユガク, 湯掻, *i.v.* To cook slightly by pouring boiling water over, to scald.

YUGAME, *-ru, -ta*, ユガメル, *t. v.* To turn from a straight line, or right direction, to incline, to bend, crook. *Take wo* —, to bend a bamboo. Syn. KAGAMERU, MAGERU.

YUGAMI, *-mu, -nda* ユガム, 歪, *i.v.* To be awry, inclined from the right direction, crooked, bent, distorted, askew. *Hata-zao ga yuganda*, the flag-staff is not perpendicular. *Katana ga* —, the sword is bent. Syn. MAGARU, KAGAMU.

YŪGAO, ユフガホ, 夕顔, *n.* The flower of a species of gourd that opens in the night.

YUGE, ユゲ, 汽, *n.* Steam, vapor of boiling water. Syn. JŌKI.

†YŪGE, ユウゲ, 晩飯, *n.* Supper. Syn. YŪMESHI.

YŪ-GEI, ユウゲイ, 遊藝, *n.* Amusing arts or performances, such as music, and the drama.

YUGU, ユグ, 湯具, *n.* The inside garment worn by women, from the waist to below the knee, originally worn on entering a bath. Syn. YUMOJI.

YŪ-GUN, ユウグン, 遊軍, *n.* The reserve corps of an army. Syn. YUHEI.

YŪ-GURE, ユフグレ, 夕暮, *n.* The period just after sun-set, twilight.

YŪ-HEI, ユウヘイ, 遊兵, *n.* The reserved corps of an army.

YUI, *-ū, -ūta*, ユフ, 結, *t.v.* To tie, used only of the hair. *Kami wo* —, to dress and tie up the hair.

†YUI-GAI, ユヰガイ, 遺骸, *n.* A dead body, corpse. Syn. SHIGAI.

YUI-GEN, or YUIGON, ユヰゲン, 遺言, *n.* The verbal will, or last directions of a dying person; (in Japan it is not a custom to write a will, nor has a *Yuigon* any legal authority). — *szru.*

YUI-KAI, ユヰカイ, 遺誡, (*nokosz imashime*). *n.* The dying instructions, or exhortations, as of a parent, or teacher. *Oya no — wo mamoru.*

YUI-KOTSZ, ユヰコツ, 遺骨, (*nokoru hone*). *n.* The pieces of bone left after burning a dead body.

YUI-MOTSZ, ユヰモツ, 遺物, (*nokosz mono*). *n.* The things left by a deceased person; or a present made by a person about to die, a legacy, bequest.

YŪ-IN, *-szru*, ユウイン, 誘引, (*izanau*). To persuade to go along with. Syn. IZANAU.

YUI-NŌ, ユヒナフ, 結納, *n.* The present made to a woman at the time of espousal, (customarily of fish, *sake*, a belt, and money.)

YUI-SEKI, ユヰセキ, 遺跡, (*nokoru ato*). The writing left by a deceased person, the ruins, or remains of an ancient place, house, castle, &c. Syn. KOSEKI, KIUSEKI.

YUI-SHO, ユイシヨ, 由緒, *n.* Pedigree, lineage, descent. — *tadashii h'to.* — *wo tadasz*, to examine into the pedigree. Syn. YURAI, RAIREKI.

YUI-TSZKE, *-ru, -ta*, ユヒツケル, 結付, *t.v.* To bind fast to, to tie something on another. Syn. MUSZBI-TSZKERU.

†YŪ-JIN, ユウジン, 友人, *n.* A friend, companion. Syn. TOMODACHI.

YŪ-JIN, ユウジン, 遊人, *n.* A man of leisure; one who lives without business, or occupation.

YŪ-JO, ユウヂヨ, 遊女, (*asobime*). *n.* A harlot. Syn. JŌRO.

†YU-JUN, ユジユン, 由旬, *n.* A measure of distance of uncertain length, used by the Buddhists. Paradise is said to be 84,000 *yujun* to the west of this world.

YUKA, ユカ, 床, *n.* The floor; used only of the ground-floor. — *no sh'ta*, beneath the floor.

YŪ-KAGE, ユウカゲ, 夕影, *n.* The evening shadows, twilight.

YUKA-JITA, ユカジタ, 牀下, *n.* Under the floor of a house, beneath the house.

YUKARE, *-ru, -ta*, ユカレル, 被行, pass. and poten. of *Yuki*. Can go. *Michi ga nai kara yukarenu*, as there is no road you cannot go. *Kono michi wa yukareru ka*, can I go along this road?

YUKARI, ユカリ, 緣, *n.* Relation, affinity, connection, acquaintance. Syn. YEN, CHINAMI, YOSZGA.

YUKASE, *-ru, -ta*, ユカセル, 令行, caust. of *Yuki*. To cause to, or let go.

†YUKASHII, -KI, -KU, -U, -SA, ユカシイ, That which is absent or past, and is tenderly thought of, or yearned after. Syn. NATSZKASHII, KOISHII.

YUKATA, ユカタ, 涼衣, *n.* A thin garment of a single thickness worn in summer.

YŪ-KATA, ユフカタ, 夕方, *n.* The evening, about sundown.

YUKE, ユケ, imper. of *Yuki*. Go.

YŪ-KEI, ユフケイ, 夕景, *n.* The evening.

†YŪ-KEN, ユウケン, 勇健, Well, in good

health. *Go — ni on kurashi nasare o medetaku zonji soro.*

YUKI, ユキ, *n.* The same as *Katayuki.*

YUKI,*-ku,-ita*, ユク, 行, *i.v.* To go. *Yedo ye —*, to go to Yedo.
Syn. IKU, MAIRU.

YŪ-KI, ユウキ, 勇氣, *n.* Courage, bravery, boldness. *— ga tszyoi.*

YUKI, ユキ, 雪, *n.* Snow. *— ga furu*, it snows.

YUKI-AI,*-au,-atta*, ユキアフ, 行合, *i. v.* To meet in the way from opposite directions.

YUKI-AKARI, ユキアカリ, 雪光, *n.* Snow light, or light caused by the snow. *— de aruku.*

YUKI-ATARI,*-ru,-tta*, ユキアタル, 行當, *t. v.* To walk against, to strike against while going.

YUKI-BOTOKE, ユキボトケ, 雪佛, *n.* An image made of snow.

YUKI-DAMA, ユキダマ, 雪玉, *n.* A snowball.

YUKI-DOKE, ユキドケ, 雪消, *n.* The thawing of the snow.

YUKI-DOKORO, ユキドコロ, 行所, *n.* The place to which one is going; the place where any one has gone. *— ga shirenu*, don't know where he is gone.

YUKI-DOMARI, ユキドマリ, 行止, *n.* The end of a road, or end of one's journey.

YUKI-CHIGAI,*-au,-atta*, ユキチガフ, 行違, *i.v.* To pass each other in the way.

YUKI-GAKE, ユキガケ, 行掛, *n.* While going. *— ni cha-ya ye yoru*, to stop at a tea-house while going to any place.

YUKI-GATA, ユキガタ, 行方, *n.* The place where any one has gone. *— ga shirenai*, don't know where he has gone.

YUKIGE-NO-MIDZ, ユキゲノミヅ, 雪消水, *n.* Snow-water.

YUKI-KAI,*-au,-atta*, ユキカフ, 往來, *(ō rai)*, *i.v.* To go and come, to go to and fro. Syn. YUKIKI.

YUKI-KAYERI,*-ru,-tta*, ユキカヘル, 往反, *i.v.* To go and returu.

YUKI-KAYOI,*-ō,-ōta*, ユキカヨフ, 往通, *i.v.* To go and come often, to be in the habit of going and coming.

YUKI-KI, ユキ, 往來, (*ō-rai*). *n.* Going and coming, passing to and fro; intercourse, or visiting backward and forward.

YUKI-KOROBASHI, ユキコロバシ, 雪轉, *n.* Rolling snow into large balls. *— wo szru.*

YUKI-KŌ, ユキカフ, see *Yukikai.*

YUKI-KURE,*-ru,-ta*, ユキクレル, 行暮, *i.v.* To be belated in going.

YUKI-NO-SH'TA, ユキノシタ, 石荷, *n.* The name of a flower, the Saxifraga sarmentosa.

YUKI-OROSHI, ユキオロシ, 雪卸, *n.* A snow-slip, avalanche. Syn. NADARE.

YUKI-SZGI,*-ru,-ta*, ユキスギル, 行過, *t.v.* To go too far, go beyond. *Yukō to omō tokoro yori yukiszgita*, went beyond the place he was going to.

YUKI-TODOKI,*-ku,-ita*, ユキトドク, 行届, *i.v.* To extend, or reach to the utmost, to be thorough, complete, perfect. *Gimmi ga yuki-todoita*, the examination was thorough. *Kami no miru koto wa nani goto ni mo yuki-todokanu tokoro wa nai*, there is nothing that God does not see.

YŪ-KIYO, ユウキヨ, 幽居, *(samushiki szmai).* *n.* A lonely dwelling.

YŪ-KIYŌ, ユウキヨウ, 遊興, *n.* Pleasure and amusement.

YUKKURI-TO, ユツクリト, 緩, *adv.* Leisurely, not in haste, not in a hurry to return.

YUKŌ, ユカウ, fut. of *Yuku.* Will, or would go. *Yedo ye yukō*, I shall go, or am thinking of going to Yedo.

YUKU, ユク, *adj.* and final form of *Yuki*, 行. To go. *—h'to wa dare*, who is going? *— tokoro ga nai*, no place to go to.

†YŪ-KUN, ユウクン, 遊君, *n.* A harlot.
Syn. JŌRO.

†YUKURI-NAKU, ユクリナク, 不意, *adv.* Unexpectedly, suddenly.
Syn. FUI, F'TO, OMOWADZ-NI.

YUKU-SAKI, ユクサキ, 行先, *n.* The journey, or distance to the place one is going, the place to which one is going, destination, the future. *— ga nagai.* *— wa doko da*, where are you going to? *— wa shirenu*, don't know where I am going.
Syn. YUKUYE.

YUKU-SZYE, ユクスヱ, 行末, *n.* The future, the time to come. *— wo omō*, to think of the future.

YUKUYE, ユクヘ, 行方, *n.* The place to which one is going, or has gone, the whereabouts. *H'to no — wo tadzneru*, to inquire where a person has gone. *— wo shiranu*, d'ont know where he has gone.
Syn. YUKUSAKI.

YUKU-YUKU, ユクユク, 行行, *adv.* In future, as time elapses. Syn. NOCHI-NOCHI.

YŪ-MAGURE, ユウマグレ, 夕間暮, *n.* The evening twilight.

YUMAKI, ユマキ, 湯纏, *n.* The cloth worn by women around the loins. Syn. YUGU.

YUME, ユメ, 夢, *n.* A dream. — *wo miru*, to dream. — *ga sameru*, to wake from a dream. — *no yo no naka*, this world so like a dream. — *ni mo zonzedz*, not even dreaming of such a thing. Syn. IME.

†YUME, ユメ, 努, *obs.* always follows the neg. impert. particle *na*, to which it gives emphasis, = beware of, take heed that you do not.

YŪ-MEI, イウメイ, 有名, Having a name celebrated, famous.
Syn. NADAKAI, KŌMEI.

YUME-MI,-*ru*,-*ta*, ユメミル, 夢, *t.v.* To dream. *Nani wo yumemita*, what did you dream about?

YUME-MI, ユメミ, 夢見, *n.* Dreaming.

YŪ-MEN, ユウメン, 宥免, *n.* Pardon, forgiveness. — *szru*, to pardon.
Syn. YURUSZ, SHAMEN.

YŪ-MESHI, ユウメシ, 夕飯, *n.* Supper.

YUME-URANAI, ユメウラナヒ, 夢占, *n.* Divining one's future by means of a dream.

YUME-YUME, ユメユメ, 努努, *adv.* Positively, certainly, peremptorily. — *kono kotoba wo h'to ni morasz koto nakare*, beware that you don't tell this to any one.
Syn. KESSH'TE.

YUMI, ユミ, 弓, *n.* A bow. — *wo iru*, to shoot a bow. — *no tszru*, a bow-string.
Syn. KIU.

YUMI-DZRU, ユミヅル, 弓絃, *n.* A bow-string.

YUMI-GATA, ユミガタ, 弓形, *n.* Bow shaped, an arch.

YUMI-HARI-DZKI, ユミハリヅキ, 弓張月, *n.* The moon when three or four days old.

YUMI-TSZKURI, ユミツクリ, 弓作, *n.* A bow maker.

YUMI-YA, ユミヤ, 弓矢, *n.* Bow and arrow, arms. — *no michi*, the rules of war. — *tori*, a soldier. — *gami*, the god of war; viz. *Hachi-man.*

YUMOJI, ユモジ, *n.* The inside garment worn by women from the waist to the knee.

YUN-DE, ユンデ, 弓手, *n.* The hand in which the bow is held; viz. the left. — *mete*, the left and right hand.

YUNDZYE, ユンヅヱ, 弓杖, *n.* Using the bow as a cane. — *ni szgatte tatsz*, stood leaning on his bow.

YUN-ZEI, ユンゼイ, 弓勢, (*yumi no ikioi*). The power of a bow or the force of an arrow. — *no tszyoi h'to*, a person who draws a strong bow.

YU-NI, ユニ, 湯煮, *n.* Cooking with boiling water. — *wo szru.*

YU-NIU, ユニウ, 輸入, *n.* Imports of merchandize.

YU-RAI, ユライ, 由來, *n.* The origin and subsequent history, the rise and progress, history.
Syn. G'WAN-RAI, YENGI.

†YŪ-RAKU, ユウラク, 遊樂, (*asobi tanoshimu*). *n.* Pleasure, sport, amusement.

YURAMEKI,-*ku*,-*ita*, ユラメク, *i.v.* To move or swing to and fro, to roll or rock from side to side, as a boat; to vibrate, oscillate. *Fune ga* —, the ship rolls.

†YŪ-RAN, ユウラン, 遊覽, (*asobi miru*). Looking at for amusement, or sport. — *szru.*

YURARE,-*ru*,-*ta*, ユラレル, 被搖, pass. of *Yuri.* To be rocked, swung, shaken. *Fune, kago nado ni* —, to be rocked in a boat, or norimon.

YURARI-TO, ユラリト, *adv.* With a waving or swinging motion; like a person springing nimbly into the saddle. *Uma ni — uchi-noru*, to spring nimbly upon a horse.

YURA-YURA, ユラユラ, *adv.* Swinging, rocking, rolling, vibrating, or oscillating to and fro. *Fune ga — szru*, the boat rocks.

YURE,-*ru*,-*ta*, ユレル, 搖, *i.v.* To rock from side to side, to swing.

YŪ-REI, ユウレイ, 幽靈, *n.* A ghost, an apparition, phantom, spectre. — *ga deta*, a ghost appeared. Syn. ONRIYŌ.

YŪ-REKI, ユウレキ, 遊歷, (*asobi heru*). Travelling for pleasure. — *szru. Shokoku wo — szru.*

YŪ-RETSZ, ユウレツ, 優劣, (*masari otori*). *n.* Superiority or inferiority. *Kuni no — wo arasō*, to dispute about the comparative excellence of different countries. — *wa nai.*

YŪRI, ユウリ, 遊里, *n.* The prostitute quarters in a town. Syn. KURUWA.

YURI, ユリ, 百合, *n.* The lily.

YURI,-*ru*,-*tta*, ユル, 搖, *t.v.* To rock, to move to and fro, to swing, to shake, to sift by shaking. *Ji-shin ga yuru*, there is an earthquake. *Nami ga fune wo* —, the waves rock the ship. *Kome wo* —, to wash rice by shaking.

YURI,-*riru*,-*rita*, ユリル, 許, *i.v.* To be pardoned, forgiven, excused, to be allowed, permitted. *Tszmi ga yurita*, the crime is pardoned.
Syn. YURUSARERU.

YURI-AGE,-*ru*,-*ta*, ユリアゲル, 搖上, *t.v.* To sift out or separate by sifting.

Shinsho wo —, to run through one's property.

YŪ-RIKI, ユウリキ, 勇力, *n.* Strength. Syn. CHIKARA.

YURI-KOMI,-*mu*,-*nda*, ユリコム, 搖込, *t. v.* To pack down by shaking, as tea in a box.

YURI-KUDZSHI,-*sz*,-*sh'ta*, ユリクヅス, 搖崩, *t. v.* To shake down, to cause to fall by shaking, (as an earthquake).

YURI-WAKE,-*ru*,-*ta*, ユリワケル, 淘分, *t. v.* To separate by shaking, as with a sieve; to bolt, to clean by sifting.

YURU, ユル, see *Yuri.*

YURUBE,-*ru*,-*ta*, ユルベル, 弛, *t. v.* same as, *Yurumeru.*

YURUBI,-*bu*,-*nda*, ユルブ, see *Yurumi.*

YURUGASHI,-*sz*,-*sh'ta*, ユルガス, caust. of *Yurugu.* To cause to shake, or rock.

YURUGI,-*gu*,-*ida*, ユルグ, 動搖, (*dōyō*). *i. v.* To shake, vibrate, rock, to swing, to move to and fro, to be loose, to quake, tremble. *Jishin de iye ga* —, the house is shaken by the earthquake. *Ha ga* —, the tooth is loose. *Kugi ga* —, the nail is loose. Syn. UGOKU.

YURUI,-KI,-SHI, ユルイ, 緩, *a.* Slack, not tense nor tight, loose, easy, lax, not firm, flabby, soft, limber, nor strict, nor severe; remiss. *Nawa ga yurui*, the rope is slack. *Go hatto ga* —, the laws are not strict. *Kutsz ga* —, the shoe is loose.

YURUKASE, ユルカセ, 忽, In the phrase; — *ni szru*, to slight, disregard, neglect, despise. Syn. OROSOKA.

YURUKU, ユルク, *adv.* see *Yurui.* — *szru*, to slacken, relax, soften. — *naru*, to become slack. — *nai*, not slack, tense.

YURUMARI,-*ru*,-*tta*, ユルマル, 緩, *i.v.* To be slack, lax, loose; to become weak, lose zeal, or ardor.

YURUME,-*ru*,-*ta*, ユルメル, 緩, *t. v.* To make less tense, tight, or severe; to slacken loosen, relax one's attention or care. *Tszmi wo* —, to mitigate the punishment of crime. Syn. KUTSZROGERU.

YURUME-GUSZRI, ユルメグスリ, 緩藥, *n.* Anodyne medicines.

YURUMI,-*mu*,-*nda*, ユルム, 緩, *i. v.* To be slack, lax, loose, soft, flabby, flaccid, to be remiss, to remit zeal, activity, or attention, to flag. *Samusa ga* —, the cold has moderated. *Ki ga* —, to become remiss, or negligent. *Itami ga* —, the pain has abated. Syn. KUTSZROGU.

YURURI, ユルリ, A hearth; same as *Irori.*

YURURI-TO, ユルリト, *adv.* Not in a hurry or haste, leisurely, slowly, taking time and ease. — *yasznde iki-nasare*, take a little rest and then go on your journey. Syn. YUKKURI.

YURUSA, ユルサ, 緩, *n.* Slackness, looseness, tension.

YURUSARE,-*ru*-*ta*, ユルサレル, 被許, pass. of *Yurushi.* To be allowed, permitted, pardoned, excused.

YURUSHI,-*sz*,-*sh'ta*, ユルス, 許, *t. v.* To grant, allow, permit; to let go, set free; to accede to; to yield, to pardon, to forgive, to excuse. *Negai wo* —, to grant a petition. *Tszmi wo* —, to pardon a crime. *Ki wo* —, to refuse confidence in. *Onna ni ki wo yurusz na*, don't confide in a woman. *Yurush'te kudasare*, or *O yurushi nasare*, pardon me. Syn. SHA-MEN SZRU; SHŌCHI SZRU.

YURUSHI, ユルシ, 許, *n.* Permission, leave, forgiveness, pardon. — *wo ukeru* to receive pardon. Syn. MEN-KIYO.

YURUSHI, ユルシ, 緩, see *Yurui.*

YURUYAKA, ユルヤカ, 緩, Not strict, severe, or rigorous; slack, lax, easy, lenient, gentle.

YURU-YURU, ユルユル, 緩緩, *adv.* Leisurely, without hurry or haste, slowly. — *to aruku*, to walk leisurely. Syn. SORO-SORO.

YUSAN ユサン, 遊山, *n.* A pleasure excursion, a picnic. — *bune*, a pleasure boat. — *szru*, to go on a picnic. Syn. ASOBI.

YŪSARI, ユウサリ, 夕去, *n.* The night. Syn. YORU.

YUSAWARI, ユサハリ, 鞦韆, *n.* A swing. Syn. BURANKO.

YŪ-SEN, ユウセン, 勇戰, *n.* Fighting bravely or heroically. — *szru.*

YU-SEN, ユセン, 湯錢, *n.* The price of a bath.

YUSEN, ユセン, 湯煎, *n.* Heating by the waterbath, by placing the vessel containing the substance to be heated in boiling water. — *ni szru.*

YŪ-SHA, ユウシヤ, 勇者, *n.* A brave man.

YŪ-SHI, ユウシ, 勇士, *n.* A brave soldier.

†YŪSHI, ユウシ, 有司, *n.* A civil officer. officer of government. Syn. YAKUNIN.

†YUSHUTSZ,-*szru*, ユシユツ, 涌出, (*waki deru*). To spring, or issue forth, as water from the earth.

YU-SHUTSZ, ユシユツ, 輸出, *n.* The export of merchandize. — *ga ōi*, the exports are large.

YUSZ, ユス, 榕樹, *n.* The name of a tree, the Ficus pyrifolia.

YUSZBURI,–*ru*,–*tta*, ユスブル, 搖, *t. v.* To shake anything standing, as a tree, pole &c. *Ki wo yuszbutte mi wo otosz,* to shake off the fruit from a tree.

YŪ-SZDZMI, ユウスズミ, 夕涼, *n.* The cool of the evening.

YUSZGI,–*gu*,–*ida*, ユスグ, 潔, *t. v.* To cleanse by washing, to wash. *Te wo* —, to wash the hands. Syn. SZSZGU, ARAU.

YUSZRA, ユスラ, 珠櫻, *n.* A tree which yields a fruit something like a cherry, the Prunus tomentosa.

YUSZRI, ユスリ, *n.* Extortion of money by fraud, threat, or intimidation.
Syn. NEDARI, KATARI.

YUSZRI,–*ru*,–*tta*, ユスル, 搖, *t.v.* To shake anything standing, as a tree, pole; to extort. *Ki wo* —, to shake a tree. *Yusztte kane wo toru,* to extort money.
Syn. UGOKASZ.

YUSZRI-KOMI,–*mu*,–*nda*, ユスリコム, same as, *Yurikomi.*

YUTAKA, ユタカ, 豐, Abundance, plenty, prosperity, affluence. — *ni kurasz,* to live in plenty. — *na.* Abundant, plentiful, copious, fruitful, prolific, rich. — *na kuni,* a rich and fertile country. Syn. JŪBUN.

YUTAN, ユタン, 油單, *n.* An oil cloth for covering goods, or a large cloth used for wrapping.

YUTA-YUTA, ユタユタ, 湛湛, *adv.* In a rocking manner, as a boat.

YUTŌ, ユトウ, 油桶, *n.* An oil-can.
Syn. ABURA-TSZGI.

YUTORI,–*ru*,–*tta*, ユトル, *i. v.* To linger, to stop for a while, to delay. *Michi ni* —, to linger in the way.

YU-TSZGI, ユツギ, 湯次, *n.* A pot for holding hot water.

YUWADZ, ユハズ, 不結, neg. of *Yui.*

YUWASE,–*ru*,–*ta*, ユハセル, caust. of *Yui.*

YUWAYE,–*ru*,–*ta*, ユハヘル, pass. of *Yui.*

YUWŌ, ユワウ, 硫黄, *n.* Sulphur.

YU-YA, ユヤ, 湯屋, *n.* A public bath-house.

YŪ-YAKE, ユウヤケ, 晩霞, *n.* The red and glorious appearance of the western clouds when the sun is setting. — *ga szru.*

YŪ-YAMI, ユウヤミ, 夕闇, *n.* An evening without moonlight.

YUYE, ユヱ, 故, *n.* Reason, cause, account, sake, because, effect, consequence, result. *Hiru yoru no wakaru — wa nani,* what is the cause of day and night? *Chi wa nan no — de meguru,* what is the cause of the circulation of the blood? *Nani — konna nangi wo szru koto yara,* why am I thus afflicted? *Omaye — nara washa dokoma-demo kara tenjiku no hate made mo,* (song), for your sake I will go any-where, even to the end of India and China. *Shiranu koto — shikata ga nai,* because you were ignorant of it there is nothing more to be done. *Kono yuye ni,* on this account, therefore. *Sono yuye ni,* on that account. Syn. SEI, WAKE, SHOI, YUYEN.

YUYEN, ユヱン, 所以, *n.* Reason, cause. *Sono — wo tadznuru ni,* in inquiring into the cause of it. Syn. YUYE.

YU-YEN, ユエン, 油烟, *n.* Lamp black.

YŪ-YO, ユウヨ, 猶豫, *n.* Hesitation, doubt, quandary, perplexity. *Ikaga sen to — szru,* to hesitate what to do.
Syn. KOGI, NI-NO-ASHI WO FUMU, TAME-RAU.

YŪ-YO, ヰウヨ, 有餘, (*amari ari*). *n.* Room, space, or time remaining; redundancy, excess, more than, something over. — *ga nai,* there is no room left, or there is nothing over. *Roku-jū — no rōjin,* an old man of more than sixty years. — *no aru yō ni kiru,* cut it so that there shall be something over.

YŪ-YŪ, ユウユウ, 悠悠, *adv.* In an easy, quiet way; free from labor, want, or trouble. — *to sh'te hi wo kurasz,* to live an easy and quiet life.

YU-YU-SHII,–KI,–KU, ユユシイ, 雄雄敷, Having a gallant, grand, or martial appearance. *Yuyushiku idetatsz,* to march out in a gallant and imposing manner.

Z

ZA, ザ, 座, *n.* A seat, place to sit in. — *ni tszku,* to take one's seat. — *wo tatsz,* to rise from a seat. — *wo yudzru,* to yield a seat. — *szru,* to sit down. Syn. SEKI.

ZA-BUTON, ザブトン, 座蒲團, *n.* A rug or cushion for sitting on.

ZABU-ZABU, ザブザブ, *adv.* The sound of the splashing of water. *Midz ga — to naru. Midz wo — to kakeru.*

ZA-CHIU, ザチウ, 座中, *n.* In or of the assembly, or session, during the session.

ZAGU, ザグ, 座具, *n.* A cloth on which a Bonze sits when praying.

ZAI, ザイ, 罪, (*tszmi*). *n.* Crime, transgression of law, sin. — *wo okasz,* to commit a crime.

ZAI, ザイ, 財, (*takara*). *n.* Wealth, riches, property. — *wo musaboru,* to covet wealth.

ZAI, ザイ, 在, *n.* The country, a place away from a town. *Kanagawa no* —, the country near Kanagawa. — *no h'to*, a countryman, rustic.

ZAI-GO, ザイゴ, 在鄉, *n.* The country, or place away from a town. — *ni oru*, to live in the country. Syn. INAKA.

ZAI-GŌ, ザイガフ, 罪業, *n.* Sin, (Budd). *Zensei no* —, the sins committed in a previous state. — *ga fukai*, his sins are great. Syn. TSZMI.

ZAI-HAN, ザイハン, 在判, (*han ari*). *n.* Having a seal, sealed. — *no kakitszke*, a sealed writing.

ZAI-HŌ, ザイホウ, 財寶, *n.* Money, riches. Syn. TAKARA.

ZAI-I, ザイ井, 在位, (*kurai ni aru*). *n.* Upon the throne. — *no Tenshi*, the reigning emperor. — *wo manzai to inoru*, to pray that the reigning monarch may reign a thousand years.

†ZAI-JŌ, ザイジヤウ, 罪狀, *n.* The nature or kind of crime.

ZAI-JŪ, ザイヂユウ, 在住, Now residing, a resident. *Yedo* — *na h'to*, a person now residing in Yedo.

ZAI-KIN, ザイキン, 在勤, (*tsztome ni aru*). Discharging official duty, in office. *Yokohama* — *no mono domo*, officers doing duty in Yokohama.

ZAI-MEI, ザイメイ, 在名, (*na aru*). Having the maker's name inscribed, as a sword. — *no katana*.

ZAI-MOKU, ザイモク, 材木, *n.* Timber, for building; lumber.

ZAI-MOKU-YA, ザイモクヤ, 材木屋, *n.* A lumberyard, or a person who sells timber.

ZAI-MOTSZ, ザイモツ, 財物, (*takara mono*). Precious things, any article of value.

ZAI-NIN, ザイニン, 罪人, (*tszmibito*). *n.* A criminal, a sinner. Syn. TOGA-NIN.

ZAI-RIU, ザイリウ, 在留, Dwelling, living, residing. *Tō-ji yedo* — *no daimiyō*, the nobles now residing in Yedo.

ZAI-SE, ザイセ, 在世, (*yo ni aru*), Living in the world. *Chichi ga* — *no toki*, when my father was living. Syn. ZOM-MEI.

ZAI-SHO, ザイシヨ, 在所, *n.* Place of one's birth, native place; the country. — *wa doko da*, where were you born? — *no h'to*, a countryman, a native of a place. Syn. KOKIYŌ.

†ZAI-SHŌ, ザイシヤウ, 罪障, (*tszmi sawari*), *n.* Sins, (which are an obstruction in the way to paradise). Budd. — *wo shōmetsz szru*.

ZAI-SHUKU, ザイシユク, 在宿, (*yado ni iru*). At home. — *bi*, the days when one is at home. *Sensei wa* — *de gozarimas ka*, is Mr. —— at home?

ZAI-TAKU, ザイタク, 在宅, (*iye ni aru*). At home, in the house.

ZAI-YAKU, ザイヤク, 在役, (*yaku ni aru*). In office. — *chiu ni*, while in office.

ZAKO, ザコ, 雜魚, *n.* A general name for any small fish.

ZAKOBA, ザコバ, 雜魚塲, *n.* A fish-market.

ZAKOKU, ザコク, 雜穀, *n.* All kinds of grain.

ZAKONE, ザコ子, 雜寢, *n.* Sleeping crowded confusedly together.

ZAKURO, ザクロ, 柘榴, *n.* The pomegranate, Punica granatum.

ZAKURO-BANA, ザクロバナ, *n.* A grogblossom, the red nose of a grog-drinker.

ZAMBU-TO, or ZAMBURI-TO, ザンブト, *adv.* The sound made by any thing falling into water. — *midz ni tobi-komu.*

ZAM-BUTSZ, ザンブツ, 殘物, *n.* Any thing left over, or remaining; the residue, remnants.

ZAMOTO, ザモト, 座元, *n.* The manager of a theatre, or show.

ZAM-PEI, ザンペイ, 殘兵, *n.* The residue of a defeated army.

ZAN, ザン, 讒, *n.* Slander, calumny, false charges. — *wo kamayeru*, to get up a slander.

ZANGE, ザンゲ, 懺悔, same as *Sange.*

ZANGEN, ザンゲン, 讒言, *n.* Slander, calumny, detraction, false charges. — *wo szru*, to slander, to malign. — *wo shindzru*, to believe a slander.

†ZANGI, ザンギ, 慚愧, (*haji hajiru*). *n.* Shame. — *wo idaku*, to feel ashamed. Syn. HADZKASHII.

ZAN-GIN, ザンギン, 殘銀, (*nokoru kane*). Remaining money, remainder, or balance of the money not yet paid. — *wa ikura*, how much money is there yet due? — *wa itszka szgite haraimashō*, I will pay the balance in five days.

ZAN-GIRI, ザンギリ, 殘切, *n.* The hair worn long and combed back in the manner of some Japanese physicians.

ZAN-JI, ザンジ, 暫時, *n.* Short space of time, a little while. — *ni*, soon, quickly, in a little while. — *no aida*. — *no uchi*. Syn. SHIBARAKU, SZKOSHI NO AIDA.

ZAN-KAN, ザンカン, 殘寒, (*nokoru samusa*). *n.* The cold weather yet remaining.

ZAN-KIN, ザンキン, 殘金, *n.* same as *Zan-*

gin; used only for money of a higher denomination.

ZAN-K'WA, ザンクワ, 殘花, (nokoru hana). The flowers yet remaining.

ZAN-NEN, ザンネン, 殘念, n. Regret, sorrow, disappointment felt at the failure of hope, expectation, or desire. *Kataki wo utadz ni shinuru no ga — da*, I regret that my enemy should die without being slain. Syn. KUCHI-OSHII, KUYASHII, MUNEN.

ZAN-NIU, ザンニフ, 攙入, n. Interpolation. — *szru*, to interpolate.

†ZAN-NIN, ザンニン, 殘忍, n. Cruel, devoid of pity, inhuman. — *na h'to*, a cruel man. Syn. BŌ-AKU, NASAKENAI.

†ZAN-SETSZ, ザンセツ, 殘雪, (*nokoru yuki*). n. The snow yet remaining.

†ZAN-SHA, ザンシャ, 讒者, n. A slanderer, calumniator.

ZANSHI,–*szru*,–*sh'ta*, ザンスル, 讒, t.v. To slander, calumniate, bring false charges against.
Syn. SHIKODZRU.

ZAN-SHO, ザンショ, 殘暑, (*nokoru atszsa*). n. The remainder of the hot weather.

ZAN-SHU, ザンシュ, 殘酒, (*nokoru sake*). n. The remainder of the *sake*.

ZAN-SO, ザンソ, 讒訴, n. False charges, or complaints against another made to a ruler, official slander.

ZAN-ZAI, ザンザイ, 斬罪, n. Capital punishment. — *ni okonau*.

ZAPPI, ザッピ, 雜費, n. Expenses, disbursements of money. *Ikusa no — ga ōi*, the expenses of war are great.
Syn. NIU-YŌ.

ZARARI-TO, ザラリト, *adv.* Rough to the feel, or hearing. — *te ni sawaru*.

ZARA-TSZKI,–*ku*,–*ita*, ザラツク, i.v. To be rough, not smooth to the feel, as sand, &c. *Kona ga* —, the flour feels rough.

ZARA-ZARA, ザラザラ, *adv.* In a manner rough or harsh to the feel, or hearing. *Te-atari ga — szru*, it feels rough.

ZARE,–*ru*,–*ta*, ザレル, same as *Jare*. To sport, play, frolic.

ZAREKOTO, ザレコト, 諧謔, n. Jesting, joking, facetious or playful talk. — *wo iu*.

ZARI, ザリ, see *Jari*.

ZARU, ザル, 笊, n. A basket.

ZARU, ザル, 不, a neg. adjective suffix to verbs, formed from *dz*, and *aru*; the same as *Nu*. *Kami no shirazaru koto nashi*, God knows all things. *Omowazaru saiwai wo yeta*, have got an unexpected good fortune.

ZA-SEKI, ザセキ, 座席, n. An apartment or room, a place of meeting or assembly.

ZASHI,–*sz*,–*sh'ta*, ザス, 座, i.v. To sit in the Japanese manner. *Tatami ni* —, to sit upon a mat. Syn. SZWARU.

ZA-SHIKI, ザシキ, 座敷, n. A room, or apartment.

ZA-SHIKI-RŌ, ザシキラウ, 座敷牢, n. A room of a private house converted into a prison, or place of confinement, as for a lunatic. — *ni ireru*, to imprison in a room.

†ZA-SHŌ, ザシヤウ, 座上, n. At the time of sitting, in the chamber.

ZASSETSZ, ザツセツ, 雜說, n. Miscellaneous sayings, or writings.

ZASSHO, ザツショ, 雜書, n. Miscellaneous books, a medley of different kinds of books.

ZASZ, ザス, see *Zashi*.

ZASZ, ザス, 座主, n. The head bishop of Buddhist sects, always a son of the *Mikado*, and belonging to the *Tendai* sect.

ZATŌ, ザトウ, 座頭, n. The general name of the privileged persons among the blind; of whom there are three ranks, the *Kenjiyō*, *Kōtō*, and *Shibun*.

ZATSZ, ザツ, 雜, Coarsely, badly or roughly made, unworkmanlike, carelessly done. — *da*, it is coarsely made. — *na mono*, or — *butsz*, a coarse article.
Syn. SOMATSZ, YAKUZA.

ZATSZ-JI, ザツジ, 雜事, (*samazama no koto*). n. Many and various things to do, various engagements.

ZATSZYŌ, ザツヨウ, 雜用, n. Idem.

ZATTO, ザツト, 雜, *adv.* Coarsely, roughly, not nicely, not minutely; without care, attention, neatness, or skill. — *de yō gozarimas*, you need not be very particular in doing it. — *deki-agatta*, done coarsely, or not done with care. — *sh'ta mono*, a carelessly made thing. Syn. RIYAKU.

†ZAYŪ, ザユウ, 座右, (*za no migi*). The right side of a seat, or a place always near to where one sits. *Kono hon wa — wo hanasz bekaradz*, this book must not be removed from its place near the desk. *Tszne ni — ni oku*.

ZAZAMEKI,–*ku*,–*ita*, ザザメク, i.v. To make a noise, clamor, tumult, or clatter.
Syn. SAWAGU.

ZA-ZEN, ザゼン, 坐禪, n. Sitting in religious meditation or abstraction, as the Buddhists. — *wo szru*.

ZA-ZŌ, ザザウ, 坐像, n. An image, or idol in a sitting posture.

ZE, ゼ, 是, *n.* That which is right, that which is. *Idzre ka ze-naru wo shiradz,* don't know which is right. *Sono setsz wo ze to sz,* to regard that doctrine as the right one.

ZE, ゼ, contr. of *zo* and *ye*. A colloquial particle, used to give emphasis to what is said before, same as *zo*, and *yo;* as, *Bakimono-banashi ga ī ze,* ghost stories are the best.

ZEGEN, ゼゲン, *n.* A person who supplies prostitutes to houses of ill-fame, a pimp, procurer, pander. Syn. HANNIN.

ZE-HI, ゼヒ, 是非, *n.* Right or wrong, so or not; true or false, (*adv.*) must. — *wo arasō,* to dispute about the right or wrong, so or not so, of any subject. *Ze ka hi ka imada sadamaradz,* not determined whether it is so, or not. *Hi wo sztete ze wo toru,* to reject the false and hold to that which is true. — *ni oyobadz,* without gainsaying. — *ga nai,* no room for dispute, no remedy. — *ni tszmaru,* unable to gainsay, or deny. — *tomo sō seneba naran,* must by all means do so. — *kite kudasare,* you must come.

ZEHI-ZEHI, ゼヒゼヒ, 是非非, *adv.* Must, by all means. Syn. KANARADZ.

ZEI, ゼイ, 税, *n.* Duty, excise, customs, tax. — *wo osameru,* to pay duty, or tax. — *wo toru,* to collect duty. Syn. UNJŌ, NENGU.

†ZEI-BUTSZ, ゼイブツ, 贅物, *n.* An excrescense, a useless appendage, unnecessary or superfluous thing. Syn. YOKEI-NA-MONO.

ZEI-CHIKU, ゼイチク, 筮竹, *n.* The 50 rods, or sticks used by fortune-tellers. Syn. MEDOGI.

ZEI-GIN, ゼイギン, 税銀, *n.* Money paid for duty, or tax. Syn. UNJŌ, NENGU.

ZEI-K'WAN, ゼイクワン, 税官, *n.* A custom-house officer, a controller of customs, taxes, or excise.

ZEI-SOKU, ゼイソク, 税則, *n.* A tariff, or rate in which customs, taxes, or excise are levied.

ZEI-TAKU, ゼイタク, 贅澤, Extravagance, prodigality in the way of living. — *na h'to.*

†ZEKKEI, ゼツケイ, 絶景, *n.* An extremely fine landscape.

†ZEKKŌ, ゼツカウ, 絶交, (*majiwari wa tatsz*). — *szru,* to break off intimacy, fellowship, or friendship. Syn. NAKATAGAI, FUTS'Ū.

†ZEKKŌ, ゼツカウ, 舌耕, (*sh'ta de tagayesz*). (lit. ploughing with the tongue). — *szru,* to make a living by talking, lecturing, &c.

ZEKKU, ゼツク, 絶句, *n.* A verse, or stanza of poetry of four lines.

ZEM-BI, ゼンビ, 全備, (*mattaku sonawaru*). Full and complete in all its parts, having no deficiency, perfect. — *sh'taru,* complete, perfect. Syn. MATTAKI, MANZOKU.

ZEM-BU, ゼンブ, 全部, Complete number of volumes. *Kono hon wa — rok'satsz da,* this book is complete in six volumes.

ZEM-BU, ゼンブ, 膳夫, *n.* A person who superintends the arrangements, and preparing of a feast.

ZEM-BUN, ゼンブン, 前文, *n.* The introductory part of a letter.

ZEMMAI, ゼンマヒ, 狗脊, *n.* The shoots of young ferns.

ZEMMAI, ゼンマヒ, *n.* A circular spring for moving machinery, a mainspring. — *shikake,* a machine moved by a mainspring. — *saiku,* idem.

ZEM-PEN, ゼンペン, 前篇, *n.* The first series of a book.

ZEM-PI, ゼンピ, 前非, *n.* Former crimes, or sins, former evil practices. — *wa kuyamu,* to repent of one's crimes.

ZEM-PIYŌ, ゼンペウ, 前表, *n.* An omen, prognostic, presage. Syn. KIZASHI.

ZEN, ゼン, 善, (*yoshi*). *n.* Virtue, goodness. — *wo okonau,* to practice virtue. — *ni szszmu,* to persuade to the practice of virtue.

ZEN, ゼン, 繕, *n.* A dining table, (such as the Japanese use, low, and small, each person having a table to himself.) — *ni szwaru,* to sit at a dining table. — *wo szyeru,* to set a table.

ZEN, ゼン, 前, (*maye*). Before, in the presence of, only used in compounds. *Zen-ni,* before, previously.

ZEN-AKU, ゼンアク, 善惡, (*yoshi ashi*). Virtue and vice, good and evil. — *wo wakimayeru,* to discern between good and evil.

ZEN-CHI-SHIKI, ゼンチシキ, 善知識, *n.* A priest of eminent virtue.

ZEN-CHŌ, ゼンテウ, 前兆, *n.* A prognostic, an omen. Syn. ZEMPIYŌ.

ZEN-CHŌ, ゼンテウ, 前朝, (*maye no asa*). *n.* Yesterday morning, the previous dynasty. Syn. SAKUCHŌ.

ZEN-DAI, ゼンダイ, 前代, (*maye no yo*). *n.* Former ages, previous times. — *mi mon,* unheard of in former times.

ZEN-DANA, ゼンダナ, 膳棚, *n.* A case of shelves in which dining tables are kept.

ZEN-DŌ, ゼンダウ, 善道, (*yoki michi*). *n.* The good way, the way of virtue.

ZEN-GEN, ゼンゲン, 前言, (*maye ni iu*). *n.* A prophecy, prediction, foretelling.

ZEN-GO, ゼンゴ, 前後, (*maye ushiro*, or *saki ato*). Before and behind, before or after, front and rear. — *wo waszreru*, to be bewildered, or confused. *Tōka — ni kuru*, to come in ten days, sooner or later.

ZEN-GŌ, ゼンゴフ, 善業, *n.* Good or virtuous deeds, good works. — *no mukui*, the reward of good works.

ZEN-GON, ゼンゴン, 善根, *n.* Virtuous deeds, acts of charity and benevolence, good works. — *wo okonau.*

ZENI, ゼニ, 錢, *n.* Small copper or iron coin, cash.

ZENI-AUI, ゼニアフヒ, 錢葵, *n.* The name of a flower.

ZENI-BAKO, ゼニバコ, 錢箱, *n.* A money-box.

ZENI-GAME, ゼニガメ, 錢龜, *n.* A small kind of tortoise.

ZENI-IRE, ゼニイレ, 錢入, *n.* A purse. Syn. SAIFU.

ZENI-SASHI, ゼニサシ, 錢貫, *n.* The string on which cash are strung.

ZENI-ZA, ゼニザ, 錢座, *n.* The mint where copper coins are made.

†ZEN-JI, ゼンジ, 禪師, *n.* Buddhist priest, Bonze.

ZEN-JI, ゼンジ, 善事, (*yoki koto*). A good deed, virtuous action.

ZEN-JITSZ, ゼンジツ, 前日, (*maye no hi*). *n.* The day previous, yesterday, a previous, or former day.

ZEN-KIN, ゼンキン, 錢金, *n.* Money.

ZEN-K'WAI, ゼンクワイ, 全快, *n.* Recovery from sickness, perfect restoration to health. — *sh'ta*, restored to perfect health. Syn. HOMBUKU.

ZEN-NEN, ゼンネン, 前年, (*maye no toshi*). *n.* The previous year, the year before.

ZEN-NI, ゼンニ, 禪尼, *n.* A nun. Syn. AMA, BIKUNI.

ZEN-NIN, ゼンニン, 善人, (*yoki h'to*). *n.* A good man.

ZEN-NO-TSZNA, ゼンノツナ 緋, *n.* Two long strips of cotton cloth, attached to a coffin, and held in the hands of those walking in front of it.

ZEN-SAI, ゼンサイ, 前妻, (*maye no tszma*). *n.* The first wife, a former wife.

ZEN-SE, ゼンセ, 前世, (*maye no yo*). *n.* The previous state of existence, (Bud).

ZEN-SEI, ゼンセイ, 善政, (*yoki matszrigoto*). *n.* Good government.

ZEN-SEI, ゼンセイ, 全盛, (*mattaku sakannari*). Flourishing, or prosperous to the highest degree.

ZEN-SHIN, ゼンシン, 善心, (*yoki kokoro*). A virtuous mind.

ZEN-SHIN, ゼンシン, 全身, (*mattaki mi*). *n.* The whole body Syn. SŌSHIN.

ZEN-SHITSZ, ゼンシツ, 禪室, *n.* A Buddhist temple. Syn. TERA.

ZEN-SHŪ, ゼンシウ, 禪宗, *n.* The name of a sect of Buddhists.

ZEN-SŌ, ゼンソウ, 禪僧, *n.* A priest of the *Zenshū* sect.

ZEN-SOKU, ゼンソク, 喘息, *n.* Asthma.

ZEN-TAI, ゼンダイ, 全體, *n.* The whole body, the entire system of anything composed of parts; in com. coll. used as an adverb. Usually, generally, commonly, always, customarily, habitually, naturally, constitutionally or from birth, before. *Kiyō mo i-nai ga — rusz-gachi da*, he is out again to day, he is always out. — *shō-jiki na mono*, he has always been an honest person. *Yokohama wa — h'to no warui tokoro*, Y. is generally the place for bad men.
Syn. G'WANRAĪ, ITTAI.

ZEN-YA, ゼンヤ, 前夜, (*maye no yo*). *n.* The previous night, the night before; last night.

ZEN-ZEN, ゼンゼン, 前前, Former times, past-times.

ZEN-ZEN-NI, ゼンゼンニ 漸漸, *adv.* Gradually, by degrees. Syn. SHIDAI-SHIDAI-NI.

ZEPPEKI, ゼツペキ, 絕壁, *n.* A precipice.

ZEPPI, ゼツピ, 是非, *adv.* (coll. for *Zehi*). Must, positively, without dispute.
Syn. KANARADZ.

ZEPPIN, ゼツピン, 絕品, *n.* An article of the best quality.

†ZESSEI, ゼツセイ, 絕世, *n.* The finest in the world. — *no bijin*, the most beautiful of women.

†ZESSEN, ゼツセン, 舌戰, *n.* lit. a tongue battle. A war of words, dispute, quarrel.

†ZESSHI,-*sz*,-*sh'ta*, ゼツスル, 絕, (*tayeru*). *i.v.* To be cut off, destroyed, exterminated, to come to an end.

ZESSHOKU, ゼツショク, 絕食, Ceasing to eat from want of appetite, as in sickness.

ZESSO, ゼツソ, 舌疽, *n.* An ulcer on the tongue.

ZETCHŌ, ゼツチヤウ, 絕頂, *n.* The apex, highest peak, the summit of a mountain.
Syn. ITADAKI, CHŌJO.

ZETSZ, ゼツ, 舌, (*sh'ta*). *n.* The tongue.

ZETSZ-RIN, ゼツリン, 絕倫, The highest or

best of the kind, or amongst men; as, *Bu yū* —, the bravest of men.

ZETTAI, ゼツタイ, 舌苔, (*sh'ta no koke*). A fur, or coat on the tongue as in fever, a furred tongue. — *ga kakatta*.

ZETTAN, ゼツタン, 舌端, (*sh'ta no saki*). *n.* The tip or end of the tongue.

†ZETTŌ, ゼツトウ, 舌頭, *n.* idem.

ZO, ゾ, A particle used to give emphasis to the preceeding word or sentence. *Nani zo*, what? *Sono hako no naka ni nan zo aru ka*, is there not something in that box? *Nan to iu koto zo*, what is that you say? *Sōde wa nai zo*, it is no such thing. *Buchi ni nigon wa nai zo*, I would have you know, that a soldier never breaks his word. *Warui koto wo szru to butsz zo*, if you are bad I'll beat you. *Naku to ōkami ga kuru zo*, if you cry the wolf will catch you.

ZŌ, ザウ, 象, *n.* An elephant.

ZŌ, ザウ, 像, *n.* An image, statue, idol, a likeness. *Butsz-zō*, a Buddhist idol. *H'to no* —, a statue. *Moku-zō*, a wooden image. *Seki-zō*, a stone image.
Syn. KATA.

ZŌ, ザウ, 臟, *n.* The viscera. *Gozō*, the five viscera; viz., the heart, lungs, stomach, liver, and kidneys. *Nō no* —, the brain. *Hai no* —, the lungs. *Shin no* —, the heart.

ZŌ-BUSSHA, ザウブツシヤ, 造物者, *n.* The Creator.

†ZŌ-CHIU, ゾウチウ, 增注, *n.* Notes, or commentary added to the original notes.

ZŌ-CHŌ, *-szru*, ゾウチヤウ, 增長, To become more and more, to become greater and greater, to increase. *Ogori ga* —, to become more and more extravagant.

ZŌ-DAN, ザフダン, 雜談, *n.* Useless, or idle talk.

†ZŌ-FU, ザウフ, 臟腑, *n.* A viscera, or organ of the body, the intestines.

ZŌ-GAN, ザウガン, 象眼, Inlaid work of gold or silver.

ZŌ-GE, ザウゲ, 象牙, *n.* Ivory.

ZŌ-GEN, ゾウゲン, 增減, (*mashi herashi.*) Adding to or taking from, increasing or diminishing. — *szru*.

ZŌ-GON, ザフゴン, 雜言, *n.* Scurrilous, foul, or abusive language. — *wo iu*, to abuse. Syn. SOGON, AKKŌ.

ZŌ-GU, ザフグ, 雜具, *n.* Various articles of furniture.

ZŌ-HAN, ザウハン, 藏具, Holding, or possessing the blocks or stereotype plates on which a book has been printed.

ZŌ-HIYŌ, ザフヒヤウ, 雜兵, *n.* Common soldiers.

†ZŌ-HO, ゾウホ, 增補, (*mashi oginau*). Enlarged and deficiencies filled up, corrected and enlarged, spoken of a book.

ZŌ-KIN, ザフキン, 雜巾, *n.* A house-cloth, or coarse towel.

ZOKKON, ゾツコン, *adv.* coll. Very, exceedingly, truly, indeed. — *kokoroyaszi*, very intimate. Syn. JITSZ-NI.

ZOKU, ゾク, 俗, Common, vulgar, plebian, inelegant, uneducated, unpolished, laity, secular. — *na mono*, a vulgar person. — *ni*, vulgarly, commonly. — *no kotoba*, the vulgar dialect.

ZOKU, ゾク, 族, *n.* A family, clan, or tribe having the same surname. *Ichi-zoku*, the whole family, or tribe.

ZOKU, ゾク, 賊, *n.* A robber, bandit.
Syn. DOROBŌ.

ZOKU-BUN, ゾクブン, 俗文, *n.* The vulgar style of writing.

ZOKU-BUTSZ, ゾクブツ, 俗物, *n.* A vulgar person, one uneducated, or unrefined.

ZOKU-CHŌ, ゾクチヤウ, 賊長, *n.* The chief of a band of robbers.

ZOKU-DAN, ゾクダン, 俗談, *n.* Vulgar talk, or conversing in the vulgar dialect.

ZOKU-GEN, ゾクゲン, 俗言, or ZOKU-GO, ゾクゴ, *n.* The common, or vulgar dialect, such as is spoken by the common people; not the learned, elegant or refined language of scholars.

†ZOKU-HEN, ゾクヘン, 續編, *n.* A supplementary treatise, or additional volume.

ZOKU-JI, ゾクジ, 俗事, *n.* The common or vulgar business or affairs of life, secular business.

ZOKU-JIN, ゾクジン, 俗人, *n.* A common or unlearned person.

ZOKU-MIYŌ, ゾクミヤウ, 俗名, *n.* The secular name, or the name which a person bore while living, in contradistinction to the *Kaimiyō*.

ZOKU-NIN, ゾクニン, 俗人, *n.* same as *Zoku-jin*.

ZOKURASHII, -KI, -KU, ゾクラシイ, 俗敷, Common, vulgar, unrefined, inelegant, or unlearned in manner, style, language, &c.

ZOKU-SETSZ, ゾクセツ, 俗說, *n.* A saying story, or belief current among the vulgar, or common people; a vulgar saying.

ZOKUSHI, *-szru*, *-sh'ta*, ゾクスル, 屬, (*tszku*). *i.v.* To belomg, pertain, attached to, to be subject to, tributary, to connect one's self with, join. *Riu-kiu wa Satszma ni* —, the Lew-Chew islands belong to *Satszma*. *Mikata wo hanarete teki ni* —, to leave one's party and join the enemy. *Kujira wa nan no bu ni* —, to what class (of animals) does the whale belong? *Nichiren shū ni* —, to join the sect of *Nichiren*. Syn. SH'TAGAU.

ZOKU-SHŪ, ゾクシウ, 俗臭, (*zoku kusai*). (Lit. vulgar smell.) Having the appearance, manner, or language of a vulgar person, or thing. Syn. ZOKURASHII.

†ZOKU-TAI, ゾクタイ, 俗體, *n*. A lay-man, or one who does not belong to the Buddhist priesthood.

ZOKU-TO, ゾクト, 賊徒, (*dorobō no tomogara*). *n*. A band or company of robbers.

ZOKU-ZOKU, ゾクゾク, *adv*. — *szru*, to start, shudder, or shiver, as when cold water is poured over a person.

ZOM-BUN, ゾンブン, 存分, *n*. Mind, opinion, sentiments. — *wo nokosadz iu*, to speak one's mind without reservation. — *ni kanawanu*, not to one's liking. *Omaye no — ni shi-nasare*, do as you think best. Syn. OMOIRE.

ZOMEKI,–*ku*,–*ita*, ゾメク, *i.v.* To be noisy, uproarious, turbulent. *Zomeki-aruku*, to go along shouting, singing, or making a noise. Syn. SAWAGI.

ZOMMEI, ゾンメイ, 存命, *n*. In life, still living. *Chichi no — no uchi ni wa yempō ye yukimasen*, I cannot go to a distant country while my father is living. *Otots'-san wa — de gozarimas ka*, is your father still living? Syn. NAGARAYERU, ZAISE.

ZŌ-MOTSZ, ザウモツ, 藏物, *n*. Personal property, the things which one possesses.

ZONDZRU, ゾンズル, 存, see *Zonji*.

ZON-G'WAI, ゾングワイ, 存外, (*omoi no hoka*). Contrary to one's expectations, different from what one supposed. — *hayaku dekita*, done sooner than I expected.

ZŌNI, ザフニ, 雜煮, *n*. A kind of food.

ZON-I, ゾンイ, 雜意, *n*. Mind, opinion, sentiments, thoughts. Syn. ZOMBUN.

†ZŌ-NIN, ザフニン, 雜人, *n*. The rabble, the common herd.

ZONJI,–*dzru*,–*ta*, ゾンズル, 存, *i.v.* To think, to know, a polite word. *Arigatō-zonjimas*, thank you. *Gō-zonjika*, do you know? *Yedo wo go-zonji de gozarimas ka*, have you ever been to Yedo? *Zojite oru*, I know or I have been. Syn. SHIRU, OMŌ.

ZONJI-GAKENAI,-KI,–KU, ゾンジガケナイ, 無存掛, Unexpected, unlooked for. Syn. FURIYO.

ZON-JI-YORADZ, or ZONJIYORANU, ゾンジヨラズ, 不存寄, Unexpected, unlooked for, unthought of, incidental. Syn. OMOI-YORADZ.

ZONJI-YORI, ゾンジヨリ, 存寄, *n*. Opinion, mind, sentiments, views. *Jishin no — wo mochiyuru*, to act according to one's own opinions. Syn. ZOMBUN.

ZON-JŌ, ゾンジヤウ, 存生, *n*. In life, living. *O-jī san wa go — de gozarimas ka*, is your grand father still living? Syn. ZOMMEI.

ZON-NEN, ゾンネン, 存念, *n*. Thoughts, mind, opinion, views, sentiments.

ZONZAI, ゾンザイ, Careless, inattentive, negligent, not neat, sloven. *Ano daiku wa — da*, that carpenter does his work in a very careless manner. — *ni mono wo iu*, to speak in a careless or rude way. Syn. SOMATSZ, ZATTO.

ZŌRI, ザウリ, 草履, *n*. Sandals made of straw. — *no o*, the thong of a sandal.

ZŌRI-TORI, ザウリトリ, 草履取, *n*. The servant who carries his masters sandals. — *ni mo tarimasen*, unworthy to carry his sandals.

ZŌ-RIU,–*szru*, ザウリフ, 造立, (*tszkuri tateru*). To erect, build. *Tera wo* —, to build a temple.

ZORO-ZORO, ゾロゾロ, *adv*. Dragging or trailing like the long skirt of a robe. — *to aruku*, to walk with the skirt dragging behind.

ZŌSA, ザウサ, 造作, Always with a negative; as, *Zōsa mo nai*, not difficult, easy. *Zōsa mo naku dekita*, easily done. Syn. YASZI.

ZŌ-SAKU,–*szru*, ザウサク, 造作, (*tszkuru*). To finish off a building, to make it complete in all its parts, to repair. *Iye wo* —.

†ZŌSHIKI, ザフシキ, 雜色, *n*. An inferior servant of a *Kuge*.

ZŌ-SZI, ザフスイ, 雜炊, *n*. A kind of food.

ZŌ-TŌ, ゾウタフ, 贈答, (*okuri kotayeru*). Sending and replying to letters, correspondence. *Tegami no — mo nai*.

ZOTTO, ゾツト, *adv*. Startled, shocked, as by sudden alarm; a sudden feeling of chilliness. — *szru*.

ZŌ-YEI, ザウエイ, 造營, (*tszkuri itonami*). — *szru*, to erect, to build.

†ZŌ-YEKI, ゾウエキ, 增益, (*mashi masz*). — *szru*, to add to and complete as a book. Syn. ZŌHO.

ZŌ-YŌ, ザフヨウ, 雜用, *n*. Expenses, outlay for miscellaneous purposes. — *ga tanto kakaru*, the expenses are heavy.

APPENDIX.

AGE-BUTA, アゲブタ, 上蓋, *n.* A trap-door.

AKA-NASZ, アカナス, 赤茄, *n.* The tomato.

AKURU, アクル, 明, (same as *Akeru*). *a.* Opening, ensuing, next, following, (spoken of the day or year only). *Yo no — wo matsz*, to wait for the dawning of the day. — *hi*, the next day. — *toshi*, the following year.

AWAKI,-KU,-SHI, アハシ, 淡, *a.* and *adv.* Having a delicate flavor, or slight taste; tasteless as water. *Ajiwai ga awaki mono*, a thing of a delicate flavor. *Awaku sh'te midz ni nitaru*, tasteless as water. Syn. TAMPAKU.

AWAYAKA, アハヤカ, 淡, *a.* idem.

BADZ, バツ, *n.* A horse's hoof; or the horny part of the hoof separated from the foot, and used for making imitation shell-ware.

BARASHI,-*sz*,-*sh'ta*, バラス, *t. v.* To separate, take apart and scatter things that have been united. *Hon wo* —, to take a book to pieces and scatter the leaves. *Gunzei wo* —, to break up and disperse an army. Syn. CHIRASZ.

BRIKI, ブリキ, *n.* Tinned plates of iron; tin.

BUNSEKI, ブンセキ, 分拆, *n.* Analysis, decomposition of a compound into its constituent parts. *Midz wo — szru*, to decompose water.

||BUNYARI, ブンヤリ, *n.* A sling for throwing stones.

†CHIN-TAI, チンタイ, 鎮臺, *n.* A governor, appointed by the Shōgun to a distant port; as, *Nagasaki no* —, the governor of Nagasaki.

DA, ダ, Inferior in quality, mean, low, common, poor, cheap, coarse. *Da-mono*, an article of inferior quality. *Da-g'washi*, low priced confectionary. *Da-yak'sha*, a poor play-actor. Syn. SO, SOMATSZ, YASZ.

DANRIYOKU, ダンリヨク, 弾力, *n.* Elasticity. — *no aru mono*, things that have elasticity.

DAYEN, ダエン, 橢圓, Oval, elliptical. — *na mono.* Syn. TAMAGONARI.

DEMO, デモ, (same as *Demo*, conj. but used as an adj.) Any kind no matter what, common, poor, mean, inferior in quality. *Are — isha da*, he is a poor doctor, of no cleverness. — *yakusha*, an inferior play-actor. — *gakusha*, not much of a scholar.

DEN-KI, デンキ, 電氣, *n.* Electricity.

DEN-SEN, デンセン, 傳染, Infectious, contagious, communicating from one to another. — *biyō*, an infectious disease. — *szru*, to infect. Syn. UTSZRU.

DŌ-GAKU, ダウガク, 道學, *n.* Religious, or moral philosophy. — *no kōshaku*, lectures on moral subjects. — *sho*, a religious book.

DŌ-GAKU-SHA, ダウガクシヤ, 道學者, *n.* A moral philosopher.

DOMBURI, ドンブリ, *n.* A large porcelain bowl.

DŌ-ZEI, ドウゼイ, 同勢, *n.* The equipage or attendants of a Daimiyō.

DZI, ズイ, 蕋, *n.* The pistils of a flower.

FŪ-CHŌ, フウチヤウ, 風鳥, *n.* A humming bird.

FUCHŌFUDA, フチヤウフダ, *n.* A label, or ticket affixed to goods. — *wo tszkeru*, to affix a label.

FUKASHIGI, フカシギ, 不可思議, Miraculous, supernatural. — *na koto.*

FUKETSZ-NA, フケツナ, 不潔, *a.* Dirty, foul, unclean, impure, dishonest, unprincipled. — *midz*, dirty water. — *kokoro.*

FUROKU, フロク, 附錄, *n.* An appendix to a book. *Kotoba wo shūi sh'te — szru.*

FUSA-ZAKURA, フサザクラ, 草櫻, The Verbena.

FU-TAME-NA, フタメナ, 不爲, *a.* Not for one's interest or advantage, impolitic, prejudicial, unhealthy.

FUTTŌ, フツトウ, 沸騰, (*waki-agaru*). To effervesce, foam up.

GARI-*ru*,-*tta*, ガル, Derived from *ga*, and *aru*, to be, or have; it is used as a suffix to adjectives, and adds the idea of habitually being, possessing, or manifesting the quality of the root to which it is suffixed; as, *Itagaru*, from *itai*; complaining much of pain, making much ado about a little pain. *Hoshigaru*, from *hoshii*, wanting; much given to expressing one's desire for anything. *Mitagaru*, from *Mi*, to see; *ta*, contr. of *tai*, wish; and *garu*; wanting to see, desirous of seeing, prying and curious about. *Kitanagaru*, from *Kitanai*; complaining much of dirt, given to noticing dirt; so also of *Kikitagaru*, *Ureshigaru*, *Kuitagaru*, &c.

GATSZ-GATSZ, ガツガツ, *n.* Hungry and voracious, ravenous. — *kū*, to eat ravenously. — *szru*, to be voraciously hungry.

GEBIZŌ, ゲビザウ, *n.* A glutton, gourmand.

GEM-PON, ゲンポン, 原本, *n.* The original copy of a book or picture.

GIYŌ-JŌ-SHO, ギヤウジヤウシヨ, 行狀書, *n.* A biography, memoir,

GOKŌ, ゴクワウ, 後光, *n.* The halo that surrounds the head of an idol.

GOMA, ゴマ, *n.* Telling tales on others, talebearing, mischief making. — *wo szru*, to tell tales, make mischief.

GOMA-SZRI, ゴマスリ, *n.* A talebearer, mischief maker.

HA-DAN, ハダン, 破談, *n.* Breach of promise, breaking or violation of a contract, agreement, or engagement. *Yak'soku wo — szru*, to break a promise. *Yengumi ga — ni naru*, the marriage is broken off.

HAKKAN, *-szru*, ハツカン, 發汗, To sweat, perspire.

HAKKAN-ZAI, ハツカンザイ, 發汗劑, *n.* Diaphoretic medicines.

HAKU-RAN-K'WAI, ハクランクワイ, 博覽會, *n.* A collection of rare and curious things kept for show, an exhibition.

HAMUKI, *-ku*, *-ita*, ハムク, *t.v.* To growl, or snarl as a dog.

HANE-BASHI, ハネバシ, *n.* A draw-bridge.

HARETSZ, *-szru*, ハレツ, 破裂, To burst, explode.

HARETSZ-DAMA, ハレツダマ, 破裂玉, *n.* A bomb-shell.

HARETSZ-G'WAN, ハレツグワン, 破裂丸, *n.* idem.

HARI-FUDA, ハリフダ, 張札, *n.* A placard, a hand-bill.

HEN-JIN, ヘンジン, 變人, *n.* An eccentric person.

HERAGAYERI, ヘラガヘリ, *n.* A sprain of the ankle or foot. — *wo szru*, to sprain the ankle.

HESHI, *-sz*, *-sh'ta*, ヘス, 減, *t.v.* To lessen, diminish, reduce in number or bulk, to subtract. *Kadz wo* —, to diminish the number. Syn. GENDZRU, HERASZ.

HI-BUNE, ヒブネ, 火舩, *n.* A steamboat. Syn. JŌK'SEN.

HIMEGAKI, ヒメガキ, 女墻, *n.* A parapet.

HITSZ-YŌ, ヒツヨウ, 必用, Indispensible, important, necessary, requisite. *Fude wa — na mono*, a pen is an indispensible article.

HI-YAKU, ヒヤク, 秘藥, *n.* A secret medicine, a nostrum.

HIYOGURI, *-ru*, *-tta*, ヒヨグル, *t. v.* To squirt. *Midz wo* —, to squirt water.

HO-BUNE, ホブネ, 帆舩, *n.* A sailing ship, a sail-boat.

HŌ-KAN, ハウカン, 方鑑, *n.* A pharmacopœia, a medical formulary.

HOZO, ホゾ, *n.* The tenon of a piece of timber which fits into the mortise.

ICHI-DAI-KI, イチダイキ, 一代記, *n.* A biography, memoir.

ICHI-MATSZ, イチマツ, 市松, *n.* A kind of plaid, or checkered figure on cloth.

IJIGITANAI, イヂギタナイ, *a.* Gluttonous, fond of good eating.

ISSZMBŌSHI, イツスンボウシ, 侏儒, *n.* A dwarf, pigmy.

JAKU, ジヤク, 弱, *n.* A small fraction less than the precise quantity or measure. *Roku rin* —, a small fraction less than six *rin*. *Ichi grain Troy wa Nippon no roku rin jaku ni ataru*, one grain Troy is a fraction less than six *rin* of Japanese weight.

JŌ-BUKURO, ジヤウブクロ, 狀袋, *n.* A letter envelope.

JOREN, ジヨレン, *n.* A basket with a handle, used for shovelling earth.

JŌRIU, *-szru*, ジヤウリウ, 蒸溜, To distil. *Sake wo — sh'te shō-chiu wo toru*, to distil *sake* and make alcohol. *Jōriu-szi*, distilled water.

JŪYEN, ヂウエン, 重緣, Intermarrying, mutually giving and receiving in marriage. — *szru*, to intermarry.

KAGASHI, *-sz*, *-sh'ta*, カガス, 嚇, *t.v.* To growl, snarl. *Inu ga h'to wo* —.

KAI, カヒ, 峡, *n.* A ravine.

KAI-SHIN, カイシン, 改心, (*aratameru kokoro*). *n.* A change of heart or mind for the better, reformation. — *szru*, to experience a change of heart.

KAISHIDEI, カイシデイ, 芥子泥, *n.* A sinapism, mustard-plaster.

KAI-SŌ, *-szru*, カイサウ, 改葬, To remove a dead body from one grave to another.

KAJŌ, カゼウ, 个條, *n.* A separate item, article, particular. — *ga ōi*, the items are many. *San — no jōyaku*, an agreement or treaty having three articles. *Kono — ni yotte tszmi wo mōshi-tsekeru*, to condemn on this one count.

KAKE-HANARE,*-ru,-ta*, カケハナレル, 懸, 隔, *i. v.* To be exceedingly different, as different as possible, or very far apart. *Kake-hanareta tokoro.*

KAKUBEJISHI, カクベジジ, *n.* Young lads, clad in fancy clothes and wearing caps like a lion's head, who go about from place to place, performing summersaults, and other gymnastic feats; a tumbler.

KAKU-KAKU, カクカク, 斯斯, So, thus, this way. — *no shidai ni*, in this manner,

KAKUSHI, カクシ, *n.* A pocket.

KAMA, カマ, 窖, *n.* A furnace, kiln.

KAN-YŌ, カンエウ, 肝要, Important. *Kuni no — naru tokoro*, the important, (strategic) places of a country. — *na mono*, an important thing or matter.

KENNON, ケンノン, Dangerous, hazardous. — *da*, take care.

KEOSARE,*-ru,-ta*, ケオサレル, 氣壓, *i.v.* To be thrown into the back ground by the surpassing excellence of something else, to be thrown into the shade.

KIRIHI, キリヒ, 切火, *n.* Fire struck out with a flint and steel.

†KIYŌ, キヤウ; 强, *n.* A fraction over the precise measure or quantity. *San rin* —, a fraction over three *rin*.
Syn. SZGI, YO, AMARI.

KOBUCHI, コブチ, *n.* A kind of snare or trap for catching birds or small animals.

KO-JITA, コジタ, 小舌, *n.* Tongue-tie. *Kodomo ni — ga dekita*, the child is tongue-tied.

KORO, コロ, *n.* A cylindrical wooden roller used in moving heavy bodies.

KUDARANU, クダラヌ, 不下, (*neg.* of *Kudari*), As used in com. coll. = don't unperstand, unintelligible, useless, stupid, absurd. *Kono bun no imi ga* —, the meaning of this writing is unintelligible. — *koto wo iu*, to say something absurd or foolish.

KUJIKE,*-ru,-ta*, クヂケル, 折, *i. v.* To be discouraged, disheartened. *Ki ga* —.

KUMAGAYERI, クマガヘリ, *n.* A summerset. — *wo utsz*, to turn a summerset.

KUNIKUDZSHI, クニクヅシ, 國崩, *n.* A battering ram.

KUSHIRO, クシロ, 釧, *n.* A bracelet.

KUTSZGO, クツゴ, 口籠, *n.* An ox muzzle. *Ushi ni — wo hameru*, to muzzle an ox.

K'WAIRAISHI, クワイライシ, 傀儡師, *n.* A person who carries about a portable puppet show.

MAKUYA, マクヤ, 幕屋, *n.* A tent.

MU-GIYŌ-TAI, ムギヤウタイ, 無形體, Incorporeal, immaterial, not consisting of body or matter. *H'to no tamashii wa — na mono*, the soul of man is incorporeal.

MU-SHUKU, ムシユク, 無宿, Homeless, vagrant, outcast.

OBOYE-CHŌ, オボエチヤウ, 覺帳, *n.* A note book, memorandum book.

PAPPU, パツプ, *n.* A poultice.

RENGI, レンギ, *n.* A wooden pestle.

SHIPPO, シツポ, 尾, *n.* The tail of an animal, bird, or fish.

SHŌ-NIU-SEKI, シヨウニウセキ, 鍾乳石, *n.* A stalactite.

SHŪ-SHI, シウシ, 宗旨, *n.* A religious sect.

SON-SHŌ, ソンシヤウ, 尊稱, *n.* An honorable appellation, title.

TAI, タイ, 臺, *n.* A tower, or high terrace.

TAKA-MI-KURA, タカミクラ, 高御座, *n.* The throne of the Mikado, a throne.

THE END.

AN INDEX;

OR,

JAPANESE EQUIVALENTS

FOR THE

MOST COMMON ENGLISH WORDS.

ABO

ABACUS, Soroban.
ABAFT, Ushiro-ni.
ABANDON, Szteru; hai-szru; yameru.
ABANDONED, Hōratsz.
ABASE *one's self*, Heri-kudaru; mi wo sageru. — *another*, tori-hishigu.
ABASH, Kao wo tszbusz.
ABASHED, Hadzkashii.
ABATE, Heru; gendzru; uszrogu; yurumeru; herasz; hesz.
ABBREVIATE, Habuku; hashoru; tszdzmeru; riyaku szru.
ABBREVIATION, Riyaku-ji.
ABDICATE, Kurai wo szberu; kurai wo yudzru; jōi szru.
ABDOMEN, Hara; fuku.
ABDUCT, Kadowakasz.
ABHOR, Kirau; iyagaru; nikumu.
ABIDE, Szmu; oru; jū-szru.
ABILITY, Chikara; kiriyō; chiye.
ABJECT, Iyashii; gesen.
ABJECTLY, Iyashiku.
ABLE, Dekiru; yeru. *Not able*, Dekinu; atawadz.
ABLE-BODIED, Jōbu-na; szkoyaka.
ABOARD *ship*, Fune ni oru.
ABODE, Szmai; iye; uchi.
ABOLISH, Yameru; hai-szru.
ABOMINABLE, Nikui.
ABOMINATE, Nikumu; kirau.
ABORIGINES, Dojin; moto no h'to.
ABORTION, Riu-zan; datai. *To cause abortion*, ko wo orosz; *or*, ko wo nagasz.
ABOUND, Tak'san; tanto.

ABU

ABOUT, Mawari; gurai; tai-tei; bakari; achi-kochi; *see also under*, kakari, wo.
ABOVE, Wiye-ni; yo; koyeru; amari; szgiru; migi.
ABOVE-BOARD, Omote-muki-ni; muki-dashi-ni; meihaku.
ABRADE, Szri-muki; szri-yaburu.
ABREAST, Narabi; mukau.
ABRIDGE, Habuku; tszdzmeru; riyaku-szru; tszmeru.
ABROAD, Soto; yoso.
ABROGATE, Yame-saseru.
ABRUPTLY, Totsz-zen; sotszji; sotsz-zen.
ABSCESS, Hare-mono.
ABSCOND, Chikuten szru; nigeru; tachinokeru.
ABSENT, Inai; oranu; rusz.
ABSENT-MINDED, Mu-chiu; uchōten; uwano sora.
ABSOLVE, Yurusz.
ABSORB, Szi-komu; hikkomu.
ABSORBED IN, Kori-katamaru; hamaru; shidzmaru; fukeru; szsamu.
ABSTAIN, Tatsz; imu; imi-kirau; shō-jin szru, hikayeru.
ABSTINENCE, Mono-imi. *Religious* —, Shōjin.
ABSTEMIOUS, Shu-shoku wo hikayeme ni szru.
ABSTRACT, *v.* Nuku; nuite toru.
ABSTRUSE, Fukai.
ABSURD, Higa-koto; sakashira; ri ni somuku; tszmaranu.
ABUNDANCE, Yutaka.

ABUNDANT, Tak'san, ōi; obitadashii; jūbun.
ABUSE, *v.* Soshiru; Nonoshiru; akkō szru; waruku iu; mugoku szru. (*n*). mugoime; hidoi-me.
ACADEMY, Gakudō.
ACCELERATE, Hayameru; hayaku-szru.
ACCEDE, Shōchi szru; gatten-szru; nattoku szru; uke-hiku.
ACCEPT, Morau; uke-toru; toru; itadaku; chōdai.
ACCEPTABLE, Ki-ni-iru.
ACCIDENT, Ayamachi; kega. *Without accident*, Buji-ni.
ACCIDENTAL, Hakaradz; futo; omoi-yoranu; rinji-no; hiyoi-to.
ACCLIMATE, Jikō ni nareru.
ACCLIVITY, Saka.
ACCOMMODATE *one's self to circumstances*, Rinkiōhen ni szru; tszgo shidai ni szru.
ACCOMPANY, Tomonau; tszreru; isshō-ni yuku; tomo-ni yuku; gu-szru.
ACCOMPLICE, Dō-rui.
ACCOMPLISH, Togeru; szmu; jō-ju szru; owaru; dekiru; jū-bun-ni szru.
ACCORD, Au; awaseru; kanau; ōjiru. *With one accord*, Sorōte; ichi-dō-ni; dō-yō-ni; hitoshiku. *Own accord*, jibun-de; midzkara; onodzkara; shi-zen.
ACCORDING *to*, Shitagau; shidai; ni-yotte; tōri ni.
ACCOUNT, Kanjō; sanyō; santō; sō. *To give an account*, noberu; arisama wo iu; kikaseru. *Of no account*, kamawanu; nani mo naranu; taisetsz no nai. *On this account*, kono yuye ni. *On account of*, ...ni yotte.
ACCOUNTABLE, Mi ni kakaru; kakawaru.
ACCOUNTANT, Kanjō-kata.
ACCOUTREMENT, Shō-zoku.
ACCUMULATE, Takuwayeru; tameru; tszmu; kasamu.
ACCURATE, Chigawanu; sō-i-nai; machigai ga nai.
ACCUSE, Aitedoru; uttayeru.
ACCUSTOMED, Nareru.
ACHE, Itami.
ACID, Sz; san; szppai.
ACKNOWLEDGE, Fukusz; haku-jō szru; zange szru.
ACME, Sai-chiu; debana.
ACNE, Nikibi.
ACORN, Kashi-no-mi.
ACONITE, Udz; torikabuto.
ACQUAINT, Shiraseru; kikaseru.
ACQUAINTANCE, Chikadzki; kokoro yaszi h'to; shirube.
ADAMANT, Kongō.
ACQUIESCE, Akirameru; shōchi szru; fukusz; ubenau; yurusz; nattoku szru.
ACQUIRE, Motomeru; totonau; ukeru; yeru; mōkeru.
ACQUIT, Yurusz; mendzru; shōchi szru; yūmen-szru; shamen szru.
ACRE, = 1210 *tszbo.*
ACRID, Karai.
ACRIMONY, Karasa.
ACROSS, Yoko; wataru; koyeru.
ACROSTIC, Oriku.
ACT, *n.* Waza; koto; tokoro; totan.
ACT, *v.* Szru; itasz; nasz.
ACTION, Okonai; giyō-jo; shogiyō; hataraki; waza; shi-kata; kassen.
ACTIVE, Hayai; te-bayai.
ACTOR, Yakusha.
ACTUALLY, Jitsz-ni; hon-ni; makoto-ni.
ACUTE, Togaru; szrudoi; tszyoi.
ADAGE, Kotowaza.
ADAPT, Kanau; au.
ADD, Awaseru; soyeru; k'wa szru.
ADDICTED *to*, Hamaru; fukeru.
ADDITION, Yose-zan; mashi-zan. *In addition to*, hoka-ni; mata wa.
ADDRESS, Ate-na.
ADEPT, Jōdz; yete; tokui.
ADEQUATE, Taru.
ADHERE, Tszku; nebari-tszku; hebari-tszku.
ADHESIVE, Nebaru; nebai.
ADJACENT, Tszgi-no; tonari.
ADJECTIVE, Keiyōshi.
ADJOURN, Hinobe wo szru.
ADJUDICATE, Tori-sabaku; han-dan szru.
ADJUST, Tszkurō; naosz.
ADMINISTER, Okonau; shihai-szru. — *medicine*, fuku szru.
ADMIRABLE, Appare; shimbiyō.
ADMIRE, Kan-shin szru.
ADMIT, Yurusz; shōchi szru.
ADMITTANCE, *no*, Hairu bekaradz.
ADMONISH, Imashimeru; iken-szru; isameru.
ADOPT, Yōshi ni szru; tori-mochīru.
ADOPTED *son*, Yōshi.
ADORE, Ogamu; wiyamau; agameru; inoru.
ADORN, Kazaru; yatszsz; yosoō.
ADRIFT, Tadayō; nagareru; uki-uki.

ADROIT, Takumi; te-bayai.
ADULATION, Hetszrai; kobi.
ADULT, Otona.
ADULTERATE, Mazeru.
ADULTERER, Mippu; maotoko.
ADULTERY, Mitts'u.
ADVANCE, Szszmeru; szszmu; agaru. — *money*, Mayekin wo harau. — *the price*, Ne-age wo szru. *To go in* —, Maye ni yuku.
ADVANCEMENT, Shō-shin; shussei.
ADVANTAGE, Kai; yeki; shōri; sen. *Take — of*, tayori ni szru; tanomu; noru; jōdzru.
ADVENTURE, Koto; me; yama.
ADVERB, Fukushi.
ADVERSARY, Aite; ada; teki; kataki.
ADVERSE, Giyaku; sakarau.
ADVERSITY, Wazawai; sainan; fukō.
ADVERT, Sasz; tszkeru; tzide ni.
ADVERTISE, Fureru; hiromeru; kikaseru; fuichō; hirō.
ADVERTISEMENT, Hiki-fuda; hirome-gaki.
ADVICE, Iken; isame.
ADVISE, Iken-szru; isameru; oshiyeru. — *with*, sōdan szru.
ADVOCATE, Kujishi; tori-nasz.
ADZ, Chō-no.
AFAR, Tōi; yempō; haruka-ni.
AFFABLE, Nengoro-na.
AFFAIR, Koto; yoshi; waza; shi-kata.
AFFECT, Kandzru; fureru; ataru; kandō; kakaru.
AFFECTED, Namaiki-na.
AFFECTION, Jōai; nasake; yamai; biyōki.
AFFIANCE, Ī-nadzkeru.
AFFIDAVIT, Kōshō.
AFFINITY, Yen; chinami; shinrui; yoszga; yukari.
AFFIRM, Tash'kani iu; chikatte iu.
AFFIX, Ts'keru.
AFFLICT, Kurushimeru; komaraseru.
AFFLICTION, Nangi; nanjū; kannan.
AFFLUENCE, Yutaka; kane-wo-motsz; tomeru.
AFFORD, Dekiru.
AFFRAY, Ken'kwa.
AFFRONT, Ki ni fureru; ikaraseru.
AFLOAT, Ukamu.
AFOOT, Kachi de.
AFORESAID, Migi-no; maye-no; kudan-no.
AFRAID, Osoreru; kowai; kowagaru; okkanai; okushi.
AFRESH, Arata-ni; mata.
AFT, Fune no tomo ni. *Directly aft*, Matomo.
AFTER, Ato; nochi; go; kara.
AFTER-BIRTH, Yena; nochi-zan; hōye.
AFTERNOON, Hiru-szgi.
AFTERPAINS, Ato-bara.
AFTERWARD, Nochi-ni; ato-kara.
AGAIN, Mata; futa-tabi; kasaneru; matawa; sate-mata.
AGAINST, Sakarau; ataru; tszku.
AGATE, Menō.
AGE, Toshi; sai; toshi-baye; yowai; nenrei; nempai.
AGED, Oitaru; toshi no yotta.
AGENT, Miyōdai; tedai.
AGGRAVATE, Omoku szru.
AGGREGATE, Tszgō; awasete; shimete.
AGITATE, Ugoku; furū; urotayeru.
AGO, Ato; izen.
AGREE, Kanau; au.
AGREEABLE, Ki-ni-iru; omoshiroi.
AGREEMENT, Yak'soku.
AGROUND, Szwaru; i-szwaru; i-tszku.
AGUE, Okori; giyaku; hi-okori.
AH, Ā; satemo; ara.
AHEAD, Saki-ni; maye-ni.
AID, *v.* Taszkeru; szkeru; tetszdau.
AID, *n.* Sewa; taszke; hojo; shūsen; sariyaku.
AILMENT, Yamai; biyōki; wadzrai.
AIM, Nerau; kentō; ate.
AIR, Kūki; uta; nari; mottai.
AIR-BLADDER, Midz-bukuro.
AIR-HOLE, Kaze-nuki no ana.
AKIN, Shinrui; yen.
ALACRITY, Szmiyaka.
ALARM, Awateru; urotayeru; odoroku; osoreru.
ALARM-BELL, Haya-gane.
ALAS, Ā; satemo-satemo; ana.
ALBINO, Shiroko.
ALCOHOL, Shō chiu.
ALIEN, Yoso no h'to; ta-nin.
ALIGHT, Oriru; tomeru; kudaru.
ALIKE, Onajikoto; dō-yō; nite-oru.
ALIMENT, Shoku-motsz; tabe-mono.
ALIVE, Ikite-oru.
ALKALINE, Shioge; akuge.
ALL, Mina; nokoradz; szbete; moro-moro-no; ban; shikkai. — *over it*, Mamben-ni. — *or singly*, Sō-betsz.
ALLAY, Osameru; shidzmeru; yawarageru; nadameru.
ALLEVIATE, Karuku szru.

ALLEY, Kōji; roji.
ALLIANCE, Chinami; jōyaku; yoszga; yukari; majiwari.
ALLOT, Wari-tszkeru; ategau.
ALLOW, Yurusz; shō-chi szru; okure; kiku.
ALLOWANCE, Wari-ai.
ALLOY, Awase-gane.
ALLUDE, Ate-tszkeru; sash'te iu; tszite iu; honomekasz.
ALLURE, Izanau; sasō; hiku; yū-in szru; sosonokasz.
ALLY, Mikata.
ALMANAC, Koyomi.
ALMIGHTY, Atawazaru tokoro nashi.
ALMOND, Hadankiyō.
ALMOST, Hotondo; nan-nan; yoppodo; szde ni; hobo.
ALMS, Semotsz; segiyo; hodokoshi; hōsha.
ALOES, Ro-k'wai.
ALOFT, Wiye-ni.
ALONE, H'tori-de. *To let alone*, Mama-yo; sztete-oku; utchatte oku; kamawa-nai.
ALONG, Sōte, (*see* Soi), tszku. — *with*, issho-ni.
ALOOF, Tōzakeru.
ALOUD, Takaku; takagoye de.
ALPHABET, I-ro ha.
ALREADY, Szde-ni, mo-haya.
ALSO, Mata; yahari; mo; oyobi.
ALTAR, Dai.
ALTER, Aratameru; naosz; kawaru; henkaku.
ALTERCATION, Kenk'wa; kōron; arasoi.
ALTERNATE *days*, Kaku-jitsz; ichi nichi oki.
ALTERNATELY, Kawari gawari-ni, tagaichigai ni; kōtai.
ALTERNATIVE, *no* —, Shikata ga nai; yamu koto wo yedz; zehi ga nai; yoginai.
ALTHEA, Hachisz.
ALTHOUGH, Shikashi-nagara; keredomo; tatoi; tomo; iyedomo; totemo.
ALTITUDE, Takasa.
ALTOGETHER, Ichidō-ni; isho-ni; itchi; mattaku.
ALUM, Miyōban. *Burnt* —, yaki-miyōban, kohan.
ALWAYS, Itszdemo; itszmademo; tōshi; shijū; jōjū.
AMANUENSIS, Daihitsz.
AMASS, Takuwayeru; tameru.
AMAUROSIS, Sokohi; akimekura; kokushōgan.
AMAZE, Odoroku; bikkuri; tamageru; giyōten.

AMBER, Kohaku.
AMBIGUOUS, Fushin; fu-fummiyō; utagawashii.
AMBITION, Tai-mō.
AMBUSCADE, Fuku-hei; fuse-zei
AMEND, Aratameru, naosz; kai shin szru.
AMENORRHŒA, Kei-hei.
AMENDS, *to make* —, Tszgunau; aganau; madō.
AMERICA, Amerika.
AMETHYST, Shisekiyei.
AMIABLE, Otonashii; onjun; sznao; yasashii; onto; niuwa; h'toyaka.
AMICABLE, Mutszmajii; shitashii; wa-jun.
AMIDST, Naka; chiu; uchi.
AMISS, Ayamaru.
AMMUNITION, Tama-kuszri.
AMNESTY, Oyurushi; gosha; taisha.
AMONGST, Naka; chiu; uchi.
AMOUNT, Tszgō; sōtai; shime-daka; shimete.
AMPLE, Jūbun; hiroi.
AMPUTATE, Setszdan szru.
AMULET, Mamori.
AMUSE, Nagusameru; asobaseru; tawamureru.
AMUSEMENT, Nagusami; asobi; tawamure; kiyō.
AN, H'totsz; ichi.
ANACONDA, Mitszchi.
ANALYZE, Bunseki szru.
ANARCHY, Midare; ran.
ANATOMY, Fuwaki; kaibō.
ANCESTOR, Senzo.
ANCHOR, Ikari.
ANCHORAGE, Kakari-ba.
ANCIENT, Mukashi; inishiye; furui; kiu. — *and modern*, ko-kon. — *customs*, kofū.
ANCIENTS, Kojin.
AND, To; narabi-ni; oyobi; shikōsh'te.
ANECDOTE, Otoshi-banashi; hanashi.
ANFRACTIONS, Uneru.
ANGEL, Tennin.
ANGER, Haratachi; okori; ikari; ikidōri.
ANGLE, *n.* Kaku; szmi; kado.
ANGLE, *v.* Tszru.
ANGRY, Hara ga tatsz; okoru; ikidōru; rippuku.
ANIMAL, Kedamono; jūrui.
ANIMATE, Hagemasz; seishin wo tszkeru. — *being*, Dōbutsz. — *and inanimate*, Ujō-mujō.
ANISE-SEED, Uikiyō.

ANKLE, Kurubushi.
ANNALS, Nendaiki; rekishi.
ANNEX, Tszgu; awaseru; soyeru; tszkeru.
ANNIHILATE, Naku-szru; kesz.
ANNIVERSARY, Iwaibi.
ANNOTATE, Chiu szru; kaki-ireru.
ANNOUNCE, Tszgeru; shiraseru; kikaseru.
ANNOY, Komaraseru; ijimeru; jirasz.
ANNOYING, Urusai; mendō.
ANNUAL, Mai-nen; nen-nen; toshi-doshi; toshi-nami; rei-nen. — *payment*, nem-pu.
ANNUL, Yameru; hai-szru.
ANODYNE, Shits'uzai; yurume-guszri.
ANOINT, Abura wo tszkeru.
ANOMALOUS, Hō-g'wai; tszne-naranu.
ANONYMOUS, Na nashi; mu-mei.
ANOTHER, Hoka-no; betsz-no; ta; yoso; adashi; mata; mo-h'totsz. *One* —, tagai-ni; ai-tagai-ni.
ANSWER, Kotayeru; tō; hen-ji; hen-tō. *To — the purpose*, ma-ni-au.
ANSWERABLE, Tszgunō-hadz; madō-beki; kakawaru.
ANT, Ari.
ANTAGONIST, Aite.
ANTICIPATE, Maye-motte shiru; mi-tōsz; sen-ken; maye-motte toru; temawa-shi.
ANTIDOTE, Doku-keshi; gedokuzai.
ANTIPATHY, Kirai.
ANTIQUARY, Kobutszka.
ANTIQUITY, Mukashi; inishiye.
ANTITHESIS, Han-tai; ura-hara.
ANUS, Kōmon.
ANVIL, Kanashiki; kanatoko.
ANXIETY, Anji; kokoro-dzkai; shimpai; kidzkai; kurō.
ANY, Demo. — *person*, dare-demo. — *time*, itsz-demo. — *how*, dō-demo. — *thing*, nan-demo. — *where*, doko-demo. *Not — more*, mo nai.
APART, Betsz-betsz-ni; hanarete; wakete; hedateru.
APARTMENT, Heya; zashiki; ima.
APE, Saru.
APERTURE, Kuchi, ana.
APEX, Zetchō; chō-jo; itadaki.
APIECE, Dztsz; maye; ate-ni.
APOLOGIZE, Ayamaru; wabiru; yeshaku; shikidai szru; ĭwake wo iu; shinshaku szru.
APOSTATIZE, Daraku szru; ochiru.
APOTHECARY, Kuszri-ya.
APPARATUS, Dōgu.
APPAREL, Kimono, ifuku; meshi-mono; i-shō,
APPARENT, Miyeru; ichi-jirushi.
APPARITION, Bakemono; yūrei.
APPEAL, Uttayeru.
APPEAR, Arawareru; gosz; miyeru.
APPEARANCE, Nari; nari-furi; tei; sō; iro; keshiki; ge; miba; mikake; mi-date.
APPEASE, Nadameru; isameru.
APPEND, Tszgu; soyeru.
APPENDAGE, Soi-mono; zei-butsz.
APPENDIX, Furoku; tszika.
APPERTAIN, Soi.
APPETITE, *see* Shokumotsz; oishiku; szsz-mu; shokuji.
APPLAUD, Homeru; shōbi szru.
APPLE, Ringo.
APPLICABLE, Tszku.
APPLY, Tanomu; negau; ategau; oku, szyeru; ateru; tszkeru; haru.
APPOINT, Nindzru; mōshi-tszkeru; ĭ-tszke-ru; sadameru; sho-szru.
APPORTION, Wari-tszkeru; kubaru; wake-ru; haitō szru.
APPRAISE, Ne-uchi wo fumu; ne wo tszke-ru.
APPREHEND, Tszkamayeru; torayeru; me-shitoru; kokoroyeru; wakaru.
APPROACH, Chika-yoru; chika-dzku; yo-ru.
APPROPRIATE, *a.* Mochimaye; *(v.)* Ate-ha-meru.
APPROVE, Ki-ni-iru; homeru; nattoku szru; gatten szru.
APRICOT, Andz.
APRIL, Shi-gatsz.
APRON, Maye-kaki; maye-dare.
APT, Yoku; yaszi; gachi; *also words with the suffix*, Garu.
AQUEDUCT, Szidō; toyu; kakehi.
ARCH, Yumi-gata; tszki-gata; naka-daka.
ARCHER, Yumite.
ARCHERY, Kiujutsz; shajutsz.
ARCHITECT, Yedz-hiki.
ARDENT, Atszi. — *in pursuit of*, szszmu.
ARE, Aru; nari.
AREA, Tszbo-kadz; hirosa; taka; ba.
ARGUE, Arasō; rondzru; giron szru.
ARID, Kawaku; hiru; hashiyagu.
ARISE, Agaru; noboru; okiru; okoru; hasszru.
ARITHMETIC, Sanjutsz.
ARM, Te; ude.
ARMS, Bugu; buki; dōgu. *Fire* —, Teppō.

ARMOR, Katchiu; yoroi-kabuto; gusoku.
ARMPIT, Waki no sh'ta.
ARMY, Gunzei; hei; ikusa.
AROMATIC, Kōbashii.
AROUND, Mawari; meguri.
ARRANGE, Naraberu; tszraneru; sonayeru.
ARRANGEMENT, Ichi; sonaye; shidai.
ARREAR, Fusoku; taradz.
ARREST, Torayeru; tszkamayeru; meshitoru.
ARRIVAL, Tōchaku.
ARRIVE, Chaku szru; tszku; kuru; tōchaku szru; tōrai szru.
ARROGANT, Takaburu; jiman; manshin.
ARROW, Ya.
ARSENAL, Buki-gura.
ARSENIC, Yoseki; hisōseki.
ART, Jutsz.
ARTEMISIA, Yomogi.
ARTERY, Dōmiyaku.
ARTFUL, Kōk'watsz; szrekkarashi; takumi.
ARTICLE, Mono; shina-mono; jō; kajō.
ARTIFICE, Hakarigoto; tedate; keiriyaku; bōriyaku; bōkei; takumi.
ARTIFICIAL, Tszkuri. — *flowers*, tszkuri-bana. — *teeth*, ireba. — *nose*, tszke-bana. — *eye*, ireme. — *hair*, iregami; soyegami.
ARTILLERY, Ōdztsz; teppō; taihō. — *corps*, taihōtai.
AS, *see* Gotoku; tōri; yō; toki; hodo; ni; naru-take; nite.
ASCEND, Agaru; noboru.
ASCERTAIN, Mi-todokeru; tadasz.
ASCITES, Kochō; chōmen.
ASHAMED, Hajiru; hadzkashii.
ASHES, Hai.
ASHORE, Hama ni szwaru. *Gone* —, jōriku-sh'ta; oka ni agatta.
ASIDE, *to set* —, shimau; kata-dzkeru. *Stand* —, yokeru; waki ye yore.
ASK, Tadzneru; tō; tanomu; negau.
ASKANT, *to look* —, shirime ni miru; sobameru.
ASKEW, Nejirete iru; magaru; hidzmu; yugamu.
ASLEEP, Nete iru; nemuru.
ASPARAGUS, Temmondō.
ASPECT, Iro; keshiki; kao; muki.
ASS, Usagi'ma; rōba.
ASSAFŒTIDA, Agi.
ASSASSIN, Shikaku.
ASSASSINATE, Kiru; korosz; utsz.
ASSAULT, Semeru; utsz.
ASSAY, Tamesz; fuki-wakeru.
ASSEMBLE, Atszmeru; yoseru; tszdoyeru; matomeru.
ASSEMBLY, K'wai; seki.
ASSENT, Shōchi szru; yurusz; gaten szru; ubenau; nattoku szru.
ASSESS, Wari-tszkeru; ateru.
ASSIGN, Ategau; ate-hameru; wari-tszkeru.
ASSIST, Tetszdau; taszkeru; szkeru; sewa wo szru; shūsen szru; hojo szru; sariyaku.
ASSOCIATE, Tszki-ai; chikadzku; kumu; majiwaru.
ASSORT, Tori-wakeru.
ASSUAGE, Yurumeru; yawarageru; nadameru; nagusameru.
ASSURE, Ukeau.
ASTERN, Tomo-ni.
ASTHMA, Zensoku.
ASTONISH, Odoroku; bikkuri; akireru; tamageru; kimo wo tszbusz.
ASTONISHING, Menyōna.
ASTRAY, Mayō; madowasz.
ASTRIDE, Matagaru.
ASTRINGENT, Shibui; shūren. — *medicines*, shūrenzai.
ASTRONOMY, Temmon.
ASUNDER, Betsz-betsz-ni; hanareru; hedateru.
AT, Ni; de; ye. — *first*; hajimete; shote. — *last*, yō-yaku; tszi-ni; tō-tō.
ATHWART, Yoko-ni; yokosama; yokogiru;
ATMOSPHERE, Kūki.
ATONE, Aganau; tszgunau.
ATROCIOUS, Futoi; furachi-na; futodoki.
ATROPHY, Kiyorō.
ATTACK, Semeru; utsz.
ATTAIN, Oyobu; todoku; itaru.
ATTEMPT, Tamesz; sei wo dasz.
ATTEND, Nen wo ireru; ki wo tszkeru; kiku; tsztomeru; tomonau.
ATTENTION, Nen.
ATTENTIVELY, Toku-to; tszku-dzku; kitto.
ATTEST, Shōko szru.
ATTIRE, *n.* Kimono; ifuku; shō-zoku; idetachi.
ATTIRE, *v.* Kiru; yosoō; yatszsz; idetatsz.
ATTITUDE, Kamaye; yōsz.
ATTRACT, Hiku; hiki-yoseru.
ATTRITION, Szri-yaburu.
AUCTION, Seri; sayashi.
AUDACIOUS, Futoi; furachi-na.
AUGUST, Hachi-gatsz.
AUNT, Oba.

AUSPICIOUS, Kichi-na; saiwai-no.
AUSTERE, Genjū; kibishii; katai.
AUTHOR, Saku-sha; senja.
AUTHORITY, Ken; ikioi; isei; ikō.
AUTHORIZE, Isei wo yaru.
AUTOGRAPH, Jikihitsz.
AUTUMN, Aki; shū.
AUXILIARIES, Ka-sei.
AVAIL, Kai; yeki; yaku ni tatsz; yōnitatsz.
AVALANCHE, Nadare; yuki-ōroshi.
AVARICE, Musabori; yokubari.
AVENGE, Hōdzru; mukuyuru; kayesz.
AVERAGE, Narashi; heikin; taigai; taitei; nami.
AVERSE, Kirau; ki ni iranu; iyagaru; itō.
AVERT, Fusegu; yokeru. — *the eyes*, waki-me wo furu.
AVOID, Yokeru; sakeru; nogareru.
AWAKE, Me ga sameru; okiru.
AWAY, Rusz; inai. *To run* —, nigeru; chikuten-szru; shuppon szru. *To throw* —, szteru; utcharu. *To go* —, saru; yuku. *Look* —, yoso ni miru.
AWKWARD, Bukiyō; busaiku; buchōhō; heta; tsztanai.
AWL, Kiri.
AWNING, Hi-yoke.
AWRY, Yugamu.
AXE, Ono; maki wari; yoki.
AXIS, Shingi.
AXLE, Shingi; jiku.
AZALEA, Tsztszji.

B

BABBLE, Kuchi wo tataku; kuchisaganai.
BABY, Akambō; bō-ya; midorigo; yaya.
BACK, Senaka; ushiro; ura. *To go* —, kayeru. — *of a sword*, mune. *Turn the — on*, somuku.
BACKBITE, Soshiru; waruku iu; zangen.
BACKWARD, *a.* Yenriyo; habakaru; iyagaru; osoi; okureru.
BACKWARD, *adv.* Ato-ye; ushiromuki. *To fall* —, aomuke ni taoreru. *To go* —, atoshizari. *To look* —, kayeri-miru. *To read* —, saka-yomi.
BAD, Warui; ashii; aku. — *name*, aku-miyō. — *man*, aku-nin. — *countenance*, aku-sō.
BADGE, Mon; shirushi.
BADGER, Tanuki.

BAG, Fukuro; tawara; hiyō.
BAGGAGE, Nimotsz.
BAIL, *n.* Ukeai-nin.
BAIL, *v.* Ukeau. — *a boat*, aka wo kayedasz.
BAIT, Ye; yeba.
BAKE, Yakeru.
BALANCE, Hakari; tem-bin; nokori; amari; tszri-ai; hei-kin szru; hiki-nokori; sashi-hiki.
BALCONY, Yen; yengawa; k'wairō.
BALD, Hage.
BALE, Tsztszmi; kōri.
BALK, Sashi-yameru.
BALL, Mari; tama.
BALLAD, Uta.
BALLAST, Karuni.
BALLOON, Ki-kiu; fūsen; kūsen.
BALLOT, Ire-fuda; niu-satsz.
BALUSTRADE, Rankan; teszri; obashima.
BAMBOO, Take.
BANANA, Bashō.
BAND, Himo; nawa; seme; kumi; totō; nakama; sha.
BANDAGE, Maki-momen; hōtai.
BANDY-LEGGED, Yegomata.
BANE, Doku.
BANISH, Shima-nagashi; yentō; ruzai; tszihō.
BANK, Kishi; tszka; adzchi; kashi; kanekashi.
BANKNOTE, Tegata; satsz.
BANKRUPT, Tszbureru; botszraku.
BANNER, Hata; hata-jirushi.
BANQUET, Chisō; shuyen; sakamori.
BANTER, Yobi-dasz.
BAR, K'wan-nuki; yokogi; shirasz; sz.
BARB, Kayeri; sakaha.
BARBARIAN, Yebisz.
BARBER, Kami-yui.
BARE, Hadaka.
BARE-FOOTED, Hadashi; szashi.
BARELY, Kara-gara; karōjite; yōyaku.
BARGAIN, Yak'soku; yakujō; ukeai.
BARK, Ki no kawa.
BARK, *(as a dog)*. Hoyeru.
BARLEY, Ōmugi.
BARM, Kōji; tane.
BARN, Kura.
BARRACK, Jingoya; tamuro.
BARREL, Taru; oke; son.
BARREN-LAND, Are-chi; hinchi; yase-chi. — *woman*, umadz.
BARTER, Kōyeki.

BADGE, a. Iyashii; gooon.
BASHFUL, Hadzkashigaru; omohayui; ome-ru; hajirai; yenriyo; habakaru; ome-ome-to.
BASIN, Tarai; hachi.
BASIS, Ishidzye; dodai; yoridokoro.
BASK, Hinatabokko.
BASKET, Kago; zaru.
BASS-RELIEF, Oki-age.
BASTARD, Tetenashigo.
BAT, Kōmori; hempuku.
BATE, Makeru; habuku.
BATH, *hot* —, Yu.
BATHE, Yu ni hairu; abiru; moku-yoku szru; giyōdzi; yokusz.
BATHING-TUB, Furo; yu-oke.
BATTERING-RAM, Kuni-kudzshi.
BATTERY, Hōdai.
BATTLE, Ikusa; kassen; tatakai; sensō.
BATTLEDOOR, Hagoita.
BAWL, Naku; sakebu.
BAY, Iri-umi, Uchi-umi.
BAYONET, Ken.
BE, Aru, Oru; iru; gozaru; naru.
BEACH, Hama; nagisa.
BEAD, Tama.
BEAK, Kuchi-bashi.
BEAN, Mame.
BEAR, Kuma.
BEAR, *v.* Korayeru; ga-man; shimbō; shinobu; kan-nin; shusshō; umareru; shōdzru; shinogu.
BEARING, Hōgaku; nari-furi,
BEARD, Hige.
BEAST, Chikushō; kedamono.
BEAT, Butsz; chō-chaku; naguru; utsz; katsz.
BEAUTIFUL, Kirei; migoto; utszkushii; hanayaka; bibishii.
BECAME, *pre.* Natta; sh'ta.
BECAUSE, Ni-yotte; yuye.
BECKON, Maneku.
BECOME, Naru; szru.
BECOMING, Niau; au; kanau; sōtō.
BED, Futon. *In* —, nete iru.
BEDAUB, Darake; mabure.
BED-CHAMBER, Nema.
BED-CURTAIN, Chō.
BEDDING, Ya-gu; futon.
BEDECK, Kazaru; yosoō.
BED-SORE, Tokodzre.
BED-STEAD, Nedoko.
BEE, Hachi.
BEE-HIVE, Hachi no sz.

BEEF, Ushi no niku.
BEESWAX, Mitsz-rō.
BEFALL, Au.
BEFORE, Maye; saki; zen; sendatte; itsz-zo-ya; izen; sendo; moto.
BEFOREHAND, Maye-motte; kanete; ara-kajime; katszte; madaki; mayebiro-ni.
BEFRIEND, Sewa wo szru; tayoru.
BEG, Negau; kō; tanomu. *I — pardon,* gomen kudasare.
BEGAN, Hajimaru.
BEGET, Umu; shōdzru; mōkeru.
BEGGAR, Kojiki; hinin; katai.
BEGIN, Hajimeru; kakaru; nari-kakaru.
BEGINNER, Shoshin.
BEGINNING, Hajime; shote; okori; shoho-tsz.
BEGONE, Yuke; noke.
BEGRUDGE, Oshimu.
BEGUILE, Azamuku; damasz; taburakasz; itszwaru.
BEHAVE, Okonau.
BEHAVIOR, Okonai; tachifurumai; giyō-gi; shimuke; shi-nashi.
BEHEAD, Kubi wo kiru.
BEHIND, Ato; ushiro; go; otoru; okureru.
BEING, *ppr.* Sh'te; nite; atte.
BELCH, Okubi.
BELFRY, Shurō.
BELIEVE, Shindzru; shinko szru; makoto to omō; ukegau.
BELL, Kane; tszrigane; hayagane; rin.
BELLADONNA, Rōtō.
BELLOW, Naku; sakebu; hoyeru.
BELLOWS, Fuigo.
BELLY, Hara; fuku.
BELLYACHE, Hara-itami; fuku-ts'u.
BELONG, No; zoku szru; tszku; soyeru.
BELOVED, Kawai; aish'ta; itōshii.
BELOW, Sh'ta; sa.
BELT, Obi.
BENCH, Koshi-kake.
BEND, Mageru; kagameru; wageru; tawa-meru; shinayeru; nabiku; shidareru. — *back;* soru; aomuku;
BENEATH, Sh'ta.
BENEFIT, Kai; yeki; yō.
BENEVOLENCE, Nasake; jō-ai; fubin.
BENUMB, Shibireru; mahi szru; kogoyeru.
BEQUEATH, Yui-gon szru; yudzru.
BERRY, Ichigo.
BESEECH, Negau; kō; tanomu.
BESIDE, Soba ni; hotori.
BESIDES, Hoka-ni; wiye-ni; betszdan; shi-kamo; katawara-ni.

BESIEGE, Semeru ; utsz.
BESMEAR, Darake; mabure ; nuru ; tszkeru.
BESPATTER, Haneru.
BEST, Goku yoi; ichi-ban ; mottomo yoi; sai-jō. —*in the world*, zessei.
BESTOW, Hodokosz ; atayeru ; yaru ; tamau.
BESTRIDE, Matagaru.
BET, Kakeru ; kake wo szru.
BETEL, Binrōji.
BETRAY, Uru.
BETROTH, Ī-nadzkeru.
BETROTHAL, Yendzki.
BETTER, Yoi; masaru; ī; shiku; mashi.
BETWEEN, Aida; ma; hasamu.
BEWARE, Abunai.
BEWILDER, Mayō; urotayeru, shūshō.
BEWITCH, Tori-tszku.
BEYOND, Szgiru; achira; amaru.
BIAS, Kata-hīki; hīki; yeko; katayoru.
BICH-DE-MER, Kinko; iriko.
BID, Ī-tszkeru; meidzru; geji; maneku; yobu; ne wo tszkeru.
BIER, Rendai.
BIG, Ōkii; dai.
BIGOTED, Henkutsz, katakurushii.
BILE, I; tan.
BILGE-WATER, Aka.
BILL, Kuchi-bashi; kanjō; kakidashi; kanjō-gaki; mokuroku. *Bank* —, tegata. — *of exchange*, kawase-tegata. — *of sale*, shikiri. — *of lading*, okuri-jo.
BIND, Shibaru; muszbu; kukuru; karageru; maku; yui; membaku szru; karameru.
BINDING, Hiyō-shi; heri.
BIOGRAPHY, Ichidaiki; giyōjōsho.
BIRD, Tori.
BIRD-CAGE, Tori-kago.
BIRD-LIME, Tori-mochi.
BIRD'S *nest*, Tori-no-sz,
BIRTH, Umare; san; tan-jō.
BIRTH-DAY, Tan-jō-bi.
BIRTH-PLACE, Ko-kiyō; furusato.
BISMUTH, Jakan-seki.
BIT, Kutszwa.
BITCH, Me-inu.
BITE, Kamu; kui-tszku.
BITTER, Nigai.
BLACK, Kuroi. — *and blue*, urumu. *Blacken*, kuroku szru; kuromeru.
BLACKGUARD, Kuchigitanai.
BLACKSMITH, Kajiya.
BLACKSMITH'S *tongs*, Yattoko.
BLADDER, Shōben-bukuro; bōkō.
BLADE, Mi; hon.
BLAME, Togameru; shikaru; kadzkeru; Īkakeru.
BLANK, Kara. —*paper*, shira-kami.
BLAZE, Honō; k'wayen.
BLEACH, Shiroku szru; sarasz.
BLEAR-EYED, Tadare-me.
BLEED, Chi ga deru; chi wo toru.
BLEMISH, Kidz.
BLEND, Majiru; awaseru.
BLESS, Iwau; shuku szru.
BLESSINGS, On; megumi.
BLIND, Mekura; meshii; mō-moku. — *of one eye*, katame; mekkachi.
BLINDMAN'S-BUFF, Kakurembō.
BLINK, Majiroku.
BLISTER, Midz-bukure; hi-bukure.
BLISTERING-PLASTER, Hatsz-bō.
BLOAT, Fukureru; mukumu.
BLOCK, Ate; uchiban; hota. *To* — *up*, sasayeru; jama szru.
BLOCKHEAD, Gudon; oroka; gumai; don; nibui; baka; koppayaro.
BLOOD, Chi.
BLOODY, Chi-darake; chi-mabure.
BLOOM, Saku; sakayeru; sakan.
BLOSSOM, Hana.
BLOT *out*, Kesz; shōmetsz.
BLOT, Szmi ga tszku.
BLOW, *n*. Uchi.
BLOW, *v*. Fuku; saku; ayegu. —*the nose*, hana wo kamu. — *out*, fuki-kesz; fuki dasz. — *down*, fuki-taosz; fuki-otosz. — *away*, fuki harau; fuki-chirasz. — *up*, fuki-ageru; fukurakasz. — *over*, fuki-kayesz.
BLUE, Aoi; hana-iro.
BLUNDER, Ayamachi; shikujiru.
BLUNT, Nibui; don.
BLUSH, Sekimen; akaramu.
BOA-CONSTRICTOR, Mitszchi.
BOARD, *n*. Ita.
BOARD, *v*. Tō-riu szru; ita wo haru.
BOAST, Jiman szru, taiheiraku wo iu; kō man szru.
BOAT, Fune.
BOATMAN, Sendō; funako.
BODY, Karada; dō; tai.
BODY-GUARD, Keigo.
BOG, Numa.
BOIL, *n*. Hare-mono; nebuto.
BOIL, *v*. Wakasz; waku ; tagiru ; niyeru ; niye-tatsz; niru; taku.
BOILER, Dōko.
BOILING-WATER, Yu; nettō.

BOISTEROUS, Sawagashii; hageshii; arai; kibishii.
BOLD, Dai-tan; kimo no f'toi; yūki; otemba.
BOLT, K'wan-nuki; sen.
BOLT, *v.* Tozasz; shimeru; tojiru. *(sift)* Yuri-wakeru.
BOMB, Haretsz-dama.
BOND, Shōmon; kidzna; ruisetsz.
BONE, Hone; kotsz.
BONNET, Kaburi-mono.
BONZE, Bōdz; oshō; jūji.
BOOK, Hon; shomotsz; shojaku.
BOOK-BINDER, Seihonya.
BOOK-CASE, Hondana.
BOOK-COVER, Hiyōshi.
BOOK-KEEPER, Shoyaku.
BOOK-MARK, Shiori.
BOOK-STAND, Kendai.
BOOK-STORE, Hon-ya; shorin.
BOOM, Hogeta.
BOOR, H yak'shō; inaka-mono; yabo.
BOORISH, Bu-sa-hō; bu-kotsz-na.
BOOT, Naga-gutsz; oi; sh'ta; tashimaye.
BOOTY, Bundori.
BORAX, Hōsha.
BORDER, Sakai; heri; fuchi; hashi; kiwa.
BORE, Kuru. — *a hole*, Ana wo momu; ana wo kuru; ana wo akeru.
BORROW, Karu; shaku-yō szru; haishaku szru.
BOSOM, Mune; futokoro; k'wai-chiu.
BOSS, Kashira; oya-bun.
BOTANY, Wiye mono-gaku.
BOTH, Riyō; riyō-hō; dochira mo; futatsz nagara. — *feet*, Moro-ashi; riyō-ashi; — *hands*, riyō-te; moro-te. — *knees*, moro-hiza.
BOTHERSOME, Urusai; mendō.
BOTTLE, Tokuri; bin.
BOTTOM, Soko. *Turn — up*, Fuseru; utszmukeru.
BOUGH, Yeda.
BOUNCE, Haneru; tobu.
BOUND, *v.* Haneru; tobu.
BOUND, *n.* Kukuri; saigen.
BOUNDARY, Sakai; kagiri.
BOUNTY, Hōbi.
BOW *of a ship*, Hesaki; mioshi.
BOW, *v.* Jigi wo szru; aisatsz; yeshaku szru; utszmuku.
BOW, *n.* Yumi.
BOWELS, Harawata; chō.
BOWL, Wan; domburi. — *of a pipe*, gankubi.
BOW-SHOT, Yagoro; yaomote.
BOW-STRING, Tszru; yumi-dzru.
BOX, Hako. — *of a theatre*, Sajiki.
BOX, *v.* Uchi-au.
BOX-WOOD, Tszge.
BOY, Muszko; warambe; dōji.
BOY, *(servant)*, Kodzkai.
BRACE, *n.* Ni wa; nuki; tszka; shimbari; hijiki.
BRACE, *v.* Kau; magiru.
BRACELET, Ude-wa; tamaki.
BRACKET, San; shimbari.
BRACKISH, Shioke.
BRAG, Jiman szru; kōman szru; taiheiraku wo iu.
BRAID, *n.* Himo.
BRAID, *v.* Kumu.
BRAIN, Nō no zō.
BRAN, Nuka.
BRANCH, Yeda; shiriu.
BRAND, Yakiban.
BRANDISH, Furi-mawasz; hiramekasz.
BRASS, Shinchiu.
BRAVE, Daitan; kimo-futoi; isamu; yūki.
BRAZEN-FACED, Atszkawadzra.
BREACH, Shiri.
BREAD, Pan.
BREADTH, Haba; yoko; no.
BREAK, Kowasz; yaburu; tszbusz; kudaku; kudzsz; oru; tatsz; kiru; abaku; somuku; hishigu; tenarashi.
BREAK OF DAY, Yoake; akatszki; akebono.
BREAKFAST, Asa-gohan; asa-han; asa-meshi.
BREAKWATER, Midzyoke; namiyoke; kawayoke.
BREAST, Mune.
BREAST-PLATE, Muna-ate.
BREATH, Iki; kokiu.
BREATHE, Iki wo hiku; ikidzkai.
BREECH, Shiri.
BREECHES, Momohiki; hakama.
BREED, Yashinau; sodateru; shōdzru.
BREEZE, Kaze.
BRETHREN, Kiyōdai.
BREW, Kamosz.
BREWERY, Sakaya.
BREWER, Tōji.
BRIBE, Mainai; wairo.
BRICK, Kawara.
BRIDE, Hana-yome.
BRIDEGROOM, Hana-muko.
BRIDESMAID, Kaizoye.

BRIDGE, Hashi.
BRIDLE, Omogai.
BRIEF, Mijikai.
BRIEFLY, Ara-ara; arakajime; tai-riyaku.
BRIGAND, Dorobō; tōzoku.
BRIGHT, Hikaru; kagayaku; sayeru; tszya; teru; akiraka.
BRILLIANT, Kagayaku; tszya.
BRIMFUL, Ippai; tatayeru.
BRIMSTONE, Iwo.
BRINE, Shio.
BRING, Motte-kuru; tszrete-kuru. — *back*, motte-kayeru. — *forth*, shusshō szru; umu; san-szru; shōdzru. — *up*, motte-ageru; sodateru; shi-tateru; bu-iku szru. — *to light*, arawasz. — *to mind*, omoidasz. — *in*, motte-hairu.
BRINGING UP, Sodachi; nari-tachi; sei-iku; buiku; shi-tate.
BRINK, Kiwa; fuchi.
BRISK, Isogu; hayaku.
BRISTLE, Buta no ke.
BRITISH, Igirisz no; yei.
BRITTLE, Moroi; koware-yaszi; sakui.
BROAD, Hiroi.
BROADAXE, Yoki; masakari.
BROIL, *v.* Yakeru; aburu.
BROKER, Sai-tori; kuniu-nin.
BROKERAGE, Kōsen; buai.
BRONZE, Kara-kane.
BROOK, Tani-gawa.
BROOM, Hōki.
BROOMCORN, Morokoshi.
BROTH, Shiru.
BROTHEL, Jorōya; kutszwaya.
BROTHER, Kiyōdai. *Elder* —, ani. *Younger* —, otōto. — *in law*, ane-muko; imōto muko.
BROW, Mayu; mamige.
BROWN, Kuri-iro.
BRUISE, Uchi-kidz; uchimi.
BRUSH, *n.* Hake.
BRUSH, *v.* Haku.
BRUSHWOOD, Tszmagi; shiba.
BRUTE, Chikushō; kedamono.
BUBBLE, Awa; abuku.
BUBO, Yokone.
BUCK, Shika; saoshika.
BUCKET, Oke; te-oke; tago. *Well* —, tszrube.
BUCKLER, Tate.
BUCK-SKIN, Shika no kawa.
BUCK-WHEAT, Soba.
BUD, Me.
BUDDHA, Amida; butsz.
BUDDHISM, Buppō; butsz-dō.
BUDDHIST TEMPLE, Tera.
BUFFOON, Dōke-mono; niwaka.
BUG, Mushi.
BUGLE, Rappa; charumera.
BUILD, Tateru; fushin szru; konriu szru; kamayeru; tszkuru; tszku; zō-riu szru.
BULK, Kasa; ōkisa.
BULKY, Kasabaru; kasadaka.
BULL, O-ushi; kotoi.
BULLET, Tama.
BULL-FROG, Gama.
BULLION, Ara-gane.
BULLOCK, Ushi.
BUMBLE BEE, Kumabachi.
BUNCH, Fusa.
BUNDLE, *n.* Wa; tabane; tsztszmi; taba; kōri.
BUNDLE, *v.* Tabaneru; tsztszmu.
BUNG-HOLE, Taru no kuchi.
BUNGLING, Heta; bu-saiku; tsztana i; bu-ki yō; fu-tegiwa.
BUOY, Uke; ukegi.
BUOY, *v.* Ukaseru; ukamu.
BUOYANT, Uku.
BUOYANTLY, Uki-uki-to.
BUR, Iga.
BURDEN, Da; katszgi; ni; tszmi-daka.
BURDENSOME, Omoi.
BUREAU, Tansz.
BURLESQUE, Okashii.
BURN, *n.* Yakedo.
BURN, *v.* Taku; yaku; moyasz; kogasz; hoteru.
BURNISH, Migaku; togu.
BURROW, Horu.
BURST, Hashireru; yebiru; hazeru.
BURY, Hōmuru; udzmeru; ikeru. — *in the water*, szisō szru.
BUSHEL, *about* = Ni-to-nigō.
BUSHY, Shigeru.
BUSINESS, Yō-ji; yō; shōbai; ka-giyō; tosei. — *talk*, yōdan. *Though none of my business*, yoso-nagara. *None of my business*, watakushi no kamau koto de wa nai.
BUSTLE, Nigiyaka.
BUSY, Isogashii; yōji ga aru.
BUT, Bakari; tada; tadashi; shikashi. *Also the conjunctive affixes*, ba; tomo; temo.
BUTCHER, Niku-ya.
BUTTERFLY Chō.
BUTTS, Adzchi.

BUTTOCK, Shiri; Ishiki.
BUTTON, Botan.
BUY, Kau. *See*, kai-dashi; kai-hamari; kai-ire; kai-kaburi; kai-komi; kai-motome; kai-tai; shi-ire; shi-komi.
BUYER, Kai-te; kai-kata; kai-nushi.
BUY AND SELL, Uri-kai; bai-bai.
BY, De; ni; nite; motte. (*near*), soba; hotori; nami. — *the way*, katawara ni.
BY AND BY, Noch'hodo.
BY-ROAD, Nuke-michi.
BY-STANDER, Waki ni tatsz h'to.

C

CABIN, Heya; koya.
CABINET, Tansz.
CABLE, Tszna; nawa.
CACKLE, Hiyo-hiyo to naku.
CAGE, Kago.
CAJOLE, Hetszrau; kobiru; nei.
CAKE, Pan; mochi; k'washi; hi-g'washi.
CALABASH, Hiyōtan; fukube; hisago.
CALAMITY, Wazawai; sainan.
CALAMUS, Shōbu; ayame.
CALCINE, Yaku.
CALCULATE, Kanjō szru; kazoyeru; tszmoru.
CALCULATION, Kanjō; santō; sanyō; tszmori; hakari.
CALCULUS, Sekirin.
CALENDER, Koyomi.
CALF, Ushi no ko; yoyo. — *of leg*, komura; fukurahagi.
CALICO, Sarasa.
CALK, *see* Maihada.
CALL, *v.* Yobu; maneku; iu; tonayeru; nadzkeru; shōsz; gōsz; shōdai szru; yoru. — *together*, atszmeru; yoseru. — *to mind*, omoi-dasz. — *back*, yobi-kayesz. — *out*, yobi-dasz. — *in*, yobi-komu. — *near*, yobi-yoseru.
CALLING, Kagiyō; shōbai; tosei.
CALLOUS, Katai; katamari.
CALLUS, Mame.
CALM, Odayaka; shidzka; ochi-tszku; heiwa; nagu.
CALOMEL, Kei-fun.
CALORIC, K'waki.
CALUMNIATE, Zangen; soshiru; hihō; shīgoto.
CALYX, Utena.
CAMEL, Rakuda.
CAMELLIA, Tszbaki.
CAMERA OBSCURA, Nozoki.
CAMOMILE FLOWERS, Kuyoku; yakikk'wa.
CAMP, Jin; tamuro; jingoya.
CAMPAIGN, Ikusa.
CAMPHOR, Hennō; shōnō; riu-nō.
CAMPHOR TREE, Kusz-no-ki.
CAN, Dekiru, narō. *Formed also by the pot. mood ending*, yeru; *as*, miyeru, *can be seen.* kikoyeru, *can be heard.*
CANAL, Hori.
CANARY-BIRD, Kanariya,
CANCEL, Kesz.
CANCER, Yōso.
CANCER *of Breast*, Niuyō.
CANDLE, Rōsoku.
CANDLE *stick*, Shokudai.
CANDY, K'washi; *see* Tō.
CANE, Tszye; to.
CANGUE, Kubigase.
CANINE-TEETH, Kiba.
CANNON, Ōdztsz; teppō.
CANNONADE, Teppō de utsz.
CANNOT, Dekinu; atawadz. *Also formed by the neg. pot. mood ending*, yenu; *as*, miyenu, *cannot be seen.* Kikoyenu, *cannot be heard.* Kazoyenu, *cannot be counted.*
CANOE, Maruta-bune.
CANONICAL-BOOKS, Kiyō.
CANTER, Hashiru.
CANTHARIDES, Hammiyo.
CANTHUS, *External* —, majiri. *Internal* —, magashira.
CANVAS, Ho-momen.
CANVASS, Giron-szru; rondzru.
CAP, Dzkin; kaburi-mono; kammuri.
CAPABLE, Dekiru.
CAPACIOUS, Ōkii; hiroi.
CAPACITY Kiriyō; chiye; sai; ōkisa; hirosa; hodorai.
CAPE, Saki; misaki.
CAPER, Odoru; haneru.
CAPITAL, Motode; midzkin. — *punishment*, shizai; keiriku.
CAPITAL-CITY, Miyako.
CAPITULATE, Kōsan szru; kudasz.
CAPRICIOUS, Uwatszku; dekigokoro.
CAPSTAN, Rokuro; manriki; maki-rokuro; shachi.
CAPTAIN, Kashira.
CAPTIVATED, Mayo; jaku szru; norokeru.
CAPTIVE, Toriko. *To take* —, ikedoru.
CAPTURE, Toru; torayeru; tszkamayeru; ikedoru.

CAR, Kuruma.
CARBONIC-ACID, Tansan.
CARBUNCLE, Yō.
CARCASS, Sh'kabane; shigai
CARD, Nafuda. *Playing* —, karuta; meku-ri-fuda.
CARDAMON-SEED, Yakuchi.
CARDIAC-ORIFICE, I no jōkō.
CARDINAL, Kanyō; dai-ichi; kanjin.
CARE, Shimpai; kokorodzkai; nen; anji; kidzkai; kokorogake; kurō; tsztszshimi. *Take* —, abunai; ki wo tszkeru; yōjin szru. *Don't* —, kamawanai.
CAREEN, Katamuku; kashigu; katageru.
CAREFUL, Tsztszshimu; yōjin-bukai; mem-mitsz-na; nen wo ireru; teinei.
CARELESS, Zonzai; okotaru; yudan; metta.
CARELESSLY, Nen wo iredz-ni; ki wo tsz-kedz-ni; ukkari-to; somatsz-ni.
CARESS, Amayeru.
CARGO, Ni; nimotsz; tszmi-ni.
CARIOUS TOOTH, Mushiba.
CARNIVEROUS, Nikujiki.
CARP, *v.* Rikutsz wo iu.
CARPENTER, Daiku.
CARPET, Shiki-mono.
CARRIAGE, Kuruma; nari; nari-furi.
CARRIER, Ninsoku; karuko.
CARROT, Ninjin.
CARRY, Motsz; hakobu; hissageru. *To — on the shoulder*, katszgu; katageru. *To — with a pole across the shoulder*, nina-u. — *in the hand*, sageru; tadzsayeru. — *on the back*, ō; ombu szru; shō, or seō. — *in the belt*, obiru. — *in the bosom*, daku. — *a chair*, kaku. *To — on*, szru; nasz. — *away*, motte-yuku. — *back*, motte-kayeru. — *up*, motte-agaru. — *down*, motte-oriru. — *out*, motte-deru. — *in*, motte-hairu. — *across*, motte-wataru. — *through*, motte-tōru.
CART, Kuruma.
CARVE, Horu; kiru.
CASCADE, Taki.
CASE, Tameshi; rei; yoshi; koto; arisama; yōsz; yōdai; hako; saya; tsztszmi; fuku-ro; tana. *In case*, moshi; naraba; mo-shikuba.
CASH, Zeni; kane; genkin; sokkin.
CASK, Taru; son.
CASKET, Hako.
CASSIA, Keishi; nikkei.
CAST, Nageru; hōru; utsz; iru; tojiru. — *away*, szteru; utcharu. — *out*, dasz. — *in*, ireru. — *down*, orosz; otosz. — *up*, nage-ageru; kanjō szru.
CASTANET, Yotszdake.
CASTIGATE, Butsz; imashimeru.
CASTLE, Shiro.
CASTOR-OIL, Himashi no abura
CASTRATE, Kintama wo nuku,
CASUAL, Omowadz; hakaradz; futo; rinji-no.
CASUALTY, Kega; ayamachi.
CAT, Neko.
CATALOGUE, Mokuroku.
CATAMENIA, Tszki-no-mono; sawari; kei-szi; g'wasszi.
CATARACT, Taki. — *of eye*, sokohi.
CATARRH, Fūja; kaze; hikikaze.
CATCH, Toru; torayeru; tszkamayeru. — *up to*, oi-tszku. — *cold*, kaze wo hiku. — *disease*, utszru; tszku. — *rain-water*, tameru. — *fire*, tszku.
CATECHISE, Seme-tō; mon-dō szru.
CATER, Makanau.
CATERPILLAR, Shaku-tori-mushi.
CATHARTIC, Gezai; kudashi-guszri.
CATTY, Kin.
CAULK, *see Calk.*
CAUSE, *n.* Wake; yuye; shisai; sei; dōri; szji; yuyen.
CAUSE, *v.* Saseru; *formed by the caust. form of the verb ; as,* miseru, *to cause to see, to show.* Kikaseru, *to cause to hear, to tell.* Yukaseru, *to cause to go, to send.*
CAUSTIC, Fuyaku; kusarakashi.
CAUTERIZE, Kusarakasz.
CAUTION, Tsztszshimi; yōjin; tashinami; yōi; imashime.
CAVALRY, Kiba-musha.
CAVE, *n.* Ana; hora.
CAVE, *v.* Kudzreru.
CAVIL, Rikutsz; hi wo utsz.
CAVITY, Ana; kubomi.
CAYENNE PEPPER, Tōgarashi.
CAW, Kā-kā.
CEASE, Yameru; yosz; todomeru; tayeru.
CEDAR, Szgi.
CEDE, Yudzru; yurusz.
CEILING, Tenjō.
CELEBRATE, Iwau; matszru; shuku szru.
CELEBRATED, Nadakai; kōmei; mei.
CELERITY, Hayasa; szmiyaka.
CELESTIAL, Ten no.
CELIBACY, Musai.
CELL, Kobeya; sz.
CELLAR, Anagura.
CEMENT, *n.* Nori.
CEMENT, *v.* Tszgu; awaseru; muszbu.

CEMETERY, Hakasho; hakaba; hakachi.
CENSER, Kōro.
CENSOR, O-metszke.
CENSORIOUS, Kogoto dzki; hinan-sh'tagaru.
CENSURE, Togame; imashime; kimeru; modoku; sattō.
CENSUS, Nindzu; nimbetz; h'to-kadz.
CENTIPEDE, Mukade.
CENTRE, Man-naka.
CENTURY, H'yaku nen.
CERATE, Kōyaku.
CEREMONY, Reigi; rei; reishiki. *Without* —, o jigi-nashi; yenriyo nashi; habakari nashi.
CERTAIN, *a.* Tash'ka-na; hon-no; sadaka; jitsz na; makoto; aru; saru; nanigashi; masashiki.
CERTAINLY, Tash'ka-ni; honto; makoto-ni; shika-to.
CERTIFICATE, Shō-ko-gaki; shōmon; tegata; kitte.
CERTIFY, Ukeau.
CERUMEN, Mimiaka.
CHAFE, Szru; szri-kiru; szri-yaburu; ijimeru; azakeru; naburu; karakau.
CHAFF, Nuka.
CHAFFER, Kojiru.
CHAIN, Kusari.
CHAIR, Isz; kosh'kake; k'yokuroku; za.
CHAIR, *sedan* —, Kago; norimono.
CHAIR-BEARERS, Kago-kaki.
CHALK, Gofun.
CHALLENGE, Yobi-dasz.
CHAMBER, Nema; sho.
CHAMBER-MAID, Koshi-moto; heya-kata; gejo.
CHAMBERPOT, Shi-bin.
CHAMP, Kamu.
CHAMPION *of wrestlers*, Sekitori.
CHANCE, Un; hima; szki; szkima; toki; jisetsz. *By* —, omowadz-ni; hakaradzni; futo.
CHANGE, *of money*, Tszri.
CHANGE, *v.* Aratameru; hendzru; bakeru; kawaru; kayeru. — *money*, riyō-gai szru.
CHANGEABLE, Utszrigi-na; uwatszku.
CHANNEL, Mi-o; funa-michi.
CHANT, Utau; tonayeru; gindzru.
CHAOS, Doro-umi.
CHAP, Akagire.
CHAPTER, Shō; hen; k'wai.
CHAR, Kogasz; kogareru.
CHARACTER, Ji; moji; shirushi; hiyōban; tachi.
CHARCOAL, Szmi.
CHARGE, *v.* Semeru; ī-tszkeru; tszkeru; owaseru. — *a gun*, tszmeru. *Give in* —, adzkeru.
CHARGE, *n.* Ne; nedan; mei; i-tszke; ōse.
CHARITY, Fubin; jihi; awaremi; hodokoshi; segiyō; hōsha; kōriyoku.
CHARLATAN, Namaiki; heta; yabu-isha; yōi.
CHARM, *n.* Mamori; go-fū.
CHARM, *v.* Mayowasz.
CHART, Yedz.
CHASE, *v.* O, *or* oi; karu. — *out*, oi-dasz. — *into*, oi-komu. — *around*, oi-mawaru. — *away*, oi-harau; oi-nokeru; oi-tateru; oi-yaru. — *and overtake*, oi-tszku. — *back*, oi-kayesz.
CHASE, *n.* Kari; oi.
CHASTE, Katai. — *woman*, kimuszme; teijo; teisetz.
CHASTISE, Butsz; korasz; imashimeru.
CHAT, Hanashi; iu.
CHATTEL, Nimotsz; kagu.
CHATTER, Shaberu; sayedzru.
CHEAP, Yaszi; ge-jiki.
CHEAPEN, Makeru; sagaru; yaszku szru; ne wo hiku.
CHEAT, Damasz; azamuku; itszwaru; mayakasz; taburakasz; tabakaru.
CHECK, Tomeru; todomeru; hikayeru.
CHECKERBOARD, Go-ban.
CHECKERS, Go-ishi.
CHECKERED *figure*, Benke-jima; ichi-matsz; gobanjima.
CHEEK, Hō; hōbeta.
CHEER, *v.* Toki no koye wo ageru; hagemasz; chikara wo tszkeru; kibarashi wo szru.
CHEERFUL, Kishoku ga yoi; keshiki ga yoi; kokoromochi no yoi; kigen yoi; kigarui.
CHEMISE, Jiban.
CHERISH, Yashinau; daku.
CHERRY, Sakura.
CHESS, Shōgi. — *board*, shōgi-ban. — *men*, koma.
CHEST, Hako; hitsz; mune; kiyōkaku.
CHESTNUT, Kuri.
CHEW, Kamu; kū.
CHICKEN, Hiyoko; niwatori.
CHICKEN-POX, Midzimo.
CHIDE, Imashimeru; korasz; sh'karu; togameru.
CHIEF, Chō; kashira; ichi-ban; shōgun; taishō; sen; tōdori.

CHIEFLY, Moppara; ō-kata; ta-bun; tai-han.
CHILBLAIN, Shimoyake.
CHILD, Akago; akambō; ko; kodomo; bōya; shōni; nenne; yaya; midorigo; dōji.
CHILD-BIRTH, San; ko wo umu. *A woman in* —, sampu.
CHILDHOOD, Osanai-toki; yō-nen; itoke-nai.
CHILDISH, Kodomorashii; oi-boreru; taji-reru; rōmō.
CHILDREN, Kodomo; kodomo-ra.
CHILL, *v.* Heyasz; samuku szru.
CHILL OF FEVER, Okan.
CHILLY, Samui; hiyeru.
CHIME, Chōshi.
CHIMNEY, Kemuri-dashi.
CHIN, Otogai; ago.
CHINA, Kara; morokoshi; shina.
CHINA-ROOT, San-kirai.
CHINAWARE, Setomono.
CHINK, Szkima; hima; ma.
CHINTZ, Sarasa.
CHIP, *n.* Koppa; kokera; kudz.
CHIP, *v.* Sogu.
CHISEL, Nomi.
CHIVALRY, Bushi; samurai.
CHOICE, Yerami; yori; gimmi sh'ta; goku-jō; yori-nuki.
CHOKE, *v.* Musebu; kubiru; tszmeru.
CHOLERA, Korori; k'wakuran.
CHOOSE, Yeramu; yoru; szguru.
CHOP, Kiru; tataku.
CHORD, Chōshi; shirabe; soroi.
CHRIST, Kirish'to.
CHRISTIAN, Kirisztan.
CHRONIC, Kōjiru.
CHRONIC-DISEASE, Chō-biyō.
CHRONICLE, Rekishi.
CHRONOLOGY, Nendaiki.
CHRONOMETER, Tokei.
CHRYSALIS, Sanagi.
CHRYSANTHEMUM, Kiku no hana.
CHUM, Dōkiyo.
CHURCH, Dō.
CHURLISH, Burei; shitszrei; buaisatsz; buaisō; butchōdzra.
CICATRICE, Kidz no ato.
CICATRIZE, Naoru; iyeru.
CIGAR, Maki-tabako.
CINDER, Hinoko; keshidzmi; moyekudz.
CINNABAR, Shinsha.
CINNAMON, Nikkei; keishi.
CIPHER, *v.* San wo szru.
CIRCLE, Maru; wa.
CIRCUIT, Mawari; meguri.
CIRCUITOUS, Mawari-dōi; uyen-na.
CIRCULAR, Marui.
CIRCULATE, Meguru; mawaru.
CIRCULATION, Jun-k'wan; meguri; kayoi.
CIRCUMFERENCE, Mawari.
CIRCUMSCRIBE, Kakomu; kakō.
CIRCUMSPECT, Tsztszshimu; yō-jin; ki wo tszkeru; tashinamu.
CIRCUMSTANCE, Koto; yoshi; arisama; yōsz; shigi.
CIRCUMSTANCES, Shinshō; bungen; shina; shindai. *According to* —, koto ni yoru.
CIRCUMSTANTIALLY, Kuwashiku; isai-ni; komayaka-ni.
CIRCUMVENT, Damasz; taburakasz; azamu-ku; kataru.
CIRCUS, Kiyokuba.
CISTERN, Midz-tame.
CITADEL, Shiro.
CITE, Hiku; meshidasz; mesz.
CITIZEN, H'to, chō-nin; nimbetsz.
CITRON, Bushukan.
CITY, Tok'wai. *Capital* —, Miyako.
CIVIL, Teinei; aisō no yoi.
CIVILITY, Teinei; aisō; reigi; seiji.
CLAM, Hamaguri.
CLAMOR, *v.* Sawagu; wameku; sakebu; zo-meku; zazameku.
CLAMOR, *n.* Sawagi; sōdō.
CLAMP, Kaszgai.
CLAN, Zoku.
CLANDESTINE, Hisoka-na; naishō; shinobu; sotto.
CLAP, Ateru; tataku; utsz. — *the hands*, kashiwade.
CLAPBOARD, Itabame. *To* —, ita wo ha-ru.
CLARIFY, Szmasz.
CLASP, *n.* Tome; kanagu; kohaze; seme.
CLASP, *v.* Kakeru; nigiru; daku; karamu; shigami-tszku.
CLASS, Rui; shu-rui; tagui; tōri; kurai.
CLASSIFY, Buwake; naraberu.
CLATTER, Yakamashii; sawagi.
CLAUSE, Ku; kajō.
CLAW, T'szme.
CLAY, Neba-tszchi; tszchi.
CLEAN, *a.* Kirei; isagiyoi; keppaku; shō-jō; kiyoraka.
CLEAN, *adv.* Szkkari; sappari.
CLEANSE, Kirei ni szru; arau; kiyomeru; szszgu.

CLEAR, Akiraka; kirei; szmu; szmasz; sawayaka, meihaku; kiyoraka; shōjō; hakkiri to sh'ta; fummiyō; szki-tōru. — *away*, Tori-harau; harau; hareru; akeru; nokeru; kai-hotsz szru.
CLEAT, San.
CLEAVE, Waru; tszku; hiki-tszku; nebari-tszku.
CLEFT, Wareme; szkima; hibiki.
CLEMENT, K'wannin.
CLEPSYDRA, Rōkoku.
CLERK, Bantō.
CLEVER, Jōdz; rikō; kash'koi; hatszmei; takumi.
CLEW, Atokata.
CLIFF, Gake; soba.
CLIMATE, Jikō; yōki; kikō.
CLIMAX, Sakari; tōge; debana; saichiu.
CLIMB, Noboru; yojiru.
CLINCH, Nigiru.
CLING, Szgaru; szgari-tszku; tori-tszku.
CLINKING, *sound*. Gara-gara.
CLIP, Kiru; hasande kiru; habuku; hedzru; hatszru.
CLOAK, Hiki-maki.
CLOCK, Tokei.
CLOD, Tszchi-kure.
CLOG, *n.* Geta; bokuri; ashida.
CLOG, *v.* Tszmaru; tszkayeru; fusagaru; jama szru; sasayeru; samatageru; sawaru.
CLOSE, *v.* Tateru; shimeru; tozasz; tojiru; tatamu; fusagu; shibomeru; awaseru; nigiru; owaru; shimau; szmu; yoseru; tszmeru.
CLOSE, *a.* Katai; semai; tszmeru; chikai; shiwai; komoru.
CLOSELY, Kataku; kisshiri-to.
CLOSET, Todana; nando; oshi-ire.
CLOT, Katamari.
CLOTH, Tammono; kempu. *Cotton* —, momen. *Woollen* —, rasha.
CLOTHE, Kiru; haku; chaku szru; fuku szru; chaku-yō szru.
CLOTHING, Kimono; ishō; i-fuku; shozoku.
CLOUD, Kumo.
CLOUDY, Kumoru. — *sky*, donten.
CLOVE, Chōji.
CLOVER, Umagoyashi.
CLOWN. Dōke-mono; niwaka; hiyo-kin; inakamono.
CLOWNISH, Yabo-na; bukotsz; buiki; busahō.
CLOY, Aku.
CLUB, Bō; sau; kumi; nakama; shachiu; sha; renchiu.
CLUCKING, Kukunaki.
CLUMSY, Heta; bukiyō-na; tsztanai.
CLUSTER, Fusa; mori; mura; muragaru.
CLUTCH, Nigiru; tszkamu.
COAGULATE, Katamaru; kataku naru; kogoru.
COAL, Sek'tan; ishidzmi; oki.
COAL-SCUTTLE, Szmitori.
COARSE, Futoi; arai; so; somatsz; zats; zatto. — *language*, sogon.
COAST, Kaihen; umi-bata; kaigan; umibe.
COAT, Haori.
COAX, Kudoku; szszmeru; szkasz; nadameru.
COBBLER, Naoshi.
COBWEB, Kumo no sz.
COCCYX, Kame-no-o.
COCHIN-CHINA, Annan-koku.
COCHINEAL, Yōkō.
COCK, Ondori; osz.
COCK-CROWING, Toki wo tszkuru; keimei.
COCK-FIGHTING, Ke-awaseru; tori-awase; tō kei.
COCKROACH, Abura-mushi.
COCKS-COMB, Tosaka; kei-tō.
COCOA-NUT, Yashi.
COCOON, Mayu.
COD, Tara.
COD-LIVER-OIL, Rei-furu-taran.
COFFEE, Kōhi.
COFFIN, K'wan; hitszgi; hayaoke.
COGITATE, Kangayeru; omō; kamben szru; andzru; shiriyo szru.
COHABIT, Kōgō szru; majiwaru.
COIL, *n.* Toguro.
COIL, *v.* Waganeru; wadakamaru; kanagaru; karamu.
COIN, Kane.
COITION, Kōgō; makuhai.
COLANDER, Zaru.
COLD, Samui; hiyeru; kanjiru; tszmitai; reiki; kan; samusa; kanki; utoi. *To take* —, kaze wo hiku.
COLIC, Fukuts'u; hara-itami; senshaku.
COLLAR, Yeri.
COLLATE, Kuraberu; hiki-awaseru; santei; sankō.
COLLEAGUE. Dōyaku.
COLLECT, Atszmeru; yoseru; tameru; takaru; matomeru; tori-tateru; tszdoyeru; tsznoru.
COLLECTOR, Kaketori.
COLLEGE, Gakumonjo; gakkō.
COLLISION, Tszki-ataru.

Colloquial, Zokugo; heiwa.
Collusion, Nare-ai.
Colonize, Wiyeru.
Color, *n.* Iro.
Color, *v.* Irodoru; iro wo tszkeru; saishiki.
Colt, Koma; uma no ko.
Column, Hashira.
Comb, *n.* Kushi.
Comb, *v.* Toku.
Combat, Uchiai; shiai; tataki-ai.
Combine, Awaseru; kuwaszru; mazeru; chōgō szru.
Combustible, Moyeru. — *matter*, moyekusa.
Come, Kuru; chaku-szru; kitaru; oide; mairu; tszku; tōrai szru; tōchaku. — *back*, kayeru. — *down*, kudaru; oriru. — *up*, agaru. — *in*, agaru; hairu; iru. — *near*, yoru; chika-yoru. — *on*, iza; ide; szszmu. — *out*, deru; ideru. — *over*, *or across*, wataru; koyeru. — *together*, atszmāru; yoru. — *to pass*, hatash'te; atatta. — *up with*, oi-tszku. — *at*, oyobu; todoku. — *after*, ato kara kuru; tori ni kuru. *How much does it come to?* nedan wa ikura; awasete ikura; dono-kurai. — *to himself*, honshin ga tszita. *Come to hand*, te ni todoku.
Comet, Hōki-boshi; szi-sei.
Comfort, Nagusameru.
Comic, Okashii; dōkeru.
Command, Ī-tszke; geji; mei; sashidz; shiki.
Commandant, Tōdori.
Commander in chief, Shōgun; taishō.
Commandment, Imashime; go-kai; *the ten* —, jikkai.
Commemorate, Iwau; shuku szru.
Commence, Hajimeru; okosz.
Commencement, Hajimari; okori; hottan; shote; saisho.
Commend, Homeru; tori-mochi; adzkeru; makaseru.
Comment, Toku; chiu szru; chiu-kai szru.
Commerce, Akinai; bai-bai; shōbai.
Commingle, Mazeru.
Commiserate, Awaremu; fubin ni omō.
Commiseration, Awaremi; fubin; sokuin;
Commissary, Hiōy-rō-kata.
Commission, Men-jō; choku-jō. — *money*, kōsen; buai; kaszri; uwamaye. — *merchant*, toiya.
Commissioner, Shisha; tszkai; shisetsz.
Commit, Adzkeru; makaseru; yudaneru; nindzru; szru; nasz; itasz. — *to prison* rōya ni ireru. — *crime*, tszmi wo okasz. — *to memory*, oboyeru; sorandzru; kioku szru.
Committee, Sōdai.
Commodious, Benri; tszgō; yaku ni tatsz; yō ni tatsz.
Commodity, Nimotsz; ni; shina mono.
Common, Tszne; hei zei; hei-jitsz; fudan; itszmo. — *people*, hei-min. — *person*, zokunin; heinin; bon-nin. — *soldier*, hei-sotsz. — *colloquial*, zoku-go; hei-wa. — *clothes*, hei-fuku.
Commonly, Zentai; g'wan-rai; tszne-dzne.
Commotion, Sōdō; sawagi; midare.
Commune, Hanashiai; adzkaru.
Communicate, Tamau; kudasaru; yaru; shiraseru; kikaseru; iu; hanasz.
Communication, Ts'urō; ōrai; michi; yukiki; otodzre; tayori; inshin; majiwari.
Commute, Aganau; tszgunau.
Compact, *n.* Yak'soku; yakujō.
Compact, *a.* Katai.
Companion, Tomodachi; tszre; hōbai; hōyu.
Company, Nakama; kumi; renchiu; taigo; shachiu. *Keep* —, tszki-ai; majiwaru.
Compare, Kuraberu; hi-szru; junjiru; hai-szru; yosoyeru.
Compass, Kagiri, mawari. *Mariner's* —, jishaku.
Compasses, Bunmawari.
Compassion, Awaremi; fubin; jihi; nasake; itawashii.
Compatible, Au; kanau.
Compel, Osz; saseru.
Compendiously, Aramashiku; tairiyaku; ōmune.
Compensate, Mukui; kayesz; hōdzru; tszgunau; aganau.
Compete, Kisoi; arasoi; aite ni szru.
Competitor, Aite.
Compile, Setchiu szru.
Complain, Uttayeru; shūso-szru; tang'wan; nageku; nakigoto wo iu.
Complete, Mattaku; jū-bun.
Complete, *v.* Szmasz; dekiru; deki-agaru; jō-jū szru; owaru; shimau; shi-ageru; zembi; sonawaru; jūbun; tarau; manzoku.
Complexion, Ganshoku; kao-iro.
Compliment, Iwai; shūgi; shuku; homare; aisatsz.
Comply, Sh'tagau; kanau; nabikeru.
Compose, Tszkuru; koshirayeru; ochi-tszku; shidzmaru.

COMPOSITION, Bunshō; awase; shi-kata; shi-hō; sei-hō.
COMPOSURE, Hei-ki; ochi-tszki.
COMPOUND, Awaseru; mazeru.
COMPREHEND, Wakaru; fukumu; satoru; komoru; obiru; omoi-tori; yetoku szru.
COMPRESS, Osz.
COMPRISE, Fukumu; kaneru; komoru; obiru.
COMPULSION, Shĭte; oshite; muri-ni.
COMPUNCTION, Kuyami; zannen; kuyashiku omō.
COMPUTE, Kazoyeru; tszmoru; hakaru; kanjō szru.
COMRADE, Tomodachi; hōbai.
CONCAVE, Kubomi; kuboi.
CONCEAL, Kakusz; kakumau; hisomu; shinobu.
CONCEALMENT, *without* —, akarasama-ni. *In* —, shinonde; hisoka-ni.
CONCEDE, Shōchi szru; yurusz; nattoku szru.
CONCEIT, Omoi-nashi; dekigokoro.
CONCEITED, Hokoru.
CONCEIVE, Haramu; k'wainin szru; ninshin szru; mimochi; omoi; wakaru.
CONCENTRATE, Yose-atszmeru; korasz; kōri-katamaru.
CONCERN, *v.* Tszku; kakawaru; kamau; anjiru; tonjaku szru; toriau.
CONCERN, *n.* Kidzkai; shimpai; kokorodzkai; anji; kurō; kamau-koto; sashi-kamaye.
CONCERT, *in* —, tagai-ni; dō-on.
CONCH, Horagai; hora.
CONCILIATE, Kigen wo toru.
CONCISELY, Aramashiku; tairiyaku; zatto; riyaku-sh'te.
CONCLUDE, Owaru; shimau; sadameru.
CONCORD, Sh'tashimi; mutszmajii; itchi.
CONCUBINE, Mekake; tekake; shō.
CONCUSSION, Hibiki.
CONDEMN, Tszmi ni otosz; tszmi wo sadameru; kiyokuji.
CONDENSE, Kataku szru; katameru.
CONDITION, Yōsz; yōdai; arisama; bungen; mibun.
CONDOLE, Mimai; tomorai.
CONDUCE, Tame-ni.
CONDUCT, *n.* Okonai; giyō-jō; furumai; shiuchi; shogiyō; shosa.
CONDUCT, *v.* Tszreru; michi-biku; annai szru; indō szru; tori-okonau; tori-atszkau; yaru.
CONDUIT, Toi; hi.
CONFECTIONARY, K'washi.
CONFEDERATE, Katan; satan; katode; mikata; ichi-mi.
CONFERENCE, Ō-setsz; sōdan; tai-dan.
CONFESS, Haku-jō szru; zange szru.
CONFIDE, Tanomu; makaseru; yudaneru; adzkeru; shinkō szru.
CONFINE, Kagiru; komoru; oshi-komeru; hiki-komoru.
CONFINED, Ki no-komoru; komoru.
CONFINES, Sakai.
CONFIRM, Sadameru; īkatameru.
CONFISCATE, Kessho szru; mosshu szru.
CONFLAGRATION, K'waji.
CONFLICT, *n.* Kassen; tatakai; kenk'wa.
CONFLUENCE, Ochiai.
CONFORM, Sh'tagau; kanau. *Not — to*, tagayeru.
CONFRONT, Mukau; tai szru; ai-mukai.
CONFUSE, Midareru; midasz; urotayeru.
CONFUTE, Ī-tszmeru; heikō szru.
CONGEAL, Katamaru; kōru.
CONGEE, Kayu.
CONGENIAL, Au.
CONGENITAL *disease*, Taidoku.
CONGRATULATE, Iwai; shuku szru; medetai.
CONGREGATE, Atszmaru; yoru.
CONJECTURE, Sziriyō szru; szisatsz; ateru; kumi-toru; oshi-hakaru; tszmori; *or th; verb suffixes*, de arō; shō; ō; *or final n.*
CONJUGAL, Fū-fu-no; me-oto-no.
CONJUNCTURE, Tokoro; toki; ori-fushi; orikara.
CONJURATION, Mahō.
CONJURE, Chikawaseru; chikai wo tatesaseru.
CONJURER, Mahō tszkai.
CONNECT, Awaseru; tszgu; tsznagu; tszdzkeru.
CONNECTION, Shinrui; yen; aidagara; chinami; yoszga; awaseme.
CONNIVE, Minu-furi wo szru; shiranu kao wo szru; shirabakkureru.
CONNOISEUR, Kanteisha.
CONQUER, Katsz.
CONSANGUINITY, Chiszji; kettō.
CONSCIENCE, Honshin; hara; kokoro.
CONSCIOUSNESS, — *of guilt*, ushirogurai. *Return to* —, honshō ga tszku.
CONSECRATE, Kaigen szru; ageru; agameru.
CONSECUTIVELY, Tszdzku; jun-jun-ni.
CONSEQUENTIAL, Shisairashii.
CONSENT, Yurusz; shōchi; gaten; natto-

ku. *One* —, dō shin; dō-on; ichidō-ni; ichi-do ni; ubenau.
CONSEQUENCE, Ato; daiji; taisetsz. *No* —, daiji-nai; kamawanu.
CONSERVE, *n*. Neriyaku.
CONSIDER, Kangayeru; omoi; anjiru; kamben szru.
CONSIDERABLY, Yohodo; yaya; dzibun.
CONSIDERATE, Tsztszshimu; omoi-yaru.
CONSIGN, Adzkeru.
CONSIGNEE, Adzkarite.
CONSIGNER, Adzke-nushi.
CONSIST *of*, Tszkuru; koshirayeru; shihō.
CONSISTENCE, Kosa.
CONSOLE, Nagusameru; nadameru.
CONSOLATION, Kiyaszme.
CONSOLIDATE, Awaseru; gasszru; katakuszru; katameru.
CONSPICUOUS, Akiraka; ichijirushi; meihaku; medachi.
CONSPIRE, Ī-awaseru; kumi-au; shi-kumu; kuwadateru.
CONSPIRACY, Muhon; mikkei.
CONSTABLE, Dōshin.
CONSTANCY, Setszgi.
CONSTANTLY, Taiyedz-ni; tōshi; yamedz-ni; shijū; shikiri-ni.
CONSTERNATION, Odoroki; bōzen; bikkuri; urotaye; rōbai.
CONSTIPATION, Kesszru; hiketsz; bempei.
CONSTITUTE, Tateru; sadameru; nasz; naru.
CONSTITUTION, Sei-ji; umaretszki; shō; shōai; seishitsz; mijō.
CONSTRAIN, Osz; shīru.
CONSTRAINT, *by* —, Oshite; shīte; muri-ni; muri-mutai-ni.
CONSTRICT, Chijimeru; shimeru.
CONSTRUCT, Tszkuru; koshirayeru; fushin-szru.
CONSTRUCTION, Seisaku.
CONSTRUE, Honyaku szru; toku; naosz.
CONSUL, Konshur.
CONSULT, Sōdan szru; chōji-awaseru; dankō szru; haizai szru.
CONSUME, Tsziyasz; tszkusz; yakete-shimau; shōshitsz. — *the day*, kurasz; utszsz.
CONSUMPTION, — *of the lungs*, Rōshō; rōgai.
CONTACT, Tszku; ateru.
CONTAGION, Yaku-biyō; yeki.
CONTAGIOUS *disease*, Utszri-yamai; denzembiyō.
CONTAIN, Hairu; tszmu, obiru; ireru.
CONTAMINATE, Kegareru; yogareru; fujō ni szru.
CONTEMN, Karondzŕu; anadoru; misageru; iyashimeru; sageshimu; naigashiro ni omō.
CONTEMPLATE, Kangayeru; nagameru.
CONTEMPTIBLE, Iyashii.
CONTEND, Arasō; kisō; hagemi-au; isakau.
CONTENT, Kotutaru; anshin; akirameru.
CONTENTS, Iremono.
CONTENTION, Kenk'wa; arasoi; kōron; mome; monchaku.
CONTEST, Arasoi; kenk'wa; kassen.
CONTIGUOUS, Tszgi; tszdzku.
CONTINGENT, Hakaradz; rinji; fui-no; omoi-gake nai; omoi-yoranu.
CONTINUAL, Tayedz; yamedz; tōshi; tszdzkeru.
CONTINUE, Todomaru; motsz; tamotz; tszdzku.
CONTORT, Nejireru.
CONTOUR, Szji; nari; kiwa.
CONTRABAND, Go-hatto-na mono; kinzei na shina; bahan; nuke-ni.
CONTRACT, *v*. Chijimeru; chijikamaru; habuku; szkumeru; chijimaru; semaku szru; tszmeru; tszru; tszdzmeru; bibiru; yakujō szru; yak'soku szru; hikiukeru; ukeau.
CONTRACT, *n*. Ukeoi; yakujō; yak'soku.
CONTRADICT, Ī-kesz; sakarau; ifusegu; sakō; nigon.
CONTRARY, Giyaku; sakasama; sakarau. *On the* —, kayette; kekku.
CONTRAST, Urahara; hantai.
CONTRIBUTE, Kishin szru; kifu szru; josei szru; kōriyoku; k'wanke.
CONTRIBUTION, Kishin; kifu; hōnō.
CONTRIVE, Kufu szru; takumu; hatszmē szru; hakaru; shigaku; takunamu.
CONTROL, Katsz; sei szru.
CONTROVERSY, Arasoi; kōron; sōron.
CONTUSE, Utsz.
CONUNDRUM, Nazo.
CONVALESCENT, Hombuku; zen-k'wai; heiyu.
CONVENE, Atszmeru; yoseru.
CONVENIENT, Benri; tszgō; katte; tszide; chōhō.
CONVENT, Amadera.
CONVERSE, Hanashi-au; dandzru.
CONVERSELY, Abekobe; kayette.
CONVERSION, Kedo; henk'wa.
CONVERT, Kawaru; hendzru; kedo szru; k'wa-szru; aratameru.

CONVEX, Nakadaka.
CONVEY, Hakobu; moteyuku; unsō; watasz.
CONVICT, *n.* Tszmibito; toga-nin; zai-nin; meshiudo.
CONVICT, *v.* Ī-fuseru; ī-taosz.
CONVINCE, Nattoku szru; akirameru; heikō szru; gaten-szru.
CONVOKE, Yobi-atszmeru.
CONVOLUTED, Unekure; uneru.
CONVOLVULUS, Asagao.
CONVULSED, Hiki-tszkeru.
CONVULSION, Kiyōfū.
COOK, *v.* Taku; riyōri szru.
COOK, *n.* Meshi-taki; nikata; riyōri nin.
COOL, Tszmitai; hiye; samui; szdzshi; nōriyō; sameru; szdzmu.
COOLIE, Ninsoku; karuko.
COOP, Toya; ori; togura.
COOPER, Okeya.
COOPERATE, Tetszdau.
COPIOUS, Yutaka-na; tanto; tak'san.
COPPER, Akagane; dō.
COPPERAS, Rōha; riyoku-ban.
COPPERPLATE, Dōhan.
COPULATE, Tszrumu.
COPY, *n.* Sh'ta-gaki; gesho; ammon; sōkō; sei-sho; honsho; utszshi; tehon. *Two copies of a book*, hon ni bu.
COPY, *v.* Utszsz; kakitoru.
CORAL, Sangoju; umimatsz.
CORD, Himo; ito; nawa.
CORDAGE, Nawa.
CORDIAL, *a.* Nengoro. — *medicine*, kitszke.
CORE, Shin.
COREA, Chōsen; kōrai.
CORK, *see* Kuchi.
CORMORANT, U.
CORN, Tomorokoshi; tako; iwonome.
CORNEA, Kakumaku.
CORNER, Kaku; kado; szmi.
COROLLA, Rin.
CORPS, Kumi; te; taigo.
CORPSE, Shigai; sh'kabane.
CORPULENT, Koyeru; himan; futoru; botteri-to; buta-buta to.
CORRECT, *a.* Tadashii; yoi; machigai nai; sōi nai; chigawanu; chan-to.
CORRECT, *v.* Aratameru; naosz; kaki-naosz; ī-naosz; shi-naosz; kiyōgo szru; imashime; korasz.
CORRESPOND, Au; kanau.
CORRIDOR, Rōka.
CORRODE, Kusarakasz; kui-iru; shimi-komu.

CORROSIVE SUBLIMATE, Mōko.
CORRUGATED, Chijireru.
CORRUPT, Kusaru; yokoshima; aku.
COST, Ne; nedan; atai; niuyō; iriyō; zappi; irime; irika.
COSTIVE, Kesszru.
COSTUME, Idetachi; kimono; ifuku; ishō.
COTTON, Wata; momen. — *flannel*, mompa. — *clothes*, mempuku. — *rug*, mensen. — *velvet*, menten; membirōdo.
COUCH, Nedoko.
COUGH, Seki.
COUNCIL, Hiyōjō; k'wai.
COUNCIL *of state*, Gorōjū.
COUNSEL, *n.* Iken; imashime.
COUNSEL, *v.* Iken szru; imashimeru; sōdan szru.
COUNT, Kazoyeru; kanjō szru; hakaru; tszmoru. — *on the fingers*, yubiori.
COUNTENANCE, Kao; omote; tszra; kambase; iro; keshiki; memboku; mempi.
COUNTERACT, Kesz; naku szru.
COUNTERFEIT, Nise-mono; nisegane; niseru; magayeru.
COUNTERSIGN, Aidz; Ai-kotoba.
COUNTRY, Kuni; koku; tochi; inaka; zaigō; kokka. *Native* —, kokiyō; furusato.
COUNTRYMAN, Inaka-mono; h'yak'shō; dōkoku na h'to; zaisho.
COUNTY, Kōri; gun.
COUPLE, F'tatsz, ittszi; awaseru.
COURAGE, Yūki; dai-tan; kimo-f'toi; isamashii; takeki; goyū.
COURIER, Hikiyaku; haya.
COURSE, Michi; szji; hōgaku; narabi; tszdzki; jun. *Of* —, shizen-ni; mochiron.
COURT, *n.* Seifu; yak'sho. *Court-room*, kujiba.
COURT, *v.* Īyoru; hetszrau.
COURTEOUS, Teinei; aisō; ingin; nengoro.
COUSIN, Itoko.
COVENANT, Yak'soku; yakujō; jōyaku.
COVER, *v.* Kabuseru; osou; ōu; kakusz; f'ta wo szru; tsztszmu.
COVER, *n.* F'ta.
COVET, Musaboru; hoshigaru; yokubaru; tonyoku.
COW, Ushi meushi; oname.
COWHERD, Ushikai.
COWARD, Okubiyō mono.
COWARDICE, Okubiyō; okure; hikiyō.
COWPOX, Giutō.
CRAB, Kani.

CRACK, Szkima; wareme; ware; hima; hibiki.
CRAFT, Kagiyō; takumi.
CRAMP, Tszri; komuragayeri; szkumu.
CRANE, Tszru; tadz.
CRAPE, Chirimen.
CRAVE, Kō; tanomu; negau.
CRAW, Yebukuro.
CRAWL, Hau; mukumeku.
CRAZY, Kichigai; kurui; kiyōki; hakkiyō; kiyōran; monogurui.
CREASE, Orime.
CREATE, Tszkuru.
CREATOR, Zōbusha.
CREDENTIAL, Shōko.
CREDIT, *selling on* —, kakeuri; noberu. *Buy on* —, okinoru.
CREEP, Hau.
CREST, Mon; tatemono; tosaka.
CREVICE, Wareme; ware; szkima; hima.
CRICKET, Kiri-girisz; kera.
CRIME, Tszmi; toga; zai; k'wazai.
CRIMINAL, Tszmibito; toganin; zainin; meshiudo.
CRIMINAL-CODE, Seibai-shiki-moku.
CRIMINATE, Aitedoru; togameru.
CRIPPLE, Izari; katawa; fugu; koshi-nuke.
CRISP, Sakkuri.
CRITICAL TIME, Masaka no toki; wakeme.
CRITICAL YEARS OF LIFE, Yakudoshi.
CRITICISE, Hihan szru; hi wo utsz; hiyō szru.
CROOKED, Magaru; Igamu; kagamu; nejireru.
CROP, Yebukuro; deki; saku.
CROSS, *n.* Jūmonji; jūjika.
CROSS, Yoko.
CROSS, *v.* Wataru; koyeru; sakarau; dadakeru; jireru; szneru.
CROSS-QUESTION, Toi-tszmeru.
CROSS-ROAD, Tszji; chimata.
CROSSWISE, Yoko-ni; yokosama.
CROTON-BEAN, Shiyen; hadz.
CROUCH, Udzkumaru; shagamu; sh'ta ni oru.
CROUP, Bahifū.
CROW, *n.* Karasz.
CROW, *v.* Toki wo tszkuru.
CROWBAR, Kanateko.
CROWD, Kunju; muragaru.
CROWN, Itadaki.
CRUCIBLE, Rutszbo.
CRUCIFY, Jūjika ni ageru; haritszke ni kakeru.
CRUDE, Nama; arai. — *metal*, aragane.
CRUEL, Mugoi; muzan; nasake-nai; zannin; funinjō-na; haku-jō-na; jaken; tszrai; tszrenai.
CRUMBLE, Kudzreru; momi-kudaku; boroboro-to; ugomotsz.
CRUPPER, Shirigai.
CRUSH, Oshi-tszbusz; oshi-kudaku.
CRY, Naku; sakebu; omeku; wameku; yobau.
CRYSTAL, Szishō.
CRYSTALIZE, Katamaru; kōru.
CUB, Ko.
CUCUMBER, Ki-uri.
CUE, Mage; motodori; tabusa.
CUFF, Sodekuchi.
CULMINATION, Debana; sakari; tōge.
CULTIVATE, Tszkuru; tagayesz; shitateru.
CUMBER, Jama szru; hodasareru.
CUNNING, Rikō; warujiye; sarujiye; kōk'watsz.
CUP, Wan; choku. —*for drawing blood*, szifukube.
CUPBOARD, Todana; zendana.
CUPIDITY, Musabori; yoku; tonyoku.
CURABLE, Naorareru; zen-k'wai szru; iyeru.
CURDLE, Katamaru.
CURE, Naoru; iyeru; zenk'wai szru; hombuku szru.
CURIOUS, Medzrashii; kimiyō na; kitai na.
CURL, Chijireru.
CURRENT, Ts'ūyō, hayaru; riukō; nagare; rufu. — *report*, torisata. — *usage*, ts'ūrei.
CURRY, *v.* Koszru; kedzru. —*favor with*, tori-iru.
CURSE, Nonoshiru; akkō szru; noroi; tokobu; tatari.
CURTAIL, Habuku; gendszru; mijikaku szru.
CURTAIN, Maku; tobari; chō; to-chō; nōren.
CURVE, Mageru.
CUSHION, Zabuton.
CUSTOM, Narawashi; hō; fū; narai; fūzoku; hōshiki; rei; tameshi; unjō; zeigin.
CUSTOMARY, — *way*, ari-fure.
CUSTOMER, Tokui; kaite.
CUSTOM-HOUSE, Unjōsho.
CUT, Kiru; sogu; kizamu, kedzru; horu; tachi. — *asunder*, kiri-hanasz. — *across*, yokogiru; yoko-ni kiru. — *down*,

kiritaosz; kiri-otosz. — *off*, tatsz; tayasz; sayegiru; kobamu; tayeru. — *out*, kiri-dasz. — *with scissors*, hasande kiru.
CUTICLE, Uwa-kawa.
CUTLASS, Katana.
CUTLER, Kajiya.
CUTPURSE, Kinchakkiri.
CUTTLEFISH, Ika.
CYCLE, Mawari.
CYMBAL, Niyohachi.

D

DAGGER, K'waiken.
DAILY, Nichi-nichi; mai-nichi; hibi.
DAM, Seku; seki-tomeru.
DAMAGE, *n.* Kega; kidz; son; itami; hason.
DAMAGE, *v.* Itamu, sokonau; sondzru.
DAMAGED *goods*, Sawate-mono.
DAMP, Shimeru; nureru; shitoru; shikki.
DAMPEN, Shimesz; nurasz.
DAMSEL, Muszme.
DANCE, Odoru; mau.
DANCER, Odoriko; maiko.
DANDELION, Tampo.
DANDRUFF, Fuke.
DANGER, Abunasa; kennon; ayauki.
DANGEROUS, Abunai; ayaui.
DANGLE, Buratszku; bura-bura; burari.
DAPPLED, Madara; buchi.
DARE, Ayete; yobi-dasz.
DARK, Kurai; kuramu.
DARKEN, Kuraku szru.
DARKNESS, Yami.
DARLING, Kawai.
DARN, T'szkurau; naosz.
DASH, Nageru; utsz.
DATE, Toki; jibun; koro; hidori; gappi.
DATE, *(fruit)*, Natszme.
DAUB, Darake; mabure; nuru; naszru.
DAUGHTER, Muszme. *Eldest* —, anemuszme. — *in law*, yome.
DAUNT, Osoreru. *Nothing daunted*, osoredz.
DAWN, Yoake; akebono; akatszki; shinonome. *Before* —, mimei.
DAY, Nichi; hi. *First day of the month*, tszitachi. *Last day of the month*, misoka. *First day of the year*, ganjitsz. *Another* —, tajitsz. — *after to-morrow*, miyō-go-nichi. — *before yesterday*, issakujitsz; ototoi. *Day by day*, nichinichi; hibi. *What* —? ikka. *Daytime*, hiru; hi no uchi; chiu. *All day*, shūjitsz; himemosz. *Every other day*, ichi-nichi-oki; kakujitsz. *Day and night*, hiru-yoru, chiu-ya.
DAY-BOOK, Chōmen.
DAY-BREAK, Yoake; akatszki. *Before* —, asa-madaki.
DAYLIGHT, Hiru.
DAZZLE, Mabushii; mabayui.
DEAD, Shinda; nakunatta. — *man*, shinin; h'to-jini. — *tree*, kareta ki.
DEADLY, Inochi ni kakaru.
DEAF, Tszmbo. — *in one ear*, kata-tszbo. — *and dumb*, ōshi.
DEAL, *n.* Hodo. *Great* —, yoppodo; tak'san; tanto; ōi.
DEAL, *v.* Wakeru; wari-tszkeru; haibun szru; akinau; motenasz.
DEALER, Akindo.
DEAR, Kawairashii. — *in price*, takai; kōjiki.
DEARTH, Hideri; kampatsz.
DEATH, Shi.
DEBAR, Kobamu; kindzru; kinzei.
DEBASE, Otosz.
DEBATE, Arasoi, rondzru; giron.
DEBILITATE, Yowaku szru; yowameru.
DEBILITY, Yowasa.
DEBT, Oime; kari; shakkin; kake; kashi.
DECADE, Jun. *First* —, Shōjun. *Middle* —, chiu-jun. *Last* —, ge-jun.
DECAMP, Chikuten szru; shuppun szru; nigeru; kake-ochi wo szru.
DECANT, Uwadzmi wo toru.
DECANTER, Tokkuri.
DECAPITATE, Kubi wo kiru.
DECAY, Otoroyeru; Szibi szru.
DECEASE, Shinuru; naku naru; hōgiyo; gōkiyo; seikiyo; shikiyo; sosszru; bosszru; hateru; mimakaru; yo wo saru; jaku szru.
DECEIT, Itszwari; uso.
DECEIVE, Azamuku; damasz; taburakasz; itszwaru.
DECEMBER, Jūni-gatsz.
DECIDE, Sadameru; ketszjō szru; kiwameru; tadasz; kesszru; ketchaku.
DECIDEDLY, Kessh'te; kitto; zehi.
DECIPHER, Toku.
DECISION, Mōshi-watashi; sadame; ketszdan.
DECK, *n.* Itago; kampan.

DECK, *v.* Kazaru; yosoou.
DECLARE, Arawasz; miseru; akasz.
DECLINE, Jitai szru; jijō szru; kotowaru; shōchi senu; inamu; otoroyeru; szibi szru; katamuku; soreru.
DECLIVITY, Saka.
DECOCT, Sendzru.
DECOCTION, Senyaku.
DECOMPOSE, Bunseki szru; wakeru.
DECORATE, Kazaru; yosoou; mekasz; yatszsz.
DECORUM, Rei; reigi.
DECOY, Obiku; tszridasz.
DECREASE, Heru; hesz; gendzru; genshō szru; habuku.
DECREE, Okite; sadame.
DECREPIT, Boreru; oi-boreru; rōmo.
DECRY, Kusashi; kenasz.
DEDICATE, Ageru.
DEDUCT, Hiku.
DEED, Koto; waza; gō; sagō; giyō-jō; okonai; shikata.
DEED, Shōmon; kokenjō; baikenjō.
DEEP, Fukai. *The snow is —*, yuki ga tszmoru.
DEEPEN, Fukaku szru; fukameru.
DEER, Sh'ka.
DEFACED, Mametsz.
DEFAME, Soshiru; zangen szru; hihō szru; waruku-iu.
DEFEAT, Makeru; haigun szru.
DEFECT, Fusoku; taradz; kidz; ayamachi; ochido.
DEFEND, Mamoru; katameru; fusegu; kabau. *— from*, yokeru.
DEFER, Hinobe wo szru; matsz.
DEFICIENT, Fusoku naru; taranu.
DEFICIENCY, Meri; heri; kan; kakeberi.
DEFILE, *n.* Sessho.
DEFILE, *v.* Kegasz; yogosz; kitanaku szru.
DEFILED, Kegareru; yogoreru; kitanai.
DEFILEMENT, Kegare; yogore; ye.
DEFINE, Kiwameru; sadameru; toku; tadasz.
DEFINITE, Kimari.
DEFLECT, Soreru.
DEFORM, Katachi wo sokonau.
DEFORMED, Katawa.
DEFRAUD, Kataru; kaszmeru; takuru.
DEFRAY, Harau.
DEFY, Yobi-dasz.
DEGENERATE, Otoroyeru; szibi szru.
DEGRADE, Sageru; otosz.
DEGREE, Do; hodo; kurai; dan. *By degrees*, dan-dan; shidai-ni.
DEIFY, Kami ni agameru: kami to nasz.
DEITY, Kami; shin.
DEJECT, Ki wo otosz; chikara wo otosz.
DEJECTION, Kiochi.
DEJECTED, Uttoshiku omō; utsz-utsz; urei.
DELAY, Matsz; osoku-naru; temadoru; himadoru; yen-nin; todokōru; chitai; chichi szru.
DELEGATE, Tszkawasz; yaru; tateru; yudaneru.
DELEGATE, *n.* Shisha; tszkai.
DELETERIOUS, Doku.
DELIBERATE, Kangayeru; shian szru; kufū szru; omoi-mawasz.
DELICATE, Tei-nei; kiyasha-na; fūriu; ikina; yawaraka; assari-to-sh'ta; hosoyaka; hiyowai; niu-jaku; tampaku.
DELICIOUS, Oishii; umai.
DELIGHT, Ureshii; yorokobi; tanoshimi.
DELIGHTFUL, Omoshiroi; yoi.
DELIQUESCE, Fūk'wa szru.
DELIRIUM, Uwakoto; sengo;
DELIVER, Taszkeru; szkū; adzkeru; watasz.
DELUDE, Azakeru; damasz; madowasz; bakasz.
DELUGE, Kōdzi.
DEMAND, *v.* Saisoku szru; hataru. *Demands attention*, nen wo ireneba naranu.
DEMAND, *n.* Hake-kuchi; hake; muki-kuchi.
DEMOLISH, Uchi-kowasz; horobosz.
DEMON, Akuma; oni; ma; akki; yasha.
DEMONSTRATE, Arawasz; miseru.
DEMORALIZE, Kudzsz; kegasz; midasz; otosz; otoroyeru.
DEN, Ana; sōkutsz; sz.
DENOTE, Shirusz; shiraseru.
DENSE, Katai.
DENT, Ato; kidz; kubomi.
DENTIFRICE, Hamigaki.
DENTIST, Ha-isha; irebashi; hanuki; yashi.
DENUDE, Nugaseru; hadaka ni szru; hagu; muku.
DENY, Ī-kesz; ī-fusegu; kobamu; fushōchi; uchikesz. *— one's self*, onore ni katsz; kan-nin szru.
DEPART, Yuku; saru; szteru; hanareru; deru; kayeru.
DEPEND, Sagaru; yoru; tanomu; makaseru; tayoru; shindzru; shinkō szru; szgaru; sh'tagau; ate ni szru.
DEPENDENT, *n.* Karariudo; isōrō.
DEPICT, Kaku; yegaku szru; noberu; ītoru.
DEPLORE, Kanashimu; itamu.
DEPORTATION, Shima-nagashi.

DEPORTMENT, Furumai; okonai; giyō-jō; monogoshi.
DEPOSE, Otosz; shōko szru.
DEPOSIT, *n.* Adzkari-mono; h'ki-ate; ori; kasz. — *money*, tetszke; uchi-kin.
DEPOSIT, *v.* Oku; tszmu adzkeru.
DEPOSITION, Kōsho; kuchigaki.
DEPRAVE, Kegasz; kudzsz; midasz otosz.
DEPRECIATE, Sagaru; sageru; ge-jiki ni szru; yaszku szru; kenasz.
DEPREDATE, Ubau; kaszmeru.
DEPRESS, Oshi-kudasz; ki wo fusagu.
DEPTH, Fukasa.
DERANGE, Madasz.
DERIDE, Azakeru; gurō szru; rōshi; karondzru; anadoru; azawarau;
DERIVE, Uketoru; morau; hiki-ukeru.
DESCEND, Kudaru; sagaru; oriru; gekō szru; tsztayeru. — *from heaven*, amakudaru.
DESCENDANT, Shison ; kōin. *Latest* —, basson.
DESCRIBE, Hiku; kaku; ītoru; noberu.
DESCRY, Ukagau; mi-tszkeru; midasz.
DESECRATE, Kegasz.
DESERT, *v.* Szteru; mi-szteru; mi-hanasz; furi-tszteru; chiku-ten szru; kake-ochi szru; shuppon szru; utcharu; okizari.
DESERT, *n.* Kō; gō; waza; k'wabun.
DESERT, *n.* Sznabara; sabaku; sznappa.
DESERTER, Ochi-musha; ochi-udo.
DESERVING, Atari-maye; hadz; beki.
DESICCATE, Kawakasz; hossz; hashiyagasz.
DESIGN, *v.* Kaku; hiku; kufū szru; tszmori; atehameru.
DESIGN, *n.* Kokorozashi ; kokoro ; wake ; yuye; riyōken.
DESIGNATE, Ateru; shirusz.
DESIRE, Hosszru ; nosomu ; hosshi; *also formed by the affix*, tai.
DESIST, Yameru; yosz.
DESK, Tszkuye.
DESOLATE, *a.* Samushii.
DESPAIR, Yake.
DESPERADO, Meppō na yatsz.
DESPICABLE, Iyashii.
DESPISE, Karondzru; iyashimeru; anadoru; misageru; sageshimu.
DESPOND, Ki-ochi ga szru; fusagu.
DESPONDENCY, Ki-ochi.
DESTINATION, Yuku-saki; yuku-ye.
DESTINY, Yukuszye; shijū; owari; un; temmei; yakusoku.
DESTITUTE, Madzshii; bimbō; hinkiu; konkiu; naku.
DESTROY, Horobosz; tszbusz; naku szru; arasz; metszbō; chimin.
DETACH, Hadzsz; hanasz.
DETAIL, Isai; kuwashiku; komaka-ni; tszbusa-ni.
DETAIN, Tomeru.
DETECT, *v.* Mi-tszkeru; mitodokeru; miarawasz.
DETERIORATE, Otoroyeru; szibi szru.
DETERMINE, Sadameru; kiwameru; ketszjō szru.
DETEST, Nikumu; kirau.
DETHRONE, Kurai wo szberaseru.
DETRACT, Soshiru; hihō szru; zangen szru.
DETRIMENT, Son; sokonai; itami; kidz.
DEVASTATE, Arasz.
DEVELOPE, Arawasz; toku.
DEVIATE, Hadzreru; mayō
DEVICE, Kufū; tedate; te; hakarigoto; shirushi; mon.
DEVIL, Akuma; ma; oni.
DEVISE, Kufū szru ; kuwadateru; hakaru; kamayeru ; shigaku ; takumu.
DEVOID, Nai ; kara; aku ; *also prefix*, fu ; mu ; *and affix*, dz; nu; de; ji.
DEVOTE, Hamaru; fukeru ; koru; atehameru.
DEVOTION, Shin-jin; inoru; ogamu.
DEVOUT, Shin-jin. — *person*, shinja; shinji.
DEW, Tszyu.
DEXTEROUS, Jōdz; tebayai; tebash'koi.
DIABETES, Shōkatszbiyō.
DIAGONAL, Szjikai; naname.
DIAGNOSTICATE, Mitateru.
DIAL, Hidokei.
DIALECT, Namari.
DIALOGUE, Mondō.
DIAMETER, Sashi-watashi.
DIAMOND, Kongōseki.
DIAPER, Shimeshi.
DIAPHORETIC, Hakkanzai.
DIAPHRAGM, Kakumaku.
DIARRHŒA, Hara-kudari; geri.
DIARY, Nikki.
DIATHESIS, Shō.
DICE, Sai.
DICTATE, Jogon szru.
DICTIONARY, Jibiki.
DID, Sh'ta; dekita; itash'ta.
DIE, Shinuru; nakunaru; hōgiyo; gōkiyo; seikiyo; shikiyo; sosszru; bosszru; hateru; mimakeru; jaku szru; yo wo saru.
DIET, *n.* Tabe-mono; shokumotsz.
DIET, *v.* Dokudate wo szru.

DIFFER, Chigau; kotonaru; tagau.

DIFFERENCE, Chigai; shabetsz; wakachi; kejime; waidame; kenk'wa; kōron; arasoi.

DIFFERENT, Betsz no; hoka no ; ta. — *place*, yoso; bessho; ta-sho. — *paper*, besshi. — *mind*, besshin.

DIFFICULT, Mudzkashii; katai; okkū; *also*, kaneru, *used as an affix*.

DIFFICULTY, Mudzkashisa; nan.

DIFFIDENCE, Habakari; yenriyo; jijō; omohayui; omeru; uchiki.

DIFFUSE, Chiru; hiromeru; wataru.

DIG, Horu; ugatsz.

DIGEST, Konareru; shōk'wa szru; shō szru.

DIGNIFY, Agameru; tottobu; sonkiyō szru; omondzru.

DIKE, Mizo; dote; aze.

DILAPIDATED-HOUSE, Abaraya; kōhai.

DILATE, Hiroku szru; hirogeru.

DILATORY, Himadoru; osoi; hima-iru; rachi ga akanu; mendō; okotaru; bemben.

DILEMMA, Tōwaku; tohō ni kureru.

DILIGENT, Ben-kiyō szru, tsztomeru; yudan naku; seidasz; honeoru; okotaradz; moppara ni; hagemu.

DILUTE, Uszku szru; noberu; umeru.

DIM, Kaszmu; kumoru; bonyari.

DIMENSION, Okisa; tateyoko; szmpō; nori; maguchi, okuyuki; uchi-nori; sotonori; szushaku.

DIMINISH, Habuku; heru; gendzru; szkunaku szru.

DIMINUTIVE, Chīsai; ko, *as a prefix*.

DIMPLE, Yekubo.

DINNER, Hirugohan.

DIP, Kumu; szkū; shakū; ireru; tszkeru.

DIPPER, Shaku; hishaku.

DIRECT, *a.* Masszgu; szgui; jiki.

DIRECT, *v.* Miseru; sasz; tszkasadoru; michibiku.

DIRECTION, Hōgaku; tokoro-gaki.

DIRECTLY, Szgu-ni; jiki-ni; jika-ni; tadachi-ni.

DIRK, K'wai-ken; ai-kuchi.

DIRT, Aka; gomi; okori; akuta; chiri; doro; kudz; kuso; fun.

DIRTY, Kitanai; yogoreru; akadzku; akajimu; kegareru; birō na; jijimusai; oye.

DISADVANTAGEOUS, Fu-ben; fu-benri; futszgō.

DISAGREE, Naka ga warui; fuwa; awanu; chigau; tagau.

DISAGREEABLE, Ki ni iranu; ki ni kanawanu; kirau; iya-na; awanu; funiyoi.

DISALLOW, Yurusadz; shōchisenu; fushōchi.

DISAPPEAR, Miyenu; kiyeru; useru.

DISAPPOINTED, Ate ga hadzreru; shitszbō szru; an ni sōi szru.

DISAPPOINTMENT, Zannen; munen kuyashigaru; kuchi-oshii; omoi no hoka; an g'wai.

DISAPPROVE, Fushō-chi; kirau; iyagaru; ki ni awanu.

DISARRANGE, Midasz; kudzsz.

DISASTER, Fushiawase; wazawai; fukō; kannan; nan; nangi.

DISAVOW, Ī-fusegu; ī kesz.

DISBAND, Chirasz.

DISBELIEVE, Shinzedz; shinkōsenu.

DISBURSE, Harau.

DISBURSEMENT, Niuyō; iriyō; zappi; zōyō.

DISCERN, Wakaru; wakimayeru; miyeru; bendzru.

DISCERNMENT, Fumbetsz.

DISCHARGE, *v.* — *cargo*, ni wo ageru; midzage wo szru. — *a gun*, teppō wo hanasz; *or* utsz. — *from service*, hima wo dasz; *or* itoma wo yaru. — *an office*, tsztomeru. — *from prison*, rōya kara dasz. — *pus*, umi ga deru. — *water*, midz ga deru. — *a debt*, kanjō wo harau; szmasz.

DISCIPLE, Deshi; monto; montei; monjin.

DISCIPLINE, *n.* Tori-jimari; shimari.

DISCLAIM, Ī-fusegu; ī-kesz.

DISCLOSE, Abaku; yaburu; arawasz.

DISCOLOR, Shimiru.

DISCONCERTED, Warobireru.

DISCONNECT, Wakeru; hanasz; hadzsz.

DISCONTENTED, Fuanshin; yasznzenu.

DISCONTINUE, Yameru; yosz; tatsz; tomeru.

DISCORD, Fuwa; chōshi ga awanu; naka ga warui; mutszmajiku nai.

DISCOUNT, *n.* Ri; risoku.

DISCOUNT, *v.* Kasz.

DISCOURAGE, Ki wo otosz; chikara wo otosz; ki ga fusagu; kujikeru.

DISCOURSE, Hanashi; kōshaku.

DISCOVER, Arawasz; mi-dasz; mi-tszkeru; hatszmei szru.

DISCREET, Tsztszshimu; yō-jin naru.

DISCEPRANCY, Sōi; chigai; machigai.

DISCRETION, Yōjin; tsztszshimi.

DISCRIMINATE, Wakeru; wakimayeru; benjiru; bembetsz szru.

DISCUSS, Rondzru; arasou; agetszrau.
DISDAIN, Karondzru ; iyashimeru; naigashiro ni szru; mikudasz; sageshimu.
DISEASE, Yamai; biyōki. *Symptoms of* —. biyō-shō. *Cause of* —, Biyō-kon.
DISEMBARK, Jōriku szru ; oka ni agaru.
DISENTANGLE, Toku; sabaku; hodoku.
DISGORGE, Haki-dasz.
DISGRACE, *n*. Kakin; haji; kidz; chijoku; naore; shika.
DISGUISE, Yatszsz; sama wo kayeru; shinobi.
DISGUST, Kirau; aki-hateru.
DISH, Sara.
DISHEARTEN, Ki wo otosz; ki ga fusagu; kujikeru.
DISHEVELED, Ram-patsz.
DISHONEST, Fu-jitsz-na; fu-shōjiki; shōjiki de nai.
DISHONOR, *n*. Haji; kakin; kidz; chijoku.
DISINCLINED, Szszmanu.
DISINHERIT, Kandō szru; kiuri.
DISINTERESTED, Hiki naku; ōyake-ni; watakushi naku; yosome; okame.
DISJOIN, Hanareru; hadzsz.
DISLIKE, Kirau; konomadz; szkanu; iyana; ki ni iranu; imu.
DISLOCATE, Chigau; tagau; hadzreru.
DISLOYAL, Fu-chiu; fu-gi na.
DISMAL, Uttōshii; utsz-utsz; ki-bosoi.
DISMANTLE, Tori-kudzsz.
DISMISS, Kayesz ; dasz ; yaru ; hima wo dasz; itoma wo yaru.
DISMOUNT, Geba wo szru.
DISOBEDIENT, — *to parents*, fukō.
DISOBEY, Somuku; tagau; sakarau; yaburu; sh'tagawanu.
DISORDER, *n*. Midare; sōdo; konzatsz; shidara-naki.
DISORDER, *v*. Midasz; konzatsz szru.
DISORGANIZE, Kudzsz.
DISOWN, — *a son*, kandō szru.
DISPARAGE, Karondzru ; naigashiro ni szru; soshiru.
DISPARITY, Sōi; chigai.
DISPATCH, Yaru; tszkau; tszkawasz; okuru.
DISPEL, Harau ; harai-dasz; chirasz.
DISPENSARY, Seyakujo.
DISPENSE, Hodokosz ; atayeru ; kubaru ; wari-tszkeru. — *with*, mendzru ; yurusz; yudzru.
DISPERSE, Chirasz.
DISPIRIT, Ki wo otosz; ki ga fusagu.
DISPLACE, Hadzsz; midasz.
DISPLAY, Arawasz; miseru; shiraseru.
DISPLEASE, Ikaraseru; uramiru; hara wo tateru.
DISPLEASURE, Ikari ; ikidōri ; haradachi; rippuku.
DISPOSE, Oku; narabu.
DISPOSITION, Sonaye; narabi; iji; konjō; kokorodate; shōne; kokorobaye; kishitsz; kidate; saga.
DISPROPORTION, Fu-tszri-ai; fusō-ō; niawanu; tszriawanu;.
DISPUTATIOUS, Arasoitagaru.
DISPUTE, *n*. Arasoi; sōron; kōron; kenk'wa.
DISPUTE, *v*. Arasou; rondzru.
DISREGARD, Itowadz ; oshimadz ; kayerimidz.
DISRESPECTFUL, Wiyemawanu; fukei; shitszrei; burei.
DISSATISFIED, Ki ni iranu; taru koto shiranu.
DISSECTION, Kaibō.
DISSEMBLE, Shiranu furi wo szru; tobokeru; shirabakkureru.
DISSEMINATE, Chirasz; hiromeru.
DISSENT, Shōchisenu.
DISSENSION, Arasoi; sōron; kenk'wa; naka ga warui; mome.
DISSIMILAR, Niawanu.
DISSIPATE, Chirasz.
DISSOLUTE, Hōratsz; hōtō; dōraku.
DISSOLVE, Toku.
DISTANCE, Tōkisa; aida; hodo; kaku-shin.
DISTANT, Tōi; hedateru; tōzakaru; utoi.
DISTEMPER, Yamai; biyōki; wadzrai.
DISTEND, Hirogeru; fukurasz; haru.
DISTIL Jō-riu szru.
DISTINCT, Betsz; betsz-dan; kotonaru; chigai; hoka; sayaka; hakkiri-to; fummiyō; akiraka.
DISTINCTION Shabetsz; wakachi; waidame; kejime; hedate.
DISTINGUISH, Wakeru; wakimayeru.
DISTINGUISHED, Hidetaru ; nukindetaru ; bakkun; kōmei; nadakai.
DISTORT, Igameru; nejireru; yugamu.
DISTRACTED, Tori-magireru.
DISTRESS, Kanashimi; itami; nangi; kannan.
DISTRIBUTE, Kubaru; wakeru; wari-tszkeru; haibun szru; haitō szru.
DISTRICT, Tokoro; tochi.
DISTRUST, Usan; fushin; uron; ayashimu; ginen; utagau; gatenyukanu; ibukashii.
DISTURB, Odateru; sawagasz; ugokasz.
DISTURBANCE, Sawagi; sōdo; bussō.

DITCH, Dobu; mizo; sesenagi.
DITTO, Onajiku; dōzen.
DIVE, Kuguru; muguru.
DIVERS, Iro-iro; sama-zama; shuju; kusagusa; machi-machi.
DIVERSE, Chigai.
DIVERSIFY, Irodoru.
DIVERSION, Kiyō; asobi; tawamure; nagusami.
DIVERT, Nagusameru; tawamureru; kiyō szru; asobu.
DIVEST, Toru; muku; nugu; hagu.
DIVIDEND, Wari; wariai; bun.
DIVIDERS, Bunmawashi.
DIVINE, Kami no; shin no. — *commuication*, shintaku.
DIVINE, *v.* Uranau; boku szru.
DIVISION, Warizan; wakare; wakachi; hedate.
DIVORCE, Yen wo kiru; riyen; ribetsz. *A bill of* —, riyenjō; sarijō.
DIVULGE, Arawasz; morasz; abaku; yaburu.
DIZZY, Memai; kennun; menken; tachi-gurami; kurumeku; kura-kura; kuramu.
DO, Szru; nasz; itasz; dekiru; okonau; shuttai szru. *That will do*, yoroshi. *Make do*, Maniawaseru. *Do not cry so much*; sonna ni naku na. *Do it quickly*, hayaku se yo. *I will do it*, itashimashō.
DOCILE, Otonashii.
DOCK, Habuku; gendzru; tszmeru; nozoku; mijikaku szru.
DOCTOR, Isha; ishi.
DOCTOR, *v.* Riyō-ji szru.
DOCTRINE, Dōri; oshiye.
DOCUMENT, Kaki-tszke; bunshō.
DODGE, Yokeru; sakeru.
DOE, Mejika.
DOG, Inu; chin.
DOINGS, Waza; okonai.
DOLEFUL, Uttōshi.
DOLL, Ningiyō.
DOLLAR, Doru; *or* dora; yō-gin.
DOLT, Baka; ahō; don-na h'to; gu-jin.
DOMAIN, Riyō; riyōbun; chi-giyō-sho; kuni.
DOMESTIC, — *affairs*, ka-ji. — *animals*, rokuchiku; kai-mono. — *manufacture*, jisaku; te-saku; tedzkuri; koku-san; to-san.
DOMINION, Matszrigoto; seiji; kuni; riyōbun; shoriyō.
DONE, Shi-agaru; deki-agaru; jō-ju szru; shimatta; sznda; owatta.
DOOM, Mōshi-tszkeru; temmei.
DOOR, To; mon.
DOSE, Fuku.
DOT, Ten; chobo.
DOUBLE, Futatsz; bai; nisōbai. — *dealing*, kage hinata ga aru. — *hearted*, futagokoro. — *tongued*, riyōzetsz. — *edged*, riyō-ha; moroha.
DOUBT, *v.* Utagau; ayashimu; ginen szru; ayabumu; kogi szru; tamerau; giwaku; yūyo szru; fushin ni omō; usan. — *if*, yawaka; yomoya.
DOUBTFUL, Utagawashii; obotszkanai; usan-na; uron-na; fushin-na.
DOVE, Hato.
DOVE-TAIL, Ari; musō.
DOWER, Ji-san-kin.
DOWN, Sh'ta; shimo. — *the river*, kawashimo. *Go* —, kudaru; oriru. *Fall* —, korobu; ochiru; taoreru. *Throw* —, otosz; taosz. *Hang* —, sageru; tszru. *Look* —, nozoku.
DOWNCAST, Hadzkashii; omotebuse; membokunai.
DOWNFALL, Horobi; metszbō.
DOWN-WARD, Sh'ta ni.
DOZE, Nemuru; inemuri; nemutai; madoromu.
DOZEN, Jūni.
DRAB, Ki-no-iro.
DRAFT, *v.* Hiku; kaku.
DRAFTS, Go.
DRAG, Hiku.
DRAGON, Tatsz; riu.
DRAGON-FLY, Tombō.
DRAIN, Dobu; mizo; geszi.
DRAIN, *v.* Sh'tamu.
DRAM, Hai.
DRAMA, Shibai.
DRAW, Hiku; kaku; nuku. — *water*, kumu. — *blood*, chi wo toru; shiraku szru. — *back*, shirizoku; atoshizari; szkkomu; hikikomu. — *nigh*, yoru; chikadzku; chikayoru. — *up*, sonayeru; naraberu; tszraneru.
DRAW-BRIDGE, Hane-bashi.
DRAWER, Hiki-dashi.
DRAWERS, Momohiki.
DRAWING-KNIFE, Sen.
DRAWN BATTLE, Ai-biki.
DRAY, Kuruma; dai-hachi-guruma.
DRAYMAN, Shariki.
DREAD, Osoreru; kowagaru; ojiru; ojike.
DREADFUL, Osoroshii; kowai.
DREAM, Yume.

DREARY, Szgoi; samushii; uttōshi.
DREDGE, Sarayeru.
DREGS, Kasz.
DRENCH, Nureru; shimeru.
DRESS, *v.* Kiru; haku; chaku-szru; chakuyō szru; yosoō; kazaru; yatszsz; tszkurau; tszkuru.
DRESS, *n.* Ide-tachi; kimono; i-fuku; i-shō.
DRIBBLE, Tareru; sh'tataru.
DRIFT, Tadayoi; ukamu; uku.
DRILL, *v.* Narasz; chōren szru; kei-ko szru; kiri wo momu; nereru.
DRILL, *n.* Kiri; chōren; kei-ko.
DRINK, *v.* Nomu.
DRIP, Sh'tataru.
DRIVE, Ō; osz. — *a nail,* kugi wo buchikomu. — *away,* oi-harau. — *out,* oidasz. — *in,* oi-komu; oshi-komu. — *off,* oi-harau. — *back,* oi-kayesz. — *across,* oi-kosz. — *together,* oi-atszmeru.
DRIVEL, Yodare.
DRIZZLING RAIN, Kiri-ame.
DROMEDARY, Rakuda.
DROOP, Shioreru.
DROP, *n.* Tarashi; teki; shidzku.
DROP, *v.* Tareru; ochiru; otosz; sh'tataru; tarasz.
DROPSY, Sziki.
DROSS, Kasz.
DROUGHT, Hideri; kampatsz.
DROWN, Oboreru; obore-jini; botszdeki; deki-shi. — *one's self,* mi wo nageru; minage.
DROWSY, Nemutai; inemuri; nemui.
DRUDGE, Hone-oru.
DRUG, Kuszri; yaku.
DRUM, Taiko; tszdzmi.
DRUMSTICK, Bachi.
DRUNK, Yō; yei; yopparau.
DRUNKARD, Sake-nomi; nomite; nondakure.
DRY, Kawaku; hashiyaku; kasszru; hiru; hikarabiru; hosz; aburu; kareru; kara; karabiru; karappō.
DUBIOUS, Utagau; utagawashii. *see Doubt, and doubtful.*
DUCK, *wild duck,* kamo. *Tame* —, ahiru.
DUE, Atari-maye; hadz; tō-zen; szbeki. *The money is due,* shakkin no nichi-gen ga kita. *Money yet due,* zangin; nokoru kane. *To dun for money before it is due,* nichi-gen no maye-ni kane wo saisoku szru. *More than is* —, k'wa-bun.
DUEL, Hatashi-ai; shōbu; ninjō.
DULL Nibui; don; uttōshii; yoku kirenu; noroi; toroi; fukeiki. — *of hearing,* mimi ga tōi. — *day,* don-ten. — *in seeing,* me ga botto sh'ta.
DUMB, Ōshi; damaru.
DUMPLING, Manjū.
DUN, *v.* Saisoku szru; hataru.
DUNCE, Donna h'to; gu-nin; baka; ahō.
DUNG, Kuso; fun; unko.
DUPE, Damasz; azamuku.
DURABLE, Mochi ga yoi; tamochi ga yoi; tszyoi.
DURATION, Aida; uchi.
DURING, Aida; uchi; chiu; nagara; chiu-to; buri.
DUSK, Tazokare; kureai; higure; hakubo.
DUST, *n.* Hokori; gomi.
DUST, *v.* Gomi wo harau.
DUSTPAN, Gomi-tori; chiri-tori.
DUTCH, Oranda. — *man,* oranda-jin.
DUTIFUL, Kōkō-na; chiu-gi-na; jitsz-na.
DUTY, Tsztome; yakume; hōkō; shokushō; nin; hadz; atarimaye; szbeki-koto; unjō; zei; zeigin.
DWARF, Isszmbōshi.
DWELL, Szmu; oru; jū-szru; iru; owashimasz; chinza.
DWELLING, Iye; uchi; szmai; taku; jūsho; yado.
DWINDLE, Heru; yaseru; chibiru; chīsaku naru; otoroyeru.
DYE, Someru.
DYER, Some-mono ya; kōya.
DYE-STUFF, Some-kusa.
DYING, Shinde oru; shi ni kakatte iru; shinuru.
DYNASTY, Dai; yo; chō.
DYSENTERY, Ribiyō; akahara.

E

EACH, Ono-ono; mai; goto-ni; men-men. *Eeach-other,* tagai-ni; *also formed by the suffix,* au, *to the root of verbs.* Tszkiau, *to stab each other.* Tataki-au, *to beat each other.*
EAGER, Hagemu; szszmu.
EAR, Mimi; ho.
EARLY, Hayaku; toku.
EARN, Mōkeru.
EARNEST, *n.* Hatszo. — *money,* tekin; tetszke.
EARNESTLY, Moppara; ichi-dz-ni; hitaszra-ni; isshin-ni; h'toye-ni; shikkiri-ni.
EARPICK, Mimi-kaki.

EARTH, Chi; tszchi; sekai.
EARTHENWARE, Seto-mono.
EARTHQUAKE, Jishin.
EARTHWORM, Mimidz.
EAR-WAX, Mimi no aka.
EASE, *n.* Anshin; raku; an; annon; anraku.
EASE, *v.* Kutszrogeru; yurumeru; akirameru; raku ni szru.
EASILY, Yaszku; zosamonaku; mudzkashiku-nai; tayaszku; nan-naku.
EAST, Higashi; tō; tōbō.
EASY, Yaszi; zosamonai; yōi; tayaszi; mudzkashiku-nai; raku-na.
EAT, Taberu; kū; kurō; shoku-szru.
EATING-HOUSE, Riyōri-ya.
EAVES, Noki.
EBB, *v.* Hiku; hiru.
EBB-TIDE, Hiki-shiwo.
EBONY, Kokutan.
ECCENTRIC, — *person*, henjin; chajin; kebu-na.
ECHO, Kodama; yamahiko; hibiki.
ECLIPSE, — *of sun*, nisshoku. — *of moon*, gasshoku. *Eclipsed by another*, keosareru. *Ecliptic*, sekidō.
ECONOMY, Kenyaku; kanriyaku; shimatsz; sekken; tszdzmayaku; tamaka. *Political* —, keizai-gaku.
EDDY, Udz; fuchi; yodo.
EDGE, Fuchi; kiwa; hashi. — *of a sword*, ha; yaiba.
EDGED-TOOLS, Hamono; kire-mono.
EDGING, Sasaheri.
EDIBLE, Taberareru.
EDICT, Ofure; go-hatto; okite.
EDIFY, Shitateru.
EDIT, Shuppan szru; jō-boku szru.
EDITION, Hen. *First* —, sho-hen. *Second* —, ni-hen. *New* —, shim-pan.
EDITOR, Saku-sha.
EDUCATE, Shitateru; oshiyeru; shikomu; kiyōkun szru; kiyōju; shitateru.
EDUCE, Hiku.
EEL, Unagi; anago.
EFFACE, Kesz; kedzru.
EFFECT, *n.* Sei; shoi; waza; yuye; wake; kiki.
EFFECT, *v.* Togeru; jōju szru; dekiru.
EFFEMINATE, Onnarashii; niyakeru.
EFFERVESCE, Awa ga tatsz; futō szru.
EFFICACY, Kōnō; kikime.
EFFIGY, Katashiro; h'togata.
EFFORT, Ikimi; ikkiyo; hiyōri; totan. *To make an* —, sei-dasz.
EFFULGENT, Kagayaku; hikaru.

EGG, Tamago; keiran.
EGG-PLANT, Nasz; naszbi.
EGOTISM, Unobore; jifu.
EGREGIOUS, Futoi; ōki; bakkun.
EGRESS, Deru koto.
EIGHT, Yatsz; hachi.
EIGHTEEN, Jūhachi.
EIGHTEENTH, Jūhachi ban.
EIGHTY, Hachijū.
EITHER, Dochira demo; aruiwa; idzrenari tomo.
EJECT, Dasz; oi-dasz; oshi-dasz; tszki-dasz; tanadate wo szru.
EJECTION, Tanadate.
ELAPSE, Heru; kurasz; szgiru; utszru.
ELASTIC, Danriyoku; hajiku.
ELBOW, Hiji.
ELDER, Toshi-yori; oi; rōjin; toshi ga wiye; toshi-kasa. — *brother*, ani. — *sister*, ane.
ELDEST, Toshi ga wiye. — *son*, chakushi; sōriyō. — *daughter*, ane muszme.
ELECTRICITY, Yerekiter; denki.
ELEGANT, Kirei-na; rippa-na; utszkushii; migoto; ikina; fūga.
ELEMENT, Moto; genso. *The five* —, gogiyō.
ELEPHANT, Zō; kiza.
ELEVATE, Ageru; takaku szru.
ELEVATION, Takasa.
ELEVEN, Jū-ichi.
ELEVENTH, Jū-ichi-ban; jū-ichi-me.
ELF, Tengu.
ELIDE, Habuku; riyaku szru.
ELLIPTICAL, Tamago-nari; koban-nari.
ELONGATE, Nagaku szru; noberu.
ELOPE, Nigeru; kake-ochi szru; chikuten szru.
ELOQUENT, Benzetsz-na; tatszben; kuchikiki. — *person*, bensha; kuchigōsha.
ELSE, Hoka; betsz.
ELSEWHERE, Yoso; tasho; hoka no tokoro.
ELUCIDATE, Toku; tatoyeru; akiraka ni szru.
ELUDE, Yokeru; sakeru.
ELUTRIATE, Szihi szru.
ELYSIUM, Hōrai-san; gokuraku.
EMACIATED, Yaseru.
EMANATE, Deru; hasszru.
EMANCIPATE, Hanatsz; hanashi.
EMBARK, Fune ni noru.
EMBARRASS, Hodosoreru; sashi-tszkayeru; sawaru.
EMBELLISH, Kazaru; yosoō.
EMBERS, Moyekudz.

EMBEZZLE, Kaszmeru; ubau; nuszmi-toru; hiki-oi; takuri-komu.
EMBLEM, Hanjimono; shirushi.
EMBRACE, Daku.
EMBRASURE, Sama; yazama.
EMBROIDER, Nui.
EMBROIDERER, Nuihakuya.
EMBROIDERY, Nui-tori; nui-zarasa.
EMERGENCY, Kiu-hen; fui-na-koto; dekigoto; kiu; kiu-ba; sashi-atari.
EMERY, Kongōsha.
EMETIC, Tozai; haki-guszri.
EMIGRATE, Utszru; hiki-kosz.
EMINENT, Nadakai; kōmei-na; hīdetaru.
EMISSARY, Tszkai; shisha.
EMIT, Dasz; hasszru.
EMOLUMENT, Mōke; yeki; yaku-toku.
EMOTION, Jō.
EMPEROR, Tenshi; mikado.
EMPIRE, Kuni; koku.
EMPIRIC, Yabu-isha.
EMPLOY, Tszkau; mochīru; kakayeru.
EMPLOYMENT, Kagiyō; shigoto; shōbai; tosei; yōji.
EMPORIUM, Minato.
EMPOWER, Isei wo yaru; ikō wo tszkeru.
EMPRESS, Kisaki.
EMPTY, *a.* Kara; aki; muda; munashii. — *handed*, szde, teburi.
EMPTY, *v.* Akeru; uchiakeru; buchi-makeru; kara ni szru.
EMULATE, Kisoi; arasoi; hagemi-au; hariau.
ENABLE, Dekiru; yeru; *or formed by the caust. suffix*, saseru.
ENACT, Tateru; sadameru; shioku.
ENAMEL, Kuszri; shiromi; rō.
ENAMORED, Horeru; rembō.
ENCAMP, Jin wo toru.
ENCAMPMENT, Jimba; tamuro-jo; gunjin.
ENCHANT, Mayowasz; mahō wo tszkau.
ENCHANTMENT, Chobuku.
ENCIRCLE, Kakomu; kakō; torimaku.
ENCLOSE, Kakō; kakomu; kamayeru.
ENCOMIUM, Homare.
ENCOMPASS, *see Encircle.*
ENCOUNTER, Au; de-au.
ENCOURAGE, Hagemasz; szszmeru.
ENCROACH, Ōriyō szru; muridori wo szru; ōdatsz szru; yoko-dori.
END, Owari; shimai; hate; saki; hadzre; kagiri; hateshi; yuye; szye; ate; kokorozashi. — *of life*, shūyen. *In the* —, shosen, tszi-ni. *To the — that*, yō-ni.

END, *v.* Owaru; shimau; hateru; szmu; togeru; yameru; yamu; oyobu.
ENDANGER, Kakaru; kakawaru; k'wankei szru. — *life*, inochi ni kakaru. — *one's property*, shinshō ni kakawaru.
ENDEAVOR, Seidasz; tamesz; benkiyō szru; hone-oru.
ENDLESS, Owari naki; kagiri naki; saigen naki.
ENDOW, Araseru; motaseru; atayeru; sadzkeru; sonawaru.
ENDURE, Korayeru; gaman szru; shimbō szru; shinogu; shinobu; kannin-szru.
ENEMY, Teki; kataki; ada.
ENERGY, Chikara; ikioi; riki; konki.
ENERVATE, Yowaku szru; yowameru; otoroye-saseru; yowasaseru.
ENFEEBLE, *Idem.*
ENGAGE, Hiki-ukeru; ukeau; yakusoku szru; tsztomeru.
ENGINE, Shikake; karakuri; kikai. *Fire* —, riutōszi.
ENGLAND, Igirisz; yekoku.
ENGRAFT, Tszgu.
ENGRAVE, Horu; yeru; chiribamu.
ENHANCE, Ageru; takaku szru; omoku szru.
ENIGMA, Nazo.
ENJOIN, Ītszkeru; ōse-tszkeru; mōshi-tszkeru; meidzru.
ENJOY, Tanoshimu; szku; konomu; omoshirogaru.
ENJOYMENT, Kiyō; tanoshimi; omoshiromi.
ENKINDLE, Taku; okosz.
ENLARGE, Hirogeru; tszgi-tasz; hiroku szru; shidasz.
ENLIGHTEN, Terasz; akaruku szru; satosz.
ENLIST, Ka-niu szru.
ENMITY, Urami; ikon; uppun.
ENNOBLE, Agameru; son-kiyō szru; tattobu.
ENNUI, Taikutsz; umu; tozen.
ENOUGH, Jūbun; taru; aku.
ENRICH, Tomasz; koyasz; uruosz.
ENROL, Tszkeru; noseru; kaki-ireru.
ENSANGUINED, Chi-mamire; chidarake; chimidoru.
ENSCONCED, Komoru; hikkomu.
ENSIGN, Hata; hatajirushi; aijirushi.
ENSUING, Akuru; yoku; tszgi-no.
ENTANGLED, Motszreru; muszboreru.
ENTER, Hairu; iru. — *school*, niu-gaku szru; deshi-iri wo szru. — *in a book*, kaki-tszkeru; ireru; tszkeru.
ENTERPRIZE, Yama; koto.

ENTERTAIN, Motenasz; kiyo-ō szru; furumau; go-chi-sō szru; ashirau; fukumu; idaku; nagusameru.
ENTERTAINMENT, Gochisō; shuyen; kiyo-ō.
ENTHUSIASM, Nobose.
ENTICE, Izanau; sasō; hiki-ireru; hiki-dasz; sosonokasz; obiku.
ENTIRE, Mattaku; mattai; maru-de.
ENTIRELY, Mattaku; nokoradz; h'toye ni; sappari; szkkari.
ENTRAILS, Hara-wata; zōfu.
ENTRANCE, *n.* Kuchi; mon; hairi kuchi; hajimete.
ENTRAP, Wana ni kakeru.
ENTREAT, Negau; kō; koi-negau.
ENTROPIUM, Sakamatszge.
ENUMERATE, Kazoyeru; kanjō szru.
ENVELOP, *v.* Tsztszmu; fūjiru.
ENVELOPE, *n.* Jō-bukuro.
ENVIRON, akomu; kokoi; maku; tori-maku.
ENVIRONS, Atari; hotori; kinjō.
ENVOY, Shisha; tszkai.
ENVY, *v.* Netamu; sonemu.
ENVY, *n.* Netami; shitto; sonemi.
EPIDEMIC, Hayari yamai.
EPIDERMIS, Uwa-gawa.
EPIGASTRIUM, Kiubi; midzochi.
EPILEPSY, Ten-kan.
EPISTLE, Tegami; fumi; jō.
EPOCH, Nengō.
EPSOM SALT, Shariyen.
EQUAL, Onaji; dō-yō na; ichi-yō na; soroi; biyōdō. — *quantities,* tōbun.
EQUALS, Dōhai.
EQUALIZE, Narasz; heikin szru; soroyeru.
EQUANIMITY, Heiki; ochi-tszki.
EQUATOR, Sekidō.
EQUILIBRIUM, Tszri-ai.
EQUINOX, *Vernal* —, shumbun. *Autumnal* —, shūbun.
EQUIP, Teate wo szru; shitaku szru; yōi wo szru; ide-tachi.
EQUIPAGE, Te-ate; yōi; dōzei.
EQUIPMENT, Teate; yō; sh'taku.
EQUITY, Gi.
ERA, Yo; dai; jidai.
ERADICATE, Nuku; hiki nuku; kogu.
ERASE, Kesz; kedzru.
ERE, Maye ni; izen; saki-ni.
ERECT, *v.* Tateru; konriu szru.
ERR, Mayoi; ayamaru; kokoroye-chigai; omoi-chigai.
ERRAND, Ōjō; tszkai.
ERROR, Ayamachi; machigai; sōi; sakugo.
ERUCTATION, Okubi; geppu; hedo.
ERUPTION, Deki-mono. *Syphilitic* —, yōbaisō.
ESCAPE, Sakeru; yokeru; manukareru; nogareru; nigeru; nukeru.
ESCORT, *n.* Keigo; tszki-soi.
ESCUTCHEON, Mon.
ESPECIAL, Kaku-betsz; betszdan.
ESPECIALLY, Kotoni; tori-wakete; bessh'te; kakubetsz-ni.
ESPOUSE, Īnadzkeru.
ESPY, Mi-tszkeru; midasz; ukagau.
ESSAY, *n.* Bunshō; tamashi; kokoromi.
ESSENCE, Genso; shōmi; seiki gokui; shui.
ESSENTIAL, Kan-yō; kanjin; naku te kanawanu; taisetsz; dai-ichi; yō.
ESTABLISH, Sadameru; kiwameru; katameru.
ESTATE, Bungen; mi-bun; katoku; shinshō.
ESTEEM, Tattobu; tai-setsz ni szru; wiyamau.
ESTIMATE, *v.* Hakaru; tszmoru; kanjō szru; kazoyeru.
ESTIMATE, *n.* Tszmori-gaki.
ESTRANGED, Tōzakaru; fuwa.
ET-CETERA, Unnun.
ETERNAL, Kagiri-naki; nagai.
ETERNITY, *n.* Yōgō; yei-yei; jimmiraisai.
ETIQUETTE, Reigi; reishiki; gishiki.
EULOGIZE, Homeru; shō szru; shōbi szru.
EUROPE, Yōropa; sei-yō.
EVACUATE, Kudaru; hiki-harau; akeru.
EVADE, Sakeru; yokeru; nukeru; nogareru; īnogareru; dashi-nuku.
EVANESCENT, Mujō; hakanai.
EVAPORATE, Tatsz; tateru; ni-tszmeru.
EVE, *to be on the eve of,* nozomu.
EVEN, *adv.* Demo; saye; szra; dani; saszga; sashimono. — *if,* tatoi.
EVEN, Tairaka-na; sorōta. — *numbers,* cho nō kadz. *Make* —, narasz; soroyeru. — *and odd,* chō-han; ki-gu.
EVENING, Yūbe; ban; kure; yū-gure.
EVENT, Koto.
EVENTUALLY, Tszi-ni; tōtō; hate-ni; ageku-ni; shimai-ni.
EVER, Itsz-mademo; bandai; yeitai; yeiyei.
EVERGREEN, Tokiwagi.
EVERLASTING, Kagiri-naki.
EVERY, Mai; goto-ni. — *day,* mai-nichi; nichi-nichi; hei-jitsz; tszne-no. — *body,* daredemo; dare-ni-temo; oyoso no h'to; bammin. — *other day,* ichi-nichioki; kaku-jitsz.

Every-where, Dokonitemo; dokodemo; idzku-ni-mo; amaneku; mamben, hōbō; sho-sho; shohō.

Evidence, Shōko; akashi.

Evident, Akiraka; ichi-jirushi; mei-haku; fummiyo

Evil, Aku; ashii; warui; kiyo; fu-kitsz. — *deeds*, akugō. — *spirits*, akki. — *thoughts*, aku-nen.

Evince, Shōko szru; arawasz; miseru.

Exact, Shimari; tori-shimari; tadashii; ki-chō-men-na; genjū-na.

Exactly, Chōdo; teinei-ni; shikkuri-to; yoku; sanagara.

Exaggerate, Hora wo fuku; ōkiku iu; hari wo bō ni iu; o ni o tszkete iu; ko-togotoshii; monogamashii.

Exalt, Agameru ageru.

Examine, Gimmi szru; shiraberu; arata-meru; tadasz; toi-tszmeru; kiu-mei; kem-bun; kemi. — *one's self*, kayeri-miru. — *a patient*, shinsatsz.

Example, Tehon; mihon; kibo; kagami; rei; tameshi; furiai; nottoru. *For* —, tatoyeba.

Exasperate, Ikaraseru; ikidōru; rippu-ku-saseru; taki-tszkeru; aradatsz; ara-dateru.

Excavate, Horu; kubomeru; kuru.

Exceed, Szgiru; kosz; koyeru; amaru.

Exceedingly, Itatte; shigoku; hanahada; ito; ammari.

Excel, Szgiru; kosz; koyeru; nukinderu; hīderu · katsz; masaru.

Excellence, Yosa.

Excellent, Yoi; yoki; ī.

Except, Hoka-ni; narade; nozoku; hiku; nokeru; oku; kaku-gai; hōgai.

Exception, Bekkaku.

Excess, Amari; yōkei; k'wabun; yobun; szgiru.

Exchange, *v.* Kayeru; tori-kayeru; riyō-gaye szru; tori-kawasz.

Exchange, *n.* Riyōgaye-ya; kawase. *Bill of* —, kawase-tegata.

Excise, Zei; zeigin; unjō.

Excite, Odateru; taki-tszkeru; hagemasz; okosz.

Exclaim, Sakebu; koye wo ageru.

Exclude, Nozoku; nokeru; saru; habuku; dasz; fusegu.

Excoriate, Szri-muku.

Excrement, Fun; kuso.

Excrescence, Kobu; zei-butsz.

Excruciating, Kurushii.

Exculpate, Ī-fusegu; ī-wake wo szru.

Excuse, *v.* Yurusz; kan-nin szru; go-men nasaru; īwake wo szru; kotowaru; yō-sha.

Excuse, *n.* Ī-wake; kotowari; shinshaku; ī-gusa; dashi; kakotszke.

Execrate, Nonoshiru.

Execute, Szru; nasz; itasz; okonau; tori-atszkau; shioki wo szru.

Executioner, Kubi-kiri.

Exemplify, Tatoyeru; tehon ni szru.

Exempt, Yurusz; menjiru; menk'yo szru.

Exequies, Sōshiki; sōrei; tomorai; okuri.

Exercise, Undō; hataraki; keiko; narasz.

Exert, *one's self*, Sei-dasz; shussei szru; chikara wo tszkusz.

Exhale, — *an order*, niou; kaoru.

Exhalation, Niyoi; ki.

Exhaust, Tszkusz; tszkiru; nakunaru; tszki-hateru; gakkari sh'te oru.

Exhibit, Miseru; arawasz.

Exhibition, Mise-mono; hakurank'wai.

Exhort, Hagemasz; imashimeru.

Exhume, Hori-dasz.

Exigency, Kiu-hen; rinkiōhen; kiu; kiuba.

Exile, Shima-nagase; yentō; ruzai; ru-nin; nagashi-mono; hai szru.

Exonorate, Ī-fusegu.

Exist, Oru; aru; iru; imasz. *Cause to* —, araseru, arashimeru.

Exorbitant, Messō-na.

Exorcise, Otosz; harau; gōbuku szru.

Expand, Hirogeru; hiroku szru; hiraku; fukurasz; noberu.

Expect, Nozomu; matsz. *Formed also by future suffix* ō, *or* arō.

Expectation, An; omoi; nozomi.

Expectorate, Haku.

Expedient, *n.* Tedate; jutsz; fumbetsz; saku; hakarigoto; senkata; shikata.

Expedient, *a.* Au; sō-ō; kanau.

Expedite, Hayameru; isogu; saisoku szru.

Expedition, Shimpatsz.

Expeditious, Hayai; rachi-aku

Expel, Dasz; oi-dasz; hōchiku szru; oi-harau; hamon.

Expend, Harau; tsziyasz; dasz; ireru.

Expenditure, Niu-yō; iri-yō; zappi; iri-ka; iri-me; kakari.

Expensive, Takai; kōjiki-na; ōku kakaru; takaku-tszku.

Experienced, Nareta; yeteta; jukush'ta; tokui.

Experiment, Kokoro-mi; kei-ken.

Expert, Jōdz.

Expiate, Aganau; tszgunau.

EXPIRATION, Tszki-iki; de-iki; owari; shimai.
EXPIRE, Iki wo tszku; shinuru.
EXPLAIN, Toku; toki-akasz; ge-szru; 'handan szru.
EXPLANATION, Yetoki.
EXPLETIVE, Kiyo-ji; jogo.
EXPLODE, Hanasz; haretsz szru.
EXPLOIT, Waza; kō; hataraki.
EXPLORE, Ukagau; tadzneru; sagasz.
EXPORTS, *n.* Yushutsz.
EXPORT, *v.* Yushutsz szru; dasz; hakobidasz.
EXPOSE, Sarasz; arawasz; abaku; miseru. — *one's life,* inochi wo kakeru.
EXPOSTULATE, Isameru; iken szru.
EXPOSURE, Muki; uke.
EXPOUND, Toku; kōshaku szru.
EXPRESS, *v.* Shiboru; shimeru; ī-toru; noberu; shirusz.
EXPRESS, *n.* Haya; hayabik'yaku.
EXPRESSION, Tszki.
EXPUNGE, Kesz; shometsz szru.
EXQUISITE, Kekkōna; seimiyō-na.
EXTEMPORIZE, Kuchi ni makaseru.
EXTEND, Todokeru; oyobu; nobasz hirogeru; habikoru. — *the time,* hinobe wo szru.
EXTENTION, Hinobe. — *to a house,* sashi-kamaye.
EXTENSIVE, Hiroi; tebiroi.
EXTENUATE, Kazaru.
EXTERIOR, Soto; uwabe; omote; hoka; wiye.
EXTERMINATE, Tatsz; tayasz; minagoroshi wo szru; messzru.
EXTERNAL, *see exterior.*
EXTINGUISH, Kesz; fuki-kesz; shimeru; chin-k'wa.
EXTIRPATE, Nuku; nuki-dasz.
EXTOL, Homeru; shōszru; sambi szru; santan.
EXTORT, Nedaru; yuszru; torishimeru.
EXTRACT, Hiku; nuku.
EXTRAORDINARY, Tszne-naranu; hijō-na; ki-miyō.
EXTRAVAGANCE, Ogori; zeitaku; mudadzkai.
EXTRAVAGANT, Muri; hō-g'wai; ogoru.
EXTREME, Shigoku; itatte. — *price,* seigiri.
EXTREMITY, Owari; hate.
EXTRICATE, Szkū; taszkeru.
EXUBERANT, Shigeru.
EXUDE, Deru.
EXULT, Yorokobu; ureshigaru; kiyetsz.
EYE, Me; manako; gan; moku. *Sore* —, biyō-gan; gam-biyō.
EYE-BALL, Me no tama.
EYE-BROW, Mayu; mamiye.
EYE-LASH, Matszge.
EYELID, Mabuta.
EYE-SORE, Sappūkei.
EYE-TOOTH, Kiba.
EYE-WITNESS, Mita shōkonin.

F

FABLE, Tatoye-banashi; tszkuri mono-gatari.
FABRIC, Ji; jiai; kime.
FABRICATE, Tszkuru; koshirayeru; saku szru.
FACE, Kao; tszra; kambe; omo; membu; memboku; omote. — *to face,* tai-men; mukiau; aimukai-ni; aitai szru; sashimukai. *Lose* —, memboku-nai.
FACE, *v.* Mukau; tai-szru.
FACETIOUS, Odokeru; tawamureru; fuzakeru.
FACILITATE, Hayaku szru; rachi wo akeru; yaszku szru.
FACILITY, Yaszku; tayaszku; zōsamonaki.
FACING, Muki; uke.
FAC-SIMILE, Shō utszshi.
FACT, Koto; arisama; yoshi; omomuki. *In* —, jitsz-ni; hon-ni.
FACTION, Totō; muhon.
FACTOR, Shi-hai-nin; tedai.
FACTORY, Demise; shi-komi-dokoro.
FACULTY, Hataraki; chiye.
FADE, Sameru; kareru; otoroyeru; uszku naru; kiyeru.
FAGOT, Shiba.
FAIL, Otoroyeru; szibi szru; kareru; ochiru; oyobanu; dekinu; tszbureru; tayeru; hadzsz; somuku; hadzreru.
FAILURE, Ochido; otoroye; szibi; sōi; ataranu; shubi-warui; hadzreru. — *of sight,* szigan.
FAINT, *a.* Uszi; hosoi; yowai.
FAINT, *v.* Tszkareru; kutabireru.
FAINTING, Memai; kennun.
FAIR, *a.* Kirei; yoi. — *weather,* otenki; seiten. — *wind,* jumpū.
FAIR, *n.* Ichi.
FAIRLY, Uso-naku-sh'te; damasadz ni.
FAITH, Shinjin; shinkō.

FAITHFUL, Shinjitsz-na; shōjiki-na. — *servant*, chiu-shin. — *soldier*, gihei.
FAITHFULLY, Jitsz ni.
FALCON, Taka.
FALCONER, Takajō.
FALL, *v.* Ochiru; otosz; taoreru; sagaru; kudaru. — *away*, yaseru. — *back*, ato ye yoru. — *down (humbly)*, sh'ta ni oru; hizamadzku. — *from*, somuku. — *in with*, shōchi szru; sh'tagau; au. — *backwards*, nokezoru. — *in price*, sagaru; dareru.
FALLOPIAN *tubes*, Rappank'wan.
FALLOW *ground*, Yaszmeji.
FALSE, Uso; itszwaru; makoto nai. — *hair*, iregami. — *tooth*, ireba. — *article*, nise mono. — *imprisonment*, mushitsz no tszmi. — *key*, ai-kagi.
FALSEHOOD, Uso; kiyo-gon; itszwari.
FALSIFY, Itszwaru; niseru.
FALTER, Tamerau; tayutau; yodomu; kuchigomoru.
FAME, Hiyōban; homare; kikoye.
FAMILIAR, Nareru; kokoro-yaszi; nengorona; nare-nareshii; koni.
FAMILIARIZE, Nareru; narasz.
FAMILY, Kanai; kenzoku; uchiwa.
FAMINE, Kikin.
FAMISH, Wiyeru; katszyeru.
FAMOUS, Kōmei naru; nadakai; kikoyeru.
FAN, Uchiwa; ōgi; sensz.
FAN, *v.* Aogu.
FANCY, Omoinashi; dekigoto; minashi; shinsō.
FANG, Kiba.
FANTASTIC, Okashii; hiyōkin-na.
FAR, Tōi; haruka; haru-baru; yempō.
FARE, *n.* Chin; dai; shoku-ji; unchin; dachin; funachin.
FAREWELL, Sayōnara; osaraba; go-kigenyoroshū.
FARM, *n.* Denji; jimen; dembata. — *house*, denka.
FARM, *v.* Tszkuru; tagayesz; kōsaku szru; unau.
FARMER, Hiyak'shō; nōfu.
FASCINATE, Mayō; mayowasz; norokeru.
FASHION, Katachi; szgata; hayari; fūzoku; narawashi.
FASHION, *v.* Tszkuru.
FASHIONABLE, Hayaru; riu-kō.
FAST, *a.* Hayai; szmiyaka; jiki; sassoku; katai; tszyoku; kibishiku.
FAST, *n.* Danjiki; kessai.
FASTEN, Shimeru; tojiru; tozasz.

FAT, *n.* Abura; aburami.
FAT, *a.* Koyeru; f'toru.
FATAL, Inochi tori; inochi ni kakaru.
FATE, Un; temmei; ten-un; yak'soku.
FATHER, Chi-chi; o-totsan; tete-oya. *Your* —, go-shimbu-sama. — *and child*, fushi.
FATHER-IN-LAW, Shūto.
FATHOM, Hiro.
FATIGUE, Tszkareru; kutabireru.
FATTEN, Koyasz.
FAUCET, Nomiguchi.
FAULT, Ayamachi; ochido; ībun.
FAVOR, *n.* On; nasake; megumi; hīki; katayori; yeko; katahīki; hempa.
FAVOR, *v.* Katadzmu; katayoru.
FAVORABLE, Au; kanau; shubi yoku. — *wind*, jumpū; oite.
FAWN, *v.* Hetszrau; kobiru.
FEAR, *n.* Osore; ojike.
FEAR, *v.* Osoreru; kowagaru; ojiru.
FEARFUL, Osoroshii; kowai; okkanai; abunagaru.
FEARLESS, Futeki.
FEAST, *n.* Chisō; furumai; iwai; matszri; sairei; shuyen.
FEAST, *v.* Furumau; motenasz; kiyō-ō szru.
FEAT, Koto; waza; kiyoku-mochi.
FEATHER, Hane; ke. — *brush*, ha-bōki.
FEATHER, *v.* — *an arrow*, hagu.
FEATURE, Yōbō; tszra-gamaye; omodachi.
FEBRIFUGE, Seiriyōzai; netsz samashi.
FEBRUARY, Nigatsz.
FECES, Fun; dai-ben; kuso; unko.
FECULENT, Nigoru; daiben-no.
FEE, Reikin.
FEEBLE, Yowai, niujaku.
FEED, *n.* Tabe-mono. *Horse* —, kaiba; magusa. *Chicken* —, ye; yeba.
FEED, *v.* Kau; tabesaseru; kukumeru; kuwaseru; fukumeru.
FEEL, *v.* Naderu; tszmaguru; saguru; oboyeru; omou.
FEEL, *n.* Te-atari; te-zawari.
FEELER, — *of an insect*, hige.
FEELINGS, Kokoro-mochi; kimochi; kibun; kimi; chikaku; oboye; shōne.
FEIGN, Niseru; mane wo szru; maneru; furi wo szru; sora. *Feigned sickness*, kebiyō; sakubiyō. — *madness*, nise-kichigai.
FELICITATE, Iwau; shuku szru; medetai.
FELICITY, Tanoshimi; raku.
FELL, Buchi-taosz; kiru.

FELLOW, Mono; yatsz; tomo; dōhai.
FELLOW-CITIZEN, Dōkoku-jin.
FELLOW-COUNTRYMAN, Dōkokujin.
FELLOW-FEELING, Omoi-yari.
FELLOW-LODGER, Dōshuku.
FELLOW-MINISTER, Dōyaku; dōkin.
FELLOW-SCHOLAR, Dōgaku; deshihōbai.
FELLOW-SERVANT, Dōhan.
FELLOWSHIP, Nakama; kumi; tszki-ai; majiwari.
FELLOW-SOLDIER, Dō-shi.
FELLOW-STUDENT, Dō-gaku.
FELLOW-TRAVELER, Dōhan; dōdō.
FEMALE, Niyo; me; onna; mesz.
FEMININE, Onnarashii; niyakeru; memeshii.
FEN, Numa.
FENCE, *n.* Hei; kaki.
FENCE, *v.* Shiau; kenjutsz szru.
FENCING, Kenjutsz; shiai.
FENCING-SCHOOL, Dōjō; keiko-ba.
FENCING-MASTER, Kenjutsz no shishō.
FEND, Fusegu; ukeru; yokeru;
FENDER, Yoke.
FERMENT, Waku; waki-agaru; mureru.
FERN, Warabi; zemmai; shida.
FEROCIOUS, Takeki; bōaku.
FERRY, *n.* Watashiba.
FERRY, *v.* Watasz; wataru.
FERRYBOAT, Watashi-bune.
FERRYMAN, Watashi-mori.
FERTILE, Koyeru.
FERTILIZE, Koyasz.
FERULE, Shippei.
FERVENTLY, H'toye-ni; ichidz-ni; hitaszrani.
FERVID, Atszi.
FESTIVAL, Matszri; sairei.
FESTIVITY, Kiyō; omoshirosa.
FETCH, Motekuru.
FETID, Kusai.
FETTER, Ashigane; hodashi.
FEUD, Kenk'wa.
FEUDATORY, Kerai; takatori.
FEVER, Netsz; netsz-biyō; shōkan.
FEVERISH, Hoteru.
FEW, Szkunai; shō-shō.
FICKLE, Uwa-uwa szru; uki; uwatszku; utszrigi-na.
FICTION, Tszkurigoto; tszkuri mono gatari; shōsetszmono.
FICTITIOUS, Niseru.
FIDDLE, Kokiu.
FIDELITY, Chiu-gi; chiu-shin; shinjitsz; chiu-setsz.
FIELD, Ta-hata; denji; ba; tan. *Rice* —, ta. *Wheat* —, hatake. — *of battle*, kassemba; senjō.
FIERCE, Takeki; arai; hageshii; tszyoi.
FIFE, Fuye.
FIFTH, Goban; goban-me.
FIFTEEN, Jūgo.
FIFTEENTH, Jūgo-ban; jūgoban-me.
FIFTY, Go-jū.
FIFTIETH, Gōjūban; gojūbanme.
FIG, Ichijiku.
FIGHT, *v.* Tatakau; kassen szru; buchi-au; kenk'wa szru.
FIGHT, *n.* Kenk'wa; buchiai; kassen.
FIGURATIVE, Tatoyeru; nazorayeru.
FIGURE, Kata; katachi; szgata; shirushi; tatoye.
FIGURE, *v.* Katadoru; kaku; tatoyeru; nazorayeru.
FILE, *n.* Yaszri; narabi; tszra; giyō.
FILIAL, Kōkō na.
FILINGS, Senkudz.
FILL, *v.* Mitszru; ippai ni szru; aku; tatayeru. — *up a deficiency*, tasz.
FILLIP, Tszma-hajiki.
FILM, Kawa; uwakawa.
FILTER, *n.* Midz-koshi.
FILTER, *v.* Kosz.
FILTH, Kitanai mono.
FIN, Hire.
FINAL, Hateru; owaru.
FINALLY, Tszi-ni; tōtō; ageku-ni; hate-ni; shimai-ni; sendzru tokoro.
FINANCES, Shinshō; shindai.
FIND, Au; midasz; mitszkeru.
FINE, *a.* Hosoi; komayaka; yoi; kirei-na; rippa-na; uszi.
FINE, *n.* Batszkin; k'wariyō.
FINELY, Yoku.
FINENESS, Hososa; komakasa; utszkushisa.
FINERY, Date; hade.
FINGER, Yubi. *Eating with the* —, tedzkami.
FINGER, *v.* Tszmaguru; dandzru.
FINISH, Jōju szru; togeru; dekiru; szmu; owaru; shuttai szru; hatasz; szmasz.
FINITE, Kagiru.
FIRE, Hi; k'waji.
FIRE, *v.* Hi wo tszkeru; hanasz; hidoru.
FIRE-ARMS, Teppō.
FIRE-BRAND, Moye-sashi; moyekui.
FIRE-ENGINE, Riu-tō-szi.
FIRE-FLY, Hotaru.

FIRE-MAN, Hikeshi.
FIRE-PLACE, Kotatsz; hidoko.
FIRE-PROOF, Yakenu; higotai ga yoi.
FIRE-WOOD, Takagi; maki.
FIRE-WORKS, Hanabi.
FIRKIN, Taru; oke.
FIRM, *a.* Jōbu; katai; tash'ka-na.
FIRM, *n.* Kumi; nakama.
FIRMAMENT, Sora; ame; ten.
FIRMLY, Kataku; jōbu-ni; shika-to; shikkari-to; jitto.
FIRST, Hajimari; hana; shote; hajime; ichi-ban; saisho; ui; some.
FIRST, *adv.* Hajimete; madz; saisho.
FIRST-BORN, Ui-zan; sōriyō; chakushi.
FIRSTDAY *of the month*, Tszitachi.
FIRST-FRUITS, Hatszo.
FIRST-MONTH, Shō-gatsz.
FIRST-RATE, Ichi-ban; goku-jō.
FIRST-WIFE, Sensai.
FISH, Uwo; sakana; giyo. — *oil*, giyotō.
FISH, *v.* Sakana wo toru; tszru; sznadoru; riyō szru.
FISH-BASKET, Ikesz.
FISHERMAN, Riyōshi; sznadori.
FISHGIG, Yasz.
FISH-HOOK, Tszri-bari.
FISHING, Tszri.
FISHING-BOAT, Tszri-bune.
FISHING-LINE, Tszri-ito.
FISHING-ROD, Tszri-zao.
FISH-MARKET, Sakana-ichi; zakoba.
FISH-MONGER, Sakana-ya.
FISHY, Sakana-kusai.
FISSURE, Wari.
FIST, Kobushi; nigiri-kobushi.
FISTULA *in ano*, Ana-ji.
FIT, *n.* Kiyōfū.
FIT, *v.* Au; awaseru; kanau; sō-ō; tekitō; niau. — *out*, shitaku szru; teate wo szru. — *up*, koshirayeru.
FIVE, Itsztsz; go.
FIX, Sadameru; kiwameru; itszki; kakeru; goszru. — *on a day*, hidori wo szru; nichi-gen; higiri.
FIXEDLY, Kitto; jitto.
FIXTURE, Iye tszki no mono; okitszke.
FLABBY, Yowai.
FLAG, *n.* Hata; ashi.
FLAG, *v.* Okureru.
FLAGEOLET, Hichiriki.
FLAGITIOUS, Aku; ashii; warui.
FLAIL, Kara-sao; kururi.
FLAKE, — *of fire*, tobihi.
FLAMBEAU, Taimatsz; tebi.
FLAME, Honō; k'wayen.
FLANK, Yoko.
FLANNEL, Raseita.
FLAP, *Saddle* —, aori
FLAP, *v.* Aoru; hatataki. *Sound of flapping*, bata bata.
FLASH, *v.* Hikaru. *To — in anger*, mukabaratatsz.
FLASK, Furaszko; tokkuri.
FLAT, Tairaka; hira; hirattai.
FLATTEN, Hirameru; hirattaku szru.
FLATTER, Hetszrau; kobiru; tszishō; bennei.
FLATTERER, Neijin.
FLATTERY, Neiben; hetszrai; kobi; tszishō.
FLAVOR, *n.* Ajiwai; aji; kagen; ambai; fūmi.
FLAVOR, *v.* Aji wo tszkeru.
FLAW, Kidz.
FLAY, Hagu; muku.
FLEA, Nomi.
FLEE, Hashiru; nigeru; chikuten szru; shuppon szru.
FLEET, Hayai; ashibaya.
FLEETING, Hakanai.
FLESH, Niku.
FLESH-COLORED, Nikuiro.
FLESHY, Koyeta; futotta.
FLEUR DE LIS, Shaga.
FLEXIBLE, Magerareru; tawayaka.
FLICKER, Matataku; kira-kira; chiratszku; chira-chira.
FLIGHT, Hashiri; kake-ochi; chikuten. *Put to flight*, hashiraseru.
FLIGHTY, Sora.
FLINCH, Biku-tszku; mijiroku.
FLING, Nageru; hōru. — *away*, nageszteru; furi-szteru.
FLINT, Hiuchi-ishi.
FLOAT, Uku; ukabu.
FLOCK, *v.* Muragaru; gunsan.
FLOCK, *n.* Mure.
FLOG, Butsz; utsz; muchi-utsz.
FLOOD, Kōdzi.
FLOOD-GATE, Szimon.
FLOOD-TIDE, Michi-shiwo.
FLOOR, Yuka.
FLORIST, Wiyekiya.
FLOSS-SILK, Mawata.
FLOUNDER, Agaku.
FLOUR, Ko; kona. *Wheat* —, komugi-no-ko. *Rice* —, kome-no-ko. *Buckwheat* —, soba-no-ko.

FLOURISH, Sakan-naru ; sakaru ; han-jō szru; sakayeru; yutaka; furu.
FLOW, Nagareru.
FLOWER, *n.* Hana.
FLOWER, *v.* Saku.
FLUCTUATION, Agari-sagari.
FLUE, Kemuri-dashi; kaza-ana.
FLUENT, Ben no yoi; benzetsz; kuchimame; szrari to; szra-szra to.
FLUID, Midzmono; riudōbutsz.
FLUOR-ALBUS, Koshike.
FLURRIED, Urotayeru ; atafuta; awatadashii; bikkuri.
FLUSH, Akaku naru.
FLUTE, Fuye; ōteki; shakuhachi.
FLUTTER, Hirameku; hirugayeru ; soyogu; biratszku; bira-bira; chiratszku; chira-chira.
FLUX, Harakudari; geri. *Bloody* —, geketsz.
FLY *v.* Tobu; hashiru ; kakeru ; haneru ; hajikeru. — *at*, tobi-tszku.
FLY, *n.* Hai. *Horse* —, abu. — *poison*, haidoku.
FLYING-FISH, Tobi uwo.
FOAM, Awa.
FODDER, Kaiba.
FOE, Ada; kataki; teki.
FOG, Kiri; moya.
FOIL, *n.* Haku; kise.
FOIL, *v.* Fusegu.
FOLD, *v.* Oru; tatamu. — *the arms*, komanuku.
FOLD, *n.* Ye; bai.
FOLLOW, Sh'tagau; tszite yuku; ou ; fukujū szru.
FOLLOWER, Tomo; jūsha; dzijū ; sh'tagau h'to ; monto; deshi.
FOLLOWING, Sa; akuru.
FOMENT, Musz; taderu.
FOND, Konomu; szku; tashimu ; *also formed by the suffix*, tai, *and* garu; *as*, asobitagaru, *to be fond of play.*
FONDLE, Ayasz.
FOOD, Tabemono; shoku-motsz ; shoku-ji; kui-mono.
FOOL, Baka; ahō; tawake; shiremono; chōsaibō.
FOOL, *v.* Gurō szru; naburu; baka ni szru; azamuku; damasz.
FOOL-HARDY, Mukōmidz; muteppō.
FOOLISH, Bakarashii; tawai-mo-nai; tszmara-nai; don-na; ahōrashii; gu-naru.
FOOLISHNESS, Tawakoto.
FOOT, Ashi. *On foot*, kachi.
FOOT, *in length*, Shaku.
FOOT-BALL, Kemari.
FOOT-HOLD, Ashi-gakari; ashi-damari; fumi-dome.
FOOTING, *Idem.*
FOOT-PRINT, Ashiato.
FOOT-RULE, Monosashi; kanezashi.
FOOT-SOLDIER, Kachi-musha; ashigaru.
FOOT-STALK, Kuki.
FOOT-STEP, Ashi-ato.
FOOT-STOOL, Fumidai.
FOOT-STOVE, Kiyakuro.
FOP, Date-sha.
FOR, Tame-ni; kawari-ni; sash'te; mukatte; wo; no; ni; ni-wa; uchi-ni ; maye; buri.
FORBEAR, Kannin szru; hikayeru; yameru; korayeru; shimbō szru.
FORBEARANCE, Kikayeme; kannin.
FORBID, Kindzru; kotowaru ; imashimeru; sei-kin szru; sasayeru; chōji szru.
FORCE, *n.* Chikara; ikioi; sei; seiriki; konki. *By* —, shĭte; muri-ni; oshite.
FORCE, *v.* Shĭru; osz; hesz; *also formed by the caust. suff.* shi; *or* saseru. — *out*, shi-dasz. — *open*, oshi-akeru. — *apart*, oshi-hedateru. — *into*, oshi-komu. — *back*, oshi-kayesz. — *one's way into*, oshi-iru. — *down*, oshi-kudasz. — *through*, oshi-tōsz.
FORCEPS, Nuki. *Tooth* —, ha-nuki. *Hair* —, ke-nuki.
FORCIBLY, Osh'te; shĭte; muri-ni.
FORD, Kachi-watari.
FORE, Zen; maye; saki.
FOREARM, Ude; ko-ude; te.
FOREBODE, Mitōsz; miszkasz; senken szru; zempiyō.
FORE-CAST, Hakaru; tszmoru; yōjin.
FORE-FATHER, Senzo.
FORE-FINGER, H'to-sashi-yubi.
FOREGO, Hikayeru; kan-nin szru; jitai szru.
FOREGOING, Maye-no; migi-no; sen-no; kudan.
FOREHEAD, Hitai; nuka.
FOREIGN, Yoso; ta. — *country*, g'wai koku; ikoku; yoso no kuni; takoku. *Brought from a — country*, hakurai.
FOREIGNER, G'wai-kokujin; ijin; tōjin; yoso no h'to.
FOREKNOW, Miszkasz; mi-tōsz; arakajime shiru; mayemotte shiru; senken szru.
FORELOCK, Mayegami.
FOREMAN, Kashira; tōriyō.
FOREMAST, Maye-bashira.

FORE-MENTIONED, Kudan; iwayuru.
FORE-MOST, Ichiban saki no; hana no; massaki.
FORENOON, Hiru-maye.
FORE-ORDAIN, Maye-ni sadameru ;maye-ni kiwameru.
FOREPART, Maye no hō.
FORESAID, Kudan.
FORE-SEE, Miszkasz; mitōsz.
FORESAIL, Mayebo.
FOREST, Hayashi.
FORE-STALL, Kai-shimeru; kuguru; saki-bashiru; saki-kuguru.
FORE-TELL, Mayemotte iu; kanete iu; arakajime iu.
FORETHOUGHT, Yōjin.
FORE-TOOTH, Mayeba.
FOREVER, Itszmademo; yeitai; yeiyei; bandai.
FORE-WARN, Mayemotte isameru; kanete iken szru; kanete shiraseru.
FORFEIT, *n.* Batsz-kin; k'wariyō.
FORFEIT, *v.* Kakaru.
FORGE, *v.* Niseru; utsz; kitau. *Forged seal,* bōhan. *Forged writing,* bōsho.
FORGE, *n.* Kaji; kajiya.
FORGERY, *n.* Niseru koto; nisemono; gihitsz.
FORGET, Waszreru; shitsz-nen szru; bōkiyaku szru.
FORGETFUL, Waszreppoi; waszregachi; yoku waszreru.
FORGIVE, Yurusz; mendzru;shamen szru; yūmen; yuriru.
FORK, Mata. *Forked,* futamata.
FORM, Katachi; szgata; nari; kata.
FORMALITY, *Without —,* yenriyo naku; jigi-nashi.
FORMER, Maye-no; sen; izen.
FORMERLY, Mukashi; kono-maye ni.
FORMULA, Hō; seihō.
FORNICATION, Jain; kanin; tawakeru.
FORSAKE, Szteru; utcharu; hai szru.
FORT, O-dai-ba; hōtai; toride.
FORTH, *From that day forth,* konokata; irai. *So forth,* un-nun; shika-shika. *Go forth,* deru. *Call forth,* yobi-dasz.
FORTHWITH, Tachi-machi; tachidokoro; szgu-ni; sokuza-ni.
FORTIETH, Shijū-ban.
FORTIFICATION, Toride; o-daiba.
FORTIFY, Katameru; kengo ni szru.
FORTITUDE, Gaman; shimbō; koraye-jō; kannin.
FORTUITOUS, Fui; hakaradz; futo; zonjiyoradz; onodz-to.
FORTUNE, Shinsho ; zai-hō; takara; shiawase; un.
FORTUNATE, Sai-wai-na; shiawase na; unno-yoi.
FORTUNE-TELLING, Uranai; bai-boku.
FORTUNE-TELLER, Uranaija; baiboku-shi.
FORTY, Shi-jū.
FORWARD, Bu-yenriyo-na; busahō-na; hayaku ; saki-no ; maye-no.
FORWARD, *To go —,* Szszmu; maye ye deru.
FOSSIL-WOOD, Umoregi.
FOSTER, Yashinau; sodateru; yōiku szru.
FOSTER-BROTHER, Chikiyōdai.
FOSTER-CHILD, Yashinaigo.
FOSTER-FATHER, Yōfu.
FOSTER-MOTHER, Yōbo.
FOUL, Kitanai; yogoreru; kegareru; fujō-na; musai; nigoru; warui; ashii; aku.
FOULMOUTHED, Kuchigitanai.
FOUND, *v.* Kai-ki szru; konriu szru; hajimeru; hiraku; iru; motodzku. *Have you — it?* attaka.
FOUNDATION, Dodai; ishidzye; motoi; yoridokoro.
FOUNDER, Kaiki; hottō-nin; imonoshi; soshi.
FOUNDLING, Sztego; hiroigo.
FOUNDRY, Imojiya.
FOUNTAIN, Idzmi.
FOUR, Yotsz; shi.
FOURFOLD, Yoye; shi-mai.
FOURSQUARE, Shikaku.
FOURTEEN, Jūshi.
FOURTEENTH, Jūshiban.
FOURFOOTED, Yotsz-ashi; shisoku
FOURTH, Yo-ban.
FOURTH-DAY, Yokka.
FOWL, Tori; niwatori.
FOX, Kitszne.
FRACTION, Hash'ta; bu.
FRACTURE, *v.* Oru; oreru.
FRAGILE, Koware-yaszi; moroi; sakui; yowai.
FRAGMENT, Hasz'ta; hampa.
FRAGRANT, Kōbashii; kaoru.
FRAIL, Yowai.
FRAILTY, Yowasa; ochido.
FRAME, Szdate; honegumi; waku; shōji.
FRAME, *v.* Kiri-kumu; kufū szru; kuwadateru.
FRANCE, F'ransz; futsz.

FRANK, Meihaku-na; shin-sotsz-na; okusokonai.
FRANTIC, Kurui; muchiu; gureru; monogurui.
FRATERNAL, Kiyōdai-no.
FRATERNITY, Nakama; kumi; shachiu; renchiu.
FRAUD, Itszwari; katari; hameru.
FRAY, Kenk'wa.
FREAK, Dekigokoro.
FRECKLE, Sobakasz.
FREE, Dokuriyu; h'tori-dachi; jiyū-na; jizai-na; todokōri-nai; hōdai; tada-no. *Set free*, hanatsz.
FREELY, Jiyū-jizai-ni; tada; todokōri-naku.
FREEZE, Kōru; kogoyeru. — *to death*, kogoye-jini.
FREIGHT, *n.* Ni; nimotsz; tsznda mono; funa-chin; unchin; dachin.
FREIGHT, *v.* Tszmu.
FRENZY, Monogurui; kichigai.
FREQUENT, *v.* Kayō; shiba-shiba yuku.
FREQUENTLY, Shiba-shiba; tabi-tabi; choko-choko.
FRESH, Atarashii; nama. — *water*, kumi tate no midz.
FRESHET, Kōdzi; ōmidz.
FRET *v.* Szru; szri-yaburu; szri-kiru; iratsz; iratszku; jirasz.
FRIABLE, Koware-yaszi; moroi; sakui; yowai.
FRICTION, Szre-ai; kishimu.
FRIEND, Tomodachi; hōyu; hōbai; mikata; yorube; tayori.
FRIENDLY, Nengoro-ni; kokoro-yaszi; shinsetsz-ni; mutszmajiku; koni.
FRIENDSHIP, Mutszmajii; shitashimi; konsei; yoshimi.
FRIGHT, Osore; odoroki.
FRIGHTEN, Odorokasz; odosz; obiyakasz.
FRIGHTFUL, Osoroshii.
FRINGE, Fusa; yōraku; baren.
FRISK, Haneru; jareru; tawamureru.
FRIVOLOUS, Wadzka; karui; isasaka; sasai.
FRIZZLED, Chijireru.
FROCK, Kimono; uwagi.
FROG, Kawadz; kayeru; hiki; amagayeru; gama.
FROLIC, Tawamure; asobi.
FROM, Kara; yori.
FRONT, Omote; maye; muke.
FRONT-DOOR, Omote-mon.
FRONTLET, Mabisashi.
FROST, Shimo.
FROST-BITTEN, Shimoyake.
FROTH, Awa.
FROWN, Shikameru; mayu wo hisomeru.
FROZEN, Kōtta; kogoyeta.
FRUGAL, Kenyaku; kanriyaku; shimatsz; tszdzmayaka.
FRUIT, Mi; kinomi; midz-k'washi; kudamono. *First fruits*, hashiri.
FRUITFUL YEAR, Hōnen.
FRUITLESS, Muda; munashiku.
FRUSTRATE, Naku szru; munashiku szru; sashi-yameru.
FRY, Ageru.
FUEL, Takigi; maki; takimono.
FUGITIVE, *n.* Kake-ochi-nin; shuppon nin.
FULFIL, Hatasz; szmasz; togeru.
FULL, Ippai; mitszru; aku; mattaku; jūbun. — *moon*, mangetsz. — *tide*, michi-shiwo. — *bloom*, hana-zakari.
FULLY, Mattaku; shika-to.
FUMIGATE, Fuszberu; ibusz; kuyorasz.
FUNCTION, Yaku; yakume; hataraki.
FUND, Motode; motokin; midzkin.
FUNDAMENT, Shiri; ishiki.
FUNERAL, Tomurai; sōrei; sōsō; okuri; sōshiku.
FUNGUS, Take.
FUNNEL, Jōgo.
FUR, Ke; kawa. — *coat*, ke-goromo.
FURBISH, Migaku; togu.
FURIOUS, Hageshii; tszyoi; kibishii; arai; takeki.
FURL, Maku; orosz; sageru.
FURLOUGH, Hima; yaszmi.
FURNACE, Kamado; hettszi; kama; kudo.
FURNISH, Soroyeru; sonayeru; dasz; atayeru; teate wo szru.
FURNITURE, Dōgu; kagu; kazai.
FURRED *tongue*, Zettai; hakutai.
FURROW, Mizo; saku.
FURTHER, Toi-hō; mata; mo mata; sonowiye-ni; nao.
FURTHERMORE, Sono-wiye; sono-hoka; mata; nao; nao-mata; mata-wa.
FURTIVELY, Shinonde; kakurete.
FURY, Hageshisa; arasa; tszyosa.
FUSE, Hi-nawa; tansoku.
FUSIBLE, Tokeru.
FUSS, Yakamashii; sawagi.
FUTILE, Muda; munashii; itadzra.
FUTURE, Mirai; yuku-szye; nochi; go; kōsei. — *state*, nochi no yo; gosei; goshō; gose.

G

GABLE, Hafu.
GAD, Asobu; bura-bura.
GAG, *v.* Kamaseru.
GAG, *n.* Sarugutszwa.
GAGE, *v.* Hakaru.
GAIN, *v.* Mōkeru; katsz; uru; ukeru; itaru. — *over*, katarau.
GAIN, *n.* Ri; yeki; mōke; riyeki; kai; torika.
GAINSAY, Īfusegu; ī-kesz.
GAIT, Ashi-tszki; aruki-buri; ashidori; furi.
GALAXY, Ama no kawa.
GALE, Ōkaze; arate; tai-fū.
GALL, Tan; I; kimo.
GALL-BLADDER, *Idem.*
GALL, *v.* Szreru; szru.
GALLANT, Yūki-na; isamashii; gōkina; kenage.
GALLERY, Rōka; sajiki.
GALLIPOT, Tszbo; futamono.
GALLNUT, Gobaishi; fushi.
GALLON, Maszmono, = *to about*, ni-shō roku-gō.
GALLOP, Kakeru; hashiru.
GALLOWS, Gokumon.
GAMBLING, Bakuchi; bakuyeki.
GAMBLING-HOUSE, Bakuchi-yado.
GAMBLER, Bakuchi-uchi.
GAMBOGE, Shiō; tōwō.
GAMBOL, Haneru; tawamureru; jareru.
GAME, *n.* Shōbugoto; kachi-make; kari; yemono; ban. *Two games of chess*, shōji ni ban.
GAME, *v.* Shōbugoto wo szru; bakuchi wo utsz.
GANG, Kumi; nakama; totō.
GANGRENE, Funiku. — *of the feet*, dasso.
GOAL, Rōya; h'to-ya;; agari-ya; gokuya.
GOALER, Rōban; rōmori; gokusotsz.
GAP, Ana.
GAPING, Akubi.
GARB, Nari; ide-tachi; ifuku; kimono.
GARBAGE, Akuta.
GARDEN, Hatake; sono; niwa; wiyegomi; sayen; senzai.
GARDENER, Saku-nin; wiyekiya.
GARGLE, Kuchi wo sosogu; ugai wo szru.
GARLIC, Ninniku; nira.
GARMENT, Kimono.
GARNER, Kura.
GARNISH, Kazaru.
GARRISON, *v.* Katameru.
GARRISON, *n.* Tamurō; katame.
GARRULOUS, Shaberu.
GARTER, Himo.
GASH, *n.* Kiri-kidz.
GASP, Tameiki.
GATE, Mon; kido.
GATHER, Atszmeru; yoseru; toru; tsznoru.
GAUDY, Hanayaka.
GAUGE, Hakaru.
GAUNT, Yaseta.
GAUZE, Moji; ro.
GAY, Kirei-na; hanayaka-na; hade na; date na.
GAZE, Nagameru; kiyorori to miru.
GEAR, Dōgu; bagu.
GELATINOUS, Nebai; nebaru.
GEM, Tama.
GENDER, Mesz-osz; shi-yu.
GENEALOGY, Keidz; chiszji; ketto.
GENERA, Rui; burui.
GENERAL, *n.* Taishō. — *in chief*, shōgun; shotaishō.
GENERALITY, Tabun; taihan; ōkata.
GENERALLY, Tai-tei; ōkata; sōtai; ōmune; taigai; tairiyaku; zentai; g'wanrai; oyoso.
GENERAL-NAME, Sōmiyō.
GENERATE, Shōdzru; naru.
GENERATION, Dai; yo.
GENEROUS, Ki ga hiroi; ki no ōkii; mono-oshimi senu.
GENTEEL, Teinei; fūriu; fūga; ikina; miyabiyaka; ateyakana.
GENTIAN, Rindō.
GENTLE, Otonashii; onjun; sō; yasashii.
GENTLEMAN, Kunshi.
GENTLY, Soro-soro-to; sorori-to; sotto; so-yo-soyo-to; yasra; shidzka-ni.
GENTRY, Samurai.
GENUINE, Hon; hontō; jitsz-na; makoto no; shōjin.
GEOGRAPHY, Chiri.
GERM, Kizashi; mebaye.
GERMINATE, Kizasz; me ga deru.
GESTATION, Migomori; k'wainin.
GESTICULATE, Temane wo szru.
GESTURE, Temane; monomane; mi-buri.
GET, Uru; ukeru; motomeru; mōkeru; totonoyeru. — *on*, shinogu. — *out of the way*, yokeru. — *the day*, katsz; shōri wo yeru. — *together*, atszmeru; tszmu. — *over*, szgiru. — *up*, okiru; agaru; noboru. — *away*, tatsz; saru. —

behind, okureru. — *back*, kayeru. — *clear*, sakeru; yokeru. — *out*, deru. — *in*, hairu; iru. — *loose*, hanareru. — *down*, oriru; kudaru. — *rid of*, yokeru; sakeru. — *through*, shi-agaru; szmu. — *near*, chikayoru; yoru. — *at*, todoku; oyobu. — *drunk*, sake ni yō. — *between*, hedateru. — *to*, itaru; ataru.

GHOST, Yūrei; bō-kon; tamashii; iki-riyō; shi-riyō.

GIANT, Noppō; seitaka.

GIDDY, Memai; kennun; kura-kura; kurumeku; kuramu.

GIFT, Shinjō-mono; shim-motsz; okuri-mono; immotsz; tama-mono.

GIGGLE, Warau; kutsz-kutsz warau.

GILD, *v.* Kiseru; kimpaku wo haru.

GILDING, Kimpaku.

GILL, Yera.

GIMLET, Kiri.

GIN, Wana; kobuchi; otoshi.

GIN, *v.* Kuru.

GINGER, Shōga; hajikami.

GINGLE, Gara-gara.

GINSENG, Ninjin.

GIRD, *v.* Shimeru; muszbu; maku. — *on*, obiru. — *up*, karageru; hashoru.

GIRDLE, Obi.

GIRL, Muszme; shinzō; otome.

GIRLISH, Muszme-rashii.

GIVE, Yaru; watasz; atayeru; kure; hodokosz; harau; yokosz. — *place*, yokeru. — *one's self to*, hamaru; koru. — *back*, kayesz. — *in*, makeru; yurusz; kusszru. — *over*, yameru; yosz. — *out*, hiromeru; kikaseru; dasz. — *up*, yameru yosz, yudzru. — *way*, makeru.

GIVER, Yarite.

GIVES, Ashigane.

GIZZARD, Usz.

GLAD, Yorokobu; ureshii; ureshigaru; kiyetsz szru.

GLADDEN, Yorokobasz.

GLANCE, Chirari-to miru; soreru; nagureru.

GLARE AT, Neme-tszkeru; niramu.

GLASS, Giyaman; Bīdoro.

GLEE, Yorokobi; ureshigaru; tanoshimi.

GLEN, Tani; kuki.

GLIB, Nameraka; tszru-tszru.

GLIBLY, Dzra-dzra.

GLIDE, Nagareru; hashiru; tobu.

GLIMMER, Chiratszku.

GLIMPSE, Chirarito.

GLISTEN, Kagayaku; hikaru; tszya.

GLITTER, Kirameku; kira-kira; kagayaku; hikaru.

GLOBE, Chikiu.

GLOOM, Utsz; shinki; usa. *Dispel* —, ussan; kibarashi.

GLOOMY, Uttōshi; ibusei; kokorobosoi; ui; inki.

GLORIFY, Homeru; shōbi szru; agameru.

GLORIOUS, K'wōdai; kagayaku; hikaru.

GLORY, Yeiyō; yei-gwa; ogori; kagayaki; hikari; homare; ikō.

GLOSS, *n.* Tszya.

GLOSS, *v.* Tszya wo tszkeru; īkazaru.

GLOSSARY, Jibiki.

GLOVE, Tebukuro.

GLOW, Moyeru; yaku; hikaru; atszi; akai.

GLOW-WORM, Mushi-botaru.

GLUE, Nikawa.

GLUE, *v.* Nikawadzke wo szru.

GLUEPOT, Nikawa-nabe.

GLUEY, Nebai; betatszku; beta-beta.

GLUT, Aku.

GLUTINOUS, Nebai; beta-tszku.

GLUTTON, Gebizō; ōgurai.

GLUTTONOUS, Ijigitanai; kuitagaru.

GNASH, *v.* Hagiri; hagishiri; hagami; kami-shimeru.

GNAW, Kamu; kū. *Sound of gnawing*, bori-bori-to.

GO, Yuku; iku; mairu. *Let go*, hanatsz. — *about*, mawaru. — *against*, sakarau. — *aside*, hikayeru. — *across*, koyeru; wataru. — *astray*, mayoi. — *away*, saru. — *by*, koyeru; szgiru. — *down*, kudaru; oriru; sagaru. — *forth*, deru. — *forward*, szszmu. — *in*, hairu; iru. — *in and out*, de-iri wo szru. — *off*, hanareru; saru; hanasz. — *out*, deru; kiyeru. — *over*, koyeru; wataru; yomu. — *through*, tōru; szmu; togeru. — *up*, agaru; noboru. — *with*, tomonau; dōdō szru; isshō ni yuku; dōhan szru. — *to and fro*, kayō; yukiki. *The place to which one is going or gone*, yukusaki; yuku-tokoro; yukuye. *Just about to go out*, dekakaru.

GO-BETWEEN, Nakōdo; chiu-nin; bai-shaku.

GOAD, *v.* Hagemasz

GOAL, Matoba; meate.

GOAT, Hitszji.

GOBLET, Wan; sakadzki.

GOBLIN, Akki; tengu.

GOD, — *of the Sintoo*, kami; shin. — *of the Buddhists*; hotoke.

GODDESS, Onnagami; megami.

GODLINESS, Shinjin.

GODOWN, *n.* Kura; dōzo.
GOING, Yuku; mairu; iku; *as you are going*, yuki-gakeni.
GOLD, Kin; kogane. — *beater*, haku-ya. — *color*, kinshoku; konjiki.
GOLD-FISH, Kingiyo.
GOLD-LEAF, Kimpaku.
GOLD-SMITH, Kinzaiku-nin.
GOLD-THREAD, Kinshi.
GONG, Dora.
GONORRHŒA, Rimbiyō; rinshitsz. *Female* —, shōkachi.
GOOD, Yoi; yoroshii; ī; riyō; zen. *make* —, tszgunau; oginau; madoi. *Doing* —, sazen. — *for nothing*, yōnitatanu; nani ni mo naranu. — *while*, yaya; hisashiku. — *deal*, yohodo; dzi-bun. — *and bad*, ashi-yoshi; zen-aku.
GOOD-NATURED, Otonashii; niuwa.
GOODNESS, Yosa; yoroshisa; on; megumi; awaremi; jihi; toku; nasake.
GOODS, Ni; nimotsz; kagu; shiromono.
GOOSE, *wild* —, gan; kari. *Tame* —, gochō.
GOOSE-FLESH, Tori-hada.
GORGEOUS, Kekkō na; rippa-na; hanayaka na; k'wabi; kirabiyaka.
GOUGE, *n.* Marunomi; kujiru.
GOURD, Hiyotan; fukube.
GOURMAND, Gebizō; taishoku-na mono.
GOVERN, Osameru; matszrigoto wo szru; shi-hai szru; riyō szru; shiroshimesz.
GOVERNMENT, Matszrigoto; seifu; seiji; seidō; shihai; kōhen; kōgi.
GOVERNOR, Bugiyō; chintai.
GOWN, Kimono; koromo.
GRACE, On; megumi; awaremi; jihi; fubin; nasake; on-taku.
GRACEFUL, Fūriu-na; ikina; miyabiyaka; ateyaka-na; taoyaka; adana; shinayaka.
GRACIOUS, Jihi-bukai; nasake-bukai.
GRADATION, Dan-dan; shidai.
GRADE, Kurai; kakushiki; kaku; jō-chiuge; dan.
GRADE, *v.* Narasz.
GRADUALLY, Shidai-ni; dan-dan; oi-oi; itszto-naku.
GRAFT, *n.* Tszgiho; tszgiki.
GRAFT, *v.* Tszgu.
GRAIN, Tszbu; go-koku; mokume.
GRANARY, Kura.
GRAND, Kekkō na; rippa-na; ririshii; rinrin; kōdai; szbarashii.
GRAND-CHILD, Mago.
GRAND-DAUGHTER, Mago-muszme.
GRANDEUR, Kekkō; rippa; rinrin.
GRANDFATHER, Jiji; o-ji-san. *Great* —, hijiji. *Great great* —, hījiji.
GRANDMOTHER, Baba; obăsan. *Great* —, hibaba. *Great great* —, hībaba.
GRANDSON, Mago.
GRANT, Yurusz; shōchi szru; kudasare; tamaye.
GRAPE, Budō; yebi.
GRAPPLE, Kumiau; tori-kumu; tszkami-au.
GRASS, Kusa.
GRASSHOPPER, Batta.
GRASSPLOT, Shiba.
GRASP, Tszkamu; nigiru.
GRATE, Kishiru; kishiriau.
GRATEFUL, Arigatai; katajikenai.
GRATER, Oroshi.
GRATING, *n.* Kōshi.
GRATIS, Tada; dai wo toranu.
GRATITUDE, Arigataki.
GRATUITOUSLY, Tada.
GRAVE, *a.* Majime-na; magao; kuszmu; ogosoka.
GRAVE, *n.* Haka; tszka.
GRAVE, *v.* Horu.
GRAVE-CLOTHES, Kiyō-katabira.
GRAVEL, Jari; kuri-ishi; koishi; sazare-ishi.
GRAVELY, Majime de; magao de.
GRAVER, Tagane.
GRAVE STONE, Sekitō; hakajirushi.
GRAVEYARD, Hakachi; hakasho; rantōba.
GRAVITY, Omosa.
GRAY, Shiraga; shiroi.
GRAZE, Szru; kaszru; fureru.
GREASE, Abura.
GREASE-SPOT, Abura no shimi.
GREASY, Aburake.
GREAT, Ōkii; k'wōdai; bakutai; tai; kō; dai. — *in extent*, hiroi. — *in number*, tak'san; tanto; taisō; ōku. — *distance*, tōi; haruka; yempō. — *consequence*, taizetsz; daiji. — *while*, nagaku; hisashiku. — *in degree (as love, &c)*, fukai; atszi; tszyoi; omoi; hageshii.
GREATLY, Ōki-ni.
GREATNESS, Ōkisa.
GREEDY, Tonyoku; musaboru; yokubaru; mangachi; dōyoku.
GREEN, Aoi; midori; nama; jukusanu; aomu; aomi-datsz.
GREEN-BOTTLE-FLY, Kusobaye.
GREEN-GROCER, Yao-ya.
GREEN-HOUSE, Muro.
GREENNESS, Aosa.
GREENS, Na; yasai.

GREET, Aisatsz-szru ; yeshaku szru; jigi szru.
GRIDDLE, Age-nabe.
GRIDIRON, Aburiko; tekkiu.
GRIEF, Kanashimi; urei.
GRIEVE, Kanashimu; uriō; komaru.
GRIEVOUS, Kurushii; dztsznai.
GRILL, Yakeru; ageru.
GRIMACE, Mekao.
GRIN, Warau.
GRIND, Hiku; togeru.
GRIP, *n.* Tszkami; nigiri.
GRIPE, *v.* Tszkamu; nigiru;
GROAN, Unaru; umeku.
GROG, Sake.
GROG-BLOSSOM, Zakuro-bana.
GROG-DRINKER, Sakenomi; jōgo.
GROG-SHOP, Sakaya.
GROIN, Momone.
GROOM, Betto.
GROOVE, Shikii.
GROPE, Saguru; tadoru.
GROSS, *a.* Akudoi; shitszkoi; iyashi; bukotsz; gehin; aku.
GROSS, *n.* H'wahan; tai-han; h'yaku-shijūshi. — *language*, akkō; k'wagon. *In the* —, kuchi de.
GROTTO, Ana; hora.
GROTESQUE, Okashii.
GROUND, Tszchi; tszchibeta; jimen; jigiyō; denji; tane. *Run aground*, iszwaru. — *rent*, jidai.
GROUND-FLOOR, Yuka.
GROUNDLESS, Wake ga nai; shisai ga nai.
GROUNDNUT, Rakk'washō.
GROUP, Mura.
GROVE, Mori; yabu.
GROVEL, Hau.
GROW, Hayeru; nobiru; futoru; seichō szru; chōdzru. — *in skill*, agaru; szszmu. — *(to become)*, naru; *as, to grow cold*, samuku naru. — *together*, awaseru. — *(rice &c.)*, tszkuru. — *old or late*, fukeru. — *better or stronger*, hidatsz. — *more violent*, tszyoru; tsznoru. — *late*, fukeru. — *in size*, futoru. — *of its self*, jinenbaye.
GROWL, Kagasz; hamuku; igamu.
GROWN, *Full* —, seichō; seijin.
GROWTH, Oitachi; sodachi.
GRUB, Horu; horiru.
GRUB-WORM, Szkumomushi.
GRUDGE, Oshimu; oshii.
GRUDGINGLY, Oshinde.
GRUMBLE, Butsz-butsz iu; gudo-gudo iu; tszbuyaku; kogoto wo iu.
GUARANTEE, Ukeau; hiki-ukeru.
GUARD, *v.* Mamoru; shugo szru; ban szru; yokeru; kabau; keiyei szru.
GUARD, *n.* Mamori; ban; keigo; mori; katame.
GUARDIAN, Kōken; hosa; ushiromi.
GUESS, Sziriyō szru; oshi-hakaru; īateru.
GUEST, Kiyaku; marōto.
GUIDE, *n.* Annaija; tebiki; shirube.
GUIDE, *v.* Annai szru; michibiku.
GUILD, Nakama; kabu.
GUILE, Itszwari; uso; azamuki.
GUILELESS, Meikaku.
GUILT, Tszmi; zai.
GUILTLESS, Mushitsz; tszmi nai; higō; muzai.
GUILTY, Tszmi-aru; uzai. *Not* —, muzai.
GUISE, Nari; furi; szgata.
GUITAR, Samisen.
GULF, Iriumi; uchiumi.
GULL, *v.* Azamuku; damasz.
GULL, *n.* Kamome.
GULLET, Nodo; shokudō.
GULLY, Ana; kubomi.
GUM, Yani; gom; haguki.
GUMMY, Nebari; nebai.
GUN, Teppō.
GUNNERY, Hōjutsz.
GUNPOWDER, Yensho; dōguszri.
GUNSMITH, Teppō-kaji.
GUNSTOCK, Teppōdai.
GUNWALE, Funabata.
GURGLE, Doku-doku; goto-goto.
GUSH-OUT, Waki-deru.
GUT, Harawata.
GUTTER, Toi; toyu; hi; mizo; dobu.
GYPSUM, Sekkō.

H

HABIT, Kuse; kimono.
HABITABLE, Szmawareru.
HABITATION, Szmai; jūkiyo.
HABITUAL, Tszne no; heijitsz no; itszmono; fudan-no.
HABITUALLY, Tszne-dzne; zentai; g'wanrai.
HABITUATE, Nareru.
HACK, Tataki kiru.
HACKLE, Kogu.

HADES, K'wōsen; yomi no kuni.
HÆMATURIA, Ketszrin.
HAFT, Tszka; ye.
HAGGARD, Yasegao.
HAIL, *n.* Hiyō.
HAIL, *v.* Yobu; maneku.
HAIR, Kami; ke. — *stood on end,* yodatsz — *breadth,* gōbatsz.
HAIRPIN, Kanzashi; binsashi.
HAIRY, Kebukai.
HALE, Szkoyaka; tassha; jōbu; mame; mameyaka.
HALF, Han; hambun; nakaba.
HALF-DONE, Nama-niye; nama-yake; chiudō.
HALF-MOON, Hangetsz.
HALF-WAY, Hammichi; chiudō.
HALF-YEAR, Hantoshi.
HALL, Dō.
HALLOO, *Exclam,* Oi; moshi.
HALLOW, Wiyamau; son-kiyo szru.
HALO, Gokō. — *around the moon,* tszki no kasa.
HALT, Todomeru; bikko wo hiku.
HALTER, Tsznagi nawa; hadzna.
HALVE, Futatsz ni kiru.
HALYARD, Hodzna.
HAM, Momo.
HAMLET, Mura.
HAMMER, Kanadzchi.
HAMMER, *v.* Buchi-komu; utsz.
HAMPER, *v.* Sasawaru; hodasareru.
HAND, Te *At hand.* chikai. *on hand,* deki-ai; ari-awase, ari-ai *Off hand,* dehōdai; detarame. *Lend a hand,* tedztau; te wo kash'te kudasare. *On the other hand,* kayete. *Hand to mouth, see* kurashi. *Suiting the hand,* tegoro. — *behind the back,* ushirode.
HAND, *v.* Watasz; yaru.
HANDBILL, Harifuda; hiki-fuda; chirashi; bira.
HAND-BREADTH, Tszka; soku.
HANDCUFF, Tejō; tegase; tegane.
HANDFUL, H'to tszkami.
HANDILY, Tebayaku; jōdz,
HANDLE, *v.* Sawaru; tori-atszkau; ijiru.
HANDLE, *n.* Ye; te; torite.
HANDMAID, Koshimoto.
HANDRAIL, Teszri,
HANDSAW, Nokogiri.
HANDSOME, Kirei; utszkushii ; migoto; bibishii.
HAND-SPIKE, Bō.
HANDWRITING, Tenarai; jikihitsz.
HANDY, Jōdz; tebayai; benri; tszgō ga yoi.
HANG, Kakeru; tszru; sagaru. — *a door,* to wo hameru. — *out,* nozokeru. — *down,* sageru; tareru; tarasz; tszrusz. — *up,* kakeru. — *to one side,* katasagari.
HANGER-ON, Isōrō; kakari-udo.
HANG-NAIL, Sakakure; sakamuke.
HANK, Kuri.
HAPPEN, Au; deau; dekuwaseru; aru; ataru. — *to have,* ariau.
HAPPILY, Saiwai ni.
HAPPINESS, Raku ; tanoshimi ; saiwai ; k'wanraku.
HAPPY, Raku na; saiwai naru.
HARASS, Komaraseru; nayamasz.
HARBINGER, Saki-bure.
HARBOR, Minato; funa-gakari.
HARBOR, *v.* Kakumau; tomeru.
HARD, Katai; mudzkashii ; nan; kibishii; tszyoi; *see* kaneru. — *to chew,* hagotaye.
HARDEN, Kataku szru; katameru.
HARDLY, Karōjite; yōyaku; kara-gara.
HARDNESS, Katasa; kurō; nan; nangi.
HARDSHIP, Kurō; nangi; nanjū; shinku; karai-me; konku.
HARDWARE, Kanamono.
HARDY, Kitszi.
HARE, Usagi.
HARELIP, Mitsz-kuchi; iguchi.
HARK, *imp.* Kike; kiki nasare.
HARLEQUIN, Dōkemono.
HARLOT, Jōro; oyama; yūjo.
HARM, *n.* Gai szru; sokonau; sondzru; itameru; ataru.
HARMFUL, Doku na.
HARMLESS, Doku-nai; gai-senu.
HARMONIOUS, Naka ga yoi; mutszmajii ; wajun na.
HARMONIZE, Chōshi wo awaseru ; nakanaori wo szru; waboku szru.
HARMONY, Chōshi; shirabe.
HARNESS, Bagu.
HARP, Koto.
HARPOON, Mori.
HARROW, Maguwa.
HARSH, Arai; ara-arashii.
HARSHLY, Araku; kibishiku.
HARVEST, *v.* Karu; kiru.
HARVEST-TIME, Kari-shun.
HASTE, Hayaki; isogi; kiu.
HASTEN, Hayameru; saisoku szru; isogaseru; isogu.

HASTILY, Hayaku; sassoku; kiu-ni; isoide szgu-ni; jiki-ni ; szmiyaka-ni.

HASTY, Hayai; kiu-na; sasoku no; szmiyaka-na.

HAT, Kaburi mono; yeboshi; dzkin.

HATCH, Kayeru.

HATCHEL, Inakogi; hashi.

HATCHEL, *v.* Kogu.

HATCHET, Teyoki; nata.

HATE, *v.* Nikumu; uramu; kirau.

HATEFUL, Nikui; kirawashii.

HATRED, Nikumi ; urami; ikon.

HAUGHTY, Taka-buru; ōfū; jiman; hokoru; ōhei.

HAUL, *v.* Hiku; taguru; kai-guru.

HAUNT, Tszku. *Haunted house*, bake-mono-yashiki.

HAVE, Aru ; motsz ; motomeru. *As an auxiliary, forming the perfect tense, it is formed by the verb suffix*, ta; *as*, katta, *have bought, from* kai; kita; *have heard, from* kiki.

HAVEN, Minato; kakari-ba.

HAWK, Taka; tobi.

HAWKING, Takagari; botefuri.

HAWSER, Tszna; nawa.

HAY, Hoshi-kusa.

HAY-STACK, Inamura.

HAZARD, Ayaui; abunai; kennon; inochigake; *see* kakawaru; kakeru.

HAZE, Kaszmi.

HAZY, Kaszmu; bonyari.

HE, Are; kare; ano h'to; ano okata; kono h'to; kono okata.

HEAD, Atama; kashira; kōbe; tszmuri; kubi; dz. — *of a river*, minamoto. — *of a discourse*, dai ; shui. — *of wheat*, ho. — *of a cask*, kagami. *crown of* —, dzboshi.

HEAD, *v.* Mukau; hikiyuru; hiki-tszreru.

HEADACHE, Dzts'ū.

HEADLAND, Saki; misaki; hana.

HEADLONG, Massakasama ni ; mukōmidz ni ; muteppō-ni.

HEAD-QUARTERS, Honjin.

HEAD-SEA, Sakanami.

HEADSTRONG, Waga-mama ; kimama ; wambaku; kidzi.

HEAD-WIND, G'yak'fū; mukaikaze.

HEAL, Naosz; jiszru · iyasz.

HEALED, Hombuku; zenk'wai; heiyu ; naoru; iyeru.

HEALTH, Yōjō. *In* —, jōbu; tassha; mame. *Preserving* —, yōjō szru; hoyō wo szru. *For the sake of* —, yōjō no tame ni. *Restored to* —, hom-buku; zen-k'wai heiyu. *Leaving home for the sake of* —, deyōjō szru. *Careless of* —, fūyōjō.

HEALTHY, Yōjō ni naru; yashinau.

HEAP, *n.* Kasa; tszmi; yama.

HEAP, *v.* Tszmu; kasaneru. — *up*, takuwayeru; atszmeru. — *in measuring*, yama-mori ni szru; mori-ageru.

HEAR, Kiku; chōmon szru.

HEARSAY, Fūbun; fūsetsz; hiyōban; uwasa; dembun; densetsz.

HEART, Kokoro ; shin no zō; shin; ki ; hara. *Learn by* —, sorandzru ; oboyeru. *Set the* — *at rest*, akirameru; omoi-kiru. *With the whole* —, isshin de ; shin kara ; kokoro komete.

HEARTILY, Shinkara; jitsz ni.

HEAT, Atszsa ; k'waki ; honoke; (*of animals*), sakari; tszrumu.

HEAT, *v.* Atszku szru; atatameru.

HEAVE, Nageru. — *the anchor*, ikari wo maku. — *down*, katamukeru; sobadateru. — *to*, todomeru.

HEAVEN, Ten ; ame ; sora; gokuraku; tendō; jōdo.

HEAVINESS, Omosa.

HEAVY, Omoi.

HECTOR, *v.* Ijimeru.

HEDGE, Kaki; ikegaki ; kakine.

HEED, *v.* Ki wo tszkeru ; nen wo ireru; mochiiru ; kiku; tsztszshimu.

HEEDLESS, Ki-wo-tszkenu ; sosōna; mukōmidz; bunen; buyōjin.

HEEL, Kagato.

HEIGHT, Takasa; tate; desakari; debana; tōge ; saichiu. *Past the* —, takenawa.

HEIGHTEN, Ageru; takaku szru ; takameru.

HEINOUS, Nikui.

HEIR, Sōzoku nin; iye-tszgi ; ato-tori; katoku-nin.

HEIRLOOM, Yui-motsz; arikitatta mono.

HELL, Jigoku.

HELM, Kaji.

HELMET, Kabuto.

HELMSMAN, Kajitori.

HELP, *v.* Tetszdau; taszkeru; szkeru; sewa wo szru; josei szru.

HELP, *n.* Tetszdai; taszke; sewa; shūsen; okage; rishō; hojo szru; joriki. *There is no help for it*, shikata ga nai; sen kata nashi; shiyō ga nai. *Cannot* —, yaru kata naku.

HELPER, Sewa-nin; taszkeru h'to; tetszdai nin; yorube; tayori.

HEM, Shiwabuki; sekibarai; kowadzkuri.
HEM, *n.* Heri.
HEM, *v.* Nui.
HEMIPHLEGIA, Chiubu.
HEMOPTISIS, Toketsz.
HEMORRHOIDS, Iboji.
HEMP, Asa.
HEN, Mendori.
HENCOOP, Toya; ori.
HENCE, Koko-kara; kono yuye ni; kore ni yotte. *A year* —, ichi nen tatte.
HENCE-FORTH, Kore-kara; ima-kara; ika; igo; kono-nochi; kiyōkō.
HER, Ano onna no; kano onna no; sono; are no; kare no.
HERALD, Shisha.
HERB, Kusa.
HERD, Mura; mure.
HERE, Koko; kochi; kochira. — *and there*, achi-kochi.
HERE-ABOUTS, Kono-atari; kono-hen; kono-hō.
HERE-AFTER, Kono-nochi; igo; irai; mirai; yukuszye.
HERE-AT, Kono-yuye-ni; kore-ni-yotte.
HERE-BY, Kore de.
HERE-TO-FORE, Kono-maye-ni; izen.
HEREDITARY, Mochi-tsztaye-no; oya-yudzri-no; chiszji no. — *disease*, den-zembiyō.
HERESY, Betsz no ha; michi wo somuku oshiye; gedō.
HERITAGE, Sōzoku; katoku.
HERMAPHRODITE, Futa-nari.
HERMIT, Inja.
HERO, Gōketsz; yei-yū; maszrao.
HEROIC, Tegara-na; kenage.
HESITATE, Tamerau; yūyo szru; chiu-cho szru; shiriashi wo fumu; tayutai; chichiu.
HEW, Kiru.
HEXAGON, Rok'kaku.
HICCOUGH, Shakuri.
HIDDEN, Kakureta.
HIDE, *v.* Kakusz; hisomeru; hisomu; kakureru; kakumau;
HIDE, *n.* Kawa.
HIDEOUS, Osoroshii; nikui.
HIGGLE, Kogiru; negiru.
HIGH, Takai; take; takeru. — *minded*, kedakai.
HIGHWAY-MAN, Sanzoku; oihagi; yamadachi.
HILARITY, Kiyō; omoshirosa.
HILL, Koyama; yama; oka.
HILLOCK, Tszka.
HILLSIDE, Saka.
HIM, Kare; are; anoh'to.
HIMSELF, Midzkara; onore; jibun. *By* —, h'tori de; jibun de.
HINDER, Samatageru; sasawaru; sayegiru; jama szru; kodawaru; kobamu; sasayeru.
HINDRANCE, *n.* Jama; kodawari; shōge; koshō; sawari; sashitszkai.
HINDMOST, Itchi-ato.
HINGE, Chōtszgai.
HINT, *v.* Atetszkeru.
HIRE, *n.* Kiukin; dai; chin; sonriyō; chinsen.
HIRE, *v.* Yatoi; kakayeru; oku.
HIS, Kare no; ano h'to no; are no.
HISTORIAN, Kiroku-sha.
HISTORY, Reki-shi; kiroku.
HIT, Ateru; butsz; utsz; fureru. — *upon*, au; deau; ataru.
HITCH, *v.* Tsznagu; motszreru; hikkakaru.
HITHER, Koko ye; kochi ye.
HITHER-TO, Ima-made, kore-made.
HIVE, Hachi no sz.
HOARD, Takuwayeru; tszmu.
HOAR-FROST, Shimo.
HOARSE, Koye ga kareru; karegoye.
HOARY HEAD, Shiraga.
HOAX, Szkasz; azamuku; damasz; taburakasz; chakasz.
HOBBLE, *v.* Bikko wo hiku; tobo-tobo.
HOBBY-HORSE, Take-uma.
HOBGOBLIN, Tengu; bakemono.
HODGE-PODGE, Gotani.
HOG, Buta. *Wild* —, shishi; inoshishi.
HOG-PEN, Buta-goya.
HOIST, Ageru; hiki-ageru; kakageru.
HOLD, *v.* Tomeru; motsz; tszmu; ukeru; hairu; hikayeru. — *out*, tamotsz; tayeru. — *in*, hikayeru; tomeru. — *on*, shimbō szru; tayeru. — *out*, todokeru; *(offer)*, kakeru. — *up*, ageru; sasayeru. *Lay* — *of*, tszkamu; tszkamayeru; torayeru. — *under the arm*, waki-basamu. — *in the mouth*, fukumu.
HOLE, Ana.
HOLIDAY, Matszribi; kiujitsz; iwaibi.
HOLLAND, Oranda.
HOLLOW, Kara; kubomu; uro. — *shot*, uro no tama.
HOLLOW, *v.* Kubomeru; kuru.
HOLLY, *n.* Tarayō.
HOLLYHOCK, Aoi.
HOLY, Isagiyoi; kiyoi; sei-naru.
HOMAGE, Wiyamai.

HOME, Iru-tokoro; szmai-dokoro; szmika; szmai; iye; uchi; yado.
HOMELY, Minikui; somatsz-na; bukiriyō.
HOME-MADE, Tedzkuri; tesaku; tezaiku; jisaku; tesei.
HONE, Toishi; awasedo.
HONE, *v.* Togu.
HONEST, Shōjiki; tadashii; jitsz; shinjitsz.
HONEY, Mitsz; hachi-mitsz.
HONEY-SUCKLE, Nindō.
HONOR, *n.* Toku; i; itoku; ikō.
HONOR, *v.* Tattobu; sonkiyō szru; wiyamau; agameru.
HONORABLE, Tattoki; takai; kōmei naru; nadakai; tadashii.
HOOD, Dzkin.
HOODWINK, Damasz; mayakasz; gomakasz; me wo kuramasz; īkuromeru.
HOOF, Tszme; badz; hidzme.
HOOK, Kagi; ori-kugi; tobi-guchi. *Fish* —, tszri-bari. *Pot* —, ji-zai kagi.
HOOP, Taga; wa.
HOP, Tobu; odori.
HOPE, Nozomi; kokorozashi.
HOPE, *v.* Nozomu.
HOPEFUL, Tanomoshii.
HOPELESS, Nozomi ga tszki-hateta; akiramete iru; omoi-kitte iru; senkata-nai; shiyō ga nai.
HORIZON, Kumoi.
HORN, Tszno; charumera.
HORNET, Hachi.
HOROSCOPE, Hoshi-uranai; uranai.
HORRIBLE, Osoroshii.
HORSE, Uma. —*power*, Ba-riki. —*hoof*, batei; badz.
HORSE-BOY, Betto; mago.
HORSE-CHESNUT, Tochi no ki.
HORSE-CLOTH, Baginu.
HORSE-DEALER, Bakurō.
HORSE-DOCTOR, Hakuraku; ma-isha.
HORSE-DUNG, Bafun; maguso.
HORSE-FLY, Abu.
HORSE-JOCKEY, Bakurō.
HORSE-LOAD, Da; dani.
HORSE-MAN, Kiba-musha; manori.
HORSE-MANSHIP, Bujutsz.
HORSE-RACE, Keiba.
HORSE-RADISH, Wasabi.
HORSE-SHOE, Kanagutsz.
HORSE-WHIP, Muchi.
HOSE, Tabi; kawadoyu.
HOSPITABLE, Aisō-na; ashirai no yoi; nengoro-na; motenasz.
HOSPITAL, Biyō-in.
HOSPITALITY, Aisō; ashirai; motenashi.
HOST, Shujin; motenashi-kata; kiyaku-aite; yadoya no teishu.
HOSTAGE, H'tojichi.
HOSTILE, Teki no; tekitau.
HOSTILITY, Ikusa.
HOSTLER, Betto; mago.
HOT, Atszi; karai; hoteru. — *springs*, deyu; tōjiba.
HOT-BED, Toko; nawashiro.
HOT-BLOODED, Hayari-o; kekki-no.
HOTEL, Yadoya; hatagoya.
HOT-HOUSE, Muro.
HOT-WATER, Yu; sayu.
HOUR, Toki; ji.
HOUR-GLASS, Szna-dokei.
HOURLY, Toki-toki-ni; toki-goto ni.
HOUSE, Iye; uchi; yado; szmai; ke. — *for sale*, uri-szye. *House by house*, yado-nami.
HOUSE-BREAKER, Yajirikiri.
HOUSE-CLOTH, Zōkin.
HOUSEHOLD, Kanai.
HOUSEHOLDER, Shotai.
HOUSEHOLD *stuff*, Kagu; kazai; shotai-dōgu.
HOUSELESS, Yadonashi.
HOUSE-MAID, Gejo.
HOUSE-MOVING, Ya-utszri; watamashi.
HOUSE-RENT, Yachin; tana-chin.
HOUSE-SEARCH, Ya-sagashi.
HOVER, Tobu.
HOW, Dō; ikaga; ikan; ikutsz; ikayō; donoyō; iku; idzkunzo; ikadeka; ikani. *How much more*, mash'te; iwan-ya. *How, or the way in which anything is made or done, see*, shihō; shikata. *How much? or How many?* ikura; nani-hodo; iku; ikahodo; dore-hodo; dore-dake; ikutsz; dono-kurai. *How long?* itsz-made; itsz-kara. *How can? or How shall?* dōsh'te.
HOWBEIT, Keredomo; saredomo; naredomo; iyedomo.
HOWEVER, Tomokakumo; keredomo; saredomo; shikashi; shikashi-nagara; shikaru-ni; shikaru-tokoro.
HOWL, Hoyeru; naku.
HOWSOEVER, Ikayō demo; donoyō demo.
HUB, Kuruma no koshiki; shajiku.
HUCKSTER, Botefuri.
HUG, Daku; daki-shimeru; daki-tszku.
HUGE, Ōkii.
HULL, Kara; kawa. — *of a ship*, fune no dō.

HULL, *v.* Muku; hagu.
HUM, *v.* Unaru; naru; hana-uta wo utau.
HUMAN, Ningen; h'to; bonnin. — *sacrifice*, h'tomigoku. — *form*, bon-shin.
HUMANE, Ninjō no aru; nasake no aru; jihi no aru.
HUMANITY, Bon-shin.
HUMBLE, Kenson na; wiya-wiyashii.
HUMBLE, *v.* Herikudaru ; kenson szru ; kentai szru; yenriyo szru; hige. — *another*, osayeru; heiko szru; hishigu; kujiku ; torihishigu.
HUMBLE-BEE, Kumabachi.
HUMID, Nurete iru; shimeru; shikke.
HUMIDITY, Shikki; sziki.
HUMMING-BIRD, Fūchō.
HUMMING-KITE, Unaridako.
HUMMING-TOP, Unarigoma.
HUMOR, Kibun ; kokochi ; kokoromochi ; kigen; kishoku.
HUMOR, *v.* Ki wo toru ; kigen wo toru; ayasz; amayakasz.
HUMOROUS, Okashii; dōkeru; hiyōgeru.
HUMPBACK, Semushi; kukuse.
HUNDRED, H'yaku.
HUNDRED-THOUSAND, Jūman.
HUNDREDTH, H'yaku ban.
HUNGER, *v.* Haraheru; wiyeru.
HUNGER, *n.* Hidarusa.
HUNGRY, Hidarui; himojii; katszyeru.
HUNT, *v.* Sagasz ; tadzneru ; karu ; riyō szru.
HUNT, *n.* Kari; riyō.
HUNTER, Kariudo; riyōshi; satsz-ht'o.
HURL, Nageru.
HURRAH, *v.* Toki no koye wo ageru; toki wo tszkuru.
HURRICANE, Taifū; ōkaze; arashi; shippū.
HURRY, *v.* Isogu; seku; seru ; hayameru.
HURT, *v.* Itamu; kidz wo tszkeru; itameru; sondzru; sokonau.
HURT, *n.* Itami; kega; kidz; sokonai.
HURTFUL, Doku na; gai-naru ; sokonau; sondzru.
HUSBAND, Otto; teishu; muko; tszma; tono-go. — *and wife*, fūfu; me-otto; fusai.
HUSBAND, *v.* Kenyaku szru.
HUSBANDMAN, H'yak'shō ; nōnin; dempu.
HUSBANDRY, Nōgiyō; kōsaku; saku.
HUSH, *v.* Shidzmeru. — *up. (imper.)* damare.
HUSH-MONEY, Kuchidome-kin.
HUSK, Saya.
HUSKY, Kareta.
HUT, Koya; iyori; waraya.
HUZZA, Toki no koye.
HYACINTH, Szisenk'wa.
HYGIENE, Yōjō.
HYMN, Wasan; shōmiyō; uta.
HYPOCRITE, Gizensha ; gikunshi ; maisz; neijin.
HYPOCRITICAL, Hiyōri-na ; sharakusai ; fugitsz.

I

I, watakushi; ware.
IBIS, Toki.
ICE, Kōri; hi. *Thin* —, haku hiyō.
ICE-HOUSE, Himuro.
ICICLE, Tszrara; taruki.
IDEA, Omoi; kokoro-base; riyōken.
IDENTICAL, Dōyō; onaji koto.
IDENTIFY, Mi-oboyeru ; itchi szru.
IDIOM, Namari.
IDIOT, Kinuke; baka.
IDLE, Hima de iru; asonde iru; yō-nashi; bushō-na. — *time*, hima; itoma. — *talk*, zōdan.
IDLE, *v.* Himadoru; asobu.
IDLENESS, Hima; itoma; bushō; okotaru; kedai; busei.
IDLER, Bushō-mono ; dzruke-mono ; namake-mono.
IDLY, Asonde; yōji-sedz-ni; itadzra-ni.
IDOL, Zō; moku-zō; butsz-zō; kana-butsz; do-butsz; seki-zō.
IDOLATER, Moku-zō wo ogamu h'to.
IDOLATRY, Butsz wo ogamu koto.
IDOLIZE, Kami-sama no yō ni omou; agameru ; daiji-garu.
IF, Moshi; naraba; yoshiya; ka; ya; hiyotto; nara; *also formed by conj. verb, suffix*, ba, *and* tara; *as*, yukaba, *if you go*, araba, *if there are*, mitara, *if you see.*
IGNIS-FATUUS, Kitsznebi; hidama.
IGNITE, Taku; hi wo tszkeru; moyuru ; moyasz.
IGNOBLE, Iyashii; gebiru; gehin; gesen-na.
IGNOMINIOUS, Iyashii; hadzkashii.
IGNOMINY, Haji ; chijoku; kakin; kidz.
IGNORAMUS, Mugaku; gujin.
IGNORANCE, Shiranu koto; mugaku; monmō.
IGNORANT, Shiranu; wakaranu.
IGNORANTLY, Shiradz ni; wakaradz ni.
ILL, *a.* Ambai-warui; wadzrau; fuk'wai.

ILLS, Nangi; kurō.
ILL-BLOOD, Urami.
ILL-BRED, Burei; shitszrei; busahō; sodachi ga warui.
ILLEGAL, Hōg'wai; okite ni somuku.
ILLEGIBLE, Yomenu.
ILL-HUMORED, Szneru.
ILLIBERAL, Rinshoku; semai; shiwai; shōriyō-na.
ILLIMITABLE, Kagiri naki; muhen.
ILLITERATE, Mugaku; mommō.
ILL-MANNERED, Riyo-g'wai; burei; shitszrei; bushitszke.
ILL-NATURED, Tanki-na; kataku-na; iji no warui.
ILLNESS, Yamai; biyōki; wadzrai.
ILLUMINATE, Terasz; akaruku szru.
ILLUSIVE, Itszwaru; damasz; mayakasz.
ILLUSTRATE, Toku; tatoyeru; arawasz; toki-akirameru; satosz.
ILLUSTRATION, Tatoye; yetoki.
ILLUSTRIOUS, Mei; nadakai; nukindzru; hīderu; kōmei.
ILL-WILL, Urami.
IMAGE, Zō; kata; utszshi.
IMAGINARY, Omoi-nashi-no.
IMAGINATION, Omoinashi; kokorobase; riyōken; kufū; dekigokoro; shinso.
IMAGINE, Omou; omoi-nasz; riyōken szru; kufū szru; kuwadateru.
IMBECILE, Niu-jaku; hi-niyaku; jū-jaku; yowai.
IMBIBE, Szi-komu; nomi-komu.
IMBROWN, Kogasz; kogeru.
IMBRUED, — *in blood*, chimamire ni naru.
IMBUE, Someru; somaru; sonawaru.
IMITATE, Maneru; niseru; katadoru; nazorayeru; narau; magayeru.
IMITATION, Magai; mane; nise.
IMMATERIAL, Katachi naki; mugiyō-na; daijinai; kamawanu.
IMMATURE, Mijuku; jukusenu; nama; umanu.
IMMEASURABLE, Hakararenu.
IMMEDIATE, Tachi-machi. — *relief*, sokkō.
IMMEDIATELY, Jika-ni; jiki-ni; szgu-ni; tadachi-ni; tachi-machi-ni; tachi-dokoro-ni; yaniwani.
IMMENSE, Ōkii; bakutai.
IMMERSE, Shidzmeru; hameru; tszkeru; oboreru.
IMMETHODICAL, Shimari ga nai; torishimari no nai.
IMMINENT, Kakatte iru; nozonde iru; nannan to szru.
IMMODERATE, Do ni szgiru.
IMMODEST, Haji wo shiranu; buyenriyō; atsz-kawa-dzra na.
IMMORAL, Fugi-na; fugiyōgi; fugiyōseki.
IMMORTAL, Tayenu; tszkinu; nakunaranu; fu-shi.
IMMORTALIZE, Matsz dai ni nokosz; kōsei ni tsztayeru.
IMMOVABLE, Ugokasenu.
IMMUNITY, Yurushi; menkiyo.
IMMURE, Komeru.
IMMUTABILITY, Kawaranu koto.
IMMUTABLE, Kawaradz; *or* kawaranu; tokiwa naru; fuyeki.
IMMUTABLY, Kawaradz ni.
IMPAIR, Yowaku szru; yowameru; otoroyeru.
IMPART, Hodokosz; atayeru; yaru; kudasaru; tamau; adzkaru.
IMPARTIAL, Katayoranu; ōyakena; katahīki-naku; yeko-nashi.
IMPASSABLE, Tōrarenu; watararenu; kosarenu.
IMPATIENT, Iratsz; seku; seikiu-na.
IMPATIENTLY, — *to wait*, machidōi; machi-wabiru.
IMPEDE, Sasayeru; jama szru; samatageru;
IMPEDIMENT, Jama; sawari; koshō.
IMPEL, Osz; seshimuru; saseru.
IMPENDING, Kakatte iru; nozonde iru; nan-nan to szru.
IMPENETRABLE, Tszki-tōsenu; tōranu.
IMPENITENT, Tszmi wo kuyamanu; tszmi wo zan-nen ni omowanu; kōk'wai senu.
IMPERATIVE, Somukarenu; kessh'te; zehi; kanaradz.
IMPERCEPTIBLE, Miyenu; kikoyenu.
IMPERFECT, Fusoku-na; mattakaranu; sorowanu; taranu. — *book*, hahon.
IMPERFECTION, Fu-soku; kaketaru tokoro.
IMPERIAL, Choku. — *ambassador*, choku-shi. — *letter*, choku-sho.
IMPERIOUS, Kōman-na; jiman-rashii.
IMPERISHABLE, Naku naranu; tayeru; kuchinu.
IMPERMEABLE, Tōranu.
IMPERTINENT, Burei-na; shitszrei-na; buyenriyo-na.
IMPERVIOUS, Tōranu; szkanu.
IMPETUOUS, Seikiu-na; sekkachi na; hageshii; sekatszku; sosokashii.
IMPETUS, Ikioi; hiyōshi; hiyōri; *see* dzninori.
IMPIETY, Bushinjin; kami wo wiyamawanu.

IMPINGE, Ataru; tszki-ataru.
IMPIOUS, Aku; ashii ; warui ; mottainai.
IMPLACABLE, Urami ga harenu; yawaraganu ; tokenu.
IMPLEMENT, Doku ; kikai.
IMPLICATED, Makizoye; renrui; hiki-ai.
IMPLICITLY, Utagawadz ni.
IMPLORE, Negau; kō; koi-negai; tang'wan szru.
IMPOLITE, Burei; shitszrei; busahō; bushitszke; riyo-g'wai.
IMPOLITIC, Tame ni naranu; futame-na.
IMPONDERABLE, Hakarenu; omomi naki ; mekata-naki.
IMPORT, Hakobi-komu; yuniu szru.
IMPORTANCE, Daiji ; taisetsz.
IMPORTANT, Taisetsz-na; daiji-na ; setszna; kanyō ; tai-sh'ta ; kaku-betsz.
IMPORTS, Yuniu no nimotsz.
IMPORTUNATELY, Hitaszra-ni ; hita-mono; hira-ni; ichi-dz ni; tatte ; shikiri ni.
IMPORTUNE, Kudoku.
IMPOSE, Ateru. — *on*, azamuku; damasz; kataru.
IMPOSING, — *in appearance*, yuyushii.
IMPOSSIBLE, Dekinu ; atawanu; oyobanu; kanawadz.
IMPOST, Unjō; zeigin.
IMPOSTOR, Katari-mono.
IMPOSTURE, Katari.
IMPOTENT, Yowai; niu-jaku na; hiniyaku na.
IMPOVERISH, Bimbō ni szru ; toboshiku szru.
IMPRACTICABLE, Dekinu; atawanu; nasarenu; serarenu.
IMPRECATE, Norō; tokobu; shuso szru.
IMPRECATION, Noroi; shuso.
IMPREGNABLE, Yaburarenu.
IMPRESS, *v*. Osz; oshi-komu. — *on the mind*, kimo ni meidzru.
IMPRESS, *n*. Kata.
IMPRESSION, Ato; kata; shirushi.
IMPRISON, Rōya ni ireru; jurō szru. — *in one's house*, heimon szru.
IMPROBABLE, Nasasō ; nakarō ; arumai ; arisō-mo-nai; nasō.
IMPROMPTU, Dehōdai; detarame.
IMPROPER, Fusō-ō; funiai; fu-sōtō; ni-awanu; kanawanu; ataranu; awanu; hibun.
IMPROVE, Szszmu ; agaru; jōdz ni naru ; szszmeru; ageru. — *the opportunity*, toki ni jōdzru; ki ni ōdzru. *Improving daily*, himashi-ni yoku naru.

IMPROVIDENT, Fuyōi; fuyōjin; tashinami-naki; yōi-senu.
IMPRUDENT, Tashinami naki; fuyō-jin; kamawanu; muyami; fukakugo.
IMPUDENT, Haji-shiranu; fuyenriyo; busahō-na.
IMPUGN, Īfusegu; kobamu.
IMPULSE, Ikioi; chōshi; hibiki ; kotaye.
IMPUNITY, Buji-de; bu-nan-ni; kega naku; koto-naku.
IMPURE, Kitanai; fuketsz-na; yogoreta; kegareta; mazetta; mszе-mono ga aru.
IMPUTE, Kiseru; owaseru; nuri-tszkeru; īkakeru; īoseru; kabuseru; kadzkeru.
IN, or INTO, Uchi ; ni; *also the compounds of* komu, *and* iru, *and pp. ending of verbs*, te. *To go in*, hairu. *Put* —, ireru. *Fall* —, ochi-komu; hamaru. *To be* —, iru; oru. *Jump* —, tobi-komu. *Knock* —, buchi-komu. *Throw* —, nage-komu. *Pour* —, tszgu *Pull* —, hiki-komu , hiki-ireru. *To strike in anger*, ikatte butsz. *Go in haste*, isoide yuku. *Run in fear*, kowagatte hashiru. *In my opinion*, watakushi no omō ni wa.
INABILITY, Atawanu; dekinu; oyobanu.
INACCESSIBLE, Yukarenu; oyobanu; itararenu.
INACCURATE, Machigau.
INACTIVE, Bushō-na; hone-oranu.
INADEQUATE, Fusoku; taranu; sorowanu.
INADMISSIBLE, Ukerarenu.
INADVERTENT, Okotaru ; nen wo irenu; ki wo tszkenu.
INALIENABLE, Torarenu.
INANIMATE, Mujō-na ; shi-butsz.
INAPPLICABLE, Awanu; funiai.
INAPPROPRIATE, Funiai; awanu.
INASMUCH, Kara; yuye ni.
INATTENTIVE, Nen wo irenu; ki wo tszkenu; okotaru.
INAUGURATE, Kurai ni ageru.
INAUGURATION, Sokui.
INAUSPICIOUS, Kiyō-naru; ashiki; warui; fukitsz.
INBORN, Umare-tszita; shōtoku no.
INCALCULABLE, Kazoyerarenu ; hakararenu; kanjō dekinu.
INCANTATION, Mahō; majutsz; chobuku.
INCAPABLE, Dekinu; atawanu.
INCARNATE, Nin-tai wo ukeru; niku-shin ni yadoru.
INCARNATION, Nintai wo ukeru koto.
INCASE, Tsztszmu; kiseru.
INCAUTIOUS, Yōjin naki; tashinami naki; muyami na.

INCENDIARY, Hitszke.
INCENSE, Kō.
INCENSE-STICKS, Senkō.
INCENTIVE, Hagemi; chikara.
INCESSANT, Tayedz; yamadz.
INCESSANTLY, Shikiri-ni.
INCEST, Kanin.
INCH, Sun.
INCIDENT, *n.* Koto.
INCIDENTAL, Omoi-gake-nai; futo; omoiyoranu; zonjiyoranu; fui-na; rinji-na.
INCISION, Kiru; kiri-kidz.
INCISOR-TOOTH, Mayeba; mukaba.
INCITE, Okosz; hagemasz; odateru.
INCIVILITY, Shitszrei; burei.
INCLEMENT, Kibishii; hageshii.
INCLINATION, Kokoro; ki; kokorozashi; kuse.
INCLINE, Katayoru; katamukeru; katadzmu; hidzmu; kashigu; katamuku.
INCLOSE, Kako; kakomu; tori-maku; tsztszmu.
INCLOSURE, Kakoi; kakomi.
INCLUDE, Tsztszmu; fukumu; kaneru; komeru.
INCOGNITO, Shinonde shinobi-ni.
INCOMBUSTIBLE, Hi ga tszkanu; moyenu.
INCOME, Taka; torika; shunō.
INCOMMODE, Komaraseru.
INCOMMODIOUS, Fu-benri; katte ga warui.
INCOMPARABLE, Bu-sō; tagui naki; hiruinaki; narabi-naki.
INCOMPATIBLE, Awanu; fuwa na; fugō-na; majiranu. — *medicine*, tekiyaku.
INCOMPETENT, Taranu; fusoku-na; oyobanu.
INCOMPLETE, Mattaku-nai; manzoku senu; sorowanu.
INCOMPREHENSIBLE, Wakaranu; satorarenu; gaten ga yukanu; nomi-komenu.
INCONCEIVABLE, Kakari-shirarenu; satorarenu.
INCONGRUOUS, Fusō-ō; funiai; sō-ō-senu.
INCONSIDERABLE, Wadzka-na; isasaka.
INCONSIDERATE, Omoi-yaranu; kagaye-naki; mufumbetsz-na.
INCONSISTENT, Awanu; fuwa-na; fusō-ō; funiai.
INCONSOLABLE, Nadamerarenu.
INCONSTANT, Kawari yaszi; sadamaranu; uwatszite-iru; utszrigi-na.
INCONTESTABLE, Arasowarenu; hihan-subekarazaru; rondz-bekarazaru.
INCONTINENT, Inran naru.
INCONTROVERTIBLE, Arasowarenu; rondzbekarazaru; hi wo utsz koto ga dekinu.
INCONVENIENT, Fubenri-na; futszgō; katte no warui; fuben.
INCORPOREAL, Katachi no naki; mugiyōtai.
INCORPORATE, Maze-awaseru.
INCORRECT, Chigau, machigau; tadashikaranu.
INCORRIGIBLE, Korinu; aratamenu; torinaosarenu.
INCORRUPTIBLE, Kusaranu; kuchinu.
INCREASE, Masz; fuyeru; fuyasz; futoru; ōkiku naru; tszyoku naru; tsznoru; tszyoru; zōchō; kasamu.
INCREDIBLE, Shinzerarenu; shinko-serarenu; shinjigatai.
INCRUST, Uwakawa ga hatta; mabure tszita.
INCUBUS, Unasareru; osowareru.
INCULCATE, Oshiye-komu.
INCUR, Ukeru; au; kōmuru.
INCURABLE, Naoranu; jishigataki.
INCURSION, Okasz.
INDEBTED, Oime ga aru; kari ga aru; kake ni natte oru.
INDECENT, Busahō-na; burei-na; birō na.
INDECISION, Yūyo; tamerō; kogi.
INDECISIVE, Shōbu ga tszkanu; tamerau; sadamaranu.
INDECOROUS, Busahō-na; burei-na; shitszrei-na.
INDECORUM, Busahō; burei.
INDEED, Makoto-ni; jitsz-ni; tashika-ni; honni; hon-tō ni; ge-ni.
INDEFATIGABLE, Tszkarenu; kutabirenu; yowaranu.
INDEFENSIBLE, Tamotarenu.
INDEFINITE, Kimaranu; sadamaranu; kimerarenu.
INDELIBLE, Kiyenu.
INDELICATE, Busahō-na; birō.
INDEMNIFY, Madō; tszgunau.
INDEMNITY, Madoi-kin.
INDENT, *v.* Kubomu; hekomu; hekomasz.
INDENTATION, Kubomi; hekomi; kireme.
INDENTURE, Shōmon; ukejō.
INDEPENDENT, Dokuriu; h'toridachi; jiritsz.
INDESTRUCTIBLE, Nakunaranu; messenu.
INDEX, Mokuroku.
INDIA, Tenjiku; indo.
INDIAN-INK, Szmi.
INDIAN-CORN, Tomorikoshi.
INDIAN-TURNIP, Tennanshō.

INDICATE, Shiraseru; shimesz; miseru.
INDICATION, Shirushi; kizashi; keshirai.
INDIFFERENT, Kamawanu; tonjakusenu; yosoyososhii.
INDIGENCE, Bimbō; hin-kiu; madzshiki.
INDIGENT, Bimbō-na; madzshii.
INDIGESTIBLE, Konare-gatai; shōk'wa-senu.
INDIGESTION, Teitai; shokutai; shokushō.
INDIGNATION, Ikari; ikidōri; rippuku; haradachi.
INDIGNITY, Iyashimi; naigashiro; chijoku; keibetsz.
INDIGO, Ai.
INDIRECT, Mawaridōi; tōmawashi; atetszkeru.
INDISCERNIBLE, Miyenu.
INDISCREET, Tsztszshimanu; mufumbetsz.
INDISCRIMINATE, Shabetsz-naki; wakachinaki.
INDISCRIMINATELY, Yatara-ni.
INDISPENSABLE, Nakute kanawanu; hitszyō-na.
INDISPOSE, Kirau; iyagaru; kirawaseru; fuk'wai-na.
INDISPOSITION, Kirai; fuk'wai; ambai ga warui; wadzrai; yamai.
INDISPUTABLE, Mochiron; ron ni oyobanu.
INDISSOLUBLE, Tokenu; hanarenu; kirenu.
INDISTINCT, Akiraka-naranu; kaszka-na; hakkiri-senu; fu-fummiyō-na; bonyarish'ta; honoka.
INDIVIDUAL, H'totsz; h'tori; ichi-nin.
INDIVIDUALLY, H'tori-de; h'tori-dztsz; h'tori datte.
INDIVISIBLE, Wakerarenu.
INDOLENT, Okotaru; bushō-na; fusei.
INDORSE, Uragaki wo szru; urahan wo osz.
INDORSEMENT, Uragaki; urahan.
INDORSER, Uragaki wo szru h'to; ukeainin.
INDUBITABLE, Utagai-naki; utagawashikaranu; tash'ka-na.
INDUCE, Szszmeru; kudoku; okoru; hasszru.
INDUCEMENT, Shui; tane; moto.
INDUE, Araseru; motaseru.
INDULGE, Idaku; ō-me ni miru.
INDURATE, Kataku szru; katameru.
INDURATION, Katamari; shikori.
INDUSTRIOUS, Honeoru.
INDUSTRY, Honeori.
INEBRIATE, *n.* Sake-nomi.
INEFFABLE, Ī-tszkusarenu.
INEFFECTUAL, Muda-na; munashiki; kikanu; yaku ni tatanu.
INEFFICACIOUS, Kikanu; kōnō-nashi; kikime ga nai.
INELEGANT, Buikina; utszkushiku nai.
INELIGIBLE, Toru ni taranu.
INEQUALITY, Sorowanu-koto.
INERT, Nibui; don-na.
INESTIMABLE, Hakari-kirenu.
INEVITABLE, Manukarenu; nogarenu.
INEXCUSABLE, Yurusarenu.
INEXHAUSTIBLE, Tszkusarenu; mujin.
INEXORABLE, Kiki-irenu.
INEXPEDIENT, Fusō-ō; futszgō; awanu.
INEXPERIENCED, Miren.
INEXPERT, Heta; tsztanai; buchōhō.
INEXPLICABLE, Toku koto wa dekinu; toki-akasarenu.
INEXPRESSIBLE, Iyenu; iu ni iwarenu; yemo-iwadz.
INEXTINGUISHABLE, Kesarenu.
INEXTRICABLE, Hodokarenu.
INFALLIBLE, Machigai-naki; machigawanu.
INFAMOUS, Futoi; nikui.
INFAMY, Naore; kajin; haji.
INFANCY, Wakai toki; itokenai toki; osanai toki; jaku-nen.
INFANT, Akambō; akago; midzgo; midorigo.
INFANTRY, Hohei; kachi-musha.
INFATUATE, Mayō; oboreru; hamaru.
INFECT, Utszsz; densen szru; kabureru; utszru; makeru.
INFER, *see* oshi; oshite shiru; sziriyō szru; szisatsz szru.
INFERIOR, Otoru; makeru; sh'ta; ochiru. — *quality*, gehin.
INFERNAL, — *doctrines*, madō. — *rites*, mahō. — *arts*, majutsz. — *spirits*, akuma — *regions*, makai.
INFEST, Komaraseru.
INFIDEL, Fushinjin; shinkō senu h'to.
INFINITE, Kagiri-naki; saigen-naki; kiwamari naki; muhen.
INFIRM, Yowai; jūjaku-na; hiniyaku-na; biyō-shin-na; oiboreru.
INFIRMITY, Yamai; biyōki; ayamachi; ochido.
INFLAMED, Tadareru; kinshō sh'ta; biran szru.
INFLAMMABLE, Moyeru; moye-yaszi.
INFLAMMATION, Kinshō.
INFLATE, Fukurasz; fukureru.
INFLEXIBLE, Magaranu; tawamanu.
INFLICT, Tszmi ni okonau.
INFLUENCE, Isei; ikō; ikioi; okage; szikiyo; hakiki.

INFLUENZA, Fūja; jaki.
INFORM, Kikaseru ; tszgeru ; shiraseru ; oshiyeru; todokeru; chiu-shin szru.
INFORMATION, Tayori ; otodzre ; shirase; oshiye.
INFORMER, Sonin.
INFREQUENT, Mare; tama-tama; metta-ninai; medzrashii.
INFRINGE, Somuku; yaburu.
INFUSE, Ireru.
INFUSIBLE, Tokenu.
INGENIOUS, Hatszmei-na ; rikō-na; kash'-koi; takumi.
INGENUOUS, Mei-haku-na.
INGLORIOUS, Naore-na; membokunai; hadz-kashii.
INGOT, Chōgin.
INGRAFT, Tszgu.
INGRATIATE, Kigen wo toru.
INGRATITUDE, On wo shiranu; arigataki wo shiranu.
INGREDIENT, Tane. *One* —, ichimi.
INHABIT, Szmau; oru; jū szru; iru.
INHABITABLE, Szmareru.
INHABITANT, Szmau-h'to; jū-nin.
INHALE, Szi-komu.
INHERIT, Tszgu; ato wo toru; sōzoku szru; mochi-tsztayeru.
INHERITANCE, Katoku.
INHOSPITABLE, Fuashirai; aisō no-nai.
INHUMAN, Hakujō; fu-ninjō; muzan; hidoi; mugoi.
INIMICAL, Uramiru; nikumu.
INIMITABLE, Niserarenu; oyobanu; manerarenu.
INIQUITY, Fuhō; budō; fushō.
INJECT, Sasz; sashi-komu.
INJURE, Sokonau; sondzru; gai-szru; itamu.
INJURIOUS, Warui; doku-na.
INJURY, Sokonai; gai; kidz; kega; itami.
INJUSTICE, Muri.
INK, Szmi.
INK-STAND, Szmi-ire; yatate.
INK-STONE, Szszri.
INLAND, Oku; inaka.
INLAY, *v.* Kiri-hameru.
INMATE, Dō-kiyo.
INMOST, Oku.
INN, Yadoya; hatagoya.
INNATE, Umaretszki; seishitsz.
INN-KEEPER, Yadoya no teishu.
INNOCENT, Mushitsz; muzai; higō.
INNOCUOUS, Doku no nai; gai no nai.
INNUMERABLE, Kadzyerarenu; muriyō.
INOCULATE, Tszgu; wiyeru.
INODOROUS, Nioi-naki.
INOFFENSIVE, Gai ni naranu.
INQUEST, Kenshi; kembun; gimmi.
INQUIRE, Tadzneru; tō; kiku; sensaku szru; gimmi szru.
INQUSITIVE, Monodzki; kikitagaru.
INSALUBRIOUS, Yōki ga warui.
INSANE, Kichigai; hakkiyō; kiyōran.
INSANITY, Kiyōki; ranshin.
INSATIABLE, Akanu.
INSCRIBE, Kaku.
INSCRIPTION, Uwagaki.
INSECT,. Mushi.
INSECURE, Abunai; ayaui.
INSENSIBLE, Oboye ga nai; shōne ga nai; shibireru.
INSEPARABLE, Wakerarenu.
INSERT, Ireru; hameru; kuwayeru; hasamu.
INSIDE, Naka; uchi; ura.
INSIGNIA, Shirushi; mon; mondokoro.
INSIGNIFICANT, Wadzka.
INSIDE *out*, Uragayesz.
INSINCERE, Fujitsz-na; shinjitsz nai.
INSIPID, Aji no nai; tampaku; awaki; mumi.
INSIST, Shi-iru; osz.
INSNARE, Hameru; szkasz.
INSOLENT, Ōfū; ōhei.
INSOLUBLE, Tokenu.
INSOLVENT, Shin-shō ga tszbureru.
INSPECT, Aratameru; gim-mi szru; kembun szru; shiraberu.
INSPECTION, Kembun; kemmi.
INSPECTOR, Mekiki.
INSPIRE, Szikomu; iki wo hiku.
INSPIRATION, Hiki-iki.
INSPIRIT, Hagemasz; chikara wo tszkeru; ki wo hiki-tateru.
INSTALMENT, Nashi-kudzshi. *Daily* —, higake. *Monthly* —, tszkifu. *Yearly* —, nempu.
INSTANCE, Rei; tameshi. *For* —, tatoyeba.
INSTANT, *a.* Kiu-na; niwaka; sashiataru.
INSTANT, *n.* Toki; koro; jibun; soku-ji; shuyu.
INSTANTANEOUS, Tachimachi; sokuji; niwaka.
INSTEAD, Kawari-ni.
INSTEP, Ashi no kō.
INSTIGATE, Odateru; keshi-kakeru.
INSTIGATOR, Odateru h'to.

INSTIL, Shimi-komaseru.
INSTITUTE, Tateru; hajimeru.
INSTRUCT, Oshiyeru; tszgeru; kiyōkun szru.
INSTRUCTION, Oshiye; kiyōkun; ītszke; shinan; denju.
INSTRUCTOR, Shishō.
INSTRUMENT, Dōgu.
INSUFFERABLE, Tayerarenu; korayerarenu; gaman-dekinu; shimbō dekinu.
INSUFFICIENT, Taranu; fusoku.
INSULT, Hadzkashimeru; chōrō szru; gurō szru.
INSUPERABLE, Atawanu; oyobarenu.
INSUPPORTABLE, Tayerarenu; gaman dekinu.
INSURE, Ukeau.
INSURANCE, Ukeai.
INSURGENT, Muhon-nin.
INSURMOUNTABLE, Oyobarenu.
INSURRECTION, Muhon; ikki; gekiran.
INTEGUMENT, Kawa.
INTELLECT, Chiye; sai; saichi.
INTELLIGENT, Rikō-na; kash'koi.
INTELLIGIBLE, Wakari-yaszi.
INTEMPERATE, Szgiru. — *in drink*, sake ga szgiru.
INTENSE, Hageshii; tszyoi; kibishii; kitszi.
INTENTION, Tszmori; riyōken; kokorozashi; meate. *Contrary to one's* —, kokoro naradz.
INTENTIONALLY, Waza to; koto sara in.
INTENTLY, Hitaszra-ni; moppara; hita-mono.
INTER, Hōmuru; udzmeru.
INTERCALARY-MONTH, Urūdzki.
INTERCEDE, Tori-nasz; tori-tszkurō.
INTERCESSION, Torinashi; nakadachi.
INTERCESSOR, Chiu-nin.
INTERCEPT, Sashi-tomeru; tomeru; seki-tomeru; osayeru; yokodori wo szru.
INTERCHANGE, Tori-kayeru; kayeru; kōyeki szru; kayowasz.
INTERCOURSE, Tszkiai; majiwari; ōrai; yukiki; kayoi.
INTERDICT, Kindzru; sei-kin szru; kotowaru; kobamu; kinshi; kinzei; kindan.
INTEREST, *n.* Ri; risoku; kai; yeki; wari-ai; buai.
INTERESTED IN, Omoshirogaru.
INTERESTING, Omoshiroi.
INTERFERE, Kamau; kakawaru.
INTERIOR, Naka; uchi; ura.
INTERLACE, Kumu; kagaru.
INTERLEAVE, Shira-kami wo hasamu; hasami-ireru.
INTERLINE, Hasamu; hasami-ireru.
INTERMARRY, Jūyen szru.
INTERMEDDLE, Kamau.
INTERMINABLE, Kagiri-naki.
INTERMINGLE, Mazeru; kondzru.
INTERMISSION, Aida; hima; ma.
INTERMIT, Aida wo oku.
INTERNAL, Naka; uchi; ura. — *injury*, naison. — *medicine*, naiyaku.
INTERPOLATE, Zan-niu szru; sakashira wo szru.
INTERPOSE, Hasamu; osayeru; naka ni tatsz; tori-atszkau; hedateru.
INTERPRET, Honyaku szru; naosz; handan szru; īhodoku.
INTERPRETER, T'sūji.
INTERROGATE, Tō; tadzneru; kiku.
INTERRUPT, Jama wo szru; samatageru; tomeru; sashi-tomeru; sashideguchi wo szru; togireru; todaye; chiu-zetsz; deshabaru.
INTERSECT, Yokogiru.
INTERSPERSE, Mazeru.
INTERSTICE, Szkima; hima; aida; ma.
INTERTWINE, Motszre-au; aimatō; karamiau.
INTERVAL, Aida; hima; ma.
INTERVENE, Hedateru; naka ni tatsz; tori-atsz au.
INTERVENTION, Tori-atszkai; nakadachi.
INTERVIEW, Taimen szru; ōsetsz szru.
INTERWEAVE, Ori-awaseru; ori-mazeru.
INTESTATE, Yui-gon nashi.
INTESTINE, Harawata; zōfu.
INTHRONE, Kurai ni tszkeru.
INTIMATE, Nengoro-na; kokoro-yaszi; fukai; jukkon; kon-i; majiwaru.
INTO, *see In.*
INTOLERABLE, Shimbō dekinu; gaman dekinu; korayerarenu; taye-gataki.
INTOXICATE, Yō; meitei szru.
INTOXICATED, Sake ni yotta.
INTRERCH, Hori wo horu; jingamaye wo szru; soko wo kidzku.
INTREPID, Isamashii; isamu.
INTRICATE, Motszreru; irikumu; konzatsz.
INTRIGUE, Imbō.
INTRODUCE, Tebiki wo szru; shōkai; hikiawaseru; chikadzki ni szru; hajimeru.
INTRODUCER, Nakadachi; baishaku; chiunin; tebiki.
INTRODUCTION, — *of a book*, jobun;

hashi-gaki; mayegaki. *Letter of —*, okuri-tegata.
INTRUDE, Oshikomu; deszgiru.
INTRUST, Adzkeru; yudaneru; makaseru; nindzru.
INUNDATE, Afureru; koboreru.
INUNDATION, Kodzi; ōmidz.
INURE, Nareru.
INVADE, Okasz; shimpatsz.
INVALID, *n.* Biyō-shin.
INVALUABLE, Tattoki.
INVARIABLE, Kawaranu; dōyō na; tokiwa.
INVEIGH, Nonoshiru.
INVEIGLE, Hiki-ireru; sosonokasz; tszri-komu; obiku; szkasz.
INVENT, Hatszmei szru; takumu; takunamu.
INVENTORY, Mokuroku.
INVERT, Fuseru.
INVERSELY, Sakasama; abekobeni; achikochi; urahara.
INVEST, *v.* Ire-komu; ireru.
INVESTIGATE, Shiraberu; gimmi szru; tadasz; sensaku szru.
INVETERATE, Kōjiru.
INVIGORATE, Jōbu ni szru; kengo ni szru; tszyomeru.
INVINCIBLE, Katarenu.
INVIOLABLE, Yaburarenu.
INVISIBLE, Miyenu.
INVITE, Yobu; maneku; shōdai szru; yobareru.
INVITATION, Yobare; shōdai.
INVOICE, Okuri-jō; tszmi-ni no mokuroku.
INVOKE, Negau; tanomu.
INVOLUNTARY, Onodz-to; onodzkara; shizento.
IPECACUANHA, Tokon.
IRKSOME, Mendō; taikutsz saseru; iya-na; urusai.
IRON, *n.* Tetsz; kurogane; magane.
IRON, *v.* Nosz; hinoshi wo kakeru.
IRONY, Ura wo iu; saka ni iu.
IRREGULAR, Sorowanu; midari-na; kimari no nai; mura.
IRRELIGIOUS, Bushinjin; budō.
IRREMEDIABLE, Naoranu.
IRREPARABLE, Shi-naosarenu; naoranu.
IRRESISTIBLE, Fusegi-kirenu; sasayerarenu; tekishigataki.
IRRESOLUTE, Ketszjō naki; ki ga uwatszite iru; sadamaranu.
IRRIGATE, Uruosz; midz wo kakeru.
IRRITATE, Ikaraseru; tadareru; ; iraira szru; irairashii; iratszku.

IS, Aru; gozarimasz.
ISINGLASS, Nibe; kanten.
ISLAND, Shima.
ISSUE, *v.* Deru; hassz.
ISSUE, *n.* Hate; owari; shimai; yukuszye.
IT, Are; sono.
ITCH, Shitsz; hizen.
ITCHING, Kayui; kayumi; kaii.
ITEM, Kajō; kado.
ITINERATE, Mawaru; henreki szru.
ITSELF, Onodz to; onodzkara; hitori-de; shizen-to; jibun-ni.
IVORY, Zōge.
IVY, Tszta.

J

JACK *with a lantern*, Kitsznebi; ink'wa.
JACKET, Hanten.
JADED, Tszkareru; kutabireru.
JALAP, Yarapa.
JANITOR, Momban.
JANUARY, Shōgatsz.
JAPAN, Nippon; yamato.
JAPAN-VARNISH, Yurushi.
JAR, *v.* Ugokasz; yurugasz.
JAR, *n.* Tszbo; kame.
JASMINE, Kuchinashi.
JAUNDICE, Ōdan.
JAVELIN, Teyari.
JAW, Ago.
JAY, Kasasagi.
JEALOUS, Netamu; sonemu; yakkamu.
JEALOUSY, Yaki-mochi; shitto; netami; rinki.
JEER, Naburu; chōrō szru; azakeru.
JEOPARDY, Ayauki; kennon; kinan.
JERK, *v.* Shakuru; nageru; haneru; bikutszku; biku-biku szru; hikumeku.
JEST, Jōdan wo iu; share wo iu; tawamureru *In —*, jōdan da; dōkeru.
JESTER, Taikomochi; dōkemono.
JETTY, Hatoba; sambashi.
JEWEL, Kazarimono; tama.
JEWELER, Kazariya.
JIG, Odori.
JILT, Hadan szru; hengai szru.
JINGLE, Narasz.
JOB, Shigoto. *Work done by the job*, ukeoi shigoto.
JOB'S *tears*, Bodaiju.

JOCKEY, Bakurō.
JOCOSE, Jōdan; tawamureru.
JOG Ugokasz.
JOIN, Au; awaseru; tszgu; kuwayeru; soyeru; gasszru.
JOINER, Himonoya.
JOINT, Fushi; awashime; tszgai-me. *Out of* —, chigai. — *of bamboo*, yo.
JOKE, Jōdan; share; tawamure.
JOLLY, Omoshirogaru.
JOLT, Ugoku.
JOSTLE, Osz.
JOT, Ten; chobo; mijin.
JOURNAL, Ki; nikki; roku.
JOURNEY, Tabi; riyokō.
JOVIAL, Omoshirogaru.
JOY, Yorokobi; ureshisa; tanoshimi; kiyō.
JOYFUL, Ureshii.
JUDGE, *n.* Saiban-nin; tori-sabakikata; bugiyō.
JUDGE, *v.* Sai-ban szru; gimmi szru; sabaku; sai-kiyo szru; tori-sabaku; miwakeru; hihan szru; hiyō szru.
JUDGMENT, Wakimaye; fumbetsz; wakachi; kamben; riyōken; kiyōjō; bachi; tatari; tembatsz.
JUDICIOUS, Shimatsz na; kamben aru.
JUG, Tokkuri.
JUGGLE, Tedzma wo tszkau; shinadama wo tszkau.
JUGGLER, Yashi; tedzma-tszkai; shinadama-tszkai.
JUICE, Shiru.
JULY, Sh'chi-gatsz.
JUMBLE, Konzatsz; konran; mucha-mucha; gotatszku; gota-gota sh'te iru; iregomi; iri-kumu; irimidaru.
JUMP, Tobu; haneru.
JUNCTION, Awashime; ochi ai.
JUNE, Rokugatsz.
JUNIPER, Ibuki.
JUPITER, Mokusei.
JURISDICTION, Riyō; riyōbun; shihai.
JUST, *adv.* Chōdo; adakamo; tate; sanagara. — *as it is*, ari-no-mama.
JUST, *a.* Richigi-na; shōjiki-na; ren-chokuna; seichoku-na; ōyake; atarimaye; hadz; beki; makoto-no; hontō-no; jitszno; mottomo; choku na.
JUSTICE, Gi; ri; giri; dō; dōri.
JUSTIFY, Yurusz; sha-men szru; tszmi nashi to ī-watasz.
JUT-OUT, Sashi-deru; haridasz.
JUVENILE, Wakai; itokenai.

K

KEEN, Hageshii; kibishii; tszyoi; szrudoi.
KEEP, *v.* Mamoru; motsz; tamotsz; shugo szru; kau. — *back*, nokosz; osayeru; hikayeru. — *down*, osayeru. — *alive*, ikeru; ikaru. — *under*, hikayeru. — *off*, fusegu; yokeru. — *at a distance*, tōzakeru. — *in mind*, kokoro-gakeru.
KEEPER, Bannin; mori.
KEG, Oke; taru; kodaru.
KERNEL, Mi; nin.
KETTLE, Nabe; tetszbin.
KEY, Kagi.
KICK, Keru. — *up*, Ke-ageru; ke-tateru. — *open*, ke-hanasz. — *over*, ke-taosz. — *down*, ke-kudasz; ke-otosz. — *into*, ke-komu. — *out*, kedasz.
KID, Hitszji no ko.
KIDNAP, Kadowakasz.
KIDNEY, Jin-no-zō; mirado.
KILL, Korosz; sesshō szru; chiu szru.
KILN, Kama.
KIN, Shinrui; yenja.
KIND, Tagui; rui; shurui; kurai; gara. — *of person*, h'to-gara; jimpim; jimbutsz. — *of day*, higara.
KIND, Nasake aru; nengoro-na; shinsetszna.
KINDLE, Taku; taki-tszkeru.
KINDLY, Nengoro ni.
KINDNESS, Nasake.
KINDRED, Kiyōdai; shinrui; shimmi; shinzoku; shinseki.
KING, Ō; koku-ō.
KINGDOM, Koku; kuni; riyōbun.
KING-FISHER, Kawasemi.
KINK, Yore; takureru.
KISS, *No equivalent for this word in the Japanese.*
KITCHEN, Daidokoro; katte.
KITCHEN-GARDEN, Hatake; sayen; senzai.
KITE, Tako; ikanobori.
KITTEN, Neko no ko; koneko.
KNAPSACK, Dōran.
KNAVE, Katari; ōdō.
KNAVISH, Dzrui; kataru; kō-k'watsz.
KNEAD, Koneru; neru; neyasz.
KNEE, Hiza.
KNEEL, Hizamadzku.
KNEEPAN, Hiza no sara.
KNIFE, *Pocket* —, Kokatana. *Table* —, hōchō. *Kitchen* —, deba.

Knit, Amu.
Knob, Hikite.
Knock, Butsz; utsz; tataku. — *down*, buchi-taosz. — *out*, buchi-dasz. — *in*, buchi-komu. — *off*, buchi-otosz.
Knot, Fushi; muszbime; fushime. *Full of* — fushikuredatsz.
Know, Shiru; wakaru; kokoro-yeru; zonjiru; satoru.
Knowledge, Kokoroye; jutsz.
Knuckle, Yubi no fushi; genkotsz.
Kum-kwat, Kinkan.

L

Label, Fuchō-fuda.
Labor, *n.* Shigoto; hone-ori; hataraki; san. *Day* —, hiyō.
Labor, *v.* Shigoto wo szru; honeoru; rōszru. *To be in* —, san szru.
Laborious, Honeoru.
Lace, *v.* Kagaru.
Lacerate, Saku; kakikiru.
Lachrymal-duct, Rui-k'wan.
Lack, *n.* Jūman.
Lack, *v.* Nai; kotokaki.
Lacquer, Urushi.
Lacquer, *v.* Urushi wo nuru.
Lacquer-ware, Nuri-mono; shikki.
Lad, Warambe; dōji.
Ladder, Hashigo.
Lade, *v.* Kumu; shakū; sukū. — *a ship*. tszmu. — *horse*, noseru.
Ladle, Shaku; hishaku; shakushi.
Lady, Onna; fujin.
Lag, Okureru; ato ni naru.
Laity, Zoku; hei-nin; banzoku. *Clergy and* —, sōzoku.
Lake, Midzumi; koszi.
Lamb, Hitszji no ko; kohitszji.
Lame, Chimba; bikko; katawa; fugu.
Lament, Kanashimu; nageku; naku.
Lamentable, Nagekawashii; itōshii; oshii; atara.
Lamentation, Kanashimi; nageki; naki.
Lamp, Andon; tōdai; shoku.
Lamp-black, Yuyen.
Lamp-wick, Tōshin.
Lamprey, Dojō.
Lance, *n.* Yari.
Lance, *v.* Yari de tszku.
Lancet, Habari; hirabari.
Land, Oka; riku; chi; tszchi; jimen; denji; kachiji.
Land, *v.* Oka ni agaru.
Landing-place, Hatoba; ageba.
Landlady, Hatagoya no niyōbo.
Landlord, Hatagoya no teishu; aruji.
Land-mark, Bōgui.
Landscape, Keshiki; fūkei; mirashi; chōbō.
Lane, Hoso-michi.
Language, Kotoba; monoii.
Languid, Darui; yowai; dayui; namakeru; darakeru.
Languish, Otoroyeru; szibi szru.
Languor, Darui; namakeru.
Lantern, Chōchin.
Lap, *n.* Hiza.
Lap, *v.* Nameru.
Lapse, *of time*, Heru.
Lapsus linguæ, Kuchi ga szberu.
Larboard, Fune no hidari.
Lard, Buta no abura.
Lares, Jibutsz.
Large, Ōkii; f'toi; hiroi.
Largeness, Ōkisa.
Lark, Hibari.
Lascivious, Tzkebe-na; irogonomi-na; uwakina; kōshoku.
Lash, *n.* Himo.
Lash, *v.* Moyau; shibari-tszkeru; makitszkeru; muchi-utsz.
Lass, Muszme; shinzō.
Lassitude, Darusa; taigi.
Last, *v.* Motsz; tamotsz.
Last, *a.* Owari no; shimai-no; hate-no. — *month*, atogetsz; sengetsz; maye no tszki; kiyogetsz. — *year*, saku-nen; kiyonen; maye no toshi; kiu-nen. — *night*, sakuban; saku-ya. *At last*, tszi-ni; tōtō; yōyaku; yōyō; yatto; shosen; hikkiyo. — *of life*, matszgo. — *ages*, matszdai.
Latch, Kake-gane.
Latchet, Hana-o; o.
Late, Osoi; okureru; chi-chi szru. — *years*, kinnen. — *sleeping*, asa-ne. — *in coming*, chisan. — *and early*, chisoku.
Lately, Kono-aida; chikagoro; kinrai; konogoro; kono-hodo.
Latent, Hisoka na; kakusz; nainai; naisho; hiszru.
Latest, Ichiban ato; ichiban osoi. — *generations*, matszdai.
Lath, Komaye.
Lathe, Rokuro.

LATTER, Nochi no; ato no.
LATTERLY, Kono-aida; konogoro; kinrai; chikagoro.
LATTICE-WORK, Kōshi.
LAUDABLE, Appare-na; kanshin-na.
LAUGH, Warau; yemu. — *at*, azakeru.
LAUGHABLE, Okashii; monowarai.
LAUNCH, Funa-oroshi.
LAVISH, Ōzappai; oshige mo naki.
LAW, Okite; gohatto; hō; sahō; hōshiki; nori. — *of nature*, tendō.
LAWFUL, Okite-dōri; go-jōhō-dōri; gomen-no.
LAWLESS, Furachi-na; fuhō-na.
LAWSUIT, Kuji; deiri.
LAWYER, Kujishi.
LAX, Yurui; darui.
LAXITY, Yurusa.
LAY, Oku; noseru; kakeru. — *aside*, szteru; yameru; nokeru. — *away*, katadzkeru; shimau. — *before*, sonayeru. — *by*, katadzkeru. — *down*, oku; neru; fuseru. — *hold of*, tszkamu; tszkamayeru. — *in*, takuwayeru; tszmu. — *open*, hiraku; akeru; arawasz; abaku. — *over*, kakeru; kiseru; noseru. — *out*, harau; tszkawasz. — *one's self out*, sei wo dasz. — *together*, atszmete oku. — *to heart*, ki ni kakeru. — *up*, takuwayeru; tszmu. — *siege*; semeru; kakomu. — *wait*, machi-buse wo szru. — *waste*, arasz. — *a wager*, kakeru. — *the blame on*, kiseru, nuri-tszkeru, kabuseru.
LAYER, Ye; kasane.
LAYMAN, Zoku; zokutai.
LAZY, Bushō-na.
LEAD, Namari.
LEAD, *v.* Tszreru; hiku; michibiku; hikīru; annai szru. — *a life*, kurasz. — *astray*, madowasz; mayowasz.
LEADER, Annaija; kashira; chōbon-nin.
LEADPENCIL, Seki-hitsz.
LEAF, Ki no ha. — *of a book*, hira. *Gold* —, kimpaku. — *of a door*, to.
LEAF-STALK, Kuki.
LEAFY, Shigeru.
LEAGUE, *n.* Yak'soku; keiyaku; totō.
LEAGUE, *v.* Yak'soku szru; totō wo muszbu.
LEAK, *v.* Moru.
LEAN, *n.* Yaseru.
LEAN, *v.* Katamuku; katayoru. — *on or against*, motareru; yorikakaru; motaseru; yoru.
LEAP, Tobu; odoru; haneru.
LEAP-FROG, Tobi-koshi.
LEAP-YEAR, Urū-toshi.
LEARN, Narau; manabu; keiko szru.
LEARNED *in*, Jōdz; tassh'ta. — *man*, gakusha.
LEARNING, Gakumon.
LEASE, *v.* Kasz; karu.
LEAST, *a.* ....yori mo chīsai; chīsai hō.
LEAST, *At* —, semete.
LEATHER, Kawa; tszkuri-kawa; nameshikawa.
LEATHER-DRESSER, Kawata; yeta.
LEAVE, *n.* Yurushi; menkiyo.
LEAVE, *v.* Shirizoku; taishutsz szru; saru; nozoku; hedateru; hanareru; nokosz; szteru; utcharu; adzkeru; makaseru; yudzru; nindzru; noku; shirizokeru. — *off*, yameru; yosz; tatsz. — *out*, otosz. — *over*, amasz. — *off wine*, kinshu szru.
LEAVEN, Tane; pan no tane.
LEAVINGS, Nokori-mono; amari.
LECTURE, Kōshaku; oshiyeru; seppō szru; hōdan szru; kōdan.
LECTURER, Kōshakushi
LEDGER, Chōmen.
LEE, Kazashimo; kazesh'ta.
LEE-SHORE, Kazashimo no iso; kaze uke no oka.
LEE-SIDE, *of a ship*, Fune no kazashimo no hō.
LEEWARD, Kaza-shimo no hō; kazesh'ta no hō.
LEECH, Hiru; szitetsz.
LEES, Ori; kasz.
LEFT, Hidari.
LEFT-HAND, Hidari no te.
LEFT-HANDED, Hidari-giki.
LEG, Ashi.
LEGACY, Yui-motsz; katami.
LEGAL, Okite-dōri.
LEGALIZE, Yurusz; gomen ni naru.
LEGERDEMAIN, Tedzma; shinadama.
LEGGING, K'yahan.
LEGIBLE, Yomeru.
LEGITIMATE, Jitsz; honto. — *child*, jisshi.
LEGUME, Saya.
LEISURE, Itoma; hima; ma; yori-yoku; ankan; aida.
LEISURELY, Soro-soro-to; yuru-yuru-to.
LEMON-OIL, Tōhiu.
LEND, Kasz; yōdateru.
LENGTH, Nagasa; tate. — *of life*, jōmiyō.
LENGTHEN, Tszgu; nagaku szru; noberu.
LEOPARD, Hiyō; nakatszkami.

LEPER, Raibiyō-yami; kattai.

LEPROSY, Raibiyō; tenkeibiyō; nari; kattai.

LESS, Chīsai; szkoshi; otoru.

LESSEN, *t.v.* Herasz; habuku; hesz; szkunaku szru; genshō szru; chīsaku szru; otoru; tszmeru; gendzru.

LESSEN, *i.v.* Heru; otoru; habuku; szkunaku naru; chīsaku naru; tszmaru; chijimu.

LESSON, Nikk'wa.

LEST, Moshiya; osorakuba; hiyotto; szreba.

LET, Yurusz; shōchi szru; kasz; yaru; *and the caust. form of the verb.* — *alone*, sztete oku; utchatte oku; mama yo; kamau na; nageyari sh'te oku. — *down*, orosz; tarasz. — *loose*, hanatsz,. — *in*, hairaseru. — *blood*, chi wo toru; shiraku szru. — *out*, hanasz; yurumeru; dasz. — *me have*, kudasaru; chōdai. — *me see*, mite kudasare. — *me write*, watakushi kakase nasare. — *grow*, hayasz.

LETHARGY, Nekomi.

LETTER, Tegami; fumi; jō; shokan; ji; moji; monji; shomen.

LETTUCE, Chisha.

LEVEL, *a.* Taira; tairaka; hirattai. — *ground*, hei-chi; hira-chi.

LEVEL, *v.* Narasz; tairageru; taira ni szru. — *a gun*, teppō wo tameru.

LEVEL, *n.* Midzmori.

LEVER, Teko.

LEVIGATE, Saimatsz ni szru; szru; szri-kudaku.

LEVITY, Karusa.

LEVY, Ī-tszkeru; mōshi-tszkeru; ateru; tsznoru.

LEWD, Irogonomi-na; szkebi-na; uwaki-na; kōskoku; midarana.

LEXICON, Jibiki.

LIABLE, Kakawaru; kakariai.

LIAR, Uso-tszki.

LIBEL, Zengen.

LIBERAL, Mono-oshimi senu.

LIBERALLY, Oshimadz-ni; jūbunni.

LIBERATE, Hanasz; hanareru.

LIBERTY, Jiyū ni naru koto; kokoro no mama. *At* —, hōdai.

LIBRARY, Shosai.

LICENSE, *n.* Yurushi; men-kiyo; kabu; menjō.

LICENSE, *v.* Yurusz; menkiyo szru.

LICENTIOUS, Hōtō-naru; hōratsz-na; buraina.

LICK, *v.* Nameru; neburu; butsz; utsz. — *the mouth*, kuchi-namedzri.

LICORICE-PLANT, Kanzō.

LID, Futa. *Eye* —, mabuchi.

LIE, *n.* Uso; itszwari; kiyogon; mampachi.

LIE, *v.* Uso wo tszku; itszwaru.

LIE, *v.* Neru; fuseru; heig'wa szru; ataru. — *by*, yaszmu. — *in wait*, machi-fuseru; nerau. — *down*, neru; fusz. — *in*, san wo szru; ko wo unde-iru. *Let lie*, nekasz.

LIEGE, Shujin; tono sama.

LIEU, Kawari.

LIFE, Inochi; seimei; mei; jumiyō; shōgai. *In* —, zommei; zonjō.

LIFELESS, Inochi no nai; darui; darakeru; taigi.

LIFE-TIME, Isshōgai; isshō; shō-gai; zaisei no toki; zonjō no uchi.

LIFT, *v.* Ageru.

LIGHT, *n.* Akari; hikari; tomoshibi; shoku; akarusa. *In one's* —, akari-saki. *Bring to* —, arawasz; akasz.

LIGHT, *a.* Karui; uszi; akarui. *Set* — *by*, karondzru. *Make* — *of*, naigashiro-ni; mono no kadz to mo sedz; betszjō szru.

LIGHT, *t.v.* Akari wo tszkeru; tobosz; terasz.

LIGHT, *i.v.* Tomaru. — *down*, orosz.

LIGHTEN, Hikaru; karumeru; karuku szru.

LIGHT-FINGERED, Toguse no warui.

LIGHT-FOOTED, Ashi-baya.

LIGHT-HEADED, Memai; kurumeku.

LIGHT-HEARTED, Ki no karui; kiraku-na.

LIGHTNESS, Karusa.

LIGHTLY, Karuku.

LIGHTNING, Inadzma; hikari; inabikari; denk'wa.

LIGHTNING-BUG, Hotaru.

LIGHTNING-ROD, Rai-yoke.

LIKE, Onaji; nitaru; niru; gotoku; dō; yō; tōri; mama; sama; h'toshii; ayakaru; sō; rashii. — *minded*, dōshin, dōi.

LIKE, *v.* Konomu; szku; tashimu; *also the suffix*, tai, *after the roots of verbs; as*, kaki-tai, *would like to write*, kai-tai; *would like to buy*, yuki-tai, *would like to go.*

LIKELIHOOD, *formed by suffix* sō.

LIKELY, Tabun; ōkata; *see* sō.

LIKE-MINDED, Dōi; onaji-kokoro.

LIKEN, Nazorayeru.

LIKENESS, Katachi; szgata; nigao; yezō.

LIKEWISE, Mata; mo; yappari.

LIKING, Ki ni iru; kokoro ni kanau.

LILY, Yuri.
LIMB, Yeda.
LIMBER, Yurui; nayeru; gun'ya-gun'ya; gutatszku; nayasz.
LIME, Ishibai.
LIME-KILN, Ishi-bai-gama.
LIME-WATER, Sekk'waiszi.
LIMIT, *n.* Sakai; kagiri; kiri; kiwa; kukuri.
LIMIT, *v.* Kagiru; kiwameru.
LIMP, Bikko wo hiku.
LIMPID, Kiyoki; kiyoraka; szmu.
LINCHPIN, Sen.
LINE, Ito; nawa; szji; chiszji. *A line from top to bottom*, kudari. *To strike a line*, szmi wo utsz.
LINE, *v.* Ura wo tszkeru.
LINEAGE, Chi-szji; szji; kettō; shison; szjime; szjō; kechi-miyaku; nagare.
LINEAL, *descent by the eldest son*, Chakuriu.
LINEAMENT, Kao-katachi; kao-tszki; yōbō.
LINEN, Nono.
LINGER, Himadoru; temadoru; tamerau; gudz-gudz szru; yutoru.
LINIMENT, Kōyaku.
LINING, Ura.
LINK, *n.* K'wan; wa.
LINK, *v.* Tsznagu; hameru.
LINT, Hotszki; sanshi.
LINTEL, Kamachi.
LION, Shishi.
LIP, Kuchi-biru.
LIQUEFY, Tokeru; fūk'wa szru.
LIQUID, Midzmono; riudōbutsz.
LIQUIDATE, Harau.
LIQUORICE, Kanzō; dzbōto.
LISPING, Sh'ta-motszre; sh'ta-taradz.
LIST, Mimi; mokuroku.
LIST, (*Nautical*), katayoru.
LISTEN, Kiku; chōmon szru.
LISTLESS, Ukkari-to.
LITERATI, Gak'sha.
LITERATURE, Gakumon; bun; bundō.
LITHOGRAPH, Ishidzri.
LITTER, Gomi; chiri; akuta; kudz.
LITTLE, Chisai; szkoshi; chitto; wadzka; shō-shō. — *by little*, chibi-chibi; szkoshi-dztsz.
LIVE, *v.* Oru; iru; szmau; jū-szru; ikiru; nagarayeru; kurasz. — *long*, chō-sei szru.
LIVE, *a.* Ikiteoru.
LIVELIHOOD, Kurashi-kata; kurashi; tosei; shōbai; kuchiszgi; kagiyō; nariwai; k'wakkei; kokō; yoszgi; yowatari.
LIVELY, Ki no karui; kigaru-na.
LIVER, Kimo; tan no zō; renge.
LIVERY, Shozoku.
LIVID, Aozame.
LIVING, Ikiteoru; ikeru; ikitaru; *see Livelihood*,
LIZARD, Imori; yamori;.
LOAD, *n.* Da; katszgi; ni; tszmidaka.
LOAD, *v.* Tszmu; komeru.
LOAFING, Namakeru; norakura szru.
LOAFER, Nora-kura-mono; namake-mono.
LOAN, *n.* Shakkin; kari.
LOAN, *v.* Kasz; yōdateru.
LOATHE, *v.* Kirau; iyagaru; mukadzku; muka-muka.
LOATHSOME, Kirai-na.
LOBE *of the ear*, Mimi-tabu.
LOBSTER, Kuruma-yebi.
LOCALITY, Tokoro; sho.
LOCATE, Tateru.
LOCATION, Tateru-tokoro.
LOCK, *n.* Jō; jōmaye.
LOCK, *v.* Jō wo orosz; tojiru. — *one' self in*, toji-komoru.
LOCKET, Kohaze.
LOCOMOTIVE, Jok'sha.
LOCUST, Inago.
LODESTONE, Jishaku.
LODGE, *v.* Yadoru; shuku szru; tomaru.
LODGER, Kiyaku.
LODGING, Yadori; shuku.
LOFTY, Takai; kō.
LOG, Ki; hashira.
LOIN, Koshi.
LOITER, Himadoru; temadoru; gudz-gudz szru; gudo-tszku.
LONELY, Samushii; shinshin to sh'ta; monosabishii.
LONG, Nagai; chō. — *ago*, toi. — *talk*, chō-dan. — *life*, chōju; chō-mei. — *and short*, chō-tan. — *journey*, chō-to. — *night*, chōya. — *sickness*, chō-biyō. — *time*, hisashii. — *long time since*, hisashiburi. — *delayed*, machi-dōi.
LONG, *v.* Sh'tau; koishiku omō; koi-sh'tau, koishigaru; natszkashii; yukashii.
LONGEVITY, Naga-iki; chōmei.
LONG-RUN, Hate; owari; shimai; tszi-ni.
LONG-SUFFERING, Ki no nagai.
LONG-TONGUED, Sh'ta no nagai; shaberite.
LOOK, Miru; goran; nagameru. *Formed also by the particle*, sō, *and* ranshii, *which see.* — *up*, mi-ageru; aogu; aumuite miru. *Tired of looking*, mi-aku. — *out for*, mi-awaseru; mitateru. — *down*,

mikudasz; mi-orosz; nozomu. — *about* mi-mawasz. — *after*, mi-okuru; mamoru. — *for*, matsz; sagasz; ukagau. — *into*, gimmi szru; sensaku szru. — *across*, mi-watasz; mi-kosz; mikayeru. — *back*, kayeri-miru. — *through a crack*, kaimami wo szru. — *through*, mi-tōsz; miszkasz. — *away*, yoso ni miru; yosomi.

LOOKS, Miba; midate; tei; szgata.

LOOKER-ON, Sobo kara miru h'to; kembutsz-nin.

LOOKING-GLASS, Kagami.

LOOKOUT, Monomi; mihari; tōmi.

LOOM, Hata.

LOOP, Wasa; wana.

LOOP-HOLE, Hazama; yazama.

LOOSE, *v.* Toku; yurumu; kutszrogu; darumu; tarumu; yurugu; hanareru; hiraku; akeru; yurusz.

LOOSE, *a.* Yurui.

LOOSEN, Tokeru; yurumeru; kutszrogeru; yuruku szru; tarumeru; hanasz.

LOOSENESS, Yurusa.

LOP, Kiru.

LOPSIDED, Kashigu; katamuku; katadzri.

LOQUACIOUS, Taben-na; shaberu.

LOQUAT, Biwa; rokitsz.

LORD, Shu; shu-jin; nushi; aruji; kimi; tono; danna.

LORDLY, Jiman-naru; takaburu; dannagao.

LORE, Gakumon; jutsz; oshiyo.

LOSE, *v.* Ushinau; useru; nakunaru; otosz; funjitsz; son szru; makeru; nukeru. — *the way*, mayō.

LOSER, Make-kata.

LOSE AND WIN, Kachi-make; shōbu.

LOSS, Son; sommō; sonshitsz. — *in weight*, kan; heri; meri.

LOST, Nakunatta; ushinatta; useta.

LOT, Kuji; jimen. *To draw* —, kuji wo toru. *How much for the lot?* komi de ikura.

LOTION, (*med.*) Araiguszri.

LOTTERY, Mujin.

LOTUS, Hasz no hana; ren-ge.

LOUD, Takai; ō.

LOUSE, Shirami.

LOUNGE, *v.* Bura bura sh'te iru.

LOUSY, Shirami-takari.

LOVE, *v.* Aiszru; kawaigaru; chōai szru; itsz'ushimu; konomu; szku; horeru; rembo szru; okkochiru. *Love to God, or to parents*, wiyamau. — *talk*, chiwa. — *letter*, chiwa-bumi. — *song*, koika. — *sick*, koi-wadzrau.

LOVE, *n.* On-ai; chōai; itszkushimi; ainen; jōai; koi; rembo; noroke.

LOVE-LETTER, Chiwa-bumi.

LOVELY, Kawai; kawairashii.

LOVER, Koi-bito; koi-otoko; okkochi.

LOVE-SICK, Chiwagurui; koiwadzrau.

LOVE-SONG, Koi no uta; koika.

LOVING-KINDNESS, Jihi; fubin.

LOW, *a.* Hikui. — *water*, shio ga hiru; hiki-shio; *or shallow*, asai. — *in price*, yaszi. — *in condition*, iyashii; karui; sh'ta no; hisen. — *in strength*, yowai. — *fellow*, gerō; gesz. — *employment*, geshoku.

LOW-BRED, Iyashii; gehin-na.

LOWER, *v.* Sageru; orosz. — *the price*, makeru.

LOWER, *a.* Sh'ta no. — *seat*, geza.

LOWER-MOST, Ichi-ban sh'ta no.

LOWLY, Herikudaru; kenson-na; hikayemena; hige szru; kentai.

LOW-PRICED, Gejiki; yaszi.

LOW-WATER, Hikishio.

LOYAL, Chiu-na; chiugi-na; gi.

LOYALTY, Chiugi.

LUBRICATE, Abura wo nuru.

LUCID, Akiraka-naru; teru; meihaku.

LUCK, Un; shiawase; ketai.

LUCKY, Un no yoi; saiwai; shiawashe no yoi; kichi. — *day*, kichi-nichi; kittan. — *or unlucky*, kikkiyō. — *dream*, dzimu. — *omen*, dzi-gen; dzisō.

LUCRATIVE, Mōke no aru.

LUCRE, Mōke; ri; yeki.

LUDICROUS, Okashii.

LUG, Hiku; ninau; katszgu.

LUGGAGE, Ni; nimotsz.

LUKEWARM, Nurui; noroi; nurumu.

LULL, Nagiru; shidzka; odayaka.

LUMINOUS, Hikaru; teru.

LUMP, Katamari. *Buy in the lump*, kuchi de kau; *see* oroshi; komi ni kau.

LUMPY, Tszbu-tszbu.

LUNACY, Kichigai; ranshin; monogurui.

LUNATIC, Kichigai h'to; kiyōjin.

LUNCH, Chanoko.

LUNG, Hai no zō.

LURE, Izanau; sasō; sonokasz; obiku.

LURK, Machi-buse wo szru.

LUSCIOUS, Oishii; amai.

LUST, *n.* Yoku.

LUST AFTER, Musaboru; tonyoku; yokubaru.

LUSTRE, Hikari ; kagayaku ; tszya.
LUSTRING, Kaiki.
LUSTY, Jōbu-na ; szkoyaka.
LUXATION, Hone-chigai.
LUXURIANT, Shigeru; habikoru.
LUXURIOUS, Ogoru.
LUXURY, Ogori.
LYE, Aku.
LYING *in*, San. — *woman*, sampu.

M

MACARONI, Udon.
MACERATE, Hitasz; tszkeru.
MACHINE, Shikake; karikuri.
MACKEREL, Saba.
MACULÆ, Aza.
MAD, Kurui; kichigai; ranshin.
MADAM, Kami-san; okusama; goshinzo san.
MADDER, Akane.
MADMAN, Kichigai; kiyō-jin.
MAGGOT, Uji; onaga-mushi.
MAGIC, Mahō; idzna; yōjutsz.
MAGICIAN, Mahō-tszkai; idznatszkai.
MAGIC-LANTERN, Utszshiye.
MAGISTRATE, Yakunin.
MAGNANIMOUS, Tai-riyō-na; ōmaka-na; taiyū-na.
MAGNET, Jishaku.
MAGNIFICENT, Rippa-na; kekkō-na.
MAGNIFY, Ōkiku szru; homeru; ōkiku iu; taisō ni iu.
MAGNITUDE, Ōkisa.
MAGNOLIA, Nemunoki.
MAGPIE, Kasasagi.
MAID, Muszme.
MAID-SERVANT, Gejo; hash'tame.
MAIL, *Coat of* —, yoroi.
MAIMED, Katawa; fugu.
MAIN, Hon; shu. — *object*, hon-i; shu-i. — *building of a temple*, hondō. *In the* —, taitei; tairiyaku; taigai.
MAINLY, Moppara; omo-ni.
MAIN-MAST, Nakabashira; hombashira; ō-bashira.
MAIN-SAIL, Ōbashira no sh'ta no ho.
MAINTAIN, Yashinau; hagokumu; mamoru; motsz.
MAIN-TOP, Ōbashira no saki.
MAIN-YARD, Ōbashira no sh'ta no hogeta.
MAIZE, Tomorokoshi; namba.
MAJESTIC, Kedakai; ateyaka.

MAJORITY, Tahan; ōkata; taihan; tabun.
MAKE, Tszkuru; koshirayeru; dekiru; mōkeru ; tateru. *Formed also by the caust. form of the verb; as*, motaseru, *to make another carry*. Yukaseru, *to make another go*. — *amends*, tszgunau; madō. — *account of*, taizetsz ni omō. — *free with*, buyenriyo sh'te; habakari naku. — *good*, tszgunau; madō; oginau; togeru; szmu. — *light of*, naigashiro ni szru; karondzru. — *much of*, daiji ni szru; taizetsz ni szru; tattobu. — *over*, watasz; yudzru. — *out*, wakaru; kokoroyeru. — *up*, koshirayeru; naka wo naosz. — *up a deficiency*, tasz. — *up a loss*, tszgunau. — *up one's mind*, kokoro wo sadameru. — *up a sum of money*, chōdatsz; sandan; saikaku. — *water*, shōben szru; *(of a ship)*, moru. — *for*, mukatte hashiru.
MAKER, Tszkuru h'to; saiku-nin. *Generally formed by affixing*, ya *or* shi, *to the end of the thing made; as*, fude-shi, *a pen-maker*.
MAKING, Tszkuri; shihō. *One's own* —, te-saku; tezaiku.
MALADY, Yamai; biyōki.
MALE, Nan; o; osz; yu. — *and female*, nan-niyo; me-o; mesz-osz; shi-yu.
MALARIA, Jaki; akki; shōreidoku.
MALEDICTION, Akkō; soshiri; noroi.
MALEFACTOR, Zai nin; toganin; tszmibito; meshiudo.
MALEVOLENCE, Urami; ikon.
MALICE, Urami; nikumi; ikon; ishu.
MALIGN, *v.* Zangen szru.
MALIGNANT, Aku; ja; yoko-shima-na.
MALIGNITY, Urami; ikon.
MALL, *n.* Ōdzchi; kakeya.
MALLET, Tszchi.
MALT, Moyashi; kōji.
MALTREAT, Mugoku szru.
MAMMA, Okkā-san.
MAN, H'to; nin; ningen; otoko. *Like a* —, otoko-rashii; h'torashii.
MANACLE, Tegane; tejō; tegase.
MANAGE, Atszkau; tori-atszkau; mote-atszkau; shihai szru; osameru.
MANAGEMENT, Tori-atszkai.
MANAGER, Zamoto.
MANDATE, Mikoto-nori; mei; mōshi-tszke.
MANE, Tategami.
MANES, Tamashii; kompaku; reikon.
MANŒUVER, *n.* Keiko.
MANFULLY, Kitszku; tszyoku.
MANIAC, Kichigai h'to; ranshin mono.

MANIFEST, *a.* Akiraka-na; ichijirushi; meihaku; fummiyō.
MANIFEST, *n.* Okurijō.
MANIFEST, *v.* Arawasz.
MANIFOLD, Ōku; obitadashiku.
MANKIND, Ningen; h'to; nin.
MANLIKE, H'to-rashii.
MANLY, Kitszi; otokogi; otoko-buri ga yoi.
MANNA, Kanro.
MANNER, Mama; sama; yō; tōri; kurai; rui; nari; nari-furi.
MANNERS, Furumai; giyōjō; okonai; narifuri; narawashi; fūzoku; soburi; fūtei.
MAN-OF-WAR, Gunkan; ikusa-bune.
MANSION, Yakata.
MANSLAUGHTER, H'togoroshi.
MANTIS, Kamakiri; tōrō.
MANUFACTURE, *v.* Tszkuru; koshirayeru; saku; sei szru.
MANURE, Koyashi.
MANUSCRIPT, Bunshō; sh'tagaki.
MANY, Ōi; tak'san; tanto; taisō; obitadashii. *How* —, ikura; ikutsz; nanihodo; dore-dake; nambō.
MAP, Kuni-yedz.
MAPLE, Momiji no ki.
MAR, Itamu; sokonau; sondzru.
MARASMUS, Hikan.
MARBLE, Rōseki.
MARCH, *v.* Chōren szru.
MARCH, *n.* Sangatsz.
MARE, Memma.
MARGIN, Kiwa; fuchi; hashi.
MARINE, *a.* Umi no; kai.
MARINER, Sendō; funako; funabito.
MARK, *n.* Shirushi; ato; mato; mejirushi. *Hit the* —, tekichiu.
MARK, *v.* Shirushi wo tszkeru; shirusz; *(notice)*, mi-tomeru.
MARKET, Ichi; sōba. — *price*, sōba. — *people*, ichi-bito. — *place*, ichi-ba; *None in the* —, shinagire.
MARRIAGE, Konrei; yomedori. *To give in* —, yomi ni yaru; meawaseru.
MARROW, Kotsz-dzi; dzi.
MARRY, Metoru; yome wo toru. — *off a daughter*, katadzkeru.
MARS, K'wa-sei.
MARSH, Nama; sawa.
MARTEN, Ten.
MARTIAL, Ikusa no; bu; gun.
MARVEL, *n.* Fushingi.
MARVEL, *v.* Ayashiku omō; ayashimu; fushingi ni omō; ibukashiku omō; fushin ni omō.
MARVELOUS, Ayashii; fushin-naru; ibukashii; fushingi-naru.
MASCULINE, Otokomasari.
MASH, Oshi-kudaku; oshi-tszbusz; hishigeru; hishigu.
MASK, Men.
MASON, Ishiya.
MASS, Kasa; hōji; tszizen.
MASSACRE, H'togoroshi.
MASSY, Omoi.
MAST, Hobashira; hashira. *Foremast*, maye-bashira. *Main* —, ōbashira. *Mizzen* —, atobashira.
MASTER, Danna; shujin; aruji; kashira.
MASTERY, Ri; kachi.
MASTICATE, Kami-konasz.
MASTURBATION, Sendzri.
MAT, *n.* Tatami; goza; mushiro; komo.
MAT, *v.* Tatami wo shiku; komo wo tsztszmu.
MATCH, *n.* Tszkegi; hinawa; aite.
MATCH, *v.* Au; awaseru; sorō; naraberu; hiki-ateru; hi szru; hitteki szru.
MATCHLESS, Busō; narabi-nashi.
MATCHLOCK, Teppō.
MATCH-MAKER, Nakōdo; baishaku; chiunin.
MATE, Aite. *School* —, dōgaku.
MATE, *v.* Awaseru; soroyeru.
MATERIAL, *a.* Katachi aru; u-giyōtai; taisetsz-na. — *and immaterial*, uzō-muzō.
MATERIAL, *n.* Shina; ji; jiai.
MATERNAL, Haha no.
MATHEMATICS, San-gaku; san.
MATRICE, Kata; ikata.
MATRICULATE, Niugaku.
MATRIMONY, Yengumi.
MATTER, Umi; koto; mono; ji; shina; tane; kusa. *What is the matter?* nanda; dōsh'ta. *Great* —, daiji. *Small* —, wadzka. *No* —, kamai-masen; sashi-kamaye wa nai. *No* — *what*, nanigoto ni yoradz.
MATTER, *v.* Umu; kamau.
MATTRESS, F'ton; shitone; tentoku.
MATURE, *v.* Juku szru; umu.
MATURE, *a.* Juku-sh'ta; unda; neru.
MAW, Yebukuro.
MAXIM, Dōri.
MAY, *n.* Gogatsz.
MAY, *v.* *Formed by the potent. suffix;* yeru; *or* rareru; *neg.* yenu, *or* rarenu; maszmai, *or* mai; *also by the fut. or dub. suffix;* shō; mashō; ō; dearo; *also in other ways; as. If the weather is pleasant I may go*, otenki nara yuki-mashō.

If your work is done you may go, shigoto ga szudara itte mo yoi. *May I go to Yedo?* Yedo ye itte yoroshū gozarimasz ka, *or* Yedo ye itte mo yoi ka. *May I pass through this road?* kono michi wo tōtte mo yoi ka. *You may not*, tōtte wa warui. *If the breach is not healed they may fight*, naka wo naosaneba kenk'wa wo szru darō. *It may not rain, but I will take my umbrella with me*, furu-mai keredomo kasa wo motte-ikō.

MAYOR, Machi-bugiyō.

ME, Watakushi; ore; ware.

MEAL, *n.* Meshi; gohan; gozen; jiki; ko; kona. *Wheat* —, udonko; komugi-noko; mempu. *Buckwheat* —, sobako. *Indian* —, tomorokoshi-no-ko.

MEAN, *a.* Iyashii; gesen-na; kechi na; shidz; chiu-na. — *while*, aida; ma.

MEAN, *n.* Chiu; nakaba.

MEANS, Shinsho; shindai; kane. *By — of*, de; wo motte; nite. *By all means*, zehi; kesh'te; kitto; kanaradz. *By no means, the same words with a negative verb.*

MEAN, *v.* Riyōken; tszmori; omō; naze; dō iu kokoro de.

MEANING, Kokoro; wake; imi; riyōken; tszmori.

MEANLY, Iyashiku; miszborashiku.

MEASLES, Hash'ka; mashin.

MEASURE, Monosashi; shaku; kanejaku; kujirajaku; masz; hakari; hodo; kenzao.

MEASURE, *v.* Hakaru; kenchi wo utsz.

MEASUREMENT, Nori.

MEAT, *n.* Niku; tabe-mono.

MECHANIC, Shoko-nin.

MECHANISM, Saiku.

MECONIUM, Kanibaba.

MEDDLE, Kamau; sawaru; ijiru; tonjaku szru; tori-au; deszgiru; kakawaru; k'wankei szru.

MEDDLER, Yajimma; deszgi-mono.

MEDIATE, *v.* Tori-nasz; tori-atszkau; tori-motsz; atszkau.

MEDIATION, Tori-atszkai; atszkai.

MEDIATOR, Chiu-nin; atszkai.nin; naka-dachi.

MEDICAL-ART, I-jutsz. — *fee*, yakurei. — *advertisement*, nōgaki. — *virtue*, yakuriki; kōnō. — *compound*, yakuzai. — *prescription*, ihō.

MEDICINAL, — *plant*, yakusō.

MEDICINE, Kuszri; yakushu. *Price of* —, yakudai. *Virtues of* —, kōnō; yakuriki. *Quality of a* —, yaku-hin. — *chest*, yaku-rō. *To take* —, kuszri wo nomu; fukuyaku szru.

MEDITATE, *v.* Kangayeru; zazen szru.

MEDITATION, Zazen; kagaye.

MEDIUM, Chiu. *Just* —, uchiba. — *quality*, chiu-dōri.

MEDLEY, Mucha-kucha; konzatsz.

MEEK, Ontō; onjun; niuwa.

MEET, *v.* Au. — *together*, atszmaru; yoru; k'wai szru.

MEETING, Atszmari; ai; k'wai; ochi-ai.

MEETING-HOUSE, K'waisho; atszmari-dokoro; hai-den.

MELANCHOLY, Kiutsz; ki ga fusagu; shinki; usa.

MELLOW, Yawaraka.

MELODY, Ne; oto.

MELON, Uri.

MELT, *v.* Toku; *or* tokeru.

MEMBER, Yeda; h'to; mono.

MEMENTO, Katami; yui-motsz; yudzri-mono.

MEMOIR, Giyō-jō-sho; ichi-dai-ki.

MEMORANDUM, Kaki-tome; kaki-tszke; hagaki; oboye-gaki. — *book*, tome-chō.

MEMORIAL, Katami; tsztaye.

MEMORY, Oboye; mono-oboye; kioku. *To recite from* —, sorandzru.

MEN, H'to; ningen.

MENACE, Korasz; odosz.

MEND, *v.* Naosz; tszkurō; aratameru; hidatsz; masaru.

MENDICANT, Kojiki.

MENIAL, Ge-nan; ge-jo; shimobe.

MENSES, Tszki no mono; sawari; keiszi; gekke; tszki-yaku; keikō.

MENTION, *v.* Iu; hanasz.

MERCER, Gofukuya.

MERCHANDISE, Ni; nimotsz; shina; shiromono.

MERCHANT, Akindo; akiudo; shōnin.

MERCHANT-MAN, Akinaibune; nibune; shōsen; bai-sen.

MERCIFUL, Jihi no fukai; jihi-bukai; awaremi-bukai; nasake no aru; nasake-bukai.

MERCILESS, Jihi-naki; nasake-nai.

MERCURY, Midz-gane; szigin.

MERCY, Jihi; awaremi.

MERELY, Tada; nomi; bakari.

MERIDIAN, Nitchiu; mahiru.

MERIT, Kō; isaō; kudoku.

MERIT, *v.* Atarimaye; beki; hadz; *as, a faithful servant merits praise*, chiu-naru kerai wa shō-szbeki mono da.

MERITORIOUS, Shō-szbeki ; homerareru ; kō-aru. —*deed*, kō.
MERMAID, Nin-g'yo.
MERRY, Omoshirogaru; nikoyaka.
MESH, Me.
MESS, *v.* Taberu.
MESSAGE, Kōjō; tayori; otodzre; shōsoku.
MESSENGER, Tszkai.
MESSMATE, Dō-shuku.
METAL, Kane.
METALLURGIST, Kanefuki.
METAMORPHOSE, Hendzru; hen-k'wa szru; henge szru; bakeru.
METEMPSYCHOSIS, Umare-kawari; ruten; rinden; rinye.
METEOR, Yobaiboshi; riusei.
METHOD, Shimari; torishimari.
METROPOLIS, Miyako.
METTLESOME, Kitszi.
MEW, Niya-niya.
MIASMA, Akki.
MICA, Kirara; ummo.
MICROSCOPE, Mushi megane; kembikiyō.
MIDDAY, Nitchiu; mahiru.
MIDDLE, Mannaka; nakaba; chiu-ō. —*ages*, chiu-ko; nakagoro; naka-mukashi. —*aged*, chiu-nen.
MIDDLE-MAN, Chiu-nin; nakōdo; saitori; kuaiunin.
MIDDLING, Kanari; dzibun; chiu-hin; chiu gurai; chiu-dōri.
MIDNIGHT, Yonaka.
MIDST, Naka; uchi; chiu; nakaba; saichiu; chiuto; chiu-dō.
MIDSUMMER, Chiu ka.
MIDWIFE, Toriagebaba.
MIDWINTER, Chiutō.
MIEN, Nari.
MIGHT, *n.* Chikara; ikioi; sei; tszyoki; riki.
MIGHT, *pret. of may, is thus formed: if he had called the Doctor earlier he might have recovered*, hayaku isha ni kakattara naoru de attarō. *If he had wished he might have gone*, ki-ni-ittara yuku de attarō. *I might have sold them last year*, kiyo-nen urude attarō. *Don't fire the gun, you might shoot somebody*, teppō wo hanasz na h'to ni atarō mo shirenu. *Don't cross on the log you might fall*, marukibashi wo wataru na ochiō mo shirenu.
MIGHTILY, Tszyoku; ōki-ni; hageshiku; kibishiku; hiroku.
MIGHTY, Tszyoi; hageshii; kibishii; ōkii; ikō; gōsei.

MIGRATE, Utszru.
MILD, Matai; umai; hodoyoi.
MILDEW, Kabi.
MILDLY, Mataku; umaku; hodoyoku.
MILE, Ri. *Equal to* niri-han *of English mile. Half a mile*, han-michi.
MILE-STONE, Ichiridzka.
MILITARY, Bu. —*class*, buke. —*science*, budō; bugei; gumpō; —*arms*, bugu; buki. —*power*, bui. —*merit*, budō. —*fame*, bumei.
MILK, Chichi.
MILK, *v.* Chichi wo shiboru.
MILKY-WAY, Ama-no-gawa; ginga.
MILL, Usz.
MILLET, Awa.
MILLION, H'yaku-man; oku.
MILT, Hararago.
MIMIC, *n.* Maneshi.
MIMIC, *v.* Maneru. —*others*, h'to-mane wo szru.
MINCE, *v.* Tataku.
MIND, Kokoro; shin; ki; nen; i; riyōken; omoi; tszmori; zonjiyori; zombun; zoni; zonnen.
MIND, *v.* Nen wo ireru; ki wo tszkeru; kokoro ni kakeru; itō; mochi-iru; toriau; tonjaku.
MINE, *a.* Watakushi no; waga.
MINE, *v.* Horu.
MINE, *n.* Mabu; ana.
MINER, Kane-hori.
MINERAL, Kōbutsz.
MINGLE, Mazeru; kondzru; kaki-mazeru; awazeru.
MINIATURE, Nigao.
MINISTER, *For foreign minister the English word*, Minisztor *is now universally use. Japanese minister of foreign affairs*, gaikoku-bugiyō.
MINISTER, *v.* Tsztomeru; hodokosz.
MINISTRY, Tsztome; yakume.
MINT, *n.* Gin-za.
MINT, *n.* Hakka.
MINUTE, *a.* Chīsai; komayaka-na; szkoshi.
MINUTELY, Kuwashiku; komayaka-ni; isaini; tszbusa-ni; saimitsz-ni; koma-goma to.
MIRACLE, Fushigi.
MIRACULOUS, Fushigi-na.
MIRAGE, Nago; shinkirō.
MIRE, Doro.
MIRROR, Kagami.
MIRTH, Tawamure; kiyō.

MISAPPREHEND, Kiki-chigau; kiki-sokonau; omoi-chigau.
MISBEHAVIOR, Busahō; burei; shitszrei.
MISCALCULATE, Kazoye-chigau; hakari-chigau; tszmori-chigau.
MISCALL, Yobi-chigayeru.
MISCARRY, Hadzreru; ataranu; deki-sokonau; hansan szru; nagarezan; riuzan szru.
MISCELLANEOUS, — *writings*, dzi-hitsz; mampitsz; zassho.
MISCHANCE, Fu-un; fu-shiawase.
MISCHIEF, Warusa; itadzra.
MISCHIEVOUS, Itadzra-na.
MISCHIEF-MAKER, Goma-szri.
MISCONCEPTION, Omoi-chigai; riyōken-chigai; kokoro-chigai; omoi-ayamari.
MISCONDUCT, Fugiyōgi; fugiyō-seki.
MISCONJECTURE, Sziriyō-chigai; riyōken-chigai.
MISCONSTRUE, Honyaku-chigai; toki-ayamaru.
MISDATE, Hi wo kaki-ayamaru; hidori-chigai.
MISDIRECT, Namaye-chigai.
MISER, Shiwambō; kechina h'to; rinshoku na h'to.
MISERABLE, Nanju na; nangi-na; wabishiki.
MISERLY, Shiwai; rinshoku na; yabusaka; kechi-na.
MISERY, Nangi; nanjū; kurō.
MISFORTUNE, Wazawai; sainan; fukō.
MISHAP, Fukō; ayamachi.
MISINTERPRET, Toki-ayamaru; honyaku chigai; handan chigai; geshi chigai.
MISJUDGE, Mitate-chigai; tszmori-chigai.
MISLAY, Oki-chigai; oki-waszreru.
MISLEAD, Mayowasz; madowasz.
MISLETOE, Hoya; yadorigi.
MISMANAGE, Shi-soknau; shi-kujiru.
MISPLACE, Oki-chigai; oki-waszreru.
MISPRINT, Kaki-chigau.
MISPRONOUNCE, Ī-sokonau; ī-chigau; īayamaru.
MISQUOTE, Hiki-chigau.
MISREPRESENT, Īmageru; itszwate noberu.
MISRULE, Midare.
MISS, *v.* Hadzreru; machigau; mayō; miyenakunaru; nuku.
MISS, San.
MISSING, Naku-natta; ushinatta.
MISSPELL, Kanadzkai chigai.
MISSPEND, Tsziyasz; mudadzkai.
MISSTEP, Fumi-hadzsz.
MIST, Kiriame; nuka-ame.
MISTAKE, *v.* Ayamaru; machigau; sonjiru; sokonau; sōi.
MISTAKE, *n.* Ayamachi; ochido; sakugo; shi-ochi.
MISTER, San; sama.
MISTIMED, Ori ni awanu; basho ni awanu.
MISTRESS, San; kamisan; goshinzo; iro-onna.
MISTRUST, Fushin ni omō; ibukashiku omō; utagau.
MISUNDERSTAND, Kokoroye-chigau; omoi-chigau.
MISUSE, Tszkai-sokonau; mochi-ayamaru.
MITIGATE, Nadameru; gendzru; yawarageru; karuku naru.
MIX, Mazeru; majiru; kaki-mazeru; kondzru; awaseru; konran; konzatsz.
MIZZEN-MAST, Atobashira.
MOAN, *v.* Unaru; umeku; naku; kanashimu.
MOAT, Hori.
MOB, Ikki; sōdō.
MOCK, Maneru; azakeru; azawarau; gurō szru; warau; naburu.
MOCKERY, Gurō; chōrō.
MODE, Yō; tōri; mama; sama; furi.
MODEL, Kata; tehon; mihon; hinagata.
MODEL, *v.* Katadoru.
MODERATE, *v.* Hikayeru; gendzru; habuku.
MODERATE, *a.* Chiu-gurai-no; nami-no; hodo no yoi.
MODERATION, Hikayeme; uchiba.
MODERN, Imo no; tōji-no. — *times*, konsei; konji. *Ancient and* —, ko-kon.
MODEST, Hadzkashigaru; hajirau; uchiki.
MODESTY, Yenriyo; habakaru; hige.
MODIFY, Kayeru.
MOIST, Nureta; shimetta; uruoi; urumu.
MOISTEN, *v.* Nurasz; shimesz; uruosz.
MOISTURE, Shikke.
MOLAR-TOOTH, Okuba.
MOLE, Muguramochi; hokuro; doriyō.
MOLLIFY, Yawarageru; nadameru; yurumeru.
MOMENT, Henshi; kata-toki. *In a* —, chotto; tachi-machi; shuyu; sznka; sznin. *Of* —, daiji-na; taisetsz-na; setszna. *Last* —, kiwadoi.
MOMENTOUS, Daji-na; taisetsz-naru.
MOMENTUM, Hadzmi; sei; ikioi.
MONARCH, Tenshi; ō; kashira; saishō.
MONASTERY, Tera; ji.
MONEY, Kane; kinsz; kinsen; kingin.

MONEY-BAG, Saifu; kane-ire.
MONEY-CHANGER, Riyōgaye-ya.
MONEY-LENDER, Kane-kashi.
MONEY-LESS, Kane-nai.
MONKEY, Saru.
MONOPOLY, Kabu.
MONSTROUS, Kik'wai-na; hen-na; igiyō; keshō-no mono.
MONTH, Tszki; getsz; g'watsz. — *about*, kaku-getsz.
MONTHLY, Tszki-dzki; maigetsz.
MONUMENT, Hi; seki-hi.
MOON, Tszki; getsz. *Full* —, mangetsz. *New* —, mikka-dzki.
MOON-LIGHT, Tszki-akari; tszki-kage. — *night*, tszki-yo; getsz-ya.
MOOR, No; nobara.
MOOT, Arasō; rondzru.
MORAL, — *philosophy*, shingaku.
MORALITY, Michi; dōri.
MORE, Nao; mada; yo; amari; yori; masaru; ma.
MORE *and more*, Masz-masz; iyo-iyo; zōchō; iyamasz; itodo. *How much more*, mash'te; iwanya. *A little more*, mo szkoshi; machitto.
MOREOVER, Sono wiye ni; mata; nao; naosara; nao-mata; mata wa; katsz; katszmata.
MORNING, Asa; chō; kesa; hirumaye.
MORNING-GLORY, Asagao.
MORROW, Miyō-nichi; ash'ta. — *morning*, miyō-asa. — *evening*, miyō-ban.
MORTAL, Shinuru hadz; shiszbeki; ningen. — *wound*, omode. — *disease*, shini yamai
MORTAR, Niuhachi; usz; kabe; tszchi.
MORTGAGE, *v.* Hiki-ate ni szru.
MORTIFICATION, Funiku.
MORTIFY, Kusaru.
MORTISE, Hozo-ana.
MOSS, Koke.
MOST, Ichiban; goku; itatte; mottomo; hanahada. *The most part*, taigai; ōkata; arakata; tai-tei; tairiyaku; aramashi. *At the most*, seisai.
MOSTLY, Taigai; tairiyaku; ōkata; taitei.
MOTH, Shimi; hiru.
MOTHER, Haha; okkā-san; ofukuro.
MOTHER *in law*, Shūtome.
MOTION, Undō; ugoki; hataraki.
MOTION, *v.* Maneku.
MOTIVE, Kokoro; wake; yuye; riyōken.
MOTTLED, Madara; buchi; mura.

MOULD, *n.* Kata; ikata; kabi.
MOULD, *v.* Katadoru; kabiru.
MOULDER, Kudzreru.
MOULDING, Oshi-buchi.
MOULDY, Kabitszku; kabikusai.
MOULT, Kegawari; toya.
MOUND, Tszka.
MOUNT, *v.* Ageru; nobiru; noru. — *guard*, ban wo szru.
MOUNTAIN, Yama; san.
MOUNTEBANK, Yashi.
MOURN, Kanashimu; naku; nageku.
MOURNFUL, Kanashii; urei; itamashii.
MOURNING, Imi; kichiu; mochiu. — *clothes*, mofuku. *End of* —, imiake.
MOUSE, Hatszka-nedzmi.
MOUTH, Kuchi. *Expression of* —, kuchimoto.
MOVE, Ugoku *or* ugokasz; undō szru; utszru; hikkosz; hakobu; kandzru. — *with friction*, kishimu.
MOVEMENT, Hataraki; undō; guai; ambai; hashiri.
MOW, Nagu; karu; kiru. — *down*, nagifuseru.
MOXA, Kiu; yaito.
MUCH, Tak'san; tanto; taisō; ōki-ni; yoppodo; osa-osa; hodo; dake; kurai. *How* —, ikura; ikutsz; nambō; nani-hodo; dore-dake. — *more*, mash'te; iwan-ya. *Twice as* —, bai; nisōbai. *So* —, kono kurai. *Too* —, amari.
MUCILAGE, Nori.
MUCILAGINOUS, Nebaru; neba-neba.
MUCUS, — *of nose*, hanashiru.
MUD, Doro. *Besmeared with* —, doro-darake.
MUDDY, Nigoru; nukaru; nigosz.
MUFFLE, Kaburu.
MULBERRY *tree*, Kuwa; kōdz; kaji; kōzo.
MULCT, Batszkin; k'wa-riyō.
MULE, Roba; usagi-uma.
MULTIPLICATION, Kake-zan.
MULTIPLIED, Kadz-kadz.
MULTIPLY, Masz; fuyeru; habikoru; shigeru.
MULTITUDE, Ōzei; tak'san; ōi.
MUM, Damaru; moku.
MUMPS, Hasami-bako to iu yamai.
MUNITION, Gunki; buki.
MURDER, *n.* H'togoroshi.
MURDERER, Geshinin.
MURIATIC ACID, Shiosz.
MURMUR, Tszbuyaku; unaru.

MUSHROOM, Take; kusabira.
MUSIC, Gaku; hiyōshi; ongaku. *Instruments of* —, nari-mono.
MUSIC-BOOK, Fu.
MUSK, Jakō.
MUSKET, Teppō.
MUSKMELON, Makuwauri.
MUSLIN, Momen; sarashi.
MUSQUITO, Ka. — *net*, kaya; kachō.
MUST, Kanaradz; kitto; zehi; *also formed by two negatives; as*, yukaneba naran, *must go*. Mineba naran, *must see*.
MUSTARD, Karashi.
MUSTER, *n*. Tehon; mihon.
MUSTER, *v*. Atszmeru.
MUSTY, Kabi-kusai; museru.
MUTABLE, Hen-k'wa szru; kawaru.
MUTE, *n*. Oshi.
MUTE, *a*. Damaru, mokunen.
MUTINY, Sōdō.
MUTTER, Tszbuyaku.
MUTTON, H'tszji no niku.
MUTUALLY, Tagai-ni; tomo-ni; katami-ni; komo-gomo.
MUZZLE, *n*. Kutszgo; tsztsz-guchi. *To* —, kutszgo wo hameru.
MY, Watakushi no; waga.
MYRIAD, Man; yorodz.
MYRRH, Motszyaku.
MYSELF, Jibun; jishin; onore; midzkara.
MYSTERIOUS, Satori-gataki; wakaranu; ibukashii.
MYSTERY, Inji; ōgi; himitsz; okui.
MYSTIFY, Ī-kuromeru; īmagirasz.

N

NAIL, Kugi; tszme.
NAKED, Hadaka; ratei.
NAME, *n*. Na; namaye; mei; nanori; miyōku; miyōmon.
NAME, *v*. Na wo tszkeru; nanoru; nadzkeru; sho szru; gosz.
NAMELESS, Na no nai; mumei.
NAMELY, Sznawachi.
NAPE, Chirike.
NAPKIN, Tenugui.
NARCOTIC, Mayaku; maszizai.
NARRATE, Noberu; tszgeru; kikaseru; hanasz; monogataru; chindzru.
NARRATION, Monogatari.
NARROW, *a*. Semai; hosoi.
NARROW, *v*. Semaku szru; chijimeru; sebameru; hosomeru.
NARROWLY, Semaku; karōjite.
NASAL-SOUND, Hana-goye.
NASAL-POLYPUS, Hanatake.
NASTY, Madzi.
NATION, Kuni; koku.
NATIONAL, — *customs*, kokufū. — *law*, kokuhō. — *government*, koku-sei. — *production*, kokusan.
NATIVE, *of a place*, tochi no h'to. — *place*, kokiyō; furusato; kiuri.
NATIVITY, Tanjō; umare.
NATURAL, Umaretszki-no; atarimaye; tōzen. — *disposition*, honshō.
NATURALLY, Umaretszki-ni; zentai; g'wanrai; shizen; shōtoku.
NATURE, Shō; shitsz; umaretszki; seishitsz; shō-ai; sei.
NAUGHT, Muda-ni; munashiku. *Set at* —. karondzru; naigashiro-ni szru.
NAUGHTY, Warui.
NAUSEATE, Mukadzku; muka-muka szru; haki-sō ni naru.
NAUTILUS, Hotategai.
NAVEL, Heso; hozo. — *string*, heso no o.
NAVIGABLE, Fune ga tōru.
NAVIGATE, Fune wo tszkau.
NEAR, Chikai; soba. — *way*, haya-michi.
NEAR, *adv*. Masa-ni; hotondo.
NEAR, *v*. Chikayoru; chikadzku; yoru; nozomu; sashi-kakaru; kakaru.
NEARLY, Chikaku; masa-ni; kakaru; hotondo; yoppodo; hobo. — *all*, tai-tei; taigai; ta-bun; ōkata; tai-han. — *done*, yoppodo dekita.
NEAR-SIGHTED, Chikame.
NEAT, Kirei; teinei.
NEATLY, Kirei-ni; teinei-ni.
NECESSARY, Kanaradz; nakute kanawanu; yamu koto wo yedz; yondokoronai; yoginai.
NECK, Kubi; nodo.
NECK-CLOTH, Kubi-maki.
NECKLACE, Kubitama.
NECROMANCER, Mahō-tszkai.
NEED, Yō; iriyō; yōni-tatsz. *More than one needs*, yobun; yokei. *Not needed*, fuyō.
NEEDLE, Hari.
NEEDLE-BOX, Haribako.
NEEDLE-WORK, Harishigoto.
NEEDLESSLY, Muda-ni; munashiku; itadzra-ni.
NEEDY, Madzshii; hinkiu-na; bimbō.

NEFARIOUS, Futoi; aku; ashiki; nikui.

NEGLECT, *v.* Okotaru; yudan wo szru; soriyaku ni szru; darumu; orosoka.

NEGLIGENCE, Okotari; yudan; tai-man; yurukase.

NEGLIGENTLY, Soriyaku ni; somatsz-ni; nen wo iredz-ni; orosoka-ni.

NEGOTIATE, Atszkau; tori-atszkau; hakarau; tori-hakarau.

NEGOTIATOR, Atszkai-nin.

NEGRO, Kurombō.

NEIGH, Inanaku; ibau.

NEIGHBOR, Tonari; kinjo-na-h'to. *Next — but one*, mata-donari.

NEIGHBORHOOD, Kinjo; kimpen; atari; kinzai; moyori.

NEIGHBORING, — *states*, kingoku. — *village*, kinson; kingō.

NEPHEW, Oi.

NERVE, Shinkei.

NEST, Sz.

NESTLING, Szgomori.

NET, Ami.

NETTLE, Ira-kusa.

NEUTRAL, Chiu-ritsz szru; katayoranu.

NEVER, Itszto-temo; katszte nashi; tszi-ni nai.

NEVERTHELESS, Shikashi-nagara; keredomo; saredomo; iyedomo.

NEW, Atarashii; shin. — *goods*, shintō no shina. — *edition*, shimpan.

NEWS, Shimbun; tayori; shinsetsz; chindan; chinsetsz.

NEW-COMER, Shinzan.

NEWS-PAPER, Shimbunshi.

NEW-TEA, Shincha.

NEW-YEAR, Shin-nen; kai-nen.

NEW-YEAR'S DAY, Ganjitsz. — *eve*, joya.

NEW-YEAR'S GIFT, Toshidama.

NEXT, Tszgi-no. — *day*, akuru hi; yokujitsz. — *month*, rai-getsz; yoku-tszki. — *year*, rai-nen; yoku-nen; akuru-toshi. — *world*, rai-se. — *spring*, rai-shun.

NICE, Kirei-na; teinei.

NICK, Kidz; kake. — *of time*, kiwadoi.

NICKED, Koboreru; kakeru.

NICKNAME, Ada-na.

NIECE, Mei.

NIGGARD, Shiwambō; shiwai; rinshoku-na; yabusaka.

NIGH, Chikai. — *to*, nosomu; masa-ni; hotondo.

NIGHT, Yoru; ya; ban; yabun; yo. *Whole* —, yodōshi; yomoszgara. *To-night*, kom-ban. *Last* —, saku-ban. *To-morrow* —. miyō-ban. *In the* —, yachiu. *Late at* —, yofukai. *Lasting all* —, ariake; akasz. — *about*, kakuya.

NIGHT-BLINDNESS, Torime.

NIGHT-BOAT, Yofune.

NIGHT-CLOTHES, Nemaki; yogi.

NIGHTLY, Mai-ban.

NIGHTMARE, Umasareru; osowareru.

NIGHT-SWEAT, Ne-ase.

NIGHT-SOIL, Shimogoye.

NIGHT-WATCH, Yoban.

NIMBLE, Ashibaya.

NIMBUS, Kōmiyō.

NINE, Kokonotsz; ku.

NINETEEN, Jūku.

NINETEENTH, Jūku-ban.

NINETIETH, Kujū-ban.

NINETY, Kujū.

NINTH, Ku-ban; kuban-me.

NIPPLE, Chi-mame.

NITRATE OF POTASH, Shōseki.

NITRATE OF SILVER, Shōsangin.

NITRIC ACID, Shōsekisan.

NO, Iye; iya; nai; *and neg. suff.*, nu; dz; de; mai. — *matter*, kamai-masen. *No help for it*, shikata ga nai; shiyō ga nai.

NOBLE, Tattoki; omoki; takai; kenage. — *and ignoble*, ki-sen.

NOBLEMAN, Daimiyō; kugo; samurai.

NOBLY, Appare-na.

NOBODY, Dare mo nai.

NOD, Unadzku.

NOISE, Oto; ne; sawagi; hibiki. *To make* —, yakamashii; sawagu. sōdo szru; zazameku; zomeku.

NOISE, *v.* Fure-chirasz; hiromeru.

NOISELESS, — *steps*, nuki-ashi; shinonde.

NOISOME, Doku-na; aku; warui; kusai.

NOISY, Yakamashii; sawagashii; sōzōshii.

NOMINATE, Tateru.

NONE, Mo nai.

NOON, Mahiru; nitchiu; haku-chiu.

NOOSE, Wana.

NORTH, Kita; kita no hō; hoku; ne no hō.

NORTH-EAST, Tō-hoku; ushi-tora no hō. — *wind*, narai.

NORTH-POLE, Hokkiyoku.

NORTH-STAR, Hokkiyokusei; hokushin.

NORTH-WEST, Kita-nishi; seihoku; inu-i no hō.

NORTH-WIND, Kita-kaze; hoku-fū.

NOSE, Hana. *To blow the* —, kamu. *Blow the — with the fingers*, tebana wo kamu. — *bleed*, hanaji.

NOSE-BAND, Hana-gawa.
NOSE-RING, Hanagai.
NOSTRIL, Hana no ana.
NOSTRUM, Hi-yaku.
NOT, *Is not, or have not*, Nai. *Do not*, na; nakare; muyō. *Not yet*, mada, *or* imada *with a neg. verb*. — *the least*, kaimu.
NOTABLE, Ki-miyō; miyō-naru.
NOTCH, Kiri-kata.
NOTCHED, Kakeru; koboreru.
NOTE, *n*. Shirushi; chiu; fu; tegata; tegami; kaki-tszke; kaki-tome.
NOTE, *v*. Tszkeru; kaki-tomeru; mi-tomeru; shirusz; chiu-kai szru; chiushaku szru.
NOTE-BOOK, Oboye-chō.
NOTED, Nadakai; kōmei.
NOTHING, Nani mo nai; mu-ichi-motsz. — *but this*, kore-bakari; kore kiri.
NOTICE, *v*. Miru; mi-tszkeru; mi-tomeru; kayeri-miru; kamau.
NOTICE, *n*. Fure; shirase. *Give* —, shiraseru; tszgeru. — *of others*, h'to-me
NOTIFY, Kikaseru; shiraseru.
NOTION, Kokoroye; omoi; riyōken; tszmori.
NOTIONAL, Uwatszku.
NOTORIETY, G'wai-bun; miyōmon.
NOTWITHSTANDING, Saredomo; keredomo; iyedomo, nagara.
NOUN, Tai no kotoba.
NOURISH, Yashinau; sodateru; bu-iku szru; yōiku szru.
NOURISHMENT, Tabe-mono; yashinai-mono; kui-mono; shokumotsz.
NOVEL, *n*. Kusazōshi, sakumono-gatari.
NOVEMBER, Jū-ichi-gatsz.
NOVICE, Heta; shimbochi; shami; shoshin.
NOW, Ima; tōji; imasara. — *and then*, ori-ori; ori-fushi; ō-ō.
NOWHERE, Doko ni mo nai.
NOXIOUS, Doku-na; gai ni naru; tame ni naranu; sawaru.
NOZZLE, Kuchi.
NUISANCE, Gai; jama.
NUMB, Shibireru; mahi szru.
NUMBER, *n*. Kadz.
NUMBER, *v*. Kazoyeru.
NUMBERLESS, Kazoyerarenu.
NUMERICAL, — *order*, bandate.
NUMEROUS, Ōi.
NUN, Ama; bikuni; zenni.
NUNNERY, Amadera.
NUPTIAL *presents*, Yuino.
NUPTIALS, Konrei; kon-in.
NURSE, *n*. Mori; kai-hō-nin; kambiyō-nin; togi. *Wet* —, uba; omba.
NURSE, *v*. Mori wo szru; kaihō szru; kambiyō szru; chichi wo nomaseru.
NURTURE, *v*. Yashinau; sodateru; buiku szru.
NUT, Mi.
NUT-GALL, Gobaishi; fushi.
NUTMEG, Nikudzku.
NUTRITIOUS, Yashinau.
NUT-SHELL, Kara.
NUX-VOMICA, Machin.

O

OAK, Kashi-no-ki.
OAKUM, Maihada; *or* makihada; kihada.
OAR, Ro; kai.
OATH, Chikai; seigon.
OBEDIENT, Shitagau; kōkō; kō.
OBEY, Shitagau; fuku szru; nabiku; mochīru; kifuku.
OBJECT, *n*. Ate; me-ate; kokoro-zashi.
OBJECT, *v*. Kotowaru; īfusegu; nan wo tszkeru; kobamu.
OBJECTION, Nan.
OBLATION, Kumotsz; sonaye mono.
OBLIGATION, Beki; hadz; atarimaye.
OBLIGE ME, Dōzo; nani to zo; dōka.
OBLIGED, Yamukoto wo yedz; yondokoro naku; yoginai; kanaradz; zehi naku. *Am obliged to you*, arigato; katajikenō.
OBLIGING, Nengoro-na; shinsetsz-na.
OBLIQUE, Naname; szjikai.
OBLITERATE, Kesz; mametsz.
OBLOQUY, Soshiri; hihō
OBNOXIOUS, Kakawaru.
OBSCENE, Waizatsz. — *story*, irobanashi. — *pictures*, makuraye.
OBSCURE, *a*. Akiraka naranu; fufummiyō.
OBSCURE, *v*. Magirakasz.
OBSEQUIES, Tomorai; sōrei.
OBSEQUIOUS, Hetszrau; kobiru; omoneru; raidō.
OBSERVANCE, Shitagai; mamori.
OBSERVATION, Me; miru.
OBSERVATORY, Temmondai.
OBSERVE, Miru; mitszkeru; iu; hanasz; mamoru; shitagau; okonau.
OBSOLETE, Furumekashii.

OBSTACLE, Jama; sasawari; samatage; koshō.
OBSTINATE, Henkutsz; katakuna; katakurushii; wagamama; kimama ; henshū; kataiji; jōppari.
OBSTINATELY, Kataku.
OBSTREPEROUS, Sawagashii; yakamashii.
OBSTRUCT, Jama wo szru; sasawaru; samatageru; fusagu; fusagaru; kodawaru.
OBSTRUCTION, Jama; sasawari; koshō.
OBTAIN, Yeru; uru; motomeru ; totonoyeru.
OBTRUDE, Sashideru ; deshabaru; oshikomu.
OBTUSE, Don.
OBVIOUSLY, Akiraka; fummiyō.
OCCASION, Koto ; ori ; tszide; yō; wake; yuye. *No occasion,* oyobanu.
OCCASION, *v.* Saseru.
OCCASIONALLY, Ori-fushi; ori-ori; tabi-tabi; tama-tama; tama-ni.
OCCULT, Kakuretaru.
OCCUPANT, Szmai h'to; oru-h'to.
OCCUPY, Szmau; oru; toru.
OCCUPATION, Kagiyō; tosei; shōbai; nariwai.
OCCUR, Au; aru; kakaru.
OCCURRENCE, Koto; yoshi. *Without evil* —, buji. *All the* —, ari-sama.
OCEAN, Umi; kai ; nada.
O'CLOCK, Toki. *Six — in the morning,* ake-mutsz. *Twelve* —, kokonotsz-doki.
OCTOBER, Hachi-gatsz.
OCULIST, Me-isha.
ODD, Medzrashii; mare-na; han; ki. — *and even,* ki-gū.
ODE, Shi ; uta.
ODIOUS, Nikui; kirawashii; niku-nikushii.
ODOR, Nioi.
ODORIFEROUS, Kōbashii.
OF, No. *Of course,* mochiron; shizen.
OFF, *off-hand,* dehōdai; detarame. *Off and on*; *as, off watch,* hi-ban, *on-watch,* tō-ban.
OFFENCE, Tszmi; ochido ; toga; okori.
OFFEND, Okasz; rippuku-saseru; itameru; sakarau; sawaru ; sorashi.
OFFENSIVE, Iya-na; kirai-na; kimusai; kinku; kiza na.
OFFER, *v.* Ageru ; dasz ; kubutsz szru ; tamukeru; sasageru; tatematszru; īireru; yaru. *I offered him a hundred dollars but he would not take it,* h'yaku doru yarō to iutemo toranai. *What offer do you make?* ikura dasō ka.
OFFERING, Kumotsz; tamuke.
OFFICE, Tsztome; yakume; sewa; yakusho; k'wan-shoku. *Holding* —, zai-kin; zaiyaku.
OFFICER, Yakunin.
OFFICIAL, K'wan.
OFFICIATE, Tsztomeru.
OFFICIOUS, Sewa wo yaku.
OFFSET, Yeda.
OFFSPRING, Shison.
OFTEN, Shiba-shiba; tabi-tabi; maido; maimai.
OIL, Abura.
OIL, *v.* Abura wo tszkeru.
OIL-CAKE, Abura-kasz.
OIL-CAN, Abura-tszgi.
OIL-JAR, Abura-tszbo.
OIL-PAINTING, Aburaye.
OIL-PRESS, Abura-shime.
OIL-SHOP, Aburaya.
OIL-TUB, Aburadaru.
OILY, Aburake.
OINTMENT, Kōyaku.
OLD, Furui; ro; kiu; furuberu; hine. *How old?* toshi wa ikutsz. — *times,* mukashi. — *man,* rojin; toshiyori. — *house,* furui-iye; kiu-taku. — *horse,* roba. — *clothes,* furute; furugi; kiburushi. — *rags,* furu-gire. — *furniture,* furu-dōgu. — *rice,* hine-gome. — *friend,* kiu-iu. — *custom,* kiu-rei.
OLDAGE, Oi; rōnen; rō.
OLDER, — *brother,* ani. — *sister,* ane.
OLDEST, — *son,* chaku-shi; sōriyō; chōnan. — *daughter,* ane-muszme.
OLD-FASHIONED, Ko-fū no; furukusai; furumekashii.
OLD-TESTAMENT, Kiuyaku.
OLIVE, Kanran.
OMEN, Zempiyō; kizashi; shō; shirase; yengi. *Good* —, dzigen.
OMINOUS, Fukitsz-na.
OMISSION, Ochido; shiochi; ayamachi; ochi.
OMIT, *v.* Riyaku szru; nuku; otosz; ochiru. — *to write,* kaki-morasz; kaki-otosz. — *to say,* ī-morasz; ī-otosz. — *reading,* yomiotosz.
OMNIPOTENT, Atawazaru koto nashi; dekinu koto nashi.
OMNIPRESENT, Arazaru tokoro nashi.
OMNISCIENT, Shiranu koto nashi.
ON, Wiye; ni; wo. — *foot,* kachi. — *the contrary,* kayette; kekku.
ONCE, Ichi-do; aru-hi; katszte. *At* —, soku-ji; tachi-dokoro; szgu-ni; sokkoku; sokkon.

ONE, Ichi; h'totsz. — *day (uncertain)*, aruhi. *All* —, onajikoto; kamawanu. *One by* —, h'totsz dztsz. — *o'clock*, kokonotsz-han-doki. — *(of a pair)*, kataippō; kata-kata. — *after the other*, tszgi-tszgi-ni; jun-jun-ni. — *person*, h'tori; ichi nin. — *effort*, ikkiyo. — *another*, tagai-ni.

ONE-CORNER, Kata-dzmi.

ONE EYE, Kata-me.

ONE FACE, Kata-omote.

ONE FOOT, Kata-ashi.

OND HAND, Kata-te.

ONE LEG, Kata-ashi.

ONE SIDE, Kata-ippō; katakawa.

ONE WAY, Kata-michi.

ONION, Negi; h'tomoji.

ONLY, Bakari; nomi; tada. — *son*, h'tori muszko. — *child*, h'torigo.

ONSET, Seme.

ONWARD, Szszmu.

OOZE, Deru.

OPAQUE, Tszkitōranu.

OPEN, *v.* Hiraku; akeru; aku; hirogeru; hassz.

OPEN, *a.* Hiraita; aita.

OPENING, Kuchi; ana.

OPENLY, Omote-muki; ōyake; mukidashi; kozen to.

OPERA, Shibai.

OPERATE, Kiku; setszdan szru; kiru.

OPERATION, Hataraki; kiki.

OPHTHALMIA, Gan-biyō; me no yamai.

OPINION, Iken; riyōken; omoi; kokoro; zombun; zonjiyori; zonnen; zoni.

OPIUM, Ahen.

OPPONENT, Aite.

OPPORTUNELY, Oriyoku; chōdo yoi toki.

OPPORTUNITY, Tszide; kō-bin; tayori; yoszga; bin; bingi; ki; ma; hima; ori. — *by ship*, funa-dayori.

OPPOSE, Sakarau; fusegu; tekitai szru; mukayeru; motoru.

OPPOSING, Mukai.

OPPOSITE, Mukai; taiszru; hantai; urahara; sakasama.

OPPRESS, Setageru; kurushimeru; semeru; itaburu.

OPTION, Omōmama; zom-bun; omoi-ire. *Own* —, kokoro ni makaseru; kokoro shidai.

OR, Aruiwa; ka; ya.

ORACLE, Takusen; kami no tszge.

ORAL, Kōjō no. — *instruction*, kuden; kuchidztaye.

ORANGE, Mikan; tachibana.

ORANGE-PEEL, Chimpi.

ORANG-OUTANG, Hihi; shōjō.

ORATOR, Bensha.

ORCHARD, Sono; hatake.

ORCHIS, Sekkoku.

ORDAIN, Sadameru; tateru.

ORDER, *n.* Shidai; narabi; shidara; retsz; ichi; rasshi; geji; sashidz; ītszke; mei; shiki; rei; jun; tszide; shimari; torishimari; riugi; kurai; rui; atszraye; chiu-mon. *In order to*, tame ni; yō ni.

ORDER, *v.* Osameru; ītszkeru; meidzru; atszrayeru; chiu-mon szru.

ORDERLESS, Midareru.

ORDERLY, Chanto sh'ta; tadashiku.

ORDINANCE, Okite; reishiki.

ORDINARY, Tszne no; heijitsz; heizei; fudan; itszmo-no; nabete. — *person*, bonnin. — *clothes*, heifuku.

ORE, Aragane.

ORGAN, Dōgu.

ORGANIZE, Koshirayeru.

ORIFICE, Kuchi; ana.

ORIGIN, Hajimari; moto; okori; ranshō; shohotsz; hottan; minamoto; kongen; kompon; tane; motodate.

ORIGINAL-COPY, Tane-hon; gempon.

ORIGINALLY, G'wanrai; moto-yori; zentai; hon-rai.

ORIGINATE, Hajimeru; okosz; hokki szru; okoru.

ORIGINATOR, Hottō nin; hokki nin.

ORNAMENT, Kazari.

ORPHAN, Minashigo; kodoku.

OSTENSIBLE, Omotemuki; arawa-ni; ōyake.

OSTRICH, Dachō.

OTHER, Hoka; betsz; yoso; ta; aruiwa. — *side*, ano hō; achira. — *day*, konaida. kono-goro; chika-goro.

OUGHT, Beki; hadz; atarimaye. *You ought to have written yesterday*, kinō kakeba yokatta, *or* kinō kakeba yokatta mono wo. *Ought to have bought it*, kayeba yokatta, *or*, kayeba yokatta no ni. *Ought to have gone*, yukeba yokatta mono wo, *or* yukeba yokatta no ni. *You ought to go to-day*, kiyō iku hadz no koto, *or*, kiyō iku beki koto. *Men ought to fear God*, h'to wa kami wo wiyamau hadz no mono.

OUNCE, *troy*, *equals*, hachi momme ni-fun san-rin.

OUR, Warera-no.

OUST, Oshi-nokeru.

OUT, Soto. *Formed by affixing* deru *or* dasz *to the roots of verbs, as.* Kake-dasz *to run out.* Tobi-dasz, *to jump out.* Tori-dasz, *to take out.* *To pour out*, kobosz; tszgu. *To go out (as a fire)*, kiyeru. *To put out (a fire)* kesz. *To be out (of a house)*, rusz; deta. *Out of*, kara; yori; nai. *Out of silk*, ito ga urete shimatta. *Out of oil*, abura ga shimatta. *To be fully out (as an eruption)*, desorō.
OUTCAST, Rōnin; runin; mushuku.
OUTCRY, Sawagi.
OUT-DO, Szgiru; katsz; masaru.
OUTER, Uwa; soto-no. — *darkness*, chiu-u.
OUTFIT, Teate; yōi; shitaku.
OUT-GO, Koyeru; szgiru;.
OUT-LANDISH, Bukotsz-na.
OUT-LAST, Nagaku motsz; nagaku tamotsz; mochi ga yoi.
OUTLAY, Iriyō; niuyō; zappi.
OUT-LEAP, Tobi-kosz; tobi-koyeru.
OUTLET, Deguchi.
OUTLINE, — *sketch*, suji-gaki; sh'tagaki.
OUT-LIVE, Iki-nokoru; okureru.
OUT-NUMBER, Kadz ga koyeru, kadz ga masaru.
OUT-POST, Bansho; sayaku.
OUTRAGE, Hidoime; mugoime.
OUTRAGEOUS, Futoi.
OUTRIDE, Kake-kosz.
OUT-RUN, Hashiri-kosz; kake-kosz.
OUT-SAIL, Hashiri-kosz.
OUT-SELL, Uri-katsz.
OUTSET, Hajimete; hajimari; okori.
OUTSIDE, Soto; hoka; wiye; g'wai-men; uwamuki; uwabe; omote-muki. — *garment*, uwagi. — *coat*, uwanuri.
OUT-WALK, Aruki-kosz.
OUTWARD, Soto; wiye.
OUTWARDLY, Omote-muki-ni; ōyake-ni.
OUT-WEAR, Nagaku motsz; mochi ga yoi.
OUT-WEIGH, ... yori omoi.
OVAL, Tamagonari; dayen; ibitsz.
OVEN, Kama; furo; muro.
OVER, Wiye; yo; szgiru; amaru; nokoru. *To cross* —, wataru; koyeru. *To hand* —, watasz. *To run* —, afureru; koboreru. *To have* —, amaru; nokoru. *To look* —, mi-watasz. *To roll* —, korobu. *Over and* —, kasane-gasane; jūjū. — *again*, kayeru. — *and above*, sono hoka ni; sono wiye ni. — *against*, mukai. *To give over*, yameru; yosz. *All* —, szunda; shimatta. — *the head (deep)*, take ni tatanu. *Something* —, yūyo.
OVERANXIOUS, Anji-szgiru.
OVERAWE, Osoreru; ojikeru.
OVER-BALANCE, Omoszgiru.
OVERBEARING, Ōhei-na; ōfū-na.
OVERBID, Takaku tszkeru.
OVERBOARD, Midz ni hamaru.
OVERCAST, Kumoru.
OVERCAUTIOUS, Tsztszshimi szgiru; yōjin szgiru.
OVERCHARGE, Kakene wo iu; tzke-kake wo szru; komi-szgiru.
OVERCLOUD, Kumoru.
OVERCOME, Katsz.
OVERCONFIDENT, Hokoru.
OVERDO, Shi-szgiru; ni-szgiru; yaki-szgiru; hone-ori-szgiru.
OVERDOSE, Bunriyō ni szgiru.
OVERDRAW, Tori-szgiru; morai-szgiru.
OVERDRIVE, Oi-szgiru.
OVERDUE, Nichigen wo kosz.
OVEREAT, Kui-szgiru; tabe-szgosz.
OVERESTIMATE, Tszmori-szgiru; hakari-szgiru.
OVERFATIGUE, Tszkare-szgiru
OVERFED, Kuwase-szgiru.
OVERFLOW, Afureru; koboreru.
OVERGROW, Habikoru; shigeru.
OVERHANG, Wiye kara deru; nozoku.
OVERHASTY, Amari isogu; isogi-szgiru.
OVERHAUL, Aratameru.
OVERHEAD, Wiye-ni; atama no wiye ni.
OVERHEAR, Kiki-dasz; kiki-tszkeru.
OVERJOY, Amari-yorokobu; ōyorokobi.
OVERLADE, Nose-szgiru; tszmi-szgiru.
OVERLAND, Riku; kuga; oka.
OVERLAP, Kasane-kakeru.
OVERLARGE, Amari ōkii; ōki-szgiru.
OVERLAY, Kasanaru; kakeru.
OVERLOAD, Nose-szgiru; tszmi-szgiru.
OVERLOOK, Mi-watasz; mi-harasz; mi-kosz; sairiyō szru; ōme ni miru; yurusz; kayeri-midz; mi-nogasz; mi-hadz-sz; mi-nokosz; mi-otosz.
OVERMATCH, Katsz; masaru; szgiru.
OVER-MODEST, Yenriyo szgiru; omeru; uchiki-szgiru.
OVER-MUCH, Amari na; szgiru; yokei; yobun.
OVERPAID, Yokei ni yaru; harai-szgiru.
OVERPASS, Szgiru; koyeru.
OVERPLUS, Amari; nokori.
OVERPOWER, Katsz.
OVERPROMPT, Hiya-szgiru.
OVERRATE, Takaku tszmoru; tszmori-szgiru.
OVERREACH, Damasz.

OVERRIDE, Nori-szgiru.
OVERRUN, Shigeru; habikoru; michiru; afureru.
OVERSCRUPULOUS, Kirai-gachi.
OVERSEE, Tszkasadoru; sairiyō szrū; shihai szru.
OVERSEER, Tōriyō; kashira.
OVERSET, Hikuri-kayeru; kutsz-gayeru; hikuri-kayesz.
OVERSIGHT, Mi-otoshi; ayamachi; tszkasadoru koto; shiochi.
OVERSIGHT, Mekubari.
OVERSLEEP, Ne-szgiru.
OVERSPREAD, Ōi-wataru; habikoru; michiwataru.
OVERSTEP, Yuki-kosz; yuki-szgiru.
OVERSTOCK, Mise ni szgiru.
OVERSTRAIN, Ikimi-szgiru.
OVERTAKE, Oi-tszku.
OVERTHROW, Taosz; oshi-taosz; horobosz.
OVERTOP, Wiye ni deru; hīderu.
OVERTRADE, Te ni haru akinai.
OVERTURE, *To make* —, mōshi-ireru; ī-ireru.
OVERTURN, Hikuri-kayesz.
OVERWHELM, Shidzmu.
OVERWORK, Tszkarakasz.
OVIPAROUS, Ranshō.
OWE, *v.* Oi.
OWING, Yotte (yoru); kara; yuye.
OWL, Fukurō; mimidzku.
OWN, *v.* Motsz; hakujō szru; zange szru.
OWN, *a.* Jibun no; jishin no; waga; onoga.
OWNER, Nushi; mochi-nushi.
OX, O-ushi; kotoi.
OXYGEN, Sanso.
OYSTER, Kaki.
OYSTER-SHELL, Kaki-gara.

P

PACE, Fumi.
PACIFIC, Odayaka-na; mutszmajii; shitashii.
PACIFY, Nadameru; nagusameru; shidzmeru; yawarageru.
PACK, *v.* Tszmu; tszmeru.
PACK, *n.* Tsztszmi.
PACKAGE, Tsztszmi; kōri; ba.
PACKET, *ship*, K'wai-sen.
PACK-HORSE, Ni-uma; da-uma; konida-uma.
PACK-SADDLE, Kura.
PAD, Ate; makura.
PADDLE, *n.* Kai.
PADDLE, *v.* Kai de kogu.
PADDY, Ine; kome.
PADLOCK, Jō; jō-maye.
PAGAN, Mokuzō wo ogamu mono.
PAGE, Hira; sobadzkaye.
PAGODA, Tō.
PAIL, Oke; teoke.
PAIN, Itami. *Labor* —, ikimi. *Take pains*, rōszru; tansei.
PAINFUL, Itai; ita-itashii.
PAINT, *v.* Nuru; irodoru; yedoru; saishiki szru.
PAINTING, Irodori. *Oil* —, aburaye.
PAIR, Soku; tszi; tszgai.
PALACE, Kinri; goten.
PALE, Shiroi.
PALISADE, Yarai; saku.
PALLIATE, Karuku iu; iwake wo szru; tori-tszkurau.
PALLID, Aozameru.
PALM, Tanagokoro.
PALM-TREE, Shuro.
PALMISTRY, Tesōmi.
PALPITATION, Dōki; doki-doki.
PALSIED, Shibireru.
PALSY, Chiuki; yoi-yoi; chiushō.
PALTRY, Iyashii; kitanaki.
PAN, Sara; nabe.
PANDER, Zegen; hannin.
PANE, Mai. *One pane of glass*, giyaman ichi mai.
PANIC, Odoroki; bikkuri.
PANNIER, Kago.
PANOPLY, Gusoku; katchiu; yoroi-kabuto.
PANT, Ayegu.
PANTALOON, Hakama; momohiki.
PANTOMIME, Shibai.
PANTRY, Mono-oki.
PAPER, *n.* Kami. *Wall* —, karakami. *News* —, shimbunshi. — *covers*, hiyōshi. *Waste* —, hōgu.
PAPER, *v.* Haru; hari-tszkeru.
PAPER-CUTTER, Kami-kiri.
PAPER-HANGER, Kiyōjiya.
PAPER-HANGINGS, Kara-kami.
PAPER-MAKER, Kami-szki.
PAPER-MILL, Kami-szkiba.
PAPER-STORE, Kamiya.
PAPER-WALLET, Kami-ire.
PAPER-WEIGHT, Bunchin; kesan.
PAPIER-MACHE, Harinuki.

PAPIST, Tenshukiyō na h'to.
PAR, Heikin sōba; jō-nedan.
PARABLE, Tatoye-banashi.
PARADE, Chōren.
PARADE-GROUND, Keikoba.
PARADISE, Gokuraku; tendō; jōdō.
PARAGON, Mihon; tehon; kagami.
PARAGRAPH, Ku.
PARALLEL, Soroi.
PARAMOUR, Mippu; maotoko; iro-otoko; mabu.
PARAPET, Himegaki; rui.
PARASITE, Yadorigi; hoya.
PARASOL, Higasa.
PARBOILED, Namaniye; ibiru.
PARCEL, Tsztszmi; wariai.
PARCEL, *v.* Wari-tszkeru.
PARCH, Kogasz; iru,
PARCHED, Kogeta; karabiru; kawaku.
PARCHING, Hashiyagu; hikarabiru.
PARDON, Yurusz; sha-men szru; yōsha; yūmen; yuriru. — *me*, gomen nasare; kannin kudasare. *To implore* —, wabiru.
PARE, Muku; hagu; kedzru.
PARENT, Oya; fubo; futa-oya; chichi-haha; riyō-shin.
PARISHIONER, Danke; danna; ujiko.
PARK, Niwa.
PARLOR, Zashiki; heya.
PARRICIDE, Oya-koroshi.
PARROT, Ōmu; inko.
PARRY, Ukeru; uke-tomeru.
PARSIMONIOUS, Rinshoku na; shiwai.
PART, Bu; bun; hō; kata; wari-ai; kiriyō; chiye. *For my* —, watakushi ni wa; watakushi ni tszite. *For the most* —, ōkata; taitei; zen-tai. *Take* — *in*, tadzsawaru; katan szru.
PART, *v.* Wakeru; waru; hanareru; hedateru; wakareru; saru; ribetsz szru. *The cable has parted*, tszna ga kireta.
PARTAKE, Adzkaru; kakari-au.
PARTIAL, Kata-hīki; hīki; katayori; yekona; hempa; mibīki.
PARTICIPATE, Adzkaru; tadzsayeru; kakari-au; tadzsawaru.
PARTICLE, Chitto mo; szkoshi-mo; *(in grammar)*, te-ne-wo-ha.
PARTICULAR, *a.* Kakubetsz; betszdan; kuwashii; komayaka; isai-naru; kirai-gachi-na; tashitaru.
PARTICULARS, *n.* Arisama; isai; shisai; kado.
PARTICULARLY, Kuwashiku; komaka-ni; isai-ni; tszbusa-ni; kakubetsz-ni; betsz; dan-ni; bessh'te; koto-ni; sai-mitsz-nisash'te; wakete; chiku-ichi.
PARTING, Ribetsz; hanare; wakare.
PARTITION, *n.* Hedate; shikiri.
PARTITION, *v.* Wari-tszkeru; kubaru; hedateru; shikiru.
PARTNER, Kumi no h'to; nakama.
PARTNERSHIP, Kumi; nakama.
PARTURITION, San szru; umu; shussen. *Easy or natural* —, an-zan. *Difficult or unnatural* —, nan-zan.
PARTY, Nakama; shachiu; hō; kata; k'wai; te.
PASS, *v.* Tōru; utszru; heru; kurasz; kayō; tszyō szru; koyeru; szgiru; okuru. — — *to and fro*, yukiki; kayoi; tōri; ōrai. — *away* kiyeru; nakunaru. *To let* —, tōraseru; tōsz; kayowaseru; kayeri-midz; ōme ni miru. *To come to* —, hatasz. *To* — *by*, tōru; szgiru; koyeru. *To* — *on*, szszmu. *To* — *over*, wataru; koyeru. *To* — *time*, utszru; kurasz; heru. *To* — *the cup*, sasz. — *sentence*, mōshi-tszkeru. — *a law*, sadameru.
PASS, *n.* Nanjo; sessho; tegata; kitte.
PASS-BOOK, Kayoi-chō,
PASS-WORD, Aidz; aikotoba.
PASSABLE, Tōrareru.
PASSAGE, *n.* Michi; dōro; deiriguchi.
PASSENGER, Kiyaku; noru h'to; tōru h'to.
PASSION, Jō; iji; ikiji; ki.
PASSION-FLOWER, Tokei-bana.
PASSIONATE, Tanki; ki no mijikai.
PASSPORT, Kitte; tegata; inkan; menjō.
PAST, *pret.* Szgitta; sznda; tōtta; kosh'ta sannuru; saru; sarinishi.
PAST, *n.* — *time*, koshi-kata; k'wako; izen; ato.
PASTE, Nori.
PASTE, *v.* Haru; tszkeru.
PASTEBOARD, Atszgami; itagami.
PASTIME, Nagusami; asobi; tedzsami; kibarashi.
PASTURE, Kusa.
PATCH, Tszgi; hagi.
PATCH, *v.* Tszgi wo szru; hagu; tszgu; tszdzru.
PATCH-WORK, Hagi-ko.
PATELLA, Hiza no sara.
PATENT, *n.* Kabu.
PATERNAL, Oya no.
PATH, Ko-michi; michi.
PATIENCE, Kannin; shimbō, gaman.
PATIENT, Kannin szru; shimbō szru; gaman szru; shinobu; shinogu; korayeru.

PATIENTLY, Kannin-sh'te; shimbōsh'te; gaman-sh'te; shinonde; shinoide; korayete.
PATOIS, Namari.
PARTRIDGE, Shako.
PATRIMONY, Katoku.
PATRIOT, Chiushin.
PATRIOTISM, Chiushin; chiugi.
PATROL, *n.* Yomawari; yoban; ban-nin.
PATROL, *v.* Ban-szru.
PATRONAGE Okage; sewa; shūsen.
PATRONIZE, Sewa wo szru.
PATTEN, Geta.
PATTER, Bara-bara to furu.
PATTERN, Tehon; mihon; kagami; kibo.
PAUNCH, Yebukuro.
PAUPER, Bimbō-nin; konkiu-nin; monomorai.
PAUSE, *v.* Yaszmu; tamerau.
PAUSE, *n.* Yaszmi.
PAVILLION, Tei
PAVE, Ishi wo shiku.
PAVEMENT, Shiki-ishi.
PAW, Ashi.
PAWN, Sh'chi; kata; hiki-ate; tembutsz. — *of chess*, koma; fu.
PAWN, *v.* Sh'chi ni oku.
PAWNBROKER, Sh'chiya.
PAWNED ARTICLES, Sh'chi-motsz; sh'chigusa; adzkari-mono.
PAY, *v.* Harau. — *a vow*, hodoku. — *out rope*, nawa wo taguri-dasz. — *back*, hemben; hennō; henjō; kayesz; mukuyuru.
PAY, *n.* Dai; chin; shiro; rei; kiukin; yaku-riyō. *Increasing the* —, kazō szru.
PAYABLE, Harau hadz.
PAYDAY, Harai-bi.
PAYMASTER, Kanjō kata.
PAYMENT, Harai; mukui.
PEA, Saya-yendō.
PEACE, Taihei; jisei; odayaka; anshin; raku; ando; annon; anraku; waboku; seihitsz; heian. *To make* —, waboku wo szru; naka-naori wo szru. *Hold the* —, damaru; mokunen szru.
PEACEFUL, Odayaka-na.
PEACEMAKER, Aisatsznin.
PEACH, Momo. — *tree*, momo no ki. — *blossom*, momo no hana. — *color*, momo no iro.
PEACOCK, Kujaku.
PEAK, Mine; zetchō.
PEANUT, Rakk'wanshō.
PEAR, Nashi. — *tree*, nashi no ki.
PEARL, Shinju.
PEARL-DIVER, Ama.
PEARL-OYSTER, Awabi.
PEASANT, H'yak'shō; nōmin.
PEAT, Szkumo.
PEBBLE, Koishi; jari; sazare-ishi.
PECK, (*measure*) *about* = goshō.
PECK, *v.* Tszku; tsztszku.
PECULATE, Nuszmu; kaszmeru.
PECULIAR, Mochimaye; hen-na; miyō-na; kotonaru.
PEDANTIC, Gak'sha-buru; gak'sha-rashiku szru; kōman; namaiki-na; koshaku-na.
PEDDLE, *v.* Seri-uri wo szru; hisagu.
PEDDLER, Seri-akindo; szai; furi-uri.
PEDDLING, Seriuri; seri-akinai.
PEDESTAL, Ishidzye; dodai.
PEDESTRIAN, Kachi.
PEDICLE, Kuki.
PEDIGREE, Keidz; szjime; szjō; ka-kei.
PEEL, *n.* Kawa.
PEEL, *v.* Muku; hagu; hegu.
PEEP, *v.* Nozoku; nozoki-mi wo szru; szki-mi wo szru.
PEEPING, Nozoki-mi; szki-mi.
PEER, Dōhai.
PEER, *v.* Kiyorori to miru; jiro-jiro to miru.
PEEVISH, Tanki-na; jireru; iji-iji szru.
PEG, Ki-kugi; take-kugi.
PELLICLE, Uwakawa.
PELLUCID, Reirō-naru; szki-tōru.
PELT, *v.* Nage-utsz; utsz.
PELTRY, Ke-kawa; kawa.
PEN, Fude; hitsz; ori; koya.
PEN, *v.* Kaku.
PENALTY, Keibatsz; shioki; tszmi; k'wariyō; batsz-kin.
PENANCE, Giyō; tszmi-horoboshi.
PENATES, Ji-butsz.
PENCIL, Seki-hitsz; fude.
PENDENT, Tszru; sageru.
PENDULUM, Omori.
PENETRATE, Sasz; tszki-komu; tesszru; szi-komu; shimu.
PENITENT, *a.* Kō-k'wai szru; kuyuru; kuyamu; zan-nen-garu.
PENITENTIARY, Rōya; h'toya.
PENKNIFE, Kogatana.
PENMAKER, Fudeshi.
PENMAN, Kaku-h'to; kaki-te. *Good* —, nō-hitsz. *Bad* —, aku hitsz.
PENMANSHIP, Hitszi; fudedzkai. *Learning* —, tenarai; hippō.
PENNY, Zeni; mon.

PEN-RACK, Fudenose; hikka.
PENSION, Szte-buchi.
PEN-STORE, Fudeya.
PENTHOUSE, Hisashi.
PENURIOUS, Rinshoku-na; shiwai; kechina.
PENURY, Konkiu; madzshiki; bimbō.
PEONY, Butan.
PEOPLE, H'to; tami; chō-nin; bammin; shimo-jimo; shimozama; sh'tajita.
PEPPER, *black* —, koshō. *Cayenne* —, tōgarashi.
PEPPER-BOX, Koshō-ire.
PEPPERMINT, Hakka.
PERAMBULATE, Yūreki szru; henreki szru; mawaru.
PERCEIVE, Miru; kiku; oboyeru; satoru.
PERCENTAGE, Wari; kōsen.
PERCEPTIBLE, Miyeru; shireru; oboyeru.
PERCEPTION, Shōne; satori.
PERCH, *n.* Tomarigi.
PERCH, *v.* Tomaru.
PERCHANCE, Futo; fui-ni; omoi-yoradz-ni.
PERCOLATE, Kosz; tōru.
PERCUSSION, Hibiki.
PERCUSSION-CAP, Dondor; (*a Dutch-word.*)
PERDITION, Metszbō; horobi; messzru; daraku szru.
PEREMPTORILY, Kitto; genjū ni; kataku; shikato.
PERFECT, Mattaki; ju-bun; manzoku; zembi-sh'taru; (*see* yemman).
PERFECTLY, Mattaku; jūbun-ni; sappari to.
PERFIDIOUS, Fu-chiu-na; fu-jitsz-na; akugiyaku-na.
PERFIDY, Fujitsz; fu-chiu.
PERFORATE, Tōsz; sashi-tōsz; nuke-tōru; tszki-tōsz.
PERFORATION, Ana.
PERFORM, Szru; nasz; itasz; dekiru; okonau; togeru; szmu; hatasz; tori-okonau; itonamu.
PERFUME, *n.* Kō; kaori; kōki.
PERFUME, *v.* Kaoru; niō; kunjiru.
PERHAPS, Ōkata; tabun. *Mostly by the dubit. suffix,* rō, *or* sō; *as,* kuru de arō, *perhaps he will come.* Yoku naru de arō, *he will perhaps get well.* Ari-sō na mono da, *perhaps it is so, or perhaps there are.*
PERIL, Ayauki; abunaki; kennon; kinan.
PERILOUS, Ayaui; abunai; kennon naru; inochi ni kakaru.
PERINEUM, Towatari.
PERIOD, Toki; jisetsz; jibun.
PERISH, Shinuru; messzru; horobiru; kareru; nakunaru.
PERJURE, Itszwate chikau.
PERMANENT, Kawaranu; tayedz.
PERMEATE, Tōru.
PERMISSION, Yurushi; shōchi; menkiyo. *Without* —, kotowari-nashi.
PERMIT, *v.* Yurusz; shōchi szru; menk'yo szru; kiyoyō szru.
PERNICIOUS, Doku-na; gai ni naru.
PERPENDICULAR, Masszgu-ni tatsz.
PERPETRATE, Nasz; okonau; okasz.
PERPETUAL, Tayedz; yamazaru; bandaifuyeki.
PERPETUALLY, Tayedz-ni; yamadz-ni; tayema-naku; tokoshinaye-ni.
PERPETUATE, Matsz-dai ni nokosz; bandai ni tsztayeru,
PERPLEX, Tori-komu; konzatsz; mayō; tohō ni kureru; torimagireru; urotayeru; magotszku.
PERPLEXITY, Tōwaku; kokorokubari.
PERQUISITE, Homachi.
PERSECUTE, Hidoime ni awaseru; semeru; nayamasz.
PERSEVERE, Shimbō szru; shitōsz; korikatamaru.
PERSIMMON, Kaki.
PERSIST, Ī-tōsz.
PERSISTENT, Hitaszra-ni; ichidz-ni; kujikedz.
PERSON, H'to; mono; hō; kata. *In person,* jibun de. *Received in person,* jiki-den. *Ordinary* —, bon-nin; hei-nin; h'tonami.
PERSONAL, Jiki. — *conversation;* jiki-dan. — *complaint,* jikisō.
PERSONALLY, Jibun de; jika-ni; jiki-ni.
PERSONATE, Maneru; niseru; nazorayeru.
PERSONIFY, Nazorayeru; yosoyeru.
PERSPICUOUS, Sapparito; meihaku-na; fummiyō-na; akiraka-na.
PERSPIRATION, Ase.
PERSPIRE, Ase ga deru; hakkan szru.
PERSUADE, Kudoku; szszmu; sasō; sosonokasz; nattoku szru; gaten szru; izanau.
PERTAIN, Soi; tszku.
PERTINACIOUS, Henkutsz-na; kataku-na; kataiji-na.
PERTINENT, Tszku.
PERTURBED, Urotayeru; sawadachi.
PERUSE, Yomu.
PERVADE, Tōru; michiru.
PERVERSE, Wagamama; yokoshima; henkutsz-na; higamu.

PERVERT, Mageru; kojitszkeru; fuk'wai szru.
PERVIOUS, Szku; szkitaru; szkitōru.
PESTER, Komaraseru; kurushimeru.
PESTERED, Komaru.
PESTIFEROUS, Aku; doku-na; gai-szru; itameru.
PESTILENCE, Yakubiyō; yeki; yekirei.
PESTLE, Niubō, rengi; szrikogi.
PET, *n.* Kawairashii mono.
PET, *v.* Amayakasz.
PETAL, Hanabira.
PETITION, *n.* Negai; g'wansho; kinen; meyasz.
PETITION, *v.* Negau; tang'wan szru; uttayeru.
PETRIFACTION, K'wa-seki.
PETRIFY, Ishi ni kawaru; k'waseki szru.
PETTED, Amayeru.
PETTIFOGGER, Kujishi.
PETTY, Wadzka; iyashii; chīsai.
PETULANT, Tanki-na.
PEWTER, Rō; handa; biyakurō.
PHANTASM, Maboroshi.
PHANTOM, Bakemono.
PHARMACOPŒIA, Yakuzaisho; hōkan.
PHEASANT, Kiji.
PHENIX, Hōwō.
PHENOMENON, Koto; arisama; hen-ji.
PHIAL, Bin; tokkuri.
PHILOSOPHER, Monoshiri; gakusha; hakase.
PHILOSOPHY, Gaku; jutsz; ri; dōri; michi; dō.
PHLEBOTOMY, Shiraku.
PHLEGM, Tan.
PHOTOGRAPHY, Shashinkiyō de utsz.
PHRASE, Ku.
PHTHISIS, Rōshō; rōgai.
PHYSIC, Ijutsz; kuszri.
PHYSICIAN, Isha; ishi; hondō.
PHYSIOGNOMIST, Ninsōmi; ninsōja.
PHYSIOGNOMY, Ninsō; mensō.
PIAZZA, Genk'wa.
PICK, — *off*, toru; mushiru; mogu. — *out*, nuku; toru. — *up*, hirō; kaki-tateru. *To pick (as cotton, wool)*, hogusz. *To pick (stick)*, sasz; tszku; tsztszku; seseru. *(select)*, yerabu; yoru; yeru; gimmi szru. — *the nose*, hana wo kujiru.
PICK, *n.* Tszrubashi.
PICKED, *pret.* Yeranda; yotta; gimmi sh'ta. — *soldiers*, seihei.
PICKET-FENCE, Yarai; komayose.
PICKLE, *v.* Tszkeru.
PICK-POCKET, Kinchaku-kiri.
PICNIC, Yusan; hanami; asobi.
PICTURE, Ye; dz; yedz; iki-utszshi.
PICTURE-FRAME, Gaku no fuchi; waku.
PICUL, H'yakkin.
PIEBALD, Buchi; madara.
PIECE, *n.* Kire; hashi; kake; *(of cloth)*, tan; hiki.
PIECES, Szn-szn; dzda-dzda.
PIECE, *v.* Tszgu; hagu.
PIECE-GOODS, Tammono.
PIECE-WORK, Uketori-shigoto.
PIER, Hatoba.
PIERCE, Sasz; tszku; tōsz; shimu; sashikomu; tszki-komu; tesszru. — *through*, sashi-tōsz; tszki-tōsz; nuke-tōru.
PIETY, Shinjin. *Filial* —, kōkō.
PIG, Inoka; kobuta.
PIGEON, Hato. *House* —, Iyebato.
PILE, *n.* Kui; kasa; tszmi; yama.
PILES, Iboji.
PILFER, Nuszmu.
PILFERING, Konuszmi; teguse ga warui.
PILFERER, Szri; mambiki; konuszbito.
PILGRIM, Dōsha.
PILGRIMAGE, *To go on* —, mōderu; mairu; saukei szru.
PILL, G'wanyaku. *One* —, h'to tszbu. — *box*, mage-mono.
PILLAGE, Ubau; ubai-toru.
PILLAR, Hashira.
PILLORY, Kubigase.
PILLOW, Makura.
PILOT, Midz-saki.
PIMP, Zegen; hannin.
PIMPLE, Nikibi.
PIN, Hari; tome-bari. *Wooden* —, kikuji; sen.
PINCH, *v.* Tszmeru; tszmamu; hasamu. — *off*, tszmu; tszmikiru.
PINCH, *n.* Tszmami.
PINCHERS, Kugi-nuki.
PINE, Matsz-no-ki. — *bur*, matsz-kasa.
PINE, *v.* Yaseru.
PINK, Sekichiku.
PINNACLE, Zetchō.
PINT, = *about*, nigo san shaku.
PIOUS, Shinjin naru; kami wo wiyamau.
PIPE, Kiseru; kuda; rappa.
PIRATE, Kaizoku.
PISTIL, Hana no dzi; shibe.
PISTOL, Teppō; tanegashima.
PIT, Ana; ba; kubomi. — *of the stomach*, midzochi; mune; kiubi.

PIT, *v.* Kubomu; hekomasz.
PITCH, Matsz no yani.
PITCH, *v.* Nageru; ochiru; szteru. — *a camp*, jin wo toru.
PITCH-BLACK, Makkuro.
PITCH-DARK, Makkura.
PITCHER, Midz-ire; midzsashi.
PITCH-FARTHING, Ana-ichi; zeni-nage.
PITCH-FORK, Mataki; saszmata.
PITEOUS, Wabishiki; nangi-na.
PITFALL, Otoshi-ana.
PITH, Ki no shin; dzi; gokui; shui; ōgi.
PITIABLE, Kawaisō; aware-na.
PITIFUL, Fubin-na; jihi no fukai; aware-na; shōshi; itawashii.
PITILESS, Nasake nai; fubin naki.
PITY, *n.* Fubin; awaremi; jihi; nasake; aware; sokuin.
PITY, *v.* Awaremu; fubin ni omō; itawaru; megumu.
PIVOT, Kaname.
PLACARD, Harifuda; bira,
PLACE, Tokoro; basho; tochi; za; bungen; mibun. *In the — of*, kawari ni. *Native —*, kokiyō; furusato; kiui. *In the first —*, ichi ban ni. — *where it is*, aridokoro; arisho.
PLACE, *v.* Kakeru; oku; szyeru; osameru; adzkeru; noseru.
PLACENTA, Yena.
PLACID, Odayaka-na; shidzkana; yaszraka.
PLAGUE, Yeki; yekirei; yakubiyō.
PLAID, Benke-jima; goban-jima; ichi-matsz.
PLAIN, *n.* Hirachi; heichi.
PLAIN, *a.* Taira; tairaka; hirattai; akiraka-na; fummiyō; shitszboku; jimi-na; szna-o; ubu; kōlō. — *wood*, shiraki. *To make —*, akirameru.
PLAINLY, Akiraka-ni; hakkiri.
PLAIT, *n.* Hida; shiwa; orime.
PLAIT, *v.* Kumu; hida wo toru; yoru.
PLAN, *v.* Yedz; hinagata; hakarigoto; saku; tedate; te; kufū; fumbetsz.
PLAN, *v.* Kufū szru; hakaru; kuwadateru.
PLANE, *a.* Tairaka-na; hirattai.
PLANE, *v.* Kedzru.
PLANE, *n.* Kanna.
PLANET, Hoshi.
PLANK, *n.* Atszi ita.
PLANK, *v.* Ita wo haru.
PLANT, *n.* Kusa; wiyeki; sōmoku.
PLANT, *v.* Wiyeru; udzmeru; maku; uwaru.
PLANTAIN, Bashō. *Common —*, ōbako.
PLANTATION, Denji.
PLASTER, *n.* Kabe; *(med)*, kōyaku.
PLASTER, *v.* Kabe wo nuru.
PLASTERER, Shakan.
PLASTER *of paris*, Sekkō.
PLATE, Sara; sane; kana-ita. *Copper —*, dōhan.
PLATE, *v.* Kiseru.
PLATED, Kiseta. *Gold —*, kinkise. *Silver —*, gin-kise.
PLATTER, Sahachi; bon.
PLAUSIBLE, Kuchi-sagashii.
PLAY, *v.* Tawamureru; fuzakeru; asobu; hiyōgeru; jareru; odokeru; *(drama)*, shibai wo szru. — *checkers*, go wo utsz. — *chess*, shōgi wo sasz. — *cards*, karuta wo utsz. — *the flute*, fuye wo fuku. — *the guitar*, samisen wo hiku. — *the woman*, onnakata wo szru. — *upon*, damasz; azamuku.
PLAY, *n.* Tawamure; asobi; shibai; bakuchi; gwai; ambai.
PLAYDAY, Kiujitsz.
PLAYER, Yakusha.
PLAY-HOUSE, Shibai.
PLAY-THING, Omocha; moteasobi.
PLEA, Īgusa; īwake; negai; kōjitsz.
PLEAD, Tang'wan szru; nageku; negau; iu; noberu.
PLEASANT, Yoi; omoshiroi; umai; ureshii; kokoroyoki.
PLEASE, Ki ni iru; kokoro ni kanau. *As you —*, kokoro ni makasz; dzi-i; go katte ni. *To — another*, kigen wo toru; nagusameru. *As much as one pleases*, omō sama; omo-ire; zombun.
PLEASED, Omoshirogaru; tanoshimu.
PLEASING, Yoi; kokoroyoki.
PLEASURE, Tanoshimi; omoshirosa; ureshisa; kiyō; asobi. *At pleasure*, kokoro shidai; kokoro makase; dzi-i; katte ni; kimama.
PLEBIAN, Iyashii; zoku-na.
PLEDGE, *n.* Sh'chi; hiki-ate; ate; kata; ukeai; katame; kotoba-jichi.
PLEDGE, *v.* Ukeau; sh'chi ni oku.
PLENTEOUS, Ōi; tak'san; obitadashii; yutaka-na.
PLENTIFUL, *id.* — *crop*, hōsaku. — *year*, hōnen.
PLENTY, Jūbun; tak'san.
PLIABLE, Tawayaka-na; nabiki-yaszi; shinayaka; nayeru.
PLIGHT, *v.* Ukeau;
PLIGHT, *n.* Yōsz; yōdai; sama.
PLOT, *n.* Hakarigoto; saku; tedate; kufū.

PLOT, *v.* Hakaru; kufū szru; kuwadateru.
PLOUGH, *n.* Kara-szki.
PLOUGH, *v.* Tagayesz; szku.
PLUCK, *v.* Toru; mushiru; mogu; tszmu; chigiru. — *out*, nuku.
PLUG, *n.* Tszme; sen.
PLUG, *v.* Tszmeru; fusagu.
PLUM, Ume. — *tree*, ume no ki. — *blossoms*, ume no hana.
PLUMAGE, Hane.
PLUMB, *adv.* Masszgu.
PLUMB-LINE, Sageszmi.
PLUME, Hane.
PLUNDER, *v.* Ubau; ubai-toru; toru; nuszmu; kaszmeru.
PLUNDER, *n.* Bundori; nuszmi-mono.
PLUNGE, Shidzmeru; hameru.
PLUTO, Yemma.
PLY, *v.* Honeoru; hagemu.
PLY, *n.* Ye.
POCKET, Kakushi.
POCKET-BOOK, Kami-ire.
POCKET-KNIFE, Kogatana; saszga.
POCKET-MONEY, Kodzkai.
POCK-MARK, Abata; janko.
POEM, Shi; uta.
POET, Utayomi; kajin; shijin.
POETRY, Shi; uta.
POINT, Saki; ten; chobo; kiwa; toki; tokoro; shui; honi. — *of death*, matszgo; rinjū; shinigiwa; shi ni kakaru; shigo.
POINT, *v.* Togaraseru; kedzru; sasz; nerau; tameru; kutō wo kiru.
POINTED, Togaru.
POISE, *v.* Tszriau; hakaru.
POISON, Doku. *Kill with* —, dokusatsz; dokugai.
POISON, *v.* Doku wo tszkeru; dokugai wo szru; mori-korosz.
POISONOUS, Doku-na.
POLE, Sao; bō. *North* —, hokkiyoku. *South* —, nan-kiyoku. *Coolie's* —, tembimbō; ninaibō.
POLE-STAR, Hokushin.
POLICEMAN, Yakunin; bannin.
POLISH, *v.* Migaku; togu; takuma szru.
POLISH, *n.* Tszya.
POLITE, Aisō no yoi; seji no yoi; tei-neina; fūriu-na; ikina.
POLITENESS, Rei; reigi; reishiki; shitszkegata; ingin.
POLLEN, Nioi.
POLLUTE, Kegasz; yogosz.
POLTROON, Okubiyō-mono; hikiyō mono.
POLYPUS OF NOSE, Hanatake.
POMATUM, Bintszke; abura.
POMEGRANATE, Zakuro.
POMP, Ogori; ririshiki; rin-rin.
POMPOUS, Taka-buru; ōhei-na; ōfū-na; ririshiki; ibaru.
POND, Ike; senszi.
PONDER, Kangayeru; andzru; omō; megurasz.
PONDEROUS, Omoi.
PONGEE, Tszmugi.
PONTOON-BRIDGE, Funa-bashi.
POOL, Ike.
POOP, Fune no tomo.
POOR, Bimbō; konkiu; madzshii; demo; shidz; wabishii. — *family*, hinka. — *and mean*, hin-sen.
POP, Pon-pon; patchiri-to; patchi-patchi-to.
POP-GUN, Tszki-deppō.
POPPY, Keshi. — *heads*, ōzokkoku.
POPULACE, Shimo-jimo; chōnin.
POPULATION, Nindzu; h'to-kadz; nimbetsz.
POPULOUS, H'to no ōi.
PORCELAIN, Setomono.
PORCH, Yen; genk'wa.
PORE, Keana; sōri.
PORK, Buta no niku.
PORPOISE, Fugu.
PORT, Minato; narifuri. — *the helm*, torikaji.
PORTEND, Shiraseru; arawasz.
PORTER, Momban; ninsoku; koage; karuko.
PORTERAGE, Ninsoku-chin; unchin; hakobi-chin.
PORTFOLIO, Tatōgami.
PORT-HOLE, Sama; teppōzama.
PORTICO, Yen; genk'wa; rōka.
PORTION, *n.* Wari; wariai; bun; maye.
PORTION, *v.* Wari-tszkeru; wakeru; kubaru; ategau; ate-hameru.
PORTLY, Koyeta.
PORTRAIT, Yezō; nigao.
PORTRAY, Kaku; hiku.
PORTULACCA, Hanahiyu.
POSITION, Kamaye; muki; uke; bungen; mibun; bunzai.
POSITIVELY, Kanaradz; zehi; kessh'te; kitto; tash'kani; sh'kato.
POSSESS, Motsz; motomeru; aru.
POSSESSION, Mochi-mono; mochiba; mochikitari; shinsho; shindai.
POSSESSOR, Nushi.
POSSIBLE, Ōkata; de arō, *or the dubit. suff.* ō; rō. *To God all things are possible*, kami ni atawazaru tokoro nashi.

POST, *n.* Hik'yaku; hashira; kui; mochiba; mochikuchi.
POST, *v.* Oku.
POSTAGE, Hik'yaku-chin; jō-chin.
POSTERIOR, Ato; nochi; go.
POSTERIORS, Shiri; ishiki; oido.
POSTERITY, Shison; kōin.
POSTERN, Karamete; uramon.
POST-HORSE, Shaku-ba.
POST-MAN, Hik'yaku.
POST-OFFICE, Hik'yakuya.
POSTPONE, Nobasz, shinokosz.
POSTPONEMENT, Hinobe.
POSTSCRIPT, Soyegaki; kakisoye.
POST-TOWN, Shuku; shukuba; yeki.
POSTURE, Kamaye; yōsz; arisama.
POT, Nabe; kama. — *lid*, kama-buta.
POTATO, Imo. *Irish* —, jagatara-imo. *Sweet* —, satszma-imo.
POTENT, Tszyoi; ikioi no aru.
POTHOOK, Jizai-kagi; kagi.
POTTER, Yaki-mono-shi; szye-mono-shi.
POUCH, Fukuro; kane-ire; kinchaku.
POULTICE, Pappu.
POUND, Kin. *One pound avoirdupois,* = sh'chi momme ni fun go-rin.
POUND, *v.* Butsz; utsz; tszku.
POUR, *v.* Tszgu; kobosz; kumu; shaku; moru; koboreru.
POVERTY, Bimbō; konkiu; hin; madzshiki; hinkiu.
POWDER, *n.* Ko; kona; saimatsz; san; matsz; fun. *Gun* —, yenshō; k'wayaku. *Face* —, oshiroi.
POWDER, *v.* Kona ni szru; ko ni szru; saimatsz ni szru; hiku; szri-kudaku; orosz.
POWER, Chikara; ikioi; ikō; isei; kōnō; kikime; ken; kuriki.
POWERFUL, Chikara aru; tszyoi; ikioi-no-aru; isei aru; kikime ga aru.
POWERFULLY, Tszyoku.
PRACTICE, *n.* Koto; okonai; keiko; manabi; jutsz; narai; ts'u-rei; riyōri; furi-ai; rei.
PRACTICE, *v.* Nareru; nasz; keiko szru; manabu; megurasz; tanren szru; remma; renju; okonau.
PRAIRIE, No; hara; nohara.
PRAISE, *n.* Homare; san; sambi; shō; shōbi.
PRAISE, *v.* Homeru; sambi szru; shōbi szru.
PRAISE-WORTHY, *action*, Kō.
PRANCE, Haneru; odoru.
PRANK, Jōdan; tawamure.
PRATE, Shaberu.
PRAWN, Yebi.
PRAY, *v.* Inoru; kitō szru; negau; koi-negau; tanomu.
PRAYER, Inori; kitō; negai; koi; kinen. — *for rain*, amagoi.
PREACH, *v.* Kōshaku szru; seppō szru; kōdan szru; hirogeru; hōdan szru.
PRECARIOUS, Obotszkanai; tash'kanaradz; kimara-nai.
PRECAUTION, Yōi; yōjin; tsztszshimi.
PRECEDE, Saki ni yuku; saki ni tatsz; maye ni aru.
PRECEDENCE, Sente; senguri-ni.
PRECEDENT, *n.* Senrei; sen-kaku; senki; kiu-rei.
PRECEDING, Sen; saki-no; maye-no.
PRECEPT, Imashime, kai; oshiye; iken; hō.
PRECEPTOR, Shi; shishō.
PRECINCT, Sakai; riyō-chi.
PRECIOUS, Tattoki; takara.
PRECIPICE, Kenso; zeppeki· soba.
PRECIPITANTLY, K'wa-kiu-ni; awatadashiku; isoide.
PRECIPITATE, *v.* Otosz; seku; isogu; hayamaru; sosokashii.
PRECIPITOUS, Kewashii; sagashii; sobadatsz; sobiyeru.
PRECISE, Katai; shikakubaru; katakurushii; kirikōjō; shikatszberashii.
PRECISELY, Chōdo; adakamo; shika-to,
PRECLUDE, Fusegu; kobamu; sasayeru; sayegiru.
PRE-CONCERT, Maye-motte kakaru; kanete sadameru; maye-motte kuwadateru.
PRECURSOR, Sakidachi.
PREDECESSOR, Sen-no; maye no.
PREDESTINATE, Mayemotte torikimeru; maye-ni sadameru; arakajime kimeru.
PREDICATE, Iu.
PREDICT, Mayemotte iu; arakajime iu.
PREDICTION, Mayemotte iuta koto; zengen.
PREDOMINANT, Szgitaru; katsz; gachi; ōku; masaru.
PREDOMINATE, Szgiru; masaru; katsz.
PREEMINANT, Hīderu; szgiru.
PREEIMNENTLY, Nakandzku; szgurete.
PRE-ENGAGEMENT, Senyaku.
PRE-EXIST, Zense ni oru; maye no yo ni oru; kono yo no maye ni oru.
PRE-EXISTENCE, Zense; maye no yo; kono yo no maye ni oru koto.
PREFACE, Jo; hashigaki.

PREFER, Yerabu; tattomu; ageru; szszmeru. *I — this one*, kono hō ga yoi.
PREFERABLE, Yoi; madashimo; mashi.
PREFIX, Maye ni oku; kakarikotoba.
PREGNANT, K'wai-nin; mi-mochi; ninshin; haramu; migomori.
PREJUDICE, Katahīki; yeko; katayoru; higamu.
PREJUDICIAL, Doku-na; gai-naru.
PREMATURE, Haya-szgiru; tokinaranu; tszki-taradz; mada jukusenu. *— birth*, shōsan.
PREMEDITATE, Mayemotte kangayeru; .mayemotte hakaru.
PREMISE, Mayemotte iu.
PREMIUM, Hōbi; ri; rigin.
PREMONITION, Mayemotte shiraseru; sakini shiraseru.
PREOCCUPY, Saki ni oru.
PREORDAIN, Mayemotte sadameru; arakajime kiwameru.
PREPARATION, Shitaku; yōi; sonaye; yōjin; teate; kakugo; moyōshi.
PREPARE, Shitaku szru; sonayeru; mōkeru; koshirayeru; totonoyeru; kamayeru; moyōsz.
PREPAY, Saki ni harau; mayebarai wo szru.
PREREQUISITE, Mayemotte nakereba naranu.
PREROGATIVE, Kakaru. *It is the — of the father to govern his family*, kanai-jū wo osameru koto wa teishu h'tori ni kakaru.
PRESAGE, Zempiyo; shirase; zenchō.
PRESCIENCE, Mayemotte shiru.
PRESCRIBE, Ītszkeru; kuszri wo yaru; riyōji wo szru.
PRESCRIPTION, Hōgaki. *Alter a —*, tempō szru.
PRESENCE, Oru-koto; oru-toki. *In the —*, omote; maye; gan-zen; ma no-atari. *Loose — of mind*, tohō wo ushinau; akire-hateru; ki-okure.
PRESENT, Oru; iru; genzai; ima; tadaima; tō; tōji; tōbun; *(gift)*, rei-motsz; miage; okuri mono; shinjō-mono; immotsz; shimmotsz. *For the —*, tōbun; tōji.
PRESENT, *v.* Shinjō szru; yaru; ageru; tszkawasz.
PRESENTIMENT, Mayemotte omō.
PRESENTLY, Ima-ni; ottszke; otte; nochihodo; hodonaku; szgu-ni; jiki-ni.
PRESERVE, *v.* Taszkeru; szkū; tabau; tamotsz; mamoru; shugo szru; kakō; satō ni tszkeru.
PRESERVE, *n.* Tomeba.

PRESIDE, Shihai szru; matszrigoto wo szru.
PRESS, *v.* Osz; shiboru; shimeru; isogu; seku; hayameru; shīru.
PRESS, *n. Oil —*, shimé-gi. *To put a book to —*, hon wo han ni okosz.
PRESUME, Omō; tszmoru; riyōken.
PRESUMPTUOUS, Sashi-deru.
PRETENCE, Kakotszke; īgusa; dashi.
PRETEXT, Kakotszke; īgusa; dashi.
PRETEND, Kakotszkeru; itszwaru; kotoyoseru; maneru; niseru. *— not to know*, shirabakkureru; shiranu kao wo szru.
PRETENDER, Ikiszgi; namaiki; kītafū.
PRETTY, *a.* Kirei; utszkushii; migoto; rippa.
PRETTY, *adv.* Kanari; dzibun; yaya.
PREVAIL, Katsz; hayaru; riu-kō szru; hakkō szru.
PREVENT, Kobamu; fusegu.
PREVIOUS, Saki; maye; izen; sen. *— state*, maye no yo; zense; shukusei.
PREVIOUSLY, Itszzoya; sendatte; maye-ni; mayekata; mayemotte; kanete; sakidatte; sakihodo; senkoku; katszte.
PREY, Bundori.
PREY, *v.* Toru.
PRICE, Nedan; ne; atai; dai; chin; shiro.
PRICE-CURRENT, Sōbadzke. *Tea —*, chanofu.
PRICELESS, Atainaki.
PRICK, *v.* Sasz; tszku.
PRICKLY-PEAR, Saboten.
PRIDE, Kōman; jiman; takaburi; hokori; ōfū; ōhei; manki; manshin.
PRIEST, Bōdz; ōsho; jūji; sō; hōshi; kannushi.
PRIMARILY, Madz; moto; hajimete.
PRIMARY, Moto-no. *— importance*, dai ichi; sen-ichi; sakidatsz.
PRIME, Moto; ichi-ban; dai-ichi; sakannaru. *— object*, shu; shui.
PRIMING, Kuchi-guszri.
PRIMITIVE, Moto-no. *— times*, inishiye; mukashi.
PRINCE, Daimiyō; taishi; miya; seishi.
PRINCESS, Hime; naishin-nō; hime-miya; himegimi.
PRINCIPAL, *a.* Taisetsz na; kanyō naru; omoi; k'wantaru.
PRINCIPAL, *n.* Chō; kashira; motode; motokin; sen; senichi. *— and interest*, g'wanri. *— thing*, dai-ichi; kanyō; yō; kan-jin.
PRINCIPALITY, Riyōbun; riyō.
PRINCIPALLY, Moppará; dai-ichi; omo-ni.

PRINCIPLE, Ri ; dōri ; kotowari; michi; moto; kizashi.
PRINT, *v.* Han ni okosz; szru; jōboku szru.
PRINT, *n.* Ato; kata; ji.
PRINTER, Hanszri.
PRINTING-PRESS, Hanszri-dai.
PRIOR, Saki ni; maye-ni.
PRISON, Rōya; h'to-ya.
PRISONER, Zainin ; meshiudo ; tszmibito; toriko.
PRIVACY, Inkiyo.
PRIVATE, Jibun no; jishin no; watakushi no; naishō no; naibun no; hisoka-naru. — *business*, shiyō. — *opinion*, nai-i.
PRIVATELY, Hisoka-ni ; nai-nai; naishō ni; aitai-ni.
PRIVY, Chōdzba; sets'in; kōka; kawaya.
PRIZE, *n.* Bundori; hōbi.
PRIZE, *v.* Tattomu; omondzru.
PROBABLY, Ōkata; tabun; kedashi; *also formed by the suffixes*, rashii; sō; *and* rō; darō.
PROBATION, Kokoromi; tameshi.
PROBE, *n.* Saguri.
PROBE, *v.* Saguru; gimmi szru.
PROBITY, Tadashisa.
PROBLEMATICAL, Obotszkanai ; utagawashii; tash'kanaranu.
PROBOSCIS, Hana.
PROCEED, Szszmu; deru; motenasz; toriatszkau.
PROCEEDING, *n.* Koto; shiwaza; shikata.
PROCEEDS, Taka; agari; dai.
PROCESSION, Retsz; giyōretsz.
PROCLAIM, Hirogeru ; hiromeru ; fureru; fure-chirasz.
PROCLAMATION, Ofure.
PROCLIVITY, Kuse.
PROCRASTINATE, Himadoru ; temadoru ; noberu; shi-nokosz; manurui ; madarui; madoroi.
PROCURE, Motomeru; ukeru; yeru.
PROCURER, Zegen; hannin.
PRODIGAL, Tsziyasz; oshige-naki; oshimadz ni tszkau; mudadzkai; ōzappai.
PRODIGAL, *n.* Sanzaika.
PRODIGIOUS, Okii; bakutai; k'wōdai.
PRODIGY, Hen-na koto; ayashii koto; miyō-na koto; ki-naru-koto; kik'wai-na-koto; heni.
PRODUCE, *v.* Dasz ; hiki-dasz ; miseru ; shōdzru; muszbu; naru; tszkuru; koshirayeru; saku; dekiru; tateru.
PRODUCE, *n.* Saku ; tszkuri; deki; sakumotsz.
PRODUCT, *n.* *Idem.*
PRODUCTION, Sakumotsz; sambutsz; tszkurimono.
PROFANE, *a.* Mottainai; kegaretaru.
PROFANE, *v.* Kegasz; yogosz.
PROFICIENT, Jōdz; yete; tokui ; shōtatsz.
PROFILE, Hammen no yedz.
PROFIT, Ri; riyeki; buai; yeki; kai; ribun; mōke; toku; bugin. — *and loss*, ri-gai; son-toku; toku-shitsz.
PROFITABLE, Tokuyō; rikata; ri no aru; kai no aru.
PROFLIGATE, Dōraku ; hōtō.
PROFOUND, Fukai.
PROFUSE, Tsziyasz; sanzai szru.
PROGENITOR, Senzo; kōso; shiso; g'wanso.
PROGENY, Shison.
PROGNOSTIC, Shirase; zempiyō; shō.
PROGNOSTICATE, Mi-tōsz; mi-nuku; mi-sadameru.
PROGRESS, Szszmu.
PROHIBIT, Kobamu; fusegu; kindzru; kotowaru; seikin szru; sasayeru; sei szru.
PROJECT, *n.* Kufū; saku.
PROJECT, *v.* Kufū szru; hakaru; hami-dasz; deru. *Projecting teeth*, deba. — *eyebrows*, debitai.
PROLAPSUS ANI, Dakkō.
PROLIX, Mendō; nagatarashii; shitszkoi; kudoi; kuda-kudashii.
PROLONG, Nagaku szru; nobasz; nobiru.
PROMINENT, Hīdetaru; takai; medatsz.
PROMISCUOUS, Midaretaru; konzatsz sh'ta.
PROMISCUOUSLY, Konzatsz sh'te; midarete; mazete.
PROMISE, *n.* Yak'soku; yaku-jō; ukeai; katame.
PROMISE, *v.* Yak'soku szru; ukeau.
PROMONTORY, Hana.
PROMOTE, *v.* Shussei szru; ageru; hiromeru.
PROMOTION, Shussei; shōshin.
PROMPT, *v.* Jogon szru; odateru; saseru; hagemasz.
PROMPT, Hayai; szmiyaka-na; toi; shinsotsz; sakui;
PROMPTLY, Hayaku; toku; szguni.
PROMULGATE, Hiromeru; fureru.
PRONE, Utszbushi; katamuku; szki-na.
PRONG, Mata.
PRONOUNCE, Iu; hanasz.
PRONUNCIATION, Īkata; īyō.
PROOF, Shōko; kokoromi; akashi. *Fire* —, higotaye no yoi. *Bullet* —, tama-gotaye.

PROP, *n.* Shimbari; tszka; tszppari; tszkkaibō.
PROP, *v*, Kau.
PROPAGATE, Tsztayeru; hiromeru; fuyasz; waku; shōdzru.
PROPEL, Osz.
PROPENSITY, Kuse; katamuki.
PROPER, Mochimaye; kanau; tadashii; niau; sōtō; tōzen.
PROPERLY, Tadashiku.
PROPERTY, Shinsho; shindai; kazō; mochimono; shoji; shozō; kazai. — *holder*, shotai.
PROPHECY, Zengen; yogen.
PROPHESY, Mayemotte iu; arakajime iu.
PROPHET, Yogensha.
PROPITIATE, Nagusameru; nadameru; kigen wo toru.
PROPITIATION, Aganai; tszgunai.
PROPITIOUS, Tame ni naru; wajun ni naru.
PROPORTION, *n.* Hodo; wari-ai; bun; kakkō.
PROPORTION, *v.* Awaseru; ōdzru; kanau.
PROPOSE, Tszgeru; īdasz; kakeru; īireru.
PROPRIETOR, Nushi; mochinushi.
PROPRIETY, Tadashiki.
PROSE, Bun.
PROSECUTE, Aitedoru.
PROSELYTE, *n.* Kaishū-nin.
PROSPECT, Keshiki; fūkei; chōbō; mi-watashi; nagame.
PROSPER, Sakayeru; hanjō szru.
PROSPEROUS, Sakan-naru; hanjō naru; han-k'wa-na; sai-wai-na; shiawase-na.
PROSTITUTE, Jōro; yūjo. — *quarters*, kuruwa; yūri.
PROSTRATE, Taosz; fuseru.
PROSY, Kochitaki; netszi.
PROTECT, Mamoru; shugo szru; kago szru; kabau; yokeru.
PROTECTION, Mamori; shugo; okage; yoke.
PROTEST, Kitto iu; kessh'te iu; kataku iu.
PROTRACT, Nagaku szru; nobasz; himadoru; temadoru.
PROTRUDE, Deru; dasz.
PROTUBERANCE, Kobu.
PROUD, Hokoru; takaburu; ōhei-naru; jiman; kōman; ōfū-naru.
PROVE, Tamesz; kokoro-miru; shōko wo tateru; keiken szru.
PROVERB, Kotowaza.
PROVIDE, Shitaku szru; yōi szru; teate wo szru; sonayeru; ategau. — *food*, makanau.
PROVIDENCE, Yoi; yōjin; temmei; kago.
PROVIDENT, Yōjin no yoi; tsztszshimu.
PROVINCE, Kuni; koku.
PROVINCIALISM, Namari; katakoto; kiyōdan.
PROVISION, Yoi; shitaku; teate; tabe-mono; shokuriyo; sonaye.
PROVOCATION, Ikaru wake.
PROVOKE, Ikaraseru; rippukusaseru; hara wo tataseru; naburu; jirasz; ki wo momu; okoru.
PROVOKING, Jireru; jirettai.
PROW, Mioshi; hesaki.
PROWL, Shinobi aruku; nerai-aruku; haik'wai.
PROXY, Kawari; dai; miyōdai.
PRUDENCE, Yōjin; tsztszshimi; tashinami.
PRUDENT, Tsztszshimu; yōjin-bukai; tashinamu.
PRUNE, Kari-komu; tszkuru; yeda wo szkasz.
PRY, *v.* Ukagau; nerau; kojiru. — *up*, koji-ageru. — *open*, koji-akeru. — *apart*, koji-hanasz.
PSALM, Wasan; shōmiyō.
PUBERTY, H'to to naru toki; otona; irokedzku.
PUBLIC, Ōyake. — *business*, goyō. — *and private*, kōshi.
PUBLICLY, Omote-muki ni; ōyake-ni; kōzen-to; bahareru.
PUBLICITY, G'wai-bun; tamon.
PUBLISH, Hiromeru; fureru; arawasz; shuppan szru; amu; fure-shirasz.
PUCKER, Szbomeru; hisomeru.
PUDDLE, *n.* Nukarumi.
PUERILE, Kodomorashii; osanage-na.
PUFF, *v.* Fuku. — *up*, fukureru. — *of hair*, tabo.
PUFFBALL, Metszburedake.
PUGNACIOUS, Ken-k'wa-dzki.
PUKE, Haku.
PULL, Hiku; toru; mushiru; mogu; tszmu. — *in two*, saku. — *apart*, hiki-hanasz; hiki-wakeru. — *up*, hiki-ageru; hiki-okosz; hiki-tateru; nuku. — *out*, hiki-dasz; nuku; hiki-hadzsz. — *off*, hiki-hagu. — *open*, hiki-hatakeru. — *over*, hiki-taosz. — *across*, hiki-watasz. — *in*, hiki-ireru; hiki-komu. — *back*, hiki-kayesz; hiki-modosz. — *around*, hiki-mawasz. — *opposite*, hiki-mukeru. — *down*, hiki-orosz; hiki-otosz. — *near*, hiki-yoseru; hiki-tszkeru. — *along*, hiki-tszreru.
PULLEY, Rokuro.
PULPIT, Kōza.
PULSATE, Utsz; ugoku; odoru.

PULSE, Miyaku.
PULVERIZE, Ko ni szru; saimatsz ni szru; szri-tszbusz.
PUMICE-STONE, Karu-ishi.
PUMP, Pomp'; riu-tōszi.
PUMPKIN, Kabocha; bōbura.
PUN, Share; jiguchi.
PUNCH, *n.* Uchigiri.
PUNCH, *v.* Buchi-komu; tszku.
PUNCTILIOUS, Kata-szgiru; reigi-szgiru.
PUNCTUAL, Katai; toki wo hadzsanu.
PUNCTUATE, Ku wo kiru; ten wo tszkeru; kiri wo tszkeru.
PUNGENT, Karai.
PUNISH, Tszmi szru; korasz; imashimeru; kei-batsz szru; basszru; shioki wo szru; sekkan szru.
PUNISHMENT, Shioki; kei-batsz; imashime; korashi; bachi; batsz. *Capital* —, danzai.
PUP, Ko-inu; inukoro.
PUPIL, Deshi; monjin; shosei. — *of the eye*, h'tomi.
PUPPET, Ningiyō.
PURCHASE, Kau.
PURCHASER, Kaite.
PURE, Szmi-kitta; sznda; (*pret. of* szmi); kirei-na; kiyoi; shōjō-na; muku; seichoku-na; isagiyoi; keppaku-na; kiyoraka na; sei-ketsz-na. — *heart*, tanshin. — *and impure*, zei-daku. — *stream*, sei-riu. — *water*, seiszi.
PURGATIVE, Gezai; kudashi-guszri.
PURGE, Kudasz.
PURIFY, Szmasz; kiyomeru; keppaku ni szru; kirei ni szru.
PURPLE, Murasaki.
PURPORT, Omomuki.
PURPOSE, *n.* Kokorozashi; kokoro; wake; yuye; shisai; tszmori; riyōken. *On* —, waza-to; koto-sara-ni. *To no* —, muda-ni; munashiku; itadzra-ni. *To answer the* —, kototaru; mani-awaseru.
PURPOSE, *v.* Omō; kokorozasz; sadamaru.
PURPOSELY, Waza-to; koto-sara-ni.
PURSE, Kinchaku; kane-ire.
PURSER, Kanjō-kata.
PURSUANT, Sh'tagatte; tszite; yotte.
PURSUE, *v.* Ō; (*see* oi); okkakeru; sh'tagau; tszku; karu.
PURSUER, Otte.
PURSUIT, Oi; tosei; kagiyō; shōbai.
PURULENT, Unda; umi wo motsz.
PURVEY, Makanau.
PURVEYOR, Makanai-kata.
PUS, Umi; nō.
PUSH, Osz; tszku. — *against*, oshi-tszkeru; oshi-ateru. — *across*, oshi-watasz. — *up*, oshi-ageru; oshi-tateru. — *over*, oshi-taosz; oshi-watasz; oshi-kosz. — *out*, oshi-dasz. — *in*, oshi-komu; oshi-ireru. — *down*, oshi-fuseru; oshi-taosz; oshi-otosz; oshi-sageru. — *near*, oshi-yoseru. — *apart*, oshi-hedateru; oshi-wakeru. — *open*, oshi-akeru; oshi-hiraku. — *back*, oshi-kayesz. — *aside*, oshi-nokeru. — *through*, oshi-tōsz.
PUSILLANIMOUS, Kechi-na; ki no semai; shōriyō-na; shōtan.
PUSTULE, Dekimono.
PUT, Oku; szyeru; ateru; noseru; tszkeru; kakeru. — *about ship*, fune wo mawasz. — *away*, shimau; katadzkeru; osameru. — *away a wife*, ribetsz szru; — *down*, oku; osameru; shidzmeru; osayeru. — *forth*, dasz; nobasz; noberu; kizasz; kakeru. — *into*, ireru; hairu; komeru. — *in mind*, ki wo tszkete yaru; shiraseru. — *in practice*, okonau; sh'tagau. — *off*, nugu; noberu. — *on*, kiru; haku; oku; noseru; owaseru; kiseru; kakeru. — *out*, kesz; kasz; kizasz; dasz; nobasz; shikujiru. — *to*, awaseru; kuwayeru; soyeru; kakeru. — *to death*, korosz. — *trust in*, shinko szru; tanomu; makaseru. — *together*, atszmeru; awaseru; soyeru. — *up*, tsztszmu; tszmu; takuwayeru; kakō; shimatte oku. — *up with*, kannin szru; shinogu; shinobu; shimbō szru. — *to sea*, shuppan szru. — *up to*, odateru; szszmeru; keshi-kakeru. — *in fear*, odosz; obiyakasz. — *aside, or out of the way*, dokeru; nokeru. — *on the fire*, taku; kuberu.
PUTREFY, Kusaru.
PUTRID, Kusai.
PUZZLE, Mayowasz, komaraseru.
PUZZLED, Mayō; tohō ni kureru.
PYRAMIDAL, Szginari.
PYROSIS, Riu-in; sampaiyeki; mushidz.

Q

QUACK-DOCTOR, Yabu-isha; yōi.
QUADRANGLE, Shikaku.
QUADRUPED, Yotsz-ashi; shi-soku.
QUADRUPLE, Shisōbai.
QUAIL, Shako.

QUAKE, Furu, wananaku; ononoku.
QUALIFIED, Taru; tarau.
QUALITY, Tachi; shō; shitsz; gara; hin; kurai; hodo; shina. — *of medicines*, kōnō. *Superior* —, jōhin; gokujō. — *Middling* —, chiu-hin. *Inferior* —, gehin. — *of man*, h'to-gara; jim-pin.
QUALM *of conscience*, Ushirogurai; kuyamu.
QUANDARY, Tohō ni kureru; tamerai; yūyo; magotszku.
QUANTITY, Hodo; dake; bunriyō.
QUARREL, *n.* Kenk'wa; kōron; isakai; arasoi; naka ga warui; monchaku; momc.
QUARRELSOME, Kenk'wa-dzki na.
QUARRY, *v.* Horu.
QUART, = *about*, shi-go rok'shaku.
QUARTER, Shi-bu-ichi.
QUARTER, *v.* Yotsz ni wakeru.
QUASH, *v.* Osayeru; shidzmeru.
QUAY, Hatoba.
QUEEN, Kisaki; n'yo-tei.
QUEER, Ayashii; okashii.
QUELL, Shidzmeru; osameru; tairageru; heiji szru.
QUENCH, Kesz; shimeru.
QUESTION, *n.* Toi; tadzne; ron; rongi; rondan. *Beyond all* —, mochiron; mottomo. — *and answer*, mondō.
QUESTION, *v.* Tadzneru; tō.
QUESTIONABLE, Obotszkanai.
QUIBBLE, Rikutsz wo iu.
QUICK, Hayai; sassoku-na; szmiyaka; kiuna; jiki; toi; sōsō; isogu.
QUICKLY, Hayaku; sassoku; kiu-ni; jiki-ni; isoide; toku; kiusoku.
QUICKEN, Hayameru; seku; isogu.
QUICKNESS, Hayasa.
QUICK-SIGHTED, Me-bayai.
QUICKSILVER, Midzkane; szigin.
QUIET, Skidzka; odayaka; tairaka.
QUIET, *v.* Shidzmeru; osameru; heiji szru; ochi-tszkeru; ochi-tszku.
QUIETLY, Shidzka-ni; odayaka ni; ochi-tszite; sotto; soro-soro-to; yūyū.
QUIETNESS, Anki; annon; anraku.
QUILL, Hane.
QUILT, *n.* Futon.
QUILT, *v.* Tojiru.
QUININE, Kinayen; kinakina.
QUINTESSENCE, Gokui; shui; ōgi.
QUIRE, Kami nijū-shi-mai.
QUIT, Yameru; yosz; szteru; sztete-oku; utcharu; saru; hanareru.
QUITE, Mattaku; sappari-to; sara-ni.
QUIVER, *n.* Yebira; yanagui; utszbo; yugi; yadztsz.
QUIVER, *v.* Furū; wananaku; ononoku.
QUIZ, *v.* Chōrō szru; gurō szru; naburu.
QUOTE, Hiku.

R

RABBIT, Usagi.
RACE, Chiszji; shison; hashiri-kurabe. *Horse* —, keiba. *Boat* —, keishū.
RACK, *Clothes* —, ikō. *Pen* —, hikka.
RACKET, Sawagi.
RADIATE, Deru; hasszru.
RADISH, Daikon.
RAFT, Ikada.
RAFTER, Taruki.
RAG, Boro; tszdzre.
RAGE, Ikari; kurui; ikidōri; rippuku.
RAGING, Kurū; hageshii; takeshi.
RAIL, *n.* Teszri; rankan.
RAIL, *v.* Nonoshiru.
RAIL-ROAD, Jōk'sha-michi; tetszdō.
RAILLERY, Jōdan.
RAIMENT, Ifuku; kimono.
RAIN, Ame. *Long* —, furi-tszdzki. *Prayer for* —, amagoi. — *drops*, amadare. — *hat*, amagasa. *Heavy* —, ō-ame; ō-buri. *To* —, ame ga furu; furu. *Having the appearance of*, amakedzku; amefurisō; *Detained in the house by rain*, furi-komerareru.
RAINBOW, Niji; kōgei.
RAIN-COAT, Kappa.
RAIN-DOOR, Amado.
RAINY, Uten; amefuri. — *season*, niubai.
RAIN-TUB, Midztame; tenszioke.
RAIN-WATER, Ama-midz; tenszi.
RAISE, Ageru; tateru; agameru; odateru; kakageru. — *from sleep*, samesz; okiru. — *a family*, sodateru; buiku szru. — *from death*, ikasz; yomi-gayeru. — *money*, kane wo koshirayeru. — *horses*, uma wo kau; *or*, uma wo koshirayeru. — *wheat*, mugi wo tszkuru. — *a sedition*, muhon wo okosz. — *the price*, nedan wo ageru; *or*, nedan wo takaku szru. — *bread*, pan wo fukurakasz. — *a siege*, kakomi wo toku. — *a wall*, ishi-gaki wo kidzku.
RAISIN, Hoshi-budō.
RAKE, Kumade; dōraku-mono.
RAKE, *v.* Kaku. — *together*, kaki-atszmeru. — *and level*, kaki-narasz.

RALLY, Hiki-kayesz; matomeru.
RAM, Ō-hitszji.
RAM, *v.* Tszki-komu; buchi-komu.
RAMBLE, Aruki-mawaru; bura-bura aruku; shōyō.
RAMIFY, Yeda wo dasz.
RAMROD, Hisao.
RANCID, Kusai.
RANCOR, Urami; nikumi; ikon.
RANDOM, — *shot*, magure-atari; nagare-ya. *Talk at* —, dehōdai; detarame.
RANGE, *v.* Naraberu; aruki-mawaru.
RANGE, Ya-omote; yagoro.
RANK, *n.* Narabi; retsz; sonaye; kurai; kaku; kakushiki; I; ikai; bungen; mibun; rui.
RANK, *a.* Shigeru; habikoru; kusai; akudoi; shitszkoi.
RANK, *v.* Naraberu; sonayeru; tszraneru.
RANSACK, Hōbō sagasz.
RANSOM, Aganai-kin; mi-ukekin; aganai; tszgunai.
RAP, Tataku; butsz.
RAPACIOUS, Takeki.
RAPE, Gōin.
RAPESEED, Natane.
RAPID, Hayai; kiu-na.
RAPIDS, Se; kiu-riu; kayase.
RAPIDITY, Hayasa.
RAPIDLY, Hayaku; isoide; kiu-ni.
RAPINE, Ubai-tori.
RARE, Medzrashii; mare-na; szkunai. — *thing*, chim-butsz.
RARELY, Mare-ni; tama-ni; tama-tama; tamasaka; mare-mare.
RAREFY, Uszku szru; karuku szru.
RARITY, Medzrashisa; mare-naru koto; chim-butsz; uszsa; karusa.
RASCAL, Kiyatsz; yatsz; aitsz.
RASH, Mukōmidz; ki wo tszkenu.
RASP, Yaszri.
RASP, *v.* Kedzru; orosz.
RASPBERRY, Ichigo.
RAT, Nedzmi.
RATAN, Tō.
RATE, Kurai; hodo; dake; ne; nedan. — *of interest*, wari. *Market rate*, sōba.
RATE, *v.* Shikaru; togameru.
RATHER, Yoi; kayete; mushiro; nakanaka; nama-naka; kekku; namajii; namajikka; dzibun. — *think that*, yawaka; yomoya.
RATIFY, Muszbu; sadameru.
RATIO, Hodo; kurai.
RATION, Fuchi.
RATIONAL, Dōri ni kanau.
RATIONALE, Īware; dōri.
RATIONALIST, Rigak'sha.
RATSBANE, Nedzmi-koroshi.
RATTLE, Gara-gara naru; gata-gata szru.
RAVAGE, *v.* Arasz.
RAVAGED, Areru.
RAVE, Kurū; uwa-koto wo iu; sengo wo iu.
RAVEL, Toku; tokeru.
RAVEN, Karasz.
RAVENOUS, Gatsz-gatsz.
RAVINE, Kai; tani.
RAVISH, Ubai-toru; gōin szru.
RAW, Nama; arai. — *hide*, aragawa.
RAZE, Horobosz; uchi-kudzsz.
RAZOR, Kami-sori.
RAZOR-STROP, Togi-kawa.
REACH, *v.* Todokeru; todoku; oyobu; itaru; ataru.
REACH, *n.* Atari; temoto; tejika; teatari.
REACT, Kotayeru; hibiku.
REACTION, Hadzmi; hibiki.
READ, Yomu; doku-sho szru. — *through*, yomi-tōsz; yonde shimau; yomi-ageru. *About to* —, yomi-kakeru. *Wish to* —, yomi-tai. *Do not wish to* —, yomi-taku nai. *Hard to* —, yomi-gatai; yomi-nikui. *To mistake in reading*, yomi-ayamaru; yomi-sokonau. *To pretend to* —, yomi-nasz. *To read over again*, kuri-kayesh'te yomu ; sarayeru. *Can* —, yomeru.
READILY, Hayaku; yaszku; szgu-ni; szmiyaka-ni; yoku; kokoro-yoku.
READINESS, Hayasa; yaszsa; shitaku; kakugo.
READY, Shitaku ga aru; yōi ga aru; kakugo aru; sonaye ga aru; kokoro-yoku. *To make* —, shitaku szru; yōi szru; kakugo szru; sonayeru. — *money*, genkin; sokkin. — *to perish*, shi ni kakaru. — *way*, chikai-michi. — *at hand*, temoto; tejika. —*made*, deki-ai; ariai.
REAL, Jitsz-na; hon-no; makoto no; hontō na.
REALITY, Jitsz. *In* —, hon-ni ; jitsz-ni; makoto-ni; ge-ni.
REALIZE, Jitsz to omō; hontō to omō; makoto to szru. *Do not* —, jitsz to senu; makoto to omowanu.
REALLY, Jitsz-ni; hon-ni; makoto-ni; nakanaka.
REAM, Kami shi h'yaku hachi-jū mai.

REANIMATE, Yomi gayeraseru; hagemasz; iki-kayeru; ike-kayesz.

REAP, Karu; kiru.

REAPER, Kari-te.

REAR, Ushiro; ato. — *column of an army*, gojin; shingari. — *house*, uradana.

REAR, *v.* Tateru; sodateru; buiku szru; yōiku szru; yashinau; hagokumu; moritateru.

REAR-GUARD, Shingari; gojin.

REAR-RANK, Go-jin.

REASON, Dōri; ri; kotowari; michi; rikutsz; yuye; sei; wake; waza; chiye; fumbetsz.

REASON, *v.* Kangayeru; fum-betsz szru; rondzru; dankō szru; hiyō-ron szru; giron szru.

REASONABLE, Dōri ni kanau; ri ni au; mottomo.

REASONABLY, Mottomo; dzi-bun ni; kanari.

REASONING, Ron; gi-ron; hiyō-ron.

REASSEMBLE, Sai-k'wai szru; futa-tabi atszmeru.

REBEL, *n.* Mu-hon-nin; g'yaku-shin; g'yaku-zoku.

REBEL, *v.* Mu-hon szru; hon-gyaku szru; sakarau.

REBELLION, Mukon; hon-g'yaku; gekiran.

REBELLIOUS, G'yaku-i; bōg'yaku.

REBOUND, Hajiku; hadzmi.

REBUILD, Sai-kon szru; mata-tateru.

REBUKE, Togameru; shikaru; imashimeru; korasz.

RECALL, Yobi-kayesz;. — *to mind*, omoidasz.

RECANT, Ī-kayesz; ī-kayeru; ī-naosz.

RECAPITULATE, Kuri-kayesh'te iu.

RECAPTURE, Tori-kayesz.

RECEDE, Shirizoku; ato-shizari; yameru; hiku; naikō szru.

RECEIPT, Morai; itadaki; chōdai; kōmuri; uketori; shihōgaki.

RECEIVE, Morai; itadaki; chōdai; kōmuri; uketori; shihōgaki.

RECEIVE, Morau; itadaku; chōdai szru; kōmuru; adzkaru; tamawaru; kudasaru; junō szru. — *a guest*, kiyaku wo mukau.

RECEIVER, Uketori-nin; moraite. — *of stollen goods*, nuke-mono-kai.

RECENT, Atarashii; ima; shin. — *times*, chikaki toshi.

RECENTLY, Konaida; kono-goro; senjitsz; chikagoro; kinrai.

RECESS, Kiri; yaszmi; hiki; naka-iri.

RECIPE, Shihō-gaki; hōgaki.

RECIPROCAL, Tagai; ai-tagai.

RECIPROCALLY, Aitagai-ni; tagai ni; katami-ni.

RECIPROCATE, Kayowasz; tori-kayeru; kayesz; mukuyuru; hōdzru; shiau; shikayesz.

RECITATION, Sodoku; anshō.

RECITE, Hanasz; iu; noberu; sodcku wo szru; ansho szru; chiu de yomu; tonayeru.

RECKLESS, Mukō-midz; karuhadzmi; muyami na; metta-na.

RECKON, Kanjō szru; kazoyeru; tszmoru; hakaru.

RECOIL, Hadzmi.

RECKONING, Kanjō; tszmori; kazoye.

RECLAIM, Tori-kayesz; tori-modosz; shinaosz; tame-naosz.

RECLINE, Neru; fuseru; fusz.

RECLUSE, Inkiyo; in-ja.

RECOGNITION, Mi-oboye.

RECOGNIZE, Mi-oboyeru.

RECOIL, Hajiku.

RECOLLECT, Oboyeru; omoi-dasz; kokorodzku.

RECOMMEND, Tori-motsz.

RECOMMENDATION, Torimochi. *Letter of* —, soye-bumi; tensho.

RECOMPENSE, *v.* Mukuyuru; hōdzru; hempō szru; tszgunau.

RECOMPENSE, *n.* Mukui; hempō.

RECONCILE, Naka wo naosz; nakanaori wo szru; tokeau; akirameru; sh'tagau.

RECONCILIATION, Naka-naori.

RECONDITE, Ōgi.

RECONNOITRE, Ukagau.

RECONQUER, Tori-kayesz.

RECONSIDER, Mata-kangayeru; kuri-kayesh te omō; omoikayesz; omoi-naosz.

RECONSTRUCT, Sai-kon szru; mata tateru; saikō szru.

RECONVEY, Mochi-kayesz, hakobi-kayesz; kayesz.

RECORD, *v.* Shirusz; kaki-tomeru; tszkeru; ki szru; noseru.

RECORD, *n.* Chō; chōmen; kiroku; denki; roku.

RECOUNT, Kataru; monogataru; noberu; iu; hanasz.

RECOVER, Tori-kayesz; torikayeru. —*from sickness*, hombuku szru; zenk'wai szru; heiyu szru; naoru; k'wai-fuku szru.

RECOVERY, Hombuku; zenk'wai; heiyu; oginai; k'waifuku.

RECREATION, Nagusami; asobi; kisanji; kibarashi.

RECRUIT, Oginau; tasz; hoyeki szru.
RECTIFY, Naosz; aratameru; kai-kaku szru; kaisei szru.
RECTITUDE, Shōjiki.
RECUR, Kayeru; sai-kayeru; sai-kan szru.
RECURRENT, Sai-kan-naru.
RED, Akai; kurenai.
REDDEN, Akaku szru; akameru; akaramu. *Face to* —, sekimen szru.
REDDISH, Akami.
REDEEM, Aganau; miuke wo szru; ukekayesz; kai-modosz; taszkeru; szkū.
REDEEMER, Aganai-nin.
REDEMPTION, Kai-modoshi, aganai; mi-uke.
RED-HAIRED, Akage.
RED-HOT, Hi ni naru; yakeru.
RED-LEAD, Tan.
RED-OCHRE, Taishaseki.
REDOUND, Naru.
REDRESS, Naosz; aratameru; szkū.
REDUCE, Habuku; gendzru; herasz; otosz. — *the price*, makeru; hiku. — *to subjection*, tairageru; sh'tagawaseru. — *in rank*, shikujiru.
REDUCTION, Habuki;genshō. — *in price*, nebiki.
REDUNDANT, Yokei; yobun; amari no; nokoru.
REED, Take; yoshi; aze.
REEF, *n.* Iwa.
REEF, *v.* Ho wo tszmeru.
REEL, *n.* Waku; maiba; kase.
REEL, *v.* Kuru; yoromeku.
REFER, Makaseru.
REFINE, Fuki-wakeru; yakinaosz; aratameru; naosz.
REFINED, Fūriu-na; ateyaka-na; miyabi-taru; miyabiyakana; fūga.
REFLECT, *v.* Kangayeru; omoi-mawasz; shiriyo szru; utszsz; utszru; kayerimiru.
REFLECTION, Kangaye; shiriyo.
REFORM, Aratameru; kaikaku szru; naosz; kaishin szru; henkaku szru.
REFRAIN, Hikayeru; shimbō szru.
REFRESH, Szdzmu; nagusameru; nōriyō wo szru; yaszmeru.
REFRESHING, Szdzshii.
REFUGE, Kakure-ba; tanomi-dokoro; yōgai.
REFUGEE, Ochi-udo.
REFULGENT, Kagayaku; hikaru; kira-kira szru.
REFUND, Tszgunau; kayesz; hemben szru.
REFUSAL, Kotowari.
REFUSE, Kotowaru; yurusanu; shōchi senu; ji-tai szru; inamu.
REFUTE, Ī-yaburu; ī-tszmeru; ī-katsz; ī-tszbusz.
REGARD, *v.* Itoi; kamau; kayeri-miru; tattomu; mamoru; wiyamau. *In* — *to*, ni tszite.
REGARD, *n.* Yōsha.
REGENT, Gotairo.
REGIMEN, Doku-date; yōjō.
REGION, Tochi; tokoro; atari; kai.
REGISTER, *n.* Chō; chōmen.
REGISTER, *v.* Kaki-tomeru; tszkeru.
REGRET, Zan-nen; kuchi-oshii; kuyami; oshimi; mu-nen; ki-no-doku; kō-k'wai.
REGRET, *v.* Kuyamu; kō-k'wai szru; oshimu; kinodoku ni omō; zan-nen ni omō. *To be regretted*, kuyashii.
REGULAR, Tori-shimari no yoi. — *order*, jumban; junguri; junjun ni.
REGULARITY, Tori-shimari; shimari.
REGULATE, Osameru; totonoyeru.
REGULATION, Okite; sadame; gijō.
REGURGITATE, Haku; modosz.
REHEARSE, Hanasz; kataru; noberu; monogataru.
REIGN, Kurai wo fumu; shihai szru; osameru.
REIGNING, — *emperor*, zaii; kin-jō. *One in whom avarice is the reigning passion*, ri-yoku-gachi na mono.
REIMBURSE, Tszgunau.
REIN, Tadzna.
REITERATE, Kuri-kayesz; kasane-gasane iu.
REJECT, Szteru; utcharu; kotowaru; ukenu; shōchi senu.
REJOICE, Yorokobu; kiyetsz szru.
RELAPSE, Sai-kan szru; sai-hotsz; sai-kayeru; tachi-modoru; ato-modori wo szru; temodori.
RELATE, Noberu; kataru; iu; hanasz; tszgeru; chindzru; kakawaru; tszku.
RELATION, Mono-gatari; hanashi; shinrui; yenja; aidagara; yukari; miyori; yen; chinami; chigiri; tame. *In* — *to*, ni tszite; taish'te.
RELATIVE, Shinrui.
RELAX, Yurumeru; kutszrogeru; yawarageru; yaszmeru; darumu.
RELAXATION, Nagusami; yaszmi; kibarashi.
RELAY, Kaye-uma.
RELEASE, Hanasz; yurusz.
RELENT, Tokeru; yurumu.
RELENTLESS, Jihi naki; awaremi naki.

RELIABLE, Tanomoshii; toritomeru.
RELIANCE, Tanomi; tayori; chikara; shinko.
RELIC, Ato; nokori; nagori. *Ancient* —, koseki.
RELIEF, Raku.
RELIEVE, Raku ni szru; yurumeru; taszkeru.
RELIGION, Oshiye; michi; hō; dō.
RELIGIOUS, Shin-jin-naru. — *book*, oshiye no hon; dōgakusho. — *discourses*, dōwa.
RELINQUISH, Yameru; szteru; hai szru, yudzru; shirizoku.
RELISH, Oishii; umai; konomu; szku. *Do not* —, oishiku nai.
RELUCTANT, Iyagaru; kirau; itō.
RELY, Tanomu; tayoru; szgaru; yoru.
REMAIN, Matsz; todomaru; tomaru; tō-riu szru; zairiu szru; nokoru; nokosz; amaru; amasz.
REMAINDER, Nokori; amari. — *of money*, zangin.
REMAINING, Nokoru; amaru. *None* —, nokoradz. — *money*, zangin. — *flowers*, zan-k'wa.
REMAINS, Ato; nokori; amari; naki-gara.
REMAND, Kayesz.
REMARK, *v*. Mi-tomeru; mi-tszkeru; hanasz.
REMARKABLE, Miyō-na; kimiyō-na; medzrashii; kakubetsz-no; betsz-dan-no; yerai.
REMARKABLY, Kakubetsz-ni; tori-wakete; bessh'te.
REMARRY, Saiyen szru; futatabi metoru.
REMEDIABLE, Naorareru.
REMEDILESS, Naoranu; kuszri-nai; shikata ga nai.
REMEDY, Kuszri; riyōji; oginai; tszkuroi; shi-kata; shi-yō; sen-kata. *No* —, kuszri ga nai; shi-kata ga nai.
REMEDY, *v*. Naoru; naosz; tszkurō; oginau.
REMEMBER, Oboyeru; omoidasz; kokoro ni kakeru.
REMEMBRANCE, Oboye.
REMIND, Ki wo tszkeru; oshiyeru.
REMISS, Okotaru; yudan wo szru; taiman; tarumu; darumu; nukaru; orosoka.
REMISSION, Yurushi; shamen; gomen; yurumi; yaszmi.
REMISSNESS, Okotari; yudan; kedai.
REMIT, Yurumu; uszrogu; yurusz; shamen szru; gomen szru. — *money*, yaru; okuru; tszkawasz.
REMNANT, Hash'ta; nokori; hampa; sztari; zambutsz.
REMONSTRANCE, Isame; kangen; iken.
REMONSTRATE, Isameru; kangen szru; iken szru.
REMORSE, Kuyami; zannen; kōk'wai.
REMORSELESS, Jihi-naki; awaremi naki.
REMOTE, Tōi; yempō; haruka.
REMOTENESS, Tōsa.
REMOVAL, Tori-harai; harai.
REMOVE, Utszru; utszsz; toru; hadzsz; tori-harau; tori-hadzsz.
REMUNERATE, Mukuyuru; kayesz; hōdzru; hōbi wo yaru; tszgunau.
REND, Saku; waru; hikisaku; sakeru.
RENDER, Kayesz; mukuyuru; hōdzru. *Also the caust. form of the verb:* naosz; honyaku szru.
RENDEZVOUS, Atszmeru; matomeru.
RENEW, Shi-naosz; shi-kayeru; aratameru; ire-kayeru.
RENOUNCE, Szteru.
RENOWN, Kōmei; homare; kō-miyō; nadakai.
RENT, *v*. Karu; kasz.
RENT, *n*. Tana-chin; yachin. *Ground* —, jidai.
RENTER, Kari-te; kari-kata; tanako; tanagari.
REPAIR, Naosz; tszkurō; oginau; shi-naosz; tszgunau.
REPARATION, Tszgunai; oginai; naori.
REPAY, Kayesz; mukuyuru; hōjiru; tszgunau; hemben szru; henjō szru; henkiyaku; hennō.
REPEAL, Yameru.
REPEAT, Kasanete iu; kasaneru; mata.
REPEATEDLY, Kasane-gasane; tabi-tabi; tatami-kakete; kayesz-gayesz; kure-gure.
REPEL, Fusegu; shirizokeru.
REPENT, Kuyamu; kō-k'wai szru; zan-nen ni omō.
REPENTANCE, Kō-k'wai; zan-nen; kuyami.
REPINE, Oshimu; kuchi-oshigaru; kuyamu.
REPLACE, Kayesz.
REPLY, *v*. Kotayeru; hen-tō szru; henji szru.
REPLY, *n*. Kotaye; hentō; henji.
REPORT, *v*. Mōshi-ageru; todokeru; mōshi-noberu; chiu-shin szru; gonjō szru.
REPORT, *n*. Todoke-sho; fūbun; hiyō-ban; uwasa; tori-sata; fūzetsz; hibiki; oto.
REPOSE, Neru; yaszmu.
REPREHEND, Togameru; imashimeru; korasz; korashimeru.

REPRESENT, Nazorayeru; yosoyeru; katadoru.
REPRESENTATIVE, Sōdai; miyō-dai.
REPRESS, Osameru; shidzmeru; hikayeru; tori-hishigu; osayeru.
REPRIMAND, Togameru; imashimeru; shikaru; korashimeru; kimeru.
REPRINT, Sai-han szru.
REPRISAL, Hem-pō.
REPROACH, *v.* Togameru; shikaru; nonoshiru; kimeru; kime-tszkeru.
REPROACH, *n.* Togame; nonoshiri; akkō; zōgon; sogon; haji; kakin; chijoku.
REPROBATE, Dōraku; hōtō; hōratsz.
REPROOF, Imashime; iken; isame; togame; korashime.
REPTILE, Mushi.
REPUBLISH, Sai-han szru.
REPUDIATE, Szteru; utcharu; ribetsz szru; riyen szru.
REPUGNANCE, Kirau; iyagaru; imu; itō.
REPUGNANT, Sakarau; motoru; sakō; awanu; kanawanu.
REPUTATION, Hiyōban; miyōmon; na.
REQUEST, *v.* Negau; tanomu; kō.
REQUEST, *n.* Negai; tanomi; koi. *In* —, hake-kuchi ga ōi; ure-kuchi ga aru.
REQUIRE, or REQUISITE, *Formed thus. It is required of the people that they obey the laws of the state,* tami wa koku-hō ni sh'tagawaneba naranu. *Air is requisite to life,* kūki wa nakute kanawanu mono nari.
REQUITAL, Mukui; hempō.
REQUITE, Mukuyuru; hōjiru; kayesz.
RESCIND, Yameru; haiszru.
RESCUE, Taszkeru; szkū.
RESEMBLE, Niru; niteoru; nazorayeru; yosoyeru; ayakaru; katadoru.
RESENT, Ikidōru; togameru.
RESENTMENT, Ikidōri; urami; onnen.
RESERVE, *v.* Nokosz; nokoru; kokoro wo oku; okiau.
RESERVE, *n.* Yenriyo; habakari; kokoro-oki.
RESERVED, Tottoki no.
RESERVOIR, Midz-tame.
RESHIP, Tszmi-kayesz; okuri-kayesz.
RESIDE, Szmu; oru; jū-kiyo szru; szmau; zaijū.
RESIDENCE, Szmai; jūkiyo; iye; taku.
RESIDENT, Jū-nin; szmu-h'to.
RESIDUE, Nokori; zambutsz.
RESIDUUM, Kasz; tare-kasz.
RESIGN, Yudzru; makaseru; sh'tagau; taishin szru. — *office,* tai-yaku szru. — *seat,* tai-za szru.
RESIN, Matsz no yani; chan.
RESIST, Sakarau; tekitau; sakō; bōgiyo szru.
RESISTLESS, Sakarawarenu.
RESOLUTE, Kitszi; kidzyoi; kijōna.
RESOLVE, Sadameru; ketszjō szru; ketchaku szru; toku; wakeru; handan szru; bunri szru.
RESONANCE, Hibiki.
RESORT, *v.* Mochiiru.
RESOUND, Naru; hibiku; narasz; doyomu.
RESOURCE, Shikata; shiyō; senkata.
RESOURCES, Taka; shin-sho.
RESPECT, *v.* Wiyamau; tattomu.
RESPECT, *n.* Wiyamai; tattomi. *In respect to,* ni tszite; taish'te. *No — of persons,* hedatszru kokoro nashi.
RESPECTABLE, Hodo-yoi. — *person,* h'togara no yoi h'to; jim-pin no yoi-h'to; jōhin na h'to; bungen no yoi h'to.
RESPECTFUL, Wiya-wiyashii.
RESPECTING, Ni tszite; taish'te.
RESPECTIVE, Mochimaye.
RESPIRATION, Iki-dzkai; kokiu.
RESPIRE, Iki wo szru; kokiu szru.
RESPITE, Hima; itoma; yaszmi.
RESPOND, Kotayeru; hentō szru; henji szru; ōdzru.
RESPONSE, Kotaye; hentō; henji.
RESPONSIBLE, Kakawaru; tszgunau hadz; madō-beki.
REST, *v.* Yaszmu; kiusoku szru; ikō; oku.
REST, *n.* Yaszmi; nokori.
RESTAURANT, Riyōri-ya.
RESTLESS, Ochi-tszkanu.
RESTORATION, Naori. — *to health,* hombuku;; zenk'wai; heiyu. — *of friendship,* naka-naori.
RESTORE, Kayesz; tszgunau; oginau; tszkurau; naoru. — *to health* hombuku szru. — *to life,* yomi-gayeru; saisei. — *a building,* sai-kon szru.
RESTRAIN, Hikayeru; osayeru; sashi-tomeru; tomeru; shukumeru.
RESTRAINT, Hikayeme; osaye.
RESULT, *v.* Okoru; hasszru. — *in,* hateru; shimau; owaru; oyobu; hatasz.
RESULT, *n.* Owari; hate; sei; yuye; waza; ni yotte.
RESUME, Sai-ko szru; mata-hajimeru.
RESURRECTION, Haka kara yomigayeru; sai-sei szru; iki-kayeru.
RESUSSITATE, Ike-kayesz; ikasz.

RETAIL, Ko-uri wo szru.
RETAIN, Motsz; tamotsz.
RETAINER, Kerai; shin.
RETAKE, Tori-kayesz.
RETALIATE, Kayesz; mukuyuru.
RETARD, Osoku szru; nibuku szru; sasayeru; todokōru.
RETCH, Yedzku; haku;
RETICULE, Tamoto-otoshi.
RETINUE, Tomo; dōzei.
RETIRE, Shirizoku; jitai szru; saru; hiki-toru; tonsei szru; noku.
RETIRED, Inkiyo.
RETIREMENT, *Living in* —, in-kiyo.
RETORT, *v.* Ī-kayesz.
RETORT, *n.* Rambiki.
RETRACE, Kayeru; modoru.
RETRACT, Ī-naosz; hen-gai szru; īkayeru.
RETREAT, *v.* Shirizoku; hiki-kayesz; hiki-toru. — *of an army*, taijin szru.
RETRENCH, Habuku; herasz; gendzru; seiriyaku.
RETRENCHMENT, Genshō.
RETRIBUTION, Mukui; k'wahō; in-g'wa.
RETRIEVE, Sai-ko szru; k'waifuku szru; tate-naosz.
RETROGRADE, Atoshizari wo szru; atomodori wo szru.
RETROSPECT, Kayeri-miru.
RETURN, *v.* Kayeru; modoru; hennō szru; kayesz; modosz; kizan; mukuyuru; henjō; kichaku. — *an answer*; kotayeru. — *home*, ki-taku szru. — *compliment*, henrei szru. *On returning*, kayeri-gake ni.
RETURN, *n.* Kayeri; modori; kayeshi; ribun; mōke.
REVEAL, Arawasz; arawareru; shiraseru; kikaseru; tszgeru.
REVELRY, Sakamori sawagi.
REVELATION, *divine* —, kami no tszge; kami no shirase; takusen; jigen.
REVENGE, *v.* Kayesz; mukuyuru; hōdzru.
REVENGE, *n.* Mukui.
REVENGEFUL, Mukuitagaru.
REVENGER, Uchite; kataki wo utsz h'to.
REVENUE, Taka; shu-nō; agari; tori-ka.
REVERBERATE, Hibiku; doyomu.
REVERE, Wiyamau; son-kiyō szru; tattomu.
REVERENCE, Wiyamai; tattobi; son-kiyō; kukiyō.
REVERY, Uttori-to.
REVERSE, *v.* Fuseru; guri-kayesz.
REVERSE, *n.* Wazawai; fu-un; un ga kawaru.
REVERSELY, Saka-sama; abekobe-ni; kayete.
REVERT, Kayesz.
REVIEW, *v.* Kuri-kayesh'te miru; kayerimiru; sziko szru; kemi szru; sarayeru.
REVILE, Akkō szru; nonoshiru.
REVISE, Kuri-kayesh'te miru; kayeri-miru; szi-ko szru; kai-sei szru.
REVISIT, Mata kayeru.
REVIVE, Iki-kayeru; yomi-gayeru; futatabi okoru; sai-ko szru.
REVOKE, Īkayesz; aratameru; kiri-kayeru.
REVOLT, *n.* Muhon; ikki.
REVOLT, *v.* Muhon szru; ikki wo okosz.
REVOLUTION, Muhon; junk'wan; mawari.
REVOLVE, Mawaru; meguru; mawasz; megurasz; junk'wan szru. — *in the mind*, omoi-mawasz.
REWARD, *n.* Hōbi; mukui. — *and punishment*, shō-batsz.
REWARD, *v.* Hōbi wo yaru; shō szru; mukuyuru; hōjiru.
RHEUMATISM, Fūshitsz; ts'ufū; fūdoku.
RHINOCEROS, Sai.
RHUBARB, Daiyō.
RHYME, Uta.
RIB, Abara-bone.
RIBBON, Himo.
RICE, *Unhulled* —, momi. *Clean rice*, kome; *or*, haku-mai. — *shoots*, naye. — *in the stalk*, ine. — *straw*, wara. *Cooked* —, meshi. *Early* —, wase. *Late* —, okute. *Middling* —, nakate. *Upland* —, okabo. — *bran*, nuka. — *flour* kome no ko. — *cakes*, mochi. *Old* —, komai. — *box*, komebitsz. — *bag*, kome-dawara. — *store*, komeya.
RICH, Kane-mochi; shinsho no yoi; yūfukuna; tomeru; yutaka-na; koyeru.
RICHES, Takara; zai-hō; shinsho; tomi.
RICHLY, Fukaku; omoku; ōku; jūbun-ni; makoto-ni; jitsz-ni.
RICK, Inamura.
RICOCHET, Toberu. — *firing*, toberiuchi.
RID, Toru; taszkeru; harau; oidasz.
RIDE, Noru; jōdzru; ga szru; haseru.
RIDDLE, Nazo.
RIDER, Nori-te; nori-kata; umanori.
RIDGE, Mune; mine.
RIDICULE, Azakeru; gurō szru; chōrō szru; warau; aza-warau.
RIDICULOUS, Okashii; monowarai; oko; okogamashii.

RIDING-SCHOOL, Ba-ba.
RIFLE, *n.* Teppō.
RIFLE, *v.* Ubai-toru; kaszmeru; nuszmu.
RIG, *v.* Idetachi; yosoō.
RIGGING, Fune no tszna.
RIGHT, *v.* Tadashii; yoi; makoto, jitsz; yoroshii; migi. — *side,* migi no hō. — *and wrong,* zen-aku; ri-hi; ze-hi. *All right,* yoroshi; yoshi;
RIGHT, *adv.* Yoroshiku; yoku; tadachi-ni; mottomo; tōzen.
RIGHT, *n.* Dōri; michi; ri; gi;zen; szji; hadz; beki. *To put to rights,* sōji szru. — *and left,* sa-yū.
RIGHTEOUS, *I know of no word in the Japanese language answering to this word or to the word Righteousness.*
RIGHTFUL, Szji-no.
RIGHTLY, Yoku; yoroshiku; jitsz-ni; makoto-ni.
RIGHT-HAND, Migi-no-te.
RIGID, Katai; kibishii; genjū na; kowai; kiu-kutsz na; ogosoka.
RIGOR, Katasa; kibishisa.
RIGOROUSLY, Kataku; kibishiku.
RIM, Fuchi.
RIND, Kawa.
RING, *n.* Wa; nari. — *and staple,* kakegane.
RING, *v.* Narasz; naru; hibiku.
RING-FINGER, Beni-sashi-yubi.
RING-LEADER, Kashira; chōbon; hottō-nin; hon-nin.
RING-WORM, Tamushi.
RINSE, Sosogu; arau.
RIOT, Sōdō; ikki; sawagi; ran. *To run* —, abareru.
RIOTOUS, Abareru; sawagashii.
RIP, Saku; hiki-saku; sakeru.
RIPE, Juku-sh'ta; unda; yawaraka; renjuku na.
RIPPLE, Se; joro-joro to.
RISE, *v.* Agaru; noboru; okiru; tatsz; deru; okoru; hasszru; he-agaru. *Rising up or lying down,* oki-fushi.
RISK, Kakawaru; kakeru.
RITE, Hō; rei; shiki.
RIVAL, Aite.
RIVAL, *v.* Kisō; kioi; arasoi.
RIVE, Waru; saku.
RIVER, Kawa. — *bank,* kawa-bata; kawabe; kawa-gishi. — *month,* kawagushi. *Up the* —, kawakami. *Down the* —, kawashimo.
RIVET, Me-kugi.

RIVULET, Tani-gawa; ogawa.
ROAD, Michi; dōro. *In the* —, to-chiu.
ROADSTEAD, Kakari-ba.
ROAM, Yūreki szru; aruki mawaru.
ROAR, Naku; hoyeru; sakebu.
ROAST, Yaku; iru.
ROB, Nuszmu; ubau; kaszmeru; toru.
ROBBER, Dorobō; nuszbito; tōzoku.
ROBE, Kimono. *Priest's* —, koromo.
ROBE, *v.* Yosoō; kiru.
ROBUST, Szkoyaka; tassha; jōbu; sōken-na; takumashii; mame-na; mameyaka.
ROCK, Iwa; banjaku; iwao.
ROCK, *v.* Yurugu; yurugasz; yureru; yuru; yura-yura; ugoku.
ROCK-CRYSTAL, Szishō.
ROCKET, Hanabi; noroshi.
ROCK-WORK, Tszki-yama.
ROD, Sao.
ROGUE, Yatsz; katari.
ROLL, *v.* Korobu; korobasz; korogaru; maku; mawaru; mawasz; meguru; hineru; makuru.
ROLL, *n.* Maki.
ROLLER, Koro; to-guruma.
ROLLING-PIN, Membō.
ROMP, *v.* Tawamureru ; fusakeru; jareru ; odokeru.
ROOF, *n.* Yane.
ROOF, *v.* Fuku.
ROOM, Heya; zashiki; ma. *Plan of* —, madori.
ROOMY, Hiroi.
ROOST, *n.* Tomarigi; negura.
ROOST, *v.* Tomaru.
ROOSTER, Ondori.
ROOT, *n.* Ne.
ROOT, *v. (as a pig),* Horu;. — *up,* nuku; kogu.
ROPE, Nawa; tszna.
ROPE-DANCING, Tszna-watari.
ROPE-MAKER, Tszna-uchi.
ROPE-MAKING, Tszna-uchi.
ROSARY, Judz, nenju; dzdz.
ROSE, Bara no hana. *White* —, yashōbi; dobi.
ROSIN, Chan.
ROSTRUM, Kōza.
ROT, *v.* Kusaru; kuchiru.
ROTATE, Mawaru; meguru.
ROTTEN, Kusai; kuchi-taru.
ROUGE, Beni.
ROUGH, Arai; somatsz-na; bukotsz-na; gasatsz; zaratszku. — *estimate,* ara-dzmori.

ROUGHLY, Araku; somatsz-ni; zatto; burei-ni; kibishiku; tszyoku.

ROUGHNESS, Arasa.

ROUND, Marui; madoka naru. *To go* —, mawaru; meguru. *To turn* —, mawasz; megurasz. *To wind* —, maku. *Make* —, maruku szru; marumeru. — *off the corners*, kado wo toru.

ROUNDABOUT, Mawaridōi; uyen-na.

ROUNDNESS, Marusa.

ROUSE, *v.* Mesameru; okiru; me wo samasz; okosz. — *up*, hagemasz; hagemu; fumpatsz szru.

ROUT, *v.* Oi-chirasz; seme-yaburu.

ROUTED, Hai-gun szru.

ROVE, Yūreki szru.

ROW, *n.* Narabi; tszra; retsz; kudari; giyō; tate; kawa. *To place in a* —, naraberu; narabu; tszranaru; tszraneru.

ROW, *v.* Kogu.

RUB, *v.* Koszru; szru; momu; naderu; kishiru. — *and polish*, migaku; szri-migaku. — *off*, szri-hagasz; szri-muku; szri-otosz. — *in*, szri-komu; momi-komu. — *fine*, szri-kudaku. — *out*, kesz; momi-kesz. — *up*, migaku. — *against*, szri-chigau; kishiru. — *on*, szri-tszkeru. — *off*, momi-otosz.

RUBBISH, Gomi; akuta; chiri.

RUDDER, Kaji.

RUDDY, Akai.

RUDE, Arai; somatsz; zatsz; soriyaku; burei; shitszrei; bukotsz; busahō; heta; nama.

RUDELY, Araku; ara-arashiku; ara-ara; somatsz ni; zatto; burei-ni.

RUDIMENT, Moto; dodai.

RUE, *v.* Zan-nen ni omō; kuyamu; oshimu.

RUEFUL, Kanashii.

RUFFIAN, Rambō-nin; abaremono.

RUFFLE, Shiwameru; hida wo toru; araku szru; sawagasz.

RUG, Mōsen; mensen.

RUGGED, Arai.

RUIN, *n.* Horobi; metszbō.

RUIN, *v.* Horobiru; horobosz; tszbusz; tszbureru; ha-metsz; yaburu; metszbō; botszraku; chinrin.

RUINS, Ato; koseki.

RULE, *n.* Ki-soku; kaku; rei; hō; sa-hō; sadame; hō-shiki; shi-hai.

RULE, *v.* Shi-hai szru; osameru; szji wo hiku. *Ruled paper*, kebikigami.

RULER, Osameru h'to; kashira; shi-hai szru h'to; matszrigoto szru h'to; jōgi.

RUMBLE, Naru; todoroku; doro-doro; goro-goro.

RUMOR, Fūbun; fūzetsz; hiyōban; uwasa.

RUMP, Shiri.

RUMPLE, *v.* Momu.

RUMPLED, Shiwa ga yoru.

RUN, *v.* Hashiru; kakeru. — *away*, chikuten szru; nigeru. — *(flow)*, nagareru. — *(metal)*, toku; iru. — *round*, mawaru; meguru. — *(as ink)*, ochiru. — *(as a snake)*, hau. — *after*, ō; (ōi). — *at*, tszki-kakaru. — *into*, kake-komu; hashiri-komu. — *down*, tareru; tarasz; kake-kudaru; hashiri-oriru; soshiru; waruku iu. — *over*, afureru; koboreru. — *out*, kake-dasz; nagare-deru; moru; szmu. — *riot*, abareru. — *up*, kake-agaru. — *through*, kake-tōru; tszyasz; tszki-tōsz. — *a nail into the foot*, kugi ga ashi ni tatsz.

RUNAWAY, Ochi-udo.

RUSH, *n.* Ashi.

RUST, *n.* Sabi.

RUST, *v.* Sabiru.

RUSTIC, *n.* Inaka-mono; gasatsz-mono.

RUSTIC, *a.* Inaka; bukotsz-na.

RUSTLE, *v.* Sara-sara to naru.

RUSTY, Sabita.

S

SABBATH, Zontaku; ansoku-nichi; yaszmibi.

SACK, Tawara; fukuro.

SACRED, *Formed by the prefix*, mi; on; go; *or* o; *as*, *sacred name*, mi-na. — *book*, on kiyō. — *worship*, o matszri.

SACRIFICE, *v.* Ageru; sonayeru; tamukeru; tatematszru; matszru.

SACRIFICE, *Animal* —, ikeniye. *Things offered in* —, kumotsz; tamuke.

SACRILEGIOUS, Mottainai.

SAD, Kanashii; urei; itamashii. *To feel* —, kanashimu; urei.

SADDLE, Kura.

SADDLER, Bagu-ya.

SADDLE-TREE, Kura-bone.

SADLY, Kanashiku; ureite.

SADNESS, Kanashisa; urei; utsz.

SAFE, Buji; sokusai; dai-jōbu; tassha-na; tash'ka-na; tszdzkanai.

SAFELY, Buji-ni; anzen-ni; tash'ka-ni.

SAFFLOWER, Beni no hana.

SAG, Kata-yoru; kata-dzru; tawamu.
SAGACIOUS, Kash'koi; rikō-na; chiye ga aru.
SAGACITY, Chiye; chi-riyaku.
SAGE, Seijin.
SAGO, Sagobei.
SAID, Itta *pret. of* iu; hanash'ta; kudan-no; iwayuru.
SAIL, *n.* Ho; sō. *To set* —, shuppan szru. — *boat, or ship*, hobune; hokakbeune.
SAIL, *v.* Shuppan szru; hashiru.
SAINT, *Buddhist* —, hijiri.
SAKE, Tame; yotte; (yori).
SALAD, Chisha.
SALARY, Yaku-riyō; rei; rei-kin.
SALE, Ure; hake-kuchi; hake; sabake; uriguchi; sabaki-kuchi.
SALEABLE, Ure ga yoi.
SALIVA, Tszbaki; yodare; katadz.
SALMON, Shake. *Pickled* —, shio-biki.
SALT, Shio.
SALT, *v.* Shio ni tszkeru; shio wo szru.
SALT-CELLAR, Shio-ire; teshio; shiozara.
SALTISH, Shio-ke.
SALT-MAKER, Shio-yaki.
SALT-MERCHANT, Shio-ya.
SALT-PETRE, Shō-seki.
SALT-WATER, Shio; shio-midz.
SALT-WORKS, Shiohama.
SALTY, Shio-kayui; shio-karai; shoppai.
SALUBRIOUS, Tame ni naru.
SALUTARY, Tame ni naru.
SALUTATION, Aisatsz; jigi; reigi.
SALUTE, Aisatsz szru; reigi wo szru; jigi wo szru.
SALVATION, Taszke; szkui; saido.
SALVE, Kōyaku.
SAME, Onaji; onajikoto; dō. — *as before*, moto no tōri; itszmo onaji. *Not all the* —, onajiku nai. — *as the pattern*, mihon no tōri. — *state*, dōhen.
SAMPAN, Fune; temma.
SAMPLE, Tehon; mihon.
SANCTIFY, Kiyomeru; szmasz.
SAND, Szna; isago.
SANDAL, Zōri; sekida; waraji.
SANDAL-WOOD, Biyakudan.
SAND-BAG, Do-hiyō.
SAND-BANK, Sz.
SANDY, Szna-gachi. — *desert*, sznappa; sabaku.
SANE, Tash'ka-na.
SANG-FROID, Hei-ki; magao.
SANGUINARY, H'to-jini no ōi; mugoi; muzan.

SAP, Shiru; yani; shibu.
SARDINE, Iwashi.
SARDONIC, Nigawarai.
SASH, Obi; Shōji.
SATCHEL, Dōran.
SATIATE, Aku; taru; tennō szru.
SATIETY, Aki; taikutsz.
SATIN, Shusz.
SATIRE, Rakushu; warukuchi.
SATISFACTION, An-shin; taru koto; akirame; tszgunai; oginai.
SATISFY, Aku; taru; aki-taru; tszgunau; oginau; akirameru; ki ni kanau.
SATURATE, Shimesz; nurasz; shimi-tōru.
SATURN, Dosei.
SAUCE, Shōgu; miso.
SAUCER, Sara.
SÀVAGE, Mugoi; muzan-na; yebisz.
SAVE, Taszkeru; szkū; tamotsz; saido szru; do szru. — *money*, kane wo nokosz; *or*, kane wo tameru.
SAVING, Kenyaku-na; shimatsz-na; kanriyaku na.
SAVIOUR, Szkuite; taszkete.
SAVOR, Nioi; ajiwai.
SAVORY, Oishii; umai.
SAW, *n.* Nokogiri.
SAW, *v.* Hiku.
SAWDUST, Oga-kudz.
SAY, Iu; hanasz; iwaku; danjiru; tszgeru.
SAYING, Setsz; hanashi. *Habit of* —, kuchi-kuse.
SCAB, *n.* Kasa-buta.
SCAB, *v.* Kaseru.
SCABBARD, Saya.
SCAFFOLD, Ashiba.
SCALD, *v.* Yu de yakeru; ibiru.
SCALD, *n.* Yakedo.
SCALE, Hakari; tem-bin; koke; uroko; sane.
SCALE, *v.* Noboru; agaru;
SCAMP, Kiyatsz; yatsz.
SCANDAL, Soshiri; zangen; hihō; haji.
SCANDALOUS, Hadzkashii.
SCANTY, Semai; taranu; fusoku-na; szkunai; szkoshi.
SCANTILY, Taradz-ni; szkunaku; fusoku ni sh'te.
SCAR, Ato.
SCARCE, Szkunai; fusoku; toboshii; futtei.
SCARCELY, Yōyaku; yatto; karōjite.
SCARE, Odosz; odorokasz; obiyakasz.
SCARE-CROW, Odoshi; kagashi; sōdz; hita; naruko; tori-odoshi.
SCARF, *Of a priest*, kesa.
SCARIFY, Asaku kiru.

SCARLET, Akai; hi.
SCARP, Kishi.
SCATTER, Chirasz; chiru; hai-szru.
SCATTERED, Mabara; usszri to; chiru.
SCATTERINGLY, Bara-bara; barari-to; sanzan; chiri-chiri.
SCAVENGER, Machi no sōji nin.
SCENE, Keshiki; yōsz; tei.
SCENERY, Keshiki; fūkei; keishoku; chōbō.
SCENT, Nioi; ka.
SCENT, *v.* Kagu; kaoru; kagi-dasz; kagi-tszkeru.
SCHEDULE, Mokuroku.
SCHEME, Tedate; te; hakarigoto, keiriyaku; kufū; jutsz; hōben.
SCHEME, *v.* Kufū szru; kuwadateru; hakaru.
SCHISM, Wakari; yedaha.
SCHOLAR, Deshi; monjin; gakusha.
SCHOOL, Gakudō; keiko-ba; gakumonjo; juku; ha; riu; riugi; shū-shi.
SCHOOL-FELLOW, Dō-gaku.
SCHOOL-HOUSE, Gakudō; gakumonjo.
SCHOOL-MASTER, Shishō.
SCHOOL-MATE, Dōgaku.
SCIENCE, Gaku; jutsz.
SCISSORS, Hasami.
SCLEROTIC, Haku-maku.
SCOFF, *v.* Azakeru; gurō szru; soshiru.
SCOLD, Shikaru; togameru; kogoto wo iu; kimeru.
SCOOP, *n.* Shaku.
SCOOP, *v.* Kumu; kuru; yeguru; sogu; sarayeru.
SCOOP-NET, Szkui-ami; sade.
SCOPE, Tokoro; basho.
SCORCH, Kogasz.
SCORCHED, Kogeru; yakeru.
SCORE, Shirushi.
SCORE, *v.* Shirusz.
SCORIA, Kankuso.
SCORN, Anadori; keibetsz; iyashimi. *To laugh to —*, azawarau.
SCORN, *v.* Anadoru; kei-betsz szru; misageru; karondzru; iyashimeru.
SCORPION, Sasori.
SCOUNDREL, Yatsz; me.
SCOUR, Migaku; togu; szru; szri-migaku.
SCOURGE, Muchi; shimoto; tatari; bachiatari.
SCOURGE, *v.* Muchi-utsz; basszru; keibatsz szru.
SCOUT, Monomi; tōmi.
SCOWL, Shikameru; hisomeru.
SCRABBLE-UP, Yoji-noboru; haiagaru; kaki-noboru.
SCRAMBLE-UP, *Idem.* *Scramble for*, baitorigachi.
SCRAP, Hash'ta; kire.
SCRAPE, *v.* Kedzru; kosogeru; szru; kaku.
SCRATCH, *v.* Kaku. — *off* kakiotosz; kakimushiru. — *and search for*, kakisagasz. — *out*, kaki-kesz.
SCRAWL, *n.* Aku-hitsz; ram-pitsz.
SCREAM, Sakebu.
SCREECH, *Idem.*
SCREEN, *n.* Biyōbu; shōji; fuszma; mi; jotan.
SCREEN, *v.* Ōi; kazasz; kakusz; kabau; abau; kabusaru; kadamu; mi de hiru.
SCREW, *n.* Neji.
SCREW, *v.* Nejiru. — *into*, neji-komu. — *open*, neji-akeru. — *out*, shiboru.
SCRIBBLE, Kaku; fude makase ni kaku; tedzsami ni kaku.
SCRIBE, Shoyaku; yūhitsz.
SCRIP, Fukuro.
SCRIPTURES, Sei-kiyō.
SCROFULA, Rui-reki.
SCRUB, Migaku.
SCRUPLE, *v.* Tamerō; tayutau; yūyo szru; kogi szru.
SCRUTINIZE, Sensaku szru; shiraberu; gimmi szru; tadzneru; toi-tszmeru.
SCRUTINY, Shirabe; tadzne; sensaku.
SCUFFLE, Kenk'wa.
SCULL, *v.* Kogu.
SCULL, *n.* Ro.
SCULL-PIN, Robeso.
SCULPTOR, Ishiya. — *of wood images*, busshi.
SCULPTURE, *v.* Horu.
SCUM, Uwa-kawa.
SCURF, Fuke.
SCURRILITY, Akkō; waru-kuchi.
SEA, Umi; kai; nada. *The — is rough*, nami ga arai. *Half seas over*, namayoi; horoyoi. — *and land*, kai-riku.
SEA-BOARD, Kai-gan; umi no iso; kai-hen; umite.
SEA-BREEZE, Umi-kaze; kaifū.
SEA-CAPTAIN, Fune-no kashira; sen-shō.
SEA-CHART, Umi no yedz.
SEA-COAST, Kai-gan; kai-hen.
SEA-FIGHT, Funa-ikusa.
SEA-HORSE, Umi-'ma.
SEAMAN, Sendō.
SEA-SICK, Fune ni yō.
SEA-SIDE, Kai-gan; umite; kai-hen.

SEA-WATER, Shio.
SEAL, *(fish)*, ottosei; ash'ka.
SEAL, *n.* Han; in; ingiyō; fū.
SEAL, *v.* Han wo osz; fūjiru.
SEAL-CHARACTER, Tensho.
SEAM, Nui-me; awashi-me.
SEAMSTRESS, O-hari; mono-nui.
SEAR, *v.* Yaku; kogasz.
SEARCH, *v.* Sagasz; tadzneru; motomeru; sensaku szru; shiraberu. — *a house*, ya-sagaszi.
SEARCH, *n.* Tadzne; sagashi; sensaku; shirabe.
SEASON, Toki; jisetsz; kikō. *The four* —, shiki. *Out of* —, toki-naranu.
SEASON, *v.* Aji wo tszkeru; kagen szru; narasz; tanren szru. *To season by drying*, karasz; kawakasz; hossz.
SEASONABLE, Tszgō no yoi; hodo-yoi.
SEASONING, Kagen; ambai.
SEAT, Koshi-kake; za; seki; ba-sho; tokoro; ba; sho.
SEAT, *v.* Za-szru; szwaru; oku; szyeru.
SECEDE, Shirizoku.
SECLUDE, Hiki-komoru; tonsei szru; kakureru.
SECLUSION, Inkiyo; inton; tonsei; kakureru.
SECOND, *n.* Katōdo; katan-nin.
SECOND, *a.* Ni-ban ; ni-ban-me. — *time*, futa-tabi; mata. *Buying at — hand*, mata-gai. *Borrowing at — hand*, matagari. — *son*, ji-nan. — *wife*, gosai.
SECOND, *v.* Tetszdau; katan szru.
SECOND-COUSIN, Mata-itoko.
SECRET, *a.* Kakureru ; hisoka-na ; naishō-na; mitsz-na. — *talk*; mitsz-dan.
SECRET, *n.* Mitszji; himitsz; kimitsz. — *medicine*, hi-yaku.
SECRETARY, Yūhitsz; shoyaku.
SECRETE, *v.* Kakusz.
SECRETLY, Hisoka-ni; nai-nai; naishō de; shinonde; nai-bun de; hiso-hiso; koso-koso.
SECT, Shūshi; shū; ha; riu; riugi; shūmon.
SECTION, Shō; hen. — *of country*, hō; kata.
SECULAR, Seken-no ; zoku. — *affairs*, zokuji.
SECURE, *a.* Genjū-na; kengo-na; daijōbu-na; katai; ankō; anshin; buji-naru.
SECURE, *v.* Ukeau; mamoru; katamaru.
SECURITY, Anshin; an-non; kengo; katame; ukeai; hikiate; kahan-nin; ukeai-nin.
SEDATE, Shidzka-na; heiki-na; ochi-tszite iru; butchōdzra.
SEDENTARY, Ugoka-nai. — *employment*, szwari-shigoto.
SEDIMENT, Kasz; tare-kasz; ori.
SEDITION, Muhon; ikki; sōdō.
SEDITIOUS, Bōgiyaku-na; muhō-na.
SEDUCE, Sosonokasz; izanau; hiki-komu; taburakasz.
SEDULOUS, Hone-oru, hataraku; benkiyō-na; mame-na.
SEE, Miru. *I request to see, or wish to see*, hai-ken itashitai; mitai. *See here, (polite)*, goran nasare; minasare. *(Common)*, miyo. *(Vulgar)*, miro. *Let me see*, mise-nasare. *See to it*, ki wo tszke yo. *To see, (for curiosity)*, kembutsz szru. *To mistake in seeing*, mi-ayamatsz; michigai; mi-sokonau.
SEED, Tane.
SEEDLING, Mibaye.
SEED-TIME, Shitszke-doki; wiyetszke-doki.
SEEK, Sagasz; tadzneru; motomeru; sensaku szru.
SEEM, *Formed by the suffixes*, rashii; sō; *also by*, keshiki; iro; nari-sō; nari; ke; furi.
SEETHE, Niru.
SEIGE, Kakomi.
SEINE, Hiki-ame.
SEIZE, Toru; tszkamu; nigiru; ubau. — *with the teeth*, kui-tszku.
SEIZURE, Tori; ubai.
SELDOM, Mare-ni; tama-tama ; tama-ni.
SELECT, *v.* Yerabu ; yoru ; gimmi szru ; yeru.
SELF, Ji-bun; ji-shin; onore ; midzkara; hitori de; mi. *Made by* —, jisaku ; tesaku.
SELF-ADMIRATION, Ji-man.
SELF-DENIAL, Onore ni katsz ; shim-bō; kannin.
SELF-CONCEIT, Ji-man; jifu; unubore.
SELF-DESTRUCTION, Jibō-jimetsz.
SELF-EDUCATED, Dokugaku.
SELF-EXAMINATION, Kayeri-miru.
SELF-EVIDENT, Ichi-jirushi.
SELF-INTEREST, Midame ; shi-yoku.
SELFISH, Temaye-gatte; ki-mama ; watakushi no ; waga-mama; kidzi.
SELF-LOVE, Ji-ai.
SELF-MURDER, Jigai.
SELF-PARTIAL, Mi-hīki.
SELF-POSSESSION, Hei-ki; ochi-tszki.
SELF-PRAISE, Jiman; jisan.
SELF-WILLED, Waga-mama ; kimama.
SELFISH, Unubore; midame.

SELL, Uru; sabaku; orosz.
SELLER, Urite; uri-nushi.
SELVEDGE, Mimi.
SEMEN, Tane; sei; inszi.
SEMI-ANNUAL, Han-toshi-no; han-nen-no; han-ki.
SEMINARY, Gakudō; gakumonjo.
SEND, Yaru; tszkau; okuru; tszkawasz; todokeru; okosz. *Also formed by the caust. form of the verb; as, To send rain*, ame wo furasz. *To send a messenger*, tszkai wo yukaseru. *To — forth*, hasszru. *— back*, kayesz; henjō; hemben.
SENIOR, Toshi-ori.
SENSE, Kokoro; ki; shōne; imi; wake. *Lose one's senses*, ki wo ushinau.
SENSIBILITY, Chikaku; shōne.
SENTENCE, Ku; ī-tszke; mōshitszke; mōshiwatashi; kiyōjō.
SENTENCE, *v.* Mōshi-tszkeru; ī-tszkeru.
SENTIMENT, Riyōken; iken; kokoro; tszmori; zombun; zonjiyori; zoni; zonnen.
SENTINEL, Ban-nin; mi-hari.
SENTRY, *Idem.*
SEPARATE, Wakeru; hanareru; hedateru; kiwadatsz.
SEPARATELY, Betsz-betsz-ni; mei-mei ni.
SEPARATION, Hanare; wakare; ribetsz; fuyen.
SEPTEMBER, Ku-gatsz.
SEPULCHRE, Haka.
SEPULTURE, Tomorai; sōrei; sōshiki.
SEQUEL, Yukuszye; ato.
SERENE, Akiraka-na; uraraka; nodoka; shidzka-na; odayaka-na. *— sky*, sei-ten.
SERIES, Tszdzki. *Compounds of* ren; rui. *— of years*, rui-nen; rennen. *— of days*, renjitsz; rui-jitsz. *— of dynasties*, rui-dai.
SERIOUS, Daiji-na; taisetsz-na; jitsz; hontō; ogosoka; katai; omoi.
SERIOUSLY, Omoku; magao de.
SERMON, Hōdan; dangi; seppō; kōshaku.
SERPENT, Hebi; ja. *— charmer*, hebi-tszkai.
SERVANT, Kodzkai; hōkō-nin; kerai; boku; genan; gejo; sobadzkai; kiu-ji; meshi-tszkai.
SERVE, Tsztomeru; hōkō szru; kiu-ji wo szru; tszkayeru; sh'tagau; motenasz; yō ni tatsz; ogamu; wiyamau. *— up*, sonayeru; koshirayeru. *—out*, kubaru; wakeru. *— the purpose*, ma-ni-au; yōdatsz. *To make — the purpose*, ma-ni-awaseru.
SERVICE, Tsztome; hōkō; yaku; yakume; yō. *Public —*, goyō; yaku-yō. *Of no —*, yō ni tatanu; yaku ni tatanu; kikimasen. *Time of —*, nenki.
SERVICEABLE, Yō ni tatsz; yaku ni tatsz; tokuyō; yōdatsz.
SERVILE, Iyashii.
SESSION, Seki.
SET, *v.* Oku; szyeru; osameru; tszkeru; sonayeru; sadameru. *Sun has —*, hi ga kureta. *— a day*, nichi-gen wo szru; higiri wo szru. *— a razor*, kamisori wo awaseru. *— sail*, shuppan szru. *— a sail*, ho wo ageru. *— a watch*, ban wo tszkeru; tokei wo naosz. *— a bone*, hone wo tszgu. *— apart*, ate-hameru. *To set about*, hajimeru; shikakeru; tori-kakaru. *— up*, tateru. *— up business*, kai-giyō szru. *— up shop*, mise wo dasz. *— one's self against*, teki szru; tekitau. *To set aside*, katadzkeru; sztete oku; utchatte oku; sashi-oku. *— agoing*, ugoki-dasz; hajimeru. *— by*, shimau; katadzkeru. *— down*, orosz. *— down in a day book*, chōmen ni tszkeru, *or* kaku, *or* shirusz. *— forward*, szszmeru. *— off*, kazaru; ashirau. *— on*, keshi-kakeru; odateru. *— out, (on a journey)*, tatsz. *— at naught*, naigashiro ni szru; karondzru. *— in order*, naraberu; osameru. *— eyes on*, me ni kakaru. *— the teeth on edge*, hagayui. *— at ease*, ochi-tszkeru; akirameru. *— free*, hanatsz. *— at work*, shigoto ni tszkeru. *— on fire*, hi wo tszkeru. *— a trap*, wana wo haru. *Sets well*, yoku ai-masz. *— about*, tori-kakaru. *— day*, nichigen; higiri; jōjitsz. *— up shop*, mise wo hiraku; kai-giyō szru.
SET, *n.* *— of books*, bu. *— of boxes*, ireko.
SETTING-SUN, Irihi.
SETTLE, Odomu; sadameru; kiwameru; ochi-tszku; kimaru; shidzmeru; kimeru; osameru; szmasz; aritszkeru; hitszjō; oriau; kesszru. *— an account*, kanjō szru.
SEVEN, Nanatsz; sh'chi.
SEVEN-FOLD, Sh'chi-sōbai.
SEVENTEEN, Jū-sh'chi.
SEVENTH, Sh'chi-ban; sh'chi-ban-me.
SEVENTIETH, Sh'chi-jū-ban-me.
SEVENTY, Sh'chi-jū.
SEVER, Kiru; hanareru; wakeru.
SEVERAL, Szu.
SEVERALLY, Betsz-betsz-ni; goto-ni.
SEVERE, Kibishii; kitszi; tszyoi; hageshii; omoi; ogosoka-naru; genjū-na; kiukutsz na.

SEVERELY, Tszyoku; hageshiku; kibishiku; kitszku; hishi-to; hishi-bishi-to.
SEVERITY, Tszyosa.
SEW, Nui; tojiru. — *together*, nui-awaseru. — *one thing on another*, nui-tszkeru. — *and lengthen*, nui-tszgu.
SEWER, Dobu.
SEX, Nan-niyo; mesz-osz.
SEXUAL-INTERCOURSE, Kōgō.
SHABBY, Miszborashii.
SHACKLE, Hodasz.
SHADE, Kage. *A sun shade*, hi ōi.
SHADE, *v.* Ōi; kakusz; bokasz; bokeru; kegeru.
SHADOW, Kage; kagebōshi.
SHADY, Kage aru. *Under a — tree*; mori no sh'ta.
SHAFT, Hashira; ye; nagaye.
SHAKE, Ugoku; ugokasz; furū; furu; yuru; yurugu; yurugasz; yuszburu; yuszru. — *off*, furi-harau; furi-hanatsz. — *out*, furi-dasz.
SHAKING, Furui.
SHALL, *Formed by future suffix*, ō; rō. *What — I do?*, nan to shō. — *I go or not?* yukō ka yukumai ka. *How — I do it?* dōsh'te shiyō ka. — *go to morrow?* ash'ta yukimashō.
SHALLOW, Asai.
SHAMANISM, Shamon.
SHAME, Haji; chijoku; kakin; hadzkashimi.
SHAMEFUL, Hadzkashii.
SHAMELESS, Haji wo shiranu.
SHAMPOO, Momu; ampuku; amma szru; dōin szru.
SHAMPOOER, Amma.
SHAPE, Katachi; szgata; kata.
SHAPE, *v.* Katadoru.
SHARE, *v.* Wari-tszkeru; wakeru; wari-awaseru.
SHARE, *n.* Wari-ai; wari; wappu; wari-maye; bun.
SHARER, Kakari-ai.
SHARK, Same; fuka.
SHARKS-FINS, Same no hire.
SHARP, Yoku-kireru; tszrudoi; togeru. (*fig.*) karai; kitszi; tszyoi; kibishii. — *voice*, togari-goye.
SHARPEN, Togu; togarakasz.
SHARPLY, Tszyoku; hitszku; kibishiku; karaku.
SHARP-SIGHTED, Mebayai.
SHATTER, Uchi-kudaku; buchikowasz.
SHAVE, Soru; kedzru; sogu.
SHAVINGS, Kanna-kudz.

SHE, Ano onna; are.
SHEAF, Taba; tabane.
SHEAR, *v.* Hasami-kiru.
SHEARS, Hasami; ki-basami; kana-basami.
SHEATH, Saya.
SHEATHE, Katana wo osameru.
SHED, *v.* Nagasz; otosz. — *light*, terasz. — *tears*, raku-rui szru. — *blood*, ayasz. — *skin*, kawa wo nugu. — *hair or feathers*, ke ga kawaru.
SHED, *n.* Koya.
SHEEP, Rashamen; hitszji.
SHEET, Mai; nedoko no shikimono.
SHEET-COPPER, Akagane-ita.
SHEET-IRON, Tetsz-ita.
SHEET-LEAD, Namari ita.
SHELF, Tana.
SHELL, Kara.
SHELL, *v.* Kawa wo muku.
SHELTER, Oi; yokeru. — *from rain*, amayadori.
SHIELD, *n.* Tate.
SHIELD, *v.* Kabau; mamoru; yokeru.
SHIFT, *v.* Kawaru; kayeru; utszsz; utszru.
SHIN, Hagi.
SHINE, Terasz; hikaru; kagayaku.
SHINGLE, Yane-ita.
SHINGLE-ROOFED, Ita-buki.
SHINING, Terasz, hikaru; kagayaku.
SHIP, Fune. — *of war*, gunkan; ikusabune. *Merchant* —, akinai bune; shōsen. *Steam* —, hibune; jōk'sen. — *owner*, funa-mochi. *A place where — stop*, funa-ba; funa-tszki.
SHIP, *v.* Fune ni tszmu.
SHIP-BOARD, *To go on* —, fune ni noru.
SHIP-BUILDER, Funa-daiku.
SHIP'S *carpenter*, Fune no daiku.
SHIPMENT, Funadzmi.
SHIP-WRECK, Ha-sen; nansen. *One saved from* —, funa-kobori.
SHIP-WRIGHT, Funa-daiku.
SHIRKING, Dzrui; dzrukeru.
SHIRT, Jiban; hadagi.
SHIVER, Kudaku; kudakeru; furū; wananaku; ononoku; zoku-zoku szru.
SHOAL, Asai-tokoro; sz.
SHOCK, Hibiki; kotaye; tszku; tajiroku; biku-biku szru; zoku-zoku; zotto.
SHOE, Kutsz. *One pair of* —, kutsz issoku.
SHOE-MAKER, Kutsz-ya.
SHOOT, Hanasz; utsz. — *a bow*, iru. *Of a bud*, kizasz; tatsz.
SHOOTS, Naye; me; me-baye.

SHOOTING-STAR, Yobaiboshi; riusei.
SHOP, Mise; tana.
SHOP-KEEPER, Akindo.
SHOPPING, Kaimono ni yuku.
SHORE, Iso; kishi. *Sea* —, kai-gan.
SHORT, Mijikai; tan. — *road*, chikai-michi. *To be* — *of*, taranu; fusoku; toboshii. *Come* — *of*, itaranu, todokanu. *Cut* —, habuku; herasz; riyaku szru. *Fall* —, hekomi ni naru.
SHORT-BREATHED, Kataiki; iki-gire.
SHORTEN, Mijikaku szru; habuku; herasz; gendzru; riyaku szru; tszmeru; tszmaru.
SHORT-LIVED, Tammei.
SHORTLY, Shibaraku; chotto; jiki-ni; hayaku.
SHORTNESS, Mijikasa.
SHORT-SIGHTED, Chika-me.
SHORT-WITTED, Tansai.
SHOT, Tama. *Bow* —, ya-goro; yaomote. *A good* —, tedari. — *hole*, tama-kidz. *Long* —, tōya.
SHOULD, *as*, *You should have paid the money at the time you promised*, nichi-gen ni kane wo harayeba yokatta; *or*, *if expressing regret*, nichi-gen ni kane wo harayeba yokatta mono wo. *If I had had time I should have gone*, watakushi hima ga attara yuku de attarō. *I should go if I were well*, ambai ga yoi nara yukō. *I should have gone yesterday*, kinō yukeba yokatta mono wo. *Children should obey their parents*, ko wa oya ni kōkō szru hadz no koto. *It should be done*, szru hadz no koto; *or* szru beki koto; *or* atatrimaye no koto.
SHOULDER, Kata.
SHOULDER, *v.* Katszgu; katageru.
SHOUT, *n.* Sakebi; toki no koye; sawagi. — *of victory*, kachidoki.
SHOUT, *v.* Sakebu; toki no koye wo ageru; wameku.
SHOVE, Osz.
SHOVEL, Szki. *Fire* —, jūnō. *A basket* —, joren.
SHOW, *v.* Miseru; kikaseru; oshiyeru; arawasz; shimesz. — *mercy*, awaremu.
SHOW, *n.* Mise-mono; miye; miba; midate; mikake.
SHOW-BILL, Hiki-fuda.
SHOWER, Niwaka ame; shigure; yūdachi.
SHOWY, Medatawashii, medatsz; hanayakana.
SHREWD, Rikō na; kash'koi; chiye no aru; saru-gash'koi; sarurikō; hashikoi.
SHREWDNESS, Chiye; rikō; rihatsz.
SHRIEK, Sakebi.
SHRILL-VOICE, Hosokoye; hosone.
SHRIMP, Yebi
SHRINE, Mikoshi.
SHRINK, *v.* Chijimeru; tszmaru; ijikeru; atoshizari; mijiroku; biku-biku szru.
SHRIVEL, Chijimaru; chijimu; shiwa ga yoru; shioreru; shinabiru; hinayeru.
SHROFF, *n.* Kanemi.
SHROFF, *v.* Kane wo miru.
SHROUD, Kiyō katabira.
SHRUB, Ki; wiyeki.
SHRUG, Sobiyakasz.
SHUDDER, Furū; wananaku; ononoku; zokuzoku szru.
SHUFFLE, Kiru.
SHUN, Nogareru; yokeru; manukareru; sakeru; shinobu.
SHUT, Shimeru; tateru; tojiru; fusagu; komoru; tatamu; szbomeru; tozasz; tszgumu; shibomu.
SHUTTLE, Hi.
SHUTTLE-COCK, Hane; hago.
SHY, Kowagaru.
SIAM, Shamuro.
SICK, Yamu; wadzrau; fuk'wai; ambai warui; biyōki. *Sea* —, fune ni yō. — *at stomach*, mukadzku. — *person*, biyō-nin; biyō-ja; biyō-kaku. — *bed*, biyō-shō. — *and afflicted*, biyō-nō; biyō-ku; biyō-nan.
SICKLE, Kama.
SICKLY, Biyō-shin.
SICKNESS, Biyōki; yamai. *During* —, biyō-chiu. *After* —, biyō-go. *Cause of* —, biyō-kon. *Died of* —, biyō-shi. *Kind of* —, biyō-tei.
SIDE, Kata; kata-wara; waki; kataye; soba; hotori; kawa; hen; kiwa; hata; hō. *Every* —, hōbō. *Both* —, riyō-hō. *One* —, kataippō; kata-kata; kata-hashi. *This* —, konata; kochi. *That* —, achira; achi; anata.
SIDE-DISH, *or anything eaten with rice*, O-kadz; sai.
SIDE-LONG, Yoko-ni.
SIDE-WISE, Yoko-ni; yokosama; katamukeru.
SIEVE, Furui.
SIFT, Furū.
SIGH, Tameiki.
SIGH, Tansoku szru; nageku.
SIGHT, Miru-koto; me. *To be in* —, miyeru. *The ship is not in* —, fune ga miyenu. *To take* —, nerau.

SIGHTLESS, Me-nashi; mekura.
SIGHTLY, Medatsz.
SIGHT-SEEING, Kembutsz; mono-mi.
SIGN, Shirushi; shōko; yengi; zempiyō; shirase; shō; kizashi; keshirai; kamban.
SIGN, *v.* Han wo osz; kaki-han szru; shirusz.
SIGNAL, Aidz.
SIGNATURE, Han; kaki-han.
SIGN-BOARD, Kamban.
SIGNIFICATION, Kokoro; wake; imi.
SIGNIFY, Arawasz; miseru; shiraseru; kikaseru; oshiyeru; hiyō szru.
SIGN-POST, Michi-shirube.
SILENCE, *v.* Shidzmeru; yarikomu; heikō szru; īkomeru.
SILENT, Damaru; mokuneu; shidzka; odayaka; mugon.
SILENTLY, Damatte; moku-nen to sh'te; shidzka-ni.
SILK, Kinu; ito.
SILK-WORM, Kaiko.
SILLY, Bakarashii; gu-na; don-na; guchi na; oroka.
SILVER, Gin, shirogane.
SILVER-LEAF, Gimpaku.
SILVER-WARE, Ginzaiku.
SIMILAR, Onaji; niru; dōyō; h'toshiki.
SIMILITUDE, Katachi; utszshi.
SIMPLE, Ichi-mi-na; h'toye-no; jimi-na; shitszboku; ubuoroka-na; gu-na; kōtō.
SIMPLY, Nomi; bakari.
SIMULATE, Niseru; maneru; magai; magayeru.
SIMULTANEOUS, Onaji toki; dōji.
SIN, *n.* Tszmi; zai; zai-go.
SIN, *v.* Tszmi wo okasz; kami no michi ni somuku; *or*, michi ni motoru; bonzai.
SINAPISM, Kaishidei.
SINCE, Kara; konokata; i-rai; yori; imamade; ato; yuye; aida; yotte.
SINCERE, Jitsz; makoto; hon-na, shinjitszna; hontō.
SINCERELY, Jitsz-ni; makoto-ni; hon-ni; hontō.
SINCERITY, Jitszi; magokoro.
SINEW, Szji.
SINFUL, Tszmi aru.
SING, Utau; gindzru; yeidzru. *To lead in singing*, ondo wo toru.
SINGE, Yaku.
SINGING-BOOK, Uta no fu.
SINGING-WOMAN, Gei-sha; tori oi; geiko.
SINGLE, H'totsz; ichi; h'toye; ichimi. — *person*, h'tori; doku-shin. *To — out*, megakeru.
SINGLY, H'tori-de; jishin; jibun.
SINGULAR, Medzrashii; miyō-na; betsz-dan; kaku-betsz.
SINGULARITY, Kuse.
SINGULARLY, Kaku-betsz ni; betsz-dan ni.
SINK, *n.* Nagashi; dobu; geszi.
SINK, *v.* Shidzmu; hamaru; oboreru; otoroyeru; sagaru; kubomu. — *a well*, ido wo horu.
SINNER, Tszmi aru h'to; zai-nin; tszmi-bito.
SIN-OFFERING, Tszmi wo aganau ikeniye; tszmi wo aganau kumotsz.
SIP, Szu; (szi); nomu.
SIR, Sama; san.
SISTER, Kiyōdai; onna-kiyōdai. *Older* —, ane. *Younger* —, imōto. — *in law*, ani-yome; kojūtome.
SIT, Szwaru; za-szru; koshi wo kakeru. — *up all night*, yodōshi; tetszya; yo-akashi. — *up with the sick*, yotogi. — *in a ring*, kurumaza; madoi.
SITE, Basho; tokoro.
SITUATION, Basho; tokoro; yakume.
SIX, Mutsz; roku.
SIX-FOLD, Muye; roku-mai; rok'sōbai.
SIXTEEN, Jūroku.
SIXTEENTH, Jūroku-bam-me.
SIXTH, Roku-ban; rokubam-me.
SIXTIETH, Roku jū-ban.
SIXTY, Rokujū.
SIZE, Ōkisa; kasa.
SKELETON, Gaikotsz.
SKETCH, *n.* Ye; dz; yedz.
SKETCH, *v.* Kaku; yegaku.
SKILL, Tegiwa; takumi.
SKILLFUL, Jōdz; takumi-no; tegiwa no yoi.
SKIN, Kawa.
SKIN, *v.* Muku; hagu.
SKIP, Tobu; haneru.
SKIRMISHERS, Sampei.
SKIRT, Szso. *To hold up the* —, tszmadoru.
SKIRT, *v.* Kakō.
SKULL, Atama no hone; dokuro; sharikōbe.
SKY, Sora; ame; ten. *Clear* —, sei-ten.
SKYLARK, Hibari.
SLACK, Yurui; tarui; tarumu; amai; okotaru; kutszrogu.
SLACKEN, Yurumeru; kutszrogeru; tayumeru.
SLAKE, Kesz; tomeru.

SLAM, *v.* Hato to shimeru; pisshari to shimeru.
SLANDER, *v.* Zanszru; shikodzru; soshiru.
SLANDER, Zangen; shīgoto; gomaszri.
SLANDERER, Neijin; zansha.
SLANTING, Naname; szjikai; nazoye.
SLAP, Haru; utsz; tataku.
SLATTERN, Szbeta.
SLAUGHTER, Hofuru; kiri-korosz.
SLAY, Korosz; kiru; setsz-gai szru; kiri-korosz; ayameru; chiu-riku szru.
SLED, Sori.
SLEDGE, Tszchi.
SLEEK, Nameraka.
SLEEP, *v.* Nemuru; neru; ne-iru; netszku. — *together*, soine; soibushi. — *in the daytime*, hirune.
SLEEP, *n.* Nemuri. *Position in* —, nezō.
SLEEPLESS, Nemuradz; nedz.
SLEEPY, Nemutai; nemui.
SLEET, Mizore.
SLEEVE, Sode.
SLEIGHT, *of hand*, tedzma; shinadama; hayawaza.
SLENDER, Hoso-nagai; hosoi.
SLICE, *n.* Mai; kire.
SLICE, *v.* Kizamu; hayasz.
SLIDE, Szberu; dzru. — *down*, dzri-ochiru.
SLIGHT, Karui; yowai; wadzka.
SLIGHT, *v.* Naigashiro ni szru; karondzru; tenuke wo szru; yurukase.
SLIGHTLY, Karuku; yowaku; zatto; somatsz-ni; uszku; usz-usz.
SLILY, Shinonde; hisoka-ni; sotto.
SLIM, Hosonagai.
SLIME, Doro.
SLIMY, Nebari tszku.
SLING, Bunyari; wana.
SLING, *v.* Nageru; hōru.
SLINK AWAY, Ome-ome to nigeru.
SLIP, Dzru; szberu; fumihadzsz. — *out*, tsztto deru; piyoi-to deru. — *in*, dzrikomu. — *down*, szberi-korobu. *To give one the slip*, h'to wo hadzsz. — *of the tongue*, kuchi ga szberu.
SLIPPERY, Dzru-dzru; szberu; nameraka; nume-nume; numeru; nuratszku.
SLOPE, Saka; kōbai.
SLOPING, Naname; szjikai.
SLOTHFUL, Bushō-na; randa-na; fusei.
SLOVENLY, Musai; musakurushii; miszborashii; jidaraku.
SLOW, Osoi; yurui; shidzka-na; himadoru; tema wo toru; rachi ga akanu; madarui. — *and fast*, chisoku.
SLOWLY, Osoku; yuruku; soro-soro-to; shidzka-ni; yuru-yuru-ni; bem-ben.
SLUG, Name-kuji.
SLUGGISH, Gudz-gudz; nibui; yodomu; namakeru.
SLUICE, Szi-mon.
SLY, Ōchakuna; dzrui.
SMALL, Chīsai; hosoi; szkunai; komayaka-na; wadzka-na.
SMALLNESS, Chīsasa; hososa.
SMALL-POX, Hōso.
SMART, Piri-piri-itamu; biri-tszku; hiritszku.
SMASH, Uchi-kudaku; buchi-kowasz.
SMATTERING, Namaiki; namagaten.
SMEAR, *v.* Nuru; mabureru; mamireru.
SMEARED, Darake; mabure; midoro.
SMELL, *v.* Kagu.
SMELL, *n.* Nioi.
SMELT, *v.* Fuki-wakeru.
SMILE, *v.* Niko-niko szru; hoyoyemu. — *in derision*, azawarau.
SMILING-FACE, Nikoyaka-na kao; yegao.
SMITE, Butsz; utsz; tataku.
SMITH, Kaji.
SMOKE, *n.* Kemuri.
SMOKE, *v.* Ibusz; fuszberu; kuyorasz. — *tobacco*, tabako wo nomu.
SMOKING, Iburu; kuyoru; fuszboru.
SMOKY, Kemutai.
SMOOTH, Nameraka-na.
SMOOTH, *v.* Narasz; nosz; nobasz; naderu.
SMOOTHING-IRON, Hinoshi.
SMOOTHLY, Nameraka-ni; tszru-tszru.
SMOTHER, Iki wo tszmeru.
SMOULDER, Iburu; kayoru.
SMUGGLE, Bahan szru; mitszbai szru; nuke-uri wo szru.
SMUGGLED *goods*, Nuke-ni; bahammono.
SMUGGLER, Bahan-nin.
SNAIL, Maimaitszbura; tanishi; dedemushi.
SNAKE, Hebi; kuchi-nawa.
SNAP, *v.* Oru; hajiku; shakuru. — *the fingers*, tszmahajiki.
SNARE, Wana.
SNARL, Kagasz; īgamu.
SNATCH, Hitakkuru; ottoru.
SNEAKINGLY, Ome-ome-to.
SNEER, Aza-warau.
SNEEZE, *n.* Kusame.
SNIPE, Shigi; chidori.
SNIVEL, *v.* Hana ga tareru.
SNORE, *v.* Ibiki wo kaku.
SNOT, Aobana; hana.

SNOUT, Hana; kuchi.
SNOW, Yuki.
SNOW-BALL, Yuki-dama.
SNOW-SHOE, Kanjiki.
SNOW-SLIP, Yuki-nadare.
SNOW-STORM, Fu-buki.
SNUFF, *n.* Kagi tabako.
SNUFF, *v.* Kagu. — *a candle*, shin wo kiru.
SNUFFERS, Shinkiri.
SO, Sō; sayō; shika; sa; yō. *See also*, shikadz; shikaji; shikaku; shikaradz; shikarashimuru; shikarazaru; shikareba; shikaredomo; shikari; shikari to iyedomo; shikarubeki; shikaru-ni; shika-shika; sareba; sare-domo; saritomo; saritote.
SO MUCH, Kono-kurai; kore-dake; kore-hodo; sa-hodo; kahodo.
SO AS, Yōni.
SOAK, Hitasz; tszkeru; kasz.
SOAP, Shabon; sekken.
SOBER, Magao; majime; geko. *Become* —, sameru; yeisameru.
SOCIABLE, Aisō no yoi; nengoro-na.
SOCIETY, Nakama; kumi; renchiu; shachiu.
SOCK, Tabi.
SOD, Shiba.
SODOMY, Nanshoku.
SOFT, Yawaraka.
SOFTEN, Yawaraka ni szru; yawarageru.
SOFTLY, Yawaraka-ni; sorori-to; shidzkani; sotto; yaora.
SOIL, *n.* Tszchi; doro; koyashi; yogore.
SOIL, *v.* Yogosz; kegasz; aka ga tszku.
SOILED, Yogoreru; kegareru; akajimita.
SOJOURN, Tomaru; yadoru; tōriu szru; shuku szru; kishuku.
SOJOURNER, Kiyaku; kiyakujin; tabibito; kishuku-nin.
SOLACE, Nagusami.
SOLDER, Biyakurō.
SOLDIER, Tszwamono; hosotsz; shisotsz; heisotsz; gunsotsz; samurai; bushi; heishi.
SOLE, Ashi no ura.
SOLE-FISH, Hirame.
SOLELY, Bakari; nomi; tada; moppara-ni.
SOLEMN, Omo-omoshii; wiya-wayashii; oshi-tszita.
SOLEMNIZE, Okonau; szru; muszbu.
SOLEMNLY, Omo-omoshiku; wiya-wiyashiku; oshi-tszite.
SOLICIT, Negau; tanomu; kō.
SOLICITATION, Negai; tanomi; koi.
SOLICITOUS, Anjiru; anjite oru; kidzkai szru; kokorodzkai szru.
SOLICITUDE, Shimpai; anji; kurō; kigakari; kidzkai.
SOLID, Katai.
SOLIDIFY, Kataku szru; katameru.
SOLIDITY, Katasa.
SOLIDLY, Kataku; shikkari to.
SOLILOQUY, H'torigoto.
SOLITARY, Samushii; hanareru; tada h'totsz; h'torimi.
SOLSTICE, *Summer* —, geshi. *Winter* —, tōji.
SOLUBLE, Tokeru.
SOLVE, Toku; toki-wakeru; hodoku; handan szru; ihodoku.
SOME, Aru; aruiwa; saru. *There must be some reason for it*, nan zo wake ga arō, *or* nani yuye darō.
SOMEBODY, Aru h'to; nani-gashi.
SOME-HOW, Tokaku; kare-kore.
SOMERSET, Kumagayeri. *To turn a* —, hikkuri-kayeru; kumagayeri wo utsz.
SOMETHING, Nan zo; nani ka; nani-goto. *I will go to-morrow unless something prevents*, ash'ta sashi-tszkaye ga nakattara yuki-mashō. *There must be something the matter*, nan zo wake ga aru de arō.
SOMETIMES, Toki-doki; ori-ori; orifushi; toki to sh'te; itszka.
SOME-WHERE, Aru-tokoro; dokozo.
SOMNAMBULATION, Nebokeru.
SON, Ko; muszko, segare; shisoku; shison. *Oldest* —, sōriyo; chakushi. *Second* —, jinan. *Third* —, san-nan. *Youngest* —, basshi. — *in law*, muko.
SONG, Uta.
SONOROUS, Naru. — *bodies*, naru-mono.
SOON, Hayaku; jiki-ni; szgu-to; chika-uchi ni; chika-jika; kinjitsz; tōkaradz; hodo-naku; ma mo naku. *As* — *as*, shidai.
SOOT, Szsz.
SOOTHE, Nadameru; szkasz.
SOOTHSAYER, Uranaija; boku szru.
SOOTHSAYING, Uranau.
SOPHISTRY, Rikutsz; sakashiragoto; higakoto.
SORCERER, Mahō-tszkai; idznatszkai.
SORCERY, Mahō; idzna; majutsz.
SORE, *n.* Deki-mono.
SORE, *a.* Itai; itamu; tadareru; hidoi.
SORELY, Hidoku; ita-itashiku; hanahada.
SORGHUM, Sato-kibi.

SORROW, *n.* Urei; kanashimi; itami; zannen; kinodoku.
SORROW, *v.* Kanashimu; nageku; kuyamu.
SORROWFUL, Urei; kuyashii; kanashimu.
SORRY, Kinodoku; zannen; kuchi-oshii; itami-iru.
SORT, Tagui; rui; shurui; yō; tōri; kurai; nami; gara. *Out of sorts*, ambai warui; fuk'wai. *Many* —, iro-iro; sama-zama.
SORT, *v.* Buwake wo szru; yori-wakeru.
SOT, Sake-nomi; nomi-nuke; tawake.
SOUL, Tamashii; rei-kon; mitama; seishin; kompaku.
SOUND, *n.* Oto; hibiki; nari; ne; on.
SOUND, *v.* Naru; narasz; hibiku; todoroku.
SOUND, *a.* Tassha; mattaki; jōbu-na; mansoku-na; yoi; szkoyaka-na. *Sound* —, jukuszi.
SOUNDLY, Yoku; hidoku; tszyoku.
SOUP, Shiru; shitaji.
SOUR, Szppai; szi.
SOURCE, *n.* Mina-moto; moto; kongen; kompon.
SOURNESS, Szppasa; szsa.
SOUTH, Minami; uma no hō. — *wind*, minami kaze; nampū. — *east*; tatszmi; tōnan. — *west*, hitszjisaru; seinan.
SOVEREIGN, Tszkasa; kashira; ō.
SOW, *n.* Mebuta.
SOW, *v.* Maku; chirasz.
SOY, Shōyu.
SPACE, Aida; ma; hima; kūchiu; kokū; chiu.
SPACIOUS, Hiroi.
SPADE, Szki.
SPAN, *v.* Nigiru.
SPANK, *v.* Shiri wo haru.
SPAR, *v.* Shiai szru.
SPAR, *n.* Maruta; shiai.
SPARE, Yaru; yurusz; oshimu. *To be sparing*, kenyaku szru.
SPARE, Szkunai. — *time*, hima; itoma.
SPARING, Kenyaku; oshimu; shimatsz; shiwai; rinshoku.
SPARK, Hibana; hinoko.
SPARKLE, *v.* Hikaru; chiradzku; kirameku; kagayaku.
SPARKINGLY, Kira-kira.
SPARROW, Szdzme.
SPARSE, Mabara.
SPASM, Tszru; hiki-tszkeru.
SPATTER, Haneru; hodobashiru; tobashiru; chiru.
SPATULA, Hera.
SPAWN, Uwo no ko.
SPEAK, Iu; hanasz; tszgeru; kataru. — *to one's self*, chingin szru.
SPEAR, Yari. — *exercise*, sōjutsz.
SPEAR, *v.* Tszku.
SPECIAL, Kakubetsz-na; betsz-dan-na; sashitaru.
SPECIALLY, Koto-ni; koto-sara-ni; bessh'te; kakubetsz-ni; betszdan-ni; tori-wakete.
SPECIALITY, Yete; tokui; semmon.
SPECIE, Kane; kingin; kinsen.
SPECIES, Rui; tagui; shurui.
SPECIFIC, *a.* Mochimaye-no.
SPECIFY, Kuwashiku iu.
SPECIMEN, Tehon; mihon.
SPECK, Ten; chobo.
SPECKLED, Chobo-chobo; madara; fu.
SPECTACLE, Mise; mikake; miba.
SPECTACLES, Megane.
SPECTATOR, Kembutsz-nin; okame.
SPECTRE, Bake-mono; yūrei.
SPECULATE, Kangayeru; omoimawasz; shian szru; yama wo szru; mokuromu.
SPECULATION, Kangaye; yama; mokuromi.
SPECULATOR, Yamashi.
SPEECH, Kotoba; monoī; hanashi.
SPEECHLESS, Mokunen.
SPEED, *v.* Hayameru; seku; isogu.
SPEED, *n.* Hayasa. *With* —, hayaku; toku; kiu-ni.
SPEEDILY, Hayaku; toku; jiki-ni; szmiyaka ni; isoide.
SPELL, *n.* Iu; gofu; majinai.
SPELLING, Kanadzkai.
SPELTER, Totan.
SPEND, *v.* Tszkau; harau; tsziyasz; tszkaihatasz; tszkai-kiru; tszkusz. — *time*, utszsz, heru, kurasz; tatsz; szgiru. — *the night*, yo wo akasz.
SPERM, Tane; sei; inszi.
SPERMACITI, Kujira no abura.
SPEW, Haku.
SPHERE, Chi-kiu; bungen; mibun; kurai.
SPHERICAL, Marui.
SPICE, *n.* Yakumi. *To* —, yakumi wo kakeru.
SPICY, Kōbashii.
SPIDER, Kumo.
SPIGOT, Kuchi; taru-guchi; sen.
SPIKE, Kugi.
SPILE, *n.* Kui; sen.
SPILL, Koboreru; kobosz; otosz; ayasz.
SPIN, *v.* Tszmugu. — *a top*, koma wo mawasz.

SPINACH, Horensō.
SPINDLE, Tszmu.
SPINE, Sebone; toge.
SPINNING-WEEL, Itoguruma.
SPIRE, Roban.
SPIRIT, Ki; kokoro; chikara; seishin; ki-kon; sei-riyoku; konjō; rei-kon; kompa-ku; kishoku; kigen; kokoro-mochi; ki-bun; yū-rei; bake-mono. *Evil spirits*, akki; akuma; ma; oni.
SPIRITED, Ki-tszyoi; gōki-na.
SPIT, *v.* Haku.
SPIT, *n.* Tszbaki; yodare; katadz.
SPIT-BOX, Haifuki.
SPITE, *n.* Urami; ikon; nikumi,
SPITEFUL, Urameshii.
SPLASH, *v.* Kakeru; hane-kakeru; hodoba-shiru; tobashiru; chiru.
SPLEEN, Hi no zō.
SPLENDID, Kekkō-na; rippa-na; appare-na; hikaru.
SPLENDOR, Hikari; kagayaki; tszya; ha-ye.
SPLICE, Tszgu.
SPLINTER, Toge.
SPLIT, *v.* Waru; hegu; saku; wakeru. — *the difference*, ayumi au; aibiai.
SPLIT, *n.* Wari; hibiki.
SPOIL, Ubau; arasz; ubai-toru; itamu; ku-saru; azareru; sokonau; dainashi.
SPOIL, *n.* Bundori.
SPOKE, *n.* Ya.
SPONGE, Umi-wata.
SPONGE-CAKE, Kasztera.
SPONTANEOUSLY, Onodzto; onodzkara; shizen; h'tori-de-ni; jibun de; jinen.
SPOOL, Itomaki.
SPOON, Saji.
SPORT, *n.* Tawamure; jōdan; odoke.
SPORT, *v.* Tawamureru; fuzakeru; hiyōge-ru; odokeru.
SPORTSMAN, Kariudo.
SPOT, Ten; shimi.
SPOTTED, Madara; shimita; buchi-na; ki-rifu.
SPOUT, *n.* Kuchi; toyu.
SPOUT, *v.* Fuki-deru.
SPRAIN, Haragayeri; kujiru.
SPRAY, Shira-nami; awa.
SPREAD, *v.* Shiku; haru; noberu; hirome-ru; hiromaru; hirogaru. — *as disease*, hayaru; utszru. — *as grass*, habikoru; shigeru. — *as ink*, nijimu.
SPRING, *n.* Haru; shun; idzmi; hajiki; ha-jiki-gane; zemmai; kizashi; hadzmi. — *like*, harumeku. *Hot* —, onsen, ideyu; tōji.
SPRING, *v.* Hayeru; hasszru; shōdzru; oko-ru; kizasz; deru; hajiku; haneru; tobu. — *on*, tobi-tszku; tobi-kakeru. — *in*, tobi-komu. — *out*, tobi-dasz. — *a leak*, moru.
SPRINKLE, *v.* Sosogu; kakeru; maku; utsz; chirasz.
SPROUT, *v.* Kizasz; hayeru; mebuku; me-datsz; moyeru.
SPROUT, *n.* Me; naye; mebaye.
SPRUCE, Tei-nei-na.
SPUME, Awa.
SPUR, *n.* Kedzme.
SPURIOUS, Niseru. — *thing*, nisemono; gambutsz; gibutsz.
SPURN, *v.* Oshimodosz; tszkikayesz; shiri-zokeru.
SPY, *v.* Ukagau; nerau; mitszkeru; mi-dasz.
SPY, *n.* Shinobi; kanja; yokome; ommitsz; metszke; meakashi; monomi; okappiki.
SPY-GLASS, Tōmegane.
SQUABBLE, *v.* Arasō; sōron; kōron; ken-k'wa.
SQUADRON, Kumi; te.
SQUALID, Miszborashii; kitanai.
SQALL, *n.* Yūdachi,
SQUALL, *v*, Naku; sakebu.
SQUANDER, Tsziyasz; mudadzkai wo szru; sanzai szru.
SQUARE, Shikaku-na.
SQUARE, *carpenters*, Kanezashi.
SQUASH, *n.* Tōnasz.
SQUASH, *v.* Oshi-tszbusz; hishigeru.
SQUAT, *v.* Tszkubau; udzkumaru.
SQUEAK, *v.* Kishiru; kishimu.
SQUEAL, *v.* Sakebu; naku.
SQUEEZE, Shimeru; shiboru. — *out*, shi-bori-dasz.
SQUEEZE-MONEY, Kaszri; uwamaye.
SQUINT, Yabu-nirami; higarame.
SQUIRM, Notakuru.
SQUIRREL, Risz.
SQUIRT, *n.* Midz-teppo.
SQUIRT, *v.* Hiyoguru; tszku
STAB, *v.* Tszku; sasz.
STABLE, *a.* Tash'ka-na; sadamatta; katai; shikkari to sh'ta.
STABLE, *n.* Uma-ya.
STABLE-BOY, Bettō.
STACK, *n.* Inamura.
STAFF, Tszye.
STAG, Sh'ka.

STAGE, *n.* Butai; dan; kōza; tomari; shukuba.
STAGGER, Hiyoro-hiyoro to aruku; yoro-yoro to aruku; yorobō; yoromeku; tajiroku.
STAGGERINGLY, Hiyoro-hiyoro to.
STAGNANT, Tamaru; yodomu; todokōru.
STAIN, *v.* Shimu; somaru; mabureru; nuru; yogareru.
STAIN, *n.* Shimi.
STAIR, *n.* Hashigo.
STAKE, *n.* Kui; hashira; kakemono; kakegoto.
STAKE, *v.* Kakeru.
STALACTITE, Shōnuiseki.
STALE, Furu-kusai; kusai. *To grow* —, mizame szru.
STALK, *n.* Kuki; jiku.
STALLION, Ouma.
STAMEN, Shibe; hana no dzi.
STAMMER, *v.* Domoru; koto-osoi; kuchigomoru.
STAMP, *n.* Han; in.
STAMP, *v.* Han wo osz.
STANCH, Jōbu-na; katai; shikato sh'ta.
STANCH, *v.* — *blood*, chi wo tomeru.
STANCHION, Tszppari; shimbari; tszka.
STAND, *v.* Tatsz; korayeru; shinogu; tomaru. — *by*, soba ni tatsz.
STAND, *n.* Tomari.
STANDARD, Hata.
STANDARD-BEARER, Hatamochi.
STANDING, Tatsz.
STAND-POINT, *see* wakime; okame; yosome.
STANZA, Zekku.
STAPLE, Sambutsz; ji; shina.
STAR, Hoshi.
STARBOARD, Fune no migi no hō. — *the helm*, omo-kaji wo toru.
STARCH, Nori.
STARE, Nagameru; kiyororito miru; kiyorotszku; mi-tszmeru.
STARK, *adv.* — *naked*, mappadaka.
STARLIGHT, Hoshi no hikari.
START, *v.* Biku-biku szru; biku-tszku; bikkuri szru; tatsz. — *on a journey*, tabidachi wo szru; detachi. *Get the* — *of*, sakigake wo szru.
STARTLE, *v.* Biku-biku szru; odoroku; tamageru; zatto; gikkuri-to; odosz.
STARTLING, Monoszgoi; odoro-odoroshii
STARVE, *v.* Wiye-jini szru; gashi szru; hijini; katszyeru.
STATE, Kuni; koku; yōsz; yōdai; arisama; sama; mama.
STATE, *v.* Iu; hanasz; mōsz; tszgeru; noberu; chindzru.
STATED, Kimaru; sadamaru; kimatte oru.
STATEMENT, Kōjō; kakitori.
STATION, Ba; tokoro; mochiba; kurai; dan. — *in life*, mibun; bungen. *Official* —, yaku; yakume. *Post* —, shukuba.
STATION, *v.* Oku; mōshi-tszkeru; sonayeru.
STATIONER, Kamiya.
STATUE, Ningiyō; zō.
STATURE, Take; sei.
STATUTE, Okite; sadame.
STAVE, *n.* Kure.
STAVE, *v.* Tszki-kowasz.
STAY, *v.* Matsz; tomaru; todomaru; tōriu szru; oru; osayeru; hikayeru; yameru; yamu; tanomu.
STEAD, Kawari.
STEADFASTLY, Kataku; shikkari; tash'kani; kitto; jitto.
STEADILY, Jitto; kitto.
STEADY, Shikato sh'ta; tash'ka-na; katai; shikkari to sh'ta.
STEAL, Nuszmu; ubau; toru; kaszmeru. — *away*, hisokani nigeru; nukete deru.
STEALTH, Nuszmi. *By* —, hisoka-ni; shinonde.
STEALTHILY, Hisokani; hiso-hiso; naishō; shinonde; kossori-to; nukete.
STEAM, Jōki; yuge.
STEAM, *v.* Musz; fukasz.
STEAM-BOAT, Hi-bune; jōk'sen.
STEAM-BOILER, Kama.
STEAM-CAR, Jōk'sha.
STEAM-ENGINE, Jōki no shikake.
STEEL, Hagane; hiuchi.
STEELYARD, Tembin; hakari.
STEEP, *n.* Soba; gake; zeppeki; nanjo.
STEEP, *a.* Kewashii; sagashii; kittatsz.
STEEP, *v.* Hitasz; tszkeru.
STEEPLE, Roban.
STEER, Kaji wo toru.
STEERSMAN, Kaji-tori.
STEM, *n.* Jiku; kuki.
STEM, *v.* Sakarau; saka noboru.
STEP, *v.* Fumu; aruku. — *into*, fumi-komu; yoru. — *back*, atoshizari; ushiro-ashi. — *across*, fumi-koyeru; fumi-watasz; matageru; matagu. — *aside*, yokeru. — *upon and break*, fumi-kudaku; fumi-tszbusz. — *on*, fumi-tszkeru.
STEP, *n.* Dan. *One* —, h'to ashi. *Step by step*, dan-dan; shidai-ni; oi-oi.

STEPS, Agaridan; hashigo; fumi-dan; fumi-tszgi.
STEP-BROTHER, Tane-gawari no kiyōdai; beppuku no kiyōdai; chi-kiyōdai.
STEP-CHILD, Mama-ko.
STEP-DAUGHTER, Mamako.
STEP-FATHER, Mama-chichi.
STEP-LADDER, Fumi-dan; fumi-tszgi; kiyatatsz.
STEPMOTHER, Mama-haha.
STEPSON, Muko.
STEPSTONE, Kutsznugi; dan.
STERILE, Yaseru.
STERN, *n.* Fune no tomo.
STERN, *a.* Arakenai; kibishii.
STERNLY, Kataku; kibishiku.
STERN-MOST, Itchi ato no.
STERNUM, Mune no hone.
STEW, Niru; yuderu.
STEWARD, Makanai-kata; katte-kata.
STICK, Bō, sao; tszye; ki.
STICK, *v.* Sasz; tszku; haru; tszkeru; koberi-tszku; nebari-tszku; kishimu; hebari-tszku. —*fast*, hittszku; kakaru; itszku.
STICKY, Nebai; nebaru; beta-beta; betatszku.
STIFF, Katai; katamaru; kowai; kowabaru; katakuna; henkutsz-na.
STIFFEN, Kataku szru; katameru; kowaku szru.
STIFFNESS, Katasa; kowasa; kataki; henkutsz; kataiji.
STIFLE, *v.* Iki wo tomeru; kesz.
STIGMA, Haji; kakin; chijoku; kidz.
STILL, *v.* Shidzmeru; osameru; tomeru; todomeru.
STILL, *a.* Shidzka-na; odayaka-na; shidzmaru; ochi-tszku; damaru; moku-nen.
STILL, *n.* Rambiki.
STILL, *adv.* Mada; ima-made; nao; h'toshiwo; keredomo; naosara; sh'kashi-nagara; yahari. — *more*, iyo-iyo; masz-masz.
STILL-BORN, Shinde umareru.
STILT, Take-uma.
STIMULATE, Hagemasz; odateru.
STING, *v.* Sasz.
STING, *n.* Hari.
STINGY, Shiwai; rinshoku-na; kechi-na; yabusaka; mimitchii; mono-oshimi.
STINT, Herasz.
STIPULATE, Yak'soku szru.
STIPULATION, Yak'soku; jōyaku; kajō.
STIR, *v.* Ugoku; ugokasz; undō szru; kakimawasz; kaki-mazeru. — *up*, hagemasz; odateru; okosz.
STIR, *n*, Nigiyaka; sawagi; sōdō.
STIRRUP, Abumi. — *leather*, chikara-gawa.
STITCH, *v.* Nū; tojiru.
STOCK, Jiku. — *of a gun*, teppō no dai. — *(capital)*, moto de; motokin; midzkin. — *(supply)*, takuwaye.
STOCKS, Ashigase; hota.
STOCK, *v.* Takuwayeru.
STOCKADE, Yarai; saku.
STOCKING, Tabi.
STOLEN-GOODS, Nuke-mono.
STOMACH, Ibukoro; i.
STONE, Ishi; seki. *precious* —, tama. — *in the bladder*, sekirin. — *image*, sekizō; ishi-botoke. — *step*, seki-dan. — *wall*, ishi-gaki. — *chips*, ishiko.
STONE, *v.* Ishi de butsz.
STONE-CUTTER, Ishiya; ishi-kiri,
STOOL, Koshi-kake; shōgi; fumidan; daiben.
STOOP, *v.* Kagamu; kuguru; kagameru.
STOP, *v.* Tomaru; tomeru; yameru; yaszmu; yosz; osayeru; todomeru; fusagu; udzmeru; sasayeru; seki-tomeru; hikayeru; kindzru; sashi-tomeru; tszmaru. *Not stopping to do*, ayedz; tori-ayedz.
STOP, *n.* Todome; yaszmi; sasaye; kinzei; jama; tszmari.
STORAGE, Kurashiki; kura ni tszmu.
STORE, *n.* Mise.
STORE, *v.* Tszmu; takuwayeru; kodzmu.
STORE-HOUSE, Kura.
STORM, Ōkaze; arashi; taifū.
STORM, *v.* Semeru; osou; utsz.
STORMY, Areru.
STORY, *n.* Hanashi; setsz; mono-gatari; kai.
STORY-TELLER, Hanash'ka.
STOUT, Szkoyaka-na; jōbu-na; tassha; sōken.
STOW, *v.* Tszmu; tszmi-komu.
STOWAGE, Tszmi.
STRADDLE, Matagaru; fumbaru; hadakaru; matageru.
STRAGGLE, Mayō.
STRAIGHT, *a.* Mattszgu; szgui; semai. — *face*, magao.
STRAIGHT, *adv.* Szgu-ni; mattszide.
STRAIGHTEN, *v.* Mattszgu ni szru; nobasz.
STRAIGHTWAY, Tachi-dokoro ni; tachi-machi ni; szgu-ni.
STRAIN, *v.* Ikimu; ki wo haru; chikara wo ireru; sei wo dasz; hipparu. — *(as water)*, kosz.
STRAINER, *n.* Midz-koshi.
STRAIT, *n.* Seto; nanjō; nangi; nanjū.
STRAIT, *a.* Semai.

STRAITEN, Semaku szru; setsznai; komaru; semaru.
STRANGE, *a.* Kotonaru; medzrashii; ayashii; hen-na; kawatta; miyō-na; fushigi-na; fushin-na; hiyon-na; ihen na; kitai na; otszna.
STRANGELY, Ayashiku.
STRANGER, Shiranu; h'to; yoso no h'to; kiyaku; tabi no h'to.
STRANGLE, Musebu; kubiru; kubiri-korosz; shime-korosz; museru.
STRAP, Kawa-himo.
STRATAGEM, Hakarigoto; keiriyaku; bōkei.
STRAW, Wara. — *bag*, hiyō; kamasz; tawara.
STRAWBERRY, Ichigo.
STRAW-CUTTER, Oshikiri
STRAW-ROOF, Wara-yane.
STRAY, Mayō.
STREAK, *n.* Szji.
STREAM, Nagare.
STREAM, *v.* Nagareru.
STREET, Machi; tōri.
STRENGTH, Chikara; riki; ikioi; tszyosa; yūriki.
STRENGTHEN, Tszyoku szru; jōbu ni szru; katameru.
STRENUOUS, Tszyoi; hageshii.
STRESS, *lay — on*, Taizetsz ni szru.
STRETCH, Nobasz; nobiru; haru; todoku; hipparu; noberu; oyobu.
STREW, Chirasz; maku.
STREWED, Chiru.
STRICT, Kibishii; katai; genjū, kiukutsz na; kengo; monogatai; ogosoka.
STRIFE, *n.* Arasoi; kōron; sōron; kenk'wa.
STRIKE, *v.* Utsz; butsz; tataku; chōchaku szru; ateru; ataru; naguru; tszku; sasz. — *in*, naikō szru. *The lightning has struck*; kaminari ga ochita (ochi).
STRING, *n.* Ito; nawa; sashi; koyori; o.
STRING, Sasz; tszranuku; tōsz.
STRIP, *v.* Nugu; hagu; muku; hegu; toru; ubau; kogu; hageru. — *naked*, hadaka ni szru.
STRIP, *n.* Hegi.
STRIPE, Shima.
STRIPED, Shima no.
STRIPLING, Wakashu; shōnen.
STRIVE, Sei wo dasz; hagemu; haru. — *together*, kisō; arasō; kumi-au; momi-au; hagemi-au.
STROKE, K'wakn. — *of the sun*; atszke-atari; shoki-atari.
STROKE, *v.* Naderu.
STROLL, Asobu; yūreki szru.
STRONG, Jōbu; tszyoi; szkoyaka; kengo-na; katai; tash'ka-na; kibui. — *or weak*, kiyō-jaku.
STROP, Togi-kawa.
STRUCTURE, Tszkuri-kata; koshiraye-yō; tszkuri; koshiraye; seisaku.
STRUGGLE, *n.* Momi-ai; agaki; aseri.
STRUGGLE, *v.* Momi-au; sei wo dasz; agaku; aseru.
STRUMPET, Jōro.
STRUT, Fumbaru; bakko szru.
STUBBLE, Kabu; kari-kabu.
STUBBORN, Henkutsz; kataku-na; wagamama.
STUDENT, Deshi; shosei.
STUDIOUS, Benkiyo szru; sei-dasz; kingaku szru.
STUDY, *n.* Gakumon; keiko; manabi.
STUDY, *v.* Manabu; narau.
STUFF, Shina; mono; shina-mono; orimono.
STUFF, *v.* Tszmeru; tszme-komu; fusagu.
STUMBLE, Tszmadzku; fumi-hadzsz.
STUMP, Kabu.
STUMP, *v.* Tszmadzku.
STUPEFIED, Shibireru; mahi szru; bōzen to sh'te iru.
STUPID, Don; gu; oroka-naru; manuke; tomma; tonchiki; nibuki.
STURDY, Szkoyaka; jōbu.
STUTTER, Domoru.
STY, Butagoya; monomorai.
STYLE, Yō; te; fū; nari; tei; kamaye; szgata; sama; tszki; kata; riu; riugi.
STYLISH, Ikina; fūriu na; shareru.
STYPTIC, Chi-tome.
SUBDUE, Osameru; tairageru; taiji szru; shidzmeru; sh'ta-gayeru; nabikeru; fuku szru; heiji szru.
SUBJECT, Sh'tagau; fuku szru; fukujū szru; zoku szru.
SUBJECT, *v.* Tairageru; osameru; sh'tagayeru.
SUBJECT, *n.* Koto; omomuki; yoshi; wake; sh'tagau mono; tami; haika. — *for thought*, omoi-gusa.
SUBJUGATE, Tairageru; osameru; sh'tagayeru; nabikeru; fuku-saseru.
SUBLET, Mata-gashi wo szru.
SUBLIME, *v.* Sei szru; sei-hō szru.
SUBLIME, *a.* Bakkun; miyō-na; taye-naru; zetsz-miyō.
SUBMERGE, Shidzmeru; oboreru.

SUBMISSION, Sh'tagai; kōsan.
SUBMIT, Sh'tagau ; kudaru; kōsan szru ; makaseru; zoku szru; tszku; fukusz.
SUBPŒNA, *v.* Yobi-dasz; meshi-dasz; meshi-yoseru.
SUBPŒNA, *n.* Meshijō.
SUBSCRIBE, Na wo kaku; kishin szru; kifu szru.
SUBSCRIPTION, Kishin ; kifu ; hōnō. — *paper*, kishin fuda.
SUBSEQUENT, Ato no; nochi no; tszgi no; go.
SUBSEQUENTLY, Nochi ni; ato de.
SUBSIDE, Shidzmu ; odomu ; shidzmaru ; ochi-tszku.
SUBSIST, Kurasz; inochi wo tsznagu; oru.
SUBSISTENCE, Kuchiszgi; kate.
SUBSTANCE, Mono; shina ; shitsz ; shui; honi.
SUBSTANTIAL, Utsztsz ; jitsz; makoto-no; hon-tō; jōbu-na.
SUBSTANTIALLY, Jitsz-ni; makoto-ni; honni; tai-riyaku-ni.
SUBSTITUTE, *v.* Kawarini szru; dai ni szru.
SUBSTITUTE, *n.* Miyōdai; kawari no h'to; migawari.
SUBTERFUGE, Īgusa; kakotszke
SUBTERRANEOUS, Tszchi no naka; chi-chiuno.
SUBTILE, Kash'koi; rikō-na.
SUBTRACT, Hiku; nozoku; hesz; habuku.
SUBTRACTION, Hikizan.
SUBURBS, Jōka; hadzre; bōbana.
SUBVERT, Horobosz; katamukeru.
SUCCEED, Tszgu; tszdzku; togeru; dekiru; kanau.
SUCCEEDING, Nochi no; tszdzku. — *years*, kōnen.
SUCCESSFUL, Ataru; shubiyoi; kanau; au.
SUCCESSION, Tszdzki.
SUCCESSIVE, Tszdzku. — *days*, renjitsz. — *years*, rennen. — *generations*, rendai.
SUCCESSOR, Ato-tszgi; tszgi no h'to; ato-tori.
SUCCINTLY, Ara-ara; tairiyaku; zatto.
SUCCOR, Taszkeru; szkū.
SUCCOR, Taszke; szkui.
SUCCUMB, Kōsan szru; sh'tagau; kusszru; kuppuku.
SUCH, Kono-yō-na; kon-na; kayō-na; sono-yō-na; son-na; ano-yō-na; anna; āyu; sayō-na; kono-kurai-na; kono tōri-no; sono-kurai-na; sono-tōri-no; saszga-no; sa-hodo-no; sabakari-no; kaku-nogotoki.
SUCK, Sū; nomu; shaburu. — *in*, szi-komu. — *out*, szidasz.
SUCKLE, Chi-chi wo nomaseru.
SUCKLING, Chi-nomi-go.
SUDDEN, Kiu-na; niwaka-na; fui-na; tachimachi-na. — *death*, tonshi. — *riches*, deki-bugen. — *notion*, deki-gokoro.
SUDDENLY, Niwaka-ni; kiu-ni; futo; tachimachi-ni ; ton-ni; soku-ji-ni; fui-ni ; h'yoito.
SUDORIFIC-MEDICINES, Hakkan-zai.
SUE, *v.* Uttayeru; todokeru; so-shō szru; negai dasz.
SUET, Ushi no abura.
SUFFER, Ukeru; au; yurusz; gaman szru; kandzru; tayeru; shinogu.
SUFFERING, Setsznai; kurushimi; kutszu.
SUFFICIENT, Taru; aku; jūbun-na; kanau.
SUFFICIENTLY, Jūbun-ni.
SUFFOCATE, Iki ga tszmaru.
SUGAR, Satō.
SUGAR-CANDY, Kōrizatō; satōg'washi.
SUGAR-CANE, Satō-kibi; kansha.
SUGAR-BOWL, Satō-ire.
SUGAR OF LEAD, Yentō.
SUGGEST, Iu; hanasz; oshiyeru.
SUICIDE, Jigai; jisatsz.
SUIT, *n.* Koto; kuji. *One — of clothes*, kimono h'to kasane.
SUIT, *v.* Au; kanau; ōjiru. — *one's taste*. ki ni iru; ki ni kanau. *Exactly* —, chōdo yoi. *Does not suit*, ki ni iranu.
SUITABLE, Au; kanau; sōō.
SULKY, Szneru.
SULLEN, Butchōdzra.
SULLY, Yogosz; kegasz.
SULLIED, Kumoru; yogareru.
SULPHATE OF COPPER, Tampan.
SULPHATE OF IRON, Riyoku-ban.
SULPHATE OF ZINC, Kōhan.
SULPHUR, Iwo.
SULTRY, Mushi-atszi; atszi; homeku.
SUM, Tszgō; shime-daka; awasete; mina.
SUM, *v.* Shimeru; yoseru; kanjō szru; awaseru. *The sum of the matter*, shosen; hikkiyō; tszmari.
SUMMARILY, Ara-ara; zatto; tairiyaku; riyaku-sh'te; arakajime.
SUMMARY, Riyaku; tszdzme.
SUMMER, Natsz; ka.
SUMMERSET, Kumagayeri.
SUMMIT, Zetchō; itadaki; chōjo; sai-chiu; debana; desakari; tōge.

SUMMON, Mesz; meshi-dasz. — *together*, meshi-atszmeru; meshi-yoseru.
SUMMONS, Ī-tszke; meshi-bumi; meshi-jō.
SUMPTUOUSNESS, Ogori; yeig'wa.
SUN, Hi; nichi-rin; taiyō. — *dried*, amaboshi.
SUN, *v.* Sarasz.
SUNBURNT, Yakeru; kogeru.
SUNDAY, Ansoku-nichi; yaszmi-bi; dontaku.
SUNDER, *v.* Hanareru; wakeru; wakareru; hedateru; kireru; kiru; tatsz.
SUNDIAL, Hidokei.
SUNFLOWER, Himawari; oguruma.
SUNLIGHT, Hikage.
SUNKEN, Kuboi; kubomu.
SUNNY, — *place*, hinata.
SUNRISE, Hi no de.
SUNSET, Hi no iri; higure.
SUNSHINE, Hinata.
SUP, Szu; nomu; szszru.
SUPERABUNDANCE, Yokei; k'wabun; yobun; amaru.
SUPERANNUATED, Oiboreru; rōmō.
SUPERB, Rippa; kekkō.
SUPERCARGO, Uwanori.
SUPERCILIOUS, Ōfū; ōhei; takaburu.
SUPER-EMINENT, Nukinderu; hīderu.
SUPER-EXCELLENT, Goku-jō; tobikiri; daigoku-jō.
SUPERFICIAL, Uwamuki; omotemuki; uwabe; asai; namaiki-na.
SUPERFICIALLY, Omote-muki-ni.
SUPERFICIES, G'wai-men; omote; uwatszra.
SUPERFINE, Goku-hin; gokujō.
SUPERFLUITY, Yokei; yobun; amaru; tak'san.
SUPERFLUOUS, Szgiru; yaye ni naru; yokei-na.
SUPER-HUMAN, H'to no oyobanu; jin-riki ni atawanu; fushigina; fukashigi.
SUPER-IMPOSED, Kasanaru.
SUPERINTEND, Sairiyō szru; tszkasadoru; sahai szru.
SUPERINTENDENT, Kimo-iri; sairiyō-nin; bugiyō.
SUPERIOR, Masaru; szgureru; katsz; nukinderu; hīderu; jō; wiye no; kami.
SUPERIOR-MAN, Kunshi.
SUPERIORS, Me-wiye no h'to; kami ni tatsz h'to; jōhai.
SUPERLATIVE, Nukindeta; masatta; szgureta. *Words used to form the — degree are*, mottomo; hanahada; ittatte; goku; ito; shigoku.
SUPERNATURAL, Fushigi-na; shimben-na; fukashigi-na.
SUPERNUMERARY, Kadz no hoka.
SUPERSCRIPTION, Uwagaki.
SUPERSEDE, Oshi-nokeru; nokeru; fuyō ni szru; yaszmeru.
SUPERSTITION, Gohei-katszgi.
SUPERVISE, Sai-riyō szru; sahai szru; tszkasadoru.
SUPERVISOR, Sai-riyō-nin.
SUPINE, Aomuki.
SUPPER, Yumeshi; yugohan; yashoku.
SUPPLANT, Oshi-nokeru.
SUPPLE, Shinayaka; taoyaka.
SUPPLEMENT, Furoku; tszika; tszketari.
SUPPLICATE, Negau; tanomu; tang'wan szru; kitō wo szru.
SUPPLICATION, Negai; tanomi; kig'wan; g'wan; kitō.
SUPPLIES, Teate.
SUPPLY, *v.* Atayeru; yaru; teate wo szru. — *a deficiency*, tasz; oginau. — *the wants of the poor*, bimbō-nin wo szkū.
SUPPORT, *v.* Motsz; ukeru; tayeru; shinobu; korayeru; shinogu; yashinau; hagokumu; kotayeru; shimbō szru; gaman szru; tetsztau; taszkeru; katan szru.
SUPPORT, *n.* Dodai; tszka; taszke; yashinai.
SUPPORTER, Katōdo; katannin; satan-nin.
SUPPOSE, *v.* Omō; darō; de arō; *or the dub. form of the verb.* Tszmoru; tatoyeru.
SUPPOSING, Moshi; moshikuba; tatoyeba; yoshimba; yoshiya; hiyotto.
SUPPOSITION, Tszmori; omoi; hakari.
SUPPRESS, *v.* Osameru; tairageru; shidzmeru; taiji szru; hisomeru; hikayeru; kakusz; tomeru.
SUPPURATE, Umu; ibō.
SUPREME, Ichi-ban wiye; jō.
SURE, Tash'ka; katai; jōbu; utagai-naki; sōi-naki; shikkari to sh'ta; hitszjō; masashii. *Not* —, obotszkanai.
SURELY, Tash'ka-ni; sōi-naku; makoto-ni; jitsz-ni; kitto.
SURETY, Ukeai-nin; hikiukenin.
SURF, Nami.
SURFACE, Omote; tszra; hira; soto; g'waimen; men.
SURFEITED, Aku; aki-hateru.
SURGEON, Ge-k'wa-isha.
SURGERY, Gek'wa.
SURMISE, Szi-riyō szru; szisatsz szru; oshihakaru.
SURMOUNT, Katsz; masaru.

SURNAME, Sei; uji.
SURPASS, Szgiru; masaru; katsz; kosz.
SURPLUS, Amari;nokori.
SURPRISE, . Odorokasz; odoroku; akireru; obiyakasz. *By* —, futo; fui-ni; omoigake naku; dashi-nuke ni.
SURPRISE, *n.* Odoroki; fui.
SURRENDER, Kōsan szru; kudaru; yudzru.
SURROUND, *v.* Kakomu; torimaku.
SURVEY, *v.* Kenchi wo utsz; soku-riyō szru; hakaru; kembun szru; bunken wo szru. *Surveying instruments*, bunkendōgu.
SURVEYOR, Fushin-yaku; jikata-yakunin.
SURVIVE, Okureru; iki-nokoru.
SURVIVOR, Iki-nokoru-mono.
SUSCEPTIBLE, Makeru.
SUSPECT, Utagau; ayashimu; sziriyō szru; ayabumu; ibukaru; fushin ni omō; kedoru.
SUSPEND, Kakeru; sageru; tszru; yaszmeru; tomeru.
SUSPENSE, Tayutai; tamerau; tadayō; utagau.
SUSPICION, Utagai; usan; uron; ginen; gishin; fushin; giwaku.
SUSPICIOUS, Utagawashii; uron-na; usanrashii; gaten-yukanu; ayashii; fushinna; ibukashii.
SUSTAIN, *see support.*
SUSTENANCE, Yashinai; shokumotsz.
SUTURE, Awashime.
SWAB, Yezōkin; zōkin.
SWAB, *v.* Fuku.
SWADDLE, Tsztszmu; maku.
SWAGGER, Takaburu; rikimi-kayeru; rikimi-chirasz; bakko szru; fumbatakaru.
SWALLOW, *n.* Tszbame; tszbakura.
SWALLOW, *v.* Nomu; nomi-komu. —*whole*, maru-nomi.
SWAMP, Numa.
SWAN, Hishikui.
SWAP, Tori-kayeru; kōyeki szru.
SWARD, Shiba.
SWARM, *v.* Waku; takaru; uza-uza szru.
SWARM, *n.* Mura.
SWAY, Shihai szru.
SWEAR, Chikau; nonoshiru; akkō szru.
SWEAT, Ase. *To* —, ase ga deru; hakkan-szru.
SWEEP, Haku; sōji szru.
SWEEPINGS, Gomi.
SWEET, Amai; kawairashii.
SWEETEN, Amaku szru.
SWEET-FLAG, Shōbu; ayame.
SWEETMEATS, K'washi.
SWEETNESS, Amasa.
SWEET-POTATOE, Satszma-imo.
SWELL, *v.* Hareru; fukureru; tszmoru; tszyoru; bōchō szru.
SWELLING, *n.* Haremono.
SWERVE, Hadzreru.
SWIFT, Hayai; kiu-na; szmiyaka-na.
SWIFTNESS, Hayasa.
SWIM, Oyogu; ukamu. *Head* —, me ga mau; kennun szru.
SWINDLE, Damasz; kataru; mayakasz.
SWINDLER, Katari; mayashi.
SWINE, Buta.
SWINE-HERD, Butakai.
SWING, *v.* Yurugu; furu; mawaru; yuru.
SWING, *n.* Buranko; yusawari.
SWITCH, *n.* Szmoto.
SWITCH, *v.* Muchi-utsz.
SWOON, Memai; tachi-gurami.
SWORD, Katana; tszrugi. — *rack*, katana-kake. — *cut*, katana kidz.
SWORD-BLADE, Katana no mi; yaiba.
SWORD-EXERCISE, Ken-jutsz.
SWORD-FIGHT, Shi-ai.
SYCOPHANT, Neijin; nejikebito.
SYMBOL, Hanjimono.
SYMMETRICAL, Tszriau. *Not* —, tszriawanu.
SYMPATHIZE, Omoi-yaru; awaremu; itchi szru.
SYMPTOM, Shirushi; shōko.
SYNONYMOUS-WORD, Nitaru kotoba.
SYHPILIS, Kasa; sōdoku.
SYHPILITIC ERUPTION, Yōbaisō.
SYRINGE, *n.* Midz-deppō.
SYRINGE, *v.* Tszku.
SYSTEM, Dō; riu; riugi; michi; shidara; shidai.
SYSTEMATIC, Kimari no yoi; torishimari no yoi.

T

TABLE, Dai; tszkuye; zen: *Dining* —, handai.
TABLE-BOY, Kiu-ji.
TABLE-CLOTH, Handai-shiki; shokusen.
TABLET, *Ancestral* —, ihai.
TACITURN, Mukuchi.
TACK, *n.* Biyō.
TACK SHIP, Fune wo magiru.

TACT, Yete; tokui; jōdz. *No* —, heta.
TACTICS, Kei-ko; hei-jutsz; gun-gaku; heihō; gumpō.
TAEL, Ichi-riyō.
TAIL, Shippo; o.
TAILOR, Shitateya.
TAINT, Tszku; utszru; kusaru; azareru.
TAKE, Toru; ukeru; uke-toru; tszkamayeru. — *in the arms*, daku. — *in the fingers*, tszkamu. — *food*, taberu; kū. — *one's choice*, yerabu; yoru. — (*accept*), uke-toru. — *medicine*, kuszri wo nomu. — *the liberty*, habakari nagara. — *for granted*, mochiron. *Taken sick*, yami-tszku. *Take a house*, iya wo karu. — *a likeness*, zō wo utszsz. — *a castle*, shiro wo semetoru. — *a seat*, koshi-kakeru; szwaru; chakuza szru. *How much will it take?* ikura kakarimashō. — *away*, tori-harau; tori-nokeru; tori-hanasz. — *care*, abunai; ki wo tszkeyo. — *care of* mamoru. — *your own course*, katte ni se-yo; omaye no kokoro-mochi shidai. *Take down*, orosz; tori-kudzsz. — *out*, tori-dasz; hadzsz. — *out of the way*, tori-harau; tori-nokeru. — *hold of*, tszkamayeru; nigiru. — *back*, tori-kayesz. — *apart*, tori-kudzsz. — *in*, ukeru; hairu. — *notice*, mi-tszkeru. — *an oath*, chikau. — *off*, toru; nugu; orosz. — *out a stain*, shimi wo nuku, — *part in*, kumi szru; issho ni naru; nakama ni hairu. — *place*, ga atta (aru). — *effect*, kiku. — *root*, ne ga tszku. — *up*, hirō; ageru; tszkamayeru. — *time*, himadoru; temadoru. — *up room*, ba wo toru. — *to heart*, ki ni motsz. — *advantage of*, tszke-konde; dz ni notte; jōdzru. — *the air*, asobu. — *leave*, itoma-goi wo szru. — *breath*, yaszmu. — *aim*, nerau. — *along*, tszreru; tomonau. *The child takes after his father*, kodomo ga chichi ni niteoru. *To take for*, michigayeru. — *to*, konomu; szku. *Take to one's heels*, nigeru. *Take cold*, kaze wo hiku. *Take without restraint*, tori-hōdai. *Take all*, tori-kiru.
TALC, Kirara; ummo.
TALE, Hanashi; monogatari. *To tell* —, tszgeguchi wo szru.
TALE-BEARER, Tszge-guchi; gomaszri.
TALENT, Chiye; sainō; kiriyō; riyō.
TALK, *v.* Mono wo iu; iu; hanasz; kataru; shaberu; dankō szru.
TALK, *n.* Mono-ī; hanashi; katari; danwa; kotoba; uwasa; setsz. — *about others*, h'togoto wo iu. — *to one's self*, h'torigoto wo iu. — *in sleep*, negoto wo iu.
TALL, Sei-takai.
TALLOW, Ushi no abura.
TALLOW-TREE, Rō no ki.
TALLY, Te-ita; shirushi-ita.
TALON, Tszme.
TAME, *a.* Otonashii; matai.
TAME, *v.* Natszkeru.
TAN, *v.* Namesz.
TANGLE, *v.* Motszreru; muszboreru.
TANK, Midz-oke; midz-tame.
TANNED-HIDE, Nameshi-kawa.
TANNER, Kawa-nameshi; kawata; kawaya.
TANTALIZE, Mise-birakasz.
TAP, *v.* Tataku; dashi-guchi wo akeru.
TAPE-WORM, Sanada-mushi.
TAR, Chan.
TARDY, Osoi; okureru; yen-nin; osonawaru; chichi szru.
TARE, Hagusa; fūtai. — *of weight*, kan.
TARGET, Mato; kaku. — *shooting*, kakuuchi.
TARIFF, Unjō; zeisoku.
TARNISH, Kumoru; sabiru.
TARO, Satoimo.
TARRY, Matsz; todomaru; tomaru; tōriu szru.
TART, *a.* Szppai.
TARTAR-EMETIC, Toshuseki.
TARTARIC ACID, Shuseki-san.
TARTARUS, Jigoku.
TASK, H'to kiri no; bun; nikk'wa.
TASSEL, Fusa.
TASTE, *n.* Aji; ajiwai; fūmi; mi. *Bitter* —, nigami. *Acrid* —, kara-mi.
TASTE, *v.* Ajiwau; nameru; aji wo miru; aji wo kiku.
TASTELESS, Aji no nai.
TATTERED, Yabureta.
TATTLE, *v.* Shaberu; kuchi-saganai.
TATTLER, Oshaberi.
TATTOO, *n.* Hori-mono.
TATTOO, *v.* Horu.
TAUGHT, *a.* Katai.
TAUNT, Nonoshiru.
TAVERN, Yadoya; hatagoya.
TAX, *n.* Nengu; unjō; denso; men. *Pay* —, nengu wo osameru.
TAX, *v.* Nengu wo toru.
TEA, Cha.
TEA-CANISTER, Cha-ire.
TEA-CHEST, Cha-bako.
TEA-CUP, Chawan.

TEA-DEALER, Cha-akindo.
TEA-GARDEN, Chayen.
TEA-GROUNDS, Cha-gara; cha-kasz.
TEA-HOUSE, Chaya.
TEA-JAR, Cha-tszbo.
TEA-PLANT, Cha no ki.
TEA-PLANTATION, Cha-batake.
TEA-POT, Dobin; cha-bin.
TEACH, *v.* Oshiyeru; kiyōkun szru; michibiku, kiyōju szru; satosz.
TEACHING, Oshiye; kiyōkun; kiyō-ju; shinan.
TEACHER, Shishō.
TEAL, Kamo.
TEAR, *n.* Namida. *Shed* —, raku-rui.
TEAR, *v.* Saku; yaburu; hiki-saku; hikiyaburu; chigireru. — *off*, hittakuru; nuku; hiki-hadzsz; hiki-hagu. — *up*, hiki-nuku.
TEASE, Naburu; jirasz; ijimeru; komaraseru; nedaru; gudzru.
TEDIOUS, Urusai; nagatarashii; mendō; taikutsz; kochitaki; kudoi.
TEDIUM, Taikutsz.
TEEM, Mitszru.
TEETH, Ha. *Front* —, maye-ba. *Back* —, okuba. *Canine* —, kiba. *Gnashing of* —, hagami; higishiri.
TEGUMENT, Kawa.
TELESCOPE, Tōmegane.
TELL, Kikaseru; tszgeru; kataru; hanasz; iu; noberu; shiraseru; oshiyeru; wakaru; chiushin. — *to others*, tagon.
TELL-TALE, Tszge-guchi.
TEMERITY, Mukōmidz.
TEMPER, *n.* Ki; kokoro; iji; kishitsz; shōne; ki-date.
TEMPER, *v.* Kitau; neru; tanren szru; nereru; nerikitau.
TEMPERAMENT, Shō; shōai; seishitsz; umaretszki.
TEMPERANCE, Hikayeme; uchiba.
TEMPERATE, Hodoyoi.
TEMPERATURE, Yōki; kan-dan.
TEMPEST, Arashi; ōkaze.
TEMPESTUOUS, Areru.
TEMPLE, Tera; miya; yashiro; dō.
TEMPORAL, Yo no; seken no.
TEMPORARY, Kari ni; tōbun; tōji. — *residence*, karidzmai. — *sewing*, karinui.
TEMPT, Sosonokasz; hiku; kokoro-miru; ki wo hiku; ki wo hīte miru.
TEMPTATION, Sosonokashi; sasoi; kokoromi.
TEMPTED, Hikareru; sosonokasareru.
TEN, Jū; tō. — *hundred*, issen. — *thousand*, man.
TENACIOUS, Kataku-na; katai; kataiji-na; henkutsz; nebai, nebaru.
TENACIOUSLY, Kataku; nebaku.
TENACITY, Nebasa.
TENANT, *Of land*, ji-kari. — *of a house*, tanako; tanagari.
TEND, *v.* Mamoru; ban wo szru; ki wo tszkeru; kaihō szru; muku; mukau; yoru; sasz.
TENDER, *a.* Yowai; yawaraki; tayowai; ki no yowai; yasashii; onjun-na.
TENDER-HEARTED, Jihi-bukai; nasake aru.
TENDERLY, Yawaraka-ni.
TENDON, Szji; kinkon.
TENDRIL, Tszru no te; te.
TENEMENT, Iye; tana.
TENESMUS, Shiburu.
TENET, Oshiye; setsz.
TENFOLD, Jissōbai; toye.
TENON, Hozo.
TENOR, Omomuki; shui; imi.
TENSE, *a.* Katai; shimaru.
TENSE, *n.* (*in grammar*), *past* —, k'wako. *Present* —, genzai. *Future* —, mirai.
TENSENESS, or TENSION, Katasa; shimari.
TENT, Makuya.
TENTH, Jū-ban; jūbam-me. — *part*, jūbu-ichi.
TENUITY, Hososa; uszsa.
TEPID, Nurui; nurumu.
TEPIDNESS, Nurusa.
TERM, Nichi-gen; miyō-moku; kotoba; ji; shirushi; yak'soku. *Come to terms*, yak'soku szru.
TERMINATE Shimau; owaru; kagiru.
TERMINATION, Owari; shimai; hate; kagiri.
TERRACE, Utena; dai.
TERRIBLE, Osoroshii; mezamashii.
TERRIBLENESS, Osoroshisa.
TERRIBLY, Osoroshiku.
TERRIFY, Odosz; obiyakasz.
TERRITORY, Riyōbun.
TERROR, Osore; kiyōfu.
TEST, *v.* Tamesz; kokoromiru.
TESTAMENT, Yuigon.
TESTICLE, Kintama; kin; innō; fuguri.
TESTIFY, Shōko wo tatsz.
TESTIMONY, Shōko.
TETHER, *v.* Tsznagu.
TEXT, Hom-mon; dai.

TEXTURE, Jiai; hada; ji; kime.
THAN, Kara; yori.
THANK, Arigatō; katajikenai; sha-szru; rei wo iu.
THANKFUL, Aragatai; katajike-nai; arigatagaru.
THANKLESS, Arigataku omowanu; on wo shiranu; arigatagaranu.
THANK-OFFERING, G'wan-hodoki.
THAT, Sore; are; kare; sono; kano; to; yō ni. *Also formed as follows; they — love others*, h'to wo aiszru mono. *The person — struck me*, watakushi wo butta h'to.
THATCH, *v*. Wara wo fuku.
THATCHED-HOUSE, Waraya.
THATCHER, Yane-ya.
THATCHING, Wara-fuki.
THAW, *v*. Toku.
THE, *has no equivalent*.
THEATRE, Shibai.
THEFT, Nuszmi.
THEIR, Are no; sono h'to no; sono; karerano.
THEM, Karera wo; sono h'to wo; are wo.
THEME, Dai.
THEMSELVES, Onore; ji-shin; jibun.
THEN, Sono-toki; ano-toki; sōsh'te; shikaraba; kara; sono ato de.
THENCE, Soko kara.
THENCEFORTH, Sono nochi; sono-go.
THEOLOGY, Shingaku; shintō.
THEOLOGIAN, Shingakusha.
THEORY, Omoi-nashi.
THERE, Achi; achira; soko; sochi; sochira; aszko. *Here and* —, achi kochi.
THEREABOUT, Gurai; bakari.
THEREAFTER, Sono-nochi.
THEREAT, Sokoni; sokode.
THEREBY, Sono-yuye-ni; kono yuye ni; kore ni yotte.
THEREIN, Sono uchi ni.
THERMOMETER, Kandankei.
THESE, Kore; korera.
THESIS, Dai.
THEY, Sorera; sore.
THICK, Koi; atszi; shigei; shigeru; futoi; nigoru.
THICKEN, Atszku szru; koku szru; shigeru.
THICKET, Mori; yabu; odoro.
THICKLY, Atszku; koku.
THICKNESS, Atszsa; kosa; f'tosa; shigeisa.
THIEF, Nuszbito; dorobō; tōzoku; yotō; mambiki.
THIGH, Momo.
THIMBLE, Yubinuki.
THIN, Uszi; hosoi; yaseru.
THIN, *v*. Uszku szru; mabiku; szkasz; mabara ni szru; manuku.
THING, Mono; koto; shina; motsz. *All things*, bam-motsz. *Any* —, nandemo. *No such* —, sō de wa nai.
THINK, Omō; kangayeru; tszmoru; shian szru. — *much of*, tattomu. — *of each other*, Omoi-au. *To cease to — of*, omoi-szteru; omoi-yaru; omoi-kiru. — *of*, omoi-dasz; omoi-tszku. — *more and more of*, omoi-tszmoru. — *of only*, omoi-tszmeru. — *too much of*, omoi-szgosz. — *meanly of*, omoi-sageru; karondzru. — *better of*, omoi-naosz. — *of again*, omoi-kayesz.
THINKING, Mono-omoi.
THINLY, Uszku; hosoku; mabara-ni.
THINNESS, Uszsa.
THIRD, Samban; sambam-me. *One* —, sambu-ichi.
THIRST, *v*. Nodo-kawaku; kawaku; kasszru.
THIRST, *n*. Katsz; kawaki.
THIRSTY, Kawaku; kasszru.
THIRTEEN, Jū-san.
THIRTEENTH, Jūsamban.
THIRTIETH, Sanjūban.
THIRTY, Sanjū.
THIS, Kore, kono; kon. — *year*, kon-nen; ko-toshi. — *morning*, kon-chō; kesa. — *day*, konnichi; kiyō. — *evening*, komban; koyoi. — *night*, konya; komban. — *month*, kono tszki; kongetsz. — *world*, kono-yo. — *time*, kondo; kono-tabi. — *manner*, kono tōri; konomama; konobun.
THISTLE, Azami.
THITHER, Aszko; achira.
THONG, Himo; o.
THORACIC-DUCT, Niubik'wan.
THORAX, Mune.
THORN, Toge; hari.
THOROUGH, Mattaku; maru-de; jūbun-na; yuki-todoku. *Not* —, fuyukitodoki; futemawari.
THOROUGH-FARE, Tōri-michi; ōrai; kaidō; michi.
THOROUGHLY, Mattaku; marude; jūbunni; sappari.
THOUGH, Keredomo; naredomo; iyedomo; tatoi; tomo; domo; shikashi.
THOUGHT, *n*. Omoi; riyōken; kangaye; tszmori; zoni; shiriyo; shian; kufū; an; kokoro-gake.

THOUGHTFUL, Yōjin no yoi; tashinami no yoi; ki wo tszkeru.
THOUGHTLESS, Ki no tszkanu; ukkari to sh'ta.
THOUSAND, Sen; chi. *Ten* —, man.
THOUSAND-FOLD, Sembai.
THOUSANDTH, Semban. — *part*, sembu-ichi.
THRASH, *v.* Utsz; konasz.
THRASHING, Konashi.
THRASHING-FLOOR, Konashi-ba.
THREAD, Ito. *Ball of* —, heso.
THREAD, *v.* Ito wo tōsz; tszranuku; szgeru.
THREAT, Imashime; korashi; odoshi.
THREATEN, Korasz; imashimeru; odosz. — *rain*, furisō. — *to fall*, taore-sō.
THREE, Mitsz; san; mi.
THREE-CORNERED, San-kaku.
THREE-FOLD, Sambai; sansōbai; mitsz-gake; miye.
THREE-LEAVED, Mitszba.
THREE-PLY, Miye.
TEREESCORE, Rokujū.
THRESHOLD, Shikimi; shikii.
THRICE, Sando; mitabi.
THRIFTY, Hanjō szru; sakayeru.
THRILL, *v.* Tesszru; kotayeru; hibiku.
THRIVE, Sakayeru; hanjō szru.
THROAT, Nodo. *Clear the* —, kowadzkuri; seki-barai; shiwabuki.
THROB, *v.* Dōki ga utsz. — *with pain*, dzki-dzki itamu.
THRONE, Takamikura; kurai.
THRONG, *n.* Ozei; kunju.
THRONG, *v.* Kunju szru; yoru; atszmaru; nigiwai; nigiwashii; nigiyaka.
THROTTLE, Nodo wo shimeru.
THROUGH, Tōru; nite. *To pass* —. tōsz. *Go* —, tōru. *Blow* —, fuki-tōsz. *Run — with a thread (string)*, tszranuku; sasz. *Run — (with a spear)*, sashi-tōsz. *Shoot — (with an arrow)* i-tōsz. *Shoot — (with a ball)*, uchi-tōsz. *To carry —, (accomplish)*, togeru; dekiru. *Died through starvation*, wiyete shinda.
THROW, Nageru; hōru. — *down*, taosz; otosz; nage-orosz. — *away*, szteru; utcharu; nage-szteru. — *into*, nage-komu; nage-ireru. — *up*, nage-ageru; haku. — *out*, nage-dasz. — *across*, nage-kosz. — *aside*, nage-yaru. — *against*, nage-tszkeru. — *and hit*, nage-utsz.
THRUM, *v.* Hiku.
THRUST, *v.* Tszku; sasz; osz. — *through*, tszki-tōsz. — *out*, oshi-dasz. — *in*, oshi-komu; oshi-ireru. — *open*, oshi-akeru; oshi-hiraku. — *against*, oshi-ateru; oshi-tszkeru. — *apart*, oshi-hedateru; oshi-wakeru. — *back*, oshi-kayesz. — *down*, oshi-fuseru; oshi-ku-dasz; oshi-sageru. — *aside*, oshi-nokeru.
THUMB, Oya-yubi.
THUMP, *v.* Butsz; utsz.
THUNDER, Kami-nari; rai. — *and lightning*, rai-den.
THUNDER, *v.* Kami-nari ga naru, *or*, todoroku; hatameku.
THUNDER-BOLT, Raijū.
THUNDER-STRUCK, Bōzen; bikkuri.
THUS, Kono-tōri; kono-mama; ka-yō; kaku-no-gotoku.
THWART, Sakarau; teki-szru; sasayeru; samatageru.
TICK, *n.* Dani.
TICKET, Fuda; tegata.
TICKLE, Kosoguru.
TICKLISH, Kuszguttai; kosobayui; kosobaigaru.
TIDE, Shio.
TIDINGS, Tayori; otodzre; inshin; sata.
TIDY, Kirei; tei-nei.
TIE, *n.* Muszbime; yen.
TIE, *v.* Muszbu; shibaru; tsznagu; karageru; kukuru; yū; yuwayeru.
TIER, Narabi.
TIFFIN, Hirugohan; chiu-han.
TIGER, Tora.
TIGHT, Katai; shimaru.
TIGHTEN, Kataku szru; haru; shimeru.
TIGHTLY, Kataku; shika-to; tszyoku; hittari to; shikkari to; kisshiri to.
TILE, Kawara. — *kiln*, kawara-gama. *To roof with* —, kawara wo fuku. — *roof*, kawara-yane.
TILER, Shakan.
TILING, Kawara-yane.
TILL, *prep.* Made. — *now*, ima-made. — *then*, sono toki made; sono maye ni.
TILL, *v.* Tagayesz; kōsaku szru.
TILLAGE, Kōsaku; tagayeshi.
TILLER, Kaji no ye; h'yak'shō.
TILT, *v.* Katamukeru.
TILTED, Katamuku.
TIMBER, Zai-moku.
TIMBER-YARD, Zaimoku-ya.
TIME, Toki; jisetsz; koro; koro-oi; jikoku; ji-bun; jidai; jigi; ori; hodo; yo; dai; k'woin; tszki-hi; go; do; tabi; ma; hen.

Spare —, hima; itoma. *Ancient* —, mukashi; inishiye. *Set* —, nichigen; kokugen. *Three times five are fifteen*, san go no jūgo. — *(of music)*, fushi. *Any* —, itszdemo. *What* —, itsz. *To be in* —, ma ni au. *Not in* —, ma ni awanu. *At times he rides and at other times he walks*, kago ni nottari aruitari. *Have time enough*, ma ga aru. *To loose* —, osoku naru; hima ga iru. *Long* —, hisashii; nagai. *Short* —, shibaraku; chitto; szkoshi. *Many* —, shibashiba; toki-doki.

TIMELY, Tszgō-yoi toki; hayaku.

TIME-PIECE, Tokei.

TIME-SERVING, Tszishō wo iu; kigen wo toru; hetszrau.

TIMID, Okubiyō na; abunagaru; kimo no chīsai; ayabumu; omeru.

TIMIDITY, Okubiyō; hi-kiyō.

TIN, Szdz; briki; handa.

TINCTURE, *v.* Someru.

TINDER, Hokuchi.

TINFOIL, Szdz-haku.

TINKER, Ikakeya.

TINKLE, *v.* Narasz; rin-rin to naru.

TINSEL, Kazari; date.

TINT, *formed by adding* mi *to the name of the color; as, red tint.* aka-mi. *Green tint*, aoi-mi.

TINY, Chīsai.

TIP, Saki.

TIPPET, Kubimaki.

TIPPLE, *v.* Sake wo nomu.

TIPPLER, Sake-nomi.

TIPPLING-HOUSE, Sakaya.

TIPTOE, *To stand on* —, tszmadateru; choriu szru.

TIRE, *v.* Tszkareru; umu; tszkarakasz; kutabireru; taikutsz; agumu; taigi.

TIRESOME, Taikutsz-naru; umu; tszkareru; honeori.

TIT, Chichi.

TITHE, Jūbu-ichi.

TITLE, Gedai; miyō-moku; k'wan-miyō; sonshō; szji.

TO, Ni; ye; made; oyobu; taish'te.

TOAD, Kawadz; kayeru.

TOAD-STOOL, Take.

TOAST, Yaki-pan.

TOBACCO, Tabako.

TOBACCONIST, Tabako-ya.

TOBACCO-PIPE, Kiseru.

TOBACCO-POUCH, Tabako-ire.

TO DAY, Konnichi; kiyō.

TOE, Ashi no yubi.

TOGETHER, Isshō-ni; tomo-ni; dōshi; ichidō; itchi. *Also formed by the suffix*, au, *to the root of a verb, as, Talk together*, hanashi-au. *Fight* —, tataki-au. *To join* —, awaseru. *To mix* —, mazeru.

TOIL, *n.* Hone-ori; ku-rō; wana.

TOIL, *v.* Hone-oru; kurō szru; rō szru; shinku szru.

TOILET, Yosooi. *To make one's* —, migoshiraye wo szru.

TOILSOME, Kurō-na; hone no oreru; rō szru.

TOKEN, Shirushi; shirase.

TOLERABLE, Kanari; dzi-bun; korayerareru.

TOLERATE, *v.* Yurusz; menkiyo szru; kannin szru.

TOLERATION, Yurushi; menkiyo; kan-nin.

TOLL, *v.* Narasz.

TOLL, *n.* Chin; dai; unjō.

TOMATO, Aka-nasz.

TOMB, Haka; tszka; fumbo.

TOMB-STONE, Haka-jirushi; sekitō.

TONE, Ne; neiro; koye; oto; kowane.

TONGS, Hi-bashi.

TONGUE, Sh'ta; kotoba.

TONGUE-TIE, Kojita.

TONIC MEDICINES, Hoyaku.

TONSURE, Teihatsz; rak'shoku; chi-hatsz; kashira-orosz.

TOO, Szgiru; amaru; mo; mata. — *many*, tak'san.

TOOL, Dōgu.

TOOTH, Ha; me; *see Teeth. Carious* —, mushiba. *Artificial* —, ire-ba.

TOOTH-ACHE, Ha-itai; ha ga itai.

TOOTH-BRUSH, Yōji.

TOOTHDYE, Haguro.

TOOTH-EDGE, Hagayui.

TOOTH-FORCEPS, Ha-nuki.

TOOTHLESS, Hanaki.

TOOTHPICK, Koyōji.

TOOTH-POWDER, Hamigaki.

TOP, *n.* Itadaki; zetchō; chōjo; wiye; kashira. *Spinning* —, koma.

TOPHEAVY, Atamagachi.

TOPHET, Jigoku.

TOPSPINNING, Koma-mawashi.

TOPSY-TORVY, Sakasama; mucha-kucha.

TORCH, Taimatsz; tebi. — *light*, kagaribi.

TORMENT, *v.* Semeru; kurushimeru; kashaku szru; nayameru; nayamu.

TORMENT, *n.* Seme; kashaku.

TORN, *pret.* Sakeru; yabureru.

TORNADO, Taifū.
TORPID, Shibireru; don-ni naru; mahi szru; kikanu.
TORPOR, *n.* Shibire; mahi; don.
TORREFY, Yaku; kawakasz.
TORRENT, Kiu-riu; hayase.
TORRID, Atszi; yakeru.
TORTOISE, Kame.
TORTOISE-SHELL, Bekkō.
TORTUOUS, Magaru; unekuru; uneru.
TORTURE, *v.* Semeru; kurushimeru; kashaku szru; gōmon szru; sainamu.
TORTURE, *n.* Seme; kashaku; gōmon.
TOSS, *v.* Nageru; hōru; yuru. — *up*, nage-ageru.
TOSSED, Yureru; tadayō.
TOTAL, *n.* Tszgō; sōtaka; shime.
TOTAL, *a.* Mina; mattaki; nokoradz.
TOTALLY, Issai; mattaku; szbete; sappari; szkkari.
TOTTER, Hiyoro-hiyoro szru; yoromeku; yorobō; furatszku.
TOTTERINGLY, Yoro-yoro-to; hiyoro-hiyoro to; gura-gura.
TOUCH, *v.* Ataru; fureru; sawaru; kamau; kanjiru. *To — at*, yoru.
TOUCH, *n.* Teatari; tezawari.
TOUCH-HOLE, K'wamon.
TOUCHING, Kandzru; ugokasz.
TOUCH-STONE, Tszke-ishi.
TOUGH, Katai; jōbu; nebaru.
TOUGHNESS, Katasa; nebasa.
TOUR, Mawari; yūreki.
TOURNIQUET, Chi-tome dōgu.
TOW, Hiku.
TOWARD, Mukau; sasz; taish'te (taishi); tszite (tszki).
TOWBOAT, Hikifune.
TOWEL, Tenugui; fukin.
TOWER, Tō; tai.
TOWN, Machi; jōka; chō.
TOWN-HALL, K'waisho.
TOWNSHIP, Kōri.
TOWNSMAN, Chō-nin.
TOY, *n.* Omocha; moteasobi.
TOYSHOP, Omocha-ya.
TRACE, Ato; kata.
TRACE, *v.* Kaku; hiku.
TRACK, *n.* Ato; michi.
TRACK, *v.* Ato wo tszkeru; ato wo sh'tau.
TRACT, Tochi; tokoro.
TRACTABLE, Otonashi.
TRADE, *n.* Akinai; kōyeki; baibai; shōbai; urikai; tori-hiki. — *is dull*, akinai fukeiki da.
TRADE, *v.* Akinau.
TRADER, Akindo; akibito; shōnin.
TRADITION, Tsztaye; dempō; kuden; ī-tsztaye; den. *Secret* —, hiden. *Come down by* —, denrai.
TRADITIONAL, Tsztayeru; den-rai. — *receipt*, dempō. — *doctrines*, dempō.
TRADUCE, Soshiru; hihō szru; zangen szru.
TRAFFIC, Akinai; kōyeki; baibai; shōbai; urikai.
TRAFFIC, *v.* Akinau; kōyeki wo szru.
TRAIL, *n.* Ato; ashiato.
TRAIL, *v.* Hiki-dzru.
TRAIN, *v.* Keiko szru; oshiyeru; narasz; kiyō-kun szru; sodateru.
TRAIN, *n.* Dōzei; giyō-retsz.
TRAINING, Kei-ko; narai; sodachi.
TRAITOR, Muhon-nin; hongiyaku-nin; giyaku-nin; giyaku-shin; giyaku-zoku.
TRAITOROUS, Aku-giyaku-na; bō-giyaku-na; fuchiu-na.
TRAMPLE, Fumu; fumi-tszkeru. — *to death*, fumi-korosz.
TRANQUIL, Odayaka-na; shidzka-na; taira; annon; ochi-tszku; heiki.
TRANQUILIZE, Osameru; shidzmeru; tairageru; heiji szru; ochi-tszkeru; otoshi-tszkeru.
TRANQUILLITY, Anshin; ando; odayaka; heian.
TRANSACT, Tori-atszkau; atszkau; szru; tori-hakarau; hakarau.
TRANSACTION, Tori-atszkai; koto; yoshi.
TRANSCEND, Szgiru; masaru; koyeru.
TRANSCENDENT, Szguretaru; nukindetaru; hīdetaru; bakkun-na.
TRANSCRIBE, Utszsz; kaki-utszsz; naki-toru.
TRANSCRIPT, Utszshi; kakitori.
TRANSFER, *v.* Utszru; utszsz; watasz; hakobu.
TRANSFIGURE, Hendzru; hengeru; kawaru.
TRANSFIX, Tszki-tōsz.
TRANSFORM, Hendzru; kawaru; henge szru; bakeru.
TRANSFORMATION, Henk'wa.
TRANSFUSE, Utszsz.
TRANSGRESS, Somuku; yaburu; okasz.
TRANSGRESSION, Tszmi; zai; toga.
TRANSGRESSOR, Zainin; tszmibito; toganin.
TRANS-SHIP, Ni wo utszsz.
TRANS-SHIPMENT, Ni no utszshi; utszshi.
TRANSIENT, Kari-no; karisome naru; zanji no.

TRANSIT, Watari; hakobi.
TRANSITION, Kawari; utszri; hen.
TRANSITORY, Mujō; tszne-naranu; sadame-naki. *This — world*, utsztsz no yo.
TRANSLATE, Hon-yaku szru; naosz; yaku szru.
TRANSLUCENT, Mitōsz; szki-tōsz.
TRANSMIGRATE, Umare-kawaru; ruten szru.
TRANSMIGRATION, Rinye; rinden; ruten.
TRANSMIT, Yaru; okuru; watasz; tsztayeru; tōsz; denrai.
TRANSMUTE, Hendzru; hengeru; kawaru.
TRANSPARENT, Mitōsz; szkitōsz.
TRANSPIRE, Moreru; arawareru; roken szru.
TRANSPLANT, Utszsh'te wiyeru; utszsz.
TRANSPORT, *v.* Hakobu; mochi-hakobu; unsō szru. — *a criminal*, shima ye nagasz; yentō szru; nagasz; ruzai szru.
TRANSPORTATION, Hakobi; unsō; yentō; shima-nagashi; ruzai.
TRANSPOSE, *v.* Oki-kayeru; ire-kayeru.
TRANSVERSE, Yoko; yokogiru; yokotawaru; yokotayeru.
TRAP, *n.* Wana; otoshi; hago.
TRAP, *v.* Wana de toru; toru.
TRAP-DOOR, Age-buta.
TRAPPINGS, Kazari.
TRASH, Kudz.
TRAVAIL, Hone-ori; kurō; rō; san szru. *Severe* —, nan-san. *Easy* —, anzan.
TRAVEL, *v.* Aruku; tabi szru; yūreki szru; hen-reki szru; hemeguru.
TRAVEL, *n.* Tabi.
TRAVELER, Tabi-bito.
TRAVERSE, *adv.* Yoko-ni.
TRAVERSE, *v.* Yūreki szru; henreki szru; mawaru.
TRAY, Bon.
TREACHEROUS, Futagokoro. — *servant*, giyakushin.
TREACHERY, Yashin; giyaku-i.
TREAD, *v.* Fumu; aruku. — *on*, fumi-tszkeru. — *on and kill*, fumi-korosz. — *on and break*, fumi-kudaku; fumi-tszbusz.
TREADLE, Fumigi.
TREADMILL, Fumi-guruma.
TREASON, Yashin; f'tagokoro; giyaku-i.
TREASURE, Takara; zai-hō.
TREASURE, *v.* Takuwayeru; tszmu; atszmeru.
TREASURER, Kanjō kata.
TREASURY, Kane-gura.
TREAT, Motenasz; ashirau; atszkau; toriatszkau; rondzru; noberu. — *disease*, riyōji szru.
TREATISE, Kaki-mono; hon.
TREATMENT, Shi-muke; shi-uchi; tori-atszkai; ashirai. *Medical* —, riyō-ji.
TREATY, Jōyaku; yakujō.
TREBLE, Sambai; sansōbai.
TREE, Ki; jumoku.
TREE-FROG, Ama-gayeru.
TREFOIL, Uma-koyashi.
TRELLIS-WORK, Kōshi.
TREMBLE, *v.* Furū; wananaku; ononoku; zoku-zoku szru; dōburui.
TREMBLINGLY, Buru-buru; wana-wana.
TREMENDOUS, Tszyoi; hanahadashii.
TRENCH, *n.* Mizo; dobu.
TREPIDATION, Furui; wananaki.
TRESPASS, *v.* Tszmi wo okasz; ōdatsz wo szru; yokodori wo szru.
TRESPASS, *n.* Tszmi; toga; zai.
TRESTLE, Dai.
TRIAL, Kokoromi; tameshi; gimmi; sainan; nangi.
TRIANGLE, Sankaku.
TRIBE, Zoku.
TRIBULATION, Sai-nan; nangi
TRIBUNAL, Shirasz; sai-ban-sho.
TRIBUTARY, Zoku szru.
TRIBUTE, Mitszgi.
TRICK, *n.* Tedate; hōben; takumi; jōdan; tawamure.
TRICK *v.* Damasz; taburakasz; azamuku; chakasz.
TRICKLE, *v.* Tareru; sh'tataru.
TRIFLE, Tawamureru; jōdan szru.
TRIFLING, Wadzka; shō-shō; karu-garushii; isasaka.
TRIGGER, Hikigane; hibuta.
TRIM, *v.* Yosoō; kazaru; tszkurō; tszkuru.
TRINKET, Kazari-mono.
TRIP, *v.* Tszmadzku; fumihadzsz. — *up another*, komata wo toru.
TRIPLETS, Mitszgo.
TRIPOD, Mitsz-ashi; gotoku.
TRITURATE, Tszri-kudaku; konasz; szritszbusz.
TRIUMPH, *n.* Kachi; yorokobi; shōri. *Shout of* —, kachidoki. *To celebrate a* —, kachi wo iwau.
TRIUMPH, *v.* Katsz; kachi-hokoru; shōri wo yeru.
TRIVIAL, Wadzka; shō-shō; sasai.
TROOP, *n.* Kumi; hei-sotsz.
TROPHY, Bundori.

TROT, Jinori.
TROUBLE, *n.* Shimpai; kurō; kidzkai; kokorodzkai; meiwaku.
TROUBLE, *v.* Komaraseru; meiwaku saseru; wadzrawasz.
TROUBLED, Komaru; meiwaku szru.
TROUBLESOME, Urusai; mendō; wadzrawashii.
TROUGH, Toi; toyu.
TROUT, Yamame.
TROWEL, Kote.
TROWSERS, Momohiki; hakama; patchi.
TRUE, Makoto; jitsz; hontō shinjitsz; ma. — *or false*, jippu; kiyō-jitsz.
TRULY, Makoto-ni; jitsz-ni; hon-ni; hon-tō; ge-ni-mo; ari-no-mama; naka-naka.
TRUMPET, Rappa; charumera.
TRUNK, Hako; hitsz; dō; *(of a tree)*, miki; *(of an elephant)*, hana.
TRUST, *v.* Shindzru; shinko szru; tayoru; tanomu; makaseru; adzkeru. *To sell on* —, kaki-uri wo szru. *To buy on* —, oginoru.
TRUSTEE, Adzkari-nin; sewa-nin.
TRUST-WORTHY, Shōjiki; shikkari-to sh'ta.
TRUSTY, Shōjiki; chiugi.
TRUTH, Makoto; jitsz; hontō; arisama.
TRUTHFUL, Tadashii; shōjiki.
TRUTHFULLY, Tadashiku; itszwari-naku; masszgu-ni; aritei-ni.
TRY, Tamesz; kokoro-miru; sabaku; saiban szru; tadasz; gimmi szru.
TUB, Oke. *Bathing* —, furo.
TUBE, Kuda; tsztsz.
TUCK, *v.* Hashoru; tszmeru; age wo szru; makuru.
TUFT, Fusa.
TUG, *v.* Hiku; hone wo oru.
TUITION, *n.* Oshiye. *Price of* —, rei-kin.
TUMBLE, *v.* Taoreru; korobu; ochiru; kokeru. —*from a horse*, raku-ba.
TUMBLER, Kakube-jishi, midz-nomi.
TUMID, Hareru; fukureru.
TUMOR, Katamari; kobu; funriu.
TUMULT, Sawagi; sōdō; midare; ran.
TUMULTUOUS, Sawagashii; sōzōshii; yakamashii; midareru; hishimeku; kamabiszshi.
TUNE, Chōshi; uta. *To put in* —, chōshi wo awaseru.
TUNNAGE, Fune no tszmi-daka.
TUNNY-FISH, Iruka.
TURBAN, Dzkin.
TURBID, Nigoru; nigosz.
TURBULENT, Sawagashii; zomeku.
TURF, Szkumo; matszchi.
TURGID, Hareru.
TURN, *v.* Mawasz; megurasz; kuru; mawaru; meguru; kayeru; furi-kayeru; kawaru; hendzru; bakeru. — *inside out*, ura-gayesz. — *aside*, yokeru; waki ye yoru. — *off, or away*, hima wo dasz; shikujiru; yokeru. — *back*, kayeru; modoru. — *down*, ori-kayesz. — *out*, oshi-dasz; oi-dasz; oi-harau. — *over*, watasz; yudzru; fuseru; kayesz. — *the back*, ushiro wo miseru. — *loose*, hanasz. — *and face.* furi-muku. — — *away from*, furi-tszkeru; mi-szteru. — *bottom up*, fuseru; hikkuri-kayesz; utszmukeru.
TURN, *n.* Mawari; meguri; kawari; jun; ban. *By turns*, jumban-ni; junguri-ni; kawaru-gawaru; kōtai.
TURNIP, Kabura.
TURPENTINE, Matsz-yani.
TURTLE, Kame.
TURTLE-DOVE, Hato.
TUSK, Kiba.
TUTELARY-GOD, Ubuszna.
TUTOR, Shishō.
TWAIN, *cut in* —, Futatsz ni kiru.
TWEEZERS, Kenuki.
TWELFTH, Jū-ni-ban. — *month*, jū-ni-gatsz.
TWELVE, Jū-ni.
TWENTIETH, Ni-jū-ban. — *day of the month*, hatszka.
TWENTY, Ni-jū. — *years*, hatachi.
TWENTY-FOLD, Nijūbai; nijissōbai; hataye.
TWICE, Nido; f'ta-tabi. — *as much*, bai; ni-sōbai.
TWIG, Koyeda.
TWILIGHT, Tazokare; higure; yūguru.
TWINS, Futago.
TWINE, *n.* Ito; hoso-nawa.
TWINE, *v.* Matō; karamu; matoi-tszku; karami-tszku.
TWINKLE, *v.* Kirameku; kiratszku; matataku.
TWIRL, *v.* Mawasz; hineru.
TWIRLING, Mawaru; mawatte oru; hinekuri-mawasz.
TWIST, *v.* Yoru; hineru; nejiru; nau.
TWIT, *v*, Togameru.
TWITCH, *v.* Hiku; tszru; bikutszku; hikumeku.
TWITTER, *v.* Sayedzru.
TWO, Futatsz; ni; riyō. — *by two*, futatsz dztsz. — *or three men*, riyō-san nin.

One or — days, ichi riyō-nichi. — *swords*, riyō-tō.
TWO-EDGED, Riyō-ha.
TWO-FOLD, Ni-sō-bai; bai.
TWO-PLY, Futa-ye.
TWO-SIDED, Riyō-tan.
TWO-SIDES, Riyō-hō.
TWO-TONGUED, Riyō zetsz.
TWO-WAYS, Riyō-yō.
TYPE, Shirushi. *Printing* —, k'watsz-ji.
TYPHOON, Taifū.
TYRANNICAL, Bōgiyaku-na.
TYRO, Shogaku; shoshin; mijuku.

U

UBIQUITY, Imasazaru tokoro nashi.
UGLY, Mi-nikui; nikui; kitanai; bukiriyō; mitomonai.
ULCER, Deki-mono.
ULTIMATE, — *object or end*, tszmari. *The — end of labor is ease*, hone-ori no tszmari wa anraku da.
ULTIMATELY, Hate-ni; tszi-ni; szye; tszmari; hikkiyō; shosen; ageku-ni; shimai-ni.
UMBRELLA, Amagasz; kara-kasa; kasa.
UMPIRE, Giyō-ji; chiu-nin; adzkari-nin.
UN, *Words commencing with the negative prefix* un, *are formed in Japanese by suffixing the negative particles*, dz; nu; zaru; nai; masen; de; ji; and mai; *also by prefixing*, fu; mu; *and* bu.
UNABLE, Dekinu; atawadz. *Also the negative potential form of the verb.*
UNACCEPTABLE, Ki ni iranu.
UNACCOMPANIED, Tomo nashi.
UNACCOUNTABLE, Wakaranu.
UNACCUSTOMED, Nareru. — *to seeing*, minarenu. — *to hearing*, kiki-narenu. — *to wearing*, ki-narenu. — *to living in*, i-narenu.
UNACQUAINTED, Shiranu; zonji-masen; mi-shiranu.
UNADULTERATED, Maze-mono ga nai; junszi.
UNADVISEDLY, Kamben naku; midari-ni.
UNALLOWABLE, Yurusarenu.
UNALTERABLE, Kawaranu; henzenu.
UNAMBIGUOUS, Akiraka-naru; meihaku-na.
UNANIMOUS, Dōshin; itchi szru; dō-i.
UNANSWERABLE, Ī-kayesarenu; arasowarenu; ronzerarenu.
UNANTICIPATED, Omoigakenai; zonjiroranu; futo; zon-g'wai.
UNAPPROACHABLE, Yori-tszkarenu; chikadzkarenu.
UNAPT, Heta; bukiyō.
UNARMED, Szde; marugoshi; mutō.
UNASKED, Negawadz-ni; tanomadz-ni.
UNASSORTED, Wakedz ni aru.
UNATTAINABLE, Oyobanu; todokanu; yerarenu.
UNAUTHENTIC, Hontō-naki.
UNAVAILABLE, Yō-ni-tatanu; muda ni naru; munashii.
UNAVENGED, Mukuidz; kayesadz; kataki wo utadz.
UNAVOIDABLE, Yondokoro-nai; yamu koto wo yedz; senkata nashi; shigata ga nai.
UNAWARES, Omoi-gake-naku; omoi-yoradz; futo.
UNBALANCED, Futszriai.
UNBEARABLE, Korayerarenu; tayerarenu; shinobarenu; shimbō-dekinu.
UNBECOMING, Niawanu; utszranu; kanawanu; fusō-ō-na; funiai; hibun; masanai.
UNBELIEF, Bu-shin-jin.
UNBELIEVING, Shinkō senu; shinzenu; makoto to omowanu; bushinjin.
UNBEND, Yurumeru; kutszrogeru; yaszmeru.
UNBIASED, Katayoranu; hedate-naki.
UNBIDDEN, Yobadz ni; manekadz ni.
UNBLAMABLE, Mushitsz; toga-naki; tszmi nashi.
UNBLEMISHED, Kidz nashi; kegare nashi.
UNBOLT, Hiraku; akeru.
UNBOSOM, Uchi-akeru; akasz.
UNBOUND, Shibara-nai. — *of books*, hiyōshi no nai.
UNBOUNDED, Kagiri nashi.
UNBROKEN, Tagawanu; hadzrenu; mattaki; ara.
UNBUCKLE, Hadzsz.
UNBURNT, Yakanu.
UNBUTTON, Hadzsz.
UNBUTTONED, Hadzreru.
UNCALCULABLE, Kazoyerarenu.
UNCALLED, Yobadz; manekadz.
UNCANCELED, Kiyenu; yamanu; szmanu;
UNCASE, Tsztszmi wo akeru; *or* toku.
UNCAUSED, Shizen; onodzto; onodzkara.
UNCEASING, Tayedz; tōshi; tszdzku; ma mo naki; tayema naki; yaszmadz.
UNCEASINGLY, Tayedz-ni; ma mo naku; tōsh'te; tszdzite.

UNCEREMONIOUS, Rei ni kakawaranu.
UNCERTAIN, Obotszka-nai; tash'kanaradz; sadamaranu; kokoro-moto-naku omō.
UNCHAIN, Kusari wo toku; hanatsz.
UNCHAINED, Kusari ga tokeru.
UNCHANGEABLE, Kawararenu; henzenu.
UNCHANGING, Kawaranu.
UNCIVIL, Aisō-mo-nai; burei.
UNCIVILIZED, Hirakenu.
UNCLARIFIED, Szmanu.
UNCLASP, Tome wo hadzsz.
UNCLE, Oji; oji-san.
UNCLEAN, Kegareru; yogoreru; kitanai; fujō; oye.
UNCLOSE, Akeru; hiraku.
UNCLOTHE, Kimono wo nugu.
UNCLOUDED, Kumoranu; hareta.
UNCOIL, Toku.
UNCOLORED, Nuranu; somenu.
UNCOMBED, Tokanu.
UNCOMFORTABLE, Ki ni kanawanu.
UNCOMMON, Medzrashii; mare-na; hijōna; mu-rui na; kitai na; koto-no-hoka.
UNCONCERNED, Kamawanu; tonjaku senu; ki ni kakenu; nome-nome to.
UNCONSCIONABLE, Muri; dōri ni somuku.
UNCONSCIOUS, Oboyo nashi; shiranu; oboyenu.
UNCONSPICUOUS, Midate no nai; miba ga nai.
UNCONSTITUTIONAL, Koku hō ni awanu.
UNCONSTRAINEDLY, Jiyū-ni; ji-zai ni; katte-ni.
UNCORK, Kuchi wo nuku; kuchi wo akeru.
UNCOURTEOUS, Burei; busahō; aisō-naki; buashirai-na.
UNCOUTH, Bukotsz na; yabo na.
UNCOVER, Arawasz; akeru; hiraku; hagureru; haguru. — *the head*, kaburimono wo toru. — *a house*, yane wo toru.
UNCREATED, Shizen.
UNCTUOUS, Aburake ga aru.
UNCULTIVATED, Tagayesanu; tszkuranu.
UNCURL, Nejire wo nobasz.
UNCURRENT, Tszyō senu; tōranu.
UNDECAYED, Otoroyenu; yowaranu; kuchinu.
UNDECEIVE, Mayoi wo toku.
UNDECIDED, Sadamaranu; ketchaku senu.
UNDECISIVE, Shōbu nashi.
UNDEFILED, Kegarenu; isagiyoi.
UNDEFINED, Tokenu.
UNDENIABLE, Ī-kesarenu; utagawanu.
UNDER, Sh'ta; uchi. *Will not sell under five dollars*, godoru no uchi de wa urimasen. *Under fifty years old*, gojissai no uchi.
UNDER-DONE, Namaniye.
UNDERGO, Au; ukeru. *This meaning is included in the intrans. form of the verb; as.* Tszkareru, *to undergo, or suffer fatigue.* Itamu, *to undergo, or feel pain.*
UNDER-HAND, Naisho; hisokani.
UNDERMINE, Sh'ta wo horu.
UNDERMOST, Ichiban sh'ta; goku sh'ta.
UNDERNEATH, Sh'ta.
UNDERRATE, Kenasz; mi-sageru.
UNDERSELL, Yaszku uru.
UNDERSTAND, Wakaru; geseru; sastoru; yetoku szru; gaten szru; nomi-komu.
UNDERSTANDING, Chiye; riyōken; fumbetsz; wakimaye.
UNDERTAKE, Hiki-ukeru; ukeau.
UNDERTAKING, Koto; waza; shigoto.
UNDERVALUE, Kenasz; misageru; karondzru; iyashimeru.
UNDERWORK, Shigoto wo yaszku szru.
UNDESERVING, Taranu; k'wabun; mi ni amaru. — *of praise*, homeru ni taranu. — *of reward*, hōbi wo yaru ni taranu.
UNDESIGNEDLY Kokoronaku; futo; nani ge naku; tszi.
UNDESIRABLE, Hoshiku nai; konoma nai.
UNDETERMINED, Sadamaranu; kiwamaranu; ketchaku senu.
UNDEVOUT, Bushinjin.
UNDIMINISHED, Heranu; otoroyenu.
UNDISCERNIBLE, Miyenu.
UNDISCERNING, Waki-mayenu; wakatanu.
UNDISCIPLINED, Tori-shimari naki; mijuku-na; tanren senu.
UNDO, Hadzsz; tori-hadzsz; hodoku; hiraku; akeru; toku.
UNDONE, Hadzreru; hodokeru; tokeru; aita (aku); hiraita (hiraku).
UNDOUBTED, Utagai naki; mōshi-bun nashi; tash'ka naru.
UNDRESS, *n.* Fudan-gi.
UNDRESSED, Hadaka-naru; kimono nashi; kimono wo nuite iru.
UNDRIED, Kawakanu; hinu; nurete iru; shimette iru. — *wood*, nama-ki.
UNDRINKABLE, Nomarenu.
UNDUE, Szgiru; amaru; hodo ni szgiru.
UNDULATE, Uneru; n'yoki-n'yoki to; n'yoro-n'yoro to.
UNDUTIOUS, Fu-kō naru; sh'tagawanu; fuchiu na.
UNDYING, Shinanu.

UNEASY, Fu-anshin; anjiru; ochi-tszkanu; shidzmaranu; yaszmaranu.
UNEATABLE, Taberarenu; kuwarenu
UNEMBARRASSED, Sashi-tszkaye ga nai; sawari nashi.
UNEMPLOYED, Yō no nai; yōji ga nai; hima na; hima ga aru; hatarakanu.
UNENGAGED, Yak'soku nashi; yōji nashi.
UNEQUAL, Sorowanu; fu-soroi-na; fudō-na; onajiku nai; taranu; todokanu; tszri-awanu.
UNEQUALED, Busō na; tagui nashi; narabi naki.
UNEQUIVOCAL, Utagai naki; akiraka naru; meihaku na.
UNERRING, Machigawanu; ayamari naki; tash'ka naru.
UNESSENTIAL, Taisetsz ni nai; omoku nai.
UNEVEN, Sorowanu; fusoroi; tairaka naranu; futszriai.
UNEXAMPLED, Tagui nashi; tameshi naki; narabi naki.
UNEXCEPTIONABLE, Mōshi-bun nashi; ī-bun nashi.
UNEXHAUSTED, Tszkinu; tszkusarenu; kiwamerarenu.
UNEXPECTED, Fui no; futo; omoi-yoranu; omoi-gakenai; zonji-yoranu; hiyoi to.
UNEXPLORED, Shirabenu; mi-todokenu; shiranu.
UNEXTINGUISHABLE, Kiyenu; kesarenu.
UNFADING, Samenu; hagenu; kawaranu; ochinu.
UNFAILING, Tszkinu; naku-naranu; otoroyenu; tayenu; tagawanu.
UNFAIR, Tadashikaranu; fu-shōjiki-na; muri na; fu-shō na.
UNFAITHFUL, Fu-chiu na; fu-jitsz na; fugi na; jitsz no nai; futagokoro.
UNFAMILIAR, Narenu.
UNFASHIONABLE, Hayaranu; toki ni awanu.
UNFASTEN, Akeru; hiraku; toku; hadzsz.
UNFATHOMABLE, Fukasa ga hakararenu.
UNFAVORABLE, Kanawanu; tame ni naranu; awanu.
UNFEELING, Nasake no nai; omoi-yaranu; mugoi.
UNFEIGNED, Nise de nai; uso de nai; itszwaranu; jitsz na; hontō na.
UNFILIAL, Fu-kō na.
UNFINISHED, Szmanu; deki-agaranu; jōjusenu; togenu; shimawanu.
UNFIT, Awanu; kanawanu; futszgō; ni-awanu.
UNFIX, Hadzsz.
UNFLAGGING, Tszkarenu; yowaranu; otoroyenu.
UNFOLD, Hirogeru; arawasz; kikaseru.
UNFORTIFIED, Yō-gai naki.
UNFORTUNATE, Fushiawase; fu-un; fukō.
UNFRIENDLY, Naka ga warui; mutszmajiku nai; futszki-ai.
UNFRUITFUL, Yutakanaranu; mi-noranu. — *year*, kiyō-nen. — *soil*, yase-tszchi.
UNFURL, Ho wo ageru.
UNFURNISHED, Dōgu nashi; kazai nashi.
UNGENTEEL, Bukotsz na; buiki na; yabu na; bu-sahō na.
UNGOVERNABLE, Te ni awanu.
UNGRATEFUL, Arigataki wo shiranu; on wo shiranu.
UNGUENT, Kōyaku.
UNHANDY, Heta; futegiwa; tsztanai; bukiyō; fubenri; futszgō.
UNHAPPILY, Fushiawase ni; fu-kō ni sh'te.
UNHAPPY, Tanoshimi nashi; ajikinai; fu-anshin; fu-kitsz; fu-shiawase.
UNHEALTHY, Yōjō no tame ni naranu.
UNHEARD, Kikanu; kikoyenu.
UNHINGE, Hadzsz.
UNIFORM, Dōyō; onaji; sorōte oru.
UNIMPARED, Otoroyenu; yowaranu.
UNIMPORTANT, Taisetsz ni nai; daiji nai; omoku nai; kamawanu.
UNINHABITED, Szmu h'to nashi; h'to nashi. — *house*, aki-ya; aki-dana.
UNINTENTIONALLY, Kokoro naku; nanige naku; nani-gokoro naku; waza to de nai.
UNINTERESTING, Omoshiroku nai.
UNINTERMITTING, Tayedz; tszdzku; ma mo nai; tayema naku; yamedz.
UNION, Mutszmajii; shitashimi; chigiri.
UNITE, Awaseru; gasszru; au; k'wa szru.
UNIVERSAL, Amaneku-no; ittō no.
UNJUST, Fugi; fuszji; hidō; muri; higi; mutai.
UNKIND, Nasake no nai; fushinsetsz na.
UNLACE, Toku.
UNLADE, Ni wo orosz.
UNLAWFUL, Fu-hō na; go hatto ni somuku; okite ni somuku.
UNLEARNED, Mugaku no; mommō na.
UNLESS, Moshi. *Also formed by the neg. sub. suffix*, zareba, *or* neba; *as, unless you eat you will die*, tabeneba shinimasz. — *we take a boat we cannot go*, fune ni noraneba yukarenu. — *you believe you cannot be saved*, shinkō seneba taszkaranu.

UNLICENSED, Kabu ga nai; yurusarenu.
UNLIKE, Chigau; kotonaru; ninu; onajikaranu; fudō na; onajiku nai; kawaru; kotokawaru; tagau; nigenai.
UNLMITED, Kagiri nashi; kiwamaranu; kiri ga nai.
UNLOAD, Ni wo orosz. — *a gun*, teppō no tama wo toru.
UNLOCK, Jō wo akeru.
UNLUCKY, Fukitsz na; kiyō na; fushiawase; warui; fu-un.
UNMANAGEABLE, Te ni awanu; te ni amaru. *Ship is* —, fune ga kaji ni awanu.
UNMARRIED, Yome ni ikanu; teishu motanu.
UNMARRIAGEABLE, Yome ni ikarenu.
UNMERCIFUL, Awaremi nashi; fu-bin no nai; nasake nashi.
UNMERITED, Taranu; k'wabun.
UNMINDFUL, Ki ga tszkanu; omowanu.
UNMOLESTED, Kamawarenu; tonjaku nashi.
UNMOVEABLE, Ugokarenu; ugokasarenu.
UNNATURAL, Arumajiki; dōri de nai.
UNNECESSARY, Oyobanu; yō ni tatanu; muda.
UNNOTICED, Me ni tszkanu; mitszkeraredz.
UNNUMBERED, Kazoyenu.
UNOBSTRUCTED, Jama nashi; todokōri nashi; sasawaranu.
UNOCCUPIED, Aku. — *time*, hima; itoma. — *house*, aki-ya; aki-dana.
UNPAID, Harawanu.
UNPALATABLE, Umaku nai; oishiku nai; madzi.
UNPARALLELED, Busō; tagui nashi; narabi nashi.
UNPARDONABLE, Yurusarenu; kamben-naranu.
UNPERCEIVED, Me ni tszkanu; mi-tszkerarenu.
UNPLEASENT, Ki ni iranu; fujiyū; omoshiroku nai; fushō-na; funiyoi; iya na; kiza.
UNPOLISHED, Migakanu; ara.
UNPOLITE, Burei; shitszrei; busahō.
UNPOPULAR, Hayaranu; riukō senu.
UNPREJUDICED, Katayoranu; ōyake-na.
UNPREPARED, Sh'taku senu; yōi naki; kakugo nai.
UNPROFITABLE, Kai naki; yeki nashi; munashii; yōni tatanu; ri nashi.
UNRAVEL, Toku; hodoku; hogureru; hogusz.
UNREASONABLE, Muri; dōri nashi; hibun.
UNREMITTING, Tayema naki; yaszmi naki; ma naki.
UNRESERVED, Nokoradz; nokosadz; aritei; ari no mama.
UNRESISTING, Tekitai senu; temukai senu; fusegadz.
UNREVENGED, Ada wo kayesadz; kataki wo utanu.
UNRIPE, Juku-senu; umanu.
UNRULY, Te ni awanu; te ni amaru.
UNSAFE, Abunai; ayauki; jōbu ni nai.
UNSALEABLE, Ure-kuchi ga nai.
UNSATISFACTORY, Ki ni kanawanu; taranu.
UNSATISFIED, Aki-taranu; fusoku ni omō; taru-koto shiranu.
UNSEAL, Fū wo hiraku.
UNSEASONABLE, Toki-naranu; jisets ni awanu; basho ni awanu.
UNSEASONED, Nama; narenu; kagen ga warui; fu-ambai na.
UNSEEN, Miyenu.
UNSERVICEABLE, Yō ni tatanu; yaku ni tatanu.
UNSETTLED, Sadamaranu; kimaranu; ochitszkanu.
UNSIGHTLY, Mi-nikui; bu-kiriyō.
UNSKILLFUL, Heta; bukiyō; busaiku; tsztanai; futegiwa.
UNSOCIABLE, Majiwaranu; tszki-awanu.
UNSOLD, Urenai.
UNSOLICITED, Negawadz; tanomadz.
UNSOUND, Jōbu ni nai; tassha ni nai; mattaku nai; sorowanu.
UNSPEAKABLE, Īwarenu; ī-tszkusarenu.
UNSTABLE, Sadamaranu.
UNSTOP, Kuchi wo akeru.
UNSUCCESSFUL, Togenu; dekinu; hatasanu.
UNSUITABLE, Fu-sōō-na; fu-niai-na; futszgō-na.
UNSURPASSABLE, Kosarenu; szgirarenu; katarenu.
UNSUSPICIOUS, Utagawanu.
UNTANGLE, Toku.
UNTAUGHT, Manabanu; narawanu; keiko senu; mu-gaku.
UNTHANKFUL, Arigatagaranu; on wo shiranu.
UNTHINKING, Ki wo tszkenu; nen wo irenu.
UNTIE, Toku; hodokeru; hodoku; hogureru.
UNTIL, Made.
UNTIMELY, Toki naranu ni.

UNTO, Made.
UNTRUE, Makoto nai; uso; itszwari no; jitsz de nai; mujitsz.
UNUSED, Narenu.
UNUSUAL, Tszne-naranu; rei-naranu; mare-na; igi; kaku-betsz; betszi; betszjo. *Nothing* —, bui; buji; igi-nashi.
UNUSUALLY, Itsz ni naku; koto no hoka.
UNUTTERABLE, Īwarenu; ī-tszkusarenu.
UNVENTILATED, Ki no komoru; kimusai.
UNWELL, Ambai-warui; fuk'wai.
UNWHOLESOME, Tame ni naranu.
UNWIELDY, Tszkai-nikui; fubenri.
UNWILLING, Iya; szkanu; nozomanu; kirau.
UNWILLINGLY, Iya nagara; konomadz-ni; fushō-bushō ni.
UNWIND, Maki-kayesz; hodoku; toku.
UNWISE, Chiye no nai; orokanaru.
UNWITTINGLY, Shiradz-ni; ki ga tszkandz-ni; oboyedz ni.
UNWOMANLY, Onnarashiku nai.
UNWORTHY, Mi ni amaru; bun ni szgiru; k'wabun na; taranu.
UNYIELDING, Katai; kataku na; yurusanu; shōchi senu; kataiji-na.
UP, Wiye; kami; *also by* ageru, *and* agaru, *in compound verbs; as, to throw up*, nage-ageru. *To jump up*, tobi-ageru. *To pull up*, hiki-ageru. *To lift up*, ageru; tateru; okosz. *To get up*, okiru; tatsz. *To go up*, agaru; noboru. *To blow up*, fukurasz. *To grow up*, sodatsz; nobiru. *Up the river*, kawa kami. *To go into the water up to the chin*, kubi-take midz ni hairu. *Sun is up*, hi ga deru. *Not come up to*, oyobanu. *The time is up*, toki ga kita. *Up and down*, wiye sh'ta; achi kochi. *Ups and downs*, daka-boku.
UPBRAID, Togameru; shikaru; soshiru.
UPHEAVE, Oshi-ageru.
UPHOLD, Sasayeru.
UPLAND, Hatake; yama.
UPON, Wiye ni; yotte; ni; tszite; nochi. — *the whole*, shosen; hikkiyō.
UPPER, Wiye no.
UPPER-MOST, Ichi-ban wiye no.
UPRIGHT, Shōjiki, tadashii; tate.
UPROAR, Sawagi; sōdō.
UPRORIOUS, Sawagashii; sōzōshii; yakamashii; hishimeku.
UPROOT, Nenuki wo szru.
UPSET, Hikuri-kayesz; hikuri-kayeru; kutszgayesz.
UPSHOT, Hate; shimai; ageku ni.
UPSIDE-DOWN, Saka-sama; abekobe
UPWARD, Wiye ni; yo; amari; kami. *To look* —, aomuku; aogu. — *of a hundred men*, h'yaku yo nin. — *of five years*, go nen amari.
URGE, Seku; seru; saisoku szru; hagemasz; szszmeru; isogaseru; hayameru; kudoku; izanau; shīru.
URGENT, Kiu na; isogi; aseru; kiusoku na.
URGENTLY, Shikiri-ni; ichidz-ni; hitaszra ni; h'toye ni; hira-ni.
URINAL, Shibin.
URINE, Shōben; shōyō; ibari.
URINATE, Shōben szru.
US, Warera; watakushi-domo.
USAGE, Rei; narawashi; shimuke; tori-atszkai; furiai.
USE, *v.* Tszkau; mochīru; nareru; motenasz.
USE, *n.* Tszkai; tszkai-kata; yō; iriyō; kai. *To be of* —, yō ni tatsz; yaku ni tatsz. *Have no further use of this*, kore wa mo iri-masen.
USEFUL. Yō ni tatsz; yaku ni tatsz.
USELESS, Yō ni tatanu; muyō; yaku ni tatanu; muda; munashii; fu-yō na; kainaki; muyeki; muyaku; dame.
USELESSLY, Muda-ni; itadzra ni; munashiku.
USHER, Tori-tszgi.
USHER, *v.* Annai szru.
USUAL, Hei-zei; hei-jitsz; atarimaye; fudan; itsz; itsz-mo no; rei no. *As* —, itsz-mo no tōri.
USUALLY, Taitei; tszne-ni; hei-zei; zentai.
USURER, Kōri-kashi.
UTENSIL, Utszwa; dōgu.
UTILITY, Yō; riyō; hentetsz.
UTERUS, Shikiu; kobukuro.
UTMOST, Kagiri; tszkushi; aritake; hanahadashii; itari.
UTTER, *v.* Iu; hanasz; akasz; tagon szru.
UTTERANCE, Kotoba-dzki.
UTTERLY, Maru de; mattaku. — *consumed*, yake-hateru; tszki-hateru; yake-shimau.
UTTERMOST, Itatte; shigoku.
UVULA, Hiko.

V

VACANCY, Aida; ma; szkima; hima.
VACANT, Aku; kara. — *time*, hima; itoma. — *house*, akiya; aki-dana. — *land*, kūchi.

VACANTLY, Ukkari; muchiu.
VACATE, Akeru.
VACATION, Yaszmi; kiu-soku.
VACCINATE, Wiye-bōso wo szru.
VACCINATION, Wiye-bōso; shu-tō; giutō.
VACILLATE, Tayutau; tamerau; sadamaranu.
VACUITY, Kū; kokū; chiu.
VAGABOND, Gorotszki; mushuku; yadonashi; dembō.
VAGRANT, *n.* Rōnin.
VAGUE, Sadamaranu.
VAIN, Muda; munashii; dame; muyeki; muyaku; muyō; itadzra; jiman; hokoru; takaburu; hakanai; mujō.
VAIN-GLORIOUS, Jiman; hokoru; unubore; jifu.
VAINLY, Muda-ni; munashiku; itadzra ni.
VALE, Tani.
VALIANT, Yū naru; gō-yū-na; yūki no tszyoi; kitszi; takeki.
VALID, Yoi.
VALLEY, Tani.
VALOR, Yūki; gōki.
VALUABLE, Tattoi; takai. — *thing*, takara-mono; hōmotsz.
VALUE, Atai; yō; nedan; ne; riyō.
VALUE, *v.* Tattomu; takara to szru; oshimu; taisetsz ni omō; omondzru.
VALUELESS, Ne-uchi ga nai; fuyō na; iranu.
VAN, Saki-te; senjin; sembō; saki.
VANE, Kazami
VANISH, Kiyeru; useru; nakunaru.
VANITY, Takaburi; hokori; jiman; unubore; munashisa; hakanasa.
VANQUISH, Katsz; īfuseru.
VAPOR, Sziki; yuge; jōki; ki. — *of blood*, chi-kemuri.
VARIABLE Sadamaranu; kawari-yaszi; yoku kawaru; kimari no nai.
VARIANCE, Arasoi; fuwa. *At* —, naka ga warui.
VARIATION, Kawari; kawaru koto; shabetsz.
VARIEGATE, Irodoru; saishiki szru.
VARIOUS, Iro-iro; sama-zama; shuju; machi-machi; tori-dori.
VARNISH, *n.* Urushi. *To* —, urushi wo nuru.
VARNISHER, Urushi-ya.
VARNISH-TREE, Urushi-no-ki.
VARY, Kawaru; hendzru; kotonaru.
VASE, Hana-ike; k'wa-bin.
VASSAL, Kerai.
VAST, Hiroi; ōki; ōi; k'wo-dai; baku-tai; taisō.
VASTNESS, Hirosa; ōkisa; ōsa.
VAT, Fune; oke.
VAULT, *n.* Muro; anagura.
VAULT, *v.* Tobu; haneru.
VAUNT, *v.* Takaburu; jiman szru; tai-heiraku wo iu; ibaru.
VEER, *v.* Kawaru; mawaru.
VEGETABLE, Yasai; kusa. — *kingdom*, sōmoku.
VEGETATE, Hayeru; shōdzru.
VEGETATION, Ki-kusa; sōmoku.
VEHEMENCE, Tszyosa; hageshisa; hidosa.
VEHEMENT, Tszyoi; hageshii; arai; hidoi.
VEHEMENTLY, Tszyoku; hageshiku; hidoku.
VEIL, *n.* Katszgi; fukumen.
VEIL, Kakusz; ō; sayegiru.
VEIN, Jō-miyaku; szji; shibe; mokume.
VELOCITY, Hayasa.
VELVET, Birōdo.
VEND, *v.* Uru.
VENDUE, Seri.
VENEER, *v.* Hagu; kiseru.
VENERABLE, Rō; toshi wo totta.
VENERATE, *v.* Wiyamau; sonkiyo szru.
VENERATION, Wiyamai.
VENERIAL *disease*, Kasa; yōbaisō; baidoku.
VENERY, Iro; szkebei.
VENESECTION, Shiraku.
VENGEANCE, Kataki-uchi; tegayeshi; mukui; kayeshi; hempō. *To take* —, kataki wo utsz; fuku-shū szru; ada wo kayesz; ada wo mukuyuru.
VENISION, Sh'ka no niku.
VENOM, Doku.
VENOMOUS, Doku na. — *snake*, dokuja.
VENT, Ana; kuchi; k'wa-mon; ure-kuchi. *Give* — *to*, dasz; haki-dasz.
VENTILATE, Kaze wo tōsz.
VENTRILOQUISM, Hachi-ningei.
VENTURE, *v.* Kakeru; yatte miru; ayete.
VENTURE, *n.* Kake-goto. *Mercantile* —, yama.
VENTURESOME, Mukōmidz; muyami na.
VENUS, Kinsei; miyōjō.
VERANDA, Yen; rōka.
VERB, Hataraki kotoba.
VERBAL, — *message*, kō-jō; dengon; ī-tszgi; kotodzte; kōdatsz. — *dispute*, kōron.
VERBATIM, Kotoba-utszshi ni.
VERBENA, Fusa-sakura.

VERDANT, Aoi; midori-na.
VERDICT, Mōshi-watashi.
VERDIGRIS, Rokushō.
VERGE, Kiwa; hashi.
VERIFY, Sadamaru; kiwamaru; tash'ka ni naru.
VERILY, Makoto ni; jitsz ni; ge ni;
VERISIMILAR, Makotorashii.
VERITY, Makoto; jitsz.
VERMIFUGE, Mushi-osaye; satchiu-zai.
VERMILION, Shu. — *ink*, shu-dzmi.
VERMIN, Mushi.
VERNAL, Haru no; shun. — *equinox*, shumbun. — *showers*, haru-sama.
VERSE, Ku; uta; shi. *To write verses*, uta wo yomu.
VERSED, Nareru; tokui; jōdz; yete. *Not — in*, heta; futokui.
VERTEX, Zet-chō; kashira.
VERTIGO, Memai; kennun; tachi-gurami.
VERY, *adv.* Taisō; hanahada; itatte; goku; shigoku; ito; dzndo.
VERY, *a.* Jitsz no; makoto no. *That — day*, soku-jitsz.
VESICLE, Midz-bukure.
VESSEL, Utszwa; kibutsz.
VEST, Sode-nashi.
VESTIBULE, Gen k'wa.
VESTIGE, Ato; seki; nagori. — *of antiquity*, koseki
VESTURE, Kimono.
VETERAN-SKILL, Rō-kō.
VETO, Seishi; kindzru.
VEX, Ijimeru; kurushimeru; komaraseru; ikaraseru; ijiru; jirasz.
VEXED, Komaru; ikidōru.
VIAL, Tokuri; bin.
VIBRATE, Yurugu; yurameku.
VICARIOUS, Kawari no; dai no. — *agent*, miyōdai.
VICE, Aku; ashiki.
VICE-AGENT, Miyō-dai; tedai.
VICE-VERSA, Kayette; abekobe ni.
VICINITY, Atari; kinjo; kimpen; moyori.
VICIOUS, Yokoshima; aku; ashiki; fuhō; furachi. — *custom*, aku-fū. — *company*, akutō.
VICISSITUDE, Hen-k'wa; kawari; seiszi.
VICTIM, Ikeniye.
VICTOR, Kachi-te; katta-h'to.
VICTORIOUS, Kachitaru.
VICTORY, Kachi; shōri. *Puffed up by —*, kachi-hokori.
VICTUAL, *v.* Makanau.
VICTUALER, Makanai-kata; hiyō-rō-kata.
VICTUALS, Tabemono; shokumotsz; kuimono; hiyōrō; kate.
VIE, Kisō; arasō; hari-au.
VIEW, *n.* Keshiki; fūkei; chōbō; me. *Not in —*, miyenu. *To take a —*, kembun szru. *With a — to*, meate ni szru.
VIEW, *v.* Miru; kem-bun szru; nagameru.
VIGIL, Himachi; ts'uya.
VIGILANCE, Yōjin; tsztszshimi.
VIGILANT, Tsztszshimu; ki wo tszkeru.
VIGOR, Chikara; kiriyoku; konki; seikon; genki; seishin; shinki.
VIGOROUS, Jōbu na; szkoyaka na; sō-ken na; tszyoi.
VIGOROUSLY, Tszyoku.
VILE, Iyashii; gesen na; ashiki; hiretsz na.
VILENESS, Iyashisa; ashisa; aku.
VILIFY, Nonoshiru; akkō szru; zangen szru; zan szru; shiyuru (shii).
VILLAGE, Mura.
VILLAIN, Yatsz; yatszme; akunin; akutō.
VILLAINOUS, Ashiki; warui; aku; bō-aku; futoi
VINDICATE, Īfusegu; īwake wo szru; mamoru; abau; kabau.
VINDICTIVE, Uramiru; ikidōru.
VINE, Budō-kadzra; kadzra; tszru.
VINEGAR, Sz.
VINEYARD, Budō badake.
VIOLATE, Yaburu; somuku; motoru; sakarau; tagayeru; gō-in szru.
VIOLENCE, Tszyosa; arasa; hageshisa; ikiyoi; hidosa; hidoi-me; mugoi-me. *By —*, muri ni; shīte.
VIOLENT, Tszyoi; hageshii; arai; hidoi; mugoi; ikatszi; satsz-batsz.
VIOLENTLY, Tszyoku; araku; hageshiku; hidoku; muri ni; shīte.
VIOLET, Szmire; szmō-tori-bana.
VIOLIN, Kokiu.
VIPER, Mamushi; hami.
VIRAGO, Akuba.
VIRGIN, Ki-muszme.
VIRTUE, Toku; zen; yosa; yoroshisa; kōnō; kikime; chikara; kuriki. *In virtue of*, ni yotte; yuye ni.
VIRTUOUS, Zen naru; yoi; yoroshii.
VIRULENT, Tszyoi; hidoi.
VIRUS, Doku.
VISAGE, Tszra; kao.
VISCERA, Hara-wata; zōfu; zō.
VISCID, Nebai; nebaru; nebari-tszku; betatszku.
VISCIDITY, Nebasa; nebari.

VISIBLE, Miyeru; me ni kakaru; akiraka naru.
VISION, Me; me de miru koto; maboroshi.
VISIONARY, Yume no; maboroshi no.
VISIT, *n.* Mimai.
VISIT, *v.* Mimau; mamiyeru.
VISITOR, Kiyaku; kiyaku-jin.
VITAL, Yashinau; ikasz. — *power*, seishin.
VITIATE, Sokanau; waruku szru; yaburu; kudzsz.
VIVIFY, Ikasz.
VIVIPAROUS, Taishō.
VOCABULARY, Jibiki.
VOCATION, Kagiyō; tosei; shōbai; nariwai.
VOCIFERATE, Sakebu; omeku; wameku; donaru; ganaru.
VOCIFEROUS, Sawagu; yakamashii; sōzōshii; sawagashii.
VOGUE, Hayaru; riukō szru.
VOICE, Koye; ne; oto.
VOID, Kara; kū; aku; kukiyo; munashii; muda; nai; kūgumoru. *Make* —, yaburu; sakarau.
VOLCANO, Yake-yama; k'wazan; hi no yama.
VOLUMN, Maki; satsz; ōkisa.
VOLUMINOUS, Tai-bu na.
VOLUNTARILY, Midzkara; jibun de; kokoro kara; dziini; kononde; nozonde.
VOMIT, Haku.
VORACIOUS, Gatsz-gatsz szru; bōshoku.
VORTEX, Udz.
VOTE, *n.* Ire-fuda.
VOUCHER, Hikaye-gaki.
VOUCHSAFE, Tamau.
VOW, *n.* G'wan; g'wandate; kisei.
VOW, *v.* G'wandate wo szru; g'wan wo kakeru.
VOWEL, Jibo; boin.
VOYAGE, Funaji.
VULGAR, Iyashii; zoku na; hiretsz; bukotsz na; gesen na; buiki na; gebiru; saganai. — *person*, zoku-butsz. — *tongue*, zokugo. — *style of writing*, zoku-bun. — *appearance*, zokurashii. — *class*, shimo-jimo.
VULGARLY, Iyashiku; zoku ni; zokurashiku.

W

WABBLE, Yoromeku; yoro-yoro szru.
WADDING, Naka wata. *Waded clothes*, wata-ire.
WADDLE, Yego-yego sh'te aruku.
WADE, Kachi watari.
WAGE, *v.* Kakeru; yatte miru. — *war*, ikusa szru.
WAGER, *n.* Kake-mono; keibutsz.
WAGER, *v.* Kakeru; yatte miru.
WAGES, *n.* Kiu-kin; temachin; chin; yakuriyō; chinsen.
WAGGISH, Odokeru.
WAGON, Kuruma.
WAIL, *v.* Naku; kanashimu.
WAIST, Koshi.
WAIT, *v.* Matsz. — *upon*, tsztomeru; au. — *upon the table*, kiuji wo szru. *To lay in* —, machibuse wo szru. — *all night*, machi-akasz. — *impatiently for*, machi-kaneru; machi-wabiru. — *all day*, machi-kurasz.
WAITER, Kiuji-nin; shaku-tori; bon.
WAITING-MAID, Koshi-moto.
WAKE, *v.* Sameru; okiru; *(t. v.)*, okosz; samasz.
WAKE, *n.* Himachi; tszya.
WALK, Aruku; ayumu; fumu; kachi de yuku; hokō szru. *Please — in*, o agari nasare; *or*, o hairi nasare. — *to and fro*, tachi-motōru.
WALKING-STICK, Tszye.
WALL, Ishi-gaki; kabe.
WALLOW, *v.* Notaru; nota-uchi-mawaru.
WALL-PAPER, Kara-kami.
WALNUT, Kurumi.
WANDER, Samayō; bura-bura aruku; rurō szru; madō; *(in mind)*, uwakoto wo iu.
WANE, Heru; kakeru; otoroyeru.
WANT, *n.* Hin-kiu; bimbō. *To be in — of a servant*, kodzkai ni kotokagu.
WANT, *v.* Iru; nai; toboshii; taranu; fusoku; kakeru; koto-kagu; hoshii. *Also the suffix*, tai. *Do you — to buy any fish?* sakana wa yoroshū gozarimasz ka.
WAR, Ikusa. *To make* —, ikusa szru; tatakau. *Man of* —, ikusa-bune. — *stories*, gundan. — *expenses*, gunyōkin. — *chariot*, heisha.
WARBLE, *v.* Naku.
WARD, *n.* Chō.
WARD-OFF, Fusegu; yokeru.
WARDEN, Ban-nin.
WARDROBE, Todana; ifuku.
WARES, Shina-mono; ni; nimotsz.
WAREHOUSE, Kura.
WARFARE, Ikusa.
WARILY, Ki wo tszkete; tsztszshinde; yōjin sh'te.

WARM, *a.* Atatakai; danki na.
WARM, *v.* Atatakaku szru.
WARMTH, Atatakasa; danki.
WARN, Korasz; imashimeru; iken wo szru; koriru.
WARP, *v.* Soru; magaru; higamu; hizoru.
WARP, *n.* Tate-ito.
WARRANT, *v.* Ukeau.
WART, Ibo.
WARY, Yōjin szru; ki wo tszkeru.
WAS, *pret.* Atta.
WASH, *v.* Arau; sentaku szru; szszgu; kiyomeru.
WASH, *n.* (*Medical*), arai-guszri.
WASHERMAN, Sentakuya.
WASHING, Arai; sentaku.
WASP, Koshi-boso; jigabachi.
WASTE, *v.* Tsziyasz; tsziyeru; heru; arasz; yaseru; chibiru.
WASTE, *n.* Kudz; tsziye; heri. — *land*, arechi; no-hara. — *paper*, hōgu. *Laid* —, arasz.
WASTEFUL, Muda ni tszkau; tszyasz.
WATCH, *v.* Mamoru; ban szru; ki wo tszkeru; me wo tszkeru; ukagau; matsz. — *with the sick*, yotogi wo szru.
WATCH, *n.* Tokei; ban; bannin; kō. *Off* —, hiban. *On* —, tō-ban.
WATCHFUL, Yō-jin szru; ki wo tszkeru; tsztszshimu.
WATCHFULNESS, Yōjin.
WATCH-HOUSE, Bansho.
WATCHMAKER, Tokei-shi; tokeiya.
WATCHMAN, Ban-nin; mihari. *Night* —, yoban.
WATCH-TOWER, Monomi; yagura. *Fire* —, hi no miyagura.
WATCHWORD, Ai-kotoba.
WATER, Midz; szi. *To* —, midz wo kakeru. — *a horse*, uma ni midzkau.
WATER-BLISTER, Midz-bukure.
WATERBRASH, Riuin; mushidz.
WATER-CLOCK, Midz-dokei.
WATER-CLOSET, Chōdzba; setszin.
WATERCRESS, Midztade.
WATER-CUP, Midz-nomi.
WATER-DRAIN, Midz-nuki.
WATER-ENGINE, Riutoszi.
WATER-FALL, Taki.
WATER-FOWL, Midz-dori.
WATER-JAR, Midz-kame.
WATER-LEVEL, Mikz-mori.
WATER-LILY, Hasz; renge.
WATERMAN, Sendō.
WATER-MELON, Szika.
WATER-PAIL, Teoke.
WATER-POT, Jōro.
WATER-PROOF, Midz wo hajiku.
WATER-TORTURE, Midz-zeme.
WATER-WHEEL, Midz-guruma.
WATER-WILLOW, Yanagi.
WAVE, *n.* Nami.
WAVE, *v.* Hirameku; hiramekasz; hirugayeru; furu; yudzru.
WAVER, Tamerō; tayutau; sadamaranu.
WAVING, Hempon; hempen.
WAVY, Uneru.
WAX, *n.* Rō. *Bees* —, mitsz-rō. *White* —, hakurō.
WAX, *v.* Tsznoru; tszyoru; masaru; iyamasz; futoru; chōjiru. *Waxing and waning of the moon*, tszki no michi-kake.
WAY, Michi; dō; dōro; ts'ūro; ji; ōrai; tōri; yō; kurai; hō; shihō; shikata. *One's own way*, waga-mama; kimama. *To make* —, yokeru; waki ye yoru. *To give* —, makeru; shirizoku; yudzru. *By the* —, katawara ni. *In the* —, tochiu ni. *Any* —, dōdemo; ika yō demo. *To be in the* —, jama. *To lose the* —, mayō.
WAYFARER, Tabibito.
WAYLAY, Machi-buse.
WAYMARK, Michi-shirube.
WAYWARD, Kimama; wagamama; kidzi.
WE, Warera; watakushi-domo; ware-ware.
WEAK, Yowai; jū-jaku na; hin'yaku; uszi.
WEAKEN, Yowameru; yowaku szru; yowaraseru; yowaru; uszku szru.
WEAKLY, Yowaku.
WEAKNESS, Yowasa; yowami; kiyo.
WEALTH, Zaihō; shinsho; shindai; tomi.
WEALTHY, Yūfuku na; fukki; tomeru; tomu. — *person*, kanemochi; chōja; daijin; bugensha.
WEANING, Chibanare.
WEAPON, Ikusa no dōgu; buki; heiki.
WEAR, *v.* Kiru; chaku szru; chaku-yō szru; mesareru; mesz. — *on the head*, kaburu; itadaku. — *away*, heru; herasz; chibiru. *To* — *out*, ki-yaburu. *To* — *a ring*, yubiwa wo hameru.
WEAR, *n.* Yana.
WEARIED, Tszkareru; kutabireru; agumu; umu.
WEARINESS, Tszkare; kutabire; taikutsz.
WEARY, Tszkareru; kutabireru; agumu; itō; taikutsz szru; umu. — *of waiting*, machi-kaneru.
WEASEL, Itachi.

WEATHER, Tenki; hiyori; jikō.
WEATHER-BOARD, Hame.
WEATHER-COCK, Kazami.
WEAVE, Oru.
WEAVER, Hata-ori.
WEB, *Spiders* —, kumo-no-sz.
WED, Metoru.
WEDDING, Konrei; yengumi; konin; yomedori.
WEDDING-FEAST, Konrei-burumai.
WEDGE, Ya; kusabi.
WEED, *n.* Kusa.
WEED, *v.* Kusagiru; kusa wo toru.
WEEK, Mawari.
WEEP, Naku; nageku; kanashimu.
WEEPING-WILLOW, Shidare yanagi.
WEEVIL, Kome-mushi.
WEIGH, Hakaru; kakeru. — *anchor*, ikari wo ageru. — *in the mind*, kangayeru; kamben szru.
WEIGHT, Mekata; kakeme; omosa; bunriyō; kimme; fundō; omori; omomi.
WEIGHTY, Omoi; tai-setsz na; omoru; omotai; daiji na.
WELCOME, *v.* Mukayeru; aisō wo iu; motenasz; aisatsz szru.
WELCOME, *a.* Yoi; ureshii; ki ni iru.
WELD, *v.* Tszgu; awaseru.
WELFARE, Ampi; anshin.
WELL, *n.* Ido. — *bucket*, tszrube. — *crib*, ido-gawa; igeta. — *digger*, idohori. *cleaning a* —, idogaye.
WELL, *a.* Tassh'ya-na; jōbu-na; mubiyō; szkoyaka-na; saiwai na. *Are you well?* gokigen yoroshii ka.
WELL, *adv.* Yoku; yoroshiku; shika-to. *To speak well of* —, homeru.
WEN, Kobu.
WEST, Nishi; sai; nishi no hō; tori no hō.
WESTERN, Nishi no.
WESTWARD, Nishi no hō ye.
WET, *v.* Nureru; shimeru; uruō; nurasz; shimesz; uruosz. —*from head to foot*, dzbunure.
WETNURSE, Uba; omba; menoto.
WHALE, Kujira. — *bone*, kujira. —*fishing*, kujira-gari.
WHARF, Hatoba; ageba.
WHAT, Nani, *and its compounds.* Idzre; ikan; ikani; dono. — *manner*, dō. — *time*, itsz. — *place*, doko; dochira. — *kind*, donna; dono yō na; ikanaru. — *day*, ikka. — *person*, dare; dono h'to.
WHEAT, Komugi. — *flour*, komugi-no-ko; udonko.

WHEEDLE, Hetszrau; kobiru; tszishō wo iu.
WHEEL, Kuruma.
WHEELWRIGHT, Kurumashi.
WHEN, Itsz; toki; itszkara; itszmade. *Whenever*, itszdemo.
WHENCE, Doko kara.
WHENCESOEVER, Doko kara demo.
WHERE, Doko; dochira; tokoro; idzchi; idzku; idzkata; idzre. *Every* —, doko ni mo. *Any* —, dokodemo. *No* —, doko ni mo nai.
WHEREABOUTS, Yuku-ye; ikidokoro; arika.
WHEREAS, ---- ni yotte; yuye ni.
WHEREFORE, Sono yuye ni; nani yuye; naze.
WHEREVER, or WHERESOEVER, Dokodemo; doko ni demo.
WHET, Togu.
WHETHER, Dochira; ka. — *or not*, inaya.
WHETSTONE, Toishi; to.
WHICH, Dochira; dore; dono. *This is the pencil* — *he made*, kore wa ano h'to no koshirayeta fude da. *What is the name of the book* — *he is reading?* ano h'to no yomu hon no na wa nan da.
WHICHEVER, Dochira demo.
WHILE, Toki; ori; koro; katagata; nagara; tsztsz; gatera. — *in the way*, tochiu; dō-chiu. — *going*, ikegake ni.
WHIM, Dekigokoro.
WHIMPERING, Nakigoto.
WHIMSICAL, Uwatszku; uwa-uwa sh'te iru.
WHINING, Nakigoto.
WHIP, *v.* Butsz; muchi-utsz; utsz.
WHIP, *n.* Muchi.
WHIRL, *v.* Mawaru; meguru; mau.
WHIRLPOOL, Udz.
WHIRLWIND, Tszmuji; maikaze.
WHISK, Hōki.
WHISKER, Hōhige.
WHISPER, *v.* Sasayaku; hisomeku.
WHISTLE, *v.* Usobuku.
WHISTLE, *n.* Fuye; usobuki; kuchi-buye.
WHIT, *Not a* —, chitto mo nai; szkoshi mo nai; mijin mo nai.
WHITE, Shiroi; haku. — *of the eye*, shirome; hakumaku. — *of an egg*, shiromi.
WHITEBEAR, Haguma.
WHITEN, *v.* Shiroku szru; shiromu.
WHITE-WAX, Hakurō.
WHITENESS, Shirosa.
WHITHER, Doko ye; dochira ye.

WHITHERSOEVER, Doko ye demo; doko護 mademo.
WHITLOW, Hiyōsō.
WHIZZING, Piyō to; hiyō to; riu-riu.
WHO, Dare; dono h'to; donata; dochira.
WHOEVER, Daredemo.
WHOLE, Mina; szbete; issai; sō; mattaki; maru de; nokoradz. — *night*, yodōshi; yomoszgara. — *life*, isshōgai; isshō. — *year*, nenjū; marutoshi. — *body*, isshin; sōshin. — *empire*, tenka ittō. — *world*, sekai ittō; henkai. — *day*, shūjitsz; himemosz. — *heart*, isshin; h'tomuki-ni. — *family*, kanai-jū. *Swallow* —, maru-nomi ni szru.
WHOLESALE, Kuchi de uru; oroshi. — *dealer*, toiya; nakagai.
WHOLESOME, Tame ni naru; yoi.
WHOLLY, Mattaku; maru de; issai; ichigai; ichidz; kaimoku; kaishiki.
WHOM, Dare.
WHOOP, Sakebu; toki no koye wo ageru; yobu.
WOOPING-COUGH, H'yaku-nichi-zeki.
WHOOP, Hata to.
WHORE, Jōro; oyama; yūjo. — *monger*, jōro-kai. — *house*, jōro-ya.
WHOSE, Dare no; dono h'to no.
WHY, Naze; nani yuye; dōsh'te; dōyu wake.
WICK, Shin.
WICKED, Aku; warui; ashiki; fugi. — *man*; aku-nin.
WIDE, Hiroi; haba; yoko.
WIDELY, Hiroku.
WIDEN, Hiroku szru; hiromaru.
WIDOW, Goke; yamome.
WIDOWER, Yamome.
WIDTH, Hirosa; haba; yoko.
WIELD, Furu.
WIFE, Tszma; kanai; niyōbō; naigi; kami-san; oku-sama; sai. *Former* —, sensai. *Second* —, nochi-zoye; gozai. — *and children*, saishi.
WIG, Kadzra.
WILD, No; arai; kurū. — *horse*, no'ma. — *dog*, no-inu. — *flower*, no-bana. *Growing* —, jinen-baye.
WILDBOAR, Inoshishi.
WILD-GOOSE, Gan; kari.
WILD-LAND, Are-chi.
WILDERNESS, Nobara; no; hara.
WILDLY, Araku.
WILDNESS, Arasa.
WILD-OATS, Hagusa.
WILE, Te; tedate; tekuda.
WILL, *n.* Ki; kokoro; nozomi; kokoro-zashi; riyōken; omoi. *Verbal* —, yuigon. *Ill* —, urami. *Good* —, shinsetsz; nengoro. *As you* —, dzii; omō-mama.
WILL, *v.* Sadameru; iru; hosszru; negau; nozomu. *As expressing an inclination of mind, it is formed by the terminal suffix* ō; shō; dearō; n. *as*, yukō, *or* yuki-mashō, *I will go*; *or*, *would like to go*; *or*, *am thinking of going*. *Will you, or will you not?* Iru ka iranu ka. *Will he go?* yuku de arō ka. *He will not go*, yuki-masen, *or* (*if there is some doubt*), yuki-maszmai.
WILLFUL, Kimama; wagamama; kataiji na; hoshī-mama.
WILLFULLY, Waza to; kokoro kara; wagamama ni; kimama ni.
WILLINGLY, Shinkara; shinsetsz ni; nengoro ni.
WILLOW, Yanagi.
WILT, *v.* Hinayeru; shioreru; shinabiru; shibomu.
WIN, *v.* Katsz; yeru; toru.
WINCE, *v.* Tajiroku; biku-tszku; biku-biku szru.
WIND, Kaze; fū. *Fair* —, jumpū. *Contrary* —, giyakufū. *State of* —, kazenami.
WIND, *v.* Maku; kuru; matō; mawaru.
WINDLASS, Shachi; manriki.
WINDOW, Mado. — *sash*, shōji. — *glass*, giyaman. — *shade*, misz; szdare.
WINDPIPE, Nodobuye.
WINDWARD, Kazakami.
WINE, Sake; budōshu.
WINE-BIBBER, Sake-nomi.
WINE-CASK, Sakadaru.
WINE-GLASS, Sakadzki; hai.
WINE-MERCHANT, Sakadoiya.
WINE-PARTY, Saka-mori; shuyen.
WING, T'szbasa; hane; hagai.
WINK, *v.* Matataku; me wo utsz; majiroku. *To beckon by winking*, meguwase.
WINNER, Kachi-te; yeru h'to.
WINNOW, Hiru; hi-dasz.
WINTER, Fuyu; tō. — *solstice*. tōji.
WINTER-QUARTERS, Fuyu-gomori.
WINTERY, Fuyumeku; fuyurashii.
WIPE, Fuku; nugū. — *away a reproach*, haji wo szszgu. — *out*, nugui-otosz.
WIRE, Harigane. — *drawer*, harigane-shi. — *gauze*, kana-ami.
WISDOM, Chiye; sai; sainō; saichi; chishiki. — *tooth*, osoiba.

WISE, *a.* Kash'koi; rikô na; chiye aru.

WISH, *v.* Hoshii; hosszru; nozomu; negau; *also the suffix*, tai. *I wish to go*, yukitai. *Do not wish to go*, yuki-taku nai. *I wish you much joy*, omedetō.

WISTERIA, Fuji.

WIT, Chiye; saichi. *To wit*, sznawachi.

WITCH, Matszkai onna; ichiko.

WITCHCRAFT, Mahō-tszkai.

WITH, De; nite; ni; wo motte; tomo ni; issho ni; dōshi; wo.

WITHDRAW, *v.* Shirizoku; hiku; noku; hiki-toru; tori-modosz; kayeru.

WITHE, Heida.

WITHER, *v.* Kareru.

WITHHOLD, Hanasanu; dasanu; hikkomu; yaranu.

WITHIN, Uchi; naka; chiu.

WITHOUT, Soto; hoka; nai; nakute; nakereba; *also formed by the neg. suff.*, dz *followed by* ni ; *as*, *He returned the pen without using it*, fude wo tszkawadz ni kayesh'ta. *Died without seeing it*, midz ni shinda. *Better without it*, nai hō ga yoi. *Cannot do without it*, nakute kanawanu.

WITHSTAND, Fusegu; kobamu ; sakarau; tekitau.

WITNESS, *n.* Shōko; shōko-nin; shō-nin.

WITNESS, *v.* Shōko szru; miru.

WITTICISM, Share.

WIZARD, Mahōtszkai.

WOE, Sai-nan; kanashimi; wazawai.

WOEFUL, Kanashii.

WOLF, Ōkami.

WOMAN, Onna; fujin; jo. *An old* —, rōba; obāsan.

WOMANLIKE, Onnarashii.

WOMB, Shikiu ; kobukuro.

WONDER, *v.* Ayashimu; odoroku; ibukaru; fushin ni omō; kanshin szru.

WONDER, *n.* Ayashimi; odoroki; fushigi; heni; henji. *To be struck with* —, bikkuri szru.

WONDERFUL, Ayashii; fushigi na; kimiyō na; miyō naru; medzrashii; kitai na; keu na; hen-na; kik'wai na; kidoku; shimbiyō.

WON'T, Iya da yo.

WONT, *v.* Nareru.

WOO, Yendan szru.

WOOD, Ki; takigi; maki; moku; hayashi; zai-moku. *quality of* —, kiji.

WOOD-CUTTER, Kikori.

WOODEN, Moku; ki. — *house*, mokuba. — *idol*, mokubutsz; mukuzō. — *bowl*, kibachi. — *sword*, kidachi; bokutō, — *taste*, kiga. — *ware*, kigu. — *nail*, kikugi. — *pillow*, kimakura. — *ticket* kan-satsz.

WOODPECKER, Kitsztszki.

WOOF, Yoko; nuki.

WOOL, Ke.

WORD, Ji; moji; kotoba; gon; gengon; gongo; tayori; otodzre; inshin. — *for word*, kotoba-utszshi ni.

WORK, *n.* Shigoto; hataraki; shita mono; saiku; waza; shi-waza. *To set to* —, shigoto ni tszkeru. *The time spent in* —, tema.

WORK, *v.* Shigoto szru; hataraku; szru; nasz; itasz; saiku szru; nereru; neru.

WORKING, Guai; ambai. — *day*, shigotobi.

WORKMAN, Shoku-nin; shigotoshi; saikunin.

WORKMANLIKE Tegiwa na; yoku dekita; jōdz na.

WORKMANSHIP, Tegiwa.

WORKSHOP, Shoku-ba.

WORLD, Sekai; chikiu; tenchi; tenka; seken; yo; sejō; seji.

WORM, *n.* Mushi. *Earth* —. mimidz. — *eaten*, mushi-kui. — *hole*, mushi-ana. — *medicine*, mushi-guszri; mushi-osaye.

WORRY, *v.* Komaru; komaraseru.

WORRIED, Komaru; wadzrawashii.

WORSE, Nao warui; ---- yori warui; otoru.

WORSHIP, *v.* Ogamu; matszru; hai szru; wiyamau; agameru; son-kiyo szru; inōru; kitō szru.

WORSHIP, *n.* Matszri; hairei; sairei; inori ; kitō.

WORST, Goku warui.

WORST, *v.* Katsz; makasz.

WORSTED, Makeru; fukaku szru.

WORTH, *n.* Atai; nedan; ne; riyō; dai. *A man of great* —, kō no aru h'to.

WORTH, *v.* Ataru. *How much is one day's labor* —? ichi nichi no shigoto wa ikura ni ataru; *or*, ichi nichi no temachin wa ikura. *It is* — *half an ichibu*, ni-shu ni ataru. *Not* — *a cent*, ichi mon ni ataranu. *How much is he* —? ano h'to no shinsho wa ikura. *Not* — *speaking of*, iu ni taranu; toru ni taranu.

WORTHLESS, Ne-uchi ga nai; yō ni tatanu; yaku ni tatanu; yakuza-na.

WORTHY, Sō-ō; tattobu; kō no aru. *Not worthy of praise*, homeru ni taranu.

WOULD, *If it were me I* — *go*, Watakushi

nara yuki-mashō. *It — have been better if I had not come*, koneba yokatta mono wo; *or*, koneba yokatta ni. *If I could I — do it*, dekiru nara shimashō.
WOUND, *n.* Teoi; kidz; kega; itade; omode.
WOUND, *v.* Teoi ni szru; te wo owaseru; kidz wo tszkeru; kidztszku.
WRANGLE, *v.* Arasō; kōron szru; sōron szru; serifu wo iu.
WRAP, Tsztszmu; matō; maku.
WRAPPER, Tsztszmi; furoshiki.
WRATH, Ikari; doki; ikidōri; fundo.
WREATH, Hana-katszra.
WREATHE, *v.* Kumu.
WRECKED, *v.* Kowareru; yabureru. *Shipwreck*, hasen.
WRENCH, *v.* Neji-toru; nejiru; kanaguru.
WREST, *v.* Nejitoru; fuk'wai szru; kojitszkeru.
WRESTLE, *v.* Szmō wo toru; kumi-au; nejiau; jidori wo szru.
WRESTLER, Szmōtori.
WRESTLING, Szmō; jidori; yawara; jūjutsz.
WRETCH, Yatsz.
WRETCHED, Nangi na; nanjū na; iyashiki; kitanai.
WRIGGLE, Agaku; furu.
WRING, *v.* Shiboru; nejiru. — *off*, neji-kiru; neji-oriru. — *out*, neji-shiboru. — *from*, yuszru.
WRINKLE, *n.* Shiwa.
WRINKLE, *v.* Shiwa wo yoseru; hisomeru; shiwamu; shiwameru; shikameru; shikamu.
WRIST, Tekubi.
WRISTBAND, Sodeguchi.
WRITE, Kaku; shitatameru; sho szru. — *in*, kaki-ireru. — *over again*, kaki-kayeru; kaki-naosz. *To omit to* —, kakimorasz; kaki-otosz. *To correct by writing*, kaki-naosz.
WRITER, Kakite; sakusha; hissha.
WRITHE, Modayeru.
WRITING, *n.* Tenarai; kakimono; kaki-tszke. *Hand* —, te. — *master*, tenaraijishō. — *school*, terakoya.
WRONG, Ashii; warui; mutai; yoku nai; hi; machigai; sokonai; chigai; sondzru; ayamaru. — *end uppermost*, saka-sama; abekobe ni. — *side out*, ura-gayeshi ni; abekobe ni. — *written*, kaki-sokonai. *Done* —, Shi-sokonau; shiayamaru; shi-sonjiru. *Speak* —, Ī-sokonau; ī-chigai. *Hear* —, kiki-sokonau.
WRONG, *v.* Sokonau; gai-szru; muri wo szru.
WRONGFULLY, Muri ni; midari ni; muhō ni.
WROUGHT, *pret.* Sh'ta; dekita. — *iron*, kitaigane.
WRY, *a.* Nejireru. — *face*, shikami-dzra.

Y

YARD, Niwa. — *of a sail*, hogeta, ketabō. — *measure*, = san-jaku.
YARD-STICK, Monosashi.
YARN, Ito.
YAWN, Akubi.
YEAR, Toshi; nen; sai. *New* —, shin-nen. *This* —, kotoshi; tōnen. *Last* —, kiyo-nen; saku-nen. — *before last*, otodoshi; issakunen. *Next* —, rai-nen; miyō-nen. — *after next*, sarai-nen. — *by year*, toshi-nami; toshi-doshi; nennen. *Altenate* —, kaku-nen. *Whole* —, nenjū. *Fixed* —, nengen; nenkiri. *Within the* —, nennai. *For years past*, nenrai. *Number of* —, nenszu.
YEARLY, Toshi-doshi; nen-nen mai-nen.
YEAST, Tane; kōji.
YELK, Kimi.
YELL, *v.* Sakebu; naku; wameku.
YELLOW, Ki-iro; ki; kibamu.
YES, Sayō; hei.
YESTERDAY, Kinō; sakujitsz. — *morning*, kinō no asa; saku-chō. — *evening*, sakuban.
YET, Mada; nao; mata; imada; sono wiye. *Not* —, mada. *Not yet come*, mada konu.
YIELD, *v.* Yudzru; kōsan szru; sh'tagau; shōdzru; fukusz; kuppuku szru; kusszru; nabiku.
YIELD, *n.* Deki.
YOKE, *n.* Kubi-ki.
YONDER, Aszko; achira; soko.
YOU, Anata; omaye; nanji; temaye; kisama; sokka; sonohō; sonata; kiden; go; o.
YOUNG, *a.* Wakai; itokenai; osanai.
YOUNG, *n.* Ko.
YOUR, Anata no; omaye no.
YOURSELF, Anata-jibun; go-jibun; jibun; jishin; midzkara.
YOUTH, *n.* Wakai toki; itokenai toki; yōshō.
YOUTHFUL, Wakai; itokenai; osanai; jakunen.

Z

ZEALOUS, Hagemu; fumpatsz szru.
ZIGZAG, Une-kune; chidori-gake.
ZINC, Totan. *Sulphate of* —, kōhan.

THE END.